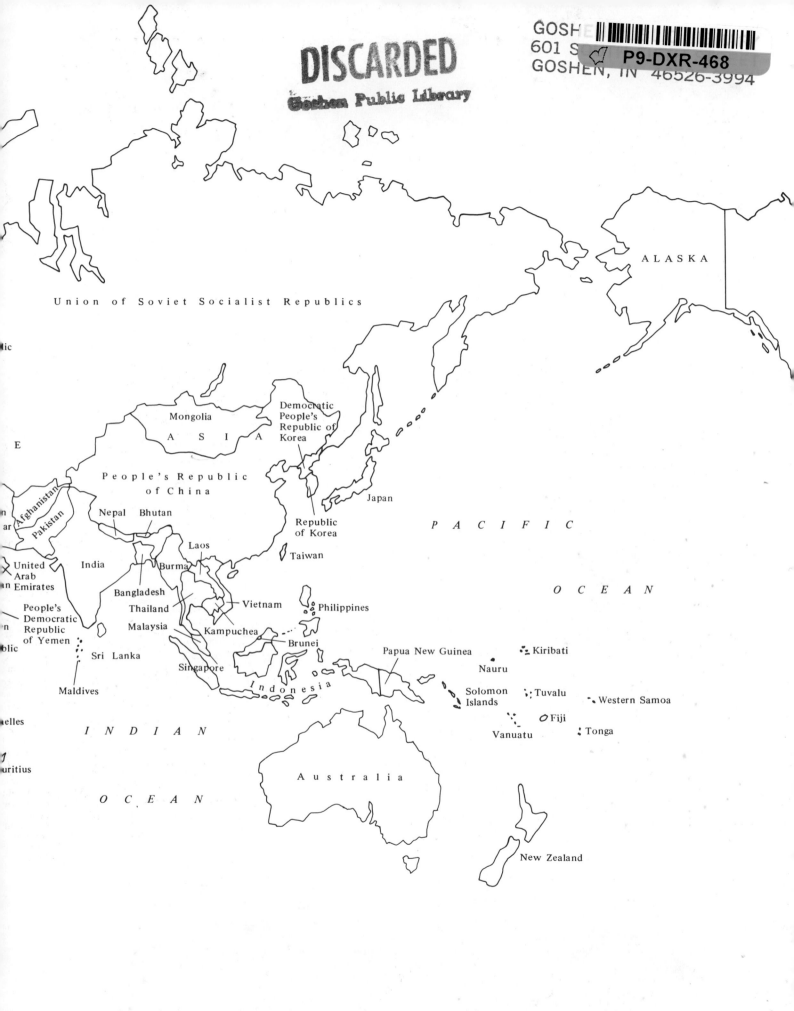

ALASKA

Union of Soviet Socialist Republics

Mongolia

Democratic People's Republic of Korea

A S I A

People's Republic of China

Japan

Afghanistan

Pakistan

Nepal

Bhutan

Republic of Korea

Taiwan

India

Laos

Burma

United Arab Emirates

Bangladesh

Vietnam

People's Democratic Republic of Yemen

Thailand

Malaysia

Kampuchea

Philippines

Sri Lanka

Singapore

Brunei

Papua New Guinea

Kiribati

Maldives

Indonesia

Nauru

Solomon Islands

Tuvalu

Western Samoa

Vanuatu

Fiji

Tonga

P A C I F I C

O C E A N

I N D I A N

O C E A N

Australia

New Zealand

Antarctica

POLITICAL HANDBOOK OF THE WORLD: 1988

*Governments and Intergovernmental Organizations
as of March 15, 1988*

(with major political developments noted through July 1, 1988)

EDITED BY

Arthur S. Banks

ASSISTANT EDITORS
Thomas C. Muller, Katherine F. Sheahan

PRODUCTION EDITOR
Elaine Tallman

*Published for the Center for Education and Social Research
of the State University of New York at Binghamton*

CSA Publications
State University of New York
Binghamton, New York 13901

PUBLISHING HISTORY OF THE *Political Handbook*

A Political Handbook of Europe, 1927, ed. Malcolm W. Davis. Council on Foreign Relations.

A Political Handbook of the World: 1928, ed. Malcolm W. Davis and Walter H. Mallory. Harvard University Press and Yale University Press.

Political Handbook of the World: 1929, ed. Malcolm W. Davis and Walter H. Mallory. Yale University Press.

Political Handbook of the World: 1930–1931, ed. Walter H. Mallory. Yale University Press.

Political Handbook of the World: 1932–1962, ed. Walter H. Mallory. Harper & Brothers.

Political Handbook and Atlas of the World: 1963–1967, ed. Walter H. Mallory. Harper & Row.

Political Handbook and Atlas of the World: 1968, ed. Walter H. Mallory. Simon and Schuster.

Political Handbook and Atlas of the World: 1970, ed. Richard P. Stebbins and Alba Amoia. Simon and Schuster.

The World This Year: 1971–1973 (supplements to the *Political Handbook and Atlas of the World: 1970),* ed. Richard P. Stebbins and Alba Amoia. Simon and Schuster.

Political Handbook of the World: 1975, ed. Arthur S. Banks and Robert S. Jordan. McGraw-Hill.

Political Handbook of the World: 1976–1979, ed. Arthur S. Banks. McGraw-Hill.

Political Handbook of the World: 1980–1983, ed. Arthur S. Banks and William Overstreet. McGraw-Hill.

Political Handbook of the World: 1984–1988, ed. Arthur S. Banks. CSA Publications.

ISSN   0193-175X
ISBN   0-933199-04-X

This edition of the *Political Handbook*

is dedicated to

ROBERT BAYARD TEXTOR

The man in the golden robe

CALENDAR COVERAGE FOR THE 1988 *Handbook*

Textual Material: updated through March 15, 1988; major late-breaking developments noted through July 1.

Currency Exchange Rates: March 1, 1988.

Cabinet Lists: March 15, 1988, or later (as noted).

Media: radio and television data generally for mid-1987; newspaper circulation figures for 1986 or earlier, with some later data (as noted).

Diplomatic Postings: March 1, 1988.

CONTENTS

INTERGOVERNMENTAL ORGANIZATIONS

APPENDICES

INDEX

PREFACE

The present volume continues a publishing tradition extending from 1928, when the Council on Foreign Relations issued *A Political Handbook of the World,* edited by Malcolm W. Davis and Walter H. Mallory. Mr. Mallory became the sole editor in 1929 and continued in that capacity until 1968. The essential structure of the work is based on the format introduced by Richard P. Stebbins and Alba Amoia in the 1970 edition. Since 1975 the *Handbook* has been assembled at the State University of New York at Binghamton, which, as of 1985, also assumed the role of publisher.

The editors have attempted to make the information current as of March 15, 1988, with important later-breaking developments — particularly leadership changes — updated through July 1 (see page iv for additional details on calendar coverage).

A major problem facing the compilers of a global compendium turns on the rendering of both geographic and proper names. Despite a number of international conferences on the subject, the problem is becoming more, rather than less acute, in part because of an increasing tendency toward linguistic "nationalization". Thus cities once known as Leopoldville, Lourenço-Marques, and Salisbury are now styled Kinshasa, Maputo, and Harare, respectively, while the former Republic of Upper Volta is now known as Burkina Faso; in addition, throughout the Third World (particularly in Africa) Christian given names are commonly — and understandably — being abandoned as lingering relics of colonialism.

In rendering proper names based on the Roman alphabet, we have included relevant diacritics, where known. The indexing of Spanish names has been keyed to the paternal component; in the case of Portuguese names, however, the increasingly prevalent practice (to which we largely adhere) is to key to the terminal component, even if maternal. In some cases, the "family" name in the western sense may be rarely, if ever, used, while the given name may be foreshortened (see, for example, the headnote under Tonga).

In the transliteration of names derived from non-Western languages, we have attempted to strike a reasonable balance between the customary usage of the country under treatment and that of the international press. We have made a particular effort to achieve some degree of standardization in the transliteration of Arabic names, although complete uniformity appears to be approachable only in the rendering of Gulf Arabic. Symptomatic of the problem

is the fact that at least eight Romanized variants of Colonel Qadhafi's name are extant, including two (Gaddafy and Qathafi) used by the Libyan government, neither of which appears to be favored by journalists. In accordance with currently prevailing practice, mainland Chinese names are given in *pinyin,* although Wade-Giles and other variants are utilized elsewhere. On occasion, consistency must yield to an individual's preference (if known), as, in the case of Greek, chosing between Constantine, Constantinos, or Konstantinos.

The post-World War II march toward independence by the world's dependent peoples is now virtually completed. Thus, during 1987, for the third year in a row (but only the seventh time since 1946) no newly independent territory entered the community of nations.

The articles on individual countries are presented in alphabetical order of their customary names in English, followed by their official names in both English and the national language or languages. Where no official name is given, the latter is identical with the customary name that appears in the section heading. Each country's "related territories" (if any) are treated together at the end of the country article. In the case of politically divided countries (China, Germany, and Korea), a discussion of matters pertaining to the country as a whole is followed by more detailed description of the distinct political entities established within its territory. The inclusion in the main country sequence of Namibia (South West Africa) and the "independent" Black homelands of South Africa is motivated solely by practical considerations and is not intended to prejudge the legal status of these territories. We have elected to include one territory without a permanent population and government (Antarctica) as well as a number of political entities whose international status may, by choice or tradition, be somewhat impaired (Liechtenstein, Monaco, and San Marino being among the more conspicuous examples). In addition, we have included an article on the Palestine Liberation Organization, even though it has no juridically recognized territorial base. The PLO is accorded such treatment because of its importance in contemporary Middle Eastern affairs; other groups that might have been so treated are the South West African People's Organisation (SWAPO) of Namibia and the Popular Front for the Liberation of Saguia el Hamra and Rio de Oro (Polisario) of Western Sahara.

At initial citation within each country section, the surname (or important part of the name) of most persons in public life is rendered in full capitals to distinguish it from given names and titles. In most cases, two population figures are presented at the beginning of each country listing: a 1988 estimate, together with an official census figure if a census has been conducted since 1970. In a few cases, figures for 1988 differ substantially from collateral figures in the immediately preceding edition. This is usually due to the availability of new census data which have necessitated estimation revision. The monetary exchange rates that also appear at the beginning of each country section are, for the most part, IMF market rates, although in some cases, including most of the Communist bloc, other rates have been used.

The intergovernmental organizations selected for treatment are presented in a separate alphabetical sequence based on their official (in a few cases, customary) names in English. Where an organization is conventionally referred to by initials, these are appended to the official name. A list of member countries of most organizations is printed in the body of the relevant article; for the United Nations and its principal associated agencies, the memberships are given in Appendix B. Non-UN intergovernmental organization memberships for individual countries are listed at the end of each country section, in conformity with a list of abbreviations given on page 2. While we are quite aware of the political significance of various nongovernmental organizations (particularly multinational corporations), we have explicitly limited this section to groups whose memberships are composed of more than two states, whose governing bodies meet with some degree of regularity, and which possess permanent secretariats or other continuing means for implementing collective decisions. The IGO component, as a whole, has been quite substantially revised for this edition, although for some groups timely information has been difficult (in one or two cases, impossible) to obtain. The line maps are, for the most part, intended to illustrate instances of disputed territorial sovereignty.

The preparation of a large-scale reference work of this kind entails a multitude of obligations, few of which can be acknowledged adequately in a brief prefatory statement. Although no longer associated with either its assembly or publication, the Council on Foreign Relations sponsored the *Handbook* for nearly a half-century, guided by a

standard of excellence that we have striven to emulate. The editors are deeply indebted to senior officers at SUNY-Binghamton, including President Clifford D. Clark, former Vice President Arthur K. Smith, and Vice Provost Nathan W. Dean, who have provided institutional resources and encouragement without which we would long ago have foundered.

A number of academic colleagues, at SUNY-Binghamton and elsewhere, have served as a panel of area consultants, collectively reviewing a sizable portion of the manuscript. These "co-editors" include Panayote E. Dimitras (Greece), Üstün Ergüder, Dankwart A. Rustow, and Müberra Yüksel (Turkey), Kunihiko Imai (Japan), Sondra Koff (Italy), Don Peretz (Israel), Edwin H. Rutkowski (Soviet Union), James Savarimuthu (Malaysia), Otto Ulč (Czechoslovakia and South Africa), Thomas Uthup (India), and Tianchi Woongchaisuwan (Thailand). Fred Radewagen, publisher of the *Washington Pacific Report*, provided invaluable insight into late-breaking developments in the South Pacific. We are also indebted to a large number of diplomatic, governmental, and intergovernmental personnel (both US and foreign), who responded with remarkable patience to innumerable appeals, by mail and telephone, for vitally needed information.

Invaluable staff assistance at Binghamton was provided by our indefatigable and supremely resourceful business manager, Benjamin R. Surovy; by our sales fulfillment expeditor, Lynne A. Datto; by Paul C. Parker, Director, Sponsored Funds Administration; and by Carol McLain and Kenneth A. Wilson, information processing specialists. Also making important contributions were Jennie Cheng, Theresa J. diPierno, Kevin Gieg, Christopher M. Jones, Stanley B. Kauffman, Herman Paikoff, Arlene M. Sahr, Jason Scherr, Thomas E. Sheahan, David Skyrea, Thomas Tallman, and MaryAnn Verhoeven. The maps were rendered by Burton C. Rush of Visual Services, Briarcliff Manor, New York; the cover design is by Christopher Bidlack Creative Service, Ann Arbor, Michigan, and the printing and binding by Braun-Brumfield, Inc., Ann Arbor, Michigan.

The dedication of the present edition reflects a friendship of nearly 40 years with a remarkable individual whom many will remember as the co-author and principal inspiration of a volume entitled *A Cross-Polity Survey*.

GOVERNMENTS

INTERGOVERNMENTAL ORGANIZATION ABBREVIATIONS

Country membership in an intergovernmental organization is given in one of two locations. Appendix B lists membership in the United Nations and its Specialized and Related Agencies; non-UN memberships are listed at the end of each country section, under Intergovernmental Representation, the abbreviations given in the list below being used. An asterisk indicates a nonofficial abbreviation; a dagger following an IGO name indicates a primarily economic agency, in most cases a commodity organization, that is not separately referenced in the present edition. In the individual country sections, associate or special memberships are given in italics.

ACCT	Agency for Cultural and Technical Cooperation
ADB	Asian Development Bank
ADF	African Development Fund
*AfDB	African Development Bank
*AFESD	Arab Fund for Economic and Social Development
AGC	African Groundnut Council †
ALADI	Latin American Integration Association
AMF	Arab Monetary Fund
Ancom	Andean Group
ANRPC	Association of Natural Rubber Producing Countries †
ANZUS	Australian, New Zealand, and US Security Treaty
APCC	Asian and Pacific Coconut Community †
APEF	Association of Iron-Ore Exporting Countries †
ASEAN	Association of Southeast Asian Nations
BADEA	Arab Bank for Economic Development in Africa
BCIE	Central American Bank for Economic Integration
BIS	Bank for International Settlements
*BLX	Benelux Economic Union
BOAD	West African Development Bank
CACM	Central American Common Market
*CAEU	Council of Arab Economic Unity
Caricom	Caribbean Community and Common Market
CCC	Customs Cooperation Council
CDB	Caribbean Development Bank
CEAO	West African Economic Community
CEEAC	Economic Community of West African States
*CENT	Council of the Entente
CEPGL	Economic Community of the Great Lakes Countries
CERN	European Organization for Nuclear Research
*CEUR	Council of Europe
CILSS	Permanent Inter-State Committee on Drought Control in the Sahel
CIPEC	Intergovernmental Council of Copper Exporting Countries †
CMEA	Council for Mutual Economic Assistance
Copal	Cocoa Producers' Alliance †
*CP	Colombo Plan for Cooperative Economic and Social Development in Asia and the Pacific
*CWTH	The Commonwealth
EADB	East African Development Bank
EC	The European Communities
ECOWAS	Economic Community of West African States
*EEC(A)	Associate Member, European Economic Community
*EEC(L)	African, Caribbean, or Pacific country affiliated with the EEC under the Lomé Convention
EFTA	European Free Trade Association
EIB	European Investment Bank
ESA	European Space Agency
Eurocontrol	European Organization for the Safety of Air Navigation
GCC	Gulf Cooperation Council
Geplacea	Group of Latin American and Caribbean Sugar Exporting Countries †
G-10	Group of Ten
IACO	Inter-African Coffee Organization †
IADB	Inter-American Development Bank
IATTC	Inter-American Tropical Tuna Commission †
IBA	International Bauxite Association †

IBEC	International Bank for Economic Cooperation
*IC	Islamic Conference
ICAC	International Cotton Advisory Committee †
ICCAT	International Commission for the Conservation of Atlantic Tunas †
ICCO	International Cocoa Organization †
ICES	International Council for the Exploration of the Sea †
ICM	Intergovernmental Committee for Migration
ICO	International Coffee Organization †
IDB	Islamic Development Bank
IEA	International Energy Agency
IIB	International Investment Bank
IIC	International Institute for Cotton †
*ILZ	International Lead and Zinc Study Group †
Inmarsat	International Maritime Satellite Organization
INRO	International Natural Rubber Organization †
Intelsat	International Telecommunications Satellite Organization
Interpol	International Criminal Police Organization
IOOC	International Olive Oil Council †
ISO	International Sugar Organization †
ITC	International Tin Council †
ITPA	International Tea Promotion Association †
IWC	International Whaling Commission †
IWSG	International Wool Study Group †
*IWTC	International Wheat Council †
LAS	League of Arab States (Arab League)
*MRU	Mano River Union
*NAM	Nonaligned Movement
NATO	North Atlantic Treaty Organization
*NC	Nordic Council
NIB	Nordic Investment Bank
OAPEC	Organization of Arab Petroleum Exporting Countries
OAS	Organization of American States
OAU	Organization of African Unity
OCAM	Common African and Mauritian Organization †
ODECA	Organization of Central American States
OECD	Organization for Economic Cooperation and Development
OECS	Organization of Eastern Caribbean States
OPANAL	Agency for the Prohibition of Nuclear Weapons in Latin America
OPEC	Organization of Petroleum Exporting Countries
*PCA	Permanent Court of Arbitration
SAARC	South Asian Association for Regional Cooperation
SADCC	Southern African Development Coordination Conference
SELA	Latin American Economic System
SPC	South Pacific Commission
SPEC	South Pacific Bureau for Economic Cooperation
SPF	South Pacific Forum
UDEAC	Central African Customs and Economic Union
UPEB	Union of Banana Exporting Countries †
WEU	Western European Union
WTO	Warsaw Treaty Organization

AFGHANISTAN

Republic of Afghanistan
De Afghanistan Jamhuriat (Pushtu)
Jomhuri-ye Afghanestan (Dari)

Political Status: Republic established following military coup which overthrew traditional monarchy in July 1973; constitution of 1977 abolished following coup of April 27, 1978; present regime established following coup of December 27, 1979; current constitution adopted November 30, 1987.

Area: 249,999 sq. mi. (647,497 sq. km.).

Population: 15,551,400 (1979C). The 1979 census, the first ever undertaken, yielded a figure approximately 20 percent lower than previous estimates. Assuming the accuracy of the count, the population in mid-1988 would total about 19,252,000, including some 3 million Nomads (excluded from the census) and 3–5 million refugees temporarily domiciled in western Pakistan and northern Iran.

Major Urban Centers (1982E): KABUL (urban area, 1,036,000); Khandahar (191,000); Herat (150,500); Mazar-i-Sharif (110,400). The eight-year civil war has resulted in major shifts in urban settlement. The population of Kabul has substantially increased as a result of refugee influx, while Khandahar and Herat have undergone major decreases (inhabitants of the former being estimated at less than 50,000 in late 1985).

Official Languages: Pushtu, Dari (Persian).

Monetary Unit: Afghani (official rate March 1, 1988, 50.60 afghanis = $1US). The effective rate of the afghani has fallen steadily since 1979, reaching a low of more than 175 afghanis to the dollar in late 1987.

President of the Republic, President of the Revolutionary Council, and General Secretary of the People's Democratic Party of Afghanistan: Dr. (formerly Maj. Gen) Mohammad NAJIBULLAH Ahmadzai [also referenced simply as Najibullah or Najib]; assumed post of General Secretary of the PDPA upon the resignation of Babrak KARMAL on May 4, 1986; named President of the Ruling Council on September 30, 1987, succeeding Acting President Haji Mohammad CHAMKANI; named President of the Republic by the Grand National Assembly on November 30, 1987.

Prime Minister: Soltan Ali KESHTMAND; appointed by former President Babrak Karmal upon the latter's resignation as Prime Minister on June 11, 1981.

THE COUNTRY

Strategically located between the Middle East, Central Asia, and the Indian subcontinent, Afghanistan is a land marked by physical and social diversity. Physically, the landlocked country ranges from the high mountains of the Hindu Kush in the northeast to low-lying deserts along the western border. Pushtuns (alternatively Pashtuns or Pathans) comprise about 55 percent of the population, while Tajiks, who speak Dari (an Afghan variant of Persian), comprise about 30 percent; other groups include Uzbeks, Hazaras, Baluchis, and Turkomans. Tribal distinctions (except among the Tajiks) may cut across ethnic cleavages, while religion is a major unifying factor: 90 percent of the people profess Islam (80 percent Sunni and the remainder, mostly Hazara, Shi'ite).

In 1980, women constituted approximately 19 percent of the paid work force, with a higher percentage engaged in unpaid agricultural labor. Female participation in government is minimal, although there is a women's branch of the ruling party and one female politburo member; among the various *mujaheddin* resistance groups, female participation is nonexistent.

Economically, Afghanistan is one of the world's poorest countries, with a per capita GNP of less than $250 a year in 1985. Nearly 80 percent of the labor force is employed in agriculture (largely at a subsistence level), but opposition to a land-reform program (substantially modified since its original introduction in 1978) has contributed to a lack of self-sufficiency in food, despite increased use of fertilizer and planting of such grains as "miracle" wheat. The country's extensive mineral deposits are largely unexploited except for natural gas, which presently ranks with fruit products and cotton as a leading export commodity. Since its military intervention in late 1979, the Soviet Union has been Afghanistan's leading trade partner, while development aid from the West and from such international agencies as the Asian Development Bank has been suspended in protest against the Soviet presence or because of uncertainties attributable to insurgent activities.

GOVERNMENT AND POLITICS

Political background. The history of Afghanistan reflects the interplay of a number of political forces, the most important of which traditionally have been the monarchy, the army, religious and tribal leaders, and foreign powers.

The existence of Afghanistan as a political entity is normally dated from 1747, when the Persians were overthrown and the foundations of an Afghan Empire were established by Ahmad Shah DURANI. Ahmad's successors, however, proved relatively ineffective in the face of dynastic and tribal conflicts coupled, in the nineteenth century, with increasingly frequent incursions by the Russians and British. The latter wielded decisive influence during the reign of ABDUR RAHMAN Khan and in 1898 imposed acceptance of the Durand line, which established the country's southern and eastern borders but which, by ignoring the geographic distribution of the Pushtun tribes, also laid the foundation for subsequent conflict over establishment of a Pushtunistan state. Emir AMANULLAH succeeded in forcing the British to relinquish control over Afghan foreign affairs in 1919 and attempted to implement such reforms as modern education, women's rights, and increased taxation before being forced to abdicate under pressure from traditional leaders.

The outbreak of World War II severely damaged the economy — markets were lost and access to imports and credit was cut off — and subsequent dissent among intellectuals and failure to resolve the Pushtunistan issue led to a crisis of leadership. Prince Sardar Mohammad DAOUD, designated prime minister in 1953, succeeded in obtaining economic aid from both the United States and the Soviet Union, while modernization of the army helped to alleviate the threat posed by tribes hostile to the government. Politically, however, Daoud was quite conservative, ignoring the legislature, jailing his critics, and suppressing opposition publications. His dismissal in 1963 was followed by a series of moves toward a more modern political system, including the promulgation of a new constitution in 1964 and the holding of a parliamentary election in 1965. Nevertheless, problems encountered by subsequent governments — recurrent famine; a worsening financial situation; increased restiveness on the part of the small, educated middle class; and a sense of impatience with civilian rule — led in 1973 to a military coup, the overthrow of King Mohammad ZAHIR Khan, and the return of Daoud as president of a newly proclaimed republic.

On April 27, 1978, in the wake of unrest stemming from the assassination of a prominent opposition leader at Kabul, the Daoud regime was overthrown in a left-wing coup led by the deputy air force commander, Col. Abdul KHADIR. On April 30, a newly constituted Revolutionary Council designated Nur Mohammad TARAKI, secretary general of the formerly outlawed People's Democratic Party of Afghanistan (PDPA), as its president and announced the establishment of the Democratic Republic of Afghanistan, with Taraki as prime minister. Eleven months later, on March 27, 1979, Taraki yielded the office of prime minister to party hard-liner Hafizullah AMIN while remaining titular head of state by virtue of his Council presidency.

It was officially announced on September 16 that the PDPA Central Committee had unanimously elected Amin as its secretary general and, shortly thereafter, that the Revolutionary Council had designated Amin to succeed Taraki as president. While Kabul radio reported on October 9 that Taraki had died after "a severe and prolonged illness", it was generally assumed by foreign observers that the former president had succumbed on September 17 to wounds received three days earlier during an armed confrontation at the presidential palace. Subsequent reports suggested that a Soviet-backed effort by Taraki to remove the widely disliked Amin as part of a conciliatory policy toward rebel Muslim tribesmen had, in effect, backfired. Such suspicions heightened when Moscow, on December 25–26, airlifted some 4,000–5,000 troops to Kabul, which culminated in Amin's death and replacement on December 27 by his longtime PDPA rival Babrak KARMAL, theretofore living under Soviet protection in Czechoslovakia. Karmal, however, proved scarcely more acceptable to the

rebels than Amin, his regime being supported primarily by the continued presence of Soviet military personnel (estimated to number more than 110,000 by mid-1982). During the ensuing three years, the level of Soviet military involvement increased marginally because of continued resistance throughout the country by *mujaheddin* ("holy warrior") guerrillas, operating largely from rural bases and supplied from Pakistan, where more than 3 million Afghans had sought refuge. In 1985, a semblance of constitutional government was restored. A partially elected Grand National Assembly (*Loya Jirga*) was convened on April 23 for the first time in eight years and promptly endorsed the Soviet presence, while elections for local village councils were held from August through October, despite disruptions attributable to *mujaheddin* activity.

On May 4, 1986, after a visit to the Soviet Union for what were described as medical reasons, Karmal stepped down as general secretary of the People's Democratic Party in favor of the former head of the state intelligence service (KhAD), Mohammad NAJIBULLAH (Najib). On November 20, Karmal asked to be relieved of his remaining government and party posts, being succeeded as head of the Revolutionary Council by Haji Mohammad CHAMKANI, who was, however, designated only on an acting basis.

Najibullah assumed the Council presidency on September 30, 1987, and was named president of the Republic ("Democratic" being deleted from the country's official name) under a new constitution approved by the Grand National Assembly on November 30. Seven months later, on April 14, 1988, Afghanistan, Pakistan, the Soviet Union, and the United States concluded a series of agreements providing for the withdrawal of Soviet troops commencing May 15; however, the *mujaheddin* were unrepresented and vowed to continue their resistance until an Islamic regime had been installed at Kabul (see Foreign relations and Current issues, below).

Constitution and government. On April 30, 1978, the Revolutionary Council proclaimed the abrogation of Mohammad Daoud's "self-created" constitution of February 1977 and announced that it would rule by decree until a new constitution, based on "the promotion of Islam and its human values", had been adopted. Four years later, on April 14, 1980, the Council ratified a provisional basic law that assigned a "leading" role to the PDPA. The 1980 document was superseded by a new constitution on April 21, 1985, that identified the party as the country's "guiding force", while reaffirming the Council's authority, subject to action by a revived Grand National Assembly as "the highest organ of state power". The Assembly convened on November 29–30, 1987, to approve the current constitution, which provides for an executive president and a bicameral National Assembly, while describing the PDPA as "the guardian . . . of national reconciliation" within a national front that would provide a role for other parties.

The country has long been divided into 29 provinces nominally administered by elected local councils (*jirgas*), although Kabul announced in March 1988 that it had decided to create a new northern province (Sari Pull) from portions of Balkh and Juzjan that appeared to be designed to provide Soviet military forces with a buffer zone should the projected withdrawal break down.

Foreign relations. Afghan foreign policy historically reflected neutrality and nonalignment, but by the mid-1970s Soviet economic and military aid had become pronounced. Following the April 1978 coup, the Taraki government, while formally committed to a posture of "positive nonalignment", solidified relations with what was increasingly identified as "our great northern neighbor". Following what was, for all practical purposes, Soviet occupation of the country in late 1979, the Karmal regime asserted that Soviet troops had been "invited" because of the "present aggressive actions of the enemies of Afghanistan" (apparently an allusion to the United States, China, Pakistan, and Iran, among others)—a statement which proved singularly unconvincing to most of the international community. On January 14, 1980, the UN General Assembly, meeting in special session, called by a vote of 104–18 (with 18 abstentions) for the immediate and unconditional withdrawal of the Soviet forces, while Afghanistan's membership in the Islamic Conference was suspended two weeks later. Subsequently, the General Assembly and other international bodies reiterated their condemnation, most nations refusing to recognize the Kabul regime; exceptions to the latter included Mozambique and, of greater consequence, India, which participated in a joint Indo-Afghan communiqué in early 1985 expressing concern about "the militarization of Pakistan".

In early 1986, following the accession to power of economy-conscious Mikhail Gorbachev, Moscow indicated a willingness to consider a timetable for withdrawal of Soviet troops, conditioned on withdrawal of international support for the *mujaheddin*. The immediate result was a new round of "proximity talks" (first launched in 1982) involving UN mediation between Afghan and Pakistani representatives at Geneva, Switzerland. The Geneva talks bore fruit on April 14, 1988, with the signature of an Afghan-Pakistani agreement (guaranteed by the Soviet Union and the United States) on mutual noninterference and nonintervention. Accompanying accords provided for the voluntary return of refugees and took note of a time frame established by Afghanistan and the Soviet Union for a "phased withdrawal of foreign troops" over a nine-month period commencing May 15. However, the agreements did not provide for a cease-fire, with both the United States and Pakistan reserving the right to provide additional military supplies to the Afghan guerrillas if Moscow continued to provide arms to the Kabul regime.

Current issues. The conclusion of the April agreement on Soviet military disengagement from Afghanistan raised at least as many questions as it answered, many of them concerning the future activities of the *mujaheddin* guerrillas who had not been represented at the Geneva talks. The resistance fighters had long been deeply divided between fundamentalist and moderate groups, some of the latter favoring return of the monarch, Mohammad Zahir Khan, currently living in exile at Rome; the former, by contrast, had been committed to the creation of an Islamic revolutionary regime for nearly a decade prior to the 1979 Soviet incursion. Both groups had endorsed a prospective coalition that might include some degree of PDPA representation, while excluding leading members of the existing Kabul

government—a scenario manifestly at variance with the latter's insistence on a PDPA—dominated "national front". One fact, however, was abundantly clear: the Najib administration could not survive, or even maintain a posture of parity vis-à-vis the *mujaheddin,* without continued Soviet support. This cast doubt on whether the withdrawal, however deeply desired by the current Moscow leadership, could be fully implemented within the announced time span, with most observers agreeing that conflict between Kabul and the guerrillas, as well as within the Islamic Alliance, would continue for the foreseeable future.

POLITICAL PARTIES

A National Fatherland Front (NFF) was formally launched at Kabul on June 15, 1981, as a broad alliance of political parties, mass organizations, and tribal bodies, with the PDPA as its "guiding force". The 940 members of the Front's founding National Congress designated a 95-member National Committee, which in turn elected a 23-member Executive Board. Future congresses were to have been convened at no more than five-year intervals, but one scheduled for November 18, 1986, was postponed until January 14–15, 1987, apparently because of differences within the PDPA following the designation of Dr. Najib as general secretary. At the 1987 session the grouping's name was changed to the **National Front** (NF).

Chairman: Abdorrahim HATEF.

Government Party:

People's Democratic Party of Afghanistan—PDPA (*Jamaat-i-Demokrati Khalq-i-Afghanistan*). The pro-Communist PDPA was initially organized in January 1965 as the *Khalq* ("Masses") party under the leadership of Nur Mohammad Taraki. A *Parcham* ("Banner") faction withdrew in 1973 following *Khalq* defiance of a Soviet directive to support the Daoud regime. The two factions were reunited in opposition to Daoud in 1977, but most prominent *Parcham* followers of former defense minister Abdul Khadir were purged in the wake of an abortive coup on August 17, 1978. Longtime *Parcham* leader Babrak Karmal, installed as president of the Republic in December 1979, at first attempted to reunite the two factions within both government and party, but by mid-1980 most *Khalq* leaders had been removed from the cabinet and high party posts. As initially reconstituted under Karmal, the chief PDPA organs were a 36-member Central Committee, a 7-member Politburo, and a 3-member Secretariat; as of late 1985, the Central Committee had been increased to at least 46 full members and the Politburo and Secretariat to 8 members each. During 1986, membership on the Central Committee nearly doubled, while the Politburo was increased to 14 (exclusive of 6 alternates) and the Secretariat to 13 at the second national PDPA conference on October 18–20, 1987.

General Secretary: Dr. Mohammad NAJIBULLAH Ahmadzai.

Other Members of Politburo: Lt. Gen. Sayed Mohammad GHULAB-ZOI (Interior Minister), Najmoddin KAWIANI (member, Secretariat), Soltan Ali KESHTMAND (Prime Minister), Solayman LAEQ (Minister of Nationalities and Tribal Affairs), Haydar MASUD (member, Secretariat), Niaz Mohammad MOHMAND (member, Secretariat), Nur Ahmed NUR (member, Revolutionary Council Presidium), Lt. Gen. Mohammad RAFI (Defense Minister), Abdul Zaher RAZMJO (Secretary, Kabul City Committee), Lt. Col. Mohammad WATANJAR (Minister of Communications), Abdul WAKIL (Minister of Foreign Affairs), Lt. Gen. Ghulam Faruq YAQUBI (Minister of State Security), Dr. Saleh Mohammad ZIRAY (member, Revolutionary Council Presidium).

Alternates: Mahmud BARIALAY, Mohammad Ismail DANESH, Mir Saheb KARWAL, Farid Ahmad MAZDAK, Gen. Abdul QADER Ashna, Shahnawaz TANAY

Central Committee Secretariat: Mahmud BARIALAY, Mohammad Anwar ESAR, Mir Saheb KARWAL, Najmoddin KAWIANI, Haydar

MASUD, Niaz Mohammad MOHMAND, Dr. Mohammad NAJIBUL-LAH Ahmadzai, Nur Ahmed NUR, Gen. Abdul QADER Ashna, Mohammad Daud RAZMYAR, Mohammad Khalil SEPAHI, Mohammad SHARIF, Dr. Saleh Mohammad ZIRAY.

Insurgent Organizations:

Opposition to the Kabul regime and its Soviet backers has been characterized since 1980 by sporadic infighting among dozens of guerrilla groups (the largest of which are listed below), alternating with generally unsuccessful efforts at integration. The principal cleavage has been between Islamic fundamentalist groups with military structures growing out of traditional tribal militias and more modern Islamic moderates dedicated to national unification but lacking widespread popular support. The most recent unity formation, the Islamic Alliance (below), hoped to avoid the collapse of its predecessors (a 1980 grouping of the same name that was followed in 1981 by a Supreme Council of Islamic Unity) by foregoing ideological controversy in order to concentrate on military and financial cooperation.

Islamic Alliance of Afghan Holy Warriors (*Hedadia-i-Islami Muja-heddin Afghanistan*). The Alliance, composed of the seven leading *mujaheddin* groups based at Peshawar, Pakistan, was formed in May 1985 to serve both as "the true representative of the Afghan people" in international forums and as a means of strategic coordination among its component parties. The following September it sent the radical fundamentalist, Gulbuddin Hekmatyar, as its spokesman to the UN General Assembly. In October 1987 it embarked on the establishment of an administrative infrastructure with the designation of a central secretariat and appointed Mawlali Khalis of the *Hizb-i-Islami Khalis* (below) as its leader (*rais*) for an eighteen-month period. The process of institutionalization was further advanced in February 1988 with an announcement that the alliance would shortly name a coalition cabinet to replace the Communist government of President Najib.

Leader: Mawlawi Mohammad Yunis KHALIS.

Islamic Afghan Association (*Jamaat-i-Islami Afghanistan*). The Afghan Association is a fundamentalist group that draws most of its support from Tajiks and Uzbeks in the northern part of the country. It has proven to be the most effective rebel force in the Panjsher Valley. Like the Islamic Party (below), it is based in Peshawar, Pakistan, and maintains offices at Teheran, Iran; following numerous clashes, the two groups have cooperated more closely since August 1984, and lead a fundamentalist bloc within the Alliance. The *Jamaat* engaged in heavy combat with Soviet forces in 1985, including sporadic invasions of Soviet Tadzhikistan, while in early 1986, a number of Afghan military officers were convicted of passing intelligence to the group.

Leaders: Burhanuddin RABBANI, Ahmed Shah MASOUD (Military Commander).

Islamic Party (*Hizb-i-Islami*). Drawing most of its support from Pushtuns in the eastern part of the country, the Islamic Party is the largest and most radical of the fundamentalist groups, and has often engaged in internecine clashes with erstwhile Alliance allies including, most notably, the *Jamaat-i-Islami*. Its principal leader Gulbuddin Hekmatyar, has been known to have ties to both Iran and Libya, although they are believed to have been reduced in recent years.

Leader: Gulbuddin HEKMATYAR.

Islamic Party–Khalis (*Hizb-i-Islami Khalis*). Based largely in Nangarhar Province, the Islamic Party–Khalis is a splinter of *Hizb-i-Islami* that has been somewhat less hostile to the moderate groups than its parent party.

Leader: Mawlawi Mohammad Yunis KHALIS.

Islamic Unity (*Ittihad-i-Islami*). Like the other fundamentalist formations, *Ittihad-i-Islami* has long opposed Westernizing influences in pursuing what it views largely as an Islamic holy war (*jihad*) against Soviet forces. Its leader, Abdul Rasul Sayaf, headed the Alliance at its inception in 1985.

Leader: Abdul Rasul SAYAF.

Islamic Revolutionary Movement (*Harakat-i-Inqilab-i-Islami*). The largest of the moderate insurgent groups, the Islamic Revolutionary Movement has participated in all of the major coalition efforts; within the Supreme Council, it was formerly linked with the two parties below in a moderate opposition bloc that received substantial CIA funding. In 1981, two dissident factions, led by Nasrallah MANSOUR and Rafiullah al-MOUSIN (both claiming the *Harakat-i-Inquilab-i-Islami* name) joined the fundamentalist bloc.

Leaders: Mohammad Nabi MOHAMMADI, Nasrullah MAN-SUR.

National Liberation Front (*Jibbeh Nijat-i-Milli*). The National Liberation Front is committed to Afghan self-determination and the establishment of a freely elected government. Its leader, Sebratullah Mojadidi, was chairman of the moderate opposition bloc.

Leaders: Sibghatullah MOJADDIDI, Hashimatullah MOJAD-DIDI.

National Islamic Liberation Front (*Shora-ye-Milli Inqilab-i-Islami*). The most leftist of the moderate groups, the National Revolutionary Front had refused to join the Supreme Council in 1981 because not all of the participants had agreed to the election of people's representatives to a provisional government.

Leader: Sayed Ahmed GAILANI.

Among the other active opposition parties and groups are the following: the **Social Democratic Party,** a secular organization which, led by Mohammad Amin WAKMAN, was reported to have engaged in bitter fighting against elements of the *Hizb-i-Islami* in August 1980; the **Afghanistan Islamic and Nationalist Revolutionary Council,** chaired by Zia Khan NASSRY, a US citizen born in Afghanistan; the **Alliance of Islamic Fighters,** formed under Wali BEG in May 1979 and consisting mainly of Hazara tribesmen; and the **Islamic Movement of Afghanistan,** led by Mohammad Assef Mohseni QANDAHARI from exile in Iran, which joined seven other Iranian-based groups in mid-1987 to form an **Islamic Revolution United Front for Afghanistan.**

LEGISLATURE

A **Grand National Assembly** (*Loya Jirga*) consisting of 1,796 delegates met for the first time since 1977 on April 23, 1985. Although Kabul claimed that 1,400 of the members had been elected by provincial councils, it appeared that the majority of the delegates were PDPA appointees. The Assembly again met on November 29–30, 1987, to approve a new constitution (see Constitution and government, above), under which Dr. Najibullah was designated as president of the Republic.

CABINET

Prime Minister	Soltan Ali Keshtmand
First Deputy Prime Minister	Lt. Gen. Nazar Mohammad
Deputy Prime Ministers	Sayed Amanuddin Amin
	Mohammad Aziz
	Pohanmal Guldad
	Mohammad Hakim
	Mahbubullah Koshani
	Sayed Mohammad Nasim Mayhanparast
	Abdul Hamid Mohtat
	Mohammad Hasan Sharq
Ministers	
Agriculture and Land Reform	Ghulam Faruq Kobakiwal
Civil Aviation	Mohammad Aziz Negahban
Commerce	Mohammad Khan Jalalar
Communications	Brig. Gen. Mohammad Aslam Watanjar
Construction Affairs	Nazar Mohammad
Domestic Trade	(Vacant)
Education	Abdul Samad Qayyumi
Electrical Energy	Raz Mohammad Paktin
Finance	Dr. Mohammad Kabir
Foreign Affairs	Abdul Wakil
Foreign Trade	(Vacant)

Higher Education	Abdul Wahid Sorabi
Interior	Lt. Gen. Sayed Mohammad Gulabzoi
Irrigation	Ahmad Shah Sorkhabi
Islamic Affairs and Endowment	Maulawi Abdul Jamil Zarifi
Justice	Mohammad Bashir Baghlani
Light Industry and Foodstuffs	Najibullah Masir
Mines and Industries	Mohammad Ishaq Kawa
National Defense	Lt. Gen. Mohammad Rafi
Nationalities	Mohammad Akbar Shormach
Public Health	Dr. Sher Bahadur
State Security	Lt. Gen. Ghulam Faruq Yaqubi
Transport	Lt. Col. Sher Jan Mazdooryar
Tribes	Solayman Laeq
Without Portfolio	Faqir Mohammad Yaqubi

Ministers of State

Direct Cooperation	Sayed Akran Paiger
Foreign Affairs	Shah Mohammad Dost
Islamic Affairs	Abdul Ghafur Baher
Nationalities and Tribal Affairs	Sargang Khan Jaji
Without Portfolio	Nemattulah Pazhwak
President, Central Bank	Abdul Basir Ranjbar

NEWS MEDIA

All domestic information media are rigorously controlled by the government, and access by foreign journalists to areas outside the major cities is officially discouraged. On January 19, 1980, US reporters were expelled from the country because of "slanderous" and "biased" accounts.

Press. The following are government dailies published at Kabul: *Haqiqat-i-Inqilab-i-Sawr* (Truth of the April Revolution, 50,000), in Pushtu and Dari, PDPA organ founded 1980; *Anis* (Friendship, 25,000), in Pushtu and Dari; *Kabul New Times* (formerly *Kabul Times*, 5,000), in English.

News agencies. The domestic facility, the Bakhtar News Agency, operates under the Ministry of Information and Culture; among the foreign bureaus located at Kabul are those representing the Soviet agencies TASS and *Novosti*.

Radio and television. Radio Afghanistan, which operates under the supervision of the Ministry of Communications, broadcasts domestically in Pushtu, Dari, Uzbeki, Nuristani, Turkmani, and Baluchi to approximately 150,000 receivers. In August 1981, it was reported that Radio Free Afghanistan, a Pakistan-based clandestine radio service, was broadcasting within Afghanistan from a portable transmitter. People's Television Afghanistan broadcasts over one station at Kabul; in 1987 there were an estimated 20,000 TV sets.

INTERGOVERNMENTAL REPRESENTATION

Ambassador to the US: (Vacant).

US Ambassador to Afghanistan: (Vacant).

Permanent Representative to the UN: Shah Mohammad DOST.

IGO Memberships (Non-UN): ADB, CP, IC, IDB, Intelsat, NAM.

ALBANIA

Socialist People's Republic of Albania
Republika Popullore Socialiste e Shqipërisë

Political Status: Independent state since 1912; under Communist regime established in 1946.

Area: 11,100 sq. mi. (28,748 sq. km.).

Population: 2,594,600 (1979C), 3,151,000 (1988E).

Major Urban Centers (1983E): TIRANA (206,100); Durrës (72,400); Shkodër (71,200); Elbasan (69,900); Vlonë (61,100); Korçë (57,100).

Official Language: Albanian.

Monetary Unit: Lek (noncommercial rate March 1, 1988, 7.00 lekë = $1US).

President of the Presidium of the People's Assembly (Head of State) and First Secretary of the Central Committee of the Albanian Party of Labor: Ramiz ALIA; elected President by the People's Assembly on November 22, 1982, succeeding Haxhi LLESHI; reelected on February 19, 1987; designated First Secretary by the APL on April 13, 1985, following the death of Enver HOXHA on April 11; redesignated at 13th APL Congress on November 3–8, 1986.

Chairman of the Council of Ministers (Premier): Adil ÇARÇANI; designated by the People's Assembly on January 14, 1982, to succeed Mehmet SHEHU, who died on December 17, 1981; reappointed in 1982 and on February 19, 1987.

THE COUNTRY

The Socialist People's Republic of Albania, one of the smallest and least advanced of European nations, is located at the mouth of the Adriatic, where it is flanked by Yugoslavia on the north and east and by Greece on the east and south. A mountainous topography has served to isolate its people and retard both national unity and development. The two main ethnic-linguistic groups, the Ghegs north of the Shkumbin River and the Tosks south of that river, together embrace 97 percent of the population. Albanian (*shqip*) is an independent member of the Indo-European language group. There are two dialects corresponding to the ethnic division, the Tosk dialect being in official use. A majority of the population has traditionally been Muslim, but since 1967 Albania has claimed to be an atheist state.

The Communist regime has collectivized agriculture, but efforts to persuade the peasants to adopt modern farming methods have not been completely successful. Imports are primarily goods needed for industrialization: machinery, spare parts, metals, and construction materials. Exports—including petroleum and other mineral products, such as chromium (the leading foreign exchange earner), ferronickel, and copper—go primarily to other socialist countries, although trade has been expanding with Austria, Greece, Italy, France, Turkey, and other Western states. While economic modernization has made considerable progress, Albania still has the lowest per capita GNP (approximately $946 in 1985) of any European country. On the other hand, many years of autarky (only recently being somewhat relaxed) have yielded an economy with no foreign debt, no unemployment, and virtually no inflation.

GOVERNMENT AND POLITICS

Political background. Following almost 450 years of Turkish suzerainty, Albania was declared independent in 1912 but remained in a state of confusion until a monarchy was proclaimed in 1928 by President Ahmad Bey Zogu, who ruled as King ZOG I until Albania was invaded and annexed by Italy in 1939. During the later stages of World War II, the Communist-led National Liberation Front under Gen. Enver HOXHA was able to assume control of the country, proclaiming its liberation from the Axis powers on November 29, 1944. Hoxha's provisional government obtained Allied recognition in November 1945 on the condition that free national elections be held. Subsequently, on December 2, 1945, a Communist-controlled assembly was elected, and the new body proclaimed Albania a republic on January 11, 1946. The Albanian Communist Party, founded in 1941, became the only authorized political organization in a system closely patterned on other Communist models. Renamed the Albanian Party of Labor (APL) in 1948, its Politburo and Secretariat have continued to wield decisive control.

Despite extensive second-echelon purges in 1972–1977, very little turnover in the top political leadership occurred prior to a number of Politburo changes announced on November 7, 1981, at the conclusion of the Eighth Congress of the APL. Shortly thereafter, on December 17, Mehmet SHEHU, who had served as chairman of the Council of Ministers since 1954, was officially reported to have committed suicide at "a moment of nervous distress". (Three years later, party officials declared that Shehu had been "liquidated because he met with the unbreakable unity of the party with the people".) On January 14, 1982, First Deputy Chairman Adil ÇARÇANI, who pledged adherence to the political line established by party First Secretary Hoxha, was designated by the People's Assembly to succeed Shehu. Subsequently, on November 22, a newly elected People's Assembly named Ramiz ALIA to succeed Haxhi LLESHI as president of its Presidium (head of state), while an ensuing reorganization of the Council of Ministers was widely interpreted as a purge of former Shehu supporters.

On April 11, 1985, after a prolonged illness which had kept him from public view for nearly a year, Hoxha died of a heart condition at Tirana. Two days later, Alia (who had assumed a number of Hoxha's functions during the party leader's illness) became only the second individual to be named APL first secretary since World War II.

Constitution and government. A new constitution formally adopted on December 27, 1976, did not significantly alter the system of government detailed in its 1946 predecessor. Under its provisions, the former People's Republic of Albania was redesignated as the Socialist People's Republic of Albania and the APL was identified as "the sole directing political power in state and society". Private property was declared to be abolished, as were the "bases of religious obscurantism", and financial dealings with "capitalist or revisionist monopolies or states" were outlawed.

Nominally, the supreme organ of government is the unicameral People's Assembly, which in practice meets for only a few days twice each year to ratify actions taken by its Presidium, whose president is the head of state. Responsibility for day-to-day administration rests with the Council of Ministers and its chairman, who serves as prime minister. The Council of Ministers reflects the penetration of the governmental infrastructure by the party, since most ministers are also members of the Politburo and/or the Central Committee of the APL. The judiciary consists of a Supreme Court and district and local courts. Members of the Supreme Court are elected for four-year terms by the People's Assembly or, between sessions, by its Presidium, while lower-court judges are elected directly for three-year terms.

For purposes of local administration, Albania is divided into 26 districts (*rrethët*), over 200 localities, and 2,500 villages. People's Councils, elected by direct suffrage for three-year terms, are the local governing bodies in each subdivision.

Foreign relations. Albania's pursuit of an antirevisionist and anti-imperialist foreign policy has been conditioned by geography and shifting relationships between external Communist powers. There have been four principal phases in its dealings with the outside world. The period immediately after World War II was marked by a dependence upon Yugoslavia that lasted until the latter's expulsion from the Cominform in 1948. The second phase was one of accord with the Soviet Union, Albania remaining a close ally of the USSR until the softening of Soviet policy toward Yugoslavia following the death of Stalin. Hoxha flouted Khrushchev in a 1957 speech praising Stalin, thereby opening an ideological cleavage between the two countries. Three years later, Soviet efforts to enlist support in its dispute with the People's Republic of China were rebuffed, and in 1961 Albania severed diplomatic relations. The third phase was one of dependence on China. Tirana, which was instrumental in gaining United Nations membership for the People's Republic, accepted Peking's view of world affairs until the post-Maoist regime moved toward détente with the West. In mid-1977, Albania severely criticized Chinese foreign policy toward both the United States and the Third World, the estrangement culminating in Peking's suspension on July 7, 1978, of all economic and military assistance (reportedly totaling $5 billion over a 24-year period). Formal diplomatic relations were, however, retained.

In the wake of the rupture with "imperialist-revisionist" China, the Hoxha regime sought new trade links with a variety of socialist and nonsocialist countries, exclusive of the two superpowers, both of whose policies have consistently been branded by Tirana as inimical to its independence and security. Improved relations with Yugoslavia, whose Kosovo province contains in excess of 1 million ethnic Albanians (more than three-quarters of the province's population), were jolted by a wave of riots involving Serbian security forces in March-May 1981 and by widespread unrest in Kosovo in 1984. During the same period, ferry service was initiated with Greece and Italy, while a number of barter agreements were concluded with France, Italy, and several African countries, among others. In 1985, negotiations were initiated with London on the status of Albania's prewar gold reserves (acquired by Britain from the Germans at the end of World War II) — an issue that continues to inhibit both diplomatic and trade relations between the two countries. Collateral negotiations with the Federal Republic of Germany yielded an agreement in September 1987 to establish diplomatic links after Tirana had abandoned its insistence on reparations for World War II damage. During the same month, Greece announced the end of a state of war that had technically existed since an Italian invasion from Albania in October 1940. The action was preceded by a settlement of border issues that effectively voided Athens' long-standing claim to a portion of southern Albania populated by a sizeable Greek community.

Current issues. The elevation of Ramiz Alia to the party leadership in April 1985 came as no surprise, many observers noting that Alia, a longtime Hoxha confidante, had taken over many of his ailing mentor's de facto duties in recent years. Once in office, Alia reaffirmed his country's opposition to both "American imperialism" and "Soviet social-imperialism", while asserting that discussions with West European diplomatic and trade representatives should not be interpreted as "opening up" Albania. Concurrently, however, Alia emphasized his country's "cultural affinities" with Greece and Turkey, while expressing hope for better relations with Belgrade as a Yugoslav railway link neared completion. Despite a further exchange of polemics on the Kosovo Albanian and other issues, a five-year trade agreement with Yugoslavia was concluded at Tirana in November 1985, while the Shkodër-Titograd rail line was formally opened to nonpassenger transport in August 1986.

At the ninth quinquennial party congress on November 3-8, 1986, three candidates were elevated to full Politburo status, while a new five-year plan (1986-1990) was announced that envisioned a 35-37 percent growth in national income, with increases of 29-31 percent and 35-37 percent, respectively, in industrial and agricultural output. However, First Secretary Alia, in his keynote speech, was openly critical of failures under the previous plan, some (but not all) of which were blamed on prolonged drought and unforeseen energy shortages. In international affairs, Alia reiterated the country's determination to avoid economic or political linkages with the superpowers, while seeming to dampen prospects for improved relations with Yugoslavia by renewed complaints of Belgrade's treatment of ethnic Albanians.

Following pro forma balloting for a new People's Assembly on February 1, 1987, a reorganized Council of Ministers was installed that, coupled with numerous party leadership changes the previous November, appeared to complete a purge of Shehu supporters.

POLITICAL PARTIES

As a one-party Communist state, Albania accords a monopoly position to the Albanian Party of Labor, with the party's Politburo and Secretariat also serving as de facto governing bodies of the state. The **Democratic Front of Albania** (*Fronti Demokratik e Shqipërisë*) is a mass organization to which all adult Albanians theoretically belong;

its principal function is to present candidates for local and national elections, at which no other electoral lists are tolerated. Its current chairperson is Nexhmije HOXHA, widow of the former APL first secretary.

Albanian Party of Labor (*Partia ë Punës ë Shqipërisë* — APL). Founded in November 1941 under the supervision of Yugoslav emissaries, the APL claimed a membership of 147,000 in 1986. Its leading organs are a Central Committee, presently composed of 85 full and 46 alternate members, a Politburo of 13 full and 5 candidate members, and a five-member Secretariat. Party congresses are held every five years, most recently on November 3-8, 1986.

First Secretary: Ramiz ALIA.

Other Members of Politburo: Muho ASLLANI (Party Chief, Shkodër District), Besnik BEKTESHI (Deputy Prime Minister), Adil ÇARÇANI (Prime Minister), Foto ÇAMI (Member, Secretariat), Hajredin ÇELIKU (former Minister of Industry and Mines), Lenka ÇUKO (Member, Secretariat), Hekuran ISAI (Minister of Interior), Rita MARKO (Deputy Chairman, Presidium of People's Assembly), Pali MISHKA (Chairman, People's Assembly), Prokop MURRA (Minister of People's Defense), Manush MYFTIU (Deputy Chairman, Council of Ministers), Simon STEFANI (Member, Secretariat).

Candidate Members: Vangjel ÇERRAVA (Member, Secretariat), Llambi GEGPRIFTI (Minister of Industry and Mines), Pirro KONDI (Party Chief, Tirana District), Qirjako MIHALI (Party Chief, Durrës District), Gen. Kiço MUSTAQI (Chief, General Staff).

Central Committee Secretariat: Ramiz ALIA, Foto ÇAMI, Vangjel ÇERRAVA, Lenka ÇUKO, Simon STEFANI.

LEGISLATURE

The **People's Assembly** (*Kuvënd Popullore*) is a unicameral body of 250 deputies, all elected for four-year terms on a single list of the party-controlled Democratic Front. One deputy is elected for every 8,000 of the population on the basis of universal, direct suffrage of all citizens over 18. The last election was held February 1, 1987.

President: Petro DODE.

CABINET

Chairman, Council of Ministers (Premier)	Adil Çarçani
Deputy Chairmen	Besnik Bekteshi
	Vangjel Çerrava
	Hekuran Isai
	Manush Myftiu

Ministers

Agriculture	Themie Thomai
Communal Economy	Xhemal Tafaj
Construction	Farudin Hoxha
Domestic Trade	Osman Murati
Education	Skender Gjinushi
Energy	Lavdosh Hametaj
Finance	Andrea Nako
Food Industry	Jovan Bardhi
Foreign Affairs	Reis Malile
Foreign Trade	Shane Korbeci
Health	Dr. Ahmet Kamberi
Industry and Mines	Llambi Gegprifti
Internal Affairs	Hekuran Isai
Light Industry	Lavdosh Hametaj
People's Defense	Prokop Murra
Transportation	Luan Babametu

Ministerial Chairmen

Committee for Culture and Arts	Alfred Uci
State Committee for Science and Technology	Ajet Ylli

State Control Commission	Enver Halili
State Planning Commission	Niko Gjyzari
Director, Albanian State Bank	Andrea Nako

NEWS MEDIA

All media of mass communication are controlled by the state or by the APL.

Press. The following are published at Tirana: *Zëri i Popullit* (Voice of the People, 105,000), daily organ of the APL Central Committee; *Bashkimi* (Unity, 30,000), daily organ of the Democratic Front; *Rruga ë Partisë* (People's Road, 9,000), monthly theoretical organ of the APL Central Committee; *Puna* (Labor), twice-weekly organ of the Central Council of Trade Unions; *Laiko Vema* (People's Step), twice-weekly organ of the Greek minority; *Zëri i Rinisë* (Voice of Youth), twice weekly.

News agency. The principal source for both domestic and foreign news is the official Albanian Telegraph Agency (ATA).

Radio and television. Radio and Television of Albania (*Radiotelevisione Shqiptar*), a government facility, controls all broadcasting. Radio Tirana transmits internationally in 19 languages, while television is broadcast in four districts. There were approximately 218,000 radio and 52,000 television receivers in 1987.

INTERGOVERNMENTAL REPRESENTATION

Diplomatic relations with the United States were severed in 1946.

Permanent Representative to the UN: Bashkim PITARKA.

IGO Memberships (Non-UN): CMEA (withdrew from active participation in 1961).

ALGERIA

Democratic and Popular Republic of Algeria
al-Jumhuriyah al-Jaza'iriyah
al-Dimuqratiyah al-Sha'biyah

Political Status: Independent republic since July 3, 1962; under one-party rule established by military coup July 5, 1965, and confirmed by constitution adopted November 19, 1976.

Area: 919,590 sq. mi. (2,381,741 sq. km.).

Population: 17,780,000 (1977C), 23,505,000 (1988E), excluding nonresident nationals (estimated at more than 1 million).

Major Urban Centers (1984E): EL DJAZAIR (Algiers, 1,860,000); Wahran (Oran, 670,000); Qacentina (Constantine, 450,000); Annaba (350,000). In May 1981, the government ordered the "Arabizing" of certain place names which did not conform to "Algerian translations".

Official Language: Arabic (French is also widely used).

Monetary Unit: Dinar (market rate March 1, 1988, 5.29 dinars = $1US).

President: Col. Bendjedid CHADLI; elected February 7 and sworn in February 9, 1979, following the death on December 27, 1978, of Col. Houari BOUMEDIENNE and the interim presidency of Rabah BITAT; reelected unopposed for a second five-year term on January 12, 1984.

Prime Minister: Abdelhamid BRAHIMI; designated by the President on January 22, 1984, to succeed Col. Mohamed Ben Ahmed ABDELGHANI.

THE COUNTRY

Located midway along the North African littoral and extending southward into the heart of the Sahara, Algeria is a Muslim country of Arab-Berber population, Islamic and French cultural traditions, and an economy in which, until recently, the traditional importance of agriculture had been replaced by reliance on hydrocarbons. Women constitute only 7 percent of the paid labor force, concentrated in the service sector (particularly health care). In the parliamentary election of February 1987, 7 of 60 women candidates were elected.

The objectives of the country's second development plan (1985–1989) include restoration of the agricultural self-sufficiency lost following the 1963 expropriation of French colonial estates and subsequent forced collectivization; improvements in health, education, housing, and infrastructure (ports, roads, irrigation and power facilities); and continued industrial diversification in the context of diminishing oil and natural gas reserves. Most of the large industries have been nationalized, and foreign companies must have 51 percent Algerian participation. France, long Algeria's leading trading partner, remains the leading source of imports, while the United States receives about half of the country's exports—chiefly crude petroleum.

GOVERNMENT AND POLITICS

Political background. Conquered by France in the 1830s and formally annexed by that country in 1842, Algeria achieved independence as the result of a nationalist guerrilla struggle that broke out in 1954 and yielded eventual French withdrawal on July 3, 1962. The eight-year war of liberation, led by the indigenous National Liberation Front (FLN), caused the death of some 250,000 Algerians, the wounding of 500,000, and the uprooting of nearly 2 million others, as well as the emigration of some 1 million French settlers. The new Algerian regime was handicapped by deep divisions within the victorious FLN, particularly between the chiefs of the revolutionary army and a predominantly civilian political leadership headed by Ahmed BEN BELLA, who formed Algeria's first regular government and was elected to a five-year presidential term in September 1963. Despite his national popularity, Ben Bella's extravagance and flamboyant style antagonized the army leadership, and he was deposed in June 1965 by a military coup under Col. Houari BOUMEDIENNE, who assumed power as president of the National Council of the Algerian Revolution.

During 1976, the Algerian people participated in three

major referenda. The first, on June 27, resulted in overwhelming approval of a National Charter that committed the nation to the building of a socialist society, designated Islam as the state religion, defined basic rights of citizenship, singled out the FLN as the "leading force in society", and stipulated that party and government cadres could not engage in "lucrative activities" other than those afforded by their primary employment. The second referendum, on November 17, approved a new constitution which, while recognizing the National Charter as "the fundamental source of the nation's policies and of its laws", assigned sweeping powers to the presidency (see Constitution and government, below). The third referendum, on December 10, reconfirmed Colonel Boumedienne as the nation's president by an official majority of 99.38 percent. On February 25, 1977, in the first legislative election since 1964, a unicameral National People's Assembly was established on the basis of a candidate list presented by the FLN.

President Boumedienne died on December 27, 1978, after a lengthy illness, and was immediately succeeded by the president of the National People's Assembly, Rabah BITAT, who was legally ineligible to serve as chief executive for more than a 45-day period. Following a national election on February 7, 1979, Bitat yielded the office to Col. Bendjedid CHADLI, who had emerged as the FLN presidential designee during an unprecedented six-day meeting of a sharply divided party congress held in January.

In June 1980, in a move that effectively marked the end of the Boumedienne era, an FLN congress granted Chadli authority to select members of the party's Political Bureau, and on July 15 the president revived the military General Staff, which had been suppressed by his predecessor after a 1967 coup attempt led by Col. Tahir ZBIRI. As a further indication that he had consolidated his control of state and party, Chadli on October 30 pardoned the exiled Zbiri and freed from house detention former president Ben Bella, who had been released from 14 years' imprisonment in July 1979.

At the presidential election of January 12, 1984, Chadli was reelected unopposed for a second five-year term, subsequently being sworn in on January 16. On January 22, he appointed Abdelhamid BRAHIMI as prime minister to replace Col. Mohamed Ben Ahmed ABDELGHANI, who became minister of state for the presidency.

Constitution and government. The 1976 constitution established a single-party state with the FLN as its "vanguard force". Executive powers are concentrated in the president, who embodies "the unity of the political leadership of the party and the state". He serves additionally as president of the High Security Council and of the Supreme Court, as well as commander in chief of the armed forces. He is empowered to appoint one or more vice presidents and, under a 1979 constitutional amendment that reduced his term of office from six to five years, is obligated to name a prime minister. The president also officiates at joint meetings of the party and the executive, and may initiate legislation. Members of the National People's Assembly are nominated by the party and elected by universal suffrage for five-year terms (save in the event of presidential dissolution). The Assembly, which meets for no more than six months of the year, may legislate in all matters except those involving national defense. The judicial system is headed by a Supreme Court, to which all lower magistrates are answerable.

In late 1983, as part of a decentralization move, the number of regional administrative units (*wilayaat*) was increased from 31 to 49, each continuing to be subdivided into districts (*da'iraat*) and communes. At both the *wilaya* and communal levels there are provisions for popular assemblies, and each *wilaya* has an appointed governor (*wali*). The various administrative units are linked vertically to the minister of the interior. Party organization parallels the administrative hierarchy.

A special congress of the FLNR in late 1985 reaffirmed the commitment to a one-party state, branding dissidents calling for a multiparty system as "destructive elements". More importantly, a new National Charter was advanced (approved by public referendum on January 16, 1986) which, while maintaining allegiance to socialism and Islam, accorded President Chadli greater leeway in his approach to social and economic problems, particularly in regard to partial privatization of the "inefficient" public sector.

Foreign relations. Algerian foreign relations have gone through a series of changes that date back to the pre-independence period, formal contacts with many countries having been initiated by the provisional government (*Gouvernement Provisoire de la République Algérienne* — GPRA) created in September 1958. Foreign policy in the immediate postindependence period was dominated by Ben Bella's anti-imperialist ideology. The period immediately following the 1965 coup was essentially an interregnum, with Boumedienne concentrating his efforts on internal affairs and Foreign Minister Abdelaziz BOUTEFLIKA carrying on a low-profile policy. Following the Arab-Israeli War of 1967, Boumedienne became much more active in foreign policy, with a shift in interest from Africa and the Third World to a more concentrated focus on Arab affairs. After the 1973 war the theme of "Third World liberation" reemerged, reflecting a conviction that Algeria should be in the forefront of the Nonaligned Movement. Subsequently, Algeria joined with Libya, Syria, the People's Democratic Republic of Yemen, and the Palestine Liberation Organization to form the so-called "Steadfastness Front" in opposition to Egyptian-Israeli rapprochement.

A major controversy erupted following division of the former Spanish Sahara between Morocco and Mauritania in early 1976. In February, the Algerian-supported Polisario Front (see Political Parties, below) announced the formation of a Saharan Arab Democratic Republic (SADR) in the Western Sahara that was formally recognized by Algeria on March 6; subsequently a majority of other nonaligned states accorded the SADR similar recognition. However, the issue split the Organization of African Unity, with Morocco withdrawing from the grouping in 1984 in protest at the seating of an SADR delegation. Concurrently, relations between Algeria and Morocco continued to deteriorate, with President Chadli pledging full support for Mauritania's "territorial integrity" and Morocco referring to the Polisarios as "Algerian mercenaries" (see Morocco, Foreign relations). Nonetheless, negotiations between the two states have taken place, the latest being a tripartite summit (with Saudi Arabia) in May 1987, at which a prisoner exchange was arranged.

Relations with Libya worsened in response to Tripoli's "unification" Treaty of Oujda with Rabat in August 1984 (see entries under Libya and Morocco) and plummeted further as a result of Libya's expulsion of Tunisian workers in the summer of 1985. Algiers felt obliged, however, to defend the Qadhafi regime in the events leading up to the US attacks on Tripoli and Benghazi in April 1986. On January 28, President Chadli met with Colonel Qadhafi to deplore, *inter alia,* the "continuing conflict in the Western Sahara", with Libyan authorities subsequently calling for "amalgamation" of the two countries. Although Algeria resisted political union with the Qadhafi regime, economic benefits inherent in joint energy and water projects yielded the proposed establishment by Algeria, Libya, and Tunisia of a Maghreb gas transport company; shortly thereafter, Algeria invited Libya to join the friendship treaty it had concluded with Tunisia and Mauritania in 1983.

Ties with France were temporarily strained by French legislation passed in July 1986 making visas mandatory for all North Africans seeking entry into the country; however, swift action by French authorities against Algerian opposition activists later in the year led to an improvement in relations. Earlier, in April 1985, President Chadli became the first Algerian head of state since independence to visit Washington, utilizing the occasion to secure Algeria's removal from a list of countries prohibited from purchasing US weapons.

Current issues. The major domestic issue presently confronting the Chadli regime is a massive unemployment rate arising from a rapidly expanding population (half of Algeria's inhabitants are under 25) and an economic growth rate that has fallen to only half of the 6 percent registered in 1985. In early November 1987 the cabinet was reorganized, with the Planning Ministry, which had "supervised" the economy, being eliminated. The action, along with others to give more autonomy to state-owned farms and nationalized industries, was seen as a comprehensive attempt to break with the "socialist revolution" of the late Houari Boumedienne.

POLITICAL PARTIES

Government Party:

National Liberation Front (*Front de Libération Nationale*—FLN). Founded November 1, 1954, and dedicated to socialism, nonalignment, and pan-Arabism, the FLN successfully conducted the war of independence against France but was subsequently weakened by antagonism between moderate and radical factions and by disputes over the role of the army in political affairs. The highest party organ is the FLN Congress, which convenes in ordinary session every five years and to which a Central Committee (currently 160 members) is responsible. At an extraordinary congress held June 15–19, 1980, at Algiers and attended by 3,993 delegates (including 800 from the armed forces), the Central Committee's Political Bureau was reduced in size from 17–21 members to 7–11 members, all to be nominated by President Chadli in his capacity as FLN secretary general. On June 29, the president named 7 persons, broadly representative of the party's factions, to the body; its membership was increased to 10 in 1981, but again declined to 9, exclusive of 5 alternates, at the fifth party congress in January 1984.

Secretary General: Col. Bendjedid CHADLI (President of the Republic).

Other Members of Politburo: Col. Mohamed Ben Ahmed ABDELGHANI, Boualem BAKI, Col. Abdallah BELHOUCHET, Boualem BENHAMOUDA, Rabah BITAT, Dr. Ahmed Taleb IBRAHIMI, Mohamed Cherif MESSAADIA, Mohamed Hadj YALA.

Alternates: Mustafa BENLOUCIF, Cmdt. Rachid BENYELLES, Abdelhamid BRAHIMI, Abdallah KHALAF (alias Col. Kasdi Merbah), Bachir ROUIS.

Proscribed Parties:

Movement for Democracy in Algeria (*Mouvement pour la Démocratie d'Algérie*—MDA). The MDA was formed in May 1984 by former president Ahmed Ben Bella (released in 1979 after 14 years of prison and house arrest), its expressed purpose being to "achieve pluralism and begin Algeria's apprenticeship in democracy". The founding congress of the new party was held at an unspecified location in France, where Ben Bella himself resided, although insisting that most of the leadership would be based in Algeria. In December 1985 Ben Bella and Hocine Aït-Ahmed, an ally in the Algerian revolution but subsequently a political opponent, announced in London that they had formed a "united front" to oppose the FLN, which they charged with depriving Algerians of basic rights.

Leader: Ahmed BEN BELLA.

Several parties, all outlawed and most operating from exile, exert only minimal political influence. These include the predominantly Berber **Socialist Forces Front** (*Front des Forces Socialistes*—FFS) and a pro-Soviet Communist group, the **Socialist Vanguard Party** (*Parti de l'Avant-Garde Socialiste*—PAGS).

Sahrawi Front:

Popular Front for the Liberation of Saguia el Hamra and Rio de Oro (*Frente Popular para la Liberación de Saguia el Hamra y Rio de Oro*—Polisario). Established in 1973 to win independence for Spanish (subsequently Western) Sahara, the Polisario Front was initially based in Mauritania, but since the mid-1970s its political leadership has operated from Algeria. Collateral with Spain's withdrawal from the disputed territory in February 1976, Polisario proclaimed a Saharan Arab Democratic Republic (SADR), but the area was annexed by Mauritania and Morocco. When the former concluded a peace agreement with the Front in August 1979, Rabat quickly laid claim to the entire Western Sahara. (For additional background, see the discussion under Morocco: Annexed Territory). Although rumors surfaced in late 1980 that Algeria was conducting secret negotiations with Morocco to resolve their differences, there was no subsequent evidence that Algiers had lessened its support for the Polisario cause. At Polisario's Sixth Congress, held December 7–9, 1985, somewhere "in liberated territories", the Front's Political Bureau was expanded from 25 to 27 members, while the seven members of the Executive Committee were reelected.

Secretary General: Mohamed 'ABD AL-AZZIZ (President of the SADR).

Other Members of Politburo Executive Committee: Mohamed Lamine OULD AHMED (Prime Minister of the SADR), Mohamed Amin OULD BAHALI, Ibrahim GHALI, Ayyub HABIB, Bachir Mustapha SAYED, Mahfuz Ali TIBAH.

LEGISLATURE

The unicameral **People's National Assembly** (*Assemblée Nationale Populaire*) currently consists of 295 members serving five-year terms. At the most recent election of February 26, 1987, deputies were selected from a list of 885 candidates (3 for every seat) which had been drawn up by the National Liberation Front.

President: Rabah BITAT.

CABINET

Prime Minister	Abdelhamid Brahimi
Minister of State for the Presidency	Mohamed Ben Ahmed Abdelghani
Ministers	
Agriculture	Mohamed Rouighi
Commerce	Mohand Amokrane Cherifi

Culture and Tourism	Col. Boualem Bessaieh
Education and Training	Mostefa Benamar
Energy, Chemical and	
Petrochemical Industries	Belkacem Nabi
Finance	Abdelazziz Khellef
Foreign Affairs	Dr. Ahmed Taleb Ibrahimi
Heavy Industry	Faysal Boudraa
Higher Education	Aboubaker Belkaid
Hydraulics, Forests and	
Fishing	Ahmed Benfreha
Information	Bachir Rouis
Interior and Localities	El-Hadi Khediri
Justice	Mohamed Cherif Kherroubi
Labor and Social Affairs	Mohamed Nabi
Light Industry	Zitouni Messaoudi
National Defense	Col. Bendjedid Chadli
Posts and	
Telecommunications	Mustafa Benzaza
Public Health	Col. Kasdi Merbah
Public Works	Aissa Abdellaoui
Regional Development,	
Town Planning and	
Construction	Abdel Malek Nourani
Religious Affairs	Boualem Baki
Transportation	Gen. Rachid Benyelles
Veterans	Mohamed Djeghaba
Youth and Sports	Abdelhak Rafik Bererhi
Governor, Central Bank	Badredine Nouioua

NEWS MEDIA

Press. Both national and foreign press activities are subject to strict government control. The following are dailies published at El Djazaire (Algiers) unless otherwise noted: *el-Moudjahid* (395,000), FLN organ in French; *Algérie Actualité* (240,000), government weekly in French; *an-Nasr* (Qacentina, 120,000), in Arabic; *el-Massa* (100,000), in Arabic; *Horizons 2000* (100,000), in French; *al-Chaab* (80,000), government information journal in Arabic; *al-Jumhuriyah* (Wahran, 70,000), FLN organ in Arabic.

News agencies. The domestic agency is *Algérie Presse Service* (APS). A number of foreign agencies maintain offices at Algiers.

Radio and television. The government-controlled *Radiodiffusion Télévision Algérienne* (RTA) maintains a television network (*Télévision Algérie*) servicing about a dozen stations, and four radio networks; broadcasts were received by about 1.6 million TV and 3.6 million radio receivers in 1987.

INTERGOVERNMENTAL REPRESENTATION

Ambassador to the US: Mohamed SAHNOUN.

US Ambassador to Algeria: L. Craig JOHNSTONE.

Permanent Representative to the UN: Hocine DJOUDI.

IGO Memberships (Non-UN): ADF, AfDB, AFESD, AMF, APEF, BADEA, CCC, *EIB,* IC, IDB, ILZ, Inmarsat, Intelsat, Interpol, IOOC, IWTC, LAS, NAM, OAPEC, OAU, OPEC.

ANDORRA

Valleys of Andorra
Valls d'Andorrà (Catalan)
Les Vallées d'Andorre (French)
Principado de Andorra (Spanish)

Political Status: Co-Principality under joint suzerainty of the President of the French Republic and the Spanish Bishop of Urgel.

Area: 180 sq. mi. (467 sq. km.).

Population: 30,600 (1979C), 51,000 (1988E).

Major Urban Center (1985E): ANDORRA LA VELLA (16,600).

Official Language: Catalan (French and Spanish are also used).

Monetary Units: There is no local currency. The French franc and the Spanish peseta are both in circulation.

French Co-Prince: François Maurice MITTERRAND; became Co-Prince May 21, 1981, upon inauguration as President of the French Republic.
    Permanent French Delegate: Maurice JOUBERT.
    Viguier de France: Louis DEBLE.

Spanish Episcopal Co-Prince: Mgr. Joan MARTI y Alanís; became Co-Prince January 31, 1971, upon induction as Bishop of Seo de Urgel.
    Permanent Episcopal Delegate: Nemesi MARQUES Oste.
    Vegeur Episcopal: Francesc BADIA Batalla.

Syndic General: Fransesc CERQUEDA i Pascuet; elected by the General Council on January 4, 1982; reelected on January 10, 1986.

Head of Government (*Cap del Govern*): Josep PINTAT Solens; appointed by the General Council on May 21, 1984, following the resignation of Oscar RIBAS Reig on April 30; reappointed on January 10, 1986.

THE COUNTRY

A rough, mountainous country of limited dimensions, Andorra is set in a large drainage area of the Pyrenees between France and Spain. The main stream is the Riu Valira, which has two branches and six open basins. It is from this peculiar geographic configuration that the country derives its name. The approximately 15,000 indigenous residents are of Catalan stock but are now substantially outnumbered by more than 29,000 Spaniards, 3,000 Frenchmen, and 4,000 others. Virtually all of the inhabitants are Roman Catholic. The traditional mainstays of the economy were farming and animal husbandry, but tourism and the transshipment of goods are presently the most important sources of income. Most trade is with Spain and France, the main exports being foodstuffs, cattle, timber, and such manufactured goods as furniture and tobacco products; in addition, Andorra's status as a duty-free principality led, prior to the admission of Spain to the European Community (EC), to a certain amount of smuggling between her neighbors. Most of the power produced by the hydroelectric plant at Les Escaldes is exported to southern France and the Spanish province of Barcelona.

GOVERNMENT AND POLITICS

Political background. The unique political structure of Andorra dates from 1278, when an agreement on joint suzerainty (a *paréage*) was reached between the French count of Foix, whose right ultimately passed to the president of the French Republic, and the Spanish bishop of the nearby See of Urgel. The first personal meeting between co-princes since 1278 occurred on August 25, 1973, when President Georges POMPIDOU and Bishop Joan MARTI y Alanís met at Cahors, France, to discuss matters affecting the future of the Principality, while on October 19, 1978, President Valéry GISCARD D'ESTAING and Mgr. Martí y Alanís attended 700th anniversary ceremonies at Andorra la Vella.

On December 29, 1978, the General Council elected as chief executive officer (*syndic procureur général*) Estanislau SANGRA Font, an independent from the parish of Les Escaldes-Engordany, to succeed the two-term first syndic, Julià REIG Ribo, who was ineligible for reelection. The defeat of Carlos RIBAS Reig, a nephew of the outgoing first syndic, by a 12–11 vote meant that for the first time in over a century Andorra's chief executive was not resident in the parish of Sant Julià de Lòria.

Under new constitutional arrangements (see below) that included, on December 9, 1981, the Principality's first nonstaggered legislative election, the General Council, on January 8, 1982, named another Reig nephew, Oscar RIBAS Reig, to a four-year term as Andorra's first head of government. Ribas Reig resigned on April 30, 1984, as the result of a lengthy dispute over tax policy, the Council electing Joseph PINTAT Solens as his successor on May 21. Pintat Solens was redesignated on January 10, 1986, following a general election on December 12, 1985.

Constitution and government. Andorra does not have a written constitution, and the rights of the co-princes vis-à-vis local political institutions have never been conclusively established. As joint suzerains, the French president and the bishop of Urgel are represented respectively by the prefect of the French department of Pyrenees-Orientales and the vicar general of the Urgel diocese. Their resident representatives in Andorra bear the titles of *viguier de France* and *veguer Episcopal*.

Prior to 1981, no clear definition of powers existed, legislative and some administrative authority being exercised, subject to the approval of the co-princes, by the General Council of the Valleys, a 28-member assembly encompassing 4 representatives from each of the Principality's present seven parishes, the former joint parish of Andorra La Vella and Les Escaldes-Engordany (which together accounted for 70 percent of the population) having been divided into separate parishes in June 1978. Under a Political Reform Law approved after a stormy legislative debate in November 1981, a head of government (*cap del govern*) was, for the first time, created, while the former first and second syndics were redesignated as syndic general (chairman) and sub-syndic (sub-chairman) of the General Council, with the *syndic général* remaining, by protocol, the higher-ranked official. Legislators were formerly elected every two years for staggered four-year terms; under the 1981 reform, the Council as a whole sits for four years, designating the head of government (who appoints an Executive Council of up to six members) for a like term.

Women were enfranchised in 1970 and in 1973 were permitted to stand for public office. Second-generation Andorrans were allowed to vote in 1971 and first-generation Andorrans over the age of 28 were accorded a similar right in 1977.

The judicial structure is relatively simple. The *viguiers* each appoint two civil judges (*battles*), while an appeals judge is appointed alternately by each co-prince. Final appeal is either to the Supreme Court at Perpignan, France, or to the Ecclesiastical Court of the Bishop of Seo de Urgel, Spain. Criminal law is administered by the *Tribunal de Corts,* consisting of the *battles,* the appeals judge, the *viguiers,* and two members of the General Council (*parladors*).

Local government functions at the district level through parish councils, whose members are selected by universal suffrage. At the lower levels there are *communs* and *corts.* The former are ten-member bodies elected by universal suffrage; the latter are submunicipal advisory bodies that function primarily as administrators of communal property.

Foreign relations. President Pompidou and Bishop Martí y Alanís agreed in 1973 that Andorra could send indigenous representatives to international meetings. However, the understanding was subsequently repudiated by President Giscard d'Estaing, and the Principality's external relations continue to be handled largely by France. A recent exception was the participation of an Andorran delegation at a conference of French and Spanish Pyrenean regions held at Jaca, Spain, under the auspices of the Council of Europe on June 7–10, 1982.

On January 1, 1986, Spain joined France as a member of the European Community. A determination of Andorra's status in regard to the EC had not been made as of early 1988.

Current issues. In the wake of the 1981 changes (enacted in accordance with a decree issued by the co-princes on January 15), further reforms, particularly in regard to electoral procedure, were to have been submitted to the voters in a nonbinding referendum scheduled for January 14, 1982. In part because of appeals from radical quarters that favored the introduction of "authentic democracy", the balloting was postponed until May 28, when a plurality of 42.2 percent of participating voters approved the introduction of a system of proportional representation at both the national and parish levels. For a number of reasons, including a 48 percent absention rate and the fact that voters in all but the two largest parishes favored retention of the existing system, the co-princes have not yet acted on the "consultation".

In August 1983, the Ribas Reig administration introduced a wide-ranging tax bill to alleviate recurrent budgetary deficits and resigned in April 1984 because of the Council's failure to approve the legislation. The underlying justification for the bill stemmed from what has been termed an "ultracapitalist economy" in an "ultrafeudalistic state", where there is no penal code, no domestic customs bureau, no land registry, uncontrolled speculation in real estate, and unregulated foreign-owned companies and banks that reportedly engage in the laundering of various European currencies. This issue also has not yet been resolved.

Prior to the 1985 election, the voting age was lowered to 18. As a result, a group of younger, more progressive individuals (*Los Jóvenes*) entered the political arena, who did not, however, secure representation in the General Council. Although formerly a member of the Council, Pintat Solens did not seek reelection in 1985, such affiliation not being a requirement for designation as head of government.

POLITICAL PARTIES

Although political parties are technically illegal, an Andorran Democratic Association (*Agrupament Democràtic Andorrà* – ADA) was organized in 1976 as a merger of former moderate and "Democracy and Progress" groupings within the General Council. The ADA campaigned actively against the "intransigence" of the co-princes' commitment to the existing system of representation at the election of December 14, 1977, and sponsored referenda proposals calling for national elections on the basis of proportional representation. In 1979 the ADA was reorganized as the **Andorran Democratic Party** (*Partit Demòcrata Andorrà* – PDA), which urged abstention at the 1981 balloting. Also calling for a boycott of the 1981 election was a previously unknown "independentist" group, **Free Andorra** (*Andorrà Lliure*).

All members of the present Council are essentially conservative, supporters of Ribas Reig reportedly being drawn largely from the banking and tobacco sectors, those of Sangrà Font from tourism and real estate, and those of the present *cap del govern* from commerce.

LEGISLATURE

The **General Council of the Valleys** (*El Consell General de las Valls d'Andorrà*) is a unicameral body consisting of 28 members (4 each from 7 parishes) elected for four-year terms. At the most recent election of December 12, 1985, the group headed by Oscar Ribas won 16 seats, while those headed by Josep Pintat and Estanislau Sangrà obtained 6 seats each.

Syndic General: Francesc CERQUEDA i Pascuet.
Sub-Syndic: Antoni GARRALLA Rossell.

CABINET

Head of Government	Josep Pintat Solans
Councillors	
Agriculture, Commerce and Industry	Luís Molné Armengol
Education and Culture	Roc Rossell Dolcet
Finance	Bonaventura Riberaygua Miquel
Public Services	Merçé Sansá Renyé
Social Welfare	Magi Maestre Campderos
Tourism and Sports	Josep Miño Guitart

Secretaries General	
Tourism and Sports	Montserrat Roncheras Santacreu
Finance	Jordi Aleix Camp

NEWS MEDIA

Press. Joining French and Spanish newspapers, which have long circulated in Andorra, the weekly *Poble Andorrà* (3,000) began publication at Andorra la Vella in 1974.

Radio and television. In 1981 the question of control over Andorran airwaves resulted in the government ordering the Principality's two radio stations, the French-owned *Sud-Radio* and the commercial, privately owned Spanish *Radio Andorra*, off the air. The dispute arose over the co-princes' refusal to permit effective nationalization of the broadcast facilities, which had extensive audiences in both France and Spain. Under a compromise approved by the General Council in September, the right of the Andorran people to operate (but not necessarily own) radio stations was acknowledged, and the General Council was granted full sovereignty over any stations broadcasting solely within Andorra. In February 1983, an Andorran-owned public radio and television facility, the *Entitat Nacional Andorrana de Radiodifusio* (ENAR) was established to provide broadcasting services pending resolution of the dispute with the French and Spanish companies.

As of 1987, there were approximately 8,000 radio and 4,000 television receivers in use.

INTERGOVERNMENTAL REPRESENTATION

Andorra does not send or receive ambassadors and, although a member of UNESCO and Interpol, is not a participant in any other major treaty or intergovernment organization. Most of its quite limited foreign relations are conducted through the French co-prince.

ANGOLA

People's Republic of Angola
República Popular de Angola

Political Status: Formally independent upon the departure of the Portuguese High Commissioner on November 10, 1975; government of the Popular Movement for the Liberation of Angola (MPLA) recognized by the Organization of African Unity on February 11, 1976.

Area: 481,351 sq. mi. (1,246,700 sq. km.).

Population: 5,646,166 (1970C), 8,665,000 (1988E). The results of a census begun in 1982 have not yet been announced and some estimates for 1985 were in excess of 8.7 million.

Major Urban Centers (1983E): LUANDA (urban area, 1,250,000); Huambo (90,000); Lobito (75,000); Benguela (50,000).

Official Language: Portuguese (most Angolans speak tribal languages).

Monetary Unit: Kwanza (official rate March 1, 1988, 29.92 kwanza = $1US).

President and Head of Government: José Eduardo dos SANTOS; designated by the Central Committee of the Popular Liberation Movement of Angola–Party of Labor (MPLA-PT) and sworn in September 21, 1979, following the death of Dr. Antônio Agostinho NETO on September 10; confirmed by an extraordinary congress of the MPLA-PT on December 17, 1980; reconfirmed on December 9, 1985.

THE COUNTRY

The largest of Portugal's former African possessions, Angola is located on the Atlantic south of the Congo River. The greater part of its territory is bounded on the north and east by Zaire, on the southeast by Zambia, and on the south by Namibia (South West Africa). It also includes the small exclave of Cabinda in the northwest (bordered by the Congo Republic and Zaire), where important offshore oil deposits are being exploited. The overwhelming proportion of Angola's people are Bantus, who comprise four distinct tribal groups: the Bakongo in the northwest, the Kimbundu in the north-central region inland from Luanda, the Ovimbundu in the south-central region, and the Chokwe in eastern Angola. No native language is universally spoken, Portuguese being the only tongue not confined to a specific tribal area.

While no specific data on female economic participation are available, women have traditionally experienced equality with men in subsistence activities, and their role in agriculture has expanded in recent years due to male employment in the petroleum industry. While women currently hold 14 percent of the seats in the National People's Assembly, with several who were active in the independence struggle holding high government and party positions, overall female influence is minimal.

The port of Lobito, because of its rail links with Zaire, Zambia, Zimbabwe, Mozambique, and South Africa, served as a leading outlet for much of Central Africa's mineral wealth until independence was declared in 1975. Since then, civil war has crippled the Benguela Railway and devastated much of the formerly prosperous economy, including the export of diamonds and coffee. Guerrilla activity has resulted in massive migration of peasant farmers to cities or neighboring countries and, despite its potential as a breadbasket for southern Africa, Angola relies heavily on food imports to stave off widespread famine. Black market activity flourishes with the local currency having become nearly worthless. Although the government has attempted to stimulate the economy by reducing state control over industry and agriculture, its efforts are hampered by corruption, bureaucratic inefficiency, and the allocation of more than half of its revenue to military expenditure. Only oil, of which Angola is the second leading sub-Saharan exporter, keeps the economy afloat, generating more than 85 percent of revenue and attracting private foreign investment despite US support for antigovernment forces.

GOVERNMENT AND POLITICS

Political background. Portuguese settlements were established in eastern Angola in the late fifteenth century by navigators seeking trade routes to India, but the territory's present boundaries were not formally established until the Berlin Conference of 1884–1885. In 1951 the colony of Angola became an Overseas Province of Portugal and was thus construed as being an integral part of the Portuguese state.

Guerrilla opposition to colonial rule broke out in 1961 and continued for 13 years, despite a sizable Portuguese military presence. At the time of the 1974 coup in Lisbon, there were three principal independence movements operating in different parts of Angola. The National Front for the Liberation of Angola (FNLA), which had established a government-in-exile in Zaire in 1963 under the leadership of Holden ROBERTO, controlled much of the north. The Soviet-backed Popular Movement for the Liberation of Angola (MPLA), led by Dr. Agostinho NETO, controlled much of the central region plus Cabinda. The third group, the National Union for the Total Independence of Angola (UNITA), operated in eastern and southern Angola under the leadership of Dr. Jonas SAVIMBI. On January 15, 1975, the three leaders signed an agreement with Portuguese representatives calling for the independence of Angola on November 11, 1975 (the 400th anniversary of the founding of Luanda). The pact provided for interim rule by a Portuguese high commissioner and a Presidential Collegiate consisting of one representative from each of the three liberation movements. During succeeding months, however, the FNLA and UNITA formed a tacit alliance against the MPLA, whose forces at the time of independence controlled the capital. On November 10 the Portuguese high commissioner departed after a brief ceremony at Luanda, and at midnight Dr. Neto announced the establishment, under MPLA auspices, of the People's Republic of Angola. On November 23 the FNLA-UNITA announced the formation of a rival Democratic People's Republic of Angola, with the central highlands city of Huambo (formerly Nova Lisboa) as its capital.

By late November some two dozen nations had recognized the MPLA government, although the Organization of African Unity had urged all countries to withhold recognition until formation of a coalition government. Meanwhile, Cuba had dispatched upwards of 18,000 troops in support of the MPLA, while both Uganda and Zaire had threatened to break diplomatic relations with the Soviet Union because of its involvement in the Angolan war. The revelation that American money and equipment were being channeled to FNLA forces through Zaire posed the additional risk of a US-Soviet confrontation. By late December the Cuban troops, equipped with Soviet armored vehicles and rocket launchers, had helped turn the tide in favor of the MPLA, and some 4,000–5,000 South African troops operating in support of the Huambo regime were substantially withdrawn a month later. In early February 1976 the MPLA launched a southern offensive that resulted in the capture of Huambo and other key cities, prompting declarations by the FNLA and UNITA that their forces would henceforth resort to guerrilla warfare. On February 11 the Organization of African Unity announced that the MPLA government had been admitted to membership, following formal recognition of the Neto regime by a majority of OAU member states.

Although the FNLA and UNITA continued to resist government and Cuban forces during 1976–1978 and announced in early 1979 the formation of a joint military force, it appeared that Roberto's FNLA forces had been virtually annihilated in the north and that only UNITA was offering organized opposition to the Luanda regime.

On September 10, 1979, President Neto died at Moscow, USSR, where he had been undergoing medical treatment, and on September 21 was succeeded as chief of state, head of government, MPLA-PT chairman, and commander in chief by Minister of Planning José Eduardo dos SANTOS.

In September 1984 the remaining 1,500 guerrillas and 20,000 civilian members of Comira (*Conselho Militar por Resistancia de Angola*), which had been founded by former FNLA members, surrendered to the Luanda government under a 1979 amnesty provision, its military members being integrated into the MPLA forces. The demise of the movement long led by Holden Roberto left the South Africa-supported UNITA as the only substantial domestic threat to Luanda.

Constitution and government. Under the 1975 constitution as amended, the government is headed by a president who also serves as chairman of the MPLA-PT. In the event of presidential disability, the MPLA-PT Central Committee is authorized to designate an interim successor, thus reinforcing the role of the party as the people's "legitimate representative". In December 1978 the positions of prime minister and deputy prime minister were abolished, while in November 1980 the legislative Council of the Revolution was replaced as the "supreme organ of state power" by a National People's Assembly, whose members are indirectly designated at meetings of locally elected provincial delegates. Prior to the 1980 national and provincial elections, suffrage was extended to all adults except criminals and those "who are active members of factionalist, puppet groups" (i.e., the FNLA and UNITA), although the system had not been completely implemented by 1986 because of continued insurgency and a lack of adequate census information.

The country is divided into 18 provinces (*províncias*) administered by centrally appointed commissioners, with legislative authority vested in provincial assemblies. The provinces are further divided into councils (*concelhos*), communes (*comunas*), circles (*círculos*), neighborhoods (*bairros*), and villages (*povoações*).

Foreign relations. On June 23, 1976, the United States exercised its right of veto in the Security Council to block Angolan admission to the United Nations. The stated reason for the action was the continued presence in Angola of a sizable Cuban military force. On November 19, however, the United States reversed itself, citing "the appeals of its African friends", and Angola was admitted on December 1. Senegal, the last Black African state to withhold recognition of the MPLA-PT government, announced the establishment of diplomatic relations with Angola in February 1982, while the People's Republic of China, long an opponent of the Soviet-supportive regime, established relations in late 1983.

Relations with Portugal were suspended briefly in late 1976 and remained relatively cool prior to a June 1978 agreement providing for the mutual repatriation of Angolan and Portuguese nationals. More recently, relations have again been strained by allegations of Portuguese-based exile support for UNITA rebels, although efforts have been made to restore previously substantial trade links between the two countries.

Relations have fluctuated with neighboring Zaire, which charged the Neto government with providing support for rebel incursions into Shaba (formerly Katanga) Province in March 1977 and May 1978. Shortly thereafter, President Mobutu agreed to end his support for anti-MPLA forces based in Zaire, in return for a similar pledge from President Neto in regard to Zairian dissidents operating from Angola. In October 1979 a more extensive trilateral non-aggression pact was signed at Ndola, Zambia, by the presidents of Angola, Zaire, and Zambia. Despite these agreements and a Kinshasa-Luanda security pact signed in early 1985, sporadic accusations of Zairian support for Angolan insurgents have continued to issue from Luanda (see Current issues, below).

In the south, Luanda's support for the South West African People's Organisation (SWAPO), which has operated from Angolan bases since the mid-1970s, has resulted in numerous cross-border raids by South African defense forces deployed in Namibia. On the other hand, despite periodic encouragement of UNITA and an unwillingness to establish formal relations prior to the withdrawal of Cuban troops, both the Carter and Reagan administrations have made overtures to Luanda, citing the need for Angolan involvement in the Namibian independence process. In early 1985, statements by dos Santos indicating a willingness to negotiate on Cuban troop withdrawal were cited by Washington as evidence of its "constructive engagement" policy in southern Africa; however, all contacts were suspended by Angola later in the year following US congressional repeal of the "Clark Amendment" banning military aid to the insurgents, with repeated military activity by Pretoria having already reduced Luanda's willingness to negotiate. Relations with Washington deteriorated further in 1986, following a US decision to give UNITA $15 million in military aid, including ground-to-air missiles.

Current issues. By late 1987, amid growing evidence of a military standoff, attention again focused on the possibility of a negotiated settlement of the protracted civil war. Talks with Washington resumed at mid-year despite the Reagan administration's pro-UNITA posture. "Careful consideration" was reportedly being given to a Luandan peace place that offered "flexibility" in regard to the Cuban troop presence, assuming withdrawal of South African troops from southern Angola and progress in resolution of the Namibian question. However, the government continued to reject, at least in its official statements, the idea of a direct political settlement with UNITA.

For his part, UNITA's Savimbi suggested negotiations might lead to normalization of Benguela rail traffic, which would substantially benefit the Angolan economy and boost efforts by neighboring African countries to reduce dependence on trade routes through South Africa. In April, presidents Kaunda of Zambia and Mobutu of Zaire joined dos Santos in declaring their intent to rehabilitate the railway at a projected cost of $280 million. Nonetheless, relations with Kinshasa remained tense, with Luanda charging that Zaire had become the main conduit for US arms to UNITA. Despite Mobutu's denials, observers noted the continued shift of UNITA operations from southern and eastern provinces to northern provinces bordered by Zaire. Possibly linked to the shift, South Africa stepped up its troop deployment in the southern provinces. Often heavy fighting did little to alter the military balance. UNITA continued to prevail in much of the countryside, while government forces, equipped with a new supply of Soviet arms, maintained control of the cities, in addition to vital oil-producing areas and diamond mines. The wave of displaced persons, "fleeing both sides" according to one report, spread into neighboring countries, with international relief agencies attempting to supply those that remained with food via air drops.

In economic affairs, the dos Santos administration pursued privatization measures, hoping that cooperation with foreign corporations, successful in the oil industry, could be extended to diamond mining and coffee production. Acknowledging the ongoing inefficiency of the economy, dos Santos said Angola would apply for membership in the International Monetary Fund. The government also mounted a campaign to broaden its Third World ties, particularly in Latin America, where Brazil had emerged as a leading trade partner.

POLITICAL PARTIES

Government Party:

Popular Liberation Movement of Angola–Party of Labor (*Movimento Popular de Libertação de Angola–Partido Trabalhista* — MPLA-PT). Organized in 1956, the Soviet-backed MPLA provided the primary resistance to Portuguese colonial rule in central Angola prior to independence. During its first national congress, held at Luanda on December 4–11, 1977, the party was formally restructured along Marxist-Leninist lines and redesignated as the MPLA-Labor Party. At the party's second congress in December 1985, a new Central Committee, with membership increased to 90, was elected. The committee subsequently selected a Political Bureau of 11 full and 2 alternate members, as well as an 8-member Secretariat. Several longstanding members were dropped from the former, reportedly to strengthen the position of dos Santos who was elected to a further five-year term as party chairman.

Reflecting the dos Santos administration's increasingly pragmatic approach to economic problems, the congress adopted a resolution promoting several "Western-style" reforms, without, however, altering its alliance with Cuba and the Soviet Union and its hostility to the United States and South Africa regarding the UNITA insurgency. By late 1987, on the other hand, dos Santos appeared to have solid party backing for his pursuit of a settlement with Washington and Pretoria that aimed at reducing "external involvement" in the civil war.

Leader: José Eduardo dos SANTOS (President of the Republic and Chairman of the Party).

Insurgent Groups:

National Union for the Total Independence of Angola (*União Nacional para a Independência Total de Angola* — UNITA). Active primarily in southern Angola prior to the Portuguese withdrawal, UNITA joined with the FNLA (below) in establishing an abortive rival government at Huambo in November 1975 and since early 1976 has been engaged in guerrilla operations against Luanda. Although its ideology is of Maoist derivation, the party's image within Black Africa has suffered because of US and South African military assistance. In late 1982 UNITA leader Savimbi asserted that no basic ideological differences separated UNITA and the MPLA-PT, and that the removal of all Cuban troops would lead to negotiations with the government. Although, his subsequent avowals of "anti-communism" and increased solicitation of aid from Pretoria and Washington reportedly generated internal dissent, Savimbi, drawing strength from his Ovimbundu ethnic group, has remained in strong control. During a much-publicized visit to Washington in 1986 he was accorded treatment normally reserved for heads of state and his successful solicitation of US arms has greatly enhanced UNITA's military strength and negotiating position.

Leaders: Dr. Jonas SAVIMBI (President), Jeremiah CHITUNDA (Vice President), Miguel N'Zau PUNA (Secretary General).

Most other insurgent formations appear now to be dormant. The National Front for the Liberation of Angola (*Frente Nacional de Libertação de Angola* — FNLA), which had been active since 1962 in northern Angola, was consistently the most anticommunist of the resistance groups until the collapse of its forces in the late 1970s. Longtime FNLA leader Holden Roberto, having been expelled from Zaire in 1979 (and apparently from Senegal and Gabon shortly thereafter), was subsequently granted political asylum in France, from whence a group of dissidents announced in September 1980 that the FNLA apparatus had been dismantled in favor of a Military Council for Angolan Resistance (*Conselho Militar por Resistancia de Angola* — Comira) to continue operations against the MPLA-PT. While the official Angolan News Agency claimed in December 1981 that some 2,000 Comira guerrillas were being trained by mercenaries from Zaire, it appeared by late 1984 that most of its leaders had surrendered to government forces.

Following Washington's 1986 decision to increase its military aid to UNITA, Roberto appeared before a US congressional panel seeking, without apparent success, similar support for a rejuvenation of FNLA activity. Late in the year, another prominent FNLA leader, Daniel CHIPENDA, who had been living in exile at Lisbon since 1979, declared his support for the government.

Formerly headquartered at Kinshasa, Zaire, the Front for the Liberation of the Cabinda Enclave (*Frente de Libertação do Enclave de Cabinda* — FLEC) was initially affiliated with the FNLA. Founded in 1963, it split in 1975 into rival factions headed by Luis Ranque Franque and Henrique N'Zita Tiago (who was killed in December 1979 during a clash with Cuban troops). In November 1977 a splinter group styling itself the Military Command for the Liberation of Cabinda was organized, while on June 1, 1979, the Armed Forces for the Liberation of Cabinda established another splinter, the **Popular Movement for the Liberation of Cabinda** (*Movimento Popular de Libertação de Cabinda* — MPLC), which charged FLEC with "irresponsible and overtly imperialist acts". A **Movement for the Liberation of Cabinda** (*Movimento de Libertação de Cabinda* — Molica) had been formed earlier, but the status of it and the other FLEC splinters is presently unclear.

Other Groups:

During 1987, foreign press sources reported the activities of several minor opposition groups, including the **Democratic Independents,** described as conducting a campaign to end the civil war and free political prisoners, and the hitherto unknown **Movement for Socialist Unity in Angola,** members of which were said to have been imprisoned for their activity. In addition, **Unangola,** a Lisbon-based expatriate formation headed by André Franco de SOUSA, was reported to be urging negotiations between UNITA and the MPLA-PT as well as peace talks with South Africa.

LEGISLATURE

In accordance with the 1975 constitution, as amended, a 223-member **National People's Assembly** (*Assembléia Nacional Popular*) with a three-year term of office was elected in 1980 as successor to the Council of the Revolution, which had served as a legislature since formation of the Republic. Subsequent balloting was deferred until late 1986, when the legislative term was extended to five years and the number of deputies increased to 289. The list of candidates, all members of the MPLA-PT, was drawn up by the Assembly's Permanent Commission. The new Assembly convened on January 30, 1987.

First Secretary: Lucio LARA.

CABINET

President	José Eduardo dos Santos

Ministers of State

Economic and Social Affairs	José Eduardo dos Santos
Inspection and State Control	Kundi Paihama
Production and Economic Coordination	Lt. Col. Pedro de Castro Van Dúnem ("Loy")

Ministers

Agriculture and Forestry	Fernando Faustino Muteka
Construction and Housing	João García (Cabelo Branco)
Defense	Col. Pedro Maria Tonha
Education	Augusto Lopes Teixeira
External Relations	Alfonso Van Dúnem
Finance	Augusto Teixeira de Matos
Fisheries	Francisco José Ramos Da Cruz
Foreign Trade	Domingo Das Chagas Simoes Rangel
Health	António José Ferreira Neto
Industry	Henrique de Carvalho dos Santos
Interior	Lt. Col. Manuel Alexandre Duarte Rodrigues
Internal Trade	Joaquim Guerreiro Dias
Justice	Fernando Franca Van Dúnem
Labor and Social Security	Diogo Jorge de Jesus
Petroleum and Energy	Lt. Col. Pedro de Castro Van Dúnem
Planning	António Henriques da Silva
Provincial Coordination	(Vacant)
State Security	José Eduardo dos Santos
Transport and Communications	Carlos António Fernandes
Governor, National Bank	António Inácio

NEWS MEDIA

Press. Since nationalization of the press in 1976, the government has required all news disseminated by the media to conform to official policy. The following are Portuguese-language dailies published at Luanda: *Jornal de Angola* (40,000), official newspaper; *Diário da República* (8,500), government news sheet.

News agencies. The domestic facility is the government-operated Angolan News Agency (Angop). *Agence France-Presse,* Cuba's *Prensa Latina,* and some East European agencies also maintain offices at Luanda.

Radio and television. The principal broadcasting services are *Radio Nacional de Angola* and *Televisão Popular de Angola,* both controlled by the government. There were 410,000 radio receivers in 1987. Television service, which was introduced in 1976, broadcasts on a limited basis to some 33,000 receivers.

INTERGOVERNMENTAL REPRESENTATION

There are at present no diplomatic relations between Angola and the United States.

Permanent Representative to the UN: Manuel Pedro PACAVIRA.

IGO Memberships (Non-UN): ADF, AfDB, BADEA, IACO, ICCAT, ICO, Intelsat, Interpol, NAM, OAU, SADCC.

ANTARCTICA

Political Status: Normally uninhabited territory, subject to overlapping claims of national sovereignty that remain in suspense under provisions of Antarctic Treaty signed December 1, 1959.

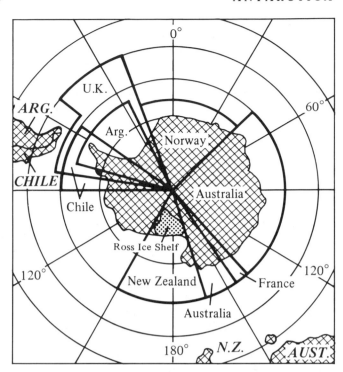

Area: 4,826,000 sq. mi. (12,500,000 sq. km.).

Population: A transient population of some 3,000 (during the Antarctic summer) is maintained by various nations operating research stations under terms of the Antarctic Treaty.

Political Institutions: None.

Political background. The most isolated and inhospitable of the world's continents, Antarctica remained outside the mainstream of exploration and colonial exploitation until the early twentieth century. Captain Cook first sailed south of the Antarctic Circle in 1773, and in the following century coastal areas were visited by ships from such countries as Britain, France, Russia, and the United States. Between 1900 and 1914 the interior of the continent was penetrated by Amundsen (the first, in 1911, to reach the South Pole), Scott, Shackleton, Mawson, and others. This era saw the first territorial claims and the start of commercial Antarctic whaling. Competition for Antarctic territory increased in the interwar decades, while scientific exploration was aided by new technology, chiefly the airplane. Contention over territorial claims was further intensified during and after World War II, but the coming of the International Geophysical Year (1957–1958) brought the beginnings of a new, cooperative, nonpolitical approach to Antarctic problems.

Territorial claims. Prior to the conclusion of the Antarctic Treaty of 1959, the political geography of Antarctica followed the conventional nineteenth-century pattern of national claims to sovereignty over areas largely unexplored and unsettled. Such claims, advanced by seven governments, took the form of wedge-shaped sectors extending inward from the coast to the South Pole (see map).

The overlapping claims of Great Britain, Argentina, and

Chile in the area of the Antarctic Peninsula, the most northerly and accessible area of the continent, have been in dispute since the 1940s. The British claim is based upon prior discovery and occupation, while those of Chile and Argentina are based upon the "contiguity" principle, involving a southward extension of their national territories. The two latter claims overlap, but Argentina and Chile have consistently presented a united front in opposition to the British claim.

The remaining sector claims have occasioned no serious disputes. Norway's is based upon coastal reconnaissance in the 1930s, France's on the d'Urville expedition of 1840. The Australian claim, assigned by the United Kingdom in 1936, is based on both exploration and "contiguity", while the "contiguous" area claimed by New Zealand resulted from conveyance by Britain in 1923. This sector provides the best access to the interior of the continent by way of the Ross Ice Shelf.

The unclaimed "Pacific Sector" (sometimes called Marie Byrd Land) has the most inaccessible coastline of the entire continent and was tacitly awarded to the United States because of Admiral Byrd's work there. US personnel are located primarily in the vicinity of the Palmer Peninsula in the northwest and at McMurdo Station near the Ross Ice Shelf. As originally enunciated by Secretary of State Charles Evans Hughes in 1924, however, US Antarctic policy has consistently denied the principle of valid sovereignty without actual settlement. While reserving all rights accruing from its discoveries and exploration, Washington has made no territorial claims and has refused to recognize those of any other nation.

The Soviet Union, which returned to the area during the International Geophysical Year (IGY), has established seven year-round scientific bases, including those in the Australian and Norwegian areas and in the Antarctic Peninsula. Like the United States, it has not recognized any claims to territorial sovereignty, which are tabulated (roughly clockwise from the Greenwich meridian) below:

Queen Maud Land (Norway)	20°W	to	45°E
Australian Antarctic Territory (Australia)	45°E	to	136°E
Adélie Land (France)	136°E	to	142°E
Australian Antarctic Territory (Australia)	142°E	to	160°E
Ross Dependency (New Zealand)	160°E	to	150°W
"Pacific Sector" (unclaimed)	150°W	to	90°W
Antártida Chilena (Chile)	90°W	to	53°W
British Antarctic Territory (UK)	80°W	to	20°W
Antártida Argentina (Argentina)	74°W	to	25°W

The Antarctic Treaty. The International Geophysical Year (July 1, 1957, to December 31, 1958) shifted the emphasis in Antarctic development to international cooperative scientific research. Under the IGY program 11 nations operated research stations: Argentina, Australia, Belgium, Chile, France, Japan, New Zealand, Norway, the Soviet Union, the United Kingdom, and the United States. Between 200 and 300 scientists and technical personnel participated in Antarctic projects in the fields of geology, terrestrial and upper atmosphere physics, biology, glaciology, oceanography, meteorology, and cartography. Following this effort, a conference of the same 11 nations and South Africa was held at Washington, DC, on US initiative in October 1959 to formalize continued scientific coopera-

tion in Antarctica and to prohibit military use of the area. The resulting treaty, which was signed December 1, 1959, and entered into force June 23, 1961, set forth the following major principles applicable to the area south of 60 degrees South Latitude:

1. *Peaceful purposes.* Article I of the treaty specifies that "Antarctica shall be used for peaceful purposes only" and specifically prohibits such measures as the establishment of military bases, the carrying out of military maneuvers, and the testing of weapons. Other articles prohibit nuclear explosions and the disposal of radioactive waste material (Article V) and confer on each contracting party a right to have duly designated observers inspect Antarctic stations, installations and equipment, and ships and aircraft (Article VII).

2. *Freedom of scientific investigation.* Articles II and III provide for continued freedom of scientific investigation and for cooperation toward that end, including the exchange of information, personnel, and scientific findings, and the encouragement of working relations with United Nations Specialized Agencies and other interested international organizations. There are also provisions for periodic consultations among the signatory powers.

3. *"Freezing" of territorial claims.* Article IV stipulates (1) that the treaty does not affect the contracting parties' prior rights or claims to territorial sovereignty in Antarctica, nor their positions relative to the recognition or nonrecognition of such rights or claims by others; and (2) that activities taking place while the treaty is in force are not to affect such claims, while no new claims may be asserted (or existing claims enlarged) during the same period.

The treaty is open to accession by any UN member state or any other state acceptable to the signatory powers, although a distinction is made between "consultative parties" (signatories that engage in Antarctic scientific activities and participate in biennial consultative meetings) and "nonconsultative parties" (those that have only acceded to the treaty and do not attend biennial meetings). As of March 1, 1988, the 20 consultative parties included the original 12 signatories plus Poland (1977), the Federal Republic of Germany (1981), Brazil (1983), India (1983), China (1985), Uruguay (1985), the German Democratic Republic (1987), and Italy (1987), while the 17 acceding parties included Austria, Bulgaria, Cuba, Czechoslovakia, Denmark, Ecuador, Finland, Greece, Hungary, the Democratic People's Republic of Korea, the Republic of Korea, the Netherlands, Papua New Guinea, Peru, Romania, Spain, and Sweden.

The duration of the treaty is indefinite, but provision is made for modification by unanimous consent at any time and for an optional review of its operation after 30 years. The United States, among others, has carried out a number of inspections under Article VII and has declared itself satisfied that the provisions of the treaty are being faithfully observed.

Economic potential. It was long assumed that Antarctica's mineral resources (including coal, oil, gold, platinum, tin, silver, molybdenum, antimony, and uranium) would remain technologically unexploitable for an indefinite period, but the discovery of iron deposits in the Prince Charles Mountains bordering on the Indian Ocean, coupled with the possibility that similar deposits may lie in the Shackleton Range near the Weddell Sea, led to concern that political cooperation might yield to economic rivalry.

Attention has also been focused on potential offshore oil and natural gas deposits and on the harvesting of krill, a small crustacean that is the major living marine resource of the region and a potentially important source of protein. A number of governments and private corporations have expressed interest in pressing the search for petroleum, although the technology required to tap any reserves has been estimated as being at least 10–20 years away. Those states already fishing for krill include East Germany, West Germany, Japan, Poland, Taiwan, and the Soviet Union.

Recent developments. At a meeting held May 7–20, 1980, at Canberra, Australia, 15 treaty members (the original 12 plus Poland and the two Germanies) approved the final draft of a Convention on the Conservation of Antarctic Marine Living Resources, which was signed on September 11 and, having been ratified by a majority of the participating governments, came into force on April 7, 1982. The accord called for the establishment at Hobart, Tasmania, of both a scientific committee to set quotas for the harvesting of krill, and an international commission responsible for conducting studies of Antarctic species and the food chain, recommending conservation measures, and supervising adherence to the convention. The area covered by the document extends beyond that specified in the 1959 treaty to roughly the "Antarctic Convergence" — where warm and cold waters meet and thus form a natural boundary between marine communities. The convention did not, however, meet the expectations of conservationists. In particular, in a report issued concurrently with the Canberra meeting, the International Institute for Environment and Development criticized the accord for requiring consensus decisions, which may hinder effective action; for being unenforceable with regard to nonsignatories; and for failing to recognize that even minimal harvesting of krill may do irreparable harm to the Antarctic ecosystem.

The establishment of an International Minerals Regime was discussed at the Eleventh Consultative Meeting at Buenos Aires, Argentina, from June 23 to July 7, 1981; at the Twelfth Consultative Meeting at Canberra on September 13–27, 1983; and at a series of special consultative sessions during 1981–1987, with final action expected by mid-1988. Concurrently, Third World countries have increasingly demanded full international control over the region, a proposal to such effect being advanced by Malaysia at the 1982 session of the UN General Assembly. The matter was further debated at the Assembly's 1983 session, culminating on December 15 in a directive to Secretary General Pérez de Cuéllar to prepare "a comprehensive, factual and objective study on all aspects of Antarctica, taking fully into account the Antarctic Treaty system and other relevant factors".

At the Thirteenth Consultative Meeting at Brussels, Belgium, from October 4 to 18, 1985, most of the discussion focused on the growing environmental impact of scientific activity in the region. Specifically, the group decided to limit access to 13 special scientific zones and 3 environmental areas — a 75 percent increase in such restricted areas. Subsequently, in a series of votes on December 3 that was boycotted by most treaty nations, the UN General Assembly approved three resolutions calling for the expulsion of South Africa from the treaty organization, "international management and equitable sharing of the benefits" of any future minerals regime, and continued UN monitoring of issues related to the Antarctic area.

Earlier in the year, the London-based Greenpeace environmentalist group had called for the designation of Antarctica as a "World Heritage Park" and in September joined with the ecological Southern Ocean Coalition in urging the Commission for the Conservation of Marine Living Resources to impose stringent fishing quotas in the area. In response, a Commission spokesman stated that the Treaty governments had long been committed to sound conservation policies.

During the Fourteenth Consultative Meeting at Rio de Janeiro, Brazil, in October 1987 it was agreed that acceding states and nongovernmental groups from nonacceding states could attend consultative sessions as observers. A wide variety of other actions were also taken, including authorization for the release of documents to the public, the provision of human impact safeguards for scientific drilling, and the establishment of additional sites of special scientific interest.

ANTIGUA AND BARBUDA

Political Status: Former British dependency; joined West Indies Associated States in 1967; independent member of the Commonwealth since November 1, 1981.

Area: 171.5 sq. mi. (444 sq. km.), encompassing the main island of Antigua (108 sq. mi.) and the dependent islands of Barbuda (62 sq. mi.) and Redonda (0.5 sq. mi.).

Population: 65,525 (1970C), 83,700 (1988E), including 81,900 on Antigua and 1,800 on Barbuda. Redonda is uninhabited.

Major Urban Center (1984E): St. JOHN'S (36,000).

Official Language: English.

Monetary Unit: East Caribbean Dollar (market rate March 1, 1988, 3.67 EC dollars = $1US).

Sovereign: Queen ELIZABETH II.

Governor General: Sir Wilfred Ebenezer JACOBS; named Governor of the Associated State in 1967, becoming Governor General upon independence.

Prime Minister: Vere Cornwall BIRD, Sr. (Antigua Labour Party); served as Chief Minister, 1960–1967, and as Premier of the Associated State, 1967–1971; returned as Premier, succeeding George WALTER, in 1976; redesignated in 1980, continuing as Prime Minister upon independence; formed new government April 19, 1984, following election of April 17.

THE COUNTRY

Located in the northern part of the Caribbean's Lesser Antilles, the islands of Antigua and Barbuda are populated

largely by Blacks whose ancestors were transported as slaves from Western Africa in the seventeenth and eighteenth centuries. Minorities include descendants of British colonial settlers, Portuguese laborers, and Lebanese and Syrian traders. Anglican Protestantism and Roman Catholicism claim the largest number of adherents, although a wide variety of other denominations exist and complete religious freedom prevails.

Agriculture dominated the economy until the 1960s, when a pronounced decline in sugar prices led to the abandonment of most cane fields and increased reliance on tourism, which currently accounts for about 60 percent of GDP. The harbor at St. John's, long used as a dockyard for the British Navy, is a port of call for 11 major shipping lines, while a modern air facility, featuring a new Canadian-financed terminal complex, is served by 6 international carriers. The country nonetheless faces a variety of economic problems, including high external debt. Efforts are under way to promote agriculture, particularly livestock raising and produce cultivation, expand the fishing industry, and assist the growth of light manufacturing through infrastructural improvements.

GOVERNMENT AND POLITICS

Political background. Colonized by Britain in the early seventeenth century after unsuccessful efforts by Spain and France, Antigua became a founding member of the Federation of the West Indies in 1958, following the introduction of ministerial government two years earlier. Together with its northern dependency, Barbuda, it joined the West Indies Associated States in 1969 as an internally self-governing territory with a right of unilateral termination, which it exercised on November 1, 1981. At independence, Premier Vere C. BIRD, Sr., whose Antigua Labour Party (ALP) had returned to power in 1976 and was victorious at the early election of April 1980, became prime minister. Concurrently, the colonial governor, Sir Wilfred E. JACOBS, was redesignated as governor general.

At another early election on April 17, 1984, the ALP swept all 16 of the Antiguan seats in the House of Representatives, with Bird forming a new government two days later.

Constitution and government. Although the opposition Progressive Labour Movement (PLM) had campaigned for a unicameral legislature elected by proportional representation, the independence constitution retained the existing bicameral legislature composed of an appointed Senate and a House of Representatives elected from single-member constituencies (16 on Antigua and 1 on Barbuda) for a five-year term, subject to dissolution. The governor general consults with both government and opposition leaders in the selection of senators, who review all legislation but are essentially limited to delaying powers. Executive power is exercised by a Council of Ministers headed by a prime minister and responsible to Parliament. The constitutional independence of the judiciary is reinforced by the fact that Antigua and five neighboring states (Dominica, Grenada, St. Kitts-Nevis, St. Lucia, and St. Vincent) participate equally in a Supreme Court, which encompasses a Court of Appeal with a High Court, one of whose judges is resident in Antigua and presides over a Court of Summary Jurisdiction. District courts deal with minor offenses and civil actions involving not more than EC $500.

While Antigua and Barbuda collectively constitute a unitary state, secessionist sentiment has long been pronounced on the smaller island, and Premier Bird initiated, prior to independence, a limited devolution of powers to the Barbuda Council, which contains 9 directly elected members in addition to a government nominee and the Barbuda parliamentary representative.

Foreign relations. In 1965, (then) Chief Minister Bird, a strong believer in regional cooperation, played a leading role in organizing the Caribbean Free Trade Association (Carifta), predecessor of the Caribbean Community and Common Market (Caricom). Upon independence, Antigua became a member of the Commonwealth and, shortly thereafter, the 157th member of the United Nations. Subsequently, St. John's accepted observer status within the Nonaligned Movement, viewing the latter as a "viable alternative [to] . . . confrontation between the superpowers". However, in January 1982 the prime minister called on the United States to "protect" the Caribbean against foreign "subversive elements". Antigua is also an active member of the Organization of Eastern Caribbean States (OECS), which provided troops in support of the US invasion of Grenada in October 1983. The swing to the right continued in 1985, St. John's agreeing to the establishment of a US-backed regional military training base on the main island and the use of existing US bases for regional security exercises.

Current issues. Bird's sweeping victory in the April 1984 balloting yielded an opposition in disarray, only the left-wing Antigua Caribbean Liberation Movement (ACLM) continuing to function as a viable antigovernment grouping through its local and trade union affiliates. Subsequently, the government concentrated on attempts to stimulate an economy suffering from a growing trade deficit and a large external debt. A freeze was imposed on government hiring, limitations were placed on foreign ownership of land, plans were announced to double the number of tourist accommodations, and Washington was asked to increase its aid.

However, the initiatives did little to stifle opposition charges of corruption and maladministration.

By early 1986 Dr. Ivor HEATH, leader of the newly formed United National Democratic Party (UNDP), had emerged as a leading opposition spokesman, while the ACLM continued to denounce the government through its widely read weekly, *The Outlet.* In mid-1987 US authorities strongly denied an *Outlet* report that American Air Force personnel were involved in a major cocaine operation "supplying a vast network of local dealers". Meanwhile, Prime Minister Bird resisted demands for the ouster of his son, Vere BIRD, Jr., in the wake of an official inquiry that had charged him with conduct "unbecoming a minister of government" in connection with the funding of an airport rehabilitation project. The issue led to a split within the Bird family, the prime minister's second son, deputy prime minister Lester BIRD joining a "dissident majority" of eight officials, including education minister Reuben HARRIS, who announced a campaign to rid the country of "family government". The prime minister's fourth son, Ivor BIRD, thereupon announced that he would contest Harris' parliamentary seat at the next election, although his prospective party affiliation remained unclear since Harris had already been endorsed by the ALP.

For its part, the opposition seemed unable to capitalize on the intra-ALP cleavage. Late in the year, the UNDP leadership rejected a proposal by ACLM leader and *Outlet* editor Tim HECTOR that the two groups form an electoral coalition, countering with a suggestion (branded by Hector as "insulting") that the UNDP contest all seats "with the ACLM's support and endorsement".

POLITICAL PARTIES

Government Parties:

Antigua Labour Party (ALP). In power from 1967 to 1971 and a decisive victor in subsequent balloting in 1976, 1980, and 1984, the ALP has long been affiliated with the Antigua Trades and Labour Union (AT&LU). Recently, however, questions have risen as to the viability of its grass-root linkages. At a party convention in June 1984, the prime minister's son, Lester Bird, in accepting redesignation as party chairman, adopted a posture of appealing over the heads of the older leadership to women's, youth, and other groups for "modern approaches" and "a proper philosophical base" for party activity. In doing so, he appeared to be solidifying his own claim to political succession.
Leaders: Vere C. BIRD, Sr. (Prime Minister), Lester Bryant BIRD (Deputy Prime Minister and Party Chairman), J.E. ST. LUCE (Secretary).

Organization for National Reconstruction (ONR). Formed in June 1984 as a pro-Bird force against anti-St. John's sentiment on Barbuda, the ONR has been quite vocal in its support of efforts to end the island's "isolation" and further economic development. In March 1985 by-elections, the ONR ended four years of domination of the Barbuda Council by the Barbuda People's Movement (below), gaining all five of the seats contested and thus a majority of nine elective seats on the eleven-member Council. However, it lost all four of the seats contested in March 1987 to the BPM.
Leader: Arthur NIBBS (President).

Opposition Parties:

Progressive Labour Movement (PLM). In power during 1971–1976 under the leadership of George Walter (see UNDP, below), the PLM was organized in 1970 as the political affiliate of the Antigua Workers' Union (AWU), which had emerged in the wake of a 1967 split in the AT&LU. The PLM delegation to the December 1980 independence talks at London refused to sign the conference report following rejection of proposals that included guarantees related to human rights and the right to strike, the adoption of proportional representation and a unicameral legislature, and assurances of greater local autonomy for Barbuda. In 1984, the party lost the 3 parliamentary seats it had won four years earlier, but with no non-ALP parties represented in the lower house insisted that it remained the "official opposition". It was reported that its leader, Robert Hall, favored entering the UNDP, but was outvoted within the party executive by colleagues who felt that other opposition parties should dissolve and merge with the PLM.
Leader: Robert HALL (former Leader of the Opposition).

United National Democratic Party (UNDP). The UNDP was formed in early 1986 by merger of the National Democratic Party (NDP) and the United People's Movement (UPM). The UPM was organized in 1982 by former PLM leader George Walter, who had been forced to withdraw from active politics in February 1979 upon conviction of mishandling state finances while premier in 1971–1976. The decision was reversed several days after the 1980 election, Walter subsequently accusing the new PLM leadership of efforts to exclude him. With considerable support from AWU members, who had been omitted from the PLM delegation to the independence talks, Walter announced that the UPM would be devoted to social democracy and to returning the country "to the hands of Antiguans"—a reference to extensive foreign participation in the economy. Ironically, in late 1982 a government official accused Walter of accepting financial support from Venezuela in return for a pledge of greater cooperation with Caracas should the UPM win power. The UPM secured no parliamentary representation in 1984 and Walter assumed no public role in formation of the UNDP, reportedly because of the negative impact it might have in launching the new formation.

The NDP was organized by a group of business leaders in early 1985. Initially perceived as a conservative alternative to both the ALP and the ACLM (below), it subsequently attempted to forge links with the leftist opposition in an effort to soften its image as a "middle-class party". However, elements within the NDP, as well as within the ACLM, were reportedly opposed to the latter's inclusion in the UNDP.
Leaders: Dr. Ivor HEATH (NDP), Baldwin SPENCER (UPM).

Antigua Caribbean Liberation Movement (ACLM). Originally known as the Afro-Caribbean Liberation Movement, the ACLM is a "new Left" organization that contested the 1980 election, winning less than 1 percent of the vote and obtaining no parliamentary seats. In 1982, ACLM accusations of government corruption in regard to the sale of passports and the alleged "disappearance" of loan funds resulted in a police raid on the offices of the party's newspaper, *The Outlet,* where classified documents were discovered, in violation of the Official Secrets Act. Subsequently, party leader Tim Hector and a number of others were arrested and fined for violations of the Newspaper Registration Act and the Public Order Act. In 1985, Hector was sentenced to six months imprisonment on charges of "undermining confidence in a public official", after publishing criticism of several government ministries; he remained free on bail while his appeal was heard and in May 1986 his conviction was overturned by the High Court, which ruled the relevant section of the Public Order Act to be unconstitutional. The ACLM presented no candidates for the 1984 balloting.
Leader: Tim HECTOR (Chairman).

Barbuda People's Movement (BPM). A separatist party which presently controls the local Barbuda Council, the BPM has criticized the island's sole parliamentary deputy for failure to represent Barbudan interests. Having rejected the independence agreement, party leader Hilbourne Frank asserted in early 1982 that Parliament's passage of a bill altering land-tenure practices and permitting individual ownership "erodes the traditional, customary and constitutional authority handed down to the Council and the people of Barbuda". At the most recent Council balloting on March 23, 1987, the BPM won all four of the contested seats.
Leader: T. Hilbourne FRANK (former Chairman of the Barbuda Council).

Barbuda Committee. Following the local poll of March 1987, the Barbuda Committee held one elective Council seat in addition to appointive representation by Committee leader Eric Burton, the Barbuda parliamentary deputy.
Leader: Eric BURTON.

LEGISLATURE

The **Parliament** is a bicameral body consisting of an appointed Senate and a directly elected House of Representatives.

Senate. The upper house has 17 members named by the governor general: 11 (including at least 1 from Barbuda) appointed on advice of the prime minister, 4 named after consultation with the leader of the opposition, 1 recommended by the Barbuda Council, and 1 chosen at the governor general's discretion.
President: Bradley CARROTT.

House of Representatives. The lower house has 17 members chosen every five years (subject to dissolution) from single-member constituencies. At the most recent election of April 17, 1984, the Antigua Labour Party captured all 16 seats from the main island, the remaining seat being won by the Barbuda Committee.
Speaker: Casford MURRAY.

CABINET

Prime Minister	Vere C. Bird, Sr.
Deputy Prime Minister	Lester B. Bird
Ministers	
Agriculture, Fisheries, Lands and Fisheries	Hilroy Humphreys
Defense	Vere C. Bird, Sr.
Economic Development, Tourism and Energy	Lester B. Bird
Education, Culture, Youth Affairs and Sports	Reuben Harris
External Affairs	Lester B. Bird
Finance	John St. Luce
Health and Labor	Adolphus Freeland
Home Affairs	Christopher O'Mard
Information	Vere C. Bird, Sr.
Legal Affairs	Keith Ford
Public Utilities and Aviation	Robin Yearwood
Public Works and Communications	Vere C. Bird, Jr.
Without Portfolio	Douglas Christian
	Eustace Cochran
	Molwyn Joseph
	Hugh Marshall
	Henderson Simon
	Donald Sheppard
Attorney General	Keith Ford

NEWS MEDIA

Press. Freedom of the press is constitutionally guaranteed. The following are published at St. John's: *The Outlet* (5,500), ACLM weekly, *The Worker's Voice* (3,300), twice-weekly organ of the ALP and AT&LU; *The Herald* (2,500), progovernment. The ACLM announced in late 1987 that financing had been obtained to convert *The Outlet* into a daily — the only such paper in an OECS state.

Radio and television. Radio ZDK is a private station broadcasting from St. John's. The government-operated Antigua and Barbuda Broadcasting Service (ABS) transmits over one radio station and one TV facility, the latter providing the most sophisticated full color service in the Commonwealth Caribbean. Other radio facilities include Voice of America, BBC Caribbean, and Deutsche Welle relays, plus a religious station, Caribbean Radio Lighthouse. There were approximately 36,000 radio and 27,500 television receivers in 1987.

INTERGOVERNMENTAL REPRESENTATION

Ambassador to the US: Edmund Hawkins LAKE.

US Ambassador to Antigua: Paul A. RUSSO (resident in Barbados).

Permanent Representative to the UN: Lloydstone JACOBS.

IGO Memberships (Non-UN): Caricom, CDB, CWTH, EEC(L), *EIB,* IWC, *NAM,* OAS, OECS, OPANAL.

ARGENTINA

Argentine Republic
República Argentina

Political Status: Independent republic proclaimed 1816; under military regimes 1966–1973 and 1976–1983; constitutional government restored December 10, 1983.

Area: 1,072,358 sq. mi. (2,777,407 sq. km.), excluding territory claimed in Antarctica and the South Atlantic.

Population: 27,949,480 (1980C), 31,940,000 (1988E).

Major Urban Centers (1980C): BUENOS AIRES (2,922,829; urban area, 9,969,826); Córdoba (983,969); Rosario (957,301); La Plata (564,750); San Miguel de Tucumán (498,579); Mar del Plata (414,696). In May 1987 the Chamber of Deputies (acting on a measure previously approved by the Senate) endorsed a presidential proposal to transfer the federal capital nearly 400 miles to the south to Viedma in Río Negro province.

Official Language: Spanish.

Monetary Unit: Austral (principal rate March 1, 1988, 4.60 australs = $1US). The austral, linked to the US dollar and equal to 1,000 peso argentinos, was introduced in June 1985; the peso argentino, equal to 10,000 old pesos, had been introduced in June 1983.

President: Dr. Raúl ALFONSIN Foulkes (Radical Civic Union); designated for a six-year term by the electoral college on November 30, 1983, following general election of October 30; sworn in December 10, succeeding junta-appointed Gen. Reynaldo Benito Antonio BIGNONE.

Vice President: Víctor MARTINEZ; designated by the electoral college on November 30, 1983, for a term concurrent with that of the President.

THE COUNTRY

Second in size among the countries of South America, the Argentine Republic includes the national territory of Tierra del Fuego and claims certain South Atlantic islands (including the Falklands/Malvinas) as well as portions of Antarctica. The country extends 2,300 miles from north to south and exhibits varied climate and topography, including the renowned *pampas,* the fertile central plains. The population is largely Caucasian but of varied national origin. Spaniards and Italians predominate, but there are also large groups from other West and East European countries, as well as Middle Easterners of both Arab and Jewish descent. Although Spanish is the official language, English, Italian, German, and French are also spoken. Over 90 percent of the population is Roman Catholic. Women constitute less than 30 percent of the paid labor force and are concentrated in the service sector, where 40 percent are engaged as domestics. With the exception of both wives of former president Perón, women have been minimally represented in government, although a women's group called *"La Madres de la Plaza de Mayo"* was at the forefront of opposition to the former military regime.

Argentinians enjoy one of the highest per capita incomes in South America but in recent years have been subject to rampant inflation that exceeded 100 percent annually after 1975 and escalated to more than 1000 percent in early 1985, necessitating a drastic currency revision as part of a series of "war economy" measures by mid-year. A year later, the *Plan Austral* appeared to have achieved its immediate goals, with inflation plunging to an annualized rate of 50 percent, before surging again to more than 200 percent for 1987. Food grains and livestock account for about two-thirds of the country's export earnings; industry is growing but remains dependent upon the importation of machinery and raw materials.

GOVERNMENT AND POLITICS

Political background. Following the struggle for independence from Spain in 1810–1816, Argentina experienced a period of conflict over its form of government. The provinces advocated a federal system to guarantee their autonomy, while Buenos Aires favored a unitary state in which it would play a dominant role. A federal constitution was drafted in 1853, but Buenos Aires refused to ratify the document until its 1859 defeat in a brief war. Following a second military defeat in 1880, the territory was politically neutralized by being designated a federal district.

The initial years of the federation were dominated by the Conservatives. In 1890, however, widespread corruption prompted organization of the reformist *Unión Cívica Radical* (UCR), which in 1912 successfully pressed for enactment of a liberal electoral law that resulted in the election of Radical leader Hipólito IRIGOYEN as president in 1916. Faced with mounting economic problems, the Irigoyen government was overthrown and replaced by the nation's first military regime in 1930.

With the election of Augustín P. JUSTO to the presidency in 1932, a second period of Conservative rule was launched that lasted until 1943, when the military again intervened. Juan Domingo PERON Sosa was elected chief executive in 1946, inaugurating a dictatorship that was eventually overthrown in 1955. Peronism, however, continued to attract widespread support and Argentina entered an era of chronic political instability and repeated military intervention.

At a general election held in March 1973, the Peronist Dr. Héctor J. CAMPORA emerged victorious. Four months later, Cámpora resigned to force a new election in which Perón would be eligible as a candidate. The new round of balloting, held in September, returned the former president to power with an overwhelming majority after 18 years of exile. Following his inauguration, Perón was plagued by factionalism within his own movement and by increasingly widespread opposition from guerrilla groups. Upon his death on July 1, 1974, he was succeeded by his wife, Isabel (born María Estela) Martínez de PERON, who had been elected vice president the preceding September. Mrs. Perón's turbulent presidency was terminated on March 24, 1976, by a three-man military junta, which on March 26 designated Lt. Gen. Jorge Rafael VIDELA as president.

In December 1976 General Videla stated that his government was "very close to final victory" over left-wing terrorists, most prominently the so-called *Montonero* guerrillas and the People's Revolutionary Army. Earlier, in an apparent consolidation of power by Videla, a number of rightist officers were retired and replaced by moderates. On May 2, 1978, however, it was announced that while Videla had been redesignated as president for a three-year term retroactive to March 29, he would cease to serve as a member of the junta following his military retirement on August 1. The pattern was repeated with the retirement of Lt. Gen. Roberto Eduardo VIOLA as army commander and junta member as of December 31, 1979, and his designation to succeed Videla in March 1981. Buffeted by health problems and an inability to deal with a rapidly deteriorating economy, Viola stepped down as chief executive on December 11 and was succeeded 11 days later by the army commander, Lt. Gen. Leopoldo Fortunato GALTIERI, who continued as a member of the junta, along with Adm. Jorge Isaac ANAYA and Lt. Gen. Basilio Arturo LAMI DOZO, commanders, respectively, of the navy and air force.

The region and the world were shaken by a brief but intense conflict with Britain that erupted in 1982 as the result of a 149-year dispute over ownership of the Falkland Islands (*Islas Malvinas*), located in the South Atlantic some 400 miles northeast of Tierra del Fuego. Argentina invaded the islands on April 2, prompting the dispatch of a British armada that succeeded in regaining control with the surrender of some 15,000 Argentine troops at the capital, Stanley, on July 15 (see Contested Territory, below). Branded as having "sold out" the country by his conduct of the war, Galtieri resigned on June 17, being succeeded immediately as army commander by Maj. Gen. Cristino NICOLAIDES and on July 1 as president by Gen. Reynaldo Benito Antonio BIGNONE. On June 22 the junta was effectively dissolved, President-elect Bignone conceding the following day that the country had been ruled by an "abnormal regime" since the 1976 coup and promising to hold nationwide elections by March 1984. On September 21, following the replacement on August 17 of General Lami Dozo by Brig. Gen. Augusto Jorge HUGHES, the junta was reestablished, with Admiral Anaya retiring in favor of Vice Adm. Rubén Oscar FRANCO on October 1. However, in the face of an economic crisis and mounting pressure from the nation's political parties, Bignone announced in February 1983 that elections for a civilian government would be advanced to the following October.

At balloting for national, provincial, and municipal authorities on October 30, the UCR, under the leadership of Raúl ALFONSIN Foulkes, scored a decisive victory, winning not only the presidency, but a majority in the Chamber of Deputies. Following pro forma designation by the electoral college, Alfonsín and his vice-presidential running mate, Víctor MARTINEZ, were sworn in for six-year terms on December 10.

On November 3, 1985, at the first renewal of the lower house in 20 years, the UCR marginally increased its majority, largely at the expense of the *oficialista* wing of the Peronist party (see Political Parties, below). On September 6, 1987, on the other hand, the Radicals were reduced to plurality status, with most of the Peronist gains again being registered by the Movement's *renovadores* faction, whose principal leaders Antonio CAFIERO (governor of Buenos Aires) and Carlos Saúl MENEM (governor of La Rioja) emerged as leading candidates for the presidency in 1989.

Constitution and government. Upon returning to civilian rule, most of the constitutional structure of 1853 was reintroduced. The president and vice president are designated for six-year terms by an electoral college chosen on the basis of proportional representation, with each electoral district having twice as many electors as the combined number of senators and deputies. The National Congress currently consists of a 46-member Senate, one-third being replenished every three years, and a 254-member Chamber of Deputies, one-half being elected every two years. The judicial system encompasses a Supreme Court, federal appeals courts, and provincial courts that include supreme and subsidiary judicial bodies.

There are 22 provinces, plus the Federal District of Buenos Aires and the National Territories of Tierra del Fuego, the Antarctica, and the South Atlantic Islands. The provinces elect their own governors and legislatures, and retain those powers not specifically delegated to the federal government. In practice, however, there has been a history of substantial federal intervention in provincial affairs.

Province and Capital	Area (sq. mi.)	Population (1980C)
Buenos Aires (La Plata)	118,843	10,865,408
Catamarca (Catamarca)	38,540	207,717
Córdoba (Córdoba)	65,161	2,407,754
Corrientes (Corrientes)	34,054	661,454
Chaco (Resistencia)	38,468	701,392
Chubut (Rawson)	86,751	263,116
Entre Ríos (Paraná)	29,427	908,313
Formosa (Formosa)	27,825	295,887
Jujuy (San Salvador de Jujuy)	20,548	410,008
La Pampa (Santa Rosa)	55,382	208,260
La Rioja (La Rioja)	35,649	164,217
Mendoza (Mendoza)	58,239	1,196,228
Misiones (Posadas)	11,506	588,977
Neuquén (Neuquén)	36,324	243,850
Río Negro (Viedma)	78,383	383,354
Salta (Salta)	59,759	662,870
San Juan (San Juan)	33,257	465,976
San Luis (San Luis)	29,632	214,416
Santa Cruz (Río Gallegos)	94,186	114,941
Santa Fé (Santa Fé)	51,354	2,465,546
Santiago del Estero (Santiago del Estero)	52,222	594,920
Tucumán (San Miguel de Tucumán)	8,697	972,655

Territory and Capital		
Tierra del Fuego (Ushuaia)	8,074	29,392

Federal District		
Distrito Federal (Buenos Aires)	77	2,922,829

Foreign relations. Argentina has traditionally maintained an independent foreign policy and has been reluctant to follow US leadership in hemispheric and world affairs. It claims territory in the Antarctic (see section on Antarctica) and despite the outcome of the 1982 war continues to assert its long-standing claim to sovereignty over the Falklands. The latter claim has won support at the UN General Assembly which, since the cessation of hostilities, has called annually on the claimants to initiate negotiations on peaceful resolution of the dispute.

Relations with Chile became tense following the announcement in May 1977 that a panel of international arbitrators had awarded Chile the ownership of three disputed islands in the Beagle Channel, just north of Cape Horn (see map). As in the case of the Falklands, there is evidence of petroleum in the area. The award also permitted Chile to extend its nominal jurisdiction into the Atlantic, thereby strengthening its Antarctic claims, which overlap those of Argentina. Having expected a "political" rather than a purely legal judgment, with at least one island being awarded to each country, Argentina, in January 1978, formally repudiated the decision. A subsequent 19-month mediation effort by Pope John Paul II resulted in a proposal that endorsed the awarding of the three islands to Chile while limiting the assignment of offshore rights on the Atlantic side of the Cape Horn meridian. The proposal was rejected by the Argentine junta, but accepted by Alfonsín prior to his election as president, and a treaty ending the century-old dispute was narrowly ratified by the Argentine Senate in March 1985.

For nearly a decade Argentina was embroiled in a dispute with Brazil over water rights on the Paraná River. In October 1979, however, both countries joined Paraguay in signing an agreement that not only resolved differences over Brazil's Itaipú dam, the world's largest, but freed the way for cooperative exploitation of the Uruguay River. Economic linkage between the continent's two largest states was further enhanced on December 10, 1986, with the signing by presidents Alfonsín and Sarney of 20 accords launching an ambitious integration effort intended, in the words of the Brazilian chief executive, "eventually to create a Latin American common market". Under the plan, a cus-

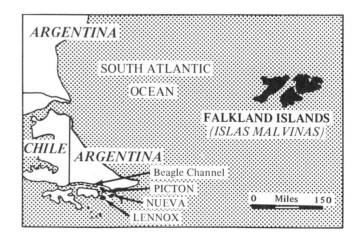

toms union was established for most capital goods as of January 1, 1987, with cooperation in the exchange of food products, the promotion of bilateral industrial ventures, the establishment of a $200 million joint investment fund, and joint energy development (including a new $2 billion hydroelectric facility) to follow. President Sanguinetti of Uruguay, who was present at the meeting, pledged his "determined support" for the move and agreed to a series of ministerial-level talks designed to pave the way for his country's participation in the integration process.

Current issues. Campaigning on the slogan "*basta con el pasada*" ("away with the past"), the UCR's Raúl Alfonsín not only led a return to constitutional government after more than seven years of military rule, but tendered the *peronistas* their first electoral loss in nearly four decades. Scarcely more than a year after his inauguration, the president called a rally "in defense of democracy" at the Plaza de Mayo in Buenos Aires and subsequently presented a 12 percent across-the-board spending cut to Congress, while resisting pressure for wage increases. In mid-1985 he again appeared at the Plaza de Mayo to announce a "war economy", formally styled the *Plan Austral,* that included the introduction of a new currency unit, a freeze on wages and prices, and further spending cuts. The immediate results were encouraging, but during 1986 the economy came under increased strain, with a return to rising inflation at midyear yielding an erosion of support for the reform program. In June the country's labor federation called a 24-hour general strike, claiming that worker buying power had fallen by 12 percent since the plan's introduction, while farmers had embarked on a series of protests that severely disrupted trading in their products. Concurrently, a public opinion poll indicated that popular support for the plan had fallen by more than half, to 38 percent. Undaunted, the president embarked on a number of economic initiatives, including a package of joint undertakings with Brazil (see Foreign relations, above) and, with input from Japanese consultants, a four-point domestic strategy encompassing privatization of state-owned enterprises, export promotion, investment in technology, and reconstruction of capital markets.

Politically, the president ran into difficulty in coping with recovery from the "dirty war" waged against opponents of the former military regime. In late 1986, despite strong leftist opposition, he signed into law a Full Stop (*Punto Final*) bill that imposed, with certain exceptions, a 60-day deadline for the initiation of court proceedings against alleged human rights violators. Subsequently, in mid-1987, the Supreme Court upheld the constitutionality of a "due obedience" (*obediencia debida*) measure that exempted most junior officers from responsibility for acts committed under military rule on the ground that they were merely acting under orders from superiors. The prosecution of senior officers nonetheless continued, provoking two attempted military uprisings in the course of the year.

The substantial reverses suffered by the Alfonsín government at the September 1987 election (including the loss of all but two provincial governorships) appeared to dash any hope of an extended period of UCR rule and raised the possibility of a Peronist victory in the 1989 presidential balloting. The prospect was enhanced by realignment within the Peronist ranks: given the strong showing of the *renovadores* faction, the more conservative *oficialistas* agreed to a "reunification" of the leadership under the new governor of Buenos Aires province, Antonio Cafiero.

POLITICAL PARTIES

A ban on political activity, imposed by the military on its return to power in March 1976, was relaxed in December 1979 in favor of all parties save those professing "totalitarian ideologies". Subsequently, a series of essentially ad hoc groupings of varying orientation emerged. In mid-1980 a Union of the Democratic Center (*Unión de Centro Democrático* — UCD), embracing eight minor parties and modeled after the Spanish ruling party of the same name, was announced. Other alliances included the seven-party "Forum for the Defense of Sovereignty, Democracy, and the National Heritage" and a five-party front (*multipartidaria*), dedicated to opposing far-right elements within the military. The ban on party activity was formally lifted by President Bignone at his inauguration on July 1, 1982, and over 300 national and regional groups participated in the general election of October 30, 1983; however, two formations, the Radical Civic Union and the (Peronist) Justicialist Liberation Front shared 92 percent of the vote. At the legislative balloting of November 3, 1985, the combined vote share of the UCR and Peronists dropped to 77 percent, with "orthodox" and "renovating" factions of the latter (alone or in alliance with smaller parties) presenting separate lists in most districts. At the mid-term lower house poll of September 6, 1987, the two major groups drew more than 79 percent of the vote, although the UCR slipped from majority to plurality status by retaining only 117 of 254 seats.

Leading Parties:

Radical Civic Union (*Unión Cívica Radical* — UCR). The UCR, whose history dates from the late nineteenth century, represents the moderate Left in Argentine politics. In the period following the deposition of Juan Perón, the party split into two factions, the People's Radical Party (*Unión Cívica Radical del Pueblo* — UCRP) and the Intransigent Radical Party (*Unión Cívica Radical Intransigente* — UCRI), led by former presidents Arturo Illia and Arturo Frondizi, respectively. The UCR reemerged following the legalization of parties in 1971 and remained relatively unified during the 1973 presidential candidacy of Dr. Ricardo Balbín, but suffered a number of internal cleavages thereafter. Balbín was instrumental in organizing the 1981 five-party alignment to press for a return to civilian rule, but died on September 9, leaving the party without a unified leadership. Largely because of the personal popularity of its presidential candidate, the party led the 1983 balloting with 51.8 percent of the vote, winning, in addition to the presidency, a majority in the Chamber of Deputies. Subsequently internal dissention diminished, the *balbínista* faction concluding a late 1984 alliance with left-leaning elements, while the long-standing policy of incompatibility between government and party roles was abandoned with the designation of President Alfonsín as ex officio party leader. In early 1986, as the issue of presidential succession loomed, a new rivalry emerged between former labor minister Juan Manuel Casella, the apparent *alfonsinista* front-runner, and the influential governor of Córdoba province, Eduardo Angeloz. There is also an increasingly influential youth wing known as the National Coordinating Union (*Junta Coordinadora Nacional* — JCN).

Leaders: Dr. Raúl ALFONSIN Foulkes (President of the Republic), Dr. Víctor MARTINEZ (Vice President of the Republic), Juan Manuel CASELLA, Eduardo ANGELOZ (Governor of Córdoba province),

Osvaldo ALVAREZ Guerrero (Governor of Río Negro province), César JAROSLAVSKY (Congressional Bloc President), Edison OTERO (Senate Bloc President).

Justicialist Nationalist Movement (*Movimiento Nacionalista Justicialista*—MNJ). The MNJ grew out of the extreme nationalist *Peronista* (also known as *Laborista*) movement led by General Perón during 1946–1955. Formally dissolved after its leader went into exile, it regrouped, in alliance with a number of smaller parties, as the **Justicialist Liberation Front** (*Frente Justicialista de Liberación*—Frejuli) prior to the 1973 election. Frejuli's victorious candidate, Héctor Cámpora, subsequently resigned to permit the reelection of Perón, who had returned in 1972. The Movement's nominal leader, Isabel Martínez de Perón, who was ousted as her husband's successor in 1976 and confined to prison and house arrest for five years thereafter, was permitted to go into exile in July 1981. The MNJ has more than 3 million registered members, with additional support from affiliated trade unions, and won 40.2 percent of the vote in October 1983.

The Peronists (as they are still popularly known) have experienced a number of internal cleavages, the most recent occasioned by the *corrientes renovadores* ("current of renewal"), which was initially launched by a group of moderate trade unionists and students calling for a more democratic party structure. Although both factions asserted their allegiance to Mrs. Perón at separate congresses in February 1985, she withdrew as MNJ leader; subsequently, dissent within the *renovadores* faction led to their defeat at a unified party congress in July, which ignored Mrs. Perón's resignation and reelected her as titular president. At the same congress, the crucial position of secretary general was given to Buenos Aires party chairman Herminio Iglesias, a powerful figure with links to conservative unions.

For the 1985 legislative balloting, the two factions presented separate lists in alliance with smaller parties in most districts. The *oficialistas* revived Frejuli in coalition with the MID (below) and the following minor formations: the **Popular Left Front** (*Frente de Izquierda Popular*—FIP), the **Revolutionary National Front** (*Frente Nacional Revolucionario*—FNR), the **Constitutional Nationalist Movement** (*Movimiento Nacionalista Constitucional*—MNC), the **Independence Party** (*Partido de la Independencia*—PI), the **Labor Party** (*Partido Laborista*—PL), the **Authentic Socialism** (*Socialismo Auténtico*), the **Principista Civic Union** (*Unión Cívica Principista*—UCP), and the **Popular Union** (*Unión Popular*—UP). In critical Buenos Aires province they were, however, substantially outpolled by the **Front of Revewal, Justice, Democracy, and Participation** (*Frente Renovador, Justicia, Democracia y Participación*—Frejudepa), an alliance of *renovadores* and Christian Democrats; at the federal capital, they won no seats, as contrasted with 4 captured by a *renovador* list presented by the **Justice Party** (*Partido Justicialista*—PJ).

Senator Vicente Saadi, an *oficialista,* resigned as MNJ first vice president following the 1985 election, reportedly because of the movement's poor showing. On December 10, Herminio Iglesias, also an *oficialista,* stepped down as secretary general, while the *renovadores,* 11 days later, appointed a leadership of their own, headed by Antonio Cafiero, Carlos Grosso, and Saúl Menem. In November 1986, the *renovadores* boycotted the movement's national congress, at which Isabel Perón and Senator Saadi were elected honorary and "effective" presidents, respectively. However, a cleavage subsequently developed within the dissident troika, Cafiero boycotting a *renovador* congress at Tucumán, while Grosso withdrew from the meeting because of a dispute over the timing of internal party elections in Córdoba and Buenos Aires provinces. Following the relatively poor showing of the *oficialistas* at the 1987 election, Senator Saadi resigned as *Justicialista* president, paving the way for a "unity slate" that awarded the presidency and vice presidency to Cafiero and Menem, respectively.

Leaders: María Estela ("Isabelita") Martínez de PERON (former President of the Republic and Honorary President of the Party); Antonio CAFIERO (President), Carlos Saúl MENEM (Vice President), Vicente Leónidas SAADI (Senate *oficialista* Bloc President), José Luis MANZANO (Congressional *oficialista* Bloc President), Herminio IGLESIAS (former Secretary General), Carlos GROSSO.

Lesser Parties:

Movement of Integration and Development (*Movimiento de Integración y Desarrollo*—MID). Previously the Frondizi wing of the UCR, the MID consistently opposed the policies of former economics minister José Martínez de HOZ, which, it contended, had brought the country to the brink of a fiscal "explosion". It participated in the Frejuli alliance during the 1985 campaign.

Leaders: Arturo FRONDIZI (former President of the Republic and President of the Party), Rogelio FRIGERIO (Vice President of the Party).

Intransigent Party (*Partido Intransigente*—PI). The PI is a left-of-center splinter of the UCR. It won six lower house seats in 1985, losing one in 1987.

Leaders: Dr. Oscar ALENDE (Congressional Bloc President), Lisandro VIALE, Mariano LORENCES (Secretary).

Union of the Democratic Center (*Unión de Centro Democrático*—UCD). Founded in 1980 as an alliance of eight right-of-center parties, the UCD refused to join a number of opposition groups that concluded a mid-1984 pact with the UCR on a variety of policy issues, including economic recovery and the Beagle Channel and Falkland Island disputes. It increased its lower house representation from three to seven in 1987.

Leaders: Alvaro ALSOGARAY (Congressional Bloc President), Jorge AGUADO.

Christian Democratic Party (*Partido Demócrata Cristiano*—PDC). The PDC is a traditional grouping of Christian Democrats with a relatively limited membership of less than 70,000.

Leaders: Carlos AUYERO (President), Augusto CONTE (Congressional Bloc President), Francisco CERRO, Gabriel PONZATTI.

Federal Alliance (*Alianza Federal*—AF). The rightist AF was formed in mid-1983 as a coalition of the Democratic Concentration (*Concentración Demócrata*), the Federal Party (*Partido Federal*), the Popular Federalist Force (*Fuerza Federalista Popular*), and the Popular Line Movement (*Movimiento Línea Popular*).

Leaders: Francisco MANRIQUE, Guillermo Belgrano RAWSON.

Democratic Left Front (*Frente de Izquierda Democrática*—FID). The FID was created in June 1983 as an alliance of the **Progressive Democratic Party** (*Partido Demócrata Progresista*—PDP) and the **Democratic Socialist Party** (*Partido Socialista Democrático*—PSD).

Leaders: Rafael MARTINEZ Raymonda (PDP), Américo GHIOLDI (PSD).

Communist Party of Argentina (*Partido Comunista de la Argentina*—PCA). Founded in 1918, the pro-Moscow PCA operated semilegally under the former military regime, in part because of the latter's relatively cordial relations with the Soviet Union, which had become the country's largest purchaser of grain, as well as a strategic ally during the intensely anti-Western phase occasioned by the Falklands war. Although a registered party, the PCA backed the Peronist slate in the 1983 balloting. At its 16th party congress in November 1986, delegates engaged in harsh self-criticism of 40 years of "reformist" policies and ousted a number of old guard figures, including longtime leaders Rubens ISCARO and Irene RODRIGUES, from both the Politburo and Central Committee.

In June 1987 the PCA joined with the **Humanist Party** (*Partido Humanista*—PH) and ten other small groups to form the **Broad Front of Liberation** (*Frente Amplio de Liberación*—FAL) as an electoral alternative to the UCR and Peronists.

Leaders: Patricio ETCHEGARY, Luis HELLER, Jorge PREYRA, Ernesto SALGADO, Athos FAVA (General Secretary).

Other minor parties include the conservative **National Center Party** (*Partido Nacional de Centro*—PNC), launched in 1980; the center-right **Union for the New Majority** (*Unión para la Nueva Mayoría*—UNM), formed in 1986 by José Antonio ROMERO Feris; the **Democratic Integration Party** (*Partido de Integración Democrática*—PID), led by Ricardo HILLEMAN; the **Popular Christian Party** (*Partido Popular Cristiano*—PPC), led by José Antonio ALLENDE; the **Social Democracy** (*Democracia Social*—DS), organized in 1981 by former junta member Adm. Emilio MASSERA; the Peronist-Trotskyite **Movement to Socialism** (*Movimiento al Socialismo*—MAS), led by Rubén VISCONTI and Luis ZAMORA; the **Popular Socialist Party** (*Partido Socialista Popular*—PSP), led by Edgardo ROSSI and Guillermo ESTEVEZ Boero; the Trotskyite **Workers' Party** (*Partido Obrero*—PO), led by Juan Carlos VENTURINI and Gregorio FLORES; the Maoist **Marxist-Leninist Communist Worker's Party** (*Partido Obrero Comunista Marxista-Leninista*—POCML, led by Elías SEMAN and Roberto CRISTINA; and the **Workers' Socialist Party** (*Partido Socialista de los Trabajadores*—PST), led by Nora CIAPPONI. Regional parties include the **Corrientes Autonomous Party** (*Partido Autonomista de Corrientes*—PAC), the **Corrientes Liberal Party**

(*Partido Liberal de Corrientes*— PLC), the **Jujeño Popular Movement** (*Movimiento Popular Jujeño*— MPJ), the **Mendoza Democratic Party** (*Partido Demócrata de Mendoza*— PDM), the **Neuguén Popular Movement** (*Movimiento Popular Neuquino*— MPN), the **Popular Catamarca Movement** (*Movimiento Popular Catamarqueño*— MPC), the **Salta Renewal Party** (*Partido Renovador de Salta*— PRS), and the **San Juan Bloc Party** (*Partido Bloquista de San Juan*— PBSJ).

Terrorist Groups:

Revolutionary Peronist (*Peronista Revolucionario*— PR). The *Peronista Revolucionario* is the name assumed in mid-1986 by the Peronist Montonero Movement (*Movimiento Peronista Montonero*— MPM), which was formally launched at Rome, Italy, in April 1977 by merger of the *Montonero* guerrilla movement and the Authentic Peronist Party (*Partido Peronista Auténtico*— PPA). The *Montoneros* were organized as a Peronist terrorist movement in 1969 and merged with the Revolutionary Armed Forces (*Fuerzas Armadas Revolucionarias*— FAR) in 1972. The PPA was established as a faction within Frejuli on March 12, 1975, but following the ouster of its leaders on April 4, it went into opposition as an independent party pledged to "fight monopolies" and to "promote worker participation in the planning and control of the national economy". It was banned by the Peronist government on December 24, 1975. In late 1979, the MPM announced a major "counter offensive" against the Videla regime which failed to materialize; in April 1980, it declared its support for the left-wing guerrillas in El Salvador as part of a campaign for solidarity among Latin American insurrectionist groups.

Announcing that the Montoneros had been formally dissolved, PPA leader Oscar Bidegaín was arrested in December 1983 upon his return to Argentina in a bid to regain legal status for his party. In February 1984, the Montonero commander Mario Eduardo Firmenich, was arrested by Brazilian authorities and subsequently extradited to Argentina after assurances had been tendered that he would not be subjected to more than 30 years' imprisonment. In August 1986, *La Nación* reported that Firmenich had agreed with MNJ leader Vicente Saadi to help finance Peronist candidates in the 1987 congressional campaign if a PR representative were included in their list.

Leaders: Dr. Oscar BIDEGAIN (former PPA leader, currently imprisoned), Mario Eduardo FIRMENICH (former MPM Secretary General, currently imprisoned).

Revolutionary Labor Party/People's Revolutionary Army (*Partido Revolucionario de los Trabajadores/Ejército Revolucionario del Pueblo*— PRT/ERP). The founder of the Trotskyite PRT/ERP, Roberto Santucho, and his principal subordinate, Enrique Gorriaran, were both killed in a clash with army security forces in July 1976. In a press conference at Rome a year later, the new PRT/ERP leader, Luis Mattini, called for "democratic unity" based on respect for human rights and equality for all Argentinians. The PRT/ERP has been less successful as a political force than the *Montoneros* because of its lack of a strong Peronist base, and much of its effectiveness as a guerrilla organization was believed destroyed by the end of 1977.

Leader: Luis MATTINI.

Argentine Anticommunist Alliance (*Alianza Anticomunista Argentina*— AAA). Originally an army-linked paramilitary organization thought to have conducted much of the "dirty war" of the 1970s, the Alliance was reported to have been revived after police raids on several residences in May 1985 yielded firearms, explosives, and three arrests. The group has since been linked to a number of terrorist acts, including several kidnappings and the destruction of the facilities of the moderate Radio Belgrano station. It's alleged founder José López Rega surrendered to US authorities at Miami in March 1986 and was extradited to Argentina in July to face a variety of charges, including fraud and murder.

Leaders: José LOPEZ Rega (under indictment), Raúl GUGLIAMINETTI, Aníbal GORDON.

LEGISLATURE

Argentina's bicameral **National Congress** (*Congreso Nacional*) was dissolved in March 1976 and reconstituted after the election of October 30, 1983.

Senate (*Senado*). In its present form, the upper house consists of 2 members elected by each of the 23 provincial legislatures. Senators are renewed by thirds every three years, the thirds elected in 1986 and 1989

determined by lot. Following the 1986 balloting, the Justicialist Liberation Front held 20 seats; the Radical Civic Union, 18; the Movement of Integration and Development, 1; regional parties, 6 (Neuguén Popular Movement, 2; San Juan Bloc Party, 2; Corrientes Autonomous Party, 1; Corrientes Liberal Party, 1); with 1 vacancy from Santiago del Estero.

President: Víctor MARTINEZ (Vice President of the Republic).
President Pro Tempore: Dr. Edison OTERO.

Chamber of Deputies (*Cámara de Diputados*). The lower house currently consists of 254 deputies, directly elected for four years, with one-half reelected every two years. Following the election of September 6, 1987, the Radical Civic Union held 117 seats; the Peronists, 105; the Union of the Democratic Center, 7; the Intransigent Party, 5; the Christian Democratic Party, 3; regional parties, 17.

Speaker: Dr. Juan Carlos PUGLIESE.

CABINET

President	Raúl Alfonsín
Vice President	Víctor Martínez
Ministers	
Defense	José Horacio Jaunarena
Economy	Juan Vital Sourrouille
Education and Justice	Jorge Sábato
Foreign Relations and Worship	Dante Caputo
Interior	Enrique Nosiglia
Labor and Social Security	Ideler Tonelli
Public Health and Social Action	Ricardo Barrios Arrechea
Public Works and Services	Rodolfo Terragno
Secretary General of the Presidency	Carlos Becerra
President, Central Bank	José Luis Machinea

NEWS MEDIA

The impact of Argentina's traditionally influential news media has been substantially reduced in recent years. There were numerous newspaper closings during the Peronist revival, while official censorship and personal attacks on journalists further inhibited the media prior to the restoration of civilian rule in 1983. More recently, economic recession has severely curtailed the circulation of most leading papers.

Press. Unless otherwise noted, the following are Spanish-language dailies published at Buenos Aires: *Crónica* (520,000 daily, 430,000 Sunday); *Clarín* (490,000 daily, 740,000 Sunday); *La Nación* (205,000 daily, 275,000 Sunday), founded 1870; *La Razón* (160,000); *Diario Popular* (140,000); *El Cronista Comercial* (100,000); *La Prensa* (65,000 daily, 145,000 Sunday), founded 1869; *Buenos Aires Herald* (21,000), in English.

News agencies. The domestic agencies include *Agencia "Los Diarios"*, TELAM (official news agency), and TelPress International. There are also a number of foreign agencies with bureaus at Buenos Aires.

Radio and television. All broadcasting is supervised by the secretary of state for communications and the *Comité Federal de Radiodifusión* (Comfer). There are approximately 150 radio stations and 35 television stations. *Radio Nacional* is an official government service providing local, national, and international programming. Government-owned commercial radio and television stations are grouped under the *Dirección General de Radio y Televisión,* while privately owned stations belong to the *Asociación Radiodifusoras Privadas Argentinas* and the *Asociación de Teleradiodifusoras Argentinas.* During 1987 approximately 19.8 million radio and 6.0 million television receivers were in use.

INTERGOVERNMENTAL REPRESENTATION

Ambassador to the US: Enrique José Alejandro CANDIOTI.

US Ambassador to Argentina: Theodore E. GILDRED.

Permanent Representative to the UN: Dr. Marcelo E.R. DELPECH.

IGO Memberships (Non-UN): ADF, AfDB, ALADI, CCC, G77, Geplacea, IADB, ICAC, ICCO, ICM, IIC, ILZ, Inmarsat, Intelsat, Interpol, ISO, IWC, IWSG, IWTC, NAM, OAS, PCA, SELA.

CONTESTED TERRITORY

Falkland Islands (*Las Malvinas*). First sighted by an English vessel in the late sixteenth century and named after the incumbent treasurer of the Royal Navy, the Falkland Islands were later styled *Les Malouines* (from which the Spanish *Las Malvinas* is derived) by a group of French settlers who transferred their rights to Spain in 1766. A British settlement, recognized by Spain in 1771, was withdrawn in 1774, the islands being uninhabited at the time of Argentine independence in 1816. The new government at Buenos Aires claimed the territory by right of colonial succession in 1820, although a group of its nationals were forcibly expelled in 1832, prior to a reaffirmation of British sovereignty in 1833. Argentine claims to the smaller South Georgia and South Sandwich islands, several hundred miles to the southeast, were not formally advanced until 1927 and 1948, respectively. The question of the legal status of the territories, collectively encompassing some 6,000 square miles (16,058 sq. km.), became the subject of extensive negotiations initiated under United Nations auspices in 1966 and extending to early 1982. The British claim is based on continuous occupation since 1833 and the manifest sentiment of the 1,800 inhabitants (primarily sheepherders domiciled on East and West Falkland) to remain British subjects.

The immediate precipitant of the 1982 conflict was the arrival at South Georgia on March 19 of a group of workers to dismantle an old whaling station, in the course of which the Argentine flag was raised. Following a British protest to the UN Security Council, Argentinian troops landed on the Falklands on April 2 and quickly overcame resistance by a token force of Royal Marines. South Georgia and South Sandwich were seized on April 3. Two days later, the lead ships of a British armada sailed from Portsmouth, England, participating in the recovery of South Georgia on April 25–26. On May 21, some 5,000 British troops began landing at San Carlos Bay on the northwest coast of East Falkland, initiating an operation that culminated in surrender of the main Argentine force at Stanley on June 14. Overall, the campaign cost 254 British and 750 Argentinian lives and heavy material losses, including that of Argentina's only heavy cruiser, the *General Belgrado,* and, on the British side, of two destroyers and two frigates. Subsequently, Argentina and 19 other Latin American countries submitted the Falkland issue to the UN General Assembly, although no de jure resolution of the sovereignty issue has yet been achieved.

During 1985, President Alfonsín repeatedly expressed alarm at the construction of an airport (approximately the size of that at Point Salines in Grenada) on Mount Pleasant, while naming as his government's priority "the demilitarization of the South Atlantic". A more serious problem arose in 1986, with a British announcement in late October that it would establish a 200-mile "exclusive economic zone", measured from the shore of the islands, as of February 1, 1987, thereby overlapping a 200-mile zone previously claimed by Argentina off its continental mainland. However, the effect of the action was subsequently diluted by a British foreign ministry declaration that it would police the new policy (impinging largely on fishing) only up to the limit of a previously established 150-mile "protective zone" measured from the center of the islands. (For additional details on the Falklands issue, see United Kingdom: Related Territories.)

AUSTRALIA

Commonwealth of Australia

Political Status: Original member of the Commonwealth; established as a federal state under democratic parliamentary regime in 1901.

Area: 2,966,136 sq. mi. (7,682,300 sq. km.).

Population: 14,923,300 (1981C), 16,354,000 (1988E).

Major Urban Centers (urban areas, 1984E): CANBERRA (264,000); Sydney (3,355,000); Melbourne (2,888,000); Brisbane (1,145,000); Perth (983,000); Adelaide (979,000); Hobart (176,000); Darwin (66,000).

Official Language: English.

Monetary Unit: Australian Dollar (market rate March 1, 1988, 1.39 dollars = $1US).

Sovereign: Queen ELIZABETH II.

Governor General: Sir Ninian STEPHEN; succeeded Sir Zelman COWEN on July 29, 1982.

Prime Minister: Robert James Lee HAWKE (Australian Labor Party); sworn in on March 11, 1983, following parliamentary election of March 5, succeeding John Malcolm FRASER (Liberal-National Coalition); reappointed following election of December 1, 1984.

THE COUNTRY

Lying in the Southern Hemisphere between the Pacific and Indian oceans, Australia derives its name from the Latin *australis* (southern). A nation of continental dimensions, with an area slightly less than that of the contiguous United States, Australia includes the separate island of Tasmania in the southeast. It is the driest of the inhabited continents, with the inner third of its territory a desert ringed by another third of marginal agricultural lands. The population is concentrated in the coastal areas, particularly in the southeastern states of New South Wales and Victoria. These states account for nearly two-thirds of the total population, with their capitals alone accounting for nearly one-third. Persons of British extraction now comprise only about one-half of the total, while the remainder includes a sizable group of immigrants, of predominantly Western and Southern European origins, but with a growing proportion of Asians, primarily refugees from Indochina. There are also an estimated 300,000 aborigines who have won government support in their campaign for better treatment, although land-rights legislation on their behalf was shelved in 1986 due to lack of public support. Women comprise 40 percent of the labor force; over 50 percent of the adult female population was employed full time outside the home in 1984, concentrated mainly in clerical, sales, and lower-level health care occupations.

Traditionally dependent upon exports of wool and wheat, the Australian economy industrialized rapidly after World War II with subsequent expansion based on extensive mineral discoveries. Although agriculture continues to account for two-fifths of exports, manufactured goods and such natural resources as iron ore, bauxite, coal, nickel, gold, silver, copper, uranium, oil, and natural gas have increased in importance, with approval being granted in mid-1984 for the largest uranium mine in the world to commence operations at Roxby Downs, South Australia.

GOVERNMENT AND POLITICS

Political background. The Commonwealth of Australia was formed on January 1, 1901, by federation of the former British colonies of New South Wales, Queensland, South Australia, Tasmania, Victoria, and Western Australia, all of which became federal states. Two territorial units were added in 1911: the vast, underpopulated, and undeveloped area of the Northern Territory and the Australian Capital Territory, an enclave created within New South Wales around the capital city of Canberra. Political power since World War II has been exercised largely by three leading parties: the Australian Labor Party on the one side and the Liberal Party, in alliance with the National Party (formerly the National Country Party), on the other. The Liberal–National Country coalition ruled from 1949 to 1972, when the Labor Party narrowly toppled the regime headed by Liberal Prime Minister William McMAHON.

In the wake of the 1972 election, the government of E. Gough WHITLAM moved quickly to eliminate military conscription, withdraw remaining Australian forces from Vietnam, and establish closer links with other Asian governments — in particular, that of the People's Republic of China. On the domestic scene, it lowered the voting age to 18, established a representative body for the aborigines, and attempted to expand federal power vis-à-vis the states. It proved incapable, however, of resolving a number of economic problems and was forced to call a general election in May 1974 after failing to obtain approval for key money bills in the opposition-dominated Senate. The result was an even narrower Labor victory in the House of Representatives, coupled with a failure to gain control of the Senate. During 1975 the Labor Party's problems intensified. Following Senate rejection of the government's annual budget, Governor General John R. KERR, in an unprecedented action on November 11, dismissed the prime minister, named minority leader Malcolm FRASER as his successor, and dissolved both houses of Parliament. In an election held on December 13, the electorate turned decisively to Fraser, giving his Liberal–National Country coalition its most impressive victory ever.

In an election called one year early, on December 10, 1977, the coalition defied predictions and succeeded in retaining its better than two-thirds majority in the House of Representatives. On the other hand, its showing at the October 18, 1980, general election was less impressive: although retaining a three-to-two advantage in the House, the Fraser government fell two seats short of a majority in the Senate, with the balance of power in the hands of five senators from the Australian Democratic Party.

The Liberal-National coalition continued to decline in popular support over the next three years, in part because of a series of disputes with trade unions over austerity measures to combat severe economic recession. On February 3, 1983, Fraser called a general election for March 5, with William G. HAYDEN stepping down as Labor leader on February 8 in favor of Robert (Bob) J.L. HAWKE, former head of the Australian Council of Trade Unions and "the most admired public figure in the country" on the basis of opinion polls. Led by Hawke, Labor achieved a decisive victory in the House balloting, although unable to win effective control of the Senate.

In an apparent upsurge of popularity accompanying economic recovery, Hawke called for a new election on December 1, 1984, which, however, yielded a reduced majority in the House and failure to obtain a majority in the Senate. By contrast, amid disarray within opposition ranks (see Current issues, below), Labor increased its House margin by four seats while retaining its plurality in the Senate at the balloting of July 11, 1987.

Constitution and government. The Federal Constitution of July 9, 1900, coupled a bicameral legislative system patterned after that of the United States with the British system of executive responsibility to Parliament. The governor general, most of whose actions are circumscribed by unwritten constitutional convention, represents the Crown. Responsibility for defense, external affairs, foreign trade, and certain other matters is entrusted to the federal government, residual powers being reserved to the states. The prime minister, who is leader of the majority party (or coalition) in the Federal Parliament, is assisted by a cabinet selected from the membership of the House and Senate. The Senate is composed of no less than 6 (currently 12) senators from each of the six states, with two additional senators each from the Australian Capital Territory and the Northern Territory. Apart from the territorial incumbents, senators are elected for six years, the elections being staggered so that approximately one-half of the Senate is renewed every three years. The House of Representatives is to have, as nearly as possible, twice as many members as the Senate. Membership is proportional to population, although no state can be allotted fewer than five representatives; almost two-thirds of the House seats are held by the heavily populated states of New South Wales and Victoria. The House is elected for a period of three years, unless dissolved sooner, and must initiate all measures dealing with revenue and taxation. The entire Senate may be elected in the event of a double dissolution, normally on the advice of the prime minister following upper house intransigence in regard to government measures (as occurred in both 1983 and 1987), while either double dissolution (with mandatory back-dating of senatorial terms) or early dissolution of the House may result in scheduled elections for the two bodies falling at different times. (Referenda providing for the abandonment of fixed senatorial terms so that Senate and House elections would always be held simultaneously were defeated in 1974, 1977, and 1984.)

The judicial system embraces the High Court of Australia, the Federal Court of Australia, state and territorial courts, and lower (magistrates') courts. Under legislation enacted in 1976, the High Court, consisting of a chief justice and 6 other justices, remains responsible for interpreting the Constitution while also maintaining original and appellate jurisdiction in certain areas. A 25-member Federal Court, established in 1977, has assumed jurisdiction in a number of matters previously under the purview of the High Court and has replaced both the Australian Industrial Court and the Federal Court of Bankruptcy.

For the most part, state governments are patterned after the federal government. Each state has an elected premier, an appointed governor, and (with the exception of Queensland) a bicameral legislature. The more important activities of the state governments are in the areas of health, public safety, transportation, education, and public utilities. In 1974 the partially elected advisory councils of the Northern and Capital territories were replaced by fully elected legislative assemblies, and in July 1978 a wide range of internal authority was transferred to the Northern Territory government, although the territory's chief minister declared in mid-1979 that statehood was still "years away".

State and Capital	Area (sq. mi.)	Population (1984E)
New South Wales (Sydney)	309,498	5,407,000
Queensland (Brisbane)	666,872	2,505,000
South Australia (Adelaide)	379,922	1,352,000
Tasmania (Hobart)	26,177	437,000
Victoria (Melbourne)	87,876	4,075,000
Western Australia (Perth)	975,096	1,383,000

Territory and Capital		
Capital Territory (Canberra)	927	245,000
Northern Territory (Darwin)	519,768	139,000

During a visit in March 1986, Queen Elizabeth gave royal assent to the Australia Act, which terminated most residual links to the monarchy. Court cases could not, thenceforth, be referred to Britain's Privy Council on final appeal and the queen would no longer tender ceremonial approval for gubernatorial appointments, although state governments wishing to do so might continue to bestow knighthoods on New Year's and the queen's birthday.

Foreign relations. Australia's foreign policy, traditionally based upon its position as an isolated outpost of Great Britain, has been adjusted to the realities of declining British power and close geographic proximity to Asia, while a long-standing commitment to internationalism has been expressed by membership in the Commonwealth and the United Nations, in such regional security organizations as ANZUS, and in such cooperative efforts as the Colombo Plan and the Asian Development Bank.

During the 1970s Australia sought to delineate a foreign policy more independent of Britain and the United States. Almost immediately after assuming office, Prime Minister Whitlam, an outspoken critic of US Vietnamese policy, established diplomatic relations with the People's Republic of China, East Germany, and North Vietnam. Under Prime Minister Fraser, relations with Washington improved, while ratification of a major cooperation treaty with Japan (an outgrowth of negotiations initiated by Whitlam in 1973) was completed in July 1977. Responding to the Soviet intervention in Afghanistan, Canberra in 1980 supported an increased ANZUS naval presence in the Indian Ocean and granted US air and naval forces increased access to Australian bases. Following the accession of the Labor government in March 1983, Prime Minister Hawke normalized relations with the Soviet Union, while reaffirming Australia's ANZUS commitment in a June visit to the United States.

Australia's position on nuclear power and weapons, long controversial because of the country's possession of 30 percent of global uranium reserves, attracted international attention following the February 1985 refusal by New Zealand to allow docking privileges to a US naval ship without a determination that no nuclear weapons were on board. Wellington's policy created a rupture in the ANZUS

alliance (see articles on ANZUS and New Zealand), although the Hawke administration restated its allegiance to the pact. After the United States suspended its security obligations to New Zealand over the issue in 1986, joint US-Australian military exercises were held and bilateral security cooperation was reinforced, the legal framework of ANZUS being left intact pending resolution of the dispute between Washington and Wellington.

While refusing to deny port access to nuclear-armed US vessels, the government, in December 1986, responded to widespread antinuclear sentiment by ratifying the South Pacific Forum's Treaty of Rarotonga, which proposes a "nuclear-free zone" in the region. In addition, while continuing to export uranium to nuclear powers, including France, the government's vocal opposition to French nuclear testing in the South Pacific contributed to growing friction between the two countries. The rift widened in late 1986, when France reduced the size of its diplomatic mission in response to Australian support at the United Nations of measures requested by the independence movement on New Caledonia.

The Hawke administration has sought a role in resolving the Kampuchean question, having suggested a joint Australian-Japanese peace-keeping force to facilitate a Vietnamese withdrawal; however, Canberra's refusal to back the Democratic Kampuchea coalition at the United Nations and Hawke's overtures to Hanoi have precluded action in concert with the Association of Southeast Asian Nations (ASEAN). In another area of regional concern, Canberra discontinued economic assistance to Fiji following the September 1987 coup (see article on Fiji), but resumed the program in February 1988.

Current issues. The Labor Party's first retention of office for three successive terms was largely the result of disagreements within and between the National and Liberal parties in the months preceding the July 1987 election. In late 1986 the highly conservative leader of Queensland's National Party administration, Sir Johannes (Joh) BJELKE-PETERSEN had severely castigated the leadership of both opposition groups and in April 1987 ordered Queensland's MPs to withdraw from the coalition that had been in effect at the federal level since 1949. Sir Joh did not, however, act upon an earlier threat to mount an "assault on Canberra" by campaigning for the post of federal executive, since he would thereby have been obliged to resign his state premiership. Although agreeing not to "stand in the way of defeating the Hawke government", Sir Joh declared his opposition to a successor regime headed by either the NP's Ian SINCLAIR or the LP's John HOWARD, while asserting that the latter's long time opponent, former Liberal leader Andrew PEACOCK, was "someone I can work with". Following the election, Howard withstood a leadership challenge from Peacock, as did Sinclair from Queensland MP Ray BRAITHWAITE, and on August 6 the two announced a restoration of the coalition between their respective parties.

The parliamentary double dissolution had been occasioned by the failure of a number of government proposals in the Senate, including a controversial attempt to introduce national identity cards that would allegedly curtail welfare fraud and tax evasion. While the measure was effectively killed by Labor's failure to improve its strength in the upper house, Prime Minister Hawke announced a variety of cost-cutting administrative changes upon his return to office, including a reduction in the number of senior cabinet ministers from 27 to 16.

By early 1988, despite a substantial economic revival, the Labor Party was being buffeted by a number of political scandals (one of which had forced the resignation of its national president, Michael YOUNG) and in a stunning electoral upset in March lost control of New South Wales, the country's most populous state.

POLITICAL PARTIES

Government Party:

Australian Labor Party (ALP). The oldest of the existing political parties, with a continuous history since the 1890s, Labor began as the political arm of the trade-union movement and is still closely linked with the unions in both structure and orientation. Its traditional advocacy of extensive social services and expanded immigration (which trade-union elements only grudgingly endorsed) has now largely been accepted by the Liberal and National parties. Present policies include the pursuit of racial and sexual equality, increased rights for the aborigines, and a more independent foreign policy. The party has long been divided between a moderate, pragmatic wing, which commands a majority in terms of parliamentary representation, and a dogmatically socialist, trade-union-oriented left wing, which tends to be more strongly entrenched in the party organization. This dichotomy has become more visible under Hawke's leadership, the trade union faction claiming "we are in danger of losing our heart" because of economic deregulation and governmental neglect of Labor's antinuclear platform. Left-wing parliamentarians were held largely responsible for Labor's sudden refusal to cooperate with American MX missile testing in February 1985, although the party in July 1986 rejected a left-wing proposal to endorse the barring of US nuclear armed ships from Australian ports.

Leaders: Robert J.L. HAWKE (Prime Minister), William G. HAYDEN (Minister for Foreign Affairs), John BUTTON (Government Leader in the Senate), Robert McMULLAN (National Secretary).

Major Opposition Parties:

Liberal Party of Australia (LP). Founded in 1944 by Sir Robert Menzies as a successor to the United Australia Party, the Liberal Party represents an amalgamation of traditional liberals and conservatives with strong ties to the business community. Liberals generally espouse private enterprise and deprecate government ownership of commercial operations exclusive of power and other utilities, irrigation, communications, and certain transport facilities. The Liberals have a record of conservative financial policies, economic stability, counterinflationary measures, and cooperation with the Commonwealth and the United States. While losing its legislative majority in 1983, the party recouped some of its losses in the 1984 election and popular support for its leader, Andrew Peacock, appeared to be rising prior to his resignation because of the rejection of his candidate for deputy leader in September 1985. Peacock failed by a 41–28 vote to regain the leadership after the 1987 election and indicated, after accepting the post of deputy leader, that he had not abandoned his effort to do so.

Leaders: John W. HOWARD (Leader of the Opposition in the House), Neil BROWN (Deputy Leader), Andrew PEACOCK (Deputy Leader), Frederick M. CHANEY (Leader of the Opposition in the Senate).

National Party of Australia (NPA). Founded in 1920 as the Country Party and subsequently known as the National Country Party, the National Party assumed its present name in October 1982 in an effort to widen its appeal. Conservative in outlook, its policies have traditionally reflected a concern with rural and farming issues, such as guaranteed farm prices, tax rebates for capital investment and conversion to electricity, and soil conservation. Precluded by its size from winning a majority in the House, it has a long history of alliance with the United Australia Party and its successor, the Liberal Party. Recently, however, a conflict emerged within

the coalition over an implicit agreement that the parties would not compete with each other for safe seats. In 1986, the NPA retained its control of the Queensland state house, conservative Premier Bjelke-Petersen's strong showing provoking disagreement with the federal leadership and breakdown of the opposition coalition during the 1987 parliamentary campaign. Subsequently, it was reported that the Bjelke-Petersen faction had styled itself the **New National Party of Australia.**

Leaders: Ian SINCLAIR (Parliamentary Leader), Bruce LLOYD (Deputy Leader), Johannes BJELKE-PETERSEN (Premier of Queensland), Paul DAVEY (Federal Director).

Australian Democrats Party (AD). The mildly socialist AD was organized in May 1977 by former Liberal cabinet minister Donald L. CHIPP and some members of the Australia Party, a small reformist group. It has declared its intention to avoid identification with existing interests and to concentrate on specific current issues as they arise. By increasing its Senate representation from 2 seats to 5 at the October 1980 national election, it secured the balance of power in the upper house, a position that it maintained at the 1983, 1984, and 1987 balloting.

Leaders: Sen. Janine HAINES (Parliamentary Leader), Heather SOUTHCOTT (National President).

Minor Parties:

Western Australia Anti-Nuclear Party (WAANP). The WAANP was launched initially as the Nuclear-Free Australia Party (NFAP) in December 1985 by a group of individuals who had withdrawn from the **Nuclear Disarmament Party** (NDP) at its First National Conference in April because of alleged infiltration by members of the Socialist Workers' Party (below). The NDP had been organized in mid-1984 to oppose the mining and export of uranium, the docking of US nuclear-powered or armed ships in Australian ports, and nuclear defense ties with the United States. At the 1984 election it gained one upper house seat from Western Australia, but lost it when the senator, Jo Vallentine, joined the dissidents and sat as an independent prior to formation of the NFAP. The NDP and the WAANP obtained one Senate seat each in 1987.

Leader: Jo VALLENTINE.

Communist Party of Australia (CPA). Established in 1920 and with a current membership of less than 2,000, the CPA has never held a seat in the Federal Parliament. Pro-Moscow in the early years of the Sino-Soviet dispute, it subsequently adopted a neutralist position that included criticism of both Chinese and Russian influence in Southeast Asia. In May 1983, for the first time in nearly two decades, a CPA delegation visited China, where "differing assessments" of the Indochinese situation were discussed.

Leader: Judy MUNDEY (General Secretary).

Other minor parties, also unrepresented in the legislature, include the **Rural Australia Party** (formerly the Farm and Town Party); the **Communist Party of Australia–Marxist-Leninist** (CPA-ML), led by Edward Fowler HILL, which split from the CPA in 1967; the pro-Moscow **Socialist Party of Australia** (SPA), led by Peter Dudley SYMON, which broke with the CPA in 1971 after the latter had condemned the Soviet invasion of Czechoslovakia; the **Socialist Workers' Party,** led by James PERCY, which broke with the Trotskyite Fourth International in August 1985; and two additional Trotskyite formations, the **Socialist Labor League** (SLL) and the **Spartacist League of Australian and New Zealand** (SLANZ).

LEGISLATURE

The Australian **Federal Parliament** is a bicameral legislature with an upper chamber (Senate) and a lower chamber (House of Representatives), both elected by direct universal suffrage. In a May 1977 constitutional referendum, the electorate approved an amendment specifying that a casual Senate vacancy should be filled by a person of the same political party as the member being replaced.

Senate. The Senate currently consists of 76 members (12 from each state plus 2 each from the Australian Capital Territory and the Northern Territory), who are elected from state or territorial lists by proportional representation. Balloting is normally conducted every three years, with members of the state delegations serving staggered six-year terms; however, a full Senate was elected on July 11, 1987, following a "double dissolution" of Parliament on June 5. Following the 1987 poll the Australian Labor Party held 32 seats; the Liberal Party, 28; the Australian Democrats Party, 7; the National Party, 6; the Western Australia Anti-Nuclear Party, 1; the Nuclear Disarmament Party, 1; independent, 1.

President: Kerry SIBRAA.

House of Representatives. The present House consists of 148 representatives elected from single-member constituencies by preferential balloting (progressive elimination of lowest-ranked candidates with redistribution of preferences until one candidate secures a majority). Members are elected for three-year terms, subject to dissolution. Following the election of July 11, 1987, the Australian Labor Party held 86 seats; the Liberal Party, 43; and the National Party, 19.

Speaker: Joan CHILD.

CABINET

Prime Minister	Robert J.L. (Bob) Hawke
Deputy Prime Minister	Lionel Bowen
Senior Ministers	
Administrative Services	Stewart West
Arts, Sports, Environment, Tourism and Territories	Graham Richardson
Assisting the Prime Minister for Commonwealth-State Relations	Lionel Bowen
Community Services and Health	Dr. Neal Blewett
Defense	Kim C. Beazley
Employment, Education and Training	John Dawkins
Finance	Peter Walsh
Foreign Affairs and Trade	William (Bill) Hayden
Immigration, Local Government and Ethnic Affairs	Clyde Holding
Industrial Relations	Ralph Willis
Industry Technology and Commerce	John Button
Primary Industries and Energy	John Kerin
Social Security	Brian Howe
Trade Negotiations	Michael Duffy
Transport and Communications	Gareth Evans
Attorney General	Lionel Bowen
Treasurer	Paul Keating
Junior Ministers	
Aboriginal Affairs	Gerry Hand
Arts and Territories	Gary Punch
Consumer Affairs and Prices	Nick Bolkus
Defense Science and Personnel	Ros Kelly
Employment and Education Services	Peter Duncan
Home Affairs	Robert Ray
Housing and Aged Care	Peter Staples
Justice	Michael Tate
Local Government and Status of Women	Margaret Reynolds
Resources	Peter Cook
Science, Customs and Small Business	Barry O. Jones
Transport and Communications Support	Peter Morris
Veterans' Affairs	Ben Humphreys
Governor, Central Bank	Robert Alan Johnston

NEWS MEDIA

In recent years an increasing number of newspapers and broadcasting stations have been absorbed by media groups, the three principal ones being the John Fairfax Group, the Herald and Weekly Times, Ltd., and News Corporation, Ltd. The chief executive and principal shareholder of News Corporation, Ltd., Australian-born Rupert Murdoch, has extended his corporate holdings to include leading overseas publications, including *The Times* (United Kingdom) which in 1981 became one of a number of papers controlled by News International, a UK subsidiary of News Corporation, Ltd.

Press. Newspapers are privately owned and almost all are published in the state capitals for intrastate readers; circulation figures for most have declined in recent years, those that follow being for September 1987. *The Australian* and the *Australian Financial Review* are the only genuinely national daily newspapers. The leading dailies are as follows: *Sun* (Melbourne, 558,900), sensationalist; *Daily Mirror* (Sydney, 284,100); *Daily Telegraph* (Sydney, 274,500), conservative; *Sydney Morning Herald* (Sydney, 258,700), oldest morning newspaper (founded 1831), conservative; *The West Australian* (Perth, 238,100), conservative; *The Age* (Melbourne, 235,200), independent; *The Sun* (Sydney, 231,800); *The Advertiser* (Adelaide, 216,300), conservative; *Courier Mail* (Brisbane, 213,900), conservative; *The Herald* (Melbourne, 213,100); *News* (Adelaide, 155,800); *The Australian* (Sydney, Adelaide, Perth, Melbourne, Brisbane, 139,300), first national daily, independent; *Sun* (Brisbane, 125,800); *Telegraph* (Brisbane, 112,500); *Daily News* (Perth, 91,000); *Australian Financial Review* (Sydney, 77,800); *The Mercury* (Hobart, 53,900), conservative; *The Canberra Times* (Canberra, 43,300), conservative; *Northern Territory News* (Darwin, 18,900). The leading Sunday papers are: *Sun-Telegraph* (Sidney, 575,800); *Sun-Herald* (Sidney, 565,000); *Sunday Sun* (Brisbane, 359,500); *Sunday Mail* (Brisbane, 316,900); *Sunday Times* (Perth, 288,600); *Sunday Mail* (Adelaide, 238,700); *Sunday Press* (Melbourne, 164,900); *Sunday Observer* (Melbourne, 97,300); *Sunday Tasmanian* (Hobart, 40,000); *Sun Territorian* (Darwin, 20,202).

News agencies. The domestic agencies are the Australian Associated Press, a Reuters-affiliated international news service owned by the principal metropolitan dailies of Australia, and Australian United Press, a news service controlled by country papers.

Radio and television. Radio and television services are provided both by private stations and by those of the Australian Broadcasting Corporation, whose status is comparable to that of the British Broadcasting Corporation. The Australian Broadcasting Control Board is a government body that determines and guarantees technical and programming standards for radio and television stations. The Federation of Australian Radio Broadcasters is an association of privately owned radio stations; its television counterpart is the Federation of Australian Commercial Television Stations. There were approximately 27.3 million radio and 6.0 million television receivers in 1987.

INTERGOVERNMENTAL REPRESENTATION

Ambassador to the US: Frederick Rawdon DALRYMPLE.

US Ambassador to Australia: Laurence William LANE, Jr.

Permanent Representative to the UN: Richard A. WOOLCOTT.

IGO Memberships (Non-UN): ADB, ANZUS, APEF, BIS, CCC, CIPEC, CP, CWTH, IBA, ICAC, ICCO, ICO, IEA, ILZ, Inmarsat, INRO, Intelsat, Interpol, ITC, IWC, IWSG, IWTC, OECD, PCA, SPC, SPEC, SPF.

RELATED TERRITORIES

Ashmore and Cartier Islands Territory. The Ashmore Islands (comprising Middle, East, and West islands) and Cartier Island, all uninhabited, are situated in the Indian Ocean about 200 miles off the northwest coast of Australia. Under the Ashmore and Cartier Islands Acceptance Act (effective May 10, 1934) it was intended that the territory be administered by Western Australia, but by a 1938 amendment to the Act it was formally annexed to the Northern Territory. Since July 1978, Ashmore and Cartier have been under the direct administration of the Australian government, initially under the Minister for Home Affairs and presently under the Minister for Territories.

Australian Antarctic Territory. A British legacy, the Australian Antarctic Territory encompasses two sectors of Antarctica extending from

45 to 136 degrees East Longitude and from 142 to 160 degrees East Longitude. Together these sectors comprise almost 2.5 million square miles, or nearly 50 percent of the continent. The provisions of the Antarctic Treaty of 1959 have placed the area in a state of suspended sovereignty, although nominally the laws of the Australian Capital Territory are in effect.

Christmas Island. Australia took over administration of Christmas Island from Singapore in 1958. The former British Crown Colony, with an area of about 52 square miles, is located in the Indian Ocean about 230 miles south of Java and is governed by an administrator responsible to the Minister for Territories. As of June 1983 the population was 3,214, over three-fourths of whom were Chinese and Malays. The only industry on the island, the extraction of phosphates (deposits are expected to be depleted in the late 1980s), is under management of the British Phosphate Commission, the shareholders being Australia, New Zealand, and the United Kingdom.

Administrator: A.D. TAYLOR.

Cocos (Keeling) Islands. The Cocos Islands, discovered in 1609 by Capt. William Keeling of the British East India Company, consists of 2 copra-producing atolls of 27 islands that were detached from Singapore in 1955. They are located in the Indian Ocean about 580 miles southwest of Java and have an area of about 5.5 square miles. In September 1978, John Clunies-Ross, the descendant of a Scottish sea captain who was granted authority over the islands by Queen Victoria in 1886, yielded his claim after agreeing in June to financial compensation of $7 million. While an Australian-appointed administrator remained the chief executive officer of the islands, a Cocos (Keeling) Islands Council with limited powers was established in July 1979. The population of the islands in June 1984 was 584.

In a referendum conducted on April 6, 1984, an overwhelming majority of the inhabitants voted for integration with Australia (as opposed to free association or independence), the Canberra government subsequently announcing that the islands would, for voting purposes, thenceforth be treated as part of Australia's Northern Territory.

Administrator: Carolyn STUART.
Chairman of the Islands Council: Parson bin YAPAT.

Coral Sea Islands Territory. The Coral Sea Territory was created in 1969 as a means of administering a number of very small islands east of Queensland. The islands, none permanently inhabited, are under the jurisdiction of the Minister for Territories.

Heard Island and McDonald Islands. Heard and McDonald, located about 2,500 miles southwest of Fremantle in Western Australia, serve primarily as scientific stations. There are no permanent inhabitants and the islands are the responsibility of the Minister for Science.

Norfolk Island. Located about 1,000 miles east of Queensland, Norfolk Island has an area of 14 square miles and a population (1985) of 1,850. The island is the second-oldest British settlement in the South Pacific, having been discovered by Captain Cook in 1774 and occupied as a penal colony a few weeks after the founding of Sydney in 1788. Many of its inhabitants are descendants of *Bounty* mutineers who moved from Pitcairn in 1856. Under the Norfolk Island Act passed by the Australian Parliament in 1979, a nine-member Norfolk Island Legislative Assembly first convened in August 1979, its leadership constituting an Executive Council with cabinet-like functions. The chief executive is an Australian administrator named by the governor general and responsible to the Minister for Territories.

Administrator: Cmdr. John A. MATTHEW.
Assembly President and Chief Minister: John Terence BROWN.

AUSTRIA

Republic of Austria
Republik Österreich

Political Status: Federal republic established in 1918; reestablished in 1945 under Allied occupation; independence restored under Four-Power Treaty of July 27, 1955.

Area: 32,376 sq. mi. (83,853 sq. km.).

Population: 7,555,338 (1981C), 7,564,000 (1988E).

Major Urban Centers (1981C): VIENNA (1,531,346); Graz (243,166); Linz (199,910); Salzburg (139,426); Innsbruck (117,287).

Official Language: German.

Monetary Unit: Schilling (market rate March 1, 1988, 11.85 schillings = $1US).

Federal President: Dr. Kurt WALDHEIM; elected on June 8, 1986, to succeed Rudolf KIRCHSCHLÄGER for a six-year term commencing July 8.

Federal Chancellor: Dr. Franz VRANITZKY (Austrian Socialist Party); sworn in on June 16, 1986, following the resignation of Dr. Fred SINOWATZ (Austrian Socialist Party) on June 9; formed new government on January 14, 1987, following election of November 23, 1986.

THE COUNTRY

Situated at the crossroads of Central Europe, Austria is topographically dominated in the south and west by the Alps, while its eastern provinces lie within the Danube basin. The vast majority of the population is of Germanic stock, but there is an important Slovene minority in the province of Carinthia. Approximately 90 percent of the population is Catholic, although religious freedom is guaranteed. Women comprise approximately 40 percent of the official labor force, concentrated in sales, agriculture and unskilled manufacturing; females have held about 10 percent of Federal Assembly seats in recent years, with more than twice as many serving in provincial government.

Austria possesses a mixed economy; the state owns or holds major shares in most large industries, including mineral extraction, iron and steel, heavy machinery, utilities, finance, and broadcasting. Although limited in scope by the mountainous terrain, agriculture still provides over 80 percent of domestic food requirements, with an emphasis on grains, livestock, and dairy products. During the 1970s Austria's overall economic growth rate was exceeded among industrialized countries only by that of Japan. During the 1980s Austrian business attempted to garner a larger share of world trade, while by 1986 Austrian investment abroad exceeded capital inflow for the first time. Nonetheless, exports on a per capita basis remained well below those of Western European countries of comparable size and the nation continued to register a trade deficit in excess of $5 billion.

GOVERNMENT AND POLITICS

Political background. Austria was part of the Hapsburg-ruled Austro-Hungarian Empire until the close of World War I, the Austrian Republic being established in

November 1918. Unstable economic and political conditions led in 1933 to the imposition of a dictatorship under Engelbert DOLLFUSS, while civil war in 1934 resulted in the suppression of the Social Democratic Party and Dollfuss' assassination by National Socialists, who failed in their attempt to seize power. Hitler invaded Austria in March 1938 and formally incorporated its territory into the German Reich.

With the occupation of Austria by the Allies in 1945, a provisional government was established under the Socialist Karl RENNER. Following a general election in November 1945, Leopold FIGL formed a coalition government based on the People's (Catholic) and Socialist parties. The coalition endured under a succession of chancellors until 1966, when the People's Party won a legislative majority and Josef KLAUS organized a single-party government. In 1970 the Socialists came to power as a minority government under Dr. Bruno KREISKY. Subsequent elections in 1971, 1975, and 1979 yielded majority mandates for Chancellor Kreisky.

Following legislative balloting on April 24, 1983, in which the Socialists failed to retain clear parliamentary control, Kreisky, in accordance with a preelection pledge, resigned in favor of Vice Chancellor Fred SINOWATZ, who formed a coalition government on May 24 that included three members of the third-ranked Austrian Freedom Party.

In a runoff election on June 8, 1986, that attracted world attention because of allegations concerning his activities during World War II, former UN secretary general Kurt WALDHEIM defeated the Socialist candidate, Kurt STEYRER, for the Austrian presidency. In protest, Chancellor Sinowatz and three other cabinet members resigned, a new Socialist government being formed under the former finance minister, Dr. Franz VRANITZKY, on June 16.

The government collapsed in mid-September, after the Freedom Party had elected Jörg HAIDER, a far-right nationalist, as its chairman, thereby rendering it unacceptable as a coalition partner for the Socialists. At the ensuing lower house election of November 23, the Socialists lost 10 seats, though retaining a slim plurality, and on January 14, Vranitzky formed a new "Grand Coalition" with Dr. Alois MOCK of the People's Party as vice chancellor and foreign minister.

Constitution and government. Austria's constitution, adopted in 1920 and amended in 1929, provides for a federal democratic republic embracing nine provinces (*Länder*) including Vienna, which also serves as the capital of Lower Austria. Although most effective power is at the federal level, the provinces have considerable latitude in local administration. The national government consists of a president whose functions are largely ceremonial, a cabinet headed by a chancellor, and a bicameral legislature. The chancellor is appointed by the president from the party with the strongest representation in the lower house, the National Council (*Nationalrat*); the upper house, the Federal Council (*Bundesrat*), which represents the provinces, is restricted to a review of legislation passed by the National Council and has only delaying powers. The two houses together constitute the Federal Assembly (*Bundesversammlung*), whose approval in full sitting is required in certain contingencies.

Each province has an elected legislature (*Landtag*) and an administration headed by a governor (*Landeshauptmann*) designated by the legislature. The judicial system is headed by the Supreme Judicial Court (*Oberster Gerichtshof*) and includes 2 other high courts, the Constitutional Court (*Verfassungsgerichtshof*) and the Administrative Court (*Verwaltungsgerichtshof*). There are also 4 higher provincial courts (*Oberlandesgerichte*), 17 provincial and district courts (*Landes- und Kreisgerichte*), and numerous local courts (*Bezirksgerichte*).

Land and Capital	Area (sq. mi.)	Population (1981C)
Burgenland (Eisenstadt)	1,531	272,568
Carinthia (Klagenfurt)	3,681	537,212
Lower Austria (administered from Vienna)	7,402	1,439,609
Salzburg (Salzburg)	2,762	442,506
Styria (Graz)	6,327	1,184,175
Tirol (Innsbruck)	4,883	586,297
Upper Austria (Linz)	4,625	1,274,307
Vorarlberg (Bregenz)	1,004	305,612
Vienna	160	1,517,154

Foreign relations. The Austrian State Treaty of 1955 ended the four-power occupation of Austria, reestablished the country as an independent, sovereign nation, and forbade any future political or economic union with Germany. In October 1955, the Federal Assembly approved a constitutional amendment by which the nation declared its permanent neutrality, rejected participation in any military alliances, and prohibited the establishment of any foreign military bases on its territory. While generally sympathetic to the West in foreign policy, Austria has established friendly relations with most Communist governments and has promoted Vienna as a neutral meeting ground between East and West for international conferences and summit meetings.

The Kreisky government drew criticism from Israel and some Western leaders in March 1982 by hosting Libyan leader Mu'ammar al-Qadhafi in his first visit to the West, while five months later, writing in a West German periodical, Chancellor Kreisky accused Israel of "gigantic crimes" in connection with its invasion of Lebanon. Relations with the Jewish state had been volatile for over a decade — Kreisky was the first Western leader to extend recognition to the Palestine Liberation Organization — and the situation was further exacerbated by the circumstances surrounding the election of Kurt Waldheim as Austrian president in 1986 (see Current issues, below).

Current issues. Dominating recent events have been echoes of Austria's linkage with Germany during World War II. In January 1985, Defense Minister Friedhelm FRISCHENSCHLAGER, a member of the right-wing Freedom Party, was obliged to tender a public apology for having met with convicted Nazi war criminal Walter REDER upon the latter's release from 40 years of confinement in an Italian prison. The action was termed a "serious political mistake" by Chancellor Sinowatz, whose government survived a no-confidence vote at a special parliamentary session on February 1.

Far more damaging to the country's international image were charges leveled against former UN secretary general

Kurt WALDHEIM after he had announced as a candidate for the state presidency. At issue was a highly selective account of Waldheim's activities during 1938–1945 in his autobiography, *In the Eye of the Storm*. The author claimed, *inter alia*, to have been studying at Vienna during a period when he was, in fact, serving as an officer in a German force engaged in demonstrable atrocities in the Balkans. Documents published by the Austrian magazine *Profil* in March 1986 did not implicate Waldheim personally in war crimes, but raised serious questions that constituted, according to the World Jewish Congress, "a 40-year pattern of falsification and deception". Waldheim himself branded the accusations "pure lies", while Alois Mock, leader of the conservative Austrian People's Party, insisted that they represented external interference in Austrian domestic politics. Waldheim captured 49.64 percent of the vote at balloting on May 4, falling just short of the absolute majority required to avoid a run-off election on June 8 against the Socialist candidate, Kurt Steyrer. Chancellor Sinowatz reacted to the Waldheim victory by submitting his resignation, being succeeded on June 16 by Dr. Franz Vranitzky, a noted economist.

At a stormy Freedom Party convention in September 1986, Vice Chancellor STEGER was defeated for reelection as party chairman by Jörg Haider, leader of the group's so-called "national wing", who had earlier rebuked Frischenschlager for his apology in the Reder affair. Insisting that the junior coalition partner's "liberal element had been shoved into the background", Chancellor Vranitzky, who had been attempting to refurbish the country's image, called for a new election, with results that were sufficiently inconclusive as to necessitate revival of the "Grand Coalition" in January 1987.

Three months later, Waldheim's wartime record again captured the world's headlines as Washington, after a year-long inquiry based partly on Yugoslavian archive materials placed the former UN secretary general on its list of undesirable aliens barred from entering the United States. The Austrian president immediately branded the action as "dismaying and incomprehensible", later declaring that he would resign his office if the charges against him could be substantiated. Vranitzky, during a May visit to Washington, requested that the entrance ban be "modified", but the request was denied. A subsequent Waldheim audience with Pope John Paul II, coupled with official visits to Arab countries, elicited further criticism, while the Vienna section of the Socialist party, at a congress on June 27, called for the president to step down. The pressure on the beleaguered president intensified as the 50th anniversary of Germany's annexation of Austria approached in March 1988, with elements of both the army and the business community expressing their "deep concern" at the adverse impact of the affair on "the international and national prestige of Austria".

POLITICAL PARTIES

Government Coalition:

Austrian Socialist Party (*Sozialistische Partei Österreichs* – SPÖ). Formed in 1889 as the Social-Democratic Party, the SPÖ represents the overwhelming majority of workers and part of the lower middle class. The party has stressed neutrality, the nationalization of major industries, development of nuclear power, and economic planning. Former chancellor Bruno Kreisky resigned as honorary president upon reformation of the "Grand Coalition" in January 1987, claiming that Chancellor Vranitzky had turned his back on socialism in support of the "banks and bourgeoisie".

Leaders: Dr. Franz VRANITZKY (Federal Chancellor), Dr. Fred SINOWATZ (Chairman), Karl BLECHA and Dr. Heinz FISCHER (Vice Chairmen), Heinrich KELLER (First General Secretary); Peter SCHIEDER (Second General Secretary).

Austrian People's Party (*Österreichische Volkspartei* – ÖVP). Catholic in origin, the ÖVP developed out of the former Christian Social Party. Dominated by farmers and businessmen, it advocates a conservative economic policy and expansion of foreign trade.

Leaders: Dr. Alois MOCK (Vice Chancellor and Chairman of the Party), Helmut KUKACKA (Secretary General).

Other Parties:

Austrian Freedom Party (*Freiheitliche Partei Österreichs* – FPÖ). Formed in 1956 as a successor to the League of Independents, which drew much of its support from former National Socialists, the Freedom Party in the early 1970s moderated its extreme right-wing tendencies in favor of an essentially liberal posture. Its coalition with the SPÖ after the 1983 election, the first time that it had participated in a federal administration, collapsed as the result of a resurgence of far-right sentiment in 1986. Nonetheless, the FPÖ made substantial gains at the expense of both the SPÖ and the ÖVP in the November 1986 balloting.

Leaders: Jörg HAIDER (Chairman), Dr. Norbert STEGER (former Chairman), Friedhelm FRISCHENSCHLAGER (Parliamentary Leader), Helmut GUGGERBAUER (General Secretary).

Green Alternatives (*Grüne Alternativen* – GA). The GA was organized during a congress at Klagenfurt on February 14–15, 1987, of three groups that had jointly contested the 1986 election: the Austrian Alternative List (*Alternative Liste Österreich* – ALÖ), a left-wing formation with links to the West German Greens; the Citizens' Initiative Parliament (*Bürgerinitiative Parlament* – BIP), and the VGÖ (below). After failing in a bid to retain its organizational identity, the UGÖ withdrew, leaving the GA, with 7 *Nationalrat* deputies, one seat short of the minimum needed to qualify as a parliamentary group.

Leader: Freda MEISSNER-BLAU.

United Greens of Austria (*Vereinte Grünen Österreich* – VGÖ). Founded in 1982, the VGÖ is an essentially conservative grouping that is concerned with air pollution and nuclear power safety, but has taken no stand on armaments issues. It contested the 1986 election in coalition with the ALÖ (below), but refused to enter the AD in 1987. It holds one National Council seat.

Leaders: Josef BUCHNER (Chairman), Herbert FUX, Eva HAUK (General Secretary).

Austrian Communist Party (*Kommunistische Partei Österreichs* – KPÖ). The KPÖ, founded in 1918, supports nationalization, land reform, and a neutralist foreign policy. Its strength lies mainly in the industrial centers and in trade unions, but it has not been represented in the legislature since 1959 and obtained only .72 percent of the vote in 1986. The majority of the party leadership is pro-Moscow and opposed to Eurocommunism.

Leaders: Franz MUHRI (Chairman), Hans KALT, Karl REITER, Dr. Walter SILBERMAYR (Secretaries).

National Democratic Party (*Nationale Demokratische Partei* – NDP). The NDP is an extreme right-wing group, whose controversial leader, convicted terrorist Dr. Norbert Burger, won 3 percent of the vote in the 1980 presidential balloting, but did not campaign in 1983. The party's youth wing, New Right Action (*Aktion Neue Rechte*), has been described as "undoubtedly the most militant" of the far-right formations.

Leader: Dr. Norbert BURGER (Chairman).

Fringe parties include the **Austria Party** (*Österreich-Partei*), led by Franz OLAH and Hans KLECATZKY; the **Stop the Foreigners Party** (*Ausländer Halt*), which is active at Vienna; and the **Austrian Family Party** (*Österreichische Familienpartei* – ÖFP), organized in mid-1982 by Leopold KENDÖL, longtime president of the Austrian Catholic Family Association. In November 1984, a Neo-Nazi **National Front** (*Nationale Front*) was banned from holding a founding meeting at the capital.

LEGISLATURE

The bicameral **Federal Assembly** (*Bundesversammlung*) consists of a Federal Council (upper house) and a National Council (lower house).

Federal Council (*Bundesrat*). The upper chamber currently consists of 63 members representing each of the provinces on the basis of population, but with each province having at least 3 representatives. Chosen by provincial assemblies in proportion to party representation, members serve for terms ranging from four to six years, depending on the life of the particular assembly. The presidency of the Council rotates among the nine provinces for a six-month term. In the present Council, the Austrian People's Party holds 33 seats and the Austrian Socialist Party, 30.

National Council (*Nationalrat*). The lower chamber consists of 183 members elected by universal suffrage from 25 electoral districts for maximum terms of four years. At the most recent election of November 23, 1986, the Austrian Socialist Party won 80 seats; the Austrian People's Party, 77; the Austrian Freedom Party, 18; and the United Greens/Alternative List, 8 (subsequently, Green Alternatives, 7; United Greens, 1).

President: Leopold GRATZ.

CABINET

Chancellor	Dr. Franz Vranitzky
Vice Chancellor	Alois Mock
Ministers	
Agriculture and Forestry	Joseph Riegler
Economic Affairs	Robert Graf
Education and Arts	Hilde Hawlicek
Family, Sports and Environment	Marilies Flemming
Finance	Ferdinand Lacina
Foreign Affairs	Dr. Alois Mock
Interior	Karl Blecha
Justice	Egmont Foregger
National Defense	Robert Lichal
Science and Research	Hans Tuppy
Social Affairs	Alfred Dallinger
Transport and Nationalized Industries	Rudolf Streicher
State Secretaries	
Chancellery	Johanna Dohnal
	Franz Löschnak
Finance	Stummvoll Gunther
President, Austrian National Bank	Stephen Koren

NEWS MEDIA

All news media operate freely and without government restrictions.

Press. The following (circulation figures for 1987) are published at Vienna, unless otherwise noted: *Neue Kronen-Zeitung* (958,100 daily, 1,294,000 Sunday), independent; *Kurier* (402,300 Monday-Thursday, 567,100 Friday, 523,600 Sunday), independent; *Kleine Zeitung* (Graz, 155,600 daily, 194,600 Friday), independent; *Oberösterreichische Nachrichten* (Linz, 98,100 daily, 139,300 Saturday), independent; *Tiroler Tageszeitung* (Innsbruck, 95,200 daily, 108,600 Saturday), independent; *Neue Zeit* (Graz, 78,400 daily, 84,400 Friday), Socialist; *Neue AZ* (72,500 Monday-Thursday, 129,200 Friday, 78,300 Saturday), Socialist; *Die Presse* (68,500 Monday-Thursday, 87,900 Friday, 87,300 Saturday), independent business appeal; *Salzburger Nachrichten* (Salzburg, 67,000 daily, 107,300 Saturday), independent; *Kärtner Tageszeitung* (Klagenfurt, 65,400 daily, 68,500 Friday); *Vorarlberger Nachrichten* (Bregenz, 63,400 daily, 65,900 Saturday); *Wiener Zeitung* (50,000), government organ, world's oldest daily (f. 1703); *Volksstimme* (39,600 daily, 72,700 Sunday), Communist.

News agencies. The domestic agency is *Austria Presse-Agentur* (APA); numerous foreign agencies also maintain bureaus at Vienna.

Radio and television. The Austrian Broadcasting Company (*Österreichischer Rundfunk* — ORF), which controls both media, is state owned but protected in its operation from political interference under the broadcasting law. In 1987 the ORF broadcast three radio programs to 2.6 million receivers and two television programs to 2.7 million receivers over a network encompassing over 500 radio and 800 television transmitters (including relays).

INTERGOVERNMENTAL REPRESENTATION

Ambassador to the US: Dr. Friedrich HOESS.

US Ambassador to Austria: Henry Anatole GRUNWALD.

Permanent Representative to the UN: Peter HOHENFELLNER.

IGO Memberships (Non-UN): ADB, ADF, AfDB, CCC, CERN, CEUR, EFTA, *ESA,* IADB, ICM, ICO, IEA, ILZ, Intelsat, Interpol, ISO, IWTC, OECD, PCA.

BAHAMAS

Commonwealth of the Bahamas

Political Status: Independent member of the Commonwealth since July 10, 1973.

Area: 5,380 sq. mi. (13,935 sq. km.).

Population: 209,505 (1980C), 244,900 (1988E).

Major Urban Centers (1982E): NASSAU (115,000; New Providence Island, 137,000); Freeport (25,000; Grand Bahama Island, 35,000).

Official Language: English.

Monetary Unit: Bahamian Dollar (market rate March 1, 1988, 1.00 dollars = $1US).

Sovereign: Queen ELIZABETH II.

Governor General: Sir Gerald C. CASH; appointed on an acting basis September 2, 1976, following the incapacitation of Sir Milo B. BUTLER; formally invested on September 29, 1979.

Prime Minister: Sir Lynden Oscar PINDLING (Progressive Liberal Party); first appointed Prime Minister in 1967; reappointed following general elections in 1972, 1977, 1982, and on June 19, 1987.

THE COUNTRY

The Commonwealth of the Bahamas comprises a group of flat, coral islands stretching from the Western Atlantic near Florida to the Caribbean Sea. Geomorphically an extension of the Little and Great Bahama banks, the archipelago consists of approximately 700 islands, the most important of which are New Providence, Grand Bahama, and Abaco. The islands have a temperate climate with modest rainfall but lack sufficient fresh water, much of which must be imported. Most Bahamians (85 percent) are descendants of former slaves. The most important religious denominations are Anglican, Baptist, Methodist, and Roman Catholic.

Banking and tourism have long been mainstays of the Bahamian economy. One of the first — and the largest — of the offshore "tax havens", the country has over 300 financial institutions, including over 100 Eurocurrency branches of foreign banks; there are currently no corporate, capital gains, or personal income taxes. Extensive resort facilities typically attract in excess of 2.5 million tourists annually, providing over two-thirds of the islands' employment, while oil refining and transshipment has emerged as an important industry. Economic growth since 1984 has averaged a respectable 3.7 percent, although unemployment has hovered at 18 percent (35 percent among young people).

GOVERNMENT AND POLITICS

Political background. First discovered by Columbus in 1492 and subsequently inhabited by a series of private settlers, the Bahamas suffered harassment by the Spanish and by pirates until becoming a British Crown Colony in 1717. During the American Civil War it enjoyed a degree of prosperity as a base for blockade runners. Similar periods of prosperity occurred during the prohibition era and following World War II.

After more than two centuries of colonial rule, constitutional changes were negotiated in 1964 which called for the establishment of internal self-government with a bicameral legislature and a prime minister. These changes were implemented following an election in 1967 that resulted in a victory for the Progressive Liberal Party (PLP) under the leadership of Lynden O. PINDLING. Local government authority was broadened in 1969, and independence, which was not supported by the opposition Free National Movement (FNM), was formally granted on July 10, 1973. At the two most recent parliamentary elections of 1982 and 1987, the PLP retained control of the House of Assembly, although falling short of the three-fourths majority it had previously enjoyed.

Constitution and government. Under the 1973 constitution, executive authority is vested in the queen (represented by a governor general with largely ceremonial powers) and the prime minister, who serves at the pleasure of the House of Assembly. Legislative authority is concentrated in the lower house of the bicameral Parliament; the upper house, or Senate, has limited functions.

Internal administration is based on the natural division into island groupings. Islands other than New Providence and Grand Bahama are administered by centrally appointed commissioners. The judicial system is headed by a Supreme Court and a Court of Appeal, although certain cases may be appealed to the Privy Council of the United Kingdom; there are also local magistrates' courts. On the outer islands the local commissioners have magisterial powers.

Foreign relations. Bahamian foreign relations have been determined in large part by the islands' proximity to Cuba, Haiti, and the United States. A long-standing dispute with Cuba over territorial fishing rights led in May 1980 to the sinking by Cuban MiG aircraft of a Bahamian patrol vessel that had apprehended two Cuban fishing boats for poaching. Havana subsequently agreed to pay compensation of $5.4 million and apologized for the "involuntary violation" of Bahamian sovereignty. In regard to Haiti, the Pindling government since 1978 has periodically attempted to deport illegal aliens, most of whom are Haitian refugees estimated to constitute more than 10 percent of the resident population; some progress was reported to have been made with Port-au-Prince on the issue prior to the fall of the Duvalier regime, although criticism of treatment accorded the aliens continued through 1987. Relations with the United States have been generally cordial, although periodically strained by accusations of high-level participation in drug trafficking.

A member of the United Nations, the Commonwealth, and a number of regional organizations, the Bahamas was admitted to the Organization of American States (OAS) in March 1982.

Current issues. In 1986, following a somewhat inconclusive two-year inquiry into the problem of cocaine smuggling, a number of anti-drug efforts were launched. US Drug Enforcement Agency officials were granted free access to the islands and talks were initiated on the creation of a joint US-Bahamian task force on drug interdiction. In addition, legislation was introduced to increase penalties for drug dealers and freeze the assets of convicted offenders. In mid-1987 it was reported that the Bahamas had concluded a formal agreement with Washington for cooperative efforts to suppress the drug trade and in January 1988 the government announced that it would increase its drug enforcement personnel from a team of 18 to one of 270.

The June 1987 election was expected to be close, given the somewhat tarnished reputation of the Pindling administration on the drug issue. The PLP nonetheless won 31 of 49 legislative seats after the prime minister had counterattacked, claiming that the opposition was "supported by almost every major or reputed drug dealer in the country". FNM leader Kendall ISAACS immediately charged that the outcome reflected "massive fraud", although conceding that his party had not been "in tune with the electorate".

POLITICAL PARTIES

Government Party:

Progressive Liberal Party (PLP). A predominantly Black-supported party, the PLP was formed in 1953 in opposition to the policies of businessmen who then controlled the government. It was a leading supporter of the independence movement and endorses policies promoting tourism and foreign investment while at the same time preventing land speculation and providing more opportunity for indigenous Bahamians. Although subject to some internal dissent, the party secured commanding parliamentary majorities in 1972, 1977, 1982, and 1987.

Leaders: Lynden O. PINDLING (Prime Minister), Sean McWEENEY (Chairman), Clement MAYNARD (Parliamentary Leader).

Opposition Parties:

Free National Movement (FNM). The FNM was founded in 1972 by amalgamation of the United Bahamian Party (UBP) and a number of anti-independence dissidents from the PLP. In 1979 it was reconstituted as the Free National Democratic Movement (FNDM) by merger with the Bahamian Democratic Party (BDP), which had been organized in late 1976 when five FNM parliamentary deputies withdrew from the parent group. Prior to the 1982 election, which it contested under its original name, it was joined by the two remaining representatives of the Social Democratic Party (SDP), which had been founded by BDP dissidents in late 1979 and had been recognized thereafter as the official opposition. Following the 1987 balloting, Kendall G.L. Isaacs resigned as parliamentary leader, the party's chairman (and founder), Cecil Wallace-Whitfield being designated his successor.

Leaders: Cecil WALLACE-WHITFIELD (Chairman and Parliamentary Leader), John Henry BOSTWICK (Senate Leader), Arthur FOULKES, Kendall G.L. ISAACS.

Vanguard Socialist Party (VSP). Founded in 1971 and committed to establishment of a socialist state, the VSP contested 18 seats in the 1982 Assembly election, winning none with only 173 votes (0.2 percent of the total).

Leader: Lionel CAREY (Chairman).

LEGISLATURE

The **Parliament** consists of an appointed Senate with limited powers and a directly elected House of Assembly.

Senate. The upper house consists of 16 members, 9 of whom are appointed on the advice of the prime minister, 4 on the advice of the leader of the opposition, and 3 on the advice of the prime minister and others whom the governor general may wish to consult.

President: Edwin COLEBY.

House of Assembly. The lower house presently consists of 49 members directly elected on the basis of universal suffrage for five-year terms (subject to dissolution). The most recent election was held on June 19, 1987, when the Progressive Liberal Party won 31 seats; the Free National Movement, 16; and independents, 2.

Speaker: Sir Clifford DARLING.

CABINET

Prime Minister	Lynden O. Pindling
Deputy Prime Minister	Clement T. Maynard
Ministers	
Agriculture, Trade, and Industry	Ervin Knowles
Education	Paul L. Adderley
Employment and Immigration	Alfred T. Maycock
External Affairs and Tourism	Clement T. Maynard
Finance	Lynden O. Pindling
Health	Dr. Norman Gay
Housing and National Insurance	George W. Mackey
Transport and Local Government	Philip M. Bethel
Works and Utilities	Darrell Rolle
Youth, Sports and Community Affairs	Peter Bethel
Attorney General	Paul L. Adderley
Governor, Central Bank	James H. Smith

NEWS MEDIA

Press. The following are published daily at Nassau, unless otherwise noted: *The Tribune* (12,000); *Nassau Guardian* (11,000); *Freeport News* (Freeport, 5,000); *Official Gazette,* weekly government publication.

Radio and television. The government-owned Broadcasting Corporation of the Bahamas, which operates two commercial radio stations at Nassau and one at Freeport, transmitted to approximately 120,000 receivers in 1986. Bahamas Television began broadcasting from Nassau in 1977; the nation's 51,000 sets also receive American television direct from Florida.

INTERGOVERNMENTAL REPRESENTATION

Ambassador to the US: Margaret Evangeline McDONALD.

US Ambassador to the Bahamas: Carol Boyd HALLETT.

Permanent Representative to the UN: Dr. Davidson L. HEPBURN.

IGO Memberships (Non-UN): Caricom, CCC, CDB, CWTH, EEC(L), *EIB,* IADB, Interpol, OAS, OPANAL.

BAHRAIN

State of Bahrain
Dawlat al-Bahrayn

Political Status: Independent emirate proclaimed August 15, 1971; under constitution adopted December 6, 1973.

Area: 240 sq. mi. (622 sq. km.).

Population: 350,798 (1981C), 475,000 (1988E). Both figures include non-nationals (approximately 180,000 in 1987).

Major Urban Centers (1981C): MANAMA (121,986); Muharraq (61,853).

Official Language: Arabic.

Monetary Unit: Dinar (market rate March 1, 1988, 1 dinar = $2.66US).

Sovereign (Emir): Sheikh 'Isa ibn Salman AL KHALIFA, descendant of a ruling dynasty which dates from 1782; succeeded to the throne November 2, 1961; assumed title of Emir on the death of his father, Sheikh Salman ibn Hamad Al KHALIFA, on December 16, 1961.

Heir Apparent: Sheikh Hamad ibn 'Isa AL KHALIFA, son of the Emir.

Prime Minister: Sheikh Khalifa ibn Salman AL KHALIFA, eldest brother of the Emir; appointed January 19, 1970, continuing in office upon independence.

THE COUNTRY

An archipelago of 35 largely desert islands situated between the Qatar peninsula and Saudi Arabia, the State of Bahrain consists primarily of the main island of Bahrain plus the smaller Muharraq, Sitra, and Umm-Nassan. Summer temperatures often exceed 100 degrees (F) and annual rainfall averages only about four inches, but natural springs provide sufficient water. The predominantly Arab population is about two-thirds indigenous Bahraini, with small groups of Saudi Arabians, Omanis, Iranians, Asians, and Europeans. At the 1981 census, 60 percent consisted of Shi'ite Muslims, while most of the remainder, including the royal family, adhere to the Sunni sect.

Oil, produced commercially since 1936, and natural gas now account for some 65 percent of the government's income, although recoverable petroleum reserves may be exhausted by the year 2000. Additional revenue is derived from operation of the Aluminum Bahrain smelter, which is the largest nonextractive enterprise in the Gulf area, and from one of the Middle East's largest oil refineries, mainly devoted to processing crude from Saudi Arabia. In recent years Bahrain has emerged as the "banking and business capital" of the region with some 75 offshore banking units (OBUs) having been licensed since 1975. Many other foreign financial institutions and commercial enterprises operate from Manama because of a less restrictive social atmosphere than in other Arab states.

Aided by fiscal support from Saudi Arabia, Kuwait, and the United Arab Emirates, the government has established an extensive network of social services, including free education and medical care, and in 1982 mounted an ambitious program for infrastructure development and improvements in agriculture and education. However, falling oil prices and worldwide recession have led to budget deficits since 1984 and official forecasts of impending austerity.

GOVERNMENT AND POLITICS

Political background. Long ruled as a traditional monarchy, Bahrain became a British protectorate in 1861 when Britain concluded a treaty of friendship with the emir as part of a larger effort to secure communication lines with its Asian colonies. The treaty was modified in 1892, but little evolution in domestic politics occurred prior to the interwar period. In 1926, Sir Charles BELGRAVE was appointed adviser to the emir, providing guidance in reform of the administrative system—an especially important step in light of accelerated social change following the discovery of oil in 1932. Belgrave continued to have a direct and personal effect on Bahraini policy until 1957, his departure coming as the result of Arab nationalist agitation that began in 1954 and reached a peak during the 1956 Anglo-French action in Egypt. Incipient nationalists also provoked disturbances in 1965 and in 1967, following the second Arab-Israeli conflict.

In 1968, Britain announced that it would withdraw most of its forces east of Suez by 1971, and steps were taken to prepare for the independence of all of the British-protected emirates on the Persian Gulf. Initially, a federation composed of Bahrain, Qatar, and the seven components of the present United Arab Emirates was envisaged. Bahrain, however, failed to secure what it considered an appropriate allocation of seats in the proposed federation's ruling body and declared for separate independence on August 15, 1971.

Despite nominal efforts at modernization, such as the creation of an Administrative Council following the 1956 disturbances, virtually absolute power remained in the hands of the emir until the adoption of the country's first constitution in 1973. Even today, nearly all advisory bodies are controlled by members of the royal family.

Although less intense than in other regional countries, rebellious sentiments among some of the majority Shi'ites, resentful of Sunni rule, precipitated conflict following the Iranian revolution of 1979 and the accompanying spread of Islamic fundamentalism. In December 1981 the government declared that it had thwarted a conspiracy involving the Iranian-backed Islamic Front for the Liberation of Bahrain, while the plot and the discovery in February 1984 of a rebel arms cache resulted in numerous arrests, the banning of a Shi'ite religious organization (the Islamic Enlightenment Society), and the issuance of compulsory identity cards to nationals and resident aliens. In May 1986 the Labor and Social Affairs Ministry announced that all expatriates would be required to leave the country upon expiry of their contracts, unless they were to be rehired.

Constitution and government. In December 1972, the emir convened a Constituent Council to consider a draft constitution that provided for a National Assembly composed of the cabinet (which replaced the Council of State in 1971) and 30 members elected by popular vote. The constitution was approved in June 1973 and became effective December 6, 1973, with an election being held the following day. However, the Assembly was dissolved in August 1975, with the emir suspending the constitutional provision for an elected legislative body.

The legal system is based on *Shari'a* (canonical Muslim law); the judiciary includes separate courts for members of the Sunni and Shi'ite sects. The six main towns serve as bases of administrative divisions that are governed by partly elected municipal councils.

Foreign relations. Since independence, Bahrain has closely followed Saudi Arabia's lead in foreign policy but has been more moderate than most other Arab states in its support of the Palestine Liberation Organization and in condemning the Israeli-Egyptian peace treaty of 1979.

Generally regarded as the most vulnerable of the Gulf sheikhdoms, Bahrain has been a target of Iranian agitation and territorial claims since the overthrow of the late shah. Although Manama adopted a posture of noncommitment at the outbreak in 1980 of the Iran-Iraq war, it subsequently joined the other five members of the Gulf Cooperation Council (GCC), established in March 1981, in voicing support for Iraq. A security treaty with Saudi Arabia was concluded in December 1981 and in February 1982 the foreign ministers of the GCC states announced that they would actively oppose "Iranian sabotage acts aimed at wrecking the stability of the Gulf region". To this end, Bahrain has joined with the other GCC states in annual joint military maneuvers. The spirit of cooperation was jolted in April 1986, however, by conflict with Qatar over a small uninhabited island, Fasht al-Dibal, that had been reclaimed from an underlying coral reef for use as a Bahraini coastguard station. Following a brief takeover by Qatari armed forces, an agreement was reached to return the site to its original condition.

Relations with Washington have long been cordial and the US administration is currently assisting in the construction of a major air base on Bahrain's southern coast. As a result, Bahraini officials were dismayed by US Senate action in late 1987 in blocking the planned purchase of a number of stringer antiaircraft missiles because similar weapons supplied to the Afghan guerrillas had fallen into Iranian hands. Eventually a compromise was reached, whereby the shipment was approved under an 18-month lease arrangement.

Current issues. During 1986 the government concentrated on plans to revitalize the economy as slumping oil prices and the effects of the Gulf war forced even the banking industry into recession. Continuing its programs to promote industrial diversity while maintaining a high level of social services, Manama for the first time issued treasury bonds to help counter a budgetary deficit, and in August approved plans for creation of the country's first official stock exchange to replace the "telephone market" theretofore maintained by licensed brokers. Like other countries in the region that relied on foreign workers during the oil boom years, Bahrain increased efforts to replace them with its own nationals. Meanwhile, the economic impact of the completion of a $900 million causeway linking Manama with Saudi Arabia remained unclear. Following the November opening to private travel of the 20-mile combination of bridges and embankments, vacationing Saudis flocked to the more relaxed Bahrainian atmosphere. Although the enhanced tourist revenue was welcomed, the causeway remained closed to commercial traffic as negotiations continued with Bahrainian businessmen fearful of a massive influx of more competitive Saudi products.

POLITICAL PARTIES

Political parties are proscribed in Bahrain. At the first National Assembly election in 1973, however, voters elected ten candidates of a loosely organized Popular Bloc of the Left, while such small clandestine groups as a Bahraini branch of the **Popular Front for the Liberation of Oman and the Arab Gulf,** apparently consisting mainly of leftist students, have continued to engage in limited activity. Among the proscribed political groups, the most militant is the **Islamic Front for the Liberation of Bahrain,** consisting mainly of Shi'ites aligned with the Iranian regime.

LEGISLATURE

The first election to fill 30 nonnominated seats in the National Assembly was held December 7, 1973. In addition to the elected members, who were to serve four-year terms, the Assembly contained 14 cabinet members (including 2 ministers of state). The Assembly was dissolved on August 26, 1975, on the ground that it had indulged in debates "dominated by ideas alien to the society and values of Bahrain".

CABINET

Prime Minister	Khalifa ibn Salman Al Khalifa
Ministers	
Commerce and Agriculture	Habib Qasim
Development and Industry	Yusuf Ahmad al-Shirawi
Education	Dr. 'Ali Muhammad Fakhru
Finance and National Economy	Ibrahim 'Abd al-Karim
Foreign Affairs	Muhammad ibn Mubarak Al Khalifa

Health	Jawad Salim al-'Urayid
Housing	Khalid ibn 'Abdallah Al Khalifa
Information	Tariq 'Abd al-Rahman al-Mu'ayyid
Interior	Muhammad ibn Khalifa ibn Hamid Al Khalifa
Justice and Islamic Affairs	'Abdallah ibn Khalid Al Khalifa
Labor and Social Affairs	Khalifa ibn Salman ibn Muhammad Al Khalifa
Public Works, Electricity and Water	Majid al-Jishi
Transportation and Communication	Ibrahim Muhammad Hasan Humaydan
Chairman, Central Bank	Khalifa Salman al-Thani

NEWS MEDIA

Press. The following newspapers are published at Manama unless otherwise noted: *Akhbar al-Khalij* (18,000), first Arabic daily, founded 1976; *Gulf Mirror* (16,000), English weekly; *al-Adhwaa* (13,000), Arab weekly; *Gulf Daily News* (12,500), in English; *Sada al-Usbu* (9,000 domestic, 16,000 foreign), Arabic weekly; *al-Bahrain al-Yawm* (4,000 domestic, 3,000 foreign), Arabic weekly, published by the Ministry of Information; *Akhbar al-Bahrain,* daily Arabic news sheet, published by the Ministry of Information.

News agencies. There is no domestic facility; *Agence France-Presse,* the AP, the Gulf News Agency, and Reuters maintain offices at Manama.

Radio and television. The Bahrain Broadcasting Station, a government facility that transmits in Arabic and English, and Radio Bahrain, an English-language commercial station, are the principal sources of radio programs and were received by 200,000 sets in 1986. The government-operated Bahrain Television, which has provided commercial programming in Arabic since 1973, added an English-language channel in 1981. In addition, broadcasts by the Arabian-American Oil Company (Aramco) and the US Air Force at Dhahran can be monitored. Approximately 135,000 television sets were in use during 1987.

INTERGOVERNMENTAL REPRESENTATION

Ambassador to the US: Ghazi Muhammad AL GOSAIBI.

US Ambassador to Bahrain: Sam H. ZAKHEM.

Permanent Representative to the UN: Karim Ebrahim al-SHAKAR.

IGO Memberships (Non-UN): AFESD, AMF, BADEA, GCC, IC, IDB, Inmarsat, Interpol, LAS, NAM, OAPEC.

BANGLADESH

People's Republic of Bangladesh
Ganaprojatantri Bangladesh

Political Status: Independent state proclaimed March 26, 1971; de facto independence achieved December 16, 1971; admitted to the Commonwealth April 18, 1972; republican constitution of December 16, 1972, most recently suspended following coup of March 24, 1982, restored on November 10, 1986.

Area: 55,598 sq. mi. (143,999 sq. km.).

Population: 89,940,000 (1981C), 104,671,000 (1988E).

Major Urban Centers (urban areas, 1981C): DHAKA (Dacca; 3,458,602); Chittagong (1,388,476); Khulna (623,184).

Official Language: Bengali. English is still widely spoken in urban areas.

Monetary Unit: Taka (market rate March 1, 1988, 31.35 takas = $1US).

President: Lt. Gen. Hossain Mohammad ERSHAD (National Party); assumed office of Chief Martial Law Administrator following military coup of March 24, 1982; assumed title of President on December 11, 1983, following the resignation of Abul Fazal Mohammad Ahsanuddin CHOWDHURY; confirmed by referendum of March 21, 1986; reelected on October 15 and sworn in for a five-year term on October 23, 1986.

Vice President: A.K.M. Nurul ISLAM (National Party); appointed by the President on November 30, 1986.

Prime Minister: Mizanur Rahman CHOWDHURY (Awami League-Mizan faction); sworn in July 9, 1986, following appointment by the President.

THE COUNTRY

Located in the east of the Indian subcontinent, Bangladesh comprises a portion of the historic province of Bengal (including Chittagong) in addition to the Sylhet district of Assam. Except for a short boundary with Burma in the extreme southeast, the country's land frontier borders on India, while its southern coast on the Bay of Bengal exposes it to periodic cyclones. Endowed with a tropical monsoon climate and rich alluvial plains dominated by the Ganges and Brahmaputra, Bangladesh has one of the world's highest population densities. The country is ethnically quite homogeneous, since 98 percent of the people are Bengali and speak a common language. Urdu-speaking, non-Bengali Muslim immigrants from India, largely Bihari, comprise 1 percent; the remaining 1 percent includes assorted tribal groups. Bangladesh contains more Muslim inhabitants than any other country except Indonesia, 85 percent of its people professing Islam; Hindus constitute most of the remainder. Although an estimated 50 percent of the food crops are produced by rural women, little more than 12 percent of the official labor force is female and is concentrated in domestic service. Traditionally unrepresented in Bangladesh politics, a number of women have nonetheless become influential within groups opposed to the present regime (see Political Parties, below).

With a GNP per capita income of barely $130, Bangladesh was listed by the World Bank in 1984 as, next to Ethiopia, the world's poorest country; its economy is particularly vulnerable to natural disasters, including a 1985 cyclone that caused 15,000 deaths and severe monsoon flooding in August-September 1987 that left nearly one-quarter of the population homeless or without food. About three-fourths of the labor force is engaged in agriculture; rice is the principal food crop and jute (of which Bangladesh produces half the world's supply) the leading export. Although significant hydrocarbon reserves exist, the country is deficient in most other natural resources. The present government has moved to divest itself of a large number of industries that were nationalized in 1972.

GOVERNMENT AND POLITICS

Political background. When British India was partitioned into independent India and Pakistan in August 1947, Bengal was divided along communal lines. Predominantly Hindu West Bengal was incorporated into India, while predominantly Muslim East Bengal was joined with the Sylhet district of Assam as the Eastern Province of Pakistan.

In the postindependence period, a comparative lack of economic progress in East Pakistan accentuated political problems caused by cultural and linguistic differences between the two provinces. In the early 1950s, Bengalis successfully agitated for the equality of Bengali and Urdu as official languages. During the next decade, however, Bengali resentment over major disparities in development expenditure and representation in the public services intensified, and in 1966 Sheikh Mujibur RAHMAN, president of the East Pakistan branch of the Awami League, called for a constitutional reallocation of powers between the central government and the provinces. The sheikh's subsequent arrest helped coalesce Bengali opinion against Pakistani President Ayub Khan, who was forced from office in March 1969.

Ayub's successor, Gen. Yahya Khan, endorsed a return to democratic rule, and during the 1970 electoral campaign Mujib and his party won 167 of 169 seats allotted to East Pakistan in a proposed National Assembly of 313 members. When fundamental constitutional questions regarding the distribution of powers between the center and the provinces yielded postponement of the National Assembly session on March 1, 1971, massive civil strife broke out in East Pakistan. Three weeks later, Mujib was again arrested and his party banned, most of his colleagues fleeing to India, where they organized a provisional government. Martial law was imposed following disturbances at Dhaka, and civil war ensued. India, having protested to Pakistan about suppression of the Eastern rebellion and the influx of millions of refugees into India, declared war on Pakistan on December 3, 1971, and the allied forces of India and Bangladesh defeated Pakistani forces in the East on December 16. The new but war-ravaged nation of Bangladesh emerged on the same day.

Upon his return from imprisonment in West Pakistan, Sheikh Mujib assumed command of the provisional government and began restructuring the new state along socialist but non-Marxist lines that featured a limitation on large landholdings and the nationalization of banks, insurance companies, and major industries. During July and August 1974 the already fragile economy was devastated by floods that led to famine and a cholera epidemic from which thousands died. Following a period of near-anarchy, a state of emergency was declared on December 28. Four weeks later, on January 25, 1975, the Constituent Assembly revised the constitution to provide for a presidential form of government and the adoption of a one-party system.

On August 15, 1975, a group of pro-Pakistan, Islamic right-wing army officers mounted a coup, in the course of which the president's house was attacked and Mujib, his wife, and five of their children were killed. Immediately thereafter the former minister of trade and commerce, Khandakar MOSHTAQUE Ahmed, was sworn in as president and on August 20 assumed the power to rule by martial law. On November 3 the new president was himself confronted with a rebellion led by Brig. Khalid MUSHARAF, the pro-Indian commander of the Dhaka garrison. Three days later, President Moshtaque vacated his office in favor of the chief justice of the Supreme Court, Abu Sadat Mohammad SAYEM, while on November 7 Musharaf was killed during a left-wing mutiny led by Col. Abu TAHER. As a result, President Sayem announced that he would assume the additional post of chief martial law administrator, with the army chief of staff, Maj. Gen. Ziaur RAHMAN, and the heads of the air force and navy as deputies. In April 1976 "mujibist" and pro-Indian officers who had been implicated in the Musharaf coup were released from custody; on the other hand, vigorous action was taken against those implicated in the November 7 mutiny, Colonel Taher himself being hanged on July 21.

Although President Sayem announced in mid-1976 that his government would honor former president Moshtaque's pledge to hold a general election by the end of February 1977, he reversed himself on November 21 on the ground that balloting would "endanger peace and tranquility" and "strengthen the hands of the enemy". Eight days later, he transferred the office of chief martial law administrator to Ziaur Rahman and on April 21, 1977, resigned the presidency, nominating the general as his successor. President Zia was confirmed in office by a nationwide referendum on May 30, designating the former special assistant to President Sayem, Abdus SATTAR, as the nation's vice president on June 3.

Despite a coup attempt by senior air force officers in early October, President Zia announced in April 1978 that a presidential election would be held on June 3 and would be followed by a parliamentary election in December. Opposition allegations of polling irregularities notwithstanding, Zia was credited with a near three-to-one margin of victory over his closest rival in the presidential balloting and was sworn in for a five-year term on June 12. After two postponements, necessitated by discussions with opposition leaders who threatened a boycott if martial and other "repressive" laws were not revoked, a new Parliament dominated by Zia's Bangladesh Nationalist Party (BNP) was elected on February 18, 1979, and on April 15 a civilian cabinet with Shah Azizur RAHMAN as prime minister was announced.

Despite some success in a forceful campaign to address the country's interrelated problems of population increase and food deficiency, the Zia government encountered continuing unrest, including several coup attempts and a major uprising by tribal guerrillas in the southeastern Chittagong Hill Tracts in early 1980. On May 30, 1981, long-standing differences within the army precipitated the assassination of the president in the course of an attempted coup at Chittagong. The alleged leader of the revolt, Maj. Gen. Mohammad Abdul MANZUR, was killed while fleeing the city on June 1, most of the army having remained loyal to Acting President Sattar. The former vice president was elected to a five-year term as Zia's successor on November 15, subsequently designating Mirza Nurul HUDA as his deputy while retaining Azizur Rahman as prime minister.

Following a period in which the military, led by its chief of staff, Lt. Gen. Hossain Mohammed ERSHAD, pressed for a campaign to counter "political indiscipline, unprecedented corruption, a bankrupt economy, [and] administrative breakdown", the armed forces again intervened on March 24, 1982, suspending the constitution, ousting the Sattar government, and installing Ershad as chief martial law administrator. Three days later, on Ershad's nomination, Abul Fazal Mohammad Ahsanuddin CHOWDHURY, a retired Supreme Court judge, was sworn in as the nation's eighth president.

In March 1983, General Ershad authorized a resumption of partisan activity and on November 11 announced a timetable for local, parliamentary, and presidential elections under an amended version of the 1972 constitution that would afford an enhanced role for the military. Two weeks later, a regime-supportive People's Party (*Jana Dal*) was formed under President Chowdhury, who resigned his office on December 11 in favor of Ershad. While the local (union council) balloting went forward on December 27, neither opposition or government-supportive parties nominated candidates. Following a protracted struggle with opposition leaders, which resulted in cancellation of presidential and parliamentary balloting scheduled for April 1, 1985, the government reimposed martial law on March 1, with General Ershad reconfirmed as president in a referendum three weeks later. Rural subdistrict elections in late May were boycotted by the leading opposition parties, while the promotion of a "transition to democracy" was announced by a *Jana Dal*-centered National Front in August.

On January 1, 1986, coincident with revocation of a ban on political activity, it was announced that the National Front had been converted into a pro-regime National Party (*Jatiya Dal*) and on March 2 President Ershad scheduled parliamentary balloting for late April. The immediate reaction of the leading opposition groups was a refusal to participate short of a full lifting of martial law. Subsequently, both the Awami League alliance and the fundamentalist *Jama'at-i-Islami* (see Political Parties, below), but not the BNP (headed by Ziaur Rahman's widow, Begum Khaleda ZIA), agreed to compete in an election rescheduled for May 7.

Under conditions of unrest that a British observer group termed a "tragedy for democracy", the *Jatiya Dal* won a narrow majority of legislative seats and a new government was sworn in on July 9 that included Mizanur Rahman CHOWDHURY, leader of a minority conservative faction of the Awami League, as prime minister. On September 1, General Ershad formally joined the government party to permit his nomination as its presidential candidate and was credited with winning 83.6 percent of the vote on October 15. On November 10, having secured parliamentary ratification of actions taken by his administration since March 1982, Ershad announced the lifting of martial law and restoration of the (amended) 1972 constitution.

In January 1987 the Awami League, which had returned briefly after a six-month boycott of parliamentary proceedings, again withdrew in response to President Ershad's projection of an enhanced political role for the military.

Subsequently the League joined with the BNP, *Jama'at-i-Islami,* and a group of Marxist parties in supporting a series of strikes to protest economic conditions as well as the passage at midyear of a Local Government Bill that authorized the armed forces to share administrative responsibilities with civilians in the country's 64 district councils. While the controversial measure was effectively rescinded on August 1, the unrest continued, prompting the government to declare a nationwide state of emergency in late November. On December 6 the president dissolved Parliament, but none of the leading opposition parties presented candidates for the legislative balloting of March 3, 1988, the official results of which yielded a government sweep of more than 80 percent of the seats.

Constitution and government. The constitution of December 1972 (replacing a provisional document of the previous March) was subjected to numerous revisions, the most important (apart from martial law suspensions in August 1975 and March 1982) involving the return to a presidential system in January 1975. The version to which the Ershad regime has returned provides for a president who is popularly elected for a renewable five-year term and who appoints (and can dismiss) the prime minister and other ministers. The unicameral National Parliament (*Jatiya Sanqsad*) is composed of 330 members of whom 300 are directly elected from single territorial constituencies for five-year terms, subject to presidential dissolution. The legislature must approve a declaration of war, although the president has full emergency powers in the event of actual or threatened invasion; constitutional amendments require a two-thirds majority. The judiciary is headed by a presidentially appointed Supreme Court, which is divided into a High Court, with both original and appellate jurisdiction, and an Appellate Division that hears appeals from the High Court. Other courts are established by law. A division of the country into five martial law zones, with deputy martial law administrators and High Court judges assigned to each, was rescinded in March 1986.

Local government has long been conducted under a three-tiered system of committees (*parishads*) operating at district (*zilla*), town (*thana*), and union levels. Under administrative reforms proposed in 1982 and implemented beginning in 1983, a subdistrict (*upa-zilla*) level was added, as the basic unit for administrative, economic, and judicial functions, and elections for 460 *upa-zillas* were held on May 16 and 20, 1985.

Foreign relations. The government of Mujibur Rahman committed itself to policies of neutralism and nonalignment in dealing with its neighbors and other foreign powers. At the same time, Bangladesh exhibited natural ties of geography, culture, and commerce with India, and in March 1972 the two countries signed a 25-year treaty of friendship, cooperation, and peace. Relations with Pakistan, initially characterized by mutual hatred and suspicion, slowly improved, with Islamabad according Bangladesh diplomatic recognition in February 1974.

The Soviet Union initially enjoyed cordial relations with Bangladesh as a corollary of its support of India in the 1971 war but in 1979–1980 Dhaka's opposition to the Vietnamese invasion of Kampuchea and to the Soviet incursion in Afghanistan resulted in a cooling of relations. In late 1983,

amid accusations of involvement in civil unrest, 14 Soviet embassy personnel were expelled and Moscow was requested to cut its diplomatic and cultural staff by half. The People's Republic of China never recognized the Mujibur Rahman regime and because of its close ties with Pakistan frustrated Bangladesh's efforts to enter the United Nations until 1974. However, relations improved considerably in the late 1970s, with a series of trade and cooperation accords being concluded in March and May 1980. President Ershad visited Beijing in July 1985, Chinese President Li Xiannian reciprocating by a visit to Dhaka in March 1986.

In 1976 Bangladesh lodged a formal complaint at the United Nations alleging excessive Indian diversion of water from the Ganges at the Farakka barrage, while in 1980 India's unilateral seizure of two newly formed islands in the Bay of Bengal further complicated relations. Progress was reported on the river waters dispute during a meeting between President Ershad and Indian Prime Minister Rajiv Gandhi at a Nassau (Bahamas) Commonwealth summit meeting in October 1985, the two leaders agreeing to a three-year extension, with effect from the 1986 dry season, of an interim water-sharing pact concluded in 1982. Meanwhile, additional tension had been generated by protests in India's Assam state against illegal immigration from Bangladesh, culminating in New Delhi's initiation of work on a fence at the disputed border in mid-1984. In the wake of a number of subsequent border incidents, particularly in the Muhuri River area, India threatened to resume construction of the fence in January 1985 and again in February 1986.

Relations with the country's eastern neighbor, Burma, noticeably improved following UN mediation of a complaint registered by Dhaka in connection with an influx in 1977 of over 200,000 Muslim refugees, most of whom had established residence in Burma during the period of British rule. Rangoon subsequently agreed in principle to repatriation of the refugees, while in 1980 a number of boundary and cooperation agreements were negotiated.

Current issues. During 1986 General Ershad presided over a nominal return to civilian rule in the face of a divided and somewhat hesitant opposition. The Bangladesh National Party was the only major formation that consistently rebuffed government overtures to participate in both the parliamentary election in May and the presidential poll in October, thereby gaining a measure of popular support that was of insufficient magnitude to deter Ershad, who — remarkably — had encountered no major coup threat during his four years of power, as contrasted with some 21 (the last successful) against President Zia. In March, the Awami League's Sheikh Hasina WAJED had agreed to join the BNP's Begum Khaleda in a boycott of the legislative balloting, but ultimately reversed herself, only to be refused entry to the parliament at its opening session on July 9. The conservative *Jama'at-i-Islami* participated, as did the Bangladesh Communist party and the leading factions of the leftist National Awami and *Jatiya Samajtantrik* parties; some members of the Marxist-oriented Bangladesh *Krishak Sramik* Awami League (Baksal) defied their leadership and competed, although the three who won seats were subsequently expelled from the party.

In 1987 the opposition gradually coalesced, Sheikh Hasina and Begum Khaleda meeting in October to coordinate plans (endorsed by both right-wing fundamentalists and left-wing Marxists) for the assembly of some 2 million supporters to immobilize the government in a so-called "siege of Dhaka" on November 10. While prompt government action (including the arrest of numerous opposition leaders) succeeded in curtailing the protest, disorders continued thereafter, with President Ershad proclaiming a state of emergency on November 27 to cope with a call for a three-day general strike commencing November 29. While Ershad appeared to retain the crucial backing of the military, the opposition continued to press for his resignation as a precondition for its participation in any form of electoral activity. Subsequently, the ineffectual outcome of the March 1988 poll attested to the emergence of a political stalemate and the likely prospect that martial law would be reimposed.

POLITICAL PARTIES

Political party activity was banned following the coup of August 1975 and only a limited number of parties were permitted to contest the presidential election of June 1978. Following opposition threats to boycott the 1979 parliamentary balloting, martial law restrictions governing parties were lifted and a large number of political groups contested the election. Subsequently, most of the opposition parties splintered into factions, some of which organized as independent groups.

A new proscription on party activity, imposed in the wake of the March 1982 coup, remained in effect until March 1983, following General Ershad's call for a "national dialogue" to pave the way for a return to civilian rule. Subsequently, three major opposition blocs emerged. In April 1983, a National United Front (NUF) of 11 right-wing and Islamic parties was organized by former president and Democratic League head Khandakar Moshtaque Ahmed. The following September, a 22-party alliance called the Movement for the Restoration of Democracy (MRD) was announced that included a 7-party coalition led by the Bangladesh Nationalist Party and a 15-party formation headed by the Awami League (Hasina). By mid-1984, however, the NUF had declined in importance, while the MRD had, for all practical purposes, dissolved into its component groups. In August, following the opposition parties' rejection of Ershad's call for national elections and the president's subsequent referendum victory, a government-supportive, five-party National Front, subsequently the National Party, was organized that included numerous defectors from the 7-party alliance.

Government Party:

National Party (*Jatiya Dal*). The *Jatiya Dal* was initially launched in August 1985 as the National Front, a somewhat eclectic grouping of right-wing Muslims and Beijing-oriented Marxists, who rejected the confrontation politics of their former alliance partners in favor of cooperation with Ershad. The coalition announced as its immediate purpose "peaceful transition from military rule to constitutional democracy through national elections", to be facilitated by lifting of the ban on political activity. In addition to the four groups listed below, the Front included a dissident faction of the Bangladesh Nationalist Party (below) led by former prime minister Azizur Rahman; it was declared to have been converted into a unified party on January 1, 1986, in anticipation of the parliamentary

balloting that was subsequently held on May 7. As of late 1986, the *Jatiya Dal* held 178 of 300 directly elective legislative seats, plus all 30 indirectly elected women's seats (see Legislature, below). Amid numerous charges of electoral impropriety, it was awarded 250 of the 300 directly elective seats at the subsequent balloting of March 3, 1988.

Leaders: Lt. Gen. Hossain Mohammad ERSHAD (President of the Republic and Chairman of the Party), Shah Moazzam HOSSAIN (Deputy Prime Minister and General Secretary of the Party).

People's Party (*Jana Dal*). Formed in January 1983, by (then) President Chowdhury and drawing its membership from civilian "implementation committees" set up by the army in support of Ershad's policies, the *Jana Dal* claims adherence to nationalism, Islamic values, and democracy. Its leadership includes a number of government officials, in addition to defectors from the Bangladesh Nationalist Party and other groups. In late 1985, party leaders asserted that *Jana Dal's* membership had expanded to encompass a "party nucleus" in every *upa-zilla.*

Leaders: Mizanur Rahman CHOWDHURY (Prime Minister and General Secretary of the Party), Abul Fazal Mohammad Ahsanuddin CHOWDHURY (Chairman).

United People's Party (UPP). Originally a pro-Beijing offshoot of the National Awami Party (below), the UPP experienced considerable fractionalization in early 1978, when some members refused to join in supporting Ziaur Rahman's presidential candidacy. During 1978–1980 some of its leaders defected to the BNP, while others joined the DP (below). The UPP was a member of the BNP-led faction of the MRD until August 1985, when it joined the National Front, with party leader Ahmed appointed to Ershad's cabinet.

Leader: Kazi Jafar AHMED (former Deputy Prime Minister).

Democratic Party – DP (*Ganatantric Dal*). The *Ganatantric Dal* was formed in December 1980 by members of the NAP-Bhashani, a dissident faction of the UPP, and two other participants in the 1979 Democratic Front: the Jatiya Gana Mukti Union and the Gonofront (itself an alliance of seven leftist splinter groups). Its original leader, Mirza Nurul Huda, subsequently joined the BNP and was named vice president of the Republic in November 1981. Within the MRD, the DP was a member of the BNP-led grouping, until its inclusion in the Front in August 1985.

Leader: Sirajul Hossain KHAN.

Bangladesh Muslim League (BML). A coalition of conservative Islamic parties that had opposed independence from Pakistan in 1971 and was banned under the Mujibur Rahman regime, the BML has long been prone to factionalism. Some of its members joined the BNP in 1980, while a number of splinter groups formed during the same year. In 1986, it obtained 4 parliamentary seats in its own right, despite being a member of the government coalition.

Leader: Tofazzal ALI (Chairman).

Opposition Parties:

Bangladesh Nationalist Party – BNP (*Bangladesh Jatiyabadi Dal*). The BNP was formally launched in September 1978 by a number of groups that had supported President Zia in his election campaign. During 1978–1980, a number of defectors from other parties, including elements of the National People's Party (below), joined the government formation. According to official returns, the BNP candidate, Abdus Sattar, captured nearly 66 percent of the vote in a field of over 30 candidates at the November 1981 presidential balloting. Unlike most pro-Awami parties, which favor a return to parliamentary government, the BNP supports a strong presidential system and is not unwilling to concede a permanent role to the military. Indeed, one of the basic problems for the BNP is that it is basically similar in ideology and outlook to the *Jatiya Dal,* albeit derived from President Ershad's military predecessor.

The breakaway faction that followed Azizur Rahman into the National Front in July 1985 included Sultan Ahmed CHOWDHURY and A.K.M. Mayedul ISLAM (as its general secretary). The main body of the party, led by the widow of General Zia, refused to participate in the parliamentary poll of May 1986, the presidential balloting of October 1986, or the legislative election of March 1988.

Leaders: Begum Khaleda ZIA (Chairwoman), Badruddoza CHOWDHURY (Vice Chairman), K.M. Obaidur RAHMAN (Secretary General).

National People's Party – NPP (*Jatiya Janata Dal*). A social-democratic party organized in 1978, the NPP supported the candidacy of its founder, Gen. Mohammad Ataul Osmani, at the 1981 presidential election.

Leaders: Ferdaus Ahmed QUARISHI (Chairman); Yusuf ALI, Abdul Matin CHOWDHURY, A.K. Mujibur RAHMAN (General Secretaries).

Awami League. A predominantly middle-class party organized in East Pakistan during 1948 under Sheikh Mujibur Rahman, the Awami (People's) League was, with Indian support, a major force in the drive for independence. Although formally disbanded by President Moshtaque Ahmed in 1975, it remained the best-organized political group in the country and served as the nucleus of the Democratic United Front (*Ganatantrik Oikya Jote*), which supported the presidential candidacy of General Osmani in June 1978.

During 1980 a major cleavage developed between a majority faction led by Abdul Malek Ukil and a right-wing minority faction led by Mizanur Rahman Chowdhury, the former electing Mujibur Rahman's daughter, Hasina Wajed, as its leader in February 1981, while Chowdhury accepted appointment as prime minister of the Ershad government in July 1986. A further split in 1983 resulted in the expulsion of Abdul Razzak and six others, who announced formation of the Bangladesh Krishak Sramik Awami League (below). The major ideological differences between the Awami League and both of its major rivals (the BNP and the National Front) are its advocacy of a "Westminster-style" parliamentary system and its Indian-influenced commitment to "secularism and socialism". It participated in the legislative balloting of May 1986, but boycotted most subsequent parliamentary proceedings, as well as the general election of March 1988.

Leaders: Sheikh Hasina WAJED (Hasina faction), Begum Sajeda CHOWDHURY (General Secretary).

Bangladesh Krishak Sramik Awami League (Baksal). Initially a left-wing faction within the Awami League, the Razzak group rejected the principle of parliamentary democracy in favor of the one-party system established by Sheikh Mujib during his 1975 "Second Revolution". Strongly pro-Soviet, it has long worked closely with the Bangladesh Communist Party (below). The Baksal designation was the original name of the parent formation.

Leader: Abdul RAZZAK.

National Socialist Party (*Jatiya Samajtantrik Dal*—JSD). The JSD originated as a Scientific Socialists (*Boigyanik Samajtantrabadi*) faction within the Awami League in the early post independence period. The largely student group, led by Abdul Rab and Shajahan Siraj, defected from the League in 1972. Following President Zia's assumption of power, many of its members were arrested. It was reinstated as a legal entity in November 1978, although several leaders, including Maj. M.A. Jalil, were not released from detention until March 1980.

Differences within the JSD over participation in a loosely formed 10-party opposition alliance contributed to a November 1980 split that resulted in formation of the **Bangladesh Socialist Party** (*Bangladesh Samajtantrik Dal*—BSD). Two months earlier, dissatisfaction with the alliance had led over 500 members of the JSD student wing to join the BNP. In 1983–1985, the party was a prominent member of the 15-party coalition led by the Awami League; in May 1986, separate electoral lists were presented by supporters of Rab and Siraj, respectively.

Leaders: Abdul RAB, Shajahan SIRAJ, Maj. M. Abdul JALIL (1981 presidential candidate).

National Awami Party (NAP). Founded by the late A.H.K. Bhashani, the NAP was the principal opposition party prior to the 1975 coup. It subsequently underwent numerous cleavages, the main splinters being the National Awami Party (Muzaffar), a pro-Moscow but noncommunist participant in the 10-party opposition alliance of 1980; and the National Awami Party (Bhashani), a pro-Beijing but likewise noncommunist faction that participated in a 5-party left-wing Democratic Front (*Ganatantrik Jote*), which was organized in October 1979 and subsequently helped form the Democratic Party (above). Competing for the national presidency in 1981 were Muzaffar Ahmed of the NAP's pro-Moscow faction and Selina Mazumdar of the pro-Beijing group. Both factions joined the Awami League alliance within the MRD.

Leaders: Muzaffar AHMED (NAP-Muzaffar), Abu Nasser Khan BHASHANI and Abdus SUHANI (NAP-Bhashani).

Communist Party of Bangladesh (CPB). Although the pro-Moscow CPB was permitted to resume a legal existence in November 1978, over 50 of its members were arrested in March-April 1980. The party held its first congress since 1974 in February 1980 and participated in the opposi-

tion alliance of the same year. It supported the presidential candidacy of the NAP's Muzaffar Ahmed in 1981 and joined the Awami League faction of the MRD in 1983. Its long-time general secretary, Mohammad Farhad, died at Moscow in October 1987.

Leaders: Moni SINGH (President), Saifuddin Ahmed MALIK, Abdur SALAM.

Equalitarian Party (*Samyabadi Dal*). Initially a pro-Beijing grouping, the *Samyabadi Dal* was the only Communist party to win a legislative seat at the 1979 balloting. Its leader, Mohammad Toaha, served as head of the 1979 Democratic Front and in 1983 adopted a pro-Soviet posture in support of the 15-party alliance.

Leader: Mohammad TOAHA (1981 presidential candidate).

Islamic Assembly (*Jama'at-i-Islami*). A pro-Pakistani grouping that was revived in May 1979 after seven years of inactivity, the *Jama'at-i-Islami* is the most fundamentalist of the religious parties and has branded General Ershad as "the enemy of Islam". It has been relatively quiescent since a series of mass rallies in late 1984.

Leader: Abbas Ali KHAN (President).

Ganatantric League. Founded in 1976, the *Ganatantric* (Democratic) League experienced a resurgence following the release from prison in 1980 of its leader, former president Khandakar Moshtaque Ahmed. In April 1983, Moshtaque Ahmed organized a National United Front (*Jaitya Oikya Jote*) of opposition right-wing parties.

Leader: Khandakar MOSHTAQUE Ahmed.

Freedom Party. Formation of the Freedom Party was announced in August 1987 by two of the participants in the 1975 coup that had resulted in the death of Sheikh Mujibur Rahman. Ousted in the November 1975 counter-coup, the two had subsequently gone into exile in Libya, although one of them, Sayeed Farook Rahman, after returning to Bangladesh in 1985, stood unsuccessfully as a presidential candidate against General Ershad in 1986.

Leaders: Sayeed Farook RAHMAN, Khandakar Abdur RASHID.

Other parties include the **Bangladesh People's League,** led by Dr. Alim Al-RAZEE; the **Islamic Democratic League,** headed by Maulana Abdur RAHIM; the **Bangladesh Jatiya League,** led by Ataur Rahman KHAN; the **Bangladesh Democratic Movement,** led by Rashed Khan MENON; and the **Bangladesh Workers' Party,** a Communist grouping.

Chittagong Insurgents:

The armed opposition to Dhaka and to the influx of Bengali settlers into the Hill Tracts has been led since 1975 by the **Shanti Bahini** ("Army of Peace"), consisting of some 2,000 guerrillas (mainly Chakma tribesmen) under Manabendra LARMA, a former member of Parliament. Smaller resistance groups have included the **Kaderia Bahini,** under Kader SIDDIQI, a Mujibist living in India; and the **Mukti Parishad,** headed by Sudharta TANGCHAINGA. Although sporadic insurgent attacks occurred through 1987, a major military threat appeared to have receded.

LEGISLATURE

The National Parliament (*Jatiya Sangsad*), a unicameral body of 300 seats filled by direct election and 30 additional seats reserved for women, was dissolved following the coup of March 24, 1982. An election for a new body of the same size and composition was held on May 7, 1986, with the following results: *Jatiya Dal,* 153 seats; Awami League, 76; *Jama'at-i-Islam,* 10; Communist Party of Bangladesh, 5; National Awami Party (Bhashani), 5; Bangladesh Muslim League, 4; *Jatiya Samajtantrik Dal* (Rab), 4; *Jatiya Samajtantrik Dal* (Siraj), 3; Bangladesh *Krishak Sramik* Awami League, 3; Bangladesh Workers' Party, 3; National Awami Party (Muzaffar), 2; independents, 32. Following party realignments and a number of by-elections on August 20, it was reported that the ruling party's majority had risen to 208, including the 30 indirectly elected women's seats.

At the most recent election of March 3, 1988, which was boycotted by the leading opposition parties, the *Jatiya Dal* was credited with winning 250 of the 300 elective seats.
Speaker: Shamsul Huda CHOUDHURY.

CABINET

Prime Minister	Mizanur Rahman Chowdhury
Deputy Prime Ministers	Moudad Ahmed
	Dr. M.A. Matin
	Shah Moazzam Hossain

Ministers

Agriculture	M. Mahbubuzzam
Commerce	Lt. Gen. Hossain Mohammad Ershad
Communications	Mohammad Matiur Rahman
Defense	Lt. Gen. Hossain Mohammad Ershad
Education	Mahbubur Rahman
Energy and Mineral Resources	Anwar Hossain
Establishment and Reorganization	Lt. Gen. Hossain Mohammad Ershad
Finance	Maj. Gen. Mohammad Abdul Munim
Fisheries and Livestock	Mirza Ruhul Amin
Foreign Affairs	Humayun Rashid Chowdhury
Health and Family Planning	Salahuddin Kadir Chowdhury
Home Affairs	Dr. M.A. Matin
Industries	Moudad Ahmed
Information	Lt. Gen. Hossain Mohammad Ershad
Irrigation, Water Development, and Flood Control	Anisul Islam Mahmud
Jute	Lt. Col. (Ret.) Zafar Imam
Labor and Manpower	Anwar Zahid
Land Administration and Land Reform	Sirajul Hossain Khan
Law and Justice	A.K.M. Nurul Islam
Local Government, Rural Development and Cooperatives	Shah Moazzem Hossain
Planning	Air Vice Mar. (Ret.) A.K. Khandker
Ports, Shipping and Inland Water Transport	A.K.M. Moyeedul Islam
Post and Telecommunications	Mizanur Rahman Chowdhury
Relief and Rehabilitation	Maulana M.A. Mannan
Religious Affairs	Maulana M.A. Mannan
Social Welfare and Women's Affairs	Maj. Gen. (Ret.) Mohammad Shamsul Huq
Textiles	Sunil Kumer Gupta
Works	Lt. Gen. Hossain Mohammad Ershad
Youth and Sports	(Vacant)

Ministers of State

Agriculture	Abus Salam
Civil Aviation and Tourism	A. Sattar
Defense	Qazi Jalaluddin Ahmed
Energy and Mineral Resources	Iqbal Hossain Chowdhury
Food	Maj. Sardar Amzad Hossain
Labor and Manpower	(Vacant)
Local Government, Rural Development and Cooperatives	B.K. Dewan
Works	Sheikh Shahidul Islam
Youth and Sports	Mustafa Jamal Haider
Governor, Central Bank	Mohammad Nurul Islam

NEWS MEDIA

Press. Censorship was imposed following the 1982 coup. Press curbs were formally abandoned with the revocation of martial law in November 1986; earlier in the year, five weeklies (including the London-based *Janamat*) were banned for printing "objectionable" or "slanderous" material. Another weekly was banned in January 1987, as was the Bengali-language daily *Banglar Bani* the following August. The following are published at Dhaka in Bengali, unless otherwise noted: *Ittefaq* (230,000); *Sangbad* (60,000); *Bangladesh Observer* (32,000), in English; *Azad* (20,000); *Dainik Bangla* (18,000); *Morning Post* (17,000), in English; *Bangladesh Times* (10,000), in English.

News agencies. There are two domestic news agencies located at Dhaka: the Bangladesh News Agency (*Bangladesh Sangbad Sangsta*) and the Eastern News Agency (ENA).

Radio and television. The government-controlled Radio Bangladesh operates domestic radio stations at Dhaka, Chittagong, Khulna, and other leading cities while providing overseas service in six languages. Bangladesh Television, operated by the government since 1971, broadcasts from some dozen stations. There were 4.3 million radio and 304,000 television receivers in 1987.

INTERGOVERNMENTAL REPRESENTATION

Ambassador to the US: A.H.S. Ataul KARIM.

US Ambassador to Bangladesh: Willard Ames DE PREE.

Permanent Representative to the UN: Justice B.A. SIDDIQUI.

IGO Memberships (Non-UN): ADB, CCC, CP, CWTH, IC, ICAC, IDB, Intelsat, Interpol, ISO, ITPA, NAM, SAARC.

BARBADOS

Political Status: Independent member of the Commonwealth since November 30, 1966.

Area: 166 sq. mi. (431 sq. km.).

Population: 246,082 (1980C), 257,000 (1988E).

Major Urban Center (1980C): BRIDGETOWN (7,517).

Official Language: English.

Monetary Unit: Barbados Dollar (market rate March 1, 1988, 2.01 dollars = $1US).

Sovereign: Queen ELIZABETH II.

Governor General: Sir Hugh SPRINGER; appointed February 24, 1984, to succeed Sir Deighton Harcourt Lisle WARD, who died January 9.

Prime Minister: Dr. Lloyd Erskine SANDIFORD (Democratic Labour Party); sworn in on June 2, 1987, following the death of Errol Walton BARROW (Democratic Labour Party) on June 1.

THE COUNTRY

Geographically part of the Lesser Antilles, Barbados is also the most easterly of the Caribbean nations (see map, p. 22). The island enjoys an equable climate and fertile soil, approximately 85 percent of the land being arable. Population density is among the world's highest, although the birth rate has declined in recent years. Approximately 80 percent of the population is of African origin, and another 15 percent is of mixed blood, with Europeans representing only 5 percent of the total; nonetheless, there is a strong and pervasive sense of British tradition and culture. The Anglican Church enjoys official status, but other Protestant, Roman Catholic, and Jewish groups are also active. Sugar, upon which the island was historically dependent, is still a major contributor to the economy, while tourism is the leading source of foreign exchange; manufacturing, especially that geared toward fellow members of the Caribbean Community, is also an important source of income.

GOVERNMENT AND POLITICS

Political background. Historically a planter-dominated island, and often called the "Little England" of the Caribbean, Barbados has been molded by a British tradition extending back to 1639. In 1937 economic problems caused by the fluctuating price of sugar led to demonstrations in Bridgetown, which resulted in the establishment of a British Royal Commission to the West Indies. The Commission proved instrumental in bringing about social and political reform, including the introduction of universal adult suffrage in 1951. The island was granted full internal sovereignty ten years later.

Barbados played a leading role in the short-lived West Indies Federation (1958–1962) and supplied its only prime minister, Sir Grantley ADAMS. The collapse of the Federation and the inability of Barbadian leaders to secure the establishment of an Eastern Caribbean Federation as a substitute left independence within the Commonwealth, which was achieved on November 30, 1966, as the only viable alternative. An election held November 3, 1966, confirmed the dominant position of the Democratic Labour Party (DLP), whose leader, Errol Walton BARROW, had been named premier in 1961 and was reappointed prime minister in 1971.

In an election held September 2, 1976, the opposition Barbados Labour Party (BLP) upset the DLP, and Barrow's 15-year rule ended the following day with the designation of Sir Grantley's son, J.M.G.M. ("Tom") ADAMS, as prime minister. In voting that was extremely close in many constituencies, the BLP retained its majority on June 18, 1981. Adams died in March 1985 and was succeeded by his deputy, H. Bernard ST. JOHN, who was unable to contain rising fissures within the BLP. As a result, the DLP won a decisive legislative majority of 24–3 at balloting on May 28, 1986, with a new Barrow administration being installed the following day. Barrow died suddenly on June 1, 1987, and was succeeded on the following day by Lloyd Erskine SANDIFORD.

Constitution and government. The governmental structure is modeled after the British parliamentary system. The queen remains titular head of state and is represented by a governor general with quite limited governmental functions. Executive authority is vested in the prime minister and his cabinet, who are collectively responsible to a bicam-

eral legislature. The upper house of the legislature, the Senate, is appointed by the governor general after consultation with the government, the opposition, and other relevant social and political interests. Members of the lower house, the House of Assembly, are elected for a maximum term of five years. The franchise is held by all persons over the age of 18, and voting is by secret ballot.

The judicial system embraces lower magistrates, who are appointed by the governor general with the advice of the Judicial and Legal Service Commission, and a Supreme Court, encompassing a High Court and a Court of Appeal. The chief justice is appointed by the governor general on the recommendation of the prime minister after consultation with the leader of the opposition.

Previously elected local government bodies were abolished in 1969 in favor of a division into 11 parishes, all of which (in addition to the municipality of Bridgetown) are now administered by the central government.

Foreign relations. Barbados has striven to pursue an active, but nonaligned, posture in United Nations, Commonwealth, and hemispheric affairs. After participating for some years in the general OAS ostracism of Cuba, it reestablished relations with Havana in 1973, though still enjoying cordial relations with the United States. In December 1979, in a move characterized by Prime Minister Adams as an act of "East Caribbean defence cooperation", it dispatched troops to St. Vincent to help maintain order while St. Vincent police were deployed in containing an uprising on the Grenadines' Union Island. Relations with neighboring Grenada, on the other hand, deteriorated following installation of the leftist regime of Maurice Bishop at St. George's in March 1979 and the Adams government participated in the US-led invasion precipitated by the coup of October 1983. This action, while strengthening Bridgetown's relations with Washington, strained its links with Britain and, perhaps more seriously, with Trinidad, which claimed that the operation was undertaken without properly consulting all members of the Caribbean community. Despite these difficulties, Prime Minister Adams was widely perceived as a regional leader, his death being described as "leaving a power vacuum in the Caribbean". Subsequently, Barbados moved even closer to the United States: despite outspoken dissatisfaction with the level of aid provided by the US Caribbean Basin Initiative, the island was designated in early 1985 as the center of the Washington-funded Regional Security System (RSS) and coordinated RSS military maneuvers in the Eastern Caribbean the following September. However, even prior to Adams death, the idea of providing the RSS with a 1,000-man rapid deployment force had quietly been dropped. Following the DLP's 1986 victory, Prime Minister Barrow joined James Mitchell of St. Vincent in opposing the conclusion of a formal RSS treaty, stating in a letter of September 2 to six regional chief executives that his government would rely instead on a 1982 memorandum of understanding that provided for cooperation in a number of nonmilitary activities such as drug control, prevention of smuggling, and maritime conservation and training.

Current issues. At the death of Prime Minister Adams in March 1985, Bernard St. John inherited a fractious government, a divided ruling party, and a deeply troubled economy. Nonetheless, buoyed by improving public poll results and the introduction of an expansionary budget, St. John decided to call an early 1986 election, which most observers expected to be close. The magnitude of the ensuing DLP victory was attributed to a variety of factors, including Barrow's emphasis on the need for combatting unemployment while pursuing a foreign policy more independent of Washington.

Upon his return to office, Prime Minister Barrow moved to implement the DLP's "alternative budget", which featured an attempt at economic stimulation by the abolition of income taxes on earnings below B$15,000; cuts in public-sector borrowing and expenditure; and privatization of a number of state enterprises, including Caribbean Airways (which terminated scheduled services on April 1, 1987). However, despite a significant increase in tourism, little economic improvement was registered: by late 1987 unemployment, reflecting stagnation in the manufacturing sector, remained in excess of 19 percent, while the country continued in deficit with most of its trading partners.

POLITICAL PARTIES

The two principal parties, the Barbados Labour Party and the Democratic Labour Party, traditionally exhibited similar labor-oriented philosophies, differing little on policies and programs, with political contests turning mainly on considerations of personality. Recently, however, the DLP has appeared to have adopted a somewhat right-of-center posture (see below).

Government Party:

Democratic Labour Party (DLP). A moderate party founded in 1955 by dissident members of the Barbados Labour Party (below), the DLP has, for most of its existence, been closely allied with the country's principal labor group, the Barbados Workers' Union. In the election of 1971, the DLP obtained 18 out of 24 legislative seats, but retained only 7 in 1976; its representation rose to 10 in 1981. Former prime minister Errol W. Barrow resigned as DLP leader following the 1976 defeat but returned to the party presidency in mid-1980. After the 1981 defeat, he again stepped down as president, while remaining in Parliament as leader of the opposition.

In 1985, in the wake of Prime Minister Adams' death, continued recession, and the likelihood of an early election, Barrow advanced an essentially conservative program including privatization of state enterprises, cutbacks in public works, sale of the government's share in a number of corporate sectors, and the introduction of business incentives. However, the new platform also deplored Bridgetown's involvement in US strategic interests and called for dissolution of the Regional Security System.

Following Barrow's own death in June 1987, his deputy, Erskine Sandiford, was named prime minister and assumed leadership of the party.

Leaders: Dr. Lloyd Erskine SANDIFORD (Prime Minister), Branford Mayhew TAITT (President), Cora CUMBERBATCH (General Secretary), David THOMPSON (Assistant General Secretary).

Opposition Parties:

Barbados Labour Party (BLP). Founded in 1938, the BLP is the older of the leading parties. After dominating Barbadian politics in the 1950s under the leadership of Sir Grantley Adams, it went into opposition, winning 9 seats in 1966 and only 6 in 1971. It returned to power in 1976 and retained its majority at the election of June 18, 1981. Long led by Tom Adams, the BLP split into a number of factions upon his death in 1985, thereby contributing to the defeat of the St. John government a year later. Parliamentary leader Henry Forde, named to succeed St. John as BLP chairman in October 1986, declared that the party would have

to be rebuilt as a "highly decentralized" organization featuring "mass democracy in the formation of policy".

Leaders: Henry FORDE (Leader of the Opposition and Chairman of the Party), Patricia SYMMONDS (General Secretary).

Minor parties include the **People's Progressive Movement** (PPM), founded in 1979 and led by Eric SEALY, the left-wing **Workers' Party of Barbados,** founded in 1985 by Dr. George BELLE, and the leftist **Movement for National Liberation** (Monali), led by Bobby CLARKE. The last grouping was briefly the center of a controversy in early 1982 as the result of a Cuban offer to extend, through the party, three scholarships in agronomy and audio-visual technology to Barbadian students. Although Monali initially accepted the offer, it was withdrawn following a formal protest by Bridgetown to Havana, which subsequently announced that any such scholarships would be handled through government-to-government channels.

LEGISLATURE

The bicameral **Parliament** consists of an appointed Senate and an elected House of Assembly.

Senate. The Senate consists of 21 members appointed by the governor general; 12 are appointed on advice of the prime minister, 2 on advice of the leader of the opposition, and 7 to represent social, religious, and economic interests.
President: Frank L. WALCOTT.

House of Assembly. The House currently consists of 27 members elected for five-year terms by direct popular vote. At the last election, held on May 28, 1986, the Democratic Labour Party won 24 seats and the Democratic Labour Party won 3.
Speaker: Lawson A. WEEKS.

CABINET

Prime Minister	Dr. Lloyd Erskine Sandiford
Deputy Prime Minister	Philip Marlowe Greaves
Ministers	
Agriculture, Food and Fisheries	Warwick Franklin
Economic Affairs, Information and National Insurance	Dr. Lloyd Erskine Sandiford
Education and Culture	Cyril Walker
Employment, Labor Relations and Community Development	Neville Keith Simmons
Finance	Dr. Lloyd Erskine Sandiford
Foreign Affairs	Sir James Cameron Tudor
Health	Branford Mayhew Taitt
Housing and Lands	Harold Blackman
Industry, Trade and Commerce	Evelyn Greaves
International Transport, Telecommunications and Immigration	Philip Marlow Greaves
Legal Affairs	Maurice Athelstan King
Public Works and Transport	Don George Blackman
Tourism and Sports	Wesley Winfield Hall
Ministers of State	
Civil Service	L.V. Harcourt Lewis
Finance	Carl Clarke
Attorney General	Maurice Athelstan King
Governor, Central Bank	Kurleigh King

NEWS MEDIA

All news media are free of censorship and government control.

Press. The following are privately owned and published at Bridgetown: *The Nation* (22,000 daily, 35,000 Sunday, published as *Sunday Sun*); *Advocate-News* (19,000 daily, 30,300 Sunday), independent; *The Beacon*

(15,000), weekly BLP organ. In addition, an *Official Gazette* is issued on Monday and Thursday.

News agencies. The Caribbean News Agency (Cana) is located at St. Michael; Spain's *Agencia EFE* is also represented in Barbados.

Radio and television. Barbados Rediffusion Service, Ltd., has operated a wired radio system since the 1930s, and the government-owned Caribbean Broadcasting Corporation (CBC) has offered a wireless system since 1963. The Voice of Barbados, privately owned, began broadcasting in 1981, while Barbados Broadcasting Service (BBS), also private, began transmission in late 1982. In addition, a multidenominational religious system has sought licensing. At present, the CBC operates the only television station, but a Canadian-based cable TV company is proceeding with plans to enter the market. There were approximately 62,000 television receivers in 1987.

INTERGOVERNMENTAL REPRESENTATION

Ambassador to the US: Sir William R. DOUGLAS.

US Ambassador to Barbados: Paul A. RUSSO.

Permanent Representative to the UN: Dame Ruth Nita BARROW.

IGO Memberships (Non-UN): Caricom, CDB, CWTH, EEC(L), *EIB,* Geplacea, IADB, Intelsat, Interpol, ISO, IWTC, NAM, OAS, OPANAL, SELA.

BELGIUM

Kingdom of Belgium
Koninkrijk België (Dutch)
Royaume de Belgique (French)
Königreich Belgien (German)

Political Status: Independence proclaimed October 4, 1830; monarchical constitution of 1831 most recently revised in 1970.

Area: 11,781 sq. mi. (30,513 sq. km.).

Population: 9,848,647 (1981C), 9,862,000 (1988E).

Major Urban Centers (1985E): BRUSSELS (urban area, 970,500); Antwerp (urban area, 482,000); Ghent (233,000); Charleroi (211,000); Liège (202,000); Bruges (118,000); Namur (102,000).

Official Languages: Dutch, French, German.

Monetary Unit: Belgian Franc (principal rate March 1, 1988, 35.28 francs = $1US).

Sovereign: King BAUDOUIN (BOUDEWIJN, BALDUIN); succeeded to the throne July 17, 1951, on the abdication of his father, King LEOPOLD III.

Heir to the Throne: Prince ALBERT of Liège, brother of the King.

Prime Minister: Dr. Wilfried MARTENS (Christian People's Party); served as Prime Minister from April 1979 to March 1981; returned to office on December 17, 1981, following election of November 8, succeeding Mark EYSKENS (Christian People's Party); most recently reinstalled on May 6, 1988, following parliamentary election of December 13, 1987.

THE COUNTRY

Wedged between France, Germany, and the Netherlands, densely populated Belgium lies at the crossroads of Western Europe. Its location has contributed to a history of ethnic diversity, as manifested by linguistic and cultural dualism between the Dutch-speaking north (Flanders) and the French-speaking south (Wallonia). The Walloons constitute 32 percent of the total population (another 10 percent being effectively bilingual) and the Flemings 56 percent, most of the remainder comprising a small German-speaking minority located along the eastern border. In contrast to the linguistic division, a vast majority of the population is Roman Catholic, with small minorities of Jews and Protestants.

The economy is largely dominated by the service sector, which provides 61 percent of the GDP and employs 66 percent of the nation's labor force. Belgium's industry, responsible for 36 percent of the GDP, is concentrated in metal fabrication, food, and chemicals, with de-emphasis on the traditional textile, steel, and glass sectors. Agriculture occupies only about 3 percent of the labor force, although supplying three-quarters of food requirements.

Moderate but steady economic growth prevailed during most of the two decades after World War II, but the annual increase in GDP fell to an average of less than 2 percent in the decade following the OPEC-induced "oil shock" of 1973–1974, one of the lowest rates among industrialized nations. Unemployment consistently exceeded 12 percent during 1982–1987, although austerity measures succeeded in reducing inflation from 8.7 to 1.5 percent during the same period. A substantial regional imbalance also exists: most major industry is disproportionately concentrated in Flanders, a factor that has heightened regional and ethnic tension.

GOVERNMENT AND POLITICS

Political background. After centuries of Spanish and Austrian rule and briefer periods of French administration, Belgium was incorporated into the Kingdom of the Netherlands by the Congress of Vienna in 1815. Independence was proclaimed on October 4, 1830, and Prince LEOPOLD of Saxe-Coburg was elected king in 1831, although Belgian autonomy was not formally recognized by the Netherlands until 1839. The only subsequent challenges to the nation's integrity occurred in the form of German invasion and occupation during the two world wars.

Since World War II, Belgium has been governed by a series of administrations based on one or more of its three major political groups: Christian Democratic, Social Democratic, and Liberal. By the early 1960s, however, the traditional system was threatened by ethnic and linguistic antagonism. In addition to a proliferation of minor parties, divisions arose within the previously national parties, and in 1963 linguistic tension resulted in division of the country into Dutch- and French-speaking sections. By constitutional amendment in 1970, three cultural communities (Dutch, French, and German) were recognized and four linguistic areas (the fourth embracing 19 bilingual boroughs of Brussels) established. The new arrangement also called for assignment of powers over economic and social affairs to the three communities. Implementation of the plan was, however, slow. While linguistic parity within the central government was achieved in 1973, it was not until mid-1975 that Parliament approved legislation authorizing the establishment of community executives and assemblies.

Under the so-called "Egmont pact" of 1977, Belgium's major parties agreed, in effect, on the establishment of a federal system. Subsequently, however, Flemish extremists argued that an autonomous Brussels would give the French-speaking minority control of two of the country's three districts and insisted that the capital remain bilingual. In August 1978 the issue was further complicated by a ruling of the Supreme Court that certain aspects of the plan were unconstitutional, and on October 11 the government of Prime Minister Léo TINDEMANS was forced to resign. His caretaker successor, Paul vanden BOEYNANTS, continued in office following a national election on December 17 at which the distribution of seats in the Chamber of Representatives remained virtually unchanged. On April 3, 1979, after more than three months of extended negotiations, a new government was formed under Dr. Wilfried MARTENS that included five of the six parties (CVP, PSC, SP, PS, FDF, discussed under Political Parties, below) that had participated in the outgoing government.

In mid-July, royal assent was secured for the establishment of transitional bodies in preparation for the election of three regional parliaments between January 1, 1980, and January 1, 1982. A powerful group within the Christian People's Party (CVP), led by party president Tindemans, argued, however, that Brussels should be granted only limited autonomy, and at its National Conference in mid-December the CVP endorsed the Tindemans position. In early January 1980, Prime Minister Martens announced postponement of self-government for Brussels while committing his government to the establishment of regional bodies for Flanders and Wallonia. In response, representatives of the French-Speaking Front (FDF) withdrew on January 16, leaving the government without the two-thirds majority needed for constitutional revision and forcing its resignation on April 9. Martens succeeded, however, in forming a new government on May 18 that included representatives of the two Liberal parties (PRL, PVV) as well as of four members of the earlier coalition (CVP, PSC, SP, PS). Requisite constitutional majorities thus having been restored, the government was able to secure parliamentary approval during July and August to establish councils for the Dutch- and French-speaking regions.

Alleviation of the constitutional crisis brought to the fore a number of long-simmering and ultimately unresolvable differences on economic and defense policies, the Liberals opposing the Socialists in calling for an increase in the defense budget and cuts in the social-security and pension systems. As a result, the government resigned on October 4, and 12 days later Martens announced the formation

of a non-Liberal coalition (CVP, PSC, SP, PS) that was subsequently approved by extraordinary congresses of the parties involved.

Dr. Martens was forced to tender his government's resignation on March 31, 1981, following opposition by both Socialist parties to CVP proposals for economic reform. He was succeeded on April 8 by Mark EYSKENS, heading a government that was virtually unchanged except for Martens' own departure. The Eyskens government, in turn, was obliged to resign on September 21, while a general election on November 8 yielded little in the way of party realignment in either legislative house. Following the inability of either Willy de CLERCQ (PVV) or Charles-Ferdinand NOTHOMB (PSC) to organize an acceptable coalition, Martens succeeded, on December 17, in securing approval of a four-party government that included both Liberal parties while excluding the Socialists.

Despite implementation of an economic austerity program, the coalition marginally increased its majority at parliamentary balloting on October 13, 1985, a new government (Dr. Martens' sixth) being sworn in on November 28. By May 1986, however, the country was plagued by a series of one-day strikes, and on May 31, over 100,000 demonstrated in Brussels in protest against the austerity package with its massive spending cuts and anticipated staff reductions in education, health, public transportation, and telecommunications. The new budget, approved by the cabinet on May 20, 1986, was intended to reduce the public sector's share of the GNP from 10.3 percent in 1985 to 7 percent by 1990, but by November 1986 the cabinet was forced to advance a new 10-point plan, providing for 18,000 more jobs, in compensation for those lost through the austerity measures.

Dr. Martens was again forced to resign in October 1987 in the wake of renewed linguistic controversy (see Current issues, below) and at the election of December 13 the Christian Democrats lost seven Chamber seats to the Socialists, the latter achieving a plurality for the first time since 1936. A 144-day impasse followed, with Martens responding on May 6, 1988, to the king's request to form a new five-party government (Belgium's 34th since World War II) that encompassed the Christian Democrats, the Socialists, and the Flemish Nationalist People's Union, while excluding the Liberals.

Constitution and government. Under the constitution of 1831 (as amended), Belgium is a constitutional monarchy with a parliamentary form of government. Executive power theoretically rests with the king, who is head of state, but actual power rests with the prime minister and his cabinet, both being responsible to a bicameral legislature. The judicial system, based on the French model, is headed by the Court of Cassation, which has the power to review any judicial decision; it may not, however, pass on the constitutionality of legislation, for which advisory opinions may be sought from a special legal body, the Council of State. There are also nine assize courts (one in each province), three courts of appeal, and numerous courts of first instance and justices of the peace.

As of early 1988, Belgium remained divided into nine provinces, each with a directly elected legislature and a governor appointed by the king. In mid-1977, however, the government had proposed the abandonment of the provincial structure in favor of an ethnic-linguistic reorganization plan (see Political background, above) that was formally adopted by the cabinet on February 22, 1978. The plan was significantly advanced by a series of constitutional reforms approved by the Parliament in mid-1980 that permitted Flanders and Wallonia to establish directly elected regional assemblies with authority over a variety of specified activities, including public health, road transport, and urban redevelopment. Brussels, on the other hand, continues to be administered by a three-member executive.

Foreign relations. Originally one of Europe's neutral powers, Belgium since World War II has been a leader in international cooperation. It is a founding member of the United Nations, NATO, the Benelux Union, and all of the major West European regional organizations. Its only overseas possession, the former Belgian Congo, became independent in 1960, while the Belgian-administered UN Trust Territory of Ruanda-Urundi became independent in 1962 as the two states of Rwanda and Burundi. Belgium has a substantial technical-assistance program aimed primarily, but not exclusively, at its former African territories.

One of the most difficult foreign policy issues of the last decade has concerned the stationing of intermediate-range cruise missiles on Belgian territory, as decided by NATO in December 1979. Despite strong pressure from the US Reagan administration, the Martens government postponed a decision in the matter until after the resumption of East-West arms talks in early 1985, with the Chamber of Representatives endorsing deployment by the relatively narrow margin of 116–93 in a confidence vote on March 20. In June 1986, on the other hand, Belgium joined the Netherlands and Denmark in refusing to have chemical weapons stationed in their respective countries.

Current issues. During 1986 intense controversy arose over the nomination of José HAPPART as mayor of Voeren (Les Fourons), a group of largely French-speaking villages northeast of Liège that had been transferred to the Flemish-speaking district of Limburg in the early 1960s. The dispute, centering on Happart's refusal to take a mandated competency test in Flemish (though he was known to be fluent in the language), led Prime Minister Martens to submit his government's resignation on October 14; the tender was rejected by King Baudouin, although the interior minister, Charles-Ferdinand NOTHOMB, was forced from office because of his handling of the affair. In September 1987 the Court of Cassation dismissed Happart from office, although the controversial mayor continued in an acting capacity, generating a crisis within the Marten coalition that forced its collapse in October and a new election in December. Under a compromise that broke a five-month stalemate and permitted Marten to form a center-left administration in May 1988, it was agreed that Happart would remain in office pending local balloting in October and subsequent inquiry by a bipartisan panel. The new coalition (which, with the inclusion of the People's Union, commanded the two-thirds majority required for constitutional revision) also agreed to continue the prime minister's economic austerity program.

POLITICAL PARTIES

Belgium's leading parties were long divided into French- and Dutch-speaking sections, which tended to subscribe to common programs for general elections. Beginning in the late 1960s, the cleavages became more pronounced, with the sections typically holding separate conferences while maintaining loose alliances with their homologues on the other side of the linguistic border. Thus they are typically listed by "family" rather than as homogeneous or composite parties. Collaterally, the dominance of the three principal groupings has been eroded somewhat by an increase in the strength of numerous smaller ethnic and special-interest groups. At the 1977 election, for example, some 17 parties presented lists in the Brussels area alone, with only about half obtaining the minimum quota of votes needed to secure parliamentary representation.

Christian Democratic Family:

Christian People's Party (*Christelijke Volkspartij* — CVP). The CVP and the PSC (below) are joint heirs to the former Catholic Party, which traditionally upheld the position of the Catholic Church in Belgium and included representatives of commercial and manufacturing interests as well as of the working classes. Both groups are now nondenominational and, with substantial representation from the Catholic Trade Union Federation (the country's largest labor organization), favor a variety of social and economic reforms. They are, however, deeply divided on regional and constitutional issues, the CVP representing Flemish interests at Brussels and in the north.

Leaders: Wilfried MARTENS (Prime Minister), Léo TINDEMANS (former Prime Minister), Frank SWAELEN (President), Ludo WILLEMS (Secretary).

Social Christian Party (*Parti Social Chrétien* — PSC). The PSC is the French-speaking (Walloon) counterpart of the CVP.

Leaders: Gérard DEPREZ (President), Charles-Ferdinand NOTHOMB, Joseph MITCHELL, Jacques LEFEVRE (Secretary).

Social Democratic Family:

Socialist Party (*Socialistische Partij* — SP). Until October 1978 the SP was the Dutch-speaking wing of the historic Belgian Socialist Party (BSP), an evolutionary Marxist grouping organized in 1885 as the *Parti Ouvrier Belge*. Both the SP and the PS (below) are essentially pragmatic in outlook, concentrating on social welfare and industrial democracy issues within a free enterprise context. Both are associated with the Belgian Federation of Labor, the country's second-largest trade union organization.

Leaders: Karel Van MIERT (President), Willy CLAES, Carla GALLE (Secretary).

Socialist Party (*Parti Socialiste* — PS). Long the dominant force within the traditional party because of its strength in Walloon industrial centers, the French-speaking PS formally split with the SP prior to the 1978 election.

Leaders: Guy SPITAELS (President), Roger GAILLIEZ (Secretary).

Liberal Family:

Party for Freedom and Progress (*Partij voor Vrijheid en Vooruitgang* — PVV). In 1961 Belgium's traditional Liberal Party changed its name to the Party for Freedom and Progress. During the 1974 campaign the party's French- and Dutch-speaking wings supported a common free-enterprise program emphasizing the need for a strong central government and tightened controls on public spending. Prior to the 1977 election, the French-speaking wing (*Parti pour la Liberté et le Progrès* — PLP) under André Damseaux merged with part of the Walloon Rally to form the Party of Walloon Reform and Liberty (see PRL, below).

Leaders: Anne-Marie NEYTS-UYTTEBROECK (President), Guy VERHOFSTADT (former President), Willy de CLERCQ.

Liberal Reformation Party (*Parti Réformateur Libéral* — PRL). The PRL was formed on May 19, 1979, by merger of the Party of Walloon

Reform and Liberty (*Parti des Réformes et de la Liberté en Wallonie* — PRLW) and the Liberal Party (*Parti Libéral* — PL). The PRLW had been organized in November 1976 by members of the Walloon Rally (see Walloon Party, below) who were opposed to the RW's leftward drift after the municipal elections of the previous month. They were joined by the former Walloon wing of the PLP. The PL was a Brussels-area group which, although allied with the French-Speaking Front (below) in 1974, presented a separate list in 1977. At its inaugural congress the PRL announced that it would seek to cooperate with the PVV. At the 1981 election its lower-house representation rose from 15 to 24 seats, while its elected Senate representation nearly doubled, from 6 to 11 seats. Its parliamentary strength was largely unchanged in 1985 and 1987.

Leaders: Louis MICHEL (President), Jean GOL (former PRLW leader), André DAMSEAUX (former PLP President), Etienne KNOOPS (PRLW), Georges MUNDELEER (former PL President), François-Xavier de DONNEA, Edouard C. KLEIN (General Secretary).

Other Parties:

The People's Union (*De Volksunie* — VU). A Flemish nationalist party founded in 1953, *Volksunie* favors an autonomous Flanders within a federal state. The party also gained substantially at the 1981 election, its lower-house representation rising from 14 to 20 seats; 4 of the latter were, however, lost in 1985 and remained at 16 in 1987.

Leaders: J. GABRIELS (President), P. van GREMBERGEN (Secretary).

French-Speaking Front (*Front Démocratique des Bruxellois Francophones* — FDF). The FDF, a formation of French-speaking Brussels interest groups, is loosely connected with Walloon regional parties. It retained its existing 1 Chamber and 3 Senate seats in 1987.

Leaders: Georges CLERFAYT (President), Georges VERZIN (General Secretary).

Walloon Party (*Parti Wallon* — PW). The PW was formed in 1985 by amalgamation of the former Walloon Rally (*Rassemblement Wallon* — RW) with the smaller Popular Walloon Rally (*Rassemblement Populaire Wallon* — RPW) and the Independent Walloon Front (*Front Indépendantiste Wallon* — FIW). The RW was linked with the French-Speaking Front from 1968 until after the 1974 election. Centrist on economic issues, it broke with the FDF on June 10, 1974, when, upon joining the earlier Tindemans coalition, it became the first federalist party to accept governmental responsibility. After experiencing severe losses (largely to the Socialists) in the municipal elections of October 10, 1976, the party leadership proposed that the Rally "return to its sources" and establish itself as a left-wing party located between the Socialists and the Communists. The move was opposed by a centrist group headed by François Perin and Jean Gol, both of whom urged that the party should remain committed to "ideological pluralism". Rebuffed on the issue, the centrists withdrew on November 24 to enter the PRLW. Prior to the 1981 election, the RW renewed its alliance with the FDF, but the joint list yielded only 8 Chamber seats, as contrasted with a total of 15 formerly held by the two parties. It failed to secure parliamentary representation in either 1985 or 1987.

Leader: Jean-Claude PICCIN (President).

Flemish Bloc (*Vlaams Blok* — VB). The VB contested the election of December 1978 as an alliance of the National Flemish Party (*Vlaamse Nationale Partij* — VNP) and the Flemish People's Party (*Vlaamse Volkspartij* — VVP). It was formally constituted as a unified party in May 1979. Winning 1 Chamber seat in 1981 and 1985, it obtained a Senate seat and an additional Chamber seat in 1987.

Leader: Karel DILLEN (Chairman).

Democratic Union for the Respect of Labor (*Respect voor Arbeid en Democratie/Union Démocratique pour le Respect du Travail* — RAD/UDRT). The *Poujadiste* RAD/UDRT contested both the 1978 and 1981 elections on a platform of "total economic freedom" based on a major reduction in taxes. Its lower house representation dropped from 3 to 1 in 1985, the last being lost in 1987.

Leaders: Robert HENDRICK (President), Michel van HOUTTE (Dutch-speaking Secretary), Pascal ROUBAIX (French-speaking Secretary).

Belgian Communist Party (*Parti Communiste de Belgique/Kommunistische Partij van België* — PCB/KPB). The PCB/KPB was founded in 1921, but, in recent years, has shifted away from a pro-Moscow to an essentially Eurocommunist posture. It has been highly critical of the Soviet

presence in Afghanistan and in 1983 resumed contacts with the Chinese Communist Party. Although it won only 2 Chamber seats in 1977, when its popular vote dropped to its second-lowest level since World War II, its representation increased to 4 in 1978; it fell again to 2 in 1981, both seats being lost in 1985.

Leaders: Louis Van GEYT (President), Claude RENARD (French-speaking Vice President), Jef TURF (Dutch-speaking Vice President), Daniel FEDRIGO (Parliamentary Leader), Jan DEBROUWERE (National Secretary).

German-Speaking Party (*Partei der Deutschsprachigen Belgier* — PDB). The PDB was formed in 1972 to further the interests of the German-speaking community. Campaigning under the slogan "We want to remain Belgians, but not to become Walloons", it has yet to secure parliamentary representation.

Leader: Alfred KEUTGEN (President).

Ecologists (*Ecologistes* — Ecolo). Formed prior to the 1981 election, Ecolo won 5 Chamber seats in 1985, 2 of which were lost in 1987.

Leaders: J.M. VERHERTBRUGGEN and J. HUMBLET (Federal Secretaries).

Live Differently (*Anders gaan leven* — Agalev). A Flemish counterpart to Ecolo, Agalev obtained 4 lower house seats in the 1985 balloting, increasing its representation to 6 in 1987.

Leader: Léo COX (Political Secretary).

United Feminist Party (*Vereenigde Feministiche Partij/Parti Féministe Unifié* — VFP/PFU). The VFP/PFU was founded in 1972 to promote women's rights, enhance feminine participation in public life, and press for the inclusion of more women on party electoral lists. It is unrepresented in Parliament.

Leaders: Nina ARIEL, Claire BIHIN, Renée WATY-FOSSEPREZ.

Other parties participating, without success, in recent elections included the **Belgian Party of Labor** (*Partij van de Arbeid/Parti du Travail de Belgique* — PvdA/PTB); the **Socialist Workers' Party** (*Socialistische Arbeiders Partij* — SAP); and **Solidarity and Participation** (*Solidarité et Participation* — SEP), a group by members of the Walloon Christian labor movement.

LEGISLATURE

The bicameral **Parliament** consists of a Senate and a Chamber of Representatives, both elected for four-year terms and endowed with virtually equal powers. The last election was held December 13, 1987. The king may dissolve either or both chambers.

Senate (*Sénat/Senaat*). The upper house consists of both directly and indirectly elected members. The number of directly elected members (presently 106) is equal to half the number of members of the Chamber of Representatives. Of the indirectly elected senators, two-thirds (presently 51) are elected by the Provincial Councils on a population basis, while one-third (presently 26) are co-opted by the Senate itself in secret balloting. One of the nondirectly elected seats is constitutionally assigned to the heir to the throne. The breakdown of elected members by family and party in the wake of the 1987 balloting was as follows: Social Democratic, 37 (PS, 20; SP, 17); Christian Democratic, 31 (CVP, 22; PSC, 9); Liberal, 23 (PVV, 11; PRL, 12); People's Union, 8; Ecologists, 5 (Agalev, 3; Ecolo, 2); French-Speaking Front, 1, Flemish Bloc, 1. The full membership, by party, was PS, 36; SP, 29; CVP, 39; PSC, 16; PVV, 18; PRL, 21; VU, 13; FDF, 2; Ecolo and Agalev, 8; VB, 1.

President: Roger LALLEMAND.

Chamber of Representatives (*Chambre des Représentants/Kamer van Volksvertegenwoordigers*). The size of the lower house is proportional to the population but cannot exceed 1 member for every 40,000 inhabitants. After the 1987 election, its current membership of 212 was distributed, by family and party, as follows: Social Democratic, 72 (PS, 40; SP, 32); Christian Democratic, 62 (CVP, 43; PSC, 19); Liberal, 48 (PVV, 25; PRL, 23); People's Union, 16; Ecologists, 9 (Agalev, 6; Ecolo, 3); French-Speaking Front, 3; Flemish Bloc, 2.

President: Erik van KEIRSBILCK.

CABINET

Prime Minister	Wilfried Martens
Vice Prime Ministers	Willy Claes
	Jean-Luc Dehaene
	Philippe Moureaux
	Hugo Schiltz
	Melchior Wathelet

Ministers

Brussels Affairs	Philippe Moureaux
Budget	Hugo Schiltz
Civil Service	Michel Hansenne
Development Cooperation	André Geens
Economic Affairs and Planning	Willy Claes
Employment and Labor	Luc Van den Brande
Finance	Philippe Maystadt
Foreign Commerce	Robert Urbain
Foreign Relations	Léo Tindemans
Institutional Reforms (Flemish)	Jean-Luc Dehaene
Institutional Reforms (Francophone)	Philippe Moreaux
Interior, Modernization of Public Services, Scientific and Cultural National Institutions	Louis Tobback
Justice	Melchior Wathelet
Middle Classes	Melchior Wathelet
National Defense	Guy Coeme
National Education (Flemish)	Willy Claes
National Education (Francophone)	Yvan Ylieff
Pensions	Alain Van der Biest
Postal Service, Telegraph, and Telephone	Freddy Willockx
Public Works	Paula D'Hondt-Van Opdenbosch
Science Policy	Hugo Schiltz
Social Affairs	Philippe Busquin
Governor, National Bank of Belgium	Wivina De Meester

NEWS MEDIA

Press. The following are published daily at Brussels, unless otherwise noted: *Krantengroep De Standaard* (378,000), in Dutch, independent; *Het Laatste Nieuws* (304,000), in Dutch, independent; *Le Soir* (215,000), in French, independent; *Het Volk* (Ghent, 193,000), in Dutch, Christian Democratic; *Gazet van Antwerpen* (Antwerp, 183,000), in Dutch, Christian Democratic; *La Meuse* (Liège, 132,000), in French, independent; *La Dernière Heure* (97,000), in French, Liberal; *La Libre Belgique* (90,000), in French, independent.

News agencies. The official agency is *Agence Télégraphique Belge de Presse/Belgisch Pers-telegraaf-agentschap* (*Agence Belga/Agentschap Belga*); private facilities include *Centre d'Information de Presse* (Catholic) and *Agence Day*. Numerous foreign agencies also maintain bureaus in Belgium.

Radio and television. The French-language *Radiodiffusion-Télévision Belge de la Communauté Culturelle Française* (RTBF), the Dutch-language *Belgische Radio en Televisie* (BRT), and the German-language *Belgisches Rundfunk- und Fernsehzentrum* (BRF) are government-owned systems operated by Cultural Councils, under grants made by the Parliament. In 1987 there were 23 main television stations and more than 3.0 million sets in use, while radio receivers numbered approximately 4.6 million. Programming is normally left to the board of directors of each station. Under the basic law of May 18, 1960, information transmission (i.e., news and current affairs) cannot be censored by the government.

INTERGOVERNMENTAL REPRESENTATION

Ambassador to the US: Herman DEHENNIN.

US Ambassador to Belgium: Geoffrey SWAEBE.

Permanent Representative to the UN: Paul NOTERDAEME.

IGO Memberships (Non-UN): ACCT, ADB, ADF, AfDB, BIS, BLX, CCC, CERN, CEUR, EC, EIB, ESA, Eurocontrol, G10, IADB, ICAC, ICCO, ICES, ICM, ICO, IEA, ILZ, Inmarsat, INRO, Intelsat, Interpol, IOOC, ITC, IWSG, NATO, OECD, PCA, WEU.

BELIZE

Political Status: Former British dependency; became independent member of the Commonwealth on September 21, 1981.

Area: 8,867 sq. mi. (22,965 sq. km.).

Population: 144,857 (1980C), 180,500 (1988E).

Major Urban Centers (1985E): BELMOPAN (4,500); Belize City (47,000).

Official Language: English. Spanish is the country's second language.

Monetary Unit: Belize Dollar (market rate March 1, 1988, 2.00 dollars = $1US).

Sovereign: Queen ELIZABETH II.

Governor General: Elmira Minita GORDON; assumed office upon independence, succeeding Governor James P.I. HENNESSY.

Prime Minister: Manuel A. ESQUIVEL (United Democratic Party); assumed office following election of December 14, 1984, succeeding George Cadle PRICE (People's United Party).

THE COUNTRY

Located on the Caribbean coast of Central America, bordered by Mexico's Yucatan Peninsula on the north and by Guatemala on the west and south, Belize is slightly larger than El Salvador but with less than 3 percent of the latter's population. Most of the inhabitants are of mixed ancestry: Carib Blacks (*Garífunas*), Creole descendants of African slaves and English settlers, and mestizos of Spanish and Mayan Indian derivation. Roman Catholics constitute the largest religious group (50 percent), with roughly equal numbers (14 percent each) of Anglicans and Methodists.

Approximately three-quarters of the country is forested, but the quality of its timber has been depleted by more than two centuries of exploitation by British firms. Less than a fifth of its arable land, located primarily in the south, is under cultivation. The principal export commodities are sugar, molasses, fruit, and fish, with the economy subject to chronic trade deficits. Although living conditions at Belize City, which contains more than one-quarter of the population, are poor, school attendance is high and adult literacy is upwards of 90 percent. Average income is little more than $1,000 a year, in part because of widespread unemployment that has induced tens of thousands of Belizeans to emigrate, principally to the United States.

GOVERNMENT AND POLITICS

Political background. Initially colonized in the early seventeenth century by English woodcutters and shipwrecked seamen, the territory long known as British Honduras became a Crown dependency governed from Jamaica in 1862 and a separate colony in 1884. The frontier with Guatemala was delineated in an 1859 convention that was formally repudiated by Guatemala in 1940 (see Foreign relations, below). Internal self-government was granted under a constitution effective January 1, 1964, while the official name was changed to Belize in June 1973. Although the dispute with Guatemala remained unresolved, independence was granted on September 21, 1981, Britain agreeing to provide for the country's defense "for an appropriate period". At independence, George Cadle PRICE, who had served continuously in an executive capacity since his designation as first minister in 1961, was named prime minister.

At the country's first post-independence election of December 14, 1984, the electorate expressed its apparent weariness of more than three decades of rule by Price's People's United Party (PUP), turning, by a substantial margin, to the more conservative United Democratic Party (UDP), led by Manuel A. ESQUIVEL.

Constitution and government. With modifications appropriate to Britain's yielding of responsibility in the areas of defense, foreign affairs, and the judiciary, Belize's 1981 constitution is structured after its 1964 predecessor. The Crown is represented by a governor general of Belizean citizenship who must act, in most matters, on the advice of a cabinet headed by a prime minister. The National Assembly, with a normal term of five years, is a bicameral body encompassing an 18-member House of Representatives elected by universal adult suffrage and a Senate of 8 members, 5 of whom are appointed on the advice of the prime minister, 2 on the advice of the leader of the opposition, and 1 after consultation with the Belize Advisory Council, an independent body of no less than 6 members charged with advising the governor general in regard to a number of essentially judicial prerogatives. Cabinet members may be drawn from either house, save that the finance minister must sit in the House of Representatives, where all money bills originate.

The governor general may, at his own discretion, appoint a five-member Elections and Boundaries Commission and, on the advice of the prime minister, 8 members of a 13-member Public Services Commission (the remaining members serving ex officio). The judicial system includes, as superior courts of record, a Supreme Court, whose chief justice is appointed on the advice of the prime minister after consultation with the leader of the opposition, and a Court of Appeal, from which final appeal may, in certain cases, be made to the judicial committee of the UK Privy Council. There are also courts of summary jurisdiction and civil courts in each of the six districts into which the country is divided for administrative purposes.

Since taking office, the Esquivel administration has established a network of district councils, consisting of individuals selected by inhabitants of village clusters to oversee development projects at the local level. By late 1987, the political implications, if any, of the new bodies had not yet been determined.

Foreign relations. Belize became a full member of the Commonwealth upon independence and was admitted as the 156th member of the United Nations in September 1981, despite a Guatemalan protest that the "unilateral creation" of an independent state in disputed territory constituted "an invitation to third powers to become protectors of Belize" and thus to make Central America "an area for ambitions and confrontation". Although formally requesting membership in the Organization of American States in October, the Price government indicated its willingness to have action on the matter deferred in view of an OAS rule prohibiting the admission of a state involved in territorial disputes with existing members. Belmopan further announced that its foreign policy would be that of a "middle course" in working for regional "peace, stability, and prosperity" while eschewing relations with Cuba and the Soviet Union.

Guatemala had long contended that its dispute was with Britain, not with Belize, and that its repudiation in 1940 of the boundary set forth in the 1859 convention was justified because of Britain's failure to fulfill certain treaty obligations, including a commitment to construct a road from Belize City to the border to provide northern Guatemala with access to the Caribbean. Thus, under its 1945 constitution, Guatemala claimed British Honduras as part of its national territory.

Progress toward resolution of the problem appeared to have been registered in a tripartite "Heads of Agreement" document drafted at London on March 11, 1981, with Guatemala yielding on the territorial issue and Belize abandoning maritime claims — beyond waters surrounding a number of southern cays — as a means of granting Guatemala "permanent and unimpeded access" to its relatively isolated port of Puerto Barrios on the Gulf of Honduras. However, the agreement angered elements within both Belize and Guatemala, as well as serving to revive a longstanding Honduran claim to the Sapodilla Cay group (see map). Further talks held at New York in late May were reported to have "succeeded in turning a large bulk of the . . . agreement into treaty language", but Guatemalan intransigence thereafter led to a British announcement that it would proceed with independence on September 21, despite the lack of formal settlement.

The immediate post-independence period yielded further negotiations between the three countries and an increase in external support for Belize. In 1982, Guatemala called for renewed discussions with Britain, and tripartite talks were reopened in January 1983, but broke down immediately because of Belize's continued refusal to cede any territory. Rumors of an impending British troop withdrawal (the presence being guaranteed only until 1985) surfaced in the wake of the talks, and, in August 1983, after

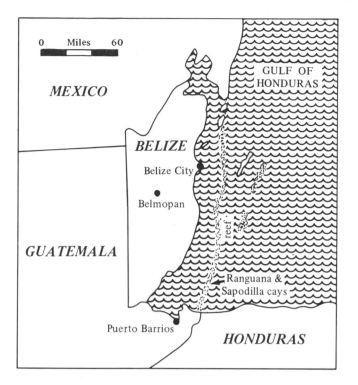

the ouster of Ríos Montt, the new Guatemalan leadership insisted that it would press for sovereignty over all of Belize. However, the Vinicio Cerezo administration which took office in late 1985 adopted a conciliatory posture and new, albeit inconclusive discussions were held at Miami, Florida, in April 1987, after which Belizean Foreign Minister Dean BARROW declared that "an incremental approach and patient diplomacy are what will be required to find a way forward".

Current issues. Faced with declining revenue after closure of one of the country's two major sugar mills, the Esquivel administration advanced a plan in early 1986 to offer Belizean citizenship to persons willing to buy $25,000 in interest-free government bonds. A consulate was opened in Hong Kong to publicize the scheme to individuals concerned about the prospect of the colony's takeover by the People's Republic in 1997. The plan drew immediate opposition criticism, which was partially blunted by the revelation that a similar proposal had been endorsed by PUP leaders during the previous administration. The government has also attempted to halt the problem of a growing trade deficit by promoting private-sector initiative in areas such as oil exploration, foreign investment, and increased tourism. One such initiative — the sale of 686,000 acres in the northwest (approximately 12 percent of Belize's land area) to a consortium of citrus developers including Coca-Cola Foods — has, however, been attacked for inadequate environmental planning as well as for the magnitude of the potential economic intrusion.

During 1987 the UDP was criticized for the enactment of legislation creating a Security and Intelligence Service (SIS). Responding to opposition charges that it was fomenting a "police state", UDP spokesmen insisted that the SIS was necessary both to deal with illegal immigrants and to counter large-scale drug activity. The controversy was intensified late in the year by an arson attack on the home of the minister responsible for the SIS, Curl THOMPSON, involvement with which was vehemently denied by opposition leaders. Subsequently, the PUP's political fortunes, which had plummeted at the 1984 general election, revived in March 1988 with victories in four of seven Town Board contests.

POLITICAL PARTIES

Government Party:

United Democratic Party (UDP). The UDP was formed in 1974 by merger of the People's Democratic Movement, the Liberal Party, and the National Independence Party. An essentially conservative, Creole grouping, the party boycotted the preindependence constitutional discussions and the independence ceremonies on the ground that assurances of continued support by Britain were "vague and uncertain". The UDP includes an extremist youth wing, the Belize Action Movement, whose adherents engaged in numerous clashes with police during the preindependence period. In January 1983, Manuel Esquivel was named party leader in succession to Theodore Aranda, who withdrew from the UDP while retaining his parliamentary seat and later formed the center-right Christian Democratic Party before joining the People's United Party (below) in mid-1987. After securing an unexpectedly lopsided victory at the balloting of December 14, 1984, Esquivel became head of the first non-PUP government since independence. In December 1986, the UDP registered another triumph by winning all 9 seats at the Belize City Council.

Leaders: Manuel A. ESQUIVEL (Prime Minister and Party Leader), Curl THOMPSON (Deputy Prime Minister), Dean LINDO (Chairman).

Opposition Parties:

People's United Party (PUP). Founded in 1950 as a Christian Democratic group, the PUP has been dominant for most of the period since the achievement of internal self-government in 1964. After 34 years in office (largely under colonial administration), the PUP was decisively defeated at the December 1984 election, former president and party leader George C. Price being among those losing their legislative seats. Following the election, PUP chairman and right-wing faction leader Louis Sylvestre resigned from the party and formed the PPB (below). At a January 1986 "Unity Congress", the leader of the left-wing faction, Said Musa, was elected party chairman, while the leader of the rump right-wing faction, Florencio Marín, was elected deputy chairman.

Leaders: George Cadle PRICE (former Prime Minister), Said MUSA (Chairman), Florencio MARIN (Deputy Chairman and Leader of the Opposition), Theodore ARANDA.

Belize Popular Party (BPP). Formally constituted in July 1985, the BPP consists largely of the former right wing of the PUP led by Louis Sylvestre. The new group was launched following Sylvestre's defection from the ruling party in early 1985 on the ground that it had been "taken over by communists" intending to overthrow the government. Included in its membership are a number of UDP dissidents.

Leaders: Mark CUELLAR (Chairman), Louis SYLVESTRE (Leader), Fred HUNTER (Deputy Leader).

LEGISLATURE

The Belize **National Assembly** is a bicameral body consisting of an appointed Senate and a directly elected House of Representatives, both serving five-year terms, subject to dissolution.

Senate. The upper house has 8 members, 5 of whom are appointed on the advice of the prime minister, 2 on the advice of the leader of the opposition, and 1 after consultation with the Belize Advisory Council.

President: Doris GARCIA.

House of Representatives. The lower house currently has 28 members elected by universal adult suffrage. At the election of December 14, 1984, the United Democratic Party won 21 seats, while the People's United Party won 7. The withdrawal of Louis Sylvestre from the PUP in January 1985 reduced the party's parliamentary representation to 6, Sylvestre retaining his seat as leader of the Belize Popular Party.

Speaker: Carla CASTILLO.

C A B I N E T

Prime Minister	Manuel A. Esquivel
Deputy Prime Minister	Curl Thompson
Ministers	
Agriculture	Dean Lindo
Commerce, Industry and Tourism	Eduardo Juan
Defense	Manuel A. Esquivel
Economic Development	Dean O. Barrow
Education, Youth and Sports	Elodio Aragon
Electricity, Transport and Communications	Derek Aikman
Finance	Manuel A. Esquivel
Foreign Affairs	Dean O. Barrow
Health	Israel Alpuche
Home Affairs and Local Government	Curl Thompson
Housing and Public Works	Hubert Elrington
Labor and Social Services	Philip Goldson
Natural Resources	Charles Wagner
Social Security	Manuel A. Esquivel
Attorney General	Dean Barrow
Governor, Central Bank	Allan Slusher

N E W S   M E D I A

Press. Freedom of the press is constitutionally guaranteed. The following are published at Belize City: *Amandala* (6,000), independent weekly; *The Reporter* (6,500), pro-UDP weekly; *The Belize Sunday Times* (5,500), PUP organ; *The Beacon* (4,200), UDP weekly; *Government Gazette,* official weekly.

Radio and television. Radio Belize is a government-operated service that provides daily programming on a semicommercial basis in English and Spanish. In August 1981, the government agreed to introduce party political broadcasts as a means of "building national unity". In mid-1986, licenses were issued to eight operators for 14 privately owned television channels retransmitting US satellite programs, all of which had theretofore been technically illegal. There were approximately 90,000 radio and 12,000 television receivers in 1987.

INTERGOVERNMENTAL   REPRESENTATION

Ambassador to the US: Edward A. LAING.

US Ambassador to Belize: Robert G. RICH, Jr.

Permanent Representative to the UN: Kenneth E. TILLETT.

IGO Memberships (Non-UN): Caricom, CDB, CWTH, EEC(L), *EIB,* IADB, Interpol, ISO, IWC, NAM.

BENIN

People's Republic of Benin
République Populaire du Bénin

Political Status: Independent Republic of Dahomey established August 1, 1960; military regime established October 26, 1972, becoming Marxist one-party system 1972–1975; present name adopted November 30, 1975, and retained under constitution of August 1977.

Area: 43,483 sq. mi. (112,622 sq. km.).

Population: 3,338,240 (1979C), 4,275,000 (1988E).

Major Urban Centers (1981E): PORTO NOVO (144,000); Cotonou (383,300).

Official Language: French.

Monetary Unit: CFA Franc (market rate March 1, 1988, 285.80 francs = $1US).

President: Ahmed (Mathieu) KEREKOU; assumed power by coup d'état October 26, 1972; designated President by Council of Ministers the following day; reconfirmed by the Revolutionary National Assembly in 1980 and on July 31, 1984; relinquished military title of Brigadier General on January 1, 1987.

THE   COUNTRY

The elongated West African state of Benin (formerly Dahomey) lies between Togo and Nigeria, with a southern frontage on the South Atlantic and a northerly bulge contiguous with Burkina Faso (formerly Upper Volta) and Niger. The country's population exhibits a highly complex ethnolinguistic structure, the majority falling within four major tribal divisions: Adja, Bariba, Fon, and Yoruba. The principal tribal languages are Fon and Yoruba in the south, and Bariba and Fulani in the north. Approximately 70 percent of the people are animists, the remainder being almost equally divided between Christians (concentrated in the south) and Muslims (concentrated in the north). The labor force includes nearly three-quarters of the adult female population, concentrated primarily in the cultivation of subsistence crops.

Benin is primarily an agricultural country, with cotton, cocoa, and various oilseeds serving as principal sources of foreign exchange. The little industrial development that exists mainly supports cotton and palm oil production. In October 1986, as part of an effort to stimulate local industry, the importation of a number of consumer goods was sharply curtailed, while by mid-1987 deepening recession had forced a restructuring of the country's industries and the adoption of a privatization program. Benin has relied heavily on France, its major external market, to subsidize current expenses as well as basic development.

GOVERNMENT   AND   POLITICS

Political background. Under French influence since the mid-nineteenth century, the territory then known as Dahomey became self-governing within the French Community in December 1958 but permitted its Community status to lapse upon achieving full independence on August 1, 1960. During the next 12 years, personal and regional animosities generated five military coups d'état, most of them interspersed with short-lived civilian regimes.

The country's first president, Hubert MAGA, was overthrown in October 1963 by Col. Christophe SOGLO, who served as interim head of state until the election in January 1964 of a government headed by President Sourou-Migan APITHY. In December 1965, after a series of political crises and a general disruption of civilian government, Soglo again assumed power as president of a military-backed regime. Another military coup led by Maj. Maurice KOUANDETE on December 17, 1967, ousted Soglo and established an interim regime under Lt. Col. Alphonse ALLEY. Following an abortive attempt at a new election in May 1968, the former foreign minister, Dr. Emile-Derlin ZINSOU, was appointed president of a civilian regime. In December 1969 the Zinsou government was overthrown by Kouandété and military rule was reinstituted. After another attempt at election in March 1970, the military established a civilian regime based on the collective leadership (Presidential Council) of the country's three leading politicians: Justin AHOMADEGBE, Apithy, and Maga. After an abortive coup led by Kouandété in February 1972, the ruling triumvirate was overthrown by (then) Maj. Mathieu KEREKOU on October 26, 1972. The new president abolished the Presidential Council and Consultative Assembly and established a Military Council of the Revolution committed to a division of posts on the basis of regional equality.

On December 3, 1974, President Kérékou declared that Dahomey was to become a "Marxist-Leninist state" and two days later announced that the nation's banks, insurance companies, and oil-distribution facilities would be nationalized. Subsequently, he ordered the establishment of "Defense of the Revolution Committees" in all businesses to "protect the revolution from sabotage". On November 30, 1975, the country was styled a "people's republic" to reflect the ideology officially embraced a year earlier, and was renamed Benin, after an African kingdom that had flourished in the Gulf of Guinea in the seventeenth century. The Benin People's Revolutionary Party (PRPB) was established as the nucleus of a one-party system that December. In August 1977 a new basic law was promulgated to reflect a commitment to three stages of development: a "revolutionary national liberation movement", a "democratic people's revolution", and a "socialist revolution".

In January of the same year, a group of mercenaries had been repulsed by government forces in a brief, but pitched, battle at Cotonou. A UN mission of inquiry subsequently reported that the invaders had been flown in from Gabon under the command of an adviser to Gabonese President Bongo. The incident provoked an angry exchange between presidents Kérékou and Bongo at an OAU summit meeting in July 1978, after which Bongo ordered the expulsion of some 6,000 Benin nationals from Gabon. Most of the mercenaries as well as 11 Benin "traitors" (including former president Zinsou in absentia) were condemned to death in May 1979.

President Kérékou accepted conversion to Islam (changing his first name from Mathieu to Ahmed) in September 1980, during a state visit by Libya's Colonel Qadhafi. He was redesignated for a five-year term as head of state and government on July 31, 1984.

Constitution and government. The 1977 *Loi Fondamentale* provides for a National Revolutionary Assembly made up of people's commissioners, who are popularly elected from a single party list and in turn elect the president of the People's Republic. Under a constitutional amendment of February 1984, the number of commissioners was reduced from 336 to 196, while their terms were extended from 3 to 5 years. The president designates both cabinet ministers and provincial prefects, who collectively constitute a National Executive Council. Ideological and policy direction is determined by the PRPB, to which the armed forces are directly responsible. In September 1981 President Kérékou announced the creation of a new judicial system headed by a Central People's Court that would be responsible to the president, the National Executive Council, and the National Revolutionary Assembly, and would supervise the activities of people's courts at various lower levels.

The country is administered through six provinces, each of which is subdivided into prefectures and arrondissements. There are also elected provincial, district, town, and village councils.

Foreign relations. While its earlier relations were primarily with other francophone Africa countries, Benin has recently sought to consolidate its interests with the broader African community, in particular with Nigeria. These efforts were undermined by the Nigerian expulsion of over three million foreign workers in 1983–1984, which strained neighboring economies and was characterized as "a blow to the spirit of ECOWAS [the Economic Community of West African States]". In addition the January 1985 summit at Ouagadougou, Burkina Faso, which was also attended by representatives of Ghana and Libya, was pronounced a failure after Libyan leader Qadhafi was charged with supporting "only a regime that would do his bidding". Despite such setbacks Benin has actively entered into cooperative ventures with a number of African states: the new Nangheto dam over the Mano River, scheduled to open in January 1988, is a joint project with Togo; a new commission for the exchange of scientific and cultural information has been established with Mauritania; and Benin is currently investigating the possibility with Ghana of increased oil exploration in the two countries (Benin's present output of some 7,000 barrels per day is adequate only for domestic use). Following the tenth ECOWAS summit in mid-1987, Benin and other member nations agreed to set up a health organization merging the resources of franco- and anglophone Africa and discussed the possible formation of a single monetary zone.

Benin has long adhered to a nonaligned posture and maintains relations with a variety of both Communist and Western governments; traditionally strong military and economic ties with France were reaffirmed during meetings in 1981 and 1983 between presidents Kérékou and Mitterrand, following a revision of treaty relations in 1975, while in late 1986 President Kérékou visited the USSR, Bulgaria, Yugoslavia, and China for a series of talks with key leaders.

Current issues. Following directives from the party congress for the rejuvenation of the economy, the national assembly early in 1986 agreed to open up the transportation and consignment of goods, under state control for 10 years, to the private sector, including multinational corporations. To increase traffic from nearby landlocked countries to the port of Cotonou, loans were negotiated for the construction and improvement of roads and bridges. With a total foreign debt in excess of $500 million, the government also began to work with the IMF on proposals for the rescheduling of external debt payments.

A major cabinet reshuffle in February 1987, involving the appointment of "pragmatists" to most economic portfolios, was seen as an effort to respond to the difficult economic circumstances that the country had recently encountered. Subsequently, a judicial commission of inquiry was set up to investigate the role of officials and police during a series of prison riots that resulted in 24 deaths, while in May the University of Benin was closed to avoid student protest demonstrations and boycotts in remembrance of students who had died during disturbances the year before. Meanwhile, the Porto Novo government was charged by Amnesty International with illegally detaining some 88 persons accused of supporting the banned Dahomey Communist Party (PCD), despite the release of 50 detainees in September 1986.

POLITICAL PARTIES

Ruling Party:

Benin People's Revolutionary Party (*Parti de la Révolution Populaire du Bénin* — PRPB). Organized in December 1975, the PRPB is committed to a policy of "democratic centralization". It features a Communist-style Central Committee of 45 members, an 11-member Political Bureau, and associated youth and women's groups. Its second ordinary congress was held on November 18–24, 1985.

Leader: Ahmed (Mathieu) KEREKOU (President of the Republic and Chairman of the Central Committee).

Illegal Opposition:

Front for the Liberation and Rehabilitation of Dahomey (*Front de Libération et Réhabilitation du Dahomey* — FLRD). The FLRD, whose leadership has announced its opposition to Kérékou's "dictatorial regime", was accused of complicity in one of the 1975 coup attempts and in the 1977 mercenary attack at Cotonou. The leadership (currently composed of "voluntary exiles" in Paris) denied the former allegation but remained silent in regard to the latter.

Leaders: Dr. Emile-Derlin ZINSOU (former President of the Republic), Gratien POGNON.

A long-banned, pro-Albanian **Communist Party of Dahomey** (*Parti Communiste Dahoméen* — PCD) appears recently to have been active. A number of students involved in the 1985 university disturbances were charged with being PCD activists, while Amnesty International announced that some 100 reported PCD members were under detention (see Current issues, above).

LEGISLATURE

The most recent balloting for the **National Revolutionary Assembly** (*Assemblée Nationale Révolutionnaire*) was held on June 10, 1984. The present 196 deputies, styled "people's commissioners", were elected on a single list (reportedly favored by 93.5 percent of those participating) to represent social-professional classes rather than geographical constituencies.

President of Permanent Committee: Romain Vilon GUEZO.

CABINET

President	Brig. Gen. Ahmed Kérékou
Ministers Delegate	
Interior, Security and Territorial Administration	Edouard Zodehougan
Planning and Statistics	Ibrahim Souradjou
Ministers	
Commerce, Crafts and Tourism	Girigissou Gado
Culture, Youth and Sports	Ousmane Batoko
Defense and Armed Forces	Brig. Gen. Ahmed Kérékou
Equipment and Transport	Soulé Dankoro
Finance and Economy	Barnabé Bidouzo
Foreign Affairs and Cooperation	Guy Landry Hazoumé
Information and Communication	Ali Houdou
Justice and Inspection of Public and Semi-Public Enterprises	Saliou Aboudou
Labor and Social Affairs	Lt. Col. Nathanaël Mensah
Nursery and Primary Education	Maj. Philippe Akpo
Public Health	Col. André Atchade
Rural Development and Cooperatives	Martin Dohou Azonhiho
Secondary and Higher Education	Lt. Col. Vincent Guezodje
Director, Central Bank	Guy Pognon

NEWS MEDIA

Press. Benin's press law provides for advance censorship of all periodicals, films, and records. *Ehuzu* (10,000) is a government daily published at Cotonou; other organs include *Bénin-Magazine* (15,000), a government monthly dealing with social, cultural, and economic affairs; a government weekly, *Bénin-Presse Information;* and a Catholic fortnightly, *La Croix du Bénin*. In addition, a privately owned bimonthly, *La Gazette du Golfe* was launched in early 1988.

News agency. The *Agence Bénin-Presse* operates as a section of the Ministry of Information.

Radio and television. The government's *Office de Radiodiffusion et de Télévision du Bénin* broadcasts in French, English, and a number of indigenous languages throughout the country. There were approximately 300,000 radio receivers in 1986. Television service, introduced in late 1978, was received by 15,000 sets in 1987.

INTERGOVERNMENTAL REPRESENTATION

Ambassador to the US: (Vacant).

US Ambassador to Benin: Walter Edward STADTLER.

Permanent Representative to the UN: Gratien Tonakpon CAPO-CHICHI.

IGO Memberships (Non-UN): ACCT, ADF, AfDB, BADEA, BOAD, CEAO, CENT, ECOWAS, EEC(L), *EIB*, G77, IACO, ICCAT, ICO, Intelsat, Interpol, NAM, OAU, OCAM.

BHUTAN

Kingdom of Bhutan
Druk-yul

Political Status: Independent monarchy; under Indian guidance in international affairs since 1949.

Area: 18,147 sq. mi. (47,000 sq. km.).

Population: 1,524,000 (1988E).

Major Urban Center (1985E): THIMPHU (20,000).

Official Language: Dzongkha.

Monetary Unit: Ngultrum (market rate March 1, 1988, 13.08 ngultrums = $1US). The ngultrum is at par with the Indian rupee, which circulates freely within the country.

Monarch: Druk Gyalpo Jigme Singye WANGCHUK; proclaimed King on July 24, 1972, following the death on July 22 of his father, Druk Gyalpo Jigme Dorji WANGCHUK.

THE COUNTRY

The Kingdom of Bhutan is situated in the eastern Himalayas between Tibet and India. Mountainous in the north and heavily forested in the south, the country's terrain has served to isolate it from the rest of the world and to inhibit any large population concentrations. The people are predominantly Bhutanese or Bhotes with about 20 percent of Nepalese extraction, although Nepalese immigration has been prohibited since 1959. Four main languages are spoken: Dzongkha (the official language) in the north and west, Bumthangkha in the central section, Sarachapkha in the east, and Nepali in the west. The *Druk Kargue* sect of Mahayana Buddhism is the official state religion, and Buddhist priests (*lamas*) exert considerable political influence. The *lamas,* numbering about 6,000, are distributed in 8 major monasteries (*dzongs*) and 200 smaller shrines (*gompas*). Most of the Nepalese are Hindu.

The economy is largely agrarian, but diversification is being attempted. Timber and mineral resources, including deposits of coal, iron, copper, and gypsum, are potentially valuable economic assets. A series of five-year plans have attempted to exploit these resources and to modernize infrastructure. The fifth plan (1981–1986) emphasized hydroelectric power development, geological exploration, transportation, and telecommunications. The sixth plan (1987–1991) is designed to improve the availability of public services and generate greater popular participation in government development programs.

GOVERNMENT AND POLITICS

Political background. A consolidated kingdom since the mid-sixteenth century, Bhutan is presently governed by a fourth-generation hereditary monarch styled the dragon king (*druk gyalpo*). Previously the country was ruled by a diarchy of temporal and spiritual rajas, but in 1907 Ugyan WANGCHUK was established on the throne with British assistance. British guidance of Bhutan's external affairs, which began in 1865 in exchange for a financial subsidy, was confirmed by treaty in 1910. India succeeded to the British role by a treaty concluded August 8, 1949, in which India pledged not to interfere in Bhutanese internal affairs, while Bhutan agreed to be "guided" by Indian advice in its external relations.

The post-World War II era has witnessed increased social and political change, primarily at the initiative of King Jigme Dorji WANGCHUK. Considerable unrest resulted from some of these policies, and in 1964 Prime Minister Jigme Polden DORJI was assassinated. Nonetheless, the king pursued his policy of modernization, establishing a Royal Advisory Council in 1965 and a Council of Ministers three years later, when a High Court (*Thimkhang Gongma*) was also created and the king gave the National Assembly (*Tsongdu*) authority to remove ministers as well as their chairman (the monarch) by a vote of no confidence. The Assembly, however, subsequently abrogated the latter right.

The present monarch, Jigme Singye WANGCHUK, who succeeded his father on July 24, 1972, continues to face resistance from traditional elements as well as from a militant Nepalese minority. The most noteworthy development of his reign has been an effort to exert greater independence from India while broadening international contacts.

Constitution and government. There is no written constitution, but in the post-World War II period the infrastructure of a constitutional monarchy was established. Ultimate executive authority continues to be vested in the king, who appoints and is assisted by a Council of Ministers and a nine-member Royal Advisory Council. The latter consists of one member to represent the king, two to represent religious authorities, and six to represent the people. Legislative authority is nominally vested in the National Assembly (*Tsongdu*), from which all members of the Council of Ministers and eight members of the Royal Advisory Council are selected. The *Tsongdu,* which in practice does little but approve bills initiated by the monarch, consists of 150 members. The judicial system encompasses a High Court, an appellate court, and district magistrates' courts, with citizens conventionally accorded the right of ultimate appeal to the king through the royal chamberlain (*gyalpön zimpon*).

The country is divided into 18 administrative districts (*dzongs*), each governed by a district officer (*dzongda*) and an appointed magistrate (*thrimpon*).

Foreign relations. Bhutan's external relations continue to be conducted largely through the Indian government, although the 1949 treaty that requires Thimphu to seek "advice" from New Delhi in foreign affairs has come under periodic criticism, particularly in the wake of India's formal absorption of neighboring Sikkim in 1974. The question of the Kingdom's international status was revived in February 1980, following the establishment of diplomatic relations with Bangladesh. The action was Thimphu's first effort to deal directly with a third country, although it had acted independently of India in several international forums, including the 1979 UNCTAD-V trade meeting at Manila, the Havana nonaligned summit in September 1979, and the United Nations General Assembly. Since then, Bhutan has joined a number of multilateral bodies, including the World Bank, the International Monetary Fund, and the Asian Development Bank, and has engaged in direct negotiations with China to settle a border controversy that is linked to the Chinese-Indian dispute over portions of Arunachal Pradesh (see map under India entry). In August 1983, it participated with Bangladesh, India, the Maldives, Nepal, Pakistan, and Sri Lanka in the establishment of a committee that subsequently evolved into the South Asian Association for Regional Cooperation (SAARC), with an "integrated program of action" in such areas as agriculture, rural development, and telecommunications. In mid-1984 the kingdom established relations with the Maldives and in 1985, subsequent to a May meeting at Thimphu of SAARC ministers, extended its diplomatic contacts to include Denmark, Norway, Sweden, Switzerland, and the European Community. During 1986–1987 relations were further extended to include Finland, Japan, and Sri Lanka.

During a September 1985 visit to Thimphu, Indian Prime Minister Rajiv Gandhi, in the first address by a visiting dignitary to a special session of the National Assembly, announced that his government would finance a number of new development projects in Bhutan, including improvements in electricity distribution at the capital and the construction of an additional broadcasting facility.

Current issues. In recent years, Bhutan's principal domestic concern has been the status of both the Nepalese minority and a sizable number of Tibetan refugees that were originally resettled with Indian assistance following the 1959 Lhasa revolt. The Tibetans were offered Bhutanese citizenship but many refused, evidently because the Dalai Lama wished them to remain stateless to facilitate their eventual return to China. Following the issuance of an expulsion order in 1979, most of the aliens became citizens, with India agreeing to accept the rest. The Nepalese nonetheless continue to argue that they suffer discrimination, in part because government officials favor investment in businesses closely allied with the royal family.

The most recent round of border discussions with China concluded at Beijing in June 1987, with a further round scheduled for 1988. New Delhi's tacit acceptance of the direct talks was viewed as stemming from a hope that they might establish a basis for resolution of the larger Sino-Indian dispute, though Thimphu's expansion of diplomatic relations since 1985 was in itself construed as a weakening of India's capacity to speak for its neighbor in foreign affairs.

POLITICAL PARTIES

Bhutan has no organized, legal parties. The **Bhutan National Congress** operates in northeastern India but is primarily a spokesman for the Nepalese minority. Its goals include the liberalization of immigration for Nepalese, more checks on the rule of the king, and increased elected representation in government.

LEGISLATURE

The 150-member **National Assembly** (*Tsongdu*) meets twice a year for sessions rarely lasting more than two weeks. Two-thirds of the members are elected every three years from village constituencies; of the remainder, 10 represent religious bodies and 40 are designated by the king to represent government and other secular interests.

Speaker: Lyonpo Tamji JAGAR.

CABINET

Chairman	Druk Gyalpo Jigme Singye Wangchuk
King's Representatives	
Agriculture	Ashi Dechen Wangmo Wangchuk
Finance	Ashi Sonam Chhoden Wangchuk
Ministers	
Communications, Tourism and Social Services	Dr. T. Tobgyal
Foreign Affairs	Lyonpo Dawa Tsering
Home Affairs	HRH Namgyel Wangchuk

NEWS MEDIA

Press. *Kuensel* (5,000) is a government weekly in Dzongkha, Nepali, and English; the Department of Information has indicated that it plans to issue the paper on a daily basis by mid-1988. There are also two English-language monthlies: *Kuenphen Digest* and *Kuenphen Tribune.*

Radio and television. There were more than 25 radio stations transmitting in Dzongkha, Sarachapkha, Nepali, and English to approximately 14,000 receivers in 1987; there is no television service.

INTERGOVERNMENTAL REPRESENTATION

Diplomatic relations between Bhutan and the United States are conducted through the government of India.

Permanent Representative to the UN: Jigmi Yoser THINLEY.

IGO Memberships (Non-UN): ADB, CP, NAM, SAARC.

BOLIVIA

Republic of Bolivia
República de Bolivia

Political Status: Independent republic proclaimed 1825; civilian government reestablished in October 1982 after virtually constant military rule since September 1969.

Area: 424,162 sq. mi. (1,098,581 sq. km.).

Population: 4,613,486 (1976C), 6,991,000 (1988E).

Major Urban Centers (1982E): LA PAZ (administrative capital, 881,000); Sucre (judicial capital, 80,000); Santa Cruz (377,000); Cochabamba (282,000); Oruro (132,000).

Official Languages: Spanish, Aymará, Quechua (Aymará and Quechua were adopted as official languages in 1977).

Monetary Unit: Boliviano (market rate March 1, 1988, 2.20 bolivianos = $1US); the peso was replaced by the boliviano in February 1987 at a ratio of 1,000,000:1.

President: Dr. Víctor PAZ Estenssoro (Historical Nationalist Revolutionary Movement); elected by the Congress on August 5, 1985, and inaugurated for a four-year term on August 6, succeeding Dr. Hernán SILES Zuazo (Leftist Nationalist Revolutionary Movement).

Vice President: Julio GARRET Ayllón (Historical Nationalist Revolutionary Movement); elected by the Congress on August 5, 1985, for a term concurrent with that of the President; had served as Acting Vice President since the resignation of Jaime PAZ Zamora (Leftist Revolutionary Movement) on December 14, 1984.

THE COUNTRY

A land of tropical lowlands and *pampas* flanked by high mountains in the west, landlocked Bolivia is noted for a high proportion of Indians (predominantly Aymará and Quechua), who constitute over 60 percent of the population, although their integration into the country's political and economic life has been progressing very slowly. Women constitute approximately 25 percent of the labor force with roughly equal numbers in agricultural, manufacturing, clerical, and service activities. Spanish, the sole official language until 1977, is the mother tongue of less than 40 percent of the people, while Roman Catholicism is the predominant religion.

Although agriculture now provides only one-sixth of Bolivia's gross national product, it employs about half of the population, mostly on a subsistence level. The main crops are cotton, coffee, sugar, wheat, barley, and corn. A mainstay of the economy is tin mining, although the state-owned mines have long been wracked by labor difficulties and the fluctuation of tin prices on the international market has led to economic instability. Other significant metal exports include silver, zinc, and tungsten. Petroleum production peaked in 1974, while natural gas has increased in importance and in 1982 surpassed tin as the country's leading export.

The leading contributor to the underground economy has long been coca leaf production, with the overwhelming proportion of an annual output of more than 100,000 tons entering the cocaine trade. At present, some 400,000 persons in the Chapare region alone are engaged in coca cultivation, with total income from drug trafficking estimated at more than $2.5 billion. Sporadic efforts to curb the trade have been thwarted by overall economic conditions that reached disastrous levels with suspension of payments on a massive foreign debt in early 1984 and inflation that exceeded 16,000 percent in July 1985 before falling to 10 percent in mid-1987 in response to drastic austerity measures. Success in curbing inflation has not, however, been equalled by gains in employment: in late 1987 it was estimated that 25 percent of the economically active population was unemployed, with an additional 39 percent underemployed.

GOVERNMENT AND POLITICS

Political background. Bolivia's history since its liberation from Spanish rule in 1825 has been marked by recurrent domestic instability and frequent conflicts with neighboring states, especially Chile, Peru, and Paraguay. Increased unrest in the mid-twentieth century culminated in April 1952 in a seizure of power by the reform-minded Nationalist Revolutionary Movement (MNR), which proceeded to carry out a thoroughgoing social and political revolution under the leadership of presidents Víctor PAZ Estenssoro and Hernán SILES Zuazo, who alternately dominated the political scene in four-year terms from 1952 to 1964. MNR rule was cut short in November 1964, when the vice president, Gen. René BARRIENTOS Ortuño, acting in the midst of widespread disorder, assumed power by a military coup d'état. After serving with Gen. Alfredo OVANDO Candía as copresident under a military junta, Barrientos resigned to run for the presidency and was elected in July 1966. Supported by the armed forces and a strong coalition in Congress, his regime encountered intense opposition from the tin miners, who charged repression of workers' unions. A southeastern jungle uprising led by Castroite revolutionary Ernesto "Ché" GUEVARA in 1967 resulted in Guevara's death at the hands of government troops and the capture of guerrilla ideologist Régis DEBRAY.

Barrientos was killed in a helicopter crash in April 1969 and Vice President Luis Adolfo SILES Salinas succeeded to the presidency. Siles was deposed the following September by the military, who installed Barrientos' former copresident, General Ovando, as chief executive. "Back-to-back" coups occurred in October 1970, the first led by Gen. Rogelio MIRANDA and the second by Gen. Juan José TORRES. The Torres regime came to power with the support of students, workers, and leftist political parties. It was accompanied by continuing instability, the nationalization of properties (both foreign and domestic), and the creation in 1971 of an extraconstitutional "Popular Assembly" of trade-union leaders, Marxist politicians, and radical students led by Juan LECHIN Oquendo of the tin-miners' union. In August 1971 the armed forces, in alliance with the MNR and the Bolivian Socialist Falange (FSB), deposed Torres and appointed a government under (then) Col. Hugo BANZER Suárez. Two years later, the MNR withdrew from the coalition, and, after an abortive revolt the following November, Banzer rescinded an earlier pledge to return the nation to civilian rule in 1975.

In November 1977 President Banzer again reversed himself, announcing that a national election would be held on July 9, 1978. After balloting marked by evidence of massive fraud, the military candidate, Gen. Juan PEREDA Asbún, was declared the winner over his closest competitor, former president Siles Zuazo. However, faced with a suddenly unified opposition, Pereda was forced to call for an annulment. President Banzer then declared that he would not remain in office beyond August 6, and on July 21 Pereda was installed as Bolivia's 188th head of state. Pereda was himself ousted on November 24 by Brig. Gen. David PADILLA Arancibia, who promised to withdraw following an election on July 1, 1979.

At the 1979 election, Siles Zuazo of the center-left Democratic and Popular Unity coalition (see Political Parties, below) obtained a bare plurality (36.0 percent to 35.9 percent) over Paz Estenssoro, the leader of a new MNR coalition that included a number of leftist groups. Called upon to decide the outcome because of the lack of a majority, the Congress was unable to choose between the leading candidates and on August 6 designated Senate President

Walter GUEVARA Arze to serve as interim executive pending a new presidential election in May 1980.

Guevara was ousted on November 1 in a military coup led by Col. Alberto NATUSCH Busch, who was himself forced to resign 15 days later in the face of widespread civil disorder, including a paralyzing general strike at La Paz. On November 16 the Congress unanimously elected the president of the Chamber of Deputies, Lidia GUEILER Tejada, to serve as the country's first female executive for an interim term expiring August 6, 1980.

At a national election on June 29, 1980, Dr. Siles Zuazo again secured the largest number of votes while failing to win an absolute majority. As a result, before the new Congress could meet to settle on a winner from among the three leading candidates, the military, on July 17, once more intervened, forcing the resignation of Gueiler the following day in favor of a "junta of national reconstruction" that included Maj. Gen. Luis GARCIA MEZA Tejada (sworn in as president on July 18), Maj. Gen. Waldo BERNAL Pereira, and Vice Adm. Ramiro TERRAZAS Rodríguez.

During the following year the regime remained internally divided because of differences within the military, and internationally isolated because of charges that certain of its members were actively engaged in the drug trade. In early 1981 revolts broke out at the military academy at La Paz and at Cochabamba, southeast of the capital, while former presidents Natusch and Banzer were both exiled in mid-May for plotting against the government. On May 26 García Meza resigned as army commander and as junta member, naming Gen. Humberto CAYOJA Riart as his successor in both posts; three days later Admiral Terrazas resigned as navy commander and junta member in favor of (then) Capt. Oscar PAMMO Rodríguez. On June 27, General Cayoja was arrested for involvement in a plot to remove García Meza from the presidency, Brig. Gen. Celso TORRELIO Villa being designated his successor. On August 4, following a rebellion at Santa Cruz, the president resigned in favor of General Bernal, who, in turn, yielded the office of chief executive to General Torrelio on September 4.

Amid growing economic difficulty, labor unrest, pressure from the parties, and lack of unity within the military, Torrelio announced that a constituent assembly election would be held in 1984. While a decision in April 1982 to move the date ahead to 1983 was reversed a month later, the increasingly beleaguered government, in late May, issued a political amnesty and authorized the parties and trade unions to resume normal activity. On July 19, General Torrelio was ousted in favor of Gen. Guido VILDOSO Calderón, who announced, following a meeting of armed forces commanders on September 17, that the Congress elected in 1980 would be reconvened to name a civilian president. The lengthy period of military rule formally ended on October 10 with the return to office of Siles Zuazo and the concurrent installation of Jaime PAZ Zamora as vice president.

During the ensuing two years, numerous government changes proved incapable of reversing steadily worsening economic conditions, and in November 1984 Siles Zuazo announced that he would retire from the presidency following a general election in mid-1985. At the balloting on July 14, former president Banzer Suáres of the right-wing Nationalist Democratic Action obtained a narrow plurality (28.6 percent) of the votes cast, while the Historic Nationalist Revolutionary Movement of runner-up Paz Estenssoro won a plurality of congressional seats. In a second-round legislative poll on August 5, Paz Estenssoro secured a clear majority over his ADN competitor and was inaugurated for his fourth presidential term on August 6 in the country's first peaceful transfer of power since his succession of Siles Zuazo exactly 25 years earlier.

While successful in virtually eliminating one of history's highest rates of inflation, the new administration proved unable to resolve a wide range of other economic difficulties that included massive unemployment (generated, in part, by a crippling decline in world tin prices) and an illegal cocaine trade that provided half of the country's export income. The public responded by rejecting most government candidates on December 6, 1987, in municipal balloting that yielded impressive gains for both the rightist ADN and the Leftist Revolutionary Movement (MIR).

Constitution and government. The constitution of February 1967 was Bolivia's 16th since independence. It vested executive power in a popularly elected president and legislative authority in a bicameral Congress. Suspended in 1969, it was reinstated in 1979, the country having been ruled during the intervening decade by presidential decree; it remained technically in effect following the 1980 coup subject to military contravention of its terms, and was restored to full force upon the return to civilian rule in October 1982.

Under the 1967 basic law, the president is directly elected for a four-year term if the recipient of an absolute majority of votes; otherwise, Congress makes the selection from among the three leading contenders. The bicameral legislature consists of a 27-member Senate and a 130-member Chamber of Deputies, both directly elected for four-year terms. The judicial system is headed by a Supreme Court whose twelve members divide into four chambers: two for civil cases, one for criminal cases, and one for administrative cases. There is a District Court in each department as well as provincial and local courts to try minor offenses.

There are nine territorial departments, each administered by a prefect appointed by the central government. The departments are subdivided into provinces, which are also headed by centrally appointed officials. Although the 1967 constitution called for the biennial election of municipal councils (empowered to supplant the president in the designation of mayors) implementing legislation was deferred until 1986, with local balloting being conducted on December 6, 1987, for the first time in 39 years.

Foreign relations. Throughout most of the modern era, Bolivia's relations with its immediate neighbors have been significantly influenced by a desire to regain at least a portion of the maritime littoral that was lost to Chile in the War of the Pacific (1879–1884). In February 1975 relations with Chile were resumed after a 12-year lapse, Santiago announcing that an "agreement in principle" had been negotiated between the two countries whereby Bolivia would be granted an outlet to the sea (*salida al mar*) along the Chilean-Peruvian border in exchange for territory elsewhere. Definitive resolution of the issue was, however, complicated in late 1976 by a Peruvian proposal that the

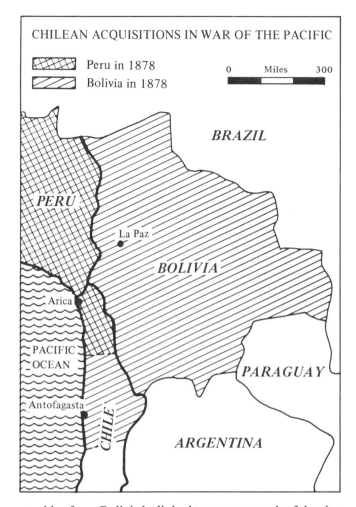

CHILEAN ACQUISITIONS IN WAR OF THE PACIFIC

Peru in 1878
Bolivia in 1878

0   Miles   300

PERU

BRAZIL

La Paz

BOLIVIA

Arica

PACIFIC
OCEAN

PARAGUAY

Antofagasta

CHILE

ARGENTINA

corridor from Bolivia be linked to an area north of the city of Arica (obtained by Chile as a consequence of the war) that would be under the three nations' joint sovereignty (see map). The proposal was based on a 1929 treaty which provided that any cession of former Peruvian territory must be approved by Lima. In March 1978 the Banzer government again broke relations with Santiago on the ground that Chile had displayed insufficient sincerity and flexibility in its negotiating posture, while in April 1979 the Bolivian foreign minister proposed that a corridor be carved out of historically non-Peruvian territory. The latter proposal, widely interpreted as placing the burden on Chile to reject a solution on which both Peru and Bolivia could agree, nonetheless proved unacceptable to Santiago. A continuing impasse in the matter was partially breached in February 1986 by Bolivia's announcement that it would reopen a consular office at Santiago, while in September the Bolivian and Chilean foreign ministers concluded a 30-point agreement intended to promote political and economic rapprochement between their two countries.

Under the Banzer regime, Bolivia pursued an anti-Communist and pro-US line in inter-American affairs, although links with Washington were tenuous during most of the period of military rule because of the alleged involvement of senior officials in the cocaine trade. Relations with Colombia, Ecuador, Peru, and Venezuela were severed after the 1980 coup, and in December of the same

year the García Meza government announced its intention to withdraw from the Andean Pact, although reversing itself four months later. Significantly, the presidents of Colombia, Ecuador, and Peru attended the Siles Zuazo inauguration on October 10, 1982, while Washington demonstrated its unhappiness at the inclusion of the Bolivian Communist Party in the new government coalition by sending a relatively low-ranking delegation headed by its representative to the Organization of American States. Despite expressions of concern by the military, diplomatic relations with Cuba were reestablished in May 1985, while relations with Taiwan were severed upon recognition of the People's Republic of China immediately prior to the July election.

Current issues. Few if any countries have matched Bolivia's unhappy record of political instability, which has yielded nearly 200 chief executives in somewhat more than a century and a half of independence. There were 13 presidents from 1969 to 1982 alone, the most durable incumbency being that of General Banzer (1971–1978).

Upon assuming office, Paz Estenssoro, declaring that "without a new policy . . . Bolivia will die on us", abandoned his longtime populist image and advanced a more radical austerity package than even his harshest critics had anticipated. Prices were permitted to rise by 400 percent for bread to more than 1,000 percent for electricity and gas, wages and salaries were frozen, government spending was slashed, and the peso was devalued by 95 percent. By 1987 the austerity program, strongly backed by the IMF and World Bank, had succeeded beyond all expectations in curbing theretofore rampant inflation, with economic growth (albeit a modest 2.2 percent) recorded for the first time in seven years. However, both business and labor had ranged themselves against the administration, the former insisting that a failure to include a restoration of traditional subsidies as a component of economic revitalization had driven many firms to the brink of bankruptcy and the latter charging that increased unemployment and a decline in real wages had demonstrated a lack of concern for the poor. The result (reflected in the 1987 municipal poll) was an emerging polarization between rightist and leftist forces, with the incumbent MNRH seen as unlikely to rebound as a major contender at the next nationwide balloting in 1989.

POLITICAL PARTIES

There are upwards of 60 political parties in Bolivia, of which 18 (including the leftist FPU coalition, below) offered presidential candidates at the 1985 election. The principal alignments in 1978 were the National People's Union (*Unión Nacionalista del Pueblo*—UNP), a hastily organized group of various rightist elements favoring General Pereda's candidacy, and two centrist coalitions, the Democratic and Popular Unity (*Unidad Democrática y Popular*—UDP) and the Historical Nationalist Revolutionary Movement (*Movimiento Nacionalista Revolucionario Histórico*—MNRH), supporting former presidents Siles Zuazo and Paz Estenssoro, respectively. The leading contenders in 1979 and 1980 were the UDP, a realigned MNR coalition called the Alliance of the Nationalist Revolutionary Movement (*Alianza de Movimiento Nacionalista Revolucionario* — A-MNR), and General Banzer Suárez' newly formed Nationalist Democratic Action (*Acción Democrática Nacionalista* — ADN). The 1985 campaign was largely a two-way race between the ADN and the MNRH. The principal components of these and other groupings are listed below, by general political tendency from right to left.

Right-Wing Parties:

Bolivian Socialist Falange (*Falange Socialista Boliviana* — FSB). Modeled at its founding in 1937 after the Spanish Socialist Falange, the FSB was the principal government party throughout the Banzer era. Virtually eliminated as an electoral force in 1980, a number of its members joined the García Meza government following the July 17 coup, while one of its leaders, Gonzalo Romero Alvarez García, was named foreign minister in the Torrelio government of September 1981.

Leaders: David AÑEZ Pedraza (President), Dr. Mario GUTIERREZ, Gastón MOREIRA Ostría.

Nationalist Democratic Action (*Acción Democrática Nacionalista* — ADN). The ADN was formed in early 1979 by former president Hugo Banzer Suárez under the slogan "peace, order, and work". Banzer ran third in presidential balloting in both 1979 and 1980. He secured a plurality of the popular vote in 1985, but was defeated by Paz Estenssoro in a congressional runoff. Following the election, the ADN concluded a somewhat fragile legislative alliance, the Democratic Pact (*Pacto pour la Democracia*) with the MNRN, which was reaffirmed after both parties had experienced losses at municipal balloting in December 1987.

Leaders: Gen. Hugo BANZER Suárez (former President of the Republic and President of the Party), Guillermo FORTUN (Deputy Leader).

Nationalist Democratic Front (*Frente Democrático Nacionalista* — FDN). The FDN was formed in February 1987 by Eudoro Galindo, formerly the second-ranked leader of the ADN, who had criticized the Democratic Pact and was expelled from the party in November 1986 for being a "fascist".

Leaders: Eudoro GALINDO, Jorge BLECHNER.

Other right-wing groups include the **Committee of National Unity** (*Comité de Unidad Nacional* — CUN), a self-styled "technocratic" organization of business and government leaders formed in early 1978; two *barrientista* parties, the **Popular Christian Movement** (*Movimiento Popular Cristiano* — MPC) and the **National Barrientista Movement** (*Movimiento Nacional Barrientista* — MNB); and two traditional groups, the **Republican Socialist Union Party** (*Partido de la Unión Republicana Socialista* — PURS) and the **Liberal Party** (*Partido Liberal* — PL).

Center-Right Parties:

Historical Nationalist Revolutionary Movement (*Movimiento Nacionalista Revolucionario Histórico* — MNRH). Founded in 1941 by Víctor Paz Estenssoro, the original *Movimiento Nacionalista Revolutionario* (MNR) ruled from 1952 and 1964 but was outlawed for a time after the 1964 coup. It joined with the FSB and others in a *Frente Popular Nacionalista* (FPN) in support of the Banzer coup in 1971 but withdrew two years later. It has spawned a number of other parties as a result of leadership disputes and contested the 1978 election as the leading component of the MNRH (initially an electoral alliance) after failing to negotiate an accord with the UDP. The MNRH in turn contested the 1979 and 1980 elections as the core party of the A-MNR. Although tendered left-wing congressional support in defeating General Banzer for the presidency in August 1985, Paz Estenssoro subsequently concluded a political accord with the ADN to facilitate implementation of a hard-line economic stabilization program (see Current issues, above). The MNRH was decisively defeated in most of the municipal contests of December 6, 1987, with most observers concluding that it had little chance of substantial recovery at the next general election in 1989.

Leaders: Dr. Víctor PAZ Estenssoro (President of the Republic and of the Party), José Luis HARB (Secretary General).

Authentic Revolutionary Party (*Partido Revolucionario Auténtico* — PRA). The PRA originated as a dissident MNRH faction, whose leader, former interim president Walter Guevara Arze, has called, without success, for reunification of the traditional MNR.

Leader: Dr. Walter GUEVARA Arze.

Center-Left Parties:

Christian Democratic Party (*Partido Demócrata Cristiano* — PDC). The PDC is a somewhat left-of-center Catholic party, a right-wing faction of which supported the Banzer regime. It joined the A-MNR prior to the 1979 election. In early 1982, PDC leader Benjamín Miguel, in an apparent reference to right-wing elements within the MNR, indicated that the party would henceforth refuse to cooperate with other parties that "lack a democratic vocation". In November, the party joined the UDP coalition, one of its members accepting the housing portfolio in the Siles Zuazo government. It withdrew from the coalition in October 1984.

Leaders: José Luis ROCA (President), Dr. Luis OSSIO Sanjines (1985 presidential candidate), Miguel ROCHAS (Secretary).

Leftist Nationalist Revolutionary Movement (*Movimiento Nacionalista Revolucionario de Izquierda* — MNRI). An offshoot of the MNR, the MNRI was the principal element in the organization of the UDP prior to the 1978 balloting. Its presidential candidate, Hernán Siles Zuazo, obtained electoral pluralities in 1979 and 1980, and returned as the country's chief executive in October 1982. Faced with insurmountable economic problems, the president announced in November 1984 that he would cut short his term by one year. The party, which had suffered the defection of its secretary general three months earlier, thereupon split into a number of factions, including the center-right **Nationalist Revolutionary Movement–April 9 Revolutionary Vanguard** (*Movimiento Nacionalista Revolucionario–Vanguardia Revolucionaria 9 de Abril* — MNR-V) and the **Leftist Nationalist Revolutionary Movement–One** (*Movimiento Nacionalista Revolucionario Izquierdo–Uno* — MNRI-1), each of which campaigned separately in 1985.

Leaders: Dr. Hernán SILES Zuazo (former President of the Republic), Roberto JORDAN Pando ("official" 1985 presidential candidate), Carlos SERRATE Reiche (MNR-V 1985 presidential candidate), Federico ALVAREZ Plata (Secretary General).

Leftist Revolutionary Movement (*Movimiento de la Izquierda Revolucionaria* — MIR). The MIR is a non-Communist Marxist party that organized as a splinter of the PDC and has a history of cooperation with the MNRI. It joined the UDP coalition prior to the 1978 election, its leader, Jaime Paz Zamora, running for the vice presidency in 1979 and 1980, and assuming the office in 1982. The MIR withdrew from the government in January 1983, but returned in April 1984. In mid-December, Paz Zamora resigned as vice president in order to qualify as a presidential candidate in 1985. The MIR's surprising success at the December 1987 municipal poll suggested that it and the rightist ADN would be the principal contestants at the next nationwide balloting in 1989.

Leaders: Jaime PAZ Zamora (former Vice President of the Republic and President of the Party), Guillermo CAPOBIANCO, Oscar EID Franco (General Secretary).

Left-Wing Parties:

Tupaj Katari Revolutionary Liberation Movement (*Movimiento Revolucionario Tupaj Katari-Liberación* — MRTK-L). Both the MRTK-L and the group from which it split, the *Movimiento Revolucionario Tupaj Katari* (MRTK) are among a number of small *campesino* formations. The MRTK joined the A-MNR in 1979, while the MRTK-L obtained 2 congressional seats in 1985.

Leaders: Juan CONDURI Uruchi (President), Genaro FLORES Santos (1985 presidential candidate).

Socialist Party–One (*Partido Socialista-Uno* — PS-1). The PS-1 was organized in 1971 by a group seeking a return to the policies of former president Ovando Candía. A relatively small party, it nonetheless obtained about 7 percent of the vote in 1979 and 8 percent in 1980. Its presidential candidate on both occasions, Marcelo Quiroga Santa Cruz, was murdered during the 1980 coup. It won 5 congressional seats in 1985, although credited with only 2.2 percent of the vote.

Leaders: Ramiro VELASCO (1985 presidential candidate), Roger CORTEZ, Walter VAZQUEZ.

United People's Front (*Frente del Pueblo Unido* — FPU). The FPU was organized prior to the 1985 electoral campaign as a coalition of some 12 left-wing groups, including those listed below. By 1987 it was essentially moribund, the PCB (below) joining with the MNRI (above) and a number of other groups in a leftist Patriotic Alliance (*Alianza Patriótica* — AP) to contest the municipal balloting of December 6.

Leader: Antonio ARANIBAR Quiroga (1985 presidential candidate).

National Leftist Revolutionary Party (*Partido Revolucionario de la Izquierda Nacionalista*—PRIN). PRIN was founded in 1964 as an offshoot of the MNR by the country's most influential labor leader, Juan Lechín Oquendo, who announced in mid-1986 that he was stepping down as president of the miners' federation (*Federación Sindical de Trabajadores Mineros Bolivianos*—FSTMB) and as executive secretary of the Bolivian workers' confederation (*Central Obrera Boliviano*—COB), being succeeded in the latter position by the Communist Party's general secretary, Simon Reyes (PCB, below) in July 1987.

Leader: Juan LECHIN Oquendo.

Bolivian Communist Party (*Partido Comunista de Bolivia*—PCB). Formally organized in 1952, the PCB is a Moscow-line group that lost much of its influence because of a failure to support the *guevarista* insurgents in the mid-1960s. Subsequently, it joined the UDP coalition, losing further support within the labor movement because of its participation in the Siles Zuazo government. At a contentious party congress in February 1985, Simón Reyes Rivera was named to succeed Jorge Kolle Cueto as PCB secretary general. Shortly thereafter a minority faction, also styling itself the *Partido Comunista de Bolivia,* split from the parent group under the leadership of Carlos SORIA Galvarro.

Leader: Simón REYES Rivera (Secretary General).

Workers and Masses Front (*Frente Obrero y de Masas*—FOM). Also known as MIR-*Masas,* the FOM is a dissident MIR group linked to the Bolivian Workers' Central (COB).

Leader: Walter DELGADILLO Terceros.

Leftist Revolutionary Movement–Free Bolivia (*Movimiento de Izquierda Revolucionaria-Bolivia Libre*—MIR-BL). The MIR-BL is also an MIR splinter, formed in January 1985.

Leader: Antonio ARANIBAR Quiroga.

Marxist-Leninist Bolivian Communist Party (*Partido Comunista Boliviano Marxista-Leninista*—PCB-ML). The PCB-ML, a pro-Peking offshoot of the PCB, supported Paz Estenssoro as a member of the A-MNR in 1979 and 1980. A splinter group, the *Partido Communista Boliviano Marxista-Leninista Disidente,* refused to accept the legitimacy of the post-Maoist Chinese leadership, and in May 1984 finally broke with the parent party because of its continued relationship with Paz Estenssoro's MNRH.

Leader: Oscar ZAMORA Medinacelli (First Secretary).

Revolutionary Workers' Party (*Partido Obrero Revolucionario*—POR). The POR is a Trotskyite party whose quite limited membership is spread over three factions.

Leaders: Guillermo LORA Escobar, Hugo GONZALEZ Moscoso, Amadeo ARZE.

Workers' Vanguard (*Vanguardia Obrera*—VO). The VO, also a Trotskyite party, obtained one legislative seat at the 1979 election.

Leaders: Ricardo CATOIRA, Filemón ESCOBAR.

LEGISLATURE

The bicameral Bolivian **Congress** (*Congreso*) normally sits for four years. The Congress elected in June 1980 was suspended in the wake of the July coup and did not convene until October 1982, when it voted to confirm Siles Zuazo as president. A new election was held on July 14, 1985, after the chief executive had announced his intention to serve for only three years. Of the 157 seats in the two houses at the 1985 balloting, the Historical Nationalist Revolutionary Movement won 59; the Nationalist Democratic Action, 51; the Leftist Revolutionary Movement, 16; the Leftist National Revolutionary Movement, 8; the Vanguard Nationalist Revolutionary Movement, 6; the Socialist Party — One, 5; the United People's Front, 4; the Christian Democratic Party, 3; the Bolivian Socialist Falange, 3; and the Tupaj Katari Revolutionary Liberation Movement, 2.

President: Julio GARRET Ayllón.

Senate (*Senado*). The upper house consists of 27 members, 3 from each department, elected for terms concurrent with those of the Chamber of Deputies. In each department delegation, 2 seats are held by the majority party or group, while 1 is reserved for the minority.

President: Ciro HUMBOLT Barrerro.

Chamber of Deputies (*Camara de Diputados*). The lower house currently consists of 130 members elected by universal and direct suffrage for four-year terms, with proportional representation for minorities.

President: Willy VARGAS Vacaflor.

CABINET

President	Víctor Paz Estenssoro
Vice President	Julio Garrett Ayllón
Ministers	
Air Force	Gen. Jaime Zegada Hurtado
Agriculture, Livestock and Campesino Affairs	José Guillermo Justiniano Pastor
Education and Culture	Enrique Ipiña Melgar
Energy and Hydrocarbons	Fernando Illanes
Finance	Juan Luis Cariaga Osorio
Foreign Affairs and Worship	Guillermo Bedregal Gutiérrez
Housing and Urban Affairs	Juan Franklin Anaya Vásquez
Industry, Commerce and Tourism	Fernando Jaime Moscoso Salmón
Information	Hernán Antelo Laughlin
Interior, Migration and Justice	Juan Carlos Durán Saucedo
Labor and Labor Development	Alfredo Franco Guachalla
Mining and Metallurgy	Jaime Villalobos Chávez
National Defense	Alfonso Revollo Thenier
Planning and Coordination	Gonzalo Sánchez de Lozada Bustamante
Revenue	Ramiro Cabezas
Social Services and Public Health	Carlos Pérez Gúzman
Transport and Communications	Andrés Petricevic Raznatovic
Secretary General of the Presidency	Walter Zuleta Roncal
President, Central Bank	Javier Nogales

NEWS MEDIA

All news media are privately owned; however, strict censorship was often enforced under recent military governments.

Press. The following papers are published daily at La Paz, unless otherwise noted: *Presencia* (85,000), Catholic; *El Diario* (45,000); *Ultima Hora* (36,000), independent; *Hoy* (25,000), independent; *El Mundo* (Santa Cruz, 20,000), business oriented; *Los Tiempos* (Cochabamba, 18,000), independent.

News agencies. The domestic press associations are the *Asociación Nacional de Periodistas* and the *Asociación Nacional de Prensa;* a number of foreign agencies, including AFP, ANSA, AP, and UPI, maintain bureaus at La Paz.

Radio and television. The *Asociación Boliviana de Radiodifusoras* encompasses nearly 150 short- and medium-wave stations, which transmits to approximately 500,000 radio receivers. The *Empresa Nacional de Televisión Boliviana* services some 390,000 television sets.

INTERGOVERNMENTAL REPRESENTATION

Ambassador to the US: (Vacant).

US Ambassador to Bolivia: (Vacant).

Permanent Representative to the UN: Hugo NAVAJAS-MOGRO.

IGO Memberships (Non-UN): ALADI, Ancom, ANRPC, Geplacea, IADB, ICM, ICO, Intelsat, Interpol, ISO, IWTC, NAM, OAS, OPANAL, PCA, SELA.

BOTSWANA

Republic of Botswana

Political Status: Independent republic within the Commonwealth since September 30, 1966.

Area: 231,804 sq. mi. (600,372 sq. km.).

Population: 941,027 (1981C), 1,215,000 (1988E). Both figures are de jure.

Major Urban Centers (1981C): GABORONE (59,657); Francistown (31,065); Selebi-Pikwe (29,469); Serowe (23,661). In 1985, the population of Gaborone was estimated at 100,000.

Official Language: English (SeTswana is widely spoken).

Monetary Unit: Pula (market rate March 1, 1988, 1.68 pula = $1US).

President: Dr. Quett K.J. MASIRE (Botswana Democratic Party); appointed Vice President in 1966; became Acting President upon the death of Sir Seretse M. KHAMA (Botswana Democratic Party) on July 13, 1980, and President upon election by the National Assembly on July 18; reappointed following election of September 8, 1984.

Vice President: Peter S. MMUSI (Botswana Democratic Party); appointed by the President upon the death of Lenyeleste M. SERETSE on January 3, 1983; reappointed following election of September 8, 1984.

THE COUNTRY

Landlocked Botswana, the former British protectorate of Bechuanaland, embraces a substantial area of desert, swamp, and scrubland situated on a high plateau in the heart of southern Africa. The country is bordered on three sides by the traditionally White-ruled territories of South Africa and Namibia (South West Africa), but with Black-ruled Zimbabwe to the northeast. The population is divided into eight main tribal groups, the largest of which is the Bamangwato. A majority of the people follow ancestral religious practices, but about 15 percent are Christian. Due in part to the large-scale employment of males in neighboring South African mines, 80 percent of households are headed by women who, however, cannot hold land title or control their crops, and therefore are denied access to funds and equipment under rural development programs. Female representation among senior officials is at present limited to the incumbent foreign minister.

At the time of independence Botswana was one of the world's poorest countries, dependent on stock-raising for much of its income because of an extremely dry climate that made large scale farming difficult. Subsequent mineral discoveries initiated economic growth that has recently averaged about 10 percent a year. At present, Botswana is one of the world's top three producers of diamonds, which provide 75 percent of foreign exchange and 60 percent of government revenue. While extractive activity (also involving copper-nickel matte and coal) has yielded infrastructural gains, food production has remained a problem. While 80 percent of the work force is involved in subsistence agriculture, two-thirds of the population is currently dependent on food relief. The government's free-enterprise orientation and conservative monetary policies have attracted substantial foreign aid, although private foreign investors have been wary of the country's economic dependence on South Africa. Current government programs focus on economic diversification to deal with growing unemployment, agricultural improvements, educational expansion, and the promotion of tourism.

GOVERNMENT AND POLITICS

Political background. A British protectorate from 1885, Botswana (formerly Bechuanaland) achieved independence within the Commonwealth on September 30, 1966, under the leadership of Sir Seretse KHAMA and has subsequently been regarded as a showplace of democracy in Africa. Following the National Assembly election of October 20, 1979, at which his Botswana Democratic Party (BDP) won 29 of 32 elective seats, President Khama was redesignated for a fourth five-year term. His death on July 13, 1980, led to the selection of Dr. Quett K.J. MASIRE, vice president and minister of finance and development planning, to fill the remainder of the presidential term. Both Masire and Vice President Peter S. MMUSI were reappointed following the most recent legislative election of September 8, 1984.

Constitution and government. The 1966 constitution provides for a president who serves as head of state and government, a Parliament consisting of a National Assembly and a consultative House of Chiefs, and a judicial structure embracing a High Court and a Court of Appeal. Thirty-four members of the National Assembly are directly elected by universal adult suffrage and then select four additional members. Sitting as an electoral college, the Assembly elects the president for a term coincident with its own. The House of Chiefs acts as a consultative body on matters of native law, customs, and land, and also deliberates constitutional amendments. The president can delay for up to six months, but not veto, legislation.

At the local level, Botswana is divided into nine districts and four towns, all governed by councils. Chiefs head five of the District Councils, elected leaders the remaining four. The districts impose personal income taxes to generate revenue, the local funding being supplemented by central government grants.

Foreign relations. Although generally pro-Western in outlook, Botswana belongs to the Nonaligned Movement and has established diplomatic relations with the Soviet bloc and the People's Republic of China.

Botswana's relations with South Africa, its major trading partner and the employer of over half its nonagricultural work force, have been problematic. While maintaining no formal diplomatic relations with Pretoria and participating as one of the six Front-Line States (also including Angola, Mozambique, Tanzania, Zambia, and Zimbabwe) opposing minority rule in southern Africa, it has attempted to maintain peaceful coexistence with the Pretoria regime. Tensions heightened in 1985, however, when South African Defense Forces mounted a cross-border attack on alleged havens for the African National Congress, killing 15 people. Despite assurances from Botswana that it would not condone any "terrorist activity" from its territory, the SADF engaged in a similar action near Gaborone in May 1986 as part of its policy of "hot pursuit" of alleged ANC guerrillas. After strongly condemning the raids as naked aggression, the Masire government informed the other Front-Line States that it "would not stand in the way" of those who might wish to initiate economic sanctions against South Africa.

In late 1986, Botswana was obliged to postpone a long-planned acquisition of the domestic portion of a Zimbabwe-South African rail line because of a demand by the neighboring tribal homeland of Bophuthatswana that a customs post be set up at the border. Botswana refused, since such action would constitute de facto recognition of a territory acknowledged to be "independent" only by Pretoria, and the dispute remained unresolved through 1987.

Current issues. Bowing to South African pressure, the Masire administration in 1986 agreed to interdict ANC political and military activity, forcing numerous ANC adherents to leave the country. Collaterally, Botswanan troops received training from Britain's Special Air Services to increase their ability to combat future South African incursions, while the United States sent helicopters and experts in counterintelligence as part of a $10 million military aid package. Although there was no repetition of the 1985 and 1986 SADF attacks in 1987, South African commandos killed four people in a house at Gaborone during a cross-border incursion in late March 1988.

Internally, Masire's BDP, although still solidly in control of the government, faced increased opposition and sporadic social unrest. Critics cited growing unemployment as well as a concentration of wealth among the economic elite. The opposition Botswana National Front, which had surprised observers with its 1984 election advances (see BNF, below), was the primary beneficiary of antiadministration sentiment. However, BNF leaders charged that the controversial National Security Act passed in 1986 inhibited their activities. The act gave law enforcement officials broad powers to arrest without warrant and to impose 30-year sentences on those deemed guilty of security violations. President Masire promoted the act as "anti-terrorist" and necessary to counter spies and saboteurs, while the US and other Western governments viewed it as diminishing Botswana's longstanding democratic reputation.

POLITICAL PARTIES

Government Party:

Botswana Democratic Party (BDP). Founded in 1962 as the Bechuanaland Democratic Party, the BDP has been the majority party since independence. It advocates self-development on a Western-type democratic basis, cooperation with all states, multiracialism, and the maintenance of equitable relations with South Africa. In June 1984, Masire announced measures to "democratize" party nominations through a revamped primary system. However, all candidates remained subject to approval by a Central Committee, which is dominated by government ministers. Although still dominant in rural areas where educational advances have been well received, the BDP has recently lost support in the cities.

Leaders: Dr. Quett K.J. MASIRE (President of the Republic and of the Party), A.M. TSOEBEBE (Vice President), Daniel KWELAGOBE (Secretary General).

Opposition Parties:

Botswana National Front (BNF). The BNF is a leftist party organized after the 1965 election. Its principal leader, Dr. Kenneth Koma, was the only candidate to oppose Sir Seretse for the presidency in 1979, but failed to retain his Assembly seat. The party's share of the vote increased to 20 percent at the 1984 election, with its legislative representation growing from 2 to 4; it also won control of the Gaborone city council. Although the BNF in the past has been categorized as pro-Communist, Koma has recently characterized its activists as "social democrats" who are "not Marxist".

Leaders: Dr. Kenneth KOMA, BATHOEN II Gaseitsiwe (Parliamentary Leader), Mareledi GIDDIE (Secretary General).

Botswana People's Party (BPP). Formerly the principal minority party, the northern-based BPP advocates social democracy and takes a pan-Africanist line. It retained its single legislative seat in 1984.

Leaders: Dr. Knight MARIPE (President), Kenneth MKHWA (Chairman), John MOSOJANE (Secretary General).

Botswana Independence Party (BIP). The BIP, formed in 1964 by a dissident BPP faction, espouses a program similar to that of the BPP. It lost its only legislative seat at the 1979 election.

Leaders: Motsamai K. MPHO (President), J.G. GUGUSHE (Vice President), Emmanuel R. MOKOBI (Secretary General).

Botswana Progressive Union (BPU). The BPU was formed in 1982.

Leaders: D.K. KWELE (President), G.G. BAGWASI (Chairman), R.K. MONYATSIWA (Secretary General).

Other Party:

Botswana Liberal Party (BLP). The BLP was formed in February 1984, its founder declaring that the socio-economic development of the country had "stagnated" since independence, but declining to align his new grouping with other opposition parties because of their alleged lack of popular appeal.

Leader: Martin CHAKALISO (President).

LEGISLATURE

The bicameral **Parliament** consists of an elective National Assembly with legislative powers and a consultative House of Chiefs.

House of Chiefs. The House of Chiefs is a largely advisory body of 15 members: the chiefs of the 8 principal tribes, 4 elected subchiefs, and 3 members selected by the other 12.

Chairman: Chief SEEPAPITSO.

National Assembly. The National Assembly, which sits for a five-year term, currently consists of 34 directly elected and 4 indirectly elected members, in addition to the speaker and the (nonvoting) attorney general; the president serves ex officio. The most recent general election was held September 8, 1984, with the Botswana Democratic Party winning 29 seats; the Botswana National Front, 4; and the Botswana People's Party, 1. At a subsequent by-election, the BDP lost 1 seat to the BNP.

Speaker: James G. HASKINS.

C A B I N E T

President	Dr. Quett K.J. Masire
Vice President	Peter Mmusi

Ministers

Agriculture	Daniel K. Kwelagobe
Commerce and Industry	M.P. Kwako Nwako
Education	Kebatlamang P.S. Morake
Finance and Development Planning	Peter Mmusi
Foreign Affairs	Gaositwe K.T. Chiepe
Health	Lesedi Mothibamele
Labor and Home Affairs	Englishman Kgabo
Local Government and Lands	Patrick Balopi
Mineral Resources and Water Affairs	Archibald M. Mogwe
Presidential Affairs and Public Administration	Ponatshego Kedikilwe
Works, Transport and Communications	Colin Blackbeard
Attorney General	M.D. Mokama
Governor, Central Bank	Quill Hermans

N E W S   M E D I A

Press. All papers are published at Gaborone, except as noted: *Botswana Daily News/Dikgang Tsa Gompieno* (30,000), published by the Department of Information and Broadcasting in English and SeTswana; *Botswana Guardian* (14,000), weekly; *Kutlwano* (8,000), published monthly by the Department of Information and Broadcasting in English and SeTswana; *Business Gazette* (8,000), weekly; *Botswana Advertiser,* weekly; *Northern Advertiser* (Francistown), weekly.

News agency. The Botswana Press Agency (Bopa) was established at Gaborone in 1981.

Radio and television. The government-owned Radio Botswana operates six stations broadcasting in English and SeTswana. In 1985, there were 80,000 radio receivers. The TV Association of Botswana operates two low-power transmitters near Gaborone that relay programs from South Africa, although plans have been announced for an independent station broadcasting from Botswana.

INTERGOVERNMENTAL   REPRESENTATION

Ambassador to the US: Serara T. KETLOGETSWE.

US Ambassador to Botswana: Natale H. BELLOCCHI.

Permanent Representative to the UN: Legwaila Joseph LEGWAILA.

IGO Memberships (Non-UN): ADF, AfDB, BADEA, CCC, CWTH, EEC(L), *EIB,* Interpol, NAM, OAU, SADCC.

BRAZIL

Federative Republic of Brazil
República Federativa do Brasil

Political Status: Independent monarchy proclaimed 1822; republic established 1889; currently functioning under constitution adopted in 1967 but extensively revised on October 20, 1969.

Area: 3,286,470 sq. mi. (8,511,965 sq. km.).

Population: 119,098,992 (1980C), 144,925,000 (1988E).

Major Urban Centers (1985E): BRASILIA (federal district, 1,577,000); São Paulo (10,099,000); Rio de Janeiro (5,615,000); Belo Horizonte (2,122,000); Recife (1,290,000); Pôrto Alegre (1,275,000); Belém (1,121,000).

Official Language: Portuguese.

Monetary Unit: Cruzado (market rate March 1, 1988, 98.50 cruzados = $1US). The cruzado, introduced in February 1986, is equal to 1,000 cruzeiros.

President: José SARNEY Costa (Liberal Front Party); named Vice President by the electoral college on January 15, 1985; became Acting President on March 15, due to the incapacitation of the President-Elect, Tancredo NEVES (Party of the Brazilian Democratic Movement; succeeded to the presidency following Neves' death on April 21.

Vice President: Vacant, upon assumption of the presidency by José SARNEY.

THE   COUNTRY

The population of South America's largest country, which occupies nearly half the continent, is approximately 55 percent Caucasian, with at least 35 percent of mixed blood and less than 0.5 percent pure Indian. The Caucasians are mainly of Portuguese descent but include substantial numbers of Italian, German, Dutch, and Belgian immigrants. There are small African Negro, Japanese, and Chinese minorities. The population is overwhelmingly Roman Catholic in religious belief, but other faiths are permitted. Women make up 27 percent of the paid labor force, a majority in domestic service, with one-quarter of adult females estimated to be unpaid agricultural workers. Although women are minimally represented in political life, a few from powerful families have managed to occupy high-level government and party positions.

The Brazilian economy was traditionally based on one-crop agriculture under the control of a landed aristocracy. In recent years, however, the economy has been substantially diversified, and coffee, which once accounted for 50 percent of the nation's exports, now contributes about 10 percent. Soybeans, cotton, sugar, and cocoa are other important agricultural commodities. In industry, textiles remain important, while iron, steel, petroleum, and paper production have grown significantly; in addition, Brazil's arms industry has doubled since 1977, accounting for an increasing share of export income. Numerous minerals are mined commercially, including quartz, chromium, manganese, gold, and silver. However, recent depressed commodity prices have had a highly adverse effect on Brazil's balance of payments, and by late 1983 the country was experiencing severe economic difficulty, including the developing world's highest external debt (in excess of $100 billion) and inflation approaching 200 percent. While subsequent refinancing efforts, largely under IMF auspices, substantially improved Brazil's foreign trade situation and produced a trade surplus of over $12 billion for 1984, inflation continued its upward spiral, exceeding 233 percent for

1985. The economy responded positively to austerity measures mandated by the Sarney administration's "Cruzado Plan" in February 1986, but again plummeted with a relaxation of price and wage controls late in the year. By January 1987, inflation had spiraled to an annualized rate of 500 percent and, in what was termed a "technical moratorium", the government in late February temporarily suspended payments on its foreign debt (see Current issues, below).

GOVERNMENT AND POLITICS

Political background. Ruled as a Portuguese colony until 1815, Brazil retained its monarchical institutions as an independent state from 1822 until the declaration of a republic in 1889. Constitutional democratic rule was overturned in 1930 by a military coup d'état led by Getúlio VARGAS, whose dictatorship lasted until 1945. Enrico DUTRA, Vargas, Juscelino KUBITSCHEK, and Jânio QUADROS subsequently served as elected presidents, but in 1961 Quadros resigned and was succeeded by Vice President João GOULART. Goulart's leftist administration, after being widely criticized for inflationary policies, governmental corruption, and prolabor and alleged pro-Communist tendencies, was overturned by the military in March 1964. Marshal Humberto de Alencar CASTELLO BRANCO, who served as president from 1964 to 1967, vigorously repressed subversive and leftist tendencies, instituted a strongly anti-inflationary economic policy, and reestablished governmental authority on a strictly centralized basis. Brazil's 13 political parties were dissolved in 1965, and political freedom was drastically curtailed by an "institutional act" whose main provisions were later incorporated into a constitution adopted under presidential pressure in 1967 and substantially revised in 1969. Direct presidential elections were abolished, the president was given sweeping powers to restrict freedom of the press, and formal political activity was limited to the formation of two newly authorized parties, the progovernment *Aliança Renovadora Nacional* (Arena) and the opposition *Movimento Democrático Brasileiro* (MDB).

The policies of Castello Branco were continued under Arthur da COSTA E SILVA (1967–1969) and Emílio Garrastazú MEDICI (1969–1974), rising political dissatisfaction with authoritarian rule being countered in December 1968 by the president's assumption of virtually unlimited powers that were retained for nearly a decade thereafter. Despite periodic disturbances, the ease with which power was passed to President Ernesto GEISEL in early 1974 suggested that the military and its allies were still firmly in control. However, at a legislative election in November, the opposition MDB captured approximately one-third of the seats in the Chamber of Deputies and 16 of 20 seats to be filled in the Senate. Four years later, the MDB won a clear majority of votes cast but failed to capture either house because of electoral arrangements favoring the government party.

On March 15, 1979, João Baptista FIGUEIREDO was sworn in for a six-year term as Geisel's hand-picked successor, after electoral-college designation five months earlier by a vote of 355–226 over the MDB candidate, Gen.

Euler Bentes MONTEIRO. In November Arena and the MDB were dissolved under a policy of political relaxation (*abertura*) that permitted the emergence of a more broad-ranged party spectrum (see Political Parties, below).

Under electoral procedures that favored its newly established Democratic Social Party (PDS), the government failed to capture a majority of lower-house seats at the legislative election of November 15, 1982. Subsequently, Tancredo NEVES, of the Party of the Brazilian Democratic Movement (PMDB), outpolled Paulo MALUF in the electoral college balloting of January 15, 1985, but was unable to assume office because of illness. His vice presidential running mate, José SARNEY Costa, of the Liberal Front Party (PFL) became acting president on March 15 and succeeded to the presidency at Neves' death on April 21. Upon entering office, Sarney negotiated a somewhat fragile coalition between the PMDB and the PFL, the former securing a 53 percent majority and the coalition 77 percent of lower house seats at the legislative election of November 15, 1986.

Constitution and government. The revised constitution of 1969 maintained Brazil's status as a federal republic in which the central government retained broad powers but the states were permitted to establish congruent constitutions and governments. In addition to the powers formally granted to the central government, the financial dependency of states and municipalities has, in recent years, contributed to increased centralization.

Executive authority is currently vested in a president and vice president, elected for six-year terms by an electoral college consisting of members of the bicameral National Congress and delegates from the state legislatures. However, in May 1985, four months after the selection of Neves, Congress approved a constitutional amendment restoring direct election for a four-year term, suggesting (in the wake of a pledge by President Sarney to limit his incumbency) that balloting under the new arrangement would be held in late 1988. Subsequently, however, a five-year term was incorporated into the draft of a new basic law (see below) that would appear to call for an election in 1989. The judicial structure is headed by a Supreme Court, whose justices are appointed by the president with the approval of the Senate. There are also federal courts in the state capitals, a Federal Court of Appeals, and special courts for dealing with military, labor, and electoral issues.

Brazil is presently divided into 23 states, 3 federal territories, and the Federal District of Brasília. The states, which have their own constitutions, legislatures, and judicial systems, may divide or join with others to form new states. Thus the former state of Guanabara merged with Rio de Janeiro in 1975, while in 1977 the new state of Mato Grosso do Sul was formed out of the southern part of Mato Grosso. The most recent addition resulted from elevation of the southwest Amazon territory of Rondônia to statehood in December 1981.

State and Capital	Area (sq. mi.)	Population (1987E)
Acre (Rio Branco)	58,915	377,000
Alagoas (Maceió)	10,707	2,344,000
Amazonas (Manaus)	604,032	1,848,000
Bahia (Salvador)	216,612	11,216,000

Ceará (Fortaleza)	58,158	6,121,000
Espírito Santo (Vitória)	17,605	2,391,000
Goiás (Goiânia)	247,912	4,681,000
Maranhão (São Luís)	126,897	4,889,000
Mato Grosso (Cuiabá)	n.a.	1,618,000
Mato Grosso do Sul (Campo Grande)	n.a.	1,697,000
Minas Gerais (Belo Horizonte)	226,707	15,059,000
Pará (Belém)	482,904	4,514,000
Paraíba (João Pessôa)	21,765	3,110,000
Paraná (Curitiba)	77,048	8,240,000
Pernambuco (Recife)	37,946	7,014,000
Piauí (Teresina)	96,886	2,542,000
Rio de Janeiro (Rio de Janeiro)	17,092	13,332,000
Rio Grande do Norte (Natal)	20,469	2,210,000
Rio Grande do Sul (Pôrto Alegre)	108,951	8,755,000
Rondônia (Pôrto Velho)	93,839	838,000
Santa Catarina (Florianópolis)	37,060	4,272,000
São Paulo (São Paulo)	95,713	31,460,000
Sergipe (Aracajú)	8,492	1,345,000

Territory and Capital

Amapá (Macapá)	54,161	229,000
Fernando de Noronha	10	1,300
Roraima (Boa Vista)	88,843	113,000

Federal District

Distrito Federal (Brasília)	2,245	1,745,000

In mid-1980 the government named a working group to draft a new constitution. Although originally scheduled for promulgation in March 1982, the text was never approved by Congress, and several measures were proposed by mid-1985 to empower the Congress elected in 1986 to act as a constituent assembly. In October, the Congress established November 15, 1986, as the date for legislative and gubernatorial balloting and empowered its successor, following its convening on February 1, 1987, to act as a constituent assembly for purposes of constitutional revision, including definition of the length of the current presidency. On March 22, 1988, following a year of sharp disputes and major shifts in party alliances, the Constituent Assembly voted 344 to 212 (with three abstentions) in favor of the presidential form of government and a five-year term of office for "future" presidents, leaving technically undecided the duration of President Sarney's incumbency.

Foreign relations. Long a leader in the inter-American community, Brazil has traditionally been aligned in international affairs with the United States, which is its major trading partner. The conclusion of a 1975 nuclear-plant agreement with West Germany in the wake of the Geisel government's refusal to sign the 1968 UN Treaty on the Non-Proliferation of Nuclear Weapons, coupled with problems arising from increased coffee prices and the Carter administration's stand on human rights, led, however, to a degree of estrangement between the two countries. In March 1977, largely in reaction to the human-rights criticism, Brazil canceled a 25-year-old military assistance treaty with the United States. As a result of the cancellation, Brazil's arms industry became one of the fastest-growing sectors of the economy, with international customers including Libya and Saudi Arabia. While improved Washington-Brasília relations under the Reagan administration led to the signing of a military cooperation agreement in February 1984, controversy continued over an "understanding" that Washington would be allowed to monitor the sale of Brazilian arms using US technology.

On July 3, 1978, a Treaty of Amazon Cooperation (Amazon Pact) was signed with Bolivia, Colombia, Ecuador, Guyana, Peru, Suriname, and Venezuela. Although concluded in the relatively short period of 15 months, the Pact has been criticized as lacking in detail on substantive development of the Amazon basin.

Relations with Argentina, which had been strained because of a series of disputes over utilization of the hydroelectric potential of the Paraná River, improved in late 1979 with the conclusion of a tripartite accord involving the two countries and Paraguay. More conclusive evidence of realignment within the Southern Cone was provided by a visit of President Figueiredo to Buenos Aires in May 1980 (the first by a Brazilian head of state in 30 years), during which a total of ten intergovernmental agreements were signed, embracing such traditionally sensitive areas as arms manufacture, nuclear technology, and exploitation of the hydroelectric resources of the Río Uruguay.

During the 1982 Falkland Islands war Brazil joined with its regional neighbors in supporting Argentina, while the Brazilian embassy at London represented Argentine interests in the British capital. However, its posture throughout was distinctly muted, partly because of traditional rivalry between the continent's two largest countries and partly because of an unwillingness to offend British financial interests, which were viewed as critical to resolution of Brasília's foreign debt problems. The 1983 election of Raul Alfonsín to the Argentine presidency served to dampen rapprochement with Buenos Aires because of the new chief executive's well-publicized links to Brazilian opposition leaders; however, by mid-1984 the situation had improved and a number of trade and cooperation agreements were concluded after Brazil's return to civilian rule in early 1985. Economic ties between the continent's two largest states were further enhanced on December 10, 1986, with the signing by presidents Sarney and Alfonsín of 20 accords launching an ambitious integration effort intended, in the words of the Brazilian chief executive, "eventually to create a Latin American common market". Under the plan, a customs union was established for most capital goods as of January 1, 1987, with cooperation in the exchange of food products, the promotion of bilateral industrial ventures, the establishment of a $200 million joint investment fund, and joint energy development (including a new $2 billion hydroelectric facility) to follow.

Diplomatic relations were restored with Cuba in June 1986, after a 22-year rupture, while in September 1987 talks were held on peace, nuclear disarmament, and bilateral trade with visiting Soviet Foreign Minister Eduard Shevardnadze in what was widely believed to be a demonstration of heightened Soviet interest in the region.

Current issues. Largely through the strength of his personality, Tancredo Neves had formed a highly effective coalition of quite diverse political elements for the 1984 presidential campaign. His successor, José Sarney (who, as former president of the promilitary PDS, had been selected mainly for ticket-balancing purposes) was obliged, during his early months in office, to forge a political base for himself, while contending with a variety of pressing problems that included massive foreign indebtedness, the extreme poverty of nearly half of the Brazilian population (the so-called "social debt"), escalating inflation, a bloated bureaucracy, and constitutional questions raised by the circumstances of his own accession to office.

One of the most divisive issues encountered by Sarney was agrarian reform, with a presidential proposal in June 1985 to reassign over a million acres of state and private land to landless peasants meeting such intense resistance that the legislation ultimately approved in October was limited to the distribution of publicly owned land in remote northern areas of the country. However, even the revised measure became the object of persistent lobbying by the country's most powerful interest group, the landowners' Democratic Rural Union (*União Democrática Ruralista* — UDR), which in May 1988 succeeded in inducing the Congress to include an exemption for all "productive" land in the proposed new constitution.

The most conspicuous feature of the Cruzado Plan, launched in February 1986, was a price and wage freeze, which succeeded in reducing the monthly inflation rate of nearly 16 percent in January to less than 1 percent for some of the ensuing months. The seeming success of the Plan yielded a surge in popular support for the president and a massive victory for the PMDB/PFL alliance at the November 15 congressional and gubernatorial balloting. Immediately after the election, however, many of the controls were lifted and Sarney's popularity visibly eroded because of the turnabout, in addition to its apparent political timing. Even prior to the near-total abandonment of the measures in January 1987, many PMDB elements were seen as distancing themselves from the administration, while a return to double-digit monthly inflation led to a debt moratorium in late February. By March, trapped in an unremitting economic and political crisis, Sarney attempted to press the newly inaugurated Congress (sitting as a Constituent Assembly) to define the length of his mandate, considerable uncertainty existing as to whether he would be permitted to serve the full six years to which his predecessor had been elected. In November the Assembly's constitutional drafting committee endorsed a modified presidential system and a reduced presidential term of four years. However, in March 1988 the full body, by an unexpected 2–1 margin, voted for retention of the presidential system, with the chief executive to serve a five-year term. While the action did not specifically apply to the incumbent, it was widely believed thereby that Sarney's mandate would not be cut short.

With inflation soaring to 366 percent, Luíz Carlos BRESSER Pereira, Sarney's third finance minister, resigned in December 1987 after failing to secure full presidential approval for proposed tax changes and limits on government spending. However, his successor, Mailson Ferreira da NOBREGA succeeded in reopening talks with the IMF in early 1988 after partial debt repayments to creditor banks had been resumed and in April announced a two-month freeze on public-sector wages as part of a seven-point deficit reduction plan.

POLITICAL PARTIES

All of Brazil's existing parties were dissolved by decree in 1965, clearing the way for establishment of a single government party, the National Renewal Alliance (*Aliança Renovadora Nacional* — Arena), and a single opposition party, the Brazilian Democratic Movement (*Movimento Democrático Brasileiro* — MDB), which began organizing in 1969. At the election of November 1978, the Alliance retained control of both houses of Congress but was substantially outpolled in the popular vote by the MDB. Both groups were formally dissolved on November 22, 1979, upon the enactment of legislation sanctioning a more liberal party system. Under the new arrangement, parties were required to swear allegiance to the "democratic system", give six months prior notice of a national congress, and win 5 percent of the total vote in order to retain legal status. For the indirect presidential balloting in 1985, a **Democratic Alliance** (*Aliança Democrática*) was formed, composed of the PMDB and PFL (below), in support of the candidacy of Tancredo Neves. However, neither of the Alliance partners was firmly committed to the leadership of Neves' successor, while President Sarney called for a "National Pact" centered on the non-*Malufista* wing of his own preelection Social Democratic Party (see below).

The bill enacted by Congress on May 9, 1985, which restored direct presidential elections, also legalized all political parties, a move presumed to be directed mainly at the theretofore proscribed Brazilian Communist Party (PCB), which had been publicly running candidates under the PMDB banner.

Party of the Brazilian Democratic Movement (*Partido do Movimento Democrático Brasiliero* — PMDB). Rejecting government strictures against the adoption of names implying continuity with earlier party groups, the PMDB was launched in 1979 by some 100 federal deputies and 20 senators representing the more moderate elements of the former MDB. In late 1981 it was enlarged by merger with the Popular Party (*Partido Popular* — PP), a center-right grouping of some 70 deputies and 8 senators, most of whom had also been affiliated with the MDB. As the party reorganized to prepare for the 1986 congressional balloting, a conservative faction, *Grupo Unidade*, insisted that PP elements (which opposed recent PMDB initiatives for land reform and tax revision) were underrepresented in the party and issued an unsuccessful challenge to Ulisses Guimarães for the party presidency. The PMDB won a majority in both houses of Congress and 22 of 23 state governorships in the November 1986 election.

During 1987 the party became increasingly divided, with leftists, organized as the **Progressive Unity Movement** (*Movimento da Unidade Progressiva* — MUP), proposing a "grand leftist front" that would include "nonradicalized" factions of the PDT and the PT (below) to campaign for truncation of Sarney's term and an immediate presidential election. By early 1988 the *históricos* (constituting a majority within the party, but not within the Constituent Assembly) were also pressing for a break with the Sarney government, following the Assembly vote in favor of the presidential system and a five-year term for the incumbent (see Current issues, above).

Leaders: Ulisses GUIMARÃES (President of the Constituent Assembly, President of the Chamber of Deputies and President of the Party), Alfredo CAMPOS (PMDB Bloc Leader in the Senate), Pimenta da VIEGA (PMDB Bloc Leader in the Chamber of Deputies), Miquel ARRAES de Alencar, José FREITAS Nobre, Teotônio VILELA, Alfonso CAMARGO, Milton REIS (Secretary General).

Social Democratic Party (*Partido Democrático Social* — PDS). The PDS emerged in late 1979 as the principal successor to Arena, augmented in the Congress by a number of right-wing members of the former MDB. The party lost its majority in the Chamber of Deputies at the November 1982 election but retained its control of the electoral college as a result of its representation in the Senate and state governorships. In mid-1984, the party split over the nomination of Paulo Maluf as PDS candidate for president in 1985, José Sarney resigning as party leader over the issue in

June and, after formation of the Liberal Front Party (below), running as vice-presidential candidate on the *Aliança Democrática* ticket.

Leaders: Jarbas PASSARINHO (President), Paulo MALUF (1985 presidential candidate), Aloysio CHAVES, Antônio DELFIM Netto (former Planning Minister), Amaral PEIXOTO, Virgilio TAVORA (General Secretary).

Liberal Front Party (*Partido da Frente Liberal* — PFL). The *Frente Liberal* was formed in 1984 as a faction within the PDS that was opposed to the presidential candidacy of Paulo Maluf. It organized as a separate entity prior to the 1985 electoral college balloting, at which it supported Tancredo Neves as a member of the *Aliança Democrática*. At present it is the second largest party in Congress, although its co-founder, José Sarney, withdrew in March 1988 to form a new presidential coalition involving elements of the PMDB and PDS (see BTD, below).

In September 1987 the PFL announced its withdrawal from the *Aliança Democrática,* thus formally terminating its linkage with the PMDB, although it decided the following month to continue its support of President Sarney until after approval of the new constitution.

Leaders: Marco MACIEL (Chairman), Dr. Antônio Aureliano CHAVES de Mendonça (former Vice President of the Republic), Carlos CHIARELLI (PFL Bloc Leader in the Senate), José LORENÇO (PFL Bloc Leader in the Chamber of Deputies), Saulo QUEIROZ (Secretary General).

Democratic Transition Bloc (*Bloco de Transição Democrática* — BTD). Formed in early 1988 by President Sarney as a projected multiparty, government-supportive formation, the BTD is composed primarily of disgruntled PMDB members angered by the overtly proparliamentarist and anti-Sarney posture of the party mainstream. Both PMDB President Ulisses Guimarães and PFL Chairman Marco Maciel have rejected overtures by the new group.

Leaders: José SARNEY (President of the Republic), Carlos SANT'ANA.

Democratic Labor Party (*Partido Democrático Trabalhista* — PDT). The PDT is a left-wing party organized by Leonel da Moira Brizola, a former governor of Rio Grande do Sul and the leader of the pre-1965 Brazilian Labor Party, following his return on September 5, 1979, after 15 years in exile. At the 1982 balloting Brizola, a man of known presidential aspirations, won the state governorship of Rio de Janeiro; prior to Neves' election, he attempted unsuccessfully to form a new socialist party and after the president-elect's death led the campaign for direct presidential balloting in 1988. At the November 1985 municipal balloting, the PDT won mayoralties at Porto Alegre and — more importantly — Rio de Janeiro, although a Brizola protégé was defeated in his bid for the state governorship in 1986.

Leaders: Doutel de ANDRADE (President), Leonel da Moira BRIZOLA, Brandão MONTEIRO (Parliamentary Leader), Carmen CYNIRA (General Secretary).

Brazilian Labor Party (*Partido Trabalhista Brasileiro* — PTB). The PTB was organized in 1980 by a niece of former president Getúlio Vargas. It attained greater visibility in 1985 through the widely supported candidacy of Jânio Quadros for mayor of São Paulo.

Leaders: Luíz GONZAGA de Paiva Muniz (President), Ivete VARGAS, Jânio QUADROS (former President of the Republic), Celso PEÇANHA, José CORREIA Pedroso (General Secretary).

Workers' Party (*Partido dos Trabalhadores* — PT). Also a party of the Left, the PT endorses "a pure form of socialism" that rejects orthodox Marxism. It made important gains in the 1985 municipal balloting, electing Maria Luisa FONTONELLE as one of the country's first two women mayors at Ceará's capital, Fortaleza, and winning 20 percent of the vote at São Paulo. It increased its lower house representation from 14 to 19 in 1986, while retaining its single Senate seat. During the 1987–1988 controversy over the duration of President Sarney's mandate and the possible introduction of a parliamentary system of government, the PT came out strongly in favor of immediate presidential elections with the avowed intention of running PT president Luis da Silva as its candidate.

Leaders: Luís Inácio Lula da SILVA (President), Jacó BITTAR (Vice President), Olivio DUTRA (General Secretary).

Brazilian Revolutionary Communist Party (*Partido Comunista Brasileiro Revolucionario* — PCBR). The PCBR is an extreme-left party "harbored" by the PT, though its exact relationship to the larger organization remains unclear.

Leader: Antônio PRESTES de Paulo.

Brazilian Communist Party (*Partido Comunista Brasileiro* — PCB). A pro-Moscow party, the PCB has been relatively active in recent years despite being officially banned prior to the 1986 balloting. Luís Carlos PRESTES, one of the party's leading figures for over 50 years, was removed from his post as secretary general in May 1980 after having opposed a "broad front" policy of alignment with all opposition groups, and in October 1981 joined the Workers' Party. At its January 1984 party congress, the PCB declared its commitment to "nationalist democracy based on a multiparty system". In early 1985 PCB leaders disagreed over the advantages of legalization, some claiming that it would make the party more vulnerable by depriving its candidates of the electoral umbrella of the PMBD. It currently holds 2 seats in the Chamber of Deputies.

Leaders: Giocondo DIAS, Salomão MALINA (Secretary General).

Communist Party of Brazil (*Partido Comunista do Brasil* — PCdoB). Founded in 1961 as an offshoot of the PCB, the PCdoB is a Maoist group that has been active in support of rural guerrilla operations against the military. In August 1978 it publicly expressed its support for the Albanian Communist Party in its break with the post-Maoist Chinese leadership. It also won 2 Chamber seats in 1986.

Leaders: João AMAZONAS (President), Diógenes de Arruda CÂMARA, Renato RABELO.

Three additional parties currently hold congressional seats: the **Liberal Party** (*Partido Liberal* — PL), the **Christian Democratic Party** (*Partido Democrata Cristão* — PDC), and the **Brazilian Socialist Party** (*Partido Socialista Brasileiro* — PSB).

LEGISLATURE

The bicameral **National Congress** (*Congresso Nacional*) consists of a Senate and a Chamber of Deputies, both of which are directly elected by universal suffrage. The two houses, sitting together, form a Constituent Assembly for purposes of constitutional revision.

Senate (*Senado*). The upper house currently consists of 72 members (3 for each state, plus 1 for each territory) elected for eight-year terms, with one-third and two-thirds, respectively, named every four years. Following the election of two-thirds on November 15, 1986, the Party of the Brazilian Democratic Movement held 44 seats; the Liberal Front Party, 16; the Social Democratic Party, 5; the Democratic Labor Party, 2; the Brazilian Socialist Party, 2; and the Christian Democratic Party, the Liberal Party, and the Brazilian Labor Party, 1 each.

President: Humberto LUCENA.

Chamber of Deputies (*Câmara dos Deputados*). Seats in the lower house are allocated on a population basis, save for the territories, each of which is entitled to one deputy. There are presently 487 members serving four-year terms. At the election of November 15, 1986, the Party of the Brazilian Democratic Movement won 259 seats; the Liberal Front Party, 115; the Social Democratic Party, 36; the Democratic Labor Party, 24; the Workers' Party, 19; the Brazilian Labor Party, 19; the Liberal Party, 7; the Christian Democratic Party, 3; the Brazilian Communist Party, 2; the Communist Party of Brazil, 2; and the Brazilian Socialist Party, 1.

President: Ulisses GUIMARÃES.

CABINET

President	José Sarney Costa
Vice President	(Vacant)
Ministers	
Administration	Aluízio Alves More
Agriculture	Iris Rezende Machado
Air Force	Gen. Octávio Júlio Moreira Lima
Army	Gen. (Ret.) Leónidas Pires Gonçalves
Communications	Antônio Carlos Magalhães
Culture	Celso Monteiro Furtado
Education	Hugo Napaleão do Rego Neto
Finance	Mailson Ferreira da Nóbrega

Foreign Affairs	Roberto Costa de Abreu Sodré
Health	Dr. Luíz Carlos Borges da Silveira
Housing and Urban Affairs	Luíz Humberto Prisco Vianna
Industry and Trade	José Hugo Castelo Branco
Interior	João Alves
Irrigation Affairs	Vincente Fialho
Justice	Paulo Brossard de Souza Pinto
Labor	Almir Pazzianotto Pinto Urban
Land Reform and Development	Jader Fontenelle Barbalho
Mines and Energy	Dr. Antônio Aureliano Chaves de Mendoça
Navy	Adm. Henrique Saboia
Planning Secretariat of the Presidency	Aníbal Teixeira
Science and Technology	Luíz Henrique da Silveira
Transportation and Public Works	José Reinaldo Carneiro Tavares
Welfare and Social Security	Renato Archer Bayma da Silva
Chief, Civilian Household of the Presidency	Ronaldo Costa Couto
Chief, Military Household of the Presidency	Gen. Rubens Bayma Denys
Chief, National Intelligence Service	Gen. Ivan de Souza Mendes
President, Central Bank	Elmo de Arauio Camoës

NEWS MEDIA

Brazil has a vigorous and extensive news media network, which was subject to censorship, though somewhat relaxed after 1978, during the period of military rule. The present government announced the end of political constraints in March 1985.

Press. No Brazilian paper enjoys truly national distribution. The following are Portuguese-language dailies, unless otherwise noted: *O Globo* (Rio de Janeiro, 350,000), conservative; *O Dia* (Rio de Janeiro, 340,000), popular labor; *O Estado de São Paulo* (São Paulo, 230,000), independent; *Fôlha de São Paulo* (São Paulo, 215,000); *Jornal do Brasil* (Rio de Janeiro, 200,000), Catholic conservative; *Notícias Populares* (São Paulo, 145,000); *Ultima Hora* (Rio de Janeiro, 60,000); *Latin American Daily Post* (Rio de Janeiro, 36,000), only English-language daily; *Diário de Pernambuco* (Recife, 34,000), oldest paper in Latin America (founded 1825), independent; *Jornal de Brasília* (Brasília, 30,000).

News agencies. There are a number of domestic agencies, including *Agência Globo* and *Agência JB*, both headquartered at Rio de Janeiro; *Agência Estado* and *Agência Fôlhas*, headquartered at São Paulo; and *Agência ANDA* and *Empresa Brasileira de Notícias,* headquartered at Brasília. Numerous foreign agencies also maintain bureaus at Brasília, Rio de Janeiro, and São Paulo.

Radio and television. The government's National Telecommunications Department (*Departamento Nacional de Telecomunicações*) oversees television and radio broadcasting. Most of the radio stations are commercial, but several are owned by the government or the Catholic Church. Commercial broadcasting is organized into a national association, *Associação Brasileira de Emissoras de Rádio e Televisão*, and a number of regional groups. In 1986 there were approximately 50.5 million radio and 36.0 million television receivers.

INTERGOVERNMENTAL REPRESENTATION

Ambassador to the US: Marcilio Marques MOREIRA.

US Ambassador to Brazil: Harry W. SHLAUDEMAN.

Permanent Representative to the UN: Paulo NOGUEIRA-BATISTA.

IGO Memberships (Non-UN): ADF, AfDB, ALADI, Copal, CCC, Geplacea, IADB, ICAC, ICCAT, ICCO, ICO, IIC, Inmarsat, INRO, Intelsat, ISO, IWC, IWTC, OAS, OPANAL, PCA, SELA.

BRUNEI

Negara Brunei Darussalam

Political Status: Former constitutional monarchy in treaty relationship with the United Kingdom; independent sultanate proclaimed January 1, 1984.

Area: 2,226 sq. mi. (5,765 sq. km.).

Population: 193,832 (1981C), 246,500 (1988E).

Major Urban Centers (1986E): BANDAR SERI BEGAWAN (69,000), Seria (26,000).

Official Language: Malay (English is widely used).

Monetary Unit: Brunei Dollar (official rate March 1, 1988, 2.01 dollars = $1US).

Head of State and Prime Minister: Sultan Muda HASSANAL BOLKIAH Mu'izzaddin Waddaulah; ascended the throne October 5, 1967, upon the abdication of his father, Sultan Omar ALI SAIFUDDIN; crowned August 1, 1968; assumed office of Prime Minister at independence, succeeding former Chief Minister Pehin Dato Haji ABDUL AZIZ bin Umar.

THE COUNTRY

Brunei consists of two infertile jungle enclaves on the north coast of Borneo. About 60 percent of its population is Malay; the remainder is composed of other indigenous tribes and of Chinese, many of whom are merchants and traders. Malay is the official language, but the use of English is widespread. A majority of the inhabitants follow Islam, the official religion; smaller groups are Buddhist, Confucian, Christian, and pagan.

Brunei's per capita income, approximately $20,000 in 1986, is one of the highest in the world. Its wealth is derived from royalties on oil produced by Brunei Shell Petroleum and Brunei Shell Marketing, in both of which the government now holds a 50 percent interest, and on liquefied natural gas produced by Brunei LNG, in which the government, Shell, and Mitsubishi of Japan hold equal shares. Brunei's balance of trade is consistently favorable, and government revenue typically exceeds expenditure, with some of the surplus being used to finance improvements in roads, schools, and other public services; to augment the country's already large overseas investments; and to reduce dependence on imported food by augmenting agricultural output.

Despite constitutional restrictions upon ethnic Chinese citizenship, very little emigration took place after independence. Nonetheless, with an eye to eventually eliminating the need for all "foreign" labor, the government has placed special emphasis on raising Malay literacy and technical education. In addition, concern over reduced oil revenue has led the government to accelerate economic diversification efforts, particularly the exploitation of silica for a microchip and optics industry.

GOVERNMENT AND POLITICS

Political background. Brunei became a British protectorate in 1888 and was administered from 1906 to 1959 by a British resident. Sultan Omar ALI SAIFUDDIN, twenty-eighth in a line of hereditary rulers dating from the fifteenth century, promulgated Brunei's first written constitution in 1959, creating a framework for internal self-government while retaining British responsibility for defense and external affairs. At balloting in August-September 1962, all 10 elective seats in a 21-member Legislative Council were won by the left-wing Brunei People's Party (PRB), led by A.M.N. AZAHARI, which sought a unitary state that would include the adjacent British territories of North Borneo (subsequently Sabah) and Sarawak. In December a rebellion was launched by the PRB-backed North Borneo Liberation Army which, with Indonesian support, proclaimed a "revolutionary State of North Kalimantan". However, the revolt was quickly suppressed, Azahari being granted political asylum by Malaya.

A plan to join the Federation of Malaysia was accepted by the sultan during preliminary talks in 1963 but was subsequently rejected because of disagreements regarding Brunei's position within the Federation and the division of its oil royalties. Following talks with the British Commonwealth secretary in 1964, the sultan introduced constitutional reforms to allow a limited form of ministerial government, and a new general election was held in March 1965. Britain continued to press for a more representative government, however, and on October 4, 1967, the sultan, personally unwilling to accept further change, abdicated in favor of his 22-year-old son, Crown Prince HASSANAL BOLKIAH, who was crowned on August 1, 1968.

In early 1970, the constitution was suspended and the Legislative Council was reconstituted as an entirely appointive body, the sultan subsequently ruling primarily by decree. In 1971 renegotiated arrangements with Great Britain gave the sultan full responsibility for internal order but left the British with responsibility for external affairs, while an agreement on formal independence, concluded at London on June 30, 1978, following 12 days of discussions between the UK government and Sultan Hassanal Bolkiah (who was assisted by his father), specified that Britain's responsibilities for Brunei's defense and foreign affairs would terminate at the end of 1983. Formal treaty signing on January 7, 1979, came only after Indonesia and Malaysia had given assurances that Brunei's sovereignty would be respected, that the sultan's opponents would not be allowed to maintain guerrilla bases in either country, and that both would support ASEAN membership for Brunei.

On January 1, 1984, after proclaiming independence, the sultan assumed the office of prime minister and announced a cabinet dominated by the royal family; official ceremonies marking independence were subsequently held on February 23.

Constitution and government. Many provisions of the 1959 constitution have been suspended since 1962; others were effectively superseded upon independence. Under its terms, the sultan, as head of state, presides over a Council of Ministers and is advised by a Legislative Council, a Privy Council to deal in part with constitutional issues, and a Religious Council; it also provides for a Council of Succession. At present, the cabinet is composed chiefly of members of the royal family, while the Legislative Council, to which a portion of the membership was elected in 1962 and 1965, is (as originally projected in 1959) wholly appointive. The judicial system includes a High Court, a Court of Appeal, and magistrates' courts; there are also religious courts from which the Religious Council hears appeals.

For administrative purposes Brunei is divided into four districts, each headed by a district officer responsible to the sultan. District councils with a minority of elected members advise the district officers on local affairs.

At independence only ethnic Malays were accorded an unchallenged right to Bruneian citizenship; Chinese residents, theretofore protected by Bruneian-British passports, could acquire similar status only after 20 years' residence and passage of a stringent Malay language test.

Foreign relations. The future status of British Army Gurkhas became a major policy issue during the independence negotiations. A series of lengthy discussions culminated inconclusively at London in April 1983 because of the sultan's insistence that the troops be placed under his command. British representatives, however, argued that this would pave the way for the troops to be used as internal security forces in the advent of opposition activities, while neighboring states expressed concern about the prospect of a "mercenary" army in the region. In September it was agreed that the troops would remain under British command for a five-year period, their only function being to protect the gas and oil fields, and would be available for duty in Hong Kong, if so needed. Earlier, in July, the sultan announced that Britain's Crown Agents would no longer manage the bulk of Brunei's investment portfolio rumored to be worth $4.58 billion, the securities being turned over to the newly established Brunei Investment Agency, which acts on advice from American and Japanese firms. In early 1985, on the other hand, there were reports that Sir Hassanal had transferred large sums of money to Britain to help shore up the declining pound sterling.

Relations with Indonesia and Malaysia were long marred by territorial claims and support offered to the sultan's political opponents. In addition, Malaysia regularly called upon Britain to "decolonize" Brunei and backed UN resolutions pressuring London to sponsor UN-supervised elections in the sultanate. Brunei, meanwhile, continued to claim sovereignty over Limbang, the area of Sarawak separating the nation's two regions. Following the selection of Hussein bin Onn as Malaysian prime minister in 1976, however, relations between the neighbors improved, and, in July 1980, Hassanal Bolkiah paid the first official visit by a sultan to Malaysia in 17 years. In October

1984 he met at Jakarta with Indonesian President Suharto who asserted that his government had no territorial ambitions in regard to the sultanate.

Upon independence, Brunei became a member of the Commonwealth and in January 1984 joined ASEAN as its sixth member. Soon after, it was admitted to the Islamic Conference, where the sultanate has been a vocal supporter of the Palestine Liberation Organization. In September 1984 it became the 159th member of the United Nations.

Current issues. As it entered its fourth year of independence, Brunei remained largely unchanged from the days of colonial rule. There was little evidence of social unrest, although power continued to be concentrated in the royal family. Two previously government-sanctioned parties, neither construed as a serious challenge to royal prerogative, had reportedly ceased to exist by early 1988 (see Political Parties, below).

In late 1986 a major financial scandal erupted with the failure of the National Bank of Brunei, which had been controlled by Malaysian financial tycoon Tan Sri KHOO Teck Puat. However, Khoo, an Australian permanent resident, remained beyond the immediate reach of Brunei authorities and the numerous charges lodged against him in the year following the bank's collapse served largely as testimony to weakness in the sultanate's long-outmoded banking and company laws.

POLITICAL PARTIES

Political parties were essentially moribund for most of the quarter century after the failed 1962 rebellion. A Brunei People's Independence Front (*Barisan Kemerdeka'an Ra'ayat*—Baker), formed in 1966 by amalgamation of a number of earlier groups, was deregistered because of inactivity in early 1985; a Brunei People's National United Party (*Partai Perpaduan Kebangsa'an Ra'ayat Brunei*—Perkera), founded in 1968, also appeared to be no longer functioning. Despite the absence of an electoral process, the following two parties were accorded legal recognition in 1985 and 1986, respectively: the Brunei National Democratic Party (*Partai Kebangsa'an Demokratik Brunei*—PKDB), a moderate Islamic group led by Haji Abdul LATIF Chuchu; and the Brunei National United Party (*Partai Perpaduan Kebangsa'an Brunei*—PPKB), a late 1985 offshoot of the PKDP led by Hatta Haji ZAINAL Abiddin. However, in early 1988 the *Far Eastern Economic Review* reported that the government had dissolved the PKDP, there being, at the time, "no other political parties". Reportedly, the PKDP had called upon the sultan to step down as prime minister, lift the 26-year-old state of emergency, and hold nationwide elections.

Exile Formation:

Brunei People's Party (*Partai Ra'ayat Brunei*—PRB). Formerly a legal party that was deeply involved in the 1962 insurgency, the PRB has since been supported by a somewhat shadowy membership of about 100 individuals, most of them living as exiles in Indonesia or Malaysia. In April 1986, the government released seven PRB detainees, six of whom had been held without trial since 1966.

LEGISLATURE

The **Legislative Council** (*Majlis Meshuarat Negeri*) is, at present, a wholly nonelective body of 21 members, 6 ex officio, 5 "official" (public office holders), and 10 nominated (individuals who do not hold public office).

CABINET

Prime Minister	Sultan Hassanal Bolkiah
Ministers	
Communication	Pehin Dato Haji Abdul Aziz bin Umar
Culture, Youth and Sports	Pehin Dato Haji Hussein
Defense	Sultan Hassanal Bolkiah
Development	Pengiran Dr. Ismail
Education	Pehin Dato Abdul Rahman bin Taib
Finance	Prince Jefri Bolkiah
Foreign Affairs	Prince Mohamed Bolkiah
Health	Dato Dr. Haji Nordin Johar
Internal Affairs	Pehin Dato Haji Isa bin Ibrahim
Law	Pengiran Bahrin bin Abbas
Religious Affairs	Pehin Dato Haji Mohamad Zain

NEWS MEDIA

Press. The following newspapers are published in Brunei: *Pelita Brunei* (Bandar Seri Begawan, 45,000), weekly in Romanized Malay; *Borneo Bulletin* (Kuala Belait, 36,000), progovernment weekly, in English; *Salam* (Seria, 9,000), fortnightly, in English, Chinese, and Romanized Malay, published by the Brunei Shell Petroleum Co., Ltd.

Radio and television. The government-controlled Radio and Television Brunei, with broadcasts in Malay, English, Chinese, and local dialects, transmitted to approximately 75,000 radio and 48,000 television receivers in 1987.

INTERGOVERNMENTAL REPRESENTATION

Ambassador to the US: Dato Paduka Haji MOHD SUNI bin Haji Idris.

US Ambassador to Brunei Darussalam: Thomas C. FERGUSON.

Permanent Representative to the UN: Awang Haji JAYA bin Abdul Latif.

IGO Memberships (Non-UN): ASEAN, CWTH, IC, Interpol.

BULGARIA

People's Republic of Bulgaria
Narodna Republika Bŭlgariya

Political Status: Communist People's Republic established December 4, 1947; present constitution promulgated May 18, 1971.

Area: 42,823 sq. mi. (110,912 sq. km.).

Population: 8,942,976 (1985C), 9,009,000 (1988E). The results of the 1985 census are preliminary.

Major Urban Centers (1983E): SOFIA (1,069,900); Plovdiv (372,000); Varna (300,000); Bourgas (182,000); Roussé (180,000).

Official Language: Bulgarian.

Monetary Unit: Lev (noncommercial rate February 1, 1988, 1 lev = $1.31US).

President of the State Council and General Secretary of the Communist Party: Todor ZHIVKOV; served as Chairman of the Council of Ministers from 1962 to 1971; elected President of the State Council by the National Assembly on July 7, 1971; reelected by the Assembly in 1976, 1981, and on June 17, 1986; named First Secretary of the Communist Party on March 8, 1954; designated General Secretary on April 4, 1981; redesignated on April 5, 1986.

Chairman of the Council of Ministers (Premier): Georgi Ivanov ATANASOV; named on March 21, 1986, to succeed Georgi (Grisha) Stanchev FILIPOV; reappointed on June 17.

THE COUNTRY

Extending southward from the Danube and westward from the Black Sea, Bulgaria occupies a key position in the eastern Balkans adjacent to Romania, Yugoslavia, Greece, and Turkey. Like Greece and Yugoslavia, the country includes portions of historic Macedonia, and tensions with neighboring states have long existed because of the Bulgarian tendency to consider all Slavic-speaking Macedonians as ethnic Bulgarians; more than 88 percent of Bulgaria's population is so classified, with a sizable minority (about 9 percent) of Turks and scattered groups of gypsies and Romanians. The predominant language is Bulgarian, a component of the southern Slavic language group. Religious observances are discouraged, but the principal faith remains that of the Bulgarian Orthodox Church, with small percentages of other Christians, Muslims, and Jews.

Traditionally an agricultural country, Bulgaria has industrialized since World War II under a series of five-year plans; as a result, machine building, ferrous and nonferrous metallurgy, textile manufacturing, and agricultural processing have grown in importance. In 1979, following the example of Hungary, the government introduced a "New Economic Mechanism" (NEM) in agriculture that was extended the following year to industry, transport, and tourism. A distinct departure from the Soviet model of economic organization, which had been rigorously followed for over a decade, the NEM has emphasized decentralized decisionmaking, accountability on the part of state enterprises, and the gradual elimination of subsidies for non-self-supporting operations. Early results of the policy were encouraging, with industrial output increasing by more than 4 percent in both 1982 and 1983, although major reverses in 1985 contributed to a series of structural economic reforms in early 1986, most of which were themselves substantially revised in late 1987 (see Political background and Current issues, below). Bulgaria

remains highly dependent upon the Soviet Union which takes 60 percent of its exports, with another 20 percent going to other members of the Council for Mutual Economic Assistance (CMEA).

GOVERNMENT AND POLITICS

Political background. Bulgarian kingdoms existed in the Balkan Peninsula during the Middle Ages, but the Ottoman Turks ruled the area for 500 years prior to the Russo-Turkish War of 1877–1878, and full independence was achieved only with the proclamation of the Bulgarian Kingdom in 1908. Long-standing territorial ambitions led to Bulgarian participation on the losing side in the Second Balkan War and in both world wars. Talks aimed at Bulgaria's withdrawal from World War II were interrupted on September 5, 1944, by a Soviet declaration of war, followed by the establishment four days later of a Communist-inspired "Fatherland Front" government. The monarchy was rejected by a 92 percent majority in a referendum held September 8, 1946, and a "People's Republic" was formally established on December 4, 1947, under the premiership of the "father of Bulgarian Communism", Georgi DIMITROV, who died in 1949. Communist rule was consolidated under the successive leadership of Vulko CHERVENKOV and Anton YUGOV. Since 1954, Todor ZHIVKOV, occupying various positions within the government and party hierarchies, has maintained his status as Bulgaria's leader while continuing the pro-Soviet policies instituted by his predecessors.

In the wake of what reporters termed "an unusual absence of warmth" between Zhivkov and Soviet party chief Gorbachev during a meeting at Belgrade in October 1985, there were rumors that the 74-year-old Bulgarian leader might step down at the Thirteenth Party Congress in April 1986. Instead, Zhivkov embarked on a major "rejuvenation" of leading government and party posts, beginning in late January. Two older Politburo members were dropped and Georgi ATANASOV, theretofore a candidate member, was elevated to full status and named to succeed Georgi FILIPOV as premier on March 21. Subsequently, a number of economic ministries were abolished and replaced by government corporations reporting to an umbrella Council for Economic Affairs; less than two years later, the Economic Council and three sister "superministries", together with several other bodies (including the State Planning Commission), were scrapped in an even more drastic reorganization (see Current issues, below).

Constitution and government. Under the 1971 constitution the Presidium of the National Assembly was replaced by a Council of State, most of whose members are drawn from the Communist Party. The present Council president is party general secretary Todor Zhivkov, who thus holds the highest position in both state and party organizations. Legislative authority is vested in the National Assembly, which sits for a five-year term and nominally elects the Council of State and the Council of Ministers. The Assembly meets at least three times a year but serves primarily to ratify decisions made by other state and party bodies.

The judicial system is headed by a Supreme Court and a chief prosecutor (attorney general). Charged with governing the behavior of all lower courts, the Supreme Court is elected by the National Assembly; local courts include lay assessors as well as judges. The chief prosecutor, elected by the National Assembly for a five-year term, is responsible for ensuring the lawful behavior of all citizens, including government officials, and appoints and discharges all other prosecutors.

In August 1987 the National Assembly appeared to pave the way for constitutional revision by endorsing a number of changes that included the substitution of 9 provinces for the previous 28 districts as the basic units of regional administration. At the local level there are 283 municipal units and some 4,000 towns and villages.

Foreign relations. Bulgaria's close alignment with the Soviet Union in foreign policy reflects not only the two countries' economic and ideological ties but also a traditional friendship stemming from Russian assistance in Bulgarian independence struggles. Fidelity to Soviet policy has characterized Bulgarian participation in the United Nations, the CMEA, and the Warsaw Treaty Organization. Indicatively, its ambassador to the USSR is accorded ministerial status. In January 1977 Bulgaria's network of relations with West European governments was completed by an exchange of ambassadors with post-Franco Spain. While shunning contact with Beijing, Sofia has pursued close relations with North Korea, as evidenced by a visit to Bulgaria by Kim Il Sung in July 1984. Relations with Third World nations include strong trade links with Ethiopia, Libya, Nigeria, and South Yemen.

Bulgarian relations with Yugoslavia have been periodically complicated by a contention that all Macedonians (including those resident in Yugoslavia) are ethnically Bulgarian. Relations with Albania and Greece have improved in recent years, with President Zhivkov calling in 1979 for full normalization of relations with Tirana and agreeing, during an April visit to Corfu, to participate in multilateral Balkan discussions on specific issues. Since 1982, Zhivkov has received support from Greece, Romania, Turkey, and Yugoslavia for the concept of a Balkan "nuclear-free zone", which was discussed during a meeting at Athens in early 1984. Bulgarian-Turkish relations have fluctuated. Although under a ten-year agreement (1968–1978) Bulgaria permitted over 100,000 ethnic Turks to emigrate, recent efforts toward assimilation of ethnic Turks (reportedly including the forced adoption of Bulgarian names) have generated pronounced tensions with Ankara. In early 1985, Turkey's ambassador to Sofia was recalled for consultation, while Prime Minister Turgut Özal offered to reopen its borders to as many as 500,000 new immigrants. Sofia's official position was a scathing rejection of all "Turkish accusations", calling the Bulgarian Turks "a fictitious minority" and claiming that the name changes were merely those of Bulgarians voluntarily reversing a process mandated during Ottoman rule.

Current issues. The extensive ministerial restructuring undertaken during the first half of 1986 came in the wake of highly adverse weather conditions in 1985 that contributed to a severe shortfall in plan fulfillment for the year and pointed up what were described as "failures in economic management and too much caution" in implementing the 1979 NEM. In May the National Assembly approved a series of measures intended to "totally liquidate the departmental structure and departmental work" of the government. Under the reform, four new bodies were established within the Council of Ministers: an Economic Council, an Agriculture and Forestry Council, a Social Council, and a Council for Intellectual Development.

After a period of apparent hesitation following Mikhail Gorbachev's accession to power in the Soviet Union, President Zhivkov, acknowledging that the party had become "uncontrollably omnipotent" in some spheres, proposed an even more comprehensive restructuring in July 1987 that entailed abolition of the recently established Councils in favor of economic "self-management". Under the new plan, industrial enterprises would be accorded broad discretion in regard to production, sales, revenue distribution, and local management. Central planning would continue, but the State Planning Commission (as well as state committees for prices, social and labor affairs, and science) would be dropped and the acceptance of plan requirements would be voluntary. Implementation of the program was to have been discussed at an extraordinary party conference in December. However, in October President Zhivkov was summoned to Moscow for talks with General Secretary Gorbachev, amid indications that the Soviets were alarmed at the projected pace of the reforms. Subsequent to Zhivkov's return, the Bulgarian press noticeably toned down its references to *perestroistvo* (the Bulgarian equivalent of the Russian *perestroika,* or "restructuring") and the party conference that eventually met on January 28–29, 1988 (its raison d'être apparently having been rescinded), confined itself to endorsement of the party's "leading role" in providing for change, with no specifics being advanced.

POLITICAL PARTIES

Bulgaria's only authorized political parties, the Bulgarian Communist Party and the Bulgarian National Agrarian Union, form the backbone of the **Fatherland Front** (*Otechestven Front*), a Communist-controlled mass organization that also includes the trade unions, the Communist youth movement, and individual citizens. Chairman of the Fatherland Front's National Council is Pencho KUBADINSKI.

Bulgarian Communist Party (*Bulgarska Komunisticheska Partiya*— BKP). The Bulgarian Communist Party traces its origins to an ideological split in the old Social Democratic Party. In 1903 the radicals split to form the Bulgarian Workers' Social Democratic Party, which became the Communist Party in 1919. Party congresses meet every five years to elect a Central Committee, which in turn elects the party's highest executive bodies. The Politburo, which has fluctuated in size since the Eleventh Party Congress in 1976, became an 11-member body (exclusive of candidates) at the Thirteenth Congress, held at Sofia on April 2–5, 1986.

General Secretary: Todor ZHIVKOV (Chairman, State Council).

Other Members of Politburo: Chudomir ALEKSANDROV (Secretary, Central Committee), Georgi ATANASOV (Premier), Milko BALEV (Secretary, Central Committee), Ognyan DOINOV (Deputy Premier), Gen. Dobri DZHUROV (Defense Minister), Georgi (Grisha) FILIPOV (Secretary, Central Committee), Pencho KUBADINSKI (Member, State Council), Petur MLADENOV (Foreign Minister), Stanko TODOROV (Chairman, National Assembly), Yordan YOTOV (Secretary, Central Committee).

Candidates: Petur DYULGEROV, Andrei LUKANOV, Stoyan MARKOV, Grigor STOICHKOV, Lt. Gen. Dimitur STOYANOV, Georgi YORDANOV.

Central Committee Secretariat: Chudomir ALEKSANDROV, Milko BALEV, Georgi (Grisha) FILIPOV, Emil KHRISTOV, Stoyan MI-KHAILOV, Dimitur STANISHEV, Vasil TSANOV, Yordan YOTOV, Kiril ZAREV, Todor ZHIVKOV.

Bulgarian Agrarian People's Union (*Bulgarski Zemedelski Naroden Soyuz*—BZNS). A rump of Bulgaria's prewar agrarian party with a membership of approximately 120,000, the BZNS is allowed pro forma representation in the government but does not compete with the BKP. In September 1984, BZNS was the official sponsor of an International Peace Meeting at Sofia, attended by 76 left-wing parties from 45 countries.
Secretary: Nicolai GEORGIYEV.

LEGISLATURE

The **National Assembly** (*Narodno Sobranie*) is a unicameral body of 400 members last elected June 8, 1986, from the Fatherland Front ticket for a five-year term. The Bulgarian Communist Party obtained 276 seats; the Bulgarian National Agrarian Union, 99; and nonparty elements, 25.
Chairman: Stanko TODOROV.

CABINET

Chairman, Council of Ministers (Premier)	Georgi Ivanov Atanasov
Deputy Chairman	Grigor Georgiev Stoichkov
Ministers	
Agriculture and Forestry	Aleksi Ivanov
Culture, Science and Education	Georgi Momchev Yordanov
Economics and Planning	Stoyan Kostov Ovcharov
Foreign Affairs	Petur Toshev Mladenov
Foreign Economic Relations	Andrey Karlov Lukanov
Internal Affairs	Col. Gen. Dimitur Ivanov Stoyanov
Justice	Svetla Raykova Daskalova
National Defense	Gen. Dobri Marinov Dzhurov
Public Health and Social Welfare	Radoy Petrov Popivanov
Transportation	Vasil Ivanov Tsanov
Minister Extraordinary and Ambassador Plenipotentiary to USSR	Georgi Tsankov Pankov
Chairman, State and People's Control Committee	Georgi Dimitrov Georgiev
Chairman, Bulgarian National Bank	Vasil Georgiev Kolarov

NEWS MEDIA

All information media belong to the government or its supporting organizations and are used to further official policy.

Press. The following are dailies published at Sofia: *Rabotnichesko Delo* (850,000), organ of the Central Committee of the BKP; *Trud* (300,000), organ of the trade unions; *Otechestven Front* (280,000), organ of the Fatherland Front; *Narodna Mladezh* (250,000), organ of the Youth Union; *Kooperativno Selo* (190,000), published by the Ministry of Agriculture; *Zemedelsko Zname* (165,000), organ of the BZNS; *Vecherni Novini* (125,000), organ of the Sofia People's and District Front committees; *Narodna Armiya* (55,000), published by the Ministry of Defense.

News agencies. The official facility is the Bulgarian Telegraph Agency (*Bŭlgarska Telegrafna Agentsiya*—BTA). A number of foreign agencies, including *Agence France-Presse* and Reuters, maintain offices at Sofia.

Radio and television. Radio and television are controlled by the Committee for Television and Radio of the Committee for Culture of

the Council of Ministers. Bulgarian Television transmits over ten main stations, while Bulgarian Radio offers four domestic programs and broadcasts internationally in twelve languages. In 1987 there were approximately 2.5 million radio and 2.2 million television receivers.

INTERGOVERNMENTAL REPRESENTATION

Ambassador to the US: Stoyan Iliev ZHULEV.

US Ambassador to Bulgaria: Sol POLANSKY.

Permanent Representative to the UN: Alexander STREZOV.

IGO Memberships (Non-UN): BIS, CCC, CMEA, IBEC, ICCO, IIB, ILZ, Inmarsat, ISO, PCA, WTO.

BURKINA FASO

Political Status: Became independent as the Republic of Upper Volta on August 5, 1960; under largely military rule 1966–1978; constitution of November 27, 1977, suspended upon military coup of November 25, 1980; present name adopted August 4, 1984.

Area: 105,869 sq. mi. (274,200 sq. km.).

Population: 7,976,019 (1985C), 8,625,000 (1988E).

Major Urban Centers (1985C): OUAGADOUGOU (442,223); Bobo-Dioulasso (231,162).

Official Language: French.

Monetary Unit: CFA Franc (market rate March 1, 1988, 285.80 francs = $1US).

Chairman of the Popular Front, Head of State, and Head of Government: Capt. Blaise COMPAORE, leader of military coup that overthrew the former President of the Republic and Chairman of the National Revolutionary Council, Cdr. Thomas SANKARA, on October 15, 1987.

THE COUNTRY

A land of arid savannas drained by the Mouhoun (Black), Napinon (Red), and Nakambe (White) Volta rivers, Burkina Faso occupies a bufferlike position between the landlocked states of Mali and Niger on the west, north, and east, and the coastal lands of Côte d'Ivoire, Ghana, Togo, and Benin on the south. The most prominent of its numerous African population groups is the Mossi, which encompasses almost two-thirds of the population and has dominated much of the country for centuries. Other tribal groups include the Bobo, most of whom are settled around the western city of Bobo-Dioulasso, and the Samo. Mossi resistance to outside influence has contributed to the retention of tribal religion by a majority of the population, while 20 percent has embraced Islam and 10 percent, Christianity. Women have traditionally constituted over half the labor force, producing most of the food crops, with men responsible for cash crops. While customary law has been described as "unfavorable" to female property and political rights, the Sankara government appointed a number of women to ministerial and other politically influential posts.

The former Upper Volta is one of the poorest countries in Africa, with an average per capita income estimated at $140 in 1985 and over 80 percent of the population engaged in subsistence agriculture. While most agricultural products are consumed domestically, cotton, karité nuts, livestock, and peanuts are exported. Mineral deposits, mainly manganese, remain largely unexploited due to a lack of transportation facilities. Industry, consisting mainly of the production of textiles and processed agricultural goods, makes only a small contribution to the GNP. Drought cut deeply into food production, creating a cereal deficit of over 300,000 tons and prompting the establishment of the first Ministry of Water Resources in Africa in 1984; however, good harvests in 1985 and in 1986 returned the country to self-sufficiency in grain production.

GOVERNMENT AND POLITICS

Political background. Under French control since 1896, the country established its separate identity in March 1959, when it became an autonomous state of the French Community under Maurice YAMEOGO of the Voltaic Democratic Union (UDV), a political disciple of President Félix Houphouët-Boigny of the Côte d'Ivoire. Under Yaméogo's leadership, Upper Volta became fully independent on August 5, 1960. Though reelected for a second term by an overwhelming majority in 1965, Yaméogo was unable to cope with mounting student and labor dissatisfaction and was compelled to resign in January 1966. Lt. Col. Sangoulé LAMIZANA, the army chief of staff, immediately assumed the presidency and instituted a military regime.

Faithful to his promise to restore constitutional government within four years, Lamizana submitted a new constitution for popular approval in December 1970 and sponsored a legislative election in which the UDV regained its pre-1966 majority. Gérard Kango OUEDRAOGO was invested as prime minister by the National Assembly in February 1971, while Lamizana was retained as chief executive for a four-year transitional period, after which the president was to be popularly elected. On February 8, 1974, however, the army, under General Lamizana, again seized control to prevent the political rehabilitation of ex-president Yaméogo. Declaring that the takeover was aimed at saving the country from the threat of squabbling politicians, Lamizana suspended the 1970 constitution, dissolved the National Assembly, and dismissed the cabinet. A new government was formed on February 11, with Lamizana continuing as president and assuming the office of prime minister.

In the wake of a ministerial reorganization in January 1977, the president announced that a constitutional referendum would take place by midyear, followed by legislative and presidential elections at which he would not stand as a candidate. The referendum was held November 27, with a reported 97.75 percent of the voters endorsing a return to democratic rule. Lamizana reversed himself, however, and announced his candidacy for the presidency in 1978. Rejecting an appeal by three opponents on April 13 that he abandon his military rank and campaign as a civilian, Lamizana retained his office at a runoff election on May 29 after having obtained a plurality at first-round balloting on May 14. Earlier, on April 30, the regime-supportive UDV-RDA (see Political Parties, below) obtained a near-majority in a reconstituted National Assembly, which on July 7 designated Dr. Joseph Issoufou CONOMBO as prime minister.

Despite restrictions imposed on all but the leading political groups, Upper Volta remained only one of two multiparty democracies (the other being Senegal) in former French Africa until November 25, 1980, when the Lamizana regime was overthrown in a military coup led by former foreign minister Col. Sayé ZERBO. Officials of the ousted government, including the president and the prime minister, were placed under arrest, while a Military Committee of Recovery for National Progress (*Comité Militaire de Redressement pour le Progrès National* — CMRPN) suspended the constitution, dissolved the legislature, and banned political activity. A transitional cabinet of civil servants was named by the Committee and served until a 17-member Council of Ministers headed by Colonel Zerbo as both president and prime minister was announced on December 7.

Accusing Zerbo of having "made the paramilitary forces an agent of terror", a group of noncommissioned officers mounted a coup on November 7, 1982, that installed Maj. Jean-Baptiste OUEDRAOGO, a former army medical officer, as head of what was termed the People's Salvation Council (*Conseil de Salut du Peuple* — CSP). On August 4, 1983, Ouédraogo was in turn overthrown in a brief rebellion led by (then) Capt. Thomas SANKARA, who had been named prime minister in January, only to be arrested, along with other allegedly pro-Libyan members of the CSP, in late May. Immediately after the August coup, Sankara announced the formation of a National Revolutionary Council (*Conseil National de la Révolution* — CNR) with himself as chairman. A year later, following two failed counter-coup attempts, the name of the country was changed to Burkina Faso, a vernacular blend meaning "democratic and republican land of upright men".

In the wake of a state visit by Col. Mu'ammar al-Qadhafi in December 1985, Cdr. Sankara declared that his country had "gone beyond the era of republics" and proclaimed the establishment of a Libyan-style "Jamahiriya" system aimed at linking national government policy to the wishes of the population as expressed through local people's committees.

Sankara was overthrown in yet another coup led by his second-in-command, Capt. Blaise Compaoré, on October 15, 1987. Charged with being a "madman", Sankara was executed the following day, along with 12 governmental associates. Faced with substantial domestic hostility, Compaoré pledged to continue the "people's revolution" as head of a new "Popular Front" that was nonetheless hailed as being of essentially moderate outlook by neighboring conservative regimes.

Constitution and government. The 1977 constitution, which was suspended in November 1980, called for a president and a National Assembly to be elected separately for five-year terms on the basis of a multiparty system. A period of uncertain military rule followed, yielding, in August 1985, a revised government structure intended to promote "the Burkinabe identity".

Under the new arrangement, President Sankara as head of the National Revolutionary Council (CNR), the supreme political body, assumed responsibility for the proclamation of laws (*zatu*) in accordance with "the will of the people". The "revolutionary executive" was placed under the supervision of a People's Commission, acting in concert with a Ministerial Administrative Committee, and a Ministerial Council. Within the villages, Revolutionary Defense Committees (*Comités pour la Défence Révolutionnaire* — CDR), which were established in the wake of the 1983 coup and took over the function of tax collection from local chiefs in 1984, were designated as the ultimate repositories of "popular and insurrectional power". Earlier, a judicial reorganization had been announced, under which Popular Revolutionary Tribunals (*Tribunaux Populaires de la Révolution* — TPR) were established under the jurisdiction of Appeals Courts at Ouagadougou and Bobo-Dioulasso. The precise status of these institutions remained unclear in the immediate wake of the 1987 coup, although Captain Compaoré was reported in March 1988 to have ordered the formation of new "Revolutionary Committees" to replace the former CDRs.

Administratively, the country is divided into 25 provinces, which are subdivided into departments, arrondisements, and villages.

Foreign relations. Upper Volta had consistently adhered to a moderately pro-French and pro-Western foreign policy while stressing the importance of good relations with neighboring countries; however, after the 1983 coup relations between Burkina Faso and France cooled, a result primarily of France's unease over Sankara's vigorous attempts to rid the country of all vestiges of its colonial past (made manifest by the 1984 change in country name, the adoption of radical policies modeled on those of Ghana and Libya, and the heavily publicized arrests of allegedly pro-French former government officials and trade unionists accused of plotting against the Sankara regime).

Subsequent relations with francophone neighbors remained hesitant, partly because of Sankara's blunt style in attacking perceived government corruption throughout the region and his strong ideological opinions. Fears, voiced most strongly by the Côte d'Ivoire, that Burkina Faso might become a Libyan satellite were, on the other hand, partially blunted by Ouagadougou's emphasizing its ties and proposed future union with Ghana.

On December 25, 1985, a 20-year-long controversy involving the so-called Agacher Strip at Burkina's northern border with Mali led to four days of fighting that left approximately 300 dead on both sides. However, a ruling from the International Court of Justice on December 22, 1986, that awarded the two countries roughly equal portions of the disputed territory, largely terminated the unrest. Relations with another neighbor, Togo, were strained in 1987 over expressed suspicion of Burkinabe complicity (heatedly denied) in a September 1986 coup attempt against President Eyadema.

The coup of October 1987 was manifestly welcomed by the region's most respected elder statesman, President Houphouët-Boigny of the Côte d'Ivoire, with whom Captain Compaoré had long enjoyed close personal relations; other observers agreed that the new Burkinabe regime would, in all likelihood, be less pro-Libyan and less anti-Western than its immediate predecessor.

Current issues. The overthrow of President Sankara yielded a distinctly mixed reaction within Burkina Faso. Widely hailed as a remarkably incorruptible leader who had striven to improve the status of rural dwellers in one of the world's poorest countries, he had alienated trade union leaders, the urban elite, and most civil servants by branding them "enemies of the revolution". He had attempted to outlaw polygamy and otherwise improve the status of women in an essentially male-dominated society and, during the latter period of his rule, had generated resentment by a number of policies such as requiring officials to wear uniforms of homemade cotton while donating their free time to public-service projects. Seemingly surprised by Sankara's charismatic legacy, Compaoré felt obliged to vilify his former colleague as one who had betrayed the ideals to which both had once been committed by an addiction to "bureaucratization, militarization, and the assertion of political power".

POLITICAL PARTIES

Formal party activity, proscribed by the military government in February 1974, was resanctioned in October 1977 pending the legislative election of April 30, 1978, after which only the three strongest parties were constitutionally permitted to sit in the National Assembly. More stringent legislation passed by the Assembly in May 1979 called for the dissolution of all but the three leading parties. Political party activity was again suspended following the 1980 coup, although several groups that were represented in the Sankara government at its inception have maintained a visible political identity.

Leftist Groups:

The most prominent of the still-vocal Marxist-Lenist groups is the Moscow-oriented **Patriotic League for Development** (*Ligue-Patriotique pour la Développement* — Lipad), some of whose members held ministerial portfolios until their ouster in August 1984. A number of Lipad leaders, including former foreign minister Arba DIALLO and trade unionist Soumane TOURE, have been detained on corruption charges. Although Diallo, like Touré, was subsequently released, Touré was arrested again in May of 1987 on charges of subversion. **The Union for Communist Struggle** (*Union de la Lutte Communiste* — ULC) appears to have recently undergone a split with the creation of a splinter group, the **Burkinabe Communist Union** (*Union des Communistes Burkinabe* — UCB), led by Clement OUEDRAOGO, which was rumored to have been created by the army as a way of checking on the activities of the ULC. Also tolerated by the Sankara government were the **Marxist-Leninist Union of Burkina** (*Union des Marxistes-Léninistes du Burkina* — UMLB) under Bamou Paulin BAMOUNI and the **Burkinabe Communist Group** (*Groupe Communiste Burkinabe* — GCB), a splinter of the banned **Voltaic Revolutionary Communist Party** (*Parti Communiste Revolutionnaire Voltaïque*). Leftist groups not associated with the regime included the pro-Albanian **Voltaic Revolutionary Communist Party** (*Parti Communiste Révolution-*

naire Voltaïque—PCRV) and remnants of Lipad's pan-African parent party, the **African Party for Independence** (*Parti Africain pour l'Indépendence*—PAI *Voltaïque*).

Other Groups:

Prior to the 1980 coup, the governing party was the Voltaic Democratic Union–African Democratic Rally (*Union Démocratique Voltaïque–Rassemblement Démocratique Africain*—UDV-RDA), an outgrowth of the Ivoirian RDA which won 28 seats in the 1978 National Assembly election and was led by Malo TRAORE and Gerard Kango OUEDRAOGO. In opposition were the National Union for the Defense of Democracy (*Union Nationale pour la Défense de la Démocratie*—UNDD), organized by Herman YAMEOGO, and the Voltaic Progressive Front (*Front Progressiste Voltaïque*—FPV), a socialist grouping led by Joseph KI-ZERBO that contained some former UDV-RDA dissidents, most significantly Joseph OUEDRAOGO. Most such individuals subsequently left the country, Ki-Zerbo having been accused of planning a coup against Sankara in May 1984. Following the coup of October 1987, followers of former president Sankara formed a clandestine resistance movement styled the **Democratic and Popular Rally–Thomas Sankara** (*Rassemblement Démocratique et Populaire–Thomas Sankara*).

LEGISLATURE

The unicameral National Assembly (*Assemblée Nationale*) was dissolved following the November 1980 coup.

CABINET

Head of Government	Capt. Blaise Compaoré
Ministers	
Agriculture and Livestock	Albert Guigma
Commerce and People's Supply	Frederic Assomption Korsaga
Economic Promotion	Capt. Henri Zongo
Environment and Tourism	Noelle Marie Béatrice Damiba
Equipment	Badiel Balao
External Relations	Jean-Marc Palm
Finance	Guy Some
Health and Social Affairs	Alaine Zoubga
Higher Education and Scientific Research	Clement Oumarou Ouédraogo
Hydrology	Alfred Nombre
Information and Culture	Serge Theophile Balima
Justice	Salif Sampebogo
Labor, Social Security and Civil Service	Albert D. Milogo
Mines	Jean Yado Toe
National Education	Philippe Some
Planning and Development	Youssouf Ouédraogo
Popular Defense and Security	Maj. Jean-Baptiste Boukari Lingani
Rural Development	Jean-Leonard Compaoré
Sports	Lt. Theodore Hien Kilimite
Territorial Administration	Leopold Ouédraogo
Transport and Communication	Dominique Issa Konate
Secretaries General	
Committees for the Defense of the Revolution	Capt. Arsene Bognessan Ye
Government and Council of Ministers	Prosper Vokouma
Secretaries of State	
Budget	Celestin Tiendrebeogo
Culture	Alimata Ouédraogo Salembere
Livestock	Amadou Diao
Social Affairs	Alice Tiendrebeogo
Governor, Central Bank	Boukary Ouédraogo

NEWS MEDIA

Press, radio, and television are owned and operated by the government.

Press. Under the present regime, there is a Written Press Board (*Direction de la Presse Ecrite*) charged with overseeing the media. The following are published at Ouagadougou: *Carrefour Africain* (6,000), published weekly by the government; *Sidwaya* (5,000), government daily; *Bulletin Quotidien d'Information* (1,500), published daily by the *Direction de la Presse Ecrite; Dunia,* daily; *Journal Officiel du Burkina,* government weekly. A new satirical newspaper, *L'Intrus,* was introduced by the government in mid-1987.

News agencies. *Agence Burkinabê de Presse* (AVP) is the domestic facility; *Agence France-Presse* and TASS maintain offices at Ouagadougou.

Radio and television. *Radiodiffusion-Télévision du Burkina* operates a number of radio and television stations, the latter concentrating on educational programming during the school year. There were approximately 120,000 radio and 41,500 television receivers in 1987.

INTERGOVERNMENTAL REPRESENTATION

Ambassador to the US: (Vacant).

US Ambassador to Burkina Faso: David H. SHINN.

Permanent Representative to the UN: Michel Monvel DAH.

IGO Memberships (Non-UN): ACCT, ADF, AfDB, BADEA, BOAD, CCC, CEAO, CENT, CILSS, ECOWAS, EEC(L), *EIB,* IC, IDB, Intelsat, Interpol, NAM, OAU, OCAM, PCA.

BURMA

Socialist Republic of the Union of Burma
Pyidaungsu Myanma Nainggan-Daw

Political Status: Independent republic established January 4, 1948; military-backed regime instituted March 2, 1962; present one-party constitution adopted January 4, 1974.

Area: 261,789 sq. mi. (678,033 sq. km.).

Population: 35,300,000 (1983C), 38,391,000 (1988E).

Major Urban Centers (1983E): RANGOON (2,459,000); Mandalay (533,000); Bassein (335,000); Moulmein (220,000).

Official Language: Burmese.

Monetary Unit: Kyat (market rate March 1, 1988, 6.32 kyats = $1US).

President of the Republic and Chairman of the State Council: U SAN YU; elected by the State Council and confirmed by the People's Assembly for a four-year term on November 9, 1981, following the resignation of U NE WIN; reconfirmed on November 4, 1985.

Vice President: U AYE KO; elected Secretary of the State Council for a four-year term on November 9, 1981; elected Vice President for a term concurrent with that of the President on November 4, 1985.

Prime Minister: U MAUNG MAUNG KHA; designated by the People's Assembly on March 29, 1977, succeeding U SEIN WIN; redesignated in 1978, 1981, and on November 4, 1985.

Chairman of the Burma Socialist Program Party: U NE WIN; assumed power as Chairman of the Revolutionary Council following military coup of March 2, 1962; leader of the BSPP since its formation on July 4, 1962; inaugurated as President of the Republic and Chairman of the State Council on March 2, 1974; redesignated on March 2, 1978; resigned the state positions as of November 9, 1981; most recently reconfirmed as BSPP Chairman at Party Congress of August 1-7, 1985.

THE COUNTRY

Burma is the largest country on the Southeast Asian mainland. Its extensive coastline runs along the Bay of Bengal and the Andaman Sea, while it shares a common border with Bangladesh and India in the west, China in the north, and Laos and Thailand in the east. Dominating the topography are tropical rain forests, plains, and mountains that range from 8,000 to 15,000 feet and rim the frontiers of the east, west, and north. Major rivers include the Irrawaddy, the Chindwin, and the Sittang; nearly three-quarters of the population is concentrated in the Irrawaddy basin in the south.

The dominant ethnic group is the Burman, which encompasses more than 70 percent of the inhabitants. The Karens (about 7 percent) are dispersed over southern and eastern Burma, while the Shans (6 percent), Thai in origin, are localized on the eastern plateau; Chins, Kachins, Mons, and Arakanese, totaling about one million, are found in the north and northeast. In addition, about 400,000 Chinese and 120,000 Indians and Bangladeshi are concentrated primarily in the urban areas. The various ethnic groups speak many languages and dialects, but the official Burmese, which is related to Tibeto-Chinese, is spoken by the vast majority. The use of English, long the second language of the educated elite, declined substantially after the 1962 coup, but is now being revived. About 85 percent of the population professes classical Buddhism (Theravada Buddhism), the state religion; minority religions include Islam, Christianity, Hinduism, and primitive animism. Less than 33 percent of women are in the official labour force, with a larger proportion estimated to be unpaid family workers; female representation in the military-dominated government is virtually nonexistent.

Although Burma is rich in largely unexploited mineral resources (including hydrocarbons, silver, zinc, copper, lead, nickel, antimony, tin, and tungsten), its economy, like that of most South Asian nations, is heavily dependent on agriculture. Rice, teak and other hardwoods, rubber, pulses, and cotton are among the country's exports, with agriprocessing the leading industry. Officially, most economic activity other than food production is conducted by state-owned enterprises, but routine shortfalls, stemming in part from bureaucratic inefficiency and corruption among public officials, have made black market trade the main source of consumer goods (largely smuggled in through border areas controlled by ethnic insurgents). There is also a thriving trade in opium, over half the world's supply of which is grown in the "Golden Triangle" at the juncture of Burma, Laos, and Thailand. Despite its wealth of resources, Burma remains a poor country with a per capita income of less than $190 per year and severe problems in health care, education, housing, and employment. Falling commodity prices since the early 1980s, especially for rice, and the government's long-standing antipathy to foreign investment have precipitated a current financial crisis marked by a nearly unmanageable external debt, the depletion of foreign exchange, and import constraints that have exacerbated the shortages of goods and spare parts for manufacturing.

GOVERNMENT AND POLITICS

Political background. Modern Burma was incorporated into British India as a result of the Anglo-Burmese wars of 1824–1886 but in 1937 was separated from India and granted limited self-government. During World War II, Japan occupied the country and gave it nominal independence under a puppet regime led by anti-British nationalists, who subsequently transferred their loyalties to the Allied war effort.

The Anti-Fascist People's Freedom League (AFPFL), a coalition of nationalist forces, emerged as the principal political organization in 1945. Under the AFPFL, various groups and regions joined to form the Union of Burma, which gained full independence from the British in January 1948 and for a decade maintained a parliamentary democracy headed by Prime Minister U NU. In May 1958 the AFPFL dissolved into factional groups, precipitating a political crisis that four months later forced U Nu to resign in favor of a caretaker government headed by Gen. NE WIN, commander in chief of the armed forces. Ne Win scheduled elections in February and March of 1960, and the U Nu faction of the AFPFL returned to power on April 4 under the name of the Union Party. However, growing differences within the party and problems of internal security, national unity, and economic development contributed to government ineffectiveness. As a result, Ne Win mounted a coup d'état in March 1962, organized a Revolutionary Council of senior army officers to run the government, and abolished the national legislature. A Burma Socialist Program Party (BSPP) was launched by the Council the following July. In January 1974, after 12 years of army rule, the Ne Win government adopted a new constitution and revived the legislature as a single-chambered People's Assembly.

At a special BSPP congress in October 1976, the party's general secretary, SAN YU, severely castigated his colleagues for the economic malaise that the country had long endured, and 16 leading party members, including Prime Minister U SEIN WIN and Deputy Prime Minister U LWIN, were denied reelection to the Central Committee in February 1977. On March 29 a new cabinet was organized with U MAUNG MAUNG KHA as prime minister, while a new People's Assembly was elected in January 1978.

At its inaugural session on March 2, the Assembly designated an enlarged State Council chaired by Ne Win, who was thereby reconfirmed as president, and approved a new cabinet headed by the incumbent prime minister.

In 1980, while continuing its military efforts to weaken the country's rebel groups, the Ne Win regime offered a general amnesty to political opponents as well as to Communist and ethnic insurgents (see Political Parties, below). Most notable among those taking advantage of the amnesty was the first leader of independent Burma, U Nu, who was permitted to return to Rangoon after 12 years of exile.

At the BSPP's fourth congress in August 1981, Ne Win announced his intention to resign as president while retaining his post as party chairman. Accordingly, a legislative election was held on October 4–18, the new Assembly approving San Yu as his successor on November 9. In a move evidently intended to demonstrate government continuity, Maung Maung Kha was reappointed prime minister on the same day.

San Yu's status as Ne Win's heir apparent was further enhanced at the party's fifth congress in August 1985 by appointment to the newly created post of BSPP vice chairman. On November 9, following pro forma legislative balloting a month earlier, the regime's third most powerful figure, party general secretary U AYE KO (already second in line to the presidency as secretary of the State Council) was formally designated vice president. Since both San Yu and U Aye Ko are former generals, continued military dominance of the government in the post-Ne Win period seems likely.

Constitution and government. The 1974 constitution was adopted with the stated objective of making Burma a "Socialist Republic" under one-party rule. It provides for a unicameral People's Assembly as the supreme organ of state authority, and for a State Council comprising 14 representatives from the country's major political subdivisions and 15 additional members (including the prime minister) elected from the Assembly. The Council and its chairman, who is also state president, serve four-year terms, concurrent with that of the Assembly. The prime minister is designated by the Council of Ministers, which is elected by the Assembly from its own membership, following nomination by the State Council. Government employees, including members of the armed forces, can stand for election to the Assembly and to the People's Councils at lower levels. The BSPP nominates the only institutionally backed candidates for popularly elected offices. Judicial, legal, and investigatory functions are supervised by Councils of People's Justices, People's Attorneys, and People's Inspectors, members of which are also elected by the Assembly from lists submitted by the State Council.

The country's principal political components are seven states (Arakan, Chin, Kachin, Karen, Kayah, Mon, Shan) and seven divisions (Irrawaddy, Magwe, Mandalay, Pegu, Rangoon, Sagaing, Tenasserim). The states and divisions are divided into townships, which are subdivided into urban wards and village tracts.

Foreign relations. Nonalignment has been the cornerstone of Burmese foreign policy since 1948, and the present regime's participation in most intergovernmental organization activity, including that of the United Nations and its Specialized Agencies, until quite recently, has been marginal. Following the Sixth Summit Conference of the Nonaligned Movement at Havana in September 1979, Burma announced its withdrawal from the group, indicating that it would consider participation in an alternative organization committed to "genuine nonalignment".

In 1949 Burma became the first non-Communist country to recognize the People's Republic of China, with which it shares a 1,200-mile border. The two signed a Treaty of Friendship and Mutual Nonaggression in 1960 following settlement of a long-standing border dispute. By 1967, however, leftist terrorism, aimed at instituting a Chinese-style "Cultural Revolution", was increasingly resented by the Burmese, and widespread riots broke out at Rangoon, causing a severe deterioration in Sino-Burmese relations. During 1970–1971 relations again improved and a suspended economic assistance agreement was revived. Another aid pact was concluded in July 1979, with a resultant increase in Chinese funding for Burmese industrial development. Subsequently, tension over support for the insurgent Burmese Communist Party (see Political Parties, below) decreased and in May 1985 Ne Win visited Beijing in his capacity as chairman of the BSPP, following a March visit to Rangoon by Chinese President Li Xiannian. Diplomatic relations with North Korea, on the other hand, were severed in late 1983, following a bomb attack at Rangoon which killed 17 South Koreans, including four cabinet ministers, two North Korean army officers subsequently being sentenced to death for the incident.

Relations with Bangladesh worsened in mid-1978 because of an exodus from Burma of some 200,000 Muslims, who, according to Dhaka, had been subjected to an "extermination campaign" by Burmese government troops. Later, it appeared that Muslim leaders had encouraged the flight in part to publicize their desire to establish the Arakan region as an Islamic state, and repatriation was begun at the rate of several thousand per week. Although Burma agreed to guarantee the safety of the returnees, it also insisted that those without acceptable credentials would be denied entry, leaving the status of as many as 50,000 persons in doubt. In 1979 the two neighbors agreed to commission a new survey of their common border, the results of which were formally accepted in August 1985. A year later, Burma concluded a maritime boundary agreement with India.

In 1980, having already modified its policy of rejecting foreign economic and technical assistance by accepting aid from West Germany and Japan, Burma also obtained aid from OPEC and, for the first time in 17 years, from the United States. In 1987 negotiations commenced with the Asian Development Bank (ADB) for a $55 million loan to overcome a severe shortfall in crude oil, other fuels, and equipment required to reverse a decline in domestic oil production.

Current issues. In August 1987, at the first of two unprecedented joint meetings of the party Central Executive Committee and the State Council, Ne Win openly acknowledged "flaws" in the "Burmese way to Socialism". Subsequently, on September 1, Rangoon officially lifted restrictions on internal trade, making it possible for Burmese citizens to freely buy, sell, transport, or store staples for the first time since Ne Win took office. In a concomitant attempt at monetary reform, all currency notes except those of small denomination were withdrawn. The latter action spawned the first student demonstration at Rangoon since 1974 and on September 6 the government closed all educational institutions until further notice.

Throughout 1987 the regime remained preoccupied with the ethnic and Communist insurgencies in the northern and eastern border regions. Faced with the formation of a loose alliance among rebel groups (see Political Parties and Groups, below), Rangoon intensified its military campaign, entering areas formerly held by the insurgents and cutting into their income from "tariffs" assessed on smugglers.

Increasingly, the ethnic formations (though not the Communists) appeared to favor a "fourth alternative" for resolution of the nearly 40-year-old conflict. In an interview with a Western journalist, BRANG SENG, chairman of the Kachin Independence Organization (KIO), rejected unitarism, federalism, and fragmentation into small states, in favor of ethnic "autonomy". Under the somewhat vaguely detailed plan, a territorial unit such as Kachin State would become autonomous within the Union of Burma, while non-Kachin peoples would be permitted to establish autonomous districts on a sub-state basis, with the principle of autonomy extending downward, where appropriate, to the local township level.

POLITICAL PARTIES AND GROUPS

Immediately prior to the 1962 coup, the most important Burmese parties were U Nu's Union Party (*Pyidaungsu*); the opposition Anti-Fascist People's Freedom League; and the pro-Communist National Unity Party, with its major affiliate, the Burmese Workers' Party. Although a number of their leaders were imprisoned, the parties continued to exist until March 1964, when the Revolutionary Council banned all parties other than its own Burma Socialist Program Party.

Government Party:

Burma Socialist Program Party (BSPP). Formed in July 1962 by the Revolutionary Council to organize mass participation in its programs, the BSPP champions rigid socialism, tight central control, and continuation of the single-party system. At its Fifth Congress, which met August 2–7, 1985, Gen. Ne Win was reelected party chairman, while Union President San Yu was elected to the newly established post of deputy chairman. Concurrently, the Central Committee was increased from 260 to 280 members and the Central Executive Committee from 15 to 17 members.

Leaders: U NE WIN (Chairman), U SAN YU (Deputy Chairman), U AYE KO (General Secretary), U SEIN LWIN (Joint General Secretary).

Illegal Opposition Groups:

The Burmese Communists, in open rebellion since 1948, were long divided into two major factions. The **Communist Party of Burma** (Red Flags), a Trotskyite group outlawed in 1947, was led by Thakin SO until his capture in 1970, while the small **Arakan Communist Party** (ACP) had emerged as a Red Flag splinter group. The more important **Burmese Communist Party** (White Flags, or BCP), a doctrinaire Peking-oriented group outlawed in 1953, was led by Thakin Than Tun until his assassination in September 1968, little more than a year after Peking had officially acknowledged its support of the BCP's efforts to overthrow Ne Win.

Though considerably weakened by Maoist purges in 1966 and by a disastrous series of setbacks in 1968, the party maintained an alliance with pro-Communist Karens until increasingly fanatic emulation of the White Flags of the Chinese "Cultural Revolution" yielded the loss of most Karen supporters. In March 1975, Thakin Zin and Thakin Chit, the BCP chairman and secretary general, respectively, were killed during an engagement with the Burmese army, the party's Central Committee announcing that Thakin BA THEIN TIN, the head of its delegation at Peking, had been elected Thakin Zin's successor. Since the late 1970s Chinese aid has diminished, with the BCP turning to drug trafficking (as well as "taxing" opium caravans passing through territory under its control) as a means of financing its insurgency. Unconfirmed reports of Soviet aid to the BCP, channeled through Vietnam and Laos, began circulating in mid-1984. Current BCP strength is estimated at 10,000–20,000.

Except for several ACP leaders and one member of the BCP Politburo, relatively few Communists took advantage of the amnesty offered by Rangoon in May 1980, although in a remarkable act of clemency, Thakin So, whose death sentence had earlier been voided, was named a recipient of the National Order of Merit (*Naing Ngant Gon-Yi*), an award theretofore bestowed on persons who had distinguished themselves in the struggle for an independent Burma. In early 1984 it was reported that, in the face of serious illness on the part of the BCP party chairman, effective leadership had devolved to vice-chairmen Thakin PE TINT and KHIN MAUNG GYI.

In May 1975, five minority insurgent groups – the **Arakan Liberation Party** (ALP), the **Karen National Union** (KNU), the **Karenni National Progressive Party** (KNPP), the **New Mon State Party** (NMSP), and the **Shan State Progressive Party** (SSPP) – agreed to form a **National Democratic Front** (NDF) to "overthrow Ne Win's one-party military dictatorship" and to found a Burmese federal union based on national self-determination. The NDF held its first congress in mid-1982 at an undisclosed location, having expanded its membership to include the **Lahn National United Party** (LNUP), the **Palaung State Liberation Organization**, and the **Pa-O National Organization**. The front agreed to assemble a common fighting force (dominated by the 4,000-strong KNU) and to present itself as a "third force" alternative to both the Rangoon government and the BCP. Two new groups were added to the coalition in September 1983: the **Wa National Organization** (WNO) and, more importantly, the **Kachin Independence Organization** (KIO). The Kachins were admitted despite a tactical alliance with the BCP that was first reported in April 1983 and confirmed in early 1984. Also reported to be cooperating with the Communist forces was the 3,000-member Shan State Army, the military wing of the SSPP, despite an earlier decision by the SSPP to sever all formal links with the BCP.

By mid-1985, the NDF had, for all practical purposes, become dormant, the KNU reporting formal cooperation only with the **Kawthoolei Muslim Patriotic Front** (KMPF), a Muslim autonomist group formed in 1983. However, it was revived as the result of a conference held at the KIO's Pa Jan headquarters from December 16 to January 20, when it was decided to establish three regional commands encompassing Kachin, Shan, and Palaung forces in the north; Pa-O, Wa, and Karenni formations in the center; and Karen, Mon, and Arakan units in the south. Front members also agreed to open a dialogue with the BCP, whose Central Committee had stated in October that it was prepared to abandon its commitment to a one-party system of government in favor of "freedom and democracy".

Also reported to be active against Burmese forces in 1985 were the **Thailand Revolutionary Army**, composed of elements from both the Shan State Army and the Shan United Revolutionary Army (below), and the Arakan Muslim **Rohingya Patriotic Front**. In addition, a number of groups continued to operate in the southwest primarily for the purpose of drug trafficking; most visible among these was the **Shan United Army**, which was initially formed in 1963 as a militia unit to combat Shan insurgents; in 1982, after having been driven from its Thai base, it reportedly formed an alliance with elements of the LNUP, but in mid-1984 was accused by the KNU of having been recruited by the Burmese Army to aid in the suppression of other insurgent groups. Also engaged in drug trafficking was the 800-member **Shan United Revolutionary Army**, composed of tribal mercenaries and remnants of the Kuomintang Third Army, which fled China's Yunnan Province in 1949 and, operating from bases along the Thai border, the recipient of support from the US Central Intelligence Agency into the 1960s. In August 1980 LO Hsing-minh and some 145 followers from the **Shan State Revolutionary Army** – yet another significant source of illegal drugs – accepted amnesty, while the LNUP surrendered in 1984.

In August 1986 the NDF concluded a formal alliance with the BCP, despite strong opposition from the KNU, while the KIO reiterated its long-standing position that cooperation with the Communists should be construed strictly as a military pact directed against a common enemy. On November 16, in the alliance's first major operation, elements of the BCP, the Kachin Independence Army, the Shan State Army, and the Palaung State Liberation Army inflicted heavy casualties on government troops in northeastern Shan province. However, in a series of subsequent encounters through March 1987, Burmese army forces reported a number of victories against the rebels and claimed to have substantially improved security in the northern areas.

Along the northern portion of the Indian border in the west, the government has long faced opposition from two Naga groups: the **National Socialist Council of Nagaland** (NSCN) and the **Naga National Council** (NNC), while in the west-central border region it was reported in mid-1987 that the Zomis of Chin State (theretofore Burma's only ethnic group not to have organized a rebel army) had formed a **Zomi Liberation Front.**

Burmese Communist Party and Affiliated Groups:

Burmese Communist Party (BCP). Based along Chinese border in eastern Kachin State and northeastern Shan State.
Leaders: Thakin BA THEIN TIN (Chairman), Thakin PE TINT (Vice Chairman), KHIN MAUNG GYI (Central Committee Secretary), TIN YEE (Chief of Staff, People's Army).

Karenni People's Liberation Organization (KPLO). Also known as "Red Karennis"; based in Kayah State, across from northwest border of Thailand.
Leader: NYA MAUNG MAE.

Kayan Newland Council (KNLC). Based in southwest Shan State.
Leader: SHWE AYE (aka NAING LU HTA).

Shan State Nationalities Liberation Organization (SSNLO). Based in south-central Shan State.
Leader: THA KALEI (Chairman).

National Democratic Front (Northern Command):

Kachin Independence Organization (KIO). Operates throughout Kachin State and in northern Shan State.
Leaders: BRANG SENG (Chairman), Maj. Gen. ZAU MAI (Chief of Staff, Kachin Independence Army—KIA).

Palaung State Liberation Organization (PSLO). Based in northwest Shan State.
Leaders: KHRUS SANGAI (Acting Vice Chairman), Maj. AI MONG (Chief of Staff, Palaung State Liberation Army—PSLA).

Shan State Progress Party. Active in several areas of central Shan State.
Leaders: Col. SAI LEK (General Secretary), Lt. Col. GAW LIN DA (Chief of Staff, Shan State Army—SSA).

National Democratic Front (Central Command):

Karenni National Progressive Party (KNPP). Based along the Thai border in Kayah (Karenni) State.
Leaders: BYA REH (Chairman), Brig. Gen. BEE HTOO (Chief of Staff, Karenni Army—KA).

Pa-O National Organization (PNO). Based in west-central Shan State.
Leaders: AUNG KHAM HTI (Chairman), Col. HTOON YI (Chief of Staff, Pa-O National Army—PNA).

Wa National Organization (WNO). Based in Shan State along northwest Thai border.
Leader: AI CHAU HSEU (Chairman of the Organization and Chief of Staff, Wa National Army—WNA).

National Democratic Front (Southern Command):

Arakan Liberation Party (ALP). Operates from KNU bases in Karen State; it is not currently active in Arakan State.
Leader: Maj. KHAING YE KHAING (Chairman of the Party and Chief of Staff, Arakan Liberation Army—ALA).

Karen National Union (KNU). Active in Karen along Burmese-Thai border.
Leader: BO MYA (President of the KNU and Chief of Staff, Karen National Liberation Army—KLNA).

New Mon State Party (NMSP). Operates along Thai border in Mon State.
Leader: NAI NOL LAR (President of the Party and Chief of Staff, Mon National Liberation Army—MNLA).

[**Note:** The above listing is based primarily on "An Insurgency Who's Who", *Far Eastern Economic Review,* 28 May 1987, pp. 48–49.]

Exile Group:

Committee for the Restoration of Democracy in Burma. The Committee for the Restoration of Democracy was formed at Washington, DC, in early 1987. The organization seeks to forge a common front leading to peace talks between the Rangoon government and ethnic rebel leaders. The group's leader, Ye Kyaw Thu, met with NDF leaders in July 1987, securing their agreement on most issues except that of a face-to-face meeting with General Ne Win.
Leader: YE KYAW THU (General Secretary).

LEGISLATURE

A new 489-member **People's Assembly** (*Pyithu Hluttaw*) convened November 4, 1985, following a general election, held October 6–20, in which all candidates were nominated by the Burma Socialist Program Party. The normal term of the Assembly is four years, the 1981 election being held one year early to ensure an orderly transition upon the retirement of President U Ne Win. All senior members of the executive branch are selected from among the legislators. Assembly sessions are headed, in rotation, by members of a panel of chairmen.

CABINET

Prime Minister	U Maung Maung Kha
Deputy Prime Ministers	U Tun Tin
	Gen. Kyaw Htin
Ministers	
Agriculture and Forests	Brig. Gen. Than Nyunt
Construction	Maj. Gen. Myint Lwin
Cooperatives	U Than Hlaing
Culture	U Aung Kyaw Myint
Defense	Gen. Kyaw Htin
Education	(Vacant)
Energy	U Sein Tun
Foreign Affairs	U Ye Gaung
Health	U Tun Wai
Home and Religious Affairs	Maj. Gen. Min Gaung
Industry No. 1	U Tint Swe
Industry No. 2	U Maung Cho
Information	U Aung Kyaw Myint
Labor	U Ohn Kyaw
Livestock Breeding and Fisheries	Rear Adm. Maung Maung Win
Mines	U Than Tin
Planning and Finance	U Tun Tin
Social Welfare	U Ohn Kyaw
Trade	U Khin Maung Gyi
Transport and Communications	U Saw Pru

NEWS MEDIA

Press. The Revolutionary Council banned all publication of privately owned foreign newspapers in early 1966, and 13 printing presses were taken over by the government in early 1969. A 10-member group headed by a central press chief controller was formed to manage them. Under the 1974 constitution, all newspapers remain heavily censored. The following, unless otherwise noted, are dailies published at Rangoon in Burmese:

Loketha Pyithu Neizin / Working People's Daily (155,000), official government organ, in Burmese and English; *Kyemon* (Mirror, 140,000), official government organ; *Botahtaung* (Vanguard, 138,000), official government organ; *Myanma Alin* (New Light of Burma, 50,000), nationalized in 1969; *Working People's Daily* (25,000), in English; *Guardian* (19,000), in English, nationalized in 1964.

News agencies. The domestic facility is the government-sponsored News Agency of Burma (NAB). Several foreign agencies maintain offices at Rangoon.

Radio and television. Programming is controlled by the state-owned Burma Broadcasting Service, which broadcasts in Burmese, English, and a variety of local languages. There were approximately 800,000 radio and 64,000 television receivers in 1986.

INTERGOVERNMENTAL REPRESENTATION

Ambassador to the US: U MYO AUNG.

US Ambassador to Burma: Burtin LEVIN.

Permanent Representative to the UN: U Maung Maung GYI.

IGO Memberships (Non-UN): ADB, CP, Interpol.

BURUNDI

Republic of Burundi
Republika y'u Burundi (Kirundi)
République du Burundi (French)

Political Status: Independent state since July 1, 1962; under military control from November 28, 1966; one-party constitution adopted by referendum of November 18, 1981; military control reimposed following coup of September 3, 1987.

Area: 10,747 sq. mi. (27,834 sq. km.).

Population: 3,992,130 (1979C), 5,305,000 (1988E).

Major Urban Centers: BUJUMBURA (1979C, 172,201); Gitega (1978E, 16,000).

Official Languages: Kirundi, French (Swahili is also used).

Monetary Unit: Burundi Franc (market rate March 1, 1988, 131.49 francs = $1US).

President: Maj. Pierre BUYOYA; designated September 9, 1987, by the Military Committee for National Salvation following ouster of Col. Jean-Baptiste Bagaza on September 3.

THE COUNTRY

Situated in east-central Africa, bordered by Rwanda, Tanzania, and Zaire, Burundi is a country of grassy uplands and high plateaus. It is one of the most densely populated countries in Africa, with over 400 persons per square mile. The population embraces three main ethnic groups: the Hutu (Bahutu), who constitute 84 percent of the population; the Tutsi (Batutsi, Watutsi), who are numerically a minority (15 percent) but dominate the country politically, socially, and economically; and the Twa, or pygmies (1 percent). More than half of the population is nominally Christian, the majority being Roman Catholic. Women account for more than half of the labor force, although concentrated in subsistence activities, with men predominant in paid labor; women cannot, however, hold title to the land they work, and are barred from holding paid employment without consent of their husbands. Female representation in politics and government is minimal.

One of the world's least-developed countries, with a per capita GNP of $240 in 1985, Burundi remains dependent on agriculture: more than 90 percent of its inhabitants are farmers, primarily at the subsistence level, while coffee typically accounts for about 80 percent of export earnings. The small industrial sector consists for the most part of agricultural processing. At present, small quantities of cassiterite, bastnasite, gold, colombite-tantalite, and wolframite are extracted, while exploitation of a major deposit of nickel (and potentially significant reserves of phosphate, petroleum, and uranium) awaits construction of transport infrastructure.

GOVERNMENT AND POLITICS

Political background. Established in the sixteenth century as a feudal monarchy ruled by the Tutsi, Burundi (formerly Urundi) was incorporated into German East Africa in 1895 and came under Belgian administration as a result of World War I. From 1919 to 1962 it formed the southern half of the Belgian-administered League of Nations mandate, and later United Nations Trust Territory, of Ruanda-Urundi. Retaining its monarchical form of government under indigenous Tutsi rulers (*mwami*), Urundi was granted limited self-government in 1961 and achieved full independence as the Kingdom of Burundi on July 1, 1962.

Rivalry between Tutsi factions and between the Tutsi and the Hutu resulted in the assassination of Prime Minister Pierre NGENDANDUMWE in January 1965 and an abortive Hutu coup the following October. The uprising led to repressive action by government troops under the command of (then) Capt. Michel MICOMBERO. Named prime minister as the result of military intervention in July 1966, Micombero suspended the constitution, dissolved the National Assembly, and on November 28 deposed King NATARE V. In addition to naming himself president of the newly proclaimed republic, Micombero took over the presidency of Unity and National Progress (Uprona), the Tutsi-dominated political party, which was accorded monopoly status.

Despite antigovernment plots in 1969 and 1971, the Micombero regime was generally able to contain conflict in the immediate postcoup era. In 1972, however, the mysterious death of the former king and another attempted Hutu uprising provoked renewed reprisals by Micombero's Tutsi supporters. At least 100,000 deaths ensued, largely of Hutus, with countless thousands fleeing to neighboring countries.

On November 1, 1976, Micombero was overthrown in a bloodless coup led by (then) Lt. Col. Jean-Baptiste BAGAZA, who suspended the constitution and announced that formal power under the "Second Republic" would be assumed by a 30-member Supreme Council of the Revolution with himself as head of state. At an Uprona congress convened in December 1979, the Council was abolished, effective January 1980, and its functions transferred to a party Central Committee headed by the president. On October 22, 1982, elections were held for a new National Assembly and for pro forma reconfirmation of Bagaza as chief executive. Following his redesignation as party leader at the Uprona congress of July 25–27, 1984, Bagaza was named to a third presidential term (the first by direct election), obtaining a reported 99.6 percent of the vote in a referendum on August 31.

On September 3, 1987, while attending a francophone summit in Canada, Bagaza was overthrown in a "palace coup" led by Maj. Pierre BUYOYA, who announced that provisional authority would be exercised by a 31-member Military Committee for National Salvation (CMSN), which on September 9 designated him as president of the Republic. On October 1, Buyoya announced the formation of a new government, declaring that Uprona organs and the National Assembly would subsequently be restored.

Constitution and government. The 1981 constitution provided for a National Assembly, 52 of whose 65 members were directly elected for five-year terms from a group of candidates endorsed by Uprona's Central Committee; it further provided that the president of Uprona would be the sole candidate for election, also for a five-year term, as chief executive. Under a 1986 reform that replaced provincial courts with public prosecutor's offices, the formal judiciary encompassed a Supreme Court, a Court of Appeal, and county courts; added in 1986 was an auxiliary institution, the "Council of Worthies of the Hill", which was to perform a mediation and conciliation role in regard to rural disputes. As of late 1987, pending constitutional redefinition, ultimate authority was lodged in the CMSN, headed by Major Buyoya.

For administrative purposes the country is divided into 15 provinces, each headed by an appointed governor. The provinces are subdivided into districts and communes.

Foreign relations. Internal conflicts have significantly influenced Burundi's relations with its neighbors. During the turmoil of the Micombero era, relations with Rwanda (where the Hutu are dominant), as well as with Tanzania and Zaire, were strained. Under President Bagaza, however, a new spirit of regional cooperation led to the formation in 1977 of a joint Economic Community of the Great Lakes Countries (CEPGL), within which Burundi, Rwanda, and Zaire have agreed to organize a development bank, exploit gas deposits under Lake Kivu, and establish a fishing industry on Lake Tanganyika.

Burundi is a member, along with Rwanda, Tanzania, and Uganda, of the Organization for the Management and Development of the Kagera River Basin. In February 1984 a revised plan for a 2,000 kilometer rail network linking the four countries was approved, thereby addressing Bujumbura's concern about Burundi's lack of access to reliable export routes; hydroelectric and communications projects by the organization also signaled greater economic cooperation, as did Burundi's entrance (along with the rest of CEPGL) into the recently formed Central African Economic Community.

Current issues. The overthrow of President Bagaza was reportedly welcomed by Burundians, many of whom had been alienated by his antichurch campaign. Although Tutsi leaders had long been wary of links between the Catholic hierarchy and the Hutu community, many Tutsis joined in condemning the expulsion and imprisonment of Church leaders, the proscription of weekday masses, and other "dictatorial" anticlerical measures.

President Buyoya moved quickly to address the issue, religious leaders being included in the release of more than 200 political prisoners. He also accused Bagaza of having concentrated too much power in his own hands and conducting an "incoherent" economic policy. Announcing that "the military will not remain in power long", the new chief executive promised that "all sections" of society would be consulted on decisions regarding a return to civilian government. The pledge appeared to be directed at the politically deprived Hutus, although Buyoya charged that outsiders had overemphasized tribal rivalry in Burundi. Nonetheless, observers noted that Bagaza, himself a Tutsi, displayed little zeal for bringing Hutus into the government.

In international affairs the Belgian- and German-educated Buyoya was expected to be more pro-Western than his predecessor, although Burundi remained formally nonaligned. Regional leaders appeared to welcome the change of administration and most borders were promptly reopened.

POLITICAL PARTIES

Of the 24 political parties that contested Burundi's preindependence elections in 1961, only Unity and National Progress (Uprona) survived to serve as the political base of the Micombero and Bagaza regimes.

Former Government Party:

Unity for National Progress (*Unité pour le Progrès National—*Uprona). Founded in 1958 as *Union et Progrès National,* Uprona was dissolved after the 1976 coup but subsequently reestablished as the country's only authorized party. In December 1979, at its first National Congress, the party elected a Central Committee of 48 members, adopted a charter for economic development, and pledged to return the country to civilian rule under President Bagaza's leadership. At its second Congress on July 25–27, 1984, Bagaza was reelected party president, thus becoming the sole candidate for reelection as president of the Republic on August 31. Following the 1987 coup, all Uprona leaders were dismissed and formal party activity ceased, pending a promised "restoration" by President Buyoya, who had previously been a little-known Central Committee member.

LEGISLATURE

A National Assembly (*Assemblée Nationale*), successor to an earlier such body dissolved by Mwami Natare V in 1966, was named in October 1982. It consisted of 65 members, 13 nominated by the president and 52 directly elected from 104 candidates endorsed by Uprona. In August 1987 it was announced that forthcoming balloting would be for an expanded membership of 100. Although suspended following the September 1987 coup, President Buyoya promised to revive the body within "one to two years".

CABINET

President	Maj. Pierre Buyoya
Ministers	
Agriculture and Animal Husbandry	Jumaine Hussein
Civil Service	Charles Karikurubu
Energy and Mines	Victor Ciza
External Relations and Cooperation	Cyprien Mbonimpa
Family and Women's Affairs	Dorothée Cishahyo
Finance	Pierre Binoba
Information	Frederic Ngenzebuhoro
Interior	Lt. Col. Aloys Kadoyi
Justice	Evariste Niyonkuru
Labor and Professional Training	Gamaliel Ndaruzaniye
National Defense	Maj. Pierre Buyoya
National Education	Lt. Col. Jean-Claude Ndiyo
Planning	Gerard Niyibigira
Public Health	Tharcisse Nyunguka
Public Works and Urban Development	Evariste Simbarakiye
Rural Development	Gabriel Toyi
Social Affairs	Pia Ndayiragije
Trade and Industry	Bonaventure Kidwingira
Transport, Posts and Telecommunications	Maj. Simon Rusuku
Youth, Sports and Culture	Adolphe Nahayo

NEWS MEDIA

Press. The following are published at Bujumbura: *Ubumwe* (20,000), weekly, in Kirundi; *Le Renouveau du Burundi,* (20,000), government daily, in French; *Burundi Chrétien,* weekly publication of the Gitega Archbishopric, in French.

News agency. Daily bulletins are issued by the official *Agence Burundaise de Presse.*

Radio and television. The government radio facility, *La Voix de la Révolution,* broadcasts in French, Kirundi, and Swahili; *Télévision Nationale du Burundi* offered programming from a station at Bujumbura to approximately 4,500 television receivers in 1987.

INTERGOVERNMENTAL REPRESENTATION

Ambassador to the US: Edouard KADIGIRI.

US Ambassador to Burundi: James Daniel PHILLIPS.

Permanent Representative to the UN: Jonathas NIYUNGEKO.

IGO Memberships (Non-UN): ACCT, ADF, AfDB, BADEA, CCC, CEEAC, CEPGL, EEC(L), *EIB,* IACO, ICO, Interpol, NAM, OAU.

CAMEROON

Republic of Cameroon
République du Cameroun

Political Status: Independence proclaimed 1960; federation established 1961; one-party unitary republic declared June 2, 1972.

Area: 183,568 sq. mi. (475,442 sq. km.).

Population: 7,663,246 (1976C), 10,362,000 (1988E).

Major Urban Centers (1984E): YAOUNDE (650,000); Douala (850,000).

Official Languages: French, English.

Monetary Unit: CFA Franc (market rate March 1, 1988, 285.80 francs = $1US).

President: Paul BIYA; served as Prime Minister 1975–1982; installed as President on November 6, 1982, to serve the remaining term of Ahmadou Babatoura AHIDJO, who resigned on November 4; reelected without opposition on January 14, 1984 and April 24, 1988.

THE COUNTRY

Situated just north of the equator on the Gulf of Guinea, and rising from a coastal plain to a high interior plateau, Cameroon is the product of a merger in 1961 between the former French and British Cameroon trust territories. Its nearly 100 tribes speak 24 major languages and represent a diversity of traditional African (45 percent), Christian (35 percent), and Muslim (20 percent) religious beliefs. Reflecting its dual colonial heritage, Cameroon is the only country in Africa in which both French and English are official languages. Women constitute 40 percent of the official labor force, producing over half of the country's food crops. Approximately 14 percent of the National Assembly is female, although a similar level of representation does not obtain at either the cabinet or local-provincial levels.

Cameroon's economy has long been primarily rural and, despite the discovery of major oil deposits in 1973, agriculture continues to provide half of the country's export earnings while employing three-quarters of its population. Coffee, cocoa, and timber are among the most important agricultural products, but bananas, cotton, rubber, and palm oil are also produced commercially. Oil production declined from a high of 9.2 million tons in 1985 to 8.2 million tons in 1987, with the World Bank predicting an annual output of no more than 2.0 million tons by 1996. Apart from oil-related activity, industrial development has focused on agricultural processing and aluminum smelting that utilizes both domestic and imported bauxite. The fourth five-year plan (1976–1982) emphasized hydroelectric expansion and completion of the Transcameroonian Railway as a means of overcoming a long-standing transportation problem, whereas the fifth plan (1982–1987) called for the maintenance of self-sufficiency in agriculture and further exploitation of mineral and energy resources. The current plan (1986–1991) focuses on the development of medium-sized farms to stanch the steady exodus of rural youth to urban areas. France has traditionally been Cameroon's most important business partner, although liberal investment policies have recently attracted capital from other Western sources, particularly the United States.

Nevertheless, by 1987 concern over depressed oil and other commodity prices, coupled with a crippling foreign debt, had led to a new, more pessimistic assessment of Cameroon's economy.

GOVERNMENT AND POLITICS

Political background. A German protectorate before World War I, Cameroon was divided at the close of that conflict into French and British mandates, which became United Nations trust territories after World War II. French Cameroons, comprising the eastern four-fifths of the territory, achieved autonomous status within the French Community in 1957 and, under the leadership of Ahmadou Babatoura AHIDJO, became the independent Republic of Cameroon on January 1, 1960. The disposition of British Cameroons was settled in February 1961 by a UN-sponsored plebiscite in which the northern and southern sections voted to merge with Nigeria and with the former French territory, respectively. On October 1, 1961, the Federal Republic of Cameroon was formed, with Ahidjo as president and John Ngu FONCHA, prime minister of the former British region, as vice president.

The federal structure was designed to meet the challenge posed by Cameroon's racial, tribal, religious, and political diversity. It provided for separate regional governments and political organizations, joined at the federal level. A transition to unitary government began in 1965–1966 with the merger of the regional political parties to form the Cameroon National Union (UNC) under the leadership of President Ahidjo and was formally instituted on June 2, 1972, following a referendum on May 20 that indicated overwhelming support for the adoption of a new constitution. Subsequently, President Ahidjo faced no organized opposition and on April 5, 1980, was reelected to a fifth successive term. However, in an unanticipated move on November 4, 1982, Ahidjo announced his retirement, effective two days later, in favor of his longtime associate, Prime Minister Paul BIYA. Immediately following his installation as president, Biya, a southerner, named a northern Muslim, Maigari BELLO BOUBA, to head a new government designed to retain the somewhat tenuous regional and cultural balance that had been established by the former head of state. Bello Bouba was dismissed in August 1983, following a coup attempt that allegedly involved Ahidjo, then resident in France.

President Biya was unopposed for reelection on January 14, 1984, and immediately following his inauguration on January 21 the National Assembly voted to abolish the post of prime minister and to abandon "United Republic of Cameroon" as the country's official name in favor of the pre-merger "Republic of Cameroon". Biya was returned to office on April 24, 1988, one year prior to the expiry of his existing term, to permit simultaneous presidential and legislative balloting.

Constitution and government. The 1972 constitution provides for a unitary state headed by a strong executive. The president, directly elected by universal suffrage for a five-year term, is assisted by a cabinet drawn from the civil service rather than the legislature. Members may return to their former positions upon termination of their ministerial duties. Under a constitutional revision of January 1984, the president of the Assembly becomes, in the event of a vacancy, chief executive, pending the outcome, within 40 days, of a presidential election at which he cannot stand as a candidate. Legislative authority is vested in a National Assembly whose normal five-year term may be lengthened or shortened at the discretion of the president. Under legislation enacted in June 1987, "Any political party existing legally can present one or several lists each including as many candidates as there are seats." The judicial system is headed by a Supreme Court and a High Court of Justice; there are also provincial magistrates and a court of appeal.

Cameroon is administratively divided into ten provinces, each headed by a provincial governor appointed by the president. The provinces are subdivided into regions and districts.

Foreign relations. Formally nonaligned, Cameroon maintains relations with a wide variety of both Western and Eastern nations, although ties with France remain especially strong. Dominating recent foreign policy concerns has been the civil war in neighboring Chad, which has resulted in an influx of some 100,000 refugees into Cameroon's northern provinces. Thus the Ahidjo government took part in several regional efforts to mediate the dispute prior to the ouster of the Libyan-backed Woddei government in mid-1982; more recently, Cameroon has served as a staging ground for France's support of the Habré government.

Relations with other neighboring states have been uneven. In May 1981 Cameroon was forced to evacuate nearly 10,000 of its nationals from Gabon following a sports-related riot. Border incidents with Nigeria, resulting in a seven-month suspension of diplomatic relations in May 1981, continued into early 1987, with Lagos threatening "to take military reprisals" against alleged incursions by Cameroonian *gendarmes* into Borno State. However, relations improved markedly thereafter, the first session of a new joint economic, scientific, and technical commission was held in August with the aim of "reinforcing" African unity, while in December Nigerian President Ibrahim Babangida was warmly received during his first visit to Cameroon.

Current issues. A 1986 visit by President Biya to West Germany in search of economic "diversification" stirred resentment in France, where Cameroon's image had recently been tarnished by the hiring of a French journalist to write articles favorable to the regime and to "track" the activities of former president Ahidjo. These events were dramatically overshadowed, however, by the August release of poisonous gas from Lake Nyos, which resulted in more than 2,000 deaths.

In June 1987 President Biya responded to severe economic decline by implementing "draconian" measures as the only alternative to going to the IMF, which he described as "the bane of Third World countries". Under the new program, state-supplied service abuses were curtailed, selected state and parastatal businesses privatized, and "bloated" civil service ranks trimmed. In addition, personal and business taxes were reduced by 25 percent.

Electoral reforms were enacted at the June 1987 Assembly session and on October 27 local elections were held which, for the first time, sanctioned competitive balloting for legislative seats. A similar practice was observed in balloting for National Assembly seats on April 24, 1988, although each of the two lists was restricted to candidates presented by the Cameroon People's Democratic Movement.

POLITICAL PARTIES

Government Party:

Cameroon People's Democratic Movement — CPDM (*Rassemblement Démocratique du Peuple Camerounais* — RDPC). Formerly the Cameroon National Union (*Union Nationale Camerounaise* — UNC), the RDPC is the only officially recognized party. It was formed in 1966 as a composite of the Cameroon Union (*Union Camerounaise*), the former majority party of East (French) Cameroons, and of several former West (British) Cameroons parties, including the governing Kamerun National Democratic Party (KNDP), the Kamerun United National Congress (KUNC), and the Kamerun People's Party (KPP). The RDPC acquired its present name at its fourth party congress, March 21–24, 1985. Called a "congress of renewal", the March meeting reelected President Biya as party leader; approved the proposed name change over significant anglophone resistance; expanded the party's Central Committee from a maximum of 60 members (42 elected by the congress) to 90 (65 elected); and discussed means to "democratise" party structure by strengthening village representation. In implementation of "authentic democracy", balloting for representation on local and regional party bodies was conducted during January-March 1986, although most decisions are controlled by a 12-member Political Bureau, headed by the president.

Leaders: Paul BIYA (President of the Republic and of the Party), François Sengat KUO (Political Secretary).

Other Groups:

In the absence of official opposition parties, most dissent has been voiced by Paris-based exile groups. The most prominent, the **Cameroon People's Union** (*Union des Peuple de Cameroun* — UPC), which contains both a centrist faction and a Marxist-Leninist element led by Secretary General Woungly MASSAGA, claims thousands of "militants" in both France and Cameroon. Continued proscription of the UPC, which had been formally dissolved in 1955, was upheld by the Cameroon Supreme Court in June 1986. Earlier, in February 1985, a proposed "national discussion" among all exiles, proposed by a rival group, the **Cameroonian Organization To Fight for Democracy** (*Organisation de Cameroun Latter pour Democratie* — OCLD), had been banned by French authorities.

LEGISLATURE

The **National Assembly** (*Assemblée Nationale*) currently consists of 150 members elected for five-year terms. At the most recent election of April 24, 1988, voters were permitted to choose between two lists (or, in the case of single-member constituencies, two candidates) presented by the Cameroon People's Democratic Union.

President: Solomon Tandeng MUNA.

CABINET

President	Paul Biya
Director of Civil Cabinet	Samuel Libock
Deputy Director of Civil Cabinet	Rene Sadi

Ministers Delegate to the Presidency

Computer Services and Public Contracts	Paul Kamga Njike
Defense	Michel Meva'a Meboutou
Relations with the Assemblies	Francis Nkem
Stabilization Plan	Emmanuel Zoa Oloa
State Inspection and Administrative Reform	Mohamadou Labarang

Ministers

Agriculture	Jean-Baptiste Yonke
Animal Husbandry, Animal Industries and Fisheries	Hamadjoda Adjoudji
Civil Service	André Booto N'Gon
Commerce and Industry	Joseph Tsanga Abanda
Equipment	Herman Maimo
Finance	Sadou Hayatou
Foreign Affairs	Philippe Mataga
Foreign Affairs (Delegate)	Papa Sale
Higher Education and Scientific Research	Abdoulaye Babale
Information and Culture	Ibrahim Mbombo Njoya
Justice	Benjamin Itoe
Labor and Social Welfare	Adolphe Moudiki
Mines and Power	Michael Kima Tabong
Missions at the Presidency	Titus Edzoa
	Joseph Charles Doumba
National Education	Georges Ngango
Planning and Regional Development	René Zé Nguélé
Posts and Telecommunications	Leonard-Claude Mpouma
Public Health	Victor Anomah Ngu
Social Affairs	Rose Zang Nguele
Territorial Administration	Jérôme Emielin Abondo
Transport	André-Bosco Cheoua
Urbanism and Town Planning	Ferdinand-Léopold Oyono
Women's Affairs	Boubakary Yaou Aissatou
Youth and Sports	Joseph Fofe
Governor, Central Bank	Casimir Oye Mba

NEWS MEDIA

Press. Prior censorship is practiced in Cameroon, while editors and proprietors are frequently cautioned against indulging in "sensationalism". The principal newspapers are the *Cameroon Tribune* (Yaoundé), government daily (65,000) in French and weekly (30,000) in English; *The Gazette* (Limbe, 65,000), weekly in English; *La Gazette* (Douala, 35,000), French edition of *The Gazette*, weekly; *Cameroon Outlook* (Victoria, 7,500), thrice weekly in English. The English-language *Cameroon Times*, the country's only Sunday newspaper, was suspended in 1983 and permanently banned in late 1984 for publishing articles deemed unacceptable by the government.

News agencies. The former *Agence Camerounaise de Presse* (ACAP) was replaced in 1978 by the *Société de Presse et d'Edition du Cameroun* (Sopecam), which, under the Ministry of Information, is responsible for the dissemination of foreign news within Cameroon and also for publication of the *Cameroon Tribune*. The principal foreign agency is *Agence France-Presse;* Reuters, TASS, and Xinhua also maintain bureaus at Yaoundé.

Radio and television. *Radiodiffusion Nationale du Cameroun* is a government network operating under the control of the Ministry of Information and Culture. *Radio Yaoundé* is the national station; local facilities broadcast from Bafoussam, Bamenda, Bertoúa, Buea, Douala, and Garoua. A national television service, launched in early 1985, currently transmits to some 4,500 receivers. Financial and technical constraints have led the government to consider the possibility of introducing solar energy receivers, which could make Cameroon a leader in visual broadcasting.

INTERGOVERNMENTAL REPRESENTATION

Ambassador to the US: Paul PONDI.

US Ambassador to Cameroon: Mark L. EDELMAN.

Permanent Representative to the UN: Paul Bamela ENGO.

IGO Memberships (Non-UN): *ACCT,* ADF, AfDB, BADEA, BDEAC, CCC, Copal, EEC(L), *EIB,* IACO, IC, ICAC, ICCO, ICO, IDB, Intelsat, Interpol, NAM, OAU, PCA, UDEAC.

CANADA

Political Status: Granted Dominion status under British North America Act of 1867; recognized as autonomous state within the Commonwealth in 1931; constitution "patriated" as of April 17, 1982.

Area: 3,851,809 sq. mi. (9,976,185 sq. km.), including inland water.

Population: 24,343,180 (1981C), 26,081,000 (1988E).

Major Urban Centers (urban areas, 1986E): OTTAWA (796,100); Toronto (3,292,600); Montreal (2,873,114); Vancouver (1,372,800); Edmonton (665,800); Calgary (591,100); Winnipeg (609,100); Quebec (606,900); Hamilton (567,200).

Official Languages: English, French.

Monetary Unit: Canadian Dollar (market rate March 1, 1988, 1.26 dollars = $1US).

Sovereign: Queen ELIZABETH II.

Governor General: Jeanne SAUVE; appointed by Queen Elizabeth II on the advice of the Prime Minister and sworn in for a five-year term May 14, 1984, succeeding Edward SCHREYER.

Prime Minister: (Martin) Brian MULRONEY (Progressive Conservative Party); assumed office September 17, 1984, in succession to John Napier TURNER (Liberal Party), following general election of September 4.

THE COUNTRY

Canada, the largest country in the Western Hemisphere and the second-largest in the world, extends from the Atlantic to the Pacific and from the Arctic to a southern limit near Detroit, Michigan. Because of its northerly location, severe climate, and unfavorable geographic conditions, only one-third of its total area has been developed and over two-thirds of its people inhabit a 100-mile-wide strip of territory along the US border. Colonized by both English and French settlers, it retained throughout a long period of British rule a cultural and linguistic duality that continues as one of its most serious internal problems. Of the more than six million French-speaking Canadians, approximately four-fifths are concentrated in the province of Quebec, where demands for political and economic equality or even separation from the rest of Canada persist. A major step toward linguistic equality was taken in July 1969 with the enactment of an official-languages bill pro-viding for bilingual districts throughout the country. Despite this concession, Quebec enacted legislation establishing French as its sole official language in 1977, certain portions of which were voided by a series of court rulings in 1984–1986.

In recent years, the status of the vast Northwest Territories, comprising more than one-third of the country's land area, has been the subject of constitutional debate. In early 1987, the *Inuit,* an Eskimo people accounting for some 16,000 of the sparse overall population of 51,000, won tentative concessions that could lead to the formation of their own province (Nunavut) in the larger, eastern portion of the NWT by 1991; the smaller western region is home to a more mixed population that includes some 8,000 Athapaskan-speaking *Déné* Indians and nearly 3,000 *Métis* (mixed Indian and European), but with a narrow White majority (see Current issues, below).

Women constitute approximately half of the Canadian labor force, concentrated largely in service, sales, and teaching. In government, they occupy less than 10 percent of elected and appointed positions, although they have long taken an active role in political party affairs and the federal cabinet, as of March 1988, included six females among its 40-odd members.

Canada holds a prominent position among the world's manufacturing nations, but development has also made the economy increasingly dependent on foreign sources for investment capital and markets that can absorb surpluses of both agricultural and manufactured goods. Mineral wealth plays an important part in Canadian economic success. Possessing significant petroleum reserves, it is also one of the leading producers of asbestos, nickel, zinc, and potash as well as a major source of uranium, aluminum, titanium, cobalt, gold, silver, copper, platinum, iron ore, lead, and molybdenum. The country's forests supply over one-third of the world's newsprint, and its farms and ranches produce vast quantities of wheat and beef, substantial proportions of which are also available for export. As in cultural, political, and military affairs, proximity to the United States has led to a degree of economic dependence (nearly three-fourths of foreign investment is from US sources) while simultaneously heightening the sense of Canadian nationalism and the determination to preserve a distinctly Canadian identity.

GOVERNMENT AND POLITICS

Political background. United under British rule in 1763 following France's defeat in the Seven Years War, Canada began its movement toward independence in 1867 when the British North America Act established a federal union of the four provinces of Quebec, Ontario, Nova Scotia, and New Brunswick. The provinces reached their present total of ten with the addition of Newfoundland in 1949.

Under the 1867 act, executive authority was vested in the British Crown but was exercised by an appointed governor general; legislative power was entrusted to a bicameral Parliament consisting of a Senate and a House of Commons. Canada's growing capacity to manage its own affairs won formal recognition in the British Statute of Westminster of 1931, which gave Canada autonomous status within the Commonwealth. The political system, like the institutional structure, was closely modeled on British precedents, and for all practical purposes the country has been governed for over a century by alignments equivalent to today's Liberal and Progressive Conservative parties. Liberal governments, headed successively by W.L. MacKenzie KING and Louis ST. LAURENT, were in office from 1935 to 1957, when the Conservatives (later renamed Progressive Conservatives) returned to power under John DIEFENBAKER, prime minister from 1957 to 1963. Lester B. PEARSON, leader of the Liberal Party, headed minority governments from 1963 until his retirement in 1968, when he was succeeded by Pierre Elliott TRUDEAU. The new prime minister secured a majority for the Liberals in the election of June 1968 and was returned to power with a reduced majority in October 1972. Contrary to preelection forecasts, the Trudeau government won decisive control of the House of Commons in July 1974.

On May 22, 1979, the 16-year Liberal reign ended, the Progressive Conservatives winning a plurality of House seats in a general election called by Trudeau on March 26. Although his party remained six shy of an absolute majority, obtaining 136 of 282 seats in the newly expanded body, Charles Joseph CLARK was sworn in as prime minister on June 4, Trudeau becoming leader of the opposition.

On November 21, Trudeau announced his resignation as Liberal Party leader, calling for a convention in March 1980 to elect a successor. However, the Clark government experienced a stunning parliamentary defeat on December 13 in an effort to enact a series of stringent budgetary measures, necessitating a dissolution of the House the following day and the calling of a new election for February 18, 1980. Given an evident resurgence of Liberal popularity, Trudeau agreed to withdraw his resignation and returned to office on March 3 as head of a new Liberal government that commanded a majority of six seats in the Commons. However, continued economic difficulties combined with accusations of political patronage to erode the governing party's popularity, the Progressive Conservatives gaining a number of House seats in 1983 byelections. On February 29, 1984, Prime Minister Trudeau again resigned the leadership of his party, and was replaced at a party convention in mid-June by John Napier TURNER, a former MP and businessman who had served as finance minister from 1972 to 1975. Turner was sworn in as prime minister on June 30; a week later, heartened by polls indicating that the transfer of power had aided his party's popularity, he called a general election for September 4. The balloting produced instead a decisive reversal, the Progressive Conservatives winning 211 of 284 House seats. On September 17 a Conservative cabinet took office, led by PCP leader Brian MULRONEY.

Constitution and government. During 1981, Prime Minister Trudeau's lengthy effort to "patriate" the Canadian constitution moved toward realization, the Parliament completing action in December on a measure calling for its London counterpart to convert the British North America Act, which had served as the country's basic law since 1867, into a purely Canadian instrument. Earlier, in response to actions brought by the provinces, the move had

secured mixed construction in the courts: a Manitoba court ruled in favor of the government in February, while a Newfoundland court ruled in March that Ottawa could not install a new charter binding on the provinces without their consent. Confronted with an "opting out" proposal by the dissidents, whereby a province could avoid applying a constitutional amendment affecting its rights and powers, the prime minister agreed not to press the issue prior to review by the Supreme Court.

On September 28 the high court, in a somewhat ambiguous ruling, held that the government's effort to secure a new constitution was "legal" but "offends the federal principle" by proceeding without overall provincial consent. Trudeau responded by convening a meeting with the premiers in early November, at the conclusion of which all but Quebec's René LEVESQUE agreed to a compromise that included a bill of rights and an amending formula but permitted the provinces to nullify bill-of-rights provisions within their own boundaries, should they so wish. On this basis, the Canada Bill (the Constitution Act 1982) was approved by the British Parliament in March 1982 and was formally signed by Queen Elizabeth II in a ceremony at Ottawa on April 17.

As sovereign, the British monarch is represented by a governor general, now a Canadian citizen appointed on the advice of the prime minister. The locus of power is the elected House of Commons, where the leader of the majority party is automatically designated by the governor general to form a cabinet and thus become prime minister. The House may be dissolved and a new election called in the event of a legislative defeat or no-confidence vote. The Senate, appointed by the governor general along both geographic and party lines, must also approve all legislation but tends largely to limit itself to the exercise of a secondary, restraining influence.

Provincial governments operate along comparable lines. Each of the provinces has its own constitution, a lieutenant governor appointed by the governor general, and a legislative assembly whose principal leader is the provincial premier. Municipalities are governed by elected officials and are subject to provincial, rather than federal, authority. The Yukon Territory and the Northwest Territories (comprising the districts of Keewatin, Franklin, and Mackenzie) are governed by appointed commissioners with the assistance of elected and/or appointed council members. In late 1982 Ottawa announced a willingness to divide the Northwest Territories into two regions with greater autonomy, assuming resolution of boundary claims; however, despite extensive negotiations within the framework of a constitutional alliance comprising representatives of both indigenous and non-indigenous populations, significant progress toward resolution of the issue was not registered until early 1987 (see Current issues, below). Each province has its own judicial system, with a right of appeal to the Supreme Court of Canada.

Province and Capital	Area (sq. mi.)	Population (1987E)
Alberta (Edmonton)	255,285	2,393,200
British Columbia (Victoria)	366,255	2,924,300
Manitoba (Winnipeg)	251,000	1,096,000
New Brunswick (Fredericton)	28,354	730,500

Newfoundland (St. John's)	156,185	584,100
Nova Scotia (Halifax)	21,425	895,400
Ontario (Toronto)	412,582	9,303,400
Prince Edward Island (Charlottetown)	2,184	131,100
Quebec (Quebec)	594,860	6,665,900
Saskatchewan (Regina)	251,700	1,036,000

Territory and Capital

Northwest Territories (Yellowknife)	1,304,903	54,100
Yukon Territory (Whitehorse)	207,076	25,600

Foreign relations. Canadian foreign policy in recent decades has reflected the varied influence of historic ties to Great Britain, geographical proximity to the United States, and a growing national strength and self-awareness that have made Canada one of the most active and influential "middle powers" of the post-World War II period. Staunch affiliation with the Western democratic bloc and an active role in NATO and other Western organizations have been accompanied by support for international conciliation and extensive participation in United Nations peacekeeping ventures and other constructive international activities.

While maintaining important joint defense arrangements with the United States, Canada has shown independence of US views on a variety of international issues. In addition, anti-US sentiment has been voiced in connection with the extensive US ownership and control of Canadian economic enterprises and the pervasive US influence on Canadian intellectual and cultural life. A general review of Canada's international commitments begun in the late 1960s resulted in diversification of the nation's international relationships. In line with this trend, Canada reduced the number of troops committed to NATO, and Prime Minister Trudeau made state visits to the Soviet Union and the People's Republic of China. Canada is a member of the Inter-American Development Bank and has Permanent Observer status at the Organization of American States. Its representatives have been active in the Conference on Security and Cooperation in Europe and in the mutual and balanced force reduction (MBFR) talks, and in 1976 it approved a major economic cooperation agreement with the European Community which Canadians hoped would provide an economic "Third Option" vis-à-vis the Commonwealth and the United States.

Since assuming office, Prime Minister Mulroney has sought to improve relations with Washington in both economic and foreign policy matters. One of the first initiatives of his administration was to change the name of the watchdog Foreign Investment Review Board to Investment Canada, in an attempt to encourage US capital inflow; subsequently, although having campaigned in 1984 against a free trade agreement with the United States, he signed such a pact with President Reagan in January 1988 as a means of ensuring continued Canadian access, during a period of rising protectionist sentiment, to the crucial US market. While increasing defense spending, Mulroney has continued much of the international moderation of his predecessor: Ottawa declined to participate formally in President Reagan's Strategic Defense Initiative, has diverged from US policy on Central America, and has threatened to break all diplomatic relations with South Africa "if there is no progress on the dismantling of apartheid".

Recent disputes with the United States have centered on fishing rights off the two countries' east and west coasts, delimitation of maritime boundaries in the Gulf of Maine, and the effects of "acid rain" from US industries on Canadian forests. While the fishing and boundary issues were largely resolved following a World Court decision in October 1984, the "acid rain" issue has remained an area of contention between Ottawa and Washington through both the Trudeau and Mulroney administrations. However, in early 1986 the Reagan administration appeared to have moved away from its position that the problem "requires more study" by agreeing to negotiations on the reduction of sulfur dioxide emissions. Immediately prior to the third annual US-Canadian summit on April 5–6, 1987, President Reagan announced that his government would spend $2.5 billion over five years on demonstration projects aimed at cleaner coal burning, although at the talks themselves he went no further in regard to a possible bilateral accord than to reaffirm his earlier willingness to "consider" the matter. In another area of contention with Washington, the Canadians hailed the conclusion in early 1988 of an agreement on Arctic cooperation, although the pact fell short of long-sought US recognition that waters adjacent to the Arctic archipelago are subject to Canadian sovereignty.

Current issues. The impressive victory of the Progressive Conservatives in the 1984 general election reflected deep dissatisfaction with former prime minister Trudeau's economic policies, including an inability to reduce 11 percent unemployment. Although economic growth rose to 4 percent in 1985, unemployment remained unacceptably high and the succeeding Mulroney administration encountered widespread resistance to its trade, tax, and defense policies, while suffering the embarrassment of a series of scandals involving cabinet members. In September 1985, Fisheries Minister John FRASER left the government because of a scandal involving the canning of rancid tuna; within days, Communications Minister Marcel MASSE also resigned following charges of electoral misconduct in his home district. A month later, Transport Minister Suzanne BLAIS-GRENIER, who had been demoted from the environment ministry after allegations that she had "courted" logging and mining interests, was charged with having misused government funds in her former post and in December also resigned from the cabinet. In January 1986, (then) Deputy Prime Minister Erik NIELSEN revealed that the PCP had eavesdropped on meetings of Liberal MPs during the 1960s; in May, Minister for Regional and Industrial Expansion Sinclair STEVENS resigned following allegations of conflict of interest in regard to a business loan obtained by his wife, while in January 1987, Transport Minister André BISSONNETTE was dismissed in the wake of inquiries into a land transaction involving a government defense project. The pattern continued into 1988 with the dismissal in early February of Supply and Services Minister Michel COTE for violation of conflict-of-interest rules, while the prime minister himself was criticized for failure to report a Conservative Party loan to redecorate his official residence at Ottawa. Collaterally, the government was buffeted by a series of Liberal victories in Ontario in May 1985, in Quebec the following December, and in Prince Edward Island in April 1986, followed by New Democratic

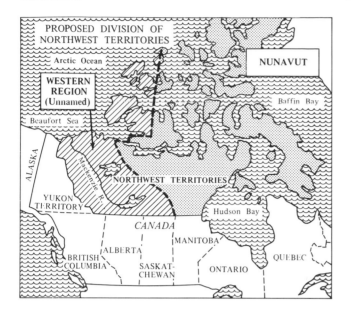

PROPOSED DIVISION OF
NORTHWEST TERRITORIES

victories in PCP strongholds in Newfoundland and Yukon in July 1987. The losses, reflecting a decline in the Conservatives' public opinion rating by late 1987 to 23 percent (as contrasted with 35 percent for the Liberals and a surprising 41 percent for the New Democrats), did not bode well for the incumbent party's prospects at the next general election, which, following marginal improvement in PCP poll standing by March 1988, was expected by many observers to be scheduled for as early as September or October.

In early 1987, a long-standing controversy involving the rights of native inhabitants of the Northwest Territories appeared to be moving toward resolution as the result of agreement between the Nunavut Constitutional Forum (representing *Inuit* Eskimo interests) and the Western Constitutional Forum (representing a number of indigenous and nonindigenous groups). Under the accord, the NWT would be divided into two regions that would eventually become Canada's 11th and 12 provinces, the proposed boundary between the two reflecting an approximate line of demarcation between the *Inuit* and non-*Inuit* peoples (see map). The two forums and the federal government must, however, reach agreement on a constitution for each region, with difficult bargaining expected over control of natural resources because of recent oil discoveries in the Mackenzie River delta and the Beaufort Sea.

POLITICAL PARTIES

Canada's traditional two-party structure, based on the alternating rule of the Conservative (now Progressive Conservative) and Liberal parties, has been diversified since the 1930s by the emergence of such populist and socialist movements as the Social Credit (Socred) and New Democratic parties, separatist feeling in Quebec, and an increase in the variety of French-Canadian groupings outside the regular party system. In addition, the electoral fortunes of the historic parties have shifted dramatically in the course of the last two national elections. In February 1980, the Liberals won 147 seats and the PCP, 103; in September 1984 an overwhelming Conservative victory left the Liberals with only 10 seats more than the third-ranked New Democrats.

As of January 1987, the PCP controlled 5 provincial governments (Alberta, New Brunswick, Newfoundland, Nova Scotia, Saskatchewan), the Liberals, 3 (Ontario, Prince Edward Island, Quebec); Socred, 1 (British Columbia); and the NDP, 1 (Manitoba). The NDP (a junior partner of the Liberals in Ontario) was also in power in the Yukon Territory, with the assembly of the Northwest Territories consisting entirely of independent members.

Governing Party:

Progressive Conservative Party (PCP). More nationalist in outlook than the Liberals — and traditionally less willing to compromise with the Quebec separatists — the Progressive Conservatives lay greater stress on Canada's British and Commonwealth attachments while actively promoting programs of social welfare and assistance to farmers. Despite its federal election defeat in 1980, the party remained in control of 7 of the 10 provincial governments, and following the replacement of Charles Joseph Clark by Brian Mulroney as party leader in June 1983, climbed steadily in the polls before winning decisive control at the federal level on September 4, 1984. It lost control of Prince Edward Island to the Liberals in April 1986.

Leaders: Brian MULRONEY (Prime Minister), Charles Joseph CLARK (Secretary of State for External Affairs), Bill JARVIS (President of the Party), Donald Frank MAZANKOWSKI (Government Leader in the House), Lowell MURRAY (Government Leader in the Senate), Jean Carol PELLETIER (National Director).

Opposition Parties:

Liberal Party of Canada. Historically dedicated to free trade and gradual social reform, the Liberal Party in recent decades has promoted expanded social-welfare measures, federal-provincial cooperation, and an international outlook favoring an effective United Nations, cooperation with the United States and Western Europe, and a substantial foreign economic aid program. In power at the federal level for 19 of the previous 21 years, the Liberals suffered a disastrous defeat in September 1984, losing nearly two-thirds of their former representation. However, in the ensuing year the party won control of both the Ontario and Quebec provincial legislatures (the former in coalition with the NDP), while substantially improving its standing in the polls.

Leaders: John Napier TURNER (Leader of the Opposition), Allan MacEACHEN (Leader in the Senate), Michel ROBERT (President of the Party), Paul ROUTHIER (Party leader in Quebec), Marie-André BASTIEN (Secretary General).

New Democratic Party (NDP). A democratic socialist grouping founded in 1961 by merger of the Cooperative Commonwealth Federation and the Canadian Labour Congress, the New Democratic Party favors economic nationalism and domestic control of resources, a planned economy, broadened social benefits, and an internationalist foreign policy. It currently controls the provincial government of Manitoba and helped to bring down the Conservative Party government of Ontario in 1985, thereafter becoming a junior coalition partner with the Liberals. The NDP lost only one of its 31 House seats in the 1984 general election, despite previous indications that the party was declining in popular support. In July 1987, on the other hand, reflecting what was viewed as widespread voter dissatisfaction with the mainstream parties, the NDP won a series of three critical by-elections on the basis of a popularity rating that had catapulted to a record 41 percent. In April 1988, with public opinion polls showing that more than 70 percent of Canadians favored retention of NATO membership, the NDP announced indefinite postponement of its long-standing pledge to withdraw from the alliance if voted into office.

Leaders: John Edward BROADBENT (Parliamentary Leader), Johanna den HERTOG (President), Bill William KNIGHT (Secretary).

Social Credit Party (Socred). The Social Credit Party, which controlled Alberta from its founding in 1935 to 1971, and has been the governing party of British Columbia since 1975, has not been represented at the federal level since 1980. It advocates adjustments in monetary policy as the key to general economic welfare.

Leaders: Harvey G. LAINON (National Leader), Bill VANDER ZAHN (Premier of British Columbia).

Minor parties active at the federal level, but holding no parliamentary seats, include **The Green Party,** an environmentalist grouping led by Seymour TRIEGER; the **Communist Party**, led by William KASHTAN; and the **Libertarian Party,** led by Dennis CORRIGAN and Chris BLATCHLEY.

Regional Parties:

Quebec Party (*Parti Québécois*). Running on a platform of French separatism, the *Parti Québécois* won control of the provincial assembly from the Liberals in the election of November 15, 1976. In a referendum held May 20, 1980, it failed to obtain a mandate to enter into "sovereignty-association" talks with the federal government. In April 1981, it increased its majority in the 122-member assembly to 80; however, a number of by-election defeats had reduced that number to 72 by January 1984.

On October 3, 1985, Pierre-Marc JOHNSON was sworn in as provincial premier in succession to longtime party leader René Lévesque, who was in poor health and whose influence had waned because of divisiveness over the sovereignty issue. However, neither Johnson's conciliatory posture on federalism nor an emerging conservatism on economic issues sufficed to avert a crushing defeat in provincial balloting on December 2, at which the PQ obtained only 23 seats to the Liberals' 99. Lévesque died on November 1, 1987, and ten days later, amid a resurgence of pro-independence sentiment, Johnson stepped down as party president, being succeeded by Jacques Parizeau.

In March 1985, a group of separatist dissidents led by Dr. Camille LAUREN formed a **Democratic Rally for Independence** (*Rassemblement Démocratique pour l'Independence),* although indicating that "the umbilical cord with the PQ has not yet been cut". The group is presently led by Sylvie SCHIRM.

Leaders: Jacques PARIZEAU (President), Nadia ASSIMOPOULOS (Vice President).

Other parties active in Quebec include the **Independentist Party** (*Parti Indépendantiste*), founded in August 1985 by a group of PQ separatists, but which, under the interim leadership of Denis MONIÈRE, obtained only 1 percent of the vote in the December poll; the **Nationalist Party** (*Parti Nationaliste*), founded in 1983 by hard-line separatist, Marc LEGER; the **National Union** (*Union Nationale*), a reconstruction of the former Conservative Party, led by Jean-Marc BÉLIVEAU; the **Creditist Rally** (*Ralliement des Créditistes*), an offshoot of the Social Credit Party; and the **Popular National Party** (*Parti Nationale Populaire*).

A **Party for an Independent Newfoundland,** led by Charles DEVINE, was founded in 1983, while a **Representative Party** was founded in Alberta by former Social Credit legislator Ray SPEAKER in 1985. There is also a **Western Canada Concept,** led by Douglas CHRISTIE, active in British Columbia.

LEGISLATURE

Influenced by British precedent (though without a peerage), Canada's bicameral **Parliament** consists of an appointed Senate and an elected House of Commons.

Senate. The upper house consists of 104 individuals appointed to serve until 75 years of age by the governor general and selected, on the advice of the prime minister, along party and geographic lines. (In 1975 the membership was increased by the addition of one senator each from the Yukon and Northwest Territories.) As of 1986, approximately 70 percent of the members were Liberals and 25 percent were Conservatives; geographically, Ontario and Quebec are most heavily represented, with 24 senators each. The powers of the Senate are coextensive with those of the Commons, save that all money bills must originate in the lower house.
Speaker: Guy CHARBONNEAU.

House of Commons. The lower house consists of 282 members elected for five-year terms (subject to dissolution) by universal suffrage on the basis of direct representation. Selected prior to 1986 by the prime minister with the approval of the opposition parties, the speaker is now elected by secret ballot of all Commons members. At the election of September 4, 1984, the Progressive Conservative Party won 211 seats; the Liberal Party, 40; the New Democratic Party, 30; independent, 1.
Speaker: John FRASER.

CABINET

[as of March 31, 1988]

Prime Minister	Brian Mulroney
Deputy Prime Minister	Donald Frank Mazankowski
Secretary of State	Lucien Bouchard
Secretary of State for External Affairs	Charles Joseph Clark

Ministers

Agriculture	John Wise
Communications	Flora Isabel MacDonald
Consumer and Corporate Affairs	Harvie Andre
Employment and Immigration	Barbara McDougall
Energy, Mines and Resources	Marcel Masse
Environment	Thomas McMillan
External Relations	Monique Landry
Finance	Michael Holcombe Wilson
Fisheries and Oceans	Thomas Edward Siddon
Indian Affairs and Northern Development	William McKnight
International Trade	John Carnell Crosbie
Justice and Attorney General	Ramon John Hnatyshyn
Labor	Pierre Cadieux
National Defense	Perrin Beatty
	Paul Wyatt Dick (Associate Minister)
National Health and Welfare	Arthur Jacob Epp
National Revenue	Elmer Mackintosh MacKay
Privatization, Regulatory Affairs and Operations	Donald Frank Mazankowski
Public Works	Stewart D. McInnes
Regional Industrial Expansion	Robert de Cotret
Revenue	Elmer MacKay
Status of Women	Barbara McDougall
Supply and Services	Otto John Jelinek
Transport	Benoît Bouchard
Veterans Affairs	George Harris Hees

Ministers of State

Agriculture	Pierre Blais
Canadian Wheat Board	Charles James Mayer
Employment and Immigration	Monique Vézina
Federal-Provincial Relations	Lowell Murray
Finance	Thomas Hockin
Fitness and Amateur Sports	Jean Charest
Forestry and Mines	Gerald S. Merrithew
Grains and Oil Seeds	Charles James Mayer
Indian Affairs and Northern Development	Bernard Valcourt
Multiculturalism	Gerry Weiner
Science and Technology	Robert de Cotret
Senior Citizens	George Harris Hees
Small Business and Tourism	Bernard Valcourt
Transport	Gerry St. Germaine
Treasury Board	Douglas Lewis
Youth	Jean Charest
Without Portfolio	Douglas Lewis
Solicitor General	James Francis Kelleher
Government Leader in the House	Donald Frank Mazankowski
Government Leader in the Senate	Lowell Murray
President, Queen's Privy Council	Donald Frank Mazankowski
President, Treasury Board	Patricia Carney
Governor, Bank of Canada	John W. Crow

NEWS MEDIA

News media are free from censorship or other direct government control.

Press. There are no national press organs; of the 908 provincial newspapers in 1986, 724 were weeklies and 112 were dailies, about one-third of the latter being owned by Thomson Newspapers, Ltd., the largest of

Canada's major chains. The following (circulation figures for 1987) are English-language dailies, unless otherwise noted: *Star* (Toronto, 523,500 daily, 527,000 Sunday); *Le Journal de Montréal* (Montreal, 327,500 daily, 344,100 Sunday), in French; *Globe and Mail* (Toronto, 317,000); *Toronto Sun* (Toronto, 308,000 daily, 456,200 Sunday); *Sun* (Vancouver, 230,300); *La Presse* (Montreal, 201,900 daily, 169,800 Sunday), in French; *Gazette* (Montreal, 199,000), oldest Canadian newspaper, founded 1788; *Ottawa Citizen* (Ottawa, 188,500); *Free Press* (Winnipeg, 174,700 daily, 151,100 Sunday); *The Province* (Vancouver, 173,000 daily, 219,300 Sunday); *Edmonton Journal* (Edmonton, 171,000 daily, 150,800 Sunday); *The Spectator* (Hamilton, 142,700); *Free Press* (London, 128,100); *Le Soleil* (Quebec, 117,800 daily, 93,500 Sunday), in French; *Windsor Star* (Windsor, 86,300). In February 1988 Toronto's *Financial Post,* theretofore a weekly, commenced daily publication in competition with the *Globe and Mail;* shortly thereafter it was announced that the *Montreal Daily News* would shortly be launched as the *Gazette's* only English-language competitor in Quebec.

News agencies. In January 1985, The Canadian Press, a cooperative of over 100 daily newspapers, became Canada's only wire service after buying out its only competitor, United Press Canada. Numerous foreign agencies maintain offices in the leading cities.

Radio and television. Radio and television broadcasting is supervised by the Canadian Radio-Television and Telecommunications Commission (CRTC), which was formed by the 1968 Broadcasting Act. The publicly owned Canadian Broadcasting Corporation (CBC) provides domestic radio and television service in both English and French. Most major television stations not associated with the CBC are affiliated with the CTV Television Network, Ltd., although there are several other smaller services, some emphasizing French-language and/or educational programming. There were approximately 15.7 million television receivers in 1988.

INTERGOVERNMENTAL REPRESENTATION

Ambassador to the US: Allan E. GOTLIEB.

US Ambassador to Canada: Thomas Michael Tolliver NILES.

Permanent Representative to the UN: Stephen LEWIS.

IGO Memberships (Non-UN): ACCT, ADB, ADF, AfDB, BIS, CCC, CDB, CP, CWTH, G10, IADB, IATTC, ICCAT, ICES, ICO, IEA, ILZ, Inmarsat, INRO, Intelsat, Interpol, ISO, ITC, IWTC, NATO, OECD, PCA.

CAPE VERDE ISLANDS

Republic of Cape Verde
República de Cabo Verde

Political Status: Former Portuguese dependency; became independent July 5, 1975; first constitution adopted September 7, 1980.

Area: 1,557 sq. mi. (4,033 sq. km.).

Population: 296,093 (1980C), 337,000 (1988E).

Major Urban Centers (1979E): PRAIA (São Tiago, 37,000); Mindelo (São Vicente, 35,000).

Official Language: Portuguese.

Monetary Unit: Cape Verde Escudo (market rate February 1, 1988, 68.06 escudos = $1US).

President: Aristides María PEREIRA; elected by the National People's Assembly on July 5, 1975; reelected for five-year terms, in 1981 and on January 13, 1986.

Prime Minister: Gen. Pedro Verona Rodrigues PIRES; assumed office July 15, 1975; reconfirmed by the National People's Assembly in 1981 and on January 13, 1986.

THE COUNTRY

Cape Verde embraces ten islands and five islets situated in the Atlantic Ocean some 400 miles west of Senegal. The islands are divided into a northern windward group (Santa Antão, São Vicente, Santa Lucia, São Nicolau, Sal, and Boa Vista) and a southern leeward group (Brava, Fogo, São Tiago, and Maio). About 60 percent of the population is composed of *mestiços* (of mixed Portuguese and African extraction), who predominate on all of the islands except São Tiago, where they are outnumbered by Black Africans; Europeans constitute less than 2 percent of the total. Most Cape Verdeans are Roman Catholics and speak a Creole version of Portuguese that varies from one island to another. Partly because of religious influence, women have traditionally been counted as less than 25 percent of the labor force, despite evidence of greater participation as unpaid agricultural laborers; female representation in party and government affairs is virtually nonexistent.

The islands' economy has traditionally depended on São Vicente's importance as a refueling and resting stop for shipping between Europe and Latin America. The airfield on Sal had previously served a similar function for aircraft, with South African planes alone providing some $10 million per year in direct income; however, by mid-1987 political controversy had deeply cut into this source of revenue (see Current issues, below). Corn is the major subsistence crop, but persistent drought since the late 1960s has forced the importation of it and other foods; fish, bananas, and salt are the leading export commodities. In an unusual effort to counter the effects of the drought, the government in 1987 bought 10,700 hectares of land in Paraguay for intensive cultivation.

GOVERNMENT AND POLITICS

Political background. Cape Verde was uninhabited when the Portuguese first occupied and began settling the islands in the mid-fifteenth century; a Portuguese governor was appointed as early as 1462.

During the 1970s several independence movements emerged, the most important being the mainland-based African Party for the Independence of Guinea and Cape Verde (PAIGC), which urged the union of Cape Verde and Guinea-Bissau, and the Democratic Union of Cape Verde (*União Democrática de Cabo Verde*—UDCV), which was led by João Baptista MONTEIRO and rejected the idea of a merger.

An independence agreement signed with Portuguese authorities on December 30, 1974, provided for a transitional government prior to independence on July 5, 1975. A 56-member National People's Assembly was elected on June 30, 1975, but only the PAIGC participated; the results indicated that about 92 percent of the voters favored the PAIGC proposal of ultimate union with Guinea-Bissau.

Upon independence the Assembly elected Aristides PEREIRA, the secretary general of the PAIGC, as president of Cape Verde. On July 15, (then) Maj. Pedro PIRES, who had negotiated the independence agreements for Guinea-Bissau (effective September 10, 1974) as well as Cape Verde, was named prime minister.

The question of eventual unification with Guinea-Bissau remained unresolved, however, both governments promising to hold referenda on the issue. In January 1977 a Unity Council composed of six members from each of the national assemblies was formed, although in December the two governments asserted that it was necessary to move cautiously, with initial emphasis to be placed on establishing "a common strategy of development". Both countries continued to be ruled through the PAIGC, President Pereira serving as its secretary general and President Luis Cabral of Guinea-Bissau as its deputy secretary.

On September 7, 1980, Cape Verde's first constitution was adopted by the National People's Assembly, the expectation being that a new basic law under preparation in Guinea-Bissau would be virtually identical in all key aspects. On November 14, however, the mainland government was overthrown, and on February 12, 1981, the Cape Verdean Assembly voted to expunge all references to unification from the country's constitution. Formal reconciliation between the two governments was announced in mid-1982 (see Foreign relations, below), both sides agreeing, however, that there would be no immediate resumption of unification efforts.

Constitution and government. The constitution of September 7, 1980, declares Cape Verde to be a "sovereign, democratic, unitary, anti-colonialist and anti-imperialist republic" under single-party auspices. Guaranteed rights include those of free association, religion, and speech. Legislative authority is vested in the National People's Assembly, which also elects the president of the Republic for a five-year term. The prime minister is designated by the Assembly and responsible to it. The Assembly's own president, who is to serve as interim president of the Republic in the event of a vacancy, is prohibited from simultaneously holding a ministerial position. The basic law was amended on February 12, 1981, to revoke provisions designed to facilitate union with Guinea-Bissau, thus overriding, inter alia, a 1976 judiciary protocol calling for the merger of legal procedures and personnel. The likelihood of a merger was virtually eliminated by adoption of the mainland constitution of May 1984, which emulated its Cape Verdean counterpart by lack of reference to the sister state.

Foreign relations. Formally nonaligned, Cape Verde has established diplomatic relations with some 50 countries, including most members of both the European Economic Community, with which it is associated under the Lomé Convention, and the Soviet bloc. In 1980, however, it rejected a Soviet overture for the use of naval facilities at the port of São Vicente as a replacement for facilities formerly available at Conakry, Guinea. The Pereira government has since reaffirmed its opposition to any foreign military accommodation within its jurisdiction. In March 1984 Cape Verde became one of the few noncommunist countries to establish relations with the Heng Samrin government of Kampuchea and, following a visit by Yasir 'Arafat in August 1986, exchanged ambassadors with the Palestine Liberation Organization (PLO).

The country's closest regional links have been with Guinea-Bissau (despite a 20-month rupture following the ouster of the Cabral government in November 1980) and the other three lusophone African states, Angola, Mozambique, and Sao Tome and Principe. Relations with Bissau were formally reestablished in July 1982 prior to a summit meeting of the five Portuguese-speaking heads of state at Praia on September 21–22, at which a joint committee was set up to promote economic and diplomatic cooperation. In June 1987, foreign ministers from the five states met at Lisbon for a series of high-level talks with Portuguese government officials on the destabilization activities of Unita and Renamo in Angola and Mozambique, respectively.

Current issues. Unlike the first national development plan, whose focus on redistribution of land to the peasantry had precipitated a series of riots on Santa Antão in August 1981, the current plan (1986–1990), adopted in December 1986, calls for reform in three areas: agriculture, education, and the civil service. An earlier version of the plan that had encouraged the repatriation of an estimated 600,000 Cape Verdeans abroad had met with disappointing results.

A November 1986 ban against South African air landings threatened an already fragile economy: refueling and rest stops by South African planes had long provided the country with a major source of income. But despite a projected revenue loss of $7 million for 1987, the government continued to back the sanction as a matter of "morality and solidarity with the rest of Africa".

POLITICAL PARTIES

Although a number of parties existed prior to independence, the only party that participated in the 1975 and 1980 legislative elections was the African Party for the Independence of Guinea-Bissau and Cape Verde (PAIGC). The reference to Guinea-Bissau was dropped, insofar as the Cape Verdean branch was concerned, on January 20, 1981, in reaction to the mainland coup of the previous November.

Government Party:

African Party for the Independence of Cape Verde (*Partido Africano da Independência do Cabo Verde* – PAICV). The PAICV's predecessor party, the PAIGC, was formed in 1956 by Amílcar Cabral and others to resist Portuguese rule in both Cape Verde and Guinea-Bissau. Initially headquartered at Conakry, Guinea, the PAIGC began military operations in Guinea-Bissau in 1963 and was instrumental in negotiating independence for that country. Following the assassination of Cabral on January 20, 1973, his brother Luis and Aristides María Pereira assumed control of the movement, Luis Cabral serving as president of Guinea-Bissau until overthrown in the 1980 coup.

Leaders: Aristides María PEREIRA (President of the Republic and Secretary General of the Party), Gen. Pedro PIRES (Prime Minister of the Republic and Deputy Secretary General of the Party).

Exile Opposition:

Cape Verdean Independent Democratic Union (*União Caboverdiana Independente Democrática* – UCID). The UCID is a right-wing opposition group active among the 500,000 Cape Verdean emigrants in Portugal and elsewhere. In mid-1982, 16 of its alleged adherents were arrested and sentenced to prison terms of varying duration on charges of conspiring to overthrow the PAICV government.

LEGISLATURE

The unicameral **National People's Assembly** (*Assembléia Nacional Popular*), currently encompassing 83 deputies, was most recently redesignated on December 7, 1985. The nominees were single listed by the party from some 200 potential candidates, some of whom were not PAICV members.

President: Abílio Augusto Monteiro DUARTE.

CABINET

Prime Minister	Gen. Pedro Verona Rodrigues Pires
Ministers	
Armed Forces and Security	Col. Julio de Carvalho
Education	André Corsino Tolentino
Finance	Gen. Pedro Verona Rodrigues Pires
Foreign Affairs	Col. Silvino Manuel da Luz
Health, Labor and Social Affairs	Dr. Ireneu Gomes
Industry and Energy	Adão Silva Rocha
Information, Culture and Sports	David Hopffer Cordeiro de Almada
Interior	Cortino Cortes
Justice	Col. José Eduardo Figueiredo Araujo
Local Administration and Urbanism	Tito Livio Santos de Oliveira Ramos
Plan and Cooperation	Gen. Pedro Verona Rodrigues Pires
Public Works	Adriano de Oliveira Lima
Rural Development and Fishing	Maj. João Pereira Silva
Transport, Commerce and Tourism	Maj. Osvaldo Lopes da Silva
Governor, Central Bank	Amaro Alexandre Daluz

NEWS MEDIA

Press. The Cape Verdean press includes the following, all published at Praia: *Boletim Oficial,* government weekly; *Unidade e Luta,* PAICV organ; *Voz di Povo,* government weekly.

Radio and television. There are two government radio stations: on São Vicente, the *Voz de São Vicente,* and at Praia, São Tiago, the *Emissora Oficial da República de Cabo Verde.* In 1987 there were approximately 49,000 radio receivers. Television has recently commenced, on a limited basis, from a transmitter at Praia.

INTERGOVERNMENTAL REPRESENTATION

Ambassador to the US: José Luis FERNANDES-LOPES.
US Ambassador to Cape Verde: Vernon Dubois PENNER, Jr.
Permanent Representative to the UN: Humberto Bettencourt SANTOS.
IGO Memberships (Non-UN): ADF, AfDB, BADEA, CILSS, ECOWAS, EEC(L), *EIB,* ICCAT, Intelsat, NAM, OAU.

CENTRAL AFRICAN REPUBLIC

République Centrafricaine

Political Status: Became independent August 13, 1960; one-party military regime established January 1, 1966;

Central African Empire proclaimed December 4, 1976; republic reestablished September 21, 1979; military rule reimposed September 1, 1981; present constitution adopted November 21, 1986.

Area: 240,534 sq. mi. (622,984 sq. km.).

Population: 2,054,610 (1975C), 2,919,000 (1988E).

Major Urban Centers (1982E): BANGUI (350,000); Berberati (100,000); Bouar (55,000).

Official Language: French. The national language is Sango.

Monetary Unit: CFA Franc (market rate March 1, 1988, 285.80 francs = $1US).

President: Gen. André-Dieudonne KOLINGBA; assumed power as head of the Military Committee for National Recovery, following the resignation of President David DACKO on September 1, 1981; assumed the offices of President and Prime Minister upon dissolution of the CMRN on September 21, 1985; sworn in as President for a six-year term on November 29, 1986, following referendum of November 21.

THE COUNTRY

The Central African Republic is a landlocked, well-watered plateau country in the heart of Africa. Its inhabitants are of varied ethnic, linguistic, and religious affiliations. In addition to French and many tribal dialects, Sango is used as a lingua franca. About 60 percent of the population is Christian, 35 percent animist, and 5 percent Muslim.

Nearly 90 percent of Central Africans are employed in farming and animal husbandry, primarily at a subsistence level. Leading exports include diamonds, coffee, timber, and cotton. Most of the small industrial sector is engaged in food processing, while uranium resources are being developed with French and Swiss partners. Economic diversification has been hindered by a lack of adequate transportation facilities, but an even greater hindrance to development was personal aggrandizement during 1976–1979 of self-styled Emperor Bokassa, a virtually empty national treasury at the time of his ouster in September 1979 being only partially mitigated by marginal increases in commodity exports in ensuing years. France remains the country's main source of imports, chief market for exports, and principal aid donor.

GOVERNMENT AND POLITICS

Political background. Formerly known as the territory of Ubangi-Shari in French Equatorial Africa, the Central African Republic achieved independence on August 13, 1960, after two years of self-government under Barthélemy BOGANDA, founder of the Social Evolution Movement of Black Africa (MESAN), and his nephew David DACKO, the Republic's first president. As leader of MESAN, President Dacko rapidly established a political monopoly, dissolving the principal opposition party in December 1960 and banning all parties except MESAN in 1962. Dacko was ousted on January 1, 1966, in a military coup led by Col. Jean-Bédel BOKASSA, who declared himself president. Bokassa abrogated the constitution, dissolved the Assembly, assumed power to rule by decree, took over the leadership of MESAN, and became chief of staff and commander in chief of the armed forces.

Following his assumption of power, Bokassa survived a number of coup attempts (including one involving his son-in-law), often relying on French military intervention. Elected president for life by MESAN in 1972, he assumed the additional office of prime minister in April 1976, but relinquished it to Ange PATASSE the following September, when a new Council of the Central African Revolution (CRC) was established. In the context of widespread government and party changes, Bokassa further enhanced his image as Africa's most unpredictable leader by appointing former president Dacko to be his personal adviser.

On October 18, during a state visit by Libyan leader Mu'ammar al-Qadhafi, Bokassa revealed that he had been converted to Islam and would henceforth be known as Salah al-Din Ahmad Bokassa. On December 4 he announced that the Republic had been replaced by a parliamentary monarchy and that he had assumed the title of Emperor Bokassa I. On December 7 the emperor abolished the CRC and the next day abandoned his Muslim name because of its incompatibility with the imperial designation.

In the wake of a lavish coronation ceremony at Bangui on December 4, 1977, the Bokassa regime became increasingly brutal and corrupt. In mid-1979, Amnesty International reported that scores of schoolchildren had been tortured and murdered after protesting against compulsory school uniforms manufactured by the Bokassa family. In August, an African judicial commission confirmed the report, the emperor responding with a series of arrests and executions of those who had testified before the commission.

On the night of September 20–21, while on a visit to Libya, the emperor was deposed by former president Dacko with French military assistance. While several prominent members of the Bokassa regime were arrested, the "government of national safety" that was announced on September 24 drew widespread criticism for including a number of individuals—among them, in addition to Dacko, the new vice president, Henri MAIDOU, and the new first deputy prime minister, Alphonse KOYAMBA—who had held high-ranking posts in the previous administration. Koyamba was among the ministers replaced in a major cabinet reshuffle in July 1980, while Maidou and Prime Minister Bernard Christian AYANDHO were dismissed in August and placed under house arrest. Ayandho's successor, Jean-Pierre LEBOUDER, was named on November 12, the vice presidency remaining vacant.

In a presidential election on March 15, 1981, Dacko was credited with 50.23 percent of the votes cast, as contrasted with 38.11 percent for his closest competitor, former prime minister Patassé. Alleged balloting irregularities triggered widespread violence at the capital prior to Dacko's inaugu-

ration and the naming of Simon Narcisse BOZANGA as prime minister on April 4. In mid-July, opposition parties were temporarily banned after a bomb explosion at a Bangui theater, and on July 21 the army, led by Gen. André-Dieudonne KOLINGBA, was asked to restore order. Six weeks later, on September 1, it was announced that Dacko, known to be in failing health, had resigned in favor of a Military Committee for National Recovery (CMRN) that, headed by General Kolingba, suspended the constitution, proscribed political party activity, and issued a stern injunction against acts of public disorder.

Patassé and a number of senior army officers were charged with an attempted coup against the Kolingba regime on March 3, 1982, after which the former prime minister took refuge in the French Embassy at Bangui and a month later was flown out of the country. In mid-October, General Kolingba made an official trip to Paris, where he was praised for introducing "rigorous" economic recovery and for restoring "legitimate authority in the Central African Republic".

Internal security merged with regional concerns in late 1984, after an opposition group led by Alphonse M'BAIKOUA, who had been involved in the 1982 coup attempt, joined with Chadian *codo* rebels in launching border insurgency operations. The following April, Bangui and Ndjamena began a joint counterinsurgency campaign which failed to curb the rebels, most of whom sought temporary refuge in Cameroon, while the destruction of civilian villages in the "combing" action heightened local hostility against government forces.

In keeping with promises to launch a gradual return to civilian rule, Kolingba dissolved the CMRN in September 1985 and placed himself, in the dual role of president and prime minister, at the head of a cabinet numerically dominated by civilians, although military men remained in the most powerful positions. At a referendum on November 21, 1986, a reported 91 percent of the electorate approved a new single-party constitution, under which General Kolingba was continued in office for a six-year term.

Constitution and government. The imperial constitution of December 1976 was abrogated upon Bokassa's ouster, the country reverting to republican status. A successor constitution, approved by referendum on February 1, 1981, provided for a multiparty system and a directly elected president with authority to nominate the prime minister and cabinet. The new basic law was itself suspended on September 1, 1981, both executive and legislative functions being assumed by a Military Committee for National Recovery, which was dissolved on September 21, 1985. The constitution approved in November 1986 is a revised version of the 1981 document. The most important modification was the substitution of a one-party "assembly" system for Dacko's pluralistic arrangement, which General Kolingba characterized as inviting "division and hatred as well as tribalism and regionalism".

Local government is currently administered through 16 provinces, under which are grouped subprovinces and numerous rural communes.

Foreign relations. As a member of the French Community, the country has retained close ties with France throughout its changes of name and regime. A defense pact between the two states permits French intervention in times of "invasion" or outbreaks of "anarchy", and French troops, in the context of what was termed "Operation Barracuda", were prominently involved in the ouster of Bokassa. By contrast, in what appeared to be a deliberate shift in policy by the new government of President Mitterrand, some 1,100 French troops remained in their barracks during General Kolingba's assumption of power and, despite debate over alleged French involvement in the Patassé coup attempt, the French head of state declared his support of the regime in October 1982. Economic aid to the CAR has continued, as has concern over the civil war in neighboring Chad, with 2,000 troops posted to the French base at Bouar by August 1983. The Chadian war has preoccupied the CAR leadership since 1980, partly because of the numbers of refugees that have sought refuge in the country's northern region. In addition, trepidations about Libyan intentions not only in Chad but throughout Central Africa prompted Bangui in 1980 to sever diplomatic ties with Libya and the Soviet Union, both of which had been accused of fomenting internal unrest. Relations with the former, although subsequently restored, remained tenuous, with two Libyan diplomats declared *persona non grata* in April 1986.

Current issues. In a remarkable and largely unexplained move, Jean-Bedel Bokassa, who was under sentence of death for offenses committed while the country's "emperor", returned to Bangui from exile in France on October 23, 1986, and was immediately arrested. A retrial on charges that included murder, cannibalism, and corruption concluded on June 12, 1987, with a guilty verdict on 4 of 14 charges; however, the death sentence and trial itself were immediately challenged by Bokassa's lawyers who maintained that a head of state could be legally prosecuted only for treason. The appeal was rejected by the Supreme Court in November; however, in February 1988 President Kolingba, who was reportedly opposed to capital punishment, commuted the sentence to life imprisonment in solitary confinement.

Demonstrations against the continued presence of French troops broke out in Bangui in March 1986 after the crash of a French military jet that killed 35 Centrafricans. Increased French military involvement in the Chadian conflict and its use of the CAR as a base of operations supported the popular perception (endorsed by various internal and exile opposition groups) that the Kolingba regime was preoccupied with the furtherance of French strategic concerns.

The anti-French hostility came in the wake of unrest among students decrying the lack of economic opportunity for graduates. After the circulation at Bangui University of leaflets calling for Kolingba's ouster, student leaders were arrested, provoking a widespread student strike. The administration blamed the turmoil on outside elements, particularly pro-Libyan factions determined to destabilize the government. President Kolingba pardoned the student leaders and other political prisoners later in the year.

In March 1987 the commander of the French military forces in the CAR was requested to leave following two separate incidents involving French soldiers in which Centrafricans had been seriously injured or killed. For many CAR citizens the French presence continued to be viewed as "foreign interference".

POLITICAL PARTIES

The constitution of December 1980, suspended following the 1981 coup, called for the establishment of a multiparty system. General Kolingba specifically banned political parties upon taking power and did not include their legalization in his promise of future civilian rule since to do so would invite "weakening and paralysis of the state and make it prey to individualistic demands". In late 1983, the three main opposition parties formed a coalition, four others that had participated in the 1981 election no longer being active; no opposition grouping was recognized upon formation of the regime-supportive RDC (below) in 1986.

Governing Party:

Central African Democratic Assembly (*Rassemblement Démocrate Centrafricaine*—RDC). The RDC was launched in May 1986 as the country's sole legal party. General Kolingba declared that the new formation would represent "all the various tendencies of the whole nation" but would deny representation to those who "seek to impose a totalitarian doctrine". During its first congress at Bangui on February 6–7, 1987, President Kolingba nominated 44 members of a provisional political bureau.

Leaders: Gen. André-Dieudonne KOLINGBA, Jean-Paul NGOU-PANDE (Executive Secretary).

Illegal Opposition:

Central African Revolutionary Party (*Parti de la Révolution Centrafricaine*—PRC). Organized in 1983 during a secret meeting at Moyenne-Sido near the Chadian border, the PRC has condemned the policies of the Kolingba regime, while advocating a "strongly progressive" program. Its founding groups, not consistently referenced thereafter as operating under the PRC umbrella, are listed below.

Movement for the Liberation of the Central African People (*Mouvement pour la Libération du Peuple Centrafricaine*—MLPC). The MLPC was organized at Paris in mid-1979 by Ange Patassé, who had served as prime minister from September 1976 to July 1978, and was runner up to Dacko in the presidential balloting of March 1981. At an extraordinary congress on September 14–18, 1983, Patassé was accorded a vote of no confidence and replaced with a nine-member directorate as part of a move from "nationalism" to "democratic socialism". A communiqué released at Paris in July 1986 announced that the MLPC had joined forces with the FPO-PT (below) to present a united front against the Kolingba government.

Leaders: Francis Albert OUKANGA (Secretary-General), Raphaël NAMBELE (Secretary for External Relations).

Ubangi Patriotic Front—Labor Party (*Front Patriotique Oubanguien—Parti Travaillaiste*—FPO-PT). Founded by Abel Goumba and long Congo-based, the FPO-PT repudiated the Dacko government in 1981, has called for the withdrawal of French troops and the establishment of "true democracy", and has forged links with a number of European socialist parties. Its leaders have been periodically placed in detention and released in subsequent amnesties, most recently in mid-1985 when the president and secretary general were allowed to return from internal exile in the north. Formal linkage with the MLPC (above) was announced in 1986.

Leaders: Abel GOUMBA (President), Patrice ENDJIMOUNGOU (Secretary General).

Central African Movement for National Liberation (*Mouvement Centrafricaine pour la Liberté Nationale*—MCLN). The pro-Libyan MCLN, organized at Paris by Idi Lala, a former member of the FPO-PT, claimed responsibility for the July 1981 theater bombing at Bangui, in the wake of which it was outlawed. Lala, who was condemned to death in absentia by a military court in May 1982, was deposed as leader in late 1983 by elements within the party which declared the bombing "off target"; at the time of its entry into the PRC, its leadership included former members of the Kolingba government who had been involved in the 1982 coup attempt. These leaders, especially Gen. Alphonse M'baikoua, have been involved in guerrilla action in the north, with the assistance of Chadian insurgents.

On December 10, 1984, a number of MCLN leaders announced the formation of an exile Provisional Government for National Salvation, triggering a vehement denunciation by General Kolingba in mid-January of "embittered" individuals dedicated to the creation of a "phantom" republic. No leading members of either the MLPC or the FPO-PT were associated with the announcement, which was somewhat inexplicably issued in the name of the MLPC Provisional Executive Council.

Leaders: Gen. François BOZIZE, Gen. Alphonse M'BAIKOUA.

LEGISLATURE

The 1981 constitution provided for a multiparty National Assembly (*Assemblée Nationale*), whose members were to have been elected within three months of the presidential balloting on March 15, 1981; no such election was held prior to General Kolingba's assumption of power on September 1. On July 31, 1987, the first legislative elections in 23 years were held, with 142 RDC-nominated candidates vying for 52 seats.

Secretary General: Emile Nicaise MBARI.

CABINET

President	Gen. André-Dieudonné Kolingba
Ministers	
Cabinet Affairs	Capt. Justin Ndjapou
Civil Service, Labor, Social Security and Professional Training	Daniel Sehoulia
Commerce and Industry	Timothee Marboua
Communications, Arts and Culture	David N'Guindo
Defense and War Veterans	Gen. André-Dieudonne Kolingba
Economy, Finance, Planning and International Cooperation	Dieudonné Wazoua
Energy, Mines and Water Resources	Michel Salle
Foreign Affairs	Jean Louis Psimhis
Interior and Territorial Administration	Lt. Col. Christophe Grelombe
Justice and Keeper of the Seals	Michael Gbezera Bria
National and Higher Education	Pierre Sammy Mackfoy
Posts and Telecommunications	Thomas Matouka
Public Health	Jean Willyboro Sacko
Public Works and Territorial Development	Capt. Jacques Kitte
Rural Development	Theodore Bagayombo
Transport and Civil Aviation	Pierre Gonifei-Ngaibonanou
Waters, Forests, Fish, Wildlife and Tourism	Raymond Mbitikon
Secretaries of State	
Economy, Finance, Budget and Debt Management	Louis H. Papeniah
Planning, Statistics and International Development	Syriaque Samba Panza
Rural Development	Georges Assas Mbilault
Director, Central Bank	Alphonse Koyamba

NEWS MEDIA

Press. The following are published at Bangui: *E Le Songo,* daily tabloid in Sango, launched in June 1986; *Journal Officiel de la République Centrafricaine,* fortnightly in French; *Renouveau Centrafricaine,* weekly in French.

News agency. *Agence France-Presse* was nationalized in 1974 as *Agence Centrafricaine de Presse* (ACAP).

Radio and television. The government-controlled *La Voix de la République Centrafricaine* broadcasts in French and Sango. The country's one television station also operates under government supervision.

INTERGOVERNMENTAL REPRESENTATION

Ambassador to the US: Christian LINGAMA-TOLEQUE.

US Ambassador to the Central African Republic: David C. FIELDS.

Permanent Representative to the UN: Michel GBEZERA-BRIA.

IGO Memberships (Non-UN): ACCT, ADF, AfDB, BADEA, BDEAC, CEEAC, EEC(L), *EIB,* IACO, ICO, Intelsat, Interpol, NAM, OAU, OCAM, UDEAC.

CHAD

Republic of Chad
République du Tchad

Political Status: Independent since August 11, 1960; military regime instituted in 1975, giving way to widespread insurgency and ouster of Transitional Government of National Unity in 1982.

Area: 495,752 sq. mi. (1,284,000 sq. km.).

Population: 5,530,000 (1988E).

Major Urban Centers (1979E): N'DJAMENA (400,000); Sarh (120,000); Mondou (85,000); Abéché (54,000).

Official Language: French.

Monetary Unit: CFA Franc (market rate March 1, 1988, 285.80 francs = $1US).

President: Hissein HABRE; sworn in October 21, 1982, following overthrow of the government of Goukhouni OUEDDEI (Goukouni WEDDEYE, Goukouni WODDEI) on June 7.

THE COUNTRY

Landlocked Chad, the largest in area and population among the countries of former French Equatorial Africa, extends from the borders of the equatorial forest in the south to the Sahara Desert in the north. Its unevenly distributed population is characterized by overlapping ethnic, religious, and regional cleavages; the more populous south is largely Negroid and animist, while the north is overwhelmingly Sudanic and Muslim. There is a Christian minority of about 5 percent. Of the country's 12 major ethnic groups, the largest are the Saras in the south and Arabs in the center, north, and east. French is the official language, but Chadian Arabic has recognized status in the school system and the major Black tribes have their own languages. Women constitute roughly 30 percent of the official labor force and more than 65 percent of unpaid family workers; female participation in government and politics is virtually nonexistent.

The economy is almost exclusively agricultural, nearly one-half of the gross national product being derived from subsistence farming, livestock-raising, and fishing. Cotton accounts for over 70 percent of export earnings, with cotton-ginning being the most important industry. Attempts at locating significant mineral resources have largely been unsuccessful, although uranium and other mineral deposits are believed to be located in the extreme northern Aozou Strip, occupied by Libya in 1973–1975. Despite aid from such sources as the UN Development Programme, the World Bank, and the African Development Fund, widespread civil war has, in recent years, precluded measurable economic development, with the per capita GNP less than $200 and about one-quarter of the population existing at a near-starvation level.

GOVERNMENT AND POLITICS

Political background. Brought under French control in 1900, Chad became part of French Equatorial Africa in 1910 and served as an important Allied base in World War II. It became an autonomous member state of the French Community in 1959, achieving full independence under the presidency of François (subsequently N'Garta) TOMBAL-BAYE one year later. Tombalbaye, a southerner and leader of the majority Chad Progressive Party (*Parti Progressiste Tchadien*—PPT), secured the elimination of other parties prior to the adoption of a new constitution in 1962.

The northern (Saharan) territories—historically focal points of resistance and virtually impossible to govern—remained under French military administration until 1965, when disagreements led Chad to request the withdrawal of French troops. Dissatisfaction with Tombalbaye's policies generated progressively more violent opposition and the formation in 1966 of the Chad National Liberation Front (Frolinat), led by Aibrahim ABATCHA until his death in 1969, and then by Dr. Abba SIDDICK. French troops returned in 1968 at the president's request, but despite the French presence and reconciliation efforts by Tombalbaye, the disturbances continued, culminating in an attempted coup by Frolinat in 1971 (allegedly with Libyan backing). In a further effort to consolidate his regime, Tombalbaye created the National Movement for Cultural and Social Revolution (*Mouvement National pour la Révolution Culturelle et Sociale*—MNRCS) in 1973 to replace the PPT.

On April 13, 1975, Tombalbaye was fatally wounded in an uprising by army and police units. Two days later, Brig. Gen. Félix MALLOUM, who had been in detention since 1973 for plotting against the government, was designated chairman of a ruling Supreme Military Council. The new regime, which banned the MNRCS, was immediately endorsed by a number of former opposition groups, although Frolinat remained aloof.

Following a major encounter between Libyan and Frolinat forces in the Tibesti Mountains in June 1976, Frolinat military leader Hissein HABRE attempted to negotiate a settlement with the Malloum regime but was rebuffed. In September Habré lost control of the main wing of the movement to Goukhouni OUEDDEI, who elected to cooperate with the Libyans. In early 1978 Frolinat launched a major offensive against government forces at Faya-Largeau, about 500 miles northeast of the capital, while on February 5 the government announced that it had concluded a ceasefire agreement with a rebel group, the Armed Forces of the North (FAN), loyal to Habré. In the course of talks involving representatives of Chad, Niger, Libya, and Sudan at Sebha, Libya, on February 23–24 and March 23–27, a ceasefire agreement was concluded with Oueddei's People's Armed Forces (FAP), the largest Frolinat faction. In April, however, the FAP resumed military operations and was repulsed only with major French assistance; nevertheless, in early June Frolinat remained in effective control of the northern two-thirds of the country. On August 29 President Malloum announced the appointment of Habré as prime minister under a "basic charter of national reconciliation".

In late 1978 a serious rift developed between Malloum and Habré, and an abortive coup on February 12, 1979, by forces loyal to the prime minister was followed by a month of bloody, but inconclusive, confrontation between the rival factions. On March 16 a four-party agreement was concluded at Kano, Nigeria, involving Malloum, Habré, Oueddei, and Aboubakar Mahamat ABDERAMAN, leader of a "Third Army", the Popular Movement of Chadian Liberation (MPLT). Under the Kano accord, Oueddei on March 23 became president of an eight-member Provisional State Council, which was composed of two representatives from each of the factions and was to serve until a new government could be constituted. French troops were to be withdrawn under a truce guaranteed by Cameroon, the Central African Empire, Libya, Niger, Nigeria, and Sudan. At a second Kano conference held April 3–11, however, the pact broke down, primarily because agreement could not be reached with five other rebel groups, one of which, the "New Volcano", headed by the Revolutionary Democratic Council (*Conseil Démocratique Revolutionaire*—CDR) of ACYL Ahmat, had apparently become a leading beneficiary of Libyan support in the north. Meanwhile, former Malloum supporter Lt. Col. Wadal Abdelkader KAMOUGUE, commander of the Chadian Armed Forces (FAT), had launched a secessionist uprising in the south, also with Libyan backing.

On April 29 a second provisional government was announced under Lol Mahamat CHOUA of the MPLT, with Gen. Djibril Negue DJOGO, former army commander under President Malloum, as his deputy. The Choua government was, however, repudiated by the six "guarantor" states during a third meeting at Lagos, Nigeria, on May 26–27, no Chadian representatives being present. In early June fighting erupted at N'Djamena between Frolinat and MPLT contingents, while other altercations occurred in the east, south, and north (where an invasion by a 2,500-man Libyan force, launched on June 26, met stiff resistance).

In another effort to end the turmoil, a fourth conference convened at Lagos on August 20–21, attended by representatives of 11 Chadian groups and 9 external states (the original 6, plus Benin, Ivory Coast, and Senegal). The August meeting resulted in the designation of Oueddei and Kamougue as president and vice president, respectively, of a Transitional Government of National Unity (*Gouvernement d'Union National de Transition* — GUNT) whose full membership, announced on November 10, included 12 northerners and 10 southerners.

Although the Lagos accord had called for demilitarization of N'Djamena by February 5, 1980, fighting resumed at the capital on March 21 between Defense Minister Habré's FAN and President Oueddei's FAP, the latter subsequently being reinforced by Kamougue's FAT and elements of Acyl's Front for Joint Action (FAC). The coalescence of all other major forces against the FAN occurred primarily because of the perception that Habré, contrary to the intent of the Lagos agreement, had sought to expand his sphere of influence. While the FAN, clearly the best-organized of the military units, continued to maintain control of at least half the city, the OAU and such regional leaders as Togo's President Eyadéma arranged several short-lived ceasefires in late March and April.

On June 15 Libya, moving into the vacuum created by the removal of the last French military contingent on May 17, concluded a military defense treaty with the Oueddei government. By early November, 3,000–4,000 Libyan troops had moved into northern Chad and had also established a staging area within 40 miles of N'Djamena. Habré's position in the capital came under attack by Libyan aircraft, and fighting in the countryside spread as the government attempted to sever the FAN's link to its main base at Abéché, near the Sudanese border. An assault against FAN-controlled sectors of the capital was launched by government and Libyan forces on December 6, after Habré had rejected an OAU-sponsored ceasefire. Five days later the FAN withdrew from the city, some elements retreating toward Abéché and others crossing into Cameroon.

On January 6, 1981, the governments of Chad and Libya announced a decision to achieve "full unity" between their two countries. The action prompted (then) OAU Chairman Siaka Stevens of Sierra Leone to convene an extraordinary meeting of the Organization's Ad Hoc Committee on Chad at the Togolese capital of Lomé, where, on January 14, representatives of 12 governments repudiated the proposed merger, reaffirmed the validity of the 1979 Lagos accord, called on Libya to withdraw, and authorized the formation of an OAU peacekeeping force. Subsequently, it was reported that President Oueddei had been opposed to unification and had signed the agreement at Tripoli under duress, the Libyans expressing their disenchantment with his lack of "Islamic fervor" and calling for his replacement by Acyl Ahmat. Both Vice President Kamougue and Dr. Siddick vehemently opposed the plan, the former terming it an "impossible marriage" and the latter fleeing to Sudan in April after resigning as health minister.

In late May the Transitional Government announced that several faction leaders had agreed to disarm and join in the formation of a "national integrated army" in anticipation of a Libyan withdrawal. Nonetheless, factional conflict continued, while at midyear a revitalized FAN mounted an offensive against Libyan and Libyan-backed government troops in the east. In mid-September, during a two-day meeting at Paris with Oueddei, French authorities agreed to provide logistical support to an OAU force to supplant the Libyans, and in November most of the latter were withdrawn after Benin, Gabon, Nigeria, Senegal, Togo, and Zaire had undertaken to form a 5,000-man contingent to maintain order, supervise elections, and assist in establishing a unified Chadian army.

During early 1982 FAN forces regained control of most of the eastern region and began advancing on N'Djamena, which fell on June 7, GUNT President Oueddei fleeing to Cameroon before establishing himself at the northern settlement of Bardai on the border of the Libyan-controlled Aozou Strip. Upon entering the capital, the Council of the Commander in Chief of the FAN (*Conseil du Commandement en Chef des FAN* — CCFAN) assumed political control and on June 19 named Habré to head a 30-member Council of State. Earlier, on June 11, OAU Chairman Daniel arap Moi ordered the withdrawal of the OAU force, which, at maximum strength, had scarcely exceeded 3,000 men, two-thirds from Nigeria. During the ensuing four months the FAN, with assistance from FAT units, succeeded in gaining control of the south, and on October 21 Habré was sworn in as president of the Republic. Following his investiture, the new chief executive dissolved the Council of State in favor of a 31-member government that included Dr. Siddick; DJIDINGAR Dono Ngardoum, who had served briefly as prime minister under Oueddei in May; and Capt. Routouane YOMA, a former aide of Colonel Kamougue. Two months later N'Djamena announced that the FAN and FAT would be consolidated as the Chadian National Armed Forces (*Forces Armées Nationales Tchadiennes* — FANT).

After the declaration at Algiers in October 1982 of a "National Peace Government" by eight of the eleven signatories of the 1979 Lagos accord, Oueddei forces regrouped at Bardai with renewed support from Tripoli. By May 1983 GUNT units were advancing south, and with the aid of 2,000 troops and several MIG fighters supplied by Libya, captured the "northern capital" of Faya-Largeau on June 24. Habré immediately called for international assistance and received aid from Egypt, Sudan, and the United States, with France avoiding direct involvement despite a 1976 defense agreement (see Foreign relations, below). FANT troops recaptured Faya-Largeau on June 30, only to lose it again on August 10, while France, under mounting pressure from the United States and a number of francophone African countries, began deploying troops along a defensive "red line" just north of Abéché on August 14. The French — who eventually numbered some 3,000, in addition to 2,000 Zäirean troops — maintained an effective ceasefire for the remainder of the year, while calling for a negotiated solution between the two factions. In November, the OAU announced that it would sponsor "reconciliation talks" at Addis Ababa and issued invitations to all participants in the Lagos conference, but protocol demands by Habré led to their eventual cancellation. While Habré continued to urge France to aid him in a full-scale offensive against Oueddei, the Mitterrand government refused, at one point urging "a federation of Chad" as a means of ending the conflict. Meanwhile, in the wake of renewed fighting, the "red line" was moved 60 miles north.

Following Colonel Qadhafi's April 1984 offer of a mutual withdrawal of "Libyan support elements" and French forces, talks were initiated between Paris and Tripoli that yielded a withdrawal accord on September 17. The French pullout was completed by the end of the year; Libya, however, was reported to have withdrawn less than half of its forces from the north and the political-military stalemate continued.

In a statement issued at Tripoli on October 15, 1985, Oueddei was declared dismissed as FAP leader. The GUNT president repudiated the action and on November 5 announced the release of Acheikh Ibn OUMAR, leader of the GUNT-affiliated Revolutionary Democratic Council (*Conseil Démocratique Revolutionnaire*—CDR), who reportedly had been arrested a year earlier. On November 11, N'Djamena responded by concluding a "reconciliation agreement" with a breakaway faction of the CDR, the Committee for Action and Concord (*Comité d'Action et de Concord*—CAC).

In February 1986, GUNT forces mounted an offensive against FANT troops at the center of the "red line", but by early March had been repulsed, reportedly with heavy losses. On June 19, FAT leader Kamougue announced from Paris his resignation as GUNT vice president, while in August Oumar declared that the CDR had "suspended collaboration" with the GUNT, but would "maintain solidarity with all anti-Habré factions." Clashes between CDR and GUNT units followed, the latter offering to open peace talks with N'Djamena; however, the Habré government insisted that the GUNT would first have to repudiate the Libyan intervention. Subsequently, during a meeting of GUNT factions at Cotonou, Benin, in mid-November, Oueddei was "expelled" from the grouping, with Oumar being named its president. In late December, as FANT forces were reported to be moving north, fighting broke out between FAP units loyal to Oueddei and what Libyan sources characterized as Oumar's "legitimate" GUNT.

On March 22, 1987, in what was seen as a major turning point in the lengthy Chadian conflict, FANT troops captured the Libyan air facility at Ouadi Doum, 100 miles northeast of Faya-Largeau. Deprived of its air cover, the Libyans thereupon withdrew from Faya-Largeau, its most important military base in northern Chad, abandoning an estimated $1 billion worth of sophisticated weaponry. On August 8 Chadian government troops captured the town of Aozou, administrative capital of the northern strip; however, it was retaken by Libyan forces three weeks later. Chad thereupon entered southern Libya in an unsuccessful effort to deprive it of air support in the continuing struggle for the disputed territory. A ceasefire was then negotiated by OAU chairman Kenneth Kaunda of Zambia, although further fighting had broken out by late November, with skirmishes continuing into 1988.

Constitution and government. The 1964 constitution was abrogated in April 1975 by the Malloum government,

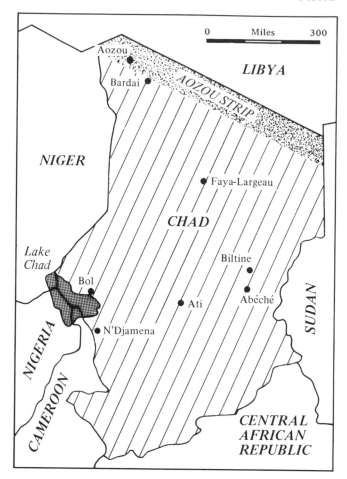

which issued a provisional replacement in August 1978. The latter was in turn superseded by the Kano agreement of March 1979. The Transitional Government of National Unity named in November 1979 was to remain in existence until February 1981, at which time a national election was to have been held.

A new basic law, derived from the Malloum charter, was promulgated by the CCFAN in mid-1982. Pending the adoption of a permanent constitution, it assigned full powers to the president, who could be appointed or dismissed only by the FAN Council. Coincident with the absorption of CCFAN into the National Union for Independence and Revolution (see Political Parties, below) in June 1984, ultimate authority was vested in UNIR's Central Committee. The legal system, based on French civil and Chadian customary law, was headed by a Supreme Court until April 1975, when the court was abolished.

Administratively, the country is divided into 14 prefectures, each with an appointed governor.

Foreign relations. Chad's internal unrest has long been exacerbated by conflict with Libya over delineation of their common border. The dispute was intensified in 1975 by Libya's annexation of an area of some 27,000 square miles in northern Chad (the Aozou Strip) that is said to contain substantial iron ore and uranium deposits (see map). Since 1977, Libyan representatives have consistently identified the territory in question as part of "southern Libya", largely on the basis of a 1935 agreement between France and Italy that the latter had failed to ratify.

The country's relations with France have been complicated since the mid-1970s by intermittent French involvement in the civil war. In October 1975, France, for the second time, evacuated its military bases in Chad, having angered the Malloum government because of its negotiations with the Habré-led Frolinat wing that had kidnapped French ethnologist Françoise Claustre in April 1974. In March 1976 new cooperation agreements were concluded, Paris agreeing to come to Chad's defense in the event of an external attack but not to intervene directly with regard to the rebels. Despite this assertion, French forces aided government troops in the northern Tibesti region subsequent to the release of Mme. Claustre in January 1977 and played a crucial role in stemming the Frolinat offensive in April-May 1978. More recent interventions have been justified at annual Franco-African summits as within the scope of French commitments to francophone states.

Despite the fact that disagreement over Chadian representation had contributed to a serious crisis within the OAU in 1981–1983, the Habré government was eventually seated at the 1983 regular session at Addis Ababa, as well as at the non-aligned summit at New Delhi in 1984.

Current issues. The unexpected, but crushing defeat of Libyan forces in March 1987 was viewed as a major humiliation — both domestically and internationally — for Col. Mu'ammar Qadhafi, while offering hope that President Habré might be close to unifying his long divided country. In the course of the action, an estimated one-third of an occupying force of 14,500 was either killed or wounded, while N'Djamena's losses were minimal. Even more impressive was the capture of a vast arsenal of Soviet-supplied equipment that Libyan bombers attempted to destroy, with imperfect success, in the wake of the troop withdrawal.

Even before its military victory, the Habré regime had succeeded in winning over or neutralizing much of the domestic opposition, with most of Goukhouni Oueddei's followers transferring their loyalties to N'Djamena. However, reconciliation talks at Algiers between Oueddei and government representatives broke down in late July, apparently because of pressure exerted by Tripoli on the former GUNT president.

POLITICAL GROUPS

The formation of the regime-supportive National Union for Independence and Revolution (below) marked the first legally recognized political party to have existed in Chad since the Movement for Social and Cultural Revolution was banned in 1975. Both the government party and a number of opposition groups have long claimed to represent the Chad National Liberation Front (*Front de Libération National Tchadien* — Frolinat), an organization which suffered such extensive fractionalization subsequent to its founding in 1966 that by 1986 it had become little more than a generic name for various groups originally based in the north.

Governing Party:

National Union for Independence and Revolution (*Union Nationale pour l'Indépendance et la Révolution* — UNIR). The UNIR was formed on June 22, 1984, during the first extraordinary congress of Frolinat-FAN, consisting largely of Habré's wing of Frolinat, the Armed Forces of the North, which voted to disband. In addition to the FAN, the party incorporates the Assembly for Unity and Democracy in Chad, led by Djingar Dono Ngardoum; the National Democratic Popular Assembly, led by Kassire Koumakoye; the Democratic Movement of Chad, led by Ngarina Mbaikel; the wing of Original Frolinat led by Habré's former minister of education, Abba Siddick; and factions of the Popular Party of Chad-Democratic Assembly. Its structure includes a Central Committee and a 14-member Executive Bureau; its ideology, expressed at the 1984 congress, includes a commitment to democracy and opposition to "religious fanaticism". Recent UNIR working sessions have emphasized a commitment to national reconciliation.

Leaders: Hissein HABRE (President of the Republic and Chairman of the Party), Capt. Gouara LASSOU (Executive Secretary).

Other Groups:

Following Habré's capture of N'Djamena in 1982, most of the factions opposed to the FAN coalesced under a reconstituted GUNT. During 1983–1984, dissent between GUNT factions over the extent of Libyan involvement led to reported dissolution of the coalition, although pronouncements continued to be issued in its name. During a meeting at Sebha, Libya, on August 7, 1984, most of the pro-Libyan military components of GUNT joined in forming the National Council of Liberation (*Conseil National de la Libération* — CNL), which was succeeded by a more inclusive Supreme Revolutionary Council (*Conseil Suprême de la Révolution* — CSR) a year later. By 1986, however, anti-Libyan sentiment appeared to have gained the ascendancy, with Oueddei being removed as CSR chairman (and president of GUNT) in November. Thereafter, the CSR declined in importance, many of its component groups having announced their dissolution and acceptance of integration into the UNIR by early 1988.

LEGISLATURE

The National Assembly (*Assemblée Nationale*) was dissolved on April 13, 1975.

CABINET

President	Hissein Habré
Minister of State	Dono Ngardoum Djidingar

Ministers

Agriculture and Rural Development	Col. Wadal Abdel Kader Kamougué
Civil Service	Routouang Yoma Golom
Commerce and Industry	Soubiane Bilal
Culture, Youth and Sports	Djibrine Hissein Grinki
Finance and Data Processing	Ngarnayal Mbailem Bana
Food Security and Afflicted Groups	Ahmed Senoussi Wadak
Foreign Affairs	Gouara Lassou
Information and Civic Orientation	Adoum Moussa Seïf
Interior and Territorial Administrative	Ibrahim Mahamat Itno
Justice and Keeper of Seals	Gen. Djibril Négué Djogo
Labor and Employment	Oudalbaye Naham
Livestock and Rural Water	Seid Bauche
Mines and Energy	Col. Alphonse Kotiga Guérina
National Defense, Veterans and War Victims	Hissein Habré
National Education	Mahamat Nour Malaye
Planning and Cooperation	Mahamat Soumaïla
Posts and Telecommunications	Assileck Halata
Public Health	Mahamat Senoussi Khatir
Public Works, Housing and Urbanism	Kassiré Delwa Koumakoye
Social Affairs and Promotion of Women	Yaneko (Ruth) Romba

Tourism and Environment	M'Bailao Lossimian Naïmbaye
Transportation and Civil Aviation	Abdoulaye Douto
Counsellor to the President	Ouangmoutching Homsala
Director, Central Bank	Madje Adam

NEWS MEDIA

The Ministry of Information controls all media.

Press. The following are published at N'Djamena: *Info-Tchad* (1,500), daily bulletin of the official news agency, ATP; *Al-Watan,* government weekly; *Journal Officiel de la République du Tchad,* official organ.

News agencies. The domestic agency is *Agence Tchadienne de Presse* (ATP). *Agence France-Presse* and Reuters also maintain offices at N'Djamena.

Radio and television. *Radiodiffusion Nationale Tchadienne* broadcasts in French, Arabic, and local languages. One television station transmits from N'Djamena to a limited number of receivers.

INTERGOVERNMENTAL REPRESENTATION

Ambassador to the US and Permanent Representative to the UN: Mahamat Ali ADOUM.

US Ambassador to Chad: John BLANE.

IGO Memberships (Non-UN): ACCT, ADF, AfDB, BADEA, BDEAC, CILSS, EEC(L), *EIB,* IC, ICAC, IDB, Intelsat, Interpol, NAM, OAU.

CHILE

Republic of Chile
República de Chile

Political Status: Independent republic since 1818; present "transitional" constitution approved September 11, 1980 (with effect from March 11, 1981), partially superseding military regime instituted in 1973.

Area: 292,256 sq. mi. (756,945 sq. km.).

Population: 8,884,768 (1970C), 12,686,000 (1988E).

Major Urban Centers (1985E): SANTIAGO (urban area, 4,318,000); Viña del Mar (316,000); Valparaíso (267,000); Talcahuano (221,000); Concepción (218,000); Antofagasta (175,000).

Official Language: Spanish.

Monetary Unit: Peso (market rate March 1, 1988, 242.79 pesos = $1US).

Head of State: Gen. Augusto PINOCHET Ugarte; leader of four-man junta which assumed power by coup d'état September 11, 1973; officially designated Head of State on June 26, 1974; proclaimed President on December 17, 1974; named by plebiscite of September 11, 1980, to a further eight-year term as President, commencing March 11, 1981.

Other Junta Members: The other members of the junta, now serving in a consultative capacity, are Adm. José Toribio MERINO Castro, Gen. Fernando MATTHEI Aubel (replaced Maj. Gen. Gustavo LEIGH Guzmán on July 24, 1978), Gen. Rodolfo STANGE Oelcker (replaced Gen. César MENDOZA Durán on August 2, 1985), and Lt. Gen. Humberto GORDON Rubio (replaced Lt. Gen. Julio CANESSA Robert on October 8, 1986).

THE COUNTRY

Occupying a narrow strip along some 2,700 miles of South America's west coast, the Chilean national territory also includes Easter Island, the Juan Fernández Islands, and other smaller Pacific islands. The population is predominantly mestizo (mixed Spanish and Indian) but also includes German, Italian, and other small foreign groups. Roman Catholicism, which was disestablished in 1925, is the religion of 85 percent of the people. Women constitute nearly 40 percent of the paid labour force, a majority in domestic service with the rest concentrated in agriculture, education and health care; save during the Allende regime of 1970–1973, when women were prominent both in government and the opposition, female political representation has been minimal.

Chile is the world's leading copper producer, the commodity accounting for over two-fifths of export earnings. Other commercially mined minerals include gold, silver, coal, and iron. In addition, there are large-scale nitrate deposits in the north and some oil reserves in the south. Since World War II, the country has suffered from lagging agricultural production, with a reliance on food imports contributing to record balance-of-payment deficits in the early 1980s. The economy has recently begun to recover, despite unacceptably high unemployment and a foreign debt burden of $20 billion. Most economic advisers to the current regime have come from the "Chicago school" of free-market economics, thus promulgating extreme budgetary austerity, lax import restrictions, privatization of state enterprises, and pro-business tax structures.

GOVERNMENT AND POLITICS

Political background. After winning its independence from Spain in 1810–1818 under the leadership of Bernardo O'HIGGINS, Chile experienced a period of alternating centralized and federal constitutions. The political struggles between conservative and liberal elements culminated in the civil war of 1829–1830, the conservatives emerging victorious. Conflicts with Peru and Bolivia in 1836–1839 and in 1879–1884 (the War of the Pacific) resulted in territorial expansion at the expense of both (see map, p. 67).

Liberal elements prevailed in the presidential balloting following World War I. The election of Arturo ALESSANDRI was a victory for the middle classes, but the reforms he advocated were never implemented because of parliamentary intransigence. Left-Right antagonism after World War II occasioned widespread fears for the future of the democratic regime, but the election in 1964 of

Eduardo FREI Montalva appeared to open the way to fundamental economic and social reforms. The failure of the Frei regime to accomplish these goals led to the election of Salvador ALLENDE Gossens in 1970, Chile thus becoming the first of the American republics to choose an avowedly Marxist president by constitutional means. Allende immediately began to implement his openly revolutionary "Popular Unity" program, which included the nationalization of Chile's principal foreign-owned enterprises, a far-reaching redistribution of social benefits, and the pursuit of a more independent foreign policy. Despite the very real benefits which began to accrue to the lower classes as a result of these and other policies, Allende gradually alienated the middle class, a sizable portion of the legislature, the judiciary, and finally the military. He was killed during a right-wing coup on September 11, 1973, which resulted initially in rule by a four-man junta. On June 26, 1974, Maj. Gen. Augusto PINOCHET Ugarte was designated as head of state, the other junta members gradually assuming subordinate roles.

Pinochet, proclaimed president on December 17, 1974, has governed on the basis of unwavering army support, despite widespread domestic and foreign criticism centering on human rights abuses, including the "disappearance", arbitrary arrest and detention, torture, and exiling of opponents. Citing the need for harsh measures to combat communism, the regime, since its installation, has typically operated under either a state of siege or a somewhat less restrictive state of emergency.

In a national referendum on January 4, 1978, Chileans were reported, by a three-to-one majority, to have endorsed the policies of the Pinochet government, although the significance of the poll was lessened by the inability of opposition groups to mount an effective antireferendum campaign.

On September 11, 1980, the electorate, by a two-to-one margin, endorsed a new constitution which, over an eight-year period that commenced March 11, 1981, is to serve as the framework for "slow and gradual evolution" toward a democratic order. Antigovernment agitation has, however, grown throughout the 1980s, propelled in part by economic decline during 1983–1985. The government has responded with a mixture of liberalization and repression, while refusing to accelerate its timetable or alter its carefully circumscribed procedures for a return to elected government.

Constitution and government. Under the present regime, effective power remains concentrated in the military. The judicial system, headed by a Supreme Court, continues to operate (supplemented by military courts), but the former National Congress has been dissolved and competitive political activity has been proscribed. On December 31, 1975, a consultative Council of State, composed of leading citizens drawn from various sectors of society, was organized as a first step toward "a new constitutional order", which was subsequently described by General Pinochet as being based on the principle of "authoritarian democracy". The basic law drafted by the Council and adopted by plebiscite in September 1980 provides for a 120-member Chamber of Deputies to be elected in 1990 and for a Senate of 35 members (exclusive of former presi-

dents), 26 of whom are also to be elected. Prior to expiration of the chief executive's current term, the junta is mandated to nominate a successor for approval by plebiscite. If confirmed, he will serve until 1997, at which time free and open presidential balloting will be conducted. Should the junta's candidate be rejected, the incumbent will serve for an additional year, during which an open election will be held.

In 1975 the country's 25 historic provinces were grouped into 12 regions plus the metropolitan region of Santiago, each headed by a governor (*governador*), and were further subdivided into 40 new provinces and approximately 300 municipalities, headed by intendents (*intendentes*) and mayors (*alcaldes*), respectively. Except at Santiago and Viña del Mar, the mayors were formerly elected; at present, officials at all three levels are appointed by the president.

Foreign relations. Chile has traditionally followed a pro-Western foreign policy, but under the Allende regime contacts with Communist states were strengthened, including the establishment of diplomatic relations with Cuba. Concomitantly, US-Chilean relations cooled, primarily as a result of the nationalization of US business interests. Following the 1973 coup, US relations improved, diplomatic ties with Cuba were severed, and links with other Communist-bloc nations were curtailed. However, the assassination at Washington, DC, on September 21, 1976, of Orlando LETELIER del Solar, a prominent government official under the Allende regime, became a festering bilateral issue. In May 1979 the Chilean Supreme Court refused a US Justice Department request for the extradition of three army officers who had been charged in the case, including the former chief of the Chilean secret police, while in November, Washington moved to curtail diplomatic, economic, and military relations with Santiago after the Court also ordered the closing of investigations into possible criminal charges against the three in Chile.

In 1981, the US Congress passed legislation linking cooperation in the Letelier case with any economic or military aid to Chile, while also requiring certification of Santiago's progress on human rights. Recent US policy has been mixed, combining praise for Pinochet's hard-line anticommunism with pressure to end press censorship and initiate a dialogue with opposition leaders.

A lengthy dispute with Argentina over the ownership of three islands in the Beagle Channel north of Cape Horn was technically resolved in May 1977, when a panel of international arbitrators awarded all three islands to Chile (see map, p. 26). The award was, however, repudiated by Argentina since it permitted Chile to extend its territorial limits into the Atlantic, thereby strengthening its claims to contested territory in the Antarctic. Subsequent mediation initiated by Pope John Paul II in 1981 yielded a 1984 agreement based on a "bi-oceanic" principle proposed by Buenos Aires, under which Chile still received the islands but claimed only Pacific Ocean territory, conceding all Atlantic rights to Argentina.

In September 1977, in ceremonies at Washington, DC, that accompanied the signing of the Panama Canal treaties, Pinochet met with the presidents of Bolivia and Peru in regard to Bolivia's long-sought outlet to the Pacific (see Bolivia: Foreign relations), but no definitive settlement emerged and in March 1978 Bolivia severed diplomatic relations because of alleged Chilean inflexibility in the negotiations. The impasse appeared to have been breached in 1986 when Bolivia reopened its consular office at Santiago, but no resolution of the issue had been achieved by mid-1988. .

During the 1982 Falkland Islands conflict, Chile attempted to maintain a low profile while cautiously endorsing regional support for Argentina and helping to rescue survivors from its sunken cruiser *General Belgrano*. However, its posture of formal neutrality was compromised by the crash-landing, on Chilean territory, of a British helicopter that appeared to be far out of range of its mother ship in the South Atlantic. More damaging were British press reports in the wake of the Argentine defeat, which claimed that London and Santiago had participated in joint electronic intelligence-gathering throughout the period of the hostilities.

Current issues. On August 25, 1985, acting on the initiative of Santiago's newly appointed cardinal, Juan Francisco FRESNO, 11 center and center-right parties signed an Accord for the Transition to Full Democracy (*Acuerdo para la Transición a la Plena Democracia*) that called for lifting the state of emergency, the restoration of civil liberties, and more liberal electoral procedures than had been advanced by the government for the 1990 parliamentary poll. President Pinochet responded that "we would betray the Chilean people if we returned to a formal and hollow democracy". A seemingly more serious threat to the regime was presented by a 48-hour general strike on July 2–3, 1986, organized by the Civic Assembly (*Asamblea de la Civilidad*), a grouping of more than 20 professional, student, and labor organizations. The 1986 action was endorsed by virtually all of the country's political parties, including the Communist Party and other leftist groups that had not participated in the 1985 Accord. Although its leaders hoped that the strike would stimulate a crescendo of dissent that would force concessions, the opposition's momentum stalled under a renewed government crackdown that included the arrest of many prominent politicians. Thereafter, the question of the use of violence by anti-Pinochet forces again isolated the Communists, particularly in the wake of the president's narrow escape from a motorcade attack on September 7 and the earlier discovery of a large arms cache, which, according to authorities, was intended for use by leftist guerrillas.

During 1987 political party activity, while remaining technically illegal, intensified in anticipation of the plebiscite that was expected to be conducted by the end of the ensuing year. In January 1988 the right-wing *Renovación Nacional* (see Political Parties, below), having become the first group to secure electoral status, announced that it would back the candidate advanced by the armed forces — expected to be President Pinochet, although some sentiment within the junta (particularly on the part of its naval representative) appeared to favor a civilian nominee. Subsequently, in the wake of two public opinion polls (one conducted by a pro-opposition firm) that showed marginal support for the government, some 14 center and center-left parties agreed to campaign jointly for a "no" vote. Four members of the recently organized United Left (*Izquierda Unida*) indicated that they would support the action, although three IU formations, including the Communist Party, refused to participate in what they foresaw as a "fraudulent plebiscite".

POLITICAL PARTIES

Chile's traditional multiparty system ran the gamut from extreme Right to extreme Left, and parties have historically played an important role in the nation's political life. Following the 1973 coup, however, the military government, declaring party politics to be inappropriate, outlawed those groups which had supported the Allende government and forced the remainder into "indefinite recess". In 1977, following the alleged discovery of a "subversive plot" by the Christian Democrats, it formally dissolved all of the existing parties and confiscated their assets. In the early 1980s, as opposition to the Pinochet regime crystallized, the traditional formations resurfaced, most of them, although still illegal, being tolerated by the government within unstated but generally understood limits. A number of somewhat fluctuating coalitions followed and in March 1987 legislation was approved that would recognize groups "which share the same political doctrine of the government" and proved capable of obtaining 0.5 percent of the vote in 8 of Chile's 13 regions.

Rightist Groups:

Prior to its dissolution in June 1985, a coalition known as the National Democratic Accord (*Acuerdo Democrático Nacional* — Adena) offered "critical support" to the regime and tried to mediate a compromise with the centrist *Alianza Democrática* (below). It encompassed a number of right-wing parties, including the **Movement for National Union** (*Movimiento de Unión Nacional* — MUN), led by Andrés ALLAMAND; the **Radical Democracy** (*Democracia Radical* — DR), led by Jaime TORMO; the **National Action Movement** (*Movimiento de Acción Nacional* — MAN), led by Federico WILLOUGHBY and Pablo RODRIGUEZ Grez; the **Christian Social Movement** (*Movimiento Social Cristiano* — MSC), led by Juan de DIOS Carmana; and the **National Democratic Party** (*Partido Democrático Nacional* — PDN or Padena), led by Mateo FERRER and Apolonides PARRA. Following Adena's demise, occasioned by what leaders cited as "intransigence" by both government and opposition, the MUN moved toward rapprochement with the AD, becoming a signatory of the 11-party Accord for Transition to Full Democracy, while in early 1987 it joined the right-wing *Renovación Nacional* alliance (below).

Rightist parties that did not affiliate with Adena included the **National Advance Guard** (*Avanzada Nacional* — AN), led by César HIDALGO and reported to have close links to the military; the **Independent Democratic Union** (*Unión Democrática Independiente* — UDI), another military-linked group currently led by Jaime GUZMAN; the **National Party** (*Partido Nacional* — PN), formerly headed by Interior Minister Sergio JARPA Reyes and more recently by Carmen SAENZ and Fernando OCHAGAVIA; and the **Project for National Development** (*Proyecto de Desarrollo Nacional* — Proden), a business-oriented grouping formed in 1982 by Jorge LAVANDERO, which was active in 1983 but relatively quiescent thereafter. The PN, Chile's largest right-wing party and one of the major anti-Allende formations, participated in the 11-party Accord of August 1985.

In early 1987 the UDI joined with the MUN (above) and the National Labor Front (*Frente Nacional del Trabajo* — FNT), led by Sergio ONOFRE Jarpa, to form a new right-wing coalition, the **National Renovation** (*Renovación Nacional* — RN). Although under strong pressure to join the new group, the PN reportedly broke off talks with RN leaders in March to concentrate on relations with the Christian Democrats and right-wing Socialists, with whom it had been associated in the 1985 pact. The RN was registered as a national party in December, although by March 1988 a pronounced internal cleavage had developed, with the MUN/FNT leadership ranged against that of the UDI.

In January 1987, a new right-wing terrorist group surfaced, the **September 7 Command** (*Commano 7 de Septiembre*). The organization claimed responsibility for the murder of several government opponents following the September 7, 1986, attempt on President Pinochet's life, from which it took its name.

Centrist Groups:

Democratic Alliance (*Alianza Democrática* — AD). The most visible and cohesive of the revived opposition, the AD was formed in early 1983 as the *Multipartidaria,* assuming its present designation at mid-year. It includes two of the leading pre-Pinochet formations, the non-Marxist but formerly Allende-supportive **Radical Party** (*Partido Radical* — PR), led by Enrique SILVA Cimma, and the **Christian Democratic Party** (*Partido Demócrata Cristiano* — PDC), currently under the leadership of Patricio AYLWIN. Other coalition members include the **Liberal Republican Party** (*Partido Republicano Liberal* — PRL), led by Armando JARAMILLO Lyón; the **Liberal Movement** (*Movimiento Liberal* — ML), led by Pedro ESQUIVEL and Gastón URETA; the **Social Democracy** (*Social Democracia* — SD), led by Mario SHARPE; the **Popular Socialist Union** (*Unión Socialista Popular* — Usopo), led by Ramón SILVA Ulloa; and a moderate faction of the **Chilean Socialist Party** (*Partido Socialista de Chile* — PSCh), led by Carlos BRIONES Olivos.

The AD, dominated by the PDC (Chile's largest political party), was a major component of the August 1985 Accord. The PDC, under right-wing pressure, agreed to the exclusion of Marxist groups from the pact. However, in the wake of government unwillingness to yield on constitutional revision, AD contact with the Left was reported in 1986 and the PDC, in early 1987, endorsed "single party" opposition to the regime that would include center-right and moderate leftist formations, while disavowing association with groups advocating the use of violence.

In mid-1986, a group headed by industrialist Orlando SAENZ was reported to have formed the **Democratic Intransigence** (*Intransigencia Democrática* — ID) to serve as a bridge between right- and left-wing opposition parties, while in November a new center-left coalition, the Democratic National Accord (*Acuerdo Nacional Democrático* — Ande, not to be confused with Adena, above) was formed in support of the Accord for Transition to Full Democracy, which encompassed the PDC, PN, Padena, PR, PSCh, Usopo, BSCh (below), MAPU (see under IU, below), and the **Social Democratic Party** (*Partido Social Demócrata* — PSD).

Leftist Groups:

Chilean Socialist Bloc (*Bloque Socialista Chileno* — BSCh). The BSCh was formed in late 1983 by a variety of Socialists and leftist Catholics who had split from the Christian Democrats in the late 1960s and early 1970s. Unlike the MDP (see under IU, below), the Bloc committed itself to nonviolent transition to democratic government and offered the AD (of which it was a member until December 1986) limited support toward that end. Its founding members included the **Socialist Convergence** (*Convergencia Socialista*), led by Angel FLISHFISH and Manuel Antonio GARRETON, and the **Christian Left** (*Izquierda Cristiana* — IC), led by Luis MAIRA, which subsequently joined the IU.

United Left (*Izquierda Unida* — IU). The IU was launched in June 1987 under the presidency of Clodomiro ALMEYDA Medina, who had been foreign minister in the Allende government and subsequently led a Marxist-Leninist faction of the PSCh from exile until returning clandestinely to Chile in March. The IU superseded the Communist-centered Popular Democratic Movement (*Movimiento Democrático Popular* — MDP, below), broadening it to include the non-Marxist IC, a leftist faction of the PR, and the **United Popular Action Movement** (*Movimiento de Acción Popular Unitaria* — MAPU), led by Oscar GARRETON.

The MDP, led by Germán COREA, had been formed in September 1983. Due to the advocacy of violent overthrow of Pinochet by most of its component groups, including the **Communist Party of Chile** (*Partido Comunista de Chile* — PCC), headed by Luís CORVALAN Lepe and José SANFUENTES, a constitutional tribunal ruled in January 1985 that the MDP was not legally acceptable; three months later, in response, the PCC proclaimed a strategy "to make Chile ungovernable" and endorsed the actions of the FPMR (below), which has generally been regarded as the PCC's military wing, although maintaining a separate clandestine leadership. Despite constant repression from the Pinochet regime, the PCC retains considerable influence, particularly among the poor and within some labor organizations. In early 1987, internal dissent was reported

over the endorsement of violence, which had alienated centrist opposition groups that might otherwise have welcomed the MDP into an anti-Pinochet coalition. Other MDP members included two factions of the Socialist Party (Almeyda's PSCh-ML and a non-Leninist group — which did not join the IU — led by Ricardo NUÑEZ Munoz) and the **Movement of the Revolutionary Left** (*Movimiento de Izquierda Revolucionaria* — MIR), a quasi-guerrilla organization formed by PSCh elements in the mid-1960s that has been led for the last decade by Andrés PASCAL Allende, a nephew of the late president who was reported to have returned secretly from exile in August 1986.

Independent leftist groups in early 1988 included the Nuñez faction of the PSCh; the moderate **Party for Democracy** (*Partido por la Democracia* — PPD), organized by a group of Nuñez faction dissidents under the leadership of Ricardo LAGOS in December 1987; and the recently formed **Humanist Party** (*Partido Humanista* — PH), led by José Tomás SAENZ. Prominent at the extreme Left was the **Manuel Rodríguez Patriotic Front** (*Frente Patriótica Manuel Rodríguez* — FPMR), an urban insurgent group that claimed responsibility for a number of bombings during 1984–1986 and achieved notoriety as a result of the 92-day kidnapping of army colonel Carlos CARREÑO in 1987.

LEGISLATURE

The former National Congress (*Congreso Nacional*) consisted of a Senate and Chamber of Deputies, each elected by universal suffrage and proportional representation. Both houses were dissolved in the wake of the 1973 coup. The constitution approved in September 1980 calls for reactivation of a bicameral legislature, balloting for which is currently scheduled in 1990.

CABINET

President	Gen. Augusto Pinochet Ugarte
Ministers	
Agriculture	Jorge Prado Aránguiz
Defense	Rear Adm. (Ret.) Patricio Carvajal
Economy, Development and Reconstruction	Brig. Gen. Manuel Concha Martínez
Finance	Hernán Büchi Buc
Foreign Relations	Ricardo García Rodríguez
Health	Dr. Juan Giacone Gandolf
Housing and Urbanization	Miguel Angel Poduje
Interior	Sergio Fernández Fernández
Justice	Hugo Rosende
Labor and Social Welfare	Alfonso Márquez de la Plata Irarrázaval
Land and Colonization	Gen. Jorge Hernán Veloso Bastias
Mining	Samuel Lira Ovalle
Public Education	Juan Antonio Guzmán Molinare
Public Works	Maj. Gen. Bruno Siebert Held
Transportation	Gen. Jorge Massa Armijo
Secretary General of Government	Orlando Poblete Iturrate
Secretary General of the Presidency	Gen. Sergio Valenzuela Ramírez
President, Central Bank	Brig. Gen. Enrique Seguel Morel

NEWS MEDIA

Until 1973 the Chilean news media enjoyed freedom of expression and were among the most active on the South American continent. Since then, policies adopted by the military junta have severely depleted the ranks of both press and broadcasting facilities while sharply curtailing the freedom of those that remain. In summarizing his government's attitude, General Pinochet stated in September 1976 that the dissemination of any material based on Marxist ideology or other doctrines opposed to the nation's "basic institutions" would be considered offenses against the state. Although prior censorship is not employed, the government has regularly seized press runs of critical publications and temporarily shut down opposition magazines, most recently during a state of siege in late 1986.

Press. In the wake of the 1973 coup, a number of papers, including *La Prensa, El Siglo, Puro Chile, La Tribuna,* and *La Segunda,* were closed down, although the last was subsequently permitted to resume publication. The following are dailies at Santiago: *La Tercera de la Hora* (210,000); *Las Ultimas Noticias* (140,000); *El Mercurio* (120,000 daily, 250,000 Sunday), world's oldest Spanish-language paper (founded 1827), conservative; *La Nación* (50,000), government owned; *La Segunda* (40,000); *¿Qué Pasa?* (30,000), weekly; *El Diario Oficial* (15,000). The principal opposition daily, *La Epoca,* which was launched under Christian Democratic auspices in March 1987, has attained only a third of its target circulation of 60,000, while the left-wing *Fortín Mapocho,* converted from a weekly to a daily in April, has a circulation of no more than 10,000. *El Siglo,* a clandestine Communist Party organ, claims a circulation of 25,000.

News agencies. The domestic facility is *Agencia Informativa Orbe de Chile;* a number of foreign bureaus, including ANSA, AP, Reuters, TASS, and UPI, maintain offices at Santiago.

Radio and television. In 1976 the government announced the establishment of a National Radio and Television Council (*Consejo Nacional de Radio y Televisión*) to prevent the broadcasting media from being used as "negative instruments or disrupters of the community". In January 1977, under a decree prohibiting political parties from operating radio stations, the highly respected Christian Democratic station, *Radio Balmaceda,* was closed down. The *Asociación de Radiodifusoras de Chile* and the *Radio Difusoras Australes Sociedad, Ltda.,* both operate short- and medium-wave stations. *Televisión Nacional de Chile* operates some two dozen stations; each of Santiago's three major universities operates at least one noncommercial television station. During 1987 there were approximately 2.6 million television sets in use.

INTERGOVERNMENTAL REPRESENTATION

Ambassador to the US: Hernan Felipe ERRAZURIZ.

US Ambassador to Chile: Harry George BARNES, Jr.

Permanent Representative to the UN: Pedro DAZA.

IGO Memberships (Non-UN): ALADI, CCC, CIPEC, IADB, ICCO, ICM, Inmarsat, Intelsat, Interpol, IWC, OAS, OPANAL, PCA, SELA.

CHINA

Zhongguo (Chung-kuo)

Political Status: Politically divided since 1949; mainland under (Communist) People's Republic of China; Taiwan under (Nationalist) Republic of China.

Area: 3,705,387 sq. mi. (9,596,961 sq. km.), including Taiwan.

Population: 1,134,407,000 (1988E), including Taiwan.

THE COUNTRY

The most populous and one of the largest countries in the world, China dominates the entire East Asian land mass but since 1949 has been divided between two governments. The Communist-ruled People's Republic of China (PRC) controls the Chinese mainland, including Manchuria, Inner Mongolia, Sinkiang (Chinese Turkestan), and Tibet. The anti-Communist government of the Republic of China (Nationalist China) administers the island province of Taiwan and some smaller islands, including Quemoy (Kinmen), Matsu, and the Pescadores.

Climatically and geographically, the vast and varied expanse of mainland China ranges from tropical to far-northern temperate, from desert to extremely wet-humid, from river plains to high mountains. Population density varies from less than 1 to over 200 per square kilometer. Of the mainland population, 93 percent is ethnically Han Chinese, but there are 15 minority peoples of over 1,000,000, including Uigurs, Tibetans, Manchus, and Mongols, and many smaller groups. Agriculture is still the predominant occupation, with 80 percent of the population living in the countryside, although the PRC has had considerable success in developing both light and heavy industry. In 1984, 90 percent of adult women were employed full-time outside the home; female representation in party and government averaged about 20 percent, with a concentration in lower levels.

Taiwan, a semitropical island 100 miles off China's southeast coast, has small plains suitable for agriculture in the west and towering mountains along its east-central spine. About 98 percent of the population is ethnically Chinese, the remainder being of aboriginal Malayo-Polynesian stock. The Chinese may be divided into three groups: numerically predominant Amoy Fukienese, whose ancestors arrived before the Japanese occupation of Taiwan in 1895, minorities of the Hakka, whose ancestors likewise arrived before 1895, and "Mainlanders", who arrived after 1945 from various parts of China. The major occupations are farming, light and hi-tech industry, commerce, fishing, and the processing of agricultural goods. Economic advance has been rapid in recent years; the standard of living is now one of the highest in East Asia, and half of Taiwan's people live in urban areas. Approximately 75 percent of women over age 15 are salaried or wage workers, mainly in the textile and garment industry; low "women's wages" are viewed as crucial to the economy's competitiveness in the world market. Female representation in government is minimal.

Political background. China's history as a political entity is less ancient than its cultural tradition but extends at least back to 221 BC, when north China was unified under the Ch'in dynasty. In succeeding centuries of alternating unity and disunity, the domain of Chinese culture spread from north to south until it covered what is today considered China proper. After the fall of the Manchu Dynasty in 1912, a republic was established under the leadership of SUN Yat-sen, who abdicated the presidency in favor of the northerner YUAN Shih-kai but subsequently formed a rival regime in the south following Yuan's attempt to establish a new dynasty. During the Northern Expedition of 1926–1928 (an attempt by the southern government, after Sun's death, to reunify China), CHIANG Kai-shek defeated his rivals, gained control of the Kuomintang (Nationalist Party), and expelled the Communists from participation in its activities. With the capture of Peking in June 1928, the Kuomintang regime gained international recognition as the government of China. Many warlord regimes continued to exist, however, while the Communists set up local governments in Kiangsi Province and later, after the Long March of 1934–1935, at Yenan, Shensi Province. In a remarkable display of Chinese unity, most such groups, including the Communists accepted the leadership of the central government following the Japanese invasion of July 1937.

Communist strength increased during World War II, and the failure of postwar negotiations on establishment of a coalition government was followed by full-scale civil war in which the Communists rapidly won control of the entire mainland. In December 1949 the Nationalists moved their capital to Taipei on the island of Taiwan, whence they continued to claim legal authority over the whole of China. The Communists established their own government, the People's Republic of China, at Peking (Beijing) on October 1, 1949, and have since maintained a parallel claim to sovereignty over all of China, including Taiwan. While each of the two governments has sought diplomatic recognition from as many states as possible, a decisive breakthrough for the PRC occurred on October 25, 1971, when the UN General Assembly voted to recognize its delegation as comprising "the only legitimate representatives of China" to the world body. This action also encouraged increased acceptance of the People's Republic by individual governments, an overwhelming majority of which now recognize the PRC. At the conclusion of US President Nixon's visit to the People's Republic on February 21–28, 1972, a joint communiqué included a US acknowledgment that "all Chinese on either side of the Taiwan Strait maintain that Taiwan is a part of China", together with an assertion that the United States "does not challenge that position". It was not, however, until December 15, 1978, that Washington agreed to severance of diplomatic relations with Taipei and the formal recognition of the People's Republic, effective January 1, 1979.

PEOPLE'S REPUBLIC OF CHINA

Zhonghua Renmin Gongheguo
(Chung-hua Jen-Min Kung-ho Kuo)

Note: As of January 1, 1979, the People's Republic of China officially adopted a system known as *pinyin* for rendering Chinese names into languages utilizing the Roman alphabet. The system is not in use in Taiwan, where the older Wade-Giles form of transliteration has been retained. In the material that follows, mainland personal and place names — such as Mao Zedong (Mao Tse-tung) and Beijing (Peking) — are rendered in *pinyin*, with occasional parenthetical reference to Wade-Giles or other English equivalents for purposes of clarification.

Political Status: Communist People's Republic established October 1, 1949; present constitution adopted December 4, 1982; controls mainland China and represents China in the United Nations.

Area: 3,691,795 sq. mi. (9,561,758 sq. km.), excluding Taiwan.

Population: 1,008,175,288 (1982C), 1,114,056,000 (1988E), excluding Taiwan.

Major Urban Centers (1987E): BEIJING (Peking, 6,082,000; urban area, 9,765,000); Shanghai (8,673,000; urban area, 12,440,000); Tianjin (Tientsin, 5,630,000; urban area, 8,421,000); Shenyang (4,242,000); Wuhan (3,455,000); Guangzhou (Canton, 3,289,000); Chongqing (Chungking, 2,687,000); Harbin (2,568,000); Nanjing (Nanking, 2,460,000); Dalian (Dairen, 1,811,000).

Official Language: Northern (Mandarin) Chinese (*putung hua*).

Monetary Unit: Renminpiao (People's Bank Dollar) or Yuan (principal rate March 1, 1988, 3.72 yuan = $1US). The overall currency is known as Renminbi (People's Currency).

President: YANG Shangkun; elected by the National People's Congress on April 8, 1988, succeeding LI Xiannian.

Vice President: WANG Zhen; elected by the National People's Congress on April 8, 1988, succeeding Gen. ULANHU (ULANFU).

Premier of the State Council: LI Peng; named to succeed Premier ZHAO Ziyang (CHAO Tzu-yang), on an acting basis following the latter's confirmation as General Secretary of the Chinese Communist Party, effective November 24, 1987; confirmed as Premier by the National People's Congress on April 9, 1988.

GOVERNMENT AND POLITICS

Political background. Following its establishment in 1949, the government of the People's Republic of China (PRC) devoted major attention to the consolidation of its rule in China and outlying territories and to socialization of the Chinese economy. Within China proper, Communist rule was firmly established by the early 1950s. Xizang (Tibet), over which China has historically claimed suzerainty, was brought under military and political control in 1950–1951 and, after a nationalist revolt and the flight of the Dalai Lama to India in 1959, was incorporated as an Autonomous Region of the PRC in 1965. Occupation of Taiwan, on the other hand, was prevented by a protective role assumed by the United States in 1950, although the offshore islands of Quemoy and Matsu were sporadically shelled in subsequent years as an ostensible prelude to the "liberation" of Taiwan itself.

The internal policy and economic planning of the PRC, originally modeled on Soviet experience and supported by Soviet technical aid and loans, began to deviate markedly from Soviet models with the proclamation in 1958 of the "Great Leap Forward", a new system of economic development based on the organization of the peasant population into rural communes and the use of labor-intensive as opposed to capital-intensive methods of production. The failure of the "Great Leap Forward" was followed by a period of pragmatic recovery in 1961–1965 that coincided with growing ideological differences between the Chinese and Soviet Communist parties. Apparently believing that the revolutionary ardor of the Chinese Communist Party (CCP) had succumbed to bureaucratization, Chairman MAO Zedong (MAO Tse-tung) launched the "Great Proletarian Cultural Revolution" in 1965–1966 to reassert the primacy of Marxist-Leninist doctrine against "revisionist" tendencies imputed to leading elements within the CCP. A period of internal turmoil and civil strife in 1966–1968 found Mao, Defense Minister LIN Biao (LIN Piao), and others denouncing the influence of PRC Chairman LIU Shaoqi (LIU Shao-ch'i), whose ouster was announced in October 1968, and other alleged revisionists, some of whom — including former CCP secretary general DENG Xiaoping (TENG Hsiao-p'ing) — were subsequently "rehabilitated". After causing vast internal turbulence that reached a peak in 1967, the Cultural Revolution diminished in intensity during 1968 and early 1969 amid indications that one of its main results had been an increase in the power of the military. At the CCP's Ninth Congress, held in April 1969, Marshal Lin Biao was hailed as the "close comrade in arms and successor" of Chairman Mao. Two years later, however, Lin disappeared from public view and was subsequently branded as an inveterate opponent of Mao who had been largely responsible for the excesses of the Cultural Revolution (he was later reported to have perished in a plane crash in Mongolia on the night of September 12–13, 1971, while en route to the Soviet Union after failing in an attempt to seize power). In early 1974, "counterrevolutionary revisionism" of the Lin variety was indirectly, but vigorously, attacked by means of a campaign directed against China's ancient sage Confucius, with some arguing that the true target was Premier ZHOU Enlai (CHOU En-lai). By the end of the year, however, increasing numbers of senior officials, including many military men who had been purged during the Cultural Revolution, had reappeared.

A subsequent period of relative quiescence was shattered by the deaths of Premier Zhou on January 8, 1976, and of Chairman Mao on September 9. Shortly after Zhou's death, Vice Premier HUA Guofeng (HUA Kuo-feng) was named acting premier. The appointment came as a surprise to foreign observers, who had anticipated the elevation of the rehabilitated Deng Xiaoping. As first vice premier, Deng had performed many of Zhou's functions during the latter's long illness, but on April 17, following demonstrations at Beijing and elsewhere in support of Deng, it was announced that he had again been dismissed from all government and party posts and that Hua had been confirmed as premier. A widespread propaganda campaign was subsequently launched against Deng and other "unrepentant capitalist-roaders".

Mao's death precipitated a renewed power struggle that resulted in a victory for the "moderate", or "pragmatic", faction within the Politburo over the "radical" faction composed of Vice Premier ZHANG Chunqiao (CHANG Ch'un-ch'iao), JIANG Qing (CHIANG Ch'ing, Mao's

widow), WANG Hongwen (WANG Hung-wen), and YAO Wenyuan (YAO Wen-yüan), who had called for a return to the principles of the Cultural Revolution. Stigmatized as the "gang of four", the radicals were arrested on October 6, one day before Hua's designation as chairman of the CCP Central Committee, and were later indicted on charges that included plotting to overthrow the government. The trial of the four (plus six associates of Lin Biao) began at Beijing on November 20, 1980, and concluded with convictions (including deferred death sentences for Zhang and Jiang) on January 25, 1981.

In July 1977 Deng Xiaoping, for the second time, was rehabilitated and restored to his former posts of CCP deputy chairman, vice premier of the State Council, and chief of staff of the armed forces. Though the Fifth National People's Congress (NPC), which met at Beijing on February 25–March 5, 1978, reconfirmed Hua as premier and named CCP Deputy Chairman YE Jianying (YEH Chien-ying) as NPC chairman — a post vacant since the 1976 death of Marshal ZHU De (CHU Teh) — most observers considered Deng to be at least as powerful as Hua. The vice premier's ascendancy was further manifested during what appeared to be another leadership struggle in the last quarter of the year, culminating in late December in a CCP Central Committee meeting at which four of Deng's close supporters were named to the party Politburo while several "Maoists" were, without losing their Politburo seats, effectively stripped of key governmental and party responsibilities.

Of more far-reaching consequence than the personnel changes at the December meeting was a sweeping reform in agricultural policy that, as implemented in 1979–1980, progressively nullified the Maoist commune system by permitting a return in many areas to farming on a family basis, despite occasional condemnation at the provincial level of production teams that had "divided up the land . . . for individual farming or disguised individual farming". Subsequently, some land was converted to cash and industrial crop production, while additional acreage was taken out of agriculture entirely for the construction of local workshops and plants. Collaterally, the state farms were transformed into integrated enterprises operating on the basis of long-term, low-interest loans, rather than state subsidies, and assigned responsibility for their own profits and losses.

At a plenum of the CCP Central Committee, held at Beijing on February 23–29, 1980, a number of Deng's opponents were removed from the Politburo, while two of his supporters were promoted to the latter's Standing Committee. Furthermore, the party Secretariat, which had been abolished during the Cultural Revolution, was reinstated with HU Yaobang (HU Yao-pang), a Deng ally, named as general secretary, while Liu Shaoqi was posthumously rehabilitated as "a great Marxist and proletarian revolutionary". The trend continued at an August 30–September 10 session of the National People's Congress, which at its concluding meeting accepted Hua's resignation as premier of the State Council, naming Vice Premier ZHAO Ziyang (Chao Tzu-yang) as his successor. In an apparent effort to ease the transition, Deng also resigned as vice premier, while Hua retained titular status as party chairman. Hua subsequently retired from public view and was replaced as CCP chairman by Hu at a Central Committee plenum on June 27–29, 1981, the general secretaryship being vacated. Although remaining a member of the Politburo's Standing Committee, Hua was also removed as chairman of the party's Military Commission, with Deng being named his successor.

During the Twelfth CCP Congress, which met September 1–11, 1982, a new party constitution was adopted that abolished the posts of chairman and vice chairman while reinstating that of general secretary (to which former chairman Hu was named). Although a number of leadership changes (generally strengthening the dominance of Deng's "reformist" faction) were subsequently announced, the membership of the Standing Committee remained unchanged, save for the dropping of Hua, whose sole remaining position was membership on the Central Committee.

The restructuring of the upper CCP echelon was accompanied by a program of widespread personnel "rectification" at the provincial and municipal levels in late 1982 and early 1983. The following October, a three-year "consolidation" campaign was announced to eliminate vestiges of "leftist factionalism" among party cadres. One year later, the party's Central Committee unanimously approved an unprecedented program on *Reform of the Economic Structure,* which urged reliance "on the world's advanced methods of management, including those of developed capitalist countries". The new urban policy distinguished between state ownership of enterprises and "the power of operation" and sought to couple the requirements of a planned economy with those of a "commodity economy based on the law of value" by reducing the degree of "mandatory planning" in favor of "guidance planning", under which noncritical sectors would be increasingly subject to market forces. Specifically, the document called for rejection of an "irrational price system" that frequently reflected neither the true value of commodities nor "the relation of supply to demand". However, a remarkable comment in the December 7 issue of *People's Daily* that "one cannot expect the works of Marx and Lenin to solve today's problems" was subsequently amended to read ". . . to solve all of today's problems".

On the personnel front, the "rectification" campaign continued into 1985, with General Secretary Hu Yaobang announcing on April 9 that some 70 percent of the leaders in 107 party and State Council departments, as well as in 29 regional, provincial, and municipal governments, were to be replaced. However, the most dramatic implementation of the policy came in September, when an extraordinary National CCP Conference of Party delegates (less amenable to local influence than a Congress) was convened for the first time since 1955 and proceeded to abolish "de facto lifelong tenure" by retiring nearly one-fifth of the Central Committee; the latter body then met to accept the resignation of approximately 40 percent of the ruling Politburo. While further consolidating the position of Deng Xiaoping, the shake-up at the senior level did not, however, consist entirely of a purge of those with misgivings about his policies, a number of individuals with little obvious enthusiasm for market economics or an "open door" to the

West being permitted to retain their positions. Conspicuous among the latter was Hua Guofeng, who remained a member of the Central Committee, despite a four-year period of political eclipse.

Domestically, political relaxation reached a zenith during 1986. Early in the year, General Secretary Hu endorsed open criticism of party pronouncements and subsequently revived a short-lived 1957 appeal by Chairman Mao to "Let a hundred flowers bloom", promising that the policy, this time, would not be reversed. In December, student demonstrations broke out in at least a dozen cities, including Beijing, calling for the election of more genuinely representative people's congresses. The situation generated bitter resentment by conservative party leaders and on January 16, 1987, Hu was forced to resign as party leader. Named as his successor, on an acting basis, was Premier Zhao, whose spokesmen insisted that while intellectuals should not be considered targets of a campaign against "bourgeois liberalization", they should refrain from airing "new views" inappropriate to Chinese society. Zhao stepped down as premier coincident with confirmation of his status as CCP general secretary on November 24, LI Peng, being designated to fill the vacated post.

Earlier, on December 4, 1982, the National People's Congress approved a new PRC constitution (see below), which reinstated the post of head of state (abolished under the 1975 constitution), with the incumbent to bear the title of president, rather than that of chairman. LI Xiannian (LI Hsien-nien) was named to fill the new position on June 18, 1983, following elections to the Sixth NPC in March-April, the prominent Inner Mongolian leader, Gen. ULANHU (ULANFU), being named vice president. Subsequently, in the course of an extensive government reorganization at the opening session of the Seventh NPC in March-April 1988, the two leaders were replaced by YANG Shangkun and WANG Zhen, respectively.

Constitution and government. The constitution adopted by the First National People's Congress on September 20, 1954, defined the PRC, without reference to the Communist Party, as "a people's democratic state led by the working class and based on the alliance of workers and peasants"; by contrast, both the 1975 and 1978 constitutions identified the PRC as "a socialist state of the dictatorship of the proletariat", while specifically recognizing the CCP as "the core of leadership of the whole Chinese people". Article 1 of the most recent (1982) constitution defines the PRC as "a socialist state under the people's democratic dictatorship led by the working class and based on the alliance of workers and peasants." Like its immediate predecessor, it seems designed in part to guard against abuses attributed to proponents of the Cultural Revolution. Thus, for example, its civil-rights provisions are somewhat more circumscribed and it does not revive a guarantee (dropped from the 1978 document in September 1980) that citizens may "speak out freely, air their views fully, hold great debates, and write big-character posters"—"rights" that were viewed as being abused in political campaigns during the Cultural Revolution. On the other hand, arrests must still be sanctioned by appropriate authorities and carried out by "public security" organs, while rights to a defense and to a public trial are retained, save in cases "involving special circumstances as prescribed by law". Minority rights are defined, equal pay for equal work is mandated, and deputies may be recalled at all legislative levels. Among the enumerated responsibilities are those involving the observation of "labor discipline", the payment of taxes, and the exercise of family planning.

The National People's Congress is identified as "the highest organ of state power". Deputies are elected by lower-level legislative bodies and by units of the armed forces for five-year terms. Sessions are held once a year. Among the NPC's functions are constitutional amendment and the election of most leading government officials, including the president and vice president of the PRC, whose terms are concurrent with that of the legislature; state councillors (including premier and vice premiers); and ministers. Judicial authority is exercised by a hierarchy of "people's courts" under the supervision of the Supreme People's Court. There is a collateral hierarchy of "people's procuratorates" under the supervision of a Supreme People's Procuratorate, with both the courts and the procuratorates accountable to legislative bodies at relevant levels. The principal regional and local organs are Provincial and Municipal People's Congresses (elected for five-year terms); Prefecture, City, and County Congresses (elected for three-year terms); and Town Congresses (elected for two-year terms). In mid-1985, it was reported that a five-year campaign to dismantle some 56,000 rural communes in favor of 92,000 local township governments had been completed.

Administratively, the PRC is divided into 21 provinces: Anhui (Anhwei), Fujian (Fukien), Gansu (Kansu), Guangdong (Kwangtung), Guizhou (Kweichow), Hebei (Hopei), Heilongjiang (Heilungkiang), Henan (Honan), Hubei (Hupeh), Hunan (Hunan), Jiangsu (Kiangsu), Jiangxi (Kiangsi), Jilin (Kirin), Liaoning (Liaoning), Qinghai (Tsinghai), Shaanxi (Shensi), Shandong (Shantung), Shanxi (Shansi), Sichuan (Szechwan), Yunnan (Yunnan), Zhejiang (Chekiang); 5 autonomous regions: Guangxi Zhuang (Kwangsi Chuang), Nei Monggol (Inner Mongolia), Ningxia Hui (Ningsia Hui), Xinjiang Uygur (Sinkiang Uighur), Xizang (Tibet); and 3 centrally governed municipalities: Beijing (Peking), Shanghai (Shanghai), Tianjin (Tientsin).

Foreign relations. Historically a regional hegemon periodically weakened by dynastic and other internal difficulties, China's capacity to withstand external intrusion reached a nadir with the Japanese occupation of Manchuria in 1931–1932, after nearly a century of coastal penetration by Britain and other Western powers. Technically a victor at the conclusion of World War II, it received substantial Soviet assistance after the Maoist takeover in 1949, but was progressively estranged from Moscow in the wake of Stalin's death in 1953 and the alleged "revisionist" posture of his successors. For a lengthy period extending from the Soviet cancellation of its technical aid program in 1960 to the lapse of a 30-year friendship treaty in 1980, the ideological hostility persisted, aggravated by conflicting territorial claims, Moscow's invasion of Afghanistan in 1979, and what Beijing viewed as a threatening Soviet military presence in Mongolia. In the more recent context of leadership changes in both countries, tensions have measurably

subsided; low-level normalization talks were initiated in October 1982 and continued at six-month intervals thereafter. During 1984–1985 a number of economic accords were concluded, while upon taking office in March 1985 Soviet General Secretary Gorbachev called for "a serious improvement in relations with China". Subsequently, although two rounds of negotiations on the border issue were held, after a nine-year lapse, in 1987, the possibility of a Sino-Soviet summit continued to be precluded by the presence of Vietnamese troops in Kampuchea.

An ally of Hanoi during the Vietnam War, China denounced Vietnam as Moscow's "Asian Cuba" in mid-1978 and continued its support for Kampuchea (Cambodia) in the border dispute that culminated in a Vietnamese invasion of its western neighbor at the end of the year. A Chinese incursion into northern Vietnam in February 1979, triggered by the Vietnamese action in Kampuchea but rooted in a series of border disputes going back to the mid-nineteenth century, proved to be an embarrassment to the ostensibly more powerful participant. While local successes were registered, serious personnel and equipment shortcomings were evident as the relatively inexperienced Chinese encountered strong resistance from battle-hardened Vietnamese militiamen bearing Soviet and captured American weapons. There was no evidence that Hanoi was forced to reassign any substantial number of regular army units from Kampuchea, and the Chinese withdrew in mid-March, claiming that they had succeeded in their objective of "teaching Hanoi a lesson". Sporadic border clashes continued thereafter, some of the more serious in April-June 1984 during a Vietnamese dry-season offensive against Kampuchean guerrillas, with further encounters in 1985.

For more than a quarter-century relations with India have been strained because of a territorial dispute that resulted in full-scale fighting between the two countries in October 1962, with China occupying some 14,500 square miles of territory adjacent to Kashmir in the west, while claiming some 36,000 square miles bordering Bhutan in the east (see map under entry for India). In 1979, China declared that it would not seek Indian withdrawal in the east (south of the so-called McMahon line drawn by the British in 1915) if India would recognize its claim in the west, which involves a portion of its strategically important Sinkiang-Tibet highway; New Delhi responded by calling for Chinese withdrawal from both sectors as a precondition of settlement talks. The first direct negotiations on the issue were held at Beijing in late 1981, but proved abortive; a further round of discussions at New Delhi in November 1985 also failed to end the impasse, although the two parties continued the dialogue at Beijing in mid-1986 and at New Delhi in late 1987.

Contrasting with regional rivalry has been a striking improvement in relations with the West, highlighted by visits to the People's Republic by US presidents Nixon and Ford in February 1972 and December 1975, respectively. The United States and the PRC established de facto diplomatic relations in 1973 by agreeing to set up "liaison offices" in each other's capitals and moved to complete the exchange, on a de jure basis, as of January 1, 1979. Japan, long China's leading trading partner, recognized the PRC as the "sole legal government of China" in 1972, and on August 12, 1978, the two signed a treaty of peace and friendship, culminating six years of intermittent talks.

Foreign affairs occupied center stage during 1984, including an exchange of visits by CCP General Secretary Hu Yaobang and Japanese Prime Minister Nakasone, and by Chinese and American defense ministers, in addition to an 18-day West European tour by Premier Zhao Ziyang. By far the most important visiting dignitary was US President Ronald Reagan, who engaged in extensive talks with Chinese leaders from April 26 to May 1. Of possibly greater importance was the initialing on September 26 of a "Sino-British Declaration on the Question of Hong Kong". Under the slogan "one country and two systems", China will regain full sovereignty over Hong Kong in 1997, when the 99-year lease of the New Territories expires, while agreeing to maintain the enclave as a capitalist "Special Administrative Region" for at least 50 years thereafter. A lengthy series of guarantees tendered by Beijing to facilitate reversion of the colony has been construed both as a means of assuaging the fears of business interests upon which China depends for an estimated one-third of its foreign exchange and as a signal of Chinese intention in regard to the future of Taiwan, in presumed reference to which the category of Special Administrative Region was included in the 1982 constitution. The agreement on Hong Kong was followed on April 13, 1987, by a joint Sino-Portuguese declaration on the future of Macao, which is to revert to Chinese sovereignty in 1999 (see Portugal: Related Territories).

The People's Republic was admitted to the United Nations as the sole representative of China in 1971, succeeded Taiwan as Chinese member of the International Monetary Fund and World Bank group in 1980, and joined the International Criminal Police Organization (Interpol) in 1984. One of the world's nuclear powers since the mid-1960s, the PRC is reported to possess ballistic missiles capable of reaching key Soviet targets and, despite a denunciation of Moscow's endorsement of détente as "fraudulent rhetoric" during its first appearance at the Geneva Disarmament Conference in February 1980, has since endorsed arms control as a matter of historic necessity. Although not a signatory to the 1968 UN Treaty on the Non-Proliferation of Nuclear Weapons, China joined the International Atomic Energy Agency in early 1984 and at a Vienna meeting of the organization's General Conference in September 1985 announced its willingness to permit IAEA inspection of certain of its nuclear installations.

Current issues. The sweeping domestic changes of 1982–1985 were followed in 1986 by an effort to resolve the intrinsic tension between individual accountability and state control in both rural and urban sectors. In the countryside, replacement of the commune system by "contract responsibility" had yielded somewhat diminished grain output because of a shift into more lucrative, but less essential crops, accompanied by an officially sanctioned loss of marginal land to animal husbandry and forestry. In addition, conflict emerged in some areas between farmers and party cadres, some of whom sought to retain a semblance of the earlier system by diverting earnings to the provision of local amenities. In some 27,000 urban enterprises, the introduction of "factory director responsibility" formally trans-

ferred decision-making authority to unit managers, without absolving local party officials of responsibility for "guaranteeing and supervising". Symptomatically, the launching at Shenyang in August of a quite modest "stock market" experiment in the sale of transferable industrial bonds — the first public trading of commercial paper in China since 1949 — was followed in September by a Central Committee attack on "bourgeois liberalism" as a capitalist affront to socialist values.

At the forefront of the liberalization drive was party secretary Hu Yaobang, who issued a lengthy attack on Mao's Cultural Revolution that was interpreted as supportive of greater academic and artistic freedom. Hu also disturbed conservative party officials by spearheading draft legislation that would have formally prevented CCP functionaries, particularly at the local level, from interfering with the day-to-day management of state factories and other economic enterprises. However, student demonstrations that erupted in December provided an opportunity for the hardliners to reassert their influence. In January 1987 Hu was forced to step down as party chief because of "mistakes on major issues of political principles", Premier Zhao being named his acting successor. In March, immediately prior to the convening of the National People's Congress, its Standing Committee, chaired by 85-year-old PENG Chen, voted to withdraw the proposed legislation on the party's economic activities. However, in a somewhat contradictory opening address to the NPC on March 25, Zhao reiterated the need to grant "full authority" to enterprise managers, while denouncing "pernicious" Western ideas and demanding a tight rein on intellectual and artistic expression.

A period of intense intraparty maneuvering appears to have followed, in the course of which the liberals regained much of the ground lost early in the year. In a lengthy report to the Thirteenth Party Congress in October, Zhao argued that China was in the "primary stage of socialism", during which a distinction between the ownership and management of state and collective enterprises was justified and certain economic practices "not peculiar to capitalism" could be tolerated. Significantly, as noted by Stanley Rosen in *Asian Survey,* the sweeping personnel changes approved by the Congress (see Political Parties, below) yielded a leadership which "although balanced between cautious and more thoroughgoing reformers, no longer contained open critics of reform".

The process of "rejuvenation" was extended to government ranks at the conclusion of the Seventh NPC's opening session in April 1988, which yielded the confirmation of LI Peng as premier (a post occupied on an acting basis since the previous November) and extensive changes in other senior posts in favor of what the official New China News Agency termed "a group of technocrats, who are younger in age, pragmatic, and [committed to China's] current policies for reform and opening to the outside world".

POLITICAL PARTIES

Although established essentially as a one-party Communist state, the PRC has preserved some of the characteristics of a "United Front" regime by permitting the continued existence of eight small minority parties, some of whose leaders hold high government office along with Communists and nonparty personnel. In addition, the **China People's Political Consultative Conference** (CPPCC), which originally included representatives of all bodies adopting the 1949 constitution, reemerged in 1978, its last previous meeting having been held in January 1965. Among the groups represented were the All-China Federation of Trade Unions, the All-China Women's Federation, and the Communist Youth League (all three denounced during the Cultural Revolution); political parties; minority nationalities; religious groups; and an assortment of other social, scientific, artistic, and cultural interests. During the most recent CPPCC session, held at Beijing on March 24–April 10, 1988, numerous reports for presentation to the NPC were approved and new officers installed including, as president, Li Xiannian (former PRC president).

Leading Party:

Chinese Communist Party — CCP (*Zhongguo Gongchan Dang*). The previously unquestioned political dominance of the CCP was substantially weakened as a result of the Cultural Revolution and the disruptive activities of "Red Guard" forces in the mid-1960s. However, reconstruction of the party organization, begun in late 1969, was largely completed by late 1973, with the revolutionary committees created during the Cultural Revolution being made subordinate to party committees. The CCP's resurgence was formalized in 1975, when, for the first time, it was constitutionally recognized as the "vanguard" of state and society; by contrast, the party is unreferenced in the 1982 document, save in the preamble, where, at several points, its "leadership" role is acknowledged.

The party's highest organ is the National Party Congress, whose Central Committee elects a Political Bureau as well as other top figures. In theory, party congresses are elected every five years and hold annual sessions; however, the Eighth Congress held only two sessions (in 1956 and 1958), while the Ninth Congress did not convene until 1969. The Twelfth Congress, which met September 1-11, 1982, adopted a new party constitution, under which the posts of CCP chairman and vice chairman were abolished, and elected a 348-member Central Committee (210 full and 138 alternate members), which in turn elected a 28-member Politburo (25 full and 3 alternate members).

On September 16, 1985, the retirement of 64 Central Committee members, including 10 senior Politburo figures, was announced. Subsequently, at the conclusion of a special party conference on September 17-23, a replenished Central Committee of 210 full members and 133 alternates was presented, while 6 Deng protégés (including a former alternate) were subsequently named to a restructured Politburo of 20 full members and 2 alternates. Concurrently, the party Secretariat was expanded to 14 full members, with the addition of 3 new members and promotion of 2 existing alternates.

On January 16, 1987, Hu Yaobang was dismissed as general secretary (although remaining on the five-member Politburo Standing Committee) and replaced, on an acting basis, by Premier Zhao Ziyang.

The process of internal reform was further advanced at the Thirteenth Congress on October 25-November 1, 1987, the 1,997 delegates electing a substantially reduced Central Committee of 175 full and 110 alternate members, a new Central Discipline Inspection Commission of 69 members, and a 200-member Central Advisory Commission. Among those retiring was Deng Xiaoping (who continued, however, as chairman of the party's Military Commission), in addition to most remaining survivors of the "founding generation" of CCP leaders. At its first plenary session on November 2, the new Central Committee confirmed Zhao Ziyang (who subsequently resigned the premiership) as general secretary and named a restructured Politburo of 17 full members and one alternate (including a five-member Standing Committee) that encompassed only half of the previous incumbents. The new Standing Committee thereupon appointed an even more drastically curtailed Secretariat of four full members and one alternate.

General Secretary: ZHAO Ziyang (First Vice Chairman, CCP Military Commission).

Other Members of Politburo Standing Committee: HU Qili (Member, CCP Secretariat), LI Peng (Premier, State Council), QIAO Shi (Member, CCP Secretariat, and First Secretary, Central Discipline Inspection Commission), YAO Yilin (Vice Premier, State Council, and Chairman, State Planning Commission).

Other Members of Politburo: HU Yaobang (former General Secretary), JIANG Zemin (Mayor of Shanghai), LI Ruihuan (Mayor of Tianjin), LI Tieying (Member, State Council), LI Ximing (Beijing Municipal Party Secretary), Gen. QIN Jiwei (Defense Minister and Member, CCP Military Commission), SONG Ping (former Member, State Council), TIAN Jiyun (Vice Premier, State Council), WAN Li (Vice Premier, State Council), WU Xueqian (Vice Premier), YANG Rudai (Sichuan Party Secretary), YANG Shangkun (Permanent Vice Chairman, CCP Military Commission).

Alternate: DENG Guangen (Minister of Railways).

Secretariat: HU Qili (Member, Politburo Standing Committee, and Secretary of Secretariat), QIAO Shi (Member, Politburo Standing Committee), RUI Xingwen (Shanghai Municipal Party Secretary), YAN Mingfu (Head, CCP United Front Work Department).

Alternate: WEN Jiabao (Secretary, Party Committee of Departments under Central Committee).

Minority Parties:

While expected "to work under the leadership of the Communist Party", the following largely middle-class and/or intellectual groups were permitted, in October 1979, to recruit new members and to hold national congresses for the first time in two decades: the **Revolutionary Committee of the Kuomintang** (*Zhongguo Guomin Dang Geming Weiyuanhui*), founded in 1948; the **China Democratic League** (*Zhongguo Minzhu Tongmeng*), founded in 1941; the **China Democratic National Construction Association** (*Zhongguo Minzhu Jianguo Hui*), a business-oriented group founded in 1945; the **China Association for Promoting Democracy** (*Zhongguo Minzhu Cujin Hui*), a Shanghai cultural and educational group founded in 1945; the **Chinese Peasants and Workers' Democratic Party** (*Zhongguo Nong Gong Minzhu Dang*), founded in 1947; the **September 3, 1945 (V-J Day) Society** (*Jiu San Xuehui*); the **Taiwan Democratic Self-Government League** (*Taiwan Minzhu Zizhi Tongmen*), founded in 1947; and the **China Party for Public Interests** (*Zhongguo Zhi Gong Dang*), an outgrowth of a nineteenth-century secret society organized by overseas Chinese.

L E G I S L A T U R E

National People's Congress — NPC (*Quanguo Renmin Daibiao Dahui*). The NPC is a unicameral body indirectly elected for a five-year term with one session scheduled annually, although the Second Congress (1959–1963) did not meet in 1961 and the Third met only once (from December 20, 1964, to January 4, 1965). No subsequent election was held until 1974, the Fourth Congress convening in complete secrecy at Beijing in January 1975.

Meetings became regularized with the Fifth Congress, elected at a series of municipal and provincial congresses held during November 1977–February 1978 and holding its first session February 25–March 5. At its fifth session, which convened on November 26, 1982, the fourth PRC constitution was adopted by a vote of 3,037–0. The election of 2,978 deputies to the Sixth Congress took place during March-April 1983, while the same number of deputies were elected to the Seventh Congress, whose first session was held from March 25-April 13, 1988.

Chairman of the Standing Committee: WAN Li.

CABINET

[as of April 15, 1988]

Premier	Li Peng
Vice Premiers	Tian Jiyun
	Wu Xueqian
	Yao Yilin
State Councillors	Chen Junsheng
	Chen Xitong
	Li Guixian
	Li Tieying
	Qin Jiwei
	Song Jian
	Wang Bingqian
	Wang Fang
	Zou Jiahua

Ministers

Aeronautics and Astronautics Industry	Lin Zongtang
Agriculture	He Kang
Astronautics	Li Xu'e
Chemical Industry	Qin Zhongda
Civil Affairs	Cui Naifu
Coal Industry	Yu Hongen
Commerce	Hu Ping
Communications	Qian Yongchang
Construction	Lin Hanxiong
Culture	Wang Meng
Electronics Industry	Li Tieying
Energy Resources	Huang Yicheng
Finance	Wang Bingqian
Foreign Affairs	Qian Qichen
Foreign Economic Relations and Trade	Zheng Tuobin
Forestry	Gao Dezhan
Geology and Mineral Resources	Zhu Xun
Justice	Cai Cheng
Labor	Luo Gan
Light Industry	Zeng Xianlin
Machine Building and Electronics Industry	Zou Jiahua
Materials	Liu Suinian
Metallurgical Industry	Qi Yuanjing
National Defense	Qin Jiwei
Nuclear Industry	Jiang Xinxiong
Personnel	Zhao Dongwan
Petroleum Industry	Wang Tao
Posts and Telecommunications	Yang Taifang
Public Health	Chen Minzhang
Public Security	Wang Fang
Radio, Film and Television	Ai Zhisheng
Railways	Li Senmao
State Security	Jia Chunwang
Supervision	Wei Jianxing
Textile Industry	Wu Wenying
Urban and Rural Construction and Environmental Protection	Ye Rutang
Water Resources	Yang Zhenhuai
State Commission of Science, Technology, and Industry for National Defense	Ding Henggao
State Education Commission	Li Tieying
State Family Planning Commission	Peng Peiyun
State Nationalities Affairs Commission	Ismail Amat
State Physical Culture and Sports Commission	Li Menghua
State Planning Commission	Yao Yilin
State Restructuring of Economic System Commission	Li Peng
State Science and Technology Commission	Song Jian
State Scientific and Technological Commission	Song Jian
Auditor General	Lu Peijian
Chairman, Central Military Commission	Deng Xiaoping
Governor, People's Bank of China	Li Guixian
Secretary General, State Council	Chen Junsheng

NEWS MEDIA

All media are under rigid government control. There are no reliable news circulation figures, those provided below being recent estimates.

Press. The following are published daily at Peking, unless otherwise noted: *Renmin Ribao* (People's Daily, 5,000,000), official CCP Central Committee organ; *Quingdao Ribao* (Quingdao Daily, Shandong Province, 2,600,000); *Gongren Ribao* (Workers' Daily, 1,800,000); *Guangming Ribao* (Brightness Daily, 1,500,000), organ of minority parties; *Nanfang Ribao* (South China Daily, Guangdong Province, 1,000,000); *Beijing Ribao* (Beijing Daily, 1,000,000), organ of Peking CCP Municipal Committee; *Jiefang Ribao* (Liberation Daily, 1,000,000), organ of Shanghai CCP Municipal Committee; *Beijing Wanbao* (Beijing Evening News), 550,000; *Guangzhou Ribao* (Canton Daily), 500,000; *Jiefang Junbao* (Liberation Army Daily, 100,000), PLA organ; *Liaowang* (Outlook), influential Xinhua weekly. *China Daily* (140,000) began publication in July 1981 as the country's only English-language newspaper; a New York edition was launched in June 1983 and a London edition in September 1986.

News agencies. The leading official facility is *Xinhua* (New China News Agency — NCNA), which is attached to the State Council and has offices around the world; a number of other agencies service PRC-sponsored papers abroad. Some two dozen foreign agencies maintain offices at Peking.

Radio and television. The Central People's Broadcasting Station provides service in *putung hua* and various local dialects; the Central People's Television Broadcasting Section offers programming via some 40 main and 125 satellite stations. In September 1984, the Ministry of Radio and Television reported that television reached nearly 60 percent of the population (more than 600,000 people).

INTERGOVERNMENTAL REPRESENTATION

Ambassador to the US: HAN Xu.

US Ambassador to China: Winston LORD.

Permanent Representative to the UN: LI Luye.

IGO Memberships (Non-UN): ADB, AfDB, Inmarsat, INRO, Intelsat, Interpol, IWC, PCA (de jure).

CHINA: TAIWAN

Political Status: Chinese province; controlled by the government of the Republic of China (established 1912), whose authority since 1949 has been limited to the island of Taiwan (Formosa), P'enghu (the Pescadores), and certain offshore islands, including Quemoy (Kinmen) and Matsu.

Area: 13,592 sq. mi. (35,203 sq. km.).

Population: 16,260,000 (1975C), 20,012,000 (1988E).

Major Urban Centers (1986E): TAIPEI (2,567,000) Kaohsiung (1,321,000); Taichung (695,000); Tainan (648,000); Keelung (350,000).

Official Language: Mandarin Chinese.

Monetary Unit: New Taiwan Dollar (market rate March 1, 1988, 28.63 dollars = $1US).

President: LEE Teng-hui; elected Vice President by the National Assembly on March 22, 1984; sworn in as President on January 13, 1988, upon the death of CHIANG Ching-kuo, who had been inaugurated for a second six-year term on May 20, 1984.

Vice President: Vacant, following the inauguration of LEE Teng-hui as President.

President of Executive Branch (Premier): YÜ Kuo-hua; appointed by the President on May 20, 1984, and confirmed by the Legislative *Yuan* on May 25, succeeding SUN Yün-hsüan.

GOVERNMENT AND POLITICS

Political background. Since its establishment on Taiwan in 1949, the Chinese Nationalist regime has continued to declare itself the government of all China, vowing to return eventually to the mainland but devoting its main attention to ensuring its own survival and economic development. The danger of Communist conquest, which appeared very real in 1949–1950, was averted primarily by the decision of US President Truman to interpose the protection of the American Seventh Fleet upon the outbreak of the Korean War in 1950. Since that time, the Nationalist government has continued under the domination of the Nationalist Party, or Kuomintang (KMT), led by CHIANG Kai-shek until his death on April 5, 1975. Many of the individuals who were in control in 1949 continued to hold important positions thereafter, although the government in recent years has been retiring older people and infusing "new blood" into the bureaucracy. In a major reorganization in June 1969, the post of vice premier was awarded to the president's son, CHIANG Ching-kuo, who was subsequently named premier in May 1972. Chiang was selected by the National Assembly in March 1978 to succeed C.K. YEN as president and was sworn in on May 20. Following his inaugural, he designated SUN Yün-hsüan as premier.

President Chiang was reelected on March 21, 1984, while LEE Teng-hui, an islander who had served since 1981 as governor of Taiwan, was elected vice president the following day, in succession to HSIEH Tung-min, who had not sought reappointment. On May 20, YÜ Kuo-hua was named to succeed Sun as premier and was formally installed as head of a new government on June 1. Lee succeeded to the presidency following Chiang's death on January 13, 1988.

Constitution and government. The pervasive authority of the Kuomintang, originally founded by SUN Yat-sen, is exercised within a complicated constitutional framework that combines Western and traditional Chinese elements and was established in its present form by a constitution promulgated January 1, 1947. A popularly elected National Assembly, designed to represent the will of the people, stands at the apex of the system and includes among its powers the election and recall of the president and vice president, amendment of the constitution, and exercise of the rights of initiative and referendum. The president, elected for a six-year term, has wide powers of appoint-

ment, can declare war and peace, and acts as mediator and arbiter among the government's five specialized branches, or *yüan* (Executive, Legislative, Judicial, Examination, and Control), each of which has its own head, or president. The Executive Branch is headed by the premier and includes most of the ministries. The popularly elected Legislative Branch enacts the laws but cannot increase the budget. The Judicial Branch, consisting of 15 grand justices appointed by the president, is responsible for interpreting the constitution; the Examination Branch has charge of civil-service examinations; and the indirectly elected Control Branch is responsible for auditing and general administrative surveillance.

Because of an inability to replenish its mainland representation, the terms of members of the National Assembly elected in 1947, along with those of the Legislative and Control branches, were extended indefinitely, but substantially less than half of the original members of these bodies are now alive in Taiwan. Elections to fill Taiwanese seats in the Legislative Branch were held in 1969, 1972, and 1975. A scheduled reelection of Taiwanese members in 1978 was postponed following announcement of the impending break in diplomatic relations with the United States. Partial elections to the Assembly and Legislative Branch were subsequently held in 1980, to the Legislative Branch alone in 1983, and to both bodies on December 6, 1986.

The territorial jurisdiction of the Republic of China currently extends to one Chinese province (Taiwan) and part of a second (Fukien's offshore islands) as well as to two directly administered municipalities (Taipei and Kaohsiung). Skeleton governments for the Communist-occupied areas of China are maintained against the day of "recovery of the mainland". The province of Taiwan, which has its own provincial assembly, is subdivided into 16 counties and four municipalities.

Foreign relations. The most important factor in the foreign policy of the Taiwan government has been the existence on the mainland of the Communist regime, which was awarded the Chinese seat at the United Nations on October 25, 1971. Reflecting its diminished political status, the Republic of China is today recognized by relatively few governments, though its trade relations are extensive. Diplomatic relations with Japan were severed in 1972, following Japanese recognition of the PRC. Relations with the United States, once extremely close, cooled after President Nixon's visit to the mainland in February 1972. The communiqué issued at the conclusion of the Nixon visit contained the following expression of Washington's posture on the Taiwan question: "The United States acknowledges that all Chinese on either side of the Taiwan Strait maintain that there is but one China and that Taiwan is part of China. The United States Government does not challenge that position. It reaffirms its interest in a peaceful settlement of the Taiwan question by the Chinese themselves. With this prospect in mind, it affirms the ultimate objective of the withdrawal of all U.S. forces and military installations from Taiwan."

Concurrent with the announcement on December 15, 1978, that the United States and the PRC would establish diplomatic relations on January 1, 1979, Washington issued a statement saying that both diplomatic relations and (upon expiration of a required one-year's notice) the Mutual Defense Treaty with the Republic of China would be terminated. It also indicated that all US military personnel would be withdrawn from Taiwan within four months. It subsequently stated, however, that all remaining agreements with Taipei would remain in effect. In particular, arms shipments would be permitted to continue "on a selective basis".

Current issues. In late 1986 Chiang Ching-kuo had embarked on a program of political reform that was by no means completed at the time of his death in January 1988. While opposition parties remained technically illegal, the Democratic Progress Party (see Political Parties, below) was allowed to contest the December 1986 National Assembly and Legislative Branch elections, winning 19 percent of the vote in the former and 22 percent in the latter. In July 1987 martial law, which had been in effect for nearly 40 years, was lifted (though a tough "National Security Law for the Period of Rebellion Suppression" was concurrently enacted); a long-standing ban on travel to the PRC was lifted in November (effective only in regard to the island's "mainlander" minority); while press restrictions were eased (but not completely abandoned) at the end of the year. During the same period, indirect trade with the mainland increased substantially (the PRC becoming, in effect, Taiwan's third-largest trading partner), while inducements were extended to surviving mainland legislators to resign their seats in anticipation of greater native Taiwanese representation at the balloting scheduled for 1989. The regime remained adamantly opposed, however, to Beijing's "one country, two systems" tender of reunification, as well as to the advocacy of formal independence from China, for which two in a lengthening series of dissidents were given extended prison terms in early 1988.

While Vice President Lee Teng-hui, an islander, constitutionally acceded to the presidency at Chiang's death, his acceptability as KMT leader was expected to be severely challenged by the party's old guard, with the likely support of the 74-year-old premier, Yü Kuo-hua. Somewhat surprisingly, despite manifest evidence of disagreement between conservative and reformist factions, the Kuomintang's Central Standing Committee designated Lee as acting chairman on January 27, pending confirmation by the full Central Committee at a session scheduled for July. After some apparent wavering, the action was endorsed by Premier Yü, with the reformist KMT secretary general, LEE Huan, emerging as the new president's most conspicuous political ally.

POLITICAL PARTIES

Prior to 1986, two non-Kuomintang (*tang-wai*) political groups were occasionally successful in Taiwanese elections, although their representatives were obliged to run as independents, since opposition parties, as such, were not allowed to compete for public office. In a major concession to opposition sentiment, the government in May 1986 permitted an umbrella Tangwai Public Policy Association to open offices at Taipei and elsewhere; four months later, two new dissident groups were formed, one of which,

though technically illegal, was permitted to participate in the December 1986 election.

Governing Party:

Nationalist Party (*Kuo-min Tang* or *Kuomintang* — KMT). Dominating all levels of government in the Republic of China, the KMT is organized on principles similar to the Soviet Communist Party, with a National Congress, a Central Committee, party cells, etc. It has never been a completely disciplined formation, although all elements support its deep-rooted anti-Communist posture. In November 1976, at its first national congress since 1969, the party elected (then) Premier Chiang Ching-kuo to succeed his father as chairman and expanded the Central Committee from 99 to 130 full members. In 1984, as the result of a party "rejuvenation" campaign, it was reported that 70 percent of an estimated 2 million party members were native Taiwanese.
Leaders: LEE Teng-hui (President of the Republic and Acting Chairman of the Party), LEE Huan (Secretary General); KAO Ming-huey, MA Ying-chiu, James C.Y. SOONG (Deputy Secretaries General).

Unrecognized Parties:

Young China Party (*Ch'ing-nien Tang*). Formed in 1923 and more frequently supportive of the government than other non-Kuomintang groups, the Young China Party is staunchly democratic and anti-Communist.
Leader: LI Huang (Chairman).

Democratic Socialist Party (*Min-chu She-hui Tang*). The Democratic Social Party resulted from the 1932 merger of the National Socialist and Democratic Constitutionalist parties. Although also anti-Communist, the group has typically distanced itself from the Kuomintang on most issues. It currently holds one seat in the National Assembly.
Leaders: YANG Yu-tse (Chairman), LIU Yi-ping (Secretary General).

Democratic Progress Party (*Min-chu Chin-pu Tang*). Despite the ban on organization of new parties, a group of dissidents, advocating trade, tourist, and communications links with the mainland, met at Taipei in September 1986 to form the DPP (sometimes rendered as Democratic Progressive Party). Although remaining legally unrecognized, the group won 11 National Assembly and 12 Legislative Branch seats on December 6, 1986. On February 10, 1988, in its first meeting with representatives of the KMT, it agreed to abandon a call for island independence.
Leaders: YAO Chia-wen (Chairman), YU Ching, CHIOU I-jen.

Taiwan Democratic Party (*Taiwan Min-chu Tang*). Organization of the Taiwan Democratic Party was announced at Washington, DC, in September 1986 by three Taiwanese exiles, including Hsu Hsin-liang, founder of the banned opposition magazine, *Formosa*. The three indicated that they planned to return to Taipei "to struggle, through open, peaceful and legal means, for the legitimate rights of the [Taiwanese] people", but have not, as yet, been permitted to do so.
Leaders: HSU Hsin-liang, LIN Shui-Chuan, HSIEH Tsung-min.

Labor Party (*Kung Tang* or *Kungtang*). The *Kungtang* (most accurately rendered as Workers' Party) was launched in December 1987 in the hope of becoming the principal spokesman for Taiwan's 7.5 million-member workforce. It has also addressed a number of nonlabor issues, such as environmentalism, feminism, and the rights of ethnic minorities.
Leaders: WANG Yi-hsiung (Chairman), SU Chin-li (Secretary General).

During 1987 a number of other new groups were formed, including the **Chinese Freedom Party,** which called for free elections and improved relations with the mainland; the Kaohsiung-based **Democratic Liberal Party;** the extreme right wing **Democratic Freedom Party,** and the **China Democratic Justice Party.**

LEGISLATURE

Under the unusual constitutional system of the Republic of China, parliamentary functions are performed by the National Assembly, the Legislative Branch, and even the Control Branch. The KMT dominates all of these bodies, and only 5–10 percent of their members belong to minority groups.

National Assembly (*Kuo-min Ta-hui*). Originally elected in November 1947 for a term of six years, the Assembly is a unicameral body with a nominal membership of 3,045. It has been periodically reconvened in Taiwan (most recently in March 1984), primarily for the purpose of electing a president and vice president. Although only 1,105 seats were filled as of mid-1983, the constitution has been interpreted so that a quorum is defined as one-third-plus-one of those members present at a plenary session, instead of as a fraction of the original membership. Meetings are chaired through a system of rotation within an 85-member Presidium. At the most recent election for 84 Taiwan Province members, held December 6, 1986, the KMT won 68 seats; the Democratic Progress Party, 11; Democratic Socialist Party, 1; independents, 4.

Legislative Branch (*Li-fa Yüan*). Originally elected in May 1948 for a term of three years, the Legislative Branch is the formal lawmaking organ of the Republic of China. It is a unicameral body nominally composed of 760 members popularly elected on a regional and occupational basis. Surviving mainland members (now less than 300) have had their terms of office extended indefinitely, while Taiwan Province members were most recently elected on December 6, 1986, with the KMT winning 59 of the 73 contested seats; the Democratic Progress Party, 12; independents, 2.
President: NIEH Wen-ya.

Control Branch (*Chien-ch'a Yüan*). The Control Branch is elected by local councils and serves as a watchdog agency vis-à-vis the Executive Branch and the administration. It may impeach or censure officials and holds powers of consent regarding the president and vice president of the Republic, and the members of the Examination and Judicial branches.
President: YU Chun-hsien.

CABINET

The cabinet is known as the Executive Branch Council (*Hsing-cheng Yüan Hu-yi*). The premier is chosen by the president with the consent of the Legislative Branch, and the vice premier and ministers are appointed by the president upon recommendation of the premier. Ministers are chosen individually; the cabinet is not responsible collectively. All ministers are members of the Kuomintang.

President, Executive Branch (Premier)	Yü Kuo-hua
Vice President, Executive Branch (Vice Premier)	Lien Chan
Ministers	
Communications	Kuo Nan-hung
Economic Affairs	Li Ta-hai
Education	Mao Kao-wen
Finance	Chi'en Ch'un
Foreign Affairs	Ding (Ting) Mou-Shih
Interior	Wu Po-hsiung
Justice	Shih Ch'i-yang
National Defense	Gen. Cheng Wei-Yuan
Without Portfolio	Chang Feng-hsü
	Chao Yao-tung
	Chou Hung-t'ao
	Hsiao T'ien-tsan
	Kao Yü-shu
	Kuo Wei-fan
	Li Kuo-ting
Commission Chairmen	
Mongolian and Tibetian Affairs	Wu Hua-peng
Overseas Chinese Affairs	Tseng Kuang-shun

NEWS MEDIA

Prior to the easing of long-standing press restrictions on December 31, 1987, the total number of newspapers was limited to 31, nearly half of which were either government- or party-owned, with several of the remainder controlled by individuals with close ties to the KMT. As of January 1, 1988, the government indicated that it would accept applications for new papers for the first time since 1951 and would lift the page limit from 12 to 24. Under the current press law it continues to be illegal for journalists to "advocate communism" or to support independence for the island. Under the latter stipulation, the monthly *Formosa,* which had attained a circulation of over 100,000, was closed down in December 1979 and most of its staff arrested; two other opposition magazines, *The Eighties* and *Spring Wind,* were suspended shortly thereafter, as was *The Asian* in April 1980.

Press. Of Taiwan's daily newspapers, 2 are in English and the remainder in Chinese. The following are published at Taipei, unless otherwise indicated: *Lieh-ho Pao* (United Daily News, 1,400,000), relatively independent; *Chung-kuo Shih-pao* (China Times, 1,200,000), relatively independent; *Chung-yang Jih-pao* (Central Daily News, 600,000), official KMT organ; *Taiwan Hsin-sheng Pao* (New Life Daily, 300,000), Taiwan provincial government paper; *Chung-hua Jih-Pao* (China Daily News, southern edition, Tainan, 270,000); *Chung-hua Jih-pao* (China Daily News, northern edition, 200,000); *Ta-hua Wan-pao* (Great China Evening News, 200,000); *Hsin-wen Pao* (Daily News, Kaohsiung, 130,000); *China Post* (80,000), in English; *Chung-kuo Wan-pao* (China Evening News, Kaohsiung, 66,000); *China News* (30,000), in English.

News agencies. The most important domestic news agency is the reorganized, privately owned *Chung-yang T'ung-hsün She* (Central News Agency—CNA). *Agence France-Presse,* AP, East Asia News, Naigai News, Pan-Asia Newspapers Alliance, Reuters, and UPI also maintain bureaus or stringers at Taipei.

Radio and television. There are three major domestic radio networks broadcasting in both Mandarin and Taiwanese; additional stations broadcast to the mainland and overseas in a large number of languages and dialects. There are three television networks broadcasting from a dozen main stations to about 6.1 million receivers.

INTERGOVERNMENTAL REPRESENTATION

A founding member of the United Nations, the Republic of China lost its right of representation in that body's major organs on October 25, 1971, while diplomatic relations with the United States terminated on January 1, 1979. Informal relations continue to be maintained through the American Institute in Taiwan and its Nationalist Chinese counterpart, the Coordination Council for North American Affairs.

IGO Memberships (Non-UN): ADB (listed as "Taipei, China"), ICAC.

COLOMBIA

Republic of Colombia
República de Colombia

Political Status: Independent Gran Colombia proclaimed 1819; separate state of New Granada established 1831; republican constitution adopted 1886; bipartisan National Front regime instituted in 1958 but substantially terminated in 1974.

Area: 439,734 sq. mi. (1,138,914 sq. km.).

Population: 22,551,811 (1973C), 28,963,000 (1988E).

Major Urban Centers (urban areas, 1986E): BOGOTA (4,453,000); Medellín (2,213,000); Cali (1,416,000); Barranquilla (1,192,000); Bucaramanga (635,000); Cartagena (549,000).

Official Language: Spanish.

Monetary Unit: Peso (market rate March 1, 1988, 273.64 pesos = $1US).

President: Virgilio BARCO Vargas (Liberal Party); elected May 25, 1986, and inaugurated August 7 for a four-year term, succeeding Belisario BETANCUR Cuartas (Conservative Party).

Presidential Substitute: Víctor MOSQUERA Chaux (Liberal Party); elected by the Congress to succeed Francisco POSADA de la Peña (Conservative Party) for the first two years of the presidential term.

THE COUNTRY

Situated at the base of the Isthmus of Panama, with frontage on both the Caribbean and the Pacific, Colombia is divided geographically into three main regions defined by ranges of the Andes mountains: a flat coastal area, a highland area, and an area of sparsely settled eastern plains drained by tributaries of the Orinoco and Amazon rivers. In terms of population, Colombia is more diverse than most other Latin American countries. About 75 percent is of mixed blood, including both mestizos and mulattoes; groups of ethnically pure Spanish, Indian, and Negro are small. Spanish is the language of most of the people, except for isolated Indian tribes. Women constitute approximately 26 percent of the official labor force, with a substantial additional proportion engaged in unpaid agricultural labor; in the urban sector, women are concentrated in domestic service and informal trading. Female participation in government is numerically minor, but quite visible.

Colombia's economy remains dependent on agriculture, especially coffee, which accounts for over half of officially recorded exports. Equally important, however, is the smuggling of cocaine and marijuana. Petroleum products, chiefly fuel oil, are the second-largest official export, while efforts to develop alternative agricultural exports—cotton and sugar, in particular—have been partially successful. Recent indicators have been mixed: exports increased by 55 percent in 1986, largely because of high coffee prices, while the economy grew by 4.5 percent overall, with inflation falling to 20 percent (from 22.5 percent in 1985); on the other hand, unemployment remained above 12 percent, while severe maldistribution of wealth continued to be a major source of political dissatisfaction.

GOVERNMENT AND POLITICS

Political background. Colombia gained its independence from Spain in 1819 as part of the Republic of Gran Colombia, which also included what is now Ecuador, Panama, and Venezuela. In 1830, Ecuador and Venezuela separated, the remaining territory, New Granada, being designated the Granadan Confederation in 1858, the United States of Colombia under a federal constitution promulgated in 1863, and the Republic of Colombia under a unitary constitution adopted in 1886. Panamanian independence, proclaimed in 1903, was not recognized by Bogotá until 1909.

The critical nineteenth-century issues of centralism versus federalism and the role of the Catholic Church gave rise to the Liberal and Conservative parties, which still dominate Colombian politics. Relative calm extended from 1903 to the early 1940s, when domestic instability emerged, culminating in a decade (1948–1958) of internal violence (*la Violencia*) that may have taken as many as 300,000 lives. This period included a coup d'état in 1953 which resulted in a four-year dictatorship under Gen. Gustavo ROJAS Pinilla. To avert a resumption of full-scale interparty warfare after the fall of Rojas Pinilla, the two major parties agreed in July 1957, in the so-called Pact of Sitges, to establish a National Front (*Frente Nacional*) under which they would participate equally in government until 1970. However, the Front's existence was extended to 1974 by a constitutional reform of December 1968 that provided for its gradual dismantling, beginning at the local and subsequently extending to the national level, with the partial exception of the executive branch (see Constitution and government, below). Thus Misael PASTRANA Borrero, although a Conservative, ran in 1970 with Liberal support, whereas Dr. Alfonso LOPEZ Michelsen ran in 1974 only as a Liberal and was opposed by a Conservative candidate, Dr. Alvaro GOMEZ Hurtado.

Fears that the end of the National Front would work to the advantage of supporters of former dictator Rojas Pinilla proved to be unwarranted in the aftermath of the 1974 balloting, at which López Michelsen captured 56 percent of the vote, Liberals and Conservatives together securing 80 percent as well as an overwhelming majority of legislative seats. The presidential election of June 4, 1978, was much closer, the Liberal candidate, Dr. Alfonso César TURBAY Ayala, defeating his Conservative opponent, Dr. Belisario BETANCUR Cuartas, by a paper-thin margin. In view of the outcome, Turbay Ayala, adhering to a continuing vestige of the *Frente Nacional,* awarded 5 of 12 cabinet posts to the Conservatives, with whom a formal leadership pact (opposed by dissident factions within both parties) was concluded in May 1979.

In 1982, the Liberals captured a majority of lower-house seats in a legislative election held March 14; however, an intraparty dispute between orthodox and New Liberalism factions resulted in the nomination of ex-president López Michelsen by the former and of Dr. Luis Carlos GALAN Sarmiento by the latter for the presidential balloting on May 30. As a result of the Liberal split, Dr. Betancur, who had been renominated by the Conservatives, emerged as the victor with 46.8 percent of the valid votes and was inaugurated as the new chief executive on August 7.

The Liberal cleavage proved less costly at the congressional balloting of March 7, 1986, the mainstream group securing a majority in both houses. As a result, Galán, who had been renominated by the NL, withdrew from the presidential poll of May 25, at which the mainstream candidate, Virgilio BARCO Vargas, decisively defeated the Conservative's 1974 nominee, Gómez Hurtado.

Constitution and government. The 1886 constitution has been extensively revised, the most notable amendment being that of 1957 which instituted the *Frente Nacional*. Under the National Front system, the presidency alternated between Liberals and Conservatives, with equal numbers of offices held by members of the two parties. The rule of parity and alternation also applied to the judicial and legislative branches, membership in both houses of the bicameral Congress being equally divided between the two parties.

Under a constitutional amendment adopted in 1968, elections were held without regard to Liberal-Conservative parity at the local level, while the National Front was to continue in force at the national level until 1974, when a new president and all legislative bodies were to be elected on a nonrestrictive basis. Local, departmental, and national executive branches were to continue under the parity arrangement until 1978, after which the chief executive was mandated to name members of the leading nonpresidential party to administrative positions on an "equitable" basis. While there is, strictly speaking, no vice president, the Congress elects for a two-year term a presidential substitute (*designado*), of the same party as the chief executive, who is to occupy the presidency should the office become vacant.

The organization of the judicial system is based on districts, each of which contains a number of municipal courts and a district court. At the apex of the system is the Supreme Court of Justice, which is divided into civil, criminal, labor, and general sections. The Supreme Court has the power to declare legislative acts unconstitutional and exercised that right by invalidating a congressional act of December 1977 which had called for the election of a constitutional assembly concurrent with the 1978 presidential balloting.

Colombia is presently divided into 23 departments, 9 national territories, and the capital district of Bogotá. The departments have elected assemblies but are headed by governors appointed by the central government. The departments have the authority to establish municipal districts with elected councils and mayors who served as gubernatorial agents until March 1988, when the country's first mayoral elections were held. The national territories, encompassing nearly 50 percent of the country's land area but less than 2 percent of its population, include 4 intendencies (*intendencias*) and 5 commissaries (*comisarías*).

Foreign relations. Colombia's activity on the international scene has recently centered on regional affairs. An active member of the Andean Pact, it became, in 1976, the first Latin American country to forgo all economic assistance from the United States. Relations with Nicaragua, already strained because of deportations of Colombian migrant workers, were further exacerbated in late 1979 by Managua's decision to revive a series of long-standing claims to the Caribbean islands of San Andrés and Providencia, both acquired by Colombia under a 1928 treaty, and the uninhabited cays of Quita Sueño, Ron-

cador, Serrana, and Serranilla, which were assigned to Colombia under a 1972 agreement with the United States that was ratified in 1981 by the US Senate. In February 1980 Nicaragua formally denounced the 1928 accord as having been concluded under US military occupation, while arguing that the cays were located on its continental shelf and thus constituted part of its national territory. (Honduras, which had also been a party to the dispute, recognized Colombia's claim to the islands in an accord concluded in August 1986.) Since 1979, relations with the country's northeastern neighbor have also been strained because of a dispute involving the maritime boundary through the Gulf of Venezuela; little progress has thus far been registered in resolving the dispute, which a former Colombian foreign minister somewhat cryptically termed "an aspect of secret foreign policy". The two governments did, however, initiate talks in early 1987 on issues involving contraband trade and the containment of guerrilla activity along their common border.

In recent years, Colombia has been actively involved in efforts to promote peace in Central America, primarily as a member of the "Contadora Group" (also including Mexico, Panama, and Venezuela), which first met at Contadora Island, Panama, on January 7–8, 1983. However, the five years of intermittent talks that followed were largely unrelated to the *contra-sandinista* cease-fire that was negotiated in early 1988.

Current issues. In recent years Colombia has become an increasingly bloody battleground involving government forces, left-wing guerrillas, drug traffickers, and right-wing death squads. By mid-1987 a series of tenuous cease-fire accords negotiated three years earlier between the government and leftist insurgents had largely broken down, with some rebel units supporting themselves by participating in the drug trade, while the so-called "Medellín cartel" (estimated to be realizing $6 billion a year from cocaine and marijuana sales) had infiltrated all elements of the political spectrum and had succeeded in thwarting most official efforts to counter its influence. In early February Carlos LEHDER Rivas, reportedly a leading cartel member, was arrested and extradited to the United States to face prosecution on cocaine distribution and racketeering charges. However, an even more important drug figure, Jorge Luís OCHOA Vasquez (son of the reputed Medellín "godfather", Fabio OCHOA Restrepo), was freed following his arrest in November on technical constitutional grounds. Meanwhile, more than 1,000 political leaders, including 14 left-wing congressmen, had been killed by right-wing extremists, with total homicides for the year estimated at 11,000. The turmoil continued into early 1988, with the assassination of the country's attorney general and the kidnapping of Andrés PASTRANA Arango, the son of former president Misael Pastrana Borrero. Responsibility for both actions was claimed by a group known as *Los Extraditables,* which had declared "total war" on the extradition of Colombian citizens.

Colombia's first-ever mayoral elections on March 15, 1988 (preceded by some 250 political and drug-related deaths) resulted in a major setback for the ruling Liberals, who, despite the magnitude of their 1986 congressional victory, won only 420 of 1,008 contests, with Conservatives emerging as victors in the two largest cities, Bogotá and Medellín.

POLITICAL PARTIES

The Liberal and Conservative parties dominate Colombian politics and, until 1974, shared power under the National Front system. Constitutionally, the leading minority group is still entitled to representation in the executive branch; however, following the 1986 balloting, the Conservative Party directorate voted to move into formal opposition.

Government Party:

Liberal Party (*Partido Liberal* — PL). A traditional party that tends to reflect the interests of the more commercialized and industrialized sector of the electorate, the PL has endorsed moderately paced economic and social reform. In May 1979, following the conclusion of a seven-point agreement between the majority (*Grupo de los 90*) faction headed by President Turbay Ayala and the Conservative Party leadership, a formal opposition movement, the *Unión Liberal Popular* (ULP), was launched within the party, with the dissident *Democratización Liberal* faction of former president Lleras Restrepo at its center.

At a party convention in September 1981, former chief executive López Michelsen was designated Liberal candidate for the presidency in 1982, as a result of which his arch rival, Lleras Restrepo, and another former president, Alfonso Lleras Camargo, threw their weight to an independent center-left campaign launched by Dr. Luis Carlos Galán of the New Liberalism (below). Running on a platform that called for abandonment of the de facto two-party system and of the constitutional provision permitting ex-presidents to seek reelection after only four years out of office, Galán drew enough Liberal votes from López Michelsen to throw the May presidential election to the Conservative candidate, Belisario Betancur.

For the 1986 campaign, the mainstream leadership, including the still-influential Lleras Camargo, joined in supporting the former mayor of Bogotá, Virgilio Barco Vargas, a political centrist, whose capture of the presidency on May 25 was preceded by a PL victory at the congressional poll on March 9.

Leaders: Virgilio BARCO Vargas (President of the Republic), Dr. Alfonso LOPEZ Michelsen, Dr. Julio César TURBAY Ayala, Alfonso LLERAS Camargo (former Presidents of the Republic).

Opposition Parties:

New Liberalism (*Nuevo Liberalismo* — NL). Formed prior to the 1982 election, the center-left *Nuevo Liberalismo* is largely the vehicle of PL dissident Luis Carlos Galán. Despite a series of televised debates between Galán and Conservative presidential candidate Alvaro Gómez Hurtado, the NL suffered a decisive defeat at the congressional balloting of March 9, 1986, with Galán subsequently withdrawing from presidential contention.

Leader: Dr. Luis Carlos GALAN Sarmiento.

Conservative Party (*Partido Conservador* — PC). A traditional party formerly based in the agrarian aristocracy, the PC was long divided between National Front conservatives and an independent faction composed of followers of the late president Laureano Gómez. The essentials of the split continued until November 1981, when the *ospina-pastranistas*, led by Dr. Misael Pastrana Borrero (president, 1970–1974), concluded an agreement with the *alvaristas*, led by Dr. Alvaro Gómez Hurtado (unsuccessful 1974 candidate), that set the stage for the 1982 upset victory of Dr. Belisario Betancur Cuartas, a party moderate who had failed in a challenge to NF candidate Pastrana in 1970. In 1986, Dr. Gómez Hurtado was presented as the Conservative nominee, but was decisively beaten by the PL's Barco, in part because of close association with his dictatorial father, Laureano, during the period of *la Violencia*.

Leaders: Dr. Misael PASTRANA Borrero (former President of the Republic), Dr. Alvaro GOMEZ Hurtado (1986 presidential candidate), Dr. Belisario BETANCUR Cuartas (former President of the Republic), Bertha HERNANDEZ de Ospina Pérez, Fernando SANCLEMENTE.

Patriotic Union (*Unión Patriótica* — UP). The UP was formed in May 1985 as the political arm of the Colombia Revolutionary Armed Forces (FARC, below), which has itself been viewed as the paramilitary wing of the Communist Party of Colombia (PCC, below). Advancing a program that included political and trade union freedom, agrarian reform, and opposition to US interference in Latin America, the UP won 1 Senate and 10 Chamber seats in March 1986. It mounted a major effort on behalf of its initial presidential nominee, FARC leader Jacobo Arenas, although Arenas withdrew his candidacy in January following the alleged discovery of a plot to assassinate him. A number of prominent UP members have recently been murdered (reportedly by paramilitary police units), including the organization's (then) president, Jaime Pardo Leal, on October 11, 1987.

Leaders: Bernardo JARAMILLO Ossa (President), Obido SALINAS (Executive Secretary).

Other Parties and Party Groups:

Christian Democratic Party (*Partido Democracia Cristiana* — PDC). The PDC is a small and relatively ineffectual Christian Democratic grouping. It was banned from participation in the 1986 elections because of fraudulent electoral registration.

Leaders: José AGUSTIN Linares (President), Francisco PAULA Jaramillo, José ALBENDEA (Secretary General).

National Popular Alliance (*Alianza Nacional Popular* — Anapo). Organized in 1971 as the personal vehicle of ex-dictator Gustavo Rojas Pinilla, who died in 1975, Anapo once commanded substantial lower-class support, especially in the larger urban areas. By late 1977, however, it had split into a number of distinct factions. One group joined two small radical parties, the **Workers' Movement of the Revolutionary Left** (*Movimiento Obrero Izquierdo Revolucionario* — MOIR) and the **Broad Colombian Movement** (*Movimiento Amplio Colombiano* — MAC), in the formation of a People's United Front (*Frente por la Unidad del Pueblo* — FUP) that obtained one lower-house seat in the February 1978 congressional election and then joined the PCC-ML (see under PCC, below) in supporting the presidential candidacy of Jaime Pedrahita Cardona. A second Anapo group joined the UNO (see under PCC, below) in supporting the 1978 presidential candidacy of Julio César Pernía. A third group, led by Carlos Toledo Plata, campaigned in 1978 as the *Anapo Socialista*, while a rump group under María Eugenia Rojas de Moreno Díaz supported the candidacy of Betancur Cuartas and reaffirmed its backing of the latter in 1982.

Leaders: María Eugenia ROJAS de Moreno Díaz (1974 presidential candidate), Joaquín MEJIA.

Communist Party of Colombia (*Partido Comunista de Colombia* — PCC). Colombia's historic pro-Moscow party, the PCC experienced a split in 1965 when a Maoist faction withdrew to form the **Communist Party of Colombia–Marxist-Leninist** (*Partido Comunista de Colombia Marxista-Leninista* — PCC-ML). The PCC participated in the 1978 campaign as a member of the National Opposition Union (*Unión Nacional de Oposición* — UNO), a coalition of dissidents from other parties that had been organized prior to the 1974 balloting and was additionally augmented in 1978 by the small **Independent Liberal Movement** (*Movimiento Independiente Liberal* — MIL) and an Anapo group.

In 1982 the PCC joined with the **Attention** (*Firmes*) movement and two other minor left-wing groups, the **Socialist Revolutionary Party** (*Partido Socialista Revolucionario* — PSR) and the **Colombian Labor Party** (*Partido Obrero Colombiano* — POC), in a coalition styled the Democratic Unity of the Left (*Unidad Demócrata de Izquierda* — UDI) that supported the presidential candidacy of Dr. Gerardo Molina. Although a legal party, the PCC did not participate directly in the 1986 balloting, presumably supporting candidates of the Patriotic Union (above).

Leader: Dr. Gilberto VIEIRA (General Secretary).

Socialist Workers' Party (*Partido Socialista de los Trabajadores* — PST). The PST was organized in September 1977 by members of a former Trotskyite party, the *Bloque Socialista*.

Leader: María Socorro RAMIREZ (1978 presidential candidate).

Paramilitary Groups:

In September 1981 most of the groups listed below formed a loosely structured guerrilla alliance. During 1984 the main components of FARC, M-19, and the EPL reached agreement on a cease-fire with the government;

however, M-19 formally repudiated the accord in June 1985, while the EPL followed suit in November. By early 1987 at least 10 rebel organizations, with a total strength of more than 27,000 militants, were reported to be active in various parts of the country. Subsequently, M-19 proposed an alliance with FARC that would effectively terminate the latter's adherence to the truce accord and in early October it was reported that FARC and most members of the CNG (M-19, the Quintín Lame Commando, the PRT, the ELN, and the EPL) had established a joint **Simón Bolívar Guerrilla Coordinating Board** (*Coordinadora Guerrillera Simón Bolívar*—CGSB).

Colombia Revolutionary Armed Forces (*Fuerzas Armadas Revolucionarias de Colombia*—FARC). FARC is a Moscow-line group affiliated with the PCC. In late 1983 it indicated a willingness to conclude a ceasefire agreement, which was formalized in March 1984. The agreement was renewed on March 2, 1986, in return for which the Betancur government guaranteed (without conspicuous fulfillment) the safety of electoral candidates advanced by FARC's political affiliate, the Patriotic Union (above). A dissident FARC group, the **Ricardo Franco Front** (*Frente Ricardo Franco*), led by Javier DELGADO and José FEDOR Rey, refused to participate in the accord and by late 1987 FARC itself was reported to have returned to a posture of "total insurrection".
Leaders: Jacobo ARENAS, Manuel MARULANDA Vélez.

National Guerrilla Coordination (*Coordinadora Nacional Guerrillera*—CNG). The CNG was formed in late 1985 by the three groups below, plus the smaller **Quintín Lame Commando** (*Comando Quintín Lame*) and **Free Homeland** (*Patria Libre*) formations operating in Cauca and Sucre departments, respectively, and the **Workers' Revolutionary Party** (*Partido Revolucionario de los Trabajadores*—PRT). In early 1986, the CNG was reported to have joined with guerrillas in Ecuador, Panama, Peru, and Venezuela in forming a *Batallón América* as the core of an eventual Bolivarian army (*ejército bolivariano*) composed of rebels from the countries freed by Simón Bolívar in the early nineteenth century.

April 19 Movement (*Movimiento 19 de Abril*—M-19). A self-proclaimed armed branch of Anapo which shocked the military establishment by a daring raid on an army arsenal north of the capital in January 1979, M-19 was subsequently responsible for the two-month occupation of the Dominican Embassy at Bogotá in early 1980 and the 27-hour seizure of the Palace of Justice at the capital in November 1985. In 1981, it appeared that the party had split into two factions: a moderate group led by Jaime Bateman Cayón, who announced in January that he favored a legal role for the organization, and a hard-line faction styling itself the *Coordinadora Nacional de Bases* (CNB), which advocated continued armed resistance and was reported to have established operational links with FARC. Prior to his death in a plane crash in April 1983, Bateman repudiated a truce agreement concluded six months earlier; a new dialogue with the government, undertaken by his successors in 1984, was repudiated in mid-1985. Carlos Pizarro, commander of the *Battalón América,* became head of the Movement in March 1986, following the killing by government forces of its two principal leaders, Iván Marino Ospina and Alvaro Fayad; in August 1986, the group's new second-in-command, Gustavo Londoño Arias, was also killed, while reports circulated that Pizarro may have met the same fate.
Leader: Carlos PIZARRO León Gómez.

National Liberation Army (*Ejército de Liberación Nacional*—ELN). Once the largest and most militant of the insurgent organizations, the Cuban-line ELN was responsible for the November 1983 kidnapping of the (then) president's brother, Dr. Jaime Betancur Cuartas, but released him after Cuban President Fidel Castro characterized the act as "unrevolutionary". Alleged to have links with guerrilla forces in El Salvador, Venezuela, and Peru, the group's leadership has consistently termed offers of amnesty a "sham", although some of its rank and file were reported to have accepted the government's terms.
Leader: Fabio VASQUEZ Castaño.

Popular Army of Liberation (*Ejército Popular de Liberación*—EPL). Formed as a guerrilla arm of the PCC-ML, the ELP initially rejected amnesty offers by the government, but accepted a truce in September 1984. It repudiated the accord following the assassination at Bogotá of its (then) leader, Oscar William Calvo, on November 20, 1985. Calvo was succeeded by his brother, Jairo de Jesús Calvo ("Commander Rojas"), who was killed in a shootout with police near Bogotá in February 1987.
Leader: Francisco CARABALLO.

Movement for Workers' Self-Defense (*Movimiento de Autodefensa Obrera*—MAO). A Trotskyite group, the MAO surfaced initially in 1978 as a perpetrator of a number of urban kidnappings and assassinations. Its leadership also accepted a truce in September 1984, although a splinter faction rejected the decision. The Movement was reported to have become affiliated with the Popular Union in July 1985.
Leader: Adelaida ABADIA Rey.

Minor leftist formations include the **Disaffected Youths of Colombia** (*Juventudes Inconformes de Colombia*—JIC), which has called for the elimination of drug dealers and kidnappers, and the **Student Revolutionary Movement** (*Movimiento Revolucionario Estudiantil*—MRE).

In early 1982, a right-wing group calling itself **Death to Kidnappers** (*Muerte a Secuestradores* —MAS) emerged in self-proclaimed response to leftist forces that engaged in abductions to finance their activities. Subsequently, President Betancur ordered an official investigation into the activities of the organization, which was reported to have links to drug traffickers as well as the nation's armed forces; another extreme-right group, about which little is known, is the **White Eagles Legion** (*Legión Aguilas Blancas*).

LEGISLATURE

The Colombian **Congress** (*Congreso*) is a bicameral legislature consisting of a Senate and a Chamber of Representatives, each elected for a four-year term. From 1958 to 1974 both houses were theoretically divided equally between Liberals and Conservatives, although members of other groups could run as nominal candidates of one of the two major parties and thus gain representation. At each of the last four elections, the Liberals obtained majorities in both houses, although they retained control of the Chamber in 1986 by only one seat.

Senate (*Senado*). The upper house is presently composed of 114 members, each department being represented by at least two senators. Following the election of March 9, 1986, the Liberal Party held 60 seats; the Conservative Party, 45; the New Liberalism, 8; and the Patriotic Union, 1.
President: Humberto PELAEZ Gutiérrez.

Chamber of Representatives (*Cámara de Representantes*). The lower house is presently composed of 199 members, each department being entitled to at least two representatives. Following the election of March 9, 1986, the Liberal Party held 100 seats; the Conservative Party, 82; the Patriotic Union, 10; and the New Liberalism, 7.
President: Román GOMEZ Covallo.

CABINET

President	Virgilio Barco Vargas
Presidential Designate	Víctor Mosquera Chaux

Ministers

Agriculture and Livestock	Luis Guillermo Parra Durán
Communications	Dr. Fernando Cepada Ulloa
Economic Development	Dr. Fuad Char Abdala
Education	Dr. Antonio Yepes
Finance	Luis Fernández Alarcón
Foreign Affairs	Col. Julio Londoño Paredes
Government	Dr. César Gaviria Trujillo
Justice	Dr. Enrique Low Murtra
Labor	Dr. Diego Younes Merino
Mines and Energy	Guillermo Eduardo Perry Rubio
National Defense	Gen. Rafael Samudio Molina
Public Health	Dr. José Granada Rodríguez
Public Works	Dr. Luis Fernando Jaramillo Correa
President, Central Bank	Francisco Ortega Acosta

NEWS MEDIA

Press. The press in Colombia is privately owned and enjoys complete freedom. Most newspapers function as the organs of political parties or factions. The following are dailies published at Bogotá, unless otherwise noted: *El Tiempo* (225,000 daily, 340,000 Sunday), *llerista* Liberal; *El Espectador* (218,000), *llerista* Liberal; *El Colombiano* (Medellín, 124,000), Conservative; *El Espacio* (98,000), *turbayista* Liberal; *El País* (Cali, 73,000 daily, 108,000 Sunday), *ospina-pastranista* Conservative; *El Heraldo* (Barranquilla, 66,000 daily, 51,000 Sunday), *turbayista* Liberal; *El Siglo* (65,000 daily, 72,000 Sunday), *alvarista* Conservative; *Occidente* (Cali, 53,000), *ospina-pastranista* Conservative; *El Pueblo* (Cali, 50,000), Liberal; *Voz Proletaria* (46,000), PCC weekly; *La República* (30,000), *ospina-pastranista* Conservative; *La Patria* (Manizales, 26,000), Conservative.

News agencies. The domestic agency is the Colombia Press; a number of foreign agencies maintain offices at Bogotá.

Radio and television. Broadcasting is supervised by the Ministry of Communications, although stations are both publicly and privately owned and operated. The official radio network is *Radio Cadena Nacional, S.A.;* most of the nearly 300 commercial stations belong to one of the six private networks. Television facilities are owned by *Instituto Nacional de Radio y Televisíon* (Inravisíon), a state monopoly; there were about 5.5 million television receivers in 1987.

INTERGOVERNMENTAL REPRESENTATION

Ambassador to the US: Víctor MOSQUERA Chaux.

US Ambassador to Colombia: Charles A. GILLESPIE, Jr.

Permanent Representative to the UN: Dr. Enrique PEÑALOSA.

IGO Memberships (Non-UN): ALADI, Ancom, CDB, Geplacea, IADB, ICAC, ICM, ICO, Inmarsat, Intelsat, Interpol, ISO, OAS, OPANAL, PCA, SELA, UPEB.

COMORO ISLANDS

Federal Islamic Republic of the Comoros
Jumhuriyat al-Qumur al-Ittihadiyah al-Islamiyah (Arabic)
République Fédérale Islamique des Comores (French)

Political Status: Former French dependency; proclaimed independent July 6, 1975; present government established on basis of constitution adopted October 1, 1978, following coup d'état of May 12–13.

Area: 718 sq. mi. (1,860 sq. km.), excluding the island of Mahoré (Mayotte), which has been retained as a "Territorial Collectivity" by France.

Population: 356,000 (1980C), excluding 52,000 residents of Mahoré; 420,000 (1988E), excluding Mahoré.

Major Urban Centers (1980C): MORONI (Njazidja, 18,000), Mutsamudu (Nzwani, 13,000), Fomboni (Mwali, 5,400).

Official Languages: Arabic, French (a majority speaks Comoran, a mixture of Arabic and Swahili).

Monetary Unit: CFA Franc (market rate March 1, 1988, 285.80 francs = $1US).

President: Ahmed ABDALLAH Abderemane; installed, with Mohamed AHMED, as Co-President of Political-Military Directorate following overthrow of President Ali SOILIH on May 12–13, 1978; approved as sole President for a six-year term at election of October 22, 1978, following the resignation of Co-President Ahmed on October 3; unopposed for reelection on September 30, 1984.

THE COUNTRY

Located in the Indian Ocean between Madagascar and the east coast of Africa, the Comoro Republic consists of three main islands: Njazidja (formerly Grande-Comore), site of the capital, Moroni; Nzwani (Anjouan); and Mwali (Mohéli). A fourth component of the archipelago, Mahoré (Mayotte), is claimed as national territory but remains under French administration (see France: Related Territories). The indigenous inhabitants derive from a mixture of Arab, Malagasy, and African strains; Islam is the state religion.

Volcanic in origin, the islands are mountainous, with a climate that is tropical during the rainy season and more temperate during the dry season. There are no significant mineral resources, and soil conditions vary, being comparatively rich on Mahoré and substantially poorer on the more populous islands of Nzwani and Njazidja. Economically, the islands have long suffered from an emphasis on the production of export crops, such as vanilla and perfume essences—the latter shipped primarily to France—and an insufficient cultivation of foods, particularly rice, needed for local consumption. Less than 10 percent of the population is engaged in salaried work, and the government remains highly dependent on foreign assistance to cover administrative and developmental expenses as well as trade deficits.

GOVERNMENT AND POLITICS

Political background. Ruled for centuries by Arab sultans and first visited by Europeans in the sixteenth century, the Comoro archipelago came under French rule in the nineteenth century: Mayotte became a French protectorate in 1843; Anjouan, Grande-Comore, and Mohéli were added in 1886. In 1912, the islands were joined administratively with Madagascar, from where they were governed until after World War II. Because of the lengthy period of indirect rule, the Comoros suffered comparative neglect, as contrasted with the nearby island of Reunion, which became an overseas French Department in 1946.

In the wake of a 1968 student strike that was suppressed by French police and troops, France agreed to permit the formation of legal political parties in the archipelago. Four years later, in December 1972, 34 of the 39 seats in the Comoran Chamber of Deputies were claimed by a coalition of pro-independence parties: the Democratic Rally of the Comoran People, led by Prince Saïd Mohamed JAFFAR; the Party for the Evolution of the Comoros, which was linked to the Tanzania-based National Liberation Movement of the Comoros (Molinaco); and the Democratic

Union of the Comoros, led by Ahmed ABDALLAH Abderemane. The other 5 seats were won by the anti-independence Popular Movement of Mahoré, headed by Marcel HENRY. As a result of the election, the Chamber named Abdallah president of the government, succeeding Prince Saïd IBRAHIM, co-leader, with Ali SOILIH, of the People's Party (*Umma-Mranda*), which had campaigned for a more gradual movement toward independence. The new government immediately began negotiations with Paris, and an agreement was reached in July 1973 providing for a five-year transition period during which France would retain responsibility for defense, foreign affairs, and currency. The only unresolved issue appeared to be the status of Mahoré, whose inhabitants remained strongly opposed to separation from France.

In a referendum held December 22, 1974, 95 percent of participating voters favored independence, despite a negative vote from Mahoré (where 25 percent of the registered electorate abstained). On July 6, 1975, a unilateral declaration of independence was voted by the territorial Chamber of Deputies, which designated Abdallah as head of state and prime minister. The action was timed to preempt the passage of legislation by the French National Assembly calling for an island-by-island referendum on a Comoran constitution—a procedure designed to allow Mahoré to remain under French jurisdiction. Having announced his intention to sever economic as well as political ties with France, the increasingly dictatorial Abdallah (who was visiting Nzwani at the time) was ousted on August 3 in a coup d'état led by Ali Soilih and supported by a National United Front of several parties. On August 10 governmental power was vested in a 12-member National Executive Council headed by Prince Jaffar, who was appointed president and prime minister, while in September, following an armed invasion of Nzwani by forces under Soilih, Abdallah surrendered and was subsequently exiled. At a joint meeting of the National Executive Council and the National Council of the Revolution on January 2, 1976, Soilih was named to replace Jaffar as head of state and the NCR was redesignated as the National Institutional Council. The presidency was also divorced from the premiership, and on January 6 Abdellahi MOHAMED was named to the latter post.

As president, Soilih encountered substantial resistance in attempting to mount a Chinese-style program designed to "abolish feudalism". During a month-long *"Periode Noire"* in 1977, civil servants were dismissed, the regular governmental machinery temporarily dismantled, and the "people's power" vested in a 16-member National People's Committee of recent secondary-school graduates. The "revolution" also included establishment of people's committees at island, district, and local levels, despite numerous skirmishes between people's militia forces and Islamic traditionalists. Between April 1976 and January 1978, at least three unsuccessful coups against the regime were mounted.

During the night of May 12–13, 1978, President Soilih was ousted by a group of about 50 mercenaries under the command of Col. Bob DENARD (the alias of Gilbert BOURGEAUD), a Frenchman previously involved in rebellions elsewhere in Africa and in southern Arabia. The suc-

cessful coup resulted in the return of Ahmed Abdallah, who joined Mohamed AHMED as co-president of a Political-Military Directorate that also included Denard. It was subsequently reported that Soilih had been killed on May 29 in an attempt to escape from house arrest. An exclusively "political directorate" was announced on July 22 in view of the "calm" that had resulted from a decision to return to traditional Islamic principles.

Co-President Ahmed resigned on October 3, following the approval by referendum two days earlier of a new constitution (see below). Abdallah was thus enabled to stand as sole candidate for president in balloting held October 22. Following a legislative election that concluded on December 15, Salim Ben ALI was designated prime minister, a post he continued to hold until dismissed by the president on January 25, 1982. His successor, Foreign Minister Ali MROUDJAE, was appointed on February 8, with the rest of the cabinet being named a week later. President Abdallah was unopposed in his bid for reelection to a second six-year term on September 30, 1984.

Amid evidence of serious dissent within the government leadership, Abdallah, following his reelection, secured a number of constitutional amendments that abolished the position of prime minister and reduced the powers of the Federal Assembly. These actions precipitated a coup attempt by junior members of the presidential guard on March 8, 1985, while the chief executive was on a private visit to Paris. Subsequently, the Democratic Front, a Paris-based opposition group (see Political Parties, below) was charged with complicity in the revolt, many of its domestic supporters being sentenced to life imprisonment in early November, although some were granted presidential amnesty at the end of the year.

At the most recent legislative balloting of March 22, 1987 (termed "a grotesque masquerade" by regime opponents), the entire slate of 42 candidates presented by President Abdallah was declared elected. Subsequently, in December, the president (again in France to attend a Franco-African heads-of-state meeting) survived another coup attempt with the assistance of Colonel Denard who, although officially retired, had remained in control of the country's small security force.

Constitution and government. The constitution of October 1, 1978, provides for a federal Islamic state headed by a president, who is elected by universal suffrage for a maximum of two six-year terms. The post of prime minister was abolished by a constitutional amendment adopted December 31, 1984. Legislative authority resides in a unicameral Federal Assembly, whose members are popularly elected for five-year terms. The country's judiciary is headed by the Supreme Court/High Court of Justice, located at Moroni. There are also courts of the first instance, a state security court, and 16 *qadi* courts, or courts of Muslim law.

Each of the islands elects its own governor and a Council that possesses limited powers of financial autonomy. If the functioning of the constitutional order is "interrupted by force", each island may "provisionally exercise in its territory all powers previously held by the Federal Republic". As adopted, the constitution applies to the three islands currently under government control but is intended to apply to Mahoré when that island "returns to the Comoro community".

Foreign relations. Comoran foreign relations continue to be dominated by the Mahoré issue. On November 21, 1975, French military personnel resisted an "invasion" by Ali Soilih and an unarmed contingent that attempted to counter the Mahori "secession". At the end of the year, France recognized the sovereignty of the other three islands, but referenda held on Mahoré in February and April 1976 demonstrated a clear preference for status as a French Department. On December 16, the French Senate ratified a measure according the island special standing as a *collectivité territoriale,* with that status being extended on December 6, 1979, for another five years. In mid-October 1981, President Abdallah pressed for French withdrawal during a Paris meeting with President Mitterrand, who, he noted, had opposed detachment of the island from the rest of the archipelago in 1975. He repeated the argument during a visit to France in June 1984, the French government responding that a further referendum on the issue would be deferred because the inhabitants of Mayotte were not sufficiently "well informed" on the options open to them. Postponement of the referendum was officially confirmed by the French National Assembly in a bill approved on December 19.

The Comoros was formally admitted to the Indian Ocean Commission, a regional grouping theretofore comprised of Madagascar, Mauritius, and the Seychelles, in January 1985. The Organization of African Unity, which the Comoros joined shortly after independence, has repeatedly called upon France to withdraw from Mayotte.

Current issues. Since assuming power, the Abdallah regime has consistently suppressed all political opposition, with the leading exile groups accusing the president of "repressive actions, intimidation and violations of all constitutional measures" in seeking reelection.

In December 1983, the French government announced that it would double its aid to Comoros and assume full responsibility for the islands' defense, its unwillingness to proceed with another referendum on Mayotte being attributed to no discernible change in sentiment by the latter's inhabitants. Indeed, the French secretary of state for overseas territorities declared, during a visit to the island in May, that his government now viewed *departement* status as "unsuited to the situation of Mayotte", thus reducing the options to two: continuance of the existing arrangement or incorporation of Mayotte into the Comoran Republic. Subsequently, on July 24, some 70 members of a pro-integration group were physically prevented from returning to Mayotte after having attended a political meeting on Nzwani.

At the Federal Assembly election of March 1987 (ostensibly open to any citizen wishing to compete as an independent), voters on two of the islands (Anjouan and Moheli) were presented only with presidential nominees. By contrast, opposition candidates were advanced in 20 constituencies on Grande Comore, none of whom was elected. The regime attributed the outcome to extensive preelectoral consultation with leading citizens in regard to the selection of presidential candidates, which, it was argued, constituted "a form of direct democracy". In July, amid reports

that Abdallah would seek a constitutional revision permitting him to run for a third term in 1990, the president announced that civil servants who had been dismissed for political reasons would be rehired; however, a "clarification" issued in August indicated that the policy would apply only to those suspected of complicity in the 1985 coup attempt—not to those supporting opposition candidates at the 1987 balloting.

By early 1988 the circumstances surrounding the December coup attempt were unclear, although there were reports that Madagascan authorities had been concerned with averting a possible South African-supported attack by French mercenaries recruited by Colonel Denard.

POLITICAL PARTIES

Although the 1978 constitution sanctioned multiparty activity, the Federal Assembly voted in 1979 for the establishment of a single-party system and a regime-supportive **Union for Comoran Progress** (*Union pour le Progrès Comorien*—UPC) was launched in February 1982. Earlier, in mid-1981, two Paris-based opposition groups, the **Comoran National United Front** (*Front National Uni des Komores*—FNUK) and the **Union of Comorans** (*Unions des Komoriens*—Unikom) had formed a coalition (FNUK-Unikom) under the leadership of Abubakar Ahmed NURDIN. Subsequently, they joined a third group, the **National Committee for Public Salvation** (*Comité National de Salut Public*), led by Saïd Ali KEMAL, in a more comprehensive "patriotic alliance to fight the anti-democratic regime of Ahmed Abdallah".

During a meeting at Marseilles in June 1987, FNUK-Unikom and two other exile groups, the **Comoran Students' Association** (*Association des Etudiantes Comoriens*) and the **Comoran Liberation Movement** (*Mouvement pour la Libération des Comores*—MLC) announced that they were merging into a single party, subsequently identified as the **Rally of Comoran Opposition Movements** (*Rassemblement des Mouvements de l'Opposition Comorien*—RMOC). Also active in France is the **Union for a Democratic Republic in the Comoros** (*Union pour une République Démocratique des Comores*—URDC), led by Mouzaoir ABDALLAH, and the **Democratic Front** (*Front Démocratique*—FD), represented in exile by Mohamed MONJOIN and within the Comoros by its secretary general, Moustapha Said CHEIKH, who was, however, sentenced to life imprisonment for complicity in the 1985 coup attempt.

LEGISLATURE

The unicameral **Federal Assembly** (*Assemblée Fédérale*), currently encompassing 42 members, is directly elected for a five-year term. Each electoral ward names one deputy, there being no fewer than five wards per island. Balloting for the present Assembly was conducted on March 22, 1987, all of the victors having been nominated by President Abdallah as de facto representatives of the Union for Comoran Progress.

President: Mohamed Taki ABDULKARIM.

C A B I N E T

President	Ahmed Abdallah Abderemane

Ministers

Economy, Finance, Domestic Commerce and State Enterprises	Saïd Ahmed Saïd Ali
Foreign Affairs, Cooperation and Foreign Commerce	Saïd Madi Kafe
Health and Population	Ali Hassan Ali
Interior, Information and Press	Omar Tamou
Justice, Employment, Professional Training and Manpower	Ben Ali Bacar
National Education, Culture, Youth and Sports	Salim Idarousse
Plan, Equipment, Environment, Urbanism and Housing	Mickidache Abdel-Rahim
Production, Rural Development, Industry and Crafts	Mohamed Ali
Director General, Central Bank	Mohamed Halifa

Secretaries of State

Interior	Abdul Aziz Hamadi
Post and Telecommunications	Ahmed Ben Daoud
Transportation and Tourism	Athoumane Abdou

N E W S   M E D I A

Press. As of late 1988, there were no domestic print media, save for a newsletter, *La Lettre des Comores.*

News Agency. There is an *Agence Comores Press* (ACP), located at Moroni.

Radio and television. Domestic and international radio service is provided by the government-operated *Radio-Comores.* In 1986 the French government announced that it would provide funding for the construction of a television station.

INTERGOVERNMENTAL   REPRESENTATION

Ambassador to the US: Ali MLAHAILI (resident in the Comoros).

US Ambassador to the Comoros: Patricia Gates LYNCH (resident in Madagascar).

Permanent Representative to the UN: Amini Ali MOUMIN.

IGO Memberships (Non-UN): ACCT, ADF, AfDB, BADEA, EEC(L), *EIB,* IC, IDB, NAM, OAU.

CONGO

People's Republic of the Congo
République Populaire du Congo

Political Status: Independent since August 15, 1960; one-party People's Republic proclaimed December 31, 1969.

Area: 132,046 sq. mi. (342,000 sq. km.).

Population: 1,912,429 (1984C), 2,121,000 (1988E).

Major Urban Centers (1980E): BRAZZAVILLE (422,400); Pointe-Noire (185,110); Kayes (formerly Jacob, 31,500); Loubomo (formerly Dolisie, 30,200).

Official Language: French.

Monetary Unit: CFA Franc (market rate March 1, 1988, 285.80 francs = $1US).

President: Col. Denis SASSOU-NGUESSO; named Interim President by the Central Committee of the Congolese Labor Party (PCT) following the resignation of Brig. Gen. Joachim YHOMBI-OPANGO on February 5, 1979; confirmed as President at an extraordinary congress of the PCT on March 27; reelected for a five-year term on July 30, 1984.

Prime Minister: Ange-Edouard POUNGUI; designated by the President on August 11, 1984, succeeding Col. Louis-Sylvain GOMA.

THE   COUNTRY

The People's Republic of the Congo is a narrow 800-mile-long strip of heavily forested territory extending inland from the Atlantic along the Congo and Ubangi rivers. It is bordered on the east by Gabon, on the north by Cameroon and the Central African Republic, and on the west and south by Zaire. The members of the country's multitribal society belong mainly to the Bakongo, Matéké, M'bochi, and Vili tribal groups and include numerous pygmies, who are thought to be among the first inhabitants of the area. Linguistically, the tribes speak related Bantu languages; French, although the official language, is not in widespread use. There is, however, a lingua franca, Mouman Koutouba, which is widely employed in commerce. In the past decade there has been substantial rural-to-urban migration, with close to 50 percent of the population now living in or near Brazzaville or Pointe Noir. Partly because of its level of urbanization, the Congo has a 93 percent literacy rate, the highest in Black Africa. About half of the population adheres to traditional religious beliefs, while the remainder is Roman Catholic, Protestant, and Muslim.

Although the country possesses exploitable deposits of manganese, copper, lead-zinc, and gold, oil and timber are its leading resources, with the first accounting for more than 93 percent of export earnings in 1985. Since 1983, however, the world oil glut has drastically curtailed revenue. As a result, the government is presently committed to redirection of the largely state-controlled economy into rural development, with particular emphasis on expansion of the traditionally minor cash crops of coffee and cocoa.

GOVERNMENT   AND   POLITICS

Political background. Occupied by France in the 1880s, the former colony of Middle Congo became the autonomous Republic of the Congo in 1958 and attained full independence within the French Community on August 15, 1960. The country's first president, Fulbert YOULOU, established a strong centralized administration but resigned in 1963 in the face of numerous strikes and labor demonstrations. His successor, Alphonse MASSAMBA-DEBAT, was installed by the military and subsequently reelected for a five-year term. Under Massamba-Débat the regime embraced a Marxist-type doctrine of "scientific socialism", and the political system was reorganized on a one-party basis. In 1968, however, Massamba-Débat was stripped of authority as a result of differences with both left-wing and military elements. A military coup led by (then) Capt. Marien NGOUABI on August 3 was followed by the establishment of a National Council of the Revolution to direct the government.

Formally designated as head of state in January 1969, Ngouabi proclaimed a "people's republic" the following December, while a constitution adopted in January 1970 legitimized a single political party, the Congolese Labor Party (PCT). Three years later, a new basic law established the post of prime minister and created a National Assembly to replace the one dissolved in 1968.

President Ngouabi was assassinated on March 18, 1977, and the PCT immediately transferred its powers to an 11-member Military Committee headed by (then) Col. Joachim YHOMBI-OPANGO, which reinstituted rule by decree. Former president Massamba-Débat, who was accused of having plotted the assassination, was executed on March 25. On April 3, it was announced that (then) Maj. Denis SASSOU-NGUESSO had been named first vice president of the Military Committee and that (then) Maj. Louis-Sylvain GOMA, who retained his post as prime minister, had been named second vice president.

Responding to pressure from the Central Committee of the PCT after having made disparaging remarks about the condition of the country's economy, General Yhombi-Opango, as well as the Military Committee, resigned on February 5, 1979. The Central Committee thereupon established a ruling Provisional Committee and named Colonel Sassou-Nguesso, the minister of defense and security, as interim president. At an extraordinary congress on March 26–31, the party confirmed Sassou-Nguesso as president, while on July 8 the voters approved a new constitution and elected a People's National Assembly in addition to district, regional, and local councils. On July 30, 1984, the president was elected for a second term and on August 11, as part of a reshuffling aimed at "strengthening the revolutionary process", named Ange-Edouard POUNGUI to succeed Louis-Sylain Goma as prime minister.

Constitution and government. The 1979 constitution established the Congolese Labor Party as the sole legal party, with the chairman of its Central Committee, elected for a five-year term by the party Congress, serving as president of the Republic. Under a constitutional revision adopted at the third PCT congress (July 27–31, 1984), the president was named chief of government as well as head of state, with the authority to name the prime minister and members of the Council of Ministers. The legislature is elected from a list prepared by the PCT, while the judicial system is headed by a Revolutionary Court of Justice whose judges are appointed by the PCT Central Committee. The judiciary further encompasses a Supreme Court; a court of appeal; and criminal, county, magistrates', and labor courts. In August 1984, the Constitutional Chamber of the Supreme Court was replaced by a separate Constitutional

Council to rule on the constitutional validity of legislation and to supervise balloting in elections and referenda.

Local administration is based on nine regions, each with an elected Popular Regional Council and Executive Committee. Representing the national government are commissars named by the PCT Central Committee.

Foreign relations. The People's Republic of the Congo withdrew from the French Community in November 1973 but remains economically linked to Paris. In June 1977, it was announced that diplomatic ties with the United States would be resumed after a 12-year lapse, although the US embassy at Brazzaville was not reopened until November 1978 and ambassadors were not exchanged until May 1979.

The Congo has long maintained close relations with Communist nations, including the People's Republic of China, Cuba, and the Soviet Union, signing a 20-year Treaty of Friendship with the latter in May 1981. It is on relatively good terms with its neighbors, although recurrent border incidents have strained relations with Zaire despite the conclusion of a number of economic cooperation agreements. As an active member of the Organization of African Unity, the Congo has hosted a number of meetings aimed at resolving the civil war in Chad, although it tacitly supported the claims of Hissein Habré by serving as a staging area in 1983 for Habré-supportive French troops. In 1986, President Sassou-Nguesso was selected as the OAU's chief mediator in the Chadian negotiations. In early 1987 he embarked on a nine-nation European tour to emphasize the gravity of the economic situation facing sub-Saharan Africa and the need for effective sanctions against South Africa.

Current issues. In 1986 a continued shortfall in oil revenue and the lessened value of the dollar forced the government to accept IMF-inspired austerity measures, including a 42 percent budget cut, the abandonment of numerous development projects, and a 6 percent levy on the salaries of public officials; in addition, taxes on non-oil income were increased and 1400 "fictitious" civil servants were dismissed. By early 1987 the PCT Central Committee had approved measures to counteract deforestation and the decline of agricultural productivity, and had endorsed the rescheduling of $500 million in debt servicing charges.

The bleak economic outlook was compounded by rebellion in the north. In July 1987, 20 military officers linked to the MPC (see Political parties, below) were arrested on charges of plotting a coup. Subsequently, the army, aided by French forces, attacked the north Congo home village of Lt. Pierre ANGA, who had been named by some of the arrested officers as a co-conspirator. Following a purge of leading government and party officials, Anga, who had eluded capture during a disturbance in which some 60 persons were killed, released a tape alleging that Sassou-Nguesso had participated in the murder of former president Ngouabi. Former president Yhombi-Opango, a close friend of Anga, was reimprisoned in August in an attempt to halt the unrest; nonetheless, reports of attacks by rebel forces in the north continued to circulate.

POLITICAL PARTIES

The People's Republic of the Congo became a one-party

state in 1963 when the National Revolutionary Movement (*Mouvement National Révolutionnaire* — MNR) supplanted the two parties that had been politically dominant under the preceding administration: the Union for the Defense of African Interests (UDDIA) and the African Socialist Movement (MSA). The MNR was in turn replaced by the Congolese Labor Party in 1969, coincident with the declaration of the People's Republic.

Congolese Labor Party (*Parti Congolais du Travail* — PCT). The Marxist-Leninist PCT is organized along hierarchical lines and is buttressed by auxiliary organizations. At the third National Party Congress on July 27–31, 1984, the size of the PCT Central Committee was enlarged from 60 to 75 members and that of its Politburo from 8 to 13. On November 28, 1986, in what was billed as a "cost-cutting" move, the latter body was reduced to 10, while the party Secretariat was cut from 10 to 8 members. Among those losing their Politburo posts was former foreign minister, Pierre NZE, who had been considered one of the PCT's leading theoreticians.
Leaders: Col. Denis SASSOU-NGUESSO (President of the Republic and Chairman of the PCT Central Committee), Ange Edouard POUNGUI (Prime Minister), André Obami ITOU (General Secretary).

February 22 Movement (*Mouvement du 22 Fevrier* — M-22). M-22 is a factional grouping of PCT hardliners from the northern Congo.
Leaders: Camille BONGOU (former PCT General Secretary), Benoit NGOLLO, Ambroise NOUMAZALAYE.

There are also two Paris-based formations: the Marxist **Congolese Patriotic Movement** (*Mouvement Patriotique Congolais* — MPC) and the free-enterprise **Congolese Democratic Party** (*Parti Démocratique Congolais* — PDC).

LEGISLATURE

The unicameral **People's National Assembly** (*Assemblée Nationale Populaire*) sits for a five-year term. The most recent election to the 153-member body took place on September 23, 1984, all of the candidates being nominated by the PCT.
President: Jean BANGA-ZANZOU.

CABINET

Prime Minister	Ange Edouard Poungui
Ministers	
Basic Education and Literacy	Pierre Damien Bassoukou-Boumba
Commerce, Small and Medium Enterprises	Alphonse Poaty-Souchlaty
Defense and Security	Col. Emmanuel Elenga
Foreign Affairs and Cooperation	Antoine Ndinga-Oba
Forestry	Ossebi Douniam
Higher Education and Culture	Jean-Baptiste Tati-Loutard
Industry, Fishing and Crafts	Ambroise Edouard Noumazalaye
Information, Posts and Telecommunications	Christian Gilbert Bembet
Justice and Keeper of the Seals	Dieudonné Kimbembé
Labor and Social Security	Dieudonné Kimbembé
Mines and Energy	Rodolphe Adada
Planning and Finance	Pierre Moussa
Public Health and Social Affairs	Bernard Combo-Matsiona
Public Works, Construction, Housing and Urbanism	Lt. Col. Benoît Moundele-Ngollo
Rural Development	Justin Lekoundzou Itihi-Ossetoumba
Scientific Research and Environment	Christophe Bouramoue

Territorial Administration and Local Government	Col. Raymond Damase-Ngollo
Tourism, Sports and Leisure	Jean-Claude Ganga
Transport and Civil Aviation	Hilaire Mounthault
Director, Presidential Cabinet	Basile Ikouebe
Director, Central Bank	Gabriel Bokilo

NEWS MEDIA

The news media are subject to government censorship.
Press. The following are French dailies published at Brazzaville: *Mweti* (8,000); *ACI* (1,000), government bulletin.
News agencies. The official news agency is *Agence Congolaise d'Information* (ACI); *Agence France-Presse, Novosti*, and TASS are represented at Brazzaville.
Radio and television. *La Voix de la Révolution Congolaise* offers radio programming in French, English, Portuguese, and a variety of indigenous languages, while *Radiodiffusion-Télévision Nationale Congolaise* operates one television station. There were approximately 5,500 television receivers in 1987.

INTERGOVERNMENTAL REPRESENTATION

Ambassador to the US: Benjamin BOUNKOULOU.

US Ambassador to the People's Republic of the Congo: Leonard Grant SHURTLEFF.

Permanent Representative to the UN: Dr. Martin ADOUKI.

IGO Memberships (Non-UN): ACCT, ADF, AfDB, BADEA, BDEAC, CCC, EEC(L), *EIB*, IACO, ICO, Intelsat, Interpol, NAM, OAU, UDEAC.

COSTA RICA

Republic of Costa Rica
República de Costa Rica

Political Status: Independence proclaimed September 15, 1821; republic established in 1848; democratic constitutional system instituted in 1899.

Area: 19,575 sq. mi. (50,700 sq. km.).

Population: 2,417,226 (1984C), 2,682,000 (1988E).

Major Urban Centers (1984C): SAN JOSE (245,370); Puntarenas (47,851); Limón (43,158); Alajuela (33,929); Cartago (23,884); Heredia (20,867); Liberia (14,093).

Principal Language: Spanish (there is no "official" language).

Monetary Unit: Colón (market rate March 1, 1988, 73.70 colones = $1US).

President: Oscar ARIAS Sánchez (National Liberation Party); elected February 2 and inaugurated May 8, 1986, for a four-year term, succeeding Luis Alberto MONGE Alvarez (National Liberation Party).

First Vice President: Jorge Manuel DENGO Obregón (National Liberation Party); elected February 2, 1986, for a term concurrent with that of the President, succeeding Armando ARAUZ Aguilar (National Liberation Party), who had become sole Vice President upon the resignation of First Vice President Alberto FAIT Lizano in July 1984.

Second Vice President: Victoria GARRON de Doryan (National Liberation Party); elected February 2, 1986, for a term concurrent with that of the President.

THE COUNTRY

One of the smallest of the Central American countries, Costa Rica lies directly north of Panama and combines tropical lowlands, high tableland, and rugged mountainous terrain. Its people, known as *Costarricenses,* are overwhelmingly of European (predominantly Spanish) descent. This unusual homogeneity is broken only by mestizo and Negro minorities, which are concentrated in the provinces of Guanacaste and Limón, respectively. Roman Catholicism is the state religion, but other faiths are permitted. The country's literacy rate, over 90 percent, is one of the highest in Latin America. In 1983, women constituted 29 percent of the paid work force, concentrated in service and agricultural occupations; female representation in elected bodies averages about 6 percent.

In 1948 Costa Rica embarked on the establishment of what has become one of the world's most progressive welfare states, providing a complete program of health care and education for workers and their families. Substantial economic growth, yielding one of the region's highest standards of living, continued through most of the 1970s before giving way to depressed prices for coffee, beef, bananas, and sugar exports, accompanied by increased oil import costs. By the early 1980s, the country was experiencing deep recession, marked by high inflation, unemployment, budget deficits and trade imbalances. Bankruptcy was averted by means of aid from the United States, the World Bank, and the International Monetary Fund, although several IMF agreements have been compromised by Costa Rica's inability to meet fund conditions. By 1986, austerity measures were credited with having stabilized the economy, although strains continued because of a large foreign debt, an influx of some 250,000 refugees from neighboring Nicaragua, and continued low prices for commodity exports (see Current issues, below).

GOVERNMENT AND POLITICS

Political background. Costa Rica declared its independence from Spain in 1821 but accepted inclusion in the Mexican Empire of 1822–1823. It was a member of the United Provinces of Central America from 1824 to 1839, when its autonomy was reestablished. A republic was formally declared in 1848 during a period characterized by alternating political conflict and rule by the leading families, who monopolized the indirect electoral system. In 1897 it joined El Salvador, Honduras, and Nicaragua in the Greater Republic of Central America, but the federation was dissolved in 1898. A year later, President Bernardo SOTO sponsored what is considered to be the country's first free election, inaugurating a democratic process that has survived with only two major interruptions, one in 1917 and the other in 1948. Since the uprising led by José FIGUERES Ferrer, following annulment of the 1948 election by President Teodoro PICADO, transfer of power has been accomplished by constitutional means, further securing Costa Rica's reputation as what has been called "perhaps the most passionately democratic country in Latin America". At the most recent election, held February 2, 1986, Oscar ARIAS Sánchez of the National Liberation Party defeated his closest competitor, Rafael Angel CALDERON Fournier of the Social Christian Unity Party by a 52 to 46 percent vote margin.

Constitution and government. The constitution of 1949 provides for three independent branches of government: legislative, executive, and judicial. The legislative branch enjoys genuinely coequal power, including the ability to override presidential vetoes. Members of the legislature are elected by direct popular vote and may not be reelected for successive terms. The president serves as chief executive and is assisted by two elected vice presidents in addition to a cabinet of his own selection. By Latin American standards the president's powers are limited, and a 1969 constitutional amendment prohibits the reelection of all previous incumbents.

The judicial branch is independent of the president, its members being elected for eight-year terms by the legislature. The judicial structure encompasses the Supreme Court of Justice, which may rule on the constitutionality of legislation; four courts of appeal; and numerous local courts distributed among the judicial districts. One of the unique features of the Costa Rican governmental system is the Supreme Electoral Tribunal (*Tribunal Supremo de Elecciones*), an independent body of three magistrates and three alternate magistrates elected by the Supreme Court of Justice for staggered six-year terms. The Tribunal oversees the entire electoral process, including the interpretation of electoral statutes, the certification of parties, and the adjudication of alleged electoral irregularities.

For administrative purposes the country is divided into seven provinces and 81 *municipios,* the former administered by governors appointed by the president. The latter are governed by councils that have both voting and nonvoting members, and by executive officials appointed by the president. The executive officers may veto council acts, but all such vetoes are subject to judicial review.

Costa Rica is one of only a handful of countries that constitutionally proscribes the raising of a national army, save under strictly limited circumstances of public necessity.

Foreign relations. A founding member of the United Nations and of the Organization of American States, Costa Rica has typically been aligned with the liberal, democratic wing in Latin American politics and has opposed dictatorships of both the Right and the Left. On May 11, 1981, it broke relations with Havana after a protest regarding the treatment of Cuban political prisoners had elicited an "insulting" response by Cuba's representative to the United Nations. In 1982 it endorsed proposals for negotiations between the newly installed government in El Salvador and the insurgent Democratic Revolutionary Front.

In recent years an overriding external concern has been the Nicaraguan *sandinista-contra* conflict and concurrent US involvement in regional affairs. Although formally neutral on the issue, San José has at times expressed strong criticism of Managua's Marxist orientation, while accepting over $730 million in economic aid from the United States since 1982. The presence of US-backed *contra* insurgents in the northern border area has been particularly controversial, yielding skirmishes between Costa Rica's civil guard and Nicaraguan forces. Fearful of being dragged more deeply into the conflict, San José has ordered periodic raids of *contra* camps, vowing to prevent Costa Rica from being used "as a base for any foreign military operations".

Current issues. Popular concern over the Nicaraguan problem appeared to play a major role in the February 1986 presidential victory of Oscar Arias Sánchez, who was perceived as less "hawkish" than his opponent. Following the election Arias reaffirmed Costa Rica's "strict neutrality" in regional disputes, emphasizing that friendship with the United States would not mean "servitude" to its pro-*contra* policies. In early 1987 he introduced a peace plan that served as the basis of intensive effort to negotiate a settlement to fighting in Nicaragua, El Salvador, and Guatemala. The initiative earned him the 1987 Nobel Peace Prize, with his reputation further enhanced by the *sandinista-contra* ceasefire in early 1988.

Arias was less successful during 1987 in addressing Costa Rica's economic difficulties. Despite attempts to stimulate agricultural production and accelerate privatization of state-run industries, the growth rate slowed to about 2.5 percent and the government was able to meet only one-half of its external debt repayment obligations. In April the administration announced a recovery program encompassing foreign trade liberalization and a projected reduction in the public deficit. However, the opposition forced a delay in legislative action until November, when a compromise was reached on proposed tax increases. Subsequently, the IMF released a $64 million standby loan, paving the way for negotiations on debt rescheduling. However, the collapse of a number of private financial institutions in early 1988 generated new fiscal problems, as did resistance to proposed cuts in spending by the four state universities.

POLITICAL PARTIES

Government Party:

National Liberation Party (*Partido de Liberación Nacional*—PLN). Founded by former president José Figueres Ferrer in the aftermath of the 1948 revolution, the PLN has traditionally been the largest and best-organized of the Costa Rican parties and is a classic example of the democratic Left in Latin America. Affiliated with the Socialist International, it has consistently favored progressive programs. In July 1976 President Figueres precipitated a crisis within the party leadership by calling for revocation of the constitutional requirement that a president may not serve more than one term, thereby contributing to the defeat of Luis Alberto Monge as PLN presidential candidate in 1978. Subsequently, the cultivation of a network of predominantly regional and local support, coupled with a "return to the land" (*volver a la tierre*) campaign slogan, enabled Monge to secure a decisive victory in 1982. Although Oscar Arias Sánchez

won a primary election over the more conservative Carlos Manuel Castillo in early 1985, disagreement between their supporters (largely abated during the 1986 campaign) continued in the Assembly. By 1987 Castello was seen as a strong contender for the 1990 presidential nomination, his principal competitor appearing to be former PLN secretary general Rolando Araya Monge.

Leaders: Oscar ARIAS Sánchez (President of the Republic); Luis Alberto MONGE Alvarez, José FIGUERES Ferrer, Daniel ODUBER Quirós (former Presidents of the Republic); Carlos Manuel CASTILLO; Guido GRANADOS; Rolando ARAYA Monge, Walter COTO (Secretary General).

Opposition Groups:

Social Christian Unity Party (*Partido Unidad Social Cristiana*—PUSC). A loose alliance of the essentially conservative parties, listed below, plus the former Democratic Renovation Party (see National Union, below), the PUSC campaigned prior to the 1978 election as the *Partido Unidad Opositora* (PUO) and as the *Coalición Unidad* in 1978, adopting its present name in December 1983. Partly because of conflict within the PLN leadership, it won the presidency in 1978 but was defeated in both 1982 and 1986.

Leaders: Cristián TATTEMBACH Yglesias (President), Rodrigo CARAZO Odio (former President of the Republic), Roberto TOVAR Faja (Secretary General).

Calderonist Republican Party (*Partido Republicano Calderonista*—PRC). Named after former president Rafael Angel Calderón Guardia, the PRC was formed in 1976 by a breakaway group of the PUN (below).

Leaders: Alvaro CUBILLO Aguilar (President), Rafael Angel CALDERON Fournier (1986 PUSC presidential candidate), Gerardo BOLANOS Alpizar (Secretary).

Christian Democratic Party (*Partido Demócrata Cristiano*—PDC). The PDC is a traditional Christian Democratic group formed in 1962.

Leaders: Rafael Alberto GRILLO Rivera (President), Claudio GUEVARA Barahona (Secretary).

Popular Union Party (*Partido Unión Popular*—PUP). The PUP is a coalition of right-wing interests.

Leaders: Cristián TATTEMBACH Yglesias (President), Juan Rafael RODRIGUEZ Calvo (Secretary).

National Union (*Unión Nacional*—UN). The UN was formed in April 1985 by the leader of the previously PUSC-affiliated Democratic Renovation Party (*Partido Renovación Democrática*—PRD), Oscar Aguilar Bulgarelli, who opposed Rafael Calderón's "absolute and anti-democratic control" of the parent coalition, including an alleged effort to change its posture from social democratic to liberal.

Leader: Oscar AGUILAR Bulgarelli.

National Unification Party (*Partido Unificación Nacional*—PUN). The PUN is a remnant of the *Unificación Nacional* organized prior to the 1966 election as a coalition of two conservative groups, the Republican Party (*Partido Republicano*—PR) and the National Union Party (*Partido Unión Nacional*—PUN), which were subsequently joined by the Revolutionary Civic Union (*Partido Unión Civico Revolucionaria*—PUCR) and the Authentic Republican Union Party (*Partido Unión Republicana Auténtica*—PURA). The PUN was not registered for the 1982 or 1986 elections.

Leaders: Guillermo VILLALOBOS Arce (President), Rogelio RAMOS Valverde (Secretary).

National Movement (*Movimiento Nacional*—MN). An outgrowth of the former National Union Party (see PUN, above), the MN is a conservative grouping whose leader obtained 3.7 percent of the vote at the 1982 presidential balloting.

Leaders: Mario ECHANDI Jiménez, Rodrigo SANCHO Robles (Secretary).

Democratic Party (*Partido Demócrata*—PD). The PD is a small grouping that supported the 1982 presidential candidacy of Edwin Retana Chávez.

Leaders: Edwin RETANA Chavez (President), Alvaro GONZALEZ Espinosa (Secretary).

People United (*Pueblo Unido* — PU). The PU was organized prior to the 1978 election as a coalition of left-wing groups that included the Popular Vanguard Party (see Popular Alliance, below), the Costa Rican Socialist Party (PSC), and the Workers' Party (PT). The coalition supported the presidential candidacy of Dr. Rodrigo Gutiérrez Sáenz in 1978 and 1982, but subsequently fell into disarray because of a leadership dispute within the PVP, which resulted in the formation by ex-PVP leader Manuel Mora Valverde of the rival Costa Rican People's Party (PPC). In 1985, the PPC, the PSC and the MNR (below) secured official registration under the PU inscription, the PVP charging the PPC with involvement in the "theft" of the rubric.

Costa Rican People's Party (*Partido del Pueblo Costarricense* — PPC). The PPC originated as a Havana-oriented Popular Vanguard splinter led by Manuel Mora Valverde; the group initially presented itself as the "real" PVP, but was rebuffed in February 1984 when the Civil Registry recognized the mainstream (Vargas-Ferreto) faction as being in legitimate possession of the traditional party name. In 1984, it joined with the MNR and a number of other groups as the Patriotic Alliance (*Alianza Patriótica*) — a name that was also claimed briefly by the PVP and its allies in 1985 (see Popular Alliance, below).
Leaders: Eduardo MORA Valverde, Manuel Enrique DELGADO Cascante, Manuel MORA Valverde (Secretary General).

Costa Rican Socialist Party (*Partido Socialista Costarricense* — PSC). The PSC is a pro-Cuban Marxist party, which was a member of the 1978-1982 PU electoral alliance.
Leaders: Alvaro MONTERO Mejía (President of the Party and 1986 PU presidential candidate), Alberto SALOM Echeverría (Secretary).

New Republican Movement (*Movimiento Nueva Republica* — MNR). The MNR is a moderate splinter of the MRP (see Workers' Party, below).
Leader: Sergio Erick ARDON Ramírez.

Workers' Party (*Partido de los Trabajadores* — PT). The PT has long been the political wing of the Revolutionary People's Movement (*Movimiento Revolucionario del Pueblo* — MRP), a Maoist extremist group that endorsed revolutionary activity in 1978-1980, although its leadership appeared to moderate its position in mid-1981, declaring that "popular struggles can . . . be waged [in Costa Rica] without the unjust violence of terrorist actions".
Leaders: José Francisco ARAYA Monge (President), Ilse ACOSTA Polonio (Secretary).

Radical Democratic Party (*Partido Radical Demócrata*). The Radical Democratic Party was formed in mid-1982 by a number of avowedly left-of-center members of the former Carazo Odio administration.
Leaders: Juan José ECHEVERRIA Brealey, Rodrigo ESQUIVEL Rodríguez (Secretary).

Popular Alliance (*Alianza Popular*). The Popular Alliance was launched prior to the 1986 balloting with the former PU standard bearer, Dr. Rodrigo Gutiérrez Sáenz of the FAD (below) as its presidential candidate. At its formation, denied access to the old People United label, the group styled itself the Popular Democratic Union (*Unión Democrática Popular* — UDP) and for a time in 1985 presented itself as the *Alianza Patriótica* in an apparent effort to cloud the electoral prospects of the PPC.

Popular Vanguard Party (*Partido Vanguardia Popular* — PVP). Founded in 1931 as the Costa Rican Communist Party (*Partido Comunista Costarricense* — PCC), the PVP adopted its present name in 1943 and regained legal status in 1975, following the lifting of a long-standing proscription of nondemocratic political organizations. During the 1978 and 1982 campaigns, it participated in the *Pueblo Unido* coalition. In 1983, a struggle erupted between the essentially moderate "old guard" leadership headed by longtime secretary general Manuel Mora Valverde and a younger hard-line group headed by Humberto Vargas Carbonell and Arnaldo Ferreto Segura. In the course of the dispute, Mora was "elevated" to the newly created post of party president, before withdrawing, in 1984, as leader of the newly formed Costa Rican People's Party (above).
Leaders: Arnoldo FERRETO Segura (President), Humberto Elías VARGAS Carbonell (Secretary General), Oscar MADRID Jiménez (Undersecretary General).

Broad Democratic Front (*Frente Amplio Democrático* — FAD). Initially formed within the PU, the FAD was withdrawn by its founder in May 1985 to enter into the (then) UDP alliance with the PVP.
Leader: Dr. Rodrigo GUTIERREZ Sáenz.

Costa Rican Popular Front (*Frente Popular Costarricense* — FPC). The FPC is a small anti-Soviet party of the extreme Left. It lost its only legislative seat at the 1982 election.
Leaders: Rodolfo CERDAS Cruz (President), Wilbert Ezequiel SOLANO Rojas (Secretary).

National Christian Alliance Party (*Alianza Nacional Cristiana*). The National Christian Alliance Party was one of the four minor parties to contest the 1986 presidential election.
Leaders: Victor Hugo GONZALEZ Montero (President), Alejandro MADRIGAL (1986 presidential candidate), Juan RODRIGUEZ Venegas (Secretary).

Costa Rican Ecology Party (*Partido Ecológico Costarricense* — PEC). The PEC was formed in June 1984, participating without success in the 1986 balloting.
Leader: Alexander BONILLA.

There are about a dozen other minor parties; in addition, limited legislative representation is occasionally secured by regional or provincial groups. Thus the **Cartago Agricultural Union** (*Unión Agrícola Cartaginesa* — UAC) won a single seat in 1978, as did the **Alajuela Democratic Party** (*Partido Alajuela Demócrata* — PAD) in 1982 and the **Independent Cartago** (*Cartago Independiente*) in 1986.

Extremist Groups:

In early 1981 the government claimed to have evidence of a new left-extremist organization called the **Carlos Aguero Echeverría Command,** named after a Costa Rican who had been killed while participating in the *sandinista* insurgency in Nicaragua. Subsequently, it was reported that the group had claimed credit for a bazooka attack on a US embassy car on March 17. In 1984, there were reports of activity by a right-wing group known as the **Army of the Costa Rican People** (*Ejército del Pueblo Costarricense* — EPC).

LEGISLATURE

The **Legislative Assembly** (*Asamblea Legislativa*) is a unicameral body whose 57 members, representing the provinces in proportion to population, are elected for four-year terms by direct popular vote and may not be immediately reelected. Following the election of February 2, 1986, the National Liberation Party held 29 seats; the Social Christian Unity Party, 25; and the People United, the Popular Alliance, and Independent Cartago, 1 each.
President: Rosemary KARPINSKI Dodero.

CABINET

President	Oscar Arias Sánchez
Frist Vice President	Jorge Manuel Dengo Obregón
Second Vice President	Victoria Garrón de Doryan
Ministers	
Agriculture and Livestock	Antonio Alvarez Desanti
Culture	Carlos Francisco Echeverría Salgado
Economy	Luis Diego Escalante
Education	Francisco Antonio Pacheco
Finance	Fernando Naranjo Villalobos
Foreign Affairs	Rodrigo Madrigal Nieto
Foreign Trade	Muñi Figueres de Jiménez
Government and Police	Rolando Ramírez Paniagua
Health	Dr. Edgar Mohs Villalta
Housing	Fernando Zumbado Jiménez
Industry, Energy and Mines	Alvaro Umaña Quesada
Information	Guido Fernández Saborio
Justice	Luis Paulino Mora
Labor and Social Security	Edwin León Villalobos

National Planning and Economic Policy	Otón Solís Fallas
Presidency	Rodrigo Arias Sánchez
Public Security	Hernán Garrón Salazar
Public Works and Transport	Guillermo Constenela Umaña
Science and Technology	Rodrigo Zeledon
President, Central Bank	Dr. Eduardo Lizano Fait

NEWS MEDIA

All news media are free of censorship.

Press. Except as noted, the following are published daily at San José: *La Nación* (91,000), conservative; *La República* (60,000), independent; *La Prensa Libre* (50,000), independent; *Libertad* (25,500), pro-Moscow Communist weekly; *Eco Católico* (15,500), Catholic weekly; *La Gaceta* (5,300), official government gazette.

News agencies. There is no domestic facility. *Agence France-Presse, Deutsche Presse-Agentur, Prensa Latina,* and Tass maintain offices at San José.

Radio and television. Broadcasting is supervised by the government's *Departamento Control Nacional de Radio-televisión.* Television and radio stations are commercial, except for several offering religious or cultural programming. The *Sistema de Radio y TV Cultural* network was organized by the government in 1978 to transmit news and cultural programs. There were 470,000 television receivers in 1987.

INTERGOVERNMENTAL REPRESENTATION

Ambassador to the US: Danilo JIMENEZ.

US Ambassador to Costa Rica: Deane Roesch HINTON.

Permanent Representative to the UN: Dr. Carlos José GUTIERREZ.

IGO Memberships (Non-UN): BCIE, CACM, CCC, CDC, Geplacea, IADB, ICM, ICO, Intelsat, Interpol, ISO, IWC, IWTC, OAS, ODECA, OPANAL, SELA, UPEB.

COTE D'IVOIRE

République de Côte d'Ivoire

Note: In November 1985, the United Nations responded affirmatively to a request from the Ivoirian government that *Côte d'Ivoire* be recognized as the sole official version of what had previously been rendered in English as Ivory Coast and in Spanish as *Costa de Marfil.*

Political Status: Independent since August 7, 1960, under one-party presidential regime; present constitution adopted October 31, 1960.

Area: 124,503 sq. mi. (322,463 sq. km.).

Population: 6,709,600 (1975C), 11,556,000 (1988E).

Major Urban Centers (1976E): ABIDJAN (951,000); Bouaké (175,000), Yamassoukro (100,000, designated as future capital in March 1983). In 1987 the population of Abidjan was estimated at 2 million.

Official Language: French.

Monetary Unit: CFA Franc (market rate March 1, 1988, 285.80 francs = $1US).

President: Félix HOUPHOUET-BOIGNY; first elected in 1960; most recently reelected October 27, 1985, for a sixth five-year term.

THE COUNTRY

A land of forests and savannas, with a hot, humid climate, the Côte d'Ivoire is the richest and potentially the most nearly self-sufficient state of former French West Africa. Indigenous peoples fall into five principal ethnic groups: Ashanti-Agni-Baoule, Kru, Malinké, Mandé, and Lagoon dwellers, while as much as 30 percent of the population consists of migrant workers, mostly from Burkina Faso, Ghana, and Mali. There is also a sizable White population that includes about 100,000 Lebanese and 60,000 French. Although a majority of the people adhere to traditional religious practices, about 25 percent are Muslim and 13 percent are Christian. Women constitute approximately 38 percent of the adult labor force, primarily in agriculture; female representation on government and party levels is minimal.

The economy has undergone rapid growth since the 1950 completion of the Vridi Canal, which transformed Abidjan into a deepwater port. Although agriculture now accounts for only one-fourth of total GDP, the Côte d'Ivoire is the world's leading producer of cocoa and Africa's primary exporter of coffee, bananas, and tropical woods. The country's agricultural success has enabled the government to promote economic diversification, particularly with regard to agriprocessing and textile production. Development yielded an annual average real growth rate of about 7.5 percent during 1960–1980, although a variety of factors yielded a severe five-year recession thereafter. Although maintaining its reputation as a model African economy (the annual per capita income of more than $700 is one of Black Africa's highest), the Côte d'Ivoire continues to be buffeted by falling world prices for its agricultural exports. Debt repayment problems in 1987 (see Current issues, below) were attributed to the failure of offshore oil production to meet expectations, against which the government had borrowed heavily in the 1970s.

GOVERNMENT AND POLITICS

Political background. Established as a French protectorate in 1842, the Côte d'Ivoire became part of the Federation of French West Africa in 1904, an autonomous republic within the French Community in 1958, and a fully independent member of the Community in August 1960, although its membership was abandoned with the adoption of its present constitution two months later. Its main political leader since the 1940s has been Félix HOUPHOUET-BOIGNY, who in 1944 organized the *Syndicat Agricole Africain,* an African farmers union, and was one of the founders of the African Democratic Rally (RDA), an international political party with branches in numerous French African territories. As leader of the RDA's Ivorian branch, the Democratic Party of the Ivory Coast (PDCI), Houphouët-Boigny served in the French National Assembly from 1946 to 1959, became prime minister of the autonomous republic in 1959, and has been president since the general election held shortly after independence.

The postcolonial era has been relatively stable by African standards. Most vocal opposition to the regime has come from students, and there have been periodic demonstrations and university closings. Another source of tension has been the presence of many foreign workers, with whom indigenous Ivorians have sporadically clashed in competition for jobs. An alleged antigovernment conspiracy in 1963 resulted in the arrest and imprisonment of numerous party and government officials; however, subsequent evidence indicated that the plot was not a serious threat, and a majority of the prisoners were released. Additional attempts at subversion were suppressed in 1970 and 1973, the sentences of most of those involved being commuted in 1975.

The election of an enlarged National Assembly on November 9 and 23, 1980, marked the first time since independence that no single list of PDCI candidates was presented. Although all 649 office-seekers were party members, incumbents captured only 26 of 147 seats, while a similar infusion of new representatives occurred at municipal balloting later in the month. On November 25, the Assembly approved a constitutional amendment creating the post of vice president, which was to have been left vacant until the next presidential election. However, the provision was repealed immediately prior to the balloting of October 27, 1985, the succession reverting to the National Assembly president.

Constitution and government. The 1960 constitution provided the framework for a one-party presidential system based on the preeminent position of President Houphouët-Boigny and the PDCI. Although other parties are not proscribed, the PDCI is in fact the only party and all who vote are considered members. The president, elected by universal suffrage for a five-year term, has wide authority. There is no prime minister, and the cabinet (selected from outside the legislature) is responsible only to the chief executive. A presidential veto can theoretically be overridden by a two-thirds vote of the unicameral National Assembly, the membership of which was increased from 147 to 175 in 1985. Upon the death or incapacitation of the chief executive, the president of the Assembly will head an interim government for up to 60 days, pending balloting for a successor.

The judicial system is headed by the Supreme Court, which has four divisions: constitutional, judicial, administrative, and audit and control. The president of the Supreme Court is appointed by the president for a five-year term. Other tribunals include the Court of Appeal at Abidjan, the State Security Court, 26 courts of the first instance, and courts of assize.

The country is divided for administrative purposes into 26 departments, each with an elected Council; in November 1985, 3,908 councillors and 420 deputy mayors were elected in 135 municipalities.

Foreign relations. In line with its generally pro-French orientation, the Côte d'Ivoire has adhered to a moderate policy in African affairs and a broadly pro-Western posture. Relations with Ghana have periodically been strained,

most recently following a soccer match in September 1985 when a wave of attacks on Ghanaian nationals provoked charges from Accra that the fighting was officially sanctioned. Although ties with neighboring Burkina Faso have also been problematic, a visit to Abidjan in early 1985 by Col. Thomas Sankara served to ease tensions, despite his country's Libyan and Ghanaian ties. Relations with the Central African Republic, cool since the provision of sanctuary to former emperor Bokassa, improved once the ex-sovereign departed for Paris in late 1983. Relations with Israel, which had been broken off in 1973, were reestablished in December 1985 (an Arab League threat in late 1986 to break ties with Abidjan over the matter resulted in transfer of the Ivoirian embassy from Jerusalem to the less controversial location of Tel Aviv). Relations with the Soviet Union, severed in 1969, were resumed in February 1986, while relations were also established with Cuba in 1986 and Nicaragua in 1987.

Current issues. In May 1987 the government announced a moratorium on repayments of its $8 billion external debt, citing price reverses for cocoa, coffee, and other commodity exports. Although the most recent round of negotiations with the International Monetary Fund and the World Bank had been completed in 1986, President Houphouët-Boigny called for "a rescheduling of the rescheduling". World attention focused on the subsequent discussions (which eventually yielded agreement in October 1987) because of the effect that debt problems for the relatively healthy Ivoirian economy could have throughout the Third World. Some internal development programs were also cut back as a result of the revenue shortfalls. However, plans proceeded for a large rice-growing project in the north and the creation of a specially trained force to combat growing "gangsterism" in Abidjan.

Political speculation centered on the succession to President Houphouët-Boigny, his advancing years forcing consideration of a future without the guidance that has won him internal veneration and worldwide respect. Some observers felt that Henri KONAN-BEDIE had become virtual heir apparent with his January 1986 reelection as president of the National Assembly, which would make him interim president in the event of a presidential vacancy. Philippe YACE, the legislative leader from 1960 to 1980 and in the process of making a political comeback, declined to challenge Bédié but maintained his position as third senior statesman by assuming the presidency of the influential Economic and Social Council. However, Houphouët-Boigny has divorced himself from the issue, citing the Baoule tradition that "the chief must not know his successor".

In keeping with his efforts to avoid "an atmosphere of *fin de regne*" Houphouët-Boigny has maintained a high international profile, calling, inter alia, for "dialogue with no exceptions" on the South African question. While he is still accorded widespread deference as "the wise man of Africa" (seven heads of state of neighboring countries attended his sister's funeral in March 1987), his regional influence has nonetheless been viewed by some as waning.

POLITICAL PARTIES

Government Party:

Democratic Party of the Ivory Coast (*Parti Démocratique de la Côte d'Ivoire* — PDCI). Established in 1946 as a section of the African Democratic Rally (*Rassemblement Démocratique Africain* — RDA), the PDCI has held a monopoly position since independence, even though other parties are not formally banned. During the Seventh Congress of the PDCI, held September 29–October 1, 1980, the position of secretary general was abolished and the membership of both the Central Committee and Political Bureau was reduced — from 200 to 100 in the case of the former, and from 75 to 25 for the latter. In addition, an Executive Committee of 9 (subsequently 13) members was established to assist the party president.

The party's predominant role in determining Ivoirian policy was manifested at the Eighth Congress on October 9–12, 1985, at which a previous constitutional amendment establishing the post of vice president was effectively voided (formal repeal being subsequently voted by the National Assembly).

Leader: Félix HOUPHOUET-BOIGNY (President of the Republic and of the Party).

LEGISLATURE

The **National Assembly** (*Assemblée Nationale*) consists of a single chamber whose present 175 members, all belonging to the PDCI and serving five-year terms, were most recently elected by direct universal suffrage in multicandidate balloting on November 10, 1985.

President: Henri KONAN-BEDIE.

CABINET

President	Félix Houphouët-Boigny
Ministers of State	Camille Alliali
	Lazeni Coulibaly
	Auguste Denise
	Lamine Diabate
	Paul Gui Dibo
	Mathieu Ekra
	Emile Kei-Boguinard
	Maurice Seri Gnoléba
	Amadou Thiam

Ministers

Agriculture, Rural Development and Civil Defense	Denis Bra Kanon
Animal Husbandry	Christophe Gboho
Budget	Moise Koumauo Koffi
Civil Service	Jean-Jacques Bechio
Commerce	Nicolas Kouandi-Angba
Construction and Town Planning	Vamomussa Bamba
Defense and Marine	Jean Konan Banny
Economy and Finance	Abdoulaye Koné
Foreign Affairs	Siméon Aké
Industry	Bernard Ehui Koutoua
Information, Culture, Youth and Sports	Laurent Dona-Fologo
Interior	Léon Konan Koffi
Internal Security	Maj. Gen. Oumar N'Daw
Justice and Attorney General	Noel Nemin
Labor	Albert Vanié-Bi-Tra
Mines	Yed Esaie Angoran
National Education in Charge of Higher Education	Dr. Balla Keita
Planning	Oumar Diarra
Posts and Telecommunications	Vincent Tieko Djédjé
Primary Education	Odette Kouame Nguessan
Public Health and Population	Alphonse Djédje-Mady
Public Works and Transport	Koffi Aoussou
Relations with the National Assembly	Emile Brou
Scientific Research	Alhassane Salif N'Diaye
Social Affairs	Yaya Ouattara
Technical Education and Professional Training	Ange François Barry-Battesti
Tourism	Duon Sadia
Water and Forest Resources	Vincent Pierre Lokrou
Women's Promotion	Hortense Aka Anghui
Director, Central Bank	Charles Konan Banny

NEWS MEDIA

Press. The following are published daily at Abidjan, unless otherwise noted: *Fraternité-Matin* (80,000), official PDCI organ; *Ivoire Dimanche* (75,000), weekly; *Abidjan 7 Jours* (10,000), weekly; *Journal Officiel de la Côte d'Ivoire,* published weekly by the Ministry of the Interior; *Fraternité-Hebdo,* weekly PDCI organ. A new daily, *Reveil de l'Afrique Noire,* commenced publication in late 1986 with a projected circulation of 20,000 intended to serve as a catalyst of francophone African unity. Another daily, *Ivoire Soir,* was launched in 1987 to concentrate on social and cultural life as a complement to *Fraternité Matin.*

News agencies. The domestic agency is *Agence Ivoirienne de Presse* (AIP). Agence France-Presse, ANSA, and Reuters maintain offices at Abidjan.

Radio and television. The government-operated Ivoirian Radio (*Radiodiffusion Ivoirienne*) and Ivoirian Television (*Télévision Ivoirienne*) transmitted to approximately 1.3 million radio and 625,000 television receivers in 1987.

INTERGOVERNMENTAL REPRESENTATION

Ambassador to the US: Charles Providence GOMIS.

US Ambassador to the Côte d'Ivoire: Dennis KUX.

Permanent Representative to the UN: Amara ESSY.

IGO Memberships (Non-UN): ACCT, ADF, AfDB, BADEA, BOAD, CCC, CEAO, CENT, Copal, ECOWAS, EEC(L), *EIB,* IACO, ICAC, ICCAT, ICCO, ICO, IIC, INRO, Intelsat, Interpol, ISO, NAM, OAU, OCAM.

CUBA

Republic of Cuba
República de Cuba

Political Status: Independent republic founded in 1902; under Marxist-inspired regime established January 1, 1959; designated a Communist system in December 1961; present constitution adopted February 16, 1976, with effect from February 24.

Area: 44,218 sq. mi. (114,524 sq. km.).

Population: 9,723,605 (1981C), 10,553,000 (1988E).

Major Urban Centers (1986E): HAVANA (2,034,000); Camagüey (369,000); Santiago de Cuba (362,000); Holguín (198,000); Santa Clara (179,000), Guantánamo (174,000).

Official Language: Spanish.

Official Language: Spanish.

Monetary Unit: Peso (noncommercial rate March 1, 1988, 1 peso = $1.25US).

President of the Council of State and of the Council of Ministers, and First Secretary of the Communist Party of Cuba: Fidel CASTRO Ruz; assumed office of Prime Minister in 1959; became First Secretary of the Communist Party on October 2, 1965; named President of the Council of State and of the Council of Ministers by the National Assembly on December 2, 1976; reappointed in 1981 and on December 28, 1986.

First Vice President of the Council of State and of the Council of Ministers: Gen. Raúl CASTRO Ruz; designated by the National Assembly on December 2, 1976; reappointed in 1981 and on December 28, 1986.

Vice Presidents of the Council of State: Juan ALMEIDA Bosque, Osmany CIENFUEGOS Gorriarán, Carlos Rafael RODRIGUEZ Rodríguez, José Ramón MACHADO Ventura, Pedro MIRET Prieto. Almeida and Rodríguez have served since 1976; Cienfuegos, Machado, and Miret were designated on December 28, 1986.

THE COUNTRY

The largest of the Caribbean island nations, Cuba lies at the western end of the Greater Antilles, directly south of Florida. Its varied terrain, with abundant fertile land and a semitropical climate, led to early specialization in the production of sugar as well as tobacco, coffee, and other crops. Its ethnic composition is an admixture of Caucasian and Negro. The vast majority of the population has traditionally been Roman Catholic, but freedom of worship is now restricted. Women constitute about one-third of the labor force and provide close to half of the country's administrators; more than one-third of the current National Assembly is female, with female representation on the party's Central Committee reported as 18.2 percent in February 1986, including one full and two alternate Politburo members.

The Cuban economy was in difficulty following the revolution of 1959. Production lagged, dependence upon foreign assistance (mainly from the Soviet Union) increased, and real per capita income declined. Despite sporadic attempts at industrialization, the Castro regime emphasized agricultural development, and sugar remained the principal export. The 1976–1980 economic plan failed to achieve many of its goals, in part because a decline in sugar prices necessitated the renegotiation of imports in light of reduced hard-currency earnings. By contrast, economic growth surged by a record 12 percent in 1981, although much of the increase was attributed to an unusually poor performance in 1980, when production of both sugar and tobacco was drastically curtailed because of plant disease. Depressed world prices for sugar and oil (reexported from the Soviet Union) led to economic decline thereafter, despite the introduction of liberalization measures, which were abandoned

in favor of a rigid austerity program in 1986 (see Current issues, below).

GOVERNMENT AND POLITICS

Political background. Liberated from Spanish rule as a result of the Spanish-American War of 1898, Cuba was established as an independent republic on May 20, 1902, but remained subject to US tutelage until the abrogation of the so-called Platt Amendment in 1934. Subsequent political development was severely limited by the antidemocratic influence of Fulgencio BATISTA, who ruled the country directly or indirectly from 1933 to 1944 and maintained a repressive dictatorship from 1952 to 1959. Weakened by army and middle-class disaffection, Batista's regime was overthrown on January 1, 1959, by a revolutionary movement under Fidel CASTRO Ruz that had commenced guerrilla operations in 1956.

After a brief period of moderation, the Castro government embarked upon increasingly radical internal policies, which gradually developed into a full-scale social revolution purportedly based on the adaptation of Marxist-Leninist ideas to Latin American conditions. Relations with the United States deteriorated rapidly as the result of Castro's strident anti-Americanism, culminating in October 1960 with the expropriation of all US business interests in Cuba. The United States responded by severing diplomatic relations, imposing a trade embargo, and supporting an ill-fated invasion by anti-Castro Cuban exiles (the Bay of Pigs) in April 1961.

Concurrent with the decline in US-Cuban relations, Castro cultivated increasingly close ties with the Communist countries, particularly the Soviet Union, whose emplacement of offensive missiles in Cuba precipitated the US-Soviet "missile confrontation" of October 1962. Since that time, the Castro government has maintained and consolidated its internal authority, aided in part by the departure of thousands of disaffected Cubans, most of whom have settled in the United States.

The fourth general election of municipal councillors under the 1976 constitution was held in two stages on October 19 and 26, 1986, with 13,257 seats in the 169 local governing bodies being contested. Subsequently, the municipal representatives selected delegates to the 14 provincial assemblies and, on November 27, 510 delegates to the National Assembly, which convened on December 27 to redesignate the president and other government leaders. Earlier, a drastic shakeup had occurred at the opening session of the third quinquennial party congress in February 1986, with a collateral restructuring of the State Council by the new Assembly in December.

Constitution and government. A new constitution, which had been under preparation for nearly a decade, was approved at the first congress of the Cuban Communist Party in December 1975, adopted by popular referendum on February 16, 1976, and declared in effect eight days later, on the anniversary of the commencement of the 1898 war of Cuban independence. It provides for an indirectly elected National Assembly that designates a Council of State from among its membership. The Council of State appoints a Council of Ministers in consultation with its president, who serves as head of state and, in his role of president of the Council of Ministers, as chief of government. The judiciary consists of a People's Supreme Court in addition to intermediate and local courts. Members of the judiciary (as well as of the State Council and cabinet) are subject to legislative recall.

Under the 1976 constitution, Cuba's six traditional provinces were abandoned in favor of a 14-province structure, with provincial assemblies designed to encourage greater popular involvement in government. Members of the provincial assemblies, like those of the National Assembly, are drawn from 169 popularly elected municipal assemblies, an earlier constitutional provision for intra-provincial regional assemblies having been dropped following a "popular power" experiment in Matanzas Province in June 1975. Members of the municipal and provincial assemblies serve for terms of two and one-half years, while the National Assembly sits for five years.

Foreign relations. Partly because of its attempt to promote Castro-type revolutions throughout Latin America, Cuba was for a number of years ostracized by most other Latin American governments. It was excluded from participation in the Organization of American States in 1962, and the OAS imposed diplomatic and commercial sanctions in 1964. However, following the death of the Argentine-born revolutionary Ernesto ("Ché") GUEVARA in Bolivia in 1967, the Castro regime scaled down its support of external guerrilla activity, and by 1974 a number of OAS states had moved to reestablish relations. In July 1975, the OAS itself, while not formally lifting the sanctions, adopted a resolution stating that its members would henceforth be "free to normalize" relations with Havana.

While Cuba no longer stands out as a self-proclaimed nemesis of other Latin American governments, its foreign relations have typically been shaped by an ingrained hostility toward the United States and other established governments in the Americas, and by a corresponding affinity for the Communist-bloc nations and revolutionary movements around the world. In March 1969, it became the first country to accord formal recognition to the National Liberation Front of South Vietnam and during 1975 initiated a major program of military assistance to the Soviet-backed MPLA regime in Angola. As host of the Sixth Conference of Heads of State of the Nonaligned Movement in September 1979, it sought, with some success, to identify the "socialist camp" as the "natural ally" of the Third World movement. During the same year, Havana provided assistance for the new *sandinista* government in Nicaragua, although dwindling fiscal resources have since limited its commitment, with Castro repeatedly stating that Cuba would be "unable" to support Managua militarily in the event of a US invasion.

During 1981, Havana's international posture was dominated by a massive emigration of Cuban citizens largely orchestrated by the Castro regime. Precipitating the exodus was the influx, in early April, of some 10,000 Cubans onto the grounds of the Peruvian Embassy at Havana after the government had withdrawn its police guard in a dispute over the right of political asylum. Subsequently, President Castro indicated that Cuban exiles in the United States would be permitted to pick up anyone who wished to leave from the port of Mariel, more than 114,000 thereupon departing by boat for Florida. Concurrently, most of those at the embassy were flown to a variety of foreign destinations, including some 3,500 to the United States. In response to US government complaints that large numbers of common criminals and other undesirables were among the exiles, Castro asserted, in a May Day speech, that Washington had provoked the exodus and was obliged to "swallow the dagger whole".

In the wake of the Grenada crisis in October 1983 (see Grenada article), Cuban relations with the United States and the region at large fell to their lowest ebb in years, with Cuba in a "state of national alert". Although there were some indications of a thaw in 1984, with formal talks on the status of the Mariel refugees leading to a December 1984 immigration agreement, the accord was suspended by Havana in May 1985 after Radio Martí, an "alternative" radio station directed at Cuba, had commenced transmissions from Florida.

President Castro's much-publicized failure to attend the funeral of Konstantin Chernenko in March 1985 suggested a desire to distance Cuba from Soviet policy, while overtures to the United States were communicated through visiting US bishops, congressmen, and news reporters. Following a war of words surrounding Radio Martí and abrogation of the immigration agreement, the door to rapprochement was left open with the September announcement of the release of 75 of the 200 prisoners scheduled for emigration under the suspended accord.

During 1986, relations between Havana and Washington again hardened, the US State Department somewhat incongruously linking reestablishment of the migration accord to Cuban acquiescence to the return of the *Marielito* "undesirables". The situation was further aggravated in December by a protest outside the Swiss embassy at Havana against an overflight by a US reconnaissance plane during Cuban military maneuvers. Although the flight was described by a Western diplomat as "clumsy provocation", Washington responded by withdrawing the head of its interests section at the embassy in mid-January 1987.

Current issues. A number of cabinet changes in 1984–1985 suggested a gradual shift of power from 1959-era ideologues to younger technocrats under the leadership of the increasingly powerful Raúl Castro. The most significant loss of power was experienced by Vice President Rodriguez, whose economic responsibilities were assigned to fellow Politburo member Osmany CIENFUEGOS Gorriarán. Subsequently, after a lengthy period of structural stability, extensive "renovation" of the party leadership was announced at the third PCC congress in February 1986. The move, formally described by President Castro as an effort to increase representation by young people, women, and Blacks, yielded, in emulation of prevailing Soviet practice, a diminution of influence by government ministers and enhanced status for regional party leaders. Collaterally, additional powers were assigned to a Cienfuegos "central group", with speculation that the latter might evolve into an "umbrella ministry" to provide coordination across a variety of economic sectors, as had recently been undertaken in a number of East European states.

Faced with a manifestly worsening economic situation, President Castro launched a major campaign against bureaucratic corruption and inefficiency in July 1986. He returned to the theme at the reconvened session of the party congress in late November, and a month later announced a major austerity program to compensate for a severe decline in foreign exchange earnings and Soviet subsidies, which had earlier been estimated at some $6 billion a year. A similar note was sounded in late 1987, with President Castro warning of continued hardships that would require the maintenance of austerity measures through 1988.

POLITICAL PARTIES

The only authorized political party is the Communist Party of Cuba.

Communist Party of Cuba (*Partido Comunista Cubano* — PCC). The PCC is a direct descendant of the Rebel Army and the 26th of July Movement (*Movimiento 26 de Julio*), which constituted Fidel Castro's personal political following during the anti-Batista period. The organizational revolution began in 1961 with the formation of the Integrated Revolutionary Organizations (*Organizaciones Revolucionarias Integradas* — ORI), which included the Popular Socialist Party (*Partido Socialista Popular* — PSP), the 26th of July Movement, and the Revolutionary Directorate (*Directorio Revolucionario* — DR). The ORI was transformed into the United Party of the Cuban Socialist Revolution (*Partido Unido de la Revolución Socialista Cubana* — PURSC) in 1963, the latter being redesignated as the Communist Party of Cuba in 1965. The first PCC congress was held on December 17–22, 1975, and the second on December 17–20, 1980. Major personnel changes were approved at the first session of the third congress, held February 4–7, 1986, including the replacement of 10 of 24 full and alternate Politburo members and approximately one-third of the 146-member Central Committee. The congress reconvened on November 30–December 2, primarily to discuss a campaign aimed at the "rectification of mistakes and negative tendencies" that had been launched by President Castro in July.

First Secretary: Fidel CASTRO Ruz (President, State Council and Council of Ministers).

Second Secretary: Gen. Raúl CASTRO Ruz (First Vice President, State Council and Council of Ministers).

Other Members of Politburo: Juan ALMEIDA Bosque (Vice President, State Council), Julio CAMACHO Aguilera (First Secretary, Santiago de Cuba), Osmany CIENFUEGOS Gorriarán (Vice President, State Council and Council of Ministers), Gen. Abelardo COLOME Ibarra (Deputy Armed Forces Minister), Vilma ESPIN Guilloys de Castro (President, Federation of Cuban Women), Armando HART Dávalos (Member, State Council), Estebán LAZO Hernández (First Secretary, Matanzas), José Ramón MACHADO Ventura (Vice President, State Council), Pedro MIRET Prieto (Vice President, State Council and Council of Ministers), Jorge RISQUET Valdés-Saldaña (Member, Secretariat), Carlos Rafael RODRIGUEZ Rodríguez (Vice President, State Council and Council of Ministers), Roberto VEIGA Menéndez (General Secretary, Cuban Workers' Federation).

Alternate Members: Luis ALVAREZ de la Nuez (First Secretary, Havana), Gen. Senén CASAS Reguero (Deputy Armed Forces Minister), José Ramón FERNANDEZ Alvarez (Vice President, Council of Ministers), Yolanda FERRER Gómez (Secretariat, Federation of Cuban Women), Raúl MICHEL Vargas (First Secretary, Guantánamo), José RAMIREZ Cruz (President, Small Farmers' Association), Julián RIZO Alvarez (Member, Secretariat), Ulises ROSALES del Toro (Chief, Armed Forces General Staff), Rosa Elena SIMEON Negrin (President, Academy of Sciences), Lazaro VAZQUEZ García (First Secretary, Camagüey Province).

Secretariat: Carlos ALDANA Escalante, José Ramón BALAGUER Cabrera, Gen. Sixto BATISTA Santana, Fidel CASTRO Ruz, Gen. Raúl CASTRO Ruz, Jamie CROMBERT Hernández-Baquero, José Ramón MACHADO Ventura, Jorge RISQUET Valdés-Saldaña, Julián RIZO Alvarez, Pedro ROSS Leal, Lionel SOTO Prieto.

LEGISLATURE

A unicameral **National Assembly of People's Power** (*Asamblea Nacional del Poder Popular*) was convened, with a five-year mandate, on December 2, 1976, following elections (the first since 1958) to municipal assemblies, which in turn had elected delegates to both provincial and national legislative bodies. A similar procedure was used to elect assemblies that convened in December 1981 and December 1986.

Acting President: Severo AGUIRRE del Cristo.

CABINET

President, Council of Ministers	Fidel Castro Ruz
First Vice President, Council of Ministers	Gen. Raúl Castro Ruz
Vice Presidents, Council of Ministers	Osmany Cienfuegos Gorriarán
	Homero Crabb Valdés
	Joel Domenech Benítez
	Antonio Esquivel Yedra
	José Ramón Fernández Alvarez
	José López Moreno
	Pedro Miret Prieto
	Antonio Rodríguez Maurell
	Carlos Rafael Rodríguez Rodríguez
	Diocles Torralba González

Ministers

Agriculture	Adolfo Díaz Suárez
Basic Industries	Marcos Portal León
Communications	Manuel Castillo Rabassa
Construction	Homero Crabb Valdés
Construction Materials Industry	Levi Farah Balmaseda
Culture	Armando Hart Dávalos
Domestic Trade	Manuel Vila Sosa
Education	José Ramón Fernández Alvarez
Fishing Industry	Ship Capt. Jorge A. Fernández Cuervo-Vinent
Food Industry	Alejandro Roca Iglesias
Foreign Relations	Isidoro Octavio Malmierca Peoli
Foreign Trade	Ricardo Cabrisas Ruiz
Higher Education	Fernando Vecino Alegret
Interior	José Abrantes Fernández
Justice	Juan Escalona Reguera
Light Industry	Antonio Esquivel Yedra
Public Health	Dr. Julio Tejas Pérez
Revolutionary Armed Forces	Gen. Raúl Castro Ruz
Steelworking Industry	Marcos Lage Coello
Sugar Industry	Juan Ramón Herrera Machado
Transportation	Diocles Torralba González
Without Portfolio	José Alberto Naranjo Morales

State Committee Presidents

Economic Cooperation	Ernesto Meléndez Bachs
Finance	Rodrigo García Leon
Labor and Social Security	Francisco Linares Calvo
Material and Technical Supply	Sonia Rodríguez Cardona
Prices	Arturo Guzmán Pascual
Standardization	Ramón Darias Rodés
Statistics	Fidel Vascós González
President, Central Planning Board	José López Moreno
President, National Bank of Cuba	Héctor Rodríguez Llompart
Secretary, Council of State	José Miyar Barruecos
Secretary, Council of Ministers	Osmany Cienfuegos Gorriarán

NEWS MEDIA

The press is censored and all channels of communication are under state control.

Press. The following are daily newspapers published at Havana, unless otherwise noted: *Granma* (705,000), official PCC organ, morning and weekly editions; *Juventud Rebelde* (300,000), organ of the Communist Youth; *Los Trabajadores* (152,000), labor oriented; *Tribuna de la Habana* (60,000); *Adelante* (Camagüey, 32,000); *Sierra Maestra* (Santiago de Cuba, 25,000); *Vanguardia* (Santa Clara, 24,000).

News agencies. The domestic facilities are the government-controlled *Prensa Latina* and *Agencia de Información Nacional* (AIN). A number of Communist-bloc agencies (including TASS) maintain offices at Havana, as do *Agence France-Presse* and Reuters.

Radio and television. Broadcasting is controlled by the Ministry of Communications and the *Instituto Cubano de Radio y Televisión*. There are 5 national radio networks (classical music, drama, general entertainment, news and sports, 24-hour news) in addition to short-wave service provided by *Radio Habana, Cuba;* some 50 TV stations operate throughout the country. There were approximately 2.0 million television sets in 1987.

INTERGOVERNMENTAL REPRESENTATION

There are, at present, no diplomatic relations between Cuba and the United States. On September 1, 1977, however, a US interest section was established in the Swiss Embassy at Havana, while a Cuban interest section was established in the Czech Embassy at Washington.

Permanent Representative to the UN: Oscar ORAMAS Olivia.

IGO Memberships (Non-UN): CMEA, Geplacea, IBEC, ICCAT, IIB, Interpol, ISO, IWTC, NAM, OAS, PCA, SELA.

CYPRUS

Republic of Cyprus
Dimokratia Kyprou (Greek)
Kıbrıs Cumhuriyeti (Turkish)

Political Status: Independent republic established August 16, 1960; member of the Commonwealth since March 13, 1961; under ethnic Greek majority regime until coup led by Greek army officers and subsequent Turkish intervention on July 20, 1974; Turkish Federated State proclaimed February 13, 1975, in Turkish-controlled (northern) sector; permanent constitutional status in process of negotiation between Greek and Turkish representatives, despite proclamation of independent Turkish Republic of Northern Cyprus on November 15, 1983.

Area: 3,572 sq. mi. (9,251 sq. km.), embracing approximately 2,172 sq. mi. (5,625 sq. km.) in Greek-controlled (southern) sector and 1,400 sq. mi. (3,626 sq. km.) in Turkish-controlled (northern) sector.

Population: 688,000 (1988E), embracing approximately 530,000 Greeks, 150,000 Turks, and 8,000 of other nationality groups. Although population transfers have been extensive, the figures for the principal ethnic communities should not be taken as definitive of population by sector.

Major Urban Centers (1982E): NICOSIA (149,100, excluding Turkish sector); Limassol (107,200); Larnaca (48,300); Famagusta (39,500).

Official Languages: Greek, Turkish.

Monetary Unit: Cyprus Pound (market rate March 1, 1988, 1 pound = $2.18US).

President: George VASSILIOU (Independent); elected February 21, 1988, and inaugurated for a five-year term on February 28, succeeding Spyros KYPRIANOU (Democratic Party).

Vice President: (Vacant). Rauf R. DENKTAŞ, current President of the Turkish Republic of Northern Cyprus (see Cyprus: Turkish Sector), was elected Vice President by vote of the Turkish Community in February 1973, but there has been no subsequent vice-presidential election.

THE COUNTRY

Settled by Greeks in antiquity, conquered by Turkey in 1571, and taken over by Great Britain in 1914, Cyprus is the largest island in the eastern Mediterranean and supports diverse and often antagonistic races and traditions. Approximately 80 percent of the population speaks Greek and belongs to the Orthodox Church, while 18 percent is Turkish-speaking Muslim; the remaining 2 percent is composed of adherents of other religions.

Although Cyprus was traditionally an agricultural country, the rural sector presently employs no more than 25 percent of the total labor force and contributes less than 20 percent of GDP. A higher percentage of women (34 percent) than men (18 percent) work in agriculture and other subsistence activities. Nonetheless, vegetables, fruits, nuts, and wine rank with clothing and footwear as leading exports. Following the de facto partition of the island into Greek and Turkish sectors in 1974, rebuilding in the south emphasized manufacturing of nondurable consumer goods, while the more severely damaged north has relied on its citrus groves, mines, and tourist facilities as well as on direct budgetary assistance from Turkey.

GOVERNMENT AND POLITICS

Political background. The conflict between Greek and Turkish Cypriot aspirations has shaped the political evolution of Cyprus both before and after the achievement of formal independence on August 16, 1960. Many Greek Cypriots had long agitated for *enosis,* or the union of Cyprus with Greece; most Turkish Cypriots, backed by the Turkish government, consistently rejected such demands, opposed the termination of British rule in 1960, and advocated division of the island into Greek- and Turkish-speaking sectors. Increased communal and anti-British violence after 1955 culminated in the Zürich and London compromise agreements of 1959, which provided for an independent Cyprus guaranteed by Greece, Turkey, and

Britain, and instituted stringent constitutional safeguards for the protection of the Turkish minority. These agreements expressly prohibit either union with Greece or partition of the island between Greece and Turkey.

The government of Archbishop MAKARIOS proposed 13 constitutional changes in November 1963, including changes in those portions of the constitution considered inviolable by the Turkish Cypriots. The proposals led to a renewal of communal conflict, the withdrawal of Turkish Cypriots from the government, and, in 1964, the establishment of a United Nations peacekeeping force. Further conflict broke out in 1967, nearly precipitating war between Greece and Turkey.

Following the 1967 violence, Turkish Cypriots moved to implement an administration for their segment of the island. This organization, known as the Turkish Cypriot Provisional Administration, constituted de facto government in the Turkish communities. Withdrawal of Turkish Cypriots from the government of Archbishop Makarios also meant that from 1967 until the Turkish military intervention in July 1974, the prime conflicts were between the Makarios regime and radicals in the Greek community that were led (until his death in January 1974) by Gen. George GRIVAS.

On July 15, 1974, the Greek Cypriot National Guard, led by Greek army officers, launched a coup against the Makarios government and installed a Greek Cypriot newspaper publisher and former terrorist, Nikos Giorgiades SAMPSON, as president following the archbishop's flight from the island. Five days later, Turkish troops were dispatched to northern Cyprus, bringing some 1,400 square miles (39 percent of the total area) under their control before agreeing to a cease-fire. On July 23 the Sampson government resigned and the more moderate presiding officer of the Cypriot House of Representatives, Glafcos CLERIDES, was sworn in as acting president. On the same day, the military government of Greece fell, and on July 25, representatives of Britain, Greece, and Turkey met at Geneva in an effort to resolve the Cyprus conflict. An agreement consolidating the cease-fire was concluded on July 30, but the broader issues were unresolved when the talks collapsed on August 14. Upon his return to Cyprus and resumption of the presidency on December 7, Makarios rejected Turkish demands for geographical partition of the island although he had earlier indicated a willingness to give the Turks increased administrative responsibilities in their own communities.

On February 13, 1975, Turkish leaders in the occupied northern sector proclaimed a Turkish Federated State of Cyprus with Rauf DENKTAŞ, the nominal vice president of the Republic, as president. Describing the state as the "Turkish Cypriot federal wing of the Cyprus Republic", Denktaş indicated that the Turks were not seeking international recognition but were merely reconstituting their "internal administration to be ready for the birth of a federal state". Although the action was immediately denounced by both President Makarios and Greek Prime Minister Caramanlis, the formation of a Turkish Cypriot Legislative Assembly was announced on February 24.

Several sessions of talks between Denktaş and Glafcos Clerides, representing the Greek Cypriots, were held at

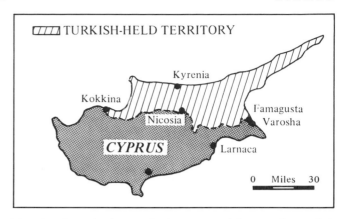

New York and Vienna during 1975 without substantial progress toward a constitutional settlement, and the United Nations Security Council on June 13 extended the mandate of the UN Force in Cyprus (UNFICYP) for an additional six months. At a Vienna meeting from July 31 to August 2, agreement was, however, reached on the transfer of 9,000 Turkish Cypriots from the south to the north of the island, the transfer subsequently being effected under UNFICYP supervision. (The UNFICYP mandate was further extended at six-month intervals through June 1988).

Extensive negotiations between Greek and Turkish representatives were held at Vienna in April 1977, following a meeting between Makarios and Denktaş in February. Although it was revealed that the more recent Greek proposals embraced the establishment of a bicommunal federal state, the Makarios government insisted that only 20 percent of the island's area be reserved for Turkish administration, while the Turks countered with demands that would entail judicial parity and a presidency to rotate between Greek and Turkish chief executives. In view of these differences, a statement issued at the conclusion of the Vienna meeting simply stated that a "considerable gap between the views of the two sides" remained.

Archbishop Makarios died on August 3, 1977, and was succeeded, as acting president, by Spyros KYPRIANOU, who was elected on August 31 to fill the remaining six months of the Makarios term. Following the kidnapping of Kyprianou's son on December 14 by right-wing extremists, Glafcos Clerides withdrew as a contender for the presidency and Kyprianou became the only candidate at the close of nominations on January 26, 1978. As a result, the election scheduled for February 5 was canceled, Kyprianou being installed for a five-year term on March 1. In April 1982 the two government parties, the Democratic Party and the Progressive Party of the Working People (AKEL) agreed to support Kyprianou for reelection in February 1983.

In a three-way race that involved Clerides and Socialist Party leader Vassos LYSSARIDES (who technically withdrew on January 4), Kyprianou won reelection on February 13, 1983, securing 57 percent of the vote. Nine months later, on November 15, the Turkish Cypriot Legislative Assembly unanimously approved the declaration of an independent "Turkish Republic of Northern Cyprus".

After a series of separate "proximity" talks with UN Secretary General Javier Pérez de Cuéllar in late 1984, President Kyprianou and Turkish Cypriot leader Denktaş met at United Nations headquarters on January 17–20, 1985, for their first direct negotiations in five years. Prior to the meeting, the two had endorsed a draft proposal to establish a federal republic that entailed substantial territorial concessions by the Turks and the removal of foreign troops from the island. Although Pérez de Cuéllar declared that "the gap [had] never been so narrow" between the two sides, the talks collapsed after Kyprianou had reportedly characterized the plan as no more than an "agenda", pending "clarification" of a number of matters, including a timetable for the withdrawal of Turkish forces and the tender of firm international guarantees that the agreement would be honored. Subsequently, the government's pro-Moscow coalition partner, AKEL, joined with the opposition Democratic Rally in blaming Kyprianou for the breakdown in the talks and calling for his resignation as president.

At the conclusion of a bitter debate on the president's negotiating posture, the House of Representatives voted unanimously on November 1 to dissolve itself, paving the way for an early legislative election. In the balloting on December 8, Kyprianou's Democratic Party gained marginally (though remaining a minority grouping), while the opposition failed to secure the two-thirds majority necessary to enact a constitutional revision that would require the chief executive to conform to the wishes of the House.

Deprived of the backing of the AKEL, which normally commands about one-third of the Greek Cypriot vote, Kyprianou ran third in first-round presidential balloting on February 14, 1988. In a runoff election one week later, George VASSILIOU, a millionaire businessman running with Communist backing, defeated Clerides by securing a 51.53 percent majority.

Constitution and government. The constitution of 1960, based on the Zürich and London agreements, provided for a carefully balanced system designed to protect both Greek Cypriot and Turkish Cypriot interests. A Greek president and a Turkish vice president, both elected for five-year terms, were to name a cabinet composed of representatives of both groups in specified proportions. Legislative authority was entrusted to a unicameral House of Representatives with 35 Greek and 15 Turkish members to be elected by their respective communities. In addition, Greek and Turkish Communal Chambers were established to deal with internal community affairs. Collateral arrangements were made for judicial institutions, the army, and the police. Following the original outbreak of hostilities in 1963 and the consequent withdrawal of the Turkish Cypriots from the government, there were a number of changes, including merger of the police and gendarmerie, establishment of a National Guard, abolition of the Greek Communal Chamber, amendment of the electoral law, and modification of the judicial structure.

Subsequent to withdrawal, the Turkish community practiced a form of self-government under the Turkish Cypriot Provisional Administration, an extraconstitutional entity not recognized by the government. The Turkish Cypriot Provisional Assembly was composed of the 15 Turkish members of the national legislature and the 15 representatives to the Turkish Cypriot Communal Chamber. In early 1975 the Provisional Administration was reorganized as a Turkish Federated State in the northern

sector of the island, followed by a unilateral declaration of independence in November 1983 (see Cyprus: Turkish Sector, below).

Prior to the Turkish intervention, the island was divided into six administrative districts, each headed by an official appointed by the central government. Municipalities were governed by elected mayors.

Foreign relations. Cyprus is a member of the United Nations and several other intergovernmental organizations. On a number of occasions Archbishop Makarios made diplomatic overtures toward Third World countries, although even prior to the 1974 conflict internal problems made it difficult for him to follow up on such initiatives.

As a result of the events of 1974, the domestic situation became in large measure a function of relations with Greece and Turkey, two uneasy NATO partners whose range of disagreement has by no means been confined to Cyprus. Britain, because of its treaty responsibilities in the area, has played a major role in attempting to mediate the Cyprus dispute, while the United States has played a less active role. The intercommunal talks, which have been held intermittently since 1975, were initiated at the request of the United Nations Security Council, which has assumed the principal responsibility for truce supervision through the UNFICYP.

Current issues. In March 1986, UN Secretary General Pérez de Cuéllar submitted a revised reunification proposal to the Greek and Turkish Cypriot leaders, which was accepted by the Turks, but elicited no immediate reaction from President Kyprianou, who proceeded to consult with Greek Prime Minister Papandreou. Subsequently, the latter met with the Soviet ambassador to Athens, whose government had called earlier in the year for an international conference on the Cyprus question.

The UN plan provided for a two-state federation with a Greek president and a Turkish vice president, coupled with a territorial allocation to the Turks of 29 percent, as contrasted with the near-40 percent held since 1974. The plan addressed Turkish troop withdrawal as a matter that should "be agreed upon prior to the establishment of a transitional federal government". The Kyprianou government responded by calling for a firm timetable for Turkish withdrawal, a revision of existing international guarantees to avert the possibility of another Turkish intervention, assurances that would preclude independent foreign contacts by the Turkish component of the federation, a limitation on Turkish veto power over certain areas of federal decision making, and guaranteed freedom of movement, settlement, and property ownership in either zone.

The continuance of a hard-line posture in the wake of a manifestly conciliatory meeting between the Greek and Turkish prime ministers at Davos, Switzerland, in January 1988 was a prime factor in Kyprianou's defeat on February 14. By contrast, President Vassiliou ushered in his administration with a pledge to seek direct talks with Turkey on reunification. However, the "peace offensive" that he had pledged to lead suffered from the subsequent lack of an overture to Prime Minister Özal to such effect; in addition, he declined to meet with his Turkish Cypriot counterpart, reportedly because a tender from Denktaş, issued prior to the election, carried the implication that the two would confer as equals. As a result, while the prospects for resolving the lengthy dispute appeared to have been marginally advanced, most observers felt that further progress would turn on enhancement of the "spirit of Davos" between Greece and Turkey.

POLITICAL PARTIES

Throughout the 14 years preceding the Turkish intervention, the Cypriot party system was divided along communal lines. As a result of population transfers, the Greek parties now function exclusively in the south, while the Turkish parties function in the north. All are headquartered within the divided city of Nicosia. The Greek parties are listed below, while the Turkish parties are listed in the next section (Cyprus: Turkish Sector).

Democratic Party (*Demokratiko Komma* — Diko). The Democratic Party is a center-right grouping organized in 1976 as the Democratic Front to support President Makarios' policy of "long-term struggle" against the Turkish occupation of northern Cyprus. The leading component of the government alliance in the House of Representatives after the 1976 election, at which it won 21 seats, its representation fell to 12 seats in 1981. In December 1985, it obtained 16 seats (28 percent) in an enlarged House of 56 members, after its former coalition partner, AKEL (below), had joined the Democratic Party in an attempt to force President Kyprianou's resignation.

Leader: Spyros KYPRIANOU (former President of the Republic).

Progressive Party of the Working People (*Anorthotikon Komma Ergazomenou Laou* — AKEL). Organized in 1941 as the Communist Party of Cyprus, AKEL dominates the Greek Cypriot labor movement and claims a membership of about 15,000. Its support of President Kyprianou, withdrawn for a period in 1980 because of the latter's handling of "the national issue", was renewed in September when the government agreed to a renewal of intercommunal talks. Its support was again withdrawn as a result of the breakdown in talks at UN headquarters in January 1985.

Leaders: Ezekias PAPAIOANNOU (General Secretary), Andreas FANDIS (Deputy General Secretary), Dinos KONSTANTINOU (Organizing Secretary).

Democratic Rally (*Demokratikos Synagermos* — Disy). The Democratic Rally was organized in May 1976 by Glafcos Clerides following his resignation as negotiator for the Greek Cypriots in the intercommunal talks at Vienna. The Rally has long favored a strongly pro-Western orientation as a means of maintaining sufficient pressure on the Turks to resolve the communal dispute. It secured 24.1 percent of the vote in 1976 but won no legislative seats. Its fortunes were dramatically reversed in the 1981 balloting, at which it obtained twelve seats with seven more being added in 1985.

Leaders: Glafcos CLERIDES (Chairman), Alekos MARKIDIS (General Secretary).

Unified Democratic Union of Cyprus/Socialist Party (*Eniea Demokratiki Enosis Kyprou* — EDEK/*Sosialistiko Komma*). The EDEK is a moderately left-of-center grouping which supports a unified and independent Cyprus. It concluded an electoral alliance with the Democratic Front and AKEL in 1976 but campaigned separately in 1981, its three representatives refusing to support the government after the new House convened. Its chairman, Dr. Vassos Lyssarides, campaigned for the presidency in 1983 as leader of a National Salvation Front, although announcing his withdrawal prior to the actual balloting as a means of reducing "polarization" within the Greek Cypriot community. The party obtained six seats in 1985.

Leader: Dr. Vassos LYSSARIDES (Chairman).

Three minor parties that emerged prior to the 1981 election, but have been unable to secure legislative representation are the **Pan-Cyprian Renewal Front** (*Pangiprio Ananeotiko Metopo* — Pame), led by former education minister Chrysostomos SOFIANOS; the **Center Union** (*Enosi Kentrou* — EK), led by Tassos PAPADOPOULOS, chief Greek Cypriot negotiator in the intercommunal talks from 1976 to 1978; and the **New Democratic Camp** (*Nea Demokratiki Parataxi* — Nedipa), led by Alecos

MICHAELIDES, former president of the House of Representatives. A **Liberal Party** (*Komma Phileleftheron*), led by Nikos A. ROLANDIS, was organized in 1986.

LEGISLATURE

The Cypriot **House of Representatives** (*Vouli Antiprosópon/Temsilciler Meclisi*) is a unicameral body formerly encompassing 35 Greek and 15 Turkish members, although Turkish participation ceased in December 1963. At the most recent balloting on December 8, 1985, for an enlarged House of 56 members, the Democratic Rally won 19 seats; the Democratic Party, 16; the Progressive Party of the Working People, 15; and the Socialist Party, 6.

President: Dr. Vassos LYSSARIDES.

CABINET

President	Spyros Kyprianou
Minister to the President	(Vacant)
Ministers	
Agriculture and Natural Resources	Andreas Gavrielides
Commerce and Industry	Takis Nemitsas
Communications and Works	Nakos Protopapas
Defense	Andreas Aloneftis
Education	Andreas Philippou
Finance	George Syrimis
Foreign Affairs	George Iacovou
Health	Panicos Papageorghiou
Interior	Christodoulos Veniamin
Justice	Christodoulos Chrysanthou
Labor and Social Insurance	Takis Christofides
Governor, Central Bank	Afxendis Afxendiou

NEWS MEDIA

The material that follows encompasses Greek-sector media only; for Turkish media see Cyprus: Turkish Sector, below.

Press. The following newspapers are published daily at Nicosia in Greek, unless otherwise noted: *Phileleftheros* (Liberal, 20,000), independent; *Havavghi* (Dawn, 14,000), AKEL organ; *Simerini* (Today, 12,000), right-wing; *Apogevmatini* (Afternoon, 11,000), progovernment; *Agon* (Struggle, 7,500), right-wing; *Alithia* (Truth, 5,000); *Ta Nea* (The News, 6,300), EDEK organ; *Eleftherotypia* (Free Press, 6,000), Diko organ; *Cyprus Mail* (2,600), independent, in English.

News agencies. A Greek-sector Cyprus News Agency was established in 1976; numerous foreign bureaus maintain offices at Nicosia.

Radio and television. Prior to the 1974 conflict, broadcasting was controlled by the semigovernmental Cyprus Broadcasting Corporation and the government-owned *Radyo Bayrak* and *Radyo Bayrak Televizyon*. CBC presently maintains television service from its station at Mount Olympus, while the RB and the RBT stations broadcast from the Turkish sector. Radio service is also provided by the BBC East Mediterranean Relay and by the British Forces Broadcasting Service, Cyprus. There were approximately 89,000 television receivers in the Greek sector in 1987.

INTERGOVERNMENTAL REPRESENTATION

Ambassador to the US: Andrew J. JACOVIDES.

US Ambassador to Cyprus: Bill K. PERRIN.

Permanent Representative to the UN: Constantine MOUSHOUTAS.

IGO Memberships (Non-UN): CEUR, CWTH, EEC(A), *EIB*, ICM, ICO, Intelsat, Interpol, NAM.

CYPRUS: TURKISH SECTOR

Turkish Republic of Northern Cyprus
Kuzey Kıbrıs Türk Cumhuriyeti

Political Status: Autonomous federal state proclaimed February 13, 1975; independent republic (thus far recognized only by Turkey) declared November 15, 1983; TRNC constitution approved by referendum of May 6, 1985.

Area: Approximately 1,400 sq. mi. (3,626 sq. km.).

Population: 158,000 (1988E). See population note under Republic of Cyprus; a 1986 estimate by Turkish sector authorities was in excess of 162,000.

Principal Language: Turkish.

Monetary Unit: Turkish Lira (market rate March 1, 1988, 1179.39 liras = $1US). Use of the Cyprus pound as an alternative unit of exchange was terminated on May 16, 1983.

President: Rauf R. DENKTAŞ (National Unity Party); designated President by joint meeting of the Executive Council and Legislative Assembly of the Autonomous Turkish Cypriot Administration on February 13, 1975; continued in office by popular elections in 1976, 1981, and on June 9, 1985.

Prime Minister: Dr. Derviş EROĞLU (National Unity Party); nominated by the President on July 10, 1985, and confirmed by the Assembly of the Republic on July 30, succeeding Nejat KONUK (Independent); formed new government on September 2, 1986.

GOVERNMENT AND POLITICS

Political background. The Turkish Cypriots withdrew from participation in the government of the Republic of Cyprus in January 1964, in the wake of communal violence precipitated by Archbishop Makarios' announcement of proposed constitutional changes in November 1963. In 1967 a Turkish Cypriot Provisional Administration was established to provide governmental services in the Turkish areas, its representatives subsequently engaging in sporadic constitutional discussions with members of the Greek Cypriot administration. Meanwhile, an uneasy peace between the two communities was maintained by a UN peacekeeping force that had been dispatched in 1964. The constitutional talks, which ran until 1974, failed to bridge the gulf between Greek insistence on a unitary form of government and Turkish demands for a bicommunal federation.

A Turkish Federated State of Cyprus was established on February 13, 1975, following the Greek army coup of July 15, 1974, and the subsequent Turkish occupation of northern Cyprus. Rauf DENKTAŞ, nominal vice president of the Republic of Cyprus, was designated president of the Federated State and retained the office as the result of a presidential election on June 20, 1976, in which he defeated the Republican Turkish Party nominee, Ahmet Mithat BERBEROĞLU, by a majority of nearly four to one. He was reelected for a five-year term in June 1981, remaining in office upon proclamation of the nominally independent Turkish Republic of Northern Cyprus in November 1983.

Intercommunal discussions prior to the death of Archbishop Makarios on August 3, 1977, yielded apparent Greek abandonment of its long insistence on unitary government but left the two sides far apart on other issues, including Greek efforts to secure a reduction of approximately 50 percent in the size of the Turkish sector, and Turkish demands for virtual parity in such federal institutions as the presidency (to be effected on the basis of communal rotation) and the higher judiciary.

Prior to the breakdown in discussions between Denktaş and Greek Cypriot leader Spyros Kyprianou at UN headquarters in January 1985 (see previous article), the Turks had made substantial concessions, particularly in regard to power sharing and territorial demarcation of the projected federal units. Specifically, they had abandoned their earlier demand for presidential rotation and had agreed on a reduction of the area to be placed under Turkish local administration to approximately 29 percent of the island total. However, the two sides were unable to agree on a specific timetable for Turkish troop withdrawal, the identification of Turkish-held areas to be returned to Greek control, or a mechanism for external guarantees that the pact would be observed. Expressing his disappointment that the impasse had not been fully resolved, UN Secretary General Pérez de Cuéllar pledged that efforts would be made to address the remaining points of disagreement. For his part, in announcing, on January 25, that presidential and legislative elections would be held in June, President Denktaş insisted that neither the balloting nor the adoption of the TRNC constitution should be construed as efforts to "close the door to a federal solution".

The constitution was approved by 70 percent of those participating in a referendum on May 5, with the leftist Republican Turkish Party (CTP, below) actively campaigning for a "no" vote. At the presidential poll on June 9, Denktaş was accorded a like margin, while the National Unity Party (UBP) fell two seats short of a majority at the legislative balloting of June 23. On July 30, a coalition government involving the UBP and the Communal Liberation Party (TKP), with Dervis EROĞLU as prime minister, was confirmed by the Assembly.

The Eroğlu government fell on August 11, 1986, after the TKP had refused to endorse a proposal to expand the scope of trade and investment in the sector. However, the prime minister was able to form a new administration on September 2 that included the center-right New Dawn Party (YDP) as the UBP's coalition partner.

Constitution and government. The constitution of the present Turkish Republic provides for a presidential-parliamentary system headed by a popularly elected chief executive, who serves a five-year term and cannot lead a party or be subject to its decisions. The president appoints a prime minister, who (unlike other ministers) must be a member of the legislature and whose government is subject to legislative recall. The 50-member Assembly of the Republic sits for five years, and its president, who is elected at the beginning of the first and fourth year of each term, becomes acting head of state in the event of presidential death, incapacity, or resignation. The Supreme Court, composed of a president and 7 additional judges, also sits as a Constitutional Court (5 members) and as a Court of Appeal and High Administrative Court (3 members each). Lesser courts and local administrative units are established by legislative action.

Current issues. In early June 1986, Turkish Prime Minister Turgut Özal visited the TRNC, announcing that his government would undertake a program of economic support to the breakaway Republic that would lead to the latter's international recognition. The visit was protested by both Washington and Moscow, whose otherwise divergent views on communal reconciliation were viewed as linked to Greek Cypriot President Kyprianou's intransigence on the unity issue. During Özal's three-day stay, President Denktaş, in a self-proclaimed "slap in the face of the Greek Cypriot leadership", ordered the closure of crossing points between the two sectors. Subsequently, however, the TRNC head of state continued his appeal for political "partnership" with the Greeks, adding that by continuing to recognize the Kyprianou government, Western nations had offered it little incentive to come to terms with his own administration. (For recent developments in Greek-Turkish Cypriot relations, see previous article).

POLITICAL PARTIES

Most of the Turkish Cypriot parties share a common outlook regarding the present division of the island. The National Unity Party fell two seats short of a majority at the election of June 23, 1985, and has been the dominant force in successive coalition administrations.

Government Parties:

National Unity Party (*Ulusal Birlik Partisi* — UBP). The UBP was established in 1975 as an outgrowth of the former National Solidarity (*Ulusal Dayanı*) movement. Committed to the establishment of a bicommunal federal state, it captured three-quarters of the seats in the Turkish Cypriot Legislative Assembly at the 1976 election but was reduced to a plurality of 18 seats in 1981 and survived a confidence vote in the Assembly on September 11 only because the motion failed to obtain an absolute majority. The UBP's former leader, Rauf Denktaş, is precluded by the constitution from serving as president of the party or from submitting to party discipline while president of the Republic. His successor, Mustafa Çağatay, withdrew from the party leadership upon resigning as prime minister in November 1983.
Leaders: Dr. Dervis EROĞLU (Prime Minister), Olgun PAŞALAR (Secretary General).

New Dawn Party (*Yeni Doğuş Partisi* — YDP). The YDP is a center-right grouping formed in January 1984, primarily to represent persons immigrating from Turkey during the previous decade. Its name is variously translated as "Revival", "Renaissance", and "New Birth". The party won 4 Assembly seats in 1985. It joined the Eroğlu administration in September 1986.
Leaders: Aytaç BEŞEŞLER, Vural ÇETIN (Secretary General).

Other Parties:

Republican Turkish Party (*Cumhuriyetçi Türk Partisi* — CTP). The CTP is a Marxist formation that campaigned against the 1985 constitution because of its alleged repressive and militaristic content. The party captured 2 Assembly seats in 1976, 6 in 1981, and 12 in 1985.
Leaders: Özer ÖZGÜR (1981 and 1985 presidential candidate), Nacı Talat USAR.

Communal Liberation Party (*Toplumcu Kurtuluş Partisi* — TKP). Also known as the Socialist Salvation Party, the TKP is a left-of-center grouping organized in 1976. The 6 Assembly seats won by the party in 1976 were doubled in 1981, 2 of which (for an enlarged chamber) were lost in 1985. The TKP joined the Eroğlu government in July 1985, but withdrew in August 1986.
Leaders: İsmail BOZKURT, Alpay DURDURAN (1985 presidential candidate), Mustafa AKINCI, Erdal SURECH (Secretary General).

Progressive People's Party (*Atilimci Halk Partisi* — AHP). The AHP resulted from the merger in early 1986 of the Democratic People's Party (*Demokratik Halk Partisi* — DHP) and the Communal Endeavor Party (*Toplumsal Atılım Partisi*TAP). The DHP, which advocated the establishment of an independent, nonaligned, and biregional Cypriot state, was organized in 1979 by former prime ministers Nejat Konuk and Osman Örek, both of whom had left the UBP because of dissention within the party. In January 1982 Konuk announced that he would thenceforth sit in the Assembly as an independent and subsequently returned as head of a new coalition government from December 1983 to July 1985. The TAP, led by İrsen KÜCÜK, was a centrist party formed in 1984. Neither the DHP nor the TAP won Assembly representation in 1985.
Leaders: İsmet KOTAK, İrsen KÜCÜK.

New Turkish Unity Party (*Yeni Türk Birlik Partisi* — YTBP). The YTBP is a revival of the right-wing Turkish Unity Party (*Türkiye Birlik Partisi* — TBP) formed by İsmail Tezer prior to the 1981 election.
Leader: İsmail TEZER.

Social Democratic Party (*Sosyal Demokrat Parti* — SDP). The SDP is a left-of-center party founded in 1982 by a group that included the son of the president, Raif Denktaş, who died in an automobile accident in early 1986.
Leader: Hasan MESUTOĞLU.

Cyprus Democratic Party (*Kıbrıs Demokrasi Partisi* — KDP). The KDP is a social democratic formation organized in January 1985. It did not contest the June 1985 election.
Leaders: Fuat VEZIROĞLU, Ekrem URAL.

Working People's Party (*Çalışan Halkın Partisi* — CHP). The ÇHP is an extreme left-wing party organized in 1983.
Leader: Bekir AZGIN.

North Cyprus Socialist Party (*Kuzey Kıbrıs Sosyalist Partisi* — KKSP). The KKSP was officially registered in August 1985.
Leader: Doğan HARMAN.

LEGISLATURE

A Turkish Cypriot Legislative Assembly, formerly the Legislative Assembly of the Autonomous Turkish Cypriot Administration, was organized in February 1975. Styled the **Assembly of the Republic** (*Cumhuriyet Meclisi*) under the 1985 constitution, it currently contains 50 members, who are elected for five-year terms. Following the election of June 23, 1985, the National Unity Party held 24 seats; the Republican Turkish Party, 12; the Communal Liberation Party, 10; and the New Dawn Party, 4.
President: Hakkı ATUN.

CABINET

Prime Minister	Dr. Derviş Eroğlu

Ministers

Agriculture and Forests	Ataç Beşeşler
Economy, Industry and Commerce	Erdal Onurhan
Finance and Customs	Mehmet Bayram
Foreign Affairs and Defense	Dr. Kenan Atakol
Health and Social Welfare	Dr. Mustafa Erbilen
Housing	Onay Fadil Demirciler
Interior, Rural Affairs and Natural Resources	Taşkent Atasayan
Labor, Youth and Sports	Günay Caymaz
National Education and Culture	Salih Coşar
Public Works, Communication and Tourism	Nazif Borman

NEWS MEDIA

Press. Freedom of the press is guaranteed under the 1985 constitution, save for legislative restrictions intended to safeguard public order, national security, public morals, or the proper functioning of the judiciary. The following are published daily at Nicosia in Turkish, unless otherwise noted: *Halkın Sesi* (Voice of the People, 6,200); *Kıbrıs Postası* (Cyprus Post, 4,600); *Kıbrıs* (formerly *Special News Bulletin*, 4,000), official weekly in English; *Bozkurt* (Grey Wolf, 3,000); *Birlik* (Unity, 2,400), UBP organ; *Günaydın Kıbrıs* (Good Morning, Cyprus, 1,900).

News agency. The Turkish-sector facilities are Turkish News Cyprus (*Türk Ajansı Kıbrıs* — TAK) and the Northern Cyprus News Agency (*Kuzey Kıbrıs Haber Ajansi*).

Radio and television. Broadcasting in the Turkish sector is controlled by *Radyo Bayrak* and *Radyo Bayrak Televizyon*. There were approximately 75,000 television receivers in the sector in 1987.

INTERGOVERNMENTAL REPRESENTATION

The Turkish Federated State did not seek general international recognition and maintained no missions abroad, except for a representative at New York who was recognized by the United Nations as official spokesman for the Turkish Cypriot community; it did, however, participate in an Islamic Conference meeting on economic cooperation at Ankara, Turkey, November 4–6, 1980. The present Turkish Republic of Northern Cyprus has proclaimed itself independent, but has been recognized, as such, only by Turkey, with whom it exchanged ambassadors on April 17, 1985.

IGO Memberships (Non-UN): IC.

CZECHOSLOVAKIA

Czechoslovak Socialist Republic
Československá Socialistická Republika

Political Status: Independent republic established 1918; Communist People's Republic established 1948; declared a Socialist Republic 1960; federal system established January 1, 1969.

Area: 49,370 sq. mi. (127,869 sq. km.).

Population: 15,283,095 (1980C), 15,639,000 (1988E).

Major Urban Centers (1985E): PRAGUE (1,195,000); Bratislava (410,000); Brno (385,000); Ostrava (326,000).

Official Languages: Czech, Slovak.

Monetary Unit: Koruna (noncommercial rate March 1, 1988, 8.96 korunas = $1US).

President of the Republic: Gustáv HUSÁK; elected President by the Federal Assembly on May 29, 1975, succeeding Gen. Ludvík SVOBODA; reelected for a third term on May 22, 1985; elected First Secretary of the Communist Party in 1969, succeeding Alexander DUBČEK; reelected (with the title of General Secretary) in 1971, 1976, 1981, and 1986; resigned as party leader on December 17, 1987.

Chairman of the Government (Prime Minister): Lubomír ŠTROUGAL; appointed by the President in 1970, succeeding Oldřich ČERNÍK; reappointed following elections in 1971, 1976, 1981, and on May 23–24, 1986.

Prime Minister of the Czech Socialist Republic: Ladislav ADAMEC; appointed by the Presidium of the Czech National Council on March 20, 1987, succeeding Josef KORČÁK.

Prime Minister of the Slovak Socialist Republic: Petr COLOTKA; appointed by the Slovak National Council in 1969; reappointed following elections in 1971, 1976, 1981, and on May 23–24, 1986.

General Secretary of the Communist Party of Czechoslovakia: Miloš JAKEŠ; elected by the Central Committee on December 17, 1987, succeeding Gustáv HUSÁK.

THE COUNTRY

Born from the dismemberment of the former Austro-Hungarian Empire at the close of World War I, Czechoslovakia is generally considered to be the most Western oriented among the Communist-ruled countries of Eastern Europe. As its name implies, its principal ethnic components are Czechs (65 percent) and Slovaks (30 percent), the former concentrated in the western and central regions of Bohemia and Moravia, the latter in the eastern region of Slovakia. Magyars, constituting less than 5 percent of the total population, are the only substantial minority remaining since the virtual elimination of the Jewish community during the Nazi occupation of 1939–1945, the flight and expulsion of over three million Germans after World War II, and the annexation of Ruthenia by the USSR at the close of that conflict. About three-quarters of Czechoslovakia's population was formerly listed as Roman Catholic, and most of the remainder as Protestant. Both faiths have persisted despite the antireligious policies of the Communist regime. Ninety percent of the adult female population is employed outside the home, concentrated in lower-paying clerical and service sectors; a pronatalist policy with incentives for working mothers has been relatively ineffective. In political life, women hold 28 percent of the Federal Assembly seats, but are unrepresented on the ruling party Politburo; by contrast, a number of women are leaders of the prominent dissident group Charter 77.

Among CMEA member states, Czechoslovakia ranks second only to the German Democratic Republic in per capita income and industrialization, although Slovakia has long been less affluent than Bohemia and Moravia. The industrial sector, virtually all of which is run by some form of collective management, supports about one-half of the labor force and is a major producer of machinery and machine tools, chemical products, textiles, and glassware. Agriculture is likewise highly collectivized; the principal crops are wheat, potatoes, barley, and sugar beets. A series of economic reforms aimed at greater flexibility, decentralization, and responsiveness to market forces within a framework of overall planning was cut short by the invasion and partial occupation of Czechoslovakia by forces of the Warsaw Pact in August 1968. By 1980, however, the government was calling for greater efficiency, reduced budgetary aid to state enterprises, linkage between wages and productivity, and improved quality control to make Czechoslovak goods more marketable in the West. A serious recession, resulting from energy shortages and aid to neighboring Poland, was followed in 1983–1985 by a modest rebound, with growth in national income of 3.2 percent in the latter year. However, industrial exports continue to lag behind those of raw materials, and the domestic market has been depressed by a number of recent consumer price increases.

GOVERNMENT AND POLITICS

Political background. From its establishment in 1918 until its dismemberment following the Munich agreement of 1938, Czechoslovakia was the most politically mature and democratically governed of the new states of Eastern Europe. Due mainly to the preponderant role of Soviet military forces in the liberation of the country at the close of World War II, however, the Communists gained a leading position in the postwar government headed by President Eduard BENEŠ, and assumed full control in February 1948.

The trial and execution of such top Communist leaders as Vladimír CLEMENTIS and Rudolf SLÁNSKÝ during the Stalinist purges in the early 1950s exemplified the country's posture as a docile Soviet satellite under the leadership of Antonín NOVOTNÝ, first secretary of the Communist Party and (from 1957) president of the Republic. By 1967 growing unrest among intellectuals and students had produced revolutionary ferment which led in early 1968 to Novotný's ouster and his replacement by Alexander DUBČEK as party first secretary and by Gen. Ludvík SVOBODA as president. Dubček, a prominent Slovak Communist, rapidly emerged as the leader of a popular movement for far-reaching political and economic change.

A reformist cabinet headed by Oldřich ČERNÍK took office in April 1968 with a program that included strict observance of legality, broader political discussion, greater economic and cultural freedom, and increased Slovak autonomy under new constitutional arrangements designed in part to provide for redress of economic disadvantages. Widely hailed within Czechoslovakia, these trends were sharply criticized by the Soviet Union, which, on August 20–21, 1968, invaded and partially occupied the country in concert with the other Warsaw Pact nations, except Romania.

The period after the invasion was characterized by the progressive entrenchment of more conservative elements within the government and the party, and by a series of pacts which specified Czechoslovakia's "international commitments", limited internal reforms, and allowed the stationing of Soviet troops on Czech soil. For a time, the pre-August leadership was left in power, but Dubček was replaced by Gustáv HUSÁK as general secretary in 1969, removed from his position in the Presidium, and in 1970 expelled from the party. Oldřich Černík retained his post as chairman of the government until 1970, when he was replaced by Lubomír ŠTROUGAL and also expelled from the party. The actions against the two leaders were paralleled by widespread purges of other reformers during 1969–1971, some 500,000 party members ultimately being affected. President Svoboda, although reelected by the Federal Assembly to a second five-year term in 1973, was replaced on May 29, 1975, by Husák, who retained his party posts. Husák was unanimously reelected president in 1980 and again in 1985.

The 74-year-old Husák, who had been reported to be in failing health, resigned as party general secretary on December 17, 1987, while retaining his Politburo membership and the largely ceremonial office of president; the Central Committee immediately appointed as his successor Miloš JAKEŠ, a cautious *apparatchik* who had overseen party economic policy since 1981 and was viewed by some as an interim incumbent.

Constitution and government. While President Husák called for the drafting of a new constitution at the Seventeenth Party Congress in March 1986, the basic principles of the 1960 constitution, as amended in 1968 to establish a federal state, remained in effect at the end of the year. All power purports to emanate from the working people, the Communist Party being designated as the vanguard of the working class and the guiding force in society and the state.

The principal administrative division is between the federal government and the two national governments, the Czech Socialist Republic in Bohemia and Moravia, with Prague as the seat of government, and the Slovak Socialist Republic in Slovakia, with Bratislava as the seat of government. Each of the component republics has its own executive and National Council (legislature), which operate concurrently with (but within the framework of their jurisdictions, independently of) the federal organs at Prague.

Nominally, the supreme organ of state power is the bicameral Czechoslovak Federal Assembly, which consists of the House of Nations and the House of the People. The Federal Assembly elects the president, who in turn appoints a cabinet that includes the chairman of the government (prime minister); both executives remain, in theory, dependent upon the Assembly. The judicial system is headed by a Supreme Court, whose judges are also elected by the Federal Assembly. Judges for regional and district courts are elected by the National Councils; there are also military tribunals and local people's courts.

Foreign relations. Since 1968, Czechoslovakia has maintained the posture of an obedient Soviet satellite state, adhering to Moscow's line on such events as the Vietnamese invasion of Kampuchea in late 1978, the Soviet intervention in Afghanistan in December 1979, and the imposition of martial law in Poland in 1981. Formal diplomatic relations with the Federal Republic of Germany were not established until December 1973, although a number of economic and cultural agreements between the two countries were subsequently concluded. The status of Sudeten Germans (*Landsmannschaften*), traditionally a sensitive issue between the two countries, has clouded Bonn-Prague relations in recent years: the presence of West German officials at *Landsmannschaften* rallies in 1984 and 1985 led to condemnation by Prague of "German revanchism", coinciding with Soviet efforts to prevent strengthened ties between East and West Germany. More recently, there have been incidents involving Communist neighbors: in November 1986 Polish authorities protested extensive Czech pollution of the Oder (Odra) river, while in early 1987 there were complaints of economic and cultural oppression, including threats of violence, against ethnic Hungarians in Slovakia, which had been part of Hungary until 1918.

For more than three decades, relations with the United States and Britain were strained by an inability to resolve compensation claims against property seized in 1948 as well as by the holding at Washington and London of 18.4 metric tons of Czechoslovak gold confiscated by Germany in World War II. Compensation was finally made and the gold returned in February 1982, but relations, instead of improving, subsequently worsened: reciprocal diplomatic protests were lodged by Prague and Washington in April 1984 after a US Army helicopter strayed into Czechoslovak airspace and was allegedly fired on, while Czech officials have frequently charged British embassy personnel with espionage. In May 1986, charges of espionage were also exchanged with Sweden, Stockholm expelling five Czech nationals (including four diplomats) and Prague responding by expelling two Swedish embassy personnel.

Current issues. Emulating the policies of reconstruction (*perestroika*) advanced in the Soviet Union following Mikhail Gorbachev's assumption of power has been particularly difficult for the Czech leadership, since it appears to be called upon to implement reforms that it had been charged with eradicating in 1968. At a Central Committee meeting in March 1987, President Husák felt obliged to reject the "slander" that his government was adverse to change by asserting that "We attentively follow the measures being undertaken in the Soviet Union". Somewhat petulantly he added that "no one is forcing Soviet ideas on Czechoslovakia" and, while alluding to a number of reforms that were under consideration, advanced no specific proposals. However, a draft bill to "restructure the economic mechanism" was introduced in July (with effect from January 1, 1989), while a similar bill dealing with agricultural reorganization was presented in September.

The designation in mid-December of Miloš Jakeš to succeed Husák as party leader seemed to represent a short-term compromise between hardline conservatives and Gorbachev-oriented liberals. Somewhat more flexible than his predecessor, Jakeš had been an advocate of moderate reform in the early 1970s and had played a key role in the country's transformation into a net exporter of food. Politically he represented the past: as head of the party's Central Control and Auditing Commission he had been responsible for the widespread purge mounted in the wake of the Soviet invasion. Nonetheless, in a congratulatory message following his appointment, Gorbachev urged the new general secretary to proceed not only with reform of the Czech economy, but with the "democratization of public and political life". Opposition spokesmen were far from persuaded that Jakeš himself could implement such a mandate, human-rights leader Václav HAVEL likening his role to that of Konstantin Chernenko, Gorbachev's immediate predecessor in the Soviet Union. Evidence to such effect surfaced shortly thereafter: numerous members of Charter 77 (see under Political Parties, below) were arrested in January 1988, while in March hundreds of Roman Catholics were taken into custody following a demonstration against the government's failure since 1973 to reach agreement with the Vatican on the filling of vacant bishoprics.

POLITICAL PARTIES AND GROUPS

Despite undisputed Communist Party control since 1948, Czechoslovakia has retained some elements of a multiparty system through the institution of the **National Front of the Czechoslovakian Socialist Republic** (*Národní Fronta*), which is led by the Communist Party but includes four minor parties in addition to trade-union, farmer, and other groups. Since 1968, however, public disenchantment with authorized political institutions has remained high, the majority of the population offering little more than ritualistic support for party and government.

Government Party:

Communist Party of Czechoslovakia (*Komunistická Strana Československa* – KSČ). Formed in 1921, the KSČ was the only Communist party in Eastern Europe to operate legally prior to World War II. The party Congress, which normally convenes every five years and last met March 24–28, 1986, elects the Central Committee, which in turn elects a Presidium and Secretariat, both headed from April 1969 until his resignation on December 17, 1987, by Gustáv Husák. The membership of the KSČ (including candidates) was reported in 1986 to total more than 1.67 million. The **Communist Party of Slovakia** (*Komunistická Strana Slovenska* – KSS) has traditionally been permitted a separate status within the formal structure of the KSČ as a concession to Slovak sentiment. The KSS holds its own congresses and has a separate Central Committee.

Secretary General: Miloš JAKEŠ.

Other Members of Presidium of the Central Committee: Ladislav ADAMEC (Deputy Prime Minister and Chairman, Czeck National Council), Vasil BIĽAK (Secretary, Central Committee), Petr COLOTKA (Deputy Prime Minister; Chairman, Slovak National Council), Karel HOFFMAN (Secretary, Central Committee), Gustáv HUSÁK (President of the Republic), Alois INDRA (Chairman, Federal Assembly), Antonín KAPEK (former First Secretary, Prague KSČ Committee), Josef KEMPNÝ (former Deputy Prime Minister), Jozef LENÁRT (First Secretary, KSS), Lubomír ŠTROUGAL (Prime Minister).

Candidate Members: Jan FOJTÍK, Josef HAMAN, Vladimír HERMAN, Miloslav HRUŠKOVIČ, Ignác JANÁK, František PITRA.

Central Committee Secretariat: Mikuláš BEŇO, Vasil BIĽAK, Jan FOJTÍK, Josef HAMAN, Josef HAVLÍN, Karel HOFFMAN, Zdeněk HOŘENÍ, Miloš JAKEŠ, Marie KABRHELOVÁ, František PITRA, Jindřich POLEDNÍK, Miroslav ZAVADIL.

National Front Parties:

Serving mainly as transmission belts to segments of the population that reject doctrinaire communism, the other National Front parties are the **Czechoslovak Socialist Party;** the **Czechoslovak People's Party,** a Catholic group; the **Slovak Reconstruction Party;** and the **Slovak Freedom Party.** Also affiliated with the Front are the Revolutionary Trade Union Movement and the Socialist Union of Youth.

Dissident Group:

Charter 77 (*Charta 77*). The leading Czechoslovak dissident group, Charter 77 was organized to oversee government adherence to the civil and human rights specified in the constitution and in such documents as the 1948 UN Declaration of Human Rights; the 1975 Final Act of the Helsinki Conference on Security and Cooperation in Europe; and the UN Covenants on Civil and Political Rights, and on Economic, Social and Cultural Rights. The group's manifesto, dated January 1, 1977, was initially signed by 242 individuals, but its adherents subsequently numbered more than 1,000, many of whom have been subject to arrest, imprisonment, and official harassment for such activities as issuing statements regarding specific violations of human rights, publishing unauthorized works through the underground "padlock press", participating in the semiclandestine Jan Potočka University (named after the group's first spokesman), and forming in May 1978 the **Committee for the Defense of the Unjustly Persecuted** (*Výbor pro Obranu Nespravedlivě Stíhaných* – VONS). Charter 77 has also called for the withdrawal of all Soviet troops from the country.

Leading members of Charter 77 include Jiří HÁJEK, foreign minister during the "Prague Spring" of 1968; Pavel KOHOUT, a well-known writer deprived of his citizenship and denied reentry from Austria in October 1979; Václav HAVEL, a noted playwright whose October 1979 sentence for activities "against the state" and "in collusion with hostile forces from abroad" was commuted in 1983 because of ill health; Jaroslav ŠABATA, regional leader of Moravia during the Dubček administration; and Rudolf BATTĚK, a sociologist who helped found both Charter 77 and VONS and who was imprisoned in July 1981 on charges of subversion.

Despite police harassment, spokesmen held a news conference at Prague on January 6, 1987, to mark the tenth anniversary of the group's founding; during a two-week period in January 1988, on the other hand, at least 20 Charter 77 members, including most of its leaders, were arrested.

Spokespersons for 1988: Stanislav DEVÁTÝ, Miloš HÁJEK, Bohumír JANÁT.

LEGISLATURE

The **Federal Assembly** (*Federální Shromáždění*), a bicameral body, replaced the National Assembly on January 1, 1969.

Chairman: Alois INDRA.

House of Nations (*Sněmovna Národů*). The upper house comprises 150 members (75 from each Republic) directly elected for five-year terms. The most recent election was held May 23–24, 1986.

Chairman: Ján JANÍK.

House of the People (*Sněmovna Lidu*). The lower house consists of 200 members elected on the basis of population for five-year terms. The most recent election was held May 23–24, 1986, when 134 deputies were elected from the Czech Socialist Republic and 66 from the Slovak Socialist Republic.

Chairman: Vladimír VEDRA.

CABINET

Prime Minister	Lubomír Štrougal
First Deputy Prime Minister	Rudolf Rohlíček
Deputy Prime Ministers	Ladislav Adamec
	Petr Colotka
	Ladislav Gerle
	Pavol Hrivnák
	Karol Laco
	Matej Lúčan
	Jaromír Obzina
	Svatopluk Potáč
	Miroslav Toman

Ministers

Agriculture and Food	Miroslav Toman
Communications	Jiří Jíra
Electrotechnical Industry	Milan Kubát
Finance	Jaromir Žák
Foreign Affairs	Bohuslav Chňoupek
Foreign Trade	Jan Sterba
Fuels and Power	Vlastimil Ehrenberger
General Engineering	Ladislav Luhový
Interior	Vratislav Vajnar
Labor and Social Affairs	Miroslar Boďa
Metallurgy and Heavy Engineering	Eduard Saul
National Defense	Gen. Milan Václavík
Transportation	Vladimír Blažek

Minister Chairmen

Federal Price Office	Michal Sabolčík
People's Control Commission	František Ondřich
State Commission for Research and Development and Investment Planning	Jaromír Obzina
State Planning Commission	Svatopluk Potáč
	Vladimir Janza (Deputy)
Chairman, Czechoslovak State Bank	Jan Stejskal

NEWS MEDIA

The media are subject to censorship by the Government Press and Information Committee; private ownership is forbidden.

Press. The following dailies are published in Czech at Prague, unless otherwise noted: *Rudé Právo* (950,000), central organ of the KSČ; *Zemědělské Noviny* (342,000), organ of the Ministry of Agriculture and Food; *Pravda* (Bratislava, 330,000), in Slovak, organ of the KSS; *Práce* (320,000), organ of the Central Trade Union Council; *Mladá Fronta* (318,000), organ of the Socialist Union of Youth; *Práca* (Bratislava, 230,000), in Slovak, organ of the Slovak Committee of Trade Unions; *Svobodné Slovo* (228,000), organ of the Czechoslovak Socialist Party; *Lidová Demokracie* (216,000), organ of the Czechoslovak People's Party; *Nová Svoboda* (Ostrava, 198,000), organ of the KSČ regional committee; *Večerní Praha* (120,000), organ of the Prague City Committee of the KSČ; *Rovnost* (Brno, 114,000), organ of the South Moravian Regional Committee of the KSČ.

News agencies. The government-controlled domestic service is the Czechoslovak News Agency (*Československá Tisková Kancelář* – CTK, or *Četeka*). Numerous foreign agencies also maintain bureaus at Prague.

Radio and television. Radio and television are under government control. Czechoslovak Radio (*Československý Rozhlas*) operates parallel broadcasting organizations in both the Czech and Slovak republics while also offering foreign broadcasts in a dozen languages. Czechoslovak Television (*Československá Televize*) and Czechoslovak Television in Slovakia (*Československá Televize na Slovensku*) are responsible for television broadcasting. There were 4.7 million radio and 4.4 million television receivers in 1987.

INTERGOVERNMENTAL REPRESENTATION

Ambassador to the US: Miroslav HOUSTECKY.

US Ambassador to Czechoslovakia: Julian Martin NIEMCZYK.

Permanent Representative to the UN: Evžen ZÁPOTOCKÝ.

IGO Memberships (Non-UN): BIS, CCC, CMEA, IBEC, ICCO, IIB, ILZ, INRO, PCA, WTO.

DENMARK

Kingdom of Denmark
Kongeriget Danmark

Political Status: Constitutional monarchy since 1849; under unicameral parliamentary system established in 1953.

Area: 16,629 sq. mi. (43,069 sq. km.).

Population: 5,123,989 (1981C), 5,119,000 (1988E). Area and population figures are for mainland Denmark; for Greenland and the Faroe Islands, see Related Territories, below.

Major Urban Centers (1985E): COPENHAGEN (urban area, 1,357,000); Århus (193,000); Odense (137,000); Ålborg (114,000).

Official Language: Danish.

Monetary Unit: Krone (market rate March 1, 1988, 6.49 kroner = $1US).

Sovereign: Queen MARGRETHE II; proclaimed Queen on January 15, 1972, following the death of her father, King FREDERIK IX, on January 14.
Heir to the Throne: Crown Prince FREDERIK, elder son of the Queen.

Prime Minister: Poul SCHLÜTER (Conservative People's Party); sworn in September 10, 1982, following the resignation of the government of Anker JØRGENSEN (Social Democratic Party) on September 3; formed new governments after the elections of January 10, 1984, and September 8, 1987; resigned to head caretaker administration following election of May 10, 1988; formed present minority government on June 3, 1988.

THE COUNTRY

Encompassing a low-lying peninsula and adjacent islands strategically situated at the mouth of the Baltic, Denmark has a homogeneous and densely settled population, the vast majority (95 percent) belonging to the state-supported Evangelical Lutheran Church. Approximately 45 percent of the wage labor force is female, with 40 percent of working women concentrated in "female intensive" service and textile manufacturing jobs; in government, women hold between 20 and 30 percent of national legislative seats with significantly less representation at the local level.

About three-fourths of the country's terrain is devoted to agriculture, and roughly two-thirds of the agricultural output is exported (chiefly meat, dairy products, and eggs).

However, industrial expansion has been substantial since World War II, with manufactures (principally machinery and electrical equipment, processed foods and beverages, chemicals and pharmaceuticals, textiles, clothing, and ships) now accounting for about two-thirds of total exports. Fluctuating market conditions and the escalating cost of imported fuel led to severe trade deficits in the late 1970s, but despite such economic pressures the government remained committed to an extensive social welfare system, which absorbs over half the gross national product.

GOVERNMENT AND POLITICS

Political background. The oldest monarchy in Europe, Denmark has lived under constitutional rule since 1849 and has long served as a model of political democracy. Its multiparty system, reflecting the use of proportional representation, has resulted since World War II in a succession of minority and coalition governments in which the Social Democratic Party held the preponderant position from 1953 to 1968 under the leadership of Jens Otto KRAG. Despite the return of Krag as head of a minority government following an early election called by Prime Minister Hilmar BAUNSGAARD in 1971, the Social Democrats for a time declined in importance.

After overseeing the installation of Queen MARGRETHE II on January 15, 1972, and Denmark's entry into the Common Market, Krag stunned the Danes by resigning and withdrawing from public life. Anker JØRGENSEN succeeded Krag but was forced to call a new election in 1973 following a dispute with Erhard JAKOBSEN, who subsequently formed the Center Democrats. Voter discontent was reflected in the election of December 4, 1973, by considerable defection from the traditional parties.

Prime Minister Poul HARTLING, heading a minority government since the 1973 election, called for a new election on January 9, 1975. The Social Democrats secured a plurality of seats and Jørgensen returned as head of a minority administration on February 13. Dwindling support for economic reform, particularly from the Left, forced Jørgensen to call for a new election on February 12, 1977, at which both the Social Democrats and the Conservatives made substantial advances, allowing the incumbent to form a new government with support from center-right parties. Following successive resignations, Jørgensen was returned to office in 1979 and 1981, as head of minority governments. A further resignation in 1982 yielded the installation of Poul SCHLÜTER of the Conservative People's Party as head of a new minority government that included Liberals, Center Democrats, and the Christian People's Party. The first Conservative prime minister since 1901, Schlüter faced heavy opposition to his proposed austerity measures: for the first time since 1929, the budget failed, and he was forced to call an election 23 months prior to expiry of the constitutional mandate.

The balloting of January 10, 1984, yielded a decrease in class-alliance voting with Danes supporting the traditional Conservative outlook on economic issues, including lowered interest rates. As a result, Schlüter remained in office as head of the existing four-party coalition. The coalition's minority status was further eroded at an early election on September 8, 1987, although Schlüter was able to form a new administration with the continued support of two other nonsocialist parties.

On April 14, 1988, the opposition Social Democrats secured legislative approval for a resolution requiring that NATO vessels be formally "reminded" of Denmark's 31-year ban on nuclear weapons. Prime Minister Schlüter responded by calling a snap election for May 10, at which the socialist bloc suffered a marginal loss, while the rightist Progress Party (theretofore unacceptable as a government coalition partner) registered a 43 percent gain in representation. Since the anti-NATO forces nonetheless retained a narrow majority, the prime minister submitted his resignation and moved into caretaker status, ultimately forming a minority three-party government encompassing the Conservatives, Liberals, and Radical Liberals on June 3.

Constitution and government. The constitution adopted in 1953 abolished the upper house of Parliament while leaving intact the main outlines of the Danish political system. Executive power is nominally vested in the monarch but is exercised by a cabinet responsible to the (*Folketing*), a legislative body that includes representatives from the Faroe Islands and Greenland. The judicial system is headed by a 15-member Supreme Court and encompasses two high courts, local courts, specialized courts for labor and maritime affairs, and an ombudsman who is appointed by the *Folketing*. Judges are appointed by the Crown on the advice of the minister of justice.

Under a major reform enacted in 1970, the former 25 regional districts were reduced to 14 counties (*amtskommuner*), each governed by an elected council (*amtsiåd*) and mayor (*amtsborgmester*). The counties in turn are divided into 277 local administrative units, each featuring an elected communal council (*kommunalbestyrelse*) and mayor (*borgmester*). The city of Copenhagen is governed by a city council (*borger repræsentation*) and an executive consisting of a head mayor (*overborgmester*), 5 deputy mayors (*borgmestie*), and 5 aldermen (*rådmænd*).

Foreign relations. Danish foreign policy, independent but thoroughly Western in outlook, emphasizes support for the United Nations, the economic integration of Europe, and regional cooperation through the Nordic Council and other Scandinavian programs. Formerly a member of the European Free Trade Association (EFTA), Denmark was admitted to the European Communities (EC) on January 1, 1973; dissatisfaction with fishing agreements led to the withdrawal of newly autonomous Greenland from the EC in 1982, followed by sporadic conflict with individual community members, particularly the United Kingdom, over North Sea fishing rights. Although committed to collective security, the Danish government has consistently resisted pressure by NATO to increase in real terms its defense appropriations; indeed, responding to widespread popular agitation, the Social Democrats and their allies were able, in May 1984, to force legislation making Denmark the first NATO member to withdraw completely from missile deployment.

Danish voters in February 1986 endorsed by popular referendum continued participation in the EC, while a major cabinet shuffle in March helped to reinforce the coalition government's pro-EC position; however, leftist opposition parties in the *Folketing* succeeded in enacting measures that would further reduce Denmark's full participation in NATO, including, in April 1988, the passage of legislation reiterating a long-standing (but theretofore unenforced) ban on visits by nuclear-equipped vessels.

Current issues. The election of May 10, 1988, resulted from a complex set of alignments within the *Folketing,* whereby the Schlüter coalition enjoyed a majority on domestic, but not NATO-related foreign issues. The swing vote, both before and after the 1988 poll, was held by the Radical Liberals, whose leader, Niels Helvig PETERSEN, was proved unable to form a new government. The three-party Schlüter administration that ultimately emerged on June 3 controlled only 67 of 179 *Folketing* seats, virtually assuring that another election would be required, possibly as early as the fall.

POLITICAL PARTIES

Because of Denmark's multiparty system, no single group has been able to secure more than a plurality of the popular vote in recent decades, the most common practice being for the leading party to form a minority government supported by legislative agreements with other parties. For most of the period, preponderant influence has been exercised by the Social Democratic Party, which obtained 30.7 percent of the vote at the 1988 election, down from 32.9 percent in 1981. However, the governments formed since September 1982 have been based on Conservative-led coalitions.

Government Parties (as of June 3, 1988):

Conservative People's Party (*Konservative Folkeparti*). Founded in 1915 as an outgrowth of an earlier Conservative grouping (*Højre*), the Conservative People's Party mainly represents financial, industrial, and business groups. It supports adequate defense, protection of private property, sound fiscal policy, and lower taxation. Under the leadership of Poul Schlüter, the party recovered from a low of 5.5 percent of the vote in 1975 to 23.4 in 1984, before dropping to 20.8 in 1987. Although winning only 38 *Folketing* seats in 1987 (five less than in 1984), Schlüter was able to form a new minority government after the Radical Liberals had refused to form a coalition with the Social Democratic and Socialist People's parties (below). The party lost three additional seats (for a total of 35) in 1988.

Leaders: Poul SCHLÜTER (Chairman); Hans Tustrup HANSEN, Kristian KJAER, Maj. S.E. ANDERSEN (Vice Chairmen); Torben RECHENDORF (Secretary General).

Liberal Party (*Venstre*). Founded in 1872 as the Agrarian Party but currently representing some trade and industrial groups as well as farmers, the Liberal Party (commonly referenced in Danish as *Venstre* [Left] rather than *Liberale Parti*) stands for individualism as against socialism in industry and business, reduction of taxation through governmental economy, relaxation of economic restrictions, and adequate defense. Its parliamentary representation dropped from 22 in 1984 to 19 in 1987, but returned to 22 in 1988.

Leaders: Uffe ELLEMANN-JENSEN (Chairman), Anders Fogh RASMUSSEN (Vice Chairman), Claus Hjort FREDERIKSEN (Secretary General).

Radical Liberal Party (*Det Radikale Venstre*). The Radical Liberal Party was founded in 1905 and represents mainly small landowners and urban intellectual and professional elements. In domestic affairs, the party advocates strengthening of private enterprise in a socio-liberal context;

in foreign affairs, it is pacificist in outlook. In the past it has endorsed Social Democratic governments, but more recently has supported the Schlüter coalition in the *Folketing*. Following the September 1987 election, parliamentary leader Niels Helvig Petersen rebuffed Anker Jørgensen's appeal to re-align with the Social Democratic and Socialist People's parties, thereby precluding the establishment of a new Socialist administration. The party was awarded five cabinet posts in the Schlüter government formed in June 1988.

Leaders: Thorkild MØLLER (Chairman), Keld Anker NIELSEN and Karen NØHR (Vice Chairmen), Niels Helvig PETERSEN (Parliamentary Leader), Jens CLAUSAGER (Secretary General).

Other Parties:

Center Democrats (*Centrum-Demokraterne*). The Center Democrats grouping was formed in November 1973 by the dissident Social Democrat Erhard Jakobsen to protest "leftist" tendencies in the government and plans for increased taxation. In addition to believing that traditional "Left" and "Right" political distinctions are no longer appropriate in contemporary Denmark, Jakobsen also heads the **European Center Democrats** (*Europæiske Centrum-Demokrater*), which supports cooperation within the European Community.

Leaders: Erhard JAKOBSEN (Chairman), Yvonne Herløv ANDERSEN (Secretary General).

Christian People's Party (*Kristeligt Folkeparti*). The Christian People's Party was formed in 1970 in opposition to abortion and liberalization of pornography regulations. It achieved representation in the *Folketing* for the first time in 1973.

Leaders: Flemming KOFOD-SVENDSEN (Chairman), Nils Chr. ANDERSEN (Secretary General).

Progress Party (*Fremskridtspartiet*). The right-wing Progress Party was formed in 1972 by Mogens Glistrup, who was convicted in February 1978 of tax evasion after the longest trial in Danish legal history. In 1983 he was sentenced to a three-year prison term. The party advocates gradual dissolution of the income tax and abolition of the diplomatic service and the military. The second largest parliamentary group after the 1973 balloting, it had slipped to eighth place by 1984, with one of its six representatives subsequently joining the Conservatives and another becoming an independent. In an unexpected recovery, it won nine seats in 1987, but was unable to join in what would have yielded a six-party Schlüter majority because of a Radical Liberal refusal to ally itself with a party viewed as not only extremist, but racist because of a strong anti-immigrant posture. It registered the largest single-party gain at the 1988 balloting, winning 16 seats.

Leader: Johannes SØRENSEN (Chairman).

Social Democratic Party (*Socialdemokratiet*). Founded in 1891, the Social Democratic Party represents mainly industrial labor and advocates economic planning, full employment, extensive social security benefits, and closer Nordic cooperation. Although the plurality grouping (with 54 legislative seats from a 29.3 percent vote share) after the 1987 balloting, it was unable to form a government under former prime minister Anker Jørgensen, who resigned as party leader on September 10.

Leaders: Svend AUKEN (Party Chairman and Parliamentary Leader), Birte WEISS (Vice Chairman), Steen CHRISTENSEN (Secretary General).

Socialist People's Party (*Socialistisk Folkeparti*). The Socialist People's Party was formed in 1958 by former Communist Party chairman Aksel Larsen, who had disagreed with Moscow over the suppression of the 1956 Hungarian Revolution. With a membership that has increased significantly in recent years, it advocates left-wing socialism independent of the Soviet Union, unilateral disarmament, opposition to NATO and Danish membership in the EEC, and Nordic cooperation. It has often acted as an unofficial left wing of the Social Democrats, concentrating on influencing the platform and voting patterns of the larger party.

Leaders: Gert PETERSEN (Chairman), Aage FRANDSEN (Vice Chairman), Lillian UBBESEN (Secretary).

Left Socialist Party (*Venstresocialisterne*). The Left Socialists split from the Socialist People's Party in 1967 and achieved representation in the legislature for the first time in 1975. In 1984 the party's "revolutionary" wing, informally known as the "Leninist" faction, broke with the leadership over its unwillingness to organize cadres along traditional communist lines. Two members defected to the Socialist People's Party

in July 1986. Subsequently the party was weakened by growing factionalization, with the "Red Realists" favoring cooperation with the Socialist People's Party and the "Left Oppositionists" following a rigid Marxist-Leninist line. It is currently unrepresented in the *Folketing*.

Leaders: Preben WILHJELM (founder), Thor TEMTE (Secretary). There is no titular chairman, the principal leadership being regarded as being collective.

Justice Party (*Retsforbund*). The Justice Party (also known as the Single-Tax Party) was founded in 1919. It subscribes to the beliefs of US economist Henry George, its adherents sometimes being referred to as "Georgists". At the 1981 election, it lost all five of the seats won in 1979 and has since been unrepresented in the *Folketing*.

Leaders: Poul Gerhard C. KRISTIANSEN (Chairman), Herluf K. MUNKHOLM (Secretary).

Communist Party of Denmark (*Danmarks Kommunistiske Parti*). The Danish Communist Party was formed in 1919, achieved parliamentary representation in 1932, and participated in the immediate post-war coalition government. The party was greatly weakened by the 1945 Hungarian revolt and the schism that subsequently led to the formation of the Socialist People's Party. It supports the Soviet political line despite some reservations with regard to Eastern Europe. Its representation in the *Folketing* following the 1973 election was its first since 1956. It lost all of its 7 legislative seats at the 1979 balloting and has since been unsuccessful in securing parliamentary representation.

Leaders: Ole SOHN (Chairman), Poul EMANUEL (Secretary).

Common Course (*Fælles Kurs*). An anti-immigration, pro-trade union grouping, Common Course was the only far-left grouping to secure parliamentary representation in 1987, but lost all of its four seats in 1988.

Leaders: Preben Møller HANSEN, Ib JAKOBSEN (Secretary General).

Several minor parties exist, mainly leftist in nature. The Maoist **Communist Workers' Party of Denmark** (*Danmarks Kommunist-Arbeiderparti*), long led by Benito SCOCOZZA, having never achieved parliamentary representation, has explored the possibility of affiliation with the Left Socialists. Also active are the Albanian-oriented **Marxist-Leninist Party** (*Marxistik-Leninistik Parti*); the former Leninist wing of the Left Socialists, the **Union Common List** (*Faglig Faellesliste*); and the environmentalist **Green Party** (*De Grønne*).

LEGISLATURE

The *Folketing* is a unicameral legislature whose members are elected every four years (subject to dissolution) by universal suffrage under a modified proportional representation system. Of its present membership of 179, 135 are elected in 17 districts, with 40 additional seats divided among those parties that have secured at least 2 percent of the vote but whose district representation does not accord with their overall strength. Following the most recent election of May 10, 1988, the Social Democratic Party held 55 seats; the Conservative People's Party, 35; the Socialist People's Party, 24; the Liberal Party, 22; the Progress Party, 16; the Radical Liberal Party, 10; the Center Democrats, 9; and the Christian People's Party, 4. In addition, 2 representatives each were elected from the Faroe Islands and Greenland.

President: Svend JAKOBSEN.

CABINET

[as of June 3, 1988]

Prime Minister	Poul Schlüter
Ministers	
Agriculture	Laurits Tørnæs
Church Affairs	Torben Rechendorff

Cultural Affairs	Ole Vig Jensen
Defense	Knud Enggaard
Economic Affairs	Niels Helveg Petersen
Education and Research	Bertel Haarder
Energy	Jens Bilgrav-Nielsen
Environment	Lone Dybkjaer
Finance	Palle Simonsen
Fisheries	Lars P. Gammelgaard
Foreign Affairs	Uffe Ellemann-Jensen
Health	Elsebeth Kock-Petersen
Housing	Agnete Laustsen
Industry	Nils Wilhjelm
Interior and Nordic Cooperation	Thor Pedersen
Internal Revenue	Anders Fogh Rasmussen
Justice	Erik Ninn-Hansen
Labor	Henning Dyremose
Transport and Communication	H.P. Clausen
Social Affairs	Aase Olesen
Governor, Central Bank of Denmark	Eric Hoffmeyer

NEWS MEDIA

Press. Freedom of the press is constitutionally guaranteed and newspapers and magazines are privately published. No newspaper, with the exception of the Communist *Land og Folk,* is directly owned by a political party, although many reflect party viewpoints. The following newspapers are published daily at Copenhagen, unless otherwise noted: *Ekstra Bladet* (250,000), independent Radical Liberal; *B.T.* (213,000), independent Conservative; *Politiken* (158,000 daily, 227,000 Sunday), independent Radical Liberal; *Berlingske Tidende* (130,000 daily, 202,000 Sunday), independent Conservative; *Ålborg Stiftstidende* (Ålborg, 73,000 daily, 105,000 Sunday), independent; *Fyens Stiftstidende* (Odense, 72,000 daily, 110,000 Sunday); *Århus Stiftstidende* (Århus, 70,000 daily, 91,000 Sunday), independent; *Aktuelt* (58,000 daily, 113,000 Sunday), Social Democratic.

News agencies. The domestic agency, owned by the Danish newspapers, is *Ritzaus Bureau;* numerous foreign bureaus also maintain offices at Copenhagen.

Radio and television. Radio and television stations have traditionally been controlled by the government-owned, noncommercial Danish State Radio and Television Service (*Danmarks Radio*). The monopoly was terminated by the *Folketing* in 1986, which sanctioned the immediate establishment of independent local radio broadcasting, with a nationwide commercial television channel to commence operation in 1988. There were approximately 2.3 million radio and 2.0 million television receivers in 1987.

INTERGOVERNMENTAL REPRESENTATION

Ambassador to the US: Eigil JØRGENSEN.

US Ambassador to Denmark: Terence A. TODMAN.

Permanent Representative to the UN: Ole BIERRING.

IGO Memberships (Non-UN): ADB, ADF, AfDB, BIS, CCC, CERN, CEUR, EC, EIB, ESA, IADB, ICAC, ICCO, ICES, ICM, ICO, IEA, ILZ, Inmarsat, INRO, Intelsat, Interpol, IOOC, ITC, IWC, IWSG, NATO, NC, NIB, OECD, PCA.

RELATED TERRITORIES

Faroe Islands (*Faerøerne,* or *Føroyar*). The Faroe Islands in the North Atlantic have been under Danish administration since 1380. Their area is 540 square miles (1,399 sq. km.), the population is 46,250 (1987E), and the capital is Tórshavn (population 13,400 − 1984E). The principal language is Faroese, with most inhabitants also Danish-speaking. Fishing and sheep raising are the most important economic activities.

The islands, which send two representatives to the *Folketing,* constitute a self-governing territory within the Danish state. A 32-member local legislature (*Løgting*) elects an administrative body (*Landsstyre*) headed by a chairman (*løgmadur*). The Crown is represented by a national ombudsman (*ríkisumbodsmadur*). The islands have been represented on the Nordic Council since 1969 and demands for greater internal autonomy are increasing.

The principal political groups are the **Union Party** (*Sambandsflokkurin*), which urges the retention of close links to metropolitan Denmark; the **Social Democratic Party** (*Javnatharflokkurin*); the **Republican Party** (*Tjóveldisflokkurin*); the **People's Party** (*Fólkaflokkurin*); the **Moderate Self-Rule Party** (*Det Moderate Selvstyreparti*); and the **Progressive and Fisheries Party** [and] **Christian People's Party** (*Fremskridts − og Fisheripartiet Kristeligt Folkeparti*).

National Ombudsman: Niels BENTSEN.
Prime Minister: Atli DAM (Social Democratic Party).

Greenland (*Grønland,* or *Kalaallit Nunaat*). Encompassing 840,000 square miles (2,175,600 sq. km.), including an extensive ice cover, Greenland is the second-largest island in the world, after Australia. The population, which is largely Eskimo, totals 53,800 (1987E), with residents of the capital, Nuuk (Godthåb), totaling 11,200. The indigenous language is Greenlandic. Fishing, mining, and seal hunting are the major economic activities. A number of oil concessions were awarded to international consortia in 1975, but most were subsequently abandoned.

Although under Danish control since the fourteenth century, the island was originally colonized by Norsemen and only through an apparent oversight was not detached from Denmark along with Norway at the Congress of Vienna in 1815. It became an integral part of the Danish state in 1953 and was granted internal autonomy, effective May 1, 1979, on the basis of a referendum held January 17. The island continues, however, to elect two representatives to the Danish *Folketing*. Since achieving autonomy, the island government has sought compensation from the United States for the 1953 relocation of indigenous villagers during the construction of US airbases in the northwest.

At a pre-autonomy general election held April 4, 1979, the socialist **Forward** (*Siumut*) party obtained 13 of 21 seats in the new parliament (*Landsting*), and *Siumut* leader Jonathan Motzfeldt subsequently formed a five-member executive (*Landsstyre*). Three other participating groups were the **Feeling of Community** (*Atassut*) party, led by Lars CHEMNITZ, which obtained the remaining 8 seats; the **Wage Earners** (*Sulissartut*); and the Marxist-Leninist **Eskimo Brotherhood** (*Inuit Ataqatigiit*), led by Arqaluk LYNGE.

At the balloting of April 1983 for an enlarged *Landsting* of 26 members, the *Siumut* and *Atassut* parties won 12 seats each, Motzfeldt again forming a government with the support of 2 *Inuit Ataqatigiit* representatives. A further election on June 6, 1984, necessitated by a nonconfidence vote two months earlier, yielded a formal coalition of the *Siumut* and *Inuit Ataqatigiit* parties, which had obtained 11 and 3 seats respectively. However, a disagreement ensued regarding the prime minister's alleged "passivity" over the projected installation of new radar equipment at the US airbase at Thule, forcing another early election on May 26, 1987, the results of which were: *Siumut* and *Attasuk,* 11 seats each; *Inuit Ataqatigiit,* 4; and a new political party, *Issittrup Partii* (Polar Party), representing the business community and fishing industry, 1. On June 9 Motzfeldt succeeded in forming a new administration based on the previous coalition.

In 1985, following a 1982 decision to withdraw from the EEC, an agreement with the Common Market came into effect whereby Greenland guarantees EEC members access to its Arctic waters in return for $23 million in annual aid for five years.

Prime Minister: Jonathan MOTZFELDT (Forward Party).

DJIBOUTI

Republic of Djibouti
République de Djibouti (French)
Jumhuriyah Djibouti (Arabic)

Political Status: Former French dependency; proclaimed independent June 27, 1977.

Area: 8,880 sq. mi. (23,000 sq. km.).

Population: 445,000 (1988E), including nonnationals.

Major Urban Center (1981E): DJIBOUTI (200,000).

Official Languages: French and Arabic.

Monetary Unit: Djibouti Franc (market rate March 1, 1988, 176.83 francs = $1US).

President: Hassan GOULED Aptidon; elected President by the Chamber of Deputies on June 24, 1977; popularly reelected for six-year terms in 1981 and on April 24, 1987.

Prime Minister: Barkat GOURAD Hamadou; designated by the President on September 30, 1978, following dissolution of the government of Abdallah Mohamed KAMIL on September 21; reappointed in 1981, 1982, and on November 23, 1987.

THE COUNTRY

Formerly known as French Somaliland and subsequently as the French Territory of the Afars and the Issas, the Republic of Djibouti is strategically located in East Africa just south of the Bab el Mandeb, a narrow strait that links the Gulf of Aden to the Red Sea. Djibouti, the capital, was declared a free port by the French in 1949 and has long been an important communications link between Africa, the Arabian peninsula, and the Far East. The largest single population group (40 percent) is the ethnically Somalian Issa tribe, which is concentrated in the vicinity of the capital, while the Afar tribe (35 percent) is essentially nomadic and ethnically linked to the Ethiopians. The remaining 25 percent consists largely of Yemeni Arabs and Somalis from Somalia.

Serviced by a number of international airlines and heavily dependent on commerce, Djibouti also provides Ethiopia with its only railroad link to the sea, with the port currently undergoing extensive rehabilitation. The country is largely barren, with less than 1 percent of its land under cultivation, few known natural resources and little industry. More than 60 percent of the population is unemployed and the government is heavily dependent on foreign aid from France and other western donors, several Arab countries, and various multilateral organizations.

GOVERNMENT AND POLITICS

Political background. The area known as French Somaliland was formally demarcated by agreement with Emperor Menelik II of Ethiopia in 1897 following a half-century of French penetration that included a series of treaties with indigenous chiefs between 1862 and 1885. Internal autonomy was granted in 1956, and in 1958 the voters of Somaliland elected to enter the French Community as an Overseas Territory. Proindependence demonstrations during a visit by President de Gaulle in August 1966 led to a referendum on March 19, 1967, in which a majority of the registered (predominantly Afar) voters opted for continued association with France. Somali protest riots were severely repressed, and the name of the dependency was changed to Territory of the Afars and the Issas to eliminate exclusive identification with the Somali ethnic group.

On December 31, 1975, a UN General Assembly resolution called on France to withdraw from the Territory, and during 1976 extensive discussions were held at Paris between leading tribal representatives and the French government. In the course of the talks, France tacitly agreed that the Afar president of the local Government Council, Ali ARIF Bourhan of the National Union for Independence (UNI), no longer represented a majority of the population, and approved a new nationality law governing eligibility for a second referendum on independence. Subsequently, Arif resigned, and on July 29 a new ten-member Council, composed of six Issas and four Afars, was formed.

On May 8, 1977, 98.8 percent of the electorate voted for independence while simultaneously approving a single list of 65 candidates for a Chamber of Deputies. Following the passage of relevant legislation by the French Parliament, the territory became independent as the Republic of Djibouti on June 27. Three days earlier, Issa leader Hassan GOULED Aptidon of the African People's League for Independence (LPAI) had been unanimously elected president of the Republic by the Chamber. On July 12, President Gouled named Afar leader Ahmed DINI Ahmed to head a 15-member Council of Ministers.

On December 17, Prime Minister Dini and four other Afar cabinet members resigned amid charges of "tribal repression", the duties of prime minister being assumed by the president until the designation of a new government headed by Mohamed Abdallah KAMIL on February 5, 1978. Kamil was in turn succeeded by Barkat GOURAD Hamadou on September 30, 1978. Gourad, an Afar advocate of "detribalization", formed subsequent governments on July 7, 1981 (following the reelection of President Gouled on June 12), and on June 5, 1982, after a legislative election held May 21.

Although all of the cabinets formed since independence have ostensibly been designed to strike a careful balance in tribal representation and all three prime ministers named by President Gouled have been Afars, charges of Issa domination have persisted, and most members of the opposition Djibouti People's Party (PPD) formed in August 1981 were from the ethnic minority. The regime's immediate response was to arrest PPD leader Moussa Ahmed IDRIS and the party's entire 12-member executive committee. All were released, however, by early January 1982, after the enactment of legislation establishing Gouled's Popular Rally for Progress (RPP) as the sole authorized party.

Despite a limit of presidential tenure to two terms (see Constitution and government, below), Gouled was permitted to run again in 1987 on the ground that he was initially appointed by the Chamber of Deputies rather than being popularly elected. As sole candidate, the incumbent was reported to have secured 90 percent of the vote in the April 24 poll.

Constitution and government. As of March 15, 1988, a formal constitution for Djibouti had not yet been adopted, although the Chamber of Deputies established under the 1977 independence referendum was empowered to act as a constituent assembly. In this capacity it approved a number of measures in 1981 dealing with the presidency and the legislature. On February 10, it decreed that candidates for the former could be nominated only by parties holding at least 25 Chamber seats, with balloting by universal suffrage and election for a six-year term that could be renewed only once. Following the presidential election of June 12 (at which the incumbent was the only candidate), the opposition PPD was organized, but was denied legal status on the basis of a "National Mobilization" law approved on October 19 that established a one-party system. As a result, all of the candidates at the parliamentary elections of 1982 and 1987 were presented by the government-supportive RPP.

The colonial judicial structure, based on both French and local law, was technically abolished at independence, although a successor system based on Muslim precepts remains imperfectly formulated. For administrative purposes the Republic is divided into five districts.

Foreign relations. Djibouti's small size and its mixed population of Ethiopian-oriented Afars and Somali-oriented Issas make it highly vulnerable in the context of continuing friction between its two neighbors. Both have recognized Djibouti's independence, but each has threatened to intervene in the event of military action in the area by the other. Despite bilateral accords in 1986 and 1987, Somalia has long regarded Djibouti as a "land to be redeemed", while the nearly 500-mile railroad between the port of Djibouti and Addis Ababa is viewed by Ethiopia as vital to its export-import trade, given the continuing revolt in its Red Sea province of Eritrea. The country's security depends on a French garrison of over 4,500 troops, which underscores Djibouti's strategic position given the Soviet military presence in Ethiopia and South Yemen.

In January 1986, Gouled hosted a six-nation conference to set up a Permanent Intergovernmental Authority on Drought and Development in East Africa (PIGADD), which marked the first meeting between the Ethiopian head of state, Lt. Col. Haile-Mariam, and President Siad Barre of Somalia since the two countries went to war in 1977. The other states participating in the conference as PIGADD members were Kenya, Sudan, and Uganda. Subsequently, peace talks between the 1977 combatants, mediated by Djibouti, were held at Addis Ababa in May, with Gouled reaffirming his country's role in the peace negotiations during a state visit to Ethiopia in September.

The repatriation of some 50,000 Ethiopians who had fled to Djibouti during the Ogaden conflict began in 1983, but was subsequently halted by the drought; it was resumed in December 1986 amid charges that the "voluntary" program would in fact expose the refugees to potential mistreatment. By 1987 it was estimated that fewer than 20,000 expatriates remained, with Djibouti insisting that they too must leave since resources were lacking for their assimilation.

Relations with Egypt (severed following the 1979 Egypt-Israel peace accord) were resumed in September 1986. By contrast, relations with another neighbor, the People's Democratic Republic of Yemen, had become strained because of the interception on August 17 of an Air Djibouti Boeing-720 on a flight from North Yemen to Addis Ababa. Forced to land at Aden, the plane was searched for supporters of former South Yemen president Ali Nasser Mohammed, who had been charged with murder following his ouster in January. Although Djibouti authorities charged the Yemenis with "an act of piracy", air and sea links were subsequently re-established between the two countries.

Current issues. In March 1987 a bomb exploded in a Djibouti cafe, killing 11 persons and giving rise to the prospect of domestic turmoil. However, it was determined that the action was directed largely against the French presence and the single-party balloting in April proceeded calmly, despite external objections by a newly formed opposition group (see MNDID, below). Domestic speculation centered on whether Gouled would complete his six-year term, some observers suggesting that he might withdraw in favor of a handpicked successor such as his nephew Ismail Omar GUELLAH.

POLITICAL PARTIES

Negotiations with the French that culminated in the referendum of May 8, 1977, were conducted by a United Patriotic Front representing five of the territory's major political groups. In preparing a list of candidates for the assembly election that accompanied the referendum, the Front acted under the name of the Popular Independence Rally (*Rassemblement Populaire pour l'Indépendance* — RPI). Its successor, the Popular Rally for Progress, was the only participant in the presidential election of June 1981 and was subsequently declared to be the country's only legal political party.

Government Party:

Popular Rally for Progress (*Rassemblement Populaire pour le Progrès* – RPP). The RPP was launched on March 4, 1979, its leading component being the socialist African People's League for Independence (*Ligue Populaire Africaine pour l'Indépendance* – LPAI). Long the principal spokesman for the Issa majority, the LPAI was not represented in the Afar-dominated preindependence Chamber of Deputies, although two of its members held ministerial posts. The RPP is directed by a Political Bureau appointed by Hassan Gouled in his capacity as party chairman.

Leaders: Hassan GOULED Aptidon (President of the Republic and Chairman of the Party), Gen. Moumin BAHDON Farah (Secretary General).

Illegal Opposition:

National Djibouti Movement for the Installation of Democracy (*Mouvement National Djiboutien pour l'Instauration de la Démocratie* – MNDID). The MNDID was formed in early 1986 under the leadership of Aden Robleh Awaleh, a former Gouled cabinet member and vice-president of the RPP, who had fled Djibouti after denying government allegations he had been a "silent partner" in a bombing during the January 1986 PIGADD meeting. Robleh, who accused the government of harassing him out of fear that he might become a presidential contender, called on supporters of the FLCS (below), of which he was once a member, and other antigovernment exiles to join the MNDID and create unified opposition to the "tyranny" of President Gouled. The party's initial communiqué called for promulgation of a constitution that would terminate the single-party system and usher in a "true liberal democracy". Robleh who traveled widely during 1986–1987 in search of support for the MNDID, established his headquarters at Paris, with a reported branch at Addis Ababa.

Leaders: Aden ROBLEH Awaleh, Moussa HUSSEIN, Omar Elmi KHAIREK.

Front for the Liberation of the Somali Coast (*Front de Libération de la Côte des Somalis* — FLCS). An Issa group currently headquartered at Mogadishu, Somalia, the FLCS has consistently urged that Djibouti be incorporated into a greater Somalia. While participating in the negotiations with the French and not actively opposing independence, none of its members was presented for election to the assembly in the list of May 1977.

Leaders: Abdallah WABERI Khalif (Chairman), Omar OSMAN Rabeh (Vice Chairman).

Democratic Front for the Liberation of Djibouti (*Front Démocratique pour la Libération de Djibouti* — FDLD). Organized on June 1, 1979, as a merger of two Afar groups — the National Union for Independence (*Union Nationale pour l'Indépendance* — UNI) and the Popular Movement for Liberation (*Mouvement Populaire pour la Libération* — MPL) — the FDLD accused the Hassan Gouled regime of repression, of collusion with the "imperialist enemy" (France), and of favoring annexation by Somalia. It denounced the 1981 presidential balloting as an "electoral masquerade" because of the absence of opposition candidates.

Prior to independence, the UNI had been split into majority and minority factions, the former (led by Ali Arif Bourhan) electing to boycott the negotiations with the French. In April 1977, however, Arif announced his "unconditional support" for Hassan Gouled's leadership and urged his followers to participate in both the referendum and the election of May 8. The MPL, composed of a group of young Marxists who boycotted the preindependence negotiations and campaigned for abstention at the May 8 election, was declared illegal following the resignation of Prime Minister Dini Ahmed in December.

On November 2, 1981, former MPL leader Shehem DAOUD announced from Paris that because of "the gravity of the situation in the Horn of Africa region", he was prepared to join forces with President Gouled, while some two dozen other FDLD adherents were reported to have returned from Ethiopia to accept an offer of amnesty in September 1982.

Leader: Mohamed KAMIL Ali.

Djibouti Liberation Movement (*Mouvement pour la Libération de Djibouti* — MLD). A Marxist group based in Ethiopia, the MLD supported independence but also boycotted the preindependence negotiations with the French as well as the legislative election of May 8, 1977.

Leader: Shehem DAOUD.

Djibouti People's Party (*Parti Populaire Djiboutien* — PPD). Organized on August 15, 1981, the PPD was immediately banned, with 13 of its leaders arrested. A further 40 supporters were imprisoned on September 9, although virtually all were released by early 1982. Composed largely of Afars, the party also attracted some Issas, of whom the best known was Omar OSMAN Rabeh, former vice chairman of the FLCS. Two founding PPD leaders, former prime minister Moussa Ahmed Idris and Mohamed Ahmed Issa, were elected to the Chamber of Deputies in 1987 by inclusion on the PRP list.

Leaders: Ahmed DINI Ahmed and Mohamed Abdallah KAMIL (former Prime Ministers).

LEGISLATURE

The **Chamber of Deputies** (*Chambre des Députés*) is a unicameral body whose 65 members are elected from a single list presented by the Popular Rally for Progress. The first balloting since independence was conducted on May 21, 1982; at the most recent poll of April 24, 1987, more than 85 percent of those voting were reported to have approved the official list.

President: Abdukader WABERI Askar.

CABINET

Prime Minister	Barkat Gourad Hamadou
Ministers	
Agriculture and Rural Development	Mohammed Moussa Chehem
Civil Service and Administrative Reform	Ismail Ali Youssouf
Finance and National Economy	Mohamed Djama Elabe
Foreign Affairs and Cooperation	Moumin Bahdon Farah
Health and Social Affairs	Ougoure Hassab Ibrahim
Industry	Salem Abdou Yahya
Interior, Posts and Telecommunications	Youssouf Ali Chirdon
Justice and Islamic Affairs	Helaf Orbis Ali
Labor and Social Welfare	Ahmed Ibrahim Abdi
National Defense	Hussein Barkad Siraj
National Education	Suleiman Farah Lodon
Planning and Land Development	Barkat Gourad Hamadou
Port and Maritime Affairs	Bourhan Ali Warki
Public Works, Urban Affairs and Housing	Ahmed Aden Youssouf
Sports, Youth and Culture	Omar Chirdon Abbas
Trade, Transport and Tourism	Moussa Bouraleh Robleh
Governor, Central Bank	Luc Aden Abdi Mohamed

NEWS MEDIA

Press. There are no daily newspapers. *La Nation de Djibouti* (4,000) appears weekly, while *Carrefour Africain* (500), a Roman Catholic publication, is issued twice monthly.

News agency. *Agence France-Presse* maintains an office at Djibouti.

Radio and television. *Radiodiffusion-Télévision de Djibouti* broadcasts in French, Afar, and Arabic to approximately 32,000 radio and 14,000 television receivers.

INTERGOVERNMENTAL REPRESENTATION

Ambassador to the US and Permanent Representative to the UN: Roble OLHAYE Oudine.

US Ambassador to Djibouti: (Vacant).

IGO Memberships (Non-UN): ACCT, ADF, AfDB, AFESD, EEC(L), *EIB,* IC, IDB, Interpol, LAS, NAM, OAU.

DOMINICA

Commonwealth of Dominica

Political Status: Former British dependency; joined West Indies Associated States in 1967; independent member of the Commonwealth since November 3, 1978.

Area: 290.5 sq. mi. (752.4 sq. km.).

Population: 73,795 (1981C), 90,000 (1988E).

Major Urban Centers (1981C): ROSEAU (8,279), Portsmouth (2,200).

Official Language: English (a French patois is widely spoken).

Monetary Unit: East Caribbean Dollar (market rate March 1, 1988, 2.70 EC dollars = $1US).

President: Clarence Augustus SEIGNORET; elected by the House of Assembly and inaugurated for a five-year term on December 19, 1983, succeeding Aurelius MARIE.

Prime Minister: Mary Eugenia CHARLES (Dominica Freedom Party); sworn in following election of July 21, 1980, succeeding James Oliver SERAPHINE (Dominica Democratic Labour Party); reappointed on July 4, 1985, following election of July 1.

THE COUNTRY

The largest of the West Indies Associated States as constituted in 1967, Dominica is located between Guadeloupe and Martinique in the Windward Islands of the eastern Caribbean (see map, p. 22). Claimed by both France and England until coming under the latter's exclusive control in 1805, it continues to reflect pronounced French influence. Most of its inhabitants are descended from West African slaves who were imported as plantation laborers in the seventeenth and eighteenth centuries, although a few hundred members of the Carib Indian tribe, which once controlled the entire Caribbean and gave the area its name, remain. Roman Catholicism is the dominant religion, but there are also long-established Anglican and Methodist communities.

One of the poorest and least developed of Third World countries, Dominica was devastated by hurricanes in 1979 and 1980, which struck the island with such force that it virtually destroyed the economy. Particularly hard hit was banana production, which typically accounts for some 70 percent of the country's exports. An increase in tourist arrivals, some inflow of foreign capital in support of labor-intensive export industry, and improved banana output have since yielded a measure of economic recovery, although sustained development is hindered by poor infrastructure, including an inadequate road system.

GOVERNMENT AND POLITICS

Political background. An object of contention between Britain and France in the eighteenth century, Dominica was administered after 1833 as part of the British Leeward Islands. In 1940, it was incorporated into the Windward Islands, which also included Grenada, St. Lucia, and St. Vincent. It participated in the Federation of the West Indies from 1958 to 1962 and became one of the six internally self-governing West Indies Associated States in March 1967.

The West Indies Act of 1966 stipulated that the islands' external dependency on Britain was completely voluntary and could be terminated by either party at any time. Thus, having failed to agree on a plan for regional unity, the Associated States declared in December 1975 that each would separately seek full independence. The details of an independence constitution for Dominica were discussed at a London conference in May 1977, and in July 1978 both

houses of Parliament approved an Order in Council terminating the association as of November 3. Pending a new election, the existing premier, Patrick Roland JOHN, was designated prime minister, while the incumbent governor, Sir Louis COOLS-LARTIQUE, continued as interim chief of state.

Following government rejection of an opposition nominee for president, the speaker of the House, Fred E. DEGAZON, was elected to the largely ceremonial post by the legislature and was sworn in December 22, 1978. Subsequently, in the wake of an extended general strike and a series of opposition demonstrations at Roseau, President Degazon retired to Britain, his successor, Sir Cools-Lartique, also being forced to resign only 24 hours after his return to office on June 15, 1979. On June 21, Prime Minister John was obliged to resign after a number of his legislative supporters had moved into opposition, the interim president, Jenner ARMOUR, designating former agriculture minister James Oliver SERAPHINE as his successor. At legislative balloting on July 21, 1980, both Seraphine and John were denied reelection, and Mary Eugenia CHARLES of the victorious Dominica Freedom Party (DFP) was asked by President Aurelius MARIE (who had succeeded Armour in late February) to form a new government.

There were two attempts by apparent supporters of former prime minister John to overthrow the government in 1981, the second of which included an effort to free John, who had been jailed under a state of emergency. Following his acquittal and release from prison in June 1982, John moved to reunify the opposition Democratic Labour Party, from which Seraphine had withdrawn in 1979. The effort succeeded in mid-1983, Seraphine being designated DLP leader and John his deputy. In early 1985, opposition forces further closed ranks as the DLP joined with the United Democratic Labour Party (UDLP) and the Dominica Liberation Movement Alliance (DLMA) to form the Labour Party of Dominica (LPD), which, however, failed to oust the DFP at the parliamentary election of July 1. Subsequently, John was convicted on retrial of the 1981 conspiracy charge, being sentenced in October to 12 years' imprisonment.

Constitution and government. Under the constitution which became effective upon independence, the Commonwealth of Dominica is a "sovereign democratic republic" based upon a respect for the principles of social justice. The head of state is a president who is elected for a five-year term by the legislature upon joint nomination by the prime minister and the leader of the opposition, or by secret ballot in the event of disagreement between the two. The president may not hold office for more than two terms. Parliament consists of the president and a House of Assembly, which includes one representative from each electoral constituency (as defined by an Electoral Boundaries Commission) and nine senators who, according to the wishes of the legislature, may be either elected or appointed (five on the advice of the prime minister and four on the advice of the leader of the opposition). The term of the House is five years, subject to dissolution. The president appoints as prime minister the elected member who commands a majority in the House; in addition, he may remove the prime minister from office if, following a no-confidence vote, the latter does not resign or request a dissolution. Provision is made for a Public Service Commission to make appointments to and exercise disciplinary control over the public service, as well as for a Police Service Commission and a Public Service Board of Appeal. The court system embraces the Supreme Court of the West Indies Associated States (redesignated, in respect of Dominica, as the Eastern Caribbean Supreme Court), courts of summary jurisdiction, and district courts (the latter dealing with minor criminal offenses and civil cases involving sums of not more than $EC500). Partially elected local-government bodies function in the principal towns and villages, with Roseau and Portsmouth controlled by town councils consisting of both elected and nominated members.

Foreign relations. Although Dominica was admitted to the Commonwealth at independence and to the United Nations shortly thereafter, its diplomatic ties are extremely limited. It maintains only token representation at Washington, most official contacts with the United States being maintained through the US ambassador to Barbados, who is also accredited to Roseau. Regional memberships include the Organization of American States and various Caribbean groupings, including the Organization of Eastern Caribbean States.

Closely allied with the United States, upon which it relies heavily for foreign aid, Dominica joined the multinational force that participated in the US-led invasion of Grenada in October 1983 (see article on Grenada), and supported the United States' bombing of Libya in April 1986.

Current issues. By 1986 banana production had rebounded strongly from the devastating hurricanes of 1979–1980 and the government announced plans to increase exports further by distributing 2,000 acres of agricultural land to small farmers. In addition, a program to stimulate private investment, improve the balance of payments, and reduce civil service expenditure was endorsed by the IMF, which agreed to provide $1.9 million in assistance through 1989. In mid-1987 Prime Minister Charles announced the conclusion of a major fisheries agreement with the European Community and late in the year indicated that her government would go ahead with construction of a major cardboard box factory, despite protests from St. Lucia, where the region's only existing such facility was located.

The major political developments during 1987 concerned allegations (emphatically denied by the government) that Prime Minister Charles had accepted a payment of $100,000 by the US Central Intelligence Agency for her support of the invasion of Grenada in 1983 and an apparent gerrymandering of electoral arrangements at Portsmouth to permit the DFP to take control of a town council that had traditionally been an opposition stronghold.

POLITICAL PARTIES

The Dominican party system has been in a state of considerable flux since independence. In early 1979 a number of parliamentary members of the original Dominica Labour Party (DLP) withdrew under the leadership of Oliver Seraphine to form the Democratic Labour Party (subse-

quently the Dominica Democratic Labour Party — DDLP), while the cabinet named by Seraphine on June 21 drew upon a recently organized Committee of National Salvation (CNS) — an alliance of former opposition groups that included the Dominica Freedom Party (DFP), headed by Eugenia Charles. The CNS was, however, divided between a left-wing faction, representing trade-union interests, and the traditionally conservative DFP. Another component of the CNS, the National Alliance Party (NAP), had recently been formed by Michael Douglas, who subsequently became finance minister in the Seraphine government.

The 1980 election was contested by a rump of the DLP, led by Patrick John; the DDLP; the DFP; and a recently organized Dominica Liberation Movement Alliance (DLMA). The principal contenders in 1985 were the DFP and the Labour Party of Dominica (LPD).

Government Party:

Dominica Freedom Party (DFP). A right-of-center grouping long associated with propertied interests at Roseau, the DFP won 17 of 21 elective House of Assembly seats in 1980, and 15 of 21 in 1985.

Leader: Mary Eugenia CHARLES (Prime Minister).

Opposition Parties:

Labour Party of Dominica (LPD). The LPD was formed in early 1985 by merger of the Dominica Labour Party (DLP), the United Dominica Labour Party (UDLP), and the Dominica Liberation Movement Alliance (DLMA). The dominant party after the 1975 election, the DLP was weakened by the defection of Oliver Seraphine and others in 1979 as well as by a variety of charges against party leader Patrick John, including an allegation that, as prime minister, he had attempted to secure South African backing for a number of developmental projects. The DLP won no seats at the 1980 election, and John was subsequently charged with attempting to overthrow the government.

Upon his withdrawal from the DLP, Seraphine launched the Democratic Labour Party, restyled the Dominica Democratic Labour Party (DDLP) prior to the 1980 election, at which it secured two Assembly seats without, however, returning its leader. In late 1981, the opposition parliamentarian, Michael Douglas, who claimed to have been designated DDLP leader at a meeting in September, was expelled from the party and organized the UDLP, while Seraphine brought the DDLP back into the DLP in mid-1983.

A self-proclaimed "new left" grouping, the DLMA was organized by Atherton MARTIN following his dismissal from the Seraphine government in October 1979, allegedly for advocating closer links to Cuba. In January 1984, an investigation was launched into the activities of the group's general secretary, William REVIERE, following the discovery, during the Grenada invasion, of letters from him requesting aid from Eastern-bloc countries.

In a contest for the LDP leadership, Douglas defeated Seraphine at a merger conference by a vote of 12-3, Seraphine and Henry Dyer, former minister of communications and works in the Charles government, being elected deputy leaders. Concurrently, John was named LDP general secretary, a post he was obliged to vacate, along with his Assembly seat, when he was reimprisoned in October. (John resigned from the party in September 1987 in a move that was interpreted as aimed at securing his freedom.)

Despite a dispute as to who would stand in a by-election to replace John, Douglas was reelected party leader at an August 1986 LPD convention; a new constitution was also approved which created a National Council as the party's governing body.

Leaders: Michael A. DOUGLAS (Leader of the Opposition), R.E. HENRY (Deputy Leader), Oliver J. SERAPHINE, Henry DYER, Jerome BARZEY (General Secretary).

Dominica Progressive Force (DPF). The left-wing DPF was organized in 1983 by a former member of the DLP. It contested 9 seats at the July 1985 election, winning none.

Leader: Lennard BAPTISTE.

LEGISLATURE

Parliament consists of the president, ex officio, and a **House of Assembly** that encompasses 21 elected representatives and 9 senators who, at the discretion of the House, may be either appointed or elected. Following the election of July 1, 1985, the Dominica Freedom Party held 15 representative seats and the Labour Party of Dominica, 5. A sixth opposition seat was held by Rosie DOUGLAS, who, reportedly because of links to Cuba and Libya, had been denied a place on the LPD list headed by his brother and, somewhat inexplicably, ran as a candidate of the United Dominica Labor Party, despite inclusion of the UDLP in the preelection merger. The DFP gained a seat at a May 1986 by-election to replace John, and another in August 1987, when a former LPD member who had declared as an independent 14 months earlier joined the majority. At present, the DFP is represented by 5 nominated senators and the LPD by 4.

Speaker: Marie Davies PIERRE.

CABINET

Prime Minister	Mary Eugenia Charles
Deputy Prime Minister	Charles Maynard
Ministers	
Agriculture, Industry, Lands and Surveys	Charles Maynard
Communications, Public Works, and Road Construction	Alleyne John Carbon
Community Development, Housing and Social Affairs	Heskeith Alexander
Defense	Mary Eugenia Charles
Economic Affairs	Mary Eugenia Charles
Education and Sports	Henry George
Finance	Mary Eugenia Charles
Foreign Affairs	Mary Eugenia Charles
Health, Water and Sewage	Ronan David
Legal Affairs, Immigration and Labor	Brian Alleyne
Tourism and Trade	Charles Maynard
Attorney General	Brian Alleyne

NEWS MEDIA

Press. The following are published at Roseau: *New Chronicle* (4,000), progressive weekly; *Official Gazette* (600), government weekly.

Radio and television. The government-operated Dominica Broadcasting Corporation provides radio service in English and French patois, while the privately owned Radio Jumbo offers programming in French. There were approximately 36,000 radio receivers in 1987. There is also a television relay station which offers programming from CBC Barbados for a limited number of local receivers.

INTERGOVERNMENTAL REPRESENTATION

Ambassador to the US: McDonald Phillip BENJAMIN.

US Ambassador to Dominica: Paul A. RUSSO (resident in Barbados).

Permanent Representative to the UN: Franklin Andrew BARON.

IGO Memberships (Non-UN): ACCT, Caricom, CDB, CWTH, EEC(L), *EIB,* ICCO, Interpol, IWC, OAS, OECS, UPEB.

DOMINICAN REPUBLIC

República Dominicana

Political Status: Independent republic established in 1844; under constitutional regime reestablished July 1, 1966.

Area: 18,816 sq. mi. (48,734 sq. km.).

Population: 5,647,977 (1981C), 6,694,000 (1988E).

Major Urban Centers (1981C): SANTO DOMINGO (1,313,172); Santiago de los Caballeros (278,638); La Romana (91,571).

Official Language: Spanish.

Monetary Unit: Peso (principal rate March 1, 1988, 5.30 pesos = $1US).

President: Joaquin BALAGUER Ricardo (Social Christian Reformist Party); elected May 16, 1986, and inaugurated for a four-year term on August 16, succeeding Salvador JORGE Blanco (Dominican Revolutionary Party).

Vice President: Carlos A. MORALES Troncoso (Social Christian Reformist Party); elected May 16 and inaugurated on August 16, 1986, the office having been vacant since the death on January 20, 1983, of Manuel FERNANDEZ Mármol (Dominican Revolutionary Party).

THE COUNTRY

The Dominican Republic occupies the eastern two-thirds of the Caribbean island of Hispaniola, which is shared with Haiti. The terrain is varied, including mountains, fertile plains, and some desert. About 70 percent of the population is of mixed ancestry, both mestizo and mulatto, with small minorities (about 15 percent each) of pure Caucasian (Spanish) and Negro origin. The cultural tradition is distinctly Spanish, and 98 percent of the people profess allegiance to the Roman Catholic Church, although other religions are permitted. In 1982, 22 percent of the adult female population was in the official labor force, not counting unpaid agricultural family workers. Female representation in government has long been virtually nonexistent.

The economy is primarily agricultural, the leading cash crops being sugar, coffee, cocoa, and tobacco. The agricultural sector employs nearly 50 percent of the labor force. Manufacturing is largely oriented toward agricultural processing, but deposits of gold, silver, ferronickel, and bauxite contribute significantly to export earnings. Since 1981, spiralling foreign indebtedness and plummeting commodity prices have severely crippled the economy, with austerity measures further inhibiting the capacity of most individuals to meet basic food and shelter needs. During 1986 unemployment was estimated at about 30 percent, while inflation declined to about 10 percent (from nearly 38 percent in 1985), largely because of the elimination of food subsidies and a substantial drop in the value of the peso; by contrast, substantial food price increases in 1987 yielded a reescalation in inflation to an estimated 40 percent by the end of the year.

GOVERNMENT AND POLITICS

Political background. Since winning its independence from Spain in 1821 and from Haiti in 1844, the Dominican Republic has been plagued by recurrent domestic conflict and foreign intervention. Controlled by an American military governor from 1916 to 1924, the country entered into a 30-year period of rule under Gen. Rafael Leonidas TRUJILLO Molina in 1930. Trujillo ruled personally from 1930 to 1947 and indirectly thereafter until his assassination in 1961, his death giving rise to renewed political turmoil. An election in December 1962 led to the inauguration of Juan BOSCH Gaviño, a left-of-center democrat, as president in February 1963. Bosch was overthrown in September 1963 by a military coup led by (then) Col. Elías WESSIN y Wessín. Subsequently, the military installed a civilian triumvirate which ruled until April 1965, when civil war erupted. US military forces (later incorporated into an OAS-sponsored Inter-American Peace Force) intervened on April 28, 1965, and imposed a truce while arrangements were made to establish a provisional government and prepare for new elections. Dr. Joaquín BALAGUER, a moderate who had been president at the time of Trujillo's assassination, defeated Bosch at an election held in June 1966. Emphasizing material development and political restraint, Balaguer was reelected in 1970 and successfully dealt with an attempted coup in 1971. In 1974 he was virtually unopposed for election to a third term, all of his principal opponents having withdrawn in anticipation of election irregularities. After the election, Silvestre Antonio GUZMAN Fernández, speaking on behalf of the opposition coalition, demanded annulment of the results; however, he agreed not to press the demand after securing Balaguer's assurance that he would not seek further reelection in 1978. Despite his pledge, Balaguer contested the 1978 election but was defeated by Guzmán Fernández by a three-to-two majority. The inauguration of the new president on August 16 was the first occasion in Dominican history that an elected incumbent yielded power to an elected successor.

In late 1981 three-time former chief executive Balaguer surprised many observers by announcing that he would seek to regain the presidency in 1982, despite his age (74) and failing eyesight. The announcement came in the wake of mounting economic problems and a significant weakening of President Guzmán's influence within the ruling Dominican Revolutionary Party (PRD). At midyear, Guzmán declared that he would not seek reelection and formally endorsed Vice President Jacobo MAJLUTA Azar

as his successor. However, at a PRD convention in November Majluta was decisively rejected in favor of Guzmán's arch rival, Salvador JORGE Blanco, who had been defeated for the 1978 nomination and whom Guzmán had succeeded in ousting from the party presidency in late 1979.

At the May 1982 election, Jorge Blanco defeated Balaguer by a 10 percent margin, while the PRD retained its majority in both houses of Congress. On July 4, President Guzmán died of an apparently self-inflicted gunshot wound, being succeeded on an acting basis by Majluta Azar until Jorge Blanco's inauguration on August 16.

At the balloting of May 16, 1986, Balaguer was elected to a fourth term, narrowly defeating Majluta after the PRD had succumbed to severe internal friction attributed primarily to a left-wing faction led by José Francisco PEÑA Gómez.

Constitution and government. The constitution of November 28, 1966, established a unitary republic consisting of 26 provinces and a National District. Executive power is exercised by the president, who is elected (together with the vice president) by direct vote for a four-year term. Members of the bicameral National Congress, consisting of a Senate and a Chamber of Deputies, are likewise elected for four-year terms. The judicial system is headed by a Supreme Court of Justice, which consists of at least nine judges elected by the Senate. The Supreme Court appoints judges of lower courts operating at the provincial and local levels. All three branches of government participate in the legislative process. Bills for consideration by the legislature may be introduced by members of either house, by the president, and by judges of the Supreme Court.

For administrative purposes the provinces are divided into municipal districts and townships. Provincial governors are appointed by the president, while the municipalities are governed by elected mayors and municipal councils.

Foreign relations. A member of the United Nations and most of its Specialized Agencies, the Dominican Republic also participates in the Organization of American States. It maintains diplomatic relations with most Western countries but not with the Communist nations. Relations with the United States were long strained by the latter's history of intervention but have substantially improved since the reestablishment of constitutional government in 1966. Recurring tensions and frontier disputes with Haiti have also influenced Dominican external affairs, periodically resulting in closing of the 193 miles of common border.

Current issues. The Blanco administration, which inherited an external debt of more than $1.1 billion, was consistently plagued by unrest stemming from IMF-mandated austerity measures and other efforts to resolve the country's economic difficulties. During 1985, the GDP declined by 1.2 percent, while foreign indebtedness, despite controls, rose to $2.9 billion. Following his return to office, President Balaguer leveled charges of corruption against his predecessor and in early 1987 stated that the government would be unable to meet repayment obligations to the IMF and other creditors on a debt that had escalated further to $3.8 billion. Although coffee prices were high, sugar — upon which 40 percent of the country's income depended — had sunk to a record low of $0.05 on the world market, with the United States threatening to cut preferential purchases by more than one-third. In an effort to ward off such an eventuality, the government indicated that it would act on US demands to curb drug trafficking. In October, the president ordered the retirement of 23 generals (some accused of involvement in the drug trade). Earlier, he had pledged to "clean up" the judiciary and the state bureaucracy. In response to suggestions that poor health might impair his capacity to govern, he intimated that Vice President Morales, a former Gulf and Western executive, would be a capable successor, should the need arise.

By early 1988 expectations that the aging chief executive might be able to rescue the country from its economic malaise had substantially dimmed. During February and March a wave of strikes, rioting, and looting erupted in response to a government announcement of major food price increases. The disturbances came in the wake of mounting business opposition to the president's fiscal policies, which included a campaign against tax evasion and currency trafficking, in addition to increased import duties, a 6 percent value-added tax on services, and the introduction of property taxation.

POLITICAL PARTIES

The shifting political groupings that have appeared in the Dominican Republic since the fall of Trujillo reflect diverse ideological viewpoints as well as the influence of specific personalities. Party divisions and splinter groups are common.

Presidential Party:

Social Christian Reformist Party (*Partido Reformista Social Cristiano* — PRSC). Created in 1963 by Joaquín Balaguer, the PRSC stresses a policy of economic austerity, national reconstruction, and political consensus. Drawing heavily on peasant and middle-class support, it won the elections of 1966, 1970, and 1974, but lost in 1978 after its leader had withdrawn a pledge not to become a candidate for a fourth term. It lost again in 1982, Balaguer being defeated in the presidential poll by a 37–47 percent margin; however, public recollection of a strong economy under Balaguer gave the ex-president a narrow victory over his PRD opponent in May 1986.

Leaders: Dr. Joaquín BALAGUER Ricardo (President of the Republic), Carlos A. MORALES Troncoso (Vice President of the Republic), Joaquín RICARDO (Secretary General).

Other Parties:

Dominican Revolutionary Party (*Partido Revolucionario Dominicano* — PRD). Founded as a left-democratic grouping by former president Juan Bosch Gaviño in 1939, the PRD rejects communism and Castroism but has been critical of American "imperialism" and "neo-colonialism". A member of the Socialist International since 1966, the party boycotted both the 1970 and 1974 elections but won the presidency and a majority in the Chamber of Deputies under the relatively conservative leadership of Antonio Guzmán Fernández in 1978, repeating the performance under Salvador Jorge Blanco in 1982. A three-way split within the PRD in the run-up to the 1986 balloting raised two distinct possibilities: that former vice president Majluta Azar might compete as the nominee of his right-wing *La Estructura* faction, and that Blanco supporters, unhappy with the president's endorsement of left-leaning José Peña Gómez, would rally for reelection of the incumbent. In July 1985, Majluta registered *La Estructura* as a separate party, but in January 1986 was named the PRD candidate with Peña Gómez succeeding him as party president. Majluta attributed his defeat in the May balloting to Peña Gómez, many of whose followers were reported to have supported Juan Bosch of the PLD (below). Lacking a congressional majority after the election, President Balaguer

named a number of PRD/*La Estructura* members to the cabinet formed in late August.

Leaders: José Francisco PEÑA Gómez (leader of *Bloque Institucional* faction and President of the Party), Salvador JORGE Blanco (former President of the Republic), Jacobo MAJLUTA Azar (leader of *La Estructura* faction), Andrés van der HORST (*La Estructura*), Hatuey DECAMPS (Secretary General).

Dominican Liberation Party (*Partido de la Liberación Dominicana* — PLD). The PLD, a breakaway faction of the PRD, organized as a separate party under PRD founder Juan Bosch Gaviño during the 1974 campaign. Bosch ran unsuccessfully as PLD presidential candidate in both 1978 and 1982, securing 9.8 percent of the vote on the latter occasion. Subsequently, he was highly critical of the Blanco regime's economic policies as well as its often harsh anti-protest tactics. Although popular opinion polls showed Bosch running second to Balaguer in late 1985, the PLD nominee placed third, with 18.4 percent of the vote, in the 1986 presidential balloting.

Leaders: Juan BOSCH Gaviño, Jesús Antonio PICHARDO, Lidio CADET (Secretary General).

Quisqueyan Democratic Party (*Partido Quisqueyano Demócrata* — PQD). A right-wing group, the PQD was formed by Gen. Elías Wessín y Wessín following his departure into exile in the United States after the civil disturbances of 1965; two years earlier, the general had led the military coup that overthrew President Juan Bosch. The PQD supported Wessín y Wessín in the 1970 presidential campaign and participated in the coalition which boycotted the 1974 election. In September 1977 General Wessín announced his candidacy for the 1978 presidential election but subsequently withdrew in favor of MID candidate Francisco Augusto Lora. Wessín ran a distant fourth in the 1982 presidential balloting. In November 1986 he was named interior minister in the Balaguer administration.

Leaders: Gen. (Ret.) Elías WESSÍN y Wessín (President), Juan Manuel TAVERAS (Secretary General).

Democratic Integration Movement (*Movimiento de Integración Democrática* — MID). Organized as the *Movimiento de Integración Nacional* in support of the 1970 presidential candidacy of Francisco Augusto Lora, the right-wing MID was joined by several other parties in promoting Lora's candidacy in 1978.

Leader: Dr. Francisco Augusto LORA.

Movement of National Conciliation (*Movimiento de Conciliación Nacional* — MCN). Formed in late 1968 to sponsor the presidential candidacy of Héctor GARCIA Godoy, former Dominican ambassador to the United States and provisional president of the Republic after the 1965 revolution, the MCN also boycotted the 1974 election and joined the coalition supporting Francisco Augusto Lora in 1978.

Leaders: Dr. Jaime M. FERNANDEZ (President), Víctor MENA (Secretary).

Revolutionary Social Christian Party (*Partido Revolucionario Social Cristiano* — PRSC). A party of the democratic Left which rejects both capitalism and communism, the PRSC is patterned after other Christian Democratic parties of Latin America and draws most of its supporters from young professionals as well as from youth and labor. Its youth wing is considerably more radical in its approach than is the party mainstream.

Leaders: Dr. Claudio Isidoro ACOSTA (President), Alfonso Moreno MARTINEZ, Dr. Alfonso LOCKWARD (Secretary General).

Dominican Communist Party (*Partido Comunista Dominicano* — PCD). The PCD, a pro-Moscow group, was outlawed in 1964 but permitted to resume a legal existence in November 1977. At a National Convention on January 1, 1978, the party nominated Narciso Isa Conde as the first Communist presidential candidate in Dominican history. In 1982 it renominated Isa Conde; it did so again in 1986, although formally a member of a **Dominican Leftist Front** (*Frente de Izquierda Dominicana* — FID), formed in 1983, which called for an electoral boycott.

Leaders: José Israel CUELLO, Silvano LORA, Narciso ISA Conde (Secretary General and 1986 presidential candidate).

Dominican Popular Movement (*Movimiento Popular Dominicano* — MPD). Organized in 1965 as a pro-Peking extremist group, the MPD subsequently assumed a measure of respectability as part of the coalition that attempted to prevent President Balaguer from winning a third term in 1974.

Leader: Julio de PEÑA Valdés.

Joining the PRSC, PLD, PQD, and PCD in presenting presidential candidates in recent elections have been the **Social Democratic Alliance** (*Alianza Social Demócrata*—ASD); the **Christian Popular Party** (*Partido Popular Cristiano*—PPC) backed by representatives of the Unification Church; and the **Progressive National Force** (*Fuerza Nacional Progresivo-*—FNP). In addition, the far-right **Constitutional Action Party** (*Partido Acción Constitucional*—PAC) captured one seat in the Chamber of Deputies in 1982. In late 1985 the vice-president of the PPC, Martin BAUER, who had been accused of funneling party funds to right-wing groups in other Latin American countries, was found murdered near Santo Domingo.

LEGISLATURE

The **National Congress** (*Congreso Nacional*) consists of a Senate and a Chamber of Deputies, both directly elected for four-year terms. Anticipating fraud, all major opposition parties boycotted the 1974 balloting, but presented candidates thereafter.

Senate (*Senado*). The Senate consists of 30 members, 1 from each province and the National District. Following the election of May 16, 1986, the Social Christian Reformist Party held 21 seats; the Dominican Revolutionary Party, 7; and the Dominican Liberation Party, 2.
President: Florentino CARAVAJAL Suero.

Chamber of Deputies (*Cámara de Diputados*). The Chamber presently consists of 120 members elected on the basis of 1 deputy for every 50,000 inhabitants, with at least 2 from each province. As a result of the election of May 16, 1986, the Social Christian Reformist Party held 56 seats; the Dominican Revolutionary Party, 48; and the Democratic Liberation Party, 16.
President: Ramón EDILIO Vargas.

CABINET

President	Joaquin Balaguer Ricardo
Vice President	Carlos A. Morales Troncoso
Secretaries of State	
Agriculture	Miguel de Jesus Amezquita
Armed Forces	Lt. Gen. António Imbert Barreras
Education, Fine Arts and Public Worship	Pedro C. Pichardo
Finance	Roberto Martínez Villanueva
Foreign Relations	Donald Reid Cabral
Industry and Commerce	Rafael Conrado Marion-Landais
Interior and Police	Elias Wessin y Wessin
Labor	Mario Read Vittini
Presidency	Rafael Bello Andino
Public Health and Social Welfare	Dr. Ney Arias Lora
Public Works and Communications	Marcos A. Subero Sajuin
Sports, Physical Education and Recreation	Temistocles Metz
Tourism	Fernando Rainieri Marranzini
Without Portfolio	Simón Tomás Fernández
	Francisco Augusto Lora
Attorney General	Pura Núñez
Governor, Central Bank	Roberto Saladín

NEWS MEDIA

Press. The following privately owned newspapers are published at Santo Domingo, unless otherwise noted: *Listín Diario* (55,000), moderate independent; *El Nacional* (45,000), leftist nationalist; *El Caribe* (28,000), moderate nationalist; *La Noticia* (18,000); *La Información* (Santiago, 14,500), conservative independent.
News agencies. There is no domestic facility; several foreign agencies maintain bureaus at Santo Domingo.

Radio and television. Broadcasting is supervised by the *Dirección General de Correos y Telecomunicaciones.* There are over 100 radio stations as well as 7 commercial television networks, 2 of which also offer educational programming. There were approximately 700,000 radio and 450,000 television receivers in 1987.

INTERGOVERNMENTAL REPRESENTATION

Ambassador to the US: Eduardo A. LEON.

US Ambassador to the Dominican Republic: Lowell C. KILDAY.

Permanent Representative to the UN: Juan Aristides TAVERAS Guzmán.

IGO Memberships (Non-UN): Caricom, Geplacea, IADB, IBA, ICM, ICO, Intelsat, Interpol, ISO, IWTC, OAS, OPANAL, PCA, SELA, UPEB.

ECUADOR

Republic of Ecuador
República de Ecuador

Political Status: Gained independence from Spain in 1822 (as part of Gran Colombia); independent republic established in 1830; present constitution approved January 15, 1978, with effect from August 10, 1979.

Area: 109,482 sq. mi. (283,561 sq. km.).

Population: 8,060,712 (1982C, not adjusted for under-enumeration), 10,981,000 (1988E, adjusted).

Major Urban Centers (1986E): QUITO (1,093,000); Guayaquil (1,509,000); Cuenca (193,000); Ambato (122,000).

Official Language: Spanish.

Monetary Unit: Sucre (market rate March 1, 1988, 244.50 sucres = $1US).

President: León FEBRES Cordero Rivadeneira (Social Christian Party); elected May 6 and inaugurated August 10, 1984, for a four-year term, succeeding Dr. Osvaldo HURTADO Larrea (Popular Democracy-Christian Democratic Union).

President Elect: Rodrigo BORJA Cevallos (Democratic Left); elected May 8, 1988; to be inaugurated for a four-year term on August 10.

Vice President: Blasco Manuel PEÑAHERRERA Padilla (Radical Liberal Party); elected May 6, 1984, for a term concurrent with that of the President, succeeding León ROLDOS Aguilera (Democratic Party).

Vice President Elect: Luis PARODI (Democratic Left); elected on May 8, 1988, for a term concurrent with the President Elect.

THE COUNTRY

South America's third-smallest republic has four main geographic regions: the Pacific coastal plain (*Costa*), the Andes highlands (*Sierra*), the sparsely populated eastern jungle (*Oriente*), and the Galapagos Islands (*Archipélago de Colón*) in the Pacific. The population is roughly 40 percent Indian, 40 percent mestizo, 10 percent Caucasian, and 10 percent Negro. Although Spanish is the official language, numerous Indian languages are spoken, the most important of which is Quechua. Approximately 90 percent of the population professes Roman Catholicism, but other religions are practiced, including tribal religion among the Indians. In 1980, 26 percent of the paid labor force was female, primarily in domestic service, market trade, and transient agricultural labor; female participation in government is virtually nonexistent.

Adverse climate, jungle terrain, volcanic activity, and earthquakes limit the country's habitable area and have slowed its economic development. The economy is primarily agricultural, with approximately one-half of the population engaged in farming, mainly on a subsistence level. The most important crops are bananas (of which Ecuador is the world's largest exporter), coffee, and cocoa. Hardwoods and balsa are harvested from the forests, while Ecuadorian Pacific waters are a prime tuna-fishing area. Gold, silver, and copper continue to be mined, and production from Amazonian oil fields has placed Ecuador second only to Venezuela in petroleum output among South American countries. Other energy resources include natural gas deposits in the Gulf of Guayaquil and considerable hydroelectric potential.

GOVERNMENT AND POLITICS

Political background. Charismatic individuals rather than political platforms have dominated Ecuador's political life through most of the period since the country's liberation from Spanish rule in 1822 and its establishment as an independent republic in 1830. An historical division between Conservatives and Liberals (now of little practical significance) emerged in the nineteenth century, the Conservatives being based in the highlands and the Liberals on the coast.

A bright spot in Ecuadorian political life occurred in 1948 with the election of Galo PLAZA Lasso to the presidency. The first chief executive since 1924 to complete his full term in office, Plaza Lasso created a climate of stability and economic progress, while his successor, José María VELASCO Ibarra, stood out in a lengthy catalog of interrupted presidencies and military juntas. Prior to his election in 1952 (his only full term), Velasco had served twice as president, in 1934–1935 and in 1944–1947. He was subsequently elected in 1960 and in 1968, but both terms were prematurely ended by coups, the first in 1961. His replacement, Carlos Julio AROSEMENA Monroy, was himself ousted by a military junta in July 1963. During his last term in office, Velasco dissolved the National Congress and assumed dictatorial powers in mid-1970 to cope with a financial emergency. He was deposed for a fourth time in

February 1972, the stimulus to military intervention being the approach of a presidential election in which Assad BUCARAM Elmhalim, a populist politican, appeared the likely winner. The military leadership, under Gen. Guillermo RODRIGUEZ Lara, canceled the election, nominally restored the Liberal constitution of 1945, and advanced a "nationalist, military, and revolutionary" program emphasizing the objectives of social justice and popular welfare.

In December 1975, President Rodríguez announced his intention to make way for a return to civilian rule, but his actual departure in January 1976 was precipitated by a government crisis during which the entire cabinet resigned. A three-man junta headed by Vice Adm. Alfredo POVEDA Burbano which succeeded Rodríguez stated that the 1972 program of the armed forces would be honored and that the nation would be returned to civilian leadership within two years; however, it was not until July 16, 1978, that a presidential election, in which no candidate obtained a majority of votes, was held. At a runoff on April 29, 1979, the center-left candidate, Jaime ROLDOS Aguilera, defeated his conservative opponent, Sixto DURAN Ballén, by a more than two-to-one majority and was inaugurated, without incident, on August 10.

Roldós, his minister of defense, and a number of others were killed in a plane crash on May 24, 1981, and the Christian Democratic vice president, Osvaldo HURTADO Larrea was immediately sworn in to complete the remainder of his five-year term. On June 2 the late president's brother, León ROLDOS Aguilera, by a legislative margin of one vote, was elected to the vice presidency.

A dispute between the president and vice president in early 1982, ostensibly over rapprochement with neighboring Peru (see Foreign relations, below), led to the resignation of two *roldosista* ministers and, amid mounting economic problems, a period of uncertain legislative support for Hurtado, who was constitutionally precluded from reelection in 1984. At the balloting on January 29, with 17 parties competing, the opposition Democratic Left won 24 of 71 legislative seats, while its presidential candidate, Rodrigo BORJA Cevallos, obtained a slim plurality. However, at a second-round poll on May 6, Borja was narrowly defeated by the nominee of the conservative National Reconstruction Front, León FEBRES Cordero. Subsequently, a major constitutional struggle erupted between the executive and legislative branches over control of the judiciary, with the president refusing to recognize a new Chamber-appointed Supreme Court. The issue was eventually resolved in December, when the Chamber agreed to the resignation of both judicial panels and the appointment of a new court composed of both progovernment and opposition members.

In June 1985, five deputies of the independent Radical Alfarista Front (FRA) and two from the opposition Democratic Left (ID) shifted their allegiance to the president, thereby, with the support of the Concentration of Popular Forces (CFP), providing the government with its first legislative majority since the 1984 balloting. However, the fragility of the president's legislative support led him to issue a call in February 1986 for a June constitutional plebiscite on whether independent candidates should be permitted to stand for elective office; collaterally, while Febres was known to seek the creation of a third, "independent" force as a means of retaining his majority, spokesmen indicated that he had no intention of resigning his party membership to head a new "national front".

The government was shaken in mid-March as the result of a brief revolt led by Lt. Gen. Frank VARGAS Pazzos, who had been dismissed as armed forces chief of staff after demanding the discharge and imprisonment of Defense Minister Luis PIÑEIROS Rivera and army commander Gen. Manuel ALBUJA for alleged misuse of public funds. Although both submitted their resignations, forces loyal to Vargas subsequently occupied the Quito air base, claiming that the government had broken an agreement to place the two under arrest.

At mid-term legislative balloting in June (postponed from January to allow for voter recertification), the pro-government parties again lost control of the Chamber by a decisive margin of 27–43, while the referendum on independent candidatures was defeated by an even more massive 58.8–25.2 percent vote. The result was a reescalation of friction between the two branches, with the president rejecting a congressional amnesty granted to General Vargas in September.

On January 16, 1987, Febres Cordero was kidnapped by dissident paratroopers at Taura air base and held for 11 hours, until agreeing to the release of Vargas. The Congress thereupon approved a nonbinding resolution calling on the president to resign. The chief executive responded by declaring that he intended to remain in office until the expiration of his term in August 1988.

At the general election of January 31, 1988, PSC presidential candidate Sixto Durán Ballén ran a poor third to the ID's Borja Cevallos and Abdalá BUCARAM Ortiz of the Ecuadorian Roldosist Party (PRE). Buttressed by a comfortable legislative majority, Borja went on to defeat Bucaram in runoff balloting on May 8.

Constitution and government. In a referendum held January 15, 1978, Ecuadorians approved a new constitution that came into force with the retirement of the military junta and the inauguration of Jaime Roldós Aguilera in August 1979. The new basic law provided for a unicameral legislature and a single four-year presidential term, extended the vote to illiterates (presumed to number some 30 percent of the population), and established a framework of social rights for citizens. The judicial system is headed by a Supreme Court, which is responsible for supervising superior courts. The superior courts in turn supervise lower (provincial and cantonal) courts.

Administratively, the country is divided into 19 provinces plus the Galapagos Islands. The provinces are subdivided into municipalities.

Foreign relations. The most enduring foreign-affairs issue is a boundary dispute with Peru that dates back to the sixteenth century and involves a 125,000-square-mile tract of land between the Putumayo and Marañón rivers, both tributaries of the upper Amazon. The dispute has resulted in periodic conflict and in a number of agreements (none of which has permanently resolved the problem), including the Rio Protocol of January 1942, which awarded the greater part of the area to Peru and was formally repu-

CLAIMED BY ECUADOR
— — FRONTIER ESTABLISHED BY RIO PROTOCOL
•••• EXACT FRONTIER NOT FIXED BY RIO PROTOCOL

diated by Velasco Ibarra in 1960 on the ground that Ecuador had been pressured into acceptance of its terms by the guarantor states (Argentina, Brazil, Chile, and the United States). The frontier established by the Rio Protocol was itself never fully delineated, a 50-mile stretch in the vicinity of the Condor Mountains remaining to be charted along the presumed watershed of the Zamora and Santiago rivers, in an area where a new tributary of the Marañón was subsequently discovered (see map).

In January 1981 Ecuador and Peru engaged in five days of fighting in the Condor region, while representatives of the guarantor states convened at Brasília for negotiations on a ceasefire that was accepted by the combatants on February 2. However, further skirmishes were reported, and it was not until March 17 that the two sides began to withdraw their forces from the disputed area.

Current issues. The remarkable spectacle of a legislature locked in bitter conflict with an elected president only recently subjected to the humiliation of a kidnapping was attributed, in large part, to Febres Cordero's commitment to economic conservatism, coupled with what critics viewed as a lack of regard for constitutional process. The abortive electoral reform measure was widely construed as contrary to basic law, while the chief executive's hasty capitulation to his kidnappers contradicted a machismo-type image that he had previously cultivated. By March 1987, an impasse between the executive and legislative branches had clearly emerged: the Congress lacked the two-thirds majority required for impeachment, while President Febres vehemently rejected appeals that he resign in favor of Vice President Peñaherrera, to allow political passions to subside prior to the 1988 electoral campaign.

With the inauguration of Borja Cevallos on August 10 the constitutional impasse will have been resolved. Although a social democrat, the president-elect has assured the business community that he will not seek expanded state intervention in the economy, being described by his vice-presidential running mate as an advocate of an "ideological, pragmatic equilibrium . . . removed from extremes".

POLITICAL PARTIES

Historically dominated by the Conservative and Liberal parties and long complicated by pronounced personalist tendencies, the Ecuadorian party system has recently been in a state of considerable flux. The principal coalitions formed for the 1984 elections were a right-of-center National Reconstruction Front (*Frente de Reconstrucción Nacional* — FRN), which supported the presidential candidacy of Febres Cordero, and a left-of-center Progressive Front (*Frente Progresista* — FP). Both groups subsequently underwent a degree of restructuring, ultimately constituting a minority presidential bloc (PSC, PC, PLR, PD, CFP, FRA) and a majority opposition bloc (ID, DP, PRE, PSE, FADI, MPD) after the mid-term congressional balloting of June 1986. In the second-round presidential balloting of May 1988, Rodrigo Borja was supported by the ID, DP, CFP, FRA, FADI, and MPD, which had collectively obtained 60 of 71 legislative seats in January.

Legislative Parties:

Democratic Left (*Izquierda Democrática* — ID). The ID, a moderate social-democratic party, named Rodrigo Borja Cevallos as its presidential candidate in 1978, endorsed Roldós Aguilera at the 1979 runoff, and offered partial support to the Hurtado Larrea government after Roldós' death. It narrowly lost the presidency at the May 1984 runoff after having captured a substantial legislative plurality in January. Borja Cevallo was the front-runner at the first-round presidential balloting in January 1988 and defeated Abdalá Bucaram of the PRE at a runoff on May 8.

Leaders: Rodrigo BORJA Cevallos (President-elect of the Republic), Efrán COCIOS (National Director), Xavier LEDESMA, Jorge WASHINGTON Cevallos, Raúl BACA Carbo (Secretary General).

Popular Democracy (*Democracia Popular* — DP). In late 1977, the Christian Democratic Party (*Partido Demócrata Cristiano* — PDC) joined with the Progressive Conservatives (see PC, below) in organizing the Popular Democratic Coalition (*Coalición Popular Democrática*), which, having been denied separate registration by the Supreme Electoral Tribunal, joined with the CFP (below) in supporting the 1978/1979 presidential candidacy of Jaime Roldós Aguilera. In August 1981, the Popular Democratic legislative group (subsequently identified as the *Democracia Popular*) joined with a number of other members in a government-supportive alliance styled the Democratic Convergence (*Convergencia Democrática*). During the 1984 presidential race, the group (also identified as *Democracia Popular* — *Unión Demócrata Cristiana*) campaigned under the Popular Democracy label in support of former PCP leader Julio César Trujillo. It supported Borja Cevallo at second-round balloting in 1988.

Leaders: Dr. Osvaldo HURTADO Larrea (former President of the Republic), Dr. Julio César TRUJILLO (1984 presidential candidate), Jamil MAHUAD Witt (1988 presidential candidate), Wilfrido LUCERNO Bolaños.

Ecuadorian Roldosist Party (*Partido Roldosista Ecuatoriano* — PRE). The PRE is a *roldosista* party organized in December 1982. It won three chamber seats in 1984 and five in 1986. Its leader, Abdalá Bucaram, fled the country in 1986 after being indicted on charges of embezzlement and of defaming the armed forces while mayor of Guayaquil; however, the Febres Cordero government allowed him to return in August 1987 to present himself as a candidate in the 1988 presidential balloting, at which he ran second to the ID's Borja Cevallos.

Leader: Abdalá BUCARAM Ortiz.

Social Christian Party (*Partido Social Cristiano* — PSC). Moderately right-of-center, the PSC was launched in 1951 by former president Camilo Ponce Enríquez. Subsequently, it served in coalition with the PC (below) and the Equadorian Nationalist Revolutionary Action (*Acción Revolucionaria Nacionalista Ecuatoriana* — ARNE), a clerically oriented rightist group that was denied electoral registration in 1978 and was thereafter dissolved. Sixto Durán Ballén, the PSC's 1988 presidential candidate, ran third in the first-round balloting on January 31 and was thus excluded from the May 8 runoff.

Leaders: León FEBRES Cordero Rivadeneira (President of the Republic), Camilio PONCE (President of the Party), Sixto DURAN Ballén (1988 presidential candidate).

Concentration of Popular Forces (*Concentración de Fuerzas Populares* — CFP). Formed in 1946 by Carlos Guevara Moreno, the CFP is committed to broad-based socioeconomic change. Its longtime leader, Assad Bucaram, was the front-running candidate in the abortive 1972 presidential campaign and was conceded to be the leading contender in 1978 until declared ineligible on the basis of foreign parentage. Bucaram's protégé and nephew-in-law, Jaime Roldós Aguilera, the candidate of a coalition of the CFP and Popular Democrats, obtained a plurality of ballots cast on July 16 and defeated Durán Ballén in a runoff election on April 29, 1979. Following the CFP victory, a pronounced breach emerged between Roldós and his former mentor, most party leaders remaining loyal to Bucaram. In 1980 Roldós formally broke with the CFP by organizing a new group called People, Change and Democracy (below). Further defections occurred, and on November 6, 1981, Bucaram died, leaving the rump CFP with no firm leadership. The party ranked third after the legislative balloting of January 1984, with seven congressional seats, and currently ranks fifth, with five.

Leaders: Angel DUARTE Valverde (1984 presidential candidate), Averroes BUCARAM Saxida, Galo VAYAS.

Ecuadorian Socialist Party (*Partido Socialista Ecuatoriano* — PSE). Founded in 1925 as part of the Communist International, the PSE is a Marxist party that gave birth to the PCE and later to the PSR (see FADI, below). The party supports a moderate socialist program.

Leaders: Enrique AYALA Mora, Fabian JARAMILLO Davila, Fernando MALDONADO, Héctor SORIA (Secretary).

Alfarista Radical Front (*Frente Radical Alfarista* — FRA). The FRA was founded by Abdón Calderón Muñoz, a maverick Guayaquil businessman who was assassinated on November 29, 1978. The party's legal recognition was withdrawn in early 1979, after which its supporters were reported to have joined the Democratic Left in order to participate in the congressional election of April 29. Its legal status restored, the FRA made an unexpectedly strong showing at local and provincial elections in December 1980, winning more than 20 percent of the national vote, but currently holds only two Chamber seats.

Leaders: Jaime AZPIAZU (1984 presidential candidate), Iván CASTRO Patiño, Cecilia CALDERON de Castro.

Left Broad Front (*Frente Amplio de Izquierda* — FADI). FADI is a six-party formation of the far Left that supported the first-round candidacy of René Maugé Mosquera for each of the last three presidential campaigns. The Front's core group is the **Ecuadorian Communist Party** (*Partido Comunista Ecuatoriano* — PCE), whose pro-Moscow majority faction is led by Maugé (named PCE general secretary in December 1981). The other five parties are the **Committee for the People** (*Comité del Pueblo* — CDP), a splinter group of the Maoist **Marxist-Leninist Communist Party** (*Partido Comunista Marxista-Leninista* — PCML); the **Socialist Revolutionary Party** (*Partido Socialista Revolucionario* — PSR), a pro-Cuban group which withdrew from the Ecuadorian Socialist Party in 1962; the **Revolutionary Movement of the Christian Left** (*Movimiento Revolucionario de Izquierda Cristiana* — MRIC), supported by a number of left-wing Catholics; the **Movement for Leftist Unity** (*Movimiento por la Unidad de la Izquierda* — MUI); and the **Second Independence Movement** (*Movimiento Segunda Independencia* — MSI), led by Jaime GALARZA Zavala.

Leader: René MAUGE Mosquera.

Democratic Popular Movement (*Movimiento Popular Democrático* — MPD). The Maoist MPD, which was banned from participation in the 1978 election, has since been represented in the Chamber (currently by two representatives).

Leaders: Dr. Jaime HURTADO González, Jorge MORENO.

Radical Liberal Party (*Partido Liberal Radical*—PLR). The PLR is the principal heir to the traditional Liberal Party (*Partido Liberal*—PL), which was dominant in Ecuadorian politics for a half century after 1895, but subsequently split into a number of factions. Historically based on the coastal plain, the party strongly favors agrarian reform, separation of church and state, social security, and popular education. In recent years it has secured only marginal legislative representation.

Leaders: Blasco Manuel PEÑAHERRERA Padilla (Vice President of the Republic), Carlos Julio PLAZA.

Conservative Party (*Partido Conservador*—PC). Formed in 1855, the PC is Ecuador's oldest political party. It is based on a traditional alliance between church and state and has historical roots in the Andean highlands. In early 1976, the party split into right- and left-wing factions, the latter subsequently organizing as the Progressive Conservative Party (*Partido Conservador Progresista*—PCP), which joined with a number of other parties, including the Christian Democrats (see Popular Democracy, above), in a 1978 alliance styled the Popular Democratic Coalition that supported the presidential candidacy of Jaime Roldós Aguilera. By 1986 its Chamber representation had been reduced to a single seat, which it retained in 1988.

Leader: José TERAN Varea.

Other Parties:

Democratic Party (*Partido Demócrata*—PD). The PD was organized in 1981, initially as the Radical Democratic Party (*Partido Radical Demó-crata*—PRD), by a number of dissident Liberals, including Francisco Huerta Montalvo, who had been the PLR presidential candidate prior to his disqualification in 1978 because of alleged financial irregularities. They were joined by deserters from other parties, including León Roldós Aguilera, who was elected vice president of the Republic by the Chamber of Representatives in June 1981. In early 1982 Roldós was excluded from cabinet meetings after a public dispute with the president, although the party continued to support the Hurtado administration in the Chamber. Prior to the 1984 balloting Roldós joined the People, Change and Democracy (below). It won five Chamber seats in 1984, one in 1986 and none in 1988.

Leaders: Dr. Francisco HUERTA Montalvo (1984 presidential candidate), Heinz MOELLER, Luis PIANA.

People, Change and Democracy (*Pueblo, Cambio y Democracia*—PCD). Intended as the personal vehicle of President Roldós Aguilera, the PCD had not been legally recognized at the time of Roldós' death on May 24, 1981, and was subsequently characterized as "an inchoate political force" which had "lost its raison d'être". It secured one Chamber seat in 1986, which was lost in 1988 after the party had chosen to ally itself with neither government or opposition blocs.

Leaders: Dr. León ROLDOS Aguilera (former Vice President of the Republic), Ernesto BUENANO Cabrera.

Nationalist Revolutionary Party (*Partido Nacionalista Revolucionario*—PNR. The PNR is a populist-oriented vehicle of former president Arosemena Monroy. Its leader was declared ineligible to stand for reelection in 1978 and the party subsequently endorsed the candidacy of Huerta Rendón. The party lost its sole legislative seat in 1988.

Leaders: Dr. Carlos Julio AROSEMENA Monroy, Dr. Mauricio GANDARA.

National Velasquista Party (*Partido Nacional Velasquista*—PNV). Originally formed in 1952, the PNV was long the personal vehicle of José María Velasco Ibarra and remained committed to Velasco's promises of economic and social reform after the former president went into exile. In March 1977 Velasco informed his followers that he would not run again for the presidency, formally repudiating the party that claimed allegiance to him; he died on March 30, 1979, little more than a month after returning to Ecuador from Argentina.

Leaders: Juan Carlos FAIDUTTI, Alfonso ARROYO Robelly.

Ecuadorian Popular Revolutionary Action (*Acción Popular Revolucionaria Ecuatoriana*—APRE). APRE resulted from a rivalry within the Concentration of Popular Forces in the 1950s between a majority faction led by Assad Bucaram and a leftist minority led by José Hanna Musse. The split was partially personal. Both Bucaram and Hanna Musse were of Lebanese extraction, the former having retained dual nationality, while the latter had not. In 1958, Hanna Musse formally broke with the CPF, his new organization being known until 1978 as the National

Guevarista Party (*Partido Nacional Guevarista*). Although legally recognized, APRE has not contested recent presidential or legislative elections.

Leaders: Lt. Gen. Frank VARGAS Pazzos, José HANNA Musse, Antonio HANNA Musse.

Guerrilla Groups:

During 1985 the **Eloy Alfaro Popular Armed Forces**—**Alfaro Lives** (*Fuerzas Armadas Populares Eloy Alfaro*—*Alfaro Vive*), ostensibly affiliated with the *Izquierda Democrática,* was active, while a new group, the **Free Country Montoneros** (*Montoneros Patria Libre*—MPL), surfaced in early 1986. During 1986, the two top *Alfaro Vive* leaders were reportedly killed in skirmishes with police.

LEGISLATURE

The bicameral legislature dissolved by the military junta in 1970 has been replaced by a unicameral **National Chamber of Representatives** (*Cámara Nacional de Representantes*) that currently consists of 71 popularly elected members, 12 of whom are elected on a national list for four-year terms and 59 on provincial lists for two-year terms. Although center-right supporters of Febres Cordero were unable to win control of the Chamber at the election of January 29, 1984, a realignment (including the defection of two opposition deputies) yielded a slim government majority of one seat in June 1985. A more conclusive reversal occurred at the biennial balloting of June 1, 1986 (deferred from January), with the opposition bloc winning a majority of 43 seats. The distribution after the election of January 31, 1988 (an overwhelming majority supporting the presidential candidacy of Rodrigo Borja) was as follows: Democratic Left, 31; Popular Democracy, 8; Ecuadorian Roldosist Party, 8; Social Christian Party, 7; Concentration of Popular Forces, 5; Ecuadorian Socialist Party, 4; Alfarista Radical Front, 2; Left Broad Front, 2; Democratic Popular Movement, 2; Radical Liberal Party, 1; Conservative Party, 1.

President: Jorge ZABALA.

CABINET

President	León Febres Cordero Rivadeneira
Vice President	Blasco Manuel Peñaherrera Padilla
Ministers	
Agriculture and Livestock	Marcel Laniado de Wind
Education and Culture	Ivan Gallegos Domínguez
Finance and Credit	Eduardo Cabezas Molina
Foreign Relations	Rafael García Velasco
Industry, Commerce, Fishing, and Integration	Ricardo Noboa Bejarano
Interior and Justice	Heinz Moeller Freile
Labor	Guillermo Chang Durango
National Defense	Gen. Medardo Salazar Navas
Natural Resources and Energy	Fernando Santos Alvite
Public Health	Dr. José Tohme Amador
Public Works and Communications	César Rodrígues Baquerizo
Social Welfare	Aquiles Regail Santisteban
Secretary General of Administration	Patricio Quevedo Terán
President, Central Bank	Fernando Herrero Sevilla

NEWS MEDIA

Press. The following are daily newspapers published at Guayaquil, unless otherwise noted: *El Universo* (180,000 daily, 250,000 Sunday), independent; *El Comercio* (Quito, 132,000), commercial, independent; *Ultimas Noticias* (Quito, 90,000), independent; *El Tiempo* (Quito, 35,000), Conservative; *El Telégrafo* (36,000 daily, 51,000 Sunday), Liberal; *La Razón* (28,000), Liberal.

News agencies. There is no domestic facility. A number of foreign agencies maintain bureaus at either Quito or Guayaquil.

Radio and television. Broadcasting is supervised by the nongovernmental *Asociación Ecuatoriana de Radiodifusión* and the *Instituto Ecuatoriano de Telecomunicaciones* (Ietel). Of the approximately 270 radio stations (the most numerous, on a per capita basis, in Latin America), about two dozen are facilities of the religious *La Voz de los Andes*. There are 10 television stations, most of which are commercial. There were approximately 1.9 million radio and 620,000 television receivers in 1987.

INTERGOVERNMENTAL REPRESENTATION

Ambassador to the US: Mario RIBADENEIRA.

US Ambassador to Ecuador: Fernando Enrique RONDON.

Permanent Representative to the UN: Carlos TOBAR Zaldumbide.

IGO Memberships (Non-UN): ALADI, Ancom, Copal, Geplacea, IADB, ICCO, ICM, ICO, Intelsat, Interpol, ISO, IWTC, NAM, OAS, OPANAL, OPEC, PCA, SELA.

EGYPT

Arab Republic of Egypt
Jumhuriyat Misr al-'Arabiyah

Political Status: Nominally independent since 1922; republic established in 1953; joined with Syria as the United Arab Republic in 1958 and retained the name after Syria withdrew in 1961; present name adopted September 2, 1971; under limited multiparty system formally adopted by constitutional amendment approved in referendum of May 22, 1980.

Area: 386,659 sq. mi. (1,001,449 sq. km.).

Population: 40,500,000 (1979C), 52,661,000 (1988E), including more than 1.5 million Egyptian nationals living abroad.

Major Urban Centers (1976C): CAIRO (al-QAHIRA, 5,084,463; urban area, 6,818,318); Alexandria (al-Iskandariyah, 2,318,655); al-Giza (1,246,713); al-Mahalla al-Kubra (292,853); Tanta (284,636); Port Said (Bur Sa'id, 262,620); al-Mansura (257,866). Greater Cairo was estimated in 1986 to have a population in the vicinity of 12 million.

Official Language: Arabic.

Monetary Unit: Egyptian Pound (principal rate March 1, 1988, 1 pound = $1.43US).

President: Muhammad Husni MUBARAK; appointed Vice President on April 15, 1975; succeeded to the presidency upon the assassination of Muhammad Ahmad Anwar al-SADAT on October 6, 1981; confirmed by national referendum of October 13 and sworn in for a six-year term on October 14; served additionally as Prime Minister from October 14, 1981, to January 2, 1982; sworn in for a second term on October 13, 1987, following reconfirmation in referendum of October 5.

Prime Minister: Dr. 'Atif Muhammad Najib SIDQI (Atef SIDKI, SEDKI); appointed by the President and sworn in November 12, 1986, following the resignation of Dr. 'Ali Lutfi Mahmud LUTFI.

THE COUNTRY

Situated in the northeast corner of Africa at its juncture with Asia, Egypt occupies a quadrangle of desert made habitable only by the waters of the Nile, which bisects the country from south to north. Although the greater part of the national territory has traditionally been regarded as wasteland, Egypt is the most populous country in the Arab world: 99 percent of the people are concentrated in 3.5 percent of the land area, with population densities in parts of the Nile Valley reaching 6,000 per square mile. Arabic is universally spoken, and 92 percent of the ethnically homogeneous people adhere to the Sunni sect of Islam, most of the remainder being Coptic Christian. Women are listed as 8 percent of the paid labor force, with 70 percent of rural women engaged in unpaid agricultural labor; urban employed women tend to be concentrated in health care and education, although on the lower levels.

Completion of the Aswan High Dam in 1971 permitted the expansion of tillable acreage and of multiple cropping, while the use of fertilizers and mechanization have also increased production of such crops as cotton, wheat, rice, sugarcane, and corn, although Egypt still imports 60 percent of its food. Much of the population continues to live near the subsistence level, high rural to urban migration increasing the number of urban unemployed. A growing industrial sector, which employs 30 percent of the labor force, is centered on textiles and agriprocessing, although the return by Israel of Sinai oil fields permitted Egypt to become a net exporter of petroleum. At the same time, the reopened Suez Canal (closed from the 1967 war until 1975) also helped stimulate the economy, which averaged an annual real growth rate in gross domestic product of 9 percent from mid-1979 to mid-1983. By 1985 economic conditions had sharply deteriorated as the decline in world oil prices not only depressed export income but severely curtailed remittances from Egyptians employed in other oil-producing states; in addition, tourism, another important source of revenue, declined because of regional terrorism and domestic insecurity. Compounding the difficulties are rapid population growth (an increase of approximately one million every nine months) and an inefficient and bloated bureaucracy of some 12 million civil servants. During 1987 on the other hand, the Cairo metro, Africa's first subway system was formally inaugurated, while the Mubarak administration reached agreement with the Paris Club and the United States for the rescheduling of debt payments that, accompanied by a flexible package of economic reforms, paved the way for the infusion of new IMF credits.

GOVERNMENT AND POLITICS

Political background. The modern phase of Egypt's long history began in 1882 with the occupation of what was then an Ottoman province by a British military force, only token authority being retained by the local ruler (khedive). After establishing a protectorate in 1914, the United Kingdom granted formal independence to the government of King FU'AD in 1922 but continued to exercise gradually dwindling control, which ended with its evacuation of the Suez Canal Zone in 1956. The rule of Fu'ad's successor, King FAROUK (FARUK), was abruptly terminated as the result of a military coup on July 23, 1952. A group of young officers (the "Free Officers"), nominally headed by Maj. Gen. Muhammad NAGIB, secured Farouk's abdication on June 18, 1953, and went on to establish a republic under Nagib's presidency. Col. Gamal Abdel NASSER (Jamal 'Abd al-NASIR), who had largely guided these events, replaced Nagib as prime minister and head of state in 1954, becoming president on June 23, 1956.

The institution of military rule signaled the commencement of an internal social and economic revolution, growing pressure for the termination of British and other external influences, and a drive toward greater Arab unity against Israel under Egyptian leadership. Failing to secure Western arms on satisfactory terms, Egypt accepted Soviet military assistance in 1955. In July 1956, following the withdrawal of a Western offer to help finance the High Dam at Aswan, Egypt nationalized the Suez Canal Company and took possession of its properties. Foreign retaliation resulted in the "Suez War" of October-November 1956, in which Israeli, British, and French forces invaded Egyptian territory but subsequently withdrew under pressure from the United States, the Soviet Union, and the United Nations.

On February 1, 1958, Egypt joined with Syria to form the United Arab Republic under Nasser's presidency. Although Syria reasserted its independence in September 1961, Egypt retained the UAR designation until 1971, when it adopted the name Arab Republic of Egypt. (A less formal linkage with North Yemen, the United Arab States, was also established in 1958 but dissolved in 1961.)

Egypt again incurred heavy losses in the six-day Arab-Israeli War of June 1967, which resulted in the closing of the Suez Canal, the occupation by Israel of the Sinai Peninsula, and an increase in Egypt's military and economic dependence on the USSR. Popular discontent resulting from the defeat was instrumental in bringing about a subsequent overhaul of the state machinery and a far-reaching reconstruction of the Arab Socialist Union (ASU), the nation's only authorized political party.

A major turning point in Egypt's modern history occurred with the death of President Nasser on September 28, 1970, power subsequently being transferred to Vice President Anwar al-SADAT. The new president successfully weathered a government crisis in 1971 that included the dismissal of Vice President 'Ali SABRI and other political figures accused of involvement in a plot to repudiate his leadership. A thorough shake-up of the party and government followed, with Sadat's control being affirmed at a July ASU congress and, two months later, by voter approval of a new national constitution as well as a constitution for a projected Federation of Arab Republics involving Egypt, Libya, and Syria. At the same time, the pro-Soviet leanings of some of those involved in the Sabri plot, combined with Moscow's increasing reluctance to comply with Egyptian demands for armaments, generated increasing tension in Soviet-Egyptian relations. These factors, coupled with Sadat's desire to acquire US support in effecting a return of Israeli-held territory, culminated in the expulsion of some 17,000 Soviet personnel in mid-1972.

The apparent unwillingness of US President Nixon to engage in diplomatic initiatives during an election year forced Sadat to return to the Soviet fold to prepare for another war with Israel, which broke out in October 1973. After 18 days of fighting, a ceasefire was concluded under UN auspices, and US Secretary of State Henry Kissinger ultimately arranged for peace talks that resulted in the disengagement of Egyptian and Israeli forces east of the Suez Canal. Under an agreement signed on September 4, 1975, Israel withdrew to the Gidi and Mitla passes in the western Sinai and returned the Ras Sudar oil field to Egypt after securing political commitments from Egypt and a pledge of major economic and military support from the United States.

Although he had intimated earlier that he might step down from the presidency in 1976, Sadat accepted designation to a second six-year term on September 16. On October 26, in the first relatively free balloting since the early 1950s, the nation elected a new People's Assembly from candidates presented by three groups within the Arab Socialist Union. Two weeks later, the president declared that the new groups could be termed political parties but indicated that they would remain under the overall supervision of the ASU. The role of the ASU was further reduced in June 1977 by promulgation of a law that permitted the formation of additional parties under carefully circumscribed circumstances, while its vestigial status as an "umbrella" organization was terminated a year later.

On October 2, 1978, Sadat named Mustafa KHALIL to head a new "peace" cabinet that on March 15, 1979, unanimously approved a draft peace treaty with Israel. The People's Assembly ratified the document on April 10 by a 328–15 vote, while in a referendum held nine days later a reported 99.95 percent of those casting ballots voiced approval. At the same time, a series of political and constitutional reforms received overwhelming support from voters. As a result President Sadat dissolved the Assembly two years ahead of schedule and called for a two-stage legislative election on June 7 and 14. Sadat's National Democratic Party (NDP) easily won the multiparty contest — the first such election since the overthrow of the monarchy in 1953 — and on June 21 Prime Minister Khalil and a substantially unchanged cabinet were sworn in. On May 12, 1980, however, Khalil resigned, with President Sadat assuming the prime ministership two days later.

By 1981, Egypt was increasingly reliant on the United States for military and foreign policy support, while growing domestic unrest threatened the fragile political liberalization initiated in 1980. In an unprecedented move in early September, the government imprisoned over a thousand opposition leaders, ranging from Islamic fundamentalists to journalists and Nasserites.

On October 6, 1981, while attending a military review at Cairo, President Sadat was assassinated by a group of Muslim militants affiliated with *al-Jihad* ("Holy Struggle"). The Assembly's nomination of Vice President Muhammad Husni MUBARAK as his successor was confirmed by a national referendum on October 13, the new president naming a cabinet headed by himself as prime minister two days later. On January 2, 1982, Mubarak yielded the latter office to First Deputy Prime Minister Ahmad Fu'ad MUHI al-DIN.

The NDP retained overwhelming control of the Assembly at the March 1984 election, the right-wing New Wafd Party being the only other group to surpass the eight percent vote total needed to gain direct representation. However, popular discontent erupted later in the year over measures to combat economic deterioration and numerous opposition leaders, accused of "fomenting unrest", were arrested. Meanwhile, Islamic fundamentalists continued a campaign for the institution of full *shari'a* law that provoked a new wave of arrests in mid-1985.

At his death in June 1984, Muhi al-Din was succeeded as prime minister by Gen. Kamal Hasan 'ALI, who was himself replaced on November 12, 1986, by Dr. 'Atif Muhammad SIDQI, a lawyer and economist whose appointment appeared to signal a willingness to institute drastic reform measures sought by the IMF and World Bank. Anticipating a resurgence of opposition and facing court challenges to the legality of an Assembly that excluded independent members, the president confounded his critics by mounting a referendum in February 1987 on the question of legislative dissolution. The subsequent election of April 6 reconfirmed the NDP's control, and on October 5 Mubarak received public endorsement for a second term.

Constitution and government. Under the 1971 constitution, executive power is vested in the president, who is nominated by the People's Assembly and elected for a six-year term by popular referendum. The president may appoint vice presidents in addition to government ministers and may rule by decree when granted emergency powers by the 458-member Assembly, which functions primarily as a policy-approving rather than as a policy-initiating body. At present, all but 10 presidentially appointed assemblymen are directly elected from 48 constituencies under a complex system of proportional representation that favors the majority party. There is also a Consultative Council (*Shura*), formerly the Central Committee of the ASU, that is currently composed of 140 elected and 70 appointed members. The judicial system is headed by a Supreme Court (the Court of Cassation) and includes six Courts of Appeal in addition to courts of first instance. A Supreme Judicial Council is designed to guarantee the independence of the judiciary.

For administrative purposes Egypt is divided into 26 governorates, each with a governor appointed by the president, while most functions of the Ministry for Local Government are shared with regional, town, and village officials.

Constitutional amendments passed by the Assembly on April 30, 1980, and approved by referendum on May 22 included the following: designation of the country as "socialist democratic" rather than "democratic socialist"; identification of the Islamic legal code (*shari'a*) as "the" rather than "a" principal source of law; and deletion of reference to the ASU as the sole conduit for political activity, thus validating the limited multiparty system already in existence.

Foreign relations. As the most populous and most highly industrialized of the Arab states, Egypt has consistently aspired to a leading role in Arab, Islamic, Middle Eastern, African, and world affairs and has been an active participant in the United Nations, the Arab League, and the Organization of African Unity. For a number of years, its claim to a position of primacy in the Arab world made for somewhat unstable relations with other Arab governments, particularly the conservative regimes of Jordan and Saudi Arabia, although relations with those governments improved as a result of the 1967 and 1973 wars with Israel. Relations with the more radical regimes of Libya and Syria subsequently became strained, largely because of the interim settlement with Israel that yielded alleged plots against the Sadat regime. Thus a January 1, 1972, agreement by the three states to establish a loose Federation of Arab Republics was never implemented.

Formally nonaligned, Egypt has gone through four phases: the Western orientation of the colonial period and the monarchy, the anti-Western and increasingly pro-Soviet period initiated in 1955, a period of flexibility dating from the expulsion of Soviet personnel in 1972, and a renewed reliance on the West—particularly the United States—following widespread condemnation of Egyptian-Israeli rapprochement by most Communist and Arab governments.

On November 19, 1977, President Sadat began a precedent-shattering three-day trip to Jerusalem, the highlight of which was an address to the Israeli *Knesset*. While he offered no significant concessions in regard to the occupied territories, was unequivocal in his support of a Palestinian state, and declared that he did not intend to conclude a separate peace with Israel, the trip was hailed as a "historic breakthrough" in Arab-Israeli relations and was followed by an invitation to the principals in the Middle Eastern dispute and their great-power patrons to a December meeting in Egypt to prepare for a resumption of the Geneva peace conference. Israeli Prime Minister Begin responded affirmatively but all of the Arab invitees declined, and on December 5 Egypt broke relations with five of its more radical neighbors (Algeria, Iraq, Libya, Syria, and South Yemen). The December 26 meeting at Ismailia, Egypt, between Sadat and Begin yielded potential bases of accord in regard to Sinai, in addition to an agreement to continue discussions at the ministerial level on both political issues (at Jerusalem) and military issues (at Cairo).

Little in the way of further progress toward an overall settlement was registered prior to a dramatic ten-day "summit" convened by US President Carter at Camp David, Maryland, in September 1978. The meeting yielded two documents—a "Framework for Peace in the Middle East" and a "Framework for a Peace Treaty between Israel and Egypt"—that were signed by President Sadat and Prime Minister Begin at the White House on September 17. By mid-November details of a peace treaty and three annexes had been agreed upon by Egyptian and Israeli representatives. Signing, however, was deferred beyond the target date of December 17 primarily because of Egyptian insistence on a specific timetable for Israeli withdrawal from the West Bank and Gaza, in addition to last-minute reservations regarding Article 6, which gave the document precedence over treaty commitments to other states. Negotiations held February 21–25, 1979, at Camp David by Prime Minister Khalil and Israeli Foreign Minister Dayan failed to resolve the differences. Thus, on March 8, US President Carter flew to the Middle East for talks with leaders of both countries, and within six days compromise proposals had been accepted. The completed treaty was signed by Begin and Sadat at Washington on March 26, and on April 25 the 31-year state of war between Egypt and Israel officially came to an end with the exchange of ratification documents at the US surveillance post at Um-Khashiba in the Sinai. On May 25 the first Israeli troops withdrew from the Sinai under the terms of the treaty and negotiations on autonomy for the West Bank and Gaza opened at Beersheba, Israel.

In reaction, the Arab League convened at Baghdad, Iraq, and by the end of the month had approved resolutions calling for the diplomatic and economic isolation of Egypt. By midyear, all League members but Oman, Somalia, and Sudan had severed relations with the Sadat regime, and Cairo's membership had been suspended from a number of Arab groupings, including the League, the Arab Monetary Fund, and the Organization of Arab Petroleum Exporting Countries. Egypt succeeded in weathering the hard-line Arab reaction largely because of increased economic aid from Western countries, including France, West Germany, Japan, and the United States, which alone committed itself to more aid on a real per capita basis than had been extended to Europe under the post-World War II Marshall Plan.

Although Egypt and Israel formally exchanged ambassadors on February 26, 1980, a month after opening their border at El Arish in the Sinai to land traffic, no progress has since been made on the question of Palestinian autonomy, negotiations being impeded, in part, by continued Jewish settlement on the West Bank, the Israeli annexation of East Jerusalem in July 1980, and the invasion of Lebanon in June 1982. Following the massacre of Palestinian refugees at Sabra and Chatila in September 1982, Cairo recalled its ambassador from Tel Aviv. (Relations at the ambassadorial level were ultimately reestablished in September 1986, despite tension over Israel's bombing of the PLO headquarters at Tunis in October 1985.)

The Soviet intervention in Afghanistan in December 1979 generated concern in Egypt, with the government ordering the USSR in February 1980 to reduce its diplomatic staff at Cairo to seven, while offering military assistance to the Afghan rebels. In 1981, accusing the remaining Soviet embassy staff of aiding Islamic fundamentalist unrest, Cairo broke diplomatic relations and expelled the Soviet ambassador. Diplomatic relations were resumed in September 1984, as the Mubarak government departed from the aggressively pro-US policy of the later Sadat years, while a three-year trade accord was signed by the two governments in late 1987.

Relations with most of the Arab world also changed during Mubarak's first term, Egypt's stature among moderate neighbors being enhanced by a virtual freeze in dealings with Israel after the 1982 Lebanon invasion. Although relations with radical Arab states, particularly Libya, remained strained, Egypt's reemergence from the status of Arab pariah allowed it to act as a "silent partner" in negotiations between Jordan and the PLO that generated a 1985 peace plan (see entries on Jordan and the PLO). However, the subsequent collapse of the plan left the Mubarak administration in an uncomfortable middle position between its "good friend" King Hussein and the PLO, whose Cairo offices were closed in May 1987 after the passage of an "anti-Egyptian" resolution by the Palestine National Council.

During an Arab League summit at 'Amman, Jordan, in November, the prohibition against diplomatic ties with Egypt was officially lifted, although the suspension of League membership remained in effect. It was widely believed that the threat of Iranian hegemony in the Gulf was the principal factor in Cairo's rehabilitation. Egypt, which had severed relations with Iran in May upon discovery of a fundamentalist Muslim network allegedly financed by Iran, possessed the largest and best-equipped armed force in the region. Following the 'Amman summit, Egypt authorized reopening of the PLO facility, instituted joint military maneuvers with Jordan, increased the number of military advisors sent to Iraq, and arranged for military cooperation with Kuwait, Saudi Arabia, and the United Arab Emirates.

Current issues. President Mubarak's call for early Assembly balloting in April 1987 was seen as an effort to minimize political fallout from impending economic reform. Opposition parties, which had boycotted a partial election to the *Shura* in October 1986 because of procedural constraints, participated in a relatively "clean" campaign that was hailed as reflecting Mubarak's commitment to democratization. It was also hoped that providing a new legislative role for the more moderate fundamentalists would serve to limit civil disturbances by religious militants. However in January 1988, in the course of what Mubarak himself had characterized as "brutal, oppressive measures against the Palestinian people in the occupied territories", hundreds of fundamentalist protesters were beaten by Egyptian police. The spread of fundamentalism, albeit linked to the events in Israel, has also been fueled by the failure of Egyptian authorities to address adequately the needs of an increasingly poor population. Collaterally, "democratization" is perceived as incompatible with Islam by growing numbers of the religious militants.

In international affairs, the president reportedly declined an invitation to visit Washington in early 1987 because of US arms sales to Iran, which he described as destroying American credibility among Arabs "and maybe in the whole world". Regionally, he continued his pursuit of a comprehensive peace settlement, joining in the call for an international conference on the matter after a February

1987 meeting with Israel's foreign minister, Shimon Peres. However, obstacles to such a conference, including the unshakable opposition of Israeli Prime Minister Yitzhak Shamir, the lack of American support for Soviet participation, and the "estrangement" between Jordan and the PLO, continued to block any real progress towards a meeting. In January 1988 Mubarak, following state visits to Western and Persian Gulf states, met with President Reagan to offer a new mid-East peace initiative that called for a six-month "cooling off" period and freeze on Jewish settlements, guarantees on Palestinian fundamental rights, a more visible American role, and definite movement towards an international peace conference. In exchange for Cairo's demonstrated commitment to Arab-Israeli peace and its support of the Gulf states against Iranian aggression, Mubarak called for Washington's forgiveness of some of its foreign debt, additional fiscal aid, and support of its appeal to the IMF for leniency in domestic economic reforms.

POLITICAL PARTIES

Egypt's old political parties were swept away with the destruction of the monarchy in 1953. Efforts by the Nasser regime centered on the creation of a single mass organization to support the government and its policies. Following unsuccessful experiments with two such organizations, the National Liberation Rally and the National Union, the Arab Socialist Union—ASU (*al-Ittihad al-Ishtiraki al-'Arabi*) was established as the country's sole political party in December 1962. Major reorganizations were mandated in 1967, following the war with Israel, and in 1971, following the Sabri plot.

Prior to the legislative election of October 1976, President Sadat authorized the establishment of three "groups" within the ASU—the leftist National Progressive Unionist Assembly (NPUA), the centrist Egyptian Arab Socialist Organization (EASO), and the rightist Free Socialist Organization (FSO)—which presented separate lists of Assembly candidates. Following the election, Sadat indicated that it would be appropriate to refer to the groups as distinct parties, though the ASU would "stand above" the new organizations. A law adopted on June 27, 1977, authorized the establishment of additional parties under three conditions: (1) that they be sanctioned by the ASU; (2) that, except for those established in 1976, they include at least 20 members of the People's Assembly; and (3) that they not have been in existence prior to 1953.

On February 4, 1978, the ASU Central Committee modified the impact of the 1977 legislation by permitting the *Wafd,* the majority party under the monarchy, to reenter politics as the New Wafd Party—NWP. Less than four months later, however, representatives of the NWP voted unanimously to disband the party to protest the passage of a sweeping internal security law on June 1. Subsequently, President Sadat announced the formal abolition of the ASU, the conversion of its Central Committee into a Consultative Council to meet annually on the anniversary of the 1952 revolution, and the establishment of a new centrist group which, on August 15, was named the Na-

tional Democratic Party (NDP). In an April 1979 political referendum, the voters overwhelmingly approved removal of the first two conditions of the 1977 law, thus clearing the way for the formation of additional parties. In May 1980 a constitutional amendment, also approved by referendum, removed reference to the defunct ASU as the sole source of political activity, thus formally legitimizing the limited multiparty system. In July 1983, the Assembly approved a requirement that all parties obtain 8 percent of the vote to gain parliamentary representation. One month later, the New Wafd Party announced that it was "resuming public activity", a government attempt to force the NWP to re-register as a new party being overturned by the State Administrative Court the following October.

At the 1984 election, only the NDP and the NWP won elective seats, the former outdistancing the latter by a near 6–1 margin. In 1987, the NDP obtained a slightly reduced majority of 77.2 percent, the remaining seats being captured by the NWP and a coalition composed of the Socialist Labor Party, the Liberal Socialist Party, and "Islamists" representing the Muslim Brotherhood (see below).

Government Party:

National Democratic Party—NDP (*al-Hizb al-Watani al-Dimuqrati*). The NDP was organized by President Sadat in July 1978 as the principal government party, its name being derived from that of Egypt's historic National Party formed at the turn of the century by Mustapha Kamel. In late August it was reported that 275 deputies in the People's Assembly had joined the new group, all but 11 having been members of the Egyptian Arab Socialist Party—EASP (*Hizb Misr al-'Arabi al-Ishtiraki*), which, as an outgrowth of the EASO, had inherited many of the political functions earlier performed by the ASU. The EASP formally merged with the NDP in October 1978. President Mubarak, who had served as deputy chairman under President Sadat, was named NDP chairman at a party congress on January 26, 1982. In the wake of the May 1984 Assembly balloting, fewer than three dozen of the 390 elected NDP representatives were new to their posts, most observers continuing to characterize the NDP as "Sadat's party". The NDP retained overwhelming control of the Assembly in 1987, winning 346 elective seats.

Leaders: Muhammad Husni MUBARAK (President of the Republic and Chairman of the Party),), Dr. Yusuf Amin WALI (Secretary General).

Opposition Parties:

New Wafd Party—NWP (*Hizb al-Wafd al-Gadid*). Formed in February 1978 as a revival of the most powerful party in Egypt prior to 1952, the NWP formally disbanded the following June, but reformed in August. In 1980, a "new generation of *Wafd* activists" instigated demonstrations in several cities, prompting the detention of its leader, Fuad Serageddin, until November 1981. A rightist formation in alliance with a number of Islamic groups, the *Wafd* won 15 percent of the vote in the May 1984 election, thus becoming the only opposition party with parliamentary representation. Part of its electoral support came from the proscribed **Muslim Brotherhood** (*Ikhwan*), which secured indirect Assembly representation by running a number of its candidates under the *Wafd*'s aegis. In 1987, the Brotherhood entered into a de facto coalition with the SLP and the LSP (below), its candidates winning 37 of the coalition's 60 seats. The NWP, by contrast, won 35 seats (23 less than in 1984).

Leaders: Fuad SERAGEDDIN, Ibrahim FARRAG (Secretary General).

Socialist Labor Party—SLP (*Hizb al-'Amal al-Ishtiraki*). The SLP was officially organized in November 1978 by former minister of agriculture Ibrahim Shukri to provide "loyal and constructive opposition" to the NDP. While affirming the need for Islamic law to serve as the basis of Egyptian legislation, the party has called for a democratic regime with a more equal sharing of wealth between urban and rural areas. It failed to obtain the required eight percent of the vote to secure direct Assembly representation in May 1984, but four of its members were subsequently appointed by President Mubarak. For the 1987 Assembly balloting, the SLP joined with the LSP (below) and representatives of the Muslim Brotherhood in an alliance which netted 60 elective seats, 20 of which it held in its own right.

Leader: Ibrahim Mahmud SHUKRI.

Liberal Socialist Party—LSP (*Hizb al-Ahrar al-Ishtiraki*). The principal objective of the LSP, which was formed in 1976 from the right wing of the ASU, is that of securing a greater role for private enterprise within the Egyptian economy. The party's Assembly representation fell from twelve to three seats at the June 1979 election, and was eliminated entirely at the 1984 election, gaining less than one percent of the vote. It obtained three elective seats in 1987 as a member of the SLP-led coalition.

Leader: Mustafa Kamal MURAD.

National Progressive Unionist Party—NPUP (*Hizb al-Tajammu' al-Watani al-Taqaddumi al-Wahdawi*). Although it received formal endorsement as the party of the Left in 1976, the NPUP temporarily ceased activity in 1978 following the enactment of restrictive internal security legislation. It contested the June 1979 Assembly election on a platform that, alone among those of the four sanctioned parties, opposed the Egyptian-Israeli peace treaty, and failed to retain its two parliamentary seats. In both 1979 and 1984 the party leadership charged the government with fraud and harassment, although on the latter occasion, Mubarak included a NPUP member among the presidential nominations. Party supporters have frequently been detained for alleged antigovernment or Communist activities, most recently following food riots at Kafr el Dawwar in October 1984. The NPUP failed to win parliamentary representation in the 1987 election, securing less than two percent of the vote.

Leaders: Khalid MUHI al-DIN (MOHIEDDIN), Qabbari 'ABDAL-LAH, Abu al-'Izz al-HARIRI, Dr. Rif'at el-SA'ID (Secretary).

Umma Party (*Hizb al-'Umma*). A tiny Muslim organization, the Umma Party based in Khartoum, Sudan, won only miniscule support in the 1987 Assembly election.

Leader: Sadiq al-MAHDI (Prime Minister of Sudan).

Party of Social and Democratic Construction (PSDC). The PSDC was founded by Sami Mubarak, the brother of the President, in December 1986. Mubarak had been elected to the Assembly in 1984 as a member of the New Wafd Party.

Leader: Sami MUBARAK.

Two groups were reportedly seeking recognition in 1986 as "Nasserite" parties, one establishing itself as the **Arab Socialist Nasserite Party** under the leadership of Farid Abdel KARIM, a former member of the ASU, and the other organizing under the leadership of lawyer and former ASU member Kamal AHMED.

Illegal Groups:

In recent years the government has moved energetically against a number of clandestine left-wing formations, the most important of which, the **Egyptian Communist Party** (*al-Hizb al-Shuyu'i al-Misri*), was founded in 1921 but has experienced numerous cleavages that have yielded, *inter alia,* the **Egyptian Communist Labor Party**, the Maoist **Revolutionary Current**, the **Revolutionary Egyptian Communist Party**, and the **Organization of the Egyptian Communist Party–January 8,** whose name records the merger in 1975 of the extremist Workers and Peasants' Organization and the Egyptian Communist Party Organization.

Also subject to government crackdowns have been a variety of Islamic fundamentalist groups, including **Survivors from Hell** (*Al-Najoun Min al-Nar*), **Egypt's Revolution,** implicated in the 1987 shooting of two American officials, **Denouncement and Holy Flight** (*Takfir wa al-Hijra*) and the **Holy Struggle** (*al-Jihad*), a secret organization blamed for attacks against Copts in 1979 and 1980, and the assassination of Sadat in October 1981.

LEGISLATURE

The **People's Assembly** (*Majlis al-Sha'ab*) is a unicameral legislature elected for a five-year term. As sanctioned by a popular referendum, President Sadat dissolved the existing Assembly (which had two years remaining in its term) on April 21, 1979, and announced expansion of the

body from 350 to 392 members, in part to accommodate representatives from the Sinai. Prior to the election of May 27, 1984, the Assembly was further expanded to 458 members, 10 of whom are appointed by the president. At the election of April 6, 1987, held after a February referendum had endorsed an early dissolution, the results were as follows (the 1984 results in brackets): the National Democratic Party, 346 [390]; the Socialist Labor Party and its coalition partners, 60 [0] ("Islamists", 37; SLP, 20; Liberal Socialist Party, 3); New Waft Party, 35 [58]; independents, 7 [0].

President: Dr. Rifa'at al-MAHGOUB.

CABINET

Prime Minister	Dr. 'Atif Muhammad Najib Sidqi
Deputy Prime Minister for Agriculture	Dr. Yussef Amin Wali
Deputy Prime Minister for Defense and Military Production	Field Mar. Muhammad 'Abd al-Halim Abu Ghazala
Deputy Prime Minister for Foreign Affairs	Ahmad Esmet 'Abd al-Meguid
Deputy Prime Minister for Planning	Dr. Kamal Ahmad al-Ganzouri
Ministers	
Cabinet Affairs and Administrative Development	'Atif Muhammad 'Ubayd
Culture	Faruq Husni
Economy and Foreign Trade	Dr. Yusri 'Ali Mustafa
Education	Dr. Ahmad Fathi Surur
Electricity and Energy	Muhammad Mahir Muhammad Abaza
Finance	Dr. Muhammad Ahmad al-Razzaz
Health	Dr. Muhammad Raghib al-Duwaydar
Housing, Utilities and New Communities	Hasaballah Muhammad al-Kafrawi
Industry	Muhammad Mahmud Faraj 'Abd al-Wahhab
Information	Muhammad Safwat Muhammad Yusuf al-Sharif
Interior	Zaki Mustapha 'Ali Badr
International Cooperation	Dr. 'Atif Muhammad Najib Sidqi
Justice	Faruq Saif al-Nasr
Manpower and Training	'Asim 'Abd al-Haq Salih
People's Assembly and Consultative Council Affairs	Ahmad Salama Muhammad
Petroleum and Mineral Resources	'Abd al-Hadi Muhammad Qandil
Public Works and Irrigation	'Isam Radi 'Abd al-Hamid Radi
Religious Trusts	Dr. Muhammad 'Ali Mahjub
Social Insurance and Social Affairs	Amal 'Abd al-Rahim 'Uthman
Supply and Internal Trade	Dr. Muhammad Jalal Abu al-Dahab
Tourism and Civil Aviation	Fuad 'Abd al-Latif Sultan
Transport, Communication and Maritime Transport	Sulayman Mitawalli Sulayman
Ministers of State	
Emigration and Egyptians Abroad	Fuad Iskandar
Foreign Affairs	Butrus Butrus Ghali
International Cooperation	Maurice Makramallah

Military Production	Maj. Gen. Gamal al-Din al-Sayyid Ibrahim
People's Assembly and Consultative Council Affairs	(Vacant)
Scientific Research	Dr. 'Adil 'Abd al-Hamid 'Izz
Governor, Central Bank	Dr. Mahmud Salah al-Din al-Hamid

NEWS MEDIA

The Supreme Press Council, established under a constitutional amendment in May 1980 to assure freedom of the press, oversees newspaper and magazine activity while government boards also direct the state information service, radio, and television. Although the government retains 51 percent ownership (exercised through the *Shura*) of major newspapers and consequent editorial influence, it has in recent years permitted the development of an active and often highly critical opposition press.

Press. The following are Cairo dailies published in Arabic, unless otherwise noted: *al-Ahram* (900,000 daily, 1,100,000 Friday), semiofficial; *al-Akhbar* (790,000), Saturday edition published as *Akhbar al-Yawm* (1,090,000); *al-Jumhuriyah* (650,000); *al-Misaa* (105,000); *Le Journal d'Egypte* (72,000), in French; *Egyptian Gazette* (36,000), in English; *Le Progrès Egyptien* (21,000), in French. Party organs include the National Democratic daily *Mayo* (500,000), the Socialist Labor weekly *al-Shaab* (50,000), the Liberal Socialist weekly *al-Ahrar,* and the National Progressive Unionist weekly *al-Ahali.*

News agencies. The domestic agency is the Middle East News Agency; numerous foreign bureaus also maintain offices at Cairo.

Radio and television. The Arab Republic of Egypt Broadcasting Corporation operates numerous radio stations broadcasting in Arabic and other languages, and some three dozen television stations transmitting in two programs. Commercial radio service is offered by Middle East Radio. There were approximately 15.0 million radio and 3.9 million television receivers in 1987.

INTERGOVERNMENTAL REPRESENTATION

Ambassador to the US: Abdel Raouf al-Sayyed al-REEDY.

US Ambassador to Egypt: Frank G. WISNER.

Permanent Representative to the UN: 'Abd al-Halim BADAWI.

IGO Memberships (Non-UN): ADF, AfDB, AFESD, AMF, BADEA, CCC, *EIB,* IC, ICAC, IDB, Inmarsat, Intelsat, Interpol, IOOC, ISO, IWC, IWTC, LAS, NAM, OAPEC, OAU, PCA.

EL SALVADOR

Republic of El Salvador
República de El Salvador

Political Status: Part of Captaincy General of Guatemala, 1821; independence declared in 1841; republic proclaimed in 1859; constitution of 1962 suspended following military coup of October 15, 1979; provisional government superseded following promulgation of new constitution on December 20, 1983, and presidential election of March 25 and May 6, 1984.

Area: 8,260 sq. mi. (21,393 sq. km.).

Population: 3,554,648 (1971C), 5,026,000 (1988E).

Major Urban Center (1987E): SAN SALVADOR (484,000).

Official Language: Spanish.

Monetary Unit: Colón (official rate March 1, 1988, 5.00 colones = $1US).

President: José Napoleón DUARTE Fuentes (Christian Democratic Party); elected May 6, 1984, and sworn in June 1 for a five-year term, succeeding Provisional President Alvaro Alfredo MAGAÑA Borja (Independent).

Vice President: Rodolfo Antonio CASTILLO Claramount (Christian Democratic Party); elected May 6, 1984, and sworn in June 1 for a term concurrent with that of the President, succeeding Pablo Mauricio ALVERGUE (Christian Democratic Party), Gabriel Mauricio GUTIERREZ Castro (Nationalist Republican Alliance), and Raúl MOLINA Martínez (National Conciliation Party).

THE COUNTRY

The smallest of the Central American countries and the only one whose territory does not touch the Caribbean Sea, El Salvador is oriented geographically and, to some extent, psychologically toward the Pacific and the other isthmus countries. Its population density is the highest in the Americas, while its per capita income is one of the lowest. Although there is a small Indian minority, the people are largely of mixed Spanish and Indian descent, with 90 percent classified as mestizo. The Catholic Church is predominant, but Protestant and Jewish faiths are represented. Women constitute approximately 35 percent of the paid labor force, concentrated largely in domestic and human service sectors and in manufacturing; female participation in government is minimal, with women being most visibly represented in the insurgent Democratic Revolutionary Front (see Parties and Paramilitary Groups, below).

While remaining heavily dependent on agriculture, with coffee as the primary cash crop, El Salvador — prior to the domestic instability generated by the coup of October 1979 — had become the region's leading exporter of manufactured goods. The industrial sector as a whole employed about 20 percent of the work force, with most external sales to the United States and neighboring Central American nations.

During 1979–1987 all major economic indicators steadily declined, counterinsurgency being described by one analyst as the country's "only growth sector". Most severely affected was agriculture, with production of coffee, cotton, and sugar each falling by approximately 50 percent from 1979–1982, while capital flight has been estimated at one billion since 1979. Inflation exceeded 38 percent in 1986, with more than 70 percent of the work force under- or unemployed. In addition, despite land-redistribution efforts in the early 1980s, no more than 15 percent of the rural population currently holds land title.

GOVERNMENT AND POLITICS

Political background. After six decades of turbulence following its proclamation of independence in 1841, El Salvador enjoyed periods of relative calm during the first three decades of this century and again from 1950 to 1960. Lt. Col. Oscar OSIRIO ruled from 1950 to 1956 and was succeeded by an elected president, Lt. Col. José María LEMUS, but a coup d'état in 1960 overthrew Lemus and inaugurated a period of renewed instability.

A new constitution was promulgated in January 1962 and an election was held the following April, although the opposition did not participate. Col. Julio Adalberto RIVERA, candidate of the recently organized National Conciliation Party (PCN), was certified as president and served a five-year term; subsequent PCN victories brought Gen. Fidel SANCHEZ Hernández and Col. Arturo Armando MOLINA Barraza into power in 1967 and 1972, respectively, but announcement of the 1972 results provoked an unsuccessful coup by leftist forces, in the wake of which their candidate, José Napoleón DUARTE Fuentes, was exiled.

Following the election of February 20, 1977, the PCN candidate, Gen. Carlos Humberto ROMERO Mena, was declared president-elect with a majority of 67 percent of the votes cast, although the opposition, as in 1972, charged the government with massive electoral irregularities. The PCN won 50 of 54 seats at the legislative election of March 18, 1978, which was boycotted by most of the opposition on the ground that there were inadequate assurances that the tabulation of results would be impartial.

In the wake of rapidly escalating conflict between right- and left-wing groups, including numerous kidnappings and assassinations, arbitrary arrests by government authorities, and occupations of public buildings by opposition forces, General Romero was ousted on October 15, 1979, in a coup led by Col. Jaime Abdul GUTIERREZ and Col. Adolfo Arnoldo MAJANO Ramos, who were joined by three civilians on October 17 in a five-man ruling junta. While appealing to extremist forces to respect "the will of the majority" and aid in the installation of a "true democracy", the junta was actively opposed by leftist elements protesting military rule, and a state of siege, lifted on October 23, was reimposed three days later.

Two of the three civilian members of the junta, as well as all civilian cabinet members, resigned on January 3, 1980, in protest at a "swing to the Right" for which the remaining civilian junta member, Mario Antonio ANDINO, was allegedly responsible. Andino himself resigned the following day, three prominent Christian Democrats joining the junta on January 9 after obtaining assurances that rightist influence would be contained and a dialogue initiated with leftist organizations. One of the three, Héctor DADA Hirezi, withdrew on March 3 and was replaced by former PDC presidential candidate José Napoleón Duarte, who had returned from exile after the October coup. The most widely publicized terrorist act of the year was the assassination of the liberal Msgr. Oscar Arnulfo ROMERO y Galdames, archbishop of San Salvador, on March 24. While the junta initially blamed leftist forces for the act, the actual perpetrators were widely assumed to be rightist elements.

Earlier, three major mass organizations, in concert with the Salvadoran Communist Party, had announced the formation of a Revolutionary Coordination of the Masses (CRM) to oppose the PDC-military coalition. The CRM was superseded in late April by the Revolutionary Democratic Front (FDR), a coalition of some 18 leftist and far-leftist groups, including a dissident faction of the PDC (see Parties and Paramilitary Groups, below). Subsequently, the major guerrilla organizations formed the Farabundo Martí National Liberation Front (FMLN) to serve, in conjunction with the FDR, as the basis of a projected "democratic revolutionary government" following a leftist victory. In the wake of these and other developments, including the apparent complicity of government security forces in the murder of three American nuns and a lay worker on December 2, the junta was reorganized on December 3, with Duarte and the increasingly hard-line Gutiérrez being sworn in as its president and vice president, respectively, on December 22.

Although the intensity of FMLN activity increased substantially in early 1981, President Duarte on March 5 named a three-member commission to update electoral registers for Constituent Assembly balloting in March 1982. By midyear the Christian Democrats and four rightist parties had been registered, subsequently being joined by the Nationalist Republican Alliance (Arena) of former army major Roberto D'AUBUISSON, who was reported to have been implicated in the murder of Archbishop Romero. The FDR, on the other hand, refused to participate, continuing efforts initiated in January to secure external support for its revolutionary program.

At the election of March 28, 1982, the Christian Democrats secured the largest number of seats (24) in the 60-member Assembly. However, four right-wing parties collectively constituted a majority and refused to permit Duarte to continue as president. The ensuing interparty negotiations resulted in a deadlock, with the Christian Democrats insisting on representation in the new government proportional to their share in the vote. On April 22 the Assembly convened for its first session and elected Major d'Aubuisson as its president by a vote of 35–22. After further negotiations that were reportedly influenced by pressure from the United States, the armed forces presented the Assembly with a list of individuals that it considered acceptable as candidates for provisional chief executive, pending a direct presidential election. One of those listed, the independent Dr. Alvaro MAGAÑA Borja, was accepted by the Assembly on April 29 and sworn in on May 2 together with three vice presidents representing the PDC, the PCN, and Arena. Two days later a 14-member government was formed that included three Christian Democrats, four members from each of the two leading right-wing groups, and three independents.

These events generated no reprieve from insurgent activity. Nonetheless, the five parties represented in the Constituent Assembly agreed in August 1983 to establish a multiparty commission to prepare a timetable for new elections. Following promulgation of a revised constitution on December 20, the Assembly approved presidential balloting for March 1984 and legislative and municipal elections for March 1985.

The 1984 poll was contested by eight candidates, the acknowledged front-runners being d'Aubuisson and Duarte, neither of whom secured a majority. At a runoff on May 6, Duarte emerged the clear winner, with 53.6 percent of the vote, and was inaugurated on June 1.

The FDR-FMLN, refusing to participate in the presidential campaign, stepped up their military activity, although agreeing to peace talks with Duarte in late 1984. The talks, at the guerrilla-held town of La Palma on October 15, were hailed as "historic", but FMLN insistence on a "purification" of the armed forces through the integration of guerrilla elements proved a stumbling block for future talks, which were suspended altogether in January 1985.

In something of a surprise victory, the Christian Democrats swept the March 1985 election, winning 33 seats in the National Assembly and control of 200 of the country's 262 municipalities. The defeat of Arena, which had inhibited land reform measures and blocked Duarte's efforts in the areas of human rights and peace negotiation, was taken as evidence that traditional rightists in the business sector and the military had gone over to the PDC, the former heartened by negotiations with the International Monetary Fund and the latter welcoming US military aid funds and training that had measurably enhanced the armed forces' firepower and counterinsurgency tactics. Duarte, viewing the election results as a "mandate for peace", pledged to reopen negotiations with the insurgents while rebuilding the collapsed Salvadoran economy. Within a year of the election, however, efforts at negotiation had largely been abandoned; economic measures had managed to alienate both the business community and Duarte's traditional grassroots and trade union support; and the military stalemate which had prevailed since 1981 (in the words of a US observer, "due to the high quality and dedication of both sides") continued to sap the country's economy and infrastructure.

The rebels' capacity to act with relative impunity was dramatized by the kidnapping of the president's daughter, Inés Guadalupe DUARTE Durán, by FMLN-affiliated forces in September 1985. The bombardment of insurgent areas was suspended while the bishop of San Salvador negotiated the release of Sra. Duarte and a group of abducted bureaucrats in exchange for 34 political prisoners, including a number of guerrilla commanders, with 98 wounded insurgents given safe passage to Mexico City. The agreement provoked resentment on the part of the armed forces, as well as a widespread perception that only Inés Duarte's abduction had prevented the indefinite detention of the kidnapped officials. Public discontent was further fueled by the government's 1986 economic austerity plan, which included a 100 percent currency devaluation, limited wage concessions, tax increases, and a doubling of gasoline prices. Business leaders charged Duarte with "bowing to the dictates of the IMF", while labor unrest intensified. On February 21, thousands marched at San Salvador to protest sharp increases in the cost of living, which had risen by more than 125 percent since 1980.

Through the mediation of Peruvian President Alan García, the first meeting in more than a year between government and rebel representatives was held at Lima in May 1986. However, Duarte's close advisor, Minister of Culture Julio REY Prendes, insisted that the administration had been "deceived" into believing that the opposition leaders would be speaking for their individual parties rather than on behalf of the FMLN, and the talks were quickly suspended. Subsequently, the country experienced a series of disasters. An earthquake in mid-October that caused massive destruction and more than 1,200 fatalities was followed by the most severe drought in 30 years. The latter yielded a loss of one-quarter of the country's basic grain production and intensification of a hydroelectric shortfall that had been precipitated by insurgent destruction of power pylons and substations.

On the basis of a peace plan advanced by the five Central American presidents in August 1987, discussions with FDR-FMLN representatives were resumed at San Salvador in early October. However, the government insisted that the rebels lay down their arms as a precondition for inclusion in the "democratic" process and the talks again foundered. Subsequently, at legislative balloting in March 1988, Arena won a near majority of 30 seats, with the PDC and PLC winning 23 and 7, respectively.

Constitution and government. The constitution adopted by the Constituent Assembly on December 6, 1983, provides for a president and vice president, both elected by direct popular vote for five-year terms, and for a unicameral National Assembly elected for a three-year term. The judicial system is headed by a Supreme court, whose 13 members are elected by the Assembly. The country is divided into 14 departments headed by governors appointed by the chief executive.

Foreign relations. El Salvador belongs to the United Nations, the Organization of American States, and to their subsidiary bodies. It is an active member of the Organization of Central American States, whose secretariat is located at San Salvador, and of the Central American Common Market.

A period of stability in foreign affairs was shattered by the outbreak of war with Honduras in July 1969. The conflict was generated by incidents in Honduras involving some 300,000 Salvadoran immigrant laborers, whose presence was widely resented by the Hondurans. The immediate precipitant, however, was an international soccer series played between the two countries; consequently, the conflict has been labeled the "Soccer War". Hostilities were ended on July 18 as the result of a ceasefire worked out by OAS intermediaries. Nonetheless, sporadic border incidents continued until the signing of a peace treaty at Lima, Peru, on October 30, 1980, which Salvadoran opposition forces immediately branded as designed to coordinate "repressive policies" by the two governments.

In the early 1980s, following allegations of aid to the FMLN by the *sandinista* regime in Nicaragua, cooperation between El Salvador, Guatemala, and Honduras increased. In October 1983, at the urging of the United States, a revival of the Central American Defense Council (Condeca), originally a four-member group that included Nicaragua, was announced in support of a joint approach to "extracontinental aggression of a Marxist-Leninist character". Although no formal action was undertaken by the truncated Council, San Salvador and Tegucigalpa subsequently cooperated during US military maneuvers in the region in

1983–1984, as well as in attempts to interdict alleged Nicaraguan arms shipments to Salvadoran rebel forces.

The recognition of the FDR-FMLN as a "representative political force" by France and Mexico in a 1981 joint declaration accompanied acceptance of the FDR as a member of the Socialist International and a number of other international organizations. While Mexico subsequently withdrew to a posture of mediation as a member of the Contadora Group, France maintained its position even after a Paris visit by President Duarte in June 1984. Duarte's European tour did, however, result in expressions of support from Belgium and the United Kingdom, as well as in a more tangible $18 million aid pledge from West Germany's Helmut Kohl, a fellow Christian Democrat.

Current issues. The severity of the Christian Democratic defeat in March 1988, which many viewed as consigning Duarte to lame duck status for the remaining year of his presidential term, was attributed to voter weariness at the government's continued inability to come to terms with the rebels, coupled with a sense that Arena, under the seemingly moderate leadership of Alfredo CRISTIANI, had overcome its extremist origins. In addition, observers pointed out that Arena had drawn strong support from conservative peasants and urban slum-dwellers, whose livelihood had been imperiled by the prolonged insurgency. Also damaging to the PDC was the emergence of a bitter intraparty feud between former planning minister Fidel CHAVEZ Mena and former culture and communications minister Julio REY Prendes, each hoping to succeed Duarte, who is ineligible for reelection.

PARTIES AND PARAMILITARY GROUPS

At present, the leading parties in El Salvador are grouped as follows: the Christian Democrats, supporting President Duarte since his election in May 1984, but holding a parliamentary majority only from March 1985 to March 1988; conservative anti-administration parties, some of which have the backing of clandestine right-wing "death squads"; and a coalition of left-wing organizations, most with paramilitary affiliates, that has boycotted every election since 1980 and continues to engage in guerrilla warfare against the Duarte government.

Presidential Party:

Christian Democratic Party (*Partido Demócrata Cristiano* — PDC). A moderately left-of-center grouping, the PDC was the core component of the National Opposition Union (*Unión Nacional Opositora* — UNO), which won 8 legislative seats in 1972 and 14 in 1974 but boycotted the 1976 and 1978 balloting. Its best-known figure, José Napoleón Duarte, returned from exile following the October 1979 coup, joined the junta on March 3, 1980, and became junta president on December 22. He was succeeded by Provisional President Alvaro Magaña in May 1982 after the PDC had failed to secure a majority at the March Constituent Assembly election. Although Duarte was continued as president under the new constitution in May 1984, the PDC did not win legislative control until March 1985; it returned to minority status following the election of March 20, 1988.
Leaders: José Napoleón DUARTE Fuentes (President of the Republic), Dr. José Antonio MORALES Erlich (former member, Ruling Junta), Julio Adolfo REY Prendes (President of the Party), Fidel CHAVEZ Mena, Rodolfo Antonio CASTILLO Claramount (Secretary General).

Other Recognized Parties:

Nationalist Republican Alliance (*Alianza Republicana Nacionalista* — Arena). Arena was launched in 1981 as an outgrowth of the Broad National Front (*Frente Amplio Nacional* — FAN), an extreme right-wing party organized a year earlier by ex-army major Roberto d'Aubuisson. D'Aubuisson was arrested briefly in May 1980 as the instigator of an attempted coup against the junta, which he had accused of "leading the country toward communism". Runner-up at the 1982 election with 19 Assembly seats, the Alliance formed a conservative bloc with the PCN (below), which succeeded in scuttling most of the post-coup land-reform program and secured the appointment of a right-wing judiciary. Although remaining second-ranked at the 1985 balloting, Arena's legislative representation dropped to 13 on the basis of a 29 percent vote share. The party's defeat was both preceded and followed by charges from within that both d'Aubuisson's leadership and reputation were proving a liability to the party. In May, former vice-presidential candidate Hugo Barrera led a splinter out of the party to form the PL (below), while at Arena's national convention in September d'Aubuisson formally resigned as secretary general and accepted appointment as honorary president. The party's new leader, Alfredo Cristiani, was widely regarded as a "technocratic" representative of the coffee and business communities. Arena was awarded 30 of 60 Assembly seats in March 1988, being denied a formal majority by an Electoral Commission decision that awarded one of two disputed seats to the PDC.
Leaders: Maj. Roberto D'AUBUISSON (Honorary President), Alfredo CRISTIANI (President), Mario REPDAELI (Secretary General).

National Conciliation Party (*Partido de Conciliación Nacional* — PCN). At the time of its founding in 1961, the PCN enjoyed a fairly broad range of political support and displayed some receptivity to social and economic reform. Over the years, however, it became increasingly conservative, serving the interests of the leading families and the military establishment. Following the declared willingness of its leadership to support peace talks with the rebels in mid-1982, 9 of its 14 assemblymen withdrew to form PAISA (below). The PCN's Francisco Guerrero, running as a candidate of moderation, placed third in the March 1984 presidential balloting, and his refusal to back d'Aubuisson in the runoff was considered crucial to Duarte's victory. The party won 12 legislative seats in March 1985, five of which were lost in the 1988 poll.
Leaders: Francisco José GUERRERO (1984 presidential candidate), Hugo CARRILLO (former Secretary General), Raúl MOLINA Martínez (Secretary General).

Salvadoran Authentic Institutional Party (*Partido Auténtico Institucional Salvadoreño* — PAISA). Formed in October 1982 as a right-wing offshoot of the PCN, PAISA was a dependable ally of Arena in the Constituent Assembly. Its presidential candidate, Col. Roberto Escobar, won only 1.2 percent of the vote in March 1985, while its Assembly representation dropped from nine seats to one; it secured no seats in 1988.
Leaders: Col. Roberto ESCOBAR García (1984 presidential candidate and Secretary General of the Party), Julia Maria CASTILLO.

Democratic Action (*Acción Democrática* — AD). The AD was organized in 1981 as a moderately reformist group committed to the defense of private enterprise. It won two Assembly seats in 1982 and subsequently supported the PDC in its talks with the rebels. In 1988 it lost the single seat won in 1985.
Leaders: René FORTIN Magaña (1984 presidential candidate), Ricardo GONZALEZ Camacho.

Smaller recognized parties include the **Stable Republican Centrist Movement** (*Movimiento Estable Republicano Centrista* — Merecen), a Conservative group led by Juan Ramón ROSALES; the **Popular Salvadoran Party** (*Partido Popular Salvadoreño* — PPS), led by Francisco QUIÑONEZ Avila, which functioned as the PCN's only formal opposition in the 1978 election; and the business-supported **Popular Orientation Party** (*Partido de Orientacion Popular* — POP) led by Gilberto TRUJILLO.

Unrecognized Groups:

In the wake of the 1985 legislative balloting, a number of new parties sought official registration, most significantly the **Free Fatherland** (*Patria Libre* — PL), also identified as the New Fatherland (*Patria Nueva*), formed by Hugo BARRERA, d'Aubuisson's 1984 running mate, upon his departure from Arena in May 1985; others included the **Independent Democratic Party** (*Partido Independiente Democrático* — PID), led by Eduardo

GARCIA Tobar, and the student-backed **Salvadoran Centrist Party** (*Partido Centrista Salvadoreño* — PACES), founded by Tomás CHAFOYA Martínez.

Democratic Convergence (*Convergencia Democrática* — CD). The CD was organized in November 1987 as an alliance of the following three groups, two of which (the MNR and the MPSC) had long been core components of the FDR (below). The new coalition, characterized as part of an effort by the theretofore clandestine formations to resume open political activity within El Salvador, was ranked third (behind Arena and the PDC) in a public opinion poll conducted prior to the 1988 balloting, at which the CD did not attempt to present candidates. Despite their participation in the CD, the MNR and MPSC indicated that they did not intend to withdraw from the FDR or sever their links to its military wing, the FMLM.

Leaders: Mario Reni ROLDAN (PSD), Guillermo Manuel UNGO Revelo (MNR), Dr. Rubén ZAMORA Rivas (MPSC).

Social Democratic Party (*Partido Social Demócrata* — PSD). The PSD is a left-wing grouping formed in 1987 by Mario Reni Roldán, a participant in the government-rebel peace talks.

Leader: Mario Reni ROLDAN (Secretary General).

National Revolutionary Movement (*Movimiento Nacional Revolucionario* — MNR). The MNR is a social-democratic party that participated in the *Unión Nacional Opositora* from 1972 to 1978. It was a founding member of the FDR (below), following the resignation of Guillermo Manuel Ungo from the junta in January 1980.

Leaders: Guillermo Manuel UNGO Revelo (President), Eduardo CALLES (Vice President), Héctor OQUELI Colindres.

Social Christian Popular Movement (*Movimiento Popular Social Cristiano* — MPSC). Also a founding component of the FDR, with a substantially larger political base than the MNR, the MPSC has tended to waver somewhat in its degree of commitment to the rebel cause.

Leader: Rubén Ignacio ZAMORA Rivas.

Left-Wing Dissident and Paramilitary Groups:

Democratic Revolutionary Front (*Frente Democrático Revolucionario* — FDR). The FDR was formed in April 1980 as an umbrella organization of the dissident political groups listed below. Its paramilitary affiliate is the **Farabundo Martí National Liberation Front** (*Frente Farabundo Martí para la Liberación Nacional* — FMLN), organized in October 1980 under the leadership of Salvador CAYETANO Carpio. The FMLN is headed by a National Revolutionary Directorate (*Dirección Revolucionaria Nacional* — DRN) composed of representatives of participating paramilitary organizations. On April 12, 1983, Cayetano Carpio died, apparently a suicide, at Managua, Nicaragua.

On January 14, 1981, the FDR announced the formation of a seven-member diplomatic-political commission which would seek external support for the establishment of a "democratic revolutionary government" in El Salvador. Expelled from their headquarters at Managua, Nicaragua, in December 1983 following the US invasion of Grenada, the FDR leadership relocated to Mexico City. In late 1985, MPSC leader Rubén Zamora confirmed reports that a number of FDR activists were moving back to El Salvador in order to engage in legal political organization. However, the FDR-FMLN directorate immediately issued a denial that friction between the coalition's political and military wings had resulted in a split of any kind, stating instead that the activists would be "building a mass base" for the insurgents in urban areas.

Leaders: Guillermo Manuel UNGO Revelo (FDR President), Mario AGUIÑADA Carranza (UDN), Jorge Shafik HANDAL (UDN-PCS), Ana Guadalupe MARTINEZ (ERP), José Napoleón RODRIGUEZ Ruiz (FAPU), Salvador SAMAYOA (FPL), Joaquím VILLALOBOS (FMLN Commander), Dr. Rubén Ignacio ZAMORA Rivas (MPSC).

National Revolutionary Movement (see under Democratic Convergence, above).

Social Christian Popular Movement (see under Democratic Convergence, above).

Christian Democratic Party–Popular Faction (*Partido Demócrata Cristiano–Facción Popular* — PDC-FP). The PDC-FP is a dissident PDC group led by Hectór Antonio Dada, who served as a member of the junta during the period January 9–March 3, 1980.

Leader: Hectór Miquel Antonio DADA Hirezi.

National Democratic Union (*Unión Demócrata Nacional* — UDN). Serving prior to the 1979 coup as a legal front for the **Salvadoran Communist Party** (*Partido Comunista Salvadoreño* — PCS), the UDN participated in the *Unión Nacional Opositora* during the 1977 presidential campaign. The PCS (also known as the *Partido Comunista de El Salvador* — PCES) is a small pro-Moscow group that was long repudiated by most mass and guerrilla organizations for its "revisionist" tendencies. In early 1980 it adopted a more militant posture, becoming, under its secretary general, Jorge Shafik Handal, the equivalent of the UNO's paramilitary wing.

Leaders: Mario AGUIÑADA Carranza, Dr. Gabriel GALLEGOS Valdés, Jorge Shafik HANDAL.

Popular Revolutionary Bloc (*Bloque Popular Revolucionario* — BPR). Espousing a blend of Marxist and Christian teachings, the BPR was formed in 1975 as a largely peasant front, with the well-organized Federation of Field Workers (*Federación de Trabajadores del Campo* — FTC) as one of its key components. Subsequently, it was broadened to include a large number of peasant, student, trade-union, and other groups. Its increased urban militancy was reflected in occupations of the Costa Rican, French, and Venezuelan embassies as well as the Catholic cathedral at San Salvador during 1979.

What eventually became the paramilitary wing of the BPR, the **Popular Liberation Forces** (*Fuerzas Populares de Liberación* — FPL), was organized in 1970 as a Trotskyite breakaway faction of the PCS by the latter's former secretary general, Salvador Cayetano Carpio. The largest of the left-wing guerrilla groups (currently accounting for about 50 percent of the FMLN's total forces), the FPL claimed responsibility for numerous reprisals against the former government's militia force (Orden) in the rural areas as well as for a series of urban assassinations, including those of the minister of education and a government legislative deputy in mid-1979. In late 1979 it announced that it had entered into a tactical alliance with FARN (see FAPU, below), and, increasingly identified as the *Fuerzas Populares de Liberación-Farabundo Martí* (FPL-FM), joined with FARN and the ERP (see LP-28, below) in forming the FMLN in October 1980.

Following the 1979 coup, the BPR announced that it had entered into a "tactical alliance" with FAPU, and, in concert with FAPU and LP-28, in January 1980 organized the **Revolutionary Coordination of the Masses** (*Coordinadora Revolucionaria de Masas* — CRM), which in turn became a component of the FDR in late April.

Leaders: Facundo GUARDADO, Oscar MEJIA, Marco Antonio PORTILLO, Francisco REBOLLA, Carlos GOMEZ (Secretary General).

Unified Popular Action Front (*Frente de Acción Popular Unificado* — FAPU). Somewhat similar to the BPR but with a more distinctly Marxist orientation, FAPU was established as a coalition of student, peasant, and trade-union groups in 1974 and participated in a number of demonstrations at the capital, including occupation of the Mexican Embassy in early 1979. Its military wing is the **Armed Forces of National Resistance** (*Fuerzas Armadas de Resistencia Nacional* — FARN), led by Fermán CIENFUEGOS, who may have been killed during a clash with government troops in early 1988. FARN has been one of the most visible of the terrorist groups since engaging in the abduction of numerous Salvadoran and foreign businessmen in 1978–1979, most of whom were released following payment of substantial ransoms.

As a member of the CRM, FAPU participated in the launching of the FDR and is presently represented in its diplomatic-political commission, while FARN's Cienfuegos was a FMLN representative at the La Palma talks in October 1984.

Leaders: Saúl VILLALTA, José Napóleon RODRIGUEZ Ruiz.

February 28 Popular Leagues (*Ligas Populares del 28 de Febrero* — LP-28). The LP-28 is a relatively small political organization that participated in formation of both the CRM and the FDR. Its paramilitary affiliate, the **People's Revolutionary Army** (*Ejercito Revolucionario del Pueblo* — ERP), is, on the other hand, the second-largest component of the FMLN, its leader, Joaquín Villalobos, being widely regarded as the FMLN's chief military strategist. Possibly the most extreme of the guerrilla groups, the ERP has experienced a number of internal cleavages since its formation in 1972, one of the most crucial (which led to the creation of FARN) stemming from the murder of one of its founders, Roque Dalton García. There have also been sporadic differences with the FPL over military strategy, stemming in part from the fact that the two forces are largely based in different provinces (Morazán and Chalatenango, respectively). Perhaps significantly, the ERP is represented directly on the FDR diplomatic-political commission, while LP-28 is not so represented.

Leader: Leoncio PICHINTE, Joaquín VILLALOBOS (Secretary General).

Two additional mass organizations are the **Political Antifascist Detachment** (*Destacamento Político Antifascista*—DPA) and the **Liberation Leagues** (*Ligas Liberaciones*—LL), whose paramilitary wings are the **People's Revolutionary Armed Forces** (*Fuerzas Revolucionarias Armadas del Pueblo*—FRAP) and the **Revolutionary Party of Central American Workers** (*Partido Revolucionario de Trabajadores Centroamericanos*—PRTC), respectively. The PRTC gained substantial visibility in 1985: early in the year one of its top commanders, Nidia DIAZ, was captured by government forces with most of the group's records in her possession, in what was described by army sources as a "substantial victory". On June 19, the group claimed responsibility for the bombing of a San Salvador cafe which killed four US Marines. Díaz was one of the highest-ranking guerrilla leaders to be included in the controversial prisoner exchange of November 1985, which led to the release of Inés Duarte Durán.

Two small groups that have been cited as responsible for terrorist attacks within San Salvador, as well as the Inés Duarte kidnapping, are the **Pedro Pablo Castillo Front** and the **Clara Elizabeth Ramírez Front,** both of which subsequently appeared to function primarily as tactical units of the FMLN.

Right-Wing Terrorist Groups:

Extreme right-wing groups include the **Falange,** an organization with reputed links to the military and the "14 families"; the **Union of White Warriors** (*Unión de Guerreros Blancos*—UGB), a self-styled "death squad" that has acknowledged responsibility for killing numerous individuals, including Jesuit priests believed to be associated with left-wing terrorists; the **Salvadoran Anti-Communist Army** (*Ejército Salvadoreño Anticomunista*—ESA), led by Cdr. Aquiles BAIRES, an increasingly visible "death squad" responsible for death threats against Duarte, the Electoral Commission, and various trade unionists; the **Knights of Christ the King** (*Caballeros de Cristo Rey*), organized by the bishop of San Vincent; the **Independent Society of Nocturnal Vigilantes** (*Sociedad Independiente de Vigilantes Nocturnos*), originally established as a private security force; and the **Maximiliano Hernández Martínez Brigade,** named after a former president who was reportedly responsible for the death of 30,000 peasants in a 1932 uprising.

LEGISLATURE

At balloting for the present 60-member **Legislative Assembly** (*Asamblea Legislativa*), elected for a three-year term on March 20, 1988, the Nationalist Republican Alliance won 30 seats; the Christian Democratic Party, 23; and the National Conciliation Party, 7.

President: Guillermo Antonio GUEVARA Lacayo.

CABINET

President	José Napoleón Duarte Fuentes
Vice President	Rodolfo Antonio Castillo Claramount
Ministers	
Agriculture and Livestock	Antonio Morales Ehrlich
Culture and Communications	Roberto Edmundo Viera
Defense and Public Security	Gen. Carlos Eugenio Vides Casanova
Economy	José Ricardo Perdomo
Education	Carlos Cruz Alvarez
Finance	Ricardo López Cabezas
Foreign Affairs	Ricardo Acevedo Peralta
Foreign Trade	Carlos Aquilino Duarte Funes
Interior	Edgar Ernesto Belloso Funes
Justice	Julio Alfredo Samayoa
Labor and Social Welfare	Lázaro Tadeo Bernal Lizama
Planning	Remo Bardi
Presidency	Col. Carlos Reynaldo López Nuila
Public Health and Social Services	Benjamin Valdéz
Public Works	Luis López Cerón
Presidential Commissioners	
Administrative Reform	Rafael José Pleytez Menéndez
Economic Affairs	Atilio Viéytez Cañas
President, Central Bank	Mauricio Choussy Rusconi

NEWS MEDIA

News media, with the exception of one official journal and certain broadcasting facilities, are nominally free of censorship and government control. Most commercial media are, however, owned by right-wing interests.

Press. The following newspapers are published daily at San Salvador, unless otherwise noted: *La Prensa Gráfica* (96,000 daily, 116,000 Sunday), conservative; *El Diario de Hoy* (76,000 daily, 76,000 Sunday), ultraconservative; *El Mundo* (58,000 daily, 63,000 Sunday); *Diario Latino* (25,000), conservative; *Diario Oficial* (2,100), government owned.

News agencies. The Spanish *Agencia EFE* maintains an office at San Salvador; AP, Reuters, and UPI are also represented.

Radio and television. Broadcasting is supervised by the official *Administración Nacional de Telecomunicaciones.* Virtually all of the licensed radio stations are commercial, one exception being the government-operated *Radio Nacional de El Salvador.* In 1981 the government attempted to link all radio outlets to the national network to silence guerrilla broadcasts, although they continued over "Radio Liberation" and "Radio Venceremos" (the latter launched by the ERP, but subsequently serving as the voice of the FMLN). Two of San Salvador's five television channels feature educational programming and are government operated. There were approximately 1.2 million radio and 425,000 television receivers in 1987.

INTERGOVERNMENTAL REPRESENTATION

Ambassador to the US: Ernesto RIVAS Gallont.

US Ambassador to El Salvador: Edwin G. CORR .

Permanent Representative to the UN: Roberto MEZA.

IGO Memberships (Non-UN): BCIE, CACM, CDC, Geplacea, IADB, ICAC, ICM, ICO, Intelsat, ISO, IWTC, OAS, ODECA, OPANAL, SELA.

EQUATORIAL GUINEA

Republic of Equatorial Guinea
República de Guinea Ecuatorial

Political Status: Former Spanish Guinea; independent republic established October 12, 1968; military rule imposed following coup of August 3, 1979; present constitution adopted August 15, 1982.

Area: 10,830 sq. mi. (28,051 sq. km.).

Population: 304,000 (1983C), 352,000 (1988E); both figures exclude an estimated 100,000 people who fled the country prior to the 1979 coup.

Major Urban Centers (1984E): MALABO (Bioko, 42,000); Bata (Río Muni, 53,000).

Official Language: Spanish.

Monetary Unit: CFA franc (market rate March 1, 1988, 285.50 CFA francs = $1US). The CFA franc replaced the former currency, the epkwele, upon Equatorial Guinea's admission to the Central African Customs and Economic Union in December 1983.

President: Col. Teodoro OBIANG Nguema Mbasogo; assumed power as President of a Supreme Military Council following the ouster of MACIE (formerly Francisco Macías) Nguema Biyogo Ñegue Ndong on August 3, 1979; inaugurated October 12, 1982, following confirmation for a seven-year term by referendum on August 15.

Prime Minister: Capt. Cristino SERICHE Bioko; designated Second Vice President by the Supreme Military Council on December 7, 1981, succeeding Capt. Eulogio OYO Riquesa; named Prime Minister under constitution of August 15, 1982.

THE COUNTRY

The least populous and the only Spanish-speaking Black African nation, Equatorial Guinea consists of two sharply differing regions: the mainland territory of Río Muni, including Corisco, Elobey Grande, and Elobey Chico islands as well as adjacent islets; and the island of Bioko (known prior to 1973 as Fernando Póo and from 1973 to 1979 as Macías Nguema Biyogo), including Pagalu (known prior to 1973 as Annobón) and adjacent islets in the Gulf of Guinea. Río Muni, whose area is 10,045 square miles (26,017 sq. km.), accounts for more than nine-tenths of the country's territory and about three-quarters of its total population; Bata is the principal urban center. Bioko's area covers 785 square miles (2,034 sq. km.); Malabo is the chief town and the capital of the Republic.

The two basic ethnic groups, both Bantu subgroupings, are the Fang in Río Muni and the Bubi in Bioko. Other elements include the Kombe and various coastal tribes in Río Muni, and Fernandinos (persons of mixed racial descent) in Bioko. While Spanish is the language of administration and education, various African dialects are spoken and pidgin English serves as a commercial lingua franca. Roman Catholicism is the religion of approximately 80 percent of the population.

The economy, in which the island of Bioko has enjoyed undisputed leadership, is based largely on timber, coffee, palm products, bananas, and cocoa, the last traditionally being the principal export. Industry consists primarily of small-scale agriprocessing operations; recent offshore exploration for oil has failed to locate commercially exploitable reserves. Since the August 1979 coup, aid has been tendered by Spain, France, and other international donors to help Equatorial Guinea recover from the economic devastation of the Macie era, during which most skilled workers were killed or fled the country, cocoa production

and per capita GNP plummeted, and such essential urban services as power and water were disrupted. By 1983, exports had begun to rise, although nowhere near pre-1968 levels, but the overall process of recovery has been slow.

GOVERNMENT AND POLITICS

Political background. The former territory of Spanish Guinea, with Spanish sovereignty dating from 1778, was granted provincial status in 1959 and internal autonomy in 1964, achieving full independence under the name of Equatorial Guinea on October 12, 1968. The preindependence negotiations with Spain had been complicated by differences between the mainland Fang, whose representatives sought the severance of all links with Spain, and the island Bubi, whose spokesmen advocated retention of some ties with Spain and semiautonomous status within a federal system. A compromise constitution and electoral law, submitted for popular approval in a UN-supervised referendum on August 11, 1968, was accepted by 63 percent of the people, the substantial adverse vote reflecting Bubi fears of mainland domination as well as Fang objections to the degree of self-rule accorded the islanders. In presidential balloting a month later, MACIAS Nguema Biyogo, a mainland Fang associated with the Popular Idea of Equatorial Guinea (*Idea Popular de Guinea Ecuatorial* – IPGE), defeated the head of the preindependence autonomous government, Bonifacio ONDO Edu of the Movement for the National Unity of Equatorial Guinea (*Movimiento de Union Nacional de Guinea Ecuatorial* – MUNGE). Along with other Equatorial Guineans, Macías dropped his Christian name (Francisco) on September 26, 1975; in 1976 he also changed his surname from Macías to Macie.

In 1969 President Macías seized emergency powers during a major international crisis involving tribal rivalries, personality conflicts, allegations of continued Spanish colonialism, and conflicting foreign economic interests. Following an unsuccessful coup d'état led by Foreign Minister Atanasio N'DONGO Miyone of the National Movement for the Liberation of Equatorial Guinea (*Movimiento Nacional de Liberación de la Guinea Ecuatorial* – Monalige), the president arrested some 200 individuals, most of whom (including N'Dongo) were executed. An accompanying panic, aggravated by the extralegal activities of Macías' youth militia, provoked the flight of the country's Spanish population. Subsequently, a highly centralized, single-party state was instituted, Macie's control being formalized by his assuming the presidency for life in July 1972.

Macie's 11-year rule (during which the country became widely known as the "Auschwitz of Africa") was terminated on August 3, 1979, in a coup led by his nephew, (then) Lt. Col. Teodoro OBIANG Nguema Mbasogo, who assumed the presidency of a Supreme Military Council that later in the month named Capt. Florencio MAYE Elá and Capt. Salvador ELA Nseng as first and second vice presidents, respectively. In February 1980 Elá Nseng was succeeded by Capt. Eulogio OYO Riquesa, presiding officer of the military tribunal that had ordered Macie's execution on September 29, 1979, for crimes that included genocide, treason, and embezzlement. The government was further reshuffled in early December 1981, the first vice presidency becoming vacant in the wake of Mayé Elá's assignment to the United Nations, and Capt. Cristino SERICHE Bioko succeeding Oyo Riquesa as second vice president.

Concurrent with the adoption, by referendum, of a new constitution on August 15, 1982, Colonel Obiang was confirmed as president for a seven-year term. Subsequently, Captain Seriche was named prime minister, the two vice-presidential roles being eliminated. The first National Assembly election mandated by the new constitution was held on August 28, 1983.

An attempted coup of unclear origin (the third since 1981) failed to unseat Colonel Obiang in 1986 while he was in France attending July 14th celebrations. Reports indicated that some 30 military and civilians attempted to take over the presidential palace but were arrested by government loyalists. At first, the government denied a revolt had occurred; a month later, however, Eugenio ABESO Mondu, a former diplomat and a member of the National Assembly, was executed for his involvement, with 13 others, including prominent cabinet members and military officers, sentenced to jail terms.

Constitution and government. The 1973 constitution, which assigned virtually unlimited powers to the president, was abrogated following the 1979 coup. The 1982 document provides for an elected president serving a seven-year term, and for a Council of State, one of whose functions is to screen candidates for presidential nomination. A National Council for Economic and Social Development serves the administration in a consultative capacity, while legislative functions are assigned to a unicameral National Assembly, whose members are elected for five-year terms. The judiciary is headed by a Supreme Court at Malabo, which acts as the country's highest court of appeals.

In late 1980, as part of a process of administrative reform, the country was divided into six provinces (four mainland and two insular). Subsequently, while local functionaries continued to be appointed from Malabo, some decentralization of government occurred, and plans were announced for the establishment of local government councils.

Foreign relations. While officially nonaligned, the Macie regime tended to follow the lead of the more radical African states. Diplomatic relations were established with — and aid received from — several Communist regimes, including the Soviet Union, the People's Republic of China, Cuba, and North Korea. Relations with Gabon and Cameroon were strained as a result of territorial disputes, while by 1976 the mistreatment of Nigerian contract workers had led Lagos to repatriate some 25,000, most of them cocoa plantation laborers. Since 1979, however, Colonel Obiang has increased cooperation with his country's neighbors, with a Nigerian consulate opening at Bata in 1982 and a joint defense pact concluded during a three-day official visit to Lagos by President Obiang in January 1987. Economic agreements were signed with Cameroon and the Central African Republic in 1983, and Obiang was active in the formation of the Central African Economic Community, announced in October 1983. Two months later,

Equatorial Guinea became the first non-French-speaking member of the Central African Customs and Economic Union (UDEAC).

At the time of Macie's ouster, France was the only Western power maintaining an embassy at Malabo, although Spain had long been purchasing export commodities at above-market prices. Madrid made its first overture to the new regime in December 1979 with a state visit by King Juan Carlos, in the wake of which economic and military assistance was tendered; in 1983, it played a leading role in renegotiating the country's $45 million foreign debt. At present, despite Equatorial Guinea's admission to UDEAC and the franc zone, Spain remains a major aid source and trade partner.

Current issues. In late 1987 President Obiang issued a pardon for 50 political prisoners, many of whom had been convicted for complicity in the 1986 coup attempt. Meanwhile, economic adversity continued to thwart government efforts to revive the cocoa industry and improve the transportation infrastructure, despite IMF approval for rescheduling of payments on the country's large external debt.

POLITICAL PARTIES

Political parties were banned in the wake of the 1979 coup. In August 1987, on the eighth anniversary of his seizure of power, President Obiang announced the launching of a **Democratic Party of Equatorial Guinea** (*Partido Democrática de Guinea Ecuatorial* — PDGE). The new formation was described as a "government party" rather than a "single party", with a prospect that other parties might eventually be sanctioned, depending on the country's "experience and stage of development".

Exile Groups:

National Alliance for the Restoration of Democracy (*Alianza Nacional de Restauración Democrática* — ANRD). Founded in 1974 and now the oldest of the external groups, the Swiss-based ANRD announced in August 1979 that it would regard the ouster of Macie Nguema as nothing more than a "palace revolution" unless a number of conditions were met, including the trial of all individuals for atrocities under the former dictator and the establishment of a firm date for termination of military rule. It repudiated the 1982 constitutional referendum and in April 1983 joined with the **Movement for the Liberation and Future of Equatorial Guinea** (*Movimiento de Liberación y Futuro de Guinea Ecuatorial* — Molifuge) and two smaller groups in establishing a **Coordinating Board of Opposition Democratic Forces** (*Junta Coordinadora da las Fuerzas de Oposición Democrática*), which denounced the August legislative balloting as a "sham" and called for an economic embargo of the Obiang regime by regional governments.

Leader: Martín NSOMO Okomo (Secretary General).

Democratic Movement for the Liberation of Equatorial Guinea (*Reunión Democrática para la Liberación de Guinea Ecuatorial* — RDLGE). Formed in 1981, the Paris-based RDLGE announced a provisional government-in-exile following the failure of reconciliation talks between its leader and Colonel Obiang in late 1982. In 1984 it joined with the Spanish-based **Socialist Party of Equatorial Guinea** (*Partido Socialista de Guinea Ecuatorial* — PSAGE) in an alliance styled the **Social Democratic Convergence** (*Convergencia Social Democrática* — CSD).

Leader: Manuel Rubén NDONGO.

Other formations include the **April 1 Bubi Nationalist Group**, which has issued a number of manifestos calling for an end to alleged human rights abuses against the Bubi people and independence for the island of Bioko.

LEGISLATURE

The present constitution provides for a unicameral **House of People's Representatives** (*Cámara de Representantes del Pueblo*) to meet for a five-year term. In balloting held August 28, 1983, 41 unopposed candidates, chosen by Colonel Obiang, were elected by 50,000 voters.

CABINET

Prime Minister	Capt. Cristino Seriche Bioko
Deputy Prime Minister	Alejanro Envoro Ovono
Ministers	
Agriculture	Alfredo Abero Nvono
Civil Service	Massoko Mecheba Ikaka
Communications and Transport	Demetrio Elo Ndongo Nsefumu
Defense	Col. Teodoro Obiang Nguema Mbasogo
Economic Planning	Hilario Nsue Alene
Education and Sports	Fortunato Nzambi Machinde
Energy	Olo Mba
Finance	Felipe Inestroka Ikaka
Foreign Affairs	Marcelino Nguema Onguene
Health	Sisinio Nsoro M'Bana
Industry and Commerce	Francisco Pascual Obama Eyegue
Information and Tourism	Leandro Mbomio Nsue
Justice and Religion	Angel Ndongo Micha
Labor	Anacleto Ejapa Bolekia
Public Works and Territorial Administration	Alejanro Envoro Ovono
Water Resources and Forestry	Angel Alongo Nchama

NEWS MEDIA

Press. The following are published at Malabo, unless otherwise noted: *Ebano* (1,000), official daily in Spanish; *Poto Poto* (Bata), daily in Spanish and Fang; *Hoja Parroquial,* weekly. An additional publication, *Unidad de la Guinea Ecuatorial,* is issued on an irregular basis.

News agency. The only facility currently operating at Malabo is Spain's *Agencia EFE.*

Radio and television. *Radio Nacional de Guinea Ecuatorial* broadcasts over two stations at Bata and one at Malabo in Spanish and vernacular languages; the government's *Television Nacional* transmits over one channel at Malabo. There were approximately 100,000 radio and 2,500 television receivers in use in 1987.

INTERGOVERNMENTAL REPRESENTATION

Ambassador to the US and Permanent Representative to the UN: (Vacant).

US Ambassador to Equatorial Guinea: Chester E. NORRIS, Jr.

IGO Memberships (Non-UN): ADF, AfDB, BADEA, BDEAC, CEEAC, EEC(L), *EIB,* Interpol, NAM, OAU, UDEAC.

ETHIOPIA

People's Democratic Republic of Ethiopia
Hizbawit Democrasiawi Republik Ityopia

Political Status: Former monarchy; provisional military government formally established September 12, 1974, cul-minating a gradual assumption of power begun in February 1974; Marxist-Leninist one-party system instituted September 6, 1984; Communist constitution approved by referendum of February 1, 1987, with effect from September 12.

Area: 471,799 sq. mi. (1,221,900 sq. km.).

Population: 42,169,203 (1984C); 46,728,000 (1988E).

Major Urban Centers (1980E): ADDIS ABABA (1,277,000); Asmara (425,000); Dire Dawa (82,000); Gondar-Azezo (77,000); Dessie (76,000); Nazret (70,000); Jimma (64,000); Harar (63,000).

Official Language: Amharic.

Monetary Unit: Birr (market rate March 1, 1988, 2.82 birr = $1US).

President of the Republic and General Secretary of the Workers' Party of Ethiopia: Lt. Col. MENGISTU Haile-Mariam; named chairman of the Provisional Military Administrative Council (PMAC) on February 11, 1977, following the death of Brig. Gen. TEFERI Banti on February 3; named Secretary General of the WPE on September 10, 1984; elected to a five-year term as President of the Republic by the National Assembly on September 10, 1987.

Vice President: Lt. Col. FISSEHA Desta; elected by the National Assembly on September 10, 1987.

Prime Minister: Lt. Col. FIKRE-SELASSIE Wogderes; appointed by the President on September 10, 1987.

THE COUNTRY

One of the oldest countries in the world, Ethiopia exhibits an ethnic, linguistic, and cultural diversity that has impaired its political unity and stability in spite of the preponderant position long occupied by the Christian, Amharic- and Tigrinya-speaking inhabitants of the central highlands. Among the more than 40 different tribes and peoples, the Amhara and the closely related Tigrai number about 33 percent of the population, with the largely Muslim Galla accounting for 40 percent. Amharic, the official language, is spoken by about 60 percent of the people; Galla, Tigrinya, Arabic, Somali, and Tigre are also prominent among the country's 70 languages and over 200 dialects, while English, Italian, and French have traditionally been employed within the educated elite. The Ethiopian Orthodox (Coptic) Church embraces about 40 percent of the population, as does Islam. Women supply about one-quarter of the labor force, the vast majority as unpaid agricultural workers; although females have traditionally influenced decisionmaking among the Amhara and Tigres peoples, their representation in the Mengistu government is minimal.

One of the world's half-dozen poorest countries in terms of per capita GNP, Ethiopia remains dependent on agriculture, with over 80 percent of its rapidly expanding population engaged in farming and livestock-raising. The principal export is coffee, which accounts for more than 60 percent of export earnings. Industrial development, primarily concentrated in nondurable consumer goods, has been hampered by the quarter-century-old civil war in Eritrea and guerrilla activity in other regions. Gold is mined commercially, and deposits of copper, potash, and natural gas have recently been discovered. A National Revolutionary Development Campaign was launched in February 1979 to centralize economic planning, including increased collectivization of land and formation of producer cooperatives. Following abolition of the monarchy, Communist sources became the leading suppliers of military and economic aid, although severe drought-induced famine, which caused an estimated one million deaths in 1984–1985, spurred large-scale emergency contributions of food by Western nations.

The government has recently concluded the first phase of a controversial "villagization" program, under which some 30–35 million peasants are to be moved by 1991 from isolated farms to newly created villages, where it is contended that health, education, communication, and energy services will be more readily available. The program also reflects the regime's commitment, contrary to the prevailing trend in most of Africa, to increased state intervention (implicitly yielding collectivization) in agricultural production, which Western critics argue will hinder, rather than facilitate the attainment of development goals.

An ostensibly distinct program of "resettlement" was launched in 1985 to move 1.0–1.5 million persons from the northern highlands to the more fertile south. The latter program was suspended for most of 1986 because of charges that relocation was occurring at gunpoint, with many deaths en route. It was resumed in 1987, allegedly on a voluntary basis. As in the case of villagization, the peasants are required to form villages rather than dispersing throughout the countryside.

GOVERNMENT AND POLITICS

Political background. After centuries of medieval isolation, Ethiopia began its history as a modern state with the reign of Emperor MENELIK II (1889–1913), who established a strong central authority and successfully resisted attempts at colonization by Italy and other powers. Emperor HAILE SELASSIE I (Ras TAFARI Makonnen) succeeded to the throne in 1930 on the death of his cousin, the Empress ZAUDITU. Confronted with a full-scale invasion by Fascist Italy in 1935, Haile Selassie vainly appealed for assistance from the League of Nations and remained abroad until Ethiopia's liberation by the British and the liquidation of Italy's East African Empire in 1941. In accordance with a decision of the UN General Assembly, the former Italian colony of Eritrea was joined to Ethiopia in 1952 as an autonomous unit in an Ethiopian-Eritrean federation. Abandonment of the federal structure by formal incorporation of Eritrea into Ethiopia in 1962 fanned separatist sentiment, which became the basis of protracted guerrilla warfare.

Although the post-World War II period witnessed a movement away from absolute monarchy, the pace of liberalization did not meet popular expectations, and in early 1974 an uprising among troops of Ethiopia's Second Army Division gradually escalated into a political revolt. As a result, Prime Minister Tshafe Tezaz AKLILU Habte-Wold resigned on February 28 and was replaced by ENDALKACHEW Makonnen, who also was unable to contain discontent among military, labor, and student groups. By late spring many aristocrats and former government officials had been imprisoned, and on July 22 Endalkachew was forced to resign in favor of Mikael IMRU.

On September 12 the military announced that the emperor had been officially deposed in favor of his son, ASFA WOSSEN, who would have only a ceremonial role, and that a Provisional Military Government (PMG) had been formed under Lt. Gen. AMAN Mikael Andom. Initially, the military presented a united front, but rival factions soon emerged. On November 24 approximately 60 officials, including two former prime ministers and Aman Andom, were executed, apparently on the initiative of (then) Maj. MENGISTU Haile-Mariam, strongman of the little-publicized Armed Forces Coordinating Committee, or *Dergue,* as it was popularly known. After November 28, the *Dergue* acted through a Provisional Military Administrative Council (PMAC), whose chairman, Brig. Gen. TEFERI Banti, served concurrently as acting head of state and government.

Former emperor Haile Selassie, in detention since his deposition, died in August 1975. Earlier, on March 21, the PMAC had decreed formal abolition of the monarchy while declaring its intention to organize a new national political movement "guided by the aims of Ethiopian socialism".

On February 3, 1977, following reports of a power struggle within the *Dergue,* General Teferi and six associates were killed in an armed encounter in the Grand Palace at Addis Ababa. Eight days later, Mengistu and Lt. Col. ATNAFU Abate were named chairman and vice chairman, respectively, of the PMAC in a proclamation that also modified the *Dergue* structure (see Constitution and government, below). However, Colonel Atnafu was executed on November 11 for alleged "counter-revolutionary crimes". Collaterally, antigovernment violence, dubbed the "white terror", flared at Addis Ababa amid indications of growing coordination between several opposition groups, including the Marxist Ethiopian People's Revolutionary Party (EPRP) and the more conservative Ethiopian Democratic Union (EDU). The Mengistu regime responded by mounting in December 1977–February 1978 an indiscriminate "red terror" based in part on the arming of civilians in urban dweller associations (*kebeles*).

The struggle for control at Addis Ababa was accompanied by military challenges on three major fronts. By March 1977 virtually all of northern Eritrea was under rebel administration, while government forces were being subjected to increased pressure by EDU guerrillas in the northwest. In late July the government conceded that the greater part of the eastern region of Ogaden had fallen to insurgents of the Western Somalia Liberation Front (WSLF), who were supported by Somali regular forces, and on September 7 Addis Ababa severed relations with Mogadishu

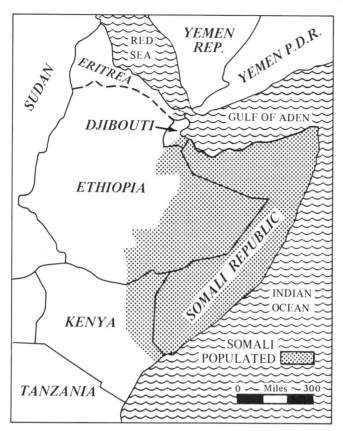

YEMEN REP.
RED SEA
ERITREA
SUDAN
YEMEN P.D.R.
DJIBOUTI
GULF OF ADEN
ETHIOPIA
SOMALI REPUBLIC
KENYA
INDIAN OCEAN
SOMALI POPULATED
TANZANIA
0 ~ Miles ~ 300

because of the "full-scale war" that existed between the two countries (see map of ethnically Somali territory). By mid-December, however, a massive influx of Cuban personnel and Soviet equipment had shifted the military balance in Ethiopia's favor, and most of the region was recovered prior to formal Somali withdrawal in March 1978. A renewed offensive was then mounted in Eritrea, and in late November government forces recaptured the last two major cities held by the rebels, the strategically important Red Sea port of Massawa and the provincial capital, Keren.

Despite the success of the 1978 anti-insurgent campaigns, a major offensive in mid-1979 to wipe out remaining resistance in Eritrea proved ineffectual, with government control remaining limited to the principal towns and connecting corridors. Similar conditions prevailed in the Ogaden, where the WSLF and its ally, the Somali Abo Liberation Front (SALF), persisted in launching guerrilla attacks. In response, Ethiopia was reported to have initiated a "scorched-earth" policy — poisoning water supplies, killing herds of livestock, strafing settled areas — that further aggravated what the UN Office of High Commissioner for Refugees had earlier described as the world's worst refugee problem.

In early 1982 the Ethiopian government launched a "final" offensive against the Eritrean rebels, paralleled by a multipurpose campaign known as "Red Star" that was designed to "alleviate the bitter problems of the people" in the war-torn province. However, neither proved conspicuously successful, the military situation becoming essentially stalemated at midyear in the wake of severe casualties inflicted on government forces.

Following a number of unsuccessful attempts to unite existing Marxist parties, a Commission for Organizing the Party of the Working People of Ethiopia (COPWE) was formed in December 1979 to pave the way for establishment of a Soviet-style system of government. On September 10, 1984, COPWE's work was declared to have been completed, with Colonel Mengistu being designated secretary general of a new Workers' Party of Ethiopia (WPE); however, the PMAC remained in effective control, pending completion of a civilian governing structure.

A commission appointed and chaired by Colonel Mengistu presented the draft of a new constitution in early 1987. The only major change resulting from an estimated 20,000 "question and answer" sessions throughout the country was the excision (in deference to Muslim sentiment) of a clause outlawing polygamy. A reported 81 percent of voters approved the document at a referendum on February 1, the government announcing three weeks later that the country would thenceforth be styled the People's Democratic Republic of Ethiopia (PDRE).

A unicameral national legislature (*Shengo*), elected June 14, convened September 9 and on the following day selected Colonel Mengistu as the country's first president. The *Shengo* also named Lt. Col. FISSEHA Desta, theretofore deputy secretary general of the PMAC Standing Committee, as PDRE vice president and elected a 24-member State Council, headed by Mengistu and Fisseha as president and vice president, respectively. The former deputy chairman of the PMAC Council of Ministers, Lt. Col. FIKRE-SELASSIE Wogderes, was designated prime minister of a new government whose composition, announced on September 20, was largely unchanged from that of the outgoing administration.

Constitution and government. An imperial constitution, adopted in 1955, was abrogated when the military assumed power in 1974. The political reorganization of the PMAC in February 1977 included provision for a quasi-legislative Central Congress, encompassing all 60–70 members of the *Dergue;* the Congress was empowered to name a Central Committee, with a Standing Committee as its executive organ. The chairman of the PMAC (Colonel Mengistu) headed all three bodies as well as the Council of Ministers.

The 1987 constitution provides for a Communist system of government based on "democratic centralism". Nominally, the highest organ of state power is a popularly elected national *Shengo* (the Amharic rendition of "soviet") that designates leading officials, including a president, a vice president, and a Council of State, which is to exercise legislative power when the *Shengo* is not in session. The president, who serves a five-year term, is assigned wide-ranging powers, including the designation of government ministers and higher court judges. The WPE is identified as the "leading force of the state and society", with responsibility to "serve the working people and protect their interests". Some private ownership is to be tolerated, although the new basic law emphasizes central planning based on socialist principles. Freedom of speech, press, assembly, and peaceful demonstration are to be respected, as is freedom of religion as long as it is not "exercised in a manner contrary to the state and the revolution".

The country has long been divided into 15 administrative regions, including the capital. Under the Mengistu regime, local administration has been conducted through some 1,200 *kebeles* and 30,000 peasant associations, all exercising, through 15-member committees, judicial as well as administrative powers. Under the current basic law, provincial *shengos* are to be established to "ensure implementation of laws, decisions, and directives of the state". In late 1987, in an apparent effort to placate separatists, a plan was advanced to establish "autonomous regions" in five areas of long-standing rebel activity, including Eritrea in the north and Ogaden in the east.

Foreign relations. A founding member of both the United Nations and the Organization of African Unity (OAU), Ethiopia under Emperor Haile Selassie was long a leading advocate of regional cooperation and peaceful settlement in Africa. Addis Ababa was the site of the first African summit conference in 1963 and remains the seat of the OAU Secretariat and the UN Economic Commission for Africa.

As a result of Selassie's overthrow, Ethiopia shifted dramatically from a generally pro-Western posture to one of near-exclusive dependence on the Soviet bloc. Moscow guided Addis Ababa in the formation of a Soviet-style ruling party and provided weapons and other assistance to military units (including some 11,000 Cuban troops) during the Ogaden war in 1977–1978; while initially maintaining a low profile in regard to the Eritrean secessionist movements (the two most important of which are Marxist inspired), it subsequently increased its support of counterinsurgency efforts.

Because of ethnic links to Somalia and the presence of virtually equal numbers of Muslims and Christians in Eritrea, most Arab governments (with the exception of Marxist South Yemen) have remained neutral or have provided material support to the guerrilla movements. Most Black African governments, on the other hand, have supported Addis Ababa, although the OAU has adopted a posture of formal neutrality.

In recent years, relations with neighboring countries have been strained by refugees fleeing Ethiopia because of famine or opposition to the Mengistu regime's resettlement policies. Some hope for rapprochement with Mogadishu was raised by discussions between Colonel Mengistu and Somali President Siad Barre during a January 1986 drought summit in Djibouti. Renewed border fighting was reported in early 1987, but both leaders described it as "isolated" and high level talks continued throughout the year.

Relations with Sudan have also fluctuated since the Sudanese coup of April 1985. In mid-1986, Khartoum announced that it had ordered the cessation of Eritrean rebel activity in eastern Sudan, apparently expecting that Addis Ababa would reciprocate by reducing its support for the Sudanese People's Liberation Army (SPLA). Subsequently, Khartoum angrily denounced continued Ethiopian support of the SPLA as "aggression".

Although Ethiopia remained strongly linked to the Soviet Union, anti-American rhetoric became manifestly subdued during an influx of US food aid, valued at more than $430 million, from 1984 through 1986.

Current issues. The transfer from military to civilian government in 1987 had little practical effect on Ethiopia's leadership or its policies. The villagization program (see

The Country section, above) remained a top priority with 10 million persons scheduled for inclusion by the end of the year. However, the government reportedly failed to provide the wide-ranging services it promised for the villages, concentrating instead on political indoctrination; in addition, the program is seen as fostering dependence on the government, thereby curbing antiregime sentiment.

Severe drought returned in the second half of the year, generating fears of a return to the famine conditions of 1984–1985, which resulted in the death of an estimated one million persons. Western countries responded quickly to an appeal for emergency food relief, although many expressed concern over continuing reports of widespread human rights abuses by the Mengistu government. Distribution of food supplies remained a difficult problem, especially in Eritrea, where insurgents, rejecting the new constitution for failing to provide meaningful self-determination, continued their guerrilla activity. Late in the year the rebels mounted a series of offensives in the north that yielded a reported rout of government forces in early December, while two key food distribution centers and two other towns in Tigre region were captured in March 1988.

POLITICAL PARTIES

Political parties were not permitted under the monarchy. Movement by the PMAC toward the formation of a socialist one-party system began in 1977, when the Marxist All-Ethiopian Socialist Movement (Meison) was launched by the government as the political arm of the *Dergue*. Following the declaration by a number of Meison members of a posture of "revolutionary opposition" to the PMAC, the party was dissolved; official attempts in 1978–1979 to consolidate existing Marxist groups under the leadership of the Revolutionary Torch (*Abyot Seded*) also failed, most constituent groups being banned by early 1979. In December 1979, the PMAC established the Commission for Organizing the Party of the Working People of Ethiopia (COPWE), a quasi-party organization encompassing a 1,500 member General Assembly, a 93-member Central Committee, and a 7-member Executive Committee that included Colonel Mengistu and 6 other PMAC officials. When COPWE was replaced by the Workers' Party of Ethiopia (see below), continued PMAC authority was ensured by the inclusion of all 7 executive committee members in the new Politburo.

Government Party:

Workers' Party of Ethiopia — WPE (*Ye Ityopia Seratepnotch Parti*). After five years of preparation by COPWE, the WPE held its founding congress on September 6–10, 1984, at which time it elected a 136-member Central Committee and an 11-member Politburo. In a speech opening the congress, Colonel Mengistu declared that the party would work toward "balanced development", literacy, and local self-administration. The 1987 constitution endorses the WPE's position as the "leading force of the state and society", granting it wide authority, including the right to approve all candidates for the National Assembly. The party's membership is estimated at 50,000, although exact figures are not released and many members reportedly prefer not to publicize their party affiliation.

General Secretary: Lt. Col. MENGISTU Haile-Mariam (President of the Republic and of the State Council).

Other Full Members of Politburo: ADDIS Tedla (Member, State Council, and Deputy Prime Minister), ALEMU Abebe (Member, State Council, and Deputy Prime Minister), AMANUEL Amde-Mikeil (Vice

President, State Council), BERHANU Bayih (Member, State Council, and Minister of Foreign Affairs), Lt. Col. FIKRE-SELASSIE Wogderes (Member, State Council, and Prime Minister), Lt. Col. FISSEHA Desta (Vice President of the Republic and of the State Council), HAILU Yimanu (Member, State Council, and Deputy Prime Minister), LEGESSE Asfaw (Member, Secretariat), SHIMELIS Mazengia (Member, Secretariat), Lt. Gen. TESFAYE Gebre-Kidan (Member, State Council).

Alternates: FASIKA Sidelil, KASSA Gebre, SHEWANDAGN Belete, TEKA Tulu, TESFAYE Dinka, TESFAYE Wolde-Selassie.

Central Committee Secretariat: ASHAGRE Yigletu, EMBIBEL Ayele, FASIKA Sidelil, Lt. Col. FISSEHA Desta, LEGESSE Asfaw, Lt. Col. MENGISTU Haile-Mariam, SHEWANDAGN Belete, SHIMELIS Mazengia, WUBESET Desie.

Eritrean Separatist Groups:

Eritrean People's Liberation Front (EPLF). Launched in 1970 as a breakaway faction of the Marxist-oriented Eritrean Liberation Front (ELF) formed in 1958, the EPLF is an avowedly nonsectarian left-wing group supported by both Christians and Muslims. The largest of the separatist organizations, with as many as 40,000–60,000 men and women under arms, the EPLF has remained committed to "the principle of self-determination". In addition to inflicting thousands of Ethiopian army casualties during a 1984 spring offensive, it announced that it had set up schools, hospitals, and a taxation system in areas under its control. In 1985, it was reported that the EPLF had held secret talks with the government, straining its relations with other insurgent groups. However, there have been no subsequent reports of negotiations and EPLF-government military encounters have intensified. The Front refused to take part in formation of the EUNC (below) in January 1985, but merger with a small ELF faction, the ELF-Central Leadership was announced in November 1986. Subsequently, the EPLF reportedly sought to absorb other ELF factions, as mandated by its second congress (the first since 1977) held at an undisclosed location on March 12–19, 1987. Other congress resolutions served to distance the Front from the Soviet Union while reducing the virulence of its anti-American posture. In an apparent response for calls for internal democratization, the EPLF enlarged its central committee from 31 to 78 and agreed to schedule future congresses on a triennial basis.

Leader: Isaias AFEWERKI (Secretary General).

Eritrean Unified National Council (EUNC). The formation of the EUNC in January 1985 at Khartoum, Sudan, was the latest in a series of guerrilla unification efforts since 1980; however, in contrast to previous coalitions, it included only the Muslim Eritrean groups, which (unlike the EPLF) receive support from conservative Arab governments. EUNC activity was reportedly hampered in 1986 by disagreement among faction leaders, some being committed to Eritrean independence, with others willing to consider a return to federalism as a means of resolving the lengthy conflict. Little concerted activity has since been reported by ELF factions, one having merged with the EPLF (above) and another, the ELF-Revolutionary Command, led by Ahmed Muhammed NASSER, sending observers to the EPLF congress.

Leader: Yohannes ZERE Mariam (President).

Other Guerrilla Groups:

Western Somalia Liberation Front (WSLF). The WSLF, established in 1975, long advocated the incorporation of the Somali-speaking Ogaden region into a "Greater Somalia". During late 1977, with support from Somalian regular forces, the WSLF gained control of the greater part of the area, but since conclusion of the Ethiopian offensive in March 1978 has been forced to operate primarily from bases inside Somalia. At its most recent congress in February 1981, the Front elected a new Central Committee that committed itself to the establishment of a "free state of Western Somalia" independent of both Ethiopia and Somalia. WSLF activity declined in 1986, some of its leaders apparently having shifted their allegiance to the newly formed ONLF (below).

Leader: Abdi ESMAIL (Secretary General).

Ogaden National Liberation Front (ONLF). The ONLF was organized in January 1986, allegedly by militant WSLF members opposed to Ethiopian-Somali talks on the future of the Ogaden that did not involve participation by regional representatives.

Tigre People's Liberation Front (TPLF). A Marxist group that has claimed control of the countryside and several towns in Tigre Province

south of Eritrea, the TPLF is one of the most active antigovernmental groups in Ethiopia. It has strongly criticized the EPLF for rejecting a union of opposition groups, while the recent ascendancy within the Front of a pro-Albanian **Marxist-Leninist League of Tigre** (MLLT) has seemingly dimmed the prospect of such an alliance in the future.

Ethiopian People's Democratic Movement (EPDM). An Amhara-based formation which in recent years has invited participation by other ethnic groups, the EPDM waged a number of pitched battles with government troops during November 1986 in Wollo Province. It is the only group to have accepted the appeal for unity by the TPLF, upon which it depends for supplies and military support. In mid-1986 it decided to launch a Marxist-Leninist political wing similar to the MLLT.

Oromo Liberation Front (OLF). Initially centered in the eastern and mid-country regions, the OLF has recently expanded its activities to the west and south. Some observers have argued that the government targeted the eastern province of Hararghe as the initial locus of its controversial villagization program because of concern over the OLF's capacity to draw on nationalist sentiment among Ethiopia's nearly 14 million Oromo Muslims.

Smaller groups include the **Afar Liberation Front** (ALF), which has been active in Hararghe and Wollo provinces; the **Somali Abo Liberation Front** (SALF), which has long been an independent source of Somali opposition in the mountainous southern region; and the **Ethiopian People's Revolutionary Army** (EPRA), which was little known prior to a series of kidnappings and other guerrilla acts in Gojam Province in early 1987.

Right-Wing Opposition:

Ethiopian People's Democratic Alliance (EPDA). Founded in 1982, the EPDA was an attempt by right-wing opponents of the PMAC to regroup elements of the Ethiopian Democratic Union (EDU), which had collapsed in 1978 as the result of a leadership crisis. The EPDA comprises an "internal" wing, headquartered in Sudan, and an "external" wing operating in Britain and the United States. The EPDA is not known to be conducting military operations within Ethiopia, where its support among the Ethiopian populace is apparently minimal, despite a strongly anti-Communist propaganda campaign reportedly financed with $500,000 annually from the United States.

Leaders: Commodore Eskinder TASSEW (Chairman), Adam ABDO (Deputy Chairman), Dereje DERESSA (Secretary General).

LEGISLATURE

Balloting was conducted on June 14, 1987, for an 835-member National Assembly (*Shengo*) under the new constitution. The more than 2,500 candidates were nominated by the Workers' Party of Ethiopia, the armed forces, and selected mass organizations. Although party affiliation was not mandated, all members of the WPE Politburo and Central Committee were elected, some, including Colonel Mengistu, running unopposed. On September 10, the *Shengo* accepted a transfer of power from the PMAC's Central Congress (which had served in a legislative capacity since 1977), the PMAC itself being dissolved.

CABINET

Prime Minister	Lt. Col. Fikre-Selassie Wogderes
Deputy Prime Ministers	Addis Tedla
	Alemu Abebe
	Hailu Yimenu
	Tefere Wonde
	Tesfaye Dinka
Ministers	
Agriculture	Geremew Debele
Coffee and Tea Development	Cdr. Tekola Dejene

Communications and Transport	Assegid Wolde-Ammanuel
Construction	Kassa Gebre
Culture, Sports and Youth Affairs	Maj. Girma Yilma
Defense	Maj. Gen. Haile Giorgis Hapte-Mariam
Domestic Trade	Mersha Wodajo
Education and Fine Arts	Dr. Yayehrad Kitlaw
Finance	Wole Chekol
Foreign Affairs	Berhanu Bayih
Foreign Trade	Tadesse Gebre-Kidan
Health	Brig. Gen. Gizaw Tsehay
Industry	Maj. Gen. Fanta Belay
Internal Affairs	Col. Tesfaye Wolde-Selassie
Information and National Guidance	Abdulhafez Yusuf
Justice	Wondayen Mehretu
Labor and Social Affairs	Shimellis Adugna
Mines, Energy and Water Resources	Tekeze-Shoa Ayetnfisu
State Farms	Yousouf Muleta
Urban Development and Housing	Tesfaye Maru
Chairman, National Committee for Central Planning	Lt. Col. Mengistu Haile-Mariam
Coordinator of Regional Affairs	Tsegaw Ayele
Coordinator of Religious Affairs	Dibekulu Zewde
Head, Institute of Nationalities	Hailu Wolde-Ammanuel
Governor, National Bank	Tadesse Gebre-Kidan

NEWS MEDIA

Communications media are strictly controlled by the government and present the official version of international and domestic events to a small circle of governmental officials, teachers, army officers, and other members of the educated elite.

Press. Except as noted, the following are published daily at Addis Ababa by the Ministry of Information and National Guidance: *Serto Ader* (100,000), weekly WPE organ; *Addis Zemen* (37,000), in Amharic; *Yezareitu Ityopia* (30,000), weekly, in Amharic; *Ethiopian Herald* (6,000), in English; *Hibret* (Asmara, 4,000).

News agencies. The domestic facility is the Ethiopian News Agency (ENA); a number of foreign bureaus maintain offices at Addis Ababa.

Radio and television. The Voice of Revolutionary Ethiopia broadcasts locally and internationally in Amharic, English, Arabic, and a number of other languages. In 1977 the World Lutheran Federation's Radio Voice of the Gospel, at that time the most powerful medium- and short-wave facility in Africa, was nationalized. The Ethiopian Television Service has been broadcasting under government auspices since 1964. There were approximately 3.0 million radio and 70,000 television receivers in 1987.

INTERGOVERNMENTAL REPRESENTATION

Ambassador to the US: (Vacant).

US Ambassador to Ethiopia: (Vacant).

Permanent Representative to the UN: Tesfaye TADESSE.

IGO Memberships (Non-UN): ADF, AfDB, BADEA, CCC, EEC(L), *EIB,* IACO, ICO, Intelsat, Interpol, NAM, OAU.

F I J I

Political Status: Voluntarily assumed the status of a British dependency in 1874; became independent member of the Commonwealth on October 10, 1970; lapse of membership in the grouping announced by Commonwealth Heads of Government on October 16, 1987, following declaration of Republic on October 15.

Area: 7,055 sq. mi. (18,272 sq. km.).

Population: 714,548 (1986C), 746,000 (1988E).

Major Urban Center (1986C): SUVA (69,481).

Official Language: English (Fijian and Hindustani are also widely spoken).

Monetary Unit: Fiji Dollar (market rate March 1, 1988, 1.46 dollars = $1US).

President: Ratu Sir Penaia Kanatabatu GANILAU; appointed by the Queen to succeed Ratu Sir George CAKOBAU as Governor General on February 12, 1983; resignation from the position accepted on October 15, 1987; appointment as President announced by the Head of the Interim Military Government, Brig. Sitiveni Rabuka, on December 5.

Prime Minister: Ratu Sir Kamisese MARA; appointed by the President on December 5, 1987.

THE COUNTRY

Situated in the Southern Pacific between New Caledonia and Western Samoa, Fiji consists of a group of some 330 principal islands, many of them mountainous and only about one-third inhabited, together with 500 islets spread over an area of 250,000 square miles of ocean. Viti Levu, the largest island, accommodates close to 80 percent of the population and is the site of Suva, the capital, and of the airport at Nadi, an important hub of South Pacific air communications. Native Fijians (a mixture of Melanesian and Polynesian stock) became a minority of Fiji's mixed population in consequence of the introduction of numerous Indian indentured laborers following the establishment of British rule in 1874. At the 1976 census, Fijians constituted about 44 percent of the population; Indians, 50 percent; other Pacific islanders, 2 percent; Europeans and part-Europeans, 3 percent; and Chinese, 1 percent. Virtually all native Fijians are Christian, approximately 85 percent being Methodist and 12 percent Roman Catholic. The Indian population is predominantly Hindu, with a Muslim minority. In 1982, 17 percent of adult women were counted in the official labor force, with about twice that percentage assumed to be engaged in subsistence activities.

Fiji is economically dependent upon agriculture, with sugar and coconut oil accounting for 70–80 percent of all local product exports in recent years. Gold is the most important of the minerals currently being mined, while fishing and tourism (the latter declining sharply in the wake of recent political events) are also significant sources of income.

GOVERNMENT AND POLITICS

Political background. Discovered by the Dutchman Tasman in 1643 and visited by Captain Cook in 1774, Fiji became a British possession in 1874, when it was unconditionally ceded to the United Kingdom by the paramount chief in order to ensure internal peace. The beginnings of modern Fijian administration came with implementation of the Fijian Affairs Ordinance in 1945, which laid the foundations for local government. A ministerial system was introduced in 1966 under a British constitutional order providing for a Legislative Council elected in such a way as to ensure adequate Fijian representation. Indian demands for the introduction of the "one man, one vote" principle delayed further constitutional progress until early 1970, when Indian leaders agreed to postpone their demands until after independence. Following an April-May constitutional conference at London, Fiji became independent on October 10, 1970.

The Alliance Party, led since before independence by Ratu Sir Kamisese K.T. MARA, lost its parliamentary majority in a stunning upset at the election that concluded on April 2, 1977. However, the opposition National Federation Party (NFP) was unable to form a government and Prime Minister Mara continued to serve in a caretaker capacity until his party recovered its majority at the election of September 17–24. Following a bitterly fought campaign, the Alliance retained power, with a substantially reduced majority, at the election of July 10–17, 1982.

Prior to the 1987 balloting, the NFP formed a coalition with the Fiji Labour Party (FLP), which had been launched in mid-1985 with trade-union backing. In an apparent effort to dampen momentum generated by the coalition, Prime Minister Mara called for an early election on April 4–11, at which the Alliance obtained only 24 of 52 legislative seats. On April 14 the coalition (a majority of whose representatives were Indians) formed a government headed by the FLP's ethnic Fijian leader, Dr. Timoci BAVADRA. Demonstrations were thereupon mounted by Fijians demanding constitutional changes that would preclude Indian political domination and on May 14 an army unit led by (then) Lt. Col. Sitiveni RABUKA stormed the Parliament building and arrested Bavadra and his fellow ministers. Declaring that he had assumed control pending elections under a new constitution, Rabuka announced the appointment of a new 17-member interim ruling council composed largely of former Alliance officials, including Ratu Mara as foreign minister.

A confusing sequence of events followed. Initially the governor general, Ratu Sir Penaia GANILAU, refused to recognize the new regime, insisting that "in the temporary absence of Ministers of the Crown" it was his duty to exercise executive authority on behalf of the queen. He reversed himself on May 17, swearing in Colonel Rabuka as chief minister, but reversed himself again on May 19 by refusing to officiate at the installation of Rabuka's ministerial colleagues. Two days later, after extensive consultation with the (native Fijian) Great Council of Chiefs, it was reported that Rabuka would be assigned responsibility for home affairs and the armed forces in a 19-member council charged with advising the governor general as head of an interim

government. The new body was, however, reduced to 16 members at its inaugural meeting on May 25 because of the withdrawal of Dr. Bavadra and two Indian associates. Four days later Rabuka was reported to have been confirmed as commander in chief of Fiji's armed forces, with the rank of colonel.

On September 25, in the wake of inconclusive constitutional discussions and mounting racial violence, Rabuka (identified as having been further promoted to the rank of brigadier) mounted a second coup that yielded formal abrogation of the 1970 constitution and replacement of the existing civilian administration by a military council. On October 7 Brigadier Rabuka proclaimed the establishment of a republic and announced the appointment of a largely nonmilitary government of 23 members. On October 15 the queen accepted Ratu Ganilau's resignation as governor general. On December 5 Ganilau was designated president of Fiji, stating that his principal objective was to effect "a return to parliamentary democracy and the reestablishment of links with Her Majesty the Queen". Subsequently he swore in a new cabinet that included Ratu Mara as prime minister and Brigadier Rabuka as home minister.

Constitution and government. Fiji's 1970 constitution established Fiji as a fully sovereign and independent state with a titular head, the British monarch, represented locally by a governor general. Executive authority was vested in a prime minister and cabinet appointed by the governor general and responsible to a bicameral Parliament consisting of an appointed Senate and an elected House of Representatives. A complex electoral system was advanced to ensure adequate representation for the Fijian community, encompassing both communal and national electoral rolls. Separate communal rolls were established for the Fijian and Indian ethnic groups, in addition to a general communal roll for the European and Chinese segments of the population. The national rolls were designed to elect members representing the three basic groups, but without communal segregation of voters. The judicial system included a Fiji Court of Appeal, a Supreme Court (the superior court of record), magistrates' courts, and provincial and district courts. Judicial appointments were assigned to the governor general, with provision for an ombudsman to investigate complaints against government officials.

Following independence, local government organization equalled the electoral system in complexity. Fiji was divided into four administrative divisions, each headed by a divisional commissioner assisted by district officers, with main urban areas governed by local authorities. In addition, a separate Fijian Administration, headed by a Fijian Affairs Board, was established to oversee 14 communal provinces, each with a partially elected Council. At the apex of the provincial councils, a Great Council of Chiefs was empowered to advise the government on Fijian affairs. A National Land Trust Board was given administrative responsibility for over four-fifths of the nation's land, which could not be alienated, on behalf of village groups. Indians were restricted to leasing holdings for up to ten years, a situation that, along with the system of representation, remained the object of persistent Indian dissatisfaction.

The 1970 basic law was abrogated after the second coup of September 1987; a successor document had not been approved as of March 1988.

Foreign relations. Fiji is a member of the United Nations and many of its associated agencies as well as of several regional organizations, including the South Pacific Commission and the South Pacific Forum. In June 1978 it made a 500-man contribution to the UN peacekeeping force in Lebanon, the expenses of which have been assumed by the United Nations. In November 1984, Prime Minister Mara was received by President Reagan in the first official visit to Washington by the leader of an independent Pacific Island nation, and subsequently secured substantial US aid commitments. These commitments were, under US law, suspended as a result of the 1987 military takeovers, although diplomatic relations were reaffirmed with the appointment of a new US ambassador in March 1988.

The republican proclamation of October 1987 occurred during a Commonwealth Heads of Government Meeting at Vancouver, Canada, prompting a declaration that Fiji's membership in the grouping had "lapsed". The joint statement went on to say that Fiji's status might be reconsidered should "the circumstances warrant", with British Prime Minister Thatcher pointedly noting that the Commonwealth currently encompassed 26 other republics and at least four military governments; however, readmission would require the unanimous endorsement of the members, with India viewed as reluctant to give its assent prior to constitutional resolution of Fiji's ethnic impasse.

Current issues. The bewildering panorama of six governments in the period April-December 1987 was the result of a number of deeply divisive cross-currents in Fijian society and politics. Most native Fijians, including virtually all members of the Great Council of Chiefs, were adamantly opposed to a government dominated by Indians, since the latter represented a potential challenge to constitutionally entrenched ethnic Fijian rights, particularly in regard to land tenure. Some chiefs, including the former governor general, were, however, disturbed at the antidemocratic implications of entrenchment and were less than enthusiastic at the termination of the historic link to the Crown. In addition, a Constitutional Review Committee established by Ratu Ganilau at midyear heard testimony from representatives of a recently formed "Back to Early May Movement" which claimed the support of some 35 percent of the electorate in urging the formation of a government of "national unity" to explore the possibility of political change under the 1970 basic law. On the other hand, the events leading to both of the coups were profoundly influenced by the *Taukei* movement, led by Ratu Meli VESIKULA, which served as the principal vehicle of radical Melanesian nationalism. *Taukei* members were prominently represented in the several ministerial groupings named by Brigadier Rabuka, although its involvement in the Mara government formed in December was substantially reduced, giving rise to speculation that Rabuka himself wished to give more moderate politicians an opportunity to address the nation's difficulties. Significantly, following his reinvestiture, Mara joined with Rabuka and Ganilau in a centuries-old ritualistic exchange of whales' teeth, whereas *Taukei*'s Vesikula castigated the prime minister as a dictator that had lost the support of his people. Subsequently, in March, it was reported that President Ganilau and Prime Minister Mara would be travelling to London to seek "an acceptable arrangement which would allow the entire people of Fiji the opportunity to show in the most direct way their continuing loyalty to the British Crown". However, the timetable for adoption of a new constitution remained uncertain, while the mounting of a new election appeared remote.

POLITICAL PARTIES

Political Party activity was formally suspended in October 1987.

Alliance Party. The Alliance Party, a multiracial coalition which led the country to independence, was formed in 1968 by the Fijian Association, the General Electors' Association, and the Indian Alliance. Its unity was subsequently disrupted by disputes within the Indian Alliance, including a personal rivalry between James Shankar Singh and Sir Vijay Singh, both of whom left the cabinet in 1979. Sir Vijay, having been dismissed as minister of economic planning and as attorney general following allegations of conflict of interest in a fraud case, subsequently joined the NFP (below); prior to the April 1987 election, on the other hand, Irene Jai Narayan, a leading Indian representative who had been narrowly defeated in a bid for the NFP parliamentary leadership, joined the Alliance. At the 1987 balloting the party won only 24 of 52 lower house seats, becoming, for the first time, a minority grouping.

Leaders: Ratu Sir Kamisese K.T. MARA (President of the Party), James Shankar SINGH (President of the Indian Alliance), Irene Jai NARAYAN, Jone BANUVE (Secretary General).

National Federation Party (NFP). The NFP was formed in 1963 as a union of two parties: the Federation, a predominantly Indian party, and the National Democratic Party, a Fijian party. Most of its support came from the Indian community because of its advocacy of the "one man, one vote" principle, which would give greater political strength to the Indian population.

At the election of March 19–April 2, 1977, the NFP increased its parliamentary strength from 19 to 26 seats, but because of internal leadership problems was unable to form a government. Divisions between the so-called "dove" (NFP-D) and "flower" (NFP-F) factions proved disastrous in the September 1977 election, overall representation dropping to 15, with former parliamentary leader Siddiq Koya among the defeated. Koya returned to the House in 1982, when the party won a total of 22 seats. In 1984, NFP-F leader Jai Ram Reddy was elected party president, but resigned his parliamentary seat after an "emotional dispute" with speaker Tomasi Vakatora that prompted a four-month NFP parliamentary boycott. The party subsequently returned to Parliament under Koya, whose somewhat authoritarian style further fragmented the leadership. In early 1985, Koya dismissed the flower faction's Irene Narayan as deputy leader, while a major electoral challenge was presented later in the year by a "youth wing" led by Anil Singh. Narayan resigned from the party in December 1985 to sit as an independent and, in a somewhat surprising move, joined the Alliance in early 1987 after having served briefly as a Labour representative.

The NFP successfully contested the 1987 election in coalition with the FLP (below) but was ousted from ministerial participation by the coup of May 14.

Leaders: Harish Chandra SHARMA (President), Siddiq KOYA (former Leader of the Opposition), Jai Ram REDDY (NFP-F leader), Anil SINGH and Navendra SINGH ("youth wing").

Fiji Labour Party (FLP). Launched in July 1985 by leaders of the Fiji Trades Union Congress (FUTC), the FLP presented itself as a "multiracial political vehicle . . . for all working people", although drawing most of its support from the Indian community. It outpolled the NFP in winning eight Suva city Council seats in November 1985, but failed to obtain parliamentary representation at a by-election in early 1986. Subsequently, it gained three seats held by NFP defectors.

Partly to neutralize potential Alliance claims that an Indian might become prime minister as a result of the 1987 balloting, the FLP's ethnic Fijian leader, Dr. Timoci Bavadra, was named to head the coalition slate, with the Alliance's Harish Sharma as his deputy. Both were forced from office by the Rabuka coup.

Leaders: Dr. Timoci BAVADRA (President), Krishna DATT (Secretary General).

Western United Front (WUF). The WUF was organized in mid-1981 by Ratu Osea Gavidi, theretofore the only independent in the House of Representatives. The party committed itself to bringing ethnic Fijians into greater prominence in both government and business. Although viewed as a serious threat to the Alliance Party, it secured only 2 House seats in 1982, none in 1987.

Leaders: Ratu Osea GAVIDI (President), Isikeli NADALO (Secretary).

National Labour and Farmers' Party (NLFP). The NLFP was formed in early 1982 by three former members of the National Federation Party with the avowed purpose of safeguarding the interests of farmers and laborers, particularly sugarcane workers, who, it was argued, had not been sufficiently protected either by the Alliance Party or the NFP.

Leader: Gurubux SINGH (President).

Fijian Nationalist Party (FNP). The FNP was organized in 1974 as a strongly anti-Indian communal organization. Its strenuous campaigning drew many votes from the Alliance and contributed to the latter's reversal in the election of March-April 1977. The party won no seats in 1982 or 1987, many of its candidates losing their deposits. In early 1988 it sent a telegram to Indian Prime Minister Gandhi asking him to repatriate the Fijian Indian population.

Leaders: Waisale BAKALEVU (Chairman), Sakiasi BUTADROKA (Secretary General).

Taukei Liberation Front (TLF). The TLF is a recently organized extremist group dedicated to indigenous Fijian nationalism.

Leader: Ratu Meli VESIKULA.

LEGISLATURE

Under the 1970 Constitution, Parliament consisted of an appointed Senate of 22 members serving staggered six-year terms and an elected House of Representatives of 22 Fijian, 22 Indian, and 8 "general" members serving five-year terms, subject to dissolution. Both bodies were suspended in the wake of the May 1987 coup.

CABINET

Prime Minister	Ratu Sir Kamisese Mara
Ministers	
Communications, Transport and Works	Apisai Tora
Cooperative and National Marketing Authority	Iswari Bajpai
Education	Felipe Bole
Employment and Industrial Relations	Taniela Veitata
Fijian Affairs	Vatiliai Navunisaravi
Finance and Economic Planning	Josefata Kamikamica
Foreign Affairs	Ratu Sir Kamisese Mara
Forests	Josaia Tavaiqia
Health	Dr. Apenisa Kurisaqila
Home Affairs, National Youth Service and Auxiliary Army Service	Brig. Sitiveni Rabuka
Housing and Urban Development	Tomasi Vakatora
Indian Affairs	Irene Jai Narayan
Information	Charles Walker
Justice	Sailosi Kepa
Lands and Mineral Resources	William Tongiavalu
Primary Industries	Viliame Gonelevu
Responsible for Public Service	Ratu Sir Kamisese Mara
Rural Development and Rural Housing	Apolosi Buivakaloloma
Tourism, Civil Aviation and Energy	David Pickering
Trade and Commerce	Apolosi Buivakaloloma
Women's Affairs and Social Welfare	Finau Tabakaucoro
Youth and Sport	Ilaisa Kakisolomone
Attorney General	Sailosi Kepa
Governor, Reserve Bank	Jone Kubuabola

NEWS MEDIA

Press. The following are published at Suva, unless otherwise noted: *The Fiji Times* (27,000), founded in 1869, in English; *Nai Lalakai*, (18,000), Fijian weekly; *Shanti Dut* (8,000), Hindi weekly; *Islands Business* (8,000), English monthly; *Fiji Royal Gazette,* government weekly in English. The *Times* and the *Fiji Sun* were suspended in the wake of the May 1987 coup, which both had criticized; subsequently the *Sun* formally ceased publication.

Radio and television. The Fiji Broadcasting Commission operates two radio networks broadcasting in English, Fijian, and Hindustani to approximately 420,000 receivers; in addition, the government in 1985 approved its first private license to a SUVA-based company, Communications Fiji, Ltd. Currently, there is no television broadcasting, although an agreement with a subsidiary of Australia's Publishing and Broadcasting, Ltd., was to have led to the establishment of a Fijian network by early 1988.

INTERGOVERNMENTAL REPRESENTATION

Ambassador to the US: (Vacant).

US Ambassador to Fiji: Leonard ROCHWARGER.

Permanent Representative to the UN: Winston THOMPSON.

IGO Memberships (Non-UN): ADB, CP, EEC(L), *EIB*, Intelsat, Interpol, ISO, PCA, SPC, SPEC, SPF.

FINLAND

Republic of Finland
Suomen Tasavalta (Finnish)
Republiken Finland (Swedish)

Political Status: Independent since 1917; republic established July 17, 1919; under presidential-parliamentary system.

Area: 130,119 sq. mi. (337,009 sq. km.).

Population: 4,784,710 (1980C), 4,948,000 (1988E).

Major Urban Centers (1984E): HELSINKI (484,000; urban area, 887,000); Tampere (168,000; urban area, 243,000); Turku (162,000; urban area, 240,000).

Official Languages: Finnish, Swedish.

Monetary Unit: Markka (market rate March 1, 1988, 4.07 markkaa = $1US).

President: Dr. Mauno KOIVISTO (Social Democratic Party); became Acting President on September 11, 1981, upon the incapacitation of Urho Kaleva KEKKONEN, who resigned on October 27; inaugurated January 27, 1982, for a six-year term following designation by an electoral college on January 26; reelected on February 15, 1988.

Prime Minister: Harri HOLKERI (National Coalition); formed four-party government on April 30, 1987, succeeding Kalevi SORSA (Social Democratic Party), after legislative election of March 15–16.

THE COUNTRY

A land of rivers, lakes, and extensive forests, Finland is, except for Norway, the northernmost country of Europe. Over 93 percent of the population is Finnish-speaking and belongs to the Evangelical Lutheran Church. The once-dominant Swedish minority, numbering about 7 percent of the total, has shown occasional discontent but enjoys linguistic equality; there is a Lapp minority in the north. Women constitute 47 percent of the labor force, concentrated in textile manufacture, clerical work, and human services; in recent years, female participation in elective bodies has averaged 30 percent.

Wood, paper, and other forestry-related products continue to account for over two-fifths of Finland's exports, but the metal and machinery industries together have become the country's leading employer and producer. The industrial sector as a whole employs about 35 percent of the labor force, while agriculture (including forestry and fishing) accounts for only 12 percent. Nevertheless, Finland is self-sufficient in dairy products and also produces most of its own meat and grains. Private enterprise remains dominant, but the government operates firms in such key areas as mining, oil refining, forest products, chemicals, and engineering.

GOVERNMENT AND POLITICS

Political background. The achievement of Finnish independence followed some eight centuries of foreign domination, first by Sweden (until 1809) and subsequently as a Grand Duchy within the prerevolutionary Russian Empire. The nation's formal declaration of independence dates from December 6, 1917, and its republican constitution from July 17, 1919, although peace with Soviet Russia was not formally established until October 14, 1920. Soviet territorial claims led to renewed conflict during World War II, when Finnish troops distinguished themselves both in the so-called Winter War of 1939–1940 and again in 1941–1944 (the "Continuation War"). Under the peace treaty signed at Paris in 1947, Finland ceded some 12 percent of its territory to the USSR (the Petsamo and Salla areas in the northeast and the Karelian Isthmus in the southeast) and assumed reparations obligations that totaled an estimated $570 million upon their completion in 1952. A Treaty of Friendship, Cooperation, and Mutual Assistance with the Soviet Union, concluded under Soviet pressure in 1948 and renewed in 1955, 1970, and 1983, precludes the adoption of an anti-Soviet foreign policy.

Finnish politics since World War II has been marked by the juxtaposition of a remarkably stable presidency under J.K. PAASIKIVI (1946–1956) and Urho K. KEKKONEN (1956–1981) and a volatile parliamentary system that has yielded a sequence of short-lived coalition governments based on shifting alliances. A series of "redsoil" (*punamulta*) governments in 1950–1959 was followed by a variety of minority agrarian and majority nonsocialist regimes, while a new structure of "popular front" representation that emerged in 1966 included Communist and non-Communist, center, and center-left parties.

In September 1972, a new government without Communist participation was formed under Kalevi SORSA, who served as prime minister until mounting economic problems forced his resignation in June 1975. A "nonpolitical" interim cabinet headed by Keijo LIINAMAA was appointed pending a parliamentary election called for September 21–22, but the balloting resulted in only minor party realignment. A year later, on September 17, 1976, the five-party government of Prime Minister Martti MIETTUNEN resigned after failing to secure legislative approval for the 1977 budget; however, Miettunen was reappointed 12 days later as head of a three-party minority coalition that excluded the Social Democratic and Communist parties. Following legislative resolution of a land-reform issue over which the Socialists had differed with the minority coalition, a five-party government (the 60th in 60 years) was formed under Kalevi Sorsa on May 15, 1977.

The election of March 18–19, 1979, saw significant gains by the conservative National Coalition (*Kokoomus*) at the expense of the Communist-dominated Finnish People's Democratic League (SKDL), but, in late May, Dr. Mauno KOIVISTO of the Social Democratic Party (SSDP) formed a four-party coalition government from which the conservatives were excluded. Koivisto succeeded to the acting presidency as a result of Kekkonen's incapacitation on September 11, 1981, and was named on January 26, 1982, to a regular six-year term by an electoral college that had been constituted by nationwide balloting on January 17–18. On February 25, former prime minister Sorsa was sworn in as head of a new government based, like its predecessor, on a coalition of the SSDP, the SKDL, the Center Party (KP), and the Swedish People's Party (SFP). The SKDL withdrew on December 29 in a dispute over the 1983 defense budget, but Sorsa was able to maintain his parliamentary majority on a three-party basis for the duration of the legislative term. The existing coalition was enlarged by the addition of the Finnish Rural Party (SMP) in an administration sworn in on May 6, 1983, following parliamentary balloting on March 20–21.

At the election of March 15–16, 1987, the Conservatives gained 9 seats, drawing to within 3 of the plurality Social Democrats, and on April 30, for the first time in 20 years, a *Kokoomus* leader, Harri HOLKERI, became prime minister, heading a new four-party coalition that included the SSDP, the SFP, and the SMP.

Constitution and government. The constitution of 1919 provides for a parliamentary system in combination with a strong presidency, which in practice has tended to grow even stronger because of the characteristic division of the legislature (*Eduskunta/Riksdagen*) among a large number of competing parties. The president, elected for a six-year term by an electoral college chosen through universal suffrage and proportional representation, is directly responsible for foreign affairs and shares domestic responsibilities with the prime minister and the cabinet, the composition of which reflects the political makeup of the *Eduskunta*. The latter, a unicameral body of 200 members, is elected by proportional representation for a four-year term, subject to dissolution by the president. The judicial system includes a Supreme Court, a Supreme Administrative Court, courts of appeal, and district and municipal courts.

Administratively, Finland is divided into 12 provinces (*läänit*), which are subdivided into municipalities and rural communes. The 11 mainland provinces are headed by presidentially appointed governors, while the Swedish-speaking island province of Åland has enjoyed local autonomy since 1951.

Foreign relations. Proximity to the Soviet Union and recognition of that country's security interests have been decisive factors in the shaping of postwar Finnish foreign policy, although Helsinki has followed a course of strict neutrality and abstention from participation in military alliances. The desire "to remain outside the conflicting interests of the Great Powers", formally recorded in the Soviet-Finnish treaty of 1948, has not prevented active and independent participation in such multilateral organizations as the United Nations, the Nordic Council, and the OECD. During meetings held January 6–9, 1987, agreements were signed with the Soviet Union on cooperation in trade and space research; agreement was also reached on the exchange of information on nuclear accidents. Subsequently, nuclear safety accords were also concluded with Denmark, Norway, and Sweden.

Joining the European Free Trade Association at its inception in 1960 as an associate member, Finland, on a similar basis, became in 1973 the first free-market economy to be linked to the Council for Mutual Economic Assistance. In 1985, it became a full member of EFTA.

Finland enjoys traditionally close and sympathetic relations with the United States, in part because of its unique record in settlement of its post-World War I indebtedness, the final payment having been made in 1975, nine years ahead of schedule.

Current issues. At the 1983 election, both the Conservatives and the Communists had lost ground, while the Finnish Rural Party, capitalizing on rising provincial unrest, more than doubled its representation. In 1987, the Conservatives gained substantially, while the Rural Party and the deeply divided Communists (see Political Parties, below) experienced major reverses. The new government coalition that emerged on April 30, with *Kokoomus* leader Holkeri as prime minister and SSDP leader Sorsa as foreign minister, was not as ideologically diverse as its formal membership might suggest, since both the Conservatives and Social Democrats had been moving toward the center of the Finnish political spectrum in recent years. In particular, the new government was not expected to alter the close relations with the Soviet Union that had prevailed since World War II, as a function of both history and geographic proximity. In September 1985, President Koivisto had visited Moscow for discussions with the new Soviet leader Mikhail Gorbachev, while in June 1986, at the conclusion of a visit to Helsinki by the Soviet foreign trade minister, the two countries had concluded an accord whereby Soviet exports would be increased by $330 million a year during 1987–1990 to help reduce Finland's trade surplus with its eastern neighbor. Not surprisingly, the 1987 electoral campaign had focused almost entirely on domestic issues, with all of the major parties singling out unemployment and housing as the country's foremost problems.

In second-round electoral college balloting on February 15, 1988, President Koivisto easily won election to a second six-year term; two weeks earlier he had secured a popular plurality of 48 percent (2 percent less than needed for direct election) in a field of five candidates that included Prime Minister Holkeri.

POLITICAL PARTIES

Finland's multiparty system, based on proportional representation, prevents any single party from gaining a parliamentary majority. The 18-member coalition government formed on April 30, 1987, contained the following party distribution: Social Democratic Party, 8; National Coalition, 7; Swedish People's Party, 2; Finnish Rural Party, 1.

Socialist Parties:

Finnish Social Democratic Party (*Suomen Sosialidemokraattinen Puolue* – SSDP). The SSDP, a predominantly socialist party, is supported mainly by skilled laborers and lower-class white-collar workers, with additional support from small farmers and professionals. It has been the largest party in the legislature following virtually every election since 1907. It suffered a net loss of one parliamentary seat in March 1987, with its leader, Kalevi Sorsa, yielding the office of prime minister to the Kok (below) in a new four-party government formed on April 30. Sorsa announced his resignation as SSDP chairman on April 29, effective as of the party's congress held June 4–6, 1987.

Leaders: Pertti PAASIO (Chairman), Pertti HIETALA (Chairman of Parliamentary Group), Kalevi SORSA (Foreign Minister and former Prime Minister), Ulpu IIVARI (Secretary).

Finnish People's Democratic League (*Suomen Kansan Demokraattinen Liitto* – SKDL). A leftist electoral and parliamentary alliance founded in 1944 by both Communists and non-Communists, the SKDL ended 18 years in opposition when three of its members were given posts in a coalition government in 1966. It withdrew from the Sorsa coalition on December 29, 1982. Wrent by factionalism, the SKDL's legislative strength fell from 33 to 26 at the 1983 balloting and, following a formal rupture within the SKP (below), expelled 10 minority deputies from its parliamentary group in June 1986. The truncated League obtained 16 *Eduskunta* seats in 1987.

Leaders: Esko HELLE (Chairman), Jarmo WAHLSTRÖM (Chairman of Parliamentary Group), Reijo KÄKELÄ (Secretary General).

Finnish Communist Party (*Suomen Kommunistinen Puolue* – SKP). The leading component of the SKDL, the SKP sided with the Soviet Union in the early years of the Sino-Soviet dispute but underwent a split at its April 1969 congress between a majority "revisionist" faction led by Aarne Saarinen and a minority "Stalinist" faction led by Taisto Sinisalo. The dispute continued into 1984, with minority members formally ousted from leadership positions at the party's twentieth Congress in May. The two factions presented separate lists at local elections the following October, as a result of which the SKDL lost substantial ground.

At an Extraordinary Congress in March 1985 (which the minority faction had demanded, but eventually boycotted), party chairman Arvo Aalto called for "socialism with a Finnish face". In November, the Stalinists organized a dissident "Committee of SKP Organizations" and in mid-April 1986 announced the formation of a separate electoral front, the Democratic Alternative (below). In late April, the minority faction elected a rival Central Committee and secretary general. On June 5, its deputies were expelled from the SKDL parliamentary group and proceeded to form their own Democratic Alternative group within the *Eduskunta*.

Leaders: Arvo AALTO (Chairman), Heljä TAMMISOLA (Deputy Chairman), Esko VAINIONPÄÄ (General Secretary).

Democratic Alternative (*Demokraattinen Vaihtoehto* – Deva). Deva was formed in April 1986 to present candidates of the SKP's minority faction at the 1987 election. Within the legislature it became a grouping encompassing the 10 dissidents expelled by the SKDL in June 1986. It secured four *Eduskunta* seats at the balloting of March 1987. Subsequently, claiming that it represented the "true SKP", it adopted the title

Communist Party of Finland–Unity (*Suomen Kommunistinen Puolue–Yhdenäisyys*–SKP-Y), although the parliamentary group continued to employ the Deva designation.

In November 1987, arguing that the SKP-Y had itself become "conciliatory" toward Eurocommunism, an "ultra-orthodox" group, led by Markus KAINULAINEN formed a 33-member council to pave the way for the formation of a third, strictly "Marxist-Leninist" party by mid-1988.

Leaders: Kristina HALKOLA (Chairman), Ensio LAINE (Chairman of Parliamentary Group), Seppo TIMONEN (General Secretary).

Non-Socialist Parties:

National Coalition (*Kansallinen Kokoomus*–Kok). A conservative party formed in 1918, the Kok is the prime spokesman for private enterprise and the business community as well as for landowners. At the March 1979 general election, it displaced the SKDL as the second-largest parliamentary party, retaining this position in 1983 and 1987.

Leaders: Harri HOLKERI (Prime Minister), Ilkka SUOMINEN (Chairman), Tapani MORTTINEN (Chairman of Parliamentary Group), Aarno KAILA (Secretary).

Center Party (*Keskustapuolue*–KP, or Kepu). Formed in 1906 as the Agrarian Union (its present name was adopted in 1965), the Center Party has traditionally represented rural interests, particularly those of the small farmers. Because of major population shifts within the country, it now draws additional support from urban areas. It won 40 legislative seats in March 1987, retaining its previous status as the third-ranked party.

Leaders: Paavo VÄYRYNEN (Chairman), Kauko JUHANTALO (Chairman of Parliamentary Group), Seppo KÄÄRIÄINEN (Secretary).

Liberal People's Party (*Liberaalinen Kansanpuolue*–LKP). The LKP was formed in 1965 as a merger of the former Finnish People's Party and the Liberal Union. At a national congress on June 18–20, 1982, the party, which espouses a moderate social-liberal program, voted to merge with the Center Party while retaining its own identity.

Leaders: Kyösti LALLUKKA (Chairman), Helvi SIPILÄ (1982 presidential candidate), Jari P. HAVIA (Secretary).

Finnish Rural Party (*Suomen Maaseudun Puolue*–SMP). The SMP was formed in 1956 by a small faction that broke from the Center Party. As a protest group representing farmers and merchants, the SMP made substantial gains at the 1983 election, winning 17 seats and subsequently joining the government coalition; its representation fell to 9 in 1987 and was awarded only one cabinet post as a member of the Holkeri coalition.

Leaders: Pekka VENNAMO (Chairman), Urpo LEPPÄNEN (Chairman of Parliamentary Group), Aaro M. NIIRANEN (Secretary).

Swedish People's Party (*Ruotsalainen Kansanpuolue/Svenska Folkpartiet*–RKP/SFP). Liberal in outlook, the SFP has represented the political and social interests of the Swedish-speaking population since 1906. It holds two ministries in the present coalition government.

Leaders: Christoffer TAXELL (Chairman), Elisabeth REHN (Chairman of Parliamentary Group), Jan Magnus JANSSON (1982 presidential candidate), Peter STENLUND (Secretary).

Constitutional Party of the Right (*Perustuslaillinen Oikeistopuolue/Konstitutionella Högerpartiet*–POP). A conservative party organized in 1973 as the Finnish Constitutional People's Party (SPKP) by dissident members of the Kok and SFP, the party opposed extension of Kekkonen's term, favoring the French system of direct election of the president. It lost its only parliamentary seat in March 1979.

Leaders: Georg C. EHRNROOTH (Chairman), Panu TOIVONEN (Secretary).

Finnish Christian League (*Suomen Kristillinen Liitto*–SKL). The SKL was formed in 1958 to advance Christian ideals in public life. It gained two legislative seats, for a total of five, at the 1987 election.

Leaders: Esko ALMGREN (Chairman), Eeva-Liisa MOILANEN (Chairman of Parliamentary Group), Jouko JÄÄSKELÄINEN (Secretary).

Finnish Pensioners' Party (*Suomen Eläkeläisten Puolue*–Eläk). Registered in December 1985, Eläk is not currently represented in the *Eduskunta*.

Leaders: Kauko LAIHANEN (Chairman), Pauli KOIVULA (Secretary).

Unregistered Party:

The Greens (*Vihreäp*). Although not officially registered as a party, Finland's Greens elected two parliamentary deputies in 1983 and four in 1987.

Leader: Pekka HAAVISTO (Chairman of Parliamentary Group).

LEGISLATURE

The *Eduskunta/Riksdagen* is a unicameral body of 200 members elected by universal suffrage on the basic of proportional representation. Its term is four years, although the president may dissolve the legislature and order a new election at any time. Following the election of March 15–16, 1987, the Social Democratic Party held 56 seats; the National Coalition Party, 53; the Center Party, 40; the Finnish People's Democratic League, 16; the Swedish People's Party, 12; the Finnish Rural Party, 9; the Finnish Christian League, 5; the Democratic Alternative, 4; the Greens, 4; Åland Islands (affiliated with Swedish People's Party), 1.

Speaker: Matti AHDE.

CABINET

Prime Minister	Harri Holkeri
Ministers	
Agriculture and Forestry	Toivo T. Pohjala
Commerce and Industry	Ilkka Suominen
Communications	Pekka Vennamo
Defense	Ole Norrback
Education, 1st Ministry	Christoffer Taxell
Education, 2nd Ministry	Anna-Liisa Piipari
Environment	Kaj Bärlund
Finance, 1st Ministry	Erkki Liikanen
Finance, 2nd Ministry	Ulla Puolanne
Foreign Affairs	Kalevi Sorsa
Foreign Trade	Pertti Salolainen
Interior	Jarmo Rantanen
Justice	Matti Louekoski
Labor	Matti Puhakka
Social Affairs and Health, 1st Ministry	Helena Pesola
Social Affairs and Health, 2nd Ministry	Tarja Halonen
Without Portfolio	Ilkka Kanerva
Chancellor of Justice	Jorma S. Aalto
Governor, Bank of Finland	Rolf Kulborg

NEWS MEDIA

Finland enjoys complete freedom of the press; broadcasting is largely over government-controlled facilities.

Press. Newspapers are privately owned, some by political parties or their affiliates; many others are controlled by or support a particular party. The following (circulation figures for 1987) are dailies published at Helsinki in Finnish, unless otherwise indicated: *Helsingin Sanomat* (429,800 daily, 512,000 Sunday), independent; *Ilta-Sanomat* (189,700, daily, 228,600 Sunday), independent; *Aamulehti* (Tampere, 141,900 daily, 146,700 Sunday), National Coalition; *Turun Sanomat* (Turku, 133,900 daily, 138,700 Sunday), independent; *Maaseudun Tulevaisuus* (130,900), independent; *Uusi Suomi* (91,800 daily, 98,000 Sunday), independent; *Kaleva* (Oulu, 86,700), independent; *Savon Sanomat* (Kuopio, 85,200), Center Party; *Keskisuomalainen* (Jyväskylä, 75,400), Center Party; *Kauppalehti* (73,000), independent commercial; *Nykypäivä* (67,000), conservative; *Hufvudstadsbladet* (65,100 daily, 68,500 Sunday), in Swedish, independent; *Etelä-Suomen Sanomat* (Lahti, 64,100), independent; *Pohjalainen* (Vaasa, 64,000), National Coalition; *Satakunnan Kansa* (Pori, 60,800), National Coalition; *Ilkka* (Seinäjoki, 53,500), Center Party; *Karjalainen* (Joensuu, 53,400), National Coalition; *Kansan Uutiset* (45,700), Finnish People's Democratic League; *Suomen Sosiali-demokraatti* (formerly *Demari*, 34,000), Social Democratic; *Suomenmaa* (32,000), Center Party; *Tiedonantaja* (25,000), minority Communist.

News agencies. *Oy Suomen Tietotoimisto/Finska Notisbyrån Ab* (STT/FNB) is a major independent agency covering the entire country; major international bureaus also maintain offices at Helsinki.

Radio and television. Broadcasting is largely controlled by the state-owned Finnish Broadcasting Company (*Oy Yleisradio Ab*), which offers radio programming in both Finnish and Swedish and services two television systems. In addition, an independent commercial television company, *Oy Mainos-TV-Reklam Ab,* transmits on a limited basis. There were approximately 2.5 million radio and 1.8 million television receivers in 1987.

INTERGOVERNMENTAL REPRESENTATION

Ambassador to the US: Paavo Illmari RANTANEN.

US Ambassador to Finland: Rockwell Anthony SCHNABEL.

Permanent Representative to the UN: Dr. Keijo KORHONEN.

IGO Memberships (Non-UN): ADB, ADF, AfDB, BIS, CCC, *CMEA,* EFTA, IADB, ICAC, ICCO, ICES, ICO, ILZ, Inmarsat, INRO, Intelsat, Interpol, ISO, ITC, IWSG, IWTC, NC, NIB, OECD, PCA.

FRANCE

French Republic
République Française

Political Status: Parliamentary republic under presidential regime established 1958–1959.

Area: 211,207 sq. mi. (547,026 sq. km.).

Population: 54,334,871 (1982C), 55,823,000 (1988E). Area and population figures are for metropolitan France (including Corsica); for Overseas Departments and Territories, see Related Territories, below.

Major Urban Centers (1982C): PARIS (2,176,000; urban area, 8,707,000); Marseilles (874,000; urban area, 1,111,000); Lyons (413,000; urban area, 1,221,000); Toulouse (348,000; urban area, 541,271); Nice (337,000); Strasbourg (249,000); Nantes (241,000); Bordeaux (208,000); Saint-Etienne (205,000); Le Havre (199,000).

Official Language: French.

Monetary Unit: Franc (market rate March 1, 1988, 5.72 francs = $1US).

President: François MITTERRAND (Socialist Party); elected May 10, 1981, and inaugurated May 27 for a seven-year term, succeeding Valéry GISCARD D'ESTAING (formerly Independent Republican); reelected on May 8, 1988.

Premier: Michel ROCARD (Socialist Party); formed minority government on May 12, 1988, following the resignation of Jacques CHIRAC (Rally for the New Republic)

on May 10; formed new government on June 28, 1988, following National Assembly election of June 5 and 12.

THE COUNTRY

The largest nation of Western Europe and once the seat of a world empire extending into five continents, France today is largely concentrated within its historic frontiers, maintaining its traditional role as the cultural center of a world civilization but retaining only a few vestigial political footholds in the Pacific and Indian oceans and the Americas. While the population of metropolitan France, which includes the island of Corsica, remains largely native born (93.2 percent in 1982), immigration has, in recent years, become a major political issue, the principal foreign ethnic groups being of Portuguese, Italian, Spanish, and North African origins. French is the universal language, though Breton, Basque, Alemannic, and other languages and dialects are spoken to some extent in outlying regions. The Roman Catholic Church, officially separated from the state in 1905, is predominant, but there are substantial Protestant and Jewish minorities, and freedom of worship is strictly maintained. Women constituted 40 percent of the labor force in 1983, concentrated in clerical, sales, and human service sectors; female representation in elected bodies, most prevalent at the local level, has been estimated at 10 percent.

In addition to large domestic reserves of coal, iron ore, bauxite, natural gas, and hydroelectric power, France leads the Western European countries in the production and export of agricultural products; it is also an important exporter of chemicals, iron and steel products, automobiles, machinery, precision tools, aircraft, ships, textiles, wines, perfumes, and *haute couture.* Post-World War II economic planning, associated particularly with the name of Jean MONNET, contributed to the strengthening and expansion of an economy that was traditionally characterized by fractionalization of industry and inefficient production techniques.

A currency devaluation in 1958 and an economic stabilization program instituted in 1963 were instrumental in achieving domestic monetary stability, a buildup of large reserves, and a strengthening of the franc which yielded an average annual economic growth rate of 5.9 percent in the ten-year period 1959–1969. However, economic performance fluctuated thereafter. Domestic turmoil in mid-1968 resulted in production losses, a decline in currency reserves, and increased speculation against the franc. Devaluation was momentarily averted by the imposition of a severe austerity program, but renewed losses of gold and dollars necessitated an 11.1 percent devaluation in August 1969. Despite subsequent improvement, particularly in export performance, the economy slowed again by 1974, due primarily to increases in petroleum prices and an unacceptably high rate of inflation that fluctuated between 8.4 and 13.4 percent during 1975–1984, before dropping to an average of 3.9 percent in 1985–1987. Under the European Monetary System (EMS) the franc was devalued (against the West German mark) by 8.5 percent in October 1981 and another 10.0 percent in July 1982, while its value vis-à-vis the US dollar declined by more than 100 percent in 1980–1984 before recovering by nearly 80 percent in 1985–1987.

GOVERNMENT AND POLITICS

Political background. For most of the century after its Revolution of 1789, France experienced periodic alternation between monarchical and republican forms of government, the last monarch being NAPOLEON III (Louis Napoleon), who was deposed in 1870. Overall, the republican tradition has given rise to five distinct regimes: the First Republic during the French Revolution; the Second Republic after the Revolution of 1848; the Third Republic from 1870 to 1940; the Fourth Republic, proclaimed in October 1946 but destined to founder on dissension occasioned by the revolt in Algeria; and the Fifth Republic, established by Gen. Charles DE GAULLE in 1958.

Reentering public life at a moment of threatened civil war, de Gaulle agreed on May 13, 1958, to accept investiture as president of the Council of Ministers on the condition that he be granted decree powers for six months and a mandate to draft a new constitution that would be submitted to a national referendum. Following adoption of the constitution and his designation by an electoral college, de Gaulle took office on January 8, 1959, as president of the Fifth Republic, naming as premier Michel DEBRE, who served in that capacity until 1962. De Gaulle's initially ambiguous policy for Algeria eventually crystallized into a declaration of support for Algerian self-determination, leading in 1962 to the recognition of Algerian independence in spite of open opposition by French army leaders in Algeria and widespread terrorist activities in Algeria and metropolitan France.

Debré's resignation in April 1962 marked the end of the decolonization phase of the Fifth Republic and was followed by the induction as premier of Georges POMPIDOU, who resigned in October but remained as caretaker premier and subsequently headed the government formed in the wake of a November election that gave the Gaullists an absolute majority in the National Assembly. Pompidou's premiership, which continued until mid-1968, was marked by heavy stress on the independent development and modernization of French economic and military power, as well as a gradual reduction in France's commitments to its Western allies and a movement toward a more independent foreign policy that featured improved relations with the Soviet Union, recognition of Communist China, and opposition to United States policy in Vietnam and elsewhere.

Under a 1962 constitutional amendment calling for direct election of the president, de Gaulle won a second term in December 1965 over a variety of opposition candidates. The closeness of the election, which required a runoff ballot between de Gaulle and François MITTERRAND, leader of the newly formed Federation of the Democratic and Socialist Left (FGDS), reflected a marked decline in the president's earlier popularity. The Gaullists were further set back by the parliamentary election of March 1967, in which they lost their majority in the National Assembly and became dependent on the support of the Independent Republicans (RI), led by Valéry GISCARD D'ESTAING.

The Fifth Republic was shaken in May and June 1968 by a period of national crisis that began with student demonstrations and led to a nationwide general strike and an overt bid for power by leftist political leaders. After a period of indecision, de Gaulle dissolved the National Assembly and called for a new election, which yielded an unexpectedly strong Gaullist victory. The Gaullist Union of Democrats for the Republic (UDR) won 292 seats in the 487-member National Assembly, with the allied Independent Republicans winning 61 seats. Traditionally marginal Gaullist strength in the Senate was maintained in a partial Senate election held in September.

Maurice COUVE DE MURVILLE, who succeeded Pompidou as premier in July 1968, was entrusted by de Gaulle with responsibility for directing a program of far-reaching internal reconstruction. Based on the concept of "participation", it stressed political and social reforms through labor-management cooperation and profit sharing, accompanied by plans for broad decentralization of the French political and economic structure. Despite continuing labor and student unrest, political confidence in President de Gaulle was further revived by his dramatic decision to resist monetary devaluation during the European financial crisis of late 1968 and a remarkable, if short-term, recovery of the French economy during the winter of 1968–1969.

As part of the reform program, a series of constitutional amendments were advanced that, inter alia, would have limited the Senate to an essentially advisory role while providing that interim responsibility in the event of a presidential vacancy would devolve upon the premier rather than upon the Senate president. Following popular rejection of the plan in a referendum held April 27, 1969, de Gaulle immediately resigned, and the president of the Senate, Alain POHER, succeeded him as interim president of the Republic on April 28.

Former premier Pompidou, the Gaullist candidate, emerged as front-runner in first-round presidential balloting on June 1, 1969, and defeated Poher in a runoff election on June 15. Inaugurated for a seven-year term five days later, Pompidou appointed Jacques CHABAN-DELMAS, president of the National Assembly, as premier in a cabinet that included Debré as minister of defense and Giscard d'Estaing as minister of economy and finance.

During the 18-month period following de Gaulle's retirement, France regained a measure of tranquillity and self-assurance under an intentionally low-key Pompidou regime. The death of the former president on November 10, 1970, was thus an occasion for national homage but by no means for panic. On the other hand, the emergence of rivalries and jealousies among de Gaulle's successors, the abatement of overt revolutionary threats, a recrudescence of corruption and scandal in French public life, and a growing feeling that it was "time for a change" after 15 years of Gaullist rule began to erode the electoral basis of the majority coalition.

In the face of the widest display of leftist unity since 1965, the Gaullists were held to a virtual standoff in the municipal elections of March 1971, although they registered some gains in the senatorial election the following September. In late 1971, however, the government was embarrassed by a series of real-estate and financial scandals, while the revelation in early 1972 that Premier Chaban-Delmas had utilized tax loopholes to personal advantage contributed to circumstances that led to his resignation and replacement by Pierre MESSMER on July 5. The appointment of Messmer, a committed Gaullist, was interpreted as an attempt to strengthen the hand of President Pompidou in rallying the party faithful for the forthcoming legislative election.

Despite a loss of some 100 seats, the Gaullists succeeded in retaining an assured parliamentary majority of 31 in the election of March 1973, and Messmer was redesignated as premier. In the face of recurrent rumors that he was seriously ill, President Pompidou denied that he would resign for the purpose of securing a renewed electoral mandate but did not rule out the possibility of stepping down before the expiration of his term in 1976. In November a still-dominant, but divided Gaullist party concluded its biennial convention with a clear endorsement of former premier Chaban-Delmas as its next candidate for president.

President Pompidou's death on April 2, 1974, led to what was essentially a three-way race between François Mitterrand, candidate of the combined Socialist and Communist Left, and Chaban-Delmas and Giscard d'Estaing, each contending for Gaullist support. On April 7 the Gaullist party formally renewed its support of Chaban-Delmas. In the first round of the election on May 5, Giscard d'Estaing, the candidate of the Gaullist-allied Independent Republicans, outpolled Chaban-Delmas and went on to defeat Mitterrand in the runoff on May 19 with 50.7 percent of the vote.

By mid-1976 the government faced mounting problems, including renewed demonstrations by students opposing educational reform, substantial gains by the Left in recent cantonal elections, one of the most devastating droughts in West European history, a mounting export deficit, and spiraling inflation. On August 25, Premier Jacques CHIRAC resigned, charging that the president would not grant him sufficient authority to deal with the nation's problems, and was immediately replaced by the politically independent economist Raymond BARRE. Earlier, President Giscard d'Estaing indicated that he had severed his Independent Republican party affiliation in an effort to generate a "presidential majority" of centrists, including—but no longer dominated by—Gaullists.

The resignation of Premier Chirac left France for the first time in nearly three decades without a Gaullist as either president or premier. By mid-1977 widespread doubt had emerged that Giscard d'Estaing could establish the broad personal mandate that would permit him to govern "above parties", as did the founder of the Fifth Republic. Earlier, in late 1976, Chirac had reorganized the Gaullist party into the new Rally for the Republic (RPR), and in March 1977 had defeated Giscard's candidate, Michel D'ORNANO, in a Parisian mayoral election. Following the latter setback, the president asked Premier Barre to form a new government to spur economic recovery and the formulation of a program to defeat the Left alliance at the next parliamentary election. By September, however, a serious crisis had emerged within the alliance itself in the course of interparty negotiations to revise the leftists' 1972 common program. On September 14, Left Radical leader Robert FABRE walked out of an alliance "summit meeting" after objecting

to Communist proposals for more extreme nationalization than had been called for by the 1972 document, while deep cleavages subsequently emerged between the Communists and Socialists.

Despite last-minute agreement by the left-wing parties to close ranks and enforce "republican discipline" for second-round legislative balloting in March 1978, the "government majority", comprising the RPR and a new Giscardian coalition, the Union for French Democracy (UDF), staged a remarkable comeback that yielded a substantially larger margin of victory than in 1973. On April 5, Premier Barre formed a new cabinet that included virtually all members of the previous administration, and in late May the government embarked on a radical economic program aimed at removing price controls, reducing subsidies to private enterprises, and giving France "modern means of management". However, the program proved less than conspicuously successful, and by late 1980 public opinion polls indicated that Giscard d'Estaing would have difficulty in defeating the Socialist challenger, Mitterrand, in the 1981 presidential election. The ensuing campaign was complicated by former premier Chirac's announcement in February 1981 that he would seek the presidency as the RPR candidate, following earlier Gaullist declarations by former premier Debré and Marie-France GARAUD.

At the first round of the presidential balloting on April 26, Giscard d'Estaing led a field of 10 candidates in outpolling Mitterrand by less than 2.5 percent of the vote, but was defeated by the Socialist contender at a runoff on May 10 by a 3.5 percent margin. In subsequent National Assembly balloting on June 14 and 21, the Socialists received a commanding legislative majority of 269 seats, and on June 23 Pierre MAUROY, who had succeeded Barre as premier on May 22, announced a new Socialist government that included four Communist representatives.

In the face of increasingly overt criticism by the Communist Party and of substantial left-wing losses in balloting for the European Parliament on June 17, 1984, Premier Mauroy felt obliged to submit his resignation on July 17 and was succeeded two days later by Laurent FABIUS as head of a new administration in which the Left Radical Movement (MRG) and the small Unified Socialist Party (PSU) continued to be represented. While declining to participate in the Fabius government, the Communists did not withdraw their parliamentary support until the following September, when the alliance was formally terminated.

During 1985, the need for "cohabitation" between a Socialist president and a rightist government loomed as former premier Chirac forged a conservative alliance between the RPR and the UDF. While the Socialists remained the largest single party in the Assembly after the ensuing election of March 16, 1986, the RPR/UDF grouping drew within a few seats of an absolute majority and with Chirac's redesignation as premier two days later « la République à deux têtes » became a reality. The delicate balance persisted until the 1988 presidential election, for which a divided Communist Left presented two candidates, while the rightist vote was split between Chirac, former premier Barre of the UDF, and the National Front's Jean-Marie LE PEN. Campaigning on the slogan "France united", Mitterand obtained a decisive plurality of 34.1 percent in first-round balloting on April 24 and secured a 54.3 percent majority in the May 8 runoff, becoming the first incumbent in the 30-year history of the Fifth Republic to win reelection by popular vote.

Despite Mitterand's triumph, the Socialists, while gaining 61 new seats at an early legislative poll in June, fell short of a majority. However, Michel ROCARD, who had been named to head a minority administration on May 12, was able to form a new government on June 28 with the support of a number of centrists and independents.

Constitution and government. The constitution of the Fifth Republic, accepted by a national referendum on September 28, 1958, retained many traditional features of France's governmental structure, while significantly enhancing the powers of the presidency in a mixed presidential-parliamentary system. The president, originally chosen by an electoral college but now directly elected in accordance with a 1962 constitutional amendment (Article 6), holds powers expanded not only by the terms of the constitution itself but also by de Gaulle's broad interpretation of executive prerogative, especially under the provision (Article 5) designating the president as guardian and arbiter of the basic law. In addition to his power to dissolve the National Assembly with the advice (but not necessarily the concurrence) of the premier, the president may hold national referenda on some issues (Article 11) and is granted full legislative and executive powers in times of emergency (Article 16). A partial check on his authority is the existence of a Constitutional Council, which supervises elections, passes on the constitutionality of organic laws, and must be consulted by the president in the use of his emergency powers. In France's first major constitutional revision in 11 years, the Senate and National Assembly voted on October 21, 1974, to permit, on petition by 60 senators or 60 deputies, a challenge to the Council of laws that might infringe on individual liberties.

The broad scope of presidential authority has curtailed the powers of the premier and the Council of Ministers, whose members are named by the president and over whose meetings he is entitled to preside. The cabinet has, however, been strengthened vis-à-vis the National Assembly by limiting the conditions under which the government can be defeated and by forbidding ministers to hold seats in Parliament.

The legislative capacity of the once all-powerful National Assembly is now greatly circumscribed. No longer permitted to set its own agenda, the Assembly must give priority to bills presented by the government, which can open debate on a bill and propose amendments. The Assembly can pass specific legislation in such fixed areas as civil rights and liberties, liability to taxation, the penal code, amnesty, declaration of war, electoral procedure, and the nationalization of industries; however, it can only determine "general principles" in the areas of national defense, local government, education, property and commercial rights, labor, trade unions, social security, finance, and social and economic programs. Unspecified areas remain within the jurisdiction of the executive, and no provision is made for the Assembly to object to a government decree on the ground that it is within a parliamentary mandate.

Under the 1958 electoral law, deputies to the National Assembly were elected under a single-member constituency system with provision for a runoff when failing to achieve a majority on the first ballot. In 1985 (effective, save for three overseas constituencies, in March 1986), a system of proportional representation was adopted, with seats allocated within departments in the order in which they appear on lists presented by parties obtaining at least 5 percent of the vote; in addition, the 1985 legislation increased the size of the chamber from 491 to 577, yielding a ratio of approximately one deputy for every 100,000 inhabitants. In 1986 the Chirac government, over strong Socialist opposition, secured parliamentary approval of a bill restoring the majoritarian system. The Assembly term is five years, assuming no dissolution.

The Senate, most of whose members are indirectly elected by an electoral college (see Legislature, below), was reduced by the Fifth Republic to a distinctly subordinate status, with little power other than to delay the passing of legislation by the National Assembly. The 1958 constitution further provided that if the presidency of the Republic becomes vacant, the president of the Senate will become president ad interim, pending a new election. A separate consultative body, the Economic and Social Council, represents the country's major professional interests and advises on proposed economic and social legislation.

The judicial system was reorganized in December 1958. Trial procedure was modified and the lower courts were redistributed by abolishing the judges of the peace (*juges de paix*) and replacing them with *tribunaux d'instance*. The higher judiciary consists of courts of assize (*cours d'assises*), which handle major criminal cases; courts of appeal (*cours d'appel*), for appeals from lower courts; and the Court of Cassation (*Cour de Cassation*), which judges the interpretation of law and the procedural rules of the other courts.

The territory of metropolitan France (outside Paris) is divided into 96 departments (*départements*), which in turn are subdivided into 3,708 communes (Corsica, originally a single department, was divided into 2 in 1974); in addition, there are 4 Overseas Departments: French Guiana, Guadeloupe, Martinique, and Reunion. The administrative structure is identical in all departments; each is headed by a commissioner of the Republic (*commissaire de la République*) who, prior to the enactment of decentralization legislation in March 1982, was known as a prefect (*préfet*). While the incumbent continues to be appointed by and responsible to the central government, certain of his traditionally dominant administrative and financial functions have been transferred to locally elected departmental assemblies (*conseils généraux*) and regional assemblies (*conseils régionaux*). The smallest political unit, the commune, has a popularly elected municipal council (*conseil municipal*) headed by a mayor.

Foreign relations. French foreign policy as developed under de Gaulle was dominated by the single aim of restoring France's former leading role and its independence of action on the international scene. Within France itself, these aims resulted in an emphasis on furthering military power at the expense, if necessary, of social objectives. This was particularly evident in de Gaulle's strenuous effort to establish an independent nuclear force and his collateral refusal to sign nuclear test-ban and nonproliferation treaties. Within the Europe of "the Six", France accepted the economic provisions of the Treaty of Rome but consistently resisted all attempts at political integration on a supra-national basis and, prior to de Gaulle's death, twice vetoed British membership in the European Communities (EC). Within the Atlantic community, France accepted the provisions of the North Atlantic Treaty but withdrew its own military forces from NATO control and refused the use of its territory for Allied military activities. Denouncing the United States for alleged "hegemonic" tendencies in international political, economic, and financial affairs, de Gaulle sought to restrict US capital investment in France, assailed the "privileged" positions of the dollar and pound as international reserve currencies, and reduced French cooperation in international monetary arrangements. In world politics, France under de Gaulle's leadership tended to minimize the significance of the United Nations and its agencies and initiated a variety of foreign-policy ventures of a more or less personal character, among them a rapprochement with the Federal Republic of Germany in 1962–1963, recognition of Communist China in 1964, intermittent attempts to establish closer relations with the Soviet Union, persistent criticism of US actions in Vietnam, condemnation of Israeli policy during and after the 1967 Arab-Israeli conflict, and cultivation of French-speaking Canadian separatist elements.

The most pronounced foreign-policy change under President Pompidou was the adoption, as early as December 1969, of a more flexible attitude toward the problem of British admission to the EC. While as late as January 1971 the French president termed British policy on conditions of entry "unrealistic", he announced, after a meeting with Prime Minister Heath the following May, that the two leaders were in basic agreement regarding the future of Western Europe, and in April 1972 called for a massive "yes" vote in a national referendum on the issue. While the referendum was not strictly necessary because of the Gaullist legislative majority, 68 percent of the participating voters responded affirmatively, and the EC was enlarged in early 1973.

President Giscard d'Estaing introduced a more positive posture of cooperation with the United States and other Western powers, based in part on a close personal relationship with (then) West German Chancellor Helmut Schmidt. Rapidly emerging as one of the world's most traveled heads of state, he became in 1976 the first French president in 16 years to visit Britain, while a 1979 trip to West Berlin was the first such visitation by a postwar French leader.

Although viewed at the outset of his incumbency as a consummate statesman, President Mitterand's image subsequently became tarnished because of terrorism by pro-independence Melanesians in New Caledonia (see Related Territories below) and a military withdrawal from Chad in 1984 that was not accompanied by a promised Libyan withdrawal. Even more embarrassing was the sinking, by French agents, of the antinuclear Greenpeace vessel *Rainbow Warrior* at Auckland harbor, New Zealand, in July 1985 (see New Zealand article), for which an international arbitration tribunal in October 1987 assessed damages of $8.1 million. The settlement, resulting from what was apparently the first arbitration between a sovereign nation and a private organization, was separate from a UN-negotiated award of $7 million to New Zealand and the payment of unspecified damages to the family of a Greenpeace photographer who had been killed in the incident.

In a historic ceremony at the northern French city of Lille on January 20, 1986, President Mitterrand and British Prime Minister Thatcher announced their support for a long-discussed, cross-channel tunnel to be constructed during 1987–1993. The projected undertaking, as contrasted with a scheme that had been abandoned in 1975, is to provide for rail-only traffic, with provision for a road link "as soon as [its] technical feasibility is assured".

Since 1970 the principal vehicle for cooperation with other French-speaking nations has been the Agency for Cultural and Technical Cooperation (*Agence de Coopération Culturelle et Technique*—ACCT), which by the conclusion of its eighth general conference at Libreville, Gabon, on December 9, 1981, had admitted 32 full and 6 associate members, plus (as "participating governments") the Canadian provinces of Quebec and New Brunswick. Subsequently, French-speaking summits were convened at Paris, France, in February 1986 and Quebec, Canada, in September 1987, with the announced goal of establishing "a full-fledged Francophone Commonwealth".

Annual Franco-African summit conferences are also convened, the fourteenth such meeting being held at Antibes, France, on December 10–12, 1987, with representatives of 37 African countries in attendance.

Current issues. Following the absolute majority obtained by the Socialists in the June 1981 legislative balloting, President Mitterrand set in motion a program of economic and political change unequalled in the 23 years of the Fifth Republic. In accordance with its campaign manifesto, the new administration moved to nationalize five major industrial groups and most of the country's remaining private banks; the death penalty was abolished, while the centralized prefectural system instituted by Napoleon in 1793 was dismantled, turning significant local decisionmaking authority over to town and regional councils.

By mid-1984, French socialism was retreating in disarray from its triumph of three years earlier. In the face of mounting unemployment, persistent inflation, and widening trade and budget deficits, the combined forces of the Left captured only 30 percent of the vote at the European Parliament election on June 17, the far-rightist National Front emerging as the only clear gainer with a startling 11 percent. On July 19, Laurent Fabius was installed as premier of a new Socialist-led government that, indicatively, was charged by President Mitterrand to "represent no political party".

The election of March 16, 1986, yielded a situation that had clearly not been anticipated by the framers of the 1958 constitution: a president and a premier of radically opposed political ideologies. Somewhat surprisingly, "cohabitation" resulted in neither political stalemate or institutional paralysis, although a concerted (and largely successful) effort by Premier Chirac to reverse the Socialists' 1982 nationalization program was impeded by the president's consistent refusal to accede to relevant decrees.

In keeping with his posture of firmness in dealing with economic and social issues, Chirac urged a tough anti-terrorist posture following a series of bombings at Paris in September 1986, and was reported to be the author of a number of moves that included the imposition of visa requirements for visitors from non-European countries, including the United States. In February 1987 George Ibrahim ABDALLAH, a pro-Syrian Christian Maronite from Lebanon, was sentenced to life imprisonment for complicity in the attacks and in August France severed relations with Iran as the result of incidents involving both the Iranian embassy at Paris and the French embassy at Teheran. In mid-December, on the other hand, two French hostages in Lebanon were released after France had expelled 17 Iranian political exiles, while three additional hostages were freed four days before the second-round presidential balloting in May 1988, Premier Chirac asserting that a restoration of relations with Iran was imminent. However, the action failed to turn the tide in favor of the premier, whose resignation on May 10 marked the return of both executive positions to Socialist control.

POLITICAL PARTIES

Events since World War II have altered France's traditional multiparty system almost beyond recognition. Its major elements continue to manifest themselves within a continually changing pattern of electoral and parliamentary alliances. The principal groupings after the 1973 election were (1) the Gaullist Union of Democrats for the Republic (UDR), which had joined the National Federation of Independent Republicans (FNRI) and the Democratic and Progressive Center (CDP) in an electoral coalition called the Union of Progressive Republicans for the Support of the President of the Republic (URP); (2) a group of centrist parties—including the Democratic Center (CD), the Radical Party (RRRS), the Republican Center (CR), and the Democratic Socialist Movement (MDSF)—which fought the election as the Reform Movement (MR) and subsequently organized in the Assembly as the Federation of Reformers, most of whose leadership joined the government coalition after the presidential election of 1974; (3) a group of Socialists and Left Radicals; and (4) the French Communist Party (PCF). The Socialists, Left Radicals, and Communists had contested the election of 1973 in an alliance styled the Left Union (UG).

In December 1976 the UDR was transformed into a new organization called the Rally for the Republic (RPR) under the leadership of former premier Chirac, while in May 1977 the FNRI joined with a number of smaller "Giscardian" groups to form the Republican Party (PR). The PR, in turn, formed the core of the Union for French Democracy (UDF), a somewhat loosely structured centrist alliance organized in March 1978 to counterbalance Chirac's RPR, despite the fact that maintenance of a government majority in the National Assembly was contingent upon partial RPR support.

Following the Socialist victory at the May 1981 presidential election, the RPR and the UDF formed a short-lived alliance styled the Union for the New Majority (UMN), while the leading leftist groups (see below) concluded a series of bilateral accords also aimed primarily at closing ranks for second-round legislative balloting on June 21, at which the Socialists obtained an absolute majority. While remaining the largest single party after the 1986 Assembly election, the Socialists were forced to yield con-

trol of the government (save for the presidency) to a new RPR/UDF alliance that had been concluded a year earlier under the leadership of Jacques Chirac. While the resurgent Socialists fell 13 seats short of an absolute majority at the Assembly balloting of June 1988, they were able to form a government with the support of other leftists (excluding the Communists) and right-centrists.

Leading Leftist and Left-Centrist Parties:

France's principal left-center grouping from 1965 until late 1968 was the Federation of the Democratic and Socialist Left (FGDS), a combination formed by representatives of the Socialist Party (SFIO), the Radical Party (RRRS), and the Republican Institutions Convention (CIR). Anticlerical in domestic policy, the FGDS advocated broad social and economic reforms and supported European integration while opposing integration with the Atlantic alliance. Despite its anti-Communist outlook, the Federation formed an electoral alliance with the Communists in the elections of 1965, 1967, and 1968. The loss of more than half of its Assembly seats in the June 1968 election provoked an internal crisis that led in October 1968 to the alliance's formal dissolution, although its representatives in the National Assembly continued to operate as a distinct parliamentary group. Subsequent attempts to form a new Socialist party composed largely of FGDS members were set back by the 1969 presidential election, in which the non-Communist Left was further fractured by its inability to agree on a common candidate for president.

Prior to the 1973 campaign, most of the Socialists and a Radical splinter group formed an alliance with the Communists called the Left Union (UG). Following the election, the Socialists and Left Radicals, and the Communists organized themselves into separate parliamentary groups that subsequently reunited for the 1974 presidential campaign. During 1977 a number of disagreements arose between the Communists and their Socialist allies, thus precluding the adoption of a common program for the 1978 legislative election.

In 1981 most parties of the Left presented separate candidates for first-round presidential balloting, at which the Communist share of the vote fell to its lowest level since the legislative election of 1936. In the second round, the Socialist candidate, François Mitterrand, was endorsed by the Communists, the United Socialists, and the Left Radicals, defeating the incumbent, Giscard d'Estaing, with 51.76 percent of the vote. The four parties subsequently agreed to support the best-placed leftist candidates in the National Assembly runoff balloting, which, for the first time in French political history, gave the Socialists outright parliamentary control.

Socialist Party (*Parti Socialiste*—PS). Originally established in 1905 and known for many years as the French Section of the Workers' International (SFIO), the French Socialist Party was, under Guy Mollet's leadership, the principal component of the FGDS. As a step toward the hoped-for reorganization of the non-Communist Left, a party congress which met in July 1969 adopted a new party name and elected a new leadership in which, however, supporters of former secretary general Mollet continued to hold a commanding position. Under the leadership of François Mitterrand, a dissident group, the Republican Institution Convention (CIR), held itself aloof from the 1969 reorganization. Subsequently, Mitterrand rejoined the party as first secretary and was the candidate of the combined Left in the 1974 presidential election, losing to Giscard d'Estaing in the runoff by less than 1 percent of the popular vote. In a rematch that concluded on May 10, 1981, Mitterrand was victorious by a margin of more than 3.5 percent, while the PS completed its domination of the executive establishment by its Assembly sweep of June 21. However, as the result of a Socialist defeat at the Assembly election of March 16, 1986, the president was forced to accept the appointment of a rightist administration headed by Jacques Chirac for the remaining two years of his initial term.

Leaders: François Maurice MITTERRAND (President of the Republic), Michel ROCARD (Prime Minister), Laurent FABIUS (President of the National Assembly), Lionel JOSPIN (First Secretary).

French Communist Party (*Parti Communiste Français*—PCF). An offshoot of the Socialist Party, the PCF assumed a separate identity in 1920. It was the largest party of the Fourth Republic and in 1983 claimed a membership of 710,000. The single-member constituency system introduced by the Fifth Republic limited its parliamentary representation, and it suffered severe losses in the June 1968 election. However, it made a startling comeback in the presidential election of 1969, at which its candidate, Jacques Duclos, won 21.5 percent of the total vote on the first ballot. It won an identical proportion of the vote in 1973, securing 73 seats in the Assembly. In 1978 it slipped from third to fourth place, although its representation rose to 86 seats.

The party remains a powerful and effective force in local government, dominates the largest French labor organization, the *Confédération Générale du Travail* (CGT), and has gathered wide support among the dissatisfied French peasantry. Although opposed to NATO and European integration, and in favor of closer relations with the East, it publicly disapproved the Soviet intervention in Czechoslovakia in 1968 and in 1976 formally abandoned the theory of the "dictatorship of the proletariat" while endorsing a policy of "socialism in the colors of France". A "reconciliation" occurred during a four-day visit to Moscow by Secretary General Marchais in January 1980, immediately prior to which the PCF had endorsed the Soviet intervention in Afghanistan on the ground that the Afghan people had the right to seek help in quelling a rebellion supported by "US imperialism". In October 1982, Marchais also led a delegation to China for a renewal of relations between the French and Chinese parties that had been suspended for more than two decades.

The party suffered a major setback in the 1981 legislative balloting, its 44 elected deputies constituting little more than half of the former representation. On the other hand, it was awarded four portfolios in the Mauroy government of June 23—the first such participation since 1947.

Following its formal break with the Socialists in September 1984, the PCF experienced a major rupture between "traditionalists", led by Marchais and André LAJONIE, and a group of dissident "renovators", led by Pierre JUQUIN, who insisted that the party's decline stemmed from a failure to adapt to fundamental changes in French society. In 1987 Juquin announced that he would stand as an independent presidential candidate in 1988 and was subsequently expelled from the PCF, which, with Lajonie as its standard-bearer, slipped to a record postwar low of 7 percent at the first-round balloting on April 24.

Leaders: Georges MARCHAIS (Secretary General), André LAJONIE, Gaston PLISSONNIER.

Left Radical Movement (*Mouvement des Radicaux de Gauche*—MRG). The MRG, a splinter from the Radical Party (see under UDF, below), organized to participate in the 1973 election as part of the Left Union. Its parliamentary strength rose from 10 seats to 14 at the election of June 1981, after having entered the government in May. It secured only two Assembly seats in 1986, which increased to nine in 1988.

Leaders: François DOUBIN (President), Michel CREPEAU (former Minister of Commerce), Roger-Gérard SCHWARTZENBERG.

Leading Rightist and Right-Centrist Parties:

Rally for the Republic (*Rassemblement pour la République*—RPR). The RPR was established in late 1976 as successor to the Union of Democrats for the Republic (UDR), which had been formed in 1967 as heir to the Gaullist Union for the New Republic (UNR). The legislative strength of the UDR had declined from an absolute majority in the election of June 1968 to a plurality in the election of March 1973. The RPR emerged as the largest single party in the election of March 1978, though with some 30 fewer seats than its predecessor. Remaining technically "within the majority" that supported the government in the Assembly, the RPR was essentially the personal vehicle of Jacques Chirac in the political rivalry with President Giscard d'Estaing that resulted in Chirac's resignation as premier in August 1976.

After placing third in first-round presidential balloting on April 26, 1981, Chirac announced that his supporters should vote "according to their conscience" in the runoff, thus denying a critical measure of support to Giscard d'Estaing in the contest with Mitterrand on May 10. At the legislative election in June the RPR ran second to the Socialists, its representation falling from 153 to 85.

In April 1985, the RPR concluded an alliance with the UDF (below) to "govern together and together alone" in the event the two were able to command an Assembly majority after the 1986 election. Though the 286 seats ultimately controlled by the two groups fell marginally short of the goal because a number of nonalliance rightist deputies chose to remain unaffiliated, the pact was, for all practical purposes, implemented in formation of the Chirac government.

Leaders: Jacques CHIRAC (President), Claude LABBE, Jacques TOUBON (Secretary General).

Union for French Democracy (*Union pour la Démocratie Française*—UDF). The UDF is composed of a number of right-centrist parties plus several smaller groups that backed Giscard d'Estaing personally within the former governing coalition. It supported Giscard d'Estaing in the 1981 campaign, albeit unofficially since the incumbent voiced a desire to stand as a "citizen candidate" unidentified with any specific grouping. Collaterally, it became possible for individuals to become "direct affiliates" of the UDF without holding membership in one of its constituent groups. In implementation of its 1985 accord with the RPR (above), the UDF was awarded 5 senior cabinet posts in the government formed after the March 1986 balloting.

Leaders: Jean LECANUET (President), Jean-Claude GAUDIN, Michel PINTON (Secretary General).

Republican Party (*Parti Républicain*—PR). The PR was organized in May 1977 as a merger of the former National Federation of Independent Republicans (FNIR) and several smaller pro-Giscard groups. The FNIR, founded by Giscard d'Estaing in 1966, was made up primarily of independents originally affiliated with the National Center of Independents and Peasants (see below). Though more conservative than the Gaullists in domestic policy, it was more pro-NATO and "European" in its international outlook. In 1974 Giscard formally severed his affiliation with the FNIR in his search for a new "presidential majority".

Leaders: Michel PONIATOWSKI (Honorary President), François LEOTARD (Secretary General).

Social Democratic Center (*Centre des Démocrates Sociaux*—CDS). The CDS was organized in May 1976 by merger of the Democratic Center (CD) and the Democratic and Progressive Center (CDP), both of which were members of the legislative Federation of Reformers. The CD had been organized in 1966 by Jean Lecanuet from among members of the former Popular Republican Movement (MRP), the Democratic Assembly (RD), the National Center of Independents and Peasants (CNIP), and an earlier Democratic Center (CD) group in the National Assembly. It was similar to the former Federation of the Democratic and Socialist Left (FGDS) on most domestic issues while strongly supporting the Atlantic alliance and European integration in foreign affairs. The predominantly Christian Democratic CDP was originally constituted in 1969 as the Modern Democracy and Progress (PDM) in support of the presidential candidacy of Georges Pompidou in preference to the official centrist candidate, Alain Poher. Allied with the UDR in the 1973 election, it subsequently organized with others as the Centrist Union in the National Assembly.

Leaders: Pierre MEHAIGNERIE (President), Jean-Marie DAILLET (Vice President), Jacques BARROT (Secretary General).

Radical Party (*Parti Républicain Radical et Radical-Socialiste*—RRRS). The leading party of the prewar Third Republic and a participant in many Fourth Republic governments, the Radical Party maintains its traditional anticlerical posture but is more conservative than the Socialists in economic and social matters.

On July 20, 1977, the **Movement of Social Liberals** (*Mouvement des Sociaux Libéraux*—MSL), which had been organized in February 1977 by Olivier STIRN, former secretary of state for overseas departments and territories, announced its incorporation into the Radical Party. Stirn, who had resigned from the RPR in an effort to rally Gaullists and moderate socialists to Giscard d'Estaing, indicated at the time of the merger that he viewed the Radical program as representing the preferable alternative to the conservatism of the Right and the common program of the Left. Stirn relaunched the MSL as a separate group in October 1981, though declaring that he continued to regard himself as a Radical. The RRRS is also known as the *Parti Radical Valoisien,* after its rue de Valois address at Paris.

Leaders: André ROSSINOT (President), Didier BARIANI (Secretary General).

Social Democratic Party (*Parti Social-Démocrate*—PSD). The Social Democratic Party was adopted as the new name of the former Democratic Socialist Movement (MDS) in October 1982. The MDS was a centrist group which participated in the 1973 election as part of the Reform Movement and was a founding member of the UDF in 1978.

Leaders: Max LEJEUNE (President), Charles BAUR (Secretary General).

National Center of Independents and Peasants (*Centre National des Indépendants et Paysans*—CNIP). Historically a rightist group strongly supporting the free-enterprise system, the CNIP has endorsed the North Atlantic alliance and European integration. Although not directly linked to either the RPR or the UDF, it joined the UMN grouping formed prior to the second-round legislative balloting in 1981.

Leaders: Jacques FERON (President), Yvon BRIANT (Secretary General).

National Front (*Front National*). The National Front is an extreme right-wing formation, organized in 1972 on an anti-immigration program, that startled observers in June 1984 by winning 10 of the 81 French seats in the European Parliament. It made a scarcely less impressive showing in 1986 by winning 35 Assembly seats, while its leader, Jean-Marie Le Pen secured 15 percent of the vote in first-round presidential balloting on April 24, 1988. Its loss of all but one of its Assembly seats at the legislative balloting only two months later was attributed to the fact that the June election was conducted under majoritarian rather than proportional representation.

Leaders: Jean-Marie LE PEN (President), Jean-Pierre STIRBOIS (Secretary General).

Minor Parties:

Unified Socialist Party (*Parti Socialiste Unifié* — PSU). An assemblage of various Socialist splinter groups that was established in 1960, the PSU, advocating policies somewhat more radical than those of the earlier FGDS, decided in 1967 not to join the Federation, nor did it formally join the Left Union in 1973. In 1974 the party rejected a minority proposal to merge with the Socialist Party, but cooperated with the latter in second-round presidential and legislative balloting in 1981 and joined the Mauroy government in March 1983.

Leader: Jean-Claude LE SCORNET (Secretary).

French Democratic Party (*Parti Démocrate Française* — PDF). The PDF was organized in June 1982 by Guy Gennesseaux, a former Radical vice president, who had urged withdrawal of the RRRS from the UDF. The new formation was described as "neither liberal nor socialist", but dedicated to the construction of "a modern society of the third type".

Leader: Guy GENNESSEAUX.

The Greens (*Les Verts*). The Greens organized as a unified ecologist party in 1984 as an outgrowth of an Ecology Today (*Aujourd'hui l'Ecologie*) movement that had presented a total of 82 candidates at first-round National Assembly balloting in June 1981. The Greens have yet to win legislative representation.

Leader: Guy MARMOT (National Secretary).

Popular Gaullist Movement (*Mouvement Gaulliste Populaire* — MGP). The MGP was formed in April 1982 by merger of two small left-oriented Gaullist groups, the Democratic Union of Labor (UDT) and the Federation of Progressive Republicans (FRP).

Leaders: Jacques DEBU-BRIDEL (UDT), Pierre DABEZIES (FRP).

Workers' Struggle (*Lutte Ouvrière* — LO). The LO is a small Trotskyite party whose leader entered the presidential races of both 1974 and 1981 "not at all to be elected" but to "make heard the workers' voice amid the . . . hypocritical declarations" of the leading candidates, including those of the Socialist and Communist parties, who were accused of being preoccupied with electoral politics.

Leader: Arlette LAGUILLER.

New Forces Party (*Parti des Forces Nouvelles* — PFN). A party of the extreme Right that has attempted to serve as an umbrella for a number of like-minded groups, the PFN put up a total of 86 candidates in the first round of the 1981 legislative balloting. It did so on the basis of an agreement with the National Front (above) not to oppose each other in any constituency. However, relations between the two were strained because of failure to agree on a common candidate for the May presidential election.

Leader: Félix BUSSON (President of General Council).

Other minor parties include the **New Royalist Action** (*Nouveau Action Royaliste* — NAR), led by Bertrand RENOUVIN; the **Movement of Democrats** (*Mouvement des Démocrates* — MD), organized in 1975 by former minister of foreign affairs Michel JOBERT in an effort to rally orthodox Gaullists against the Giscard d'Estaing government's alleged departure from the policies of presidents de Gaulle and Pompidou; the **Left Reform Movement** (*Mouvement de la Gauche Réformatrice* — MGR), a centrist party formed in 1975 and currently led by Aymar ACHILLE-FOULD; two Trotskyite groups, the **Revolutionary Communist League** (*Ligue Communiste Révolutionnaire* — LCR), led by Alain KRIVINE, and the **Communist Committees for Self-Management** (*Comités Comunistes pour l'Autogestion* — CCA); and two Maoist groups, the **Marxist-Leninist Communist Party** (*Parti Communiste Marxist-Léninist* — PCML) and the **Revolutionary Marxist-Leninist Communist Party** (*Parti Communiste Révolutionnaire-Marxist-Léninist* — PCRML).

There are also a number of regional organizations of varying degrees of militancy, including the **Breton Democratic Union** (*Union Démo-*

cratique Breton — UDB), a socialist-oriented group seeking autonomy for Brittany by nonviolent means; the separatist **Liberation Front of Brittany–Breton Republican Army** (*Front Libération de la Bretagne–Armée Republicain Breton* — FLB-ARB); the French Basque **Those of the North** (*Iparretarrak*), which was outlawed in July 1987 following the conviction of its leader, Philippe BIDART, for murder; the autonomist **Union of the Corsican People** (*Unione di u Populu Corsu* — UPC); the separatist **Corsican National Liberation Front** (*Front de Libération Nationale de la Corse* — FLNC), which was formally outlawed in January 1983, following a lengthy series of terrorist incidents for which the group claimed responsibility; and the **Corsican Movement for Self-Determination** (*Mouvement Corse pour l'Autodétermination* — MCA), which was banned in February 1987 after a series of bomb attacks.

LEGISLATURE

The bicameral **Parliament** (*Parlement*) consists of an indirectly chosen Senate and a directly elected National Assembly.

Senate (*Sénat*). The French Senate, which under the Fifth Republic has been reduced to a limiting and delaying role, currently consists of 319 members selected by thirds every three years for nine-year terms. The 296 senators from metropolitan France (including Corsica) are designated by an electoral college of National Assembly deputies and regional and municipal council members; in addition, 13 are elected to represent the overseas departments and territories, excluding a seat for the former French Territory of the Afars and the Issas (now Djibouti), which has never been legally vacated; while 10 are named by the Higher Council of French Abroad (*Conseil Supérieur des Français à l'Etranger*) to represent French nationals overseas (the latter to increase to 12 in 1989). Following the most recent partial election of September 28, 1986, the distribution of seats by senatorial grouping was as follows: Union for French Democracy and affiliated, 154; Rally for the Republic, 77; Socialist, 64; Communist, 15; Left Radical Movement, 9.

President: Alain POHER.

National Assembly (*Assemblée Nationale*). The French Assembly presently consists of 577 deputies elected by two-round majority voting for five-year terms (subject to dissolution). The most recent election, held on June 5 and 12, 1988, resulted in a total of 305 seats for parties of the Left and 272 for parties of the Right, distributed as follows: Socialist Party, 262; Communist Party, 27; Left Radical Movement, 9; other leftist, 7; Union for French Democracy, 130 (including Republican Party, 58; Social Democratic Center 49; Radical Party, 3; Social Democratic Party, 3; others, 17); Rally for the Republic, 129; National Front, 1; other rightist, 12.

President: Laurent FABIUS.

CABINET

[as of June 28, 1988]

Prime Minister	Michel Rocard
Ministers of State	
Economy, Finance and Budget	Pierre Bérégovy
Equipment and Lodging	Maurice Faure
Foreign Affairs	Roland Dumas
National Education, Research and Sports	Lionel Jospin
Ministers	
Agriculture and Forests	Henri Nallet
Cooperation and Development	Jacques Pelletier
Culture and Communication, Large Works and Bicentennial	Jack Lang
Defense	Jean-Pierre Chevènement
European Affairs	Edith Cresson

Foreign Commerce	Jean-Marie Rausch
Industry and Territorial Management	Roger Fauroux
Interior	Pierre Joxe
Justice and Keeper of the Seals	Pierre Arpaillange
Labor, Employment and Professional Training	Jean-Pierre Soisson
Overseas Departments and Territories	Louis Le Pensec
Post, Telecommunications and Space	Paul Quilès
Public Employment and Administrative Reform	Michel Durafour
Relations with Parliament	Jean Poperen
Research and Technology	Hubert Curien
Solidarity, Health, Social Protection and Government Spokesman	Claude Evin
Transport and Sea	Michel Delebarre

Ministers Delegate

Culture and Communication in charge of Communication	Catherine Tasca
Economy, Finance and Budget in charge of Budget	Michel Charasse
Foreign Affairs	Edwige Avice
Foreign Affairs in charge of Francophone Affairs	Alaine Decaux
Industry and Territorial Management in charge of Commerce and Crafts	François Doubin
Industry and Territorial Management in charge of Territorial Management and Reconversions	Jacques Chérèque
Industry and Territorial Management in charge of Tourism	Oliver Stirn
Solidarity, Health and Social Protection in charge of the Aged	Théo Braun
Solidarity, Health and Social Protection in charge of Health	Léon Schwarzenberg
Transport in charge of the Sea	Jacques Mellick

Secretaries of State

Culture in charge of Large Works	Emile Biasini
Economy in charge of Consumption	Véronique Neiertz
Foreign Affairs in charge of International Cultural Relations	Thierry de Beaucé
Humanitarian Action	Bernard Kouchner
Interior in charge of Territorial Collectivities	Jean-Michel Baylet
Labor in charge of Professional Training	André Laignel
National Education in charge of Teaching Technique	Robert Chapuis
National Education in charge of Youth and Sports	Roger Bambuck
Prime Minister's Office in charge of Environment	Brice Lalonde
Prime Minister's Office in charge of Plan	Lionel Stoléru
Prime Minister's Office Without Charge	Tony Dreyfus
Solidarity in charge of the Family	Hélène Dorlhac
Solidarity in charge of the Handicapped	Michel Gillibert
Technological and Natural Risk Prevention	Gérard Renon
Transport in charge of Waterways and Transport Routes	Georges Sarre
Veteran's Affairs	André Meric
Women's Rights	Michèle André
Governor, Bank of France	Jacques de Larosière

NEWS MEDIA

Press. France's traditional freedom of the press has been maintained

under the Fifth Republic, subject to the restriction that offensive criticism may not be directed against the head of state. This formal freedom has, however, been partially offset by rapidly declining circulation and recent trends in ownership of the nation's newspapers. There are now only 10 major Parisian dailies (as contrasted with 28 following World War II and 80 prior to World War I) and a major political issue erupted in mid-1976 with regard to the takeover of *France-Soir* by the conservative Hersant chain, which had acquired *Le Figaro* a year earlier despite legislation that, in principle, banned press monopolies. More stringent antimonopoly legislation was approved in September 1984, although the Constitutional Council ruled that it could not be applied retroactively to Hersant.

The following newspapers are published daily at Paris, unless otherwise noted: *Ouest-France* (Rennes, national circulation, 44 editions, 780,000); *La Dépêche du Midi* (Toulouse, 600,000, including national distribution), Radical management; *Le Figaro* (440,000), founded 1826, leading morning independent and standard-bearer of the moderately rightist liberal bourgeoisie; *France-Soir* (415,000), leading evening paper, pro-Gaullist orientation; *La Voix du Nord* (Lille, 375,000); *Le Dauphiné Libéré* (Grenoble, 368,000 daily, 370,000 Sunday), leading provincial; *Le Monde* (360,000), independent evening paper with international readership and weekly edition in English, left-of-center; *Le Progrès* (Lyon, 352,000 daily, 440,000, Sunday); *Sud-Ouest* (Bordeaux, 350,000 daily, 230,000 Sunday); *Le Parisien Libéré* (338,000), popular morning independent with Gaullist management but large Communist readership; *L'Est Républicain* (Nancy, 310,000 daily, 320,000 Sunday); *La Nouvelle République du Centre-Ouest* (Tours, 270,000); *Nice-Matin* (Nice, 262,000); *Centre-France* (Clermont-Ferrand, 250,000 combining former *La Montagne, Populaire du Centre, Journal du Centre*), independent; *L'Equipe* (240,000); *Le Républicain Lorrain* (Metz, 216,000); *Le Provençal* (Marseilles, 180,000), largest southeastern daily, Socialist; *International Herald Tribune* (170,000), American, absorbed European edition of *New York Times* in 1967; *Libération* (167,000), politically independent, but culturally leftist; *L'Aurore* (120,000), conservative; *L'Humanité* (120,000), Communist; *La Croix* (115,000), liberal Catholic, popular with left-wing intelligentsia; *Le Quotidien de Paris* (76,000), pro-RPR; *Les Echos* (66,000), financial and economic; *Le Nouveau Journal* (59,000), financial. In January 1985, a new centrist daily, *Le Soir* was launched at Paris, in addition to an international business daily, *Tribune de l'Economique*.

News agencies. The principal French news agency is the semiofficial *Agence France-Presse* (AFP), which operates in most countries and many overseas territories in French, English, and Spanish; other agencies include *Agence Parisienne de Presse* and *Agence Républicaine d'Information*. The leading foreign news agencies also maintain bureaus in France's principal cities.

Radio and television. Until 1972 the government-owned French Radio and Television Organization (*Office de Radiodiffusion et Télévision Française* — ORTF) held a monopoly of both domestic and international services. Granted fiscal and administrative autonomy under the Ministry of Education in 1959, the ORTF was reorganized in May 1972 following a scandal involving clandestine advertising. In July 1974 legislation was enacted breaking up the ORTF in favor of seven state-financed but independent companies: one with overall supervisory responsibility for broadcasting (*TéléDiffusion de France*), one with operational responsibility for radio broadcasting (*Société Nationale de Radiodiffusion*), three television companies (one for each of the nation's TV channels), a radio and television production company (*Société Française de Production*), and an Audio-Visual Institute (*Institut de l'Audiovisuel*). There were approximately 52 million radio and 23 million television receivers in 1987.

INTERGOVERNMENTAL REPRESENTATION

Ambassador to the US: Emmanuel Jacquin de MARGERIE.

US Ambassador to France: Joe M. RODGERS.

Permanent Representative to the UN: Pierre-Louis BLANC.

IGO Memberships (Non-UN): ACCT, ADB, ADF, AfDB, BDEAC, BIS, CCC, CERN, CEUR, EC, EIB, ESA, Eurocontrol, G10, IADB, IATTC, ICAC, ICCAT, ICCO, ICES, ICO, ILZ, Inmarsat, INRO, Intelsat, Interpol, IOOC, ITC, IWC, NATO, OECD, PCA, SPC, WEU.

RELATED TERRITORIES

The former French overseas empire has been in a state of constitutional and political transformation since World War II as a majority of its component territories have achieved independence and most of the others have experienced far-reaching modifications in their relationships to the home country. The initial step in this process of readjustment was the establishment in 1946 of the French Union (*Union Française*) as a single political entity designed to encompass all French-ruled territories. As defined by the constitution of the Fourth Republic, the French Union consisted of two elements: (1) the "French Republic", comprising metropolitan France and the Overseas Departments and Territories; and (2) a second group encompassing all those "associated territories and states" that chose to join. Vietnam, Laos, and Cambodia became associated states under this provision; Tunisia and Morocco declined to do so. However, the arrangement proved ineffective in stemming the tide of nationalism, which led within a decade to the independence of the Indochinese states, Tunisia, and Morocco; the commencement of the war of independence in Algeria; and growing pressure for independence in other French African territories.

In a further attempt to accommodate these pressures, the constitution of the Fifth Republic as adopted in 1958 established the more flexible framework of the French Community (*Communauté Française*), the primary purpose of which was to satisfy the demand for self-government in the African colonies while stopping short of full independence. Still composed of the "French Republic" on the one hand and a group of "Member States" on the other, the Community was headed by the president of the French Republic and endowed with its own Executive Council, Senate, and Court of Arbitration. Initially, 12 French African territories accepted the status of self-governing Member States, although Guinea declined and opted for complete independence in 1958. In anticipation of the independence still sought by other Member States, the French constitution was amended in 1960 to permit continued membership in the Community even after independence. However, no such state subsequently participated in Community institutions and its Senate was formally abolished on March 16, 1961, at which time the organization became essentially moribund.

The present French Republic encompasses, in addition to mainland France, four Overseas Departments, two Territorial Collectivities, and four Overseas Territories, each of whose present status is indicated below.

Overseas Departments:

The Overseas Departments all have similar political institutions. Like the metropolitan Departments, their administrative establishments are headed by commissioners of the Republic (formerly prefects) who are appointed by the French Ministry of the Interior. Each Overseas Department elects a General Council (*Conseil Général*) to which many of the earlier prefectural powers, particularly in financial affairs, were transferred in 1982. General councilors are elected to represent individual districts (*cantons*). Voters also elect, from party lists, a Regional Council (*Conseil Régional*) to which enhanced powers in economic, social, and cultural affairs were accorded in 1983. (In contrast to metropolitan France, the overseas regions and departments are geographically coterminous; nonetheless, a 1983 attempt to provide each with a single General and Regional Council was invalidated by the Constitutional Council.) There are also directly elected mayors and municipal councils for the various townships (*communes*).

French Guiana (*Guyane*). Situated on the east coast of South America between northern Brazil and Suriname (see map, p. 242), French Guiana, after an early period of alternating colonial rule, became a French possession in 1816 and was ruled as a colony until 1946, when it was accorded Department status. From 1852 to 1947 it was utilized as a penal colony, the most notorious installation of which was on Devil's Island (one of the Salut group), where political prisoners were incarcerated. Its territory covers an area of 35,135 square miles (91,000 sq. km.). Of its population (1987E) of 87,000, 90 percent inhabit the coastal region and are mainly Negroes interspersed with some Caucasians and Chinese, while the 10 percent living in the interior are largely Indian and Negro. The capital, Cayenne, has a population (1987E) of 40,000. The two main parties are the Gaullist **Rally for the Republic** (RPR), which supports the status quo, and the **Guianese Socialist Party** (PSG), whose longtime advocacy of internal self-rule has recently been augmented by a demand for autonomy as a "necessary and preparatory stage" for full independence. The shift by the PSG was occasioned, in part, by the emergence of the **Guianan Unity** (UG) as an announced catalyst for nonviolent proindependence opinion within the Department, as well as of the terrorist **Guiana National Liberation Front** (FNLG), several of whose members were arrested in 1981 and flown to Paris for trial before the State Security Court. The Department elects two deputies to the French National Assembly and one senator to the Senate.

Commissioner of the Republic: Jacques DEWATRE.
President of the General Council: Elie CASTOR.
President of the Regional Council: Georges OTHILY (PSG).

Guadeloupe (*Guadeloupe*). A group of Caribbean islands situated in the Lesser Antilles southeast of Puerto Rico (see map, p. 22), Guadeloupe was first occupied by the French in 1635, was annexed as a colonial possession in 1815, and became a French Department in 1946. It has an area of 687 square miles (1,780 sq. km.) and a population (1987E) of 340,000, of whom 15,000 are residents of the capital, Basse-Terre. Guadeloupians are predominantly Negro and mulatto, with a few native-born Caucasians and many metropolitan French. The Department's economy, based principally on sugar, rum, and bananas, is plagued by poverty and unemployment. Fairly widespread discontent among the population is also focused on such problems as the dominance of White landowners and alleged government corruption. A left nationalist formation, the Group of National Organizations of Guadeloupe (GONG), received notoriety at a trial in 1968 when 19 of its members were given suspended sentences for advocating independence. The organization was superseded by the semiclandestine **Popular Union for the Liberation of Guadeloupe** (UPLG) in 1978, while the more extremist **Armed Liberation Group** (GLA) claimed credit for a series of bombings commencing in March 1980. In May 1984, authorities formally outlawed a new group, the Caribbean Revolutionary Alliance (ARC), which had gained prominence through a series of some 30 bombing incidents over a 12-month period. Apart from the **Communist Party of Guadeloupe** (PCG), which has rejected "independence at any price" and normally secures about 25 percent of the vote, the leading parties are the **Rally for the Republic** (RPR) and the **Socialist Party** (PS). Most of the militant groups, including the UPLG, boycotted the 1986 elections. The Department elects four deputies to the French National Assembly and two senators to the Senate.

Commissioner of the Republic: Bernard SARAZIN.
President of the General Council: Dominique LARIFA (PS).
President of the Regional Council: Félix PROTO (PS).

Martinique (*Martinique*). Another island in the Lesser Antilles (see map, p. 22), Martinique was also occupied by the French in 1635, was annexed as a colonial possession in 1790, and became a Department in 1946. It has an area of 425 square miles (1,100 sq. km.). Its population (1987E) of 329,000 is predominantly Negro with a small number of native-born Caucasians and many metropolitan French. The capital, Fort-de-France, has a population of approximately 100,000. Martinique's economy, based largely on the processing of sugarcane products, is, like that of the other Overseas Departments, heavily dependent on direct and indirect subsidies from the French government. Since the eruption in

October 1965 of riots organized to protest the hardships of chronic over-population and economic underdevelopment, there has been increasing sentiment for local autonomy as a precursor of independence. The leading parties are the **Rally for the Republic** (RPR), the **Martinique Progressive Party** (PPM), and the **Martinique Communist Party** (PCM). While both the PPM and the PCM advocate autonomy for the island, the former rejects close ties with either the French Communist Party or the Soviet Union. Martinique is represented in the French Parliament by four deputies and two senators.

Commissioner of the Republic: Jean JOUANDET.
President of the General Council: Emile MAURICE (RPR).
President of the Regional Council: Aimé CESAIRE (PPM).

Reunion (*Réunion*). The island of Reunion, located in the Indian Ocean about 600 miles east of Madagascar, has been a French possession since 1642 and an Overseas Department since 1946. The island has an area of 970 square miles (2,510 sq. km.). Its rapidly growing population of 561,000 (1987E), located mainly on the coast, is composed of Malabar Indians, Caucasians, Negroes, Malays, Annamites, and Chinese. The capital, Saint-Denis, has a population of approximately 111,000. The economy is based primarily on sugarcane cultivation. A manifesto issued by the **Socialist Party** (PS) and the **Reunion Communist Party** (PCR) in May 1968 demanded self-determination and economic and social development programs. The only formation currently committed to full independence is the **Movement for the Independence of Reunion** (MIR), which stems from the Marxist-Leninist Communist Organization of Reunion (OCMLR), a Maoist group organized by PCR dissidents in 1975, while a number of parties favoring the retention of Department status are loosely grouped into the **French Reunion Association** (ARF). The island is represented in the French Parliament by four deputies and two senators.

Commissioner of the Republic: Jean ANCIAUX.
President of the General Council: Auguste LEGROS (RPR).
President of the Regional Council: Pierre LAGOURGUE (PS).

Territorial Collectivities:

Mahoré (*Mayotte*). One of the four principal islands of the Comoros archipelago northwest of Madagascar, Mahoré has an area of 145 square miles (375 sq. km.) and a population (1985C) of 67,138. The chief towns are Mamoudzou and Dzaoudzi, with populations of 12,119 and 5,675, respectively. In two referenda held in 1976, the largely Christian residents rejected inclusion in the Muslim-dominated Republic of the Comoros in favor of French Department status. The following December it was made a Territorial Collectivity (*Collectivité Territoriale*) of France, a category construed as being midway between an Overseas Department and an Overseas Territory. In December 1979, this status was extended by the French National Assembly for another five years, at the conclusion of which a third referendum was to have been held; however, the Assembly in December 1984 adopted a bill that indefinitely postponed a final decision in the matter. The UN General Assembly, on the other hand, has on three occasions voted in support of Comoran sovereignty over the island and has called on Paris to settle its dispute with Moroni in accordance with UN resolutions. The economy is almost entirely agricultural, the principal products being vanilla, ylang-ylang, and copra. The territory is administered by a commissioner and an elected General Council of 17 members; it is represented in the French Parliament by one deputy and one senator. The local parties are the **Mahoran Popular Movement** (MPM), which has called for full departmental status; the **Party for the Mahoran Democratic Rally** (PRDM), which has demanded unification with the Comoros; and the **Mahoran Rally for the Republic** (RMPR).

Commissioner of the Republic: Akli KHIDER.
President of the General Council: Younoussa BAMANA (MPM).

St. Pierre and Miquelon (*Saint-Pierre et Miquelon*). Located off Newfoundland in the North Atlantic, St. Pierre and Miquelon consists of eight small islands covering 93 square miles (242 sq. km.). The population at the 1982 census totaled 6,041, approximately 90 percent of whom lived at the capital, St. Pierre. Formerly an Overseas Territory, the islands were raised to the status of an Overseas Department in July 1976 following a referendum on March 7; by 1982, on the other hand, popular sentiment clearly favored the status of a Territorial Collectivity, which came into effect in June 1985. There is an elected General Council in addition to elected municipal councils. The Territory is represented in the French

Parliament by one deputy and one senator.

Commissioner of the Republic: Bernard LEURQUIN.
President of the General Council: Mark PLANTEGENEST.

Overseas Territories:

The four French Overseas Territories (except for the French Southern and Antarctic Lands) have similar administrative structures headed by a high commissioner or administrator appointed by the central government and sharing authority in varying degrees with local representative bodies. The former Territory of the Comoro Islands became independent on July 6, 1975, although France has not yet yielded its de jure claim to sovereignty over the island of Mahoré (see above).

French Polynesia (*Polynésie Française*). Scattered over a wide expanse of the South Pacific, the 120 islands of French Polynesia (comprising the Austral [Tubuai] Islands, the Gambier Islands, the Marquesas Archipelago, the Society Islands, and the Tuamotu Archipelago) have a combined area of 1,622 square miles (4,200 sq. km.) and a population (1983C) of 166,700, of whom approximately 23,500 are settled at the territorial capital, Papeete (Tahiti). Long-standing concern over French underground nuclear tests on Mururoa Atoll was heightened by a controversial accident on July 25, 1979, that caused a major tidal wave and provoked charges that the adjacent seabed had been contaminated. Three years earlier, Francis SANFORD, the Tahitian leader of the **United Front Party** (*Te Ea Api*), left the Gaullist group in the French National Assembly when Paris refused the request of the former Polynesian Territorial Assembly for internal autonomy, and subsequently campaigned for independence. In May 1977, a new Territorial Assembly was elected in which the **United Front for Internal Autonomy** (FUAI), embracing the *Te Ea Api* and four other parties, obtained 14 of the 30 seats, while the Popular Union Party — PUP (**Tahoeraa Huiraatira**), the Polynesian section of the French RPR, obtained 10 seats. At the following election in May 1982, Sanford himself was the only *Te Ea Api* candidate to be returned, while *Tahoeraa Huiraatira,* campaigning on a platform of internal self-government based on the Cook Islands model, increased its representation to 13; on the Left, a group of nine small parties that campaigned for full independence obtained approximately 15 percent of the vote. At the most recent balloting, called one year early in March 1986, *Tahoeraa* won a majority of 24 seats in an enlarged house of 41 members.

In 1977 Assembly representatives of the leading parties accepted a compromise Territorial Statute whereby the French high commissioner would remain president of the Government Council but most internal affairs would be handled by an elected vice president. In August 1984 the French Parliament approved a new government structure, under which local executive responsibilities were assigned to an Assembly-elected president of a Council of Ministers. The Territory is represented in France by one senator and two National Assembly deputies.

High Commissioner: Jean MONTPEZAT.
President of the Council of Ministers: Alexandre LEONTIEFF.

French Southern and Antarctic Lands (*Terres Australes et Antarctiques Françaises*). The Southern and Antarctic Lands comprise the Antarctic Continent between 136 and 142 degrees East Longitude and south of 60 degrees South Latitude (see map, p. 19), together with the islands of Saint Paul, Amsterdam, and the Kerguelen and Crozet archipelagos. The total area embraces some 150,000 square miles (390,000 sq. km.). The seat of administration is at Paris, where a Consultative Council that assists the Territory's administrator meets twice yearly. The legal status of the Antarctic portion of the Territory, in which French scientific research stations are currently operating, remains in suspense under the Antarctic Treaty of 1959 (see Antarctica in main alphabetical listing).

High Administrator: Adm. Claude PIERI.

New Caledonia (*Nouvelle-Calédonie*). A group of islands covering 7,375 square miles (19,000 sq. km.) in the Pacific Ocean east of Queensland, Australia, New Caledonia has a population (1983C) of 145,400, of whom about 60,000 reside at Nouméa, the Territory's capital. An important mining center, the Territory possesses the world's largest nickel reserves and is the second-largest nickel producer outside the Communist bloc. A long-term economic development plan, which included a proviso that the Territory could not become independent for at least 19 years, was approved by the Territorial Assembly in February 1979. In an Assembly election the following July that was widely interpreted as a referendum on the independence issue, the Independence Front (FI), encompassing a group of parties demanding the severance of all links to France, obtained a little over one-third of the vote. An increased degree of militancy was reported at the FI's first territorial convention in March 1981, in part because of the accession to independence of neighboring Vanuatu eight months earlier. Subsequently, the FI succeeded in concluding a legislative coalition with the autonomist Federation for a New Caledonian Society (FNSC), which had theretofore been allied with the anti-independence **Rally for Caledonia in the Republic** (RPCR). On June 15, 1982, the new de facto majority ousted the RPCR-led government and three days thereafter installed an FI-led "government of reform and development" headed by Jean-Marie TJIBAOU. The change in government without an intervening election precipitated widespread demonstrations by right-wing elements that culminated in an invasion of the Territorial Assembly chamber on July 22, in the course of which three FI deputies were injured. Following a restoration of order, the high commissioner announced that a new constitution for New Caledonia, to be promulgated by mid-1983, would give the Territory increased internal autonomy.

The proposed statute of autonomy, as presented by the French government in March 1983, contained a number of concessions to the native Melanesian (*Kanak*) people, including the return of tribal land to customary owners and the addition of Melanesian "assessors" to the judicial system. Under the plan, substantial powers would be transferred from the French high commissioner to a new territorial government headed by a president who would be elected by the Territorial Assembly and empowered to name his own ministers. At the conclusion of an all-party conference near Paris in mid-July, the FI and the FNSC accepted the French offer on the basis of an anticipated vote on self-determination that would be confined to Melanesians and other New Caledonians with at least one parent born in the territory. The planter-dominated RPCR, on the other hand, declared its opposition to any reform that excluded persons other than French military and civil service personnel from the franchise.

In July 1984 the French National Assembly approved the autonomy statute, which provided for an Assembly election by the end of the year and a referendum on independence by 1989, without, however, calling for electoral reform. As a result, the FI position hardened into a demand that the vote be confined exclusively to Melanesians (approximately 45 percent of the total population). Subsequently, the FI joined with a number of other proindependence groups in forming a **Kanaka Socialist National Liberation Front** (FLNKS). The FLNKS boycotted the legislative balloting on November 18, at which the RPCR won 71 percent of the vote and 34 of 42 seats. One week later, amid mounting acts of terrorism that yielded the deaths of a number of separatists, the FLNKS announced the formation of a provisional Kanaki government under Tjibaou's presidency.

During 1985 a number of new proposals for resolving the controversy were advanced, including, on April 25, a plan advocated by French Premier Fabius, whereby four regional councils would be established, the members of which would sit collectively as a Territorial Congress, replacing the existing Territorial Assembly. The Fabius plan was immediately condemned as "iniquitous" by the RPCR, but tentatively accepted by the FLKS (without, however, dismantling its provisional regime) as strengthening the movement toward independence. The plan was subsequently approved by the French National Assembly and balloting for the regional bodies was conducted on September 29, with the RPCR (which agreed to participate) securing 25 of 46 seats in the Congress, although securing a majority only in the heavily populated, but largely non-Melanesian Nouméa region.

Following the Socialist loss in the French National Assembly balloting of March 1986, the situation changed dramatically. Criticizing the regional council arrangement as "badly conceived, badly organized, and badly prepared, Bernard PONS, the new minister for Overseas Departments and Territories, advanced a "Pons Plan", under which the councils would be limited to responsibility for local public works and cultural matters. After extensive debate, the proposal to return effective political and economic authority to the high commissioner received parliamentary approval and in August the South Pacific Forum, supported by the FLNKS, recommended that New Caledonia be restored to the United Nations list of non-self-governing territories. Despite intense pressure by France (which indicated that it would ignore such action), the General Assembly voted overwhelming to do so in December.

In the face of an FLNKS boycott, the independence referendum conducted on September 13, 1987, yielded a 98 percent vote in favor of remaining within the Republic. A month later, Pons introduced a new

"autonomy statute" that by means of boundary redefinition left the FLNKS dominant in two, rather than three, of the four regions. Subsequently, in balloting for a new territorial Congress (conducted in conjunction with the first-round French presidential poll on April 24, 1988), the RPCR won 35 of 48 seats. The FLNKS reaction was, however, relatively subdued in the wake of the metropolitan Socialist victories in May and June, which were almost certain to prompt further alteration of the territory's constitutional status.

New Caledonia is presently represented in the French Parliament by two deputies and one senator.

High Commissioner: Clément BOUHIN.
President of the Territorial Congress: Dick UKEIWE (RPCR).

Wallis and Futuna Islands (*Wallis et Futuna*). The inhabitants of these former French Protectorates voted in 1959 to exchange their status for that of a French Territory. The Territory covers 106 square miles (274 sq. km.) in the South Pacific just west of Samoa and has a population (1983E) of 12,400, excluding some 10,000 Wallisians residing in New Caledonia. Political activity is basically conservative, most voters favoring local affiliates of the metropolitan RPR and UDF. The islands are governed by a high administrator and an elected Territorial Assembly, and are represented in the French Parliament by one deputy and one senator.

High Administrator: Gérard LAMBOTTE.
President of the Territorial Assembly: Falakiko GATA (UDF).

Insular Possessions:

France also has a number of small insular possessions which are not recognized as components of the French Republic. These include **Clipperton Island** (*Ile Clipperton*), geographically located in, but not part of, French Polynesia; **Tromelin Island** (*Ile Tromelin*), situated off the northeast coast of Madagascar; and several islands located in the Mozambique Channel between Madagascar and the west coast of Africa: **Bassas da India** (*Bassas da India*), **Europa Island** (*Ile Europa*), **Juan de Nova Island** (*Ile Juan de Nova*), and the **Glorioso Islands** (*Iles Glorieuses*).

GABON

Gabonese Republic
République Gabonaise

Political Status: Independent since August 17, 1960; present republican constitution adopted February 21, 1961; under one-party presidential regime since March 1968.

Area: 103,346 sq. mi. (267,667 sq. km.).

Population: 1,027,529 (1972C), 1,545,000 (1988E). There is some evidence that both the 1972 census figure and subsequent estimates may be substantially inflated.

Major Urban Centers (1975E): LIBREVILLE (251,000); Port-Gentil (78,000); Lambaréné (23,000).

Official Language: French.

Monetary Unit: CFA Franc (market rate March 1, 1988, 285.80 francs = $1US).

President: El Hadj Omar (formerly Albert-Bernard) BONGO; elected Vice President on March 19, 1967; succeeded to the presidency December 2, 1967, upon the death of Léon M'BA; reelected for seven-year terms in 1973, 1979, and on November 9, 1986.

Prime Minister: Léon MEBIAME; appointed Vice President in December 1967; reelected February 25, 1973; designated Prime Minister by President Bongo on April 16, 1975, under constitutional amendment of April 12.

THE COUNTRY

A tropical, heavily forested country on the west coast of Central Africa, Gabon is inhabited by a sparse population whose largest components, among over 40 distinct ethnic groups, are the Fang and Eshira tribes. A sizable European (predominantly French) community is also resident. Indigenous Gabonese speak a variety of Bantu languages, with Fang predominating in the north. About 60 percent of the population is Christian, with most of the rest adhering to traditional beliefs; there is also a small Muslim minority. Women constitute over half of salaried workers in the health and trading sectors, although female representation in party and government bodies is minimal.

Abundant natural resources that include oil, manganese, uranium, and timber have given Gabon the highest per capita GNP in Black Africa, estimated at about $4,250 in 1983. In addition, it has reserves of approximately one billion tons of high-grade iron ore, although inadequate transport facilities have hindered exploitation. Oil output tripled during the mid-1970s and until 1986 had accounted for about three-fourths of Gabon's export earnings. Most of the country's food must be imported, even though half of the labor force is employed (mainly at a subsistence level) in agriculture.

GOVERNMENT AND POLITICS

Political background. Colonized by France in the latter half of the nineteenth century and subsequently administered as a part of French Equatorial Africa, Gabon achieved full independence within the French Community on August 17, 1960. Its longtime political leader, President Léon M'BA, ruled in a conservative yet pragmatic style and supported close political and economic relations with France. However, M'Ba's attempts to establish a one-party state based on his Gabon Democratic Bloc (BDG) were resisted for several years by the Gabonese Democratic and Social Union (UDSG), led by Jean-Hilaire AUBAME. Only after an attempted coup by Aubame's army supporters had been thwarted by French military intervention in February 1964, and after M'Ba's party had gained a majority in legislative elections two months later, was the UDSG formally outlawed.

M'Ba was reelected to a seven-year presidential term in March 1967 but died the following November and was succeeded by Vice President Albert-Bernard (subsequently

El Hadj Omar) BONGO. Officially declaring Gabon a one-party state in March 1968, Bongo announced a "renovation" policy that included conversion of the former ruling party into a new, nationwide political grouping, the Gabon Democratic Party (PDG). The incumbent was unopposed for reelection to a fourth term on November 9, 1986, after surviving a coup plot by military officers in mid-1985.

Constitution and government. At a six-day Special Congress of the PDG in January 1979, a variety of resolutions aimed at injecting "a limited dose of democracy" into party and governmental procedures was endorsed, including constitutional changes normally requiring approval by means of national referenda. In late February, however, President Bongo declared that the measures would be implemented without public endorsement, in furtherance of the government's program of financial austerity. The changes included shortening the legislative term from seven to five years, holding presidential and parliamentary elections on different dates, permitting independents to stand against party nominees in legislative contests, and forbidding public officials to hold more than one administrative position.

The constitution of 1961, as amended, stipulates that the president and all but nine members of the unicameral National Assembly be directly elected by universal suffrage for terms of seven and five years, respectively; popular approval is, however, pro forma, since all candidates must be approved by the PDG (see Legislature, below). The president appoints a prime minister, who serves as head of government, and other members of a Council of Ministers, all of whom must in theory resign following a vote of no confidence; however, no legislator has ever moved such a vote. The judiciary includes a Supreme Court appointed by the president, a High Court of Justice (appointed by and from the National Assembly) with the authority to try the president and other government officials, a Court of Appeal, a Superior Council of Magistracy headed by the president, and lesser courts.

For administrative purposes Gabon is divided into nine provinces and subdivided into 37 departments, all headed by presidentially appointed executives. Libreville and Port-Gentil are governed by elected mayors and Municipal Councils, while four smaller municipalities have partly elected and partly appointed administrations.

Foreign relations. Following his accession to power, President Bongo sought to lessen the country's traditional dependence on France by cultivating more diversified international support. In early 1981, on the other hand, Gabon's foreign minister announced closing of the country's embassies in Cuba and Libya as an "economy measure", asking that reciprocal steps be taken by Havana and Tripoli. Regionally, Gabon withdrew in 1976 from membership in the Common African and Mauritian Organization (OCAM), while relations with Benin have been cool since Gabon's alleged involvement in a mercenary attack at Cotonou in 1977 and the expulsion in 1978 of some 6,000 Beninese workers following civil disturbances. Relations with neighboring Equatorial Guinea suffered until the overthrow of the Macie regime in August 1979, by which time as many as 80,000 Equatorial Guinean refugees had fled to Gabon.

Relations with Cameroon deteriorated in May 1981 with the expulsion of nearly 10,000 Cameroonians in the wake of violent demonstrations at Libreville and Port-Gentil. The demonstrations were in response to an incident during a soccer match at Douala, Cameroon, which the Cameroonian government branded as a "premeditated act" designed to justify exclusion of its nationals from the Gabonese economy and the ensuing expropriation of their assets.

More recently, an overt campaign against immigrant workers has further strained ties between Gabon and its neighbors. Libreville nonetheless continues to participate in the ten-member Economic Community of Central African States (CEEAC), hosting its third summit meeting in August 1987.

During the same month, a presidential visit to the United States served to strengthen relations between the two countries, with Bongo pledging to protect American investments of more than $200 million and Washington agreeing to debt-restructuring of some $8 million owed by Gabon for military purchases. Earlier, during a visit to Tunis, Prime Minister Mebiame met with Yasir 'Arafat, reiterating his government's support of the PLO reaffirming its opposition to apartheid, Zionism, and neocolonialism.

Current issues. In mid-1986, President Bongo announced deep budget cuts and a freezing of funds for most state investment projects as part of an effort to revitalize the economy. The government also proposed the privatization of four state-owned companies and in June 1987 decreed obligatory "solidarity" loan Subscriptions totaling 27 billion CFA over an 18-month period by individuals, businesses, and parastatal bodies with incomes in excess of 100,000 CFA. Partly in response to such measures, the World Bank in August agreed to support a structural adjustment program to reduce the country's dependence on oil exports. Economic diversification had earlier been aided by the completion in December 1986 of the 700-kilometer Transgabonais Railway.

POLITICAL PARTIES

Officially declared a one-party state in March 1968, Gabon in practice had been under one-party government since the banning of the former opposition group, the Gabonese Democratic and Social Union (*Union Démocratique et Sociale Gabonaise* — UDSG), in 1964.

Government Party:

Gabon Democratic Party (*Parti Démocratique Gabonais* — PDG). Officially established by President Bongo in 1968, the PDG is the successor to the earlier Gabon Democratic Bloc (*Bloc Démocratique Gabonais* — BDG) of President M'Ba. The PDG's Political Bureau, appointed by the secretary general, is empowered to issue decrees having the force of law, although the Congress is technically the highest party organ. There is also an advisory Central Committee. In September 1986 the Third PDG Congress expanded the Central Committee from 253 to 297 members and the Political Bureau from 27 to 44 members to give "young militants" more access to leadership roles.

Leaders: El Hadj Omar BONGO (President of the Republic and Chairman of the Party), Léon MEBIAME (Prime Minister and Secretary General of the Party).

Illegal Opposition:

Movement for National Renewal (*Mouvement de Redressement Nationale* — Morena). Organized in 1981, Morena operates clandestinely within Gabon and, with support from the French Socialist Party, has formed a self-proclaimed government-in-exile at Paris. In 1981–1982, its domestic leaders were repeatedly arrested for distributing leaflets calling for a multiparty system. Many were sentenced to long prison terms, but by 1986 all had been released under a general amnesty that had been urged by French President Mitterrand. In June 1987 a report that Paul Mba-Adessole had been removed as Morena's president was formally denied.

Leaders: Paul MBA-ADESSOLE (President), Flavien EDOU (General Treasurer), Marcel Ogoula RENOMBO (General Secretary).

LEGISLATURE

The **National Assembly** (*Assemblée Nationale*) is a unicameral legislature that currently consists of 120 members, 111 directly elected for five-year terms and 9 nominated by the president. Balloting is in two stages, at the first of which only PDG activists participate. Thus, at the most recent poll of February 17, 1985, the 111 elective nominees were selected from 268 candidates previously "validated" by the party leadership, all of whom were confirmed in a referendum on March 3 that reportedly involved 95.4 percent of the electorate.

President: Augustin BOUMAH.

CABINET

Prime Minister	Léon Mébiame
1st Deputy Prime Minister	Georges Rawiri
2nd Deputy Prime Minister	Etienne Guy Mouvagha-Tchioba
3rd Deputy Prime Minister	Emile Kassa-Mapsi
4th Deputy Prime Minister	Simon Essimengane

Ministers of State

Culture, Arts and Popular Education	François Owono-Nguema
Foreign Affairs and Cooperation	Martin Bongo
Higher Education and Scientific Research	Jules Bourdès-Ogouliguende
Industries and State Companies	Etienne Moussiron
Information, Posts and Telecommunications	Zacharie Myboto
Public Land, Surveys and Law of the Sea	Henri Minko
Territorial Administration, Local Communities and Immigration	Richard Nguema-Bekale
Tourism, Leisure and National Parks	Alexandre Sambat
Trade, Technology Transfer and Rationalization	Jean-François Ntoutoume-Emane
Secretary General of the Presidency	René Radembino-Coniquet

Ministers

Agriculture, Livestock and Rural Development	Michel Anchouey
Civil and Commercial Aviation	Michel Essonghe
Civil Service, Administrative Reform and Mixed Economy Enterprises	Emile Kassa-Mapsi
Economy and Finance	Mamadou Diop
Energy and Hydraulic Resources	Divungui Di-Ndinge
Environment and Conservation	Dr. Hervé Mountsinga
Finance, Budget and Participation	Jean-Pierre Lemboumba-Lepandou
Habitation and Housing	Albert Yangari
Immigration and National Disasters	Gen. Barthelmy Mbia
Justice and Keeper of the Seals	Sophie Ngwamassana
Labor, Employment and Human Resources	Maitre Louis-Gaston Mayila
Merchant Marine	Paulin Obame Nguema
Mines and Petroleum	Guy-Etienne Mouvagha-Tchioba

National Defense, War Veterans and
    Public Security   Julien Mpouho-Epigat
National Education   Guy Nzouba Ndama
Planning and Economy   Pascal Nzé
Professional Training and
    Promotion of Handicrafts   José Joseph Amiar-Nganga
Public Health and Population   Dr. Jean-Pierre Okias
Public Relations   Georges Rawiri
Public Works, Equipment,
    Construction and Territorial
    Development   Gen. Jean-Boniface Assélé
Relations with Assemblies   Bonjean François Ondo
Small and Medium Businesses   Emmanuel Nze-Bekale
Social Affairs, Social Security and
    Welfare   Sylvestre Oyouomi
State Control   Jean-Mile Mbot
Territorial Administration and Local   Antoine Mboumbou-
    Collectivities   Miyakou
Transport, Water and Forests, and
    Social Communication   Georges Rawiri
Urban Housing and Development   Simon Essimengane
Youth and Sports   Victor Affene

Director, Central Bank   J.P. Leyimangoye

NEWS MEDIA

All news media are owned and operated by the government.

Press. The following are published at Libreville: *Gabon-Matin* (18,000), published daily by the *Agence Gabonaise de Presse; L'Union* (15,000), published by the *Société Nationale de Presse et d'Edition; Dialogue* (3,000), monthly PDG organ; *Gabon d'Aujourd'hui,* published weekly by the Ministry of Information.

News agency. The domestic facility is the *Agence Gabonaise de Presse.*

Radio and television. The government-controlled *Radiodiffusion-Télévision Gabonaise* broadcasts national and regional radio programs in French and local languages, plus educational television programming from Libreville and Port-Gentil. The most powerful radio station in Africa, called "Africa No. 1", began transmitting in February 1981 from Moyabi. There were approximately 145,000 radio and 37,200 television receivers in 1987.

INTERGOVERNMENTAL REPRESENTATION

Ambassador to the US: Jean-Robert ODZAGA.

US Ambassador to Gabon: Warren CLARK, Jr.

Permanent Representative to the UN: Laurent-Marie BIFFOT.

IGO Memberships (Non-UN): ACCT, ADF, AfDB, BADEA, BDEAC, CCC, CEEAC, Copal, EEC(L), *EIB,* IACO, IC, ICCAT, ICCO, ICO, IDB, Intelsat, Interpol, NAM, OAU, OPEC, UDEAC.

GERMANY

Deutschland

Political Status: Politically divided since World War II; existing boundaries confirmed by normalization treaty concluded November 8, 1972, between the German Democratic Republic and the Federal Republic of Germany.

THE COUNTRY

Germany's commanding position in Central Europe and its industrious population have made it a significant factor in modern European and world affairs despite the political fragmentation that has characterized most of its history. Flat and low-lying in the north and increasingly mountainous to the south, the country combines abundant agricultural land with rich deposits of coal and other minerals and a strategic position astride the main European river systems. Ethnically and culturally the population is remarkably homogeneous, with no numerically significant national minorities except for large numbers of foreign workers who have entered West Germany since World War II. (Germany's once substantial Jewish population was virtually destroyed during the Nazi period in 1933–1945 and presently numbers only about 35,000.) Protestantism, chiefly Evangelical Lutheranism, is the religion of about half of the West Germans and four-fifths of the East Germans; Roman Catholicism accounts for roughly 45 percent in the West and 8 percent in the East.

In East Germany, women are estimated at 50 percent of the labor force, although most are engaged in sales and textile or chemical manufacturing; female participation in party and legislative bodies averages 25 percent, with no Politburo representation. In the Federal Republic, women constitute 38 percent of the paid labor force, concentrated in clerical, sales, and service sectors in urban areas and as unpaid agricultural workers in rural areas; female representation in elected bodies ranges from 10 to 22 percent, with two female cabinet members in March 1988.

Although highly industrialized prior to World War II, the German economy exhibited major regional variations which, coupled with quite dissimilar occupation policies, yielded divergent patterns of postwar reconstruction and development. West Germany, with a greater resource base, substantial financial assistance from the Western allies, and a strong commitment to the free-enterprise system, recovered rapidly, greatly expanded its industry, and by the 1960s had become the strongest economic power in Western Europe. East Germany, denied access to many of its traditional raw materials, plundered by the Soviets of as much as 50 percent of its prewar industrial fixed capital, and committed to a vast land-redistribution program, recovered more slowly, though experiencing over the last quarter-century a surge in development that has placed it among the top dozen nations in industrial output and second only to the USSR among Communist states.

POLITICAL HISTORY

Germany's history as a modern state dates from the Franco-Prussian War of 1870–1871 and the proclamation in 1871 of the German Empire, the result of efforts by Otto von BISMARCK and others to convert a loose confederation of German-speaking territories into a single political entity led by the Prussian House of Hohenzollern. Defeated by a coalition of powers in World War I, the German Empire disintegrated and was replaced in 1919 by the Weimar Republic, whose chronic economic and political instability paved the way for the rise of the National Socialist (Nazi) Party and the installation of Adolf HITLER as chancellor in 1933. Under a totalitarian ideology stressing nationalism, anti-Communism, anti-Semitism, and removal of the disabilities imposed on Germany after World War I, Hitler converted the Weimar Republic into an authoritarian one-party state (the so-called "Third Reich") and embarked upon a policy of aggressive expansionism that led to the outbreak of World War II in 1939 and, ultimately, to the overthrow of Nazi Germany by the Allies in 1945.

Following Germany's unconditional surrender on May 8, 1945, the country was divided into zones of military occupation assigned to forces of the United States, Britain, France, and the Soviet Union, whose governments assumed all powers of administration pending the reestablishment of a German governmental authority. Berlin, likewise divided into sectors, was made a separate area under joint quadripartite control with a view to its becoming the seat of the eventual central German government, while the territories east of the Oder and Neisse rivers were placed under Polish administration, East Prussia was divided into Soviet and Polish spheres, and the Saar was attached economically to France.

At the Potsdam Conference in July-August 1945, the American, British, and Soviet leaders agreed to treat Germany as a single economic unit and ensure parallel political development in the four occupation zones, but the emergence of sharp differences between the Soviet Union and its wartime allies soon intervened. The territories east of the Oder and Neisse were incorporated into Poland and the USSR, while Soviet occupation policies prevented the treatment of Germany as an economic unit and prompted joint economic measures in the Western occupation zones. Protesting a proposed currency reform in the US and British occupation zones, Soviet representatives withdrew from the Allied Control Council for Germany in March 1948. Three months later the USSR instituted a blockade of the land and water routes to Berlin that was maintained until May 1949, forcing the United States and United Kingdom to resort to a large-scale airlift to supply the city's Western sectors.

Having failed to agree with the USSR on measures for the whole of Germany, the three Western powers resolved to merge their zones of occupation as a step toward establishing a democratic state in Western Germany. A draft constitution for a West German federal state was approved by a specially elected parliamentary assembly on May 8, 1949, and the Federal Republic of Germany (FRG), with its capital at Bonn, was proclaimed on May 23. The USSR protested these actions and on October 7 announced the establishment in its occupation zone of the German Democratic Republic (GDR), with East Berlin as its capital.

In West Germany the former occupation regime was gradually converted into a contractual relationship based on the equality of the parties involved. Under the London and Paris agreements of 1954, the FRG was granted sovereignty and admitted to the North Atlantic Treaty Organization (NATO) and the Western European Union (WEU), while on January 1, 1957, the Saar was returned as the result of a plebiscite held in 1955. The Soviet-

sponsored GDR was also declared fully sovereign in 1954 and was accorded formal recognition by Communist, though not by Western, governments. Although Berlin has remained technically under four-power control, East Berlin has been incorporated into the GDR, while West Berlin, without being granted parliamentary voting rights, has been accorded status similar to that of a *Land* (state) of the FRG. Both German regimes were admitted to full membership in the United Nations in the fall of 1973.

Until the early 1970s the FRG and its Western allies advocated reunification of Germany on the basis of an internationally supervised all-German election to choose a government empowered to conclude a formal peace treaty with the country's wartime enemies. The Soviet Union and the GDR, however, insisted that unification be based on recognition of the existence of "two German states" and achieved by negotiation between the two regimes, which would then form a government to conclude a treaty. A new constitution adopted by the GDR in 1968 further implied that reunification could take place only when West Germany became a "socialist" state. With regard to Germany's frontiers, the USSR, Poland, and the GDR insisted that the territorial annexations carried out at the end of World War II were definitive and irreversible, while the FRG maintained that under the 1945 Potsdam agreement Germany's territorial frontiers could be established only by a formal peace treaty. Beginning in 1967, however, the FRG gave indications of increased readiness to accept the Oder-Neisse line as Germany's permanent eastern frontier, ultimately recognizing it as such in a December 1970 treaty with Poland. The "two Germanies" concept, in turn, acquired legal standing with the negotiation in November 1972 of a "Basic Treaty" (*Grundvertrag*) normalizing relations between the FRG and the GDR. While the agreement stopped short of a mutual extension of full diplomatic recognition, it affirmed the "inviolability" of the existing border and provided for the exchange of "permanent representative missions" by the two governments, thus effectively ruling out the possibility of German reunification within the foreseeable future.

GERMAN DEMOCRATIC REPUBLIC

Deutsche Demokratische Republik

Political Status: Communist regime established in Soviet occupation zone of Germany on October 7, 1949; present constitution adopted April 9, 1968.

Area: 41,768 sq. mi. (108,178 sq. km.).

Population: 16,705,635 (1981C), 16,670,000 (1988E).

Major Urban Centers (1984E): (East) BERLIN (1,160,000); Leipzig (558,000); Dresden (521,000); Karl-Marx-Stadt (317,000); Magdeburg (290,000); Halle (242,000).

Official Language: German.

Monetary Unit: DDR-Mark (noncommercial rate March 1, 1988, 1.67 marks = $1US).

Chairman of the Council of State and General Secretary of the Socialist Unity Party: Erich HONECKER; designated Chairman of the Council of State by the People's Chamber on October 29, 1976, succeeding Willi STOPH; redesignated in 1981 and on June 16, 1986; became First Secretary of the Socialist Unity Party on May 3, 1971, succeeding Walter ULBRICHT; designated General Secretary on May 22, 1976; redesignated in 1981 and on April 21, 1986.

Chairman of the Council of Ministers (Premier): Willi STOPH; designated by the People's Chamber on October 29, 1976, succeeding Horst SINDERMANN; redesignated in 1981 and on June 16, 1986.

GOVERNMENT AND POLITICS

Political background. Communist rule was established in East Germany soon after World War II through the ascendancy of the Socialist Unity Party (SED), a Soviet-sponsored political organization created by a forced merger of the preexisting Communist and Social Democratic parties. A faithful adherent of the Soviet political line, the SED achieved political leadership in the five East German states (*Länder*) as a result of elections held in October 1946. Its influence likewise predominated in the elected People's Congress and the Soviet-sponsored People's Council, which proclaimed the establishment of the German Democratic Republic (GDR) on October 7, 1949. While Soviet authorities retained ultimate control through a Soviet Control Commission, the powers of the Soviet military administration were nominally handed over to the new government, with Wilhelm PIECK serving as president.

The Soviet system of administration, including reorganized district and local governments, collectivized agriculture, and a revised judicial system, was introduced in 1952. Coupled with severe food shortages, the increased Sovietization led on June 17, 1953, to uprisings and strikes that were forcibly put down by the Soviet army, although the USSR subsequently ended the collection of reparations from East Germany and announced the attainment of full sovereignty by the GDR on March 25, 1954. This new status was not recognized by the Western powers, and the internal discontent that persisted produced massive emigration to West Germany until the main escape route was cut off by the building of the Berlin Wall in 1961.

After the death of Pieck in 1960, the office of president was abolished and superseded by a 23-man Council of State chaired by Walter ULBRICHT. Otto GROTEWOHL, designated the GDR's first minister-president in 1949, held the technically subordinate position until his death and succession by Willi STOPH in 1964. In October 1972 the status and functions of the Council of Ministers were redefined and the office of minister-president became that of chairman of the Council of Ministers. Following the death of Ulbricht in August 1973, Stoph was named chairman of the State Council and Horst SINDERMANN succeeded Stoph as premier.

Even before the death of Ulbricht, a proponent of orthodox communism who long opposed the trend toward a more "liberal" order in Czechoslovakia and other Communist states, the East German regime had grown more flexible with regard to the *Ostpolitik* of West German Chancellor Willy Brandt. As a result, in 1973 a normalization treaty with the Federal Republic was concluded and the two Germanies were admitted to the United Nations as separate states (see Foreign relations, below).

On October 17, 1976, the East German leadership was reshuffled, SED Secretary Erich HONECKER becoming chairman of the State Council in place of Stoph, who returned to his former position as premier. Sindermann in turn was reassigned to the considerably less prestigious position of president of the legislature. Honecker's added designation as head of state replicated the consolidation of top party and government posts that had prevailed under Ulbricht.

Constitution and government. The constitution promulgated April 9, 1968, gave formal sanction to a political structure that had long ago outgrown the constitution of 1949, itself based on the Weimar Constitution of 1919. The new basic law established the GDR as a "socialist German state"; announced the socialist ownership of the means of production as the foundation of its economy; and set as its goal the union of the two German states on the basis of "democracy and socialism" — a reference that was deleted from the constitution in September 1974.

Political power is theoretically exercised by the workers, led by the National Front of the German Democratic Republic and its component parties and mass organizations. The supreme organ of state power is the unicameral legislature, the People's Chamber (*Volkskammer*), which is elected by universal suffrage on the basis of a list (containing a limited number of multiple candidatures) presented by the National Front. The People's Chamber elects the Council of State and its chairman, who serves as head of state, and designates the chairman of the Council of Ministers on the latter's recommendation. In practice, all political power in the GDR is wielded by the Communist-dominated Socialist Unity Party (SED), whose hierarchy parallels the state organization at all levels. The judicial system, charged with the maintenance of "socialist legality", is headed by a Supreme Court that is responsible to the People's Chamber. In mid-1987 a new appellate court, styled the Grand Bench, was established to hear appeals against Supreme Court decisions. There are also county, district, military, social, and labor courts. A penal code based upon the Soviet model was introduced in 1968, and a new Soviet-style civil code was adopted in 1976. In June 1978, the *Volkskammer* approved 48 amendments to the penal code, many in effect restricting Western access to information by stiffening criminal penalties for internal security violations or by making illegal such activities as communicating nonsecret but "treasonous" information.

Provincial administration is conducted through 14 districts (*Bezirke*), which replaced the traditional states in 1952; district and local government is based on a system of elected assemblies, councils, and committees.

Foreign relations. Prior to 1969 the GDR was accorded diplomatic recognition only by other Communist governments, and its participation in multilateral organizations was limited primarily to the Soviet-backed Council for Mutual Economic Assistance and Warsaw Pact. In 1969–1970, however, the GDR was recognized by a number of Arab governments, and in August 1972, after a year of informal talks, it was announced that the East and West German regimes would enter into formal negotiations on normalization of relations. A Basic Treaty to such effect was ratified by the West German legislature on December 21, 1972, and by the East German legislature on June 13, 1973. The following September both East and West Germany were admitted to the United Nations. Although Britain and France recognized the GDR in February 1973, the United States did not agree to recognition and an exchange of ambassadors until September 5, 1974, immediately prior to the GDR's formal abandonment of reunification as a constitutional objective.

Even before the signing of the 1972 Basic Treaty, SED Secretary Honecker had asserted that "history has already made the decision" in favor of two separate German states, adding that the Berlin Wall and the heavily guarded frontier would be retained as "existing realities". Nevertheless, the GDR has refused to acknowledge any claim by the Federal Republic to authority in West Berlin, while Bonn has refused to acknowledge the GDR's national sovereignty or to remove from the FRG's Basic Law reference to the goal of reunification. Periodic problems involving espionage and political defections have also strained relations, although the two governments have succeeded in reaching a number of trade and cultural exchange agreements. In addition, East Germany has benefited from West Germany's insistence that trade between the two is intra-national, thus enabling the GDR to obtain duty-free access to European Community (EC) markets.

In world affairs, the GDR has echoed the Soviet line on most international issues, while maintaining the most active foreign-aid program of any East European country other than the USSR. By 1984, it had concluded economic agreements with 63 developing nations and had dispatched more than 200,000 "expert advisers" to Third World countries.

Current issues. During 1985, Mikhail Gorbachev's first year as Soviet leader, the highly centralized East German economic system was hailed as a model for socialist revitalization. By early 1986, although the GDR remained, on a per capita basis, the most prosperous East European country, it was increasingly being viewed as moving against the trend toward more market-oriented policies within the Soviet bloc. Collaterally, there were virtually no references in the East German press to Gorbachev's calls for "openness" and "democratization".

On the diplomatic front, an irony emerged. In 1983–1984, during a period of relaxation in relations with the FRG, Chairman Honecker had twice been forced to cancel scheduled visits to Bonn because of manifest Soviet displeasure, although a meeting with Chancellor Kohl did occur during the funeral of Konstantin Chernenko in March 1985. By 1987, Moscow itself was keenly interested in consolidating the Kohl government's support for the so-called "zero option" European missile plan, and in Septem-

ber Honecker embarked on the first official visit to West Germany by an East German head of state, holding extensive talks with Kohl and other FRG leaders, in the course of which a number of agreements were concluded between the two governments. The rapprochement occurred during year-long observances in both East and West Berlin marking the divided city's 750th anniversary.

POLITICAL PARTIES

The one-party system dominated by the Socialist Unity Party (SED) is partially masked by the existence of other parties and mass organizations which, though separately represented in the People's Chamber, are controlled by the SED through the instrumentality of the **National Front of the German Democratic Republic** (*Nationale Front der Deutschen Demokratischen Republik*).

Socialist Unity Party of Germany (*Sozialistische Einheitspartei Deutschlands* – SED). Pressure exerted by Soviet occupation authorities led in April 1946 to the formation of the SED by merger of the Communist and Social Democratic parties. The executor of Communist policy, the SED controls all East German organizations except the churches and provides leadership and generates public support for government programs. During the SED's Eleventh Congress, which met at East Berlin, April 17–21, 1986, the party Politburo was increased in size from 19 to 22 (exclusive of candidate members), while the Secretariat, with one member being replaced, remained at 11. The SED has an allotment of 127 seats in the People's Chamber.

General Secretary: Erich HONECKER.

Other Members of Politburo: Hermann AXEN (member, Secretariat), Hans-Joachim BOEHME (First Secretary, Halle Party Executive), Horst DOHLUS (member, Secretariat), Werner EBERLEIN (First Secretary Magdeburg Party Executive), Werner FELFE (member, State Council), Kurt HAGER (member, State Council), Joachim HERRMANN (member, Secretariat), Dr. Werner JAROWINSKY (member, Secretariat), Gen. Heinz KESSLER (Defense Minister), Günther KLEIBER (Deputy Chairman, Council of Ministers), Egon KRENZ (member, Secretariat), Werner KROLIKOWSKI (First Deputy Chairman, Council of Ministers), Siegfried LORENZ (First Secretary, Karl Marx Stadt Party Executive), Gen. Erich MIELKE (Minister of State Security), Dr. Günter MITTAG (Deputy Chairman, State Council), Erich MÜCKENBERGER (Chairman, Central Party Control Commission, and member, Presidium of People's Chamber), Alfred NEUMANN (First Deputy Chairman, Council of Ministers), Günther SCHABOWSKI (First Secretary, East Berlin Party Executive), Horst SINDERMANN (Deputy Chairman, State Council, and President, People's Chamber), Willi STOPH (Deputy Chairman, State Council, and Chairman, Council of Ministers), Harry TISCH (member, State Council).

Candidate Members: Ingeburg LANGE (member, Secretariat), Gerhard MÜLLER (First Secretary, Erfurt Party Executive), Margarete MÜLLER (member, State Council), Gerhard SCHÜRER (Deputy Chairman, Council of Ministers, and Chairman, State Planning Commission), Werner WALDE (First Secretary, Cottbus Party Executive).

Central Committee Secretariat: Hermann AXEN, Horst DOHLUS, Werner FELFE, Kurt HAGER, Joachim HERRMANN, Erich HONECKER, Dr. Werner JAROWINSKY, Egon KRENZ, Ingeburg LANGE, Dr. Günter MITTAG, Günter SCHABOWSKI.

Four other parties, each with 52 representatives in the People's Chamber, are the **Christian Democratic Union of Germany** (*Christlich-Demokratische Union Deutschlands* – CDU), the **Democratic Peasants' Party of Germany** (*Demokratische Bauernpartei Deutschlands* – DBD), the **Liberal Democratic Party of Germany** (*Liberal-Demokratische Partei Deutschlands* – LDPD), and the **National Democratic Party of Germany** (*National-Demokratische Partei Deutschlands* – NDPD). These parties are Communist controlled and have nothing to do with their present-day counterparts in the Federal Republic. Also represented in the People's Chamber are four Communist-controlled mass organizations: the Confederation of Free German Trade Unions (*Freier Deutscher Gewerkschafts-*

bund), 68 seats; the Free German Youth (*Freie Deutsche Jugend*), 40 seats; the Democratic Women's League (*Demokratischer Frauenbund Deutschlands*), 35 seats; and the German Cultural League (*Deutscher Kulturbund*), 22 seats.

LEGISLATURE

The **People's Chamber** (*Volkskammer*) is a unicameral body elected for a five-year term by universal suffrage from a single list of candidates presented by the Communist-controlled National Front. The last election was held on June 8, 1986. The 66 previously nonvoting East Berlin delegates were incorporated into the Chamber as full members on June 28, 1979, thus raising the membership to 500.
President: Horst SINDERMANN.

CABINET

Chairman, Council of Ministers (Premier)	Willi Stoph
First Deputy Chairmen	Werner Krolikowski
	Alfred Neumann
Deputy Chairmen	Manfred Flegel
	Hans-Joachim Heusinger
	Günther Kleiber
	Wolfgang Rauchfuss
	Hans Reichelt
	Gerhard Schürer
	Rudolph Schulze
	Horst Sölle
	Herbert Weiz

Ministers

Agriculture, Forestry and Foodstuffs	Bruno Lietz
Chemical Industry	Günther Wyschofsky
Coal and Energy	Wolfgang Mitzinger
Construction Industry	Wolfgang Junker
Construction of General Machinery, Agricultural Machinery and Vehicles	Gerhard Tautenhahn
Construction of Heavy Machinery and Equipment	Hans-Joachim Lauck
Construction of Machine Tools and Processing Machinery	Rudi Georgi
Culture	Hans-Joachim Hoffmann
District Managed Industry and Foodstuffs Industry	Udo-Dieter Wange
Electrical Engineering and Electronics	Felix Meier
Environmental Protection and Water Management	Hans Reichelt
Finance	Ernst Höfner
Foreign Affairs	Oskar Fischer
Foreign Trade	Gerhard Beil
Geology	Manfred Bochmann
Glass and Ceramics Industry	Karl Grünheid
Health	Ludwig Mecklinger
Interior	Gen. Friedrich Dickel
Justice	Hans-Joachim Heusinger
Light Industry	Werner Buschmann
Materials Management	Wolfgang Rauchfuss
National Defense	Gen. Heinz Kessler
Ore Mining, Metallurgy and Potash	Kurt Singhuber
Post and Telecommunications	Rudolph Schulze
Public Education	Margot Honecker
Science and Technology	Herbert Weiz
State Security	Gen. Erich Mielke
Trade and Supply	Gerhard Briksa
Transportation	Otto Arndt
University and Technical School Affairs	Hans-Joachim Böhme
Chairman, State Contract Court	Manfred Flegel
Chairman, State Planning Commission	Gerhard Schürer
Chairman, Workers' and Peasants' Inspectorate Committee	Albert Stief
Director, Office for Prices	Walter Halbritter
Director, Office of Youth Affairs	Hans Sattler
State Secretary for Labor and Wages	Wolfgang Beyreuther
State Secretary, State Planning Commission	Wolfgang Gress
	Heinz Klopfer
Permanent Representative, CEMA	Günther Kleiber
President, State Bank	Horst Kaminsky

NEWS MEDIA

The 1968 constitution guarantees freedom of the press, but broadcasting is under state control and all major daily newspapers are affiliated with political parties. Accordingly, they follow a Communist line.

Press. There are some 40 dailies and 30 weeklies, with a combined circulation of over 18 million. The following are dailies published at East Berlin, unless otherwise noted: *Junge Welt* (1,300,000), youth organ; *Neues Deutschland* (1,100,000), SED organ; *Freie Presse* (Karl-Marx-Stadt, 652,000), SED organ; *Freiheit* (Halle, 580,000), SED organ; *Sächsische Zeitung* (Dresden, 562,000), SED organ; *Leipziger Volkszeitung* (Leipzig, 480,000), SED organ; *Volksstimme* (Magdeburg, 447,000), SED organ; *Tribüne* (411,000), organ of Trade-Union League; *Das Volk* (Erfurt, 397,000), SED organ; *Berliner Zeitung* (393,000), SED organ; *Märkische Volksstimme* (Potsdam, 342,000), SED organ; *Ostee Zeitung* (Rostock, 289,000), SED organ; *Lausitzer Rundschau* (Cottbus, 287,000), SED organ; *BZ am Abend* (199,000), SED organ; *Neue Zeit* (105,000), CDU organ; *Bauern-Echo* (92,000), DBD organ; *Der Morgen* (57,000), LDPD organ; *National-Zeitung* (56,000), NDPD organ.

News agencies. The official news agency is the government-owned *Allgemeiner Deutscher Nachrichtendienst* (ADN); numerous foreign agencies, most representing Communist nations, also maintain offices at East Berlin.

Radio and television. State committees for radio and television broadcasting (*rundfunk* and *fernsehen*) coordinate all radio and television activity. The principal radio organizations are *Radio DDR, Berliner Rundfunk,* and *Stimme der DDR* for domestic broadcasts, and Radio Berlin International for foreign transmissions. There were approximately 6.7 million radio and 6.2 million television receivers in 1987.

INTERGOVERNMENTAL REPRESENTATION

Ambassador to the US: Dr. Gerhard HERDER.

US Ambassador to the German Democratic Republic: Francis J. MEEHAN.

Permanent Representative to the UN: Harry OTT.

IGO Memberships (Non-UN): CMEA, IBEC, ICCO, ICES, IIB, Inmarsat, ISO, PCA, WTO.

INCORPORATED TERRITORY

East Berlin. Following a breakdown in cooperation between the Soviet Union and the other occupying powers and the subsequent removal of Greater Berlin's municipal government to the Western sector in September 1948, a city government for East Berlin was installed in November 1948. Subsequently, on October 7, 1949, East Berlin became the capital of the newly proclaimed German Democratic Republic.

Unlike West Berlin, East Berlin has no separate constitutional status and has been administratively integrated into the GDR. It is politically controlled by the Socialist Unity Party (SED) and governed by a mayor (*Bürgermeister*) and a Municipal Council (*Magistrat*) elected for a four-year term.

In June 1979 the Soviet Union, affirming that East Berlin was a constituent part of the GDR, ceded responsibility for the city, thus violating a September 3, 1971, four-power agreement under which no change in the status of Greater Berlin was to have been unilaterally initiated. On June 28, East Berlin's previously nonvoting representatives to the East German People's Chamber (*Volkskammer*), all 66 of whom had been nominated by the Municipal Assembly, were incorporated into the Chamber as full delegates. At the 1981 and 1986 balloting, the representatives from East Berlin were elected under the same procedures employed throughout the rest of the country.

Mayor: Erhard KRACK.

FEDERAL REPUBLIC OF GERMANY

Bundesrepublik Deutschland

Political Status: Federal republic established May 23, 1949; under democratic parliamentary regime.

Area: 95,987 sq. mi. (248,606 sq. km.).

Population: 60,650,599 (1970C), 60,740,000 (1988E). Area and population figures include West Berlin.

Major Urban Centers (1985E): BONN (293,000); (West) Berlin (1,852,000); Hamburg (1,586,000); Munich (1,266,000); Cologne (919,000); Essen (622,000); Frankfurt am Main (598,000); Dortmund (575,000); Düsseldorf (563,000); Stuttgart (562,000); Bremen (529,000); Duisburg (521,000); Hannover (511,000).

Official Language: German.

Monetary Unit: Deutsche Mark (market rate March 1, 1988, 1.69 marks = $1US).

Federal President: Dr. Richard von WEIZSÄCKER (Christian Democratic Union); elected by the Federal Assembly on May 23, 1984, to succeed Dr. Karl CARSTENS (Christian Democratic Union); inaugurated July 1, 1984, for a five-year term.

Federal Chancellor: Dr. Helmut KOHL (Christian Democratic Union); formed coalition government on October 4, 1982, following passage of constructive vote of no confidence against government of Helmut SCHMIDT (Social Democratic Party) on October 1; reappointed in 1983, and on March 11, 1987, following general election of February 25.

GOVERNMENT AND POLITICS

Political background. During the eight years following proclamation of the Federal Republic of Germany on May 23, 1949, the Christian Democratic Union (CDU) under Chancellor Konrad ADENAUER maintained coalition governments with the Free Democrats and other minor parties, thereby excluding the Social Democratic Party (SPD) from power. In 1957 the CDU and its Bavarian affil-

iate, the Christian Social Union (CSU), won a clear majority of legislative seats, but in 1961 and again in 1965 were forced to renew their pact with the Free Democrats. In 1966 disagreements on financial policy led the FDP to withdraw from the coalition, and Ludwig ERHARD, who had succeeded Adenauer as chancellor three years earlier, was obliged to resign. On December 1, a Christian Democratic-Social Democratic "grand coalition" government was inaugurated, with Kurt-Georg KIESINGER of the CDU as chancellor.

As a result of the election of September 1969, Willy BRANDT, leader of the Social Democrats as well as vice chancellor and foreign minister of the CDU-SPD government, became chancellor at the head of an SPD-FDP coalition. Though the coalition was renewed after the November 1972 election, widespread labor unrest early in 1974 attested to the increasing inability of the Brandt government to cope with domestic economic difficulties, including a record postwar inflation of more than 7.5 percent; however, the revelation that one of the chancellor's personal political aides had been found to be an East German espionage agent was the crucial factor leading to his resignation on May 6 and his replacement shortly thereafter by former finance minister Helmut SCHMIDT. Former foreign minister Walter SCHEEL, who had served briefly as interim chancellor following Brandt's resignation, was elected federal president on May 15 and was sworn in on July 1, succeeding Gustav HEINEMANN.

At a close election on October 3, 1976, the SPD-FDP coalition obtained a substantially reduced majority of 253 out of 496 seats in the *Bundestag* and on December 15 Schmidt was reconfirmed as chancellor. Conservatives, however, constituted the largest bloc of state delegates and therefore held an overall majority at the 1979 Federal Convention; as a result, Karl CARSTENS, the CDU candidate and president of the *Bundestag,* was elected on May 23 to succeed President Scheel, who had decided not to seek a second term after being denied all-party support.

Chancellor Schmidt was returned to office following the *Bundestag* election of October 5, 1980, at which the SPD gained 4 seats and the FDP, 14, while the CDU/CSU, led in the campaign by Franz-Josef STRAUSS, ministerpresident of Bavaria and CSU chairman, lost 17.

An extensive reorganization of the Schmidt government in April 1982 pointed up increasing disagreement within the SPD-FDP coalition on matters of defense and economic policy. On September 17 all four FDP ministers resigned, precipitating a "constructive vote of no confidence" on October 1 that resulted in the appointment of Dr. Helmut KOHL as head of a CDU/CSU-FDP government. Subsequently, in mid-December, Kohl called for a nonconstructive confidence vote that was deliberately lost by CDU abstentions, thus permitting the chancellor to call an early election. At the balloting on March 6, 1983, the three-party coalition won 278 of 498 lower house seats, allowing Kohl to form a new government on March 29.

The coalition's mandate was renewed on January 25, 1987, although the Christian Democrats' share of the vote (44.3 percent) was its poorest showing since the founding of the West German state in 1949. The Social Democrats did marginally better than opinion polls had predicted, drawing 37.0 percent, compared with 38.2 percent in 1983 (which had, however, been its most severe loss since 1961). Gaining strength at the expense of the major parties were the FDP, which was awarded an additional ministry (for a total of four) in the government formed on March 11, and the Greens, whose parliamentary representation increased from 27 to 42.

Constitution and government. Under the Basic Law (*Grundgesetz*) of May 23, 1949, West Germany is a Federal Republic in which areas of authority are both shared and divided between the component states (*Länder*) and the Federal Government (*Bundesregierung*). Responsibility in such areas as economic, social, and health policy is held jointly, with Bonn establishing general guidelines, the states assuming administration, and both typically providing funds. Each state (*Land*) has its own parliament elected by universal suffrage, with authority to legislate in all matters — including education, police, and broadcasting — not expressly reserved to the Federal Government. The latter is responsible for foreign affairs, defense, and such matters as citizenship, migration, customs, posts, and telecommunications.

The major federal components are the head of state, or federal president (*Bundespräsident*); a cabinet headed by a chancellor (*Bundeskanzler*); and a bicameral legislature consisting of a *Bundesrat* (Federal Assembly) and a *Bundestag* (National Assembly). *Bundesrat* members are appointed and recalled by the state governments; their role is limited to those areas of policy that fall under joint responsibility, although they have veto powers where state interests are involved. The *Bundestag,* elected by universal suffrage under a mixed direct and proportional representation system, is the major legislative organ. It elects the chancellor by an absolute majority but cannot overthrow him except by electing a successor. The president, whose functions are mainly ceremonial, is elected by a special Federal Convention (*Bundesversammlung*) made up of the members of the *Bundestag* and an equal number of members chosen by the state legislatures. Ministers are appointed by the president on the advice of the chancellor.

The judiciary is headed by the Federal Constitutional Court (*Bundesverfassungsgericht*), with the two houses of Parliament each electing half its judges, and also includes a Supreme Federal Court (*Bundesgerichtshof*) as well as Federal Administrative, Financial, Labor, and Social courts. While the constitution guarantees the maintenance of human rights and civil liberties, certain limitations in time of emergency were detailed in a controversial set of amendments adopted in 1968. The Federal Constitutional Court is authorized to outlaw political parties whose aims or activities are found to endanger "the basic libertarian democratic order" or its institutional structure. An equally controversial decision was made in July 1979 when the Parliament revoked the statute of limitations on genocide and murder, thereby permitting prosecution of Nazi war criminals discovered after December 31, 1979. The action was largely of symbolic value, however, given the difficulty of successfully prosecuting crimes committed decades ago.

The Federal Republic encompasses ten *Länder,* excluding West Berlin, which technically remains under tripartite Allied control and sends only nonvoting representatives to plenary sessions of both houses of Parliament.

Land and Capital	Area (sq. mi.)	Population (1987E)
Baden-Württemberg (Stuttgart)	13,803	9,303,000
Bavaria (Munich)	27,238	11,002,000
Bremen (Bremen)	156	649,000
Hamburg (Hamburg)	291	1,560,000
Hesse (Wiesbaden)	8,151	5,508,000
Lower Saxony (Hannover)	18,311	7,173,000
North Rhine-Westphalia (Düsseldorf)	13,149	16,540,000
Rhineland-Palatinate (Mainz)	7,658	3,601,000
Saarland (Saarbrücken)	992	1,038,000
Schleswig-Holstein (Kiel)	6,053	2,611,000
West Berlin	185	1,869,000

Foreign relations. The division of Germany and the anti-Soviet and anti-Communist outlook of most West Germans have resulted in very close relations between the Federal Republic and the Western Allies, whose support was long deemed essential both to the survival of the FRG and to the eventual reunification of Germany on a democratic basis. The FRG is a key member of NATO and the EC as well as of the WEU, the OECD, the Council of Europe, and other multilateral bodies aimed at closer political and economic cooperation among the countries of Western Europe and the North Atlantic area.

A genuine dialogue with the nations of Eastern Europe was opened up during the chancellorship of Willy Brandt. In March 1970, in response to an earlier appeal from East German leader Walter Ulbricht for the establishment of diplomatic relations, Brandt met with GDR Minister-President Stoph and detailed a 20-point program of accommodation that stopped just short of diplomatic recognition. While the treaty that was eventually concluded on November 8, 1972, committed the signatories to "respect the independence and sovereignty of each of the two States", the FRG, in a note transmitted the same day, declared that the action did not conflict with its long-term objective of working "for a state of peace in Europe in which the German nation will recover its unity in free self-determination". The GDR, however, officially denied that it had received any such communication.

In August 1970 Brandt signed a nonaggression treaty with the Soviet Union and the following December concluded a treaty with Poland by which the Federal Republic formally recognized Polish acquisition of nearly one-fourth of Germany's prewar territory. A preliminary agreement governing access to Berlin was concluded with the East Germans in December 1971, while a treaty voiding the 1938 Munich Agreement was negotiated with Czechoslovakia in June 1973 and ratified a year later. The initiation of this program of post-World War II "reconciliation" earned a Nobel Peace Prize for Chancellor Brandt in October 1971, while its territorial implications were reaffirmed by the Final Act of the 1975 Helsinki Conference on Security and Cooperation in Europe.

Under Chancellor Schmidt, the FRG continued to pursue both détente with the East and maintenance of the Western alliance. Despite occasional differences with the United States, particularly over the Carter administration's "unpredictability" and its alleged failure to consult in a timely fashion with its Western European allies, Bonn offered firm support for the US position in the North-

South dialogue on economic development, and on the November 1979 seizure of the American embassy at Teheran, Iran. It adopted a somewhat more moderate posture than that of the United States in response to the December 1979 Soviet intervention in Afghanistan, but joined France in warning the USSR that détente "could not withstand another shock".

Current issues. During 1986, marked improvement was registered in détente between the two Germanies. In contrast to the earlier tensions that had resulted in erection of the Berlin wall, ever-increasing numbers of East Germans (over 200,000 in the course of the year) visited the West, with less than 1 percent refusing to return home, while GDR authorities, as of October 1, abandoned a major source of irritation to Bonn: the pass-through of alleged "political refugees" from Third World countries, such as Ghana and Sri Lanka. (The mechanism employed to halt the flow was the simple one of requiring that passengers heading for West Berlin through the East Berlin airport have valid West German visas.) Part of the relaxation was attributed to arrangements for the dual year-long celebration of Berlin's 750th anniversary, which the Honecker regime hoped to utilize as a means of legitimizing its claim to East Berlin as an integral component (and capital) of the Democratic Republic, while providing the Soviets with an avenue of communication with the FRG during the debate on removal of medium-range missiles from Europe. Honecker did not attend the opening of the West Berlin ceremony on April 30, 1987, although his visit to the Federal Republic in September was the first by an East German head of state.

There were no clear victors at the West German parliamentary balloting in January 1987. Chancellor Kohl was returned to office, but with a disappointingly reduced majority that increased the CDU's dependency on its coalition partners. The Social Democrats did better than anticipated, given gloomy preelection opinion forecasts, but remained divided between leftist and centrist factions, particularly following the second (and presumably final) resignation of its longtime "Grand Old Man", Willy Brandt, as the result of his somewhat bizarre effort to secure the appointment of a woman who was neither a party member nor a German citizen as SDP spokesperson. The group displaying the greatest electoral advance, the Greens, was even more divided between "pragmatists" and Marxist-Leninist ideologues, its most conspicuous effort at cooperation with the SDP (a coalition in Hesse) collapsing in February.

At *Land* balloting on September 7, the CDU lost its absolute majority in what had theretofore been its stronghold of Schleswig-Holstein, largely because of farmer resistance to the Kohl government's support of EC agricultural policy. Two weeks later, the CDU minister president of Schleswig-Holstein, Uwe BARSCHEL, resigned in the wake of allegations that he had been involved in attempts to discredit the *Land* SPD and its leader, Björn ENGHOLM; subsequently, Barschel committed suicide and the FDP withdrew from its coalition with the CDU until the circumstances surrounding his death had been clarified. Earlier, in balloting at Bremen, the SPD retained control of the city parliament (*Bürgerschaft*), with the Greens doubling their representation from five to ten.

POLITICAL PARTIES

There were approximately 60 parties and political groups active in 1987. The most important of these are listed below.

Governing Parties:

Christian Democratic Union (*Christlich-Demokratische Union* — CDU). Founded in 1945 and dominated from 1949 to 1963 by Chancellor Konrad Adenauer, the CDU and its Bavarian affiliate, the Christian Social Union (below), continued as the strongest party alignment within the Federal Republic until 1969. A middle-of-the-road grouping with a generally conservative policy and broad political appeal, the party stands for united action by Catholics and Protestants to sustain German life on a Christian basis, while guaranteeing private property and freedom of the individual. With a list headed by CSU Chairman Franz-Josef Strauss, who had threatened to sever the CDU/CSU bond if denied coalition support in opposing incumbent Chancellor Helmut Schmidt, the CDU suffered a loss of 16 of its 190 *Bundestag* seats at the October 1980 election. However, following a transfer of support by the Free Democratic Party (below) to the CDU on October 1, 1982, Schmidt was obliged to step down as federal chancellor in favor of the CDU's Dr. Helmut Kohl. Kohl continued as the head of three-party administrations following the *Bundestag* elections of March 6, 1983, and January 25, 1987.

Leaders: Dr. Helmut KOHL (Federal Chancellor and Party Chairman), Dr. Gerhard STOLTENBERG (Finance Minister), Dr. Heiner GEISSLER (General Secretary).

Christian Social Union (*Christlich-Soziale Union* — CSU). The Bavarian affiliate of the CDU espouses policies similar to its federal partner but tends to be more conservative. In November 1976 the CSU voted to terminate its 27-year alliance with the CDU but reversed itself in December, when it agreed to continue the parliamentary grouping for another four years. Party Chairman Franz-Josef Strauss became minister-president of Bavaria following the *Land* election of October 15, 1978, and nine months later was selected as CDU/CSU candidate for chancellor at the 1980 national election. The party's *Bundestag* representation of 53 after the March 1983 election was reduced to 49 by the withdrawal of two deputies to form the Republicans Party (below) the following November; it lost two additional seats at the balloting of February 1987.

Leaders: Dr. Franz-Josef STRAUSS (Minister-President of Bavaria and CSU Chairman), Dr. Theodore WAIGEL (Parliamentary Leader), Gerold TANDLER (General Secretary).

Free Democratic Party (*Freie Demokratische Partei* — FDP). A moderately rightist party that inherited the tradition of economic liberalism, the FDP stands for free enterprise without state interference but advocates a program of social reform as well as a policy of conciliation in Central Europe. At the 1980 parliamentary election it won 53 seats (14 more than in 1976), in part because of the defection of Christian Democratic voters dissatisfied with candidate Franz-Josef Strauss. Its representation fell to 34 in 1983, but rose to 46 in 1987.

The FDP formed a governing coalition with the Social Democratic Party (below) following the elections of 1972, 1976, and 1980, but shifted its support to the CDU in October 1982 after a dispute over the size of the 1983 budgetary deficit, thereby causing the fall of the Schmidt government. FDP Chairman Hans-Dietrich Genscher retained his positions as vice chancellor and foreign minister under the successor government of Helmut Kohl, while former FDP secretary general Günter Verheugen defected to the Social Democrats and a number of other left-of-center members withdrew to form an opposition Liberal Democratic Party (below).

Leaders: Hans-Dietrich GENSCHER (Vice Chancellor and Foreign Minister), Dr. Martin BANGEMANN (Economics Minister and Party Chairman), Wolfgang MISCHNICK (Deputy Chairman), Dr. Helmut HAUSSMANN (General Secretary).

Opposition Parties:

Social Democratic Party (*Sozialdemokratische Partei Deutschlands* — SPD). Founded in the nineteenth century and reestablished in 1945, the SPD was the principal opposition party before joining in a coalition with the CDU/CSU from 1966 to 1969. After the election of October 1969, it formed a governing coalition with the FDP that continued until October 1982, when the latter transferred its support to the CDU, thus forcing the SPD into opposition. The party's original Marxist outlook was largely discarded in 1959, although sentiment exists, particularly within the party's youth organization, for a return to a more doctrinal posture in opposition to reformist forces long led by former chancellor Willy Brandt. With a powerful base in the larger cities and the more industrialized states, the SPD lays major stress on a strong central government and social-welfare programs, and has long advocated normalization of relations with Eastern Europe.

Brandt resigned as SPD chairman at a stormy leadership meeting on March 23, 1987, after his colleagues had refused to endorse his choice for party spokesperson. Parliamentary leader Hans-Jochen Vogel was thereupon designated as his interim successor, with confirmation to the post occurring at a party convention in July.

Leaders: Hans-Jochen VOGEL (Chairman and Parliamentary Leader), Oskar LAFONTAINE and Johannes RAU (Deputy Chairman).

Green Party (*Die Grünen*). Constituted as a national "antiparty party" during a congress held January 12–14, 1980, at Karlsruhe, *Die Grünen* is an amalgamation of several ecology-oriented groups formed in the late 1970s, including the Green Action Future (*Grüne Aktion Zukunft* – GAZ), the Green List Ecology (*Grüne Liste Umweltschutz* – GLU), and the Action Group of Independent Germans (*Aktionsgemeinschaft Unabhängiger Deutscher* – AUD). During a March 22–23 conference, the new party adopted a basically leftist program that called for the dissolution of NATO and the Warsaw Pact, economic reorganization, an unlimited right to strike, and a 35-hour workweek. Internal divisiveness and the defection of some conservatives contributed to a poor showing at the October federal election, when the party won only 1.5 percent of the vote. At the 1983 balloting, on the other hand, it won 27 *Bundestag* seats on the basis of a 5.6 percent vote share, and by late 1987 had secured representation in eight of the 11 *Lander* parliaments.

In 1985, in the wake of serious electoral losses in the Saarland and North Rhine-Westphalia, a split emerged between the fundamentalist (*Fundi*) wing of the party, which rejects participation in coalition governments and advocates a purist ideological posture, and the realist (*Realo*) faction composed largely of *Bundestag* members. With Green participation in the Hesse state government augmented late in the year, the *Realo* tendency appeared to be in the ascendancy, although the group's overall public support – largely drawn from former SPD voters – was reported to have declined.

During what was described as a "chaotic" congress at Nuremberg in September 1986, the *Realos* consolidated their hold over the group, which came close to overtaking the Free Democrats at the federal balloting of January 1987, winning 8.3 percent of the vote and 42 *Bundestag* seats. On February 9, however, its Hesse coalition with the SPD collapsed in the wake of a dispute over increased consumption of plutonium at a nuclear processing plant.

Leaders: Jutta DITFURTH, Regina MICHALIK, Christian SCHMIDT, Eberhard WALDE (General Secretary).

Republicans Party (*Die Republikaners*). Primarily a Bavarian formation, the Republicans party was formed on November 25, 1983, by two former CSU deputies who objected to Strauss' "one-man" leadership, particularly in regard to East-West relations. The manifestly right-wing group was described as a "conservative-liberal people's party" that favored a reunited Germany, environmental protection, and lower business taxes.

Leaders: Franz HANDLOS (Chairman), Franz SCHÖNHUBER, Ekkehard VOIGT.

Liberal Democratic Party (*Liberaldemokratische Partei* – LDP). The LDP was organized in November 1982 by some 1,500 left-of-center Free Democrats who opposed the shift in affiliation from the SPD to the CDU. Concurrently, delegates of the Young Democrats, the FDP's youth organization, voted to secede from the parent body in favor of the LDP.

Leaders: Ralf BARTZ (Chairman), Georg HUNDT (General Secretary).

National Democratic Party (*Nationaldemokratische Partei Deutschlands* – NPD). Formed in 1964 by a number of right-wing groups, the NPD has been accused of neo-Nazi tendencies but has avoided giving clear-cut grounds for legal prohibition. Unrepresented in the *Länder* parliaments as well as in the *Bundestag*, its appeal at the federal level slipped to a record low 0.2 percent of the popular vote in 1980 and failed to recover in either 1983 or 1987.

Leader: Martin MUSSGNUG (Chairman).

German Communist Party (*Deutsche Kommunistische Partei* – DKP). West Germany's former Communist Party, led by Max REIMANN, was banned as unconstitutional in 1956, though Reimann returned from exile in East Germany in 1969. Meanwhile, plans to establish a new Communist party consistent with the principles of the Basic Law had been announced in September 1968 by a 31-member "federal committee" headed by Kurt BACHMANN. At its inaugural congress in April 1969, the new party claimed 22,000 members, elected Bachmann as chairman, and announced its intention to seek a common front with the SPD in the 1969 *Bundestag* election (an offer that was promptly rejected by the SPD). The DKP is currently unrepresented in *Länder* governments and won only 0.2 percent of the vote in each of the last three federal elections; it claims approximately 50,000 members and receives substantial financial support from the East German SED, with which the DKP cooperated in a series of "alternative" postwar anniversary celebrations in 1985. A number of "New Left" and Maoist parties continue to compete with the DKP.

Leaders: Herbert MIES (Chairman), Hermann GAUTIER (Deputy Chairman).

Extremist Groups:

Although terrorist activity has receded since the 1970s, armed groups both of the Right and Left have remained active. Neo-Nazi groups, whose membership was estimated in early 1985 at 22,000, were charged with close to 100 violent incidents in 1984. They included the **National Socialist Action Front/National Action** (*Aktionsfront Nationaler Sozialisten/Nationale Aktion* – ANS/NA) and various "military sport groups" (*Wehrsportgruppen*), including the *Wehrsportgruppe Hoffman* led by Odfried HEPP and allegedly supported by the Palestine Liberation Organization. On the left, the **Red Army Faction** (RAF), an outgrowth of the Baader-Meinhof group of the early 1970s, has an estimated strength of 500 and has recently reactivated itself after a relatively quiescent period following a series of bombings in 1977. With the emplacement of Pershing missiles in 1984, the RAF declared an "anti-imperialist war" and claimed responsibility for over 20 bombings in 1985, mainly at US military and diplomatic installations, which left four dead; the group also claimed credit for the assassination of arms manufacturer Ernst ZIMMERMAN in February. None of the groups commands significant popular support, although some RAF activists have been endorsed by radical Green Party members.

LEGISLATURE

The bicameral **Parliament** (*Parlament*) consists of an indirectly chosen upper chamber, the *Bundesrat*, or Federal Assembly, and an elective lower chamber, the *Bundestag*, or National Assembly.

Federal Assembly (*Bundesrat*). The upper chamber consists of 41 members appointed by the *Länder* governments, each of whose 3–5 votes (depending on population) are cast *en bloc*, plus 4 representatives with nonvoting status appointed by the West Berlin government. Lengths of term vary according to state election dates. The presidency rotates annually among heads of the state delegations, usually *Länder* minister-presidents.

National Assembly (*Bundestag*). Deputies to the lower chamber are elected for four-year terms (subject to dissolution) by direct popular vote under a complicated electoral system combining direct and proportional representation. There are also 22 representatives from West Berlin whose votes are recorded but are counted only in procedural matters. The election of January 25, 1987, yielded the following distribution of seats: Christian Democrats, 223 (Christian Democratic Union, 174; Christian Social Union, 49); Social Democratic Party, 186; Free Democratic Party, 46; Green Party, 42.

President: Dr. Philipp JENNINGER.

CABINET

Chancellor	Dr. Helmut Kohl (CDU)
Vice Chancellor	Hans-Dietrich Genscher (FDP)
Chief, Federal Chancellery	Wolfgang Schäuble (CDU)

Ministers

Agriculture and Forestry	Ignaz Kiechle (CSU)
Defense	Dr. Manfred Wörner (CDU)
Economic Cooperation	Hans Klein (CSU)
Economics	Martin Bangemann (FDP)
Education and Science	Jürgen Mölleman (FDP)
Environment, Nature	
Conservation and Reactor	
Safety	Klaus Töpfer (CDU)
Finance	Dr. Gerhard Stoltenberg (CDU)
Foreign Affairs	Hans-Dietrich Genscher (FDP)
Inner-German Relations	Dr. Dorothée Wilms (CDU)
Interior	Dr. Friedrich Zimmermann (CSU)
Justice	Hans A. Engelhard (FDP)
Labor and Social Affairs	Dr. Norbert Blüm (CDU)
Post and Telecommunications	Dr. Christian Schwarz-Schilling (CDU)
Regional Planning, Housing and	
City Planning	Oscar Schneider (CSU)
Research and Technology	Dr. Heinz Riesenhuber (CDU)
Transport	Jürgen Warnke (CSU)
Youth, Family, Women and	
Health Affairs	Rita Süssmuth (CDU)
President, German Federal Bank	Karl Otto Pöhl

NEWS MEDIA

Freedom of speech and press is constitutionally guaranteed except to anyone who misuses it in order to destroy the democratic system.

Press. Newspapers are numerous and widely read, and many of the principal dailies have national as well as local readerships. No newspaper is directly owned by a political party and only about 10 percent support party lines. There are, however, some very large publishing concerns, notably the giant Axel Springer Group, which accounts for some 40 percent of the country's daily newspaper circulation and is Europe's largest publishing conglomerate. Springer's four major dailies are *Die Welt, Hamburger Abendblatt, Bild-Zeitung,* and *Berliner Morgenpost.* Except for those published at West Berlin (see below), the highest circulation dailies (figures for 1987) are as follows: *Bild-Zeitung* (Hamburg and a number of other cities, 4,902,800), sensationalist independent tabloid; *Westdeutsche Allgemeine* (Essen, 1,278,000); *Hannoversche Allgemeine* (Hanover, 507,000); *Express* (Cologne, 438,000); *Rheinische Post* (Düsseldorf, 401,000); *Süddeutsche Zeitung* (Munich, 378,000); *Frankfurter Allgemeine* (Frankfurt-on-Main, 377,000); *Südwest Presse* (Ulm, 366,000); *Augsburger Allgemeine* (Augsburg, 351,000).

News agencies. The domestic news agency is *Deutsche Presse-Agentur* (DPA), which supplies newspapers and broadcasting stations in the Federal Republic and West Berlin. It also transmits news overseas in German, English, French, Spanish, and Arabic. Numerous foreign bureaus maintain offices throughout the country.

Radio and television. Broadcasting networks are independent, nonprofit, public corporations chartered by the *Länder* governments, and efforts to institute commercial and cable television, including transmissions from Luxembourg, met with firm opposition from the Schmidt government. The coordinating body is the Association of Public Broadcasting Organizations of the Federal Republic of Germany (*Arbeitsgemeinschaft der Öffentlich-rechtlichen Rundfunkanstalten der Bundesrepublik Deutschland*—ARD). In addition, the American Forces Network, the British Forces Broadcasting Service, Radio Free Europe, Radio Liberty, and the Voice of America operate numerous transmitting facilities. There were approximately 25.8 million radio and 23.0 million television receivers in 1987.

INTERGOVERNMENTAL REPRESENTATION

Ambassador to the US: Juergen RUHFUS.

US Ambassador to the Federal Republic of Germany: Richard R. BURT.

Permanent Representative to the UN: Count YORK von Wartenburg.

IGO Memberships (Non-UN): ADB, ADF, AfDB, BDEAC, BIS, CCC, CERN, CEUR, EC, EIB, ESA, Eurocontrol, G10, IADB, ICAC, ICCO, ICES, ICM, ICO, IEA, ILZ, Inmarsat, INRO, Intelsat, Interpol, IOOC, ITC, IWC, IWSG, NATO, OECD, PCA, WEU.

WEST BERLIN

Governing Mayor: Eberhard DIEPGEN (Christian Democratic Union); designated by the House of Representatives on February 8, 1984, to succeed Dr. Richard von WEIZSÄCKER (Christian Democratic Union), following the latter's resignation to contest the federal presidency; sworn in for a full term (normally four years) on April 18, 1985, following redesignation by the House of Representatives elected on March 10.

GOVERNMENT AND POLITICS

Political background. Originally occupied by Soviet forces in the concluding phase of World War II, the former German capital of Berlin was subsequently declared a separate area of occupation under the joint control of the United States, the United Kingdom, France, and the Soviet Union, each of which assumed responsibility for one of the occupation sectors into which the city was divided. An Allied *Kommandatura* (Control Council) was established to provide for quadripartite governance, and a citywide representative Assembly with a non-Communist majority was elected in September 1946. Joint administration broke down in the following months as a result of various inter-Allied disagreements and the exclusion of the Western powers from any influence on the administration of the Soviet-controlled Eastern sector. Following Soviet protests against Western economic and political measures in West Germany, the Soviet representative walked out of the *Kommandatura* on June 16, 1948, and the USSR established a land and water blockade of Berlin's Western sectors which was maintained until May 1949. The municipal government, minus its SED members, transferred its seat to West Berlin in September 1948, with a new city government being installed in East Berlin two months later.

Beginning in 1958, the USSR and the GDR repeatedly demanded the withdrawal of Allied troops from West Berlin and its establishment as a Soviet-guaranteed "free city", but the division of the city was completed in August 1961 when the Russians constructed a wall between East and West Berlin to stop the flow of refugees from East to West Germany. Since then, pressures have somewhat abated, with a Quadripartite Agreement of 1971 guaranteeing access to the city from the West. Although the four-power administration and the *Kommandatura* have long ceased to function, the Western powers regard them as technically still in existence and continue to uphold the ultimate authority of the occupying powers under the original agreements.

Despite its isolation and its vulnerability to Communist harassment, West Berlin displayed a remarkable sense of public solidarity and enjoyed a considerable measure of internal political stability under a series of Social Democratic mayoralties, notably those of Ernst REUTER (1947–1953) and Willy BRANDT (1957–1966). In 1967, however, a serious internal crisis arose when student demonstrations led to the resignation of Mayor Heinrich ALBERTZ and his replacement by Klaus SCHÜTZ. Meanwhile, the sense of mission of the late 1940s and the 1950s had slackened, and West Berlin began to suffer a net loss of population as younger people sought wider opportunities in the West. Economically, the city has remained heavily dependent on West Germany for trade and investment as well as for financial grants to cover its budget deficit and social-insurance payments.

The danger of renewed Communist harassment was vividly brought home to West Berliners by East Germany's attempt to block the convening of the West German Federal Convention at West Berlin for the presidential election of March 5, 1969. The election ultimately took place without incident, but subsequent East German and Soviet complaints about alleged violations of the 1971 four-power agreement laid a basis for intermittent interference with the city's overland communications, including a half-day delay of traffic on July 15, 1978, to protest the visit to Berlin by FRG Chancellor Schmidt and US President Carter.

Following the resignation of Schütz in the wake of a series of political scandals, Dietrich STOBBE was elected governing mayor on May 2, 1977. Although named to a regular four-year term following the *Land* election of March 18, 1979, Stobbe became embroiled in charges of financial irregularities and was also forced to resign on January 15, 1981. His successor, Hans-Jochen VOGEL, proved unable to restore public confidence in the ruling SPD-FDP coalition, and in a premature election held on May 10 the opposition CDU obtained a plurality of 65 House seats. On May 31, 4 of 7 FDP deputies announced that they would "tolerate" a CDU minority administration, which, headed by Richard von WEIZSÄCKER, was approved on June 11. On November 28, 1983, Weizsäcker was nominated as CDU candidate for the federal presidency and was succeeded as mayor by Eberhard DIEPGEN on February 8, 1984.

A House election on March 10, 1985, yielded increased representation for both the CDU and the FDP, the new House reconfirming Diepgen's incumbency. In response to a near-doubling of the FDP representation, Diepgen assigned three ministries to the smaller party.

Constitution and government. With a few exceptions, West Berlin enjoys complete self-government under a 1950 constitution that defines its special position under technical three-power control. Although Berlin is regarded in West German constitutional law as a state (*Land*) of the Federal Republic of Germany, Allied reservations have prevented this status from being fully realized and the three occupying powers still retain certain rights of intervention.

West Berlin delegates sit without vote in the *Bundestag* and *Bundesrat,* and West German legislation must be specifically adopted in West Berlin to be valid there. The local legislative body is the directly elected House of Representatives (*Abgeordnetenhaus*); it elects the governing mayor (*Regierender Bürgermeister*) and, on his recommendation, the Senate (*Senat*), which exercises cabinet responsibilities. Local administration is carried out through a democratically organized system of local districts and mayors.

Current issues. In 1986, amid muted expressions of concern by Britain, France, and the United States, preparations were launched for observances during 1987 in both the eastern and western sectors marking the 750th anniversary of the pre-World War II German capital. The misgivings increased after Mayor Diepgen and the East German leader, Erich Honecker, exchanged invitations to participate in the festivities to begin on April 30 in West Berlin, with the official East German observance scheduled for October. While the Western powers approved the invitation to Honecker as a means of defusing the political implications of a Diepgen trip to the East, they were relieved that he chose not to attend the opening ceremony, at which Chancellor Kohl referred to the Berlin Wall as symbolizing the lack of freedom in the East and as a "wound from which all people suffer".

POLITICAL PARTIES

West Berlin's political party system is similar to that elsewhere in the Federal Republic, the **Christian Democratic Union** (CDU), the **Social Democratic Party** (SPD), and the **Free Democratic Party** (FDP) all being represented in the city legislature. Also contesting the 1979, 1981, and 1985 House elections was the **Alternative List for Democracy and Ecology** (*Alternative Liste für Demokratie and Umweltschutz* — AL), which campaigned on a platform attacking unemployment, government economic policies, environmental mismanagement, and pornography. Since the dissolution in 1985 of the local chapter of the Green Party due to allegations that it had been infiltrated by neo-Nazis, the Alternative List has had the support of the federal Green organization.

LEGISLATURE

The **House of Representatives** (*Abgeordnetenhaus*) currently consists of 144 members (12 more than in 1981) elected by direct popular vote for what are normally four-year terms. At the election of March 10, 1985, the Christian Democratic Union won 69 seats; the Social Democratic Party, 48; the Alternative List, 15; and the Free Democratic Party, 12.

President: Peter REBSCH.

SENATE

Governing Mayor	Eberhard Diepgen (CDU)
Senators	
Construction and Housing	George Wittwer (CDU)
Cultural Affairs	Dr. Volker Hassemer (CDU)
Economics and Labor	Elmar Pieroth (CDU)

Education, Vocational Training	
and Sports	Dr. Hanna-Renate Laurien (CDU)
Finance	Dr. Günter Rexrodh (FDP)
Health and Social Affairs	Ulf Fink (CDU)
Interior	Dr. Wilhelm A. Kewenig (CDU)
Justice and Federal Affairs	Dr. Rupert Scholz (CDU)
Science and Research	Dr. George Turner (Ind.)
Transportation and Public	
Utilities	Edmund Wronski (CDU)
Urban Development and	
Environment	Dr. Jürgen Starnick (Ind.)
Youth and Family Affairs	Cornelia Schmalz-Jacobsen (FDP)

NEWS MEDIA

Press. Normal freedom of the press prevails in West Berlin. The two largest papers are published by the Springer Group. The following are dailies, unless otherwise noted: *BZ* (307,000), independent; *Berliner Morgenpost* (182,000 weekdays, 300,000 Sunday), independent; *Der Tagesspiegel* (120,000 daily, 128,000 Sunday), independent.

GHANA

Republic of Ghana

Political Status: Independent member of the Commonwealth since March 6, 1957; under military control 1966–1969 and 1972–1979; Third Republic overthrown by military coup of December 31, 1981.

Area: 92,099 sq. mi. (238,537 sq. km.).

Population: 12,205,574 (1984C), 14,878,000 (1988E). The 1984 figure is provisional and is believed to reflect substantial underenumeration.

Major Urban Centers (1984C): ACCRA (964,879); Kumasi (348,880); Tamale (136,828); Tema (99,608).

Official Language: English.

Monetary Unit: New Cedi (market rate March 1, 1988, 181.82 cedi = $1US).

Chairman, Provisional National Defense Council: Flt. Lt. (Ret.) Jerry John RAWLINGS; formally designated Chairman of the PNDC on January 11, 1982, following military overthrow of government of President Hilla LIMANN (People's National Party) on December 31, 1981.

THE COUNTRY

Located on the west coast of Africa just north of the equator, Ghana's terrain includes both a tropical rain forest running north about 170 miles from the Gulf of Guinea and a grassy savanna belt that is drained by the Volta River. While the official language of the country is English, the inhabitants are divided among more than 50 linguistic and ethnic groups, the most important being the Akans (includ-ing Fanti), Ashanti, Ga, Ewe, and Mossi-Dagomba. About 40 percent of the population is Christian, and 12 percent is Muslim, with most of the rest following traditional religions. Over 40 percent of households are headed by women, who dominate the trading sector and comprise nearly 50 percent of agricultural labor; a smaller proportion of salaried women is concentrated in the service sector. Under the current military government, women are represented in both the ruling council and cabinet.

Still primarily an agricultural country, Ghana exhibits a mixed economy in which state enterprises and boards play significant roles. Cocoa, the most important cash crop, accounts for a majority of the country's export earnings, although production declined steadily from 1971 to 1984 before responding to an intense government effort at revival in 1985–1986. Other export commodities are timber, coconuts, palm products, sheanuts, and coffee. Industry is diversified and includes an aluminum smelter, a steel mill, and an oil refinery. Gold is the leading mineral resource, followed by manganese, diamonds, and bauxite.

GOVERNMENT AND POLITICS

Political background. The first West African territory to achieve independence in the postwar era, Ghana was established on March 6, 1957, through consolidation of the former British colony of the Gold Coast and the former UN Trust Territory of British Togoland. The drive to independence was associated primarily with the names of J.B. DANQUAH and Kwame N. NKRUMAH. The latter became prime minister of the Gold Coast in 1952, prime minister of independent Ghana in 1957, and the country's first elected president when republican status within the Commonwealth was proclaimed on July 1, 1960. Subsequently, Nkrumah consolidated his own power and that of his Convention People's Party (CPP), establishing a one-party dictatorship that was increasingly viewed with apprehension by neighboring states.

In 1966 the military ousted Nkrumah in response to increasing resentment of his repressive policies and financial mismanagement, which had decimated the country's reserves and generated an intolerably large national debt. An eight-man National Liberation Council (NLC) headed by Lt. Gen. Joseph A. ANKRAH was established to head the government. Promising an eventual return to civilian rule, the NLC carried out a far-reaching purge of Nkrumah adherents and sponsored the drafting of a new constitution. The NLC era was marked, however, by a series of alleged plots and corruption charges, Ankrah resigning as head of state in April 1969 after admitting to solicitation of funds from foreign companies for campaign purposes. He was replaced by Brig. Akwasi Amankwa AFRIFA, who implemented plans for a return to civilian government.

Partial civilian control returned following a National Assembly election in August 1969 that resulted in the designation of Kofi A. BUSIA as prime minister. Presidential power was exercised by a three-man Presidential Commission, made up of members of the NLC, until August 31, 1970, when Edward AKUFO-ADDO was inaugurated as head of state. The Busia administration was unable to deal with economic problems generated by a large external debt and a drastic currency devaluation, and in January 1972 the military, under (then) Col. Ignatius Kutu ACHEAMPONG, again seized control. The National Redemption Council (NRC), which was formed to head the government, immediately suspended the constitution, banned political parties, abolished the Supreme Court, and dissolved the National Assembly. In 1975 the NRC was superseded by the Supreme Military Council (SMC).

In the wake of accusations that "governmental activity had become a one-man show", General Acheampong was forced to resign as head of state on July 5, 1978, and was immediately succeeded by his deputy, (then) Lt. Gen. Frederick W.K. AKUFFO. Akuffo promised a return to civilian rule by mid-1979 and, in late July 1978, reconstituted a Constitution Drafting Commission, which subsequently presented its recommendations to an appointed, but broadly representative, Constituent Assembly that convened in mid-December.

In the wake of an effort to secure constitutional immunity from future prosecution for existing government officials, Akuffo was ousted on June 4, 1979, by a group of junior military officers. The next day, an Armed Forces Revolutionary Council (AFRC) was established under Flight Lt. Jerry John RAWLINGS, who had been undergoing court-martial for leading an unsuccessful coup on May 15. Having dissolved the SMC and the Constituent Assembly, the AFRC launched a "house-cleaning" campaign, during which former presidents Acheampong, Afrifa, and Akuffo, in addition to a number of other high-ranking military and civilian officials, were executed on grounds of corruption. Although the AFRC postponed promulgation of a new constitution until autumn, it did not interfere with scheduled presidential and legislative balloting on June 18. In a runoff presidential poll on July 9, Dr. Hilla LIMANN of the People's National Party, which had won a bare majority in the new National Assembly, defeated Victor OWUSU of the Popular Front Party, and was inaugurated on September 24.

The Limann government proved unable to halt further deterioration of the nation's economy and, in the wake of renewed allegations of widespread corruption, was overthrown on December 31, 1981, by army and air force supporters of Lieutenant Rawlings, who was returned to power as head of a Provisional National Defense Council (PNDC). In early January, two special bodies were created: a National Investigations Committee to evaluate charges of impropriety by members of the previous administration and a Citizens' Vetting Committee to review the assets of any individual whose life-style appeared inconsistent with declared income. On January 21, a 17-member cabinet was appointed that included a number of prominent individuals known for their "spotless integrity".

Since the 1981 coup, the Rawlings regime has been under pressure on several fronts: economically, a steady decline in the world price of cocoa and population expansion resulting from the expulsion of Ghanaians from Nigeria have led to food shortages and profiteering; politically, numerous attempted countercoups and clashes between pro- and antigovernment forces have resulted in radical state policy changes, including reorganization of the judicial and administrative structures.

Constitution and government. The Provisional National Defense Council, constituted on January 11, 1982, assumed authority for an indefinite period to "exercise all the powers of government". While the PNDC contained both military and civilian representatives, the cabinet appointed on January 21 was composed entirely of civilians. On May 1, a major judicial reorganization was launched, with the functions of existing bodies (including a Supreme Court, a Court of Appeal, and a High Court of Justice) partially superseded by public and military tribunals. In June 1983, an Interim People's Tribunal Council was created with the authority, not subject to appeal, to try individuals in absentia and to hand down death sentences.

Although Rawlings announced in early 1982 that local government institutions would continue to function, all district and city councils were subsequently abolished, preparatory to the establishment of "people's defense committees" (PDCs) to "deal with corruption and other counter-revolutionary activities at members' workplaces and in their communities . . . and afford everyone the opportunity to participate in the decision-making process in the country". Collaterally, an Interim National Coordinating Committee (INCC) was named to delineate a role for the PDCs within "the people's armed forces" and provide linkage with the PNDC. In March, an INCC spokesman indicated that in due course a People's Constituent Assembly would be established on the basis of election by the PDCs, while in December the government published plans for a three-tiered system encompassing PDC-guided local councils, district councils elected by the first tier, and regional councils chosen by the district bodies. In December 1984, it was announced that the PDCs would thenceforth be known as Committees for the Defense of the Revolution (CDRs), their mission by 1986 expanding "beyond political rhetoric" to the launching of development projects such as schools and health clinics. Concurrently, a seven-member National Commission for Democracy (NCD) was appointed to develop future political structures, although it has thus far declined to endorse either a single or multiparty system.

Foreign relations. External relations under recent military regimes have been pragmatic rather than ideological, the government unilaterally renouncing certain portions of the foreign debt and further disturbing creditor nations by taking partial control of selected foreign enterprises.

Relations with neighboring Togo have been strained since the incorporation of British Togoland into Ghana at the time of independence. In 1977, Ghana accused Togo of smuggling operations aimed at "sabotaging" the Ghanaian economy, while Togo vehemently denied accusations that it was training Ghanaian nationals to carry out acts of subversion in the former British territory. Following the downfall of the Limann government, Togolese leaders reacted to widely circulated newspaper reports of Togolese involvement in countercoup activity by assuring the Rawlings administration of their determination to maintain a posture of "good neighborliness, brotherhood, and cooperation". The border between the two countries has nonetheless been periodically closed. Accra has repeatedly charged Togolese officials with spreading "vicious lies" about the Rawlings regime and "providing a sanctuary" for its opponents. The complaints of border violations continued into 1987, with the Lomé regime being subjected to further criticism at mid-year for its restoration of ties with Israel.

Relations with other regional states have been mixed since the 1981 coup. The PNDC moved quickly to reestablish links with Libya (severed by President Limann in November 1980 because of the Qadhafi regime's presumed support of Rawlings), thereby clearing the way for shipments of badly needed Libyan oil. In April 1987 an agreement was signed with Iran for the delivery of 10,000 barrels of crude per day. Additionally, joint ventures between the two nations were proposed in agriculture and shipping, with plans for formal diplomatic relations at the ambassadorial level in 1988. On the other hand, relations with neighboring Nigeria and with Liberia remained cool because of the forced return of over two million workers, primarily from Nigeria.

In September 1985, following violence over a soccer match, Accra recalled its ambassador to the Ivory Coast, the avoidance of a formal rupture being attributed, in part, to the two countries' common sociolinguistic roots. By contrast, Ghana had moved in 1984 to forge closer links with its northern neighbor, Burkina Faso (formerly Upper Volta), which, prior to the October 1987 assassination of Burkina president, Thomas Sankara, had yielded an agreement to work toward political union within the next decade.

Current issues. During its six years in power, the Rawlings regime has survived numerous coup attempts, including at least two in 1985. A further antigovernment plot was apparently thwarted in March 1986 when Brazilian authorities arrested 18 persons and seized a shipload of armaments allegedly bound for dissidents in Ghana. In March 1987, in a gesture of goodwill, Accra suspended charges against 12 persons being held for subversion; however, in June, following a series of student demonstrations and the closing of three major universities, arrests were made in connection with yet another coup plot. Subsequent intimations of a link between student protest groups and dissident organizations in a series of editorials by the state-run media were widely believed to have been the cause of the July bombing of the New Times Corporation building in Accra. Related signs of discontent were reflected in persistent criticism by Ghana's powerful Trade Unions Congress (TUC) of the austerity measures necessitated by the Economic Recovery Program.

Despite potential destabilization, the Rawlings administration has won strong support from the World Bank and the International Monetary Fund for its effort to overcome persistent economic stagnation. Austerity measures, unpopular with some of the PNDC's early supporters, succeeded in reducing inflation from a high of 123 percent in 1983 to approximately 25 percent in 1987. Nonetheless, a critical budgetary imbalance remains, which the government hopes to reduce with comprehensive tax reform, further restructuring of the external debt, more productive use of IMF standby credit, and privatization of state enterprises.

POLITICAL PARTIES

Political parties, traditionally based more on tribal affiliation than on ideology, were banned in 1972. The proscription was lifted in early 1979, with six groups formally contesting the June election. During 1981, four of the five opposition parties formed a somewhat fragile coalition that was accorded legal status immediately prior to the coup of December 31. Following the coup, parties were again outlawed.

In April 1982, the PNDC announced that a "United Front" of groups supporting the objectives of the regime would shortly be established; however, no action on the proposal had been taken by the end of 1986.

There are numerous external opposition groups, largely based in Britain, including the **Ghana Democratic Movement** (GDM), whose chairman, Joseph Henry MENSAH, was released after a 1986 mistrial in a US court on charges that he conspired to buy weapons to be used in a coup attempt against the Rawlings government. Limited domestic opposition has been voiced by the **New Democratic Movement** (NDM) and the **Kwame Nkrumah Revolutionary Guards,** most of whose leaders were detained in May 1987 after announcing the formation of a **National Committee for the Defence of Democratic Rights.**

LEGISLATURE

The unicameral National Assembly elected in June 1979 was dissolved following the coup of December 31, 1981. In March 1982, a spokesman for the PNDC's Interim National Coordinating Committee (INCC) announced that a People's Constituent Assembly would meet to draft a "People's Constitution" following "thorough organization and establishment of the People's Defense Committees throughout the country."

CABINET

[as of April 4, 1988]

Chairman, Provisional National Defense Council	Flt. Lt. (Ret.) Jerry John Rawlings
Chairman, Committee of Secretaries	P.V. Obeng

Secretaries

Agriculture	Cmdr. Steve Obimpeh
Committees for the Defense of the Revolution	William Yeboah
Chieftancy Affairs	Emmanuel Tanoh
Education and Culture	K.B. Asante
Finance and Economic Planning	Dr. Kwesi Botchwey
Foreign Affairs	Dr. Obed Asamoah
Fuel and Power	Ato Ahwoi
Health	Nana Akuoko Sarpong
Industry, Science and Technology	Dr. Francis Acquah
Information	Mohammed Ben Abdallah
Internal Affairs	Nii Okaijah Adamafio
Justice and Attorney General	G.E.K. Aikins
Lands and Natural Resources	Kwame Peprah
Local Government and Rural Development	Kwamena Ahwoi
Mobilization and Productivity	Hundu Yahaya
Roads and Highways	Lt. Col. Mensah Gbedemah

Trade and Tourism	Kofi Djin
Transport and Communications	E.O. (Yaw) Donkor
Works and Housing (Acting)	Charles Boadu
Youth and Sports	K. Saarah-Mensah
Governor, Central Bank	John S. Addo

NEWS MEDIA

Under the 1979 constitution, state-owned media were required to "afford equal opportunities and facilities for the representation of opposing or differing views", and the Ghanaian press was one of the freest and most outspoken in Western Africa. Since the 1981 coup, not only radio and television but also the leading newspapers have become little more than propaganda organs of the government.

Press. The following are English-language dailies published at Accra, unless otherwise noted: *People's Daily Graphic* (200,000), government owned; *The Mirror* (180,000), government-owned weekly; *Weekly Spectator* (165,000), government owned; *The Ghanaian Times* (100,000), government owned; *The Pioneer* (Kumasi, 98,000); *People's Evening News* (60,000). The independent weekly, *Free Press,* ceased publication in April 1986, after complaining that its personnel had been subjected to government harassment.

News agencies. The domestic facility is the official Ghana News Agency. AFP, AP, *Xinhua,* UPI, DPA, and TASS maintain offices at Accra.

Radio and television. Radio and television service is provided by the autonomous statutory Ghana Broadcasting Corporation. The two home service radio networks, one of which is commercial, transmitted to 3.0 million receivers in 1987, while the four television stations were received by approximately 150,000 sets.

INTERGOVERNMENTAL REPRESENTATION

Ambassador to the US: Eric Kwamina OTOO.

US Ambassador to Ghana: Stephen R. LYNE.

Permanent Representative to the UN: James Victor GBEHO.

IGO Memberships (Non-UN): ADF, AfDB, BADEA, CCC, Copal, CWTH, ECOWAS, EEC(L), *EIB,* IACO, IBA, ICCAT, ICCO, ICO, Intelsat, Interpol, NAM, OAU.

GREECE

Hellenic Republic
Elleniki Demokratia

Political Status: Gained independence from the Ottoman Empire in 1830; under military rule 1967–1974; civilian control reinstituted July 23, 1974; present republican constitution adopted June 7, 1975.

Area: 50,944 sq. mi. (131,944 sq. km.).

Population: 9,740,417 (1981C), 10,097,000 (1988E).

Major Urban Centers (1981C): ATHENS (885,136, urban area, 3,027,331); Thessaloniki (406,300, urban area, 706,180); Patras (142,200); Larissa (102,426); Iraklion (102,398).

Official Language: Greek.

Monetary Unit: Drachma (market rate March 1, 1988, 135.26 drachmas = $1US).

President: Christos SARTZETAKIS; elected by Parliament on March 29, 1985, and sworn in March 30, succeeding Ioannis ALEVRAS, who had become Interim President following the resignation of Constantine (Konstantinos) KARAMANLIS on March 10.

Prime Minister: Dr. Andreas PAPANDREOU (Panhellenic Socialist Movement); assumed office following election of October 18, 1981, succeeding George John RALLIS (New Democracy); formed new government following election of June 2, 1985.

THE COUNTRY

Occupying the southern tip of the Balkan Peninsula and including several hundred islands in the Ionian and Aegean seas, the Hellenic Republic is peopled overwhelmingly by Greeks but also includes minority groups of Turks and others. Some 98 percent of the people speak modern (*dimotiki*) Greek, a more classical form (*katharevoussa*) no longer being employed in either government or university circles. The vast majority of the population belongs to the official Eastern Orthodox Church, which has been granted increased autonomy in its internal affairs by a government charter issued in 1969. In 1981, women constituted 27 percent of the paid work force, with three-fifths of those classed as "economically active" in rural areas performing unpaid agricultural family labor; urban women are concentrated in the clerical and service sectors. In government, women's legislative representation has long hovered at about 4 percent.

Traditionally based on agriculture, with important contributions from shipping and tourism, the Greek economy during the last two decades has witnessed substantial increases in the industrial sector, notably in chemical, metallurgical, plastics, and textile production. This expansion has, however, been accompanied by severe inflationary pressures, the consumer price index rising by an average of more than 20 percent annually during 1980–1986, with a marginal abatement to 16.4 percent in 1987.

GOVERNMENT AND POLITICS

Political background. Conquered by the Ottoman Turks in the later Middle Ages, Greece emerged as an independent kingdom in 1830 after a protracted war of liberation conducted with help from Great Britain, France, and tsarist Russia. Its subsequent history has been marked by championship of Greek nationalist aspirations throughout the Eastern Mediterranean and by recurrent internal upheavals reflecting, in part, a continuing struggle between royalists and republicans. The monarchy, abolished in 1924, was restored in 1935 and sponsored the dictatorship of Gen. John METAXAS (1936–1941) before the royal family took refuge abroad upon Greece's occupation by the Axis powers in April 1941. The restoration of the monarchy in 1946 took place in the midst of conflict between Communist and anti-Communist forces that had erupted in 1944 and was finally terminated when the Communists were defeated with US military assistance in 1949. A succession of conservative governments held office until 1964, when the Center Union, a left-center coalition led by George PAPANDREOU, achieved a parliamentary majority. Disagreements with the young King CONSTANTINE on military and other issues led to the dismissal of Papandreou in 1965, initiating a series of crises that culminated two years later in a coup d'état and the establishment of a military junta. An unsuccessful attempt by the king to mobilize support against the junta in December 1967 was followed by the appointment of a regent, the flight of the king to Rome, and a reorganization of the government whereby (then) Col. George PAPADOPOULOS, a member of the junta, became prime minister.

In May 1973 elements of the Greek navy attempted a countercoup in order to restore the king, but the plot failed, resulting in formal deposition of the monarch and the proclamation of a republic on June 1. Papadopoulos' formation of a civilian cabinet and the scheduling of an election for early 1974 resulted in his ouster on November 25 by a conservative military group under the leadership of Brig. Gen. Dimitrios IOANNIDES. The new regime, insisting that Papadopoulos had been moving much too quickly, canceled the election and reinstituted curbs on civil liberties. In the face of increased restiveness, growing inflation, and a crisis in Cyprus, it was forced, however, to reverse itself and in July 1974 called on Constantine KARAMANLIS to form a caretaker government preparatory to a return to civilian rule. Karamanlis was confirmed as prime minister following a parliamentary election on November 17, and Michael STASINOPOULOS was designated provisional president a month later. Stasinopoulos was succeeded as president by Konstantinos TSATSOS on June 19, 1975. On November 28, 1977, eight days after an early election in which his New Democracy party retained control of the legislature by a reduced majority, Karamanlis formed a new government. He resigned as prime minister on May 6, 1980, following his parliamentary designation as president the day before, and was succeeded on May 10 by George RALLIS, who came under increasing attack during the ensuing 14 months for his lack of success in dealing with a variety of economic problems.

At the general election of October 18, 1981, the Panhellenic Socialist Movement (Pasok) swept to victory with a majority of 22 seats, and Andreas PAPANDREOU formed Greece's first socialist administration three days later. Despite ongoing complaints that the Pasok leadership had failed to make good on its election promises, the government was given a vote of confidence at the European Parliament election in June 1984, winning 41.6 percent of the vote and capturing 10 of the 24 available seats.

President Karamanlis resigned on March 10, 1985, after Papandreou had withdrawn an earlier pledge to support his reelection, and was succeeded, on an interim basis, by the president of Parliament, Ioannis ALEVRAS. In a legislative poll on March 29 that stirred controversy because of the use of color-coded ballots and an allegedly improper tie-breaking vote by Alevras, the Pasok nominee, Christos SARTZETAKIS, was named to a regular five-year term as head of state. Subsequently, Pasok remained in power, with a somewhat reduced majority, as the result of an early popular election on June 2.

Constitution and government. The possibility of a return to monarchy was decisively rejected at a plebiscite on December 8, 1974; the Greek people, by a two-to-one margin, expressed their preference for an "uncrowned democracy". The republican constitution adopted on June 7, 1975, provided for a parliamentary system with a strong presidency. Under the new basic law (branded as "Gaullist" by political opponents of Karamanlis), the president had the power to name and dismiss cabinet members (including the prime minister), to dissolve Parliament, to veto legislation, to call for referenda, and to proclaim a state of emergency. These powers were lost by a constitutional amendment that secured final parliamentary approval on March 7, 1986. The action restored full executive power to the prime minister, assuming retention of a legislative majority. The unicameral Parliament, whose normal term is four years, elects the president by a two-thirds majority (three-fifths on a third ballot). A requirement that the head of state be elected by secret ballot was rescinded by a second amendment, also effective in March 1986. (A year earlier, the government had withdrawn a proposal that the amending process itself be simplified by dropping a requirement for a third reading after an intervening election.) The judicial system is headed by the Supreme Court and includes magistrates' courts, courts of the first instance, and justices of the peace.

Traditionally administered on the basis of its historic provinces, Greece is currently divided into 51 prefectures (plus the self-governing monastic community of Mount Athos), with Athens further divided into 4 subprefectures. In January 1987, the government approved a plan to divide the country into 13 new administrative regions to facilitate planning and coordinate regional development.

Foreign relations. Greece has historically displayed a Western orientation and throughout most of the post-World War II era has been heavily dependent on Western economic and military support. The repressiveness of the military regime was, however, a matter of concern to many European nations, and their economic and political sanctions were instrumental in Greece's withdrawal from the Council of Europe in 1969. Relations with the United States remained close, primarily because Greece continued to provide a base for the US Sixth Fleet, but the return to democratic rule was accompanied by increased evidence of anti-American feeling.

The most important issue in Greek foreign affairs is relations with Turkey, including the Cyprus question, which has been a source of friction since the mid-1950s. The Greek-inspired coup and subsequent Turkish intervention in Cyprus in July 1974 not only exacerbated tension between the two countries but served to bring down the military regime of General Ioannides; it also precipitated Greek withdrawal from military participation in NATO. The return of civilian government, on the other hand, brought a renewal of cooperation with Western Europe. Greece announced in September 1974 that it was rejoining the Council of Europe and subsequently applied for full, as distinguished from associate, membership in the EEC, with preliminary agreement being reached at Brussels in December 1978 and entry achieved on January 1, 1981.

Greece returned to the NATO military command structure, after a six-year lapse, in October 1980. The action was accepted by Turkey's recently installed military regime, although a lengthy dispute between the two countries over continental-shelf rights in (and air channels over) the Aegean Sea remained unresolved.

Prior to the 1981 electoral campaign, Pasok had urged withdrawal from NATO and the EC, in addition to cancellation of the military bases agreement with the United States. During the campaign these positions were modified, Dr. Papandreou calling only for "renegotiation" of the terms of membership in the two international groupings.

Although continuing his criticism of the US military presence, the prime minister signed an agreement on September 9, 1983, permitting US military bases to continue operation until the end of 1988. However, on September 29, he cancelled a NATO exercise scheduled for October, claiming violations of Greek airspace by US aircraft. In August 1984 joint biennial maneuvers with the United States in northern Greece were called off on the ground that there was no discernible Communist threat in the area, whereas Turkey was a "visible danger". Four months later, Turkey vetoed a proposal by Papandreou to assign Greek forces on Lemnos to NATO, invoking a long-standing contention that militarization of the island was forbidden under the 1923 Treaty of Lausanne. As a result, no Greek or Turkish forces were committed to the alliance for 1985, with Greece withdrawing from the NATO Defense College at Rome in January because of a simulated exercise aimed at the hypothetical overthrow of a recently installed leftist regime. In early 1986, Dr. Papandreou reiterated his intention to "rid the country of foreign bases" and in September declared, without indicating a timetable, that "our decision to remove . . . nuclear weapons from our country is final and irrevocable".

Controversy with Turkey continued throughout 1987, with Athens maintaining its boycott of NATO exercises because of Lemnos and related issues, although Papandreou declared in January that Greece would remain a member of the alliance as a means of averting war with its neighbor. Meanwhile, in November 1986, the Greek foreign minister had condemned the election of Turkey to the presidency of the Council of Europe. Relations with Washington improved somewhat during the period, despite a brief rift occasioned by US charges of a "deal" with the Abu Nidal terrorist organization, and in late 1987 talks on the military bases accord were resumed.

Current issues. Pasok, which had been slipping in the public opinion polls, was returned to power in June 1985 by what was viewed as more of a vote against the New Democracy and its conservative policies than of support for the Socialists. By contrast, at nationwide municipal balloting in October 1986, the government party was severely shaken by losses that included the country's three largest cities. The setback was attributed largely to a lack of traditional second-round support by the pro-Soviet Communist

Party, which had denounced the prime minister's fiscal policies as a violation of his 1985 campaign promises and had sought a revision of the electoral law in favor of a more genuinely proportional system (see Legislature, below).

After taking power, the Papandreou government embarked on an austerity program that included devaluation of the drachma, price increases for essential goods and services, and a two-year freeze (save for inflationary adjustments) on salaries and wages. The program yielded approval of a $1.7 billion loan package from the European Community, although the EC insisted on further belt-tightening before releasing the second half of the loan in 1986. The result was a series of major work stoppages in the wake of the October elections, culminating in a 24-hour general strike in mid-January 1987.

By October 1987, partly in reaction to a series of scandals involving both government and public-sector company officials, popular support for the PASOK administration had fallen to its lowest point (35 percent) since 1981. However, polls also revealed that a majority of the voters did not favor an election prior to expiration of the existing parliamentary term in 1999.

POLITICAL PARTIES

The Greek party system is complex and somewhat fluid, with some of its components being essentially personalist in nature. The parties below are ordered largely on the basis of their strength at the 1985 election.

Government Party:

Panhellenic Socialist Movement (*Panellenio Sosialistiko Kinema*— Pasok). Founded in 1974 by Andreas Papandreou, Pasok endorses republicanism and socialization of the economy. In foreign affairs it is formally committed to the dissolution of both NATO and the Warsaw Pact, strict control of US military installations in Greece, and renegotiation of Greek membership in the European Community. In 1975 the party was weakened by the withdrawal of members who disagreed with Papandreou's refusal to endorse the creation of a "broad Left" alliance of opposition socialist parties. However, most of the dissidents, including, most prominently, Lady Amalia Fleming and Melina Merkouri, rejoined Pasok prior to the 1977 election, at which it won 93 parliamentary seats. The 1981 balloting yielded a Pasok majority, permitting Papandreou to form the country's first socialist government.

On March 10, 1985, Pasok announced that it would not support the reelection of President Karamanlis, offering as its candidate Christos Sartzetakis, who was elected to a five-year term by the legislature in procedurally controversial balloting on March 29. Its forces augmented by supporters of the **Union of the Democratic Center** (*Enosis Demokratikou Kentrou*) and the **Christian Democracy** (*Christianike Demokatia*), neither of which had secured representation in 1981, Pasok was returned in early parliamentary balloting on June 2 with a somewhat diminished majority that permitted Papandreou to continue as prime minister. On September 25 the establishment of a new minor formation, the **People's Militant Unity** (*Laiki Agonistiki Enotita*—LAE), was announced by a number of Pasok dissidents.

At local balloting in October 1986, Pasok suffered major reverses, the percentage of municipalities under its control falling to 48.8 from 62.4 in 1982.

Leader: Andreas PAPANDREOU (Prime Minister).

Other Parties:

New Democracy (*Nea Demokratia*—ND). Formed in 1974 as a vehicle for Constantine Karamanlis, the New Democracy was, under Karamanlis, a broadly based pragmatic party committed to parliamentary democracy, social justice, an independent foreign policy, and free enterprise. George

Rallis, generally viewed as a moderate centrist, was elected party leader on May 8, 1980, and was designated prime minister the next day, following Karamanlis' election as president of the Republic. In the wake of the ND's defeat at the 1981 election, Rallis lost an intraparty vote of confidence and, in a move interpreted as reflecting the ascendancy of right-wing influence within the parliamentary group, was succeeded in December by the leader of the party's conservative wing, Evangelos AVEROFF-TOSSIZZA. Averoff resigned as leader of the opposition in August 1984, following the ND's poor showing at the European Parliament balloting in June, the moderates rallying to elect Constantine Mitsotakis as his successor over Constantine Stefanopoulos. Stefanopoulos, in turn, withdrew with a number of his center-right supporters to form the Democratic Renewal (below) in September 1985, after Mitsotakis' August redesignation as ND leader, despite the party's legislative loss to PASOK two months earlier.

During the 1985 campaign, the ND was supported by the **Democratic Socialist Party** (*Komma Demokratikou Sosialismou* — Kodeso), a centrist alliance whose former leader, Ioannis PESMAZOGLOU, had announced his "temporary" withdrawal from politics in the wake of the 1984 Euroelection results and subsequently declared as an independent; Kodeso's current leader is Charalambos PROTOPAPAS.

The ND experienced a significant resurgence in the 1986 municipal elections, winning control of the country's three largest cities, Athens, Piraeus, and Salonika.

Leader: Constantine MITSOTAKIS (Leader of the Opposition).

Democratic Renewal (*Demokratike Ananeose* — Diana). Launched in September 1985 by a group of self-styled ND "purists" dedicated to maintenance of the parent party's true ideals, Diana has been construed largely as the outcome of a personality clash between the ND's Constantine Mitsotakis and the more conservative Constantine Stefanopoulos.

Leader: Constantine (Kostis) STEFANOPOULOS.

Communist Party of Greece (*Kommounistiko Komma Elladas* — KKE). During the 1967–1974 military dictatorship what was initially styled the Communist Party–Exterior evolved from the pro-Moscow faction of the earlier but long-divided Greek Communist Party, in opposition to the nationalist-oriented Communist Party–Interior (below). It became the third-largest party in Parliament following the 1977 election, but experienced numerous membership defections during 1980 in reaction to leadership support of the Soviet intervention in Afghanistan. Increasingly recognized as the official KKE, it recovered to become the only group other than Pasok and the New Democracy to secure parliamentary representation in 1981.

Following the 1984 Europarliamentary election, the KKE distanced itself from Pasok, seeking to attract voters from the latter's left wing and hoping to increase its leverage in the next parliament, should Pasok fail to secure a majority. Prior to the 1985 balloting, at which it won 12 seats, it absorbed the United Socialist Alliance of Greece (*Eniea Socialistiki Parataxi Ellados* — ESPE), formed in February 1984 by Pasok dissident Stathis PANAGOULES, who had resigned as deputy interior minister in August 1982. The KKE's continued unwillingness to support Pasok in second-round balloting contributed to the governing party's poor showing in 1986.

Leader: Kharilaos FLORAKIS (General Secretary).

Greek Left (*Elleniki Aristera*). The Greek Left was formally launched in 1987 during an April 21–26 constituent congress of the majority faction of the Communist Party of Greece — Interior (*Kommounistiko Komma Elladas-Esoterikou* — KKE-*Esoterikou*). The action implemented a decision of the KKE-*Esoterikou's* fourth national conference in May 1986 to reorganize as a more broadly based party of the Left, thereby rejecting an appeal by its (then) general secretary, Yiannis Banias, that a longstanding specific identification with Marxism-Leninism be retained.

Founded in 1968, the Communist Party–Interior provided most of the leadership of the **United Democratic Left** (*Eniea Demokratiki Aristera* — EDA), a Communist-front organization that operated while both wings of the KKE were outlawed and subsequently evolved into a separate party. The two KKE formations joined with the EDA to contest the 1974 election as members of a United Left coalition.

Ultimately emerging as Greece's principal "Eurocommunist" group, the KKE-*Esoterikou* participated in the 1977 election as a member of the Alliance of Progressive and Left-Wing Forces, splitting the Alliance's two seats with the EDA. Unsuccessful in 1981, it regained its single seat in 1985.

Leader: Leonidas KYRKOS (General Secretary).

Communist Party of Greece–Interior — Renewal Left (*Kommounistiko Komma Elladas-Esoterikou — Ananeotiki Aristera*). Upon formation of the Greek Left, the minority Banias faction of the KKE-*Esoterikou* regrouped, adding Renewal Left to the former party label.

Leader: Yiannis BANIAS (General Secretary).

National Political Union (*Ethniki Politiki Enosis* — Epen). The right-wing Epen held its first assembly on January 29, 1984, designating George Papadopoulos, former dictator of Greece from 1967–1973 who is serving a life term in prison, as its leader. At a mass rally to celebrate the birth of the party, a taped message from Papadopoulos (subsequently confiscated by the government) was aired. Following the rally a government spokesman asserted that the nominal party head would be ineligible to stand for office in any future election. The party ran fifth in the 1985 balloting, but secured no parliamentary representation; earlier, it had obtained one seat in the 1984 European Parliament election.

Leader: George PAPADOPOULOS.

Liberal Party (*Komma Fileleftheron* — KF). The KF was formed prior to the 1981 election by former Democratic Center deputy Nikitas Venizelos in an electorally unsuccessful effort to "revive the political heritage" of his grandfather, former prime minister Eleftherios Venizelos. It has thus far been unable to achieve legislative representation.

Leader: Nikitas VENIZELOS.

Greek Socialist Party (*Elleniko Socialistiko Komma* — ESK). The ESK was formed in April 1987 by former national economy minister Gerassimos Arsenis, who had been expelled from PASOK in February 1986.

Leader: Gerassimos ARSENIS.

Minor leftist formations that participated in the 1985 balloting included the **Militant Socialist Party of Greece** (*Agonistiko Sosialistiko Komma Elladas* — ASKE), organized by Pasok dissident Nikos KARGOPOULOS; the Maoist **Revolutionary Communist Party of Greece** (*Epanastatiko Kommounistiko Komma Elladas* — EKKE); the **Communist Left** (*Kommounistike Aristera* — KA), formerly the Revolutionary Left; and the Trotskyite **Workers International Union** (*Ergatiki Diethnistiki Enosi* — EDE).

LEGISLATURE

The unicameral **Parliament** (*Vouli*) consists of 300 members elected by direct universal suffrage for four-year terms, subject to dissolution. Since 1926, the procedure for allocating seats, usually a form of proportional representation, has tended to vary from one election to another. At the most recent legislative balloting of June 2, 1985, a system of "reinforced proportional representation" (a variation on a procedure introduced in 1951 to provide the leading party with a working majority) was employed, with the following results: the Panhellenic Socialist Movement, 161 seats; the New Democracy, 126; the Communist Party of Greece, 12; and the Communist Party of Greece–Interior, 1. However, at the ceremonial opening of Parliament on June 17, 10 deputies (4 each from Pasok and the ND, and 2 from the KKE declared themselves as independents. Further changes, resulting in part from formation of the Democratic Renewal, yielded the following distribution by late 1987: Pasok, 157; ND, 111; KKE, 9; Diana, 8; Greek Left, 1; independent, 14.

President: Ioannis ALEVRAS.

CABINET

Prime Minister	Andreas Papandreou
First Deputy Prime Minister	Ioannis Charalambopoulos
Second Deputy Prime Minister	Agamemnon Koutsogiorgas
Ministers	
Agriculture	Yiannis Pottakis
Commerce	Nikolaos Akritidis

Culture and Sciences	Melina Merkouri
Environment, City Planning and Public Works	Evangelos Kouloumbis Emmanuel Papastefanakis (Alternate)
Finance	Dimitrios Tsovolas Georgios Petsos (Alternate)
Foreign Affairs	Karolos Papoulias Ioannis Kapsis (Alternate) Theodoros Pangalos (Alternate for EEC)
Health, Welfare and Social Insurance	Ionnis Floros
Industry, Energy and Technology	Anastassios Peponis Costas Papanayiotou (Alternate)
Interior	Akis Tsohatzopoulos Kosmas Sfiriou (Alternate)
Justice	Agamemnon Koutsogiorgas
Labor	Georgios Gennimatas
Merchant Marine	Evangelos Yiannopoulos
National Defense	Ioannis Charalambopoulos Efstathios Yiotas (Alternate)
National Economy	Constantine Simitis
National Education and Religious Affairs	Antonios Tritsis
Northern Greece	Stelios Papathemelis
Public Order	Antonis Drossoyiannis
Transportation and Communication	Costas Badouvas Spyros Sarantitis (Alternate)
Without Portfolio for Earthquake Stricken Kalamata	Althanassios Filippopoulos
Minister for the Aegean	Petros Valvis
Minister to the Prime Minister	Apostolos Kaklamanis
Governor, Bank of Greece	Dimitris Halkias

NEWS MEDIA

The news media operated under severe constraints while the military was in power. Since the return to civilian rule, censorship has been lifted, and a number of papers banned by the military have reemerged.

Press. The following are published daily at Athens (circulation figures for November 1987): *Ethnos* (161,383), center-left; *Eleftheros Typos,* center-right, (135,044); *Eleftherotypia* (129,855), center-left; *Ta Nea* (121,911), center-left; *Avriani* (100,581), center-left; *Apogevmatini* (91,459), center-right; *Rizospastis* (48,703), KKE organ; *Vradyni* (47,876), center-right; *Mesimvrini* (34,592), center-right; *I Proti,* left-wing (33,617); *Kathimerini* (24,461), center-right; *Demokratikos Logos,* center-left (9,693); *Acropolis* (9,178), center-right; *Estia* (6,819), far-right; *Avgi,* left-wing (4,597); *Eleftheri Ora* (1,195), far-right.

News agencies. The major domestic service is the Athens News Agency (*Athinaiko Praktorio Idisseon*). Several foreign bureaus maintain offices at Athens.

Radio and television. In 1987 Hellenic Radio-Television (*Elleniki Radiophonia Tileorassi* – ERT) became a joint stock company by merger of ERT-1 (the original ERT, which had been state-controlled since 1939) and ERT-2 (the former Information service of the Armed Forces (*Ypiresia Enimeroseos Enoplon Dynameon* – Yened), which had been turned over to civilian operation in 1982. The restructuring yielded two television channels, ET-1 and ET-2, and the First, Second, Third, and Fourth programs of *Elleniki Radiophonia.* Concurrently, the state radio monopoly ended with the creation of municipal stations at Athens, Piraeus, and Salonica. Completing the process of deregulation, a number of private local stations are scheduled to commence operation in 1988. There were approximately 4.3 million radio and 1.8 million television receivers in 1987.

INTERGOVERNMENTAL REPRESENTATION

Ambassador to the US: George D. PAPOULIAS.

US Ambassador to Greece: Robert Vossler KEELEY.

Permanent Representative to the UN: Constantine ZEPOS.

IGO Memberships (Non-UN): BIS, CCC, CERN, CEUR, EC, EIB, ICAC, ICCO, ICM, ICO, IEA, IIC, Inmarsat, Intelsat, Interpol, IOOC, ITC, NATO, OECD, PCA.

GRENADA

State of Grenada

Political Status: Independent member of the Commonwealth since February 7, 1974; constitution suspended following coup of March 13, 1979; restored November 9, 1984.

Area: 133 sq. mi. (344 sq. km.).

Population: 93,858 (1970C), 126,000 (1988E).

Major Urban Center (1980E): ST. GEORGE'S (7,500).

Official Language: English.

Monetary Unit: East Caribbean Dollar (market rate March 1, 1988, 2.70 EC dollars = $1US).

Sovereign: Queen ELIZABETH II.

Governor General: Sir Paul SCOON; assumed office in September 1978, succeeding Sir Leo Victor DE GALE.

Prime Minister: Herbert Augustus BLAIZE (New National Party); sworn in December 4, 1984, following parliamentary election of December 3 and dissolution of provisional government chaired by Nicholas A. BRAITHWAITE.

THE COUNTRY

Grenada, the smallest independent nation in the Western hemisphere, encompasses the southernmost of the Caribbean's Windward Islands, some 90 miles north of Trinidad (see map, p. 22). The country includes the main island of Grenada, the smaller islands of Carriacou and Petit Martinique, and a number of small islets. The population is approximately 75 percent Black, the balance being largely mulatto, with a small White minority. English is the official language, while a French patois is in limited use. Roman Catholics predominate, with Anglicans constituting a substantial minority. Women held a number of influential positions during the Marxist era (1979–1983), but currently hold no legislative or ministerial posts.

Grenada's economy is based on agriculture; bananas, cocoa, nutmeg, and mace are its most important products. Tourism, an important source of foreign exchange, declined substantially in the mid-1970s but has since shown signs of revival. Unemployment has long been a major problem, encompassing an estimated 25 percent of the adult population in 1986.

GOVERNMENT AND POLITICS

Political background. Discovered by Columbus on his third voyage in 1498, Grenada was alternately ruled by the French and British until 1783, when British control was recognized by the Treaty of Versailles. It remained a British colony until 1958, when it joined the abortive Federation of the West Indies. In 1967 Grenada became a member of the West Indies Associated States, Britain retaining responsibility for external relations. Eric M. GAIRY, who had been removed from office by the British in 1962 for malfeasance, was redesignated prime minister upon the assumption of internal autonomy.

On February 7, 1974, Grenada became a fully independent member of the Commonwealth, two years after an election which the British interpreted as a mandate for independence. Many Grenadians, however, were opposed to self-rule under Gairy, whom they compared to Haiti's "Papa Doc" Duvalier. United primarily by their disdain for Gairy, the nation's three opposition parties — the Grenada National Party (GNP), the New Jewel Movement (NJM), and the United People's Party (UPP) — contested the election of December 7, 1976, as a People's Alliance. Although failing to defeat the incumbent prime minister, the Alliance succeeded in reducing the lower-house strength of Gairy's Grenada United Labour Party (GULP) to 9 of 15 members.

In the early morning of March 13, 1979, while the prime minister was out of the country, insurgents destroyed the headquarters of the Grenada Defense Force, and a People's Revolutionary Government (PRG) was proclaimed by opposition leader Maurice BISHOP. Joining Bishop in the new government were 11 other members or supporters of the NJM plus 2 members of the GNP.

In September 1983, disagreement arose between Bishop (who reportedly favored rapprochement with the United States) and Deputy Prime Minister Bernard COARD (who sought a clear-cut alignment with the Soviet bloc), Bishop being forced to accept an NJM Central Committee decision calling for joint leadership. On October 13, Bishop was removed from office and placed under house arrest by Gen. Hudson AUSTIN, commander of the People's Revolutionary Army (PRA). Six days later, after having momentarily been freed by rioting supporters, Bishop was recaptured and executed, with General Austin being installed as head of a 16-member Revolutionary Military Council (RMC). On October 25, after the governor general, Sir Paul SCOON, had requested the Organization of Eastern Caribbean States (OECS) to intervene and restore order, US military forces, with OECS endorsement and limited personnel support, invaded the island, seizing Austin and others involved in the coup. Subsequently, a provisional administration under Nicholas A. BRAITHWAITE was established, which held office until the installation of Herbert A. BLAIZE as prime minister of a new parliamentary regime on December 4, 1984.

Constitution and government. Grenada's constitution, originally adopted in February 1967 and modified only slightly on independence, was suspended following the March 1979 coup, but restored in November 1984, the legitimacy of laws enacted in the interim being confirmed by Parliament in February 1985. The British monarch is the nominal sovereign and is represented by a governor general. Executive authority is exercised on the monarch's behalf by the prime minister, who represents the majority party in the House of Representatives, the lower house of the bicameral legislature. The House is popularly elected for a five-year term, while the upper chamber, the Senate, consists of 13 members appointed by the governor general: 10 on the advice of the prime minister (3 to represent interest groups) and 3 on the advice of the leader of the opposition. The judicial system includes a Supreme Court composed of a High Court of Justice and a two-tiered Court of Appeal, the upper panel of which hears final appeals from the High Court. There are also eight magistrates' courts of summary jurisdiction.

Grenada is administratively divided into six parishes encompassing 52 village councils on the main island, with the minor islands organized as separate administrative entities.

Foreign relations. The United Kingdom and the United States recognized the Bishop government on March 1979, but relations subsequently deteriorated, with Washington condemning St. George's midsummer signing of a two-year technical-assistance pact with Havana, and London deploring "the unattractive record of the Grenada government over civil liberties and democratic rights." Relations with Washington worsened further in the wake of US and NATO naval maneuvers off Puerto Rico in July 1981, Grenada branding the exercises as a rehearsal for invasion of its territory. Nine months later, after Grenada had become the only English-speaking Caribbean state to declare its support for Argentina in the Falkland Islands war, US President Reagan opened a four-day visit to nearby Barbados by charging that St. George's had joined with Cuba, Nicaragua, and the Soviet Union in an effort to "spread the virus of Marxism" in the area.

Regional reaction to the Bishop regime was initially somewhat mixed, but by mid-1982 all of the other six members of the OECS (Antigua, Dominica, Montserrat, St. Kitts-Nevis, St. Lucia, and St. Vincent) were generally hostile, although the most vocal regional criticism of the PRG came from Prime Minister Adams of Barbados. Bishop's murder provoked even more widespread condemnation, including that of the Cuban government, which announced on October 20, 1983, that "no position claimed as revolutionary . . . can justify savage methods such as the elimination of Maurice Bishop and the outstanding group of honest and moral leaders who died". The ensuing military intervention by US and Caribbean forces, coupled with President Reagan's assertion that Grenada had become "a Soviet-Cuban colony being readied for use as a major military bastion to export terror", left little opportunity for an improvement in relations between St. George's and Havana under either the interim administration of Nicholas Braithwaite or the restored parliamentary government of Herbert Blaize. Thus, the last Cuban diplomat remaining in Grenada (a chargé d'affaires) departed in March 1984, with relations between the two countries being further strained during the ensuing year by Havana's attempt to recover $6 million for equipment used to construct an airport at Port Salines that Washington had earlier characterized as a military threat to the region. Since then Grenada has participated in the US-backed regional security plan designed to avert future leftist takeovers, Prime Minister Blaize remaining one of the strongest supporters of US Caribbean policy.

President Reagan was warmly received during a visit on February 20, 1986, which included a "mini-summit" with other English-speaking Caribbean leaders. Earlier, on October 31, 1985, Queen Elizabeth II was reported to have been given a "subdued welcome" because of Britain's failure to assist in the 1983 intervention and the relatively modest dimensions of its subsequent aid program.

Current issues. While the 1983 invasion of Grenada was completed in little more than three days, Washington subsequently experienced difficulty in disengaging itself from the economic and political life of the island. Although US troops withdrew by mid-1985, the government remained heavily dependent on US aid in dealing with extensive infrastructure damage, a large foreign debt, high unemployment, and a deteriorating agricultural base.

The United States also played a major role, along with Caribbean sources, in supporting the New National Party (NNP) in its successful 1984 campaign. Internal cohesion however, proved lacking, with GDM and NDP factions protesting their exclusion from policy decisions by Prime Minister Blaize and his former GNP followers. The rupture became final with the resignation in April 1987 of three government ministers because of a planned retrenchment of half of the country's 3,600 civil servants, with most major opposition leaders joining in formation of the National Democratic Congress (see Political Parties, below). Although the NDC encompassed a variety of divergent interests, its prospects for survival were enhanced by the government's adoption of sweeping emergency powers at midyear and the disclosure in November of an internal NNP report that called for the establishment of a party intelligence unit to monitor the activities of other political groups.

Throughout the year, local and international attention focused on judicial proceedings against Coard, Austin, and 16 associates for their complicity in the murder of Prime Minister Bishop and others prior to the American intervention. After a controversial trial involving prolonged constitutional debate and protests from the defendants that they were scapegoats in a post facto attempt to justify the invasion, Coard, his wife, Austin, and 11 others were found guilty of murder and sentenced to death. Numerous appeals were immediately filed, including a demand, rejected by the government, for review by London's Privy Council.

POLITICAL PARTIES

Prior to the 1979 coup, Eric Gairy's Grenada United Labour Party (GULP) had consistently dominated the country's politics, although its majority in the House of Representatives was substantially reduced at the election of December 1976, which the leftist New Jewel Movement (NJM), the centrist United People's Party (UUP), and the conservative Grenada National Party (GNP) contested as a People's Alliance. For the 1984 balloting, only the GULP campaigned under its original name.

Government Party:

New National Party (NNP). The NNP was launched in August 1984 as an amalgamation of the Grenada National Party (GNP), led by Herbert Blaize; the National Democratic Party (NDP), led by George Brizan and Robert Grant; the Grenada Democratic Movement (GDM), led by Dr. Francis Alexis; and the Christian Democratic Labour Party (CDLP), led by Winston Whyte. The center-right GNP was founded by Blaize in 1956, but became essentially moribund during its leader's retirement from politics after the 1979 coup. The NDP, organized in early 1984, became the most liberal component of the NNP. The GDM was formed in 1983 by a group of right-wing exiles resident in Barbados and elsewhere, who reportedly benefited from substantial US support. The CDLP (see National Democratic Congress, below) withdrew from the coalition in September 1984, after a series of policy disputes with the other groups.

In its campaign manifesto, the NNP formally endorsed the 1983 military intervention and urged that foreign military and police units not be withdrawn. It dominated the balloting of December 3, 1984, winning 14 of 15 lower house seats. However, by mid-1985 the coalition was in substantial disarray, GNP elements holding most of the government portfolios. Infighting continued throughout 1986, Brizan and Alexis reportedly mounting an unsuccessful challenge to Blaize's leadership prior to a December convention at which the GNP faction gained virtually complete control, with Ben Jones, reputedly the prime minister's heir apparent, defeating Brizan for the post of deputy leader. In April 1987 Brizan and Alexis left the government and moved into opposition leaving the NNP little more than a "reborn GNP", with a diminished legislative majority of 9 members.

Leaders: Herbert A. BLAIZE (Prime Minister and NNP Political Leader), Ben JONES (Deputy Political Leader), Lawrence JOSEPH (Chairman), Dr. Keith MITCHELL (General Secretary).

Other Parties:

National Democratic Congress (NDC). The NDC was launched in April 1987 by former NNP leaders George Brizan and Francis Alexis, who were subsequently joined by a variety of anti-Blaize figures, including leaders of the Grenada Democratic Labour Party (GDLP) and the Democratic Labour Congress (DLC). Launched in March 1985 by (then) opposition leader Marcel Peters, the GDLP had expressed concern about unemployment, a lack of "Christian values", and Grenada's security in the wake of the US withdrawal. The DLC had been formed in August 1986 by Kenny Lalsingh, a legislative representative who had left the NNP earlier in the year, in a realignment that included the former Christian Democratic Labour Party (CDLP), a centrist formation of ex-UPP members that competed unsuccessfully in the 1984 balloting. The NDC held its inaugural conference on December 18, 1987.

Leaders: Kenny LALSINGH (Chairman), George BRIZAN (Leader of the Opposition), Dr. Francis ALEXIS and Phinsley ST. LOUIS (Deputy Leaders), Albert FORSYTHE, Terrence GRIFFITH, Marcel PETERS, Oliver JOSEPH (General Secretary), Tillman THOMAS (Deputy General Secretary).

Grenada United Labour Party (GULP). The GULP was founded in 1950 as the personal vehicle of Eric M. Gairy, who headed governments in 1951–1957, 1961–1962, and 1967–1979. Having acquired a reputation for both corruption and repression while in office, Gairy did not present himself for election in 1984, when the GULP secured 36 percent of the popular vote compared to the NNP's 59 percent. The party's only successful candidate, Marcel Peters, after being formally designated leader of the opposition, announced his withdrawal in protest at alleged electoral irregularities, but later reversed himself and secured the appointment of three associates as opposition senators. In early 1985, Peters formed the GDLP (see under NDC, above) after being expelled from GULP, which was thus left with no parliamentary representation.

In December 1987 Sir Eric announced that he was retiring from active politics, while remaining GULP president. His deputy, Raphael Fletcher, was expected to succeed him as leader in April at a party convention, which was, however, postponed to June.

Leaders: Sir Eric M. GAIRY (President and Party Leader), Raphael FLETCHER (Deputy Leader).

Maurice Bishop Patriotic Movement (MBPM). The MBPM was formed prior to the 1984 balloting by former members of the NJM who had supported Prime Minister Bishop against the radical military faction that was responsible for his ouster and murder. Currently without legislative representation, the MBPM announced in early 1988 that it would shortly hold a convention in an effort to rebuild its strength.

Leaders: Kendrick RADIX, George LOUISON.

Grenada Federated Labour Party (GFLP). The GFLP is a small formation whose sole parliamentary candidate in 1984 garnered a total of 10 votes.

Leader: Fenderson J. FELIX.

LEGISLATURE

The bicameral **Parliament**, embracing an appointed Senate of 13 members and a popularly elected 15-member House of Representatives, was dissolved by the People's Revolutionary Government following the March 1979 coup. It was reconvened on December 28, 1984, following the general election of December 3.

Senate. The upper house contains 13 members, 10 nominated by the government and 3 by the Leader of the Opposition.

President: (Vacant, following the resignation of Alphonsus ANTOINE on March 31, 1988).

House of Representatives. At the December 1984 election, the New National Party won 14 seats and the Grenada United Labour Party won 1; however, the GULP representative was expelled from the party in February 1985, subsequently sitting as a member of the Grenada Democratic Labour Party. By early 1988 NNP representation had been reduced to 9 seats, all of the defectors, plus the GDLP member, having joined the recently organized National Democratic Congress.

Speaker: Sir Hudson SCIPIO.

CABINET

Prime Minister	Herbert Blaize
Ministers	
Agriculture, Forestry, Lands and Tourism	Ben Jones
Carriacou and Petit Martinique Affairs	Herbert Blaize
Community Development, Women's Affairs and Cooperatives	Dr. Keith Mitchell
Education, Culture and Fisheries	George McGuire
Energy	Herbert Blaize
External Affairs	Ben Jones
Finance	Herbert Blaize
Health, Housing and Physical Planning	Daniel Williams
Home Affairs	Herbert Blaize
Information	Herbert Blaize
Labor	George McGuire
Legal Affairs	Daniel Williams
Local Government, Social Security, Youth Affairs and Sports	George McGuire
National Security	Herbert Blaize
Trade, Industry and Planning	Herbert Blaize
Works, Communications, Public Utilities and Civil Aviation	Dr. Keith Mitchell
Ministers of State	
Agriculture and Tourism	Pauline Andrews
Education, Culture, Youth Affairs and Fisheries	Ben Andrews
Legal Affairs and National Security	Lawrence Joseph
Social Security, Local Government and Labor	Norton Noel
Women's Affairs and Community Development	Grace Duncan
Works and Cooperatives	Alleyne Walker
Attorney General	Daniel Williams

NEWS MEDIA

Press. There are no daily newspapers. The *Grenadian Voice* is issued twice weekly; weeklies include the *Grenada Guardian,* a GULP publication; the *Informer;* and the *West Indian.* An opposition *Grenadian Tribune* was launched in June 1987.

Radio and television. Radio Grenada (formerly Radio Free Grenada) is a government-owned enterprise which broadcasts throughout the Grenadines. Approximately 55,000 receivers were in use in 1987. Television Grenada provides limited programming, primarily on a booster basis from Barbados and Trinidad.

INTERGOVERNMENTAL REPRESENTATION

Ambassador to the US: Albert O. XAVIER.

US Ambassador to Grenada: (Vacant).

Permanent Representative to the UN: Dr. Lamuel A. STANISLAUS.

IGO Memberships (Non-UN): Caricom, CDB, CWTH, EEC(L), *EIB,* ICCO, NAM, OAS, OECS, OPANAL, SELA.

GUATEMALA

Republic of Guatemala
República de Guatemala

Political Status: Independent Captaincy General of Guatemala proclaimed 1821; member of United Provinces of Central America, 1824–1838; separate state established 1839; most recent constitution adopted May 31, 1985, with effect from January 14, 1986.

Area: 42,042 sq. mi. (108,889 sq. km.).

Population: 6,043,559 (1981C, excluding adjustment for underenumeration), 9,173,000 (1988E).

Major Urban Centers (1981C): GUATEMALA CITY (749,784); Quezaltenango (72,745); Escuintla (73,688).

Official Language: Spanish.

Monetary Unit: Quetzal (official rate March 1, 1988, 2.50 quetzales = $1US).

President: Mario Vinicio CEREZO Arévalo (Guatemalan Christian Democratic Party); selected in run-off election of December 8, 1985, and inaugurated for a five-year term on January 14, 1986, succeeding Gen. Oscar Humberto MEJIA Victores.

Vice President: Roberto CARPIO Nicolle (Guatemalan Christian Democratic Party; inaugurated on January 14, 1986, for a term concurrent with that of the President).

THE COUNTRY

The northernmost of the Spanish-speaking Central American countries, Guatemala is also the most populous, with an annual growth rate close to 3 percent. The population, which is noted for its high proportion (more than 50 percent) of Indians, is concentrated in the southern half of the country. The other major population group, the *ladinos,* is made up of mestizos and assimilated Indians. Although Spanish is the official language, many of the Indians speak traditional languages, of which the most important are Caribe, Pocomam, Chol, Mam, Maya, and Quiché. The dominant religion is Roman Catholicism, but other faiths are permitted. Women constitute 14 percent of the official labor force, not including subsistence farming and unreported domestic service; employed women are concentrated in sales, clerical, and the service sector, and make up 40 percent of professionals. Female participation in government has traditionally been virtually nonexistent, although there are two women in the present cabinet.

The Guatemalan economy is still largely agricultural and coffee remains by far the single most important source of foreign revenue; cotton, bananas, and sugar are also exported. Significant progress has recently been registered in manufacturing, which, like commercial farming, is predominantly in the hands of *ladinos* and foreign interests. On the other hand, severe budgetary difficulties have persisted since the early 1980s, and a standby credit agreement concluded by the Ríos Montt regime with the International Monetary Fund was suspended following the 1983 coup. The economy was in severe decline during 1985, with inflation at a record average rate of nearly 40 percent for the 12 months prior to July 1986. Conditions thereafter improved measureably thereafter due in part to exceptionally high world coffee prices, with inflation dropping to less than 13 percent in 1987.

GOVERNMENT AND POLITICS

Political background. Guatemala, which dates its liberation from Spanish rule from 1821 and its independence as a nation from the breakup of the United Provinces of Central America in 1839, has existed through much of its national history under a series of prolonged dictatorships, one of the more recent being that of Gen. Jorge UBICO in 1931–1944. The deposition of Ubico in 1944 by an alliance of students, liberals, and dissident members of the military known as the "October Revolutionaries" inaugurated a period of reform. Led initially by President Juan José AREVALO and then by his successor, Jácobo ARBENZ Guzmán, the progressive movement was aborted in 1954 by rightist elements under Col. Carlos CASTILLO Armas. The stated reason for the coup was the elimination of Communist influence, Castillo Armas formally dedicating his government to this end until his assassination in 1957. Still another coup in 1963 overthrew the government of Gen. Miguel YDIGORAS Fuentes. A new constitution drawn up under Ydígoras' successor, Col. Enrique PERALTA Azurdia, paved the way for the election in 1966 of a civilian president, Julio César MENDEZ Montenegro, and the restoration of full constitutional rule with his inauguration on July 1, 1966. Méndez was succeeded as president by (then) Col. Carlos ARANA Osorio in an election held March 1, 1970, amid widespread terrorist activity that included the kidnapping of the nation's foreign minister.

The 1974 presidential and legislative balloting presented a confusing spectacle of charges and countercharges. Ini-

tially, it appeared that Gen. Efraín RIOS Montt, the candidate of the National Opposition Front (a coalition of the Christian Democrats and two minor parties) had placed first in the presidential race by a wide margin. Subsequently, however, the government declared that Gen. Kjell Eugenio LAUGERUD García, the candidate of the ruling right-wing coalition, had obtained a plurality of the votes cast. Since neither candidate was officially credited with a majority, the Congress, controlled by the conservatives, was called upon to designate the winner and named General Laugerud.

Similar confusion prevailed at the election of March 5, 1978, which evoked numerous allegations of fraud and threats of violence during a five-day period of indecision by the National Electoral Council, which eventually ruled that the center-right candidate, Maj. Gen. Fernando Romeo LUCAS García, had narrowly outpolled his right-wing opponent, Colonel Peralta Azurdia, with the latter's nephew, Gen. Ricardo PERALTA Méndez, in third place as the candidate of a center-left coalition. On March 13 the Congress, after intense debate, formally endorsed Lucas García as president-elect by a 34–27 vote.

At the election of March 7, 1982, Gen. Angel Aníbal GUEVARA, the candidate of a new center-right grouping styled the Popular Democratic Front, was declared the victor over three opponents separately representing center-left, centrist, and far-right interests, with no left-wing organizations participating. Two days later, the defeated candidates joined in a public demonstration protesting the conduct of the election and calling for annulment of the results. The appeal was rejected by outgoing President Lucas García and on March 23 a group of military dissidents seized power in a bloodless coup aimed at the restoration of "authentic democracy". On March 24 formal authority was assumed by a three-member junta consisting of General Ríos Montt, Brig. Gen. Horacio Egberto MAL-VONADO Schaad, and Col. Francisco Luis GORDILLO Martínez. Subsequently, on June 9, Ríos Montt dissolved the junta and assumed sole authority as president and military commander.

Although taking office with strong military and business support, Ríos Montt became increasingly estranged from both by a series of anticorruption and economic reform proposals, while incurring mounting opposition from the Catholic Church because of overt proselytizing by a US Protestant sect to which he belonged. Following a number of apparent coup attempts, he was ousted on August 8, 1983, by a group of senior army officers under Brig. Gen. Oscar MEJIA Victores, who promised that an election would be held in 1984 to pave the way for "a return to civilian life".

The balloting of August 1, 1984, in which 17 parties participated, was for a National Constituent Assembly, which drafted a new basic law (adopted on May 31, 1985) modeled largely on its 1965 predecessor. At the subsequent general election of November 3, the Christian Democratic Party obtained a slim majority of legislative seats and in a run-off presidential poll on December 8, its candidate, Mario Vinicio CEREZO Arévalo, defeated the National Center Union candidate, Jorge CARPIO Nicolle, by a 68–32 percent margin.

Since the early 1960s, Guatemala has been beset by guerrilla terrorism. Initially, two groups, the Rebel Armed Forces and the 13th of November Movement, operated in the country's rural northeast. After 1966, counterinsurgency actions drove them into the cities, generating urban violence which claimed the lives of many Guatemalans as well as some members of the foreign diplomatic community. In 1976 a new left-wing group, the Guerrilla Army of the Poor, claimed credit for a wave of increased terrorism following a devastating earthquake in February. Both left- and right-wing extremism intensified after the 1978 balloting, with the principal left-wing groups forming in January 1981 a unified military command called the Guatemalan National Revolutionary Unity (see Political Parties, below). By late 1983, a vigorous offensive launched by Ríos Montt and continued by his successor was reported to have substantially weakened the guerrillas, although at the cost of driving some 500,000 rural Guatemalans from their homes.

Constitution and government. The present constitution provides for the direct election for five-year, nonrenewable terms of a president and a vice president, with provision for a runoff between the two leading slates in the absence of a majority. The president is responsible for national defense and security, and names his own cabinet. Legislative power is vested in a unicameral National Congress, whose members can be reelected once after the passage of an intervening five-year term. The seven members of the Supreme Court are selected by the Congress for four-year terms, with the president of the Court supervising the judiciary throughout the country. Local administration includes the municipality of Guatemala City and 22 departments, each headed by a governor appointed by the president. In December 1986 Congress approved legislation organizing the departments into eight regions.

Foreign relations. The principal focus of Guatemalan foreign affairs has long been its claim to Belize (formerly British Honduras), which became independent in 1981. Guatemalan intransigence in the matter not only delayed Belizean independence but adversely affected relations with Britain, which dispatched military reinforcements to the area in 1975 after receiving reports that Guatemala was massing troops at the border. Despite talks in 1975 and 1976 and a joint commitment in 1977 to a "quick, just and honorable solution" to the controversy, no agreement was reached; when Britain granted independence to Belize in September 1981, the Lucas García government severed all diplomatic ties with London and appealed unsuccessfully to the UN Security Council to intervene (see entry under Belize). In August 1984, representatives of the three leading groups offering presidential candidates for the forthcoming election met in Washington with US officials to formulate a policy that would permit formal recognition of Belize and withdrawal of the British "trip wire" force. While no immediate results were forthcoming, the conciliatory posture was continued by the Vinicio Cerezo administration, which took office late in the year, and direct discussions were held with Belizean representatives at Miami, Florida, in April 1987. Meanwhile, consular relations with Britain were resumed in August 1986, with full diplomatic ties restored the following January.

Generally cordial relations with the United States yielded crucial military and other aid that supported relatively successful counterinsurgency efforts during the late 1960s. Subsequently, however, Washington evidenced concern over the diminishing effectiveness of such assistance in a context of increased polarization between Right and Left. In March 1977 Guatemala repudiated US military support after the Carter administration had announced that human-rights considerations would be utilized in setting allocation levels. Although military and economic assistance was resumed under the Reagan administration, all aid (except for cash sales) was suspended by Congress in November 1983 following publication of the Kissinger Commission report on Central America, which attributed thousands of recent civilian deaths to "the brutal behavior of the security forces". The program was again reinstituted in mid-1984, although Guatemalan officials complained that "the most important country in Central America", was receiving a fraction of the aid given to Honduras and El Salvador because of its neutrality in the Central American conflict.

Current issues. Upon assuming office on January 14, 1986, Vinicio Cerezo became the first civilian president of Guatemala since the administration of Méndez Montenegro in 1966–1970. Only days before, General Mejía had introduced a major economic reform program in accord with IMF guidelines and the new chief executive asserted in his inaugural speech that the country faced a period of "great austerity and sacrifice". In May the Congress approved a National Social and Economic Reform Plan, intended to curb excessive inflation and alleviate widespread unemployment, while in June the government announced an Integral Rural Development Plan to aid peasants in the acquisition of land, in addition to technical skills for its productive utilization.

In October 1986 President Cerezo signalled his willingness to enter into peace talks with the country's guerrilla organizations, including the Guatemalan National Revolutionary Unity (see under Political Parties, below). However, no formal contacts were made with the rebels prior to a series of "exploratory talks" at Madrid under Spanish government auspices in October 1987.

POLITICAL PARTIES

Political power in Guatemala has traditionally been personal rather than institutional, with parties developing in response to the needs or ambitions of particular leaders. In accordance with an electoral law enacted in January 1984, all parties wishing to contest the July 1984 Constituent Assembly elections were required to present 40,000 signatures in order to qualify for official registration. The first 15 groups below (grouped roughly from rightist to center-leftist) were thus recognized, the center-leftist PSD and the leftist CGUP choosing not to participate. Following the November 1985 balloting, 9 parties were accorded legal registration, 7 (MLN, CAN, PID, UCN, PR, PDCG, PDCN) for having obtained more than 4 percent of the popular vote and 2 (PNR, PSD) for having won congressional representation, despite lesser vote shares. In early

1986 two previously registered right-wing formations, the anti-Communist Unification Party (*Partido de Unificación Anticomunista*— PUA) and the Emergent Movement for Harmony (*Movimiento Emergente de Concordia*— MEC), were disbanded.

Right-Wing Parties:

National Liberation Movement (*Movimiento de Liberación Nacional* — MLN). The origins of the MLN date back to the "Liberation Movement", headed by Carlos Castillos Armas, which ousted the Arbenez government in 1954. Retaining its early anti-Communist orientation, it favors close ties with the Roman Catholic Church but disclaims a reactionary philosophy, despite links to El Salvador's Nationalist Republican Alliance (Arena). MLN leader Mario Sandoval Alarcón was officially declared to be the runner-up in the 1982 presidential balloting; in 1984, the party formed an alliance with the CAN (below), which placed third in the popular vote, while obtaining a plurality in the Constituent Assembly. It obtained 6 congressional seats in 1985.

Leaders: Mario SANDOVAL Alarcón (former Vice President of the Republic and Secretary General of the Party), Julio AGUILAR (Assistant Secretary General).

Nationalist Authentic Central (*Central Auténtica Nacionalista*— CAN). Formerly known as the Organized Aranista Central (*Central Aranista Organizada*— CAO), the CAN is a right-wing group that joined with the PID and PR (below) in endorsing Lucas García for the presidency in 1978. It emerged as a significant political force by electing 35 mayors— more than any other party— at municipal balloting in April 1980, although running a distant fourth in the 1982 presidential race. It contested the 1984 Assembly election in coalition with the MLN and won 1 congressional seat in 1985.

Leaders: Mario DAVID García (1985 presidential candidate), Carlos ARAÑA Osorio, Héctor MAYORA Dawe (Secretary General), Danillo PARINELLO (Assistant Secretary General).

Institutional Democratic Party (*Partido Institucional Democrático* — PID). The PID was formed in 1965 as a vehicle of conservative business interests led by former president Ydígoras Fuentes. It cooperated with the MLN during the 1970 and 1974 presidential campaigns but entered into a Broad Front (*Frente Amplio*) coalition with the PR (below) and the Organized Aranista Central in support of the 1978 candidacy of Lucas García. It supported the MLN's Mario Sandoval in the 1985 presidential campaign and obtained 6 seats in the congressional balloting.

Leaders: Donaldo ALVAREZ Ruíz, Jorge LAMPORT Rodil, Oscar Humberto RIVAS García (Secretary General), René ARENAS (Assistant Secretary General).

Center-Right Parties:

National Unity Front (*Frente de Unidad Nacional*— FUN). The FUN was organized as a coalition of the Christian Democrats (PDCG, below) and two smaller groups, the Authentic Revolutionary Party (*Partido Revolucionario Auténtico*— PRA) and the Popular Participation Front (*Frente de Participación Popular*— FPP), in support of the 1978 presidential candidacy of General Peralta Méndez. In early 1981, it endorsed Alejandro Maldonado Aguirre of the PNR (below) as its 1982 nominee. Subsequently, it formally declared for Gen. Angel Guevara, most of the Christian Democrats having withdrawn to continue their support of Maldonado. In 1985, it joined the MEC in endorsing the PUA's Leonel Sisniega.

Leaders: Col. Enrique PERALTA Azurdia (former President of the Republic), Gabriel GIRON Ortiz.

Union of the National Center (*Unión del Centro Nacional*— UCN). Founded in late 1983 by newspaper publisher Jorge Carpio Nicolle, the UCN expanded rapidly in 1984 and received substantial US media coverage. Its program is business oriented and opposes the inclusion of Guatemala in any US Central American military strategy. There were indications prior to the July 1984 balloting that the party had widespread support within the Guatemalan armed forces. After the UCN had placed second in the popular vote, Carpio Nicolle launched an active "American-style" campaign for the presidency in 1985, being defeated in run-off balloting by the PDCG's Vinicio Cerezo.

Leaders: Jorge CARPIO Nicolle (Secretary General), Ramiro de LEON Carpio (Assistant Secretary General).

National Renewal Party (*Partido Nacionalista Renovador*— PNR). Legally recognized in 1978, the PNR was organized by a number of MLN moderates after the parent party had endorsed the presidential candidacy of Peralta Azurdia. Its principal leader, Alejandro MALDONADO Aguirre, was credited with running third in the 1982 balloting, but fared poorly in 1985, winning only 3.2 percent of the vote, and was subsequently named to the Constitutional Court.

Leaders: Renán QUIÑONEZ Sagastume (Secretary General), Fermín GOMEZ (Assistant Secretary General).

Popular Democratic Force (*Fuerza Democrática Popular*— FDP). Organized in 1983 by former FUN leader, Francisco Reyes Ixcamey, the FDP unsuccessfully contested the 1984 election in coalition with the CND (below).

Leader: Francisco REYES Ixcamey.

National Democratic Coordination (*Coordinadora Nacional Democrática*— CND). The CND was formed in early 1984 by supporters of Gen. Angel Guevara, the declared winner of the 1982 presidential contest.

Leaders: Gen. Angel Aníbal GUEVARA, José Miguel BARRIOS.

Center Parties:

Revolutionary Party (*Partido Revolucionario*— PR). Advocating land reform, administrative change, and more rapid national development, the PR became the government party under President Méndez Montenegro in 1966, but its influence waned as Méndez became increasingly subjected to pressure from both Right and Left. Subsequently, it endorsed the unsuccessful candidacies of Mario Fuentes Pieruccini in 1970 and Col. Ernesto Paiz Novales in 1974. While the bulk of the party supported Lucas García in 1978, a faction led by Alberto Fuentes Mohr endorsed the Christian Democratic nominee, Gen. Ricardo Peralta Méndez. Fuentes Mohr was assassinated, reportedly by the right-wing ESA (below), in January 1979. In 1982, the PR joined with the PID and the FUN (below) in support of General Guevara; it ran fourth in the popular vote in 1984, electing 10 assemblymen. In 1985, it supported Jorge Serrano of the PDCN (below) for president.

Leaders: Jorge GARCIA Granados, Mario FUENTES Pieruccini (Secretary General), Victor Hugo GODOY (Assistant Secretary General).

Guatemalan Christian Democratic Party (*Partido Democracia Cristiana Guatemalteca*— PDCG). A party of liberal and reformist views, the PDCG was a member of the FUN in support of the 1978 presidential candidacy of Peralta Méndez. In 1982, most of its members joined with the PNR in a National Opposition Union (*Unión Nacional Opositora*— UNO) that endorsed Maldonado Aguirre. In 1984 the PDCG obtained a plurality of the popular vote, which yielded 20 Assembly seats. It secured a majority of 51 congressional seats in 1985, with its longtime leader, Vinicio Cerezo Arévalo defeating the UCN's Jorge Carpio in a run-off for the presidency.

Leaders: Mario Vinicio CEREZO Arévalo (President of the Republic), Dr. Francisco VILLAGRAN Kramer (former Vice President of the Republic), Alfonso CABRERA Hidalgo (Secretary General), Ricardo GOMEZ Gálvez and Catalina SOBERANIS Reyes (Assistant Secretaries General).

Populist Party (*Partido Populista*— PP). The PP is a small formation that failed to secure Assembly representation in 1984.

Leader: Asisco VALLADARES.

Center-Left Parties:

Civic Democratic Front (*Frente Cívico Democratico*— FCD). The FCD was formed in February 1984 by PDCG dissident Danilo Barillas and a number of social democratic political committees that were unable to secure individual registration; its members also include the Indian members of Ríos Montt's Council of State. It formed an electoral coalition with the parent party in January 1985.

Leaders: Danilo BARILLAS, Jorge GONZALEZ del Valle.

Democratic Party of National Cooperation (*Partido Democrático de Cooperación Nacional*— PDCN). Like the FCD, the PDCN was organized as an umbrella for a number of political groups unable to register separately as parties prior to the 1984 balloting. In 1985, it joined the PR in an electoral alliance that won 11 congressional seats. Subsequent to the poll, its presidential candidate, Jorge SERRANO Elias, a prominent evangelical Protestant, withdrew from the party to form a new group, the **Movement for Social Action** (*Movimiento de Acción Social*— MAS).

Leaders: Rolando BAQUIX Gómez (Secretary General), Miguel Angel SOLORZANO (Assistant Secretary General).

Democratic Alliance (*Alianza Democrática* — AD). The AD is a left-oriented grouping of otherwise uncertain political commitment that was formed by former congressional deputy Leopoldo Urrutia and a number of university figures in 1983.

Leader: Leopoldo URRUTIA.

United Revolutionary Front (*Frente Unido de la Revolución* — FUR). The FUR is the successor to the former Revolutionary Democratic Union (*Unión Revolucionaria Demócratica* — URD), founded by Francisco Villagrán Kramer as a breakaway group from the PR. The Front, although not officially registered as a participant in the 1978 election, supported the candidacy of Lucas García. In March 1979, only a few days after the FUR had joined with the PR and a number of center-left groups in forming the Democratic Front against Repression (see under CGUP, below), FUR leader Manuel Colom Argueta was assassinated. Following the subsequent killing of other leaders and activists, including Supreme Court Justice Alfonso Rodríguez Serrano, who had been proposed as a moderate-left presidential candidate, the FUR refused to participate in the 1982 election. It regrouped as a coalition that included the **Humanistic Movement of Democratic Integration** (*Movimiento Humanista de Integración Demócratica* — MHID), led by Victoriano ALVAREZ; the **October 20 Movement** (*Movimiento 20 de Octubre*), led by Marco Antonio VILLAMAR Contreras; and the **New Force** (*Fuerza Nueva* — FN), led by Carlos Rafael SOTO in supporting the presidential candidacy of Mario Solórzano of the PSD (below).

Leaders: Edmundo LOPEZ Duran, Augusto TOLEDO Peñate.

Democratic Socialist Party (*Partido Socialista Demócratico* — PSD). The PSD is a center-left grouping affiliated with the Socialist International that had gone underground in 1979 after the murder of many of its leaders and did not participate in the 1984 Assembly election. It won 2 congressional seats in 1985.

Leaders: Mario SOLORZANO Martínez (Secretary General and 1985 presidential candidate), Luis ZURITA Tablada (Assistant Secretary General).

Left-Wing Front:

Guatemalan Committee of Patriotic Unity (*Comité Guatemalteco de Unidad Patriótica* — CGUP). The CGUP was organized at Mexico City, Mexico, in February 1981 as an opposition front consisting primarily of (1) the **Democratic Front against Repression** (*Frente Democrático contra la Represión* — FDCR), formed initially in cooperation with the FUR but subsequently, under the leadership of Rafael GARCIA, with close links to the guerrilla organization ORPA (see under URNG, below); (2) the **January 31 Popular Front** (*Frente Popular 31 de Enero* — FP-31), with links to the EGP (see also URNG, below); and (3) a number of individual members of the FUR, the PDS, and the **Committee for Peasant Unity** (*Comité de Unidad Campesina* — CUC).

While denying that the organization was designed to serve as the political arm of any guerrilla group, the CGUP leadership endorsed the basic program of the URNG; it has refused to take part in recent elections because of anticipated "fraud and corruption" in addition to fears for the safety of its members.

Leader: Luís TEJERA Gómez.

Clandestine and Guerrilla Groups:

Guatemalan Labor Party (*Partido Guatemalteco del Trabajo* — PGT). In effect the Communist Party of Guatemala, the PGT has been banned since the overthrow of the Arbenz government in 1954. With virtually no influence on national elections, but with considerable appeal to students and intellectuals, it has endorsed the strategy of the Rebel Armed Forces (see URNG, below) while supporting its own "action arm", the *Fuerzas Armadas Revolucionarias*. A dissident faction, the **PGT-Leadership Nucleus** (PGT-LN), headed by Mario SANCHEZ, insists that the party itself must be the principal organ for armed struggle, and is formally aligned with the UNRG.

Leader: Carlos GONZALEZ (General Secretary).

Guatemalan National Revolutionary Unity (*Unidad Revolucionaria Nacional Guatemalteca* — URNG). The URNG was formed in January 1981 as an umbrella organization designed to provide various guerrilla groups, primarily those listed below, with a unified military command. In early 1985, it announced a program of intensified action, with numerous army casualties being reported during the remainder of the year.

Leader: Raúl MOLINA Mejía.

Rebel Armed Forces (*Fuerzas Armadas Rebeldes* — FAR). Founded in 1963 by dissidents of the extremist "13th of November Movement", the FAR claimed credit for the assassination of US Ambassador John Gordon Mein in August 1968. After being relatively quiescent for a number of years, the group resumed guerrilla activity in early 1978. Its most publicized recent actions were the 1983 kidnapping of the sisters of Ríos Montt (in June) and of Mejía Victores (in September), both of whom were released in late October.

Leaders: Pablo MONSANTO, Nicolas SIS.

Guerrilla Army of the Poor (*Ejército Guerrillero de los Pobres* — EGP). The EGP began functioning in the west-central department of Quiché in December 1975. Subsequently, it acknowledged responsibility for a variety of terrorist activities, including the kidnapping of the Salvadoran ambassador to Guatemala, Col. Eduardo Casanova Sandoval in May 1977 and of former interior minister Roberto Herrera Ibargüen the following December. In mid-1980 it announced the formation of a spin-off unit, the **Ernesto Guevara Guerrilla Front** (*Frente Guerrillero Ernesto Guevara* — FGEG), operating in the department of Huehuetenango on the Mexican border.

Leaders: Rolando MORAN, Carmelo DIAZ.

Armed People's Organization (*Organización del Pueblo en Armas* — Orpa). Emerging formally in September 1979 after what it termed "several years of preparation" in the departments of Solalá and San Marcos, Orpa had become, by late 1980, second only to the EGP in the scope of its antigovernment guerrilla activity.

Leader: Rodrigo ASTURIAS (a.k.a. "Comandante Gaspar ILOM").

Anti-Communist Secret Army (*Ejército Secreto Anticomunista* — ESA). A right-wing group presumed to be an outgrowth of the former White Hand (*La Mano Blanca*), the ESA is reportedly linked to the more extreme faction of the MLN. It is known to maintain a "death list" of numerous left-wing activists and has been prominently involved in the escalation of political assassinations that began in late 1978. In early 1980 it issued a communiqué in which it threatened to kill 20 leftists for each assassination of a rightist.

Another right-wing formation, the **Squadron of Death** (*Escuadrón de la Muerte* — EM) is also active.

LEGISLATURE

The present legislative body is a unicameral **National Congress** (*Congreso Nacional*) of 100 members, 75 of whom are directly elected, with the remaining 25 selected on the basis of proportional representation. The Chamber sits for five years, with members eligible for reelection to one additional term only, after a five-year lapse. At the election of November 3, 1985, the Guatemalan Christian Democratic Party won 51 seats; the Union of the National Center, 22; the Revolutionary Party/Democratic Party of National Cooperation, 11; the National Liberation Movement and the Democratic Institutional Party, 6 each; the Democratic Socialist Party, 2; and the Nationalist Authentic Central and the Nationalist Renewal Party, 1 each.

President: José Ricardo GOMEZ Gálvez.

CABINET

President	Gen. Vinicio Cerezo Arévalo
Vice President	Roberto Carpio Nicolle
Ministers	
Agriculture	Rodolfo Augusto Estrada
Communications, Transport and Public Works	Mario López Estrada
Culture and Sports	Ana Isabel Prera Flores de Lobo

Defense	Gen. Héctor Alejandro Gramajo Morales
Economy	Lizardo Arturo Sosa López
Education	Eduardo Meyer Maldonado
Energy and Mines	Roland Castillo Contoux
Finance	Rodolfo Paiz Andrade
Foreign Relations	Alfonso Cabrera Hildago
Interior	Juan José Rodil Peralta
Labor and Social Security	Rodolfo Maldonado
Public Health and Social Welfare	Carlos Armando Soto Gómez
Urban and Rural Development	René Armando de León Schlotter
Special Affairs	Sara Mishaan Rossell
President, Central Bank	José Miguel Gaitan

NEWS MEDIA

Press. The following newspapers, all published at Guatemala City, are privately owned Spanish dailies, unless otherwise noted: *Prensa Libre* (69,000); *El Gráfico* (60,000); *Diario La Hora* (20,000); *Diario de Centroamérica* (15,000), official government publication; *Central American Report,* English-language weekly.

News agencies. The only domestic facility is the independent *Inforpress Centroamericana;* a number of foreign agencies maintain bureaus at Guatemala City.

Radio and television. Broadcasting is supervised by the government's *Dirección General de Radiodifusión y Televisión Nacional.* Of the approximately 90 radio stations, five are government operated and six offer educational programming. There are four commercial television stations. There were approximately 350,000 radio and 400,000 television receivers in 1987.

INTERGOVERNMENTAL REPRESENTATION

Ambassador to the US: Oscar PADILLA Vidaurre.

US Ambassador to Guatemala: James H. MICHEL.

Permanent Representative to the UN: Fernando ANDRADE-DIAZ Durán.

IGO Memberships (Non-UN): BCIE, CACM, Geplacea, IADB, ICAC, ICM, ICO, Intelsat, Interpol, ISO, IWTC, OAS, ODECA, OPANAL, PCA, SELA, UPEB.

GUINEA

Republic of Guinea
République de Guinée

Political Status: Independent republic since October 2, 1958; under one-party presidential regime until military coup of April 3, 1984.

Area: 94,925 sq. mi. (245,857 sq. km.).

Population: 5,781,014 (1983C), 6,279,000 (1988E).

Major Urban Centers (1972C): CONAKRY (525,671); Labé (418,648); N'Zérékoré (290,743); Kankan (264,684); Siguiri (253,758). There are no recent estimates and there is evidence that the 1972 figures may have been substantially inflated.

Official Language: French, pending adoption of Soussou or Malinké. (Six other tribal languages are also spoken).

Monetary Unit: Guinea Franc (market rate March 1, 1988, 300.00 francs = $1US). In January 1986, the currency was devalued by more than 90 percent, with the Guinea franc replacing the syli.

President of the Republic and Head of the Military Committee for National Recovery: Brig. Gen. Lansana CONTE; named president by the CMRN on April 5, 1984, following the deposition on April 3 of Lansana BEAVOGUI, who had been named Acting President upon the death of Ahmed Sékou TOURE on March 26.

THE COUNTRY

Facing the Atlantic on the western bulge of Africa, Guinea presents a highly diversified terrain that ranges from coastal flatlands to the mountainous Foutah Djallon region where the Niger, Gambia, and Senegal rivers originate. The ethnic groups composing the predominantly Muslim population include over 2 million Fulani (Fulah); over 1.25 million Malinké (Mandingo); over 500,000 Soussou; 350,000 Kissi; and 250,000 Kpelle. Although the Malinké have long been the dominant tribe, the current administration has been carefully balanced in ethnic representation. While women are responsible for an estimated 48 percent of food production, female participation in the military government is nonexistent.

The majority of the population is dependent upon subsistence agriculture. While bananas, coffee, peanuts, palm kernels, and citrus fruits are important cash crops, most foreign exchange is derived from mining. Guinea is the world's second largest producer of bauxite, its reserves being exploited largely with the assistance of foreign companies. There are also valuable deposits of iron ore, gold, diamonds, uranium, and oil, in addition to substantial hydroelectric capability. Despite these resources, the GNP per capita was only $320 in 1985, reflecting an economy weakened by a quarter of a century of Marxist-inspired management. In the last two years before his death, limited private enterprise was encouraged by Sékou Touré in an effort to alleviate the situation; following its post-Touré takeover, the CMRN announced a free-market economic policy and a series of economic liberalization measures involving banking and foreign investment. Development aid has since been obtained from a number of regional and European sources, notably France and Belgium.

GOVERNMENT AND POLITICS

Political background. Historically part of the regional kingdom of Ghana, Songhai, and Mali, Guinea was incorporated into the French colonial empire in the late nineteenth century. Post-World War II colonial policy led to increasing political activity by indigenous groups, and in 1947 the Democratic Party of Guinea (PDG) was founded. Under the leadership of Ahmed Sékou TOURE, the PDG pushed for independence and, following rejection of membership in the French Community in a referendum held September 28, 1958, Guinea became the first of France's African colonies to achieve complete independence. Since the PDG already held 58 of the 60 seats in the Territorial Assembly, Sékou Touré automatically became president upon establishment of the Republic on October 2, 1958. Although the Soviet Union came to Guinea's aid following the abrupt withdrawal of French technical personnel and a collateral crippling of the new nation's fragile economy, its nationals were expelled in 1961 after being charged with involvement in a teachers' strike.

Plots and alleged plots have dominated Guinea's history; at one time or another the United States, Britain, France, West Germany, the Soviet Union, and other countries have been accused of conspiring against the regime. The most dramatic incident occurred in November 1970 when Guinea was invaded by a force composed of Guinean dissidents and elements of the Portuguese army. The action was strongly condemned by the United Nations and resulted in a wave of arrests and executions. In July 1976, Diallo TELLI, the minister of justice and former secretary general of the Organization of African Unity (OAU), was arrested on charges of organizing an "anti-Guinean front" supported financially by France, the Ivory Coast, Senegal, and the United States. Observers viewed Telli's possible complicity in a conspiracy, coupled with evidence of discontent within the people's militia, as indicative of a potentially serious threat to the Touré regime (the severity of which reportedly prompted the flight of nearly one-quarter of Guinea's population to neighboring countries). Subsequently, French sources reported that Telli had been assassinated in prison while awaiting trial.

President Touré was sworn in for the fifth time on May 14, 1982, after an election five days earlier in which he was credited with close to 100 percent of the votes cast. Two years later, on March 26, 1984, Africa's longest-serving chief executive died while undergoing heart surgery in a Cleveland, Ohio, hospital. Prime Minister Lansana BEAVOGUI immediately assumed office as acting president, but on April 5 a group of junior military officers siezed power in a bloodless coup and announced the appointments of (then) Col. Lansana CONTE as president of the Republic and Col. Diarra TRAORE as prime minister. Despite Touré's legendary status, the military found themselves in control of what had been described as a "police state", with widespread corruption in the government and party bureaucracy and an economy "in shambles". While immediate action was taken by the postcoup administration to reduce political repression — over 1,000 political prisoners were released, press censorship was lifted, and freedom of speech and travel restored — the malfunctioning state-controlled economy presented a more intractable challenge.

In subsequent months, power struggles were reported between President Conté and the internationally visible Traoré, the former consolidating his power by abolishing the prime minister's post and demoting Traoré to education minister in a December cabinet reshuffle. Seven months later, on July 4, 1985, while President Conté was out of the country, army elements led by Traoré declared the dis-

solution of the "corrupt" Conté administration and occupied sections of Conakry. The coup attempt was quelled by loyalist forces prior to the president's return on July 5, most of those involved being arrested, pending trial by military courts. Although there was no official confirmation, it was widely assumed by mid-1986 that Traoré and his coconspirators had been executed.

Constitution and government. The 1982 constitution was suspended and the Democratic Party of Guinea dissolved by the Military Committee for National Recovery (*Comité Militaire de Redressement National* — CMRN) in the wake of the April 1984 coup. Guinea has since been ruled by a president and Council of Ministers named by the CMRN.

In a decree issued in May 1984, President Conté ordered that the name "People's Revolutionary Republic of Guinea", which had been adopted in 1978, be dropped in favor of the country's original name, the Republic of Guinea. Subsequently, he announced the formation of a "truly independent judiciary" and revival of the formerly outlawed legal profession. In August 1985, a Court of State Security was established, encompassing a supreme court judge, two military officers, and two attorneys, to try "crimes against the state".

The country is administratively organized into four main geographic divisions — Maritime, Middle, Upper, and Forest Guinea — that are subdivided into 33 regions and 175 districts; each region and district was formerly governed by a decision-making congress of the PDG. In April 1986, district council elections were held at Conakry as prototypical of a system of "truly representative" similar structures to be established throughout the country. Each council is to have six elected members, assisted by four elders designated by the local religious leader.

Foreign relations. President Touré's brand of militant nationalism and his frequent allegations of foreign-provoked conspiracy led to strained international relations, including diplomatic ruptures with France (1965–1975), Britain (1967–1968), and Ghana (1966–1973). By January 1978, however, Conakry had moved to ease long-standing tensions with its immediate neighbors. Shortly thereafter, during a meeting at Monrovia, Liberia, attended by the presidents of Gambia, Guinea, the Ivory Coast, Liberia, Senegal, and Togo, diplomatic relations with Senegal and the Ivory Coast were restored, with the participants pledging bilateral and multilateral cooperation in both political and economic spheres. In October 1980, Guinea acceded to the Mano River Union, formed seven years earlier to promote economic cooperation between Liberia and Sierra Leone, while in March 1982 Touré called for the unification of Guinea and Mali, arguing that economically the two countries were "two lungs in a single body". In recent years Conakry has also increased its visibility in the Economic Community of West African States (ECOWAS); in July 1985, despite an insurgent takeover of the Guinean capital, President Conté remained at the head of states' meeting at Lomé, Togo, long enough to deliver a scheduled address before returning home to restore order.

In December 1978, French President Giscard d'Estaing visited Guinea, the first Western leader to do so in over two decades. The extremely warm reception he received was viewed as part of a broad effort to scale down assistance from Soviet and other Eastern Bloc countries in favor of Western aid and investment. In keeping with the policy shift, President Touré made a number of trips to the United States, Canada, and Western Europe during 1979–1983. However, distrust of the "father of African socialism" and an overvalued local currency discouraged large-scale Western involvement. By contrast, in the wake of the April 1984 coup Prime Minister Traoré negotiated a broad aid package with France, while French and other foreign investment increased significantly upon the adoption of monetary and fiscal reforms recommended by the IMF.

Current issues. The Conté government's commitment to economic reform met with international praise in 1986 but drew domestic criticism. Following the closure of state-owned banks in favor of French commercial institutions, the administration announced that many state businesses would also be privatized or abandoned. The IMF responded by approving standby credit and rescheduling external debt payments. A three-year development plan was advanced, emphasizing small rural projects and help for locally owned enterprises, while a late-1987 bauxite pricing arrangement involving sales by the *Compagnie des Bauxites de Guinée* (CBG) is expected to reflect more accurately the free market price of the commodity.

In the face of unrebutted charges by Amnesty International that the Conté government was in flagrant violation of human rights because of the secret summary trial and summary execution of 60 former Sékou Touré supporters and relatives, domestic opposition to the Conakry regime continued to mount. In a defensive response to antigovernment activity Conté likened his predecessor to Hitler and accused "intellectuals" of fomenting discontent.

POLITICAL PARTIES

Prior to the April 3 coup, Guinea was a typical one-party state, according a monopoly position to the Democratic Party of Guinea (PDG) in all aspects of public life. Although the CMRN initially promised an eventual return to "democracy", all political party activity remained proscribed as of early 1987. Exile groups include the **Unified Organization for the Liberation of Guinea** (*Organisation Unifiée pour la Libération de la Guinée*—OULG), based mainly in the Ivory Coast, and a half-dozen formations headquartered in France.

LEGISLATURE

The 210-member People's National Assembly (*Assemblée Nationale Populaire*), elected from a single PDG list for a seven-year term on January 27, 1980, was dissolved in April 1984.

CABINET

President	Brig. Gen. Lansana Conté
Resident Ministers	
Forest Guinea (N'Zérékoré)	Maj. Mamadou Baldet
Maritime Guinea (Kindia)	Capt. Joseph Bagbo Zoumanigui
Middle Guinea (Labé)	Lt. Col. Sory Doumbouya
Upper Guinea (Kankan)	Maj. Kerfalla Camara
Delegate Ministers	
Economic and Financial Control	Kemoko Keita
Information, Culture and Tourism	Maj. Zaïnoul Abdiné Sanoussi
Missions	Capt. Abdou Rahmane Diallo
National Defense	Maj. Babacar N'Diaye
Ministers	
Administrative Reform and Civil Service	Mamouna Bangoura
Agriculture and Animal Resources	Maj. Alhousseny Fofana
Economy and Finance	Lamine Bolivogui
Foreign Affairs	Maj. Jean Traoré
Industry, Commerce and Crafts	Maj. Ousmane Sow
Interior and Decentralization	Maj. Henri Tofani
Justice	Basirou Barry
National Education	Dr. Saliou Koumbassa
Natural Resources and Environment	Ousmane Sylla
Plan and International Cooperation	Edouard Benjamin
Posts and Telecommunications	Hervé Vincent Bangoura
Public Health and Population	Dr. Pathe Diallo
Social Affairs and Employment	Maj. Jean Kolipé Lama
Transport and Public Works	Maj. Faciné Touré
Urbanism and Habitat	Bana Sidibé
Youth and Sports	Amadou Binani Diallo
Permanent Secretary of CMRN	Maj. Abou Camara
Governor, Central Bank	Kabine Kaba

NEWS MEDIA

All mass media are owned or controlled by the government.

Press. The press is subject to rigorous government censorship. The following are published at Conakry: *Horoya,* weekly, in French and local languages; *Journal Officiel de Guinée,* fortnightly government organ; *Le Travailleur de Guinée,* monthly organ of the National Confederation of Guinean Workers.

News agencies. The official news agency is *Agence Guinéenne de Presse* (AGP), which became operational in July 1986 as part of the UNESCO-supported West African News Agencies Development (WANAD) project. *Xinhua,* APN, and TASS are represented at Conakry.

Radio and television. The government-operated *Radiodiffusion Télévision Guinéenne* operates eight radio transmitting stations, with broadcasts in French, English, Portuguese, Arabic, and local languages; in 1987 there were approximately 200,000 receivers. Television broadcasting, introduced in 1977, reaches some 12,000 TV sets.

INTERGOVERNMENTAL REPRESENTATION

Ambassador to the US: Tolo BEAVOGUI.

US Ambassador to Guinea: Samuel Eldred LUPO.

Permanent Representative to the UN: Mohamed TRAORE.

IGO Memberships (Non-UN): ACCT, ADF, AfDB, BADEA, ECOWAS, EEC(L), *EIB,* IACO, IBA, IC, ICO, IDB, Intelsat, Interpol, MRU, NAM, OAU.

GUINEA-BISSAU

Republic of Guinea-Bissau
República da Guiné-Bissau

Political Status: Achieved independence from Portugal on September 10, 1974; under rule of Revolutionary Council following coup of November 14, 1980; present constitution adopted May 16, 1984.

Area: 13,948 sq. mi. (36,125 sq. km.).

Population: 767,739 (1979C), 924,000 (1988E).

Major Urban Center (1979C): BISSAU (109,486).

Official Language: Portuguese (several local languages are also spoken).

Monetary Unit: Guinea Peso (market rate March 1, 1988, 650.00 pesos = $1US).

President of the Council of State: Brig. Gen. João Bernardo (Nino) VIEIRA; served as Vice President of the Republic, 1977–1978; designated Principal Commissioner (Prime Minister) by the former Council of State on September 28, 1978; leader of military coup that deposed President Luis de Almeida CABRAL on November 14, 1980; elected by the National Assembly to a five-year term as President of revived Council of State on May 16, 1984.

Vice President: Col. Iafai CAMARA; designated Second Vice President by the Council of State on May 16, 1984; named Vice President following the arrest of First Vice President Col. Paulo Alexandre Nunes CORREIA on November 7, 1985.

THE COUNTRY

Situated on the west coast of Africa between Senegal on the north and Guinea on the south, the Republic of Guinea-Bissau also includes the Bijagóz Archipelago and the island of Bolama. The population is primarily of African descent (principal tribes include the Balante, Fulani, Mandyako, and Malinké), but there are smaller groups of mulattoes, Portuguese, and Lebanese. The majority continues to follow traditional religious beliefs; however, there is a significant Muslim population and a small Christian minority.

Agriculture continues to employ the vast majority of the population, with peanuts typically producing two-thirds of export earnings. Other important exports are palm products, fish, and cattle, while such crops as cotton, sugar, and tobacco have recently been introduced in an effort to diversify the country's output. Industry is dominated by state enterprises and mixed ventures, while the chief mineral resource may be petroleum (the extent of on- and offshore reserves is uncertain, although a number of Western oil companies have signed contracts with the government for continuing exploration). Economic development has been hindered by insufficient capital, skilled labor, and transport facilities. Real GNP has been estimated to have declined by an average of 2.1 percent a year since the mid-1970s, and the country remains one of the poorest in the world, with a per capita income of approximately $220 in 1985.

GOVERNMENT AND POLITICS

Political background. First discovered by the Portuguese mariner Nuno Tristão in 1446, the territory long known as Portuguese Guinea did not receive a final delimitation of its borders until 1905. Initially, the country was severely exploited by slave traders, and consequent hostility among the indigenous peoples resulted in uprisings in the early twentieth century. The area was eventually pacified by military means and in 1952 was formally designated as an Overseas Province of Portugal.

In 1956 a group of dissatisfied Cape Verdeans under the joint leadership of Amílcar CABRAL, Luis de Almeida CABRAL, Aristides PEREIRA, and Ralph BARBOSA formed the African Party for the Independence of Guinea and Cape Verde (PAIGC). Failing to win concessions from the Portuguese, the PAIGC, with assistance from Warsaw Pact nations, initiated an armed struggle in 1963 and by the early 1970s claimed to control two-thirds of the mainland territory. On January 20, 1973, Amílcar Cabral was assassinated at Conakry, Guinea, allegedly by PAIGC dissidents but with the apparent complicity of the Portuguese military. Six months later, Cabral's brother Luis and Aristides Pereira were confirmed as party leaders by a PAIGC congress.

A government was formally organized and independence declared on September 23–24, 1973. The Portuguese authorities claimed the move was a "propaganda stunt", but the coup in Portugal in April 1974 led to an informal ceasefire and negotiations with the rebel leaders. Although the talks failed to resolve the status of the Cape Verde Islands, an agreement signed August 26, 1974, provided for the independence of Guinea-Bissau as of September 10, 1974, and the removal of all Portuguese troops by October 31.

In the first balloting since independence, 15 regional councils were elected during December 1976 and January 1977, the councils in turn selecting delegates to a second National People's Assembly, which convened in March 1977; Cabral was reelected president of the Republic and of the 15-member Council of State, while (then) Maj. João Bernardo VIEIRA was designated vice president of the Republic and reconfirmed as president of the Assembly. Vieira became principal commissioner (prime minister) on September 28, 1978, succeeding Maj. Francisco MENDES, who had died accidentally on July 7.

The principal political issue of the late 1970s was a projected unification of Cape Verde with Guinea-Bissau, many mainland leaders — including President Cabral and other high officials of the binational PAIGC — being Cape Verdean *mestiços*. On November 10, 1980, an extraordinary session of the National People's Assembly adopted a new constitution that many Black Guineans saw as institutionalizing domination by islanders, and four days later a coup led by Vieira, a native Guinean, deposed the president. On November 19 the Council of State and the Assembly were formally dissolved by a Revolutionary Council that designated Vieira as head of state and, on the following day, announced a provisional cabinet, all but one of whose members had served in the previous administration. Shortly thereafter, President Vieira identified the basic reasons for Cabral's ouster as the country's social and economic difficulties, including severe food shortages; "progressive abandonment of the principle of democratic centralism"; and "corruption of the meaning of unity between Guinea-Bissau and Cape Verde".

At a PAIGC conference in November 1981, it was announced that presidential and legislative elections under a new constitution would be held in early 1982 and that the party would retain its existing name, despite the fact that in the wake of the coup its Cape Verdean wing had formally repudiated the goal of unification with the mainland (see entry under Cape Verde Islands). In May 1982, President Vieira instituted a purge of reputed left-wingers within the government and the PAIGC, and named Victor SAUDE Maria as prime minister, a post that had been vacant since the 1980 takeover. Continued instability persisted for the next two years, culminating in the ouster of Saúde Maria on March 8, 1984, for alleged anti-state activity. The return to constitutional rule followed on March 31 with the election of eight regional councils which, in turn, chose 150 deputies to a new National People's Assembly. The Assembly convened on May 14 and two days later approved a new basic law that combined the offices of head of state and chief of government into the presidency of a revived Council of State, to which Vieira was unanimously elected.

A further attempt to overthrow the Vieira regime was reported on November 7, 1985, when security forces arrested some 50 individuals, including the first vice president, Col. Paulo Alexandre Nunes CORREIA, and a number of other prominent military and civilian officials, who were apparently opposed to economic austerity moves and upset by a military anticorruption drive. Despite international appeals for clemency, Correia and five of his associates were executed in July 1986.

Constitution and government. The constitution of May 1984 gives the PAIGC the right to define "the bases of state policy in all fields"; for legislative purposes it recreates the National People's Assembly, members of which are designated by eight regional councils. The Assembly elects a 15-member Council of State, whose president serves as head of state and commander in chief of the armed forces. The president and vice presidents are members of the government, along with ministers, secretaries of state, and the governor of the National Bank.

A 1976 merger of the Guinea-Bissau legal structure with that of Cape Verde was effectively voided in the wake of the 1980 takeover, although participation in a number of interministerial commissions involving all five of the lusophone African states has continued.

Foreign relations. During the struggle for independence, Guinea-Bissau received economic and military assistance from many Communist countries, including the Soviet Union, Cuba, and China. A subsequent deterioration in relations with the USSR because of alleged encroachment upon the country's fishing grounds appeared to have been reversed in early 1978 with a promise of Soviet assistance in modernizing the country's fishing industry. In May 1982, on the other hand, President Vieira replaced two strongly pro-Soviet cabinet ministers with Western-trained "technocrats" and appealed for development aid from non-Communist sources.

In November 1980, Guinea was the first country to recognize Guinea-Bissau's Revolutionary Council; earlier disputes over offshore oil exploration rights had been defused by former Guinean President Sékou Touré's announcement that Guinea would cooperate with other African states in developing on- and offshore resources. Similar controversy with Senegal erupted in early 1984, involving questions about the legality of offshore borders drawn by the French and Portuguese governments before independence. In February 1985, the World Court offered a settlement of the Bissau-Conakry border question which was accepted by both governments, while in March a meeting between Vieira and Senegalese President Diouf resulted in assignment of the latter dispute to an ad hoc international tribunal.

A meeting with President Pereira of Cape Verde in Mozambique on June 17–18, 1982, yielded an announcement that diplomatic relations would be restored. Subsequently, both leaders participated in annual Portuguese African summit meetings. Despite "reconciliation", the unification sought by Cabral became more and more distant as island influence was purged from the mainland party, with no reference to eventual merger being mentioned in the 1984 Guinea-Bissau constitution. At the seventh summit meeting of the five lusophone African states in May 1987, the major issue was the continued, united opposition to South African *apartheid*.

Current issues. President Vieira, his popular support apparently undiminished by an uneasy political situation and by international outcries over the execution of those charged with complicity in the 1985 coup attempt, tried to strengthen his position further with a major cabinet shakeup in July 1986. In May 1987 Bissau officially denied rumors that 20 army officers had been arrested for involvement in another potential coup. President Vieira, returning to the capital on August 4 after extended medical treatment in Europe, called the rumors "unfounded".

The IMF, which has been working with the Vieira regime for four years, renewed its call for reforms to deal with a "deteriorating" economic situation. The government responded by lifting trade restrictions and privatizing import and export activity. Plans were also announced to promote agricultural modernization in villages, with local committees being given more leeway in implementing official policies.

On May 3, 1987, the Vieira government announced that it would devalue the peso by 145 percent in order to "reflect its real value", and, as part of a continuing austerity program, would dismiss over 5,000 civil servants by the end of 1989. Concurrently, the government's latest four-year plan (1988–1991) targeted agricultural development as the country's top priority, while an agreement was announced with the World Bank for a structural adjustment loan of $15 million.

POLITICAL PARTIES

Government Party:

African Party for the Independence of Guinea and Cape Verde (*Partido Africano da Indepêndencia da Guiné e Cabo Verde* — PAIGC). Formed in 1956 by Amílcar Cabral and others, the PAIGC established external offices at Conakry, Guinea, in 1960 and began armed struggle against the Portuguese authorities in 1963. The only lawful party since independence, the PAIGC is formally committed to the principle of "democratic centralism". Its policy-making and administrative organs include a Central Committee (the Supreme Council of the Struggle), a National Council, a Permanent Committee, and a Secretariat.

Until the coup of November 1980, the party leadership was binational, with Aristides Pereira, president of Cape Verde, serving as secretary general and President Luis Cabral of Guinea-Bissau as deputy secretary. On January 19, 1981, the Cape Verdean branch decided to break with the mainland organization, proclaiming, on the following day, an autonomous African Party for the Independence of Cape Verde (PAICV).

At the fourth PAIGC congress on November 10–14, 1986, General Vieira was elected to a new four-year term as secretary general; also elected was a new Central Committee of 60 regular and 10 alternate members and a restructured Politburo of 12 full and 4 alternate members.

Leaders: Brig. Gen. João Bernardo VIEIRA (Chairman of the Council of State and Secretary General of the Party), Dr. Vasco CABRAL (Permanent Secretary of Central Committee).

Opposition Groups:

Prior to the 1980 coup there were no opposition groups known to be operating within the country, although the remnants of a Front for the Liberty and Independence of Guinea-Bissau (*Frente para à Libertação e Indepêndencia da Guiné-Bissau* — Fling), a group opposed to the unification of Cape Verde and the mainland, were headquartered at Dakar, Senegal. In March 1981 it was announced that Fling had been dissolved, its militants being accepted into the PAIGC.

In November 1981, it was reported that a group of politicians ousted in the coup had organized a **Front for National Unity and Development** (*Frente para Unidade Nacional e Desenvolvimento* — FUND). FUND accused the Vieira regime of "incompetence" and of yielding to "external pressures", while declaring its loyalty to the original principles of the PAIGC, as expounded by Amílcar Cabral.

In November 1986, the formation of a **Guinea-Bissau Bafata Resistance Movement** under the leadership of Dr. Domingos Fernandes GOMES, a former director of Bissau's central hospital, was announced at Lisbon. According to Gomes, the group would fight "for the creation of a lay state, inspired by the merits of a state of democratic law and a pluralist democracy in Guinea-Bissau".

LEGISLATURE

The 150-member National People's Assembly (*Assembléia Nacional Popular*) was dissolved by the Revolutionary Council on November 19, 1980, but revived on May 14, 1984, with members designated by eight popularly elected regional councils.

President: Carmen PEREIRA.

CABINET

President	Brig. Gen. João Bernardo Vieira
Vice President	Col. Iafai Camara

Ministers of State

Armed Forces	Col. Iafai Camara
Justice	Nicandro Pereira Barreto
Presidency (Economic Affairs)	Tiago Aleluia Lopes
Rural Development and Fisheries	Carlos Correia

Ministers

Civil Service, Labor and Social Security	Henriqueta Godinho Gomes
Commerce and Tourism	Col. Manuel Dos Santos
Economic Coordination, Planning and Interantional Cooperation	Bernard Cardoso
Education, Culture and Sports	Dr. Fidelis Cabral d'Almada
Finance	Victor Freire Monteiro
Foreign Affairs	Julio Semedo
Information and Telecommunications	Mussa Djassi
National Security and Public Order	Maj. José Alfaia Pinto Pereira
Natural Resources and Industry	Filinto de Barros
Planning	Bartolomeu Simões Pereira
Public Health	Alexandre Nunes Correia
Public Works	Maj. Avito da Silva

Resident Ministers

Eastern Province	Malam Bacai Sanha
Northern Province	Mario Cabral
Southern Province	Luis Oliveira Sanca
Minister-Governor, Central Bank	Pedro Godinho Gomes

NEWS MEDIA

Press. The following are published at Bissau: *Voz da Guiné* (6,000), daily; *Nô Pintcha,* (6,000), thrice-weekly official government publication.

Radio and television. Radio programming is offered by the government's *Radiodifusão Nacional da República da Guiné-Bissau;* broadcasts are principally in Portuguese. In 1987 there were approximately 26,000 radio receivers. Television service is expected to begin in June 1988, with initial broadcasting capability limited to Bissau.

INTERGOVERNMENTAL REPRESENTATION

Ambassador to the US and Permanent Representative to the UN: Alfredo Lopes CABRAL.

US Ambassador to Guinea-Bissau: John Dale BLACKEN.

IGO Memberships (Non-UN): *ACCT,* ADF, AfDB, AGC, BADEA, CILSS, ECOWAS, EEC(L), *EIB,* IC, IDB, NAM, OAU.

GUYANA

Cooperative Republic of Guyana

Political Status: Formerly the colony of British Guiana; independent member of the Commonwealth since May 26, 1966; under republican regime instituted February 23, 1970; present constitution approved February 11, 1980, with effect from October 6.

Area: 83,000 sq. mi. (214,969 sq. km.).

Population: 758,619 (1980C), 801,000 (1988E).

Major Urban Center (1976E): GEORGETOWN (72,000; urban area, 187,600).

Official Language: English.

Monetary Unit: Guyana Dollar (market rate March 1, 1988, 20.00 dollars = $1US).

Executive President: Hugh Desmond HOYTE (People's National Congress); appointed First Vice President on August 12, 1984, succeeded to the presidency on August 6, 1985, upon the death of Linden Forbes Sampson BURNHAM (People's National Congress); elected to a full five-year term on December 9.

First Vice President and Prime Minister: Hamilton GREEN (People's National Congress); appointed Vice President for Public Welfare on December 31, 1980; reappointed as Vice President for Social Infrastructure on August 12, 1984; succeeded Hugh Desmond HOYTE as First Vice President and Prime Minister on August 6, 1985.

Vice President and Deputy Prime Minister for Education and Social Development: Viola BURNHAM (People's National Congress); appointed on August 17, 1985.

Vice President and Deputy Prime Minister for National Development: Ranji CHANDISINGH (People's National Congress); appointed on August 12, 1984.

THE COUNTRY

Noted for its dense forests and many rivers, Guyana, whose name is an Amerindian word meaning "land of waters", is situated on the northern Atlantic coast of South America, with Venezuela and Suriname on the west and east, and Brazil on the south and southwest. The majority of inhabitants are concentrated along the narrow coastal belt, the only area suitable for intensive agriculture. Most of their ancestors arrived during the centuries of British colonial rule: Negro slaves before 1800 and East Indian plantation workers during the nineteenth century. At present, about 50 percent of the population is of East Indian origin, mainly engaged in agriculture; 31 percent is African, primarily urban-dwelling; 12 percent is of mixed blood; 4 percent is indigenous Indian; and the remainder is European. The principal religions are Christianity (50 percent), Hinduism (30 percent), and Islam (15 percent). In 1982, 27 percent of adult women were in the paid labor force, mainly concentrated in agriculture and cottage industry; female participation in national government is close to 20 percent, with substantially less representation at the local level.

The economy is based primarily on agriculture, with sugar and rice being the principal crops, but exploitation of mineral resources, including bauxite, alumina, gold, diamonds, and manganese, has become increasingly important. Bauxite mining and the sugar industry were nationalized in the mid-1970s and about 80 percent of the country's productive capacity was within the public sector

(with cooperatives accounting for another 10 percent) by 1982, when a reversal of the trend began. Since 1975, Guyana has experienced severe economic difficulty, with falling export prices generating large balance-of-payments deficits and shortages of basic commodities creating a vast underground economy supported by widespread smuggling. Faced with one of the lowest per capita GNP rates in the Western Hemisphere, an external debt in repayment arrears, and extensive corruption and inefficiency, Prime Minister Hoyte launched an economic liberalization program in 1986 with "reconstruction" tactics that departed significantly from his predecessor's socialist policies.

GOVERNMENT AND POLITICS

Political background. Guyana's political history during its first decade of independence was largely determined by an unusual ethnic structure resulting from the importation of African slaves and, subsequently, of East Indian laborers to work on the sugar plantations during the centuries of British colonial rule. The resultant cleavage between urbanized Africans and rural East Indians was reflected politically in an intense rivalry between the Communist-led, East Indian-supported People's Progressive Party (PPP) of Dr. Cheddi B. JAGAN and the African-backed People's National Congress (PNC), led by Forbes BURNHAM, a former PPP leader who broke with Jagan in 1955. Jagan's party, with a numerically larger constituency, came to power in British Guiana under a colonial constitution introduced in 1953, but was removed from office later that year because of British concern over a veer toward communism. Jagan's party again emerged victorious in general elections held in 1957 and 1961, but was defeated in 1964, when the introduction of a new system of proportional representation made possible the formation of a coalition government embracing Burnham's PNC and the small United Force (UF). In spite of earlier internal disorders, Burnham's administration successfully negotiated with the British for independence and remained in office following the achievement of full Commonwealth status in 1966 and the adoption of a republican form of government in 1970. However, the reelection of the Burnham government in 1968 and 1973 generated widespread controversy. Contributing to opposition charges of fraud and withdrawal of the UF from the governing coalition was a revision of the electoral law to allow Guyanans residing overseas to vote.

The 1970 redesignation of Guyana as a "cooperative republic" attested to the PNC's increased commitment to socialism. In his "Declaration of Sophia", published on the tenth anniversary of his premiership, Burnham referred to the PNC as a "socialist party" committed to government land control, the nationalization of foreign business interests, and a domestic economy of three sectors, "public, cooperative, and private", with the cooperative sector predominant. He also called for revision of the nation's constitution to expunge the "beliefs and ideology of our former imperialist masters". Subsequently, in a referendum held July 10, 1978, over 97 percent of those voting were said to have approved extension of the legislature's term beyond its July 23 expiration date so that the PNC-dominated National Assembly could serve, additionally, as a constituent body to consider a series of drastic changes in the nation's basic law.

World attention focused on Guyana in late 1978 with the bizarre suicide-murder of over 900 members of the People's Temple commune at Jonestown following an investigation by US Congressman Leo J. Ryan, whose party was ambushed by cult members as it prepared to enplane at a northwestern airstrip on November 18. Subsequent reports indicated that the Burnham government had been unusually hospitable to a variety of dissident religious sects, including the House of Israel, a 7,000-member group of Black converts to Judaism headed by David HILL (known locally as "Rabbi Washington"). A number of the sects had been granted extensive tracts of land in the largely undeveloped interior, and some, including the House of Israel, had been politically active in support of the ruling PNC. (The favored status of the sects waned in 1986, after Hill and 3 others pled guilty to manslaughter in the 1977 death of a sect-member's husband and were sentenced to 20-years' imprisonment.)

Guyana's new constitution was declared in effect on October 6, 1980, with Burnham assuming the office of executive president and designating Ptolemy A. REID as prime minister. On December 15, in an election branded by an international team of observers as "fraudulent in every possible respect", the PNC was credited with an overwhelming popular mandate, and on January 1, 1981, the government was substantially expanded to include five vice presidents and additional ministers.

In the wake of worsening fiscal conditions, the regime faced mounting internal and external political challenges, culminating in the arrest by Canadian authorities in December 1983 of six persons, including a member of the Toronto-based right-wing Conservative Party of Guyana, who were charged with plotting to assassinate Burnham and other key officals. A number of subsequent leadership changes included the appointment, in August 1984, of Vice President Hugh Desmond HOYTE to succeed the reportedly ailing Reid as first vice president and prime minister, and the designation of pro-Soviet Ranji CHANDISINGH to succeed Reid as PNC general secretary.

President Burnham died on August 6, 1985, while undergoing surgery at Georgetown, and was succeeded by Vice President Hoyte, who was accorded a regular five-year mandate on December 9 in balloting that, as in 1980, yielded allegations of widespread fraud.

Constitution and government. The constitution of 1966 established Guyana as a parliamentary member of the Commonwealth under the sovereignty of the British queen. The monarchical structure was abandoned in 1970 in favor of a titular president elected by the National Assembly for a six-year term.

The 1980 constitution provides for a popularly elected chief executive with virtually unlimited powers, including the authority to appoint and dismiss an unspecified number of vice presidents (one serving as prime minister) and the right to veto all legislative enactments. The National Assembly includes 53 popularly elected members plus 12 members designated indirectly to represent regional and local interests. The judicial system consists of a Supreme

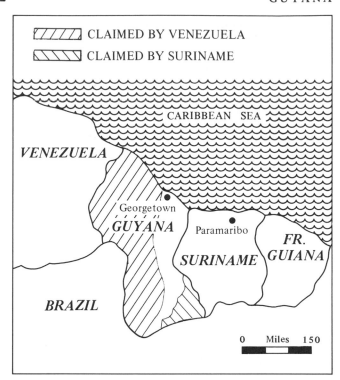

Court, encompassing a High Court and a Court of Appeal, and ten magistrates' courts, one for each judicial district. There are elected councils in the country's ten regions, including municipal administrations at Georgetown and New Amsterdam. Local councillors elect from their own membership a National Congress of Local Democratic Organs, which, together with the National Assembly, constitutes a deliberative body known as the Supreme Congress of the People of Guyana.

Foreign relations. In recent years Guyana has established diplomatic relations with the Soviet Union, the People's Republic of China, and other Communist countries while also strengthening its ties with nations in Sub-Saharan Africa. The country's major foreign-policy problem stems from boundary disputes with both its eastern and western neighbors. The disagreement with Suriname centers on the delineation of a riparian boundary between the two countries: Guyana claims that the boundary follows the Courantyne, while Suriname claims it follows the New River. The dispute with Venezuela is the most serious: Venezuela has long claimed all territory west of the Essequibo River, which amounts to more than half of Guyana's total area (see map). In 1966, the two countries agreed to settle the issue by diplomatic means, while in 1970, after talks had failed, Venezuela agreed to a 12-year moratorium on its claim. The 1970 protocol provided that if the dispute should not be resolved by September 18, 1982, it would be referred to an "appropriate international organ" or, failing agreement on such an organ, to the secretary general of the United Nations. In the wake of a series of border incidents that accompanied expiration of the moratorium, Venezuela rejected a Guyanan request to seek a ruling from the International Court of Justice and formally requested the mediation of UN Secretary General Javier Pérez de Cuéllar. In March 1983, Caracas announced that Guyana had acquiesced in the action, but no further progress was reported until February 1985, when the Venezuelan foreign minister indicated that his government was prepared to adopt a conciliatory attitude in furtherance of a "new spirit of friendship and cooperation" between the two countries. Although still unresolved at the conclusion of a November 1987 meeting of presidents Hoyte and Lusinchi at Georgetown, the issue was described as one that would continue to be addressed "with flexibility and understanding".

Current issues. Acknowledging that the economy was "virtually bankrupt", the administration implemented policy changes in 1986 to encourage private investment, relieve the foreign currency shortage, and stimulate the potentially lucrative gold, oil, and timber sectors. The immediate results were meager, however, with GDP increasing only 0.3 percent through the period.

In January 1987 a 56 percent devaluation of the Guyanan dollar yielded substantial price increases, while President Hoyte's efforts to negotiate an international "rescue package" were branded by the PPP as "genuflecting before the International Monetary Fund and the World Bank at the expense of the working people". Opposition sentiment was further inflamed by a major fuel crisis in October and a delay in revealing the recommendations of an Integrity Commission that had been established in 1986 to consider the need for a code of conduct in public life. The Commission identified electoral reform as one of Guyana's "acutely sensitive issues" and called for a dialogue between government and opposition leaders to enact needed reforms.

POLITICAL PARTIES

Government Party:

People's National Congress (PNC). The PNC was created by Forbes Burnham in 1957 after he had broken with PPP leader Cheddi Jagan. Primarily an urban-based party, it represents the African racial bloc of about one-third of the population, including most of the nation's intellectuals. Initially, it advocated a policy of moderate socialism, anticommunism, and hospitality to private investment, but an increasing swing to the Left, culminating in Prime Minister Burnham's 1974 "Declaration of Sophia" (see Political background, above), brought the PNC close to the opposition People's Progressive Party on most domestic issues. In 1987 President Hoyte rejected allegations of a shift to the Right, insisting that the PNC remained committed to socialism, while arguing that the latter, given local conditions, must follow an "innovative course". The PNC drew heavily on the overseas vote in securing a two-thirds legislative majority in 1973 and was accused of massive fraud in obtaining better than three-quarter majorities in 1980 and 1985.

Leaders: Hugh Desmond HOYTE (Executive President of the Republic), Hamilton GREEN (First Vice President and Prime Minister of the Republic), Viola BURNHAM (Vice President and Deputy Prime Minister of the Republic), Ranji CHANDISINGH (Vice President and Deputy Prime Minister of the Republic, and General Secretary of the Party).

Opposition Groups:

Patriotic Coalition for Democracy (PCD). The PCD was organized after the 1985 election by the following five parties, who promised to restore the "elective principle" in opposition to the PNC's alleged "defiance of the will of the overwhelming majority of the population".

People's Progressive Party (PPP). Launched in 1950 by Dr. Cheddi B. Jagan and his wife, Janet Jagan, the PPP began as an anticolonial party speaking for the lower social classes, but has come to represent almost exclusively the large East Indian racial group. It has consistently followed a pro-Soviet line, and at a June 1969 Moscow meeting of Communist party leaders, Dr. Jagan formally declared the PPP to be a communist party. It has long advocated state ownership of indus-

try but not collectivization of agriculture. While the PPP and other opposition groups charged that the PNC fraudulently manipulated the overseas vote in the 1973 election, Dr. Jagan offered his "critical support" to the PNC in August 1975. The PPP Central Committee narrowly approved participation in the December 1980 legislative balloting, at which the party was officially credited with winning 10 seats. It was awarded 8 seats in 1985.

Leaders: Dr. Cheddi B. JAGAN (General Secretary), Janet JAGAN (Executive Secretary), Ram KARRAN.

Working People's Alliance (WPA). Organized in late 1976 following the tender of PPP support to the ruling PNC, the WPA began as an alliance of left-wing groups that included the African Society for Cultural Relations with Independent Africa (ASCRIA), founded by Eusi Kwayana during his affiliation with the PNC. Three of its principal leaders, Dr. Omawale, Dr. Rupert Roopnarine, and Dr. Walter Rodney, were indicted on arson charges in July 1979, the last being killed by a bomb explosion in June 1980. The party has been described as having "the appearance of a genuine bridge across the racial barrier in Guyana" in that its membership is drawn from both the African and Indian ethnic communities. It refused to participate in the December 1980 election on the ground of anticipated irregularities. It campaigned in 1985, winning 1 seat.

Leaders: Eusi KWAYANA, Dr. Rupert ROOPNARINE, Moses BHAGWAN.

Democratic Labour Movement (DLM). Founded in 1982 as an affiliate of the small National Workers' Union, the DLM is a largely centrist formation that has called for a more integrated PCD structure than has been favored by either the PPP or WPA.

Leader: Paul Nehru TENNASSEE.

People's Democratic Movement (PDM). The PDM is a small centrist group founded in 1973.

Leader: Llewellen JOHN.

National Democratic Front (NDF). The NDF was formed in November 1985.

Leader: Joseph BACCHUS.

United Force (UF). A small party that represents conservative business and other interests, the UF favors racial integration and has found support from White, Amerindian, and other minority groups. Its programs have favored economic orthodoxy, closer ties to Western nations, and encouragement for private investment and foreign loans. The UP withdrew from the governing coalition in 1968 to protest the enfranchisement of the overseas voters. It failed to win any seats in the 1973 election but was credited with winning 2 seats in 1980, both of which it retained in 1985.

Leader: Marcellus Feilden SINGH.

Liberator Party (LP). The LP is a right-wing party formed in 1972 by a group of UF dissidents. In the 1973 balloting it obtained 2 seats, which were reassigned to the UF when the LP refused to participate in legislative sessions as a protest against alleged electoral fraud. It won no seats in 1980 or 1985.

Leaders: Dr. J.K. Makepeace RICHMOND (Chairman), Dr. Gunraj KUMAR.

Berbice Progressive Party (BPP). The BPP was launched in the central Corentyne area in September 1987 with a platform calling for a "new Guyana" under "genuine East Indian leadership". Its founders were not immediately revealed.

External Groups:

Conservative Party of Guyana (CPG). The CPG is a Canadian-based right-wing organization, whose leader was allegedly involved in a December 1983 plot to assassinate President Burnham.

Leader: Keshava Keith MOONASAR.

United Republican Party (URP). Also a right-wing group, the URP was reported to have been launched in early 1987 by a US-based former member of the UF.

Leader: Robert GANGADEEN.

LEGISLATURE

Under Guyana's present constitution, the unicameral **National Assembly,** which sits for five years barring dissolution by the president, consists of 65 members: 53 are directly elected under a system of proportional representation, 10 are separately elected by each of the regional councils, and 2 are designated by the National Congress of Local Democratic Organs. At the election of December 15, 1985 (the results of which, as in 1980, were disputed), the People's National Congress was awarded 54 seats (42 directly elective and all of the indirectly elective); the People's Progressive Party, 8; the United Force, 2; and the Working People's Alliance, 1.

Speaker: Sase NARAIN.

CABINET

Prime Minister	Hamilton Green
Deputy Prime Minister for Education and Social Development	Viola Burnham
Deputy Prime Minister for National Development	Ranji Chandisingh
Deputy Prime Minister for Planning and Development	William Haslyn Parris
Deputy Prime Minister for Public Utilities	Robert H.O. Corbin

Senior Ministers

Agriculture	Dr. Patrick Mackenzie
Communications and Works	Jules Ranenburg
Education, Environment and Food Policy	Deryck Bernard
Finance	Carl Greenidge
Foreign Affairs	Rashleigh Esmond Jackson
Health	Dr. Noel Blackman
Trade and Tourism	Winston Murray

Ministers

Agriculture	Vibert Parvattan
Forestry	Dharamdeo Sawh
Information and Public Service	Yvonne Harewood-Benn
Labor, Housing and Cooperatives	Seeram Prashad
Medical Education, Environment and Food Policy	Jaillal Kissoon
National Development	Urmia E. Johnson
Office of the President	Pandit Chintaman Gowkarran Sharma
Regional Development	Jeffrey Thomas
Governor, Bank of Guyana	Patrick Matthews

NEWS MEDIA

Press. Newspapers are indirectly censured through government control of newsprint, which was relaxed somewhat in 1986. The following are published at Georgetown: *Guyana Chronicle* (61,000 daily, 102,000 Sunday), state owned; *New Nation* (26,000), weekly PNC organ; *Mirror* (20,000 Sunday), PPP organ; *Stabroek News,* (15,000), independent weekly launched in December 1986; *The Catholic Standard* (10,000), weekly; *Guymine News* (8,000), weekly publication of Guyana Mining Enterprises, Ltd.

News agencies. The state-owned Guyana News Agency was established in 1981, following termination of an agreement with the Barbados-based Caribbean News Agency. TASS, *Prensa Latina,* and the Associated Press maintain bureaus at Georgetown.

Radio and television. There are two radio broadcasting stations, the government-controlled Guyana Broadcasting Service and Radio Demerara (a local associate of Rediffusion, Ltd., London). In 1987, there were approximately 360,000 radio receivers. There is no television service.

INTERGOVERNMENTAL REPRESENTATION

Ambassador to the US: Dr. Cedric Hilburn GRANT.

US Ambassador to Guyana: Theresa Anne TULL.

Permanent Representative to the UN: Samuel R. INSANALLY.

IGO Memberships (Non-UN): Caricom, CCC, CDB, CWTH, EEC(L), *EIB,* Geplacea, IADB, IBA, Interpol, ISO, NAM, SELA.

HAITI

Republic of Haiti
République d'Haïti

Political Status: Independent state proclaimed in 1804; republic since 1859; presently under military-civilian regime instituted in February 1986, pending implementation of constitution approved by referendum on March 29, 1987.

Area: 10,714 sq. mi. (27,750 sq. km.).

Population: 5,053,742 (1982C), 5,457,000 (1988E).

Major Urban Center (1983E): PORT-AU-PRINCE (721,000).

Official Languages: French, Creole.

Monetary Unit: Gourde (market rate March 1, 1988, 5.00 gourdes = $1US).

President: Lt. Gen. Henri NAMPHY; assumed power following ouster of Leslie F. MANIGAT (Assembly of National Progressive Democrats) on June 19, 1988.

THE COUNTRY

The poorest country, on a per capita basis, in the Western Hemisphere, Haiti occupies the western third of the mountainous Caribbean island of Hispaniola, which it shares with the Dominican Republic. Approximately 95 percent of the largely illiterate population is of pure African descent, with a small percentage of mulattoes and Whites. Roman Catholicism, which coexists with a folk religion based on various voodoo cults, is the official religion, but other faiths are permitted. Women constitute close to 50 percent of the agricultural labor force and 60 percent of the urban work force, concentrated in domestic service and manufacturing; female representation under the Duvalier regime was minimal, with the exception of the reputed "influence" of Jean-Claude Duvalier's wife, Michèle.

The economy has been handicapped by an underdeveloped social infrastructure and a paucity of mineral resources, the extraction of limited amounts of bauxite having ceased in 1983. Although the manufacturing sector has grown recently, with an emphasis on plants for assembly and reexport of imported components, agriculture remains the country's mainstay. Important crops include sugarcane, cacao, sisal, and especially coffee, the principal commodity, which accounts for about 30 percent of export earnings. In recent years, unemployment has frequently exceeded 50 percent, while declining coffee revenues have strained finances in a country in which much of the annual budget is normally derived from foreign aid.

GOVERNMENT AND POLITICS

Political background. Since a slaves' revolt that established Haiti in 1804 as the first independent republic in Latin America, the nation's history has been marked by violence, instability, and mutual hostility between Negroes and mulattoes. After a period of US military occupation (1915–1934), mulatto presidents held office until 1946, when power passed to a Black president, Dumarsais ESTIME. His moderate administration was terminated in 1950 by an army coup that prepared the way for the regime of another Black, Gen. Paul MAGLOIRE, who was also overthrown, in December 1956. Five interim regimes followed before François DUVALIER won the presidency in the election of September 1957. Contrary to expectations, the Duvalier administration quickly degenerated into a dictatorship, with Duvalier forcing an unconstitutional reelection in 1961 and being designated president for life in May 1964.

Throughout his reign Duvalier maintained a tight grip over the country. With most opponents in exile, the regime maintained a balance of terror using a blend of persuasion, voodoo symbolism, and a personal army of thugs and enforcers, the so-called *Tontons Macoutes* (Creole for bogeymen). In early 1971, Duvalier had the constitution amended to allow him to designate a successor; his son, Jean-Claude, was promptly named to the position and assumed the presidency following his father's death on April 21.

Beginning in mid-1977, the younger Duvalier appeared to yield somewhat under continuing US pressure to ameliorate the more corrupt and repressive aspects of his family's two decades of rule. Thus in November 1978, in return for substantially increased US aid, he ordered a series of budgetary and ministerial reforms. At the election of February 11, 1979, an independent candidate running on a human-rights platform (despite offering "critical support" for the regime) won an overwhelming victory against a government-endorsed opponent, while in an unprecedented act of public defiance, some 200 intellectuals issued a manifesto in June protesting censorship of plays and films. Most startling of all was the appearance at midyear of three new political parties (see Political Parties, below) after publication of a book by Grégoire EUGENE, a law professor, pointing out that such organizations were technically permissible under the Haitian constitution. By the end of the year, however, the period of liberalization appeared to have ended with the passage of a repressive press law

and increased attacks on dissidents by former members of the *Tontons Macoutes.*

The first municipal elections in 26 years were held in mid-1983. No opposition candidates presented themselves, several potential nominees having disappeared prior to the balloting. In August, the national legislature dissolved itself after accepting a new, presidentially drafted constitution. While balloting for a new chamber on February 12, 1984, witnessed the defeat of numerous Duvalierists, foreign observers were convinced that the government, wishing to create the appearance of change, had asked former incumbents not to campaign vigorously. Six months later, a regime-supportive National Progressive Party (PNP) was launched under legislation permitting partisan activity by groups agreeing to accept the life presidency. Earlier, extensive rioting had erupted in response to government misuse of food aid and manifest police brutality, yielding a press crackdown and the detention of several opposition politicians. In November, the government announced the discovery of a "communist" plot against the regime, in what was widely perceived as a bid for support from anticommunist donor nations, particularly the United States.

In early 1985, under visible pressure from both the United States and France (another substantial aid donor), the government released a number of political prisoners and in April President Duvalier announced a series of "democratic" reforms. These included the legalization of political parties, increased power for the National Assembly, and provision for a new post of prime minister, to be filled by presidential appointment from the parliamentary majority. However, restrictions on party registration ensured the exclusion of known regime opponents, while the life presidency remained intact.

Renewed rioting broke out in late November after several teenagers had been killed during an antigovernment demonstration at Gonaïves and in December a government reshuffle was announced that suggested a shift in the balance of power to an inner circle of Duvalierist hardliners. On January 8, 1986, all schools and universities were closed in response to a widespread student boycott movement, while the first major protest demonstration at the capital was dispersed by police ten days later. However, the disturbances intensified, and on January 31 a US White House spokesman told reporters that Duvalier had fled the country. The announcement proved premature, and it was not until February 7 that the president departed, with an entourage of family and close associates, on a US plane to France. The army chief of staff, Gen. Henri NAMPHY, immediately assumed power as head of a five-member National Council of Government (*Conseil National du Gouvernement* — CNG) that included two other officers and two civilians. On February 10, a 19-member provisional government was announced which, however, contained a number of prominent Duvalierists. On March 20, the one prominent anti-Duvalierist in the new administration, Haitian human rights leader Gérard GOURGUE, resigned from both the CNG and the justice ministry, alleging "resistance" to liberalization. General Namphy responded by excluding the Duvalierists from a reconstituted Council that included himself, (then) Col. Williams REGALA (the interior and defense minister), and Jacques FRANÇOIS (succeeded as foreign minister in a cabinet reshuffle on March 24 by retired general Jean-Baptiste HILAIRE).

In the face of continued unrest that, in the words of General Namphy, left the country "on the verge of anarchy . . . and civil war", it was announced on June 6 that municipal elections would be held in July 1987 and that a new government would be installed in February 1988, following presidential and legislative balloting the preceding November. In September an election was held for 41 of 61 members of a Constituent Assembly charged with drafting Haiti's 23rd constitution since independence. The new basic law, incorporating a number of safeguards to prevent the return of a Duvalier-type dictatorship, was overwhelmingly approved by a referendum on March 29, 1987.

By mid-1987 the Namphy regime had proven to be unwilling or unable to curb a mounting campaign of terror by former members of the *Tontons Macoutes* and the promised local elections were postponed. Presidential and legislative balloting commenced on the morning of November 29, but within hours was also called off because of widespread violence and voter intimidation. The four principal opposition leaders thereupon withdrew as presidential candidates and Leslie MANIGAT, a self-proclaimed "democratic centralist" who was widely believed to have the backing of the CNG, emerged from the rescheduled poll of January 17, 1988, with a declared majority of 50.3 percent.

On June 17 President Manigat attempted to remove General Namphy as army commander, but was himself overthrown by a military coup two days later. On June 20 Namphy announced the formal deposition of the Manigat administration, declaring that he would thenceforth rule by decree as the country's chief executive.

Constitution and government. The 1987 constitution provided for the sharing of power between a directly elected president who would serve no more than two five-year terms, a prime minister responsible to a legislature composed of a Senate and House of Representatives, and an independent judiciary. It divided the traditionally monolithic armed forces into distinct military and police components; accorded the universally spoken Creole language official status in addition to French; banned Duvalierists from public office for ten years; authorized an independent commission to supervise elections; asserted the previously nonexistent rights of free education, decent housing, and a fair wage; and eliminated official, but generally ignored sanctions against the practice of voodoo. The new basic law was effectively suspended by the coup of June 19, 1988.

Haiti is presently divided into nine departments, each headed by a presidentially appointed prefect and subdivided into *arrondisements* and communes.

Foreign relations. Despite its membership in the United Nations and a number of other international bodies, Haiti maintains no close ties with neighboring countries and has participated in few of the recent moves toward Caribbean economic and political integration. Haiti's most sensitive foreign affairs issue, the border relationship with the Dominican Republic, has been periodically aggravated by activities of political exiles from both countries. Port-au-Prince has exchanged ambassadors with many European and Latin American governments but does not have formal diplomatic relations with any Communist nation. Relations with the United States, which were briefly suspended in 1963, have fluctuated, the Duvalier government frequently using its votes in international bodies to bargain for increased foreign assistance from Washington.

In early 1983 long-standing litigation regarding the rights of Haitian refugee "boat people" being detained in Florida was resolved by a US landmark decision, which allowed some 1,700 detainees to apply for political asylum while establishing constitutional protection for those remaining incarcerated. In September 1985 Haiti concluded an agreement with the Bahamas that would require all illegal immigrants to register with Bahamian authorities, with only those resident in the islands before December 30, 1980, married to Bahamians, or owning real estate being permitted to remain; under the agreement, it was estimated that as many as 40,000 Haitians would be subject to expulsion.

Current issues. The visible circumstances surrounding General Namphy's ouster of President Manigat in June 1988 were not without irony. On June 14 Namphy ordered the reassignment of Col. Jean-Claude PAUL, a powerful infantry commander who had been indicted by a US grand jury for involvement in cocaine smuggling. Paul refused the order, which Namphy rescinded following presidential intervention. Three days later Manigat, evidently believing that he had Paul's support, directed that the general be placed under house arrest. However, Paul appears to have sided with Namphy in the showdown with Manigat, who was permitted to leave the country shortly after the coup of June 19. Namphy subsequently justified the action as arresting a "path toward dictatorship in its most brutal form".

Manigat, although described as a "passionate advocate of democracy" during an academic career that spanned 23 years of previous exile, had himself declared that there could be no viable resolution of Haiti's problems without the support of the army. Partly for this reason, but also because of the dubious validity of the January election, his inauguration on February 7 was boycotted by most opposition leaders and no foreign heads of state were in attendance, the United States and France being represented by their ambassadors to Port-au-Prince. Most American aid had been suspended following the abortive balloting of November 1987, although a State Department spokesman condemned the 1988 coup as a "serious blow to hopes for democracy [in Haiti]".

During 1986–1987 the CNG had made a strenuous effort to regain possession of the former dictator's fiscal plunder: upwards of $800 million that had been derived from the pocketing of tax revenues, kickbacks on government contracts, and siphoning from foreign loan funds. However, it was evident that Duvalier could not be forced to return in the absence of an extradition treaty between Haiti and France, while a French court dismissed a civil suit in June 1987 on the ground that its jurisdiction did not extend to misappropriation of funds by officials of foreign governments.

POLITICAL PARTIES

All parties were outlawed during the first six years of the François Duvalier dictatorship. In 1963 a regime-supportive National Union Party (*Parti de l'Unité Nationale*— PUN) was organized with an exclusive mandate to engage in electoral activity. Its Jean-Claudiste successor, the National Progressive Party (*Parti Nationale Progressiste* — PNP), was launched in September 1985. Six years earlier, three unofficial groups had surfaced: the first two opposition parties listed below, plus a Haitian National Christian Party (*Parti Chrétien National d'Haïti*— PCNH) organized by Rev. René des RAMEAUX. All of the latter were subjected to intermittent repression for the remainder of the Duvalier era.

In March 1987 it was reported that more than 60 new parties had been formed. Two months earlier, a **National Congress of Democratic Movements** (*Congrès National des Mouvements Démocratiques*— CNMD) had been organized in opposition to the Namphy regime by delegates from nearly 300 political groups, trade unions, peasants' and students' organizations, and human rights associations. Subsequently, the CNMD became the core of a loosely organized "Group of 57" that organized a variety of anti-government protests (including a general strike at Port-au-Prince on June 29) before being amalgamated into the National Front for Concerted Action (FNC, below) in September.

All political party activity was suspended in the wake of the June 1988 coup.

Former Government Party:

Assembly of National Progressive Democrats (*Rassemblement des Démocrates Nationaux-Progressistes*— RDNP). The RDNP was organized by Leslie Manigat while an exile in Venezuela during the 1970s. Strongly anti-Communist, Manigat called in mid-1986 for a "solidarity pact" between centrist parties. The lack of an effective response was attributed, in part, to Manigat's reputation as a *noiriste,* hence a threat to the country's powerful mulatto elite. Manigat was credited with securing a bare majority of the presidential vote at the highly controversial balloting of January 17, 1988.
Leader: Leslie MANIGAT (in exile).

Former Opposition Parties:

Haitian Social Christian Party (*Parti Social Chrétien d'Haïti*— PSCH). The PSCH was launched on July 5, 1979, as one of two parties styling themselves the Haitian Christian Democratic Party (see PDCH, below). Subsequently it added the issue date of its manifesto, becoming known as the PDCH-27 Juin, before being more commonly identified by the Social Christian label. Its leader, Grégoire Eugène, was deported to the United States in December 1980 and prohibited from returning until after the February 1984 election, when he resumed his position as professor of Constitutional and International Law at Haiti University. For the remainder of the Duvalier era, he and his daughter, Marie, were sporadically subjected to either detention or house arrest. Eugène was credited with running fourth in the 1988 presidential poll.
Leader: Grégoire EUGENE.

Haitian Christian Democratic Party (*Parti Démocratique Chrétien d'Haïti*— PDCH). The PDCH was also formed on July 5, 1979, by Silvio Claude, who had been arrested and deported to Colombia after standing unsuccessfully for election to the legislature in February. Rearrested upon his return to Haiti, he was sentenced in August 1981 to a 15-year prison term for attempting to create "a climate of disorder". Although the sentence was annulled in February 1982, periods of arrest and/or detention continued for the remainder of the Duvalier era. The PDCH refused to participate in the election of January 1988.
Leaders: Silvio CLAUDE, Nicolas ESTIVERNE.

National Front for Concerted Action (*Front National de Concertation* — FNC). The FNC was organized in September 1987 by merger of the Group of 57 (above) with a number of other moderate left-wing formations. Led by Gérard Gourgue, a prominent human rights lawyer who had resigned as minister of justice in the Namphy administration in March 1986, the party joined the PDCH in boycotting the January 1988 balloting.
Leader: Gérard GOURGUE.

Movement for the Installation of Democracy in Haiti (*Mouvement pour l'Instauration de la Démocratie en Haïti*— MIDH). The MIDH was founded by Marc Bazin, a former World Bank official, who also boycotted the 1988 election.
Leader: Marc BAZIN.

National Agricultural and Industrial Party (*Parti Agricole et Industriel National*— PAIN). PAIN was formed by Louis Déjoi II, the son of a prominent Duvalier opponent, who joined in the 1988 boycott.
Leader: Louis DEJOI II.

United Party of Haitian Communists (*Parti Unifié des Communistes Haïtiens*— PUCH). The original Communist Party of Haiti was formed in 1934, reorganized as the Haitian Party of National Unity in 1959, and adopted its present name in 1968. At its first congress, convened at an undisclosed location in late 1978, the pro-Moscow PUCH called for a united opposition front to bring down the Duvalier regime. Subsequently, it operated mainly as an exile grouping, its secretary general residing in Havana before returning to Haiti in March 1986. The party has recently been weakened by the withdrawal of a group of former exiles in New York and Montreal to form a rival **Haitian Liberation Party** (*Parti de la Libération Haïtienne*— PLH) that urges closer regional solidarity with Cuba and Nicaragua. PUCH was the only major party to boycott the CNMD Conference in January 1987.
Leader: René THEODORE (Secretary General).

Other parties include the **Mobilization for National Development** (*Mobilisation pour le Développement National*— MDP), whose leader, Hubert de RONCERAY, was runner-up to Manigat in the presidential balloting of January 1988; the **Movement for Organization of the Country** (*Mouvement d'Organisation du Pays*— MOP), led by the third-ranked presidential candidate, Gérard Philippe AUGUST; the **National Party of Labor** (*Parti National du Travail*— PNT), led by Thomas DESULME; and the **Haitian National Popular Party** (*Parti Populaire National Haïtien* — PPNH), led by Bernard SANSARICQ, who narrowly escaped death in a shooting incident with government troops in August 1987.

LEGISLATURE

The 1987 constitution provided for a bicameral legislature consisting of a 27-member **Senate** and a 77-member **House of Representatives.** Four of the leading parties campaigned for a boycott of the January 17, 1988, balloting, at which the turnout may have been as low as 5–10 percent. Most of those elected, primarily as independents, were thought to be former Duvalier office holders. The legislature was dissolved on June 20, 1988.

CABINET

The 15-member government named by President Manigat in February 1988 was dismissed following the coup of June 19. On June 20 General Namphy was reported to have appointed an administration of eleven military officers and one civilian.

NEWS MEDIA

The Duvalier government controlled all media, though limited opposition sentiment emerged with the establishment of the weekly newspapers *Le Petit Samedi Soir* and *Hebdo Jeune Presse.* The Namphy administration issued a press decree in mid-1986 that guaranteed "freedom of expression" but prohibited the publication of material deemed damaging to "morality or public order". It also mandated the licensing of all journalists.

Press. The following are French-language dailies published at Port-au-Prince, unless otherwise noted: *Le Petit Samedi Soir* (10,000), weekly; *Le Nouvelliste* (6,000); *Le Matin* (5,000); *Panorama* (3,000); *Le Moniteur* (2,000), twice-weekly official gazette; *Hebdo Jeune Presse,* liberal weekly.

News agencies. A Haitian Press Agency (*Agence Haïtienne de Press*), to operate in collaboration with *Agence France-Presse,* was launched in 1981.

Radio and television. Government, commercial, and religious radio facilities include approximately 40 radio stations (counting relays). *Télé Haïti,* a private commercial company, broadcasts over two channels, one in French and the other in English. There were some 200,000 radio and 25,000 television receivers in 1987.

INTERGOVERNMENTAL REPRESENTATION

Ambassador to the US: (Vacant).

US Ambassador to Haiti: Brunson McKINLEY.

Permanent Representative to the UN: Yves L. AUGUSTE.

IGO Memberships (Non-UN): ACCT, CCC, Geplacea, IADB, IBA, ICCO, ICO, Intelsat, Interpol, ISO, OAS, OPANAL, PCA, SELA.

HONDURAS

Republic of Honduras
República de Honduras

Political Status: Part of the independent Captaincy General of Guatemala, 1821; member of United Provinces of Central America, 1824–1838; separate republic established 1839; present constitution promulgated January 20, 1982, following a decade of military rule.

Area: 43,277 sq. mi. (112,088 sq. km.).

Population: 2,653,857 (1974C), 4,878,000 (1988E).

Major Urban Centers (1985E): TEGUCIGALPA (571,000); San Pedro Sula (373,000).

Official Language: Spanish.

Monetary Unit: Lempira (official rate March 1, 1988, 2.00 lempiras = $1US).

President: José Simeon AZCONA Hoyo (Liberal Party); inaugurated for a four-year term on January 27, 1986, in succession to Dr. Roberto SUAZO Córdova (Liberal Party), following election of November 24, 1985.

Vice Presidents: Jaime Rolando ROSENTHAL Oliva, Alfredo FORTIN Inestroza, José PINEDA Gómez (Liberal Party); elected November 24, 1985, for a term concurrent with that of the President.

THE COUNTRY

Honduras, the second-largest of the Central American republics, is mountainous, sparsely inhabited, and pre-dominantly rural. Approximately 90 percent of the population is racially mixed; Indians constitute about 7 percent, and Blacks and Whites the remainder. Roman Catholicism is the religion of the majority of the people. Women constitute about 7 percent of the rural labor force, exclusive of unpaid family workers, and 32 percent of the urban work force, primarily in domestic service; in a break with tradition, a female serves in the present cabinet as education minister.

The nation's economy is dependent on agriculture; bananas, coffee, beef, and timber are the most important exports. Industrial growth has been slow, and most production is limited to nondurable consumer goods. Unprecedented coffee price increases fueled GDP growth during the last half of the 1970s, but the economy has since plummeted because of regional insecurity, severe trade imbalances, mounting public-sector deficits, and a large external debt, while unemployment, illiteracy, poverty, landlessness, and disease place Honduras only slightly above Haiti in regional development status. Conditions have been exacerbated by the influx of refugees from neighboring El Salvador and Nicaragua and the disruption of economic and social activity by the presence of *contra* bases within Honduras.

GOVERNMENT AND POLITICS

Political background. Honduras declared its independence from Spain in 1821 as part of the Captaincy General of Guatemala. After a brief period of absorption by Mexico, the states of the Captaincy General in 1824 organized as the Central American Federation, which broke up in 1838. Decades of instability, revolution, and governmental change followed, with Honduras experiencing 67 different heads of state between 1855 and 1932, and US military forces intervening on three occasions between 1912 and 1924. A measure of internal stability, accompanied by a minimum of reform and progress, was achieved between 1932 and 1954 under the presidencies of Tiburcio CARIAS Andino and Juan Manuel GALVEZ. Three years after a military coup in 1954, Ramón VILLEDA Morales was installed as constitutional president and served until his 1963 overthrow in another military coup mounted by (then) Col. Oswaldo LOPEZ Arellano. Subsequently, a Constituent Assembly, with a National Party (PN) majority, approved a new constitution and designated López Arellano as president.

Immediately prior to the 1971 election, López Arellano organized the groundwork for a new government under a Pact of National Unity, which called for the sharing of governmental posts by the two major parties. Although reminiscent of the National Front arrangement in Colombia, the Pact was not nearly as successful. After 18 months in office, the government of President Ramón Ernesto CRUZ was overthrown by the military under former president López Arellano, who was designated to serve the remainder of Cruz's presidential term. López was weakened, however, by charges of inept response to conditions created by a disastrous hurricane that ravaged the northern part of the country in September 1974. On March 31, 1975, he was replaced as military commander in chief by (then) Col. Juan Alberto MELGAR Castro after a group of dissatisfied junior officers had seized control of the Supreme Council of the Armed Forces, and on April 22 was further supplanted by Melgar Castro as head of state. The new president was in turn ousted on August 7, 1978, by a three-man junta headed by Brig. Gen. Policarpo PAZ García.

On July 25, 1980, a Constituent Assembly that had been elected on April 20 named Paz García to serve as sole executive pending the adoption of a new constitution and the popular election of a successor. Despite last-minute rumors of a new coup, Dr. Roberto SUAZO Córdova led the Liberal Party (PLH) to a surprisingly conclusive victory in nationwide balloting on November 29, 1981, and assumed office on January 27, 1982, promising "a revolution of work and honesty".

At his inauguration, President Suazo Córdova referenced the Honduran record of 16 constitutions, 126 governments, and 385 armed rebellions in 161 years of independence and declared that "the time had come for rectifications". It was obvious, however, that a peaceful transition had been achieved by mortgaging the incoming administration to an "iron circle" of military hard-liners headed by Gustavo ALVAREZ Martínez, who was promptly promoted from colonel to general.

On March 31, 1984, General Alvarez was dismissed and sent into exile, following charges of plotting a coup and misappropriating government funds. The latter allegations turned largely on the activities of the Association for the Progress of Honduras (*Asociación para el Progreso de Honduras* — APROH), a right-wing grouping of military and business leaders which, a year earlier, had accepted a $5 million contribution from the intensely anti-Communist Unification Church of Sun Myung Moon for the purpose of countering Honduran "subversives". APROH, which was formally outlawed in November 1984, had also advocated direct US military intervention against the Nicaraguan *sandinistas* as a necessary precondition of regional economic development.

Late in the year, amid deepening fissures within the ruling PLH, President Suazo Córdova endorsed controversial businessman Carlos FLORES Facussé as his successor. Flores was, however, viewed as a stalking-horse for the president, who was ineligible for reelection, and withdrew his candidacy. The *suazocordovistas* thereupon shifted their support to former interior minister, Oscar MEJIA Arrellano. A majority of the party's congressional delegation, on the other hand, backed Chamber president Efraín BU Girón, leaving the chief executive with the minority support of only 29 deputies. The split yielded a constitutional crisis in early 1985, with Congress removing five of the nine Supreme Court justices on grounds of corruption and the president responding by ordering the arrest of the new chief justice. The crisis was resolved in April by reinstallation of the "old" court after the leading parties had agreed to an "open contest" in the forthcoming presidential balloting that would permit any faction of a recognized party to present a presidential candidate; an electoral change approved later in the year declared that the winner would be the leading candidate within the party that secured the most votes. Under the new arrangement (ulti-mately challenged, without success, by the *nacionalistas*), José AZCONA Hoyo, an anti-*suazocordovista* Liberal was declared president-elect after the election of November 24, despite placing second to the leading National Party nominee, Rafael Leonardo CALLEJAS.

Azcona's victory in what was hailed as a remarkably "clean" election yielded the first transition involving elected civilians in more than half a century. However, because of party fissures, he could look forward to controlling only 46 of 132 legislative seats. As a result, prior to his inauguration on January 27, 1986, the incoming chief executive concluded a "National Accord" (reminiscent of the 1971 pact) with the Nationalists that gave the opposition effective control of the judiciary and representation in the cabinet and other influential bodies, thus dimming prospects for major policy changes, including meaningful land reform. Although the accord subsequently deteriorated (see PN under Political Parties, below), PLH-PN cooperation at mid-year yielded the indefinite suspension of municipal elections scheduled for November, neither party apparently favoring a public test prior to the presidential and legislative balloting scheduled for 1989.

Constitution and government. The constitution promulgated in January 1982 provides for a directly elected president and a unicameral legislature whose members serve four-year terms concurrent with that of the chief executive. The judiciary includes a Supreme Court and five courts of appeal, each of which designates local justices within its territorial jurisdiction.

Internal administration is based on 18 departments headed by centrally appointed governors. The departments are subdivided into a total of 283 municipalities, each with an elected mayor and municipal assembly (including the capital, which prior to 1985 had been denied such status for 47 years).

Foreign relations. A member of the Organization of American States (OAS) and the United Nations, Honduras has long inclined toward a conservative position in inter-American and world affairs. It is nominally active in the Organization of Central American States (ODECA) and the Central American Common Market (CACM), although it no longer accepts the agreements on which these institutions are based. It also participated in the 1982, US-sponsored formation of a Central American Democratic Community (Condeca), which included Costa Rica, El Salvador, and Guatemala, while excluding Nicaragua; however, the alliance (promulgated with a variety of economic and security objectives) quickly became moribund.

A series of disagreements with neighboring El Salvador in 1969 led to an undeclared "soccer" war, in the course of which invading Salvadoran forces inflicted hundreds of casualties before a ceasefire was arranged by the OAS on July 18. Renewed hostilities broke out in July 1976 and it was not until October 30, 1980, that a formal peace treaty was signed at Lima, Peru. Despite the treaty, conditions along the border remained tense because of continuing clashes between Salvadoran government forces and guerrilla groups operating from sanctuaries in the ostensibly demilitarized *bolsones territoriales*. The two countries agreed in mid-1986 to have the International Court of Justice rule on the dispute after bilateral discussions failed to yield a permanent settlement.

The most pressing foreign-policy problem in recent years has stemmed from the presence of several thousand Nicaraguan exiles in border camps, many of them former members of the *somocista* National Guard. Evidence of collusion between the so-called *contras* and elements of the Honduran armed forces emerged as early as 1981, followed by charges in mid-1982 of a clandestine plan for "confrontation" with Managua. By 1984, the Nicaraguan rebels, with substantial US funding, were operating openly from southern Honduras, despite occasional denials from Tegucigalpa. The *contra* presence has served to complicate traditionally strong relations with the United States; despite a tenfold increase in economic aid since 1981, Honduran nationalism has been aroused by the disparity between economic and military assistance and by perceptions that the country was being used as a "platform" for US action against the *sandinistas*.

Current issues. In his inaugural address President Azcona expressed the desire to concentrate on economic and social, rather than military issues, but Honduras subsequently became even more involved in the *contra-sandinista* conflict. Nicaraguan troops reportedly attacked *contra* bases in Honduras in March 1986, Washington responding with $20 million in emergency aid to repel the "invasion". A second incursion late in the year involved minor contact between Honduran and Nicaraguan forces, prompting Tegucigalpa to threaten air strikes deep within Nicaragua.

In 1987 President Azcona successfully lobbied for the return of most *contra* units to Nicaragua and joined other Central American presidents in extended negotiations on a regional peace plan. A crisis loomed in March 1988 when a cross-border operation by Nicaragua elicited additional US troop deployments. However, tension eased thereafter with the signing of the *sandinista-contra* ceasefire (see Nicaragua article).

The Azcona administration also encountered numerous difficulties in other areas during 1987 and early 1988. Investigations continued into charges that military and security forces had supported "death squads" responsible for the killing of some 200 leftists in 1980–1984, with international concern being voiced over the subsequent human rights climate in Honduras. Opponents also attacked Azcona for failing to promote meaningful land reform and for rejecting a proposed national reconciliation commission. In January 1988 the International Monetary Fund, World Bank, and Inter-American Development Bank suspended disbursements because of the country's failure to meet external debt repayments. Further problems developed in April, when rioters set fire to the US embassy at Tegucigalpa to protest the arrest and apparently unconstitutional extradition to the United States of a suspected international drug dealer.

POLITICAL PARTIES

Under the Pact of National Unity concluded prior to the 1971 election, the country's two major political parties, the National Party and the Liberal Party, agreed to put up separate candidates for the presidency but to accept equal representation in the Congress, the cabinet, the Supreme Court, and other government organs. The Pact became moot upon the resumption of military rule in late 1972 and was not renewed for the election of November 1981, at which the two traditional parties shared 94.2 percent of the vote. At the November 1985 balloting the continuance of an essentially two-party system was reaffirmed, the smaller parties collectively being limited to less than 5 percent of the vote.

Presidential Party:

Liberal Party of Honduras (*Partido Liberal de Honduras* – PLH). Tracing its political ancestry to 1890, the PLH is an urban-based, center-right grouping that has historically favored social reform, democratic political standards, and Central American integration. With the active support of a social-democratic faction, Alipo (below), it secured an impressive victory over the nationalists in the 1981 balloting, winning the presidency and a clear majority in the National Assembly. Following the inauguration of President Suazo Córdova in January 1982, Alipo influence waned, while the non-*alipista* group split into an "old guard" *rodista* tendency (named after former Liberal leader Modesto Rodas Alvarado), composed primarily of traditionally antimilitarist conservatives, and a presidential tendency (*suazocordovistas*), encompassing right-wing technocrats with close links to the business community and the armed forces. The latter cleavage resulted in the president's loss of legislative support in early 1985 and the generation of a major constitutional crisis (see Political background, above).

One of four PLH candidates, José Azcona Hoyo, with partial *rodista* and Alipo support, won the presidency in 1985 without the backing of Suazo Córdova, who, with the remaining *rodistas,* supported Oscar Mejía Arellano. The PLH candidates obtained 51 percent of the votes, Azcona being the individual leader with a 28 percent vote share. In 1987 rightist Carlos Flores Facussé, a strong supporter of US policy, was elected PLH president and thus became a leading contender for 1989 presidential nomination. Carlos Orbín Montoya, the president of the National Assembly and a close associate of President Azcona, was runner-up in the balloting, which once again underscored widespread division within the ruling party.

Leaders: José AZCONA Hoya (President of the Republic), Dr. Roberto SUAZO Córdova (former President of the Republic), Carlos FLORES Facussé (President of the Party), Oscar MEJIA Arellano (1985 *suazocordovista* presidential candidate), Carlos Roberto REINA (1985 presidential candidate of the M-Líder, below), Carlos ORBIN Montoya (President of Congress), Efraín BU Girón (former President of Congress and 1985 presidential candidate).

Popular Liberal Alliance (*Alianza Liberal del Pueblo* – Alipo). Technically a left-of-center tendency within the PLH, Alipo has a separate organizational structure, but is itself divided into a number of factions, the most important of which are a financial and agro-export oriented tendency led by Edmond Bogran, and a strongly antimilitary tendency, also known as the Revolutionary Liberal Democratic Movement (*Movimiento Liberal Democrático Revolucionario* – M-Líder), led by Carlos and Jorge Reina.

Leaders: Edmond BOGRAN, Jorge BUESO Arias, Gustavo GOMEZ Santos, Carlos Roberto REINA, Jorge Arturo REINA.

Other Parties:

National Party (*Partido Nacional* – PN). Created in 1923 as an expression of national unity after a particularly chaotic period, the PN is a right-wing party with close ties to the military. While traditionally dominated by rural landowning interests, it has, in recent years, supported programs of internal reform and favors Central American integration. Factionalism within the PN was evidenced in the wake of November 1982 balloting for the party executive, former president Gen. Juan Melgar Castro accusing the *oficialista* faction, led by former president Ricardo Zúñiga, of perpetrating a "worthless farce". In July 1983, two separate PN conventions were held, and three presidential candidates were nominated in 1985. Rafael Leonardo Callejas, supported by most of the party, led all contenders in the 1985 balloting with 43 percent of the total votes. However, the other two PN candidates garnered less than 2 percent each. As a result, under existing electoral procedure, the presidency was awarded to the Liberals, whose nominees had collectively obtained a 51 percent vote share.

The PN quickly reached a power-sharing agreement with the PLH (see Political background, above), but Callejas, after declaring the accord's commitments no longer binding, announced in January 1987 that the PN would move into "more critical" opposition.

Leaders: Rafael Leonardo CALLEJAS (President of the Party), Ricardo ZUÑIGA Augustinus and Gen. Juan Alberto MELGAR Castro (former Presidents of the Republic), Fernando LARDIZABAL, Juan Pablo URRUTIA (1985 presidential candidates).

National Innovation and Unity Party (*Partido de Innovación Nacional y Unidad* — PINU). A centrist group, the PINU was granted legal status in 1977. It ran third in the 1981 balloting, although securing only 2.5 percent of the vote, and was fourth in 1985 with 1.9 percent. In mid-1986, the party announced that it had become a social democratic formation, although several other groups indicated that they intended to seek recognition under the same rubric, including one formally launched the following October (see PSDH, below).

Leaders: German LEITZELAR (President), Dr. Miguel ANDONIE Fernández, Enrique AGUILAR Cerrato (1985 presidential candidate).

Christian Democratic Party of Honduras (*Partido Demócrata Cristiano de Honduras* — PDCH). The PDCH, another small centrist party with some trade union support, was accorded legal recognition by the Melgar Castro government in December 1977. The action was reversed in November 1978 after complaints by the PN that it had broken the electoral law by receiving funds from abroad. The party was permitted to contest the 1981 election, at which it ran fourth, with 1.6 percent of the vote. In 1985, it barely secured the 1.5 percent vote share needed to maintain registration.

Leaders: Wilfredo LANDAVERTE (President), Rubén PALMA (former President), Dr. Hernán CORRALES Padilla (1985 presidential candidate).

Democratic Action Party (*Partido de Acción Democrática* — PAD). The centrist PAD was reported to have been established in late 1986 by Gen. Walter López Reyes, who had resigned the previous February as commander of the Honduran armed forces amid reports of fractionalization within the military over *contra* policy. In early 1987 López charged that the US Central Intelligence Agency had "infiltrated" Honduran security forces and that "*contra* death squads" had killed Hondurans considered subversive by the government. López has announced his intention to run as PAD presidential candidate in 1989.

Leader: Gen. (Ret.) Walter LOPEZ Reyes.

Honduran Social Democratic Party (*Partido Socialista Democrático de Honduras* — PSDH). The PSDH was reportedly established in October 1986 with the goal of modernizing the Honduran state through tax, educational, and land reform.

Leaders: Jorge ILLESCAS Oliva, Amado GOMEZ Tercero.

Clandestine Groups:

Honduran Revolutionary Movement (*Movimiento Hondureño Revolucionario* — MHR). Although refusing to present a presidential candidate, the principal leftist coalition during the 1981 electoral campaign was the Honduran Patriotic Front (*Frente Patriótico Hondureño* — FPH), an alliance of some 30 small groups that included the Communist Party of Honduras (below) and the **Communist Party of Honduras–Marxist-Leninist** (*Partido Comunista de Honduras–Marxista-Leninista* — PCH-ML), which had been organized some years earlier by a number of Maoist-oriented PCH dissidents. In April 1983, the PCH joined with a number of guerrilla organizations, exclusive of the PCH-ML, to form the MHR, under a National Unified Directorate (*Directorio Nacional Unificado* — DNU) to coordinate "the struggle for national liberation" in Honduras. The tangible results of the organization have been quite limited, however, with some observers describing it as "nonfunctioning" by 1986. Subsequently, in early 1987, a reorganized FPH was reported to have applied for recognition as a legal party.

Communist Party of Honduras (*Partido Comunista de Honduras* — PCH). The PCH is a Moscow-oriented group originally formed in 1927 and reorganized in 1954. Outlawed in 1957, it regained legal status in 1981, but two years later was again functioning as a clandestine formation. In 1984 Rigoberto Padilla Rush, PCH secretary general although resident in Cuba since 1982, was officially expelled from the Central Committee. However, he continued to lead a radical external wing, which advocated revolutionary violence, while a more moderate faction, headed by Mario Sosa Navarro, dominated PCH

activity within Honduras. That split was apparently healed at the Fourth Congress (the first since 1977), held "in conditions of clandestinity" in January 1986, at which Padilla was reelected to his former post. Resolutions approved by the Congress deemphasized military activity in favor of an anti-US, anti-*contra* political platform to be presented in the 1989 election campaign.

Leaders: Mario SOSA Navarro, Rigoberto PADILLA Rush (Secretary General).

Cinchonero Popular Liberation Movement (*Movimiento Popular de Liberación Cinchonero* — MPLC). Formed in 1978, the Marxist MPLC was responsible for the hijacking of a Honduran airliner in March 1981 as well as a hostage seizure at San Pedro Sula in September 1982 of more than 100 prominent business and government leaders, all of whom were subsequently freed. In November 1986, the Honduran government claimed to have suppressed a minor Cinchonero insurgency in the northeast. The MPLC, which has reportedly received arms and training from Cuba and Nicaragua, has at various times been linked to antigovernment guerrilla organizations active in Colombia and El Salvador.

Leader: Raul LOPEZ.

Morazanista Front of Honduran Liberation (*Frente Morazanista de Liberación Hondureña* — FMLH). Reportedly organized in 1979, the FMLH is named after Francisco Morazan, a nineteenth-century revolutionary leader. In September 1984, members of the group, after planting a number of bombs about the city, seized a Tegucigalpa radio station to denounce the Suazo government as "treacherous and corrupt".

Leaders: Fernando LOPEZ, Octavio PEREZ (both names are reportedly aliases).

Lorenzo Zelaya People's Revolutionary Front (*Frente Popular Revolucionario–Lorenzo Zelaya* — FPR-LZ). Allegedly linked to the Nicaraguan *sandinistas,* the FPR-LZ claimed responsibility for shooting two US military advisors at the Tegucigalpa airport in September 1981. In March 1987 the government reported that security forces had killed two of its leaders in San Pedro Sula.

Leader: Efraín DUARTE.

Revolutionary Party of Central American Workers-Honduras (*Partido Revolucionario de los Trabajadores Centroamericanos-Honduras* — PRTC-H). The PRTC-H is the Honduran branch of the rebel PRTC of El Salvador, which is supported by Nicaragua and Cuba.

Leader: Wilfredo GALLARDO Museli.

Movement of Revolutionary Unity (*Movimiento de Unidad Revolucionario* — MUR). The MUR was unknown prior to the announcement of its inclusion in the MHR.

Another leftist group known as *Froylan Turcios* claimed responsibility for two acts of violence in Tegucigalpa in 1987 to protest the presence in Honduras of US and *contra* troops.

Paramilitary right-wing groups include the **White Hand** (*Mano Blanca*) and the **Honduran Anti-Communist Movement** (*Movimiento Anticomunista de Honduras* — Macho).

LEGISLATURE

Under the constitution advanced by the Constituent Assembly elected on April 20, 1980, the former Congress of Deputies has been replaced by a **National Assembly** (*Asamblea Nacional*) that currently consists of 134 members elected for four-year terms. At the most recent election of November 24, 1985, the Liberal Party won 67 seats; the National Party, 63; the Christian Democratic Party, 2; and the Innovation and Unity Party, 2.

President: Carlos ORBIN Montoya.

CABINET

President	José Simeon Azcona Hoyo

Ministers

Communications, Public Works and Transport	Juan Fernando López
Economy and Commerce	Reginaldo Panting Penalba
Finance	José Efraín Bu Girón
Foreign Affairs	Carlos López Contreras
Health and Social Aid	Rubén Antonio Villeda Bermúdez
Interior and Justice	Romualdo Bueso Peñalba
Labor and Social Security	Adalberto Discua Rodríguez
National Defense and Public Security	Col. Wilfredo Sánchez Valladares
Natural Resources	Rodrigo Castillo
Presidency	Celeo Arias Moncada
Public Education	Elisa Estela Valle de Martínez Pavetti
Tourism and Culture	Arturo Rendon Pineda
Executive Secretary, Higher Council of Economic Planning	Mario Espiral
President, Central Bank	Gonzalo Carías Pineda

NEWS MEDIA

Press. Except as noted, all newspapers are privately owned and published daily at Tegucigalpa: *El Tiempo* (San Pedro Sula, 71,000), left-of-center; *La Tribuna* (50,000); *La Prensa* (San Pedro Sula, 38,000); *El Tiempo* (30,000), liberal; *La Gaceta* (3,000), official government organ.

News agencies. *Deutsche Presse-Agentur* and the Spanish *Agencia EFE* maintain offices at Tegucigalpa.

Radio and television. Broadcasting is under the supervision of the *Empresa Hondureña de Telecomunicaciones* (Hondutel). Many of the more than 100 radio stations are operated by religious groups. Commercial television is provided by the *Compañia Televisora Hondureña, S.A.* There were approximately 145,000 television receivers in 1987.

INTERGOVERNMENTAL REPRESENTATION

Ambassador to the US: Roberto MARTINEZ Ordonez.

US Ambassador to Honduras: Everett Ellis BRIGGS.

Permanent Representative to the UN: Ramón HERNANDEZ Alcerro.

IGO Memberships (Non-UN): BCIE, CACM, CDC, Geplacea, IADB, ICAC, ICM, ICO, Intelsat, Interpol, ISO, OAS, ODECA, OPANAL, PCA, SELA, UPEB.

HUNGARY

Hungarian People's Republic
Magyar Népköztársaság

Political Status: Independent kingdom created in 1000; republic proclaimed in 1946; Communist People's Republic established August 20, 1949.

Area: 35,919 sq. mi. (93,030 sq. km.).

Population: 10,709,463 (1980C), 10,580,000 (1988E).

Major Urban Centers (1986E): BUDAPEST (2,075,000); Miskolc (212,000); Debrecen (212,000); Szeged (182,000); Pécs (177,000); Győr (129,000).

Official Language: Hungarian.

Monetary Unit: Forint (principal rate March 1, 1988, 47.95 forints = $1US).

Chairman of the Presidential Council (Head of State): Károly NÉMETH; elected by the National Assembly on June 25, 1987, to succeed Pál LOSONCZI.

Chairman of the Council of Ministers (Premier) **and General Secretary of the Hungarian Socialist Workers' Party:** Károly GRÓSZ; designated Chairman of the Council of Ministers by the Presidential Council and confirmed by the National Assembly on June 25, 1987, to succeed György LÁZÁR; named to succeed János KÁDÁR as General Secretary at National Conference of the Hungarian Workers' Party on May 22, 1988.

THE COUNTRY

Masters for over 1,000 years of the fertile plain extending on either side of the middle Danube, the Hungarians have long regarded their country as the eastern outpost of Western Europe in cultural pattern, religious affiliation, and political structure. Over 95 percent of the present Hungarian population is of Magyar origin; Germans, Slovaks, Southern Slavs, and Romanians are the only sizable ethnic minorities. Despite the antireligious policies of the Communist regime, about half of the population is classified as Roman Catholic; there are also Protestant, Eastern Orthodox, and Jewish adherents. In 1980, women accounted for 45 percent of the labor force, concentrated in manufacturing services and the professions; at present, females hold approximately one-third of government and party posts.

Although the Hungarian economy was traditionally dependent on the agricultural sector, which was largely collectivized following the Communist assumption of power after World War II, industry currently employs over half of the labor force and accounts for the majority of export earnings. The country remains, however, a net food exporter, with the largest agricultural trade surplus in Eastern Europe. Leading industrial products, almost all of which require imported raw materials (iron ore, petroleum, copper, crude fibers), include machinery, transportation equipment, electrical and electronic equipment, chemicals, and textiles. Bauxite, coal, and natural gas are the chief mineral resources.

Despite a series of Western-inspired economic policies, including the creation of numerous private and semiprivate ventures, most objectives of the sixth five-year plan (1981–1985) were not met, with the government in each of the years 1984–1987 feeling obliged to increase prices for basic commodities. In addition, a Western-style value tax was introduced in 1987, along with the Soviet bloc's first income tax (see Current issues, below).

GOVERNMENT AND POLITICS

Political background. As part of the polyglot Austro-Hungarian Empire, the former Kingdom of Hungary lost much of its territory and the bulk of its non-Magyar population at the end of World War I. A brief and bloody Communist dictatorship under Béla KUN in 1919 was followed by 25 years of right-wing authoritarian government under Adm. Miklós HORTHY, who bore the title of regent. Hungary joined Germany in the war against the Soviet Union in June 1941 and was occupied by Soviet forces in late 1944, a definitive peace treaty with the Allied Powers not being signed until 1947. Communists obtained only 17 percent of the vote in a free election held in November 1945 but with Soviet backing assumed key posts in the coalition government that proclaimed the Hungarian Republic on February 1, 1946. Seizing de facto control in May-June 1947, the Communists proceeded to liquidate most opposition parties and to establish a dictatorship led by Mátyás RÁKOSI. The remaining parties and mass organizations were grouped in a Communist-controlled "front", while the Hungarian People's Republic was formally established in 1949.

The initial years of the Republic were marked by purges and the systematic elimination of domestic opposition, which included the 1949 treason conviction of the Roman Catholic primate, József Cardinal MINDSZENTY. In the post-Stalin era, on the other hand, gradual liberalization led to the outbreak in October 1956 of a popular revolutionary movement, the formation of a coalition government under Imre NAGY, and the announcement on November 1 of Hungary's withdrawal from the Warsaw Pact. Massive Soviet military force was employed to crush the revolt, and a pro-Soviet regime headed by János KÁDÁR was installed on November 4.

Concerned primarily with consolidating its position, the Kádár government was initially rigid and authoritarian. However, the Eighth Party Congress (1962) marked the beginning of a trend toward pragmatism in domestic policy combined with strict adherence to Soviet pronouncements in foreign affairs. Three years later, Kádár resigned the premiership, though remaining first secretary of the Hungarian Socialist Workers' Party. His successor as premier, Gyula KÁLLAI, was in turn succeeded by Jenő FOCK in 1967.

Hungary's subservience to the USSR in foreign affairs was most dramatically demonstrated by the participation of its troops in the Warsaw Pact invasion of Czechoslovakia in August 1968. At the same time, its domestic pragmatism was demonstrated by implementation of a program known as the New Economic Mechanism (NEM), which allowed for decentralization, more flexible management strategies, incentives for efficiency, and expanded production of consumer goods. Although given full support by the Tenth Party Congress (1970) and endorsed by Soviet party secretary Leonid Brezhnev during a 1972 state visit, the NEM was derailed in 1973 following an ideological victory by its opponents. The call for a return to more orthodox Communist centralization resulted in the removal of Rezső NYERS, the "father" of the economic reform, from the party Politburo in March 1975, while Premier Fock was replaced by planning expert György LÁZÁR the following May. In the late 1970s, however, responding to escalating prices for imported materials and the need to make Hungarian goods more competitive on the world market, the government began to reintroduce NEM policies.

At the Thirteenth Party Congress in March 1985, longtime Kádár loyalist Károly NÉMETH was named to the newly created post of deputy general secretary and assigned new administrative responsibilities, although party spokesmen resisted speculation that he was being groomed as Kádár's successor. In a governmental realignment in June 1987, Németh succeeded Pál LOSONCZI as head of state, while the "Gorbachev era" (56-year-old) Károly GRÓSZ replaced Lázár as premier. These events were dramatically overshadowed by sweeping changes at a national party conference (the first in 31 years) on May 19–22, 1988, which concluded with the designation of Grósz as general secretary, Kádár (named to the newly created but ceremonial party presidency) being dropped, along with six associates, from the Politburo. Concurrently, six new Politburo members were named, including the now manifestly rehabilitated Rezső Nyers.

Constitution and government. The constitution of 1949 (as amended in 1972) declares the Hungarian People's Republic to be a state in which all power belongs to the working people and the bulk of the means of production is publicly owned. In practice, Communist control is exercised at all levels by the Hungarian Socialist Workers' Party, either directly or through the Communist-dominated People's Patriotic Front. The highest state authority is nominally the unicameral National Assembly, which is elected by secret ballot and universal suffrage. In December 1983, the Assembly adopted a law mandating a choice of candidates for most parliamentary and all local council seats; however, all nominees, including independents, are required to declare their support for People's Patriotic Front policies. The Assembly in turn elects a 21-member Presidential Council, which acts as an interim legislative body between Assembly sessions and whose chairman serves as head of state. The Assembly also elects the Council of Ministers, whose chairman functions as prime minister. The judicial system is jointly administered by the Supreme Court, whose president is named by the legislature, and the Ministry of Justice. Below the Supreme Court are county, district, and municipal courts. There is also a chief public prosecutor, as well as a Constitutional Law Council, established by the National Assembly in April 1984 to rule on the constitutionality of proposed legislation.

The country is administratively divided into 19 counties and the city of Budapest (which has county status), districts, towns, and villages. Council members at the local levels are directly elected, while those at the county level are elected by the members of the lower-level councils. Each council elects an executive committee and a president.

Foreign relations. Since the failure of the 1956 revolution, Hungary has faithfully followed the Soviet lead in international questions, voting with the Soviet bloc in the United Nations, adhering to the Brezhnev Doctrine of the limited sovereignty of Communist states, and serving as a reliable member of the Warsaw Pact, the CMEA, and other multilateral Communist organs. It has provided limited aid to a number of Soviet-supportive Third World states, including Angola, the Congo, and Mozambique. However, relations with its closest Eastern-bloc neighbors have not always been smooth. Disputes over the treatment of ethnic Hungarians in Romania have caused tension with Bucharest, while Czechoslovak authorities have expressed disapproval of Budapest's improved relations with the West since the 1960s. Reflecting the thaw, a US-Hungarian agreement on most-favored-nation status was concluded in 1978, while Western leaders to visit Hungary since 1979 include West Germany's Helmut Schmidt, British Prime Minister Margaret Thatcher, and Italy's Bettino Craxi. In addition, relations with Austria have been close, Vienna providing much of the external capital for new Hungarian economic ventures.

During 1987 Hungary joined Poland in agreeing to an exchange of quasi-diplomatic "interest-sections" with Israel. The year also witnessed a polemic exchange unprecedented in Eastern Europe over the treatment of ethnic Hungarians in Romanian-held Transylvania, with Budapest also accusing its neighbor of permitting gross pollution of the Sebes-Körös/Crisul RepedeRiver at the border town of Oradea. A three-volume history of the territorial dispute, published by the Hungarian Academy of Sciences, was bitterly attacked by Romanian authorities as "a conscious forgery of history".

Current issues. Following the introduction of the NEM in 1979, Hungary developed the most market-oriented economy in Eastern Europe, as evidenced by an upward movement in consumer prices, the gradual elimination of subsidies for industrial imports, and a liberal atmosphere for small-scale private investment and product innovation. While productivity increased and the consumer goods shortages of other Eastern-bloc countries were avoided, concern was increasingly voiced at a growing income differential between "forint millionaires" (encompassing professionals, managers, and some party officials) and an estimated two-thirds of the population experiencing visible decline in its standard of living. Complaints were also lodged against the sanctioning of "economic work collectives", which allowed groups of workers to utilize the facilities of their enterprises for more remunerative activity outside of regular work hours. By 1987 consumerism, coupled with state regulation that included support of nonprofitable enterprises, had generated widespread economic malaise. A foreign debt of $13 billion translated into Europe's highest on a per capita basis, inflation had reached double-digit levels, and real wages continued to slide. Of equal significance were indications that the quality of life, as indexed by suicide, alcoholism, and similar negative indicators, had plummeted because of the consumer-driven effects of excessive work schedules. Both government economists and the still widely respected Rezcö Nyers argued that the immediate objectives were to achieve a balance in the country's international accounts, a halt in the rise of the national debt, and a gradual reduction in the budget deficit. To this end, the new government of Károly Grósz advanced a number of belt-tightening measures, including further price increases and both personal income and value-added taxes (the two latter virtually unprecedented for a Communist country). Initially, however, it resisted the adoption of a key element in Nyers' longer-term agenda, withholding subsidies for inefficient enterprises, on the ground that it would result in massive layoffs under a regime committed ideologically to full employment.

The May 1988 purge of the old guard, including the removal of both Kádár and Németh from Politburo membership, provided clear evidence that the proponents of economic reform had won the day. Most Hungarians appeared elated at the "housecleaning" that accorded political primacy to an individual who, although basically conservative, had acquired a reputation for organizational skill and decisiveness. It was also the first time in more than two decades that the top positions in party and government had been combined, although there were indications that Grósz might step down as premier by the end of the year.

POLITICAL PARTIES

The sole political party is the Hungarian Socialist Workers' Party. As in other Communist-ruled states of Eastern Europe, its operations are supported by a Communist-controlled "front" organization, known in Hungary as the **People's Patriotic Front** (*Hazafias Népfront*), which embraces virtually all organized groups and associations in the country. Established in October 1954, it succeeded the Hungarian People's Independence Front of 1949, which had included the remnants of former non-Communist political parties. The People's Patriotic Front is led by former premier Gyula KÁLLAI (President) and Imre POZSGAY (Secretary General).

Hungarian Socialist Workers' Party (*Magyar Szocialista Munkáspárt*). Established in June 1948 by merger of the Communist Party and the left-wing Social Democratic Party, Hungary's dominant group was known until 1956 as the Hungarian Workers' Party; it was reorganized under its present name when János Kádár took over the leadership in the wake of the 1956 revolution. The Thirteenth Congress, held at Budapest on March 25–28, 1985, concluded with the election of a 105-member Central Committee, which, in turn, designated a 13-member Politburo (3 existing members being replaced) and an 8-member Secretariat (2 members being replaced and 1 added). Membership in the latter two bodies was reduced to 11 and 6, respectively, as a result of the drastic reorganization approved at the national party conference in May 1988.

General Secretary: Karoly GRÓSZ.

Other Members of Politburo: János BERECZ (Secretary, Central Committee), Dr. Judit CSEHÁK (Health and Social Welfare Minister), Csaba HÁMORI (First Secretary, HSWP Youth League), Pál IVANYI (Mayor of Budapest), János LUKACS (Secretary, Central Committee), Miklos NEMETH (Secretary, Central Committee), Rezső NYERS (former Finance Minister), Ilona PATAI (Member, Political Economy Committee, Central Committee), Imre POZSGAY (Secretary General, People's Patriotic Front), István SZABÓ (Chairman, National Council of Producers' Cooperatives).

Central Committee Secretariat: János BERECZ, György FEJTI, Karoly GRÓSZ, János LUKACS, Miklos NÉMETH, Lénárd PÁL, Mátyás SZÜRÖS.

LEGISLATURE

Under new electoral arrangements adopted in December 1983, the **National Assembly** (*Országgyülés*) is a unicameral body of 387 members elected by direct universal suffrage for five-year terms. There are 352 contested seats, in addition to 35 filled on a single "national list" prepared by the PPF. At the balloting of June 8, 1985, 345 individuals were declared elected, no candidates in 42 constituencies having secured a sufficient number of votes; at a second-round poll on June 22, 41 of the remaining seats were filled, a later by-election being necessitated in one district due to withdrawal of the nominees.

President: István SARLÓS.

CABINET

Chairman, Council of Ministers (Premier)	Károly Grósz
Deputy Chairmen	József Marjai
	Péter Medgyessy

Ministers

Agriculture and Food	Jeno Váncsa
Construction and Urban Development	László Somogyi
Culture and Education	Béla Köpeczi
Defense	Col. Gen. Ferenc Kárpáti
Domestic Trade	Dr. Zoltán Juhár
Environmental Protection and Water Management	Dr. László Maróthy
Finance	Miklos Villanyi
Foreign Affairs	Péter Várkonyi
Health and Social Welfare	Dr. Judit Csehák
Industry	Frigyes Berecz
Interior	István Horváth
Justice	Dr. Imre Markója
Trade	József Marjai
Transportation	Lajos Urbán

Minister-Chairmen

Central Statistical Office	Ferencné Nyitrai
National Planning Office	János Hoós
National Technological Development Commission	Pál Tétényi
State Office for Church Affairs	Imre Miklós
State Office for Wages and Labor	Csaba Halmos
President, National Bank	Mátyás Timár

NEWS MEDIA

All information media are either state owned or under effective government or party control.

Press. Although freedom of the press is constitutionally guaranteed, its scope is curtailed by extensive legislation as well as by administrative practice. Most newspapers are organs of political groups, trade unions, and youth and social (including religious) organizations. The major Budapest papers circulate nationally, but there are also nearly two dozen provincial dailies, all with circulations under 100,000. The following are issued daily at Budapest, unless otherwise noted: *Népszabadság* (People's Freedom, 700,000 daily, 800,000 Sunday), organ of Hungarian Socialist Workers' Party; *Szabad Föld* (Free Soil, 580,000), political weekly of the People's Patriotic Front; *Népszava* (Voice of the People, 293,000 daily, 300,000 Sunday), organ of the Trades Union Council; *Esti Hirlap* (Evening Journal, 200,000), Budapest Party Committee organ; *Magyar Nemzet* (Hungarian Nation, 106,000), People's Patriotic Front daily; *Magyar Hirlap* (Hungarian Journal, 55,000), government publication; *Daily News* (15,000), in English and German.

News agencies. The Hungarian Telegraph Agency (*Magyar Távirati Iroda*—MTI) is the official facility. It is the sole receiver and distributor of news but maintains working relationships with several resident foreign bureaus, including Reuters and UPI.

Radio and television. Domestic radio and television service is provided by *Magyar Rádió*, which also transmits abroad in seven languages, and *Magyar Televizió*. There were approximately 5.7 million radio and 3.5 million television receivers in 1987.

INTERGOVERNMENTAL REPRESENTATION

Ambassador to the US: Dr. Vencel HAZI.

US Ambassador to Hungary: Robie Marcus Hooker PALMER.

Permanent Representative to the UN: Ferenc ESZTERGALYOS.

IGO Memberships (Non-UN): BIS, CCC, CMEA, IBEC, ICAC, ICCO, ICO, IIB, ILZ, Interpol, ISO, PCA, WTO.

ICELAND

Republic of Iceland
Lýthveldith Ísland

Political Status: Independent republic established June 17, 1944; under democratic parliamentary system.

Area: 39,768 sq. mi. (103,000 sq. km.).

Population: 240,443 (1984C), 246,000 (1988E).

Major Urban Center (1984E): REYKJAVÍK (93,200; urban area, 130,700).

Official Language: Icelandic.

Monetary Unit: Króna (market rate March 1, 1988, 39.46 krónur = $1US).

President: Vigdís FINNBOGADÓTTIR (nonparty); elected June 29 and inaugurated August 1, 1980, for a four-year term, succeeding Kristján ELDJÁRN; sworn in for second term August 1, 1984, having been unopposed at close of nominations on June 2.

Prime Minister: Thorsteinn PÁLSSON (Independence Party); sworn in as head of three-party government on July 8, 1987, after election of April 25, succeeding Steingrímur HERMANNSSON (Progressive Party).

THE COUNTRY

The westernmost nation of Europe, Iceland lies in the North Atlantic Ocean just below the Arctic Circle. Although one-eighth of the land surface is glacier, the warm Gulf Stream assures a relatively moderate climate and provides the country's richest resource in the fish that abound in its territorial waters. The population is quite homogeneous, the preponderant majority being of Icelandic descent. The language is an old form of Norwegian. Virtually the entire population (98 percent) adheres to the official Evangelical Lutheran Church, although other faiths are permitted. Approximately 80 percent of adult women work outside the home, mainly in clerical and service sectors; the male-female wage differential averages 40 percent, and women own only 10 percent of total property. While female representation averages only 15 percent, a number of women are politically influential, including the current president of the Republic, the social affairs minister, and six legislators elected by the Women's Alliance party.

Although fishing and fish processing employ only about 13 percent of the labor force, marine products account for nearly three-fourths of Iceland's export trade. Other leading activities include dairy farming and sheep raising, while development efforts have focused on exploiting the country's considerable hydroelectric and geothermal energy supply. As a result, aluminum smelting has become a significant industry, producing 10–15 percent of export earnings. Numerous devaluations of the króna since 1981, chronic inflation that peaked at 86 percent in 1983, a foreign debt amounting to nearly half of the GNP, and decline of the fishing industry due to high costs and depleting stocks have all contributed to economic adversity; however, a potential for more efficient exploitation of both maritime resources and domestic industrial capacity offers hope for long-term recovery.

GOVERNMENT AND POLITICS

Political background. Settled by disaffected Norsemen in the last quarter of the ninth century, Iceland flourished as an independent republic until 1262, when it came under Norwegian rule. In 1381, it became (along with other Scandinavian countries) a Danish dominion and for 500 years stagnated under neglect, natural calamities, and rigid colonial controls. The island achieved limited home rule in 1874 under the leadership of Jón SIGURDSSON and in 1918 became an internally self-governing state united with Denmark under a common king. Iceland's strategic position in World War II resulted in British occupation after the fall of Denmark, with military control subsequently being transferred to American forces. Full independence was achieved on June 17, 1944.

Coalition government has dominated Icelandic politics, there having been few single-party governments in the nation's history. The most significant change in the postwar era was the defeat of a 12-year centrist coalition of the Independence and Social Democratic parties in 1971. The election of June 1974 resulted in a coalition involving the Independence and Progressive parties, while that of June 1978 yielded (on August 31) a center-left government headed by Ólafur JÓHANNESSON and containing three representatives each from the Progressive, Social Democratic, and People's Alliance parties. The latter government fell on October 12, 1979, after withdrawal of the Social Democratic ministers in protest against what they regarded as inadequate measures to curb mounting inflation. Three days later, Benedikt GRÖNDAL formed a minority Social Democratic government that remained in office on an interim basis following an inconclusive legislative election on December 2–3.

A series of unsuccessful efforts to form a new government led President Kristján ELDJÁRN to threaten the nomination of a nonparty cabinet. On February 8, however, Gunnar THORODDSEN, vice chairman of the Independence Party, formed a coalition with the Progressive and Alliance parties despite the opposition of Indepen-

dence leader Geir HALLGRÍMSSON and most of the IP parliamentary delegation. Subsequently, on June 29, Vigdís FINNBOGADÓTTIR, director of the Reykjavík Theatre since 1972, became the world's first popularly elected female head of state when she defeated three other candidates seeking to succeed President Eldjárn, who had announced on January 1 his decision not to run for a fourth term.

On March 14, 1983, Prime Minister Thoroddsen requested dissolution of the *Althing* and announced that he would not be a candidate for reelection. After generally inconclusive balloting on April 23, unsuccessful efforts by each of the three major party leaders to form a viable coalition, and a new presidential threat to name a nonparty administration, Steingrímur HERMANNSSON of the Progressive Party succeeded, on May 26, in organizing a cabinet of his own and Independence Party members.

At the election of April 26, 1987, marked by an Independence Party loss of five seats and a doubling (to six) of representation by the feminist Women's Alliance, the coalition fell one seat short of a majority, with the prime minister moving into caretaker status, pending installation of the IP's Thorsteinn PÁLSSON as head of a new administration that included Progressive and Social Democratic representatives on July 8.

Constitution and government. Iceland's constitution, adopted by referendum in 1944, vests power in a president (whose functions are mainly titular), a prime minister, a legislature, and a judiciary. The president is directly elected for a four-year term. The (now) 63-member legislature (*Althing*), also elected for four years (subject to dissolution), encompasses an upper house (*Efri deild*) of 21 members selected by and from the elected deputies and a lower house (*Nedri deild*) containing the other 42 members. The prime minister, who performs most executive functions, is appointed by the president but is responsible to the legislature. The two houses sit as a unicameral body for certain purposes, including deliberation of no-confidence motions. District magistrates (*sýslumenn*) and town magistrates (*baejarfógetar*) occupy the lower levels of the judicial system, while the Supreme Court sits at the apex. There are also special courts to deal with such areas as labor disputes and impeachment of government officials.

Iceland is divided into 17 provinces (*sýslur*), which are subdivided into municipalities. Each province is administered by a centrally appointed administrative officer (*sýslumadur*), who is assisted by an elected council. The rural and urban municipalities, which also elect councils, are headed by officers known as *sveitarstjóri* and *baejarstjóri*, respectively.

Foreign relations. Isolation and neutrality, together with an economic dependence on fishing, are the principal determinants of Icelandic foreign relations. Successive attempts to extend its territorial waters from 4 miles in 1952 to 200 miles in 1975 embroiled the country in disputes with a number of maritime competitors. The first "cod war" resulted from the proclamation of a 12-mile limit in 1958 and was terminated by agreements with Britain, Ireland, and West Germany in 1961; a second period of hostilities followed the proclamation of a 50-mile limit in 1973 and was ended by a temporary agreement with Britain the same year. In 1975, a third "cod war" erupted following Iceland's extension of the limit to 200 miles despite an adverse ruling in 1974 by the International Court of Justice on the 50-mile limit. In June 1980, problems arose when Denmark extended its jurisdiction to 200 miles off Greenland's eastern coast. A month earlier, on the other hand, Iceland and Norway reached an agreement on fishing within an overlapping 200-mile zone and, in October 1981, concluded a related agreement on possible exploitation of mineral resources in the vicinity of Jan Mayen Island.

Traditionally opposed to maintenance of an indigenous military force, the government, in 1973, announced its intention to close the US-maintained NATO base at Keflavík in order "to ensure Iceland's security". The decision was reversed in August 1974 by the conservative-led Hallgrímsson coalition, although the government requested that Icelanders be employed for nonmilitary work previously done by Americans at the base.

The Hermannsson government was generally conciliatory toward the US and NATO, although relations with Washington were momentarily strained in March 1985 by press reports that Pentagon contingency plans included the movement of nuclear depth charges to the Keflavík base. Shortly thereafter, US officials assured Reykjavík that no such weapons would be deployed without Icelandic approval while in May the *Althing,* by unanimous vote, declared the country to be a nuclear-free zone.

Iceland received world attention in October 1986 as the venue of a meeting between US President Reagan and Soviet leader Mikhail Gorbachev. While the Reykjavík summit yielded no discernible progress toward resolution of East-West differences, it was of measurable value to a country that had been attempting to encourage tourism as an alternative to near-exclusive dependency on fishing as a source of foreign exchange.

Current issues. The defeat of the Hermannsson coalition at the 1987 balloting was not due to a poor showing by the prime minister's Progressive Party, but to a preelection split in the Independence Party (see Political Parties, below), coupled with a strong showing by the Women's Alliance. The program of the three-party government installed on July 8 called for new duties on nonessential imports, a 12–20 percent increase in family and pension benefits, and a review of maritime, agricultural, and fiscal policies. No major changes in foreign affairs were announced, although Fisheries Minister Halldór ÁSGRÍMS-SON (one of only two incumbents to retain office under the Pálsson administration) had announced in June that Iceland might withdraw from the International Whaling Commission if the United States continued to complain that it was engaged in commercial whaling under the guise of "scientific research".

POLITICAL PARTIES

Former Government Coalition:

Independence Party (*Sjálfstaedisflokkurinn*). Formed in 1929 by a union of conservative and liberal groups, the Independence Party has traditionally been the strongest party and has participated in most governments since 1944. Although primarily representing commercial and fishing interests, it draws support from all strata of society and is especially strong in the urban areas. It stands for a liberal economic policy, economic stabilization, and the continued presence of NATO forces. A major split occurred in February 1980 when Vice Chairman Thoroddsen, backed by several Independence MPs, broke with the regular party leadership and formed a coalition government with the Progressive and People's Alliance parties. Thoroddsen did not seek parliamentary reelection in 1983, while former prime minister and party chairman Geir Hallgrímsson accepted the foreign affairs portfolio in the coalition government announced in May 1983. Hallgrímsson stepped down as party leader the following October, although remaining in the government until January 1986. The party lost 5 of its 23 seats at the election of April 26, 1987, largely because of the defection of Albert Gudmundsson, who had been forced to resign as industry minister in March because of a tax scandal and subsequently formed the Citizens' Party (below). The government installed on July 8 included 4 Independence Party ministers.

Leaders: Thorsteinn PÁLSSON (Prime Minister and Party Chairman), Ólafur G. EINARSSON (Parliamentary Leader), Geir HALL-GRÍMSSON (former Prime Minister), Sigurbjörn MAGNÚSSON (Parliamentary Secretary), Kjartan GUNNARSSON (Party Secretary).

Progressive Party (*Framsóknarflokkurinn*). Founded in 1916 as a representative of agrarian interests, the Progressive Party has been responsible for many social and economic reforms benefiting agriculture and the fisheries. In the past it has expressed qualified support for NATO while advocating the withdrawal of military forces as soon as possible. Although placing second in the 1983 balloting, its chairman, Steingrímur Hermannsson, succeeded in forming a new coalition government in which 6 of the 10 cabinet posts were allocated to the Independence Party. The party did better than anticipated at the 1987 balloting, retaining 13 of its 14 seats (the net loss attributable to the defection of a Progressive legislator prior to the election). Unable to form a new government, party leader Steingrímur Hermannsson submitted his resignation on April 28. The party was awarded 4 ministries in the Pálsson government of July 8, with Hermannsson assuming the Foreign Affairs portfolio.

Leaders: Steingrímur HERMANNSSON (Party Chairman and former Prime Minister), Páll PÉTURSSON (Parliamentary Leader), Ólafur JÓHANNESSON (former Prime Minister), Kristján BENEDIKTSSON (Parliamentary Secretary), Haukur INGIBERGSSON (Party Secretary).

Social Democratic People's Party (*Althýduflokkurinn*). Formed in 1916, the Social Democratic People's Party advocates state ownership of large enterprises, increased social-welfare benefits, and continued support for NATO forces, with eventual replacement by Icelanders when conditions permit. At the April 1987 election, the party's legislative strength rose from 6 seats to 10. It controls 3 ministries in the present administration, including the Finance portfolio.

Leaders: Jón Boldvin HANNIBALSSON (Party Chairman), Eidur GUDNASON (Parliamentary Leader), Jón GUDMUNDSSON (Parliamentary Secretary).

Other Parties:

Citizens' Party (*Borgariflokkurinn*). The Citizens' Party was formed in March 1987 by Independence Party veteran Albert Gudmundsson, who had been obliged to leave the Hermannsson cabinet after being charged with failure to report income from a failed shipping firm. The new party won 7 seats at the April poll, forcing the resignation of the coalition government.

Leader: Albert GUDMUNDSSON.

People's Alliance (*Althýdubandalag*). Formerly styled the Labor Alliance, the People's Alliance was launched in 1956 as an electoral front of Communists and disaffected Social Democrats. The Communists form its principal element. The Alliance has advocated a radical socialist domestic program and a neutralist policy in foreign affairs, including Icelandic withdrawal from NATO. Its parliamentary representation fell from 10 to 8 in 1987.

Leaders: Svavar GESTSSON (Party Chairman), Ragnar ARNALDS (Parliamentary Leader), Kristján VALDIMARSSON (Parliamentary Secretary).

Social Democratic Alliance (*Bandalag Jafnadarmanna*). The Social Democratic Alliance was formed prior to the 1983 election, at which it won 4 seats, by a number of dissident Social Democrats dissatisfied with worsening economic conditions. It is unrepresented in the current *Althing*.

Leaders: Gudmundur EINARSSON (Party Chairman), Stefán BENEDIKTSSON (former Parliamentary Leader).

Women's Alliance (*Samtoek um Kvennalista*). The Women's Alliance was organized prior to the 1983 balloting, for which it presented 8 candidates, seating 3. Said to be the only feminist group in the world to secure such representation, it doubled its seats to 6 in 1987. It has no formal leadership, the role of parliamentary leader being subject to rotation among its legislative members.

Leaders: Gudrún AGNARSDÓTTIR (Parliamentary Chairman), Bergljót BALDURSDÓTTIR (Parliamentary Secretary).

LEGISLATURE

The **Parliament** (*Althing*) currently consists of 63 members normally elected for four-year terms by a mixed system of proportional and direct representation. The members elect one-third of their number to constitute the Upper Chamber (*Efri deild*), while the remainder make up the Lower Chamber (*Nedri deild*). At the election of April 26, 1987, the Independence Party won 18 seats; the Progressive Party, 13; the Social Democratic People's Party, 10; the People's Alliance, 8; the Citizens' Party, 7; and the Women's Alliance, 6. The remaining seat was won by a Progressive Party dissident.

Speaker of the Combined Houses: Thorvaldur G. KRISTJÁNSSON.

CABINET

Prime Minister	Thorsteinn Pálsson
Ministers	
Agriculture	Jón Helgason
Commerce	Jón Sigurdsson
Communications	Mathías Á. Mathíesen
Education	Birgir Ísleifur Gunnarsson
Finance	Jón Baldvin Hannibalsson
Fisheries	Halldór Ásgrímsson
Foreign Affairs	Steingrímur Hermannsson
Health and Social Security	Gudmundur Bjarnason
Industry	Fridrik Sophusson
Justice and Ecclesiastical Affairs	Jón Sigurdsson
Social Affairs	Jóhanna Sigurdardóttir
Chairman, Board of Directors, Central Bank of Iceland	Jonas G. Rafnar

NEWS MEDIA

Press. The following are dailies published at Reykjavík: *Morgunbladid* (45,000), Independence Party; *DV* (*Dagbladid-Visir*, 39,000), independent; *Timinn* (17,000), Progressive Party; *Thjodviljinn* (12,000), People's Alliance; *Althydubladid* (5,200), Social Democratic.

Radio and television. The Icelandic State Broadcasting Service (*Ríkisútvarpid*) operates 47 radio transmitting and relay stations. Its television division (*Ríkisútvarpid-Sjónvarp*) provides service about 24 hours a week. In addition, the US Navy broadcasts from the NATO base at Keflavík. There were approximately 79,000 radio and 71,000 television receivers in 1987.

INTERGOVERNMENTAL REPRESENTATION

Ambassador to the US: Ingvi S. INGVARSSON.

US Ambassador to Iceland: Nicholas RUWE.

Permanent Representative to the UN: Hans G. ANDERSEN.

IGO Memberships (Non-UN): BIS, CCC, CEUR, EFTA, ICES, Intelsat, Interpol, IWC, NATO, NC, NIB, OECD, PCA.

INDIA

Republic of India
Bharat

Political Status: Independent member of the Commonwealth since August 15, 1947; republican system instituted January 26, 1950.

Area: 1,222,480 sq. mi. (3,166,240 sq. km.), excluding approximately 32,350 sq. mi. (83,787 sq. km.) of Jammu and Kashmir presently held by Pakistan and 14,500 sq. mi. (37,555 sq. km.) held by China.

Population: 685,185,700 (1981C), 792,615,000 (1988E), including population of Indian-controlled portion of Jammu and Kashmir. The 1981 figure does not include an adjustment for underenumeration.

Major Urban Centers (1981C): DELHI (4,865,077; urban area, 5,713,581); Calcutta (3,291,655; urban area, 9,165,650); Bombay (urban area, 8,227,332); Madras (3,266,034); Bangalore (2,482,507); Hyderabad (2,142,087); Ahmedabad (2,024,917); Kanpur (1,531,345).

Official Languages: Hindi, English (in addition to other languages which are official at state levels).

Monetary Unit: Rupee (market rate March 1, 1988, 13.08 rupees = $1US).

President: Ramaswamy VENKATARAMAN; elected July 13, 1987, and inaugurated July 25 for a five-year term, succeeding Giani Zail SINGH.

Vice President: Dr. Shankar Dayal SHARMA; elected August 21, 1987, and inaugurated September 3 to post vacated by designation as President of Ramaswamy VENKATARAMAN.

Prime Minister: Rajiv GANDHI (Indian National Congress–I); sworn in October 31, 1984, upon the assassination of Indira GANDHI (Indian National Congress–I); reconfirmed following election of December 24–27, 1984.

THE COUNTRY

Forming a natural subcontinent between the Arabian Sea and the Bay of Bengal, and stretching from the Himalayas in the north to the Indian Ocean in the south, the Republic of India encompasses a mélange of ethnic, linguistic, and socioreligious groups which together constitute a national population second in size only to that of mainland China. Although about 83 percent of the people profess Hinduism, the Muslim component (over 11 percent) makes India the world's third-largest Muslim country, after Indonesia and Bangladesh. Smaller religious groups include Christians, Sikhs, Buddhists, and Jains. Despite Hindu predominance, independent India has rigorously adhered to the concept of a secular state in which all religions enjoy equal status under the constitution. Caste discrimination, though still practiced in rural areas, is legally outlawed by the Indian constitution. In 1984, women constituted 21 percent of the paid labor force, 90 percent of whom were in agriculture and the rest spread evenly through manufacturing, education, and health care; female representation averages about 5 percent overall in elected bodies.

India embraces over 1,600 different languages and dialects. Most are of Indo-European derivation, followed in importance by Dravidian, Austro-Asiatic, and Sino-Tibiti. The states, the federal units of India, are delimited by major linguistic groups, the official language of a given state being that spoken by the majority of its inhabitants.

Agriculture employs over 70 percent of the Indian labor force; the principal crops are rice, cotton, and jute (fall harvest); wheat and barley (summer harvest); and tea, oil-seeds, coffee, and sugarcane. Beginning with the advent of the "green revolution" in the late 1960s, agricultural productivity improved markedly from an historically low level characterized by antiquated farming practices and poor varieties of seed. Industrial activity has traditionally centered on the production of cotton textiles, jute, tea, and food products, but substantial investments under a series of five-year plans have provided impetus to the expansion of heavy industry.

Like its predecessors, the sixth plan projected an annual economic growth rate that India had never achieved for a sustained period. However, upon plan completion, its target of 5.2 percent had been met, primarily by increased productivity in the agricultural and tertiary sectors, with self-sufficiency in the critical area of crude oil production having risen from 34 to 73 percent.

Until quite recently, India was heavily dependent on concessional multilateral financing, leading aid sources being the World Bank and the International Monetary Fund. In November 1981 the IMF approved a record three-year loan of some $5.8 billion, the rights to $1.1 billion of which were relinquished in early 1984 because of improvement in the country's foreign exchange position.

The seventh five-year plan, introduced in late 1985, called for 4 percent annual growth in agriculture and 7 percent growth in industry. While the former target has thus far been met or surpassed, agricultural output declined substantially in 1987 because of severe drought in 21 of 35 rainfall subdivisions; high releases of food grains were nonetheless maintained because of substantial reserves built up in previous years.

Overall policy aims at a "socialist pattern of society", with provision for a mixed economy embracing both public and private sectors. Railroads, aviation, armaments, and atomic energy are exclusively government controlled, and the state dominates a range of other specified activities, including iron and steel, shipbuilding, oil, chemicals, certain types of mining, banking, and foreign trade.

GOVERNMENT AND POLITICS

Political background. After a prolonged struggle against colonial rule, India attained independence within the Commonwealth on August 15, 1947, when Britain put into effect the Indian Independence Act, thereby dividing the subcontinent into the sovereign states of India and Pakistan. However, the act applied only to former British India, thus setting the stage for confrontation between the two new nations over accession of various princely states and feudatories, including the still-disputed Jammu and Kashmir.

Mohandas Karamchand GANDHI, an advocate of nonviolence and internal reform of Indian society who had led the country's quest for independence, was assassinated on January 30, 1948, provoking widespread rioting that claimed the lives of countless members of the *Mahasabha,* the Hindu politico-religious group to which his assassin belonged. Jawahar Lal NEHRU, leader of the politically dominant Indian National Congress (INC), served as India's first prime minister, enunciating its basic principles of democracy, secularism, socialism, and economic development at home; nonalignment in world power conflicts; and nonparticipation in military blocs. Congress rule within a democratic framework was successfully maintained throughout Nehru's 17-year premiership, which began in the course of armed hostilities with Pakistan over the status of Kashmir and was marked by such subsequent events as the annexation of Hyderabad in 1949, the adoption of a republican form of parliamentary government in 1950, the transfer of Pondicherry and other colonial territories by France in 1954, the constitutional incorporation of Jammu and Kashmir into the Indian Union in 1957, the annexation of Goa and other Portuguese possessions in 1961, and a limited armed conflict with the People's Republic of China in 1962.

Nehru died on May 27, 1964, and was succeeded by Lal Bahadur SHASTRI, under whose leadership India fought a second major war with Pakistan (August-September 1965) that ended without territorial gain for either side. Shastri died on January 11, 1966, while attending a peace conference at Tashkent, USSR. His successor as prime minister was Indira GANDHI, Nehru's daughter, whose early period in office saw a partial normalization of relations with Pakistan, a marked growth in food production following acute shortages in 1966-1967, and a decline in the political ascendancy of the Congress, which split in 1969 into conservative and Gandhi factions.

Mrs. Gandhi's late-1970 political gamble of dissolving the lower house of Parliament was vindicated when her "New Congress" group, which had held 228 of 520 seats, swept the election of March 1971 with a record majority of 352, sufficient to amend the constitution. The combined strength of Mrs. Gandhi's principal adversaries, a "Grand Coalition" of the conservative "Old Congress", the right-wing *Jana Sangh* and *Swatantra* parties, and a group of extreme leftists, was reduced to 49. The pro-Soviet Communist Party of India had earlier entered into a loose coalition with the ruling Congress, whereas the Communist Party of India–Marxist, remaining nonaligned on the national scene, had entered into a major electoral alliance with local and translocal parties in its stronghold, West Bengal.

Immediately after the election, a deteriorating political situation in East Pakistan occasioned a massive influx of some ten million refugees into India. Subsequently, India and Pakistan were drawn into a third major military engagement, which resulted in a decisive Indian victory and conversion of East Pakistan into the independent state of Bangladesh.

Internal developments in India during this period included the abolition of constitutionally guaranteed privileges of the British-trained Civil Service; the withdrawal of privy purses to the erstwhile rulers of princely India; the upgrading of Himachal Pradesh, a former Union Territory administered by the central government, to the status of a full state of the Indian Union; reorganization of the Assam region, resulting in creation of the states of Assam, Meghalaya, Manipur, and Tripura, and of the Union Territories of Mizoram and Arunachal Pradesh (components of the former North East Frontier Agency); enactment of legislation authorizing the use of preventive detention as an antiterrorism measure; and the adoption of constitutional amendments permitting parliamentary restriction of fundamental rights and the exemption of nationalization laws from constant legal challenges.

A major constitutional change occurred on September 4, 1974, when the House of the People (*Lok Sabha*) passed a Constitutional Amendment Bill altering the status of Sikkim from that of a protectorate to that of an associated state of the Indian Union. The change had earlier been unanimously endorsed by all 32 members of the Sikkim National Assembly and received the assent of the king (*chogyal*) of Sikkim, although the latter did not personally favor the change. On May 16, 1975, following the passage of another Constitutional Amendment Bill on April 26, Sikkim became the 22nd state of the Indian Union, the office of *chogyal* being abolished.

Of far greater constitutional significance were the events leading up to and following a High Court ruling on June 12, 1975, that Mrs. Gandhi's election to the *Lok Sabha* in 1971 was null and void. On March 6 a growing anticorruption campaign led by Jaya Prakash NARAYAN, who had founded the Indian Socialist Party in 1948 but had subsequently withdrawn from politics to become a leader of the *Sarvodaya* movement, culminated in a massive demonstration at Delhi and the presentation of a "charter of demands" for reform to the presiding officers of Parliament. A number of Congress Party leaders expressed sympathy with Narayan's views, while Mrs. Gandhi declared that a conspiracy was being mounted to force her from office. At a crucial state election in Gujarat on June 8 and 11, the Congress lost its former overwhelming majority to the Janata (People's) Front, a multiparty coalition that supported Narayan's program. The following day, the High Court of Allahabad ruled in favor of a petition filed by Raj NARAIN, Mrs. Gandhi's Samyukta Socialist opponent in 1971, that charged election irregularities. The ruling disqualified Mrs. Gandhi from membership in the *Lok Sabha,* but she was granted a 20-day stay to appeal to the Supreme Court. Opposition party leaders immediately launched a civil-disobedience campaign to force the prime minister's

resignation, and on June 26 President Fakhruddin 'Ali AHMED declared a state of emergency. Nearly 700 opposition leaders were promptly arrested, press censorship was introduced for the first time since independence, and on July 1 Mrs. Gandhi announced a 20-point program of economic reform designed to curb inflation, liquidate rural indebtedness, stimulate production, and increase employment opportunities. The state of emergency was approved by both houses of Parliament on July 22, a majority of the opposition members subsequently withdrawing from the lower house in protest. On November 7 the Indian Supreme Court unanimously upheld the prime minister's appeal against the ruling of the Allahabad High Court, and on December 29 the Congress Party postponed until 1977 the parliamentary election scheduled for early 1976, Mrs. Gandhi vowing to maintain the state of emergency until a sense of national unity and discipline had been restored. The decision to continue the existing *Lok Sabha* was formally affirmed by Parliament in February 1976, while the government's capacity to amend the constitution was assured by its regaining a two-thirds majority in the March election to the Council of States (*Rajya Sabha*).

Mrs. Gandhi startled the nation and the world by announcing in January 1977 that a parliamentary election would be held the following March. Although India had achieved a degree of economic recovery since the declaration of emergency, the arbitrary arrest of opposition leaders, the favoritism displayed toward the prime minister's younger son, Sanjay GANDHI, in an apparent effort to groom him as her successor, and discontent with the frequently capricious implementation of the government's birth-control program had led to a major erosion of Congress' popularity as well as to defections from its leadership. With only six weeks allotted for the campaign, Janata forces quickly organized at the national level under Narayan and opposition Congress leader Morarji R. DESAI. Campaigning on a platform of ending the emergency and restoring democracy, the Janata coalition swept the election, Mrs. Gandhi herself being among the defeated. On March 24 Desai was designated prime minister, and the state of emergency was revoked on March 27.

The new government strengthened its position in a series of state contests in June, the Janata Party winning control in 8 of the 11 legislatures for which elections were held. These victories permitted the unopposed election of the Janata candidate, Neelam Sanjiva REDDY, as president of India on July 18. In late December Mrs. Gandhi, followed shortly by seven supporters, resigned from the INC Working Committee and, in January 1978, organized the Indian National Congress–Indira (INC-I), which by midyear had become the nation's major opposition party. Mrs. Gandhi returned to the *Lok Sabha* after winning a November by-election in a rural district of southern India, but in late December was stripped of her seat and imprisoned for the duration of the parliamentary term by action of the Janata majority.

The fragility of the Janata coalition was increasingly manifested from mid-1978 to mid-1979 in a major leadership dispute between Prime Minister Desai and Charan SINGH that involved charges of corruption leveled against relatives of both, and by a series of communal riots in a number of states that effectively split the party into Hindu and secular factions. Singh was removed from the home ministry in June 1978 but returned as deputy premier and finance minister in January 1979. Meanwhile, the communal riots provoked demands by Raj Narain and others that Janata adopt the posture of a secular "third force" opposed to both Hindu extremism and the "authoritarianism" of Indira Gandhi. Removed from Janata's national executive on grounds that he had called for a change in government, Narain resigned from the party on June 23, 1979, to establish "a real Janata Party". In mid-July, Singh and a number of others also resigned to join Narain's Janata Party–Secular (JP-S), thus depriving the government of its majority in the *Lok Sabha* and forcing Desai's resignation as prime minister on July 15. Invited by President Reddy to form a new government on July 26, Singh was sworn in two days later, but submitted his own resignation on August 20 following the defection of a number of INC members and an announcement that the INC-I would not support him in a confidence vote. Although Jagjivan RAM, Janata parliamentary leader following Desai's resignation from the party on July 27, insisted that Singh's advice to dissolve the lower house was not binding because his government had never survived a confidence vote, Reddy nonetheless dissolved the *Lok Sabha* on August 22 and asked Singh to remain in office in a caretaker capacity pending a new election. After Janata announced that it would introduce a motion in the *Rajya Sabha* for impeachment of the president on grounds that he had called for dissolution to prevent Ram, a Harijan (untouchable), from becoming prime minister, Reddy prorogued the upper house on August 25.

In a dramatic reversal of her defeat in 1977, Mrs. Gandhi swept back into power at the *Lok Sabha* election of January 3–6, 1980, her party's majority (enhanced by a by-election win in February) precisely equaling that of her 1971 triumph: 352 seats. Following a series of similarly impressive state assembly victories on May 28–31, indirect biennial balloting for approximately one-third of the *Rajya Sabha* seats on July 4 yielded an INC-I plurality of 121 seats, 12 more than that of the breakaway Congress a decade earlier. The personal popularity of Mrs. Gandhi was further evidenced when a longtime supporter, Giani Zail SINGH, a Sikh, easily won election as India's seventh president on July 15, 1982. However, her administration proved unable to curb mounting domestic violence. A continuing influx of illegal Bengali immigrants generated reprisals in Assam, while riots broke out in Karnataka over a recommendation that Kannada be adopted as the language of instruction. Muslims and Hindis battled sporadically in Uttar Pradesh and Gujarat, and untouchables were targets for numerous atrocities. Maoists, Naxalites, and other extremists continued their frequently violent activities in Manipur, Mizoram, Nagaland, and West Bengal, while demands for autonomy by Sikhs in Punjab led to the storming of Parliament in October 1982 by several thousand individuals as part of a continuing *morcha* ("mass agitation").

The Sikh agitation had been led by the relatively moderate leader of the Akali Religious Party (*Shiromani Akali Dal*), Harchand Singh LONGOWAL, who sought, in addition to greater political and religious autonomy for his followers, the incorporation into Punjab of Chandigarh (a union territory that served as the state capital of both Punjab and Haryana), and the abolition of controversial language in the Indian constitution that was construed as classifying the Sikh religion as a sect of Hinduism. In March 1984, as Hindu-Sikh violence intensified, the government charged Longowal with sedition, thus driving many of his supporters closer to the extremists led by Sikh fundamentalist Jarnail Singh BHINDRANWALE, who operated from sanctuary within the Golden Temple at Amritsar. In early April, New Delhi indicated a willingness to accept the Akali demand for separate religious recognition, but a series of subsequent assassinations, reportedly ordered by Bhindranwale, yielded an assault on the Golden Temple during the night of June 5–6, in the course of which upwards of 1,000 persons, including Bhindranwale, were killed. Although four of the six officers in charge of the operation were Sikhs and the government ordered immediate repairs to the heavily damaged shrine, the action provoked an even deeper resentment within the Sikh community that reached a climax on October 31 with Mrs. Gandhi's assassination by two Sikh members of her personal bodyguard.

Mrs. Gandhi's younger son, Rajiv, was immediately sworn in as prime minister (Sanjay having been killed in a June 1980 plane crash). The ensuing parliamentary campaign lasted only six weeks (the shortest since independence), but featured an extremely well-financed effort by the INC-I that was launched with heavy emphasis on the need for national unity and concluded with an appeal to "Give Rajiv a chance". The turnout of voters was a record 63.6 percent, with the INC-I, in a victory of unprecedented magnitude, capturing 401 of 508 contested seats. The fateful year concluded with mankind's worst industrial accident: a gas leak at Union Carbide's Bhopal chemical facility in early December that resulted in some 2,000 deaths, with many more thousands seriously injured. While precise responsibility for the accident was unclear, a number of less serious accidents in 1985, including a chlorine gas leak at Bombay in late August, contributed to rising popular clamor for more effective regulation of several hundred establishments utilizing or producing hazardous chemicals.

On July 25, 1985, the government concluded a peace accord with Harchand Singh that provided for a devolution of power to local Punjab authorities and paved the way for state elections in late September. Sikh extremists responded by assassinating Longowal on August 20, although the balloting to fill both Punjabi and national legislative seats proceeded on September 25, with the *Akali Dal* registering an overwhelming victory under its new leader, Surjit Singh BARNALA.

Violence in Punjab and elsewhere persisted through 1986. At midyear, the prime minister ruled out the transfer of Chandigarh without a simultaneous conveyance of Punjabi territory to Haryana; meanwhile radicals had proclaimed a separate Sikh state, Khalistan, the exact boundaries of which were unspecified. The approval of measures conferring statehood on Arunachal Pradesh and Mizoram failed to satisfy local separatists, while others continued their activities in Assam, Nagaland, Tripura, and Jammu and Kashmir (despite a lifting of president's rule in the last on December 7).

At indirect balloting on July 13, 1987, the (then) vice president and nominee of the Congress (I), Ramaswamy VENKATARAMAN, defeated the opposition candidate for president by an overwhelming margin and was sworn in as President Singh's successor on July 25. On September 3 Dr. Shankar Dayal SHARMA, theretofore governor of Maharashtra, was inaugurated as vice president, after having been elected unopposed on August 21.

Constitution and government. India's frequently amended constitution of January 26, 1950, provides for a republican form of parliamentary government in a union which currently embraces 25 states and 7 centrally administered territories. The national government is headed by a president, who is chosen for a five-year term by an electoral college (under a weighted voting system) composed of the elected members of both the bicameral Parliament and the state legislatures. The vice president is chosen by an electoral college consisting of the members of the full Parliament; he serves as ex officio chairman of the upper house of the legislature, the Council of States (*Rajya Sabha*), and presides over its meetings. The lower House of the People (*Lok Sabha*) is presided over by a speaker elected by its members. He must be a member of Parliament but by convention divests himself of party affiliation while serving as presiding officer. The prime minister is elected by the parliamentary members of the majority party and heads a government that is collectively responsible to the legislature.

Each of the states has a governor, who is appointed by the president for a term of five years, and a popularly elected legislature. The legislatures may be bicameral or unicameral, but all are subject to maximum terms of five years. Administration is carried out by a chief minister heading a cabinet subject to parliamentary responsibility. In the event that constitutional processes in a state are rendered inoperative, the Union constitution provides for the institution of direct presidential rule. The president can also appoint an agent to act in his name, while the prime minister can call for new state elections.

The Union Territories, some of which are former foreign territories or located in outlying regions, are administered by appointed officials responsible to the president. Such officials are generally referred to as lieutenant governors. For all practical purposes, the entire administration of the Union Territories is directed by the central government at New Delhi.

State and Capital	Area (sq. mi.)	Population (1981C)
Andhra Pradesh (Hyderabad)	106,877	53,592,605
Arunachal Pradesh (Itanagar)	32,269	628,050
Assam (Dispur)	30,318	19,902,826E
Bihar (Patna)	67,133	69,823,154
Goa (Panaji)	1,429	1,003,136
Gujarat (Gandhinagar)	75,699	33,960,905
Haryana (Chandigarh)	17,074	12,850,902
Himachal Pradesh (Simla)	21,495	4,237,569
Jammu and Kashmir (Srinagar)	85,805	5,954,010
Karnataka (Bangalore)	74,043	37,043,451
Kerala (Trivandrum)	15,005	25,403,217
Madhya Pradesh (Bhopal)	170,980	52,138,467
Maharashtra (Bombay)	118,826	62,715,300
Manipur (Imphal)	8,631	1,411,375
Meghalaya (Shillong)	8,683	1,328,343
Mizoram (Aizawl)	8,142	487,774
Nagaland (Kohima)	6,381	773,281
Orissa (Bhubaneswar)	60,147	26,272,054
Punjab (Chandigarh)	19,448	16,669,755
Rajasthan (Jaipur)	132,129	34,108,292
Sikkim (Gangtok)	2,744	314,999
Tamil Nadu (Madras)	50,220	48,297,456
Tripura (Agartala)	4,045	2,047,351
Uttar Pradesh (Lucknow)	113,673	110,885,874
West Bengal (Calcutta)	33,920	54,485,560

Union Territory and Capital		
Andaman and Nicobar Is. (Port Blair)	3,202	188,254
Chandigarh (Chandigarh)	44	450,061
Dadra and Nagar Haveli (Silvassa)	189	103,677
Daman and Diu (Daman)	43	78,981
Delhi (Delhi)	573	6,196,414
Lakshadweep (Kavaratti)	12	40,237
Pondicherry (Pondicherry)	185	604,182

Foreign relations. India's policies as a member of the Commonwealth, the United Nations, and other multilateral organizations have been governed by a persistent belief in nonalignment, peaceful settlement of international disputes, self-determination for colonial peoples, and comprehensive efforts to ameliorate conditions in the developing nations. In conformity with this outlook, it has avoided participation in regional defense pacts and has avoided exclusive alignment with either Western or Communist powers, although it has accepted economic and, since 1962, military aid from members of both groups. More specific foreign-policy preoccupations have, since independence, focused on Pakistan. The centuries-old rivalry between Hindus and Muslims in the subcontinent was directly responsible for the partition in 1947. This rivalry continued to embitter Indo-Pakistani relations, particularly in regard to the long-standing dispute over Jammu and Kashmir. Fighting over that territory in 1947–1948 resulted in a de facto division into Pakistani- and Indian-held sectors (see map under Pakistan entry). The Indian portion was subsequently absorbed as a separate state of the Indian Union. The action was strongly protested by Pakistan, and renewed armed conflict between the two countries erupted in 1965. In December 1971, following a political crisis in East Pakistan and the flight of millions of Bengali refugees to India, the two nations again went to war. The brief conflict ended with Pakistani acceptance of a ceasefire on the western front and the emergence in the east of the independent state of Bangladesh. (In March 1972 India and Bangladesh concluded a 25-year Treaty of Friendship and Cooperation, and relations remain close despite recent disagreements over boundaries, diversion of Ganges water, and conflicting claims to newly formed islands in the Bay of Bengal.)

India and Pakistan agreed to resume normal relations during talks at Simla, India, in mid-1972, but ambassadors were not exchanged until July 1976, two months after a meeting at Islamabad, Pakistan, that also led to resumed Pakistani overflights of Indian territory and to renewed commercial relations (supplementing a government-to-government trade pact concluded in November 1974). Despite differences in 1981–1982, generated in large part by

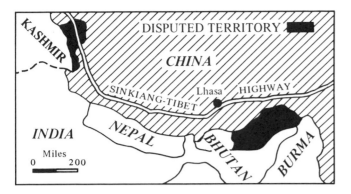

US decisions to approve Pakistani purchase of advanced F-16 fighter aircraft and to grant some $3.2 billion in aid and military credits to Islamabad, Prime Minister Indira Gandhi and Pakistani President Zia met on November 1, 1982, and agreed to the establishment of a permanent joint commission to discuss economic, educational, cultural, and technical (but not military) cooperation. More recently, following a prime ministerial meeting at Bangalore, India, in November 1986, representatives of the two governments met at Lahore, Pakistan, to formulate measures aimed at controlling illegal crossings, drug trafficking, smuggling, and terrorism along their border.

In its relations with the People's Republic of China, India initially attempted to maintain a friendly posture; however, border tensions between the world's two most populous nations had developed by the end of the 1950s and escalated into military conflict in October 1962. At issue are 14,500 square miles of territory in the Aksai Chin area of eastern Kashmir (through which the Chinese have constructed a strategic highway linking Sinkiang with Tibet) and some 36,000 square miles of Arunachal Pradesh in the northeast (below the so-called McMahon line, dating from 1913–1914), from which China withdrew after the 1962 war (see map). Following a thaw in relations during 1976, ambassadors were exchanged for the first time in nearly 14 years, while respective ministerial visits to China in 1979 and to India in 1981 represented the first such exchange in over 20 years. Formal, but still inclusive talks on the border issue were most recently held at New Delhi at Beijing in mid-1986 and New Delhi in late 1987.

Relations between India and the Soviet Union have reflected a general coincidence of views on international political problems, mutual proximity to China, Soviet support for the Indian position on the Kashmir issue, and Soviet economic and military aid. In August 1971 the two countries entered into a 20-year Treaty of Peace, Friendship, and Cooperation. Although the Charan Singh caretaker government denounced the Soviet intervention in Afghanistan in December 1979, the successor Gandhi administration labeled the Afghan situation "an internal affair of that country". Furthermore, in July 1980, India became the first non-Communist state to recognize the pro-Soviet Heng Samrin government of Kampuchea. In his first official foreign trip as prime minister, Rajiv Gandhi visited the Soviet Union in May 1985, while Soviet leader Mikhail Gorbachev was accorded a well-orchestrated welcome to India in November 1986.

The United States was a strong supporter of Indian independence, and US aid for some years thereafter far exceeded that received by any other nation. Politically, relations have fluctuated, the most severe strain having occurred during the 1971 conflict between India and Pakistan. Differences also arose over India's explosion of an underground nuclear device in May 1974 and a subsequent refusal to accept a provision of the 1978 US Nuclear Non-Proliferation Act requiring those countries receiving enriched US fuel to permit international inspection. The latter problem was apparently resolved during Mrs. Gandhi's mid-1982 visit to the United States, when it was announced that France was willing to supply reactor fuel, thereby permitting both Washington and New Delhi to skirt the issue and yet fulfill the terms of a 30-year nuclear aid agreement concluded in 1963. Three months earlier, India had announced plans to reprocess potentially weapons-grade plutonium, although the government remains publicly committed to the development of nuclear capability for peaceful purposes only. A variety of nuclear and arms supply issues (particularly as they involved Pakistan) were reportedly discussed with President Reagan at the beginning of a four-day US visit by Rajiv Gandhi on June 12, 1985; on the following day, the Indian leader, in an address to a joint session of Congress, expressed his country's gratitude for US economic input to the "green revolution" of the 1960s.

During 1987 India became directly involved in the ethnic strife that had engulfed its southern neighbor, Sri Lanka. Sri Lanka's Tamil dissidents had long enjoyed the tacit support of compatriots in the south Indian state of Tamil Nadu and it was not until 1985 that Rajiv Gandhi retreated from the overtly pro-Tamil posture of his recently assassinated mother by declaring that he opposed any attempt by the Tamil minority to establish an autonomous state in Sri Lanka. In late 1986 he dispatched emissaries to Colombo to propose the merger of Sri Lanka's largely Tamil Northern and Eastern provinces as a basis of settling the dispute and in July 1987, during his first official visit to Sri Lanka, offered military assistance to the Jayawardene government in support of the regionalization plan. Within days, 3,000 Indian troops were dispatched to the island's Jaffna peninsula to assist in the disarming of the guerrillas. Eventually, most of the rebels agreed to surrender their weapons in accordance with the Indian-backed peace accord, although numerous outbreaks of violence continued for the remainder of the year, despite an increase in Indian troop strength to at least 15,000. (For further details see article on Sri Lanka.)

Current issues. Despite his party's electoral triumph in late 1984, Prime Minister Gandhi was buffeted by a wide variety of ethnic, religious, and political challenges to his leadership during the ensuing three years. Conditions remained tense in much of the northeast, where the Gurkha National Liberation Front (GNLF), led by Subhash GHISING, was pitted against a state government controlled by the Communist Party of India—Marxist (CPI-M) in demanding a separate Gurkhaland (*Tarun Gorkha*) for India's Nepali-speaking minority. Throughout the region other tribal elements displayed mounting disillusionment with the state administrations of Bihar, Madhya Pradesh,

Orissa, and West Bengal, while in eastern Tripura numerous clashes were reported involving migrants from neighboring Bangladesh. Elsewhere, fighting persisted between Hindus and Muslims in Gujerat and Uttar Pradesh, while economic inequities sparked conflict between landowners and landless in Andhra Pradesh. Perhaps the most intractable problem, however, was that of Punjab. In August 1986 Gen. Arun VAIDYA, who had led the 1984 raid on the Golden Temple, was assassinated. In January 1987 some 400 troops mounted a fresh assault (the tenth since 1984) on the Golden Temple complex and in May central government rule was reimposed, with more than 1200 persons meeting violent deaths during the remainder of the year. (With no amelioration of the disturbances by early 1988, the government secured a constitutional amendment extending the one-year limit on central rule for upwards of three years.) Meanwhile, unrest persisted in the southern state of Tamil Nadu, whose longtime chief minister, Maruthur Gopala RAMACHANDRAN, had strongly supported intervention in Sri Lanka, but whose death in December 1987 provoked an intense power struggle that led to the imposition of presidential rule in January 1988.

In early 1987, the prime minister became embroiled in a series of scandals involving possible kickbacks on defense and other procurement from foreign suppliers. The most serious turned on a Swedish report that Indian officials had been paid $5 million in bribes on a $1.3 billion contract for field artillery during the previous year; additional charges involved possible improprieties in connection with the purchase of four West German submarines some years earlier. On April 12 the popular but controversial defense minister, Vishwanath Pratap SINGH, submitted his resignation because of an inquiry he had launched into illegal overseas activities by Indian businessmen, without having cleared the action with his cabinet colleagues. In his letter of resignation, Singh proclaimed his loyalty to the government, but was expelled from the INC-I at mid-year for "anti-party activities". The political fallout from the alleged "dirty deals" triggered a number of major cabinet changes and a poor showing by the Congress at state elections through early 1988.

POLITICAL PARTIES

Although a count during the first general election in 1952 revealed that there were over 100 parties and political groups contesting seats throughout the country, the undivided Indian National Congress (INC) dominated the political scene until 1969, when it split into ruling (Gandhi) and opposition factions (the latter, though repudiating the designation, subsequently being styled the Indian National Congress–Organization by the Election Commission). The Gandhi Congress swept the election of 1972 but became increasingly divided after its defeat in March 1977, and on January 1, 1978, those remaining loyal to Mrs. Gandhi organized separately as the Indian National Congress–Indira (INC-I), or Congress (I).

Following the declaration of emergency in June 1975, it was announced that a national Janata (People's) Front, comprising the Organization Congress, the Indian People's

Party, the Socialist Party, and the Indian People's Union, had been formed to oppose the Gandhi Congress in both houses of the national legislature. In May 1976 the widely respected Jaya Prakash Narayan announced that the Front would be converted into a unified political party in order to present a "democratic national alternative" to Congress rule. Narayan's subsequent arrest, coupled with his assertion that he would withdraw from opposition activity unless the projected merger materialized, contributed to the establishment of the Janata Party in early 1977 and to its remarkable success in defeating the Congress by a near two-to-one majority of lower-house seats at the election of March 16–20.

Precipitated initially by a fissure resulting from the expulsion of Charan Singh from the government in mid-1978 and exacerbated by communal riots and intraparty conflict in a number of states, the Janata Party split in July 1979, a breakaway faction organizing in the *Lok Sabha* as the Janata Party–Secular (JP-S) and thereafter forming the core of the People's Party (*Lok Dal*) in preparation for the 1980 election, which was called following the resignation of Prime Minister Desai on July 15 and Singh's subsequent inability to organize a parliamentary majority.

At the lower-house election of January 3–6, 1980, the Congress (I) secured a near two-thirds majority of legislative seats, exclusive of those won by allied groups, while falling only 2 seats short of a majority at a partial upper-house election on July 4. In the wake of Mrs. Gandhi's assassination, the INC-I swept nearly 80 percent of contested seats at the *Lok Sabha* balloting of December 24–27, 1984.

In early 1985, a constitutional amendment was approved that would, under most circumstances, disqualify members of parliament or of state legislatures upon changing party allegiance. Known as the "anti-defection bill", the measure was defended by the prime minister as helping to overcome the evil of "politics without principles".

Governing Party:

Indian National Congress–Indira (INC-I). Founded in 1885 and led from 1966 to 1977 by Indira Gandhi, the original Indian National Congress (INC) experienced the withdrawal in 1969 of an anti-Gandhi conservative faction that became India's first recognized opposition party, the Indian National Congress–Organization (INC-O)), prior to joining the Janata Party (below). The INC was further weakened by the defection and/or expulsion of numerous leaders both before and after the March 1977 election, at which Mrs. Gandhi lost her own parliamentary seat. On December 18 she resigned from the party's Executive Committee, and on January 1–2, 1978, her supporters designated the former prime minister as the president of a new national opposition party, the INC-I, or Congress (I). Building from a political base in the traditionally pro-Gandhi south, the INC-I had displaced the rump INC as the principal opposition force in both houses of Parliament by May. On July 23, 1981, the Election Commission ruled that the INC-I was the "real" Congress in that the majority of INC leaders and legislative officeholders at the time of the 1978 division had since become members of Mrs. Gandhi's party. By late 1982 the anti-Gandhi Congress had, for all practical purposes, disintegrated (see INC-S, below).

Under the leadership of Mrs. Gandhi's son, Rajiv, the INC-I won 401 of 508 contested lower house seats in December 1984 (adding 11 others by late 1986). It was marginally less successful at the state level in March 1985, winning control of 8 of the 11 state assemblies for which elections were held.

Leaders: Rajiv GANDHI (Prime Minister and President of the Party); A.K. ANTHONY, Ghulam Nabi AZAD, Naresh Chandra CHATUR-

VEDI, Oskar FERNANDES, Najma HEPTULLA, G. Karuppiah MOOPANAR, Ram RATTAN, Kedar Nath SINGH (General Secretaries).

Other Parties:

Indian National Congress–Socialist (INC-S). Following the 1980 general election, at which the anti-Gandhi INC won a mere 13 seats in the *Lok Sabha,* the party was increasingly identified as the INC-U, or Congress (U), after its president, Devaraj URS. In 1981, in the wake of numerous defections, including that of Yeshwantrao Balwantrao CHAVAN, the INC-U leader in the lower house (who subsequently joined the INC-I), the party on August 5 suffered the loss of a faction led by Jagjivan RAM; formerly associated with the old INC and subsequently several other groups, including Janata, Ram established his own Indian National Congress–Jagjivan (INC-J), or Congress (J), which merged with the INC-I in August 1986, following Ram's death in July. In August 1981, President Urs resigned and was succeeded by Sharad Pawar, the party thenceforth being known as the INC-S, or Congress (S), a designation retained when the party adopted the "Socialist" label the following October.

Subsequently, the party continued to experience defections and splintering. In December the majority of the Kerala state party, led by A.K. Antony and identified as the Indian National Congress–Antony (INC-A), or Congress (A), joined an eight-party United Democratic Front (UDF) alliance, led by Mrs. Gandhi's Congress (I), that won the May 19, 1982, state election and subsequently merged with the INC-I. Meanwhile on April 28 the Karnataka state party, led by Urs until his death on June 6, had reorganized as the Karnataka Revolutionary Front (KRF). Thus by late 1982 the Congress (S) could claim no more than a handful of *Lok Sabha* seats and remained a significant force in only one or two states. It claimed only 4 lower house seats after the 1984 balloting (all of which were lost by either by-election or defection during the ensuing two years) and was virtually annihilated at the state level in March 1985.

Leaders: Sarat Chandra SINHA (President); V. Kishore CHANDRA, S. DEO, K.P. UNNIKRISHNAN (General Secretaries).

National Socialist Congress (*Rashtriya Samajwadi* Congress). The National Socialist Congress was launched in January 1987 under the presidency of Pranab Mukherjee, an "Indira loyalist" who had been suspended from the INC-I in April 1986 after attacking Rajiv Gandhi for deviating from his mother's socialist principles and establishing a "neofascist oligarchy" in India.

Leader: Pranab MUKHERJEE (President).

Janata Party (JP). Functioning on an ad hoc basis prior to the March 1977 election, the Janata Party was formally established on May 1, 1977, by merger of the Indian People's Union (*Bharatiya Jana Sangh* – BJS), the Indian National Congress–Organization (INC-O), the Indian People's Party (*Bharatiya Lok Dal* – BLD), and the Socialist Party (SP). The Congress for Democracy (CFD) agreed to join the new party on May 5.

From the outset, considerable diversity existed within the JP, the most conspicuous common denominator being shared opposition to Mrs. Gandhi. The BJS was a right-wing Hindu nationalist group, while the BLD, organized in 1974 as a coalition of parties opposed to government economic policies, included the former Freedom Party (*Swatantra*), the Samyukta Socialist Party, the Orissa-based Uktal Congress, the Indian Revolutionary Party (*Bharatiya Kranti Dal*) of Uttar Pradesh, and others. The SP came into existence in 1971 as a merger of the Praja Socialist Party and the Indian Socialist Party, joined by a number of Samyukta Socialists. The CFD was formed prior to the 1977 election by longtime INC leader Jagjivan Ram, who broke with Mrs. Gandhi over the suspension of civil rights and the increasingly authoritarian tendencies of her administration.

Following conflict between the *Jana Sangh* section of the party and supporters of former BLD president Charan Singh, the latter withdrew in mid-1979 (see Dalit Mazdoor Kisan Party, below), forcing the resignation of Prime Minister Desai and the subsequent dissolution of the *Lok Sabha* on August 22. After Janata's defeat at the 1980 general election the party suffered the defection of Jagjivan Ram, who briefly formed his own Janata Party (J) before joining the Congress (U) – see INC(S), above – in April 1980. Its representation in the lower house fell from 21 to 10 at the election of December 1984, although it had regained 3 of those lost by early 1987.

Leaders: Chandra SEKHAR (President); Madhu DANDAVATE (Leader in *Lok Sabha*); M.S. GURUPADASWAMY (Leader in *Rajya Sabha*); Anantram JAISWAL, Indubhai PATEL, S. Jaipal REDDY, Syed SHAHABUDDIN, Yashwant SINHA, Bhai VAIDYA (General Secretaries).

Bharatiya Janata Party (BJP). The BJP was formed in April 1980 by the bulk of Janata's *Jana Sangh* group, which opposed efforts by the JP leadership to ban party officeholders from participation in the activities of the *Rashtriya Swayamsevak Sangh* (RSS), a paramilitary Hindu communal group. By 1982 the BJP was generally regarded as the best-organized non-Communist opposition party and in fact held more *Lok Sabha* seats than Janata. In August 1983, the party entered into a National Democratic Alliance with the *Lok Dal* (below), which remained in effect through the *Rajya Sabha* elections of March 1984, but was abandoned prior to the *Lok Sabha* balloting in December, at which the BJP's representation was reduced to 2 seats.

Leaders: Atal Bihari VAJPAYEE (President), Sikandar BAKHT (Vice President), Krishanlal SHARMA (General Secretary)

People's Party (*Lok Dal*). The *Lok Dal* was organized on September 26, 1979, by merger of a number of dissident Janata groups, including the Janata Party–Secular (JP-S), which had been formed by Raj Narain on July 10 after his expulsion from the Janata national executive for criticizing links between the *Jana Sangh* faction and the RSS. Charan Singh, designated leader of the JP-S upon leaving the government on July 16, was elected president of *Lok Dal* at its founding convention, while the JP-S was revived as a separate party by Narain following his expulsion from the *Lok Dal* in March 1980 for "anti-party activities".

In early 1982 the *Lok Dal,* Janata, and the Congress (S) discussed a future merger and proposed a common platform on which to contest the May state elections, but both efforts proved abortive. On July 29 party President Charan Singh expelled a Haryana state legislative leader for allegedly working against party candidates in the May balloting, which in turn precipitated the resignation of four *Lok Dal* general secretaries. On August 9 a convention of dissidents, claiming the support of a majority of the party's *Lok Sabha* and state assembly representatives, voted to remove Singh and asserted their identity as the "real" *Lok Dal.* Subsequently, in January 1983, the dissidents rejoined Janata. In 1987 another split occurred, yielding a minority faction, *Lok Dal* (*A*), and a larger group, *Lok Dal* (*B*), that objected to Ajit Singh assuming the presidency after his father's death in May.

Leaders: Ajit SINGH (President, *Lok Dal* [*A*]), Hemvati Nandan BAHAGUNA (President, *Lok Dal* [*B*]), Satya Prakash MALAVIYA (Secretary General, *Lok Dal* [*B*]).

Communist Party of India (CPI). Though the CPI-M (below) took with it the majority of CPI members when it broke away in 1964, most of the party bureaucracy, legislative representatives, and trade unionists remained in the CPI. Loyal to the international goals of the USSR, the CPI favors large-scale, urban, capital-intensive industrialization, and "democratic centralism". Loosely allied with the INC, the party initially supported the 1975–1977 emergency. Unable to form a left-wing coalition (the CPI-M having allied itself with Janata), some state CPI organs remained associated with the INC at the March 1977 election, and the party as a whole suffered severe losses. After heated debate at its April 1978 convention, the CPI condemned its own support of the state of emergency. In opposition after the 1977 election, it supported the Singh government in August 1979, subsequently joining with the CPI-M and other groups in a Left Front coalition that contested the 1980 election and currently governs in West Bengal.

Former CPI chairman S.A. Dange (see AICP, below) was formally expelled from the party and the position of chairman was abolished at a CPI congress held March 22–28, 1982. At that time the party condemned the Gandhi government's "reactionary and authoritarian" domestic policies but voiced support for its continued adherence to nonalignment and friendship with the Soviet Union. Four months later, the CPI's Hirandra Nath MUKHERJEE, presidential nominee of the anti-Gandhi opposition, was disqualified from contesting the election against Zail Singh because of failure to register as a voter. The party's *Lok Sabha* representation fell from 13 to 6 in December 1984.

Leaders: C. Rajeswara RAO (General Secretary), Indrajit GUPTA (General Secretary, Trade Union Front).

All India Communist Party (AICP). The AICP was formed in April 1980 by supporters of S.A. Dange, who had resigned the CPI chairmanship in November 1979 after his appeal for support of the Congress (I) had been rejected by the party's National Council. It is unrepresented in the *Lok Sabha.*

Leader: Shripad Amrit DANGE (General Secretary).

Communist Party of India–Marxist (CPI-M). Organized in 1964 by desertion from the CPI of "Leftists" favoring a more radical line, the CPI-M supports small-scale, rural-oriented, labor-intensive development as well as political decentralization. Allied with Janata in the March 1977 election primarily to insure the defeat of the INC, the CPI-M won control of West Bengal three months later and of Tripura in January 1978. In 1969 some of its more extreme and overtly pro-Chinese members had withdrawn to form the CPI-ML (below). Although supporting the Desai government after the 1977 election, it joined with the CPI in endorsing Charan Singh's efforts to establish a parliamentary majority in 1979 and participated in the 1980 Left Front coalition. It currently holds 22 seats in the *Lok Sabha*.

Leaders: Jyoti BASU (Chief Minister of West Bengal), E.M. Sankaran NAMBOODIRIPAD (General Secretary).

Communist Party of India–Marxist-Leninist (CPI-ML). As the result of disagreement over operational strategy for the spread of communism in rural India, an extreme faction within the CPI-M organized the CPI-ML in the spring of 1969. Committed to Maoist principles of people's liberation warfare, the party was actively involved in the "Naxalite" terrorist movement in North Bengal and was banned during the state of emergency. Some members, including a group led by Satya Narain Singh, have since rejected revolutionary Marxism and now support parliamentary democracy. Others, retaining a revolutionary stance, have severely criticized the present policies of the People's Republic of China. The party failed to secure *Lok Sabha* representation in 1977, 1980, or 1984.

Leaders: Satya Narain SINGH, Ram Pyara SARAF.

Akali Religious Party (*Shiromani Akali Dal*—SAD). While contesting elections nationally, the *Akali Dal*'s influence is confined primarily to Punjab, where it campaigns against excessive federal influence in Sikh affairs. It campaigned as a Janata Party ally at the 1980 election, losing 8 of its 9 lower-house seats; in the same year, it lost control of the Punjab legislature to the INC-I.

During 1981–1982 the *Akali Dal* became increasingly militant with regard to demands for greater state autonomy, designation of the city of Amritsar as a Sikh holy site, and the transfer to Punjab of the city of Chandigarh, currently a Union Territory as well as the administrative capital of both Punjab and Haryana states. While the party has remained aloof from extremist acts, such as hijackings, undertaken by separatist groups that include the *Dal Khalsa* ("Association of the Pure"), its leaders lent support to a *morcha* ("mass agitation") that resulted in the arrest of up to 30,000 Sikhs leading up to and following the October 11, 1982, storming of the Parliament House at New Delhi. A number of party leaders were among the hundreds detained in November as the government attempted to avoid another *morcha* at the Asian Games, held at New Delhi.

Prior to the June 1984 storming of Amritsar's Golden Temple, leadership of the Sikh agitation had effectively passed from the *Akali Dal* to the more extremist followers of Jarnail Singh Bhindranwale. In July 1985, a year after Bhindranwale's death, the moderate *Akali Dal* leader, Harchand Singh Longowal, concluded a peace agreement with Prime Minister Rajiv Gandhi, but was assassinated on August 20. In accordance with the agreement, state legislative balloting was nonetheless held on September 25, at which the *Akali Dal* secured an overwhelming majority of 73 out of 117 Assembly seats, while capturing 7 of 13 seats in the *Lok Sabha*. In early November, a militant breakaway faction, the United *Akali Dal*, which had boycotted the September poll, was itself weakened by the "dictatorial and undemocratic" response of its president, Joginder SINGH, to an appeal from the radical All India Sikh Student Federation (AISSF) that its members "unite under the banner of the *Damdami Taksal* [a radical religious organization] and the AISSF".

In May 1986, a number of leaders, including Prakash Singh Badal, a former chief minister, withdrew to form a separate party under Badal's presidency that was recognized as a distinct 27-member formation within the state assembly. In February 1987 the two breakaway factions agreed to unite as the Unified *Akali Dal* under the leadership of Simranjit Singh Mann, a former police official.

Leaders: Surjit Singh BARNALA (former Chief Minister of Punjab and President of the Party); Prakash Singh BADAL, Harbans Singh GHUMAN, Simranjit Singh MANN, Harbhajan Singh SANDHU (Unified *Akali Dal*).

All India Forward Bloc (AIFB). The AIFB is a leftist party confined primarily to Bengal, where it won 2 lower-house seats in 1984. Its program calls for land reform and nationalization of key sectors of the economy.

Leaders: Prem Dutta PALIWAL (Chairman), Chitta BASU (General Secretary).

Dravidian Progressive Federation (*Dravida Munnetra Kazhagam*—DMK). The DMK is an anti-Brahmin regional party dedicated to the promotion of Tamil interests. It opposes the retention of Hindi as an

official language and seeks more autonomy for the states. In the 1977 election it lost control of Tamil Nadu to the ADMK (below). In September 1979 it formed an alliance with the INC-I for the 1980 election, and, like the ADMK, supported the presidential candidacy of Zail Singh in 1982. It secured 2 lower house seats in 1984.

Leaders: Dr. Muthuvel KARUNANIDHI (former Chief Minister of Tamil Nadu), Nanjil K. MANOGARAN (General Secretary).

All India Dravidian Progressive Federation (*Anna Dravida Munnetra Kazhagam*—ADMK). The ADMK is a Tamil party which split from the DMK in 1972. It won control of Tamil Nadu, with Congress support, in 1977 and joined the Singh government in August 1979. Subsequently, it entered into an electoral agreement with Janata for the 1980 campaign. Its founder, former matinee idol Maruthur Gopala Ramachandran, died on December 24, 1987, provoking a succession struggle that yielded the brief incumbency as chief minister of his widow, Janaki Ramachandran, prior to the imposition of presidential rule on January 30, 1988. The Federation currently holds 11 *Lok Sabha* seats.

Leaders: Janaki RAMACHANDRAN, V.R. NEDUNCHEZHIAN (leader of dissident faction).

All India Muslim League (AIML). The AIML is a remnant of the pre-partition Muslim League led by Mohammad Ali Jinnah. It won 3 lower house seats in 1980 and 2 in 1984.

Leader: C.H. Muhammad KOYA.

Kerala Congress (KC). The KC won 2 *Lok Sabha* seats in 1980, though they were split between two factions that emerged in July 1979 and subsequently campaigned as allies of the INC-I and Left Front, respectively; a third group, led by R.B. Pillai, also supported the Left Front. The Joseph Faction controls both of the seats won in 1984.

Leaders: P.J. JOSEPH (INC-I faction), K.M. MANI (Left Front faction), R. Balakrishna PILLAI.

Revolutionary Socialist Party (RSP). The RSP is a Marxist-Leninist grouping that won 4 *Lok Sabha* seats in 1980, all from West Bengal as a participant in the Left Front. Its representation dropped to 3 in 1984.

Leader: Tridib CHOWDHURY (General Secretary).

Republican Party of India (RPI). The RPI is essentially a scheduled caste party committed to the realization of the equalitarian objectives of the preamble to the Indian constitution.

Leaders: Bala Sahib PRAKASH (President), J. ISHWARIBAI (General Secretary).

National Conference (NC). The dominant party in Jammu and Kashmir since independence, the NC continued to be led by Sheikh Mohammed ABDULLAH, who was primarily responsible for the 1947 decision to become part of India rather than Pakistan, until his death on September 9, 1982. He was succeeded as party leader and chief minister by his son, Dr. Farooq Abdullah, who was, however, dismissed from the latter post in July 1984 by Mrs. Gandhi, following a series of violent clashes with INC-I supporters and the loss of his majority in the State Assembly. Two months earlier, a group of NC dissidents had "expelled" Farooq from the party, naming his sister, Khaleda Shah, as president. However, Dr. Farooq returned as chief minister on March 27, 1987, following balloting four days earlier at which the NC in coalition with the INC-I won 62 of 76 Assembly seats.

Leaders: Dr. Farooq ABDULLAH (Chief Minister of Jammu and Kashmir), Sheikh Nazir AHMAD (General Secretary), Khaleda SHAH (dissident faction).

Peasants and Workers' Party of India (*Bharatiye Krishi Kamghar Paksha*—BKKP). The BKKP is a Marxist party whose influence is confined primarily to Maharashtra. In addition to nationalization of the factors of production, the party advocates the redrawing of state boundaries on an exclusively linguistic basis. It obtained 1 lower house seat in 1984, but is currently unrepresented in the *Lok Sabha*.

Leader: Dajiba DESAI (General Secretary).

All India Hindu Association (*Akhil Bharat Hindu Mahasabha*). A once-powerful Hindu group, the *Mahasabha* claims two million members but currently holds no seats in the *Lok Sabha*.

Leaders: Vikram SAVARKAR (President), Madhav Rao PATHAK (General Secretary).

Land of Telugu (*Telugu Desam*). Based in Andra Pradesh and organized in March 1982 by N.T. Rama Rao, a well-known film actor, the

Telugu Desam announced that it would support whatever party was in power at New Delhi, but would put forward its own program at the state level. It captured 28 *Lok Sabha* seats in 1984 and added 2 more during the following two years.

Leaders: N.T. Rama RAO, P. UPENDRA (General Secretary).

National Sanjay Platform (*Rashtriya Sanjay Manch* — RSM). The RSM was formed in March 1983 by the widow of the prime minister's brother, Sanjay. Committed to moderate socialism and a secular and democratic state, the party failed to secure *Lok Sabha* representation in 1984.

Leader: Maneka GANDHI.

Muslim Legislative Union (*Majlis-Ittehad-ul-Mussalman*). The *Majlis* is an Andhra Pradesh-based Muslim group that is currently unrepresented in the *Lok Sabha*.

Assam People's Council (*Asom Gana Parishad* — AGP). The AGP was launched in October 1985 as a coalition (but not a merger) of the **All-Assam Students' Union** (AASU) and the **All-Assam Gana Sangram Parishad** (AAGSP), which had initially urged the deportation of (largely Bangladeshi) "aliens" from Assam, but had agreed in August 1985 to a compromise, whereby only those arriving in the state after March 1971 would be subject to expulsion. The coalition won 64 of 126 state assembly seats and 7 of 14 *Lok Sabha* seats in December 1985, one of which it subsequently lost.

Leaders: Prafulla Kumar MAHANTA (AASU), Biraj SARMA (AAGSP).

Other Assam groups include the **United Minorities Front** (UMF), whose president, Kalipada SEN, was assassinated in September 1986, and the **Plains Tribal Council of Assam** (PTCA), both of which opposed the Assam accord.

LEGISLATURE

The Union-level **Parliament** is a bicameral body consisting of an indirectly elected upper chamber (*Rajya Sabha*) and a directly elected lower chamber (*Lok Sabha*). Under the Indian constitution, all legislative subjects are divided into three jurisdictions: the Union list, comprising subjects on which the Union Parliament has exclusive authority; the State list, comprising subjects on which the state assemblies have authority; and the concurrent list, comprising subjects on which both may legislate, with a Union ruling predominating in the event of conflict and where state questions assume national importance.

Council of States (*Rajya Sabha*). The upper chamber is a permanent body of not more than 250 members, up to 12 of whom may be appointed for six-year terms by the president on the basis of intellectual preeminence; the remainder are chosen for staggered six-year terms (approximately one-third retiring every two years) by the elected members of the state and territorial assemblies, according to quotas allotted to each. As of early 1988, there were 245 seats, distributed as follows: Indian National Congress-Indira, 149; Communist Party of India-Marxist, 14; All India Dravidian Progressive Federation, 11; Telugu Desam, 11; Janata Party, 10; Bharatiya Janata Party, 9; People's Party, 9; Communist Party of India, 4; Dravidian Progressive Federation, 3; Akali Religious Party, 2; Assam People's Council, 2; All India Forward Bloc, 1; National Conference, 1; independents and others, 9; nominated, 6; vacant, 4.

Chairman: Dr. Shankar Dayal SHARMA.

House of the People (*Lok Sabha*). The lower chamber currently consists of 544 directly elected members from the states and Union Territories. If the president is convinced that any minorities are not adequately represented in the House, he can nominate additional members. Under a constitutional amendment adopted in November 1976, the House has a term of six years, unless dissolved earlier. There is also a constitutional provision (exercised in March 1976) allowing the delay of a scheduled election for one year during a state of emergency.

At the election of December 24–27, 1984, members were elected from 508 constituencies, 27 seats from Assam and Punjab remaining tempo-

rarily unfilled because of unsettled conditions, while polling in 7 other constituencies was also deferred for miscellaneous reasons. In early 1987, as a result of the 1984 balloting, elections for the Assam and Punjab seats in 1985, and a series of by-elections, the Indian National Congress–Indira held 412 seats (including the speaker); Telugu Desam, 30; Communist Party of India–Marxist, 22; Janata Party, 13; All India Dravidian Progressive Federation, 11; Communist Party of India, 6; Assam People's Council, 6; National Conference (Farooq Group), 3; Revolutionary Socialist Party, 3; Akali Religious Party (Badal Group), 3; Akali Religious Party, 2; All-India Forward Bloc, 2; Bharatiya Janata Party, 2; Kerala Congress (Joseph), 2; People's Party, 2; All India Muslim League, 2; Dravidian Progressive Federation, 2; independents, 16, vacancies, 5.

Speaker: Dr. Balram JAKHAR.

CABINET

Prime Minister	Rajiv Gandhi

Ministers

Agriculture	Bhajan Lal
Atomic Energy and Space	Rajiv Gandhi
Civil Aviation	Motilal Vora
Communications	Vasant Puroshottam Sathe
Defense	Krishna Chandra Pant
Energy	Vasant Puroshottam Sathe
External Affairs	Rajiv Gandhi
Finance and Commerce	Narain Dutt
Health and Family Welfare	Motilal Vora
Home Affairs	Buta Singh
Human Resources Development	P.V. Narasimha Rao
Industry	J. Vengal Rao
Information and Broadcasting	Har Kishan Lal Bhagat
Law and Justice	Bindeshwari Dubey
Parliamentary Affairs	Har Kishan Lal Bhagat
Planning and Program Implementation	P. Shiv Shanker
Science and Technology	Rajiv Gandhi
Steel and Mines	Makham Lal Fotedar
Textiles	Ram Niwas Mirdha
Tourism	Mohsina Kidwai
Urban Development	Mohsina Kidwai
Water Resources	Dinesh Singh

Ministers of State (Independent Charge)

Environment and Forests	Z.R. Ansari
Food and Civil Supplies	Sukh Ram
Labor	Jagdish Tytler
Petroleum	Brahm Dutt
Railways	Madhavrao Scindia
Surface Transport	Rajesh Pilot
Welfare	Dr. Rajendra Kumari Bajpai

Other Ministers of State

Agricultural Research and Education	Hari Krishna Shastri
Agriculture	Shyamlal Yadav
Banking and Economic Affairs	Eduardo Faleiro
Chemicals and Petrochemicals	P.K. Jaichandra Singh
Coal	C.K. Jaffer Sharief
Commerce	P.R. Das Munshi
Defense	Santosh Mohan Dev
Defense Production	Shiv Raj Patil
Education and Culture	L.P. Sahi
Expenditure	B.K. Gadhvi
External Affairs	K. Natwar Singh
Fertilizers	R. Prabhu
Health	Saroj Khaparde
Home Affairs	Chintamani Panigrahi
Home Affairs (Interior)	P. Chidambaram
Industrial Development	M. Arunachalam
Law and Justice	H.R. Bhardwaj
Mines	Ramanand Yadav

Parliamentary Affairs	Sheila Dikshit
	M.M. Jacob
Personnel, Public Grievances and Pensions	P. Chidambram
Planning and Program Implementation	Biren Singh Engti
Power	Sushila Rohatgi
Revenue	Ajit Kuman Panja
Rural Development	Janardhana Poojary
Science and Technology	K.R. Narayanan
Steel	Yogendra Makwana
Tourism	Girdhar Gomango
Urban Development	Dalbir Singh
Water Resources	Krishna Sahi
Youth Affairs, Sports and Child Development	Margaret Alva
Governor, Reserve Bank	Ram Nath Malhotra

NEWS MEDIA

Traditionally among the freest in Asia, Indian news media were subjected to rigid government control following the declaration of emergency in June 1975. Most of the emergency legislation was rescinded in April 1977, and a constitutional amendment passed in August 1978 guaranteed the right to report parliamentary proceedings.

In a report submitted in April 1982, a government press commission recommended, inter alia, that precensorship be limited to extreme situations involving the national interest, that journalists should be compelled to disclose sources only in exceptional circumstances, that limitations be placed on newspaper ownership by interests engaged in other businesses, that foreign ownership be proscribed, and that a joint public-private Newspaper Development Commission, funded by taxes on newsprint and advertising, be created to facilitate expansion of Indian-language, local, and small publications. In addition, the press commission opposed the public takeover of failing newspapers while endorsing governmental initiative in launching papers in areas where none exist.

Press. There are more than 1,000 daily newspapers published in India. Although the Hindi press claims the greatest number of publications, the English-language press is dominant in both political influence and readership. The (then) largest English paper, *Indian Express* (New Delhi and elsewhere, 600,000), announced in November 1981 the closing of its Bombay edition and seven related publications because of political pressure (following a corruption investigation against the chief minister of Maharashtra) as well as labor and financial difficulties. The other leading dailies are as follows: *Malayala Manorama* (Kottayam and Kozhikode, 590,000), in Malayalam; *Times of India* (Bombay, New Delhi, and Ahmedabad, 580,000), founded 1838, in English; *Navbharat Times* (Bombay and New Delhi, 490,000), in Hindi; *Mathrubhumi* (Kottayam, Kozhikode, and Cochin, 440,000), in Malayalam; *The Hindu* (Madras, 420,000), founded 1878, in English; *Ananda Bazar Patrika* (Calcutta, 408,000), in Bengali; *Jugantar* (Calcutta, 302,000), in Bengali; *Gujarat Samachar* (Ahmedabad and Surat, 302,000), in Gujarati; *Eenadu* (Hyderabad and elsewhere, 290,000), in Telugu; *Thanti* (Madras and elsewhere, 285,000), in Tamil; *Loksatta* (Bombay, 262,000), in Marathi; *Hindustan Times* (New Delhi, 260,000), in English; *Statesman* (Calcutta and New Delhi, 214,000), founded 1875, in English; *Prajavani* (Bangalore, 198,000), in Kannada; *Hindustan* (New Delhi, 170,000), in Hindi; *Dinakaran* (Madras and elsewhere, 145,000), Tamil.

News agencies. India's four news agencies (the English-language Press Trust of India and United News of India, plus the Hindi-language *Samachar Bharati* and *Hindustan Samachar*) merged, under government pressure, in February 1976 but were permitted to reestablish as separate entities in 1978. Numerous foreign agencies maintain offices at New Delhi and other principal cities.

Radio and television. The Ministry of Information and Broadcasting supervises two separately operated facilities, All India Radio (AIR) and *Doordarshan* India (Television India — TVI). There were approximately 50 million radio and 5.0 million television receivers in 1987.

INTERGOVERNMENTAL REPRESENTATION

Ambassador to the US: Pratap Kishan KAUL.

US Ambassador to India: John Gunther DEAN.

Permanent Representative to the UN: Chinmaya Rajaninath GHAREKHAN.

IGO Memberships (Non-UN): ADB, ADF, AfDB, ANRPC, APCC, APEF, CCC, CP, CWTH, ICAC, ICO, IIC, ILZ, Inmarsat, Intelsat, Interpol, ISO, ITC, ITPA, IWC, IWTC, NAM, PCA, SAARC.

INDONESIA

Republic of Indonesia
Republik Indonesia

Political Status: Independent republic established August 17, 1945; under modified military regime instituted March 12, 1966.

Area: 741,117 sq. mi. (1,919,494 sq. km.).

Population: 147,490,298 (1980C), 173,284,000 (1988E).

Major Urban Centers (1980C): JAKARTA (6,503,000); Surabaya (2,027,000); Bandung (1,461,000); Medan (1,376,000); Semarang (1,027,000); Palembang (787,000); Ujung Pandang (formerly Makassar, 709,000); Malang (512,000); Padang (481,000); Yogyakarta (399,000).

Official Language: Bahasa Indonesian (a form of Malay).

Monetary Unit: Rupiah (market rate March 1, 1988 1660.00 rupiahs = $1US).

President: Gen. (Ret.) SUHARTO (SOEHARTO); assumed emergency executive powers on behalf of President SUKARNO on March 12, 1966; named Acting President in 1967; elected President by the People's Consultative Assembly in 1968; reelected to a fifth five-year term on March 10, 1988.

Vice President: Lt. Gen. (Ret.) SUDHARMONO; elected by the People's Consultative Assembly on March 11, 1983, for a term concurrent with that of the President, succeeding Gen. (Ret.) Umar WIRAHADIKUSUMAH.

THE COUNTRY

The most populous country of Southeast Asia, Indonesia is an archipelago of over 13,500 islands that fringes the equator for a distance of 3,000 miles from the Asian mainland to Australia. Java, Sumatra, and Borneo (whose territory Indonesia shares with Malaysia and Brunei) are the principal islands and contain most of the population, which is predominantly of Malay stock but includes some 3.5–4 million ethnic Chinese. The country contains the world's largest single Muslim group, in addition to small minorities of Christians (9 percent) and of Hindus and Buddhists (1 percent). In 1982, two-thirds of adult women were included in the official labor force, the majority in a combination of agriculture and cottage industries in rural areas; due partly to the predominance of the armed forces, coupled with Islamic strictures, female representation in government has been minimal.

Agriculture employs nearly 60 percent of the labor force and provides about one-third of the gross domestic product. Rubber, lumber, sugar, coffee, and tea are the major agricultural exports, while rice, corn, cassava, and sweet potatoes are grown mainly for domestic consumption. As the principal oil producer in the Far East, Indonesia was cushioned by high oil prices in the late 1970s. Following the March 1983 OPEC price cut, the rupiah was devalued 27.5 percent against the dollar and several major development projects were modified to conserve foreign exchange. With no significant recovery in oil, the economic slump has continued, bringing rising unemployment and calls for structural reform, particularly in regard to state trade monopolies, which have long been a basis of official patronage. The country's fourth five-year plan, Repelita IV (1984–1989), emphasizes the development of agribusiness and non-oil industry.

GOVERNMENT AND POLITICS

Political background. Colonized by the Portuguese in the sixteenth century and conquered by the Dutch in the seventeenth, the territory formerly known as the Netherlands East Indies was occupied by the Japanese in World War II. Upon Japanese withdrawal, Indonesian nationalists took control, proclaiming the independent Republic of Indonesia in August 1945. After four additional years of war and negotiation, the Netherlands government recognized the new republic on December 27, 1949, and relinquished claim to all its former East Indian possessions except West New Guinea (Irian Jaya), which came under Indonesian control in 1963. A Netherlands-Indonesian Union under the Dutch Crown had been established by the 1949 agreements but was dissolved in 1956. In December 1975 Indonesian troops occupied the Portuguese Overseas Territory of East Timor and on July 17, 1976, formally incorporated the region into Indonesia (see Annexed Territories, below).

SUKARNO, one of the leaders of the nationalist struggle, served as constitutional president from 1949 until the late 1950s, when he responded to a series of antigovernment rebellions by proclaiming martial law and, in 1959, imposing a so-called "guided democracy" under which he exercised quasi-dictatorial powers. The Indonesian Communist Party (PKI) assumed an increasingly prominent role and by 1965 had embarked, with Sukarno's acquiescence, on the establishment of a "Fifth Armed Force". The campaign to arm its supporters was actively resisted by the army, and on October 1, 1965, the PKI attempted to purge the army leadership. In retaliation, the military and the Indonesian masses assaulted their perceived opponents by the thousands in rural areas, killing numerous Chinese and virtually eradicating what had been the world's third-largest Communist party. In succeeding months President Sukarno attempted to restore order, but public confidence in his leadership had seriously eroded. In March 1966 he was forced to transfer key political and military powers to General SUHARTO, who had achieved prominence by turning back the attempted Communist takeover.

A year later, the People's Consultative Assembly removed Sukarno from office and he retired to Java, where he remained until his death in June 1970. Suharto, who had been named acting president, was elected by the Assembly in 1968 for a five-year term as chief executive. Although curbing many of the excesses of his predecessor, Suharto faced widespread discontent over steadily rising prices, domination of important sectors of the economy by foreign (particularly Japanese) capital, and pervasive military influence in government. Thus his election to a third term in 1978 was preceded by six months of student demonstrations directed in part against alleged government corruption and a structure of political representation that permits an overwhelming majority of the Assembly to be members of Golkar, the government-supportive coalition of functional groups (see Political Parties, below), or of the military. On the other hand, some 30,000 political detainees, including most of those held since the abortive 1965 coup, were freed under a government program that concluded in December 1979.

In nationwide balloting on April 23, 1987, that the government termed a "feast of democracy", Golkar's proportion of elected legislators rose from two-thirds to nearly three-quarters, while the strength of the Islamic-based United Development Party declined by nearly 12 percent; the smaller Indonesian Democratic Party, on the other hand, improved its showing by 2.4 percent over 1982.

On March 10, 1988, the People's Consultative Assembly unanimously elected President Suharto to a fifth five-year term. Eleven days later the chief executive announced a new cabinet, more than four-fifths of whose members were new appointees.

Constitution and government. In the wake of unsuccessful efforts to draft a permanent constitution in 1950 and 1956, the government in 1959 readopted by decree the provisional constitution of 1945, which allocated most powers to the president under a strong executive system. The five guiding principles (*pancasila*) identified in the preamble are monotheism, humanitarianism, national unity, democracy by consensus, and social justice.

The present structure of government is that of a highly centralized state whose principal components are the presidency, the Supreme Advisory Council (*Dewan Pertimbangan Agung* — DPA), the People's Representation Council (*Dewan Perwakilan Rakyat* — DPR), and the People's Consultative Assembly (*Majelis Permusyawaratan Rakyat* — MPR). The Assembly is the highest state organ, with sole competence to interpret the constitution and to elect the president and vice president. Meeting at least once every five years, it includes all members of the ordinary legislature, the People's Representation Council, in addition to regional delegates and representatives of assorted functional groups. As a practical matter, however, the presidency (including the Supreme Advisory Council and the National Planning Council) and the military remain the dominant political forces. At the apex of the judicial system is the Supreme Court (*Mahkamah Agung*), whose members are appointed by the president. Nominally independent of the executive, the court is essentially a review body and does not pass on the constitutionality of laws.

Indonesia is presently divided into 27 provinces, the most recent (East Timor) having been added in 1976. Provincial governors and regents are appointed by the central government from among nominees submitted by the regional and regency legislatures.

Foreign relations. Indonesia initially sought to play a prominent role in Asian affairs while avoiding involvement in conflicts between major powers. In the early 1960s, however, President Sukarno, asserting that a basic world conflict existed between the "old established forces" and the "new emerging forces", attempted to project Indonesia as the spearhead of the latter. While officially nonaligned in foreign policy, his regime formed close ties with the Soviet Union and the People's Republic of China; obtained the surrender of West New Guinea by the Netherlands; and instituted a policy of "confrontation", supported by guerrilla incursions, against the new state of Malaysia. Most of these trends have been reversed under Suharto's leadership, and although still formally nonaligned, Indonesia has drawn markedly closer to the West. Relations with Communist China deteriorated drastically and were formally suspended in October 1967; the three-year "confrontation" with Malaysia was terminated in 1966; diplomatic relations were established with Malaysia and Singapore; and Indonesia took the lead in forming the Association of Southeast Asian Nations (ASEAN) as an instrument of regional cooperation. Membership in the United Nations and many of its related agencies, from which Indonesia had withdrawn in 1965, was resumed in 1966. Relations with the United States, although strained by a year-long vacancy in the post of US ambassador to Jakarta, have recently been strengthened, the Reagan administration regarding Indonesia as an important anticommunist presence in the region; thus, the US chief executive met with President Suharto and the leaders of other ASEAN nations while en route to the Tokyo economic summit in May 1986.

Dutch interests dominate European investment, while Japan is by far the nation's leading trade partner, despite sporadic demonstrations against alleged economic imperialism and exploitation of Indonesian workers on the part of resident Japanese nationals. Anger has also been directed at Japanese investors who have met government requirements for joint ventures by taking ethnic Chinese instead of Indonesians as their partners. Problems with the Netherlands have turned less on economic issues than on South Moluccan aspirations for independence. Political leaders of the South Moluccan Islands had reserved the right of secession when their territory was incorporated into the Indonesian Republic in 1949; however, subsequent resistance to Indonesian rule was suppressed, and the "president" of a self-proclaimed Republic of South Moluccas was executed in 1966.

During 1979 the government fluctuated in its response to an influx of Indochinese refugees, most of them ethnic Chinese from Vietnam. More than 50,000 "boat people" had landed on islands of Indonesia's Anambas chain and the Riau Archipelago alone by June; in mid-July, Indonesia announced that the "boat people" would be permitted to stay in compounds on offshore islands, pending resettlement in other countries, and by the end of the year, the inflow of refugees had slowed to a trickle.

Relations with neighboring Australia worsened in 1983–1984 because of protests by Canberra's newly elected Labor Party government against large-scale antiguerrilla offensives in East Timor, although in August 1985 Prime Minister Hawke emulated his Liberal predecessor by recognizing Indonesian sovereignty in the territory. Tension again flared in April 1986, following publication in the *Sydney Morning Herald* of an article suggesting possible corruption within the Suharto administration.

Current issues. Despite continued economic difficulty, the 1987 balloting for national, provincial, and local legislators was remarkably uneventful, the heightened degree of Golkar domination assuring Suharto's assumption of a fifth presidential term in March 1988. Observers interpreted the modest gains by the Indonesian Democratic Party as indicative of a growing perception of social injustice by younger, urban voters, particularly those responding to Western influences. Neither of the minor parties is, however, an "opposition" group in the usual sense of the word; both are government-funded and support the president for reelection. Most recent criticism of the regime has come from a dissident group, the "Petition of 50", which was formed in 1980 by disaffected army officers and political activists, and is currently led by Slamet BRATANATA. Bratanata and others, while conceding that major advances have been registered under Suharto (particularly in education and health care), see further change as inhibited by a "cult of stability" that arose initially in reaction to the turmoil of the 1950s and early 1960s, but has yielded vastly enhanced central government power by ethnic Javanese at the expense of traditional regional and local authorities. In September 1986 H. Muhammed SANUSI, a prominent Islamic leader who had previously been convicted of subversion, was given a 20-year concurrent sentence for conspiring with Petition associates to assassinate President Suharto and overthrow the government.

By late 1987, speculation focused on who would emerge as heir apparent during the concluding years of the Suharto era, the most likely candidate appearing to be Golkar chairman SUDHARMONO, who was designated vice president on March 11, 1988, despite being viewed as somewhat left of center because of his advocacy of strong central government control.

POLITICAL PARTIES

The present government has long been supported by a coalition of social groups called Golkar, the traditional parties being outside the mainstream of political life.

Governing Coalition:

Joint Secretariat of Functional Groups (*Sekretariat Bersama Golongan Karya*—Sekber Golkar). A government-sponsored coalition organized in 1964, Golkar captured 64.3 percent of the popular vote in the 1982 election and 73.1 percent in 1987. Essentially a loose alliance of groups representing such functional interests as those of farmers, laborers, veterans, women, and youth, with preeminently military leadership, the organization is technically not a party and, by appealing to individual membership, has recently attempted to divest itself of its semi-corporativist structure. Jakarta's firm control over Golkar's activities was exhibited in September 1985 when intervention by its general chairman, Sudharmono, and armed forces chief Murdani prevented a civilian bureaucrat from challenging the incumbent, Maj. Gen. Imam MUNANDAR, for the governorship of Riau province.

Leaders: SUHARTO (President of the Republic), SUDHARMONO (Vice President of the Republic and Golkar General Chairman), Sarwono KUSUMAATMADJA (Secretary General).

Other Recognized Groups:

United Development Party (*Partai Persatuan Pembangunan*—PPP). In the face of sustained pressure from the government to simplify Indonesia's party system through fusion, four Islamic groups—the Muslim Scholars' Party (*Nahdatul-'Ulama*—NU), the Indonesian Islamic Party (*Partai Muslimin Indonesia*—PMI), the United Islamic Party of Indonesia (*Partai Sjarikat Islam Indonesia*—PSII), and the Muslim Teachers' Party (*Persatuan Tarbijah Islamijah*—Perti)—merged into the PPP in 1973. Although the party remained highly faction-ridden, its leadership generally supported government policies while seeking to suppress both radical elements and the more conservative *Nahdatul-'Ulama* faction. It won 16.0 percent of the popular vote in 1987, as contrasted with 27.8 percent in 1982.

During its first national congress, held at Jakarta on August 20–22, 1984, the PPP formally adopted *pancasila* as its sole ideology. However, elements within the *Nahdatul-'Ulama* demanded that the group withdraw from "practical politics", while expressing dissatisfaction with the leadership of (then) PPP chairman, John NARO, who had formerly led the PMI and was viewed as favoring the latter within the coalition. As a result, not only the NU, but also the less influential *Sjarikat Islam* severed their links with the PPP the following December, insisting that henceforth they would concentrate exclusively on social and religious activities.

Leaders: Jailani NARO (President), MARDINSYAH (Secretary General).

Indonesian Democratic Party (*Partai Demokrasi Indonesia*—PDI). The PDI also came into existence as a result of the government's exhortation to "simplify" Indonesia's party system. The party was organized on January 10, 1973, through merger of the following five minority parties: the Indonesian Nationalist Party (*Partai Nasional Indonesia*—PNI), the Upholders of Indonesian Independence (*Ikatan Pendukung Kemerdekaan Indonesia*—IPKI), the Catholic Party (*Partai Katolik*), the Protestant Party (*Partai Kristen Indonesia*—Parkindo), and the People's Party (*Partai Murba*—PM). No more unified than the PPP, the PDI won 10.9 percent of the popular vote in 1987, as contrasted with 7.9 percent in 1982; much of the gain has been attributed to an energetic campaign conducted by former president Sukarno's eldest daughter, Megawati SUKARNOPUTRI, who is increasingly being viewed as appealing to "Youth Power" within opposition ranks.

Leaders: SURYADI (General Chairman), Nico DARYANTO (Secretary General).

Illegal Parties and Groups:

Banned in 1966, the **Communist Party of Indonesia** (*Partai Komunis Indonesia*—PKI) subsequently split into pro-Peking and pro-Moscow factions; the former is nominally led from Peking by Jusuf ADJITOROP, while Satiadjaya SUDIMAN, resident in Eastern Europe, speaks for the latter. A number of long-imprisoned party leaders were executed in 1985 and 1986 (some 15 years after being sentenced for their involvement in the 1965 revolt) and, at present, there appears to be only a handful of underground PKI activists operating within the country. Regional insurgent movements include the Free Papua Organization and Fretilin (see below, under Irian Jaya and East Timor, respectively) as well as the Muslim **National Liberation Front of Acheh** (NLFA), a northern Sumatra group which has claimed responsibility for a number of terrorist acts, including a 1978 raid against the Arun natural gas facility. The Front's leader, Hasan di Tiro, was reported killed by Indonesian forces in December 1979, and the group had been all but eliminated by the end of 1980. Other small Muslim extremist groups include the **Holy War Command** (*Komando Djihad*), which claimed responsibility for a March 1981 airplane hijacking that ended with Indonesian commandos freeing the hostages at Bangkok, Thailand.

LEGISLATURE

Indonesia has two parliamentary bodies, the People's Consultative Assembly, which meets infrequently to establish broad policy guidelines and elect the president and vice president, and the People's Representation Council, which performs normal legislative functions.

People's Consultative Assembly (*Majelis Permusyawaratan Rakyat*—MPR). The MPR is an outgrowth of the Provisional People's Consultative Assembly (*Majelis Permusyawaratan Rakyat Sementara*—MPRS) originally appointed by President Sukarno in 1960. Its present membership includes the 500 members of the DPR (see below), plus another 500 comprising additional Golkar and military representatives, unaffiliated regional delegates, and, in proportion to their respective shares of DPR seats, appointed PPP and PDI members. Government-supportive members, including those elected by regional parliaments, hold about 80 percent of the seats; all decisions must be unanimous. The MPR normally meets once every five years, most recently on March 1–11, 1988.

Chairman: Kharis SUHUD.

People's Representation Council (*Dewan Perwakilan Rakyat*—DPR). An outgrowth of the Mutual Cooperation House of Representatives (*Dewan Perwakilan Rakyat-Gotong Rojong*—DPRGR) appointed by President Sukarno in 1960, the DPR currently consists of 400 elected and 100 appointed members. At the general election of April 23, 1987, Golkar obtained 299 seats; the United Development Party, 61; and the Indonesian Democratic Party, 40.

Speaker: Kharis SUHUD.

CABINET

[as of March 21, 1988]

President	Gen. (Ret.) Suharto
Vice President	Lt. Gen. (Ret.) Sudharmono
Coordinating Ministers	
Economics, Finance and Industry	Radius Prawiro
Political Affairs and Security	Adm. (Ret.) Sudomo
Public Welfare	Soepardjo Rustam
Ministers	
Agriculture	Wardoyo
Cooperatives	Maj. Gen. (Ret.) Bustanil Arifin
Defense and Security	Gen. Leonardus B. (Benny) Murdani
Education and Culture	Dr. Faud Hassan
Finance	Dr. J.B. Sumarlin
Foreign Affairs	Ali Alatas
Forestry	Hasjrul Harahap
Health	Dr. Adhyatma
Home Affairs	Rudini
Industry	Hartarto
Information	Harmoko
Justice	Ismail Saleh
Manpower	Cosmas Batubara
Mining and Energy	Ginandjar Kartasasmita
Public Works	Radinal Moochtar
Religious Affairs	Munawir Sjadzali
Social Affairs	Dr. Haryati Soebadio
Tourism, Post and Telecommunications	Soesilo Soedarman
Trade	Dr. Arifin Siregar
Transmigration	Soegiarto
Transportation	Azwar Anas
State Ministers	
Administrative Reform	Sarwono Kusumaatmadja
Housing	Siswono Judo Husodo
National Development Planning	Dr. Saleh Afiff
Population and the Environment	Dr. Emil Salim

Research and Technology	Dr. B.J. Habibie
State Secretary	Moerdiono
Women's Roles	A.S. Moerpratomo
Youth Affairs and Sports	Akbar Tanjung
Attorney General	Rear Adm. Sukarton
	Marmosudjono
Commander, Armed Forces	Gen. Try Sutrisno
Governor, Bank of Indonesia	Dr. Adrianus Mooy

NEWS MEDIA

Press. The Indonesian press, rigidly controlled under the Sukarno regime, was accorded relative freedom under President Suharto until early 1974, when riots in Jakarta triggered a government crackdown during which the army closed a dozen newspapers and prohibited some of their employees from working for other publications. A number of papers were banned briefly in early 1978 for similar reasons, while in May 1982 the Muslim paper *Pelita* was temporarily suppressed for not adhering to a preelection agreement that security considerations necessitated "free but responsible" coverage. A month earlier, publication of *Tempo,* the country's largest-circulation weekly, had also been stopped. During 1986, one of the country's largest dailies, *Sinar Harapan,* had its license suspended for publishing "speculative" articles about government policy, while *Suara Merdeka* received a warning for a similar offense; in mid-1987, the 14-month-old Jakarta daily, *Prioritas,* was banned for publishing "incorrect and tendentious" reports on the economy, while the license of the independent *Merkeda* was revoked in November. All newspapers are members of the National Press Council, the chairman of which is the minister of information. The following are dailies published at Jakarta in Indonesian, unless otherwise noted: *Kompas* (418,000), liberal Catholic; *Pos Kota* (250,000); *Berita Buana* (150,000); *Suara Merdeka* (Semarang, 140,000); *Suara Karya* (100,000); *Surabaya Post* (Surabaya, 85,000); *Harian Umum AB* (80,000), official army paper; *Pelita* (80,000), Muslim; *Pikiran Rakyat* (Bandung, 80,000), independent; *Analisa* (Medan, 75,000); *Berita Yudha* (60,000), official army publication; *Waspada* (Medan, 50,000); *Indonesia Times* (36,000), in English; *Indonesia Tze Pao* (40,000), in Chinese. Among Jakarta's weeklies, the well-established (but once suspended) *Tempo* (150,000) was challenged by the launching in August 1987 of *Editor* (135,000).

News agencies. The principal domestic service is the Indonesian National News Agency (Antara); the KNI News Service also covers national news. A number of foreign bureaus maintain offices at Jakarta.

Radio and television. Broadcasting is government controlled and under the supervision of the Directorate General of Posts and Telecommunications. *Radio Republik Indonesia* broadcast to 33.2 million sets in 1987, while *Yayasan Televisi Republik Indonesia* transmitted to approximately 5.0 million television receivers.

INTERGOVERNMENTAL REPRESENTATION

Ambassador to the US: SOESILO Soedarman.

US Ambassador to Indonesia: Paul Dundes WOLFOWITZ.

Permanent Representative to the UN: (Vacant, following the designation of Ali ALATAS as foreign minister on March 21, 1988).

IGO Memberships (Non-UN): ADB, ANRPC, APCC, ASEAN, CCC, CIPEC, CP, IBA, IC, ICO, IDB, Inmarsat, INRO, Intelsat, Interpol, ISO, ITC, ITPA, NAM, OPEC.

ANNEXED TERRITORIES

Irian Jaya (West New Guinea). The western half of the island of New Guinea, long known as Netherlands New Guinea, is a former Dutch possession which was administered by Indonesia after May 1, 1963, under a UN-sponsored agreement. With an area of 159,375 square miles (412,781 sq. km.) and a mainly Papuan population of 1.17 million (1980C), the territory had been retained by the Netherlands upon recognition of Indonesian independence in 1949 but was subsequently turned over to the United Nations on the understanding that administrative authority would

be transferred to Indonesia pending self-determination before the end of 1969. Although Papuan representatives complained of oppression by Indonesia and expressed a desire to form an independent state, Indonesia staged an "act of free choice" during July and August 1969 by convening eight regional consultative assemblies, all of which voted for annexation to Indonesia.

In 1971 a "Provisional Revolutionary Government of West Papua New Guinea" was established by insurgents who in 1976 claimed to control about 15 percent of the territory in the eastern sector, adjacent to Papua New Guinea. Though Port Moresby has banned all anti-Jakarta movements, it has sought the help of the UN High Commissioner for Refugees (UNHCR) in an effort to find third countries willing to grant Irian insurgents asylum. An offensive by the Indonesian Army against the **Free Papua Organization** (*Organisasai Papua Merdeka*—OPM) in February 1984 provoked the flight of hundreds of Irian villagers into Papua New Guinea, damaging relations with Port Moresby, while the shooting of Irian intellectual Arnold AP in a Jayapura prison occasioned international criticism. However, relations with Papua New Guinea stabilized in 1985, with a border cooperation agreement being signed in October. Additional difficulties have been presented by the resettlement of Javanese farmers in Irian Jaya; the settlements, part of an ambitious transmigration program, have provoked conflicts between the Javanese and the native Melanesian population.

East Timor. Administered by Portugal for nearly four centuries, East Timor occupies approximately half of the island of Timor, at the eastern tip of the Malay Archipelago; the western half, with the exception of the former Portuguese enclave of Ocussi Ambeno, has historically been Indonesian. The area of East Timor is 5,763 square miles (14,925 sq. km.) and its population numbers 555,350 (1980C). Principal exports are coffee, copra, rubber, and wax.

After the 1974 coup in Portugal, Australia and Indonesia announced that they favored annexation of the territory by Indonesia but that they would respect the desires of the Timorese people. In September 1974, Dr. Mário Soares, the Portuguese foreign minister, met his Indonesian counterpart, Adam Malik, at New York, and the two agreed that the Timorese should decide their own future, Portugal offering to conduct a referendum on the subject in 1975.

Within East Timor, the Timorese Democratic People's Association (*Associação da Populaça Democrática de Timor*—Apodeti) had campaigned for autonomous status within Indonesia, while the Democratic Union of Timor (*União Democrática de Timor*—UDT) had advocated looser ties to Portugal and eventual independence. In January 1975 the UDT and the left-wing **Revolutionary Front for an Independent East Timor** (*Frente Revolucionário de Este Timor Independente*—Fretilin) agreed to unite in opposition to integration with Indonesia, but the alliance broke up four months later. On August 11, the UDT launched a coup against the colonial administration at Dili, the capital, while Fretilin responded on August 15 by mounting its own insurrection. On November 28, Fretilin declared the formation of a "Democratic Republic of East Timor", but on December 7 an invasion by Indonesia, in support of a pro-Jakarta alliance that included Apodeti, the UDT, and several smaller parties, drove Fretilin from Dili. By the end of the year, Indonesia had annexed Ocussi Ambeno and had occupied virtually all of East Timor, which it annexed on July 17, 1976. The annexation was not recognized by Portugal, which has remained committed to self-determination for the Timorese, and has been repeatedly condemned by the UN General Assembly. At the May 1982 election, East Timor for the first time chose four DPR representatives, all of whom ran as Golkar candidates.

While major guerrilla activity persisted through 1977, resistance by remaining Fretilin elements has since been restricted to remote areas. Meanwhile, a major international relief effort, financed largely by the United States and administered by the Red Cross and the Catholic Relief Services, was initiated in the fall of 1979 to avert mass starvation. The effort was terminated at Indonesia's request in December 1980, by which time the crisis had abated. Estimates placed the death toll during 1975–1979 at 100,000 or more, although lack of access by the outside world continues to make it difficult to verify not only the number of fatalities but allegations that Indonesia had engaged in genocide and the systematic destruction of croplands in order to starve the islanders into submission. In August 1983, a new anti-Fretilin offensive was launched involving 20,000 Indonesian troops, with continued fighting reported through mid-1984; by 1985, however, the guerrillas appeared to have retreated, and Jakarta's primary goals in East Timor focused on education, agriculture, and infrastructure development.

During 1987 Lisbon was reported to have adopted a more flexible attitude toward negotiations over East Timor in an effort to achieve a settlement that would lead to the reestablishment of diplomatic relations with Jakarta. It indicated, however, that it would continue to oppose Indonesian claims to sovereignty over the territory.

IRAN

Islamic Republic of Iran
Jomhori-e-Islami-e-Irân

Political Status: Former monarchy; Islamic Republic proclaimed April 1–2, 1979, on basis of referendum of March 30–31; present constitution adopted at referendum of December 2–3, 1979.

Area: 636,293 sq. mi. (1,648,000 sq. km.).

Population: 49,700,000 (1986C), 53,750,000 (1988E).

Major Urban Centers (1982E): TEHERAN (urban area, 5,800,000); Mashhad (1,150,000); Isfahan (927,000); Tabriz (860,000); Shiraz (801,000); Inamshahr (previously Kermanshah, 532,000); Karaj (527,000); Ahwaz (471,000); Qom (425,000). The population of the oil refining center of Abadan, formerly close to 300,000, has been greatly reduced as a result of the Iran-Iraq war.

Official Language: Persian (Farsi).

Monetary Unit: Rial (principal rate March 1, 1988, 67.83 rials = \$1US).

Religious Leader (*Velayat Faghi*): Ayatollah Ruhollah Musavi KHOMEINI; became de facto leader of the Islamic Revolution upon departure of the former sovereign, Muhammad Reza PAHLAVI Shahanshah Aryamehr, on January 16, 1979; formally designated *Velayat Faghi,* with political authority superior to the President and other government officials, in constitution adopted on December 2–3, 1979.

President: Hojatolislam Sayed Ali KHAMENEI; elected October 2, 1981, and sworn in October 13, following the assassination of Mohammad Ali RAJAI on August 30 and establishment of a provisional Presidential Council of Hojatolislam Hashemi RAFSANJANI, Ayatollah Abdolkarim Musavi ARDEBILI, and (upon his endorsement by the *Majlis* as Prime Minister on September 1) Hojatolislam Mohammad Reza MAHDAVI-KANI; reelected August 16, 1985, and sworn in for a second four-year term on October 10.

Prime Minister: Mir Hossein MUSAVI-KHAMENEI; nominated by the President on October 27, 1981, to succeed Hojatolislam Mohammad Reza MAHDAVI-KANI, who had resigned on October 15; appointed October 31, following confirmation by the *Majlis* on October 29; reappointed on October 17, 1985, following reconfirmation on October 13.

THE COUNTRY

A land of elevated plains, mountains, and deserts that is semiarid except for a fertile area on the Caspian coast, Iran is celebrated both for the richness of its cultural heritage and for the oil resources that have made it a center of world attention in the twentieth century. Persians make up about two-thirds of the population, while the principal minority groups are Turks and Kurds, who speak their own languages and dialects. English and French are widely spoken in the cities. More than 90 percent of the people belong to the Shiʻa sect of Islam, the official religion. Prior to the 1979 revolution, women constituted approximately 10 percent of the paid labor force, with substantial representation in government and the professions; since 1979, female participation in most areas of government has been banned, with most working women serving as unpaid agricultural laborers on family landholdings.

Despite a steady increase in petroleum production, both the economy and the society remained basically agricultural until the early 1960s, when a massive development program was launched. During the next decade and a half, the proportion of gross domestic product (exclusive of oil revenue) contributed by agriculture dropped from nearly 50 percent to approximately 20 percent, and Iran became a net importer of food. A major population shift to the urban areas also occurred, reducing the once overwhelmingly rural population to little more than 50 percent and the work force in agriculture to less than 40 percent. Under a 1973–1978 five-year plan, agriculture was to expand annually by 7 percent, industry by 17 percent, and oil and gas production (the principal source of investment for the plan) by 51 percent. For a variety of reasons, including plan inefficiencies, severe inflation, and a substantial outflow of capital, these goals were not realized, while dislocations caused by the Islamic Revolution resulted, according to official sources, in a 12 percent contraction in goods and services, accompanied by a 40–70 percent falloff in the manufacturing sector, by mid-1979. Conditions continued to deteriorate following the outbreak of war with Iraq in September 1980, with petroleum exports dropping by nearly 85 percent from 1978 to 1981 before recovering to approximately 40 percent of the 1978 volume in 1983. Concurrently, domestic shortages and rising prices for imports contributed to an inflation rate that exceeded 24 percent in 1981, followed by a steady decline to near zero in 1986.

GOVERNMENT AND POLITICS

Political background. Modern Iranian history began with nationalist uprisings against foreign economic intrusions in the late nineteenth century. In 1906 a coalition of clergy, merchants, and intellectuals forced the shah to grant a limited constitution. A second revolutionary movement, also directed largely against foreign influence, was initiated in 1921 by REZA Khan, an army officer who seized power and four years later ousted the Qajar family and established the Pahlavi dynasty. Although Reza Shah initiated forced modernization of the country with Kemalist Turkey as his model, his flirtation with the Nazis led to the occupation of Iran by Soviet and British forces in 1941 and his subsequent abdication in favor of his son, Muhammad Reza PAHLAVI. The end of World War II witnessed the formation of separatist Azerbaijani and Kurdish regimes under Soviet patronage; however, these crumbled in 1946 because of pressure exerted by the United States and the United Nations. A subsequent upsurge of Iranian nationalism resulted in expropriation of the British-owned oil industry in 1951, during the two-year premiership of Mohammad MOSSADEQ.

In the wake of an abortive coup in August 1953, Mossadeq was arrested by loyalist army forces with assistance from the American Central Intelligence Agency. The period following his downfall was marked by the shah's assumption of a more active role, culminating in systematic efforts at political, economic, and social development that were hailed by the monarchy as a "White Revolution". However, the priorities established by the shah, which included major outlays for sophisticated military weapon systems and a number of "showcase" projects (such as a subway system for the city of Teheran), coupled with a vast influx of foreign workers and evidence of official corruption, led to criticism by traditional religious leaders, university students, labor unions, and elements within the business community.

In March 1975 the shah announced dissolution of the existing two-party system (both government and opposition parties having been controlled by the monarchy) and decreed the formation of a new National Resurgence Party to serve as the country's sole political group. In the face of mounting unrest and a number of public-service breakdowns in overcrowded Teheran, Emir Abbas HOVEYDA, who had served as prime minister since 1965, was dismissed in August 1977 and replaced by the National Resurgence secretary general, Dr. Jamshid AMOUZEGAR.

By late 1977 both political and religious opposition to the shah had further intensified. On December 11 a Union of National Front Forces was formed under the leadership of Dr. Karim SANJABI (a former Mossadeq minister) to promote a return to the constitution, the nationalization of major industries, and the adoption of policies that would be "neither communist nor capitalist, but strictly nationalist". Conservative Muslim sentiment, on the other hand, centered on the senior mullah, Ayatollah Ruhollah KHOMEINI, who had lived in exile since mounting a series of street demonstrations against the "White Revolution" in 1963, and the more moderate Ayatollah Sayed Kazem SHARIATMADARI, based in the religious center of Qom. Both leaders were supported politically by the long-established National Liberation Movement of Dr. Mehdi BAZARGAN.

By mid-1978 demonstrations against the regime had become increasingly violent, and Prime Minister Amouzegar was replaced on August 27 by the Senate president, Ja'afar SHARIF-EMAMI, whose parliamentary background and known regard for the country's religious leadership made him somewhat unique within the monarch's inner circle of advisers. Unable to arrest appeals for the shah's abdication, Sharif-Emami was forced to yield office on November 6 to a military government headed by the chief of staff of the armed forces, Gen. Gholam Reza AZHARI. The level

of violence nonetheless continued to mount; numerous Kurds in northwest Iran joined the chorus of opposition, and the oil fields and major banks were shut down by strikes, bringing the economy to the verge of collapse. Thus, after an effort by Golam-Hossein SADIQI to form a new civilian government had failed, the shah on December 29 named a prominent National Front leader, Dr. Shahpur BAKHTIAR, as prime minister designate.

Ten days after Bakhtiar's formal investiture on January 6, 1979, the shah left the country on what was termed an extended "vacation". On February 1, amid widespread popular acclaim, Ayatollah Khomeini returned from exile and a week later announced the formation of a provisional government under a Revolutionary Council, whose membership was not divulged but which was subsequently reported to be chaired by Ayatollah Morteza MOTAHARI. On February 11, Prime Minister Bakhtiar resigned, Dr. Bazargan being invested as his successor by the National Consultive Assembly immediately prior to the issuance of requests for dissolution by both the Assembly and the Senate.

Despite a series of clashes with ethnic minority groups, a referendum on March 30–31 approved the proclamation of an Islamic Republic by a reported 97 percent majority. A rising tide of political assassinations and other disruptions failed to delay the election on August 3 of a constituent assembly (formally titled a Council of Experts) delegated to review a draft constitution that had been published in mid-June. The result of the Council's work was subsequently approved in a national referendum on December 2–3 (see Constitution and government, below).

The most dramatic event of 1979 was the November 4 occupation of the US Embassy at Teheran and the seizure of 66 hostages (13 of whom — five White women and eight Black men — were released on November 17, while another was freed for health reasons in early July 1980), apparently in an effort to secure the return for trial of the shah, who had been admitted to a New York hospital for medical treatment. The action, undertaken by militant students, was not disavowed by the Revolutionary Council, although the government appeared not to have been consulted, and Prime Minister Bazargan felt obliged to tender his resignation the following day, no successor being named. On December 4 the United Nations Security Council unanimously condemned the action and called for release of the hostages, while the World Court handed down a unanimous decision to the same effect on December 15. Both judgments were repudiated by Iranian leaders despite the departure of the shah for Panama and an implicit threat to the Islamic government by the Soviet invasion of neighboring Afghanistan on December 27.

Notwithstanding the death of the shah in Egypt on July 27 and the outbreak of war with Iraq in late September (see Foreign relations, below), no resolution of the hostage issue occurred in 1980. American frustration at the lengthy impasse was partially evidenced by an abortive helicopter rescue effort undertaken by the US Air Force on April 24, and it was not until November 2 that Teheran agreed to formal negotiations with Washington, proposing the Algerian government as mediator. The remaining 52 hostages were ultimately freed, after 444 days of captivity, on

January 20, 1981, coincident with the inauguration of US President Reagan. In return for their freedom, Washington agreed (1) to abstain from interference in internal Iranian affairs; (2) to freeze the property and assets of the late shah's family pending resolution of lawsuits brought by the Islamic Republic; (3) to "bar and preclude" pending and future suits against Iran as a result of the 1979 revolution or the hostage seizure, with an Iran–United States Claims Tribunal to be established at The Hague, Netherlands; (4) to end trade sanctions against Teheran; and (5) to unfreeze some $7.97 billion in Iranian assets, including $2.87 billion to be transferred outright, $3.7 billion to be used as repayments for US bank loans, and $1.4 billion to be held in escrow to meet other commitments.

Internal developments in 1980 were highlighted by the election of the relatively moderate Abol Hasan BANI-SADR, a former advisor to Ayatollah Khomeini, as president on January 25 and the convening of a unicameral Assembly (*Majlis*) on May 28, following two-stage balloting on March 14 and May 9. On August 9, Bani-Sadr reluctantly agreed to nominate Mohammad Ali RAJAI, an Islamic fundamentalist, as prime minister after three months of negotiations had failed to yield parliamentary support for a more centrist candidate.

Despite the support of secular nationalists, political moderates, much of the armed forces, and many Islamic leftists, Bani-Sadr was increasingly beleaguered by the powerful fundamentalist clergy centered around the Islamic Republican Party (IRP) and its (then) secretary general, Chief Justice of the Supreme Court Ayatollah Mohammad Hossein BEHESHTI. The IRP had emerged from the 1980 legislative balloting in firm control of the *Majlis,* enabling the clergy, ultimately with the support of Ayatollah Khomeini, to undermine presidential prerogatives during the first half of 1981. Moreover, on June 1 an arbitration committee, which had been established in the wake of violent clashes on March 5 between fundamentalists and Bani-Sadr supporters, declared that the president had not only incited unrest, but had violated the constitution by failing to sign into law bills passed by the *Majlis.* Nine days later, Khomeini removed Bani-Sadr as commander in chief, and on June 22, following a two-day impeachment debate in the Assembly that culminated in a 177–1 vote declaring him incompetent, Bani-Sadr was dismissed as chief executive.

On June 28 a bomb ripped apart IRP headquarters at Teheran, killing Ayatollah Beheshti, four government ministers, six deputy ministers, 27 *Majlis* deputies, and 34 others. Prosecutor General Ayatollah Abdolkarim Musavi ARDEBILI was immediately appointed chief justice, while on July 24 Prime Minister Rajai, with over 90 percent of the vote, was elected president. Having been confirmed by the *faghi* on August 2, Rajai named Hojatolislam Mohammad Javad BAHONAR, Beheshti's successor as leader of the IRP, as prime minister, the *Majlis* endorsing the appointment three days later. Meanwhile, in late July deposed president Bani-Sadr, accompanied by Massoud RAJAVI of the *Mujaheddin* (see Political Parties and Groups, below), had fled to Paris, where he announced the formation of an exile National Resistance Council.

On August 30, President Rajai and Prime Minister Bahonar were assassinated by an explosion at the latter's offices, and on September 1 the minister of the interior, Hojatolislam Mohammad Reza MAHDAVI-KANI, was named interim prime minister. On October 2, Hojatolislam Sayed Ali KHAMENEI, Bahonar's replacement as secretary general of the IRP and a close associate of Khomeini, was elected president with 95 percent of the vote. Sworn in on October 13, he accepted the resignation of Mahdavi-Kani on October 15, with Mir Hossein MUSAVI-KHAMENEI, the foreign minister, being named the Islamic Republic's fifth prime minister on October 31, following confirmation by the *Majlis.*

President Khamenei was elected to a second four-year term on August 16, 1985, defeating two IRP challengers. On October 13, following nomination by the president, Musavi-Khamenei was reconfirmed as prime minister.

Constitution and government. The constitution adopted on December 2–3, 1979, established Shi'ite Islam as the official state religion, placed supreme power in the hands of the Muslim clergy, and named Ayatollah Ruhollah Khomeini as the nation's religious leader (*velayat faghi*) for life. The *faghi* is supreme commander of the armed forces and the Revolutionary Guard, appoints the majority of members of the National Defense Council, can declare war (on recommendation of the Council), and can dismiss the president following a legislative vote of no confidence or a ruling of the Supreme Court. An Assembly of Experts, composed of 83 mullahs, was elected in December 1982 to select a successor to the *faghi.* The president, the country's chief executive officer, is popularly elected for a four-year term, as is the unicameral *Majlis,* to which legislative authority is assigned. Although the president selects the prime minister, legislative approval is required. In the event of a presidential vacancy, a Presidential Council is constituted, the members being the speaker of the *Majlis,* the chief justice of the Supreme Court, and the prime minister; an election to fill the vacancy must be held within 50 days. A Council of Guardians of the Constitution (successor to the Revolutionary Council), encompassing six specialists in Islamic law appointed by the *faghi* and six lawyers named by the High Council of the Judiciary and approved by the legislature, is empowered to veto presidential candidates and to nullify laws considered contrary to the constitution or the Islamic faith. Political parties are authorized to the extent that they "do not violate the independence, sovereignty, national unity, and principles of the Islamic Republic", although no candidates at either the 1984 or 1988 *Majlis* balloting were permitted to declare partisan affiliation.

The judicial and legal system remains in a state of flux. With the civil courts instituted under the monarchy having been replaced by Islamic Revolutionary Courts, judges are mandated to reach verdicts on the basis of precedent and/or Islamic law. The legal code itself continues to undergo frequent changes, and on several occasions Ayatollah Khomeini has called for the purging of judges who are deemed unsuitable or overstep their authority. On August 22, 1982, it was announced that all laws passed under the former regime would be annulled if contrary to Islam, while on September 23 homosexuality and consumption of alcohol

TURKEY
USSR
SYRIA
Kirkuk · Sanandaj
IRAQ · Teheran
Kermanshah
Baghdad
Dezful
IRAN
Basra · Khorramshahr
Fao — Abadan
KUWAIT
SAUDI ARABIA
Strait of Hormuz
QATAR
▨▨▨ AREA OF
FIGHTING
UAE
0   Miles   300
OMAN

were added to the extensive list of capital offenses. Marriage and family laws were also revised, the practice of temporary marriage being reinstituted and the legal age of marriage for females being reduced to 13; in 1983 the wearing of the *chador* (veil) in public became mandatory. Although individuals are guaranteed the right to counsel by the constitution, summary trials and executions remain common, most victims being either suspected leftists and guerrillas or women found guilty of adultery, prostitution, or failure to wear the *chador*.

Iran is administratively divided into 23 provinces (*ostans*); in addition, there are nearly 500 counties (*shahrestan*) and a similar number of municipalities (*bakhsh*).

Foreign relations. Although a charter member of the United Nations, Iran momentarily curtailed its participation in the world body upon the advent of the Islamic Revolution. It boycotted the 1979 Security Council debate on seizure of the US Embassy at Teheran but joined in UN condemnation of the Soviet presence in Afghanistan late in the year.

Regionally, Iran and its western neighbor, Iraq, have long been at odds over their borders, principally over control of the Shatt al-'Arab waterway linking the Persian Gulf to the major oil ports of both countries. Although the dispute was ostensibly resolved by a 1975 accord dividing the waterway along the *thalweg* (median) line, Iraq abrogated the treaty on September 17, 1980, and invaded Iran's Khuzistan Province on September 22. Despite early reversals that included the loss of Khorramshahr, Iran succeeded in retaining control of most of the larger towns, including the beseiged oil center of Abadan, and by the end of the year the conflict had resulted in a military stalemate. The war had the immediate effect of accentuating disunity within the Islamic world, the more radical regimes of Libya, Syria, and South Yemen supporting Teheran, and the more conservative governments of Jordan, Egypt, and the Gulf states favoring Baghdad.

Despite mediation efforts by the United Nations, the

Islamic Conference, the Nonaligned Movement, and various individual countries, fighting continued, with Iran recapturing Khorramshahr in May 1982 and advancing into Iraqi territory for the first time in July. Rejecting a ceasefire overture, Teheran demanded $150 billion in reparations, ouster of the Saddam Hussein government, and Iraqi repatriation of expelled Shi'ites. By early 1984 Iranian forces had made marginal gains on the southern front with the capture of the bulk of the Majnoon oil fields north of Basra, with what was essentially a stalemate prevailing thereafter.

A major international drama erupted in late 1986 with the revelation that members of the US Reagan administration had participated in a scheme involving the clandestine sale of military equipment to Iran, the proceeds of which were to be used to support anti-Sandinista *contra* forces in Nicaragua. Within Iran the affair appeared to involve three distinct groups: a radical faction including Prime Minister Musavi-Khamenei that sought to obtain the arms to gain advantage in the war with Iraq; a group of moderates surrounding Ayatollah Montazeri, who had taken the initiative in making contact with the Americans in mid-1985; and supporters of the Assembly speaker, Hojatolislam Hashemi RAFSANJANI, who, despite some uncertainty as to their leader's own position, appeared sincerely interested in reestablishing good relations with the West. In mid-November President Reagan defended the dealings with Teheran as helping to further a variety of US policy goals, including not only support for the *contras,* but also the possibility of securing the release of Shi'ite-held hostages in Lebanon. Only a week later, it became apparent that the "small amounts of defensive weapons and spare parts" to which he alluded actually included more than 2,000 TOW antitank missiles and 235 Hawk antiaircraft missiles. Subsequently, it was reported that the Iranians themselves had terminated the shipments upon learning that some of the arms were defective and had been priced at approximately 500 percent of basic cost.

An active member of the Organization of Petroleum Exporting Countries (OPEC), Iran under both the shah and the ayatollah has been in the forefront of those urging aggressive pricing policies, as opposed to the more moderate posture of Saudi Arabia and other conservative members. After 1980, however, a combination of the world oil glut and the need to finance its war effort forced Iran to sell petroleum on the spot market at prices well below those set by OPEC; concurrently, it joined Algeria and Libya in urging a "fair share" strategy aimed at stabilizing prices through drastic production cutbacks.

Current issues. In contrast to the tide of assassinations and executions in 1981–1982, when the country appeared on the verge of political and administrative disintegration, relative stability in the upper echelon of government subsequently prevailed, with basic leadership cleavages somewhat blurred by the commanding presence of the aging Ayatollah Khomeini. Many observers viewed Hojatolislam Rafsanjani as the regime's most influential cleric after Khomeini. His priestly title, however, was not of the first rank, and Rafsanjani publicly endorsed Khomeini's own choice, Ayatollah Hussein Ali MONTAZERI for the succession. Though displaying little capacity for charismatic leadership, Montazeri was formally designated by the Council of Experts in November 1985 as future surrogate for the Hidden or Twelfth Imam, who disappeared eleven centuries ago, but is to reappear as the Mahdi (redeemer) to lead the perfect society. Despite the Council's action, a strongly right-wing group, originally drawn from the mullahs of Mahshad, is deeply committed to collective leadership. An even more conservative faction, also opposed to individual succession, is led by former prime minister Mahdavi-Kani, currently chairman of the Council of Guardians.

In October 1986 Mehdi HASHEMI, a radical fundamentalist, and his brother Hadi (Ayatollah Montazeri's son-in-law) were arrested and charged with a variety of criminal acts, including murder, torture, and a series of abductions. The action provoked outcries by the Teheran Militant Clergy Association, an anti-Rafsanjani formation with which the brothers had been associated and which was subsequently reported to have leaked information regarding the Iran-*contra* affair. Montazeri allegedly attempted to intercede on behalf of Mehdi Hashemi, who was nonetheless executed in September 1987 for "waging war against Islam". These events caused renewed speculation in regard to the succession, particularly in the wake of a June 1988 report that Khomeini was expected to succumb in the near future to a terminal illness.

POLITICAL PARTIES AND GROUPS

The principal groups active since the revolution of 1978–1979 are listed below.

Former Leading Party:

Islamic Republican Party (*Hezb-e-Jomhori-e-Islami*). Essentially a ruling party by late 1979, the Islamic Republican Party was led by a group of clergymen described as "fanatically loyal to the Ayatollah Khomeini". Its membership was a frequent target of assassins, both its first and second secretaries general, Ayatollah Mohammad Hossein Beheshti and Mohammad Javad Bahonar, falling victim to bomb explosions. The former died on June 28, 1981, along with 71 others when an explosion ripped through party headquarters.

During 1981–1982 two principal factions emerged within the party: the *Maktabi* group, which advocated the export of revolution to other Muslim countries and remained committed to the close interrelationship of politics and religion; and the *Hodjatieh* group, which supported greater separation of church and state, the adoption of a collegiate leadership after Khomeini, and a pronounced anticommunist posture. Partly because, in his view, the party had become "an excuse for discard and factionalism", Khomeini announced its dissolution in June 1987, although President Khamenei declared to "an exceptional party plenum" in March 1988 that he had dedicated himself to its reorganization.

Closely associated with the Islamic Republicans has been the *Hezbollahi* ("Party of God"), which has engaged in street fighting against leftists and, during the impeachment hearings of June 1981, against supporters of President Bani-Sadr, who labeled the group "club-wielding thugs of the clergy".

Leaders: Hojatolislam Sayed Ali KHAMENEI (President of the Republic and former Secretary General of the Party), Hojatolislam Hashemi RAFSANJANI (Speaker of the *Majlis* and leader of *Hodjatieh* group).

Association for the Defense and Sovereignty of the Iranian Nation. An opposition grouping, the Association was formed in March 1986 by Dr. Mehdi Bazargan of the National Liberation Movement (below) and a number of others who had participated in the 1979 provisional government. During its first meeting in early May, the group's 20-member Central

Committee indicated that it supported the revolution, but was opposed to continuation of the war with Iraq.

Leaders: Dr. Mehdi BAZARGAN, Ali ARDALAN, Nasser MINACHI, Dr. Assadollah MOBASHERI.

National Liberation Movement of Iran (*Nehzat-e-Azadi-e-Irân*). Established in 1961 by Dr. Mehdi Bazargan, the National Liberation Movement supported the opposition religious leaders during the anti-shah demonstrations of 1978. Named prime minister in February 1979, Dr. Bazargan resigned in the wake of the US Embassy seizure the following November. Subsequently, he remained one of the most outspoken critics tolerated by the government. In a letter authored in November 1982, the former prime minister accused the regime of responsibility for an "atmosphere of terror, fear, revenge, and national disintegration". *Nehzat-e-Azadi*, which is linked to the Paris-based National Resistance Council (see Exile Groups, below), boycotted the legislative balloting in both 1984 and 1988 because of government-imposed electoral restrictions.

Leaders: Dr. Ibrahim YAZDI, Dr. Mehdi BAZARGAN (Secretary General).

National Front (*Jebhe-e-Melli*). The National Front was established in December 1977 as an essentially secular antiregime coalition of nationalist factions, including followers of former prime minister Mohammad Mossadeq. One of its founders, Dr. Shahpur Bakhtiar, was formally expelled upon designation as prime minister by the shah in late 1978; another founder, Dr. Karim Sanjabi, resigned as foreign minister of the Islamic Republic in April 1979 to protest a lack of authority accorded to Prime Minister Bazargan. The Front called upon voters to boycott the 1981 presidential election. Together with all of the parties listed below, it is not now officially recognized.

Leader: Dr. Karim SANJABI.

National Democratic Front (*Jebhe-e-Democratic-e-Melli*). An offshoot of the National Front, the Democratic Front was founded in February 1979 by Heydayatollah Matine-Daftari, a grandson of Mohammad Mossadeq. Four months later it accused Ayatollah Khomeini of attempting to establish a religious dictatorship, while in August it called for a boycott of the constituent assembly election. In late 1981, after two years in hiding, Matine-Daftari fled to France, where he announced his support for former president Bani-Sadr's National Resistance Council (below). Less than a month later, party cofounder Shokrollah PAKNEJAD was executed as a result of charges ranging from having contact with antigovernment guerrillas to "deceptive influence over the younger generation".

Leader: Hedayatollah MATINE-DAFTARI (in exile).

Muslim People's Republican Party (*Hezb-e-Jomhori-e-Khalq-e-Mosalman*). Established by followers of the opposition religious leader Ayatollah SHARIATMADARI, the Muslim People's Party favors a strong secular government within the context of the Islamic Republic. Its principal base is in Azerbaijan, where the majority of its supporters (estimated at over 3 million) reside.

Already under virtual house arrest at Qom, Shariatmadari was placed under armed guard in April 1982, having been accused of participating, with former foreign minister Sadeq Qotbzadeh and several dozen others, in a plot to assassinate Ayatollah Khomeini. He died on April 3, 1986.

Leader: Hossein FARSHI (Secretary General).

Clandestine, Guerrilla, and Separatist Groups:

Party of the Masses (*Hezb-e-Tudeh*). Traditionally pro-Soviet, the Communist *Tudeh* was formed in 1941, was declared illegal in 1949, and went underground in 1953. A number of its leaders returned from exile in East Germany in early 1979. At a March 1981 Central Committee plenum, the party aligned itself with Ayatollah Khomeini's "anti-imperialist and popular line", while ending its support for separatist movements. Because of *Tudeh*'s conservatism, a number of more radical communist groups have emerged since the late 1970s (see below); on the other hand, a faction of the militant *Fedayeen-e-Khalq* (below) joined *Tudeh* in support of the revolution. *Tudeh* was formally banned in April 1983 after several party officials had confessed to providing the USSR with military and political information. Its founder, Iraj ESKENDARI, died in East Germany in April 1985.

Leaders: Dr. Nureddin KIANOURI (under arrest), Eshan TABARI (under arrest), Ali KHAVARI (First Secretary).

A combination of censorship, shifting alliances and loyalties, factionalism, and active suppression by the military and paramilitary organs has made it virtually impossible to ascertain the status of other small opposition parties and groups, several dozen of which have operated—some briefly, some informally—since the 1979 revolution. Marxist parties include the **Communist Party of Iran** (*Hezb-e-Komunist-e-Iran*), organized in 1979 as an alternative to the pro-Soviet posture of *Tudeh;* the **Revolutionary Workers' Party** (*Hezb-e-Kargaran-e-Inqilabi*—HKI), established in 1978 and committed to separation of church and state, women's equality, and self-determination for ethnic minorities; the **Workers' Unity Party** (*Hezb-e-Vahdat-e-Kargaran*—HUK), which, like the HKI, supports regional autonomy for Kurds, Turkomans, Baluchis, and others; and the **Socialist Workers' Party** (*Hezb-e-Kargaran-e-Sosialist*—HKS), a Trotskyite group formed after the revolution.

The largest guerrilla group, which claims some 100,000 members, is the **Mujaheddin-e-Khalq** ("People's Warriors"), founded in 1965 and long in opposition to the shah. Leftist but also Islamic, the *Mujaheddin* have recently focused their activities on urban areas, frequently engaging in street battles with the *Hodjatieh* as well as the Revolutionary Guards and the regular army; many of the political assassinations of 1979–1982 were apparently carried out by its members, thousands of whom have been executed by the Khomeini regime. The political leader of the *Mujaheddin,* Massoud RAJAVI, accompanied former president Bani-Sadr into exile at Paris in July 1981, but subsequently came under pressure from French authorities and left, with 1,000 of his followers, for Iraq in June 1986; within Iran, guerrilla leader Mussa KHIABANI was killed in February 1982, his successor being Ali ZARKESH. The other leading guerrilla organization is the **Fedayeen-e-Khalq** ("People's Strugglers"), founded in 1971 in opposition to the monarchy. Committed to Marxism and atheism (and thus the establishment of a secular state), the *Fedayeen* have been prone to factionalism, with one splinter in fact joining *Tudeh* in support of the Islamic Revolution. Another faction emerged as the **Organization Struggling for the Freedom of the Working Class** (*Sazmane Peykar dar Rahe Azadieh Tabaqe Kargar*); its leaders, Alizara ASHTIYANI and Hossein AHMADI, were captured in February 1982, and three months later *Peykar* was reportedly wiped out by government forces.

On the far Right, one of the leading underground groups has been **Forqan**, encompassing extreme fundamentalists opposed to political involvement by religious leaders. *Forqan* has claimed responsibility for a number of assassinations, including those of Army Chief of Staff Vali Ullan Qarani and Ayatollah Morteza Motahari in April-May 1979, and a June 1981 bomb attack against Ali Khamenei, the future president.

Of the separatist groups, the largest is the **Kurdish Democratic Party of Iran** (KDPI), outlawed since August 1979 and led by Dr. Abdur Rahman QASSEMLOU. Campaigning under the slogan "Democracy for Iran, Autonomy for the Kurds", the *KDPI*, like the *Mujaheddin*, has been a principal target of government forces; its guerrilla wing is often referred to as the *Pesh Mergas* (as is a similar Kurdish group in Iraq). Led by Sheikh Azedin HUSSEINI, the **Party of Toilers** (*Hezb-e-Kumelah*) has also fought for Kurdish autonomy in opposition to the Khomeini regime. In February 1982, Djaffar CHAFFII, identified as a *Kumelah* spokesman, stated at Paris, France, that his organization would remain aloof from the National Resistance Council of Bani-Sadr (see below), which did not represent the form of social revolution sought by Kurds. The following month, Mahmoud Hussein BACHRARI announced, also at Paris, that an **Arab Liberation Front of Ahwaz**, committed to self-determination for Iran's Arabic-speaking population, was being revived with assistance from Iraq.

Principal Exile Groups:

National Resistance Council for Liberty and Independence. The National Resistance Council was established in 1981 at Paris, France, by deposed president Bani-Sadr and *Mujaheddin* leader Massoud Rajavi. The two leaders were known to have different views in regard to relations with Iraq and in March 1984 Bani-Sadr announced his withdrawal from the Council, despite having been backed by it as a potential president-in-exile.

Leader: Massoud RAJAVI.

National Movement of Iranian Resistance. The National Movement, "neither monarchist nor republican", based at Paris and led by former prime minister Shahpur Bakhtiar, is apparently the best-organized and best-financed exile organization. It resorted to violence for the first time within Iran in September 1984, with a series of car bombings at Teheran and a rocket attack on a regional militia headquarters at Rezaiyeh.

Leaders: Dr. Shahpur BAKHTIAR, Abdol-Rahman BOROUMAND.

Freedom Fighters (*Azadegan*). A paramilitary group committed to restoration of the monarchy following the establishment of a transitional military regime, *Azadegan* has apparently received support from members of the late shah's family. Its most widely publicized act was the August 1981 seizure of an Iranian gunboat that was ultimately surrendered to French authorities.

Leaders: Gen. Bahram ARYANA, Adm. Kamal Ed-Din HABIBOL-LAHI.

LEGISLATURE

The most recent two-stage election was held on April 8 and May 13, 1988, to the unicameral **Islamic Consultative Assembly** (*Majlis-e-Shoura-e-Islami*), whose 270 members serve four-year terms. None of the more than 1,400 candidates ran under party labels, with 188 securing an absolute majority on the first ballot and 82 being designated in the runoff.

Speaker: Hojatolislam Hashemi Ali Akbar RAFSANJANI.

CABINET

Prime Minister	Mir Hossein Musavi-Khamenei
Ministers	
Agriculture and Rural Development	Dr. Abbas Ali Zali
Commerce	Hasan Abedi-Jafari
Construction Jihad	Bijan Namdar-Zangeneh
Culture and Higher Education	Dr. Mohammad Farhadi
Defense	Brig. Gen. Mohammad Hossein Jalali
Economic Affairs and Finance	Mohammad Javad Iravani
Education and Training	Dr. Kazem Akrami
Energy	Abol Hasan Khamoushi
Foreign Affairs	Dr. Ali Akbar Velayati
Health Care and Training	Dr. Ali Reza Marandi
Heavy Industries	Behzad Nabavi
Housing and Urban Development	Seraj-ed-Din Kazeruni
Industries	Qolam Reza Shafei
Intelligence and Security	Mohammad Mohammadi-Reyshahri
Interior	Ali Akbar Mohtashemi-Pur
Islamic Guidance	Dr. Sayed Mohammad Khatami-Ardekani
Justice	Dr. Hasan Habibi
Labor and Social Affairs	Abol Qasem Sarhadizadeh
Mines and Metals	Mohammad Reza Ayatollahi
Petroleum	Qolam Reza Aqazadeh-Khol
Plan and Budget	Masud Roqani-Zanjani
Post, Telegraph and Telephone	Mohammad Qarazi
Revolutionary Guard	Mohsen Rafiq-Dust
Roads and Transport	Mohammad Sayyed-Kia
Governor, Central Bank	Majid Qasemi

NEWS MEDIA

Freedom of the press is provided for in the 1979 constitution, except in regard to violations of public morality and religious belief, or impugning the reputation of individuals. Nevertheless, the opposition press has been stifled. Over 20 newspapers were shut down in August 1979 and drastic curbs were imposed on foreign journalists, including a ban on unsupervised interviews with government officials and a requirement that reporters apply for press cards every three months. In August 1980, Ayatollah Khomeini called for increased censorship, and on June 7, 1981, an additional 7 publications were banned. Among them were *Mizan,* the largest opposition paper, run by Mehdi Bazargan; *Inqilib Islami,* owned by Abol Hasan Bani-Sadr; and *Nameh Mardum,* organ of the *Tudeh* Party. Furthermore, on August 25, 1981, the *Majlis* passed a law making it a criminal offense to use "pen and speech" against the government. The most recent banning was that of the radical daily *Azadegan* in June 1985.

Press. The following are among the dailies published at Teheran: *Kayhan* (Universe, 350,000); *Ettela'at* (Information 250,000); *Khorassan* (40,000); *Jomhori Islami* (Islamic Republic), organ of former Islamic Republican Party; *Teheran Times,* in English; *Abrar* (Rightly Guided), founded 1985 as successor to *Azadegan.*

News agencies. In December 1981 the domestic facility, Pars News Agency, was renamed the Islamic Republic News Agency (IRNA); following the July 1981 closing of Reuters' Teheran office, *Agence France-Presse* and Italy's ANSA were the only remaining Western bureaus maintaining operations in Iran. The Soviet agency TASS, East Germany's ADN, and the New China News Agency (*Xinhua*) are also represented at Teheran.

Radio and television. Islamic Republic of Iran Broadcasting provides television service over two networks and home-service radio broadcasting in a variety of indigenous and foreign languages. Broadcasting services are also provided by the government-controlled *Radio Naft-e-Melli.* There were approximately 2.3 million television receivers in 1987.

INTERGOVERNMENTAL REPRESENTATION

The United States severed diplomatic relations with Iran on April 4, 1980.

Permanent Representative to the UN: (Vacant).

IGO Memberships (Non-UN): CCC, CP, IC, ICAC, Intelsat, Interpol, IWTC, NAM, OPEC, PCA.

I R A Q

Republic of Iraq
al-Jumhuriyah al-'Iraqiyah

Political Status: Independent state since 1932; declared a republic following military coup which overthrew the monarchy in 1958. The present constitution is a substantially amended version of a provisional document issued September 22, 1968.

Area: 167,924 sq. mi. (434,923 sq. km.).

Population: 16,278,316 (1987C), 16,778,000 (1988E).

Major Urban Centers (1977C): BAGHDAD (3,236,000); Basra (1,540,000); al-Mawsil (1,220,000); Kirkuk (535,000).

Official Languages: Arabic, Kurdish.

Monetary Unit: Dinar (market rate March 1, 1988, 1 dinar = $3.22US).

President of the Republic, Prime Minister, and Chairman of the Revolutionary Command Council: Saddam HUS-

SEIN (HUSAYN); designated by the RCC on July 12, 1979, succeeding Ahmad Hasan al-BAKR on July 16.

Vice President of the Republic: Taha Muhyi al-Din MA'RUF; designated by the RCC on April 21, 1974.

Vice Chairman of the Revolutionary Command Council: 'Izzat IBRAHIM; designated by the RCC on July 16, 1979, succeeding Saddam HUSSEIN.

THE COUNTRY

Historically known as Mesopotamia ("land between the rivers") from its geographic position centering in the Tigris-Euphrates Valley, Iraq is an almost landlocked, partly desert country whose population is overwhelmingly Muslim and largely Arabic-speaking, but includes a Kurdish minority of well over a million in the northeastern region bordering on Syria, Turkey, and Iran. More than 50 percent of the Muslims are Shi'ite, although the regime has long been Sunni-dominated. Women comprise about 25 percent of the paid labor force, 47 percent of the agricultural work force, and one-third of the professionals in education and health care; traditionally minimal female representation in government was partially reversed at the 1984 National Assembly balloting, when the number of women deputies rose from 14 to 80 (32 percent). In addition, a moderate interpretation of Islamic law has given women equal rights in divorce, land ownership, and suffrage.

Agriculture, which was characterized by highly concentrated land ownership prior to the introduction of land-reform legislation in 1958, occupies about two-fifths of the population but produces under one-tenth of the gross national product. The most important crops are dates, barley, wheat, rice, and tobacco. Oil is the leading natural resource and accounts for over half of GNP. Other important natural resources include phosphates, sulphur, iron, copper, chromite, lead, limestone, and gypsum. Manufacturing industry, largely nationalized since 1964, is not highly developed, although petrochemical, steel, aluminum, and phosphate plants were among heavy-industrial construction projects undertaken in the 1970s. In recent years the country has experienced severe economic difficulty as the result of depressed oil prices and the heavy cost (including shortfalls in oil output) attributable to war with Iran. In early 1987, on the other hand, it was reported that approximately half of its $50 billion foreign debt would be rescinded in the form of "gifts" of oil and cash transfers from other Arab Gulf states.

GOVERNMENT AND POLITICS

Political background. Conquered successively by Arabs, Mongols, and Turks, the region now known as Iraq became a British mandate under the League of Nations following World War I. British influence, exerted through the ruling Hashemite dynasty, persisted even after Iraq gained formal independence in 1932; the country continued to fol-

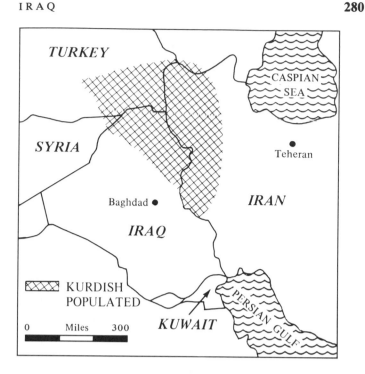

low a generally pro-British and pro-Western policy until the overthrow of the monarchy in July 1958 by a military coup that cost the lives of King FAISAL II and his leading statesman, Nuri al-SA'ID. Brig. Gen. 'Abd al-Karim KASSEM (QASIM), leader of the revolt, ruled as head of a left-wing nationalist regime until he too was killed in a second coup on February 8, 1963, that brought to power a new military regime led by Lt. Gen. 'Abd al-Salam 'AREF ('ARIF) and, after his accidental death in 1966, by his brother, Gen. 'Abd al-Rahman 'AREF. The 'Aref regime terminated in a third, bloodless coup on July 17, 1968, which established (then) Maj. Gen. Ahmad Hasan al-BAKR, a former premier and leader of the right wing of the *Baath* Socialist Party, as president and prime minister.

Under the Bakr regime, a number of alleged plots were used as excuses to move against internal opposition; the most prominent took place in June 1973 when a coup attempt by Col. Nazim KAZZAR, head of national security, led to numerous arrests and executions. Domestic instability was further augmented by struggles within the *Baath* and by relations with the Kurdish minority. The Kurds, under the leadership of Gen. Mustafa al-BARZANI, resisted most Baghdad governments in the two decades after World War II and, with Iranian military support, were intermittently in open rebellion from 1961 to 1975. A 1970 settlement with the Kurds broke down over distribution of petroleum revenues and exclusion of the oil-producing Kirkuk area from Kurdistan. In May 1974 Iraq and Iran agreed to a mutual withdrawal of troops along their common frontier, pending a settlement of outstanding issues, but the Iraqi army subsequently launched a major offensive against the rebels and over 130,000 Kurds fled to Iran to escape the hostilities. Concessions were ultimately made on both sides in an agreement concluded between the two governments in March 1975 during an OPEC meeting at Algiers, with a "reconciliation" treaty being signed at Baghdad the following June. Iraq agreed to abandon a

long-standing claim to the Shatt al-'Arab waterway at its southern boundary with Iran and accepted a delimitation of the remaining frontier on the basis of agreements concluded prior to the British presence in Iraq; Iran, in return, agreed to cease all aid to the Kurds, whose resistance momentarily subsided. In mid-1976, however, fighting again erupted between Iraqi forces and the Kurdish *Pesh Merga* guerrillas, ostensibly because of the government's new policy of massive deportation of Kurds to southern Iraq and their replacement by Arabs.

On July 16, 1979, President Bakr announced his resignation from both party and government offices. His successor, Saddam HUSSEIN, had widely been considered the strongman of the regime, and his accession to the top posts of the *Baath* and the Revolutionary Command Council (RCC) came as no surprise. Earlier in the year, the Iraqi Communist Party (ICP) had withdrawn from the six-year-old National Progressive Front (see Political Parties, below) following what Hussein himself had termed a purging of Communists from the government, while reports in late July of a failed "conspiracy" against the new president provided further evidence that he had effectively eliminated opponents from the RCC.

Although former president Bakr was known to be experiencing health problems, his resignation was apparently linked to differences within the RCC in regard to three policies: (1) the campaign not only against the Kurds but, in the aftermath of the Iranian Revolution, the increasingly restive Shi'ite community, led by Ayatollah Muhammad Baqir al-SADR until his execution in April 1980; (2) an Iraqi-Syrian unification plan (see Foreign relations, below), aspects of which President Hussein found objectionable; and (3) the suppression of the Iraqi Communist Party, including the removal from the cabinet of its two ministers. Although a broad amnesty was proclaimed on August 16, 1979, Kurdish, Shi'ite, and Communist opposition to the Hussein government persisted and appeared to expand following Baghdad's September 17, 1980, abrogation of the 1975 Algiers agreement and the invasion five days later of Iran's Khuzistan Province.

Despite overwhelming air superiority and early ground successes, including the capture in late October of the Iranian port of Khorramshahr and the destruction of the key oil refinery at Abadan (see map, p. 276), the Iranian military offered unexpectedly stiff resistance, and the brief campaign projected by Hussein had, by the end of the year, been reduced to a stalemate. By September 1981 the momentum had shifted, with Iran lifting the siege of Abadan and gradually recapturing other territory in Khuzistan. In May 1982 Khorramshahr was retaken, several Iraqi ceasefire proposals having been rejected by Teheran, which called, inter alia, for the payment of $150 billion in reparations and Hussein's ouster. In late June Iraqi forces withdrew from most captured territory still under its control, while in July Iranian forces moved across the border and advanced on the Iraqi city of Basra. That and subsequent offensives proved costly to both sides, however, and a lengthy war of attrition ensued that continued into 1988.

Constitution and government. Constitutional processes were largely nonexistent during the two decades after the 1958 coup, despite the issuance of a provisional basic law in 1968, followed, in 1971, by a National Action Charter that envisaged the establishment of local governing councils and the reconvening of a legislature. It was not until June and September 1980 that elections were held for a unicameral National Assembly and a Kurdish Legislative Council, respectively. The RCC was not, however, dissolved, effective power remaining concentrated in its chairman, who serves concurrently as president of the Republic. Assisted by a vice president and a Council of Ministers, the president has broad powers of appointment and is also commander in chief of the Armed Forces. The judicial system is headed by a Court of Cassation and includes five courts of appeal, courts of the first instance, religious courts, and revolutionary courts that deal with crimes involving state security.

As a concession to northern minority sentiment, the Kurds in 1974 were granted "autonomy [as] defined by law", and in 1976 the country's 16 provincial governorates were expanded to 18, three of which were designated as Kurdish Autonomous Regions.

Foreign relations. After following a broadly pro-Western policy that included participation in the Baghdad Pact and its successor, the Central Treaty Organization (CENTO), Iraq switched abruptly in 1958 to an Arab nationalist line that has since been consistently maintained. Relations with the Soviet Union and other Communist-bloc countries became increasingly cordial after 1958, while diplomatic links with the United States (and temporarily with Britain) were severed in 1967. In 1979, however, Baghdad moved against Iraqi Communists, veering somewhat toward the West, particularly France, for military and development aid. The change in direction was reinforced in 1981–1982. Following a June 7, 1981, Israeli air raid against Iraq's Osirak nuclear reactor, then being built outside Baghdad, France indicated that it would assist in reconstructing the facility, while on November 17, 1982, President Hussein stated that his regime might be willing to reestablish diplomatic relations with the United States should Washington end its pro-Israeli bias and demonstrate an interest in resolution of the Persian Gulf war.

Relations with Teheran have long been embittered by conflicting interests in the Gulf region, including claims to the Shatt al-'Arab and to three islands (Greater and Lesser Tunb, and Abu Musa) occupied by Iran in 1971, as well as by Iranian support for Iraq's Kurdish rebels. Following the advent of the Khomeini regime, Iraq bombed a number of Kurdish villages inside Iran, and on September 22, 1980, having repudiated the 1975 reconciliation treaty, invaded its eastern neighbor.

Relations with other Arab states have fluctuated, although Iraq has remained committed to an anti-Israel policy. A leading backer of the "rejection front", it bitterly denounced the 1977 peace initiative of Egyptian President Sadat and the Camp David accords of September 1978, after which, on October 26, Syria and Iraq joined in a "National Charter for Joint Action" against Israel. This marked an abrupt reversal in relations between the two neighbors, long led by competing *Baath* factions. The "National Charter" called for "full military union" and talks directed toward its implementation were conducted in January and June 1979. At the latter session, held at Baghdad,

presidents Assad of Syria and Bakr of Iraq declared that their two nations constituted "a unified state with one President, one Government and one Party, the *Baath*", but the subsequent replacement of Bakr by Saddam Hussein, whom the Syrians had long considered an instigator of subversion in their country, coupled with Hussein's accusations of Syrian involvement in an attempted coup, abruptly terminated the rapprochement.

The onset of the Iran-Iraq war led to a sharp division within the Arab world, with the other Gulf states, Jordan, Morocco, Mauritania, the Yemen Arab Republic, and eventually Egypt and Sudan supporting Baghdad, while the more radical Arab states — Libya, Syria, and the People's Democratic Republic of Yemen — backed Iran. Jordan soon emerged as Iraq's most vocal ally, providing vital supply lines (as did Kuwait) and announcing in January 1982 the formation of a volunteer brigade committed to fighting alongside Iraqi troops. A month earlier, Saudi Arabia and Iraq had concluded an agreement reaffirming an unratified 1975 treaty evenly dividing their oil-rich "Neutral Zone" (some 3,180 square miles), which had been created in the early 1920s to permit the free migration of nomadic inhabitants.

In response to their support for Iran, Baghdad withdrew its diplomatic personnel from Libya and Syria in October 1980 and in April 1982 severed relations with the latter. On the other hand, diplomatic relations were restored with South Yemen in January 1982, following a three-year estrangement, and with the United States, after a 17-year lapse, in November 1984.

Current issues. Despite external assistance, the lengthy Gulf war appeared during 1986 to be exacting a greater toll on Iraq's resources than on those of its enemy. In August, President Hussein called for an "honorable peace" in an open letter broadcast on Iraqi radio and television, repeating the appeal at the end of the year. On both occasions, Teheran demanded Hussein's overthrow and the payment of reparations for Iraq's "aggression". In December, Iranian forces launched a major offensive on the southern front and by early 1987 had advanced to Basra, which, however, remained under Iraqi control.

Little subsequent change occurred until April 1988, when Iraq, in a surprising victory, recaptured the strategically important port city of Fao (occupied by Iranian forces in February 1986), thereby substantially reducing the threat to Basra. While analysts continued to view the overall balance as being in Iran's favor because of its larger size and population, the Fao action was seen as improving Iraq's bargaining position should a negotiated end to the conflict prove possible.

POLITICAL PARTIES AND GROUPS

Since the 1968 coup, the dominant force within Iraq has been the *Baath,* which under the National Action Charter of 1973 became allied with the Iraqi Communist Party (ICP) and, in 1974, with three Kurdish groups in a **National Progressive Front.** In March 1979 the Front became largely moribund when the Communists withdrew.

Following the onset of war with Iran in September 1980, various opposition elements announced the formation of several antigovernment groupings, all receiving support from abroad. On November 28 the ICP, the Democratic Party of Kurdistan (DPK), and the Unified Socialist Party of Kurdistan (USPK) signed a charter establishing a **Democratic Iraqi Front** committed to establishment of a coalition government and Kurdish autonomy, the severance of ties to the "world capitalist market", and solidarity with anti-Zionist and socialist governments. Two weeks before, on November 12, a **National Pan-Arab Democratic Front**, reportedly encompassing seven different groups, including the Patriotic Union of Kurdistan (PUK) as well as *Baath* and ICP dissidents, was formed at Damascus, Syria. Finally, on November 17, 1982, opposition elements based at Teheran, Iran, established a **Supreme Council of the Islamic Revolution of Iraq,** led by Hojatolislam Sayyid Muhammad Baqir HAKIM, to work for Hussein's overthrow. The Supreme Council was believed to encompass a variety of Shi'ite factions, the most prominent of which was the extremist *al-Da'wah.*

During a meeting at Teheran in November 1986, representatives of the DPK and the PUK announced that they had concluded an agreement to coordinate their efforts against Baghdad, the DPK indicating that it had also discussed the possibility of cooperation with the Supreme Council.

Participants in National Progressive Front:

Arab Socialist Renaissance Party (*Hizb al-Baath al-Arabi al-Ishtiraki*). The *Baath,* founded in 1947, is an Arab nationalist movement with branches in Syria and other Arab countries. The Iraqi leadership, known as the Regional Command and closely associated with the Revolutionary Command Council, presently encompasses 17 members and is headed by President Hussein, who was most recently reconfirmed as regional secretary general at an extraordinary National Congress on July 10, 1986.
Leaders: Saddam HUSSEIN (President of the Republic and Regional Secretary General of the Party), 'Izzat IBRAHIM (Deputy Regional Secretary General), Michael AFLAQ (Secretary General of the Party).

Kurdish Democratic Party — KDP (*al-Hizb al-Dimuqraati al-Kurdi*). The original KDP, founded in 1946 by Mullah Mustafa al-Barzani, experienced a number of cleavages (see below), both before and after the ceasefire of March 1975. Thus the group that joined the National Front in 1974 was essentially a Marxist rump of the original party. In September 1978 it reaffirmed its support of the Front and of the *Baath*'s "revolutionary struggle". In what was largely viewed as a symbolic gesture of support for the government, in February 1982 the leadership volunteered to help fight the "racist Persian enemy".
Leader: 'Aziz Hashim AQRAWI (Secretary General).

Kurdistan Revolutionary Party (KRP). The KRP originated in 1972 as a secessionist offshoot of the original KDP and in 1974 joined the National Progressive Front along with the neo-KDP and another offshoot, the Progressive Kurdistan Movement. At a conference in January 1978, KRP members remaining at Baghdad reiterated their support of the National Front, and in August 1981 reaffirmed their commitment to President Hussein's policies.
Leader: 'Abd al-Sattar Tahir SHARIF (Secretary General).

Participants in the Democratic Iraqi Front:

Iraqi Communist Party — ICP (*al-Hizb al-Shuyu'i al-'Iraqi*). Founded in 1934, the Communist Party was legalized upon its entrance into the National Front in 1973. Pro-Moscow in orientation, it occasionally criticized the regime on both domestic and foreign policy grounds, including the latter's pro-Somalian posture in the Ethiopian conflict and its handling of the Kurdish insurgency, with which some elements of the party have been associated. In May 1978 the government executed 21 Communists for engaging in political activities within the armed forces (a right reserved exclusively to *Baath* members), and by March 1979 several hundred ICP members had either fled the country or relocated in Kurdish

areas. With the party having withdrawn from the National Front, (then) RCC Vice Chairman Hussein confirmed in April that Communists were in fact being purged.

Since the onset of war with Iran, First Secretary 'Aziz Muhammad has voiced both support for the Kurdish minority and opposition to the Gulf hostilities, which he characterized, at the February-March 1981 Soviet Communist Party Congress, as a "destructive military adventure".
Leader: 'Aziz MUHAMMAD (First Secretary, in exile).

Democratic Party of Kurdistan (DPK). The DPK evolved from a KDP offshoot, the Kurdish Democratic Party (Provisional Leadership), that was formed in late 1975 following the Algiers agreement between Iraq and Iran and the collateral termination of aid to the Kurds by Iran and the United States. With Mullah Barzani having withdrawn from the Kurdish insurgency, thereby completing dismemberment of the original KDP, the Provisional Leadership declared itself the legitimate successor to the mullah's party. Having refused to cooperate with the National Front, it undertook renewed guerrilla activity through what had been the military wing of the old party, the *Pesh Mergas* ("Those Who Face Death"). Subsequently, the Provisional Leadership consistently opposed government efforts to "resettle" Kurds in southern Iraq and engaged in clashes with both the Iraqi army and the rival PUK (below).

Mullah Barzani died at Washington, DC, on March 1, 1979. In late 1979, by which time the DPK designation had been adopted, a party congress failed to resolve differences between so-called "traditionalist" and "intellectual" factions.

In mid-July 1979 several hundred party members returned to Iraq from Iran, where they had resided since 1975. In the spring of 1980, however, there were reports that Iraqi Kurds (*Faili*), who had emigrated from Iran in the first half of the century, were being expelled from Iraq at the rate of 2,000 a day. Collaterally, on April 9 Massud Barzani, a leader of the DPK Iranian wing, voiced support for the Teheran regime at a time when "US imperialism and its lackeys are conducting their final trench warfare and the *Baath* regime of Iraq is relentlessly fighting against . . . our Shi'a brethren". An August 1981 party congress concluded with a denunciation of the "fascist regime" at Baghdad and its "imperialist war".

In November 1986, the DPK was reported to have entered into a coalition with the PUK (below).
Leaders: Massud BARZANI, 'Idris BARZANI.

Unified Socialist Party of Kurdistan (USPK). The smallest component of the Democratic Iraqi Front, the USPK claimed credit in February 1981 for holding nine foreigners hostage pending Baghdad's release of Kurdish detainees.

Leading Participant in the National Pan-Arab Democratic Front:

Patriotic Union of Kurdistan (PUK). The PUK, which is based at Damascus and has received support from the Syrian *Baath,* resulted from the 1977 merger of Jalal Talabani's Kurdish National Union (KNU) with the Socialist Movement of Kurdistan and the Association of Marxist-Leninists of Kurdistan. The KNU was formed in mid-1975 when Talabani, a left-wing member of the original KDP, refused to accept Mullah Barzani's claim that the Kurdish rebellion had come to an end. Supported by *Pesh Merga* units, Talabani subsequently attempted to unify guerrilla activity under his leadership, but the PUK suffered significant losses in June 1978 during 10 days of skirmishes in northern Iraq with the DPK, which Talabani accused of links to both the shah of Iran and the US Central Intelligence Agency.

In January 1984, it was reported that an agreement had been concluded between the PUK and government forces that called for a ceasefire, assurances of greater Kurdish autonomy, and the formation of a 40,000-member Kurdish army to counter Iranian incursions into Iraqi Kurdistan. The agreement, if actually undertaken, was never implemented and Iran's Islamic Republic News Agency asserted in November 1986 that the PUK had entered into an alliance with the DPK (above) to undertake a joint struggle against Baghdad.
Leader: Jalal TALABANI.

Shi'ite Groups Linked to the Supreme Council of the Islamic Revolution:

Holy Warriors (*al-Mujahidin*). Founded in early 1979 and with direct ties to the militant *Mujahidin* of Iran, the Holy Warriors have claimed responsibility for a variety of anti-Baghdad terrorist attacks. In March 1980 the RCC decreed the death penalty for members of the organization.

Islamic Call (*al-Da'wah al-Islamiyah*). *Al-Da'wah* was established in the 1960s with the support of the Shi'a leader Muhammad Baqir al-Sadr, who was executed by the Hussein regime in April 1980. Closely allied with the *Mujahidin, al-Da'wah* claimed responsibility in August-September 1982 for bomb attacks on the Iraqi Ministry of Planning and an airline office.

Organization for Islamic Action (*Munadhdhamat al-'Amal al-Islami*). The Organization, a splinter from *al-Da'wah,* was formed in 1980.

LEGISLATURE

The former bicameral Parliament ceased to exist with the overthrow of the monarchy in 1958, legislative functions subsequently being assumed by the Revolutionary Command Council. On the basis of a bill approved by the RCC on March 16, 1980, an election to a 250-member **National Assembly** (*Majlis al-'Umma*) was held on June 20. Although candidates do not register by political affiliation within the National Progressive Front, it was reported that the Arab Baath Socialist Party obtained approximately 73 percent of the seats at the most recent election of October 20, 1984.

An election for a separate Kurdish Legislative Council of 50 members took place in the northern Autonomous Regions of Arbil, D'hok, and Sulaimaniyah in September 1980. Balloting for an enlarged Council of 57 members occurred on August 6, 1983.

Speaker of National Assembly: Dr. Sa'adoun HAMMADI.

Chairman of Kurdish Legislative Council: Ahmad 'Abd al-QADIR al-Naqshabandi.

CABINET

[as of March 23, 1988]

Prime Minister	Saddam Hussein
First Deputy Prime Minister	Taha Yasin Ramadan
Deputy Prime Ministers	Tariq Mikhayl 'Aziz
	Gen. 'Adnan Khayrallah

Ministers

Agriculture and Irrigation	Karim Hasan Rida
Awqaf and Religious Affairs	'Abdallah Fadil 'Abbas
Culture and Information	Latif Nusayyif Jasim
Defense	Gen. 'Adnan Khayrallah
Education	'Abd al-Qadir 'Izz al-Din
Finance	Hikmat 'Umar Mukhaylif
Foreign Affairs	Tariq Mikhayl 'Aziz
Health	Dr. Sadiq Hamid 'Allush
Higher Education and Scientific Research	Mundhir Ibrahim al-Shawi
Housing and Construction	Muhammad Fadil Hussein
Industry and Minerals	Col. Hussein Kamil
Interior	Samir Muhammad 'Abd al-Wahab Shaykhli
Justice	Akram 'Abd al-Qadir 'Ali
Labor and Social Affairs	Babakr Mahmud Rasul
Local Government	'Adnan Daud Salman
Oil	Isam 'Abd al-Rahim al Shalabi
Planning	Samal Majid Faraj
Trade	Muhammad Mahdi Salih
Transport and Communications	Muhammad Hamza al-Zubaydi

Ministers of State

Military Affairs	Gen. 'Abd al-Jabbar Khalil Shanshall
Without Portfolio	'Abdallah Isma'il Ahmad
	Hashim Hasan 'Aqrawi
	Arshad Muhammad Ahmad al-Zibari
Chief, President's Cabinet	Ahmad Hussein al-Samarra'i
Governor, Central Bank	(Vacant)

NEWS MEDIA

Press. Although the 1968 constitution provides for freedom of the press, all news media are rigidly controlled by the government. Thus a ban against the publication of privately owned newspapers was lifted in 1968 but reimposed in 1969. *Tarik al-Sha'ab* (People's Path), founded in 1973 as the organ of the Iraqi Communist Party, was indefinitely suspended on April 5, 1979, although it subsequently appeared clandestinely. The following are government-regulated dailies published at Baghdad: *al-Thawra* (The Revolution, 250,000), *Baath* organ, in Arabic; *al-Jumhuriyah* (The Republic, 220,000), in Arabic; *al-'Iraq* (30,000), Kurdish Democratic Party organ; *Baghdad Observer* (20,000), in English.

News agencies. The domestic facility is the Iraqi News Agency (*Wikalat al-Anba al-'Iraqiyah*); foreign bureaus with offices at Baghdad include the Middle East News Agency, *Deutsche Presse-Agentur,* East Germany's ADN, Spain's EFE, and TASS.

Radio and television. The government Broadcasting Service of the Republic of Iraq (*Idha'at al-Jumhuriyah al-'Iraqiyah*) transmits domestically in Arabic, Kurdish, Syriac, and Turkoman; foreign broadcasts are in various European languages as well as in Persian, Swahili, Turkish, and Urdu. Baghdad Television (*Mahattat Talafizyun Baghdad*), broadcasting from 15 transmitters throughout Iraq, is controlled by the Ministry of Information. There were approximately 2.8 million radio and 610,000 television receivers in 1987.

INTERGOVERNMENTAL REPRESENTATION

Ambassador to the US: 'Abd al-Amir 'Ali al-ANBARI.

US Ambassador to Iraq: April Catherine GLASPIE.

Permanent Representative to the UN: Ismat Taha KITTANI.

IGO Memberships (Non-UN): AFESD, AMF, BADEA, *CMEA,* ICAC, IDB, Inmarsat, INRO, Intelsat, Interpol, ISO, IWTC, LAS, NAM, OAPEC, OPEC, PCA.

IRELAND

Republic of Ireland
Éire

Political Status: Independent state since 1921; under republican constitution effective December 29, 1937.

Area: 27,136 sq. mi. (70,283 sq. km.).

Population: 3,537,000 (1986C), 3,575,000 (1988E). The 1986 result is provisional; net emigration during 1982–1986 was reported to be 76,000.

Major Urban Centers (1981C): DUBLIN (urban area, 915,115); Cork (149,792); Limerick (75,520).

Official Languages: Irish (Gaelic), English.

Monetary Unit: Irish Pound (Punt) (market rate March 1, 1988, 1 pound = $1.58US).

President: Dr. Patrick J. HILLERY (Pádraig Ó HIRI-GHILE); elected November 9, 1976, following the resignation of Carroll O'DALY (Cearbhall Ó DALAIGH) on October 22; unopposed upon nomination and declared reelected for a second seven-year term on October 21, 1983.

Prime Minister (*Taoiseach*): Charles James HAUGHEY (*Fianna Fáil*); confirmed by the *Dáil* on March 10, 1987, to succeed Dr. Garret FITZGERALD (*Fine Gael*), following legislative election of February 17.

THE COUNTRY

The present-day Irish Republic, encompassing 26 of Ireland's 32 historic counties, occupies all but the northeastern quarter of the Atlantic island lying 50 to 100 miles west of Great Britain. Animated by a powerful sense of national identity, the population is overwhelmingly Roman Catholic and retains a strong sense of identification with the Catholic minority in Northern Ireland. However, a constitutional provision according a privileged position to the Church was repealed by public referendum in 1972. In 1986, women constituted 29.4 percent of the paid labour force, concentrated in the clerical and service sectors; female participation in government, traditionally minimal, currently includes one cabinet member and a leader of the recently organized Progressive Democratic Party.

Historically dependent on agricultural activities, Ireland now possesses a significant industrial sector that accounts for more than three-quarters of export earnings. The principal manufactured goods include textiles, chemicals, metals, and machinery as well as beverages; tourism is also a significant source of foreign exchange.

Largely unfavorable fiscal trends in recent years have yielded extreme contrasts indicative of an emerging dual economy. In late 1983, following the adoption of austerity measures, unemployment reached 16 percent and the foreign debt $10 billion. In 1984, more drastic action was taken to curtail public expenditure, while the Industrial Development Authority combined a vigorous advertising campaign with cash grants for plant construction and a maximum corporate tax of 10 percent to attract foreign investors. The response by a number of American, British, and Canadian firms was encouraging and contributed to the reversal of a severe trade imbalance that had crested in 1981. Collaterally, the balance of payments improved, though remaining in deficit because of profit repatriation and service obligations on a steadily increasing foreign debt that by March 1987 had reached $35 billion, with a total public-sector debt at 133 percent of GNP, the highest of any OECD country. Meanwhile, indigenous industry lagged, with the unemployment rate having climbed to more than 30 percent.

GOVERNMENT AND POLITICS

Political background. Ireland's struggle to maintain national identity and independence dates from the beginnings of its conquest by England in the early Middle Ages. Ruled as a separate kingdom under the British Crown and, after 1800, as an integral part of the United Kingdom, Ireland gave birth to a powerful revolutionary movement whose adherents first proclaimed the Republic of Ireland during the Easter Week insurrection of 1916 and, despite initial failure, reaffirmed it in 1919. A measure of national independence was accorded by Great Britain through a treaty of December 1921. Under its terms, the 26 counties of Southern Ireland were granted Dominion status, the 6 counties of Northern Ireland electing to remain within the United Kingdom. The partition is regarded as provisional by the Irish Republic, which remains formally committed to incorporation of the northern counties into a unified Irish nation.

Officially known as the Irish Free State from 1922 to 1937, Southern Ireland became the Irish Republic, or simply Ireland (*Éire*), with the entry into force of its present constitution on December 29, 1937. Its association with the British Commonwealth was gradually attenuated and finally terminated on April 18, 1949. For most of the next decade governmental responsibility tended to alternate between the Republican (*Fianna Fáil*) and United Ireland (*Fine Gael*) parties, while from 1957 to 1973 the former ruled under the successive prime ministries of Éamon DE VALÉRA (1957–1959), Sean F. LEMASS (1959–1966), and John M. LYNCH (1966–1973). After calling a surprise election in February 1973, the *Fianna Fáil* failed to retain its majority, and a coalition government of the *Fine Gael* and Labour parties was installed under the leadership of Liam COSGRAVE. Lynch returned as prime minister following a *Fianna Fáil* victory in an election held June 16, 1977, but on December 5, 1979, announced his intention to resign and six days later was succeeded by Charles J. HAUGHEY. Haughey's investiture was widely regarded as the most remarkable comeback in Irish political history: although ultimately acquitted, he had been dismissed as Lynch's finance minister in 1970 and tried on charges of conspiring to use government funds to smuggle arms to the outlawed Irish Republican Army (IRA).

At the election of June 11, 1981, *Fine Gael* gained 21 lower-house seats over its 1977 total, and on June 30 Dr. Garret FITZGERALD, by a three-vote margin, succeeded in forming a government in coalition with Labour. With all major parties having voiced support for IRA hunger strikers incarcerated at Maze prison in the North, the key issue in the campaign had been the faltering economy. The new administration quickly increased taxes, announced spending cuts, and permitted higher interest rates, but on January 27, 1982, its first full budget was defeated by a single vote. Following a new election on February 8, the Haughey-led *Fianna Fáil,* backed by three Workers' Party deputies and two independents, returned to office on March 9. Eight months later, unable to reverse the economic decline and buffeted by a series of minor scandals within his official family, Haughey lost a no-confidence motion by two votes. The balance of power again shifted at an election on November 24, yielding the installation of another *Fine Gael*–Labour government under FitzGerald on December 14.

During 1986, FitzGerald, whose promises to reduce unemployment, emigration, and government spending had yielded scant results, faced rising political discontent. In

October, he survived a no-confidence motion by two votes, but lost his parliamentary majority on December 10 with the resignation of a conservative member of the *Fine Gael*. On January 21, the four-year-old coalition government fell over the issue of budget cuts, which Labour felt would impinge inequitably on welfare programs.

At the general election of February 17, 1987, *Fianna Fáil* fell three seats short of a majority, a third Haughey administration being approved on March 10 by the barest possible margin of 83–82, with one abstention.

Constitution and government. The Irish constitution, adopted by plebiscite on July 1, 1937, is theoretically applicable to the whole of Ireland; thus, residents of Northern Ireland are considered citizens and can run for office in the South. In June 1984, voters approved by referendum a measure permitting resident noncitizens to participate in national elections.

The constitution provides for a president directly elected for a seven-year term and for a bicameral legislature (*Oireachtas*) consisting of a directly elected lower house (*Dáil*) and an indirectly chosen upper house (*Seanad*) with power to delay, but not to veto, legislation. The cabinet, which is responsible to the *Dáil*, is headed by a prime minister (*taoiseach*), who is the leader of the majority party or coalition and is appointed by the president for a five-year term on recommendation of the *Dáil*. The president has the power to dissolve the *Dáil* on the prime minister's advice. The judicial system is headed by the Supreme Court and includes a Court of Criminal Appeal, a High Court, and circuit and district courts. Judges are appointed by the president with the advice of the government and may be removed only by approval of both houses of the legislature.

Local government is based on 27 counties (Tipperary counting as 2 for administrative purposes) and 4 county boroughs (Dublin, Cork, Limerick, and Waterford), each with elected governing bodies.

Foreign relations. Independent Ireland has consistently adhered to an international policy of nonalignment, having remained neutral throughout World War II and subsequently avoiding membership in any regional security structure. It has, however, been an active participant in the United Nations (since 1955), the European Community (since 1973), and other multinational organizations.

Dublin remains committed to the goal of a united Ireland, and since 1969 its relations with the United Kingdom have been complicated by persistent violence in Ulster and terrorism committed by both the IRA and ultra-unionists. Since the late 1970s, the two governments have cooperated in security matters, but on July 18, 1981, some 15,000 IRA supporters, protesting the deaths of hunger strikers at Maze prison near Belfast and London's refusal to grant IRA prisoners political standing, rioted outside the British Embassy at Dublin. In an effort to improve relations, prime ministers FitzGerald and Thatcher, at a meeting on November 6, agreed to the formal establishment of an Anglo-Irish Inter-Governmental Conference (AIIC) to discuss a range of mutual concerns. The Conference initially met in January 1982, but encountered a number of obstacles including the Haughey government's opposition to UK proposals for devolution of power to the North, disagreement over sanctions against Argentina during the Falklands crisis,

and renewed IRA bombings at London. Further progress was, however, registered in discussions between the two prime ministers in November 1983, leading two years later to an Anglo-Irish Agreement that was subsequently ratified by the Irish and UK parliaments. The pact established a "framework" within which Dublin would have an advisory role in the devolution of power to Northern Ireland, while acknowledging British sovereignty for as long as such status should be desired by a majority of the territory's inhabitants (see Current issues, below, and entry under UK: Northern Ireland).

Relations between the two governments again worsened in the context of the Dáil's December 1987 ratification of the 1977 European Convention on the Suppression of Terrorism, which sanctioned the extradition of individuals charged with terrorist activity. Irish public opinion had opposed the Convention because of British reluctance to modify its Diplock court system, whereby suspected terrorists could be summarily tried without juries in Belfast courts—often, it was contended, with insufficient evidence of guilt. Although sentiment had shifted somewhat in reaction to civilian fatalities during the November IRA bombing at Enniskillen in Ulster, "safeguards" to the Convention were attached by the Dáil, including a stipulation that the Irish attorney general approve all extradition proceedings. Prime Minister Thatcher immediately rejected the modifications, arguing that they reduced Britain to "least favored nation" status.

Earlier, in a June 26 referendum, Irish voters approved ratification of the European Community's Single European Act, despite arguments that the Act's reference to "closer cooperation on questions of European security" threatened the Republic's neutrality (Ireland being the only EC country that was not also a member of NATO).

Current issues. The Anglo-Irish Agreement of November 1985 established guidelines for cross-border cooperation on security, judicial, and legal issues, and gave the Republic a role in the evolution of internal Northern political structures. Prime Minister FitzGerald defended the Agreement as an interim measure designed to "establish peace" in the area prior to eventual reunification and, although generating anger and cynicism among northern Unionists as well as IRA-affiliated groups, the measure received overwhelming parliamentary confirmation and a 59 percent approval rating in a subsequent public opinion poll.

While the February balloting marked the end of a decade of coalition rule, the *Fianna Fáil* government was confirmed only because a Marxist independent, Tony GREGORY, had abstained in the vote (Gregory's previous relations with the prime minister had caused embarrassment for *Fianna Fáil* because of evidence that in 1982 Haughey had promised more than $100 million in urban renewal funds for his district in return for parliamentary support). The principal surprise of the election was that the recently organized Progressive Democratic Party, a center-right formation, had surpassed Labour to become third-ranked in the House of Representatives, with 14 seats.

POLITICAL PARTIES

Government Party:

Republican Party (*Fianna Fáil*). Founded in 1926 by Éamon de Valéra, *Fianna Fáil* ("Soldiers of Destiny") previously held governmental responsibility in 1932–1948, 1951–1954, 1957–1973, 1977–1981, and March–November 1982. It advocates the peaceful ending of partition, the promotion of social justice, and the pursuit of national self-sufficiency. Since 1982, Charles Haughey has survived a number of challenges to his leadership, most notably from Desmond O'Malley (see PDP, below), who subsequently withdrew from the party. O'Malley, voting as an independent, was joined by a *Fianna Fáil* representative in voting to approve the Anglo-Irish Agreement in November 1985, the remainder of the party voting in opposition.

Leaders: Charles J. HAUGHEY (Prime Minister and Leader of the Party), Brian LENIHAN (Foreign Affairs Minister and Deputy Leader of the Party), Frank A. WALL (General Secretary).

Opposition Parties:

United Ireland Party (*Fine Gael*). *Fine Gael* ("Family of the Irish") was formed in September 1933 through amalgamation of the Cosgrave Party (*Cumann na nGaedheal*), the Center Party, and the National Guard. It advocates friendly relations and ultimate union with Northern Ireland, financial encouragement of industry, promotion of foreign investment, and full development of agriculture. Its failure to win a majority in the *Dáil* led to formation of coalition governments with the Labour Party (below) after elections in 1973, June 1981, and December 1982.

Following the surprise resignation of Garret FitzGerald on March 11, 1986, former justice minister Alan Dukes, who has been described as "being on the liberal wing of an essentially conservative party", was named opposition leader. Dukes, an economist who had also served for three years as finance minister in the second FitzGerald government, pledged to support the Haughey administration if it introduced an austerity budget of sufficient strength to improve the country's debt-ridden economy.

Leaders: Alan DUKES (President and Parliamentary Leader), John BRUTON (Deputy Leader), John DONNELLAN (Chairman, National Executive), Edward O'REILLY (General Secretary).

Progressive Democratic Party (PDP). The PDP was organized in December 1985 by former *Fianna Fáil* legislator Desmond O'Malley as an alternative to a "party system . . . based on the civil war divisions of 65 years ago". Accused by critics of being a "Thatcherite", O'Malley, who repeatedly stressed the need for new leadership in Ireland, called for fundamental tax reform, government tax cuts, and support for private enterprise. In recent public opinion polls, O'Malley's personal rating has consistently exceeded that of the prime minister. The party won 14 *Dáil* seats in the February 1987 balloting.

Leaders: Desmond O'MALLEY (Parliamentary Leader), Michael KEATING (Deputy Leader), Mary HARNEY, Patrick COX (General Secretary).

Labour Party (*Páirtí Lucht Oibre*). Originating in 1912 as an adjunct of the Trades Union Congress (TUC), the Labour Party became a separate entity in 1930. It advocates far-reaching social security and medical services, public ownership of many industries and services, better working conditions and increased participation of workers in management, expanded agricultural production, protection of the home market, and cooperation and ultimate union with Northern Ireland. At the February 1987 election, its parliamentary strength fell from 16 seats to 12.

In October 1982, its leader in Parliament, Michael O'LEARY, resigned from the party following its rejection of his proposal that Labour commit itself to formation of a coalition government with *Fine Gael* should the Haughey government fall. On November 3, one day before Haughey lost a no-confidence vote, O'Leary joined the *Fine Gael* parliamentary party, and it was left to his successor, Richard Spring, to negotiate an interparty agreement that permitted a *Fine Gael*–Labour coalition to assume office on December 14. The coalition collapsed because of Labour's objection to budget cuts advanced by Prime Minister FitzGerald in January 1987.

Leaders: Mervyn TAYLOR (Chairman), Emmett STAGG (Vice Chairman), Richard SPRING (Parliamentary Leader), Raymond KAVANAGH (General Secretary).

The Workers' Party (WP). The WP is a product of the independence and unification movements that have spanned most of the twentieth century (see *Sinn Féin,* below). Marxist in outlook and dedicated to establishment of a united, socialist Ireland, the party captured its first *Dáil* seat in 20 years at the June 1981 election and expanded its representation to 3 at the February 1982 balloting. The following November, objections to the Haughey government's proposed five-year economic plan led the party's *Dáil* members to side with the opposition on a no-confidence motion, which the government lost by 2 votes. At the November 24 election, the WP lost 1 of its 3 seats; the remaining two representatives joined the government in endorsing the Anglo-Irish Agreement. It won 4 seats in February 1987.

Leaders: Tomas MacGIOLLA (Parliamentary Leader), Prionsias DeROSSA (Deputy Leader), Sean GARLAND (General Secretary).

Sinn Féin. The islandwide *Sinn Féin* ("Ourselves Alone") currently serves as the political arm of the Provisional Irish Republican Army (see *Sinn Féin* and Provisional IRA under Political Parties and Groups in section on United Kingdom: Northern Ireland). The original *Sinn Féin* was formed in 1905 to promote Irish independence. In conjunction with the Irish Republican Army (IRA), which had been created in 1919 to conduct a guerrilla campaign against British forces, *Sinn Féin* helped to lead the revolutionary movement which produced the Irish Free State. Many members left both *Sinn Féin* and the IRA at the formation in 1922 of the *Cumann na nGaedheal* (see United Ireland Party, above) and in 1926 of the *Fianna Fáil* (see Republican Party, above). Its influence substantially reduced, *Sinn Féin* continued its strident opposition to partition while serving as the political wing of the outlawed IRA. A long-standing policy dispute within the IRA eventually led traditional nationalists, committed to continued violence, to form the Provisional IRA in 1969, while the Marxist-oriented rump, primarily devoted to nonviolent political action, continued to represent the "Official" IRA. The rump changed its name to *Sinn Féin* — The Workers' Party in 1977 to differentiate itself from the Provisional *Sinn Féin* created by the Provisional IRA. In 1982 the Marxists relinquished the *Sinn Féin* identification entirely to the "Provos" and became the Workers' Party (above).

In supporting the Provisional IRA's goal of establishing a unified "democratic socialist republic", *Sinn Féin* contested some legislative seats — though announcing that no successful candidate would sit in the *Dáil,* which it did not consider legitimate. At the February 1982 balloting, none of *Sinn Féin*'s seven candidates was successful, and it did not contest the subsequent national election, in November. In June 1985, it won its first seat on the Dublin city council.

On November 2, 1986, at the conclusion of a three-day party conference at Dublin, the delegates voted 429 to 161 in favor of ending the policy against taking up seats in the *Dáil.* Party president Gerald Adams was supported in the action by other leaders, including the Army Council of the Provisional IRA, while a splinter group, led by Ruari O'Bradaigh, left the conference in protest (see Republican *Sinn Féin,* below). The party won no seats in the election of February 1987.

Leader: Gerard ADAMS (President).

Republican Sinn Féin. The Republican *Sinn Féin* was formed by some 30 dissidents at the parent party's 1986 conference, who were vehemently opposed to participation in a *Dáil* that did not include representatives from Northern Ireland.

Leaders: Daithi O'CONNELL (Chairman), Ruari O'BRADAIGH (former *Sinn Féin* President).

Democratic Socialist Party (DSP). The DSP contested the November 1982 election in seven constituencies but failed to win any *Dáil* seats. One of its unsuccessful candidates, Jim Kemmy, had been elected to the two preceding houses as an "Independent Socialist" from Limerick; his vote against the proposed *Fine Gael*–Labor budget in January 1982 was the margin in the government's defeat.

Leaders: James KEMMY (President), Seamus RATIGAN (Chairman), Jan O'SULLIVAN (Vice Chairman), Martin McGARRY (Secretary).

Irish Republican Socialist Party (IRSP). Founded in 1974, the IRSP seeks to establish a democratic socialist republic throughout all of Ireland's 32 counties.

Leaders: Jim LAINE (Chairman), Francis BARRY (General Secretary).

Communist Party of Ireland (CPI). An islandwide grouping first formed in 1921 and reestablished in 1933, the CPI split during the Second World War, with reunification of its southern and northern elements not occurring until 1970. In recent years the party has concentrated on largely unsuccessful efforts to divert support from the Labour Party, whose participation in the coalition government was characterized as "betrayal". Staunchly pro-Moscow, the CPI leadership has unsuccessfully promoted closer coordination with other leftist groups, including the WP, Sinn Fein, the DSP, and the IRSP.

Leaders: Michael O'RIORDAN (National Chairman), Seán NOLAN (National Treasurer), James STEWART (General Secretary).

Green Alliance (*Comhaontas Glas*). Formerly styled the Ecology Party, *Comhaontas Glas* is an Irish expression of the European Green movement.

Coordinator: Kevin STANLEY.

LEGISLATURE

The Irish **Parliament** (*Oireachtas*) is a bicameral body composed of an upper chamber (Senate) and a lower chamber (House of Representatives).

Senate (*Seanad Éireann*). The upper chamber consists of 60 members serving five-year terms. Eleven are nominated by the prime minister and 49 are elected — 6 by the universities and 43 from candidates put forward by five vocational panels: (1) cultural and educational interests, (2) labor, (3) industry and commerce, (4) agriculture and fishing, and (5) public administration and social services. The electing body, a college of some 900 members, includes members of the *Oireachtas* as well as county and county borough councillors. The power of the Senate extends only to delaying for a period of 90 days a bill passed by the *Dáil*. Technically, the house does not function on the basis of party divisions.

Following a postal election for vocational and university members during January 1983 and the designation of nominated members on February 7, *Fine Gael* held 25 seats; *Fianna Fáil,* 18; Labour Party, 7; independents, 10 (the 6 university representatives, 3 nominees from Northern Ireland, and a trade-union representative).

Chairman (*Cathaoirleach*): Patrick J. REYNOLDS.

House of Representatives (*Dáil Éireann*). The *Dáil* currently has 166 members elected by direct adult suffrage and proportional representation for five-year terms, assuming no dissolution. At the most recent general election, held February 17, 1987, *Fianna Fáil* won 81 seats; *Fine Gael,* 51; the Progressive Democratic Party, 14; the Labour Party, 12; the Workers' Party, 4; independents, 4.

Speaker (*Ceann Comhairle*): Sean TREACY.

CABINET

Prime Minister	Charles Haughey
Deputy Prime Minister	Brian Lenihan
Ministers	
Agriculture	Michael O'Kennedy
Defense	Michael Noonan
Education	Mary O'Rourke
Energy, Communications and Forestry	Ray Burke
Environment	Padraig Flynn
Finance and Public Service	Ray MacSharry
Foreign Affairs	Brian Lenihan
Health	Rory O'Hanlon
Industry and Commerce	Albert Reynolds
Justice	Gerard Collins
Labor	Bertie Ahern
Marine	Brendan Daly
Social Welfare	Michael Woods
Tourism and Transport	John Patrick Wilson
Attorney General	John Murray
Governor, Central Bank of Ireland	Maurice Doyle

NEWS MEDIA

Although free expression is constitutionally guaranteed, a five-member Censorship of Publications Board under the jurisdiction of the Ministry of Justice is empowered to halt publication of books. Moreover, under the Broadcasting Act 1960, as amended in 1976 and interpreted by the Supreme Court in a July 1982 decision involving a ban against the Provisional *Sinn Fein,* individuals and political parties committed to undermining the state may be denied access to the public broadcasting media.

Press. All newspapers are privately owned and edited, but the Roman Catholic Church exerts considerable restraining influence. The following are English-language dailies published at Dublin, unless otherwise noted: *Sunday World* (370,000); *The Sunday Press* (267,000), independent; *Sunday Independent* (225,000), pro-*Fine Gael; Irish Independent* (175,000), pro-*Fine Gael; Evening Herald* (133,000), pro-*Fine Gael; Evening Press* (130,000), pro-*Fianna Fáil; The Irish Times* (90,000), independent; *The Irish Press* (87,000), independent; *Cork Examiner* (Cork, 64,000), independent; *Cork Evening Echo* (Cork, 37,000); *Limerick Leader* (Limerick, 34,000), independent triweekly.

News agencies. There is no domestic facility, although several foreign bureaus, including UPI, maintain offices at Dublin.

Radio and television. *Radio Telefís Éireann,* an autonomous statutory corporation, operates all radio and television stations, including *Radió na Gaeltachta,* which broadcasts to Irish-speaking areas. There were approximately 1 million radio and 800,000 television receivers in 1987.

INTERGOVERNMENTAL REPRESENTATION

Ambassador to the US: Padraic N. MacKERNAN.

US Ambassador to Ireland: Margaret M. O'Shaughnessy HECKLER.

Permanent Representative to the UN: Robert McDONAGH.

IGO Memberships (Non-UN): BIS, CCC, CEUR, EC, EIB, ESA, Eurocontrol, ICCO, ICES, ICO, IEA, ILZ, INRO, Intelsat, Interpol, IOOC, ITC, IWSG, OECD.

ISRAEL

State of Israel
Medinat Yisra'el (Hebrew)
Dawlat Isra'il (Arabic)

Political Status: Independent republic established May 14, 1948; under multiparty parliamentary regime.

Land Area: 8,291 sq. mi. (21,475 sq. km.). The Dead Sea and the Sea of Galilee encompass an additional 145 sq. mi. (375 sq. km.).

Population: 4,037,620 (1983C), 4,547,000 (1988E). Area and population figures include the Old City of Jerusalem (and surrounding area), which Israel effectively annexed in 1967 in an action not recognized by the United Nations or the United States (which maintains its embassy at Tel Aviv). Also included is a 444-square-mile (1,150 sq. km.) sector of the Golan Heights to which Israeli forces withdrew under a 1974 disengagement agreement with Syria, and which was placed under Israeli law in December 1981. The figures do not include the "administered territories" of the Gaza Strip and the West Bank (Judaea and Samaria), which encompass an area of about 2,410 square miles (6,242 sq. km.) and a population of approximately 1,400,000 (some 900,000 on the West Bank).

Major Urban Centers (1983E): JERUSALEM (426,000, including East Jerusalem); Tel Aviv/Jaffa (327,000); Haifa (236,000); Ramat Gan (119,000).

Official Languages: Hebrew, Arabic. English, an official language under the Mandate, is taught in the secondary schools and is widely spoken.

Monetary Unit: New Shekel (market rate March 1, 1988, 1.58 shekels = $1US). The new shekel, valued at 1,000 of the old, was introduced on September 4, 1985.

President: Chaim HERZOG; elected by the *Knesset* on March 22 and sworn in May 5, 1983, for a five-year term, succeeding Yitzhak NAVON.

Prime Minister: Yitzhak SHAMIR (*Likud*); served as Prime Minister from October 10, 1983, to September 13, 1984; became Vice Prime Minister and Foreign Minister following legislative election of July 23, 1984, and extensive inter-party discussions that yielded a national unity government to be headed by Shimon PERES for the ensuing 25 months; returned as Prime Minister on October 20, 1986, for the balance of the parliamentary term.

Vice Prime Minister: Shimon PERES (Israel Labor Party); served as Prime Minister of national unity government from September 13, 1984, to October 20, 1986, at which time he succeeded Yitzhak SHAMIR as Vice Prime Minister and Foreign Minister.

THE COUNTRY

The irregularly shaped area constituting the State of Israel is not completely defined by agreed boundaries, its territorial jurisdiction being determined in part by military armistice agreements entered into at the conclusion of Israel's war of independence in 1948–1949. Furthermore, the territory under de facto Israeli control increased substantially as a result of military occupation of Arab territories in the Sinai Peninsula (since returned to Egypt), the Gaza Strip, the West Bank of the Jordan (including the old city of Jerusalem), and the Golan Heights following the Arab-Israeli War of 1967. Those currently holding Israeli citizenship encompass a heterogeneous population that is approximately 84 percent Jewish but includes important Muslim, Christian, and Druze minorities. Women constitute 36 percent of the paid work force concentrated in agriculture, teaching and health care; at present, despite Golda Meir's service as prime minister (1969–1974) there are only 10 female legislators, one of whom is serving as minister of health.

Since independence, Israel has emerged as a technologically progressive, highly literate, and largely urbanized nation in the process of rapid development based on scientific exploitation of its agricultural and industrial potentialities. Agriculture has diminished in importance but remains a significant economic sector, its most important products being citrus fruits, field crops, vegetables, and export-oriented nursery items. The industrial sector includes among its major components hi-tech manufactures, cut diamonds, textiles, processed foods, chemicals, and military equipment. US financial assistance, tourism, and direct aid from Jews in the United States and elsewhere are also of major economic importance. Defense requirements have, however, generated a highly adverse balance of trade and a rate of inflation that escalated to more than 400 percent prior to the imposition of austerity measures in mid-1985 that yielded a dramatic reduction to less than 20 percent in 1987.

GOVERNMENT AND POLITICS

Political background. Israel's modern history dates from the end of the nineteenth century with the rise of the World Zionist movement and establishment of Jewish agricultural settlements in territory that was then part of the Ottoman Empire. In the Balfour Declaration of 1917, the British government expressed support for the establishment in Palestine of a national home for the Jewish people. With the abrogation of Turkish rule at the end of World War I, the area was assigned to Great Britain under a League of Nations mandate that incorporated provisions of the Balfour Declaration. British rule continued until May 1948, despite increasing unrest on the part of local Arabs during the 1920s and 1930s, and Jewish elements during and after World War II. In 1947 the UN General Assembly adopted a resolution calling for the division of Palestine into Arab and Jewish states and the internationalization of Jerusalem and its environs, but the controversial measure could not be implemented because of Arab opposition. Nonetheless, Israel declared its independence coincident with British withdrawal on May 14, 1948. Though immediately attacked by Egypt, Syria, Lebanon, Jordan, and Iraq, the new state was able to maintain itself in the field, and the armistice agreements concluded under UN auspices in 1949 gave it control over nearly one-third more territory than had been assigned to it under the original UN resolution. A second major military encounter between Israel and Egypt in 1956 resulted in Israeli conquest of the Gaza Strip and the Sinai Peninsula, which were subsequently evacuated under US and UN pressure. In two further Arab-Israeli conflicts, Israel seized territories from Jordan (1967) and from Egypt and Syria (1967 and 1973). Subsequent ceasefire disengagements resulted, however, in partial Israeli withdrawal from territory in the Syrian Golan Heights and the Egyptian Sinai. Withdrawal from the remaining Sinai territory was completed in April 1982 under a peace treaty with Egypt concluded on March 26, 1979. The Israeli sector of the Golan Heights, on the other hand, was placed under Israeli law on December 14, 1981.

The internal governmental structure of modern Israel emerged from institutions established by the British administration and the Jewish community during the mandate. For three decades after independence, a series of multiparty coalitions built around the moderate socialist Israel Workers' Party (MAPAI) governed with relatively little change in policy and turnover in personnel. Save for a brief period in 1953–1955, David BEN-GURION was the dominant political figure until his retirement in 1963. He was succeeded by Levi ESHKOL (until his death in 1969), Golda MEIR (until her retirement in 1974), and Yitzhak RABIN, the first native-born Israeli to become prime minister.

Prime Minister Rabin tendered his resignation in December 1976, following his government's defeat on a parliamentary no-confidence motion, but remained in office in a caretaker capacity pending a general election. On April 8, 1977, prior to balloting scheduled for May 17, Rabin was forced to resign his party post in the wake of revelations that he and his wife had violated Israeli law concerning overseas bank deposits. His successor as party leader and acting prime minister, Shimon PERES, proved unable to reverse mounting popular dissatisfaction with a deteriorating economy and evidence of official malfeasance. In a stunning electoral upset, a new reform party, the Democratic Movement for Change, captured much of Labor's support and the opposition *Likud* party, having obtained a sizable legislative plurality, formed the nucleus of a coalition government under Menachem BEGIN on June 19.

As the result of a fiscal dispute that provoked the resignation of its finance minister, the Begin government was deprived of a committed legislative majority on January 11, 1981, and the *Knesset* approved a bill calling for an election on June 30. Despite predictions of an opposition victory, the *Likud* front emerged with a one-seat advantage, and Begin succeeded in forming a new governing coalition on August 4.

The prime minister's startling announcement on August 28, 1983, of his intention, for "personal reasons", to resign both his governmental and party positions was believed by many observers to have been triggered by Israel's severe losses in the 1982 war in Lebanon (see below). The Central Committee of *Likud's* core party, *Herut,* thereupon elected Yitzhak SHAMIR as its new leader on September 1 and the constituent parties of the ruling coalition agreed to support Shamir, who, after failing in an effort to form a national unity government, was sworn in as prime minister on October 10.

Amid increasing criticism of the Shamir administration, particularly in its handling of economic affairs, five deputies of the *Likud* coalition voted with the opposition on March 22, 1984, in calling for legislative dissolution and the holding of a general election. At the balloting on July 23, Labor marginally outpolled *Likud,* securing 44 seats to *Likud's* 41. Extensive inter-party discussion followed, yielding agreement on August 31 to form a national unity coalition on the basis of a rotating premiership. Thus, Labor's Shimon PERES was approved as the new prime minister on September 13, with the understanding that he would exchange positions with Vice Prime Minister Shamir midway through a full parliamentary term of four years; thus, on October 20, 1986, Shamir became prime minister, with Peres assuming his former posts of vice prime minister and minister of foreign affairs.

Constitution and government. In the absence of a written constitution, the structure of the Israeli government is defined by fundamental laws that provide for a president with largely ceremonial functions, a prime minister serving as effective executive, and a unicameral parliament (*Knesset*) to which the government is responsible and whose powers include the election of the president. The role of Judaism in the state has not been formally defined, but the Law of Return of 1950 established a right of immigration for all Jews. The judicial system is headed by a Supreme Court. There are five district courts in addition to magistrates' and municipal courts. Specialized courts include labor courts and religious courts with separate benches for the Jewish, Muslim, Christian, and Druze communities, while military courts are important in the occupied areas.

Israel is divided into six administrative districts, each of which is headed by a district commissioner appointed by the central government. Regions, municipalities, and rural municipalities are the principal administrative entities within the districts.

Foreign relations. During most of the country's years of independence, Israeli foreign relations have been dominated by the requirements of survival in an environment marked by persistent hostility on the part of neighboring Arab states, whose harassing measures have ranged from denying Israel use of the Suez Canal (wholly mitigated upon ratification of the 1979 peace treaty) to encouraging terrorist and guerrilla operations on Israeli soil. Once committed to "nonidentification" between East and West, Israel has encountered hostility from the Soviet Union and most other Communist governments (Romania and Yugoslavia being the most conspicuous exceptions) and has depended primarily on Western countries for political and economic support and arms shipments. A member of the United Nations since 1949, it has frequently incurred condemnation by UN bodies because of its reprisals against Arab guerrilla attacks and its refusal both to reabsorb Arab refugees from the 1948–1949 war and to accept the internationalization of Jerusalem as envisaged in the 1947 UN resolution. Enactment on July 30, 1980, of a law reaffirming a unified Jerusalem as the nation's capital evoked additional condemnation.

In May 1974 a Golan disengagement agreement was concluded with Syria, while Sinai disengagement accords were concluded with Egypt in January 1974 and September 1975. Under the latter, Israel withdrew its forces from the Suez Canal to an irregular line bordered on the east by the Gidi and Mitla passes, and evacuated the Abu Rudeis and Ras Sudar oil fields. Both Egypt and the United States agreed to make a "serious effort" to bring about collateral negotiations with Syria for further disengagement on the Golan Heights, but no such negotiations have yet occurred. On the other hand, in what was hailed as a major step toward peace in the Middle East, Egyptian President Anwar Sadat startled the world in November 1977 by accepting an Israeli invitation to visit Jerusalem. While Sadat yielded little during a historic address to the *Knesset* on November 20, his very presence on Israeli soil kindled widespread hopes that the lengthy impasse in Arab-Israeli relations might somehow be breached. Subsequent discussions yielded potential bases of settlement in regard to the Sinai but no public indication of substantial withdrawal from established positions, on either side, in regard to the West Bank and Gaza. Israel, in responding to Egyptian demands for a meaningful "concession", announced a willingness to grant Palestinians in Gaza and the West Bank "self-rule", coupled with an Israeli right to maintain military installations in the occupied territories. Egypt, on the other hand,

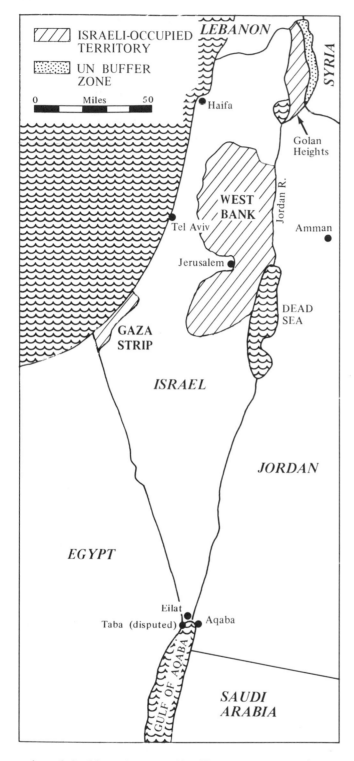

ISRAELI-OCCUPIED TERRITORY

UN BUFFER ZONE

0 Miles 50

LEBANON

SYRIA

Haifa

Golan Heights

WEST BANK

Jordan R.

Tel Aviv

Amman

Jerusalem

DEAD SEA

GAZA STRIP

ISRAEL

JORDAN

EGYPT

Eilat

Taba (disputed)

Aqaba

GULF OF AQABA

SAUDI ARABIA

White House on September 17. In the course of subsequent negotiations at Washington, representatives of the two governments agreed on the details of a treaty and related documents, but the signing was deferred beyond the target date of December 17 because of disagreement about linkage to the second of the Camp David accords, which dealt with autonomy for the inhabitants of the West Bank and Gaza and provided for Israeli withdrawal into specified security locations. In addition, Egypt wished to modify an important treaty provision by an "interpretive annex", stating that prior commitments to other Arab states should have precedence over any obligations assumed in regard to Israel. Progress toward breaking the impasse was registered in early March 1979, and the treaty was formally signed at Washington on March 26, followed by an exchange of ratifications on April 25. In a set of minutes accompanying the treaty, the parties agreed that "there is no assertion that this treaty prevails over other treaties or agreements" and that, within a month after the exchange of instruments of ratification, negotiations would be instituted to define "the modalities for establishing the elected self-governing authority" for the Gaza Strip and West Bank. No significant progress on autonomy for the two regions has yet been registered, although the sixth and final phase of withdrawal from the Sinai (involving about one-third of the peninsula's area) was completed on schedule in April 1982.

On June 6, 1982, Israeli forces invaded Lebanon. While the immediate precipitant of the incursion appeared to be the shooting on June 3 of Israel's ambassador to the United Kingdom, the attack was far from unanticipated in view of a substantial buildup of Israeli military strength along the border in May. Code-named "Peace for Galilee", the attack was justified initially in support of a need to establish a PLO-free zone extending 40–50 kilometers inside Lebanon. By June 14, however, Israeli forces had completely surrounded Beirut, shortly after US President Reagan had announced that he would approve the dispatch of 800–1,000 US marines to participate in an international force that would oversee the evacuation of Palestinian forces from the Lebanese capital. On August 6 US envoy Philip Habib reached agreement, through Lebanese intermediaries, on the PLO withdrawal, which commenced on August 21.

In what was officially described as a "police action" necessitated by the assassination of Lebanese President-elect Bashir Gemayel on September 14, Israeli contingents entered West Beirut and took up positions around the Chatila and Sabra Palestinian refugee camps, where a substantial number of terrorists were alleged to have been left behind by the PLO. On the morning of the 18th it was revealed that a large-scale massacre of civilians had occurred at the hands of right-wing Phalangist militiamen, who had been given access to the camps by Israeli authorities. While the Israeli cabinet expressed its "deep grief and regret" over the atrocities, the affair generated widespread controversy within Israel, with Prime Minister Begin resisting demands for the ouster of Defense Minister Ariel SHARON as well as for the establishment of a commission of inquiry into the circumstances of the massacre. Following the largest protest rally in Israeli history at Tel Aviv on September 25,

rejected the idea of an Israeli military presence and continued to press for Palestinian self-determination.

The prospects for a meaningful accord fluctuated widely during the first eight months of 1978, culminating in a historic summit convened by US President Carter at Camp David, Maryland, on September 5. The unusually lengthy discussions yielded two major agreements, a "Framework for a Peace Treaty between Egypt and Israel" and a "Framework for Peace in the Middle East", which were signed by President Sadat and Prime Minister Begin at the

the prime minister reversed himself and asked the chief justice of the Supreme Court to undertake a full investigation. The results of the inquiry (published in February 1983) placed direct responsibility for the slaughter on the Phalangists, but faulted Sharon and several senior officers for permitting the militiamen to enter the camps in disregard of the safety of the inhabitants. In addition, while absolving the prime minister of foreknowledge of the entry, the commission expressed surprise, in view of "the Lebanese situation as it was known to those concerned", that a decision on entry should have been taken without his participation.

Talks between Israeli and Lebanese representatives on military withdrawal commenced in late December, but became deadlocked on a number of issues, including Israeli insistence that it should continue to man early-warning stations in southern Lebanon. Subsequently, a number of attacks by Palestinian guerrilla groups were mounted against Israeli troops and contingents of the international peace-keeping force, culminating in the destruction of the consular section of the US embassy at Beirut on April 18, 1983. On May 17, however, an agreement was concluded between Israeli, Lebanese, and US negotiators that provided for Israeli withdrawal, an end to the state of war between Israel and Lebanon, and the establishment of a jointly supervised "security region" in southern Lebanon. Although unable to secure a commitment from Syria to withdraw its forces from northern and eastern Lebanon, Israel redeployed its forces in early September to a highly fortified line south of the Awali river. In March 1984, following departure of the multinational force from Beirut, the Lebanese government, under pressure from Syria, abrogated the troop withdrawal accord, although the Israeli cabinet in January 1985 approved a unilateral three-stage withdrawal that was implemented in several stages over the ensuing six months.

Despite the withdrawal announcement, Shi'ite militants mounted a terror campaign against the departing Israelis, who retaliated with an "iron-fist" policy that included the arrest and transfer to a prison camp in Israel of hundreds of Shi'ites. On June 14, the militants hijacked an American TWA jetliner, demanding release of the prisoners in exchange for their hostages. After two weeks of negotiations, the Americans were freed and Israel began gradual release of the Lebanese, both Israel and the United States insisting that the two events were unrelated.

Early in the year, negotiations had been renewed with Egypt to resolve the Taba dispute (see Occupied Areas, below)—a move that was condemned by Likud and further threatened by the assassination of an Israeli diplomat at Cairo in August, by a September air attack on the PLO's Tunis headquarters (in retaliation for the murder of three Israelis in Cyprus), and by the killing of seven Israeli tourists in Sinai during October.

Although Egypt joined in UN condemnation of the Tunis attack, President Mubarak commended Peres' overtures to Jordan's King Hussein during 1985. The most significant was Peres' speech to the UN General Assembly in October proposing direct negotiations with 'Amman and the Palestinians. The speech was considered novel because of Peres' willingness to negotiate in an international forum

that included the Soviet Union, if Moscow would renew the diplomatic relations broken in 1967. King Hussein welcomed the "spirit" of the speech, stating that it was "movement in the right direction" by "a man of vision". However, several Likud cabinet members attacked the proposals, Industry and Commerce Minister Sharon accusing Peres of abandoning government guidelines by engaging in secret negotiations, although subsequently averting a government crisis by apologizing for his remarks.

During 1986 Peres (as prime minister until October 30 and as foreign minister thereafter) continued his efforts on behalf of a comprehensive peace settlement. An unprecedented public meeting in July with King Hassan of Morocco was described as "purely exploratory", but was viewed as enhancing the position of moderate Arab leaders, including Jordan's King Hussein, whose peace discussion with the PLO's Yasir 'Arafat had broken down in January. Late in the year, the government was hard-pressed to defend its role in the US-Iranian arms affair, Peres insisting that Israel had transferred arms to Iran at Washington's request and was unaware that some of the money paid by Teheran had been diverted to Nicaraguan *contras*. The government was also embarrassed by the March 1987 conviction in a Washington court of Jonathan Jay Pollard on charges of having spied for Israel. Defense Minister Yitzhak Rabin insisted that Pollard was part of a "rogue" spy operation set up without official sanction and that no one else had engaged in such activity since Pollard's arrest in 1985. However, the case aroused deep popular feeling within Israel and it was reported that "state elements" had paid approximately two-thirds of Pollard's legal expenses.

In July Moscow's interest in renewing contacts with Israel prior to new peace initiatives was demonstrated by the first visit in 20 years of a Soviet diplomatic delegation. Other harbingers of better relations with the Soviet bloc were contacts outside Israel between the Soviet and Israeli foreign ministers and the reopening of consular relations with Hungary in September.

Current issues. Tensions caused by foreign and domestic policy disagreements between the *Likud* and Labor coalition partners continued throughout 1987 and into 1988. Prime Minister Shamir attacked a proposal for an international peace conference by Foreign Minister Peres at the September session of the UN General Assembly as a "perverse and criminal" idea that had to be "wiped off" the cabinet agenda, while subsequent efforts by US Secretary of State George Shultz to secure Israeli participation in such a conference proved equally fruitless.

In August 1987 the cabinet voted to scrap Israel's most costly defense project, the Lavi jet-fighter plane. The seven-year-old project had been viewed as crucial to the government's defense plans, while serving to benefit high-tech industry. In protest at the decision, *Likud* minister without portfolio Moshe ARENS resigned in September. Disagreements within the coalition also precipitated a withdrawal of *Knesset* support by *Shinui* (Change) party representatives and the resignation of Minister of Communications Amnon RUBINSTEIN, who charged that the cabinet had become a "two-headed monster" speaking for the country "in two voices".

The government's problems were further exacerbated by divergent views over the Palestinian violence that commenced in December. The initially spontaneous demonstrations quickly assumed the form of an organized uprising (*intifada*) demanding termination of the Israeli occupation of Gaza and the West Bank. Inhabitants of the territories, supported by many Israeli Arab citizens, engaged in strikes, non-payment of taxes, and stoning of occupation troops. The government responded with curfews, economic sanctions, arrests and deportations, widespread use of tear gas, and physical abuse of demonstrators. By April 1988 over 150 Palestinians had been killed and several hundred hospitalized, with the *intifada* certain to become a crucial political issue in the forthcoming *Knesset* campaign.

POLITICAL PARTIES

A multiplicity of parties has characterized the Israeli political scene since the state's inception, and government has been based on shifting alliances of party groups reflecting a variety of social, economic, and religious interests. Prior to the merger that yielded the Israel Labor Party (ILP) in 1968, the Israel Workers' Party (Mapai) served as the pivot around which several other groups tended to orient themselves in government coalitions. In 1969 the ILP became the nucleus of an even more inclusive Labor Alignment, which served in a governing coalition with the orthodox religious parties until displaced in 1977 by an opposition coalition formed in 1973 and organized around *Likud*.

In May 1982 the government coalition technically lost its parliamentary majority when two *Likud* deputies joined the Labor opposition in a dispute over economic policy. In mid-June, on the other hand, the State Renewal List (*Tenuat le-Israel Mehadashet* — Telem), organized prior to the 1981 election by Moshe Dayan (who died October 16), was disbanded, its two deputies joining *Likud* to compensate for the loss of the two deputies in May. Subsequently, on July 23, the extreme right-wing Tehiya (see below) entered the Begin coalition, which thereby increased its strength to 64 of 120 *Knesset* seats.

At the election of July 26, 1984, the Labor Alignment and *Likud* obtained 44 and 41 seats, respectively. The national unity government formed on September 13 initially encompassed 98 deputies representing nine parties, Mapam, a left-wing Labor Party with 6 seats, having withdrawn from the Alignment (see ILP, below), and a Labor member having defected to the opposition Civil Rights Movement, while Shas (below), with 4 deputies, and Shinui (below), with 3, withdrew from the coalition in February and May 1987, respectively.

National Unity Coalition:

Israel Labor Party — ILP (*Mifleget Ha'avoda Hayisre'elit*). The ILP was formed in January 1968 through merger of the Israel Workers' Party (*Mifleget Poalei Eretz Israel* — Mapai), a Western-oriented socialist party established in 1930 and represented in the government by prime ministers Ben-Gurion, Moshe Sharett, Eshkol, and Meir; the Israel Workers' List (*Reshimat Poalei Israel* — Rafi), founded by Ben-Gurion as a vehicle of opposition to his successor as prime minister, Levi Eshkol; and the Unity of Labor-Workers of Zion (*Achdut Ha'avoda-Poalei Zion*), which advocated a planned economy, agricultural settlement, and an active defense policy.

In January 1969, the ILP joined with Mapam (see United Workers' Party, below) in a coalition known initially as the Alignment (*Ma'arakh*)

and subsequently as the Labor Alignment (*Ma'arakh Ha'avoda*). The latter was technically dissolved upon Mapam's withdrawal in protest at formation of the national unity government, although the term has occasionally been used to reference a current linkage between Labor and *Yahad* (below).

Leaders: Shimon PERES (Vice Prime Minister, Foreign Minister, and Chairman of the Party), Yitzhak NAVON (former President of Israel), Abba EBAN (former Foreign Minister), Shoshana ARBELI-ALMOZLINO, Yitzhak RABIN (former Prime Minister), Mordechai GUR (former Army Chief of Staff), Uzi BARAM (General Secretary).

Together (*Yahad*). *Yahad* was formed in March 1984 by Ezer Weizman, *Likud* minister of defense until May 1980. It has urged that direct talks be initiated with Arab leaders, including representatives of the PLO. In effectively merging with Labor, the latter was partially compensated for the loss of Mapam's 6 seats. *Yahad* obtained 3 *Knesset* seats in July 1984, Weizman being awarded a cabinet post in the national unity government.

Leaders: Ezer WEIZMAN, Brig. Gen. (Res.) Binyamin BEN-ELIEZER.

Unity (*Likud*). Its name reflecting its contention that Israel is entitled to all land between the Jordan River and the Mediterranean, *Likud* was formed under the leadership of Menachem Begin in September 1973 in an effort to break the legislative monopoly of the Labor Alignment. Joining in the grouping were the **Herut-Liberal Bloc** (*Gush Herut-Liberalim* — Gahal), composed of the *Herut* (Freedom) and Liberal parties; the **Integral Land of Israel** movement; and the **Peace to Zion** (*Schlomzion*), a small right-wing party that entered *Likud* after the 1977 election. Apart from their common outlook in regard to captured territory, the constituent parties have differed somewhat on domestic policy, though tending theoretically to favor the denationalization of certain industries in the context of a free-enterprise philosophy.

In September 1985, *La'am* (For the Nation), a *Likud* faction that had originally been organized by former prime minister David Ben-Gurion as the State List, a splinter group from Rafi, merged with *Herut*.

Leaders: Yitzhak SHAMIR (Prime Minister and *Herut* chairman), Avraham SHARIR (*Likud* Chairman and Liberal leader), Ariel SHARON (Chairman, *Herut* Central Committee), David LEVI (Deputy Prime Minister and *Herut* Deputy Chairman), Yitzhak MODA'I (Liberal), Gideon PATT (Liberal).

National Religious Party — NRP (*Mifleget Datit Leumit* — Mafdal). Dedicated to the principles of religious Zionism, Mafdal was formed in 1956 through the union of two older organizations, *Mizrahi* and the Mizrahi Workers (*Hapoel Hamizrahi*). Formerly allied with Labor, the party went into opposition following the 1973 election because of a dispute over religious policy, but subsequently reentered the government. In December 1976, Prime Minister Rabin ousted its three cabinet members after 9 of its 10 legislative deputies had abstained on a no-confidence vote, thus precipitating a government crisis that led to a call for the May 1977 election. On the eve of the 1977 balloting, at which it obtained 12 *Knesset* seats, the party concluded an alliance with *Likud*, subsequently participating in the Begin government formed on June 20. The arrangement continued after the 1981 election, at which its representation fell to 6 seats. It holds 4 seats in the present *Knesset*.

Leaders: Dr. Yosef BURG, Zevulun HAMMER (Secretary General).

Union of Israel (*Agudat Israel*). A formerly anti-Zionist orthodox religious party, the *Agudat Israel* was allied prior to the May 1977 election with the *Poalei Agudat Israel* (see Morasha, below) in the United Torah Front, which called for strict observance of religious law and introduced the no-confidence motion that led to Prime Minister Rabin's resignation in December 1976. Its *Knesset* representation fell from 4 in 1981 to 2 in 1984 as a result of the loss of Oriental Jewish votes to the recently organized Shas (below).

Leaders: Shlomo LORINCZ, Menahem PORUSH, Avraham Yosef SHAPIRA.

Heritage (*Morasha*). *Morasha* is a religious grouping formed prior to the 1984 election by merger of the Rally of Religious Zionism (*Mifleget Tzionut Dati* — Matzad) with the Agudat Israel Workers (*Poalei Agudat Israel*). Matzad had been organized in February 1983 by former Mafdal leader, Rabbi Haim Druckman, while the *Poalei Agudat Israel* originated as a labor offshoot of *Agudat Israel* that participated with its parent party in the United Torah Front during 1973–1977, but failed to secure legislative representation in 1981. Calling for an active settlement policy in the occupied territories, *Morasha* won 2 *Knesset* seats in 1984.

Leaders: Rabbi Haim DRUCKMAN, Rabbi Avraham VERDIGER.

Movement for Economic Recovery/Courage (*Ometz*). *Ometz* was organized in early 1984 by Yigael Hurwitz, who had served as finance minister in the Begin government and was a member of Moshe Dayan's State Renewal List prior to its dissolution in 1982, at which time he rejoined *Likud.* The only member of his group to win election in 1984, Hurwitz has long urged severe austerity as an antidote to spending of what he has termed "gluttonous" proportions.
Leader: Yigael HURWITZ.

Opposition Parties:

United Workers' Party (*Mifleget Hapoalim Hameuchedet* — Mapam). Created in 1948 as a left-wing Zionist and socialist formation that originally included the Unity of Labor — Workers of Zion and the Young Guard (*Ha-Shomer Ha-Tzair*), Mapam had traditionally endorsed a neutralist foreign policy in addition to greater equality for the Arabs and fewer restrictions on the labor movement. It was a component of the Labor Alignment until after the 1984 election, when its Central Committee, opposed to the alliance with *Likud,* voted to withdraw. Its 6 deputies presently constitute the largest opposition group in the *Knesset.*
Leader: Elazar GRANOT (Secretary General).

Rebirth Movement (*Hatehiya-Tzomet* — Tehiya). Tehiya was organized in October 1979 by dissident members of *Likud* and a number of right-wing and nationalist groups that continue to exist outside the party structure. The party advocates formal annexation of the Gaza Strip, the West Bank, and the Golan Heights, without their inhabitants becoming Israeli citizens. It joined the Begin coalition in July 1982 after securing exemption from support of government policies calling for Palestinian autonomy in the occupied areas. Its *Knesset* representation rose from 3 to 5 in 1984.
Leaders: Yuval NE'EMAN, Geula COHEN, Rabbi Eliezer WALD-MAN.

Sephardi Torah Guardians (*Shomrei Torah Sephardiim* — Shas). An offshoot of *Agudat Israel,* Shas was formed prior to the 1984 balloting, at which it won 4 seats. It is an orthodox religious party drawing support from Jews of Oriental (Sephardi) descent. In December 1984, the group withdrew from the national unity coalition in a dispute with the NRP over the allocation of portfolios, Shas leader Yitzhak Peretz subsequently returning to the Interior Ministry with a budget enhanced by the transfer of funds from Religious Affairs. It withdrew again in February 1987 over the registration as Jewish of a US convert.
Leader: Rabbi Yitzhak PERETZ.

Center Movement. Also referenced as the New Liberal Party (NLP), the Center Movement was formed in mid-1987 as an alliance of the two parties below, plus a number of former *Likud* Liberals, led by Yitzhak Berman, who had briefly organized as the Liberal Center in 1986 under an essentially conservative platform that nonetheless favored giving up part of the West Bank in a peace treaty with Jordan. The three groups indicated that they would cooperate, rather than formally merge, pending the next *Knesset* campaign, at which a joint list would be presented.
Leaders: Amnon RUBENSTEIN, Moshe KOL, Yitzhak BERMAN.

Change (*Shinui*). The original *Shinui* movement under Amnon Rubinstein joined in November 1976 with the Democratic Movement of former army chief of staff Yigael Yadin to form the Democratic Movement for Change (DMC), which, with 15 seats, emerged as the third largest party at the 1977 election, after which it supported the Begin government. Following a split in the DMC in September 1978, the *Shinui* group and supporters of (then) Transport and Communications Minister Meir Amit withdrew to form the opposition Change and Initiative (*Shinui Ve Yozma* — Shai). The DMC was formally dissolved in February 1981, its remnants regrouping with supporters of *Shai* to contest the June election under the *Shinui* label. The formation won 2 *Knesset* seats in 1981 and 3 in 1984. A member of the national unity government after the 1984 balloting, Shinui withdrew from the coalition in May 1987.
Leaders: Amnon RUBENSTEIN, Zaidan ATSHE, Mordechai VIRSHUBSKI.

Independent Liberal Party. The Independent Liberal Party was organized in 1965 by a number of Liberal members of the *Knesset* in response to formation of the *Herut*-Liberal bloc.
Leaders: Moshe KOL (Chairman), Nissim ELIAD (General Secretary).

Civil Rights Movement (*ha-Tenua le-Zechouot ha-Ezrakh* — Ratz). The Civil Rights Movement, whose leader, Shulamit Aloni, was formerly a member of the Labor Party, has campaigned for women's rights, electoral reform, and reduction of the power of the religious establishment. It participated in the Rabin coalition from May 1974 until Mafdal reentered the cabinet the following November, at which time it went into opposition. It subsequently joined the *Ya'ad* group (see PLP, below) in the *Knesset* until the latter party's dissolution in late 1975. It presently holds 4 *Knesset* seats, 1 of which resulted from the defection of a Labor deputy after the 1984 balloting.
Leaders: Shulamit ALONI, Mordechai BAR-ON, Yossi SARID.

Other Parties:

Movement for Israel's Tradition (*Tenuat Masoret Israel* — Tami). Tami was organized shortly before the 1981 election by Aharon Abu-Hatzeira, formerly a member of the NRP, following his acquittal on corruption charges in connection with the distribution of state funds to religious institutions. The new group was explicitly intended as a conduit for grievances by Oriental Jewish leaders, who felt that they had not been accorded sufficient representation in the NRP electoral list. Its *Knesset* strength dropped from 3 to 1 in 1984.
Leaders: Aharon ABU-HATZEIRA, Ben-Zion RUBIN, Aharon UZAN.

Centrist Religious Movement (*Tnua Mercazit Datit* — Tamid). Tamid was launched in early 1988 by a group of Orthodox centrists, most with an NRP background, who evidenced concern with what they viewed as a growing breakdown in religious-secular relations.
Leaders: Rabbi Yehuda AMITAL, Dr. Daniel TROPPER.

Progressive List for Peace (PLP). A self-proclaimed "joint Jewish-Arab movement", the PLP was formed prior to the 1984 election by a number of radical activists who, advocating establishment of a Palestinian Arab state coexisting with Israel, were opposed to the government's settlement program in the occupied West Bank. It includes elements of the former Peace/Equality for Israel (*Shalom/Shivayon le-Israel* — Sheli). Sheli was organized as a left-wing electoral list in March 1977 by Arye Eliav, a former secretary general of the Labor Party who had formed a legislative group known as Aim (*Ya'ad*) in May 1975 to fill what he termed a void in Israeli political life occasioned by "the ideological death of the Labor Party". Following the demise of *Ya'ad,* Eliav had remained in the *Knesset* as an independent deputy, but failed in a bid for reelection in 1984. Sheli embraced the former Compass (*Moked*), which consisted of a wing of the Communist Party of Israel (*Mifleget Kommunistit Israelit* — Maki), the New Israel Left (*Smol Israeli Hadash* — Siah), and other leftist elements. It secured no representation at the 1981 election.
Having survived a challenge by the Central Electoral Committee, which branded it a subversive organization, the PLP competed vigorously with the DFPE (below) for Arab votes, winning 2 *Knesset* seats.
Leaders: Muhammad MIARI, Maj. Gen. (Ret.) Matityahu PELED (former member, General Staff).

Democratic Front for Peace and Equality — DFPE (*Hazit Democratit le-Shalom ve-Shivayon* — Hadash). The Democratic Front was organized prior to the 1977 election to present candidates drawn from the former New Communist List (*Rashima Kommunistit Hadasha* — Rakah), a section of the "Black Panther" movement of Oriental Jews, and a number of unaffiliated local Arab leaders. Rakah, a pro-Soviet and largely Arab-supported group, broke away from Maki (see PLP, above) in 1965 following a dispute over Soviet foreign policy in the Middle East. The DFPE won 4 *Knesset* seats in 1984.
Leaders: Meir VILNER, Tawfiq TOUBI.

Thus (*Kach*). A political vehicle of Rabbi Meir Kahane, founder of the US-based Jewish Defense League, *Kach* also survived a challenge from the Central Electoral Committee to elect its leader to the *Knesset* in 1984, after having competed unsuccessfully in 1977 and 1981. Linked to the activities of the anti-Arab "Jewish underground", the group advocates the forceable expulsion of Palestinians from the occupied territories.
Leader: Rabbi Meir KAHANE.

Eleven minor groupings competed unsuccessfully at the 1984 balloting, including **Eliav,** in support of former Labor Secretary General Lova ELIAV; the **Movement for Zionist Renewal,** led by Labor defector Mordechai BEN-PORAT; **Independence** (*Atzmaut*), led by Ezra ZOHAR; **Flatto-Sharon,** led by Samuel FLATTO-SHARON, the former financier whose election to the *Knesset* in 1977 had secured him immunity from extradition to France on grounds of fraud and tax evasion; **Amkha,** led by Victor TAYAR; **Youth and Aliya,** representing Georgian Jews; **Integration-Shiluv,** representing Indian Jews; the **Organization for the Defense of Tenants;** the **Movement for the Homeland; The Disabled;** and the **Has-Mas Movement to Abolish Income Tax.**

LEGISLATURE

The *Knesset* (Assembly or Congregation) is a unicameral legislature of 120 members elected by universal suffrage for four-year terms on the basis of proportional representation from national party lists. Of the 26 lists presented at the election of July 23, 1984, the following obtained representation: Labor Alignment, 44 seats (Labor Party, 38; Mapam, 6); *Likud,* 41; Tehiya, 5; National Religious Party, 4; Democratic Front for Peace and Equality, 4; Shas, 4; Shinui, 3; Civil Rights Movement, 3; *Yahad,* 3; Progressive List for Peace, 2; *Agudat Israel,* 2; *Morasha,* 2; Tami, 1; *Kach,* 1; *Ometz,* 1. Following the election, the Alignment lost 6 seats because of Mapam's withdrawal, in addition to the defection of 1 member from Labor to the CRM; the loss was partially compensated by the affiliation of Yahad with Labor in the *Knesset.*

By May 1987, the National Unity Coalition had been reduced to a seven-party grouping of 91 deputies by the withdrawal of Shas and Shinui.

In the present *Knesset,* 81 members are of Ashkenazi (European) origin, 32 are of Sephardi (Mediterranean) origin, and 7 are members of Arab or Druze communities. *Speaker:* Shlomo HILLEL.

CABINET

Prime Minister	Yitzhak Shamir
Vice Prime Minister	Shimon Peres
Deputy Prime Ministers	David Levi
	Yitzhak Navon

Ministers	
Agriculture	Aryeh Nehemkin
Communications	Gad Yaacobi
Construction and Housing	David Levi
Defense	Yitzhak Rabin
Economic Planning	Gad Yaacobi
Education and Culture	Yitzhak Navon
Energy and Infrastructure	Moshe Shahal
Finance	Moshe Nissim
Foreign Affairs	Shimon Peres
Health	Shoshana Arbeli-Almoslino
Immigrant Absorption	Yaacov Tzur
Industry and Commerce	Ariel Sharon
Interior	Yitzhak Shamir
Justice	Avraham Sharir
Labor and Social Welfare	Moshe Katzav
Police	Haim Bar-Lev
Religious Affairs	Zevulun Hammer
Science and Development	Gideon Patt
Tourism	Avraham Sharir
Transport	Haim Corfu
Without Portfolio	Yigal Hurvitz
	Yitzhak Moda'i
	Yitzhak Peretz
	Yosef Shapiro
	Ezer Weizman
Governor, Bank of Israel	Michael Bruno

NEWS MEDIA

Israeli newspapers are numerous and diversified, although many of the leading dailies reflect partisan or religious interests. Censorship is largely on national security grounds, several Arabic organs recently being closed because of alleged links with the Palestine Liberation Organization. Radio and television are government owned and operated.

Press. The following are dailies published in Hebrew at Tel Aviv, unless otherwise noted: *Yedioth Aharonoth* (170,000 daily, 350,000 Friday), independent; *Ma'ariv* (120,000 daily, 230,000 Friday), independent; *Ha'aretz* (50,000 daily, 70,000 Friday), independent liberal; *Davar* (50,000 daily, 70,000 Friday), General Federation of Labor organ; *al-Quds* (Jerusalem, 40,000), in Arabic; *Jerusalem Post* (Jerusalem, 30,000 daily, 50,000 Friday, not including North American edition published weekly at New York), in English; *Hatzofeh* (16,000), National Religious Front organ; *Hamodia* (Jerusalem, 12,000), *Agudat Israel* organ; *Al Hamishmar* (10,000), Mapam organ. There are also smaller dailies published in Arabic, Bulgarian, French, German, Hungarian, Polish, Romanian, Russian, voweled Hebrew, and Yiddish.

News agencies. The domestic agency is the News Agency of the Associated Israel Press (ITIM); numerous foreign bureaus also maintain offices in Israel, including the Jewish Telegraphic Agency of New York. The small Palestine Press Services, closely monitored by government censors, operates in East Jerusalem.

Radio and television. The commercial, government-controlled Israel Broadcasting Authority provides local and national radio service over 4 programs, international radio service in 11 languages, and television service in Hebrew and Arabic. *Galei Zahal,* the radio station of the Israeli defense forces, broadcasts from Tel Aviv, as does the Instructional Television Center, the nation's educational network. There were approximately 2.8 million radio and 665,000 television receivers in 1987.

INTERGOVERNMENTAL REPRESENTATION

Ambassador to the US: Moshe ARAD.

US Ambassador to Israel: Thomas R. PICKERING.

Permanent Representative to the UN: Benjamin NETANYAHU.

IGO Memberships (Non-UN): CCC, *EIB,* IADB, ICAC, ICM, ICO, Inmarsat, Intelsat, Interpol, IWTC, PCA.

OCCUPIED AREAS

The largely desert Sinai Peninsula, encompassing some 23,000 square miles (59,600 sq. km.), was occupied by Israel during the 1956 war with Egypt but was subsequently evacuated under US and UN pressure. It was reoccupied during the Six-Day War of 1967 and, except for a narrow western band bordering on Suez, was retained after the Yom Kippur War of 1973. The Egyptian-Israeli peace treaty, signed at Washington, DC, on March 26, 1979, provided for a phased withdrawal, two-thirds of which — to beyond a buffer zone running roughly from El Arish in the north to Ras Muhammad in the south — was completed by January 1980. Withdrawal from the remainder of the Sinai, to "the recognized international boundary between Egypt and the former mandated territory of Palestine", was completed on April 25, 1982 (three years from the exchange of treaty ratification instruments), "without prejudice to the issue of the status of the Gaza Strip".

Title to Taba, a small Israeli-occupied area adjoining the southern port of Eilat has long been disputed. A 1906 Anglo-Egyptian/Turkish agreement fixed the border as running through Taba itself. However, a 1915 British military survey (admitted to be imperfect) placed the border some three-quarters of a mile to the northeast. A decision to submit the matter to arbitration was made during talks between Egyptian President Mubarak and (then) Prime Minister Peres at Alexandria on September 10, 1986.

Gaza Strip. The Gaza Strip consists of that part of former Palestine contiguous with Sinai that was still held by Egyptian forces at the time of the February 1949 armistice with Israel. Encompassing some 140 square miles (363 sq. km.), the territory was never annexed by Egypt and since 1948 has never been legally recognized as part of any state. In the wake of the 1967 war, nearly half of its population of 356,100 (1971E) was living in refugee camps, according to the UN Relief and Works Agency for Palestinian Refugees in the Near East (UNRWA).

Judaea and Samaria. Surrounded on three sides by Israel and bounded on the east by the Jordan River and the Dead Sea, Judaea and Samaria encompasses the Jordanian (West Bank) portion of former Palestine. With an area of 2,270 square miles (5,879 sq. km.) and a largely Arab population of approximately 900,000, it has been occupied by Israel since the 1967 war, although claimed by the Palestine Liberation Organization (PLO) and others as a potentially independent state. In November 1974, following an Arab summit conference at Rabat, Morocco, King Hussein of Jordan assigned responsibility for the area to the PLO, without formally relinquishing his kingdom's claim to the territory.

Golan Heights. The mountainous Golan Heights, embracing a natural barrier of some 600 square miles (1,550 sq. km.) at the juncture of Israel and Syria southeast of Lebanon, was occupied by Israel during the 1967 war. Its interim status (including demarcation of an eastern strip under UN administation) was set forth in a disengagement agreement concluded with Syria in May 1974. In an action condemned by many foreign governments, including those of the Soviet Union and the United States, the area under Israeli military control was formally made subject to Israeli "law, jurisdiction and administration" on December 14, 1981.

ITALY

Italian Republic
Repubblica Italiana

Political Status: Unified state proclaimed in 1861; republic established by national referendum in 1946; under parliamentary constitution effective January 1, 1948.

Area: 116,303 sq. mi. (301,225 sq. km.).

Population: 56,556,911 (1981C), 57,536,000 (1988E).

Major Urban Centers (1985E): ROME (2,826,000); Milan (1,515,000); Naples (1,206,000); Turin (1,035,000); Genoa (735,000); Palermo (720,000).

Official Language: Italian.

Monetary Unit: Lira (market rate March 1, 1988, 1244.40 lire = $1US).

President of the Republic: Francesco COSSIGA; selected by an electoral college June 24 and inaugurated July 3, 1985, for a seven-year term, in succession to Alessandro PERTINI.

President of the Council of Ministers (Prime Minister): Ciriaco DE MITA (Christian Democratic Party); sworn

in as head of five-party coalition government on April 13, 1988, succeeding Giovanni Guiseppe GORIA (Christian Democratic Party).

THE COUNTRY

A peninsula rooted in the Alps and jutting into the Mediterranean for a distance of some 725 miles, the Italian Republic includes the large islands of Sicily and Sardinia and other smaller islands in the Tyrrhenian and Adriatic seas. Rugged terrain limits large-scale agriculture to the Po Valley, the Campagna region near Rome, and the plain of Foggia in the southeast. Among numerous socioeconomic cleavages, there is a vast difference between the industrialized North and the largely underdeveloped South. Ethnically, however, the Italians form a relatively homogeneous society, the only substantial minority being the approximately 250,000 German-speaking persons in the province of Bolzano whose more activist leaders sporadically agitate for total autonomy of the Trentino–Alto Adige region. Although Italian is the official language, regional variations of the standard Tuscan dialect exist, and in various parts of the country small minorities speak French, German, Ladin (similar to Romansch), Slovene, and Sard (Sardinian). Roman Catholicism is nominally professed by 99 percent of the population, but religious freedom is constitutionally guaranteed and in March 1985 the Chamber of Deputies ratified a revised concordat with the Holy See that terminated Roman Catholicism's status as the state religion. In 1980, women constituted 29 percent of the paid labor force, concentrated mainly in education and the service sector and earning approximately 74 percent of the comparable male wage; female participation in politics and government has been estimated at 10 percent.

Despite the ending of an "economic miracle" that characterized a boom period immediately after World War II, Italy's real GDP increased at an average of 4.3 percent and its population at only 0.7 percent, allowing per capita income to double during the 1960s and 1970s. Inflation, on the other hand, averaged more than 17 percent a year during 1973–1983, before receding to 4.2 percent in late 1986 after implementation of an economic austerity program; unemployment, however, remained at 11 percent, while the public debt stood at 88 percent of GDP.

GOVERNMENT AND POLITICS

Political background. Unified in the nineteenth century as a parliamentary monarchy under the House of Savoy, Italy fought with the Allies in World War I but succumbed in 1922 to the Fascist dictatorship of Benito MUSSOLINI, entering World War II on the side of Nazi Germany and switching to the Allied side only after Mussolini's removal from office in 1943. Following a period of provisional government, the monarchy was abolished by popular referendum in 1946 and a new, republican constitution went into effect January 1, 1948. A Communist bid for national power under the leadership of Palmiro TOGLIATTI was defeated in the parliamentary election of April 1948, which established the Christian Democrats (DC), then headed by Alcide DE GASPERI, as Italy's strongest political force; for 14 years thereafter, the DC led a succession of right-center coalition governments. The first important modification in this pattern occurred in 1962 with the formation by Christian Democrat Amintore FANFANI of a center-left coalition that, under a policy of an "opening to the Left" (*apertura a sinistra*), depended on Socialist parliamentary support.

Of the fifteen consecutive DC-led governments between June 1963 and April 1976, only those of Giovanni LEONE (June to December 1963 and June to November 1968), Mariano RUMOR (August 1969 to February 1970), Giulio ANDREOTTI (June 1972 to June 1973), and Aldo MORO (February to April 1976) did not include the Socialists as a coalition partner. Center-left governments, on the other hand, included four by Moro (three in 1963–1968, one in 1974–1976), five by Rumor (one in 1968–1969, one in 1970, three in 1973–1974), and one by Emilio COLOMBO (1970–1972). Most of the coalition governments fell because of disagreements between the partners over economic policy, although the early 1970s also yielded crises over the country's first divorce and abortion reform laws.

At the bitterly contested election of June 21–22, 1976, the Communists registered unprecedented gains at the expense of the smaller parties, securing 228 seats in the 630-seat Chamber (only 34 less than the Christian Democrats) and 116 seats in the 315-member Senate (only 19 less than the Christian Democrats). While another Christian Democratic–Socialist government could technically have been formed, the Socialists had indicated during the campaign that they would no longer participate in a coalition that excluded the Communists. For their part, the Communists, although they had stressed the need for a "national unity" government prior to the election, agreed to abstain on confirmation of a new cabinet in return for a "government role" at less than the cabinet level. As a result, former prime minister Andreotti succeeded in organizing an all-Christian Democratic minority government that survived Chamber and Senate confidence votes in August. Earlier, on July 5, Pietro INGRAO had become the first Communist in 28 years to be elected president of the lower house.

In January 1978 the Communists, Socialists, and Republicans withdrew their support following rejection by the Christian Democrats of a renewed Communist demand for cabinet-level participation. Negotiations conducted by DC President Moro resulted, however, in a compromise whereby the Communists settled for official inclusion in the ruling parliamentary majority and a guarantee that they would be consulted in advance on government policy. Andreotti, directed by President Leone to form a new government, organized a cabinet which, with only two changes from the preceding one, took office on March 13. Three days later, five-time prime minister Moro was abducted by the extremist Red Brigades, and on May 9 his body was found in Rome, the government, with substantial opposition support, having refused to negotiate with the terrorists. Moro had been considered a likely successor to President Leone, who on June 15, six months before the

end of his term, resigned in the wake of persistent accusations of tax evasion and other irregularities. Following the interim presidency of Amintore Fanfani, Alessandro PERTINI of the Italian Socialist Party was sworn in as head of state on July 8.

On January 26, 1979, accusing the DC of reneging on its March 1978 consultation commitments and of "wrong and intemperate" decisions in such areas as economic and agrarian policy, the Communists officially withdrew their support, and five days later the government was obliged to resign. Although Andreotti succeeded in forming a new administration on March 7, the coalition of Christian Democrats, Social Democrats, and Republicans was unable to survive a confidence motion ten days later. President Pertini thereupon dissolved Parliament and called for new elections.

The balloting of June 3–4 proved inconclusive, with Francesco COSSIGA eventually forming a "transitional" centrist government of 17 Christian Democrats, 4 Social Democrats, 2 Liberals, and 2 nonparty members that survived a confidence vote in the Chamber only because of abstentions by the Republicans and Socialists. Cossiga subsequently came under strong pressure from the trade unions because of his intention to modify Italy's manifestly inflationary wage indexation system (*scala mobile*), and in late February 1980 the Socialists withdrew their tacit parliamentary support, forcing resignation of the government on March 19. Within days, however, the Socialists agreed to participate in a new DC-led administration, and a three-party cabinet that included the Republicans was sworn in on April 4. The second Cossiga government survived until September 17, when it was forced to resign after being defeated on an economic reform package that had been introduced by decree two months earlier, subject to legislative approval.

On October 7, 1980, the Socialists and Social Democrats concluded a "third force" agreement that did not, however, preclude a dialogue to "reconcile Christian and socialist values"; accordingly, the two parties joined the Christian Democrats and Republicans in forming a DC-led government under Arnaldo FORLANI that was sworn in on October 19. Subsequently, it was revealed that a large number of leading officials, including several cabinet members, belonged to a secret Masonic lodge known as "P-2", which had been implicated in a variety of criminal activities. As a result of the scandal, Forlani was forced to submit his government's resignation on May 26, 1981, and on June 28 Giovanni SPADOLINI of the small Republican Party became the first non-Christian Democrat since 1945 to be invested as prime minister. The Spadolini coalition (encompassing the four participants in the previous government plus the Liberals) lasted until August 7, 1982, when the Socialists withdrew, claiming that Christian Democratic parliamentary deputies, in a secret ballot, had voted against a measure designed to curb tax benefits for the oil industry. Spadolini was able to form a new government that included the Socialists on August 23, but differences over economic policy persisted, forcing a second collapse on November 13.

On December 1, former prime minister Amintore Fanfani returned as head of a four-party coalition that included the Christian Democrats, Socialists, Social Democrats, and Liberals. Although Fanfani succeeded in enacting a number of much-needed tax reforms, friction arose during the 1983 regional election campaign, and on April 22, Socialist leader Bettino CRAXI withdrew his party from the coalition, forcing a new parliamentary dissolution.

At the election of June 26–27, 1983, the Christian Democrats suffered their most severe setback since the party's formation, losing 37 seats in the Chamber of Deputies and 18 in the Senate; the vote shift did not benefit the PCI, which also lost seats, but the smaller parties, most notably the Republicans. The Socialists gained 11 Chamber and 6 Senate seats, and on July 21 Craxi was asked to form Italy's first Socialist-led administration. Rejecting repeated appeals from PCI leader Enrico BERLINGUER to join the Communists in a "democratic alternative" of the Left, Craxi assembled a five-party government encompassing the Fanfani coalition plus the Republicans that was sworn in August 4. The new administration was able to enact substantial budget cuts, accompanied by unprecedented modification in the *scala mobile,* and sustained its economic program despite a series of strikes in late 1984 and early 1985. The coalition was further bolstered by regional, provincial, and municipal elections on May 12–13, 1985, at which most of the ruling parties scored gains, in some localities rendering coalitions with the PCI no longer necessary. A month later, a PCI-backed referendum to lift the ceiling on the *scala mobile* was defeated by a bare majority of 51 percent. On June 24 the DC's Francesco Cossiga won electoral college confirmation as President Pertini's successor on the first ballot, the first such occurrence since 1946.

On October 16, amid intense controversy surrounding the hijacking of a Genoa-based cruise ship (see Foreign relations, below), Defense Minister Spadolini led a PRI withdrawal from the cabinet, precipitating Craxi's resignation two days later. However, an accommodation was reached with Spadolini on October 31 that permitted retroactive rejection of the government's resignation and earned Craxi the distinction of becoming the longest-serving chief executive in postwar Italian history. Craxi again felt obliged to resign on June 27, 1986, after an unexpected defeat on a local finance bill in which numerous coalition deputies played the role of secret-ballot defectors (*franchi tiratori* or "snipers"). On August 1, however, he was able to form a new government on the basis of the previous five-party alignment.

In February 1987 the Socialists circulated a series of proposals on reform of the Italian political system that included direct election of the president and a requirement that no party could elect legislators without obtaining a minimum 5 percent of the vote. Shortly thereafter, Craxi declared that a 1986 pact with the Christian Democrats that would have permitted them to lead the government for the last year of the parliamentary term had been "liquidated" and on March 3 offered to resign. Former prime minister Andreotti was invited, but failed to form a new government, while the Communist president of the Chamber of Deputies, Nilde IOTTI, was unable to fulfill a more restricted "exploratory mandate" directed toward the same end. After a further failed effort by the DC's Luigi SCAL-

FARO, former prime minister Fanfani succeeded in organizing a minority administration that lasted only ten days until April 28, when, in a highly unusual move, the Christian Democrats voted to bring down their own government, with President Cossiga thereupon calling for an early general election on June 14–15.

The principal result of the 1987 balloting was a shift of 21 Chamber seats from the Communists to the Socialists, with a marginal gain for the Christian Democrats. The Socialists, however, strongly objected to the proposed choice of DC secretary general Ciriaco DE MITA as prime minister and President Cossiga somewhat unexpectedly called on the outgoing treasury minister, Giovanni GORIA, to head a revived five-party government that was sworn in July 29. During the ensuing seven months Goria twice submitted his resignation, primarily because of secret-ballot defections by fellow Christian Democrats on budget bills, but managed to retain coalition support until March 11, 1988, when the Socialists and Social Democrats abstained on a controversial nuclear-power vote. Subsequently, after negotiating a record 200-page government program (see Current issues, below), De Mita succeeded in forming the country's 48th postwar administration.

Constitution and government. The 1948 constitution, which describes Italy as "a democratic republic founded on work", established a parliamentary system with a president, a bicameral legislature, a responsible ministry, and an independent judiciary. The president, elected for a seven-year term by national and regional legislative deputies, is responsible for nominating the prime minister and may dissolve Parliament at any time prior to the last six months of a full term. The Parliament consists of a Senate and a Chamber of Deputies. Both houses, which have equal legislative power, are chosen by direct universal suffrage under proportional representation (partial, for the Senate), and both are subject to dissolution and the holding of new elections. The prime minister is nominated by the president and forms the Cabinet, which must be separately approved by both the Senate and Chamber.

The judiciary is headed by the Constitutional Court (*Corte Costituzionale*) and includes (in descending order of superiority) the Supreme Court of Cassation (*Corte Suprema di Cassazione*), assize courts of appeal (*corti di assize d'appello*), courts of appeal (*corti d'appello*), tribunals (*tribunali*), district courts (*preture*), and justices of the peace (*giudici conciliatori*).

Italy's historically centralized system was substantially modified under the 1948 basic law, which called for the designation of 19 (later 20) administrative regions. The *regioni* were not formally established, however, until June 1970 and were not endowed with meaningful powers until April 1972. Each region has its own administration, including a Regional Assembly. There are also 92 provinces and some 6,500 municipalities, all administered by locally elected bodies.

Foreign relations. Italian rule outside the country's geographical frontiers was terminated by World War II and the Paris Peace Treaty of 1947, by which Italy renounced all claims to its former African possessions and ceded the Dodecanese Islands to Greece, a substantial northeastern region to Yugoslavia, and minor frontier districts to France.

A dispute with Yugoslavia over the Free Territory of Trieste was largely resolved in 1954 by a partition agreement whereby Italy took possession of Trieste city and Yugoslavia acquired the surrounding rural area (the essentials of the 1954 agreement were retained in a formal settlement concluded on October 1, 1975). The Alto Adige region, acquired from Austria after World War I, has remained a source of tension between the two countries because of dissatisfaction on the part of the German-speaking inhabitants with the limited autonomy accorded them by the Italian government. A recent constitutional amendment has conferred increased rights of self-government on the region, thus helping to alleviate earlier tensions.

Internationally, Italy has been a firm supporter of European integration, the Atlantic alliance, the European Communities, and all other key Western institutions. Both the Fanfani and Craxi governments approved the deployment of US cruise missiles at Comiso, Sicily, despite internal opposition, and the first 16 were installed in March 1984. In 1983 and early 1984, Italy participated in the UN multinational force in Lebanon, with special responsibility for the protection of refugee camps at Sabra and Chatila. Rome accords diplomatic privileges to the Palestine Liberation Organization, and has attempted to forge a "special" relationship with the Arab world, a policy which was a major contributor to the crisis stemming from the October 1985 hijacking of the Genoa-based cruise ship *Achille Lauro* by Palestinian terrorists. Following an Egyptian and PLO-negotiated release of the hostages, consisting largely of Italian crew members and American tourists, US naval planes intercepted the Egyptian airliner carrying the hijackers and PLO officials, forcing it to land on Sicily; in the wake of the US action, the government agreed to the release of Mohammed Abbas, an Arafat aide suspected of directing the hijacking, saying there was "insufficient evidence" to detain him. Abbas' release worsened relations with Washington, already strained by a brief standoff between Sicilian and US armed forces at the time of the plane's landing.

The government's Mideast policy again came under scrutiny following airport terrorism at Rome and Vienna on December 27 which left 19 dead and over 100 injured. In the wake of the attacks, allegedly aided by Tripoli, Craxi agreed to an arms embargo against Libya and, while rejecting broader economic sanctions, moved to restrict the presence of Palestinian students in Italy. Although the prime minister affirmed a need for "action against terrorism", the April 1986 bombing raid on Libya by US forces, which precipitated widespread anti-American street demonstrations, received only a guarded response from Rome.

A leading foreign policy issue by early 1988 turned on whether Italy would accept the stationing of some 72 F-16 fighter-bombers that the United States was required to relocate from Spain because of the latter's decision in November not to renew a 1982 bilateral military accord. The prospect had drawn strong opposition from leftist parliamentarians as well as from elements with the government coalition.

Current issues. The complexity of the government crisis during the first half of 1987 turned in part on the demon-strable achievements of Craxi's record-setting tenure as prime minister. Although the leader of a Socialist group that had obtained only an 11 percent vote share in the 1983 election, he adopted a basically pro-business economic agenda that succeeded in reducing inflation from more than 20 to less than 5 percent, largely by trimming back the *scala mobile* wage indexing system. He was also actively involved in foreign affairs, becoming a favorite with Washington, while becoming the first Western leader to meet with the new Soviet party secretary, Mikhail Gorbachev. Critics, on the other hand, compared his activism to that of the Fascist dictator, Benito Mussolini, and argued that contemporary Italians were "wary about having too powerful a leader". The most immediate precipitant of the crisis, however, was Craxi's unwillingness to honor the 1986 rotation-of-leadership "pact" with the Christian Democrats without securing from them a pledge to proceed with referenda scheduled for mid-June on judicial reform and the future of Italy's nuclear energy program—issues that the DC leadership viewed as threatening the coalition's viability.

Giovanni Goria's installation as prime minister in late July was widely construed as an interim move unlikely to yield resolution of the basic cleavage within the coalition leadership. Indeed, Goria during his eight-month incumbency addressed himself primarily to what he termed "the lack of a sense of responsibility" by erstwhile parliamentary supporters on budgetary issues. Meanwhile, the government was overwhelmingly rebuffed in the nuclear and judicial reform referenda on November 8–9, with the collapse of the Goria administration occurring in March 1988, after the cabinet had voted to defy public sentiment by resuming construction of a nuclear power plant north of Rome.

The lengthy government program forged by Ciriaco De Mita over a 33-day period prior to his appointment on April 13 preserved the coalition by acceding to most of the Socialist demands, including cessation of work on the nuclear facility and a commitment to limit the secret legislative voting system that had been the bane of his predecessor.

POLITICAL PARTIES

Italy's three major political groupings are the Christian Democratic Party, the core of virtually all post-World War II Italian governments; the Italian Communist Party, the largest in Western Europe and widely supported by the electorate, although unrepresented in the government since 1947; and the various Socialist parties, which have experienced repeated division, reunification, and redivision in recent decades. Two smaller, moderate parties that have participated in many postwar coalitions are the Italian Republican Party and the Italian Liberal Party. Reorganization of the Fascist Party is forbidden by the constitution, but various minority parties, notably the Italian Social Movement, serve as vehicles for continuing pro-Fascist sentiment.

Government Parties:

Christian Democratic Party (*Partito Democrazia Cristiana*—DC). Heir to a pioneer Christian Democratic movement known as the Popular

Party (*Partito Popolare*), founded by Don Luigi Sturzo in the early twentieth century, the DC was primarily associated for many years with Prime Minister Alcide de Gasperi, under whose leadership it served as the mainstay of a succession of governments after 1948. Nominally centrist in outlook, the party has always been susceptible, in varying degrees, to clerical influence on the one hand and to ideas of social reform on the other. Embracing a spectrum of opinion that currently ranges from ultraconservative nostalgia for the center-right alliances of the past to a diffusion of vocal left-wing minorities, the party has continued to appeal to many voters of all classes but came within 5 percentage points of yielding its traditional plurality to the Communists in the 1976 election. The DC failed to register significant gains in the 1979 balloting, and came close to losing its plurality again in 1983. It regained some of its lost ground in the May 1985 regional, provincial, and municipal elections (particularly by winning control of the Rome city council, which had been held for nine years by the Communists), while its national vote share increased marginally in 1987.

Leaders: Arnaldo FORLANI (President); Ciriaco DE MITA (Prime Minister), Giulio ANDREOTTI and Amintore FANFANI (former Prime Ministers); Severino CITARISTI (Administrative Secretary).

Italian Socialist Party (*Partito Socialista Italiano* — PSI). Originally founded in the nineteenth century, Italy's historic Socialist Party has undergone a series of factional cleavages. In 1947 a major split developed over the question of collaboration with the Communists. While the bulk of the party, led by Pietro Nenni, allied itself with the Communists under a "unity of action" pact, a centrist faction led by Giuseppe Saragat formed the Italian Workers' Socialist Party (PSLI). In 1952 the latter group merged with other dissident factions to form the Italian Social Democratic Party (PSDI). The PSDI and the PSI merged in 1966 but split again in July 1969, with the more conservative elements regrouping under the PSDI label. Consistently the third-largest party in both houses of Parliament, the PSI has participated in most recent coalition governments. It more than held its own at the 1985 regional, provincial, and municipal balloting, while an improvement of three percent in its share of the national vote in 1987 raised its lower-house representation from 73 to 94.

Leaders: Bettino CRAXI (former Prime Minister of the Republic and Secretary General of the Party); Claudio MARTELLI (Deputy Secretary General), Claudio SIGNORILE (left-wing faction).

Italian Social Democratic Party (*Partito Socialista Democratico Italiano* — PSDI). The PSDI, which has periodically merged with its parent party, the PSI, has steadfastly opposed electoral and governmental collaboration with the Communists. The party lost almost half of its parliamentary seats in the election of June 1976 but reversed its losses three years later, increasing its Senate and Chamber membership by one-half and one-third, respectively. It joined the Cossiga government in August 1979 after four years in opposition and has participated in all subsequent ruling coalitions.

Leaders: Giuseppe SARAGAT (President for Life), Antonio CARIGLIA (Secretary).

Italian Liberal Party (*Partito Liberale Italiano* — PLI). Founded in 1848 by Count Camillo di Cavour, the conservative PLI espouses free enterprise (with workers' participation in capital and management), laicism, and strong support for NATO. The party's greatest appeal in recent times has been to the small businessman. Although it lost three-quarters of its parliamentary seats in the 1976 election, the PLI increased its Chamber representation from five to nine in June 1979 and in August joined the Cossiga government coalition. It did not participate in either of the DC-led governments organized in 1980, but supported the Spadolini and Fanfani governments of 1981–1982 and joined the Craxi coalition in 1983.

Leaders: Giovanni MALAGODI (Honorary President), Renato ALTISSIMO (President), Alfred BIONDI.

Italian Republican Party (*Partito Repubblicano Italiano* — PRI). Founded in 1897, the PRI follows Giuseppe Mazzini's moderate leftist principles of social justice in a modern free society. In foreign policy, it favors a pro-Western stance and continued membership in the Atlantic alliance. From June 1981 to November 1982, PRI Political Secretary Giovanni Spadolini served as the first non-DC prime minister in 37 years. Three years later, as defense minister, Spadolini led a PRI withdrawal from the Craxi government, claiming lack of consultation in regard to the *Achille Lauro* affair. Although he was tendered an assurance of greater cooperation in future foreign policy decisions prior to the government's

restoration, the PRI's popularity declined as a result of the crisis and Spadolini was subsequently somewhat conciliatory on most matters of external security.

Leaders: Bruno VISENTINI (President), Giovanni SPADOLINI (former Prime Minister), Giorgio LA MALFA (Political Secretary).

Opposition Parties:

Italian Communist Party (*Partito Comunista Italiano* — PCI). Formerly a staunch advocate of far-reaching nationalization, land redistribution, and labor and social reforms, the PCI has sought to achieve power by parliamentary means and has consistently been the second-leading party in both voting power and parliamentary representation. Strongest in central Italy and the industrialized areas of the North, the party registered impressive gains in the 1976 legislative election but saw its support fall 4 percent (to 30.4 percent of the total) at the June 1979 balloting. Despite the loss of 27 Chamber seats, Enrico Berlinguer remained in firm control of the PCI following a July 3–10 Central Committee meeting at which he reaffirmed that the party would refuse to participate in future government coalitions unless offered cabinet posts. At the 1983 party congress, a strategy of "democratic alternative", i.e. seeking to establish a ruling coalition with the Socialists, was announced, which has thus far been rejected by the PSI.

The PCI membership includes supporters from all classes but consists primarily of urban workers (40 percent) and agricultural laborers, tenants, and small owners (25 percent). The party controls, in assorted coalitions, about 35 percent of Italy's municipalities and has traditionally participated in over half of the nation's regional governments. It experienced a number of setbacks in the May 1985 balloting, losing control of the Rome city council for the first time in nine years and being ejected from a number of regional coalitions, although the so-called "red belt" (Emilia Romagna, Umbria, and Tuscany) remained largely unaffected. Other difficulties followed the defeat in June of a PCI-sponsored referendum to lift the *scala mobile* ceiling; while party leaders called the 46 percent favorable vote a "moral" victory, the apparent approval of Craxi's policies made more elusive the pursuit of a "democratic alternative". The party's national voting power had, however, been increased somewhat in 1984 when the Party of Proletarian Unity for Communism (*Partito d'Unità Proletaria per il Comunismo* — PDUP) chose to merge with its former parent party.

In foreign policy matters, the PCI has long maintained an attitude of considerable independence toward the Soviet Union as one of the leading advocates of "Eurocommunism"; no indication of change in this policy was evidenced by the appointment of Alessandro Natta as secretary general after the death of Berlinguer, his longtime mentor, in June 1984. The party suffered a major reversal in the 1987 balloting, losing 21 of its 198 seats in the Chamber of Deputies and 8 of its 107 seats in the Senate.

Leaders: Luigi LONGO (President), Giovanni AMENDOLA, Armando COSSUTTA (Pro-Moscow wing), Nilde IOTTI (President of the Chamber of Deputies), Gian Carlo PAJETTA, Luciana CASTELLINA (former PDUP leader), Alessandro NATTA (General Secretary), Achille OCCHETTO (Deputy General Secretary).

Proletarian Democracy (*Democrazia Proletaria* — DP). The DP was formed in 1977 by members of the PDUP who had belonged to the Italian Socialist Party of Proletarian Unity (PSIUP) prior to its 1972 merger with the PCI, plus the Workers' Vanguard (*Avanguardia Operaia* — AO). In 1979, it joined with the **Continuous Struggle** (*Lotta Continua* — LC) in an electoral alliance styled the New United Left (*Nuova Sinistra Unità* — NSU), which failed to obtain parliamentary representation. The DP took its name from that of a 1976 *Democrazia Proletaria* electoral alliance that had encompassed the PDUP as well as the LC and AO.

Leaders: Mario CAPANNA, Russo SPENA (Secretary).

Radical Party (*Partito Radicale* — PR). A leftist, predominantly middle-class grouping, the PR advocates civil and human rights. Its membership in the Chamber jumped from 4 seats in 1976 to 18 following the June 1979 election — by far the largest gain of any party. In November its (then) secretary general, Jean FABRE, a French citizen, was sentenced at Paris to a month in jail for evading conscription. In 1984, after having fled to France, PR deputy Antonio NEGRI was sentenced to 30 years' imprisonment for complicity in a variety of terrorist acts, although he and seven others were acquitted in January 1986 of being "moral leaders" of the Red Brigades and other extremist groups.

Leaders: Marco PANNELLA (President), Sergio STANZANI (Secretary General).

Italian Social Movement–National Right (*Movimento Sociale Italiano –Destra Nazionale*–MSI-DN). The resurgence of the MSI, a neo-Fascist group that merged with the former Italian Democratic Party of Monarchical Unity (PDIUM) prior to the 1972 election, has been undercut by internal division as well as by terrorist activities linked with the far Right. Committed to an extreme nationalist and anti-communist orientation, the party lost over a third of its representation in both the Chamber and Senate at the election of June 1976. Approximately half of the remainder withdrew the following December to form the National Democratic Assembly of the Right (*Democrazia Nazionale Costituente di Destra*– DN), which obtained no seats in its own right in 1979 and subsequently realigned with the parent group. In a somewhat unusual effort to gain wage-earner support, the MSI-DN allied itself with the PCI in support of the June 1985 referendum on the *scala mobile,* without measurable political benefit. The party lost 7 of its 42 chamber seats in the 1987 balloting.

Leaders: Pino ROMUALDI (President), Vittorio MUSSOLINI (son of the former Fascist leader), Gianfranco FINI (Secretary General).

National Federation for the Green List (*Federazione Nazionale per Le Liste Verdi*). The Italian branch of the European Green movement was formally launched on an environmentalist and anti-nuclear platform prior to the June 1987 election, at which it won one Senate and 13 Chamber seats.

Leaders: Gianni MATTIOLI (President of Parliamentary Group), Rosa FILIPPINI and Laura CIMA (Vice Presidents), Sergio ANDREAS (Secretary).

South Tyrol People's Party (*Südtiroler Volkspartei*–SVP). The SVP is a moderate autonomist grouping representing the German-speaking inhabitants of the South Tyrol (Alto Adige). Within the region it has been challenged by the radical **Fatherland Front** (*Heimatbund*), founded in 1971 by Hans STIELER and currently led by Eva KLOTZ.

Leaders: Dr. Silvius MAGNANO (President), Dr. Bruno HOSP (General Secretary).

Three other regional groupings that have participated in recent parliamentary elections are the **For Trieste** (*Per Trieste*), an autonomist group from the special statute region of Friuli–Venezia Giulia that includes members of the MSI and the PR; the **Valdostan Union** (*Union Valdôtaine*), a joint autonomist list from the special statute region of Val d'Aosta; and the **Sardinian Action Party** (*Partito Sardo d'Azione*).

Terrorist Groups:

Italy has long been buffeted by political terrorism, over 200 names having been used over the last two decades by groups committed to such activity. The most notorious of the left-wing formations, the **Red Brigades** (*Brigate Rosse*), was founded in 1969, reportedly in linkage with the West German Red Army Faction terrorists. The *Brigate Rosse* engaged in numerous killings during the late 1970s, including that of former prime minister Aldo Moro; more recently one of its offshoots, the **Union of Fighting Communists** (*Unione dei Comunisti Combattenti*–UCC), claimed responsibility for the March 1987 murder of Air Force Gen. Licio Giorgieri and the April 1988 assassination of Sen. Roberto Ruffilli, a leading ally of Prime Minister De Mita. Right-wing groups include the neofascist **Armed Revolutionary Nuclei** (*Nuclei Armati Rivoluzionari*– NAR). Regionally, a paramilitary **Protection League** (*Schutzverein*), believed to be linked to the Fatherland Front (see under SVP, above), has been active in the South Tyrol.

LEGISLATURE

Members of the bicameral **Parliament** (*Parlamento*) were most recently elected June 14–15, 1987, for five-year terms (subject to dissolution).

Senate (*Senato*). The upper house consists of 315 members elected by universal suffrage on a regional basis, in addition to 7 senators (2 of them ex officio) appointed for life by the head of state. At the election of June 14–15, 1987, the Christian Democratic Party won 124 seats; the Communist Party, 99; the Socialist Party, 38; the Italian Social Movement, 16; the Republican Party, 9; the Social Democratic Party, 5; the South Tyrol People's Party, 3; the Radical Party, 3; the Liberal Party, 2; the Proletarian Democracy, 1; the Green List, 1; PSI/PSDI/PR lists, 11; other, 3.

President: Giovani SPADOLINI.

Chamber of Deputies (*Camera dei Deputati*). The lower house consists of 630 members elected by universal suffrage and proportional representation. At the 1987 election the Christian Democratic Party won 234 seats; the Communist Party, 177; the Socialist Party, 94; the Italian Social Movement, 35; the Republican Party, 21; the Social Democratic Party, 17; the Green List, 13; the Radical Party, 13; the Liberal Party, 11; the Proletarian Democracy, 8; others, 7.

President: Nilde IOTTI.

CABINET

[as of April 13, 1988]

Prime Minister	Ciriaco De Mita
Deputy Prime Minister	Gianni De Michelis

Ministers

Agriculture	Calogero Mannino
Budget	Amintore Fanfani
Civil Protection	Vito Lattanzio
Cultural Assets	Vincenza Bono Parrino
Defense	Valerio Zanone
Education	Giovani Galloni
Environment	Giorgio Ruffolo
European Community Affairs	Antonio La Pergola
Finance	Emilio Colombo
Foreign Affairs	Guilio Andreotti
Foreign Trade	Renato Ruggiero
Health	Carlo Donat Cattin
Industry	Adolfo Battaglia
Interior	Antonio Gava
Justice	Guiliano Vassali
Labor	Rino Formica
Merchant Marine	Giovanni Prandini
Posts	Oscar Mammi
Public Administration	Paolo Cirino Pomicino
Public Works	Enrico Ferri
Regions and Institutional Problems	Antonio Maccanico
Relations with Parliament	Sergio Mattarella
Scientific and Technological Research	Antonio Ruberti
Social Affairs	Rosa Jervolino Russo
Southern Affairs	Remo Gaspan
Tourism	Franco Carraro
Transport	Giorgio Santuz
Treasury	Guiliano Amato
Urban Problems	Carlo Tognoli
Governor, Bank of Italy	Carlo Azeglio Ciampi

NEWS MEDIA

Although freedom of speech and press is constitutionally guaranteed, the collection and release of official news is centered in the Information Service of the Presidency of the Council of Ministers, in accordance with a law of September 15, 1952.

Press. Italy's approximately 80 daily papers have a relatively low combined circulation. Several of the papers are owned or supported by political parties. Editorial opinion, influenced by the Church and various economic groups, leans heavily to the right of center. Most of the newspapers are regional, notable exceptions being the nationally circulated *Corriere della Sera, La Stampa,* and *Il Giorno.* The following papers are published daily at Rome, unless otherwise noted: *Corriere della Sera* (Milan, 633,000), centrist; *La Stampa* (Turin, 587,000; evening edition *Stampa Sera*), center-left; *La Repubblica* (490,000), center-left; *Il Messaggero* (315,000), center-right; *Il Resto del Carlino* (Bologna, 313,000) independent conservative; *L'Unità* (300,000), PCI organ; *Il Giorno* (Milan, 295,000), independent; *La Nazione* (Florence, 290,000), right-wing; *Il Giornale* (Milan, 270,000), independent center-right; *Il Tempo* (218,000), center-right; *Il Secolo XIX* (Genova, 178,000), independent; *Il Gazzettino* (Venice, 139,000), independent; *Avvenire* (Milan, 118,000), Catholic; *Paese Sera* (63,000), left-wing; *Avanti!* (55,000), PSI organ; *Il Popolo* (43,000), DC organ.

News agencies. The leading domestic service is *Agenzia Nazionale Stampa Associata* (ANSA); numerous foreign bureaus maintain offices in the leading Italian cities.

Radio and television. Three nationwide radio broadcasting networks and two television channels are operated by *Radiotelevisione Italiana* (RAI), which is responsible to the Ministry of Post and Telecommunications. Almost 100 percent of RAI, a joint-stock company, is held by the autonomous governmental agency IRI (Institute for Industrial Reconstruction). The standards and political objectivity of all programs are regulated by a government-appointed director general, a committee appointed by the Ministry of Post and Telecommunications, and a parliamentary commission. In addition, in the wake of a 1975 court decision, over 1,000 private radio stations now broadcast locally. There were approximately 15.1 million radio and 14.9 million television receivers in 1987.

INTERGOVERNMENTAL REPRESENTATION

Ambassador to the US: Rinaldo PETRIGNANI.

US Ambassador to Italy: Maxwell M. RABB.

Permanent Representative to the UN: Maurizio BUCCI.

IGO Memberships (Non-UN): ADB, ADF, AfDB, BIS, CCC, CERN, CEUR, EC, EIB, ESA, G10, IADB, ICAC, ICCO, ICM, ICO, IEA, ILZ, Inmarsat, INRO, Intelsat, Interpol, IOOC, ITC, NATO, OECD, PCA, WEU.

JAMAICA

Political Status: Independent member of the Commonwealth since August 6, 1962; under democratic parliamentary regime.

Area: 4,244 sq. mi. (10,991 sq. km.).

Population: 2,095,878 (1982C), 2,405,000 (1988E).

Major Urban Centers (1970C): KINGSTON (111,879; urban area, 475,548); Montego Bay (42,800).

Official Language: English.

Monetary Unit: Jamaican Dollar (principal rate March 1, 1988, 5.51 dollars = $1US).

Sovereign: Queen ELIZABETH II.

Governor General: Florizel A. GLASSPOLE; assumed office June 27, 1973, following the retirement of Sir Clifford CAMPBELL on March 2.

Prime Minister: Edward Philip George SEAGA (Jamaica Labour Party); assumed office November 7, 1980, succeeding Michael Norman MANLEY (People's National Party) following parliamentary election of October 30; remained in office following election of December 15, 1983.

THE COUNTRY

Jamaica, whose name is derived from the Arawak Indian word *Xaymaca,* is a mountainous island located 90 miles south of Cuba. The third-largest island in the Caribbean, it is the largest and most populous of the independent Commonwealth nations in the area. About 77 percent of the population is of African descent; another 15 percent is of mixed Afro-European heritage. Population density is high, particularly in metropolitan Kingston, which contains more than 30 percent of the national total. The Anglican and Baptist creeds claim the most adherents, but numerous other denominations and sects are active. Approximately 34 percent of adult women are in the official labor force, concentrated in agriculture and civil service, with a large proportion of the remainder serving as unpaid agricultural workers. As a consequence of male urban migration, over one-third of all households are headed by women, with 70 percent of all children being born to single mothers. Female representation in government is proportionately higher than in other Caribbean and Latin American countries, with 30 female legislators in the national assembly elected in 1983.

The Jamaican economy is based on sugar, bauxite mining, and tourism. Important agricultural products also include rum, molasses, bananas, and citrus fruits. Under both the Manley and Seaga governments the last decade has been one of severe economic difficulty, marked by high inflation, 25 percent unemployment, a large foreign debt with stifling debt service costs, and depression of the bauxite and sugar industries. Except for a brief recovery in 1982, the Seaga administration's acceptance of IMF-mandated austerity has not yielded the desired economic stability, generating instead growing public dissatisfaction with loss of services and decreased buying power.

GOVERNMENT AND POLITICS

Political background. A British colony from 1655 to 1962, Jamaica developed a two-party system before World War II under the leadership of Sir Alexander BUSTAMANTE and Norman W. MANLEY, founders, respectively, of the Jamaica Labour Party (JLP) and the People's National Party (PNP). A considerable measure of self-government was introduced in 1944, but full independence was delayed by attempts to set up a wider federation embracing all or most of the Caribbean Commonwealth territories. Jamaica joined the now defunct West Indies Federation in 1958 but withdrew in 1961 because of disagreements over taxation, voting rights, and location of the federal capital.

Bustamante became the nation's first prime minister at independence in 1962 and on his retirement in 1967 was succeeded by Donald SANGSTER, who died within a few weeks. His replacement, Hugh L. SHEARER, led the country until the 1972 election gave a majority to the PNP for the first time since independence and permitted Michael Norman MANLEY, son of the PNP's founder, to become prime minister. Manley remained in office following an impressive PNP victory at the election of December 1976 but, confronted by an economic crisis and mounting domestic insecurity, was forced to call an early election in October 1980 that returned the JLP to power under the conservative leadership of Edward SEAGA. Benefiting from a surge of popularity occasioned by Jamaican participation in the invasion of Grenada, Seaga called an early parliamentary election for December 15, 1983, at which the JLP swept all seats in the wake of a boycott by the PNP which charged that outdated voter rolls favored the government party.

Constitution and government. Under the 1962 constitution, the queen is the titular head of state. Her representative, a governor general with limited powers, is advised, in areas bearing on the royal prerogative, by a six-member Privy Council. Executive authority is centered in a cabinet of no fewer than 12 members (including the prime minister), who are collectively responsible to the House of Representatives, the elected lower house of the bicameral Parliament; the upper house (Senate) is entirely appointive. The judicial system is headed by a Supreme Court with both primary and appellate jurisdiction. Judges of both the Supreme Court and a Court of Appeal are appointed by the governor general on the advice of the prime minister. There are also several magistrates' courts.

For administrative purposes Jamaica is divided into 12 parishes and the Kingston and St. Andrew Corporation, a special administrative entity encompassing the principal urban areas.

Foreign relations. Jamaica is a member of the United Nations and the Commonwealth as well as a number of regional organizations. Previously cordial relations with the United States were marred in July 1973 by Prime Minister Manley's declaration of US Ambassador Vincent W. de Roulet as *persona non grata*. They were further exacerbated by Jamaican support for Cuban intervention in Angola in 1975 and by subsequent allegations of US involvement in "destabilization" activities similar to those that had led to the ouster of the Allende regime in Chile.

The designation of Edward Seaga as prime minister in November 1980 signified a return to a pro-US posture, the Cuban ambassador, in turn, being declared *persona non grata* and departing the country four days prior to the formal installation of the new government. Seaga was widely regarded as a prime mover behind the Reagan administration's 1981 Caribbean Basin Initiative (CBI), and ties to Washington were further strengthened by Jamaica's participation in the US-led action in Grenada in October 1983.

Current issues. A massive repudiation of administration-backed candidates at local elections in mid-1986 (the PNP gaining control of 11 of 13 parishes) was attributed to widespread dissatisfaction over the government's economic policies, with the JLP's immediate prospects resting on the hope of quick results from a major policy reversal in the 1986–1987 budget. After years of austerity, Seaga presented a "good news" expansionary program which doubled capital expenditure, reduced interest rates, and imposed price controls on basic foods. The shift immediately put him at odds with USAID, the World Bank, and the IMF, to which the country was already $70 million in arrears. Vowing that "Jamaica has no intention of being added to the tombstone of IMF failure", Seaga nevertheless secured a surprise agreement in January 1987 with the IMF, which backed off from its earlier demand for further devaluation and retrenchment. Economic indicators for the remainder of the year were mixed: while the government reported in August that business confidence had "rebounded" with private sector investment attaining "unprecedented levels", the trade deficit worsened (largely because of increased demand for raw materials and capital goods), a 1986 balance-of-payments surplus was reversed, and unemployment remained above 20 percent.

On the political front, a four-month illness of opposition leader Manley disrupted PNP plans to mount mass demonstrations in support of its call for an early election, while the JLP appeared unwilling to risk a sympathy backlash by reversing itself and advancing the ballot date to take advantage of the momentary vacuum in PNP leadership. A public opinion poll in early 1988 revealed that the JLP had countered marginally against the popularity of the PNP, but that the latter would probably prevail in the balloting that would have to be held by the end of the year.

POLITICAL PARTIES

Jamaica's two leading parties, the Jamaica Labour Party and the People's National Party, have similar trade-union origins. Both are well organized and institutionalized, but personal leadership within them remains very important.

Government Party:

Jamaica Labour Party (JLP). Founded in 1943 by Alexander Bustamante, the JLP originated as the political arm of his Bustamante Industrial Trade Union. The more conservative of Jamaica's two leading parties, the JLP relies on business as well as labor support, while its traditional strength in rural areas appears to have dissipated somewhat as rural MPs have accepted government posts at Kingston. It supports private enterprise, economic expansion, and a generally pro-Western international stance, but also identifies with Black African and other Third World nations. Opposition to Prime Minister Seaga's leadership, particularly in regard to economic policy, has surfaced in recent years although the party rallied behind him in late 1986, convincing him to withdraw his offer to resign as prime minister and endorsing the dismissal or reassignment of his critics within the cabinet.

Leaders: Edward SEAGA (Prime Minister), Bruce GOLDING (Chairman), Ryan PERALTO (General Secretary).

Opposition Party:

People's National Party (PNP). Organized in 1938 by Norman W. Manley, the PNP became affiliated in 1943 with the Trade Union Council. After losing elections in 1945 and 1949 but winning those of 1955 and 1959, it came to power for the first time since independence in March 1972, following ten years in opposition. Headed by the son of its late founder, the PNP is based on the National Workers' Union and draws its principal support from middle-class, intellectual, and urban elements. Committed to a program of "democratic socialism", the party was decisively defeated at the October 1980 election. In recent years it has moved toward the center, its leadership eliminating the word "socialism" from its manifesto for the 1986 municipal elections and rejecting a future electoral alliance with the WPJ (below). Since its boycott of the 1983 balloting, the party has functioned as an extraparliamentary opposition; initially eschewing mass demonstrations in favor of "public forums", the PNP claimed a major role (along with the WPJ) in the fuel-price unrest of January 1985, which was followed by mass PNP rallies in tourist areas and a successful campaign for the preparation of revised voter lists. In August 1985, Manley unveiled a "shadow government program" encompassing import restrictions, restoration of currency controls, stimulation of domestic agriculture, and low-income housing. Encouraged by its victory in 11 of 13 parish councils in July 1986 (winning 126 of 187 seats overall, with a 58 percent vote share), the PNP pressed the government to advance the date — not mandated until late 1988 — of the next general election.

Leaders: Michael Norman MANLEY (President of the Party), P.J. PATTERSON (Chairman), Dr. Paul ROBERTSON (General Secretary).

Minor Parties:

Workers' Party of Jamaica (WPJ). Formerly organized as the Workers' Liberation League, the WPJ is a communist group that held its first congress on December 17, 1978, at which time it gave its "critical support" to the Manley government. It won no legislative seats in 1980 and joined the PNP in boycotting the 1983 election. The WJP registered only 2 percent support in a 1986 public opinion poll and captured no seats in the 13 local council seats that it contested.

Leader: Dr. Trevor MUNROE (General Secretary).

Other minor parties include two left-wing groups, the **Jamaica Communist Party,** led by Chris LAWRENCE, and the Trotskyite **Revolutionary Marxist League,** in addition to the **Republican Party**, the **Christian Conscience**, and the extreme right-wing **Jamaica United Front**; the last three participated, without success, in the 1983 balloting.

In May 1986, a **Jamaica-American Party** was launched by businessman James CHISHOLM, with the goal (unsupported by discernible public opinion) of making Jamaica the 51st US state.

LEGISLATURE

The bicameral **Parliament** consists of an appointed Senate and an elected House of Representatives. All money bills must originate in the lower chamber.

Senate. The upper house consists of 21 members appointed by the governor general; 13 are normally appointed on advice of the prime minister and 8 on the advice of the leader of the opposition. After the 1983 election, the PNP rejected a government offer to nominate opposition senators and expelled two party members who had accepted such appointment from Prime Minister Seaga.

President: Rev. Ephraim MORGAN.

House of Representatives. The lower house is now at its constitutional limit of 60 members, all of whom are elected by universal adult suffrage for five-year terms, subject to dissolution. Because of the PNP boycott of the election of December 15, 1983, all 60 seats were won by the Jamaica Labor Party, although 2 representatives resigned from the JLP in mid-1986 to sit as independents.

Speaker: Alva Edison ROSS.

CABINET

Prime Minister	Edward Philip George Seaga
Deputy Prime Minister	Hugh Lawson Shearer
Ministers	
Agriculture	Dr. Percival Broderick
Construction	Bruce Golding
Education	Neville Gallimore
Finance and Planning	Edward Philip George Seaga
Foreign Affairs and Industry	Hugh Lawson Shearer
Health	Dr. Kenneth Baugh
Justice	Oswald G. Harding
Labor	James A.G. Smith, Jr.
Local Government	Neville Lewis
Mining, Energy and Tourism	Hugh Hart
National Security	Errol Anderson
Public Service	Clifton Stone
Public Utilities and Transport	Pearnel Charles
Social Security and Consumer Affairs	Dr. Mavis Gilmour
Youth and Community Development	Edmund Bartlett
Ministers of State	
Agriculture	Anthony Johnson
Construction (Housing)	Robert Marsh
Construction (Works)	Brascoe Lee
Education	Hugh Dawes
Foreign Affairs	Jeannette Grant-Woodham
Health	Karl Samuda
National Security	Ryan Pearalto
Prime Minister's Office (Culture)	Lester Michael Henry
Prime Minister's Office (Information)	Olivia Grange
Public Utilities and Transport	Pat Stephens
Social Security and Consumer Affairs	Enid Bennett
Tourism	Dr. L. Henry Marco Brown
Youth and Community Development	Kingsley Sangster
Attorney General	Oswald G. Harding
Governor, Central Bank	Headly Brown

NEWS MEDIA

Press. The press has traditionally been free of censorship and government control. During 1977, however, there were left-wing appeals for nationalization of the island's newspapers, and in September the government intervened to secure reinstatement of the editor of the *Jamaica Daily News,* who had been dismissed by the paper's owners for printing a radical article in defiance of their instructions. Subsequently, the financially troubled *News* came under state control and was closed down in April 1983 after the government had rejected a purchase tender from a cooperative of its employees. The following are published at Kingston: *Star* (46,000 Monday-Thursday, 92,000 Friday); *Gleaner* (42,000 daily, 91,000 Sunday).

News agencies. There is no domestic facility; AP, the Caribbean News Agency, and Reuters are among those with bureaus at Kingston.

Radio and television. Most broadcasting is government controlled. The Jamaica Broadcasting Corporation (JBC) operates commercial radio and television facilities, while the Educational Broadcasting Service of the Ministry of Education provides radio and television service for the public schools. The JBC has long been publicly owned but the Seaga government in July 1987 introduced a revised version of a plan for substantial divestiture to the private sector. A controlling interest in Radio Jamaica, the island's only independent station, was purchased from the British Rediffusion group in September 1977 but returned to private ownership by the Seaga administration. There were approximately 1.2 million radio and 387,000 television receivers in 1987.

INTERGOVERNMENTAL REPRESENTATION

Ambassador to the US: Keith JOHNSON.

US Ambassador to Jamaica: Michael SOTIRHOS.

Permanent Representative to the UN: Lloyd M.H. BARNETT.

IGO Memberships (Non-UN): Caricom, CCC, CDB, CWTH, EEC(L), *EIB,* Geplacea, IADB, IBA, ICCO, ICO, Intelsat, Interpol, ISO, IWC, NAM, OAS, OPANAL, SELA.

JAPAN

Nippon

Political Status: Constitutional monarchy established May 3, 1947; under multiparty parliamentary system.

Area: 143,750 sq. mi. (372,313 sq. km.).

Population: 121,047,196 (1985C), 123,243,000 (1988E). The 1985 figure is provisional.

Major Urban Centers (1985C): TOKYO (8,353,674; urban area, 11,828,262); Yokohama (2,992,644); Osaka

(2,636,260); Nagoya (2,116,350); Sapporo (1,542,979); Kyoto (1,479,125); Kobe (1,410,843); Fukuoka (1,160,402); Kawasaki (1,088,611); Kitakyushu (1,056,400).

Official Language: Japanese.

Monetary Unit: Yen (market rate March 1, 1988, 129.16 yen = $1US).

Sovereign: Emperor HIROHITO; ascended throne December 25, 1926, on death of his father, Emperor YOSHI-HITO; assumed status of constitutional sovereign May 3, 1947.
Heir to the Throne: Prince AKIHITO; designated Crown Prince on November 10, 1952.

Prime Minister: Noboru TAKESHITA (Liberal Democratic Party); elected by the Diet on November 6, 1987, succeeding Yasuhiro NAKASONE (Liberal Democratic Party).

THE COUNTRY

Situated off the coast of Northeast Asia and stretching some 2,000 miles, the Japanese archipelago consists of over 3,000 islands, although the four main islands of Honshu, Hokkaido, Kyushu, and Shikoku account for 98 percent of the land area. While mountainous terrain has limited the acreage available for cultivation, the country's location has provided a stimulus to fishing and other maritime pursuits (despite a paucity of good harbors) as well as trading. The thickly settled, basically Mongoloid population is remarkably homogeneous; the only distinct ethnic minority consists of some 650,000 Koreans, mainly descendants of those brought to Japan as laborers in the period 1910–1945. Population growth, a serious problem until recent years, has been effectively slowed by the use of modern birth-control techniques and fell to an all-time low of 0.6 percent in 1984. Buddhism and Shintoism are the two major religions, with various new sects of Buddhism, e.g., *Soka Gakkai, Tenrikyo,* and *Rissho Koseikai,* currently attracting numerous adherents. In 1983, women constituted approximately 40 percent of the labor force (70 percent of agricultural workers).

Japan's most remarkable achievement over the past century has been its unique industrial development, which gave it undisputed economic primacy in Asia even before World War II and, by 1969, had placed it ahead of West Germany and second only to the United States among non-Communist industrial nations. Economic growth between 1954, when prewar economic levels were first regained, and 1970 proceeded at an average rate, in real terms, of at least 10 percent annually. By 1967, Japan was the world's third-largest producer of crude steel and aluminum; its sixth-largest exporter (machinery, iron and steel, and textiles are the leading commodities); and far and away its biggest shipbuilder, with gross tonnage on order and under production exceeding that of its four closest competitors combined. By 1980, automobile production had exceeded that of the United States, with the latter, Japan's leading trade part-

ner, taking 37 percent of exports and supplying 19 percent of imports in 1985 (up from 29 percent of exports in 1983, with no significant percentage change in imports); overall, Japan stands second only to Canada as a US trading partner. The role of agriculture in the Japanese economy has shrunk as that of industry has grown; agricultural labor has declined since 1960 from 33 percent to about 10 percent of the national work force and now produces less than 4 percent of the gross national product. In addition to its large national output, Japan is growing rapidly in GNP per capita, which exceeded $15,000 in 1986.

GOVERNMENT AND POLITICS

Political background. The armistice signed by Japan on September 2, 1945, concluded the military phase of World War II and ended the era of modernization and imperial expansion that had begun with the Meiji Restoration in 1867. Stripped of its overseas territorial acquisitions, including Manchuria, Korea, Formosa (Taiwan), southern Sakhalin, and the Kuril Islands (including de facto loss of "Northern Territories" to the Soviet Union [see Foreign relations, below]), Japan was occupied by Allied military forces under Gen. Douglas MacARTHUR and entered upon a period of far-reaching social, political, and economic reforms under the guidance of US occupation authorities. A constitution promulgated November 3, 1946, and effective May 3, 1947, deprived Emperor HIROHITO of his claim to divine right and transformed Japan into a constitutional monarchy that expressly renounced war and the maintenance of military forces. The Allied occupation was formally ended by a peace treaty signed at San Francisco on September 8, 1951, effective April 28, 1952; by its terms (still not recognized by the Soviet Union), the United States retained control of the Bonin and Ryukyu islands while informally recognizing Japan's "residual sovereignty" in those territories. Concurrently, a Security Treaty between Japan and the United States (later modified by a Treaty of Mutual Cooperation and Security, effective June 23, 1960) gave the latter the right to continue maintaining armed forces in and around Japan.

Since 1946, Japan's political development has rested mainly with a small group of conservative politicians, civil servants, and businessmen identified with the ruling Liberal Democratic Party (LDP), established in 1955 through a merger of the preexisting Liberal and Democratic parties. Dedicated both to free-enterprise economics and to continued close association with the United States, the LDP has been periodically (but as yet unsuccessfully) challenged by leftist forces associated primarily with the Japanese Socialist Party (JSP), the small Japanese Communist Party (JCP), and a wide but volatile extraparliamentary opposition, including trade-union, student, and intellectual groups.

The government headed from 1964 to 1972 by Eisaku SATO stressed continued economic expansion combined with increased independence in foreign policy, especially in Southeast Asia. Discussions with US President Johnson resulted in the return of the Bonin Islands to Japanese administration in 1968, while reversion of the Ryukyus (including Okinawa) in 1972 represented the crowning achievement of Sato's long premiership. Kakuei TANA-KA, who in July 1972 succeeded Sato as president of the ruling party and as prime minister, encountered mounting pressure from the Left. The LDP lost additional lower-house seats to the Socialists and Communists in December 1972 and barely succeeded in retaining its majority in the upper chamber at a partial election in July 1974. In the wake of these reverses, a number of ministers resigned, while Prime Minister Tanaka returned from a 12-day trip to Australia, Burma, and New Zealand in November to find his political standing substantially eroded by charges of personal and financial irregularities. He officially tendered his resignation on November 25, following a state visit by US President Ford, and Takeo MIKI was formally invested as his successor on December 6.

In July 1976, former prime minister Tanaka was indicted on charges of foreign-exchange abuses and of having accepted a $1.6 million bribe from the US Lockheed Aircraft Corporation, his subsequent arrest and pretrial release on bail generating shockwaves throughout the LDP. Collaterally, Prime Minister Miki refused to resign prior to the December 5 election but stepped down immediately thereafter, accepting responsibility for his party's poor performance, which (with independent support) yielded a bare majority of seats in the House of Representatives. On December 23, Takeo FUKUDA was elected party president, paving the way for his designation as prime minister the following day.

In a move designed to enhance public support for the party and its leadership in the wake of the Lockheed scandal, the LDP implemented an advisory party primary in 1978. Under the plan as initially implemented, party voting around the country would limit the field of candidates to two individuals, one of whom would subsequently be chosen party president (and hence prime minister) by the parliamentary delegation. Although preprimary polls gave Prime Minister Fukuda a commanding lead over his principal rival, Masayoshi OHIRA, the challenger registered a stunning upset victory in balloting on November 27. Fukuda, who had made the tactical mistake of asserting in the final week of the campaign that the runner-up should not attempt to challenge the preference of the voters, thereupon withdrew from contention, and Ohira was formally confirmed as prime minister on December 8.

Less than a year later, Ohira himself nearly fell victim to a tactical error. Responding to a series of LDP victories in local and regional balloting earlier in the year, and hoping to establish a clear LDP majority in the House of Representatives, the prime minister called for a legislative election a year ahead of schedule. The October 7 poll resulted, however, in a net loss of one seat for the Liberal Democrats, and Ohira immediately found himself challenged for the premiership by faction leaders of his own party. When the House convened in special session on October 30 to elect a prime minister, the LDP was still embroiled, and as mandated by the constitution, Ohira became head of a caretaker government that served until he finally defeated his chief rival, former prime minister Fukuda, in a close House vote on November 6.

The Ohira government fell as a result of the abstention of two major LDP factions on a no-confidence motion on May 16, 1980, and an unprecedented "double election" for the upper and lower chambers was called for June 22. However, Ohira died on June 12, Zenko SUZUKI assuming office as his successor (following the acting incumbency of Chief Cabinet Secretary Masayoshi ITO) after the LDP had been returned to power with an absolute majority in both houses. In a surprise move on October 12, 1982, Suzuki announced that he would not seek reelection as party president when his two-year term expired on November 25, thus effectively resigning as prime minister. After considerable political maneuvering, a field of four candidates presented themselves at a party primary on November 24 that resulted in a decisive victory for the "mainstream" contender, Yasuhiro NAKASONE.

In October 1983, Tanaka was convicted on the Lockheed charges and sentenced to a four-year prison term. Although the former prime minister had formally withdrawn from the LDP, continuing in the Diet as an independent, his refusal to vacate his seat pending appeal of his conviction proved embarrassing to Nakasone, who felt obliged to call for an early dissolution of the lower house on November 28. At the election of December 18, the LDP lost its absolute majority, winning only 250 of 511 seats; two days later, however, 8 independents were induced to join the party and on December 26 Nakasone formed a coalition government encompassing the LDP and the small New Liberal Club (NLC).

The LDP won a stunning victory at the election of July 6, 1986, increasing its majority in the House of Councillors and winning commanding control of the House of Representatives, largely at the expense of the opposition Japanese Socialist and Democratic Socialist parties. A reorganization of the party leadership on July 21 and the formation of a new government on July 22 that reflected a careful balancing of factional strength within the LDP paved the way for a crucial one-year extension of Nakasone's incumbency in September. While the prime minister's political fortunes encountered major setbacks in late 1986 and early 1987 (see Current issues, below), he retained office until November 6 when the Diet elected Noboru TAKESHITA, who had taken over as LDP president on October 30, as his successor.

Constitution and government. The constitution of May 3, 1947, converted Japan from an absolute to a constitutional monarchy by transferring sovereign power from the emperor to the people and limiting the former to a "symbolic" and ceremonial role. The peerage was abolished, and legislative and fiscal authority was vested in a bicameral parliament (Diet) consisting of a House of Representatives and an upper chamber, the House of Councillors, with limited power to delay legislation. The cabinet is headed by a prime minister who is leader of the majority party; it is collectively responsible to the Diet and must resign on a no-confidence vote in the House of Representatives unless the House is dissolved and a new election held. Judicial power is vested in an appointive Supreme Court and in lower courts as established by law. Administratively, Japan is divided into 47 major units (Tokyo, Osaka, Kyoto, Hokkaido Island, and 43 prefectures), each with an elected mayor or governor and a local assembly. Smaller municipal units have their own elected assemblies.

An extensive enumeration of civil rights includes freedom of thought and conscience, free and equal education, an absence of censorship, and impartial and public judicial procedure. Amendments require a two-thirds majority of both houses and subsequent ratification by a majority vote in a popular referendum. A constitutional article renouncing war and the maintenance of armed forces and other war potential (Article 9) has impeded the assumption of mutual defense responsibilities but has been interpreted by the government as permitting the maintenance of "Self-Defense Forces", which now total approximately 250,000 men.

Foreign relations. Since World War II, Japan has relied heavily on the United States for its security. This association, with the resultant presence of American forces in Japan, was long criticized by the political and extraparliamentary opposition, which urged a policy of nonalignment and made a major, but unsuccessful effort to secure abrogation of the 1960 Mutual Security Treaty on the expiration of its initial ten-year term.

Japan was admitted to the United Nations in 1956 and also participates in such "Western" organizations as the OECD and the Group of Ten. It has hosted two of the 12 annual economic summit meetings, the most recent, at Toyko on May 4–6, 1986, being hailed as "the most successful . . . to date". It joined the Inter-American Development Bank as a nonregional member in July 1976.

Japan's policies in East and Southeast Asia are closely linked to aid, trade, and reparations issues; it is a member of the Asian Development Bank and the Colombo Plan but has opposed the formation of any regional security organization in the Western Pacific.

With regard to China, Tokyo for many years pursued a policy of "separating politics from economics" by trading extensively with both Taiwan and the mainland while according diplomatic recognition only to the former. However, during a pathbreaking visit to Peking on September 25–30, 1972, Prime Minister Tanaka agreed to immediate recognition of the People's Republic as the sole legal government of China; a prompt establishment of diplomatic relations between the two governments; and as a corollary, the severance of Japanese diplomatic (but not economic) relations with Taiwan. After a lengthy series of intermittent talks, the rapprochement was formalized by the signing of a treaty of peace and friendship at Peking on August 12, 1978.

Normal relations with the Republic of Korea were established in 1965–1966 after many years of hostility, which, in muted form, persists because of resentment over the Japanese occupation, coupled with alleged discrimination against Koreans born and living in Japan. While under some domestic pressure to accord recognition to North Korea, the government has not yet done so, although relations with East Germany and North Vietnam were established in 1973. Both moves were undertaken as part of a larger effort to bolster relations with China and the Soviet Union while asserting a degree of independence of US policy.

The normalization of relations with the Soviet Union has proceeded slowly. Bilateral talks on a Japanese-Soviet peace treaty were instituted in January 1972, but Soviet re-

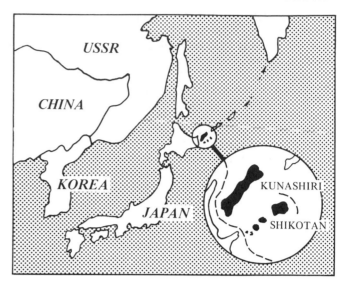

fusal to return the northern islands of Kunashiri, Etorofu, Habomai, and Shikotan, which were annexed after World War II (see map), has prevented any significant progress toward a treaty. The "Northern Territories" dispute was discussed during a visit by Soviet Foreign Minister Edvard Shevardnadze to Japan on January 15–19, 1986 (the first such visitation since that of Andrei Gromyko in 1976), at the conclusion of which the Soviet official simply asserted that "the two sides do not see a coincidence of views" on the Kuriles. A short-term fisheries agreement was, however, concluded, while Soviet leader Mikhail Gorbachev announced at Vladivostok in July that an exchange of visits "at the highest level" was under discussion. Relations again chilled in 1987 with the revelation in May that the Toshiba Machine Company had engaged in the illegal sale of computer-controlled milling equipment to the Soviet Union, followed by a mutual expulsion of Soviet and Japanese nationals on grounds of espionage in August.

In recent years, the Japanese economy has been buffeted by heightened resistance in the export sector from both the United States and Western Europe. The American automobile industry, including both labor and management, has been particularly vocal about encroachment in the domestic market, where Japanese sales now exceed 20 percent of the total, while European countries have moved to curtail increases in the importation of both motor vehicles and electronic equipment. In April 1987, following a unanimous resolution by the US Congress, the Reagan administration approved a 100 percent tariff levy on a range of Japanese electronic goods in retaliation for alleged dumping practices by Japanese semiconductor manufacturers in third country markets; subsequently, at mid-year, the European Commission was authorized to extend existing anti-dumping duties to so-called "screwdriver" operations that involved the establishment by foreign companies of assembly plants in EC member countries.

Current issues. During the 1986 legislative campaign, Prime Minister Nakasone had pledged not to introduce a "large scale indirect tax" and in an October agreement with Washington had undertaken to implement a tax reform program that would include reductions in marginal tax rates for both personal and corporate income as a means of stimulating the economy. As a result, he was accorded a favorable public opinion rating of well over 50 percent at the end of the year. Subsequently, despite manifest recession, he advanced plans for a new 5 percent sales tax, with his poll popularity plummeting to less than 25 percent. At local elections in April 1987 Liberal Democratic candidates were generally successful, but with substantially reduced majorities, as compared with the previous such balloting in 1983. Most importantly, the gubernatorial contest in the western prefecture of Fukuoka, which had been construed as a referendum on the tax proposal, yielded a stunning defeat for the ruling party. By late April, after almost a third of the LDP legislators had signed a petition demanding withdrawal of both the sales tax measure and a companion bill that would have abolished a long-standing general exemption on interest from small savings, the prime minister was forced to yield on the issue of fiscal reform. Three months earlier, in another area that had drawn substantial political opposition, the government officially abandoned a policy in effect since 1976 that had limited defense spending to less than 1 percent of GNP. Subsequently, in moves that partially offset continuing friction with Washington over trade issues, the cabinet cleared the way for Japanese participation in the US Strategic Defense Initiative (SDI) and abandoned a plan for exclusively domestic design and production of the country's next generation of fighter-bombers.

By late summer, buoyed by an upturn in economic indicators (including evidence that Japan had become the world's leading creditor nation), Nakasone had recovered much of his lost popularity and in October the LDP, which had been girding itself for a divisive four-way leadership primary, succeeded in uniting behind the incumbent's choice of Noboru Takeshita as its next president (hence, prime minister designate). Meanwhile, however, a major development within the trade union movement appeared likely to have a profound effect on the balance of Japanese politics. The Japanese Private Sector Trade Union Confederation (*Zen Nihon Minkan Rodokumiai Rengokai-Zenminroren* or *Rengo*), originally formed in 1982, had emerged by early 1987 as the country's largest trade union organization, with 5.1 million members. By November the theretofore second-ranked Japanese Confederation of Labor (*Zen Nihon Rodo Sodomei-Domei*), whose members had long supported the opposition Democratic Socialists, had agreed to merge with *Rengo,* while the public-sector General Council of Trade Unions of Japan (*Nihon Rodo Kumiai Sohyogikai–Sohyo*), from which the Japanese Socialist Party drew much of its strength, announced that it would follow suit within three years. The emergence of such a "super union", with potential influence similar to that of the American AFL-CIO, was seen by some observers as a powerful catalyst for close cooperation, if not formal merger, on the part of previously divided opposition groups (see Political Parties, below).

POLITICAL PARTIES

Throughout most of the postwar era, Japan's multiparty political structure has featured the predominance of a single government party, the Liberal Democratic Party (LDP), over a diversified opposition that includes the "clean government" *Komeito* party and three other groups: the Japanese Socialist Party (JSP), the Democratic Socialist Party (DSP), and the Japanese Communist Party (JCP). Despite internal divisions, one of which led to the establishment in 1976 of the breakaway New Liberal Club (NLC), the LDP has consistently led both houses of Parliament. Although it lost its formal majority in the House of Representatives in December 1976 and fell two seats short of a majority in the House of Councillors in July 1977, it continued to receive crucial support from independent members and regained outright control of both houses in June 1980. It suffered a major setback at lower house balloting in December 1983, but was able to remain in power in coalition with the NLC. The party secured an unprecedented majority of 304 seats in the House of Representatives on July 7, 1986, gaining five additional lower House seats upon dissolution of the NLC in August.

Government Party:

Liberal Democratic Party—LDP (*Jiyu-Minshu-to*). Born of a 1955 merger between the former Liberal and Democratic parties, the LDP attaches more importance to organization and financial power than to ideology. Particularly strong in rural areas, it is generally favorable to private enterprise, the alliance with the United States, and expansion of Japanese interests in Asia. The party leadership, generally drawn from the bureaucratic and business elites, has traditionally been distributed among some dozen "faction leaders", each of whom has controlled from 10 to 50 votes in the Diet. In 1978, however, the party implemented a primary system for selecting candidates for its presidency, and on November 6, in the first runoff between two members of the same party in the Diet's history, Masayoshi Ohira defeated Takeo Fukuda for the leadership. (Following his defeat, Fukuda secured approval of a rules change requiring at least four candidates, each supported by a minimum of 50 parliamentarians, before a primary can be held.) Ohira was succeeded, subsequent to his death on June 12, 1980, by Zenko Suzuki, who in October 1982 announced that he would not seek reelection because of a rising level of dissent within the party. Four candidates thereupon presented themselves, and in a primary conducted on November 24 Yasuhiro Nakasone secured 58 percent of the vote, thus ensuring his designation as prime minister two days later. Despite a net loss of 36 LDP seats at the 1983 lower house election, Nakasone was able to form a new government on December 26 with the support of the NLC and 8 previously independent deputies.

In October 1984 Nakasone became the first LDP president in twenty years to secure reelection. Ineligible, under party rules, for a further term, he was granted a one-year extension in September 1986, following the LDP's overwhelming parliamentary victory in July. He stood down from the party position on October 30, 1987, and retired as prime minister on November 6, being succeeded in both positions by the party's theretofore secretary general, Noboru Takeshita.

Leaders: Noboru TAKESHITA (Prime Minister and President of the Party), Kiichi MIYAZAWA (Deputy Prime Minister and Vice President of the Party), Shintaro ABE (Secretary General).

Opposition Parties:

Japan Socialist Party—JSP (*Nihon Shakai-to*). Backed by the multi-million-member *Sohyo,* Japan's largest trade-union organization, and with an estimated 75 percent of its grassroots followers adhering to Marxist principles, the JSP long appeared to be more radical than its principal rival, the Japanese Communist Party. A platform adopted in 1966 favored nonalignment, a nonaggression pact among the great powers, and a democratic transition from capitalism to socialism. Since 1983, however, extreme leftist representation among JSP Diet members has been minimal, and at the party's 50th convention in December 1985 a policy proposal called the "New Declaration" was presented by the secretary general that called for formal abandonment of Marxist-Leninist doctrine. Vehemently opposed by the party's left wing, the document was ultimately approved at a reconvened meeting on January 22, 1986. Subsequently much of its membership base was threatened by the *Sohyo* decision to disband in favor of the recently organized Private Sector Trade Union Confederation *Rengo*) by 1990. The JSP lost nearly a third of its lower house representation at the July 1986 balloting, its chairman, Masashi Ishibashi, and all 32 members of its Executive Committee thereupon resigning because of the "crushing defeat". On being named Ishibashi's successor on September 6, Takako Doi became the first woman to head a major Japanese party. Subsequently, in the course of intraparty discussions during 1987, it appeared likely that the JSP would move toward informal alignment with the DSP (below) and possibly the CGP (below) prior to the next election.

Leaders: Takako DOI (Chairwoman), Makoto TANABE (former Secretary General).

Democratic Socialist Party — DSP (*Minshu-Shakai-to*). Formed by dissident right-wing members of the JSP in 1961, the DSP espouses a moderate domestic program and a relatively independent foreign policy. Its traditional political base was the formerly second-ranked labor organization, *Domei,* which voted to merge with *Rengo* in 1987. The party's legislative effectiveness has long depended on bids from LDP and JSP leaders for support on specific issues. In September 1979, the DSP and *Komeito* (below) agreed to present joint candidates in 28 legislative constituencies and not to compete with each other in 48, with the result that the number of DSP representatives rose from 29 to 35 at the October 7 balloting. It held 37 lower house seats prior to the 1986 poll, at which 11 were lost.

Leaders: Saburo TSUKAMOTO (Chairman), Kasuga IKKO (former Chairman), Keigo OUCHI (Secretary General).

Japan Communist Party — JCP (*Nihon Kyosan-to*). With a restricted popular base of about 400,000 members, the JCP relies on tight discipline to maximize its role in united front operations. "Eurocommunist" in orientation, the party is basically directed toward domestic affairs, with an emphasis on the antinuclear issue. JCP strength in the House of Representatives crested at 39 in 1979 and stood at 27 after the 1986 election.

Leaders: Tetsuzo FUWA (Chairman, Central Committee), Kenji MIYAMOTO (Chairman, Presidium), Mitsuhiro KANEKO (General Secretary).

Clean Government Party — CGP (*Komeito*). Organized as a political society in 1962 and as a political party in 1964, *Komeito* is an affiliate of the *Soka Gakkai* Buddhist organization but has deemphasized this connection in order to broaden its political appeal. Advancing a "clean government" program and youthful slates of candidates, the party's representation in the lower house rose from 33 in 1980 to 59 in 1983, with 2 of the latter being lost in 1986. *Komeito* has long opposed the government on foreign-policy issues, particularly with regard to retention of the Japan-US Mutual Security Treaty, but has recently shifted its position in regard to the country's Self-Defense Forces, which it now regards as necessary for "protection of the territory".

Leaders: Junya YANO (Chairman), Naohiko OKUBO (Secretary General).

Social Democratic Federation — SDF (*Shaminren*). The successor to the Socialist Citizens' League, which was formed in March 1977 by former members of the JSP's right wing, *Shaminren* won 4 lower house seats in 1986.

Leader: Hideo DEN.

Second Chamber Club (*Ni-In Club*). Formed as a successor to the Green Wind Club, which originated in the House of Representatives in 1946–1947, the *Ni-In Club* won 2 upper house seats in June 1983 and 3 in July 1986.

Leader: Isamu YAMADA (Secretary).

Salaried Workers' Party (*Salaryman Shin-to*). Organized in 1983 to promote reform of the tax system, which it claims is unfair to salaried workers, the *Salaryman Shin-to* secured 2 seats in the June House of Councillors balloting, both of which were lost in 1986.

Leader: Shigeru AOKI.

Welfare Party (*Fukushi-to*). Campaigning largely on the basis of improved services for the disabled, *Fukushi-to* obtained 1 upper house seat in June 1983, but is presently unrepresented in the Diet.

Leader: Eita YASHIRO.

Other parties participating in the recent elections include the **New Politics Club** (*Shin-Sei Club*), which won 4 upper house seats in 1986;

the **Tax Party** (*Zeikin-to*), which won a House of Councillors seat in 1983; and the anti-nuclear **Japan Reform Party** (*Nihon Yonaoshi-to*).

LEGISLATURE

The bicameral **Diet** (*Kokkai*) is composed of an upper chamber (House of Councillors) and a lower chamber (House of Representatives). Real power resides in the lower chamber, although amendments to the constitution require two-thirds majorities in both houses.

House of Councillors (*Sangiin*). The upper chamber, which replaced the prewar House of Peers, consists of 252 members serving six-year terms. It is renewed by halves every three years, 100 members being elected from the nation at large and the balance from prefectural districts. The chamber cannot be dissolved. After the last election on July 6, 1986, the Liberal Democratic party held 143 seats; the Socialist Party, 42; *Komeito*, 25; the Communist Party, 16; the Democratic Socialist Party, 12; the New Politics Club, 4; the Second Chamber Club, 3; the New Liberal Club, 2; others, 4; vacant, 1. On August 11, the NLC announced that it had decided to disband and seek "reunion" with the LDP; however, one of its two councillors chose to retain his seat as an independent. Concurrently, two of the JSP members withdrew to sit as independents.

Speaker: Masaaki FUJITA.

House of Representatives (*Shugiin*). The lower chamber presently consists of 512 members elected from 130 constituencies every four years, unless the House is dissolved earlier. Historically, the number of members elected per constituency has varied from 1 to 5; at present, there is 1 single-member constituency, with the remaining 129 electing between 3 and 5 members each. Following the election of July 6, 1986, the Liberal Democratic Party held 304 seats; the Socialist Party, 86; the Clean Government Party, 57; the Communist Party, 27; the Democratic Socialist Party, 26; the New Liberal Club, 6; the Social Democratic Federation, 4; independents, 2. Upon disbandment of the NLC in August, 5 of its representatives joined the LDP, while one retained his seat as an independent.

Speaker: Kenzaburo HARA.

CABINET

Prime Minister	Noboru Takeshita
Deputy Prime Minister	Kiichi Miyazawa
Ministers	
Agriculture, Forestry and Fisheries	Takashi Sato
Construction	Ihei Ochi
Education	Gentaro Nakajima
Finance	Kiichi Miyazawa
Foreign Affairs	Sosuke Uno
Health and Welfare	Takeo Fujimoto
Home Affairs	Seiroku Kajiyama
International Trade and Industry	Hajime Tamura
Justice	Yukio Hayashida
Labor	Taro Nakamura
Posts and Telecommunications	Masaaki Nakayama
Transport	Shintaro Ishihara
Directors General	
Economic Planning Agency	Eiichi Nakao
Environmental Agency	Toshio Horiuchi
Hokkaido Development Agency	Shigeru Kasuya
Japan Defense Agency	Tsutomu Kawara
Management and Coordination Agency	Osamu Takatori
National Land Agency	Seisuke Okuno
Okinawa Development Agency	Shigeru Kasuya
Science and Technology Agency	Soichiro Ito
Chief Cabinet Secretary	Keizo Obuchi
Governor, Central Bank	Satoshi Sumita

NEWS MEDIA

News media are privately owned and are free from government control.

Press. The Japanese press exerts a strong influence on public policy. The large newspapers publish more than a dozen main editions a day as well as several subeditions, and per capita circulation figures are among the highest in the world. The first three of the following dailies constitute the "big three" national newspapers: *Asahi Shimbun* (Tokyo, Osaka, Nagoya, Sapporo, and Kitakyushu, 11,600,000 morning, 6,700,000 evening), independent; *Yomiuri Shimbun* (Tokyo, Osaka, Takaoka, Kitakyushu, and Sapporo, 8,900,000 morning, 4,800,000 evening), independent; *Mainichi Shimbun* (Tokyo, Osaka, Nagoya, Kitakyushu, and Sapporo, 6,800,000 morning, 3,400,000 evening), independent; *Nihon Keizai Shimbun* (Tokyo, Osaka, Fukuoka, and Sapporo, 2,200,000 morning, 1,800,000 evening), leading economic journal; *Chunichi Shimbun* (Nagoya and Kanazawa, 2,100,000 morning, 800,000 evening), independent; *Sankei Shimbun* (Tokyo and Osaka, 1,992,000 morning, 1,100,000 evening), independent; *Nishi Nippon Shimbun* (Fukuoka, 770,000 morning, 217,000 evening), independent.

News agencies. The leading domestic agencies are the Jiji Press, the Kyodo News Service, and Radiopress, Inc. In addition, some 20 foreign agencies maintain offices at Tokyo and other leading cities.

Radio and television. There are two separate radio and television broadcasting systems. The Japanese Broadcasting Corporation, a public entity operating three nationwide radio networks (one each for general, educational, and FM stereophonic programs) and two nationwide television networks (one general, the other educational), is financed by subscription fees provided for under the Japanese Broadcasting Law. This system supplies over 7,700 stations, which reach approximately 99 percent of the population. In addition, there are more than 130 independent members of the National Association of Commercial Broadcasters in Japan, who operate over 6,300 radio and television stations financed solely through advertising revenues. Multiple ownership of broadcasting companies by a single concern is prohibited. There were approximately 95.0 million radio and 30.3 million television receivers in 1987.

INTERGOVERNMENTAL REPRESENTATION

Ambassador to the US: Nobuo MATSUNAGA.

US Ambassador to Japan: Michael J. MANSFIELD.

Permanent Representative to the UN: Hideo KAGAMI.

IGO Memberships (Non-UN): ADB, ADF, AfDB, BIS, CCC, CP, G10, IADB, IATTC, ICAC, ICCAT, ICO, IEA, ILZ, Inmarsat, INRO, Intelsat, Interpol, ISO, ITC, IWC, IWSG, IWTC, OECD, PCA.

JORDAN

Hashemite Kingdom of Jordan
al-Mamlakah al-Urduniyah al-Hashimiyah

Political Status: Independent constitutional monarchy established May 25, 1946; present constitution adopted January 8, 1952.

Area: 37,737 sq. mi. (97,940 sq. km.), including Israeli-occupied West Bank territory of 2,270 sq. mi. (5,879 sq. km.).

Population: 2,152,273 (1979C), 3,964,000 (1988E). The 1987 figure includes approximately 900,000 under Israeli military control on the West Bank.

Major East Bank Urban Centers (1984E): 'AMMAN (744,000); Zarqa' (255,000).

Official Language: Arabic.

Monetary Unit: Dinar (market rate March 1, 1988, 1 dinar = $2.96US).

Sovereign: King HUSSEIN ibn Talal; proclaimed King on August 11, 1952; crowned May 2, 1953.
 Heir to the Throne: Crown Prince HASAN ibn Talal, brother of the King; designated April 1, 1965.

Prime Minister: Zaid al-RIFA'I; designated by the King upon the resignation of Ahmed 'Abd al-Majid 'OBEIDAT on April 4, 1985.

THE COUNTRY

Jordan, a nearly landlocked kingdom in the heart of the Arab East, is located on a largely elevated, rocky plateau that slopes downward to the Jordan Valley, the Dead Sea, and the Gulf of 'Aqaba. Most of the land is desert, providing the barest grazing for the sheep and goats of Bedouin tribesmen, whose traditional nomadic lifestyle has largely been replaced by village settlement. With Israeli occupation in June 1967 of the territory on the west bank of the Jordan River, the greater part of the country's arable area was lost. The population is mainly Arab, but numerous ethnic groups have intermixed with the indigenous inhabitants. Islam is the state religion, the majority being members of the Sunni sect. Reflecting religious stricture, less than 10 percent of Jordanian women are in the work force, mainly in subsistence activities and trading; over half are illiterate (as compared with 16 percent of men), with the percentage of women enrolled in school dropping dramatically at marriage age. Female representation in government is virtually nonexistent.

Jordan's economy and its political life have been dominated over the past three decades by dislocations and uncertainties stemming from the Arab conflict with Israel. The original East Bank population of some 400,000 was swollen in 1948–1950 by the addition of large numbers of West Bank Palestinian Arabs and refugees from Israel, most of them either settled agriculturalists or townsmen of radically different background and outlook from those of the seminomadic East Bankers. Additional displacements followed the Arab-Israeli War of June 1967. The society has also been strained by a high natural increase in population, rapid urbanization, and the frustrations of the unemployed refugees, many of whom have declined assimilation in the hope of returning to Palestine.

Although it is not an oil-producing country, Jordan was greatly affected by the oil boom of the 1970s and early 1980s. An estimated 350,000 Jordanians, including many professionals trained in one of the most advanced educational systems in the region, took well-paying jobs in wealthy Gulf states, their remittances contributing significantly to the home economy. Lower-paying jobs in Jordan were filled by foreign laborers, primarily Egyptians. However, the recent oil recession has led to the repatriation of many Jordanians in addition to reduced aid from other Arab countries.

Agricultural production is insufficient to feed the population and large quantities of foodstuffs (especially grain) have to be imported, while many of the refugees are dependent on rations distributed by the UN Relief and Works Agency for Palestine Refugees in the Near East (UNRWA). Major exports include phosphates, fruits, and vegetables. Manufacturing is dominated by production of import substitutes — mainly cement, some consumer goods, and processed foods.

GOVERNMENT AND POLITICS

Political background. Carved out of the Ottoman Empire in the aftermath of World War I, the territory then known as Trans-Jordan became a British League of Nations mandate under the rule of the Hashemite Emir 'ABDALLAH. Full independence came when 'Abdallah was proclaimed king and a new constitution was promulgated on May 25, 1946, but special treaty relationships with Britain were continued until 1957. Following the assassination of 'Abdallah in 1951 and the deposition of his son TALAL in 1952, Talal's son HUSSEIN ascended the throne at the age of 16 and was crowned king on May 2, 1953.

Hussein's turbulent reign has been marked by the loss of all territory west of the Jordan River in the 1967 Arab-Israeli War, assassination and coup attempts by more intransigent Arab nationalist elements in Jordan and abroad, and intermittent efforts to achieve a limited *modus vivendi* with Israel. The most serious period of internal tension after the 1967 war stemmed from relations with the Palestinian commando (*fedayeen*) organizations, which began to use Jordanian territory as a base for operations against Israel. In the "black September" of 1970 a virtual civil war broke out between commando and royalist armed forces, the *fedayeen* ultimately being expelled from the country in mid-1971. The expulsion led to the suspension of aid to Jordan by Kuwait and other Arab governments; it was restored following Jordan's nominal participation in the 1973 war against Israel.

In accordance with a decision reached at the October 1974 Arab summit conference at Rabat, Morocco, to recognize the Palestine Liberation Organization as the sole legitimate spokesman for the West Bank Palestinians, King Hussein announced on November 3 that the PLO would henceforth have responsibility for the area, but he stopped short of formally relinquishing his Kingdom's claim to the territory. The Jordanian government was subsequently reorganized to exclude most Palestinian representatives, and the National Assembly on November 9 approved a constitutional amendment authorizing the king to dissolve the lower house and to postpone a new election for as much as a year. In February 1976 the Assembly was briefly reconvened to approve indefinite postponement of the election scheduled for the following March.

In a move toward reconciliation with Palestinian elements, King Hussein met at Cairo in March 1977 with PLO leader Yasir 'ARAFAT, with a subsequent meeting occurring in Jordan immediately after the September 1978 Camp David accords. In March 1979, the two met again near 'Amman and agreed to form a joint committee to coordinate opposition to the Egyptian-Israeli peace treaty, while in December the king named Sharif 'Abd al-Hamid SHARAF to replace Prime Minister Mudar BADRAN as head of a new government that also included six West Bank Palestinians. Sharaf's death on July 3, 1980, resulted in the elevation of Deputy Prime Minister Dr. Qasim al-RIMAWI, whose incumbency ended on August 28 by the reappointment of Badran. Following a breakdown of negotiations with 'Arafat in April 1983 over possible peace talks with Israel and a continued deceleration in economic growth, the king reconvened the National Assembly on January 9, 1984, and secured its assent to the replacement of deceased West Bank deputies in the lower house. The next day the king appointed Interior Minister and former intelligence chief Ahmed 'OBEIDAT to succeed Badran as prime minister in a cabinet reshuffle which increased Palestinian representation to nine members out of 20. Balloting to fill eight unoccupied East Bank seats was conducted on March 12.

Prime Minister 'Obeidat resigned on April 4, 1985, the king naming Zaid al-RIFA'I as his successor.

Constitution and government. Jordan's present constitution, promulgated in 1952, provides for the sharing of authority between the king and a bicameral National Assembly. Executive power is vested in the king, who is also supreme commander of the armed forces. He appoints the prime minister and cabinet; orders general elections; convenes, adjourns, and dissolves the Assembly; and approves and promulgates laws. The Assembly, in joint session, can override his veto of legislation and must also approve all treaties. The judicial system is headed by the High Court of Justice. Lower courts include courts of appeal, courts of first instance, and magistrates' courts. There are also special courts for religious (both Christian and Muslim) and tribal affairs.

In April 1978, during the lengthy legislative recess, the king created by decree a National Consultative Council of 60 appointed members serving two-year terms to advise the prime minister and cabinet, while permitting "citizens to share responsibility" in defining national policy. The Council, renewed in 1980 and 1982, was dissolved by the January 1984 decree that recalled the National Assembly.

Local government administration is now based on the five East Bank provinces (*liwas*) of 'Amman, Irbid, Balqa, Karak, and Ma'n, each headed by a commissioner. The *liwas* are further subdivided into districts (*aqdiyas*) and subdistricts (*nawahin*). The towns and larger villages are governed by municipal councils, while the smaller villages are often governed by traditional village headmen (*mukhtars*).

Foreign relations. Historically reliant on aid from Britain and the United States, Jordan has maintained a generally pro-Western orientation in foreign policy while showing somewhat less intransigence toward Israel than have most of its Arab neighbors. Although PLO inflexibility prompted Hussein's rejection of an Israeli peace initiative in April 1983, talks continued with 'Arafat to establish a basis for future negotiation with the Jewish state until the king announced a break with the PLO leadership in February 1986. Diplomatic relations with Egypt, suspended in 1979 following conclusion of the latter's accord with Israel, were reestablished on September 25, 1984.

Relations with Saudi Arabia and other Middle Eastern monarchies have remained more cordial than have those with such left-wing republics as Libya, primarily because of Jordan's continuing refusal to permit the return of *fedayeen* groups. Relations with Syria have been particularly volatile, a period of reconciliation immediately after the 1967 war deteriorating because of differences over guerrilla activity. In September 1970 a Syrian force that came to the aid of the *fedayeen* against the Jordanian army was repulsed, with diplomatic relations being severed the following July but restored in the wake of the 1973 war. Despite numerous efforts to improve ties, relations deteriorated in the late 1970s and early 1980s, exacerbated by Jordanian support for Iraq in the protracted Gulf war with Iran. A trade and military cooperation agreement signed in September 1984 was immediately threatened by Syria's denunciation of the resumption of relations with Egypt; earlier, on February 22, relations with Libya had been broken because of the destruction of the Jordanian embassy at Tripoli, an action termed by 'Amman as a "premeditated act" by the Qadhafi regime. In September and October, on the other hand, consultation on a variety of Middle Eastern problems was renewed between Jordan and Syria, with relations further enhanced as the result of state visits by Hussein to Damascus in December 1986 and June 1987. The rapprochement with Syria, followed by a resumption of diplomatic relations with Libya in late September, paved the way for a minimum of controversy during a November Arab League summit at 'Amman, which (with neither Libya's Colonel Qadhafi or Saudi Arabia's King Fahd personally in attendance) yielded a unanimous resolution urging support for Iraq and expressing vigorous condemnation of Iran in the Gulf war.

Current issues. In February 1986 King Hussein announced that he had abandoned efforts to reach an agreement with PLO leader Yasir 'Arafat on a possible Middle East peace accord, subsequently closing the offices of *Fatah* and expelling its members from the country. The break with 'Arafat accelerated improved relations with Syria, whose president, Hafiz al-Assad, made a state visit to 'Amman in May. The realignment gained added strength from a US government decision to deny Jordan's request for purchase of an estimated $1.6 billion in fighter planes and antiaircraft equipment; because of the rebuff, Hussein turned to Britain, France, and the Soviet Union to assist in his planned military modernization.

Hostility toward the United States, which increased late in the year with the revelation of covert US sales to Iran, prompted King Hussein to take a more active role in regard to the Palestinian question. Jordan's proposal that a Jordan-Palestinian delegation meet with representatives of Israel, Egypt, Syria, and the five permanent members of the UN Security Council was eventually rejected by both Washington and Tel Aviv after months of negotiation with both European and Arab states. Washington's counter proposal in October 1987, which called for substantially

reduced participation by parties not directly involved in the dispute, was deemed unacceptable by 'Amman, with Hussein stating that his acceptance of a peace conference without the participation of other Arab states would be tantamount to "political suicide". Given the impasse, Jordan quietly shelved plans for a general election that would have yielded representation for both the West Bank and the Palestinian refugee camps.

By early 1988 talks with American special envoy Philip Habib and US Secretary of State George Schultz had been given new urgency by the uprising (*intifadah*) of Palestinians in Israeli-occupied territories. Jordan was hopeful that the unrest would help resolve the peace conference issue, while evidencing concern as to the impact of a more radical Palestinian leadership on its own population.

POLITICAL PARTIES AND GROUPS

Conditions in Jordan have not been favorable to the emergence of strong and stable political parties, which were outlawed prior to the 1963 election. In 1971 an "official" political organization, the Arab National Union (initially known as the Jordanian National Union) was established; it was abolished, however, by legislation approved on February 18, 1976.

Although outlawed in 1957, the small, pro-Moscow **Communist Party of Jordan** (*al-Hizb al-Shuyu'i al-Urduni*) maintains an active organization that supports the establishment of a Palestinian state on the West Bank, where other, smaller Communist groups also continue to operate. About 20 of its leaders, including Secretary General Fa'ik (Fa'iq) WARRAD, were arrested in May 1986 on government charges of "security violations", but released the following September.

The principal Palestinian commando (*fedayeen*) groups were driven from Jordan in 1970–1971, but in 1979 King Hussein agreed to the reopening at 'Amman of an official office of the quasi-governmental **Palestine Liberation Organization** (see segment on the PLO following Zimbabwe entry). In 1986, on the other hand, Hussein ordered the closing of the offices of Fatah, the PLO's large mainstream faction, and the expulsion of its members from Jordan following a rift with PLO leader Yasir 'Arafat (see Current issues, above). Since late 1985 the government has also cracked down on the activities of the **Popular Front for the Liberation of Palestine** (PFLP) and the **Democratic Front for the Liberation of Palestine** (DFLP), both PLO splinter groups (see PLO article). In 1985 the king also ordered the disbanding of the **Muslim Brotherhood** (*al-Ikhwan al-Muslimin*) declaring that it had used bases within Jordan, without his knowledge, to launch attacks within Syria against the government of President Hafiz al-Assad.

LEGISLATURE

The bicameral **National Assembly** (*Majlis al-'Umma*) consists of an appointed Senate (House of Notables) and an elected House of Representatives. Prior to the opening of its most recent sitting on January 9, 1984, the Assembly had not met since convening in extraordinary session in February 1976. A quasi-legislative National Consultative Council of 60 members was appointed by the King in 1978, reappointed in 1980 and 1982 (being increased to 75 members on the latter occasion), and dissolved on January 5, 1984.

House of Notables (*Majlis al-A'yaan*). The upper house currently consists of 30 members appointed by the king from designated categories of public figures, including present and past prime ministers, twice-elected former representatives, former senior judges and diplomats, and retired officers of the rank of general and above. The stated term is four years, although the most recent appointments were made on January 12, 1984. At the next replenishment, the size of the House is to be increased to 71.

President: Ahmad al-LOUZI.

House of Representatives (*Majlis al-Nuwwab*). The lower house presently consists of 60 members (30 from East Jordan and 30 from West Jordan) who, by constitutional prescription, are popularly elected for four-year terms. Most current members, however, were elected in April 1967, with seven vacant West Bank seats filled by appointment on January 18, 1984, and eight vacant East Bank seats filled at a by-election (the first in which women were accorded the franchise) on March 12. In March 1986 the House approved a government measure that at the next general election will raise its membership from 60 to 142, equally divided between the West and East Banks, including, for the first time, 11 representatives elected from within Palestinian refugee camps.

Speaker: Akef al-FAYEZ.

C A B I N E T

Prime Minister	Zaid al-Rifa'i
Deputy Prime Minister	Dhuqan al-Hindawi
Ministers	
Agriculture	Marwan al-Hamud
Culture and National Heritage	Muhammad al-Hammuri
Defense	Zaid al-Rifa'i
Education	Dhuqan al-Hindawi
Energy	Dr. Hisham al-Khatib
Finance	Dr. Hanna 'Odeh
Foreign Affairs	Tahir Nash'at al-Masri
Health	Dr. Zaid Hamzah
Higher Education	Nasir al-Din al-Asad
Industry, Trade and Supply	Hamdi al-Tabba
Information	Hani al-Khasawnah
Interior	Raja'i Dajani
Islamic Affairs, Holy Places and Religious Trusts	'Abd al-'Aziz al-Khayyat
Justice	Riyad al-Shaka'ah
Labor and Social Development	Rashid 'Urayqat
Municipal, Rural and Environmental Affairs	Yusif Hamdan al-Jabir
Occupied Territories' Affairs	Marwan Dudin
Planning	Tahir Kan'an
Public Works and Housing	Shafiq al-Zawayidah
Tourism	Zuhayr al-'Ajluni
Transport and Communications	Khalid al-Haj Hasan
Water and Irrigation	Ahmad Dakhqan
Youth	'Awad Khulayfat
Ministers of State	
Cabinet Affairs	Fayiz al-Tarawnah
Parliamentary Affairs	Dr. Sami Jawdah
Governor, Central Bank	Hussein al-Qasim

N E W S   M E D I A

Press. The press, largely privately owned, is subject to censorship, with publication of most papers having been suspended at various times for printing stories considered objectionable by the government. The following are Arabic dailies published at 'Amman, unless otherwise noted: *al-Ra'i* (Opinion 80,000), independent; *al-Dustur* (The Constitution, 65,000); *Sawt al-Sha'ab* (Voice of the People, 30,000); *al-Akhbar* (News 15,000); *The Jordan Times* (15,000), in English.

News agencies. The domestic facility is the Jordan News Agency (PETRA). *Agence France-Presse,* AP, Reuters, TASS, and UPI are among the foreign bureaus maintaining offices at 'Amman.

Radio and television. Both radio and television are controlled by the government. In 1987 transmissions from the Hashemite Jordan Broadcasting Service were received by 800,000 radio sets, while the Jordan Television Corporation, which provides educational and commercial programs, was received by 250,000 television sets.

INTERGOVERNMENTAL REPRESENTATION

Ambassador to the US: Mohammed KAMAL.

US Ambassador to Jordan: Roscoe Seldon SUDDARTH.

Permanent Representative to the UN: 'Abdallah SALAH.

IGO Memberships (Non-UN): AFESD, AMF, BADEA, CCC, *EIB,* IC, IDB, Intelsat, Interpol, LAS, NAM.

K A M P U C H E A

People's Republic of Kampuchea/Democratic Kampuchea

Sathearanakrath Pracheachon Kampuchea (Khmer)
République Populaire du Kampuchea (French)
Kampuchea Pracheatipateyy (Khmer)
Kampuchea Démocratique (French)

Note: Following the invasion of Kampuchea in late 1978 and the subsequent occupation of most of the country by Vietnamese and dissident Kampuchean forces, a number of pro-Soviet governments recognized the Heng Samrin regime of the People's Republic of Kampuchea, while others continued to recognize the Democratic Kampuchean regime, then headed by Khieu Samphan. A US spokesman stated on January 3, 1979, that "although the United States takes great exception to the human rights record" of Democratic Kampuchea, "as a matter of principle, we do not feel that a unilateral intervention against that regime is justified." The United Nations General Assembly, by substantial majorities, permitted the Democratic Kampuchean representative to retain his seat during the 1979–1987 sessions.

We retain the designation Kampuchea since it is the rendering employed by the United Nations and both of the territory's contending regimes; it should be noted, however, that the U.S. Board on Geographic Names in January 1985 approved changing United States Government usage to the French-derived "Cambodia", a style (preferred by DK leader Sihanouk) to which much of the world's press has also returned.

Political Status: Became independent as the Kingdom of Cambodia on November 9, 1953; Khmer Republic proclaimed October 9, 1970; renamed Democratic Kampuchea by constitution of January 5, 1976, following Communist (*Khmer Rouge*) takeover on April 17, 1975; de jure authority contested by governments of Democratic Kampuchea and the People's Republic of Kampuchea (formed January 8, 1979) following Vietnamese invasion of December 1978.

Area: 69,898 sq. mi. (181,035 sq. km.).

Population: In November 1980, UN officials announced that they would use a population figure of 6,000,000 for relief estimation purposes. Assuming the accuracy of a mid-1974 UN estimate of nearly 8,000,000, the population would appear to have declined by approximately 25 percent (as contrasted with a PRK claim of more than 37 percent) as a result of the mass murders of the *Khmer Rouge* era. On the basis of an official estimate of 7,200,000 in 1984, some subsequent recovery would appear to have occurred.

Major Urban Center (1972E): PHNOM PENH (1,800,000). Following the 1975 Communist takeover, virtually the entire population of the capital was evacuated. The present population of the city is unknown, although substantial reverse migration has occurred since early 1979, some 700,000 inhabitants (many presumed to be Vietnamese) being reported in 1986.

Principal Languages: Khmer, French.

Monetary Unit: Riel. There is virtually no current trading in the riel, which in 1983 circulated at less than $.05 on the black market.

Chairman of the Council of State of the People's Republic of Kampuchea and General Secretary of the Kampuchean People's Revolutionary Party: HENG SAMRIN; named President of the People's Revolutionary Council of the People's Republic of Kampuchea on January 8, 1979; designated Chairman of the Council of State by the PRK National Assembly on June 27, 1981; elected General Secretary by the KPRP Central Committee in succession to PEN SOVAN on December 5, 1981; reelected by the Fifth Party Congress on October 16, 1986.

Chairman of the Council of Ministers of the People's Republic of Kampuchea: HUN SEN; confirmed by the PRK National Assembly on January 14, 1985, in succession to CHAN SI, who died on December 26, 1984.

President of the Coalition Government of Democratic Kampuchea: Prince NORODOM SIHANOUK (Sihanoukist); assumed office upon formation of the CGDK on June 22, 1982; resigned on January 30, 1988, but withdrew the resignation on February 29.

Vice President of the Coalition Government of Democratic Kampuchea: KHIEU SAMPHAN (*Khmer Rouge*); assumed office June 22, 1982.

Prime Minister of the Coalition Government of Democratic Kampuchea: SON SANN (Khmer People's National Liberation Front); assumed office June 22, 1982.

THE COUNTRY

The smallest of the French Indochinese states to which independence was restored in 1953, Kampuchea (formerly Cambodia) is bounded by Thailand on the west and northwest, Laos on the north, and Vietnam on the east and southeast. The southwestern border of the country is an irregular coastline on the Gulf of Thailand. It is a basically homogeneous nation, with Khmers (Cambodians) constituting approximately 85 percent of the total population. Ethnic minorities were estimated in 1970 to include 450,000 Chinese, 400,000 Vietnamese, 80,000 Cham-Malays (Muslims descended from the people of the ancient kingdom of Champa), 50,000 Khmer Loeus (tribals), and 20,000 Thais and Laotians. Many of the Chinese and most Cham-Malays and Vietnamese were reported to have been massacred during the period of *Khmer Rouge* rule; since 1979, on the other hand, there has been substantial (though not wholly voluntary) resettlement by Vietnamese, largely in the Mekong region from Phnom Penh to the southeastern border.

Social cohesion and stability were traditionally derived from a common language (Khmer), a shared sense of national identity, and the pervading influence of Theravada Buddhism, the national religion. About 90 percent of the population has historically professed Buddhism, most of the remainder embracing Islam and Roman Catholicism. However, only a handful of Muslims and Christians are said to have survived the 1975–1979 holocaust. Women have long played a major economic role as agricultural laborers and have also been prominent as local traders; female participation in government is minimal, although a woman, Men Sam-On, was among those named to the KPRP Politburo in October 1985.

Kampuchea's economy is based on agriculture, which in 1984 employed approximately 80 percent of the labor force. The chief foodcrops are rice (accounting for 80 percent of the cultivated area), corn, palm sugar, sugarcane, and tobacco. Although under normal conditions rice is a leading export commodity, production plummeted during the *Khmer Rouge* era and by 1982 the area sown still remained well below the acreage needed for self-sufficiency. Between late 1979 and the end of 1980 an unprecedented $1 billion in foreign relief assistance (about equally divided between Western and Communist sources) was credited with rescuing the Khmer people from near annihilation. Virtually no economic progress has subsequently been reported, UN sources estimating per capita GDP at no more than $80 in late 1987.

GOVERNMENT AND POLITICS

Political background. Increasing pressure from Siam (Thailand) and Vietnam had almost extinguished Cambodian independence prior to the establishment of a French protectorate at the request of King ANG DUONG in 1863. In the early 1940s Japan, in furtherance of its "Greater East Asia Co-prosperity Sphere", seized de facto control of Cambodia. A Thai claim to the western portion of the region had been resisted by the French; however, on the intervention of Japan the provinces of Battambang and Siem Reap were ceded to Thailand, while the French were permitted to retain nominal control in the rest of the country. After the surrender of Japan in World War II, Cambodia was recognized as an autonomous kingdom within the French Union, and the two northwestern provinces were returned by Thailand. In 1949 Cambodia signed an accord with France that brought it into the French Union as an Associated State.

Political feuds within the governing Democratic Party having hampered negotiations with the French, King NORODOM SIHANOUK dissolved the National Assembly in January 1953 and personally negotiated his country's full independence, which was formally announced on November 9. Independence was reinforced by the Geneva Agreement of 1954, which called for the withdrawal from Cambodia of all foreign troops, including Vietminh elements that had entered as a "liberation" force. To enhance his status as national leader, Sihanouk abdicated in 1955 in favor of his father, NORODOM SURAMARIT. Reverting to the title of prince, Sihanouk organized his own mass political movement, the People's Socialist Community, or *Sangkum Reastr Niyum*. In an election held in September 1955, *Sangkum* candidates chosen by Sihanouk won 82 percent of the popular vote and all seats in the National Assembly. Opposed only by the pro-Communist People's Party (*Pracheachon*), the *Sangkum* again captured all 82 Assembly seats in an election held in September 1966. In the latter case the candidates were not handpicked, and the conservative tendencies of the resultant government, headed by (then) Lt. Gen. LON NOL, prompted Sihanouk to set up a "countergovernment" of moderates and leftists to act as an extraparliamentary opposition. Subsequent rivalry between the conservative and radical groups, coupled with a localized revolt in Battambang Province in April 1967 in which Communists played a leading role, led Sihanouk to assume special powers as head of a provisional government in May 1967. The new cabinet resigned in January 1968, and Sihanouk appointed another headed by PENN NOUTH, one of his most trusted and moderate advisers. Penn Nouth resigned in July 1969, and Gen. Lon Nol returned to the premiership. In March 1970, Prince Sihanouk was deposed as head of state, and on October 9 the monarchy was abolished and Cambodia proclaimed the Khmer Republic. An election initially scheduled for the same year was postponed because of military confrontation with the Vietcong and North Vietnamese.

Impelled by a desire to counterbalance charges by Sihanouk (from Chinese exile) of a lack of popular rule, the Lon Nol government, under a new constitution adopted in April 1972, allowed political parties to organize and held a presidential election in the spring of 1972. The balloting, distributed among three candidates, was unexpectedly close, with a final tally on June 4 giving Lon Nol 55 percent of the vote. In a legislative election held in September 1972, however, opposition parties, claiming unfair electoral procedures, declined to participate, and all seats in the Senate and National Assembly fell to the progovernment Social-Republican Party.

During 1974 the four-year war between government forces and the *Khmers Rouges* ("Red Khmers") gained in intensity, and at midyear Lon Nol offered to engage in peace negotiations with the Communist-affiliated National United Front of Cambodia (FUNC), nominally headed by Prince Sihanouk, who promptly rejected the offer in a statement issued at Peking. Following *Khmer Rouge* advances to the vicinity of the capital, on March 22, 1975, Prime Minister LONG BORET presented the president with a request, signed by a number of military and civilian leaders, that he leave the country. On April 10, Lon Nol

flew to Indonesia, the president of the Senate, Maj. Gen. SAUKHAM KHOY, being named interim president of the Republic. Two days later, US Embassy personnel evacuated Phnom Penh. Saukham Khoy having departed with the Americans, a temporary Supreme Committee of the Republic was organized and subsequently surrendered to the FUNC on April 17. The Communist-controlled government that followed included Prince Sihanouk, who was reinstated as head of state, and Penn Nouth, who returned as prime minister.

On December 14, 1975, the FUNK (formerly the FUNC), meeting at Phnom Penh for its third national congress, approved a new constitution which came into effect January 5, 1976. An election of delegates to a new People's Representative Assembly was held on March 20, and on April 2 Prince Sihanouk resigned as head of state, receiving a life pension and the honorary title of "Great Patriot". Subsequently, at its opening session on April 11, the Assembly designated KHIEU SAMPHAN as chairman of the State Presidium and POL POT as prime minister. During its period of rule, the Pol Pot regime launched a massive effort at social change, in the course of which most urban dwellers were forced to relocate in rural areas under conditions of such brutality that at least 2 million are estimated to have perished.

The traditional hostility between the Khmer and Vietnamese peoples reached a climax in late 1978 with an expansion of many months of border conflict into a full-scale invasion by the Vietnamese, supported by a small force of dissident Khmers styling themselves the Kampuchean National United Front for National Salvation (KNUFNS). Phnom Penh fell to the invaders on January 7, 1979, and the establishment of a People's Revolutionary Council under the presidency of HENG SAMRIN, a former assistant chief of the Kampuchean General Staff, was announced the following day. Remnants of the defending forces withdrew to the western part of the country, where guerrilla-type operations against the Vietnamese-supported People's Republic of Kampuchea have since been maintained by the *Khmers Rouges* as well as by right-wing *Khmers Serei* ("Free Cambodians") and smaller units claiming allegiance to Prince Sihanouk.

On June 22, 1982, after more than 18 months of negotiations, the three principal anti-Vietnamese groups concluded an agreement at Kuala Lumpur, Malaysia, on a Coalition Government of Democratic Kampuchea (CGDK). Under the agreement, Prince Sihanouk would serve as president, Khieu Samphan as vice president in charge of foreign affairs, and SON SANN, the *Khmer Serei* leader, as prime minister. It was further agreed that existing diplomatic appointees would, for the time being, retain their assignments, while the *Khmers Rouges* could resume their administration of the government of Democratic Kampuchea if the coalition should prove unworkable.

On December 26, 1984, the chairman of the PRK Council of Ministers, CHAN SI, died of an unidentified ailment in a Moscow hospital, and was succeeded on January 14, 1985, by Vice Chairman and Foreign Minister HUN SEN. A reportedly abrasive former Khmer Rouge official who had defected to the Vietnamese in 1977, Hun Sen was relieved of his foreign affairs post in December 1986, although retaining his ministerial chairmanship as well as his membership in the party Politburo.

Citing continued abuse of refugees by *Khmer Rouge* forces, Prince Sihanouk announced on May 7, 1987, that he was taking a year's "leave of absence" from the CGDK presidency. Subsequently, on January 30, 1988, he formally resigned as nominal leader of the three party coalition after having engaged in two rounds of talks in France with the PRK's Hun Sen (see Current issues, below); however, he withdrew the resignation on February 29, stating that the year-long leave would remain in effect.

Constitution and government. The constitution of Democratic Kampuchea, adopted in January 1976, was effectively abrogated upon the fall of Phnom Penh in early 1979 and the assumption of control over all but a series of western border enclaves by the KNUFNS. Until mid-1981 the KNUFNS (subsequently known as the Kampuchea United Front for National Construction and Development —KUFNCD) governed through a 14-member People's Revolutionary Council headed by Heng Samrin. On May 1, 1981, a 117-member National Assembly was elected which, at its first session on June 24–27, approved a PRK constitution that provided for a Council of State (its chairman serving as head of state) elected from the membership of the Assembly, a Council of Ministers, and a judicial system in which judges would be assisted by people's assessors. In addition, the PRK was divided into provinces (further divided into districts and communes) and municipalities (divided into wards). Direct election was specified for revolutionary committees at the commune and ward levels, with committees at higher levels elected by representatives at the next lowest levels.

The Kuala Lumpur agreement establishing a rival Coalition Government of Democratic Kampuchea provided for an "inner cabinet" comprising Prince Sihanouk, Khieu Samphan, and Son Sann, in addition to four "coordinating committees" dealing with Culture and Education, Economy and Finance, National Defense, and Public Health and Social Affairs, on each of which the Sihanoukists, the *Khmers Rouges,* and the political affiliate of Son Sann's *Khmer Serei,* the Khmer People's National Liberation Front (KPNLF), were accorded equal representation. [The impact of Sihanouk's withdrawal on these arrangements was unclear as this edition of the *Handbook* went to press.]

Foreign relations. By late 1980, some 30 governments had recognized the PRK, although India, on July 7, was the only major non-Communist country to do so. The Association of Southeast Asian Nations (ASEAN), which had earlier condemned Vietnam's "aggression" in Kampuchea, immediately issued a statement deploring New Delhi's "untimely decision".

In October 1980, the UN General Assembly, by an overwhelming majority, approved an ASEAN-sponsored resolution calling for an international conference to arrange for a phased withdrawal of Vietnamese forces and the holding of UN-supervised free elections. The resultant International Conference on Kampuchea that convened at New York in July 1981 was attended by delegates from 94 countries, although the Soviet Union, Vietnam, Laos, and a number of nonaligned countries, including India, refused

to participate. Because of the boycott, little was achieved beyond reaffirmation of the Assembly's previously stated goals. Subsequent Indochinese summit conferences attended by the foreign ministers of Vietnam, Laos, and the PRK expressly rejected the ICK agenda, proposing instead a gradual withdrawal over a ten-year period. Support for the ASEAN position within the United Nations has, however, marginally increased, the 1987 bellwether vote being 117-21-16, with the General Assembly continuing to recognize the delegation from Democratic Kampuchea. By contrast, the Nonaligned Movement has maintained an "open chair" policy, refusing to seat representatives of either Kampuchean regime during its three most recent summits (1979, 1983, and 1986).

The ASEAN country most directly affected by events in Kampuchea—and the one most deeply opposed to recognition of the PRK—is Thailand, whose eastern region has provided sanctuary for some 250,000 Khmer refugees. In March 1980 an overture from Phnom Penh to engage in bilateral talks on the refugee issue was rebuffed by Bangkok as a maneuver to obtain de facto recognition. Subsequently, Thai authorities refused offers from Phnom Penh to negotiate a border security agreement without a Vietnamese withdrawal.

An unusually intense dry season offensive by Vietnamese and PRK forces in 1984–1985 involved over 80 incursions into Thai territory and left most major CGDK border camps either destroyed or badly damaged. Immediately thereafter, PRK troops and conscript civilian labor began fortifying the border with trenches, barbed wire, and land mines. The result was a near-doubling of the civilian refugee population on both sides of the border, and in January 1987, following a split between UN Secretary General Pérez de Cuéllar and donor governments over administration of the multi-million-dollar UN Border Relief Operation (UNBRO), Bangkok announced that it would close its sprawling Khao I Dang refugee camp to stem the influx of Khmers into its territory.

Current issues. During 1987, the ninth year of Vietnam's military involvement in Kampuchea, a number of initiatives, centering largely on Prince Sihanouk, offered a glimmer of hope that an accommodation could be found between the PRK regime at Phnom Penh and the guerrilla factions that continued in uneasy coalition along the Thai border. In May, Sihanouk implicitly distanced himself from his Chinese patrons by citing continued *Khmer Rouge* human rights abuses as prompting his projected year-long "leave of absence" from the CGDK presidency. However, the action was interpreted primarily as an effort to increase his bargaining position at a December meeting, outside Paris, France, with the PRK's Hun Sen. While the meeting itself was considered a milestone, the two leaders agreed on virtually nothing. Sihanouk was reportedly prepared to split with his CGDK associates and enter into a provisional government with PRK, but the latter refused to dissolve itself as a precondition, insisting, instead, that no progress was possible until the *Khmer Rouge* units had been disbanded. Nor could the two parties agree on whether a Vietnamese troop withdrawal should be completed before the new government could be formed. Significantly, with an apparent eye toward Beijing, Sihanouk referred to problems with the non-Communist KPLNF, rather than with the *Khmers Rouges,* as precipitating his month-long withdrawal as CGDK president in early 1988.

POLITICAL AND GUERRILLA GROUPS

People's Republic of Kampuchea:

Kampuchean United Front for National Construction and Defense (KUFNCD). The KUFNCD was organized initially as the Kampuchean National United Front for National Salvation (KNUFNS) in December 1978 by Khmer opponents of the Democratic Kampuchea regime. Four of the 14 members of its Central Committee were included in the People's Revolutionary Council established as a provisional government at Phnom Penh on January 8, 1979. During its Second Congress, held at Phnom Penh on September 29–30, 1979, the Front elected a new Central Committee of 35 members, including all of the original 14. The organization adopted its present name at its Third Congress, which was attended by 430 delegates at Phnom Penh on December 20–22, 1981. A declaration adopted at the 1981 session identified the Kampuchean People's Revolutionary Party (below) as the Front's "leading nucleus".

Leaders: CHEA SIM (Chairman, National Council), HENG SAMRIN (Chairman, Presidium), YOS POR (Secretary General).

Kampuchean People's Revolutionary Party (KPRP). The KPRP was founded in early 1951, when the Indo-Chinese Communist Party, led by Ho Chi Minh, was divided into separate entities for Cambodia, Laos, and Vietnam. Following the 1954 Geneva Agreement, it was composed of three factions: a group called the *Khmer Vietminh,* which was controlled largely by North Vietnamese; an underground force that served as the ideological core of the *Khmers Rouges;* and adherents of the People's Party (*Pracheachon*), which operated legally in Cambodia. At its Second Congress, held secretly at Phnom Penh in 1960, the organization changed its name to the Communist Party of Kampuchea (PCK) but continued to be divided, largely between supporters of the North Vietnamese and a Maoist contingent led by Pol Pot (then known as Saloth Sar). In 1962 the incumbent PCK general secretary was assassinated, allegedly on order of Pol Pot, who assumed the general secretaryship the following year. The two factions were nominally reunited during 1970–1975, although most pro-Vietnamese went into exile in the wake of a purge that commenced in 1974. Following the overthrow of the *Khmer Rouge* government in 1979, the Hanoi-supported exiles staged a "reorganization Congress" at which Pen Sovan was elected general secretary and the KPRP label was readopted to distinguish the Phnom Penh group from the *Khmer Rouge* faction that continued to be led by Pol Pot until its formal dissolution on December 6, 1981. Two days earlier, on December 4, the KPRP Central Committee, in what appeared to be the outcome of a power struggle, elected Heng Samrin as its general secretary so that Pen Sovan could "take a long rest in order to recover from illness". The fifth KPRP congress on October 13–16, 1985, yielded a Politburo shakeup and a doubling of the Central Committee to 45 members (including 14 candidates), most of the new appointees being from younger, more "technocratic" cadres than their older, military counterparts.

General Secretary: HENG SAMRIN (Chairman, PRK Council of State).

Other Members of Politburo: BOU THANG (Deputy Chairman, Council of Ministers), CHEA SIM (Chairman, National Assembly and KUFNCD), CHEA SOTH (Deputy Chairman, Council of Ministers), HUN SEN (Chairman, Council of Ministers), MAT LY (Chairman, Kampuchean Federation of Trade Unions), MEN SAM-ON (Chief, KPRP Propaganda and Training Commission), NEY PENA (First Deputy Minister of Interior), SAY PHUTHANG (Chairman, KPRP Central Control Commission).

Alternates: CHAN SENG, NGUON NHEL.

Central Committee Secretariat: BOU THANG, HENG SAMRIN, HUN SEN, MEN SAM-ON, NEY PENA.

Coalition Government of Democratic Kampuchea:

Red Khmers (*Khmers Rouges*). The *Khmers Rouges* originated as the military arm of the Communist Party of Kampuchea (*Parti Communiste du Kampuchea — PCK/Kanapak Kumunist Kampuchea*) that ruled the country from 1975 to 1979, when it was ousted by Vietnamese forces that subsequently installed the Heng Samrin regime. In December 1981, the PCK was declared to have been dissolved, the *Khmers Rouges* joining with the non-Communist KPLNF and Sihanoukist forces (below) in CGDK guerrilla actions against the new government at Phnom Penh from bases in western Kampuchea. Although former DK prime minister Pol Pot was officially replaced as Khmer Rouge military commander by Son Sen in mid-1985, he is believed by some to have retained significant military and political influence. During 1985–1986, the *Khmers Rouges,* like the other two CGDK formations, experienced factionalism over the issue of military cooperation with coalition partners: Khieu Samphan-led units conducted joint operations with the KPNLAF (below), while Pol Pot loyalists, in particular Chhit Choeun (also known as Ta Mok), engaged in gun battles with elements of other CGDK armies. On the political front, the CGDK image has been tarnished by reports of human rights abuses in *Khmer Rouge*-controlled areas, while the faction's adoption, in mid-1985, of a "new ideology of democratic socialism" was received with skepticism. The *Khmers Rouges* have been the principal beneficiaries of Chinese military and other assistance to the CGDK.

Leaders: KHIEU SAMPHAN (CGDK Vice President), POL POT (former DK Prime Minister), IENG SARY (former DK Deputy Prime Minister for Foreign Affairs), SON SEN (Military Commander).

Khmer People's National Liberation Armed Forces (KPNLAF). The KPNLAF is the military wing of the *Khmer Serei* **Khmer People's National Liberation Front,** which has achieved prominence as the strongest non-Communist faction of the CGDK, with a proclaimed fighting force of 16–20,000 men, and is the primary recipient of ASEAN and US aid. However, factional infighting and the Vietnamese-PRK dry-season offensive of 1984–1985 substantially weakened the group's effectiveness. Moves in 1985 toward formation of a joint military command with Sihanoukist forces (below) were emphatically rejected by the KPNLAF's longtime leader, Son Sann, and by year's end Son Sann loyalists had expelled two pro-merger colleagues, who formed a "Provisional Committee for the Salvation of the KPLNF" in cooperation with KPNLAF military commander Sak Sutsakhan. By March 1986, both groups were claiming control of the formation, which, in the interim, was reported to have lost some 5,000 men.

Leaders: SON SANN (CGDK Prime Minister); PRUM VIT, CHEA CHHUT, KEO CHAN (loyalist group); Gen. SAK SUTSAKHAN, DIEN DEL, Abdul Gaffar PEANG METH, HING KUTHON (Provisional Committee).

Sihanoukist National Army (*Armée Nationale Sihanoukiste* — ANS). The ANS, with a fighting strength of 7–8,000 and a substantial civilian support base, is a successor to earlier pro-Sihanouk groups, such as In Skhan's National Liberation Front (FLN) and the National Liberation Movement of Kampuchea (Moulinaka), led by current Son Sann supporter Chea Chhut. Although more cohesive than the other two CGDK formations, the ANS suffered an internal shakeup in July 1985, when Sihanouk dismissed military commander Teap Ben for "corruption and incompetence" and appointed his son, Prince Norodom Rannarith, as successor. Long before Sihanouk's January 1988 resignation as CGDK president, the PRK had consistently attempted to win him and his supporters away from their alliance with the *Khmers Rouges.* Despite his withdrawal as president, the former monarch indicated that the ANS would remain within CGDK coalition.

Leaders: Prince NORODOM SIHANOUK (CGDK President), Prince NORODOM RANNARITH (Military Commander).

LEGISLATURE

A unicameral People's Representative Assembly of 250 members was elected, under Democratic Kampuchean auspices, on March 20, 1976. It has not met since the Vietnamese invasion of December 1978. Balloting for a PRK **National Assembly** was conducted on May 1, 1981, a total of 117 deputies being elected from 148 candidates advanced by the KNUFNS. Under the PRK constitution, the legislative term is five-years; however, in February 1986 the Assembly formally postponed the next general election until 1991.

National Assembly Chairman: CHEA SIM.

CABINETS

People's Republic of Kampuchea

Chairman, Council of Ministers	Hun Sen
Deputy Chairmen	Bou Thang
	Chea Soth
Director of the Cabinet	Ung Phan

Ministers

Agriculture	Say Chhum
Communication, Transport and	
Posts	Tea Banh
Defense	Koy Buntha
Economic and Cultural	
Cooperation with Foreign	
Countries	Taing Sarim
Education	Pen Navouth
Finance	Chhay Than
Foreign Affairs	Kong Korm
Health	Dr. Yit Kim Seng
Industry	Meas Samnang
Information, Press and Culture	Chheng Phon
Interior	Ney Pena
Justice	Ouk Bun Choeun
Planning	Chea Chanto
Social Welfare and Veterans	Sar Bun
State Affairs	Sin Song
Trade	Ho Noan
Without Portfolio	Khun Chhy
	Kong Samol
Attorney General	Chan Min
Cabinet Director	Ung Phan
Chairman, National Bank of	
Kampuchea	Cha Rieng

Coalition Government of Democratic Kampuchea

President	Prince Norodom Sihanouk
Vice President in Charge	Khieu Samphan
of Foreign Affairs	*(Khmer Rouge)*
Prime Minister	Son Sann (KPNLF)

Coordinating Committeemen

Culture and Education	Chak Saroeun (Sihanoukist)
	Chhoy Vi (KPNLF)
	Thuch Rin *(Khmer Rouge)*
Economy and Finance	Buon Say (KPNLF)
	Buor Hell (Sihanoukist)
	Ieng Sary *(Khmer Rouge)*
Military Affairs	Ea Chuor King Meng (KPLNF)
	Hul Sakada (Sihanoukist)
	Long Don (Khmer Rouge)
National Defense	Norodom Chakrapong (Sihanoukist)
	Sak Sutsakhan (KPNLF)
	Son Sen *(Khmer Rouge)*
Press and Information	
Affairs	Meak Lanh (KPLNF)
	Peth Bounreth (Khmer Rouge)
	Troung Mealy (Sihanoukist)
Public Health and	Bou Kheng (KPLNF)
Social Affairs	Khek Vandy
	(Sihanoukist)
	Thiounn Thioeun *(Khmer Rouge)*

NEWS MEDIA

Press. The following newspapers circulate at Phnom Penh: *Pracheachon* (The People, 45,000), KPRP weekly; *Kampuchea* (40,000); *Kaset Kangtoap Padivoat* (Revolutionary Army); *Moha Samakki Kraom Tong Ranakse* (Great Solidarity under the Front Banner).

News agency. A Kampuchea Information Agency (*Saporamean Kampuchea*) was established by the KNUFNS in late 1978.

Radio and television. The Voice of the Kampuchean People (*Samleng Pracheachon Kampuchea*) transmits by radio from Phnom Penh on behalf of the People's Republic; limited television service was initiated in 1984. A clandestine Voice of Democratic Kampuchea (*Samleng Kampuchea Pracheatipathay*) is also in operation. There were approximately 30,000 television receivers in 1987.

INTERGOVERNMENTAL REPRESENTATION

As of June 1, 1987, the United States had not established formal diplomatic relations with either Democratic Kampuchea or the People's Republic of Kampuchea, while the United Nations continued to recognize the former.

Democratic Kampuchean Representative to the UN: THIOUNN PRASITH.

IGO Memberships (Non-UN): ADB, CP, Interpol, NAM, PCA.

KENYA

Republic of Kenya
Djumhuri ya Kenya

Political Status: Independent member of the Commonwealth since December 12, 1963; republic established in 1964; de facto one-party system, established in 1969, recognized as de jure by constitutional amendment on June 9, 1982.

Area: 224,960 sq. mi. (582,646 sq. km.).

Population: 15,332,000 (1979C), 22,924,000 (1988E).

Major Urban Centers (1984E): NAIROBI (urban area, 1,103,000); Mombasa (450,000).

Official Language: Kiswahili (English is widely spoken and was the official language until 1974).

Monetary Unit: Kenya Shilling (market rate March 1, 1988, 17.16 shillings = $1US).

President: Daniel Teroitich arap MOI; became Acting President upon the death of Jomo KENYATTA on August 22, 1978; designated President on October 10 and inaugurated to fill the remaining year of Kenyatta's term on October 14, following uncontested nomination by the Kenya African National Union; named to a regular five-year term in November 1979; unopposed for redesignation in 1983 and on February 27, 1988.

Vice President: Dr. Josephat KARANJA; appointed by the President on March 24, 1988, to succeed Mwai KIBAKI.

THE COUNTRY

An equatorial country on the African east coast, Kenya has long been celebrated for its wildlife and such scenic attractions as the Rift Valley. The northern part of the country is virtually waterless, and 85 percent of the population and most economic enterprises are concentrated in the southern highlands bordering on Tanzania and Lake Victoria. The African population, mainly engaged in agriculture and stock-raising, embraces four main ethnic groups: Bantu (Kikuyu, Kamba), Nilotic (Luo), Nilo-Hamitic (Masai), and Hamitic (Somali). Non-African minorities include Europeans, Asians (mainly Indians and Pakistanis), and Arabs. In addition to Kiswahili and English, the most important languages are Kikuyu, Luo, and Somali. The majority of the people is Christian (mostly Protestant), but approximately 35 percent adheres to traditional religious beliefs; there is also a small Muslim minority.

With few known mineral resources, Kenya has remained a largely agricultural country despite the fact that only 12 percent of its land area is suited to intensive cultivation. The leading activity is subsistence agriculture, some 60–80 percent of the output being produced by women. The main cash crops are coffee, tea, sisal, pyrethrum, and sugar. Wheat, maize, and livestock are also produced, largely for domestic consumption. The manufacturing sector has been growing; important industries include food processing, the production of textiles and clothing, and oil refining. In addition, tourism continues to play an important part in the economy.

In recent years, Kenya has been subject to economic pressures, caused in part by drought and fluctuating fuel costs, necessitating financial assistance from the International Monetary Fund and the World Bank, in addition to food aid from a variety of UN agencies. The economy is further strained by the world's highest rate of natural population increase (currently estimated at more than 4 percent annually).

GOVERNMENT AND POLITICS

Political background. Kenya came under British control in the late nineteenth century and was organized in 1920 as a colony (inland) and a protectorate (along the coast). Political development after World War II was impeded by the Mau Mau uprising of 1952–1956, which was inspired primarily by Kikuyu resentment of the fact that much of the country's best land was controlled by Europeans. Further difficulties arose in the early 1960s because of tribal and political rivalries, which delayed agreement on a constitution and postponed the date of formal independence within the Commonwealth until December 12, 1963. An election held in May 1963 had already established the predominant position of the Kenya African National Union (KANU), led by Jomo KENYATTA of the Kikuyu tribe, who had previously been imprisoned and exiled on suspicion of leading the Mau Mau insurgency. Kenyatta accordingly became the country's first prime minister and subsequently, upon the adoption of a republican form of government on December 12, 1964, its first president. The principal opposition party, the Kenya African Democratic Union (KADU), dissolved itself and merged with KANU in 1964. However, a new opposition party, the Kenya Peo-

ple's Union (KPU), made its appearance in 1966 under the leadership of the leftist Ajuma Oginga ODINGA, whose forced resignation as vice president in April 1966 caused a minor split in the ruling party and led to a special election in which the new group won limited parliamentary representation.

In mid-1969 Tom J. MBOYA, the Luo secretary general of KANU and the expected successor to Kenyatta, was assassinated, generating a period of civil strife and the proscription of the KPU, several of whose leaders, including Odinga, were detained. Opposition to the Kenyatta regime continued into the 1970s, however, with a plot to overthrow the government being reported in 1971.

Both President Kenyatta and Vice President Daniel T. arap MOI, a member of the minority Kalenjin tribe, were unopposed for reelection in September 1974, but balloting held the next month repeated the outcome of the 1969 National Assembly election: although only KANU-endorsed candidates were allowed to contest seats, a substantial proportion of incumbent MPs, including several ministers, were defeated. Another political crisis occurred the following March, when Josiah Mwangi KARIUKI, leader of the unofficial parliamentary opposition, was assassinated, with a number of Kenyatta opponents subsequently being detained.

Kenyatta died on August 22, 1978, and was immediately succeeded, on an interim basis, by Moi, who, as the sole KANU candidate, was declared president on October 10 to fill the remainder of Kenyatta's five-year term. Two months later, the government announced a release of political detainees, several of whom were named to high administrative positions following President Moi's election to a full term on November 8, 1979. The concurrent National Assembly election saw nearly 750 candidates compete for 158 elective seats, with almost half the incumbents, including 7 cabinet ministers, being defeated.

A veneer of apparent stability was shattered with an attempted coup by members of the Kenyan Air Force on August 1, 1982. The rebellion was quickly crushed by loyal military and paramilitary units, and on August 21 the government announced the disbanding of the existing Air Force of some 2,100 individuals, approximately 650 of whom were subsequently convicted of mutiny. Earlier, a number of prominent members of the Luo community, including Raila ODINGA, son of the former vice president, had been arrested and charged with treason. Although many, including Odinga, were later released, trials continued well into 1983, accompanied by an atmosphere of suspicion culminating in the "traitor affair" of May 1983, in which unspecified charges by Moi led to the dismissal of Constitutional Affairs Minister Charles NJONJO, the dissolution of the National Assembly on July 22, and the calling of a premature general election. In the balloting of September 26, 1983, Moi was returned, unopposed, to the National Assembly, having previously been declared KANU's sole candidate for the presidency. Thereafter, he dealt harshly with rebel leaders, 12 of whom were executed in 1985. In 1987 Moi declared that the party had become "paramount" to the Assembly, amid charges that efforts to stifle dissent in both organizations were effectively prompting growth in political opposition (see Current issues, below).

Constitution and government. The 1963 constitution has been amended several times, mainly in the direction of increased centralization and the abrogation of checks and balances that were originally introduced on the insistence of the tribal and party opposition. The president, in addition to the vice president and all cabinet members, must be a member of the National Assembly. Originally designated by the Assembly, he is now popularly elected for a five-year term. In case of a presidential vacancy, the vice president (a presidential appointee) serves pending a new election, which must be held within 90 days. The National Assembly, initially bicameral in form, was reduced to a single chamber in 1967 by merger of the earlier Senate and House of Representatives. The president can dissolve the body and call a new election; a nonconfidence vote also results in dissolution, with both presidential and legislative balloting mandated within 90 days. The judicial system is headed by the Kenya Court of Appeal and includes the High Court of Kenya, provincial and district magistrates' courts, and Muslim courts at the district level.

Administratively, Kenya is divided into 40 rural districts grouped into 7 provinces, exclusive of the Nairobi Extra Provincial District, which comprises the Nairobi urban area.

Foreign relations. Generally avoiding involvement in "big power" politics, Kenya has devoted its primary attention to continental affairs, supporting African unity and liberation movements in southern Africa. Regionally, it once worked closely with Tanzania and Uganda, joining with them to establish the East African Community (EAC) in 1967. However, ideological differences with socialist Tanzania and a variety of disputes with Uganda long inhibited the operation of common services, and the Community was formally terminated in mid-1977. Final agreement on the distribution of EAC assets was reached on November 17, 1983, and the Kenya-Tanzania border (closed since 1977) was reopened the same day; relations with Dar es Salaam were further stabilized by the reestablishment of diplomatic relations in December. Relations with Uganda also improved in the immediate wake of the November 17 agreement, although new tensions arose in 1986, with each country accusing the other of harboring insurgents. The mutual hostility continued through most of 1987, culminating in a three-day border clash in mid-December. Kenya thereupon ordered the expulsion of the Ugandan high commissioner and closure of the Libyan embassy at Nairobi on the ground that Tripoli was using Uganda to undermine the Moi regime. The situation eased, however, as the result of a hastily called border meeting between presidents Moi and Musevini at the end of the month.

Kenyan-Somali relations have been frequently strained by the activities of nomadic Somali tribesmen (*shiftas*) in Kenya's northeastern provinces and by long-standing Somalian irredentist claims (see map, p. 185). They reached a nadir in mid-1977 with the outbreak of hostilities between Somalia and Ethiopia in the latter's Ogaden region, a Kenyan spokesman declaring that an Ethiopian victory would be "a victory for Kenya". It was not until July 1984 that President Moi paid his first state visit to Mogadishu, in the course of which an agreement was concluded on border claims and trade cooperation, with Moi offering

to help Somalian President Siad Barre "find a peaceful solution" to the dispute with Addis Ababa. The following September, several hundred ethnic Somali members of an exile group, the Northern Frontier District Liberation Front (NFDLF), responded to a government amnesty and returned to Kenya, declaring that the organization's headquarters at Mogadishu, Somalia, had been closed. Subsequently, in early December, Kenyan and Somalian representatives concluded a border security agreement, while other top *shifta* leaders responded to a second general amnesty in July 1985, declaring an end to the years of "banditry".

In June 1980, Kenya and the United States initialed an agreement that allowed US forces access to Kenyan air and naval facilities, particularly at Mombasa, in exchange for greatly increased military and economic aid. Subsequently, while maintaining the OAU line on most regional and global affairs, including the Middle East question, Nairobi quietly sought Israeli financial and technical assistance for rural development projects, in an effort to combat drought and rising unemployment.

Current issues. In early 1986 the government launched a crackdown on dissidents, especially pamphleteering supporters of the Mwakenya movement (see Political Parties, below). Despite the arrest of more than 100 persons, the campaign failed to stifle opposition, generating instead persistent accusations of human rights abuses. Initially perceived as having little mass support, the anti-Moi movement by late 1987 was considered a genuine threat to the stability of the government. Underlying some of the foment was resentment by Kikuyu tribesmen of the political ascendancy of Moi's numerically inferior Kalenjin group. Other factors included enhanced presidential power and evidence that members of the political elite had amassed large fortunes despite deepening national poverty.

As the only candidate presented by the ruling Kenya African National Union on February 27, 1988, President Moi was declared reelected without the formality of a public vote. Earlier, on February 22, primaries were held to select candidates for legislative balloting on March 21. While the latter poll was conducted by secret ballot, as mandated by the constitution, candidate selection was by means of open queuing (see Legislature, below). Subsequently, Moi indicated that the constitution would be amended to abolish the secret ballot on the ground that the open queuing procedure "enhances peace and not corruption"; opponents, on the other hand, argued that the change would replace democracy "with totalitarianism and autocracy".

POLITICAL PARTIES

The ruling Kenya African National Union (KANU) dominates both the government structure and political life. KANU's principal rival, the Kenya People's Union (KPU), was proscribed in 1969, although a one-party system was not formally mandated until June 1982.

Kenya African National Union (KANU). Originally drawing most of its support from Kenya's large Kikuyu and Luo tribes, KANU was formed in 1960, established its leading position at the election of May

1963, and subsequently broadened its constituency through the absorption of the Kenya African Democratic Union (KADU) and the African People's Party (APP), both supported by smaller tribes. KANU principles include "African Socialism", centralized government, racial harmony, and "positive nonalignment". In September 1984 President Moi announced that all civil service positions would thereafter be filled by party members and, on July 1, 1985, that a KANU "disciplinary committee" had been formed to ensure adherence to the party line. On July 2, at the party's first national election in 7 years, a number of longtime KANU leaders, including both the national chairman and the secretary general, lost their positions, thus solidifying Moi's control over the party apparatus.

Leaders: Daniel T. arap MOI (President of the Republic and of the Party), David Okiki AMAYO (National Chairman), Barudi NABWERA (Secretary General).

Illegal Opposition:

Union of Nationalists to Liberate Kenya (*Muungano wa Wazalendo wa Kukomboa Kenya*—Mwakenya). Although reportedly active since 1983, in part as a carryover of the 1982 coup attempt, supporters of Mwakenya did not emerge as active opponents of the Moi government until early 1986 when they became the primary targets of a government crackdown on dissent. By late 1987 growing support was reported both among intellectuals aiming to establish a socialist system as well as ethnic groups, including Kikuyu farmers, opposed to Moi but not necessarily committed to changing the country's capitalist orientation. Some observers estimate that the movement has attracted hundreds of thousands of sympathizers in its campaign to eliminate the corruption and civil rights abuses attributed to the incumbent administration. However, firm information on membership and leadership has proven elusive because of Mwakenya's use of forest meetings, blood oaths, and a highly secret "cell" structure seemingly derived from the Mau Mau insurgency of the 1950s.

Exile Opposition:

Movement for Unity and Democracy in Kenya (Ukenya). Ukenya was launched in February 1987 by a number of London-based Kenyans who accused the Moi government of the arrest and torture of hundreds of Kenyan peasants, workers, and intellectuals. Calling for an end to "many years of oppression", the group indicated that it would attempt to establish domestic links with Mwakenya adherents.

Leader: Yussuf HASSAN (Chairman).

LEGISLATURE

The unicameral **National Assembly** currently consists of 188 members elected by universal suffrage for five-year terms. At present, candidates are selected by open queuing behind photographs of nominees approved by the Kenya African National Union. Those receiving at least 70 percent of the primary vote are unopposed in the general election, which is by secret ballot. The most recent poll was on March 21, 1988, with only 127 of the seats being contested.

Speaker: F.M.G. MATI.

CABINET

[as of March 24, 1988]

President	Daniel T. arap Moi
Vice President in Charge of Home Affairs and National Heritage	Dr. Josephat Karanja
Ministers	
Agriculture	Elijah W. Mwangale
Commerce	K.K. arap Sego
Cooperative Development	Noah Katanga Ngala
Culture and Social Services	Paul J. Ngei
Energy	Nicholas Kiprono Biwott
Environment and Natural Resources	Jeremiah J. Nyagah
Finance	George Saitoti
Foreign Affairs	Dr. Robert J. Ouko
Health	Mwai Kibaki
Home Affairs	Mwai Kibaki
Industry	Dr. W. Koinage
Labor	Peter H. Okondo
Lands and Housing	Darius Mbela
Local Government and Physical Planning	Moses B. Mudavadi
Manpower Development and Employment	A.K. Magugu
National Guidance and Political Affairs	J.G. Kiti
Planning and National Development	Dr. Zachary Onyonka
President's Office	Jackson Angaine
	L. Kitele
	Hussein Maalim Muhammad
	B. Nabwera
Public Works	J.K. Koech
Regional Development	D. Mboya
Research, Science and Technology	Sospeter Arasa
Supply and Marketing	Richard Adero
Technical Training and Applied Technology	N.E. Hiribae
Tourism and Wildlife	G.K. Muholo
Transport and Communications	Kenneth Matiba
Water Development	D. Ndolo Ayah
Attorney General	Matthew Guy Muli
Governor, Central Bank	Philip Ndegwa

NEWS MEDIA

Freedom of the press prevails in principle; broadcasting is a government monopoly.

Press. Newspapers are privately owned and many are financially controlled by Europeans. There is no official censorship, but an unwritten set of rules bars criticism of the government and its policies, and of Black nationalism, by the White press. In addition, foreign newsmen have been threatened with expulsion if they file stories that the government finds offensive. The following are English-language dailies published at Nairobi, unless otherwise noted: *Nation* (147,000 daily, 145,000 Sunday), independent; *Taifa Leo* (59,000), in Kiswahili; *The Standard* (40,000 daily, 45,000 Sunday), moderate; *Kenya Times* (30,000), KANU organ; *Chemsha Bongo* (30,000), weekly, in Kiswahili.

News agencies. The domestic facility is the Kenya News Agency; a number of foreign agencies also maintain bureaus at Nairobi.

Radio and television. The Voice of Kenya is the national radio broadcasting agency, while the Voice of Kenya Television operates over an area extending from Nairobi to Kisumu, as well as from the coastal city of Mombasa. Both are under the control of the Ministry of Information and Broadcasting. There were approximately 700,000 radio and 193,000 television receivers in 1987.

INTERGOVERNMENTAL REPRESENTATION

Ambassador to the US: Dennis Daudi AFANDE.

US Ambassador to Kenya: Elinor Greer CONSTABLE.

Permanent Representative to the UN: Raphael Muli KIILU.

IGO Memberships (Non-UN): ADF, AfDB, BADEA, CCC, CWTH, EADB, EEC(L), *EIB,* IACO, ICO, Intelsat, Interpol, ISO, ITPA, IWC, IWTC, NAM, OAU.

KIRIBATI

Republic of Kiribati

Political Status: Formerly the Gilbert Islands; became a British protectorate in 1892; annexed as the Gilbert and Ellice Islands Colony in 1915, the Ellice Islands becoming independent as the state of Tuvalu in 1978; present name adopted upon becoming an independent member of the Commonwealth on July 12, 1979.

Area: 335 sq. mi. (868 sq. km.).

Population: 63,848 (1985C), 67,000 (1988E).

Major Urban Center (1985C): BAIRIKI (Tarawa, 21,393).

Official Languages: English, Gilbertese.

Monetary Unit: Australian Dollar (market rate March 1, 1988, 1.39 dollars = $1US). The British Pound is also in circulation.

President (*Beretitenti*): Ieremia T. TABAI; assumed office upon independence; reelected on May 4, 1982; resigned following legislative vote of no confidence on December 10, 1982; reelected on February 17, 1983, succeeding interim Council of State chaired by Rota ONARIO, and on May 12, 1987.

Vice President (*Kauoman-ni-Beretitenti*): Teatao TEAN-NAKI; appointed by the President on July 20, 1979; reappointed in May 1982; left office upon fall of government on December 10; reappointed by the President in 1983 and on May 19, 1987.

THE COUNTRY

Apart from Ocean Island (Banaba) in the west, Kiribati consists of three widely dispersed island groups scattered over 2 million square miles of the central Pacific Ocean: the Gilbert Islands on the equator; the Phoenix Islands to the southeast; and the Line Islands still farther east, and north of the equator. The Gilbert group comprises Abaiang, Abemama, Aranuka, Arorae, Beru, Butaritari, Kuria, Maiana, Makin, Marakei, Nicunau, Nonouti, Onotoa, Tabiteuca, Tamana, and Tarawa. The Phoenix group encompasses Birnie, Canton, Enderbury, Gardner, Hull, McKean, Phoenix, and Sydney. The Line group embraces Kiritimati (Christmas), Fanning, Malden, Star-buck, Vostock, and Washington, as well as Caroline and Flint, which in 1951 were leased to commercial interests on Tahiti. Not all of the islands are inhabited and several attempts at settlement have been abandoned because of drought conditions, with potable water throughout the area often described as being "as precious as gasoline". In 1978, women constituted one-third of the paid workforce, primarily in trade and service sectors; there is virtually no female participation in government.

Most of the country's national income was traditionally derived from phosphate mining on Ocean Island. By the time of independence, however, the phosphate supply was largely exhausted, although some $70 million in mining royalties had been invested in Europe. At the end of 1979, mining ceased, causing the loss of some 500 jobs; new employment opportunities being explored include expanded copra production, tuna harvesting, tourism, and labor agreements with neighboring islands. Fishing grounds in the area are said to be among the richest in the world, although the first commercial fishing vessel, built in Japan, was not put into service until 1979.

GOVERNMENT AND POLITICS

Political background. The Gilbert and Ellice Islands Colony was under the jurisdiction of the British High Commissioner for the Western Pacific until 1972, when a governor was appointed from London. In 1975 the Ellice Islands became the separate territory of Tuvalu, prior to the achievement of independence in 1978. At a constitutional conference at London in early 1979, the British government refused a request by the Banabans, most of whom had been resettled on Rabi (Rambi) Island in the Fiji group during World War II and had since become Fijian citizens, that Ocean Island be separated from the Gilberts, and the latter became independent as a republican member of the Commonwealth on July 12.

Upon independence the former chief minister, Ieremia T. TABAI, assumed office as president of the Republic and on July 20 appointed Teatao TEANNAKI as vice president. Following the first postindependence legislative election of March 26, 1982, Tabai was returned to office in presidential balloting conducted May 4. The government fell, however, on December 10 when the House of Assembly rejected, for the second time in two days, a bill that would have retroactively legitimized 5 percent salary raises for six public officials who, through an oversight, had erroneously benefited from a pay hike granted civil servants earlier in the year. As mandated by the constitution, interim administration was assumed by a three-member Council of State chaired by the chairman of the Public Service Commission, Rota ONARIO. Tabai was reelected on February 17, 1983, following legislative balloting on January 12 and 19, and on February 18 reappointed most members of his previous administration.

On May 12, 1987, following the election of a new House of Assembly on March 12 and 19, Tabai was elected to a further term, defeating his vice president, Teatao TEAN-NAKI and opposition candidate Teburoio TITO with a 59 percent share of the vote.

Constitution and government. For a small country, Kiribati has a relatively complex constitution (part of the UK Kiribati Independence Order 1979) that includes a number of entrenched provisions designed to safeguard individual and land rights for the Banabans. It provides for an executive president (*beretitenti*) who must command the support of a legislative majority. Upon passage of a no-confidence motion, the president must immediately resign, transitional executive authority being exercised by a Council of State composed of the chairman of the autonomous Public Service Commission, the chief justice, and the speaker of the House of Assembly, pending a legislative dissolution and the holding of a general election. Subsequent to each such election, the House must propose no fewer than three and no more than four candidates for the presidency from its own membership, the final selection being made by nationwide balloting. If the presidency is vacated for reasons other than a loss of confidence, the vice president (*kauoman ni beretitenti*), originally appointed by the president from among his cabinet associates, becomes chief executive, subject to legislative confirmation. The cabinet includes the president, the vice president, and no more than eight other ministers (all drawn from the Assembly), plus the attorney general, and is collectively responsible to the legislature.

The unicameral House consists of 35 members representing 23 electoral districts, an additional member named by the Banaban Rabi Council of Leaders, and the attorney general, ex officio if he is not an elected member. The speaker has no voting rights and must be elected by the House from outside its membership. The normal legislative term is four years. The judicial system encompasses a High Court, a Court of Appeal, and local magistrates' courts, the last representing consolidation of former island, lands, and magistrates' courts. There is a right of appeal to the Judicial Committee of the UK Privy Council in regard to the High Court's interpretation of the rights of any Banaban or the Rabi Council. The nominated Banaban member of the House need not be a Kiribati citizen, while all expatriates with ancestors born in Banaba before 1900 may register as electors or stand for election as if resident on the island.

Foreign relations. Kiribati became a member of the Commonwealth upon independence, but its international contacts are otherwise quite limited. In March 1984 diplomatic relations (backdated to 1979) were established with Tuvalu, augmenting links established earlier with Australia and the United Kingdom, while New Zealand indicated in late 1987 that it would open a diplomatic mission by early 1989. The country joined the International Monetary Fund (IMF) in June 1986, but as of mid-1988 had not applied for admission to the United Nations.

Modest developmental assistance has been provided by Britain, Australia, Japan, New Zealand, the United Kingdom, the United States, and the Asian Development Bank. A 1985 agreement allowing Russian fishing boats within the archipelago's continental shelf lapsed in October 1986 (see Current issues, below).

Under a 1979 treaty, the United States agreed to relinquish all claims to territory in the Phoenix and Line island groups, except for Palmyra. Included were Canton and Enderbury, previously under joint US-UK administration, but from which the British had already withdrawn. The parties also agreed that no military use of the islands by third parties would be permitted without joint consultation and that facilities constructed by the United States on Canton, Enderbury, and Hull islands would not be so used without US approval.

Current issues. Kiribati politics in 1985 were dominated by a treaty which allowed Soviet vessels fishing rights within the archipelago's territorial waters. Moscow had made similar overtures to a number of South Pacific countries, including Fiji and Vanuatu, but the Tabai government—frustrated by deadlocked talks with the American Tuna Boat Association—was the first to respond, engaging in talks with Soviet representatives at Canberra in April and May. Internally, the issue prompted media criticism as well as a petition by church leaders in the predominantly Catholic northern islands to delay conclusion of the agreement. However, the efforts failed, President Tabai insisting that the move enjoyed widespread support and that other countries should consider it no more dangerous than US grain sales to the Soviets. In August, the prime minister survived a parliamentary no-confidence vote on the issue by a narrow four-vote margin; following the vote, which effectively ratified the accord, opposition legislators announced the formation of a new political party which would, if the treaty were not put to a national referendum, advocate the partition of Kiribati. Undaunted, the government entered into discussions during 1986 for renewal of the treaty, which, however, broke down. The official explanation was that the Soviets had reduced the magnitude of their tender (reportedly from $1.5 to $1.0 million), although Moscow signed a similar treaty with Vanuatu in January 1987 that apparently included access to shore facilities, which had not been included in the Kiribati accord. Significantly, the latter agreement was concluded shortly after the United States had agreed to underwrite a five-year $60 million tuna pact with the South Pacific Forum Fisheries Agency, of which both Kiribati and Vanuatu were members. By mid-1987 a new issue had surfaced in the form of possible construction of an $8 billion Japanese space center on Christmas Island, President Tabai arguing that if quick action were not taken in the matter Kiribati would be bested by US interests seeking location of the facility in Hawaii.

The 1987 renewal of Tabai's presidential mandate came amid allegations that he would be in violation of a constitutional provision limiting an incumbent to three terms. The chief executive argued, however that he had not served three full terms, since the second had lasted for less than a year, and the opposition was unable to obtain a court order prior to the May balloting to block his candidacy.

POLITICAL PARTIES

Traditionally, there were no formally organized parties in Kiribati; instead, ad hoc opposition groups tended to form in response to specific issues. Thus, a grouping known as the Mouth of the Kiribati People (*Wiia I-Kiribati*), was significantly involved in the 1982 defeat of the Tabai government, but subsequently became moribund. At present, the only recognizable party is the opposition CDP (below).

Christian Democratic Party (CDP). The CDP was organized in August 1985 by a number of opposition legislators following the failure of a no-confidence motion against President Tabai on the Soviet fishing treaty.

More than half of the assemblymen elected in March 1987 were reported to be "sympathetic" toward CDP leader Harry Tong. Tong, while reelected in the 1987 balloting, was runner-up in a multimember constituency to party secretary Teburoio Tito, who, as one of three subsequent presidential candidates, was defeated by the incumbent chief executive.

Leaders: Dr. Harry TONG, Teburoio TITO (Secretary).

LEGISLATURE

The unicameral **House of Assembly** (*Maneaba ni Maungatabu*) currently consists of 39 elected members plus a nominated representative of Banabans resident on Rabi and the attorney general, ex officio. The normal legislative term is four years, the most recent election being held in two rounds on March 12 and 19, 1987.

Speaker: Bereteitari NEETI.

CABINET

President	Ieremia Tabai
Vice President	Teatao Teannaki
Ministers	
Education	Ataraoti Bwebwenibure
Finance	Teatao Teannaki
Foreign Affairs	Ieremia Tabai
Health and Family Planning	Rotaria Ataia
Home Affairs and Decentralization	Babera Kirati
Line and Phoenix Groups	Tekinaiti Kaiteie
Natural Resources and Development	Taomati Iuta
Trade, Industry and Labor	Raion Batoroma
Transport and Communications	Vera Rabaua
Works and Energy	Ieruru Karotu
Attorney General	Michael Takabwebwe

NEWS MEDIA

Press. The following are published on Tarawa: *Te Uekera* (2,000), published weekly in English and Gilbertese by the government's Broadcasting and Publications Authority; *Te Itoi ni Kiribati* (1,900), Catholic monthly newsletter in Gilbertese; *Te Kaotan te Ota* (1,700), Protestant monthly newsletter in Gilbertese.

Radio and television. The government-operated Kiribati Broadcasting Service transmits in Gilbertese, Tuvaluan, and English to approximately 10,000 radio receivers. There is no television service.

INTERGOVERNMENTAL REPRESENTATION

As of June 1, 1988, Kiribati had not applied for membership in the United Nations, nor had it opened an embassy at Washington, although a "roving ambassador", Atanraoi BAITEKE, remained accredited to a number of countries, including the United States.

US Ambassador to Kiribati: Leonard ROCHWARGER (resident in Fiji).

IGO Memberships (Non-UN): ADB, CWTH, EEC(L), *EIB*, Interpol, SPC, SPEC, SPF.

KOREA

Chosŏn
Alternate Name: *Hankuk*

Political Status: Politically divided; Democratic People's Republic of Korea under Communist regime established September 9, 1948; Republic of Korea under anti-Communist republican regime established August 15, 1948.

THE COUNTRY

Korea is a mountainous peninsula projecting southeastward from Manchuria between China and Japan. Whether viewed in terms of race, culture, or language, the population is extremely homogeneous; the literacy rate is more than 90 percent. For further details see the separate discussions of the Democratic People's Republic of Korea and the Republic of Korea which follow.

POLITICAL HISTORY

A semi-independent state associated with China from the seventh century AD, Korea was annexed by Japan in 1910 and tightly controlled by that country until its defeat in World War II. The northern half of Korea was integrated with the Japanese industrial complex in Manchuria, while the southern half remained largely agricultural. Although the restoration of an independent Korea "in due course" was pledged by Roosevelt, Churchill, and Chiang Kai-shek at the Cairo Conference in 1943, the need for prompt arrangements to receive the surrender of Japanese military forces in 1945 led to a temporary division of the country into Soviet (northern) and US (southern) occupation zones along the line of the 38th parallel. Efforts by the two occupying powers to establish a unified Korean provisional government shortly became deadlocked, and the issue of Korea's future was referred to the UN General Assembly on US initiative in 1947. A UN Temporary Commission was set up to facilitate elections and the establishment of a national government but was denied access to the Soviet-controlled zone. UN-observed elections were accordingly held in the southern half of Korea alone in May 1948, and the Republic of Korea (ROK) was formally established on August 15, 1948; a separate, Communist-controlled government, the Democratic People's Republic of Korea (DPRK), was established in the North on September 9. The UN General Assembly refused to recognize the latter action and declared that the ROK was the lawful government of the nation. Soviet troops withdrew from the DPRK in December 1948, and US forces left the ROK in June 1949.

On June 25, 1950, five months after US Secretary of State Dean Acheson, as the culmination of a process of American retrenchment in Asia, had delineated a Pacific "defense perimeter" that did not include Korea, DPRK troops invaded the ROK in an attempt to unify the peninsula by force. US forces promptly came to the assistance of the southern regime and the UN Security Council, meeting without the USSR, called on all member states to aid the ROK as the sole legitimate government in Korea. A total of 16 UN members subsequently furnished troops to a UN Unified Command established by the Security Council in July 1950 and headed initially by US Gen. Douglas MacArthur (later by generals Matthew B. Ridgway and Mark Clark). The intervention of some 300,000 Chinese Communist "volunteers" on the side of the DPRK in late 1950 produced a military stalemate, and an armistice agreement was eventually signed at Panmunjom on July 27, 1953, establishing a ceasefire line and a four-kilometer-wide demilitarized zone which bisects Korea near the 38th parallel.

Political negotiations at Geneva in 1954 failed to produce a settlement, and relations between the two countries are still governed by the 1953 agreement, under which a Military Armistice Commission representing the former belligerents (including China) continues to meet at Panmunjom. Chinese military forces withdrew from the DPRK in 1958, but UN forces (now exclusively American) remain in the South. The United States proposed to the UN Security Council in June 1975 that the UN Command in Korea be dissolved, but no action was taken on the proposal, presumably because it would preclude further UN discussion of the American presence. In February 1977, following earlier cutbacks in 1970–1972, the Carter administration announced a "phased withdrawal" of US combat personnel, but reversed itself in mid-1979 because of reports that the DPRK army held a numerical superiority in men and tanks far in excess of earlier estimates.

Relations between North and South have alternated between mutual tolerance and overt hostility. Contacts regarding the problem of families separated by the political division of the country began in August 1971 and have been conducted under the auspices of the Red Cross societies of the respective countries. Talks directed toward peaceful reunification were initiated in 1972 and resulted in the establishment of a North-South Coordinating Committee, which convened on October 12, 1972, and continued to meet on a regular basis until August 1973, when negotiations were unilaterally broken off by the DPRK.

Following the North's acceptance of an appeal by ROK President Park to reopen discussions, representatives of the two Koreas met at Panmunjom on February 17, 1979, in preparation for broader negotiations. After three brief sessions, however, the talks ended over differences regarding representation and the level at which future negotiations should be conducted: the DPRK delegates, all representing the Democratic Front for the Reunification of the Fatherland, insisted that a "whole-nation congress" of representatives from all Korean social and political organizations should be convened, while the ROK delegates refused to recognize the legitimacy of the technically nongovernmental Democratic Front and called for a reconvening of the 1972 Coordinating Committee. On July 1 presidents Park and Carter jointly called for tripartite talks with the North, but the DPRK flatly rejected the overture on July 10.

In January 1980, Pyongyang and Seoul agreed to a series of working-level talks designed to prepare for a first-ever meeting of their prime ministers. Ten such sessions were held during the ensuing eight months without agreement on an agenda for a high-level meeting, the discussions being terminated by North Korea on September 24, following the inauguration of South Korean President Chun on September 1. In 1981–1982 overtures by the ROK were rejected by the DPRK, which called instead for a conference of private citizens, excluding political party representatives. A number of social and economic issues were addressed following a resumption of working-level discussions in 1983, with little substantive result, save for a limited number of family reunions conducted at Seoul and Pyongyang under Red Cross auspices in September 1985. Inconclusive economic cooperation talks were also held in 1984–1985, in addition to a series of preliminary interparliamentary discussions in July-September 1985. During 1985–1986, contacts between the two regimes included several meetings at Lausanne, Switzerland, between their Olympic committees in regard to the 1988 summer games scheduled for Seoul (which Pyongyang sought unsuccessfully to cohost), while sporadic political-military talks were ritualistically suspended by the North during annual US-South Korean "Team Spirit" military exercises.

DEMOCRATIC PEOPLE'S REPUBLIC OF KOREA

Chosŏn Minchu-chui Inmin Konghwa-guk

Political Status: Communist People's Republic established September 9, 1948.

Area: 46,450 sq. mi. (120,538 sq. km.).

Population: 21,925,000 (1988E).

Major Urban Centers (1976E): PYONGYANG (1,500,000); Chongjin (300,000); Hungnam (260,000); Kaesong (240,000).

Official Language: Korean.

Monetary Unit: Won. The won is not readily convertible, the basic rate typically being set at slightly less than the US dollar, with a noncommercial rate somewhat in excess of 2 won per $1US.

President of the DPRK and Secretary General of the Korean Workers' Party: Marshal KIM Il Sung (KIM Il-sŏng); became First Secretary of the Communist Party in 1945 and Secretary General of the Korean Workers' Party in 1966; reelected to the latter post by the Sixth Party Congress, held October 10–14, 1980; made Chairman of the governing People's Committee in 1946, continuing as

Prime Minister on establishment of the DPRK in 1948; elected President by the Supreme People's Assembly in 1972; reelected in 1977, 1982, and on December 29, 1986.

First Vice President: PAK Sung Chul (PAK Sŏng-ch'ŏl); designated Prime Minister on April 30, 1976; elected Vice President by the Supreme People's Assembly on December 15, 1977, succeeding KIM Tong Kyu; reelected in 1982 and on December 29, 1986.

Second Vice President: RIM Chun Chu (Yim Ch'un-ch'u); elected by the Supreme People's Assembly on April 7, 1983, succeeding KANG Ryang Uk (KANG Yang-uk), who died January 10; reelected on December 29, 1986.

Third Vice President: LI Jong Ok (Yi Chong-ŏk); designated Prime Minister on December 15, 1977; elected Vice President by the Supreme People's Assembly on January 25, 1984; reelected on December 29, 1986.

Premier: LI Gun Mo (Yi Kŭn-mo); designated by the Supreme People's Assembly on December 29, 1986, succeeding KANG Sung San (KANG Song-san).

THE COUNTRY

A land of mountains and valleys, the Democratic People's Republic of Korea (DPRK) is located in northeastern Asia, bordering on the People's Republic of China and the Soviet Union. Its people, like those in the Republic of Korea (ROK), are characterized by ethnic and linguistic homogeneity, tracing their origins to the Mongols and the Chinese. Traditionally, Koreans have followed Buddhism and Shamanism, but since the establishment of the Communist regime, religion has declined as a factor in North Korean life. Information on women's economic participation is not currently available, although the DPRK claims full employment for all its citizens.

The DPRK has more plentiful natural resources than the ROK and inherited a substantial industrial base from the Japanese occupation, but the Korean conflict of 1950–1953 destroyed much of its economic infrastructure. The Soviet-type economy was reconstructed at a high rate of growth with substantial Soviet and Chinese aid. At present, more than 90 percent of the economy is socialized, agricultural land and production are totally collectivized, and state-owned industry is said to produce over 95 percent of manufactured goods by value. Figures on the economy since the 1970s are difficult to obtain, but the gross national product appeared to be under $1,000 per capita in 1985 (less than half that of the South), while severe trade and budgetary deficits have led Pyongyang to default on most of its international debt (presumed to exceed $2 billion). In 1985, the Seven Year Plan launched in 1978, which had called for an overall increase in industrial production of 220 percent, was pronounced a "success", although only modest gains were evident. Significantly, nearly two years of "transition" ensued before its successor, promising to propel the DPRK into the ranks of the world's economically advanced nations, was presented to the Eighth Supreme People's Assembly in April 1987.

GOVERNMENT AND POLITICS

Political background. A provisional People's Republic was established in the northern half of Korea under Soviet auspices in February 1946, and the Democratic People's Republic of Korea was formally organized on September 9, 1948, following the proclamation of the Republic of Korea in the South. Both the government and the ruling Korean Workers' Party (KWP), which superseded the Communist Party in 1949, have been headed since their inception by KIM Il Sung, a Soviet-trained Communist. Domestic political events in the wake of the 1953 armistice centered around the consolidation of Kim's power through the elimination of rival factional groups. Initially, the DPRK appeared to favor the Chinese side in the Sino-Soviet dispute, and Moscow suspended its assistance in 1964. A subsequent purge of pro-Chinese elements in the DPRK, at the time of China's "Cultural Revolution" and the fall of Nikita Khrushchev, resulted in a more independent political stance and a limited restoration of Soviet aid. By October 1966, when Kim changed his party title from chairman to secretary general, he had established undisputed leadership at home as well as a recognized position of independence within the Communist movement.

Kim Il Sung was appointed to the newly created office of president by the Supreme People's Assembly on December 28, 1972, yielding the office of prime minister to KIM Il. On April 30, 1976, Kim Il resigned his ministerial post for health reasons and was designated first vice president, being succeeded by PAK Sung Chul. On December 15, 1977, Pak was replaced as prime minister by economic expert LI Jong Ok. In a move that resulted in cabinet appointments for a number of younger contemporaries of the president's son and heir-apparent, KIM Jong Il, KANG Sung San was named prime minister on January 25, 1984, Li becoming the country's fourth vice president prior to Kim Il's death on March 9.

On December 29, 1986, the Eighth Assembly (constituted on the basis of pro forma voting in November) reelected Kim Il Sung as president and named former vice premier LI Gun Mo to succeed Kang as premier.

Constitution and government. From 1948 to 1972 the DPRK's nominal head of state was the chairman of the Presidium of the Supreme People's Assembly, who was assisted by two vice chairmen; the office was, however, of substantially less consequence than that of prime minister. Under the constitution of December 1972, executive authority was vested in the president of the Republic, who is currently assisted by three vice presidents. In addition, a 13-member "super cabinet", the Central People's Committee, oversees operation of the State Administration Council, a cabinet-like body headed by a premier. Nominally, the highest organ of authority is the Supreme People's Assembly, but the full membership rarely meets and most of its work is carried out by a 15-member Standing Committee. (The constitutional term of both president and Assembly is four years, save "[w]hen unavoidable circumstances render [an] election impossible"; however, no election since 1972 has been held on schedule, the actual Assembly sittings averaging 4.7 years.) The judicial system is headed by the Central Court and includes a People's

Court and local courts. Judges are elected by the Supreme People's Assembly.

Administratively, the DPRK is divided into nine provinces and includes three special urban districts as well as communal districts. Each of the local government units has its own People's Assembly.

Foreign relations. The foreign relations of the DPRK are for the most part determined by two factors: its relations with the ROK and its posture vis-à-vis relations between China and the Soviet Union. The most important foreign-policy problem continues to be reunification of the peninsula, but the promising initiatives of the early 1970s failed to bear fruit and relations with the ROK deteriorated. By 1979, the ROK had alleged 43,000 violations by the DPRK of the 1953 armistice, while the DPRK had in turn charged the ROK with over 217,000 violations.

The most striking rupture in North-South relations came in October 1983 after a bomb attack at Rangoon, Burma, which killed four South Korean cabinet ministers. After two captured DPRK army members confessed to having been ordered to attack the South Korean delegation, including President Chun Doo Hwan, Burma withdrew recognition of the DPRK and both Seoul and Washington demanded a public apology. Pyongyang, however, has persisted in denying any responsibility for the incident.

North Korea has gone through a number of phases in relations with its powerful Communist neighbors. Close links with the Soviet Union were cultivated until 1964, while a generally pro-Chinese period came to an end during the Maoist "Cultural Revolution". Subsequently, the Kim regime maintained a somewhat independent position, depending on both the USSR and PRC for aid (though internationally proclaiming a policy of *Juche,* or self-reliance). During 1986, ties with Moscow visibly warmed, while those with Beijing remained formally correct, with intimations of North Korean unhappiness at the growing Chinese rapprochement with Seoul and Washington. Significantly, Sino-North Korean trade gradually declined during 1981–1986, while trade with the Soviets increased over the same period, the latter becoming twice that of the former (38 percent of the DPRK total, as contrasted with 19 percent).

Although the DPRK condemned the "dominationism" evidenced by Vietnam's invasion of Kampuchea in December 1978, no similar statement was made regarding the subsequent Chinese invasion of Vietnam. Initially silent regarding the Soviet incursion into Afghanistan, it expressed its solidarity with the Soviet-supported Afghan regime in April 1980, arguing that, in contrast to the Kampuchean situation, the intervention had been at the request of the Afghan government. Recently, as relations with Moscow have become more cordial, the DPRK appears to have modified its Kampuchean policy. Although Kim Il Sung has long been a close personal friend of Prince Norodom Sihanouk and has provided the prince with a lavish North Korean residence, the DPRK leader appeared by 1986 to be distancing himself from support for the anti-Vietnamese coalition nominally headed by Sihanouk within Kampuchea.

The DPRK has consistently rebuffed proposals whereby it and the ROK would recognize each other and simultaneously be admitted to the United Nations, stating in 1979 that such an "insidious scheme" would legitimize the division of the peninsula. Pyongyang does, however, maintain a permanent observer at UN headquarters and participates in a limited number of UN-affiliated agencies. It is also an active, albeit somewhat ineffectual, member of the Nonaligned Movement, and in recent years has increased arms sales and military training to a number of Third World countries, including Ethiopia, Iran, Nicaragua, and Zimbabwe.

Current issues. By 1985, due to the manifest ascendance of the president's son, Kim Jong Il, the DPRK was widely understood to be under a "dual leadership". Believed by some to have instigated the Rangoon bombing, the younger Kim had been designated *Tang Chungang* ("center of the party"), and thus his father's most likely successor, in 1980. In February 1987 Kim Jong Il's 45th birthday was marked by considerable fanfare, although the festivities were somewhat less lavish than those reserved for Kim Il Sung's 75th birthday in April.

Throughout 1987 there was considerable sparring in regard to sponsorship of the 1988 summer Olympics, the DPRK eventually declaring that it would boycott the Games after being denied co-host status by the International Olympic Committee. Meanwhile, the November 29 bombing of a (South) Korean Air Lines plane by North Korean terrorists drew universal condemnation. According to the confession of one of the perpetrators, explosives had been placed in the plane shortly before takeoff for a flight from Bahrain to Seoul as part of an effort to destabilize Olympic travel. Both Washington and Tokyo responded by imposing sanctions against Pyongyang, including revocation by the former of a policy announced in March that authorized its diplomats to conduct "substantive conversations" with North Korea officials "at receptions and parties and in other 'neutral' locations".

On the economic front, observers were highly skeptical as to the likelihood that the new seven-year plan could attain goals that include termination of the country's food, clothing, and housing shortages, and a doubling of factory output by 1994. According to the *Far Eastern Economic Review,* a major reorganization of key ministries fell short of addressing the most serious industrial problem: the DPRK's effective exclusion from access to advanced Western technology.

POLITICAL PARTIES

North Korea is for all practical purposes a one-party state under the exclusive domination of the Korean Workers' Party, which is the core component of an umbrella grouping known as the **Democratic Front for the Reunification of the Fatherland.** Specialized political activity is carried out through some 16 authorized mass organizations and auxiliary parties, including the General Federation of Trade Unions, the Korean Democratic Youth League, the **North Korean Social Democratic Party,** and the **Religious Chungu Party.**

Korean Workers' Party — KWP (*Chosun No-dong Dang*). Founded in 1949 through merger of the existing Communist Party and the recently established National Party, the KWP controls all political activity in the

DPRK through an overlapping of party, executive, and legislative posts. The party's Sixth Congress convened on October 10–14, 1980, nearly a decade after the last such meeting. Major structural and personnel changes were announced, including an enlargement of the Central Committee from 172 to 248 (145 full and 103 candidate) members; redesignation of the former Political Committee as the Politburo, with an increase from 16 to 34 (19 full and 15 candidate) members; and establishment of a new 5-member Presidium. Appointments were also made to two other important party organs: a 12-member Secretariat and a 19-member Military Commission. Further changes occurred at subsequent Central Committee plenums, the most recent (December 27, 1986) yielding a Politburo of 32 members (including a three-member Presidium and 18 alternates) and a Secretariat of 14.

General Secretary: KIM Il Sung (KIM Il-sŏng), President of the People's Republic.

Other Members of Politburo Presidium: KIM Jong Il (KIM Chŏng-il), member KWP Military Commission, KWP Secretariat; Vice Mar. O Jin U (Oh Jin-wu), former Defense Minister, member KWP Military Commission.

Other Members of Politburo: HO Dam, KANG Song San, HONG Song Nam, KIM Hwan, KIM Yong Nam, LI Gun Mo, LI Jong Ok, O Guk Ryol, PAK Sung Chol, RIM Chun Chu, SO Chol, SO Yun Sok, YON Hyong Muk.

Central Committee Secretariat: CHAE Hui Chong, CHOE Tae Pok, CHON Pyong Ho, HO Chong Suk, HWANG Jang Yop, HYON Mu Kwang, KANG Song San, KIM Il Sung, KIM Jong Il, KIM Yong Nam, KYE Ung Tae, SO Kwang Hui, YON Hyong Muk.

LEGISLATURE

The unicameral **Supreme People's Assembly** (*Choe Ko In Min Hoe Ui*) is elected from a single slate of KWP members and party-approved nominees. The 615-member Eighth Assembly was named on November 2, 1986, previous elections having been held in 1948 and at approximately five-year intervals during 1957–1982. Between sessions, Assembly business is conducted by a 15-member Standing Committee.

Chairman of Standing Committee: YANG Hyong Sop.

CABINET

Premier	Li Gun Mo
First Vice Premier	Hong Song Nam
Vice Premiers	Chong Jun Gi
	Kim Chang Ju
	Kim Bok Sin
	Kim Hwan
	Kim Yong Nam
	Kim Yun Hyok

Ministers	
Atomic Power Industry	Choe Hak Gun
Commerce	Han Jang Gun
Culture and Art	Chang Chol
External Economic Affairs	Chong Song Nam
Finance	Yun Gi Jong
Foreign Affairs	Kim Yong Nam
Foreign Trade	Choe Jong Gun
Forestry	Kim Jae Ryul
Labor Administration	Kim Bong Ul
Machine Industry	Kye Hyong Sun
Metal Industry	Choe Man Hyon
Natural Resources Development	Kim Se Yong
Post and Telecommunications	Kim Yong Chae
Public Health	Li Jong Yul
Public Security	Lt. Gen. Paek Hak Rim
Railways	Pak Yong Sok
Shipbuilding Industry	Li Sok

Commission Chairmen	
Agriculture	Kim Chang Ju
Chemical and Light Industry	Kim Hwan
Construction and Building Materiels	Kim Yun Hyok
Education	Pyon Yong Rip
Fisheries	Choe Bok Yon
Mining Industry	Cho Chang Dok
People's Services	Kong Jin Tae
Physical Culture and Sports Guidance	Kim Yu Sun
Power Industry	Li Ji Chan
State Construction	Kim Ung Sang
State Planning	Kim Tal Hyon
State Science and Technology	Li Ja Bang
Transport	Li Gil Song
President, Academy of Sciences	Kim Gyong Bong
President, Central Bank	Yong Song U

NEWS MEDIA

All news media are censored by the KWP and staffed by KWP-approved personnel.

Press. The following are dailies published at Pyongyang, unless otherwise noted: *Rodong Shinmun,* (1,000,000), organ of the KWP Central Committee; *Rodongja Shinmun* (700,000), organ of the General Federation of Trade Unions; *Minju Chosun,* organ of the Supreme People's Assembly and the Administration Council; *Jokuk Tongil,* monthly organ of the Democratic Front for the Reunification of the Fatherland; *Joson Inmingun,* organ of the Korean People's Army; *Saenal,* biweekly Youth League organ; *Korea Today,* monthly in Chinese, English, French, Russian, and Spanish.

News agencies. The Korean Central News Agency is the official governmental news agency; *Xinhua, Novosti,* and TASS maintain bureaus at Pyongyang.

Radio and television. The Korean Central Broadcasting Committee is responsible for radio and television service. As of 1987, 16 medium-wave and 14 shortwave radio stations, as well as 11 television stations, were reported to be broadcasting to approximately 2 million radio and 180,000 television receivers.

INTERGOVERNMENTAL REPRESENTATION

There are no diplomatic relations between the United States and the Democratic People's Republic of Korea.

Permanent Observer to the UN: PAK Gil Yon.

IGO Memberships (Non-UN): NAM.

REPUBLIC OF KOREA

Taehan-min'guk

Political Status: Independent republic established August 15, 1948; present constitution approved in national referendum of October 27, 1987, with effect from February 25, 1988.

Area: 38,025 sq. mi. (98,484 sq. km.).

Population: 40,466,577 (1985C), 42,725,000 (1988E). The 1985 figure is provisional.

Major Urban Centers (1985C): SEOUL (9,645,824); Pusan (3,516,768); Taegu (2,030,649); Inchon (1,387,475); Kwangju (905,896); Taejon (866,303).

Official Language: Korean.

Monetary Unit: Won (market rate March 1, 1988, 760.80 won = $1US).

President: ROH Tae Woo (Democratic Justice Party); secured plurality of popular vote in direct election of December 16, 1987; inaugurated February 25, 1988, for a five-year term, succeeding CHUN Doo Hwan (Democratic Justice Party).

Prime Minister: LEE Hyun Jae, named by the President to head government installed on February 25, 1988, succeeding KIM Chong Yol.

THE COUNTRY

Characterized by mountainous terrain in the north and east and broad plains in the south, the Republic of Korea is densely settled, with a majority of its population concentrated in the southern section, although approximately one-quarter are residents of the capital, Seoul, which is located within 30 miles of the demilitarized zone (DMZ). The people are ethnically homogeneous, tracing their heritage to Mongol and Chinese origins. Buddhism, Shamanism, and Christianity are the important religions; the ROK has one of the largest Christian populations in Asia, numbering in excess of eight million. Women constitute nearly 40 percent of the labor force, approximately one-third working unpaid on family farms. The remainder are concentrated in services, health care, and textile and electronics manufacture, where the work force is 70–90 percent female. Female participation in politics is minimal.

Unlike the DPRK, the Republic of Korea did not begin the post-World War II period with a substantial industrial base, and postwar growth was cut short by the Korean conflict of 1950–1953. Since that time, industrial expansion has been rapid, although agriculture and fishing continue to occupy 35 percent of the work force and presently account for approximately 15 percent of the gross domestic product. Agriculture is devoted primarily to grain production, but available supplies fall below what is needed to feed the large population. As a consequence of the need to import 25 percent of its foodstuffs, self-sufficiency in food is an important goal in present economic planning. Mineral deposits include coal and iron, although industrialization has been concentrated in textiles, electronics, food processing, and chemicals. By the late 1970s, the lengthy period of economic acceleration, coupled with dramatic fuel price increases, began to take its toll, with inflation approaching 30 percent at the end of the decade, although by 1985, it had been reduced to less than 3 percent by strict monetarist policies. Unemployment has recently hovered around 4 percent and per capita GNP (now in excess of $2,800) grew by 12.5 percent in 1986 and by 12.2 percent (the world's highest) in 1987. Government economists in recent years have promoted deceleration and the diversion of some resources from the export market in order to meet domestic needs, despite the fact that exports remain crucial because of a foreign debt which, although reduced by a surprising 21 percent during the previous year, remained high at $35 billion in December 1987.

GOVERNMENT AND POLITICS

Political background. Syngman RHEE, a conservative president, dominated ROK politics from the establishment of the Republic in 1948 until student-led demonstrations against ballot tampering forced his resignation on May 3, 1960. Plagued by administrative chaos, the liberal successor government of President YUN Po Sun and Prime Minister CHANG Myon was overthrown in a bloodless military coup staged by (then) Maj. Gen. PARK Chung Hee and four other officers on May 16, 1961. The National Assembly was dissolved, the constitution suspended, and all political parties disbanded, with General Park assuming executive powers under a military junta called the Supreme Council for National Reconstruction. Although authoritarian, the junta proved relatively incorruptible and sympathetic to the needs of a largely agrarian but modernizing society. As a step toward the reestablishment of civilian rule under a revised constitution, General Park and other leading officers retired from the army preparatory to seeking elective office. Park and his newly formed Democratic Republican Party (DRP) won the presidential and legislative elections held in 1963, and constitutional rule was formally restored with Park's inauguration as president on December 17.

President Park was reelected in 1967, but a legislative election the same year was marked by charges of irregularities which led to renewed demonstrations. Following a presidentially inspired constitutional change permitting him to run for a third term, Park was reelected in 1971, winning a narrow victory over opposition candidate KIM Dae Jung. Shortly thereafter, Park declared a state of national emergency and extracted from the National Assembly, over strong opposition, an emergency-powers law that gave him virtually unlimited authority to regulate the economy and limit constitutional freedoms in the interest of national security.

Responding to increased political tension, Park abruptly proclaimed martial law on October 17, 1972, and called for the preparation of a new constitution. The latter, approved in a referendum held under martial-law restrictions, provided for a powerful president designated by a directly elected National Conference for Unification (NCU), and a weak legislature with one-third of its membership appointed by the NCU. Park was reconfirmed by the NCU on December 22, and a legislative election held February 27, 1973, completed the nominal return to constitutional government. Park was returned for a second six-year term on July 6, 1978, and the DRP, although failing to capture a plurality of votes in balloting on December 12, retained control of the National Assembly.

Opposition to the so-called *Yushin* ("Revitalizing") Constitution of 1972 grew slowly, with the government responding to recurring protests, both peaceful and violent, by increasingly repressive measures; thus, in May 1975 the regime issued a decree making it a crime to criticize the president and his policies, banning reports of any such criticism, and prohibiting rallies called to urge constitutional revision. (Earlier, in August 1974, Park's wife had been killed by an apparent North Korean agent during an attempted assassination of the president.) Although periodically granting amnesties to common criminals and decree violaters, Park continued to wield dictatorial power and symptomatically, on July 5, 1978, the day before his redesignation by the NCU, placed all opposition leaders under house arrest.

Although South Korea had become accustomed to economic progress under the Park administration (the GNP increasing at an annual rate of 10 percent since the late 1960s), inflation, escalating energy costs, and a decline in real wages had, by the summer of 1979, contributed to an economic downturn. In August some 200 women employees of a recently bankrupt textile company occupied the headquarters of the opposition New Democratic Party (NDP), demanding that they be allowed to take over management of the firm. On August 11, police and members of the Korean Central Intelligence Agency (KCIA) stormed the building, injuring and arresting several hundred demonstrators as well as a number of NDP assemblymen and journalists. Two days later, intraparty opponents of KIM Young Sam went to court in an effort to have his mid-May election as NDP president thrown out, the court ruling in their favor on September 7. Following Kim's expulsion from the National Assembly on October 4 for having criticized the regime in a *New York Times* interview, the entire legislative opposition resigned in protest. At that point, student demonstrations, begun in the aftermath of the labor protest, expanded into riots, and within a week the cities of Pusan and Masan were under martial law.

On the evening of October 26, 1979, Park was assassinated by the director of the KCIA, KIM Jae Kyu, while dining at a KCIA safehouse restaurant. Kim was subsequently reported to have been severely criticized by Park for incompetence and had been disturbed by violent tactics ordered against demonstrators by presidential security chief CHA Chi Choul (one of five others killed by Kim and his accomplices). Although anticipating military backing for a government takeover, Kim was instead arrested by army authorities within hours of the assassination.

Park was immediately succeeded by the prime minister, CHOI Kyu Hah, who was elected by the NCU on December 6 to complete Park's term. Having revoked his predecessor's emergency decrees and declared an amnesty that freed 1,646 prisoners, the new president stated, at his inauguration on December 21, that he anticipated the enactment of a new constitution "in about a year's time, unless unexpected contingencies arise".

A widespread series of labor strikes in April 1980 in support of wage increases to compensate for inflation gradually assumed a political character, with mass student demonstrations calling for the resignations of Prime Minister SHIN Hyon Hwak and Army Security Commander CHUN Doo Hwan, who had been appointed acting KCIA director on April 14. The government responded by arresting Kim Dae Jung and a number of other opposition leaders on May 18, provoking a popular uprising in the southern city of Kwangju the following day. On May 20 the Shin government resigned, PARK Choong Hoon being designated acting prime minister, and on May 27, after heavy fighting, the Kwangju insurrection was suppressed by government forces.

President Choi resigned on August 16 and was succeeded, as acting head of state, by Prime Minister Park. On August 27 Chun Doo Hwan (who had resigned his commission six days before) was elected president by the NCU, designating NAM Duck Woo as prime minister the day after his inauguration on September 1. A new constitution, approved by a reported majority of 91.6 percent in a referendum held October 22, came into effect five days later, the existing National Assembly being dissolved and its functions assumed, on an interim basis, by an appointive Legislative Council for National Security. Meanwhile, on September 17, Kim Dae Jung had been condemned to death, but his execution was deferred and, after worldwide appeals for clemency, was on January 23, 1981, commuted to life imprisonment. (In March 1982 the sentence was further reduced to 20 years, with Kim being permitted to seek medical treatment in the United States the following December.)

On January 21, 1981, President Chun rescinded martial law, which had been in effect since the Park assassination, and announced that a presidential election would be held on February 25, following balloting for an electoral college on February 11. In the electoral college, Chun's newly formed Democratic Justice Party (DJP) secured 3,676 of 5,278 seats, and the incumbent was reinstalled on March 3 after being credited with more than ten times as many electoral votes as his closest competitor. Shortly thereafter, on March 25, a new National Assembly was elected, with the DJP obtaining 151 of 276 seats.

In a move interpreted as reflecting dissatisfaction with management of the nation's economy as well as a desire to recruit senior officials not closely associated with the Park regime, President Chun accepted the resignation of Prime Minister Nam on January 3, 1982, appointing YOO Chang Soon as his successor. Four months later the country was rocked by a major financial scandal involving the manipulation of a sizeable portion of the country's money supply by a leading money market operator who, in collusion with a number of government officials, had forced several large firms into bankruptcy. On June 24, the Yoo government, accepting "moral and political responsibility" for the affair, submitted its resignation, the widely respected former president of Korea University, KIM Sang Hyup, being asked to form a new administration.

In October 1983, following a new series of banking scandals, the downing of a Korean commercial airliner that had apparently strayed into Soviet air space, and a bomb attack at Rangoon, Burma, that killed four South Korean cabinet members, Prime Minister Kim resigned, President Chun appointing a new Council of State headed by DJP chairman CHIN Iee Chong. Earlier, former NDP leader Kim Young Sam initiated a hunger strike to press for constitutional reform, while clashes between police and campus demonstrators occurred throughout the year.

In an effort to defuse the situation, Chun ordered police off the college campuses in early 1984 and lifted the ban on political activity of most of those blacklisted in 1980 (excluding Kim Dae Jung and Kim Young Sam). In December a number of opposition politicians formed the New Korea Democratic Party (NKDP), which, following Kim Dae Jung's return from the United States, won nearly 25 percent of the seats at the National Assembly balloting on February 12. Six days later, Chun again reshuffled the Council of State, replacing the ailing Prime Minister Chin with former intelligence chief LHO Shin Yong.

On May 26, 1987, Prime Minister Lho assumed "moral and political responsibility" for a reported police cover-up of the torture death of an antigovernment student demonstrator and was succeeded by LEE Han Key. Public disorder nonetheless gained in intensity and on June 29 ROH Tae Woo, who had been formally endorsed by the DJP nine days earlier as its choice to succeed Chun, announced, in an unexpected reversal of policy, that virtually all of the opposition's reform demands would be met, including the call for direct presidential balloting. On July 10 Chun resigned as DJP leader in favor of Roh so that he could carry out his remaining official duties from a "supra-partisan position" and in a cabinet reshuffle three days later removed all of the party incumbents, with KIM Chong Yol, a former air force general and ambassador to the United States, replacing Lee as prime minister.

On August 31 an eight-member committee of government and opposition representatives reached agreement on the essentials of a new constitution, which was overwhelmingly approved by the National Assembly on October 12 and by South Korean voters in a referendum on October 27. While there was substantial evidence that a unified opposition could have won the December 16 presidential poll, neither of the two Kims was willing to defer to the other. As a result, Roh obtained 35.9 percent of the vote, with Kim Young Sam and Kim Dae Jung winning 27.5 percent and 26.5 percent, respectively; KIM Jong Pil, a former prime minister under President Park, ran fourth with 7.9 percent. Following his victory, Roh named LEE Hyun Jae, a respected educator, as prime minister, while surprising observers by retaining seven incumbents (including the Interior, Finance, Foreign, and Justice ministers). DJP spokesmen suggested, however, that the new government was intended to be transitional in nature and that extensive changes could be expected after the legislative balloting in March and also after the Olympic Games in September.

The Assembly poll (postponed until April 26 because of disagreement regarding electoral procedure) yielded only a plurality (125 of 299 seats) for the DJP. While it was the first time that a South Korean presidential party had failed to win outright legislative control, a preelection agreement by the two main opposition leaders to merge their forces had again failed, with Kim Jong Pil's recently organized National Democratic Republican Party securing the balance of power with 35 seats.

Constitution and government. The present constitution (technically the ninth amendment of the country's 1948 basic law) sets forth a variety of basic rights, including freedom of press and assembly, the principle of habeas corpus, labor's right to organize and strike against employers, and the outlawing of detention without a court order. In addition, the armed forces are enjoined to observe "political neutrality". The president is directly elected for a single five-year term; there is no requirement that he obtain a popular majority and no provision for a vice president. The president appoints a prime minister and other cabinet officials; his powers vis-à-vis the National Assem-

bly have, however, been curtailed, including loss of the former right of legislative dissolution. The powers of assemblymen (who continue to sit for four-year terms) have been substantially strengthened; lawmakers are specifically authorized to investigate government affairs and enjoy complete immunity for activity inside the House. The chief justice is appointed for a five-year term by the president, with the concurrence of the Assembly; other Supreme Court judges are appointed on recommendation of the chief justice, who himself names lower-court judges.

Administratively, the country is divided into nine provinces, each headed by a presidentially appointed governor. Local government, a matter of concern to recent democratic activists, receives little constitutional attention, although Roh Tae Woo, in his statement of June 29, 1987, had committed himself to the election of local, municipal, and provincial councils.

Foreign relations. Although not a member of the United Nations, the Republic of Korea maintains a permanent observer at the world organization's New York headquarters and participates in the activities of many of its Specialized Agencies. It is also a member of the Asian Development Bank and the Colombo Plan. The designation of Seoul as the site for both the 1986 Asian Games and the 1988 Olympics reflects South Korea's growing acceptance as a member of the international community, while a thriving export program has strengthened economic ties with a variety of trading partners.

Relations with the Democratic People's Republic of Korea (DPRK) and the United States have long been the most sensitive areas of external concern for the ROK. Communication between Seoul and Pyongyang has fluctuated widely in recent years, sporadic talks alternating with hostile exchanges on a variety of issues, with closure—to say nothing of resolution—proving largely elusive. Both sides are formally committed to reunification, but have adopted differing (and occasionally shifting) positions on whether negotiations should be bilateral or trilateral (involving Washington), whether the participants should be governmental or other (the former generally favored by the south and the latter by the north), and the priority to be accorded to security considerations. After failing to agree on a face-saving formula that would permit the North to share in Olympic sponsorship, links between the two regimes reached a nadir in November 1987 with the destruction by North Korean agents of a South Korean airliner enroute from Bahrain to Seoul (see previous article).

Relations with the United States were strained in the late 1970s not only by the repressive policies of the Park regime, but by revelations of widespread Korean influence peddling in US congressional circles. More recently, US support has been reaffirmed, President Reagan pledging continued military and economic aid during a 1984 visit to Seoul and while hosting his Korean counterpart at Washington in 1985. Anti-American sentiment in the ROK, most dramatically symbolized by arson attacks on US cultural centers at Kwangju and Pusan in the early 1980s and occupation of the US Information Service library at Seoul in 1985, came mainly from opposition politicians, students, and religious leaders, who argued that support for President Chun inhibited the emergence of a truly democratic system.

By contrast, Chun's acceptance of constitutional reform in mid-1987 was reported to have stemmed in part from strong US diplomatic pressure.

Relations with Japan, formally restored in 1965 after 14 years of negotiation, have been constrained by Korean bitterness over the pre-1945 occupation and Tokyo's treatment of resident Koreans, while Japanese officials long criticized Seoul's record on human rights, curtailing economic assistance after the abduction of Korean opposition leader Kim Dae Jung from Japan in 1973. Further tension resulting from the issuance of "revisionist" Japanese historical texts in 1982 was partially eased by Prime Minister Nakasone's visit to the ROK in early 1983 (another such visit occurring in 1985), while a state visit to Japan by Chun in September 1984, the first by a South Korean president, elicited a ritual apology from Emperor Hirohito for "the unfortunate past between us" as well as a tender of support for Seoul's proposal that both Koreas be admitted to the United Nations.

Normalization of relations with the Soviet Union, long of lesser priority, was severely impaired by the destruction of a civilian Korean airliner in September 1983, after the plane had strayed off course and passed over Soviet missile installations on the island of Kamchatka. By contrast, informal relations with Beijing have greatly improved since the return to the PRC of a hijacked Chinese airliner in May 1983, with aircraft piloted by military defectors being returned in 1984 and 1985, and a torpedo boat found drifting in international waters after an apparent mutiny also being returned in the latter year.

Current issues. Few would deny that 1987 was a most remarkable year for the Republic of Korea. On April 13, after supporters of the two Kims had withdrawn from the NKDP to form what was subsequently styled the Reunification Democratic Party (RDP), President Chun announced that there would be no further constitutional discussion, thereby seeming to ensure that the 1988 presidential balloting would be conducted under the existing indirect procedure. Little more than two months later, Chun's hand-picked heir-apparent, Roh Tae Woo, made a dramatic eight-point announcement that represented virtual capitulation to opposition demands: 1) bipartisan constitutional amendment to permit direct presidential election and a peaceful transfer of power in February 1988; 2) revision of electoral procedure to ensure fair competition; 3) amnesty and the restoration of political rights for Kim Dae Jung and other political prisoners; 4) government promotion of basic human rights, including the right of habeas corpus; 5) elimination of constraints on freedom of the press; 6) greater institutional autonomy for local government and educational bodies; 7) promotion of a political climate "conducive to dialogue" among political parties and groups; 8) a national campaign against crime and corruption. Two days later President Chun publicly accepted the mandate, most observers feeling that his only viable alternative was the imposition of martial law, which would have irreparably damaged the country's international image on the eve of the Olympics.

Equally astonishing was the deterioration in relations between the two opposition leaders following Kim Dae Jung's return to active politics in early August. Both Kims had earlier given assurances that they would not split the opposition vote by standing as separate presidential candidates. Nonetheless, the more radical Kim Dae Jung withdrew from the RDP shortly after the new constitution had been approved, subsequently presenting himself as the nominee of the Peace and Democracy Party (PDP). Hoping to avert a further electoral disaster, the two Kims agreed in February 1988 to merge their respective parties into a unified opposition formation, but failed to implement the accord.

Widespread demonstrations erupted on May 18, the anniversary of the bloody Kwangju uprising eight years earlier. Far more serious disturbances broke out in early June, with thousands of student activists, in a major confrontation with riot police, being prevented from travelling to the demilitarized zone for a "unification" rally with North Korean youth.

POLITICAL PARTIES

Prior to 1972, competition between the Democratic Republican Party (DRP), formed in 1963 as an electoral mechanism for the ruling military junta, and the New Democratic Party (NDP), organized in 1967 as a coalition of opposition elements, had yielded what was essentially a two-party system. The imposition of emergency decrees and alteration of the electoral system under the 1972 constitution strongly favored progovernment groups, with the DRP becoming a personal vehicle for the late President Park. In the wake of Park's assassination, the NDP took the lead in calling for a new constitution and appeared to be the likely beneficiary of such action, having won a plurality in the 1978 balloting. However, the existing parties were dissolved following the constitutional referendum of October 1980, President Chun having announced that he favored the establishment of a multiparty system prior to the presidential election of February 1981.

At the March 1981 Assembly balloting, eight parties obtained legislative representation, the Democratic Korea Party (DKP) emerging as the largest single group in opposition to Chun's Democratic Justice Party (DJP). In February 1985, the New Korea Democratic Party (NKDP) displaced the DKP as the principal opposition formation, the two subsequently merging under the NKDP label in early April.

In April 1987 the two leading dissidents, Kim Dae Jung and Kim Young Sam, joined a majority of the NKDP legislators in announcing the formation of a new opposition group, the Reunification Democratic Party (below); however, Kim Dae Jung withdrew from the RDP in October to launch the Peace and Democracy Party (below) in support of his bid for the presidency.

Government Party:

Democratic Justice Party (DJP). The DJP was organized in early 1981 by former members of the DRP and NDP. Its candidates swept 90 of 92 electoral districts in the subsequent legislative balloting, obtaining nearly half of the 184 seats decided by popular vote and being allocated 61 of the 92 proportional seats. At the 1985 Assembly election, the DJP won 87 directly elective seats, retaining, as the largest single grouping, its 61 indirect seats. Its 35 percent share of the vote was, however, viewed as a setback, prompting the replacement of party chairman Lee Chai Hyung by Roh Tae Woo, who captured the national presidency in December 1987. At the legislative poll of April 26, 1988, the DJP won only 125 of 299 seats, although it was by no means clear that the opposition would be able to forge an antigovernment majority.

Leaders: ROH Tae Woo (President of the Republic and of the Party), YOON Giel Jong (Chairman), KIM Yoon Hwan (Majority Floor Leader in Assembly), PARK Jun Pyung (Secretary General).

Other Parties:

Reunification Democratic Party (RDP). The RDP was organized in April 1987 by Kim Young Sam and (indirectly) by Kim Dae Jung, who had been under house arrest since early March. The new party represented a hard-line posture by the dissidents in response to President Chun's unwillingness to agree to direct presidential balloting in 1988, coupled with an expressed fear that the opposition New Korea Democratic Party was being "manipulated" by the government. Initially, some 74 NKDP lawmakers participated in the action, although their number had fallen to 66 by the time of the new party's inaugural convention on May 1. Following adoption of the new constitution in October, Kim Dae Jung formed his own Peace and Democracy Party (below), splitting the opposition vote and throwing the presidency to Roh Tae Woo in December. Having failed in his own presidential bid, Kim Young Sam resigned as RDP president in February 1988, but has continued to dominate party affairs. The RDP emerged as the third-ranked party at the National Assembly election of April 26, winning 59 seats.

Leaders: KIM Myung Yoon (President), KIM Young Sam (former President).

Party for Peace and Democracy (PPD). The PPD was formed by Kim Dae Jung in October 1987, primarily as a vehicle to support his unsuccessful candidacy at the December presidential balloting. It was runner-up to the DJP at the legislative balloting of April 1988, winning 70 seats.

Leaders: KIM Dae Jung (President), PARK Young Sook (Vice President).

National Democratic Republican Party (NDRP). The NDRP was formed prior to the December 1987 presidential poll by the "third Kim", Kim Jong Pil. Although placing fourth in both the presidential and (subsequent) legislative balloting, it surprised observers on the latter occasion by winning 35 Assembly seats.

Leader: KIM Jong Pil.

Four minor parties offered presidential candidates in December 1987: the **Hanist Unification Party** (HUP), the **Social Democratic Party** (SDP), the **Unified Democratic Party** (UDP), and the **United Minjung Movement for Democracy and Unification** (UMMDU).

LEGISLATURE

The present **National Assembly** (*Kuk Hoe*) is a unicameral body of 299 members elected for four-year terms. Three-quarters of the assemblymen are chosen by direct and secret ballot from 224 single-member electoral districts; of the remaining 75 seats, 38 are allocated to the party winning the largest number of elective contests, with 37 divided among all other parties in proportion to the number of seats obtained. The distribution by party following the election of April 26, 1988 (proportional allocations in parentheses), was as follows: Democratic Justice Party, 125 (38); Party for Peace and Democracy, 70 (16); Reunification Democratic Party, 59 (13); New Democratic Republican Party, 35 (8); independents, 10.

Speaker: KIM Jae Soon.

CABINET

[as of May 15, 1988]

Prime Minister	Lee Hyun Jae
Deputy Prime Minister	Rha Woong Bae

Ministers

Agriculture and Fisheries	Yun Kun Hwan
Communications	Oh Myung
Economic Planning	Rha Woong Bae
Education	Kim Young Shik
Energy and Resources	Lee Bong So
Finance	Sa Kong Il
Foreign Affairs	Choi Kwang Soo
Government Administration	Kim Yong Kap
Health and Social Affairs	Kwon E Hyok
Home Affairs	Lee Chun Ku
Information and Culture	Chong Han Mo
Justice	Chung Hae Chang
Labor	Choi Myung Hon
National Construction	Choe Tong Sop
National Defense	Gen. (Ret.) Oh Ja Bok
National Unification	Lee Hong Koo
Science and Technology	Lee Kwan
Sports	Cho Sang Ho
Trade and Industry	Ahn Byung Hwa
Transportation	Lee Bom Choon
Minister of State for Political Affairs	Lee Jong Chan
Director, Agency for National Security Planning	Bae Mung
Director, Office of Legislation	Hyun Hong Choo
Director, Veterans Administration	Chon Sok Hong
Governor, Central Bank	Park Sung Sang

NEWS MEDIA

Press. The most influential newspapers are privately owned but during the Chun era were subject to pervasive government control; thus in late 1980 *Shin-A Ilbo* was absorbed by the pro-government *Kyunghyang Shinmun* and six provincial newspapers were closed down, limiting the provinces to one newspaper each. Most of the restrictions were eased in mid-1987 and virtually eliminated by early 1988. The following are Korean-language dailies published at Seoul, unless otherwise noted: *Chosun Ilbo* (1,800,000); *Joong-ang Ilbo* (1,600,000); *Dong-A Ilbo* (1,100,000), independent; *Hankook Ilbo* (900,000); *Kyunghyang Shinmun* (730,000), government influenced; *Seoul Shinmun* (700,000), government owned; *Maeil Kyungje Shinmun* (155,000), economic daily; *Korea Herald* (150,000), in English; *Korea Times* (140,000), in English; *Pusan Ilbo* (Pusan, 100,000). In early 1988 a number of prominent journalists (many of whom had been prohibited from media employment under presidents Park and Chun) were completing plans to launch the country's first "truly independent" newspaper, *Hangyoreh Shinmun*.

News agencies. The principal domestic facility is the United (*Yonhap*) News Agency, formed in November 1980 by forced merger of the former Hapdong News Agency with the Orient Press and several smaller agencies. A number of foreign agencies maintain offices at Seoul.

Radio and television. The publicly owned Korean Broadcasting System is a nationwide, noncommercial radio and television network which in December 1980 absorbed two of the country's four independent broadcasting services. The remaining private facilities are the progovernment Munhwa Broadcasting Corporation (MBC) and the Christian Broadcasting System (CBS), which is restricted to religious programming. There were approximately 8.6 million television receivers in 1987.

INTERGOVERNMENTAL REPRESENTATION

Ambassador to the US: KIM Kyung Won.

US Ambassador to Republic of Korea: James Roderick LILLEY.

Permanent Observer to the UN: Dr. PARK Kun.

IGO Memberships (Non-UN): ADB, ADF, AfDB, CCC, CP, ICAC, ICCAT, Intelsat, Interpol, ISO, IWC, IWTC.

K U W A I T

State of Kuwait
Dawlat al-Kuwayt

Political Status: Constitutional hereditary emirate; independent since June 19, 1961.

Area: 6,880 sq. mi. (17,818 sq. km.).

Population: 1,697,301 (1985C), 1,933,000 (1988E). The 1985 census figure includes 1,016,013 resident non-Kuwaitis (60 percent of the total).

Major Urban Centers (1985C): KUWAIT CITY (44,424); Salmiya (153,220); Hawalli (145,215).

Official Language: Arabic.

Monetary Unit: Dinar (market rate March 1, 1988, 1 dinar = $3.62US).

Sovereign (Emir): Sheikh Jabir al-Ahmad al-Jabir Al SABAH; appointed Prime Minister in 1965 and Heir Apparent in 1966; reappointed Prime Minister in 1971, 1975, and 1976; became Emir upon the death of his cousin, Sheikh Sabah al-Salim Al SABAH, on December 31, 1977.

Prime Minister and Heir Apparent: Sheikh Sa'd al-'Abdallah al-Salim Al SABAH; appointed February 8, 1978, to vacancy created by elevation of Sheikh Jabir al-Ahmad al-Jabir Al SABAH; most recently reappointed on July 13, 1986, following legislative dissolution of July 3.

T H E   C O U N T R Y

Located near the head of the Persian Gulf, Kuwait is bordered on the north and west by Iraq, and on the south by Saudi Arabia. It shared control of a 2,500-square-mile Neutral Zone with the latter until the area was formally partitioned in 1969, with revenues from the valuable petroleum deposits in the zone being divided equally by the two states. An extremely arid country, Kuwait suffered from acute water supply problems until 1950, but the installation of a number of desalination plants has since alleviated the problem.

Native Kuwaitis, who now constitute fewer than half the country's population, are principally Muslims of the Sunni sect, with a small minority of Shi'ites. The noncitizen population, upon which the sheikhdom depends for a labor pool, is composed chiefly of other Arabs, Indians, Pakistanis, and Iranians who have settled in Kuwait since World War II. In recent years the government has limited immigration and fostered the repatriation of some foreign workers in a Kuwaitization drive. Women comprise ap-

proximately 13 percent of the paid labor force; the 23 percent who are native Kuwaitis are concentrated in health care and education, with the remainder primarily employed as teachers and domestic servants.

Kuwait's petroleum reserves, estimated at 100 billion barrels in 1986, are the world's third largest, with the government in recent years striving to gain control not only of exploration and production but of "downstream" operations: refining, transport, and marketing. As a result of oil income, Kuwait has become a highly developed welfare state, providing its citizens with medical, educational, and other services without personal income taxes or related excises. The GDP per capita, one of the highest in the world, declined by nearly 20 percent in 1985–1986 because of continued recession in the oil industry, while budgetary deficits, which commenced in late 1984, are expected to continue through 1988; the latter, however, are largely technical in nature because of current account surpluses stemming from investment income.

GOVERNMENT AND POLITICS

Political background. Kuwait's accession to complete independence in 1961 was preceded by a period of close association with Great Britain that began in the late nineteenth century when the then semiautonomous Ottoman province sought British protection against foreign invasion and the extension of Turkish control. By treaty in 1899, Kuwait ceded its external sovereignty to Britain in exchange for financial subsidies and defense support, and in 1914 the latter recognized Kuwait as a self-governing state under its protection. Special treaty relations continued until the sheikhdom was made fully independent by agreement with reigning Emir 'Abdallah al-Salim Al SABAH on June 19, 1961. Iraqi claims to Kuwaiti territory were rebuffed shortly afterward by the dispatch of British troops at Kuwait's request, and were subsequently reduced to a border dispute that was substantially resolved in 1975.

On August 29, 1976, the government of Sheikh Jabir al-Ahmad Al SABAH resigned in the wake of alleged "unjust attacks and denunciations against ministers" by members of the National Assembly. Sheikh Sabah al-Salim Al SABAH, who had become emir upon the death of Sheikh 'Abdallah in 1965, responded on the same day by dissolving the Assembly, suspending a constitutional provision that would have required a new election within two months, and instituting severe limitations on freedom of the press. On September 6, a new government, virtually identical in membership to the old one, was formed by Sheikh Jabir, who became emir upon the death of Sheikh Sabah in 1977.

Observers attributed the drastic measures of 1976 to the impact of the Lebanese civil war upon Kuwait, which then counted some 270,000 Palestinians among its nonnative population. The continuing exclusion of immigrant elements from political life accounted in large part for the lack of significant political change during the remainder of the decade, despite growing dissatisfaction among the various groups—most noticeably, Shi'ite Muslims upon commencement of the Iranian revolution in early 1979.

Following a return to the earlier constitutional practice, nonparty balloting for a new National Assembly was held on February 23, 1981. Five days later, the heir apparent, Sheikh Sa'd al-'Abdallah al-Salim Al SABAH, who had first been appointed in 1978, was redesignated as prime minister. He was reappointed on March 3, 1985, after balloting on February 20 for a new Assembly which was itself dissolved on July 3, 1986, after a series of confrontations between elected and ex officio government members over fiscal and internal security issues. Echoing the events of 1976, the emir postponed new elections and implemented strict press controls (see News Media, below).

Constitution and government. The constitution promulgated in 1962 vests executive power in an emir selected from the Mubarak line of the ruling Sabah family, whose dynasty dates from 1756. The emir rules through an appointed prime minister and Council of Ministers, while the constitution calls for legislative authority to be shared by the emir and a National Assembly which is subject to dissolution by decree. The judicial system, since its revision in 1959, is based on the Egyptian model and includes courts of the first degree (criminal assize, magistrates', civil, domestic, and commercial courts) as well as a Misdemeanors Court of Appeal. The domestic court, which deals with cases involving such personal matters as divorce and inheritance, is divided into separate chambers for members of the Sunni and Shi'ite sects, with a third chamber for non-Muslims. Civil appeal is to a High Court of Appeal and, in limited cases, to a Court of Cassation.

The country is administratively divided into four districts, each headed by an official appointed by the central government.

Foreign relations. As a member of the Arab League, Kuwait has closely identified itself with Arab causes and, through such agencies as the Kuwait Fund for Arab Economic Development and the Organization of Arab Petroleum Exporting Countries, has contributed to the economic development of other Arab countries. Since 1967, it has provided direct aid to those countries that have suffered as a result of conflict with Israel. In addition, Kuwait has emerged as a leading mediator within the Arab League: in 1979, Foreign Minister Sabah al-Ahmad al-Jabir Al SABAH was instrumental in resolving a dispute within the United Arab Emirates over the distribution of governmental powers, while an attempt was also made to mediate a dispute between Oman and South Yemen over the Dhofar region. In 1981 Kuwait joined five other regional states in forming the Gulf Cooperation Council (GCC).

Dominating all other external concerns since its outbreak in 1979 has been the Iran-Iraq war, which has curtailed oil exports and generated fear of Iranian expansionism should the Khomeini regime prove victorious. Following a number of attacks on shipping by both participants and a decision by Washington to increase its naval presence in the Gulf, Kuwait, which had previously declined an offer of American tanker escort, proposed in April 1987 that a number of its vessels be transferred to US registry. The reflagging, completed by midyear, provided enhanced security for oil shipments, but was interpreted as solidifying the sheikdom's pro-Iraqi posture. A number of Iranian Silkworm missile firings ensued thereafter, including three in October that hit two tankers in Kuwaiti territorial waters and a supertanker loading facility at Sea

Island. In December another of the Chinese-made missiles, apparently aimed at the country's main oil terminal at Mina al-Ahmadi, exploded harmlessly by hitting a decoy vessel.

Current issues. In addition to threatening Kuwait's oil lifeline, the Gulf conflict has generated mounting tension within the country's resident population, more than a third of which is of Iranian extraction. Numerous acts of terrorism have erupted since 1983, including a May 1985 car bomb attack on a motorcade containing the Amir and other senior officials. In 1987 there were more than a dozen such incidents, many directed at US-related businesses.

On the economic front, the government persevered with a controversial program to prop up the commercial banks, which were still recovering from a 1982 collapse of the country's unofficial stock exchange. By early 1987 financial confidence had been visibly strengthened by the successful rescheduling of most nonperforming debts arising from the crash. However, most development projects remained in abeyance because of the shortfall in oil revenue.

POLITICAL PARTIES

Political parties as such are not permitted in Kuwait. As in other Middle Eastern countries, however, sympathizers are found for various Palestinian organizations and for foreign-based transnational parties, such as the *Baath* and the Arab Nationalist Movement, members of the latter having won five seats in the 1985 National Assembly balloting in a loosely knit "Democratic Alliance" with left-wing elements critical of the government. In addition there are a number of Islamic fundamentalist groupings, the most important being the **Islamic Social Reform Society** (*Jam'iyat al-Islah al-Ijtima'i*).

Fundamentalists won a block of seats in the 1981 National Assembly election but lost ground in 1985.

LEGISLATURE

A National Assembly (*Majlis al-'Umma*) was organized in 1963 to share legislative authority with the emir, although its impact has been limited by dissolution and suspension of constitutional prerogatives (see Political background and Current issues, above). Under the 1962 basic law, the Assembly encompasses 50 representatives (2 each from 25 constituencies) elected for four-year terms, in addition to ministers who, if not elected members, serve ex officio. Only literate, adult, native-born males whose families have resided in Kuwait since 1920 are allowed to vote, an increasingly vocal call by some women for suffrage being rebuffed by the Assembly in July 1985.

The Assembly was most recently dissolved by the emir on July 3, 1986, with no indication of when new balloting would occur.

CABINET

Prime Minister	Sa'd al-'Abdallah al-Salim Al Sabah
Deputy Prime Minister	Sabah al-Ahmad al-Jabir Al Sabah

Ministers

Amiri Diwan Affairs	Khalid al-Ahmad al-Jabir Al Sabah
Awqaf and Islamic Affairs	Khalid Ahmad al-Jasar
Commerce and Industry	Faysal 'Abd al-Razaq Khalid
Communications	'Abdallah 'Abd al-Mushin Al Sharhan
Defense	Nawwaf al-Ahmad al-Jabir Al Sabah
Education	Anwar 'Abdallah Nuri
Electricity and Water	Dr. Hamud 'Abdallah Al Ruqba
Finance	Jasim Muhammad al-Khurafi
Foreign Affairs	Sabah al-Ahmad al-Jabir Al Sabah
Information	Jabir Mubarak al-Hamad Al Sabah
Interior	Salim al-Sabah al-Salim Al Sabah
Justice and Legal Affairs	Dhari 'Abdallah Uthman
Oil	'Ali al-Khalifa al-Athbi Al Sabah
Planning	Dr. 'Abd al-Rahman 'Abdallah al-'Awadi
Public Health	Dr. 'Abd al-Razak Yusif al-Abdul Razak
Public Works	'Abd al-Rahman al-Huati
Social Affairs and Labor	Nasir Muhammad al-Ahmad Al Sabah

Ministers of State

Cabinet Affairs	Rashid 'Abd al-Aziz al-Rashid
Foreign Affairs	Sa'ud Muhammad al-'Usaymi
Housing Affairs	Nasir 'Abdallah al-Rudan
Municipal Affairs	Muhammad 'Abd al-Muhsin Al Rifai
Services Affairs	'Isa Muhammad Ibrahim al-Mazidi
Governor, Central Bank	'Abd al-Wahab Tammar

NEWS MEDIA

Press. Constitutional guarantees of freedom of the press were suspended by Emir Sabah on August 29, 1976. In June 1979, the government halted publication of two weeklies after they printed "articles considered harmful to Kuwait's relations with other Persian Gulf states". On July 12, 1980, the offices of *al-Ra'i al-'Amm* were bombed, apparently by dissidents, resulting in 2 deaths and 17 other casualties. Following the National Assembly election of 1981, censorship was relaxed, permitting the reemergence of what the *New York Times* called "some of the most free, and freewheeling newspapers in the region". However, in conjunction with the dissolution of the Assembly on July 3, 1986, the government imposed new press restrictions, subjecting periodicals to prior censorship and announcing it would suspend any newspapers or magazines printing material "against the national interest". The government also continued its drive to Kuwaitize the news media, with an estimated 40 journalists from other Arab countries being deported to open jobs for nationals. The following are published daily at Kuwait City in Arabic, unless otherwise noted: *al-Qabas* (90,000); *al-Siyasah* (81,000); *al-Anbaa* (74,000); *al-Ra'i al-'Amm* (al-Shuwaykh, 70,000); *al-Watan* (60,000); *Arab Times* (al-Shuwaykh, 44,000), in English; *Kuwait Times* (43,000), in English.

News agencies. The domestic facility is the Kuwait News Agency (KUNA); the Middle East News Agency, ANSA, *Xinhua,* Reuters, and TASS are among the foreign agencies maintaining bureaus at Kuwait City.

Radio and television. The Kuwait Broadcasting Service and Television of Kuwait, both controlled by the government, transmitted to 1.1 million radio and 700,000 television receivers, respectively, in 1987.

INTERGOVERNMENTAL REPRESENTATION

Ambassador to the US: Sheikh Sa'ud Nasir Al SABAH.

US Ambassador to Kuwait: W. Nathaniel HOWELL.

Permanent Representative to the UN: Muhammad A. ABULHASAN.

IGO Memberships (Non-UN): ADF, AfDB, AFESD, AMF, BADEA, BDEAC, GCC, IC, IDB, Inmarsat, Intelsat, Interpol, LAS, NAM, OAPEC, OPEC.

LAOS

Lao People's Democratic Republic
Sathalanalat Paxathipatai Paxaxôn Lao

Political Status: Fully independent constitutional monarchy proclaimed October 23, 1953; Communist-led People's Democratic Republic established December 2, 1975.

Area: 91,428 sq. mi. (236,800 sq. km.).

Population: 3,584,803 (1985C); 3,694,000 (1988E).

Major Urban Center (1985C): VIANGCHAN (formerly Vientiane, 377,409).

Official Language: Lao (French is still widely used in government circles).

Monetary Unit: New Kip (official rate March 1, 1988, 350.00 new kips = $1US). A "liberation kip", worth 20 old kips, was introduced in 1976; the present currency, valued at 100 liberation kips, was introduced in December 1979.

Acting President: PHOUMI VONGVICHIT; assumed office on October 29, 1986, following the resignation of SOUPHANOUVONG.

Chairman of the Council of Ministers: KAYSONE PHOMVIHAN; designated Prime Minister by the People's Congress of the Lao Patriotic Front on December 2, 1975, concurrent with the resignation of Prince SOUVANNA PHOUMA; title changed to chairman of the Council of Ministers in July 1982.

THE COUNTRY

The wholly landlocked nation of Laos is situated between Vietnam and Thailand but also shares borders with Burma, Kampuchea, and China. Apart from the Mekong River plains adjacent to Thailand, the country is largely mountainous, with scattered dense forests. Tropical monsoons provide a May-October wet season that alternates with a November-April dry season. The population is divided among four major groups: about 40 percent Lao-Lum (valley Lao); 34 percent Lao-Theung (mountainside Lao); 16 percent Lao-Tai (tribal Lao); and 10 percent Lao-Soung (mountaintop Lao). Tribal minorities include non-Khmer-speaking groups in the southern uplands and Meo and Yao in the northern mountains. Although most ethnic Lao, especially the valley Lao, follow Hinayana (Theravada) Buddhism, the tribals practice animism. Lao is the primary official language, but French is still common within government circles. Pali, locally known as *Nang Xu Tham*, a Sanskrit language of Hindu origin, is generally used by the priests.

Laos remains one of the world's three or four poorest countries, with an estimated per capita GNP of little more than $100 in 1986. About 80 percent of the population is engaged in agriculture. Rice, the principal food staple, grows on about 90 percent of the farmed land; other crops include maize, tobacco, cotton, citrus fruits, and coffee, while opium, nominally subject to state control, is an important source of income in Meo hill areas. Mining is presently confined almost entirely to tin, but there are rich deposits of high-quality iron ore in Xieng Khouang Province. Exports of timber, green coffee, electricity, and tin provide most of the country's foreign-exchange earnings. Despite recent government efforts to speed modernization, development has been hampered by poor communication facilities and an inadequate transport and distribution system.

GOVERNMENT AND POLITICS

Political background. Laos became a French protectorate in 1893 and gained limited self-government as an Associated State within the French Union on June 19, 1949. Although the French recognized full Lao sovereignty on October 23, 1953, the Communist-led Vietminh — supported within Laos by the so-called *Pathet Lao* (Land of Lao), the military arm of the Lao Communist movement — mounted a war of "national liberation" in 1954 in conjunction with its operations in Vietnam. Hostilities were ended by the Geneva accords of 1954, and the last French ties to Laos lapsed in December of that year.

Pro-Western or conservative governments held power from 1954 to 1960, except for a brief interval in 1957–1958 when neutralist Prime Minister SOUVANNA PHOUMA formed a coalition with (then) Prince SOUPHANOU-VONG, his half-brother and leader of the pro-Communist Lao Patriotic Front (*Neo Lao Hak Xat* — NLHX). In April 1960 the Lao army, headed by Gen. PHOUMI NO-SAVAN, gained control of the government through a fraudulent National Assembly election. A coup in August by a group of neutralist officers under Capt. KONG LE led to the reinstatement of Souvanna Phouma as prime minister, but a countercoup led by General Phoumi brought about the installation four months later of a rightist government headed by Prince BOUN OUM NA Champassak. In an effort to defuse the fighting and avoid deeper involvement by the great powers, a 14-nation conference was convened at Geneva in May 1961, and the rightists, neutralists, and NLHX eventually agreed to join a coalition government under Souvanna Phouma that took office in June 1962. Renewed factional feuding nevertheless led to the withdrawal of the NLHX ministers over the next two years and the continuation, with North Vietnamese support, of Communist insurgency based in the north. The NLHX refused to participate in an election held July 18, 1965, the results of which left Souvanna Phouma in control of the National Assembly. Military encounters between the government and the *Pathet Lao* (renamed the Lao People's Liberation Army in October 1965) continued thereafter, with the Liberation Army retaining control of the northeast and working closely with North Vietnamese forces concentrated in the area.

Peace talks between the *Pathet Lao* and the Souvanna Phouma government resumed in 1972, and in February 1973 ceasefire proposals put forward by the government were accepted. A political protocol signed the following September provided for a provisional coalition government (comprising 2 neutral ministers and 11 cabinet members from each of the opposing groups) and a joint National Political Consultative Council (NPCC) empowered to advise the cabinet. On April 5, 1974, King SAVANG VATTHANA signed a decree appointing the coalition government, formally marking the end of a decade of bitter warfare. Prince Souvanna Phouma was redesignated prime minister, while *Pathet Lao* leader Prince Souphanouvong was named president of the NPCC.

In May 1975, following the fall of Cambodia and South Vietnam to Communist insurgents, *Pathet Lao* forces moved into the Laotian capital of Vientiane and began installing their own personnel in government posts while subjecting both military and civilian supporters of the neutralist regime to political "reeducation" sessions. Three months later, on August 23, the formal "liberation" of Vientiane was announced. On December 2, at a People's Congress called by the Lao Patriotic Front, the monarchy was abolished, the 19-month-old coalition government of Prince Souvanna Phouma was terminated, and a People's Democratic Republic was established. Concurrently, Souphanouvong was designated head of state and president of a newly established Supreme People's Assembly, while KAYSONE PHOMVIHAN, secretary general of the Lao People's Revolutionary Party (LPRP), was named prime minister. Both the former king, Savang Vattahana, who had formally abdicated on November 29, and Prince Souvanna Phouma, prior to his death in January 1984, remained nominally in public life as "advisers" to the regime.

Souphanouvong resigned his state posts after reportedly having suffered a stroke in September 1986; he was succeeded as head of state (on an acting basis) by PHOUMI VONGVICHIT, a deputy chairman of the Council of Ministers, and as president of the Assembly by SISOMPHON LOVANSAI, theretofore one of the body's three vice presidents.

Constitution and government. Upon its establishment in 1975, the 45-member Supreme People's Assembly was charged with drafting a new Laotian constitution, but the document is yet to be issued. Following the resignation of Souphanouvong in October 1986, the presidency of the Republic was separated from that of the Assembly. The present chairman of the Council of Ministers has served since his 1975 designation by the National Congress of People's Representatives. In the wake of the Communist takeover, judicial functions were assumed by numerous local "people's courts", with a Supreme Court subsequently being added. The country is currently divided into 17 provinces (*khouengs*), each administered by a committee associated with the Lao People's Revolutionary Party. Subdivisions, also administered by People's Revolutionary Committees, include districts, cantons, and villages.

Foreign relations. As mandated by the Geneva accords of 1962, the royal government of Laos avoided military alliances but joined the United Nations as well as a number of international economic organizations, including the Colombo Plan and the Asian Development Bank. All such affiliations have been retained by the present government, although the influence of Hanoi (which maintains 40,000–50,000 troops in Laos) has reversed the country's pre-1975 neutrality in major-power issues. In late 1978, Laos strongly supported Soviet-backed Vietnam's ouster of the Pol Pot government in Kampuchea, subsequent reports indicating that Laotian troops had joined Vietnamese forces in fighting the remaining *Khmers Rouges*. Although Laos condemned China's incursion into Vietnam in February 1979, it backed the USSR's intervention in Afghanistan ten months later.

Despite the issuance of a Lao-Thai communiqué in January 1979 calling for the Mekong to become a "river of genuine peace, friendship and mutual benefit", border incidents and ideological warfare have since divided the two countries (see Current issues, below). One of the most critical issues has been the status of the Mekong River Committee, originally established in 1957 by the governments of Cambodia, Laos, Thailand, and the Republic of Vietnam to coordinate development of the water resources of the Lower Mekong basin. In 1978, representatives of Laos, Thailand, and Vietnam — without the participation of the *Khmer Rouge* government of Democratic Kampuchea — agreed to serve on an Interim Mekong Committee, while in 1980 delegates from the national Mekong committees of Laos, Vietnam, and the recently installed People's Republic of Kampuchea (PRK) initiated a series of twice-yearly meetings in protest at the exclusion of the Hanoi-backed PRK from the Interim Committee. With neither riparian group commanding full regional participation, little progress has since been registered toward implementing the goals of the original Mekong organization; however, both bodies have served to facilitate development aid to Laos, the purely Indochinese group serving as a conduit for some $50 million yearly from socialist countries while Australia and the Netherlands, among others, contribute through the Interim Committee. Japan and Sweden have also been important sources of economic assistance.

Although relations with the United States have remained cool since 1975, the Lao government has periodically assisted Washington in its search for servicemen listed as missing in action during the Vietnam war. In July 1985, the remains of 13 such persons were recovered by a US-Lao evacuation team, with excavation at other crash sites occurring in 1986 and a joint technical meeting on MIAs being convened at Vientiane in November 1987.

During 1987 attempts were made to mend relations with China, despite reports (denied by Beijing) of continued activity by China-backed "reactionaries" in Laos' northern provinces. In November, following a visit to Beijing by the Laotian deputy foreign minister (the first such high-level meeting since 1978), it was announced that the two states would reestablish links at the ambassadorial level.

Current issues. At the Fourth Congress of the LPRP in November 1986, a number of leadership changes (none involving Politburo incumbents) were made and a second (1986–1990) five-year plan was approved. The latter, a substantially revised version of a draft introduced early in the year, focused on enhanced agricultural output as its first priority, while calling for a substantial increase in timber production and a total ban, as of January 1, 1988, on unprocessed timber exports, despite complaints that such action would heighten the existing trade deficit.

During 1987, in emulation of both Moscow and Hanoi, attention was directed to the cultivation of a New Economic Management System featuring a relaxation in regard to private trade and the redesignation of nearly half of the 300 state-owned production units into "autonomous economic enterprises". Despite resistance by some party cadres to the reforms, inflation declined to a respectable 10 percent for the year.

Continuing a lengthy series of skirmishes with Thai forces, the "most serious border incident" in 12 years erupted in December 1987 in an area claimed by both Laos and Thailand on the basis of a 1907 treaty between Thailand and France. The outbreak followed an exacerbation of tension during bipartite talks in March and a subsequent Laotian claim to have shot down three Thai aircraft. However, despite uneven relations at the diplomatic level, Bangkok adopted a conciliatory economic posture, increasing the number of "strategic goods" that could be sold to Laos, pledging increased rice donations to the World Food Program for its neighbor, and agreeing to a price rise for increased electricity purchases, which constituted Laos' most lucrative hard-currency export.

POLITICAL PARTIES

In 1979, the **Lao Front for National Reconstruction** (LFNR) succeeded the Lao Patriotic Front (*Neo Lao Hak Xat* — NLHX) as the umbrella organization for various social as well as political groups committed to national solidarity.

Chairman: SOUPHANOUVONG.

Lao People's Revolutionary Party — LPRP (*Phak Pasason Pativat Lao* — PPPL). Known prior to the Communist seizure of power as the People's Party of Laos (*Phak Pasason Lao*), the LPRP is the Communist core of the LFNR. At its Fourth Congress, held at Viangchan in November 1986, the 303 delegates (representing a reported membership of 44,000) affirmed their commitment to a "strategic alliance" with Vietnam and elected a Central Committee of 51 full and 9 alternate members, in addition to an expanded Politburo of 11 full and 2 candidate members, and a 9-member Secretariat.

Secretary General: KAYSONE PHOMVIHAN.

Other Members of Politburo: Gen. KHAMTAI SIPHANDON, NOUHAK PHOUMSAVAN, and Gen. PHOUN SIPASEUT (Deputy Chairmen, Council of Ministers); MAICHANTAN SENGMANI (Minister in the Office of the Council of Ministers); PHOUMI VONGVICHIT (Acting President of the Republic), SALI VONGKHAMSAO (Chairman, State Planning Committee); Lt. Gen. SAMAN VI-GNAKET (Deputy Minister of Defense); Gen. SISAVAT KEOBOUNPHAN (Interior Minister and Secretary, Viangchan City Party Committee); SISOMPHON LOVANSAI (President, Supreme People's Assembly); SOUPHANOU-VONG (former President of the Republic).

Candidates: Brig. Gen. CHOUMMALI SAI-GNAKONG (Chief, Army Logistics), OUDOM KHATTI-GNA (Secretary, Xiang Khouang Province Party Committee).

Central Committee Secretariat: Brig. Gen. CHOUMMALI SAI-GNAKONG, KAYSONE PHOMVIHAN, Gen. KHAMTAI SIPHANDON, MAICHANTAN SENGMANI, OUDOM KHATTI-GNA, SALI VONGKHAMSAO, Lt. Gen. SAMAN VI-GNAKET, SOMLAK CHANTHAMAT, Gen. SISAVAT KEOBOUNPHAN.

In late 1980, it was reported that a number of rightists, neutralists, and tribals had met at Champassak, Thailand, to form an anticommunist **Lao People's National Liberation United Front.** Among those present at the meeting was exiled Gen. Kong Le, who had led the August 1960 coup. Two years later, on August 18, 1982, former defense minister Gen. Phoumi Nosavan announced the formation at Bangkok of a Royal Lao Democratic Government (RLDG) committed to the overthrow of the existing Lao regime in cooperation with guerrilla forces opposing the Vietnamese in Kampuchea. United Front leaders repudiated the action by Phoumi, who died on November 3, 1985.

LEGISLATURE

A 264-member National Congress of People's Representatives was convened by the Lao Patriotic Front on December 1–2, 1975, to approve the transition to a people's republic. The government had announced earlier that an election of delegates to a new National Assembly would be held by April 1976; by the end of 1986, however, no such election had been held. Thus the **Supreme People's Assembly,** established by the Congress in 1975 to draft a new constitution, continued to serve as an interim legislature.

President: SISOMPHON LOVANSAI.

CABINET

Chairman, Council of Ministers	Kaysone Phomvihan
First Deputy Chairman	Nouhak Phoumsavan
Deputy Chairmen	Gen. Khamtai Siphandon
	Phoumi Vongvichit
	Phoun Sipaseut
	Sali Vongkhamsao
Ministers	
In the Office of the Council of	
Ministers	Chanmi Duangboutdi
	Ma Khaikhamphithoun
	Gen. Sisavat Keobounphan
	Thongsavath Khaikhamphithoun
Agriculture, Irrigation and	
Cooperatives	Bounpheng Soundala
Commerce	Vanthong Sengmuang
Culture	Thongsing Thammavong
Education, Sports, Physical	
Education and Fine Arts	Bountiem Phitsamai
Equipment and Technical Supply	Thongsouk Saisankhi
Finance	Yao Phonvantha
Foreign Affairs	Phoun Sipaseut
Industry, Handicrafts and	
Forestry	Maisouk Saisompheng
Interior (Acting)	Asang Laoli
Justice	Kou Souvannamethi
National Construction	Gen. Khemphon Phovipasert
National Defense	Gen. Khamtai Siphandon
Public Health	Dr. Khamliang Phonsena
Transport, Posts and	
Communications	Col. Phao Bounnaphon
Without Portfolio	Kamsouk Saignaseng
	Ma Khaikhamphithoun
	Sot Phetlasi
	Thongchan Uplavan
Committee Chairmen	
Ethnic Affairs	Nhiavu Lobaliayao
National Social Welfare and War	
Veterans	Khambou Sounisay
News Agencies, Newspapers,	
Radio and Television	Son Khamvanvongsa
State Bank	Nouphan Sithphasay
State Planning	Sali Vongkhamsao

NEWS MEDIA

Press. Laotian newspapers, most of which have traditionally been government controlled or published by persons associated with the government, are of limited circulation and scope. Existing newspapers were suspended upon establishment of the People's Republic. Current publications include *Pasason* (The People, 30,000), PPPL organ; *Noum Lao* (Lao Youth, 6,000), Youth Union fortnightly; *Vientiane May* (New Vientiane, 2,500), organ of the local PPPL; *Aloun Mai* (New Dawn), PPPL publication.

News agencies. *Kaosan Pathet Lao* (KPL), the domestic agency, is a government organ issuing daily bulletins in Lao and French. TASS is one of the few foreign services currently operating at Vientiane.

Radio and television. National and international radio service is provided by National Radio of Laos, which broadcasts in Khmer, English, French, Lao, Thai, Vietnamese, and numerous dialects. Television transmission, which commenced on a limited basis in late 1983, is provided by Lao National Television and reaches approximately 32,000 receivers.

INTERGOVERNMENTAL REPRESENTATION

Ambassador to the US: (Vacant).

US Ambassador to Laos: (Vacant).

Permanent Representative to the UN: (Vacant).

IGO Memberships (Non-UN): *ACCT,* ADB, CP, Interpol, NAM, PCA.

LEBANON

Republic of Lebanon
al-Jumhuriyah al-Lubnaniyah

Political Status: Independent parliamentary republic proclaimed November 26, 1941, with acquisition of de facto autonomy completed upon withdrawal of French troops in December 1946.

Area: 4,015 sq. mi. (10,400 sq. km.).

Population: 3,447,000 (1988E). Estimates vary widely; the most recent official figure (2,126,325 in 1970), which excluded Palestinian refugees, was based on a population sample and was believed to reflect substantial underenumeration; some recent figures appear to be extrapolations based on the 1970 report.

Major Urban Centers (1980E): BEIRUT (702,000); Tripoli (175,000); Zahlé (47,000); Saida (Sidon, 25,000); Tyre (14,000).

Official Language: Arabic (French is widely used).

Monetary Unit: Lebanese Pound (market rate March 1, 1988, 370.00 pounds = $1US).

President: Amin Pierre GEMAYEL (Maronite Christian); elected by the National Assembly on September 21, 1982, and sworn in for a six-year term on September 23 in succession to Elias (Ilyas) SARKIS (Maronite Christian), following the assassination on September 14 of Bashir GEMAYEL, who had been designated President-elect on August 23.

Acting Prime Minister: Salim Ahmad al-HUSS (Sunni Muslim); appointed by the President, following the assassination of Rashid KARAMI (Sunni Muslim) on June 1, 1987.

THE COUNTRY

Lebanon is bounded on the west by the Mediterranean Sea, on the north and east by Syria, and on the south by Israel. A long-standing presumption of roughly equal religious division between Christians and Muslims is no longer valid because of a high birthrate among the latter. The largest Muslim sects are the Shi'ite and the Sunni, each traditionally encompassing about one-fifth of the permanent population, although recent estimates place the number of Shi'ites at over one third. Druses number nearly 200,000, and Christian sects include Maronites, Orthodox Greeks, Greek Catholics, Orthodox Armenians, and Armenian Catholics. Women comprise 25 percent of the paid labor force, concentrated in lower administrative, commercial, and educational sectors.

Because of a commercial tradition, Lebanon's living standard until the mid-1970s was high in comparison to most other Middle Eastern countries and developing nations in general. The leading contributor to national income was the service sector, encompassing banking, insurance, tourism, transit trade, income from petroleum pipelines, and shipping. Industrial development, though largely limited to small firms, was also important, the principal components being food processing, textiles, building materials, footwear, glass, and chemical products. However, the 1975–1976 civil war severely damaged the economy, with the 1976 GNP showing a 60 percent loss compared to 1974. In addition, casualties and dislocations among the civilian population yielded an estimated loss of two-thirds of skilled industrial workers. While nearly half of the GNP loss was regained by 1978, renewed turmoil contributed to further decline prior to the full-scale Israeli invasion of mid-1982.

Lebanon's economy continues to deteriorate under the impact of domestic turmoil. By 1985, some 70 percent of the country's productive capacity had come to a halt, 35 percent of all factories had been destroyed, 80 percent of industrial workers had been laid off, and the national debt had grown by 700 percent in four years to $30.4 billion. The budget deficit grew from $1 billion in 1981 to $10 billion in 1984, absorbing one-third of the gross national product. The agricultural sector in Lebanon declined by 36 percent in 1984 alone, while most government income from customs duties disappeared, and the once-stable Lebanese pound had lost approximately 95 percent of its 1982 value by March 1987.

GOVERNMENT AND POLITICS

Political background. Home to the Phoenicians in the third millenium B.C., Lebanon was later subjected to invasions by the Romans and the Arabs, with Turkish control being established in the sixteenth century. During the nineteenth century Mount Lebanon, the core area of what was to become the Lebanese Republic, acquired a special status as a result of European intervention on behalf of various Christian factions. Following disintegration of the Ottoman Empire after World War I, the country became a French mandate under the League of Nations, France adding to Mount Lebanon areas detached from Syria to enlarge the country's area and its Muslim population. Independence, proclaimed in 1941 and confirmed in an agreement with Free French representatives in 1943, was not fully effective until the withdrawal of French troops in 1946, following a series of national uprisings during the tenure of the Republic's first president, Bishara al-KHURI. The so-called National Pact of 1943, an unwritten understanding reflecting the balance of religious groups within the population at that time, provided for a sharing of executive and legislative functions throughout the governmental structure in the ratio of six Christians to five Muslims. Although this arrangement helped moderate the impact of postwar Arab nationalism, the country was racked by a serious internal crisis in the summer of 1958 that occasioned the temporary landing of US Marines at the request of President Camille CHAMOUN. The disturbances, most of them involving a rising of Muslims and Druses under Sa'eb SALAM, Kamal JUMBLATT, and Rashid 'Abd al-Hamid KARAMI, were precipitated by President Chamoun's decision to remove from the government Arab nationalist critics of Lebanon's pro-Western policies. The crisis was alleviated in July 1958 by the election of a compromise president, Gen. Fu'ad CHEHAB, who was acceptable to the dissident leadership. Internal stability was further consolidated by the peaceful election of Charles HELOU as president in 1964.

Although Lebanon was an active participant only in the first Arab-Israeli war, Palestinian guerrilla groups based in southern Lebanon began launching attacks on Israel in the mid-1960s. In November 1969, Yasir 'ARAFAT, who had emerged as chairman of the Palestine Liberation Organization (PLO) the previous February, met with representatives of the Lebanese Army at Cairo, Egypt, to conclude a secret pact under which Lebanon recognized the right of Palestinians to engage in action against the Jewish state, with the military agreeing to facilitate movement of commandos through border zones. Although the so-called Cairo Agreement was subsequently amended to restrict Palestinian activity, a sharp increase in the number of cross-border raids, particularly after the expulsion of the Palestinian guerrilla groups from Jordan in 1970–1971, generated Israeli reprisals and, in turn, demands from the Christian Right that the Lebanese government restrain the commandos.

In February 1973 Israeli troops in civilian dress raided Beirut and killed three top-ranking guerrilla leaders. The attack contributed to the resignation of a Salem-led government in April, while a feeling within the Sunni community that it lacked effective representation permitted Dr. Amin al-HAFIZ to retain office for only two months thereafter. Hafiz' successor, Taqi al-Din SULH, resigned in late September after a cabinet crisis stemming from a security dispute, but remained as head of a caretaker government until the confirmation of Rashid al-SULH in early December.

Serious fighting between the Maronite right-wing Phalangist Party and Palestinian guerrilla groups erupted at

Beirut in April 1975, exacerbated by growing tensions between status quo and anti-status quo factions. The status quo forces, mainly Maronite, opposed demands by largely Muslim nationalists, who wanted the government to identify more closely with the Palestinian and other pan-Arab causes. They also demanded revisions in Lebanon's political system to reflect Muslim population gains. As a result of the conflict, the Rashid al-Sulh government fell on May 15 and was succeeded by an emergency all-military cabinet headed by Brig. Noureddin RIFAI which, however, made no effort to intervene in the fighting and was itself forced to resign on May 26. On June 30, following the death of nearly 3,000 persons, Rashid Karami announced the formation of a "rescue" cabinet that succeeded in arranging a ceasefire on July 1. Nonetheless, fighting was soon renewed with increased intensity; by the end of the year, a full-scale civil war between the religious communities had prompted talk of possible partition into separate Christian and Muslim states.

The conflict escalated further in 1976, causing widespread destruction and virtual collapse of the economy. In March a group of Muslim army officers, calling for the resignation of President Sulayman FRANJIYAH, mounted an abortive coup and on April 9 regular Syrian army units intervened in support of the Lebanese leadership following its break with the leftists headed by Kamal Jumblatt. The Syrian intervention permitted the election by the Lebanese parliament on May 8 of Elias SARKIS to succeed President Franjiyah, who, however, refused to leave office prior to the expiration of his term on September 23, by which time Syrian and Maronite Christian forces had overcome leftist-Palestinian resistance in most sectors.

During a meeting at Riyadh, Saudi Arabia, on October 17–18, Syrian President Assad and Egyptian President Sadat agreed on the establishment of a definitive ceasefire, commencing October 21, to be maintained by a 30,000-man Arab Deterrent Force (ADF) theoretically under the authority of President Sarkis but actually under Syrian control. Despite appeals from Iraq and Libya for a limit on Syrian participation, the plan was approved during an Arab League summit meeting at Cairo on October 25–26. By late November hostilities had largely ceased and on December 9 President Sarkis designated Salim Ahmad al-HUSS to form a new government (Prime Minister Karami having tendered his resignation on September 25).

Notwithstanding the assassination of Muslim Druse leader Kamal Jumblatt on March 16, which negated efforts by President Sarkis and Prime Minister Huss to secure agreement on constitutional reform, an uneasy truce prevailed throughout much of the country during 1977. The principal exception was the southern region, where fear of Israeli intervention prevented deployment of Syrian-led peacekeeping units. Thus insulated, rightist forces made a strenuous effort to bring the entire border area under their control but were rebuffed in the coastal sector, which remained in Palestinian hands.

The formation of a new Israeli government under *Likud*'s Menachem Begin in June 1977 resulted in an escalation of support for the Phalange-led Maronite militia, which now called for withdrawal of the Syrian-led ADF from Lebanese territory. As a result, the political situation

during 1978 became more complex and the level of conflict intensified. On March 15, Israeli forces invaded southern Lebanon in an attempt to "root out terrorist bases" that had supported a guerrilla raid four days earlier on the highway between Haifa and Tel Aviv. Less than a month later the UN Security Council authorized the dispatch of an Interim Force in Lebanon (UNIFIL) to assist in restoring peace to the area, although Israeli troops did not withdraw completely until mid-June. Meanwhile, fighting broke out in the north between Christian militiamen and the ADF. Although Syrian troops had originally intervened to suppress attacks by Palestinian guerrillas and their Muslim leftist allies against Maronite right-wing militias, the Syrian government rejected partition plans sponsored by some Christian groups and in the ensuing weeks some of the most intense fighting since 1975 occurred in the Beirut area between militiamen and ADF forces.

Intrarightist conflict had also erupted at Beirut in mid-May between the Phalangists and the National Liberal Party led by former president Camille Chamoun. Subsequently, on June 13, Phalangists and supporters of former president Franjiyah engaged in a pitched battle north of Beirut, in the course of which the former president's son, Tony FRANJIYAH, and several members of his immediate family were killed. The attack came after the pro-Syrian Sulayman Franjiyah had quit the Lebanese Front (see Political Parties and Groups, below), which he had helped found, in opposition to increased NLP and Phalangist conflict with the ADF.

The Huss government twice resigned during 1978–1979 in efforts to promote a political solution. The resignation of April 19, 1978, was withdrawn in mid-May, Huss commenting that an attempt to bring together "all the active political trends in the Lebanese arena" had "regrettably clashed with contradictory attitudes and obstacles". The effort had begun on April 23 with the approval by a 13-member multifactional parliamentary committee of a six-point "national accord" that was adopted by the Chamber of Deputies four days later but rejected first by the leftist National Movement (see below) and subsequently by rightist supporters of former president Chamoun. Another proposal put forward on October 17 by Arab foreign ministers meeting at Beiteddine was also denounced by NLP leader Chamoun, who called it "nothing but words". Both proposals had called for an end to armed Palestinian action within Lebanon and the restructuring of the Lebanese Army on a more ethnically balanced basis so as to permit the eventual withdrawal of both ADF and UNIFIL forces. The second cabinet resignation occurred on May 16, 1979, with Huss forming a new government of six Muslim and six Christian ministers on July 16.

Three months earlier, on April 18, Maj. Saad HADDAD, commander of some 2,000 Christian militiamen loyal to the rightist Lebanese Front, proclaimed an "independent free Lebanese state" consisting of an eight-mile-wide strip of southern Lebanon along the Israeli border. The move was prompted by the deployment of units of the Lebanese Army, which Haddad had accused of complicity with both Syria and Palestinian guerrillas, alongside UNIFIL forces in the south. A week later, the Israeli government, which was providing matériel to Haddad's troops, announced that it would initiate preemptive strikes against terrorists in response to continuing infiltration from Lebanon. On June 6, in the context of increased Israeli shelling, "search-and-destroy" missions, and air strikes, the PLO and the National Movement stated that they would remove their forces from the port city of Tyre as well as villages throughout the south in order to protect the civilian population. In both June and September Israeli and Syrian jet fighters dueled south of the Litani River (below the so-called "red line", beyond which Israel refused to accept a Syrian presence), while UNIFIL forces were, at various times throughout the year, attacked by all sides, despite a series of UN-sponsored ceasefires. The situation was no better at Beirut and farther north. On the Right, Phalangist, NLP, Armenian, and Franjiyah loyalists clashed; on the Left, intrafactional fighting involved Nasserites, members of the Arab Socialist Union, 'Arafat's *al-Fatah* and other Palestinian groups, and forces of the Syrian Nationalist Socialist Party. Meanwhile, Syrian troops found themselves fighting elements of the Right, the Left, and increasingly militant pro-Iranian Shi'ites.

On June 7, 1980, Prime Minister Huss again tendered his resignation in order to permit formation of a unity cabinet; however, discussions conducted over the next six weeks failed to produce agreement among the various parties, and on July 20 President Sarkis named former prime minister Taqi al-Din Sulh to form a new government. On August 9, Sulh informed the president that his effort had not succeeded, and Huss continued to serve in a care-taker capacity until October 25, when former minister of justice Shafiq al-WAZZAN concluded arrangements for an administration that secured a vote of confidence from the National Assembly on December 20.

By mid-1981, in addition to the largely emasculated Lebanese military, the Syrian presence, and the sporadic incursion of Israeli units, it was estimated that some 43 private armies were operating throughout the country, in-cluding *al-Amal,* the military wing of the Shi'ite commu-nity, which had grown to a force of some 30,000 men engaged largely in operations against the Palestinians and Lebanese leftist groups sympathetic to Iraq. The most important engagements during the first half of the year, however, occurred between Syrian forces and Phalangist militiamen at Beirut and at the strategically important town of Zahlé in the central part of the country. In the course of the fighting at Zahlé, the Israeli air force intervened to assist Phalangist forces against Syrian air attacks. As Israeli attacks in Lebanon intensified and PLO guerrilla actions increased in Israel, US presidential envoy Philip Habib arranged a ceasefire between Israeli and PLO forces. The uneasy peace ended on June 6, 1982, when Israel again attacked PLO forces in Lebanon, supposedly in retaliation for an unsuccessful assassination attempt by a Palestinian gunman on the Israeli ambassador to Britain. In little more than a week the Israeli army succeeded in encircling PLO forces in West Beirut while driving the Syrians back into the eastern Bekaa Valley. Subsequently, on August 6, US envoy Habib announced that agreement had been reached on withdrawal of the PLO from Lebanon, the actual evac-uation commencing on August 21 and concluding on Sep-tember 1.

On August 23, Maronite leader Bashir GEMAYEL was designated by the Lebanese Assembly to succeed President Sarkis; however, the president-elect was assassinated in a bombing of the Phalangist Party headquarters on Septem-ber 14. His brother, Amin Pierre GEMAYEL, was named on September 21 as his replacement and was sworn in two days later. The new president promptly reappointed Prime Minister Wazzan, whose new government was announced on October 7.

The assassination of Bashir Gemayel was followed, on September 16–18, 1982, by the massacre of numerous inhabitants of the Chatila and Sabra Palestinian refugee camps at Beirut, where a group of terrorists had allegedly been left behind by the PLO. While the perpetrators of the massacre were right-wing Phalangist militiamen, they had been given access to the camps by Israeli authorities, whose de facto complicity generated intense controversy within Israel and widespread condemnation from abroad.

During late 1982 and early 1983, the presence of a multi-national peacekeeping force of US, French, Italian, and British units helped to stabilize the situation in the vicinity of Beirut, while direct negotiations between Israeli and Lebanese representatives (the first since conclusion of the 1949 war) yielded, with US participation, a troop with-drawal agreement on May 17, 1983, that included provision for the establishment of a "security region" in southern Lebanon to inhibit cross-border raids by Palestinians. The agreement was strongly opposed by Lebanese Arab nation-alists and by Syria, which refused to discuss the withdrawal of its own forces from northern and eastern Lebanon, and Israel began construction in August of a defense line along the Awali river, to which it redeployed its troops in early September. The action was followed by a resurgence of militia activity in West Beirut, clashes between pro- and anti-Syrian groups in the northern city of Tripoli, and fighting between Druse and Phalangist forces in the Chouf mountains and elsewhere.

A series of "national reconciliation" talks, involving all of the leading factions, commenced at Geneva in late Sep-tember, but were adjourned six weeks later, following simultaneous bomb attacks on the headquarters of the US and French peacekeeping contingents at Beirut. On Febru-ary 4, 1984, the Wazzan cabinet resigned, although the incumbent prime minister agreed to remain in office in a caretaker capacity. Subsequently, the Western peacekeep-ing forces were withdrawn and on March 5 Lebanon, under strong pressure from Syria, abrogated the unratified with-drawal accord concluded ten months earlier. Despite a generally unproductive second round of reconciliation dis-cussions at Lausanne in mid-March, former prime minister Karami, with Syrian endorsement, accepted reappoint-ment and on April 30 announced the formation of a ten-member government that included leaders of most of the contending parties.

Despite the Israeli withdrawal, there was no decrease in the range and intensity of violence during 1985. In March a rebellion broke out within the Lebanese military against the political leadership of the Phalange and its ostensible leader, Amin Gemayel. Deeply opposed to the president's close ties to Syria and particularly to his newly formed friendship with Syrian Vice President Khaddam, the anti-

Gemayel forces seized much of the Maronite-held sector of Beirut, the area around the port of Junieh, and the mountains north of the capital. The rebellion was led by Samir GEAGEA, a young Phalangist commander who had led the raid in which Tony Franjiyah had been slain in 1978. Geagea's forces, styled the "Independent Christian Decision Movement", called for a confederation of sectarian based mini-states and rejected an appeal in April by 50 of Lebanon's senior Christian leaders for intercommunal talks to achieve national reconciliation. In May, reportedly under pressure from Syria, Phalangist officials removed Geagea as head of their executive committee; his successor, Elie HOBEIKA, who reportedly had commanded the forces that perpetrated the Sabra and Chatila massacres in 1982, immediately affirmed the "essential" Syrian role in Lebanon and Lebanon's place in the Arab world.

Within Muslim-controlled West Beirut, the Shi'ite *al-Amal* militia fought several battles against *al-Murabitun*, the Palestinians, and its former ally, the Druse-led PSP (see Political Parties, below); it also continued the struggle against government forces across the Green Line in East Beirut. In April, a coalition of *al-Amal* and PSP forces defeated *al-Murabitun* and seized control of West Beirut. In protest against the fighting, Prime Minister Karami resigned, but reversed himself after consulting at Damascus with Syrian President Assad. Subsequently, *al-Amal* opened a campaign against Palestinian forces in Beirut and laid seige to two Palestinian refugee camps. The renewed "war of the camps" precipitated an emergency session of the Arab League Council in June, which called for a ceasefire and, under pressure from Syria, *al-Amal* agreed to withdraw its forces.

While the siege of the camps was momentarily lifted, *al-Amal* and the PSP repeatedly clashed during the ensuing three months for control of Beirut. Syria attempted to end the fighting between its Lebanese allies with a security plan drawn up under the auspices of Syrian Vice President Khaddam in September. According to the plan, the Lebanese army and police would end the rule of sectarian militias in Beirut under supervision of Syrian observers. Earlier, although the various militias continued their struggle for control of the city, PSP leader Walid Jumblatt and *al-Amal* chief Nabi Berri had launched a National Unity Front that included the Lebanese Communist Party, the *Baath,* the SSNP, and 50 independent political leaders, several of them Christian. Formed under Syrian auspices, the Front called for a political program rejecting partition, confessionalism, or other division of the country.

In mid-September the northern city of Tripoli became the scene of some of the most violent clashes in the civil war. The chief protagonists were the Islamic Unification Movement, allied with pro-Arafat Palestinians against the pro-Syrian Arab Democratic Party. Although surrounded by Syrian forces, Tripoli had become the base of an anti-Syrian coalition that Damascus wished to destroy. As a result of the fighting, 80 percent of the city's 400,000 inhabitants fled; another of its effects was the seizure at Beirut of four Soviet diplomats by Muslim fundamentalists who demanded that Moscow pressure Assad to order a ceasefire. One of the Russian diplomats was killed; the others were released on October 30 after a respite in the Tripoli battle.

Events in southern Lebanon were dominated by the withdrawal of Israeli troops and its consequences. During the phased departure, militant Shi'ites stepped up guerrilla activity against the Israelis. In retaliation, as part of its "iron fist" policy, Israel seized several hundred men from Shi'ite villages and imprisoned them in Israel. To obtain their release, a fundamentalist Shi'ite faction hijacked an American TWA airliner en route from Athens to Rome, forced the plane to land at Beirut, and removed the passengers to various locations throughout the city. After 17 days, the hostages were released through the intercession of *al-Amal* leader Berri. Concurrently, Israel began a gradual release of the Shi'ites, both the United States and Israel denying that there was any link between the two actions.

The departure of the Israelis precipitated bloody clashes between Shi'ite, PSP, Palestinian and Maronite forces seeking to gain control of the evacuated areas. However, most Maronite and Palestinian forces were defeated, the southern part of the country falling largely under Shi'ite control, with PSP forces confined to traditionally Druse enclaves.

Although Israeli occupation of Lebanon officially ended on June 6, numerous Israeli security advisors remained with the South Lebanese Army, which retained control of a narrow border strip, with Israel continuing its policy of hot pursuit of forces that continued their attacks on the SLA.

During 1986, the military alignments within Lebanon underwent substantial (in some cases remarkable) change. In January, following the conclusion of a December 28 "peace agreement" at Damascus between Druse leader Jumblatt, Shi'ite leader Berri, and Phalangist leader Hobeika, Lebanese Forces units commanded by Hobeika were decisively defeated in heavy fighting north and east of Beirut by hard-line Phalangists loyal to his predecessor, Samir Geagea. After Hobeika had fled to Paris (although returning within days to Damascus), both Jumblatt and Berri called for the removal of President Gemayel, who declared that he was "not the problem" and would refer the accord to the National Assembly, which contained a Christian majority. In the south, numerous clashes occurred in ensuing months between Palestinian and Lebanese groups, on the one hand, and the Israeli-backed SLA on the other, with increased anti-Israeli guerrilla activity by an "Islamic Resistance Front" that included the pro-Iranian *Hezbollah,* a radical Shi'ite group that had refused to endorse the December agreement. By the end of the year, it was apparent that the more moderate *al-Amal* had lost many of its militiamen to *Hezbollah*. Of greater consequence, however, was the reappearance of numerous PLO guerrillas, many of whom had returned via the Phalangist-controlled port of Junieh, north of Beirut. In November the Palestinians surged from refugee camps near Sidon and, in heavy fighting, forced *al-Amal* units to withdraw from hillside positions around the adjacent town of Maghdousheh. Druse leader Jumblatt, who had previously supported the Palestinians, immediately announced that his forces would join with other pro-Syrian leftist groups to "confront jointly any attempt by the Palestinians to expand outside their camps". By early 1987, the "war of the camps" had returned in the north, while fighting broke out at Beirut between Shi'ites and their intermittent Druse allies, prompting a renewed intervention by Syrian army forces to restore a semblance of order to the battle-scarred capital.

Constitution and government. Lebanon's constitution, promulgated May 23, 1926, and often amended, established a unitary republic with an indirectly elected president, a unicameral legislature elected by universal suffrage, and an independent judiciary. In accordance with the National Pact of 1943, the principal offices of state are divided among members of the different religious sects. The president, who is traditionally a Maronite Christian, is elected by a two-thirds majority of the legislature, while the prime minister is a Sunni Muslim nominated by the president after consultation with political and religious leaders. Parliamentary seats are allotted primarily through a system of proportional representation based on religious groupings, with five Muslims for every six Christians; thus the number of members in Parliament has traditionally been based on a multiple of eleven.

Lebanon is administratively divided into six provinces (*muhafazat*), each with a presidentially appointed governor who rules through a Provincial Council. The judicial system is headed by 4 courts of cassation and includes 11 courts of appeal and numerous courts of the first instance. Specialized bodies deal with administrative matters (Council of State) and with the security of the state (Court of Justice) and also include religious courts and a press tribunal.

At a special session of the National Assembly on May 31, 1984, Prime Minister Karami outlined a Syrian-backed program of constitutional reform that would increase the number of deputies from 99 to 120, to provide for equal representation for Christians and Muslims, and end the practice of appointing civil servants on the basis of sectarian criteria. The plan was endorsed by Christian, Druse, and Shi'ite militia representatives the following December, but was opposed by many Phalangist leaders, including President Gemayel, and became essentially moribund in the wake of severe intra-Christian conflict in January 1986.

Foreign relations. A member of the United Nations and accorded special status by the Arab League because of its sizeable Christian population, Lebanon traditionally maintained good relations with the West and followed a policy of comparative restraint with respect to Israel. The principal aim of Lebanon's foreign policy has long been to safeguard its own independence while maintaining its broad commitment to Arab nationalism. During the 1967 Arab-Israeli War the US and British ambassadors were asked to leave as a gesture of solidarity with other Arab countries, but they returned shortly thereafter.

Efforts by foreign sources to stem the conflict in Lebanon have included the Syrian intervention against leftist and Palestinian forces in April 1976, which, opposed by the Soviet Union, enjoyed Egyptian, Saudi, and US support, as well as the muted acquiescence of Israel. The action was construed as reflecting Damascus' unwillingness to permit the installation of a regime that, potentially more radical than its own, might precipitate a major military response by Israel. Shortly thereafter, the Arab League authorized emplacement of a "symbolic" peacekeeping

force that proved inadequate to the task, thus leading to the October 1976 decision to introduce the 30,000-man Arab Deterrent Force. In 1979, however, Kuwaiti, Saudi Arabian, Sudanese, and UAE contingents withdrew, leaving ADF responsibility almost exclusively in the hands of Syrian troops. Meanwhile, in April 1978 a United Nations Interim Force in Lebanon (UNIFIL) had been organized to supervise withdrawal of Israeli forces who had entered southern Lebanon in an anti-Palestinian campaign the month before.

Despite clashes with both Palestinians and Christian militiamen in which a number of its members were killed, the UNIFIL mandate was renewed at six-month intervals until the Israeli invasion of June 1982, when it was given a two-month extension, with additional two- and three-month renewals in August and October. Meanwhile, on July 6, President Reagan announced that 800–1,000 US Marines would be dispatched as part of a multinational force to assist in the evacuation of Palestinians from Beirut. While it was originally indicated that the foreign presence would be "comparatively brief", the US contingent, in addition to French and Italian units, remained in the wake of the Gemayel assassination despite forceful objection by the Soviet Union, which initially called for the deployment of additional UN forces and subsequently moved to augment its logistical support of Syrian troops in the Bekaa Valley. The multinational force was eventually withdrawn in February–March 1984, while the essentially token UNIFIL presence in the south was most recently renewed for a six-month term in January 1988.

Current issues. A country once noted for its capacity to accommodate sharply divergent political and religious cleavages, Lebanon in the last 13 years has become a microcosm of virtually every tendency for conflict within the strife-torn Middle East. While the 1982 evacuation of PLO units from West Beirut resolved a portion of the security threat to Israel, Syrian forces remained entrenched in the northeast, with remnants of Palestinian groups scattered throughout the country. Tactically advantaged by the Israeli victory and the induction of Amin Gemayel as head of state, the Maronite Christians had long been opposed not only by the Palestinians but by a variety of left-wing, nationalist and other groups, notably Druse militia based in the Chouf Mountains north of Beirut and Shi'ite forces in the south. In addition, conflict has sporadically broken out between Lebanese supporters of the Iraqi and Syrian *Baath* parties, between Sunni and Alawite Muslims at Tripoli, between pro-Iraqi and pro-Iranian groups in the course of the Gulf war, between Shi'ites and other Muslim forces at Beirut, between Phalangists and other Maronites, and between right- and left-wing elements within the Shi'ite community. In the south, the largely Maronite South Lebanese Army has given no indication of a willingness to accept reintegration of its enclave into the Lebanese state, the unit's celebrated commander, Major Haddad, who died in January 1984, being replaced by a former Lebanese army general, Antoine LAHAD.

Despite the bitter enmity that had long characterized relations between the Muslim PLO and the Christian Phalangists, the two groups became tacit allies during 1986. The astonishing volte-face was attributed to an increasing perception by Maronite leaders that the Shi'ites presented the most severe long-term threat to their traditional domination of Lebanese politics. Collaterally, some Israeli experts urged their government to consider abandoning their ties to the Christians (and institute a blockade of the Phalangist-controlled port of Junieh) in the hope of cultivating better relations with moderate Shi'ites. As one such observer put it, "Everybody knows how to switch sides in Lebanon but Israel".

The assassination, in a helicopter bombing on June 1, 1987, of Prime Minister Karami reportedly shocked a country already traumatized by seemingly endless bloodshed. Although Karami, a month earlier, had declared his wish to resign because of an inability to resolve the nation's political and economic crises, he had been one of Lebanon's most durable and widely respected Muslim leaders.

The most important development during the latter half of 1987 was the increased influence of *Hezbollah,* which, with substantial Iranian support, had supplanted *al-Amal* in many of the poorer Shi'ite areas, particularly in the south. During early 1988 the Iranian-backed group also moved to augment its strength in the suburbs of West Beirut, provoking violent clashes with *al-Amal* that were contained in May by the second deployment of Syrian army units to the area in fifteen months.

POLITICAL PARTIES AND GROUPS

Lebanese parties have traditionally been ethnic and denominational groupings rather than parties in the Western sense, with seats in the National Assembly distributed primarily on a religious, rather than on a party, basis. Until the mid-1970s, the principal political cleavage was between two personalist groups popularly known as "Chehabists" and "Chamounists", from their identification with two former presidents of the Republic. Although Chehab himself was a Maronite, his followers were largely Muslim, left of center, and inclined towards pan-Arabism, while the pro-Western and predominantly Christian Chamounists stood largely to the right of center, strongly supported the political and social status quo, and tended to be aloof from Arab concerns.

The 1975–1976 civil war generated a more pronounced cleavage, a **National Movement** of leftist, reformist, and/or Muslim parties being formed under the leadership of Kamal Jumblatt of the Progressive Socialist Party (PSP), and a **Lebanese Front** being organized by predominantly rightist, Christian parties. In March 1976 the former grouping split over the issue of Syrian intervention in Lebanon, with the pro-Syrian parties withdrawing to form a **Nationalist Front** (sometimes referred to as the National Front or the Patriotic Front).

The National Movement originated in the Progressive and National Parties and Forces (PNPF), a coalition organized by Jumblatt in 1969 in support of the Palestinian cause as well as constitutional reform. In August 1975 the Movement proposed a Transitional Reform Program entailing abolition of the confessional system of parliamentary representation and the complete secularization of government — perhaps the only issues on which most of the

component Muslim, communist, and socialist parties have consistently agreed. The formation of the Nationalist Front seven months later involved the withdrawal of several Movement parties, including the pro-Syrian faction of the *Baath* and the Syrian Nationalist Socialist Party. Beginning in 1977, however, the Movement and the Nationalist Front were gradually reconciled, initially as a result of Syria's dissociation from rightist forces but, later, by their joint opposition to the Egyptian-Israeli peace proposals and Israel's intervention in southern Lebanon.

The rightist Lebanese Front was constituted on March 26, 1976, its principal founders being former president Sulayman Franjiyah, Pierre Gemayel of the Phalangist Party, former president Camille Chamoun of the National Liberal Party (NLP), and Fr. Sharbel Kassis of the Order of Maronite Monks. Although the constituent groups were united by their opposition to the activities of Palestinian guerrillas in Lebanon and by their support for constitutional pluralism (or, failing that, Christian autonomy), Franjiyah withdrew on May 11, 1978, because of his support for the Syrian presence and his objection to growing ties between the Lebanese Front and Israel. He was also embittered by the killing of his son in fighting with the Phalange during 1978 (see Marada Brigade, below).

At present, there are several dozen political parties and groups active in Lebanon, while both the National Movement and the Lebanese Front have been increasingly subject to intrafactional violence.

Largely Christian or Right-Wing Groups:

Phalangist Party (*al-Kata'ib al-Lubnaniyah/Phalanges Libanaises*). Founded in 1936, the Phalangist Party, a militant Maronite organization and the largest member of the Lebanese Front, was deeply involved in provoking the 1975 civil war. A 1979 party communiqué called for "positive, creative, unifying diversity" within an intact Lebanon; deployment of the Lebanese army to replace units of both UNIFIL and the Arab Deterrent Force; and separation of the issues of civil strife and political reform.

Despite periodic efforts to further unify the Christian Right, the Phalangists and the National Liberals (below) found themselves increasingly at odds following the civil war, with hostilities culminating on July 7–8, 1980, in some 300 deaths at Beirut and the surrender of the NLP militia command. The following day, Phalangist leader Pierre Gemayel and NLP President Camille Chamoun agreed to the merger of the Christian militia of East Beirut into a National Home Guard under Phalangist direction. Earlier, in October 1979, during a wave of intrarightist kidnappings that continued into 1980, an Organization of Revolutionaries of the North, which was believed to be linked to the Phalangist militia, claimed responsibility for attacks against the Franjiyah clan.

A survivor of numerous assassination attempts over the years, Pierre Gemayel died of natural causes in August 1984. Subsequently, in early 1985, the party split into two factions, yielding a revolt against the Gemayel regime that the president was able to contain with Syrian assistance.

Leaders: Amin Pierre GEMAYEL (President of the Republic), Georges SAADE (President), Charles DAHDAH (Secretary General).

National Liberal Party — NLP (*Hizb al-Ahrar al-Watani/Parti National Liberal*). The NLP, a largely Maronite right-wing grouping founded in 1958, rejects any coalition with Muslim groups that would involve the Palestinians. The second-largest party in the Lebanese Front, it has repeatedly called for the withdrawal of Syrian and other Arab troops from Lebanon and in recent years has argued that a federal system is the only way to preserve the country's unity. Periodic clashes between NLP and Phalangist militias culminated in early July 1980 in a major defeat for National Liberal forces.

In an interview on June 19, 1982, party founder Camille Chamoun claimed credit for having initiated the relationship with Israel that yielded military aid for Christian forces during the Lebanese civil war. Chamoun died in August 1987.

Leader: Dany CHAMOUN.

Marada Brigade. Based in northern Lebanon, the Marada Brigade is an essentially Maronite militia loyal to the Franjiyah clan. Since 1978, when former president Franjiyah withdrew from the Lebanese Front and his son Tony was killed in a battle with Phalangist militiamen, the Brigade has focused its attacks against supporters of Pierre Gemayel's party.

Leader: Sulayman FRANJIYAH (former President of the Republic).

National Bloc (*al-Kutla al-Wataniyah/Bloc National*). The National Bloc, a Maronite party formed in 1943, has been opposed to military involvement in politics. Its principal leader, Raymond Eddé, was the object of a number of assassination attempts during 1976 and subsequently retired to self-imposed exile in France. The Bloc has frequently been critical of other rightist groups, particularly the Phalangist Party.

Leaders: Raymond EDDE (President), Sa'id AQL (Vice President), Antoine Abu ZAID (Secretary General).

Largely Muslim or Left-Wing Groups:

Progressive Socialist Party — PSP (*al-Hizb al-Taqaddumi al-Ishtiraki/ Parti Socialiste Progressiste*). Founded in 1948, the PSP is a largely Druse group that advocates a socialist program with nationalist and anti-Western overtones. A rupture in relations between former party president Kamal Jumblatt and Syrian President Assad was followed by the Syrian intervention of April 1976. Jumblatt was assassinated in March 1977, the party leadership being assumed by his son, Walid, who subsequently became a Syrian ally and during the Israeli occupation of Lebanon established close ties with the Shi'ite *al-Amal* organization (see below). The alliance ended in early 1987, when the PSP intervened on the side of the PLO in the Beirut camps conflict.

Leaders: Walid JUMBLATT (President), Fuad SALMAN (Secretary General).

Syrian Nationalist Socialist Party. (*Parti Socialiste Nationaliste Syrien*). Organized as the Syrian Nationalist Party in 1932 in support of a "Greater Syria" embracing Iraq, Jordan, Lebanon, Syria, and Palestine, the NSSP was considered a rightist group until 1970. Also known as the Syrian People's Party, it was banned in 1962–1969 after participating in an attempted coup in December 1961. The party split into two factions in 1974, one group, led by 'Abdallah Saada, subsequently joining the National Movement and the other, led by George Kenizeh and Issam Mahayri, participating in the pro-Syrian Nationalist Front. In November 1978 its leadership announced that the party had been reunited. In recent years, NSSP forces are reported to have skirmished with both the Christian Phalangists and the leftist *Murabitun*.

Leaders: Dawoud BAZ (Chairman), Joubrah JRAYSH, Anwar al-FATAYRI (Secretary).

Arab Socialist Renaissance Party (*Hizb al-Baath al-Arabi al-Ishtiraki*). Al-Baath, a pan-Arab secular party, was divided into competing factions as a result of the Syrian intervention in 1976. Pro-Iraqi leader Musa Sha'ib was assassinated in July 1980, apparently by pro-Iranian Shi'ites.

Leaders: 'Abd al-Majid RAFI'I (Secretary General of pro-Iraqi faction), Asim QANSU (Secretary General of pro-Syrian faction).

Lebanese Communist Party — LCP (*al-Hizb al-Shuyu'i al-Lubnani/ Parti Communiste Libanais*). The pro-Moscow LCP was founded in 1924 as the Lebanese People's Party, banned in 1939 by the French Mandate Authority, but legalized in 1970. Although primarily Christian in the first half-century of its existence, the party became predominantly Muslim in the wake of the civil war. Its current secretary general, George Hawi, also serves as a vice president of the National Movement.

Leaders: Niqula al-SHAWI (President), George HAWI (Secretary General).

Organization of Communist Action in Lebanon — OCAL (*Organisation de l'Action Communiste du Liban*). OCAL was founded in 1970 by the merger of two extreme left-wing groups, the Movement of Lebanese Socialists and the Socialist Lebanon. The former had been formed by members of the Arab Nationalist Movement (below), the latter by former LCP and *Baath* members. Since the civil war, OCAL has cooperated closely with the LCP, both groups having recruited heavily from poorer members of the Shi'ite community at Beirut and during 1981–1982 engaging in sporadic clashes with *al-Amal* (below) in both the capital and southern regions.

Leaders: Muhsin IBRAHIM (Secretary General of OCAL and of the National Movement), Fawwaz TRABULSI (Assistant Secretary General).

Independent Nasserite Movement — INM (*al-Murabitun*). Founded in 1958 as a socialist party opposed to the Chamoun government, the INM is familiarly known by the name of its military branch, *al-Murabitun* ("The Vigilant"). The largest of at least 13 extant Nasserite groups in Lebanon, it has never been an exclusively Muslim organization although its main support comes from the Sunni urban poor. Reports from Beirut in 1980–1981 identified the INM as a participant in intraleftist street fighting, chiefly against the NSSP and the Arab Socialist Union (below).

Leaders: Ibrahim QULAYLAT (Vice President and Militia Leader of the National Movement), Samir SABBAGH.

Movement of the Deprived (*al-Amal*). Most familiarly known by the name of its militia, *al-Amal*, the Movement was founded by Imam Musa SADR, an Iranian, who disappeared in August 1978 while in Libya; subsequent reports indicated that Sadr had fallen from favor with Libya's Colonel Qadhafi and had been jailed, and perhaps executed. Although allied with the Palestinian Left during the civil war, *al-Amal* has become increasingly militant on behalf of Lebanon's Shi'ites — many of whom have been forced from their homes in the south — and in support of the Iranian revolution of 1979. During 1980–1982 the militia reportedly fought, at various times, the pro-Iraqi *Baath*, other pro-Palestinian Muslims, the Palestinians themselves, and the Christian Right. At the same time, the leadership has aligned itself with Syria.

After the 1982 Israeli invasion, several pro-Iranian offshoots of al-Amal emerged as well-organized guerrilla movements operating against American, French, and Israeli forces with great effectiveness. Two of these groups, the **Party of God** (*Hizb Allah*, commonly rendered as *Hezbollah*) and the **Islamic Holy War** (*al-Jihad al-Islami*) have been identified with suicide attacks such as the truck bombings of the US embassy in May 1983 and of the US Marine cantonment the following October.

Leaders: Sheikh Muhammad Mahdi Shams al-DIN (Principal Controller of the Command Council), Nabi BERRI (Militia Leader), Sadr al-Din al-SADR (Chairman), Husayn al-HUSAYNI (Secretary General).

Arab Nationalist Movement — ANM (*al-Haraka al-Qawmiyya al-'Arabiyya*). The Arab Nationalist Movement is a Marxist-oriented organization established in 1948 by the militant Palestinian leader Georges Habash and a number of colleagues who had attended the American University at Beirut. A pan-Arab party with branches throughout the Middle East, the Lebanese ANM has been closely associated with the more militant Palestinian groups.

Leader: Georges HABASH.

Among the more important smaller leftist parties are the **Arab Socialist Union,** which is divided into at least three factions but remains a member of the National Movement; the **Union of Working People's Forces,** led by Kamal SHATILA, the secretary general of the Nationalist Front; and the **Arab Liberation Front** (ALF), a pro-Palestinian extremist group that has also been closely associated with the Iraqi faction of the *Baath*. The ALF's principal leader, 'Abd al-Wahab KAYYALI, was assassinated in December 1981 following several months of street fighting at Tripoli with the Arab Red Knights militia of the **Arab Democratic Party,** a pro-Syrian Alawite group recently formed at Tripoli. Subsequently, there were clashes at Tripoli between the Red Knights and the *Tawheed* militia of the Sunni **Islamic Unification Movement,** with a Syrian-mediated peace accord between the two groups reported in late 1984.

Other Groups:

Parliamentary Democratic Front — PDF (*al-Jabha al-Dimuqratiyah al-Barlamaniyah*). The PDF advocates continuation of the governing model of former President Chehab, although its late leader, Rashid 'Abd al-Hamid Karami, attempted to conciliate differences between Christians and Muslims during 10 terms as prime minister from 1955 to 1987.

Leader: (Vacant, following the assassination of Prime Minister Karami on June 1, 1987).

Constitutional Party (*al-Dustur*). Founded in 1943, *al-Dustur* is a business-oriented party that has long supported Arab nationalism.

Leader: Michel Bishara al-KHURI.

Democratic Party (*Parti Démocrate*). The Democratic Party, a secular group formed in 1969, is strongly supportive of private enterprise.

Leader: Joseph MUGHAIZEL (Secretary General).

Armenian Revolutionary Federation — ARF (*Parti Dashnak*). The Federation, a socialist Armenian party with a past history of anti-Soviet activity, was allied with Maronite groups in 1958 but, along with a number of leftist Armenian organizations, remained politically neutral during the civil war. Fighting between Armenians and rightists, including Phalangists, broke out in Beirut during 1979, the most serious street battles occurring in April, May, and September.

Leader: Khatchig BABIKIAN.

[Note: For a discussion of Palestinian groups formerly headquartered in Lebanon, see end of National Governments section.]

LEGISLATURE

The former Chamber of Deputies, which in March 1979 changed its name to the **National Assembly** (*Majlis al-'Umma/Assemblée Nationale*), is a unicameral body of 99 members elected by universal suffrage for a four-year term (subject to dissolution) through a proportional system based on religious groupings. The National Pact of 1943 specifies that the president of the body be a Shi'ite Muslim. Although the diversity and tenuousness of political alignments in the Assembly make an analysis by party groupings impossible, the law specifies that the seats will be distributed to religious groups in the following proportions: Maronite Christian, 30; Sunni Muslim, 20; Shi'ite Muslim, 19; Greek Orthodox, 11; Greek Catholic, 6; Druse, 6; Armenian Orthodox, 4; Armenian Catholic, 1; Protestant, 1; and other, 1. The most recent election was held in May 1972, the term of the present legislature having been extended for two years in 1976 because of the civil war, with further extensions at two-year intervals thereafter.

President: Hussein al-HUSSEINI (Shi'ite Muslim).

CABINET

Acting Prime Minister	Salim al-Huss
Ministers	
Agriculture	'Adil 'Usayran
Economy and Trade	Victor Qassir
Education	Salim al-Huss
Finance (Acting)	Joseph al-Hashim
Foreign and Expatriates Affairs (Acting)	Salim al-Huss
Housing and Cooperatives (Acting)	Joseph al-Hashim
Hydroelectric Resources	Nabi Berri
Industry and Oil	Victor Qassir
Information	(Vacant)
Interior	Dr. 'Abdallah al-Rasi
Justice	Nabi Berri
Labor	Salim al-Huss
National Defense	'Adil 'Usayran
Post and Telecommunications	Joseph al-Hashim
Public Health	Joseph al-Hashim
Public Works, Transport and Tourism	Walid Jumblatt
Minister of State for the South and Reconstruction	Nabi Berri
Governor, Central Bank	Edmund Naim

NEWS MEDIA

Relative to other Middle Eastern countries, the Lebanese press was traditionally free from external controls, but Syrian troops forced suspension of a number of newspapers (including the respected *al-Nahar*) in December 1976. Following the imposition of formal censorship on January 1, 1977, most of the suspended papers were permitted to resume publication. A number of newspapers and periodicals have, however, been publishing from abroad, while numerous press employees have been murdered at Beirut in recent years.

Press. The following are published daily at Beirut in Arabic, unless otherwise noted: *al-Nahar* (85,000), independent; *al-Anwar* (76,000), independent; *al-Dustur* (currently being published from London, England, 54,000); *al-Amal* (47,000), Phalangist; *Lissan-ul-Hal* (34,000); *al-Hayat* (32,000), independent; *al-Dunia* (26,000); *Sada Lubnan* (25,000), pan-Arab; *L'Orient-Le Jour* (24,000), Christian-owned independent, in French; *al-Jarida* (23,000), independent; *Le Soir* (17,000), independent, in French; *al-Nida'* (10,000), Communist; *al-Cha'b* (7,000), Nationalist; *Ararat* (5,000), Communist, in Armenian; *al-Bayraq* (3,000), rightist; *al-Charq*, pro-Syrian. The last English-language daily, the *Daily Star,* ceased publication in August 1985.

News agencies. There is no domestic facility; however, numerous foreign bureaus maintain offices at Beirut.

Radio and television. The government-controlled Radio Lebanon broadcasts nationally in Arabic, English, French, and Armenian, and internationally to three continents. The Phalangist-controlled Radio Voice of Lebanon transmits from several stations, while the religious Voice of Hope (operated by the High Adventure Broadcasting Network) transmits from one. The *Compagnie Libanaise de Télévision* is a commercial station broadcasting over four channels, while *Télé-Liban,* also commercial, broadcasts over three. There were approximately 2.0 million radio and 500,000 television receivers in 1987.

INTERGOVERNMENTAL REPRESENTATION

Ambassador to the US: Abdallah BOUHABIB.

US Ambassador to Lebanon: John Hubert KELLY.

Permanent Representative to the UN: Rachid FAKHOURY.

IGO Memberships (Non-UN): ACCT, AFESD, AMF, BADEA, CCC, *EIB,* IC, IDB, Intelsat, Interpol, IWTC, LAS, NAM, PCA.

LESOTHO

Kingdom of Lesotho

Political Status: Traditional monarchy, independent within the Commonwealth since October 4, 1966; currently under control of Military Council sworn in by the monarch on January 24, 1986, following coup of January 20.

Area: 11,720 sq. mi. (30,355 sq. km.).

Population: 1,213,960 (1976C), 1,634,000 (1988E).

Major Urban Center (1980C): MASERU (57,500).

Official Languages: English, Sesotho.

Monetary Unit: Loti (market rate March 1, 1988, 2.09 maloti = $1US). The loti is at par with the South African rand, although under a Tripartite Monetary Area agreement concluded between Lesotho, Swaziland, and South Africa on July 1, 1986, the rand has ceased to be legal tender in Lesotho.

Sovereign: King MOSHOESHOE II; became Paramount Chief in 1960 and King on October 4, 1966.

Heir to the Throne: Letsie David SEEISO, son of the King.

Chairman of the Military Council of Lesotho: Maj. Gen. Justin Metsing LEKHANYA; sworn in by the King on January 24, 1986, following the ouster of Prime Minister Leabua JONATHAN (Basotho National Party) on January 19.

THE COUNTRY

Lesotho, the former British High Commission territory of Basutoland, is a hilly, landlocked enclave within the territory of South Africa. The Basotho people, whose vernacular language is Sesotho, constitute over 99 percent of the population, which includes small European and Asian minorities. About 70 percent of the population is nominally Christian. Although diamonds account for about two-thirds of export earnings, the economy is largely based on agriculture and stock-raising; it is also highly dependent on South Africa, Lesotho's main trading partner, which employs 80 percent of the country's wage earners and is the principal supplier of energy. Because of the unusual employment pattern, women are primarily responsible for subsistence activities, although they are unable by custom to control household wealth; female participation in government is virtually nonexistent.

GOVERNMENT AND POLITICS

Political background. United under MOSHOESHOE I in the mid-nineteenth century, Basutoland came under British protection in 1868 and was governed from 1884 by a British high commissioner. A local consultative body, the Basutoland Council, was established as early as 1903, but the decisive move toward nationhood began in the mid-1950s and culminated in the attainment of full independence within the Commonwealth as the Kingdom of Lesotho in 1966. MOSHOESHOE II, the country's paramount chief, became king of the new state, and Chief Leabua JONATHAN, whose Basutoland National Party (BNP) had won a legislative majority in the preindependence election, became prime minister.

A trial of strength between the king and prime minister occurred in 1966 when the former's attempt to gain personal control over both foreign and domestic policy led to rioting by opposition parties; after being briefly confined to his palace, the king agreed to abide by the constitution. Further internal conflict followed the 1970 election, at which the opposition Basotho Congress Party (BCP) appeared to have outpolled the BNP. Voting irregularities were cited to justify the declaration of a state of emergency, the consequent suspension of the constitution, and the jailing of opposition leaders. Subsequently, the opposition leaders were released and the king, who had gone into exile, returned.

The state of emergency was ultimately lifted in July 1973, but in the wake of a coup attempt in January 1974

against his increasingly unpopular regime, the prime minister introduced new internal security measures (patterned after similar measures in South Africa) that proscribed the transmittal of outside funds to political groups within the country and authorized the detention of individuals for 60 days without legal assistance.

During 1979–1982 numerous armed clashes were reported with the Lesotho Liberation Army (LLA), a guerrilla group affiliated with the outlawed "external" wing of the BCP under Ntsu MOKHEHLE, who claimed from exile that he was Lesotho's true leader on the basis of the election results invalidated in 1970.

In late 1984, the prime minister was mandated by an extraordinary general meeting of the BNP to call for a legislative election, and, with effect from December 31, the king dissolved an interim Assembly that had been appointed after the abortive 1970 balloting. Following refusal by the five leading opposition parties to participate in the voting scheduled for September 17–18, 1985, Chief Jonathan announced that a formal poll would be unnecessary and declared all of the BNP nominees elected unopposed.

On January 20, 1986, the manifestly unpopular Jonathan regime was toppled in a relatively bloodless coup led by Maj. Gen. Justin M. LEKHANYA, commander-in-chief of the government army, the Lesotho Paramilitary Force (LPF). Among the factors reportedly contributing to the coup were the economic blockade by South Africa (see Foreign relations, below) and power struggles within the BNP and the LPF. A decree issued on the day of the coup conferred executive and legislative powers on the king who was to act in accordance with a six-man Military Council and the Council of Ministers. On January 24 the king swore in Lekhanya as chairman of the Military Council, with a largely civilian Council of Ministers being installed three days later. In February the king declared an amnesty for political offenders, and in March banned all political activity pending the establishment of a new constitution.

Constitution and government. Under the 1966 constitution, which was suspended in January 1970, Lesotho was declared to be an independent monarchy with the king functioning as head of state and executive authority vested in a prime minister and cabinet responsible to the lower house of a bicameral Parliament. The latter consisted of a Senate of 22 chiefs and 11 nominated members, and a popularly elected 60-member National Assembly. In April 1973, an interim unicameral body was established, encompassing the 22 chiefs and 71 nominated members. A Parliament Bill approved in May 1983, but dormant until dissolution of the interim Assembly in December 1984, provided for the reinstatement of bicameralism. The Bill was voided after the 1986 coup by the Military Council, which announced the vesting of "all executive and legislative powers in HM the King", pending the adoption of "further laws". The judicial system consists of a High Court, a Court of Appeal, and subordinate courts (district, judicial commissioners', central, and local). Judges of the High Court and the Court of Appeal are appointed by the king on the advice of the government and its Judicial Service Commission.

Local government is based on nine districts, each of which is administered by a commissioner appointed by the central government.

Foreign relations. Lesotho's foreign policy has been determined less by its membership in the United Nations, the Commonwealth, and the Organization of African Unity than by its position as a Black enclave within the White-ruled Republic of South Africa. While rejecting the South African doctrine of apartheid and insisting on the maintenance of national sovereignty, the Jonathan government for some years cultivated good relations with Pretoria. Subsequent events, however, led to a noticeable stiffening in Maseru's posture. Following South Africa's establishment of the adjacent Republic of Transkei in October 1976, Lesotho requested a special UN Security Council meeting on the matter, complaining that its border had been effectively closed in an "act of aggression" designed to force recognition of Transkei. A similar request was lodged in December 1982 after 42 persons, termed "refugees" by Maseru but branded by Pretoria as African National Congress (ANC) guerrillas, had been killed in a predawn assault on the capital by South African troops. A Council resolution of December 15 requiring Pretoria to pay damages for the raid was ignored, and South African Prime Minister Pieter Botha continued to accuse Maseru of harboring ANC militants among the approximately 11,000 South African refugees living in Lesotho. Friction over Chief Jonathan's refusal to expel the ANC supporters culminated in South Africa's institution of a crippling economic blockade, ostensibly to block cross-border rebel activity, on January 1, 1986. Pretoria denied charges of complicity in the subsequent overthrow of Chief Jonathan but lifted the border controls when the new military regime flew 60 ANC members to Zimbabwe.

Since 1979, in an attempt to broaden its international support both regionally and abroad, Lesotho has been an active member of the Southern African Development Coordination Conference (SADCC), a body created to lessen members' economic dependence on the White-ruled regime. Most of the nine SADCC participants have called for sanctions against Pretoria for its apartheid policies, though none has been more vulnerable than Lesotho to South African destabilization.

Current issues. Following the January 1986 coup, General Lekhanya and the Military Council, exercising power in the king's name, quickly concluded a security pact with South Africa that precluded either country from allowing the planning and execution of "acts of terrorism" against the other. In the wake of the accord, ANC supporters continued to be expelled from Lesotho although Maseru resisted Pretoria's demand they be returned directly to South Africa for prosecution. The government reaffirmed Lesotho's commitment to SADCC economic strategy, but began to distance itself from the Communist-bloc relations courted by Chief Jonathan in his last years of rule.

The new relationship with Pretoria was illustrated by the signature in October 1986 of a treaty authorizing commencement of the Lesotho Highlands Water Project, which had been under consideration for more than two decades. In addition to benefiting from substantial royalties upon completion of the 10-year project, Lesotho will be provided with a source of hydroelectric power, offsetting electricity currently purchased from South Africa. Relations continued to improve in 1987 with the signing

of trade accords and General Lekhanya's appeal to the estimated 150,000 transient Basothos not to join the politically-active South African labor movement.

POLITICAL PARTIES

Former Governing Party:

Basotho National Party (BNP). Organized in 1959 as the Basutoland National Party, the BNP has counted many Christians and chiefs among its members. It traditionally favored free enterprise and cooperation with South Africa while opposing apartheid. In the mid-1970s, however, it began coopting policies originally advanced by the BCP (below), including the establishment of relations with Communist states and support for the ANC campaign against Pretoria. Growing internal division was reported in 1985 over who would succeed the aging Chief Jonathan as prime minister. One faction was dominated by the paramilitary Youth League, armed and trained by North Korea, which reportedly planned a government takeover. The Youth League was disarmed and officially disbanded in a confrontation with the Lesotho Paramilitary Force on January 15, 1986, prior to the LPF-led coup of January 20. Although the BNP's national chairman was named finance minister in the post-Jonathan administration, supporters of Chief Jonathan were barred from political activity. Chief Jonathan was detained briefly after the coup, released, and then placed under house arrest in August along with six BNP supporters for activities allegedly threatening national stability. They were released in September by order of the High Court with an admonition to refrain from political activity. The party's national chairman was named finance minister in the post-Jonathan administration, while the former prime minister died in April 1987.

Leader: Evaristus Retselisitsoe SEKHONYANA (National Chairman).

Former Opposition Parties:

Basotho Congress Party (BCP). Strongly antiapartheid and pan-Africanist in outlook, the BCP (formerly the Basutoland Congress Party) was split, following the abortive 1970 election, by the defection of (then) deputy leader Gerard P. Ramoreboli and several other members, who defied party policy and accepted nominated opposition seats in the interim National Assembly.

Banned in 1970, the main branch of the BCP continued to oppose the Jonathan government, claiming responsibility in the late 1970s for numerous armed attacks on police and BNP-supportive politicians. Concurrently, a Lesotho Liberation Army (LLA) of 500–1,000 operated, under external BCP direction, in the country's northern mountains and from across the border. Despite overtures from the new regime in early 1986, the LLA called for revival of the 1966 constitution as a condition of abandoning antigovernment activity.

Leaders: Gerard P. RAMOREBOLI (leader of internal parliamentary group), Geoffrey KOLISANG (Secretary General of internal group), Ntsu MOKHEHLE (leader of external group and the LLA).

Marema Tloe Freedom Party (MTFP). A royalist party, the MTFP has long been committed to enlarging the king's authority. In other respects, its position has been somewhere between the BNP and the BCP. An offshoot Marema Tloe Party (MTP), formed in 1965 and led by S.S. Matete, remerged with the MTFP in 1969. One of its members, Patrick Lehloenya, accepted a cabinet post as minister to the prime minister in late 1975, subsequently becoming minister of health and social welfare. MTFP President Bennett Makalo Khaketla was appointed minister of justice and prisons in the cabinet formed after the 1986 coup.

Leaders: Bennett Makalo KHAKETLA (President), Edwin LENAYA (Vice President).

United Democratic Party (UDP). The UDP was formed in 1967 by two progovernment members of the BCP. However, in a 1982 manifesto the party called for the establishment of full diplomatic relations with Pretoria, the expulsion from Lesotho of all South African political refugees, and opposition to trade sanctions against the Botha regime. In early 1985, UDP leader Charles Mofeli branded the projected legislative balloting as a "farce" and accused Prime Minister Jonathan of attempting to create a one-party state. Mofeli was arrested in June 1987 after attacking the new regime for "abuse of power" and calling for revocation of the ban on political party activity.

Leaders: Charles MOFELI, Ben L. SHEA (Chairman), M.J. LEPHOMA (Secretary General).

Basotho Democratic Alliance (BDA). A conservative, pro-South African group, the BDA was founded at Pretoria on January 6, 1984. Its only announced policy at the time was the severance of relations with all Communist governments. The group's founder, Charles D. MOLAPO, who had resigned as the Jonathan government's minister of information in June 1983, was expelled from the party in March 1985.

Leaders: S.C. NCOJANE (President), Phoka CHAOLANE (Chairman).

National Independence Party (NIP). The NIP was formed in late 1984 by a former cabinet member who resigned from the Jonathan government in 1972. In an election manifesto issued in March 1985, the NIP called for the establishment of diplomatic relations with South Africa and the severance of links with Communist countries.

Leader: Anthony MANYELI.

Communist Party of Lesotho (CPL). The small Communist Party, founded in the early 1960s and declared illegal in 1970, long drew its major support from Basotho workers employed in South Africa. The ban on its activities within Lesotho was reported to have been "partially lifted" by the Jonathan government in 1984. In 1986 muted activity by CPL leaders was reportedly tolerated, despite the party ban.

Leaders: R. MATAJI (Chairman), Jacob M. KENA (Secretary General).

LEGISLATURE

The bicameral Parliament established under the 1966 constitution was dissolved in the wake of alleged irregularities at the election of January 27, 1970. An interim Assembly of 22 chiefs and 71 nominated members, named on April 27, 1973, was dissolved as of December 31, 1984. Subsequent arrangements called for a Senate of 22 chiefs and an Assembly of 60 elected and up to 20 nominated members. Since none of the opposition parties nominated candidates for balloting to have been conducted on September 17–18, 1985, Chief Jonathan canceled the poll and declared the BNP candidates elected unopposed. The 1983 Parliament Act, on which the action was based, was voided following the 1986 coup.

CABINET

Chairman, Military Council	Maj. Gen. Justin Metsing Lekhanya
Ministers	
Agriculture, Cooperatives and Marketing	Dr. Daniel Rakora Phororo
Defense and Internal Security	Maj. Gen. Justin Metsing Lekhanya
Education	L. Machobane
Employment, Social Security and Pensions	Moiketse M. Tiheli
Finance	Evaristus Retselisitsoe Sekhonyana
Food Service Management Units	Maj. Gen. Justin Metsing
Foreign Affairs	Lt. Col. Thaabe Letsie
Health	Dr. Strong Thabo Makenete
Highlands Water and Energy	Mohomane Lebotsa
Information and Broadcasting	Vincent Moiketse Malebo
Interior, Chieftainship Affairs and Rural Development	Chief Mathealira Seeiso
Justice and Prisons	Bennett Makalo Khaketla

Law, Constitutional and Parliamentary Affairs	Khalaki Sello
Planning, Economic Affairs and Manpower Development	Dr. Michael Maletsitsane Sefali
Public Service, Youth and Women's Affairs	Maj. Gen. Justin Metsing Lekhanya
Tourism, Sports and Culture	Chief Lechesa Mathealira
Trade and Industry	Moletsane G. Mokoroane
Transport and Telecommunications	Col. Phillip Moyani Mokhanto
Water, Energy and Mining	Col. Alexander Lesolitjane Jane
Works	Legolo B. Monyake
Ministers of State	
Agriculture, Cooperatives and Marketing	Paul Letlala Mabathoana
Interior and Chieftainship Affairs	Phillip M. Mabathoana
Military Council	Patrick Molapo
Youth and Women's Affairs	Anna Matlelima Hlalele
Governor, Central Bank	Stefan Schoenberg

NEWS MEDIA

Press. The following are published in Sesotho at Maseru, unless otherwise noted: *Leselinyana la Lesotho* (Morija, 31,000), published fortnightly by the Lesotho Evangelical Church; *Moeletsi oa Basotho* (Mazenod, 12,000), Catholic weekly; *Lentsoe la Basotho* (2,500), government organ; *Lesotho Today,* (2,500), government organ in English. Lesotho's first daily, *The Nation,* began publication at Maseru in June 1985.

Radio and television. The Lesotho National Broadcasting Service operates the government-owned, commercial Radio Lesotho, which broadcasts in Sesotho and English. Limited television service to about 1,500 receivers has recently been initiated at Maseru.

INTERGOVERNMENTAL REPRESENTATION

Ambassador to the US: William Thabo VAN TONDER.

US Ambassador to Lesotho: Robert M. SMALLEY.

Permanent Representative to the UN: (Vacant).

IGO Memberships (Non-UN): ADF, AfDB, BADEA, CCC, CWTH, EEC(L), *EIB,* Interpol, NAM, OAU, SADCC.

LIBERIA

Second Republic of Liberia

Political Status: Independent republic established in 1847; under de facto one-party system from 1878; constitution suspended and martial law imposed on April 25, 1980, following coup of April 12; new constitution approved by national referendum on July 3, 1984.

Area: 43,000 sq. mi. (111,369 sq. km.).

Population: 2,200,000 (1984C), 2,596,000 (1988E).

Major Urban Center (1978C): MONROVIA (208,629).

Official Language: English.

Monetary Unit: Liberian Dollar (market rate March 1, 1988, 1.00 dollars = $1US).

President: Samuel Kanyon DOE (National Democratic Party of Liberia); assumed leadership of the People's Redemption Council following coup of April 12, 1980, and assassination of President William Richard TOLBERT, Jr.; installed as President of Interim National Assembly on July 26, 1984; inaugurated for a four-year term as President of the Republic on January 6, 1986, following election of October 15, 1985.

Vice President: Harry S. MONIBA (National Democratic Party of Liberia); sworn in for a term concurrent with that of the president on January 6, 1986, following election of October 15, 1985.

THE COUNTRY

Facing the Atlantic along the western bulge of Africa, Liberia is a country of tropical rain forests and broken plateaus. Established as a haven for freed American slaves, it became an independent republic more than a century before its neighbors. A small "Americo-Liberian" elite (between 3 and 5 percent of the population), which traces its descent to the settlers of 1820–1840, is gradually being assimilated, while most of the inhabitants, divided into 16 principal tribes and speaking 28 native languages and dialects, adhere to traditional customs and practice indigenous religions. About 10 percent are Christians and 10–20 percent are Muslims. Women comprise approximately one-third of the paid labor force, mainly in agriculture; female participation in government, traditionally minimal, has increased marginally under the current regime.

The Liberian economy is based on exportation of iron ore, rubber, and timber, plus smaller quantities of diamonds and coffee. Iron ore, having superseded rubber in importance, now accounts for over half of the value of Liberian exports, although the industry employs only two percent of the labor force. Industrial development also includes diverse smaller enterprises producing, for example, processed agricultural goods, cement, plastic explosives, beverages, and refined petroleum. Also contributing to the economy is Liberia's status as a "flag of convenience" for about 2,450 ships, or approximately one-fifth of the world's maritime tonnage.

Although nearly three-fourths of the labor force is concentrated in the agricultural sector, subsistence activities dominate, with more than half of the country's grain requirements having to be imported. In recent years, the world drop in commodity prices, combined with mismanagement of state enterprises, has produced a severe fiscal crisis. In early 1986, with the economy described as "near bankruptcy", the International Monetary Fund suspended aid because of Monrovia's failure to make scheduled repayments on its $1.4 billion external debt.

GOVERNMENT AND POLITICS

Political background. The political origins of the Republic of Liberia stem from a charter granted by the US Congress to the American Colonization Society in 1816 to establish a settlement for freed slaves on the west coast of Africa. The first settlers arrived in 1822 with the financial assistance of US President James Monroe, and in 1847 Liberia declared itself an independent republic under an American-style constitution. During the late nineteenth and early twentieth centuries such European powers as Britain, France, and Germany became involved in the country's domestic affairs and laid claim to portions of Liberian territory. After World War I, however, American political and economic influence was reestablished, with Firestone assuming operation in 1926 of the world's largest rubber plantation at Harbel.

Relative stability characterized internal politics under the guidance of the True Whig Party, which ruled continuously for more than a century after coming to power in 1878. Political authority was strongly centralized under the successive administrations of President William V.S. TUBMAN, who served as chief executive from 1944 until his death in 1971. Tubman was elected on a platform calling for unification of the country by integrating the Americo-Liberian and tribal groups and the promotion of foreign economic investment. Although these policies were maintained by Tubman's successor, William Richard TOLBERT, Jr., limited economic imagination, insensitivity to popular feeling among indigenous Liberians, and allegations of maladministration and corruption contributed, in the late 1970s, to growing domestic opposition, including a wave of illegal strikes and widespread rioting at Monrovia in April 1979 over a proposed increase in the price of rice. Emergency powers were quickly granted to President Tolbert by the Congress, while later in the year municipal elections were postponed and tough labor laws enacted to end the strikes.

Although the administration accorded recognition in January 1980 to the People's Progressive Party (PPP), the country's first formal opposition in over two decades, President Tolbert responded to a call for a general strike by PPP leader Gabriel Baccus MATTHEWS in March by asserting that the party had planned "an armed insurrection". Matthews and other PPP leaders were arrested, but on April 12, two days before their trial was to begin, a coup led by junior officers overthrew the government, President Tolbert and over two dozen others being killed. A People's Redemption Council (PRC), chaired by (then) Master Sgt. Samuel Kanyon DOE, was established, which announced on April 13 a civilian-military cabinet that included Matthews as minister of foreign affairs. On April 22, following a series of military trials, 13 former government and True Whig officials — including the Tolbert administration's ministers of foreign affairs, justice, finance, economic planning, agriculture, and trade; the chief justice of the Supreme Court; and the presiding officers of the Congress — were publicly executed by firing squad. Three days later, the PRC suspended the constitution and instituted martial law.

During 1981 there were two alleged attempts to overthrow the new regime, one by members of the armed forces and the other by senior PRC officials, including its co-chairman, Maj. Gen. Thomas SYEN. Another alleged plot was announced in May 1983, involving the commander in chief of the armed forces, Brig. Gen. Thomas QUI-

WONKPA, but of the 13 officials charged (some, like Quiwonkpa, having fled the country),10were granted executive clemency.

In April 1981 the PRC appointed a 25-member commission to draft a new constitution, in keeping with Doe's promise of a return to civilian rule by April 1985. After a number of postponements for the avowed purpose of registering and educating voters, a constitutional referendum was held on July 3, 1984. On July 20 Doe announced that the document had been accepted and on the following day abolished the People's Redemption Council and merged its membership with 57 hand-picked civilians to form an Interim National Assembly. Although the new assembly immediately elected him as its president, Doe declared the status temporary and that he would present himself as a candidate at a national election to be held in October 1985.

Because of restrictions imposed by the government-appointed electoral commission, neither Matthews nor the chairman of the constitutional commission, Dr. Amos SAWYER, was allowed to campaign for the presidency, with their parties disqualified from presenting legislative candidates. As a result, three substantially weaker groups challenged Doe's recently launched National Democratic Party of Liberia (NDPL). Amid widespread allegations of electoral fraud and military intimidation, Doe claimed victory at the October 15 balloting on the basis of a 50.9 percent presidential vote share, while the NDPL was awarded 73 of the 90 Assembly seats.

A month later, on November 12, General Quiwonkpa and a number of other regime opponents returned to stage a coup, apparently holding the capital for several hours before being overcome and killed by government troops. In the wake of the failed uprising, President Doe ordered the arrest of prominent opposition party leaders, some of whom were released at the time of his inaugural on January 6, 1986. Subsequently all of the opposition legislators either observed an appeal for an Assembly boycott or were expelled by their parties for refusing to do so.

Constitution and government. The former Liberian constitution, adopted July 26, 1847, was modeled, save in the matter of federalism, after that of the United States. Executive authority was vested in the president, who was limited by a 1975 amendment to a single eight-year term, excluding time spent completing the unexpired term of a predecessor. The bicameral Congress consisted of an 18-member Senate and a 65-member House of Representatives.

The constitution approved in July 1984, with effect from President Doe's inaugural in January 1986, does not differ significantly from its predecessor. Rather than being elected for eight years, the president serves a maximum of two four-year terms, while the legislature is styled the National Assembly. The Senate has been increased to 26 members and the House reduced to 64. Suffrage is extended to all adults. The new basic law also provides for relatively simple registration of political parties, with prohibitions against those considered dangerous to "the free and democratic society of Liberia". Administratively, the country is divided into 13 counties.

Foreign relations. Many of the guiding principles of the Organization of African Unity (OAU) originated with President Tubman, who held a prominent position among more moderate African leaders dedicated to peaceful change and noninterference in the internal affairs of other countries. President Tolbert was similarly respected in international forums, with the result that the April 1980 coup and his assassination were widely condemned. Liberian representatives were therefore barred from the 1980 summits of the OAU and the Economic Community of West African States (ECOWAS); however, with the help of a four-member watchdog committee established by ECOWAS in May, normal relations were established with most regional states by the end of the summer.

In the wake of the November 1985 coup attempt, all borders were sealed, Gen. Quiwonkpa allegedly having returned via Sierra Leone. The borders with Guinea and the Ivory Coast were quickly reopened to facilitate trade, and relations with Sierra Leone were normalized upon the conclusion of a tripartite security agreement that included Guinea in September 1986.

Liberia's traditional friendship with the United States has been reflected both in the extent of US private investment (estimated at some $350 million in 1981) and in the existence of a bilateral defense agreement. Despite initial US criticism of the PRC takeover, neither proved to be seriously threatened. By May 1984, Liberia was receiving more US economic and military aid per capita than any other African nation, such aid constituting over one-third of the nation's budget (see Current issues, below). The new government's essentially pro-Western stance was reflected in its cool treatment of the Libyan and Soviet ambassadors (the latter being expelled in October 1983 for alleged collusion in an antigovernment conspiracy), while in July 1985 the Doe regime severed relations with Moscow for "gross interference stemming from links between student activists and the Soviet embassy at Monrovia. In May 1987, on the other hand, the Soviet embassy was permitted to reopen in the context of an overture to the eastern bloc that included the purchase from Romania of a battery of rocket launchers and anti-tank guns.

In August 1983, Liberia became the second Black African state (after Zaire) to resume diplomatic ties with Israel, thus further weakening the diplomatic boycott imposed after the 1973 war. On a state visit to Jerusalem in September (the first by an African leader since 1971), Doe expressed interest in Israeli military aid, while calling on the rest of Africa to "adopt a new and constructive attitude" toward the Jewish state. Subsequently, there were reports of Israeli weapons being used to repulse the November 1985 coup attempt.

Current issues. Despite unrelenting political pressure and an economy in crisis, President Doe has clung to power, alternating conciliatory gestures with threats to opponents. In May 1986 he pardoned all who remained in detention as a result of the November 1985 coup attempt, including Ellen JOHNSON-SIRLEAF, a former Citibank executive and LAP official. Reportedly rearrested in July, Mrs. Johnson-Sirleaf succeeded two months later in fleeing to the United States, claiming that her life was in danger.

Subsequently, Doe came under pressure to ensure Washington's continued patronage after US Senator Edward Kennedy had accused his administration of being unable to account for some $50 million of $434 million in aid during 1980–1985. The following February, he agreed to allow 17 financial experts into the country to audit government accounts and in May approved repayment on one US loan, allowing USAID to release almost $10 million in new funds.

In June 1987, as part of an apparent effort to consolidate his power base, the chief executive dismissed four Supreme Court justices, thereby drawing criticism that he had exceeded his constitutional authority. Three months earlier, a cabinet reshuffle had taken place, with two deputy ministers discharged for embezzlement. In August the foreign affairs minister, J. Bernard BLAMO, was also relieved of his post for allegedly misappropriating more than $250,000. A coup attempt, reportedly masterminded by opposition leader Gabriel Matthews, was reported in September, while a further such attempt by leaders of the banned Liberia Unification Party (below) was reported in March 1988.

POLITICAL PARTIES

Prior to the 1980 coup, an Americo-Liberian elite had dominated the country's politics since 1878 through the True Whig Party, most of whose leaders were subsequently assassinated or executed.

Upon the PRC's assumption of power, political party activity was suspended, a ban that was extended in December 1982 to any individual or group "caught making unfavorable speeches and pronouncements against the government". The ban was repealed in July 1984, although only the first four of the parties below were permitted to contest the election of October 15, 1985.

Government Party:

National Democratic Party of Liberia (NDPL). Essentially a government party, the NDPL was formed in August 1984 to support the policies and projected presidential candidacy of General Doe. Amid widespread opposition charges of fraud at the 1985 election the NDPL, in addition to electing Doe, was awarded an overwhelming majority of seats in both houses of the National Assembly.

Leaders: Samuel K. DOE (President of the Republic), Miata SHERMAN (Chairman).

Government-Supportive Party:

Liberian Liberal Party (LLP). The LLP was formed in late 1987 with the announced aim of assisting the NDLP in working for Liberia's overall development.

Leader: Paul YANSEN.

Opposition Parties:

Officials of the three following groups announced on March 17, 1986, that they were forming "a grand coalition" as the result of a "common concern" for the future of the country. The government denied the coalition's request to be designated as a distinct entity, arresting constituent party leaders for referring to themselves as members thereof. All three parties boycotted the December 1986 election of 6 deputies and 38 local government representatives.

Liberia Action Party (LAP). The LAP was organized by Tuan WREH, a former supporter and political confidant of General Doe, who was subsequently joined by a number of Tolbert-era officials, including ex-finance minister Ellen Johnson-Sirleaf. In 1985, the LAP emerged as the NDPL's primary challenger following disqualification of the UPP (below), winning 2 Senate and 8 House seats. It decided,

however, to boycott legislative proceedings because of the detention of Johnson-Sirleaf and other party leaders. In early 1986, Wreh and another LAP member were expelled from the party for agreeing to take their seats in defiance of the boycott.

Leaders: Emmanuel KOROMA (Chairman), Jackson F. DOE (1985 presidential candidate), Ellen JOHNSON-SIRLEAF (in exile in the United States), Dr. Byron TARR (Secretary General).

Liberia Unification Party (LUP). Organized in 1984 by Gabriel Kpolleh, former president of the Monrovia Public School Teachers' Association, the LUP was initially viewed as a potential "Trojan horse" by the NDLP. Kpolleh surprised many observers by backing the LAP-led legislative boycott, with all four of the party's Assembly members refusing to take their seats. In May 1987 the Electoral Commission revoked the party's registration following its refusal to pay a fine for failure to submit its accounts to audit. In March 1988 the party's leader and deputy leader were arrested on charges of plotting to overthrow the government.

Leaders: Gabriel KPOLLEH (under arrest), Harold NDANA (under arrest).

Unity Party (UP). The UP was formed by Dr. Edward B. Kesselly, who had served as local government minister in the Tolbert administration and subsequently chaired the PRC's Constituent Advisory Assembly. The party elected one senator and 2 representatives in the 1985 balloting.

Leaders: Dr. Edward B. KESSELLY, Peter Bonner JALLAH (Secretary General).

United People's Party (UPP). A centrist outgrowth of the pre-coup People's Progressive Party and viewed as the most serious threat to the NDPL, the UPP was organized by former PPP leader Gabriel Baccus Matthews, who had been dismissed as foreign minister in November 1981 because of opposition to a pro-US posture by the Doe regime and left the government again in April 1983 after serving for a year as secretary general of the cabinet. Although meeting legal requirements for registration, the UPP was not permitted to participate in the 1985 balloting because of its leader's "socialist leanings" and unofficially supported Jackson Doe of the LAP in the presidential race. After some hesitation, the UPP declined, in mid-1986, to join the "grand coalition" on the ground that its constitution precluded merger with other groups. A number of leading officials quit the party because of the exiled Matthews' position in the matter, which induced the government to permit his return from the United States and rescind its proscription of the formation in late September.

Leaders: Gabriel Baccus MATTHEWS (Chairman), Blamo NELSON (Deputy Chairman).

Liberian People's Party (LPP). The LPP was organized by former members of the Movement for Justice in Africa (Moja), whose leader, Dr. Togba-Nah TIPOTEH, had been dismissed from the cabinet for complicity in the counter-coup attempt of August 1981. LPP leader Amos Sawyer, former chairman of the PRC's national constitutional commission, was also charged with plotting against the regime in August 1984, although the allegation was widely interpreted as an attempt by General Doe to discredit a leading rival for the presidency in 1985. Reportedly in retaliation for his subsequent unwillingness to accept an offer to campaign as General Doe's running mate, an audit was initiated in early 1985 of Sawyer's finances as constitutional commission chairman, thus permitting the electoral commission to deny registration to the LPP.

Leaders: Dr. Amos SAWYER (Chairman), Dusty WOLOKOLIE (Deputy Chairman), Anthony KESSELLY (Secretary General).

Convention Democratic Party (CDP). The CDP was formed initially as the National Democratic Party of Liberia by former True Whig leader Wade Appleton in order to "prevent Liberia from becoming a socialist state". Its present name was adopted after General Doe had announced the formation of his own NDPL. It was not permitted to contest the 1985 election.

Leader: Wade APPLETON.

Two additional parties that were not permitted to register for the 1985 balloting were the **National Integration Party** (NIP), headed by former labor minister Maj. E. Sumo JONES; and the **People's Liberation Party** (LP), led by Hawa DANQUAH.

LEGISLATURE

The **National Assembly** established by the 1984 constitution is a bicameral body consisting of a Senate and a House of Representatives, both elected by universal adult suffrage.

Senate. The Senate has 26 members serving six-year terms. At the election of October 15, 1985, the National Democratic Party of Liberia was awarded 22 seats; the Liberia Action Party, 2; and the Liberian Unification and Unity parties, 1 each. However, one of the LAP senators and the LUP senator refused to occupy their seats, effectively reducing the size of the chamber to 24. In April 1986, the remaining opposition senators were expelled from party membership for refusing to withdraw. The 2 vacant seats were awarded to the NDPL as the result of a by-election on December 28.

President: John RANCY.

House of Representatives. The House consists of 64 members serving two-year terms. The allocation of seats following the 1985 balloting was National Democratic Party of Liberia, 51; Liberia Action Party, 8; Liberian Unification Party, 3; Unity Party, 2. One of the LAP and all of the LUP members joined in the opposition boycott, reducing the effective size of the body to 60. In April 1986, the remaining opposition members were expelled from their respective parties for refusing to participate in the boycott. All of the vacant seats were captured by the NDPL at the partial election in December.

Speaker: Samuel HILL.

C A B I N E T

President	Samuel K. Doe
Vice President	Harry S. Moniba
Ministers	
Agriculture	Scott Gblosuo Toweh
Commerce, Industry and Transportation	David Farhat
Education	Othello Gonga
Finance (Acting)	David Farhat
Foreign Affairs	J. Rudolph Johnson
Health and Social Welfare	Martha Sandolo-Belleh
Information, Cultural Affairs and Tourism	J. Emmanuel Z. Bowier
Internal Affairs	Col. Edward K. Sackor
Justice	Jenkins K.Z.B. Scott
Labor	Peter Naigow
Land, Mines and Energy	Maj. William Freeman
National Defense	Maj. Gen. Gray D. Allison
National Security	Patrick M. Minikon
Planning and Economic Affairs	Elijah Taylor
Posts and Telecommunications	Morris Dukuly
Public Works	Maj. Yudu S. Gray
Rural Development	Samuel D. Brownell
Transportation	Mcleod Turkeh Darpoh
Youth and Sports	Haven Grigsby
Without Portfolio	John P. Beh
Minister of State for Presidential Affairs	G. Alvin Jones
Director General of Cabinet	Momolu Getaweh
Governor, Central Bank	Paul Jeffy

N E W S   M E D I A

Press. The True Whig biweekly *Liberian Age* ceased publication at the time of the 1980 coup. The present regime has not imposed formal press censorship, although the independent *Daily Observer* has been closed and fined repeatedly since its founding in February 1981 and on March 5, 1986, unidentified arsonists attempted to destroy the paper's offices. The *Sun Times,* a daily founded in mid-1985 and occasionally critical of the Doe administration, was shut down in September 1986, but later reopened. Its managing editor is the former editor of the *New Liberian.* The following are currently issued at Monrovia: *The New Liberian* (15,000), published four times a week by the Ministry of Information; *Daily Observer* (12,000), independent, founded 1981; *The Express* (5,000),

independent biweekly; *Footprints Today,* independent daily, founded 1984; *Sunday People,* independent biweekly.

News agency. The official facility is the Liberian News Agency (Lina); *Agence France-Presse, Deutsche Presse Agentur,* Reuters, and UPI are represented at Monrovia.

Radio and television. The government-controlled Liberian Broadcasting Corporation, which oversees all broadcasting, operates one commercial radio and one commercial television station. Other radio stations are operated by the Liberian-American-Swedish Minerals Company (Lamco), the Sudan Interior Mission, and the Voice of America. There were approximately 43,000 television receivers in 1987.

INTERGOVERNMENTAL   REPRESENTATION

Ambassador to the US: Eugenia A. WORDSWORTH-STEVENSON.

US Ambassador to Liberia: James Keough BISHOP.

Permanent Representative to the UN: Sylvester JARRETT.

IGO Memberships (Non-UN): ADF, AfDB, APEF, BADEA, CCC, ECOWAS, EEC(L), *EIB,* IACO, ICO, Inmarsat, Interpol, MRU, NAM, OAU.

LIBYA

Socialist People's Libyan Arab Jamahiriya
al-Jamahiriyah al-'Arabiyah al-Libiyah al-Sha'biyah al-Ishtirakiyah

Political Status: Independent state since December 24, 1951; revolutionary republic declared September 1, 1969; name changed from Libyan Arab Republic to Libyan Arab People's Republic in 1976; present name adopted March 2, 1977.

Area: 679,358 sq. mi. (1,759,540 sq. km.).

Population: 3,637,488 (1984C), 4,229,000 (1988E).

Major Urban Centers (1984C): TRIPOLI (990,697); Benghazi (485,386); Azzawiya (220,075); Misurata (178,295). On January 1, 1987, Colonel Qadhafi announced that he was moving the capital to Hun, a small town some 300 miles southeast of Tripoli; the actual effect of the decision, however, is not yet clear.

Official Language: Arabic.

Monetary Unit: Dinar (market rate March 1, 1988, 1 dinar = $3.55US).

Revolutionary Leader (De Facto Head of State): Col. Mu'ammar Abu Minyar al-QADHAFI (Col. Moammar GADDAFY); assumed power as Chairman of Revolutionary Command Council (RCC) following coup d'état of September 1, 1969; became Prime Minister in January 1970, relinquishing the office in July 1972; designated General Secretary of General People's Congress concurrent with abolition of the RCC on March 2, 1977, relinquishing the position on March 1–2, 1979.

Secretary General of General People's Congress: Miftah al-Usta 'UMAR (Meftah al-Osta OMAR); designated at General People's Congress session of February 11–16, 1984, succeeding Muhammad al-Zarruq RAJAB (Muhammad az-Zarrouk RAGAB).

Secretary of General People's Committee (Prime Minister): 'Umar Mustafa al-MUNTASIR; appointed by the General People's Congress on March 1, 1987, to succeed Jadallah 'Azzuz al-TALHI.

THE COUNTRY

Extending for 910 miles along Africa's northern coast, Libya embraces the former Turkish and Italian provinces of Tripolitania, Cyrenaica, and Fezzan. Some 95 percent of its territory is desert and barren rockland, and cultivation and settlement are largely confined to a narrow coastal strip. The population is predominantly Arab with a Berber minority and almost wholly Sunni Muslim in religion. Arabic is the official language, but Italian, English, and French are also spoken. Although in recent years the government has made efforts to increase female literacy and education, women still comprise less than 6 percent of the official labor force; one-third of these are in unpaid agricultural labor, the rest concentrated in the civil service, health care, and education. Female representation in government appears to be minimal.

Libya's reputation as a country largely devoid of natural resources was rendered obsolete by the discovery of oil in the late 1950s; the ensuing development of export capacity resulted in its achieving the highest per capita GNP in Africa, over $8,600 in 1980. However, world market conditions subsequently reduced the country's oil revenue from a high of $20 billion in 1980 to $5 billion in 1986, with per capita GNP declining to less than $7,500 through the same period. Other industry has been limited by the weakness of the domestic market, uneven distribution of the population, and a shortage of skilled manpower. Recent large-scale development has focused on building chemical and steel complexes, in addition to a number of ambitious irrigation projects. Agriculture, which is restricted by limited rainfall and an insufficient labor pool because of migration to the cities, currently contributes only 1–2 percent of domestic output. Barley, wheat, tomatoes, olives, citrus, and dates are the primary crops.

GOVERNMENT AND POLITICS

Political background. Successively ruled by the Phoenicians, Greeks, Romans, Arabs, Spaniards, and others, Libya was under Ottoman Turkish control from the middle of the sixteenth century to the beginning of the twentieth century. It was conquered by Italy in 1911–1912 and ruled as an Italian colony until its occupation by British and French military forces during World War II. In conformity with British wartime pledges and a 1949 decision of the UN General Assembly, Libya became an independent monarchy under Emir Muhammad IDRIS al-Sanussi (King IDRIS I) on December 24, 1951. A constitution promulgated in October 1951 prescribed a federal form of government with autonomous rule in the three historic provinces, but provincial autonomy was wiped out and a centralized regime instituted under a constitutional amendment adopted in 1963.

The 1960s witnessed a growing independence in foreign affairs resulting from the financial autonomy generated by rapidly increasing petroleum revenues. This period marked the beginnings of Libyan radicalism in Third World politics and in its posture regarding Arab-Israeli relations. Increasingly, anti-Western sentiments were voiced, especially in regard to foreign-dominated petroleum companies and the presence of foreign military bases on Libyan soil. The period following the June 1967 Arab-Israeli conflict saw a succession of prime ministers, including the progressive 'Abd al-Hamid al-BAKKUSH, who took office in October 1967. His reforms alienated conservative leaders, however, and he was replaced in September 1968 by Wanis al-QADHAFI. The following September, while the king was in Turkey for medical treatment, a group of military officers led by Col. Mu'ammar al-QADHAFI seized control of the government and established a revolutionary regime under a military-controlled Revolutionary Command Council (RCC).

After consolidating his control of the RCC, Colonel Qadhafi moved to implement the goals of his regime, which reflected a blend of puritanical Islamic behavioral codes, socialism, and radical Arab nationalism. By June 1970 both the British and US military installations had been evacuated. In July the Italian and Jewish communities were dispossessed and forced from the country. In June 1971 an official party, the Arab Socialist Union (ASU), was organized, and in September of that year the Federation of Arab Republics, a union of Egypt, Syria, and Libya, was approved by separate referenda in each country. The Federation, while formally constituted at the ministerial level in December 1971 and at the legislative level in March 1972, became moribund shortly thereafter. Meanwhile, the regime had begun acquiring shares in the country's petroleum industry, resorting to outright nationalization of foreign interests in numerous cases; by March 1976, the government controlled about two-thirds of oil production.

Periodically threatening to resign because of conflicts within the RCC, Colonel Qadhafi turned over his prime-ministerial duties to Maj. 'Abd al-Salam JALLUD in July 1972 and was in seclusion during the greater part of 1974. In August 1975 his rule was seriously threatened by a coup attempt involving army officers—some two dozen of whom were ultimately executed—and a number of drastic antisubversion laws were promptly enacted. In November a quasi-legislative General National Congress (renamed the General People's Congress a year later) was created, while in March 1977 the RCC and the cabinet were abolished in accordance with "the installation of the people's power" under a new structure of government headed by Colonel Qadhafi and the four remaining members of the RCC. The political changes were accompanied by a series of sweeping economic measures, including limitations on savings and consolidation of private shops ("nests of exploitation") into large state supermarkets, which generated middle-class discontent and fueled exile-based opposition activity. The government was further reorganized at a meeting of the General People's Congress in March 1979, Colonel Qadhafi resigning as secretary general (but retaining his designation as revolutionary leader and supreme commander of the Armed Forces) in favor of 'Abd al-'Ati 'UBAYDI, who was in turn replaced as secretary of the General People's Committee (prime minister) by Jadallah 'Azzuz al-TALHI.

During the first half of 1980, some 2,000 individuals were reported to have been arrested on charges of corruption and related offenses, while an army rebellion at Tobruk claimed 200 lives before being suppressed. Two years later, in November 1982, a coup by senior army and air force officers was narrowly averted in the wake of an effort to establish an "armed people" in place of regular military forces.

At a Congress session in January 1981, Secretary General 'Ubaydi was succeeded by Muhammad al-Zarruq RAJAB, who, in February 1984, was replaced by Miftah al-Usta 'UMAR and named to succeed Talhi as secretary of the General People's Committee. Talhi was returned to the position of nominal head of government in a major ministerial reshuffle announced on March 3, 1986; in a further major reshuffle on March 1, 1987, Talhi was replaced by 'Umar Mustafa al-MUNTASIR.

Constitution and government. Guided by the ideology of Colonel Qadhafi's *Green Book,* which combines elements of nationalism, Islamic theology, socialism, and populism, Libya was restyled the Socialist People's Libyan Arab Jamahiriya in March 1977. The *Jamahiriyah* is conceived as a system of direct government through popular organs interspersed throughout Libyan society. A General People's Congress is assisted by a General Secretariat, whose secretary general serves as titular head of state. Executive functions are assigned to a cabinet-like General People's Committee, whose secretary serves as the equivalent of prime minister. The judicial system includes a Supreme Court, courts of appeal, courts of the first instance, and summary courts.

Libya is divided into ten governorates, with administration based on "Direct People's Authority" as represented in local People's Congresses, People's Committees, Trade Unions, and Vocational Syndicates.

Foreign relations. Under the monarchy, Libya tended to adhere to a generally pro-Western posture. Since the 1969 coup its foreign policy has been characterized by the advocacy of total war against Israel, a willingness to use petroleum as a political weapon, and a strong commitment to Arab unity that has given rise to numerous failed merger attempts with sister states (Libya, Egypt, Sudan, and Syria in 1969; Libya, Egypt, and Syria in 1971; Libya and Egypt in 1972; Libya and Tunisia in 1974; Libya and Syria in 1980; Libya and Chad in 1981; Libya and Morocco in 1984).

Libya's position within the Arab world has been marked by an improbable combination of ideological extremism and pragmatic compromise. Ties with its Mediterranean neighbors, Tunisia and Malta, have been strained by conflicting claims to potentially oil-rich drilling sites, as well as by accusations of hospitality to Libyan insurgents.

Following the 1978 Camp David accords, relations were severed with Egypt, both sides fortifying their common border. Tripoli has since consistently worked to block Cairo's reentry into the Arab fold (extending its condemnation to Jordan following the warming of ties between Jordan and Egypt) and has provided support to Syrian-based elements of the Palestinian Liberation Organization opposed to Yasir 'Arafat. On the other hand, relations with conservative Morocco and Saudi Arabia, broken following Tripoli's 1980 recognition of the Polisario-backed government-in-exile of the Western Sahara, resumed in 1981. Visits by Qadhafi in 1983 to both Rabat and Riyadh were followed by economic agreements, a reduction of Libyan aid to Polisario, and an August 1984 "union of states" treaty with Morocco that was abruptly cancelled by King Hassan two years later because of Libyan denunciation of a meeting with (then) Israeli prime minister Shimon Peres.

A widespread expression of international concern in recent years has centered on Libyan involvement in Chad. Libya's annexation of the Aozou Strip (see map, p. 106) in the mid-1970s was followed by active participation in the Chadian civil war, largely in opposition to the forces of Hissein Habré, who in 1982 emerged as president of the strife-torn country's latest government. By 1983 Libya's active support of the "National Peace Government" loyal to former Chadian president Goukhouni Oueddei (based in the northern Tibesti region) included the deployment of between 3,000 and 5,000 Libyan troops and the provision of air support for Oueddei's attacks on the northern capital of Faya-Largeau. Although consistently denying direct involvement and condemning the use of French troops in 1983–1984 as "unjustified intervention", Qadhafi agreed in September 1984 to recall "Libyan support elements" in exchange for a French troop withdrawal. The agreement was hailed as a diplomatic breakthrough for Paris, but was greeted with dismay by Habré, and ultimately proved to be an embarrassment to the Mitterand government because of the limited number of Libyan troops actually withdrawn. Two-and-a-half years later, in March 1987, the militarily superior Qadhafi regime suffered the unexpected humiliation of being decisively defeated by Chadian government forces, which, after capturing the air facility at Quadi Doum, 100 miles northeast of Faya-Largeau, forced the Libyans to withdraw from all but the Aozou Strip, leaving behind an estimated $1 billion worth of sophisticated weaponry (see Chad article).

Relations with the West have been problematic since the 1969 coup and the expulsion, a year later, of British and US military forces. Libya's subsequent involvement in negotiations between Malta and the United Kingdom over British naval facilities on the Mediterranean island contributed to a further strain in relations with London. In December 1979 the United States closed its embassy at Tripoli after portions of the building were stormed and set afire by pro-Iranian demonstrators, while in May 1981 the Reagan administration ordered Tripoli to shut down its Washington "people's bureau" in response to what it considered escalating international terrorism sponsored by Colonel Qadhafi. Subsequent US-Libyan relations have been characterized by what has been termed "mutual paranoia", with each side accusing the other of assassination plots amid hostility generated by US naval maneuvers in the Gulf of Sirte, which Libya has claimed as an internal sea since 1973.

Simultaneous attacks by Palestinian gunmen on the Rome and Vienna airports on December 27, 1985, brought US accusations of Libyan involvement, which Colonel Qadhafi vehemently denied. In early January 1986, President Reagan announced the freezing of all Libyan government assets in US banks, urged Americans working in Libya to depart, and ordered a new series of air and sea maneuvers in the Gulf of Sirte. Three months later, during the night of April 14, 18 F-111 bombers based in Britain, assisted by carrier-based attack fighters, struck Libyan military targets at Tripoli and Benghazi. The action was prompted by what Washington termed "conclusive evidence", in the form of intercepted cables, that Libya had ordered the bombing of a West German discotheque nine days before, in the course of which an off-duty US soldier had been killed. The US administration also claimed to have aborted a planned grenade and machine-gun attack on the American visa office at Paris, for which French authorities ordered the expulsion of two Libyan diplomats.

Current issues. Visibly shaken by the American show of force in April 1986 and the March 1987 defeat in Chad, the Qadhafi regime has continued in power through an extensive system of security police, in addition to revolutionary committees that penetrate all sectors of society. Potential opposition within the military has been curbed by frequent changes in command postings.

In contrast to his virtual disappearance from public view after the 1986 attack, Colonel Qadhafi became highly visible in the wake of the Chad fiasco, appearing to be more deeply involved in governmental affairs than at any time in recent memory. Externally, the Libyan leader reiterated his commitment to "counterterrorism" in Western Europe and elsewhere "as long as the Israelis remain in occupation of Palestine and conduct terrorist acts against the Palestinian people". In late March, a number of radical Palestinian leaders visited Tripoli for what was described as a "unity meeting", with the colonel declaring that he did not care if it was construed as a "convention of terrorists".

In early August renewed fighting commenced with Chadian forces, the latter in a surprise move capturing the town of Aozou, administrative capital of the contested border area, which was subsequently retaken by the Libyans. Six weeks earlier Qadhafi had visited Algeria, pressing for yet another multi-state union, although the prospect for its realization was viewed as unlikely in view of a long-standing Algerian conviction, bearing directly on the dispute with Chad, that African governments should accept national boundaries as delineated at the time of decolonization.

POLITICAL PARTIES

Under the monarchy, all political parties were banned. In 1971 an official government party, the Arab Socialist Union (ASU), was founded with the Egyptian ASU as its model. The party was designed primarily to serve as a "transmission belt", helping to implement government decisions at local levels and serving to channel local concerns upward to the central government. While the legislature established in November 1975 was described as an organ of the ASU, there was no subsequent public reference to the party, its functions having apparently been taken over by the General Peoples Congress and the Popular Committees.

Expatriate Opposition:

External opponents of the Qadhafi regime have established a number of small groups based not only in such neighboring countries as Egypt and Morocco but in Western Europe and the United States. While the members of these groups are most frequently students, many prominent former officials under Qadhafi, including government ministers, members of the Revolutionary Command Council, and ambassadors, have also joined, thus becoming targets for assassination. Among the exile groups are the **Libyan National Democratic Front,** established in 1977; the US-based **Free Libyan Students Union;** the **Libyan Liberation Organization** founded at Cairo, Egypt, in 1982 by former prime minister Bakkush; and the **Libyan National Salvation Front** (LNSF). Formation of the LNSF was announced at Khartoum, Sudan, on October 7, 1981, under the banner "Finding the democratic alternative". By 1984, the LNSF had established itself as the primary opposition formation, and claimed responsibility for the May gun battle at Tripoli; in September 1986 it published a list of 76 regime opponents that it claimed had been assassinated in exile and in January 1987 joined with a number of other exile formations in establishing a joint working group during a meeting at Cairo, Egypt.

LEGISLATURE

The Senate and House of Representatives were dissolved as a result of the 1969 coup, Colonel Qadhafi asserting that all such institutions are basically undemocratic, "as democracy means the authority of the people and not the authority of a body acting on the people's behalf".

A government decree of November 13, 1975, provided for the establishment of a 618-member General National Congress of the ASU to consist of the members of the Revolutionary Command Council and leaders of existing "people's congresses", trade unions, and professional groups. Subsequent to its first session on January 5–18, 1976, the body was identified as the **General People's Congress.** At a session held at the south-central city of Sebha in March 1977, some 1,100 delegates discussed a "Declaration on Establishment of People's Power", which was adopted as a constitutional document on March 2. The twelfth session of the Congress was held at Benghazi in early March 1987.

Secretary General: Mifta al-Usta 'UMAR.

CABINET

Secretary, General People's Committee	'Umar Mustafa al-Muntasir
Secretaries	
Communications and Maritime Transport	Mubarak al-Shamikh
Economy and Trade	Dr. Farhat Sharnanah
Education and Scientific Research	Ahmad Muhammad Ibrahim
Health	Dr. Mustafa Muhammad al-Zaydi
Industry	Dr. Ahmad Fathi ibn Shatwan
Information and Culture	Dr. Rajab Miftah Abu Dabbus

Marine Resources	Miftiah Mohammad Ku'aybah
Mass Mobilization and Revolutionary Orientation	'Ali al-Shaeri
People's Foreign Liaison Bureau	Jadallah Azzuz al-Talhi
Planning	Dr. Muhammad Lufti Farhat
Professional Congresses Affairs	Bashir Huwayi Huwaydi
Public Services	Fawzi al-Shakshuki
Treasury	Muhammad al-Madani al-Bukhari
Vocational Training	Matuq Muhammad Mutuq
President, People's Court	'Abd al-Raziq al-Sawsa
President, People's Prosecution Bureau	'Abd al-Salam 'Ali al-Mizighwi
Governor, Central Bank	Muhammad Zarruq Rajab

NEWS MEDIA

Press. In October 1973 all private newspapers were nationalized. Since 1978, the official Jamahiriya News Agency has published at Tripoli the country's only major daily, *al-Fajr al-Jadid* (40,000), in Arabic.

News agencies. The official facility is the Jamahiriya News Agency (Jana). East Germany's ADN, Italy's ANSA, and TASS maintain offices at Tripoli.

Radio and television. Radio and television transmission in both Arabic and English is under the administration of the Socialist People's Libyan Arab Jamahiriya Broadcasting Corporation. There were approximately 235,500 television receivers in 1987.

INTERGOVERNMENTAL REPRESENTATION

Ambassador to the US: (Vacant).

US Ambassador to Libya: (Vacant).

Permanent Representative to the UN: Dr. Ali A. TREIKI.

IGO Memberships (Non-UN): ADF, AfDB, AFESD, AMF, BADEA, IC, IDB, Intelsat, Interpol, IOOC, IWTC, LAS, NAM, OAPEC, OAU, OPEC.

LIECHTENSTEIN

Principality of Liechtenstein
Fürstentum Liechtenstein

Political Status: Independent principality constituted in 1719; established diplomatic association with Switzerland in 1919 and customs and currency association in 1923.

Area: 61 sq. mi. (157 sq. km.).

Population: 25,215 (1980C), 28,600 (1988E); both figures include more than 9,000 resident aliens.

Major Urban Centers (1985E): VADUZ (4,900); Schaan (4,700).

Official Language: German (Alemannic).

Monetary Unit: Swiss Franc (market rate March 1, 1988, 1.39 francs = $1US).

Sovereign: Prince FRANZ JOSEF II; succeeded to the throne July 25, 1938.

Deputy Head of State and Heir Apparent: Prince HANS ADAM von und zu Liechtenstein, son of the Sovereign; acceded to the executive authority of the Sovereign on August 26, 1984.

Chief of Government (Prime Minister): Hans BRUNHART (Fatherland Union); assumed office April 26, 1978, following election of February 2, succeeding Dr. Walter KIEBER (Progressive Citizens' Party); reappointed following elections of February 5 and 7, 1982, and February 2, 1986.

Deputy Chief of Government: Dr. Herbert WILLE (Progressive Citizens' Party); appointed following election of February 2, 1986, to succeed Hilmar OSPELT (Progressive Citizens' Party).

THE COUNTRY

A miniature principality on the upper Rhine between Austria and Switzerland, Liechtenstein has a predominantly Roman Catholic population whose major language, Alemannic, is a German dialect. Postwar industrialization—particularly in metallurgy and light industry—has helped raise the country's per capita GNP to one of the highest in the world while attracting substantial numbers of foreign workers. Cattle breeding and dairy production are also highly developed, but occupy only 4 percent of the population. The Principality is chiefly known as a tourist center and as the nominal headquarters of perhaps as many as 30,000 foreign business concerns that benefit from the government's liberal tax policies.

GOVERNMENT AND POLITICS

Political background. The Principality of Liechtenstein, whose origins date back to the fourteenth century, was established in its present form in 1719. Part of the Holy Roman Empire and, after 1815, a member of the Germanic Confederation, it entered into a customs union with Austria in 1852 that continued until the collapse of the Hapsburg monarchy in 1918. Formally terminating the association with Austria in 1919, Liechtenstein proceeded to adopt Swiss currency in 1921 and in 1923 entered into a customs union with Switzerland, which continues to administer Liechtenstein's customs and provide for its defense and diplomatic representation.

An unusually lengthy period of nearly 12 weeks elapsed after the legislative election of February 3, 1978, before a government could be constituted. The principal difficulty was a lack of agreement on the foreign-affairs portfolio, normally held by the chief of government. The Progressive Citizens' Party (FBP), which had lost its parliamentary majority for only the second time since 1928, declined to relinquish the post on the ground that, while losing its control of the legislature by one seat, it had received an overall majority of votes cast. The impasse was eventually resolved by acceptance of the sovereign's suggestion that the portfolio be divided, with the incoming chief of government, Hans BRUNHART of the Fatherland Union (VU), being responsible for the general management of foreign affairs and his predecessor, Walter KIEBER, being responsible for specified areas, including the monetary accord with Switzerland and relations with European economic organizations. At his retirement on July 1, 1980, Kieber was succeeded as deputy chief of government by Hilmar OSPELT. The legislative strength of the parties remained unchanged following the 1982 and 1986 elections; as a result, there were no ministerial changes on the earlier occasion, with Dr. Herbert WILLE of the FBP succeeding Ospelt as Brunhart's deputy on the latter.

The somewhat unusual action of Prince FRANZ JOSEF on August 26, 1984, in assigning his official responsibilities, without abdication of title, to Prince HANS ADAM, bestowed effective power on a business school graduate with a keen interest in both domestic and European affairs. Characterized as a "manager-prince", Hans Adam has defined his role as that of focusing on "long-term projects", while deferring to his ministers on day-to-day issues.

Constitution and government. Under the constitution adopted October 5, 1921, the monarchy is hereditary in the male line and the sovereign exercises legislative power jointly with a unicameral Diet, which is elected every four years by direct suffrage under proportional representation. The chief of government (*Regierungschef*) is appointed by the sovereign from the majority party in the Diet. The government, which is responsible to both the sovereign and the Diet, also includes a deputy chief (*Regierungschef-Stellvertreter*) appointed by the sovereign from the minority party in the Diet, and three government councillors (*Regierungsräte*) elected by the Diet itself. Elections are held in two constituencies (*Oberland* and *Unterland*), while administration is based on 11 communes (*Gemeinden*). The judicial system consists of civil, criminal, and administrative divisions: the first two include local, Superior, and Supreme courts, while the third encompasses an Administrative Court of Appeal (for hearing complaints about government officials and actions) and a State Court, both of which consider questions of constitutionality.

The enfranchisement of women at the national level, supported by both major parties and approved unanimously by the legislature, was narrowly endorsed by male voters on July 1, 1984, after having been defeated in referenda held in 1971 and 1973. Approval at the local level was also voted in eight communes, with approval in the remaining three following on April 20, 1986.

In a referendum held June 2, 1985, proposals to increase the size of the *Landtag* (to 25, as requested by the FBP, or to 21, as requested by the VU) failed to obtain necessary absolute majorities, as did a proposal to rescind the parliamentary practice (adopted in 1939) to permit a deputy to be represented by an alternate.

Foreign relations. Liechtenstein maintains an embassy at Bern but is represented elsewhere by Swiss embassies and consulates, by agreement dating from October 27, 1919. Although not a member of the United Nations, the principality belongs to a number of UN Specialized Agencies (see footnotes to Appendix B). The country does not have a standing army, but has long been preoccupied with European defense strategy and was an active participant in the Madrid and Stockholm security conferences.

Current issues. The abandonment of its distinction as the last European country to deny women the right to vote appears to have had no effect on Liechtenstein politics. On February 2, 1986, the VU again retained its one-seat legislative margin over the FBP on the basis of a fractional majority of the popular vote.

Legislation to abolish the death penalty (introduced in 1985) was approved by the *Landtag* in May 1987. Subsequently it was decided that free public transportation would be provided for a 12-month trial period, as of January 1, 1988, in an effort to reduce atmospheric pollution by discouraging private commuting.

POLITICAL PARTIES

Government Coalition:

Fatherland Union (*Vaterländische Union* — VU). Composed mainly of workers, the Fatherland Union is considered the more liberal of the two major parties. The VU won control of the government for the first time since 1928 by winning eight legislative seats in the 1970 election. It lost its majority in 1974, regained it in 1978, and held it in 1982 and 1986.
Leaders: Hans BRUNHART (Chief of Government), Dr. Otto HASLER (Chairman), Ernst HASLER (Secretary).

Progressive Citizens' Party (*Fortschrittliche Bürgerpartei* — FBP). Basically conservative in orientation, the FBP held a majority of legislative seats from 1928 to 1970 and from 1974 to 1978.
Leaders: Dr. Herbert WILLE (Deputy Chief of Government), Emanuel VOGT (Chairman), Marlene FRICK (Secretary).

Other Parties:

Christian Social Party (*Christlich Soziale Partei* — CSP). The CSP, which failed to win any seats in either 1970 or 1974, has contested none of the last three national elections.
Leaders: Fritz KAISER (Chairman), Rupert WALSER (Secretary).

The Free Electoral List (*Freie Wählerliste* — FW). Less conservative than the traditional parties, the FW was formed prior to the 1986 election, at which it narrowly failed to secure the 8 percent vote share necessary for parliamentary representation.
Leader: Helen MARXER-BULLONI (Secretary).

LEGISLATURE

The **Diet** (*Landtag*) is a unicameral body currently consisting of 15 members directly elected for four-year terms on the basis of universal suffrage and proportional representation. After four previous defeats, a proposal to increase the number of seats to 25, as of the next election, was approved in a January 1988 referendum. At the most recent balloting of February 2, 1986, the Fatherland Union retained its previous majority of 8 seats, with the Progressive Citizens' Party again winning 7.
President: Dr. Karlheinz RITTER.

CABINET

Chief of Government	Hans Brunhart
Deputy Chief of Government	Dr. Herbert Wille
Government Councillors	
Agriculture and Environmental Protection	Dr. Herbert Wille
Construction	Hans Brunhart
Culture and Sports	Dr. Herbert Wille

Economy	René Ritter
Education	Hans Brunhart
Foreign Relations	Hans Brunhart
Interior	Dr. Herbert Wille
Justice	Dr. Herbert Wille
Public Health	Dr. Peter Wolff
Social Welfare	Dr. Peter Wolff
Transportation	Wilfried Büchel
Chairman, Liechtenstein State Bank	Herbert Kindle

NEWS MEDIA

Press. The following are published at Vaduz: *Liechtensteiner Volksblatt* (8,000), issued five times a week by the Progressive Citizens' Party; *Liechtensteiner Vaterland* (7,000), issued five times a week by the Fatherland Union.

News agency. The Press and Information Office of the Liechtenstein Government (*Presse- und Informationsamt der Fürstlichen Regierung*) issues periodic press bulletins.

Radio and television. There were approximately 8,700 radio and 8,100 television receivers in 1987, although there are no broadcasting facilities within the principality.

INTERGOVERNMENTAL REPRESENTATION

Liechtenstein, which is not a member of the United Nations, conducts its foreign relations through the Swiss Foreign Ministry. The United States has no diplomatic or consular missions in Liechtenstein, the US consul general at Zürich, Switzerland, being accredited to Vaduz.

IGO Memberships (Non-UN): CEUR, Intelsat, Interpol.

LUXEMBOURG

Grand Duchy of Luxembourg
Grand-Duché de Luxembourg (French)
Grossherzogtum Luxemburg (German)

Political Status: Constitutional monarchy, fully independent since 1867; in economic union with Belgium since 1922.

Area: 998 sq. mi. (2,586 sq. km.).

Population: 364,602 (1981C), 367,000 (1988E).

Major Urban Centers (1981C): LUXEMBOURG-VILLE (78,900); Esch-sur-Alzette (25,100).

Official Languages: French, German.

Monetary Unit: Luxembourg Franc (market rate March 1, 1988, 35.28 francs = $1US); Belgian currency is also legal tender.

Sovereign: Grand Duke JEAN; ascended to the throne November 12, 1964, on the abdication of his mother, Grand Duchess CHARLOTTE.

Heir Apparent: Prince HENRI, son of the Grand Duke.

Prime Minister: Jacques SANTER (Christian Social Party); sworn in by the Grand Duke on July 20, 1984, following election of June 17, succeeding Pierre WERNER (Christian Social Party).

THE COUNTRY

Located southeast of Belgium between France and Germany, the small, landlocked Grand Duchy of Luxembourg is a predominantly Roman Catholic country whose inhabitants exhibit an ethnic and cultural blend of French and German elements. Both French and German enjoy official language status; the former predominates in government, the latter in the Church and the press. The local language, Letzeburgesch, is a West Frankish dialect.

Luxembourg is highly industrialized. Iron and steel products have long been mainstays of the economy and still account for over one-third of the gross domestic product, despite a serious downturn in 1975–1976 and the subsequent introduction of a restructuring plan that entailed the closing of obsolete plants and the eventual elimination of 45 percent of the industry's jobs. Meanwhile, economic diversification has focused on the production of such goods as rubber, synthetic fibers, plastics, chemicals, and small metal products. Luxembourg has also become an international financial center, the number of banks rising from 13 in 1955 to 115 in 1981. Agriculture, which occupies under 6 percent of the labor force, consists primarily of small farms devoted to livestock-raising. Trade is largely oriented toward Luxembourg's neighbors and fellow participants in the Benelux Economic Union and the European Community (EC).

GOVERNMENT AND POLITICS

Political background. For centuries Luxembourg was dominated and occupied by foreign powers, until the Congress of Vienna in 1815 declared it a grand duchy subject to the king of the Netherlands. The country was recognized as an independent neutral state in 1867 and came under the present ruling house of Nassau-Weilbourg in 1890. An economic union with Belgium was established in 1922, but Luxembourg retains its independent political institutions under a constitution dating back to 1868.

Since World War II, political power has been exercised by a series of coalition governments in which the Christian Social Party (PCS) has traditionally been the dominant element. For fifteen years beginning in 1959, the government was led by Pierre WERNER, who formed coalitions with both the Socialist Workers' (POSL) and Democratic (PD) parties. A month after the election of May 1974, however, the latter two formed a new government under PD leader Gaston THORN. Prior to the election of June 1979, the governing parties agreed to renew their coalition if they succeeded in gaining a parliamentary majority, but a somewhat unexpected shortfall of one seat necessitated a fairly lengthy period of intraparty negotiation that resulted in the formation of a PCS-PD government and the return of Pierre Werner as prime minister.

In the wake of the June 1984 balloting, at which the Christian Socials remained the largest party, but the Socialist Workers registered the greatest gain, a new round of negotiations led to a revived PSC-POSL coalition under former finance minister Jacques SANTER.

Constitution and government. Luxembourg's 1868 constitution has been repeatedly revised to incorporate democratic reforms, to eliminate the former status of "perpetual neutrality", and to permit devolution of sovereignty to international institutions. Executive authority is exercised on behalf of the grand duke by the prime minister and the cabinet, who are appointed by the sovereign but responsible to the legislature. Legislative authority is exercised primarily by the elected Chamber of Deputies, but there is also a nonelective Council of State, whose decisions can be reversed by the Chamber. The judicial system is headed by the Superior Court of Justice and includes a Court of Assizes for serious criminal offenses, two district courts, and three justices of the peace. There are also administrative and special social courts. Judges are appointed for life by the grand duke. The country is divided into districts, cantons, and communes. The districts function as links between the central and local governments and are headed by commissioners appointed by the central government.

Foreign relations. Luxembourg's former neutral status was abandoned after the German occupation of World War II. The country was a founding member of the United Nations and has been a leader in the postwar consolidation of the West through its membership in Benelux, NATO, the EC, and other multilateral organizations. Relations with Belgium remain particularly close.

In August 1986 Luxembourg lodged an official protest with France regarding the opening of a new nuclear plant at Cattenom on the Moselle River. Despite fears by Luxembourg and West Germany that discharges from the plant into the Moselle would endanger the safety of the duchy's citizens, the European Commission ruled in favor of its operation.

Current issues. The duchy did not appear to have suffered as much as Belgium from retrenchment in the steel industry during 1981–1986. Both output and employment remained relatively constant through the period, although the full impact of an EC-directed cutback on government subsidies to the industry remained uncertain.

By 1987 a degree of anti-Americanism was detected in the course of parliamentary debate on the proposed construction of a third US military depot, although Socialist critics within the government coalition insisted that their principal concern was that Luxembourg not become excessively dependent on military employment.

POLITICAL PARTIES

With a multiparty system based on proportional representation, Luxembourg has recently been ruled by coalition governments headed by the Christian Social Party or the Democratic Party allied with each other or with the Socialist Workers' Party. The former Social Democratic Party, organized by a number of conservative POSL dissidents in 1971, was dissolved in 1983.

Government Parties:

Christian Social Party (*Parti Chrétien Social* — PCS). Formed in 1914, Luxembourg's strongest single party draws its main support from farmers, Catholic laborers, and moderate conservatives. Often identified as a Christian Democratic grouping, the PCS endorses a centrist position that includes support for the monarchy, progressive labor legislation, assistance to farmers and small businessmen, church-state cooperation, and an internationalist foreign policy.

Leaders: Jacques SANTER (Prime Minister), Pierre WERNER (former Prime Minister), Jean SPAUTZ (President), Willy BOURG (Secretary General).

Socialist Workers' Party (*Parti Ouvrier Socialiste Luxembourgeois* — POSL). Founded in 1902, the moderately Marxist POSL draws its major support from the urban lower and lower-middle classes. It advocates extension of the present system of social legislation and social insurance, and supports European integration, NATO, and the United Nations. In 1971 a conservative wing split off to form the Social Democratic Party. In opposition prior to the June 1984 election, it subsequently joined the Santer government.

Leaders: Jacques POOS (Deputy Prime Minister), Ben FAYOT (President), Raymond BECKER (Secretary General).

Opposition Parties:

Democratic Party (*Parti Démocratique* — PD). The PD includes both conservatives and moderates and draws support from professional, business, white-collar, and artisan groups. Also referred to as the "Liberals", the party is committed to free enterprise, although it favors certain forms of progressive social legislation. It is mildly anticlerical and strongly pro-NATO. It participated in the Werner government prior to the 1984 election, after which it went into opposition.

Leader: Colette FLESCH (President).

Communist Party (*Parti Communiste de Luxembourg* — PCL). Established in 1921, the pro-Soviet PCL draws its main support from urban and industrial workers and some intellectuals. It advocates full nationalization of the economy, opposes NATO and Eurocommunism, and was the only West European Communist party to approve the Soviet invasion of Czechoslovakia in 1968. The PCL suffered a loss of 3 of its 5 parliamentary seats at the 1979 election, retaining the 2 that remained in 1984.

Leader: René URBANY (Chairman and Secretary).

Independent Socialist Party (*Parti Socialiste Indépendant* — PSI). The PSI was organized prior to the 1979 election by a small group of POSL dissenters who felt that the parent group had betrayed its ideals by participating in a government coalition with a nonsocialist partner. It lost its sole parliamentary seat in 1984.

Leader: Jean GREMLING.

The Green Alternative (*Di Gréng Alternativ*). Part of the loosely structured European environmentalist movement, the Green Alternative won 2 legislative seats in 1984. As in the case of the Greens of West Germany, the party has adopted the principle of "rotation", whereby its deputies are replaced by alternates midway through the parliamentary term.

Leader: Jean HUSS.

LEGISLATURE

Legislative responsibility is centered in the elected Chamber of Deputies, but the appointive Council of State retains some vestigial legislative functions.

Council of State (*Conseil d'Etat*). The Council consists of 21 members appointed for life; 7 are appointed directly by the grand duke, while the others are appointed by the Council itself or by the grand duke from slates proposed by the Chamber of Deputies.

Chamber of Deputies (*Chambre des Députés*). The Chamber currently consists of 64 deputies elected for five-year terms (subject to dissolution) by direct universal suffrage on the basis of proportional representation. Following the election of June 17, 1984, the Christian Socialist Party held 25 seats; the Socialist Workers' Party, 21; the Democratic Party, 14; the Communist Party, 2; and the Ecologists, 2.

President: Léon BOLENDORFF.

CABINET

Prime Minister	Jacques Santer
Deputy Prime Minister	Jacques Poos

Ministers

Agriculture	Marc Fischbach
Budget	Jean-Claude Juncker
Civil Service	Marc Fischbach
Communications	Jacques Santer
Cultural Affairs	Robert Krieps
Defense	Marc Fischbach
Education	Fernand Boden
Energy	Marcel Schlechter
Environment	Robert Krieps
Family, Housing and Social Affairs	Jean Spautz
Finance	Jacques Santer
Foreign Affairs	Jacques Poos
Foreign Trade and Cooperation	Jacques Poos
Interior	Jean Spautz
Justice	Robert Krieps
Labor	Jean-Claude Juncker
Middle Class Affairs	Jacques Poos
National Economy	Jacques Poos
Planning	Jacques Santer
Post, Telephone and Telegraph	Jacques Santer
Public Health	Benny Berg
Public Works	Marcel Schlechter
Social Security	Benny Berg
Sports	Marc Fischbach
Tourism	Fernand Boden
Transport	Marcel Schlechter
Treasury	Jacques Poos

Secretaries of State

Agriculture	René Steichen
Economies	Johny Lahure
Foreign Affairs, Foreign Trade and Cooperation	Robert Goebbels
Middle Class Affairs	Robert Goebbels
Director General, Monetary Institute of Luxembourg	Pierre Jaans

NEWS MEDIA

All news media are privately owned and are free of censorship.

Press. The following newspapers are published daily at the capital, unless otherwise noted: *Luxemburger Wort/La Voix du Luxembourg* (81,500), in German and French, Catholic, PCS organ; *Tageblatt/Le Journal d'Esch* (Esch-sur-Alzette, 24,500), in German and French, POSL affiliated; *Le Républicain Lorrain* (24,000), in French; *Letzeburger Journal* (12,000), Liberal, in German; *Letzeburger Land* (8,000), cultural weekly, in German; *Zeitung vum Letzeburger Vollek* (3,000), PCL organ, in German.

News agencies. There is no domestic facility; a number of foreign bureaus, including AP, UPI, and *Agence France-Presse,* maintain offices at Luxembourg-Ville.

Radio and television. *Radio Luxembourg* and *Télé Luxembourg,* each with several transmitters, are operated by the state-chartered, commercial *Compagnie Luxembourgeoise de Télédiffusion.* There were approximately 229,000 radio and 91,500 television receivers in 1987.

INTERGOVERNMENTAL REPRESENTATION

Ambassador to the US: André PHILIPPE.

US Ambassador to Luxembourg: Jean Broward Shevlin GERARD.

Permanent Representative to the UN: Jean FEYDER.

IGO Memberships (Non-UN): ACCT, BLX, CCC, CEUR, EC, EIB, Eurocontrol, ICCO, ICM, ICO, IEA, INRO, Intelsat, Interpol, IOOC, ITC, NATO, OECD, PCA, WEU.

MADAGASCAR

Democratic Republic of Madagascar
Repoblika Demokratika n'i Madagaskar (Malagasy)
République Démocratique de Madagascar (French)

Political Status: Established as the Malagasy Republic within the French Community in 1958; became independent June 30, 1960; military regime established May 18, 1972; present name and constitution adopted by referendum of December 21, 1975.

Area: 226,657 sq. mi. (587,041 sq. km.).

Population: 10,903,000 (1988E). A 1975 census, unevaluated for coverage error, yielded a figure of 7,568,577.

Major Urban Center (1985E): ANTANANARIVO (663,000).

Official Languages: Malagasy, French.

Monetary Unit: Malagasy Franc (market rate March 1, 1988, 1285.93 francs = $1US).

President of the Republic and Chairman of the Supreme Council of the Revolution: Adm. Didier RATSIRAKA; succeeded the former Chairman of the Military Directorate, Brig. Gen. Gilles ANDRIAMAHAZO, June 15, 1975; named President of the Republic by referendum of December 21, 1975, and inaugurated January 4, 1976, for a seven-year term; reelected on November 7, 1982.

Prime Minister: Lt. Col. Victor RAMAHATRA; appointed February 12, 1988, following the resignation of Lt. Col. Désiré RAKOTOARIJAONA.

THE COUNTRY

The Democratic Republic of Madagascar, consisting of the large island of Madagascar and five small island dependencies, is situated in the Indian Ocean off the southeast coast of Africa. Although the population includes some 18 distinct ethnic groups, the main division is between the light-skinned Mérina people of the central plateau and the more Negroid peoples of the coastal regions (*côtiers*). The Malagasy language is classified as part of the Malayo-Polynesian family, yet reflects African, Arabic, and European influences. About 36 percent of the population is classed as Christian (predominantly Roman Catholic in the coastal regions, Protestant on the plateau); about 9 percent is Muslim and 55 percent adheres to traditional beliefs. The nonindigenous population includes some 30,000 Comorans and smaller groups of French, Indians, Pakistanis, and Chinese. As in most African countries, women constitute 50 percent of the labor force, performing the bulk of subsistence activity; however, due largely to matriarchal elements in pre-colonial Malagasy culture, females are significantly better represented in the cabinet, Assembly, and in managerial urban occupations than their mainland counterparts.

Agriculture, forestry, and fishing account for about two-fifths of Madagascar's gross domestic product but employ over four-fifths of the labor force, the majority at a subsistence level. Leading export crops are coffee, cloves, and vanilla, while industry is concentrated in food processing and textiles. Mineral resources include deposits of graphite and chromium in addition to undeveloped reserves of oil shale, bauxite, iron, and nickel. Beginning in the early 1970s, a major proportion of the country's economic base, formerly dominated by foreign businesses, was taken over by the strongly socialist government. However, in the face of mounting difficulties with the external debt (currently nearing $3 billion) and worsening trade deficits, the administration of President Ratsiraka in 1980 started to reverse its policies, introducing budget austerity, currency devaluations, and measures to reduce food imports by boosting agricultural production. Although the actions have won support from international creditors, internal unrest has been generated by recurring food shortages and malnutrition within the rapidly growing population, rampant urban crime and rural banditry, escalating inflation, and persistent unemployment (see Current issues, below).

GOVERNMENT AND POLITICS

Political background. During the eighteenth and nineteenth centuries, Madagascar was dominated by the Mérina people of the plateau, but after a brief period of British influence, the French gained control and by 1896 had destroyed the Mérina monarchy. Renamed the Malagasy Republic, it became an autonomous state within the French Community in 1958 and gained full independence on June 26, 1960, under the presidency of Philibert TSIRANANA, who governed with the support of the Social Democratic Party (PSD).

Tsiranana's coastal-dominated government ultimately proved unable to deal with a variety of problems, including ethnic conflict stemming from Mérina opposition to the government's pro-French stance and their virtual exclusion from important posts. In addition, economic problems led in 1971 to a revolt by peasants in Tulear Province, while students, dissatisfied with their job prospects in a stagnating economy, initiated a rebellion in early 1972. In May, having acknowledged his growing inability to rule, Tsiranana turned over his duties as head of state and chief of government to Maj. Gen. Gabriel RAMANANTSOA, who was confirmed for a five-year term by a referendum held October 8.

An attempted coup by dissident côtier officers led to Ramanantsoa's resignation on February 5, 1975, but his successor, Col. Richard RATSIMANDRAVA, was assassinated six days later, with Brig. Gen. Gilles ANDRIAMAHAZO assuming the leadership of a Military Directorate. Andriamahazo was in turn succeeded on June 15 by Cdr.

Didier RATSIRAKA, who as foreign minister since May 1972 had been instrumental in reversing the pro-Western policies of former president Tsiranana in favor of a more Soviet-oriented and vigorously pro-Arab posture. Ratsiraka was designated president of the newly styled Democratic Republic of Madagascar on December 21, 1975, and was formally inaugurated on January 4, 1976.

While some observers attributed the period of instability to an ethnic conflict between the côtier supporters of Tsiranana and the Mérina-backed regimes of Ramanantsoa and Ratsimandrava, both Andriamahazo and Ratsiraka, although of coastal origin, took vigorous action against Ratsimandrava's assassins and acted to alleviate tribal tensions. The government formed on January 11, 1976, which was designed to reflect a regional balance of both military and civilian elements, was reconstituted on August 20 following the accidental death of Prime Minister Joël RAKOTOMALALA on July 30 and his replacement by Justin RAKOTONIAINA on August 12. Following a single-list national election on June 30, 1977, a new cabinet, headed by Lt. Col. Désiré RAKOTOARIJAONA as prime minister, was appointed. President Ratsiraka was popularly reelected to a seven-year term on November 7, 1982, securing 80 percent of the vote in a contest in which he was opposed by Monja JAONA of the National Movement for the Independence of Madagascar (Monima), who had campaigned on a platform that attempted to capitalize on growing domestic insecurity.

In August 1985 the government launched an army raid at Antananarivo that killed 19 leaders of the country's 10,000-member *kung fu* sect, which was reported to be plotting a revolution; however, the hard-line approach failed to deter burgeoning opposition to administration policies (see Current issues, below).

On February 12, 1988, Lt. Col. Victor Ramahatra (theretofore minister of public works) was named to succeed Colonel Rakotoarijaona as prime minister, following the latter's resignation for what were termed "health reasons".

Constitution and government. Under the 1975 constitution the president is elected by universal suffrage for a seven-year term; serves as chairman of a Supreme Revolutionary Council (SRC), which is charged with safeguarding the "Malagasy Socialist Revolution" and consists primarily of presidential appointees; and names a prime minister, who is an ex officio member of the SRC. A Military Development Committee advises the government on defense and development policies. Legislative functions are discharged by a Popular National Assembly elected for a five-year term by universal suffrage. The constitution also provides for an all-encompassing National Front for the Defense of the Malagasy Socialist Revolution (FNDR); a seven-member Constitutional High Court; and an administrative devolution of power to traditional village councils (*fokon'olona*).

In its constitutional restructuring, the present regime has introduced a highly "layered" form of government strongly rooted in the nation's traditional village system. Thus, the electoral procedure is extremely complex, involving a series of stages that commence with the selection of people's councils in each of the 11,000 *fokontony* (village or urban districts), followed by the indirect election of intermediate and provincial councils prior to National Assembly balloting. Government-approved parties present separate lists for all but the last of these elections, at which they are allocated places on a combined National Front list.

Foreign relations. During the Tsiranana administration, Madagascar retained close economic, defense, and cultural ties with France. In 1973, however, the Ramanantsoa government renegotiated all cooperation agreements with the former colonial power, withdrew from the Franc Zone, and terminated its membership in the francophone Common African and Malagasy Organization (OCAM). Over the next several years, a number of agreements with the Republic of South Africa were repudiated, diplomatic relations with Communist nations were established, and pro-Arab policies were announced. In 1979, the government offered the former Israeli embassy at Antananarivo to the Palestine Liberation Organization as a base for local activity, while support has consistently been offered to African liberation movements.

In recent years, there has been a drift towards the West, ambassadorial links with Washington being restored in November 1980 after a lapse of more than four years and aid agreements subsequently being negotiated with the United States, France, Japan, and a number of Scandinavian countries. On the other hand, talks were held at Moscow in 1984 and 1986 on improving trade with the Soviet Union and agreements to strengthen bilateral relations with China were announced in 1986. Regionally, Madagascar has joined Mauritius and the Seychelles in the 1982 formation of an Indian Ocean Commission (IOC), to which Australia and India were invited to accede.

Current issues. During 1987, the Ratsiraka government was viewed as facing the most severe crisis of its 12-year tenure. Serious university disturbances at Antananarivo throughout the first half of the year attested to the continued influence of student militants. In addition, widespread racial violence in February and March was aimed at members of the Indo-Pakistani ("Karana") merchant community, while other disturbances reflected what was described as a popular unwillingness to further endure "a life of quiet desperation". With the FNDR apparently breaking up (see Political Parties, below), Ratsiraka and his Vanguard of the Malagasy Revolution were expected to be severely challenged at the 1988 legislative balloting, particularly in the wake of the replacement on February 12 of Prime Minister Rakotoarijaona, who had served since 1977, but had recently given the impression of distancing himself from the president. Ratsiraka nonetheless adhered to his Western-mandated economic policies, securing further debt rescheduling and donor aid, including funds for the rehabilitation of ten of Madagascar's ports. Meanwhile, foreign businessmen, skeptical of the administration's commitment to external private investment, called for further trade liberalization.

POLITICAL PARTIES

Nominal Government Front:

National Front for the Defense of the Malagasy Socialist Revolution (*Front National pour la Défense de la Révolution Socialiste Malgache* — FNDR). The constitution of December 21, 1975, provided for the organization of the FNDR as the country's sole party. The "revolutionary associations" identified below participated in the presidential balloting of November 1982 and the legislative election of August 1983 as FNDR components. However, beginning in March 1987 the last four (Vonjy, MFM, Monima, USM) initiated joint antigovernment activity, including a refusal to vote on the state budget and in May sponsored a "change of government" demonstration in Antananarivo attended by an estimated 10,000 persons. The opposition movement was reported to be receiving support from disparate elements, including students responsible for the recent university unrest and politically active members of the Catholic hierarchy.

Vanguard of the Malagasy Revolution (*Avant-garde de la Révolution Malgache* — Arema). Organized by President Ratsiraka in March 1976 as the nucleus of the National Front, Arema won 117 of 139 seats at the 1983 National Assembly election, although its influence appeared to be waning by 1987 because of dissatisfaction with the economic policies of the Ratsiraka administration.

Leader: Adm. Didier RATSIRAKA (President of the Republic and Secretary General of the Party).

Congress Party for Malagasy Independence (*Antokon'ny Kongresy Ho An'ny Fahaleovantenan'i Madagasikara* — AKFM). The AKFM is a left-wing alliance of radical and middle- and upper-class nationalist movements in which Communist influence, largely of a pro-Soviet orientation, plays a significant role. The party won 16 seats at 1977 legislative election, but only 9 in 1983.

Leaders: Richard ANDRIAMANJATO, Rakotovao ANDRIANTIANO.

Malagasy Christian Democratic Union (*Union Démocratique Chrétien Malgache* — Udecma-KMTP). The Udecma-KMTP is a progressive Christian Democratic group formerly known as the *Rassemblement National Malgache*. It won two legislative seats in 1977, losing both in 1983.

Leader: Solo Norbert ANDRIAMORASATA.

Popular Impulse for National Unity (*Elan Populaire pour l'Unité Nationale/Vonjy Iray Tsy Mivaky* — VITM or Vonjy). Established in 1973 by followers of former president Tsiranana, Vonjy lost one of its former seven seats at the 1983 election despite speculation that it might be runner-up to Arema. Subsequently, it split into pro- and antigovernment factions, a division that was seemingly resolved at a February 1987 extraordinary congress which adopted a solid posture of opposition that cleared the way for the reported formation of an opposition front with the MFM (below) in early 1988.

Leader: Dr. Jérôme Marojama RAZANABAHINY.

Movement for Proletarian Power (*Mouvement pour le Pouvoir Prolétarien/Mpitolona ho'an ny Fanjakan'ny Madinika* — MFM). Formed in 1972 by student radicals who helped to overthrow President Tsiranana, the left-wing MFM (also known as *Pouvoir aux Petits*) initially opposed the Ratsiraka government and was not a FNDR component in the 1977 balloting. In what was called a "fitful collaboration" with the FNDR that led to internal divisiveness and "confusion", the group won three Assembly seats in 1983. Although its leaders in recent years have adopted an increasingly moderate outlook, a drive to re-establish support among student militants was reported in 1987.

Leaders: Manandafy RAKOTONIRINA, Germain RAKOTONIRAINY.

National Movement for the Independence of Madagascar/Madagascar for the Malagasy Party (*Mouvement National pour l'Indépendance de Madagascar/Madagasikara Otronin'ny Malagasy* — Monima). A left-wing nationalist party based in the south, Monima (also called *Monima Ka Miviombio*) withdrew from the National Front after the local elections of March 1977, charging it had been the victim of electoral fraud. As a result, it was awarded no places on the Front's list for the June legislative election. Its longtime leader, Monja Jaona, was under house arrest from November 1980 to March 1982, at which time he agreed to bring the group back into the FNDR and was appointed a member of the Supreme Council of the Revolution. Subsequently, he contested the 1982 presidential election as Commander Ratsiraka's only competitor, winning 20 percent of the vote. In December, it was reported that he had been stripped of his membership on the SCR and, after having issued an appeal for an "unlimited general strike", had again been placed under house arrest for activities "likely to bring about the fall of the country". He was released on August 15, 1983, after undertaking a hunger strike and was returned to the legislature at the election of August 28 as one of Monima's two representatives. The party's poor showing (less than four percent of valid votes cast) in 1983 was partly attributed to uncertainty, prior to Jaona's release, as to whether it would participate. Although the 80-year-old Jaona is not expected to be a presidential candidate again in 1989, he remains the country's most outspoken and well-known critic of government policies.

Leaders: Monja JAONA, René RANAIVOSA.

Socialist Monima (*Vondrona Sosialista Monima*—VSM). The VSM was organized in late 1977 by a group of pro-Beijing Monima dissidents. It is unrepresented in the Assembly.

Leaders: Tsihozony Maharanga RAZAFINDRABE, André Tovonaiko ARNAULT.

LEGISLATURE

The **Popular National Assembly** (*Assemblée Nationale Populaire*) is a unicameral body of 137 members directly elected for five-year terms from a single National Front list, which in 1983 encompassed more than 500 candidates. Following the balloting of August 28 the distribution of Front members was as follows: Vanguard of the Malagasy Revolution, 117; Congress Party for Malagasy Independence, 9; Popular Impulse for National Unity, 6; Movement for Proletarian Power, 3; National Movement for Independence of Madagascar, 2.

President: Lucien Xavier Michel ANDRIANARAHIN-JAKA.

CABINET

Prime Minister	Lt. Col. Victor Ramahatra
Ministers	
Agricultural Production and Agrarian Reform	Jose Michel Andrianoelison
Animal Husbandry, Fisheries, Forest and Water Resources	Joseph Randrianasolo
Civil Service, Labor and Social Law	Georges Ruphin
Commerce	Georges Solofson
Defense	Gen. (Christopher) Bienaimé Raveloson-Mahasampo
Finance and Economy	Pascal Rakotomavo
Foreign Affairs	Adrianaribone Jean Bemananjara
Health	Dr. Jean-Jacques Seraphin
Higher Education	Ignace Rakoto
Industry, Energy and Mining	Jose Rakotomavo
Information and Ideological Orientation	Simon Pierre
Interior	Augustin Ampy Portos
Justice, Keeper of the Seals	Joseph Bedo
Population, Social Condition and Youth	Jean-André Ndremanjary
Posts and Telecommunications	Andriantiana Rakotovao
Primary and Secondary Education	Charles Zeny
Public Works	Andrianaivomanana Razafindramisa
Revolutionary Art and Culture	Gisèle Rabesahala
Scientific Research and Development of Technology	Antoine Rabesa Zafera
Transportation, Meteorology and Tourism	Emile Tsaranasy
Special Counselor to the President for Financial Affairs	Nirina Andriamanerasoa
Governor, Central Bank	Richard Randriamaholy

NEWS MEDIA

Press. The following dailies are published at Antananarivo in Malagasy, unless otherwise noted: *Midi-Madagascar* (26,000), in French; *Madagascar-Matin* (17,000), in French and Malagasy; *Atrika* (13,000), government organ in French and Malagasy; *Imongo Vaovao* (10,000), AKFM organ; *Sahy* (8,000); *Maresaka* (5,000).

News agencies. In June 1977, the government replaced the existing *Agence Madagascar-Presse* with the *Agence Nationale d'Information "Taratra"* (Anta), which is responsible to the Ministry of Information and Ideological Orientation. In addition to *Agence France-Presse, Novosti* and several other Eastern-bloc services maintain offices in Madagascar, as does *Xinhua.*

Radio and television. *Radio Madagasikara,* a government-owned, commercial network, services some 2.0 million receivers, while *Télévision Madagascar* broadcasts to approximately 100,000 receivers.

INTERGOVERNMENTAL REPRESENTATION

Ambassador to the US: Leon M. RAJAOBELINA.

US Ambassador to Madagascar: Patricia Gates LYNCH.

Permanent Representative to the UN: Blaise RABETAFIKA.

IGO Memberships (Non-UN): ACCT, ADF, AfDB, BADEA, CCC, EEC(L), EIB, IACO, ICO, Intelsat, Interpol, ISO, NAM, OAU.

MALAWI

Republic of Malawi

Political Status: Independent member of the Commonwealth since 1964; republic under one-party presidential rule established July 6, 1966.

Area: 45,747 sq. mi. (118,484 sq. km.).

Population: 5,547,460 (1977C), 7,507,000 (1988E).

Major Urban Centers (1977C): LILONGWE (98,718); Blantyre (219,011); Zomba (24,234).

Official Languages: English, Chichewa.

Monetary Unit: Kwacha (market rate March 1, 1988, 2.53 kwacha = $1US).

President: Ngwazi Dr. Hastings Kamuzu BANDA; became Prime Minister of Nyasaland in 1963 and of independent Malawi in 1964; elected President by Parliament in 1966 for a five-year term; sworn in as President for Life on July 6, 1971, pursuant to a constitutional amendment adopted in November 1970.

THE COUNTRY

Malawi, the former British protectorate of Nyasaland, is a landlocked southeast African nation bordering the western side of 360-mile-long Lake Malawi (formerly Lake Nyasa). Its name is a contemporary spelling of "Maravi", which historically referenced the interrelated Bantu peoples who inhabit the area. The main tribal groups in Malawi are the Chewas, the Nyanja, and the Tumbuka. A majority of the population adheres to traditional African beliefs, although 15 percent is Muslim, 10 percent Protestant, and 10 percent Roman Catholic. A small non-African component includes Europeans and Asians. Three-quarters of adult females are unpaid agricultural workers; the number of households headed by women has increased in recent years as men move to cash-crop labor, their wives remaining responsible for subsistence activity. Female representation in government averages approximately 10 percent.

Overall, about 85 percent of the population is engaged in agriculture, the most important cash crops being tobacco, tea, peanuts, sugar, and cotton. Recent development efforts have focused on integrated rural production, diversification in light industry (particularly agriprocessing and import substitution), and improved transportation facilities. Since 1980, Malawi has faced a trade imbalance, debt interest payments that absorb one-third of export earnings, chronic unemployment, and inflation that has grown by more than 100 percent. Although credited by mid-decade with being one of the few African states with a grain surplus, Malawi continued to suffer high rates of malnutrition, infant mortality, and poverty—a paradox widely attributed to an agricultural system favoring large estate owners.

GOVERNMENT AND POLITICS

Political background. Under British rule since 1891, the Nyasaland protectorate was joined with Northern and Southern Rhodesia in 1953 to form the Federation of Rhodesia and Nyasaland. Internal opposition to the Federation proved so vigorous that a state of emergency was declared, with nationalist leaders H.B.M. CHIPEMBERE, Kanyama CHIUME, and H. Kamuzu BANDA being imprisoned. Subsequently, however, they were released, internal self-government was attained on February 1, 1963, and the Federation was dissolved at the end of that year. Nyasaland became a fully independent member of the Commonwealth under the name of Malawi on July 6, 1964, and a republic two years later with Prime Minister Banda being installed as the country's president.

The early years of the Banda presidency were marked by conservative policies, including the retention of White civil-service personnel and the maintenance of good relations with South Africa. Younger, more radical leaders soon became disenchanted. In 1965 a minor insurrection was led by H.B.M. Chipembere, while a second, led by Yatuta CHISIZA, took place in 1967. Both were easily contained, however, and Banda became firmly entrenched as the nation's political leader.

Longstanding controversy regarding President Banda's successor intensified in early 1983, amid reports of a power struggle between Dick Tennyson MATENJE, secretary general of the ruling Malawi Congress Party (MCP), and John TEMBO, governor of the Reserve Bank. On May 19, the government announced that Matenje was one of four senior politicians killed in a car accident, his party position remaining vacant with the appointment of Robson CHIRWA as administrative secretary. In April 1984, Tembo was relieved of the Bank post, although remaining politically active and in position to influence the naming of Banda's successor (see Current issues, below).

The March 1983 assassination in Zimbabwe of Dr. Attati MPAKATI of Lesoma (see Political Parties, below) left two of the three known opposition groups without leaders. In May, former Mafremo leader Orton CHIRWA, who had been jailed with his wife and son since December 1981, was found guilty of treason and sentenced to death. Subsequent appeals in December 1983 and February 1984 were denied, and Chirwa, who claimed that he and his family had been abducted from Zambia to permit their arrest, became an object of international human rights attention; bowing to the pressure, Banda commuted his sentence to life imprisonment in June 1984.

Constitution and government. The republican constitution of July 6, 1966, established a one-party system under which the MCP enjoys a political monopoly and its leader wields extensive powers as head of state, head of government, and commander in chief. Originally elected to a five-year term by the National Assembly, Banda was designated president for life in 1971. Future presidents are to be chosen, subject to popular endorsement, by an electoral college consisting of party officials. The chief executive is empowered to name a three-member Presidential Commission of cabinet ministers in the event of illness or impending absence, while death of the incumbent would lead to formation of an interim Presidential Council comprising the secretary general of the MCP and two ministers chosen by and from within the party's National Executive Committee. The judicial structure includes both Western and traditional courts. The Western system includes a Supreme Court of Appeal, a High Court, and magistrates' courts. The traditional courts, restored in 1970, are headed by chiefs.

For administrative purposes Malawi is divided into 3 regions, 24 districts, and 3 subdistricts, which are headed by regional ministers, district commissioners, and assistant district commissioners, respectively.

Foreign relations. Malawi under President Banda's leadership has sought to combine African nationalism with multiracialism at home and a strongly pro-Western and anti-Communist position in world affairs. Citing economic necessity, Malawi has been one of the few Black African states to maintain relations with South Africa. The resultant friction culminated in a September 1986 meeting at Blantyre during which the leaders of Mozambique, Zambia, and Zimbabwe reportedly warned Banda to change his policies, particularly concerning alleged Malawian support for Renamo rebels in Mozambique. Banda, while denying the allegations, nevertheless quickly concluded a joint defense and security pact with Maputo. The government also reaffirmed its commitment to an effort by the Southern African Development Coordination Conference (SADCC) to reduce dependence on South African trade routes. To that end, Malawi in 1987 agreed to increase shipments through Tanzania, with which it had established diplomatic ties in 1985 despite long-standing complaints of aid to Banda opponents. Relations with Zambia have also been strained by Malawi's claim to Zambian territory in the vicinity of their mutual border.

Current issues. In early 1987 the Banda government announced that about 300 Malawian troops had been sent to interdict Renamo attacks on crews reconstructing the Nacala Railway across northern Mozambique. The deployment underscored Banda's adoption of a stronger anti-South African posture in the face of pressure from neighboring countries (see Foreign relations, above).

Observers noted that negotiations involving the country's regional realignment had been conducted largely by former Reserve Bank governor John Tembo, whose name dominated external speculation about Banda's successor. Tembo, a leading member of the MCP executive committee, serves as the president's "official interpreter"; he is also the uncle of Banda's longtime companion and Malawi's "official hostess", Cecilia KADZAMIRA, who has been described as organizing support for possible future political aspirations of her own, although Banda (officially 82, but reportedly 89) heatedly denied at a party convention in September that he was grooming Kadzamira herself as a potential chief executive.

POLITICAL PARTIES

The Malawi Congress Party, the only authorized political party, exercises complete control of the government.

Government Party:

Malawi Congress Party (MCP). The MCP is a continuation of the Nyasaland African Congress (NAC), which was formed under President Banda's leadership in 1959. Overtly pro-Western and dedicated to multi-racialism and internal development, the party has been criticized for being excessively conservative. It has held all legislative seats since the preindependence election of 1961.

Leaders: H. Kamuzu BANDA (President of the Republic and of the Party), John TEMBO (Executive Committee Member), Robson Watayachanga CHIRWA (Adminstrative Secretary).

External Opposition:

Malawi Freedom Movement (Mafremo). Following the arrest and imprisonment of its leader, Orton Chirwa, in 1981 (see Political background, above), Mafremo was relatively inactive prior to an early 1987 attack on a police station near the Tanzanian border that was attributed to the group's newly formed military wing, the Malawi National Liberation Army. Although initially based at Dar es Salaam, Mafremo was subsequently reported to have secured Zimbabwean support through the efforts of a new leader Edward Yapwantha. Meanwhile, the continued imprisonment of Chirwa and his wife, Vera, was said to be generating increased sympathy for the movement within Malawi.

Leaders: Edward YAPWANTHA, Orton CHIRWA (imprisoned).

Socialist League of Malawi (Lesoma). Reportedly the source of an unsuccessful letter-bomb attack in 1979, the Banda government denied involvement in the 1983 assassination of Lesoma leader Dr. Attati Mpakati at Harare, Zimbabwe. Despite the 1980 formation of an affiliated People's Liberation Army of Malawi, there has been little recent evidence of Lesoma-inspired military activity, despite past claims of Soviet and Cuban support.

Leaders: Grey KAMUNYEMBENI, Kapote MWAKUSULA (Secretary General).

Congress for the Second Republic (CSR). Based at Dar es Salaam, Tanzania, the CSR is led by a former Malawian minister for external affairs.

Leader: Kanyama CHIUME.

LEGISLATURE

Members of the unicameral **National Assembly** sit for five-year terms (subject to dissolution). Since 1978 a majority of seats have been contested, although all candidates must be MCP-approved. At the most recent balloting of May 27–28, 1987, 112 elective seats were filled, with an additional 11 members being named by the president.

Speaker: Nelson P.W. KHONJE.

CABINET

President	Dr. H. Kamuzu Banda
Ministers	
Agriculture	Dr. H. Kamuzu Banda
Community Services	Eliya Katola Phiri
Education and Culture	Michael Mlambala
External Affairs	Dr. H. Kamuzu Banda
Finance	Louis Chimango
Forestry and Natural Resources	Stanford Demba
Health	Edward C.I. Bwanali
Justice	Dr. H. Kamuzu Banda
Labor	Wadson B. Deleza
Local Government	Mfunjo Mwakikunga
Trade, Industry and Tourism	Robson W. Chirwa
Transport and Communications	Dalton S. Katopola
Works and Supplies	Dr. H. Kamuzu Banda
Without Portfolio	Maxell Pashane
Governor, Central Bank	Chimwemwe Hara

NEWS MEDIA

Press. Most newspapers are privately owned and operated. There is no formal censorship, but the government's refusal to tolerate any form of criticism was reflected in a 1973 decree that journalists who printed material "damaging to the nation's reputation" were liable to life imprisonment. The following papers are published at Blantyre, unless otherwise noted: *Boma Lathu* (51,000), Department of Information monthly in Chichewa; *Moni* (39,000), monthly in English and Chichewa; *Malawi News* (22,000), weekly in English and Chichewa; *The Daily Times* (20,000), in English; *Odini* (Lilongwe, 9,000), Catholic fortnightly in English and Chichewa.

News agency. The domestic facility is the Malawi News Agency (Mana).

Radio and television. Radio service in English and Chichewa is provided to approximately 1.1 million receivers by the statutory and semicommercial Malawi Broadcasting Corporation. There is no television service.

INTERGOVERNMENTAL REPRESENTATION

Ambassador to the US and Permanent Representative to the UN: Timon Sam MANGWAZU.

US Ambassador to Malawi: (Vacant).

IGO Memberships (Non-UN): ADF, AfDB, BADEA, CCC, CWTH, EEC(L), *EIB),* IACO, ICO, Interpol, ISO, ITPA, NAM, OAU, SADCC.

MALAYSIA

Note: The capitalized portions of non-Chinese names in this article are frequently the more familiar components thereof, rather than "family" names in the Western sense.

Political Status: Independent Federation of Malaya within the Commonwealth established August 31, 1957; Malaysia established September 16, 1963, with the addition of Sarawak, Sabah, and Singapore (which withdrew in August 1965).

Area: 127,316 sq. mi. (329,749 sq. km.), encompassing Peninsular Malaysia, 50,806 sq. mi. (131,588 sq. km.); Sarawak, 48,050 sq. mi. (124,450 sq. km.); Sabah, 28,460 sq. mi. (73,711 sq. km.).

Population: 13,745,241 (1980C), including Peninsular Malaysia, 11,426,613; Sarawak, 1,307,582; Sabah, 1,011,046; 16,754,000 (1988E).

Major Urban Centers (1980C): KUALA LUMPUR (937,875); Ipoh (300,727); Johore Bahru (249,880).

Official Language: Bahasa Malaysian.

Monetary Unit: Ringgit (market rate March 1, 1988, 2.53 ringgit = $1US).

Paramount Ruler: Tunku MAHMOOD Iskandar ibni Al-Marhum Sultan Ismail (Sultan of Johore); elected February 9, 1984, by the Conference of Rulers and formally installed on November 15 for a five-year term, succeeding Tuanku Haji AHMAD SHAH ibni al-Marhum Sultan Abu Bakar (Sultan of Pahang).

Deputy Paramount Ruler: Paduka Seri Sultan Raja AZLAN Shah ibni Al-Marhum Sultan Yusuf Izzudin Shah (Sultan of Perak); elected February 9, 1984, for a term concurrent with that of the Paramount Ruler, succeeding Tuanku JA'AFAR ibni al-Marhum Tuanku Abdul Rahman (Sovereign of Negri Sembilan).

Prime Minister: Datuk Seri Dr. MAHATHIR bin Mohamad (United Malays National Organization); sworn in July 16 and formed government July 18, 1981, following the resignation of Datuk HUSSEIN bin Onn (United Malays National Organization); formed new governments on April 29, 1982, following election of April 22–26, and on August 11, 1986, following election of August 2–3.

THE COUNTRY

Situated partly on the Malay Peninsula and partly on the island of Borneo, Malaysia consists of 11 states of the former Federation of Malaya (Peninsular or West Malaysia) plus the states of Sarawak and Sabah (East Malaysia). Thailand and Singapore are the mainland's northern and southern neighbors, respectively, while Sarawak and Sabah share a common border with the Indonesian province of Kalimantan. The multiracial population is composed predominantly of Malays (46 percent), followed by Chinese (32 percent), non-Malay tribals (12 percent), Indians and Pakistanis (8 percent), and others (2 percent). Although the Malay-based Bahasa Malaysia is the official language, English, Tamil, and several Chinese dialects are widely spoken. Islam is the state religion, but the freedom to profess other faiths is constitutionally guaranteed. Minority religious groups include Hindus, Buddhists, and Christians. Female status is largely determined by ethnic group and location, urban Malay women being better educated than their rural counterparts. Overall, women comprise 42 percent of the workforce, with nearly 90 percent of female workers concentrated in agricultural and clerical sectors.

Traditionally based on the export of palm oil, rubber, and tin, the Malaysian economy is presently being expanded to emphasize recently discovered offshore petroleum deposits and timber and copper production. Diversification programs by the current regime include the dispersal of manufacturing facilities throughout the country and expansion of the population under a controversial population growth policy to provide a Japan-style guaranteed consumer market (see Current issues, below). Agriculture employs half of the labor force, but the country is not self-sufficient in foodstuffs and nearly half of the rural population subsists at the poverty level.

GOVERNMENT AND POLITICS

Political background. Malaysia came into existence as an independent member of the Commonwealth of Nations on September 16, 1963, through merger of the already independent Federation of Malaya with the self-governing state of Singapore and the former British Crown Colonies of Sarawak and Sabah. The Malay states, organized by the British in the nineteenth century, had become independent in 1957, following the suppression of a long-standing Communist insurgency. Tunku ABDUL RAHMAN, head of the United Malays National Organization (UMNO) and subsequently of the Alliance Party, became Malaya's first prime minister and continued in that capacity after the formation of Malaysia. Singapore, with its predominantly Chinese population, had been ruled as a separate British colony and became internally self-governing in 1959 under the leadership of LEE Kuan Yew of the socialist People's Action Party (PAP). Its inclusion in Malaysia proved to be temporary and was terminated in August 1965, primarily because the attempt of the PAP to extend its influence beyond the confines of Singapore was viewed as a threat to Malay dominance of the Federation. The separate colonies of Sarawak and Sabah were included in Malaysia despite strong objection from the Philippines and Indonesia, the latter maintaining an armed "confrontation" of Malaysia until after Indonesian President Sukarno's removal from power in 1965–1966.

In 1969 opposition parties showed gains in an election held in West Malaysia, but balloting was not completed in East Malaysia because of racial riots at Kuala Lumpur that resulted in the declaration of a state of national emergency. A newly created, nine-member "National Operations Council" (NOC), headed by the deputy prime minister, was given full powers to quell the disturbances, and parliamentary government was eventually restored in February 1971.

Communist guerrillas, relatively quiescent since 1960, began returning from sanctuaries across the Malaysian-

Thai border in 1968 and by early 1974 were once again posing a serious threat to domestic security. While pursuing a vigorous campaign against the insurgents, the government went ahead with plans for new legislative balloting. The August 24 election resulted in an impressive victory for Prime Minister ABDUL RAZAK bin Hussein's newly styled National Front, whose predominance left only two of the eight opposition parties with seats in the lower house of Parliament.

In January 1976, Abdul Razak died at London, where he had gone for medical treatment, and was succeeded by the deputy prime minister, Datuk HUSSEIN bin Onn, who was also designated chairman of the National Front. On July 8, 1978, in an election called one year early, the National Front retained overwhelming control of the federal House of Representatives.

In May 1981 Datuk Hussein announced that for health reasons he would not stand for reelection as UMNO president and was succeeded on June 26 by the party's deputy president, Datuk Seri Dr. MAHATHIR bin Mohamad, who formed a new government following his designation as prime minister on July 16. Subsequently, Dr. Mahathir emulated his predecessor by calling for an early election on April 22–26, 1982, which yielded an even more impressive National Front victory than in 1978, with opposition parties and independents together capturing only 22 of 154 seats in the federal House of Representatives. In another early election on August 2–3, 1986, the Front overcame predictions of a setback by winning 148 seats in an enlarged House of 177, with Dr. Mahathir forming a new government on August 11. The outcome was interpreted as a clear-cut victory for Malay nationalism, with UMNO's leading Chinese coalition partner and the opposition *Parti Islam,* a fundamentalist group, both experiencing substantial losses (see Current issues, below).

Many of the issues that had been expected to cause electoral difficulties for the Mahathir coalition in 1986 resurfaced in early 1987 to provoke a major crisis within the prime minister's own party as it prepared for a triennial leadership poll on April 24. Accusing Dr. Mahathir of tolerating corruption, mismanagement, and extravagant spending, (then) Deputy Prime Minister MUSA bin Hital joined with a number of other prominent UMNO figures in supporting the candidacy of Trade and Industry Minister RAZALEIGH Hamzah for the party presidency. After an intensely fought campaign, Mahathir defeated Razaleigh by a mere 43 of 1,479 votes, with Encik Abdul GHAFFAR bin Baba outpacing Musa by an even closer margin of 40 votes for the deputy presidency. The party thereupon divided into two factions, a so-called "Team A" headed by the prime minister and a dissident "Team B".

In late September the unheralded promotion of more than 100 non-Mandarin-trained Chinese school teachers was widely condemned as violating a 1986 government pledge that the existing character of Chinese and Tamil education would not be altered. The UMNO's leading coalition partner, the Malaysian Chinese Association (MCA), immediately joined with the opposition Democratic Action Party (DAP) in threatening a Chinese school boycott if the promotions were not rescinded. On October 27, faced with rising social tension, the government responded by ordering the detention of numerous prominent individuals from both National Front and opposition ranks; on the following day it revoked the publishing licenses of three leading newspapers, including *The Star,* an MCA-owned English language daily. While most of the detainees were subsequently released, the media suspensions remained in effect until March 1988, with a significant tightening of internal security measures.

On February 4, 1988, Peninsular Malaysia's High Court, responding to a writ filed eight months earlier by "Team B" leaders, issued a ruling that the UMNO was an illegal entity under the official Societies Act because members of 30 unregistered branches had participated in the April balloting. Former prime ministers Abdul Rahman and Hussein bin Onn, on behalf of the dissidents, thereupon filed for recognition of a new party (UMNO-Malaysia) but were rebuffed by the registrar of societies on the ground that the High Court order had not yet become effective. On the other hand, Dr. Mahathir, applying on February 13 (the date of deregistration),was granted permission to begin the process of legalizing a government-supportive "new" UMNO (UMNO-Baru). Subsequently the government secured legislation authorizing the transfer of UMNO assets to UMNO-Baru, as well as a series of constitutional amendments rescinding the right of the High Court to interpret acts of parliament. On May 21 Mahathir announced that his new formation would recommend to the supreme council of the National Front that parliamentary members of the old UMNO who refused to join UMNO-Baru would be expelled from NF ranks. In early June the lengthy dispute between the executive and judiciary reached a breaking point when, in an unprecedented move, the prime minister advised the paramount ruler to suspend the Supreme Court's lord president, Tan Sri Mohamad SALLEH bin Abas. The action was taken one day before a scheduled hearing (immediately postponed) by the Supreme Court on the High Court's February 4 decision.

Constitution and government. The constitution of Malaysia is based on that of the former Federation of Malaya, as amended to accommodate the special interests of Sarawak and Sabah, which joined in 1963. It established a federal system of government under an elective constitutional monarchy. The administration of the 13 states (11 in the west, 2 in the east) is carried out by rulers or governors acting on the advice of State Executive Councils. Each state has its own constitution and a unicameral State Assembly that shares legislative powers with the federal Parliament. The supreme head of the federation is the paramount ruler (*Yang di-Pertuan Agong*), who exercises the powers of a constitutional monarch in a parliamentary democracy. He and the deputy paramount ruler are chosen for five-year terms by and from the nine hereditary rulers of the Malay states, who, along with the heads of state of Malacca, Penang, Sabah, and Sarawak, constitute the Conference of Rulers (*Majlis Raja Raja*). Executive power is vested in a prime minister and cabinet responsible to a bicameral legislature consisting of a partially appointed Senate with few real powers and an elected House of Representatives. Judicial power is vested in a Supreme Court, with subordinate High Courts in West and East Malaysia. The pattern of local government varies to some extent from state to state.

The federal government has authority over such matters as external affairs, defense, internal security, justice (except Islamic and native law), federal citizenship, finance, commerce, industry, communications, and transportation. The states of East Malaysia, however, enjoy guarantees of autonomy with regard to immigration, civil service, and customs matters.

Under a constitutional amendment adopted in 1974, the federal capital, Kuala Lumpur, became a Federal Territory, Shah Alam replacing it as the state capital of Selangor.

State and Capital	Area (sq. mi.)	Population (1980C)
Johore (Johore Bahru)	7,330	1,601,504
Kedah (Alor Star)	3,639	1,102,200
Kelantan (Kota Bahru)	5,765	877,575
Malacca (Malacca)	637	453,153
Negri Sembilan (Seremban)	2,565	563,955
Pahang (Kuantan)	13,886	770,640
Penang (George Town)	399	911,586
Perak (Ipoh)	8,110	1,762,288
Perlis (Kangar)	307	147,726
Sabah (Kota Kinabalu)	28,460	1,002,608
Sarawak (Kuching)	48,050	1,294,753
Selangor (Shah Alam)	3,166	1,467,445
Trengganu (Kuala Trengganu)	5,002	542,280
Federal Territory		
Kuala Lumpur	94	937,875

Foreign relations. From the early 1960s, Malaysia has been a staunch advocate of regional cooperation among the non-Communist states of Southeast Asia and has been an active member of the Association of Southeast Asian Nations (ASEAN) since its inception in 1967. Although threatened by leftist insurgency in the first two decades of independence, it committed itself to a nonaligned posture by expanding relations with the Soviet Union and Eastern European countries, establishing ties with North Korea and Vietnam, and attempting to normalize relations with the People's Republic of China, which it recognized in May 1974. At the same time it maintained linkage with Western powers, Britain, Australia, and New Zealand, all pledged to defend the nation's sovereignty, assisting Malaysia against Indonesia's "confrontation" policy of 1963–1966. Relations with Singapore, which were cool following the latter's withdrawal from the Federation in August 1965, improved in subsequent years.

Despite its previous hostility, Indonesia, the world's most populous Muslim nation, supported Malaysian efforts to avoid hostilities over the Muslim rebellion that commenced during the late 1960s in the southern Philippines. In 1979, Malaysia's decision to force Indochinese refugees back to sea was condemned by Indonesia as causing the inundation of its own shores by "boat people"; however, relations improved thereafter, culminating in a joint security agreement in late 1984 that strengthened a previous accord concluded in 1972.

In May 1980, Malaysia proclaimed an exclusive economic zone (EEZ) extending for up to 200 miles from the country's territorial sea boundaries as defined in newly drawn maps. Protests were immediately registered by China, Indonesia, the Philippines, Singapore, Thailand, and Vietnam, the last having recently dispatched troops to occupy jointly claimed Amboyna Island, northeast of Sabah, in an action Kuala Lumpur gave no indication of challenging by military means. In February 1982, on the other hand, Malaysia became the first to recognize Indonesia's "archipelagic" method of defining territorial seas by means of lines drawn between the outermost extensions of outlying islands. In return, Indonesia agreed to respect Malaysian maritime rights between its Peninsular and Borneo territories.

In late 1981, the Mahathir administration made a number of controversial share purchases in the London stock exchange designed to facilitate Malaysian control over plantation enterprises theretofore subject to foreign ownership. Relations with Britain were further weakened by the announcement in January 1982 of a "Look East" posture, whereby Malaysia would increasingly strive to base its economic development policies on Japanese and South Korean, rather than Western models. However, by 1985 the latter policy had largely been abandoned, with regulations governing foreign equity participation being substantially relaxed in regard to export-oriented enterprises.

In addition to participating in most of the major global and regional intergovernmental bodies, Malaysia is also a member of the Five-Power Defense Arrangement (with Britain, Australia, New Zealand, and Singapore), which obligates its members to consult in the event of an external threat and provides for the stationing of Commonwealth forces in the area. In July 1986 Malaysia was among those boycotting the Commonwealth Games at Edinburgh as a means of protesting Britain's refusal to impose economic sanctions against South Africa and subsequently considered withdrawing from the parent grouping. In late 1987, however, it accepted the conclusion of a quasi-government report that the benefits of remaining a member outweighed the costs and announced that it would host the next Commonwealth Heads of Government Meeting in 1989.

Current issues. The 1986 federal election, called a year early and with only eight days for campaigning, had been viewed as politically risky for Prime Minister Mahathir in view of a troubled economy, a series of financial scandals involving government officials, intra- and inter-party feuds within the ruling coalition, political disarray in Sabah, and a perceived threat of "Iran-style fundamentalism" by the opposition *Parti Islam* (Pas). The outcome of the balloting on August 3 was a UMNO triumph, tempered by the poor showing of both of its Chinese allies and a near-tripling of seats by the opposition Democratic Action Party (DAP), a largely Chinese grouping. The *Parti Islam,* which had concluded an ultimately abortive electoral pact with three smaller multiracial parties, obtained only one house seat. Subsequently, despite the large number of electoral formations, evidence of a drift toward a one-party state emerged: in late November the United Sabah National Organization (USNO), which had been expelled from the Front in April 1984 but was readmitted two months prior to the election, announced that it would merge with the UMNO, which had theretofore functioned exclusively as a peninsular-based grouping (see Political parties, below).

The remarkable series of events that commenced with the near-deposition of Prime Minister Mahathir as UMNO president in April 1987 and concluded with the suspension of the Supreme Court president in June 1988 was characterized by Diane Mauzy in *Asian Survey* as reflecting substantial abandonment of the traditional "Malay way" (essentially, a consensual approach to problem resolution) in favor of the confrontational politics implicit in the "assertive style" of the incumbent chief executive. Even critics were forced to concede that Mahathir had emerged as a consummate political tactician, although his triumph, by mid-year, was not yet complete. In late May, despite the legislation on transfer of UMNO assets, delegates to the annual meeting of the investment cooperative, *Koperasi Usaha Bersatu Malaysia* (KUB), refused to dismiss supporters of Tengku Razaleigh's UMNO-Malaysia faction from the organization's board of directors and reelected Datuk HARUN Idris, a prominent dissident, to a new two-year term as chairman. Subsequently, however, charges of corruption within the KUB were filed, suggesting that Harun's tenure might be short-lived.

POLITICAL PARTIES

The major political force in Malaysia is the **National Front** (*Barisan Nasional*), a coalition of parties representing the country's major ethnic groups. The nucleus of the original coalition, organized in 1952 as the Alliance Party, was Tunku Abdul Rahman's United Malays National Organization (UMNO). With the establishment of Malaysia, the Alliance was augmented by similar coalitions in Sarawak and Sabah, the number of participating organizations totaling 10 at the 1978 election, 11 in 1982, and 13 in 1986. A number of opposition parties exist, but only two, the Democratic Action Party (DAP) and the Pan-Malaysian Islamic Party (PMIP or Pas), are currently represented in the federal Parliament.

National Front Parties:

United Malays National Organization (New) — UMNO-*Baru* (*Pertubuhan Kebangsaan Melayu Bersatu* [*Baru*]). The leading component of the ruling National Front, the UMNO has long supported the interests of the numerically predominant Malays while acknowledging the right of all Malaysians, irrespective of racial origins, to participate in the political, social, and economic life of the nation. Party officials have thus far been selected by indirect election every three years, Prime Minister Mahathir retaining the presidency in April 1987 by a paper-thin margin after an unprecedented internal contest. The intraparty struggle culminated in deregistration of the original party in February 1988, in the wake of which the pro-Mahathir faction organized the "new" UMNO (UMNO-*Baru*), the dissidents (led by the former trade and industry minister, Tengku Tan Sri Razaleigh Hamzak, and supported by former prime ministers Abdul Rahman and Hussein bin Onn) being denied an opportunity to regroup as UMNO-Malaysia (see Political background, above). UMNO-*Baru* is to hold its first annual meeting in October 1988, although its founding leadership has indicated that it will not be presenting itself for reconfirmation at that time.

Leaders: Datuk Seri Dr. MAHATHIR bin Mohamad (Prime Minister and President of the Party), Abdul GHAFFAR bin Baba (Deputy Prime Minister, Deputy President of the Party, and Secretary General of the National Front), Dato Seri Amar Wan MOKHTAR bin Ahmad, Datuk ABDULLAH bin Ahmad Badawi, ANWAR bin Ibrahim, Datuk MOHAMAD Rahmat (Secretary General).

Malaysian Chinese Association (MCA). The MCA supports the interests of the Chinese community but is committed to the maintenance of interracial goodwill and harmony. More conservative than the Chinese opposition Democratic Action Party, it withdrew from the government after the 1969 election but did not go into parliamentary opposition, and rejoined the alliance prior to the 1982 election. In 1985 the party was torn

by legal action over accusations by former deputy president Tan Koon Swan that (then) President Neo Yee Pan had padded membership lists to ensure his continued leadership. By August, it had split into three factions, the third resulting from the appointment, with the prime minister's backing, of Mak Hon Kam as acting president during an emergency general meeting of the Central Committee. In November, the party voted to install Datuk Tan as its leader, refusing to accept a tender of resignation in January 1986 upon his indictment by Singapore authorities for illegal securities transactions. A second such tender was accepted on August 27, after Tan had been sentenced to two years imprisonment, although permitted to retain his parliamentary seat since neither the offense or sentence had taken place in Malaysia.

Leaders: Datuk Dr. LING Liong Sik (President), Datuk TAN Koon Swan (former President), Datuk CHAN Kit Chee (Vice President), Datuk Dr. NEO Yee Pan and Datuk MAK Hon Kam (leaders of dissident factions), NG Cheng Kiat (Secretary General).

Malaysian Indian Congress (MIC). The leading representative of the Indian community in Malaysia, the MIC was founded in 1946 and joined the alliance in 1955. In 1984–1985, party leader Samy Vellu came under pressure from constituents claiming that the MIC was not adequately representing Indian interests, but in late 1986 was unopposed for reelection as its president.

Leaders: Datuk SAMY Vellu (President), Tan Sri S. SUBRAMANIAM, D.P. VIJENDRAN (Secretary General).

Malaysian People's Movement (*Gerakan Rakyat Malaysia*). *Gerakan* is a Penang-based social-democratic party which has attracted many intellectual supporters. It was organized in 1968 by Dr. Tan Chee Khoon, who left the party after the 1969 election to form the Social Justice Party (below). Following the 1985 MCA split, *Gerakan* leaders pressed the National Front for additional places on its list at the next election, declaring itself the more viable coalition representative of the Chinese Community. However, its parliamentary strength remained unchanged (at five) after the 1986 balloting. At the conclusion of the party's annual conference in June 1987, Datuk Lim Keng Yaik was given a mandate to proceed with a proposed confederation with the PBS (below).

Leaders: Datuk Dr. LIM Keng Yaik (President), Datuk Paul LEONG Khee Seong (Deputy President), KERK Choo Ting (Secretary General).

United Sabah Party (*Parti Bersatu Sabah* — PBS). A predominantly Kadazan party with a Roman Catholic leader, the PBS was founded by defectors from Berjaya (Sabah People's Union, below) in March 1985. Appealing to urban, middle-class voters disaffected with the Harris Salleh government, it won a majority of state assembly seats in April. It was admitted to the National Front prior to the federal balloting in 1986. In May 1988 it was announced that the "loose alliance" with *Gerakan* (above) would be called the **Pan-Malaysian Congress of Unity** (*Pehimpunan Bersatu SeMalaysia* — PBS), thus retaining the initials of the Sabah formation in an apparent effort to avoid the implication that it was to be "colonized" by the peninsular group.

Leaders: Datuk Joseph Pairin KITINGAN (Chief Minister of Sabah and President of the Party), Mark HODING (Deputy Chief Minister and Deputy President of the Party), Joseph KURUP (Secretary General).

United Sabah National Organization (USNO). The USNO was long led by Tun Mustapha bin Datuk Harun, who was ousted as chief minister of Sabah in October 1975. At the state assembly election of April 1981 it was decisively outpolled by Berjaya, obtaining only 3 of 48 elective seats. It was expelled from the United Front in February 1984 for its criticism of the government during the constitutional crisis and for opposing efforts to make the island of Labuan (part of Sabah) a federal territory. The party rebounded at the April 1985 balloting, winning 16 state assembly seats and participating in an unsuccessful court battle to resume control of the government in coalition with Berjaya.

On November 29, 1986, the party voted to disband in favor of merger with the theretofore peninsular-based UMNO, Tun Mustapha formally reiterating an announcement made seven months earlier that he would retire from active politics. However, the action gave rise to legal questions as to the status of USNO deputies in the state assembly and late in the year the UMNO indicated that, for the present, it would confine itself to absorption of grassroots components of the regional group.

Leaders: SAKARAN bin Dandai (Acting President), Tun Datu Haji MUSTAPHA bin Datuk Harun (former Chief Minister of Sabah).

Malaysian Islamic Council Front (*Barisan Jama'ah Islamiah SeMalaysia* — Berjasa). Berjasa is a Kelantan-based party organized in opposition to Pas (below) following the latter's withdrawal from the government in 1977.

Leaders: Dato Haji Wan HASHIM bin Haji Wan Achmed (President), Mahmud ZUDHI bin Haji Abdul Majid (Secretary General).

People's Progressive Party (PPP). The left-wing PPP was organized in 1955. Its strength is concentrated in Ipoh, where there is a heavy concentration of Chinese. It presented no federal election candidates in 1982 or 1986.

Leader: S.I. RAJAH (President).

United Traditional Bumiputra Party (*Parti Pesaka Bumiputra Bersatu* —PPBB). Also known as the Sarawak Alliance, the PPBB embraces **Bumiputra**, a mixed ethnic party; **Pesaka**, a Dayak and Malay party; and the **Sarawak Chinese Association.** The PPBB won a plurality of 19 seats at the Sarawak State Council election of December 1983, subsequently forming a coalition government with the PBDS and the SUPP (below). A dissident group, the **United Sarawak Natives Association** (USNA), was formed in 1986 by Tan Sri Haji ABDUL RAHMAN Yakub, a former governor of Sarawak, as the result of a dispute with his nephew, Chief Minister Taib Mahmud. Unable to secure registration for the August balloting, its candidates were forced to run as independents.

Leaders: Datuk Patinggi Amar Haji Abdul TAIB Mahmud (Chief Minister of Sarawak and President of the Party), Datuk Alfred JABU Ak Numpang (Deputy President).

Sarawak National Party (Snap). A leading Sarawak party, Snap ran in the 1974 federal election as an opposition party, capturing nine seats in the lower house. Supported largely by the Iban population of Sarawak, it joined the National Front at both the state and federal levels in March 1976 and won 16 seats in the Sarawak State Council election of September 1979, half of which were lost in December 1983.

Leaders: Datuk James WONG Kim Min (President), Encik Joseph BALAN Seling (Secretary General).

Sarawak Dayak Party (*Parti Bansa Dayak Sarawak*—PBDS). The PBDS was organized in July 1983 by a number of former Snap federal MPs, who wished to affiliate with a purely ethnic Dayak party. The new formation was accepted as a National Front partner in January 1984 and formed a coalition state government with the PPBB, SNAP, and the SUPP (below) the following March. It was dismissed from the state (but not the federal) National Front grouping prior to the April 1987 balloting for a new Sarawak assembly at which (without dislodging the coalition) it obtained a plurality of 15 seats.

Leader: Datuk Leo MOGGIE anak Inok (Acting President).

Sarawak United People's Party (SUPP). The SUPP was organized in 1959 as a left-wing Sarawak party. It won 11 seats in the Sarawak State Council elections of 1979 and 1983.

Leaders: Datuk Amar Stephen YONG Kuet Tze (President), Datuk WONG Soon Kai (Secretary General).

Muslim Front of Malaysia (*Hizbul Muslimin Malaysia*—Hamim). The Muslim Front was formed in March 1983 by Haji Mohamed Asri bin Haji Muda, the former president of Pas, who had opposed efforts to reduce the powers of the leadership and make it subordinate to a new Council of Theologians (*Majlis Ulamak*).

Leader: Datuk Haji Mohamed ASRI bin Haji Muda (President).

Opposition Parties:

Democratic Action Party (DAP). A predominantly Chinese, democratic socialist party and a 1965 offshoot of the ruling People's Action Party (PAP) of Singapore, the DAP was runner-up to the Alliance in the West Malaysian election of 1969. It won only 9 federal parliamentary seats at the 1974 election but increased its representation to 16 in 1978, although 2 of its successful candidates were detained on charges of subversion. Again limited to 9 seats in 1982, it nonetheless remained the principal opposition party at the national level. Like *Gerakan*, it mobilized in 1985 to capitalize on the disarray of the MCA and increased its lower house representation to 24 in 1986. In October 1987 a number of DAP politicians, including parliamentary opposition leader Kim Kit Sian, were arrested and held without trial for "provoking racial tensions".

Leaders: Dr. CHEN Man Hin (Chairman), LIM Kit Siang (Leader of the Opposition and Secretary General of the Party), LEE Lam Thye (Deputy Leader of the Opposition and Deputy Secretary General of the Party), Ahmad NOR (Deputy Secretary General).

Socialist Democratic Party (*Parti Sosialis Demokratik*—PSD). The PSD was formed in 1978 by a group of nonracial DAP dissidents.

Leaders: Ismail HASHIM (Chairman), FAN Yew Teng (Secretary General).

Pan-Malaysian Islamic Party (*Parti Islam SeMalaysia*—Pas or PMIP). Formerly in opposition, the *Parti Islam* joined the governing coalition on January 1, 1973. It withdrew on November 8, 1977, in protest against a government bill to impose federal rule in its principal stronghold, the state of Kelantan. An essentially fundamentalist right-wing party with a strong rural base, Pas obtained 5 seats in the 1978 federal election and an equal number in 1982. Subsequently, it launched a campaign to recruit converts from the Chinese community, while appealing to nonfundamentalist voters critical of the Mahathir government. In November 1985, one of its leaders, Ibrahim Libya, was among 18 individuals killed in a clash with police at Kampong Siong, near the Thai border. It was decisively defeated in 1986, retaining only one of the seats won four years earlier.

Leaders: Haji YUSOF Abdullah Ar Rawa (President), Dr. Fadzil NOR (Deputy President), Haji HASSAN Haji Shukri (Secretary General).

Sabah People's Union (*Bersatu Rakyat Jelata Sabah*—Berjaya). Founded in 1975, Berjaya captured 34 of 54 seats in the Sabah Assembly in 1976, precluding the return to office of former chief minister Mustapha; in 1981 it swept all but 4 of the state assembly seats. However, in April 1985 it lost all but 6 of its 50 seats, mainly to the PBS and USNO; despite a post-election attempt to retain the government with the USNO's Mustapha as chief minister, the party ultimately lost out to the PBS' Joseph Pairin Kitingan, although legally contesting the latter's victory on the grounds that Mustapha had been legally sworn in. The party withdrew from the National Front on the eve of the 1986 election.

Leaders: Datuk Haji Mohammed NOOR Mansor (President), Datuk HARRIS bin Mohammed Salleh (former Chief Minister of Sabah).

Malaysian Indian Muslim Congress (*Kongres Indian Muslim Malaysia*—Kimma). Kimma was founded in 1977 as a means of uniting Malaysia's Indian Muslims.

Leaders: Dato A.S. DAWOOD (President), Lebbai GANI bin Naina Pillai Naricar (Secretary General).

Social Justice Party (*Parti Keadilan Masyarakat*—Pekemas). A left-wing party formed in 1971 by a splinter group from *Gerakan*, Pekemas lost at the 1978 election the one House seat it had captured in 1974; it has since been unrepresented at the federal level.

Leader: Shaharyddin DAHALAN (Chairman).

Malaysian People's Socialist Party (*Parti Sosialis Rakyat Malaysia*—PSRM). The PSRM is a left-wing party that holds no legislative seats. Its former leader, Encik Kassim Ahmad, was arrested on November 3, 1976, on suspicion of having engaged in Communist activities and was not released until July 30, 1981.

Leader: Abdul RAZAK Ahmad (Secretary General).

Malaysian Nationalist Party (*Parti Nationalis Malaysia*—PNM or NasMa). A multiracial grouping, the PNM was launched in July 1985 under the banner "Malaysians for Malaysia, for justice, integrity, and progress". Envisioned by its founders as a forum for nonsectarian critics of the Mahathir regime and as a challenge to the UMNO, the party's main accomplishment by late 1985 was weakening the Pas expansion effort.

Leaders: Zainab YANG, Zainad MOHAMMED (Secretary General).

Minor opposition parties also include the largely Chinese **Sarawak People's Organization** (Sapo); the **United Sabah People's Organization**—USPO (*Pertubuhan Rakayat Sabah Bersatu*); the **National Consciousness Party** (*Kesatuan Insaf Tanah Ayer*—KITA); the **Workers' Party of Malaysia** (*Parti Pekerja-Pekerja Malaysia*—PPM); the Sabah-based **Socialist Conference Union Party** (*Parti Perhimpunan Socialis Bersatu*—Pusaka); the **Sarawak State People's Party** (*Parti Negara Rakyat Sarawak*—PNRS); the **Sabah Chinese Consolidated Party** (SCCP); the **Sabah Democratic People's Party** (Sedar); the **Sarawak Congress Party** (*Parti Kongres Sarawak*—PKS); the **United Sarawak National Association** (*Pertubuhan Bumiputra Bersatu Sarawak*—PBBS); the **Democratic Malaysia Indian Party** (DMIP); and the **United Malaysia Timor Organization** (Umat), located in Sarawak.

Illegal Opposition:

Communist Party of Malaya (CPM). A predominantly Chinese group oriented toward Beijing, the CPM was officially banned in July 1948.

It has long been committed to the merger of Peninsular Malaysia and North Kalimantan into a single state, but was weakened by the emergence of rival groups in the 1970s (see MCP, below) and now claims a membership of approximately 4,000. From bases in southern Thailand, agents have made persistent efforts to penetrate left-wing organizations in West Malaysia, where sporadic paramilitary operations have also been conducted, primarily by the CPM's military wing, the Malayan People's Army (*Tentara Rakyat Malaya*), known prior to 1982 as the Malayan National Liberation Army (MNLA). The CPM maintained close ties with the Indonesian Communist Party during the Malaysian-Indonesian "confrontation", and the **North Kalimantan Communist Party** (NKCP) of Sarawak, led by WEN Ming-chuan, has established itself in Indonesia close to the Malaysian border.

Leader: CHIN Peng (Secretary General).

Malaysian Communist Party (MCP). The MCP was formed in December 1983 by merger of the Communist Party of Malaya — Marxist-Leninist (CPM/M-L) and the Communist Party of Malaya — Revolutionary Faction (CPM/RF), both of which had split earlier from the CPM. The MCP is more urban-oriented than the largely peasant-based CPM and, unlike its rival, accepts the existence of Malaysia and Singapore as distinct entities, arguing that "under no circumstances should the [revolutionary] struggle rely upon a single nationality". It controls a small group of insurgents, organized as the Malaysian People's Liberation Army (MPLA).

Leaders: AH Leng (CPL/M-L leader and MCP Secretary General), HUANG Chen (CPL/RF).

LEGISLATURE

The federal **Parliament** is a bicameral body consisting of a Senate and a House of Representatives. Its activities were suspended during the state of emergency declared in mid-1969 but were resumed on February 20, 1971.

Senate (*Dewan Negara*). The upper chamber consists of 58 members: 32 appointed by the paramount ruler and 26 elected by the state legislatures (2 from each state) for six-year terms. The Senate is never dissolved, new elections being held by the appropriate state Legislative Assembly as often as there are vacancies among the elected members.

President: Tan Sri Benedict STEPHENS.

House of Representatives (*Dewan Rakyat*). Until 1974 the membership of the lower chamber was 144. With the designation on February 1, 1974, of the capital city of Kuala Lumpur as a Federal Territory, the membership was increased to 154, the Federal Territory returning 5 members. Currently, there are 177 members: 132 from Peninsular Malaysia (including 7 from the Federal Territory), 25 from Sarawak, and 20 from Sabah. The term of the House is five years, subject to dissolution. Elections are by universal adult suffrage, but the voting is weighted in favor of the predominantly Malay rural areas, with some urban (mainly Chinese) constituencies having three to four times as many voters as their rural counterparts.

At the most recent balloting on August 3, 1986, for Peninsular Malaysia and on August 2–3 for the east Malaysian states, the National Front won 148 seats (United Malays National Organization, 83; Malaysian Chinese Association, 17; Malaysian Indian Congress, 6; Malaysian People's Movement, 5; Sarawak affiliates, 22; Sabah affiliates, 15). The remaining 29 seats were distributed as follows: Democratic Action Party, 24; Pan-Malaysian Islamic Party, 1; independents, 4.

Speaker: Tan Sri Mohamed ZAHIR Ismail.

CABINET

Prime Minister	Datuk Seri Dr. Mahathir bin Mohamad
Deputy Prime Minister	Encik Abdul Ghaffar bin Baba
Ministers	
Agriculture	Datuk Sanusi bin Junid
Defense	Tengku Ahmad Rithauddeen al Haj bin Tengku Ismail
Education	Anwar Ibrahim
Energy, Telecommunications and Posts	Datuk Leo Moggie anak Inok
Finance	Daim Zainuddin
Foreign Affairs	Datuk Haji Abu Hassan Omar
Health	Datuk Chan Siang Sun
Home Affairs	Datuk Seri Dr. Mahathir bin Mohamad
Housing and Local Government	Ng Cheng Kiat
Information	Datuk Mohamad Rahmat
Justice	Datuk Seri Dr. Mahathir bin Mohamad
Labor and Manpower	Lee Kim Sai
Land and Regional Development	Datuk Dr. Sulaiman bin Haji Daud
National and Rural Development	Abdul Ghafar bin Baba
Primary Industries	Datuk Dr. Lim Keng Yaik
Prime Minister's Office	Datuk Dr. Mohamad Yusof Nor
Public Enterprises	Datin Napsiah Omar
Science, Technology and Environment	Datuk Amar Stephen Yong Kuet Tze
Tourism and Culture	Datuk Haji Sabaruddin Chik
Trade and Industry	Datin Paduka Rafidah Aziz
Transport	Datuk Ling Liong Sik
Welfare Services	Datuk Mustapha Mohammad
Works and Utilities	Datuk Samy Vellu
Youth and Sports	Datuk Najib Abdul Razak
Without Portfolio	Khalil bin Yaacob
Governor, Central Bank	Hussein Jaffar

NEWS MEDIA

Emergency censorship measures were imposed by the National Operations Council in May 1969. Though the emergency has long since ceased to exist, certain "sensitive" topics may not be discussed in public or in Parliament. In addition, journalists may be arrested under the Internal Security Act if suspected of Communist sympathies, or under the Official Secrets Act if deemed guilty of receiving or disseminating government information. Thus in late 1985, the local bureau chief of the *Far Eastern Economic Review* and a reporter for the *New Straits Times* were arrested and fined for possessing classified information, while the Hong Kong-based *Asian Wall Street Journal* was banned for three months in September 1986. Subsequently, in October 1987, three newspapers including *The Star* and *Sin Chew Jit Poh,* were closed down for five months for publishing material deemed "prejudicial to public order and national security". Press restrictions were tightened further in December 1987 by new legislation giving the government "absolute discretion" to restrict the issuance of any publication deemed "likely to alarm public opinion".

Press. The following, unless otherwise noted, are dailies published at Kuala Lumpur: *Utusan Malaysia/Utusan Melayu* (250,400 daily; 400,000 Sunday, published as *Mingguan Malaysia/Utusan Zaman*), in Malay; *Berita Harian* (211,000 daily; 271,000 Sunday, published as *Berita Minggu*), in Malay; *New Straits Times* (193,000 daily; 240,000 Sunday, published as *New Sunday Times*), in English; *The Star* (Selangor, 150,000 daily, 160,000 Sunday), in English; *Nanyang Siang Pao* (145,000 daily, 165,000 Sunday), in Chinese; *Sin Chew Jit Poh* (Selangor, 100,000 daily, 118,000 Sunday), in Chinese; *Shin Min Daily News* (80,000), in Chinese; *Malay Mail* (65,400 daily; 110,000 Sunday, published as *Sunday Mail*); *Kin Kwok Daily News* (Selangor, 56,000), in Chinese; *Chung Kuo Pao* (50,000), in Chinese; *Sing Pin Jih Pao* (Penang, 38,000), in Chinese; *Tamil Nesan* (30,000 daily, 60,000 Sunday), in Tamil.

News agencies. The domestic facility is the Malaysian National News Agency (Bernama); a number of foreign agencies maintain offices at Kuala Lumpur.

Radio and television. The government's Department of Broadcasting controls broadcasting through Radio Television Malaysia. Sabah and Sarawak maintain separate facilities, including one of the nation's three television networks. Additional radio programming is available through the BBC Far Eastern Relay, which recently moved from Johore to Singapore. In August 1981, Peking announced that Chinese-based broadcasts of the CPM's "Voice of the Malayan Revolution" had been discontinued; concurrently, however, a new clandestine radio station, the "Voice of Malayan Democracy", commenced operations. There were more than 1.0 million radio and 1.6 million television receivers in 1987, over 90 percent of each being concentrated in Peninsular Malaysia.

INTERGOVERNMENTAL REPRESENTATION

Ambassador to the US: Albert S. TALALLA.

US Ambassador to Malaysia: John Cameron MONJO.

Permanent Representative to the UN: Dato YUSOF M. Hitam.

IGO Memberships (Non-UN): ADB, ANRPC, APCC, ASEAN, CCC, CP, CWTH, IC, IDB, Inmarsat, INRO, Intelsat, Interpol, ITC, NAM.

MALDIVES

Republic of Maldives
Dhivehi Jumhuriyah

Political Status: Former British protectorate; independent since July 25, 1965; sultanate replaced by republican regime November 11, 1968.

Area: 115 sq. mi. (298 sq. km.).

Population: 181,453 (1985C), 195,000 (1988E).

Major Urban Center (1985E): MALÉ (46,300).

Official Language: Dhivehi.

Monetary Unit: Maldivian Rufiyaa (market rate March 1, 1988, 8.87 rufiyaa = $1US).

President: Maumoon Abdul GAYOOM; nominated by the House of Representatives on July 28, 1978, to succeed Ibrahim NASIR, who had declined to seek reelection; assumed office for a five-year term on November 11 after being confirmed by popular referendum; reelected on September 30, 1983.

THE COUNTRY

The Republic of Maldives is a 500-mile-long chain of small, low-lying coral islands extending southward in the Indian Ocean from a point about 300 miles southwest of India and 400 miles west of Sri Lanka. Grouped into 19 atoll clusters, the more than 1,200 islands have vegetation ranging from scrub to dense tropical forest. Only about 200 of the islands are inhabited by a population that displays mixed Sinhalese, Dravidian, and Arab traits. The official language, Dhivehi, is related to Sinhala. Islam is the state religion, most of the population belonging to the Sunni sect. The degree of female emancipation is highly unusual for a Muslim country; a large number of women are employed by the government and women have the same rights of divorce as men, yielding a divorce rate in 1985 almost equal to that of marriage.

The economy has traditionally been dependent on fishing; at present, processed and raw fish, sold primarily to Japan and Sri Lanka, accounts for 95 percent of exports, while shipping and tourism are of growing importance. All three activities are dominated by the government, which also conducts most import, wholesale, and retail trade.

GOVERNMENT AND POLITICS

Political background. Subjected to a brief period of Portuguese domination in the sixteenth century, the Maldives came under British influence in 1796 and were declared a British protectorate in 1887. Internal self-government was instituted in 1960, and full independence was achieved on July 26, 1965, following negotiations with the United Kingdom covering economic assistance and the retention of a British air facility on southern Gan Island. The centuries-old Maldivian sultanate was temporarily replaced by a republican form of government from 1953 to 1954 but was then reinstated until 1968, when the Maldives again became a republic, in accordance with the outcome of a national referendum.

Although Prime Minister Ahmad ZAKI (originally appointed in 1972) was redesignated on February 22, 1975, and was reported to have the support of a newly elected Citizen's Assembly, he was removed from office and placed under arrest on March 6. Executive responsibilities were assumed by President Ibrahim NASIR, and Zaki was banished. The change of government was confirmed by a constitutional revision which also empowered the president to appoint an unlimited number of vice presidents. Four such positions were subsequently established, only to be discontinued in a further government reorganization in February 1977.

After 21 years of rule, President Nasir announced in mid-1978 that he would not seek reelection, despite a parliamentary request that he continue in office. The Assembly thereupon nominated as his successor Transport Minister Maumoon Abdul GAYOOM, who had once been banished and once imprisoned for criticizing Nasir's administration but had subsequently served as his country's first permanent representative to the United Nations. Prior to Gayoom's installation on November 11, outgoing President Nasir pardoned a number of those under house arrest or banished, including former prime minister Zaki. On August 22, 1983, the Assembly renominated Gayoom as the sole presidential candidate in a referendum held September 30.

Constitution and government. Maldivian government in recent decades has combined the forms of constitutional rule with de facto control by members of a small hereditary elite. The 1968 republican constitution provides for a unicameral Citizens' Assembly (*Majlis*) that is controlled by an elected majority. The *Majlis* designates the president for a five-year term, but the action must be confirmed by popular referendum. The president appoints other leading officials, including those entrusted with overseeing the legal system, which is based on Islamic law. The country is divided into 19 administrative districts corresponding to the main atoll groups, plus the capital. Each atoll is governed by a presidentially appointed atoll chief (*verin*), who is advised by an elected committee. Each inhabited island is administered by a headman (*kateeb*), a number of assistant headmen (one for every 500 people), and a mosque functionary (*mudim*).

Foreign relations. An active participant in the Nonaligned Movement, the Republic of Maldives has long sought to have the Indian Ocean declared a "Zone of Peace", with foreign (particularly nuclear) military forces permanently banned from the area. Thus, despite the adverse impact on an already depressed economy, the government welcomed the withdrawal of the British Royal Air Force from Gan Island in March 1976 and rejected a subsequent Soviet bid to establish a base there.

Since assuming office, President Gayoom has actively sought to increase the Republic's international visibility, touring Kuwait, Libya, and the United States in autumn 1979 before attending the nonaligned summit at Havana, Cuba. In April 1980 a cultural and scientific agreement was concluded with the Soviet Union, while Gayoom subsequently visited Iraq, where technical and economic cooperation agreements were concluded and arrangements initiated for establishment of an Iraqi-Maldivian fishing venture. An economic and technical cooperation agreement was signed with India in February 1986, with Delhi agreeing to provide approximately $17 million in support of a number of development projects, including the construction of a hospital at Malé.

For economic reasons, the Maldives maintains diplomatic missions only at UN headquarters in the United States and at Colombo, Sri Lanka, where most ambassadors accredited to Malé (exceptions being those from India, Libya, Pakistan, and Sri Lanka) are resident.

The Republic became a "special member" of the Commonwealth in July 1982 and a full member in June 1985. It was a founding member of the South Asian Association for Regional Cooperation (SAARC) the following December.

Current issues. Economic difficulty experienced by the Maldives in the early 1980s was attributed to both global and regional factors: a collapse of world tuna prices and domestic turmoil on neighboring Sri Lanka, which severely affected the tourist industry. However, tourism rebounded rapidly after the completion of a new international airport on Hulule Island in 1981, with arrivals doubling by 1985; fishing output also doubled during 1982–1985 because of an increase in the number of mechanized trawlers. The result was economic overheating that was not substantially alleviated by the adoption of an import licensing scheme in early 1986 and the rufiyaa was allowed to float (yielding an effective devaluation of 30 percent) in March 1987.

POLITICAL PARTIES

There are no political parties in the Republic of Maldives.

LEGISLATURE

The Maldivian **Citizens' Assembly** (*Majlis*) is a unicameral body of 48 members: 8 appointed by the president and 40 popularly elected (2 from Malé and 2 from each of the 19 administrative districts) for five-year terms. It meets three times a year for a largely perfunctory exercise of its duties, one session in 1975 reportedly having lasted only 24 minutes. The last election was held on December 7, 1984, all candidates running as independents.

Speaker: Ibrahim SHIHAB.

CABINET

President	Maumoon Abdul Gayoom
Ministers	
Agriculture	(Vacant)
Atolls Administration	Abdulla Hameed
Defense and National Security	Maumoon Abdul Gayoom
Education	Mohamed Zahir Hussain
Fisheries	Abdul Sattar Moosa Didi
Foreign Affairs	Fathulla Jameel
Health	Abdullah Jameel
Home Affairs and Social Services	Umar Zahir
Planning and Development (Acting)	Abdul Rasheed Hussain
Trade and Industries	Ilyas Ibrahim
Transport and Shipping	Ahmed Mujuthaba
Governor, Central Bank	Maumoon Abdul Gayoom

NEWS MEDIA

Press. The following are published at Malé: *Haveeru* (1,500), daily in Dhiveli and English; *Aafathis,* daily in Dhiveli and English; *Maldives News Bulletin,* fortnightly in English.

News Agency. The Haveeru News Agency (Hana) operates at Malé.

Radio and television. The government-owned Voice of Maldives broadcasts in Dhivehi and English to approximately 13,200 receivers. TV Maldives, which initiated service in March 1978, currently broadcasts to some 3,800 receivers.

INTERGOVERNMENTAL REPRESENTATION

The Republic of Maldives does not maintain an embassy at Washington.

US Ambassador to the Maldives: James W. SPAIN (resident in Sri Lanka).

Permanent Representative to the UN: (Vacant).

IGO Memberships (Non-UN): ADB, CWTH, CP, IDB, Interpol, NAM, SAARC.

MALI

Republic of Mali
République du Mali

Political Status: Independent republic proclaimed September 22, 1960; military regime established November 19, 1968; civilian rule reestablished under constitution approved in 1974 and promulgated June 19, 1979.

Area: 478,764 sq. mi. (1,240,000 sq. km.).

Population: 6,524,650 (1976C), 8,947,000 (1988E).

Major Urban Centers (1983E): BAMAKO (522,000); Ségou (84,000); Mopti (70,000); Sikasso (61,000); Kayes (57,000).

Official Language: French. Bambara is spoken by the majority of the population.

Monetary Unit: CFA Franc (market rate March 1, 1988, 285.80 francs = $1US).

President: Gen. Moussa TRAORE; came to power as head of Military Committee of National Liberation, which deposed the government of Modibo KEITA on November 19, 1968; assumed functions of Head of State on December 6, 1968; replaced Capt. Yoro DIAKITE as President of the Government on September 19, 1969; elected President and Head of Government (Prime Minister) for a five-year term on June 19, 1979, with the presidential term subsequently extended to six years by constitutional amendment of September 1981; reelected to a second six-year term on June 9, 1985.

Prime Minister: Dr. Mamadou DEMBELE; designated by the President on June 6, 1986.

THE COUNTRY

Of predominantly desert and semidesert terrain, landlocked Mali stretches northward into the Sahara from the upper basin of the Niger and Senegal rivers. The country's lifeline is the Niger River, which flows northeastward past Bamako, Ségou, and Timbuktu, and then southeastward through Niger and Nigeria to the Gulf of Guinea. Mali's overwhelmingly Muslim population falls into several distinct ethnic groups, among which the Bambara and other southern peoples are mostly sedentary farmers, while the Peul, or Fulani, as well as the warlike Tuareg pursue a nomadic and pastoral existence on the fringes of the Sahara. Women constitute 17 percent of the rural work force and 12 percent of the urban labor force, with a larger proportion serving as unpaid family laborers. Although the present cabinet contains two women, overall female representation in the military-dominated government and ruling party is minimal.

The Malian economy has suffered since the late 1960s from drought conditions that have repeatedly pervaded the Saharan-Sahelian zone. By 1986 the lack of rainfall had caused large scale migration of the population from rural to urban areas and the desertification of many former farmlands. Tuareg herdsmen, having lost much of their livestock, were forced to make the psychologically difficult move to subsistence farming. Nearly 90 percent of the economically active population remains dependent on agriculture, with cotton, peanuts, and livestock being the leading sources of foreign exchange. Industrial activity is concentrated in agriprocessing, while extraction of such minerals as uranium, bauxite, ferronickel, and phosphates has been hindered by inadequate transport and power facilities. Progress toward economic reconstruction has been made with foreign assistance from both Eastern and Western sources, but Mali remains one of the world's dozen poorest countries, with a per capita GNP of less than $150 in 1986.

GOVERNMENT AND POLITICS

Political background. Mali, the former French colony of Soudan, takes its name from a medieval African kingdom whose capital was located near the present Bamako. As a part of French West Africa, Soudan took part in the general process of post-World War II decolonization and became a self-governing member state of the French Community in 1958. Full independence within the Community was achieved on June 20, 1960, in association with Senegal, with which Soudan had joined in January 1959 to form a union known as the Federation of Mali. Senegal, however, seceded from the Federation on August 20, 1960, and on September 22 Mali proclaimed itself an independent republic and withdrew from the French Community.

Mali's government, led by President Modibo KEITA of the Soudanese Union Party, gradually developed into a leftist, one-party dictatorship with a strongly collectivist policy at home and close ties to the Soviet bloc and the People's Republic of China. In late 1968, the Keita regime was ousted in a bloodless coup d'état led by (then) Lt. Moussa TRAORE and Capt. Yoro DIAKITE under the auspices of a Military Committee of National Liberation (*Comité Militaire de Libération Nationale* — CMLN).

Reversing collectivist economic policies of the Keita government, the military regime pledged that civil and political rights would soon be restored. However, further centralization of the military command took place in 1972 following the trial and imprisonment of Captain Diakité and two associates for allegedly plotting to overthrow the government. Subsequent coup attempts were reported in 1976 and in February 1978, the latter involving a reputed pro-Soviet faction of the CMLN that opposed a planned return to civilian rule under a constitution approved in 1974.

After a five-year period of transitional rule by the CMLN, a civilian government was formally restored on June 19, 1979, when General Traoré was elected, unopposed, to a five-year term as president and prime minister. Earlier, in March, the Mali People's Democratic Union (UDPM) had been formally constituted as the country's sole political party. In 1982, the presidential term was increased to six years, resulting in the reelection of Traoré coincident with pro forma legislative balloting on June 9, 1985. Three days earlier the president had carried out a cabinet reshuffle that included the designation of Dr. Mamadou DEMBELE as prime minister.

Constitution and government. The constitution adopted at independence was abrogated by the military in November 1968. A new constitution was approved by referendum on June 2, 1974, but did not enter into force until June 19, 1979, an article prohibiting political activity by officeholders under ex-president Keita having been rescinded three months earlier.

Under the 1979 constitution, as amended in 1981, Mali is a one-party state headed by a president who is popularly elected for a six-year term and who may nominate a prime minister while continuing to serve as chief executive. In April 1985 the basic law was further revised to permit an unlimited number of presidential terms. Members of the unicameral National Assembly are elected from a single UDPM list for three-year terms. The judicial system is headed by a Supreme Court and includes a court of appeal, magistrates' courts, and special courts to deal with labor issues. In 1976, a Special Court of State Security was created to try cases involving the misuse of public property; dissolved after seven of its members were implicated in the coup attempt of February 1978, it was reconstituted, with a partially civilian membership, later in the year.

Mali is administratively divided into seven regions, each headed by an appointed governor; the regions are subdivided into 42 districts (*cercles*), which are also administered by appointed officials. The larger municipalities have elected councils.

Foreign relations. Under Traoré's leadership, Mali has improved its relations with the West, renewing cooperation with France, the United States, Britain, and other Western nations. Reflecting his commitment to "dynamic nonalignment", the president, on the other hand, made state visits in 1986 to both China and the Soviet Union. Regionally, Mali participates in such organizations as the Economic Community of West African States (ECOWAS), the Niger and Senegal river commissions, and the Permanent Inter-State Committee on Drought Control in the Sahel (CILSS).

For two decades, Mali was locked in a dispute with Burkina Faso (formerly Upper Volta) over ownership of the 100-mile long, 12-mile wide Agacher strip between the two countries that led to a number of military encounters, including a four-day battle in December 1985. The dispute was finally settled by a World Court ruling in late 1986 that divided the disputed territory into roughly equal parts, with the border defined in accordance with traditional patterns of nomadic passage. Border clashes involving Mauritania have also erupted, the most recent, in June 1987, leaving one dead and several injured.

Relations with Libya cooled perceptibly as a result of the latter's involvement in the Chadian civil war, and, in early 1981, a number of Libyan embassy personnel at Bamako were expelled in response to an effort to convert the mission into a "people's bureau". Relations were further exacerbated by the expulsion of some 2,500 Malian workers from Libya in 1985, as part of a drive by the Qadhafi regime to reduce its dependence on foreign manpower.

Although merger discussions initiated in 1982 with Guinean President Touré failed to bear fruit, Mali's efforts at regional integration were furthered by its readmission in 1983 to the West African Monetary Union (UMDA) and by subsequent bilateral negotiations with Niger and Senegal.

Current issues. For Mali, once dubbed the potential "breadbasket of Africa" but now reeling from the effects of drought, locust infestation, and land mismanagement, a return to agricultural self-sufficiency continues to be the top priority. The Traoré administration, acknowledging the need for retreat from its former policy of state domi-

nance of the economy, has offered production incentives to farmers by loosening price and marketing controls. The liberalization, although far from producing the "free-market" strongly encouraged by the IMF, has also been extended to industry where some privatization, despite contributing to soaring unemployment, has occurred. Measures have also been adopted to fight corruption among government officials, although Soumano SACKO, appointed finance and trade minister in February 1987, resigned six months later because of "insufficient support" in addressing questionable financial practices by prominent individuals. Subsequently, on December 5, nine persons were sentenced to death and several dozen others given jail terms for embezzlement of public funds.

POLITICAL PARTIES

Government Party:

Mali People's Democratic Union (*Union Démocratique du Peuple Malien* — UDPM). The UDPM was formally launched on March 30, 1979, under a provision of the 1974 constitution that called for a single regime-supportive party upon completion of a five-year period of transition to civilian rule. Major party organs include a Congress; a National Council, whose membership was reduced from 300 to 100 at the second extraordinary congress in March 1987; and a Central Executive Bureau, which was reduced from 19 to 17 members at the third congress in March 1988.

Leaders: Gen. Moussa TRAORE (President of the Republic and Secretary General of the Party), Boubacar DIALLO (Deputy Secretary General), Djibril DIALLO (Political Secretary).

LEGISLATURE

A unicameral **National Assembly** (*Assemblée Nationale*) was elected on June 9, 1985, for a three-year term. All 82 deputies are members of the Mali People's Democratic Union.

President: Sidiki DIARRA.

CABINET

Prime Minister	Dr. Mamadou Dembélé
Ministers	
Agriculture	Moulaye Mohamed Haidara
Employment and Civil Service	Hama Ag Mahmoud
Finance and Trade	Mohamed Alhousseyni Touré
Foreign Affairs and International Cooperation	Modibo Keita
Industrial Development and Tourism	Drissa Keita
Information and Telecommunications	Gakou Fatou Niang
Justice and Keeper of the Seal	Col. Issa Ongoiba
National Defense	Gen. Sekou Ly
National Education	Oumar Ba
Natural Resources and Livestock	Omar Tall
Planning	Gen. Ousmane Mohamed Diallo
Public Health and Social Affairs	Aïssata Sidibe Cissé
Sports, Arts and Culture	Bakary Traoré
State Enterprises	Antioumane N'Diaye
Territorial Administration and Basic Development	Col. Abdourahamane Maiga
Transport and Public Works	Cheick Omar Doumbia
Manager, Central Bank	Younoussi Touré

NEWS MEDIA

The government controls all mass media.

Press. The following are published at Bamako: *L'Essor-La Voix du Peuple* (40,000), UDPM daily; *Kibaru* (5,000), rural monthly in Bambara; *Sunjata* (3,000), social, economic, and political weekly; *Bulletin Quotidièn de la Chambre de Commerce et d'Industrie du Mali* (daily).

News agencies. The National Information Agency of Mali (ANIM) and the Malian Publicity Agency (AMP) were merged in 1977 to form the official *Agence Malienne de Presse et Promotion* (Amap); *Agence France-Presse* and a number of other foreign agencies maintain bureaus at Bamako.

Radio and television. *Radiodiffusion Nationale du Mali* broadcasts regular news bulletins and programs in French, English, and the principal local languages. Color television transmission, inaugurated on a limited basis in 1983, serves about 900 sets.

INTERGOVERNMENTAL REPRESENTATION

Ambassador to the US: Nouhoum SAMASSEKOU.

US Ambassador to Mali: Robert Maxwell PRINGLE.

Permanent Representative to the UN: Noumou DIAKITE.

IGO Memberships (Non-UN): ACCT, ADF, AfDB, AGC, BADEA, BOAD, CCC, CEAO, CILSS, ECOWAS, EEC(L), *EIB,* IC, IDB, Intelsat, Interpol, NAM, OAU, UMOA.

MALTA

Republic of Malta
Repubblika ta' Malta

Political Status: Became independent within the Commonwealth on September 21, 1964; republic declared by constitutional amendment on December 13, 1974.

Area: 122 sq. mi. (316 sq. km.).

Population: 343,000 (1988E), excluding nonnationals.

Major Urban Centers (1984E): VALLETTA (14,000); Sliema (20,100); Birkirkawa (18,000).

Official Languages: Maltese, English.

Monetary Unit: Maltese Lira (market rate March 1, 1988, 1 lira = $3.07US).

Acting President: Paul XUEREB; former Speaker of the House of Representatives; succeeded Agatha BARBARA at the conclusion of her five-year term on February 15, 1987.

Prime Minister: Dr. Edward (Eddie) FENECH ADAMI (Nationalist Party); sworn in May 12, 1987, to succeed Dr. Karmenu (Carmelo) MIFSUD BONNICI (Malta Labor Party) following parliamentary election of May 9.

THE COUNTRY

Strategically located in the central Mediterranean some 60 miles south of Sicily, Malta comprises the two main is-
lands of Malta and Gozo in addition to the small island of Comino. The population is predominantly of Carthaginian and Phoenician descent and of mixed Arab-Italian cultural traditions. The indigenous language, Maltese, is of Semitic origin. Roman Catholicism is the state religion but other faiths are permitted.

Malta has few natural resources, and its terrain is not well adapted to agriculture. Historically, the country was dependent upon British military installations and expenditures, which ceased upon expiry of the 1972 Anglo-Maltese defense agreement on March 31, 1979. The most important industry is ship repair, but the government has sought to encourage diversification while at the same time seeking external budgetary support in lieu of the former British subsidy. These efforts were initially quite successful, the economy having yielded, in 1974–1979, double-digit rates of real per capita growth, comfortable current-account surpluses (public and private transfers, along with tourism, more than compensating for trade imbalances), and declining unemployment. Since then, most economic indicators have shown little real increase, although the completion of new port facilities on the southern part of the island should add significant capacity for the transshipment of bulk freight.

GOVERNMENT AND POLITICS

Political background. Malta has a long history of conquest and control by foreign powers. It first came under British control in 1800, possession being formalized by the Treaty of Paris in 1814. Ruled by a military governor throughout the nineteenth century, it experienced an unsuccessful period of internal autonomy immediately following World War I. Autonomy was abolished in 1933, and Malta reverted to its former status as a Crown Colony until a more successful attempt at internal self-government was initiated in 1947. Independence within the Commonwealth was formally requested by Prime Minister Giorgio BORG OLIVIER in 1962 and became effective September 21, 1964. The first change in government resulted from the election of 1971, which brought the Malta Labor Party (MLP) under Dominic MINTOFF into power. The MLP retained its legislative majority in the elections of September 17–18, 1976, and December 12, 1981. The results of the 1981 election were contested by the opposition Nationalist Party, which had won a slim majority of the popular vote and, after being rebuffed in an appeal for electoral reform, instituted a boycott of parliamentary proceedings.

In a counter-move to the boycott, Prime Minister Mintoff declared the 31 Nationalist-held seats vacant on April 26, 1982, with the NP subsequently refusing to make nominations for by-elections. On June 29, opposition leader Edward FENECH ADAMI called for a campaign of civil disobedience which yielded a number of work stoppages and popular demonstrations. In August, the government secured passage of a Foreign Interference bill in a largely unsuccessful effort to curtail NP transmissions from Sicily, and in January 1983 attempted to ban opposition contacts with foreign diplomats. Two months later, the political impasse appeared to have been resolved with an NP agreement to resume parliamentary activity, after securing a commitment from Mintoff to discuss changes in the electoral law. However, the talks were suspended at midyear in the wake of increasingly violent antigovernment activity and the adoption of a legislative measure that prohibited the charging of fees by private schools and indirectly authorized the confiscation of upwards of 75 percent of the assets of the Maltese Catholic Church. During 1984, the contest erupted into a major conflict between church and state, with the Catholic hierarchy ordering the closure of all schools under its jurisdiction (half of the island's total) in September. The schools reopened two months later, with Vatican officials agreeing in April 1985 to the introduction of free education over a three-year period in return for government assurances of noninterference in teaching and participation in a joint commission to discuss remaining church-state issues, including those regarding church property. Meanwhile, on December 22, 1984, Mintoff had stepped down as prime minister in favor of Dr. Karmenu MIFSUD BONNICI, who made no ministerial changes in a government sworn in two days later.

At a bitterly contested election on May 9, 1987, Labor, as in 1981, won 34 of 65 legislative seats, but, after 16 years in office, lost control of the government because of a constitutional amendment awarding additional seats, if needed, to the party obtaining a popular majority; as a result, Nationalist leader Fenech Adami was invested as prime minister on May 12. Earlier, at the conclusion of her five-year term on February 15, President Agatha BARBARA had yielded her office, on an acting basis, to the (then) speaker of the House of Representatives, Paul XUEREB.

Constitution and government. The 1964 constitution established Malta as an independent parliamentary monarchy within the Commonwealth, with executive power exercised by a prime minister and cabinet, both appointed by the governor general but chosen from and responsible to parliament. By constitutional amendment, the country became a republic on December 13, 1974, with an indirectly elected president of Maltese nationality replacing the British monarch as de jure head of state. The president serves a five-year term, as does the prime minister, subject to the retention of a legislative majority. The parliament consists of a unicameral House of Representatives elected on the basis of proportional representation every five years, assuming no prior dissolution. Under an amendment adopted in February 1987, the party winning a majority of the popular vote is awarded additional House seats, if needed to secure a legislative majority. The judicial system encompasses a Constitutional Court, a Court of Appeal, a Criminal Court of Appeal, and lower courts. There is little established local government; however, the island of Gozo is administered by an elected Civic Council in conjunction with a commissioner appointed by the central government.

Foreign relations. Subsequent to independence, Maltese foreign policy centered primarily around the country's relationship to Great Britain (and thus to NATO). A ten-year Mutual Defense and Assistance Agreement, signed in 1964, was abrogated in 1971 after installation of the Mintoff regime. Under a new seven-year agreement concluded in 1972 after months of extensive negotiation, the size of the

rental payments for use of military facilities by Britain was tripled. Early in 1973 Mintoff reopened the issue, asking additional payment to compensate for devaluation of the British pound, but settled for a token adjustment pending British withdrawal from the facilities in March 1979. Rebuffed in an effort to obtain a quadripartite guarantee of Maltese neutrality and a five-year budgetary subsidy from France, Italy, Algeria, and Libya, the Mintoff government turned to Libya, whose leader, Col. Mu'ammar al-Qadhafi, promised "unlimited" support during ceremonies marking the British departure. In the course of the following year, however, the relationship cooled because of overlapping claims to offshore oil rights, and in September 1980 an agreement was concluded with Italy whereby Rome agreed to guarantee Malta's future neutrality and provide a combination of loans and subsidies totaling $95 million over a five-year period. In 1981, Malta also signed neutrality agreements with Algeria, France, and the Soviet Union, agreeing in March to provide the latter with facilities for oil bunkering.

In December 1984, Prime Minister Mintoff announced that the defense and aid agreement with Italy would be permitted to lapse in favor of a new alignment with Libya, which would undertake to train Maltese forces to withstand "threats or acts of aggression" against the island's sovereignty or integrity. Six months later, the maritime issue was resolved, the International Court of Justice establishing a boundary 18 nautical miles north of a line equidistant between the two countries. Earlier, a $265 million pact had been concluded with the Soviet Union that included an order for the construction of a number of vessels and assistance in clearing the Grand Harbor at Valletta of warships sunk during World War II, although it was reported in July 1985 that Britain had assumed primary financial responsibility for the undertaking.

In late March 1986, Prime Minister Mifsud Bonnici met with Colonel Qadhafi at Tripoli, in what was described as an effort to ease the confrontation between Libya and the United States in the Gulf of Sidra. In August, the Maltese leader stated that his government had warned Libya of the approach of "unidentified planes" prior to the April attack on Tripoli and Benghazi, although there was no indication that Libyan authorities had acted on the information.

A member of the United Nations and a number of other international organizations, Malta is currently committed to a nonaligned posture in international affairs.

Current issues. The most recent parliamentary election, which would normally have been held in late 1986, was deferred until May 1987 because of a constitutional crisis that was resolved in February as the result of controversial concessions by both of the leading parties: Labor agreed to a revision of the basic law that would preclude governmental control by a party that failed to obtain a popular majority, while the pro-Western Nationalists agreed to a policy of neutrality in foreign affairs. Since the presidential term is coterminous with the five-year parliamentary mandate, President Barbara was obliged to step down in mid-February, no permanent successor having been named as of March 1988.

POLITICAL PARTIES

Government Party:

Nationalist Party (NP). Advocating the retention of Roman Catholic and European principles, the NP brought Malta to independence. It formerly supported alignment with NATO and membership in the European Community, but because of the constitutional pact with Labor in February 1987 is presently committed to a neutral foreign policy, including denial of air and naval facilities to both NATO and the Warsaw Pact. The party obtained 50.9 percent of the vote at the 1981 election without, however, winning control of the legislature. At the 1987 balloting it again obtained only a minority of elective seats, but under the February constitutional amendment was permitted to form a government because of its popular majority.

Leaders: Dr. Edward FENECH ADAMI (Prime Minister and Party Leader), Guido de MARCO (Deputy Prime Minister and Deputy Party Leader), Dr. Louis GALEA (General Secretary).

Opposition Parties:

Malta Labor Party (MLP). The MLP was in power from 1971 to 1987. It advocates a socialist and "progressive" policy, including anticolonialism in international affairs, a neutralist foreign policy, and emphasis on Malta's role as "a bridge of peace between Europe and the Arab world". The party has periodically complained of intrusion by the Church in political and economic affairs. At the election of December 12, 1981, its share of the popular vote fell to 49.1 percent from 51.2 percent in 1976, but without loss of its three-seat majority in the House of Representatives; its vote share fell further to 48.8 percent in 1987, resulting in a loss of government control because of the constitutional revision.

Leader: Dr. Karmenu MIFSUD BONNICI (former Prime Minister).

Progressive Constitutional Party (PCP). The PCP advocates maintenance of Malta's links to the West. It holds no seats in the House of Representatives.

Leader: Mabel STRICKLAND.

Communist Party of Malta — CPM (*Parti Kommunista Malti* — PKM). The CPM is a legal, strongly pro-Soviet group that during the Mintoff era covertly supported the government while criticizing it on selected issues. It did not offer candidates at the 1981 election in order not to "take away votes" from the MLP and secured no legislative representation in 1987.

Leaders: Anthony BALDACCHINO (Chairman), Karmenu GERADA (International Secretary), Anthony VASSALO (General Secretary).

LEGISLATURE

The **House of Representatives** is normally a 65-member body elected on the basis of proportional representation for a five-year term, subject to dissolution. At the election of May 9, 1987, the Malta Labor Party won 34 seats and the Nationalist Party won 31; however, 4 additional seats were awarded to the Nationalists because they had obtained a majority of the popular vote.

Speaker: Dr. Jimmy FARRUGIA.

CABINET

Prime Minister	Dr. Edward Fenech Adami
Deputy Prime Minister	Dr. Guido de Marco
Ministers	
Development of Infrastructure	Michael Falzon
Development of Tertiary Sector	Dr. Emmanuel Bonnici
Education	Dr. Ugo Mifsud Bonnici
Finance	Dr. George Bonello Du Puis
Foreign Affairs	Dr. Vincent (Censu) Tabone
Gozo Affairs	Anton Tabone
Internal Affairs and Justice	Dr. Guido de Marco
Productive Development	Lawrence Gatt
Social Policy	Dr. Louis Galca

NEWS MEDIA

Press. The following are Maltese-language dailies published at Valletta, unless otherwise noted: *It-Tórca* (24,000), weekly; *Il-Mument* (20,000), weekly; *Times* (18,000 daily, 23,000 Sunday), in English; *L'Orizzont* (18,000); *In-Taghna* (18,000); *Il-Hajja,* independent.

News agencies. ANSA, *Agencia EFE,* and TASS maintain bureaus at Valletta.

Radio and television. Xandir Malta, a division of the Telemalta Corporation, provides both radio and television, under supervision of the statutory Malta Broadcasting Authority. In addition, radio broadcasts in several languages are received via Deutsche Welle Relay Malta, while Italian television programs can be received by means of a booster in Sicily. There were approximately 155,000 radio and 100,000 television receivers in 1986.

INTERGOVERNMENTAL REPRESENTATION

Ambassador to the US: Alfred FALZON.

US Ambassador to Malta: Paul R. SOMMER.

Permanent Representative to the UN: Dr. Alexander BORG OLIVIER.

IGO Memberships (Non-UN): CCC, CEUR, CWTH, EEC(A), *EIB,* Interpol, IWTC, NAM, PCA.

MAURITANIA

Islamic Republic of Mauritania
al-Jumhuriyah al-Islamiyah al- Muritaniyah (Arabic)
République Islamique de Mauritanie (French)

Political Status: Independent republic since November 28, 1960; 1961 constitution suspended by the Military Committee for National Recovery (subsequently the Military Committee for National Salvation) on July 20, 1978.

Area: 397,953 sq. mi. (1,030,700 sq. km.).

Population: 1,481,000 (1976C), 1,981,000 (1988E).

Major Urban Centers (1976C): NOUAKCHOTT (134,986); Nouadhibou (21,961); Kaédi (20,848); Zouérate (17,474). As of late 1987, it was estimated that approximately one-third of the total population was resident at Nouakchott as the result of an influx of former nomads.

Official Languages: Arabic, French.

Monetary Unit: Ouguiya (market rate March 1, 1988, 73.41 ouguiyas = $1US).

President and Prime Minister of the Republic and Chairman of the Military Committee for National Salvation: Col. Muawiya Ould Sidi Ahmad TAYA; assumed office following military coup of December 12, 1984, that ousted Lt. Col. Muhammad Khouna Ould HAIDALLA.

THE COUNTRY

Situated on the western bulge of Africa, Mauritania is an impoverished, sparsely populated, predominately desert country, overwhelmingly Islamic and, except in the south, Arabic in language. The dominant Moors, descendants of northern Arabs and Berbers, have long been viewed as constituting one-third of the population, with an equal number of Haratines (mixed-race descendants of Black slaves) having adopted Berber customs. However, Black Africans, concentrated in the rich alluvial farming lands of the Senegal River valley, now claim to account for a much larger populaion share than is officially acknowledged. The most important tribal groups in the south are the Toucouleur, the Fulani, the Sarakole, and the Wolof.

Prolonged droughts in each of the last two decades have devastated the Mauritanian economy and produced disruptive lifestyle changes. Before 1970 nearly all of the northern population was engaged in nomadic cattle-raising but the proportion had shrunk to less than one-quarter by 1986. The loss of herds and relentless desertification have caused a flight to urban areas where foreign relief shipments supply most of the food, with many Mauritanians seeking livelihood in other countries.

Current development plans concentrate on the stimulation of agricultural production and the increasingly lucrative fishing industry, which recently surpassed the extraction of iron ore as the principal source of export revenue. The country's first deep water port, financed by China, opened near Nouakchott in 1986. Regionally, Mauritania participates in such economic bodies as the Organization for the Development of the Senegal River and the Permanent Inter-State Committee on Drought Control in the Sahel.

GOVERNMENT AND POLITICS

Political background. Under nominal French administration from the turn of the century, Mauritania became a French colony in 1920, but de facto control was not established until 1934. Subsequent to its membership in the Federation of French West Africa, Mauritania became an autonomous republic within the French Community in 1958 and an independent "Islamic Republic" on November 28, 1960. President Moktar Ould DADDAH, who led the country to independence, established a one-party regime with predominantly Moorish backing and endorsed a policy of moderate socialism at home combined with nonalignment abroad. Opposition to his 18-year presidency was periodically voiced by northern groups seeking union with Morocco, by others in the predominantly Black south who feared Arab domination, and by leftist elements in both student and trade-union organizations.

Under an agreement concluded in November 1975 by Mauritania, Morocco, and Spain, the Daddah regime assumed control of the southern third of Western (Spanish) Sahara on February 28, 1976, coincident with the withdrawal of Spanish forces and Morocco's occupation of the northern two-thirds (see map and discussion under entry for Morocco). However, an inability to contain Algerian-supported insurgents in the annexed territory contributed to Ould Daddah's ouster in a bloodless coup on July 10, 1978, and the installation of Lt. Col. Mustapha Ould SALEK as head of state by a newly formed Military

Committee for National Recovery (*Comité Militaire de Recouvrement National*—CMRN). Salek, arguing that the struggle against the insurgents had "nearly destroyed" the Mauritanian economy, indicated that his government would be willing to withdraw from Tiris El-Gharbia (the Mauritanian sector of Western Sahara) if a settlement acceptable to Morocco, Algeria, and the insurgents as well as Mauritania could be found. However, the overture was rejected by Morocco and in October the Algerian-backed Popular Front for the Liberation of Saguia el Hamra and Rio de Oro (Polisario) announced that the insurgency would cease only if Mauritania were to withdraw from the sector and recognize Polisario's government-in-exile, the Saharan Arab Democratic Republic (SADR).

In March 1979, while reiterating his government's desire to extricate itself from the conflict, Colonel Salek dismissed a number of CMRN members known to favor direct talks with Polisario. Subsequently, on April 6, he dissolved the CMRN itself in favor of a new Military Committee for National Salvation (*Comité Militaire de Salut National*—CMSN) and relinquished the office of prime minister to Lt. Col. Ahmed Ould BOUCEIF, who was immediately hailed as effective leader of the Nouakchott regime. On May 27, however, Bouceif was killed in an airplane crash and was succeeded (following the interim incumbency of Lt. Col. Ahmed Salem Ould SIDI) by Lt. Col. Muhammad Khouna Ould HAIDALLA on May 31.

President Salek was forced to resign on June 3, the CMSN naming Lt. Col. Muhammad Mahmoud Ould Ahmad LOULY as his replacement. Colonel Louly immediately declared his commitment to a cessation of hostilities and on August 5, after three days of talks at Algiers, concluded a peace agreement with Polisario representatives. While the pact did not entail recognition of the SADR, Mauritania formally renounced all claims to Tiris El-Gharbia and subsequently withdrew its troops from the territory, which was thereupon occupied by Moroccan forces and renamed Oued Eddahab (the Arabic form of the province's original name, Rio de Oro).

On January 4, 1980, President Louly was replaced by Colonel Haidalla, who continued to serve as chief of government. The following December, Haidalla announced that as a first step toward restoration of democratic institutions, his largely military cabinet would be replaced by a civilian government headed by Sid Ahmad Ould BNEIJARA. Only one army officer was named to the cabinet announced on December 15, while the CMSN published a draft constitution four days later that proposed establishment of a multiparty system.

The move toward civilianization was abruptly halted on March 16, 1981, as the result of an attempted coup by a group of officers allegedly backed by Morocco, Prime Minister Bneijara being replaced on April 26 by the army chief of staff, Col. Muawiya Ould Sidi Ahmad TAYA. A further coup attempt, involving an effort to abduct President Haidalla at Nouakchott airport on February 6, 1982, resulted in the arrest of Bneijara and former president Salek, both of whom were sentenced to 10-year prison terms by a special tribunal on March 5.

On March 8, 1984, in a major leadership reshuffle, TAYA returned to his former military post and the president reclaimed the prime ministry, to which was added the defense portfolio. The following December, Haidalla was ousted in a bloodless coup led by Colonel Taya, who assumed the titles of president, prime minister, and chairman of the CMSN.

On December 19 and 26, 1986, Mauritanians elected 426 municipal councillors in the country's 13 regional capitals. The government termed the balloting (the first since 1975) as the initial phase of a democratization process soon to be extended to rural and pastoral areas.

Constitution and government. The constitution of May 23, 1961, which had replaced Mauritania's former parliamentary-type government with a one-party presidential system, was formally suspended by the CMRN on July 20, 1978. A Constitutional Charter issued by the Military Committee confirmed the dissolution of the National Assembly and the Mauritanian People's Party (PPM) and authorized the installation of the Committee's chairman as head of state until such time as "new democratic institutions are established".

On December 19, 1980, the CMSN published a constitutional proposal which was to have been submitted to a referendum in 1981. Under the document as drafted, the president would be elected for a six-year term by universal suffrage, while a reconstituted National Assembly would sit for a term of four years. The prime minister would be appointed by the head of state from the majority party or coalition in the Assembly, which would have to concur in the selection. The political system would be multiparty, although the PPM, which had ruled as the sole legal party prior to the 1978 coup, would remain proscribed. However, no referendum had been held prior to the coup of December 1984. Subsequently, Colonel Taya indicated that the military would prepare for a return to democracy through a program called the Structure for the Education of the Masses that would involve the election of councillors at the local level to advise the government on measures to improve literacy, social integration, and labor productivity. At the municipal balloting of December 1986, conducted under two-round proportional representation, three lists (of a legal maximum of four) were presented in each constituency.

The legal system has traditionally reflected a combination of French and Islamic codes, with the judiciary encompassing a Supreme Court; a High Court of Justice; courts of first instance; and civil, labor, and military courts. In June 1978 a commission was appointed to revise the system according to the precepts of Islam, and in March 1980, a month after the replacement of "modern" codes by Islamic law (*shari'a*), the CMSN established an Islamic Court consisting of a Muslim magistrate, two counsellors, and two *ulemas* (interpreters of the Koran). Earlier, in October 1978, a special Court of State Security had been created.

For administrative purposes the country is divided into 12 regions plus the capital district of Nouakchott.

Foreign relations. Mauritania has combined nonalignment in world affairs with membership in such groupings as the Organization of African Unity and, since 1973, the Arab League. Following independence, economic and cultural cooperation with France continued on the basis of agreements first negotiated in 1961 and renegotiated in 1973 to exclude special arrangements in monetary and military affairs. As a consequence, French military advisers were recalled and Mauritania withdrew from the Franc Zone, establishing its own currency. In late 1979, a limited number of French troops and military instructors returned to ensure Mauritania's territorial integrity following Nouakchott's withdrawal from Western Sahara and the sector's annexation by Morocco.

Mauritania's settlement with the Polisario Front was followed by restoration of diplomatic relations with Algeria, which had been severed upon Algiers' recognition of the Saharan Arab Democratic Republic (SADR) in 1976. During 1980–1982, Nouakchott maintained formal neutrality in Polisario's continuing confrontation with Morocco, withholding formal recognition of the SADR but criticizing Rabat's military efforts to retain control of the entire Western Sahara. In 1983 Colonel Haidalla concluded a Maghreb Fraternity and Cooperation Treaty with Algeria and Tunisia that was implicitly directed against Rabat and Tripoli. On the other hand, declaring that the conflict in the Western Sahara had "poisoned the atmosphere", Colonel Taya has attempted to return Mauritania to its traditional posture of regional neutralism. While still maintaining its "moral support" for the SADR, which it officially recognized in 1984, the Taya regime has normalized relations with Morocco and Libya, thereby balancing its growing ties with Algeria, which included the signing of a border demarcation agreement in April 1986. In 1987 the government, concerned about reinvolvement in the conflict, objected to the building of Moroccan sand walls that were forcing Polisario troops to withdraw toward the Mauritanian border (see Morocco).

Current issues. Ethnic animosity, fueled by extreme poverty, led to social unrest in 1986 as southern Blacks became increasingly vocal in their opposition to Moorish domination. Following the April publication of a "Manifesto of the Oppressed Black Mauritanian", the government arrested dozens of southern leaders, including some holding public positions, for planning "violent acts" that threatened "national unity". Resentment also rose among Haratines, many of whom remained in virtual servitude despite the official abolition of slavery in 1980. There were fewer reports of disturbances in 1987 although the regime announced in October that it had foiled a coup plot by several government "insiders", which yielded death sentences for three Toucouleur (Black African) officers in early December.

On the economic front, the government secured another standby loan from the International Monetary Fund as well as further rescheduling from Paris club creditors of repayments on Mauritania's $1.7 billion external debt. A national tree planting campaign was initiated to regain usable land from the desert (now covering 75 percent of the country), while a "food for work" program was implemented to combat what was termed a growing "beggar mentality".

POLITICAL PARTIES

Mauritania became a one-party state in 1964–1965, when the Mauritanian People's Party (*Parti du Peuple*

Mauritanien—PPM/*Hizb al-Sha'h al-Muritani*) was assigned legal supremacy over all governmental organs. The PPM was dissolved following the coup of July 1978. At the Nouakchott municipal poll of December 1986, a **National Democratic Union** (*Union National Démocratique* —UND) and a **Union for Progress and Fraternity** (*Union des Progrès et Fraternité*—UPF) were identified as having won 19 and 17 seats respectively, with minority list leader Mohammad Ould MAH being elected mayor as the result of a split in the UND.

The extent of internal opposition to CMSN rule remains unclear, although there were reports in 1980 that an **Alliance for a Democratic Mauritania**, headquartered at Paris and apparently loyal to former president Ould Daddah, had been formed by several political groups, including the Senegal-based **Movement of Free Officers**, which rejected the 1979 settlement with the Polisario Front, and an **Islamic Party** and a **Movement of National Unity**, both based in Morocco. Other Alliance associates may be the Senegal-based **Mauritanian Democratic Union**, which has called for cooperative efforts by Blacks and Haratines, and the Haratine **Free Man Movement**, which has charged the Mauritanian government with racism. In May 1984, an **Organization of Mauritanian Nationalists** was formed at Dakar, Senegal, by Khadri Ould DIE, a former military officer, while the "Oppressed Black" manifesto (widely distributed at the 1986 Harare nonaligned summit) has been attributed to the clandestine **African Liberation Forces of Mauritania** (FLAM), organized in 1983.

LEGISLATURE

The National Assembly (*Assemblée Nationale/al-Majlis al-Watani*), a unicameral body consisting entirely of PPM members, was dissolved on July 10, 1978.

CABINET

[as of April 13, 1988]

Prime Minister	Col. Muawiya Ould Sidi Ahmad Taya
Ministers	
Civil Service, Administrative Training, Labor, Youth and Sports	Mohamed Ould Haimer
Commerce and Transportation	Hamdy Samba Diop
Culture and Islamic Orientation	Mohammad Saleh Ould Addoud
Defense	Col. Muawiya Ould Sidi Ahmad Taya
Equipment	Lt. Col. Oumar Dieng Harouna
Finance and Economy	Mohamed Ould Nani
Fishing and Maritime Economy	Deh Ould Cheikh
Foreign Affairs and Cooperation	Maj. Mohammad Lemine Ould N'Diayane
Information	Mohamed Haibetna Ould Sidi Haiba
Interior, Post and Telecommunications	Lt. Col. Djibril Ould Abdellahi
Justice	Cheikh Mohamed Salem Ould Mohamed Lemine
Mines and Industry	Khadija Mint Ahmad Abderrahmane
National Education	Hasni Ould Didi
Public Health and Social Affairs	Maj. N'Diaye Kane
Rural Development	Hamoud Ould Ely
State Control	Ethmane Sid'Ahmed Yessa
Water Supply and Energy	Soumare Oumar
Governor, Central Bank	Ahmed Ould Zein

NEWS MEDIA

All news media are owned and operated by the government.

Press. The following are published at Nouakchott: *Chaab,* daily in Arabic and French; *Journal Officiel,* semimonthly, in French, edited by the Ministry of Justice.

News agencies. The government facility is *Agence Mauritanienne de Presse; Agence France-Presse* also maintains an office at Nouakchott.

Radio and television. *Radiodiffusion Nationale de la République Islamique de Mauritanie* broadcasts to approximately 200,000 receivers in French, Arabic, and indigenous tribal languages; recent programming has emphasized Arabic. *Agence Mauritanienne de Télévision et de Cinéma* broadcasts in Arabic and French to a limited number of receivers.

INTERGOVERNMENTAL REPRESENTATION

Ambassador to the US: Abdallah OULD DADDAH.

US Ambassador to Mauritania: Robert L. PUGH.

Permanent Representative to the UN: Mohamed Mahjoub OULD BOYE.

IGO Memberships (Non-UN): *ACCT,* ADF, AfDB, AFESD, AMF, APEF, BADEA, CEAO, CILSS, ECOWAS, EEC(L), *EIB,* IC, IDB, Intelsat, Interpol, LAS, NAM, OAU.

MAURITIUS

Political Status: Independent member of the Commonwealth since March 12, 1968; under multiparty parliamentary regime.

Area: 790 sq. mi. (2,045 sq. km.).

Population: 1,002,178 (1983C), 1,186,000 (1988E).

Major Urban Centers (1985E): PORT LOUIS (136,000); Beau Bassin/Rose Hill (92,000); Quatre Bornes (65,000); Curepipe (63,200).

Official Language: English (French is also used, while Creole is the *lingua franca* and Hindi the most widely spoken).

Monetary Unit: Mauritian Rupee (market rate March 1, 1988, 12.84 rupees = $1US).

Sovereign: Queen ELIZABETH II.

Governor General: Sir Veerasamy RINGADOO; appointed by the Queen, with effect from January 17, 1986, to succeed Sir Seewoosagur RAMGOOLAM, who died on December 15, 1985.

Prime Minister: Aneerood JUGNAUTH (Mauritian Socialist Movement); formed government on June 15, 1982, following election of June 11 and resignation of Sir Seewoosagur RAMGOOLAM (Independence Party); formed new governments on August 27, 1983, following election of August 21, and on September 4, 1987, following election of August 30.

THE COUNTRY

The island of Mauritius, once known as Ile de France, is situated 500 miles east of Madagascar, in the southwestern Indian Ocean; Rodrigues Island, the Agalega Islands, and the Cardagos Carajos Shoals (St. Brandon Islands) are also national territory. The diversity of contemporary Mauritian society is a reflection of its history as a colonial sugar plantation. Successive importations brought African slave laborers, Indians (who now constitute two-thirds of the population), Chinese, French, and English to the island. Religious affiliations include Christianity (predominantly Roman Catholicism), Hinduism, and Islam. Women are significantly engaged in subsistence agriculture, while comprising only 18 percent of the paid labor force.

Sugar production, to which over 90 percent of the arable land is devoted, accounts for a significant proportion of the country's export earnings. However, rapidly falling prices after 1975 created severe economic difficulties that were partly overcome by expanded activity in the country's Export Processing Zone (EPZ), by means of which investors were given tax and other incentives to set up ventures aimed at production for export. Excellent sugar harvests for three successive years (1985–1987), coupled with expanding tourist activity and increased exports of manufactured goods, have since yielded substantial economic growth. Most current sales, in sugar and other commodities, are to the European Community (EC) under trade provisions of the Lomé Convention.

GOVERNMENT AND POLITICS

Political background. Its location gave Mauritius strategic importance during the age of European exploration and expansion, and the island was occupied successively by the Dutch, French, and English. France ruled the island from 1710 to 1810, when Britain assumed control to protect its shipping during the Napoleonic wars. Political evolution began as early as 1831 under a constitution that provided for a Council of Government, but the franchise was largely restricted until after World War II. The postwar era also witnessed the introduction of political parties and increased participation in local government.

An election under a system of internal parliamentary democracy initiated in 1967 disclosed a majority preference for full independence, which was granted by Britain on March 12, 1968, with Sir Seewoosagur RAMGOOLAM as prime minister, despite an outbreak of severe communal strife between Muslims and Creoles that resulted in the declaration of a state of emergency. Under constitutional arrangements agreed upon in 1969, the life of the Legislative Assembly was extended until 1976. Although the state of emergency was lifted in 1970, new disorders brought its reimposition from December 1971 to March 1978.

Following the election of December 20, 1976, the radical Mauritian Militant Movement (MMM), led by Aneerood JUGNAUTH and Paul BERENGER, held a plurality of legislative seats, but the Independence and Mauritian Social Democratic parties formed a coalition that retained Prime Minister Ramgoolam in office with a slim majority. At the country's second postindependence balloting on June 11, 1982, the incumbent parties lost all of their directly elective seats, Jugnauth proceeding to form an MMM-dominated government on June 15.

In the wake of a government crisis in March 1983 that included the resignation of Bérenger and 11 other ministers, and the repudiation of the prime minister by his own party, Jugnauth and his supporters regrouped as the Mauritian Socialist Movement and, in alliance with Ramgoolam's Mauritius Labour Party wing of the IP and the Social Democrats, won a decisive legislative majority in a new election held August 21.

In February 1984, Labour Party leader Sir Satcam BOOLELL was relieved of his post as minister of economic planning and the MLP voted to terminate its support of the MSM. However, 11 Labour deputies under the leadership of Beergoonath GHURBURRUN refused to follow Boolell into opposition and remained in the alliance as the Mauritian Workers' Movement (subsequently the Mauritian Labour Rally).

At municipal council balloting on December 8, 1985, the opposition MMM won 57.2 percent of the vote, decisively defeating the coalition parties, who captured only 36.8 percent, while the MLP was a distant third with 5.4 percent. Although insisting that the MMM victory represented a rejection of Jugnauth's policies, Bérenger did not immediately call for the government to resign. However, such an appeal was made in the wake of a major drug scandal at the end of the month (see Current issues, below). Subsequently, the MLP agreed to a reconciliation with the MSM and Boolell was awarded three portfolios as well as the post of second deputy prime minister in a cabinet reorganization of August 8.

At an early election on August 30, 1987, called largely because of favorable economic conditions, the Jugnauth coalition retained power by capturing 41 of 62 elective legislative seats.

Constitution and government. The Mauritius Independence Order of 1968, as amended the following year by the Constitution of Mauritius (Amendment) Act, provided for a unicameral system of parliamentary government. Executive authority is exercised by a prime minister who, like the Council of Ministers, is appointed by the governor general (as representative of the Crown) from among the majority members of the Legislative Assembly. The latter is composed of 60 representatives directly elected from three-member districts on the main island, plus 2 from Rodrigues; in addition, up to 8 "best loser" seats may be awarded on the basis of party or ethnic underrepresentation as indicated by shares of total vote and total population, respectively. Judicial authority, based on both French and British precedents, is exercised by a Supreme Court, four of whose five judges (excluding the chief justice) preside additionally in Appeal, Intermediate, District, and Industrial court proceedings. There are also inferior courts and a Court of Assizes. Final appeal is to the UK Privy Council.

Nine districts constitute the principal administrative divisions, with separate administrative structures governing the Mauritian dependencies: the Agalega and Cargados

Carajos groups are ruled directly from Port Louis, while Rodrigues Island has a central government under a resident commissioner and local councils. On the main island, municipal and town councils are elected in urban areas, and district and village councils in rural areas.

Foreign relations. Formally nonaligned, Mauritius maintains diplomatic relations with most Communist states as well as with the United States and the countries of Western Europe. The principal foreign policy issue in recent years has been the status of Diego Garcia Island, which was considered a Mauritian dependency until London transferred administration of the Chagos Archipelago, in 1965, to the British Indian Ocean Territory. The following year, Britain concluded an agreement with the United States whereby the latter obtained use of the island for 50 years. After independence was achieved in 1968, Mauritius pressed its claim to Diego Garcia, while international attention was drawn to the issue in 1980 when Washington announced that it intended to make the island the chief US naval and air base in the Indian Ocean. In July the Organization of African Unity unanimously backed Port Louis' claim, but efforts by Prime Minister Ramgoolam to garner support from the UK government were rebuffed.

In July 1982 Britain agreed to pay £4 million in compensation for the resettlement of families moved to Mauritius from the Chagos chain in 1965–1973. In accepting the payment, Port Louis reserved its position in regard to Diego Garcia and insisted that existence of the US base violated a 1967 commitment by the United Kingdom (denied by London) that the island would not be used for military purposes. Subsequently, during a state visit in late August, Indian Prime Minister Indira Gandhi stated that her government supported the Mauritian claim to the Chagos group.

Earlier, on June 20, 1980, the Ramgoolam government had announced that it was amending the country's constitution to encompass the French-held island of Tromelin, located some 350 miles to the north of Mauritius, thus reaffirming a claim that Paris had formally rejected in 1976.

Current issues. In December 1985 the government was rocked by the arrest of four coalition members at Amsterdam's Schipol Airport, allegedly with heroin valued at £700,000 in their luggage. Although three of the suspects were soon released, the scandal provoked the resignation of four government ministers on January 3, 1986, with a total of six assemblymen ultimately being implicated by a commission of inquiry report in March 1987. Despite its embarrassment, the government was buoyed by highly favorable economic gains in 1986–1987, which were hailed as stemming from a "textbook model" of structural readjustment under IMF/World Bank auspices. In part by shifting to manufacturing output instead of its traditional dependence on sugar (for which world prices had recently recovered), external debt servicing was cut in half, inflation was reduced to 2 percent (as contrasted with 33 percent in 1980), and a substantial reduction was achieved in unemployment. As a result, Prime Minister Jugnauth called for an early election on August 30, at which the government coalition was returned to power with a marginally reduced 2–1 majority over the opposition. Subsequent to the balloting, the government announced that it would reintroduce legislation to make Mauritius a republic within the Commonwealth (an earlier such measure having failed in late 1983).

POLITICAL PARTIES

A large number of political parties have contested recent Mauritian elections; few, however, have run candidates in most constituencies, with only a very limited number securing parliamentary representation. Since most of the groups are leftist in orientation, ideological differences tend to be blurred, with recurrent cleavages based largely on pragmatic considerations.

Government Alliance:

Mauritian Socialist Movement (*Mouvement Socialiste Mauricien* — MSM). The MSM was organized initially on April 8, 1983, as the Militant Socialist Movement (*Mouvement Socialiste Militant*), by Prime Minister Jugnauth, following his expulsion, in late March, from the Mauritian Militant Movement (below). On May 1, the MSM absorbed the Mauritian Socialist Party (*Parti Socialiste Mauricien* — PSM), led by Harish Boodhoo, which had been formed in 1979 by the withdrawal of a group of dissidents from the Mauritius Labour Party (below).

The MSM fought the 1983 election in coalition with the MLP, the Mauritian Social Democratic Party, and the Rodriguan People's Organization, winning a clear majority of legislative seats. In February 1984, the MLP withdrew from the alliance, although a number of its deputies, reorganizing as the Mauritian Workers' Movement (see under RTM, below) remained loyal to the government.

In November 1986, Boodhoo (who had earlier resigned from the government in the wake of the drug scandal) was expelled from the party.

Leader: Aneerood JUGNAUTH (Prime Minister).

Mauritius Labour Party (MLP). A Hindu-based party, the MLP, under the leadership of Seewoosagur Ramgoolam, joined the country's other leading Indian group, the Muslim Action Committee (below) in forming the Independence Party (IP) prior to the 1976 election. Collectively, the MLP and the CAM had held an overwhelming majority of 47 legislative seats after the 1967 pre-independence balloting, whereas the IP secured only 28 in 1976 and plummeted to 2 in 1982 (both awarded to the MLP on a "best loser" basis). A condition of the MLP joining the 1983 alliance was said to be the designation of Ramgoolam as president upon the country's becoming a republic; following failure of a republic bill in December 1983, the longtime MLP leader was named governor general.

In February 1984, after MLP leader Sir Satcam Boolell was relieved of his post as minister of planning and economic development, the party went into opposition. It reentered the government in August 1986, with Boolell named second deputy prime minister and assigned the external affairs, justice, and attorney general portfolios.

Leaders: Sir Satcam BOOLELL, Vijay VENKATASAMY (Secretary General).

Mauritian Labour Rally (*Rassemblement des Travaillistes Mauriciens* — RTM). The RTM was organized, initially as the Mauritian Workers' Movement (MWM), by a group of former MLP deputies who chose to remain within the government coalition following withdrawal of the parent party in early 1984.

Leader: Dr. Beergoonath GHURBURRUN.

Mauritian Social Democratic Party (*Parti Mauricien Social-Démocrate* — PMSD). Composed chiefly of Franco-Mauritian landowners and the Creole middle class, the PMSD initially opposed independence but subsequently accepted it as a *fait accompli*. Antisocialist at home and anticommunist in foreign affairs, it is most distinguished for its francophile stance. The party was part of the Ramgoolam government coalition until 1973, when it went into opposition. It held 23 legislative seats after the 1967 election, but dropped to 8 in 1976, at which time it reentered the government. Obtaining only two "best loser" seats in 1982, it won 4 on an elective basis in 1983.

Leaders: Sir Gaëtan DUVAL (Deputy Prime Minister), Nanda KISTEN (President), V. Seetanah LUTCHMEENARAIDOO (Finance Minister), Marc HEIN (Secretary General).

Rodriguan People's Organization (*Organisation du Peuple Rodriquais* – OPR). The OPR captured the two elective seats from Rodrigues Island at both the 1982 and 1983 balloting and, having earlier indicated that it would support the MSM-Labour alliance, was awarded one cabinet post in the Jugnauth government of August 1983 which it retained after the reorganization of January 13, 1986.

Leaders: Louis Serge CLAIR, France FELICITE.

Opposition Party:

Mauritian Militant Movement (*Mouvement Militant Mauricien* – MMM). The MMM has long enjoyed substantial trade union support. Its leadership was detained during the 1971 disturbances because of its "confrontational politics", which unlike that of other Mauritian parties, was intended to cut across ethnic-communal lines. Following the 1976 election, the party's leadership strength was only two seats short of a majority; in 1982, campaigning in alliance with the PSM (see MSM above), it obtained an absolute majority of 42 seats.

In March 1983, 12 members of the MMM government of Aneerood Jugnauth, led by Finance Minister Paul Bérenger, resigned in disagreement over economic policy, coupled with a contention by Bérenger supporters that Creole should be designated the national language. Immediately thereafter, Jugnauth was expelled and proceeded to form the MSM, which, with its allies, achieved a decisive victory at the August 21 election. The MMM obtained a plurality of votes at municipal council balloting on December 8, 1985.

Prior to the 1987 balloting Bérenger, who had long been viewed as a Marxist, characterized himself as a "democratic socialist". However, he was unsuccessful in securing an Assembly seat on either a direct or "best loser" basis. The party itself campaigned as the leading component of a Union for the Future alliance that included two minor groups, the **Democratic Labour Movement** (*Mouvement Travailliste Démocrate* – MTD) and the **Socialist Workers' Front** (*Front des Travailleurs Socialistes* – FTS).

Leaders: Paul BERENGER, Dr. Prem NABABSINGH (Leader of the Opposition), Dharam FOKEER (President), Allan GANOO (Secretary General).

Other Parties:

Muslim Action Committee (*Comité d'Action Musulman* – CAM). The CAM has long represented the interests of the Indian Muslim community.

Leaders: Razack PEEROO (President), Raouf BUNDHUN (Secretary General).

Independent Forward Bloc (IFB). The IFB, supported by Hindu laborers and small planters, was formed in 1958 and participated in the government until 1969.

Leaders: G. GANGARAM (President), R. JEETAH, W.A. FOONDUN (Secretary).

Mauritian Democratic Union (*Union Démocratique Mauricienne* – UDM). The UDM was formed by conservative dissidents from the PMSD.

Leaders: Bali MAHADOO (President), Guy OLLIVRY, Elwyn CHUTEL (Secretary General).

Mauritius People's Progressive Party (MPPP). The MPPP is a left-wing party that has lost many adherents to the more militant MMM. Its principal concern has been demilitarization of the Indian Ocean area.

Leader: Teekaram SIBSURUN (Secretary General).

Mauritian Social Progressive Militant Movement (*Mouvement Militant Mauricien Social Progressiste* – MMMSP). The MMMSP was organized by Maoist dissidents from the MMM.

Leader: Dev VERASWAMY.

LEGISLATURE

The Mauritian **Legislative Assembly,** as presently constituted, is a 70-member unicameral body encompassing 62 elected deputies (including 2 from Rodrigues Island) plus 8 appointed from the list of unsuccessful candidates. The legislative term is five years, subject to dissolution. At the election of August 30, 1987, the Alliance captured 41 elective seats (Mauritian Socialist Movement, 26; Mauritian Labour Party, 9; Mauritian Social Democratic Party, 4; Rodriguan People's Organization, 2) and the opposition Union's Mauritian Militant Movement, 21. In the "best loser" distribution, 5 seats were awarded to the Alliance and 3 to the MMM.

Speaker: Ajay DABY.

CABINET

Prime Minister	Aneerood Jugnauth
Deputy Prime Minister	Sir Gaëtan Duval
Ministers	
Agriculture, Fisheries and Natural Resources	Madun Murlidas Dulloo
Cooperatives	Vishwanath Sajadah
Defense and Internal Security	Aneerood Jugnauth
Economic Planning and Development	Dr. Beergoonath Ghurburrun
Education, Arts and Culture	Armoorgum Parsooramen
Energy and Internal Communications	Mahyendra Utchanah
External Affairs and Emmigration	Sir Satcam Boolell
External Communications	Aneerood Jugnauth
Finance	Seetanah Lutchmeenaraidoo
Health	Jagdishwar Goburdhun
Housing, Lands and Environment	Sir Ramesh Jeewoolall
Industry	Joseph Hervé Duval
Information	Aneerood Jugnauth
Interior	Aneerood Jugnauth
Justice	Sir Satcam Boolell
Labor and Industrial Relations	Sheilabai Bappoo
Local Government	Joseph Clarel Desiré Malherbe
Outer Islands	Aneerood Jugnauth
Regional Administration	Clarel Malhebe
Rodrigues	Louis Serge Clair
Social Security, National Solidarity and Reform Institutions	Dr. Dineshwar Ramjuttun
Tourism and Employment	Sir Gaëtan Duval
Trade and Shipping	Dwarkanath Gungah
Women's Rights and Family Affairs	Sheilabai Bappoo
Works	Ramdathsing Jaddoo
Youth and Sports	Michaël James Kelvin Glover
Attorney General	Sir Satcam Boolell
Governor, Central Bank	Induruth Ramphul

NEWS MEDIA

The traditionally free Mauritian press was subject to censorship under the state of emergency imposed in 1971, but restrictions were lifted on May 1, 1976. Radio and television are under semipublic control.

Press. The following are published daily at Port Louis in English and French, unless otherwise noted: *Le Mauricien* (22,000); *L'Express* (20,000); *Advance* (8,000); *Le Socialist* (6,000), PSM organ; *Le Nouveau Militant* (6,000), MMM weekly; *The New Nation* (5,000); *Chinese Daily News* (3,000), in Chinese; *China Times* (3,000), in Chinese.

Radio and television. The Mauritius Broadcasting Corporation operates both radio and television facilities. Broadcasts are in English, French, Hindi, and Chinese. There were approximately 210,000 radio and 128,000 television receivers in 1987.

INTERGOVERNMENTAL REPRESENTATION

Ambassador to the US: Chitmansing JESSERAMSING.

US Ambassador to Mauritius: Ronald DeWayne PALMER.

Permanent Representative to the UN: Dr. Satteeanund PEERTHUM.

IGO Memberships (Non-UN): ACCT, ADF, AfDB, BADEA, CCC, CWTH, EEC(L), EIB, Intelsat, Interpol, ISO, ITPA, IWTC, NAM, OAU, OCAM, PCA.

MEXICO

United Mexican States
Estados Unidos Mexicanos

Political Status: Independence originally proclaimed 1810; present federal constitution adopted February 5, 1917.

Area: 761,600 sq. mi. (1,972,544 sq. km.).

Population: 66,846,833 (1980C), 82,915,000 (1988E). Figures do not include adjustment for underenumeration (estimated at more than 3 percent).

Major Urban Centers (1979E): MEXICO CITY (Federal District, 9,190,000; urban area, 14,000,000); Guadalajara (1,906,000; urban area, 2,420,000); Monterrey (1,065,000; urban area, 1,900,000); Heróica Puebla de Zaragoza (711,000); Ciudad Juárez (625,000); León (625,000); Tijuana (566,000); Acapulco (462,000); Chihuahua (386,000); Mexicali (349,000).

Official Language: Spanish.

Monetary Unit: Peso (principal rate March 1, 1988, 2281.00 pesos = $1US).

President: Miguel de la MADRID Hurtado (Institutional Revolutionary Party); assumed office December 1, 1982, for a six-year term, following election of July 4, in succession to José LOPEZ Portillo y Pacheco (Institutional Revolutionary Party).

THE COUNTRY

Extending southeastward from the United States border to the jungles of Yucatán and Guatemala, Mexico ranks third in size and second in population among North American countries and holds comparable rank among the countries of Latin America. Its varied terrain encompasses low-lying coastal jungles, a broad central plateau framed by high mountain ranges, and large tracts of desert territory in the north. The people are mainly of mixed Indian and Spanish (mestizo) descent, with minority groups of pure Indians and Caucasians. Roman Catholicism predominates, though constitutional separation of church and state has prevailed since 1857. Although about one-third of the rapidly growing population is still engaged in agriculture, increasing urbanization has generated new social issues such as adequate housing and health care, while an expanding middle class has pressed for political and economic modernization. In 1980, women constituted 25 percent of the paid labor force, concentrated mainly in trade, manufacturing, and domestic service; in the export-oriented border factories (*maquiladores*), over 80 percent of the work force is female. Women's participation in national and local government ranges from zero to 20 percent, with no female representation in the present cabinet.

Industrialization has been rapid since World War II, but its benefits have been unevenly distributed and much of the rural population remains substantially unaffected. The gross national product grew by a yearly average of 16 percent during 1972–1975, with the growth rate declining to a still-respectable 8 percent in 1978–1981. Since then, the economy has been in deep recession, with an unserviceable foreign debt, massive capital flight, widespread unemployment, and rampant inflation. Successive IMF interventions slowed the decline in 1983–1984, but by mid-1986, in the wake of a disastrous earthquake at Mexico City the preceding September and a further collapse in oil prices, crisis conditions had returned, with inflation surging to more than 140 percent in 1987. Hope for recovery rested primarily on the success of a number of economic initiatives, including an innovative buy-back plan for foreign debt, undertaken in late 1987.

GOVERNMENT AND POLITICS

Political background. Conquered by Spain in the sixteenth century, Mexico proclaimed its independence in 1810 and the establishment of a republic in 1822. The country was ruled by Gen. Antonio López de SANTA ANNA from 1833 to 1855, a period that encompassed the declaration of Texan independence in 1836 and war with the United States from 1846 to 1848. Archduke MAXIMILIAN of Austria, installed as emperor of Mexico by Napoleon III in 1865, was deposed and executed by Benito JUAREZ in 1867. The dominant figure during the latter nineteenth century was Gen. Porfirio DIAZ, who served as president from 1877 to 1910.

Modern Mexican history dates from the Revolution of 1910, which shattered an outmoded social and political system and cleared the way for a generally progressive republican regime whose foundations were laid in 1917. Since 1928, political life has been dominated by a nationwide grouping whose present name, the Institutional Revolutionary Party (PRI), was adopted in 1946 and which purports to carry forward the work of the 1917 constitution.

President Luis ECHEVERRIA Alvarez, who assumed office in 1970, adopted the slogan "Upward and Forward" (*"Arriba y Adelante"*) as a rallying cry for his program of reform, which sought to overcome maldistribution of income, widespread alienation and unrest, scattered urban and rural violence, and a visible erosion in the prestige, if not the power, of the PRI. Echeverría's efforts were opposed both by the Right, because of a feeling that the traditional favoritism shown to business interests was waning, and by the Left, because of a conviction that the reform was a sham.

In the presidential election of July 4, 1976, Finance Minister José LOPEZ Portillo, running as the PRI candidate, obtained 94.4 percent of the popular vote against a field of independents, no other party having presented an endorsed candidate. Soon after his inauguration on December 1, the new chief executive introduced a far-reaching program of political reform that resulted in three additional opposition parties, including the Mexican Communist Party, being granted conditional recognition prior to the legislative election of July 1979, after which all three were granted seats in the Chamber of Deputies according to their vote totals.

A new left-wing coalition, the Unified Socialist Party of Mexico (PSUM), formed in November 1981 by the Communists and four smaller parties, failed to gain ground against the entrenched PRI in the balloting of July 4, 1982, in which the ruling party captured all but one elective congressional seat and saw its presidential candidate, former minister of programming and budget Miguel de la MADRID Hurtado, win 74.4 percent of the vote in a field of seven nominees. During the ensuing four years, the PRI was buffeted by an unprecedented, if minor, set of electoral losses to the rightist National Action Party (PAN). In the lower house election of July 7, 1985, the PAN won 9 elective seats, while in a supplementary distribution under proportional representation the leftist parties gained substantially more seats than in 1982.

At a congress in October 1987 the PRI ratified the selection of former planning and budget minister Carlos SALINAS de Gortari as its 1988 presidential candidate. Although virtually assured on victory, Salinas faces a number of challengers including former PRI dissident Cuauhtémoc CARDENAS, PAN candidate Manuel CLOUTHIER, and Herberto CASTILLO of the Mexican Socialist Party, a recently organized leftist grouping (see Political Parties, below).

Constitution and government. Under its frequently amended constitution of February 5, 1917, Mexico is a federal republic consisting of 31 states (each with its own constitution, governor, and legislative chamber) plus a Federal District whose governor is appointed by the president. The preeminent position of the chief executive, who is directly elected for a single six-year term, is enhanced by his leadership of the dominant party, his pervasive influence on legislators, and his immense powers of patronage. The bicameral Congress, consisting of an elected Senate and Chamber of Deputies (the latter under a mixed direct and proportional system), is confined by the party system to a secondary role in the determination of national policy. The judicial system is headed by a 21-member Supreme Court, which has four divisions: administrative, civil, labor, and penal. The justices of the Supreme Court are appointed for life by the president with the approval of the Senate. Lower courts include 6 circuit courts and 47 district courts. The basis of local government is the municipality (*municipio*).

State and Capital	Area (sq. mi.)	Population (1987E)
Aguascalientes (Aguascalientes)	2,158	719,000
Baja California (Mexicali)	27,071	1,198,000
Baja California, T.S. (La Paz)	24,447	278,000
Campeche (Campeche)	21,665	724,000
Chiapas (Tuxtla Gutierrez)	28,527	2,476,000
Chihuahua (Chihuahua)	95,400	2,545,000
Coahuila (Saltillo)	58,522	1,857,000
Colima (Colima)	2,106	432,000
Durango (Durango)	46,196	1,491,000
Guanajuato (Guanajuato)	11,810	3,267,000
Guerrero (Chilpancingo)	24,631	2,250,000
Hidalgo (Pachuca)	8,103	1,921,000
Jalisco (Guadalajara)	30,941	5,573,000
México (Toluca)	8,286	11,508,000
Michoacán (Morelia)	23,113	7,500,000
Morelos (Cuernavaca)	1,907	1,331,000
Nayarit (Tepic)	10,664	818,000
Nuevo León (Monterrey)	24,924	3,420,000
Oaxaca (Oaxaca)	36,820	2,189,000
Puebla (Puebla)	13,096	4,297,000
Querétaro (Querétaro)	4,544	951,000
Quintana Roo (Chetumal)	16,228	422,000
San Luis Potosí (San Luis Potosí)	24,265	2,015,000
Sinaloa (Culiacán)	22,429	2,163,000
Sonora (Hermosillo)	71,403	1,810,000
Tabasco (Villa Hermosa)	9,522	959,000
Tamaulipas (Ciudad Victoria)	30,822	2,285,000
Tlaxcala (Tlaxcala)	1,511	687,000
Veracruz (Jalapa)	28,114	6,977,000
Yucatán (Mérida)	16,749	1,423,000
Zacatecas (Zacatecas)	28,973	1,210,000

Federal District

México City	579	10,050,000

Foreign relations. A founding member of the United Nations, the Organization of American States (OAS), and related organizations, Mexico has generally adhered to an independent foreign policy based on the principles of nonintervention and self-determination. One of the initiators of the 1967 Treaty for the Prohibition of Nuclear Weapons in Latin America (Treaty of Tlatelolco), it is the only non-South American member of the Latin American Integration Association (ALADI) and the only OAS state to have continually maintained formal relations with Cuba, despite more than a decade of ostracism of the Castro regime by most of the organization's members. It also supports the *sandinista* government of Nicaragua and recognizes El Salvador's leftist FMLN-FDR as a "representative political force ready to assume its obligations and exercise the rights deriving from it." Mexican officials did, however, attend the 1984 inauguration of Salvadoran President José Napoleón Duarte and announced a full restoration of diplomatic ties with San Salvador (suspended since 1980) in August 1985.

Under President de la Madrid and Foreign Minister Bernardo SEPULVEDA Amor, the country has continued to exercise a leadership role in the region, despite a diminution of influence because of its economic difficulties. As a participant in the Contadora Group, which also included, as original members, Colombia, Panama, and Venezuela, Mexico has taken the Group's agenda for a regional peace initiative to both South America and the United States. While Washington endorsed the Group's negotiating proposals in August 1983, US military policy in Central America continues to be a major source of strain in the traditionally cordial relationship between Mexico and its northern neighbor, with President de la Madrid tending to emphasize socioeconomic bases of regional instability and President Reagan citing "Soviet-Cuban terrorism" as the source of difficulty. Other disagreement between the two countries continues to center on border issues, such as air pollution, drug trafficking, and US efforts to control illegal immigration.

Current issues. In the opinion of many analysts, the Mexican economy had plummeted to a point of desperation in 1986 as the government was forced to halve its earlier projection of $12.1 billion in oil income and the foreign debt neared $100 billion. The administration responded by negotiating a $12 billion "rescue plan" that was approved in December by a group that included the IMF, the World Bank, the United States, and commercial creditors. A year later, in the face of continued difficulty, the peso was devalued by 22 percent and an "economic solidarity pact" was concluded with business and labor representatives. Under the agreement, minimum wages were marginally increased, with wages generally to be indexed to the rate of inflation for most of 1988; the private sector promised to moderate price increases, while public-sector prices and tariffs would be substantially increased. In addition, a novel debt-reduction plan was announced, whereby foreign creditors would be invited to exchange Mexican debt holdings at discount for new zero-coupon bonds backed by the US Treasury. Initially, it was hoped that the country's overall indebtedness would be cut by some $10 billion, although by March 1988 it was evident that the reduction would be far less because the discount bids were less favorable than had been anticipated.

In November 1986 the PRI-controlled Congress enacted a number of electoral changes that included a 100-seat expansion of the lower house, with a minimum of 150 seats reserved for opposition deputies, and the creation of an elected assembly for the Federal District. Critics countered that retention of the 1.5 percent vote-share requirement for party registration and the use of proportional representation only for the reserved seats would benefit the PRI by continued proliferation of minor parties. The opposition also objected to a clause ensuring that the majority party would remain in power even if obtaining less than 51 percent of the vote, while arguing that the assembly for Mexico City was meaningless as long as the president continued to name the mayor.

Reacting to numerous allegations of impropriety, particularly by the PRI, at recent elections, a broadly-based Democratic Assembly for Effective Voting (*Asamblea Democrática por el Sufragio Efectivo*) was formed in December 1987 to monitor the 1988 balloting. Leading members of the watchdog group included PAN businessman Alejandro GURZA, PRI dissident Porfiro MUÑOZ Ledo, and 1982 leftist presidential candidate Arnoldo MARTINEZ Verdugo.

POLITICAL PARTIES

Mexican politics since the 1920s has been based on the predominance of a single party, which has enjoyed virtually unchallenged control of the presidency, the Congress, and the state governments. Other recognized parties must capture a mandated minimum of 1.5 percent of the total vote in a national election in order to maintain their registrations.

Governing Party:

Institutional Revolutionary Party (*Partido Revolucionario Institucional*—PRI). Founded in 1929 as the National Revolutionary Party (PRN) and redesignated in 1938 as the Mexican Revolutionary Party (PRM), the PRI took its present name in 1946. As a union of local and state groups with roots in the revolutionary period, it was gradually established on a broad popular base and retains a tripartite organization based on three distinct sectors (labor, agrarian, and "popular"), although in 1978 it was officially designated as a "workers' party". While the PRI's general outlook may be characterized as moderately left-wing, its membership includes a variety of factions and outlooks. In recent years, controversies surrounding electoral outcomes have led to internal turmoil, including a 1984 leadership shakeup amid allegations that state and local PRI organizations had "disregarded" policy set in Mexico City. In late 1986 the controversy yielded the formation of a Democratic Current (*Corriente Democratica*—CD) faction under the leadership of Cuauhtémoc Cárdenas and former party president Porfiro Muñoz Ledo that called for more openness in PRI affairs, including the abolition of secrecy (*tapadismo*) in the selection of presidential candidates. In June 1987, five months after another shakeup in which half of the party's 30-member Executive Committee was replaced, the PRI withdrew recognition of the CD and in October Cárdenas announced that he had accepted the presidential nomination of PARM (below).

Leaders: Miguel de la MADRID Hurtado (President of Mexico), Jorge de la VEGA Domínguez (President of the Party), Carlos SALINAS de Gortari (1988 presidential candidate), Humberto LUGO Gil (Secretary General).

Opposition Parties:

National Action Party (*Partido Acción Nacional*—PAN). Founded in 1939 and dependent on urban middle-class support, the leading opposition party has an essentially conservative, proclerical, and probusiness orientation, and favors limitations on the government's economic role. Partially due to fragmentation within the leftist opposition, PAN has been the main beneficiary of the erosion in PRI support. In 1982, although losing all but one of its directly elective Chamber seats, the party's proportional representation rose from 39 to 54; in municipal and state balloting the following year, it was awarded nine mayoralties and three governorships, party spokesmen claiming that they had been denied a number of additional municipal victories due to PRI electoral fraud. Similar claims were made after the 1985 general election, at which PAN gained nine directly elective Chamber seats and a number of mayoralties, and was widely acknowledged to have gained the majority of votes in two gubernatorial races ultimately won by the PRI. Following the July balloting, the party led a number of large demonstrations against "the lack of democracy", both in the north and at the capital. In addition to its increased electoral support, PAN has won tacit endorsement in recent years from a number of formerly PRI-supportive trade unions, as well as from portions of the business community.

Leaders: Luis ALVAREZ (President), Pablo Emilio MADERO (former President), Manuel CLOUTHIER (1988 presidential candidate), Norberto CORELLA, Abel Vincencio TOVAR (General Secretary).

Mexican Democratic Party (*Partido Demócrata Mexicano*—PDM). The PDM is a right-wing group organized in 1974 but with roots in the conservative Roman Catholic *Sinarguista* movement of the 1920s. It registered a number of victories at the municipal level in 1983 and was awarded 12 chamber seats, on a proportional basis, in 1985.

Leaders: Gumersindo MAGAÑA Negrete (President of the Party and 1988 presidential candidate), Ignacio GONZALEZ Gollaz (Secretary).

Authentic Party of the Mexican Revolution (*Partido Auténtico de la Revolución Mexicana*—PARM). A splinter of the PRI founded in 1954, PARM advocates a return to what it considers the original spirit of the 1910 revolution. Although awarded 12 Chamber seats in 1979, in July 1982 the party failed to obtain the 1.5 percent minimum vote needed for continued registration; however, it revived in 1985, gaining 2 directly elected and 7 proportionally allocated Chamber seats. In practice, the party has been largely supportive of PRI policies.

Leaders: Jesús GUZMAN Rubio (President), Cuauhtémoc CARDENAS (former PRI/CD leader and 1988 presidential candidate), Carlos CANTU Rosas (Secretary General).

Mexican Socialist Party (*Partido Mexicano Socialista*—PMS). The PMS was launched in March 1987 by merger of Mexico's two principal leftist groups, the Unified Socialist Party of Mexico (*Partido Socialista Unificado de Mexico* — PSUM) and the Mexican Workers' Party (*Partido Mexicano de los Trabajadores* — PMT), and three smaller formations, the Patriotic Revolutionary Party (*Partido Patriótico Revolucionario* — PPR), the People's Revolutionary Movement (*Movimiento Revolucionario del Pueblo* — MRP), and the Left Communist Union (*Unidad de Izquierda Communista* — UIC).

Recognized by the Soviet Union as the country's official communist party, the PSUM had been formed in November 1981 by merger of the Mexican Communist Party (*Partido Comunista Mexicano* — PCM) with four smaller groups: the Popular Action Movement (*Movimiento de Acción Popular* — MAP), the Mexican People's Party (*Partido del Pueblo Mexicano* — PPM), the Movement for Socialist Action and Unity (*Movimiento de Acción y Unidad Socialista* — MAUS), and the Revolutionary Socialist Party (*Partido Socialista Revolucionario* — PSR). (The PCM had been formed in 1919, was accorded legal recognition from 1932 to 1942, and was thereafter semiclandestine until returned, conditionally, to legal status in 1978.) The 1981 merger was followed by an intense leadership dispute, the PSUM's Central Committee in 1983 criticizing "compartmentalization" stemming from the former party alignments. In early 1984, PSR leader Roberto JARAMILLO Flores was charged with refusal to dissolve his party as a distinct formation and was subsequently reported to have sought legal registration for the group from the Federal Electoral Commission. In February 1985, PPM leader Alejandro GASCON Mercado broke with his colleagues by launching a rival PSUM faction styled the Democratic and Radical Political Current (*Corriente Política Democrática y Radical*). Meanwhile, the mainstream leadership had organized a PSUM-led electoral front for the July balloting that included the PMT, the UIC, the Popular Socialist Party (below) and the miniscule **Socialist Current** (*Corriente Socialista* — CS). None of the foregoing won directly elective Chamber seats, although the PSUM was awarded 12 proportional seats, while the PPS and PMT were allocated 11 and 6, respectively.

The PMT was a pro-Cuban formation organized in 1974. Having announced in August 1981 its intention to join the PSUM, it withdrew prior to the coalition's November constituent meeting because of what it considered an effort by the PCM to dominate the new group's ideology and structure; however, it agreed to join the PSUM's electoral alliance in 1985. PMT leader Herberto Castillo has been named 1988 PMS presidential candidate.

Leaders: Pablo GOMEZ Alvarez (PSUM), Herberto CASTILLO (PMT).

Popular Socialist Party (*Partido Popular Socialista* — PPS). Led by Vincente Lombardo Toledano until his death in 1968, the PPS is Marxist and pro-Soviet in orientation and draws support from intellectuals, students, and some labor elements. Although some of its leaders are avowedly communist, the rank and file are predominantly noncommunist. At the election of July 4, 1976, PPS leader Jorge Cruikshank became the first opposition candidate to win a Senate seat since 1929. In the wake of charges that a "deal" had been made concerning the seat, a majority of the party voted, at the annual PPS Congress in December, for more forceful opposition to the PRI. Nevertheless, the Socialists failed to present a presidential candidate in 1982, choosing instead to support PAN's Pablo Madero; in legislative balloting the PPS lost its Senate seat but retained its 11 proportionally awarded Chamber seats. In 1983, the party won a number of state legislative seats from the PRI, and maintained its 11 seats, awarded by proportional representation, as part of the PSUM-led alliance in 1985. For the 1988 presidential balloting it has joined a "mini-coalition" in support of PARM's Cuauhtémoc Cárdenas.

Leader: Jorge CRUIKSHANK García (Secretary General).

Workers' Socialist Party (*Partido Socialista de los Trabajadores* — PST). Formed in 1975, the PST has been closely associated with the PRI and still supports the "revolutionary nationalism" of former president Echeverría, though officially presenting itself as a Marxist-Leninist party. It supported López Portillo in the 1976 presidential election; its 1982 candidate, Candido DIAZ Cerecedo, captured only 1.5 percent of the vote. However, in the 1985 legislative balloting the PST, which had refused to participate in any electoral alliance, added two proportional seats to its 1982 total of 10. It also supports PARM's Cárdenas for president in 1988.

Leaders: Rafael AGUILAR Talamantes (President), Graco RAMIREZ Abreu (Secretary General).

Revolutionary Workers' Party (*Partido Revolucionario de los Trabajadores* — PRT). The Trotskyite PRT failed to win legislative representation in July 1982, its candidate for the presidency, Rosario Ibarra de la Piedra

(the first woman ever to seek the office), capturing 1.9 percent of the vote. Excluded from the PSUM-led electoral front in July 1985, the PRT allied itself with a number of state-level leftist groups, including the **League of Marxist Laborers** (*Liga Obrera Marxista* — LOM), and was awarded six Chamber seats by proportional representation. In May 1987 the PRT and LOM were reported to have merged.

Leaders: Rosario IBARRA de la Piedra (1988 presidential candidate), Pedro PEÑALOZA (Coordinator).

Other minor formations include the **Revolutionary Socialist Party** (*Partido Revolucionario Socialista* — PRS), which was registered in 1985, and the **Social Democratic Party** (*Partido Social Demócrata* — PSD), which forfeited its registration in 1982.

Paramilitary Groups:

Although neither insurgency nor "death squads" present a serious problem in Mexico, some groups have been sporadically active. On the left, the **Army of the Poor** (*Ejercito de los Pobres* — EP), a remnant of the now largely defunct Poor People's Party (*Partido de los Pobres*), has been visible since the early 1970s. In July 1985, the EP briefly kidnapped PSUM leader Arnaldo Martínez Verdugo, demanding the "refund" of 5 million pesos allegedly entrusted to the PCM in 1974; following transfer of the desired funds, Martinez Verdugo was released. On the right, *Los Tecos,* based at the University of Guadalajara, has been relatively quiescent in recent years.

LEGISLATURE

The **National Congress** (*Congreso de la Unión*) consists of a Senate and a Chamber of Deputies, both elected by popular vote. Speakers in each chamber change monthly when Congress is in session. At other times, limited legislative functions are performed by a Permanent Committee of 14 senators and 15 deputies elected by their respective houses.

Senate (*Cámara de Senadores*). The upper chamber contains 64 members elected for six-year terms; among the electoral reforms enacted in November 1986 was a provision that the body will henceforth be elected by halves every three years. At the election of July 4, 1982, the Institutional Revolutionary Party won all 64 seats.

Chamber of Deputies (*Cámara de Diputados*). The lower chamber presently contains 400 members elected for three-year terms, including 100 seats reserved for minority opposition parties on the basis of proportional representation; in 1988, the number of deputies is to increase to 500, with a minimum of 150 seats reserved for opposition members. At the election of July 7, 1985, the Institutional Revolutionary Party won 289 of the directly contested seats, while the National Action Party won 9, and the Authentic Party of the Mexican Revolution, 2. The proportional distribution was as follows: National Action Party, 32; Mexican Democratic Party, 12; Unified Socialist Party of Mexico, 12; Workers' Socialist Party, 12; Popular Socialist Party, 11; Authentic Party of the Mexican Revolution, 7; Revolutionary Workers' Party 6; Mexican Workers' Party, 6.

CABINET

President	Miguel de la Madrid Hurtado
Secretaries	
Agrarian Reform	Rafael Rodríguez Barrera
Agriculture and Hydraulic Resources	Eduardo Pesqueira Olea
Commerce and Industrial Development	Héctor Hernández Cervantes
Communications and Transport	Daniel Díaz Díaz
Education	Miguel González Avelar
Energy, Mines and Parastatal Industry	Fernando Hiriart Balderrama
Finance and Public Credit	Gustavo Petricioli Iturbide
Fisheries	Pedro Ojeda Paullada

Foreign Relations	Bernardo Sepúlveda Amor
Government	Manuel Bartlett Díaz
Health and Public Assistance	Dr. Guillermo Soberón Acevedo
Labor and Social Welfare	Arsenio Farell Cubillas
National Defense	Gen. Juan Arévalo Gardoqui
Navy	Adm. Miguel Angel Gómez Ortega
Planning and Budget	Pedro Aspe Armella
Tourism	Antonio Enríquez Savignac
Urban Development and Ecology	Víctor Manuel Camacho Solís
Attorney General	Sergio García Ramírez
Comptroller General	Ignacio Pichardo Pagaza
Director General, Bank of Mexico	Miguel Mancera Aguayo

NEWS MEDIA

The press and broadcasting media are mainly privately owned but operate under government regulation.

Press. The print media have traditionally been subsidized, both directly and indirectly, by the government. In addition to deriving 60–80 percent of their advertising revenue from official sources, newspapers and magazines have commonly published, without attribution, materials prepared by public officials. Moreover, the low salaries paid reporters have reflected an understanding by management that incomes are typically supplemented by officeholders. In late 1982, however, the government introduced legislation making such payments to reporters a criminal offense, while substantially reducing official advertising. The most important dailies, published at Mexico City unless otherwise noted, are the following: *La Prensa* (298,000), liberal; *El Heraldo de México* (230,000), conservative; *Novedades* (190,000 daily, 205,000 Sunday), independent; *El Universal* (181,000 daily, 198,000 Sunday), center-left; *Excélsior* (175,000 daily, 195,000 Sunday), conservative; *El Sol de México* (110,000 morning and Sunday, 92,300 midday, 95,300 evening), government operated since 1972; *El Norte* (Monterrey, 100,000 daily, 108,000 Sunday); *Tribuna de Monterrey* (Monterrey, 95,000); *El Heraldo de Tampico* (Tampico, 95,000); *El Occidental* (Guadalajara, 85,000); *El Sol de Tampico* (Tampico, 75,000); *El Día* (75,000), organ of PRI left wing.

News agencies. Notimex (*Noticias Mexicanas*), Amex (*Agencia Mexicana de Noticias*), and Informex (*Informaciones Mexicanas*) are the three Mexican news agencies. A number of foreign agencies maintain bureaus at Mexico City.

Radio and television. Radio and television are privately owned and operate under the supervision of several governmental regulatory bodies, including the *Cámara Nacional de la Industria de Radio y Televisión*. In 1987 there were approximately 860 radio and 200 television broadcasting stations servicing approximately 25.5 million radio and 9.5 million television receivers.

INTERGOVERNMENTAL REPRESENTATION

Ambassador to the US: Jorge ESPINOSA DE LOS REYES.

US Ambassador to Mexico: Charles J. PILLIOD, Jr.

Permanent Representative to the UN: Mario MOYA Palencia.

IGO Memberships (Non-UN): ALADI, CCC, CDB, *CMEA*, Geplacea, IADB, ICAC, ICCO, ICO, IIC, ILZ, INRO, Intelsat, Interpol, ISO, IWC, OAS, OPANAL, PCA, SELA.

MONACO

Principality of Monaco
Principauté de Monaco

Political Status: Independent principality founded in 1338; constitutional monarchy since 1911; present constitution promulgated December 17, 1962.

Area: 0.70 sq. mi. (1.81 sq. km.).

Population: 27,063 (1982C), 30,300 (1988E).

Major Urban Center (1983E): MONACO-VILLE (1,960).

Official Language: French.

Monetary Unit: French Franc (market rate March 1, 1988, 5.72 francs = $1US). A limited supply of Monégasque currency circulates at par with the franc.

Sovereign: Prince RAINIER III; acceded to the throne November 18, 1949, following the death of his grandfather, Prince LOUIS II.

Heir Apparent: Prince ALBERT Alexandre Louis Pierre, son of the Sovereign.

Minister of State: Jean AUSSEIL; appointed by the Prince on September 10, 1985, to succeed Jean HERLY.

THE COUNTRY

A tiny but celebrated enclave on the Mediterranean coast nine miles from Nice, Monaco is surrounded on three sides by France. The Principality is divided into four districts: Monaco-Ville (the capital, built on a rocky promontory about 200 feet above sea level), Monte Carlo (the tourist quarter), La Condamine (the business district around the port), and Fontvieille (the industrial district). A majority of the citizenry is of foreign origin, primarily French, but indigenous Monégasques constitute approximately 15 percent of the population and speak their own language, a combination of French and Italian. Roman Catholicism is the state religion and French is the official language, although other European languages, in addition to Monégasque, are also spoken.

The Principality's main sources of revenue are tourism, its services as a financial center, corporate and indirect taxes, and the sale of tobacco and postage stamps. Gambling, despite the renown of the Monte Carlo Casino and the success of a new American-style casino at Loew's Monte Carlo, accounts for only four percent of the country's present income. Such light industrial products as plastics, processed foods, pharmaceuticals, glass, precision instruments, and cosmetics also yield revenue. Customs, postal services, telecommunications, and banking are governed by an economic union with France established in 1956. A Franco-Monégasque convention of administrative assistance concluded in 1963 brought under French fiscal authority many Monaco-based French companies that the 1956 customs union had virtually freed from taxation.

GOVERNMENT AND POLITICS

Political background. Ruled by the Grimaldi family since the thirteenth century, the Principality of Monaco has maintained its separate identity in close association with France, under whose protection it was placed in 1861.

A 1918 treaty stipulates that Monégasque policy must be in complete conformity with French political, military, naval, and economic interests; a further treaty of July 17, 1919, provides for Monaco's incorporation into France should the reigning prince die without leaving a male heir.

Monaco's dependence on French-controlled services was further emphasized by a dispute which arose in 1962 over the Principality's status as a tax refuge under the 1918 treaty. Various pressures, including the setting up of a customs barrier, were invoked by France before a compromise in 1963 paved the way for the signature of new conventions redefining the French-Monégasque relationship. Subsequently, Prince RAINIER III embarked on a three-year struggle with shipping magnate Aristotle S. Onassis for control of the *Société des Bains de Mer* (SBM), a corporation that owns the Monte Carlo Casino, main hotels, clubs, restaurants, and considerable Monégasque real estate. Monaco gained control of the company in 1967 by buying out Onassis' majority shareholdings.

World attention focused briefly on the Principality in 1982, following the death of Princess GRACE (the former American actress, Grace Kelly) on September 13 as the result of an automobile accident in the Côte d'Azur region the day before. Subsequently, the passing of the princess was viewed as representing a fiscal as well as personal loss for Monégasques, whose economy, based in large part on tourism, had recently stagnated, with income from both real estate and gambling receding sharply over previous years.

Constitution and government. The constitution of December 17, 1962, replacing one of 1911, vests executive power in the hereditary prince, grants universal suffrage, outlaws capital punishment, and guarantees the rights of association and trade-unionism. The prince rules in conjunction with an appointed minister of state, who must be acceptable to the French government and who is assisted by government councillors and palace personnel, all appointed by the prince. Legislative power is shared by the prince with an 18-member National Council (*Conseil National*) elected by universal suffrage for a five-year term. Municipal affairs in the four *quartiers* are conducted by a 16-member elected Communal Council (*Conseil Communal*) headed by the mayor of Monaco-Ville. The judiciary includes a Supreme Tribunal (*Tribunal Suprême*) of 7 members named by the prince on the basis of nominations by the National Council; courts of cassation, appeal, and first instance; and a justice of the peace.

Foreign relations. Monaco's foreign relations are controlled by Paris. Although the Principality participates indirectly in the European Economic Community (EEC) by virtue of its customs union with France, it remains legally outside the EEC because of its refusal to sign the Treaty of Rome in order to protect its status as a tax haven. Though not a member of the United Nations, it maintains a Permanent Observer's office at UN headquarters in New York and belongs to several UN Specialized Agencies.

Current issues. In recent years, Monaco has witnessed little overt political activity, most official attention focusing on alternatives to its traditional economic dependence on foreign business enterprise and tourism. Concerted land reclamation efforts during the last two decades have suc-

ceeded in expanding the Principality's total area by more than 20 percent, with some of the new acreage sold for private development consistent with the government's urban master plan.

POLITICAL PARTIES

For some years Monaco has been essentially a one-party state dominated by the **National and Democratic Union** (*Union Nationale et Démocratique* — UND). The UND, formed in 1962 through the merger of the National Union of Independents (*Union Nationale des Indépendants*) and the National Democratic Entente (*Entente Nationale Démocratique*), won all 18 National Council seats in the elections of 1968, 1978, 1983, and 1988. The **Monaco Socialist Party** (*Parti Socialist Monégasque*), the only opposition formation to contest recent elections, has limited political influence.

LEGISLATURE

The **National Council** (*Conseil National*) is a unicameral, 18-member body elected for a five-year term. At the most recent election of January 24, 1988, the National and Democratic Union won all 18 seats.

President: Jean-Charles REY.

CABINET

Minister of State	Jean Ausseil
Councillors	
Finance and Economics	Raoul Biancheri
Interior	Michel Eon
Public Works and Social Affairs	Bernard Fautrier

NEWS MEDIA

Press. The Principality publishes an official weekly journal, *Journal de Monaco,* which contains texts of laws and decrees. French newspapers are widely read, and special "Monaco editions" of *Nice-Matin* and *L'Espoir de Nice* are published at Nice, France.

News agency. The domestic facility, *Agence Télégraphique,* is operated by *Agence France-Presse.*

Radio and television. Radio and television broadcasting is government operated, but time is sold to commercial sponsors. *Radio Monte Carlo* (RMC), in which the French government has a controlling financial interest, broadcasts in French, Italian, and various other languages. Trans World Radio, which is maintained by voluntary subscriptions and operates in conjunction with RMC, broadcasts religious programs in many languages. *Télé Monte Carlo* has been broadcasting since 1954. There were approximately 10,000 radio and 17,600 television receivers in 1987.

INTERGOVERNMENTAL REPRESENTATION

Monaco maintains consuls general at Washington and New York, while the US consul general at Nice, France, also services American interests in Monaco.

Permanent Observer to the UN: John DUBE.

IGO Memberships (Non-UN): ACCT, Intelsat, Interpol, IWC.

MONGOLIA

Mongolian People's Republic
Bügd Nayramdah Mongol Ard Uls

Political Status: Independent since 1921; Communist People's Republic established November 26, 1924.

Area: 604,247 sq. mi. (1,565,000 sq. km.).

Population: 1,594,800 (1979C), 2,016,000 (1988E).

Major Urban Centers (1986E): ULAN BATOR (500,200); Darhan (74,000).

Monetary Unit: Tugrik (basic rate March 1, 1988, 2.84 tugriks = $1US).

Official Language: Khalkha Mongol.

Chairman of the Presidium of the People's Great Hural and General Secretary of the Mongolian People's Revolutionary Party: Jambyn BATMÖNH (Dzhambin BATMUNKH); served as Chairman of the Council of Ministers from June 11, 1974 to December 12, 1984; named General Secretary of the MPRP following the retirement of Yumjaagiyn TSEDENBAL from the post, as well as from the Presidium chairmanship (which remained temporarily vacant), on August 23, 1984; reelected on May 31, 1986; elected Chairman of the Presidium by the People's Great Hural on December 12, 1984; reelected on July 1, 1986.

Chairman of the Council of Ministers (Premier): Dumaagiyn SODNOM; elected by the People's Great Hural on December 12, 1984, succeeding Jambyn BATMÖNH; reelected on July 1, 1986.

THE COUNTRY

Traditionally known as Outer Mongolia (i.e., that portion of historic Mongolia lying north of the Gobi Desert), the Mongolian People's Republic occupies a vast area of steppe, mountain, and desert between the Soviet Union on the north and the People's Republic of China on the south. Khalkha Mongols make up 76 percent of the population, and other Mongol groups (often speaking their own dialects) compose at least another 13 percent. The remainder are Turkic-speaking peoples (7 percent) and Chinese, Russian, and Tungusic minorities (4 percent). The state restricts religious functions, although freedom of religion is constitutionally guaranteed. Lamaist Buddhism is the most prevalent faith, but its leadership was largely wiped out in the antireligious activity of 1937–1939.

The Mongolian economy traditionally has been pastoral, and animal husbandry, now largely collectivized, continues to supply the majority of economic output and exports. In recent years there has been an emphasis on diversification and more rapid development, although a late start and a lack of basic skills have made the country heavily dependent on aid from the Soviet Union and other Communist countries. A major economic complex is the Industrial Combine of Ulan Bator, which produces a wide variety of consumer products, while in late 1978 one of the world's ten largest copper-molybdenum facilities—the biggest single development project in the country's history—began operating at the largely Soviet-built complex at Erdenet.

GOVERNMENT AND POLITICS

Political background. The home of such legendary figures as Genghis Khan and Tamerlane, Mongolia fell under Chinese control in the seventeenth century and continued under Chinese suzerainty for over 200 years. The fall of the Manchu dynasty resulted in a brief period of independence from 1911 to 1919, when Chinese hegemony was reestablished. Two years later, Mongolian revolutionary leaders Sukhe BATOR and Khorloin CHOIBALSAN defeated the Chinese with Soviet assistance and established permanent independence. Initially, a constitutional monarchy was created under Jebtsun Damba KHUTUKHTU, but following his death in 1924 the Mongolian People's Party (founded in 1921) was restyled as the Mongolian People's Revolutionary Party (MPRP) and the Mongolian People's Republic (MPR) was proclaimed as the first Communist state outside the Soviet Union. Rightist influences, including a major revolt in 1932, were suppressed and Choibalsan gained the ascendancy in 1934–1939, continuing to dominate both party and government until his death in 1952.

Yumjaagiyn TSEDENBAL was named chairman of the Council of Ministers in January 1952 and, after a two-year period of apparent political eclipse, succeeded Dashiyn DAMBA as MPRP first secretary in November 1958. His accession in 1974 to the chairmanship of the Presidium of the People's Great Hural (while retaining the party leadership) followed a pattern established by other Communist leaders, such as Tito, Ceauşescu, and Kim Il Sung, but occurred two years after the death of Chairman Jamsrangiyn SAMBUU. In the interval, Tsagaanlamyn DÜGERSÜREN and, subsequently, Sonomyn LUVSAN had served as acting Presidium chairmen.

On August 23, 1984, Tsedenbal was relieved of his government and party posts, reportedly because of failing health. Concurrently, Jambyn BATMÖNH was named MPRP secretary general and, upon designation as Presidium chairman on December 12, relinquished the chairmanship of the Council of Ministers to Dumaagiyn SODNOM. Both were reconfirmed on July 1, 1986, following the Nineteenth MPRP Congress on May 28–31.

Constitution and government. The constitution adopted in 1960 leaves intact the guiding role of the Communist MPRP, whose highly centralized leadership also dominates the state administration. According to the constitution, the supreme organ of government is the national legislature, or People's Great Hural, elected (as of 1981) for a five-year term by universal adult suffrage. In practice, the Hural meets briefly once a year to approve measures submitted by the Council of Ministers, the main executive organ and locus of power within the government. The Presidium of the Hural represents the legislature between sessions, and its chairman serves as head of state. The judicial system is under the supervision of the procurator of the Republic and the Supreme Court, with both the procurator and the Court elected by and responsible to the Hural and its Presidium. Regional and local courts are elected by provincial and local hurals.

The Republic is divided into 18 provinces (*aimak*) plus the city of Ulan Bator; provinces are divided into counties (*somon*), and Ulan Bator and other cities are divided into districts (*khoron*). Provincial and local governments parallel that of the central government and, as at the national level, are dominated by party organizations.

Foreign relations. Although Mongolia attempted to take a neutral stance in the early period of the Sino-Soviet dispute, it subsequently aligned itself with the Soviet Union, in part because of an inherited fear of Chinese hegemony and in part because of a dependence on Soviet military, economic, and cultural assistance. A member of the United Nations since 1961, it became a full member of the Council for Mutual Economic Assistance (CMEA) in 1962 and signed a treaty of friendship and mutual assistance with the USSR in 1966. While diplomatic relations have been established with approximately 100 Communist and non-Communist nations, they did not, until early 1987, include formal contact with the United States.

In 1981, Mongolia urged the conclusion of a regional nonaggression pact intended to curb China's allegedly expansionist impulses and continued its attacks on "hegemonism" in East Asia through the first half of 1985. On the other hand, cross-border trade with the PRC more than doubled during the year, while, in the first such encounter since 1960, the Mongolian foreign minister met with his Chinese counterpart during the UN's 40th anniversary celebration at New York in October. The thaw continued in 1986, with the two countries concluding a five-year trade agreement in April, agreeing in June (after a lapse of 19 years) to a restoration of air services between their capitals, and, in August, signing their first consular treaty since 1949.

Current issues. The major events of 1987 were an agreement to establish diplomatic relations with the United States, the withdrawal of approximately 15,000 Soviet troops (about one-quarter of the total), and improved relations with China. The accord with Washington, which both parties had sought for more than two decades, had not materialized earlier because of Soviet opposition and a US unwillingness to offend the Nationalist government on Taiwan, which had consistently maintained that Mongolia was a Chinese province. The agreement was not expected to yield an actual exchange of ambassadors for several years because of logistical and other problems associated with the establishment of a mission at Ulan Bator.

The enhanced contacts with Beijing included two protocols calling for a four-fold increase in trade, in addition to a renewal, after a 20-year lapse, of scientific and technological cooperation. Of considerable symbolic importance was a mid-year visit to Mongolia of a delegation from the PRC National People's Congress, during which invitations were extended to a number of leading Mongolian officials to visit China.

POLITICAL PARTIES

Mongolian People's Revolutionary Party — MPRP (*Mongol Ardyn Khuv'sgalt Nam*). The MPRP, Mongolia's only political party, is organized along typical Communist lines. Its tightly centralized structure features party congresses that meet at five-year intervals, most recently on May 28–31, 1986; an elected Central Committee that meets each June and December; and a Politburo and Secretariat that are the main policy-making bodies. It was reported at the 1986 congress that party membership totaled 88,150.

General Secretary: Jambyn BATMÖNH.

Other Members of Politburo: Bat-Ochirin ALTANGEREL (Chairman, People's Great Hural), Col. Gen. Bujyn DEJID (member, Secretariat), Demchigavyn MOLOMJAMTS (member, Secretariat), Tserendashiyn NAMSRAY (member, Secretariat), Bansragchiyn LAMZAV (Chairman, Party Control Commission), Dumaagiyn SODNOM (Chairman, Council of Ministers).

Candidate Members: Paabangiyn DAMDIN, Nyamyn JAGVARAL, Sonomyn LUVSANGOMBO.

Central Committee Secretariat: Tserenpilyn BALHAAJAV, Jambyn BATMÖNH, Paavangiyn DAMDIN, Bujyn DEJID, Demchigavyn MOLOMJAMTS, Tserendashiyn NAMSRAY.

LEGISLATURE

The **People's Great Hural** is a unicameral body currently consisting of 370 members elected for five-year terms. All members are affiliated with or approved by the ruling Mongolian People's Revolutionary Party, although some two dozen represent a "nonparty" bloc. The last election was held on June 22, 1986.

Chairman: Lodongiyn RINCHIN.

CABINET

Chairman, Council of Ministers	Dumaagiyn Sodnom
Deputy Chairmen	Bat-Ochiriyn Altangeral
	Paavangiyn Damdin
	Sharavyn Gungaadorj
	Puntsagiyn Jasray
	Sonomyn Luvsangombo
	Myatavyn Peljee
	Choynoryn Süren
Ministers	
Agriculture, Livestock Breeding and Food Industry	Sharavyn Gungaadorj
Communications	Irvüdziyn Norobjab
Culture	Budyn Sumyaa
Defense	Jamsrangiyn Yondon
External Economic Relations and Supply	Punsalmaagiyn Ochirbat
Finance	Demchigjavyn Molomjamts
Foreign Affairs	Mangalyn Dügersüren
Health	Choyjilavyn Tserennadmid
Justice	Origiyn Jambaldorj
Light Industry	Choynoryn Süren
Natural Environmental Protection	Uthany Mavlyet
People's Education	Byambyn Dabaasüren
Power, Mining and Geological Industry	Sodovyn Buthuyag

Public Security	Lt. Gen. Agvaanjantsangiyn Jamsranjav
Social Economy and Services	Tumengiyn Demchigdorj
Trade and Procurement	Badrachyn Sharavsambuu
Transportation	D. Yondonsüren
Water Management	Dzunduyn Janjaadorj
Without Portfolio	Oldziyhutagiyn Ganhuyag
	Tomoriyn Namjim

Commission Chairmen

State Construction	Sonomyn Lubsangombo
State Planning	Puntsagiyn Jasray

Committee Chairmen

General Committee of State Bank	Gochoogiya Hüderchuluun
People's Control Committee	Chuvaandorjiyn Molom
State Committee for Agriculture and Food Supply	Tümenbayaryn Ragchaa
State Committee for Information, Radio and Television	Lhagvajabyn Dzantav
State Committee for Physical Culture and Sports	Davaagiyn Dashdovdon
State Committee for Science, Technology and Higher Education	Monhdorjiyn Dash
Chairman, State Bank Board of Directors	Gochoogiyn Huderchuluun
President, Academy of Sciences	Choydogiyn Tseren

NEWS MEDIA

Press. The following are published at Ulan Bator: *Pionyeriyn Ünen* (Pioneers' Truth 175,000), publication of the Youth League; *Ünen* (Truth 170,000), organ of the Central Committee of the MPRP; *Shine Hödöö* (New Countryside), published weekly by the Ministry of Agriculture; *Hödölmör* (Labor), twice-weekly organ of the Central Council of Trade Unions; *Ulaan Od* (Red Star), twice-weekly publication of the Ministry of Defense; *Utga Dzohiol Urlag* (Literature and Art), weekly organ of the Writers' Union.

News agencies. The Mongolian Telegraph Agency (*Mongol Tsahilgaan Medeeniy Agentlag*—Montsame) is the government-operated facility at Ulan Bator; TASS, *Novosti,* and East Germany's ADN are represented at the capital.

Radio and television. Ulan Bator Radio is a government service, broadcasting in Mongolian, Russian, Chinese, English, French, and Kazakh. The principal television station, at Ulan Bator, transmits both locally produced programs and Soviet programs received via satellite. There were approximately 180,000 radio and 60,000 television receivers in 1987.

INTERGOVERNMENTAL REPRESENTATION

The United States and the Mongolian People's Republic established diplomatic relations on January 27, 1987, but had not exchanged ambassadors as of mid-1988.

Permanent Representative to the UN: Gendengiin NYAMDOO.

IGO Memberships (Non-UN): CMEA, IBEC.

MOROCCO

Kingdom of Morocco
al-Mamlakah al-Maghribiyah

Political Status: Independent since March 2, 1956; constitutional monarchy established in 1962; present constitution approved March 1, 1972.

Area: 269,756 sq. mi. (698,670 sq. km.), including approximately 97,343 sq. mi. (252,120 sq. km.) of Western Sahara, two-thirds of which was annexed in February 1976 and the remaining one-third claimed upon Mauritanian withdrawal in August 1979.

Population: 20,449,551 (1982C); 24,393,000 (1988E), exclusive of nearly 200,000 Western Saharan refugees in neighboring countries (primarily Algeria).

Major Urban Centers (urban areas, 1981E): RABAT (842,000); Casablanca (2,409,000); Fez (562,000); Marrakesh (549,300); Meknès (487,000).

Official Language: Arabic.

Monetary Unit: Dirham (market rate March 1, 1988, 8.06 dirhams = $1US).

Sovereign: King HASSAN II; became King on March 3, 1961, succeeding his father, MOHAMED V.

Heir to the Throne: Crown Prince SIDI MOHAMED, son of the King.

Prime Minister: Dr. Azzedine LARAKI; appointed by the King on September 30, 1986, following the resignation of Mohamed Karim LAMRANI.

THE COUNTRY

Located at the northwest corner of Africa, Morocco combines a long Atlantic coastline and Mediterranean frontage facing Gibraltar and southern Spain. Bounded by Algeria on the northeast and (following annexation of the former Spanish Sahara) by Mauritania on the south, the country is topographically divided into a rich agricultural plain in the northwest and an infertile mountain and plateau region in the east that gradually falls into the Sahara Desert in the south and southwest. The population is approximately two-thirds Arab and one-third Berber, with small French and Spanish minorities. Islam is the state religion, most of the population adhering to the Sunni sect. Arabic is the language of the majority, with most others speaking one or more dialects of Berber; Spanish is common in the northern regions and French among the educated elite. Women comprise only 16 percent of the paid labor force, concentrated mainly in textile manufacture and domestic service; overall, one-third of the female population is described as engaged in "unpaid family labor" on agricultural estates. While an increasing number of women from upper-income brackets are participating in local and national elections, they have thus far obtained only minimal representation.

The agricultural sector employs approximately half of the population; important crops include cereals and grains, oilseeds, nuts, and citrus fruits. The world's leading exporter of phosphates, Morocco also has important deposits of lead, iron, cobalt, zinc, manganese, and silver. The industrial sector, including energy, mining, and manufacturing, emphasizes import substitution (textiles, chemicals, cement, plastics, machinery) but also accounts for about 30 percent of exports. Trade is strongly oriented towards France, whose economic influence has remained substantial. In recent years the economy has suffered from drought, declining world demand for phosphates, and the drain of fighting an 11-year-old war in the Western Sahara. Budget austerity and the privatization of inefficient state-run enterprises have yielded assistance from the International Monetary Fund and rescheduling of the country's $13 billion external debt. Nonetheless, living conditions remain low by regional standards.

GOVERNMENT AND POLITICS

Political background. Originally inhabited by Berbers, Morocco was successively conquered by the Phoenicians, Carthaginians, Romans, Byzantines, and Arabs. From 1912 to 1956 the country was subjected to de facto French and Spanish control, but the internal authority of the sultan was nominally respected. Under pressure by Moroccan nationalists, the French and Spanish relinquished their protectorates and the country was reunified under Sultan MOHAMED V in 1956. Tangier, which had been under international administration since 1923, was ceded by Spain in 1969.

King Mohamed V tried to convert the hereditary sultanate into a modern constitutional monarchy but died before the process was complete. It remained for his son, King HASSAN II, to implement his father's goal in a constitution adopted in December 1962. However, dissatisfaction with economic conditions and the social policy of the regime led to rioting at Casablanca in March 1965, and three months later the king assumed legislative and executive powers.

In June 1967 the king relinquished the post of prime minister, but the continued hostility of student and other elements led to frequent governmental changes. A new constitution, approved in July 1970, provided for a partial resumption of parliamentary government, a strengthening of royal powers, and a limited role for political parties. Despite the opposition of major political groups, trade unions, and student organizations, an election for a new unicameral Chamber of Representatives was held in August 1970, yielding a progovernment majority.

The king's failure to unify the country behind his programs was dramatically illustrated by abortive military revolts in 1971 and 1972. Senior officers of the Moroccan army were deeply implicated in an attack by 1,400 cadets on the royal palace of Skhirat while the king was celebrating his 42nd birthday in July 1971. A second assassination attempt in August 1972 was led by air force officers under the apparent guidance of Gen. Mohamed OUFKIR, the defense minister, who had gained a reputation as the king's most loyal supporter.

The present constitution was overwhelmingly approved by popular referendum in March 1972, but the parties refused to enter the government because of the king's reluctance to schedule legislative elections. After numerous delays, elections to communal and municipal councils were finally held in November 1976, to provincial and prefec-

tural assemblies in January 1977, and to a reconstituted national Chamber of Representatives in June 1977. On October 10 the leading parties agreed to participate in a "National Unity" cabinet headed by Ahmed OSMAN as prime minister.

Osman resigned on March 21, 1979, ostensibly to oversee reorganization of the proroyalist National Assembly of Independents (RNI), although the move was reported to have been precipitated by his handling of the lengthy dispute over the Western Sahara (see below). He was succeeded on March 22 by Maati BOUABID, a respected Casablanca attorney who had been disavowed by his party, the National Union of Popular Forces, for accepting appointment as minister of justice under Osman in 1977.

On May 30, 1980, a constitutional amendment extending the term of the Chamber of Representatives from four to six years was approved by referendum, thus postponing new elections until 1983. Subsequently, economic pressures increased because of declining phosphate revenues, while austerity measures mandated by the International Monetary Fund (IMF) in exchange for $1 billion in standby credit provoked numerous demonstrations and riots at Casablanca in June 1981.

Despite improvement in the security situation, the king indicated in June 1983 that legislatve balloting, scheduled for early September, would be further postponed pending the results of an OAU-sponsored referendum in the Western Sahara. On November 30, a new "unity" cabinet headed by Mohamed Karim LAMRANI was announced, with Bouabid, who had organized a new moderate party eight months earlier, joining other party leaders in accepting appointment as ministers of state without portfolio.

The long-awaited balloting for a new Chamber was finally held on September 14 and October 2, 1984, with Bouabid's Constitutional Union winning a plurality of both direct and indirectly elected seats, while four centrist parties collectively obtained a better than 2–1 majority. Following lengthy negotiations, a new coalition government, headed by Lamrani, was formed on April 11, 1985. On September 30, 1986, King Hassan appointed Dr. Azzedine LARAKI, former national education minister, as prime minister, following Lamrani's resignation for health reasons.

Constitution and government. Morocco is a constitutional monarchy, the Crown being hereditary and normally transmitted to the king's eldest son, who acts on the advice of a Regency Council if he accedes before the age of 20. Political power is highly centralized in the hands of the king, who serves as commander in chief, appoints the prime minister, and presides over the cabinet; in addition, he can declare a state of emergency, dissolve the legislature, and initiate constitutional amendments. Legislative power is nominally vested in a unicameral Chamber of Representatives, one-third of whose members are indirectly designated by an electoral college. The judicial system is headed by a Supreme Court (*Majlis al-Aala*) and includes courts of appeal, regional tribunals, magistrates' courts, labor tribunals, and a special court to deal with corruption. All judges are appointed by the king on the advice of the Supreme Council of the Judiciary.

The country is currently divided into 45 provinces and prefectures (including 4 provinces in Western Sahara), with

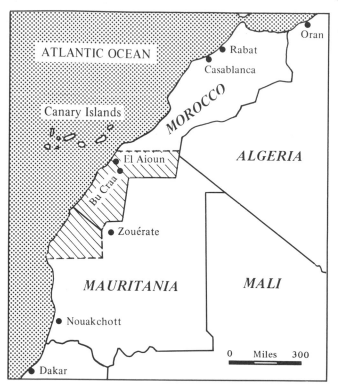

further division into administrative areas and communes. The king appoints all provincial governors, who are responsible to him.

Foreign relations. A member of the United Nations and the Arab League, Morocco has been chosen on many occasions as a site for Arab and African Islamic conferences at all levels. It has generally adhered to a nonaligned policy combining good relations with the West with support for African and especially Arab nationalism. In late 1984, however, it withdrew from the Organization for African Unity (OAU) in protest at the seating of an SADR delegation (see Annexed Territory, below). Save for some deterioration in the 1960s as a result of incidents involving French and Moroccan security services, relations with France have been cordial. Relations with the United States have also been friendly, US administrations viewing Morocco as a conservative counter to northern Africa's more radical regimes. Thus, an agreement was signed in mid-1982 that sanctioned, subjected to veto, the use of Moroccan air bases by US forces in emergency situations. Periodic joint military exercises have since been conducted, with Washington serving as a prime supplier of equipment for Rabat's campaign in the Western Sahara.

Morocco's role in regional affairs has been complicated by a variety of issues. Relations with Algeria and Mauritania have been marred by territorial disputes (until 1970, Morocco claimed all of Mauritania's territory). The early 1970s brought cooperation with the two neighboring states in an effort to present a unified front against the retention by Spain of phosphate-rich Spanish Sahara, but by 1975 Morocco and Mauritania were ranged against Algeria on the issue. An agreement reached at Madrid on November 14, 1975, excluded Algeria from the territory, and Morocco and Mauritania proceeded to occupy their assigned sectors (see map) on February 28, 1976, despite resistance from

the Polisario Front, an Algerian-backed group which had proclaimed the establishment of an independent Saharan Arab Democratic Republic (SADR). Following Mauritanian renunciation of all claims to the territory in a peace accord with Polisario on August 5, 1979, Moroccan forces entered the southern sector, claiming it, too, as a Moroccan province (see Annexed Territory, below). Relations with Algeria, although still stressed by the Saharan problem, were formally resumed in May 1988 prior to an Arab summit at Algiers on the uprising in the Israeli-occupied territories.

Traditionally strained ties with Libya (which had been accused of complicity in several plots to overthrow the monarchy) began to improve with a state visit by Qadhafi to Rabat in mid-1983. The process of rapprochement culminated in a treaty of projected union signed by the two leaders at Oujda on August 13, 1984. Described by Hassan as a vehicle for "limited cooperation and consultation", the pact seemed designed mainly to ensure withdrawal of Tripoli's support for guerrillas in the Western Sahara. An inaugural meeting of a joint parliamentary assembly was held at Rabat in July 1985 and commissions were set up to discuss political, military, economic, cultural, and technical cooperation. However, King Hassan abruptly cancelled the treaty in August 1986 after Qadhafi had denounced a July meeting with Israeli prime minister Shimon Peres.

Current issues. At the instigation of King Fahd of Saudi Arabia, King Hassan met with President Chadli of Algeria in May 1987 to seek a resolution of the Western Saharan conflict, which has long inhibited economic cooperation among regional Arab leaders. Although some observers felt "a glimmer of rapprochement" emerged from the meeting, Polisario, possibly concerned over a possible loss of negotiating leverage, stepped up its military attacks. However, the guerrillas were denied access to the coast, where they had previously attacked vessels working the rich fishing grounds, upon completion of a sixth sand wall by the Moroccan army. The wall forced Polisario soldiers to redeploy into Mauritania amid expressions of concern by the latter of being drawn back into the war.

Rabat's military position was also strengthened by a new weapons supply accord with Washington that included 100 new tanks, although the war's estimated daily cost of $1.5 million continued to limit domestic development. Morocco was admitted as a full contracting partner to the General Agreement on Tariffs and Trade (GATT), while its request for membership in the European Communities was politely rebuffed on geographic grounds. Internally, opposition to the government was muted in 1987, in contrast to the two previous years when numerous left-wing radicals and Islamic fundamentalists were arrested in a government crackdown that drew charges from Amnesty International of illegal detention and abuse of political prisoners.

POLITICAL PARTIES

Government Parties:

Constitutional Union (*Union Constitutionelle* — UC). Founded in 1983 by Maati Bouabid, the UC is a moderate party that emphasizes economic self-sufficiency. Said to have royal support, the party enjoyed surprising success in the municipal balloting of June 1983, and won a plurality of 56 directly elected seats in the September 1984 legislative election.

Leader: Maati BOUABID (former Prime Minister).

National Assembly of Independents (*Rassemblement National des Indépendants* – RNI). The RNI was launched at a Constitutive Congress held October 6–9, 1978. Although branded by left-wing spokesmen as a "King's party", it claimed to hold the allegiance of 141 of 264 deputies in the 1977 Chamber. Subsequent defections and other disagreements, both internal and with the king, resulted in the party's designation as the "official" opposition in late 1981. It won 39 directly elected seats in 1984.

Leader: Ahmed OSMAN (President of the Party and of the Chamber of Representatives).

Popular Movement (*Mouvement Populaire* – MP). Organized in 1957 as a monarchist party of Berber mountaineers, the MP was a major participant in government coalitions of the early 1960s. Since 1965, it has been weakened by feuding within the leadership. It secured the second-largest number of legislative seats at the election of June 1977 and was third-ranked after the September 1984 balloting. In October 1986, an extraordinary party congress voted to remove the MP's founder, Mahjoubi AHARDANA from the post of secretary general and transfer his responsibilities to an eight-member secretariat.

Leader: Abdelkrim KHATIB.

National Democratic Party (*Parti National Démocratique* – PND). The PND was founded as the Democratic Independents (*Indépendants Démocrates* – ID) in April 1981 by 59 former RNI deputies in the Chamber of Representatives. Five of its members were included in the government subsequently formed on November 5. At the party's first congress on June 11–13, 1982, its secretary general, Mohamed Arsalane al-Jadidi, affirmed the PND's loyalty to the monarchy while castigating the RNI for not providing an effective counterweight to the "old" parties.

Leaders: Abdelhamid KACEMI, Mohamed Arsalane al-JADIDI (Secretary General).

Other Groups:

Independence Party (*Istiqlal*). Founded in 1943, *Istiqlal* provided most of the nation's leadership before independence. It split in 1959 and its members were relieved of governmental responsibilities in 1963. Once a firm supporter of the throne, the party now displays a reformist attitude and supports the king only on selected issues. It stresses the need for better standards of living and equal rights for all Moroccans. In July 1970 it formed a National Front with the National Union of Popular Forces (below) but ran alone in the election of June 1977, when it emerged as the (then) leading party. *Istiqlal* suffered heavy losses in both the 1983 municipal elections and the 1984 legislative balloting.

Leader: Mohamed BOUCETTA (Secretary General).

National Union of Popular Forces (*Union Nationale des Forces Populaires* – UNFP). Formed in 1959 by a group of former *Istiqlal* adherents, the UNFP subsequently became a coalition of left-wing nationalists, trade-unionists, resistance fighters, and dissident members of minor parties. Weakened by internal factionalism, government repression, the disappearance of its leader Mehdi Ben Barka (while visiting France in 1965), and the neutrality of the Moroccan Labor Union (UMT), the party subsequently split into personal factions. In 1972 the National Administrative Commitee suspended the ten-man Secretariat General and the three-man Political Bureau and replaced them with a collection of five permanent committees. The Political Bureau thereupon formed its own organization, UNFP–Rabat Section, which was banned for several months in 1973 for activities against the state and subsequently reorganized as the USFP (below). The UNFP formally boycotted the legislative elections of 1977 and 1984, as well as the municipal balloting of June 1983.

Leader: Moulay Abdallah IBRAHIM.

Socialist Union of Popular Forces (*Union Socialiste des Forces Populaires* – USFP). The USFP was organized in September 1974 by the UNFP–Rabat Section, which had disassociated itself from the Casablanca Section in July 1972 and was accused by the government of involvement in a Libyan-aided plot to overthrow King Hassan in March 1973. The USFP has called for nationalization of major industries and for thorough reform of the nation's social and administrative structures. It secured the third-largest number of legislative seats at the election of June 1977 but withdrew from the Chamber in October 1981 in protest at the extension of the parliamentary term. A year later it announced that it would return

for the duration of the session ending in May 1983 so that it could participate in the forthcoming electoral campaigns. The majority of nearly 100 political prisoners released during July-August 1980 were USFP members, most of whom had been incarcerated for alleged antigovernment activities in 1973–1977. The USFP doubled its directly elected representation in the September 1984 election while being awarded only one indirectly elected seat. It refused to participate in the coalition government formed in April 1985, charging lack of official effort in regard to economic reform.

Leader: Abderrahim BOUABID (First Secretary).

Constitutional and Democratic Popular Movement (*Mouvement Populaire Constitutionnel et Démocratique* – MPCD). The MPCD (also rendered as *Mouvement Populaire Démocratique et Constitutionnel* – MPDC) is a splinter from the Popular Movement. It won 3 legislative seats in 1977, none in 1984.

Leader: 'Abd al-Karim KHATIB.

Party of Progress and Socialism (*Parti du Progrès et du Socialism* – PPS). Formed in 1968 to replace the banned Moroccan Communist Party, the PPS obtained legal status in 1974. Its single representative in the 1977 chamber, 'Ali Yata, was the first Communist to win election to a Moroccan legislature. The party gained an additional seat in 1984.

Leader: 'Ali YATA (Secretary General).

Organization for Democratic and Popular Action (*Organisation de l'Action Démocratique et Populaire* – OADP). Claiming a following of former members of the USFP and PPS, the OADP was organized in May 1983. It obtained one directly elected seat in the September 1984 balloting.

Leader: Mohamed BENSAID.

Party of Action (*Parti de l'Action* – PA). The PA was organized in December 1974 by a group of Berber intellectuals dedicated to the "construction of a new society through a new elite". It won 2 legislative seats in 1977, none in 1984.

Leader: Abdallah SENHAJI (Secretary General).

Other groups participating in the 1984 Chamber balloting included the **Moroccan Labor Union** (*Union Marocaine du Travail* – UMT), the **Democratic Confederation of Labor** (*Confédération Démocratique du Travail* – CDT), the **General Union of Moroccan Workers** (*Union Générale des Travailleurs Marocains* – UGTM), the **Social Center Party** (*Parti du Centre Social* – PCS), the **Democratic Party of Independence** (*Parti Démocratique de l'Indépendance* – PDI), and the **Party of National Union and Solidarity** (*Parti de l'Union et de la Solidarité Nationale* – PUSN).

The left-wing radicals arrested in 1985 and 1986 appeared to belong primarily to two clandestine groups: *Il al-Amam* (To the Future), formed in the 1960s by a number of PPS Maoist dissidents, and *Qa'idiyyin* (The Base), an outgrowth of a *23 Mars* group of the 1970s, most of whose members entered the OADP.

LEGISLATURE

Approximately two-thirds of the membership of the unicameral **Chamber of Representatives** (*Majlis al-Nuwab*) is elected by direct universal suffrage, the remainder by an electoral college of government, professional, and labor representatives. The most recent direct election, for 206 seats, was held on September 14, 1984. Following balloting on October 2 for 100 indirectly elected members, the distribution by party (direct election results in parentheses) was as follows: Constitutional Union, 83 (56); National Assembly of Independents, 61 (39); Popular Movement, 47 (31); *Istiqlal*, 41 (24); Socialist Union of Popular Forces, 36 (35); National Democratic Party, 24 (15); Moroccan Labor Union, 5 (0); Democratic Confederation of Labor, 3 (0); General Union of Moroccan Workers 2 (2); Party of Progress and Socialism, 2 (2); Organization for Democratic and Popular Action, 1 (1); Social Center Party, 1 (1).

President: Ahmed OSMAN.

CABINET

Prime Minister	Dr. Azzedine Laraki

Ministers of State

EEC Affairs	Mohamed Sequat
Without Portfolio	Moulay Ahmed Alaoui
	Mohamed Bahnini

Ministers

Agriculture and Agrarian Reform	Othman Demnati
Commerce and Industry	Abdullah al-Azmani
Cultural Affairs	Mohamed Benaissa
Energy and Mines	Mohamed Fettah
Equipment and Cadre Training	Mohamed Kabbaj
Finance	Mohamed Berrada
Foreign Affairs and Cooperation	Abdellatif Filali
Handicraft and Social Affairs	Mohamed Labied
Housing and Land Management	Abderrahmane Boufettas
Interior and Information	Driss Basri
Islamic Affairs	Abdelkebir Alaoui M'Dghari
Justice	Moulay Mustapha Belarbi Alaoui
Labor	Hassan Abbadi
National Education	Dr. Mohamed Hilali
Ocean Fisheries and Merchant Marine	Bensalem Smili
Posts and Telecommunications	Mohamed Laensar
Public Health	Tayeb Bencheikh
Tourism	Moussa Saadi
Transportation	Mohamed Bouamoud
Youth and Sports	Abdellatif Semlali

Ministers Delegate

Administrative Affairs	Abderrahim Ben Abdeljalil
Development of the Saharan Province	Khali Hanna Ould Errachid
Economic Affairs	Moulay Zine Zahidi
Planning	Rachid Ghazouani
Relations with the European Community	Azzedine Guessous
Relations with the Parliament	Abdul Salem Barakat
Secretary General of the Government	Abbes el Kaissi
Governor, Bank of Morocco	Ahmed Bennani

NEWS MEDIA

Press. Newspaper readership is limited by widespread illiteracy, but papers are highly outspoken and partisan. The following are published daily at Casablanca in French, unless otherwise noted: *Le Matin du Sahara* (70,000), replaced *Le Petit Marocain* following government shutdown in 1971; *al-Alam* (Rabat, 55,000), Istiqlal organ, in Arabic; *L'Opinion* (Rabat, 36,000), Istiqlal organ; *Maroc Soir* (35,000), replaced *La Vigie Marocaine* in 1971; *al-Maghrib* (Rabat, 30,000), RNI organ; *al-Mithaq al-Watani* (Rabat, 30,000), RNI organ, in Arabic; *al-Anba'a* (Rabat, 15,000), Ministry of Information, in Arabic; *al-Ittihad al-Ichtiraki,* USFP organ, in Arabic. Both *al-Mouharir,* a USFP organ, and *al-Bayane,* a PPS organ, were suspended in the wake of the June 1981 riots at Casablanca. The latter was permitted to resume publication in mid-July, but, having had a number of its issues confiscated in early 1984 because of its reporting of further Casablanca disturbances, was suspended again in October 1986 until January 1987.

News agencies. The *Wikalat al-Maghreb al-Arabi* (WMA), successor to the former *Maghreb Arabe Presse,* is an official, government-owned agency; *Agence France-Presse, Agencia EFE, Xinhua,* Reuters, ANSA, and TASS also maintain offices at Rabat.

Radio and television. Broadcasting is under the supervision of the Ministry of Information. The government-controlled *Radiodiffusion Télévision Marocaine* provides radio service over three networks (national, international, and Berber) as well as commercial television service. In addition, the Voice of America operates a radio station at Tangier. There were approximately 3.0 million radio and 1.1 million television receivers in 1986.

INTERGOVERNMENTAL REPRESENTATION

Ambassador to the US: Mohamed BARGACH.

US Ambassador to Morocco: Thomas Anthony NASSIF.

Permanent Representative to the UN: Driss SLAOUI.

IGO Memberships (Non-UN): *ACCT,* ADF, AfDB, AFESD, AMF, BADEA, CCC, *EIB,* IC, ICCAT, IDB, IIB, ILZ, Intelsat, Interpol, IOOC, IWTC, LAS, NAM.

ANNEXED TERRITORY

Western Sahara. The region known since 1976 as Western Sahara was annexed by Spain in two stages: the coastal area in 1884 and the interior in 1934. In 1957, the year after Morocco attained full independence, Rabat renewed a claim to the territory, sending irregulars to attack inland positions. In 1958, however, French and Spanish troops succeeded in quelling the attacks, with Madrid formally uniting, as the province of Spanish Sahara, the two historical components of the territory: Saguia el Hamra and Rio de Oro. Mauritanian independence in 1960 led to territorial claims by Nouakchott, with the situation being further complicated in 1963 by the discovery of one of the world's richest phosphate deposits at Bu Craa. During the next dozen years, Morocco attempted to pressure Spain into relinquishing its claim through a combination of diplomatic initiatives (the UN first called for a referendum on self-determination for the Sahrawi people in 1966), direct support for guerrilla groups, and a legal challenge in the International Court of Justice.

Increasing insurgency led Spain in May 1975 to announce that it intended to withdraw from Spanish Sahara, while a World Court ruling the following October stated that Moroccan and Mauritanian legal claims to the region were limited and had little bearing on the question of self-determination. Nevertheless, in November King Hassan ordered some 300,000 unarmed Moroccans, in what became known as the "Green March", to enter the territory. Although Spain strongly objected to the action, a tripartite agreement with Morocco and Mauritania was concluded at Madrid on November 14. As a result, Spanish Sahara ceased to be a province of Spain at the end of the year; Spanish troops withdrew shortly thereafter, and Morocco and Mauritania assumed responsibility for Western Sahara on February 28, 1976. On April 14, Rabat and Nouakchott reached an agreement under which Morocco claimed the northern two-thirds of the region, Mauritania the southern third.

The strongest opposition to the partition was voiced by the **Popular Front for the Liberation of Saguia el Hamra and Rio de Oro** (*Frente Popular para la Liberación de Saguia el Hamra y Río de Oro*—Polisario), which in February 1976 formally proclaimed a government-in-exile of the Saharan Arab Democratic Republic (SADR), headed by Mohamed Lamine OULD AHMED as prime minister. Whereas Polisario had originally been based in Mauritania, its political leadership was subsequently relocated to Algeria, with its guerrilla units, recruited largely from nomadic tribes indigenous to the region, also establishing secure bases there. Neither Rabat nor Nouakchott wished to precipitate a wider conflict by operating on Algerian soil, which permitted Polisario to concentrate militarily against the weaker of the two occupying regimes and thus to aid in the overthrow of Mauritania's Moktar Ould Daddah in July 1978. On August 5, 1979, Mauritania concluded at Algiers a peace agreement with Polisario, but Morocco responded by annexing the southern third of Western Sahara. Meanwhile, Polisario launched its first raids into Morocco itself while continuing a diplomatic offensive that by the end of 1980 had resulted in some 45 countries according recognition to the SADR.

During a summit meeting of the Organization of African Unity at Nairobi, Kenya, in June 1981, King Hassan called for a referendum on the future of the disputed territory, but an OAU special implementation committee was unable to move on the proposal because of Rabat's refusal to engage in direct negotiations or to meet a variety of other conditions advanced by Polisario as necessary to effect a ceasefire. As a result, conflict in the region intensified in the second half of the year.

At an OAU Council of Ministers meeting at Addis Ababa, Ethiopia, on February 22, 1982, an SADR delegation was, for the first time, seated, following a controversial ruling by the organization's secretary general that provoked a walkout by 18 member states, including Morocco. For the same reason, a quorum could not be found for the next scheduled Council of Ministers meeting at Tripoli, Libya, on July 26, or for the 19th

OAU summit, which was to have convened at Tripoli on August 5. An attempt to reconvene both meetings in November, following the "voluntary and temporary" withdrawal of the SADR, also failed because of the Western Sahara impasse, coupled with disagreement over the composition of a delegation from Chad. Another "temporary" withdrawal of the SADR allowed the OAU to convene the long-delayed summit at Addis Ababa in May 1983, at which it was decided to oversee a referendum in the region by the end of the year. Morocco's refusal to meet directly with Polisario representatives forced postponement of the referendum, while the 1984 Treaty of Oujda with Libya effectively reduced support for the Front's military forces. Subsequently, Moroccan soldiers crossed briefly into Algerian soil in "pursuit" of guerrillas, while extending the area under Moroccan control by 4,000 square miles. The seating of an SADR delegation at the 20th OAU summit in November 1985 and the election of Polisario secretary general Mohamed 'ABD AL-AZZIZ as an OAU vice-president prompted Morocco's withdrawal from the Organization.

At the sixth triennial Polisario congress, held in "liberated territory" on December 7–9, 1985, 'Abd al-Azziz was reelected secretary general and subsequently appointed a new 13-member SADR government that included himself as president, with Ould Ahmed continuing as prime minister. The following May, a series of "proximity talks" involving Moroccan and Polisario representatives concluded at United Nations headquarters in New York, with no discernible change in the territorial impasse. Subsequently, Rabat began construction of more than 1,200 miles of fortified sand walls that forced the rebels back toward the Algerian and Mauritanian borders. Polisario, while conceding little likelihood of victory by its 30,000 fighters over an estimated 120–140,000 Moroccan soldiers, has nonetheless continued its attacks, hoping that the economic strain of a "war of attrition" will induce King Hassan to enter into direct negotiations — a position endorsed by the 41st UN General Assembly by a vote of 98–0. The UN has also offered to administer the Western Sahara on an interim basis pending a popular referendum with Rabat insisting, as a precondition, that its forces remain in place. In 1987 the SADR reported an assassination attempt against 'Abd al-Azziz, alleging Moroccan complicity. Rabat denied the allegation and suggested that SADR dissidents may have been responsible.

Moroccan administration of the annexed territory is based on its division into four provinces: three established in 1976 (Boujdour, Essmara, Laayoune) and one added in 1979 (Oued Eddahab). The SADR administers four Algerian camps that house some 165,000 Sahrawis and claims to represent the estimated 70,000 persons remaining in the Western Sahara. The SADR also maintains an active international presence that has been officially recognized by 70 countries (see Sahrawi Front under Algeria: Political Parties).

MOZAMBIQUE

People's Republic of Mozambique
República Popular de Moçambique

Political Status: Former Portuguese dependency; became independent June 25, 1975; present constitution approved August 14, 1978.

Area: 309,494 sq. mi. (801,590 sq. km.).

Population: 12,130,000 (1980C), 14,896,000 (1988E).

Major Urban Center (1984E): MAPUTO (903,600).

Official Language: Portuguese (a number of African languages are also spoken).

Monetary Unit: Metical (market rate March 1, 1988, 454.50 meticals = $1US).

President: Joaquim Alberto CHISSANO; elected by the Central Committee of the Mozambique Liberation Front on November 4, 1986, and installed on November 6, following the death of Samora Moïsés MACHEL on October 19, 1986.

Prime Minister: Mário Fernandes da Graça MACHUNGO; designated by the President on July 17, 1986, and sworn in July 26; redesignated on January 11, 1987.

THE COUNTRY

Mozambique lies on the southeast coast of Africa, its contiguous neighbors being Tanzania on the north; Malawi and Zambia on the northwest; and Zimbabwe, South Africa, and Swaziland on the west and south. Its varied terrain comprises coastal lowlands, central plateaus, and mountains along the western frontier. The country is bisected by the Zambezi River, which flows southeastward from the Zambia-Zimbabwe border. The population, while primarily of Bantu stock, is divided into several dozen tribal groups, most speaking distinct local languages or dialects. Traditional religions are widely practiced, but there are Christian (20 percent) and Muslim (10 percent) minorities. Catholic and Anglican churches, many of which were closed following independence, are regaining influence as a result of the government's retreat from a rigidly Marxist-Leninist orientation. The 42 percent of women defined as "economically active" are almost entirely in the agricultural sector, where they exercise a degree of influence within state cooperatives. A number of women prominent in the independence struggle are active within the party-auxiliary Organization of Mozambican Women (OMM), but female representation at higher governmental levels is virtually nonexistent.

Agriculture remains the mainstay of the economy, employing two-thirds of the work force and providing the principal exports: cashew nuts, cotton, and tea, in addition to seafood. Following independence, output declined — particularly in production of sugar and cotton as well as of such minerals as coal and copper — as the government introduced pervasive state control and the Portuguese community, which possessed most of the country's technical and managerial expertise, left the country. Since the early 1980s, however, limited private ownership, foreign investment, and the development of family-owned and operated farms have again been encouraged. Industry has largely been limited to processing agricultural commodities, although significant deposits of natural gas, as well as bauxite, iron, manganese, tantalite, uranium, and other ores await exploitation.

In recent years, economic and social conditions have steadily worsened as insurgency and drought have produced widespread death and deprivation, despite massive emergency food imports and other aid.

GOVERNMENT AND POLITICS

Political background. Portuguese hegemony was established early in the sixteenth century, when Mozambican coastal settlements became ports of call for Far Eastern traders. However, it was not until the Berlin Congress of 1884–1885 that Portuguese supremacy was formally acknowledged by the European powers. In 1952 the colony of Mozambique became an Overseas Province and, as such, constitutionally incorporated into Portugal. In 1964 armed resistance to Portuguese rule was initiated by the Mozambique Liberation Front (Frelimo), led by Dr. Eduardo MONDLANE until his assassination by Portuguese agents in 1969. Following Mondlane's death, Samora MACHEL and Marcelino dos SANTOS overcame a bid for control by Frelimo Vice President Uriah SIMANGO and were installed as the movement's president and vice president, respectively. After the 1974 coup at Lisbon, negotiations at Lusaka, Zambia, called for the formation of a new government composed of Frelimo and Portuguese elements, and for the attainment of complete independence in mid-1975. The agreement was challenged by leaders of the White minority, and an attempt was made to establish a White provisional government under right-wing leadership. After the collapse of the rebellion on September 10, 1974, most of the territory's 250,000 Whites migrated to Portugal or South Africa.

On June 25, 1975, Mozambique became an independent "people's republic", with Machel assuming the presidency. Elections of Frelimo-sponsored candidates to local, district, provincial, and national assemblies were held during September-December 1977. In an apparent easing of its commitment to Marxist centralism, the government took steps in the early 1980s to separate government and party cadres. However, a government reorganization in March 1986 reestablished party domination, with the Council of Ministers being divided into three sections, each directed by a senior member of the Frelimo Political Bureau.

On July 26, 1986, Mário Fernandes da Graça MACHUNGO, an economist who had overseen a recent "liberalization" of the economy, was sworn in as prime minister, a newly created post designed to permit President Machel to concentrate on defense of the regime against the Mozambique National Resistance (Renamo) which had grown from a relatively isolated opponent to an insurgent force operating in all ten provinces.

Machel, who had remained a widely respected leader despite the country's myriad problems, died in an airplane crash on October 19, 1986, and was succeeded by his longtime associate, (then) Foreign Affairs Minister Joaquim Alberto CHISSANO, on November 6.

Constitution and government. The 1975 constitution characterized the People's Republic of Mozambique as a "popular democratic state" while reserving to Frelimo "the directing power of the state and society", with decisions taken by party organs to be regarded as binding on all government officials. The most recent constitution, adopted August 14, 1978, sets as a national objective "the construction of the material and ideological bases for a socialist society".

The president of Frelimo serves concurrently as president of the Republic and commander in chief of the armed forces. He designates members of the Council of Ministers which, since July 1986, has been headed by a prime minister responsible for routine domestic affairs. Should the president resign, die, or become incapacitated, his functions are assumed by the Frelimo Central Committee, which is entrusted with the timely designation of a successor. The "supreme organ of state power" is the People's Assembly, currently composed of 250 members, whose responsibilities between sessions are assumed by a Permanent Commission formerly headed by the president of the Republic, but now by the prime minister. The election process is pyramidal, the direct popular election of local assemblies being followed by indirect selection of district, provincial, and national assemblies. The chief executive appoints the president of the Supreme People's Court. In addition, an extensive system of local People's Tribunals has been established, while a Revolutionary Military Tribunal was formed in 1979 to hear security cases.

The governors of the country's ten provinces are appointed by the president, who may annul the decisions of provincial, district, and local assemblies; the city of Maputo (which has provincial status) is under the administrative direction of a City Council chairman. In early 1979 a corps of state inspectors was established to provide liaison between central and local government bodies. Reporting directly to the president, each of the officials in question was assigned a rank equivalent to that of a provincial governor.

Foreign relations. Avowedly Marxist in orientation, the Frelimo government has received considerable economic, technical, and security support from the Soviet Union, Cuba, East Germany, and other Moscow-line states. Since 1979, however, links with the West have increased: the United Kingdom and Brazil have extended credit, and in 1982 Portugal resumed relations that had ceased in 1977 as a result of the nationalization of Portuguese holdings. Relations with the United States, troubled since 1977 by charges of human rights abuses, reached a nadir in 1981 with the expulsion of all US embassy personnel for alleged espionage. Relations were reestablished in July 1983 and President Machel made a state visit to Washington in September 1985, securing economic aid and exploring the possibility of military assistance. In 1984, Mozambique was admitted to the World Bank and the International Monetary Fund, signifying a desire on Maputo's part to become a more active participant in the world economy.

Despite its prominence as one of the Front-Line States committed to Black majority rule in southern Africa, Mozambique maintains economic relations with South Africa as a matter of "realistic policy", with some 40,000 Mozambicans employed in South African mines and considerable revenue derived from cooperation in transport and hydroelectric power. However, relations have been severely strained by South African support for the Renamo insurgents. In a 1984 nonaggression pact, the "Nkomati Accord", Pretoria agreed to stop aiding Renamo in return for Maputo's pledge not to support the African National Congress (ANC) in its guerrilla campaign against the White minority government in South Africa. The accord proved ineffective, however, growing rebel activity fostering Mozambican suspicion of continued "destabilization" attempts by South Africa. In August 1987 the two countries agreed that the pact should be reactivated and a joint security committee established, although little amelioration of the basic conflict was anticipated.

The insurgency has also dominated Maputo's relations with other neighbors. The Zimbabwean government, declaring "If Mozambique falls, we fall", has sent an estimated 10,000 troops to combat the rebels, particularly in the transport corridor to Beira which plays a central role in the Front-Line States' effort to reduce dependence on South African trade routes. In December 1986, Tanzanian President Mwinyi also agreed to make troops available to Maputo as did Malawi following a dispute over alleged Renamo bases within its borders (see Malawi, article).

Current issues. Upon assuming office President Chissano faced a major Renamo offensive in the central provinces that threatened to "cut the country in two" prior to a Zimbabwean- and Tanganyikan-supported counteroffensive in early 1987 that restored some of the territory to government control. However, the well-equipped rebels continued to prevail in much of the countryside, amid mounting reports of terror tactics. With economic disruption exacerbated by the military statemate, Chissano devoted the remainder of the year to soliciting international aid and, from the West, private investment. He was generally well received in visits to the Soviet Union, the United States and a number of European countries. On the other hand, currency devaluations mandated by the International Monetary Fund as a condition of rescheduling the country's 3.2 billion foreign debt, further fueled an already soaring rate of inflation.

POLITICAL PARTIES

Mozambique is a one-party state in which the Mozambique Liberation Front (Frelimo) is constitutionally empowered to guide the operations of government at all levels.

Mozambique Liberation Front (*Frente da Liberatação de Moçambique* — Frelimo). Founded in 1962 by the union of three nationalist parties and led by Dr. Eduardo Mondlane until his death in 1969, Frelimo carried on armed resistance to Portuguese rule from 1964 to 1974, when agreement on independence was reached. At its third national congress, Frelimo was designated a Marxist-Leninist party directed by a Central Committee, a Political Bureau, and a Secretariat. At the fourth party congress on April 28–30, 1984, the size of the Central Committee was raised from 55 to 130 to allow more representation from rural provinces. Following the death of Samora Machel in October 1986, the Central Committee designated his longtime associate, Joaquim Alberto Chissano, as its political leader, the potential for divisiveness reportedly subsiding in 1987 as other contenders "closed ranks" behind the new president.

President: Joaquim Alberto CHISSANO.

Other Members of Political Bureau: Lt. Gen. Alberto Joaquim CHIPANDE (Defense Minister), Armando Emílio GUEBUZA (Transport and Telecommunications Minister), Col. Gen. Sebastião Marcos MABOTE (former Armed Forces Chief of Staff), Mariano de Araújo MATSINHE (Security Minister), Mário da Graça MACHUNDO (Prime Minister), José Oscar MONTEIRO (Minister for State Administration), Jorge REBELO (Central Committee Secretary for Ideological Affairs), Marcelino dos SANTOS (Secretary of Permanent Commission, People's Assembly), Jacinto Soares VELOSO (Cooperation Minister).

Secretariat: José Luis CABAÇO, Joachim Alberto CHISSANO, Armando PANGUENE, Jorge REBELO, Marcelino dos SANTOS.

Illegal Opposition:

Mozambique National Resistance — MNR (*Resistência Nacional Moçambicana* — Renamo). Also known as *Movimento Nacional da Resistência de Moçambique* (MNRM) and as the André Group, after its late founder, André Matade Matsangai, Renamo was formed in the early 1970s primarily as an intelligence network within Mozambique for the White Rhodesian government of Ian Smith. Since the declaration of Zimbabwean independence in 1980, Renamo has developed into a widespread anti-Frelimo insurgency, reportedly relying on financial support from Portuguese expatriates and heavy military aid from South Africa, the latter apparently continuing despite the Nkomati accord of 1984. The 20,000-member Renamo army, comprising Portuguese and other mercenaries, Frelimo defectors, and numerous recruits from the Shona-speaking Ndau ethnic group, operates mainly in rural areas where it has interdicted transport corridors and sabotaged food production. Widely condemned for its alleged reliance on a campaign of terror including indiscriminate killing, mutilation, and dislocation of civilians, Renamo, although now perceived as a genuine military threat to the government, has generally failed to gain internal popular support or the recognition it seeks from the West as a "legitimate" anticommunist movement. In an apparent attempt to foster its nationalist image, Renamo launched an "Africanization" program in 1987 that included replacements for White Portuguese at its Lisbon-based external headquarters.

Leaders: Gen. Alfonso DLAKAMA (President), Francisco Nota MOISES (Information Secretary), João da Silva ATAIDE and Boaventura LEMANE (external spokesmen in Europe and the United States, respectively).

In 1977 a **Revolutionary Party of Mozambique** (*Partido Revolucionário de Moçambique* — PRM), described as "an African movement not related to outside assistance", was operating as a guerrilla force in Niassa and Tete provinces. In early 1978 a **United Democratic Front of Mozambique** (*Frente Unida Democrática de Moçambique* — Fumo), led by a Frelimo founding member, Dr. Domingos AROUCA, was also reported to have been organized. There have been no recent reports of activity by either group, suggesting the possibility of absorption by Renamo. Two small Frelimo splinter groups, the **Mozambique Revolutionary Committee** (Coremo) and the **Mozambique National Independent Committee** (Conimo), are also apparently currently affiliated with Renamo as is the Kenyan-based **Democratic Party for the Liberation of Mozambique** (Padelimo).

LEGISLATURE

The **People's Assembly** (*Assembléia Popular*) consisted initially of Frelimo's (then) 57-member Central committee, which was accorded legislative status at an uncontested election in December 1977. The body was increased to 210 members in April 1983 by the addition of government ministers and vice ministers, provincial governors, representatives of the military and of each province, and 10 other citizens. While its term is not constitutionally specified, the original mandate, by law, was set at five years. The general election due in 1982 was, however, postponed because of the civil war. The lengthy poll eventually conducted in August-December 1986 was for 250 deputies, indirectly elected by provincial assemblies from a list of 299 candidates presented by Frelimo.

President of Permanent Commission: Mário da Graça MACHUNGO.

Secretary of Permanent Commission: Marcelino dos SANTOS.

CABINET

Prime Minister	Mário da Graça Machungo
Ministers	
Agriculture	João Ferreira
Construction and Water	João Mário Salomão
Cooperation	Jacinto Soares Veloso
Culture	Luis Bernardo Honwana
Education	Graça Simbine Machel

Finance	Abdul Magid Osman
Foreign Affairs	Pascoal Manuel Mocumbi
Health	Fernando Vaz
Industry and Power	António Lima Rodrigues Branco
Information	Teodato Hunguana
Interior	Manuel Jorge António
Justice	Ossumane Ali Dauto
Labor	Aguiar Real Mazula
Mineral Resources	John William Kachamila
National Defense	Gen. Alberto Joaquim Chipande
Security	Maj. Gen. Mariano de Araújo Matsinhe
Trade	Manuel Jorge Aranda da Silva
Transport and Telecommunications	Lt. Gen. Armando Emílio Guebuza

Ministers in President's Office

State Administration	José Oscar Monteiro
Without Portfolio	Felicino Gundana
Governor, Central Bank	Eneas Comiche

NEWS MEDIA

Press. The following are published at Maputo and Beira, respectively: *Notícias* (46,000), government controlled; *Diário de Moçambique* (16,000). A government-sponsored organ, the *Jornal do Povo* (People's Newspaper), recently began publication.

News agencies. The official facility is the Mozambique Information Agency (*Agência de Informação de Moçambique* — AIM); *Novosti*, Reuters, and several other European agencies are represented at Maputo.

Radio and television. All broadcasting facilities were nationalized in 1975. *Rádio Moçambique* maintains three national programs, foreign service, and a number of provincial stations. Television service, on a limited basis, served some 10,000 receivers in 1987.

INTERGOVERNMENTAL REPRESENTATION

Ambassador to the US: Valeriano FERRAO.

US Ambassador to Mozambique: Melissa Foelsch WELLS.

Permanent Representative to the UN: Manuel DOS SANTOS.

IGO Memberships (Non-UN): ADF, AfDB, BADEA, CCC, ISO, NAM, OAU, SADCC.

NAMIBIA

(South West Africa)

Political Status: Former League of Nations mandated territory, administered by South Africa since 1920; declared to be under United Nations responsibility by resolution of the General Assembly adopted October 27, 1966, but not recognized by South Africa.

Area: 318,259 sq. mi. (824,292 sq. km.).

Population: 1,039,800 (1981C), 1,246,000 (1988E). Both area and population figures include data for Walvis Bay (see Recent developments, below).

Major Urban Center (1981C): WINDHOEK (110,644).

Official Languages: Afrikaans, English, German.

Monetary Unit: South African Rand (market rate March 1, 1988, 2.09 rands = $1US).

United Nations Commissioner for Namibia: Bernt CARLSSON (Sweden), appointed to a six-month term by the UN General Assembly on December 11, 1986, succeeding Brajesh Chandra MISHRA (India), with effect from July 1, 1987; one-year extension subsequently voted through December 31, 1988.

South African Administrator General of South West Africa: Louis PIENAAR; appointed by South African Prime Minister P.W. Botha on May 30, 1985, to succeed Willem (Willie) VAN NIEKERK, effective July 1, 1985.

THE COUNTRY

Bordered on the north by Angola and Zambia, on the east by Botswana, on the southeast and south by South Africa, and on the west by the Atlantic Ocean, Namibia, which is larger than West Germany and France combined, consists of a high plateau bounded by the uninhabited Namib Desert along the Atlantic coast, with more desert land in the interior. The inhabitants are of diversified origins, although the Ovambo constitute by far the largest ethnic group (a majority of 51 percent in the 1981 census, slightly less than 50 percent on the basis of a 1986 estimate). A substantial exodus has reduced the White population, traditionally engaged in commercial farming and ranching, fish processing, and mineral exploitation, from approximately 12 to 6.6 percent. Other groups include the Kavango (9.3 percent), the Herero (7.9 percent), the Damara (7.5 percent), the Nama (4.8 pecent), and those classified as "Coloured" (4.1 percent). The country is one of the world's largest producers of diamonds, which yield about half of export earnings, although uranium, copper, lead, zinc, tin, and other minerals are available in extractable quantities. These resources yielded substantial economic growth during the 1970s; however, falling mineral prices, extended periods of drought, and internal insecurity have since yielded severe recession, marked by rising unemployment, heightened inflation, and budgetary deficits that have necessitated increased subsidization by South Africa.

GOVERNMENT AND POLITICS

Political background. South West Africa came under German control in the 1880s except for a small enclave at Walvis Bay, which had been annexed by the United Kingdom in 1878 and subsequently became a part of South Africa. Having occupied the whole of South West Africa during World War I, South Africa was granted a mandate in 1920 to govern the area under authority of the League of Nations. Declining to place the territory under the UN trusteeship system after World War II, South Africa asked the UN General Assembly in 1946 for permission to annex it; following denial of the request, Pretoria continued its rule on the strength of the original mandate.

Although the international status of the territory and the supervisory authority of the United Nations were repeatedly affirmed in advisory opinions of the International Court of Justice, the Court in 1966 declined on technical grounds to rule upon a formal complaint by Ethiopia and Liberia against South Africa's conduct in the territory. The UN General Assembly then terminated the mandate in a resolution of October 27, 1966, declaring that South Africa had failed to fulfill its obligations. A further resolution on May 19, 1967, established an 11-member UN Council for South West Africa, assisted by a UN commissioner, to administer the territory until independence (originally set for June 1968) and to prepare for the drafting of a constitution, the holding of an election, and the establishment of responsible government. The Council was, however, refused entry by the South African government, which contended that termination of the mandate was invalid. South Africa subsequently disregarded a number of Security Council resolutions to relinquish the territory, including a unanimous resolution of December 1974 that gave it five months to initiate withdrawal from Namibia (the official name adopted on December 16, 1968, by the General Assembly).

Beginning in the mid-1960s, South Africa attempted to group the Black population into a number of self-administering tribal homelands ("Bantustans"), in accordance with the so-called Odendaal Report of 1964. Ovamboland, the first functioning Bantustan, was established in October 1968, but its legitimacy was rejected by the UN Security Council. Fully implemented, the partition plan would have left approximately 88,000 Whites as the largest ethnic group in two-thirds of the territory, with some 675,000 Black inhabitants confined to the remaining third.

Both the Organization of African Unity (OAU) and the South West African People's Organisation (SWAPO) have consistently called for full and unconditional self-determination for Namibia. In May 1975, however, Prime Minister Vorster of South Africa stated that while his government was prepared to "exchange ideas" with UN and OAU representatives, it was not willing to accede to the demand that it "acknowledge SWAPO as the sole representative of the Namibian people and enter into independence negotiations with the organisation". Faced with an impasse, the UN Security Council debated a resolution calling for a mandated arms embargo against South Africa and for a UN-supervised free election not later than July 1, 1976, but the resolution was defeated because of a triple veto by France, Britain, and the United States. In January 1976, the Security Council unanimously approved a milder resolution that condemned South Africa's "illegal occupation" of Namibia and called for free elections under UN supervision.

Constitution and government. For the decade 1966–1976 the constitutional situation of Namibia involved a deep-seated conflict between the legal authority asserted by the United Nations and the actual control exercised by the South African government. During 1977 there appeared to be substantial progress toward resolution of the impasse, with the appointment by South Africa on July 6 of an administrator general to prepare for a Constituent Assembly election in 1978. The assignment to the administrator general of interim authority "to make laws by proclamation" and to "repeal or amend any legal provision"

rendered obsolete the existing 18-member Legislative Assembly, while the mandate of the former South African administrator (chosen by the Legislative Assembly) was terminated on September 30, as was representation by South West Africans in the South African Parliament. In May 1979, delegates that had been elected as constituent lawmakers the previous December voted to reorganize as a National Assembly, while a 12-member Ministerial Council was created in July 1980. In addition, the administrator general ordered elections in 1980 to 11 "second-tier" legislative assemblies based on racial and ethnic divisions—one White and ten Black—which were accorded control of health and educational affairs. However, fighting precluded voting in the north and in 1983 the National Assembly and the Ministerial Council, both manifestly unrepresentative because of a boycott by most Ovambos, were dissolved by the administrator general.

The Transitional Government of National Unity inaugurated on June 17, 1985 (see Recent developments, below), included a nonelective 62-member National Assembly and an eight-member cabinet, the chairmanship of which rotates every three months. South Africa retains control of defense and foreign affairs, while all measures enacted by the Assembly are subject to veto by the administrator general. At the time of the new government's formation, a Constitutional Council was also created which in July 1987 voted 14 to 4 to endorse a draft constitution that would have eliminated the second-tier legislative divisions and instituted a "one-man, one-vote democracy" with no entrenched protection for Whites or other minority groups. However, Pretoria rejected the document in favor of an alternative which maintained "group rights" with the issue remaining at impasse in early 1988.

Foreign relations. Under the South West Africa Constitutional Act passed by the South African Parliament in 1925, the foreign affairs of South West Africa are the responsibility of the Republic of South Africa. Namibia (represented by the UN Council for Namibia) is, however, an associate member of the World Health Oganization and in 1977 was admitted to the Food and Agriculture Organization as a full member, despite US objections that the action constituted a dangerous precedent in regard to a territory that was not yet self-governing. In 1978 it became a full member of the United Nations Educational, Scientific and Cultural Organization after some years as an associate member, and in 1982 also became a full member of the International Telecommunication Union.

Recent developments. On September 1, 1975, the South African government convened a constitutional conference at Turnhalle, Windhoek, on the future of South West Africa. SWAPO and other independence groups boycotted the conference and organized demonstrations against it. As a result, the Ovambos, with approximately half of the territory's population, were represented by only 15 out of 135 delegates. A "declaration of intent" issued on September 12 called for independence of the territory within three years under a form of government that would "guarantee to every population group the greatest possible say in its own affairs and national affairs". This position seemed to represent a compromise between the SWAPO demand for a unitary state under majority rule and the ethnic partition envisaged by the 1964 Odendaal Report.

At the second session of the conference, held March 2–19, 1976, Chief Clemens KAPUUO of the Herero-based National United Democratic Organisation (see Political Parties, below) presented a draft constitution that called for a bicameral legislature encompassing a northern chamber of representatives from Bantu areas and a southern chamber that would include representatives from the Coloured and White groups. On March 11 a SWAPO spokesman rejected the proposal, stating that its acceptance would force SWAPO to "put forward a constitution of our own" that would embrace the principle of majority rule throughout the territory. On August 18, during the third session of the conference, a plan was advanced for the creation of a multiracial interim government to prepare Namibia for independence by December 31, 1978. Despite continued opposition from SWAPO, the conference's constitution committee unanimously approved a resolution on December 3 that called for establishment of the interim government within the next six months.

Although a draft constitution calling for representation of the territory's 11 major racial and ethnic groups was approved by the Turnhalle delegates on March 9, 1977, and was subsequently endorsed by 95 percent of the White voters in a referendum on May 17, it continued to be opposed by SWAPO as well as by a "contact group" of diplomats representing the five Western members of the UN Security Council (Canada, France, the Federal Republic of Germany, the United Kingdom, and the United States). The Western delegation visited Windhoek on May 7–10 and subsequently engaged in talks with South African Prime Minister Vorster at Cape Town on June 8–10, in the course of which it indicated that the Turnhalle formula was unacceptable because it was "predominantly ethnic, lacked neutrality and appeared to prejudice the outcome of free elections". The group added, however, that the appointment of an administrator general by the South African government would not be opposed insofar as it gave promise of contributing to "an internationally acceptable solution to the Namibia question". For his part, Vorster, prior to the appointment of Marthinus T. STEYN as administrator general on July 6, agreed to abandon the Turnhalle proposal for an interim government, to accept the appointment of a UN representative to ensure the impartiality of the constituent election in 1978, and to initiate a withdrawal of South African troops to be completed by the time of independence. He insisted, however, that the South African government had no intention of abandoning its jurisdiction over Walvis Bay and certain islands off the South West African coast. (Governed as part of South Africa until 1922, when it was assigned to South West Africa for administrative purposes, Walvis Bay was, in August 1977, reincorporated into South Africa's Cape Province.)

During November and December, representatives of the "contact group" engaged in lengthy but inconclusive discussions with leaders of SWAPO and of the Black African Front-Line States (Angola, Botswana, Mozambique, Tanzania, and Zambia). The main problem concerned the South African security forces within Namibia, SWAPO asserting that their continued presence would influence the outcome of the projected election despite a UN presence. Nonetheless, Administrator General Steyn moved ener-getically to dismantle the territory's apartheid system, including abolition of the pass laws and the Mixed Marriages Act, in preparation for the 1978 balloting.

Events moved rapidly but without final resolution of Namibia's status during 1978. On March 27, Chief Kapuuo, who had assumed the presidency of the Democratic Turnhalle Alliance (see below), was shot and killed by unknown assailants on the outskirts of Windhoek. The assassination removed from the scene the best-known tribal figure apart from SWAPO leader Sam NUJOMA, who denied that his group had been involved. Three days later, the Western nations presented Prime Minister Vorster with revised proposals calling for a ceasefire between SWAPO guerrillas and the 18,000 South African troops in the territory. The latter force would be expected to withdraw from the border areas and gradually decrease to 1,500 men, with UN troops being positioned to maintain order in preparation for Constituent Assembly balloting. South Africa accepted the plan on April 25 after receiving assurances that the status of Walvis Bay would not be addressed until after the election, that the reduction of its military presence would be linked to "a complete cessation of hostilities", and that some of its troops might be permitted to remain after the election if the Assembly so requested. On May 5, SWAPO suspended negotiations because of a South African attack on a guerrilla camp in southern Angola, but on July 12 agreed to the Western plan, which had been endorsed by the Front-Line States. The UN Security Council also approved the plan, on July 27, but Pretoria reacted bitterly to an accompanying resolution calling for the early "reintegration" of Walvis Bay into South West Africa and subsequently announced that its own final approval would be deferred. In early September, South African Foreign Minister Botha denounced the size of the proposed UN military force for the territory and two weeks later indicated that his government had reversed itself and would proceed with an election of its own. SWAPO boycotted the early December balloting, and the Turnhalle Alliance was declared the victor with 82 percent of the vote. The Assembly convened on December 20 with the Alliance holding 41 of 50 seats.

In May 1979 the South African government agreed to the Constituent Assembly's request that the body be reconstituted as a National Assembly, although without authority to alter the status of the territory. Collaterally, conflict between SWAPO guerrilla forces and South African troops intensified, the latter carrying out a number of preemptive raids on SWAPO bases located in both Angola and Zambia.

By midyear, negotiations between UN and South African representatives had stalled, Pretoria having rejected a contact group proposal to establish bases for SWAPO forces in Namibia as a counter to South African installations. In an effort to break the deadlock, Angolan President Neto, a few weeks before his death in September, proposed the creation of a 60-mile-wide demilitarized zone along the Angolan-Namibian border to prevent incursions from either side. He also pledged that Angola would welcome a UN civilian presence to ensure that any guerrillas not wishing to return to Namibia to participate in an all-party election would be confined to their bases.

Although Pretoria agreed to "the concept" of a demilitarized zone, discussions during 1980 failed to yield agreement on matters of detail, and on November 24 UN Secretary General Waldheim called for the convening of a "pre-implementation meeting" at Geneva in January 1981 to discuss all "practical proposals" that might break the lengthy impasse. Earlier, DTA spokesmen had urged repeal of the General Assembly's 1973 recognition of SWAPO, arguing that the root of the problem lay in the fact that "the UN is required to play a neutral role in respect of implementation but at the same time is the most ardent protagonist of SWAPO".

During 1981–1982, units of both the South West Africa Territorial Force (SWATF) and the South African Defence Force (SADF) conducted numerous "search and destroy" raids into Angola, Pretoria insisting that the withdrawal of Cuban troops from the latter country was a necessary precondition of its own withdrawal from Namibia and the implementation of a UN-supervised election. Thus Prime Minister Botha declared at a Transvaal National Party congress in September 1982 that his government would never accede to Namibian independence unless "unequivocal agreement [could] first be reached" on the linkage issue. Subsequently, an Angolan spokesman indicated that a partial withdrawal of Cuban forces was possible if Pretoria would agree to reduce the size of its military presence to 1,500 troops and discontinue incursions into his country. The overture prompted a secret but inconclusive series of talks between Angolan and South African ministerial delegations on the island of Sal in Cape Verde in early December, the South African foreign minister subsequently asserting that responsibility for a Cuban withdrawal was "the task of the Americans".

In November 1983, a Multi-Party Conference (MPC) of seven internal groups, including the DTA, was launched at Windhoek in an effort to overcome the deadlock. Although the "Windhoek Declaration of Basic Principles" that was issued on February 24, 1984, did little more than to reaffirm the essentials of the 1979 UN plan, South African Prime Minister Botha announced in early March that his government would be willing to enter into negotiations with all relevant parties to the dispute, including the Angolan government and UNITA, the Angolan rebel movement, which enjoyed de facto SADF support. However, the overture was rejected by SWAPO on the ground that only Namibian factions should be involved in independence discussions. Collaterally, Angola offered to participate as an observer at direct negotiations between SWAPO and Pretoria. Two months later, Zambian President Kaunda and South West African Administrator General van Niekerk jointly chaired a meeting at Lusaka that was attended by representatives of South Africa, SWAPO, and the MPC, while a meeting between van Niekerk and SWAPO president Sam Nujoma was held in Cape Verde on July 25. Although unprecedented, the bilateral discussions also proved abortive, as have subsequent talks involving Washington, Luanda, SWAPO and/or Pretoria; progress on the issue was further inhibited in mid-1985 by evidence of continued US and South African support for UNITA (see entry on Angola).

After lengthy discussion with the MPC, Pretoria on June 17, 1985, installed a Transitional Government of National Unity (TGNU), with a cabinet, 62-member legislature, and Constitutional Council of representatives from the six remaining MPC parties (see Political Parties, below). Having largely excluded Ovambos, the new administration was estimated to command the support of perhaps 16 percent of the population, and was further limited by Pretoria's retention of veto power over its decisions. Not surprisingly, international support for the action was virtually nonexistent, with a formal condemnation issuing from the UN Security Council and the United States asserting that it gave rise to "the most serious questions". While its "interim" nature was stressed by Pretoria, which mandated a formal constitution within 18 months, stalled negotiations with Angola and continued SWAPO activity provoked South African intimations that the arrangement could lead to a permanent "regional alternative to independence".

In early 1986 Pretoria proposed that independence commence August 1, again contingent upon withdrawal of the Cubans from Angola. The renewed linkage stipulation, termed by the United Nations as "extraneous", prompted both Angola and SWAPO to reject the plan as nothing more than a "public relations exercise". Meanwhile, the TGNU, reportedly experiencing internal strain, was proving manifestly ineffectual. By contrast, over 10,000 persons participated in a SWAPO rally at Katutura in July (the first such event tolerated by authorities in over five years). The rally was supported by the increasingly vocal Namibian Council of Churches, whose representatives condemned South African forces for rising "brutality" against civilians. In September a UN General Assembly Special Session on Namibia strongly condemned South Africa for effectively blocking implementation of the UN plan for Namibian independence and called for the imposition of mandatory sanctions against Pretoria; however, US and UK vetoes precluded the passage of resolutions to such effect by the Security Council.

During 1987 South Africa continued to seek Western recognition of the TGNU as a means of resolving the Namibian question. However, even within the TGNU, differences emerged regarding a draft constitution and the related question of new elections to second-tier legislative bodies. Meanwhile, fighting between SWAPO and SWAFT/SADF forces in the north intensified, partly as a result of increased South African involvement in the Angolan civil war. Police also moved against SWAPO's internal political wing in August, raiding offices and confiscating materials. Several SWAPO leaders were arrested in the sweep, although the Supreme Court at Windhoek subsequently ordered their release.

POLITICAL PARTIES

The Namibian party spectrum includes nearly three dozen political and semipolitical groups representing a wide diversity of racial and tribal affiliations, the two leading forces being the South West African People's Organisation (SWAPO) and the Democratic Turnhalle Alliance (DTA). Six groups are represented in the Transitional Government of National Unity (TGNU), established in 1985;

in addition to representation in the National Assembly (see Legislature, below), the DTA was awarded three cabinet posts while the other five groups were awarded one such post each.

Members of Transitional Government of National Unity:

Democratic Turnhalle Alliance (DTA). The DTA was launched in the wake of the Turnhalle Conference as a multiracial coalition of European, Coloured, and African groups. Advocating a constitutional arrangement that would provide for equal ethnic representation, the DTA obtained an overwhelming majority (41 of 50 seats) at the Constituent Assembly balloting of December 4–8, 1978, and was instrumental in organizing the Multi-Party Conference in 1983. In addition to the two core formations listed below, it encompasses the **Bushman Alliance**, led by Geelbooi KASHE; the **Christian Democratic Union**, a Coloured group led by A.F. KLOPPER; the **Namibia Democratic Turnhalle Party**, a Nama group led by Daniel LUIPERT; the **National Democratic Party** (see also the CDA below), an Ovambo group led by Tara IMBILI; the **Rehoboth Baster Union**, led by Ben AFRICA; the **Seoposengwe Party**, a Tswana group led by Chief Constance KGOSIMANG; and the **South West Africa People's Democratic United Front**, a Damara group led by Max HARASEB.

Leaders: Chief Kuaima RIRUAKO (President of the Alliance), Dirk Frederik MUDGE (Chairman of the Alliance and Minister of Finance and Governmental Affairs), Fanuel Jariretendu KOZONGUIZI (Minister of Justice), Andrew Nick MATJILA (Minister of Education).

National United Democratic Organisation (NUDO). As the principal political vehicle of the largely Herero tribes of central and southern Namibia, NUDO has consistently favored a federal solution as a means of opposing SWAPO domination. It was led, prior to his assassination in March 1978, by Chief Clemens Kapuuo, cofounder of the DTA.

Leader: Chief Kuaima RIRUAKO.

Republican Party (RP). The RP is a White party organized in October 1977 by former members of the National Party of South West Africa (below) following the failure of Dirk Mudge to win the NP leadership on a pro-Turnhalle platform. Mudge, once considered a staunch supporter of South African policy, has recently become "a thorn in Pretoria's side" by spearheading the drive within the Transitional Government for equal ethnic representation.

Leader: Dirk Frederik MUDGE.

National Party of South West Africa – SWANP (*Nasionale Party van Suidwes Afrika*). The SWANP is a White offshoot of South Africa's ruling party and a supporter of South African policy. It won all 18 seats in the South West African Legislative Assembly balloting of 1966, 1970, and 1974, but was seriously weakened by a split during its 1977 congress, at which Abraham H. DU PLESSIS was narrowly reelected leader over Dirk Mudge, who thereupon withdrew to form the RP. The party contested the 1978 Constituent Assembly election as the Action Front for the Retention of Turnhalle Principles (Aktur), winning 6 seats, and participated in the 1983 Multi-Party Conference. In late 1986 cabinet member Ebenezer van Zijl, two assemblymen, and two representatives on the Constitutional Council resigned from the TGNU after tension had emerged between them and right-wing party leaders over recent government decisions such as the opening of schools to all races. Hardliners were subsequently named to the vacated posts and in 1987 opposed the TGNU's draft constitution because of its failure to provide for minority rights.

Leaders: Hosie PRETORIUS, Tinus BLAW, Ebenezer van ZIJL, Jan De WET (Minister of Agriculture).

Labour Party. A founding member of the DTA that was expelled from the Alliance in 1982, the Labour Party is a largely Coloured grouping that joined the MPC subsequent to the November 1983 meeting.

Leader: Dawid BEZUIDENHOUT (Minister of Transport).

Rehoboth Free Democratic Party – RFDP (*Rehoboth Bevryder Demokratiese Party* – RBDP). The RFDP is an outgrowth of the former Rehoboth Liberation Front (RLF), which endorsed the partition of Namibia along ethnic lines and obtained one Assembly seat in 1978 as representative of part of the Baster community, composed of Afrikaans-speaking people with European customs. The RFDP was an original member of the MPC. In 1987 the RFDP joined the SWANP in opposing the proposed draft constitution endorsed by other TGNU members.

Leaders: L.J.G. (Hans) DIERGAARDT (Minister of Local Government), K.G. FREIGANG.

SWAPO-Democrats. The SWAPO-Democrats was established by a number of SWAPO dissidents upon their release in May 1978 by Tanzanian authorities, who had detained them for opposing Nujoma's leadership of the parent organization. In August 1980 four of its executive members withdrew to organize separately as the **United Namibia People's Party** (UNPP). The SWAPO-Democrats participated in the MPC and party leader Shipanga was the only Ovambo named to the new "national unity" cabinet in June 1985.

In mid-1986, the SWAPO-Democrats presented a joint plan with SWANU (below) that would divide Namibia into six provinces along geographic/ethnic lines, with substantial devolution to municipality and village authorities who would be elected on a one-man, one-vote basis.

Leader: Andreas Zack SHIPANGA (Minister of Mining Affairs).

South West Africa National Union (SWANU). Formerly coordinating many of its activities with SWAPO's internal wing, the Herero-supported SWANU joined in 1978 with the Darara Council (below) and a number of smaller groups to form the Namibia National Front (NNF), a multiracial coalition in support of the Western "contact group" solution to the Namibian problem. SWANU's president, Moses Katjiuongua, participated in the 1983 MPC meeting and in September 1984 was reported to have been replaced as party leader by Kuzeeko Kangueehi, who indicated that the group would leave the MPC with a view to possible merger with SWAPO. In October, on the other hand, Katjiuongua was again identified as holding the presidency, with Kangueehi described as the leader of a dissident faction (subsequently styled SWANU-Left). The incumbent's anti-SWAPO orientation was reflected in his inclusion in the "national unity" cabinet of 1985. (See also SWAPO-Democrats, above.)

Leaders: Moses Nguesako KATJIUONGUA (President of the Party and Minister of Health), Kuzeeko KANGUEEHI (dissident leader).

Other Internal Groups:

Namibia Christian Democratic Party (NCDP). A Coloured party organized in 1978, the NCDP obtained one seat in the Constituent Assembly balloting. It withdrew from the MPC in December 1983, after having participated in the November discussions.

Leader: J.K.N. RÖHR.

Christian Democratic Action for Social Justice (CDA). Supported principally by Ovambos, the CDA was formed in January 1982 by members of the National Democratic Party who withdrew from the DTA because of the latter's failure to organize as a unified grouping.

Leader: Peter KALANGULA.

South West German-Speaking Interest Group (*Interessengemeinschaft Deutschsprachiger Südwester* – IG). Although not a member of the DTA, the IG has generally supported its objectives.

Leaders: K.W. von MAREÈS (President), Klaus J. BECKER (Chairman).

Reconstituted National Party (*Herstigte Nasionale Party* – HNP). Affiliated with the White supremacist group of the same name in the Republic of South Africa, the HNP is strongly opposed to Namibian independence. It secured one Assembly seat in 1978.

Leader: Sarel BECKER.

Namibia Unity Front (NUF). The formation of the NUF was announced in April 1987 by two ethnic Caprivi groups, the **Caprivi Alliance Party** (CAP) and the larger **Caprivi African National Union** (CANU). CANU President Siseho Simasiku, who was named chairman of the Front, said that although the constituent parties would seek joint representation through the NUF in the Transitional Government, they would retain their own central and executive committees. The NUF effectively superseded the United Democratic Party (UDP) which had been proclaimed in 1985 as a merger of the two groups by CAP leader Richard M. Mamili and CANU leader Mishake (Albert) Muyongo. Muyongo had once served as vice president of SWAPO, from which CANU withdrew in 1980, while the CAP had been a member of the DTA.

Leaders: Siseho SIMASIKU (NUF Chairman and CANU President), Mishake (Albert) MUYONGO (CANU), Richard M. MAMILI (CA), Gabriel SISEHO (CA).

Namibia People's Liberation Front (NPLF). The NPLF is supported primarily by Damaras and Namas.

Leader: Kefas CONRADIE.

Damara Council. The Damara Council also joined the MPC in November 1983, but withdrew from the grouping in March 1984.

Leader: Justus GAROËB.

Other small groups include two Herero-based formations, the Christian Democratic Coalition (CDC), led by Rehabeam UAZUKUANI, and the **Moanderu Council,** led by Chief Nguvauvu MANJUKU; the **Namibia Independence Party (NIP),** a Coloured group led by Charley HARTUNG; the Kavango-based **Namibia National Independence Party** (NNIP), led by Rudolf NGONDO, the Nama-based **Namibia Progressive Party** (NPP) led by A. VRIES; and the Rehoboth Baster **Rehoboth People's Party** (*Volksparty van Rehoboth*), led by Stellmacher Dentlinger BEUKES.

Largely External Group:

South West African People's Organisation of Namibia (SWAPO). Consisting mainly of Ovambos and formerly known as the Ovambo People's Organisation, SWAPO has long been the largest and most active South West African nationalist group and is recognized by the United Nations as the "authentic representative of the Namibian people". Founded in 1958, it issued a call for independence in 1966 and subsequently initiated guerrilla activity in the north with the support of the OAU Liberation Committee. Most recent operations have been conducted by the military arm of the country's "external wing", the People's Liberation Army of Namibia (PLAN), from bases in southern Angola. A legal "internal wing" engages in political activity within Namibia, although it has been the target of arrests and other forms of intimidation by police and South African military forces (see Recent developments, above). SWAPO's co-founder, Herman Toivo ja Toivo, was released from 16 years' imprisonment on March 1, 1984, and immediately elected to the Organization's newly created post of secretary general. In February 1988, at what was described as the largest such meeting in the movement's history, 130 delegates representing about 30 branches of SWAPO's internal wing reaffirmed their "unwavering confidence" in the exiled leadership of Sam Nujoma and their willingness to conclude a cease-fire in accordance with implementation of the UN independence plan.

Leaders: Sam NUJOMA (President), Hendrik WITBOOI (Vice President), David MERORO (National Chairman), Daniel TJONGARERO (Vice Chairman), Nathaniel MAXUILILI (leader of internal wing), Andimba (Herman) TOIVO ja TOIVO (Secretary General).

LEGISLATURE

The nonelective **National Assembly** installed on June 17, 1985, as part of the Transitional Government of National Unity, encompasses 62 members, of which 22 are nominated by the Democratic Turnhalle Alliance, and 8 each by the Labour Party, the National Party of South West Africa, the Rehoboth Free Democratic Party, the South West Africa National Union, and the SWAPO-Democrats.

CABINET

[Note: Under the present Transitional Government of National Unity, the chairman of the Council of Ministers (prime minister) rotates every three months.]

Ministers

Agriculture, Water Affairs and Sea Fisheries	Jan De Wet
Civic Affairs and Local Government	Hans Diergaardt
Commerce	Andreas Shipanga
Education	Andrew Matjila
Finance	Dirk Mudge
Governmental Affairs	Dirk Mudge
Information, Posts and Telecommunications	Fanuel Kozonguizi
Justice	Fanuel Kozonguizi
Manpower	Moses Katjiuongua
Mining Affairs	Andreas Shipanga
National Health and Welfare	Moses Katjiuongua
Nature Conservation	Andreas Shipanga
Tourism	Andreas Shipanga
Transport	Dawid Bezuidenhout

NEWS MEDIA

Press. The following newspapers are published daily at Windhoek, unless otherwise noted: *Die Republikein* (11,000), DTA organ in Afrikaans, English, and German; *Windhoek Observer* (7,000), weekly in English; *Die Suidwester* (6,000), in Afrikaans, weekly NP organ; *Allgemeine Zeitung* (6,000), in German; *The Namibian* (5,000), weekly in English; *Windhoek Advertiser* (4,000), in English.

Radio and television. The South African Broadcasting Corporation at Windhoek was redesignated as the South West Africa Broadcasting Corporation (SWABC) in May 1979. In announcing the change, SWABC officials stated that programs would still be relayed from South Africa but that henceforth emphasis would be placed on local programming "with its own South West African character". There were approximately 220,000 radio and 25,000 television receivers in 1987.

INTERGOVERNMENTAL REPRESENTATION

South West Africa has no separate diplomatic representation abroad and is not a member of the United Nations, although it is represented within the UN by the General Assembly's Council for Namibia. US interests in the territory are handled by the US Consulate General at Cape Town, South Africa.

NAURU

Republic of Nauru
Naoero

Political Status: Republic with "special membership" in the Commonwealth; independent since January 31, 1968.

Area: 8.1 sq. mi. (21 sq. km.).

Population: 8,042 (1983C), 8,700 (1988E). At the time of the 1983 census, only 4,964 were declared to be native Nauruans.

Major Urban Centers: None; the *Domaneab* ("meeting place of the people"), which is the site of the Nauru Local Government Council, is located in Uaboe District, while government offices are located in Yaren District.

Official Languages: English, Nauruan.

Monetary Unit: Australian Dollar (market rate March 1, 1988, 1.39 dollars = $1US).

President: Hammer DeROBURT; initially elected by Parliament on May 18, 1968; reelected on eight occasions thereafter, most recently on January 27, 1987, following election of January 24.

THE COUNTRY

An isolated coral island in the west-central Pacific, Nauru is located just south of the equator, between the

Marshall and Solomon islands. The present population consists of some 60 percent indigenous Nauruans (a mixture of Micronesian, Melanesian, and Polynesian stocks), 25 percent other Pacific islanders, 8 percent Chinese, and 7 percent Australians and other Caucasians. Habitation is mainly confined to a fertile strip of land ringing a central plateau composed of very high-grade phosphate deposits. This mineral wealth has yielded one of the world's highest per capita incomes, which, however, declined from a peak of over $17,000 in 1975 to an estimated $8,700 at the end of the decade. Income from the government-owned Nauru Phosphate Company provides an investment fund against the time, estimated to be in the mid-1990s, when the phosphate deposits will be exhausted.

GOVERNMENT AND POLITICS

Political background. A former German colony, Nauru became a British League of Nations mandate in 1919, with Australia as the administering power. The Japanese occupied the island during World War II and transported most of the inhabitants to Truk, where less than two-thirds survived the hardships of forced labor. In 1947, Nauru was made a UN Trust Territory under joint administration of the United Kingdom, Australia, and New Zealand, with Australia again serving as de facto administering authority. Local self-government was gradually accelerated, and in 1966 elections were held for members of a Legislative Council with jurisdiction over all matters except defense, external affairs, and the phosphate industry. Pursuant to the Council's request for full independence, Australia adopted a Nauru Independence Act in November 1967 and the trusteeship agreement was formally terminated by the United Nations, effective January 31, 1968. The arrangements for independence were negotiated by a delegation led by Hammer DeROBURT, who had been head chief of Nauru since 1956 and who became the new Republic's first president by legislative designation on May 18, 1968. Relations with the Commonwealth were defined by an agreement announced on November 29, 1968, whereby Nauru became a "special member" entitled to full participation in the organization's activities except meetings of Commonwealth heads of government. President DeRoburt, reelected in 1971 and 1973, was replaced by Bernard DOWIYOGO following a legislative election in December 1976.

Although reconfirmed on November 15, 1977, following a new parliamentary election on November 12, Dowiyogo resigned in January 1978 because of a deadlock over budgetary legislation. Immediately reelected, he resigned again in mid-April after the opposition had blocked passage of a bill dealing with phosphate royalties. He was succeeded on April 19 by Lagumot HARRIS, who in turn resigned on May 11 because of an impasse on an appropriations bill. Harris was succeeded, on the same day, by former president DeRoburt, apparently as the result of a temporary defection by an opposition representative.

The remarkable spectacle of three presidents in one month was accompanied by intense debate on the economic future of Nauru upon exhaustion of its phosphate deposits.

Exports of the commodity had been declining for several years, and both public and private groups had engaged in substantial overseas investment, including a retail and office complex on Saipan in the Marianas and a 53-story office building at Melbourne, Australia.

DeRoburt was reinvested in 1980 and 1983, but was forced to yield office to Kennan ADEANG during a ten-day loss of his parliamentary majority in October 1986 and for a four-day period in the wake of an election on December 6. He was sworn in for a ninth term on January 27, 1987, following redesignation by a new parliament elected three days earlier.

Constitution and government. Nauru's constitution, adopted by an elected Constitutional Convention on January 29, 1968, and amended on May 17 of the same year, provides for a republic whose president combines the functions of head of state and chief of government. The unicameral Parliament, consisting of 18 members popularly elected for three-year terms, selects the president from among its membership for a term corresponding to the life of the Parliament itself. The president in turn appoints a number of legislators to serve with him as a cabinet that is responsible to Parliament and is obligated to resign as a body in the event of a no-confidence vote. The judiciary consists of a Supreme Court and a District Court. The island is administratively divided into 14 districts, which are regrouped into 8 districts for electoral purposes.

Foreign relations. Nauru maintains formal diplomatic relations with about a dozen foreign governments (including, as of early 1988, the Soviet Union), primarily through representatives accredited to Australia and Fiji; its resident diplomatic corps consists of an Australian high commissioner and a Taiwanese consul general. Although it has declined to apply for membership in the United Nations, it is a member of the UN Economic Commission for Asia and the Far East, the South Pacific Commission (SPC), and the South Pacific Forum (SPF). In August 1982, it was announced that Nauru had acceded to the South Pacific Regional Trade Agreement (Sparteca), under which Australia and New Zealand have agreed to permit the duty-free entry of a wide variety of goods from SPF member countries. Its principal international tie, however, is its special Commonwealth membership, which permits participation in a wide range of Commonwealth activities and includes eligibility for technical assistance.

Current issues. As Nauru nears total depletion of its phosphate, the possibility of physical removal from the increasingly barren island has appealed to at least some of its inhabitants. Government officials have discussed the idea with a number of neighboring Pacific countries, but have thus far been rebuffed because of Nauru's insistence that it be granted legal sovereignty to any island to which its citizens might relocate.

In mid-1987 Nauru stepped up a campaign to secure compensation for the destruction of its top soil by mining interests during the previous 80 years, suggesting that it might attempt to take the matter to the UN Trusteeship Council. The former participants in the British Phosphate Commission (Australia, New Zealand, and the United Kingdom) insisted, however, that the island's inhabitants had already been adequately compensated for the loss.

In March 1988 Pacific House, a project of the Nauru Phosphate Royalties Trust, opened in Washington, DC, with the stated aim of serving as a Pacific islands' center in the US capital.

POLITICAL PARTIES

Until 1976 there were no political parties in Nauru. Following the election of December 18, 1976, at least half of the new Parliament claimed membership in the Nauru Party, a loosely structured group led by Bernard Dowiyogo and consisting primarily of younger Nauruans opposed to some of President DeRoburt's policies. The party won 9 of 18 seats in the election of November 12, 1977, but became essentially moribund thereafter.

Following the election of January 1987, it was reported that eight members of Parliament had joined an opposition **Democratic Party of Nauru** under the leadership of former president Adeang. The alignment, if firm, reduces the president's majority to one member, since the speaker does not vote.

LEGISLATURE

The unicameral **Parliament** of 18 members is popularly elected for a three-year term, subject to dissolution. Voting is compulsory for those over 20 years of age. At the election of November 12, 1977, the Nauru Party won 9 seats and, with the support of an independent member, was able to constitute a majority. It lost control on May 11, 1978, when one of its members defected and Hammer DeRoburt was reinstated as chief executive. Since 1983 all members have campaigned as independents and President DeRoburt was reelected after the most recent balloting of January 24, 1987, by a seemingly comfortable margin of 11–6; this was, however, prior to the organization of the Democratic Party (above).

Speaker: Reuben KUN.

CABINET

President	Hammer DeRoburt
Ministers	
Assistant to the President	Robidok Buraro Detudamo
Civil Aviation	Hammer DeRoburt
External Affairs	Hammer DeRoburt
Finance	Kinza Clodumar
Health and Education	Reuben Kun
Internal Affairs	Hammer DeRoburt
Island Development and Industry	Hammer DeRoburt
Justice	Bernard Dowiyogo
Public Service	Hammer DeRoburt
Works and Community Services	Robidok Buraro Detudamo

NEWS MEDIA

Press. The *Bulletin* (750) is issued weekly in English.

Radio and television. Government-owned Radio Nauru currently broadcasts in English and Nauruan to approximately 4,000 receivers. There is no television service.

INTERGOVERNMENTAL REPRESENTATION

Nauru is not a member of the United Nations.

Ambassador to the US: T.W. STARR (resident in Australia).

US Ambassador to Nauru: Laurence William LANE, Jr., (resident in Australia).

IGO Memberships (Non-UN): *CWTH,* Interpol, SPC, SPEC, SPF.

NEPAL

Kingdom of Nepal
Nepál Alhirajya

Political Status: Independent monarchy established 1769; under limited constitutional system promulgated December 16, 1962.

Area: 54,362 sq. mi. (140,797 sq. km.).

Population: 15,022,839 (1981C), 17,938,000 (1988E).

Major Urban Center (1981C): KATHMANDU (235,160).

Official Language: Nepali.

Monetary Unit: Nepalese Rupee (principal rate March 1, 1988, 22.00 rupees = $1US).

Sovereign: King BIRENDRA Bir Bikram Shah Dev; succeeded to the throne January 31, 1972, on the death of his father, King MAHENDRA Bir Bikram Shah Dev; crowned February 24, 1975.

Heir to the Throne: Crown Prince DIPENDRA Bir Bikram Shah Dev, son of the King.

Prime Minister: Marich Man Singh SHRESTHA; elected by the National Assembly on June 13, 1986, to succeed Nagendra Prasad RIJAL, who had been appointed on an interim basis following the resignation of Lokendra Bahadur CHAND on March 20.

THE COUNTRY

Landlocked between India and Tibet in the central Himalayas, Nepal is renowned for a mountainous landscape dominated by such peaks as Everest and Annapurna, and for the prowess of its Gurkha regiments, which have served in the British and Indian armies. It encompasses three distinct geographic zones: a southern plain known as the Terai, a central hill region with many rivers and valleys, and a northern section dominated by high mountains. The country is inhabited by numerous tribes that fall into two main ethnic groupings, Mongolian and Indo-Aryan. The majority of the population, particularly in the south, is Hindu in religion and linked in culture to India. The northern region, adjoining Tibet, is mainly Buddhist, but throughout the country Hindu and Buddhist practices have intermingled with each other and with Shamanism. In 1982, women constituted 67 percent of the labor force, almost entirely in agriculture; however, customary law prohibits female disposal of property, and female participation in government is minimal.

Nepal is considered one of the world's dozen least-developed nations. Its economy is primarily agricultural, with varied topography and climate allowing considerable crop diversity. Industry is oriented toward nondurable consumer goods, industrial development being hindered by rudimentary communication and transportation facilities. Natural resources include timber, mica, and coal. Over half of the export trade is with India, though efforts are being made to expand economic contacts throughout eastern Asia. Extensive foreign aid from both East and West is being used to support construction projects that include roads, railways, and a massive hydroelectric facility.

GOVERNMENT AND POLITICS

Political background. Founded in 1769 by the Gurkha ruler Prithvi NARAYAN Shah as a kingdom comprising 46 previously sovereign principalities, Nepal was ruled by Narayan's descendants until the 1840s, when the Rana family established an autocratic system that, under hereditary prime ministers, lasted until 1951. A revolution in 1950, inspired in part by India's independence, restored the power of King TRIBHUVAN Bir Bikram Shah Dev and initiated a period of quasi-constitutional rule that continued after 1955 under the auspices of Tribhuvan's son, King MAHENDRA Bir Bikram Shah Dev.

A democratic constitution promulgated in 1959 paved the way for an election that brought to power the socialist-inclined Nepali Congress Party (NCP) under Biseswar Prasad KOIRALA. In December 1960, however, the king charged the new government with misuse of power, dismissed and jailed its leaders, suspended the constitution, banned political parties, and assumed personal authority. A new constitution promulgated in 1962 and amended in 1967 established a tiered *panchayat* (assembly) system of representative bodies that was held to be more in keeping with Nepal's traditions. Nevertheless, the system encountered persistent opposition, primarily from NCP supporters and university students, who remained unsatisfied by reconciliation efforts that included Koirala's release from detention.

King BIRENDRA, who succeeded to the throne in January 1972, accorded high priority to economic development but encountered difficulty in reconciling monarchial rule with pressures for political liberalization. Confronted with mounting unrest, Prime Minister Kirti Nidhi BISTA was forced to resign in July 1973, while his successor, Nagendra Prasad RIJAL, was replaced by Tulsi GIRI in December 1975. Giri, in turn, resigned in September 1977 in the wake of corruption charges and a failure to regularize relations with India, former prime minister Bista being reinstated as head of a new Council of Ministers.

In May 1979, after prolonged demonstrations that began as a protest by students demanding changes in the system of higher education and subsequently expanded to include workers, peasants, and the middle class in a call for political reforms, King Birendra announced that a referendum would be held to determine whether the nation favored revision of the *panchayat* structure or its replacement by a multiparty system. Immediately thereafter, Bista was succeeded by Surya Bahadur THAPA, who had previously served as prime minister during 1965–1969. A year later, on May 2, 1980, Nepalese voters rejected reintroduction of a party system, and on December 15 the king proclaimed a number of constitutional changes, including direct, nonparty election to the National Assembly.

Less than a third of the Assembly members elected in May 1981 were considered strongly progovernment, and nearly two-thirds signed a nonbinding motion in mid-1982 urging Thapa to resign because of food shortages and high prices. However, the prime minister retained the king's confidence and effected a major cabinet reorganization in October that resulted in the ouster of several of his most outspoken detractors. The move followed the death on July 21 of former prime minister Koirala, who had refused to participate in the 1981 campaign but had subsequently urged a policy of accommodation between the monarchy and what he termed "democratic forces". Severe economic problems, aggravated by both flooding and drought, in addition to renewed charges of official corruption and mismanagement, resulted in parliamentary defeat of the Thapa government on July 11, 1983, and the appointment of Lokendra Bahadur CHAND as prime minister the following day.

On March 20, 1986, Prime Minister Chand submitted his resignation to concentrate on the forthcoming national election, former prime minister Rijal being named as his interim successor. In balloting that began on May 12, little more than two-thirds of the Assembly incumbents secured reelection, with a majority of the new members reportedly favoring abolition of the *panchayat* system. On June 13, the parliament elected Marich Man Singh SHRESTHA to the post of prime minister and the king, on Shrestha's recommendation, appointed a new 17-member Council of Ministers three days later.

Constitution and government. The *panchayat* system in operation prior to the May 1980 referendum provided for a hierarchically arranged parallel series of assemblies and councils encompassing four different levels: village (*gaun*) and town (*nagar*), district (*jilla*), zone (*anchal*), and national (*Rashtriya Panchayat*). The members of the village and town assemblies were directly elected, members of the other bodies being indirectly elected by bodies directly below them in the hierarchy.

The constitutional changes introduced in December 1980 provided for direct, rather than indirect, election to a nonpartisan National Assembly; designation of the prime minister by the Assembly, rather than by the king; and parliamentary responsibility of cabinet members, who would henceforth be named by the king on advice of the prime minister. Under a decentralization bill passed in 1982, considerable control over finance, development, social programs, and agriculture was devolved to district and village assemblies, which, however, can now be dissolved by the central government.

The judicial system, which has undergone a number of structural changes since the 1950s, presently consists of a Supreme Court, 15 zonal courts, and 75 district courts. Administratively, the country is divided into four development regions, each of which encompasses a hierarchy of appointed officials responsible to the central government.

Foreign relations. Although historically influenced by Britain and subsequently by India, Nepal has recently endeavored to strengthen its independence, particularly in the wake of the latter's annexation of the adjacent state of Sikkim in 1975. Thus, Kathmandu has adopted a policy of nonalignment in an effort to balance relations with India and the People's Republic of China. Indicatively, King Birendra participated in the nonaligned summit at Havana, Cuba, in September 1979 and visited both Beijing and New Delhi before returning home. Both of its immediate neighbors supply Nepal with financial aid, India being particularly interested in maintaining a buffer between itself and China. Collaterally, Nepalese leaders have moved to involve not only China but Bangladesh, Bhutan, and Pakistan in a plan for regional cooperation, with primary emphasis on water resource development.

On November 20, 1979, after 18 months of negotiation, a major issue in relations with China was apparently resolved by the signing, at Peking, of an agreement defining Nepal's northern frontier. The agreement, based on modern watershed and midstream principles as well as more conventional methods, was hailed as a model for the potential settlement of outstanding border disputes between China and the neighboring states of India and Bhutan.

Current issues. The 1986 election was boycotted by the Nepali Congress and a number of pro-Beijing Communist groups, but not by pro-Moscow Communists, who were successful in a number of constituencies, including a landslide victory at Kathmandu by Padma Ratna TULADHAR, who defeated the former home minister, Jog Meher SHRESTHA. Overall, the balloting yielded an infusion of "Young Turks" committed to reintroduction of a multiparty system. At local elections in March and April 1987, a number of proscribed groups presented nominally independent candidates, the NCP winning the posts of both mayor and deputy mayor at Kathmandu.

In June 1987 an agreement was concluded at New Delhi for enhanced economic cooperation between Nepal and India. Two months earlier, however, the government had introduced a work-permit system for foreigners that was seen as aimed primarily at the more than 1 million transient Indians entering the country each year.

POLITICAL GROUPS

Political parties were banned by royal decree in 1960, although de facto party members subsequently served as cabinet ministers and *Rashtriya Panchayat* delegates. In 1979–1980, a number of groups actively supported "collective efforts" on behalf of a party system, including a People's Party, led by former prime minister Tanka Prasad ACHARYA, and a Multi-Party Democratic Front, led by former foreign minister Rishikesh SHAH and

former home minister Kedar Man VYATHI. Most prominent among those currently active is the **Nepali Congress Party**, led by Krishna Prasad BHATTARI, Girija Prasad KOIRALA, and Ganesh Man SINGH which has long sought abolition of the *panchayat* system and defied the regime by holding a national convention at Kathmandu on March 11–13, 1985, after which it launched a civil disobedience movement (*satyagraha*) to press for the release of political prisoners and party legalization.

Nepalese Communists have been deeply divided since 1961. At present, there are eight relatively small formations that differ in attitude toward Moscow and Beijing and in their assessments of recent developments in China and India. The pro-Chinese factions include the **Nepal Communist Party–Marxist Leninist** (NCP-ML), a Maoist offspring of the Indian Naxalite movement, both of whose leaders, Radha Krishna MAINALI and Mohan Chandra ADHIKARY, are under arrest; the **Nepal Communist Party–Fourth Congress,** a Maoist group led by Mohan Bikram GHARTI that claims loyalty to the "Gang of Four"; and the **Nepal Communist Party–Mashal,** a Dengist group led by Nirmal LAMA. The pro-Moscow factions include the **Nepal Communist Party–Rayamajhi,** led by Keshar Jung RAYAMAJHI; the **Nepal Communist Party–Manandhar,** led by Bishnu Bahadur MANANDHAR; and the **Nepal Communist Party–Tulsi Lal,** led by Tulsi Lal AMATYA. There were also two previously Maoist neutralist factions, the **Nepal Communist Party–Adhikary,** led by Man Mohan ADHIKARY, and the **Nepal Communist Party–Pushpa Lal** (NCP-PL), led by Pushpa Lal's widow Sahana PRADHAM.

LEGISLATURE

A 125-member **National Assembly** (*Rashtriya Panchayat*), encompassing both indirectly elected and nominated representatives, was established under the 1962 constitution. By subsequent amendment, the Assembly was expanded to 135 members in 1975 and to 140 members in 1980. At the most recent poll of May 12, 1986, 108 members were elected for five-year terms, with balloting postponed in four constituencies because of candidate deaths and the remaining 28 members being appointed by the king.

Chairman: Nav Raj SUBEDI.

CABINET

Prime Minister	Marich Man Singh Shrestha
Ministers	
Agriculture, Law and Justice	Hari Narayan Rajauriya
Commerce	Bijay Prakash Thebe
Defense	Marich Man Singh Shrestha
Foreign Affairs and Land Reform	Shailendra Kumar Upadhyaya
Forests and Soil Conservation	Hem Bahadur Malla
Health	Gunjeshwori Prasad Singh
Panchayat and Local Development	Pashupati Shumshere J.B. Rana
Public Works, Transport and Communication	Hari Bahadur Basnet

Royal Palace Affairs	Marich Man Singh Shrestha
Supplies	Parashu Narayan Chaudhari
Water Resources	Yadav Prasad Pant

Ministers of State

Education and Culture	Keshar Bahadur Bista
Finance and Industry	Bharat Bahadur Pradhan
Home Affairs	Prakash Bahadur Singh
Tourism, Labor and Industry	Ramesh Nath Pandey

| Governor, Central Bank | Ganesh Bahadur Thapa |

NEWS MEDIA

Press. For its size, Nepal has an unusually large number of newspapers (nearly 350 dailies and weeklies). However, traditional freedom of the press was substantially abrogated by the 1975 Press and Publication Act, which resulted in the closing of a number of papers, banned material critical of the monarchy or of official policy, and subjected foreign dispatches to government censorship. In mid-1981, *Prati Dhwani,* a popular vernacular weekly, was banned for printing material deemed offensive to the Soviet diplomatic mission. In November 1982 the National Assembly approved a new Press and Publications Act that increased the degree of censorship, while in December 1985 the government suspended 99 newspapers for "irregular publication". During 1986 the *Valley News and Views,* an English-language daily, and a number of Nepalese weeklies were suppressed for publishing "objectionable material". The following are published daily at Kathmandu in Nepali, unless otherwise noted: *Gorkha Patra* (35,000), government organ; *The Rising Nepal* (20,000), government organ, in English; *New Herald* (20,000), in English; *Samaya* (18,000); *Nepali* (12,500), pro-Indian, in Hindi; *The Commoner* (6,800), independent, in English; *The Motherland* (5,000), independent, in English; *Naya Samaj* (3,000), progovernment; *Samaj* (2,000).

News agencies. The domestic facility is *Rastriya Samachar Samiti* (RSS); AP, UPI, *Agence France-Presse, Deutsche Presse-Agentur,* Reuters, TASS, and *Xinhua* also maintain bureaus at Kathmandu.

Radio and television. Radio Nepal, owned and operated by the government, broadcasts in Nepali and English. A government-operated television station, which commenced operations at Kathmandu in mid-1986, currently serves some 27,000 receivers.

INTERGOVERNMENTAL REPRESENTATION

Ambassador to the US: (Vacant).

US Ambassador to Nepal: Milton FRANK.

Permanent Representative to the UN: Jai Pratap RANA.

IGO Memberships (Non-UN): ADB, CP, Interpol, NAM, SAARC.

NETHERLANDS

Kingdom of the Netherlands
Koninkrijk der Nederlanden

Political Status: Constitutional monarchy established 1814; under multiparty parliamentary system.

Area: 13,103 sq. mi. (33,936 sq. km.).

Population: 13,060,115 (1971C), 14,721,000 (1988E).

Major Urban Centers (1986E): AMSTERDAM (677,000); The Hague (seat of government, 444,000); Rotterdam (570,000); Utrecht (230,000); Eindhoven (191,000).

Official Language: Dutch.

Monetary Unit: Guilder (market rate March 1, 1988, 1.90 guilders = $1US).

Sovereign: Queen BEATRIX Wilhelmina Armgard; ascended the throne April 30, 1980, upon the abdication of her mother, Queen JULIANA Louise Emma Marie Wilhelmina.
Heir Apparent: WILLEM-ALEXANDER, Prince of Orange.

Prime Minister: Ruud (Rudolph) F.M. LUBBERS (Christian Democratic Appeal); sworn in as head of two-party coalition on November 4, 1982, succeeding Andreas A.M. van AGT (Christian Democratic Appeal); returned as head of modified biparty administration on July 14, 1986, following general election of May 21.

THE COUNTRY

Facing the North Sea between Belgium and Germany, the Netherlands (often called "Holland", from the name of one of its principal provinces) is noted for the dikes, canals, and reclaimed polder lands providing constant reminder that two-fifths of the country's land area lies below sea level. The ethnically homogeneous, Germanic population is about equally divided between Protestants (40 percent) and Roman Catholics (40 percent), with the remainder having no religious affiliation. Church and state are separated, however, and freedom of religion is guaranteed. In 1980, women constituted 30 percent of the labor force, with over 80 percent concentrated in the human services sector; female participation in government is approximately 15 percent, decreasing substantially at the local level.

The Netherlands has experienced rapid industrialization since World War II, and the industrial sector now employs approximately 45 percent of the labor force. The traditionally important agricultural sector employs only about 6 percent but is characterized by highly efficient methods of production. With few natural resources except large natural gas deposits, most nonagricultural activity involves the processing of imported raw materials. Oil refining, chemicals, metallurgy, steel, textiles, and shipbuilding constitute the bulk of industrial output. Highly dependent upon foreign trade and beset by recurrent balance-of-payments difficulties, the economy also has relatively high levels of public expenditure and deficit financing, both of which were marginally reduced under an austerity budget in 1987.

GOVERNMENT AND POLITICS

Political background. Having won independence from Spain at the time of the Counter Reformation, the United Provinces of the Netherlands were ruled by hereditary *stadhouders* (governors) of the House of Orange until the present constitutional monarchy was established under the same house at the close of the Napoleonic period. Queen JULIANA, who had succeeded her mother, WILHELMINA, in 1948, abdicated in favor of her daughter BEATRIX on April 30, 1980.

Since World War II, the Netherlands has been governed by a succession of non-Communist coalition governments in which the large Catholic People's Party (KVP) traditionally played a pivotal role. Coalitions between the KVP and the Labor Party (PvdA) were the rule until 1958, when the latter went into opposition, the KVP continuing to govern in alliance with smaller parties of generally moderate outlook. A center-right coalition headed by Petrus J.S. de JONG assumed office in April 1967 and was followed by an expanded center-right government formed under Barend W. BIESHEUVEL in 1971.

The inability of the Biesheuvel government to cope with pressing economic problems led to its early demise in July 1972 and to an election four months later. Rather than alleviating the government crisis, the new election intensified it, yielding a 163-day interregnum before a new government could be formed. The PvdA-led government finally organized in May 1973 by Johannes M. den UYL survived until March 1977, when it collapsed in the wake of a bitter dispute between Labor and Christian Democratic leaders over compensation for expropriated land. After another extended interregnum (the longest in the nation's history), Andreas A.M. van AGT succeeded in organizing a Christian Democratic–Liberal government in late December.

At the election of May 26, 1981, the center-right coalition lost its legislative majority and, after a further extensive round of interparty negotiations, was replaced by a grouping that included the Christian Democrats, Labor, and the center-left Democrats 1966, with van Agt continuing as prime minister. The comfortable legislative majority thus achieved was offset by sharp differences in both defense and economic policy, and the new government collapsed on May 12, 1982. The principal result of further balloting on September 8 was a loss of 11 seats by the Democrats 1966 and a gain of 10 by the Liberals, Ruud F.M. LUBBERS being installed as head of another center-right government on November 4 following his succession to the Christian Democratic leadership on October 13. Contrary to opinion poll predictions, the Christian Democrats won a plurality at the lower house election of May 21, 1986, Lubbers being returned as head of a new coalition government on July 14.

Constitution and government. Originally adopted in 1814–1815, the Netherlands' constitution has been progressively amended to incorporate the features of a modern democratic welfare state in which the sovereign exercises strictly limited powers. Under a special Statute of December 29, 1954, the Kingdom of the Netherlands was defined so as to include not only the Netherlands proper but also the fully autonomous overseas territories of the Netherlands Antilles and Suriname, the latter ultimately becoming independent in 1975. On January 1, 1986, the island of Aruba formally withdrew from the Antilles federation, becoming a separate, self-governing member of the Kingdom.

Political power centers in the parliament, or States General, consisting of an indirectly elected First Chamber and a more powerful, directly elected Second Chamber. Executive authority is vested in a Council of Ministers (*Ministerraad*) appointed by the sovereign but responsible to the States General. An advisory Council of State (*Raad van State*), composed of the queen and crown prince plus a number of councillors appointed by the queen upon nomination by the Second Chamber, is consulted by the executive on legislative and administrative policy. The judicial system is headed by a Supreme Court and includes 5 courts of appeal, 19 district courts, and 62 cantonal courts.

For administrative purposes the Netherlands is divided into 12 provinces, the most recent, Flevoland, created on January 1, 1986, from land formed under the more than half-century-old Zuider Zee reclamation project. Each province has its own elected Council and a governor appointed by the queen. At the local level there are approximately 850 municipalities, each with a Council that designates aldermen to share regulatory responsibilities with a Crown-appointed burgomaster.

Foreign relations. Officially neutral before World War II, the Netherlands reversed its foreign policy as a result of the German occupation of 1940–1945 and became an active participant in the subsequent evolution of the Western community through the Benelux Union, NATO, the Western European Union, the European Communities, and other West European and Atlantic organizations. An original member of the United Nations, the Netherlands also belongs to all of its Specialized Agencies. The country's principal foreign-policy problems in the postwar period arose in connection with the 1945–1949 transition to independence of the Netherlands East Indies (Indonesia); Djakarta's formal annexation in 1969 of West New Guinea (Irian Jaya); and continued pressure, including numerous acts of terrorism, by South Moluccan expatriates seeking Dutch aid in the effort to separate their homeland from Indonesia.

A major foreign-affairs issue with profound domestic repercussions turned on the NATO decision in late 1979 to modernize and expand its nuclear arsenal. After intense debate in the Second Chamber, the Dutch acceded to the wishes of their allies but indicated that they would postpone local deployment of 48 cruise missiles in the hope that a meaningful arms-control agreement with the Soviet bloc could be negotiated; in the absence of such an agreement, a treaty with the United States authorizing deployment was finally ratified in February 1986. Subsequently, in an effort to improve relations with Eastern Europe, Queen Beatrix made a state visit to Hungary in October, while in late December Prime Minister Lubbers became the first Dutch chief executive to visit Moscow.

Current issues. The outcome of the 1986 Second Chamber poll was regarded as a personal triumph for Ruud Lubbers, whose Christian Democrats gained 9 additional seats—sufficient to offset a 9-seat loss by their Liberal coalition partner, which had recently experienced leadership difficulties. The VVD slide continued at provincial council balloting in March 1987, which significantly altered First Chamber representation following indirect elections on June 9. The PvdA, with an increase from 17 seats to 26, gained parity with the CDA, while the VVD's loss of 4 seats left the governing (CDA-VVD) coalition with a bare majority of 38 seats out of 75. Earlier, anticipating a sharp decline in North Sea gas revenues, the administration had called for the first budget reduction in 30 years. Collaterally, it hoped that Dutch unemployment (the EC's highest, at 15 percent) would begin to recede. The austerity measures were reported to have provoked two bomb attacks on public buildings at Amsterdam in September 1986, while a number of other such incidents (including an attempted firebombing of the prime minister's residence in May 1987) appeared to stem from a variety of unrelated sources, including opponents of the cruise missile deployment and of the country's (unsuccessful) bid to host the 1992 Olympic Games.

POLITICAL PARTIES

The growth of the Dutch multiparty system, which emerged from the tendency of political parties to reflect the interests of particular religious and economic groups, has been reinforced by the use of proportional representation. The two strongest groups are the Christian Democratic Appeal (CDA) and the Labor Party (PvdA), the former organized initially as an alliance of three religious parties; other parties range from the ultraconservative Political Reformed Party (SGP) to the Netherlands Communist Party (CPN). Earlier ruling coalitions tended generally to be center-right in political complexion, but the 1972 election resulted in a center-left government led by the Labor Party. After seven months of negotiations, the election of May 1977 yielded a new center-right coalition involving the Christian Democrats and Liberals (VVD). The government formed after the 1981 balloting included the CDA, the PvdA, and the Democrats 1966 (D'66), while those of November 1982 and July 1986 again involved two-party coalitions between the CDA and VVD.

Government Parties:

Christian Democratic Appeal (*Christen-Democratisch Appel* – CDA). Party organization in the Netherlands has long embraced a distinction between confessional and secular parties. In recent years the former have experienced a gradual erosion in electoral support, and partly in an effort to counter this trend the CDA was organized in December 1976 as an unprecedented alliance of the Catholic People's Party (*Katholieke Volkspartij* – KVP) and two Protestant groups, the Anti-Revolutionary Party (*Anti-Revolutionaire Partij* – ARP) and the Christian Historical Union (*Christelijk-Historische Unie* – CHU). The KVP was founded in 1945 as a centrist party supported primarily by Roman Catholic businessmen, farmers, and some workers. It endorsed many social-welfare programs while favoring close cooperation between spiritual and secular forces in the community. The ARP, founded in 1879, was the nation's oldest political organization, drawing its principal strength from Calvinist businessmen, white-collar workers, and farmers. The CHU was formed in 1908 by a dissident faction of the ARP. Traditionally more centrist than the parent party, it shared the ARP's Calvinist outlook.

The three constituent parties, which had presented joint lists at the May 1977 parliamentary election, agreed on October 11, 1980, to merge into a unified political grouping. Second to the PvdA in legislative strength after the 1982 balloting, the CDA obtained a plurality in 1986.

Leaders: Ruud F.M. LUBBERS (Prime Minister), Andreas A.M. van AGT (former Prime Minister), W.G. van VELZEN (Chairman), Dr. Bert de VRIES (Parliamentary Leader), C. BREMMER (General Secretary).

People's Party for Freedom and Democracy (*Volkspartij voor Vrijheid en Democratie* – VVD). The forerunners of the VVD included the prewar Liberal State and Liberal Democratic parties. Organized in 1948, the party draws its major support from upper-class businessmen and middle-class, white-collar workers. Although it accepts social-welfare measures, the VVD is conservative in outlook and strongly favors free enterprise and separation of church and state. The party's Second Chamber strength fell from 36 to 27 at the 1986 election, in part because of the unpopularity of its (then) parliamentary leader, Ed Nijpels, who stepped down from the post after formation of the new government in July.

Leaders: Rudolf de KORTE (Deputy Prime Minister), L. GINJAAR (Chairman), Joris VOORHOEVE (Parliamentary Leader), W.J.A. van den BERG (General Secretary).

Opposition Parties:

Labor Party (*Partij van de Arbeid* – PvdA). The Labor Party was formed in 1946 by a union of the former Socialist Democratic Workers' Party with left-wing Liberals and progressive Catholics and Protestants. It favors democratic socialism and is a strong supporter of the United Nations and an integrated European Community. The party program stresses the importance of equality of economic benefits, greater consultation in decisionmaking, and reduced defense spending. In October 1977, against the advice of its leadership, the party's national congress voted in favor of the establishment of a republican form of government for the Netherlands. The PvdA is strongly opposed to both nuclear power generation and the deployment of cruise missiles.

Leaders: C. POPPE (Acting Chairman), Willem (Wim) KOK (Parliamentary Leader), Willem (Wim) van VELZEN (Secretary).

Democrats 66 (*Democraten 66* – D66). Formed in 1966 as a left-of-center party, D66 favors the dropping of proportional representation and the direct election of the prime minister. Its stand on other domestic and foreign-policy questions is similar to that of the PvdA. The party's lower house representation declined from 17 seats to 6 in 1982, 3 of which were regained in 1986.

Leaders: Saskia van der LOO-de STEENWINKEL (Chairman), Hans van MIERLO (Parliamentary Leader), Toon de GRAFF (Secretary).

Political Reformed Party (*Staatkundig Gereformeerde Partij* – SGP). The SGP is an extreme right-wing Calvinist party that bases its political and social outlook on its own interpretation of the Bible. It advocates strong legal enforcement, including the use of the death penalty, and is against supranational government, which it feels would open society to corrupting influences. It retained its existing 3 Second Chamber seats in the 1986 election.

Leaders: Rev. D. SLAGBOOM (Chairman), B.J. van der VLIES (Parliamentray Leader), C.G. BOENDER (Secretary).

Reformed Political Union (*Gereformeerd Politiek Verbond* – GPV). A Calvinist party that resembles the SGP in outlook, the GPV argues against undue permissiveness in social behavior and in the economic sphere. It supports a strong defense policy and the Atlantic alliance but is against any subordination to a supranational governmental body.

Leaders: J. BLOKLAND (Chairman), Gert J. SCHUTTE (Parliamentary Leader), S.J.C. CNOSSEN (Secretary).

Reformational Political Federation (*Reformatorische Politieke Federatie* – RPF). Appealing to both Calvinists and interdenominational Christians, the RPF was formed in 1975 and obtained 2 Second Chamber seats in 1981 and 1982, one of which was lost in 1986.

Leaders: H. VISSER (Chairman), Meindert LEERLING (Parliamentary Leader), F.J. NIEUWENHUIS (Secretary).

Center Party (*Centrum Partij* – CP.) Despite its name, the CP is actually an extreme right-wing group that lost its only lower house seat in May 1986, after having secured 5 municipal council seats in March.

Leaders: A.W. LIER (Chairman), D.H.M. SEGERS (Secretary).

Evangelical People's Party (*Evangelische Volkspartij* – EVP). The EVP is a leftist Christian grouping that also lost its sole Second Chamber seat in 1986.

Leaders: C. OFMAN (Chairman), G. GUTOWSKI (Secretary).

Radical Political Party (*Politieke Partij Radikalen* – PPR). The PPR was formed in 1968 as a splinter group of the KVP. It advocates democratization of the political process and greater citizen participation in government, a more equitable distribution of wealth, an emphasis on détente rather than the defense capabilities of the Atlantic alliance, and increased aid to developing countries.

Leaders: Janneke van der PLAAT (Chairman), M.B.C. BECKERS-de BRUIJN (Parliamentary Leader), Lenie MULDER (Secretary).

Pacifist Socialist Party (*Pacifistisch Socialistische Partij* — PSP). A left-wing party, the PSP bases its policies on the assumption that pacifism and socialism are inseparable. The party advocates disarmament and the expansion of the United Nations into a world government with broad powers; it opposes all forms of economic imperialism and colonialism. Domestically, the PSP seeks to establish a highly socialized society. It lost 2 of its 3 lower house seats in 1986.

Leaders: M. MAZELAND (Chairman), Andrée van ES (Parliamentary Leader).

Netherlands Communist Party (*Communistische Partij van Nederland* — CPN). Appealing to left-wing intellectuals and low-income laborers, the CPN calls for the abolition of capitalism and the monarchy, a drastic cut in defense expenditure, and withdrawal from NATO. Reflecting the factional nature of Dutch politics, the CPN has been polarized since the early 1970s by a split between a social-democratic, radical feminist faction and a "workers' vanguard" led by hardline Marxists. Many of the latter left the party in 1985 to join the VCN (below). However, another orthodox faction, the "Consultation of Enhuizen", led by Marcus Bakker, continues in efforts to influence the party line. At the May 1986 balloting, following a disastrous showing at municipal elections in March, the party was denied lower house representation for the first time since 1918.

Leaders: Elli ISEBOUD (Chairman), Ina BROUWER (former Parliamentary Leader), Marius ERNSTING, Marcus BAKKER (leader, orthodox faction).

Alliance of Communists in the Netherlands (*Verbond van Communisten in Nederland* — VCN). The VCN was initially organized in February 1984 as an "advisory committee" within the CPN by orthodox Marxists ("horizontalists") who viewed the dominant "reformist" tendency as "feministic, antiworker, and anti-Russian". At its first congress on October 6–7, 1984, the new group declared its intention to organize as a separate party. Subsequently, it drew some 1,500 members from the CPN without, however, achieving the following it had hoped for.

Leaders: Laurens MEERTEN, René DAMMEN.

Other parties include the **Socialist Party** (*Socialistiese Partij* — SP) and **The Greens** (*De Groenen*), each of which secured less than .04 percent of the vote in 1986. In 1984, the Greens had joined the PSP, the PPR, and the CPN in a Green Progressive Accord (*Groenen Progressief Akkord* — GPA) that obtained 2 seats in the June European Parliament election on the basis of a 5.6 percent vote share.

LEGISLATURE

The **States General** (*Staten Generaal*) is a bicameral body consisting of an indirectly elected First Chamber and a directly elected Second Chamber. Either or both chambers may be dissolved by the sovereign prior to the holding of a new election. Compulsory voting was abolished in 1971.

First Chamber (*Eerste Kamer*). The 75 members of the upper house are indirectly elected by the country's provincial councils for staggered six-year terms, half (37 or 38, depending on the Provincial Estate groups in question) normally being elected every three years. Following the balloting of June 9, 1987, the Christian Democratic Appeal and the Labor Party each held 26 seats; the People's Party for Freedom and Democracy, 12; the Democrats 66, 5; and the Netherlands Communist Party, the Pacificist Socialist Party, the Political Reformed Party, the Radical Political Party, the Reformed Political Union, and the Reformist Political Federation, 1 each.

President: Dr. P.A.J.M. STEENKAMP.

Second Chamber (*Tweede Kamer*). The lower house consists of 150 members directly elected for four-year terms, subject to dissolution. Following the election of May 21, 1986, the Christian Democratic Appeal held 54 seats; the Labor Party, 52; the People's Party for Freedom and Democracy, 27; the Democrats 66, 9; the Political Reformed Party, 3; the Radical Political Party, 2; and the Pacific Socialist Party, the Reformed Political Union, and the Reformational Political Federation, 1 each.

President: Dr. Dirk DOLMAN.

CABINET

Prime Minister	Ruud Lubbers
Deputy Prime Minister	Dr. Rudolf W. de Korte
Ministers	
Agriculture and Fisheries	Gerrit Braks
Defense	Willem F. van Eekelen
Development Cooperation	Piet Bukman
Economic Affairs	Rudolf W. de Korte
Education	Willem (Wim) J. Deetman
Finance	Dr. Herman Onno Ruding
Foreign Affairs	Hans van den Broek
Home Affairs	Cees P. van Dijk
Housing, Physical Planning and Environment	Ed H.T.M. Nijpels
Justice	Frederik (Frits) Korthals Altes
Netherlands Antilles Affairs	Jan de Koning
Science	Willem (Wim) J. Deetman
Social Affairs and Employment	Jan de Koning
Transport and Public Works	Neelie Smit-Kroes
Welfare, Health and Culture	L.C. Brinkman
President, The Netherlands Bank	Willem Duisenberg

NEWS MEDIA

Press. Newspapers are free from censorship and are published by independent commercial establishments. There is strict separation between managerial and editorial boards. The following (circulation figures for 1986) are published daily at Amsterdam, unless otherwise noted: *De Telegraaf* (705,800), independent; *Algemeen Dagblad* (Rotterdam, 388,400), independent; *De Volkskrant* (271,100), independent Roman Catholic; *Het Vrije Volk* (Rotterdam, 197,100), Socialist; *Haagsche Courant* (Ryswyk, 182,700), independent; *NRC Handelsblad* (Rotterdam, 180,400), liberal; *De Gelderlander/De Nieuwe Krânt* (Nijmegen/Arnhem, 158,400), independent Roman Catholic; *Nieuwsblad van het Noorden* (Groningen, 135,000), independent; *De Limburger* (Maastrict/Roermond, 134,700), Roman Catholic; *Het Parool* (134,400), independent; *Trouw* (124,900), Calvinist; *Eindhovens Dagblad* (Eindhoven, 120,700), Roman Catholic; *Leeuwarder Courant* (Leeuwarden, 109,000), independent progressive; *De Stem* (Breda, 106,100), Roman Catholic; *De Courant Nieuws van de Dag* (57,000), independent.

News agencies. The Netherlands News Agency (*Algemeen Nederlands Persbureau*) is an independent agency operated at The Hague and Amsterdam on a cooperative basis by all Dutch newspapers; numerous foreign bureaus maintain offices at The Hague.

Radio and television. Radio and television services are provided by private associations under state supervision and regulation. The eight private radio and television companies are joined in the Netherlands Broadcasting Corporation (*Nederlandse Omroep Stichting* — NOS), which is directed by a 33-member Management Board comprising representatives of the media, the Crown, and cultural and social groups. There were approximately 4.8 million radio and 4.6 million television receivers in 1987.

INTERGOVERNMENTAL REPRESENTATION

Ambassador to the US: Richard H. FEIN.

US Ambassador to the Netherlands: John SHAD.

Permanent Representative to the UN: Adriaan JACOBOVITS DE SZEGED.

IGO Memberships (Non-UN): ADB, ADF, AfDB, BIS, BLX, CCC, CERN, CEUR, EC, EIB, ESA, Eurocontrol, G10, IADB, ICAC, ICCO, ICES, ICM, ICO, IEA, ILZ, Inmarsat, INRO, Intelsat, Interpol, IOOC, ITC, IWC, IWSG, NATO, OECD, PCA, WEU.

RELATED TERRITORIES

The bulk of the Netherlands' overseas empire disappeared with the accession of Indonesia to independence after World War II and the latter's subsequent acquisition of West New Guinea (Irian Jaya). Remaining under the Dutch Crown were the two Western Hemisphere territories of Netherlands Antilles and Suriname, the latter of which became independent on November 25, 1975. As of January 1, 1986, the island of Aruba was politically detached from the Antilles federation, joining it as an internally self-governing territory, with full independence scheduled for 1996 (see following articles).

ARUBA

Political Status: Formerly part of the Netherlands Antilles; became autonomous in internal affairs on January 1, 1986.

Area: 74.5 sq. mi. (193 sq. km.).

Population: 66,800 (1988E).

Major Urban Center (1986E): ORANJESTAD (17,500).

Official Language: Dutch.

Monetary Unit: Aruban Guilder (market rate March 1, 1988, 2.45 guilders = $1US). The guilder (also called the florint) is at par with the Netherlands Antilles guilder.

Sovereign: Queen BEATRIX Wilhelmina Armgard.

Governor: Felipe B. TROMP; invested on January 1, 1986, following appointment by the Queen.

Prime Minister: J.H.A. (Henny) EMAN (Aruba People's Party); sworn in January 1, 1986, following election of November 22, 1985.

THE COUNTRY

Aruba is a Caribbean island situated approximately 16 miles off the northeast coast of Venezuela and 50 miles west of Curaçao. Like other former Dutch dependencies in the area, its population is largely of mixed African ancestry, with minorities of Carib Indian and European extraction. Roman Catholicism is the dominant religion. Tourism is presently of primary economic importance, the island's only oil refinery, owned by a subsidiary of the US Exxon Corporation, having been closed down in March 1985 and its future uncertain, despite government acquisition of the facility for a nominal $1 million the following November.

GOVERNMENT AND POLITICS

Political background. Like Curaçao and Bonaire, Aruba became a Dutch possession in 1634 and remained so,

save for a brief period of British control during the Napoleonic wars, until participating in constitutional equality with the Netherlands as part of the Netherlands Antilles after 1954. However, a majority of the islanders disliked what was perceived as both political and economic domination by Curaçao, and entered into lengthy discussions with Dutch authorities that resulted in the achievement of formal parity with the Netherlands and Netherlands Antilles, under the Dutch crown, on January 1, 1986. Upon the assumption of domestic autonomy, the assets and liabilities of Aruba and the five remaining members of the federation were divided in the ratio 30:70, Aruba agreeing to retain economic and political links to the Netherlands Antilles at the ministerial level for a ten-year period. Full independence is scheduled for 1996.

Pre-autonomy balloting on November 22, 1985, yielded victory for a four-party coalition headed by J.H.A. (Henny) EMAN of the center-right Aruba People's Party (AVP) over the People's Electoral Movement (MEP), then led by "the architect of Aruba's transition to . . . eventual independence", Gilberto (Betico) CROES.

Constitution and government. The Dutch sovereign is titular head of state and is represented in Aruba by an appointed governor. Domestic affairs are the responsibility of the prime minister and other members of the Council of Ministers, appointed with the advice and approval of a unicameral *Staten* (legislature) of 21 deputies. Control of foreign affairs and defense is vested in the Council of Ministers at The Hague, with an Aruban minister plenipotentiary sitting as a voting member in matters affecting the island. Judicial authority is exercised by a local court of first instance, with appeal to a joint Court of Appeal of the Netherlands Antilles and Aruba, and ultimate appeal to the Supreme Court of the Netherlands at The Hague.

Current issues. The defeat of the MEP at the 1985 election, despite its leader's efforts on behalf of separation from Willemstad, was attributed largely to a severe drop in government income and rise in unemployment, following closure of the Exxon refinery earlier in the year, with doubt subsequently surfacing as to the island's long-term economic viability.

In early 1988 the government introduced a register of companies endowed with commercial secrecy to attract offshore financial business; however, the action drew criticism as a potential means of laundering drug money.

POLITICAL PARTIES

Government Parties:

Aruba People's Party (*Arubaanse Volkspartij* — AVP). Like the opposition MEP, the AVP advocated separation of Aruba from the Netherlands Antilles. It obtained seven *Staten* seats at the November 1985 balloting.

Leaders: J.H.A. (Henny) EMAN (Prime Minister), Armand ENGELBRECHT (Finance Minister).

Aruban Patriotic Party (*Arubaanse Patriottische Partij* — APP). Also known as the *Partido Patriótico Arubano* (PPA), the Patriotic Party has opposed full independence for the island.

Leader: Benny NISBET.

Aruba Democratic Party (*Democratische Arubaanse Partij* — DAP). A recently organized grouping, the DAP (also known as the *Partido Democratico Arubano* — PDA) won two seats in the 1985 balloting.
Leader: Leonard BERLINSKI.

National Democratic Action (*National Democratische Actie* — NDA). Also known as the *Accion Democratico Nacional* (ADN), the NDA is also a relatively new party that won two *Staten* seats in 1985.
Leaders: John BOOI, Charro KELLY (Public Works Minister).

Opposition Party:

People's Electoral Movement (*Movimentu Electoral di Pueblo* — MEP). A left-of-center member of the Socialist International, the MEP was in the forefront of the struggle for self-government and presently holds a plurality of eight seats in the *Staten*.
Leader: Nelson ODUBER (President and Parliamentary Leader).

LEGISLATURE

The unicameral *Staten* consists of 21 members elected for four-year terms, subject to dissolution. At the balloting of November 22, 1985, the People's Electoral Movement obtained 8 seats; the Aruba People's Party, 7; and the Aruban Patriotic Party, Aruba Democratic Party, and National Democratic Action, 2 each.
President: Pedro BIFLIP.

CABINET

Prime Minister	J.H.A. (Henny) Eman
Ministers	
Economic Affairs	Don Mansur
Education and Welfare	Mito Croes
Finance	Armand Engelbrecht
Justice	Watty Vos
Public Works	Charro Kelly
Transportation and Communications	Angel Bermudez

NEWS MEDIA

Press. The following are dailies published at Oranjestad: *The News* (8,000), in English; *Amigoe di Aruba* (2,900), in Dutch; *Diario* in Papiamento.

News agencies. The Netherlands News Agency (*Algemeen Nederlands Persbureau* — ANP) and the Associated Press (AP) maintain offices at Oranjestad.

Radio and television. There are five privately owned radio stations, with television provided by the commercial Tele-Aruba. There were approximately 19,000 television receivers in 1987.

INTERGOVERNMENTAL REPRESENTATION

Foreign relations are conducted through the Dutch Ministry of Foreign Affairs at The Hague.

IGO Membership (Non-UN): Interpol.

NETHERLANDS ANTILLES

De Nederlandse Antillen

Political Status: Former Dutch dependency; became autonomous in internal affairs under charter of the Kingdom of the Netherlands, effective December 29, 1954.

Area: 308 sq. mi. (800 sq. km.), encompassing Curaçao (171 sq. mi.), Bonaire (111 sq. mi.), Sint Maarten (Dutch portion, 13 sq. mi.), Sint Eustatius (8 sq. mi.), Saba (5 sq. mi.).

Population: 174,000 (1988E), including Curaçao, 149,400; Bonaire, 8,900; Sint Maarten, 13,300; Sint Eustatius, 1,400; Saba, 1,000.

Major Urban Center (1986E): WILLEMSTAD (68,000).

Official Language: Dutch. English and Spanish are widely spoken, while an Antillean patois, Papiamento, is common in the Leeward Islands.

Monetary Unit: Netherlands Antilles Guilder (market rate March 1, 1988, 2.45 guilders = $1US).

Sovereign: Queen BEATRIX Wilhelmina Armgard.

Governor: Dr. Rene A. RÖMER; invested on October 1, 1983, following the resignation of Ben LEITO.

Prime Minister: Maria LIBERIA-PETERS (National People's Party); served as Prime Minister from September 1984 to November 1985; returned to office on May 17, 1988, following collapse of government headed by Dominico (Don) F. MARTINA (New Antilles Movement).

THE COUNTRY

The Netherlands Antilles currently consists of two groups of two and three islands each, located 500 miles apart in the eastern Caribbean. The southern (Leeward) islands of Curaçao and Bonaire lie off the northwest coast of Venezuela, while the northern (Windward) islands of Sint Maarten (the northern portion of which is part of the French department of Guadeloupe), Sint Eustatius, and Saba are some 200 miles east of Puerto Rico. Approximately 85 percent of the population is of mixed African ancestry, the remainder being of Carib Indian and European derivation. Roman Catholicism is dominant in the southern islands and Saba, while Protestantism is most prevalent on Sint Eustatius and Sint Maarten. The economy has long been dependent on the refining of crude oil from Venezuela and Mexico, although most installations (centered at Curaçao) are now operating at less than 50 percent capacity because of slackened global demand; as a result, tourism and offshore banking activities are of increasing importance. Agriculture is relatively insignificant because of poor soil and little rainfall.

GOVERNMENT AND POLITICS

Political background. The Leeward Islands (including Aruba, see previous article) became Dutch possessions in 1634, while the Windward Islands passed to uninterrupted Dutch control in the early nineteenth century. Long administered as a colonial dependency, the (then) six-island

418

grouping was, in 1954, granted constitutional equality with the Netherlands and Suriname (which became independent in 1975) as an autonomous component of the Kingdom of the Netherlands.

Given the geographical range of the grouping, political differences have traditionally been island-based, necessitating highly unstable coalition governments. Thus, Prime Minister Silvio ROZENDAL, installed following an election in June 1977, was forced to resign in April 1979, in the wake of a legislative boycott by Aruban representatives. After balloting in July, a new three-party government was formed by Dominico MARTINA of the Curaçao-based New Antilles Movement (MAN), but in September 1981, the People's Electoral Movement (MEP) of Aruba again withdrew its support, as talks began at The Hague concerning the island's constitutional future. A governmental stalemate ensued that was not resolved by a general election in June 1982, although Martina remained in office until redesignation as head of a five-party coalition that excluded the MEP the following October. In March 1983 agreement was reached on the assumption of Aruban *status aparte* in January 1986, with full independence in 1996, but the Martina government was weakened by the withdrawal of the conservative National People's Party (NVP) in August and eventually collapsed in June 1984. On September 20 the NVP's Maria LIBERIA-PETERS, heading another five-party coalition that included neither the MAN or MEP, became the islands' first female prime minister. However, she was defeated at an election held November 22, 1985, in preparation for Aruba's departure on January 1, with a new Martina administration thereupon being formed.

In December 1987 Claude WATHEY, leader of the Democratic Party of Sint Maarten, resigned from the government over the issue of island independence and two months later the two remaining DPSM members also departed, leaving Martina with a one-seat legislative majority. In March 1988 a representative of the Workers' Liberation Front withdrew his support because of a proposed layoff of 1,400 public sector employees and the prime minister was again forced from office in favor of Liberia-Peters, who returned on May 17 as head of a new coalition that claimed the support of 13 of 22 *Staten* members.

Constitution and government. The Dutch sovereign is titular head of the present five-member state and is represented in the Antilles by an appointed governor. Domestic affairs are the responsibility of the prime minister and other members of the Council of Ministers, appointed with the advice and approval of a unicameral *Staten* (legislature) of 22 deputies (14 from Curaçao, 3 each from Bonaire and Sint Maarten, and 1 each from Sint Eustatius and Saba). Elections to the *Staten* are held every four years, subject to dissolution. Control of foreign affairs and defense is vested in the Council of Ministers at The Hague, with an Antillean minister plenipotentiary sitting as a voting member in matters dealing with "joint affairs of the realm". Judicial authority is exercised by a Court of Appeal at Willemstad, whose members are appointed by the queen in consultation with the Antilles government and who sit singly in island courts of first instance. Ultimate appeal is to the Supreme Court of the Netherlands at The Hague.

Each of the island territories elects an Island Council, which sits for four years and is responsible for enacting legislation regarding local affairs. A lieutenant governor is appointed by the queen for a six-year term and sits with deputies named by the elected Council as an island Executive Council.

Current issues. The departure of Aruba from the Antilles federation was occasioned in large part by an Aruban conviction that its contribution to the grouping's finances was disproportionately high, although it was obliged to enter into an "economic union" with the larger state and provide continued support of the smaller islands' economies as a condition of autonomy. The commitment appeared to be in jeopardy following a March 1986 announcement that the breakaway island would reduce or terminate preferential treatment for imports from the federation by 1990. Earlier, Prime Minister Martina had been forced to embark on an austerity program to offset a 21 percent revenue loss occasioned by Aruba's new status.

Prior to the constitutional change, the Royal Dutch/Shell Group had announced that it wished to close its refinery on Curaçao, which provided some 25 percent of the island's income. However, a "rescue package" was arranged in cooperation with the Netherlands and Venezuela that permitted the Antilles government to purchase the installation, at a token price, for lease to the Venezuelan state oil company at $11 million a year through 1990. Earlier, Willemstad's status as an offshore financial center had been weakened by Washington's repeal of a withholding tax on bond interest paid to overseas investors in US companies, for which a waiver had been granted in the case of Antilles subsidiaries. Of even greater concern was an announcement by the US Treasury Department in June 1987 that it planned to withdraw from a treaty that exempted pre-1984 Eurobonds issued by US firms through the Netherlands Antilles and Aruba to taxation. However, in July Washington reversed itself after it was discovered that upwards of 50 percent of the bonds (which some issuers were preparing to call in) were held by American investors.

A visit by Venezuelan President Jaime Lusinchi on October 31–November 2, 1987, yielded a police cooperation agreement intended to interdict drug trafficking in the islands, as well as an economic cooperation accord that included extension of the oil refinery lease through 1994 at a revised annual fee of $15 million.

Even before the fall of the Martina government in March 1988, DPSM leader Wathey appeared to draw back somewhat from his demand for full independence for Sint Maarten, although in the wake of her return to office Prime Minister Liberia-Peters felt constrained to assert that "The central structure imposed from above must be reduced to a minimum so that even Sint Maarten can feel at home within it". A potentially more serious problem for the new administration concerned the steadfast opposition of the Workers' Liberation Front to cuts in the Civil Service, for which a plan of "voluntary redundancy" was advanced, with the possibility of government employees being subjected to a "solidarity tax" to cover the wages of superfluous colleagues.

POLITICAL PARTIES

Government Parties:

National People's Party (*Nationale Volkspartij* – NVP). Also known as the *Partido Nashonal di Pueblo* (PNP), the NVP is a right-of-center Social Christian Party.
Leader: Maria LIBERIA-PETERS (Prime Minister).

Democratic Party of Sint Maarten (DPSM). Technically, an English-speaking branch of the Democratic Party (below), the DPSM supports the current government, while the DP does not.
Leader: Claude WATHEY.

Bonaire Patriotic Union (*Unión Patriótico Bonairiano* – UPB). The UPB obtained one *Staten* seat in the 1985 balloting.
Leader: C.V. WINKLAAR.

Workers' Liberation Front (*Frente Obrero de Liberashon* – FOL). The FOL is a Marxist group based on Curaçao.
Leaders: Stanley BROWN, Wilson GODETT.

West Indian People's Movement (WIPM). The WIPM won the seat from Saba at the 1985 election.
Leader: Will JOHNSON.

Opposition Parties:

New Antilles Movement (*Movimentu Antiyas Nobo* – MAN). The MAN is a left-of-center grouping that served as the core of the Martina administrations of 1982–1984 and 1985–1988, although holding only four *Staten* seats on the latter occasion.
Leader: Dominico F. MARTINA (former Prime Minister).

Democratic Party (*Democratische Partij* – DP). Prior to the 1985 election the DP was primarily a Curaçao-based party, with an English-speaking branch on Sint Maarten that currently supports the Liberia-Peters government. At present, branches on Bonaire and Sint Eustatius also have legislative representation, the former in opposition and the latter supporting the government.
Leaders: Augustín M. DIAZ, Leslie NAVARRO (former Finance Minister).

LEGISLATURE

The unicameral *Staten* presently consists of 22 members elected for four-year terms, subject to dissolution. At the most recent balloting of November 22, 1985, the National People's Party obtained 6 seats; the New Antilles Movement, 4; the Democratic Party of Curaçao, 3; the Democratic Party of Sint Maarten, 3; the Democratic Party of Bonaire, 2; the Democratic Party of Sint Eustatius, 1; the Bonaire Patriotic Union, 1; the Workers' Liberation Front, 1; the Windward Islands People's Movement, 1.
President: J.A.O. BIKKER.

CABINET

[as of May 17, 1988]

Prime Minister	Maria Liberia-Peters
Ministers	
Commerce	C.G. Smits
Development Cooperation	F.D. Crestian
Education	Ellis A. Woodley
Finance	G. De Paula
General Affairs (Defense and Foreign Affairs)	Maria Liberia-Peters
Health and Environmental Affairs	L.C. Gumbs
Industry and Employment	C.G. Smits
Internal Affairs	Maria Liberia-Peters
Justice	W.J. Knoppel
Social Affairs	S.H. Inderson
Transportation and Communication	L.C. Gumbs
Director, Bank of Netherlands Antilles	Vinny A. Servage

NEWS MEDIA

Press. The following are dailies published at Willemstad, unless otherwise noted: *Nobo* (12,000), in Papiamento; *La Prensa* (11,000), in Papiamento; *Amigoe* (10,000), in Dutch; *Beurs- en Nieuwsberichten* (8,000), in Dutch; *Saba Herald* (The Level, Saba, 500), monthly WIPM organ, in English; *Ultimo Noticia,* in Papiamento.

News agencies. The Dutch *Algemeen Nederlands Persbureau* (ANP) and the US Associated Press (AP) maintain offices at Willemstad.

Radio and television. There are a number of privately owned radio stations in operation in Curaçao, Bonaire, Sint Maarten, and Saba; commercial television service is provided at Willemstad by Tele-Curaçao. In 1987 there were 32,000 television receivers in the five-island grouping that excluded Aruba.

INTERGOVERNMENTAL REPRESENTATION

Foreign relations are conducted through the Dutch Ministry of Foreign Affairs at The Hague.

IGO Membership (Non-UN): Interpol.

NEW ZEALAND

Political Status: Original member of the Commonwealth; independence formally proclaimed 1947; under two-party parliamentary system.

Area: 103,069 sq. mi. (266,950 sq. km.).

Population: 3,261,783 (1986C), 3,296,000 (1988E).

Major Urban Centers (urban areas, 1986C): WELLINGTON (352,035); Auckland (889,225); Christchurch (333,191).

Official Languages: English, Maori.

Monetary Unit: New Zealand Dollar (market rate March 1, 1988, 1.50 dollars = $1US).

Sovereign: Queen ELIZABETH II.

Governor General: Rev. Sir Paul Alfred REEVES; assumed office November 20, 1985, succeeding Sir David Stuart BEATTIE.

Prime Minister: David R. LANGE (Labour Party); assumed office July 26, 1984, following election of July 14, succeeding Sir Robert David MULDOON (National Party); formed new government on August 19, 1987, following election of August 15.

THE COUNTRY

Extending north and south for 1,000 miles some 1,200 miles southeast of Australia, New Zealand is perhaps the most physically isolated of the world's economically advanced nations. The two main islands (North Island and South Island, separated by the Cook Strait) exhibit considerable topographical diversity, ranging from fertile plains to high mountains, but are endowed for the most part with a relatively temperate climate. The majority of the population is of British extraction, but Maori descendants of the original Polynesian inhabitants constitute about 12 percent of the total and an affirmative action program, partly in response to a growing Maori-rights movement, has recently been implemented on their behalf. There is no official religion, but the Anglican, Presbyterian, Roman Catholic, and Methodist churches claim adherents in approximately the order listed. Women constitute about 25 percent of the paid labor force, primarily in the clerical and service sectors, with numerous others in unpaid agricultural activity; female representation in elected bodies averages 10 percent, with much lower participation by Maoris.

Although the agricultural sector accounts for only about 10 percent of the gross domestic product and employs an even smaller proportion of the labor force, meat, wool, dairy, and forest products provide nearly half of New Zealand's export earnings. The country's dependence on foreign trade contributed to a major recession in the mid-1970s, in part because of a need to import most fuel. Recent development efforts have thus focused on the exploitation of significant natural gas, coal, and lignite deposits, as well as hydroelectric capacity, in order to further a policy of selective industrialization.

GOVERNMENT AND POLITICS

Political background. New Zealand was discovered by Abel Tasman in 1642, but settlement by the English did not begin until the eighteenth century. In 1840 British sovereignty was formally accepted by Maori chieftains in the Treaty of Waitangi. Recurrent disputes between the settlers and the Maoris were not resolved, however, until the defeat of the latter in the Maori wars of the 1860s. Representative institutions, including a General Assembly and a series of provincial councils, were established in 1852. Granted dominion status in 1907, New Zealand achieved full self-government prior to World War II, although independence was not formally proclaimed until 1947, when the Commonwealth assumed its contemporary form.

During the latter part of the nineteenth century, a number of labor reforms were enacted that laid the basis for further extension of the welfare state in the depression of the 1930s. Since then, New Zealand has been committed to an elaborately controlled economy and extensive programs of social welfare. Both of the main parties support the welfare state in principle, and differences between them now turn primarily on how such a system can best be administered. The more conservative National Party, which was in power from 1960 to 1972 under the leadership of

Keith J. HOLYOAKE and John R. MARSHALL, was defeated by Prime Minister Norman E. KIRK's Labour Party in the 1972 election. Following Kirk's death in August 1974, Wallace E. ROWLING was elected Labour Party leader and designated prime minister; collaterally, Robert D. MULDOON was named to succeed Marshall as National Party leader. In the midst of growing concern over increased state control of the economy and after an aggressive "presidential-style" campaign waged by Muldoon, the National Party won an unexpected landslide victory in November 1975, retaining control, with a substantially reduced majority, three years later. It continued in office after balloting on November 28, 1981, but with the precarious advantage of a single legislative seat.

Faced with intra-party defections in the wake of mounting fiscal problems, Muldoon was forced to call an early election on July 14, 1984, that yielded a Labour victory under David R. LANGE, who had succeeded Rowling as party leader in February 1983. Subsequently, action was taken to reverse decades of economic regulation through an aggressive series of tax changes and subsidy withdrawals.

Lange continued in office as head of a substantially reorganized administration following the election of August 15, 1987, at which Labour retained its majority of nearly 60 percent of legislative seats, although the popular vote gap between the two leading parties narrowed to only 2 percent.

Constitution and government. New Zealand's political system, closely patterned on the British model, has no written constitution. As in other Commonwealth states that have retained allegiance to the queen, the monarch is represented by a governor general, now a New Zealand citizen, who performs the largely ceremonial functions of chief of state. The only legally recognized executive body is the Executive Council, which includes the governor general and all government ministers; de facto executive authority is vested in the cabinet, headed by the prime minister, under a system of parliamentary responsibility. The unicameral House is elected for a three-year term by universal adult suffrage, with four seats reserved for Maori representatives being filled from a separate electoral roll. The judicial system is headed by a Supreme Court and a Court of Appeal; lower courts are known as magistrates' courts. Ultimate appeal is, at present, to the Judicial Committee of the Privy Council at London, although the Lange government has indicated that it will seek to abandon the practice by 1990. In 1962 the post of ombudsman was created to investigate citizen complaints of official actions.

Local government in urban areas is based on cities, boroughs, and town districts, while rural areas are divided into counties. Urban areas are governed by elected councils and mayors, while counties are governed by county councils, which select their own chairmen.

Foreign relations. As a small and isolated nation, New Zealand has traditionally supported collective security through the United Nations, the Commonwealth, and regional alliances such as ANZUS. The effectiveness of the last has, however, been severely crippled by the antinuclear posture of the Lange administration. Implementing a campaign pledge, the prime minister in February 1985 refused docking privileges to a US naval ship because of Washington's refusal to certify that the vessel was not nuclear armed. Fearing similar action by other allies, the Reagan administration reacted by canceling ANZUS military exercises planned for March. In June 1987 the Wellington parliament approved a Nuclear Free Zone, Disarmament and Arms Control Act that formally prohibited the entry of nuclear-armed or nuclear-powered ships into New Zealand waters. The United States, which in August 1986 had suspended its security commitment to New Zealand under the tripartite treaty, warned of punitive economic repercussions, while the British foreign minister accused Lange not only of seeking a "free lunch", but of endangering the Western alliance. Subsequently, during the 1987 legislative campaign, Labour declared its opposition to a "neither confirm nor deny" policy previously adopted by Norway, China, and Japan that would have permitted reactivation of New Zealand's ANZUS status. During the same period, relations with the Soviet Union also deteriorated. In September 1986 Wellington rejected Soviet proposals for military cooperation, landing rights for Aeroflot planes, and the use of port facilities, while in April 1987 a high-ranking Soviet embassy employee was expelled for alleged interference in domestic politics.

Earlier, Wellington found itself at odds with Paris following the arrest of two French security agents for complicity in the July 1985 sinking at Auckland harbor of the *Rainbow Warrior,* flagship of the environmental group Greenpeace, which was to have disrupted a nuclear test at Mururoa atoll. After initially denying that French personnel had been involved, Paris extended its "deep apologies" for the incident and called for the release of two of its agents, who had been convicted of manslaughter. After bitter discussions that were exacerbated by France's imposition of unofficial trade sanctions, an agreement was eventually struck, based on mediation by UN Secretary General Pérez de Cuéllar, that provided for the release of the agents upon payment of $7 million in compensation. Although disagreement continued on the issue of Pacific nuclear testing, a further rift between the two countries was seen as unlikely, given France's crucial role within the European Community, which provides the largest single market for New Zealand's commodities.

Current issues. Although polls revealed that a substantial majority of New Zealanders supported Prime Minister Lange on the nuclear issue, domestic rather than external affairs appeared to dominate the 1987 legislative campaign. Most importantly, the August 15 balloting was viewed as a referendum on the economic policies of finance minister Roger DOUGLAS, which had yielded increases in both inflation and unemployment, devaluation of the New Zealand dollar, major revision of the tax system, removal of all agricultural subsidies, and controls on interest rates and foreign exchange. While Labour achieved a sweeping victory overall, the pattern of voting indicated a "two-way verdict" with the incumbent party making significant advances in "wealthier" National strongholds and the latter gaining in less affluent constituencies normally considered safe for Labour. Following the election, both parties indicated that they might favor a change in the existing "first past the post" system of election to one based on proportional representation. Most observers felt that such a move

would necessitate enlargement of the House of Representatives, although it was unclear whether enabling legislation would be approved prior to the 1990 balloting.

POLITICAL PARTIES

The equivalent of a two-party system has long characterized New Zealand politics, traditional conservative and liberal roles being played by the National and Labour parties, respectively. However, differences between the two have narrowed considerably since World War II, with both being challenged by the social-democratic New Zealand Democratic Party (formerly the Social Credit Political League) and more recently by the libertarian New Zealand Party (see below).

Governing Party:

Labour Party. Founded in 1916 and formerly in power from 1935 to 1949, 1957 to 1960, and 1972 to 1975, the Labour Party originated much of the legislation that gave rise to an essentially welfare state. However, in an about-face, the Lange administration has introduced sweeping changes to promote free-market conditions, including economic deregulation and reduction of government subsidies. The party has nonetheless maintained its traditional antimilitaristic posture, voting in 1984 to withdraw from all alliances with nuclear powers. At the most recent election in August 1987 Labour retained its substantial legislative majority, despite some significant changes in voting pattern (see Current issues, above).

Leaders: David R. LANGE (Prime Minister and Parliamentary Leader), Geoffrey PALMER (Deputy Leader), Margaret A. WILSON (President), Anthony TIMMS (General Secretary).

Opposition Party:

National Party. Founded in 1931 as a union of the earlier Reform and United parties, the National Party controlled the government from 1960 to 1972 and 1975 to 1984. A predominantly conservative grouping drawing its strength from rural and suburban areas, the party traditionally has been committed to the support of personal initiative, private enterprise, and the removal of controls over industry. However, the orientation became clouded with Labour's shift to free-market policies, former prime minister Muldoon and his supporters defending selective state intervention in the economy. A dispute in late 1985 and early 1986 between Muldoon and his successor as party leader, James McLay (whose free-market philosophy mirrored that of the government) led to McLay's resignation in March 1986. The new leader, James Bolger, endorsed the Muldoon position, although reports of intraparty dissent continued.

In February 1983, real estate millionaire Bob Jones announced the formation of a New Zealand Party (NZP) as an overt challenge to the National Party. The free-enterprise oriented NZP called for a reduction in direct taxes, coupled with a 30 percent increase for individuals in upper-income ranges. In 1984, it drew 12 percent of the vote, mainly from National Party supporters, but failed to obtain parliamentary representation. In July 1985, citing approval of Lange's antinuclear policy and deregulatory economic program, Jones announced dissolution of the NZP, saying that "we believe a change of government to be undesirable at this time"; however, other leaders convened a party congress in August, despite the loss of their founder and financial benefactor. In March 1986, the NZP announced that it was formally merging with the National Party, although many individual members reportedly pledged their support for Labour.

During the 1987 campaign opposition leader James Bolger, while endorsing the government's antinuclear posture, nonetheless called for a restoration of the nation's military ties to Australia and the United States under the ANZUS treaty.

Leaders: Neville YOUNG (President), James (Jim) BOLGER (Leader of the Opposition), George GAIR (Deputy Leader), Sir Robert D. MULDOON (former Prime Minister), Max BRADFORD (Secretary General).

Other Parties:

New Zealand Democratic Party (NZDP). Established in May 1953 as the Social Credit Political League, the NZDP campaigns mainly on a financial platform calling for the elimination of an alleged chronic deficiency in purchasing power. In recent years it has proposed a defense posture of "armed neutrality" in the context of a nuclear-free zone, a position reaffirmed during the May 1985 congress at which the current name was adopted. Securing one House seat in the 1978 balloting, the party won an additional by-election seat in September 1980 in a district considered "safe" for the National Party. It retained its two seats in 1984, but lost both in 1987.

Leaders: J. Stefan LIPA (President), Neil J. MORRISON (former Parliamentary Leader), R. STEPHENSON (Secretary).

New Zealand Values Party. Founded in 1972, the ecology-oriented Values Party advocates reorganization of the government to meet the needs of people rather than the needs of the "system".

Leaders: Bruce SYMONDSON (President), Janet ROBORGH, Michael WARD, M. HURFORD (General Secretary).

Communist Party of New Zealand (CPNZ). Founded in 1921, the CPNZ was initially oriented toward the Soviet Union, subsequently toward China, and, since 1978, toward Albania. The CPNZ has never won parliamentary representation and its current strength is miniscule.

Leader: Richard C. WOLF.

Socialist Unity Party (SUP). A Soviet-oriented group, the SUP was founded in 1966 by CPNZ members who opposed the parent party's turn toward Peking; it boasts broad-based trade union support, including members on the ruling councils of several union federations. In January 1980, the Soviet ambassador to New Zealand was declared *persona non grata* for allegedly passing money to the SUP, full relations not being restored until February 1984.

Leaders: George Edward JACKSON (National President), Eleanor Matilda AYO (National Vice President), Ken DOUGLAS (National Chairman), Marilyn TUCKER (Acting National Secretary).

Socialist Action League (SAL). The SAL, founded in 1969 by a group of university students, is a Cuban-oriented, Trotskyite organization affiliated with the Fourth International. The party has recently sought to broaden its appeal and lent its support to Labour in the 1984 election, its youth wing actively campaigning for Lange.

Leader: Russell JOHNSON (National Secretary).

There are a number of other fringe groups, including the **Workers Communist League,** formed in 1980 by merger of two pro-Beijing groups that had split from the CPNZ, and a **New Zealand Women's Political Party,** whose sole candidate competed unsuccessfully in 1984.

LEGISLATURE

The former General Assembly of New Zealand became a unicameral body in 1950 with the abolition of its upper chamber, the Legislative Council. Now called the **House of Representatives** (although delegates are styled "members of Parliament"), the body currently consists of 97 members (93 elected by universal suffrage and 4 from Maori electoral rolls) serving three-year terms, subject to dissolution. At the election of August 15, 1987, the Labour Party won 58 seats and the National Party, 39.

Speaker: Kerry BURKE.

CABINET

Prime Minister	David Lange
Deputy Prime Minister	Geoffrey Palmer
Ministers	
Agriculture and Fisheries	Colin Moyle
Arts and Culture	Michael Bassett
Civil Aviation and Meteorological Services	Bill Jeffries
Civil Defense	Michael Bassett
Conservation	Helen Clark
Consumer Affairs	Margaret Shields
Defense	Robert Tizard
Disarmament and Arms Control	Russell Marshall
Education	David Lange
Employment	Phil Goff
Energy	David Butcher
Environment	Geoffrey Palmer
Finance	Roger Douglas
Foreign Affairs	Russell Marshall
Forests	Peter Tapsell
Health	David Caygill
Housing	Helen Clark
Immigration	Stan Rodger
Internal Affairs	Michael Bassett
Justice	Geoffrey Palmer
Labor	Stan Rodger
Lands	Peter Tapsell
Local Government	Michael Bassett
Maori Affairs	Koro Wetere
Overseas Trade and Marketing	Mike Moore
Pacific Island Affairs	Richard Prebble
Police	Peter Tapsell
Recreation and Sport	Peter Tapsell
Regional Development	David Butcher
Science and Technology	Bob Tizard
Social Welfare	Michael Cullen
State	Jonathon Hunt
State-Owned Enterprises	Richard Prebble
State Services	Stan Rodger
Statistics	Margaret Shields
Tourism	Phil Goff
Trade and Industry	David Caygill
Transport	Bill Jeffries
Women's Affairs	Margaret Shields
Works and Development	Richard Prebble
Youth Affairs	Phil Goff
Attorney General	Geoffrey Palmer
Postmaster General	Richard Prebble
Governor, Central Bank	Russell Spencer

NEWS MEDIA

Press. Complete freedom of the press prevails, except for legal stipulations regarding libel. The following (circulation figures for 1987) are dailies unless otherwise noted: *New Zealand Herald* (Auckland, 243,300); *Sunday News* (Auckland, 217,200); *The Auckland Star* (Auckland, 110,000); *Dominion Sunday Times* (Wellington, 95,800); *The Evening Post* (Wellington, 87,000); *The Press* (Christchurch, 85,500); *The Dominion* (Wellington, 72,700); *Christchurch Star* (Christchurch, 60,700); *Otago Daily Times* (Dunedin, 53,000); *Waikato Times* (Hamilton, 40,000); *Southland Times* (Invercargill, 34,500).

News agencies. The New Zealand Press Association is a cooperative, nonprofit organization established in 1879 to provide both local and international news to all New Zealand papers. There is also a South Pacific News Service (Sopac), while *Novosti* and Reuters maintain bureaus at Wellington.

Radio and television. The state-owned Broadcasting Corporation of New Zealand (BCNZ) supervises all aspects of broadcasting and controls three public, statutory bodies: Radio New Zealand, which operates numerous stations for both domestic and foreign transmission; Television One; and Television Two (South Pacific TV). In addition, there are several private commercial radio stations, although the establishment of a privately run television channel (first broached in late 1985) has not yet taken place. There were approximately 932,000 television receivers in 1987.

INTERGOVERNMENTAL REPRESENTATION

Ambassador to the US: Harold Huyton (Tim) FRANCIS.

US Ambassador to New Zealand: Paul Matthews CLEVELAND.

IGO Memberships (Non-UN): ADB, ANZUS, CCC, CP, CWTH, ICO, IEA, Inmarsat, Intelsat, Interpol, ISO, IWC, IWSG, OECD, PCA, SPC, SPEC, SPF.

RELATED TERRITORIES

New Zealand has two self-governing territories, the Cook Islands and Niue, and two dependent territories, Ross Dependency and Tokelau.

Cook Islands. Located some 1,700 miles northeast of New Zealand and administered by that country since 1901, the Cook Islands have a land area of 90 square miles (234 sq. km.) and are divided between a smaller, poorer, northern group and a larger, more fertile, southern group. The island of Rarotonga, with a population of 9,477 (1981C), is the site of the capital, Avarua. The islands' total population of 17,695 (1981C) is composed almost entirely of Polynesians, who are New Zealand citizens. Internal self-government with a 22-member Legislative Assembly and a premier was instituted in 1965, with New Zealand continuing to oversee external and defense affairs. At the election of March 30, 1978, the ruling **Cook Islands Party** (CIP) appeared to have been returned to power with 15 of 22 seats in the Assembly; however, in a remarkable turnabout, the High Court ruled on July 24 in favor of a suit brought by the opposition **Democratic Party** that CIP victories in 9 constituencies had been secured illegally (in 8 of the 9 cases because of nonresidents being flown in at government expense from New Zealand), power in the Assembly thereby shifting to 15–6 in favor of the Democrats. A year later, the former premier, Albert HENRY, pleaded guilty to criminal charges in the same case, being spared imprisonment only because of age and ill health.

A number of constitutional changes were introduced in May 1981, including the addition of two legislative seats (one providing for representation for Cook Islanders residing overseas) and extension of the parliamentary term from four to five years. Concurrently, the chief executive adopted the designation prime minister.

The CIP under Geoffrey HENRY, cousin of the former premier, was returned to power at the election of March 30, 1983, with a three-seat majority. Subsequently, however, a legislative impasse was generated by the death of one of its members and a transfer of allegiance to the DP by another. In view of the deadlock, Henry resigned on August 2, and the DP, under Sir Thomas Davis, secured a 13–11 mandate at an election held November 2. In August 1984, faced with the possible loss of its majority by defection of a member on a budget vote, the DP formed a coalition with the CIP, whose leader was named deputy prime minister; however, a failed no-confidence motion by disaffected CIP members in June 1985 led to formal abandonment of the coalition and a severe reduction in Sir Thomas' parliamentary majority. During 1986 Davis suffered a further decline in popularity by displaying sympathy for the French position in New Caledonia and by publicly differing with Wellington in the ANZUS nuclear dispute. Subsequently, questions were raised about the handling of international aid funds donated in the wake of a major cyclone in January 1987. As a result, Parliament, in a rare display of unanimity, voted to oust the unpredictable and often abrasive prime minister on July 29, with Dr. Pupuke Robati being designated his successor.

Prime Minister: Dr. Pupuke ROBATI.

Niue. An island of 100 square miles, Niue is the largest and westernmost of the Cook Islands but has been governed separately since 1903. The territory obtained internal self-government in 1974, with a premier heading a 4-member cabinet and a Legislative Assembly of 14 members elected for three-year terms. In recent years, the population has been dwindling steadily (5,194 in 1966, 4,990 in 1971, 2,530 in 1986). The exodus, largely to New Zealand, has been most pronounced since 1983 because of a prolonged drought that has affected both food and water supplies. In early 1988 the government indicated that it would seek additional aid from Wellington to stem emigration by upgrading the island's infrastructure and welfare programs.

In 1984 Sir Robert R. Rex, who had been the island's political leader since the 1950s, expressed a desire to retire, but accepted redesignation as premier following the most recent election of March 28, 1987.

Premier: Sir Robert R. REX.

Ross Dependency. A large, wedge-shaped portion of the Antarctic Continent, the Ross Dependency (see map, p. 19) extends from 160 degrees East to 150 degrees West Longitude and has an estimated area of 160,000 square miles (414,400 sq. km.). Although administered by New Zealand on behalf of the United Kingdom since 1923, its legal position is currently in suspense, in conformity with the Antarctic Treaty of 1959. The Ross Dependency Research Committee at Wellington coordinates and supervises all activity in the Dependency.

Chairman of Ross Dependency Research Committee: Dr. T. HATHERTON.

Tokelau. A small group of atolls north of Samoa with an area of 4 square miles (10.4 sq. km.) and a copra-based economy, Tokelau is claimed by the United States but has been administered by New Zealand since 1923 and was included within its territorial boundaries by legislation enacted in 1948. The population of 1,552 (1982C) exercises qualified self-government under appointed officials. Because of the islands' limited economic viability, some 100 residents a year are being resettled in New Zealand. As of November 1974, the office of administrator was transferred to the New Zealand Ministry of Foreign Affairs.

Administrator: H.H. FRANCIS.

NICARAGUA

Republic of Nicaragua
República de Nicaragua

Political Status: Independence originally proclaimed 1821; separate republic established 1838; provisional junta installed July 19, 1979; present constitution adopted November 19, 1986, with effect from January 9, 1987.

Area: 50,193 sq. mi. (130,000 sq. km.).

Population: 1,877,952 (1971C), 3,733,000 (1988E).

Major Urban Centers (1979E): MANAGUA (623,000); León (94,000); Matagalpa (88,000); Granada (56,000).

Official Language: Spanish.

Monetary Unit: New córdoba (official rate March 1, 1988, 10.00 córdobas = $1US). Prior to February 15, 1988, when the new córdoba was introduced at 1,000 of the old, Nicaragua's exchange structure was one of the most complicated in the world, encompassing eight different tiers ranging from an official parity of 70 to a free (black market) rate of more than 20,000 córdobas per $1US.

President: Cdte. (José) Daniel ORTEGA Saavedra; member of original five-member junta that assumed office July 19, 1979, following the resignation and departure from the country of President Anastasio SOMOZA Debayle on July 17 and the interim presidency of Dr. Francisco URCUYO Maliaños; assumed position of Coordinator of three-member junta on March 4, 1981; sworn in for a six-year term as President on January 10, 1985, following election of November 4, 1984.

Vice President: Sergio RAMIREZ Mercado; became member of junta on July 19, 1979; sworn in as Vice President on January 10, 1985, following election of November 4, 1984.

THE COUNTRY

Bounded by Honduras on the north and west and by Costa Rica on the south, Nicaragua is the largest but, apart from Belize, the least densely populated of the Central American states. Its numerous mountains are interspersed with extensive lowlands that make it a potential site for an interoceanic canal. The population is predominantly (69 percent) mestizo (mixed Indian and European), with smaller groups of Whites (17 percent), Blacks (9 percent), and Indians (5 percent). Roman Catholicism claims 95 percent of the inhabitants, although freedom of worship is constitutionally recognized.

In 1980, women were 22 percent of the paid labor force, concentrated in domestic service, teaching, and market vending; since that time, as a result of insurgent-induced conscription, female participation has greatly increased, particularly in agriculture (women also constitute 30 percent of the armed forces and nearly half of the civil militia). Over 40 percent of government officials are women, including, as of March 1988, one cabinet member.

The economy is essentially agricultural, coffee and cotton being the principal export crops. The extraction of mineral resources (including silver, gold, lead, gypsum, and zinc) is also important, while efforts to promote economic growth center on agricultural diversification and the stimulation of industries supporting agriculture and utilizing local raw materials. A disastrous earthquake that struck Managua in December 1972 severely disrupted development, as did the concluding phase of the *sandinista* rebellion in 1978–1979. After a period of recovery, the economy again declined because of border insurgency, floods in 1982 which devastated the cotton and coffee crops, and US blockage of an estimated $55.6 million in international development aid and sugar revenue. By early 1985, a growing fiscal crisis had prompted an 80 percent currency devaluation and the elimination of most food subsidies; following three years of negative economic growth, an even more massive devaluation of more than 99 percent was ordered in February 1988.

GOVERNMENT AND POLITICS

Political background. Nicaraguan politics following the country's liberation from Spanish rule in 1821 was long dominated by a power struggle between leaders of the Liberal and Conservative parties, punctuated by periods of US intervention, which was virtually continuous during 1912–1925 and 1927–1933. A Liberal Party victory in a US-supervised election in 1928 paved the way for the assumption of power by Gen. Anastasio SOMOZA García, who ruled the country as president from 1937 until his assassination in September 1956.

Political power remained in the hands of the Somoza family under the Liberal Party presidencies of Luis SOMOZA Debayle, the dictator's elder son (1956–1963); René SCHICK Gutiérrez (1963–1966); Lorenzo GUERRERO Gutiérrez (1966–1967); and Gen. Anastasio SOMOZA Debayle (1967–1972), the younger son of the late dictator. Constitutionally barred from a second term,

Somoza Debayle arranged an interim collegial executive (consisting of two members of the Liberal Party and one member of the Conservative Party) which oversaw the promulgation of a new constitution and administered the nation until the election of September 1, 1974, when he was formally returned to office by an overwhelming margin.

The stability of the Somoza regime was shaken by the Sandinist National Liberation Front (FSLN), which launched a series of coordinated attacks throughout the country in October 1977 in an effort to instigate a general uprising. While the immediate effort failed, far more serious disturbances erupted in 1978, including occupation of the National Palace at Managua by FSLN rebels on August 22 and a major escalation of the insurgency in early September. During the first half of 1979, the tide turned decisively in favor of the *sandinistas,* who by the end of June controlled most of the major towns as well as the slum district of the capital. Despite 12 days of intense bombardment of FSLN positions within Managua, government forces were unable to regain the initiative, and on July 17 General Somoza left the country after resigning in favor of an interim president, Dr. Francisco URCUYO Maliaños. Confronted with a bid by Dr. Urcuyo to remain in office until the expiration of his predecessor's term in 1981, three members of the FSLN provisional junta flew from Costa Rica to León on July 18 and, amid some confusion, accepted the unconditional surrender of the National Guard commander at Managua the following day.

Daniel ORTEGA Saavedra, the leader of the five-man junta and of the FSLN's nine-member Directorate, announced in August 1980 that the FSLN would remain in power until 1985, with electoral activity to resume in 1984. In addition to Ortega, the original junta included Violeta CHAMORO de Barrios, Moisés HASSAN Morales, Sergio RAMIREZ Mercado, and Alfonso ROBELO Callejas. On May 18, 1980, Rafael CORDOVA Rivas and Arturo José CRUZ Porras were named to succeed Chamoro and Robelo, who had resigned on April 19 and 22, respectively. On March 4, 1981, Hassan and Cruz also resigned, Ortega being named "coordinator" of the remaining three-member group.

On September 17, 1980, under circumstances that have not been completely explained, former president Somoza was assassinated in a bazooka attack on his limousine in central Asunción, Paraguay.

In early 1984, under diplomatic pressure from Western countries and military pressure from US-backed insurgent forces (see Current issues, below), the junta adjusted its electoral timetable to permit both presidential and legislative balloting the following November. Although attempts by the regime to reach procedural agreement with the opposition failed (most of the larger parties withdrawing from the campaign), the November 4 poll was contested by a number of small non-*sandinista* groups. In an election described as exemplary by international observers (who nonetheless objected to preelection censorship and harassment of opposition candidates), Ortega won 67 percent of the presidential vote, while the FSLN gained a like percentage of National Constituent Assembly seats.

The Assembly approved a new constitution on November 19, 1986, although the government reimposed a state of emergency upon its promulgation on January 9, 1987.

After extensive negotiations, a preliminary peace agreement for the region, based in part on proposals advanced by President Oscar Arias Sánchez of Costa Rica, was approved by the five Central American chief executives at Guatemala City, Guatemala, on August 7. Included in the plan were provisions for an effective ceasefire with rebel forces, the suspension of external aid to insurgents, the initiation of dialogue with "all unarmed internal opposition groups and those who have availed themselves of . . . amnesty", and the holding of "free, pluralistic and honest" elections. In accordance with the agreement, a series of talks between the *sandinista* government and *contra* leaders were initiated in late January 1988 that yielded a temporary truce while the talks were in progress and a 60-day ceasefire from April 1, although no conclusive resolution of the Nicaraguan conflict had been achieved by midyear.

Constitution and government. The 1974 constitution, which provided for a presidential-congressional system of government, was suspended upon installation of the ruling junta in July 1979. In 1980, a Council of State, nominally representing a broad political spectrum but dominated by the FSLN, was appointed to advise the junta on legislation.

Under a decree promulgated in January 1984, a president, vice president, and National Constituent Assembly were elected for six-year terms on November 4 and took office on January 10, 1985. The Assembly, composed of 90 proportionally elected members plus six presidential candidates obtaining a minimum of one percent of the vote, guided the drafting of a new basic law, which, adhering essentially to the particulars of the 1984 degree, was promulgated on January 9, 1988, although its extensive civil rights provisions (accounting for 69 of the 202 articles) have been severely limited by state-of-emergency regulations. Administratively, Nicaragua is divided into 16 departments and a National District (Managua), each headed by a centrally appointed official; municipalities are to be governed by locally elected bodies, initial balloting for which is expected in 1988.

Foreign relations. The conservative and generally pro-US outlook of the Somoza regime was reflected in a favorable attitude toward North American investment and a strongly pro-Western, anti-Communist position in the United Nations, the Organization of American States, and other international bodies. Washington, for its part, did not publicly call for the resignation of General Somoza until June 20, 1979, and subsequently appealed for an OAS peacekeeping presence to ensure that a successor government would include moderate representatives acceptable to "all major elements of Nicaraguan society". Although the idea was rejected by both the OAS and the FSLN, the United States played a key role in the events leading to Somoza's departure, and the Carter administration extended reconstruction aid to the new Managua government in October 1980. By contrast, President Reagan has been deeply committed to support of the largely Honduran-based rebel *contras,* despite a conspicuous lack of enthusiasm for such a policy by many US congressmen. Relations with Costa Rica, initially quite cordial, have been exacerbated by insurgent activity in the border region and the alleged killing of two Costa Rican civil guards by Nicaraguan forces in May 1985.

Prior to Somoza's ouster, the FSLN enjoyed substantial European support, particularly within the Socialist International. Since the coup, concern over Cuban and Soviet involvement, limitations on the press, and alleged mistreatment of the indigenous population have tended to erode pro-*sandinista* sentiment. The most serious rebuff came when Venezuelan President Carlos Andres Peréz, a prominent member of the International, refused to attend Ortega's inauguration, although a post-election European trip by Vice President Ramírez repaired some of the damage and facilitated the renewal of bilateral loan commitments. Regional attitudes toward the *contra* insurgency have been mixed, most South American countries professing neutrality, although Managua-Quito relations were broken in 1985 after (then) Ecuadorian President Febres Cordero called Nicaragua "a bonfire in Central America". Subsequently, members of the Contadora Group (Colombia, Mexico, Panama, Venezuela) and the Lima Group (Argentina, Brazil, Peru, Uruguay) met intermittently with Central American leaders in an effort to broker the conflict, although neither bloc directly influenced the regional accord of August 1987.

Current issues. In the nine years since the fall of Somoza, the Ortega government has confronted increased pressure from within and without. While advances in land reform, literacy, and the delivery of social services helped to generate domestic support for the regime, military incursions by the US-backed *contras* have heightened economic and political problems, while Managua's drift to the left has alienated many of its former supporters at home and abroad. The extent of US involvement became of international concern following the March 1984 mining of Nicaragua's harbors, leading Managua to file a complaint with the International Court of Justice, which ultimately ruled against the United States in a decision handed down in June 1986.

In 1985, prior to direct military assistance tendered in mid-1986, the *contras* received $27 million in "nonlethal" aid from Washington, supplemented by substantial funds from private US citizens; in response, Managua greatly increased conscription and military spending, declared a state of emergency, and called a US invasion "imminent".

During 1986 and early 1987, the *sandinista* regime displayed a number of contrasting, if not contradictory, characteristics. A new, essentially pluralistic constitution was adopted with input from five legal opposition parties. Prior to the document's adoption, however, the opposition groups had called for a "national dialogue for the sake of peace" involving six other organizations that had not participated in the 1984 elections. The constitution, as finally adopted, provided for a variety of civil guarantees, most of which remained suspended under a state of emergency that sanctioned press censorship, arbitrary detentions, and prohibition of outdoor rallies without official permission. A number of antigovernment rallies were nonetheless held, including a march of some 5,000 persons in January 1987 to commemorate the assassination of opposition newspaper owner Pedro Joaquim Chamorro. Branded by Washington as Communist dominated and refused admission to the Socialist International, the FSLN was characterized as "not even close" to Marxism by the small Communist

Party of Nicaragua which, accusing the government of "disrespect, crudeness, bribery, factionalism, and divisionism", formally moved into opposition in early 1987. Meanwhile, divisions persisted within the *contra* leadership in the wake of Washington's "Irangate" scandal (see US article), the moderate Arturo CRUZ Porras withdrawing from the movement because of a dispute with *somocista* leader Adolfo CALERO Portocarrera.

During a meeting of government and resistance leaders at the southern border town of Sapoá on March 21–23, 1988, agreement was reached on a number of key issues, including the delineation of seven enclaves to which the various rebel units would deploy during the two-month ceasefire. While the rebels proclaimed the talks a "great success", a subsequent round at Managua on April 28–30 bore little fruit, the *sandinistas* seeking a firm deadline for *contra* disarmament as a condition for their integration into civilian politics and Calero, on behalf of the insurgents, declaring that "We do not want power sharing . . . we want real political change". The standoff was to a considerable extent a reflection of ambivalent signals from Washington, with congressional leaders becoming impatient at the lack of results from a moratorium on aid to the *contras* and increasingly vulnerable to administration insistence that the Ortega regime had no intention of committing itself to genuine reconciliation.

POLITICAL PARTIES AND GROUPS

Historically, the Liberal and Conservative parties dominated Nicaraguan politics in what was essentially a two-party system. During most of the Somoza era, the heir to the liberal tradition, the Nationalist Liberal Party (*Partido Liberal Nacionalista de Nicaragua*—PLN), enjoyed a monopoly of power, while in mid-1978 the Nicaraguan Conservative Party (*Partido Conservador Nicaragüense* —PCN) joined other opposition groups in a Broad Opposition Front (*Frente Amplio de Oposición*—FAO) that called for the president's resignation and the creation of a government of national unity. In addition to the PCN, the Front included the Independent Liberal and Nicaraguan Social Christian Popular parties (see below); the Democratic Liberation Union (*Unión Democrática de Liberación*—Udel), organized in 1977 by former PCN leader and newspaper editor Pedro Joaquín Chamorro Cardenal, who was assassinated in January 1978; and the Group of 12 (*Movimiento de los Doce*), a pro-*sandinista* organization of businessmen, academics, and priests that withdrew from the FAO in October 1978 because of a proposal to include members of the PLN in a future coalition government.

Following the *sandinista* victory, the principal internal groupings were the FSLN-led Patriotic Front for the Revolution (*Frente Patriótico para la Revolución*—FPR) and the opposition Nicaraguan Democratic Coordination (below). However, by 1984 the Patriotic Front had effectively dissolved, most of its non-FSLN components having chosen to contest the November balloting as separate entities, while the *Coordinadora,* technically reduced to the status of a "citizens' association" because of its electoral boycott, was declared, somewhat prematurely, to have become "inoperative" in 1985 after several of its leaders had entered into agreements with *contra* units that included appeals for a "national dialogue".

Government Party:

  Sandinist National Liberation Front (*Frente Sandinista de Liberación Nacional*—FSLN). The FSLN was established in 1961 as a Castroite guerrilla group named after Augusto César Sandino, a prominent rebel during the US occupation of the 1920s. The Front displayed a remarkable capacity for survival, despite numerous "eradication" campaigns during the later years of the Somoza regime, in the course of which much of its original leadership was killed. In 1975 it split into three "tendencies": two small Marxist groupings, the Protracted Popular Warfare (*Guerra Popular Prolongada*—GPP) and the Proletarian Tendency (*Tendencia Proletaria*), and a larger, less extreme Third Party (*Terceristas*), a non-ideological anti-Somoza formation supported by peasants, students, and upper-class intellectuals. The three groups coordinated their activities during the 1978 offensive and were equally represented in the nine-member Joint National Directorate. Although the July 1979 junta was largely *tercerista* dominated, the withdrawal of a number of moderates since 1980 has yielded a more distinctly leftist thrust to the party leadership, hardliner Bayardo Arce reportedly characterizing the November 1984 balloting as "a bother". In an August 1985 reorganization of the Directorate, its Political Commission was replaced by a five-member Executive Commission, chaired by President Ortega, with Arce as his deputy. In addition to its control of the national government, the FSLN is supported by "defense committees" at the municipal and village levels.

  Leaders: Daniel ORTEGA Saavedra (President of the Republic and Chairman, FSLN Executive Commission); Dr. Sergio RAMIREZ Mercado (Vice President of the Republic); Bayardo ARCE Castaño (Deputy Chairman, Executive Commission); Tomas BORGE Martínez, Cdr. Humberto ORTEGA Saavedra, Cdr. Jaime WHEELOCK Roman (Members, Executive Commission).

Official Opposition Parties:

  Democratic Conservative Party (*Partido Conservador Demócrata*— PCD). Founded in 1979 by supporters of the historic PCN, the PCD has long been deeply divided, with one of its leaders, Rafael Cordova Rivas, joining the junta in May 1980 and most others in exile. Although repeatedly indicating that it would boycott the 1984 elections, the party was one of the first to register at midyear and was a surprising first runner-up on November 4, winning 14 legislative seats and a 14 percent vote share for its presidential candidate, despite last-minute pressure at a party convention to withdraw from the balloting.

  Leaders: Clement GUIDO, Enrique SOTELO, Eduardo MOLINA (General Secretary).

  Independent Liberal Party (*Partido Liberal Independiente*—PLI). Organized in 1946 by a group calling for a return to the traditional principles of the PLN, the PLI participated in the Broad Opposition Front prior to the 1979 coup. Currently led by post-coup labor minister Virgilio Godoy Reyes, the PLI was a member of the Patriotic Front, but following *Coordinadora*'s withdrawal became the most vocal opposition formation of the 1984 campaign. An October 21 decision to withdraw from the balloting was rejected by the Electoral Council, and the party won 9.6 percent of the vote and 9 Assembly seats in November. Along with the PSN (below), the PLI withdrew in December 1985 from the legislature's constitutional commission, calling restrictions on opposition activity "a sword of Damocles" precluding significant legislative participation.

  Leaders: Juan Manuel GUTIERREZ (Parliamentary Leader), Virgilio GODOY Reyes (1984 presidential candidate).

  Social Christian Popular Party (*Partido Popular Social Cristiano*— PPSC). The PPSC was formed as a splinter of the PSC (below) in 1976. Although a former member of the Patriotic Front, it has consistently criticized the FSLN's relations with the Church. It won 5.6 percent of the vote and 6 legislative seats in November 1984.

  Leaders: Mauricio DIAZ (President of the Party and 1984 presidential candidate), César DELGADILLO Machado.

  Three small leftist parties also contested the 1984 elections: the pro-Moscow **Socialist Party of Nicaragua** (*Partido Socialista Nicaragüense*— PSN), led by Luis SANCHEZ Sancho, Domingo SANCHEZ Salgado, and Gustavo TABLADA Zelaya (General Secretary); a pro-Beijing PSN splinter group, the **Communist Party of Nicaragua** (*Partido Comunista de Nicaragua* – PCN), led by Allan ZAMBRANA Zalmeron and Elí ALTAMIRANO Pérez (General Secretary); and the **Nicaraguan Marxist-Leninist Party** (*Partido Marxista Leninista de Nicaragua* – PMLN), known until 1986 as the Marxist-Leninist Popular Action Movement (*Movimiento de Acción Popular-Marxista-Leninista* – MAP-ML), a Maoist breakaway faction of the FSLN's Proletarian Tendency under the leadership of Isidro TELLEZ Toruño, one of several persons arrested in 1980 for "fomenting illegal strikes and land seizures". Each obtained two Assembly seats on the basis of a less than two percent vote share.

Unrecognized Opposition Formation:

Nicaraguan Democratic Coordination (*Coordinadora Democrática Nicaragüense* – CDN). The CDN was formed in 1981 as an opposition coalition comprised of the following two groups plus the **Liberal Constitutional Party** (*Partido Liberal Constitucionalista* – PLC), led by Alfredo REYES Estrada. A fourth opposition group, a **Conservative Party** (*Partido Conservador* – PC) rump of the traditional Nicaraguan Conservative Party, led by Mario RAPPACCIOLI, is generally viewed as a CDN ally.

Leader: Dr. Eduardo RIVAS Gasteazoro (President).

Nicaraguan Social Christian Party (*Partido Socialcristiano Nicaragüense* – PSCN). A strongly anti-*somocista* group founded in 1957, the PSCN participated in the pre-coup Broad Opposition Front but, like the PCD, refused a Council of State seat in 1980. It has links both to Venezuela's COPEI and the Christian Democratic International, describes itself as "centrist", and is supported by trade and farm union affiliates. The PSCN and the PSD (below) were core components of the pre-1985 *Coordinadora* grouping.

Leaders: Erick RAMIREZ Benevente (President), Duilio BALTODANO (Vice President), Agustín JARQUIN Anaya, Dr. Luis VEGA Miranda (General Secretary).

Social Democratic Party (*Partido Social Demócrata* – PSD). Founded in September 1979 as a splinter of the PSCN, the PSD was prohibited from styling itself the *Partido Socialdemócrata Sandinista* on the ground that it had played no part in the Sandinist revolution. Although claiming to be a party of "moderation", it was denied admission to the Socialist International after having accused the FSLN of wishing to establish a "totalitarian" government. In early 1985, the PSD leadership repudiated *Coordinadora* links to the *contra* insurgents, thus contributing to the demise of the alliance.

Leaders: Guillermo POTOY, Luis RIVAS Leiva (Secretary General).

Insurgent Groups:

Nicaraguan Resistance (*Resistencia Nicaragüense* – RN). The anti-*sandinista* RN was formally launched at Miami, Florida, on May 13, 1987, as the proclaimed fusion of a number of *contra* groups including, most importantly, the conservative United Nicaraguan Opposition (*Unidad Nicaragüense Opositora* – UNO, based in Honduras, and the smaller Southern Opposition Bloc (*Bloque Opositora del Sur* – BOS), a left-of-center formation based in Costa Rica. Under rules announced by the RN directorate, all constituent exile organizations would cease to exist and their various military wings would be integrated into a common Nicaraguan Army of Resistance.

UNO was formed in June 1985, bringing to fruition more than two years of US-backed efforts to unify both civilian and military opposition to the FSLN. The military elements, in particular the FDN and Arde (below), had joined nearly a year before in the Nicaraguan Unity for Reconciliation (*Unidad Nicaragüense de Reconciliación* – UNIR), which had been formed after the expulsion from Arde of Eden PASTORA Gomez (the former FSLN "Commander Zero"), because of his objection to the presence of Somoza-era National Guardsmen in the FDN's military command. Contacts with internal opposition leaders yielded an abortive declaration on February 12, 1985, jointly signed by Arturo Cruz Porras (former Nicaraguan ambassador to the United States and subsequent CDN presidential candidate), Pedro Joaquín Chamorro Barrios (former editor of the opposition daily *La Prensa*), and UNIR leaders, which restated longstanding *Coordinadora* demands for a "national dialogue". UNO was perceived by observers to be, like its predecessors, primarily a tactical formation to consolidate external support, conflict between the political

and military factions subsequently arising from charges by Cruz that the FDN, by maintaining a separate identity and organizational apparatus, had "rendered the organization politically powerless". In May 1986, Cruz and Arde leader Alfonso Robelo Callejas announced that former Pastora-led units of the Sandinist Revolutionary Front (see Arde, below) had agreed to join UNO under their direct leadership, thus enabling them to bid for greater power within the grouping. However, the civilian leaders' demands that UNO be "the only political organization to represent the rebels" met with stiff resistance from the FDN, leading Cruz to resign from the group in March 1987 after a lengthy dispute with FDN leader Adolfo Calero. In mid-April Robelo also withdrew, citing "periodic and consistent problems" with Calero. Robelo subsequently joined the RN directorate, although (vowing to continue the "political struggle against the Nicaraguan Marxist regime") he resigned the position on February 5, 1988, after the US House of Representatives had voted to reject President Reagan's request for additional *contra* aid.

BOS was organized in August 1985 by pro-Pastora forces opposed to affiliation with UNO (see Arde, below). Its leadership was subsequently assumed by Alfredo César Aguirre.

RN Directorate: Adolfo CALERO Portocarreraa (UNO/FDN), Pedro Joaquín CHAMORRO Barrios (UNO), Alfredo CESAR Aguirre (BOS), María AZUCENA Ferrey (former PSCN Vice President), Aristides SANCHEZ (UNO/FDN). An additional seat, reserved for a representative of the Atlantic Coast Indians, remained unfilled.

Nicaraguan Democratic Forces (*Fuerzas Democráticas Nicaragüenses* – FDN). A largely *somocista* group based in Honduras, the FDN has been a leading recipient of CIA and private US funds. It claims to command more than 12,000 insurgents in Nicaragua's northern provinces. In a series of human rights reports issued in 1985, FDN soldiers were accused of indiscriminate killing of civilians and rape and torture of prisoners, while in early 1986, US investigations were initiated into charges of drug-smuggling by FDN leaders to finance arms purchases.

Leaders: Bosco MATOMOROS, Adolfo CALERO Portocarrera, Col. Enrique BERMUDEZ Varela (Military Commander).

Democratic Revolutionary Alliance (*Alianza Revolucionaria Democrática* – Arde). Arde was organized in September 1982 by Eden Pastora, leader of the **Sandinist Revolutionary Front** (*Frente Revolucionaria Sandinista* – FRS), which served as the armed wing of the **Nicaraguan Democratic Movement** (*Movimiento Democrático Nicaragüense* – MDN), led by former junta member Alfonso Robelo. Other constituent groups included the **Nicaraguan Revolutionary Armed Forces** (*Fuerzas Armadas Revolucionarias Nicaragüenses* – FARN) and its political wing, the **Nicaraguan Democratic Union** (*Unión Democrática Nicaragüense* – UDN), both led by Fernando Chamorro Rapoccioli ("El Negro"), and the **Christian Democratic Solidarity Front** (*Frente de Solidaridad Demócrata Cristiana* – PSDC), led by José Davila Membereno. For most of 1983–1984, the largely Costa Rican-based Arde had held itself apart as a "democratic alternative" to the FDN, but military setbacks led to a vote by the Arde directorate in May 1984 to ally itself with the FDN, despite Pastora's refusal to participate in such a grouping. A few days later, Pastora was severely injured in a bomb attack which he blamed on the CIA "as punishment . . . for not joining with forces loyal to Somoza". Despite nominal alliance with the FDN, Arde received little US support, and in 1985 lost all of its base camps on the Nicaraguan side of the border to FSLN troops. Earlier, FRS units supporting Pastora's position agreed to fight "separately" but in cooperation with Arde and, following UNO's formation, organized BOS. In May 1986, it was reported that most BOS-aligned units had agreed to support the UNO, Pastora subsequently accusing the CIA of backing the "desertion" and requesting political asylum in Costa Rica.

Leaders: Alfonso ROBELO Callejas, José DAVILA Membereno, Fernando CHAMORRO Rapoccioli (Military Commander).

Exile groups that did not affiliate with the UNO included the **Third Way Movement** (M-3V), organized by Abelardo TABOADA as an "option . . . between the northern forces and Arde"; the *somocista* **Army of National Liberation** (*Ejercito de Liberación Nacional* – ELN), led by Pedro ORTEGA ("Juan Carlos"); the **Jeane Kirkpatrick Task Force** (named for the former US envoy to the United Nations); and the **Nicaraguan Anti-Communist Movement** (*Movimiento Anticomunista Nicaragüense*), which has been suspected of being a front for Arde units.

From 1982 to mid-1985, the interests of the 200,000 Miskito, Sumo, and Rama Indians in Nicaragua had been represented by two distinct groups: *Misurasata,* led by Brooklyn RIVERA, which sporadically engaged in anti-FSLN battles but refused to establish links with the FDN, and a rebel splinter of the organization, *Misura,* led by Steadman FAGOTH Muller, which did not participate in any of several Rivera-brokered truces with the government and functioned in 1984–1985 as a component of Unir and UNO. A crisis within *Misura* was precipitated by Fagoth's expulsion in August 1985 after allegedly kidnapping twelve group members for "treason"; from August 31-September 3, 895 delegates, primarily from Misura, met at Rus Rus, Honduras, and formed the **Nicaraguan Indigenous Communities Union** (Kisán). Both Fagoth and Rivera were excluded from the new formation, which, led by Diego WYKLIFFE, proclaimed itself a reunification of both native groups. Kisán's initial demand was for $3 million of $27 million in aid allocated to *contra* forces by the US government. Subsequently, Misurasata reemerged as a distinct grouping under Rivera, Kisán leaders ultimately choosing to act in concert with the larger grouping. However, hostilities between the FSLN and Rivera-led forces resumed in 1986, including gunship attacks on Miskito settlements, many of whose inhabitants had responded to the government's offer of amnesty by early 1987.

LEGISLATURE

The former bicameral Congress (*Congreso*) was dissolved following installation of the provisional junta in July 1979. A 47-member Council of State (*Consejo de Estado*), representing various *sandinista,* labor, and other organizations, was sworn in May 4, 1980, to serve in a quasi-legislative capacity. A new **National Constituent Assembly** (*Asamblea Nacional Constituyente*), charged with both ordinary and constitutional law-making functions, was elected on November 4, 1984, and convened on January 10, 1985. The distribution of its 96 seats following the November balloting was as follows: Sandinista National Liberation Front, 61; Democratic Conservative Party, 14; Independent Liberal Party, 9; Social Christian Popular Party, 6; Nicaraguan Socialist Party, Nicaraguan Communist Party, and Marxist-Leninist Popular Action Movement, 2 each.

President: Cdr. Carlos NUÑEZ Téllez.

CABINET

President	Cdte. Daniel Ortega Saavedra
Vice President	Sergio Ramírez Mercado
Ministers	
Agricultural-Livestock Development and Agrarian Reform	Cdte. Jaime Wheelock Román
Construction	Mauricio Valenzuela
Culture	Fr. Ernesto Cardenal Martínez
Defense	Cdte. Humberto Ortega Saavedra
Economy	Cdte. Luis Carrion Cruz
Education	Fr. Fernando Cardenal Martínez
Finance	William Shipman Huper Argüello
Foreign Affairs	Fr. Miguel D'Escoto Brockman
Foreign Cooperation	Cdte. Henry Ruiz Hernández
Health	Dora María Téllez Argüello
Housing and Human Services	Miguel Ernesto Vigil Icaza
Interior	Cdte. Tomás Borge Martínez
Labor	Benedicto Meneses Fonseca
Presidency	René Núñes Téllez
Tourism	Herty Lewites Rodríguez
Transportation	William Ramírez Solórazano
Attorney General	Rodrigo Antonio Reyes Portocarrero
Director, Central Bank	Joaquín Cuadra Chamorro

NEWS MEDIA

The Somoza regime severely constricted the media, particularly *La Prensa,* whose former principal editor, Pedro Joaquín Chamorro Cardenal, had received international recognition for his opposition to government policies prior to his assassination on January 10, 1978. Not surprisingly, *La Prensa* was the first Somoza-era daily to reemerge under the junta, while the extreme leftist *El Pueblo* was suspended by the new government in late July after accusing the Sandinists of "selling out the revolution" to "bourgeois groups", and in January 1980 was closed down permanently. Despite its anti-Somoza record, *La Prensa* was banned from June 1986 to October 1987, when it resumed publication after receiving government assurances that it would not have to submit to prior censorship.

Press. The 1979 guarantee of freedom of the press carried with it the stipulation that all printed matter must reflect "legitimate concern for the defense of the conquests of the revolution". The following are published daily at Managua: *Barricada* (110,000), FSLN organ; *La Prensa* (75,000), nominally independent; *El Nuevo Diario* (60,000), founded 1980 by a pro-*sandinista* group of former *La Prensa* employees.

News agencies. An official *Agencia Nicaragüense de Noticias* (ANN) was launched in September 1979; in addition, a number of foreign bureaus maintain offices at Managua.

Radio and television. There are more than 50 radio stations, including the government-controlled *La Voz de Nicaragua* and *Radio Sandino;* the church-controlled *Radio Católica,* shut down in January 1986, was permitted to resume operation in October 1987. Television service at Managua and three other locations is provided by the *Sistema Sandinista de Televisión;* there were approximately 175,000 television receivers in 1987.

INTERGOVERNMENTAL REPRESENTATION

Ambassador to the US: Dr. Carlos TUNNERMAN Bernheim.

US Ambassador to Nicaragua: Richard Huntington MELTON.

Permanent Representative to the UN: (Vacant).

IGO Memberships (Non-UN): BCIE, CACM, Geplacea, IADB, IATTC, ICAC, ICM, ICO, Intelsat, Interpol, ISO, NAM, OAS, ODECA, OPANAL, PCA, SELA, UPEB.

NIGER

Republic of Niger
République du Niger

Political Status: Former French dependency; independence declared August 3, 1960; under military regime since April 15, 1974.

Area: 489,189 sq. mi. (1,267,000 sq. km.).

Population: 5,098,427 (1977C), 6,861,000 (1988E).

Major Urban Centers (1982E): NIAMEY (370,000); Zinder (82,000); Maradi (75,000).

Official Language: French.

Monetary Unit: CFA Franc (market rate March 1, 1988, 285.80 CFA francs = $1US).

Head of State and President of the Supreme Military Council: Col. Ali SEIBOU (Saibou, Seybou) named Acting Head of State by the Supreme Military Council at the death of Maj. Gen. Seyni KOUNTCHE on November 10, 1987; designated Head of State and President of the SMC on November 14.

Prime Minister: Hamid ALGABID; named by President Kountché on November 14, 1983, to succeed Oumarou MAMANE; redesignated by President Seibou on November 21, 1988.

THE COUNTRY

A vast landlocked country on the southern border of the Sahara, Niger is largely desert in the north and arable savanna in the more populous southland, which extends from the Niger River to Lake Chad. The population includes numerous tribes of two main ethnic groups: Sudanese Negroes and Hamites. The former encompasses about 75 percent of the population, with Hausa being the predominant (56 percent) tribal group; the latter, found in the north, includes the nomadic Tuareg and Tabu. The population is largely (85 percent) Muslim, with smaller groups of animists and Christians. While French is the official language, Hausa is the language of trade and commerce. Women constitute a minority of the labor force, excluding unpaid family workers.

Agriculture and stock-raising occupy 90 percent of the work force, the chief products being millet and sorghum for domestic consumption, and peanuts, vegetables, and live cattle for export. Coal, phosphates, iron ore, and petroleum have also been discovered, but their exploitation awaits development of a more adequate transportation and communication infrastructure. The economy has declined in the 1980s, with agriculture suffering from both flooding and drought, while a decrease in demand for uranium, the country's major export, has caused a severe trade imbalance and mounting foreign debt.

GOVERNMENT AND POLITICS

Political background. An object of centuries-old contention among different African peoples, Niger was first exposed to French contact in the late nineteenth century. Military conquest of the area was begun prior to 1900 but because of stiff resistance was not completed until 1922, when Niger became a French colony. Evolution toward nationhood began under a constitution granted by France in 1946, with Niger becoming a self-governing republic within the French Community in 1958 and attaining full independence in August 1960. Although its membership in the Community subsequently lapsed, Niger has retained close economic and political ties with its former colonial ruler.

The banning of the Marxist-oriented Sawaba (Freedom) Party in 1959 converted Niger into a one-party state under the Niger Progressive Party, headed by President Hamani DIORI, a member of the southern Djerma tribe. There-

after, Sawaba elements led by Djibo BAKARY continued their opposition activity from abroad, with terrorist incursions in 1964 and 1965 including an attempt on the president's life. The Diori government, carefully balanced to represent ethnic and regional groupings, was reelected in 1965 and 1970 by overwhelming majorities but proved incapable of coping with the effects of the prolonged Sahelian drought of 1968–1974. As a result, Diori was overthrown on April 15, 1974, by a military coup led by (then) Lt. Col. Seyni KOUNTCHE and Maj. Sani Souna SIDO, who established themselves as president and vice president, respectively, of a ruling Supreme Military Council. On August 2, 1975, Colonel Kountché announced that Major Sido and a number of others, including Bakary, had been arrested for attempting to organize a second coup.

A National Development Council (*Conseil National de Développement* – CND), initially established in July 1974 with an appointive membership, was assigned quasi-leadership status in August 1983, following indirect election of 150 delegates. Earlier, on January 24, Oumarou MAMANE was appointed to the newly created post of prime minister; on August 3, he was named president of the reconstituted CND and, on November 14, was succeeded as prime minister by Hamid ALGABID.

After what was apparently a lengthy illness, President Kountché died in a Paris hospital on November 10 and was immediately succeeded by the army chief of staff, Col. Ali SEIBOU who, after being formally invested by the Supreme Military Council on November 14, named Algabid to head an otherwise substantially new government.

Constitution and government. The 1960 constitution, which provided for an elected president and National Assembly, was abrogated in the wake of the 1974 coup. Since then, the president of the Supreme Military Council has served as head of state and effective executive. An appointive prime ministerial post was established in January 1983. The CND, initially a purely advisory body, assumed some of the aspects of a legislature in August 1983 as the apex of a hierarchial structure that, at lower levels, encompasses village, local, subregional, and regional councils. The judicial system is currently headed by a military Court of State Security (superseding the former Supreme Court) and includes a Court of Appeal, assize courts, district magistrates' courts, labor courts, and justices of the peace.

In January 1984 General Kountché created a National Charter Commission, largely composed of CND members but including representatives of a cross section of other institutions, to develop the framework of a new constitution. The commission's work was suspended later in the year, the government declaring that the drought and economic problems took priority. However, charter discussions recommenced in October 1985, yielding a 100-page document that was approved by the government in January 1986 and overwhelmingly endorsed in a national referendum on June 14, 1987. On August 2 Prime Minister Algabid announced that the "constitutional normalization process" would soon begin, with the CND, replenished by national balloting, formally assuming the role of a constituent assembly.

Foreign relations. Prior to the 1974 coup, Niger pursued a moderate line in foreign affairs, avoiding involvement in East-West issues and maintaining friendly relations with neighboring states, except for a brief period of territorial friction with Benin (then Dahomey) in 1963–1964. The present government has established diplomatic links with a number of Communist states, including both China and the Soviet Union, while adopting a conservative posture in regional affairs, including a diplomatic rupture with Libya from January 1981 to March 1982. Tripoli has since been periodically charged with backing anti-Niamey forces, including those involved in a late 1983 coup attempt and a commando raid by 14 Tuareg rebels on a Niger outpost in May 1985.

A member of the United Nations and most of its Specialized Agencies, Niger at the regional level belongs to the Organization of African Unity, the Council of the Entente, the Common African and Mauritian Organization, and the Economic Community of West African States.

Current issues. The death of President Kountché represented the loss of a "quiet ally" of both Paris and Washington in their lengthy series of disputes with Libya's Mu'ammar Qadhafi, particularly in regard to the hostilities in Chad. Niger's military airport at Dirkou had been renovated by US engineers in 1984 and had been used by French aircraft to provide military supplies to Chadian forces in the Tibesti mountain region.

Upon assuming power, Colonel Seibou declared an amnesty for all political prisoners and met with the country's first president, Hamani Diori (theretofore confined to house arrest) as well as with Diori's former political opponent, Djibo Bakary, both of whom pledged their support to the new government. Perhaps most significantly, the former president's son, Abdoulaye DIORI, returned from Tripoli, where he had headed an exile formation, the Popular Front for the Liberation of Niger (FPLN), which Libyan authorities promised to disband. After years of inactivity, work was also resumed on a Libyan People's Bureau (embassy) complex at Niamey, while Tripoli agreed to pay a decade-old bill of $7.4 million for shipments of Nigerien uranium. Such moves notwithstanding, it was not immediately clear how far the rapprochement with Libya would go, Niger's foreign minister, Mahamat SANI Bako (one of the few carry-overs from the Kountché administration) declaring that "We are following a policy of good neighbors—and we didn't choose our neighbors".

POLITICAL PARTIES

Political parties in Niger have been banned since the 1974 coup.

LEGISLATURE

The functions of the National Assembly (*Assemblée Nationale*) were suspended in April 1974. In April 1982 it was announced that the **National Development Council** (*Conseil National de Développement*), established in July 1974 as an advisory body, would assume the role of a constituent assembly to draft a new constitution that would define the powers of a legislative National Council. The present Council was reconstituted as an indirectly elected body of 150 regional delegates in August 1983.

President: Oumarou MAMANE.

CABINET

Prime Minister	Hamid Algabid
Minister of State for Finance	Lt. Col. Mamadou Beidari
Ministers	
Agriculture and Environment	Amadou Mamadou
Animal and Water Resources	Mahamadou Danda
Civil Service and Labor	Abdou Aboubacar
Commerce, Industry and Crafts	Madou Mahamadou
Foreign Affairs and Cooperation	Mahamat Sani Bako
Higher Education, Research and Technology	Yahya Tounkara
Information	Sahidou Alou
Interior	Col. Ali Seibu
Justice	Soli Abdourahamane
Mines and Energy	Allele Elhadjy Habibou
National Defense	Col. Ali Seibu
National Education and Professional Training	Amadou Madougou
Planning	Almoustapha Soumaila
Posts and Telecommunications	Maj. Issa Amsa
Public Health and Social Affairs	Maj. Mainassara Bare
Public Institutions, State Farms and Parastatals	Maina Moussa Boukar
Public Works and Housing	Maj. Oumarou Coulibali
Transport and Tourism	Capt. Amadou Moussa Gross
Youth, Sports and Culture	Capt. Abdourahamane Seydou
Minister Delegate to the Interior	Amadou Fity Maiga
Secretaries of State	
Agriculture and Environment	Brigi Rafini
Interior	Boukar Elhadjy Ousmane
Public Health, Social and Women's Affairs	Moumouni Aissata
Governor, Central Bank	Abdoulaye Fadiga

NEWS MEDIA

Press. The following are published in French at Niamey: *Le Sahel* (5,000), daily news bulletin of the government Information Service; *Le Sahel Dimanche* (3,000), weekly publication of the government Information Service.

News agency. The government launched *Agence Nigérienne de Press* (ANP) in late 1986.

Radio and television. The *Office de Radiodiffusion-Télévision du Niger* (ORTN) operates *La Voix du Sahel,* a government radio service broadcasting in French, English, and indigenous languages, and also services nine television stations. There were approximately 300,000 radio and 25,000 television receivers in 1987.

INTERGOVERNMENTAL REPRESENTATION

Ambassador to the US and Permanent Representative to the UN: Joseph DIATTA.

US Ambassador to Niger: Richard Wayne BOGOSIAN.

IGO Memberships (Non-UN): ACCT, ADF, AfDB, AGC, BADEA, BOAD, CCC, CEAO, CENT, CILSS, ECOWAS, EEC(L), *EIB,* IC, IDB, Intelsat, Interpol, NAM, OAU, OCAM.

NIGERIA

Federal Republic of Nigeria

Political Status: Independent member of the Commonwealth since 1960; republic established in 1963; civilian government suspended as the result of military coups in January and July 1966; executive presidential system established under constitution effective October 1, 1979; under military rule following successive coups of December 31, 1983 and August 27, 1985.

Area: 356,667 sq. mi. (923,768 sq. km.).

Population: 100,694,000 (1988E). A 1973 census was officially repudiated as being grossly inflated insofar as the northern enumeration was concerned and some 1988 estimates run as high as 130 million. A new census is scheduled for 1991.

Major Urban Centers (1975E): LAGOS (1,061,000); Ibadan (847,000); Ogbomosho (432,000); Kano (399,000); Oshogbo (282,000); Ilorin (282,000); Port Harcourt (242,000). There are no recent data and the 1975 figure for Lagos was unquestionably conservative, at least one 1987 estimate for the capital being as high as 7 million.

Official Language: English (the leading indigenous languages are Hausa, Igbo, and Yoruba).

Monetary Unit: Naira (market rate March 1, 1988, 4.29 naira = $1US).

President of the Federal Republic and Chairman of the Armed Forces Ruling Council: Gen. Ibrahim BABANGIDA; sworn in following the ouster of Maj. Gen. Mohammadu (Muhammad) BUHARI on August 27, 1985.

THE COUNTRY

The most populous country in Africa and one of the most richly endowed in natural resources, Nigeria extends from the inner corner of the Gulf of Guinea to the border of Niger in the north and to Lake Chad in the northeast. Included within its boundaries is the northern section of the former United Nations Trust Territory of British Cameroons, whose inhabitants voted to join Nigeria in a UN-sponsored plebiscite in 1961. Nigeria's topography ranges from swampy lowland along the coast, through tropical rain forest and open plateau country, to semidesert conditions in the far north. The ethnic pattern is similarly varied, with tribal groups speaking over 250 languages. The Hausa, Fulani, and other Islamic peoples in the north, the mixed Christian and Islamic Yoruba in the west, and the predominantly Christian Ibo in the east are the most numerous groups. In the absence of reliable census information (stemming from fears of its impact on long-standing tension between north and south), it has been estimated that nearly half the population is Muslim, with 35 percent Christian and the remainder adhering to traditional religious practices. Numerous traditional rulers retain considerable influence, particularly in rural areas. Women are responsible for the bulk of subsistence farming, their involvement in the paid work force being concentrated in sales and crafts. Female representation in government is minimal.

Nigeria's important natural resources include petroleum and natural gas, hydroelectric power, and commercially exploitable deposits of tin, coal, and columbite. The oil boom of the 1970s produced rapid industrial expansion led by consumer nondurables, vehicle assembly, aluminum smelting, and steel production. However, a world glut reduced oil revenue from $26 billion in 1980 to $5.6 billion in 1986, precipitating industrial contraction and cutbacks in government and personal spending. Although petroleum continues to provide over 80 percent of export earnings, current development focuses on the revival of local food production. The leading cash crops are cocoa, peanuts, palm products, and cotton, with timber and fish also of importance.

GOVERNMENT AND POLITICS

Political background. Brought under British control during the nineteenth century, Nigeria was organized as a British Colony and Protectorate in 1914, became a self-governing federation in 1954, and achieved independence within the Commonwealth on October 1, 1960. Under the guidance of its first prime minister, Sir Abubaker Tafawa BALEWA, it became a republic three years later, with the former governor general, Dr. Nnamdi AZIKIWE of the Ibo tribe, as president. The original federation consisted of three regions (Northern, Western, and Eastern); a fourth region (the Midwest) was created in 1963.

Though widely regarded as one of the most viable of the new African states, independent Nigeria was beset by underlying tensions resulting from ethnic, religious, and regional cleavages. Weakened by strife and tainted by corruption, the federal government was overthrown on January 15, 1966, in a coup that cost the lives of Prime Minister Balewa and other northern political leaders and the establishment of a Supreme Military Council (SMC) headed by Maj. Gen. Johnson T.U. AGUIYI-IRONSI, the Ibo commander of the army. Resentment by northerners of the predominantly Ibo leadership and its subsequent attempt to establish a unitary state resulted on July 29 in a second coup, led by Col. (later Gen.) Yakubu GOWON, a northerner. Events surrounding the first coup had already raised ethnic hostility to the boiling point; thousands of Ibo who had settled in the north were massacred before and after the second, while hundreds of thousands began a mass flight back to their homeland at the urging of eastern leaders.

Plans for a constitutional revision that would calm Ibo apprehensions while preserving the unity of the country were blocked by the refusal of the Eastern Region's military governor, Lt. Col. Odumegwu OJUKWU, to accept anything less than complete regional autonomy. Attempts at conciliation having failed, Colonel Gowon, as head of the federal military government, announced on May 28, 1967, the assumption of emergency powers and the reorganization of Nigeria's 4 regions into 12 states. Intended to equalize treatment of various areas and ethnic groups throughout the country, the move was also designed to increase the influence of the Eastern Region's non-Ibo inhabitants.

The Eastern Region responded on May 30, 1967, by declaring independence as the Republic of Biafra, with Ojukwu as head of state. Refusing to recognize the secession, the federal government initiated hostilities against Biafra on July 6. Peace proposals from British, Commonwealth, and OAU sources were repeatedly rejected by Ojukwu on the ground that they failed to guarantee Biafra's future as a "sovereign and independent state". Limited external support, mainly from France, began to arrive in late 1968 and enabled Biafra to continue fighting despite the loss of most non-Ibo territory, casualties estimated at over 1.5 million, and a growing threat of mass starvation. A series of military defeats in late 1969 and early 1970 finally resulted in surrender of the rebel forces on January 15, 1970.

The immediate postwar period was one of remarkable reconciliation as General Gowon moved to reintegrate Ibo elements into Nigerian life. Not only were Ibo brought back into the civil service and the military, but the federal government launched a major reconstruction of the devastated eastern area. Normal political life remained suspended, however, and on July 29, 1975, while Gowon was attending an OAU meeting at Kampala, Uganda, his government was overthrown in a bloodless coup led by Brig. (later Gen.) Murtala Ramat MUHAMMAD.

Muhammad was assassinated on February 13, 1976, during an abortive coup apparently provoked by a campaign to wipe out widespread government corruption, as exemplified by a massive cement scandal that had yielded import orders far exceeding the unloading capacity of the country's limited port facilities. He was succeeded as head of state and chairman of the SMC by Lt. Gen. Olusegun OBASANJO, who had been chief of staff of the armed forces since the 1975 coup.

In October 1975 a 50-member committee had been charged by the SMC with the drafting of a new constitution that would embrace an "executive presidential system". Two years later, a National Constituent Assembly met to consider the draft and adjourned on June 5, 1978, the SMC subsequently making a number of changes in the Assembly-approved document. On September 21, Nigeria's 12-year-old state of emergency was terminated and the ban on political parties lifted.

A series of elections was contested in mid-1979 by five parties that had been approved by the Federal Electoral Commission (Fedeco) as being sufficiently national in representation. Balloting commenced on July 7 for the election of federal senators and continued, on successive weekends, with the election of federal representatives, state legislators, and state governors, culminating on August 11

with the election of Alhaji Shehu SHAGARI and Dr. Alex EKWUEME of the National Party of Nigeria (NPN) as federal president and vice president, respectively. Following judicial resolution of a complaint that the NPN candidates had not obtained a required 25 percent of the vote in 13 of the 19 states, the two leaders were inaugurated on October 1.

By 1983, public confidence in the civilian regime had waned in the face of sharply diminished oil income, massive government overspending, and widespread evidence of official corruption. Nonetheless, the personally popular Shagari easily won reelection in the presidential balloting of August 4. Subsequent rounds of the five-week election process, which were marred by evidence of electoral fraud and by rioting in Oyo and Ondo states, left the ruling NPN in control of 13 state houses, 13 governorships, and both houses of the National Assembly. Following the balloting, the economy continued to decline, an austerity budget adopted in November further deepening public discontent, and on December 31 a group of senior military officers (most of whom had served under Obasanjo) seized power. On January 3, 1984, Maj. Gen. Muhammadu BUHARI, formerly Obasanjo's oil minister, was sworn in as chairman of a new Supreme Military Council, which proceeded to launch a "war against indiscipline", reintroduced the death penalty, and established a number of special tribunals that moved vigorously in sentencing numerous individuals, including leading politicians, on charges of embezzlement and other offenses.

In the wake of increasing political repression by the Buhari regime and a steadily worsening economy, Buhari and his armed forces chief of staff, Maj. Gen. Tunde IDIAGBON, were deposed by senior members of the SMC on August 27, 1985. Following the coup, the new government, headed by Maj. Gen Ibrahim BABANGIDA, abolished a number of decrees limiting press freedom, released numerous political detainees, and adopted a more open style of government that included the solicitation of public opinion on future political development. There was, however, a counter-coup attempt by a group of disgruntled officers late in the year, several of whom were executed in March 1986.

Constitution and government. Prior to his assassination in February 1976, General Muhammad had announced that the 12 states created in 1967 would be expanded to 19 to alleviate the domination of subunits by traditional ethnic and religious groups, thus helping "to erase memories of past political ties and emotional attachments". A decree establishing the new states was subsequently promulgated by General Obasanjo on March 17. A centrally located area of some 3,000 square miles was also designated as a Federal Capital Territory, with the transfer of the federal administration from Lagos to the new capital of Abuja scheduled to be completed by 1990. (In September 1987 two new states, Katsina and Akwa Ibom, were created out of territory formerly in Kaduna and Cross River, respectively, President Babangida announcing that no further changes would be considered by his administration.)

Region (Pre-1967)	State (1967)	State and Capital (1987)
Northern	Benue Plateau	Benue (Makurdi) Plateau (Jos)

	Kano	Kano (Kano)
	Kwara	Kwara (Ilorin)
	North-Central	Kaduna (Kaduna)
		Katsina (Katsina)
	North-Eastern	Bauchi (Bauchi)
		Borno (Maiduguri)
		Gongola (Yola)
	North-Western	Niger (Minna)
		Sokoto (Sokoto)
Eastern	East-Central	Anambra (Enugu)
		Imo (Owerri)
	Rivers	Rivers (Port Harcourt)
	South-Eastern	Cross River (Calabar)
		Akwa Ibom (Uyo)
Mid-Western	Mid-Western	Bendel (Benin)
Western	Lagos	Lagos (Ikeja)
	Western	Ogun (Abeokuta)
		Ondo (Akure)
		Oyo (Ibadan)

The 1979 constitution established a US-style federal system with powers divided among three federal branches (executive, legislative, and judicial) and between federal and state governments. Executive authority at the national level was vested in a president and vice president, who ran on a joint ticket and served four-year terms. To be declared the victor on a first ballot, a presidential candidate was required to win a plurality of the national popular vote and at least one-quarter of the vote in two-thirds of the 19 states. Legislative power was invested in a bicameral National Assembly comprising a 95-member Senate and a 449-member House of Representatives.

Upon assuming power on December 31, 1983, the Supreme Military Council suspended those portions of the constitution "relating to all elective and appointive offices and representative institutions". A constitutional modification decree issued in January 1984 established a Federal Military Government encompassing a Supreme Military Council; a National Council of States, headed by the chairman of the SMC and including the military governors of the (then) 19 states, the chief of staff of the armed forces, the inspector-general of police and the attorney general; and a Federal Executive Council (cabinet). The decree also provided for state executive councils headed by the military governors. Following the coup of August 1985 the Supreme Military Council and the Federal Executive Council were renamed the Armed Forces Ruling Council and the Council of Ministers, respectively. The chairman of the AFRC, serving as both the head of state and chief executive, is assisted by a chief of general staff who is responsible for civilian "political affairs". Following the AFRC's announcement in September 1987 of a five-year schedule for return to civilian government (see Current issues, below), a 46-member Constitution Review Committee was created to prepare a revision of the 1979 basic law for consideration by a constituent assembly in 1988.

The existing judiciary has been left largely intact, although enjoined from challenging or interpreting "this or any other decree" of the Ruling Council. The system is headed by a Supreme Court; a Federal Court of Appeal, which includes justices expert in Islamic and customary law; and a Federal High Court. Each state has a high court, Muslim and customary appeals courts if so mandated, and local courts as established by law. Under a Special Tribunals Decree of July 1984, additional bodies were created to deal with a variety of miscellaneous offenses, including damage to public property, unlawful exportation, and drug trafficking.

Foreign relations. As a member of the United Nations, the Commonwealth, and the Organization of African Unity (OAU), Nigeria has adhered to a policy of nonalignment, opposition to colonialism, and support for liberation movements in all White-dominated African territories. It has actively participated in OAU committees and negotiations directed toward settling the Chadian civil war, the Western Sahara conflict, and disputes in the Horn of Africa. At the regional level, Nigeria was the prime mover in negotiations leading to the establishment in 1975 of the Economic Community of West African States (ECOWAS). The 1979 coup in Liberia led to a brief interruption in normal relations, while Benin and Cameroon have both challenged Nigerian territorial claims—along the Benin-Nigeria border and in offshore waters, respectively. More recently, the country's economic difficulties have resulted in additional friction with its neighbors: a January 1983 decision by the Shagari government to expel an estimated 2 million illegal aliens (primarily nationals of Benin, Ghana, Niger, and Togo) was viewed as violating "the spirit of ECOWAS", as were renewed expulsions of aliens (including famine refugees from Mali and Chad) in May 1985.

Nigeria maintains relations with both Eastern and Western governments, strong economic ties having been established with Britain, Canada, the Soviet Union, and the People's Republic of China. Its leading export partner, however, is the United States, which receives more petroleum from Nigeria than from any other country, save Saudi Arabia and Mexico.

Relations between Lagos and London, strained by the flight to Britain of a number of political associates of Shagari, were formally suspended in mid-1984, when British police arrested a Nigerian diplomat and expelled two others for the attempted kidnapping of former transport minister Umaru DIKKO, who is under indictment in Nigeria for diversion of public funds. Although Dikko's status remained unresolved, full relations with the United Kingdom were resumed in February 1986.

In January 1986 Nigeria became a full member of the Islamic Conference although intense Christian opposition yielded the appointment of a commission to evaluate the implications of membership. Muslims, on the other hand, objected strenuously to reports in October 1987 of an impending restoration of diplomatic relations with Israel.

Current issues. In September 1987 President Babangida announced that the return to civilian rule would be completed in 1992, two years later than originally scheduled. Local nonparty elections were held on December 12, 1987, and March 26, 1988, (many results of the first poll having been invalidated) to pave the way for a "new socio-political order" that the AFRC hoped would exclude the instability and corruption of previous civilian governments. The transition schedule called for promulgation of a new constitution and lifting of the ban on political parties in 1989, elections to unicameral state legislatures in 1990, and federal presidential and legislative elections in 1992. To guard against tribal and religious fractionalization, the AFRC adopted the recommendation of a university-dominated "Political Bureau" that only two political parties be sanctioned. However, it rejected Bureau suggestions that the government adopt a socialist ideology and nationalize the minority portion of the oil industry that remained in private hands. Late in the year Babangida announced that most former and current political leaders, including himself and the rest of the AFRC, would be barred from running for office in forthcoming elections.

Although the transition plan appeared to win popular support, observers cautioned that its success would depend on the continued stability of the military regime, which has encountered turbulence on several fronts. Widespread rioting in the Muslim north during March 1987 was overtly anti-Christian, but appeared to have an antiregime undercurrent. The government also faced opposition to continued budget austerity, initiated in 1986 as part of a comprehensive economic reform package. Devaluations of the naira led to an unpopular surge in prices although, as planned, food production was stimulated and many of the urban unemployed returned to farming. International response to the reforms has been highly favorable, creditors agreeing in 1987 to extensive rescheduling of payments on the country's $20 billion foreign debt.

POLITICAL PARTIES

Upon assuming power in December 1983, the Supreme Military Council banned all political parties, arrested many of their leaders, and confiscated their assets. Under the 1979 constitution, five parties had initially qualified as legal entities by maintaining offices in at least 13 of the 19 states: the National Party of Nigeria (NPN), led by Alhaji Shehu Shagari, Uba Ahmed, and Adisa Akinloye; the Nigerian People's Party (NPP), led by Nnambi Azikiwe; the Unity Party of Nigeria (UPN), led by Chief Obafemi Awolowo; the Greater Nigeria People's Party (GNPP), led by Alhaji Waziri Ibrahim; and the People's Redemption Party (PRP), led by Alhaji Aminu Kano and Abubaker Rimi. In 1982, a sixth group, the Nigerian Advance Party, led by Tunji Braithwaite, was officially registered, while the NPP (having withdrawn its legislative support of the governing NPN) joined the UPN and elements of the GNPP and PRP in a Progressive People's Alliance (PPA) that was unable to evolve into a unified party prior to the 1983 balloting because of the lack of a commonly acceptable presidential candidate.

In 1987 the government announced that the ban on political parties is to be lifted in 1989 although only two such groups will be registered.

LEGISLATURE

The bicameral National Assembly, encompassing a Senate and a House of Representatives, each popularly elected for a four-year term, was dissolved in December 1983. Indirect balloting for 450 members of a **Constituent Assembly** was conducted on April 23, 1988, votes for the 821 candidates being cast by the local government councillors selected in December and March.

CABINET

President	Gen. Ibrahim Babangida
Minister of State for External Affairs	Mohammed Z. Anka
Ministers	
Agriculture	Maj. Gen. Muhammadu Gado Nasko
Aviation	Air Vice Mar. Anthony Okpere
Communications	Col. David Mark
Defense	Lt. Gen. Domkat Ya Bali
Education	Jubril Aminu
Employment, Labor and Productivity	Alhaji Abubakar Umar
External Affairs	Maj. Gen. Ike Nwachukwu
Federal Capital Territory	Air Cmdr. Hamza Abdullahi
Finance and Economic Development	Chu S.P. Okongwu
Health	Olikoye Ransome-Kuti
Industries	Lt. Gen. (Ret.) Ipoola Alani Akinrinade
Information	Tony Momoh
Internal Affairs	Col. John N. Shagaya
Justice	Bola Ajibola
Mines, Power and Steel	Bunu Sheriff Musa
Petroleum Resources	Rilwanu Lukman
Science and Technology	Emmanuel Emovon
Social Development, Youth, Sports and Culture	Air Cmdr. Bayo Lawal
Trade	Samaila Mamman
Transport	Kalu I. Kalu
Works and Housing	Brig. Mamman Kontagora
Special Duties	Air Vice Mar. Ishaya Aboli Shekari
Governor, Central Bank	Abdulkadir Ahmed

NEWS MEDIA

The Nigerian media returned to its position as one of the freest and most active in Africa following repeal, after the coup of August 1985, of the previous regime's Decree No. 4, which had authorized numerous media suspensions and the imprisonment of journalists for "inaccurate reporting". On the other hand, the popular and outspoken weekly *Newswatch,* whose founding editor-in-chief Dele Giwa was killed by a letter bomb in 1986, was banned for several months in 1987 for publishing details of the government's political transition plan.

Press. The following are published daily at Lagos, unless otherwise noted: *Times* (475,000 daily, including evening edition, 500,000 Sunday); *Nigerian Observer* (Benin City, 150,000, 60,000 Sunday); *Nigerian Concord* (100,000 daily, 210,000 Sunday); *Nigerian Herald* (Ilorin, 100,000); *Nigerian Tribune* (Ibadan, 96,000); *Sketch* (Ibadan, 90,000 daily, 125,000 Sunday); *New Nigerian* (Kaduna, 80,000); *Nigerian Chronicle* (Calibar, 80,000); *The Renaissance* (Enugu, 50,000).

News agencies. An official News Agency of Nigeria (NAN) was established in 1978. A number of foreign agencies maintain offices at Lagos.

Radio and television. In November 1975 the government assumed control of all radio and television broadcasting facilities, placing them under a newly created National Broadcasting Authority that was itself superseded in 1978 by the Federal Radio Corporation of Nigeria (FRCN). In addition to several national stations and international service, each state also provides programming. The Nigerian Television Authority (NTV), founded in 1976 by the government, regulates all television broadcasting. There were approximately 16 million radio and 2 million television receivers in 1987.

INTERGOVERNMENTAL REPRESENTATION

Ambassador to the US: Alhaji Hamzat AHMADU.

US Ambassador to Nigeria: Princeton Nathan LYMAN.

Permanent Representative to the UN: Maj. Gen. Joseph N. GARBA.

IGO Memberships (Non-UN): ADF, AfDB, AGC, BADEA, CCC, Copal, CWTH, ECOWAS, EEC(L), *EIB*, IACO, ICAC, ICCO, ICO, IIC, Inmarsat, INRO, Intelsat, Interpol, IWTC, NAM, OAU, OPEC, SPCA.

NORWAY

Kingdom of Norway
Kongeriket Norge

Political Status: Constitutional monarchy established in 1905; under multiparty parliamentary system.

Area: 149,282 sq. mi. (386,641 sq. km.), including Svalbard and Jan Mayen (see Related Territories).

Population: 4,091,132 (1980C), 4,174,000 (1988E).

Major Urban Centers (1985E): OSLO (447,000); Bergen (206,000); Trondheim (134,000); Stavanger (95,000); Kristiansand (62,000).

Official Language: Norwegian.

Monetary Unit: Krone (market rate March 1, 1988, 6.36 kroner = $1US). (Note: The krone was devalued by 12 percent on May 11, 1986.)

Sovereign: King OLAV V; succeeded to the throne September 21, 1957, upon the death of his father, King HAAKON VII.
  Heir to the Throne: Crown Prince HARALD, son of the King.

Prime Minister: Gro Harlem BRUNDTLAND (Labor Party); served as Prime Minister from January 30 to October 31, 1981; reinstalled as head of minority government on May 9, 1986, succeeding Kåre WILLOCH (Conservative Party), whose government had lost a confidence motion on April 29.

THE COUNTRY

A land of fjords and rugged mountains, and bisected by the Arctic Circle, Norway is the fifth-largest country in Europe but the lowest in population density, except for Iceland. Three-fourths of the land area is unsuitable for cultivation or habitation, and the population, homogeneous except for a small Lapp minority in the north, is heavily concentrated in the southern sector and along the Atlantic seaboard. For historical reasons the Norwegian language exists in two forms: the Danish-inspired *Bokmål,* and *Nynorsk* (a traditional spoken tongue with a comparatively recent written form); in addition, the Lapps speak their own language, a member of the Finno-Ugrian group. The state-supported Evangelical Lutheran Church commands the allegiance of 96 percent of the population. In 1982, women constituted 42 percent of the paid labor force, concentrated mainly in clerical, sales, and human service sectors, generally in the lower pay range; about half are engaged in part-time employment. One-third of the national legislature elected in 1985 is female (the highest representation of any national assembly), while 8 of the 18 cabinet ministers installed in May 1986 were women (both a Norwegian and world record).

The Norwegian merchant fleet is one of the world's half-dozen largest and, prior to the discovery of North Sea oil, was the country's leading foreign-exchange earner. Norway continues to export considerable amounts of such traditional commodities as fish and forest products. The development of hydroelectric power in recent decades has made it Western Europe's largest aluminum producer and nitrogen products exporter. Since exports and foreign services, including shipping, account for roughly 40 percent of GNP, the economy is heavily influenced by fluctuations in the world market. While inflation has been a problem in recent years (averaging 8.6 percent from 1981 to 1987), some experts have predicted that oil and natural gas production may make Norway one of the most affluent of the world's developed nations.

GOVERNMENT AND POLITICS

Political background. Although independent in its early period, Norway came under Danish hegemony in 1380. A period of de facto independence, begun in January 1814, ended nine months later, when the *Storting* accepted the Swedish monarch as king of Norway. It remained a territory under the Swedish Crown until 1905, when the union was peacefully dissolved and the Norwegians elected a king from the Danish royal house. Though Norway avoided involvement in World War I, it was occupied by Germany from 1940 to 1945, the Norwegian government functioning in exile at London.

Norway's first postwar election confirmed the prewar ascendancy of the Labor Party and a government was formed in 1945 under Prime Minister Einar GERHARDSEN. Labor continued to rule as a majority party until 1961 and as a minority party until 1965, when a coalition of nonsocialist parties took control under Per BORTEN, leader of the Center Party. The Borten government was forced to resign in 1971, following disclosure that the prime minister had deliberately leaked information on negotiations for entering the European Communities (EC). A Labor government under Trygve BRATTELI then came to power but was forced from office in September 1972 when its agreement with the EC was rejected in a national referendum. However, when a coalition government under Lars KORVALD (Christian People's Party) failed to win the September 1973 general election, Labor returned to power as a minority government. On September 25, 1975, Prime Minister Bratteli announced his intention to resign, and on January 9, 1976, Labor Party designate Odvar NORDLI succeeded him. At the election of September 11–12, 1977, the Labor Party and its Socialist Left ally obtained a combined majority of one seat over four nonsocialist parties, enabling the Nordli government to continue in office.

Prime Minister Nordli resigned for health reasons on February 4, 1981, and was succeeded by Gro Harlem BRUNDTLAND, the country's first female chief executive. However, her government fell in the wake of a 10-seat loss by Labor at the election of September 13–14, and on October 14 Kåre WILLOCH formed a minority Conservative administration—the first such government in 53 years—with the legislative support of the Christian People's and Center parties. On June 8, 1983, in order to present a common front against Labor in municipal elections, the three parties entered into a non-socialist government coalition. Partly because of the recessionary effects of Willoch's economic policies, the legislative balloting of September 8–9, 1985, resulted in a near loss of government control. The three ruling parties obtained a total of 78 seats, as opposed to 77 for the Labor and Socialist Left parties. As a result, the Center Party, which had gained marginally in legislative representation, increased its influence within the coalition, while the right-wing Progress Party, although winning only two seats, held the balance of power.

On April 29, 1986, the Willoch government lost a confidence vote on a proposed gas tax increase, the anti-tax Progress Party voting with the opposition. Ten days later, former prime minister Brundtland formed a new Labor-Socialist Left minority administration.

Constitution and government. The Eidsvold Convention, one of the oldest written constitutions in Europe, was adopted by Norway on May 17, 1814. Executive power is exercised on behalf of the sovereign by a Council of Ministers (*Statsråd*), which is headed by a prime minister and responsible to the legislature (*Storting*). The latter presently consists of 157 members elected by universal suffrage and proportional representation for four-year terms. There are no by-elections, and the *Storting* is not subject to dissolution. Once constituted, it elects one-fourth of its members to serve as an upper chamber (*Lagting*), while the remainder serves as a lower chamber (*Odelsting*). Legislative proposals are considered separately by the two, but most other matters are dealt with by the *Storting* as a whole. Should the cabinet resign on a vote of no confidence, the chairman of the party holding the largest number of seats (exclusive of the defeated party) is asked to form a new government. The judicial system consists of town and district courts (*herredsrett, byrett*), five courts of appeal (*lagmannsrett*), and a Supreme Court (*Høyesterett*). Judges are appointed by the king on advice from the Ministry of Justice. In addition to the regular courts, there are three special judicial institutions: a High Court of the Realm (*Riksrett*), consisting of the members of the Supreme Court and the *Lagting,* that adjudicates charges against senior government officials; a Labor Relations Court (*Arbeidsretten*), which handles all matters concerning relations between employer and employee in both private and public sectors; and, in each community, a Conciliation Council (*Forliksråd*), to which most civil disputes are brought prior to formal legal action.

Local government is based on 20 counties (*fylker*); in each county, the central government is represented by an appointed governor (*fylkesmann*). The County Council (*Fylkestinget*), which elects a Board and a chairman, is the representative institution at the county level. The basic units of local government are urban municipalities and rural communes, each of which is administered by an elected Council (*Kommunestyre*), a Board, and a mayor.

In 1987 a nonlegislative *Sameting* was established, with which official bodies are expected to consult before making decisions on matters affecting the Sami (Lapp) people.

Foreign relations. A founding member of the United Nations and the homeland of its first secretary general, Trygve LIE, Norway was also one of the original members of NATO and has been a leader in Western cooperation through such organizations as the Council of Europe and the OECD. Norway participated in the establishment of the European Free Trade Association but, in a national referendum held in September 1972, rejected membership in the European Common Market. Regional cooperation, mainly through the Nordic Council, has also been a major element in its foreign policy. Internal resistance to the emplacement of US cruise and Pershing missiles, which in 1981–1983 brought about discussion of a Nordic "nuclear-free zone", had largely dissipated by 1985.

A long-standing concern has been a dispute with the Soviet Union regarding oceanbed claims in the Barents Sea. At issue is a 60,000 square-mile area of potentially oil-rich continental shelf claimed by Norway on the basis of a median line between each country's territorial coasts and by the Soviets on the basis of a sector line extending northward from a point just east of their mainland border. A collateral disagreement has centered on fishing rights in a southern "grey zone" of the disputed area, where 200-mile limits overlap. In 1977 a provisional agreement was negotiated for joint fishing in an area slightly larger than the "grey zone" proper, which has subsequently been renewed on an annual basis pending resolution of the larger controversy (see map).

Relations between the two countries were severely strained by the arrest on January 1, 1984, of Arne TREHOLT, chief of the press section of the Norwegian Ministry for Foreign Affairs, for espionage. In the wake of Treholt's arrest, the *Storting* cancelled a planned visit by Soviet politicians and expelled five Soviet diplomats, bringing the number of Soviet citizens expelled for espionage since 1970 to 20. Furthermore, frequent sightings of Soviet submarines in territorial waters have prompted Norway to bolster its northern defenses, although the December 1984 intrusion of a "target drone" Soviet missile was officially termed a "mistake", following an apology from Moscow. In July 1987 three more Soviet officials were expelled for attempting to obtain technological equipment in contravention of NATO stipulations. The issue was particularly sensitive because of an official report three months

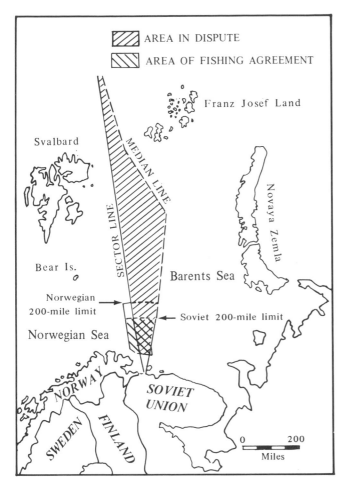

AREA IN DISPUTE

AREA OF FISHING AGREEMENT

Franz Josef Land

Svalbard

MEDIAN LINE

SECTOR LINE

Novaya Zemla

Bear Is.

Barents Sea

Norwegian
200-mile limit

Soviet 200-mile limit

Norwegian Sea

NORWAY

SOVIET
UNION

SWEDEN

FINLAND

0   200
Miles

earlier of illegal sales by the Kongsberg Vaapenfabrikk of stealth–related submarine equipment to the USSR. The United States subsequently banned all new arms contracts with the company, charging that its action had severely compromised NATO's superiority in anti-submarine warfare.

Current issues. The fall of the Willoch government in April 1986 yielded the first nonelectoral change in Norwegian administration in 23 years. On returning to office, Prime Minister Brundtland introduced a series of new austerity measures designed to limit both public spending and private consumption. Not surprisingly, the administration experienced a loss in public support, though the results of a poll in September were viewed as remarkable: a 49.5–42.9 edge for the Conservative opposition, as contrasted with a 43.9–28.8 margin for Labor only five months earlier. Equally remarkable was the outcome of local and municipal balloting on September 13–14, 1987, at which both the Labor and Conservative parties suffered declines, with the Progress Party, a right-wing anti-tax group, gaining 5.1 percent over its showing at the same level four years earlier.

POLITICAL PARTIES

Government Coalition:

Labor Party (*Arbeiderpartiet* — Ap). Organized in 1887, the Ap has been the strongest party in Norway since 1927. Its program of democratic socialism resembles those of other Scandinavian Social Democratic

parties. The Ap-controlled government supported entrance into the EEC in 1972 but was obliged to resign when the proposal was rejected in a national referendum. The party increased its parliamentary representation from 62 in 1973 to 76 (2 short of a majority) in September 1977, the Odvar Nordli government continuing in office with the support of the Left Socialists. Gro Harlem Brundtland, who had succeeded Nordli as prime minister on February 4, 1981, was forced to step down following an Ap loss of 10 seats in the September election.

Campaigning in 1985 under the slogan "New Growth for Norway", the Ap claimed that public services had declined under the conservative government and supported adoption of a job-creation program. Internationally, it called for the establishment of "non-nuclear zones" in Europe. Having declined to enter into a vote-sharing pact with the Left Socialists, the Ap nonetheless managed to gain 6 seats in the September balloting, placing the two parties' combined strength only one seat short of parity with the nonsocialist alliance. It formed a new minority government in coalition with the Left Socialists in May 1986.

Leaders: Gro Harlem BRUNDTLAND (Prime Minister and Party Chairman), Einar FØRDE (Vice Chairman and Parliamentary Leader), Thorbjørn JAGLAND (Secretary General).

Socialist Left Party (*Sosialistisk Venstreparti* — SV). Organized prior to the 1973 election as the Socialist Electoral Association (*Sosialistisk Valgforbund*), the SV was until late 1975 a coalition of the Norwegian Communist Party (below), the Socialist People's Party (*Sosialistisk Folkeparti* — SF), and the Democratic Socialist/Labor Movement Information Committee against Norwegian Membership in the Common Market (*Demokratiske Sosialister/Arbeiderbevegelsens Informasjonskomite mot Norsk Medlemskap i EF* — DS/AIK). In 1973 the coalition campaigned on a strongly anti-EEC and anti-NATO program that also called for cuts in defense expenditure and revision of the tax laws, including abolition of the value-added tax on food.

At a congress held at Trondheim on March 14–16, 1975, the members of the coalition committed themselves to the formation of the new party, although dissolution of the constituent parties was not to be considered mandatory until the end of 1976. In November 1975 the Communist Party decided against dissolution and at the September 1977 election the SV, damaged in August when 2 of its deputies leaked a secret parliamentary report on defense negotiations with the United States, retained only 2 of the 16 seats formerly held by the Socialist alliance. The party nonetheless provided the Nordli government with the crucial support needed to maintain a slim parliamentary majority prior to the 1981 balloting, at which it won 2 additional seats. Four years later, campaigning for "the struggle against nuclear weapons and unemployment" as well as equitable distribution of wealth, the party raised its parliamentary representation to 6.

Leaders: Erik SOLHEIM (Chairman), Per Eggum MAUSETH and Kjellbjørg LUNDE (Vice Chairmen), Hanna KVANMO (Parliamentary Leader).

Other Parties:

Conservative Party (*Høyre* — H). The oldest of the contemporary Norwegian parties, the *Høyre* advocates a "modern, progressive conservatism" emphasizing private investment, elimination of government control in the semipublic industries, lower taxes, and a revised tax structure that would benefit business. It favors a strong defense policy, not excluding the use of nuclear weapons. The party's parliamentary representation increased from 41 seats in 1977 to 53 in 1981, before declining marginally to 50 in 1985. During a national congress in April 1985, the party endorsed continued tax relief, as well as deregulation of the business sector; however, more attention was paid than in previous congresses to improved delivery of social welfare and educational programs. Following the local elections in September 1987, Rolf Presthus announced his resignation as party chairman, effective in January 1988.

Leaders: Kåre WILLOCH (former Prime Minister), Wenche Frogn SÆLLEG and Petter THOMASSEN (Vice Chairmen), Svein GRØNNERN (Secretary General).

Christian People's Party (*Kristelig Folkeparti* — KrF). Also known as the Christian Democratic Party, the KrF was created in 1933 with the primary object of maintaining the principles of Christianity in public life. At the 1981 election, its legislative strength dropped from 22 to 15; in 1985, despite a drop in its vote share, the party gained one seat. In addition to support of most Conservative policies, the KrF's agenda has centered on introduction of anti-abortion legislation and increased trade with developing countries.

Leaders: Kjell Magne BONDEVIK (Chairman and Parliamentary Leader), Solveig SOLLIE and Jon LILLETUN (Vice Chairmen), Odd HOLTEN (Secretary General).

Center Party (*Senterpartiet* — Sp). Formed in 1920 to promote the interests of agriculture and forestry, the Sp was originally known as the Agrarian Party. Since 1958, it has taken steps to broaden its appeal, changing its name, stressing ecological issues, and advocating reduced workdays for families with small children. Generally, however, it remains conservative on most economic, social, and religious issues. The party increased its parliamentary representation from 11 to 12 in 1985.

Leaders: Johan J. JAKOBSEN (Chairman), Anne Enger LAHNSTEIN and Kristin Hille VALLA (Vice Chairmen), John BUTTEDAL (Parliamentary Leader), John DALE (Secretary General).

Progress Party (*Fremskrittspartiet* — FrP). A libertarian group founded by Anders Lange in 1974, the Progress Party was known until January 1977 as Anders Lange's Party for a Strong Reduction in Taxes, Rates, and Public Intervention (*Anders Langes Parti til Sterk Nedsettelse av Skatter, Avgifter, og Offentlige Inngrep*). Although losing 2 of its 4 seats in the 1985 balloting, the FrP was invited to join the (then) ruling coalition to offset the Conservatives' losses. Declining to do so, the party held a subsequent balance of power in the *Storting* and provided the crucial votes needed to defeat the Willoch government in April 1986. At local and municipal balloting in September 1987, the FrP emerged as the country's third-largest party, with a 10.4 vote share.

Leaders: Carl I. HAGEN (Chairman and Parliamentary Leader), Hroar A. HANSEN and Pål Atle SKJERVENGEN (Vice Chairmen), Hans A. LIMI (Secretary General).

Liberal Party (*Venstre* — V). Formed in 1884, the Liberal Party, like the Sp, currently stresses ecological issues, while in economic policy it stands between the Conservative and Labor parties. In recent years, the Liberals have lost many of their votes to splinter groups, and lost its two remaining parliamentary seats in 1985 to the Ap, which had spurred the Liberals' offer of an election coalition.

Leaders: Arne FJØRTOFT (Chairman), Håvard ALSTADHEIM and Inger TAKLE (Vice Chairmen), Knut Erik HØYBY (Secretary General).

Liberal People's Party (*Det Liberale Folkepartiet* — DLF). Also known as the New Liberal Party, the DLF, was formed in 1972 by Liberal dissidents who favored Norway's entrance into the EEC. It lost its only parliamentary seat in 1977, at which time it was styled the New People's Party (*Det Nye Folkepartiet*). It failed to regain *Storting* representation in 1985.

Leaders: Alice RUUD (Chairman), Kristen Bade VEIRE and Åge Ragnar STORM (Vice Chairmen).

Norwegian Communist Party (*Norges Kommunistiske Parti* — NKP). The NKP participated in the Socialist Electoral Association prior to the 1973 election and was instrumental in establishing the Socialist Left Party in March 1975. At an extraordinary congress held on November 2, however, the NKP rejected its own dissolution as a precondition of formal merger with the SV. At the same congress, Party Chairman Reidar LARSEN, who was identified with the SV initiative, was replaced by Moscow "hard-liner" Martin Gunnar KNUDSEN.

The NKP held 11 seats in the *Storting* in 1945 but had lost all of them by 1961, whereas the 16 seats won by the leftist coalition in 1973 represented the balance of power between the minority Labor government and the combined opposition. Nonetheless, many party members have always opposed the strategy of coalition with other leftist groups, in accordance with Moscow's insistence that "all manifestations of opportunism of the right or left" should be rejected. The NKP has been unrepresented in the *Storting* since 1977 and won only 0.2 percent of the vote in 1985. Under chairman Hans Kleven, the party has renewed its efforts to cooperate with the SV and even the Ap, issuing a number of statements supportive of the latter in 1984.

Leaders: Kåre Andre NILSEN (Chairman), Ingerid NEGÅRD and Trygve HORGEN (Vice Chairmen), Gunnar WAHL (Secretary).

Red Electoral Alliance (*Rød Valgallianse* — RV). Originally an electoral front for the AKP (below), the RV has grown in membership to include a substantial number of self-described "independent socialists". In 1985, the party ran on a platform which asserted its independence from Moscow by expressing support for the *mujaheddin* in Afghanistan, as well as its disdain for Norway's other parties. Unlike the SV and NKP, the RV seeks

no accommodation with the Ap, calling Norway "a one-party state with two prime minister-candidates". While it has never obtained legislative representation, it has consistently outpolled the NKP, obtaining twice the latter's vote share in 1985.

Leaders: Aksel NÆRSTAD (Chairman), Arna MEISFJORD (Vice Chairman).

Workers' Communist Party (*Arbeidernes Kommunistike Parti* — AKP). The AKP was founded in 1972 by a number of Maoist groups that had emerged in the late 1960s. At the RV's Third Congress in 1983 an AKP motion urging Norway's withdrawal from NATO was defeated. At its own Fourth Congress in December 1984, the party reiterated its appeal for a Norwegian defense posture independent of both Beijing and Moscow, while reaffirming its primary commitment to armed revolution rather than electoral struggle. Women now control the top leadership posts, in the wake of a 1984 resolution that half of the Central Committee and an equal proportion of delegates to party congresses must be female.

Leaders: Kjersti ERIKSEN (Chairman), Arne LAURITZEN (Vice Chairman), Jorun GULBRANDSEN (Political Vice Chairman).

L E G I S L A T U R E

The *Storting* is a modified unicameral parliament whose 157 members are elected to four-year terms by universal suffrage and proportional representation. Once convened, it divides itself for certain purposes into two chambers by electing one-fourth of its members to an upper chamber (*Lagting*), while the remaining members constitute a lower chamber (*Odelsting*). Each *ting* names its own president. At the last election, held September 8–9, 1985, the Labor Party won 71 seats; the Conservative Party, 50; the Christian People's Party, 16; the Center Party, 12; the Socialist Left Party, 6; and the Progress Party, 2.

President of the Storting: Jo BENKOW.

C A B I N E T

Prime Minister	Gro Harlem Brundtland
Ministers	
Agriculture	Gunhild Øyangen
Church and Education	Kirsti Kolle Grøndahl
Consumer Affairs and Government Administration	Anne-Lise Bakken
Cultural and Scientific Affairs	Hallvard Bakke
Defense	Johan Jørgen Holst
Development Aid	Vesla Vetlesen
Environmental Affairs	Sissel Rønbeck
Finance and Customs	Gunnar Berge
Fisheries	Bjarne Mørk Eidem
Foreign Affairs	Thorvald Stoltenberg
Health and Social Affairs	Tove Strand Gerhardsen
Industry	Finn Kristensen
Justice and Police	Helen Bøsterud
Labor and Local Government	William Engseth
Oil and Energy	Arne Øien
Trade and Shipping	Kurt Mosbakk
Transport and Communications	Kjell Borgen
Governor, Bank of Norway	Knut G. Wold

N E W S   M E D I A

Freedom of the press is constitutionally guaranteed; radio and television are state monopolies.

Press. Newspapers, which tend to be openly partisan, are privately owned by individuals, families, corporations, and political parties. The following press organs (circulation figures for 1986) are published daily at Oslo unless otherwise noted: *Aftenposten* (427,000 morning and evening), independent Conservative; *Verdens Gang* (317,000), independent; *Dagbladet* (188,000), independent Liberal; *Bergens Tidende* (Bergen, 98,000), independent; *Adresseavisen* (Trondheim, 87,000), Conservative; *Stavanger Aftenblad* (Stavanger, 66,000), independent; *Arbeiderbladet* (58,000), Labor Party organ; *Fædrelandsvennen* (Kristiansand, 45,000), independent; *Drammens Tidende og Buskeruds Blad* (Drammen, 40,000), Conservative; *Sunnmørsposten* (Ålesund, 38,000), independent; *Haugesunds Avis* (Haugesunds, 34,000); *Nordlys* (Tromsø, 32,000), Labor Party organ; *Nationen* (21,000), Center Party organ; *Bergens Arbeiderblad* (Bergen, 18,000), Labor Party organ; *Folkets Framtid* (11,000), twice-weekly KRF organ.

News agencies. The major domestic facility is the Norwegian News Agency (*Norsk Telegrambyrå*); numerous foreign bureaus also maintain offices at Oslo.

Radio and television. A state company, *Norsk Rikskringkasting* (NRK), operates the country's one radio network, which offers local as well as national programming, and the one television network, which offers only national programming. Swedish, Danish, Finnish, Soviet, and British television is received in some border and coastal areas. There were approximately 1.6 million radio and 1.5 million television receivers in 1987.

INTERGOVERNMENTAL   REPRESENTATION

Ambassador to the US: Kjell ELIASSEN.

US Ambassador to Norway: Robert D. STUART.

Permanent Representative to the UN: Tom Eric VRAALSEN.

IGO Memberships (Non-UN): ADB, ADF, AfDB, BIS, CCC, CERN, CEUR, EFTA, IADB, ICAC, ICCO, ICES, ICM, ICO, IEA, ILZ, Inmarsat, INRO, Intelsat, Interpol, ISO, ITC, IWC, IWSG, IWTC, NATO, NC, NIB, OECD, PCA.

RELATED   TERRITORIES

Norway's principal overseas territories are the islands of the Svalbard group and Jan Mayen, both of which are legally incorporated into the Norwegian state. In addition, Norway has two dependencies in southern waters, Bouvet Island and Peter I Island, and claims a sector of Antarctica.

Svalbard. Svalbard is the group name given to all the islands in the Arctic Ocean between 10 and 35 degrees East Longitude and 74 and 81 degrees North Latitude. Spitzbergen is the most important island in the group, which became part of Norway in 1925. Coal mining is the major activity in the area and is carried on by both Norwegian and Soviet companies, with oil and gas exploration authorized to begin in 1986. Plans have been made to establish an airfield that will be open to international traffic, although protest from local residents has also yielded strict government regulations regarding the allowed number of tourist arrivals. Svalbard has a land area of 23,957 square miles (62,049 sq. km.); its resident population is approximately 3,800, of whom less than half are Norwegians, the remainder being Russians.

Governor: Leif ELDRING.

Jan Mayen. Jan Mayen is an island of 144 square miles (373 sq. km.) located in the Norwegian Sea, 555 nautical miles from Tromsø. It was incorporated as part of the Kingdom of Norway in 1930.

Bouvet Island. Located in the South Atlantic, Bouvet Island has an area of 22 square miles (58 sq. km.) and is uninhabited. It became a Norwegian dependency in 1930.

Peter I Island. Situated some 250 miles off the Antarctic Continent in the Bellingshausen Sea, Peter I Island has an area of 96 square miles (249 sq. km.) and became a Norwegian dependency in 1933. It is also uninhabited.

Queen Maud Land. The Norwegian-claimed sector of Antarctica, Queen Maud Land extends from 20 degrees West Longitude to 45 degrees East Longitude (see map, p. 19). Its legal status has been placed in suspense under terms of the 1959 Antarctic Treaty.

OMAN

Sultanate of Oman
Sultanat 'Uman

Political Status: Independent sultanate recognized December 20, 1951; present regime instituted July 23, 1970.

Area: 120,000 sq. mi. (310,800 sq. km.).

Population: 1,401,000 (1988E). No census has yet been taken, and some estimates are in excess of 1,500,000. The 1988 figure includes an estimated 300,000 foreign laborers.

Major Urban Centers (1982E): MUSCAT (capital area including Muttrah and Sib, 53,000); Salalah (17,000).

Official Language: Arabic.

Monetary Unit: Oman Rial (market rate March 1, 1988, 1 rial = $2.60US).

Head of State and Government: Sultan QABUS (QABOOS) ibn Sa'id Al Sa'id; assumed power July 23, 1970, in a coup d'état that deposed his father, Sultan SA'ID ibn Taymur.

THE   COUNTRY

The Sultanate of Oman (known prior to August 1970 as Muscat and Oman), which occupies the southeast portion of the Arabian Peninsula and a number of offshore islands, is bounded by the United Arab Emirates on the northwest, Saudi Arabia on the west, and the People's Democratic Republic of Yemen on the extreme southwest. A small, noncontiguous area at the tip of the Musandam Peninsula extends northward into the Strait of Hormuz, through which much of the world's ocean-shipped oil passes. Although the Omani population is predominantly Arab (divided into an estimated 200 tribes), small communities of Iranians, Baluchis, Indians, East Africans, and Pakistanis are also found. Ibadhis of Islam's Shi'ite sect constitute almost half of the population, while most of the remainder are Wahhabis of the Sunni branch. In addition to Arabic, English, Farsi, and Urdu, several Indian dialects are spoken.

Prior to 1970 the sultanate was an isolated, essentially medieval state without roads, electricity, or significant educational and health facilities; social behavior was dictated by the repressive and reclusive Sultan Sa'id. However, following his overthrow in 1970 (see Political background, below), the country underwent rapid modernization, fueled by soaring oil revenue. Although still a conservative Muslim regime that discourages outside visitors, Oman provides free medical facilities for its citizens and schools for more than 200,000 students. Economic growth has been concentrated in the coastal cities with an accompanying construction boom relying on a large foreign work force. The vast rural interior remains largely undeveloped, the poverty of the nonurban population attesting to an uneven distribution of income among a people of whom an estimated 70 percent still engage in farming, herding, or fishing. Over 60 percent of the country's women work as unpaid agricultural laborers on family landholdings. However, growing educational access (more than 40 percent of Omani students are females) has reduced the once large illiteracy rate among women.

Although agriculture employs a majority of the work force, most food must be imported; however, dates, nuts, limes, and fish are exported. Cattle are bred extensively in the southern province of Dhofar, and Omani camels are prized throughout Arabia. Since petroleum production began in 1967, the Sultanate has become primarily dependent on oil revenue, which currently accounts for almost all foreign-exchange earnings. More recently, reserves of natural gas and copper have been targeted for development.

GOVERNMENT AND POLITICS

Political background. Conquered by the Portuguese in 1508, the Omanis successfully revolted in 1650 and subsequently extended their domain as far south as Zanzibar. A brief period of Iranian intrusion (1741–1743) was followed in 1798 by the establishment of a treaty of friendship with Great Britain; thereafter, the British played a protective role but formally recognized the Sultanate's independence in 1951.

Oman is home of the Ibadhi sect, centered at Nazwa, which evolved from the egalitarianist Kharijite Movement of early Islam. During most of the present century, Omani politics has centered on an intra-sect rivalry between imams, controlling the interior, and sultans of the Sa'id dynasty ruling over the coastal cities of Muscat and Muttrah, although the Treaty of Sib, concluded in 1920, acknowledged the nation's indivisibility. On the death of the incumbent imam in 1954, Sultan SA'ID ibn Taymur attempted to secure election as his successor, but the post went to Ghalib ibn 'ALI. Revolts against the sultan by Imam Ghalib's followers were ended with British help in 1959, thus cementing the sultan's authority over the entire country. The foreign presence became, however, the subject of a number of United Nations debates, and remaining British bases were closed in 1977, although a number of British officers remained attached to the Omani armed forces.

The conservative and isolationist Sultan Sa'id was ousted on July 23, 1970, by his son, QABUS ibn Sa'id, the former sultan fleeing to London, where he died in 1972. Qabus, whose takeover was supported by the British, soon began efforts to modernize the country, but his request for cooperation from rebel groups who opposed his father evoked little positive response. In 1971–1972 two left-wing guerrilla groups merged to form the Popular Front for the Liberation of Oman and the Arabian Gulf (renamed in July 1974 the Popular Front for the Liberation of Oman — PFLO), which continued resistance to the sultan's regime,

primarily from bases in the People's Democratic Republic of Yemen. Qabus maintained his superiority with military assistance from Saudi Arabia, Jordan, Iran, and Pakistan, and in December 1975 asserted that the rebellion had been crushed, with a formal ceasefire being announced in March 1976. While the sultan subsequently stated his desire to introduce democratic reforms, a Consultative Assembly established in 1981 consisted entirely of appointed members and Oman remained, for all practical purposes, an absolute monarchy.

Constitution and government. In many respects the most politically underdeveloped of the Arab states, Oman has no constitution, elected legislature, or legal political parties. The sultan rules with the assistance of a cabinet of personal aides and (since 1981) a nominated Assembly that meets quarterly in a purely advisory capacity. The judicial system is based on *shari'a* (Islamic law) and is administered by judges (*qadis*) appointed by the minister of justice. Appeals are heard at Muscat. In remote areas, the law is based on tribal custom.

Administratively, the country is divided into nine regions in the north and one province in the south (Dhofar). Governors (*walis*) posted in the country's 39 *wilayats* work largely through tribal authorities and are responsible for maintaining local security, settling minor disputes, and collecting taxes. Municipal councils are presently being established in the larger towns as instruments of local government.

Foreign relations. Reversing the isolationist policy followed by his father, Qabus has fostered diplomatic relations with most Arab and Western industrialized countries, with his government indicating in 1987 that it wished to extend relations beyond Romania and Yugoslavia to include all Eastern bloc states. Britain has been deeply involved in Omani affairs since 1798, while the United States and the Sultanate signed their first treaty of friendship and navigation in 1833; in recent years Japan has also become a major trading partner. Diplomatic relations were established with the People's Republic of China in 1978 and with the Soviet Union in September 1985.

Relations with the more radical Arab states, already cool, were not improved by Sultan Qabus's endorsement of the Egyptian-Israeli peace treaty of March 1979. However, relations with the People's Democratic Republic of Yemen, long strained by that country's support of the sultan's opponents in Dhofar, improved substantially at an October 1982 "reconciliation" summit, which was followed by an exchange of ambassadors in late 1983. A PDRY deputation to a joint technical border committee session in January 1985 was the first official South Yemeni visitation to Oman since the late 1960s.

In June 1980, in the wake of statements by Sultan Qabus opposing what he viewed as Soviet efforts to destabilize the Middle East, Washington and Muscat concluded an agreement granting the United States access to Omani air and naval facilities in return for economic and security assistance. Since that time, Oman has become a base for US activities in the Persian Gulf. Fellow members of the Gulf Cooperation Council (GCC) have expressed concern over the US military involvement, preferring to concentrate on the GCC's own joint security measures. As a result of its pro-American posture and attendant coolness toward the Palestinian cause, the Qabus regime has also drawn criticism from Arab nationalists, Islamic fundamentalists, and the Iranians, although it has maintained better communications with Teheran than a number of other countries wary of ramifications of the Gulf War.

Despite its importance as an oil-producing state, Oman is not a member of either the Organization of Petroleum Exporting Countries or the Organization of Arab Petroleum Exporting Countries.

Current issues. After 15 years of rapid growth, Oman was forced to curtail development plans in 1986 as tumbling oil prices cut government revenue in half. The economic downturn forced the repatriation of some foreign workers, adding impetus to a gradual Omanization drive announced in 1985 and followed in 1986 by a decree forbidding Omani nationals to marry foreigners.

Although not a member of OPEC, Oman in 1987 announced production cuts in support of the Organization's attempt to raise world oil prices. Because of anticipated higher revenues from oil, the 1987 budget was less austere than had originally been projected, with spending cut by six percent and an announced intention to balance the budget by 1990. In addition, new tariffs on imports were introduced to stimulate local industries, although critics within the six-member GCC argued that the manifest protectionism ran counter to the GCC's trade policy of cooperation among member states.

POLITICAL PARTIES

There are no political parties in Oman. Most opposition elements are represented by the Popular Front for the Liberation of Oman (PFLO).

Illegal Opposition:

Popular Front for the Liberation of Oman (PFLO). The PFLO is descended from a line of guerrilla groups, some organized in opposition to Sultan Sa'id, others of a more regional character. In 1964 the Dhofar Liberation Front (DLF) was formed by the merger of three such groups, including the local branch of the Arab Nationalist Movement, which were closely connected to the National Liberation Front of South Yemen. In 1968 the Popular Front for the Liberation of the Occupied Arabian Gulf (PFLOAG) emerged, with an Omani faction calling itself the National Democratic Front for the Liberation of Oman and the Arabian Gulf (NDFLOAG). The fusion of the latter with other local divisions of the Popular Front produced, in February 1972, the Popular Front for the Liberation of Oman and the Arabian Gulf (also PFLOAG). In July 1974 the local components (in Oman, the United Arab Emirates, Bahrain, and Qatar) again split, at which time the PFLO designation was adopted.

Following several years of quiescence, PFLO commandos renewed their activities in Dhofar province during 1979, apparently having been encouraged not only by South Yemen but by the revolution in Iran and that country's withdrawal of its troops from Oman.

LEGISLATURE

In October 1981, Sultan Qabus issued a decree establishing an appointive **Consultative Assembly,** with a mandate restricted to "giving advice on the general economic and social policies of the country" as conveyed via its president to the sultan. The Assembly originally consisted of 45 members but the number was increased in 1983 to 55, 19 of the seats going to central government officials and the remainder to regional authorities and private sector representatives. The Assembly meets four times a year, its members appointed for two-year terms with reappointment possible.

President: Hamoud ibn Abdallah al-HARTHI.

CABINET

Prime Minister	Qabus ibn Sa'id Al Sa'id
Deputy Prime Ministers	
Financial and Economic Affairs	Qais ibn 'Abd al-Munim al-Zawawi
Governance of the Capital	Thuwayni ibn Shihab Al Sa'id
Legal Affairs	Fahd ibn Mahmud Al Sa'id
Security and Defense	Fahar ibn Taymur Al Sa'id
Ministers	
Agriculture and Fisheries	Muhammad ibn 'Abdallah ibn Zahir al-Hinai
Civil Service	Ahmad ibn 'Abd al-Nabi Makki
Commerce and Industry	Col. Salim ibn 'Abdullah al-Ghazali
Communications	Hamoud ibn 'Abdullah al-Harithy
Defense	Qabus ibn Sa'id Al Sa'id
Education and Youth Affairs	Yahya ibn Mahfudh al-Manthiri
Electricity and Water	Khalfan ibn Nasir al-Wahaybi
Environment and Water Resources	Shabib ibn Taymur Al Sa'id
Finance	Qabus ibn Sa'id Al Sa'id
Foreign Affairs	Qabus ibn Sa'id Al Sa'id
Health	Dr. Mubarak ibn Salih al-Khaduri
Housing	'Abdullah ibn Sa'id Al Busaidi
Information	'Abd al-'Aziz ibn Salim al-Ruwas
Interior	Badr ibn Sa'ud ibn Harib al-Busaidi
Justice, Religious Trusts and Islamic Affairs	Sa'id ibn Hilal ibn Sa'ud ibn Hareb
National Heritage and Culture	Faisal ibn 'Ali Al Sa'id
Petroleum and Minerals	Sa'id Ahmad al-Shanfari
Posts, Telegraphs and Telephones	Ahmad ibn Suwaydan al-Baluchi
Regional and Municipal Affairs	Muhammad ibn Ali al-Qatabi
Social Affairs and Labor	Mustahil ibn Ahmad al-Ma'ashani
President, Central Bank	'Abd al-Wahab Khayata

NEWS MEDIA

Press. Strict press censorship is maintained. The following are published at Muscat: *al-Watan* (23,000), Arabic daily; *'Uman* (20,000), daily government publication, in Arabic; *Times of Oman* (11,600), English weekly; *Akhbar Oman* (10,000), English weekly.

Radio and television. Radio Oman transmits from Muscat in Arabic and English, and Radio Salalah from Salalah in Arabic and Dhofari; both are government controlled. The BBC Eastern Relay on Masirah Island transmits Arabic, Hindi, Persian, and Urdu programming. Color television was initiated at Muscat in 1974 and at Salalah in 1975. There were approximately 150,000 television receivers in 1987.

INTERGOVERNMENTAL REPRESENTATION

Ambassador to the US: Awadh Bader al-SHANFARI.

US Ambassador to Oman: George Cranwell MONTGOMERY.

Permanent Representative to the UN: Salim ibn Muhammad al-KHUSSAIBY.

IGO Memberships (Non-UN): ADF, AFESD, AMF, BADEA, GCC, IC, IDB, Inmarsat, Intelsat, Interpol, IWC, LAS, NAM.

PAKISTAN

Islamic Republic of Pakistan
Islami Jamhuria-e-Pakistan

Political Status: Became independent August 15, 1947, as a member of the Commonwealth, from which it withdrew on January 30, 1972; republic established March 23, 1956; national territory confined to former West Pakistan with de facto independence of Bangladesh (former East Pakistan) on December 16, 1971; independence of Bangladesh formally recognized on February 22, 1974; martial law regime instituted following military coup of July 5, 1977; modified version of 1973 constitution introduced on March 2, 1985; martial law officially lifted December 30, 1985.

Area: 310,402 sq. mi. (803,943 sq. km.), excluding Jammu and Kashmir, of which approximately 32,200 sq. mi. (83,400 sq. km.) are presently administered by Pakistan.

Population: 84,253,644 (1981C), 109,307,000 (1988E), excluding population of Pakistani-controlled portion of Jammu and Kashmir (see Related Territories). The 1981 census figure does not include large numbers of refugees in the Afghan border area.

Major Urban Centers (1981C): ISLAMABAD (204,364); Karachi (5,180,562); Lahore (2,952,689); Faisalabad (1,104,209); Rawalpindi (794,843); Hyderabad (751,529); Multan (722,070); Gujranwala (658,753); Peshawar (566,248).

National Language: Urdu.

Monetary Unit: Rupee (market rate March 1, 1988, 17.55 rupees = $1US).

President: Gen. Mohammad ZIA ul-Haq; assumed office as Chief Martial Law Administrator following military coup of July 5, 1977, which deposed Prime Minister Zulfikar Ali BHUTTO (Pakistan People's Party); sworn in as President on September 16, 1978, following the resignation on September 14 of Fazal Elahi CHAUDHRY, whose five-year constitutional term had expired August 14; reconfirmed as President by referendum of December 19, 1984, and sworn in for a five-year term on March 24, 1985.

Prime Minister: Vacant, following the dismissal of Mohammad Khan JUNEJO (Pakistan Muslim League) on May 29, 1988.

THE COUNTRY

Located in the northwest of the Indian subcontinent, Pakistan extends from the Arabian Sea a thousand miles northward across eastern plains to the Hindu Kush and the foothills of the Himalayas. Its constituent political units are the North West Frontier, Punjab, Sindh, and Baluchistan provinces. Of the four, Punjab is the most densely populated, followed by Sindh. Baluchistan, largely a desert area, is very sparsely populated, and the North West Frontier is mostly tribal. The racial stock is primarily Aryan, with traces of Dravidian in part of Baluchistan. The dominant language is Punjabi (65 percent), followed by Sindhi (11 percent), and Urdu (9 percent); the remaining 15 percent encompasses Pushtu, Gujarati, and Baluchi. In addition, English is widely spoken in business and government. About 30 percent of the population is literate. Islam, the state religion, is professed by over 88 percent of the people; Hindus constitute another 10 percent, followed by small groups of Christians and Buddhists. According to official estimates, only 2.1 percent of the salaried labor force was female in 1984; other sources have attributed over 50 percent of agricultural work to rural women, with two-thirds of urban women and half of rural women also engaged in home-based or cottage industry. Recent trends toward "Islamization" on the part of the government have spurred proposals to repeal female suffrage and have nullified the legality of women's testimony in criminal court cases. However, a small percentage of seats in recent elections have been reserved for women, reinforcing the small urban elite (including opposition leader Benazir Bhutto) who are prominently involved in politics.

Although much of the country consists of mountains and deserts, some of the most fertile and best-irrigated land in the subcontinent is provided by the river system of the Indus and its tributaries. Agriculture is the major occupation of a majority of the population, the principal crops being wheat, cotton, barley, sugarcane, millet, rice, and maize, as well as fodder. In addition, the western province of Baluchistan supplies a rich crop of fruits and dates. Though not heavily endowed in mineral resources, the country has deposits of rock salt, gypsum, coal, sulphur, chromite, antimony, and limestone, in addition to some oil and gas reserves. The industrial sector, which occupies about 20 percent of the formal work force, is concentrated in the textile, cement, sugar, and rubber industries. While economic indicators displayed substantial improvement in the period immediately following the loss of the eastern region in 1971, private domestic investment declined after 1974, and severe floods in 1976 and widespread political unrest in 1977 further weakened the economy. The trend was reversed in 1979–1980, with substantial improvement in both agriculture and industry: yields of wheat, cotton, and rice set all-time records, while both public- and private-sector manufacturing output scored impressive gains. Overall, the economy has registered an average growth rate of 6–7 percent for the last decade, with remittances from Pakistanis employed in the Gulf largely offsetting a substantial trade imbalance. Future projections are, however, pessimistic because of an expected decline in remittances, a pronounced gap between savings and investment, inadequate domestic taxation, and a nonproductive budgetary commitment of approximately 70 percent to defense and civil administration.

GOVERNMENT AND POLITICS

Political background. Subjected to strong Islamic influences from the seventh century onward, the area that comprises the present state of Pakistan, together with former East Pakistan (now Bangladesh), became part of British India during the eighteenth and nineteenth centuries and contained the bulk of India's Muslim population in prepartition days. First articulated in the early 1930s, the idea of a separate Muslim state was endorsed in 1940 by the All-India Muslim League, the major Muslim political party. After the League swept the 1946–1947 election, the British accepted partition and Parliament passed the Indian Independence Act, which incorporated the principle of a separate Pakistan. The new state formally came into existence on August 15, 1947.

India's Muslim-majority provinces and princely states were given the option of remaining in India or joining Pakistan. Sindh, the North West Frontier, Baluchistan, and three-fifths of the Punjab accordingly combined to form what became West Pakistan, while a part of Assam and two-thirds of Bengal became East Pakistan. The Hindu maharaja of the predominantly Muslim state of Jammu and Kashmir subsequently acceded to India, but Pakistan challenged the action by sending troops into the territory; resultant fighting between Indian and Pakistani forces was halted by a UN ceasefire on January 1, 1949, leaving Pakistan in control of the so-called "Azad Kashmir" territory west and north of the ceasefire line. However, communal rioting and population movements stemming from partition caused further embitterment between the two countries.

Mohammad Ali JINNAH, head of the All-India Muslim League and independent Pakistan's first governor general, died in 1948. The assassination in 1951 of LIAQUAT Ali Khan, the country's first prime minister, was a second serious blow to Pakistan's political development. By 1954 the influence of the Muslim League had dwindled, particularly in East Pakistan, and Governor General GHULAM Mohammad declared a state of emergency. The installation of President Iskander MIRZA in August 1955 and the belated adoption of a constitution in February 1956 contributed little to political stability, and on October 7, 1958, Mirza abrogated the constitution, declared martial law, dismissed the national and provincial governments, and dissolved all political parties. Field Marshal Mohammad AYUB Khan, appointed supreme commander of the armed forces and chief martial law administrator, took over the presidency from Mirza on October 27 and was confirmed in office by a national referendum of so-called "basic democrats" in February 1960.

Constitutional government, under a presidential system based on indirect election, was restored in June 1962, and Ayub was designated president for a five-year term in January 1965. Despite a second war with India in late 1965, Pakistan experienced considerable economic progress during most of Ayub's tenure, but student disturbances and growing political and economic discontent, which intensified in East Pakistan, plunged the nation into renewed crisis in the fall and winter of 1968–1969. In early 1969 Ayub announced that he would not seek reelection but would per-

mit a return to decentralized parliamentary government. The announcement failed to quell the disorders, and acknowledging that his government had lost control, Ayub resigned on March 25. Gen. Agha Mohammad YAHYA Khan, army commander in chief, thereupon assumed authority as chief martial law administrator, suspended the constitution, dismissed the national and provincial assemblies, and took office as president.

On January 1, 1970, normal political activity was permitted to resume, the major unresolved issue being East Pakistani complaints of underrepresentation in the central government and an inadequate share of central revenues. In preparing for the nation's first direct election on the basis of universal suffrage (ultimately held December 7, 1970, and January 17, 1971), efforts were made to assuage the long-standing political discontent in the more populous East Pakistan by allotting it majority representation in the new Assembly, rather than, as in the previous legislature, mere parity with West Pakistan. Of the 300 seats up for direct election (162 from East Pakistan, 138 from West Pakistan), Sheikh Mujibur RAHMAN's East Pakistani Awami League won 160; the Pakistan People's Party, 82; others, 58.

After repeated postponements of the Assembly opening, originally scheduled to take place at Dacca (East Pakistan) on March 3, 1971, the government banned the Awami League and announced on August 7 the disqualification of 79 of its representatives. By-elections to the vacated seats, scheduled for December 12–23, were prevented by the outbreak of war between Pakistan and India in late November and the occupation of East Pakistan by Bengali guerrilla and Indian military forces. Following the surrender of some 90,000 of its troops, Pakistan on December 17 agreed to a cease-fire on the western front. Yahya Khan stepped down as president three days later and was replaced by Zulfikar Ali BHUTTO as president and chief martial law administrator. In July 1972 President Bhutto and Indian Prime Minister Indira Gandhi met at Simla, India, and agreed to negotiate outstanding differences. As a result, all occupied areas along the western border were exchanged, except in Kashmir, where a new line of control was drawn. On July 10, 1973, the National Assembly granted Bhutto the authority to recognize Bangladesh, and on August 14 a new constitution was adopted. The speaker of the Assembly, Fazal Elahi CHAUDHRY, was elected president of Pakistan, and Bhutto was designated prime minister.

A general election held on March 7, 1977, resulted in an overwhelming victory for the ruling Pakistan People's Party (PPP); however, the opposition Pakistan National Alliance (PNA) denounced the returns as fraudulent and initiated a series of strikes and demonstrations that led to outbreaks of violence throughout the country. Faced with impending civil war, the army mounted a coup on July 5 that resulted in the arrest of many leading politicians, including Prime Minister Bhutto, and the imposition of martial law. A proclamation issued on July 6 conferred decision-making power on the chief and local martial law administrators, while dissolving all legislative assemblies and enjoining judicial bodies from questioning executive orders. Later in the year, General Zia announced a search for a "new political system" which would reflect purely Islamic values.

President Chaudhry's constitutional term expired on August 14, 1978, although he remained in office until September 14. Two days later, General Zia assumed the presidency, announcing that he would yield to a regularly elected successor following legislative balloting in 1979.

On February 6, 1979, the Supreme Court, by a 4–3 vote, refused to overturn a death sentence imposed on Bhutto for conspiring to murder a political opponent, and on April 4, despite worldwide appeals for clemency, the former prime minister was hanged. Riots immediately erupted in most of the country's urban areas, and on April 15 PNA representatives, apparently wishing to dissociate themselves both from the execution and the disorder that followed, withdrew from the government. Earlier, President Zia had declared that "nonpartisan" elections to local government bodies would be held prior to legislative balloting on November 17. On August 30, however, he promulgated a complex party registration procedure with which the manifestly revived PPP refused to comply, and on October 16 elections were again postponed. Concurrently, asserting that "martial law will now be enforced as martial law", the president banned all forms of party activity and imposed strict censorship on the communications media.

An interim constitution promulgated in March 1981 provided for the eventual restoration of representative institutions "in conformity with Islam", while the formation the same year of the PPP-led Movement for the Restoration of Democracy (MRD) created a force against both the regime and right-wing Islamic parties. On August 4, 1983, a report by a Zia-organized commission of religious scholars concluded that a multi-party parliamentary system was not compatible with Islam; eight days later, Zia announced a "political framework" under which the 1973 constitution, amended to increase presidential power, would be restored and elections held by March 1985. The announcement helped to undercut an MRD civil disobedience campaign, which led to mass arrests of party leaders and provoked violence in Sindh and Baluchistan provinces but failed to arouse nationwide opposition to the government.

In late 1984, the president announced a December 19 referendum on his "Islamization" program, endorsement of which would also grant him an additional five-year presidential term. In the wake of an MRD call for a boycott of the balloting, the size of the turnout was hotly disputed, estimates ranging from as low as 15 to as high as 65 percent; an overwhelming margin of approval, however, led Zia to schedule parliamentary elections on a nonparty basis for February 1985.

A surprisingly large turnout of 52 percent of the electorate on February 25 was interpreted as a personal victory for General Zia in the face of another opposition call for a boycott (some terming it "Zia's second coup"), although five incumbent ministers and a number of others associated with the martial law regime failed in their bids for parliamentary seats. As a result, the president dissolved the cabinet and designated Mohammad Khan JUNEJO, of the center-right Pakistan Muslim League (PML), as the country's first prime minister in eight years. The new legisla-

ture proved more vocal than expected by either Zia or the MRD, which continued to view the government as a puppet of the military. In the absence of legal parties, the Assembly divided into two camps – a government-supportive Official Parliamentary Group (OPG) and an opposition Independent Parliamentary Group (IPG). The IPG was dominated by the moderate *Jamu'at-i-Islami,* which adopted as its primary goal the lifting of martial law and the curbing of presidential power.

The first serious disruption in the "peaceful transition" came in July, following the death of the exiled Shahnawaz Bhutto in Paris under mysterious circumstances. Allegations of involvement by Islamabad in the death of the anti-Zia insurgent leader combined with apprehension at the return from London of PPP leader Benazir Bhutto to preside over her brother's funeral. MRD activists rallied impressive crowds in response to Benazir's arrival in Pakistan; following the funeral, she was placed under house arrest for "inciting public unrest" and returned shortly thereafter to Britain. However, the disquieting effect of such visible repression was blunted by Prime Minister Junejo's mid-August announcement of the impending end of martial law.

In October, the Assembly approved a political parties law, despite objection by President Zia, who termed a multiparty system "un-Islamic". Dissent immediately ensued within the MRD, some components (including the Pakistan Muslim League and the *Jama'at-i-Islami,* which controlled the OPG and IPG, respectively) announcing their intention to register, while others termed the entire exercise "fraudulent" and continued to press for fresh elections under a fully restored 1973 constitution. Without responding to the pressure, Zia proceeded with the scheduled termination of martial law on December 30, while the second return of Benazir Bhutto in April 1986 was treated by the government as but a momentary interruption in its effort to undercut the MRD in favor of a more moderate opposition.

The increasing fragility of the opposition alliance was demonstrated at technically partyless local elections in November 1987. While the MRD had formally declared a boycott, most of its affiliates presented candidates with scant success, save for the PPP, which the PML outpolled by a better than three-to-one margin.

In what was dubbed a "constitutional coup" on May 29, 1988, President Zia abruptly dismissed the Junejo government and dissolved the National Assembly, accusing the former of corruption and the latter of a failure to provide for law and order. Also dissolved were the assemblies and local governments in the country's four provinces. Zia promised to schedule new elections within 90 days, although contrary to an assurance in a televised address to the nation on May 30 did not immediately move to name a caretaker government.

Constitution and government. Between 1947 and 1973, Pakistan adopted three permanent and four interim constitutions. In August 1973, a presidential system introduced by Ayub Khan was replaced by a parliamentary form of government. Following General Zia's assumption of power in 1977, a series of martial law decrees and an interim constitution promulgated in March 1981 progressively increased the powers of the president, as did a series of "revisions" accompanying official restoration of the 1973 document on March 2, 1985. In September, the March revisions were codified by the legislature as part of a series of constitutional amendments which included prohibition of redress for actions taken under military rule; a month later, however, further amendments appeared to temper the increase in presidential authority.

The restored Federal Assembly remained bicameral, encompassing an indirectly elected, but largely advisory Senate and a popularly elected National Assembly, only the latter being dissolved by President Zia in May 1988. The judicial system includes a Supreme Court, a Federal Shariat Court to examine the conformity of laws with Islam, and high courts in each of the four provinces.

Foreign relations. Relations between India and Pakistan reflect a centuries-old rivalry based on mutual suspicion between Hindus and Muslims. The British withdrawal in 1947 was accompanied by widespread communal rioting and competing claims to Jammu and Kashmir. A start toward improved relations was made in 1960 with an agreement on joint use of the waters of the Indus River basin, but continuing conflict over Kashmir and the so-called Rann of Kutch on the Indian Ocean involved the countries in armed hostilities in 1965, followed by a withdrawal to previous positions in conformity with the Tashkent Agreement negotiated with Soviet assistance in January 1966. After another period of somewhat improved relations, the internal crisis in East Pakistan, accompanied by India's open support of the Bengali cause, led to further hostilities in 1971. Following recognition by Pakistan of the independent nation of Bangladesh, bilateral negotiations were renewed and a number of major issues were resolved by the return of prisoners of war, a mutual withdrawal from occupied territory, and the demarcation of a new line of control in Kashmir. Further steps toward normalization were partially offset by Pakistani concern over India's explosion of a nuclear device in May 1974, formal diplomatic ties not being resumed until July 1976, after a series of agreements on transport and trade linkages had been concluded.

In 1977, General Zia initiated talks with New Delhi on a "no war" pact and concluded a technical cooperation agreement with Indian Prime Minister Indira Gandhi in late 1982; however, conflict continued to stem from the Jammu/Kashmir issue (border clashes between Indian and Pakistani soldiers left five dead in 1984), while India accused Pakistan of aiding Sikh extremists in the Punjab. Islamabad's response to the October 1984 assassination of Indira Gandhi was correct, but cautious, condemning the attack while expressing hopes that Rajiv Gandhi, despite anti-Pakistani statements made before his accession, would deal with Islamabad without his mother's inculcation of "the bitter struggle between Jinnah and her father". However, policy toward Islamabad under the younger Gandhi has remained problematic, particularly in regard to the nuclear issue.

International suspicions of the development of a "backyard bomb" by the Zia regime were heightened in August 1984 by the indictment in the United States of three Pakistani nationals for attempting to export krytron switches (used primarily to trigger nuclear devices). More tangible evidence of Pakistan's progress toward nuclear weapons capability was provided by a series of indictments by US authorities in July 1987 against individuals charged with exporting or attempting to export nuclear-related equipment, including 25 tons of a special steel alloy. The affair was of critical importance to US-Pakistan relations because of a legal requirement that Washington suspend aid to any country lacking nuclear weapons that attempts to acquire American materials illegally for producing such weapons. It also threatened to complicate the US role as a prime supplier of weapons to the Afghan resistance forces after the Soviet presence had transformed Pakistan into a "frontline" state in the eyes of the West.

Although Pakistan and Afghanistan had long been at odds over the latter's commitment to the creation of an independent "Pushtunistan" out of a major part of Pakistan's North West Frontier Province, Islamabad reacted strongly to the Soviet invasion of its neighbor in late 1979, providing Muslim rebel groups (*mujaheddin*) with weapons and supplies for continued operations against the Soviet-backed regime at Kabul. While support for the rebels occasionally provoked bombing raids into Peshawar province and the presence of over 5 million Afghan refugees proved economically burdensome, Zia's position appeared to have been strengthened as a result of the invasion.

"Proximity" talks on resolution of the Afghan conflict were initiated at Geneva, Switzerland, between Afghan and Pakistani representatives in mid-1985, but bore little fruit until November 1987, when the Soviet Union offered a 12-month timetable for withdrawal of its troops. In February 1988 Soviet General Secretary Gorbachev announced that his government would commence the withdrawal on May 15 if substantive agreement could be reached by then at Geneva. On April 14 such an agreement (involving no commitments from the *mujaheddin*, whose leaders declared that they would continue the struggle) was reached between Afghanistan and Pakistan, with the Soviet Union and the United States signing as guarantors (for details, see article on Afghanistan).

Current issues. President Zia's dramatic reassertion of full authority in May 1988 was viewed as a response to Prime Minister Junejo's insistence on forming a government party within the Assembly despite the president's known dislike of such formations, coupled with the prime minister's intrusion into areas of manifest presidential concern, including foreign policy and military affairs. By 1987 Junejo had been credited with replacing numerous military bureaucrats of the martial law period with traditional politicians and, in general, of striving for the preeminence of civilian government, with discernable tolerance of opposition sentiment. These tendencies were looked upon with disfavor by Zia and the military who, as was noted in the *Far Eastern Economic Review*, "expected to share power with civilians, not to hand it over to them".

POLITICAL PARTIES

Political parties have functioned only intermittently since Pakistan became independent. Banned in 1958, they were permitted to resume activity in 1962, and the Pakistan Muslim League, successor to Mohammad Ali Jinnah's All-India Muslim League which was responsible for Pakistan's independence, continued its dominance during Ayub Khan's tenure. Opposition parties, though numerous, were essentially sectional in character and largely ineffectual: five opposition parties which combined in 1965 to support the unsuccessful presidential candidacy of Fatima Jinnah won only 13 of 156 seats in the National Assembly. These parties also formed the nucleus of the eight-party Democratic Action Committee that conducted negotiations with President Ayub Khan prior to his removal in March 1969. Though the military government of Yahya Khan did not ban political parties as such, the lack of opportunity for overt political activity restricted their growth. The election of December 1970, on the other hand, provided a major impetus to the reemergence of parties. The Pakistan Muslim League's supremacy ended with the rise of Bhutto's Pakistan People's Party (PPP) in West Pakistan and the Awami League in East Pakistan (now Bangladesh). At the election of March 1977, the PPP faced a coalition of opposition parties organized as the Pakistan National Alliance (PNA). Although formal party activity was suspended following the coup of July 5, the ban was subsequently relaxed, and the PNA, with but minor defection from its ranks, became a de facto government party. Following General Zia's announcement in March 1979 that a general election would be held on November 17, and in the wake of widespread unrest caused by Bhutto's execution on April 4, the PNA announced that it was withdrawing from the government. On October 16 the election was indefinitely postponed and all formal party activity again proscribed.

In February 1981, nine parties agreed to form a joint Movement for the Restoration of Democracy (MRD). The composition of the alliance changed several times thereafter, but it has remained the largest opposition grouping. Despite President Zia's denunciation of political parties as "non-Islamic" and the fact that the 1985 Assembly balloting was on a nonparty basis, some party leaders who declined to participate in the boycott entered into informal legislative coalitions and immediately prior to the lifting of martial law supported legislation permitting legalization of parties under highly controlled circumstances. While most MRD participants declined to register under the new law, the prime minister's Pakistan Muslim League did so in February 1986, thus becoming the de facto ruling party. More recent realignments are discussed under the parties listed below.

Former Government Party:

Pakistan Muslim League (PML). A member of the PNA, the PML had been organized in 1962 as successor to the preindependence All-India Muslim League. It has long been ridden by essentially personalist factions. In 1984 the two main factions split over participation in the February 1985 election. The so-called "Chatta group", led by Kawaja Khairuddin, joined the MRD's boycott call (see MRD, below), while a group led by Pir Pagaro announced that it would participate "under protest". Pagaro was subsequently reported to have invited President Zia to join the PML, 27 of whose members were elected to the assembly, and to have urged the selection of Mohammad Khan Junejo, a long-time party member, as prime minister. In the absence of a party-based legislature, the PML served as the core of the government-backed Official Parliamentary Group (OPG) and was the first to register as a legal party following the lifting of martial

law in early 1986. Later in the year, a cleavage emerged between grassroots party loyalists, led by Pagaro, and office holders (many of no previous party affiliation), led by Junejo, who were charged with "becoming increasingly dependent on the administrative machinery [thus failing in effort] to make the party into a formidable political force".

Leaders: Mohammad Khan JUNEJO (former Prime Minister), Pir Sahib PAGARO, Iqbal Ahmed KHAN (Secretary General).

Former Opposition Parties:

Jama'at-i-Islami. Organized in 1941, the *Jama'at-i-Islami* (Islamic Assembly) is a right-wing fundamentalist group that has called for an Islamic state based on a national rather than a purely communalistic consensus. Members of the party ran as individuals in the 1985 Assembly election, 10 of whom were elected; subsequently, although party leaders agreed to legislative coordination with the PML, the *Jama'at* dominated the anti-martial law Independent Parliamentary Group (IPG) and, despite its unregistered status, functioned as the largest legislative opposition party.

Leader: Qazi HUSSAIN Ahmed.

Movement for the Restoration of Democracy (MRD). Although the Pakistan National Alliance had come into existence in opposition to the PPP regime headed by former prime minister Bhutto, the leaders of several of its original members joined with Bhutto's widow in lengthy discussions during 1980 that led to the formation of the antigovernment MRD in early 1981. The seven signatories of a declaration issued on February 5 (joined by the leaders of two smaller parties the following day) called for President Zia's resignation, the lifting of martial law, and national and provincial elections under a reactivated 1973 constitution. Most of the participants were later subjected to harassment or imprisonment by martial law authorities for having engaged in proscribed activities. By early 1985, the MRD, then composed of 11 members, had become badly fragmented, its components arguing over the issues of participation in Zia-sponsored elections and of appropriate opposition tactics following the end of martial law. Smaller groups also resisted perceived "domination" of the alliance by the PPP, particularly after the return from exile of Benazir Bhutto in early 1986. Khwaja KHAIRUDDIN, leader of the PML's Chatta group, was one of the MRD's founders and served as its acting secretary general until August 1986, when he resigned in an apparent disagreement with Bhutto. Subsequently, the *Tehrik-i-Istiqlal* (below) withdrew from the alignment, while an influential group of moderates under the leadership of Ghulam Mustafa Jatoi left both the MRD and the PPP to form the National People's Party (below).

Leaders: Maulana Fazlur RAHMAN, Mohammad Asghar KHAN, Qaumi Mahaz AZADI, Eqbal HAIDER (Secretary General).

Pakistan People's Party (PPP). An avowedly Islamic socialist party founded in 1967 by Zulfikar Ali Bhutto, the PPP held a majority of seats in the National Assembly truncated by the independence of Bangladesh in 1971. Officially credited with winning 155 of 200 Assembly seats in the election of March 1977, it was the primary target of a postcoup decree of October 16 that banned all groups whose ideology could be construed as prejudicial to national security. Bhutto was executed in April 1979, the party leadership being assumed by his widow and daughter, both of whom, after being under house arrest for several years, went into exile at London. In the wake of charges that she was "out of touch" with Pakistani politics despite a warm public reception (followed by brief house arrest) upon her return in July 1985 to preside over the burial of her brother, Shahnawaz, Benazir Bhutto again returned to Pakistan in April 1986. Her initial actions upon assuming the party leadership included the expulsion of her cousin, Mumtaz ALI, for advocating increased provincial autonomy, and a speaking tour at which she denounced Zia but refused to rule out the possibility of working in legal opposition to the Junejo government.

Leaders: Benazir BHUTTO, Begum Nusrat BHUTTO, Dr. Ghilam HUSAIN (Secretary General).

Pakistan National Party (PNP). The PNP is a moderately leftist group of Baluchi leadership, despite a claim to a nationwide following. It was formed by a group of dissidents from the NDP (below) in mid-1979 and joined the MRD in August 1983.

Leaders: Mir Ghaus Bakhsh BIZENJO, Syed Qaswar GARDEZI (Secretary General).

Awami National Party. The Awami (People's) National Party was formed in July 1986 by four left-of-center groups: the three listed immediately below, plus a group of PNP dissidents led by Latif

AFRIDI. As originally constituted, the grouping was unusual in that each of its constituent formations was drawn primarily from one of the country's four provinces.
Leaders: Abdul Wali KHAN, Sardar Shaukat ALI.

People's Movement (*Awami Tehrik*). The *Awami Tehrik*, organized as a Sindh-based Maoist youth group, was involved in riots that claimed over 33 lives in September 1983. It's leader, Rasul Bakhsh Paleejo, was released from prison in June 1986, after having been held without trial since 1979.
Leader: Rasul Bakhsh PALEEJO.

Mazdoor Kissan Party. The Mazdoor Kissan (Workers and Peasants) Party is a Punjab-based leftist grouping that has long been wrent by factionalism.
Leader: Sardar Shaukat ALI (Secretary General).

National Democratic Party (NDP). The NDP was organized in 1975 upon proscription of the National Awami Party (NAP), a remnant of the National Awami Party of Bangladesh that, under the leadership of Abdul Wali Khan, had endorsed a pro-Peking line and was allegedly involved in terrorist activity aimed at secession of the Baluchistan and North West Frontier provinces. Also a founding component of the PNA, the NDP withdrew from the coalition in August 1978. It was weakened by the defection of dissidents that formed the PNP in 1979.
Leaders: Abdul Wali KHAN, Sherbaz Mazari KHAN, Zahurul HAQUE (Secretary General).

All Pakistan Jammu and Kashmir Conference. Founded in 1948 by Ghulam Abbas as the Muslim Conference and known by its present name since the late 1960s, the Conference won one legislative seat at the election of March 1977 and announced the following November that it would cooperate with *Tehrik-i-Istiqlal* (below). It has long urged that the status of Jammu and Kashmir be settled by means of a plebiscite.
Leaders: Sardar Sikandar Hayat KHAN, Sardar Abdul QAYYUM.

Jama'at-i-Ulema-i-Islam. Founded in 1950, the *Jama'at-i-Ulema-i-Islam* (Assembly of Islamic clergy) is a progressive formation committed to constitutional government guided by Sunni Islamic principles.
Leader: Maulana Fazlur RAHMAN (President).

Jama'at-i-Ulema-i-Pakistan. Founded in 1968, the *Jama'at-i-Ulema-i-Pakistan* (Assembly of Pakistani Clergy) is a popular Islamic group that withdrew from the PNA in July 1978. It joined the MRD in February 1981, severed its membership the following March, then rejoined in August 1983 at the commencement of the civil disobedience campaign.
Leaders: Maulana Shah Ahmed NOORANI (President), Maulana Nasrullah KHAN, Maulana Abdus Sattar NIAZI (Secretary General).

Pakistan Democratic Party (PDP). A former component of the PNA, the PDP is a strongly Islamic party organized in 1969, which joined the MRD in early 1983.
Leaders: Nawabzada Nasrullah KHAN, Sheikh Nasim HASAN (Secretary General).

Also participating in the MRD are the following: the PML's Chatta group (see MRD, above), which characterized Pagaro and Junejo's actions as a "betrayal of Pakistan's founders"; the **Pakistan Republican Party** (PRP); and the **National Liberation Front** (NLF), a left-wing party led by Qaumi Mahaz AZADI.

National People's Party (NPP). The NPP was formed in August 1986 by a group of PPP moderates led by former Sindh chief minister Ghulam Mustafa Jatoi. Although one of her father's close associates, Jatoi accused Benazir Bhutto of "authoritarian tendencies" prior to being removed as Sindh PPP president in May. His withdrawal from the party was viewed as indicative of the younger Bhutto's inability to deal successfully with factional politics within both the PPP and the MRD.
Leaders: Ghulam Mustafa JATOI (Chairman), Ghulam Mustafa KHAN.

Tehrik-i-Istiqlal. The *Tehrik-i-Istiqlal* (Solidarity Party) is a democratic Islamic group that was a founding member of the PNA but withdrew in November 1977; one of its leaders, Mohammad Asghar Khan, was a leading proponent of both election boycotts, stating "there can be no compromise" under martial law. However, following the lifting of martial law, the party broke ranks with its coalition partners by announcing its intention to register as a legal party. It was a leading component of the MRD until September 1986 when most of its leadership withdrew in opposition to Benazir Bhutto's domination of the alliance.
Leaders: Mohammad Asghar KHAN, Ashaf VARDAG, Mian Mahmud Ali KASURI.

Khaksar Tehrik. A right-wing Islamic party advocating universal military training, the *Khaksar Tehrik* (Service Movement) is also known as *Bailcha Bardar* ("Shovel Carriers") because the group's founder, Inayatullah Khan Mashriqi, adopted the spade as its symbol to symbolize self-reliance. The PKP was a member of the PNA.
Leader: Mohammad Ashraf KHAN.

Progressive People's Party. The Progressive People's Party was organized by a group of PPP dissidents in 1978.
Leader: Maulana Kausar NIAZI.

Tehrik-i-Nifaz Fiqh Jafariya (TNFJ). As an activist group representing Pakistan's Shi'a minority, the TNFJ launched a campaign in 1980 against the government's Islamization campaign, insisting that it was entirely Sunni-based. In July 1987 it decided to reorganize as a political party committed to the principles of Iran's Ayotollah Khomeini.
Leader: Arif HUSSAINI.

Muhajir Quami Movement (MQM). Organized in 1981, the MQM is primarily concerned with the rights of Muslims migrating to Pakistan, who it would like to see recognized as constituting a "fifth nationality". The party won a majority of local council seats at Karachi, the country's largest city, in the balloting of November 30, 1987.
Leaders: Azim Ahmad TARIQ (Chairman), Dr. Imran FAROOQ (Secretary General).

Communist Party of Pakistan (CPP). Founded in 1948, the CPP is a small, illegal formation that has consistently maintained a pro-Moscow orientation. Generally supportive of the MRD and exercising some influence with the latter's leftist constituents, it was reported in mid-1987 to have applied for membership in the Movement.
Leader: Ali NAZISH.

Exile Groups:

An insurgent group known as **Al Zulfikar** (the name being derived from former prime minister Bhutto's first name and translatable as "sword") was organized after his father's execution by Shahnawaz Bhutto, originally as the Pakistan Liberation Army, based at Kabul, Afghanistan, and dedicated to the overthrow of the Zia regime. The PLA was dissolved at the request of Begum Bhutto in early 1981, but after reorganizing under its present name at the apparent urging of Col. Mu'ammar al-Qadhafi of Libya, claimed responsibility for the March 1981 hijacking of a Pakistan International Airlines plane that was diverted from a domestic flight to Kabul and, ultimately, flew to Damascas, Syria. In August 1984, 21 alleged members of *Al Zulfikar* were sentenced to 14 years' imprisonment (18, including Bhutto, in absentia) for involvement in the hijacking and various other activities. While the organization was suspected of the assassination of a number of government officials in late 1982 and mid-1984, it seemed largely dormant by the time Shahnawaz Bhutto died in July 1985; it is now headed by Shahnawaz' brother Murtaza BHUTTO. Other exile groups include the **Sind-Baluch–Pakhtun Front,** led by Abdul Hafeez PIRZADA, which advocates a federation of Pakistan to give autonomy to the provinces.

L E G I S L A T U R E

Like its pre-martial law predecessor, the present **Federal Legislature** (*Mijlis-e-Shoora*) is a bicameral body consisting of an indirectly elected Senate and a directly elected National Assembly.

Senate. The upper house serves primarily as an advisory body of 87 members, who were designated by the provincial assemblies on February 28, 1985, following election of the provincial bodies three days earlier.
Chairman: Ghulam ISHAQ Khan.

National Assembly. The lower house, to which 217 members were elected on a nonparty basis in February 1985, was dissolved on May 29, 1988.

CABINET

The government headed by Prime Minister Junejo was dismissed on May 29, 1988, no immediate successor being named.

NEWS MEDIA

Press. Although the Zia ul-Haq government endorsed the principle of a free press after the 1977 coup, a number of journalists critical of martial law were subsequently jailed and the Karachi and Lahore editions of the Bhutto family-owned *Musawat* were banned. In February 1978 newspapers were forbidden to publish any news of a political nature, while formal censorship was imposed during the last quarter of the year and reimposed in October 1979. Prior censorship of political news was lifted in January 1982, but was reimposed in July, remaining in effect until the termination of martial law in December 1985. The leading dailies include *Jang* (Karachi, Quetta, and Rawalpindi, 816,000), in Urdu, independent; *Nawa-i-Waqt* (Lahore, Multan, and Rawalpindi, 250,000), in Urdu; *Mashriq* (Karachi, Lahore, Peshawar, and Quetta, 160,000), in Urdu; *Dawn* (Karachi, 90,000), in English and Gujarati; *Imroze* (Lahore and Multan, 65,000), in Urdu; *Pakistan Times* (Lahore and Rawalpindi, 50,000), in English, liberal; *Jasarat* (Karachi, 50,000); *Daily News* (Karachi, 48,000), in English; *The Muslim* (Islamabad), in English, independent.

News agencies. There are three domestic news agencies: Associated Press of Pakistan, Pakistan Press International, and United Press of Pakistan; a number of foreign agencies also maintain offices in leading cities.

Radio and television. The government-owned Pakistan Broadcasting Corporation offers regional, national, and international programming. Additional service is provided by Azad Kashmir Radio. A public corporation, the Pakistan Television Corporation, Ltd., broadcasts to approximately 1.9 million television receivers.

INTERGOVERNMENTAL REPRESENTATION

Ambassador to the US: Jamsheed K.A. MARKER.

US Ambassador to Pakistan: Arnold Lewis RAPHEL.

Permanent Representative to the UN: S. SHAH NAWAZ.

IGO Memberships (Non-UN): ADB, CCC, CP, IC, ICAC, IDB, Intelsat, Interpol, ISO, IWTC, NAM, PCA, SAARC.

RELATED TERRITORIES

Definitive status of predominantly Muslim Jammu and Kashmir has remained unresolved since the 1949 ceasefire, which divided the territory into Indian- and Pakistani-administered sectors. While India has claimed the entire area as a state of the Indian Union, Pakistan has never regarded the portion under its control as an integral part of Pakistan. Rather, it has administered "Azad Kashmir" and the "Northern Areas" (see map) as de facto dependencies for whose defense and foreign affairs it is responsible.

Azad Kashmir. Formally styled Azad ("Free") Jammu and Kashmir, the smaller (4,200 sq. mi.) but more populous (1,980,000 – 1981C) of the Jammu and Kashmir regions administered by Pakistan is a narrow strip of territory lying along the northeastern border adjacent to Rawalpindi and Islamabad. It is divided into four administrative districts: Kotli, Mirpur, Muzaffarabad, and Poonch (with headquarters at the towns of

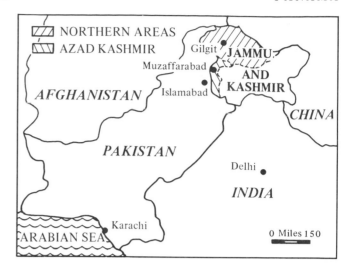

Kotli, New Mirpur, Muzaffarabad, and Rawala Kot, respectively). An Interim Constitution Act of 1974 provided for a Legislative Assembly of 42 members (40 directly elected, plus 2 women named by those directly elected) and an Azad Kashmir Council, consisting of the president of Pakistan (chairman), the president of Azad Kashmir (vice chairman), the chief executive of Azad Kashmir, five members nominated by the president of Pakistan, six members designated by the Legislative Assembly of Azad Kashmir, and the Pakistani minister of Northern Areas and Kashmir Affairs (ex officio). The Assembly was dissolved following the 1977 coup and in October 1978 the president of Azad Kashmir, Sardar Mohammad IBRAHIM Khan, was relieved of his office, the chief executive being named, additionally, as president. In November 1979, the chairmen of the Kotli, Muzaffarabad, and Poonch district councils were sworn in as a ministerial Council of Advisers for the chief executive.

Following his ouster, Muhammad Ibrahim participated in a campaign for democratic rule similar to that of the MRD and was detained in late 1982, along with a number of other prominent local leaders.

In April 1985, 13 parties, most of them affiliated with pro-Pakistani groups in Indian Kashmir, began campaigning for the first Assembly election in ten years; however, the military government in March had established a cutoff of 12 percent of the overall vote and 5 percent of the vote in each district for a party to remain legal, thus ensuring that the Islamabad-supported All-Pakistan Jammu and Kashmir Conference, led by former president Sardar Abdul Qayyum, would remain politically dominant.

President and Chief Executive: Sardar Abdul QAYYUM.

Northern Areas. The Northern Areas encompass approximately 28,000 square miles, with a population (1981C) of 562,000. There are three administrative districts: Baltistan, Diamir, and Gilgit (with headquarters at the towns of Skardu, Chilas, and Gilgit, respectively). The principal lawmaking body is a Northern Areas Council of 16 elected members. The chief executive is a commissioner appointed by the Pakistani government.

PANAMA

Republic of Panama
República de Panamá

Political Status: Became independent of Spain as part of Colombia (New Granada) in 1819; independent republic proclaimed November 3, 1903; present provisional constitutional regime established September 13, 1972.

Area: 29,208 sq. mi. (75,650 sq. km.).

Population: 1,830,175 (1980C); 2,326,000 (1988E), including approximately 36,000 residents of the Canal Zone.

Major Urban Centers (1980C): PANAMA (also known as Panama City, 389,172); Colón (59,840); David (50,016).

Official Language: Spanish.

Monetary Unit: Balboa (official rate March 1, 1988, 1.00 balboas = $1US). The US dollar is acceptable as legal tender.

President: Manuel SOLIS Palma (Independent); named by the Legislative Assembly to succeed Eric Arturo DELVALLE Henríquez (Republican Party) on February 26, 1988.

First Vice President: Vacant, by declaration of the Legislative Assembly on February 26, 1988, that Roderick Lorenzo ESQUIVEL (formerly National Liberal Party) had "abandoned" the post on September 8, 1987.

Second Vice President: Vacant, upon assumption of the office of First Vice President by Roderick Lorenzo ESQUIVEL on September 28, 1985.

Commander of the National Defense Forces: Gen. Manuel Antonio NORIEGA Morena; succeeded Gen. Rubén Darío PEREDES on August 12, 1983.

THE COUNTRY

Situated on the predominantly mountainous isthmus that links America's northern and southern continents, Panama has the second-smallest population of any Latin American country but ranks comparatively high in per capita wealth and social amenities, due mainly to the economic stimulus imparted by the interoceanic canal that was cut across its waist in 1904–1914. Population density is not high, although nearly a fourth of the people live in Panama City and Colón. About 70 percent of the populace is of mixed Caucasian, Indian, and Negro derivation; pure Caucasian is estimated at 9 percent and pure Negro at 14 percent, with the balance being of Indian and other origins. Roman Catholicism is professed by approximately 90 percent of the people, but other faiths are permitted. In 1982, approximately one-third of adult women worked outside the home, primarily in clerical work and domestic service; female participation in government is minimal.

Panama is one of the world's most important centers of entrepôt activity, its economy being based on international commerce and transit trade; since 1970, when a new banking law went into effect, it has also become a leading Spanish-language banking center. Although much of the country's income is derived from servicing the canal, a majority of the labor force is still engaged in subsistence agriculture and unemployment was estimated at close to 20 percent in 1985. Bananas are the most important export crop, although sugar and coffee are also produced commercially.

The economy is reported to have shrunk by at least 3 percent in 1987 as a result of the political crisis that began at midyear, yielding massive capital flight, a suspension of US aid, and (in February 1988) a court order freezing all government funds on deposit in US banks.

GOVERNMENT AND POLITICS

Political background. Although renouncing Spanish rule in 1821, Panama remained a part of Colombia until 1903, when a US-supported revolt resulted in the proclamation of an independent republic. Shortly thereafter, Panama and the United States signed a treaty in which the latter guaranteed the independence of Panama while obtaining "in perpetuity" the use, occupation, and control of a zone for the construction, operation, and protection of an interoceanic canal. Panama also received a down payment of $10 million and subsequent annual payments of $250,000.

In the absence of strongly rooted political institutions, governmental authority was exercised in the ensuing decades by a few leading families engaged in shifting alliances and cliques. Following World War II, however, Panamanian politics were increasingly dominated by nationalist discontent growing out of continued American control of the canal and the exclusive jurisdiction exercised by the United States in the Canal Zone. Despite increases in US annuity payments and piecemeal efforts to meet other Panamanian complaints, serious riots occurred within the Canal Zone in January 1964, and Panama temporarily broke diplomatic relations with Washington. Following a restoration of relations in April, the two countries agreed to renegotiate the treaty relationship, but progress was impeded by the internal unrest in Panama as well as by political opposition within the United States.

In early 1968, the outgoing president, Marco A. ROBLES, became involved in a major constitutional conflict with the National Assembly over his attempt to designate an administrative candidate, David SAMUDIO, for the presidential election of May 12. Samudio was defeated in the voting by Arnulfo ARIAS Madrid, a veteran politician who had already been twice elected and twice deposed (in 1941 and 1951). Inaugurated for the third time on October 1, Arias initiated a shake-up of the National Guard, a body that served both as an army and police force, and was again overthrown on October 11–12 in a coup d'état by Guard officers who felt threatened by his policies. Col. José María PINILLA and Col. Bolívar URRUTIA Parilla were installed at the head of a Provisional Junta Government, which suspended vital parts of the constitution and normal political processes, promised a cleanup of political life, and indicated that a new election would be held without military participation in 1970. Real power, however, was exercised by the high command of the National Guard under the leadership of (then) Col. Omar TORRIJOS Herrera and Col. Boris N. MARTINEZ, his chief of staff. Martínez was relieved of his command and exiled in February 1969, leaving Torrijos as the sole leader of the National Guard and of the "Revolution". In December 1969, the heads of the Provisional Junta, Colonel Pinilla and Colonel Urrutia, attempted to depose Colonel Torrijos; they failed, however, and were subsequently replaced by two civilians, Demetrio Rasilio LAKAS Bahas and Arturo SUCRE Pereira, as president and vice president. On July 15, 1975, Sucre resigned for reasons of health and was succeeded by Gerardo GONZALEZ Vernaza, the former minister of agricultural development.

Politics in the wake of the 1968 coup focused primarily on two issues: renegotiation of the Canal Zone treaty and the long-promised reactivation of normal political processes. Nationalist sentiments put increasing pressure on the United States to relinquish control over the Canal Zone, while a partial return to normalcy occurred in 1972 with the nonpartisan election of an Assembly of Community Representatives. The Assembly's primary function was to legitimize existing arrangements, and one of its first acts was the formal designation of General Torrijos as "Supreme Leader of the Panamanian Revolution".

Following a legislative election on August 6, 1978, General Torrijos announced that he would withdraw from his post as head of government and would refrain from seeking the presidency for the 1978–1984 term. On October 11 the National Assembly designated two of his supporters, Arístides ROYO and Ricardo de la ESPRIELLA, as president and vice president, respectively.

During 1979 political parties were authorized to apply for official recognition, although the leading opposition party and a number of smaller groups refused to participate in balloting on September 28, 1980, to elect one-third of an expanded Legislative Council (theretofore primarily identifiable as a nonsessional committee of the National Assembly).

General Torrijos was killed in a plane crash on July 31, 1981, and on August 1 was succeeded as National Guard commander by Col. Florencio FLORES Aguilar. On March 3, 1982, Colonel Flores retired in favor of Gen. Rubén Darío PAREDES, who was widely regarded as a leading presidential contender and whose own retirement was due on September 11. Under pressure from Paredes, President Royo on July 30 resigned, allegedly for reasons of health, in favor of Vice President de la Espriella, who reaffirmed an earlier pledge that "clean and honest" elections would be held in 1984. On September 6, it was announced that Paredes had accepted requests from the president and the military high command to remain in his post beyond the mandated retirement date.

On April 24, 1983, a series of constitutional amendments (see below) were approved in a national referendum, paving the way for a return to full civilian rule, and on August 12 General Paredes retired as military commander in favor of Gen. Manuel Antonio NORIEGA Morena to accept presidential nomination by the *torrijista* Democratic Revolutionary Party (PRD). Because of widespread opposition to his candidacy, he was, however, forced to step down as PRD standard-bearer in September.

On February 13, 1984, following the designation of Nicolás ARDITO Barletta as the nominee of a PRD-backed electoral coalition styled the National Democratic Union (Unade), President de la Espriella was obliged to resign in a second "constitutional coup". He was succeeded by Vice President Jorge ILLUECA, who was identified with more leftist elements within the PRD.

On May 6, 1984, Panama conducted its first direct presidential balloting in 15 years. From a field of seven candidates, Unade's Ardito Barletta narrowly defeated former President Arias Madrid, amid outbreaks of violence and allegations of vote rigging. The new chief executive assumed office on October 11, pledging to alleviate the country's ailing economy, expose corruption, and keep the military out of politics. The legislative election, held concurrently with the presidential poll, also yielded victory for the six-party Unade coalition, which took 45 of the 67 National Council seats.

In the second such action in 18 months, Ardito Barletta resigned on September 27, 1985, being succeeded the following day by the first vice president, Eric Arturo DELVALLE Henríquez. The move was reportedly dictated by General Noriega, who had warned a month earlier that the country's political situation was "out of control and anarchic". During his year in office, Ardito had come under increasing pressure for a series of economic austerity measures, although the more proximate cause of his downfall appeared to be an effort by the military to deflect attention from the "Spadafora scandal", involving the death of former minister of health, Hugo SPADAFORA, whose decapitated body had been found near the Costa Rican border on September 14. After leaving the government in 1978, Spadafora had joined the *sandinista* forces opposing Nicaraguan dictator Anastasio Somoza, but subsequently shifted his allegiance to the *contra* group led by Edén Pastora. Spadafora had publicly accused General Noriega of involvement in the drug trade and opposition groups charged that the president's resignation had been forced in the wake of a decision to appoint an independent investigative committee to examine the circumstances surrounding the murder.

In June 1986 the *New York Times* published a series of reports that charged General Noriega with electoral fraud, money-laundering, clandestine arms trading, and the sale of high-technology equipment to Cuba, in addition to drug trafficking. The charges were vehemently denied by Noriega, who insisted that they were part of a campaign aimed at blocking Panama's assumption of control of the Panama Canal in the year 2000. A year later, in apparent retaliation for his forced retirement as military chief of staff, Col. Roberto Díaz HERERRA issued a barrage of accusations in support of the *Times* allegations, in addition to charging his superior with complicity in the 1981 aircraft death of General Torrijos. The action prompted widespread popular unrest generated, in part, by the National Civic Crusade (*Cruzada Civilista Nacional*—CCN), a newly formed middle-class group with opposition party and church support. In July Vice President Roderik ESQUIVEL joined in an opposition call for an independent commission to investigate Hererra's claims. Although Hererra issued a retraction late in the year, a US federal grand jury handed down indictments on February 4, 1988, charging Noriega and 14 others with drug trafficking. On February 25 President Delvalle, who had previously supported Noriega, announced his intention to dismiss the general, but the following day (on the ground that he had exceeded his constitutional authority) was himself dismissed by the National Assembly, which named Education Minister Manuel

SOLIS Palma as his successor. Delvalle, whom the United States and a number of Latin countries continued to recognize as chief executive, escaped from house arrest and went into hiding, announcing that he would continue to struggle against the Noriega "puppet regime". Subsequently, Panamanian assets in US banks were frozen, further exacerbating a financial crisis linked to the fact that the US dollar was, for all practical purposes, the only circulating currency. In mid-March Noriega's forces repulsed a coup attempt by middle-ranking dissident officers, with no resolution of the political impasse in the weeks that followed.

Constitution and government. The constitutional arrangements of 1972 called for executive authority to be vested in a president and vice president designated by a popularly elected Assembly of Community Representatives for terms concurrent with the latter's own six-year span. Special powers granted to General Torrijos as extrapresidential head of state expired on October 11, 1978. Legislative authority, severely circumscribed under the Torrijos regime, was subsequently expanded, while a Legislative Council, originally established as an appendage of the Assembly under an essentially unicameral system, acquired, with the addition of directly elected members in 1980, some of the attributes of an upper chamber.

Under a series of amendments approved by national referendum on April 24, 1983, the 1972 document was substantially revised. The major changes included direct election of the president for a five-year term, the creation of a second vice presidency, a ban on political activity by members of the National Guard, and abolition of the National Assembly of Community Representatives in favor of a more compact Legislative Assembly (see Legislature, below). Under an earlier amendment introduced by General Paredes in October 1982, provincial governors and mayors, all theretofore presidential appointees, were made subject to popular election.

Headed by a nine-member Supreme Court, the judicial system embraces Superior District tribunals and Circuit and Municipal courts. The country is divided into nine provinces and one territory, the smallest administrative units, *corregimientos,* forming the basis of the electoral system.

Foreign relations. Panama is a member of the United Nations and many of its Specialized Agencies as well as of the Organization of American States and other regional bodies. Though not a member of the Organization of Central American States, it participates in some of the latter's affiliated institutions and has considered joining the Central American Common Market. Recently, it has been the center of a number of regional peace initiatives sponsored by the Contadora Group, of which it is a founding member.

The country's principal external problems have traditionally centered on the Canal Zone and its complex and sensitive relationship with the United States because of the latter's presence in the Zone (see Related Territory, below). This relationship, which eased upon conclusion of the Canal treaties, was again strained in 1983, prior to US withdrawal from Fort Gulick, which had been used as a staging area for arms shipments and intelligence missions in Central America. Relations with Washington reached a nadir in 1987–1988 as the Reagan administration committed

itself to the support of Noriega's domestic opponents — a policy complicated by evidence that the general had previously been associated with the US Central Intelligence Agency in a variety of clandestine operations.

Panama has diplomatic relations with many countries, including some East European nations; however, it does not maintain relations with the Soviet Union or the People's Republic of China. Prior to 1978, relations with neighboring Costa Rica were periodically strained by the activities of antijunta elements based in that country; relations with Cuba, on the other hand, were restored in 1974.

Current issues. While General Noriega by mid-1988 had demonstrated a capacity for survival that was, at the very least, a considerable source of embarrassment to Washington, there were increasing signs that the crisis might soon end. At a March conference in Rio de Janeiro, PRD president Rómulo ESCOBAR had indicated that his party was "aware" of the need to provide for the general's replacement, while Solís Palma subsequently spoke publicly of the possibility of a "purely Panamanian solution" that would, according to the *Latin American Weekly Report,* "assure Noriega of a 'dignified' departure". Noriega himself was reported to be willing to step down prior to the presidential balloting scheduled for May 1989 if (1) he would be permitted to designate his successor, (2) Solís Palma were to be accepted as president, and (3) the US drug charges against him were dropped. However, US opposition to the last appeared to be mounting, while the question of whether Noriega would be allowed to stay in Panama (or to return, should he leave) remained unanswered.

POLITICAL PARTIES

Political parties in Panama have traditionally tended to be personalist rather than ideological in nature. All of the ten legal parties that participated in the 1968 balloting were suspended by the ruling junta in February 1969. The ban was relaxed prior to the 1978 election, although no candidates were allowed to run on party tickets. In late 1978, the government announced that legal recognition would be accorded parties with a minimum of 10,000 members. Parties meeting this criterion were permitted to participate in the presidential and legislative elections of May 6 and the municipal elections of June 10, 1984. In mid-November, recognition was withdrawn from seven of the formations listed below for failing to gain a legal minimum of votes at the earlier balloting; the parties so affected were Frampo, Frepu, Papo, the PNP, the PP, the PPP, and the PST. The grouping below is based on alignments prior to the government crisis of June 1987, which remained unresolved for the ensuing year.

Government Coalition:

National Democratic Union (*Unión Nacional Democrática* — Unade). Unade was formed in February 1984 as a coalition of the following six parties in support of the presidential candidacy of Nicolás Ardito Barletta.

Democratic Revolutionary Party (*Partido Revolucionario Democrático* — PRD). The PRD was initially a left-of-center *torrijista* group organized as a government-supportive party in 1978. It obtained 10 of 19 elective seats at the 1980 Legislative Council balloting.

In May 1982, the PRD secretary-general, Gerardo González Vernaza, was replaced by Dr. Ernesto Pérez Balladares, a former financial advisor to General Torrijos. In November, Pérez Balladares resigned in the wake of a dispute between left- and right-wing factions within the party, subsequent speculation being that General Rubén Paredes, commander of the National Guard, would be the country's 1984 presidential candidate. Paredes announced as a candidate in mid-1983, prior to accepting retirement from military service, and was reported to have been nominated by the party in August. In the face of opposition to his candidacy, he announced his withdrawal from politics in September, but later ran as a nominee of the National People's Party (below). The PRD named Nicolás Ardito Barletta, then World Bank regional vice president for Latin America, as its candidate upon formation of the Unade coalition in February 1984. Elected chief executive in May 1984, Ardito Barletta resigned on September 27, 1985, and was succeeded by First Vice President Eric Delvalle.

Leaders: Rómulo ESCOBAR Bethancourt (President of the Party), Alfredo MACHARAVIAYA (Vice President), Dr. Carlos OZORES Typaldos (Secretary General).

National Liberal Party (*Partido Liberal Nacional* — PLN). Advocating individualism and economic policies favoring the private sector, the PLN was the leading element in the People's Alliance (*Alianza del Pueblo*) that supported the presidential candidacy of David Samudio in 1968. Samudio was removed as overall PLN leader in late 1979 for lack of effective opposition to the policies of the Royo government, subsequently joining one of two minor factions that boycotted the 1980 election. The majority faction won five Council seats in 1980.

In October 1987 the PLN's political commission approved a decision by (then) party leader Roderick Lorenzo Esquivel to withdraw from the government coalition; however, the action was challenged by members loyal to Rodolfo Chiari de Leon, who argued that such a move could only be decided by a full party convention. Subsequently Esquivel announced that he would retain his vice presidency as an independent, while continuing to participate in the campaign against General Noriega.

Leaders: Rodolfo CHIARI de Leon, Arnulfo ESCALONA Ríos, David SAMUDIO.

Broad Popular Front (*Frente Amplio Popular* — Frampo). Frampo was launched in early 1979 as a progovernment group oriented slightly to the left of the PRD. It won no Council seats in 1980 and was among the groups deregistered in November 1984 for insufficient electoral appeal.

Leader: Renato PEREIRA.

Labor Party (*Partido Laborista* — Pala). Formed in 1983, Pala is a right-of-center grouping that was an early supporter of General Paredes' candidacy.

Leaders: Justo Fidel PALACIOS (President), Carlos ELETA Almarán, Jorge Federico LEE.

Panamanian Party (*Partido Panameñista* — PP). The PP was one of the two principal pre-1969 parties, the other being the PLN. Avowedly nationalistic, it was the leading component in the National Union (*Unión Nacional*) coalition that supported the candidacy of Arias Madrid in 1968. Terming the ballot a "sham", it refused to campaign in 1980.

The present PP is a rump of the original organization, most of which regrouped as the Authentic Panamanian Party (below) in support of Arias Madrid's 1984 candidacy. It was among those from whom legal recognition was withdrawn the following November.

Leaders: Luis SUAREZ, Alonzo PINZON.

Republican Party (*Partido Republicano* — PR). A right-wing grouping, the PR supported the Robles adminstration in 1964–1968 and survived the period of suspension under Torrijos, but did not participate in the 1980 balloting. Its president, Erik Arturo Delvalle, was elected to a five-year term as first vice president of the Republic on May 6, 1985, and succeeded to the presidency on September 28, 1985, upon the resignation of Nicolás Ardito Barletta. He refused to accept the action of the National Assembly in dismissing him from the latter post on February 26, 1988.

Leader: Eric Arturo DELVALLE Henríquez (President).

Opposition Groups:

Opposition Democratic Alliance (*Alianza Democrática de Oposición* — ADO). Organized around the parties listed below, the ADO was launched in early 1984 in support of the presidential candidacy of Arnulfo Arias Madrid.

Authentic Panamanian Party (*Partido Panameñista Autentico* — PPA). The PPA represents the mainstream of the original PP, which supported the three abortive presidencies of Arias Madrid and endorsed him again in 1984.

Leader: Dr. Arnulfo ARIAS Madrid (former President of the Republic).

Christian Democratic Party (*Partido Demócrata Cristiano* — PDC). In what its leadership termed a "training exercise", the PDC participated in the 1980 balloting, winning two Council seats. Named ADO vice-presidential candidate in 1984, PDC leader Ricardo Arias Calderón has been viewed as a likely successor to Arias Madrid as principal spokesman for the opposition.

Leaders: Dr. Ricardo ARIAS Calderón (President), Guillermo COCHEZ (Vice President), Raúl E. FIGUEROA (Secretary General).

Liberal Republican and Nationalist Movement (*Movimiento Liberal Republicano Nacionalista* — Molirena). Molirena is a relatively minor conservative grouping that was legally recognized in 1981.

Leader: César ARROCHA Graell.

National People's Party (Partido Nacionalista Popular — PNP). The PNP was formed in late 1983, in support of the presidential candidacy of General Paredes, who ran a poor third in the May balloting. It was among the parties deregistered in November 1984.

Leaders: Gen. Rubén Darío PAREDES, Olimpo SAEZ.

Popular Action Party (Partido de Acción Popular — Papo). Papo is a grouping of social democrats that in July 1982 joined with a number of other small parties, including the PDC, in branding the "deposition" of President Royo by the National Guard as "going beyond the legal and institutional frameworks set up by the National Guard itself". It contested the 1984 election primarily to argue in favor of a new constituent assembly to replace the basic law formulated by the military. In an incident that he blamed on the military, Papo leader Carlos Zuñiga was kidnapped and beaten in August 1984.

Leaders: Carlos Iván ZUÑIGA (President), Miguel Antonio BERNAL (Vice President), Roberto AROSEMENA (General Secretary).

Social Democratic Party (*Partido Demócrata Socialista* — PDS). The PDS is a small leftist formation whose president was charged in mid-1987 with "subverting public order and promoting disrespect for authorities".

Leader: Carlos GONZALEZ de la Lastra (President).

People's Party of Panama (Partido del Pueblo de Panamá — PPP). Founded in 1930 as the Communist Party of Panama (*Partido Comunista de Panamá*), the PPP adopted its present name in 1943. Although declared illegal in 1953, the party adopted a generally *torrijista* outlook, particularly on the Panama Canal issue, and subsequently was permitted to operate semi-publicly. In 1979, it applied for formal recognition and, with some 77,000 members, was easily able to demonstrate the required level of support. One of its candidates, running as an independent, obtained a Legislative Council seat in 1980.

Leaders: Carlos del CID (1984 presidential candidate), Rubén DARIO Sousa (General Secretary).

Workers' Socialist Party (*Partido Socialista de los Trabajadores* — PST). The PST is a Trotskyite group that was accorded legal recognition as a party in September 1983. It sought, unsuccessfully, to enlist the support of the PPP in an electoral front against "Yankee imperialism" in 1984.

Leaders: Ricardo BARRIA (1984 presidential candidate), Virgilio ARAUZ.

Workers' Revolutionary Party (*Partido Revolucionario de los Trabajadores* — PRT). Also a Trotskyite formation, the PRT was granted legal status in October 1983. Prior to the 1984 balloting, it joined with a number of trade union organizations in a coalition styled the **United People's Electoral Front** (*Frente Electoral del Pueblo Unidos* — Frepu), which neither the PPP or the PST chose to join.

Leaders: Dr. José RENAN Esquivel (1984 presidential candidate), Gracelia DIXON (President), Dr. Egbert WETHERBORNE (General Secretary).

Other groups include the conservative **Agrarian Labor Party** (*Partido Laborista Agrario* — PLA), the **National Action Party** (*Partido Acción Nacional* — PAN), the **Popular National Federalist Party** (*Partido Federalista Nacionalista Popular* — PFNP), the **Nonaligned Revolutionary Movement** (*Movimiento Revolucionario No Alineado* — MRNA), and the **Independent Working Class Party** (*Partido Independiente de la Clase Obrera* — PICO).

LEGISLATURE

Prior to 1984, the Panamanian legislature consisted of an elected 505-member National Assembly of Community Representatives (*Asamblea Nacional de Representantes de Corregimientos*), which met on an average of only one month a year, and a de facto upper house, the National Legislative Council (*Consejo Nacional de Legislación*), consisting of 19 elected members and 37 appointed from the Assembly. Under a constitutional revision approved in April 1983, the *Asamblea Nacional* was abolished, while the Council was converted into a smaller, fully elected Legislative Assembly.

Legislative Assembly (*Asamblea de Legisladores*). The present Assembly consists of 67 members elected for five-year terms. At the election of May 6, 1984, the National Democratic Union obtained 45 seats, of which the Democratic Party won 34; the Labor Party, 7; the Republican Party, 3; and the Liberal Party, 1. The Opposition Democratic Alliance obtained 22 seats, of which the Authentic Panamanian Party won 13; the Christian Democratic Party, 6; and the Liberal Republican and Nationalist Movement, 3.

President: Ovidio DIAZ.

CABINET

[the ministerial list that follows is the one that continued to be recognized by the United States following the "dismissal" of President Delvalle and Vice President Esquivel in February 1988]

President	Eric Arturo Delvalle Henríquez
First Vice President	Roderick Lorenzo Esquivel
Second Vice President	(Vacant)

Ministers

Agriculture	Hirisnel Sucre
Commerce and Industries	José Bernardo Cárdenas de Icaza
Education	Manuel M. Solís Palma
Finance	Hector Alexander
Foreign Relations	Víctor Jorge Abadía Arias
Government and Justice	Rodolfo E. Chiari de León
Health	Dr. Francisco Sanchez Cardenas
Housing	Ricardo Bermúdez
Labor and Social Welfare	(Vacant)
Planning and Economic Policy	Ricaurte Vásquez Morales
Presidency	Nander Pitti Velásquez
Public Works	Rogelio Dumanoir
General Manager, National Bank	(Vacant)

NEWS MEDIA

Both direct and indirect media censorship is far from unknown. Following the inauguration of President de la Espriella on July 30, 1982, all of the country's newspapers were closed down for seven days, pending the establishment of rules to prevent the circulation of "slanders and insults" without "sacrificing freedom of information". Subsequently, on August 15, Panamanian broadcasters were invited to observe two weeks of "creative rest". In the wake of the government crisis that commenced in mid-1987 a number of opposition newspapers and radio stations were shut down for "inciting public disorder", while legislation was enacted in early 1988 banning the publication of material "offending the dignity" of public leaders.

Press. The following are Spanish dailies published at Panama City, unless otherwise noted: *Crítica* (37,000), progovernment; *La Repúb-* *lica/The Republic* (32,000), progovernment, in Spanish and English; *La Prensa* (31,000), independent; *La Estrella de Panamá* (28,000 daily, 36,000 Sunday), progovernment; *El Extra* (20,000), opposition tabloid; *El Matutino* (17,000), semiofficial; *Star and Herald* (10,000 daily, 14,000 Sunday), English edition of *La Estrella de Panamá*.

News agencies. There is no domestic facility; several foreign bureaus maintain offices at Panama City.

Radio and television. Most radio and television outlets are owned by government-related private groups under the supervision of the *Dirección Nacional de Medios de Comunicátion Social*. There were approximately 600,000 radio and 470,000 television receivers in 1987.

INTERGOVERNMENTAL REPRESENTATION

Ambassador to the US: Juan B. SOSA.

US Ambassador to Panama: Arthur H. DAVIS.

Permanent Representative to the UN: Dr. Jorge E. RITTER.

IGO Memberships (Non-UN): *Ancom,* Geplacea, IADB, IATTC, ICM, ICO, Inmarsat, Intelsat, Interpol, ISO, IWTC, NAM, OAS, OPANAL, PCA, SELA, UPEB.

RELATED TERRITORY

Canal Zone. Bisecting Panama in a southwesterly direction from the Atlantic to the Pacific, the Canal Zone served historically for the protection of the interoceanic waterway completed by the United States in 1914. Occupation, use, and control of a 553-square-mile area extending about five miles on either side of the canal were granted to the United States in perpetuity by Panama in a treaty concluded in 1903. Following nationalist riots within the Zone in 1964, the two countries in 1967 negotiated a new draft treaty which would have replaced the 1903 accord, recognized Panamanian sovereignty in the Zone, and enabled Panama to participate in the management of the canal. In 1970, however, following a change in government, Panama declared the draft to be unacceptable. After further extended negotiations, US and Panamanian representatives reached agreement on an amended accord that was incorporated into two treaties signed at Washington on September 7, 1977. Endorsed by Panama in a plebiscite on October 23, the treaties were barely approved by the US Senate on March 16 and April 18, 1978. Documents of ratification were subsequently exchanged during a state visit to Panama by US President Carter on June 16.

The first treaty provided for a phased assumption of control of the canal and the Canal Zone by Panama, beginning six months after ratification and concluding in the year 2000. Panama would assume general territorial jurisdiction, although until December 31, 1999, the United States would maintain control of all installations needed to operate and defend the canal. Until 1990, the canal administrator would be American, while his deputy would be Panamanian; from 1990 to 1999, the administrator would be Panamanian, with an American deputy.

The second treaty declared that "the canal, as an international transit waterway, shall be permanently neutral". It also provided that "tolls and other charges . . . shall be just, reasonable and equitable" and that vessels of war and auxiliary vessels of all nations shall at all times be entitled to transit the canal, irrespective of their internal operation, means of propulsion, origin, destination, or armament. . . ."

Implementation of the treaties was delayed because of a US Senate stipulation that ratification would not be deemed complete until the passage of enabling legislation by the Congress or until March 31, 1979, whichever came first. Thus it was not until October 1, 1979, that the American flag was lowered within the Canal Zone and administrative authority for the canal formally transferred to a binational Panama Canal Commission.

In early 1980, despite a significant increase in revenue accruing to Panama under the new arrangement, President Royo formally complained to Washington about a "unilateral" provision of the enabling legislation that effectively brought the Commission under the control of the US Defense Department. Subsequently, in the wake of an assessment that the existing facility, which is unable to offer transit to vessels in excess of 75,000 tons, would be obsolete by the year 2000, Royo and a group of high-level advisers visited Japan to discuss the possibility of Japanese involvement in the building of a new sea-level waterway.

During a meeting at Panama City in December 1982, the feasibility of a new waterway was further discussed by Panamanian, Japanese, and US representatives. Earlier, a 9.8 percent increase in canal tolls had been agreed upon to offset an anticipated shortfall of up to $5 million a month upon the opening of a new trans-isthmian oil pipeline.

In mid-1984, the canal again became the focus for anti-US sentiment, following Washington's expressed reluctance to provide a major portion of the $400–600 million needed to widen the waterway on the ground that it would be unlikely to recover its investment prior to full reversion in the year 2000. Late in the year, however, the United States and Japan agreed to a four-year program to consider canal improvements, not excluding the possibility of constructing a new facility to accommodate ships of up to 300,000 tons.

In June 1986, a tripartite commission, composed of Panamanian, Japanese, and US representatives, began a projected four-year study on the feasibility of measures to upgrade or augment the existing facility, including improved pipeline, highway, and rail transport across the isthmus. The commission has also been charged with undertaking an analysis of world shipping requirements in the twenty-first century and drafting recommendations on US-Panamanian relations upon expiration of the present Canal treaties.

Administrator: Lt. Gen. Dennis P. McAULIFFE.

Deputy Administrator: Fernando MANFREDO Bernal.

PAPUA NEW GUINEA

Political Status: Former Australian-administered territory; achieved internal self-government December 1, 1973, and full independence within the Commonwealth on September 16, 1975, under constitution of August 15.

Area: 178,259 sq. mi. (461,691 sq. km.).

Population: 3,010,727 (1980C), 3,723,000 (1988E).

Major Urban Centers: PORT MORESBY (1985E, 150,000); Lae (1979E, 45,000); Rabaul (1979E, 30,000).

Official Language: English (a pidgin variant is most commonly spoken).

Monetary Unit: Kina (market rate March 1, 1988, 1 kina = $1.11US).

Sovereign: Queen ELIZABETH II.

Governor General: Sir Kingsford DIBELA; succeeded Sir Tore LOKOLUKO on March 1, 1983.

Prime Minister: Paias WINGTI (People's Democratic Movement); appointed by the Governor General following parliamentary vote of nonconfidence against the government of Michael Thomas SOMARE (*Pangu Pati*) on November 21, 1985; reappointed following election of June 13–July 4, 1987, and parliamentary vote of August 5.

THE COUNTRY

Situated in the tropics between Asia and Australia, Papua New Guinea consists of the eastern half of the island of New Guinea — where the nation's only border is shared with the Indonesian territory of Irian Jaya — and numerous adjacent islands, including those of the Bismarck Archipelago as well as part of the Solomon group. The indigenous inhabitants, mainly of Melanesian stock, comprise over 1,000 tribes that speak more than 700 languages. Pantheism is the religion of the majority of the people, although there are numerous Christian missionary societies throughout the country. While data are unavailable on economic participation by women, their contribution to subsistence agriculture is known to be substantial; female representation in elected bodies is minimal, although "women's councils", active at both the national and provincial levels, receive significant government funding.

Much of the country's terrain consists of dense tropical forests and inland mountain ranges separated by grassland valleys. The climate is monsoonal. Roughly 70 percent of the population, living by quite primitive standards, relies upon subsistence farming and hunting for domestic needs, although some economic modernization has been achieved in recent years with government support. There are numerous mineral deposits, including silver and copper (which currently provides about one-half of export earnings), and exploitation of natural gas and hydroelectric resources has begun. Falling mineral prices, lack of private investment, and growing budget deficits have yielded economic deterioration in recent years, although major oil and gold discoveries offer hope for long-term relief.

GOVERNMENT AND POLITICS

Political background. First sighted in 1526 by a Portuguese navigator who gave it the name Papua ("woolly haired"), eastern New Guinea was colonized over the centuries by Australia and a variety of European and Asian nations, including the Netherlands, Germany, and Japan. In 1906, the British New Guinea sector, renamed the Territory of Papua, officially came under Australian administration, with Northeast New Guinea, a former German colony, being added as a League of Nations mandate in 1920. During World War II, Japan conquered most of Papua New Guinea, but Australia reassumed control in 1949 and administered the territory as a single entity until the granting of independence on September 16, 1975.

Representative government was initiated in 1964 when the House of Assembly replaced the former Legislative Council after the first common-roll election. In 1968, the territorial constitution was amended to provide for an Administrator's Executive Council, a majority of whose members were drawn from the elected members of the House of Assembly. Beginning in 1970, Papua New Guinea increasingly assumed control over its own internal affairs through the chief minister of the Council, a process that was enhanced in December 1973 by redesignation of the Australian administrator as high commissioner. On March 4, 1975, the territory acquired responsibility for its own defense, becoming independent six months later, with former chief minister Michael T. SOMARE assuming the office of prime minister. Somare was immediately confronted with a threat to national unity by a secessionist movement on the island of Bougainville, where the country's vast copper reserves are located. On September 1, Bougainville had declared unilateral independence as the "Republic of the North Solomons", claiming that the central government had been taking too much revenue from its copper industry. However, following an agreement in August 1976 that provided for substantial regional autonomy, secession leaders formally accepted provincial status for the island.

After the nation's first postindependence election, held June 18–July 9, 1977, Somare's *Pangu Pati*, the People's Progress Party (PPP), and a number of Assembly independents formed a coalition government, Somare being redesignated as prime minister on August 9. In November 1978, the PPP went into opposition and was replaced in the ruling coalition by the United Party (UP). The Somare government collapsed in the face of a nonconfidence vote on March 11, 1980, a new majority coalition being constituted two days later by Sir Julius CHAN of the PPP. Somare returned as prime minister on August 2, 1982, after intense political maneuvering that followed balloting for a new Assembly on June 5–26.

Somare survived a nonconfidence vote on March 25, 1984, after Deputy Prime Minister Paias WINGTI and a number of his followers had withdrawn from the government; he was, however, obliged to form a new coalition on April 1 that included *Pangu Pati*, the Melanesian Alliance (MA), and the National Party (NP), although the last soon returned to opposition in a dispute over the distribution of ministries. The increasingly beleaguered Somare survived two more confidence motions before succumbing to a 1986 budget vote on November 21, 1985. Opposition leader Wingti was thereupon invested as head of a coalition that included his recently organized People's Democratic Movement (PDM), the Nationalist *Papua Besena,* the NP, the PPP, and elements of the UP. Contrary to expectations, Wingti retained office as the leader of a modified six-party coalition in the wake of parliamentary balloting on June 13–July 4, 1987, securing the support of a bare majority of 54 assemblymen (3 seats of 109 being vacant) at commencement of the legislative term on August 5. On April 11, 1988, a vote on a nonconfidence motion against the Wingti administration was averted by suspending Assembly proceedings until June 27 (see Current issues, below).

Constitution and government. Under the 1975 constitution, executive functions are performed by a National Executive Council that includes a governor general, nominated by the Council itself to represent the Crown for a six-year term; a prime minister, appointed by the governor general on advice of the legislature; and other ministers who are designated on advice of the prime minister and must total no fewer than six and no more than one-quarter the number of legislators. The unicameral House of Assembly normally sits for a five-year term, dissolution not being mandated in the wake of a nonconfidence vote (which can be called by 10 percent of the members) if an alternative prime minister (previously designated by the leader of the opposition) succeeds in securing a majority. The judicial system encompasses a Supreme Court that acts as the final court of appeal, a National Court, and lesser courts (currently including district, local, warden, and children's courts) as established by the legislature.

The constitution, which can be amended by a two-thirds majority of the Assembly, also provides for the establishment of provincial governments and legislatures. At the regional level, there are 20 administrative districts, each headed by a district commissioner who is assisted by a deputy district commissioner, district officers, assistant district officers, and patrol officers. Both the Somare and Wingti administrations have advocated the dissolution and restructuring of this "Australian-style" system, three provincial administrators having been suspended for mismanagement in 1984–1985.

Foreign relations. Two issues have dominated Papuan foreign affairs since independence: somewhat sensitive relations with Indonesia stemming from the status of Irian Jaya (West New Guinea) and a dispute with Australia regarding demarcation of a maritime boundary through the Torres Strait. Though the Papuan government officially supported Jakarta in the matter of Irian Jaya, advocates of a "free Papua" called upon the United Nations to review the 1969 plebiscite that resulted in Indonesia's annexation of the territory, which contains valuable mineral deposits. More than 10,000 refugees have entered Papua New Guinea from Irian Jaya since 1983, alleging persecution by Indonesian authorities; attempts at even small-scale repatriation have thus far been unsuccessful. Jakarta has denounced the maintenance of two large border refugee camps by Port Moresby, citing the settlements as sources of aid for rebels of the Free Papua Organization (see Indonesia: Annexed Territories).

In regard to the Torres Strait, the Papuan government attempted to negotiate a boundary equidistant between its shore and that of Australia. Such an arrangement was unacceptable to Canberra because the boundary would prejudice the citizenship of Strait islanders whose interests had been vigorously championed by the government of Queensland. Thus, in June 1978 the two nations agreed upon a complex formula involving (1) a seabed line running south of a number of islands and reefs that would remain Australian enclaves, and (2) a protected zone embracing much of the waters between the two countries and to which each would have access; a treaty to such effect was ultimately ratified in February 1985.

In recent years, Australia has decreased aid to its former territory, creating tension with Port Moresby because of its strained economy. Canberra was also disturbed in 1985 by the PNG army's purchase of Israeli fighter planes, which was described as "a gesture of independence from Australia".

Although nonaligned, Papua New Guinea participates in a number of regional organizations. As a member of the South Pacific Forum, it has actively championed self-determination for French Overseas Territories, particularly New Caledonia, and in 1985, joined with Vanuatu and the Solomon Islands in a so-called "Spearhead" group within the SPF to coordinate policy on regional issues. At a summit meeting of the Association of Southeast Asian Nations (ASEAN) in December 1987, the six-member group agreed to amend its 1976 Treaty of Amity and Cooperation to permit Papua New Guinea (theretofore an observer) to join as a full member. The PNG had previously been denied membership on the grounds that it was not geographically part of Southeast Asia and because it belonged to another regional grouping, the SPF.

Current issues. Although headed by a long-time "small government" advocate with a reputation as a hard-working disciplinarian, the Wingti coalition was beset by a number of financial scandals during 1986 and early 1987, and had not been expected to survive the midyear legislative balloting. Its razor-thin retention of office was made possible by three post-electoral vacancies, with the opposition constitutionally precluded from introducing a nonconfidence motion until 1988, whatever the by-electoral results.

The House of Assembly convened on April 11 for the first time in seven months, but was immediately recessed until late June to defuse the likelihood of a successful nonconfidence vote. On May 20 Somare resigned (effective June 13) as leader of the opposition and of *Pangu Pati* in favor of his deputy, Rabbie NAMALIU. Subsequently, a "grand coalition" was broached, involving the PDM and *Pangu Pati,* with Namaliu as deputy prime minister. However, the prospect was quickly dashed—reportedly because of Somare's unwillingness to enter the government as foreign minister. Wingti thereupon announced a new alliance of the PDM and the smaller National Party, led by Michael MEL, which was alleged to have the support of 72 of the 109 assemblymen. Whatever the likelihood that short-term stability might thereby ensue, most observers were persuaded that two major reforms were necessary: a constitutional amendment (advocated by Somare during the previous campaign) that would require an MP to step down before shifting party allegiance and a tightening of rules governing the submission of nonconfidence motions.

POLITICAL PARTIES

Since independence, party loyalties have been extremely fluid, largely because the major groupings differ more over tactics than ideology. The coalition government formed in August 1987, following Paias Wingti's redesignation as prime minister, drew from the first six parties below, plus a number of parliamentary independents.

People's Democratic Movement (PDM). The PDM was organized by former deputy prime minister Paias Wingti, who broke with *Pangu Pati* in March 1985. The Wingti grouping gained ground during the ensuing months, focusing on alleged government corruption and budgetary issues; conflict over the latter led to the formation of a PDM-led government late in the year, with Wingti returning to office following the 1987 election. The party's policy statements have emphasized budget reductions, administrative restructuring, and privatization of state enterprises.
Leader: Paias WINGTI (Prime Minister).

National Party (NP). The original National Party participated in the pre-1977 National Coalition. After the 1977 election two of its leaders, Thomas Kavali and Pato Kakarya, joined the Somare government as pro-*Pangu* independents, the remainder of the party going into opposition. Kavali was subsequently dismissed from the government in January 1979, joining the opposition People's United Front (PUF) organized in November 1978 by (then) UP dissident Iambakey Okuk. The PUF adopted the NP label in early 1980 and, under the leadership of Stephen Tago, joined the Somare government on April 1, 1985. Having been allocated fewer ministries in the April government than had been demanded, the NP returned to opposition in May when Okuk, upon his return to parliament in a by-election, was not offered a cabinet post. The party was instrumental in Wingti's parliamentary victory in November, and obtained significant

cabinet representation in the post-Somare government, Okuk serving as primary industry minister until shortly before his death in November 1986.
Leaders: Michael MEL, Stephen TAGO.

People's Action Party (PAP). The PAP was formed on December 4, 1986, by (then) forestry minister Ted Diro, a staunch Wingti supporter, who was named foreign minister eight days later, but denied reappointment in August 1987 following allegations of corruption in his previous post.
Leader: Ted DIRO.

People's Progress Party (PPP). The PPP participated in the post-independence government until 1978, when it went into opposition. It became the core component of the government that succeeded the Somare administration in March 1980. It returned to opposition upon the reconfirmation of Somare as prime minister in August 1982, Sir Julius Chan being prominently involved in a number of nonconfidence motions against Somare before the latter's most recent ouster in late 1985.
Leaders: Sir Julius CHAN (Deputy Prime Minister), Hudson ARAK (National Chairman).

Papua Party (PP).Organized prior to the 1987 balloting, the PP incorporated most of the membership of the former *Papua Besena,* a Papuan nationalist movement that had long campaigned for a republican form of government. *Papua Besena* joined Okuk's PUF in November 1978, subsequently entering the Chan government as an autonomous entity. Its founder, Josephine Abaijah, failed to retain her parliamentary seat in 1982. Groups associated with it on the republican issue included the Eriwo Development Association, the Papua Black Power Movement, and the Socialist Workers' Party.
Leaders: Galeva KWARARA (Finance Minister), Josephine ABAIJAH,Gerega PEPENA.

United Party (UP). The UP is a highlands-based party organized in 1969. It favored a cautious approach to self-government and was opposed to early independence. Formerly the main opposition grouping in the House of Assembly, it entered the government in coalition with *Pangu Pati* (below) in November 1978. Technically in opposition after formation of the Chan government in March 1980, many of its members subsequently crossed the aisle to join the Chan majority. The party suffered major losses at the balloting of June 1982, after which it rejoined forces with *Pangu Pati.* It returned to opposition in April 1985. Some members supported the Wingti coalition the following November, yielding another split between government and opposition.
Leader: Paul TORATO.

Papua New Guinea United Party (*Pangu Pati*). The urban-based *Pangu Pati* was organized in 1967 and long advocated the early achievement of independence. It was the senior component of the former National Coalition and secured the largest number of legislative seats at the 1977 election. It moved into opposition following parliamentary defeat of the Somare government in March 1980 but returned to power after the election of June 1982 and the redesignation of Somare as prime minister on August 2. *Pangu* was greatly weakened by the defection of deputy prime minister Paias Wingti in April 1985, and Somare was ousted from power in a nonconfidence vote the following November; however, the party retained a significant parliamentary bloc and retained a reduced plurality of 26 Assembly seats at the election of November 1987.
Leaders: Rabbie NAMALIU (Leader of the Opposition), Michael Thomas SOMARE (former Prime Minister).

Melanesian Alliance (MA). The MA is a Bougainville-based party formed in 1978 after Fr. John Momis, a former secessionist leader, was removed as minister for decentralization by Prime Minister Somare. Its two principal leaders, Momis and John Kaputin, participated in the Chan government of March 1980. After the 1982 election, Momis became leader of the opposition, then renewed the alliance with Somare as deputy prime minister in April 1985, although disenchantment with some of Somare's policies was reported prior to the November change in government.
Leaders: Fr. John MOMIS (former Deputy Prime Minister), John KAPUTIN, Fabian Wau KAWA (General Secretary).

League for National Advancement (LNA). The LNA was formed in mid-1986 by five *Pangu Pati* assembly members who said they would compete in the 1987 elections apart from the parent formation on a "new direction" platform. Two of the founders, Tony Siaguru and Sir Barry Holloway, were described as among *Pangu Pati* leader Somare's closest advisors prior to the split.
Leaders: Tony SIAGURU, Sir Barry HOLLOWAY.

Other groups include the **Morobe Independence Group** (MIG), which won 4 Assembly seats in 1987; **One Talk** (*Wontok*), formed in November 1986 by pro-Somare UP leader Roy EVARA; the **Papuan National Alliance** (Panal), a regional group committed to the formation of a united Papua New Guinea; and the **People's Christian Alliance** (PCA), led by Tom KORAEA.

LEGISLATURE

The unicameral **House of Assembly** currently consists of 109 members (89 from open and 20 from provincial electorates) named to five-year terms by universal adult suffrage. Candidates are not obligated to declare party affiliation and postelectoral realignments are common. The following was the distribution after the most recent balloting of June 13-July 4, 1987: *Pangu Pati,* 26 seats; People's Democratic Movement, 18; National Party, 12; Melanesian Alliance, 7; People's Action Party, 6; People's Progress Party, 5; Morobe Independence Group, 4; League of National Advancement, 3; Papua Party, 3; United Party, 1, independents, 21, vacant, 3.

Speaker: Denise YOUNG.

CABINET

[as of April 1, 1988]

Prime Minister	Paias Wingti
Deputy Prime Minister	Sir Julius Chan

Ministers

Administrative Services	Johnson Maladina
Agriculture and Livestock	Gai Duwabane
Civil Aviation, Tourism and Culture	Hugo Berghuser
Communications	Gabriel Ramoi
Corrective Institutions	Tom Amaiu
Culture and Tourism	Albert Karo
Defense	James L. Pokasui
Education	Joseph Aoae
Environment and Conservation	Perry Zeipi
Finance and National Planning	Galeva Kwarara
Fishery and Marine Resources	Alan Ebu
Foreign Affairs	Akoka Doi
Forests	Tom Harik
Health	Timothy Ward
Home Affairs and Youth	Eserom Burege
Housing	Bill Ninkama
Internal Affairs	Thomas Negints
Justice	Albert Kipalan
Labor and Employment	Masket Ianqalio
Lands and Physical Planning	Kalas Swokim
Minerals and Energy	John Kaputin
Police	Peter Kuman
Provincial Affairs	Jacob Lemeki
Public Service	Utula Samana
Trade and Industry	Sir Julius Chan
Transport	Ray Yaki
Works	Aita Ivarato

NEWS MEDIA

Press. Papua New Guinea's press is considered one of the freest in the Asian-Pacific area. The following are published in English at Port Moresby, unless otherwise noted: *Papua New Guinea Post-Courier* (32,000), daily; *Niugini Nius* (Boroko, 17,000), daily; *Wantok* (Boroko, 15,000), rural weekly; *The Times of Papua New Guinea* (Boroko, 13,000), twice-weekly.

News agency. The only domestic facility is the International News Service Papua New Guinea.

Radio and television. The nation's 225,000 radio sets receive programs from the National Broadcasting Commission of Papua New Guinea and from the Papua New Guinea Service of Radio Australia. During 1987 television service was provided to some 5,000 receivers by the Niugini Television Network (NTN), which commenced operations in February following a successful legal challenge to a government decision to postpone local broadcasting as potentially detrimental to the nation's culture; in July a second channel, EM TV, went on air at Port Moresby and in March 1988 NTN was shutdown, reportedly for financial reasons.

INTERGOVERNMENTAL REPRESENTATION

Ambassador to the US and Permanent Representative to the UN: Renagi R. LONIA.

US Ambassador to Papua New Guinea: Everett E. BIERMAN.

IGO Memberships (Non-UN): ADB, ANRPC, APCC, *CIPEC,* CP, CWTH, EEC(L), *EIB,* ICCO, ICO, INRO, Intelsat, Interpol, SPC, SPEC, SPF.

PARAGUAY

Republic of Paraguay
República del Paraguay

Political Status: Independent since 1811; under presidential rule established in 1954; present constitution adopted in 1967.

Area: 157,047 sq. mi. (406,752 sq. km.).

Population: 3,035,360 (1982C), 3,603,000 (1988E).

Major Urban Centers (1982C): ASUNCION (455,517); San Lorenzo (74,359); Fernando de la Mora (66,810); Lambaré (65,145).

Official Languages: Spanish, Guaraní.

Monetary Unit: Guaraní (commercial rate March 1, 1988, 550.00 guaraníes = $1US). The free rate, on the same date, was approximately 881 guaraníes to the dollar.

President: Gen. Alfredo STROESSNER Mattiauda; assumed power by coup d'état in May 1954; elected, unopposed, on July 11 to fill the balance of his predecessor's term; reelected in 1958 and at five-year intervals thereafter, most recently on February 14, 1988.

THE COUNTRY

A landlocked, semitropical country wedged between Argentina, Bolivia, and Brazil, the Republic of Paraguay takes its name from the river that divides the fertile grasslands of the east ("Oriental") from the drier, more inhospitable Chaco region of the west ("Occidental"). The population is 95 percent mestizo, mainly of Spanish and

Indian origin, although successive waves of immigration have brought settlers from all parts of the globe, including Japan and Korea. Spanish is the official language; however, 90 percent of the population also speaks Guaraní, the language of the indigenous inhabitants. Roman Catholicism is the established religion, but other faiths are tolerated. Women constitute approximately 20 percent of the paid labor force, concentrated primarily in manufacturing and domestic service; female participation in politics is virtually nonexistent.

With 80 percent of the land owned by 1 percent of the population and without an adequate transportation network, Paraguayan development has long been retarded. Cattle-raising, agriculture, and forestry constitute the basis of the economy; cotton, timber, soybeans, and vegetable oils are the main exports. Industry is largely confined to processing agricultural, animal, and timber products, but there is a small consumer-goods industry. The government is presently embarked on exploitation of the vast hydroelectric potential of the Paraguay and Paraná rivers; the Itaipú Dam, six times the size of the Aswan Dam and jointly constructed with Brazil, was opened on November 5, 1982. As a result, Paraguay, by the early 1990s, is expected to become one of the world's leading exporters of electricity, substantially reducing—if not reversing—an adverse balance of trade that has persisted since 1973. Meanwhile, with the Itaipú construction completed and work on the even larger Yacretá complex beset with economic difficulty due to the troubled Argentine economy, economic indicators have fallen off. Between 1981 and 1986 the purchasing power of the guaraní declined by 40 percent with inflation exceeding 20 by late 1987.

GOVERNMENT AND POLITICS

Political background. Paraguay gained independence from Spain in 1811 but was slow to assume the contours of a modern state. Its initial years of independence were marked by a succession of strong, authoritarian leaders, the most famous of whom was José Gaspar RODRIGUEZ de Francia. Known as "El Supremo", Rodríguez ruled Paraguay from 1814 until 1840, during which time he sought to isolate the country from the outside world by expelling foreigners and cutting off communications. In 1865–1870 Paraguay fought the combined forces of Argentina, Brazil, and Uruguay in the War of the Triple Alliance, which claimed the lives of approximately half of the country's population and the vast majority of its males. From 1880 to 1904 the country was ruled by a series of Colorado Party presidents, while the Liberals ruled for most of the period 1904–1940. A three-year war against Bolivia over the Chaco territory ended in 1935 with Paraguay winning the greater part of the disputed region.

Since 1940, two men have successively dominated the political scene: the dictatorial Gen. Higinio MORINIGO (1940–1947) and the present chief executive, Gen. Alfredo STROESSNER Mattiauda, who came to power in 1954 through a military coup against President Federíco CHÁVEZ. Initially elected to fill the balance of Chávez' unexpired term, Stroessner has since been reelected to successive five-year terms, most recently on February 14, 1988.

Constitution and government. The revised constitution of 1967 provided for executive dominance, while conferring carefully circumscribed powers on an expanded, two-chamber legislature and the judiciary. The president is popularly elected, as are members of the Senate and the Chamber of Deputies. According to the electoral law, two-thirds of the seats in each legislative chamber are awarded to the party winning the largest number of votes, the remainder being divided among the minority parties in proportion to their electoral strength. During the legislature's annual three-month recess, the president rules by decree through the Council of State, a body composed of government ministers plus representatives from education, business, the religious community, and the military. The judicial system includes justices of the peace, courts of the first instance, appellate courts, and, at the apex, the Supreme Court of Justice. Members of the Supreme Court are appointed by the president with approval of the Senate, while appointments to the lower courts, also made by the president, require the approval of the Supreme Court.

Because the 1967 constitution did not permit General Stroessner's reelection to a sixth term in 1978, a constitutional convention was called for March 1977 to remove the proscription. All of the opposition parties boycotted the constitutional assembly election of January 6, and the legal impediment was accordingly revoked by the convention.

For administrative purposes Paraguay is divided into 19 departments (exclusive of the capital), which are subdivided into districts and municipalities. Each department is headed by an official (*delgado de gobierno*) appointed by the president. Each municipality is governed by a locally elected municipal board (*junta municipal*), which elects its own chairman; in the larger municipalities the chief executive, a mayor, is appointed by the president.

Foreign relations. A member of the United Nations, the Organization of American States, the Latin American Integration Association, and other regional organizations, Paraguay has maintained a strongly anti-Communist foreign policy, suspending relations with Nicaragua in 1980 following the assassination at Asunción of former Nicaraguan president Somoza. Relations with neighboring regimes have been relatively cordial, despite periodic tensions with Argentina and Brazil over hydroelectric issues. Recent Paraguayan fears of the possible internal effect of the rise of civilian governments in both states have, however, complicated relations, while strengthening ties with Chile.

Relations with the United States, which has long been a primary source of foreign investment, are currently strained by allegations of high-level Paraguayan involvement in narcotics trafficking, a former drug-enforcement official currently serving as ambassador to Asunción. Negative human rights reports on Paraguay have also taken their toll, as evidenced by President Reagan's inclusion of the country in a list of "unrelenting dictatorships" along with Chile, Cuba, and Nicaragua. During 1987 relations deteriorated further, the government, at one point, inviting the US ambassador to leave the country after he had attended a reception that authorities claimed was an illegal gathering of opposition leaders.

Current issues. Despite widespread corruption and the maintenance of a vast network of secret police and government informants that severely inhibits opposition, General Stroessner has long enjoyed considerable popular support, the working class in particular, if not affluent, being spared much of the widespread poverty of neighboring countries. However, in the wake of rising inflation and unemployment, a sluggish export sector, and sporadic unrest, it was anticipated that the aging chief executive might not choose to run for an unprecedented eighth term in 1988. The uncertainty gave rise to heightened factionalism within the ruling Colorado Party, while the opposition responded cautiously to a degree of political relaxation (*apertura*) proclaimed in August 1986. A leading regime opponent, Dr. Domingo LAINO of the Authentic Radical Liberal Party, was permitted to return from four years' exile in April 1987, coincident with the lifting of a long-standing state of siege in the vicinity of the capital. On the other hand, complaints that the relaxation was deceptive and intended primarily to appease foreign critics of the administration appeared to be substantiated by scattered police attacks on opposition gatherings during the remainder of the year. In August, with the president adopting a formal posture of nonintervention, the most pronounced pro-Stroessner Colorado faction, the *militantes,* swept the party convention, paving the way for an electoral victory in February of a magnitude (nearly 90 percent) that seemed disproportional to recent increases in opposition sentiment.

POLITICAL PARTIES

Paraguay's two traditional political organizations are the Liberal Party, which has been out of power since 1940 and is presently divided, and the National Republican Association (Colorado Party), which has dominated the political scene since 1947 and has sponsored the successive presidential candidacies of Gen. Alfredo Stroessner.

In August 1981 the electoral law was amended to forbid the presentation of presidential nominees by party coalitions and to require that parties have a minimum membership of 10,000 distributed among at least one-third of the country's electoral districts as a condition of registration. In addition, the Communist Party and others with "similar aims" as well as those promoting "hatred among Paraguayans" continue to be banned.

Governing Party:

National Republican Association–Colorado Party (*Asociación Nacional Republicana–Partido Colorado*). Originating in the late nineteenth century, the mainstream of the Colorado Party is conservative in outlook and has consistently supported the Stroessner regime since its inception. The party has, however, long been subject to factionalism, including most recently a cleavage between *traditionalista* and *militante* tendencies (the former favoring a change in the presidency in 1988 and the latter alternatively championing a "presidency for life" for Stroessner and the accession of his son, Col. Gustavo STROESSNER). A third faction variously styled as "renovating" (*renovadore*), "critical" (*critico*) or "moral" (*ético*), emerged in early 1986 under the leadership of State Council member Carlos Romero Arza with a commitment to both economic and political reform. At party elections in 25 districts on July 27, 1986, the *militantes* won 17 and the *tradicionalistas,* 8. A year later, at a convention on August 2, 1987, a *militante,* Interior Minister Sabino Montanaro, was elected party president. The *traditionalistas,* under the outgoing president, Dr. Juan Ramón CHAVEZ, thereupon staged a walkout, while the *éticos,* led by Carlos Romero PEREIRA, moved into opposition (see Mopoco, below).

Subsequently, President Stroessner was nominated for an eighth term and the Colorado electoral lists were purged of all but *militante* candidates for the February 1988 balloting, at which the party was officially credited with nearly 90 percent of the vote.

Leaders: Gen. Alfredo STROESSNER Mattiauda (President of the Republic), Sabino Augusto MONTANARO (Interior Minister and President of the Party), Adán GODOY Jiménez (Public Health and Social Welfare Minister), Mario PASTOR Almado, Mario Abdo BENITEZ (Secretary to the President).

Congressional Opposition:

Radical Liberal Party (*Partido Liberal Radical*—PLR). Conservative in outlook, the PLR has in recent decades been the main surviving element of Paraguay's historic Liberal Party of the nineteenth and early twentieth centuries. In January 1977 a majority of the membership joined with a majority of the Liberal Party (below) to form the Unified Liberal Party (*Partido Liberal Unificado*—PLU). The government, however, refused to accord legal recognition to the new grouping, continuing instead to recognize a minority faction of the PLR, under Justo Pastor Benítez, that was also assigned ownership of the PLR weekly, *El Radical*. In January 1985 members of a dissident wing, the **Radical Liberal Integration Movement** (*Movimiento Integración Liberal Radical*—MILR) walked out of a PLR convention in protest at the election of Persio Franco as party president. Later in the year, following the detention of a number of its leaders, the party joined the boycott of the October municipal balloting. The PLR was credited with obtaining approximately 7 percent of the vote in 1988.

Leaders: Persio FRANCO (President), Luis Maria VEGA (1988 presidential candidate), Julio BASUALDO, Justo PASTOR Benítez.

Liberal Party (*Partido Liberal*—PL). The present Liberal Party is a small but legally recognized component of the party that originally split from the PLR in 1961. Most of the PL membership joined with the majority of the PLR membership in forming the abortive PLU in January 1977. The party was credited with winning approximately 3 percent of the vote at the 1988 balloting, which its presidential candidate characterized as involving "massive, crude and scandalous fraud".

Leaders: Carlos FERREIRA Ibarra (1988 presidential candidate), Joaquín ATILIO Burgos.

Other Parties:

National Pact (*Acuerdo Nacional*). Organized in February 1979, the *Acuerdo Nacional* is a loosely organized opposition front comprising the four parties listed below. Advancing a reform program that embraces the demilitarization of politics, it suffers from internal dissension and has also been the object of sporadic repression, including the arrest of some of its adherents.

Leader: Waldino Ramón LLOVERA (President).

Authentic Radical Liberal Party (*Partido Liberal Radical Auténtico*—PLRA). The PLRA was formed by a number of center-left PLU dissidents, several of whom were subjected to police harassment and arrest following the election of February 1978. The party has since grown in strength and its leaders have been periodically arrested, including the incarceration of Secretary General Miguel Abdón Sanguier for five months in 1986–1987. Party president Domingo Laino was permitted to return from exile in April 1987.

Leaders: Dr. Domingo LAINO (President), Juan Manuel BENITEZ Florentín (Vice President), Miguel ABDON Saguier (Secretary General).

Revolutionary Febrerista Party (*Partido Revolucionario Febrerista*—PRF). Initially organized by a group of Chaco War veterans, the PRF now stands substantially to the left of the Colorados in its espousal of social and agrarian reform and is affiliated with the Socialist International. Although legally recognized, the party has boycotted all national and local elections since 1973. A discernable ideological shift has recently occurred within the party leadership, its 1985 congress replacing President Euclides Acevedo with the more moderate Fernando Vera, formerly an economist for the International Monetary Fund.

Leaders: Fernando VERA (President), Dr. Euclides ACEVEDO (former president and leader of radical wing), Adolfo FERREIRO, Ricardo LUGO Rodríguez (Secretary General).

Christian Democratic Party (*Partido Demócrata Cristiano*—PDC). The PDC, which has been refused recognition by the Electoral Commission since 1971, is one of the smallest of Paraguay's political groupings. The furthest left of the non-Communist groupings, it exercises considerable influence among the more progressive youth. In March 1986, the government lifted an order under which PDC founder Luis Resck had been forced into exile five years earlier.

Leaders: Geronimo Irala BURGOS (President), Alfredo Rojas LEON and Luis Alfonso RESCK (former Presidents), Juan Carlos DESCALZO Buongermini and Florencio RIVEROS Vásquez (Vice Presidents), Luis Manuel ANDRADA Nogues (Secretary).

Colorado Popular Movement (*Movimiento Popular Colorado* — Mopoco). Organized by a group of dissident Colorados in 1959, Mopoco has long been subject to official repression, most of its leadership operating from abroad prior to the return of Miguel Angel González and five of his associates in December 1984. Despite the subsequent imposition of either interior exile or house arrest for party leaders, non-Stroessner-dominated factions of the parent party have regularly attempted to establish links with Mopoco; thus, the *tradicionalista* Colorados sought its reincorporation as a means of simultaneously weakening both the *militantes* and the *Acuerdo Nacional*.

During a party convention at the Argentine border town of Posadas in April 1985, the party rejected violence, but committed itself to opposing the "long record of evil actions and crimes of the dictatorship". Following the 1987 *militante* takeover of the governing Colorado Party, its *ético* faction joined with Mopoco in launching an antiregime movement styled the **Colorado Convergence** (*Convergenia Colorada*).

Leaders: Waldino Ramón LLOVERA (President), Miguel Angel GONZALEZ Casabianca (former President); Enrique RIERA, Alejandro STUMPFS, Andres BOGADO (Vice Presidents).

Paraguayan Communist Party (*Partido Comunista Paraguayo* — PCP). Outlawed since 1936, the PCP claims an exile membership of 5,000. It is divided into three discernible groups: a Buenos Aires-based Miguel Soler faction, which endorses the Soviet line; a Montivideo-based Oscar Creydt faction, which champions the Chinese viewpoint; and an Obdulio Barthe faction, which has termed itself the Paraguayan Leninist Communist Party (*Partido Comunista Leninista Paraguayo* — PCLP) and is composed of Creydt faction dissidents. Barthe was nonetheless reported to have been designated PCP president at a secret Central Committee meeting in June 1978. In late 1979, Amnesty International asserted that former secretary general Miguel Soler had died while in police custody in 1975. The party's first secretary, Antonio Maidana, was arrested by Argentine authorities in 1980 and is currently imprisoned in Paraguay.

The PCP has sought, thus far without success, to gain access to the *Acuerdo Nacional* in the hope of converting it into an instrument of active resistance to the Stroessner regime within Paraguay.

Leaders: Obdulio BARTHE (President, in exile), Antonio MAIDANA (Secretary General, imprisoned), Julio ROJAS (Acting Secretary General).

LEGISLATURE

The bicameral **National Congress** (*Congreso Nacional*) currently consists of a 36-member Senate and a 72-member Chamber of Deputies, both elected concurrently with the president for five-year terms. Under Paraguayan law, the party polling the largest number of votes in a legislative election is awarded two-thirds of the seats in each chamber.

President of the Congress: Dr. Juan Ramón CHAVEZ.

Senate (*Cámara de Senadores*). Established under the revised constitution of 1967, the Senate was first organized in 1968. Following the election of February 14, 1988, the Colorado Party was awarded 24 seats; the Radical Liberal Party, 9; and the Liberal Party, 3.

Chamber of Deputies (*Cámara de Diputados*). Following the 1988 election, the Colorado Party was awarded 48 seats; the Radical Liberal Party, 17; and the Liberal Party, 7.

CABINET

President	Gen. Alfredo Stroessner
Ministers	
Agriculture and Livestock	Hernando Bertoni Agrón
Education and Worship	Carlos Ortiz Ramírez
Finance	Brig. Gen. (Ret.) César Barrientos
Foreign Relations	Carlos Augusto Saldívar Molina
Industry and Commerce	Delfín Ugarte Centurión
Interior	Sabino Augusto Montanaro
Justice and Labor	Eugenio Jacquet
National Defense	Gen. Gaspar Germán Martínez
Public Health and Social Welfare	Adán Godoy Jiménez
Public Works and Communications	Maj. Gen. (Ret.) Juan Antonio Cáceres Estigarribia
President, Central Bank	César Romero Acosta

NEWS MEDIA

Press. Newspapers do not enjoy complete freedom of the press, and a number have recently ceased publication, including the leading daily, *ABC Color*, which was shut down in April 1984. The following are published daily at Asunción, unless otherwise noted: *Ultima Hora* (45,000), liberal Colorado; *La Tribuna* (30,000), liberal Colorado; *Patria* (8,000), Colorado Party organ; *El Diario de Noticias*, commenced publication in April 1984 as a pro-government successor to *ABC Color*.

News agencies. The domestic facility is *Asociación Paraguaya de Prensa*. Several foreign bureaus maintain offices at Asunción.

Radio and television. Broadcasting is under the supervision of the *Administración Nacional de Telecomunicaciones*. All radio stations, with the exception of the government station, *Radio Nacional,* are commercial, one of them, *Radio Ñandutí*, being periodically shut down during 1984–1988 for broadcasting interviews with opposition politicians and reporting on differences within the ruling party. Approximately 650,000 radio sets were in use in 1987, while the government-controlled television channels transmitted to some 350,000 receivers.

INTERGOVERNMENTAL REPRESENTATION

Ambassador to the US: Dr. Marcos MARTINEZ Mendieta.

US Ambassador to Paraguay: Clyde Donald TAYLOR.

Permanent Representative to the UN: Alfredo CAÑETE.

IGO Memberships (Non-UN): ALADI, CCC, IADB, ICM, ICO, Intelsat, Interpol, ISO, OAS, OPANAL, PCA, SELA.

PERU

Republic of Peru
República del Perú

Political Status: Independent republic proclaimed 1821; military rule imposed October 3, 1968; constitutional government restored July 28, 1980.

Area: 496,222 sq. mi. (1,285,216 sq. km.).

Population: 17,005,210 (1981C), 21,265,000 (1988E). The 1981 figure is unadjusted for underenumeration.

Major Urban Centers (1985E): LIMA (5,008,400); Arequipa (531,800); Callao (515,200); Trujillo (438,700).

Official Languages: Spanish, Quechua.

Monetary Unit: Inti (official rate March 1, 1988, 33.00 intis = $1US). The free rate, on the same date, was approximately 107.00 intis to the dollar. The inti, at a value of 1,000 soles, was introduced on February 1, 1985.

President: Alan GARCIA Pérez (American Popular Revolutionary Alliance); declared President-elect on June 1, 1985, following election of April 14, and inaugurated for a five-year term on July 28, succeeding Fernando BELAUNDE Terry (Popular Action).

First Vice President: Luis Alberto SANCHEZ Sánchez (American Popular Revolutionary Alliance); inaugurated on July 28, 1985, for a five-year term concurrent with that of the President, succeeding Fernando SCHWALB López Aldana (Popular Action).

Second Vice President: Luis Juan ALVA Castro (American Popular Revolutionary Alliance); inaugurated on July 28, 1985, for a term concurrent with that of the President, succeeding Javier ALVA Orlandini (Popular Action).

Prime Minister: Guillermo LARCO Cox (American Popular Revolutionary Alliance); sworn in on June 29, 1987, following the resignation on June 22 of Luis Juan ALVA Castro (American Popular Revolutionary Alliance).

THE COUNTRY

The third-largest country in South America and the second after Chile in the length of its Pacific coastline, Peru comprises three distinct geographical areas: a narrow coastal plain; the high sierra of the Andes; and an inland area of wooded foothills, tropical rain forests, and lowlands which includes the headwaters of the Amazon. Although it contains only 30 percent of the population, the coastal area is the commercial and industrial center. Roman Catholicism is the state religion and Spanish has traditionally been the official language, although Quechua (recognized as an official language in 1975) and Aymará are commonly spoken by the Peruvian Indians. Of Inca descent, Indians constitute 46 percent of the population but remain largely unintegrated with the White (10 percent) and mestizo (44 percent) groups. In 1982, over 51 percent of adult women were classified as economically active, primarily in agriculture, with smaller groups in domestic service and the informal trading sector; female participation in government is less than 5 percent.

The Peruvian economy has traditionally been based on the extraction of its rich and varied mineral resources, the most important metals being copper, silver, zinc, lead, and iron. In addition, petroleum, which was discovered in the country's northeastern jungle region in 1971, is being extensively exploited and now constitutes the leading export. The agricultural sector employs approximately 40 percent of the labor force and embraces three main types of activity: commercial agriculture, subsistence agriculture, and fishing. The most important cash crops are coffee, cotton, and sugar, with fish and fishmeal also being major foreign-exchange earners.

Like most of its neighbors, Peru has recently experienced a recurrence of economic adversity, including flagging output in both agricultural and industrial sectors, a massive foreign debt, and inflation that reached a record 163 percent in 1985. In August 1985, the IMF declared the government "ineligible" for further credit after it had embarked on a somewhat unorthodox recovery program that yielded a limited degree of success by late 1986 (see Current issues, below).

GOVERNMENT AND POLITICS

Political background. The heartland of the Inca empire conquered by Francisco Pizarro in the sixteenth century, Peru held a preeminent place in the Spanish colonial system until its liberation through the efforts of José de SAN MARTIN and Simón BOLIVAR in 1821–1824. Its subsequent history has been marked by frequent alternations of constitutional civilian and extraconstitutional military regimes.

The civilian government of José Luis BUSTAMANTE, elected in 1945, was overthrown in 1948 by Gen. Manuel A. ODRIA, who held the presidency until 1956. Manuel PRADO y Ugarteche, elected in 1956 with the backing of the left-of-center American Popular Revolutionary Alliance (APRA), presided over a democratic regime that lasted until 1962, when a new military coup blocked the choice of APRA leader Víctor Raúl HAYA DE LA TORRE as president. An election in 1963 restored constitutional government under Fernando BELAUNDE Terry of the Popular Action (AP) party. With the support of the Christian Democratic Party (PDC), Belaúnde implemented economic and social reforms, although hampered by an opposition-controlled Congress and an economic crisis at the end of 1967. Faced with dwindling political support, his government was ousted in October 1968 in a bloodless coup led by Div. Gen. Juan VELASCO Alvarado, who assumed the presidency, dissolved the Congress, and formed a military-dominated leftist administration committed to a participatory, cooperative-based model that was known after mid-1974 as the Inca Plan. Formally titled the Plan of the Revolutionary Government of the Armed Forces, it aimed at a "Social Proprietorship" (*Propiedad Social*) in which virtually all enterprises—industrial, commercial, and agricultural—would be either state- or worker-owned and would be managed collectively.

Amid growing evidence of discontent within the armed forces, Velasco Alvarado was himself overthrown in August 1975 by Div. Gen. Francisco MORALES BERMUDEZ Cerruti, who had served as prime minister since the preceding February and initially pledged to continue his predecessor's policies in a "second phase of the revolution" that would make the Inca reforms "irreversible". Despite the existence of well-entrenched rightist sentiment within the military, Div. Gen. Oscar VARGAS Prieto, who had succeeded Morales Bermúdez as prime minister in September 1975, was replaced in January 1976 by a leftist, Gen. Jorge FERNANDEZ Maldonado, who was put forward as a figure capable of maintaining the policies of the revolution in the midst of growing economic difficulty. Under the new administration, Peru's National Planning Institute (INP) prepared a replacement for the Inca Plan known as the *Plan Túpac Amaru.* The document was, however, considered too radical by rightist elements. Its principal authors were deported as part of a move to clear the INP of "left-wing infiltrators" and Fernández Maldonado was replaced in July 1976 by the conservative Gen. Guillermo ARBULU Galliani, following the declaration of a state of emergency to cope with rioting occasioned by a series of austerity measures.

A considerably revised *Plan Túpac Amaru,* advanced in February 1977, formally abandoned the concept of *Propiedad Social.* While the 1977 program called for constitutional reform and an eventual general election, its principal aim was the restoration of private enterprise in a manner designed to accommodate the needs of the Peruvian business community and its foreign creditors.

Gen. Oscar MOLINA Pallochia was designated to succeed Arbulú Galliani upon the latter's retirement in January 1978, while on June 18, in Peru's first nationwide balloting in 15 years, a 100-member Constituent Assembly was elected to draft a new constitution. The Assembly completed its work in July 1979, paving the way for presidential and congressional elections on May 18, 1980, at which Belaúnde Terry's *Acción Popular* scored an impressive victory. Immediately following reinvestiture of the former chief executive on July 28, a predominantly AP government was sworn in that included Dr. Manuel ULLOA Elías as prime minister. Less than 17 months later, on December 9, 1982, Ulloa unexpectedly resigned and was succeeded by First Vice President Fernando SCHWALB López Aldana.

In March 1984, Carlos RODRIGUEZ Pastor resigned as minister of economy, finance, and commerce, following widespread criticism of an austerity program negotiated with the IMF. On April 9 Schwalb López, who supported the program, resigned as prime minister (though retaining his vice-presidency), Sandro MARIATEGUI Chiappe being named to head a new government composed entirely of AP members. However, upon being designated AP candidate for second vice president on a 1985 ticket headed by Javier ALVA Orlandini, Mariátegui was required to step down, being succeeded on October 13 by Luis PERCOVICH Roca.

The AP was decisively defeated at the election of April 14, 1985, Alva Orlandini running fourth behind APRA's Alan GARCIA Pérez; Alfonso BARRANTES Lingán, the popular Marxist mayor of Lima; and Luis BEDOYA Reyes, of the recently organized Democratic Convergence (Conde). APRA fell marginally short of a majority in the presidential poll, but second-round balloting was avoided by Barrantes' withdrawal and García was sworn in on July 28 as, at age 36, the youngest chief executive in Latin America. Enjoying control of both houses of Congress, APRA secured an unprecedented 53 percent of the vote at municipal elections in November 1986, winning 18 of 24 departmental capitals.

Constitution and government. Under the 1979 constitution, Peru is governed by a president and a bicameral Congress, both elected for five-year terms. Save at the 1980 election (for which a plurality of 36 percent was specified),

a successful presidential candidate must secure an absolute majority, with direct second-round balloting, if necessary. The chief executive, assisted by two elected vice presidents, is responsible for appointing cabinet members (who may include a prime minister) and Supreme Court judges, although the Senate must concur in the latter. The Congress may delegate lawmaking power to the president and may censure ministers, individually and collectively. Upon denial of a vote of confidence, which can be sought only by the government, the president may dissolve the Chamber of Deputies prior to the expiration of its term. The judicial system, headed by the Supreme Court and including 18 district courts, has been augmented by a nine-member Constitutional Court and a National Council for the Judiciary.

In March 1987, President García promulgated legislation that divided the country's 25 departments into 12 regions, each of which is to have an assembly of provincial mayors, popularly elected representatives, and representatives of various institutions. The move has been interpreted as paving the way for the introduction of a federal system.

Foreign relations. Peruvian foreign policy stresses protection of its sovereignty and its natural resources. After the 1968 coup, the military government expanded contacts with Communist countries, including the Soviet Union, the People's Republic of China, and Cuba. Its relations with neighboring states, though troubled at times by frequent changes of regime, are generally equable, apart from a traditional suspicion of Chile and a long-standing border dispute with Ecuador (see map, p. 166) that most recently flared into hostilities in January-February 1981. Relations with the United States have been strained by recurrent controversies over the expropriation of US businesses and the seizure of US fishing boats accused of violating Peru's territorial waters.

In December 1981 a distinguished Peruvian diplomat, Javier PEREZ de Cuéllar, became the first Latin American to be elected secretary general of the United Nations.

Current issues. The magnitude of the Belaúnde victory in May 1980 was attributed, in large part, to disarray among the left-of-center parties. APRA, scarcely recovered from the death of its founder, Víctor Haya de la Torre, in August 1979, was deeply divided between the strongly leftist following of presidential candidate Armando VILLANUEVA del Campo and the more rightward posture of a group led by Andrés TOWNSEND Ezcurra, who was expelled in early 1981. Further to the left, both of the major coalitions that had organized to contest the presidential and congressional elections collapsed before the balloting began, largely because of the intrinsically unstable blocs of Moscow-line Communists, Maoists, Trotskyites, and *velasquistas* of which they were composed. The Belaúnde forces were also aided by a remarkable economic recovery during the preceding twelve months, with substantial increases in export sales of copper, lead, silver, zinc, and oil converting a foreign reserve deficit of over $1 billion in 1978 to a surplus of more than $500 million in 1979.

Most of these circumstances were reversed in 1985. APRA had regrouped under a youthful centrist, while the leading Marxist formations had joined a United Left (UI) coalition in support of Barrantes Lingán. More importantly, economic conditions had plummeted since 1981, yielding massive inflation, underemployment estimated to encompass 60 percent of the work force, and negative growth in GNP per capita. Even the Christian Popular Party, the AP's right-wing partner, had indicated that it was "profoundly worried" at implementation of the government's public investment program for 1981–1985, as well as by lack of success in quelling insurgency by *Sendero Luminoso* guerrillas (see Political Parties, below) in the southern department of Ayacucho.

At his inauguration on July 28, 1985, President García announced that Peru would limit its payments on some $5.6 billion of foreign debt service obligations to 10 percent of export earnings (estimated at $320 million) in 1986, giving precedence to non-IMF creditors. Subsequently, he accused the IMF of being an "accomplice" of Washington in the Third World debt crisis and ordered the Fund to close its Lima office. In May 1986, the government reversed itself and agreed to pay its IMF arrears, but after unilaterally rolling over repayment of approximately $940 million in short-term debt, was cut off from further access to Fund resources. Concurrently, intense negotiations were launched with the country's more than 270 foreign creditor banks to secure 15–20 year refinancing on the basis of a "medium-term economic program" intended to reduce the country's dependence on food imports and restructure Peruvian industry, in a manner reminiscent of the Inca Plan, toward basic needs and vertical integration. The audacious effort was buoyed by short-term evidence of recovery, industrial output rising by a remarkable 7.4 percent during the first half of the year and inflation dropping to less than half (below 70 percent) of the previous year's level.

By mid-1987 the recovery appeared to have run its course, with increased inflationary pressure and a visible slackening of the 8.5 percent GDP growth registered in 1986. In late June, Luis ALVA Castro, who had served as both prime minister and foreign minister, resigned in the wake of a well-publicized rivalry with the president, leaving economic policy in the hands of García and a group styled "the bold ones" (*los audaces*) who in late July announced that the state would assume control of the country's financial system. Although bitterly condemned by the affected institutions and their right-wing political supporters, a somewhat modified version of the initial expropriation bill was promulgated in October. The action was followed by a return to triple-digit inflation and in mid-December, amid continuing rumors of possible military intervention, the government announced a currency devaluation of 39.4 percent.

POLITICAL PARTIES

Most of the political parties active before the 1968 coup were of comparatively recent vintage, the principal exception being the American Popular Revolutionary Alliance (APRA), which was alternately outlawed and legalized beginning in the early 1930s. While APRA never captured the presidency, it contributed to the success of other candidates and was the nucleus of a powerful opposition coalition that controlled both houses of Congress during Belaúnde's 1963–1968 presidency.

During the decade after 1968, the status of the parties fluctuated, many being permitted a semilegal existence while denied an opportunity to engage in electoral activity. Most, except those of the extreme Left, were permitted to register prior to the Constituent Assembly election of June 1978, with further relaxation occurring prior to the presidential and legislative balloting of May 1980, in which some 20 groups participated. By contrast, only 9 groups presented candidates in 1985, with APRA, the IU, Conde, and the AP (below) collectively capturing 96.9 percent of the valid votes.

Government Party:

American Popular Revolutionary Alliance (*Alianza Popular Revolucionaria Americana*—APRA). Best known by its initials but also referred to as the Peruvian Aprista Party, APRA was organized in Mexico in 1924 as a radical left-wing movement, subsequently generating considerable mass support throughout Peru. Over the years, it gradually mellowed into a mildly left-of-center, middle-class grouping with a strong labor base. Despite long-standing antagonism between APRA and the military, its principal figure, Víctor Raúl Haya de la Torre, was permitted to return from exile in 1969 and was designated president of the Constituent Assembly after APRA won a substantial plurality at the election of June 18, 1978. Following his death in August 1979, Haya de la Torre was succeeded as party leader by Armando Villanueva del Campo. Decisively defeated in the 1980 balloting, the party subsequently split into a left-wing faction headed by Villanueva and a right-wing faction headed by second vice-presidential candidate Andrés Townsend Ezcurra, who was formally expelled from the party in January 1981 (see under Conde, below). While he remained an influential party figure, Villanueva's control of the organization ended in 1983, with the rise of Alan García, a centrist, who in 1985 became the first APRA leader to assume the presidency of the Republic. Following his installation, García reorganized the party hierarchy, assuming the newly created post of party president and arranging for the appointment of two general secretaries, rather than one. The president's widespread popularity was viewed as the principal reason for the party's unprecedented sweep of municipal elections in November 1986.

Leaders: Alan GARCÍA Pérez (President of the Republic and of the Party), Alberto KITASONO (National Secretary), Armando VILLANUEVA del Campo (General Secretary).

Other Parties and Party Groups:

Popular Action (*Acción Popular*—AP). Founded by Fernando Belaúnde Terry in 1956, the moderately rightist AP captured the presidency in 1963 and served as the government party until the 1968 coup. Democratic, nationalist, and dedicated to the extension of social services, it sought to mobilize public energies for development on Peru's own terms. After the 1968 coup the party split, a mainstream faction remaining loyal to Belaúnde and another, headed by former vice president Edgardo Seone Corrales, collaborating with the military junta.

Belaúnde was returned to office at the 1980 election, winning 45.4 percent of the votes cast, while the AP captured 98 of 180 Chamber seats and 26 of 60 seats in the Senate. However, in a massive reversal in voting behavior, the party won only one provincial city at municipal elections in November 1983 and ran fourth in the 1985 balloting, obtaining only 12 Chamber and 7 Senate seats.

Leaders: Fernando BELAUNDE Terry (former President of the Republic), Fernando SCHWALB López Aldana (former First Vice President of the Republic), Javier ALVA Orlandini (former Second Vice President of the Republic and Secretary General of the Party), Dr. Manuel ULLOA Elías (former Prime Minister).

Christian Democratic Party (*Partido Demócrata Cristiano*—PDC). One of the many Christian Democratic parties that have sprung up in Latin America, the PDC has been identified with reform programs along lines favored by the Catholic Church. Its effectiveness has long been constricted by internal dissent: a conservative group broke away in 1967 to form the PPC (below), while the rump organization was refused official registration in 1980 after a cleavage between supporters of party president Marco Pérez and former party president Héctor Cornejo Chávez had failed to yield agreement on a single list of legislative candidates.

Leaders: Dr. Marco PEREZ (President), Héctor CORNEJO Chávez (leader of minority faction), Lily SALAZAR de Villarán (Secretary General).

Democratic Convergence (*Convergencia Democrática* — Conde). Conde was organized in 1984 as an electoral coalition of the following two groups. It placed third in the 1985 balloting, winning 12 Chamber and 7 Senate seats.

Leader: Dr. Luis BEDOYA Reyes (1985 presidential candidate).

Christian Popular Party (*Partido Popular Cristiano* — PPC). The PPC was formed in the wake of a 1967 split in the PDC, Luis Bedoya Reyes leading a conservative faction out of the parent group. The party was runner-up to APRA in the Constituent Assembly election of June 1978 and placed third in the 1980 presidential and legislative races, after which it joined the Belaúnde government by accepting two ministerial appointments. In December 1986 the PPC president ordered a reorganization of the party because of its poor showing at the November municipal balloting and a year later, in the wake of President García's expropriation of the private banks, announced that it would join with *Acción Popular* and the small **Liberty Movement** (*Movimiento Libertad*), led by Mario VARGAS Llosa, in an alliance to be known as the **Democratic Front** (*Frente Democrático* — FD).

Leaders: Dr. Luis BEDOYA Reyes (President), Felipe OSTERLING (Political Secretary).

Hayista Bases Movement (*Movimiento de Bases Hayistas* — MBH). Ostensibly subscribing to fundamental Aprista principles, the MBH was organized in December 1982 by the former leader of APRA's right-wing faction.

Leader: Andrés TOWNSEND Ezcurra.

National Integration Party (*Partido de Integración Nacional* — Padin). Padin was organized in 1982 by legislative deputy Miguel Angel Mufarech, who left the PPC because of its alliance with APRA. With leftist support, it won the Ayacucho mayoralty in November 1983. It presented no candidates in 1985, cooperating instead with the IU, without, however, becoming a formal member of the coalition.

Leaders: Leonor ZAMORA, Miguel Angel MUFARECH (Secretary General).

Odria National Union (*Unión Nacional Odriísta* — UNO). A right-wing grouping organized by supporters of former president Manuel Odría, the UNO emphasizes the need for a strong governing power but pays considerable attention to extending social services and public works. It participated in the 1980 general election without securing legislative representation and did not campaign in 1985.

Leaders: Gen. Fernando NORIEGA, Víctor FREUNDT Rosell.

Peruvian Democratic Movement (*Movimiento Democrático Peruano* — MDP). The MDP is another personalist party, long organized as the Democratic Pradista Movement (*Movimiento Democrático Pradista*) in support of the policies of former president Manuel Prado.

Leader: Marco Antonio GARRIDO Malo.

Democratic Front of National Unity (*Frente Democrático de Unidad Nacional* — FDUN). The FDUN is a rightist grouping organized to support the 1985 presidential candidacy of retired general Francisco Morales Bermúdez, the country's military ruler from 1975 to 1980. It participated, without success, in the 1985 balloting.

Leader: Gen. Francisco MORALES BERMUDEZ Cerruti.

United Left (*Izquierda Unida* — IU). The IU was originally established prior to the May 1980 election as a coalition of the first two groups listed below, plus the PCU (see PCP, below). FOCEP withdrew prior to the May balloting — ostensibly because of resurgent *velasquista* tendencies within the PSR — with PSR leader Rodríguez Figueroa replacing FOCEPS's Ledesma Izquieta as the rump group's presidential candidate. It reorganized prior to the November 1980 municipal elections, at which it captured eight departmental capitals. Subsequently, its members decided to form a permanent grouping under the leadership of Alfonso Barrantes Lingán who in November 1983 became the first Marxist to be elected mayor of Lima. The alliance ran second to APRA in 1985, winning 48 Chamber and 15 Senate seats. In May 1987 Barrantes Lingán resigned as president of the IU National Executive after doctrinaire elements had objected to either conciliation with APRA or "democratization" of the alliance; however, a public opinion poll late in the year revealed that he was the leader among the five most likely candidates for the presidency in 1990.

Leaders: Enrique BERNALES, Javier DIEZ Canseco, Manuel DAMMERT, Jorge HURTADO, Dr. Genaro LEDESMA Izquieta (Members, National Executive Committee).

Revolutionary Socialist Party (*Partido Socialista Revolucionario* — PSR). The PSR was organized in November 1976 by a group of radical army officers who had been active in the "first phase of the revolution" under Velasco Alvarado and who subsequently advocated a return to the objectives of the 1968 coup.

Leaders: Enrique BERNALES, Alfredo FILOMENO (Secretary General).

Popular Front of Workers, Peasants, and Students (*Frente Obrero, Campesino, Estudiantil y Popular* — FOCEP). An amalgamation of 13 left-wing (largely Maoist and Trotskyite) political groups, FOCEP was formed prior to the 1978 Constituent Assembly election. It obtained 1 Senate seat in 1980, several of its constituent parties having withdrawn to run separately or in coalition with other groups following FOCEP's own withdrawal from the FUI.

Leader: Dr. Genaro LEDESMA Izquieta.

Peruvian Communist Party (*Partido Comunista Peruano* — PCP). Founded in 1928, but subsequently excluded from electoral participation by the 1933 constitution, the PCP has long been active in labor, student, and intellectual groups. The main body of the party is Moscow oriented and was registered as the United Communist Party (*Partido Comunista Unidad* — PCU) prior to the 1978 Constituent Assembly election, at which it won 6 seats. The PCU joined the FUI during the 1980 campaign. A dissident Maoist faction, known as the **Peruvian Communist Party-Red Fatherland** (*Partido Comunista Peruano-Patria Roja* — PCP-PR), and a pro-Albanian group, the **Peruvian Communist Party-Red Flag** (*Partido Comunista Peruano-Bandera Roja* — PCP-BR), were both organized in 1969.

Leader: Jorge del PRADO Chávez (Secretary General).

Union of the Revolutionary Left (*Unión de Izquierda Revolucionaria* — Unir). Unir is a pro-Beijing group that participated in the abortive ARI prior to the 1980 election and subsequently obtained 2 Senate and 2 Chamber seats in its own right. Its affiliates include the **National Liberation Front** (*Frente de Liberación Nacional* — FLN), led by Dr. Angel CASTRO Lavarello, and the VR-PC and MIR-Perú (see under PUM, below).

Leaders: Sen. Rolando BREÑA Pantoja (Chairman), Jorge HURTADO (Secretary General).

Unified Mariateguista Party (*Partido Unificado Mariateguista* — PUM). The PUM was formed in 1984 as a coalition including the following two groups, plus a faction of the PCR (below).

Leader: Javier DIEZ Canseco.

Revolutionary Vanguard (*Vanguardia Revolucionaria* — VR). The VR was organized in 1966 as a revolutionary Castroite organization, whose main support was drawn from students and some labor elements. It is a small, urban-based movement, several of whose members were sentenced to lengthy prison terms following a 1975 raid on a Lima water facility. In early 1988 there were reports that it had affiliated with the UDP (below). A splinter group led by Eduardo FIGARI, the **Revolutionary Vanguard-Communist Proletarian** (*Vanguardia Revolucionaria-Proletario Comunista* — VR-PC), is a component of Unir.

Leader: Javier DIEZ Canseco.

Movement of the Revolutionary Left (*Movimiento de Izquierda Revolucionaria* — MIR). The original MIR, from which the present group derives, was a splinter from the youth wing of APRA. It was a protégé of Havana and an advocate of guerrilla warfare. Another derivative of the parent organization is the **Movement of the Revolutionary Left-Peru** (*Movimiento de Izquierda Revolucionaria-Perú* — MIR-Perú), led by Dr. Gonzalo FERNANDEZ Gasco, which is also a member of Unir.

Leader: Carlos TAPIA (Secretary General).

Revolutionary Communist Party (*Partido Comunista Revolucionario* — PCR). The PCR is a small group that split from the VR in 1974.

Leader: Manuel DAMMERT (Secretary General).

Workers' Revolutionary Party (*Partido Revolucionario de los Trabajadores* — PRT). Founded in 1978, the PRT is a Trotskyite group whose leader, Hugo Blanco, was originally designated as the ARI presidential candidate in 1980. Running separately, after the demise of the ARI, the PRT secured 2 Senate and 3 Chamber seats. It joined the IU prior to the 1985 balloting.

Leader: Hugo BLANCO Galdós.

United Left Socialists (*Socialistas Izquierda Unida*—SIU). The SIU was formed in early 1988 by former IU leader Barrantes Lingán, who was joined by a number of other moderate independents from the parent group. It was reported to be seeking recognition as a separate party within the leftist alliance.

Leader: Dr. Alfonso BARRANTES Lingán.

Popular Democratic Union (*Unión Democrático Popular*—UDP). The UDP was formed prior to the 1978 balloting by a group of 18 left-wing organizations that could not, at the time, agree on a coalition with the PCP. It joined with Unir (above) and a number of other leftist parties prior to the 1980 election in organizing an abortive Revolutionary Alliance of the Left (*Alianza Revolucionaria de Izquierda*—ARI). As of late 1987 it and other radical groups, such as **People on March** (*Pueblo en Marcha*), occupied a position to the left of the IU with reputed links to the *Sendero Luminoso* and *Tupac Amaru* guerrilla organizations (below).

Leaders: Luís BENITEZ, Edmundo MURRUGARRA.

Socialist Workers' Party (*Partido Socialista de los Trabajadores*—PST). The PST is a Trotskyite group formed in 1982 by merger of an existing party of the same name, organized in 1974, with the Revolutionary Marxist Workers' Party (*Partido Obrero Marxista Revolucionario*—POMR), organized in 1968.

Leaders: Ricardo NAPURI, Enrique FERNANDEZ Chacón.

Nationalist Left Party (*Partido de Izquierda Nacionalista*—PIN). The PIN is a coalition of groups whose main base of support is the department of Puno. Campaigning as the National Front of Workers and Peasants (*Frente Nacional de Trabajadores y Campesinos*—FNTC or Frenatraca), it captured 1 Senate and 4 Chamber seats in 1980, 3 of the latter being lost in 1985.

Leaders: Dr. Róger CACERES Velásquez (President), Pedro CACERES Velásquez, Dr. Edmundo HUNAQI Medina (Secretary General).

Socialist Party of Peru (*Partido Socialista del Perú*—PSP). The PSP is a left-wing party organized in 1979.

Leader: Dr. María CABREDO de Castillo.

Other groups of the extreme Left include the Maoist **Anti-Imperialist Revolutionary Forces for Socialism** (*Fuerzas Revolucionarias Anti-Imperialistas por el Socialismo*—FRAS) and the **Revolutionary Socialist Action** (*Acción Socialista Revolucionaria*—ASR). The extreme Right includes the **Democratic Central Front** (*Frente de Centro Democrático*—FCD) and the **Democratic Armed Forces** (*Fuerzas Armadas Democráticas*—FAD).

Guerrilla Organizations:

Luminous Path (*Sendero Luminoso*). The *Sendero Luminoso* originated at Ayacucho University as a small Maoist group led by a former philosophy instructor, Manuel Abimael Guzmán. During 1980 it was involved in a number of bombings at Lima, Ayacucho, Cuzco, and other provincial towns in southern Peru, causing property damage only. Some 170 of its followers were arrested in October 1980 and January 1981, but most were freed in a daring raid on the Ayacucho police barracks in March 1982. Thereafter, guerrilla activity in the region intensified, including the assassination of a number of local officials and alleged police informants. While the insurgency appeared to remain localized (apart from sporadic terrorist attacks at Lima), the government felt obliged to order a major sweep through the affected provinces by some 1,500 military and police units at the end of the year. During 1983–1986, the rebellion showed no sign of diminishing, despite the imposition of military rule in the departments of Ayacucho, Apurímac, Huancavelica, Huánuco, and part of San Martín. By mid-1986, more than 9,000 deaths, on both sides, had been reported since the insurgency began. In 1987 the strength of the organization was estimated to be at least 3,000.

Leaders: Maximiliano DURAND Araújo, Dr. Manuel Abimael GUZMAN Reinoso, Julio César MEZZICH Eyzaguirre, Hildebrando PEREZ Huaranga ("Comandante Caselli").

Revolutionary Tupac Amaru Movement (*Movimiento Revolucionario Tupac Amarú*—MRTA). The MRTA surfaced in September 1984 as an urban guerrilla group responsible for a number of bomb attacks at Lima. Believed to be linked to military officers loyal to the principles of the 1968–1975 left-wing government, the organization was reported to have split in early 1986, with one faction joining the *Sendero Luminoso*. On June

23, MRTA guerrillas occupied the offices of a number of foreign news agencies to protest the recent "killing of political prisoners" and on August 7 the Movement formally terminated a truce accord concluded with the government one year earlier.

Leader: Marco TURKOWSKY.

Marxist-Leninist Communist Unification Committee (*Comité Comunista Unificado Marxista-Leninista*—CCUML). The CCUML is composed of a variety of far-left insurgents, including extremists linked to the PCP-PR, the VR, and the MIR, as well as the *Sendero Luminoso*.

Leaders: Jerónimo PASACHE, Julio César MEZZICH Eyzaguirre.

In mid-1985, a previously unknown formation, the **Popular Revolutionary Commandos** (*Comandos Revolucionarios del Pueblo*—CRP), seized a Peruvian radio station to protest what it termed the country's "unjust social order".

LEGISLATURE

The bicameral **Congress** (*Congreso*), established under the 1979 constitution, encompasses a Senate and a Chamber of Deputies, both elected for five-year terms by universal adult suffrage.

Senate (*Senado*). The Senate contains 60 members elected on a regional basis, plus constitutionally elected former presidents as life members. At the election of April 14, 1985, the American Popular Revolutionary Alliance obtained 32 seats; the United Left, 15; the Democratic Convergence, 7; the Popular Action, 5; and the Nationalist Left Party, 1.

President: Armando VILLANUEVA del Campo.

Chamber of Deputies (*Cámara de Diputados*). The Chamber consists of 180 members elected by means of proportional representation. Following the election of April 1985, the American Popular Revolutionary Alliance held 107 seats; the United Left, 48; the Democratic Convergence, 12; the Popular Action, 10; the Nationalist Left Party, 1; independents, 2.

President: Luis Juan ALVA Castro.

CABINET

Prime Minister	Guillermo Larco Cox
Ministers	
Aeronautics	Lt. Gen. (Ret.) José Guerra Lorenzetti
Agriculture	Remigio Morales Bermúdez
Defense	Enrique López Albujar Trint
Economy and Finance	Gustavo Saberbein Chevalier
Education	Mercedes Cabanillas
Energy and Mines	Abel Salinas Izaguire
Fisheries	Javier Labarthe
Foreign Relations	Allan Wagner Tizón
Housing and Construction	Luis Bedoya Vélez
Industry, Commerce, Tourism and Integration	Alberto Vera de la Rosa
Interior	José Bursallo Burga
Justice	Gonzalo Durant Aspillaga
Labor	Orestes Rodríguez Campos
Navy	Vice Adm. Willy Harm Esparza
Presidency	Guillermo Larco Cox
Public Health	Ilda Urízar
Transportation and Communications	Gen. (Ret.) Germán Parra Herrera
War	Gen. Jorge Flores Torres
President, Central Bank	Pedro Coronado Labo

NEWS MEDIA

In the decade after the 1968 coup, the government assumed control of most media; it confiscated Lima's seven leading newspapers and redesignated each as spokesman for an "organized sector of the community". In July 1980 President Belaúnde announced return of the papers to their former owners and indicated that two expropriated television stations would also be denationalized.

Press. The following are published daily at Lima, unless otherwise noted: *La Cronica* (185,000), official government publication; *Ojo* (180,000), pro-PPC conservative; *El Comercio* (145,000 daily, 200,000 Sunday), pro-PPC conservative; *Expreso* (123,000), conservative; *La República* (115,000), left-wing; *El Diario de Marka* (86,000), left-wing; *Extra* (85,000), evening edition of *Expresso; El Peruano* (76,000), official government publication; *El Correo* (Arequipa, 70,000), progovernment; *El Nacional,* progovernment; *Cambio,* left-wing.

News agencies. There is no domestic facility; numerous foreign agencies maintain bureaus at Lima.

Radio and television. The government's *Empresa Nacional de Radiodifusión del Perú* operates several dozen radio and ten television stations, including repeaters. There are also numerous private radio stations (in most of which the government holds a minority interest) and three commercial TV corporations. There were approximately 4.0 million radio and 1.6 million television receivers in 1987.

INTERGOVERNMENTAL REPRESENTATION

Ambassador to the US: César Guillermo ATALA Nazzal.

US Ambassador to Peru: Alexander Fletcher WATSON.

Permanent Representative to the UN: Carlos ALZAMORA.

IGO Memberships (Non-UN): ALADI, Ancom, APEF, CCC, CIPEC, Geplacea, IADB, ICAC, ICCO, ICM, ICO, ILZ, Inmarsat, INRO, Intelsat, Interpol, IWC, IWSG, IWTC, NAM, OAS, OPANAL, PCA, SELA.

PHILIPPINES

Republic of the Philippines
República de Filipinas (Spanish)
Republika ñg Pilipinas (Pilipino)

Political Status: Independent republic since July 4, 1946; currently under constitution adopted by referendum of February 2, 1987, with effect from February 11.

Area: 115,830 sq. mi. (300,000 sq. km.).

Population: 48,098,460 (1980C), 58,867,000 (1988E).

Major Urban Centers (1980C): MANILA (de facto capital, 1,626,249); QUEZON CITY (designated capital, 1,165,990); Davao (611,311); Cebu (489,208). In November 1975 Manila, Quezon, and 15 surrounding communities were organized into an enlarged Metropolitan Manila (see Constitution and government, below).

Official Languages: English, Spanish, Pilipino.

Monetary Unit: Peso (market rate March 1, 1988, 21.01 pesos = $1US).

President: Corazon Cojuangco AQUINO; sworn in on February 25, 1986, following disputed election on February 7 and the swearing in for a second six-year term, also

on February 25, of Ferdinand Edralin MARCOS, who left the country on February 26; Mrs. Aquino's term (indefinite under the "Freedom Constitution" of March 25, 1986) is to run until June 1992 under the basic law of February 1987.

Vice President: Salvador H. LAUREL; sworn in on February 25, 1986; named Prime Minister on February 26, in succession to César E.A. VIRATA, prior to abolition of the office under the provisional constitution of March 25.

THE COUNTRY

Strategically located along the southeast rim of Asia, the Philippine archipelago embraces over 7,000 islands stretching in a north-south direction for over 1,000 miles. The largest and most important of the islands are Luzon in the north and sparsely populated Mindanao in the south. The population, predominantly of Malay stock, is largely (85 percent) Roman Catholic, although a politically significant Muslim minority is concentrated in the south. The country is not linguistically unified; English and Spanish are used concurrently with local languages and dialects, although Pilipino, based on the Tagalog spoken in the Manila area, has been promoted as a national language. Due partly to a strong matriarchal tradition (an indigenous holdover from 300 years of Spanish Catholic influence), Filipinos accord high status to women: over 70 percent possess at least secondary education and women constitute close to 50 percent of the labor force; women have also been prominent in journalism and politics, though most often with the aid of powerful men, as in the cases of Imelda Marcos and Corazon Aquino.

Rice for domestic consumption and wood, sugar, and coconut products for export are mainstays of the economy, although an industrial sector encompassing mining, food processing, textiles, and building materials is of increasing importance. Long-term balance of payments deficits and questionable management of government funds during the Marcos era led to a severe fiscal crisis, a series of devaluations of the peso, and chronic difficulty in meeting external debt repayments. In 1984–1985, the economy continued to contract, undergoing loss of foreign investment because of uncertain prospects for political stability and yielding unemployment in excess of 25 percent and inflation of approximately 33 percent. However, following Marcos' departure in February 1986, international creditors indicated a willingness to renegotiate the country's $26 billion debt, while pledges of foreign assistance, principally from the United States, exceeded $500 million.

GOVERNMENT AND POLITICS

Political background. Claimed for Spain by Ferdinand Magellan in 1521 and ruled by that country until occupied by the United States during the Spanish-American War of 1898, the Philippines became a self-governing commonwealth under US tutelage in 1935 and was accorded full independence on July 4, 1946. Manuel ROXAS, first president of the new republic (1946–1948), took office during the onset of an armed uprising by Communist-led Huk-balahap guerrillas in central Luzon that continued under his successor, the Liberal Elpidio QUIRINO (1948–1953). Quirino's secretary of national defense, Ramón MAG-SAYSAY, initiated an effective program of military action and rural rehabilitation designed to pacify the Huks, and was able to complete this process after his election to the presidency on the Nacionalista ticket in 1953. Magsaysay also dealt strongly with bureaucratic corruption and did much to restore popular faith in government, but his accidental death in March 1957 led to a loss of reformist momentum and a revival of corruption under his Nacionalista successor, Carlos P. GARCIA (1957–1961). Efforts toward economic and social reform were renewed by Liberal President Diosdado MACAPAGAL (1961–1965).

The election, under Nacionalista auspices, of former Liberal leader Ferdinand E. MARCOS in November 1965 was accompanied by pledges of support for the reform movement, but the Marcos program was hindered by congressional obstruction and a temporary renewal of the Huk insurgency. Discontent with prevailing conditions of poverty, unemployment, inflation, and corruption fostered a climate of violence that included the activities of the Maoist New People's Army (NPA), which was founded in 1969, and a persistent struggle between Muslim elements and government forces on Mindanao and in Sulu Province. In some areas the latter conflict originated in religious differences, with Muslims seeking to drive out Christian settlers from the north, but as antigovernment activities expanded under the direction of the Moro National Liberation Front (MNLF), Muslim leaders increasingly called for regional autonomy or outright independence.

In the midst of a rapidly deteriorating political situation, a Constitutional Convention began work on a new constitution in July 1971, but the scope of its deliberations was curtailed by the declaration of martial law on September 23, 1972. Strict censorship immediately followed, as did widespread arrests of suspected subversives and political opponents of the regime, most notably Liberal Party leader Benigno S. AQUINO, Jr. The new constitution, which provided for a parliamentary form of government, was declared ratified on January 17, 1973; concurrently, Marcos assumed the additional post of prime minister and announced that the naming of an interim National Assembly called for by the constitution would be deferred.

Following talks in early 1975 between representatives of the Philippine government and the MNLF at Jiddah, Saudi Arabia, and Zamboanga City, Mindanao, the Muslims dropped their demand for partition of the Republic, while the government agreed to an integration of rebel units into the Philippine armed forces. A split within the MNLF ensued, a majority of its leaders calling for continued insurgency. President Marcos nevertheless ordered a suspension of military operations in the south in late 1976, following a ceasefire agreement with representatives of the moderate faction at Tripoli, Libya. In accordance with the agreement, a referendum was held in April 1977 on the establishment of an autonomous Muslim region in the 13 southern provinces. Most Muslims boycotted the polls, however, and the proposal was defeated by an overwhelming majority of those participating.

Amid charges of widespread voting irregularity (particularly in the Manila area), balloting for the interim Assembly was conducted on April 17, 1978, the president's recently organized New Society Movement being awarded an overwhelming proportion of seats.

Martial law was lifted in January 1981, prior to the adoption by plebiscite on April 4 of a series of constitutional changes that provided, inter alia, for direct presidential election and the designation of a partially responsible prime minister. At nationwide balloting on June 16, Marcos was reelected to a six-year term and on July 27 César E.A. VIRATA secured legislative confirmation as head of a new 18-member cabinet.

The first regular Assembly election was held on May 14, 1984, with opposition candidates being credited with winning approximately one-third of the seats. However, despite the lifting of martial law, the regime continued to rule by decree. Opposition feeling was further inflamed by the assassination of Benigno Aquino upon his return from the United States in August 1983, followed by eighteen months of often violent anti-regime demonstrations. In October 1984, a government commission of inquiry concluded that the armed forces chief of staff, General Fabian VER (who was thereupon temporarily suspended from his duties), bore ultimate responsibility for Aquino's death.

A year later, in the face of mounting support for Corazon AQUINO as political surrogate for her slain husband, Marcos announced that a premature presidential election would be held in early 1986 to "restore confidence" in his administration. On December 2, having been formally acquitted of complicity in the assassination, General Ver was reinstated. Nine days later, Mrs. Aquino filed as the sole opposition candidate for the presidency, with Salvador H. LAUREL as her running mate. The balloting on February 7 was conducted amid allegations of manifest government fraud by both opposition leaders and foreign observers; Aquino was named the victor by an independent citizens' watchdog group, while official figures attesting to the president's reelection were accepted by the National Assembly on February 15. Both candidates thus claiming victory, Aquino called for an expanded program of strikes, boycotts, and civil disobedience to "bring down the usurper".

The turning point came on February 22, when Defense Minister Juan Ponce ENRILE and Lt. Gen. Fidel RAMOS (acting chief of staff during Ver's suspension and the leader of an anticorruption campaign within the military) declared their allegiance to Aquino, Ramos joining troops loyal to him at Camp Crame, the national police headquarters. In response to an appeal from Cardinal Jaime SIN to protect the rebels, the base was surrounded by thousands of Philippine citizens, effectively precluding an assault by government forces. Subsequently, much of the media passed to opposition control, while the military, including the palace guard, experienced mass defections. On February 25, following the swearing in of both claimants, Marcos and his immediate entourage were flown in US helicopters to Clark Air Force Base and departed on the following day for exile in Hawaii.

The cabinet named by President Aquino on February 26 retained Enrile in his previous post, the remaining ministries being assigned to a broad spectrum of human rights activists, politicians, and technocrats. A month later, the new chief executive dissolved the National Assembly by suspending the 1973 constitution, presenting in its place an interim document "under which our battered nation can shelter".

On February 2, 1987, more that 80 percent of those voting approved a new US-style constitution, under which President Aquino and Vice President Salvador Laurel would remain in office until 1992. At subsequent congressional balloting on May 11, Aquino supporters won more than 80 percent of 200 directly elective House seats, while defeating opposition candidates in 22 of 24 Senate races.

On August 28 the Aquino government barely survived a coup attempt led by Col. Gregorio HONASAN, who had been prominently involved in the military revolt that toppled President Marcos. Immediately thereafter a number of prominent government officials either resigned or were removed from office, including the president's closest advisor, cabinet executive secretary and former human rights lawyer Joker ARROYO, who had been openly critical of the military leadership. Concurrently, Salvador Laurel resigned as foreign minister (though retaining the vice presidency) and for all practical purposes moved into opposition by forming a de facto alliance with a number of neo-Nacionalista conservatives who declared themselves ready to assume power if Aquino were to be forced from office. The president's personal popularity was, however, reconfirmed at provincial and local balloting in January 1988, albeit in the wake of a series of electoral arrangements, some of which involved ad hoc alignment with former Marcos supporters.

Constitution and government. The basic law approved February 2, 1987, supplanting the "Freedom Constitution" of March 1986, provides for a directly elected president serving a single six-year term, a bicameral Congress consisting of 24 senators and 250 representatives (who may serve no more than two and three terms, respectively), and an independent judiciary headed by a 15-member Supreme Court. The president is specifically enjoined from imposing martial law for more than a 60-day period without legislative approval. The document contains broad civil rights guarantees, denies the military any form of political activity save voting, abolishes the death penalty, prohibits abortion, authorizes local autonomy for Muslim-dominated areas, calls for a "nuclear-free" policy (save where the national interest dictates otherwise), and requires legislative concurrence for the leasing of Filipino territory to foreign powers.

The country is divided, for administrative purposes, into 12 regions and 72 provinces. In November 1975, an enlarged Metropolitan Manila was created by merging the city with 16 surrounding communities, including the official capital (Quezon City), the small cities of Rizal and Caloocan, and 13 towns. The new metropolis, with a total population of more than 5 million, is governed by a Metropolitan Manila Commission.

Foreign relations. Philippine foreign policy has traditionally been based on strong opposition to communism, close alliance with the United States, and active participation in the United Nations and its related agencies. The Philippines is also a member of regional organizations,

such as the Association of Southeast Asian Nations and the Asian Development Bank. President Aquino's first address at an ASEAN meeting, in mid-1986, stressed the need for accelerated regional economic ties as opposed to struggle against Western protectionism.

Uncertainty about the US role in Southeast Asia after the war in Vietnam spurred greater independence in foreign policy, and diplomatic and trade relations were established with several Communist nations, including the People's Republic of China, the Soviet Union, and the Socialist Republic of Vietnam.

Washington was widely considered to have played a key role in the downfall of President Marcos: in October 1985, the Reagan administration sent Senator Paul Laxalt, a known friend of the Filipino leader, to Manila to press for political, economic, and military reforms, while congressional threats of an aid cutoff followed US observers' denunciation of the conduct of the 1986 balloting. After the events of February 22–25, Laxalt reportedly told Marcos by telephone that his flight was necessary to avert a bloodbath; subsequently, Washington has been largely supportive of the Aquino government (see Current issues, below).

Current issues. During 1987 President Aquino attempted to consolidate her power base at a time when the euphoria of the Marcos overthrow was manifestly declining and both economic and security problems were proving to be increasingly intractable. Political developments during the first half of the year were encouraging. The new constitution was overwhelming endorsed in the referendum of February 2 and government candidates secured an equally conclusive victory at the legislative balloting of May 11. However, despite the capture of a number of rebel leaders in the course of the year, the Communist insurgency continued unabated following the expiration on February 8 of a 60-day truce with the NPA. Subsequently, in response to widespread "sparrow killings" (hit-and-run assassinations) in urban areas, police increasingly offered their support to right-wing vigilantes, despite government guidelines limiting such groups to purely voluntary and unarmed action. The security problem triggered an attempted army coup by Marcos sympathizers in late January and a far more serious uprising by nominally pro-government elements in late August. Meanwhile, little was achieved in implementing land reform, which the president had consistently advocated as a primary objective of her administration. In early March she announced that the initial phase of a land-reform program would be financed by the sale of some 400 (largely bankrupt) companies expropriated from Marcos supporters, but more extensive implementation stalled because of resistance by plantation owners, some of whom were reported to be raising private armies in defense of their holdings.

The local and provincial elections of January 1988, while seemingly attesting to Aquino's continued popularity, suggested a return to more traditional patterns of Philippine politics. Despite constitutional proscription of the establishment of a political "dynasty", nepotism was clearly evident in the number of presidential family members offering themselves as candidates (a surprising number of whom were rejected by the electorate). More importantly, while Aquino continued to lead a somewhat ill-defined Laban-centered coalition of diverse groups, the historic Liberal Party resurfaced under the leadership of erstwhile Aquino supporters Jovito SALONGA and Teofisto GUINGONA (elected president and president pro tempore, respectively, of the Senate that convened in July). The far-Left, operating somewhat more discretley because of its poor showing at the legislative balloting in May, grouped itself around the reportedly NDF-linked People's Party (see under Political Parties, below), while resurgent Nacionalista sentiment was evident in a rump of the United Nationalist Democratic Organization (Unido), led by Salvador Laurel, that had participated in the original Aquino coalition but whose influence had at least temporarily waned in the wake of Laurel's resignation as foreign secretary in September.

POLITICAL PARTIES

From 1946 until the imposition of martial law in 1972, political control oscillated between the **Nacionalista Party** (NP), founded in 1907, and the **Liberal Party** (LP), organized by slightly left-of-center elements that split from the Nacionalistas in 1946. Minority parties were established from time to time, but most were short-lived. Both of the main parties concerned themselves primarily with local alliances and patronage, and their adherents readily shifted from one to the other. The only major difference was one of economic outlook: powerful sugar interests, which tended to resist foreign investment in Philippine enterprises, dominated among the Nacionalistas, while most Liberals favored a more flexible approach to foreign capital.

In early 1978, coincident with a pro forma return to party politics, the **New Society Movement** (*Kilusan Bagong Lipunan* — KBL) was organized as the personal vehicle of President Marcos. Officially credited with winning 151 of 165 elective seats at the interim National Assembly balloting of April 1978 and 88 percent of the presidential vote in June 1981, the KBL was awarded 108 of 183 elective Assembly seats in May 1984, despite losses in virtually all regions of the country. Meanwhile, in February 1980, representatives of eight opposition groups had formed a loose coalition, the United Democratic Opposition (Unido), which reorganized in April 1982 as the United Democratic Organization (also known as the United Nationalist Democratic Organization), a 12-party alignment that included the Nationalistas and Liberals; the Philippine Democratic Party (PDP), which was descended from the Christian Socialist Movement founded by the exiled Raul MANGLAPUS; and the **People's Power Movement** (*Lakas 'ng Bayan* — Laban), which was under the nominal presidency of Benigno Aquino until his assassination in August 1983 and was subsequently led by Lorenzo TANADA.

The Aquino assassination spawned a number of cross-party alliances among the opposition, which was divided on whether to boycott the May 1984 election. In late 1983, the PDP formed an alliance with Laban (PDP-Laban) under the leadership of Teofisto Guingona, while Tañada organized a separate National Alliance for Justice, Freedom and Democracy. By early 1984, three distinct opposi-

tion formations had emerged: (1) a pro-boycott "compact" group encompassing PDP-Laban; Tañada's National Alliance; Diosdado MACAPAGAL's National Union for Liberation, which had participated in a 1980 coalition with the Liberals; and a number of groups, including the Movement for Philippine Sovereignty and Democracy, associated with former senator José DIOKNO; (2) the rump of Unido, led by Salvador H. Laurel, who described the forthcoming balloting as the "last chance for Philippines democracy"; and (3) the Alliance of Metropolitan Associations (AMA), composed of a variety of formerly apolitical groups that had adopted a militantly antigovernment posture under the leadership of Agapito "Butz" AQUINO. At the actual poll, only the AMA stood firm, Guingona breaking ranks with his "compact" associates to participate under the Unido banner.

In November 1984, Corazon Aquino joined with a number of other opposition leaders in organizing a non-party Convener's Group to devise a "fast track" method of selecting an anti-Marcos candidate in the event of an early presidential election. Subsequently, in March 1985, a Unido-led National Unification Council (NUC) of opposition Assembly members was formed, largely in support of Salvador Laurel, although the fact that Laurel had not broken with Marcos until 1980 generated some friction within the grouping. In June, delegates to a Unido convention unanimously selected Laurel as their candidate for balloting expected in 1987, thus abrogating an April pledge to consult with the Convenor's Group on the choice of a nominee, while most of Unido's Laban component formally drafted Mrs. Aquino in November. Only on December 11, the closing date for the filing of nomination papers, did Aquino and Laurel agree to stand as Unido candidates for the presidency and vice presidency, respectively, at the election called for February 7, 1986.

The government landslide at the legislative balloting of May 11, 1987, was achieved without an articulated party structure, most pro-Aquino candidates running under a variety of rubrics loosely joined in a Laban-centered coalition. Opposition votes were scattered among former defense minister Enrile's **Grand Alliance for Democracy** (GAD), the remnants of Marcos' KBL, and the **People's Party** (*Partido 'ng Bayan* — PnB), which was reportedly linked to the outlawed National Democratic Front (see Illegal Groups, below).

Illegal Groups:

The Moscow-oriented **Philippine Communist Party** (*Partido Komunista ñg Pilipinas* — PKP) was outlawed in 1948 and for some time thereafter continued to support the Hukbalahap rebellion. In subsequent years, particularly after the November 1974 surrender of PKP Secretary General Felicismo MACAPAGAL and military leader Alejandro BRIONES, the party advocated political reform rather than violent change, with Macapagal actually praising President Marcos for his leadership and his "pragmatic centrist position" in a context of "imperialist" efforts to "destabilize" the government. The less-than-radical stance of the PKP (currently a legal formation) contrasts sharply with that of the larger **Communist Party of the Philippines–Marxist-Leninist** (CPP or CPP-ML), a Maoist group founded in 1968, and its military wing, the New People's Army (NPA), founded in early 1969. Until recently, the CPP was led by a three-man politburo (the "troika"), consisting of Rodolfo SALAS (Chairman), Antonio (Tony) ZUMEL, and Rafael BAYLOSIS (Secretary General). However, Salas was captured by government forces in September 1986, as was CPP-ML vice chairman Juanito RIVERA in mid-November; in

March 1988 Baylosis was also apprehended, along with NPA commander Romulo KINTANAR. The NPA, numbering 20,000–30,000 rural-based guerrillas, has been gaining strength in recent years; it is strongest in northeast and central Luzon, in the Samar provinces of the Visayas, and in southern Mindanao, although it has undertaken insurgent activity in well over three quarters of the country's 72 provinces.

In April 1973 the CPP sponsored a **National Democratic Front** (NDF) intended to unite Communist, labor, and Christian groups in opposition to the Marcos regime; declared illegal upon its formation, the Front claims close to 20,000 members. During her presidential campaign, Aquino declared that she would attempt to arrange a cease-fire with the rebels, and one of her first official acts was to release some 500 political detainees, including the CPP's founder, José Maria SISON, and Bernabe BUSCAYNO, the original leader of the NPA (who promptly joined in launching the PnB, above). Although Communist leaders insisted that "much of the fascist structures" remained from the Marcos era, talks with NPA representatives began in mid-1986 and a 60-day cease-fire was ultimately concluded effective December 10; reportedly because of a resurgence of hardline sentiment within the rebel leadership, the pact was not extended beyond its expiration on February 8, 1987.

Earlier, talks had been initiated with the country's other major insurgent group, the **Moro National Liberation Front** (MNLF). Long active on behalf of the Muslims of Mindanao, the MNLF split in 1975 into Libyan- and Egyptian-backed factions (the latter subsequently styling itself the **Moro Islamic Liberation Front** — MILF) led by Nur MISAURI and Hashim SALAMAT, respectively (see Political background, above). Originally the stronger of the two guerrilla armies, Moro forces had dwindled by 1986 to one-third their original size and in early 1987 Misauri tentatively agreed to drop his demands for an independent southern state in favor of autonomy for "Muslim Mindanao" as spelled out in the new constitution. By late 1987, despite the emergence of a new breakaway faction, the Bangsa Moro Liberation Front (BMNLF), led by Hashim SALAMAT, there were reports of renewed clashes between government and Moro units, while in early 1988 the MNLF submitted an application, in emulation of the PLO, to join the Islamic Conference as a non-state member.

LEGISLATURE

The 1987 constitution provides for a bicameral **Congress of the Philippines,** encompassing a Senate and a House of Representatives.

Senate. The upper house consists of 24 at-large members who may serve no more than two six-year terms. At the balloting of May 11, 1987, candidates supported by President Aquino won 22 seats, while the Grand Alliance for Democracy obtained 2.
President: Jovito SALONGA.
President Pro Tempore: Teofisto GUINGONA.

House of Representatives. The lower house is composed of 250 members, of whom 200 are directly elected from legislative districts; the remaining members are elected through "a party-list system of registered national, regional, and sectoral parties or organizations", save that for the first three terms under the present basic law "one-half of the seats allocated to party-list representatives shall be filled . . . by selection or election from the labor, peasant, urban poor, indigenous cultural communities, women, youth, and such other sectors as may be provided by law, except the religious sector". Representatives can serve no more than three consecutive three-year terms. At the May 1987 election, 162 of the victors were identified as being "allied one way or another to Laban", although by early 1988 nearly three dozen had realigned themselves under a resurgent Liberal Party.
Speaker: Ramon MITRA.

CABINET

President	Corazon C. Aquino
Vice President	Salvador H. Laurel
Executive Secretary	Catalino Macaraig
Secretaries	
Agrarian Reform	Philip Juico
Agriculture	Carlos Dominguez
Budget	Guillermo Carague
Education, Culture and Sports	Lourdes Quisumbing
Finance	Vicente R. Jayme
Foreign Affairs	Raul Manglapus
Health	Alfredo Bengzon
Justice	Sedfrey Ordonez
Labor and Employment	Franklin M. Drilon
Local Government	Luis Santos
National Defense	Gen. (Ret.) Fidel Ramos
Natural Resources	Fulgencio Factoran
Public Works and Highways	Juanito Ferrer
Science and Technology	Antonio Arizabal
Social Services and Development	Mita Pardo De Tavera
Tourism and Environment	José Antonio Gonzalez
Trade and Industry	José Concepcion, Jr.
Transportation and Communications	Reinerio Reyes
Director General, National Economic and Development Authority	Solita Monsod
Director General, Office of Muslim Affairs	Jiamil Dianalan
Governor, Central Bank	José B. Fernandez

NEWS MEDIA

Press. In the pre-martial law period, the Philippine press, including 19 Manila dailies and 66 provincial papers, was one of the most flourishing in Asia. Upon the imposition of martial law in September 1972, most of the leading papers, including *The Manila Times*, *The Philippine Herald*, *The Manila Chronicle*, and *The Evening News*, were shut down. With easing of the press ban in 1973–1974, some reemerged under the supervision of the Philippine Council for Print Media, but it was not until the 1983 assassination of Benigno Aquino that a true revival occurred. *The Manila Times*, formerly the largest English-language newspaper in the Orient, did not resume publication until February 1986. The following are English-language dailies published at Manila, unless otherwise noted: *Philippine Daily Inquirer* (287,000); *Bulletin Today* (255,000); *News Herald* (175,000); *Times Journal* (175,000); *Manila Times* (100,000); *Evening Post* (90,000); *Malaya* (55,000), weekly; *Business Day* (Quezon City, 54,000); *Veritas* (50,000), weekly Catholic Church publication; *Bannawag* (45,000), weekly, in Ilocano.

News agencies. The domestic facility is the Philippines News Agency; a number of foreign bureaus also maintain offices at Manila.

Radio and television. The principal broadcasting group is the Association of Broadcasters in the Philippines (*Kapisanan ñg Mga Brodkaster sa Pilipinas*). There are more than 300 radio stations broadcasting to approximately 7.8 million receivers; the five principal television networks were received by over 4.1 million TV sets in 1987.

INTERGOVERNMENTAL REPRESENTATION

Ambassador to the US and Permanent Representative to the UN: Emmanuel N. PELAEZ.

US Ambassador to the Philippines: Nicholas PLATT.

IGO Memberships (Non-UN): ADB, APCC, ASEAN, CCC, CP, ICAC, ICO, Inmarsat, Intelsat, Interpol, ISO, IWC.

POLAND

Polish People's Republic
Polska Rzeczpospolita Ludowa

Political Status: Independent state reconstituted 1918; Communist People's Republic established 1947; present constitution promulgated July 22, 1952.

Area: 120,725 sq. mi. (312,677 sq. km.).

Population: 37,026,000 (1984C), 37,634,000 (1988E).

Major Urban Centers (1985E): WARSAW (1,640,000); Łódź (844,000), Kraków (739,000); Wrocław (635,000); Poznań (573,000); Gdańsk (466,000); Szczecin (390,000).

Official Language: Polish.

Monetary Unit: Złoty (principal rate March 1, 1988, 382.08 złotys = $1US).

Chairman of the Council of State and First Secretary of the Central Committee, Polish United Workers' Party: Gen. Wojciech JARUZELSKI; elected by the *Sejm* to succeed Józef PIŃKOWSKI as Chairman of the Council of Ministers on February 11, 1981, and by the party's Central Committee to succeed Stanisław KANIA as First Secretary on October 18; elected Chairman of the Council of National Defense on November 22, 1983; relinquished chairmanship of Council of Ministers and assumed that of Council of State, succeeding Henryk JABŁOŃSKI, on November 6, 1985; reelected party First Secretary on July 3, 1986.

Chairman of the Council of Ministers (Prime Minister): Zbigniew MESSNER; elected by the *Sejm* on November 6, 1985, succeeding Gen. Wojciech JARUZELSKI.

THE COUNTRY

A land of plains, rivers, and forests uneasily situated between the German Democratic Republic in the west and the Russian, Lithuanian, Byelorussian, and Ukrainian Soviet Socialist republics in the east, Poland has been troubled throughout its history by a lack of firm natural boundaries to demarcate its territory from that of its powerful neighbors. Its present borders reflect major post-World War II adjustments that involved both the loss of some 70,000 square miles of former Polish territory to the USSR and the acquisition of some 40,000 square miles of former German territory along the country's northern and western frontiers, the latter accompanied by large-scale resettlement of the area by Poles. These boundary changes, following upon the Nazi liquidation of most of Poland's prewar Jewish population, left the country 96 percent Polish in ethnic composition and 90 percent Roman Catholic in religious faith. In 1980, women constituted approximately 46 percent of the paid labor force, concentrated mainly in the areas of sales, services, and clerical work; female participation in party and governmental affairs is estimated at about 25 percent.

On October 22, 1978, Cardinal Karol Wojtyła, archbishop of Kraków, was invested as the 264th pope of the Roman Catholic Church. The first Pole ever selected for the office, Pope JOHN PAUL II was regarded as a politically astute advocate of Church independence who had worked successfully within the strictures of a Communist regime. During a June 2–10, 1979, visit by the pope to his homeland, he was greeted by crowds estimated at 6 million. In 1980 the continuing power of the Church was perhaps best demonstrated by the influence exerted by Polish primate Stefan Cardinal WYSZYŃSKI in moderating the policies of the country's newly formed free labor unions while playing a key role in persuading the Communist leadership to grant them official recognition. Cardinal Wyszyński died on May 28, 1981, and was succeeded as primate on July 7 by Archbishop Józef GLEMP, whose efforts to emulate his predecessor were jolted on December 13 by the imposition of martial law, with a subsequent worsening in church-state relations.

Poland's economy underwent dramatic changes in the years after World War II, including a large scale shift of the work force into the industrial sector. A resource base that included coal, copper, and natural gas deposits contributed to significant expansion in the fertilizer, petrochemical, machinery, electronic, and shipbuilding industries, placing Poland among the world's dozen leading industrial nations. On the other hand, attempts to collectivize agriculture proved largely unsuccessful, with 80 percent of cultivated land remaining in private hands. Most importantly, the retention of traditional farming methods and the fragility of soil and climatic conditions led to periodic agricultural shortages which, in turn, contributed to consumer unrest.

Due in large part to work stoppages and other forms of labor protest, the country experienced an acute economic crisis during 1981, industrial production and national income falling by 19 and 13 percent, respectively, while the cost of living increased by 25 percent. During the same period, exports fell by nearly 15 percent, resulting in a trade deficit of more than $2 billion, while the total foreign debt rose to nearly $30 billion. By 1987 the external debt had risen to $36 billion, with the United States agreeing in September to provide assistance in loan consolidation and rescheduling with the "Paris Club" of Western creditors. The action came after Polish officials had agreed to both economic and political liberalization, including a reduction in central planning and the addition of consultative councils at local administrative levels (see Current issues, below).

GOVERNMENT AND POLITICS

Political background. Tracing its origins as a Christian nation to 966 AD, Poland became an influential kingdom in late medieval and early modern times, functioning as an elective monarchy until its liquidation by Austria, Prussia, and Russia in the successive partitions of 1772, 1793, and 1795. Its reemergence as an independent republic at the close of World War I was followed in 1926 by the establishment of a military dictatorship headed initially by Marshal Józef PIŁSUDSKI. The first direct victim of Nazi aggression in World II, Poland was jointly occupied by Germany and the USSR, coming under full German control with the outbreak of German-Soviet hostilities in June 1941.

After the war, a Communist-controlled "Polish Committee of National Liberation", established under Soviet auspices at Lublin in 1944, was transformed into a Provisional Government and then merged with a splinter group of the anti-Communist Polish government-in-exile in London to form in 1945 a Provisional Government of National Unity. The new government was headed by Polish Socialist Party (PPS) leader Edward OSÓBKA-MORAWSKI, with Władysław GOMUŁKA, head of the (Communist) Polish Workers' Party (PPR) and Stanisław MIKOŁAJCZYK, chairman of the Polish Peasants' Alliance (PSL), as vice premiers. Communist tactics in liberated Poland prevented the holding of free elections as envisaged at the Yalta Conference in February 1945, and the election that was ultimately held in 1947 represented the final step in the establishment of control by the PPR, which forced the PPS into a 1948 merger under the rubric of the Polish United Workers' Party (PZPR).

Poland's Communist regime has been subject to periodic crises resulting from far-ranging political and economic problems. As in many East European countries, the immediate postwar period was characterized by subservience to Moscow and the use of Stalinist methods to consolidate the regime. In 1948 Gomułka was accused of "rightist and nationalist deviations", which led to his replacement by Bolesław BIERUT and his subsequent imprisonment (1951–1954). By 1956, however, post-Stalin liberalization was generating political turmoil, precipitated by the sudden death of Bierut in Moscow and "bread and freedom" riots at Poznań, and Gomułka returned to power as the symbol of a "Polish path to socialism". The new regime initially yielded a measure of political stability, but by the mid-1960s Gomułka was confronted with growing dissent among intellectuals in addition to factional rivalry within the party leadership. As a result, Gomułka-inspired anti-Semitic and anti-intellectual campaigns were mounted in 1967–1968, with the mass emigration of some 18,000 Polish Jews (out of an estimated 25,000) by 1971. Drastic price increases caused a serious outbreak of workers' riots in December 1970, which, although primarily economic in nature, provoked a political crisis that led to the replacement of Gomułka as PZPR first secretary by Edward GIEREK, with Piotr JAROSZEWICZ succeeding Józef CYRANKIEWICZ as chairman of the Council of Ministers.

In February 1980, amid renewed economic distress, Edward BABIUCH was named to replace Jaroszewicz and, following a parliamentary election on March 23, announced a new austerity program that called for a reduction in imports, improved industrial efficiency, and the gradual withdrawal of food subsidies. In early July the government began to implement new marketing procedures for meat that effectively raised prices by some 60 percent. In plants scattered throughout Poland, workers responded by demanding wage adjustments, with over 100 brief strikes resulting from management's initial refusal to comply. By early August the stoppages had begun to assume a more overtly political character, employees demanding that they be allowed to establish "workers' committees" to replace the PZPR-dominated, government-controlled official trade unions. Among those marshaling support for the strikers was the Committee for Social Self-Defense (KOR), the largest of a number of recently established dissident groups.

On August 14 the 17,000 workers at the Lenin Shipyard at Gdańsk struck, occupied the grounds, and issued a list of demands that included the right to organize independent unions; a rollback of meat prices; higher wages, family allowances, and pensions; erection of a monument honoring the workers killed in the 1970 demonstrations; reinstatement of dismissed workers; and publication of their demands by the mass media. Three days later, workers from 21 industries in the area of the Baltic port presented an expanded list of 16 demands that called for recognition of the right of all workers to strike, abolition of censorship, and release of political prisoners. In an emergency session held the same day, the PZPR Politburo directed a commission headed by Tadeusz PYKA to open negotiations with strike committees from individual enterprises but to reject participation by "interfactory strike committees". On August 21, after the stoppage had spread beyond the Gdańsk area, notably to the port of Szczecin, the hard-liner Pyka was replaced by Mieczysław JAGIELSKI, who two days later agreed to meet with delegates of the Gdańsk interfactory committee headed by Lech WAŁĘSA, a former shipyard worker who had helped organize the 1970 demonstrations. On August 30 strike settlements were completed at Gdańsk as well as at Szczecin, where collateral discussions had been under way. Having been approved by the *Sejm,* the 21-point Gdańsk Agreement was signed by Jagielski and Wałęsa on August 31. While recognizing the position of the PZPR as the "leading force" in society, the unprecedented document stated, "It has been found necessary to call up new, self-governing trade unions which would become authentic representatives of the working class". Government concessions included a wage settlement; increased support for medical, educational, housing, and pension needs; improved distribution of consumer goods; reconsideration of censorship laws; adoption of a five-day workweek by 1982; and a commitment both to recognize the legitimacy of independent unions and to guarantee the right of workers to join them.

Although most workers along the Baltic coast returned to their jobs on September 1, strikes continued to break out in other areas, particularly the coal- and copper-mining region of Silesia, and on September 6 First Secretary Gierek resigned in favor of Stanisław KANIA. Earlier, on August 24, Józef PIŃKOWSKI had replaced Edward Babiuch as chairman of the Council of Ministers, with a number of individual ministries also changing hands.

On September 15 registration procedures to be followed by independent unions were announced, with authority to approve union statutes delegated to the Warsaw provincial court. Three days later, 250 representatives of new labor groups established at Gdańsk a "National Committee of Solidarity" (*Solidarność*) with Lech Wałęsa as chairman, and on September 24 the organization applied for registration as the Independent Self-Governing Trade Union Solidarity. The court objected, however, to its proposed governing statutes, particularly the absence of any specific reference to the PZPR as the country's leading political force, and it was not until November 10 — two days before a threatened strike by Solidarity — that the Supreme Court, ruling in the union's favor, removed amendments imposed by the lower court, the union accepting as an annex a statement of the party's role. By December, some 40 free trade unions had been registered, while on January 1, 1981, the official Central Council of Trade Unions was dissolved, virtually all of its 23 PZPR-dominated member unions having either voted to register as independents or undergone substantial membership depletion.

The unprecedented events of 1980 yielded sharp cleavages between Wałęsa and radical elements within Solidarity, and between moderate and hard-line factions of the PZPR. Fueled by the success of the registration campaign, labor unrest increased further in early 1981, accompanied by appeals from the private agricultural sector for recognition of a "Rural Solidarity", while the PZPR, which had failed to agree on a series of internal reforms necessitated by the Gierek resignation, delayed in setting a precise date for an extraordinary party congress that had been announced for late March. Amid growing indications of concern by other Eastern-bloc states, Pińkowski resigned as chairman of the Council of Ministers and was succeeded on February 11 by the minister of defense, Gen. Wojciech JARUZELSKI. Initially welcomed in his new role by most Poles, including the moderate Solidarity leadership, Jaruzelski attempted to initiate a dialogue with nonparty groups and introduced a ten-point economic program designed to promote recovery and counter "false anarchistic paths contrary to socialism". The situation again worsened following a resumption of government action against KOR and other dissident groups, although the Independent Self-Governing Trade Union for Private Farmers — Solidarity (Rural Solidarity), which claimed between 2.5 and 3.5 million members, was officially registered on May 12.

At the extraordinary PZPR congress that finally convened on July 14 at Warsaw, more than 93 percent of those attending could claim no such previous experience because of the introduction of secret balloting at the local level for the selection of delegates. As a consequence, very few renominations were entered for outgoing Central Committee members, while only four former members were reelected to the Politburo. Stanisław Kania was, however, retained as first secretary in the first secret, multicandidate balloting for the office in PZPR history.

Evidence of government displeasure at its increasingly political posture notwithstanding, Solidarity held its first National Congress at Gdańsk on September 5–10 and September 25–October 7. After reelecting Wałęsa as its chairman, the union approved numerous resolutions, including a call for wide-ranging changes in the structure of trade-union activity. Subsequently, at the conclusion of a plenary session of the PZPR Central Committee held on October 16–18 to review the party's position in light of the Solidarity congress, First Secretary Kania submitted his resignation and was immediately replaced by General Jaruzelski, who, on October 28, made a number of changes in the membership of both the Politburo and Secretariat. Collaterally, Jaruzelski moved to expand the role of the army in maintaining public order.

During the remaining weeks of 1981, relations between the government and Solidarity progressively worsened, a crisis being generated by a union announcement on December 11 that it would conduct a national referendum on January 15 that was expected to yield an expression of nonconfidence in the Jaruzelski regime. The government responded by arresting most of the Solidarity leadership, including Wałęsa, while the Council of State on December 13 declared martial law under a Military Committee for National Salvation headed by Jaruzelski. Subsequently, a number of stringent decrees were promulgated that effectively banned all organized nongovernmental activity except for religious observances, abolished the right to strike, placed major economic sectors under military discipline, closed down all nonofficial communications media, and established summary trial courts for those charged with violation of martial law regulations.

A number of the restrictive measures were eased during 1982 as opportunities for overt opposition dissipated, the most violent confrontations occurring in late August on the approach of the anniversary of the 1980 Gdańsk accord. On October 8 the *Sejm* approved legislation that formally dissolved all existing trade unions and established guidelines for new government-controlled organizations to replace them. The measures were widely condemned by the Church and other groups, and Solidarity's underground leadership called for a nationwide protest strike on November 10. However, the appeal yielded only limited public support, and Wałęsa was released from detention two days later. On December 18 the *Sejm* approved a suspension (not a lifting) of martial law that voided most of its remaining overt manifestations while empowering the government to reimpose direct military rule if it should deem such action necessary.

On July 21, 1983, State Council Chairman Jabłoński announced the formal lifting of martial law and the dissolution of the Military Committee for National Salvation, the latter body being effectively supplanted four months later by a National Defense Committee, chaired by General Jaruzelski, with overall responsibility for both defense and state security. However, these events were overshadowed by the kidnapping and murder in October 1984 of the outspoken pro-Solidarity cleric, Fr. Jerzy POPIELUSZKO of Warsaw, for which four state security officers were ultimately tried and convicted.

Following *Sejm* elections in October 1985, General Jaruzelski succeeded the aging Jabłoński as head of state, relinquishing the chairmanship of the Council of Ministers to Zbigniew MESSNER, who entered office as part of a major realignment that substantially increased the government's technocratic thrust. Jaruzelski was reelected PZPR first secretary at the party's Tenth Congress on June 29–July 3, 1986, at which nearly three-quarters of the Central Committee's incumbents were replaced.

In October 1987 Jaruzelski presented to the PZPR Central Committee a number of proposed economic and political reforms far outstripping Mikhail Gorbachev's "restructuring" agenda for the Soviet Union. Central to their implementation, however, was a strict austerity program including massive price increases that was bitterly opposed by the Solidarity leadership. In the wake of a remarkable referendum on November 29, at which the proposals failed to secure endorsement by a majority of eligible voters, the government indicated that it would proceed with their implementation, albeit at a slower pace than had originally been contemplated.

Constitution and government. As in other Eastern-bloc countries, political authority in Poland is centered in the (Communist) Polish United Workers' Party, which holds all key governmental posts. The present constitution, adopted in 1952 to replace the so-called "Little Constitution" of 1947, vests supreme authority in the unicameral Parliament (*Sejm*). The system differs from those of most other East European countries in that it permits the election of noncommunist deputies, whose candidacies must, however, be regime-approved. In addition, most seats are now nominally competitive (see Legislature, below). The Parliament elects the Council of Ministers (cabinet) and a Council of State, whose chairman exercises the mainly ceremonial functions of head of state. A Supreme Chamber of Control is responsible for supervising all activities of state administration. Under a constitutional amendment approved in October 1980, the Chamber became directly responsible to the *Sejm,* having previously been subordinate to the Council of State (until 1976) and then to the chairman of the Council of Ministers. The 1980 amendment was intended to facilitate the Chamber's investigation of governmental corruption. The 20-member Military Council of National Salvation, established in December 1981, was dissolved upon final termination of martial law in July 1983, although General Jaruzelski, withdrawing as defense minister, was named chairman of a superordinate National Defense Committee the following November. There is a Constitutional Tribunal, whose members are appointed by the *Sejm,* while the regular judiciary has three tiers: regional courts, provincial courts, and a Supreme Court. Judges of the Supreme Court are elected for five-year terms by the Council of State; the lower courts include a magistrate and two lay judges, although three professional judges sit for cases appealed to the provincial level.

As a result of constitutional and administrative reforms in 1975, the number of provinces (voivodships, or *wojewódstwo*) was increased from 22 to 49. Subdivisions include cities and towns, districts, and communes. People's councils elected for four-year terms constitute "local organs of state authority", while "local organs of State administration" include governors (*wojewodowie*) and mayors (*majorowie*).

Foreign relations. Postwar Polish foreign policy, based primarily on a close alliance with the Soviet Union, has entailed the continued stationing of Soviet troops in Poland as well as Polish participation in the Warsaw Pact and the Council for Mutual Economic Assistance (CMEA). The events of the second half of 1980 elicited harsh criticism from the Soviet Union, Czechoslovakia, and East Germany while prompting expressions of concern in the West that the Warsaw Pact might intervene militarily, as it had in Hungary in 1956 and again in Czechoslovakia in 1968. At an unannounced meeting of Pact leaders at Moscow, USSR, on December 5, First Secretary Kania, according to unconfirmed reports, was able to dissuade the more hard-line members from calling for intervention. At the time, some 500,000 troops were positioned within striking distance of the Polish border, while Warsaw Pact maneuvers in the area during March and April 1981 were widely interpreted as intended to bring pressure on both the unions and the PZPR to end clashes between police and farmers demonstrating on behalf of Rural Solidarity. Predictably, the Soviet Union and most Eastern-bloc countries endorsed the Polish government's actions of the following December, Soviet President Brezhnev declaring in the course of a March 1982 state visit to Moscow by General Jaruzelski that they were "timely measures" without which "the stability of Europe and even of the world at large would have been at risk". For its part, the United States immediately suspended food shipments to Poland and subsequently imposed a variety of economic and other sanctions against both Poland and the USSR, charging the latter with "a heavy and direct responsibility for . . . the suppression that has ensued". These measures were largely terminated with the lifting of martial law in mid-1983, and Washington withdrew its opposition to Polish membership in the International Monetary Fund at the end of 1984, facilitating the country's admission to the Specialized Agency and its sister institution, the World Bank, in June 1986.

Current issues. In July 1986 the *Sejm* approved a bill on "Special Procedure towards Perpetrators of Some Offenses", under which, by late September, numerous dissident leaders had been released from prison, with the Solidarity leadership terming the move "a spark of hope in Polish society". As an apparent *quid pro quo,* it was announced that underground activity would cease and that Lech Wałęsa, while remaining titular Solidarity chairman, would not join a new Temporary Council of Solidarity, which, viewed by some as successor to the movement's theretofore clandestine Provisional Coordinating Committee — TKK (see under Political Parties, below), was promptly branded by the government as illegal.

During 1987 Wałęsa and other dissident leaders criticized the government with relative impunity and were instrumental in generating a widespread boycott of the November 29 referendum on economic and political reform. While the Jaruzelski regime (partly in response to external pressure) appeared genuinely committed to liberalization, including the development of a market economy with an expanded role for private enterprise, a further cut in the Polish standard of living was advanced as a necessary first step. Thus, the immediate consequences would have been a freeze on wages and price increases of up to 100 percent for essential goods. In the wake of effective rejection of the program (acceptance by a majority of eligible voters being required under Polish law), the government announced that the price hikes would be phased in over a two-year period, starting with a 40 percent rise in basic food prices in late December. Collaterally, a major cabinet shakeup was announced, with nine ministries dealing with industrial matters being combined into one. In addition, "newer forms of government" were proposed, including the creation of a second legislative chamber, the legalization of opposition "clubs", and the introduction of competitive elections at the local level.

Earlier, efforts to normalize relations with the Vatican were set back by the unexpectedly uncompromising posture of John Paul II during a papal visit in June. In addition to meeting with Wałęsa, the pope appealed for an enhanced respect for human rights by Polish authorities and the restoration of an "independent and self-governing trade union".

POLITICAL PARTIES AND GROUPS

Prior to 1983, Poland's dominant Communist party, officially known since 1948 as the Polish United Workers' Party, exercised its authority through a Front of National Unity (*Front Jedności Narodnu*—FJN), which also included two nominally noncommunist groups, the United Peasants' Party and the Democratic Party, in addition to various trade-union, Catholic, women's, youth, and other mass organizations. Legislative elections were organized by the FJN on the basis of a single list which, although designed to perpetuate Communist control, offered a carefully circumscribed choice between party and independent candidates.

In 1983, the Front was superseded by the **Patriotic Movement for National Rebirth** (*Patriotyczny Ruch Odrodzenia Narodowego*—PRON), which was described in a July constitutional amendment as "a platform of joint activity by the political parties, social organizations and associations, and citizens, regardless of their outlook, on matters concerning the functioning of the socialist state. . ." In recognition of the "pluralist" nature of Polish society, only 30 percent of the seats on PRON's National Council are reserved for Communists, with 10 percent each for the United Peasants' and Democratic parties, and 50 percent for individuals of no party affiliation. However, the general secretary of PRON is Marian ORZECHOWSKI, a hard-line member of the PZPR Politburo.

A number of dissident organizations came into existence in the latter 1970s, the principal associations being listed below, under Former Dissident Groups. Although the free trade unions formed after August 1980 often explicitly disavowed any political intent, their implicitly political nature was clear both within and outside Poland. While all such organizations are now officially banned, a new, youth-oriented **Freedom and Peace** movement emerged in March 1985 to defend a student who rejected military service. Currently led by Jarasław NAKIELSKI and Jacek CZAPUTOWICZ, the formation claims to have 100 activists and 10,000 supporters for a program that couples pacifism with environmental concerns. More recently, a **Polish Socialist Party** was organized at Warsaw in November 1987 and immediately subjected to police harassment, a government spokesman warning that the organization was superfluous because of the absorption of the traditional party of the same name into the PZPR (below).

Government Parties:

Polish United Workers' Party (*Polska Zjednoczona Partia Robotnicza*—PZPR). Formed in 1948 by merger of the (Communist) Polish Workers' Party (*Polska Partia Robotnicza*—PPR) and the Polish Socialist Party (*Polska Partia Socjalistyczna*—PPS), the PZPR claimed approximately 3 million members prior to the events of 1980–1981, as a result of which enrollment declined by nearly 800,000. At the Tenth Party Congress, held June 29-July 3, 1986, at Warsaw, 1,776 delegates elected a 230-member Central Committee and a 130-member Central Control and Auditing Commission, with the former designating a Politburo of 15 full and 5 candidate members in addition to an 11-member Secretariat.

The PZPR has held a position of undisputed predominance despite internal rivalries that, in conjunction with the country's economic woes and the leadership's initial inability to contain the free labor movement, contributed to changes in the Politburo membership on five separate occasions in 1980. At the end of the year, only 5 of those who had constituted the Politburo in January remained members: President of the Re-

public Henryk Jabłoński; Deputy Premier Mieczysław Jagielski, who was chiefly responsible for negotiating the August 31 agreement with strikers at Gdańsk; Minister of Defense Gen. Wojciech Jaruzelski; Stanisław Kania, who replaced Edward Gierek as first secretary on September 6; and Stefan Olszowski, who had been dismissed from the Politburo on February 15 but was reinstated on August 24. Equally extensive changes occurred during 1980 in the administrative Secretariat.

At the reformist Ninth Congress, only four incumbent Politburo members (Jaruzelski, Kania, Olszowski, and Kazimierz Barcikowski) were retained; Kania was dropped upon being succeeded as first secretary by Jaruzelski in October 1981, while a number of other changes in late 1982 reflected hard-line sentiment that may have been dampened by the dismissal of Olszowski from both the government and Politburo in 1985. Further extensive changes occurred at the Tenth Congress with only Jaruzelski and Barcikowski remaining from the pre-1981 full Politburo membership. The reformist-oriented Mieczysław Rakowski was named as the Politburo's 16th member in December 1987.

First Secretary: Gen. Wojciech JARUZELSKI.

Other Members of Politburo: Kazimierz BARCIKOWSKI, Gen. Józef BARYŁA, Józef CZYREK, Jan GŁÓWCZYK, Gen. Czesław KISZCZAK, Zbigniew MESSNER, Alfred MIODOWICZ, Włodzimierz MOKRZYSZCAK, Zygmunt MURAŃSKI, Marian ORZECHOWSKI, Tadeusz PORĘBSKI, Mieczysław RAKOWSKI, Gen. Florian SIWICKI, Zofia STĘPIEŃ, Marian WOŹNIAK.

Candidates: Stanisław BEJGER, Bogumił FERENSZTAJN, Janusz KUBASIEWICZ, Zbigniew MICHAŁEK, Gabriela REMBISZ.

Central Committee Secretariat: Gen. Józef BARYŁA, Henryk BENARSKI, Stanisław CIOSEK, Kazimierz CYPRYNIAK, Józef CZYREK, Jan GŁÓWCZYK, Gen. Wojciech JARUZELSKI, Zbigniew MICHAŁEK, Tadeusz PORĘBSKI, Andrzej WASILEWSKI, Marian WOŹNIAK.

United Peasants' Party (*Zjednoczone Stronnictwo Ludowe*—ZSL). Formed in 1949 by a merger of the Peasant Party and the Polish Peasant Party of Stanisław Mikołajczyk, the ZSL claimed a membership of 481,000 in 1984. Its activities are based on the principle of worker-peasant alliance in the construction of socialism under the leadership of the PZPR.

Leader: Roman MALINOWSKI (Chairman of the Supreme Executive of the Party).

Democratic Party (*Stronnictwo Demokratyczne*—SD). Recruiting its members predominantly from among professional and intellectual ranks but including white-collar workers and artisans as well, the non-Marxist SD, founded in 1939, claimed a membership of 106,000 in 1984. An April 1985 party congress featured an unusually public leadership struggle between Tadeusz Młyńczak, who had been chairman of the Central Committee from 1976 to 1981, and his successor, Dr. Edward Kowalczyk, with Młyńczak being returned to his former post by a narrow margin of the almost equally divided 660 convention delegates.

Leader: Tadeusz MŁYŃCZAK (Chairman of the Central Committee).

Catholic Groups:

Although not officially recognized as parties, the following groups are active politically. **Pax,** led by Ryszard REIFF, has consistently backed regime policies (including anti-Zionism) but does not enjoy the support of the Catholic Church; the **Christian Social Association** has sought to follow a middle course between church and state; **Znak,** a liberal group founded in the 1950s, has followed more independent policies and has served the vital function of proposing alternatives to government programs. On November 21, 1980, Znak deputy Jerzy OZDOWSKI was named a deputy premier of the Council of Ministers, a position that he held until being named a deputy marshal of the *Sejm* on July 21, 1982.

Former Dissident Groups:

Committee for Social Self-Defense — "KOR" (*Komitet Samoobrony Społecznej—,,KOR"*—KSS-KOR). Organized as the Committee for the Defense of Workers (*Komitet Obrony Robotników*—KOR) in September 1976 by 14 prominent intellectuals in order to provide legal and financial aid to workers imprisoned during mid-1976 price-hike demonstrations, the Committee laid much of the original groundwork for the eventual emergence of Solidarity (below). It was renamed in September 1977 but continued to be known primarily by its original acronym. The group was formally disbanded on September 28, 1981, during the Solidarity National Congress to dispell government charges that it was operating as a counter-revolutionary enclave within the labor movement. However, as late as January 1986, police conducted a raid on the apartment of Jacek KURON, a prominent KOR leader, to break up a meeting held in conjunction with the World Congress of Individuals for Peace at Warsaw.

Movement for the Defense of Human and Civil Rights (*Ruch Obrony Praw Człowieka i Obywatela* — ROPCO). Formed in March 1977 initially to monitor compliance with the 1975 Helsinki accords, ROPCO represented no clearly defined ideology, though it tended to be more conservative and nationalistic than KOR.

Confederation of Independent Poland (*Konfederacja Polski Niezależnej* — KPN). The KPN, whose membership included a number of former ROPCO nationalists, was formed on September 1, 1979, with much the same purpose as the semiclandestine patriotic Polish Agreement on Independence (*Polskie Porozumienie Niepodległościowe* — PPN), established in 1977: to promote "freedom and independence" for Poland. Viewing itself as an unofficial political party, the KPN intended to contest the March 23, 1980, *Sejm* election, but its leaders were arrested and a February 27 meeting with the Western press was banned. On December 17 the Confederation announced that it was suspending its activities because of the country's crisis situation.

In September 1986, the KPN's former leader, Leszek MOCZULSKI, and four of his associates were released from prison under the "Special Procedure" bill enacted two months earlier.

Former Free Labor Movement:

Independent Self-Governing Trade Union Solidarity (*Niezależny Samorząd Związków Zawodowych ,,Solidarność"* — NSZZ Solidarity). Originating in a conference of independent labor groups held at Gdańsk on September 17–18, 1980, at which time a national coordinating committee chaired by Lech WAŁĘSA was established, Solidarity applied for formal recognition on September 24 and accepted registration on October 24, pending appeal of changes made to its governing statutes by the provincial court at Warsaw. On November 10 the Chamber of Labor and Social Security of the Supreme Court ruled in favor of the union, which during the next 13 months continued to press for implementation by the government of all provisions of the August 31 Gdańsk Agreement.

In structure, Solidarity was a confederation of groups from throughout Poland, with a National Coordinating Committee acting as an executive. In mid-1981 its membership was estimated at 10 million workers, or some 50 percent of the Polish labor force. It was officially banned upon the imposition of martial law in December 1981, although an underground "Provisional Coordinating Committee" (*Tymczasowy Koordynacjd Komitet* — TKK) continued to call for demonstrations in support of the restoration of independent trade union rights, issuing sporadic appeals for demonstrations on other issues. While TKK members, particularly Wałęsa, remained as a visible opposition force, by 1985 two-thirds of the union's former members had reportedly joined affiliates of the government-sponsored National Trade Union Accord, which was awarded funds impounded by the government from the *Solidarność* treasury in 1981.

Former TKK leader, Zbigniew BUJAK, who had been arrested in May 1986 after having been in hiding for five years, was among the group of dissidents released in mid-September. Subsequently, Wałęsa announced that the TKK would be disbanded to "ease the transition to legal and open undertakings". The Solidarity movement nonetheless continued to maintain a public presence. In December, at Wałęsa's urging, it sponsored the formation of an Intervention and Legality Commission, headed by Zbigniew ROMASZEWSKI, to monitor legal abuses by the Jaruzelski regime and help victims of injustice in 11 Polish cities.

Solidarity's visibility was further enhanced in 1987. Pope John Paul II, during his visit to Poland in June, termed the outlawed movement a model for the worldwide struggle for human rights and met privately with its leader. In November Wałęsa announced that the group had formed a National Executive Commission, which campaigned vigorously against the government's referendum proposals. In mid-December Wałęsa warned of the "danger of a popular explosion", while denying that there were any links between the union and a radical clandestine group, **Fighting Solidarity**, whose long-fugitive leader, Kornel MORAWIECKI, had recently been apprehended in the southwestern industrial city of Wrokław.

LEGISLATURE

The **National Assembly** (*Sejm*) is a unicameral body of

460 members chosen by universal direct suffrage for five-year terms. Under a new procedure approved in May 1985, 50 seats are reserved for a single "national list" of candidates presented by the Patriotic Movement; each of the remaining 410 are contested by two candidates put forward by electoral councils in 74 districts and approved by the PRON. At the most recent election of October 13, 1985, 53 percent of the nominations in the double-candidate constituencies were allocated to the Polish United Workers' Party; the remainder were divided equally between the Democratic and United Peasants' parties, save for 16 nominees who were formally unaffiliated. Significantly, because of strained relations with the ecclesiastical hierarchy, the present Assembly is the first in decades to lack formal representation by the Catholic Church.

Marshal: Roman MALINOWSKI.

CABINET

Chairman, Council of Ministers	Zbigniew Messner
Deputy Chairmen	Josef Kozioł
	Zdzisław Sadowski
	Zbigniew Szałajda
Ministers	
Agriculture, Forestry and Food Industries	Stanisław Zięba
Culture and Art	Aleksander Krawczuk
Environmental Protection and Natural Resources	Waldemar Michna
Finance	Bazyli Samojlik
Foreign Affairs	Marian Orzechowski
Foreign Economic Cooperation	Władysław Gwiazda
Health and Social Welfare	Janusz Komender
Industry	Jerzy Bilip
Internal Affairs	Gen. Czesław Kiszczak
Internal Trade and Services	Jerzy Jóźwiak
Justice	Lech Domeracki
Labor, Wages and Social Affairs	Ireneusz Sekula
Land Management and Construction Industry	Bogumił Ferensztajn
National Defense	Gen. Florian Siwicki
National Education	Henryk Bednarski
Office for Advancement and Application of Science and Technology	Konrad Tott
Office of Council of Ministers	Gen. Michał Janiszewski
Office of Religious Affairs	Władysław Loranc
Transport, Shipping and Communications	Janusz Kamiński
Youth Physical Culture Committee	Aleksander Kwaśniewski
Chairman, Planning Commission	Zdzisław Sadowski
President, Polish National Bank	Władysław Baka

NEWS MEDIA

Although (then) First Secretary Gierek stated in December 1977 that the Polish press is free, "the only limits being the expression of ideas contrary to Poland's unity or offensive to the Church", news media — with the notable exception of the underground press — continued under government control. For the most part, the government made little effort to halt publication of "uncensored" (*samizdat*) publications, many of which were openly distributed prior to the imposition of martial law in late 1981, when strict censorship was imposed. In July 1987 a "totally independent" monthly, *Res Publica,* commenced legal publication under a policy of "national reconciliation" proclaimed by General Jaruzelski in late 1986; however, the editor, a self-proclaimed pro-Russian conservative, was immediately branded by the clandestine press as an "opportunist" in search of personal publicity.

Press. The following are Polish-language dailies published at Warsaw, unless otherwise noted: *Trybuna Ludu* (700,000 daily, 860,000 weekend), PZPR Central Committee organ; *Trybuna Robotnicza* (Katowice, 600,000 daily, 850,000 weekend), PZPR regional organ; *Express Wieczorny* (491,000), independent; *Gromada-Rolnik Polski* (486,000), agricultural triweekly; *Polityka* (360,000), independent weekly; *Życie Warszawy* (357,600), independent; *Sztandar Młodych* (250,000 daily, 500,000 weekend), Socialist Youth Union (ZMS) organ; *Dziennik Ludowy* (171,000 daily, 450,000 weekend), ZSL organ; *Kurier Polski* (170,000), SD organ; *Zielony Sztandar* (150,000), twice weekly ZSL organ; *Słowo Powszechne* (86,000), Pax organ; *Nowe Drogi* (52,000), PZPR theoretical monthly; *Życie Literackie* (Kraków, 50,000), independent literary weekly; *Tygodnik Demokatyczny* (49,000), weekly SD organ. Several papers are also published in the languages of the national minorities (Byelorussian, German, Jewish, Russian, Ukrainian).

News agencies. The Polish Press Agency (*Polska Agencja Prasowa* — PAP), with offices in numerous Polish and foreign cities, transmits information abroad in five languages. Polish Agency Interpress (*Polska Agencja Interpress* — PAI), established to assist the PAP, issues foreign-language bulletins and aids foreign journalists. Central Press-Photo Agency (*Centralna Agencja Fotograficzna* — CAF) provides photographic services for press institutions. Numerous foreign agencies maintain bureaus at Warsaw.

Radio and television. Broadcasting operates under the supervision of Polish Radio and Television (*Polskie Radio i Telewizja*), which is responsible to the Committee for Radio and Television Affairs of the Council of Ministers. There were approximately 9.5 million radio and 9.7 million television receivers in 1987.

INTERGOVERNMENTAL REPRESENTATION

Ambassador to the US: Jan KINAST.

US Ambassador to Poland: John R. DAVIS, Jr.

Permanent Representative to the UN: Dr. Eugeniusz NOWORYTA.

IGO Memberships (Non-UN): BIS, CCC, CMEA, IBEC, ICES, IIB, ILZ, Inmarsat, PCA, WTO.

PORTUGAL

Portuguese Republic
República Portuguesa

Political Status: Independent republic proclaimed October 5, 1910; corporative constitution of March 19, 1933, suspended following military coup of April 25, 1974; present constitution promulgated April 2, 1976, with effect from April 25.

Area: 35,553 sq. mi. (92,082 sq. km.).

Population: 9,833,014 (1981C), 10,364,000 (1988E). Area and population figures include mainland Portugal plus the Azores and the Madeira Islands.

Major Urban Centers (1981C): LISBON (807,937); Porto (Oporto, 327,368).

Official Language: Portuguese.

Monetary Unit: Escudo (market rate March 1, 1988, 138.26 escudos = $1US).

President: Dr. Mário Alberto Nobre Lopes SOARES (Portuguese Socialist Party); sworn in for a five-year term on March 9, 1986, succeeding Gen. António dos Santos Ramalho EANES (nonparty), after two-stage election of January 26 and February 16.

Prime Minister: Aníbal Cavaço SILVA (Social Democratic Party); sworn in November 6, 1985, succeeding Dr. Mário Alberto Nobre Lopes SOARES (Portuguese Socialist Party); moved into caretaker status on April 28, 1987, following loss of censure motion on April 3; reinvested on August 17, 1987, following election of July 19.

THE COUNTRY

Known in antiquity as Lusitania, Portugal overlooks the Atlantic along the western face of the Iberian Peninsula, while including politically the Azores and Madeira island groups in the Atlantic. Mainland Portugal is divided by the Tagus River into a mountainous northern section and a southern section of rolling plains whose geography and climate are akin to those of northern Africa. The population, a blend of Iberian, Latin, Teutonic, and Moorish elements, is ethnically and culturally homogeneous and almost wholly affiliated with the Roman Catholic Church, which has traditionally exercised a commanding social and political influence. Portuguese, the official language, is spoken by virtually all of the population. Women comprise 40 percent of the official labor force, concentrated in agriculture and domestic service; female representation in government and politics — despite the participation of a few prominent women, including former prime minister Maria de Lourdes Pintasilgo — averages less than 10 percent.

The economy, one of the least modernized in Europe, retains a somewhat paternalistic structure characterized by limited social services and per capita income of less than $3,000. Although agriculture, forestry, and fishing engage about 24 percent of the population, they contribute only 13 percent of the gross national product, with half of the country's food needs dependent on imports. Industry, consisting primarily of small manufacturing firms, employs some 37 percent of the labor force and contributes nearly half of the GNP. Exports include textiles, clothing, and electrical machinery as well as such traditional goods as fish products, cork, and olive oil, of which Portugal is one of the world's largest producers. Unemployment, a problem since 1974 because of the influx of more than one million persons from former Portuguese colonies, has abated somewhat since entry into the European Communities on January 1, 1986.

GOVERNMENT AND POLITICS

Political background. As one of the great European monarchies of late medieval and early modern times, Portugal initiated the age of discovery and colonization and acquired a far-flung colonial empire that was one of the last to be abandoned. Interrupted by a period of Spanish rule from 1580 to 1640, the Portuguese monarchy endured until 1910, when a bloodless revolution initiated a republican era marked by chronic instability and recurrent violence. A military revolt in 1926 prepared the way for the presidency of Marshal António CARMONA (1926–1951) and the assumption of governmental authority by António de Oliveira SALAZAR, an economics professor who became finance minister in 1928 and served as prime minister from 1932 until his replacement because of illness in 1968. Salazar, mistrustful of democratic and socialist ideologies and influenced by Italian Fascism, established economic and political stability and in 1933 introduced a "corporative" constitution designed to serve as the basis of a new Portuguese State (*Estado Novo*). With the support of the Church, army, and his National Union, the only authorized political movement, Salazar completely dominated Portuguese political life and reduced the presidency to an auxiliary institution.

The later years of Salazar's regime were marked by rising, though largely ineffectual, domestic discontent and growing restiveness in the Overseas Territories. Elections were frequently boycotted by the opposition, and direct presidential elections were eliminated following a vigorous but unsuccessful opposition campaign by Gen. Humberto DELGADO in 1958. Overseas, the provinces of Goa, Damão, and Diu were seized by India in 1961; in the same year, a revolt broke out in Angola, while independence movements became active in Portuguese Guinea in 1962 and in Mozambique in 1964. The attempt to suppress the insurrections resulted in severe economic strain as well as increasing political isolation and repeated condemnation by the United Nations.

The crisis created by Salazar's nearly fatal illness in September 1968 was alleviated by the selection of Marcello CAETANO, a close associate, as the new prime minister. Although he permitted a measure of cautious liberalization, including some relaxation of secret police activity and the return from exile of a prominent opposition leader, Dr. Mário SOARES, Caetano preserved the main outlines of Salazar's policy both in metropolitan Portugal and overseas.

Prior to the parliamentary election of October 26, 1969, opposition parties were legalized, but were again outlawed after a campaign in which the official National Union won all 130 seats in the National Assembly. On December 2, 1970, the government announced a program of constitutional reform that would grant autonomy to the Overseas Territories within the framework of the Republic. The effort was nullified after Caetano failed to secure the cooperation of the country's liberal and democratic forces, and the regime returned to the rightist posture that had characterized the Salazar era. The atmosphere of repression eased again, however, after the adoption in 1971 of constitutional legislation expanding the power of the enlarged National Assembly, granting limited autonomy to the Overseas Territories, abolishing press censorship, and permitting religious freedom. Subsequently, on July 25, 1972, Rear Adm. Américo Deus Rodrigues THOMÁZ was elected to his third consecutive seven-year term as Portu-

gal's president. In the legislative election of October 28, 1973, the government party, *Acção Nacional Popular* (formerly the National Union), won all 150 seats, including 34 representing the Overseas Territories.

In a bloodless coup on April 24, 1974, a group of military officers calling themselves the Armed Forces Movement (*Movimento das Forças Armadas*—MFA) seized power, ending more than 40 years of civilian dictatorship. The president and prime minister were arrested and flown to Brazil, where they were granted political asylum. The leader of the "Junta of National Salvation", Gen. António Sebastião Ribeiro de SPÍNOLA, assumed the presidency, and on May 15 a center-left cabinet was sworn in with Adelino de Palma CARLOS as prime minister. After a dispute with the reconstituted Council of State as to the extent of his powers, Carlos resigned on July 9 and was replaced by Gen. Vasco dos Santos GONÇALVES, whose administration recognized the right of the Overseas Territories to "self-determination" with all its consequences, including independence. On September 30, General Spínola also resigned, leaving power in the hands of leftist military officers and civilians. The new president, Gen. Francisco da Costa GOMES, subsequently reappointed General Gonçalves as prime minister.

In May 1974 Costa Gomes had visited Angola, declaring upon his return that the new government was prepared to offer a ceasefire in Angola, Mozambique, and Portuguese Guinea, with the guerrilla organizations being permitted to organize political parties and to participate in democratic elections. As a result of the initiative, negotiations were undertaken that led to the independence of Guinea-Bissau (formerly Portuguese Guinea) in September 1974, while discussions with insurgent leaders in Mozambique and Sao Tome and Principe resulted in independence for both territories, as well as for the Cape Verde Islands, the following year. Although negotiations with Angolan leaders were complicated by the presence of a sizable White minority and by the existence of three major insurgent groups, the formation of a united front by the insurgents opened the way for independence. The front subsequently collapsed, but Portugal withdrew from Angola on the agreed date of November 11, 1975.

On March 11, 1975, right-wing military elements, reportedly acting at the instigation of former president Spínola, had attempted to overthrow the government. Upon failure of the coup, General Spínola flew to Brazil and the Junta of National Salvation was dissolved in favor of a Supreme Revolutionary Council (SRC). The latter, sworn in by President Gomes on March 17, was given full executive and legislative powers for the purpose of "directing and executing the revolutionary program in Portugal". Although officers constituted one-third of the cabinet announced on March 25, representatives of the Communist, Socialist, and Popular Democratic parties, as well as of the Portuguese Democratic Movement, were included.

At the election for a Constituent Assembly on April 25, the Socialists received 38 percent of the total vote, compared to 26 percent for the Popular Democrats and less than 13 percent for the Communists. The first session of the Assembly was convened on June 2, with the Socialists holding 116 of the 250 seats. Despite their commanding legislative strength, the Socialists and Popular Democrats subsequently announced their intention to resign from the government, in part because of a Communist takeover of the Socialist newspaper *República,* and on July 31 a new, essentially nonparty cabinet was formed. However, increasing opposition to Communist influence led, on August 29, to the resignation of Prime Minister Gonçalves and the appointment of Adm. José Baptista Pinheiro de AZEVEDO as head of a new cabinet (the sixth since the 1974 coup) comprising representatives of the three leading parties, as well as of the Armed Forces Movement.

In mid-November the Communist-led labor unions mounted a general strike at Lisbon, demanding the resignation of the Azevedo government and the formation of an exclusively left-wing "revolutionary government". The strike was followed on November 26 by an uprising of leftist military units which was crushed by loyalist troops responding to government pressure to restore law and order. Although the SRC had previously rebuked Azevedo for his conduct during the strike, failure of the coup was seen as a major defeat for the Communists, and in mid-December, following designation of a new army chief of staff, the Council ordered a major reorganization of the armed forces, emphasizing military discipline and the exclusion of the military from party politics.

The new constitution came into effect April 25, 1976, and an election to the 263-member Assembly of the Republic was held the same day. The Socialists remained the largest party but again failed to win an absolute majority. On June 27, Gen. António dos Santos Ramalho EANES, a nonparty candidate supported by the Socialists, Popular Democrats, and Social Democrats, was elected to a five-year term as president. The election was a major defeat for the Communists, whose candidate, Octavio PATO, finished third, behind far-left candidate Maj. Otelo Saraiva de CARVALHO. Three weeks later, on July 16, Dr. Mário Soares was invested as prime minister, heading a Socialist minority government that was, however, endorsed by the other two parties in the presidential election coalition.

During 1977 the government faced mounting difficulties caused by a faltering economy and increased party polarization. On December 8, Soares, having lost a crucial Assembly vote on an economic austerity plan needed to qualify for a $750 million loan from the IMF, was forced to resign, though he was subsequently able to form a new government (which took office on January 30, 1978) in coalition with the conservative Social Democratic Center (CDS). On July 27, however, Soares was dismissed by President Eanes after the CDS ministers had resigned over disagreements in agricultural and health policies, leaving the Socialists without a working legislative majority. His successor, Alfredo Nobre da COSTA, was in turn forced to resign on September 14 following legislative rejection of an essentially nonparty program, and a new government, also composed largely of independents, was confirmed on November 22 with Dr. Carlos Alberto da Mota PINTO, a former member of the Social Democratic Party (PSD, the renamed Popular Democratic Party), as prime minister.

With his government facing parliamentary debate on censure motions introduced separately by the Socialists and Communists, and having witnessed Assembly rejection of his proposed budget on three occasions since March, Prime Minister Mota Pinto resigned on June 6, 1979, moving to caretaker status during efforts by President Eanes to find a successor. On July 13, however, Eanes called for a new election over the objection of Socialist leader Soares, who had hoped to form a new government consisting of his party and a group of dissident Social Democratic deputies who had left the PSD in April. Six days later, Maria de Lourdes PINTASILGO, a member of several previous post-1974 governments, was named to head a caretaker, nonparty government that was sworn in on August 1. The Assembly was dissolved on September 11.

The election of December 2 confirmed Portugal's move toward the extremes of the political spectrum. Francisco SÁ CARNEIRO, a conservative Social Democrat who in July had formed a Democratic Alliance (AD) with the Center Democrats, Monarchists, and disaffected Socialists, led his electoral coalition to a clear majority (128 out of 250 seats) in the Assembly. The Socialist Party, on the other hand, lost 33 of the 107 seats it had captured in 1976, while the Communist Party (formally allied with the small Portuguese Democratic Movement) captured 47 seats, 7 more than in 1976. As a result of the election returns, and with Prime Minister Pintasilgo having resigned on December 28, Sá Carneiro was named on December 29 to organize a new government—the twelfth since 1974—that was sworn in on January 3, 1980.

The Alliance was returned to office with an increased majority at the second legislative election within a year on October 5, 1980. However, Prime Minister Sá Carneiro was killed in a plane crash on December 4, his position being assumed, on an acting basis, by Deputy Prime Minister Diogo Freitas do AMARAL. On December 13, Dr. Francisco Pinto BALSEMÃO was elected PSD leader and, upon being named prime minister designate on December 22, proceeded to organize a new AD cabinet that was sworn in on January 5, 1981.

Balsemão submitted his resignation on August 10 because of what he termed "systematic opposition" to Alliance policies within his own Social Democratic ranks. The resignation was withdrawn ten days later, following extensive intraparty discussions, and a new Balsemão government was approved on September 1. He resigned again on December 19, 1982, but the AD subsequently proved unable to nominate a new government acceptable to a majority of the Council of State.

At a general election on April 25, 1983, the Socialists obtained a substantial plurality of 101 legislative seats and Dr. Soares succeeded in organizing a cabinet of 9 Socialists, 7 Social Democrats, and 1 independent that assumed office on June 9. However, severe economic difficulties eroded the popularity of the Socialists, while the coalition partners disagreed on the extent of proposed austerity measures. On June 4, 1985, PSD parliamentary leader Anibal Cavaço SILVA announced his party's withdrawal from the government, although agreeing to a postponement until the signature of Portugal's entry into the European Communities on June 12. Two days later, Soares was named to head a caretaker administration pending a new election, while declaring himself a candidate for the January 1986 presidential poll.

The October 6 legislative balloting dealt a serious blow to the PSP, which had its representation cut nearly in half, obtaining only 57 Assembly seats. The largest vote share, 30 percent, went to the PSD, and Cavaço Silva formed a minority government based on his party's 88-seat plurality on November 6. The PSD's preferred presidential candidate, the Christian Democratic Diogo Freitas do Amaral, captured nearly half the vote in the initial presidential balloting on January 23, out of a field of 4 candidates; however, an unusual coalition of the PSP, the *Eanismo* PRD, and the Communist-led United People's Alliance (APU) succeeded in electing Soares, the remaining center-left candidate, with 51 percent of the vote in the February 16 runoff. Soares, the first civilian head of state in 60 years, was sworn in as Eanes' successor on March 9, promising to "be the president of all the Portuguese, not only those who elected me".

President Soares dissolved the Assembly on April 28, 1987, following the April 3 defeat of the Cavaço Silva government on a censure motion that had charged the administration with mismanagement of the economy. At the ensuing poll of July 19, the Social Democrats became the first party in 13 years to win an absolute majority of legislative seats, permitting the incumbent prime minister to return to office on August 17 as head of an all-PSD government. Declaring in the wake of his triumph that "the era of state paternalism will soon be over", Cavaço Silva advanced a new program emphasizing the role of free enterprise as an engine of economic growth (see Current issues, below).

Constitution and government. The constitution of April 25, 1976, stemmed from a constitutional agreement concluded two months earlier by Costa Gomes in his capacity as chief of state and president of the SRC (subsequently called the Council of the Revolution) and representatives of the leading parties. Under the pact (which superseded an earlier agreement of April 1975), the Council, while formally designated as the most important government organ after the presidency, became, in large part, a consultative body with powers of absolute veto only in regard to defense and military policy. The third most important organ, the Assembly of the Republic, was empowered to override the Council (on nonmilitary matters) and the president by a two-thirds majority.

A series of constitutional reforms that came into effect in October 1982 abolished the Council of the Revolution and distributed its powers among a Supreme Council of National Defense, a 13-member Constitutional Tribunal, and an advisory Council of State of 16 members (plus national presidents elected since adoption of the existing basic law): 5 named by the president, 5 named by the Assembly, and 6 ex officio (the prime minister, the national ombudsman, and the presidents of the Assembly, the Supreme Court, and the regional governments of the Azores and Madeira).

The president, elected for a five-year term, serves both as military chief of staff and as chairman of the Council of State, and appoints the prime minister, who is responsible to both the head of state and the Assembly. Portugal's judicial system, based on European civil law and heavily influenced by the French model, includes, in addition to the Constitutional Tribunal, a Supreme Court, courts of appeal, and district courts as well as military courts and a Court of Audit.

Administratively, metropolitan Portugal is divided into 18 districts, each headed by a governor appointed by the minister of the interior.

Foreign relations. Allied with England since 1385, Portugal declared itself neutral in World War II but has retained a Western orientation. It participates in NATO, the OECD, and the European Free Trade Association as well as the United Nations and most of its Specialized Agencies. It became a member of the Council of Europe in September 1976 and, after years of negotiation, joined Spain in gaining admission to the European Communities on January 1, 1986.

The country's foreign policy efforts prior to the 1974 coup were directed primarily to retention of its Overseas Territories at a time when other European powers had largely divested themselves of colonial possessions. Insistence on maintaining Portuguese sovereignty and combating nationalist movements in Portuguese Africa yielded mounting antagonism on the part of African, Asian, and Communist states; isolation in the United Nations and other international organizations; and occasionally strained relations with allied governments. These problems ceased with the independence of Guinea-Bissau (formerly Portuguese Guinea) in 1974 and of Angola, the Cape Verde Islands, Mozambique, and Sao Tome and Principe in 1975.

In late 1975 a dispute arose with Indonesia regarding the status of Portuguese Timor, the country's only remaining Asian possession except for Macao (for which, see Related Territories, below). On December 8, Indonesian Foreign Minister Malik announced that pro-Indonesian parties in the Portuguese (eastern) sector of the island had set up a provisional government and that Indonesian military units had occupied Dili, the capital. Portugal promptly severed diplomatic relations with Indonesia, which had also announced the annexation of Ocussi Ambeno, a small Portuguese enclave on the northern coast of West Timor. On July 17, 1976, Jakarta proclaimed the formal incorporation of the remainder of Timor into Indonesia. Lisbon's continued objection to Indonesian rule of the territory was manifested most recently in the recall of its ambassador to Australia in August 1985, after Australian Prime Minister Hawke had endorsed his predecessor's acceptance of the takeover.

Promoting its accession to the European Communities as of indirect benefit to its former colonies, Lisbon increased its economic linkages with other lusophone states in 1986, including an agreement with Brazil to establish joint commercial and industrial ventures. Domestically, the impact of EC membership is being eased by a ten-year "transitional period" during which tariffs and marketing subsidies are gradually being reduced.

Current issues. Prime Minister Cavaço Silva's success, following the July 1987 legislative balloting, in forming the first single-party majority government since the 1974 revolution was welcomed by most Portuguese as offering hope for a period of political stability that would permit a long-stagnant economy to move toward a degree of parity with those of its EC partners. The course had already been charted by the Socialists under Mario Soares who, prior to assuming the presidency in early 1986, had curtailed Communist influence while launching a number of liberalization measures. The long-term political prospect was for the emergence of an effective two-party system dominated by the Socialists and Social Democrats, both of whose platforms called for a free-market orientation and continued participation in NATO.

An eight-year economic plan advanced by Cavaço Silva prior to the election called for cuts in government spending and an emphasis on high-yielded private-sector projects controlled by domestic enterprise. Upon returning to office in August, the prime minister moved to privatize state-owned firms not of "particular importance to the public service" and to reverse a number of post-1974 measures aimed at agricultural collectivization.

POLITICAL PARTIES

Government Party:

Social Democratic Party (*Partido Social Democrata* — PSD). The PSD was founded in 1974 as the Popular Democratic Party (*Partido Popular Democrático* — PPD), under which name it won 26 percent of the vote for the Constituent Assembly on April 25, 1975, and 24 percent in the Assembly of the Republic election a year later. Although it initially advocated a number of left-of-center policies, including the nationalization of key sectors of the economy, a number of leftists withdrew in 1976 and the remainder of the party moved noticeably to the right.

An April 1979 disagreement over leadership opposition to the Socialist government's proposed budget led to a walkout of 40 PSD deputies prior to a final Assembly vote. Shortly thereafter, 37 of the 73 PSD deputies, including former party president Antônio Sousa Franco, withdrew and announced that they would sit in the Assembly as the Social Democrats Independent Action (below). The party's losses were more than recouped at the December 2 election, however, when the PSD-led Alliance won a 3-seat majority, party president Francisco Sá Carneiro being named prime minister on December 29. Dr. Francisco Pinto Balsemão was designated party leader on December 13, 1980, following Sá Carneiro's death on December 4, and became prime minister on January 5, 1981. In early 1983 Balsemão announced that he would not stand for another term as party leader, and, following the formal designation of a three-member leadership at a party congress in late February, was effectively succeeded by Carlos Mota Pinto. The party was runner-up to the PSP at the April 25 election, winning 75 Assembly seats. In June 1985 Anibal Cavaço Silva, who had succeeded Pinto as PSD leader the month before, led a withdrawal from the ruling coalition and formed a minority government on November 6 after the party had gained a slim plurality at legislative balloting on October 6. Defeated in a censure vote on April 3, 1987, the PSD became the first party since 1974 to win an absolute majority of seats at the ensuing legislative poll of July 19.

Leaders: Anibal Cavaço SILVA (Prime Minister and President of the Party), António Maria PEREIRA (Secretary General).

Other Parties:

Portuguese Socialist Party (*Partido Socialista Portuguesa* — PSP). Organized in 1973 as heir to the former Portuguese Socialist Action (*Acção Socialista Portuguesa* — ASP), the PSP won an overwhelming plurality (38 percent) of the vote in the election of April 1975, and 35 percent a year later, remaining in power under Dr. Mario Alberto Soares until July 1978. At the December 1979 balloting, the PSP lost 33 of the 107 Assembly seats it had won in 1976. Its representation returned to a plurality of 101 in 1983, with Dr. Soares being redesignated prime minister on June 9 and continuing in office until forced into caretaker status by withdrawal of the PSD from the government coalition on July 13, 1985. The party won only 57 seats at the election of October 6, although Soares succeeded in winning the state presidency in February 1986, at which time he resigned as PSP secretary general. At the June party congress Dr. Vítor Constâncio, an economist and former governor of the Bank of Portugal, was elected

secretary general over Jaime Gama, a Soares protégé. Delegates also approved wide ranging changes aimed at democratizing the party's structure and deleted all references to Marxism in its Declaration of Principles, committing the organization to an "open economy where private, public and social institutions can coexist". Despite the changes, the party's legislative strength gained only marginally (from 57 to 60 seats) at the balloting of July 16, 1987.

Leaders: Dr. Mário Alberto Nobre Lopes SOARES (President of the Republic), Manuel Tito de MORAIS (President of the Party), Dr. Vítor Manuel Ribeiro CONSTÂNCIO (Secretary General).

Democratic Renewal Party (*Partido Renovador Democrático* — PRD). Formed in February 1985 by supporters of President Eanes, the PRD advocates the establishment of an executive presidency on the French model and an ideology marginally to the left of the PSP. In the October 1985 legislative election, the PRD drew substantial numbers of dissident PSP voters, becoming the third-largest party in the Assembly with 45 seats. In the absence of constitutional change allowing Eanes to succeed himself, the self-described *eanismo* party endorsed former PSP finance minister Francisco Salgado Zenha (who had formally withdrawn from the PSP in November) as its 1986 presidential candidate. When Zenha did not survive the first-round balloting, the party endorsed Eanes' longtime political adversary, Dr. Soares, to prevent a rightist victory by Diogo Freitas do Amaral. Although Eanes returned to the party leadership in October, PRD legislative strength plummeted to 7 seats in the July 1987 balloting. Two months later, Eanes again stepped down in favor of Hermínio Martinho, pending the designation of a permanent successor by a party congress.

Leaders: Hermínio MARTINHO (Acting President), Dr. Manuela EANES, Bernardo LENCASTRE (Secretary General).

Social Democratic Center Party (*Partido do Centro Democrático Social* — CDS). The CDS is a right-of-center, Christian Democratic party. Strongest in the northern part of the country, a number of its members were named to key government posts following the 1979 and 1980 legislative elections, Diego Freitas do Amaral serving as deputy prime minister under Balsemão but resigning the party presidency on December 29, 1982, because of his objection to the naming of Dr. Pereira Crespo as prime minister designate. Following his party's serious losses (8 of 30 Assembly seats) at the October 1985 election, Francisico Lucas Pires resigned the party presidency. In January, with the center-left field split among three candidates, do Amaral won 46 percent of the vote in first-round presidential balloting, but lost to former prime minister Soares in the runoff.

Leaders: Dr. Adriano MOREIRA (President), Dr. Diogo Freitas do AMARAL, Luis de AZEVEDO Coutinho, Francisco António Lucas PIRES.

People's Monarchist Party (*Partido Popular Monárquico* — PPM). A right-of-center party advocating free enterprise and a restoration of the monarchy, the PPM contested the 1976 election without success. On March 16, 1979, PPM member Augusto Ferreira do Amaral resigned as secretary of state for agrarian reform following persistent criticism, primarily from the PCP (below), of his handling of the government land reform program, under which one-third of the farmland collectivized since 1974 was being returned to private owners. PSD leader Sá Carneiro thereupon attacked President Eanes for failing to support Amaral and the agricultural policy, and on July 5 the PPM joined the PSD and CDS in the Democratic Alliance. The party's legislative representation dropped from 6 seats in 1980 to none in 1983. It was equally unsuccessful in 1985 and 1987, obtaining only .41 percent of the vote on the latter occasion.

Leaders: Gonçalo Ribeiro TELLES, Augusto Ferreira do AMARAL.

Unified Democratic Coalition (*Coligação Democrático Unitária* — CDU). Prior to the 1979 election, the Portuguese Communist Party joined with the Popular Democratic Movement (below) in an electoral coalition known as the United People's Alliance (*Aliança Popular Unidad* or, alternatively, *Aliança Povo Unido* — APU). The APU won 47 legislative seats in 1979, 41 in 1980, and 38 in 1985, its constituent formations having campaigned separately in 1983. In the 1986 presidential race, the party formally endorsed the independent Maria de Lourdes Pintasilgo, with some dissidents reportedly supporting the PRD's Salgado Zenha; following the elimination of both from the runoff, a special Communist Party congress on February 2, 1986, urged Alliance supporters to "hold their nose, ignore the photograph" and vote for Soares.

Apparently disturbed by allegations that it was merely a PCP front, the MDP withdrew from the Alliance in November 1986. The APA was thereupon dissolved in favor of the CDU, which embraced the PCP; a group of MDP dissidents calling themselves the **Democratic Intervention** (*Intervenção Democrático* – ID); an environmentalist formation, **The Greens** (*Os Verdes*); and a number of independent leftists. The new group obtained 31 Assembly seats in 1987, 7 less than the APU in 1985.

Portuguese Communist Party (*Partido Comunista Português* – PCP). The most Stalinist of the West European Communist parties, the PCP was the dominant force within both the military and the government in the year following the 1974 coup. Its influence waned during the latter half of 1975, particularly following the abortive rebellion of November 26, and its legislative strength dropped to fourth place in April 1976, prior to organization of the APU.

Leader: Dr. Álvaro CUNHAL (Secretary General).

Popular Democratic Movement (*Movimento Democrático Popular* – MDP). Organized in 1969 and also known as the Democratic Electoral Committee (*Comissão Democrático Eleitoral* – CDE), the MDP was long linked to the PCP, with which it cooperated in events leading up to the 1974 coup. It obtained 4 percent of the vote in April 1975 but, in an unsuccessful effort to augment the appeal of its ally, did not participate in the election of April 1976. It was awarded 3 Assembly seats in 1979, 2 in 1980, and, running separately from the PCP, 3 in 1983. It won no seats with a minuscule .57 percent vote share in 1987.

Leader: José Manuel TENGARRINHA.

Popular Democratic Union (*União Democrática Popular* – UDP). The UDP was formed in 1975 by merger of three small Marxist-Leninist parties and subsequently joined a number of other left-wing groups in a Movement for Popular Unity (*Movimento de Unidade Popular* – MUP) to contest the December 1976 local elections. It retained its 1 Assembly seat in both 1979 and 1980, but gained no representation thereafter.

Leader: Mário TOMEA.

United Workers' Organization (*Organização Unida de Trabalhadores* – OUT). Formally constituted at a congress held in April 1978, OUT is an amalgamation of the far-left Popular Socialist Front (*Frente Socialista Popular* – FSP) and the Revolutionary Proletarian Party (*Partido Revolucionário do Proletariado* – PRP). Referring to the Communist Party as "completely bourgeois", the party leadership called for a mass movement of workers that would achieve socialism and oppose fascism. One of OUT's principal organizers was Lt. Col. Otelo Saraiva de Carvalho, who had been implicated in the November 1975 left-wing coup attempt, placed second in the 1976 presidential balloting, and in June 1979 was forced into retirement by the army chief of staff. Carvalho has also been identified as a founder of the extreme left-wing **Popular United Forces** (*Forças da Unidade Popular* – FUP) which, in turn, has been linked to the **Popular Forces of 25 April** (*Forças Populares de 25 Abril* – FP-25), a terrorist group that surfaced in 1980 and, along with the **Autonomous Revolutionary Groups** (*Grupos Autónomos Révolucionarios* – GAR), has been implicated in numerous bomb attacks and assassinations. In June 1984, Carvalho was one of several dozen persons arrested in connection with an inquiry into links between his FUP and the FP-25; at his trial, which began in mid-1985, he would only admit that his organization, which he described as a means of preventing a right-wing coup, had been "infiltrated" by the increasingly active terrorist group. An anonymous caller to a radio station claimed FP-25 responsibility for a bomb that exploded in the US Embassy compound in February 1986, while a previously unknown group with possible FP-25 links, the **Armed Revolutionary Organization** (*Organização Revolucionária Armada* – ORA), claimed responsibility for bombings in several cities in July.

Leaders: Lt. Col. Otelo Saraiva de CARVALHO, Isabel do CARMO (former PRP leader), Manuel SERRA (former FSP leader).

There are numerous other minor parties, most of them, save for the right-wing **Christian Democratic Party** (*Partido da Democracia Cristão* – PDC), of a far-left orientation and prone to frequent division, consolidation, and changes of name. They include two Trotskyite groups, the **Workers' Party of Socialist Unity** (*Partido Operário de Unidade Socialista* – POUS), formed in 1979 by a group of PSP dissidents, and the **Revolutionary Socialist Party** (*Partido Socialista Revolucionário* – PSR); the Maoist-oriented **Communist Party of Portuguese Workers** (*Partido Comunista dos Trabalhadores Portugueses* – PCTP), formerly called the Reorganizing Movement of the Proletarian Party (*Movimento Reorganizativo do Partido do Proletariado* – MRPP); and the pro-Albanian **Communist Party Reconstituted** (*Partido Communista: Reconstruido* – PCR).

LEGISLATURE

The unicameral **Assembly of the Republic** (*Assembléia da República*) consists of 250 members elected for four-year terms, subject to dissolution. At the most recent election of July 19, 1987, the Social Democratic Party obtained 148 seats; the Portuguese Socialist Party, 60; the Unified Democratic Coalition, 31; the Democratic Renewal Party, 7; and the Social Democratic Center, 4.

President: Dr. Fernando AMARAL.

CABINET

Prime Minister	Aníbal Cavaço Silva
Deputy Prime Minister	Enrico de Melo
Ministers	
Agriculture and Fisheries	Alvaro Roque de Pinto Bissaia Barreto
Commerce and Tourism	Joaquim Ferreira do Amaral
Defense	Enrico de Melo
Education	Roberto Carneiro
Employment and Social Security	José Silva Peneda
Finance	Miguel Ribeiro Cadilhe
Foreign Affairs	João de Deus Pinheiro
Health	Leonor Beleza
Industry and Energy	Luis Mira Amaral
Internal Administration	José Silveira Godinho
Justice	Fernando Nogueira
Parliamentary Affairs	António Capucho
Governor, Bank of Portugal	José Alberto Tavares Moreira

NEWS MEDIA

Press. After the 1974 coup, the ownership, management, circulation, and editorial policies of the nation's newspapers were in a state of flux. Eight of the leading dailies were nationalized and, following the rightist coup attempt of March 1975, Communists were permitted to take over the operation of *Diário de Notícias, Diário de Lisboa,* and *O Século,* while even more radical elements assumed the management of *A Capital* and *Diário Popular.* All of these papers subsequently suffered sharp declines in circulation.

On May 19, 1975, Communist-led printers took over the offices of the respected Socialist paper *República,* precipitating a Socialist Party withdrawal from the government in July, while a number of new papers, including the independent daily *O Dia,* began publication and (as in the case of other non-Communist papers, such as the weekly *Expresso*) experienced dramatic increases in circulation.

Following the attempted leftist revolt of November 1975, the government temporarily closed down all state-owned newspapers, charging that several had been guilty of "tendentious, distorted, and monolithic" reporting, and indicating that all politically active Communists and far-leftists would be purged from their operation. Two of the papers, *Jornal de Notícias* and *O Comércio do Porto* (both published at Porto), were subsequently permitted to reappear under their old management, while a decree law of July 1976 nationalized four publishing organizations and established two state-owned groups, which currently publish *Diário de Notícias, A Capital,* and *Diário Popular; O Século* ceased publication in 1977, but was revived in 1986.

The following are published daily at Lisbon, unless otherwise noted: *Jornal de Notícias* (Porto, 80,000); *Correio da Manhã* (78,000); *Diário Popular* (63,000); *Diário de Notícias* (59,000); *O Comercio do Porto* (Porto, 54,000); *O Dia* (47,000); *Diário de Lisboa* (42,000); *O Diário* (40,000), *O Primeiro de Janeiro* (Porto, 40,000); *A Capital* (37,000); *A Tarde* (33,000).

News agencies. The official facility is *Agência Noticiosa Portuguesa* (Anop); other domestic services include *Agência Europeia de Imprensa* (AEI) and *Agência de Representações Dias da Silva* (ADS). Numerous foreign agencies also maintain bureaus at Lisbon.

Radio and television. Until late 1975 there were, in addition to government facilities, a number of privately owned radio stations, all but one of which had come under Communist or far-left control after the 1974 coup. On December 3, 1975, the government issued decrees nationalizing television, which had theretofore been only partly state owned, and all major radio stations except *Radio Renascença,* which is owned and operated by the Catholic Church under a 1940 concordat between Portugal and the Vatican. All state-run radio facilities remain consolidated under *Radiodifusão Portuguesa* (RDP), while television broadcasting is supervised by *Radiotelevisão Portuguesa* (RTP). There were approximately 2.3 million radio and 1.6 million television receivers in 1987.

INTERGOVERNMENTAL REPRESENTATION

Ambassador to the US: João Eduardo Monteverde Pereira BASTOS.

US Ambassador to Portugal: Edward Morgan ROWELL.

Permanent Representative to the UN: João Uva de Matos PROENÇA.

IGO Memberships (Non-UN): ADF, AfDB, BIS, CCC, CEUR, EC, EFTA, *EIB, Eurocontrol,* IADB, ICAC, ICCAT, ICCO, ICES, ICM, ICO, IEA, Inmarsat, Intelsat, Interpol, IOOC, IWTC, NATO, OECD, PCA.

RELATED TERRITORIES

The Azores and the Madeira Islands have long been construed as insular components of metropolitan Portugal and, as such, are legally distinct from a group of Portuguese possessions whose status was changed in 1951 from that of "Colonies" to "Overseas Territories". Of the latter, the South Asian enclaves of Goa, Damão, and Diu were annexed by India in 1961; Portuguese Guinea became independent as Guinea-Bissau in 1974; and Angola, the Cape Verde Islands, Mozambique, and São Tomé and Príncipe became independent in 1975. Portuguese Timor was annexed by Indonesia on July 17, 1976, but the action has not yet been recognized by Portugal (see Indonesia: Annexed Territories). Macao is defined as a "collective entity" (*pessoa colectiva*) under a governing statute promulgated on February 17, 1976, although agreement was reached in March 1987 for the eventual return of Macao to Chinese sovereignty (see below). Under the 1976 constitution, the Azores and Madeira are defined as Autonomous Regions.

Azores (*Açores*). The Azores comprise three distinct groups of islands located in the Atlantic Ocean about 800 miles west of mainland Portugal. The most easterly of the islands are São Miguel and Santa Maria; the most westerly and least densely populated are Corvo and Flores; Fayal, Graciosa, Pico, São Jorge, and Terceira are in the center. There are three political districts, the capitals and chief seaports of which are Ponta Delgada (São Miguel), Horta (Fayal), and Angra do Heroísmo (Terceira). The islands' total area is 890 square miles (2,305 sq. km.) and their population (1984E), 250,700.

Following the 1974 coup, significant separatist sentiment emerged, particularly on Terceira, whose residents feared that the left-wing government at Lisbon might close the US military base at Lajes. In August 1975 a recently organized **Azorean Liberation Front** (*Frente Libertação dos Açores*—FLA) announced its opposition to continued rule from the mainland. Following the resignation of three appointed governors, the Portuguese government surrendered control of the islands' internal administration to local political leaders, and on April 30, 1976, provided for an elected Regional Assembly, which convened on September 4. A regional government had previously been established under Popular Democratic Party leadership. In 1980, the Social Democrats obtained a majority in the Assembly, which was increased on October 14, 1984, to 28 of 43 seats.

Madeira Islands (*Ilhas de Madeira*). The Madeiras consist of Madeira and Porto Santo islands, and the uninhabited islets of Desertas and

Salvages. Lying west of Casablanca, Morocco, some 500 miles southwest of the Portuguese mainland, they have a total area of 308 square miles (797 sq. km.) and a population (1984E) of 264,800. The capital is Funchal, on Madeira Island.

As in the case of the Azores, separatist sentiment exists, the **Madeira Archipelago Liberation Front** (*Frente Libertação Arquipélago de Madeira* — Flama), which advocated independence from Portugal and possible federation with the Azores and the Spanish Canaries, claiming on August 29, 1975, to have established a provisional government. However, both the government that was installed on October 1, 1976, and the elected Regional Assembly that was convened on October 23 were dominated by members of the Social Democratic Center Party. The Social Democrats have since maintained the majority, obtaining 40 of 50 seats at the most recent balloting of October 14, 1984.

Macao (*Província de Macau*). Established in 1557 as the first European enclave on the China coast, Macao comprises a peninsula and two small islets in the mouth of the Canton River, about 40 miles from Hong Kong. Its area of 6.0 square miles (15.5 sq. km.) accommodates a population of some 400,000 (1985E), mainly Chinese but with a Portuguese minority.

Western diplomats in Peking reported that the (then) governor of Macao, Col José Eduardo Martinho GARCIA Leandro, was directed in June 1974 to communicate to Chinese representatives the Lisbon government's willingness to withdraw from the enclave, but was advised that Peking had no desire to alter the status of the territory. The economy of Macao has recently been flourishing, partly as a gambling haven (yielding 42 percent of the territory's revenue in 1984) and partly as an entrepôt for trade with China (the latter being enhanced by the establishment of a Special Economic Zone in the nearby province of Zhuhai). It has also been alleged that the Chinese use the port as a means of exporting opium into the international market.

The establishment of diplomatic relations between Portugal and the People's Republic on February 9, 1979 (which followed a visit to Peking by Garcia Leandro in January), did not alter the status of Macao, (then) Prime Minister Mota Pinto declaring that it would remain "Chinese territory under Portuguese administration". Cdr. (later Rear Adm.) Vasco de ALMEIDA e Costa succeeded Gen. Nuno Viriato de MELO Egídio as governor on June 17, 1981.

In February 1984, Admiral Almeida e Costa dissolved the Legislative Assembly, which had provided the territory with a measure of self-government since 1976, after the Portuguese-dominated body had refused to approve a new electoral law giving equal representation to the Chinese community. A new Assembly, following the indirect election of 6 business representatives in July, balloting for 6 directly elected members on August 15, and the naming of 5 gubernatorial appointees on August 27, encompassed a total of 9 Chinese in the 17-member body. Policies enacted by the body included plans for infrastructural modernization and increased social services, as well as the territory's first labor law, which banned child labor and established a six-day maximum work week.

Chinese reluctance to accept reversion had been attributed to uncertainty in regard to the status of Hong Kong; with the conclusion of the agreement on Hong Kong's future in December 1984 (see article on the United Kingdom), Chinese representatives initiated discussions on Macao.

In May 1985, following the designation of Joaquim Pinto MACHADO as Admiral Almeida e Costa's successor, President Eanes visited Macao and Beijing, announcing that Sino-Portuguese talks on reversion would begin in 1986. On May 26, 1987, the two countries initialed an agreement for the return of the territory to Chinese sovereignty on December 20, 1999, under a plan similar to the "one country, two systems" approach approved for Hong Kong. China agreed to grant Macao 50 years of noninterference with its capitalist economy, with residents holding or entitled to Portuguese passports because of partial Portuguese parentage given the right to continue using the documents after reversion; Lisbon, however, has not yet indicated whether such individuals (potentially as many as 100,000) will have the option of emigration to Portugal.

On July 3, 1987, it was announced that Carlos MELANCIA had been appointed to succeed Machado as governor of the territory.

QATAR

State of Qatar
Dawlat Qatar

Political Status: Traditional sheikhdom; proclaimed fully independent September 1, 1971.

Area: 4,247 sq. mi. (11,000 sq. km.).

Population: 354,000 (1988E), including nonnationals, who have been estimated to constitute more than two-thirds of the resident population.

Major Urban Center (1980E): DOHA (al-Dawhah, 180,000).

Official Language: Arabic.

Monetary Unit: Qatar Riyal (market rate March 1, 1988, 3.64 riyals = $1US).

Sovereign (Emir) **and Prime Minister:** Sheikh Khalifa ibn Hamad Al THANI; became Prime Minister in 1970; assumed supreme power February 22, 1972, deposing his cousin, Sheikh Ahmad ibn 'Ali ibn 'Abdallah Al THANI.

THE COUNTRY

A flat, barren peninsular projection into the Persian Gulf from the Saudi Arabian mainland, Qatar consists largely of sand and rock. The climate is quite warm with very little rainfall, and the lack of fresh water has led to a reliance on desalination techniques. The population is almost entirely Arab, but indigenous Qataris (mainly Sunni Muslims of the puritanical Wahhabi sect) comprise substantially less than a majority. The nonnationals include Pakistanis, Iranians, Indians, and Palestinians, some 83,000 of whom were reported to have left the country in 1985 upon expiry of temporary work contracts.

The economy remains almost entirely dependent upon revenue from oil, which has been produced for export since 1949. Qatar assumed full control over production and marketing of its oil in 1977; most other industrialization has involved foreign participation, usually limited to 30 percent. While Qatar's output of crude is limited to about 1.7 percent of OPEC's total, exceeding only that of Ecuador and Gabon, its GNP per capita is surpassed only by that of the United Arab Emirates, according to the World Bank. Recently discovered natural gas—particularly in the offshore North Dome, one of the world's largest deposits—is expected to provide additional revenue well into the next century.

During the oil boom years of the 1970s and early 1980s, Qatar devoted most of its budget to the development of a modern infrastructure, emphasizing schools, hospitals, roads, communication facilities, and water and electric plants. Economic diversification efforts produced steel, fertilizer, and petrochemical complexes as well as expanded ports at Doha and Umm Sa'id. However, due to falling oil prices, austerity has recently been imposed, stifling further planned construction.

GOVERNMENT AND POLITICS

Political background. Dominated by Bahrain until 1868 and by the Ottoman Turks from 1878 until World War I, Qatar entered into treaty relations with Great Britain in 1916. Under the treaty, Qatar stipulated that it would not enter into agreements with other foreign governments without British consent; in return, Britain agreed to provide for the defense of the sheikhdom. Following the British government's 1968 announcement that it intended to withdraw from the Persian Gulf by 1971, Qatar attempted to associate itself with Bahrain and the Trucial Sheikhdoms in a Federation of Arab Emirates. When it became apparent that agreement on the structure of the proposed federation could not be obtained, Qatar declared for independence, which was realized in 1971.

The new state was governed initially by Sheikh Ahmad ibn 'Ali ibn 'Abdallah Al THANI, who proved to be an inattentive sovereign. In February 1972 the prime minister, Sheikh Khalifa ibn Hamad Al THANI, deposed Sheikh Ahmad, his cousin, in a bloodless coup approved by the royal family. More modernist elements have since emerged, though the present emir remains a virtually absolute monarch and most government ministers are close relatives.

Constitution and government. Qatar employs traditional patterns of authority, onto which a limited number of modern governmental institutions have been grafted. The provisional constitution of 1970 provided for a Council of Ministers and an Advisory Council of 20 (subsequently 30) members, 3 of whom were to be appointed, the rest elected. No elections have, however, been held. The Council of Ministers is led by an appointed prime minister, who is presently the sheikh himself. The judicial system embraces five secular courts (two criminal as well as civil, labor, and appeal) and religious courts, which apply Muslim law (*shari'a*).

Foreign relations. Until 1971 Qatar's foreign relations were administered by Britain. Since independence, it has pursued a policy of nonalignment in foreign affairs while eschewing diplomatic relations with most Communist regimes. Qatar belongs to the United Nations, the Arab League, and the Organization of Petroleum Exporting Countries (OPEC). On April 25, 1979, Doha severed relations with Cairo in reaction to the signing of the Egyptian-Israeli peace treaty. Shortly thereafter, the Persian Gulf Organization for Development in Egypt and the Arab Military Industries Organization, in both of which Qatar participated, were disbanded.

In 1981 Qatar joined with five other Gulf states (Bahrain, Kuwait, Oman, Saudi Arabia, and the United Arab Emirates) in establishing the Gulf Cooperation Council (GCC), and has since participated in joint military maneuvers and the formation of economic cooperation agreements; in November 1983, Doha was host to the Council's fourth annual summit, which focused on the Iran-Iraq war and cleavages within the Palestinian Liberation Organization (PLO). Qatar's long-standing support of the Palestinian cause was reaffirmed by a meeting in October 1985 between the emir and PLO Chairman Yasir 'Arafat. Recently, concern has been voiced over Soviet intentions in the Gulf and the need to protect oil routes to Japan and the West.

Following the July 1987 clash between Iranian Shi'ites and Saudi Arabian security forces at Mecca, Qatar, which had thenceforth made a more consistent effort than most of its GCC colleagues to maintain neutrality in the Iran-Iraq war, appeared to be moving closer to the pro-Iraqi posture of its Saudi neighbor.

Current issues. The government's austerity program intensified in 1987 as Qatar's economy experienced continued recession. To the dismay of the business and financial community, development of the North Dome gas fields remained stalled, although agreements were concluded in May with the US Bechtel Company and a French firm, Technip, on basic design and start-up work.

The budget for 1987–1988 provided for total expenditure of QR 12.2 million against revenue of QR 6.7 million, although the deficit was expected to be less than projected because recent outlays had generally fallen short of budgeted amounts.

POLITICAL PARTIES

There are no political parties in Qatar.

LEGISLATURE

The **Advisory Council** (*Majlis al-Shura*), created in 1972, was increased from 20 members to 30 in 1975. Although the provisional constitution stipulates that members will serve three-year terms and that all but 3 are to be elected, the present Council consists exclusively of the emir's appointees, most of them named in 1972 and subsequently reappointed.

Secretary General: 'Abd al-Aziz ibn Khalid al-GHANIM.

CABINET

Prime Minister	Sheikh Khalifa ibn Hamad Al Thani
Ministers	
Agriculture and Industry	Sheikh Faisal ibn Thani Al Thani
Commerce and Economy	(Vacant)
Defense	Sheikh Hamad ibn Khalifa Al Thani
Education	Sheikh Muhammad ibn Hamad Al Thani
Electricity and Water Resources	Sheikh Jasim ibn Muhammad Al Thani
Finance and Petroleum	Sheikh 'Abd al-'Aziz ibn Khalifa Al Thani
Foreign Affairs	(Vacant)

Information	'Isa Ghanim al-Kawari
Interior	Sheikh Khalid ibn Hamad Al Thani
Justice	(Vacant)
Labor and Social Affairs	'Ali ibn Ahmad al-Ansari
Public Health	Khalid ibn Muhammad al-Mani
Public Works	Khalid ibn 'Abdallah al-'Atiya
Transportation and Communications	'Abdallah ibn Nasir al-Suwaidi
Minister of State for Foreign Affairs	Sheikh Ahmad ibn Saif Al Thani
Director General, Monetary Agency	Majid Muhammad al-Majid al-Saad

NEWS MEDIA

Press. The following are published at Doha: *al-Rayah* (The Banner, 20,000), Arabic political daily; *al-Ouroba* (Europe 14,000), Arabic weekly; *al-'Arab* (The Arabs, 10,000), Arabic daily; *Gulf Times* (10,000 daily, 15,000 weekly), in English; *al-Doha Magazine,* monthly publication of the Ministry of Information, in Arabic; *Daily News Bulletin,* in English and Arabic.

News agency. The domestic facility is the Qatar News Agency.

Radio and television. Radio programming is provided to 130,000 sets by the government-operated Qatar Broadcasting Service, while television is provided by Qatar Television to approximately 160,000 receivers.

INTERGOVERNMENTAL REPRESENTATION

Ambassador to the US: Ahmad 'Abdallah Zaid al-MAHMOUD.

US Ambassador to Qatar: Joseph GHOUGASSIAN.

Permanent Representative to the UN: Hamad 'Abd al-Aziz al-KAWARI.

IGO Memberships (Non-UN): AFESD, AMF, BADEA, GCC, IC, IDB, Inmarsat, Intelsat, Interpol, LAS, NAM, OAPEC, OPEC.

ROMANIA

Socialist Republic of Romania
Republica Socialistă România

Political Status: Independence established 1878; People's Republic proclaimed December 30, 1947; designated a Socialist Republic by constitution adopted August 21, 1965.

Area: 91,699 sq. mi. (237,500 sq. km.).

Population: 21,559,416 (1977C), 23,022,000 (1988E).

Major Urban Centers (1986E): BUCHAREST (urban area, 1,990,000); Braşov (351,000); Constanţa (328,000); Timişoara (325,000); Iaşi (313,000); Cluj-Napoca (310,000); Galaţi (295,000).

Official Language: Romanian.

Monetary Unit: Leu (principal rate March 1, 1988, 14.05 lei = $1US; secondary rate, 8.63 lei).

President of the Republic, President of the State Council, and Secretary General of the Romanian Communist Party: Nicolae CEAUŞESCU; President of the State Council since 1967; designated President of the Republic on March 28, 1974, and reelected in 1975, 1980, and on March 29, 1985, by the Grand National Assembly; became First Secretary of the Romanian Workers' (subsequently Communist) Party in 1965 and reelected as General Secretary in 1969, 1974, 1979, and on November 22, 1984.

Chairman of the Council of Ministers: Constantin DĂSCĂLESCU; appointed by the Grand National Assembly on May 21, 1982, succeeding Ilie VERDEȚ; reappointed on March 29, 1985.

THE COUNTRY

Shaped by the geographic influence of the Carpathian Mountains and the Danube River, Romania occupies the northeastern quarter of the Balkan Peninsula and has served historically both as an outpost of Latin civilization and as a natural gateway for Russian expansion into southeastern Europe. Some 88 percent of the population is ethnically Romanian, descended from the Romanized Dacians of ancient times. The principal ethnic minorities, situated mostly in the Transylvanian lands acquired from the Austro-Hungarian Empire after World War I, are 1.8 million Magyars (Hungarians), the largest national minority in Europe, and 300,000 Germans, following the emigration, by late 1984, of some 80,000 under an agreement concluded in 1977 with West Germany. Traditionally, the Romanian (Greek) Orthodox Church has been the largest religious community. While constituting approximately half of the official labor force, women are concentrated in the agricultural sector because of male urban migration; on the other hand, female participation in political affairs has increased significantly, despite a pro-natalist campaign launched in 1984.

Although one of the world's pioneer oil producers, Romania was long a predominantly agricultural country and continues to be largely self-sufficient in food production. Most acreage is under the control of collective and state farms, while the agricultural component of the work force dropped sharply from 65 percent in 1960 to 29 percent in 1985 as the result of an emphasis on industrial development — particularly in metals, machinery, chemicals, and construction materials — under a series of five-year plans. The 1981–1985 plan called for the attainment of energy self-sufficiency by 1990 (Romania became a net importer of petroleum in the late 1970s), expansion of industrial output and exports by 50 percent each, and increased production of consumer goods. By 1984, however, it was evident that most of the plan goals, in both industry and agriculture, could not be achieved; the 1986–1990 plan set similarly ambitious targets, projecting a 34–37 percent rise in industrial output, and a 33–42 percent increase in grain production by the end of the plan period.

GOVERNMENT AND POLITICS

Political background. Originally consisting of the twin principalities of Walachia and Moldavia, the territory that is now Romania was overrun by the Ottoman Turks in the fifteenth century. Recognized as independent at the Berlin Congress in 1878, Romania made large territorial gains as one of the victorious powers in World War I but lost substantial areas to the Soviet Union (Bessarabia and Northern Bukovina) and to Bulgaria (Southern Dobruja) in 1940 under threats from its neighbors and pressure from Nazi Germany. The young King MICHAEL, who took advantage of the entry of Soviet troops in 1944 to dismiss the pro-German regime and switch to the Allied side, was forced in 1945 to accept a Communist-led coalition government under Dr. Petru GROZA and, following rigged elections won by the Communists in 1946, abdicated in 1947. The Communists promptly proceeded to eliminate the remnants of the traditional parties, and in 1952, after a series of internal purges, Gheorghe GHEORGHIU-DEJ emerged as the unchallenged party leader.

Following a decade of rigidity, Romania under Gheorghiu-Dej's leadership inaugurated a policy of increased independence from the Soviet Union in both military and economic affairs. This policy has been continued and intensified under Nicolae CEAUȘESCU, who succeeded to the party leadership on Gheorghiu-Dej's death in 1965 and became president of the Council of State in 1967. While maintaining relatively strict controls at home, the Ceaușescu regime has consistently advocated maximum autonomy in international Communist affairs. These policies were fully endorsed by Romanian Communist Party congresses in 1969, 1974, 1979, and 1984, with Ceaușescu being reelected to the top party position at all four.

On March 28, 1980, President Ceaușescu was elected to his third term as head of state by the newly convened Grand National Assembly, and the next day Ilie VERDEȚ, a close associate of the president and an experienced economic planner who had succeeded Manea MĂNESCU in March 1979, presented a new Council of Ministers that included as a first deputy Elena CEAUȘESCU, wife of the president. In the face of increasingly poor economic performance, other significant changes were subsequently made, including the replacement of Verdeț by the relatively obscure Constantin DĂSCĂLESCU on May 21, 1982.

Constitution and government. Romania's third postwar constitution, adopted in 1965 and amended in 1974, declares the nation to be a "socialist republic" whose economy is based on socialist ownership of the means of production. All power is ascribed to the people, but the Romanian Communist Party (PCR) is singled out as the society's leading political force. Supreme state power is nominally vested in the Grand National Assembly, which in turn elects the president of the Republic, a Council of State that serves as a legislative presidium, a Council of Ministers (cabinet), justices of the Supreme Court, and a chief public prosecutor (procurator general). Other executive organs are the Economic Council and the Defense Council, both of which perform advisory functions for the Council of State. In addition to the Supreme Court, the judicial system includes 39 county courts plus the Municipal Court of Bucharest, and numerous local courts, all utilizing people's assessors (lay judges appointed by the party or one of its auxiliaries) as well as regular judges.

Administratively, Romania is divided into 39 counties plus the city of Bucharest, 46 municipalities, 236 towns, and more than 2,700 communes. Elected people's councils function at all four levels.

Foreign relations. Although historically pro-Western in foreign policy, Romania during its first 15 years as a Communist state cooperated fully with the Soviet Union both in bilateral relations and as a member of the Council for Mutual Economic Assistance, the Warsaw Pact, and the United Nations. Serious differences with Moscow arose in the early 1960s over the issue of East European economic integration, leading in 1964 to a formal rejection of all Soviet schemes of supranational planning and interference in the affairs of other Communist countries. Since that time, Romania has followed an independent line in many areas of foreign policy, refusing to participate in the 1968 Warsaw Pact intervention in Czechoslovakia, rejecting efforts to isolate Communist China, remaining the only Soviet-bloc nation to continue diplomatic relations with both Egypt and Israel, condemning the Moscow-backed Vietnamese invasion of Kampuchea in 1978, and reportedly calling upon Moscow in late 1980 to withdraw its forces from Afghanistan.

Outside the Soviet bloc, Romania has cultivated relations with Yugoslavia and with such Western countries as France, West Germany, and the United States, although frequently expressing irritation with Washington because of the latter's use of trade policy to influence "domestic" concerns such as emigration. In May 1979 President Ceauşescu became the first Communist leader to visit post-Franco Spain. In addition, prior to the admission of Hungary in 1982, Romania was the only Eastern-bloc state to belong to the World Bank and the International Monetary Fund. In Third World affairs, a number of bilateral cooperative, trade, and technical agreements have recently been signed with African states, while a message from Ceauşescu read at the 1979 UNCTAD meeting at Manila, Philippines, included a call for a worldwide 10–15 percent cut in arms expenditures, with half the savings to be channeled to developing countries; a similar plea was made in an address at a Warsaw Pact meeting in May 1985. Earlier, at the Thirteenth Party Congress in November 1984, Ceauşescu had proposed the cancellation of foreign debts of all countries with per capita income of under $500–600.

Current issues. During 1987 Romanian affairs continued to be dominated by an austerity plan instituted in late 1981 in response to a debt crisis which had led the International Monetary Fund to deny scheduled withdrawals. The program included devaluation of the leu, cuts in imports, a mandatory 50 percent reduction in energy consumption, and increased exports of agricultural goods. Fiscally, the effort's results were striking, with foreign trade surpluses averaging nearly $2 billion and about half of the foreign obligation of approximately $11 billion being retired by early 1988. However, as in such "fiscal successes" elsewhere, the domestic standard of living suffered measurably, with acute food shortages and energy crises stemming from severe shortfalls in coal, oil, and hydroelectric output. The belt-tightening yielded several displays of worker unrest, as well as a rare protest on the eve of a party conference at Bucharest in mid-December, during which fires were set at the base of the city's statue of Lenin. Earlier, Romania continued to manifest its maverick role within

the Soviet bloc by rejecting suggestions by the visiting Mikhail Gorbachev that economic reforms be undertaken, one senior official declaring flatly that "We consider it unnecessary to restructure".

Externally, a number of recent disputes have involved neighboring Communist regimes. In mid-1986 Yugoslavia complained of the attempted assimilation of Serb and Croat minorities as part of en effort to create a "unified Romania nation", while an extended polemic erupted in 1987 regarding the treatment of ethnic Hungarians in Transylvania (a former Hungarian territory awarded to Romania in 1940). In an unrelated dispute, Hungary also blamed Romanian authorities for permitting excessive pollution of the Sebes-Körös/Crisul Repede river, which crossed the border downstream from the Romanian town of Oradea.

POLITICAL PARTIES

Romania's one-party system is based on the leading position of the Romanian Communist Party, which is identified by the constitution as "the leading political force of the whole society". Communist authority is exercised with the aid of the **Front of Socialist Democracy and Unity** (*Frontul Democratiei Unităţii Socialiste* — FDUS), which prepares the approved list of candidates for election to the Grand National Assembly and other bodies.

Originally formed in 1948 as the People's Democratic Front, the FDUS was reorganized in 1968 and established as a permanent political organization with a National Council made up of representatives of the PCR, various mass and professional organizations, minority nationality councils, large industrial and agricultural enterprises, and intellectual and religious leaders. Nicolae Ceauşescu has been chairman of the Executive Committee since 1968.

Romanian Communist Party (*Partidul Comunist Român* — PCR). Founded in 1921, the PCR changed its name to Romanian Workers' Party in 1948 after a merger with the left-wing Social Democrats, but resumed its original name at the Ninth Party Congress in 1965. In early 1986 the PCR had a reported membership of 3.6 million. The supreme party authority is the Congress, which convenes every five years to lay down policy guidelines and elect formally subordinate party bodies. In practice, the Congress merely ratifies appointments and policy decisions made by its Central Committee; the intermediate Executive Political Committee; and the Permanent Bureau, which was styled the Politburo until 1965 and the Permanent Presidium until 1974. In addition, a Secretariat is named by the Central Committee to coordinate party administration and personnel down to the local level.

At the Thirteenth Party Congress, held November 19–22, 1984, and attended by 3,114 delegates, General Secretary Ceauşescu praised the country's "great achievements" during the seventh five-year plan and indicated that priority would be given during the eighth plan (1986–1990) to developing a firm energy and raw materials base. At the conclusion of the Congress, appointments were made to the principal party organs, including the Permanent Bureau, which was reduced in size from 12 to 8 members, and the Secretariat, which was expanded from 8 to 10 (subsequent changes in the two bodies yielding memberships of 7 and 9, respectively, by late 1987). No major changes in policy or personnel issued from an extraordinary party conference on December 14–16, 1987.

Secretary General: Nicolae CEAUŞESCU.

Other Members of Permanent Bureau: Emil BOBU (Chairman, Council of Economic and Social Organization), Elena CEAUŞESCU (First Deputy Chairman, Council of Ministers), Constantin DĂSCĂLESCU

(Chairman, Council of Ministers), Manea MĂNESCU (Vice President, State Council), Gheorghe OPREA (First Deputy Chairman, Council of Ministers), Gheorghe RĂDULESCU (Vice President, State Council).

Central Committee Secretariat: Ștefan ANDREI, Vasile BĂRBULESCU, Emil BOBU, Nicolae CEAUȘESCU, Col. Gen. Ion COMAN, Silvin CURTICEANU, Maria GHIȚULICĂ, Constantin RADU, Ion STOIAN.

LEGISLATURE

The **Grand National Assembly** (*Marea Adunare Natională*) is the legislative body of the Socialist Republic. Members are elected by universal suffrage from single-member constituencies for five-year terms. At the most recent election of March 17, 1985, it was reported that 2.27 percent of the electorate had voted against official candidates nominated by the Front of Socialist Democracy and Unity. The directing authority of the Assembly is a five-man Bureau composed of the Assembly chairman and four vice chairmen.

Chairman: Nicolae GIOSAN.

CABINET

Chairman, Council of Ministers	Constantin Dăscălescu
First Deputy Chairmen	Elena Ceaușescu
	Lt. Gen. Ion Dincă
	Gheorghe Oprea
Deputy Chairmen	Stefan Andrei
	Lina Ciobanu
	Ion Constantinescu
	Ludovic Fazekaș
	Neculai Ibanescu
	Cornel Pacoste
	Constantin Radu
Ministers	
Agriculture	Gheorghe David
Chemical Industry	Ion Marin Nicolae
Domestic Trade	Ana Mureșan
Education and Instruction	Ion Teoreanu
Electric Power	Petre Fluture
Electrotechnical Industry	Nicolae Vaidescu
Farm Produce Contracting and Acquisition	Constantine Zanfir
Finance	Gheorghe Paraschiv
Food Industry	Paula Prioteasa
Foreign Affairs	Ioan Totu
Foreign Trade and International Economic Cooperation	Ilie Văduva
Health	Victor Ciobanu
Heavy Equipment Industry	Radu Paul Paunescu
Industrial Construction	Alexandru Dimitriu
Interior	Tudor Postelnicu
Interior, in Charge of State Security	Col. Gen. Iulian Vlad
Justice	Maria Bobu
Labor	Maxim Berghianu
Light Industry	Maria Flusca
Machine Building Industry	Serban Teodorescu
Metallurgical Industry	Marin Enache
Mines	Marin Stefanache
National Defense	Col. Gen. Vasile Milea
Petroleum Industry	Nicolae Amza
Silviculture	Eugene Tarhon
Technical-Material Supply and Control of Fixed Assets	Ione C. Petre
Tourism and Sports	Ion Stănescu
Transportation and Telecommunications	Pavel Aron
Wood Industry and Construction Materials	Gheorghe Constantinescu
Youth Affairs	Ione Toma
Chairmen	
Committee for Problems of People's Councils	Gheorghe Pana
Council for Socialist Culture and Education	Suzana Gâdea
General Trade Union Confederation	Miu Dobrescu
National Council for Science and Technology	Elena Ceaușescu
National Council for Water Resources	Ioan Badea
National Union of Agricultural Producer Cooperatives	Vasile Marin
State Committee for Nuclear Energy	Cornel Mihulecea
State Planning Committee	Ștefan Bîrlea
State Committee for Prices	Decebal Urdea
First Secretary, Union of Communist Youth	Ioan Toma
Chairman, National Bank	Florea Dumitrescu

NEWS MEDIA

Although prior censorship was formally abolished by the Grand National Assembly in March 1974, news media are enjoined from reporting that promotes internal unrest, fascist tendencies, and violations of "normal or socialist" morality. The government announced in June 1977 that it was abandoning all forms of official censorship in favor of "self-censorship" by the nation's media.

Press. Only papers controlled by or affiliated with the party or government exist at present. The following papers are Bucharest dailies published in Romanian, unless otherwise noted: *Scînteia* (Spark, 1,400,000), organ of the Central Committee of the PCR; *România Liberă* (Free Romania, 430,000), FDUS organ; *Scînteia Tineretului* (Spark of Youth, 235,000), organ of the Communist Youth Union; *Informația Bucureștiului* (Bucharest Information, 210,000), publication of the Bucharest Party Committee and People's Council; *Munca* (Labor, 170,000), weekly organ of the Central Council of Trade Unions; *Agricultura Socialistă* (Socialist Agriculture, 108,000), weekly organ of the National Union of Agricultural Production Cooperatives et al.; *Elöre* (Forward, 79,000), FDUS organ, in Magyar; *Neuer Weg* (New Way, 30,000), FDUS organ in German.

News agencies. The official organ is the Romanian Press Agency (Agerpres); ANSA, AP, Reuters, *Xinhua,* and a number of Communist-bloc agencies also maintain bureaus at Bucharest.

Radio and television. Romanian Radio and Television (*Radioteleviziunea Română*) is the state agency controlling broadcast operations. *Radiodifuziunea Română* transmits domestic programs as well as foreign broadcasts in 13 languages. There were approximately 3.2 million radio and 3.9 million television receivers in 1987.

INTERGOVERNMENTAL REPRESENTATION

Ambassador to the US: Ion STOICHICI.

US Ambassador to Romania: Roger KIRK.

Permanent Representative to the UN: Petre TANASIE.

IGO Memberships (Non-UN): BIS, CCC, CMEA, IBEC, IIB, Interpol, PCA, WTO.

RWANDA

Republic of Rwanda
République Rwandaise (French)
Republika y'u Rwanda (Kinyarwanda)

Political Status: Republic proclaimed January 28, 1961; independent since July 1, 1962; present constitution adopted December 17, 1978.

Area: 10,169 sq. mi. (26,338 sq. km.).

Population: 4,819,317 (1978C), 6,825,000 (1988E).

Major Urban Centers (1978C): KIGALI (117,749); Butare (21,691).

Official Languages: French, Kinyarwanda.

Monetary Unit: Rwanda Franc (market rate March 1, 1988, 75.48 francs = $1US).

President: Maj. Gen. Juvénal HABYARIMANA; installed as the result of a military coup on July 5, 1973, which deposed Grégoire KAYIBANDA; reconfirmed for five-year terms by referenda of December 17, 1978, and December 19, 1983.

THE COUNTRY

Situated in the heart of Africa, adjacent to Burundi, Tanzania, Uganda, and Zaire, Rwanda consists mainly of grassy uplands and hills endowed with a temperate climate. The population comprises three main ethnic groups: the Hutu, or Bahutu (90 percent); the Tutsi, or Batutsi (9 percent); and the Twa, or pygmies (1 percent). There are about equal numbers of Roman Catholics and animists, with small Protestant (9 percent) and Muslim (1 percent) minorities. In addition to French and Kinyarwanda, the two official languages, Kiswahili is widely spoken. Women account for about half of the labor force, primarily as unpaid agricultural workers on family plots; female representation in government and party posts is virtually nonexistent.

Economically poor, Rwanda has been hindered by population growth (it is the most densely populated state in Africa), inadequate transportation facilities, and distance from accessible ports. About 90 percent of the people depend on agriculture for their livelihood, and goods are produced largely for local consumption. Coffee is the leading cash crop and principal source of foreign exchange, although tea cultivation is expanding. Industry is concentrated in food processing and nondurable consumer goods, but the mining of cassiterite and wolframite ore is also important. International assistance has focused on economic diversification while the government's 1986–1990 five-year program concentrates on agricultural development.

GOVERNMENT AND POLITICS

Political background. Like Burundi, Rwanda was long a feudal monarchy ruled by nobles of the Tutsi tribe. A German protectorate from 1899 to 1916, it constituted the northern half of the Belgian mandate of Ruanda-Urundi after World War I, and of the Belgian-administered trust territory of the same name after World War II. Resistance to the Tutsi monarchy by the more numerous Hutus intensified in the 1950s and culminated in November 1959 in a bloody revolt that caused the overthrow of the monarchy and the emigration of thousands of Tutsis. The Party for Hutu Emancipation (Parmehutu), founded by Grégoire KAYIBANDA, won an overwhelming electoral victory in 1960, and Rwanda proclaimed itself a republic on January 28, 1961, under the leadership of Dominique MBONYU-MUTWA. Since the United Nations did not recognize the action, new elections were held under UN auspices in September 1961, with the Hutu party repeating its victory. Kayibanda was accordingly designated president on October 26, 1961, and trusteeship status was formally terminated on July 1, 1962. Subsequently, émigrés invaded the country in an attempt to restore the monarchy, but their defeat in December 1963 set off mass reprisals against the remaining Tutsis, resulting in 10,000–15,000 deaths and the flight of 150,000–200,000 Tutsis to neighboring countries.

The Hutu-dominated government consolidated its position in the elections of 1965 and 1969, but with President Kayibanda legally barred from seeking another term at the approaching 1973 election, the constitution was altered to assure continuance of the existing regime. The change fanned hostility between political elements from the northern region and those from the southern and central regions, the latter having dominated the government since independence. Beginning in February 1973 at the National University at Butare, renewed Hutu moves against the Tutsis spread quickly to other areas. The government, however, did not move to quell the actions of the extremists, and continued instability raised the prospect of another tribal bloodbath or even war with Burundi. In this context, a bloodless coup took place on July 5, 1973.

The new government, under Maj. Gen. Juvénal HABYARIMANA, moved quickly to dissolve the legislature, ban political organizations, and suspend portions of the constitution. A civilian-military government composed largely of younger technocrats was subsequently installed and a more centralized administrative system established. A regime-supportive National Revolutionary Movement for Development (MRND) was organized in mid-1976 and was accorded formal status as the sole legal party under a new constitution adopted by referendum on December 17, 1978; subsequently, it was announced that the same poll had confirmed Habyarimana for an additional five-year term as president.

In 1980 the administration declared that it had foiled a coup attempt allegedly involving current and former government officials, including Maj. Théonaste LIZINDE who had recently been removed as security chief after being charged with corruption. Lizinde received a death sentence, which was subsequently commuted to life imprisonment.

Single-party legislative balloting was conducted in December 1981 and December 1983, Habyarimana being elected to another term on the latter occasion.

Constitution and government. Under the 1978 constitution, executive power is vested in a president elected by universal suffrage for a five-year term. He presides over a Council of Ministers, which he appoints; the secretary general of the MRND is empowered to serve as interim president, should the incumbent be incapacitated. A unicameral National Development Council, also elected for a five-year term, shares legislative authority with the president and, by a four-fifths vote, may censure but not dismiss him. The judiciary includes magistrates', prefectural, and appeals courts; a Court of Accounts; a Court of Cassation; and a Constitutional Court composed of the Court of Cassation and a Council of State.

The country is divided into ten prefectures, each of which is administered by a prefect appointed by the central government. At the local level there are 143 communes and municipalities, each administered by a presidential appointee who is assisted by an elected council.

Foreign relations. Under President Kayibanda, Rwandan foreign policy exhibited a generally pro-Western bias while not excluding relations with a number of Communist countries, including the Soviet Union and the People's Republic of China. Following the 1973 coup, however, the country took a pronounced "anti-imperialist" turn; Rwanda became the first African nation to break relations with Israel as a result of the October 1973 war, and it has contributed to the support of liberation movements in southern Africa. At the same time, President Habyarimana has pursued a policy of "opening" (*l'ouverture*) with adjacent countries. Despite a tradition of ethnic conflict between Burundi's ruling Tutsis and Rwanda's ruling Hutus, a number of commercial, cultural, and economic agreements were concluded during a visit by Burundian President Micombero in June 1976, while similar agreements were subsequently negotiated with Tanzania and the Ivory Coast. Burundi, Rwanda, and Zaire established the Economic Community of the Great Lakes Countries in 1976; two years later, the Organization for the Management and Development of the Kagera River Basin was formed by Burundi, Rwanda, and Tanzania.

Relations with Uganda have been strained for several decades by large numbers of refugees crossing the border in both directions to escape tribal-based hostilities. Following the overthrow of President Apollo Milton Obote in 1985, about 30,000 Ugandan refugees returned from Rwanda. On the other hand, more than 200,000 Rwandan Tutsis remained in Uganda. Kigali in 1986 urged that all the refugees be given Ugandan citizenship but Kampala granted the status only to those with 10 years of official residency. Despite continued concern over the refugee issue, agreements on trade, security, and communications strengthened relations between the countries in 1986 and 1987.

Current issues. Although there has been little evidence of widespread opposition to the Habyarimana regime, some 300 members of religious sects, including the Jehovah's Witnesses, were imprisoned in 1986 on charges including disrespect of the flag, refusing to send their children

to school, and declining to pay dues to the MRND. Most, however, were pardoned as part of a mid-1987 amnesty coincident with the 25th anniversary of Rwanda's independence. Unlike the situation in neighboring Burundi, there has been no discernible schism between the government and the Roman Catholic Church, which is still strongly identified with the administration despite the withdrawal in 1985 of Mgr. Vincent NSENGIYUMA, the archbishop of Kigali, as advisor on social affairs to the MRND's Central Committee.

In 1987 the administration concentrated on the economy, forming a "crisis committee" in June in the face of plummeting coffee prices and problems in the mining industry. An austerity package introduced three years before was intensified, although an extensive AIDS-education program, necessitated by reports that Kigali had one of the highest rates of infection in the world, remained in effect.

POLITICAL PARTIES

Government Party:

National Revolutionary Movement for Development (*Mouvement Révolutionnaire National pour le Développement*—MRND). Launched on July 5, 1975, by General Habyarimana as a single national party embracing both military and civilian elements, the MRND was established to unify the Rwandan people in the face of earlier intertribal rivalry. Its fifth congress, held December 20–23, 1985, at Kigali, focused on improved ideological training for party cadres, more efficient economic management, and efforts to curb the country's excessive birth rate (currently estimated to be 3.7 percent a year).

Leaders: Maj. Gen. Juvénal HABYARIMANA (President of the Republic), Bonaventure HABYMANA (Secretary General).

LEGISLATURE

The unicameral **National Development Council** (*Conseil pour le Développement National*) currently consists of 70 members elected on December 26, 1983, from 140 candidates nominated by the MNRD.

President: Maurice NTAHOBARI.

CABINET

President	Maj. Gen. Juvénal Habyarimana
Ministers	
Agriculture, Livestock and Forests	Anastase Nteziryayo
Civil Service and Labor	François Habiyakare
Economy and Finance	Vincent Ruhamanya
Foreign Affairs and Cooperation	François Ngarukiyintwali
Health and Social Affairs	Casimir Bizimungu
Higher Education and Scientific Research	Charles Nyandwi
Industry and Handicrafts	Juvénal Uwiringiyimana
Interior	Thomas Habanabakize
Justice	Jean Marie Vianney Mugemana
National Defense	Maj. Gen. Juvénal Habyarimana
Planning	Ambroise Mulindangabo
Posts, Communications and Transport	André Ntagerura
Presidency in Charge of the Economy	Simeon Nteziryayo
Presidency in Charge of Institutional Relations	Edouard Karemera

Primary and Secondary Education   Col. Aloys Nsekalije
Public Works and Equipment   Joseph Nzirorera
Youth, Sports and Cooperative
   Societies   Maj. Augustin Ndindiliyimana

Governor, Central Bank   Augustin Ruzindana

NEWS MEDIA

Press. There are no daily newspapers. The following appear at Kigali: *Hobe* (95,000), youth monthly in Kinyarwanda and French; *Imahvo* (23,000), published weekly by the government information office, in Kinyarwanda; *Kinyamateka* (11,000), twice monthly; *La Relève*, published monthly by the government information office, in French.

News agency. The official facility is *Agence Rwandaise de Presse* (ARP).

Radio and television. The government-controlled *Radiodiffusion de la République Rwandaise* broadcasts daily in Kinyarwanda, Kiswahili, and French. Deutsche Welle Relay Kigali broadcasts in German, French, English, Hausa, Kiswahili, and Amharic. There were approximately 260,000 radio receivers in 1987. There is no television service.

INTERGOVERNMENTAL REPRESENTATION

Ambassador to the US: Aloys UWIMANA.

US Ambassador to Rwanda: Leonard H.O. SPEARMAN, Jr.

Permanent Representative to the UN: Célestin KABANDA.

IGO Memberships (Non-UN): ACCT, ADF, AfDB, BADEA, CCC, CEEAC, CEPGL, EEC(L), *EIB*, IACO, ICO, Intelsat, Interpol, NAM, OAU, OCAM.

ST. CHRISTOPHER AND NEVIS

Saint Christopher and Nevis
(St. Kitts-Nevis)

Political Status: Former British dependency; joined West Indies Associated States in 1967; independent member of the Commonwealth since September 19, 1983.

Area: 101 sq. mi. (262 sq. km.), encompassing Saint Christopher (65 sq. mi.) and Nevis (36 sq. mi.).

Population: 44,404 (1980C), 51,300 (1988E). The 1980 census results yielded 35,104 inhabitants of Saint Christopher and 9,300 of Nevis.

Major Urban Centers (1980C): BASSETERRE (Saint Christopher, 14,725); Charlestown (Nevis, 1,771).

Official Language: English.

Monetary Unit: East Caribbean Dollar (market rate March 1, 1988, 2.70 dollars = $1US).

Sovereign: Queen ELIZABETH II.

Governor General: Sir Clement Athelston ARRINDELL; named Governor General of the Associated State in November 1981, assuming office as Governor General on independence.

Prime Minister: Dr. Kennedy Alphonse SIMMONDS (People's Action Movement); installed as Premier of the Associated State in February 1980, becoming Prime Minister upon independence; redesignated following election of June 21, 1984.

Premier of Nevis: Simeon DANIEL (Nevis Reformation Party); assumed office on independence; redesignated following elections in 1983 and on December 14, 1987.

THE COUNTRY

Conventionally styled St. Kitts-Nevis, Saint Christopher and Nevis forms part of the northern Leeward Islands group of the Eastern Caribbean (see map, p. 22). The population is largely of African descent and the religion primarily Anglican. The economy is dependent on tourism, with several hotels currently under construction; agriculture on the large island is devoted primarily to sugarcane and its derivatives, and on Nevis to coconuts and vegetables. Recent economic planning has focused on the promotion of small-scale local industry and agricultural diversification to reduce the islands' dependence on food imports and fluctuating sugar prices, which by 1983 had fallen to less than half the cost of local production. Subsequently, both sugar and tourist income rose substantially, with further growth targets established under a 1986–1990 development plan.

GOVERNMENT AND POLITICS

Political background. Although one of the smallest territories of the West Indies, St. Kitts was Britain's first colony in the region, being settled in 1623. Ownership was disputed with France until 1783, when Britain acquired undisputed title in the Treaty of Versailles. The tripartite entity encompassing St. Kitts, Nevis, and the northern island of Anguilla entered the West Indies Federation in 1952 and was granted internal autonomy as a member of the West Indies Associated States in February 1967. Three months later, Anguilla repudiated government from Basseterre and, in 1976, was accorded a separate constitution that reconfirmed its status as a dependency of the United Kingdom (see United Kingdom: Related Territories).

The parliamentary election of February 18, 1980, yielded the first defeat of the St. Kitts Labour Party (LP) in nearly three decades and the formation of a government under Dr. Kenneth A. SIMMONDS of the People's Action Movement (PAM), with the support of the Nevis Reformation Party (NRP). Despite protests by the LP, which insisted that the coalition did not have an independence mandate, the Simmonds government issued a white paper on a proposed federal constitution in July 1982. A revised version of the document formed the basis of discussions at London the following December, was endorsed by the St. Kitts-Nevis House of Assembly in March 1983, and secured the approval of the British Parliament in early May. Formal independence followed on September 19.

The PAM/NRP coalition increased its legislative majority at the early election of June 21, 1984, the PAM winning

6 of 8 seats on St. Kitts and the NRP capturing all 3 seats on Nevis.

Constitution and government. The 1983 constitution describes St. Kitts-Nevis as a "sovereign democratic federal state" whose ceremonial head, the British monarch, is represented by a governor general of local citizenship. The governor general appoints as prime minister an individual commanding a parliamentary majority and, on the latter's advice, other ministers, all of whom, except for the attorney general, must be members of the legislature. He also appoints, on the advice of the government, a deputy governor general for the island of Nevis. Legislative matters are entrusted to a unicameral National Assembly, 11 of whose current members (styled "representatives") are directly elected from single-member constituencies (8 on St. Kitts and 3 on Nevis). The governor general may appoint additional members (styled "senators") who can number no more than two-thirds of the elected membership. Constitutional amendments require approval by two-thirds of the representatives, while certain entrenched provisions must also be endorsed by two-thirds of the valid votes in a national referendum. The highest court — apart from the right of appeal, in certain circumstances, to the Privy Council at London — is the West Indies Supreme Court (based on St. Lucia), which includes a Court of Appeal and a High Court, one of whose judges resides on St. Kitts and presides over a Court of Summary Jurisdiction. District courts deal with petty offenses and minor civil actions.

Nevis is provided with an island Assembly, currently consisting of 5 elected and 3 nominated members (the latter not to exceed two-thirds of the former); in addition, the governor general appoints a premier and two other members of the Nevis Assembly to serve as a Nevis Island Administration. Most importantly, the Nevis Islanders have been accorded the right of secession from St. Kitts, if a bill to such effect is approved by two-thirds of the elected legislators and endorsed by two-thirds of those voting on the matter in an island referendum.

Foreign relations. At independence, St. Kitts-Nevis became an independent member of the Commonwealth and shortly thereafter was admitted to the United Nations. It was admitted to the Organization of American States in March 1984. Regionally, it is a member of the Caribbean Community and Common Market (Caricom) and the Organization of Eastern Caribbean States (OECS). Most of its bilateral aid has come from the United Kingdom which, at independence, provided a special grant-loan package of £10 million for capital projects and technical cooperation. The Simmonds government endorsed the intervention in Grenada in October 1983, subsequently receiving modest military assistance from the United States in support of its small voluntary defense force.

Current issues. Following its reelection, the Simmonds government focused on consolidation of the sugar industry and improvements in tourism (which, catering to a largely upper-class clientele, increased substantially following completion of a number of hotel complexes). The recent five-year development plan (published in October 1987, though covering 1986–1990) seeks to reduce unemployment to below 10 percent while holding inflation to less than 5 percent, largely by increases in industrial exports and a further bolstering of tourism from 55,000 arrivals to 104,000.

The major political issue of 1987 stemmed from Dr. William HERBERT's resignation as ambassador to the United States (though not as permanent representative to the United Nations) following allegations in London's *Daily Telegraph* that he had been involved in the laundering of drug money. Declaring that he had been "grossly libelled", Herbert indicated that he intended to take legal action in both Britain and the United States (from which the reports had originally emanated).

POLITICAL PARTIES

Government Coalition:

People's Action Movement (PAM). The PAM is a moderately left-of-center party formed in 1965. It won only 3 of 9 elective seats in the 1980 preindependence balloting, but with the support of 2 members from Nevis was able to force resignation of the existing Labour government. It captured 6 of the 8 seats from St. Kitts in June 1984, thus securing an absolute majority in a new house that had been expanded to 11 elected members.

Leader: Dr. Kennedy Alphonse SIMMONDS (Prime Minister).

Nevis Reformation Party (NRP). Organized in 1970, the NRP had, prior to 1980, campaigned for Nevis' secession from St. Kitts. It won 2 National Assembly seats in 1980 and participated in the independence discussions that led to the formation of the federal state. It captured all 3 seats from Nevis in 1984, after having won all 5 seats to the Nevis Island Assembly in August 1983; it lost one of the latter to Vance AMORY, leader of the **Concerned Citizens' Movement** in a December 1987 island poll.

Leaders: Simeon DANIEL (Premier of Nevis), Levi MORTON (Secretary).

Opposition Party:

Labour Party (LP). Long the dominant grouping on St. Kitts, the LP was organized as a socialist party in 1932. It won 7 of 9 Assembly seats in 1971 and retained a plurality of 4 in 1980, but was forced from office by the PAM/NRP coalition. The party initially opposed federal status for Nevis, claiming that it made Nevis "more equal" than St. Kitts; however, this position was reversed following the LP's crushing defeat in 1984, at which it lost all but two of its legislative seats, including that of opposition leader Lee L. Moore. Subsequent changes included the ascendancy of youth leader Henry Browne as Moore's heir apparent and a distancing of the LP from the 40-year-old sugar workers' union.

Leaders: Charles E. MILLS (Chairman), Lee L. MOORE, Henry BROWNE, Jos. N. FRANCE (Secretary).

Other Parties:

People's Democratic Party (PDP). The PDP is a Nevis-based grouping that secured no representation in the Nevis Island Assembly election of 1983 or the National Assembly election of 1984, at which it contested 2 of the island's seats.

Leader: Theodore HOBSON.

United National Movement (UNM). Also a Nevis-based grouping, the UNM is unrepresented in both the island and national parliaments.

Leader: Eugene WALWYN.

LEGISLATURE

The unicameral **House of Assembly** presently consists of all 11 elected members, plus no more than 7 nominated members (two-thirds by the government, one-third by the opposition). At the most recent balloting of June 21, 1984, the People's Action Movement elected 6 members; the Nevis Reformation Party, 3; and the Labour Party, 2.

Speaker: Herman LIBURD.

CABINET

Prime Minister	Kennedy Alphonse Simmonds
Deputy Prime Minister	Michael Oliver Powell
Premier of Nevis	Simeon Daniel
Deputy Premier of Nevis	Ivor Stevens

Ministers

Agriculture, Lands, Housing, Labor and Development	Hugh Heyliger
Communications, Works and Public Utilities	Ivor Stevens
Education, Health and Community Affairs	Sydney Earl Morris
External Affairs	Kennedy Alphonse Simmonds
Finance	Kennedy Alphonse Simmonds
In the Ministry of Finance	Richard Caines
Labor and Tourism	Michael Oliver Powell
Natural Resources and Environment	Simeon Daniel
Trade and Industry	Roy Jones
Women's Affairs	Constance Mitcham
Without Portfolio	Uhral Swanston
Attorney General	Tapley Seaton

NEWS MEDIA

Press. The following are published at Basseterre: *The Labour Spokesman* (6,000), twice-weekly organ of the St. Kitts-Nevis Trade and Labour Union; *Democrat* (3,000), weekly.

Radio and television. Religious programming is provided by Radio Paradise, while the government-owned ZIZ Radio and Television broadcasts to some 22,000 radio and 7,000 TV receivers. In mid-1984, a new 12-channel television service began transmitting a wide range of US programs, received via satellite, to local subscribers.

INTERGOVERNMENTAL REPRESENTATION

Ambassador to the US: (Vacant).

US Ambassador to St. Kitts-Nevis: Paul A. RUSSO (resident in Barbados).

Permanent Representative to the UN: Dr. William HERBERT.

IGO Memberships (Non-UN): Caricom, CDB, CWTH, EEC(L), Interpol, OAS, OECS.

ST. LUCIA

Saint Lucia

Political Status: Former British dependency; joined West Indies Associated States in 1967; independent member of the Commonwealth since February 22, 1979.

Area: 238 sq. mi. (616 sq. km.).

Population: 120,300 (1980C), 150,000 (1988E).

Major Urban Center (1984E): CASTRIES (50,700).

Official Language: English.

Monetary Unit: East Caribbean Dollar (market rate March 1, 1988, 2.70 dollars = $1US).

Sovereign: Queen ELIZABETH II.

Governor General: Sir Vincent FLOISSAC; sworn in April 30, 1987, upon the retirement of Sir Allen Montgomery LEWIS.

Prime Minister: John George Melvin COMPTON (United Workers' Party); succeeded interim Prime Minister Michael PILGRIM (Progressive Labour Party) following election of May 3, 1982; returned to office following elections of April 6 and 30, 1987.

THE COUNTRY

The second-largest of the former West Indies Associated States, St. Lucia lies between Martinique and St. Vincent in the Windward Islands chain of the eastern Caribbean (see map, p. 22). As in the case of adjacent territories, most of the inhabitants are descendants of West African slaves who were imported as plantation laborers in the seventeenth and eighteenth centuries. Settlement by the French followed the conclusion of a treaty with the indigenous Carib Indians in 1660, and significant traces of French culture remain despite undisputed British control after 1803. At least 80 percent of the population is Roman Catholic.

The principal economic sectors are agriculture, with bananas and coconuts as the leading export items; tourism, which has been growing rapidly in recent years; and manufacturing, which currently embraces over 40 relatively diversified enterprises. Despite satisfactory infrastructural development and significant geothermal energy potential, the economy has been hampered by rapid population growth, which has yielded widespread unemployment (estimated at 22 percent in 1984). Inflation, on the other hand, dropped from 15 percent in 1982 to 1.3 percent in 1985 and, symptomatic of the recent economic upswing, real GDP growth of 5.8 percent was registered in the latter year.

GOVERNMENT AND POLITICS

Political background. Administered after 1833 as part of the British Leeward Islands, St. Lucia was incorporated in 1940 into the Windward Islands group, which also included Dominica, Grenada, and St. Vincent. It participated in the Federation of the West Indies from 1958 to 1962 and became one of the six internally self-governing West Indies Associated States in March 1967. As in the cases of Grenada and Dominica, St. Lucia, under Premier John G.M. COMPTON of the long-dominant United Workers' Party (UWP), applied for independence under a provision of the West Indies Act of 1966 which required only that an Order in Council be laid before the British Parliament. The opposition St. Lucia Labour Party (SLP), led by Allan LOUISY, called initially for a referendum on the issue but subsequently participated in a constitutional conference held at London in July 1978. Following approval of the proposed constitution by the St. Lucia House of Assembly on October 24 and of the draft termination order by both houses of Parliament in December, independence within the Commonwealth was proclaimed on February 22, 1979, with Premier Compton assuming the office of prime minister. Compton was succeeded by Louisy following a landslide victory by the leftist-oriented SLP on July 2.

In the wake of mounting conflict between the prime minister and a radical SLP faction led by Foreign Minister George ODLUM, Louisy resigned on April 30, 1981, in favor of the essentially centrist Winston CENAC. Cenac, in turn, was forced to step down on January 16, 1982, the governor general naming Michael PILGRIM to head an all-party administration pending a general election on May 3 at which Compton's UWP secured a decisive victory, sweeping all but three parliamentary seats. Retaining control by only one seat at the balloting of April 6, 1987, Prime Minister Compton called for a second election only three weeks later, which yielded the same outcome. On June 1, however, the UWP majority was increased to three, when the theretofore opposition leader, Neville CENAC, crossed the aisle and was promptly rewarded by being named foreign minister.

Constitution and government. Under the 1979 constitution, the St. Lucia Parliament consists of "Her Majesty, a Senate and a House of Assembly". The queen, as titular head of state, is represented locally by a governor general whose emergency powers are subject to legislative review. Senators are appointed, serve only for the duration of a given Parliament, may not introduce money bills, and can only delay other legislation. The size of the Assembly is not fixed, although the present house has not been expanded beyond the preindependence membership of 17. The prime minister must be a member of the Assembly and command a majority therein; other ministers are appointed on his advice from either of the two houses. Appointments to various public commissions, as well as the designation of a parliamentary ombudsman, require consultation with the leader of the opposition. The judicial system includes a High Court, with ultimate appeal under certain circumstances to the Privy Council at London.

In 1985, the Compton government announced a plan to divide the island into eight regions, each with its own council and administrative services; implementation of the decentralization plan began in December 1985 and was completed the following year.

Foreign relations. During St. Lucia's independence day ceremonies, Prime Minister Compton committed his government to a "full thrust towards Caribbean integration and West Indian unity", adding, however, that the island's historic links to the West precluded the establishment of diplomatic relations with Cuba. These policies were reversed under Prime Minister Louisy. In August 1979 diplomatic relations were established with the Castro regime and St. Lucia was accorded observer status at the September nonaligned conference at Havana after announcing its intention to apply for full membership in the Third World grouping. Upon returning to power in May 1982, Prime Minister Compton reaffirmed his earlier wariness of Havana while indicating that his administration would cooperate with all regional governments participating in the Organization of Eastern Caribbean States (OECS), established in June 1981. In May 1987 Compton joined with James Mitchell of St. Vincent in urging that the seven OECS members work toward the formation of a single unitary state. However, the proposal was strongly criticized as a form of neocolonialism by Prime Minister Bird of Antigua, while drawing only modest support from other regional leaders.

In early 1984, Compton headed a delegation of government and private sector representatives to Hong Kong, South Korea, and Taiwan in an effort to secure electronic and garment industry investment on the island. The overture was most successful in regard to Taiwan, with whom diplomatic relations were established in May, coincident with the signing of a number of economic accords. Subsequently, in early 1987, the government concluded a tax information exchange with the United States as a means of gaining maximal advantage of the investment potential of the Reagan administration's Caribbean Basin Initiative.

Current issues. While Prime Minister Compton's attempt to enhance his parliamentary majority by calling for a second election in May 1987 failed (the opposition gaining marginally in the popular vote), the defection of Neville Cenac measurably improved the government's position. The SLP responded angrily by accusing Cenac of "political immorality and treachery", although there had been indications of disagreement within its ranks in the allocation of shadow cabinet positions.

Early in the year the small, privately owned St. Lucia Airways had been accused of involvement in gun-running operations by the US Central Intelligence Agency and, under pressure from the government, was forced to change its name to Sky Airways. Subsequently, it ceased operations, transferring its two Boeing 707s to Caribbean Air Transport, a subsidiary of a Florida-based company.

A government decision in February 1988 to introduce casino gambling in hotels drew sharp criticism from the Catholic church, a spokesman arguing that the "evil effects" of the move would outweigh benefits derived from enhanced tourism.

POLITICAL PARTIES

Government Party:

United Workers' Party (UWP). The UWP was organized in 1964 by members of the former National Labour Movement and the People's Progressive Party. The party's basically moderate leader, John G.M. Compton, served as chief minister from 1964 to 1967 and as premier from 1967 to 1979, becoming prime minister upon independence. Decisively defeated in July 1979, the UWP returned to power on May 3, 1982. It obtained a bare majority of one Assembly seat at the election of April 6, 1987, and failed to improve its standing at a second election on April 30.

Leaders: John G.M. COMPTON (Prime Minister), George MALLET (Deputy Prime Minister).

Opposition Parties:

St. Lucia Labour Party (SLP). The SLP is a left-of-center party formed in 1946. After boycotting the independence ceremonies because they were not immediately preceded by balloting for a new Assembly, it won a landslide victory in the election of July 2, 1979. Party leader Allan Louisy resigned as prime minister in April 1981 because of intraparty conflict with "new Left" advocate George Odlum, who subsequently withdrew to form the Progressive Labour Party (below) in opposition to the government of Louisy's successor, Winston Cenac. At its 1984 annual convention, the SLP voted to assign the roles of party leader and leader of the opposition to different individuals, and, in a move interpreted as a swing to the Right, named Castries businessman Julian Hunte to the former post. Resistance from some factions to Hunte and his steadfast rejection of unity proposals from the PLP (below) seemed to have declined by 1986, but the party was unable to secure a majority at either of the 1987 elections.

Leaders: Thomas WALCOTT (Chairman), Julian R. HUNTE (Party Leader), Peter JOSIE (Deputy Leader), Allan F.L. LOUISY (former Prime Minister), Winston CENAC (former Prime Minister).

Progressive Labour Party (PLP). The PLP was formed in May 1981 by SLP dissident George Odlum. Although returning only one member (Jon Odlum, brother of George) at the 1982 Assembly election, it outpolled the SLP by a near two-to-one margin, suggesting that it might supplant the parent group as the country's principal opposition party. During 1986, amid reports of tension between party leaders, George Odlum was unsuccessful in a plea for "some form of unity" with the SLP. The party is presently unrepresented in the lower house.

Leaders: George ODLUM, Michael PILGRIM (former interim Prime Minister), Jon ODLUM.

LEGISLATURE

The **Parliament** of St. Lucia consists of an appointed Senate and an elected House of Assembly, each with a normal life of five years, subject to dissolution.

Senate. The upper house encompasses 11 members, of whom 6 are appointed on the advice of the prime minister, 3 on the advice of the leader of the opposition, and 2 after consultation with religious, economic, and social groups.

President: Henry GIRAUDY.

House of Assembly. The lower house presently consists of 17 members. At the election of April 6, 1987, the United Workers' Party won 9 seats and the St. Lucia Labour Party won 8. A second poll on April 30 yielded the same results, although the defection of Neville Cenac on June 1 gave the UWP a margin of 10 to 7.

Speaker: W. St. Clair DANIEL.

CABINET

Prime Minister	John Compton
Deputy Prime Minister	George Mallet
Ministers	
Agriculture, Land, Fisheries and Cooperatives	Ferdinand Henry
Communications, Works and Transport	Desmond Fostin
Community Affairs	Stephenson King
Education and Culture	Louis George
Finance	John Compton
Foreign Affairs	Neville Cenac
Health and Housing	Romanus Lansiquot
Home Affairs	John Compton
Information and Broadcasting	Romanus Lansiquot
Labor and National Insurance	Romanus Lansiquot
Legal Affairs	Parry Husbands
Planning and Development	John Compton
Trade, Industry and Tourism	George Mallet
Youth, Sports and Social Affairs	Stephenson King
Without Portfolio	Allan Bousquet
Ministers of State	
Agriculture, Lands and Fisheries	Gregory Avril
Housing Development and Urban Renewal	Desmond Brathwaite
Attorney General	Parry Husbands

NEWS MEDIA

Press. The following are published at Castries: *The Voice of St. Lucia* (5,000), twice weekly; *The Crusader* (3,000), weekly; *The Castries Catholic Chronicle* (2,500), monthly; *The Vanguard* (2,000), issued fortnightly by the UWP; *Etolie,* Labour Party organ.

Radio and television. The government-operated Radio St. Lucia provides service in English, while Radio Caribbean International (a subsidiary of CIRTES France) broadcasts in French, English, and Creole. Television is provided by the commercial St. Lucia Television Service, Ltd. There were approximately 95,000 radio and 4,000 television receivers in 1987.

INTERGOVERNMENTAL REPRESENTATION

Ambassador to the US and Permanent Representative to the UN: Dr. Joseph Edsel EDMUNDS.

US Ambassador to St. Lucia: Paul A. RUSSO (resident in Barbados).

IGO Memberships (Non-UN): ACCT, Caricom, CDB, CWTH, EEC(L), *EIB,* Interpol, IWC, NAM, OAS, OECS, SELA.

ST. VINCENT AND THE GRENADINES

Political Status: Former British dependency; joined West Indies Associated States in 1967; independent member of the Commonwealth since October 27, 1979.

Area: 150 sq. mi. (389 sq. km.), including the Grenadine dependencies, which encompass 17 sq. mi. (44 sq. km.).

Population: 87,305 (1970C), 136,000 (1988E).

Major Urban Center (1982E): KINGSTOWN (25,000).

Official Language: English.

Monetary Unit: East Caribbean Dollar (market rate March 1, 1988, 2.70 dollars = $1US).

Sovereign: Queen ELIZABETH II.

Acting Governor General: Henry H. Harvey WILLIAMS; assumed office upon the retirement of Sir Joseph Lambert EUSTACE on February 28, 1988.

Prime Minister: James F. MITCHELL (New Democratic Party); succeeded Robert Milton CATO (St. Vincent Labour Party) following the election of July 25, 1984.

THE COUNTRY

St. Vincent is located in the Windward group of the eastern Caribbean, south of St. Lucia and west of Barbados (see map, p. 22). Its jurisdiction encompasses the northern Grenadine islets of Beguia, Canouan, Mayreau, Mustique, Prune Island, Petit St. Vincent, and Union Island, the southern portion of the chain being part of Grenada. The population is mainly of African and mixed origin, with small numbers of Asians, Caribs, and Europeans. The economy is based almost entirely on tourism and agriculture, with bananas, arrowroot, and coconuts being the principal export commodities. An extended series of volcanic eruptions in April 1979 caused massive devastation and necessitated temporary evacuation of the northern two-thirds of the main island, although substantial recovery was reported by early 1984.

GOVERNMENT AND POLITICS

Political background. Claimed by both Britain and France during the seventeenth and eighteenth centuries, St. Vincent was definitively assigned to the former by the Treaty of Versailles in 1783. Fifty years later, it became part of the general government of Barbados and the Windward Islands and, after the separation of the two in 1885, was administered from Grenada. A founding member of the Federation of the West Indies in 1958, it joined the West Indies Associated States in 1967 as an internally self-governing territory with a right of unilateral termination, which it exercised on October 27, 1979. Upon the state's admission to the Commonwealth as a special member, Sir Sydney GUN-MUNRO, the former governor, assumed the titular role of governor general, while Premier Robert Milton CATO became prime minister and continued in office after balloting on December 5, at which his St. Vincent Labour Party (SVLP) swept 11 of 13 elective parliamentary seats.

At the most recent election, called six months early on July 25, 1984, the SVLP was defeated by the New Democratic Party (NDP), whose 9-member majority forced the resignation of Cato in favor of former premier James F. ("Son") MITCHELL.

In February 1988 Sir Joseph Lambert EUSTACE, who had succeeded Gun-Munro as governor general three years earlier, resigned and was replaced by Henry H. WILLIAMS. Earlier, in his Christmas message, Sir Joseph had expressed his unhappiness with "the glaring evils of party politics as practiced in small mini-states".

Constitution and government. An amended version of the 1969 document defining St. Vincent's status as an Associated State, the present constitution provides for a governor general who acts on behalf of the Crown and who appoints as prime minister the individual best able to command a majority within the legislature. Other cabinet members are appointed on the advice of the prime minister. The unicameral House of Assembly is currently composed of 13 representatives elected by universal adult suffrage in single-member constituencies (12 on St. Vincent and 1 encompassing the Grenadines), plus 6 senators (4 nominated by the government and 2 by the leader of the opposition). The highest court—apart from a right of appeal in certain circumstances to the Privy Council at London—is the West Indies Supreme Court (based on St. Lucia), which includes a Court of Appeal and a High Court, one of whose judges is resident on St. Vincent and presides over a Court of Summary Jurisdiction. District Courts deal with petty offenses and minor civil actions. The main island of St. Vincent is divided into five local parishes (Charlotte, St. George, St. Andrew, St. David, and St. Patrick).

Foreign relations. One of the more moderate Caribbean leaders, Prime Minister Cato declared during independence ceremonies that his government would "not succumb to pressure from any power bloc" and would not seek admission to the Nonaligned Movement because such participation "is to be aligned". Although Cato assisted in establishing the US-backed Regional Security System (RSS), his successor, Prime Minister Mitchell, has taken a strong stance against the "militarization" of the region, helping in 1986 to block the United States' effort to upgrade the RSS to a stronger alignment that would have established a centralized military force to fight "subversion" in the Eastern Caribbean. Mitchell also cancelled St. Vincent's participation in US-Eastern Caribbean joint military maneuvers late in the year.

Relations with the United States are carried on through the US ambassador to Barbados, who, prior to independence, was named special representative to St. Vincent. The island's principal sources of external aid are Britain, Canada, and the United States, which contribute both bilaterally and through donations to the World Bank, the United Nations Development Programme, and the Caribbean Development Bank. Admitted to the United Nations in September 1980, St. Vincent obtained full membership in the Commonwealth in June 1985.

Current issues. Since the NDP's generally unanticipated victory in the 1984 election, Prime Minister Mitchell's government has concentrated on economic affairs, achieving positive results such as a reduced trade deficit and substantial GDP growth from increased manufacturing, agriculture, and tourism; negative factors include shutdown of the sugar industry since 1985, difficulties in the arrowroot sector, an unemployment level of about 30 percent, and severe damage to the banana crop by tropical storm Danielle in September 1986. Despite a commitment to curtail spending and abandon financially unreliable enterprises, deficit financing continued in 1986–1987, yielding increased allotments for school building construction and expansion of educational programs. The 1987–1988 budget offered tax relief for self-employed farmers and fishermen, capital investment incentives to hoteliers, and a waiver of duty and consumption levies on raw material imports for export manufactures.

POLITICAL PARTIES

Government Party:

New Democratic Party (NDP). The NDP is a basically centrist grouping formed in 1975. It became the formal opposition party after the 1979 election, although capturing only 2 legislative seats. Its leader, James Mitchell, lost his own bid for reelection after abandonning his traditional seat from Beguia for a main-island constituency. Subsequently, his successor from the Grenadines resigned, permitting Mitchell to regain the seat at a by-election in June 1980. Following a thorough reorganization, the NDP, campaigning in July 1984 under the slogan "Time for a Change", won a commanding majority of 9 Assembly seats on the basis of 51.4 percent of the votes cast.

Leaders: James F. MITCHELL (Prime Minister), George Owen WALKER (Secretary General).

Opposition Party:

St. Vincent Labour Party (SVLP). Organized in 1955, the SVLP is a moderate socialist party that obtained 10 of 13 elective legislative seats at the preindependence balloting of 1974 and 11 seats in December 1979. It was forced into opposition after winning only 4 seats in 1984. Soon afterward, former prime minister Robert Cato, whose relatively advanced age (69) and recent ill health were viewed as contributing factors in the election reversal, announced his retirement from politics. Hudson Tannis was elected party leader at a special congress in January 1985. His rival for the party leadership, Vincent Beache, was later elected parliamentary opposition leader, indicating continued competition for control of the SVLP prior to Tannis' death in a plane crash on August 3, 1986.

Leaders: Vincent BEACHE (Leader of the Opposition), Burns BONADIE.

Other Parties:

Progressive Democratic Party (PDP). The PDP was formed in September 1981 by Randolph Russell, who had resigned as an SVLP minister in May to sit in the Assembly as an independent. In July he accepted the opposition leadership, being termed, because of his knowledge of SVLP policies, the best-qualified minority member to lead "the fight against mismanagement and corruption". The party polled less than 2 percent of the vote in 1984, returning no assemblymen.

Leader: Randolph B. RUSSELL.

United People's Movement (UPM). The UPM was organized, under the leadership of Ralph Gonsalves, as a coalition of left-wing groups prior to the 1979 election, at which it obtained no parliamentary representation. Gonsalves, once described as "the leading Marxist theoretician in the Caribbean", left the party in 1982 to form the MNU (below), his role as radical leftist advocate being assumed by Oscar Allen.

Leaders: Oscar ALLEN, Renwick ROSE.

Movement for National Unity (MNU). The MNU was organized as a moderate leftist grouping by Dr. Ralph Gonsalves, following his withdrawal from the UPM in 1982.

Leader: Dr. Ralph GONSALVES.

St. Vincent and Grenadines National Movement (SNM). Also known as the St. Vincent National Movement (SVNM), the SNM is a left-of-center party organized after a breakdown in unity talks between the UPM and NDP because of the 1983 Grenada intervention, which was opposed by Oscar Allen and endorsed by James Mitchell.

Leader: Dr. Gideon CORDICE.

LEGISLATURE

The unicameral **House of Assembly** currently consists of 6 appointed senators and 13 representatives elected from single-member constituencies for five-year terms, subject to dissolution. At the election of July 25, 1984, the New Democratic Party won 9 elective seats, while the St. Vincent Labour Party won 4. In June 1986 the House approved a constitutional amendment raising the number of elected representatives to 15.

Speaker: Douglas WILLIAMS.

CABINET

Prime Minister	James F. Mitchell
Ministers	
Communications and Works	Allan C. Cruickshank
Education	John C.A. Horne
Foreign Affairs and Finance	James F. Mitchell
Health	David E. Jack
Housing, Labor and Community Development	Jeremiah C. Scott
Information	Parnell Campbell

Legal Affairs	Parnell Campbell
Tourism and Culture	Burton B. Williams
Trade, Industry and Agriculture	Marcus P.W. Defreitas
Ministers of State	
Communications and Works	Louis Jones
Education and Health	(Vacant)
Trade, Industry and Agriculture	Herbert G. Young
Attorney General	Parnell Campbell

NEWS MEDIA

Press. The following are published at Kingstown: *The Vincentian* (3,800), independent weekly; *The New Times,* NDP weekly; *Justice,* UPM weekly; *The Star,* SVLP fortnightly.

Radio and television. St. Vincent's National Broadcasting Corporation provides local programming as well as BBC news from Kingstown to approximately 66,000 receivers. Television reception from Barbados is possible in some areas.

In May 1987 the government-owned station, Radio 705, was directed not to edit official press releases and to refrain from broadcasting "opposition propaganda" without specific authorization of its manager. The order—bitterly attacked by the PDP's political adversaries as "high-handed interference" with freedom of speech—was defended as a necessary precaution against those "who would seek to cunningly exploit" the administration's commitment to democracy. Subsequently, in April 1988, a radio phone-in program was ordered off the air on the grounds that it had become a vehicle for "blatant mischief-making".

INTERGOVERNMENTAL REPRESENTATION

Ambassador to the US: (Vacant).

US Ambassador to St. Vincent: Paul A. RUSSO (resident in Barbados).

Permanent Representative to the UN: Jonathan C. PETERS.

IGO Memberships (Non-UN): Caricom, CDB, CWTH, EEC(L), *EIB,* ICCO, Interpol, IWC, OAS, OECS, SELA.

SAN MARINO

Most Serene Republic of San Marino
Serenissima Repubblica di San Marino

Political Status: Independent republic dating from the early Middle Ages; under multiparty parliamentary regime.

Area: 23.6 sq. mi. (61 sq. km.).

Population: 22,814 (1985C), 23,600 (1988E). There are also about 20,000 Sanmarinese resident abroad.

Major Urban Center (1985E): SAN MARINO (4,200).

Official Language: Italian.

Monetary Unit: Italian Lira (market rate March 1, 1988, 1244.40 lire = $1US).

Captains Regent: Umberto BARULI (San Marino Communist Party) and Rosolino MARTELLI (San Marino Christian Democratic Party); elected by the Grand and

General Council for six-month terms beginning April 1, 1988, succeeding Gianfranco TERENZI (San Marino Christian Democratic Party) and Rossano ZAFFERANI (San Marino Communist Party).

THE COUNTRY

An enclave within the Italian province of Emilia-Romagna, San Marino is the oldest and, next to Nauru, the world's smallest republic. Its terrain is mountainous, the highest point being Mount Titano, on the western slope of which is located the city of San Marino. The Sammarinese are ethnically and culturally Italian, but their long history has created a strong sense of identity and independence. The principal economic activities are farming, livestock-raising, and some light manufacturing. Wine, textiles, varnishes, ceramics, woolen goods, furniture, and building stone are chief exports, while tourism is the leading source of foreign exchange. Other major sources of income include the sale of postage stamps and an annual budget subsidy from the Italian government.

GOVERNMENT AND POLITICS

Political background. Reputedly founded in the year 301, San Marino is the sole survivor of the numerous independent states that existed in Italy prior to unification in the nineteenth century. A treaty of friendship and cooperation concluded with the Kingdom of Italy in 1862 has been renewed and amended at varying intervals thereafter.

A Communist-Socialist coalition controlled the government until 1957, when, because of defections from its ranks, it lost its majority to the opposition Popular Alliance (composed mainly of Christian Democrats and Social Democrats), which retained power in the elections of 1959, 1964, and 1969. The Christian Democratic–Social Democratic coalition split over economic policy in January 1973, enabling the Socialists to return to power in alliance with the Christian Democrats. In the September 1974 election (the first in which women were allowed to present themselves as candidates for the Grand and General Council), the Christian Democrats and the Social Democrats each lost two seats, while the Communists and the Socialists experienced small gains.

In November 1977 the Socialists withdrew from the government, accusing the Christian Democrats of being bereft of ideas for resolving the country's economic difficulties. Following a lengthy impasse marked by successive failures of the Christian Democrats, Communists, and Socialists to form a new government, a premature general election was held on May 28, 1978, at which the distribution of legislative seats remained virtually unchanged. Subsequently, the Christian Democrats again failed to secure a mandate, and on July 17 a "Government of Democratic Collaboration" involving the Communist, Socialist, and Socialist Unity parties was approved by a bare parliamentary majority of 31 votes. The Social Democrats joined the governing coalition in 1982, but returned to opposition

after the May 1983 election, at which the ruling parties gained an additional Council seat. The leftist government fell on June 11, 1986, when the Communist and Socialist Unity parties withdrew over foreign policy and other issues. On July 26, the Council, by a 39–13 vote, approved a new program advanced by the Christian Democratic and Communist parties, the first such coalition in the country's history.

Constitution and government. San Marino's constitution, dating from the year 1600, vests legislative power in the Grand and General Council (*Consiglio Grande e Generale*) of 60 members directly elected for five-year terms, subject to dissolution. The 10-member State Congress (*Congresso di Stato*), or cabinet, is elected by the Council for the duration of its term. Two members of the Council are designated for six-month terms as executive captains regent (*capitani reggenti*), one representing the city of San Marino and the other the countryside. Each is eligible for reelection three years after the expiration of his term. Although there are civil and criminal courts in San Marino, most major cases are tried before Italian magistrates. Appeals also go initially to Italian courts, but the final court of review in some cases is the Council of Twelve (*Consiglio dei XII*), a panel of jurists chosen for six-year terms by the Grand and General Council. Administratively, San Marino is divided into nine sectors called castles (*castelli*), each of which is directed by an elected committee led by the captain of the castle, who is chosen for a term coincident with that of the captains regent.

Foreign relations. San Marino's relations with Italy (raised to the ambassadorial level in 1979) are governed by a series of treaties and conventions establishing a customs union, regulating public-service facilities, and defining general principles of good neighborly relations. The Republic is a member of several international organizations and maintains observers at both the Council of Europe and the United Nations. It was a signatory of the 1975 Final Act of the Conference on Security and Cooperation in Europe and has participated in the Conference's subsequent review sessions.

In May 1985, San Marino and China concluded a visa-exemption accord, the first such agreement between Beijing and a West European regime.

Current issues. Prior to the government collapse of June 1986, San Marino was the only Communist-dominated state in Western Europe. However, the leftist coalition's less than commanding majority had caused difficulty in securing the passage of legislation in the Grand and General Council. The only precedent for the July coalition with the Christian Democrats was the participation of Italy's Communist Party in the first two de Gasperi administrations after World War II. However, given the weakness of the smaller Sammarinese formations after the May 1988 balloting (see Legislature and Political Parties, below), it appeared likely that the seemingly implausible alliance would be revived.

POLITICAL PARTIES

San Marino's several political parties have close ties with and resemble corresponding parties in Italy.

San Marino Christian Democratic Party (*Partito Democratico Cristiano Sammarinese* — PDCS). Catholic and conservative in outlook, the PDCS came to power in 1957 and in recent years has been the strongest party in the Grand and General Council, winning 25 seats in 1974, 26 in both 1978 and 1983, and 27 in 1988. It ruled as the senior partner in a coalition with the PSS until the latter's withdrawal in December 1977, at which time it was unable to organize a new government majority and went into opposition. It returned to power in an unprecedented coalition with the PCS (below) in July 1986.

Leader: Gabriele GATTI (Secretary General).

San Marino Communist Party (*Partito Comunista Sammarinese* — PCS). A nominally independent offshoot of the Italian Communist Party, the PCS generally follows the line of its Italian parent. In the 1974 Council election the party obtained 15 seats. Subsequently, the sole deputy of the former Movement for Statutory Liberty (*Movimento per le Libertà Statutarie* — MLS) joined the PCS, raising the latter's Council strength to 16. Its representation of 15 in 1978 and 1983 rose to 18 at the election of May 29, 1988.

Leader: Gilberto GHIOTTI (Secretary General).

San Marino Socialist Party (*Partito Socialista Sammarinese* — PSS). A left-wing party, the PSS formed a coalition government with the Christian Democrats in 1973 that was continued after the 1974 election. The party, which won 8 Council seats in 1974, gained an additional deputy as the result of a split in the former San Marino Independent Social Democratic Party (*Partito Socialista Democratico Indipendènte Sammarinese* — PSDIS) in December 1975. It withdrew from the coalition in November 1977, precipitating the fall of the PDCS-led government. It won eight Council seats in 1978 and nine in 1983, entering the government on both occasions. Its exclusion in July 1986 was the first time in 40 years that it had not ruled as an ally of either the PDCS or PCS.

Leader: Antonio VOLPINARI (Secretary General).

Socialist Unity Party (*Partito Socialista Unitario* — PSU). The PSU, formed in December 1975 by the more extreme members of the former PSDIS, is close to the PCS in outlook. It won seven Council seats in 1978 and eight in both 1983 and 1988.

Leaders: Dr. Emilio DELLA BALDA, Patrizia BUSIGNANI (Secretary General).

San Marino Social Democratic Party (*Partito Socialista Democratico Sammarinese* — PSDS). The PSDS, the most moderate of San Marino's three socialist parties, is one of two groups (the other being the PSU) formed as the result of a split in the former PSDIS. It won two seats in the Grand and General Council at the 1978 election and joined the governing coalition in 1982. Its legislative representation dropped to one in the 1983 balloting, none in 1988.

Leader: Augusto CASALI (Secretary General).

San Marino Republican Party (*Partito Repubblicano Sammarinese* — PRS). The PRS is a recently formed party that lost its only Council seat in 1988.

Leader: Cristoforo BUSCARINI (Secretary General).

LEGISLATURE

The **Grand and General Council** (*Consiglio Grande e Generale*) is a unicameral body consisting of 60 members elected for five-year terms by direct popular vote. The captains regent serve as presiding officers. At the election of May 29, 1988, the Christian Democratic Party won 27 seats; the Communist Party, 18; the Socialist Unity Party, 8; and the San Marino Socialist Party, 7.

CABINET

[with the exception of the captains regent, the individuals below constituted a care-taker administration as of June 30, 1988]

Captains Regent	Umberto Baruli
	Rosolino Martelli

State Secretaries

Finance and Budget	Clara Boscaglia
Foreign and Political Affairs	Gabriele Gatti
Internal Affairs	Alvaro Selva

Ministers of State

Commmerce, Tourism and Sport	Arioso Maiani
Education, Justice and Culture	Fausta Simona Morganti
Environment and Agriculture	Fernando Bindi
Health and Social Security	Renzo Ghiotti
Industry and Handicraft	Giuseppe Amici
Labor and Cooperation	P. Natalino Mularoni
Transport and Communications	Gastone Pasolini

NEWS MEDIA

Press. Newspapers and periodicals are published by the government, by some political parties, and by the trade unions. The main publications are *Riscòssa Socialista*, PSU organ; *Il Nuovo Titano*, PSS organ; *San Marino*, PDCS organ; *La Scintilia*, PCS organ. Each has a circulation of approximately 4,000. At irregular intervals the government issues a *Bollettino Ufficiale*.

Radio and television. There is no local radio or television service. *Radio Televisione Italiano* broadcasts a daily information bulletin about the Republic under the title *Notizie di San Marino*.

INTERGOVERNMENTAL REPRESENTATION

San Marino is not a member of the United Nations and does not have diplomatic relations with the United States. It does, however, maintain consular offices at Detroit, New York, and Washington, DC, while US interests in San Marino are represented by the American consulate general at Florence, Italy.

Permanent Observer to the United Nations: Gian Nicola FILIPPI-BALESTRA.

SAO TOME AND PRINCIPE

Democratic Republic of Sao Tome and Principe
República Democrática de São Tomé e Príncipe

Political Status: Achieved independence from Portugal on July 12, 1975; current constitution adopted on December 15, 1982.

Area: 372 sq. mi. (964 sq. km.).

Population: 96,611 (1981C), 117,400 (1988E).

Major Urban Center (1981E): SÃO TOMÉ (20,000).

Official Language: Portuguese.

Monetary Unit: Dobra (market rate March 1, 1988, 72.89 dobras = $1US).

President: Dr. Manuel Pinto da COSTA; assumed office on July 12 and confirmed on December 12, 1975; most recently redesignated to a five-year term by the National Popular Assembly on September 30, 1985.

Prime Minister: Celestino Rocha da COSTA; appointed by the President on January 8, 1988.

THE COUNTRY

Located in the Gulf of Guinea approximately 125 miles off the coast of Gabon, Sao Tome and Principe embraces a small archipelago consisting of two main islands (after which the country is named) and four islets: Cabras, Gago Coutinho, Pedras Tinhosas, and Rolas. Volcanic in origin, the islands exhibit numerous craters and lava flows; the climate is warm and humid most of the year. Of mixed ancestry, the indigenous inhabitants are mainly descended from Negro plantation laborers imported from the African mainland. There is also a small European (mostly Portuguese) minority. Roman Catholicism is the principal religion. Women constituted 31 percent of the economically active population at the 1981 census and hold a limited number of leadership positions in both party and government.

Sao Tome and Principe was once the world's leading producer of cocoa, and although production has declined in recent years, cocoa still supplies over three-fourths of the country's export earnings. Other agricultural products include copra, coffee, palm kernels, sugar, and bananas, while consumables dominate the small industrial sector. Low world cocoa prices since 1980 and drought in 1982–1984 aggravated balance of-payment-deficits and hampered government efforts to revitalize an economy that had previously been depressed by the flight of Portuguese management and skilled labor at independence. Recent efforts have been directed at rehabilitating the cocoa industry (see Current issues, below) and diversifying the economy with the development of fishing and tourism.

GOVERNMENT AND POLITICS

Political background. Discovered by Portuguese explorers in 1471, Sao Tome and Principe became Portuguese territories in 1522–1523 and, collectively, an Overseas Province of Portugal in 1951. Nationalistic sentiments became apparent in 1960 with the formation of the Committee for the Liberation of Sao Tome and Principe (CLSTP). In 1972 the CLSTP became the Movement for the Liberation of Sao Tome and Principe (MLSTP), which was to remain the leading advocate of independence from Portugal as well as the paramount political force in the country. Under the leadership of Dr. Manuel Pinto da COSTA, the Gabon-based MLSTP carried out a variety of underground activities, particularly in support of protests by African workers against low wages.

In 1973 the MLSTP was recognized by the Organization of African Unity, and in the same year the country was granted local autonomy from Portugal. After the 1974 military coup at Lisbon, the Portuguese government began negotiations with the MLSTP, which it recognized as sole official spokesman for the islands. The two agreed in November 1974 that independence would be proclaimed on July 12, 1975, and that a transitional government would be formed under MLSTP leadership until that time. Installed on December 21, 1974, the transitional government council encompassed four members appointed by the MLSTP and one by Portugal. Upon independence, da Costa assumed the presidency and promptly designated his MLSTP associate, Miguel Anjos da Cunha Lisboa TROVOADA, as prime minister. In December 1978, however, Trovoada was relieved of his duties and in October 1979 arrested on charges that he had been involved in a projected coup, one of a series da Costa claimed to have foiled with the aid of Angolan troops (see Foreign relations, below). The president subsequently served as both head of state and chief executive without serious domestic challenge, despite Trovoada's release in 1981. On January 8, 1988, the office of prime minister was revived, Celestino Rocha da COSTA being appointed to the post.

Constitution and government. Under the 1982 constitution, a unicameral National Popular Assembly is the supreme organ of state and confirms the president for a five-year term upon nomination by the MLSTP. The president has sole authority to appoint and dismiss members of the cabinet and may adopt special powers by proclaiming a state of emergency. In the event of death, incapacitation, or resignation, his powers are assumed by the president of the Assembly, pending the designation of a successor. Prospective legislators have heretofore been nominated by an MLSTP-dominated Candidature Commission and elected for five-year terms by People's District Assemblies, although the MLSTP Central Committee announced in October 1987 that the election of the president, legislators, and numbers of "other leading bodies" would in the future be by direct universal and secret ballot. The judiciary is headed by a Supreme Court, whose members are proposed by the MLSTP but designated by and responsible to the Assembly.

Administratively, the country is divided into 2 provinces (coterminous with each of the islands) and 12 counties (11 of which are located on Sao Tome).

Foreign relations. Despite the exodus of much of its Portuguese population in 1974–1975, Sao Tome and Principe continued to maintain an active commercial trade with the former colonial power, generally cordial relations being somewhat strained in mid-1983 because of dissatisfaction over a projected aid package and the activities of Lisbon-based groups opposed to the da Costa regime. Following independence, diplomatic relations were established with the Soviet Union and the Eastern-bloc countries as well as the major Western states. Relations with other former Portuguese dependencies in Africa, particularly Angola, have been close; in 1978 some 1,000 troops from Angola (and a small contingent from Guinea-Bissau) were dispatched to Sao Tome to guard against what President da Costa claimed to be a series of coup plots by expatriates in Angola, Gabon, and Portugal. Most of the troops were reportedly withdrawn by early 1985 in a move toward rapprochement with the West that included the signing of a bilateral military cooperation agreement at Lisbon in February 1987.

Current issues. Since 1985, the administration of President da Costa has revised its economic strategy in favor of partial denationalization and the encouragement of foreign investment. Revival of the cocoa industry has received particular attention with foreign management skills being courted to maximize an injection of capital from Western sources. Other measures have included the privatization of "people's shops", hotel and airport construction to enhance tourism, and application for membership in the franc zone to generate much needed foreign exchange.

In April 1986 the administration's longtime concern over external destabilization was reinforced by the somewhat confusing saga of 76 nationals who, after allegedly receiving military training on the mainland in preparation for antigovernment activity, were granted temporary refuge as "boat people" by Namibian authorities. A further coup attempt was repulsed on March 8, 1988, when a group of 40 armed men, some alleged to be mercenaries, disembarked from small boats in the vicinity of the capital and attacked a police headquarters building.

POLITICAL PARTIES

Government Party:

Movement for the Liberation of Sao Tome and Principe (*Movimento de Libertação de São Tomé e Príncipe* — MLSTP). Originally known as the Committee for the Liberation of Sao Tome and Principe (*Comité de Libertação de São Tomé e Príncipe* — CLSTP), the MLSTP was founded in 1972 and gradually became the leading force in the campaign for independence from Portugal. At its first congress in 1978 the MLSTP defined itself as a "revolutionary front of democratic, anti-neocolonialist, and anti-imperialist forces". However, it did not formally adopt Marxism-Leninism despite the ideology's influence on its leaders and their economic policies. At an extraordinary congress in 1982, the MLSTP reaffirmed its position as a "democratic front" that solicited membership from those interested in contributing to the country's development "regardless of political and ideological disposition". At the most recent congress on September 26–28, 1985, the party's Central Committee was increased from 35 to 51 members, including 10 alternates; delegates also endorsed the government's decision to reduce state control of the economy (see Current issues, above). At the conclusion of an eight-day Central Committee meeting on October 18, 1988, a number of changes in party and state electoral procedures were advanced, including selection of the party president (who would continue to be the sole candidate for the national presidency) from two Committee-approved nominees.

Leader: Dr. Manuel Pinto da COSTA (President of the Republic and of the Party).

External Opposition Groups:

Two Lisbon-based groups, the **Independent Democratic Union of Sao Tome and Principe** (*União Democrática Independente de São Tomé e Príncipe* — UDISTP) and the **Sao Tome and Principe National Resistence Front** (*Frente de Resistência Nacional de São Tomé e Príncipe* — FRNSTP), announced on March 20, 1986, that they were forming a **Democratic Opposition Coalition of Sao Tome and Principe** (*Coalizão Democrática de Oposição de São Tomé e Príncipe* — CDOSTP) to combat what they called the "totalitarianism" of the da Costa government. The stated aim of the CDOSTP is to establish "a free and democratic regime" achieved through "honest elections". Although the UDISTP previously had taken the position that its goals were to be reached through "peaceful means", its association with the FRNSTP, generally considered a more radical group, led to a CDOSTP posture that did not rule out "recourse to armed struggle". The coalition, which reportedly has the support of right-wing Portuguese interests, suffered a setback in mid-year when FRNSTP chairman Carlos da GRAÇA resigned, commending the government for "initiating a new era of economic liberalization". Subsequently da Graça returned to Sao Tome and was named foreign minister in the government formed in January 1988.

LEGISLATURE

The 1982 constitution provides for a unicameral **National Popular Assembly** (*Assembléia Popular Nacional*) of 40 members indirectly elected for five-year terms by the People's District Assemblies, the most recent balloting for which was conducted on August 16–20, 1985. All of the deputies are members of and nominated by the MLSTP.

President: Alda Neves Graça do ESPÍRITO SANTO.

CABINET

Prime Minister	Celestino Rocha da Costa
Ministers	
Agriculture and Fisheries	Oscar Aguiar Sacramento e Sousa
Cooperation	Guillermo Posser da Costa
Defense and Internal Security	Raul Bragança Neto Goméz
Education and Culture	Ligia do Espirito Santo Costa
Economy and Finance in Charge of Planning and Trade	Teotonio Angelo d'Alava Torres
Foreign Affairs	Carlos Alberto Dias da Graça
Health, Labor and Social Security	Armindo Vaz de Almeida
Justice and Public Affairs	Francisco Fortunado Pires
Prime Minister's Office for the Island of Principe	Manuel Quaresma Costa
Transportation and Communications	Carlos Ferreira
Government Secretary General	Manuel Vaz Afonso Fernandes
Governor, Bank of Sao Tome and Principe	Teotonio Angelo d'Alava Torres

NEWS MEDIA

Press. The following are published intermittently at São Tomé: *Diário da República; Povo; Revolução,* government organ.

News Agency. It was reported in mid-1985 that the Angolan News Agency, ANGOP, had joined with the national radio station in establishing a Sao Tomean facility, STP/Press.

Radio and television. Radio service is provided by the official *Rádio Nacional de São Tomé e Príncipe.* There is also closed-circuit television service available two nights a week to a limited number of receivers.

INTERGOVERNMENTAL REPRESENTATION

Ambassador to the US and Permanent Representative to the UN: Joaquim Rafael BRANCO.

US Ambassador to Sao Tome and Principe: Warren CLARK, Jr., (resident in Gabon).

IGO Memberships (Non-UN): ADF, AfDB, BADEA, Copal, EEC(L), *EIB,* ICCO, NAM, OAU.

SAUDI ARABIA

Kingdom of Saudi Arabia
al-Mamlakah al-'Arabiyah al-Su'udiyah

Political Status: Unified kingdom established September 23, 1932; under absolute monarchical system.

Area: 829,995 sq. mi. (2,149,690 sq. km.).

Population: 7,012,642 (1974C); there have been no recent official figures and foreign estimates vary widely (from a low of 7.0 million to a high of 12.5 million in 1988). The previously substantial nonnational workforce has fallen by at least half, to less than 1.0 million since 1983.

Major Urban Centers (1986E): RIYADH (1,976,000); Jiddah (1,084,000); Mecca (510,000); Medina (355,000); al-Ta'if (282,000).

Official Language: Arabic.

Monetary Unit: Riyal (market rate March 1, 1988, 3.75 riyals = $1US).

Ruler and Prime Minister: King Fahd ibn 'Abd al-'Aziz Al SA'UD; confirmed by the royal court upon the death of King Khalid ibn 'Abd al-'Aziz Al SA'UD on June 13, 1982.

Crown Prince and First Deputy Prime Minister: 'Abdallah ibn 'Abd al-'Aziz Al SA'UD, half-brother of the King; appointed Crown Prince and Heir to the Throne on June 13, 1982.

THE COUNTRY

A vast, largely desert country occupying the greater part of the Arabian peninsula, the Kingdom of Saudi Arabia exhibits both traditional and contemporary modes of life. Until recently, frontiers were poorly defined and no census was undertaken prior to 1974. Some 85 percent of the indigenous inhabitants, who have traditionally adhered to patriarchal forms of social organization, are Sunni Muslim of the conservative Wahhabi sect; the Shi'ite population (15 percent) is located primarily in Eastern Province. A strict interpretation of Islam by both has limited female participation in the paid labor force to about 5 percent; paradoxically, it has also resulted in a fairly sizeable number of women in the professions, since education, banking, and health care are strictly segregated by gender. Mecca and Medina, two of the principal holy cities of Islam and the goals of an annual pilgrimage by Muslims from all over the world, lie within the western region known as the Hijaz, where the commercial center of Jiddah is also located.

Saudi Arabia is the leading exporter of oil and possesses the largest known petroleum reserves, which account for its status as one of the world's richest nations. Having acquired a 60 percent interest in the Arabian-American Oil Company (Aramco) in 1974, the government in September 1980 completed payment for the remaining 40 percent, although foreign interests continue to hold concessions for on- and offshore exploitation of oil and gas reserves in the Kuwaiti-Saudi Partitioned Zone. Dramatic surges in oil revenue permitted heightened expenditure after 1973 that focused on the development of an elaborate system of airports, seaports, and roads as well as the modernization of medical, educational, and telecommunications systems. Large-scale irrigation projects yielded agricultural self-sufficiency in a country that once produced only 10 percent of its food needs. Vast sums were also committed to armaments, particularly modern fighter planes, missiles, and air-defense systems.

Because of falling oil prices and massive support to Iraq in its war with Iran, the Saudis have experienced a major recession since 1981, with per capita GDP falling from nearly $20,000 to less than $11,000. Government reserves, estimated at $125 billion in 1983, had fallen by about one-half by 1986 because of budget deficits, although analysts continue to expect Saudi Arabia to complete successfully the transition from a construction-based to a production-based economy.

GOVERNMENT AND POLITICS

Political background. Founded in 1932, the Kingdom of Saudi Arabia was largely the creation of King 'Abd al-'Aziz Al SA'UD (Ibn Sa'ud), who devoted 30 years to reestablishing the power his ancestors had held in the eighteenth and nineteenth centuries. Oil concessions were granted in the 1930s to what later became the Arabian-American Oil Company, but large-scale production did not begin until the late 1940s.

Ibn Sa'ud was succeeded in 1953 by an ineffectual son, Sa'ud ibn 'Abd al-'Aziz Al SA'UD, who was persuaded by family influence in 1958 to delegate control to his younger brother, Crown Prince Faysal ibn 'Abd al-'Aziz Al SA'UD. Faysal began a modernization program, abolished slavery, curbed royal extravagance, adopted sound fiscal policies, and personally assumed the functions of prime minister prior to the formal deposition of King Sa'ud on November 2, 1964. Faysal was assassinated by one of his nephews, Prince Faysal ibn Musa'id ibn 'Abd al-Aziz Al SA'UD, while holding court at Riyadh on March 25, 1975, and was immediately succeeded by his brother, Crown Prince Khalid ibn 'Abd al-'Aziz Al SA'UD.

Despite a number of coup attempts, the most important occurring in the summer of 1969 following the discovery of a widespread conspiracy involving both civilian and military elements, internal stability has tended to prevail under the monarchy. The regime was visibly shaken, however, in late 1979 when several hundred members of the fundamentalist *al-Ikhwan* group seized the Grand Mosque at Mecca on November 20, during the annual period of pilgrimage to that city. Under the leadership of a *mahdi* (messiah), the Ikhwan called for an end to corruption and monarchial rule, and for a return to strict Islamic precepts. Portions of the complex were held for two weeks, with several hundred casualties being suffered by the insurgents, their hostages, and government forces. Collaterally, the Shi'ite minority in Eastern Province initiated antigovernment demonstrations. Among the 63 fundamentalists publicly beheaded on January 9, 1980, for their participation in the seizure of the Mosque were citizens of several other Islamic countries, including Egypt and South Yemen.

King Khalid died of a heart attack on June 13, 1982, and was immediately succeeded, as both monarch and prime minister, by his half-brother and heir, Crown Prince Fahd ibn 'Abd al-'Aziz Al SA'UD. On the same day, Prince 'Abdallah ibn 'Abd al-'Aziz Al SA'UD was designated heir to the throne and first deputy prime minister.

Constitution and government. Saudi Arabia is a traditional monarchy with all power ultimately vested in the king, who is also the country's supreme religious leader. No national elections have been held, there are no political parties, and legislation is by royal decree. In recent years, an attempt has been made to modernize the machinery of government by creating ministries to manage the increasingly complex affairs of state. Members of the royal family hold many sensitive posts, however, and the present king, like his immediate predecessor, serves additionally as prime minister. The judicial system, encompassing summary and general courts, a Court of Cassation, and a Supreme Council of Justice, is largely based on Islamic religious law (*shari'a*), but tribal and customary law is also applied; under both circumstances women inherit half a man's share of their father's estates, their testimony is worth half that of a man's, and purdah is enforced in business and public life.

Saudi Arabia is administratively divided into 6 major and 12 minor provinces, each headed by an appointed governor. The principal urban areas have elected municipal councils, while villages and tribes are governed by sheikhs in conjunction with their legal advisers and two other community leaders.

In March 1980, the Saudi government announced that an eight-member committee had been established to draw up a "basic system of rule" guided by Islamic principles; subsequently, in June 1983, King Fahd called upon scholars to modernize Islamic law. To date, however, no public alteration of the legal system has been evidenced.

Foreign relations. Since the late 1950s, Saudi Arabia has stood out as the leading conservative power in the Arab world. The early 1960s were marked by hostility toward Egypt over North Yemen, Riyadh supporting the royalists and Cairo backing the republicans during the civil war that broke out in 1962. By 1969, however, Saudi Arabia had become a prime mover behind the pan-Islamic movement and subsequently sought to mediate such disputes as the Lebanese conflict in 1976 and the ongoing Iran-Iraq war. The Kingdom continues to be in the forefront of Middle East peace initiatives by maintaining cordial relations with virtually all the states of the Arab League and the Islamic Conference, as well as with the Palestine Liberation Organization (PLO), which it supports financially. An influential member of the Organization of Petroleum Exporting Countries (OPEC), it was long a restraining influence in the matter of oil price increases, with Saudi refusal to endorse more than a 5 percent increase in December 1976 leading to the first major cleavage within the membership. In 1985, however, Saudi Arabia abandoned its leadership role in the face of unrestrained competition, prompted by declining oil prices, among OPEC members (see Current issues, below).

Adamantly anti-Communist, the Saudi government has been consistently allied with the United States despite opposition to the 1979 Egyptian-Israeli peace treaty. The Saudis, who provided financial support for other Arab countries involved in the 1967 and 1973 Arab-Israeli conflicts, broke diplomatic relations with Cairo in April 1979, while a subsequent decision to increase oil production temporarily in the face of supply shortages caused by the 1979 Iranian revolution was widely viewed as part of an effort to garner increased Western support for the Arab position on the Palestinian question.

The outbreak of the war between Iraq and Iran in September 1980 prompted the US Carter administration, which earlier in the year had rejected Saudi requests for equipment to upgrade its military capabilities, to announce the "temporary deployment" of four Airborne Warning and Control Systems (AWAC aircraft) to Saudi Arabia. An additional factor was the strong support given by Riyadh to Washington's plan, introduced following the Soviet intervention in Afghanistan, to increase the US military presence throughout the Gulf region. Subsequently, despite vehement Israeli objections, the Reagan administration secured Senate approval in October 1981 on a major package of arms sales to Saudi Arabia that included five of the surveillance aircraft, although delivery of the latter did not commence until mid-1986 because of controversy over US supervisory rights. Earlier, in an effort to win congressional approval for their arms purchases, the Saudis had indicated a willingness to allow American use of bases in the Kingdom in the event of Soviet military action in the Gulf. As the US Iran—*contra* scandal unfolded in late 1986 and 1987, it was alleged that the Saudis had agreed in 1981 to aid anti-Communist resistance groups around the world as part of the AWAC purchase deal, ultimately making some $32 million available to the Nicaraguan rebels between July 1984 and March 1985 when US funding for the *contra* cause had been suspended by Congress. Subsequently, plans announced by the White House in May 1987 to sell over a billion dollars' worth of planes and missiles to Saudi Arabia were delayed by congressional hearings into the "Irangate" affair.

In December 1981, Saudi Arabia concluded a treaty with Iraq confirming an unratified 1975 agreement to partition a diamond-shaped Neutral Zone that had been established in 1922 to accord nomads unimpeded access to traditional pasture and watering areas. At the signing, Saudi representatives called on all other components of "the Arab nation" to support Iraq in the conflict with its eastern neighbor. Subsequently, a number of incidents in the Persian Gulf attested to the sensitive position of the Saudis in the wake of the Iranian revolution. During 1987 the seven-year conflict yielded continued political tension between revolutionary Teheran and pro-Western Riyadh, with repercussions even extending to religious observances sacred to the Arab world (see Current issues, below).

In late 1982, an Arab League peace delegation that visited the USSR included Foreign Minister Sa'ud, the first representative of the monarchy known to have visited Moscow in several decades. Remarks made by the prince suggesting that Moscow could play a role in Mideast negotiations gave rise to speculation that bilateral relations between the two countries might improve. In 1985, there were indications that the Kingdom was moving closer to establishing formal diplomatic relations with the Soviet Union, suspended since 1937, following steps in that direction by Oman and the United Arab Emirates.

Current issues. The intertwined politics of oil, weapons, and economic retrenchment have dominated recent Saudi Arabian affairs. Angered that other OPEC countries were "cheating" on their agreements to limit production and concerned about competition by non-OPEC countries, particularly Britain, the government in early 1986 expanded output in an apparent attempt to regain control of the world oil market. However, the controversial plan failed to alter British policy, and a further plunge in prices ensued. In October, after 24 years of global economic influence, Sheikh Ahmad Zaki YAMANI was dismissed as oil minister, his successor, Hisham NAZIR, immediately calling for OPEC reconciliation in an attempt to stabilize both price and production.

The plunge in oil prices clouded the Saudi Arabian economy, yielding a standstill in construction and the collapse or restructuring of many business enterprises. However, no cuts were advanced in military spending because of possible Iranian aggression should Tehran prove victorious in its war with Iraq.

Saudi concern over the spread of revolutionary Shi'ite influence in the Gulf region and Iranian intransigence in light of it provided the spark in late July 1987 for a major confrontation at Mecca's Grand Mosque which resulted in the death of an estimated 400 Iranian pilgrims. The speaker of Iran's parliament, Hashemi Rafsanjani, called for the immediate "uprooting" of the Saudi royal family in retaliation for the incident, while King Fahd, supported by most of the Arab states, vowed to continue as "custodian" of Islam's holy shrines. In April 1988, citing the Mecca riot and increased Iranian attacks on its vessels, Saudi Arabia became the first member of the Gulf Cooperation Council to sever diplomatic relations with Teheran.

POLITICAL PARTIES

There are no political parties in Saudi Arabia.

LEGISLATURE

There is no legislature. Crown Prince Fahd stated in August 1975 that a quasi-legislative Consultative Council would soon be appointed; the assertion was repeated in early 1980, although no action in the matter had been taken by the end of 1987.

CABINET

Prime Minister	Fahd ibn 'Abd al-'Aziz Al Sa'ud
First Deputy Prime Minister	'Abdallah ibn 'Abd al-'Aziz Al Sa'ud
Second Deputy Prime Minister	Sultan ibn 'Abd al-'Aziz Al Sa'ud
Ministers	
Agriculture and Water	'Abd al-Rahman ibn 'Abd al-'Aziz ibn Hasan al-Shaykh
Commerce	Sulayman 'Abd al-Aziz al-Sulaym
Communications	Husayn Ibrahim al-Mansuri
Defense and Aviation	Sultan ibn 'Abd al-'Aziz Al Sa'ud
Education	'Abd al-'Aziz 'Abdallah al-Khuwaytir
Finance and National Economy	Muhammad 'Ali Aba al-Khayl
Foreign Affairs	Sa'ud al-Faysal Al Sa'ud
Health	Faysal 'Abd al-'Aziz Alhegelan
Higher Education	(Vacant)
Industry and Electricity	'Abd al-'Aziz ibn 'Abdallal al-Zamil
Information	'Ali Hasan al-Sha'ir
Interior	Nayif ibn 'Abd al-'Aziz Al Sa'ud
Justice	Ibrahim ibn Muhammad ibn Ibrahim al-Shaykh
Labor and Social Affairs	Muhammad 'Ali al-Fayiz
Municipal and Rural Affairs	Ibrahim ibn 'Abdallah al-'Angari
Petroleum and Mineral Resources	Hisham Muhyi al-Din Nazir
Pilgrimage Affairs and Religious Trusts	'Abd al-Wahab 'Abd al-Wasi
Planning	Hisham Muhyi al-Din Nazir
Post, Telephone and Telegraph	'Alawi Darwish Kayyal
Public Works and Housing	Mit'ib ibn 'Abd al-'Aziz Al Sa'ud
Governor, Saudi Arabian Monetary Agency	Hamad al-Sayyari

NEWS MEDIA

Most newspapers and periodicals are published by privately (but not individually) owned national press institutions. A number of periodicals are also published by the government and by Aramco. While censorship was formally abolished in 1961 and there is no official legal restriction on news coverage and expression, criticism of the king and government policy is frowned upon, and a genuinely free flow of ideas from the outside world is discouraged.

Press. The following papers are Arabic dailies published at Jiddah, unless otherwise noted: *al-Jazirah* (Riyadh, 152,000); *al-Riyadh* (Riyadh, 143,000); *Okaz* (76,000); *al-Madina al-Munawara* (55,000); *Arab News* (50,000), in English; *al-Nadwah* (Mecca, 33,000); *al-Yaum* (Dammam, 32,000); *al-Bilad* (30,000); *Saudi Gazette* (25,000), in English; *al-Sharq al-Aswat* (13,000).

News agency. The Saudi Press Agency, is located at Riyadh.

Radio and television. The Saudi Arabian Broadcasting Service, a government facility, operates a number of radio stations broadcasting in both Arabic and English, while Aramco Radio broadcasts from Dhahran in English. The Saudi Arabian Government Television Service broadcasts from a dozen locations, including Riyadh, Jiddah, and Medina. There were approximately 3.8 million television receivers in 1987.

INTERGOVERNMENTAL REPRESENTATION

Ambassador to the US: Prince Bandar ibn SULTAN.

US Ambassador to Saudi Arabia: Walter Leon CUTLER.

Permanent Representative to the UN: Samir SHIHABI.

IGO Memberships (Non-UN): ADF, AfDB, AFESD, AMF, BADEA, CCC, GCC, IC, IDB, Intelsat, Interpol, IWTC, LAS, NAM, OAPEC, OPEC.

SENEGAMBIA

Confederation of Senegambia
La Confédération de Sénégambie

Political Status: Confederation of the states of Senegal and Gambia, "each of which shall maintain its independence and sovereignty", on basis of merger agreement concluded December 17, 1981, with effect from February 1, 1982.

Area: 85,111 sq. mi. (207,487 sq. km.), encompassing Senegal, 75,750 sq. mi. (196,192 sq. km.), and Gambia, 4,361 sq. mi. (11,295 sq. km.).

Population: 8,000,000 (1988E), including 7,178,000 Senegalese and 822,000 Gambians.

Major Urban Centers (1977E): DAKAR, Senegal (818,000); BANJUL, Gambia (44,000).

Official Languages: English and French, in addition to African languages "chosen to this effect by the President and Vice President of the Confederation".

Monetary Units: As of March 1, 1988, the CFA franc (pegged to the French franc) continued to circulate in Senegal and the dalasi (pegged to the British pound) in Gambia (see separate articles, below). Under the agreement establishing the Confederation, a monetary union was projected, involving abandonment of the dalasi and adoption of the franc as a common unit of exchange.

President: Abdou DIOUF; sworn in as President of Senegal on January 1, 1981, to fill balance of five-year term expiring in February 1983; elected to a full term on February 27, 1983; reelected on February 28, 1988.

Vice President: Alhaji Sir Dawda Kairaba JAWARA; elected President of Gambia in 1970; most recently reelected for a five-year term on March 11, 1987.

THE COUNTRY

Situated on the bulge of West Africa, Senegambia is bordered by Mauritania on the north, Mali on the east, and Guinea and Guinea-Bissau on the south. Surrounded on three sides by Senegalese territory, Gambia is a narrow enclave some 6 to 10 miles wide that encompasses both shores of the Gambia River to a point some 200 miles inland from the Atlantic. Consisting largely of flat or rolling savanna, the region is peopled mainly by Africans of varied ethnic backgrounds, with the Wolof, whose language is widely used commercially, being the largest group. French, in Senegal, and English, in Gambia, are spoken only by literate minorities of less than 20 percent. There is greater uniformity in religion, Islam being professed by more than 80 percent throughout the Confederation.

Agricultural output is centered on peanuts, which in raw or processed form typically account for more than 25 percent of export earnings in Senegal and more than 80 percent in Gambia. In recent years, however, drought conditions and a succession of poor peanut harvests have contributed to widespread inflation and balance-of-payment difficulties that have been only partially offset by foreign assistance tendered largely by the former colonial powers, France and Britain.

GOVERNMENT AND POLITICS

Political background. A merger of Senegal and Gambia was advanced on August 19, 1981, following a left-wing

uprising at Banjul, Gambia, in late July that was suppressed by some 2,000 Senegalese troops acting at the Gambian president's request under a 1965 mutual defense and security accord (see Gambia article). A formal agreement launching the Confederation was signed on December 17 at Dakar, Senegal, by Presidents Abdou DIOUF and Dawda JAWARA, implementing an understanding reached at Banjul on November 12–14. The pact was approved by the legislatures of both states on December 29 and came into effect on February 1, 1982.

Following parliamentary approval by both states of protocol agreements to implement the Confederation, a joint Council of Ministers, composed of six Senegalese and five Gambians, was announced on November 4, 1982. The Confederal Assembly met for the first time on January 13, 1983, and subsequently established nine working committees dealing with defense, transport, and other areas of planned cooperation.

In 1984 Gambia began to recruit and train an army and military police in accordance with the joint defense protocol, and the Assembly authorized division of the Confederation into six regions for security purposes. However, full integration of armed forces had not occurred by early 1988, with little progress toward economic and monetary union.

Constitution and government. The agreement establishing Senegambia provides that the component states will integrate their armed and security forces and establish an economic and monetary union, while remaining politically independent entities obligated to "coordinate" their policies in foreign affairs, internal communications, and other areas. The presidents of Senegal and Gambia serve as president and vice president, respectively, of the Confederation, and as chairman and vice chairman of a joint Council of Ministers. Two-thirds of the members of a Confederal Assembly are designated by the Senegalese National Assembly and one-third by the Gambian House of Representatives. Existing governmental institutions remain in effect at the state level, including judicial bodies.

In October 1986, greater parity under a Confederal Armed Forces Defence and Integration Pact (concluded in 1983) was achieved by means of a protocol that made general mobilization, the declaration of a state of emergency, or placing Senegambian troops on the alert a joint responsibility of the two presidents, rather than of the (Senegalese) confederal president alone. Late in 1987, it was decided that the Senegambian Permanent Secretariat, largely superfluous since the Confederation's launching, would be disbanded.

Foreign relations. Since the confederal agreement provides for policy coordination rather than institutional merger in the conduct of foreign affairs, each state has retained separate representation in the various international bodies to which each belonged prior to February 1, 1982. On the other hand, in its first policy statement to the Confederal Assembly in December 1984, the Committee on External Affairs outlined a "Senegambian" position on the Western Sahara, which essentially reaffirmed that of the Organization of African Unity.

Current issues. Opposition to the establishment of Senegambia came primarily from the smaller state and one of the four parties contesting the 1987 Gambian election was organized to protest the "unequal relationship" that the Confederation was alleged to entail (see Gambia, Political Parties). Earlier, one of the few Senegalese critics, former prime minister Mamadou Dia, had termed the merger "a veritable annexation" that "does not augur well for relations between the [two] peoples".

The goal of economic and monetary union has been impeded for a variety of reasons. One has been the basic similarity of the Senegalese and Gambian economies, which has long promoted competition in both peanut and cereal production, while the establishment of a common currency has been delayed by Banjul's reluctance to enter the franc zone. Thus, "Senegambia" continues to exist, at best, as an emerging rather than an actualized entity.

POLITICAL PARTIES

Senegal and Gambia are somewhat atypical by contemporary African standards in that both currently support multiparty systems. As of early 1987, there were no reports of efforts to establish transnational party organizations. (For party groupings in the two states, see entries under Senegal and Gambia, below.)

LEGISLATURE

A unicameral **Confederal Assembly** (*Assemblée Confédérale*) consisting of 40 Senegalese and 20 Gambians, provided for under the 1981 merger agreement, met for the first time on January 13, 1983; it is required to meet at least twice yearly. The first extraordinary congress of the Confederal Assembly concluded on July 15, 1987, having adopted an "austerity" budget for 1987–1988.

Speaker: Alhaji Mamadou Baboucar N'JIE.

CABINET

[as of April 8, 1988]

President	Abdou Diouf (Senegal)
Vice President	Alhaji Sir Dawda Jawara (Gambia)
Ministers	
Defense	Médoune Fall (Senegal)
Economic Affairs	Mbemba Jatta (Gambia)
Finance	Sheriff Saikula Sisay (Gambia)
Foreign Affairs	Ibrahima Fall (Senegal)
Deputy Foreign Affairs	Omar Sey (Gambia)
Information and Telecommunications	Robert Sagna (Senegal)
Security	André Sonko (Senegal)
Deputy Security	Lamin Kiti Jabang (Gambia)
Transportation	Alasane Dialy N'Diaye (Senegal)

NEWS MEDIA

A Senegambian Information Commission, which includes media experts from the confederal states, held its most recent meeting at Dakar, Senegal, in mid-January

1987. Apart from television programming, which Gambia does not provide, it complained of a lack of media integration and called upon the Senegalese Press Agency and the Gambian Information Office to agree on a "coherent instrument for regular circulation of information between Senegal and Gambia" including the possibility of converting *Senegal Aujourd'hui* into a confederal newspaper.

INTERGOVERNMENTAL REPRESENTATION

(See entries under Senegal and Gambia, below.)

SENEGAMBIA: SENEGAL

Republic of Senegal
République du Sénégal

Political Status: Former French dependency independent since August 20, 1960; presidential system established under constitution promulgated March 7, 1963; linked with Gambia in the Confederation of Senegambia on February 1, 1982.

Area: 75,750 sq. mi. (196,192 sq. km.).

Population: 5,085,388 (1976C), 7,178,000 (1988E).

Major Urban Centers (1979E): DAKAR (850,000); Thiès (120,000); Kaolack (110,000).

Official Language: French (public instruction is now offered in English, an official language of the Confederation).

Monetary Unit: CFA Franc (market rate March 1, 1988, 285.80 francs = $1US).

President: Abdou DIOUF (Socialist Party); served as Prime Minister from February 1970 until January 1, 1981, when sworn in as President for the remainder of the five-year presidential term of Léopold Sédar SENGHOR (Socialist Party), who had resigned on December 31, 1980; popularly elected to a full term on February 27, 1983; reelected on February 28, 1988.

THE COUNTRY

Senegal is situated on the bulge of West Africa between Mauritania on the north, Mali on the east, and Guinea and Guinea-Bissau on the south. Gambia forms an enclave extending into its territory for 200 miles along one of the area's four major rivers. The predominantly flat or rolling savanna country is peopled mainly by Africans of varied ethnic backgrounds, with the Wolof, whose language is widely used commercially, being the largest group. French, the official language, is spoken only by a literate minority. Approximately 85 percent of the Senegalese profess Islam, the remainder being animists or Christians. In 1980 women constituted approximately 38 percent of the official labor force, concentrated mainly in agriculture. Their representation in government has been marginal, although the grassroots base of the ruling Socialist Party is reported to be made up primarily of female members.

About 70 percent of the population is employed in agriculture, with peanuts, the principal crop, typically accounting for one-third of export earnings. Cotton, sugar, and rice (most supplies of which have traditionally been imported) have become the focus of agricultural diversification efforts, while fishing, phosphate mining, oil refining, and tourism have grown in economic importance. In recent years, the Sahel drought has combined with other factors to curtail export earnings, necessitating cooperation with the International Monetary Fund in rescheduling the country's $1.6 million debt.

GOVERNMENT AND POLITICS

Political background. Under French influence since the seventeenth century, Senegal became a French colony in 1920 and a self-governing member of the French Community in November 1958. In January 1959 it joined with the adjacent French Soudan (now Mali) to form the Federation of Mali, which became fully independent within the Community on June 20, 1960. Two months later, Senegal seceded from the Federation, and the separate Republic of Senegal was formally proclaimed on September 5. President Léopold Sédar SENGHOR, a well-known poet and the leader of Senegal's strongest political party, the Senegalese Progressive Union (UPS), governed initially under a parliamentary system in which political rival Mamadou DIA was prime minister, but an unsuccessful coup attempt in December 1962 resulted in Dia's arrest and imprisonment (until his release in 1974) and the establishment by Senghor of a presidential form of government under his exclusive direction. In an election held under somewhat violent conditions on December 1, 1963, Senghor retained the presidency and his party won all of the seats in the National Assembly, as it also did in the elections of 1968 and 1973.

In response to demands for political and constitutional reform, Senghor in early 1970 reinstituted the post of prime minister, while a constitutional amendment adopted in 1976 sanctioned three political parties, the ideology of each being prescribed by law. In early 1979 a fourth, essentially conservative party was also accorded recognition. Additional parties were legalized under legislation enacted in April 1981.

Although he had been overwhelmingly reelected to a fourth five-year term on February 26, 1978, President Senghor resigned on December 31, 1980, and, as prescribed by the constitution, was succeeded by Prime Minister Abdou DIOUF. The new administration extended the process of political liberalization, most restrictions on political party activity being lifted in April 1981. Coalitions, however, were proscribed; thus, the opposition did not present a serious threat to the ruling Socialist Party in the presidential and legislative balloting of February 27, 1983, Diouf winning reelection by 83 percent, and the PS capturing 111 of 120 Assembly seats. At the most recent poll of February 28, 1988, Diouf was reelected by 73 percent of the vote, with the PS being awarded 103 Assembly seats.

Constitution and government. The constitution of March 1963, as amended, provides for a president elected by direct universal suffrage for a five-year term. He appoints and heads a council of ministers, the post of prime minister being abolished in 1983. Legislative power is vested in a unicameral National Assembly, whose term is concurrent with that of the president; under current procedure, half of the members are elected on a "first past the post" departmental basis, the other half by proportional representation from a national list. Only parties registered at least four months before an election are allowed to participate, and neither independent candidacies or opposition coalitions are permitted. The judicial system is headed by a Supreme Court, whose justices are appointed by the president on the advice of a Superior Court of Magistrates, which also decides questions of constitutionality. A High Court of Justice, chosen by the Assembly from among its own membership, is responsible for impeachment proceedings. A Court of Appeal sits at Dakar, with magistrates' courts at the local level.

Senegal is administratively divided into 10 regions, each headed by a presidentially appointed governor who is assisted by a Regional Assembly; the regions are divided into departments headed by prefects, which are subdivided into districts headed by subprefects.

Foreign relations. Formally nonaligned but pro-Western, Senegal has retained especially close political, cultural, and economic ties with France. An active advocate of West African cooperation, it has participated in such regional groupings as the Economic Community of West African States, the Permanent Inter-State Committee on Drought Control in the Sahel, and the Organization for the Development of the Senegal River. Preconfederal relations with Gambia were strengthened under a 1965 treaty that provided for cooperation in defense, foreign affairs, and development of the Gambia River basin. Relations with other neighbors substantially improved as the result of a "reconciliation" pact signed at Monrovia, Liberia, in March 1978 that ended five years of friction with both Guinea and the Ivory Coast.

Under President Senghor, Senegal maintained a generally conservative posture in African affairs, refusing to recognize Angola because of the presence of Cuban troops there, supporting Morocco against the claims of the insurgent Polisario Front in the Western Sahara, and breaking relations with Libya in mid-1980 because of that country's alleged efforts to destabilize the governments of Chad, Mali, and Niger as well as Senegal.

In October 1980, 150 Senegalese troops were dispatched to Banjul, Gambia, under the terms of a 1965 defense cooperation treaty, amid rumors of Libyan involvement in a projected coup against the Jawara government. A more serious challenge to the Jawara regime in July 1981 required substantially greater Senegalese assistance and was followed by an agreement to establish a Confederation of Senegambia that was consummated on February 1, 1982 (see previous article).

Reflecting the "spirit of our new diplomacy"—essentially an effort to introduce greater flexibility in its relations with other African governments—Dakar announced in February 1982 that it would reverse its long-standing support of the Angolan resistance movement and recognize the MPLA government at Luanda. Ties with Algeria were strengthened in the course of reciprocal visits by the respective heads of state in 1984–1985, while relations with Libya eased (without, however, a resumption of formal relations) as the result of a visit by Colonel Qadhafi in December 1985. The partial rapprochement with Tripoli notwithstanding, Dakar continued to grant landing rights to French planes supplying Chadian forces.

Current issues. During 1987, as in 1986, President Diouf attempted to contain internal opposition, while concentrating on efforts to rebuild the debt-plagued Senegalese economy through fiscal austerity and structural diversification. In the first endeavor he was increasingly successful, while prospects for the latter were linked to the uncertain outcome of a 1984–1989 economic plan, featuring new and extensive privatization measures, that has projected a substantial increase in domestic food production and sustained growth in fishing and tourism.

Notwithstanding the return to Senegal, after a year's absence, of Democratic Party leader Abdoulaye WADE and the formation, in July 1985, of a Senegalese Democratic Alliance (see Political Parties, below) in defiance of a constitutional ban on political coalitions, the opposition quickly fell into disarray. The Alliance was declared illegal, while three Assembly deputies were formally expelled from the PDS for opposing its formation. Disagreement also surfaced within opposition ranks in regard to the presidential and legislative elections scheduled for early 1988. In mid-1986, the PDS declared that it would boycott the balloting if a "democratic electoral code" were not adopted, including reduction of the voting age to 18 to accommodate the country's "age pyramid", fairer access to the media, and stricter procedures for both the casting and tabulation of ballots. On the other hand, the Democratic League, a Marxist formation, called for electoral participation on the basis of "disorganized alliances" that would subvert the proscription of coalitions. Subsequently, at a joint press conference in February 1987, 11 of the country's opposition groups announced their intention to organize "coordinated resistance" to the policies of the incumbent administration.

President Diouf easily won reelection with a slightly reduced majority on February 28, 1988, while the PDS, although more than doubling its Assembly representation, won only 17 of 120 seats. Opposition leader Wade immediately termed the outcome a "masquerade" and street riots erupted at Dakar, inducing the government to declare a state of emergency which, with legislative approval, was extended for an indefinite period on March 11.

POLITICAL PARTIES

In March 1976 the National Assembly approved a constitutional amendment authorizing three political parties, each reflecting a specific ideology ("current") that President Senghor had presumed to discern in Senegalese society.

Senghor's own Socialist Party thereupon adopted the centrist position of "democratic socialism", while the two other legal parties, the Senegalese Democratic Party and the African Independence Party, were assigned "liberal democratic" and "Marxist-Leninist" postures, respectively. In early 1979 the amendment was altered to permit the legal establishment of a fourth, essentially right-wing party, the Senegalese Republican Movement.

The process of liberalization reached a conclusion in April 1981, when the Assembly removed most remaining restrictions on party activity, with a number of additional groups subsequently being registered. However, six opposition parties boycotted the February 1983 election to protest the banning of political coalitions, while allegations of electoral fraud during the balloting, coupled with the coalition ban, yielded a boycott by most opposition groups of municipal elections in November 1984, the PS thereby winning control of most of the town councils.

Government Party:

Socialist Party (*Parti Socialiste*—PS). Known until December 1976 as the Senegalese Progressive Union (*Union Progressiste Sénégalaise*—UPS), the PS has consistently held a preponderance of seats in the National Assembly. A moderate, francophile party long identified with the cause of Senegalese independence, the UPS was founded by Léopold Senghor in 1949 in a secession from the dominant local branch of the French Socialist Party. From 1963 to 1974, it was the only legal party in Senegal and the only significant opposition grouping, the leftist *Parti de Regroupement Africain-Sénégal* (PRA), was absorbed in 1966 in furtherance of Senghor's "national reconciliation" policy. In November 1976, prior to its change of name, the UPS was admitted to the Socialist International. Collateral with his resignation of the presidency, Senghor withdrew as party secretary general in early 1981.

Leaders: Abdou DIOUF (President of the Republic and Secretary General of the Party), Dr. Daouda SOW (President of the National Assembly).

Opposition Groups:

Senegalese Democratic Alliance (*Alliance Démocratique Sénégalais*—ADS). Formed by the five parties listed below in July 1985, the ADS avoided styling itself an electoral coalition. However, the government declared its activities in violation of the constitutional proscription of multiparty groupings in August and pronounced it illegal in October. Nonetheless, most of the participating groups' leaders continued to affirm their support of the Alliance.

Leader: Dr. Abdoulaye BATHILY (Chairman).

Senegalese Democratic Party (*Parti Démocratique Sénégalais*—PDS). The PDS was launched in October 1974 as a youth-oriented opposition group to implement the pluralistic democracy guaranteed by the Senegalese constitution. Although standing to the left of President Senghor on certain issues, it was required by the constitutional amendment of March 1976 to adopt a formal position to the right of the government party. Having charged fraud in both the 1980 and 1983 legislative elections (although one of two opposition parties to gain representation on the latter occasion), PDS leaders participated in the 1984 municipal boycott and asserted their "regret" at having campaigned in 1983. Following the return from abroad of party leader Abdoulaye Wade in early 1985, the PDS led a number of mass prayer demonstrations for "radical change", with Wade calling for "a transitional government of national unity". In December, three anti-ADS party leaders were expelled by Wade supporters for attempting to create a "party within a party" but refused to accept the action as procedurally valid. At a national convention in January 1987 the PDS reaffirmed a decision announced seven months earlier to boycott the 1988 balloting if no action was taken on electoral reform, Wade subsequently declaring that if the demand was not met he would turn the party into a "national liberation movement" that would form its "own government". Despite its boycott threat, the PDS participated in the 1988 poll, winning 17 of 120 Assembly seats.

Leader: Abdoulaye WADE (Secretary General).

Revolutionary Movement for the New Democracy (*Mouvement Révolutionnaire pour la Démocratie Nouvelle* – MRDN). Also known as *And-Jëf*, a Wolof expression meaning "to unite for a purpose", the MRDN is a populist southern party of the extreme Left that includes both former Socialists and Maoists. It was permitted to register in June 1981, but participated in both the 1983 and 1984 election boycotts. One of its leaders, Landing Savane, ran a poor fourth in the 1988 presidential balloting.

Leaders: Abdoulaye GUEYE, Abdoulaye LY, Landing SAVANE.

Democratic People's Union (*Union pour la Démocratie Populaire* – UDP). The UDP is a Marxist grouping organized by a pro-Albanian MRDN splinter group, which has yet to contest an election.

Leader: Hamédine Racine GUISSE.

Democratic League–Labor Party Movement (*Ligue Démocratique-Mouvement pour le Parti du Travail* – LD-MPT). The LD-MPT is a self-proclaimed independent Marxist group with links to Senegal's leading teacher's union; it contested both the 1983 and 1984 elections. At its second congress in December 1986, the League's secretary general, Abdoulaye Bathily, called for "disorganized alliances" between opposition parties and presented an economic "alternative to the receipts of the International Monetary Fund and the World Bank" as a means of establishing a socialist society. In September 1987 the party pledged its party's support to PDS presidential candidate Abdoulaye Wade. Although presenting candidates, the LD-MPT secured no legislative representation in 1988.

Leaders: Babacar SANE, Mamadou DIOP, Dr. Abdoulaye BATHILY (Secretary General).

Socialist Workers' Organization (*Organisation Socialist des Travailleurs* – OST). The OST is a small, independent Marxist-Leninist formation launched in 1982.

Leader: Mbaye BATHILY.

Senegalese Democratic Party–Rénovation (*Parti Démocratique Sénégalais-Renovation* – PDS-R). The PDS-R was organized in June 1987 by an anti-ADS faction within the parent group. It has announced as its goal the establishment of a "truly secular and pluralist democracy".

Leader: Serigne DIOP.

African Independence Party (*Parti Africain de l'Indépendance* – PAI). Founded in 1957 and composed mainly of intellectuals in southern Senegal, the PAI was legally dissolved in 1960 but subsequently recognized as the "Marxist-Leninist" party called for by the 1976 constitutional amendment. Claiming to be the "real PAI", a clandestine wing of the party denounced recognition as a self-serving maneuver by the Senghor government. In March 1980 two leaders of the splinter faction, Amath Dansokho and Maguette Thiam, were charged with inciting workers to strike, but in 1981 were permitted to register the group as a distinct party (see PIT, below). Having unsuccessfully contested the 1983 election, the PAI joined the November 1984 boycott and did not present candidates in 1988.

Leaders: Majhemouth DIOP (President of the party and 1983 presidential candidate), Balla N'DIAYE (Vice President), Bara GOUDIABY (Secretary General).

Independence and Labor Party (*Parti de l'Indépendance et du Travail* – PIT). Organized by a group of PAI dissidents, the PIT is a pro-Moscow Communist party that was permitted to register in 1981. It contested both the 1983 and 1984 elections, but won no Assembly or town council seats. In 1985, while not having been invited to join the ADS, it endorsed the concept of a united front against the Diouf government. The party presented legislative candidates in 1988 without success.

Leaders: Maguette THIAM, Amath DANSOKO (Secretary General).

Senegalese People's Party (*Parti Populaire Sénégalais* – PPS). Legalized in December 1981, the PPS was also organized by a number of PAI adherents, who did not immediately delineate its program, indicating only that they aimed at the "restructuring of Senegalese society on new and scientific bases". Some of its members have been involved in demonstrations led by Casamance separatists. The party has boycotted all elections since its founding.

Leaders: Magatte LOUM, Dr. Oumar WONE (1983 presidential candidate).

Senegalese Republican Movement (*Mouvement Républicain Sénégalais* – MRS). The MRS is a self-styled "right-wing" party organized by former National Assembly vice president Boubacar Guéye. In August 1977 the party applied for legal recognition, which was not granted until February 1979. It strongly supports human rights, free enterprise, and private property. At the domestic political level, it has urged the adoption of a bicameral system and parliamentary election of the president; regionally, it has proposed the introduction of a common currency for OAU member countries. The MRS boycotted the 1983, 1984, and 1988 elections.

Leader: Boubacar GUEYE (Secretary General).

People's Democratic Movement (*Mouvement Démocratique Populaire* – MDP). The MDP, led by longtime Senghor opponent Mamadou Dia, has called for a program of socialist self-management of the economy. Dia was one of the few prominent Senegalese political figures to oppose establishment of the Senegambian Confederation. The MDP contested the 1983 general election, but boycotted the 1984 and 1988 balloting.

Leader: Mamadou DIA (former Prime Minister and 1983 presidential candidate).

National Democratic Rally (*Rassemblement National Démocratique* – RND). Established in February 1976, the RND describes itself as a "party of the masses". It applied, without success, for recognition in September 1977 and two years later its founder, Cheikh Anta Diop (died 1986), was ordered to stand trial for engaging in unauthorized party activity. It was legalized in June 1981. A possible PS-RND coalition, broached prior to the 1983 balloting, was apparently rendered moot by the magnitude of the PS victory. The party has repeatedly criticized the government for its position on Chad and for its "systematic alignment with the positions of France and the United States". It secured one Assembly seat in 1983 but did not participate in the 1988 balloting.

Leader: Ely Madiodio FALL (Secretary General).

Party for the Liberation of the People (*Parti pour la Libération du Peuple* – PLP). The PLP was founded in July 1983 by RND dissidents, who characterized the party under Diop's leadership as "the objective ally of the government". At a November press conference, Secretary General Babacar Niang stated that the new party's priorities were defense, anti-imperialism, and "a change in the fundamental direction of power". The PLP became the only leftist party with legislative representation when Niang assumed the seat to which the RND's Diop had been elected, after Diop had refused it as a protest against election irregularities. The PLP contested the 1984 municipal balloting and its secretary general ran third in the 1988 presidential poll, being credited with a vote share of less than one percent.

Leaders: Babacar NIANG (Secretary General), Abdoulaye KANE (Assistant Secretary General).

African Party for the Independence of the People (*Parti Africain pour l'Indépendance du Peuple* – PAIP). The PAIP is a Marxist-Leninist party that was legalized in August 1982, but boycotted all subsequent elections.

Leaders: Abdou BANE, Issa DIOP, Abdoulaye SLAYE, Aly NIANE (Secretary General).

Communist Workers League (*Ligue Communiste des Travailleurs* – LCT). The LCT is a small Trotskyite group formed in 1982.

Leader: Mahmoud SALEH.

Senegalese Democratic Union–Revival (*Union Démocratique Sénégalais-Renouvellement* – UDS-R). Organized in February 1985 and legally recognized in July, the UDS-R is led by Mamadou Fall, a well-known trade-union leader and former deputy, who was expelled from the PDS while in the Assembly for "divisive activities". Fall describes himself as a "progressive nationalist" seeking to promote the "unification of healthy forces". The party presented no candidates in 1988.

Leader: Mamadou FALL.

Movement of Democratic Forces of Casamance (*Mouvement des Forces Démocratiques de Casamance* – MFDC). The MFDC is a clandestine party advocating the secession of Casamance territory.

LEGISLATURE

The 120-member **National Assembly** (*Assemblée Nationale*) is a unicameral body elected by direct universal suffrage for a five-year term. At the election of February 28, 1988, the Socialist Party obtained 103 seats and the Senegalese Democratic Party, 17.

President: Dr. Daouda SOW.

CABINET

[as of April 5, 1988]

President	Abdou Diouf
Secretary General to the Presidency	Jean Collin

Ministers

Armed Forces	Médoune Fall
Civil Service and Labor	Moussa N'Doye
Commerce	Seydina Oumar Sy
Communications	Robert Sagna
Culture	Moustapha Kâ
Economy and Finance	Serigne Lamine Diop
Equipment	Alasane Dialy N'Diaye
Foreign Affairs	Cheikh Ibrahima Fall
Higher Education	Hakhir Thiam
Housing and Urban Affairs	Momodou Abbas Bâ
Industrial Development and Crafts	Famara Ibrahima Sagna
Interior	André Sonko
Justice, Keeper of the Seals	Seydou Madani Sy
National Education	Ibrahima Niam
Planning and Cooperation	Djibo Laity Kâ
Public Health	Thérèse King
Rural Development	Cheikh Abdoul Khadre Cissoko
Social Development	Ndioro N'Diaye
Tourism	El Hadj Malik Sy
Water Resources	Samba Yella Diop
Youth and Sports	Abdoulaye Makhtar Diop

Ministers Delegate

Emigration	Fatou N'Dongo Dieng
Finance and Economy	Moussa Touré
Relations with the Assembly	Farba Lo
Rural Development Responsible for Animal Resources	Mbaye Diouf
Rural Development Responsible for the Protection of Nature	Moctar Kebe
Director, Central Bank	Magatte Sene

NEWS MEDIA

Press. Newspapers are subject to government censorship and regulation, although a number of opposition papers have recently appeared, some evading official registration by means of irregular publication. The following are approved organs published in French at Dakar: *Le Soleil* (40,000), PS daily; *Afrique Nouvelle* (15,000), Catholic weekly; *Senegal Aujourd'hui* (5,000), published monthly by the Ministry of Information; *Journal Officiel de la République du Sénégal,* government weekly. Other organs include *Takusaan,* published thrice-weekly by the opposition PDS; *Le Démocrate,* PDS monthly; *Le Politicien,* satirical fortnightly; *Ande Soppi,* political monthly founded in mid-1977 by former prime minister Mamadou Dia; *Taxaw,* monthly organ of the RND; *Momsareew,* monthly PAI organ; *Construire l'Afrique,* business monthly; *Fippou,* feminist quarterly.

News agencies. *Agence de Presse Sénégalaise* is a government-operated facility; the Pan-African News Agency (PANA), as well as a number of foreign agencies, also maintain offices at Dakar.

Radio and television. Broadcasting is controlled by the *Office de Radiodiffusion-Télévision du Sénégal.* Two radio networks, *Radio Sénégal-Inter* and *Radio Sénégal II,* broadcast to the country's 455,000 receivers. There were approximately 57,000 television sets in 1987.

INTERGOVERNMENTAL REPRESENTATION

Ambassador to the US: Falilou KANE.

US Ambassador to Senegal: Lannon WALKER.

Permanent Representative to the UN: Massamba SARRE.

IGO Memberships (Non-UN): ACCT, ADF, AfDB, AGC, BADEA, BOAD, CCC, CEAO, CILSS, ECOWAS, EEC(L), *EIB,* IC, ICCAT, IDB, Intelsat, Interpol, IWC, NAM, OAU, OCAM, PCA.

SENEGAMBIA: GAMBIA

Republic of The Gambia

Political Status: Independent member of the Commonwealth since February 18, 1965; republican regime instituted April 24, 1970; joined Senegal in establishing the Confederation of Senegambia, with effect from February 1, 1982.

Area: 4,361 sq. mi. (11,295 sq. km.).

Population: 695,886 (1983C), 822,000 (1988E).

Major Urban Center (1977E): BANJUL (44,000).

Official Language: English.

Monetary Unit: Dalasi (market rate March 1, 1988, 6.64 dalasi = $1US).

President: Alhaji Sir Dawda Kairaba JAWARA (People's Progressive Party); became colonial Premier in 1962, continuing as Prime Minister after independence; elected President by members of the House of Representatives on proclamation of the Republic in 1970; reelected for five-year terms in 1972, 1977, and, by direct balloting, in 1982 and on March 11, 1987.

Vice President: Bakary Bunja DARBO (People's Progressive Party); named by the President on May 12, 1982, to succeed Hassan Musa CAMARA; reappointed following election of March 11, 1987.

THE COUNTRY

Situated on the bulge of West Africa and surrounded on three sides by Senegal, Gambia is a narrow strip of territory some 6 to 10 miles wide that borders the Gambia River to a point about 200 miles from the Atlantic. The population is overwhelmingly African, the main ethnic groups being Mandingo (40 percent), Fula (13 percent), Wolof (12 percent), and Jola and Serahuli (7 percent each); in addition, there are small groups of Europeans, Lebanese, Syrians, and Mauritanians. Tribal languages are widely spoken, though English is the official and commercial language. Islam is the religion of 80 percent of the people.

The economy has traditionally been based on peanuts, which are cultivated on almost all suitable land and which, including derivatives, typically account for upwards of 80 percent of export earnings. Industry is largely limited to peanut-oil refining and handicrafts; unofficially, smuggling into Senegal has long been important. Current development, partially channeled through the Organization for the Development of the Gambia River Basin, stresses infrastructural improvements and agricultural diversification. The country's principal aid donor is the United Kingdom.

GOVERNMENT AND POLITICS

Political background. Under British influence since 1588, Gambia was not definitively established as a separate colony until 1888. It acquired the typical features of British colonial rule, achieved internal self-government in 1963, and became fully independent within the Commonwealth on February 18, 1965. Initially a parliamentary regime, Gambia changed to a republican form of government following a referendum in 1970.

Political leadership has been exercised since independence by the People's Progressive Party (PPP), headed by President Dawda K. JAWARA, although opposition candidates secured approximately 30 percent of the popular vote in the elections of 1972, 1977, and 1982. At the May 1979 PPP Congress — the first held in 16 years — President Jawara rebuffed demands by some delegates that a one-party system be instituted, commenting that such a change could only occur through the ballot box. However, on November 1, 1980, amid allegations of a widespread anti-government conspiracy, two opposition movements described by the president as "terrorist organizations" were banned, despite protests from the legal opposition parties.

A more serious threat to the Jawara regime, involving elements of Gambia's paramilitary Field Force, resulted in a takeover of the capital, Banjul, in late July 1981 while the president was out of the country. The uprising was quelled with the aid of Senegalese troops dispatched under the terms of a 1965 mutual defense and security treaty. Subsequently, President Jawara and Senegalese President Diouf announced plans for a partial merger of their respective states in the form of a Senegambian Confederation, which came into effect on February 1, 1982 (see Senegambia article).

At the general election of March 11, 1987, President Jawara was returned to office by a majority of 59 percent, as contrasted with 73 percent in 1982, although the PPP increased its representation in the 36-member House of Representatives from 28 to 31.

Constitution and government. During the 12 years following adoption of a republican constitution in 1970, Gambia was led by a president who was indirectly elected by the legislature for a five-year term and was assisted by a vice president of his choice. The procedure was changed in 1982 to one involving direct election of the chief executive, who retained the authority to designate his deputy. The unicameral House of Representatives is popularly elected for a five-year term but may be dissolved by the president following a vote of no confidence. The judicial system is headed by a Supreme Court and includes a Court of Appeal, magistrates' courts, customary tribunals, and Muslim courts. Many judges, all of whom are appointed by the president on advice from the Judicial Service Commission, are recruited from the ranks of the Nigerian judiciary due to a shortage of domestic expertise.

At the local level, the country is divided into 35 districts administered by chiefs in association with village headmen and advisers. The districts are grouped into six regions, which are governed by presidentially appointed commissioners and area councils containing a majority of elected members, with district chiefs serving ex officio. Banjul has an elected City Council.

Foreign relations. While adhering to a formal policy of nonalignment, Gambia has long maintained close relations with the United Kingdom and the African Commonwealth states; recently it has also concluded cooperation agreements with the military governments of Liberia and Pakistan. By far the most important foreign policy question, however, has turned on relations with Senegal. In 1967 the two countries signed a treaty of association providing for a joint ministerial committee and secretariat, while other agreements provided for cooperation in such areas as defense, foreign affairs, and development of the Gambia River basin. In early 1976 a number of new accords were concluded that, coupled with the need for Senegalese military assistance in 1980 and 1981, paved the way for establishment of the Confederation of Senegambia in February 1982 (see separate article). As of early 1988, neither Gambia's external representation nor its conduct of foreign policy had been visibly affected by the partial merger of the two countries; earlier, the presence of Nigeria's (then) head of state, Maj. Gen. Mohammadu Buhari, during ceremonies marking Gambia's twentieth anniversary of independence, suggested to some that the country might have some reservations about becoming "Senegal's 11th region".

Current issues. While critics have branded the Confederation as the equivalent of annexation by Senegal, President Jawara emerged from the election of May 1982 with his capacity to speak for the Gambian people seemingly enhanced, while several members of the demonstrably divided opposition were tarnished with complicity in the abortive coup of July 1981.

By 1985 the crisis of four years before was seemingly resolved, in part by the conviction and sentence to death of one of the last coup plotters, Corp. Meta CAMARA, who had been extradited from Guinea-Bissau. The issue of confederation appeared to subside following the establishment of a permanent army and popular support for Jawara's resistance to immediate monetary union. In addition, Banjul concentrated on its own economic recovery plan (ERP), backed by the International Monetary Fund, which continued to emphasize agricultural diversification and reduced external borrowing. A decision in early 1986 to float the dalasi, which had theretofore been linked to the pound sterling and thus had been virtually non-negotiable in Senegal, together with the removal of exchange control restrictions and producer price increases contributed to a gradual economic upturn and a predicted growth rate in excess of 3 percent for 1988.

POLITICAL PARTIES

Gambia is one of the few African states to have consistently sanctioned a multiparty system, despite the predominant position held since independence by the ruling People's Progressive Party.

Governing Party:

People's Progressive Party (PPP). The moderately socialist PPP, which merged with the Congress Party (CP) in 1967, has governed the country since independence. It sponsored adoption of the republican constitution in 1970 and has long favored increased economic and cultural links with Senegal as well as maintenance of the Commonwealth association.

Leader: Alhaji Sir Dawda Kairaba JAWARA (President of the Republic).

Opposition Parties:

National Convention Party (NCP). The NCP was organized in late 1975 by Sherif Dibba, former vice president of the Republic and cofounder of the PPP. Dibba had earlier lost his post as minister for planning and economic development for supporting workers striking against the government. Although jailed in August 1981 on charges of involvement in the July coup attempt, Dibba challenged Jawara for the presidency in 1982, securing 28 percent of the vote. The five legislative seats won by the NCP in 1977 were reduced to three in 1982. A month after the election, Dibba was released from confinement, the charges against him having been vacated by a Banjul court. The party won five House seats in 1987, on the basis of a 25 percent vote share; its leader, Sherif Mustapha Dibba, failed to secure reelection, although running second to Jawara in the presidential balloting.

Leader: Sherif Mustapha DIBBA.

Gambian People's Party (GPP). The GPP was launched in early 1985 by former vice president Hassan Musa Camara and a number of other defectors from the PPP to oppose President Jawara at the 1987 general election. As the balloting approached, it was felt by many that it had overtaken the NCP as the principal opposition grouping; however, the party obtained only 13 percent of the vote and secured no legislative representation at the March poll.

Leaders: Hassan Musa CAMARA (former Vice President of the Republic), Howsoon SEMEGA-JANNEH (former Minister of Information), Alhaji Muhamadu, Lamine SAHO (former Attorney General).

People's Democratic Organisation for Independence and Socialism (PDOIS or DOY). The leftist PDOIS was formed at a congress that met from July 31 to August 19, 1986, to approve a lengthy manifesto that accused the PPP of compromising the country's sovereignty by agreeing to the establishment of Senegambia on the basis of an "unequal relationship". Both of its organizers had been imprisoned during the 1981 emergency for publishing an underground newspaper on behalf of an unlawful group.

Leaders: Halifa SALLAH, Sidia JATTA, Samuel SARR.

Illegal Opposition:

National Liberation Party (NLP). The NLP was launched in October 1975 with a program calling for radical government measures to deal with unemployment and the rising cost of living. The party, which is based primarily in rural areas, never secured parliamentary representation. In an interview published in *West Africa* in December 1980, party leader Cheyassin Papa SECKA came to the defense of the recently banned Movement for Justice in Africa (below), asserting that the organization was an expression of dissatisfaction with corruption and influence-peddling within the PPP. Secka was himself arrested in the wake of the 1981 coup attempt and was sentenced to death in June 1982.

Gambian Socialist Revolutionary Party (GSRP). Like Moja (below), the GSRP was banned on November 1, 1980, for alleged "advocacy of violence".

Leader: Pingon GEORGES.

Movement for Justice in Africa (Moja). Formed in late 1979 and taking its name from that of a similar radical party in Liberia, Moja has accused the Jawara regime of nepotism, patronage, and corruption. It has also called for an end to "foreign economic and military control" (an apparent reference to Senegal) and a more open political process. Its best-known figure, Koro SALLAH, was reported to have "almost certainly been killed" during the 1981 coup attempt, although Moja representatives continue to issue communiqués attacking the confederation as "counterfeit pan-Africanism".

Spokesman: Ousmane MANJANG.

LEGISLATURE

The unicameral **House of Representatives** currently encompasses 36 directly elected members chosen by universal adult suffrage. The term of the House is five years, unless dissolved earlier by the president. At the general election of March 11, 1987, the People's Progressive Party won 31 seats and the National Convention Party, 5.

Speaker: Alhaji Momodou B. N'JIE.

CABINET

President	Sir Dawda Kairaba Jawara
Vice President	Bakary Bunja Darbo
Ministers	
Agriculture and Natural Resources	Saikou S. Sabally
Education, Youth, Sports and Culture	Bakary Bunja Darbo
Finance and Trade	Sheriff Saikula Sisay
Foreign Affairs	Omar Sey
Health and Social Welfare	Louise N'Jie
Information and Tourism	Lamin Keba Saho
Interior	Lamin Kiti Jabang
Justice	Hassan Jallow
Lands and Local Government	Landing Jallow Sonko
Planning and Economic Affairs	Memba Jatta
National Defense	Sir Dawda Kairaba Jawara
Water Resources and Environment	Omar Amadou Jallow
Public Works and Telecommunications	Mamadou Cadi Cham
Attorney General	Hassan Jallow
Governor, Central Bank	Mamour Jagne (Acting)

NEWS MEDIA

The principal newspaper and the national radio station are government owned, but all news media operate freely.

Press. The following are English-language publications issued thrice weekly at Banjul: *Gambia News Bulletin* (2,500), published by the Government Information Office; *The Worker,* organ of the Gambia Labour Congress; *Gambia Onward. The Gambian Times,* a PPP organ, is issued four times a week; *The Nation* appears fortnightly.

Radio and television. Radio broadcasting to the country's 110,000 sets is provided by Radio Syd, a commercial outlet, and by the government-owned Radio Gambia, which relays BBC news and carries programs in English and local languages. There is no television service, but transmissions from Senegal can be received.

INTERGOVERNMENTAL REPRESENTATION

Ambassador to the US and Permanent Representative to the UN: Ousmane Amadou SALLAH.

US Ambassador to The Gambia: Herbert E. HOROWITZ.

IGO Memberships (Non-UN): ADF, AfDB, AGC, BADEA, CILSS, CWTH, ECOWAS, EEC(L), *EIB,* IC, ICCO, IDB, NAM, OAU.

SEYCHELLES

Republic of Seychelles

Political Status: Independent member of the Commonwealth since June 29, 1976; present constitution adopted March 26, 1979, with effect from June 5.

Area: 171 sq. mi. (429 sq. km.).

Resident Population: 61,898 (1977C), 66,500 (1988E); some 30,000 Seychellois live abroad, mainly in Australia and the United Kingdom.

Major Urban Center (1977C): VICTORIA (urban area, 23,334).

Official Language: Creole (replaced English and French in 1981).

Monetary Unit: Seychelles Rupee (market rate March 1, 1988, 5.32 rupees = $1US).

President: France Albert RENE; designated Prime Minister upon independence; installed as President on June 5, 1977, following coup which deposed James Richard MANCHAM; popularly elected to five-year terms in single-party balloting in 1979 and on June 17, 1984.

THE COUNTRY

The Seychelles archipelago consists of over 90 islands located in the Indian Ocean some 600 miles northeast of Madagascar. Over 85 percent of the population is concentrated on the largest island, Mahé, which has an area of approximately 55 square miles (142 sq. km.); most of the remainder is distributed between the two northern islands of Praslin and La Digue. Most Seychellois are of mixed French-African descent and adhere to Roman Catholicism. There are small minority groups of Indians and Chinese. Nearly 98 percent of adult women are classified as "economically active", largely in subsistence agriculture; women are, however, more likely than men to be literate. Female representation in government is minimal.

Excluding reexports (mainly petroleum for fueling ships and aircraft), copra currently accounts for about two-thirds of merchandise export earnings, followed by cinnamon and fish, but tourism has emerged as a significant source of national income, mainly due to the international airport opened on Mahé in 1971. The overall economy has, however, remained depressed, which has contributed to the emigration of nearly one-third of the population.

GOVERNMENT AND POLITICS

Political background. Following a half-century of French rule, the Seychelles became a British possession under the Treaty of Paris in 1814. Originally administered from Mauritius, it became a Crown Colony in 1903. A partially elected governing council was established in 1967 and limited self-government under a chief minister was introduced in 1970. Following a constitutional conference at London in March 1975, the legislative assembly established in 1970 was increased from 15 to 25 members, the 10 new members being nominated by the two parties in the government coalition. Concurrent with the achievement of independence on June 29, 1976, the former chief minister, James R. MANCHAM, was designated president and the former leader of the opposition, France Albert RENE, became prime minister.

On June 5, 1977, while the president was attending a Commonwealth conference at London, the Mancham government was overthrown in a near-bloodless coup that installed René as the new head of state. In balloting on June 23–26, 1979, conducted under a single-party socialist constitution adopted on March 26, René was confirmed in office for a five-year term. He was reelected on June 17, 1984.

Subsequent to the imposition of one-party government, President René has experienced a series of both external and internal challenges to his authority. In November 1979 he announced the discovery of an antigovernment plot "sponsored from abroad" that allegedly involved ousted president Mancham and a force of mercenaries based at Durban, South Africa. Among the 85–100 persons arrested in the wake of the allegations were the head of the country's immigration service, a former minister of finance, and a French citizen who had been advising the Seychelles Police Force. A potentially more serious threat was averted in November 1981 with the detection at Mahé's Pointe Larue airport of a group of mercenaries led by the celebrated Col. Michael ("Mad Mike") Hoare, an Irishman who had been involved in a number of African destabilization efforts during the previous two decades. In the course of a pitched battle with units of the Seychelles People's Defence Force (SPDF), some 45 of the invaders commandeered an Air India Boeing 707 and ordered the pilot to fly them to Durban, where they eventually surrendered to South African police. Released on bail in early December, the mercenaries were rearrested on January 5, 1982, in the wake of mounting international criticism. Most were given modest jail sentences under the South African Civil Aviation Offenses Act, Colonel Hoare ultimately being released in May 1985.

Additional challenges to the islands' security followed. In August 1982 some 150 lower-ranked members of the SPDF seized key installations on Mahé in an abortive protest against alleged ill-treatment by senior military officials, while in September 1986 a number of army officers loyal to the minister of defense, Col. Ogilvie BERLOUIS, were charged with plotting to assassinate the president. At London, the exile Seychelles National Movement (MNS, below) claimed knowledge of the 1986 plot, saying that the principals had been divided as to its implementation; subsequently, Colonel Berlouis resigned his post and left the country for Britain.

Despite exile opposition calls for a boycott, President René was reelected by a reported 92.6 percent of the vote on June 17, 1984, after having announced that those failing to participate would lose their right to public assistance. The Seychellois National Assembly was most recently replenished at single-party balloting on December 5, 1987.

Constitution and government. The 1979 constitution established the Republic of Seychelles as a socialist one-party state. The president, who may be elected for not more than three consecutive five-year terms, appoints an advisory Council of Ministers as well as all judges. The unicameral National Assembly, elected for a four-year term, holds legislative responsibility, while the judiciary encompasses a Court of Appeal, a Supreme Court, an Industrial Court, and magistrates' courts. Local government, seemingly necessary for geographic reasons, was abolished in 1971 following problems growing out of a district council system that had been introduced in 1948.

Foreign relations. The main objectives of Seychelles foreign policy since independence have been the "return" of a number of small islands and island groups administered since 1965 as part of the British Indian Ocean Territory, and designation of the Indian Ocean as a "zone of peace". In March 1976, prior to debate on the Seychelles independence bill in the House of Commons, the British government indicated that arrangements had been made for the return to Seychelles of the islands of Aldabra, Desroches, and Farquhar, but that the Chagos Archipelago would remain as the sole component of the British Indian Ocean Territory. Included in the archipelago is Diego Garcia, where the United States, under an agreement concluded with Britain in 1972, maintains military and communications facilities. The US also operates a space-tracking station on the island of Mahé, where, despite the Diego Garcia issue, relations between American personnel and the Seychellois have been relatively cordial. Nonetheless, in December 1979 President René imposed restrictions on foreign naval vessels visiting the islands, while in February 1980 the ruling Seychelles People's Progressive Front (SPPF) called for the dismantling of all foreign military bases in the Indian Ocean region. In September 1983, on the other hand, seven months after concluding a substantial aid agreement with the United States, the René government dropped an antinuclear requirement on British and US vessels seeking docking privileges in the islands. Little more than a year later, in October 1984, President René asserted the Seychelles was "a small country trying not to fall into any of the superpower camps" and defended the installation of Soviet-made missiles as necessary to its own defense.

Relations between the Seychelles and South Africa were by no means enhanced as a result of the 1981 coup attempt on Mahé. The South African proceedings against Colonel Hoare and his associates were confined entirely to air piracy charges on the ground that judicial notice could not be taken of activities beyond Pretoria's jurisdiction. The defendants nonetheless argued that the coup had been undertaken with arms supplied by the South African Defence Force (SADF) and with the full knowledge of the National Intelligence Service (NIS). The trial judge agreed that it would be "naive" to assume that the NIS was unaware of the plot, since one of the mercenaries was a former NIS agent. This finding was not disputed by Prime Minister P.W. Botha, who nevertheless argued that "neither the

South African Government, the Cabinet nor the State Security Council" had been informed and that "no authorization was therefore given for any action". Significantly, 34 of the mercenaries convicted on the air piracy charges were given time off for good behavior and released on November 27, 1982, after spending only four months in prison. The action was, however, preceded by an October 31 assertion in the Johannesburg *Sunday Times* that all Seychellois expatriates opposed to the René regime would be expelled from the country, while in December 1983 it was reported that Pretoria had arrested five individuals on charges of attempting to recruit mercenaries for a further coup effort against the Seychelles government.

Current issues. No serious threats to the René regime were reported during 1987, the major domestic development being an announcement in the course of the government's budget presentation late in the year that income taxation would be abolished. Subsequently, however, it was reported that revenue lost because of the reform would be regained through increased social security contributions from employers, while gross wages of employees in both the public and private sectors would be reduced by the amounts previously deducted for income tax purposes.

POLITICAL PARTIES

Prior to the coup of June 1977, government was shared by the centrist Seychelles Democratic Party (SDP), led by President James R. Mancham, and the left-of-center Seychelles People's United Party (SPUP), headed by Prime Minister France René. Following the coup, René stated that the SDP "has not been banned, it has simply disappeared". In June 1978 the recently established Seychelles People's Progressive Front (SPPF) was declared to be the sole legal party.

Government Party:

Seychelles People's Progressive Front—SPPF (*Front Populaire Progressiste des Seychelles*—FPPS). The SPPF was organized in early 1978 as successor to the SPUP. Like its predecessor, it advocates a broad spectrum of "progressive" policies while attempting to cultivate relations with Catholic clergy sympathetic to its approach to social issues. Upon the retirement of Secretary General Guy Sinon in May 1984, President René was named to succeed him as head of an expanded Secretariat of 13 members, René's former position as party president being abolished.

In an address before the SPPF annual congress in September 1985, René called for improvements in agriculture, employment, and housing, while emphasizing that "the rights of the majority come before the rights of the individual". At the 1987 congress delegates voted to "extend and strengthen the grass-roots structure of the party" and passed a resolution calling, in the future, for triennial rather than annual meetings.

Leaders: France Albert RENE (President of the Republic and Secretary General of the Party), Maj. James MICHEL (Deputy Secretary General).

Exile Groups:

A British-based organization known simply as the **Resistance Movement** (*Mouvement pour la Résistance*—MPR) appears to have been implicated in the November 1981 coup attempt, while a South African-based **Seychelles Popular Anti-Marxist Front** (SPAMF) announced late in the year that it had known of the mercenary effort but had declined to participate on the ground that it was unworkable. A third group, the **Seychelles Liberation Committee** (*Comité de la Libération Seychelles*—CLS) has been headquartered at Paris since 1979.

In November 1985, MPR leader Gérard HOAREAU was assassinated outside his London residence by an unknown assailant. Former president

Mancham charged the René government with the killing, which was vehemently denied by a spokesman for the Seychelles embassy. A year earlier, a **Seychelles National Movement** (*Mouvement National Seychellois*—MNS) was formed as a nonclandestine affiliate of the MPR, Gabriel HOAREAU (a distant relative of Gérard Hoareau) ultimately being named interim president of both groups.

In September 1985, David JOUBERT, a former Mancham cabinet official, announced the revival of the SDP as a London-based exile formation, although Mancham, who had become a British citizen, dissociated himself from the action.

LEGISLATURE

The present **National Assembly** (*Assemblée Nationale*) is a unicameral body of 23 elected members and 2 nominated members, the latter representing the small Inner and Outlying islands, which do not have fixed populations. At the election of December 5, 1987, the elected members were chosen from 36 candidates presented by the Seychelles People's Progressive Front.

Speaker: Francis MACGREGOR.

CABINET

President	France Albert René
Ministers	
Defense	France Albert René
Education, Information and Youth	James Michel
External Relations	France Albert René
Finance	France Albert René
Health and Social Services	Joseph Belmont
Internal Affairs	Rita Sinon
Labor	Jeremie Bonnelame
Legal Affairs	France Albert René
National Development	Jacques Hodoul
Planning	France Albert René
Political Organizations	Esme Jumeau
Transport and Tourism	Ralph Adam
General Manager, Central Bank	Guy Morel

NEWS MEDIA

Press. In November 1979 the islands' largest local newspaper, *Weekend Life* (3,000), was closed down for what the Ministry of Information termed "misguided reporting" and contributing to an "atmosphere of fear". The following are published at Victoria in Creole, English, and French: *The Seychelles Nation* (4,000), daily government organ; *L'Echo des Iles* (2,800), pro-SPPF Catholic fortnightly; *The People* (1,000), SPPF monthly.

News agency. The official facility is the Seychelles News Agency.

Radio and television. The government-controlled commercial station, Radio Seychelles, broadcasts locally from Victoria in English, French, and Creole; a missionary facility, the Far East Broadcasting Association, services several domestic stations and transmits in a wide variety of languages to other Indian Ocean islands, South Asia, the Middle East, and Eastern and Southern Africa. As of 1987, there were approximately 22,000 radio receivers. Television broadcasting, which commenced in 1983, is now received by some 5,500 sets.

INTERGOVERNMENTAL REPRESENTATION

Ambassador to the US and Permanent Representative to the UN: (Vacant).

US Ambassador to the Seychelles: James B. MORAN.

IGO Memberships (Non-UN): ACCT, ADF, AfDB, BADEA, CWTH, EEC(L), *EIB,* Interpol, IWC, NAM, OAU.

SIERRA LEONE

Republic of Sierra Leone

Political Status: Independent member of the Commonwealth since April 27, 1961; republic proclaimed April 19, 1971; present constitution adopted June 1978.

Area: 27,699 sq. mi. (71,740 sq. km.).

Population: 3,517,530 (1985C), 3,843,000 (1988E); the 1985 figure is unadjusted for underenumeration.

Major Urban Centers (1985C): FREETOWN (469,776); Koidu (80,000).

Official Language: English.

Monetary Unit: Leone (market rate March 1, 1988, 23.04 leones = $1US).

President: Maj. Gen. Joseph Saidu MOMOH; nominated by the All-People's Congress on August 4, 1985; assumed office on November 28, following single-party election of October 1 and resignation of Dr. Siaka Probyn STEVENS; officially inaugurated on January 26, 1986.

First Vice President: Abu Bakar KAMARA; named Second Vice President in November 1985; appointed First Vice President upon the removal of Francis Misheck MINAH on April 3, 1987.

Second Vice President: Salia JUSU-SHERIFF; appointed by the President on April 3, 1987, succeeding Abu Bakar KAMARA.

THE COUNTRY

Facing the South Atlantic and nearly surrounded by the Republic of Guinea on the northwest, north, and east, Sierra Leone ("lion mountain") may be divided into three geographic regions: a peninsula in the west; a western coastal region, which consists of mangrove swamps and a coastal plain; and a plateau in the east and northeast. The indigenous inhabitants range over 12 principal tribal groups, the most important being the Mende in the south and the Temne in the north. There are also numerous Creoles, who are descendants of freed slaves. A variety of tribal languages are spoken, with Krio, a form of pidgin English, serving as a lingua franca. Traditional religions predominate, but there are many Muslims in the north and Christians in the west.

The agricultural sector of the economy employs about two-thirds of the work force. Rice is the main subsistence crop, while cocoa, coffee, and palm kernels are the leading agricultural exports. Gold, bauxite, and rutile are among the minerals extracted, with a rapidly dwindling diamond reserve providing approximately 19 percent of export earnings in 1985 (down from 60 percent in 1980). The International Monetary Fund, the World Bank group, and the European Economic Community have been among the international agencies extending recent aid in support of efforts to revive an economy that has deteriorated markedly since the mid-1970s. The assistance has been largely ineffectual: inflation has averaged about 50 percent since 1982, while the balance of payments has been severely weakened by declining rice production and commodity smuggling.

GOVERNMENT AND POLITICS

Political background. Growing out of a coastal settlement established by English interests in the eighteenth century as a haven for freed slaves, Sierra Leone became independent within the Commonwealth in 1961. Political leadership from 1961 to 1967 was exercised exclusively through the Sierra Leone People's Party (SLPP), a predominantly Mende grouping led successively by Sir Milton MARGAI and his half-brother, Sir Albert M. MARGAI. Attempts to establish a one-party system under the SLPP were successfully resisted by the principal opposition party, the All People's Congress (APC), a predominantly Temne formation headed by Dr. Siaka P. STEVENS, a militant trade-union leader belonging to the smaller Limba tribe.

Following an unexpectedly strong showing by the APC in the election of 1967, Stevens was appointed prime minister but was prevented from taking office by Brig. David LANSANA's declaration of martial law on March 21. Two days later, Lt. Col. Andrew JUXON-SMITH assumed the leadership of a National Reformation Council (NRC) that suspended the constitution, dissolved the parties, and ruled for the ensuing 13 months. The NRC was itself overthrown in April 1968 by a group of noncommissioned officers, the Anti-Corruption Revolutionary Movement, which restored civilian government with Stevens as prime minister.

The ensuing period was marked by a series of coup attempts and government harassment of political opponents. During a state of emergency in 1970, the government banned a new opposition party, the United Democratic Party, and arrested its leaders. In 1971 the regime survived an attempted takeover by the commander of the army, John BANGURA. In 1973 official intimidation contributed to an SLPP boycott of the general election, with the APC winning all but one of the seats in the House of Representatives. In 1975 six civilians and two soldiers were executed in Freetown after being convicted of an attempt to assassinate (then) Finance Minister Christian KAMARA-TAYLOR and take over the government.

Under a new constitution adopted by referendum in early June 1978, Sierra Leone became a one-party state, President Stevens being reinvested for a seven-year term on June 14.

In early 1985, the president announced his intention to retire, naming army commander Maj. Gen. Joseph Saidu MOMOH as his successor; the new president was confirmed in single-party balloting on October 1, Stevens

transferring power to him on November 28, although formal swearing-in ceremonies were not held until January 26, 1986. The House of Representatives was renewed in a multicandidate, one-party poll held on May 29–30, a year prior to expiry of its normal term.

Constitution and government. According to the 1978 constitution (partially amended in mid-1985), Sierra Leone has a modified republican form of government. Executive authority is vested in the president who is nominated by the "recognized party" and confirmed by unopposed popular election. The president is empowered to name two vice presidents, both of whom, in the event of a vacancy, sit on an interim Presidential Council that also encompasses the attorney general, the minister of justice, the speaker of the House of Representatives, and the secretary of the ruling party. Cabinet appointments are also at the absolute discretion of the president. All members of the unicameral legislature must be members of the APC. The judicial system includes a Supreme Court and a Court of Appeal, with judges appointed by the president. The lower courts consist of high, magistrates', and native courts, the last handling cases of customary law.

Sierra Leone is administratively divided into three provinces (Northern, Eastern, Southern) and a Western Region that includes Freetown. The provinces are subdivided into 12 districts and 147 chiefdoms; the paramount chief of each district, elected by his peers, is an ex officio member of the House of Representatives, while each local unit is headed by a chief and a Council of Elders. Freetown has a partially elected city council, which elects the mayor.

Foreign relations. Sierra Leone has maintained a nonaligned but generally pro-Western foreign policy, though diplomatic relations with the USSR, several East European countries, the People's Republic of China, and North Korea have also been established. Regionally, it has been an active participant in the Organization of African Unity and a long-standing member of OAU committees established to resolve the disputes in Chad and the Western Sahara. Traditionally cordial relations with bordering states have been strained in recent years by the overthrow of civilian governments in Liberia and Guinea; however, the three countries signed a security agreement in September 1986 and revived the Mano River Union plan for economic cooperation. In the wake of his inauguration, President Momoh, a former British academy schoolmate of Lagos's military leaders, also moved to forge closer links with Nigeria and in July 1987 an agreement was reached on the direct shipment of Nigerian crude oil to Freetown, thereby eliminating costly "middleman" charges.

Current issues. The retirement of President Stevens in November 1985 was seen by most foreign observers as inevitable, following years of economic hardship, including food shortages and minimal public services. However, the "euphoria" that greeted President Momoh's accession subsided when his campaign to "instill military discipline" in fighting corruption and managing the economy failed to yield tangible results. Critics, while praising the new chief executive for his "honesty", attacked him for a lack of well-defined policies and for remaining too close to Stevens and members of the previous administration. Momoh insisted that "more time" would prove the efficacy of his initiatives, including IMF-mandated measures such as abandonment of price controls and currency devaluation; the immediate result, however, was rampant inflation. By the end of the year, Momoh promised "sterner measures" for "price-gougers" as well as for governmental officials who had not heeded his warnings about corruption.

Despite his declining popularity, Momoh has been credited with a reduction in diamond smuggling and overseeing a May 1986 legislative poll that was relatively free of the widespread violence that had marred previous elections. The anti-smuggling campaign was indirectly linked to the second major coup attempt in two years, on March 23, 1987. Although the more recent plot was reportedly conceived by Mohammed KAIKAI, a leading aide of former president Stevens, Momoh intimated that "certain big powers" had been involved. Seven months later, the country's former first vice president, Francis Misheck MINAH, was among 16 individuals sentenced to death for treason.

A communiqué denouncing Zionism was issued by Momoh following a brief visit by Yasser 'Arafat in June 1986, which resulted in the opening of a PLO office at Freetown. Earlier, however, Momoh had endorsed the local operations of the Frankfort-based Liat industrial and trading company which was accused by the nongovernmental Pan African Union (Panafu) of clandestine ties to Israel, South Africa, and right-wing banking interests in Belgium. In an act of apparent retaliation, a September police raid on Panafu's local headquarters combined with student strikes and popular demonstrations to further weaken Momoh's already beleaguered administration.

POLITICAL PARTIES

Prior to June 1978, Sierra Leone's essentially biparty system was based on a rivalry between the formerly dominant Sierra Leone People's Party (SLPP), strongest in the Mende area of the south, and the All People's Congress (APC), which, based in the Temne region of the north, gained ascendancy after the 1967 coup. Smaller parties included the United Democratic Party (UDP), which was officially banned immediately after its formation in 1970, and the Democratic National Party (DNP), which polled only 0.07 percent of the votes at the 1977 election. Under the present constitution, only the APC enjoys legal status.

Government Party:

All People's Congress (APC). Leftist and republican in outlook, the APC was formed in 1960 by Dr. Siaka Probyn Stevens in a split with a dissident group headed at that time by Albert M. Margai. Though strongest in Temne territory, the party is not exclusively tribal in character, drawing its support from wage-earning and lower-middle-class elements in both Temne and non-Temne areas. The APC won all but 1 of the legislative seats in the 1973 election, which was boycotted by the opposition SLPP; it won all but 15 seats in 1977 and was constitutionally unopposed in 1982 and 1986. At the conclusion of an APC congress on August 1–4, 1985, despite strong support for (then) first vice president Sorie Koroma, Maj. Gen. Joseph Momoh was nominated as the sole candidate to succeed Stevens as president of the Republic. While yielding the post of secretary general to Momoh, Stevens retained the title of chairman, as well as the primary loyalty of much of the party's membership.

Leaders: Maj. Gen. Joseph Saidu MOMOH (President of the Republic and Secretary General of the Party), Abu Bakar KAMARA (First Vice President of the Republic), Harry T.T. WILLIAMS (Leader of the House), Dr. Siaka Probyn STEVENS (Chairman).

Exile Groups:

A **Sierra Leone Democratic Party** (SLDP), claiming branches throughout Sierra Leone, was launched at London in August 1984. Its leaders, Adewole and Olefumi JOHN, who had been prominently associated with the APC at its accession to power, have made little headway in avoiding the organizational problems of other opposition groups. The latter include the UK-based **Sierra Leone Alliance Movement** (SLAM), led by Ambrose GANDA; the **National Alliance Party** (NAP), a left-wing, US-based group, led by former head of state Andrew Juxon-Smith; and the **Sierra Leone Freedom Council** (SLFC), consisting largely of former members of the SLPP. Upon Momoh's accession, communiqués from the SLDP and SLAM hailed the "demise of the Stevens dictatorship", while proclaiming a wait-and-see attitude toward the new administration. The SLDP was, however, implicated by French authorities in a gun-running effort to destabilize the Momoh regime in March 1986, a London spokesman subsequently insisting that charges of mercenary activity were irrelevant since "There is no legal government in Sierra Leone in accordance with the 1961 constitution."

LEGISLATURE

The unicameral **House of Representatives** presently consists of a maximum of 127 members, including 105 ordinary members, 12 district chiefs, and up to 10 members nominated by the president. The ordinary members are elected from single-member constituencies for five-year terms, subject to legislative dissolution. Under a 1981 "primary elections" law, up to four candidates per constituency may be designated by the local executives of the All People's Congress (the executives themselves, each with 21–55 members, being elected by their respective constituency memberships). Only party registrants may stand as candidates and the APC Central Committee has the authority to veto any individual whose selection is considered to be "against the national interest". At the most recent nationwide balloting of May 29–30, 1986, the 105 elective seats were contested by about 350 candidates, 7 of whom were unopposed. On June 6, new elections were held in 17 constituencies in which irregularities were alleged to have occurred. Overall, less than half of the incumbents retained their seats.

Speaker: William Niaka Stephen CONTEH.

CABINET

President	Maj. Gen. Joseph Saidu Momoh
First Vice President	Abu Bakar Kamara
Second Vice President	Salia Jusu-Sheriff
Ministers	
Agriculture, Natural Resources and Forestry	Philipson Kamara
Defense	Maj. Gen. Joseph Saidu Momoh
Education, Cultural Affairs and Sports	Moses Dumbuya
Economic Planning and National Development	Sheka Kanu
Energy and Power	Sheku R. Deen Sesay
Finance	Hasan Gbassay Kanu
Foreign Affairs	Abdul Karim Korama
Health, Social Services and Youth	Musa Kabia
Information and Broadcasting	Eya E. M'Bayo
Internal Affairs	Dr. M.L. Sidique
Justice	Abdulai Conteh

Lands, Housing and Environment	Abu Bakar Kamara
Mines	Birch Momodu Conteh
Tourism	Abdul Iscandari
Trade and Industry	Joe Amara-Bangali
Transport and Communications	Brig. Michael Abdulai
Works and Labor	V.J. Mambu
Attorney General	Abdulai Conteh
Governor, Central Bank	A.R. Turay

NEWS MEDIA

Press. In July 1980 a Newspapers Amendment Act was promulgated, under which newspaper owners are required to register with and pay an annual fee to the government. The measure was interpreted as an effort to restrict criticism of the state in that the minister of information and broadcasting (advised by a committee of government officials, lawyers, journalists, and private citizens) was given the authority to cancel, suspend, or deny renewal of registration certificates. At present, the nation's only daily newspaper is the government-controlled *Daily Mail* (Freetown, 15,000). Independent weekly organs include *For di People, Progress,* and the *Weekend Spark.*

News agencies. The domestic facility is the Sierre Leone News Agency, established in 1980 after President Stevens had complained of "the image given to Third World countries by the press in developed countries". Reuters, TASS, *Xinhua,* and *Agence France-Presse* are among the foreign agencies that maintain bureaus at Freetown.

Radio and television. The government-owned Sierra Leone Broadcasting Service operates a number of radio stations broadcasting in English, Krio, Limba, Mende, and Temne; it also provides limited commercial television service. There were approximately 230,000 radio and 25,000 television receivers in 1987.

INTERGOVERNMENTAL REPRESENTATION

Ambassador to the US: Sahr MATTURI.

US Ambassador to Sierra Leone: Cynthia Shepard PERRY.

Permanent Representative to the UN: Dr. Tom Obaleh KARGBO.

IGO Memberships (Non-UN): ADF, AfDB, APEF, BADEA, CCC, CWTH, ECOWAS, EEC(L), *EIB,* IACO, IBA, IC, ICO, IDB, Interpol, MRU, NAM, OAU.

SINGAPORE

Republic of Singapore
Hsing-chia p'o Kung-ho Kuo (Chinese)
Republik Singapura (Malay)

Political Status: Independent republic within the Commonwealth since August 9, 1965.

Area: 239 sq. mi. (620 sq. km.), including adjacent islets that encompass some 15 sq. mi. (39 sq. km.).

Population: 2,413,945 (1980C), 2,647,000 (1988E).

Major Urban Center (1983E): SINGAPORE (urban area, 2,334,000).

Official Languages: Chinese (Mandarin is now the preferred form), English, Malay, Tamil.

Monetary Unit: Singapore Dollar (market rate March 1, 1988, 2.01 dollars = $1US).

President: WEE Kim Wee; elected by Parliament on August 30, 1985, and sworn in September 1, following the resignation, for health reasons, of C.V. Devan NAIR on March 28 and the acting presidency of Dr. SENG Yeoh Ghim.

Prime Minister: LEE Kuan Yew (People's Action Party); assumed office as colonial Chief Minister in 1963, becoming Prime Minister in September 1963; reappointed after elections held in 1968, 1972, 1976, 1980, and on December 22, 1984.

THE COUNTRY

Joined to the southern tip of the Malay Peninsula by a three-quarter-mile-long causeway, Singapore consists of the single large island on which the city of Singapore is located and some 40 adjacent islets. Situated at the crossroads of Southeast Asian trade routes, the country is one of the world's most densely populated, with some two-thirds of the population—which is about 76 percent ethnic Chinese, 15 percent Malay, and 7 percent Indian and Pakistani—residing at Singapore City. Religious divisions follow ethnic divisions: the Malays and Pakistanis are Muslim, the Indians are Hindu, and the Chinese include Buddhists, Taoists, and Confucianists. Literacy is over 75 percent (more than 90 percent for those under 35 years of age). Women constitute nearly half of the labor force, a third of their number concentrated in low-wage manufacturing; female participation in government is virtually nonexistent.

The 1970s were characterized by rapid economic expansion, with real per capita growth averaging 6.7 percent a year, while per capita GDP rose from $415 in 1959 to $6,906 in 1984. The economy has traditionally been geared to the entrepôt trade, with a heavy emphasis on the processing and transshipment of rubber, timber, petroleum, and other regional products, and on related banking, shipping, insurance, and storage services. In recent years the government has spurred industrialization, with output directed to both regional and worldwide markets, while pioneer industrial legislation, investment incentives, and development plans have attracted a wide range of light and heavy industry as well as offshore commercial and investment banks.

GOVERNMENT AND POLITICS

Political background. Purchased by Great Britain in 1824 and subsequently organized as part of the Straits Settlements (with Penang and Malacca), Singapore became a Crown Colony in 1867. It was occupied by the Japanese in World War II and governed after its liberation as a separate entity, achieving internal self-rule within the Commonwealth on June 3, 1959. Led by LEE Kuan Yew of the People's Action Party (PAP), it joined in 1963 with the Federation of Malaya, Sarawak, and Sabah to form Malaysia, an arrangement designed in part to provide a political counterweight to Singapore's largely Chinese and left-oriented electorate. Malay opinion subsequently became alarmed by the efforts of Lee and his party to extend their influence into other parts of Malaysia, and Singapore was consequently excluded on August 9, 1965.

As a fully independent state with separate membership in the Commonwealth, Singapore adopted a republican form of government in 1965. The PAP, which had been seriously challenged in the early 1960s by the more radical Socialist Front (*Barisan Sosialis*), subsequently consolidated its position, obtaining a monopoly of all legislative seats in the elections of 1968, 1972, 1976, and 1980, but losing one at a by-election in October 1981 and two at the general election of December 1984. The results of the 1984 balloting, which yielded a 13-percent decline in support for the ruling party, generated widespread concern within the PAP and an intimation by Prime Minister Yew of fundamental changes in the electoral law (see Current issues, below).

In June 1979, the Lee regime announced a new industrial policy designed to promote, during the 1980s, the growth of sophisticated, capital-intensive industries, including the manufacture of computers and related components, other electronic instruments, machinery, automobile parts, and precision tools. Called by some observers a "Second Industrial Revolution", the program mandated a 1979 wage increase that amounted to over 20 percent for the lowest-paid laborers, the primary purpose being to force labor-intensive, low value-added enterprises to relocate in other countries and to decrease the city-state's dependence on foreign workers, who might cause future social problems. Collaterally, Prime Minister Lee made a strong effort to bring "new blood" into government and the PAP hierarchy, a prominent example being the designation of GOH Chok Tong, chief architect of the industrial program, as first deputy prime minister. In keeping with this strategy, a November 1982 party convention saw the election of a revamped PAP central committee in which "second-liners" (i.e., second-generation leaders) outnumbered the old guard.

On March 28, 1985, President Nair announced his resignation for reasons of health, the chairman of the Singapore Broadcasting Corporation, WEE Kim Wee being sworn in to succeed Acting President SENG Yeoh Ghim on September 1.

Constitution and government. Singapore's constitution retains the basic form established in 1959, with amendments consequent on its temporary Malaysian affiliation and its subsequent adoption of republican status. The 79-member Parliament, elected by universal suffrage and compulsory voting for a maximum term of five years, selects the president, who serves in a mainly ceremonial role for a four-year term. The prime minister, appointed by the president, heads a cabinet that is collectively responsible to the Parliament. The judicial system is headed by a High Court and includes a Court of Appeal as well as district, magistrates', and special courts. The country is administered as a unified city-state, local government bodies having been absorbed by departments of the central government, although the government in 1986 announced plans to establish town councils with strictly limited powers.

Foreign relations. Despite periodic tensions involving Malaysia and Indonesia, and with formal recognition not yet extended to the People's Republic of China, Singapore has recently taken an increasingly active role in regional affairs, especially through the Association of Southeast Asian Nations (ASEAN). In 1979, Singapore was perhaps the most vocal ASEAN critic of Hanoi's late-1978 invasion of Kampuchea and the continuing exodus of "boat people" from Vietnam. In November, Lee called on the United States, Japan, and Western Europe to impose economic sanctions against Vietnam until the latter's troops were withdrawn from Kampuchea, while earlier, at a ministerial meeting of ASEAN, (then) Foreign Minister Sinnathamby RAJARATNAM had described Hanoi's refugee policy as an "invasion" designed to create economic and racial chaos throughout the region.

In November 1986, Israeli President Chaim Herzog visited Singapore, generating an outburst of protest from neighboring Muslim countries, particularly Malaysia.

In addition to ASEAN, Singapore is a member of the Commonwealth, the United Nations and its Specialized Agencies, and the Asian Development Bank, and since 1973 has adhered to the General Agreement on Tariffs and Trade. Upon the withdrawal of most British defense forces in 1971, it became a member of the Five-Power Defense Arrangement (along with Britain, Australia, New Zealand, and Malaysia), a regional security system that calls for the maintenance of Commonwealth forces in Singapore. In December 1986, however, New Zealand announced that it would withdraw most of its 740-member force by 1989, leaving only a "modest" training contingent.

Current issues. Efforts at recovery from recent economic malaise have been directed largely by the prime minister's son, LEE Hsien Loong, whose meteoric rise has yielded speculation that he is being groomed to succeed his father, although First Deputy Prime Minister Goh remains a strong contender. In 1986, the elder Lee retreated somewhat from a 1985 announcement that he was contemplating retirement, stating he might continue beyond 1988 if he felt his leaving would cause political instability. Still being considered is a proposal to establish a directly elected presidency with enhanced powers, of which Lee would presumably be the initial incumbent.

The most publicized event of 1987 was the arrest in May and June of 22 young professionals and Catholic Church workers for conspiring to "subvert the existing social and political system" and "establish a Communist state" under the direction of TAN Wah Piow, a Singaporean exile engaged in law studies at Oxford University. Apparently embarrassed by international outcry over the action (in support of which little hard evidence was presented), the government released a number of the detainees by early September, Goh Chok Tong confessing at a PAP youth wing meeting that "Maybe we are too intolerant of differences of opinion".

In another controversial move, the government tabled two bills in November that would sanction the creation of a number of three-member group parliamentary constituencies. The GPCs were justified as permitting more adequate representation for Malay and other minority groups. However, antigovernment leader J.B. JEYARETNAM immediately charged the Lee regime with being "starkly dishonest" since opposition parties would be at a disadvantage in attracting well-qualified candidates, whereas the PAP could aid nominees in threatened constituencies by joining them to those with safer majorities.

POLITICAL PARTIES

Governing Party:

People's Action Party (PAP). Organized as a radical socialist party in 1954, the PAP under Lee Kuan Yew's leadership has been Singapore's ruling party since 1959. Some of its more militant leaders were arrested by the British in 1957, and other radicals split off in 1961 to form the Socialist Front. What remains is the more moderate, anti-Communist wing of the original party, which has supported a pragmatic socialist program emphasing social welfare and economic development. Although obtaining less than three-quarters of the vote, it won all of the parliamentary seats in 1972, 1976, and 1980; in 1984 it lost 2 seats, with an overall drop in its vote share of 12.9 percent. The PAP resigned from the Socialist International in May 1976, following accusations of repressive rule by several West European parties.

Changes in the party constitution adopted in 1982 included the designation of the PAP as a "National Movement" and the delegation of additional authority to a 14-member Central Executive Committee, most recently elected at the biennial congress in November 1986. Concern over the small but significant drop in support at the 1984 election has accelerated a PAP youth movement (headed by Lee Hsien Loong) to generate more "responsiveness" to an increasingly restive public, although party leaders have made it clear they will resist opposition efforts to dilute the PAP's monopoly of power.

Leaders: LEE Kuan Yew (Prime Minister and Secretary General of the Party), GOH Chok Tong (First Deputy Prime Minister and Assistant Secretary General of the Party), ONG Teng Cheong (Second Deputy Prime Minister and Chairman of the Party), Brig. Gen. (Res.) LEE Hsien Loong.

Opposition Groups:

Workers' Party (WP). Originally founded in 1957 and reorganized in 1971, the Workers' Party advocates a new, more democratic constitution, closer relations with Malaysia, and the establishment of diplomatic relations with the People's Republic of China. A number of its leaders have been arrested for alleged pro-Communist activities. Its secretary general, J.B. Jeyaretnam, who was convicted in late 1978 of having committed "a very grave slander" against Prime Minister Lee, attributed his defeat in a February 1979 by-election to a "deep-seated fear the people have for voting against the PAP". At a subsequent by-election in October 1981, Jeyaretnam became the first opposition member of Parliament since 1968, without, however, being accorded the status of opposition leader. Derided by the PAP for pursuing "plantation owner politics", the Sri Lanka-born Jeyaretnam retained his seat in 1984, the WP refusing an additional "non-constituency" seat (see Constitution and government, above) as being a "political gimmick". Although having been acquitted of the charge in January 1984, Jeyaretnam and party chairman Wong Hong Toy were retried in September 1985 for making a false declaration about WP finances three years before. After a series of heated parliamentary debates with Prime Minister Lee on issues relating to the trial and sentence, Jeyaretnam was fined and imprisoned for one month in late 1986, losing his legislative seat under a law which prohibits a person from serving in Parliament if assessed more than $2,000 for breaking a law.

Leaders: WONG Hong Toy (Chairman), Joshua Benjamin JEYARETNAM (Secretary General).

Singapore Democratic Party (SDP). Organized in 1980 by Chiam See Tong, a lawyer and well-known independent politician, the SDP was expected to appeal to liberal-minded Singaporeans seeking a degree of formal opposition to the PAP. Although running sixth in the total number of votes cast in the 1980 election, the party was runner-up in the three constituencies it contested. Its secretary general won the remaining seat lost by the PAP in 1984, but unlike Jeyaretnam has spoken mainly on "bread-and butter" issues such as housing, income disparity, and unemployment, while expressing a desire "not to rock the boat too much".

Leaders: LING How Doong (Chairman), CHIAM See Tong (Secretary General).

Singapore United Front (SUF). Formed in 1973, the SUF ran third in the 1984 balloting, securing 34.2 percent of the vote in the 13 constituencies it contested, but winning no parliamentary seats.

Leader: SEOW Khee Leng (Secretary General).

Socialist Front (*Barisan Sosialis* — BS). Formed in 1961 by PAP militants under the leadership of trade-unionist Lim Chin Siong, the Front gained a strong position in the Parliament and remained the leading opposition party until 1966, when 11 members resigned their seats and the other 2 went underground. Pro-Beijing, the party has had little success in carrying its revolutionary program to the people, and a number of its leaders are now in prison.

Leaders: Dr. LEE Siew Choh (Chairman), Abdul RAHIM (Secretary General).

United People's Front (UPF). Organized in late 1974, the UPF is a coalition of several small groups that won 20 percent of the vote in 8 constituencies in 1984.

Leaders: ANG Bee Lian (Chairman), Harbans SINGH Sidhu (Secretary General).

Singapore Malays National Organization (*Pertubohan Kebangsaan Melayu Singapura* — PKMS). An affiliate of the United Malays National Organization in Malaysia, the PKMS supports Malay interests and advocates reunification with Malaysia.

Leaders: Haji Abdu RAHMAN Zin (Chairman), Sahid bin SAHOOMAN (Secretary General).

Singapore Justice Party (SJP). The SJP is a small group organized in 1972. It contested only 2 parliamentary seats in 1984, winning neither.

Leaders: A.R. SUIB (President), Muthusamy RAMASAMY (Secretary General).

Islamic Movement (*Angkatan Islam*). In existence since 1958, the *Angkatan Islam* secured the least number of votes (359 in 1 constituency) of the parties (including the 8 above) that participated in the 1984 election.

Leaders: Mohd bin OMAR (President), Ibrahim bin Abdul GHANI (Secretary General).

The total of 20 officially registered parties in early 1986 also included: the **Alliance Party of Singapore**, the **National Party of Singapore**, the **People's Front**, the **People's Party** (*Partai Rakyat*), the **People's Republican Party**, the **Singapore Chinese Party**, the **Singapore Indian Congress**, the **United Democratic Party**, the **United Malays of Singapore** (*Persatuan Melayu Singapura*), the **United National Front**, and the **United People's Party**.

In April 1986, the *Far Eastern Economic Report* stated that a group of former SDP and SUF leaders (including SUF chairman TAN Chee Kien) had joined LOW Yong Nguan, a former PAP MP, to seek recognition for a **Singapore Solidarity Party** (SSP) that would "be made up mostly of young professionals [seeking] to preserve the one-man-one-vote system and [paying] more attention to the feelings of the people". However, in August the FEER reported that Low had joined the Workers' Party.

Singapore People's Liberation Organization —SPLO (*Organasi Pembebasan Singapura*—PKMS). The SPLO is an Islamic group, several of whose members were sentenced to prison terms of 2–4 years in early 1982 for possession of subversive documents.

Leader: Zainul ABIDDIN bin Mohammed Shah.

Illegal Opposition:

Communist Party of Malaya (CPM). Legally proscribed since 1948, the CPM continues to operate underground in Singapore, where it has links to the Socialist Front and the SPLO, (above). It has long advocated reintegration of Singapore within a Communist Malaysia.

Leader: CHIN Peng (Secretary General).

LEGISLATURE

The unicameral **Parliament** currently consists of 79 members elected by direct universal suffrage for five-year terms, subject to dissolution. In addition, 1–3 "non-constituency" seats may be awarded to runners-up, to permit a minimal opposition of 3 MPs. At the most recent general election, held December 22, 1984, the People's Action Party won 77 seats and the Workers' and Singapore Democratic parties, 1 each, although the Workers' Party representative was ousted in 1986 with no by-election planned to fill the vacancy.

Speaker: Dr. SENG Yeoh Ghim.

C A B I N E T

Prime Minister	Lee Kuan Yew
First Deputy Prime Minister	Goh Chok Tong
Second Deputy Prime Minister	Ong Teng Cheong
Senior Minister (Prime Minister's Office)	Sinnathamby Rajaratnam

Ministers

Communications and Information	Dr. Yeo Ning Hong
Community Development	Wong Kan Seng
Defense (First)	Goh Chok Tong
Defense (Second, Policy)	Dr. Yeo Ning Hong
Defense (Second, Services)	Brig. Gen. (Res.) Lee Hsien Loong
Education	Dr. Tony Tan Keng Yam
Environment	Dr. Ahmad Mattar
Finance	Dr. Richard Hu
Foreign Affairs (First)	Suppiah Dhanabalan
Foreign Affairs (Second)	Wong Kan Seng
Health	Yeo Cheow Tong
Home Affairs	Shunmugam Jayakumar
Labor	Lee Yock Suan
Law (First)	Edmund William Barker
Law (Second)	Shunmugam Jayakumar
National Development	Suppiah Dhanabalan
Trade and Industry	Brig. Gen. (Res.) Lee Hsien Loong
Without Portfolio	Ong Teng Cheong
	Wan Soon Bee

N E W S   M E D I A

The press is free in principle, although in practice it is restrained by continuous government monitoring and periodic crackdowns over stories or editorials which exceed official perceptions of acceptable criticism. In the 1970s a number of extremist papers were banned and minority journalists were imprisoned for alleged involvement in efforts to create a "pro-Communist Malay base in Singapore". In December 1979, two Chinese dailies, *Shin Min* and *Min Pao,* were shut down for what the government considered sensationalism and in April 1982 the *Straits Times* was ordered to divest itself temporarily of its afternoon and Sunday editions, while *Nanyang Siang Pau* and *Sin Chew Jit Poh* were obliged to merge at the corporate level, preliminary to full merger in March 1983 as *Lian He Zao Bao.* Effective competition between major newspapers ended with the merger of Singapore's three largest publishers, the Times Publishing Berhad, the Straits Times Press, and Singapore News and Publications Ltd. in mid-1984. In recent years the government has taken strong exception to stories in a number of nonlocal publications distributed in Singapore, including the *Far Eastern Economic Review* and *The Asian Wall Street Journal,* and in 1986 legislation was enacted to limit the sales of foreign publications "engaging in domestic politics". The option was first exercised late in the year against *Time* magazine

after it declined to print the complete text of a government letter responding to one of its articles; it was again invoked in December 1987, when the *Far Eastern Economic Review* was ordered to reduce its sales from about 10,000 copies to 500, the magazine deciding in February 1988 to discontinue Singapore distribution.

Press. The following newspapers are Chinese-language dailies published at Singapore, unless otherwise noted: *Straits Times* (Singapore editions, 268,000 daily; 300,000 Sunday), in English; *Lian He Zao Bao* (188,000); *Shin Min Daily News* (108,000); *Lian He Wan Bao* (81,000); *Berita Harian* (Singapore editions, 42,000 daily; 55,000 Sunday, published as *Berita Minggu*), in Romanized Malay; *Business Times* (Singapore edition, 18,000), in English; *Tamil Murasu* (8,500 daily, 10,000 Sunday), in Tamil; *International Herald Tribune* (Singapore edition, 3,000), in English.

News agencies. There is no domestic facility; the numerous foreign agencies include AP, UPI, Reuters, *Agence France-Presse,* and TASS.

Radio and television. Radio Singapore and Television Singapore are operated by the Broadcasting Division of the Ministry of Culture. Television programs are broadcast over two channels and radio programs over several networks in Chinese, Malay, Tamil, and English. The BBC Far Eastern Relay, which recently relocated from Malaysia, broadcasts in English. There were approximately 517,000 television receivers in 1987.

INTERGOVERNMENTAL REPRESENTATION

Ambassador to the US: Tommy T.B. KOH.

US Ambassador to Singapore: Daryl ARNOLD.

Permanent Representative to the UN: Kishore MAHBUBANI.

IGO Memberships (Non-UN): ADB, ANRPC, ASEAN, CCC, CP, CWTH, ICO, Inmarsat, Intelsat, Interpol, ISO, NAM.

SOLOMON   ISLANDS

Political Status: Former British-administered territory; achieved internal self-government on January 2, 1976, and full independence within the Commonwealth on July 7, 1978.

Area: 10,639 sq. mi. (27,556 sq. km.).

Population: 285,796 (1986C), 310,000 (1988E).

Major Urban Center (1986C): HONIARA (30,499).

Official Language: English (Solomons Pidgin is the effective lingua franca).

Monetary Unit: Solomon Dollar (market rate March 1, 1988, 2.04 dollars = $1US).

Sovereign: Queen ELIZABETH II.

Governor General: Baddeley DEVESI; assumed office upon independence.

Prime Minister: Ezekiel ALEBUA (Solomon Islands United Party); designated by the National Parliament on December 1, 1986, following the resignation of Sir Peter KENILOREA on November 14.

THE COUNTRY

The Solomons comprise a twin chain of Pacific islands stretching nearly 900 miles in a southeasterly direction from the Papua New Guinean territory of Bougainville to the northern New Hebrides. The six largest islands are Guadalcanal (on which the capital, Honiara, is located), Choiseul, Malaita, New Georgia, San Cristobal, and Santa Isabel. Approximately 93 percent of the inhabitants are Melanesian, with smaller groups of Polynesians (4 percent), Micronesians (1.5 percent), Europeans (0.7 percent), and Chinese (0.3 percent). Anglicans are the most numerous among the largely Christian population, followed by Roman Catholics and adherents of a variety of evangelical sects. An estimated 85 percent of the population is rural, with women bearing much of the responsibility for subsistence agriculture. Over 90 percent of the land is governed by customary land-ownership practices, creating, in combination with the strong influence of tribal nationalism, some barriers to recent development efforts. The principal export commodities are copra, timber, fish, and palm oil, while substantial bauxite deposits on the southern island of Rennell await exploitation.

GOVERNMENT AND POLITICS

Political background. Originally named on the basis of rumors that the sixteenth-century Spanish explorer Alvaro de Mendana had discovered the source of the riches of King Solomon, the islands became the object of European labor "blackbirding" in the 1870s. The excesses of the indenture trade prompted Britain to declare a protectorate over the southern islands in 1893, the remaining territory being added between 1898 and 1900. Occupied by the Japanese in 1941, some of the most bitter fighting of the Pacific war occurred near Guadalcanal and in the adjacent Coral Sea during 1942–1943. After the war, a number of changes in British administration were introduced in response to a series of indigenous political and evangelical movements. In 1960 the resident commissioner's Advisory Council was replaced by separate legislative and executive councils which, under a constitution adopted in 1970, were combined into a high commissioner's Governing Council of both elected and nominated members. Four years later, the high commissioner assumed the title of governor and the Governing Council was supplanted by an elected Legislative Council led by a chief minister, who was empowered to designate his own cabinet. The territory became internally self-governing in January 1976, following the official abandonment in 1975 of its status as a protectorate. After lengthy constitutional discussions at London in 1977, full independence was achieved on July 7, 1978, former chief minister Peter KENILOREA being designated as prime minister.

Kenilorea was redesignated following a legislative election on August 6, 1980, but was defeated 20–17 in intraparliamentary balloting on August 31, 1981, and was obliged to yield office to Solomon MAMALONI, who had served briefly as chief minister during the transition period immediately preceding independence.

Neither of the leading parties gained an absolute majority at the election of October 24, 1984, Kenilorea eventually being empowered by a 21–17 legislative vote on November 19 to form a coalition government that included members of his United Party and the recently organized *Solomone Agu Sogufenua,* in addition to a number of independents.

Although the opposition charged the ruling coalition with inefficiency and "inexplicable delays" in presenting a national development plan, Kenilorea survived a nonconfidence vote on September 6, 1985. However, he resigned on November 14, 1986, because of controversy surrounding the allocation of aid in the wake of a severe cyclone (see Current issues, below). On December 1, Deputy Prime Minister Ezekiel ALEBUA was chosen by the National Parliament as his successor.

Constitution and government. The independence agreement negotiated in September 1977 provided for a constitutional monarchy with the queen represented by a governor general of local nationality. Upon independence, the unicameral Legislative Assembly, which had been increased to 38 members in April 1976, became the National Parliament, with the authority to elect the prime minister from among its membership. The cabinet, which is appointed by the governor general on advice of the prime minister, is responsible to the Parliament. In addition, the independence agreement called for devolution of authority to local government units, within which the traditional chiefs retain formal status. The most seriously contested issue yielded a provision that nonindigenous Solomon Islanders (mainly Gilbertese, Chinese, and European expatriates) would be granted automatic citizenship upon application within two years of independence. The judicial system includes a High Court, magistrates' courts, and local courts whose jurisdiction encompasses cases dealing with customary land titles. Ultimate appeal, as in certain other nonrepublican Commonwealth nations, is to the Privy Council at London.

For administrative purposes the islands are divided into five provinces (Western, Central Islands and Santa Isabel, Guadalcanal, Malaita, and Makula and Temotu), each with an elected council.

Foreign relations. The Solomon Islands retains close links with Britain, which agreed in 1977 to provide some $43 million in nonrepayable financial assistance during 1978–1982. Additional aid has been obtained from Australia, New Zealand, Japan, and such multilateral sources as the Asian Development Bank. Regionally, Honiara has been a strong supporter of the "nuclear free zone" movement and an opponent of what former prime minister Kenilorea called French "imperialism", although stopping short of offering material aid to independence activists on New Caledonia. Despite its antinuclear posture, it has been one of the few Pacific island states to express concern about the future of ANZUS, with Australia in early 1987 extending its defense support by a tender of patrol boats (the first to be delivered in early 1988) and the deployment of long-range RAAF reconnaissance aircraft.

Current issues. Cyclone Namu, described as the worst in memory and perhaps in history, struck on May 18, 1986, killing an estimated 1,000 and leaving 90,000 homeless. Observers estimated recovery might take up to three years, particularly in light of a severe disruption of agriculture.

Reports of maldistribution of food aid began to circulate soon after an international relief effort began, critics charging that food was sold for profit or given to relatives of distributors. Prime Minister Kenilorea vehemently denied any wrongdoing, saying "all aid is welcome", but resigned on November 14, saying his administrative effectiveness had been compromised.

Economic reverses continued into 1987, with a significant reduction in export revenue, inadequate public- and private-sector investment, and a decline in real income of approximately 10 percent. In the longer term, however, the country was expected to be the "greatest beneficiary in the region" from the projected exploitation of substantial mineral deposits, including gold.

During a visit to the United States in February 1988 Deputy Prime Minister (and recently appointed Foreign Minister) Kenilorea indicated that the Solomons was considering the possibility of becoming a republic, with a president replacing the governor general.

POLITICAL PARTIES

Government Parties:

Solomon Islands United Party (Siupa). Siupa was an outgrowth of the Civil Servants' Association, which placed 10 members in the legislature in 1973 although its president, Peter Kenilorea, was defeated in his bid to sit for Honiara. Kenilorea entered the Assembly in 1976 and served as prime minister from independence until supplanted by Mamaloni in 1981. Although Kenilorea campaigned in 1976 for retention of the link to the Crown, the 1980 Siupa manifesto called for a president to replace the queen as head of state.

Leaders: Ezekiel ALEBUA (Prime Minister), Sir Peter KENILOREA (former Prime Minister).

My Land (*Solomone Agu Sogufenua* — SAS). The SAS was formed prior to the 1984 election by a group of MPs and civil servants opposed to the Mamaloni government.

Leaders: Seth LEKELALU (Parliamentary Leader), Danny PHILIP.

Nationalist Front for Progress (NFP). Formally constituted in November 1985 by PAP MP Andrew Nori, the NFP is primarily concerned with land-use issues and advocates abolition of the existing tiers of provincial government to facilitate direct cooperation between the provinces and Honiara.

Leader: Andrew NORI.

Opposition Parties:

People's Alliance Party (PAP). The PAP was formed in late 1979 by merger of the People's Progressive Party (PPP), led by former chief minister Solomon Mamaloni, and the Rural Alliance Party (RAP), led by David Kausimae. Mamaloni had urged a more cautious approach to independence than had Siupa's Peter Kenilorea. Chosen to succeed Kenilorea as prime minister in August 1981, Mamaloni was forced into opposition after the election of October 1984.

Leaders: Solomon MAMALONI (former Prime Minister and Leader of the Opposition), David KAUSIMAE, Edward KINGMELE (Secretary).

Solomon Islands Liberal Party (SILP). Formed in 1976 as the National Democratic Party (Nadepa), the SILP adopted its present name in 1986. Nadepa was the only formal party to contest the 1976 election, at which it won 5 legislative seats. Prior to independence, it campaigned vigorously for republican status and greater autonomy for district governments. It joined the Mamaloni government in September 1981. The party's legislative representation fell from 4 in 1980 to 1 in 1984, its leader being among those losing their seats.

Leader: Bartholomew ULUFA'ALU.

LEGISLATURE

The unicameral **National Parliament** consists of 38 members elected for four-year terms. The 1980 election was the first fought along party lines, though formal affiliations were blurred and Solomon Mamaloni was chosen to succeed Peter Kenilorea as prime minister a year later because of realignment by independent members. At the most recent balloting of October 24, 1984, the Solomon Islands United Party won 13 seats; the People's Alliance Party, 12; *Solomone Agu Sogu Fenua,* 4; the National Democratic Party, 1; independents, 7; vacant, 1.

Speaker: L. Mapeza GINA.

CABINET

[as of April 15, 1988]

Prime Minister	Ezekiel Alebua
Deputy Prime Minister	Sir Peter Kenilorea
Ministers	
Agriculture and Lands	Joini Tutua
Economic Planning	Paul J. Tovua
Education and Training	Daniel Sande
Finance	George Kejoa
Foreign Affairs	Sir Peter Kenilorea
Health and Medical Services	John Tepaika
Home Affairs and Provincial Government	Andrew Nori
Immigration and Labor	Jason Dorovolomo
Natural Resources	(Vacant)
Police and Justice	Swanson C. Konofilia
Post and Telecommunications	John Kaliue
Public Services	Alex Bartlett
Trade, Commerce and Industry	Augustine Rose
Transport, Works and Utilities	Alfred Maetia
Attorney General	Frank Kabui
Governor, Central Bank	Tony Hughes

NEWS MEDIA

Press. The following are published at Honiara: *Solomon Nius* (4,500), issued weekly by the government information service; *Solomon Star* (3,000), weekly; *Solomons Toktok* (1,000), independent daily in Pidgin.

Radio and television. The Solomon Islands Broadcasting Corporation provides daily radio service in Pidgin and English to an estimated 60,000 receivers. There is no television service.

INTERGOVERNMENTAL REPRESENTATION

Ambassador to the US and Permanent Representative to the UN: Francis J. SAEMALA.

US Ambassador to the Solomon Islands: Everett E. BIERMAN (resident in Papua New Guinea).

IGO Memberships (Non-UN): ADB, APCC, CWTH, EEC(L), *EIB,* SPC, SPEC, SPF.

SOMALIA

Somali Democratic Republic
Jamhuuriyada Demuqraadiga Soomaaliyeed

Political Status: Independent republic established July 1, 1960; revolutionary military regime installed October 21,

1969; one-party state proclaimed July 1, 1976; present constitution approved August 25, 1979.

Area: 246,199 sq. mi. (637,657 sq. km.).

Population: 5,167,000 (1988E), exclusive of an estimated 500,000 to 850,000 refugees from Ethiopia's Ogaden region.

Major Urban Center (1984E): MOGADISHU (570,000); Hargeisa (90,000); Kismayu (86,000).

Official Language: Somali.

Monetary Unit: Somali Shilling (principal rate March 1, 1988, 100.00 shillings = $1US.

President: Maj. Gen. Mohamed SIAD Barre; served as President of the Supreme Revolutionary Council from October 21, 1969, until its dissolution on July 1, 1976, continuing as chief executive concurrent with designation as Secretary General of Somali Revolutionary Socialist Party; elected by the People's Assembly for a constitutional term of six years on January 26, 1980; term extended to seven years by the People's Assembly on December 2, 1984; reelected for seven years by direct popular vote on December 23, 1986.

First Vice President and Prime Minister: Lt. Gen. Mohamed Ali SAMATAR (Samantar, Samater); appointed First Vice President by the President on July 31, 1970; most recently reappointed on March 1, 1982; appointed Prime Minister on January 30, 1987.

Second Vice President: Maj. Gen. Hussein KULMIE (Kulmiye) Afrah; appointed by the President on July 31, 1970; most recently reappointed on March 1, 1982.

THE COUNTRY

The easternmost country in Africa, Somalia encompasses a broad band of desert and semidesert territory extending eastward along the Gulf of Aden and continuing southwestward to a point just south of the equator. The Somalis, a people of nomadic and pastoral traditions, share a common religion (Islam) and a common language, which has only recently developed a written form. However, interclan rivalry has generated numerous economic and political cleavages, particularly between northern and southern dwellers. Nonindigenous groups include Arabs, Ethiopians, Italians, Indians, and Pakistanis.

The economy is largely undeveloped, with little real growth achieved in recent decades. For the most part, it has retained its traditional agricultural basis, which has a limited future in an area of irregular rainfall. The country possesses some mineral deposits, but none is currently being commercially exploited. Although fishing, textile, and food processing industries have been established, the bulk of the country's foreign-exchange earnings comes from livestock and livestock-related products. Somalia is the world's largest producer of incense, which is sold at around $36 a kilo to the Gulf countries, China, and France. Current development projects include the construction of a dam for hydroelectric and irrigation purposes across the Juba River in the south; further development has been hindered by the lack of supporting infrastructure and by limited private investment. Moreover, inflation, a sharp drop in exports, drought, inefficiency in state enterprises, corruption in a top-heavy bureaucracy, and the influx of refugees from neighboring Ethiopia have contributed to what has been termed a climate of "economic destitution". Recent government measures have included some degree of privatization and implementation of IMF-mandated reforms to facilitate foreign debt rescheduling.

GOVERNMENT AND POLITICS

Political background. Divided into French, British, and Italian sectors at the end of the nineteenth century, Somalia was partially reunited in 1960 when British Somaliland in the north and the Italian-administered Somaliland Trust Territory in the south achieved their independence and promptly merged to form the present republic. Large numbers of Somalis remained in Ethiopia, Kenya, and the French Territory of the Afars and the Issas (now Djibouti), and the new Somali regime announced that their inclusion in a "Greater Somalia" was a leading political objective (see map, p. 185).

The Somali Youth league (SYL) was the country's principal political party at independence and formed the Republic's initial governments. During the late 1950s and early 1960s, Somalia pursued a strongly irredentist policy toward Ethiopia and Kenya and relied increasingly on aid from the Soviet Union and other Communist states. A change of policy occurred in 1967 with the presidential election of Abdirashid Ali SHERMARKE and his appointment of Mohamed Haji Ibrahim EGAL as prime minister. Under Egal's leadership, Somalia maintained its demand for self-determination for all Somalis but emphasized reduced dependence on the Communist world, conciliation with neighboring states, and the cultivation of friendly relations with Western countries.

The Egal regime was ousted by military units under the command of Maj. Gen. Mohamed SIAD Barre on October 21, 1969, in an action that included the assassination of President Shermarke. Pledging to reduce tribalism and corruption, the military government began a reorganization of the country along socialist lines. Although briefly interrupted by antigovernment plots in 1970 and 1971, the program moved forward at a deliberate pace. In 1970, foreign banks and other foreign-controlled enterprises were nationalized, and in October 1972 local government reorganization was begun. On July 1, 1976, the Supreme Revolutionary Council (SRC) that had been established in the wake of the 1969 coup was abolished and its powers transferred to a newly created Somali Revolutionary Socialist Party (SRSP), of which Siad Barre was named secretary general. Civilian government was nominally reinstituted following popular approval of a new constitution on August 25, 1979, the one-party election of a People's Assembly on December 30, and the Assembly's election of General Siad Barre as president on January 26, 1980.

A state of emergency was declared on October 21, 1980, following a resurgence of conflict with Ethiopia (for a discussion of earlier hostilities, see Foreign relations, below), Radio Mogadishu announcing two days later that the SRC had been reconstituted. The emergency decree was rescinded on March 1, 1982, despite reports of a northern army mutiny in mid-February and sporadic border incidents that persisted thereafter.

At the most recent legislative election of December 31, 1984, 99.8 percent of the voters were reported to have cast ballots with less than 1 percent opposing the SRSP's nominees. On December 23, 1986, in the country's first direct balloting for the position, Siad Barre was the sole candidate in reelection to a seven-year presidential term.

Constitution and government. For the decade after the October 1969 coup, supreme power was vested in the Central Committee of the SRSP, whose secretary general served as head of state and chief executive. For all practical purposes these arrangements were continued under the constitution approved in 1979, which provided additionally for a People's Assembly of 177 members, 171 of whom are nominated by the party and 6 by the president. The president, formerly elected for a six-year term by the Assembly following nomination by the SRSP Central Committee, is now elected for a seven-year term through universal suffrage, although still nominated by the SRSP as the only candidate. The president may designate one or more vice presidents and a prime minister "if he shall deem it appropriate". The judicial system is based on Islamic law and is headed by a Supreme Revolutionary Court. There are also appellate, regional, and district courts in addition to specialized courts for national security and religious affairs. Administratively, the country is divided into 15 regions, which are subdivided into 78 districts.

Foreign relations. Although a member of the United Nations, the Organization of African Unity, and the Arab League, Somalia has been chiefly concerned with the problems of its own immediate area, where seasonal migrations by Somali herdsmen have long strained relations with neighboring states. The most serious dispute has been with Ethiopia, Somali claims to the Ogaden desert region precipitating conflicts beginning in 1963 that escalated into a full-scale war in 1977–1978 when government troops entered the region, eventually to be driven back by an Ethiopian counter offensive. The war had international implications, producing a reversal of roles for the Soviet Union and the United States in the Horn of Africa. Ethiopia, previously dependent on the United States for military support, was the recipient of a massive influx of arms and advisers from the Soviet Union and Cuba. Collaterally, Somalia, which had developed an extensive network of relations with Communist countries, broke with Moscow and Havana in favor of reliance on the West, eventually agreeing in 1980 to make port facilities available to the US Rapid Deployment Force for the Middle East in return for American arms. Mogadishu normalized relations with Moscow in October 1986, but continued to receive substantial military aid from Washington, Somali bases gaining added significance in 1987 as the United States increased its presence in the Persian Gulf.

Although the 1979 constitution called for "the liberation of Somali territories under colonial occupation"—implicitly referencing Somali-populated areas of Kenya as well as of Ethiopia—the Somalis promised that they would not intervene militarily in support of external dissidents. Tense relations and occasional hostilities along the border continued, however, with Ethiopia supporting the major Somali opposition groups in guerrilla operations. In January 1986 Siad Barre and Ethiopian leader Mengistu Haile-Mariam established a joint ministerial commission to resolve the Ogaden question, but no results were achieved during the ensuing year, with Somalia accusing Ethiopia of a cross-border attack in February 1987. Following major Ethiopian reverses at the hands of Eritrean secessionists in the north, the two leaders conferred during a drought conference in Djibouti on March 21–22, 1988, and agreed to peace talks at Mogadishu in early April. The discussions yielded a joint communiqué on April 4 that pledged a military "disengagement and separation", an exchange of prisoners, and the reestablishment of diplomatic relations; however, no reference was made to the long-standing border dispute.

Somali relations with Libya were severed from 1981 to 1985 because of the "continuous conspiracies of the Qadhafi regime" in support of Ethiopian-based rebels. Relations with Kenya, on the other hand, improved as the result of a visit by President Moi in July 1984, during which Siad Barre asserted that Somalia "no longer has any claim to Kenyan territory" and the two leaders reached agreement on a series of border and technical cooperation issues.

Current issues. Despite President Siad Barre's election to a new seven-year term in December 1986, his advanced age and poor health have generated intense speculation as to a successor, the selection of which could provoke domestic upheaval. A leading candidate is First Vice President Samatar, who served as de facto chief executive for several months after Siad Barre's injury in a May 1986 automobile accident. Although also named prime minister in January 1987, Samatar's candidacy is presumed to face strong opposition from Siad Barre's clan, whose members include the president's influential wife, Khadija, his brother, Abdul Rahman JAMA Barre, and his eldest son, Col. Masleh SIAD Barre.

Complicating the succession question are deteriorating economic and political conditions throughout the country and increasing guerrilla activity, particularly by the Somali National Movement (see SNM, under Political Parties, below). By early 1987, food shortages had provoked unrest in the northwest, while mass demonstrations, prompted by fuel shortages and soaring prices, were mounted at Mogadishu in August. Further difficulties were presented by a drought-induced state of emergency for the central region, a new influx of Ethiopians that compounded a decade-long refugee problem, and continued external criticism of alleged human rights abuses by the government.

POLITICAL PARTIES

Government Party:

Somali Revolutionary Socialist Party (SRSP). The SRSP held its inaugural congress on June 28 and was formally constituted on July 1, 1976, as the country's only legal party, members of the former Supreme Revolutionary Council becoming members of its Central Committee. Headed by a 47-member Central Committee and Politburo, the party is organizationally divided into 16 departments. At its third congress in November 1986, the SRSP reelected President Siad Barre as secretary general for an additional five-year term and endorsed peace talks with Ethiopia and improved relations with the Soviet Union. In a move that was interpreted as an effort to delegate authority in the light of his health problems, General Siad Barre appointed Abdelkadir Haji Mohamed assistant secretary general in early 1987.

Leaders: Maj. Gen. Mohamed SIAD Barre (President of the Republic and Secretary General of the Party), Abdelkadir Haji MOHAMED (Assistant Secretary General).

Opposition Groups:

Somali Democratic Salvation Front (SDSF). The SDSF was organized during a conference at an undisclosed location on September 19-October 5, 1982, by three dissident groups: the Somali Salvation Front (SSF), the Democratic Front for the Liberation of Somalia (DFLS), and the Somali Workers' Party (SWP). The SSF (also known as Sosaf) had been formed initially in 1976 as the Somali Democratic Action Front (Sodaf), with headquarters at Rome, Italy, the change of name and relocation to Addis Ababa occurring in early 1979. Its leader at the launching of the SDSF was Colonel Abdullahi YUSUF Ahmed, who had defected from Somalia with a group of army officers in 1978 following an abortive coup attempt. Most SSF members were drawn from the dissident Mijarteyn tribe, some of whom were executed after the coup failed.

The DFLS, another Ethiopian-backed group, was led at the time of the merger by Abderahman AYDEED Ahmed, reportedly a former chairman of the SRSP Ideological Bureau. The SWP, a Soviet-supported movement headquartered in South Yemen, was led by Hussein SAID Jama, a former member of the SRSP's Central Committee.

At the inauguration of the SDSF, Yusuf was named chairman, Said vice president, and Aydeed secretary general. A party congress in March 1983 elected a 21-member central committee and a 9-member executive committee and adopted a constitution and a political program that called for the overthrow of the Siad Barre regime, the removal of US bases from Somalia, and the establishment of "genuine peace and cooperation based on the brotherhood of the Horn of Africa". However, some DFLS and SWP members reportedly were excluded from the new formation at the 1983 congress, and Jama and Aydeed were removed from their leadership positions at a congress in November. In January 1984 it was reported that a number of SDSF members opposed to Yusuf's leadership had accepted government amnesty, as did about 200 guerrillas in May. In July 1985, Jama was reported to have founded a splinter group, the **Somali Patriotic Liberation Front** (SPLF), based, like its SWP predecessor, at Aden, South Yemen. In October 1985 Yusuf, who had been criticized for his attempts to lessen Ethiopian influence over the SDSF and for his unwillingness to facilitate further merger of Somali opposition movements, was arrested in Ethiopia and replaced as chairman on an interim basis by Mohamed Abshir. In March 1986, a party congress (attended by representatives of the SNM, below, who were investigating merger possibilities) elected Hassan Haji Ali Mireh as chairman.

The SDSF was involved in fighting along the Ethiopian border in late 1982 and in sporadic guerrilla activity within Somalia through 1984. After a period of relative quiescence, during which some of its members reportedly accepted a government amnesty offer, the SDSF in 1987 claimed responsibility for a bomb explosion in Mogadishu, as well as for several attacks on government troops.

Leader: Hassan Haji Ali MIREH (Chairman).

Somali National Movement (SNM). The SNM was organized at London, England, on April 6, 1981, by Hasan Adan Wadadi, a former Somali diplomat, who stated that the group, while committed to the overthrow of the existing Mogadishu regime, did not wish to ally itself with either the United States or the Soviet Union. Despite endorsement of the idea by several party congresses, the SNM has failed to achieve a unified front with the SDSF. In recent years the SNM, which derives most of its support from the Isaaq clan in northwestern Somalia, has become the more active of the two guerrilla groups. More than 200 SNM troops were allegedly killed in February 1987 when they assisted Ethiopian forces in an unsuccessful cross-border assault. It was announced several months later that more than 70 SNM members had been executed after being identified as government agents. Ahmed Mohamed Silyano was reelected SNM

president at the Movement's fifth congress, which was reported to have been held at Harar, Ethiopia, on February 28–March 9, 1987.

Leaders: Ahmed Mohamed SILYANO (President), Ali Mohamed Osobleh WARDIGLEY (Vice President).

Somalia First (SF). Formed at London in 1983, SF's proclaimed goal is to unite the opposition in armed struggle against the Mogadishu regime.

Leader: Mohamed AHMED.

Somali Islamic Movement (SIM). The SIM was formed at Mogadishu in May 1986 with the goal of overthrowing the Siad Barre government and introducing a "moderate and nonfanatical" *shari'a* law. In April 1987 nine of its members were given death sentences (later commuted to life imprisonment) in a secret trial before the National Security Court.

L E G I S L A T U R E

The most recent balloting for the unicameral **People's Assembly** was held on December 31, 1984. The Assembly is composed of 171 members elected from a single slate presented by the Somali Revolutionary Socialist Party, plus 6 members nominated by the president. The legislative term is five years.

Chairman of Standing Committee: Ahmed Mohamed IBRAHIM.

C A B I N E T

Prime Minister	Lt. Gen. Mohamed Ali Samatar
Deputy Prime Minister for Economic Affairs	Maj. Gen. Hussein Kulmie Afrah
Deputy Prime Minister for Social Security Affairs	Brig. Gen. Ahmed Suleiman Abdullah
Deputy Prime Minister for Political Affairs and General Services	Col. Ahmed Mohamed Farah
Ministers	
Agriculture	Abdirazak Mohamed Abubakar
Air and Land Transport	Jama Gas Mu'awiya
Commerce and Industry	Hussein Abdullah Alasow
Culture and Higher Education	Abdel Salem Sheikh Hussain
Defense	Maj. Gen. Adan Abdullahi Nur
Education	Abdullahi Mohamed Mireh
Finance	Abdul Rahman Jama Barre
Fisheries and Marine Resources	Adan Mohamed Ali
Foreign Affairs	Mohamed Ali Hamud (Acting)
Health	Mohamed Sheikh Ali Munasar
Information and Tourism	Abdirashid Sheikh Ahmed
Internal Affairs	Mohamed Abdullah Ba'Adleh
Justice and Religious Affairs	Sheikh Hassan Abdulahi Farah
Labor, Sports and Social Affairs	Mireh Aware Jama
Livestock Development and Forestry	Bile Refleh Guled
Mineral and Water Resources	Abdullahi Mohamed Hersi
Planning and Juba Valley Development	Ahmed Habib Amed
Ports and Sea Transport	Brig. Gen. Mohamed Jelle Yusuf
Posts and Telecommunications	Yussuf Hassan Elmi
Public Works and Housing	Musa Rabile Ghoud
Governor, Central Bank	Mohamoud Mohamed Nur

N E W S   M E D I A

Press. The press is relatively undeveloped and circulation is low. The only daily is the government's *October Star,* published at Mogadishu in Somali and Arabic editions as *Xiddigta Oktobar* and *Najmat Oktobar,* respectively. Other publications include *Horseid,* a private weekly in Arabic and Italian, and *Heegan* (Vigilance), a government weekly in English. In August 1985, the opposition Somali National Movement announced the launching of a monthly, *al-Moujahid* (The Fighter), to be published in Arabic, Somali, and English.

News agencies. The domestic agency is the Somali National News Agency (Sonna); Italy's ANSA is also represented at Mogadishu.

Radio and television. The government-owned Somali Broadcasting Service operates Radio Mogadishu, and the Northern Region government operates Radio Hargeisa. A mobile station, Radio *Halgan* ("Struggle"), formerly Radio *Kulmis,* broadcasts on behalf of "the united voices of the Somali opposition forces". Television service, reaching only a limited number of receivers, was introduced in 1976.

INTERGOVERNMENTAL REPRESENTATION

Ambassador to the US: Abdullahi Ahmed ADDOU.

US Ambassador to Somalia: Trusten Frank CRIGLER.

Permanent Representative to the UN: Abdullahi Said OSMAN.

IGO Memberships (Non-UN): ADF, AfDB, AFESD, AMF, EEC(L), *EIB,* IC, IDB, Intelsat, Interpol, LAS, NAM, OAU.

SOUTH AFRICA

Republic of South Africa
Republiek van Suid-Afrika
African Name: *Azania*

Political Status: Fully independent state since 1934; under republican regime established May 31, 1961, on withdrawal from the Commonwealth.

Area: 471,879 sq. mi. (1,222,166 sq. km.), including 38,679 sq. mi. (100,179 sq. km.) of the nominally independent republics of Bophuthatswana, Ciskei, Transkei, and Venda, as well as 434 sq. mi. (1,124 sq. km.) of Walvis Bay, which was administered prior to August 1977 as part of South West Africa (Namibia).

Population: 35,264,000 (1988E), including 5,814,000 (1988E) resident populations of Bophuthatswana, Ciskei, Transkei, and Venda. The official result of a 1980 census put the population of South Africa, exclusive of the nominally independent republics, at 24,885,960, including 4,528,100 Whites, 2,612,780 Coloureds, 821,320 Asians, and 16,923,760 Blacks.

Major Urban Centers (1985C): PRETORIA (administrative capital, 443,059; urban area, 822,925); Cape Town (legislative capital, 776,617; urban area, 1,911,521); Bloemfontein (judicial capital, 104,381; urban area, 232,984); Durban (634,301; urban area, 982,075); Johannesburg (632,369; urban area, 1,609,408).

Official Languages: English, Afrikaans.

Monetary Unit: Rand (market rate March 1, 1988, 2.09 rands = $1US).

State President: Pieter Willem BOTHA (National Party); designated by the majority parties in the three houses of

Parliament on September 4, 1984, and sworn in on September 14, succeeding Marais VILJOEN; continued in office following the House of Assembly election of May 6, 1987.

THE COUNTRY

Industrially the most highly developed country in Africa, the Republic of South Africa is a land of rolling plateaus within a mountainous escarpment that rims its territory on the seaward side and separates the coastal cities of Cape Town and Durban from the inland centers of Johannesburg and Pretoria. Composed of four distinct provinces—Cape of Good Hope, Natal, Transvaal, and Orange Free State—the country is peopled by four separate ethnic elements as unequal in numbers as they are in political status. The largest but least-favored group, comprising 74 percent of the total population, consists of the Xhosa, Zulu, and Sotho, who are collectively known as the Bantu; next in order of size is the dominant White community, comprising 15 percent of the population; "Coloureds", or persons of mixed blood, account for another 9 percent; and Asians, mainly Indians living in Natal Province, total 2 percent.

Some three-fifths of the Whites are "Afrikaners", who trace their descent to the Dutch, German, and French Huguenot settlers that colonized the country from the seventeenth century onward. Largely agrarian in their social traditions and outlook, they speak Afrikaans, a language closely related to Dutch; are predominantly affiliated with the Dutch Reformed Church; and have been the most resolute supporters of the official policy of separate development of the races (apartheid). The remainder of the Whites are largely English-speaking but have followed the Afrikaner lead politically, with certain reservations reflecting their closer identification with the British tradition and their greater involvement in business and industry.

South Africa has become a highly urbanized country, with half of the White population, a third of the Blacks, and most Coloureds and Asians residing in racially segregated areas in and around the dozen large cities and towns. Most of the remaining Blacks live either on White-owned farms or tribal homelands (redesignated in 1979 as "black states"). The social and economic differences between the White and non-White groups are reflected in their respective literacy rates, estimated at 98 percent for Whites and 32 percent for non-Whites.

In 1980, women constituted 35 percent of the paid labor force. White women are concentrated in the clerical and service sectors; in "White" areas, Black women work mainly as domestic servants and casual agricultural laborers. In the homelands, traditional law restricts female land ownership, although male migration to White-controlled employment sites has left women largely in control of subsistence agriculture. Female participation in government is limited to minor representation by White women in both national and provincial legislatures; however, women of all races have been prominent in the anti-apartheid movement.

The first African country to experience the full force of the industrial revolution, South Africa now has an advanced industrial economy that plays an important role in world economic affairs. The manufacturing sector, spurred by foreign investment and by governmental efforts to promote industrial self-sufficiency, presently accounts for nearly one-quarter of the gross domestic product, although real GDP plunged from an increase of 7.8 percent in 1980 to an average of 1.3 percent during the ensuing four years, while inflation through the same period hovered in the vicinity of 12 percent before climbing to more than 20 percent by late 1985, the highest in 60 years, prompting a series of reflationary efforts in early 1986. The burden of unemployment, estimated in September 1986 to be as high as 50 percent of the potentially active work force (12 times the official figure), is borne largely by the Black population.

South African gold mines supply about two-thirds of the gold produced by non-Communist countries; other important mineral products include diamonds, copper, asbestos, chrome, and platinum. The principal resource deficiency is oil, some 90 percent of annual consumption being imported from Iran prior to a formal suspension of shipments in 1979; there are, however, abundant coal reserves, from which 85 percent of primary energy needs (including 50 percent of liquid fuel requirements) are now derived. Agriculturally, the country is self-sufficient in most foods (except coffee, rice, and tea) and exports wool, maize, sugar, and fruits.

GOVERNMENT AND POLITICS

Political background. The Republic of South Africa as it exists today is the result of a long and complicated process of interaction between the African peoples and the Dutch and English colonists who came to exploit the territory. The original Cape Colony was settled by the Dutch in the seventeenth century but fell into English hands as a result of the Napoleonic wars. Discontented Dutch farmers, or Boers, trekked northward in 1836, subjugating the Zulu and other native peoples and establishing the independent republics of the Transvaal and the Orange Free State. Following the discovery of diamonds and gold in the late nineteenth century, the two Boer republics were conquered by Britain in the Anglo-Boer War of 1899–1902. In 1910 they were joined with the British colonies of the Cape and Natal (annexed in 1843) to form the Union of South Africa, which was recognized as an independent member of the Commonwealth in 1934.

Although South Africa joined with Britain in both world wars, its British and Commonwealth attachments progressively weakened as the result of domestic racial preoccupations. The National Party (NP), led by Daniel F. MALAN, came to power in 1948 with a program explicitly based on racial separation under European "guardianship" and proceeded to enact a body of openly discriminatory legislation that was further amplified under Hendrik F. VERWOERD (1958–1966). Racial segregation was strictly enforced, token political representation of non-Whites was progressively reduced, and overt opposition was severely repressed. Similar policies were applied in South West Africa, a former German territory occupied by South Africa in World War I and subsequently administered under a mandate from the League of Nations (see entry under Namibia).

Increasing institutionalization of apartheid under the Verwoerd regime led to international condemnation. External opposition was intensified by the "Sharpeville incident" of March 21, 1960, during which South African police fired on African demonstrators and caused numerous casualties. In view of the increasingly critical stand of other Commonwealth members, South Africa formally withdrew from membership in the Commonwealth and declared itself a republic on May 21, 1961.

Prime Minister Verwoerd was assassinated by a deranged White man in September 1966, but his successor, Balthazar J. VORSTER, continued Verwoerd's policies, bringing to fruition the idea of separating the Blacks into separate tribal homelands, or "Bantustans". These areas, encompassing approximately 13 percent of the country's land, were ultimately intended to house upwards of three-quarters of the population. Concurrently, a series of minor concessions to the Blacks brought about a challenge from the right-wing, or *verkrampte* (narrow-minded), faction of the National Party under the leadership of Dr. Albert HERTZOG, who formed the Reconstituted National Party (HNP) to compete in the 1970 election. The NP survived his challenge and Vorster continued in office, although the opposition United Party (UP) made some gains. At the next parliamentary election, held a year early in April 1974 to take advantage of the disorganized state of the UP and a favorable economic situation, the NP won easily, the UP losing five seats to the other opposition group, the Progressive Party (PP), which had for some years held only a single seat.

The Portuguese coup and subsequent changes in Angola and Mozambique further isolated the South African regime, leading early in 1975 to an announced policy of "ending discrimination" within South Africa and of working for détente in external affairs. The new policy was accompanied by a partial relaxation in apartheid regulations, including a repeal of "Masters and Servants" legislation, portions of which had been in existence for over a century. During the following year, however, the country experienced its worst outbreak of racial violence since the Sharpeville episode in 1960. The rioting, which began at Soweto (near Johannesburg) in mid-June, grew out of Black student protests against the compulsory use of Afrikaans as a medium of instruction. Although the government announced in early July that it would begin phasing out Afrikaans at the primary and secondary school levels, the disturbances spread to townships around Pretoria and, in late August and early September, to the heart of Cape Town. Despite the unrest, the Vorster government gave no indication of abandoning its commitment to "separate development" of the races, the official position being that the policy was not based on race but on the conviction that, within South Africa, Blacks make up distinct "nations" to which special political and constitutional arrangements should apply. It was in accordance with this philosophy that nominal independence was granted to the Transkei in October 1976, to Bophuthatswana in December 1977, to Venda in September 1979, and to Ciskei in December 1981 (see separate entries, below).

Rioting intensified during 1977 amid growing signs that the Vorster government had succumbed to a siege mentality. Drastic new security legislation was approved, including a Criminal Procedure Bill that substantially augmented the powers of the police while severely limiting the rights of individuals in judicial proceedings. On September 12, Steven BIKO, one of the country's most influential Black leaders, died under suspicious circumstances while in police detention, and on October 19 the government instituted its most drastic crackdown in two decades, closing the leading Black newspaper, arresting its editor, and banning a number of protest groups, including the Black Consciousness movement founded by Biko in 1969. Apparent White endorsement of these moves was revealed in a parliamentary election on November 30, at which the NP captured 134 of 165 lower-house seats.

On September 20, 1978, Prime Minister Vorster announced his intention to resign for reasons of health. Nine days later, he was elected by a joint session of Parliament to the essentially titular post of president, succeeding Nicolaas J. DIEDERICHS, who had died on August 21. One day earlier, the NP elected Defense Minister Pieter W. BOTHA as its new leader (hence prime minister) over Foreign Minister Roelof F. ("Pik") BOTHA and Plural Relations and Development Minister Cornelius P. MULDER. In November a long-simmering scandal involving alleged corruption and mismanagement of public funds within the Department of Information resulted in the appointment of a Commission of Inquiry. Its interim findings implicated a number of individuals, including Mulder, who was forced to resign from the government prior to formal expulsion from the NP in May 1979. On June 4 President Vorster also resigned after being formally charged with participation in a variety of clandestine propaganda activities and of giving false evidence in an effort to conceal gross irregularities in the affair. He was immediately succeeded, on an interim basis, by Senate President Marais VILJOEN, who was elected to a full term as head of state by Parliament on June 19.

Despite the scandal and increasingly vocal opposition from both the HNP and remaining *verkrampte* elements within the NP, the Botha government remained in power with an only marginally reduced parliamentary majority after the election of April 29, 1981, having campaigned on a 12-point platform, first advanced in 1979, that called for constitutional power-sharing among Whites, Coloureds, and Asians, with "full independence" for the Black homelands.

A Constitution Bill providing for an executive state president and a tricameral parliament that excluded Blacks was endorsed by 66 percent of White voters in a referendum conducted November 2, 1982, and was approved by the House of Assembly on September 9, 1983 (see Constitution and government, below). After balloting for delegates to the Coloured and Indian chambers in August 1984, Prime Minister Botha was unanimously elected president by an electoral college of the majority parties in each House on September 5 and was inaugurated at Cape Town on September 14.

Faced with mounting internal unrest and near-universal foreign condemnation, the government, in April 1985, abandoned two bastions of segregationist legislation: the Mixed Marriages Act and a portion of the Immorality Act that outlawed sex across the color line, while the prohibition of multiracial political movements was lifted in June. These moves provoked an immediate backlash by right-wing extremists, but were received by Black and moderate White leaders as "too little, too late". Clashes between police and demonstrators escalated, yielding nearly 300 deaths (mainly of Blacks) by mid-year. On July 21, in the first such action in a quarter-century, a state of emergency was declared in 36 riot-stricken Black districts and townships in the Johannesburg and eastern Cape regions. On August 15, in a speech at Durban, President Botha rejected demands for further racial concessions, insisting that they would constitute "a road to abdication and suicide" by White South Africans. In mid-September, on the other hand, he indicated that Parliament would be asked in early 1986 to consider modification of the Group Areas Act, with possible revocation of the country's pass laws and influx control into White areas. In addition, he asserted that the government was prepared to restore civil rights to nearly 10 million Blacks by permitting residents of the "independent" homelands to hold dual citizenship.

In an address at the opening of Parliament on January 31, 1986, President Botha shocked the extreme Right by declaring that "We have outgrown the outdated colonial system of paternalism, as well as the outdated concept of apartheid". In late April, he announced that a bill would be introduced terminating the pass laws, though the legislation would not affect segregation in schools, hospitals, and residential areas. Earlier, on March 7, the partial state of emergency imposed eight months before was rescinded; however, a nationwide state of emergency was declared on June 12 to quell anticipated violence on June 16, the anniversary of the Soweto uprising. Under the stringent order, the nation's security forces were authorized to take any action deemed necessary to counter perceived threats to public safety, with full exemption from subsequent legal prosecution. The order came in the wake of a proclamation issued June 4 that banned any public meeting called to commemorate the 1976 rioting.

Although the term of the House of Assembly had been extended from 1986 to 1989 to coincide with the five-year mandates of the Coloured and Indian chambers, President Botha announced in January 1987 that an early election for a new White chamber would be held on May 6. The results of the poll reflected a distinctly rightward swing by the White voters: the Nationalist Party won 123 of the 166 directly elective seats, while the far-right Conservative Party, with 22, displaced the liberal Progressive Federal Party as runner-up.

Constitution and government. The Republic of South Africa Constitution Act of 1961 provided for a president, a prime minister, and an Executive Council (cabinet) with offices at Pretoria; a bicameral legislature situated at Cape Town; an independent judiciary located at Bloemfontein; and provincial administrations in the country's four provinces. White domination of the entire structure was assured by an electoral system in which the general franchise was denied to Blacks, Coloureds, and Indians. The last two groups were accorded limited elective jurisdiction in ethnic affairs by means of a Coloured Persons' Representation Council established in 1964 and a South African Indian Council authorized in 1968; under the Bantu Authorities Act of 1951, political involvement by Blacks was confined to homeland affairs. In June 1979 the government announced that the homelands would thenceforth be known as "black states" and, with reference to the "independent" homelands, that the official distinction would be between "black states" and "independent black states".

During 1979–1980 a series of constitutional revisions were proposed, including abolition of the indirectly elected upper house of Parliament; creation of a 60-member President's Council, comprising White, Coloured, Indian, and Chinese representatives, whose chairman would occupy the new post of state vice president; formation of a separate Black advisory council; and conversion of the Coloured Persons' Representation Council into a Coloured Persons' Council of 30 nominated members. The proposal to create a Black advisory council was, however, withdrawn after being rejected by homeland leaders, while parliamentary and other criticism subsequent to passage of the Coloured Persons' Council Bill in April 1980 led to its effective demise. Agreement was, however, reached on abolition of the Senate and—not without substantial opposition—on creation of the President's Council, to which initial five-year appointments were announced on October 2, 1980.

In May 1982 the Council submitted a report on constitutional reform that recommended the selection of an executive president by an electoral college of White, Coloured, and Asian members of a new parliament from which Blacks would continue to be excluded. Subsequently, it was announced that the House of Assembly during its 1983 session would debate proposals designed to pave the way for a tricameral legislature and a triracial cabinet of members apportioned broadly in accordance with the size of the relevant population groups.

The present constitutional structure, formally enacted on September 22, 1984, features a president who serves as head of state and chief executive for a term concurrent with that of Parliament (five years, assuming no dissolution). He is designated by an electoral college of 50 Whites, 25 Coloureds, and 13 Indians chosen by majority vote of the respective communal chambers. He chairs a cabinet drawn, by his own choice, from the three houses and is assisted by a President's Council of 60 members (20 from the White chamber, 10 from the Coloured chamber, 5 from the Indian chamber, plus 15 nominated by himself and 10 by opposition parties) that serves to resolve disputes between the legislative bodies. There are also ministerial councils, whose members are chosen by the president from the majority in each chamber, that exercise executive authority over communal concerns. Each house has legislative jurisdiction over its "own" affairs, encompassing education, health, housing, social welfare, local government, and some aspects of agriculture; legislation on "general" matters, encompassing defense, finance, foreign policy, justice, law and order, transport, commerce and industry, manpower, internal affairs, and overall agricultural policy is enacted jointly by the three chambers and executed by the president, to whom is also assigned administrative responsibility for Black affairs.

The South African judicial system, based on Roman-Dutch law, is headed by a Supreme Court, whose members can be removed only on grounds of misbehavior or incapacity. There are also magistrates' courts and special courts for the application of African traditional law and custom. Numerous safeguards affecting the rights of accused persons, suspects, and legal counsel have been partially or wholly nullified by security legislation enacted during the last two decades.

The present administrative division is delimited by the four provinces of Cape of Good Hope, Natal, Transvaal, and Orange Free State. Each provincial administration is headed by an appointed provincial administrator, who formerly acted in conjunction with a Provincial Council elected on an all-White franchise. However, on July 1, 1987, the four provincial bodies were replaced by eight multiracial regional services councils (RSCs) (four in Transvaal, three in Cape Province, and one in the Orange Free State).

Province and Capital	Area (sq. mi.)	Population (1980C)
Cape of Good Hope (Cape Town)	278,380	5,091,360
Natal (Pietermaritzburg)	33,578	2,676,340
Transvaal (Pretoria)	109,621	8,350,500
Orange Free State (Bloemfontein)	49,866	1,931,860

(Note: The above census figures do not include residents of the Bantu homelands.)

Under a series of legislative enactments subsequent to the Bantu Authorities Act of 1951, a total of ten Black homelands were accorded self-governing status, with four ultimately becoming "independent" (see following articles). Each of the six states that remain "self-governing" is administered by an Executive Council headed by a chief minister who is designated by a Legislative Assembly. The South African government is represented by a commissioner general.

In 1982, the South African Supreme Court declared unconstitutional an attempt by the Botha government to transfer KaNgwane and part of KwaNdebele to the Kingdom of Swaziland, while the chief ministers of both states and of Lebowa have asserted that they will never accept "independent" status. By late 1985, the de facto distinction between the two types of homeland appeared to recede, with Botha's announcement that Pretoria would restore South African citizenship to nationals of the nominally autonomous states.

Bantu Homeland	Ethnic Group	Population (1980C)
Bophuthatswana (1972/1977)	Tswana	1,300,000
Ciskei (1972/1981)	Xhosa	677,820
Gazankulu (1973)	Shangaan/Tsonga	514,280
KaNgwane (1984)	Swazi	161,160
KwaNdebele	Ndebele	156,380
KwaZulu (1973)	Zulu	3,442,140
Lebowa (1972)	No. Sotho (Sepedi)	1,746,500
QwaQwa (1974)	So. Sotho (Seshoeshoe)	157,620
Transkei (1963/1976)	Xhosa	2,334,946
Venda (1973/1979)	Venda	513,890

(Note: Population figures include residents only; dates refer to attainment of self-government/"independence".)

In early 1987 the minister for constitutional development and planning announced that KwaZulu and the province of Natal would institute a joint body to exercise executive and administrative authority in matters affecting the two territories. Concurrently, Pretoria indicated that it welcomed a proposal of the *Indaba,* a council of Black, Indian, and White leaders in KwaZulu and Natal to create a common legislature, although by early 1988 the plan appeared to have faltered because of objections from both Black and White constituencies as to its implementation.

Foreign relations. A founding member of the United Nations, South Africa belongs to various UN-related agencies, maintains diplomatic relations with numerous Western (though not Communist) governments, and describes itself as a member of the "free world". Its international standing has nonetheless been greatly impaired as a result of racial restrictions maintained in its own territory and that of Namibia (South West Africa). Its rejection of international advice and pressure has resulted in growing restriction of South Africa's international contacts, notably through its departure from the Commonwealth in 1961, its suspension from membership in the Economic Commission for Africa in 1963, and its withdrawal or expulsion from a number of UN Specialized Agencies, including, in mid-1984, the Universal Postal Union. It has also been denied participation in the UN General Assembly, which has repeatedly condemned the policy and practice of apartheid and has advocated "universally applied economic sanctions" as the only means of achieving a peaceful solution to the problem. The UN Security Council, while stopping short of economic sanctions, called as early as 1963 for an embargo on the sale and shipment to South Africa of military equipment and materials. Relations with the United Nations were further aggravated by South Africa's refusal to apply economic sanctions against Rhodesia, as ordered by the Security Council in 1966, and its longstanding refusal to relinquish control over Namibia (see separate article), as ordered by both the General Assembly and the Security Council. Despite its political isolation on these key issues, South Africa has refrained from quitting the world body and has attempted to maintain friendly political relations and close economic ties with most Western countries. Within southern Africa, it cooperated closely with the former Ian Smith government of Rhodesia in economic and defense matters, assisting its neighbor in circumventing UN sanctions. However, in accordance with its policy of seeking détente with neighboring Black regimes, it publicly called for a resolution of the "Rhodesian question", endorsing in 1976 the principle of Black majority rule if appropriate guarantees were extended to the White minority of what became, in 1980, the Republic of Zimbabwe.

In recent years, Pretoria has mounted repeated forays into Angola in its protracted conflict with Namibian insurgents, while relations with Swaziland and Mozambique have been aggravated by the presence of African National Congress (ANC) guerrilla bases in both countries, despite the conclusion of a nonaggression pact with Mbabane in 1982 and a similar agreement with Maputo in May 1984.

During 1985, Western governments came under increased pressure to impose sanctions on the Botha regime.

US President Reagan had long opposed any action that would disrupt the South African economy but, faced in mid-September with a congressional threat to act on its own, ordered a number of distinctly modest punitive actions, with the EC countries moving in an equally restrained manner the following day. The principal American prohibitions focused on bank loans and the export of nuclear technology and computers, while the Europeans imposed an oil embargo, halted most arms sales, and withdrew their military attachés. None of these sanctions presented a serious challenge to South Africa, which was, however, sufficiently aggrieved to project the possibility of an embargo on the export of strategic metals to the United States.

During 1986, foreign pressure intensified. Despite President Reagan's appeal to the US Congress to "resist [the] emotional clamor for punitive sanctions", both the House and Senate approved measures that fell short of a total trade embargo sought by the former; the legislation became effective in early October, after the two houses, by substantial margins, had overridden a presidential veto. Earlier, European Community members had agreed to ban a variety of imports from South Africa, although failing to include a moratorium on coal, which constituted some 15 percent of South African shipments to the EC. Meanwhile, the pace of corporate divestment intensified, particularly by US firms (48 out of 311 to be fully divested by early 1987).

Pretoria's capacity to act with impunity in regard to neighboring states was amply demonstrated during 1986. On January 1, Lesotho was effectively blockaded and, three weeks later, its government overthrown by forces manifestly more malleable to South African efforts to contain cross-border attakcs by ANC guerrillas. Subsequently, on May 19, ANC targets in Botswana, Zambia, and Zimbabwe were subjected to bombing attacks by the South African Air Force, in addition to ground raids by units of the South African Defence Force (SADF). Additional raids were conducted against alleged ANC bases in Swaziland late in the year and in Zambia in early 1987.

Current issues. During the last several years, South Africa's White-dominated regime has grudgingly but steadily yielded ground in regard to the complex edifice of apartheid, while striving to retain its core: a denial of meaningful political power to the country's Black majority. What began in the mid-1970s with a limited "relaxation" in racial policy, eventually encompassed mixed participation in sporting events and the sharing of some public facilities with non-Whites; by 1985, the peripherals had been abandoned and some of the mainstays of apartheid had become vulnerable. Early in the year, President Botha formally acknowledged the existence of "urban Blacks" and indicated a willingness to treat Black communities outside the homelands as "entities in their own right", with authority to control their own affairs "at the highest level". He insisted, however, that retention of the homelands remained at the center of government policy.

The reimposition of a state of emergency in June 1986, ostensibly as a precaution against violence on the Soweto anniversary, appeared to signal the end of concessions by the Botha government, while the call, in January 1987, for an early White election was interpreted as reflecting the 70-year-old president's sense of betrayal over the foreign and domestic Black reaction to the program of cautious change that he had sought to introduce. The National Party secured a marginal increase in its legislative majority at the May poll, but the right-wing Conservative Party (contesting its first general election) emerged as its principal challenger, with the CP's Dr. Andries TREURNICHT becoming leader of the opposition.

At the opening of Parliament in February 1988 President Botha offered a package of new reforms that included multiracial balloting at municipal elections scheduled for October and the formation of a multiracial National Council to propose additional constitutional changes. Observers felt, however, that the government had exhausted most of its power-sharing options short of provoking a major White backlash. Meanwhile antiapartheid resistance grew in scope and intensity, including a one-day strike by more than a million black workers marking the 28th anniversary of the Sharpeville massacre on March 21.

POLITICAL PARTIES

In recent decades South Africa's leading party has been the predominantly Afrikaner National Party, which came to power in 1948 and steadily increased its parliamentary strength to a high of 134 (81 percent) of lower-house seats at the November 1977 election before falling marginally to 131 seats (79 percent) in 1981. While not as extremist as the Reconstituted National Party or the recently established Conservative Party of South Africa, the National Party has long been committed to the general principle of White supremacy. Parties advocating more liberal racial policies have fared poorly, with only the Progressive Party winning representation in the House of Assembly at the 1974 election; in 1977, however, a successor organization, the Progressive Federal Party, became the leading opposition party, with 17 seats, which were increased to 26 in 1981. The moderately supremacist United Party was disbanded in June 1977, while the multiracial Liberal Party had succumbed in 1968 to legislation (repealed in June 1985) prohibiting political association among members of different racial groups. The principal African organizations were banned in 1960, and Communist parties and organizations are also illegal.

Largely White Parties:

National Party (*Nasionale Party* — NP). A product of earlier splits and mergers extending back into the period before World War II, the National Party came to power under the leadership of Daniel F. Malan in 1948 and in 1951 absorbed the Afrikaner Party, then led by N.C. Havenga. Supported by the great majority of Afrikaners and by a growing number of English-speaking South Africans, it became the majority party in 1953. Its official doctrine stresses rigorous anti-Communism and separate development of the non-White races, with the Bantu homelands developing into independent states. The so-called *verligte* ("enlightened") faction under former prime minister Vorster sought to reconcile these policies with the promotion of White immigration, solidarity among all White South Africans, and the pursuit of friendly relations with the outside world, including Black African states. These ideas were rejected by the opposing *verkrampte* ("narrow-minded") faction, which tended to regard the party as a vehicle of specifically Afrikaner nationalism and opposed

the inclusion of English-speaking elements in the membership. The dismissal of *verkrampte* leader Dr. Albert Hertzog in the course of a cabinet reorganization in 1968 was generally interpreted as establishing the predominance of the Vorster faction, but the party leadership subsequently moved somewhat closer to the Hertzog position. Hertzog and other conservative elements nonetheless withdrew in 1969 to form the Reconstituted National Party (below). Vorster's influence within the party eroded sharply following the eruption of a "Watergate"–type scandal (see Political background, above) that forced his resignation as state president in mid-1979. In February 1982 the leader of the NP's conservative wing, Dr. Andries Treurnicht, was expelled from the party's parliamentary caucus in the Transvaal over the issue of power-sharing with Coloureds and Asians, and subsequently organized the Conservative Party of South Africa (below).

Leaders: Pieter Willem BOTHA (State President), Alwyn L. SCHLEBUSCH (former Vice President of the Republic), Roelof Frederik BOTHA (Foreign Minister), Frederik W. de KLERK (Leader of the House of Assembly).

Conservative Party of South Africa — CPSA (*Konserwatiewe Party van Suid-Afrika*). The CPSA was formally launched in March 1982 by a group of right-wing MPs who had been expelled from the NP for opposing the government's proposals for constitutional reform, which, it was argued, would eventually lead to power-sharing with Blacks. During its inaugural rally at Pretoria, it was announced that the National Conservative Party — NCP (*Nasionale Konserwatiewe Party*); the "Action for Our Future" (*Aksie Eie Toekoms* — AET); and the South Africa First Campaign (SAFC), a relatively obscure English-speaking group, had agreed to merge with the new movement.

The NCP had been organized in November 1979 (initially as the Action Group for National Priorities) by Dr. Connie Mulder, who had been ousted as a government minister for his role in the Information Department scandal. The AET had been formed in February 1981 by a number of Afrikaner intellectuals who favored rejection of the constitutional proposals and the establishment of separate homelands for all racial groups. Both the NCP and AET had participated in the 1981 election without securing parliamentary representation and were reported in October to have concluded a separate alliance with the *Kappie Kommando,* an Afrikaner women's group, and the extremist Afrikaner Resistance Movement (below). Dr. Mulder died on January 13, 1988.

The CPSA was runner-up to the NP at the May 1987 election, winning 22 House of Assembly seats.

Leaders: Dr. Andries TREURNICHT (Leader of the Opposition), Alkmaar SWART (AET), Brendan WILMER (SAFC).

Progressive Federal Party (PFP). The PFP resulted from the merger in September 1977 of the opposition Progressive Reform Party (PRP) and a minority of the former United Party (see NRP, below) that had argued earlier for a united opposition.

The Progressive Reform Party was formed in 1975 by merger of the Progressive Party (PP) and the Reform Party (RP), both of which had come into being as a result of defections from the UP. The PP had long been in favor of a federal solution to South Africa's multiracial political society and, although represented from 1966 to 1974 by only one parliamentary delegate (Helen Suzman), made impressive gains in the 1974 election, winning a total of seven seats. The RP was organized in early 1975 by former members of the UP's reformist wing who had opposed what they viewed as an increasingly conservative trend within the party.

PFP leader Colin Eglin stepped down as leader of the opposition in September 1979 after being criticized for not taking full advantage of the recent NP scandal. His successor, Dr. Frederick van Zyl SLABBERT, immediately reiterated PFP demands for interracial cooperation on a new constitution, which would, however, retain enforced segregation between Blacks and Whites. Japie Basson, leader of the former UP minority faction, resigned from the party on July 26, 1980, upon threat of expulsion for expressing his willingness to serve in the projected State President's Council.

The PFP campaigned against the 1983 Constitution Bill because of its exclusion of Blacks and in November 1984 announced, in a challenge to the Prohibition of Political Interference Act, that it would open its membership to individuals of all races, risking loss of its legal status, but thereby contributing to repeal of the Act seven months later. In February 1986, Dr. Slabbert announced his resignation from Parliament because of President Botha's refusal to negotiate a new, nonracial constitution with Black leaders. Shortly thereafter, Alex BORAINE, chairman of the party's Federal Council, also resigned. The PFP obtained 19 elective seats at the 1987 legislative poll.

Leaders: Colin EGLIN (former Leader of the Opposition), Peter GASTROW (National Chairman), Ken ANDREWS (Chairman, Federal Council), Harry SCHWARTZ and Helen SUZMAN (former PRP/PP leaders).

New Republic Party (NRP). The NRP was launched as a White "centrist" organization on June 29, 1977, by a majority faction of the longtime opposition United Party (UP), which had been formally disbanded the previous day in order to give "its members and supporters an opportunity to decide on their future political allegiance". The new group's manifesto was prepared in cooperation with the leader of the **Democratic National Party** (DNP), former interior minister Theo GERDENER, who, however, withdrew from the NRP on July 23 on the ground that it was simply reinstating the "mistaken" principles of the UP.

The United Party had been organized in 1934 by merger of the original Nationalist Party, led by Gen. J.B.M. Hertzog, and the South African Party, led by Gen. (later Field Marshal) Jan Christiaan Smuts. The UP, drawing most of its support from the English-speaking White community and large-scale business interests, was the chief upholder of the British tradition in South African affairs, resisting but ultimately accepting such Afrikaner-inspired actions as the establishment of the Republic and the severance of Commonwealth ties. The party lost strength through the secessions of the Progressive Party group in 1959 and the Reform Party group in 1975 (see PFP, above), as well as through defections to the National Party. Generally liberal on nonracial issues, the UP held that apartheid had been a failure, called for continued White leadership "with justice", and advocated the establishment of a federation of races governed by a central parliament in which Whites would retain effective control but other racial groups would be represented by separately elected delegates. The NRP obtained only one House of Assembly seat at the May 1987 balloting.

Leader: Bill SUTTON.

Independent Party — IP. The IP was formally launched in March 1988 by Dr. Denis Worrall, former South African ambassador to Britain, to offer White voters "a viable, workable and credible alternative to the Government of President Botha". Worrall predicted that the new group could win some 20 Assembly seats by merger with the NRP and by attracting defectors from both the PFP and the liberal wing of the NP.

Leader: Dr. Denis WORRALL.

National Democratic Movement (NDM). The NDM is an Afrikaner-dominated party organized in October 1987 with the avowed objective of developing links with Blacks "at all levels", not excluding the banned African National Congress. Its principal founder, Wynand Malan, had withdrawn from the NP because of dissatisfaction with the dominant party's slow pace of reform; he was joined by several former members of the PFP, which had been largely ineffectual in appealing to Afrikaner voters.

Leader: Wynand MALAN.

Reconstituted National Party (*Herstigte Nasionale Party* — HNP). The HNP is a right-wing Calvinist party organized by Dr. Albert Hertzog following his dismissal from the government in 1968. The party, which espouses the racist doctrine that Blacks are genetically inferior to Whites, competed in the last four elections without securing parliamentary representation. Dr. Hertzog (son of original National Party founder J.B.M. Hertzog) relinquished the HNP leadership in May 1977. In March 1979 the NP-dominated Parliament, by amendment to a 1978 electoral act, refused to register the HNP as a political party, although it was permitted to contest most constituencies (none successfully) in 1981 by producing 300 signatures in support of each nomination. It secured its first parliamentary seat, previously held by the NP, at a by-election in October 1985, but was unable to retain it in 1987.

Leaders: Jaap MARAIS, Eric LOUW.

At the extreme Right is the neofascist **National Front of South Africa**, which is allegedly linked to the National Front of Britain; there are also a number of right-wing terrorist groups, including the **White Commando** (*Wit Kommando*) and the **Afrikaner Resistance Movement** (*Afrikaanse Weerstandsbeweging* — AWB), led by Eugene TERRE'BLANCHE.

Largely Non-White Parties:

The 1968 legislation making multiracial parties illegal effectively precluded, until 1985, the emergence of any national organization cutting across racial divisions and consequently gave rise to a number of parties representing largely non-White groups.

Labour Party of South Africa (LP). Led by Sonny Leon until his resignation in September 1978, the LP is a primarily Coloured party that has long sought the establishment of a multiracial society. Originally opposed to the NP blueprint for power-sharing, it was a founding member of the South African Black Alliance (below) but was expelled from SABA in early 1983 for reversing itself and accepting the NP plan on the ground that participation was the best means of working toward eventual majority rule. It won 76 of 80 seats in the (Coloured) House of Representatives in August 1984, although losing part of its strength to the Democratic Party (below) in 1987.

Leaders: Rev. H.J. (Allan) HENDRICKSE (Party Leader), Ismail RICHARDS (Deputy Leader), Rev. Andrew JULIES (National Chairman), Jac RABIE (National Deputy Chairman).

Democratic Party (DP). Also referenced as the Democratic Alliance, the DP was organized as a grouping within the (Coloured) House of Representatives by the defection in April 1987 of seven Labour MPs, who announced that they had entered into negotiations with the PFP for the establishment of a nonracial political formation.

Leader: Trevor GEORGE.

People's Congress Party (PCP). Formerly the Congress of the People (Cope), a Coloured group, the PCP adopted its present name in January 1983. Initially, it characterized the Labour Party's acceptance of constitutional revision as a "joke", but subsequently participated in the 1984 balloting, at which it won 1 seat in the House of Representatives.

Leaders: Pieter MARAIS, Morris FYNN.

Democratic Worker's Party (DWP). Founded in 1984 by a group of PCP dissidents, the DWP is a primarily Coloured formation that rejects racial exclusivity.

Leader: Dennis de la CRUZ.

Freedom Party (FP). Also a Coloured group, the relatively moderate FP captured one House of Representatives seat subsequent to the 1984 balloting, but lost it at a by-election occasioned by the death of the incumbent in January 1987.

Leader: Charles JULIES.

National People's Party (NPP). The NPP is an Indian party whose leader, Amichand Rajbansi, formerly served as chairman of the South African Indian Council (SAIC). Rajbansi stated in 1982 that the proposed constitutional revision did "not satisfy the political guidelines" of the SAIC; subsequently, a majority of the Council voted to give the new structure a "reasonable chance" and the NPP captured a plurality of seats in the (Indian) House of Delegates in 1984.

Leader: Amichand RAJBANSI.

Solidarity Party. Solidarity is an Indian group formed prior to the 1984 balloting by Dr. J.N. Reddy, also a former SAIC chairman. It is presently the second-ranked formation in the House of Delegates.

Leaders: Dr. J.N. REDDY, Mahmoud RAJAB.

Progressive Reform Party (PRP). The PRP was formed in January 1987 by a number of dissidents from the Solidarity Party.

Leader: Pat POOVALINGHAM.

Progressive Independent Party (PIP). The PIP is a small Indian formation that won 1 House of Delegates seat in 1984.

Leader: Faiz KHAN.

United Democratic Front (UDF). The UDF was organized in May 1983 as a coalition of some 32 groups, including the **Transvaal Indian Congress** (TIC) and the Council of Unions of South Africa, to oppose the constitutional revision. A revival of an earlier Indian formation of the same name, the TIC was launched earlier in the year at the annual conference of the Transvaal Anti-SAIC Committee.

In February 1985 six leading members of the UDF were arrested on treason charges and in March all UDF meetings were proscribed for three months. In October 1986 the government declared the UDF to be an "affected organization" under a 1974 act that precluded the organization from receiving foreign funding (then estimated to be some $1 million annually, primarily from Scandinavian countries). The Front was officially banned in February 1988.

Leaders: Alberthina SISULU (President for Transvaal), Oscar MPETHA (President for Natal), Archie GUMEDE (President for Western Cape), Dr. Essop JASSAT (TIC President), Popo MOLEFE (Secretary General, under arrest), Mohamed UALLI (Acting Secretary General under arrest).

African National Congress of South Africa (ANC). The best-known Black political organization, the ANC was banned in 1960 after the Sharpeville incident. Its president, Oliver Tambo, heads an external wing operating from Zambia and other neighboring areas, while its life president, Nelson Mandela, and one of its general secretaries, Walter Sisulu, are confined to life imprisonment. (In February 1985, Mandela rejected the latest in a series of government offers to release him on condition that he renounce the use of violence, calling instead for President Botha to "renounce violence . . . by [dismantling] apartheid".) During its first major conference in 16 years, held at Kabwe, Zambia, on July 16–23, 1985, the ANC reelected its existing leadership, while expanding its national executive to 30 members that, for the first time, included one White, two Coloureds and two Indians.

In August 1978 a breakaway group that had criticized Communist influence within the ANC was organized at London as the **African National Congress of South Africa (African Nationalists)** under the chairmanship of Jonas MATLOU. There is also an **Indian National Congress of South Africa** (INC) that has cooperated with the ANC's external wing.

Leaders: Nelson MANDELA (Life President, imprisoned), Oliver TAMBO (President, in exile), Walter SISULU (imprisoned) and Alfred NZO (Secretaries General).

South African Communist Party (SACP). The SACP was formed in 1953, following dissolution, a year earlier, of the original Communist Party of South Africa (CPSA), which had been organized in 1921. The SACP has long cooperated closely with the ANC, to a number of whose senior organs SACP members have been appointed. The party's former chairman, Dr. Yusef Dadoo, died in 1983, while its former general secretary, Moses Mabhida, died at Maputo, Mozambique, in March 1986. A year later, following his appointment as Mabhida's successor, Joe Slovo resigned as chief of staff of the ANC's military wing.

Leaders: Daniel TLOOME (Chairman), Joe SLOVO (General Secretary).

Pan-Africanist Congress of Azania (PACA). A militant ANC offshoot that was also banned in 1960, the PACA seeks to unite all Black South Africans in a single national front. Based at Lusaka, Zambia, the PACA announced in May 1979 the establishment in the Sudan of a "June 16 Azania Institute" (named after the June 1976 Soweto uprising) to instruct displaced South African students in a variety of academic and artisan skills. PACA's longtime leader, John Nyati Pokela, died in June 1985.

Leaders: Zephania MTHOPENG (President, under arrest), Johnson MLAMBO (Chairman), D. MANTSHONTSHO (Administrative Secretary).

Black People's Convention (BPC). Formed in July 1972, the BPC seeks to unify all Blacks in South Africa, to expand Black consciousness, and to reorient the institutions of society to meet the needs of Blacks. The party was formally banned in 1977, its honorary president, Steven Biko, dying under suspicious circumstances on September 12 while in police custody.

Leaders: Kenneth RACHIDI (in detention), Mxolisi MVOVO (former Acting President).

South African Black Alliance (SABA). SABA was organized in early 1978 as a coalition of non-White groups committed to "working within the system", although sharing many of the aspirations of the ANC and BPC. At the time of the Alliance's formation, the leaders of its constituent parties (listed below) formally rejected merger so as not to infringe the ban on interracial parties. SABA's stated goal is a "national convention" of all population groups to draft a multiracial constitution for South Africa.

Leader: Chief Gatsha BUTHELEZI (Chairman).

Inkatha Movement. Although predominantly a Zulu organization, *Inkatha,* in response to charges of tribalism, recently revised its statutes to admit all Black applicants for membership.

Leaders: Chief Gatsha BUTHELEZI (Chief Minister of KwaZulu), Rev. Alphaeus Hamilton ZULU (National Chairman).

Indian Reform Party (IRP). The IRP was the principal opposition party within the South African Indian Council.

Leader: Y.S. CHINSAMY.

Linkoanketla Party. Formerly known as the Basotho National Party, *Linkoanketla* is a small Black party representing the Sotho tribe of the Qwaqwa tribal homeland in the Orange Free State.

Leader: Chief Kenneth MOPELI.

Azanian People's Organization (Azapo). Azapo was launched as a Black consciousness movement in early 1978, following the banning of the BPC; however, its founders, Ishmael Mkhabela and Lybon Mabasa, were immediately detained, and it did not hold its first congress until September 1979. While avowedly nonviolent, it has adopted, in opposition to SABA, a "hard line" on the possibility of negotiating with the White government.

Leaders: Nkosi MOKALA (Acting President), Curtis NKONDO, George WAUCHOPE (Secretary General).

United Christian Conciliation Party (UCCP). The UCCP is an avowedly multiracial party that was formally launched in October 1986 by a group of conservative Black community leaders, who felt obliged to deny that they were supported by the South African government.

Leaders: Bishop Isaak MOKOENA and Tamasanqa LINDA (Co-Presidents).

Federal Independent Democratic Alliance (FIDA). The FIDA was organized in July 1987 by a group of Black moderates opposed to apartheid but declaring themselves willing to participate in President Botha's proposed multiracial council as a means of giving the African majority a voice in charting the country's future.

Leader: John GOGOTYA.

Among numerous other regional and ethnic groups, there are parties based in the tribal homelands, including the **Bophuthatswana Democratic Party,** led by Chief Lucas Mangope; the **Ciskei National Independence Party,** led by Chief Lennox L. Sebe; the **Transkei National Independence Party,** formerly led by Chief George Matanzima; and the **Venda National Party,** led by Chief Patrick Mphephu prior to his death in April 1988 (see entries under Bophuthatswana, Ciskei, Transkei, and Venda, below).

LEGISLATURE

The South African **Parliament** was formerly a bicameral body consisting of a Senate and a House of Assembly, both made up exclusively of White members. The Senate (consisting largely of members designated by the provincial assemblies) was abolished, effective January 1, 1981, some of its duties being assumed by a newly created President's Council of nominated members (see Constitution and government, above). A separate South African Indian Council of 15 elected and 15 appointed members was abolished upon adoption of the 1983 constitution.

The present Parliament is a tricameral body encompassing a House of Assembly, a continuation of the former lower house; a House of Representatives, representing Coloured voters; and a House of Delegates, representing Indian voters. Each is empowered to legislate in regard to its "own" affairs, while the assent of all is required in regard to "general" affairs. The legislative term is five years, subject to dissolution.

Speaker: Johan W. GREEF.

House of Assembly. The White Chamber has 178 members, 166 of whom are directly elected (including a seat for Walvis Bay, which was added in 1981) with 8 indirectly elected by the directly elected members on the basis of proportional representation and 4 nominated by the president (1 from each province). At the balloting of May 6, 1987, the National Party won 123 of the directly elected seats; the Conservative Party, 22; the Progressive Federal Party, 19; the New Republic Party, 1; independent, 1. As of February 1988 the NP held 133 seats overall; the CPSA, 23; the PFP, 20; the NRP, 1; independent, 1; the distribution was unchanged as the result of by-elections in three constituencies on March 2, all of the seats being retained, with greatly increased majorities, by the CPSA.

Chairman: Louis le GRANGE.

House of Representatives. The Coloured chamber has 85 members, 80 of whom are directly elected, with 3 chosen by the directly elected members and 2 appointed by the president. At communal balloting on August 22, 1984, for the directly elected members, the Labour Party won

76 seats; the People's Congress Party, 1; independents, 2; undecided (due to a tie vote), 1. The Freedom Party eventually captured the undecided seat, but lost it at a by-election necessitated by the death of the incumbent in January 1987; three months later 7 Labour MPs defected to form the Democratic Party.

Chairman: P.T. SANDERS.

House of Delegates. The Indian chamber has 45 members, 40 of whom are directly elected, with 3 chosen by the directly elected members and 2 appointed by the president. At communal balloting on August 29, 1984, for the directly elected members, the National People's Party obtained 18 seats; the Solidarity Party, 17; the Progressive Independent Party, 1; independents, 4. In December 4 Solidarity members withdrew from the party to sit as independents. Four additional Solidarity MPs withdrew in January 1987 to form the Progressive Reform Party. In May, on the other hand, 2 independents joined Solidarity, while 6 MPs announced their withdrawal from the NPP; the NPP nonetheless forged a 27-member majority in June by an alliance with a group that included both dissidents and independents.

Chairman: R. BHANA.

CABINET

State President	Pieter Willem Botha
Ministers	
Agriculture	Jacob J.G. Wentzel
Commission for Administration for the South African Broadcasting Corporation	Dr. Stoffel van der Merwe
Constitutional Development and Planning	J. Christian Heunis
Defense	Gen. Magnus Malan
Economic Affairs and Technology	Daniel Steyn
Education and Development Aid	Gerrit Viljoen
Finance	Barend J. du Plessis
Foreign Affairs	Roelof F. Botha
Home Affairs and Communication	Stoffel Botha
Justice	Hendrik J. (Kobie) Coetsee
Law and Order	Adriaan Vlok
Manpower and Public Works	Pietie T.C. du Plessis
National Education	Frederik W. de Klerk
National Health and Population Planning	Willem Van Niekerk
President's Office in Charge of Administration and Privatization	Dr. Dawie de Villiers
President's Office in Charge of Information	Dr. Stoffel van der Merwe
Transport Services	Eli Nan der M. Louw
Water Affairs and Environment	Gert J. Kotze
Chairman, Ministers' Council of the House of Delegates	Amichand Rajbansi
Chairman, Ministers' Council of the House of Representatives	Frederik W. de Klerk
Governor, Central Bank	Dr. Gerhard P.C. de Kock

NEWS MEDIA

Press. Newspapers are published in both Afrikaans and English, the English-language press having by far the larger circulation despite the numerical preponderance of the Afrikaner population. There are at present a few Indian and Coloured weeklies but no Bantu-controlled newspapers. A series of laws, including the Terrorism Act of 1967 and the Publications Bill of 1974, has impeded newsgathering and restricted or silenced most overt criticism of the government, especially of its racial policies. Under legislation enacted in 1977 that grants the government virtually unlimited powers of censorship during periods of internal disorder, the nation's largest Black newspaper, *The World,* and its associated *Weekend World* were, on October 19, closed down, while in mid-1982 the Assembly appproved a Protection of Information Act that requires editors to obtain permission from the police before divulging the names

of journalists being held for interrogation. The *Rand Daily Mail,* South Africa's most influential antiapartheid newspaper ceased publication on April 30, 1985, citing a loss of $7.5 million in 1984. President Botha welcomed the paper's closing, saying he was "glad to see things develop in this direction". A strict new press code was promulgated in December 1986 under the state of emergency proclaimed six months earlier, while on January 30, 1987, the government authorized the Johannesburg police commissioner to ban the publication of "any matter" that he might deem contrary to "the maintenance of public order". Given such restrictions most newspapers have recently declined in circulation. The following are English dailies published at Johannesburg, unless otherwise noted: *The Star* (158,000 daily, 95,000 weekend); *Sowetan* (118,000); *The Argus* (Cape Town, 100,000 daily, 117,000 weekend); *Beeld* (100,000), in Afrikaans; *Daily News* (Durban, 90,000); *Cape Times* (Cape Town, 76,000); *Natal Mercury* (Durban, 62,000); *The Citizen* (60,000), progovernment; *Die Vaderland* (40,000), in Afrikaans.

News agencies. Domestic service is provided by the South African Press Association, an independent agency cooperatively owned by the country's major newspapers; a number of foreign bureaus maintain offices at Johannesburg.

Radio and television. Radio broadcasting is a monopoly of the South African Broadcasting Corporation, a public utility organization; programs are in English, Afrikaans, and Bantu languages. Television service, in English and Afrikaans only, began in 1976; a separate channel, broadcasting to Blacks in a number of native languages, commenced operations in December 1981. There were approximately 8.8 million radio and 2.6 million television receivers in 1987.

INTERGOVERNMENTAL REPRESENTATION

Ambassador to the US: Dr. Pieter Gerhardus Jacobus KOORNHOF.

US Ambassador to South Africa: Edward Joseph PERKINS.

Permanent Representative to the UN: Albert Leslie MANLEY. South Africa was denied the right to participate in General Assembly activities in 1974 but retains de jure membership in the world organization.

IGO Memberships (Non-UN): BIS, CCC, ICCAT, ILZ, Intelsat, ISO, IWC, IWSG, IWTC.

RELATED TERRITORIES

Despite United Nations action voiding its mandate, South Africa retains de facto control of South West Africa (see entry under **Namibia**), while in actions which the UN and all foreign nations have refused to recognize, it has granted formal independence to Tswana, Xhosa, and Vhavenda homelands (see following entries under **South Africa: Bophuthatswana, South Africa: Ciskei, South Africa: Transkei,** and **South Africa: Venda**).

SOUTH AFRICA: BOPHUTHATSWANA

Republic of Bophuthatswana
Repaboliki ya Bophuthatswana

Political Status: Former self-governing South African tribal homeland; recognized as independent by South Africa on December 6, 1977.

Area: 16,988 sq. mi. (44,000 sq. km.).

Population: 1,300,000 (1980C); 1,576,000 (1988E), embracing resident population only; does not include an estimated 1,700,000 Tswanas who reside outside the homeland.

Major Urban Centers (1977E): MMABATHO (10,000); Mafikeng (formerly Mafeking, 10,000).

Official Language: Setswana (English and Afrikaans are also in use for legislative, judicial, and administrative purposes).

Monetary Unit: South African Rand (market rate March 1, 1988, 2.09 rands = $1US).

President and Prime Minister: Kgosi (Chief) Lucas Lawrence Manyane MANGOPE (Bophuthatswana Democratic Party); named Chief Minister in 1972; elected President by the National Assembly on December 6, 1977; reelected, unopposed, in November 1984 to a second seven-year term beginning December 7; ousted in favor of Rocky Ismael P. MALABANE-METSING by army coup of February 10, 1988, but restored to office by South African military intervention on the same day.

THE COUNTRY

Bophuthatswana is comprised of six noncontiguous territories in north-central South Africa (see map), only one of which borders on a neighboring country (Botswana). The population consists nominally of approximately 3.1 million persons, less than half of whom are physically resident within the state, while more than one-quarter of the resident population does not speak Setswana. Despite geographic fragmentation and chronic unemployment, Bophuthatswana is endowed with substantial natural resources, including two of the world's largest platinum deposits. At present, the country is best known for "Sun City", an $85 million casino-entertainment complex which is located some 60 miles northwest of Johannesburg and is run by a consortium of South African businessmen in partnership with homeland authorities.

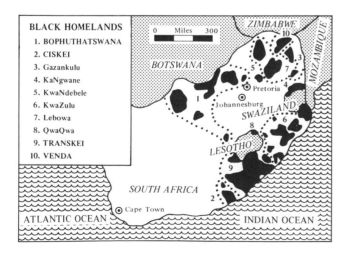

BLACK HOMELANDS
1. BOPHUTHATSWANA
2. CISKEI
3. Gazankulu
4. KaNgwane
5. KwaNdebele
6. KwaZulu
7. Lebowa
8. QwaQwa
9. TRANSKEI
10. VENDA

GOVERNMENT AND POLITICS

Political background. In June 1972 Bophuthatswana accepted internal self-government under South Africa's Bantu Homelands Constitutional Bill of the previous year, and on December 6, 1977, became the second such territory (see article on Transkei) to be designated as an independent state by South Africa. Coincident with the granting of independence, the National Assembly elected former chief minister Lucas MANGOPE president of the new republic. In accepting the office, Mangope tacitly withdrew from an earlier declaration that he would not endorse independence unless Pretoria were to grant South African citizenship to Tswanas not residing in the homeland and agree to territorial consolidation of the Bophuthatswanan state.

In the early morning of February 10, 1988, President Mangope was overthrown by members of the homeland's defense force, who installed Rocky Ismael MALABANE-METSING, leader of the Progressive People's Party, a small opposition grouping, as his successor. Less than 15 hours later, however, South African troops intervened to reinstate the deposed chief executive.

Constitution and government. Under the constitution that came into effect upon the proclamation of independence, Bophuthatswana is declared to be a republic with a president who serves a seven-year term as head of state and who appoints a cabinet over which he presides. A constitutional amendment of December 3, 1984, gave the chief executive the authority to administer any government department should he deem it necessary. The partially appointed National Assembly serves a five-year term. The judicial system is headed by a Supreme Court.

Local government consists of 76 tribal and 6 community authorities, which are grouped at the intermediate level into 12 regional authorities.

Foreign relations. On November 15, 1977, South Africa and Bophuthatswana participated in a preindependence ceremony at Pretoria during which a total of 66 bilateral treaties were approved by representatives of the two governments. The agreements included a nonaggression pact as well as arrangements for economic assistance, border movements, and the maintenance of telecommunications and aviation facilities.

Bophuthatswana is yet to be recognized by any foreign government other than South Africa and its sister independent Black homelands, although the willingness of the British to permit the opening of a "Bophuthatswana House" at London in September 1982 was viewed as a step toward establishing a semblance of foreign representation. For its part, the Organization of African Unity has condemned all four independent Bantustans as "pseudo-states" designed to "fragment South Africa" in the interest of its White minority.

Current issues. A radio broadcast by the instigators of the February 1988 rebellion charged the Mangope regime with widespread corruption and insisted that the legislative balloting of October 1987 had been rigged. Also referenced was Mangope's close relationship with Shabbtai KAL-MANOVITZ, a Soviet emigré, who had recently been arrested by Israeli authorities on suspicion of spying for Moscow. South African President P.W. Botha refused comment on his government's intervention on Mangope's behalf, save to insist that it was "opposed in principle to the obtaining of power by violence". Observers pointed out, however, that Pretoria had not responded in a similar manner to either of two recent coups in the Transkei homeland (see Transkei article, below).

POLITICAL PARTIES

Although President Mangope has rejected the idea that Bophuthatswana should become a one-party state, preferring a "free and pluralistic society", the ruling Bophuthatswana Democratic Party currently holds all seats in the National Assembly.

Government Party:

Bophuthatswana Democratic Party (BDP). Organized in November 1974, the BDP subsequently campaigned for independence on the basis of "non-racialism and justice for all".
Leaders: Kgosi Lucas L.M. MANGOPE (President of the Republic), A.M. KGOMONGWE (Secretary General).

Opposition Parties:

National Seoposengwe Party (NSP). Formed in early 1976, the NSP has opposed South Africa's homelands policy and rejected independence, save on the basis of "the consolidation of Bophuthatswana into a single unit". Formerly holding 6 legislative seats (5 elected, 1 nominated), it is unrepresented in the present Assembly.
Leader: Kgosi H.T.R. MASELOANE.

Progressive People's Party (PPP). The PPP is a small formation led by Rocky Ismael Peter Malabane-Metsing, who was named to succeed President Mangope in the abortive coup of January 1988 and subsequently, having escaped arrest, fled to Lusaka, Zambia. The PPP won six legislative seats in October 1987.
Leader: Rocky Ismael Peter MALABANE-METSING (in self-imposed exile).

LEGISLATURE

Following the pre-independence election of August 1977, the unicameral **National Assembly** contained 99 members, 48 of whom were directly elected and 51 nominated. At present, it contains 108 members, 72 of whom are directly elected for five-year terms; 24 are named by regional authorities; and 12 are nominated by the president. At the most recent balloting in October 1987 the Bophuthatswa Democratic Party was credited with winning 66 of the directly elective seats and the Progressive People's Party, 6.
Speaker: M.S.E. MOTSHUMI.

CABINET

Prime Minister	Kgosi Lucas L.M. Mangope
Ministers	
Agriculture and Forestry	Kgosi E.M. Mokgoko
Defense	Brig. H.F.P. Riekert
Economic Affairs	Kgosi Lucas L.M. Mangope
Education	L.G. Holele
Finance	L.G. Young
Foreign Affairs	S.L.L. Rathebe
Health and Social Welfare	Dr. K.P. Mokhobo
Internal Affairs	Rev. S.M. Seodi
Lands and Rural Development	D.C. Mokale
Law and Order	Kgosi B.L.M. Motsatsi
Local Government and Housing	S.L.L. Rathebe
Manpower and Coordination	Rowan Cronje
Posts and Telecommunications	K.C.A.V. Sehume
Public Works and Water Affairs	T.M. Tlhabane
Transport	G.J. Makodi

NEWS MEDIA

Press. The *Bophuthatswana Pioneer* (10,000), in English, is published monthly at Mafikeng; *The Mail* (3,600) and *The Eye Witness* are English weeklies published at Mafikeng and Mmabatho, respectively.
Radio and television. The government-controlled Radio Bophuthatswana broadcasts from Mafikeng; Bophuthatswana Broadcast Television offers limited programming in English and Setswana.

INTERGOVERNMENTAL REPRESENTATION

The Republic of Bophuthatswana is not a member of the United Nations and is not recognized by the United States.

SOUTH AFRICA: CISKEI

Republic of Ciskei
Iriphabliki Yeciskei

Political Status: Former self-governing South African tribal homeland; recognized as independent by South Africa on December 4, 1981.

Area: 3,282 sq. mi. (8,500 sq. km.).

Population: 677,820 (1980C); 852,000 (1988E), embracing resident population only; does not include an estimated 1,706,000 Ciskeian Xhosas who reside outside the homeland.

Major Urban Centers: None. A capital is being established at BISHO, adjacent to King William's Town, which, despite earlier assurances, the South African government decided in April 1981 not to include within Ciskeian territory.

Official Languages: Xhosa, English.

Monetary Unit: South African Rand (market rate March 1, 1988, 2.09 rands = $1US).

President: Chief Lennox L. SEBE; designated Chief Minister in May 1973; elected President for a five-year term by the National Assembly on December 4, 1981; named President for Life in June 1983.

THE COUNTRY

Generally regarded as the poorest and least developed of South Africa's tribal homelands, Ciskei encompasses two small territories stretching from the Indian Ocean to the vicinity of Queenstown in Cape Province (see map, p. 536). It is separated by a narrow corridor from Transkei to the northeast and, like its sister "independent Black state", is populated largely by Xhosas, many of whom have been forced to relocate from other, diverse enclaves within the surrounding White-dominated state. Most gainfully employed residents work across the border in either King William's Town or East London and provide nearly two-thirds of local income. Agricultural output is confined largely to pineapples, an extremely dry climate precluding most other forms of cultivation. More than three-quarters of the state's current income comes from South Africa in the form of direct aid. Economically, the *Africa Research Bulletin* has characterized Ciskei as "an over-populated, drought-stricken dustbowl . . . ill-equipped for independence of any kind".

GOVERNMENT AND POLITICS

Political background. In February 1973, Ciskei accepted internal self-government under South Africa's Homelands Constitutional Bill of 1971, and on December 4, 1981, joined Bophuthatswana, Transkei, and Venda as a nominally independent Black state on the basis of a lengthy series of agreements concluded at Cape Town on November 20 by Chief Minister Lennox L. SEBE and Prime Minister P.W. Botha of South Africa. Following the proclamation of independence, Sebe was elected president by the Ciskeian National Assembly (theretofore the Legislative Assembly), all of whose (then) 22 elective seats had been won in June 1978 by Sebe's Ciskei National Independence Party (CNIP). Of the 33 preindependence seats reserved for hereditary chiefs, 30 were allocated to the CNIP, with the remaining members subsequently crossing the aisle in de facto establishment of a one-party regime.

Constitution and government. Under the constitution that came into effect upon independence, Ciskei is declared to be a republic with a president who is designated by the legislature for a five-year term, although in June 1983 Chief Sebe was accorded life incumbency. The president is responsible for the appointment of an Executive Council (cabinet), all of whose members must hold legislative seats. The Assembly itself has been increased in size to 50 elected and 37 nominated members, although the nonnominated component, as of early 1988, had not yet been completely filled. The judiciary encompasses seven magistrates' courts and a Supreme Court, although appeals may be taken from the latter to the South African Supreme Court at Bloemfontein.

Foreign relations. No external government has yet recognized Ciskei as an autonomous state. In 1981, the Organization of African Unity (OAU) appealed to the international community to treat the homeland's new status as a "non-event", while the UN Security Council branded the "so-called independence" of the territory as wholly invalid. Even President Kaiser Matanzima of adjacent Transkei (see following article) announced that his government would not endorse the "pseudo independence" of "a part of Xhosaland", thus reiterating Transkei's long-standing claim to represent all of the Xhosa people. A related contention was advanced by Chief Minister Gatsha Buthelezi of KwaZulu, one of the most severe internal critics of South Africa's homeland policies, who condemned the splitting of the Xhosa-speaking people into two separate "nations" as exposing Pretoria's ethnicity posture "for the fraud it is".

Current issues. To justify his acceptance of independence, Chief Sebe cited the results of a 1980 referendum in which a reputed 98 percent of Ciskeians favored the move. However, substantial intimidation appears to have been involved, including a prereferendum warning by Sebe that anyone who "betrays the nation" by casting a negative vote would be subject to imprisonment. The action also ran counter to the recommendation of an independent commission appointed by Sebe that reported an overwhelming preference for participation in a multiracial South African state on either a unitary or federal basis. In addition, a group of Ciskeians had initiated legal proceedings in mid-1981, alleging, in a case ultimately dismissed by the Supreme Court, that the South African Parliament had acted unconstitutionally in providing for alteration of Cape Province boundaries without being petitioned to do so by the provincial legislature.

In mid-1983, President Sebe cut short a visit to Israel upon being informed that a coup was about to be launched by his brother, Lt. Gen. Charles SEBE, head of the country's Central Intelligence Service (CIS) and, on the basis of links to Pretoria, reputed to be one of the most powerful individuals in Black Africa. General Sebe was subsequently arrested, stripped of his military rank, and sentenced to 12 years' imprisonment, while the CIS was disbanded in favor of a newly created defense ministry. In September 1986, Sebe escaped and fled to Transkei, where he was granted asylum. The bizarre scenario involving the neighboring, but hostile tribal homelands, concluded in February 1987 with an abortive attack on the presidential palace led by Maj. Nkosinathi SANDILE, Ciskei's former military security chief, who had been apprehended a month earlier by Transkei authorities while on a mission to abduct Sebe.

POLITICAL PARTIES

Government Party:

Ciskei National Independence Party (CNIP). The CNIP was organized by Chief Minister Sebe in 1973. All leading governmental positions are currently filled from its ranks.

Leader: Chief Lennox L. SEBE (President of the Republic).

Other Parties:

An opposition **Ciskei National Party** (CNP) won no seats at the 1978 election and its three nominated members joined the government party in January 1980. In 1986 a new **Ciskei People's Rights Protection Party** (CPRP), led by Chief L.W. MAQOMA, met registration requirements for the projected November balloting, but was subsequently ruled ineligible on technical grounds.

LEGISLATURE

The unicameral **National Assembly** is constitutionally defined as an 87-member body encompassing 50 elected and 37 nominated members serving five-year terms. At present there are only 23 elected members, all declared elected because of unopposed nomination by the CNIP for balloting that was to have been held in November 1986.

CABINET

President	Chief Lennox L. Sebe

Ministers

Agriculture and Water Affairs	V.H. Mafani
Defense	Chief D.N. Mavuso
Education	H. Nabe
Finance and Economic Development	Chief M.E.P. Malefane
Foreign Affairs	B.N. Pityi
Health (Acting)	D.M. Takane
Internal Affairs	L.B. Williams
Justice	D.M. Takane
Manpower Utilization	G.M. Mpepo
Posts and Telecommunications	A.A. Hoyana
Public Works	Chief D.M. Jongilanga
Rural Development	W.M. Boqwana
Social Welfare and Pensions	A.M. Tapa
Transport	R.R. Mali
Youth Affairs	V.G. Ntshinga

NEWS MEDIA

There are no newspapers. The government-operated Ciskei Broadcasting Service provides radio transmissions in English, Afrikaans, and Xhosa; limited television service commenced in late 1985.

INTERGOVERNMENTAL REPRESENTATION

The Republic of Ciskei is not a member of the United Nations and is not currently recognized by the United States.

SOUTH AFRICA: TRANSKEI

Republic of Transkei
Iriphabliki Yetranskei

Political Status: Former self-governing South African tribal homeland; recognized as independent by South Africa on October 26, 1976.

Area: 15,831 sq. mi. (41,002 sq. km.).

Population: 2,334,946 (1980C); 2,911,000 (1988E), embracing resident population only; does not include an estimated 1,645,000 Transkeian Xhosas who reside outside the homeland.

Major Urban Center (1976E): UMTATA (27,000).

Official Language: Xhosa (English, Afrikaans, and Sesotho are in use for legislative, judicial, and administrative purposes).

Monetary Unit: South African Rand (market rate March 1, 1988, 2.09 rands = $1US).

President: Paramount Chief Nyangelizwe Vulindlela NDAMASE; elected by the National Assembly for a seven-year term on February 19 and installed on February 20, 1986, following the resignation of Paramount Chief Kaiser Daliwonga MATANZIMA.

Head of Military Council and of the Council of Ministers: Maj. Gen. Harrington Bantubonke HOLOMISA; assumed office following the military ouster of Prime Minister Stella SIGCAU (Transkei National Independence Party) on December 30, 1987.

THE COUNTRY

Transkei consists of three adjacent but noncontiguous territories in southeastern Africa, the largest of which borders Lesotho on the north, South Africa's Cape Province on the west and southwest, and the Indian Ocean on the east (see map, page 536). One of the smaller (northeastern) areas borders on Natal, while the other is located in a triangle bordered by the Orange Free State, Lesotho, and Cape Province. Although formally designated by South Africa as a "homeland" of the Xhosa people, Transkei contains numerous smaller ethnic groups, including Hlubis, Fingoes, Ntlangwinis, Sothos, Tembus, and Zulus, as well as some Whites and Coloureds. It counts among its natural resources some of the most fertile farmland in southern Africa, although government-supported efforts to convert from subsistence farming to a market-crop economy have met with only limited success because of a largely traditional social structure.

GOVERNMENT AND POLITICS

Political background. Those attempting to gain recognition of Transkei as an independent nation argue that it existed as a politically coherent tribal entity as early as the sixteenth century and that its territorial integrity was recognized by the British-ruled Cape Colony when it annexed the area in 1879. Indirect rule of the southern Transkei by means of the Council System was introduced in 1884 and was extended to the entire Transkei in 1926. Unlike Basutoland (now Lesotho), Bechuanaland (now Botswana), and

Swaziland, Transkei was not given the status of a protectorate when the Union of South Africa was created in 1910, although its present leaders contend that the area was never legally incorporated into the Union. In 1956 Transkei leaders accepted application of the "homelands" provision of the Bantu Authorities Act of 1951, subsequently obtaining limited internal autonomy in 1963 under the Bantu Self-Government Act of 1959. Paramount Chief Kaiser Daliwonga MATANZIMA, authority representative of the Emigrant-Tembuland, played a leading role in drafting the 1963 constitution and became chief minister when it entered into force that December. He then became prime minister upon the declaration of Transkeian independence on October 26, 1976. Both the United Nations and the Organization of African Unity repudiated the action on the ground that it served to perpetuate, rather than to diminish, racial segregation in South Africa, and to date no major government other than South Africa itself has accorded the homeland international recognition.

President Monzolwandle Botha SIGCAU died on December 1, 1978, and Chief Mantanzima was elected to a seven-year term as his successor on February 19, 1979, his brother, Chief George MANTANZIMA, being designated prime minister. In mid-January 1985, President Matanzima announced his intention to retire upon expiry of his term of office and was succeeded on February 20, 1986, by Paramount Chief Nyangelizwe Vulindlela NDAMASE, who had been elected by the National Assembly the day before.

At legislative balloting on September 25, 1986, the ruling Transkei National Independence Party (TNIP) suffered a substantial diminution of its majority as the result of a power struggle between the Mantanzima brothers (see Current issues, below) with the former president being banished to his home village of Qamata upon Chief George's reinvestiture as prime minister. A year later, on September 24, 1987, the Transkei Defense Force under the command of Maj. Gen. Harrington Bantubonke HOLOMISA seized power, charging both Mantanzimas with "deceit, massive cover-ups, fraud, and rampant corruption". President Ndamase denied, however, that an actual coup had occurred and on October 5 the (then) minister of posts and telecommunications, Stella SIGCAU became the continent's first female prime minister after succeeding her predecessor as leader of the TNIP.

Prime Minister Sigcau was herself ousted on December 30 by General Holomisa, who assumed power as head of a five-member military council; President Ndamase remained in office, despite a declaration of martial law and suspension of the constitution.

Constitution and government. A Constitutional Amendment Bill enacted by the South African legislature in 1975 provided for a parliamentary system of government for independent Transkei, with legislative power lodged in an enlarged Assembly of 75 chiefs and 75 elected members. A Transkei High Court, established in 1973 and redesignated as the Supreme Court at independence, was, in addition to other functions, assigned appellate jurisdiction in matters bearing on Bantu law and custom. For administrative purposes the country was divided into 28 districts.

Upon seizing power in late 1987, General Holomisa asserted that he had little desire to impose military rule, but that a return to civilian government would not be immediately forthcoming.

Foreign relations. Although unrecognized by any other foreign power, Transkei severed diplomatic relations with South Africa on April 10, 1978, because of Pretoria's refusal to surrender East Griqualand, a small parcel separating the bulk of Transkei's territory from a noncontiguous area in the northeast. In the wake of subsequent economic difficulties, relations were restored in February 1980.

Although obliged to tender formal recognition to Ciskei, Transkei was deeply opposed to the latter's elevation to "independence" in 1981, arguing that the action contradicted official South African policy by establishing two Xhosa homelands. The ensuing hostility led to efforts under the Mantanzima brothers to destabilize the neighboring regime (see Ciskei, Current issues).

Current issues. After retiring as president, Kaiser Mantanzima engaged in a lengthy dispute with his brother over the selection of TNIP candidates for the 1986 legislative poll. Failing in the intraparty effort, he succeeded in securing the election of 16 independent candidates and in 1987 announced the formation of a rival Transkei National Party (TNP), which was not formally registered until three days prior to Chief George's ouster in September. Both of the brothers, in addition to the detention of political opponents, had been accused of massive official corruption: Chief Kaiser of the disappearance of some $2.5 million in public funds and Chief George of accepting a $500,000 kickback on housing contracts. Other allegations involved the possible diversion of upwards of $24 million. In addition to alleged participation in irregularities by her predecessors, Chief George's successor, Stella Sigcau was charged with having accepted a $25,000 "gift" from a White-owned business to underwrite her daughter's education at a private school in Britain.

POLITICAL PARTIES

Formal party activity was suspended following the coup of December 30, 1987.

Former Government Party:

Transkei National Independence Party (TNIP). Founded in 1964, the TNIP fought for an independent Transkei after the election of 1968. At that time, Chief Kaiser Matanzima vehemently denied that the resultant convergence with a major element of South African policy implied "agreement with or support of" the latter's practice of racial discrimination. Upon his election as president of the Republic, Chief Kaiser was succeeded as TNIP leader by his brother, Chief George, who was in turn succeeded by Stella Sigcau prior to her designation as prime minister in October 1987.

Nominal Leader: Stella SIGCAU (former Prime Minister).

Former Opposition Parties:

Transkei National Party (TNP). The TNP was organized in May 1987 by former president Kaiser Matanzima following his failure, in a dispute with his brother, Chief George Matanzima, to control the selection process for the nomination of TNIP candidates of the 1986 legislative election. The new formation was not, however, recognized as a legal party until September 1987.

Nominal Leader: Chief Kaiser MATANZIMA.

Democratic Progressive Party (DPP). The DPP was organized in 1979 as a coalition of three former opposition groups: the Transkei National Progressive Party (TNPP), formed in April 1978 by 16 members of the Assembly who had defected from the TNIP; the Democratic Party (DP), which had opposed independence on the ground that it would aid Pretoria's apartheid strategy; and the New Democratic Party, a DP splinter that had favored independence. The former DPP leader, Paramount Chief Sabata DALINDYEBO, was convicted in April 1980 of violating the dignity of the president and was stripped of his tribal title, after which he went into exile, reportedly to join the African National Congress (ANC). The party won one elective legislative seat in 1981 and two (plus a nominated seat) in 1986.

Leader: Caledon MDA.

Transkei People's Freedom Party (TPFP). The TPFP was launched in October 1976 by Cromwell Diko, a former member of the TNIP, and three members of the DP. It was recognized as the official opposition party prior to the formation of the TNPP. It won no legislative seats in 1981 or 1986.

Leader: Cromwell DIKO.

LEGISLATURE

Until its suspension in December 1987, the unicameral National Assembly was composed of 150 members, including 75 co-opted members (70 chiefs and 5 paramount chiefs) and 75 elected representatives. At the most recent election of September 25, 1986, the Transkei National Independence Party won 57 of the elective seats; the Democratic Progressive Party, 2; independents, 16.

CABINET

Press reports indicate that on January 6, 1988, General Holomisa assumed the chairmanship of a 16-member Council of Ministers that included eight holdover ministers from the Sigcau administration. As of July 1, no information could be obtained from either South African or Transkei authorities as to the identity of the individuals in question.

NEWS MEDIA

Press. During 1979–1980 a number of journalists were subjected to detention, while in April 1981 the National Assembly approved a measure making it illegal to publish any news about the Transkei government without ministerial approval. *Intsimbi,* a fortnightly, and the *Transkei News,* published by the Department of Foreign Affairs and Information, are issued at Umtata.

Radio and television. The government's Transkei Broadcasting Corporation offers programing over Radio Transkei in English, as well as in Xhosa and a number of other African languages. There is no television service.

INTERGOVERNMENTAL REPRESENTATION

The Republic of Transkei is not a member of the United Nations and is not recognized by the United States.

SOUTH AFRICA: VENDA

Republic of Venda (English)
Republiek van Venda (Afrikaans)
Riphabuliki ya Venḓa (Luvenda)

Political Status: Former South African tribal homeland; recognized as independent by South Africa on September 13, 1979.

Area: 2,578 sq. mi. (6,677 sq. km.).

Population: 475,000 (1988E), embracing resident population only; does not include an estimated 210,000 Vendas who reside outside the homeland.

Major Urban Center (1979E): THOHOYANDOU (4,000).

Official Languages: English, Afrikaans, Luvenda.

Monetary Unit: South African Rand (market rate March 1, 1988, 2.09 rands = $1US).

Acting President: Gota (Chief) Frank N. RAVELE; assumed office following the death of Khosikhulu (Paramount Chief) Patrick R. MPHEPHU on April 18, 1988.

THE COUNTRY

Venda is a small enclave adjacent to Zimbabwe, at the northern tip of South Africa (see map, page 536). While the land is relatively fertile, the territory is not economically self-sufficient. Limited, but unproven, reserves of coal, graphite, copper, and magnesite are said to exist. A reported two-thirds of the job-holding men are externally employed and nearly half of the food is imported from outside the homeland.

GOVERNMENT AND POLITICS

Political background. In February 1973, Vhavenda accepted internal self-government under South Africa's Bantu Homelands Constitutional Bill of 1971, and on September 13, 1979, as the Republic of Venda, became the third such territory to be designated as an independent Black state by South Africa. On the same day, the Legislative Assembly elected Chief Patrick R. MPHEPHU, theretofore chief minister, as president of the new republic. Mphephu died on April 18, 1988, and was succeeded, on an acting basis, by Finance Minister Gota Frank N. RAVELE.

Constitution and government. Under the constitution that came into effect upon the proclamation of independence, Venda is declared to be a republic with a president who serves as head of state and who appoints an Executive Council (cabinet), over which he presides. The National Assembly of 92 members (only 45 are directly elected) serves a five-year term. The judicial system is headed by a Supreme Court.

Foreign relations. Venda is yet to be recognized by any foreign governments other than South Africa and its sister republics of Bophuthatswana, Ciskei, and Transkei. The Organization of African Unity has condemned all four Bantustans as "pseudo-states" designed to "fragment South Africa" in the interest of its White minority, while the UN Security Council on September 21, 1979, issued a statement characterizing "the so-called independence of Venda" as "totally invalid".

In the weeks preceding the declaration of independence, some 70 bilateral agreements were concluded with Pretoria. Included were support for a national security force and budgetary subsidies that are expected to continue for an indefinite period.

Current issues. Although not as geographically segmented as either Bophuthatswana or Transkei, the much smaller area assigned to Venda consists essentially of two tracts of land connected by a narrow corridor. Homeland leaders had earlier sought a more integrated territory, and Chief Mphephu stated during his independence address that he was "happy" that Venda's new status did not preclude negotiation on "further consolidation".

The legitimacy of Mphephu's designation as president was clouded somewhat by the fact that at the preindependence election the opposition Venda Independence Party had won 30 of the 42 legislative elective seats, most of the paramount chief's support coming from the ranks of the chiefs, who then held a total of 27 seats, as well as from 15 other members appointed on a tribal basis. In the period preceding independence, Mphephu had demonstrated distinctly authoritarian tendencies by detaining as many as 50 political opponents, including 12 legislators, without trial. During 1980–1982, some two dozen additional persons were detained (at least two of whom were reported to have been bludgeoned to death) by authorities of what the London *Times* has termed "arguably the most blatantly corrupt and unpopular of the four . . . ministates which have accepted internationally unrecognized independence from Pretoria".

At present, the Venda National Party holds all of the elective Assembly seats, the four opposition members elected in 1984 resigning their seats subsequent to the balloting and failing redesignation in by-elections.

POLITICAL PARTIES

Government Party:

Venda National Party (VNP). The VNP, an essentially conservative party, strongly supported formal independence from South Africa. Although winning only 12 of 42 elective seats in the preindependence balloting of July 1978, it subsequently controlled the Assembly through the allegiance of a majority of nonelected members. At the June 1984 election, it won 41 of 45 directly elective seats, capturing all of the remaining seats in subsequent by-elections.

Leader: Gota Frank N. RAVELE (Acting President of the Republic).

Opposition Party:

Venda Independence People's Party (VIPP). Despite its name, the VIPP long opposed independence, arguing that the action would further fragment Black interests in southern Africa. Its leadership formally adopted a neutral stance on the issue immediately prior to the 1978 legislative balloting, a party official complaining that the posture stemmed from "tremendous pressure" from White government officials at Pretoria. It won a majority of the elective seats in 1978, but could not control the Assembly because of a lack of support by nonelective members. It won only four seats in 1984, all of which were lost in subsequent by-elections. Former VIP leader Baldwin Mudau died unexpectedly (some reports suggesting of unnatural causes) on January 1, 1982. The formation's present status is questionable, since Venda was constitutionally declared to be a one-party state in August 1986.

Leader: Gilbert M. BAKANE.

LEGISLATURE

The unicameral **National Assembly** has 92 members, of whom 45 are directly elected, 28 are chiefs (27 chiefs and 1 paramount chief), 15 are designated by regional councils, and 4 are named by the president. At the balloting of June 1984, the Venda National Party won 41 elective seats, while the Venda Independence Party won 4. Following the election, the VIP members resigned their seats, all of which were captured by the VNP in subsequent by-elections.

Speaker: W.R. MUFAMADI.

CABINET

Acting President	Gota Frank N. Ravele
Ministers	
Agriculture, Forestry and Water Affairs	Khosi A.M. Madzivhandila
Economic Affairs	Gota F.N. Ravele
Education	G.M. Ramabulana
Foreign Affairs	Gota E.R.B. Nesengani
Health, Welfare and Pensions	Khosi M.M. Mphaphuli
Internal Affairs	A.A. Tshivhase
Justice	Khosi J.R. Rambuda
Transport, Works and Communications	Khosi C.A. Nelwamondo
Urban Affairs and Land Tenure	Khosi C.N. Makuya

NEWS MEDIA

Press. There are no regularly issued news publications.

Radio and television. The only broadcast facility is the government-controlled Radio Thohoyandou.

INTERGOVERNMENTAL REPRESENTATION

The Republic of Venda is not a member of the United Nations and is not recognized by the United States.

S P A I N

Spanish State
Estado Español

Political Status: Formerly under system of personal rule instituted in 1936; monarchy reestablished November 22, 1975, in accordance with Law of Succession of July 26, 1947, as amended in 1969 and 1971; parliamentary monarchy confirmed by constitution effective December 29, 1978.

Area: 194,896 sq. mi. (504,782 sq. km.).

Population: 37,746,260 (1981C), 48,527,000 (1988E).

Major Urban Areas (1981C): MADRID (3,188,297); Barcelona (1,754,900); Valencia (751,734); Seville (653,833); Zaragoza (590,750); Málaga (503,251); Bilbao (433,030).

Official Languages: Spanish and regional languages (principally Basque, Catalan, Galician, and Valencian). The regional languages were accorded legal recognition on November 16, 1975.

Monetary Unit: Peseta (market rate March 1, 1988, 113.87 pesetas = $1US).

Monarch: JUAN CARLOS I; invested before the Spanish Legislative Assembly in 1969; sworn in as King on November 22, 1975, following the death of the former Chief of State and President of Government, Gen. Francisco FRANCO Bahamonde, on November 20.

Heir to the Throne: Prince FELIPE; sworn in as heir apparent on January 30, 1986.

President of the Government (Prime Minister): Felipe GONZALEZ Márquez (Spanish Socialist Workers' Party); sworn in December 2, 1982, to succeed Leopoldo CALVO Sotelo y Bustelo (Union of the Democratic Center), following parliamentary election of October 28; sworn in for a second term on July 24, 1986, following election of June 22.

THE COUNTRY

Occupying more than four-fifths of the Iberian peninsula (which it shares with Portugal), Spain is separated by the Pyrenees from France and the rest of Europe, and includes within its national territory the Balearic Islands in the Mediterranean, the Canary Islands in the Atlantic, and the two small North African enclaves, or *presidios,* of Ceuta and Melilla. Continental Spain, a region of varied topography and climate, has been noted more for beauty of landscape than for wealth of resources, but possesses valuable deposits of iron, coal, and other minerals as well

as petroleum. The Spanish are a mixture of the original Iberian population with later invading peoples. The population includes several cultural groups: Castilians, Galicians, Andalusians, Basques, and Catalans. Regional feelings remain strong, particularly in the Basque and Catalan areas in the north and east, and various local languages and dialects are used in addition to the long-dominant Castilian Spanish. The population is almost entirely Roman Catholic, although religious liberty is formally guaranteed. In 1982, women comprised 29 percent of the labor force, concentrated in domestic and human services and clerical work, with only 3 percent holding administrative positions; female participation in government is presently minimal, although a Feminist Party (see Political Parties, below) has recently been organized.

The Spanish economy was transformed between 1960 and 1972, the gross national product increasing almost fivefold; however, high inflation, unemployment consistently in excess of 15 percent, and substantial balance-of-payments problems curtailed subsequent growth rates until January 1986, when entry into the European Community (EC) provided a renewed stimulus. The principal industrial products are leather, shoes, clothing, and rubber, but the shipbuilding, petroleum, and chemical industries are also of major importance. Agriculture, the traditional mainstay of the Spanish economy, has not kept pace with industrial advances despite more intensive utilization of modern techniques and materials. The most important agricultural products continue to be olives and olive oil, cereals, fruits, vegetables, and wines.

GOVERNMENT AND POLITICS

Political background. Conquered in the eighth century by North African Moors, who established a flourishing Islamic civilization in the south of the peninsula, Christian Spain completed its self-liberation in 1492 and went on to found a world empire that reached its apogee in the sixteenth century and then gradually disintegrated. Monarchical rule under the House of Bourbon continued into the twentieth century, surviving the dictatorship of Miguel Primo DE RIVERA in 1923–1930 but giving place in 1931 to a multiparty republic that became increasingly subject to leftist influences. A military uprising led by Gen. Francisco FRANCO Bahamonde began in 1936, precipitating a three-year Civil War in which the republican forces, although benefiting from Soviet Russian assistance, were ultimately defeated with aid from Fascist Italy and Nazi Germany. A fascist regime was then established, Franco ruling as leader (*caudillo*) and chief of state, with the support of the armed forces, the Church, and commercial, financial, and landed interests.

Having preserved its neutrality throughout World War II and suffering a period of ostracism thereafter by the United Nations, Spain was gradually readmitted to international society and formed particularly close ties with the United States within the framework of a joint defense agreement originally concluded in 1953. The political structure was modified in 1947 with the adoption of a Law of Succession, which declared Spain to be a monarchy (though without a monarch), and again in 1967 by an Organic Law confirming Franco's position as chief of state, defining the structure of other government bodies, and providing for strictly limited public participation in elections to the legislature (*Cortes*). Political and administrative controls in effect since the Civil War were considerably relaxed during the early 1960s, but subsequent demands for change generated increasing instability, which culminated in December 1973 with the assassination of Prime Minister Luis CARRERO Blanco by Basque separatists. The new prime minister, Carlos ARIAS Navarro, initially signaled his intent to deal harshly with dissidents; however, the April 1974 coup in Portugal, coupled with General Franco's illness in July, generated problems for the regime that resulted in some moderation of its repressive posture.

General Franco again became ill on October 17, 1975, and on October 30 Prince JUAN CARLOS de Borbón y Borbón, who had previously been designated as heir to the Spanish throne, assumed the powers of provisional chief of state and head of government. Franco died on November 20 and two days later Juan Carlos was sworn in as king, in accordance with the 1947 Law of Succession.

On July 1, 1976, Arias Navarro resigned as prime minister — reportedly at the king's request — following criticism of his somewhat cautious approach to promised reform of the political system. His successor, Adolfo SUAREZ González, moved energetically to advance the reform program, securing its approval by the National Council of the (National) Movement on October 8, by the *Cortes* on November 10, and by the public in a referendum conducted on December 15. The National Movement was abolished by cabinet decree on April 1, 1977, and on June 15 balloting took place for a new, bicameral *Cortes,* with Prime Minister Suárez González' Union of the Democratic Center (UCD) obtaining a substantial plurality in both houses. On August 22 a special lower-house subcommittee began drafting a new constitution that went into force December 29, 1978, following overwhelming approval by the *Cortes* on October 31, endorsement in a referendum on December 6, and ratification by King Juan Carlos on December 27. Suárez was formally reappointed on April 2, 1979, a general election on March 1 yielding no substantial party realignment within the legislature.

During 1979–1980 an increase in terrorist activity, particularly in the Basque region, gave rise to manifest uneasiness within military circles, while the UCD became subject to widespread internal dissent following the introduction of a liberal divorce bill that the Church and most right-wing elements bitterly opposed. On January 29, 1981, Suárez González unexpectedly resigned and on February 23, before his designated successor had been confirmed, a group of Civil Guards, led by Lt. Col. Antonio TEJERO Molina, seized control of the Congress of Deputies chamber in an attempted coup. Due largely to the prompt intervention of King Juan Carlos, the rebellion failed, Leopoldo CALVO Sotelo y Bostelo, the UCD secretary general, being approved as prime minister on February 25 and sworn in the following day. However, the fissures between moderate and rightist elements within the UCD continued to deepen, with a number of new parties being spawned in the wake of numerous leadership defections during late

1981 and the first half of 1982. As a result, lower-house UCD representation, which because of the defections had dropped from 168 to 122 by August, plummeted to a mere dozen deputies at an election held October 12. By contrast, the Socialist Workers' Party (PSOE) obtained a comfortable majority (202–106) over the Popular Alliance (AP), a resurgent right-wing group that had theretofore held only a handful of seats. Subsequently, on December 2, PSOE leader Felipe GONZALEZ Márquez was inaugurated as the first left-wing chief executive since 1936. González was sworn in for a second term on July 24, 1986, following an early election on June 22 at which the PSOE, despite marginally declining strength, retained majority control of both houses of the *Cortes.*

At his eighteenth birthday on January 30, 1986, Juan Carlos' son, Prince FELIPE, was formally invested as heir apparent, Prime Minister Gonzalez declaring that "democratic and free Spain trusts its constitutional future" to the monarchy.

Constitution and government. The present 169-article Spanish constitution, the seventh since 1812, abrogated the "fundamental principles" and organic legislation under which General Franco ruled as chief of state (*jefe del estado*) until his death in 1975. The document defines the Spanish state as a parliamentary monarchy and guarantees a variety of basic rights, including those of speech and press, association, and collective bargaining. "Bordering provinces" and "island territories and provinces" with common characteristics and/or historic regional status may, under prescribed circumstances, form "self-governing communities", but no federation of such communities is to be permitted. Roman Catholicism was disestablished as the state religion, although authorities were directed to "keep in mind the religious beliefs of Spanish society". Torture was outlawed, the death penalty abolished, and "a more equitable distribution of regional and personal incomes" advanced.

The powers of the king include naming the prime minister, after consulting the parties in the *Cortes;* serving as commander in chief of the armed forces, which are specifically recognized as guardians of the constitutional order; and calling referenda. The prime minister, who is empowered to dissolve the *Cortes* and call an election (previously prerogatives of the monarch), is assisted by a cabinet that is collectively responsible to the lower house.

Legislative authority is exercised by a bicameral *Cortes,* consisting of a territorially elected Senate of 208 members (exclusive of 49 members who, elected on a population basis, represent the "self-governing communities") and a Congress of Deputies of 300–400 (currently 350) members elected on the basis of universal adult suffrage and proportional representation. Both houses serve four-year terms, barring dissolution; each can initiate legislation, although the upper house can only delay measures approved by the lower.

The judicial system is headed by a Supreme Tribunal (*Tribunal Supremo*) and includes territorial courts, provincial courts, regional courts, courts of the first instance, and municipal courts. The country is divided into 50 administrative provinces, including the island provinces of Baleares, Las Palmas, and Santa Cruz de Tenerife. Rights of regional autonomy are recognized but must be effected by action of the *Cortes;* in addition, since no claim to autonomy may prejudice the unity of the nation, devolution can involve only a limited range of powers, such as alteration of municipal boundaries, control of health and tourism, instruction in regional languages, and the establishment (under circumscribed conditions) of local police agencies.

Draft devolution statutes were presented for the Basque and Catalan areas soon after the March 1979 election, and on October 25 were overwhelmingly approved in regional referenda. In 1980, elections for regional Legislative Assemblies were held on March 9 in the Basque provinces of Alava, Guipúzcoa, and Vizcaya, and on March 20 in the Catalan provinces of Barcelona, Gerona, Lérida, and Tarragona. Similar elections were held in Galicia on October 20, 1981, and in Andalusia on May 22, 1982. By February 1983, autonomy statutes had been approved for the remaining 13 regions, with balloting in each being conducted on May 8. The presidents of government of the Autonomous Regions are elected by the regional legislatures.

Autonomous Region	*President of Government*
Andalucía	José Rodrıguez de la Barbolla
Aragón	Hipólito Gómez de las Roces
Asturias	Pedro de Silva y Cienfuegos Jovellanos
Baleares (Balearic Islands)	Gabriel Cañellas Fons
Basque Country (Euzkadi)	José Antonio Ardanza
Canarias (Canary Islands)	Fernando Fernández Martín
Cantabria	Juan Hormaechea Cazón
Castilla y León	José María Aznar
Castilla-La Mancha	José Bono Martínez
Catalonia (Catalunya)	Jordi Pujol i Soley
Extremadura	Juan Carlos Rodríguez Ibarra
Galicia	Fernando González Laxe
Madrid	Joaquıń Leguina Herrán
Murcia	Carlos Collado Mena
Navarra	Gabriel Urralburu Tainta
La Rioja	Joaquín Espert Pérez-Caballero
Valencia	Joan Lerma

Foreign relations. Neutral in both world wars, Spain has generally sided with the anti-Communist powers since World War II but under Franco was prevented by certain democratic governments (notably those of Denmark, Norway, Belgium, and the Netherlands) from becoming a member of NATO, the European Communities (EC), and other Western organizations. It was, however, admitted to the United Nations in 1955 and, in due course, to all of the latter's Specialized Agencies. Recent years have seen a strengthening of relations with Portugal, France, and West Germany; a reduction of tension with Britain over Gibraltar, which resulted in reopening of the border in early 1985 and the prospect of sovereignty talks; and a cautious extension of economic and cultural contacts with the Soviet Union and other East European countries. Relations with the United States have remained cordial following the conclusion in 1970 of an Agreement of Friendship and Cooperation to replace the original US-Spanish defense agreement of 1953. Spain was admitted to the Council of Europe in 1977 and, in 1982, to NATO, with membership in the EC following on January 1, 1986. Continued improvement in relations with other European nations has been apparent with Spanish participation in the "Eurofighter" defense

consortium and the conclusion of a number of extradition treaties that prevent British and Italian fugitives from taking refuge in Spain and allow Madrid to extradite suspected Basque terrorists from France.

In February 1976, Spain yielded control of its North African territory of Spanish Sahara to Morocco and Mauritania. The action was taken despite strong protests by Algeria and the passage of a resolution by the UN General Assembly's Committee on Trust and Non-Self-Governing Territories in December 1975 that called for a UN-sponsored plebiscite to permit the Saharans to exercise "freely and fully" their right to self-determination. Formerly cordial relations with the Saharan representative group Polisario (see entry under Algeria) were broken and its envoys expelled following a late 1985 naval attack near the Mauritanian border, which killed two Spanish citizens.

On January 17, 1986, after months of negotiation, Madrid announced the establishment, for the first time, of full diplomatic relations with Israel. Despite recall of the Iranian ambassador, the move did not result in anti-Spanish sentiment in the Islamic world, and Madrid expressed the hope that it could thenceforth serve as a "useful intermediary" to relieve Mideast tensions.

Current issues. Although most economic indicators during early 1987 were positive, including increases in production and gross domestic product, with a continued decline in inflation (from a high of nearly 15 percent in 1982) to less than 5 percent, unemployment remained high at more than 20 percent and both the centrist and far-left opposition charged unequal social benefit from PSOE policies. At simultaneous elections on June 10 for the European Parliament and both regional and municipal government bodies, the Socialists suffered marginal losses — most severely in the municipal balloting, where their vote share fell from 43 percent in 1983 to 37 percent. Earlier, a government decree of November 1986 extending the right of abortion up to the twelfth week of pregnancy had generated intense opposition from both Church and "pro-life" groups, although an even more liberal measure proposed by United Left deputies in April 1987 was defeated.

The principal foreign affairs issue continued to be the US military presence, which Prime Minister González had promised to reduce in the course of a NATO referendum campaign in 1986. Extended negotiations on the issue finally yielded an agreement on January 15, 1988, whereby the United States would, within three years, withdraw from the Torrejón facility outside Madrid and transfer its 72 F-16 jet fighters out of the country.

POLITICAL PARTIES

The only authorized political formation during most of the Franco era was the Spanish Falange (*Falange Española Tradicionalista y de las Juntas de Ofensiva Nacional-Sindicalista* — FET y JONS), which resulted from the 1937 amalgamation of the small *Falange Española*, organized by José Antonio Primo de Rivera, and a number of traditionalist groups. It was subsequently referred to as "The National Movement", with a National Council of the Movement (*Consejo Nacional del Movimiento*) established in 1967 to serve, in a limited way, as an upper chamber of the *Cortes* and guardian of the legislative process. The latter was formally abolished in April 1977, although the Falange subsequently reemerged as a minor rightist party.

In January 1975, prior to Franco's death, a law permitting the establishment of noncommunist and nonseparatist "political associations" went into effect, and during the next two years a large number of parties, both legal and illegal, proceeded to organize. In March 1976, the Democratic Coordination (*Coordinación Democrática* — CD) was launched as a unified opposition front embracing (1) the Communist-led Democratic Junta (*Junta Democrática* — JD), which had been organized at Paris in July 1974 as a coalition of the Spanish Communist Party (PCE), trade-union and liberal monarchist elements, and other groups; and (2) the socialist Democratic Platform (*Programa Democrática* — PD), formed in June 1975 as a coalition of the Spanish Socialist Workers' Party (PSOE), several Christian Democratic groups, and others.

Following a December 1976 referendum in which voters approved the government's political reform program and the subsequent enactment of legislation simplifying the registration of political parties, the CD broke up, most of its moderate members joining with a number of non-CD parties in establishing the Union of the Democratic Center (*Unión de Centro Democrático* — UDC) which defeated the PCE and the PSOE at the June 1977 election and controlled the government for the ensuing five years. Following a disastrous showing at the October 1982 election, the UDC leadership voted in February 1983 to dissolve the party, authorizing its 12 remaining deputies to affiliate with other groups.

Government Party:

Spanish Socialist Workers' Party (*Partido Socialista Obrero Español* — PSOE). Founded in 1879 and a member of the Socialist International, the PSOE, under the young and dynamic Felipe González Márques, held its first legal congress in 44 years in December 1976 and in 1979 became the second-strongest party in the *Cortes*, winning 121 seats in the Congress of Deputies and 68 seats in the Senate at the election of March 1, in conjunction with its regional ally, the **Catalan Socialist Party** (*Partit dels Socialistes de Catalunya* — PSC). Earlier, the party had called for a "historic compromise" to obliterate the remnants of Francoism and had endorsed neutralism in foreign policy, opposing links with either NATO or the Warsaw Pact bloc. In April 1978 the Popular Socialist Party (*Partido Socialista Popular* — PSP), which had contested the 1977 election as part of the Socialist Union (*Unidad Socialista* — US), formally merged with the PSOE.

At a centennial congress in May 1979, González unexpectedly stepped down as party leader after a majority of delegates refused to abandon a doctrinal commitment to Marxism as a means of appealing to moderate voters. His control was reestablished, however, during a special congress in late September, the hard-liners being defeated by a vote of more than ten-to-one. At the 1982 election the PSOE/PSC won an absolute majority in both the Congress and Senate, González being invested as prime minister on December 2. Subsequently, the party experienced internal strain as a result of the government's pro-NATO posture, with the leaders of the youth and trade union wings both active in the Movement for Peace and Disarmament (*Movimiento por la Paz, el Desarme y la Libertad* — MPDL), a group opposed to the country's participation in any military alliance. Following popular endorsement of continued NATO membership at the March 1986 referendum, the prime minister called for an early election on June 22, at which the PSOE retained majority control of both houses, despite a loss of 18 seats in the Congress of Deputies and 10 in the Senate.

Leaders: Felipe GONZALEZ Márquez (Prime Minister and Secretary General of the Party), Ramón RUBIAL (President of the Party).

Other National Parties:

Popular Alliance (*Alianza Popular* — AP). The AP emerged in 1976 as a right-wing group that encountered internal disarray in attempting to frame policy in regard to the new constitution (8 of its congressmen voting in favor, 5 against, and 3 abstaining). In late 1978 most of its deputies joined with representatives of a number of other rightist parties in establishing the Spanish Democratic Confederation (*Confederación Democrática Española* — CDE), which contested the 1979 election as the Democratic Coalition (*Coalición Democrática* — CD), winning 9 lower-house seats. Prior to the 1982 election, the UCD national executive, by a narrow margin, rejected a proposal to form an alliance with the AP, although the Popular Democratic Party (PDP, below), a UCD constituent group, elected to do so. At the October voting the AP/PDP coalition, benefiting from the effective demise of the UCD, garnered 106 congressional seats, thus becoming the second-ranked group in the lower house. Although pro-NATO, the AP, proclaiming the poll "unnecessary", spearheaded the March 1986 referendum boycott in an effort to undermine the González government.

The AP contested the June 1986 election as part of the **Popular Coalition** (*Coalición Popular* — CP) that included the PDP and PL, below, and secured 105 congressional seats. Describing the outcome as "unsatisfactory", the PDP (with 21 deputies and 11 senators) broke with the Coalition upon convening of the new *Cortes* on July 15, while 4 members of the AP also defected in opposition to Manuel Fraga Iribarne's CP/AP leadership. Disintegration of the CP proceeded further in late October, when the AP's Catalan branch voted to exclude both PDP and LP deputies from the CP group in the regional parliament. A month later, the CP lost 5 of its 7 seats in the Basque parliament, prompting Fraga's resignation as AP president (though retaining his congressional seat) on December 2. Following the interim incumbency of Gerardo Fernández ALBOR, Antonio Hernández Mancha was named AP president (and leader of what remained of the CP) in February 1987.

Leaders: Antonio HERNANDEZ Mancha (President), Manuel FRAGA Iribarne (former President), Arturo GARCIA Tizón (Secretary General and Leader of the Opposition).

Popular Democratic Party (*Partido Democráta Popular* — PDP). The PDP was formally reconstituted as a separate party in July 1982, having previously been a component of the UCD. Allied with the AP for the 1982 electoral campaign, it also joined in boycotting the NATO referendum. A member of the PC at the time of the June 1986 balloting, it withdrew from the coalition in mid-July. In May 1987 (then) party president Oscar ALZAGA, charging the AP with bringing pressure on banks to withhold PDP campaign financing, announced his retirement from public life.

Leader: Luis de GRANDES (Secretary General).

Liberal Party (*Partido Liberal* — PL). Formed in 1977, the PL absorbed the small Liberal Union (*Unión Liberal* — UL) in 1985. Its former secretary general, José Miguel Bravo de Laguna, resigned in October 1986 after being fined for shoplifting at London. The party was also a member of the CP until mid-1986.

Leaders: José Antonio SEGURADO (President), Antonio JIMENEZ Blanco (Secretary General).

Democratic and Social Center (*Centro Democrático y Social* — CDS). The CDS was organized prior to the 1982 election by Adolfo Suárez González, who had stepped down as UCD president after resigning as prime minister in January 1981 and had subsequently been rebuffed in an effort to regain the party leadership in July 1982. The CDS returned no senators and only 2 deputies at the 1982 balloting, but secured 3 upper and 19 lower house seats in 1986.

Leaders: Adolfo SUAREZ González (former Prime Minister), Jesús María VIANA (Secretary General).

Democratic Reformist Party (*Partido Reformista Democrático* — PRD). A member of the Liberal International, the PRD was launched in early 1984 by the leader of the (thereupon dissolved) Liberal Democratic Party (*Partido Democrático Liberal* — PDL), Antonio Garrigues Walker, in conjunction with a member of the Catalan Democratic Convergence (see CiU, below). The PDL had been formed in July 1982 by members of some 60 "liberal clubs" that decided not to contest the 1982 balloting after rejecting an electoral pact with the UCD. In February 1984, Garrigues concluded an agreement to "strengthen progressive liberalism" with Ignacio Camuñas Solis of the small **Liberal Action Party** (*Partido Acción Liberal* — PAL). The PRD secured no parliamentary representation in 1986.

Leaders: Antonio GARRIGUES Walker, Miquel ROCA Junyent (CiU), Florento PEREZ (Secretary General).

Spanish Falange (*Falange Española de las JONS*). Reduced to little more than a shadow of its former significance, the Falange joined with a number of other neo-fascist groups in forming a National Union (Unión Nacional) that secured one legislative seat in 1979. It did not contest the 1982 election in order to avoid divisiveness within "the forces opposing Marxism". Subsequently, it appeared to have been largely superseded by the formation, in October 1984, of a new right-wing grouping, the **Spanish Integration Committees** (*Juntas Españolas de Integracion*), led by Antonio IZQUIERDO Ferigüela. More recently, the Falange has been bolstered by the emergence of right-wing sentiment among unemployed, working-class youth, thousands of whom marched in a "Francoist" demonstration at Madrid in November 1985 to commemorate the tenth anniversary of the former dictator's death.

Leaders: Carmen FRANCO, Diego MARQUEZ Jorrillo.

National Front (*Frente Nacional* — FN). Formation of the extreme right-wing FN was announced in October 1986 by Blas Piñar, former secretary general of the New Force (*Fuerza Nueva*), which had been dissolved in 1982.

Leader: Blas PIÑAR.

Feminist Party (*Partido Feminista* — PF). Founded in 1979 and achieving official registration in 1981, the PF has concentrated largely on non-electoral organization and education, including the publication of the journal *Poder y Libertad*.

Leader: Lidia FALCON.

Spanish Green Party (*Partido Verde Español* — PVE). Long a somewhat disparate movement of pacifists, feminists, and naturalists, the Spanish "greens" (*los verdes*) established the PVE as a formal party in June 1984, convening their first congress in February 1985. However, a number of the constituent organizations disavowed the action on the ground that it had been taken without appropriate consultation.

Leader: Luis HIDALGO.

United Left (*Izquierda Unida* — IU). The IU was formed in April 1986 as an electoral coalition involving the three parties listed below, plus the **Progressive Federation** (*Federación Progresista* — FP), led by former PCE official Ramón TAMAMES; the **Carlist Party** (*Partido Carlista* — PC); the **Humanist Party** (*Partido Humanista* — PH); and a number of small ecological and anti-NATO groups. It won a total of 7 congressional seats at the June balloting, after which the PH was asked to leave the formation.

Spanish Communist Party (*Partido Comunista de España* — PCE). The PCE, a "Eurocommunist" party that favors nonalignment and has substantial trade-union support, was legalized in April 1977, following the release from detention in December 1976 of its secretary general, Santiago Carrillo Solares. On April 19–23, 1977, it held at Madrid its first legal congress in 45 years, while on May 13 the PCE's most celebrated figure, Dolores Ibarruri ("La Pasionaria"), returned to Spain after 38 years in exile. The PCE and its regional ally, the **Unified Socialist Party of Catalonia** (*Partit Socialista Unificat de Catalunya* — PSUC), secured 20 seats in the Congress of Deputies and 12 seats in the Senate at the June 1977 election. In March 1979, with President Ibarruri having declined to seek legislative reelection for reasons of health and age, it placed 3 additional deputies in the lower house but lost all of its upper house seats. Its congressional representation declined sharply in 1982 to only 4 members, with the result that Carrillo, its longtime secretary general and the only survivor of the Civil War still to lead a major party, was forced to step down in November. Carrillo's influence was eroded still further by the decision of new party leaders to adopt internal reforms and work for a "convergence of progressive forces" with other leftist groups, both elective and nonelective; on April 19, 1985, Carrillo and 18 supporters were expelled following an emergency national congress on March 29–31, subsequently forming the Committee for Communist Unity (see under PTE-UC, below).

Immediately prior to the 1986 election, a pro-Soviet splinter group, the Spanish Communist Workers' Party (*Partido Comunista Obrero Español* — PCOE, led by Enrique LISTER, voted to disband and rejoin the PCE. Subsequently, in February 1987, a PCE delegation visited Moscow, pledging a strengthening of relations with the CPSU.

Leaders: Dolores IBARRURI Gómez (President of the Party), Fernando PEREZ Royo (Parliamentary Leader), Gerardo IGLESIAS (Secretary General).

Communist Party of the Peoples of Spain (*Partido Comunista de los Pueblos de España* — PCPE). The pro-Soviet PCPE was organized in January 1984 by Ignacio Gallego, who had resigned from the PCE Executive and Central committees the previous October, in an effort to end the "politico-ideological degeneration . . . which introduced Eurocommunism".

Leader: Ignacio GALLEGO.

Socialist Action Party (*Partido Acción Socialista* — Pasoc). Formerly known as the Spanish Socialist Workers' Party–Historical (*Partido Socialista Obrero Español-Histórico* — PSOE-H), Pasoc is a doctrinal splinter of the present governing party that remains loyal to the former PSOE secretary general, Rodolfo Llopis.

Leaders: Julián LARA Cavero (President), Alonso PUERTA (Secretary General).

Spanish Workers' Party–Communist Unity (*Partido de los Trabajadores de España–Unidad Comunista* — PTE-UC). The PTE-UC was launched at a congress held February 6–8, 1987. The new formation was an outgrowth of the Committee for Communist Unity (*Mesa para Unidad de los Comunistas* — MUC), organized by former PCE secretary general Santiago Carrillo following his expulsion in April 1985. Carrillo contested the 1986 election, without success, under the MUC label. In April 1987 he announced the PTE-UC had accepted an overture from the PCPE for unity talks.

Leaders: Santiago CARRILLO Solares (Executive President), Adolfo PIÑEDO (Secretary General).

Regional Parties:

There are numerous regional parties in addition to the regional affiliates of the PSOE and PCE listed above. The Federation of Socialist Parties (*Federación de Partidos Socialistas* — FPS), which embraced a number of regional groups, contested the June 1977 election as part of the Socialist Union but then became moribund, most of the regional organizations subsequently presenting individual lists.

Convergence and Union (*Convergència i Unió* — CiU). The center-left CiU was formed in 1979 as a coalition of the **Democratic Convergence of Catalonia** (*Convergència Democràtica de Catalunya* — CDC) and the **Democratic Union of Catalonia** (*Unió Democràtica de Catalunya* — UDC). The CiU won a majority of seats in the Catalonian legislative election of April 1984, after having secured 12 national congressional seats in 1982, and (in alliance with the ERC, below) 7 senatorial seats in 1982. It won 18 congressional and 8 senatorial seats in 1986.

Leaders: Jordi PUJOL i Soley (CDC), Miguel COLL i Alentorn (UDC).

Catalan Republican Left (*Esquerra Republicana de Catalunya* — ERC). The ERC was one of two Catalan republican parties, the other being the **Democratic Spanish Republican Action** (*Acció Republicana Democràtica Española* — ARDE), granted legal recognition in August 1977. After the 1982 balloting, the ERC shared 7 national Senate seats with the CiU while holding 1 congressional seat outright; it is presently unrepresented in the *Cortes*.

Leader: Joan HORTALA (Secretary General).

Basque Nationalist Party (*Partido Nacionalista Vasco* — PNV). A moderate party that has long campaigned for Basque autonomy, the PNV won 8 congressional and 7 senatorial seats in 1982. In February 1984 it obtained a plurality (32 of 75 seats) in the Basque Parliament, and formed a regional government headed by Carlos Garaicoetxea Urizza. Subsequently, it became embroiled in an intraparty dispute regarding devolution of power to individual Basque provinces. As a result of the dispute, Garaicoetxea was replaced as premier and party leader by José Antonio Ardanza in January 1985, after which the PNV concluded a legislative pact with the PSOE's local affiliate, the **Basque Socialist Party** (*Partido Socialista de Euzkadi* — PSE).

Leaders: José Antonio ARDANZA (Basque Premier), Xabier ARZALLUS (President).

Basque Solidarity (*Euzko Alkastasuna* — EA). The EA was formed in September 1986 by a group of PNV dissidents, subsequently joined by former premier Carlos Garaicoetxea.

Leaders: Carlos GARAICOETXEA Urizza (President), Manuel IBARRONDO.

United People (*Herri Batasuna* — HB). The HB is a Basque party with links to the political wing of the terrorist ETA (see below). It was runner-up in the Basque parliamentary election of March 1980 and obtained 2 lower-house *Cortes* seats in 1982. A decision by the Interior Ministry to withdraw legal recognition from the party was overturned by court action in January 1984. The HB won 1 senate and 5 congressional seats in 1986.

Leaders: Iñaki ESNAOLA, Jon IDIGORAS.

Basque Left (*Euzkadiko Ezkerra*—EE). The EE is a small left-wing group, also with links to the ETA. It currently holds 2 seats in the Congress of Deputies.

Leaders: Juan Maria BANDRES Molet (President), Kepa AULESTIA (Secretary General).

Andalusian Party (*Partido Andalucista*—PA). Known until early 1984 as the Andalusian Socialist Party (*Partido Socialista de Andalucía*—PSA), the PA won 5 lower-house *Cortes* seats at the 1979 election but lost them all in 1982.

Leaders: Pedro PANCHECO Herrera (President), Salvador PEREZ Bueno (Provisional Secretary General).

Aragonese Regionalist Party (*Partido Aragonés Regionalista*—PAR). The PAR is a center-right grouping allied with the CP that secured 1 congressional seat in 1986.

Leaders: Hipólito GOMEZ de las Roces (President), Emilio EIROA García (Secretary General).

Asturian Party (*Partido Asturianista*—PA). The PA is an Asturian regional group formed in September 1986.

Leader: Xuan Xosé SANCHEZ Vicente.

Galician Coalition (*Coalición Galega*—CG). Third-ranked in the Galician assembly at the 1985 election, the CG won 1 lower house *Cortes* seat in 1986. In October 1986, a rupture between conservative and progressive factions caused the momentary collapse of the regional government, the progressives, led by Pablo GONZALEZ Mariñas, subsequently withdrawing to form the **National Galician Party** (*Partido Nacionalista Galego*—PNG).

Leaders: Fernando GARCIA Agudín (President), Gen. José Manuel NOVO Rodríguez (Secretary General).

United Galicia (*Galicia Unida*—GU). The GU was formed in November 1986 to "open up a middle way in Galician politics".

Leader: José SANTOS Lago.

Valencian Union (*Unión Valenciana*—UV). The UV won a single congressional seat in 1986.

Leader: Miguel Ramón IZQUIERDO.

Other regional parties include the **Basque Revolutionary Party** (*Euskal Iraulzako Alderdia*—EIA), the **Basque Socialist Party** (*Partido Socialista de Euzkadi*—PSE), the **Canaries Independent Grouping** (*Agrupación Independiente de Canarias*—AIC), the **Canary People's Union** (*Unión del Pueblo Canario*—UPC), the **Cantabrian Regionalist Party** (*Partido Regionalista Cántabro*—PRC), the **Catalonian Centrists** (*Centristas de Cataluña*—CC), the **Communist Party of Valencian Peace** (*Partido Comunista del País Valenciano*—PCPV), the **Galician Centrists** (*Centristas de Galicia*—CG), the **Galician Left** (*Esquerda Galega*—EG), the **Galician Nationalist Block** (*Bloque Nacionalista Galejo*—PNG), the **Galician Socialist Party** (*Partido Socialista Galleqo*—PSG), the **Majorcan Assembly** (*Asamblea Majorera*—AM), the **Majorcan Union** (*Unió Mallorquina*—UM), the **Navarrese People's Union** (*Unión del Pueblo Navarro*—UPN), the **Spanish Socialist Workers' Party of Andalucía** (*Partido Socialista Obrero Español de Andalucía*—PSOEAO), the **Valencian Socialist Party** (*Partido Socialista del País Valenciano*—PSPV), and the **Valencian Union** (*Unión Valenciana*—UV). In mid-1985, the formation of a **Party of Muslim Democrats**, a group representing the Muslim community at Melilla, was announced by Aomar Mohamedi DUDU, a former provincial PSOE official, who in September 1986 accepted a position as special advisor to the minister of interior to represent the Muslim communities of Spain.

Extremist Groups:

The separatist **Basque Homeland and Liberty** (*Euzkadi ta Azkatasuna*—ETA) continued its attacks on both police officers and civilians in 1984–1987, largely through its military wing, the ETA-Militar. Other leftist groups include an ETA-M splinter, the **Autonomous Anticapitalist Commandos** (*Comandos Autónomos Anti-capitalista*—CAA) and the **Antifascist Resistance Groups of October 1** (*Grupos Resistencia Anti-fascista*

de Primero Octubre—GRAPO), although the government claimed in early 1985 that "all known members" of the latter organization had been placed under arrest. In 1987 a **Free Galician Guerrilla People's Army** (*Exército Guerrilleiro de Pobo Gallego Ceibe*—EGPGC) surfaced, claiming responsibility for a number of bomb attacks throughout Galicia. A Catalan separatist group, **Free Land** (*Terra Lliure*), has also been active, prompting the emergence in mid-1986 of a right-wing antiseparatist formation called the **Catalan Militia** (*Milicia Catalana*). Other right-wing groups include the **National Revolution** (*Revolución Nacional*—RN), **Warriors of Christ the King** (*Guerrilleros del Cristo Rey*—GCR), the **Apostolic Anticommunist Alliance** (*Alianza Apostólica Anti-comunista*—AAA), and the **Antiterrorist Liberation Groups** (*Grupos Antiterrorista de Liberacion*—GAL).

LEGISLATURE

Traditionally designated as the *Cortes* (Courts), the Spanish legislature was revived by General Franco in 1942 as a unicameral body (with strictly limited powers) and officially named *Las Cortes Españolas*. Initially, it had no directly elected members, but provision was made in 1967 for the election of 198 "family representatives". The essentially corporative character of the body was retained in 1971, when several new categories of indirectly elected and appointed members were added.

On November 19, 1976, the *Cortes* approved a long-debated Political Reform Bill, which, calling for a largely elected bicameral assembly, secured overwhelming public endorsement in a referendum held on December 15. The new *Las Cortes Generales,* consisting of a Senate and a Congress of Deputies, held its inaugural session on July 22, 1977, following a national election on June 15. The present *Cortes* was elected on October 28, 1982. Both houses serve four-year terms, subject to dissolution.

Senate (*Senado*). The upper house presently consists of 208 members: 4 from each of the 47 mainland provinces; 3 each from the larger islands of Gran Canaria, Mallorca, and Tenerife; 1 each from the islands or island groups of Ibiza-Formentera, Menorca, Fuerteventura, Gomera, Hierro, Lanzarote, and La Palma; and 2 each from the North African cities of Ceuta and Melilla. In addition, self-governing communities are entitled to elect 1 senator each, plus a further senator for each million inhabitants. The party distribution after the 1986 election was as follows: Spanish Socialist Workers' Party/Catalan Socialist Party, 124; Popular Coalition, 63; Convergence and Union, 8; Basque Nationalist Party, 7; Democratic and Social Center, 3; the Canaries Independent Grouping, 2; and the United People, 1.

President: José Federico CARVAJAL Pérez.

Congress of Deputies (*Congreso de los Diputados*). The lower house currently embraces 350 deputies elected on block lists by proportional representation. Each province is entitled to a minimum of 3 deputies, with 2 deputies each from the African enclaves of Ceuta and Melilla. At the election of June 22, 1986, the Spanish Socialist Workers' Party/Catalan Socialist Party returned 184 deputies; the Popular Coalition, 105; the Democratic and Social Center, 19; Convergence and Union, 18; the United Left, 7; the Basque Nationalist Party, 6; the United People, 5; the Basque Left, 2; and the Aragonese Regionalist Party, the Canaries Independent Grouping, the Galician Coalition, and the Valencian Union, 1 each.

President: Félix PONS Irazazabal.

CABINET

Prime Minister	Felipe González Márquez
Deputy Prime Minister	Alfonso Guerra González
Ministers	
Agriculture, Fisheries and Food	Carlos Romero Herrera
Congressional Relations	Virgílio Zapatéro
Culture and Government	
Spokesman	Javier Solana Madariaga

Defense	Narcís Serra i Serra
Education and Science	José María Maravall Herrero
Finance, Economy and Commerce	Carlos Solchaga Catalán
Foreign Affairs	Francisco Fernández Ordóñez
Health and Consumer Affairs	Julián García Vargas
Industry and Energy	Luis Carlos Croissier
Interior	José Barrionuevo Peña
Justice	Fernando Ledesma Bartret
Labor and Social Security	Manuel Chaves
Public Administration	Joaquin Almunia
Public Works and City Planning	Javier Sáenz de Cosculluela
Transportation, Tourism and Communications	Abel Caballero Alvarez
Governor, Bank of Spain	Mariano Rubio Jiménez

NEWS MEDIA

Under the 1978 constitution, the right to disseminate true information is guaranteed and prior censorship is outlawed. The most significant restriction is a 1979 law that limits the practice of journalism to those possessing a university degree in the subject.

Press. The following are dailies published at Madrid, unless otherwise noted: *El País* (348,000 daily, 613,000 Sunday), progressive; *ABC* (240,000 daily, 425,000 Sunday), Catholic monarchist; *La Vanguardia* (Barcelona, 220,000 daily, 340,000 Sunday), conservative; *El Alcázar* (145,000); *Diario-16* (128,000 daily, 180,000 Sunday); *El Correo Español y el Pueblo Vasco* (Bilbao, 108,000), independent; *Ya* (98,000 daily, 145,000 weekend), Catholic rightist; *La Gaceta del Norte* (Bilbao, 78,000 daily, 80,000 Sunday), independent; *ABC* (Seville, 57,000), monarchist; *Diario de Barcelona* (Barcelona, 30,000), founded 1792, monarchist. In October 1986, *Eguna,* the only daily ever published in Basque, resumed publication for the first time since 1937.

News agencies. Domestic agencies include *Agencia EFE,* a national agency controlled by the Ministry of Transportation and Communications; *Europa Press;* and *Logos Agencia de Información.* Numerous foreign agencies maintain bureaus at Madrid.

Radio and television. Responsibility for the regulation of broadcasting is vested in the *Dirección General de Radiodifusión y Televisión.* On October 1, 1977, the government announced that it was relinquishing its monopoly of radio news dissemination and that it would no longer be mandatory for the more than 200 stations to broadcast state news bulletins. On October 19 it was also reported that a joint government-opposition commission, *Medios de Communicación del Estado,* would assume direction of *Radiotelevisión Española* (RTVE), which operates the government radio network, *Radio Nacional Española,* and the country's state television network, *Televisión Española.* A bill that became law in April 1988 authorized three private television channels under the supervision of an independent broadcasting authority. There were approximately 14.9 million television receivers in 1987.

INTERGOVERNMENTAL REPRESENTATION

Ambassador to the US: Julian SANTAMARIA Ossorio.

US Ambassador to Spain: Reginald BARTHOLOMEW.

Permanent Representative to the UN: Don Francisco VILLAR.

IGO Memberships (Non-UN): ADB, ADF, AfDB, BIS, CCC, CEUR, EC, EIB, ESA, IADB, ICAC, ICCAT, ICES, ICM, ICO, IEA, IIC, ILZ, Inmarsat, Intelsat, Interpol, IOOC, IWC, IWSG, IWTC, NATO, OECD, PCA.

RELATED TERRITORIES

Virtually nothing remains of Spain's former colonial empire, the bulk of which was lost with the independence of the American colonies in the early nineteenth century.

Cuba, Puerto Rico, and the Philippines were lost in 1898. More recently, the West African territories of Río Muni and Fernando Póo became independent in 1968 as the state of Equatorial Guinea; Ifní was ceded to Morocco in 1969; and the Western (Spanish) Sahara was divided between Morocco and Mauritania in February 1976, the latter subsequently renouncing its claim on August 5, 1979.

Places of Sovereignty in North Africa (*Plazas de Soberanía del Norte de Africa*). These long-standing outposts on the Mediterranean coast of Morocco comprise the two enclaves of Ceuta and Melilla, officially referred to as *presidios,* or garrison towns, and three "Minor Places" (*Plazas Menores*): the tiny, volcanic Chafarinas and Alhucemas islands, and Peñón de Vélez de la Gomera, an arid garrison spot on the north Moroccan coast. Ceuta, with an area of 7.4 square miles (19.3 sq. km.), and Melilla, with an area of 4.7 square miles (12.3 sq. km.), are considered parts of metropolitan Spain and are organized as municipalities of the provinces of Cádiz and Málaga, respectively. The Minor Places are also under the jurisdiction of Málaga. In 1985, intense controversy was generated by Madrid's promulgation of a new alien residence law, which required all foreigners living in Spain to reapply for residence or face expulsion; the law, which was directed mainly at fugitives who had entered Spain prior to the conclusion of extradition treaties with a number of European countries, raised serious questions regarding the status of ethnic Moroccan Muslims, who had lived in the enclaves for generations. In February 1986, government and Muslim representatives (including members of *Terra Omnium,* a Melilla Muslim group) agreed to form a commission to conduct a census while examining "ways to integrate Muslims fully into Spanish society". In the meantime, Moroccan assertions of sovereignty over the territories has continued to irritate Rabat-Madrid relations.

SRI LANKA

Democratic Socialist Republic of Sri Lanka
Sri Lanka Prajatantrika Samajawadi Janarajaya

Political Status: Independent member of the Commonwealth since February 4, 1948; present constitution adopted August 6, 1978, with effect from September 7.

Area: 25,332 sq. mi. (65,610 sq. km.).

Population: 14,850,001 (1981C), 16,692,000 (1988E).

Major Urban Centers (1983E): COLOMBO (645,000); Dehiwala–Mount Lavinia (184,000); Jaffna (134,000); Kandy (121,000).

Official Language: Sinhala, Tamil, English. Tamil and English, formerly recognized as "national languages", became official languages under the India-Sri Lanka agreement of July 29, 1987.

Monetary Unit: Rupee (market rate March 1, 1988, 30.85 rupees = $1US).

President: Junius Richard JAYEWARDENE (United National Party); became Prime Minister following election of July 21, 1977; assumed presidency for a six-year term February 4, 1978, succeeding William GOPALLAWA; reelected October 20, 1982, under a constitutional change, approved August 26, permitting premature balloting.

Prime Minister: Ranasinghe PREMADASA (United National Party); designated by the President on February 6, 1978.

THE COUNTRY

The insular location of Sri Lanka (formerly Ceylon) off the coast of southeast India has not prevented the development of an ethnic and religious diversity comparable to that of other parts of southern Asia. Approximately 74 percent of the people are of Sinhalese extraction, descended from Aryan stock of northern India, while 18 percent are Tamil, akin to the Dravidian population of southern India; smaller minority groups, consisting primarily of Moors, Europeans, Burghers (Eurasians), and Veddah aborigines, account for the remaining 8 percent. Roughly two-thirds of the inhabitants are Buddhist, while about 19 percent are Hindu, 8 percent Christian, and 7 percent Muslim. The country's major ethnic problem has long centered on the Tamil population, which is divided into two groups: "Ceylon Tamils", whose ancestors have lived in Sri Lanka for many generations, and "Indian Tamils", whose forebears were brought to the island late in the nineteenth century as plantation laborers. The former, numbering nearly 2 million, predominate in the north and constitute about 40 percent of the population in the east. The latter, numbering about 900,000, are concentrated on the central tea plantations and, thus far, have not been prominently involved in the Tamil *eelam* (homeland) movement.

Most Ceylonese are engaged in agriculture, producing paddy, tea, coconuts, and rubber. The country's potential for heavy industry is limited by a serious deficiency of natural resources, and the economy is largely based on the export of tea, rubber, and coconut products, with tourism of increasing importance. A drop in world prices for tea and rubber in recent years has prevented significant improvement in foreign-exchange earnings, while a severe drought in 1987 necessitated a costly food import program. In response to these and other problems, the government has opened an Export Promotion Zone in the vicinity of the Colombo airport to stimulate light industry. It is also committed to a substantial increase in the hydroelectric and irrigation capability of the country's largest river, the Mahaweli Ganga. However, Tamil unrest since 1983 has adversely affected the country's economy, with widespread damage to factories, a substantial decrease in tourist arrivals (down approximately 75 percent from 1982 through 1987), and a negative foreign investment climate.

GOVERNMENT AND POLITICS

Political background. After nearly four and a half centuries of foreign domination, beginning with the Portuguese in 1505 and followed by the Dutch (1658–1815) and the British (1815–1948), Sri Lanka (then Ceylon) became an independent state within the Commonwealth on February 4, 1948. Beginning with the country's first parliamentary election in 1947, political power has oscillated between the moderate and generally pro-Western United National Party (UNP) and the Sri Lanka Freedom Party (SLFP), which has emphasized Buddhism, nationalism, "democratic socialism", and nonalignment in international affairs. Until 1956 the country was governed by the UNP, led successively by D.S. SENANAYAKE, his son Dudley SENANAYAKE, and Sir John KOTELAWALA. The SLFP, led by S.W.R.D. BANDARANAIKE, came to power in the 1956 election with an aggressively Sinhalese program reflecting the emergence of a nationalist, Sinhala-educated professional class, but a series of disorders culminated in the prime minister's assassination in 1959. The UNP formed a shaky minority government following the March 1960 general election but was unable to forestall a no-confidence vote shortly thereafter.

In July 1960 the SLFP, under the leadership of Mrs. Sirimavo R.D. BANDARANAIKE, wife of the former prime minister, won a near-majority in Parliament and organized an all-SLFP ministry. Ceylonese policy under her leadership acquired an increasingly nationalistic and anti-Western character, accompanied by allegations of rightist plots and attempted coups. The UNP, however, regained a leading position in the election of March 1965 and organized a coalition government under the premiership of party leader Dudley Senanayake. Subsequently, political power shifted back to the SLFP under Mrs. Bandaranaike, the UNP winning a bare 17 seats in a house of 157 members at balloting in May 1970.

Sri Lanka's democratic tradition received a serious setback in 1971 when a group calling itself the People's Liberation Front attempted to overthrow the government. The rank and file of the essentially Maoist Front was drawn largely from rural Sinhalese Buddhist youth. Most Ceylonese, however, declined to support the insurgents, and order was restored within a few weeks even though the underlying cause of the uprising, a deteriorating economy accompanied by a high unemployment rate, persisted.

In September 1975, Mrs. Bandaranaike reshuffled her coalition cabinet in an apparent dispute over the pace of nationalization, dropping three members of the Trotskyite *Lanka Sama Samaja* Party (LSSP), which went into opposition. The Communist Party of Sri Lanka (CPSL) also announced its intention to withdraw and work for the creation of a United Socialist Front. Throughout 1976, however, it remained a somewhat disenchanted participant in the Bandaranaike government, and the proposed USF never materialized.

An extremely bitter election campaign, in the course of which at least 9 persons were killed and nearly 60 injured in clashes between the leading parties, culminated on July 21, 1977, in an unprecedented victory for the UNP, which, led by J.R. JAYEWARDENE, obtained 142 of the 168 legislative seats with SLFP representation plummeting from 91 to 8. Following adoption by the UNP-dominated Assembly of a constitutional amendment providing for a French-style executive system (see Constitution and government, below), Jayewardene assumed the presidency on February 4, 1978, and named Ranasinghe PREMADASA prime minister two days later.

Having secured passage of a constitutional revision permitting the president to call an election after a minimum of four years in office, Jayewardene was reelected for a second six-year term on October 20, 1982 (with effect from February 4, 1983). On November 5, by a near-unanimous vote, the Parliament endorsed a government proposal that its own term be extended by six years to August 1989, subject to approval in a popular referendum. At the balloting on December 22, which occurred under a state of emergency, the measure was reported to have been approved by 54.7 percent of the participating voters.

In an apparent effort to blunt criticism of the postponement of general parliamentary renewal, the government sponsored by-elections on May 18, 1983, in 18 constituencies, most of which had shown signs of UNP decline since the 1977 vote. The UNP was credited with winning 14 of the seats, while the SLFP was awarded 3, and the small People's United Party (MEP), 1. However, the government's triumph did little to silence the increasingly restive Tamil minority. The situation reached a crisis in July, when the killing of 13 soldiers near the northern city of Jaffna set off a wave of anti-Tamil rioting that did not cease until early August. Over 400 people, mainly Tamils, died in the disturbances, which Jayewardene blamed on a "conspiracy" by socialist militants and separatists. Proscribing three leftist parties, the president also secured passage of a constitutional amendment banning all separatist activity and requiring MPs to take a loyalty oath. The 16 members of the Tamil United Liberation Front (TULF) responded by withdrawing from Parliament and were subsequently declared to have forfeited their seats.

As the violence momentarily subsided, Indian Prime Minister Indira Gandhi, under pressure from the southern Indian state of Tamil Nadu, sent an envoy to mediate between the Jayewardene government and the Tamil militants; however, most opposition leaders boycotted projected multiparty talks in October, and it was not until late December that the president agreed to invite the TULF to attend, without preconditions, a round table conference to be convened in late January 1984. A number of sessions of the "amity talks" were held during the year, with Tamil representatives advancing, as a minimal demand, the creation of an autonomus regional council encompassing the northern and eastern regions of the country, while at midyear Jayewardene countered with a proposal for a second legislative chamber. The latter was quickly rejected by the TULF, which reiterated that "We ask for an autonomous body in our own region, not for a second chamber at the center"; the president, however, indicated that he would continue to press for a solution based on bicameralism, on the ground that a national "consensus" had emerged in its favor.

During 1985, the level of violence intensified, with four of five Madras-based exile groups announcing in mid-April that they had formed a coalition to facilitate "armed revolutionary struggle for national independence" (see Political Parties, below). Meanwhile, the new Indian prime minister, Rajiv Gandhi, retreated somewhat from the overtly pro-Tamil posture of his recently assassinated mother, declaring that he opposed any attempt by the Tamils to establish an autonomous regime in Sri Lanka and launching a series of ultimately inconclusive talks between the rebels and Sri Lankan officials at Thimphu, Bhutan.

In December 1986 the government cut off essential northern services and in February 1987 mounted a major offensive against the rebels that yielded, after a lull in March and April, recapture of most of the Jaffna peninsula by late May. The Indian government, under strong domestic pressure to take action on the insurgent's behalf, responded by airlifting humanitarian supplies to the insurgents in early June, which drew a sharp diplomatic protest from Colombo. Subsequently, high-level discussion between the two governments at New Delhi yielded the remarkable announcement that Prime Minister Gandhi would fly to Colombo in late July to conclude a treaty that would bring Indian troops to Sri Lanka in support of a cease-fire and the establishment of an integrated North-East province government by an elected provincial council. On July 30, the day after conclusion of the accord, a 3,000-man Indian Peacekeeping Force (IPKF) arrived at Jaffna to assist in disarming the Tamils. However, the rebels turned over only a limited number of weapons and the IPKF found itself engaged in a major confrontation with the largest of the guerrilla groups, the Liberation Tigers of Tamil Eelam (LTTE). While the IPKF (augmented to a force of some 30,000) eventually gained control of much of the contested area, heavy fighting resumed in October. The LTTE failed to respond to an Indian call to surrender during a unilateral cease-fire in late November, and by early 1988 it was reported that IPKF troop strength had risen to 55,000, with no end in sight to a conflict that some had characterized as "India's Vietnam".

Constitution and government. In May 1972, under the country's second constitution since independence, Ceylon was redesignated the Republic of Sri Lanka, retaining independent membership within the Commonwealth. Under the present constitution (adopted August 16, 1978, as a codification and enlargement of a series of constitutional amendments approved October 20, 1977), the name was further changed to Democratic Socialist Republic of Sri Lanka and the British-style parliamentary system was abandoned in favor of a "Gaullist" presidential-parliamentary system. The most visible feature of the present system is the concentration of powers in a "strong" president who may serve no more than two six-year terms, with all but the initial incumbent to be popularly elected (currently at the expiry of no less than four years of a normal mandate). The president appoints a prime minister and, in consultation with the latter, other senior administrative officials, the only restriction being that all ministers and deputy ministers must hold legislative seats. Should Parliament reject an appropriations bill or approve a no-confidence motion, the president may appoint a new government.

The legislative term is six years, subject to presidential dissolution, although the life of the present body (elected in 1977) was extended by an additional six years in 1982. At the next election, which presumably will occur in 1988 or 1989, its size is to increase from 168 to 196 members. A constitutional amendment passed in August 1983 requires all members of Parliament to take an oath of loyalty to the unified state of Sri Lanka and bans all activity advocating "the division of the state".

Judges of the Supreme Court and the Court of Appeal are appointed by the president and are removable only on grounds of proven misbehavior or incapacity, after presentation to the president of a parliamentary motion supported by an absolute majority of members. There is also a presidentially appointed parliamentary commissioner for administration (ombudsman), who is expected to investigate complaints of wrongdoing by public officials.

Administratively, Sri Lanka is divided into 22 districts, each headed by a government agent who is a member of the National Administrative Service. Municipalities have urban or town councils, while rural areas are administered by elected village councils. In addition, the government committed itself in 1980 to the establishment of District Development Councils as vehicles of decentralized policy-making and implementation.

Foreign relations. Sri Lanka has consistently maintained a nonaligned position in world politics despite its membership in the Commonwealth and a mutual defense agreement that grants the United Kingdom the right to maintain naval and air bases, as well as land forces, in the country. While the Jayewardene government has stressed Sri Lanka's economic similarity and cultural affinity with Southeast Asia, the country's application for admission to the Association of Southeast Asian Nations (ASEAN) was rejected in 1982 on geographical grounds. The action helped to precipitate the 1985 launching of the South Asian Association for Regional Cooperation (SAARC), of which Sri Lanka was a founding member.

The island state's major foreign-policy problems since independence have involved relations with India. Conflicting claims to Kachchativu Island in the Palk Strait, which separates the two countries, were resolved in 1974, India yielding its claim and Sri Lanka agreeing to permit Indian fishermen and pilgrims access to the island without having to obtain travel documents or visas. The Palk Strait accord was supplemented on March 23, 1976, by a more general agreement on maritime economic zones.

Much more explosive has been the situation involving Sri Lanka's Tamil dissidents, who have strong ties to some 50 million Tamils in southern India. As ethnic violence on the island escalated, relations between Colombo and New Delhi became strained, largely because of the use of Indian territory as a refuge and staging area by Tamil guerrilla groups. By 1986 the activities of the LTTE in the Indian state of Tamil Nadu were encountering increased local disenchantment and the rebels transferred most of their operations to Sri Lanka's Jaffna area, thereby exposing themselves to more effective counterinsurgency action by government forces. However, neither Colombo nor its newfound Indian ally had succeeded by early 1988 in eliminating their guerrilla capability, with the extent of its military involvement constituting a growing source of embarrassment to the Gandhi administration.

Current issues. As of mid-1988 observers remained uncertain as to the true motivation for Indian involvement in the Sri Lankan conflict, though some felt that New Delhi feared a possible "spill-over" into Tamil Nadu should the insurgency succeed. There was little disagreement as to the intense pressure on President Jayewardene that the action had generated. Even before the July accord, opposition Sinhalese groups had vehemently protested Colombo's inability to end the stalemate, generating fear that the radical People's Liberation Front (see Political Groups, below)

might, as in 1971, spearhead an effort to overthrow the government. Numerous Front activists were arrested during 1987, while the organization was charged with complicity in an attempted assassination of the president in August, as well as of the killing of UNP chairman Harsha Abeywardene in December. Given the heightened degree of ethnic intransigence, a "Cyprus-style" de facto partition of the island loomed as a far from distant possibility.

POLITICAL GROUPS

Governing Parties:

United National Party (UNP). The UNP, a democratic-socialist party, advocates a moderate line and the avoidance of a narrowly "communal" posture. It strongly supported republican status and the adoption of Sinhala as the official language. Having survived virtual annihilation as a legislative force in 1970, the party swept 142 of 168 Assembly seats in July 1977 and remained in power by subsequent extension of the parliamentary term to August 1989. Its chairman and former secretary general, Harsha Abeywardene, was assassinated on the outskirts of Colombo in December 1987.

Leaders: Junius Richard JAYEWARDENE (President of the Republic and of the Party), Ranasinghe PREMADASA (Prime Minister), Nandalal FERNANDO (General Secretary).

Ceylon Workers' Congress (CWC). The CWC is a Tamil group that participated in formation of the Tamil United Front (below) in 1976. Its president and only parliamentary member, Savumyamoorthy Thondaman, joined the government in September 1978 as minister for rural industrial development. The CWC is the main spokesman for the Indian Tamils who work primarily as laborers on centrally located tea plantations and in recent years has attempted to prevent their forging links with the insurgents in the north and east.

Leaders: Savumyamoorthy THONDAMAN (President), Muthu Sangaralingam SELLASAMY (General Secretary).

Opposition Parties:

Tamil United Liberation Front (TULF). The TULF was initially organized as the Tamil Liberation Front (*Tamil Vimukthi Peramuna*—TVP) in May 1976 by a number of Tamil groups, including (in addition to the CWC) the **Federal Party** (*Illankai Tamil Arasu Kadchi*—ITAK), the **National Liberation Front** (*Jatika Vimukthi Peramuna*—JVP), the **Tamil Congress**, and the **Moslem United Front**. ITAK and the Tamil Congress had previously been partners in a coalition organized prior to the 1970 election as the Tamil United Front, while the JVP had once been in partnership with the People's United Front (below).

The TULF stated in its 1977 election manifesto that its successful candidates would serve as the constituent assembly of a proposed Tamil state (*Tamil Eelam*). At the July election the Front obtained 16 seats in the northern and eastern provinces, becoming the largest opposition group in the National Assembly. It did not present a candidate at the 1982 presidential balloting.

Having previously declared their intention to resign from Parliament in protest at the extension of the existing body beyond its normal term, the TULF MPs failed to appear for an oath renouncing separatism on August 9, 1983, and their seats were thereupon declared constitutionally vacant. Despite pressure from militants, the TULF has maintained an essentially moderate posture, engaging in talks with the government on a possible compromise settlement. During 1986, TULF participated in discussions at Colombo that ultimately failed because of its inability to influence guerrilla groups, particularly the LTTE (below).

Leaders: M. SIVASITHAMPARAM (President), R. SAMBANTHAN (Vice President), J.R.P. SURIYAPPERUMA (JVP), G.G. PONNAMBALAM (Tamil Congress), Appapillai AMIRTHALINGAM (General Secretary).

Sri Lanka Freedom Party (SLFP). The SLFP, a leading advocate of republican status prior to adoption of the 1972 constitution, stands for a neutralist foreign policy and the progressive nationalization of industry. Although winning a clear majority of seats in the House of Representatives in the election of 1970, it governed in coalition with the *Lanka Sama*

Samaja and Communist parties until September 1975. Its legislative representation plummeted from 90 seats to 8 in the election of July 1977. In October 1980 former prime minister Bandaranaike was deprived of her civil rights for a seven-year period for alleged corruption while in office. The action made her ineligible as a presidential candidate in October 1982, though she was permitted to participate in the subsequent referendum campaign. Despite the political limitation, she remained active in party affairs, causing a split between her supporters and those of the nominal president, Maithripala Senanayake. Mrs. Bandaranaike's rights were restored by means of a presidential "free pardon" issued on January 1, 1986, and she immediately launched a campaign for early general elections. In August 1986 the SLFP joined with some 20 groups, as well as prominent Buddhist leaders, in establishing the **Movement for the Defense of the Nation** (MDN) to oppose government policy that "conceded too much" on the Tamil question.

Although its parliamentary representation had dropped to 6 by late 1982, the SFLP gained 3 additional seats in the May 1983 by-election and became the formal opposition after the subsequent TULF withdrawal.

Leaders: Sirimavo R.D. BANDARANAIKE (former Prime Minister and President of the Party), Anura BANDARANAIKE (Leader of the Opposition), S. DASSANAYAKE (Secretary), Maithripala SENANA-YAKE (leader of dissident faction).

Sri Lanka People's Party (SLPP). Formed in January 1984 by the younger daughter of Sirimavo Bandaranaike, Chandrika Kumaranatunge, and her husband, Vijaya, the SLPP is a socialist grouping that accused the SLFP, under Anura Bandaranaike, of "dancing to his excellency's [the president's] tune". By 1987, however, the party, which cooperates informally with the SLCP and the LSSP (below), had become supportive of the government's approach to a negotiated settlement of the Tamil question. Vijaya Kumaranatung, a highly popular film star, was assassinated at Colombo on February 16, 1988.

Leaders: Chandrika KUMARANATUNGE, Y.P. de SILVA (General Secretary).

Communist Party of Sri Lanka (CPSL). Sri Lanka's official Communist party has consistently urged the nationalization of all banks, estates, and factories, and the use of national languages rather than English. Differences within the party membership prevented it from taking a clear position on Sino-Soviet relations, but recent trends have yielded a strongly pro-Soviet posture. During 1976 the CPSL proposed a United Socialist Front with what it called the "centralized Left" in the SLFP. The initiative resulted in the formation in April 1977 of the United Left Front (ULF), comprising the SLCP, the LSSP (below), and the PDP (below); however, the ULF obtained no Assembly seats at the July election. The party's longtime president, Dr. S.A. Wickremasinghe, died at Moscow in August 1981. The CPSL supported Hector Kobbekaduwa, the SLFP presidential candidate, in 1982.

In July 1983, four party officials were arrested on unspecified charges, and the CPSL was banned along with the NSSP and the JVP (below); however, the officials were released in late September and the ban lifted in mid-October. The CPSL is currently allied with the SLPP and the LSSP in supporting the government's posture on Tamil issues. On the other hand, in April 1986 an **Eelam Revolutionary Communist Party** (its links, if any, to the SLCP being unknown) claimed responsibility for sabotaging a dam at Kantalai in Trincomalee district.

Leaders: Pieter KEUNEMAN (Chairman), Sarath MUTTETUWE-GAMA, Kattorge P. de SILVA (General Secretary).

Ceylon Equal Society Party (*Lanka Sama Samaja* Party—LSSP). The Trotskyite LSSP, which entered into a coalition with Mrs. Bandaranaike's SLFP in 1964, opposes communalism and advocates complete nationalization, including that of foreign-owned estates and other companies. The party, which went into opposition in September 1975, lost all 19 of its former legislative seats as a member of the ULF at the election of July 1977. Its longtime leader, Dr. N.M. Perera, died in August 1979. It has joined the SLCP and the SLPP in supporting measures to negotiate a settlement with Tamil activists.

Leaders: Dr. Colvin R. de SILVA (1982 presidential candidate), Bernard SOYSA (General Secretary).

New Equal Society Party (*Nava Sama Samaja* Party—NSSP). A splinter of the LSSP, the NSSP was banned for alleged seditious activity in July 1983 and, unlike the SCLP, remains proscribed.

Leaders: Vasudeva NANAYAKKARA (1982 presidential candidate), Wickremabahu KARUNARATNE (General Secretary).

People's United Front (*Mahajana Eksath Peramuna*—MEP). The MEP, a left-wing party, was formerly allied with the JVP (see under TULF, above). Strongly Sinhalese and Buddhist, it has long advocated the nationalization of foreign estates. It gained one parliamentary seat in May 1983.

Leader: Dinesh P.R. GUNAWARDENE (General Secretary).

Democratic Workers' Congress (DWC). The DWC was formed in 1978 to promote the elimination of economic exploitation and social inequality. It has no parliamentary representation, but participated in the all-party talks of early 1984.

Leaders: Abdul AZIZ (President), Vythilingam Palanisamy GANESAN (Secretary).

People's Democratic Party—PDP (*Mahajana Prajathanthra*). The PDP was organized in March 1977 by six dissident members of the SLFP. It participated as a member of the ULF in the election of July 1977, securing no Assembly seats.

Leader: Nanada ELLSWELA.

People's Liberation Front (*Janatha Vimukthi Peramuna*—JVP). The People's Liberation Front (not to be confused with the National Liberation Front—JVP, above) is a Maoist organization that was responsible for the terrorist attacks and attempted overthrow of the government in April 1971. A variety of subsequent clandestine groups, including the "Black Lamp" and "East Wing Group", were presumed to be made up of JVP members operating under new names to disguise their connection with the earlier uprising. The Front regained legal status following the lifting of the state of emergency on February 16, 1977, and emerged as the third-ranked party at Colombo as the result of local balloting in May 1979. It was again proscribed after the July 1983 riots and was blamed for the assassination of UNP chairman Abeywardene in December 1987.

Leaders: Rohana WIJEWEERA (1982 presidential candidate), Lionel BOPAGE (General Secretary).

Sri Lanka Muslim Congress (SLMC). The SLMC, which was formed in 1980, declared itself a political party at a conference convened in December 1986 to represent Muslim interests in the negotiations for a political settlement of the Tamil question. There are about one million Muslims in Sri Lanka, 300,000 in the eastern area which Tamil militants want declared part of a Tamil province.

Leader: M. ASHRAFF.

Guerrilla Groups:

All the groups listed below are Tamil separatist, the first four joining an antigovernment coalition, the Eelam National Liberation Front—ENLF, in April 1985. Less than a year later, the Front had become essentially moribund, the LTTE having withdrawn from active participation in early 1986 and subsequently engaging in internecine conflict with its erstwhile allies.

Liberation Tigers of Tamil Eelam (LTTE). Founded in 1972 as the Tamil New Tigers, the LTTE is the largest of the guerrilla groups, with an estimated 3,000 well-armed soldiers. For many years its leadership was based in Madras, India, but by 1987 the LTTE had assumed effective control of much of northern Sri Lanka, including Jaffna, prior to the Indian military incursion at midyear.

The LTTE has proposed a socialist Tamil homeland, although ideology has recently been overshadowed by military considerations. In 1986 the LTTE, long regarded as the most hard-line of the Tamil groups, engaged in a bloody campaign against its former allies, which it charged with engaging in drug dealing and banditry. By 1987 the LTTE had become the principal champion of the Tamil cause, its intransigent posture being viewed as the major barrier to political settlement with Colombo.

In January 1987, the LTTE announced that it had launched a political party, the **Liberation Tigers of Tamil Eelam People's Front**, which would operate under the aegis of the parent group.

Leaders: Velupillai PRABAKHARAN, Anton S. BALASINGHAM.

Eelam People's Revolutionary Liberation Front (EPRLF). Among its other activities, the military wing of the EPRLF, the People's Liberation Army (PLA), was responsible for the kidnapping of two American development workers at Jaffna in May 1984. The EPRLF was the object of a full-scale LTTE offensive in the northern and eastern provinces during late 1986, although casualties appeared to be heaviest among the organization's civilian wing.

Leaders: K. PADMANABHA (General Secretary), Douglas ANAND (Military Commander).

Eelam Revolutionary Organization of Students (EROS). Organized in early 1985, EROS was subsequently charged with a number of bombings at Colombo and elsewhere. It has been reported to be courting support from Indian Tamil communities by means of grass roots education.

Leader: Velupillai BALAKUMARAN.

Tamil Eelam Liberation Organization (TELO). The TELO resulted from the merger, at Madras in April 1984, of a preexisting group of the same name with the Eelam Revolutionary Organization (ERO) and the Eelam People's Revolutionary Front (EPRF). The organization was reported to have been "virtually eliminated" in battles with the LTTE in 1986, with its principal leader, Mohan Sri SABARATNAM, apparently among the estimated 300 casualties.

Leader: A. SELYAM (General Secretary).

People's Liberation Organization of Tamil Eelam (PLOTE). PLOTE is the most important of the separatist groups not involved in the May 1985 coalition. Attempts were made on the lives of a number of its leaders at Madras in March 1985, apparently by the LTTE, whose attacks in 1986 severely curtailed PLOTE rebel activity.

Leaders: Uma MAHESHWARAM (General Secretary), T. JOTH-EASWARAM (Military Commander).

LEGISLATURE

Sri Lanka's former House of Representatives, originally elected for a five-year term on May 27, 1970, was reconstituted as a unicameral National State Assembly on promulgation of the 1972 republican constitution, which also provided for extension of the existing legislative term to 1977, with six-year terms mandated thereafter. Following the election of July 21, 1977, the United National Party held 142 seats; the Tamil United Liberation Front, 16; the Sri Lanka Freedom Party, 8; and the Ceylon Workers' Congress, 1; with 1 vacancy.

Under the 1978 basic law, the Assembly was redesignated as the **Parliament.** Future elections (of 196 members) were to have been conducted on the basis of proportional representation with a provision that parties could designate successors to members lost by death, resignation, or expulsion, making by-elections unnecessary. The latter was modified in early 1979 to permit the retention of his seat by a member changing his party affiliation.

The referendum of December 1982 extended the life of the existing Parliament by another six years to August 1989, while the constitutional amendment of February 1983 reinstated by-elections as a means of filling vacancies. Following the by-election of May 18, 1983, and the withdrawal of 16 TULF members at the conclusion of the parliamentary session in August, the UNP held 140 seats; the SFLP, 9; and the CWC, the SLCP, and the MEP, 1 each.

Speaker: E.L. SENANAYAKE.

CABINET

Prime Minister	Ranasinghe Premadasa
Ministers	
Agricultural Development and Research	D.B. Wijetunga
Cultural Affairs	E.L.B. Hurulle
Defense	J.R. Jayewardene
Education	Ranil Wickremasinghe
Emergency Civil Administration	Ranasinghe Premadasa
Energy	J.R. Jayewardene
Finance and Planning	M.N.M. Naina Marikkar
Fisheries	Festus Perera
Food and Cooperatives	D.B. Wijetunga
Foreign Affairs	A.C.S. Hameed
Health	Dr. Ranjit Atapattu
Higher Education	J.R. Jayewardene
Highways	Ranasinghe Premadasa
Home Affairs	K.W. Devanayagam
Industries and Scientific Affairs	N. Denzil Ferdinando
Janatha (People's) Estate Development	J.R. Jayewardene
Justice	Nissanka Wijeratne
Labor	Prema Chandra Imbulana
Land, Land Development and Mahaweli Development	Gamini Dissanayake
Local Government, Housing and Construction	Ranasinghe Premadasa
Manpower Mobilization and National Service	Ranil Wickremasinghe
National Security	Lalith W. Athulathmudali
Parliamentary Affairs	(Vacant)
Plan Implementation	J.R. Jayewardene
Plantation Industries	W.G. Montague Jayewickreme
Posts and Telecommunications	Sunil Abeyessundera
Power	P. Dayaratne
Private Omnibus Transport	M.H. Mohamed
Public Administration	W.G. Montague Jayewickreme
Regional Development	Chelliah Rajadurai
Rural Development	Irene Wimala Kannangara
Rural Industrial Development	Savumyamoorthy Thondaman
Security for Commercial and Industrial Establishments	M.H. Mohamed
Social Services	Asoka Karunaratne
State Plantations	J.R. Jayewardene
Textile Industries	T. Wijepala Mendis
Trade and Shipping	M.S. Amarasiri
Transport	M.H. Mohamed
Women's Affairs and Teaching Hospitals	Sunethra Ranasinghe
Youth Affairs and Employment	Ranil Wickremasinghe
Without Portfolio	Bakeer Markar
Minister of State for Information, Broadcasting and Tourism	Anandatissa De Alwis
Governor, Central Bank	Dr. Warnasana Rasaputram

NEWS MEDIA

Press. Varying degrees of censorship and other forms of media control have prevailed since 1973. Most recently, the Times of Ceylon newspaper group, which had been nationalized in 1977, was closed down in February 1985 for alleged mismanagement; immediately affected were the *Sunday Times* and *Lankadipa*, both the *Times of Ceylon* and the *Ceylon Daily Mirror* having ceased publication in 1975 and 1984, respectively. The following are Sinhalese dailies published at Colombo, unless otherwise noted: *Rivirasa* (317,000), weekly; *Silumina* (254,000), weekly; *Dinamina* (140,000); *The Island* (115,000), in English and Sinhala; *Dawasa* (108,000); *Ceylon Daily News* (65,000), in English; *Chintamani* (59,400), Tamil weekly; *Virakesari* (35,000 daily; 45,000 Sunday, published as *Virakesari Vaarveliyeedu*), in Tamil; *Aththa* (28,000), Communist Party organ; *Mithran* (18,000 daily; 25,000 Sunday, published as *Mithran Varamaler*), in Tamil; *Thinakaren* (14,000 daily; 21,000 Sunday, published as *Thinakaran Vaaramanjari*), in Tamil; *Ceylon Observer* (10,000 daily, 93,000 Sunday), in English.

News agencies. The domestic facilities are the National News Agency of Sri Lanka (*Lankapuvath*), the Press Trust of Ceylon, the Press Association of Ceylon, and the Sandesa News Agency; a number of foreign bureaus maintain offices at Colombo.

Radio and television. The public Sri Lanka Broadcasting Corporation controlled both national and commercial transmission to the nation's 3.2 million radio receivers in 1987. The Voice of America operates a station at Colombo, as does the Missionary Trans World Radio. Television programming, initiated in 1979, is received by approximately 750,000 sets.

INTERGOVERNMENTAL REPRESENTATION

Ambassador to the US: Susantha de ALWIS.

US Ambassador to Sri Lanka: James W. SPAIN.

Permanent Representative to the UN: Daya PERERA.

IGO Memberships (Non-UN): ADB, ANRPC, APCC, CCC, CP, CWTH, ICO, Inmarsat, INRO, Intelsat, Interpol, ITPA, NAM, PCA, SAARC.

SUDAN

The Republic of Sudan
Jumhuriyat al-Sudan

Political Status: Independent republic established in 1956; revolutionary military regime instituted in 1969; one-party system established in 1971; constitution of May 8, 1973, suspended following military coup of April 6, 1985.

Area: 967,494 sq. mi. (2,505,813 sq. km.).

Population: 20,564,364 (1983C), 24,205,000 (1988E).

Major Urban Centers (1983C): KHARTOUM (476,218); Omdurman (526,287); North Khartoum (341,146); Port Sudan (206,727).

Official Language: Arabic (English has been designated the "principal" language in the Southern Region).

Monetary Unit: Sudanese Pound (market rate March 1, 1988, 4.50 pounds = $1US).

Chairman of the Supreme Council (Head of State): Ahmad al-MIRGHANI (Democratic Unionist Party); designated by the Constituent Assembly on March 6, 1986, succeeding the Chairman of the Transitional Military Council, Gen. 'Abd al-Rahman Muhammad al-Hassan SIWAR AL-DAHAB (SWAREDDAHAB).

Prime Minister: Dr. Sadiq al-MAHDI (Umma Party); confirmed by the Constituent Assembly on May 6, 1986, to succeed Dr. al-Gizouli DAFALLA, following election of April 1–12; reappointed on June 3, 1987, and on April 27, 1988.

THE COUNTRY

The largest country in Africa, Sudan borders on eight neighboring states as well as the Red Sea and forms part of the transitional zone between the continent's largely desert north and its densely forested, subtropical south. The White Nile flows north for almost 2,500 miles, from the Ugandan border, past the river's union with the Blue Nile near Khartoum, to Egypt above Aswan. Approximately 70 percent of the population is Arab-Islamic and occupies the northern two-thirds of the country, while the predominantly Black south is both christian and animist. The geographic and ethnic cleavage has yielded political discord marked by prolonged periods of southern rebellion.

The economy is predominantly agricultural, although arable land is limited and only a small part of it is actually cultivated. Cotton is the most important cash crop, followed by gum arabic, of which Sudan produces four-fifths of the world supply. Other crops include sesame seeds, peanuts, castor beans, sorghum, wheat, and sugarcane. The country has major livestock-producing potential and large numbers of camels and sheep are raised for export. At present, industrial development is largely limited to the processing of agricultural products and the manufacture of light consumer goods. In recent years, the country has experienced persistent drought, while the fighting in the south has immobilized relief efforts, halted the planned exploitation of recently-discovered oil reserves, and hindered a major irrigation project. The result has been Africa's largest external debt (in excess of $13 billion) and excessive reliance on economic aid (provided largely by Saudi Arabia, West Germany, Britain, and the United States). Development programs are further hampered by a two-fold refugee crisis; more than one million persons have fled to Sudan from fighting in neighboring countries, particularly Ethiopia, while up to 400,000 have sought refuge at Khartoum from the southern insurgency.

GOVERNMENT AND POLITICS

Political background. Historically known as the land of Kush, Sudan was conquered and unified by Egypt in 1820–1821. Under the leadership of the MAHDI ("awaited religious leader"), opposition to Egyptian administration broke into open revolt in 1881; the revolt had succeeded by 1885, and the Mahdist state controlled the region until its reconquest by an Anglo-Egyptian force in 1896–1898. Thereafter, Sudan was governed as an Anglo-Egyptian condominium, becoming self-governing in 1954 and fully independent on January 1, 1956, under a transitional constitution that provided for a democratic parliamentary regime. Civilian government, led successively by Isma'il al-AZHARI and 'Abdallah KHALIL, was overthrown in November 1958 by Lt. Gen. Ibrahim 'ABBUD, whose military regime was itself dislodged following protest demonstrations in October and November 1964. The restored constitutional regime, headed in turn by Sir al-Khatim KHALIFA, Muhammad Ahmad MAHGUB, and Dr. Sadiq al-MAHDI (a descendant of the nineteenth century religious leader), was weakened both by political party instability and by revolt in the southern provinces.

Beginning in 1955 as a protest against Arab-Muslim domination, the southern insurgency rapidly assumed the proportions of a civil war. Led by the *Anyanya* (scorpion) movement under the command of Joseph LAGU, the revolt resulted in military reprisals and the flight of thousands of refugees to neighboring countries. While moderate southern parties continued to seek regional autonomy within the framework of a united Sudan, exile groups in neighboring countries worked for complete independence, and a so-called "Provisional Government of Southern Sudan" was established in January 1967 under the leadership of Agrev JADEN, a prominent exile leader.

An apparent return to normalcy under a new Mahgub government was interrupted in May 1969 by a military coup organized by a group of nationalist, left-wing officers led by (then) Col. Ja'far Muhammad NUMAYRI. With Numayri assuming the leadership of a ten-man Revolutionary Council, a new civilian administration that included a number of Communists and extreme leftists was formed by former chief justice Abubakr 'AWADALLA. Revolutionary activity continued, however, including successive Communist attempts in 1969 and 1971 to overthrow the Numayri regime. The latter effort succeeded for three days, after which Numayri regained power with Egyptian and Libyan help and instituted reprisals that included the execution of 'Abd al-Khaliq MAHGUB, the Communist Party's secretary general.

Reorganization of the government continued with the issuance of a temporary constitution in August 1971, followed by Numayri's election to the presidency in September. A month later, in an effort to consolidate his position, Numayri dissolved the Revolutionary Council and established the Sudanese Socialist Union (SSU) as the only recognized political party. Of equal significance was the ratification in April 1973 of a negotiated settlement that brought the southern rebellion to an end. The terms of the agreement, which provided for an autonomous Southern Sudan, were included in a new national constitution that became effective May 8, 1973. In November the Southern Region balloted for a Regional People's Assembly, while the first national election under the new basic law took place in May 1974 for a 250-member National People's Assembly.

In September 1975 rebel army personnel led by a paratroop officer, Lt. Col. Hassan Husayn 'USMAN, seized the government radio station at Omdurman in an attempted coup. President Numayri subsequently blamed Libya for instigating the uprising, which was quickly suppressed. The attack had been preceded by an army mutiny at Akobo on the Ethiopian border in March, and was followed by an uprising at Khartoum in July 1976 that reportedly claimed 300 lives. At a news conference in London on August 4, former prime minister Mahdi, on behalf of the outlawed Sudanese National Front (SNF), a coalition of former centrist and rightist parties that had been organized in late 1969, accepted responsibility for having organized the July rebellion but denied that it had involved foreign mercenaries.

In the months that followed, President Numayri undertook a broad-ranged effort to seek accommodation with the dissidents. In July 1977 a number of SNF leaders, including Dr. Mahdi, returned from abroad and were immediately appointed to the Central Committee of the SSU. A year later, the Rev. Philip Abbas GHABUSH, titular president of the Front, also expressed his conviction that the government was committed to the building of "a genuine democracy in Sudan" and ordered the dissolution of both the internal and external wings of the organization.

In early 1980 the north was divided into five new regions to provide for more effective local self-government, and in October 1981 the president dissolved both the National Assembly at Khartoum and the Southern Regional Assembly to facilitate decentralization on the basis of new regional bodies to which certain legislative powers would be devolved. Concurrently, he appointed Gen. Gasmallah 'Abdallah RASSA, a southern Muslim, as interim president of the Southern Region's High Executive Council (HEC) in place of Abel ALIER, who nonetheless continued as second vice president of the Republic. Immediately thereafter a plan was advanced to divide the south into three regions based on the historic provinces of Bahr al-Ghazal, Equatoria, and Upper Nile.

The projected redivision of the south yielded three regional blocs: a "unity" group led by Vice President Alier of the numerically dominant Dinka tribe, who branded the scheme a repudiation of the Addis Ababa agreement; a "divisionist" group led by the former rebel commander General Lagu of the Wahdi tribe of eastern Equatoria; and a compromise group, led by Clement MBORO and Samuel ARU Bol, that styled itself "Change Two" (C2) after an earlier "Wind for Change Alliance" that had opposed Alier's election to the HEC presidency. None of the three obtained a majority at an April 1982 election to the Southern Regional Assembly, and on June 23 a divisionist, Joseph James TOMBURA, was designated by the Assembly as regional president with C2 backing (the alliance being styled "C3"). Six days later, President Numayri named General Lagu to succeed Alier as second vice president of the Republic. Earlier, on April 11, Maj. Gen. 'Umar Muhammad al-TAYYIB (who had been designated third vice president in October 1981) was named to the first vice presidency in succession to Lt. Gen. 'Abd al-Majid Hamid KHALIL, who had been dismissed on January 25.

As expected, President Numayri was nominated for a third term by an SSU congress in February 1983, and reelected by a national plebiscite held April 15–26. In June, the tripartite division of the south was formally implemented, with both the HEC and southern assembly being abolished.

In the face of renewed rebellion in the south and rapidly deteriorating economic conditions that prompted food riots and the launching of a general strike at Khartoum, a group of army officers, led by Gen. 'Abd al-Rahman SIWAR AL-DAHAB, seized power on April 6, 1985, while President Numayri was returning from a trip to the United States. The ouster was attributed in part to opposition by southerners and some urban northerners to the adoption in September 1983 of a harsh Islamic penal code (*shari'a*), which included a ban on alcohol and mandated punishment such as amputation.

On April 9, after discussions between the officers and representatives of a civilian National Alliance for the Salvation of the Country (NASC) had proved inconclusive, General Siwar Al-Dahab announced the formation of a 14-member Transitional Military Council (TMC), with himself as chairman and Gen. Taq al-Din 'Abdallah FADUL as his deputy. After further consultation with NASC leaders, Dr. al-Gizouli DAFFALA, who had played a prominent role in organizing the pre-coup demonstrations, was named on April 22 to head an interim Council of Ministers. On May 25, a seven-member southern cabinet was appointed that included representatives of the three historic areas (henceforth to be known as "administrative regions"). Concurrently, the Sudanese People's Liberation Army (SPLA), which had become the primary rebel force in the south under the leadership of Col. John GARANG, resumed antigovernment military activity (see SPLM under Political Parties, below).

Adhering to its promise to hold a national election within a year, the TMC sponsored legislative balloting on April 1–12, 1986, despite continued insurgency in much of the south that precluded returns in 41 districts. The new body, serving as both a Constituent and Legislative Assembly, convened on April 26, but was unable to agree on the composition of a Supreme (Presidential) Council and the designation of a prime minister until May 6, with a coalition government being formed under former prime minister al-Mahdi of the Umma Party (UP) on May 15. The UP's principal partner was the Democratic Unionist Party (DUP), which had finished second in the Assembly balloting. Although several southern parties were awarded cabinet posts, most "African bloc" deputies have since boycotted Assembly activity because of alleged underrepresentation and a lack of progress toward *shari'a* repeal (see Current issues, below).

The Council of Ministers was dissolved on May 13, 1987, primarily because of a split within the DUP that had weakened the government's capacity to implement policy decisions. A new government was nonetheless formed on June 3 with little change in personnel. On August 22 the DUP formally withdrew from the coalition because of a dispute over an appointment to the Supreme Council, although indicating that it would continue to cooperate with the UP. Eight months later the DUP rejected a proposal by al-Mahdi for formation of a more broadly-based administration that would include the opposition National Islamic Front (NIF). Undaunted, the prime minister resigned on April 16, 1988, to make way for a government of "national reconciliation". Reappointed on April 27, he issued an appeal for all of the parties to join in a proposed national constitutional conference to decide on the role of Islam in a future state structure and formed a new administration that included the NIF on May 14.

Constitution and government. The constitution of 1973 provided for a strong presidential form of government. Nominated by the Sudanese Socialist Union for a six-year term, the president appointed all other executive officials and served as supreme commander of the People's Armed Forces. Legislative authority was vested in the National People's Assembly, a unicameral body that was partially elected and partially appointed.

The Southern Sudan Regional Constitution, abrogated by the June 1983 redivision, provided for a single autonomous region governed, in nonreserved areas, by the president of a High Executive Council (cabinet) who was responsible to a Regional People's Assembly. Each of the three subsequent regions in the south, like the five in the north, was administered by a centrally appointed governor, acting on the advice of a local People's Assembly. In a move that intensified southern dissent, President Numayri announced in June 1984 the incorporation into the north of a new province (*Wahdah*), encompassing territory, theretofore part of the Upper Nile region, where oil reserves had been discovered.

Upon assuming power, the Transitional Military Committee suspended the 1973 basic law, dissolved the central and regional assemblies, appointed a cabinet composed largely of civilians, and assigned military personnel to replace regional governors and their ministers. An interim constitution was approved by the TMC on October 10, 1985, to provide a framework for Assembly elections. The assemblymen chosen in April 1986 were mandated to draft a new basic law, although many southern districts were unrepresented because of rebel activity. The Assembly's charge to act as a constituent body appeared to have ceased with Prime Minister al-Mahdi's call in April 1988 for the convening of a national constitutional conference.

In January 1987 the government announced the formation of a new Administrative Council for the South, comprising representatives of six southern political parties and the governors of each of the three previously established regions. The Council, although formally empowered with only "transitional" authority, has been repudiated by both the "unity" and "divisionist" groups and its effectiveness has been minimal.

Foreign relations. Sudan has long pursued a policy of nonalignment, modified in practice by changing international circumstances, while focusing its attention on regional matters. Prior to the 1974 coup in Ethiopia, relations with that country were especially cordial because of the prominent role Haile Selassie had played in bringing about a settlement of the initial southern rebellion. Subsequently, Addis Ababa accused Khartoum of providing covert support to Eritrean rebels and, despite a number of reciprocal state visits and pledges of cooperation after 1980, relations remained strained.

Soon after taking power in 1969, Numayri forged close ties with Egyptian President Nasser within a federation scheme encompassing Sudan, Egypt and the newly established Libyan regime of Colonel Qadhafi. Although failing to promote integration, the federation yielded joint Egyptian-Libyan military support for Numayri in defeating the Communist insurgency of June 1971. However, Numayri was reluctant to join a second unity scheme — the abortive 1972 Federation of Arab Republics — because of Libyan-inspired conspiracies and opposition from the non-Arab peoples of southern Sudan. President Sadat's own estrangement from Qadhafi during 1973 led to the signing of a Sudanese-Egyptian agreement on political and economic coordination in February 1974. In subsequent years Sadat pledged to support Numayri against continued Libyan attempts at subversion and Sudan followed Egypt into close alignment with the United States. While rejecting the Egyptian-Israeli peace treaty of 1979 because of domestic opposition to Israel, Sudan was one of the few Arab states that did not break diplomatically with Cairo, and in October 1982 presidents Numayri and Mubarak concluded an agreement that provided for a Higher Council of Integration chaired by the two chief executives; an advisory Nile Valley Parliament, 40 of whose 60 members would be drawn from the two countries' legislatures (the remaining 20 being appointed); and a Joint Fund intended, according to London's *Financial Times,* to attract aid from Arab governments that "would otherwise not lend either to Sudan alone, because of fears of mismanagement, nor to Egypt, because of its peace treaty with Israel". In March 1984, an alleged Libyan air attack on the Sudanese city of Omdurman prompted the invocation by Khartoum and Cairo of a 1976 joint air defense agreement, the two governments receiving AWACS equipment and airlift assistance from the United States to monitor the Libyan-Sudanese border, despite the fact that Tripoli had denied all involvement in the incident.

In June 1980 a conference was convened at Khartoum to discuss international aid for some 500,000 refugees then living in Sudan. Most had fled Eritrea, although a significant number of Ugandans and Chadians were also involved. The situation was complicated by the presence among the Ugandans of supporters of ousted dictator 'Idi Amin who had made sporadic raids into their homeland, as well as by Khartoum's displeasure at the presence in Uganda of Tanzanian troops. The influx from Chad, where the Numayri regime had long supported Hissein Habré, helped to swell the Sudanese refugee population to more than 1 million by mid-1985.

Libya, which announced that it would terminate its support of the SPLA rebels, was the first country to recognize the post-Numayri regime, urging the TMC to sever its links with Egypt. For his part, President Mubarak assured the new government that his previous support for Numayri should not preclude continued warm relations. While close military and economic ties were reestablished with Tripoli, Sudanese relations with Cairo remained cool, in part because of Mubarak's refusal to extradite Numayri for trial by the new Khartoum government. In February 1987, however, Mubarak and Prime Minister al-Mahdi concluded a "brotherhood charter" calling for cooperation in economic, political, and cultural affairs. Collaterally, as relations between Khartoum and Tripoli waned, the United States reaffirmed its commitment to a number of Sudanese relief and development projects.

Current issues. During 1987 political deterioration coincided with continued economic decline, the government at midyear declaring an expanded state of emergency to deal with "anarchy in the marketplace". Having fallen into arrears on external debt repayments, agreement was reached "in principle" for relief from the International Monetary Fund. By October, however, price increases had generated a degree of social unrest comparable to that reached prior to the 1985 takeover. Militarily, the government remained on the defensive in the civil war, the SPLA having gained control of as much as 90 percent of the south amid mutual accusations of "food politics" involving international famine-relief shipments.

Prime Minister al-Mahdi's call in April 1988 for an all-party conference to resolve the lengthy impasse on a new constitution could be construed as a delayed reaction to a meeting at Nairobi, Kenya, in September 1987 between representatives of the SPLA and the Sudanese African parties, which had concluded with an appeal for "all Sudanese forces" to join in precisely such an undertaking. However, the Nairobi communiqué had reiterated earlier SPLA insistence that no meaningful dialogue with northern political leaders could take place prior to an abandonment of shari'a law—an issue that the prime minister had felt obliged to refer to the constitutional discussions them-

selves. The prospects for a negotiated peace were further set back by the inclusion of the fundamentalist National Islamic Front in the coalition government formed on May 14, 1988, despite a proposal by al-Mahdi that a system be devised whereby non-Muslims would be exempt from shari'a penalty provisions.

POLITICAL PARTIES

Following the 1969 coup, all political parties except the Sudanese Communist Party (see SCP, below) were outlawed. After the failure of the SCP coup in July 1971, it was also driven underground and many of its leaders were arrested. The following October, President Numayri attempted to supplant the existing parties by launching the Sudanese Socialist Union (see NSAP, below), modeled after the Arab Socialist Union of Egypt, which remained the country's only recognized political group until its suspension by the TMC in April 1985.

More than 40 parties were reported to have participated in the post-Numayri balloting of April 1986, although only the UP, the DUP, and NIF obtained substantial legislative representation.

Government Parties:

Umma (People's) Party—UP (*Hizb al-'Umma*). A moderate right-of-center formation, the UP has long been led by Prime Minister al-Mahdi. Strongest among the Ansar Muslims of the White Nile and western Darfur and Kordofan provinces, it obtained a plurality of 100 seats at the 1986 Assembly balloting. Most of its members advocate the repeal of shari'a law and are wary of sharing power with the fundamentalist NIF (below). Despite an historic pro-Libyan, anti-Egyptian posture, the party has cultivated good relations with Western countries based, in part, on al-Mahdi's personal ties to Britain.
Leaders: Dr. Sadiq al-MAHDI (Prime Minister), Idris al-BANNA (member, Supreme Council).

Democratic Unionist Party—DUP (*al-Hizb al-Ittihadi al-Dimuqratiyah*). Also right-of-center, the DUP draws its principal strength from the Khatmiya Muslims of northern and eastern Sudan. Based on its second-place showing at the 1986 poll, the DUP has been the UP's "junior partner" in recent government coalitions, although internal divisions have prevented the formulation of a clearly defined outlook. The faction led by party chairman Osman al-Mirghani, which still appears dominant, includes pro-Egyptian traditionalists once linked to the Numayri regime, who are reluctant to repeal shari'a law until an alternative code has been formulated. Younger members, on the other hand, have urged that the party abandon its "semi-feudal" orientation and become a secular, centrist formation capable of attracting nationwide support. In early 1986, the DUP reunited with an offshoot group, the Democratic People's Party (DPP), and has since appeared to have absorbed the small National Unionist Party (NUP), which had drawn most of its support from the Khartoum business community.
Leaders: Osman al-MIRGHANI (Party Chairman), Ahmad al-MIRGHANI (Chairman, Supreme Council), Sharif Zayn al-'Abidin al-HINDI (former Deputy Prime Minister), Dr. Ahmad al-Sayid HAMAD (former DDP leader), Sid Ahmad al-HUSAYN (Acting Secretary General).

National Islamic Front—NIF (*Jabhat al-Watani al-Islami*). The NIF was organized prior to the April 1986 balloting by the leader of the fundamentalist Muslim Brotherhood, Dr. Hassan 'Abdallah al-Turabi, who as attorney general had been largely responsible for the harsh enforcement of shari'a law under the Numayri government. It displayed unexpected strength by winning 51 legislative seats, but refused to enter the government until May 1988 because of the UP commitment to revise the shari'a system, which the NIF wants to strengthen rather than dilute. The Front holds five portfolios in the present "national unity" administration.
Leader: Dr. Hassan 'Abdallah al-TURABI.

Southern Sudanese Political Association (SSPA). The SSPA, the largest southern party, was formed by "old guard" politicians following the 1985 coup, its leader, Samuel Aru Bol, serving as deputy prime minister in the transitional government. Although dominated by members of the Nilotic tribes of the Upper Nile and Bahr al-Ghazal, the SSPA strongly endorses unified government for the south.

Leader: Samuel ARU Bol.

Progressive People's Party (PPP). The PPP is one of the two major "Equatorial" parties (see SAPC, below) representing Sudanese living near the Zairian and Ugandan borders. Both the PPP and SAPC, unlike the SSPA, are "pro-divisionist", calling for strong provincial governments within a weak regional administration for the south.

Leader: Elioba SURUR.

Sudanese African People's Congress (SAPC). Sudan's other "Equatorial" party, the SAPC was initially represented by Pacifico Lolik on the Supreme Council named in 1986. However, Lolik was reportedly expelled from the party in 1987 for supporting government plans for a unified southern administration.

Leader: Morris LUWIYA.

Sudanese People's Federal Party (SPFP). As in the case of several other southern parties, the SPFP was awarded a ministry in the coalition government of May 1986.

Leader: Joshua Dei WAL.

Other Parties and Groups:

Islamic Socialist Party (ISP). A little-known nonregional party, the ISP received attention in 1987 when its leader was named to the Supreme Council as a neutral candidate after a dispute between the UP and the DUP over the filling of a vacancy.

Leader: Mirghani al-NASRI.

Sudanese National Party — SNP (*al-Hizb al-Watani al-Sudani*). The SNP is a Khartoum-based party which draws most of its support from the Nuba tribes of southern Kordofan. The SNP deputies joined the southerners in boycotting the Assembly in 1986 on the ground that "African bloc" interests were underrepresented in the cabinet.

Leader: Rev. Philip Abbas GHABUSH.

Sudanese Communist Party — SCP (*al-Hizb al-Shuyu'i al-Sudani*). Founded in 1946 and a leading force in the struggle for independence, the SCP was banned under the 'Abbud regime and supported the 1969 Numayri coup, becoming thereafter the sole legal party until the abortive 1971 uprising, when it was again outlawed. The party joined the NSF in 1984 and campaigned as a recognized party in 1986, calling for opposition to Islamic fundamentalism, repeal of *shari'a* law, and the adoption of a secular, democratic constitution.

Leaders: 'Ali al-Tijani al-TAYYIB Babikar, Muhammad Ibrahim NUGUD Mansur (Secretary General).

Sudanese African Congress (SAC). A southern party based in Juba, the SAC was awarded the ministry of labor in the first post-Numayri cabinet but has since been unrepresented in the government. The SAC represents a more radical viewpoint than the SSPA, calling for a shift in the Sudanese power structure to give the south more voice in national administration. At present, the SAC appears strongly oriented toward the SPLM (below), several of its leaders having reportedly joined the movement by 1987.

Leader: Walter Kunijwok Gwado AYOKER.

Sudan African National Union (SANU). A small southern party based in Malakal, SANU (adopting the same name as a pre-Numayri party) supports the division of the south into separate regions for administration.

Leader: Andrew Wieu RIAK.

National Alliance for the Salvation of the Country (NASC). A loose coalition of professional groups, trade unions, interdenominational church groups, and political parties, the NASC was formed in 1985 as an extension of the National Salvation Front (NSF) established the year before. The NASC was instrumental in organizing strikes and other demonstrations which preceded the ouster of President Numayri, but its subsequent efforts to negotiate a north-south reconciliation through a proposed constitutional conference have been largely unproductive.

Leader: Awad al-KARIM Muhammad.

National Socialist Alliance Party (NSAP). The NSAP was declared illegal in January 1986 shortly after the announcement of its formation by supporters of former president Numayri. The NSAP had been presented as a successor to the Sudanese Socialist Union — SSU (*al-Ittihad al-Ishtiraki al-Sudani*), which had been Sudan's sole legal party from October 1971 until its suspension following Numayri's ouster in April 1985. In December 1985, 26 individuals were arrested for attempting direct revival of the SSU, which had originally been modeled after the Arab Socialist Union of Egypt.

Anyanya II Movement. *Anyanya II,* so-named in emulation of the *Anyanya* (scorpion) southern insurgency of earlier decades (see Political background, above), was formed in late 1983, when the Nuer faction broke from the recently-formed SPLA (see SPLM, below). Although the movement continued its antigovernment activity until the ouster of President Numayri, it has since become a progovernment guerrilla group, regularly engaging SPLA troops around the Upper Nile city of Malakal. However, there were reports in late 1987 of an agreement between *Anyanya II* and the SPLA to curtail hostilities arising from their longstanding ethnic rivalry.

Leaders: David Dogok PUOCH (Secretary General), Col. Gordon KONG (leader of military wing).

Sudanese Movement of Revolutionary Committees (SMRC). Established in May 1985 as an outgrowth of the Libyan-backed Sudanese People's Socialist Front (SPSF) formed the previous year, the SMRC adopted an ideology based on the "Green Book" of Colonel Qadhafi. By late 1987, however, it was reported that most "revolutionary committee" activity had ceased in the face of popular disinterest.

Insurgent Group:

Sudanese People's Liberation Movement (SPLM). The SPLM and its military wing, the Sudanese People's Liberation Army (SPLA), were formed in 1983 by Col. John Garang, until then an officer in the Sudanese army. Sent by the Numayri administration to negotiate with mutinous soldiers in southern garrisons, Colonel Garang joined the mutineers and, under his leadership, the SPLA became the dominant southern rebel force. The SPLM and SPLA were supported by Libya prior to Numayri's ouster, when Tripoli endorsed the new regime at Khartoum. The SPLA called a cease-fire immediately following the coup, but thereafter initiated military action against the Khartoum government after failing to win concessions on the southern question. Relying on an estimated 20,000 to 25,000 troops (most of them from the Dinka ethnic group), the SPLA has steadily gained control of most of the nonurban south. Downplaying its former self-description as "Marxist-Leninist", the SPLM, which nonetheless continues to train at bases in Ethiopia, does not propose secession for the south; rather, it insists that it is a national movement seeking a larger voice in national affairs for the south as well as a greater share of Sudan's economic development programs. At sporadic talks with administration representatives in 1986 and 1987, the SPLM insisted on the immediate repeal of *shari'a* law and the revocation of the state of emergency prior to negotiations on a new national poll that would include the southern districts eliminated from the 1986 balloting.

Leaders: Joseph ADOHU (former Southern Administrator), Col. John GARANG (Chairman and SPLA Commander).

LEGISLATURE

Under the Numayri regime, the size and composition of the unicameral National People's Assembly changed several times, the Assembly elected in 1974 being the only one to complete its full constitutional term of four years. All existing legislative bodies were dissolved by the TNC in April 1985.

On April 1–12, 1986, balloting was held for 260 members of a 301-member **Constituent Assembly,** voting being postponed in many southern districts because of rebel activity. Of the more than 40 groups that participated, the Umma Party won 100 seats; the Democratic Unionist Party, 63; the National Islamic Front, 51; the Progressive People's Party, 10; the Southern Sudan Political Alliance, 8; the Sudanese National Party, 8; the Sudanese African People's Congress, 7; others, 13.

Speaker: Muhammad Yousis MUHAMMAD.

C A B I N E T

[as of May 14, 1988]

Prime Minister	Dr. Sadiq al-Mahdi
Deputy Prime Minister	Aldo Ajo Deng

Ministers

Agriculture and Natural Resources	Dr. Fatih al-Tijani
Cabinet Affairs	Salah 'Abd al-Salaam al-Khalifa
Civil Service and Administrative Reform	Dr. Fadlallah 'Ali Fadlallah
Defense	Gen. 'Abd al-Majid Hamid Khalil
Economy and Foreign Trade	Mubarak 'Abdallah al-Fadil
Energy and Mining	Bakri Ahmad Adil
Finance and Economic Planning	'Umar Nur al-Da'im
Foreign Affairs	Hussein Sulaiman Abu Sailh
Health	Muhammad Musa
Higher Education and Scientific Research	Shaikh Mahjub
Industry	Dr. 'Abd al-Wahab Uthman
Information and Culture	'Abdallah Muhammad Ahmad
Internal Trade, Cooperation and Supply	Dr. 'Ali al-Haj
Irrigation and Water Resources	Mahmud Bashir Jamaa
Justice	Dr. Hasan 'Abdallah al-Turabi
Labor and Social Security	Matthew Obur
Livestock Resources	Dr. Ismail Abkar
Public Communications	Taj al-Sirr Mustafa 'Abd al-Salam
Public Works and Housing	'Uthman 'Uman 'Ali
Refugee Affairs and Relief	Hasan 'Ali Shabbu
Regional Coordination and Local Government Planning	Richard Macubi
Religious Affairs	Dr. 'Abd al-Malik al-Ju'li
Social Welfare and Refugee Affairs	Ahmad al-Rahman Muhammad
Tourism and Hotels	Amin Bashir Fallin
Transport	Aldo Ajo Deng
Youth and Sports	Joshua Dewal
Governor, Bank of Sudan	Ismail Misbah al-Meki

N E W S   M E D I A

Press. The following are dailies published at Khartoum, unless otherwise noted; the first two, nationalized by President Numayri in 1970, were closed down temporarily in August 1986, pending a return to private ownership: *al-Sahafa* (The Press, 70,000–80,000), in Arabic; *al-Ayam* (The Days, 60,000–70,000), in Arabic; *Sudan Standard*, twice-weekly government publication, in English; *Nile Mirror,* published weekly at Juba in English.

News agencies. The domestic agency is the Sudan News Agency (Suna); the Middle East News Agency, TASS, and *Xinhua* also maintain bureaus at Khartoum.

Radio and television. The Sudan Broadcasting Service is a government facility transmitting in Arabic, Amharic, Somali, and Tigrinya as well as English and the commercial. Television service is provided by the commercial, government-controlled Sudan Television Service. There were approximately 1.5 million radio and 250,000 television receivers in 1987.

INTERGOVERNMENTAL   REPRESENTATION

Ambassador to the US: Salah AHMAD.

US Ambassador to Sudan: G. Norman ANDERSON.

Permanent Representative to the UN: Amin M. ABDOUN.

IGO Memberships (Non-UN): ADF, AfDB, AFESD, AGC, AMF, BADEA, CCC, EEC(L), *EIB,* IC, ICAC, IDB, Intelsat, Interpol, LAS, NAM, OAU, PCA.

S U R I N A M E

Republic of Suriname
Republiek Suriname

Political Status: Former Netherlands dependency; granted internal autonomy December 29, 1954, and complete independence November 25, 1975; constitution of November 21, 1975, suspended on August 15, 1980, following military coup of February 25; present constitution approved by referendum of September 30, 1987.

Area: 63,036 sq. mi. (163,265 sq. km.).

Population: 352,041 (1980C), 415,000 (1988E). The 1980 figure is 27,566 less than that reported for the previous census in 1971, the difference presumably being attributable to emigration.

Major Urban Center (1980C): PARAMARIBO (67,718).

Official Language: Dutch. English, Hindi, Javanese, Chinese, and Sranan Tongo (*Taki-Taki*), a Creole lingua franca, are also widely spoken, while Spanish has been adopted as a working language to facilitate communication with Latin American neighbors.

Monetary Unit: Suriname Guilder (market rate March 1 1988, 1.79 guilders = $1US).

President: Ramsewak SHANKAR (Progressive Reform Party); elected by the National Assembly on January 12, 1988, and inaugurated for a five-year term on January 25, succeeding Acting President Lachmipersad Fred RAMDAT-MISIER.

Vice President and Prime Minister: Henck Alfonsius Eugene ARRON (Suriname National Party); elected by the National Assembly on January 12, 1988, and inaugurated on January 25 for a term concurrent with that of the President.

Commander in Chief of the National Army: Lt. Col. Dési (Daysi, Desire) Delano BOUTERSE; member of National Military Council (NMC) that ousted government of Henck A.E. ARRON on February 25, 1980; designated Head of Government on August 2, 1985; nominally yielded executive authority to administration inaugurated on January 25, 1988.

T H E   C O U N T R Y

Formerly known as Dutch Guiana, Suriname lies on the north-central coast of South America and is bordered by Guyana on the west, French Guiana on the east, and Brazil on the south. Because of the early importation of slave labor from Africa and contract labor from Asia, its society is one of the most ethnically varied in the world. The largest groups are Hindustanis (38 percent) and Creoles (31 percent), followed by Javanese, Negroes, Amerindians, Chinese, and various European minorities. Freedom of worship has traditionally prevailed among equally diverse religious groups, which adhere to Protestant (primarily Dutch Reformed, Lutheran, and Moravian), Roman Catholic, Hindu, Muslim, and Confucian faiths.

The greater part of the land area is covered with virgin forest, although the coastal region is both flat and fertile. The tropical climate yields a range of agricultural products that includes rice, various fruits, sugar, and coffee. Suriname ranks fourth among the world's producers of alumina and bauxite, which, together with aluminum, account for nearly 80 percent of the country's exports though employing only 6 percent of the work force.

Although continuing to maintain a higher standard of living than many of its neighbors, the country has experienced economic difficulty since 1980, due largely to slackened world demand for bauxite and the suspension of Dutch and US aid in reaction to a wave of official killings in December 1982. By 1986 Suriname faced what its administration termed an "economic emergency" featuring large budget deficits, mounting inflation, 25 percent unemployment, a flourishing parallel market, and disruption by rebel activity in the eastern and southern parts of the country. In early 1988, following installation of the first elected government in eight years, the country's major donors, including the Netherlands, indicated that they were prepared to enter negotiations on a resumption of aid.

GOVERNMENT AND POLITICS

Political background. First acquired by the Netherlands from Britain in 1667 in exchange for Manhattan Island, the territory now known as Suriname passed between England, France, and the Netherlands several times before Dutch authority was formally confirmed by the Congress of Vienna in 1815. Suriname remained a dependency of the Netherlands until enactment of a Statute of the Realm in December 1954 that provided the country with a parliamentary form of government and the right of local constitutional revision, thereby according it full equality with the Netherlands and the Netherlands Antilles.

A substantial portion of Suriname's Hindustani population, which constitutes the bulk of the country's skilled labor force, opposed independence, fearing economic and political repression by the Creole-dominated government of Henck ARRON, who had become prime minister in 1973. Over 40,000 Surinamese, most of them Hindustanis, subsequently emigrated, the majority settling in the Netherlands. Their relocation created a number of social and economic problems for the Netherlands while leaving Suriname with a formidable gap in such areas as commerce, medicine, and teaching. Because of the émigré problem, provisions guaranteeing certain Hindustani rights were incorporated into the independence constitution of 1975, although the government for the most part failed in its efforts to convince the expatriates to return.

Prime Minister Arron was reconfirmed following a parliamentary election in October 1977, but was ousted in an armed rebellion of some 300 noncommissioned officers on February 25, 1980, following government refusal to sanction trade-union activity within the armed forces. On March 15, the leaders of the revolt, organized as a National Military Council (NMC), designated the politically moderate Dr. Henk CHIN A Sen as prime minister while permitting the essentially titular president, Dr. Johan H.E. FERRIER, to retain his office. On August 15, the constitution was suspended and Ferrier was dismissed, Chin being named as his acting successor while continuing as prime minister. On December 3, Chin was confirmed as president, the office of prime minister being abolished.

During 1981 differences arose between President Chin, who had called for a return to democratic rule, and Lt. Col. (formerly Sgt. Maj.) Dési BOUTERSE, who had emerged as the strongman of the NMC. As a result, Chin resigned on February 4, 1982, being replaced four days later, on an acting basis, by Lachmipersad F. RAMDAT-MISIER. In the wake of an unsuccessful uprising by right-wing military elements on March 10–11, martial law was declared, while in apparent response to foreign pressure, a new government headed by Henry N. NEYHORST in the reactivated post of prime minister was announced on March 31. Following the reported discovery of a new antigovernment conspiracy on December 8, Neyhorst also resigned and the NMC ordered the execution of 15 leaders of a lobbying group called the Association for Democratic Action, claiming that they had scheduled a coup for Christmas day. On February 26, 1983, Dr. Errol ALIBUX of the leftist Progressive Workers' and Farm Laborers' Union (PALU) was chosen to head a new cabinet dominated by PALU members. Austerity measures, necessitated by the withdrawal of Dutch and American aid, provoked a strike in December by bauxite workers, who were joined by electricity workers in early January 1984. Most of the strikers returned to work following the revocation of retroactive increases in income taxes and on January 8 Colonel Bouterse announced the dismissal of the Alibux government. On February 3, an interim administration led by former Arron aide Willem (Wim) UDENHOUT was sworn in, pending "the formation of new democratic institutions". In December, the government announced a 27-month program for a "return to democracy" that included the establishment, on January 1, 1985, of an appointive 31-member National Assembly charged with the drafting of a new constitution.

On August 2, 1985, the Assembly formally designated Colonel Bouterse as "head of government", while reconfirming Ramdat-Misier as acting president. In early September, it was announced that the Assembly had appointed a commission, structured on an essentially corporative basis (including representatives of the major unions and the Association of Surinamese Manufacturers) to draft a new basic law. Subsequently, a number of party leaders accepted an invitation from Colonel Bouterse to join the NMC in formation of a Supreme Council (*Topberaad*) that would serve as the country's highest political organ. The new body approved the formation of a government headed by Prehaapnarain RADHAKISHUN on July 17, 1986, following the resignation of Prime Minister Udenhout on

June 23. Radhakishun was in turn succeeded by Jules Albert WIJDENBOSCH on February 13, 1987.

Despite an earlier announcement that a general election would not be held until March 1988, Colonel Bouterse stated on March 31, 1987, that the balloting would be advanced to independence day, November 25, 1987, preceded by a September 30 referendum on the new constitution.

The election yielded a landslide victory for the Front for Democracy and Development, a coalition of the three leading opposition parties, with Colonel Bouterse's recently organized National Democratic Front (NDF) winning only three of 51 legislative seats. On January 12, 1988, the new Assembly unanimously elected former agriculture minister Ramsewak SHANKAR to a five-year term as president, with former prime minister Arron designated as vice president and prime minister. Bouterse, however, remained commander in chief of the army and, because of a lack of constitutional specificity in regard to both the membership and functions of a revamped Military Council and a nonelective Council of State, appeared to have lost little capacity for the exercise of decisive political influence.

Constitution and government. After affirming an impressive variety of personal and public rights, the 1987 constitution sets forth a complex system of government within which the intended distribution of power is by no means clearly defined. A 51-member National Assembly, elected for a five-year term, selects a president and vice president for terms of like duration. The president serves as chairman of a nonelective State Council whose composition is "regulated by law" and whose purpose is to advise the government on public policy, ensuring that its actions are in conformity with the basic law; he also chairs a Security Council, which is empowered to assume governmental authority in the event of "war, state of siege or exceptional circumstances to be determined by law". A Military Council, also "regulated by law", is to "effect and consolidate a peaceful transition to a democratic and just society". The Assembly may amend the constitution by a two-thirds majority (although Colonel Bouterse has insisted that such action must be confirmed by plebiscite) or, lacking such a majority, may convene a People's Congress composed of its own membership plus delegates to the country's municipal and provincial councils. For electoral purposes the country is divided into ten districts, three of which at the time of the November 1987 balloting were under a state of emergency because of antigovernment guerrilla activity.

Foreign relations. Prior to the 1980 coup, Suriname's foreign relations turned on two main issues: long-standing border disputes with neighboring Guyana (see map, p. 242) and French Guiana, and a sizable development loan from the Netherlands. The border disputes result from Guyana's claim to a 6,000-square-mile tract reputedly rich in bauxite deposits, and from France's claim to a 780-square-mile tract believed to contain deposits of gold; neither controversy has yet been resolved. The aid loan, exceeding $1.5 billion to be disbursed over a period of 10–15 years, was approved by the Dutch government in order to ensure the opposition's support for independence, raise the standard of living for the Surinamese people, and compensate for termination of the preindependence right of emigration from Suriname to the Netherlands.

Considerable uncertainty followed in the wake of the Arron overthrow, the coup itself being largely unplanned, with no clear foreign policy overtones. However, a distinctly leftward thrust had become apparent by the time of President Chin's resignation, the increasingly dominant Bouterse faction within the NMC having adopted an essentially pro-Cuban posture in regional affairs, leading to a sizable increase in the flight of Surinamese to the Netherlands (despite the expiration of automatic entitlement to entry visas) and the recall of the Dutch ambassador in March 1982. The subsequent withdrawal of Dutch aid (which had provided Suriname with one of the highest standards of living in the region) was a severe blow to the country's economy. In early 1983 it appeared that the fiscal shortfall might be alleviated by commitments from Cuba and Libya. However, on June 1, coincident with reports that the US Reagan administration had considered a CIA plan to infiltrate and destabilize the self-proclaimed "socialist" regime, a substantial military and trade agreement was concluded with Brazil. Two weeks later, amid Dutch reports that Brazil had threatened to invade Suriname if efforts were not taken to curb Cuban influence, Colonel Bouterse announced that Sgt. Maj. Badressein SITAL, one of the most pro-Cuban members of the NMC, had been dismissed from both his Council and ministerial positions. In mid-October, Bouterse visited Washington and later in the month, following the Grenada action, asked Havana to withdraw its ambassador and sharply reduce its remaining diplomatic staff at Paramaribo.

In early 1984, the regime lodged official protests with the French and Netherlands governments over their alleged complicity in an invasion plot and in March 1985 Paramaribo threatened to take the Netherlands to the International Court of Justice for discontinuance of its aid program under the 1975 independence accord. The latter pronouncement came in the wake of an adverse UN Human Rights Commission report on the 1982 killings that dissuaded The Hague from reconsideration of its aid posture. On the other hand, an announcement by the government that it would proceed with ICJ action may have been rendered moot by the Hague's response to the balloting of November 25.

Current issues. Given the surprisingly poor electoral showing of the army-backed National Democratic Party, no NDP representatives were included in the 13-member cabinet announced in early 1988. Most observers were persuaded, however, that the new Council of State, guided by the military, would emerge as a major source of legislation, with the National Assembly playing a potentially ancillary role. On the other hand, there were prospects that military influence might eventually recede, depending on the attitude of the Assembly during the period of "peaceful transition" referenced by the constitution. A related consideration was the posture of the rebel Surinamese Liberation Army, led by former Bouterse aide Ronny BRUNSWIJK, which, with apparent support from bushnegro villagers, had severely disrupted bauxite mining in the eastern region prior to a government counteroffensive that had driven it back to the border with French Guiana. The military had drawn international condemnation for the alleged massacre of some 200 civilians in the area between June 1986 and August 1987, and the duration of a unilateral truce declared by the insurgents in early 1988 was expected to be linked to the evolving military-civilian balance of power at Paramaribo.

POLITICAL PARTIES

A long-standing rivalry between Creole and Hindustani groups continued to characterize the party structure of Suriname in the years following independence. The Creole-dominated National Party Alliance (*Nationale Partij Komibnatie* — NPK), organized prior to the 1977 election with the Suriname National Party as its core, controlled a bare majority in the *Staten* prior to the coup of February 25, 1980. Most of the leading opposition parties were grouped into the United Democratic Parties (*Verenigde Democratische Partijen* — VDP), a predominantly Hindu coalition dominated by the leftist Progressive Reform Party.

While traditional party activity was suspended following the 1980 coup, two leftist groups (PALU and the RVP, below) were represented in post-coup governments, initially as elements of a regime-supportive Revolutionary Front established in November 1981. The Front became moribund upon establishment of the February 25 Movement, which was itself supplanted by the army-backed National Democratic Party (below) prior to the 1987 election. Earlier, following relaxation of the party ban in the fall of 1985, the VHP, NPS, and KTPI were invited to participate in the government, their leaders joining the Supreme Council in November.

On August 2, 1987, leaders of the three leading opposition groups formed an electoral alliance, the Front for Democracy and Development, which swept the November balloting by winning 40 of 51 legislative seats.

Front for Democracy and Development:

Suriname National Party (*Nationale Partij Suriname* — NPS). A Creole grouping founded in 1946, the NPS was the leading advocate of independence from the Netherlands and the core party of the National Party Alliance prior to the 1980 coup. The NPS' Alliance partners were the predominantly Christian **Progressive Suriname People's Party** (*Progressieve Surinaamse Volkspartij* — PSV), led by Emile L.A. WIJNTUIN, and the **Reformed Progressive Party** (*Hernieuwde Progressieve Partij* — HPP), a predominantly Hindu social democratic group that split from the VHP (below) in 1975 under the leadership of Panellal PARMESSAR. The NPS won 14 Assembly seats in 1987.
Leader: Henck A.E. ARRON (Vice President and Prime Minister).

Progressive Reform Party (*Vooruitstrevende Hervormings Partij* — VHP). Long the leading Hindu party, the left-of-center VHP originally opposed independence because of anticipated repression by the Creole-dominated Alliance. Its pre-coup coalition partners included the largely Creole **Socialist Party of Suriname** (*Socialistische Partij Suriname* — SPS), led by Henk HERRENBERG; the Black **Progressive Bushnegro Party** (*Progressieve Bosneger Partij* — PBP), led by Jarien GADDEN; and the Javanese *Pendawa Lima,* led by Salam Paul SOMOHARDJO. The VHP secured a plurality of 16 legislative seats in the November 1987 poll.
Leaders: Ramsewak SHANKAR (President of the Republic), Prehaapnarain RADHAKISHUN (former Prime Minister), Jaggernath LACHMON (Chairman, National Assembly).

Party of National Unity and Solidarity (*Kerukanon Tulodo Pranatan Ingil* — KTPI). Formerly known as the Indonesian Peasants' Party (*Kaum-Tani Persuatan Indonesia*), the KTPI is a small, predominantly Javanese rural party founded in 1947. It joined the National Party Alliance prior to the 1977 election, but withdrew in December 1978. It obtained 10 legislative seats in 1987.
Leader: Willy SOEMITA.

Other Parties:

National Democratic Party (NDP). The NDP was formed prior to the 1987 election as a political vehicle for the supporters of Colonel Bouterse. As such, it succeeded the February 25 Movement, styled *Stanvaste* ("Steadfast") in Dutch, which had been characterized as a "movement, not a party" at its launching in 1984. Contrary to expectations, the NDP secured only three Assembly seats, two of which were subject to challenge and represented constituencies that had not been contested by Front nominees.
Leaders: Lt. Col. Dési BOUTERSE (Army Commander and former *Stanvaste* Chairman), Jules Albert WIJDENBOSCH (former Prime Minister), Col. Harvey NAARENDORP (former *Stanvaste* Secretary General).

Progressive Workers' and Farm Laborers' Union (*Progressieve Arbeiders en Lanbouwers Unie* — PALU). The only trade union to have retained a public role after many labor leaders were killed in December 1982, the left-wing PALU dominated the Abilux cabinet, but was not represented in subsequent administrations. It won four Assembly seats from "war zone" constituencies in 1987.
Leader: Ir Iwan KROLIS.

Revolutionary People's Party (*Revolutionaire Volkspartij* — RVP). An offshoot of the pre-coup *Volkspartij* (below) and led by a cousin of Bouterse associate Harvey Naarendorp, the RVP has been seen as a distinctly pro-Cuban formation that has consistently attempted to block negotiation with the International Monetary Fund.
Leaders: Edward NAARENDORP, Glenn SANKATSINGH, Lothar BOKSTEEN.

National Republic Party (*Partij Nationalistische Republiek* — PNR). The left-of-center PNR was a member of the Alliance until August 1977, when a dispute over representation in the government led to its withdrawal.
Leader: Robin RAVALES.

Minor parties include the left-wing **People's Party** (*Volkspartij* — VP), led by Dr. Rubin LIE Pauw Sam and Stuart MENCKEBERG; the **Progressive National Party** (*Progressieve Nationale Partij* — PNP), led by Just RENS; the **Suriname Labor Party**, led by Fred DERBY; and the **Communist Party of Suriname** (*Kommunistische Partij Suriname* — KPS), a pro-Albanian grouping that did not formally organize as a party until July 1981 and whose former leader, Bram Mehr, was executed in 1982.

Exile Group:

In January 1983 a **Movement for the Liberation of Suriname** was formed by exiles in the Netherlands under the leadership of former president Chin and former deputy prime minister André Haakmat. However, the Dutch government refused to recognize the group as a government in exile, and both subsequently declared their support for the Surinamese Liberation Army, (below).

Rebel Group:

Surinamese Liberation Army (SLA). The SLA was formed in early 1986 by former army private Ronny Brunswijk with the avowed aim of overthrowing Colonel Bouterse and "[restoring] the constitutional state" through free elections. The government charged Surinamese emigrées in the Netherlands with supporting the SLA, whose approximately 2,000 members launched a guerrilla campaign in the country's eastern and southern regions that appeared to have been largely contained by mid-1987. In the wake of the November election, the SLA's "Jungle Commando" was reported to have declared an unconditional truce, effective January 1, 1988.
Leader: Ronny BRUNSWIJK.

LEGISLATURE

The former unicameral Parliament (*Staten*) was abolished on August 15, 1980. A constituent National Assembly (*Volksvergadering*) of 31 nominated members was established on January 1, 1985, as part of the government's "return to democracy" program. In balloting for the successor **National Assembly** on November 25, 1987, the

Front for Democracy and Development won 40 seats (Progressive Reform Party, 16; Suriname National Party, 14; Party of National Unity and Harmony, 10); the Progressive Workers' and Farm Laborers' Union, 4; *Pendawa Lima,* 4; and the National Democratic Party, 3. Of the 11 non-Front results, 10 were from the country's three "war zones" and were annulled for procedural reasons by the Electoral Commission; however, the Assembly subsequently voted to admit the representatives in question, pending a review by referendum when the situation in the three areas had been "normalized".

Chairman: Jaggernath LACHMON.

C A B I N E T

Prime Minister	Henck A.E. Arron
Ministers	
Agriculture, Livestock, Fisheries and Forestry	Saimin Redjosenpono
Defense	Maj. Ahmed W. Sheikkariem
Education, Science, Culture, Sports and Youth Affairs	Ronald Venetiann
Finance and Planning	Subhas Chandra Mungra
Foreign Affairs	Edwin Sedoc
Health	Henk Ali Mahumed
Home Affairs	Evelyn Alexander-Vanenburg
Justice and Police	Jules Ajodhia
Labor	Romeo Van Russel
Natural Resources and Energy	Pretaapnarian Radhakishun
Public Works and Telecommunications	Harnarain Jankiepersadsingh
Social Affairs and Housing	Willy Soemita
Transport, Trade and Industry	Winfred A. Grep
President, Central Bank	Hendrik (Henk) O. Goedschalk

N E W S   M E D I A

All nongovernmental organs of public information were closed down in December 1982, although some were subsequently permitted to resume activity.

Press. The principal newspaper has been *De Ware Tidj* (8,000), published in Dutch and Sranan Tongo, which, however, announced in January 1988 that it was closing indefinitely because of a shortage of newsprint; others include *De Vrije Stem* (5,000), in Dutch, and several Chinese-language publications.

News agency. The official facility is the Suriname News Agency (*Surinaams Nieuws Agentschap* (SNA), which issues daily bulletins in Dutch and English.

Radio and television. There are a number of small commercial radio stations in addition to the government-owned *Stichting Radio-omroep Suriname* and *Surinaamse Televisie Stichting,* each of which broadcasts in all local languages. There were approximately 246,000 radio and 48,000 television receivers in 1987.

INTERGOVERNMENTAL   REPRESENTATION

Ambassador to the US: Arnold T. HALFHIDE.

US Ambassador to Suriname: Richard C. HOWLAND.

Permanent Representative to the UN: (Vacant).

IGO Memberships (Non-UN): EEC(L), *EIB,* IADB, IBA, Interpol, NAM, OAS, OPANAL, SELA.

S W A Z I L A N D

Kingdom of Swaziland

Political Status: Independent monarchy within the Commonwealth since September 6, 1968.

Area: 6,703 sq. mi. (17,363 sq. km.).

Population: 706,137 (1986C), 749,000 (1988E).

Major Urban Centers (1982E): MBABANE (administrative capital, 39,000); Lobamba (royal and legislative capital, 4,700); Manzini (14,000).

Official Languages: English, siSwati.

Monetary Unit: Lilangeni (market rate March 1, 1988, 2.09 emalangeni = $1US). The lilangeni is at par with the South African rand, although under a Tripartite Monetary Area agreement concluded between Swaziland, Lesotho, and South Africa on July 1, 1986, the rand has ceased to be legal tender in Swaziland.

Sovereign: King MSWATI III; installed on April 25, 1986, succeeding (as Head of State) Queen Regent Ntombi THWALA.

Prime Minister: Prince Sotsha [Sotcha, Sotja] DLAMINI, appointed by King Mswati III on October 6, 1986, to succeed Prince Bhekimpi DLAMINI.

T H E   C O U N T R Y

Bordered on the north, west, and south by South Africa and on the east by Mozambique, Swaziland is the smallest of the three former British High Commission territories in southern Africa (see map, p. 536). The country comprises a mountainous western region (Highveld), a middle region of moderate altitude (Middleveld), an eastern lowland area (Lowveld), and the so-called Lubombo plateau on the eastern border. About 97 percent of the population is Swazi African, the remainder being of European and Eurafrican (mixed) stock. English is an official language, but siSwati (akin to Zulu) prevails among the indigenous population; Afrikaans is common among the Europeans, many of whom are of South African origin. Christianity is the religion of approximately half the people; there are a few Muslims, the remainder adhering to traditional beliefs. In 1976, women were reported to constitute 37 percent of the work force and were responsible for the majority of food production. Female participation in government, with the exception of the former queens regent, is minimal.

The economy is quite diversified, given the country's small land area and population, although its composition, particularly in the mining sector, is changing. Production of iron ore, which accounted for 25 percent of export earnings in 1967, had virtually ceased by the end of the 1970s, while asbestos reserves, after 40 years of extraction, were also approaching depletion. Coal mining, on the other hand, is undergoing rapid development, while other minerals, such as tin, barites, and silica, are found in commercially exploitable quantities. Ample water supplies not only support agriculture, which yields sugar, forest products, and livestock, but constitute a potential hydroelectric power base.

GOVERNMENT AND POLITICS

Political background. Swaziland came under British control in the mid-nineteenth century, when a Swazi ruler requested protection against his people's traditional enemies, the Zulu. Kept intact when the Union of South Africa was formed in 1910, the territory was subsequently administered under native rulers by the British high commissioner for South Africa. Preparations for independence began after World War II and culminated in the promulgation of internal self-government in 1967 and the achievement of full independence within the Commonwealth in 1968 under King SOBHUZA II, who subsequently exercised firm control of the country's political institutions. Following small gains by the semiradical Ngwane National Liberation Congress in a 1972 parliamentary election and frustration of his attempts to have an opposition MP deported, the king in April 1973 repealed the constitution, abolished the legislature, introduced a detention act, and banned all opposition political activity.

Maj. Gen. Maphevu DLAMINI, who had been prime minister since 1976, died on October 25, 1979, Prince Mabandla Fred DLAMINI being designated his successor on November 23. On August 21, 1982, King Sobhuza also died, having technically reigned from the age of one in 1899, although not formally enthroned until 1921 and not recognized as paramount ruler by the British until 1966.

The naming of Prince Bhekimpi DLAMINI to succeed Prince Mabandla as prime minister in March 1983 seemed to mark the ascendancy of conservative elements within the royal house. In August, Queen Regent Dzeliwe SHONGWE was also ousted from power, reportedly because she differed over the interpretation of her role with traditionalists within the *Liqoqo,* historically an advisory council that had been elevated to the status of Supreme Council of State following Sobhuza's death. She was replaced by Ntombi THWALA, the mother of Prince Makhosetive, who was named successor to the former sovereign on August 10. Two months later, however, Prince Mfanasibili DLAMINI and Dr. George MSIBI, who were prominently involved in the palace coup that installed Queen Regent Ntombi, were dismissed from the *Liqoqo.*

On April 25, 1986, two years earlier than originally planned, Prince Makhosetive assumed the title of King MSWATI III in an apparent effort to halt the power struggle that had followed his father's death. The 19-year-old king moved quickly to consolidate his control, formally disbanding the Liqoqo in June and appointing Prince

Sotsha DLAMINI, a relatively obscure former police official, as prime minister on October 6.

Constitution and government. For some years after independence, King Sobhuza was reported to have been working on a revised Western-style constitution. However, in March 1977 he announced that he had abandoned the effort in favor of a form of traditional government based on tribal councils (*tinkhundla*). Under the *tinkhundla* system, as formally promulgated in October 1978, elections are held without political campaigns or electoral rolls, an 80-member electoral college designating one-half of a 20-member Senate and four-fifths of a 50-member House of Assembly. The remaining members of each are designated by the monarch, who also names the prime minister and other cabinet officials. The judiciary, whose members are appointed by the king, encompasses a High Court, a Court of Appeal, and district courts. There are also 17 Swazi courts for tribal and customary issues.

Swaziland is divided for administrative purposes into four districts, each headed by a commissioner appointed by the central government.

Foreign relations. Swaziland is a member of the United Nations, the Commonwealth, and the Organization of African Unity. It maintains close relations with South Africa as a result of geographic proximity, administrative tradition, and economic dependency (more than 80 percent of the kingdom's imports are from South Africa and a substantial portion of its national income consists of remittances from Swazis employed in the White-ruled state). Despite OAU strictures, Mbabane concluded a secret nonaggression pact with Pretoria in 1982 and subsequently strove to contain African National Congress (ANC) activity within its territory. Subsequently, a series of major raids on purported ANC strongholds by South African security forces in 1986 led to vehement protests by the Swazi government and a December visit by South African Foreign Minister Roelof "Pik" Botha, who reaffirmed his government's commitment to the 1982 pact and pledged that the incursions would cease. However, in July 1987 two top ANC officials and a Mozambican woman companion were murdered at Mbabane. In August, two additional killings by alleged South African agents brought the total number of ANC deaths in 1987 to eleven.

Despite its ties to South Africa, Swaziland established diplomatic relations with Mozambique during 1976. The action was prompted by a need to facilitate the movement of goods through the Mozambique port (and capital) of Maputo. The Mozambique Embassy at Mbabane was Swaziland's first resident mission from independent Africa, and a security accord was concluded between the two countries in mid-1984.

Relations with the West are friendly, despite some dissatisfaction with Britain over the amount of economic aid and the latter's unwillingness to pay financial compensation for land alienated to South African and other White concessionaires during the nineteenth century. Swaziland is also one of the few African states to maintain diplomatic ties with Israel.

Current issues. King Mswati III, at 19 the world's youngest monarch, surprised many observers with bold action during the first year of his reign, including abolition of the

Liqoqo and the installation of a new and presumably more tractable prime minister. After four years of palace intrigue that witnessed the dismissal and arrest of numerous prominent officials, most Swazis appeared to support the exercise of monarchical prerogative as a means of increased stability.

In May 1987 twelve prominent Swazis, including the former prime minister, Prince Bhekimpi DLAMINI, were arrested and charged with sedition, reportedly because of involvement with the imprisoned Prince Mfanasibili Dlamini. Most of the accused, including the two princes were found guilty and sentenced to 15 years' imprisonment in March 1988.

Economically, the new government faced persistent budgetary difficulty, although a significant rise in sugar production, and the prospect of increased international investment yielded "guarded optimism" by late 1987.

POLITICAL PARTIES

Former Government Party:

Imbokodvo National Movement. The *Imbokodvo* ("Grindstone") Movement dominated the political scene during the late 1960s and has been the only political group permitted to function openly since 1973. The leadership of the party has been vacant since the dismissal of Prince Mabandla Dlamini as prime minister in March 1983.

Illegal Opposition:

Swazi Liberation Movement (Swalimo). The avowedly revolutionary Swalimo was launched in 1978 by Dr. Ambrose Zwane of the former Ngwane National Liberatory Congress (NNLC).
Leaders: Dr. Ambrose P. ZWANE, Dumisa DLAMINI (Secretary General).

Swaziland Progressive Party (SPP). The SPP is an outgrowth of the former Swazi Progressive Association, founded in 1929.
Leader: J.J. NQUKU (President).

Swaziland United Front (SUF). The SUF was organized in 1962 as an offshoot of the SPP. Its leader, Robert Mabuza, was among 14 political detainees released in May 1980 on the personal intervention of Prime Minister Dlamini.
Leader: Robert Mpangele MABUZA.

LEGISLATURE

The bicameral **Parliament** (*Libandla*) consists of a 20-member **Senate** and a 50-member **House of Assembly.** Under procedures announced by King Sobhuza in 1977 and first implemented in 1978, an 80-member electoral college, encompassing 2 members chosen from each tribal council (*Inkhundla*), selects 40 assemblymen, who are joined by 10 Crown appointees in selecting 10 senators to join an equal number selected by the head of state. On September 28, 1987, King Mswati dissolved the existing Parliament and on November 16 the electoral college selected 40 members of a new Assembly, none of whom had served previously; the 10 Crown appointees were designated the following day.

CABINET

Prime Minister	Prince Sotsha Dlamini

Ministers

Agriculture and Cooperatives	Sipho Hezekiel Mamba
Commerce, Industry, Mines and Tourism	Douglas Ntiwane
Defense and Youth	(Vacant)
Education	Chief Sipho Shongwe
Finance	Sibusiso Barnabas Dlamini
Foreign Affairs	George Mamba
Health	Francis Friedman
Interior and Immigration	Senzenjani Enoch Tshabalala
Justice	Reginald Dhladhla
Labor and Public Service	Benjamin Nsibandze
Natural Resources, Land Utilization and Energy	Prince Nqaba Dlamini
Public Works and Communication	Wilson Mkhonta
Governor, Central Bank	H.B.B. Oliver

NEWS MEDIA

Press. Unless otherwise noted, the following are English dailies published at Mbabane: *Times of Swaziland* (10,000); *Swaziland Observer* (8,000); *Swazi News* (7,000), weekly; *The Herald* (Manzini), founded 1986.

Radio and television. The nation's 97,000 radio sets receive commercial programs from the government-controlled Swaziland Broadcasting Service and the privately owned Swaziland Commercial Radio, in addition to religious programs from Trans World Radio. The Swaziland Television Broadcasting Corporation (STBC), a subsidiary of the UK-based Electronic Rentals Group, transmits to about 12,500 receivers.

INTERGOVERNMENTAL REPRESENTATION

Ambassador to the US: (Vacant).

US Ambassador to Swaziland: Harvey Frans NELSON, Jr.

Permanent Representative to the UN: Dr. Timothy L.L. DLAMINI.

IGO Memberships (Non-UN): ADF, AfDB, BADEA, CCC, CWTH, EEC(L), *EIB,* Interpol, ISO, NAM, OAU, PCA, SADCC.

SWEDEN

Kingdom of Sweden
Konungariket Sverige

Political Status: Constitutional monarchy established June 6, 1809; under revised constitution effective January 1, 1975.

Area: 173,731 sq. mi. (449,964 sq. km.).

Population: 8,320,438 (1980C), 8,392,000 (1988E).

Major Urban Centers (1985E): STOCKHOLM (655,000; urban area, 1,549,000); Göteborg (424,000); Malmö (228,000); Uppsala (153,000).

Official Language: Swedish.

Monetary Unit: Krona (market rate March 1, 1988, 5.98 kronor = $1US).

Sovereign: King CARL XVI GUSTAF; succeeded to the throne September 19, 1973, following the death of his grandfather, King GUSTAF VI ADOLF.

Heir Apparent: Princess VICTORIA Ingrid Alice Désirée, daughter of the King.

Prime Minister: Ingvar CARLSSON (Social Democratic Labor Party); confirmed by the *Rikstag* on March 12, 1986, following interim incumbency, to succeed Olof PALME (Social Democratic Labor Party), who was assassinated on February 28.

THE COUNTRY

Situated on the Baltic side of the Scandinavian Peninsula and projecting north of the Arctic Circle, Sweden is the largest, most populous, and wealthiest of the Scandinavian countries, with a per capita GNP of nearly $13,000 in 1986. The indigenous population, almost 95 percent of which belongs to the state-supported Evangelical Lutheran Church, is homogeneous except for Finnish and Lapp minorities in the north; in addition, there are nearly 1 million resident aliens who have arrived since World War II, including some 400,000 Finns and substantial numbers from Mediterranean countries, such as Greece, Turkey, and Yugoslavia. In 1983, women constituted 47 percent of the labor force mainly in clerical work and primary education; female participation in both national and local government averages 28 percent.

Although only 7 percent of the land is cultivated and agriculture, forestry, and fishing contribute less than 4 percent of the gross domestic product, Sweden is almost self-sufficient in foodstuffs, while its wealth of resources has enabled it to assume an important position among the world's industrial nations. A major producer and exporter of wood, paper products, and iron ore, it is also a leading vehicle manufacturer and exports a variety of sophisticated capital goods. Despite socialist leadership throughout most of the postwar period, the private sector still accounts for nearly 90 percent of Sweden's output, although government outlays, primarily in the form of social security and other transfer payments, constitute about 60 percent of net national income.

GOVERNMENT AND POLITICS

Political background. A major European power in the seventeenth century, Sweden subsequently declined in relative importance but nevertheless retained an important regional position. For example, Norway was joined with Sweden in a personal union under the Swedish crown from 1814 to 1905. Neutrality in both world wars enabled Sweden to concentrate on its industrial development and the perfection of a welfare state under the auspices of the Social Democratic Labor Party, which was in power almost continuously from 1932 to 1976, either alone or in coalition with other parties.

At the *Riksdag* election of 1968, the Social Democrats, under Tage ERLANDER, won an absolute majority for the first time in 22 years. Having led the party and the country since 1946, Erlander was succeeded as party chairman and prime minister by Olof PALME in October 1969. Although diminished support for the Social Democrats was reflected in the parliamentary elections of 1970 and 1973, the party maintained control until September 1976, when voters, disturbed by a climate of increasing labor unrest, inflation, and declining economic growth, awarded the Center, Moderate, and Liberal (People's) parties a combined majority of 180 legislative seats. On October 8, a coalition government was formed under Center Party leader Thorbjörn FÄLLDIN. However, basic energy policy differences between the anti-nuclear Center and the pro-nuclear Moderates and Liberals forced the government to resign in October 1978, providing the opportunity for Ola ULLSTEN to form a minority People's Party government.

Following the election of September 16, 1979, a coalition with a bare one-seat majority was formed from a three-party center-right coalition under former prime minister Fälldin, but, on May 4, 1981, the Moderates withdrew in a dispute over tax reform, while tacitly agreeing to support the two-party government to avoid an early election and the likely return of the Social Democrats. Fälldin continued in office until the election of September 19, 1982, at which the Social Democrats obtained a three-seat plurality over nonsocialists, permitting Palme to return as head of a Social Democrat minority administration supported in parliament by the Communist Left. Although the center-right People's Party gained substantially at the balloting of September 15, 1985, reducing the SAP's representation by 7 seats, the Palme government remained in power with the support of the Communist Left's 19 members.

On February 28, 1986, Palme was assassinated at Stockholm by unidentified gunmen, the first European head of state to be killed while in office in 47 years. Deputy Prime Minister Ingvar CARLSSON assumed interim control of the government and was confirmed as Palme's successor on March 12, the nonsocialist parties abstaining from the confirmation vote out of respect for the late prime minister.

Constitution and government. The present Swedish constitution retains the general form of the old governmental structure, but the king is now only a ceremonial figure (formerly, as nominal head of government, he appointed the prime minister and served as commander in chief of the armed forces). In 1979, the *Riksdag* took final action on making women eligible for succession; thus the present king's daughter, VICTORIA, born in 1977, has become the heir apparent.

The chief executive officer is the prime minister, who is nominated by the speaker of the *Riksdag* and confirmed by the whole house. The prime minister appoints other members of the cabinet, which functions as a policy-drafting body. Routine administration is carried out largely by independent administrative boards (*centrala ämbetsverk*). Legislative authority is vested in the *Riksdag,* which has been a unicameral body since January 1971. The judicial system is headed by the Supreme Court (*Högsta Domstolen*) and includes 6 courts of appeal (*hovrätt*) and 100 district courts (*tingsrätt*). There is a parallel system of administrative courts, while the *Riksdag* appoints four *justitieombudsmen* to maintain general oversight of both legislative and executive actions.

Sweden is administratively divided into 24 counties (including Stockholm) with appointed governors and elected councils, and about 240 urban and rural communes with elected councils.

Foreign relations. Despite pro-Western sympathies, Sweden has not participated in any war nor entered any international alliance since 1814. Unlike Denmark, Iceland, and Norway, it declined to enter the North Atlantic alliance in 1949, while its determination to safeguard its neutrality is backed by an impressive defense system. As a strong supporter of international cooperation, Sweden participates in the United Nations and all its related agencies; in 1975, it became the first industrial nation to meet a standard set by the OECD, allocating a full 1 percent of its gross national product to aid for developing countries. An active member of the Nordic Council and the European Free Trade Association, it signed an industrial free-trade agreement with the European Economic Community (EEC) in 1972. Marking the end of a 450-year rupture, the Vatican announced in March 1983 that full diplomatic relations had been resumed between Sweden and the Holy See.

Stockholm's traditionally good relations with Moscow have been strained in recent years by incidents involving Soviet submarines in Swedish waters (15 such sightings being reported in 1985 alone) as well as by intrusions of Soviet planes into the country's airspace. In July 1986 a Swedish expert involved in the highly classified development of specialized submarine tracking and detection equipment was found to be missing. Subsequently, in July 1987, a major search was instituted for the presence of a foreign submarine near the Finnish border. It was presumably because of such problems that the Swedish defense budget was increased by 1.5 percent for the first time in almost a decade. Nonetheless, Sweden's commitment to positive engagement with the Soviet Union allowed talks to continue over a contested maritime area between the two nations in the Baltic Sea, which in January 1988 yielded an agreement that gave Sweden the rights to 75 percent of the 8,390-square-mile zone.

Current issues. The country's traditional sense of social peace, tolerance of foreigners, and accessibility of public officials were all seriously challenged by the Palme assassination, followed by a series of seemingly unrelated events. No fewer than four separate investigations were instituted into an arms trading scandal involving Bofors, the nation's largest arms maker. The death of the head of the War Materials Inspectorate just days before he was to testify before a special prosecutor investigating the alleged illegal sale of weapons to Iran gave credibility to speculation that Palme had been murdered for either blocking the shipments or for having acquiesced in them, thereby breaching his role as mediator in the Iran-Iraq conflict. In March 1987, following the resignation of the managing director of Bofors, the Nobel corporation, of which Bofors was a part, admitted its role in the illegal activity.

POLITICAL PARTIES

The parties below are broadly grouped, in conventional Swedish style, into bourgeois and socialist parties. A **Green Ecology Party** (*Miljöpartiet De Gröna*) was organized in 1981 by those who felt the traditional parties were too concerned with growth and status-quo economics.

Bourgeois Parties:

Moderate Coalition Party (*Moderata Samlingspartiet*—MSP). Known as the Conservative Party until after the 1968 election, the MSP was organized as a vehicle for the financial and business community and other well-to-do elements. The party advocates a tax cut and reduced governmental interference in the economy. It has long favored a strong defense policy and closer cooperation with the European Communities. Its *Riksdag* representation dropped from 86 seats in 1982 to 76 in 1985.
Leaders: Carl BILDT (Chairman), Per UNCKEL (Secretary).

People's Party (*Folkpartiet*—FP). Organized in the late 1920s as a fusion of an earlier People's Party and Sweden's traditional Liberal Party, and subsequently often referred to as the Liberal Party, the FP draws support from rural free-church movements as well as from professionals and intellectuals. Favoring socially progressive policies based on individual responsibility, the party has sought the cooperation of the Center Party (below) on many issues. It was the only party represented in the minority government of October 1978. The party lost half of its parliamentary representation at the 1982 general election, and, in July 1984, former prime minister Ola Ullsten resigned as chairman "to make way for more dynamic influences". Benefiting from a marginal loss of support for the governing Social Democrats and more substantial losses for both of the other major bourgeois parties, the FP gained 30 additional *Riksdag* seats, for a total of 51, at the September 1985 balloting.
Leaders: Bengt WESTERBERG (Chairman), Jan-Erik WIKSTRÖM (Parliamentary Leader), Gunnar BÄCKSTRÖM (Director), Peter ÖRN (Secretary).

Center Party (*Centerpartiet*—CP). Formerly known as the Agrarian Party, the CP was formed in 1922 as a political vehicle for rural interests. In return for agricultural subsidies, it began to support the Social Democrats in the 1930s, occasionally serving as a junior partner in coalition with the SAP (below). Since adopting its present name in 1957, the party has developed nationwide strength, including support from the larger urban centers. It has long campaigned for decentralization of government and industry and for reduced impact of government on the lives of individuals, while in the 1970s opposition to nuclear power became its main issue. Although the party lost 22 parliamentary seats at the election of September 16, 1979, its (then) chairman, Thorbjörn Fälldin, was returned as prime minister on October 11. It lost an additional 8 seats in the 1982 balloting, and 11 more in 1985; of its 44 remaining seats, 1 was allocated to the Christian Democrats as the result of an electoral pact signed in 1984.

At a party congress in June 1986, Karin SÖDER was elected to succeed Fälldin, who had resigned 6 months earlier because of his party's poor showing at the 1985 election. However, Ms. Söder (Sweden's first female party leader) was forced to step down in March 1987 for health reasons.
Leaders: Olof JOHANSSON (Chairman), Åke PETTERSSON (Secretary).

Christian Democratic Party (*Kristen Demokratisk Samling*—KDS). Formed in 1964 to promote Christian values in politics, the KDS claims a membership of over 20,000 but for two decades was unable to secure *Riksdag* representation. In September 1984, the group entered into an electoral pact with the Center Party, thereby securing its first and only legislative seat in 1985 despite a marginal 2.6 percent vote share.
Leaders: Alf SVENSSON (Chairman), Dan ERICSSON (Secretary).

Socialist Parties:

Social Democratic Labor Party (*Socialdemokratiska Arbetarepartiet*—SAP). Formed in the 1880s and long a dominant force in Swedish politics, the SAP has a pragmatic socialist outlook. During more than four decades of virtually uninterrupted power, it refrained from nationalization of major industries but gradually increased government economic planning and control over the business sector. When its representation in the *Riksdag* dropped to 152 in 1976, the SAP was forced, despite its sizable plurality, to move into opposition. It regained control of the government in 1982 and, despite a further reduction, maintained control in 1985 with the aid of the VPK (below). Few, if any changes in party ideology and practice were expected following the assassination of Olof Palme and the accession of his deputy, Ingvar Carlsson, to the prime ministership in March 1986.

Leaders: Ingvar CARLSSON (Prime Minister and Party Chairman), Bo TORESSON (Secretary).

Communist Left Party (*Vänsterpartiet Kommunisterna* — VPK). Originally formed in 1917, the VPK has in recent years pursued a "revisionist", or "Eurocommunist", policy based on distinctive Swedish conditions. This posture provoked considerable dissent within the party prior to the withdrawal of a pro-Moscow faction in early 1977 (see APK, below). Following the 1982 election, it agreed to support a new SAP government; its voting strength became even more vital following the SAP's loss of 7 seats in September 1985, party leader Werner pledging to use the VPK's influence to press for a more consistently leftist policy.

Leaders: Bertil MABRINK (Chairman), Kenneth KVIST (Secretary).

Communist Workers' Party (*Arbetarepartiet Kommunisterna* — APK). Formed on February 28, 1977, by three "orthodox" (neo-Stalinist) local sections of the VPK, the APK was joined by two of the VPK's parliamentary deputies but lost both seats at the 1979 election and is presently unrepresented in the *Riksdag.*

Leaders: Rolf HAGEL (Chairman), Rune PETTERSSON (Secretary).

Other leftist groups, none of which is represented in the *Riksdag,* include the **Communist Party of Sweden** (*Sveriges Kommunistiska Parti* — SKP), led by Roland PETTERSSON, which was organized in 1967 by a pro-Peking minority faction of the VPK and was known until 1973 as the Marxist-Leninist Communist League (*Kommunistiska Förbundet Marxist-Leninisterna* — KFML); the **Communist Party of Marxist-Leninist Revolutionaries** (*Kommunistiska Partiet Marxist-Leninisterna* [*revolutionärerna*] — KPML[r], a former KFML affiliate led by Frank BAUDE that broke away in 1970; and the Trotskyite **Socialist Party** (*Socialistika Partiet*), known until 1982 as the Communist Workers' League (*Kommunistiska Arbetareförbundet* — KAF).

LEGISLATURE

The unicameral *Riksdag* consists of 349 members serving three-year terms. Of the total, 310 are elected by proportional representation in 28 constituencies; the remaining 39 are selected from a national pool designed to give absolute proportionality to all parties receiving at least 4 percent of the vote. The franchise is held by all citizens over 18 years of age. Following the election of September 15, 1985, the Social Democratic Labor Party held 159 seats; the Moderate Coalition Party, 76; the People's Party, 51; the Center Party, 43; the Communist Left Party, 19; and the Christian Democratic Party, 1.

Speaker: Ingemund BENGTSSON.

CABINET

Prime Minister	Ingvar Carlsson
Deputy Prime Minister	Kjell-Olof Feldt
Ministers	
Agriculture	Mats Hellström
Civil Service Affairs	Bo Holmberg
Communications and Transport	Sven Hulterström
Culture	Bengt Göransson
Defense	Roine Carlsson
Development Aid	Lena Hjelm-Wallen
Economy and Budget	Kjell-Olof Feldt
Education	Lennart Bodström
Environment and Energy	Birgitta Dahl
Foreign Affairs	Sten Sture Andersson
Foreign Trade	Anita Gradin
Health and Social Affairs	Gertrud Sigurdsen
Housing	Hans Gustafsson
Immigration	George Andersson
Industry	Thage G. Peterson
Justice	Anna-Greta Leijon
Labor	Ingela Thalen
Wages and Salaries	Bengt K.Å. Johansson
Youth, Sport and Tourism	Ulf Lonnqvist
Chairman, Bank of Sweden	Bengt Dennis

NEWS MEDIA

Under Sweden's Mass Media Act, which entered into force in January 1977, principles of noninterference dating back to the mid-1700s and embodied in the Freedom of the Press Act of 1949 were extended to all information media.

Press. Most papers are politically oriented, and many are owned by political parties. The Press Subsidies Bill of 1966 grants state funds to political parties for distribution of their papers in case of financial difficulties. The following are published at Stockholm (circulation figures for 1985), unless otherwise noted: *Expressen* (552,100 daily, 665,300 Sunday), Liberal; *Dagens Nyheter* (400,300 daily, 497,500 Sunday), independent; *Aftonbladet* (343,400 daily, 393,200 Sunday), Social Democratic; *Göteborg-Posten* (Göteborg, 285,100 daily, 319,200 Sunday), Liberal; *Svenska Dagbladet* (225,100 daily, 227,800 Sunday), independent; *Sydsvenska Dagbladet* (Malmö, 113,700 daily, 144,900 Sunday), independent Liberal; *Arbetet* (Malmö, 108,900 daily, 131,300 Sunday), Social Democratic; *Kvällsposten* (Malmö, 103,400 daily, 133,600 Sunday), independent Liberal.

News agencies. Domestic service is provided by the Swedish Conservative Press Agency (*Svenska Nyhetsbyrån*), the Newspapers' Telegraph Agency (*Tidningarnas Telegrambyrå*), and the Swedish-International Press Bureau (*Svensk-Internationella Pressbyrån* — SIP). Numerous foreign agencies maintain bureaus at Stockholm.

Radio and television. *Sveriges Radio* is a noncommercial, state-licensed parent company providing both radio and television broadcasts. There were approximately 3.3 million radio and 3.3 million television receivers in 1987.

INTERGOVERNMENTAL REPRESENTATION

Ambassador to the US: Count Wilhelm WACHTMEISTER.

US Ambassador to Sweden: Gregory J. NEWELL.

Permanent Representative to the UN: Jan K. ELIASSON.

IGO Memberships (Non-UN): ADB, ADF, AfDB, APEF, BIS, CCC, CERN, CEUR, EFTA, ESA, G10, IADB, ICAC, ICCO, ICES, ICO, IEA, ILZ, Inmarsat, INRO, Intelsat, Interpol, ISO, ITC, IWC, IWSG, IWTC, NC, NIB, OECD, PCA.

SWITZERLAND

Swiss Confederation
Schweizerische Eidgenossenschaft (German)
Confédération Suisse (French)
Confederazione Svizzera (Italian)

Political Status: Neutral confederation from 1291; equivalent of federal system embodied in constitution of May 29, 1874.

Area: 15,941 sq. mi. (41,288 sq. km.).

Population: 6,365,960 (1980C), 6,518,000 (1988E), including approximately 900,000 noncitizens.

Major Urban Centers (1985E): BERN (135,000; urban area, 301,000); Zürich (350,000; urban area, 840,000); Basel (173,000; urban area, 363,000); Geneva (158,000; urban area, 382,000); Lausanne (124,000; urban area, 258,000).

Official Languages: German, French, Italian, Romansch.

Monetary Unit: Swiss Franc (market rate March 1, 1988, 1.39 francs = $1US).

President: Otto STICH (Social Democratic Party); elected by the Federal Assembly on December 9, 1987, to succeed Pierre AUBERT (Social Democratic Party for a one-year term beginning January 1, 1988.

Vice President: Jean-Pascal DELAMURAZ (Radical Democratic Party); elected by the Federal Assembly on December 9, 1987, to succeed Otto STICH (Social Democratic Party) for a term concurrent with that of the President.

THE COUNTRY

Situated in the mountainous heart of Western Europe, Switzerland has set an example of harmonious coexistence among different ethnic and cultural groups, and enjoys the further distinction of being a democratic country that is intimately involved in international cooperation yet has thus far declined to join the United Nations. The well-educated, politically sophisticated Swiss belong to four main language groups: German (65 percent), French (18 percent), Italian (10 percent), and Romansch (1 percent). In religious affiliation, approximately 48 percent are Roman Catholic, 44 percent Protestant. In recent years the previously large influx of foreign workers has ebbed, although in relation to total population they constitute the highest percentage (14.5) in Europe. Overall economic indicators, on the other hand, are quite favorable, with unemployment and inflation estimated at 0.8 and 1.0 percent, respectively, in 1986.

Durable goods output centers on the production of precision-engineered items and special quality products that are not readily mass-produced. Stock-raising is the principal agricultural activity; the chief crops are wheat and potatoes. Tourism, international banking, and insurance are other major contributors to the economy. Switzerland relies heavily on external transactions, and foreign exchange earned from exports of goods and services is equal to about a third of the total national income. The budget submitted in October 1987 predicted a substantial surplus (in excess of $800 million) for 1988, although deficits were forecast for the 1990s.

GOVERNMENT AND POLITICS

Political background. The origins of the Swiss Confederation date back to 1291, when the cantons of Uri, Schwyz, and Unterwalden signed an "eternal alliance" against the Hapsburgs. The league continued to expand until 1648, when it became formally independent of the Holy Roman Empire at the Peace of Westphalia. Following French conquest and reorganization during the Napoleonic era, Switzerland's boundaries were fixed by the Congress of Vienna in 1815, when its perpetual neutrality was guaranteed by the principal European powers. The present constitution, adopted May 29, 1874, superseded an earlier document of 1848 and increased the powers conferred on the central government by the cantons. With a multiparty system based on proportional representation (introduced in 1919), Switzerland has been governed in recent years by a coalition of moderate parties that jointly controls the legislature and determines the composition of the collegial executive body.

Women have had the right to vote in federal elections since 1971 and presently are accorded a similar privilege at the cantonal level in all but the two Appenzell half-cantons. Until quite recently, however, they have been denied participation in the Federal Council. In February 1984 Social Democrats narrowly defeated a leadership resolution to withdraw from the government coalition over the issue (see Political Parties, below). Subsequently, in October, the Federal Assembly reversed itself and approved the Radical Democratic nomination of Elisabeth KOPP, mayor of the Zürich suburb of Zumikon, as a member of the executive body; in so doing, they ensured, because of the principle of presidential rotation, that the position of nominal head of state will eventually fall to Ms. Kopp.

Constitution and government. Under the constitution of 1874, Switzerland is (despite the retention of "confederation" in its official name) a federal republic of 23 cantons, three of which are subdivided into half-cantons. The areas of central jurisdiction are largely detailed in the various articles of Chapter I of the 1874 basic law, as subsequently amended. The cantons retain autonomy in a range of local concerns, without the right to nullify national legislation. Responsibility for the latter is vested in a bicameral parliament, the Federal Assembly, both houses of which have equal authority. The 46-member Council of States is made up of two representatives from each undivided canton and one from each half-canton, by methods of election which vary from one canton to another. The lower house, the 200-member National Council, is directly elected by universal adult suffrage (since 1971, when women were enfranchised for federal and most cantonal elections) under a proportional representation system. Legislation passed by the two chambers may not be vetoed by the executive nor reviewed by the judiciary. In addition to normal legislative processes, the Swiss constitution provides for the use of the initiative for purposes of constitutional amendment and of the referendum as a means of ratifying or rejecting federal legislation (to go forward, the two require petitions of 100,000 and 50,000 signatures, respectively).

Executive authority is exercised on a collegial basis by a seven-member Federal Council (*Bundesrat*), whose members are elected by the entire Federal Assembly. In addition, the Assembly each year elects two of the seven to serve one-year terms as president and vice president of the Confederation. The president has limited prerogatives and serves as a first among equals. Although the Federal Council is responsible to the legislature, it has increasingly become a nonpolitical body of experts, with members usually re-elected as long as they are willing to serve.

The judicial system functions primarily at the cantonal level; the only regular federal court is the 26-member Federal Tribunal, which has the authority to review cantonal court decisions involving federal law. Each canton has civil and criminal courts, a Court of Appeal, and a Court of Cassation.

Local government is on two basic levels: cantons and municipalities or communes. In some of the larger cantons, however, the communes are grouped into districts, which are headed by commissioners. Following the federal example, there are two basic governing organs at the cantonal and communal levels: a unicameral legislature and a collegial executive. In five cantons and half-cantons (as well as in numerous smaller units) the entire voting population functions as the legislature, while in the others the legislature is elected.

After 30 years of separatist strife in the largely French-speaking, Roman Catholic region of Jura, Swiss voters in September 1978 approved cantonal status for most of the area. The creation of the 23rd canton, the first to be formed since 1815, was approved by over 82 percent of those voting in the national referendum, with Jura's full membership in the Confederation taking effect on January 1, 1979. Southern Jura, predominantly Protestant and German-speaking, remained part of Bern, while the small district of Laufen also voted, in September 1983, to remain part of Bern rather than to join the half-canton of Basel-Land.

Canton and Capital	Area (sq. mi.)	Population (1986E)
Aargau (Aarau)	542	470,000
Appenzell		
Ausserrhoden (Herisau)	94	49,300
Innerrhoden (Appenzell)	66	13,200
Basel		
Basel-Land (Liestal)	165	225,700
Basel-Stadt (Basel)	14	195,000
Bern (Bern)	2,336	923,600
Fribourg (Fribourg)	645	193,500
Genève (Geneva)	109	363,000
Glarus (Glarus)	264	36,400
Graübunden (Chur)	2,744	166,000
Jura (Delémont)	323	64,800
Luzern (Luzern)	576	304,700
Neuchâtel (Neuchâtel)	308	155,000
St. Gallen (St. Gallen)	778	402,500
Schaffhausen (Schaffhausen)	115	69,700
Schwyz (Schwyz)	351	102,700
Solothurn (Solothurn)	305	218,900
Thurgau (Frauenfeld)	391	191,500
Ticino (Bellinzona)	1,085	276,100
Unterwalden		
Nidwalden (Stans)	106	30,800
Obwalden (Sarnen)	189	27,500
Uri (Altdorf)	416	33,500
Valais (Sion)	2,018	230,600
Vaud (Lausanne)	1,243	545,700
Zug (Zug)	92	80,900
Zürich (Zürich)	667	1,128,900

Foreign relations. Switzerland's foreign policy has historically stressed neutrality and scrupulously avoids membership in military alliances. Although not a member of the United Nations, it accredits a permanent observer to the organization, is a party to the statute of the International Court of Justice, and belongs to many UN Specialized Agencies. (In 1984, both the National Council and the Council of States approved a government proposal that the country apply for UN membership; however, the action was overwhelmingly rejected by Swiss voters in a referendum held on March 16, 1986.)

A member of the European Free Trade Association (EFTA), Switzerland concluded an agreement with the European Economic Community (EEC) in 1972 which established an industrial free-trade relationship between the two parties. In the international community, Switzerland maintains cordial diplomatic relations with virtually all independent nations. It has a special relationship with the Principality of Liechtenstein, for which it handles diplomatic, defense, and customs functions.

Swiss foreign policy has recently been influenced by the principle of "solidarity", which holds that a neutral state is morally obligated to undertake social, economic, and humanitarian activities contributing to world peace and prosperity. Partly for this reason, it joined the Inter-American Development Bank in July 1976 as a nonregional member and subsequently agreed to convert into grants assorted debts owed by various developing nations. Total flow of public and private assistance to developing countries has been in excess of 3 percent of GNP in recent years.

Current issues. In recent years, a long-simmering controversy over the presence of foreigners — particularly those seeking permanent asylum — has become a major political issue, strengthening the appeal of right-wing parties and generating pressures for parliamentary action. In Geneva, where native-born Swiss have been estimated to total only two-thirds of the resident population, the anti-immigrant Vigilance Party achieved parity with the theretofore leading Liberals at cantonal balloting in October 1985, while the Federal Assembly gave final approval in June 1986 to a series of measures at curbing a refugee influx that has included a considerable number of Turks, Sri Lankan Tamils, Ugandans, and Zairians. In an April 1987 referendum Swiss voters, by a two-to-one margin, endorsed proposals restricting immigration and making political asylum more difficult to obtain. Controversy has also erupted over relaxation of traditional bank secrecy, a proposal to such effect being rejected in a May 1984 referendum. Talks were, however, initiated with the United States on closer legal cooperation between the two countries and Swiss authorities agreed in March 1986 to freeze bank deposits identified as belonging to the family of deposed Philippine president Ferdinand Marcos. Subsequently, the government blocked accounts linked to the diversion of covert Iranian arms payments to Nicaraguan "contras". Although it indicated late in the year that it might rescind the action because a formal request for assistance in the matter had not been forthcoming from Washington, most of the bank records central to the Iran-*contra* affair were released to American prosecutors by November 1987, the Federal Tribunal rejecting a defense contention that the proceedings were of a political rather than criminal nature.

The 3–1 rejection on March 16, 1986, of the proposal to join the United Nations represented one of the most severe defeats of a government proposal in Swiss history, not a single canton producing a favorable vote. According to *The New York Times,* the result stemmed from "fears that joining . . . would compromise the nation's policy of 'armed neutrality', involve its conscript army in unwanted peacekeeping missions . . . and endanger Swiss organizations such as the International Committee of the Red Cross." The report added that many Swiss have come to view the world body "as dominated by the Soviet bloc and third world nations [thus becoming] a forum of worthless and often futile politicing."

At the regional level, Switzerland was condemned by neighboring states for official negligence in connection with a fire and major chemical spill into the Rhine River at Sandoz on November 1, 1986. The disaster was particularly embarrassing to the Swiss, whose antipollution laws (some dating back to 1876) had long been considered a model of environmental self-regulation. During a meeting of Rhine ministers at Zürich in mid-November, (then) President Egli indicated that his government would consider claims for damages caused by the 30-ton spill and pledged full cooperation with the International Rhine Protection Commission in adopting measures to guard against another such catastrophe.

POLITICAL PARTIES

The Swiss political scene is characterized by a multiplicity of political parties but is dominated by a four-party coalition that controls the majority of seats in both houses of the Federal Assembly.

Government Parties:

Radical Democratic Party (*Freisinnig-Demokratische Partei der Schweiz* — FDP/*Parti Radical-Démocratique Suisse* — PRD). Leader of the historic movement that gave rise to the federated state, the FDP is liberal in outlook and stands for strong centralized power within the federal structure. At the 1987 *Nationalrat* election, it lost three of the 54 seats it had won in 1983.
Leaders: Dr. Bruno HUNZIKER (President), Ulrich BREMI (Leader of Parliamentary Group), Hans Rudolf LEUENBERGER (General Secretary).

Social Democratic Party (*Sozialdemokratische Partei der Schweiz* — SPS/*Parti Socialiste Suisse* — PSS). Organized in 1870, the SPS advocates direct federal taxation and far-ranging state control of the economy, but is strongly anti-Communist. At an extraordinary party congress in February 1984 the party rejected a proposal by its Executive Committee to withdraw from the four-party government coalition because of the Federal Assembly's unwillingness the previous November to approve its nomination of a woman to the Federal Council. At the 1987 National Council balloting its representation fell by six seats, to 41.
Leaders: Helmut HUBACHER (President); Dario ROBBIANI (Leader of Parliamentary Group); André DAGUET, Eva ECOFFEY, Jean-Pierre METRAL, Hans Kaspar SCHIESSER, Elisabeth VEYA (Secretaries).

Christian Democratic People's Party (*Christlichdemokratische Volkspartei der Schweiz* — CVP/*Parti Démocrate-Chrétien Suisse* — PDC). Formerly known as the Conservative Christian–Social Party, the CVP was formed in 1912 from elements long opposed to the centralization of national power. Appealing primarily to Catholics, it advocates cantonal control over religious education, and taxes on alcohol and tobacco, while opposing direct taxation by the federal government. At the 1987 election its lower house representation remained unchanged at 42.
Leaders: Flavio COTTI (President), Eva SEGMULLER-WEBER (Chairman), Paul ZBINDEN (Leader of Parliamentary Group), Dr. Hans Peter FAGAGNINI (General Secretary).

Swiss People's Party (*Schweizerische Volkspartei* — SVP/*Parti Suisse de l'Union Démocratique du Centre* — UDC). Formed in 1971 by a merger of the former Farmers, Artisans, and Citizens' Party and the Democratic Party, the SVP seeks a moderate course to social democracy while retaining strong agrarian and conservative social tendencies. It advocates a strong national defense as well as the protection of agriculture and small industry. In 1987 its *Nationalrat* strength increased by two to 25.
Leaders: Hans UHLMANN (President), Hans Rudolf NEBIKER (Leader of Parliamentary Group), Dr. Max FRIEDLI (Secretary).

Opposition Parties:

Independents' Alliance (*Landesring der Unabhängigen* — LdU/*Alliance des Indépendants* — AdI). Organized in 1936 by progressive, middle-class elements, the LdU represents consumers' interests and advocates liberal and social principles. In 1987 it retained its existing 8 seats in the lower house.
Leaders: Dr. Franz JAEGER (President), Dr. Sigmund WIDMER (Leader of Parliamentary Group), Peter J. AEBI (Secretary).

Liberal Party (*Liberale Partei der Schweiz* — LPS/*Parti Libéral Suisse* — PLS). With a program similar to that of the Christian Democratic Party, the LPS (formerly the Liberal Democratic Union) draws support primarily from Protestant circles. The party favors a loosely federated structure and opposes centralization and socialism. The nine seats obtained at the 1987 *Nationalrat* balloting represented an increase of one over 1983.
Leaders: Gilbert COUTAU (President), Claude BONNARD (Leader of Parliamentary Group), Philippe BOILLOD (Secretary).

National Action for People and Homeland (*Nationale Aktion Für Volk und Heimat* — NA/*Action Nationale* — AN). Formerly known as the **National Action against Foreign Infiltration of People and Homeland** (*National Aktion gegen Überfremdung von Volk und Heimat/Action Nationale contre l'Emprise et la Surpopulation Etrangères*), the NA has sought to reduce the number of resident foreign workers as well as the number of naturalizations, both proposals being overwhelmingly defeated in referenda held in October 1974 and March 1977, respectively. On the other hand, a 1981 law relaxing restrictions on foreign workers, against which the Movement had campaigned vigorously, was narrowly overturned by a referendum in June 1982. In 1983, the party presented a joint list with the Republican Movement (see RP/PRS, below), which obtained five lower house seats; running separately, it secured three *Nationalrat* seats in 1987.
Leaders: Rudolf KELLER (Chairman), Anita WILHELM (Secretary).

Republican Party (*Republikanische Partei* — RP/*Parti Républicain Suisse* — PRS). The RP was formed in 1971, initially as the Republican Movement, on a platform of preserving the Swiss way of life and opposing entry into the EEC and the UN. It obtained only 0.6 percent of the vote in 1979 and presented a joint list with the NA in 1983. The 1977 referendum on resident foreign workers was Republican-sponsored.
Leader: Franz BAUMGARTNER (President).

Evangelical People's Party (*Evangelische Volkspartei der Schweiz* — EVP/*Parti Evangélique Populaire Suisse* — PEP). The EVP is committed to a program based largely on conservative Protestant precepts. It retained its three existing lower house seats in 1987.
Leaders: Max DÜNKI (President), Hans SCHOCH (Secretary).

Workers' Party (*Partei der Arbeit der Schweiz* — PdAS/*Parti Suisse du Travail* — PST). Organized in 1921 as the Swiss Communist Party, outlawed in 1940, and reorganized under its present name in 1944, the PdAS is primarily urban based and maintains a pro-Moscow Communist posture. In June 1984, after a 20-year break caused by the Sino-Soviet dispute, the party reestablished relations with the Chinese Communist Party. It retained its single *Nationalrat* seat in 1987.
Leaders: Jean VINCENT (Honorary President), Armand MAGNIN (General Secretary).

Progressive Organizations of Switzerland (*Progressive Organisationen der Schweiz* — POCH/*Organisations Progressistes Suisses*). POCH was organized in 1972 by a group of student dissenters from the PdAS, who rejected what was viewed as an excessively doctrinaire posture by the parent group. It is nonetheless pro-Moscow in outlook and formed a legislative faction with the PdAS and the PSA (below) following the 1983 election. The party recently adopted a strongly ecologist/feminist posture that, coupled with an aggressive campaign style, has drawn support from academics and youth. Its existing lower-house strength of three increased to four in 1987.

Leaders: Georg DEGEN, Eduard HAFNER, Thomas HEILMANN (Central Secretaries).

Autonomous Socialist Party (*Autonome Sozialistische Partei/Parti Socialiste Autonome/Partito Socialista Autonomo* — PSA). The PSA was formed in 1969 as an outgrowth of an earlier split within the Socialist Party of Tessin. Viewing itself as an independent member of the Communist world movement, its influence is confined to the Italian portion of Switzerland.

Leader: Werner CAROBBIO (Secretary).

Green Party of Switzerland (*Grüne Partei der Schweiz* — GPS/*Parti Ecologiste Suisse* — PES). Then known as the Swiss Federation of Green/Ecology Parties (*Vereinigung der Grünen Partien in Schweiz/Fédération Suisse des Partis Ecologistes*), the Greens first gained representation at the cantonal level in Zürich and Luzern in April 1983 and won three seats in the October *Nationalrat* election. They won nine lower house seats in 1987, surprising many who felt that they might do better in view of recent Swiss concerns over environmental issues.

Leader: Dr. Peter SCHMID (President).

At a Geneva cantonal election in October 1985, a theretofore minor right-wing formation, the **Vigilance Party** (*Parti Vigilance* — PV), led by Eric BERTINAT, gained 12 seats (for a total of 19 out of 100) on an anti-foreign platform that claimed the influx of migrants had created a housing shortage and heightened unemployment for domestic workers. Other far-right formations include the anti-immigrant, Valais-based **Conservative and Liberal Movement** (*Mouvement Conservateur et Libéral* — MCH), launched in February 1986, and the **National Socialist Party** (*Nationalsozialistische Partei* — NSP), organized at Zürich by a former National Action vice president in August 1986. In August 1986 Valentine OEHEN, another former National Action member, formed the **Swiss Ecological Liberal Party** (*Ökologische Freiheitliche Partei der Schweiz* — ÖFPS), committed to principles of free market economy. Minor left-extremist parties include the **Socialist Workers' Party** (*Sozialistiche Arbeiterpartie* — SAP/*Parti Socialiste Ouvrière* — PSO) established in 1969 as the Marxist Revolutionary League (*Marxistische Revolutionäre Liga/Ligue Marxiste Révolutionnaire*) by dissident Trotskyite members of the PdAS, and the **Communist Party of Switzerland–Marxist-Leninist** (*Kommunistische Partei der Schweiz-Marxistische-Leninistiche/Parti Communiste Suisse-Marxiste-Léniniste*), founded in 1972. There are also a number of small interest-group parties, including the **Swiss Party for the Handicapped and Socially Disadvantaged** (*Schweizerische Partei der Behinderten und Sozialbenachteiligten* — SPBS), organized in March 1984, and the **Swiss Car Party** (*Auto Partei der Schweiz/Parti Auto Suisse*), a motorists' group formed in March 1985, which obtained two lower house seats in 1987.

LEGISLATURE

The bicameral **Federal Assembly** (*Bundesversammlung/Assemblée Fédérale*) consists of a Council of States elected in the various cantons and a National Council elected by a uniform procedure throughout the country. As a result of this dual system, the political complexion of the Council of States is more conservative than that of the National Council, which affords a closer reflection of the relative strength of the political parties.

Council of States (*Ständerat/Conseil des Etats*). The upper house consists of 46 members, 2 elected from each of the 20 cantons and 1 from each of the 6 half-cantons. Electoral procedures vary from canton to canton, but the majority hold direct elections based on the same franchise as for the National Council. Following the balloting of October 18, 1987, the Christian Democratic People's Party held 19 seats; the Radical Democratic Party, 14; the Social Democratic Party, 5; the Swiss People's Party, 4; the Liberal Party, 3; and the National Action, 1.

President: Franco MASONI (1988).

National Council (*Nationalrat/Conseil National*). The lower house consists of 200 members elected for four-year terms by direct popular

vote within each canton on a proportional representation basis. At the last election, held October 18, 1987, the Radical Democratic Party won 51 seats; the Christian Democratic People's Party, 42; the Social Democratic Party, 41; the Swiss People's Party, 25; the Green Party, 9; the Liberal Party, 9; the Independents' Alliance 8; the Progressive Organizations of Switzerland, 4; the National Action 3; the Evangelical People's Party, 3; the Swiss Car Party, 2; the Workers' Party, 1; Autonomous Socialist Party, 1; independent, 1.

President: Rudolf REICHLING (1988).

FEDERAL COUNCIL

President	Otto Stich
Vice President	Jean-Pascal Delamuraz
Department Chiefs	
Finance	Otto Stich
Foreign Affairs	René Felber
Interior	Flavio Cotti
Justice and Police	Elisabeth Kopp
Military	Arnold Koller
Public Economy	Jean-Pascal Delamuraz
Transportation, Communications and Energy	Adolf Ogi
President, Swiss National Bank	Pierre Langeutin

NEWS MEDIA

Switzerland has a long record of objective news coverage and analysis, and the press, in particular, is given close attention abroad as well as within the country.

Press. The Swiss press is privately owned and free from governmental influence, although editors are accustomed to using discretion in handling national security information. The following major publications appear daily, unless otherwise noted: *Blick* (Zürich, 380,000), in German; *Tages Anzeiger* (Zürich, 258,000), in German; *Neue Zürcher Zeitung* (Zürich, 145,000), in German, independent Liberal; *Berner Zeitung* (Bern, 121,000), in German; *Basler Zeitung* (Basel, 113,000), in German; *24 Heures* (Lausanne, 100,000), in French; *La Suisse* (Geneva, 70,500 daily, 101,000 Sunday), in French; *Der Bund* (Bern, 62,500), in German, independent; *Luzerner Neueste Nachrichten* (Luzern, 57,000), in German; *Aargauer Tagblatt/Brugger Tagblatt* (Aarau, 55,000), in German, Radical; *Le Matin* (Lausanne, 54,000 daily, 129,000 Sunday), in French; *Feuille d'Avis de Neuchâtel* (Neuchâtel, 37,000), in French; *Corriere del Ticino* (Lugano, 33,300), in Italian; *L'Impartial* (La Chaux-de-Fonds, 31,500), in French; *Giornale del Popolo* (Lugano, 21,000), in Italian, Catholic independent; *Journal de Genève* (Geneva, 20,000), in French, Liberal.

News agencies. The domestic facility is the Swiss Telegraph Agency (*Schweizerische Depeschenagentur/Agence Télégraphique Suisse*); in addition, numerous foreign agencies maintain bureaus at Geneva.

Radio and television. Broadcasting services, supported mainly by licensing fees, are operated by the postal administration, with multilingual programming from the Swiss Radio and Television Broadcasting Society (*Schweizerische Radio- und Fernsehgesellschaft/Société Suisse de Radiodiffusion et Télévision*). There were approximately 2.6 million radio and 2.3 million television receivers in 1987.

INTERGOVERNMENTAL REPRESENTATION

Ambassador to the US: Klaus JACOBI.

US Ambassador to Switzerland: Faith Ryan WHITTLESEY.

Permanent Observer to the UN: Dieter CHENAUX-REPOND.

IGO Memberships (Non-UN): ADB, ADF, AfDB, BIS, CCC, CERN, CEUR, EFTA, ESA, *G10*, IADB, ICAC, ICCO, ICM, ICO, IEA, Intelsat, Interpol, IWC, IWTC, OECD, PCA.

SYRIA

Syrian Arab Republic
al-Jumhuriyah al-'Arabiyah al-Suriyah

Political Status: Republic proclaimed in 1941; became independent April 17, 1946; under military regime since March 8, 1963.

Area: 71,586 sq. mi. (185,408 sq. km.).

Population: 9,171,622 (1981C), 11,334,000 (1988E).

Major Urban Centers (1981C): DAMASCUS (1,112,214); Aleppo (985,413); Homs (346,871); Latakia (196,791); Hama (177,208).

Official Language: Arabic.

Monetary Unit: Syrian Pound (market rate March 1, 1988, 11.23 pounds = $1US).

President: Gen. Hafiz al-ASSAD; assumed presidential powers February 22, 1971; approved as President by popular referendum March 12, and sworn in March 14, 1971; reelected by referendum in 1978 and on February 9, 1985, for a third seven-year term beginning March 12.

Vice Presidents: Col. Rif'at al-ASSAD, 'Abd al-Halim KHADDAM, Muhammad Zuhayr MASHARIQA; appointed by the President on March 11, 1984.

Prime Minister: Mahmud al-ZUBI; designated by the President on November 1, 1987, to succeed 'Abd al-Ra'af al-KASM.

THE COUNTRY

The Syrian Arab Republic is flanked by Turkey on the north; the Mediterranean Sea, Lebanon, and Israel on the west; Jordan on the south; and Iraq on the east. Its terrain is distinguished by the Anti-Lebanon and Alawite mountains running parallel to the Mediterranean, the Jabal al-Druze Mountains in the south, and a semidesert plateau in the southeast, while the economically important Euphrates River Valley traverses the country from north to southeast. Ninety percent of the population is Arab; the most important minorities are Kurds, Armenians, and Turks. Islam is professed by 87 percent of the people (most of whom belong to the Sunni sect), with the remaining 13 percent being mainly Arab and Armenian Christians. Arabic is the official language, but French and English are spoken in government and business circles.

Syria is one of the few Arab countries with adequate arable land, and one-third of the work force is engaged in agriculture (more than half of the women as unpaid family workers on rural estates). However, a lack of proper irrigation facilities makes agricultural production dependent on variations in rainfall. An agrarian reform law, promulgated in 1958 and modified in 1963, limits the size of individual holdings. Wheat, barley, and cotton are the principal crops. Major industries have been nationalized, the most important of which are food processing, tobacco, and textiles. Industrial growth has been rapid since the 1950s, with petroleum, Syria's most valuable natural resource, providing an investment base. Increased agricultural production and oil transit revenues contributed to a sharp increase in the gross national product, which expanded to an average annual rate of 10 percent in the early 1980s. However, the economy has since deteriorated because of the cost of maintaining troops in Lebanon, increased arms purchases, closure of the Iraqi pipeline at the outset of the Gulf war, a drop in oil prices, and a growing debt burden.

GOVERNMENT AND POLITICS

Political background. Seat of the brilliant Omayyad Empire in early Islamic times, Syria was conquered by the Mongols in 1400, was absorbed by the Ottoman Turks in 1517, and became a French-mandated territory under the League of Nations in 1920. A republican government, formed under wartime conditions in 1941, secured the evacuation of French forces in April 1945 and declared the country fully independent on April 17, 1946. Political development was subsequently marked by an alternation of weak parliamentary governments and unstable military regimes. Syria merged with Egypt on February 1, 1958, to form the United Arab Republic, but seceded on September 29, 1961, to reestablish itself as the independent Syrian Arab Republic.

On March 8, 1963, the Arab Socialist Renaissance Party (*al-Baath*) assumed power through a military-backed coup, Gen. Amin al-HAFIZ becoming the dominant figure until February 1966, when a second coup led by Maj. Gen. Salah al-JADID resulted in the flight of Hafiz and the installation of Nur al-Din al-ATASSI as president. With Jadid's backing, the Atassi government survived the war with Israel and the loss of the Golan Heights in 1967, but governmental cohesion was weakened by crises within the *Baath* that were precipitated by conflicts between the civilian and doctrinaire Marxist "progressive" faction led by Jadid and Atassi, and the more pragmatic and military "nationalist" faction under Lt. Gen. Hafiz al-ASSAD. In November 1970 the struggle culminated in a coup by nationalist elements, General Assad assuming the presidency and subsequently being elected to the post of secretary general of the party. The new regime established a legislature (the first since 1966) and, following a national referendum in September 1971, joined with Egypt and Libya in a now moribund Federation of Arab Republics. The first national election in 11 years was held in 1973, with the National Progressive Front, consisting of the *Baath* and its allies, winning an overwhelming majority of seats in the legislative People's Council. In 1977, the Front won 159 of 195 seats, with 36 awarded to independents, while all of the seats were distributed among Front members in 1981.

General Assad's assumption of the presidency marked the growing political and economic prominence of the Alawite Muslim sect of northwestern Syria, constituting about 13 percent of the country's population. The Alawite background of Assad and some of his top associates triggered opposition among the country's predominantly urban Sunni majority (70 percent) which had experienced economic adversity as a result of the regime's socialist policies. This opposition turned into an insurgency led by the Muslim Brotherhood (see Political Parties, below) after Syria's 1976 intervention on the Maronite side in the Lebanese civil war. The incidents perpetrated by the fundamentalist rebels included the murder of 63 Alawite military cadets at Aleppo in June 1979, another 40 deaths at Latakia in August of the same year, a series of bombings that resulted in several hundred casualties at Damascus in 1981, and numerous clashes between the dissidents and the regime's special forces led by the president's brother, Col. Rif'at al-ASSAD. The struggle reached its climax in a three-week rebellion at the northern city of Hama in February 1982, which was suppressed with great bloodshed. By 1983, the seven-year insurgency had been decisively crushed, along with the Muslim Brotherhood's stated aim of establishing an Islamic state.

In late 1983, President Assad underwent a serious illness (widely rumored to have been a heart attack) and a committee that included 'Abd al-Halim KHADDAM and Zuhayr MASHARIQA was established within the *Baath* national command to coordinate government policy. In March 1984, Khaddam and Mashariqa were named vice presidents, as was Rif'at al-Assad, a move that was interpreted as an attempt to curb the latter's ambitions as successor to the president by assigning him more carefully circumscribed responsibilities than he had theretofore exercised as commander of the Damascus-based Defense Forces. In addition, Rif'at was temporarily exiled, along with two adversaries, as apparent punishment for employing confrontationist tactics in the power struggle during his brother's illness. He returned in November to reassume responsibility for military and national security affairs.

Having recovered sufficiently to resume full leadership, President Assad was reelected to a third seven-year term in a February 1985 referendum with the reported support of 99.97 percent of the voters. Subsequently, Rif'at al-Assad was again sent into exile (still in effect as of June 1988) although technically retaining his vice presidency.

Constitution and government. According to the 1973 constitution, which succeeded provisional constitutions of 1964 and 1969, Syria is a "socialist popular democracy". Nominated by the legislature upon proposal by the Regional Command of the *Baath* Party, the president, who must be a Muslim, is elected by popular referendum for a seven-year term. The chief executive wields substantial power, appointing the prime minister and other cabinet members, military personnel, and civil servants. He also serves as commander in chief and may amend the constitution. Legislative authority is vested in a People's Council, which is directly elected for a four-year term. The judicial system, based on a blend of French, Ottoman, and Islamic legal traditions, is headed by a Court of Cassation and includes courts of appeal, summary courts, courts of first instance, and specialized courts for military and religious issues.

For administrative purposes Syria is divided into 13 provinces and the city of Damascus, which is treated as a separate entity. Each of the provinces is headed by a centrally appointed governor who acts in conjunction with a partially elected Provincial Council.

Foreign relations. Syria has consistently based its foreign policy on Arab nationalism, independence from foreign (particularly Western) influences, and opposition to Israel. Relations with other Middle Eastern states have varied, periodic disputes having erupted with Egypt, Iraq, Lebanon, Jordan, and the more conservative Arab governments. In September 1975, Syria's already strained relationship with the Sadat government worsened as a result of the Egyptian-Israeli Sinai agreement, which the Assad regime called "strange and disgraceful". Although Syrian intervention in Lebanon in 1976 (for details see entry under Lebanon) yielded a temporary reversal of the trend, the Sadat peace initiative of November 1977 and the Camp David accords of September 1978 caused the two nations to sever diplomatic relations by the end of 1978. The mutual antagonism was heightened during 1984 as a consequence of President Husni Mubarak's efforts to create an Egyptian-Jordanian-Iraqi-PLO axis directed against Syria and Libya. During 1985, on the other hand, some tentative steps were taken under Saudi Arabian auspices toward normalization of Syrian-Egyptian relations.

Syrian-Iraqi relations deteriorated in April 1975 because of a dispute over utilization of the waters of the Euphrates River and were further damaged by a long-standing rivalry between Syrian and Iraqi factions of the *Baath* Party. Relations reached a nadir in 1977 when the Syrian government accused Iraqi agents of complicity in two attempts to assassinate (then) Foreign Minister 'Abd al-Halim Khaddam, but their common opposition to the subsequent Egyptian-Israeli peace initiative helped mend the split. Though Iraq did not participate in the September 20–24, 1978, Damascus meeting of the "steadfastness" states (Algeria, Libya, South Yemen, and Syria, plus the PLO), Syria and Iraq concluded on October 26 a "National Charter for Joint Action" directed toward complete military unity against Israel and the peace plan. Further movement toward unification came to an abrupt halt in July 1979, however, when the new Iraqi president, Saddam Hussein, accused Syria of involvement in a plot to oust him. Subsequently, the two *Baath* regimes attempted to destabilize one another by providing assistance to subversive elements in each country.

During 1980 Syria became somewhat isolated within the Arab world. In the wake of the renewed estrangement from Iraq, it supported Iran (without subscribing to the latter's interpretation of Islamic ideology) in the Gulf war that broke out in September 1980, and in November appeared close to an armed confrontation with Iraq's ally, Jordan. At the same time, its defiance of Israel and the United States in Lebanon, which led to withdrawal of their forces during 1983–1985, elevated Assad to an unprecedented position of influence as military arbiter in Lebanon, while maintaining close ties with both Libya and Saudi Arabia.

The USSR has long been Syria's principal source of military equipment and economic aid, but Soviet influence, though considerable, has not been absolute. Having declined to participate in the January 1980 summit at Islamabad, Pakistan, that condemned the Soviet invasion of Afghanistan, Assad concluded a 20-year treaty of friendship and cooperation with President Brezhnev during a two-day visit to Moscow in October. Under this treaty, the Soviets replaced Syrian aircraft destroyed during Israel's invasion of Lebanon, in addition to providing a modern air defense system that included Sam-5 long-range missiles.

Syria maintains relations with all the Eastern European states, the People's Republic of China, and most nations of Western Europe. Diplomatic contacts with Britain and the United States were temporarily broken off as a result of the 1967 Arab-Israeli war, while relations with both the United States and France were strained in 1982 because of the dispatch of troops to Beirut in the wake of the Israeli invasion of Lebanon.

Current issues. The ever-shifting panorama of Lebanese internal conflict has been a major preoccupation of the Syrian leadership since regular Syrian army units intervened in Lebanon in April 1976 (see article on Lebanon). Following the departure of Western peacekeeping units in early 1984, Damascus assumed a crucial role in its neighbor's affairs. However, extensive troop deployments in the context of various "security plans" have failed to eliminate heavy fighting in and around Beirut.

Apart from the uncertainties of its role in Lebanon, Syria has encountered numerous problems, including a growing economic crisis, a wave of lethal bombings, and increased isolation from most of the Arab world over its support for Iran in the Gulf War. In addition, much of the Western bloc suspended high-level relations with Damascus and imposed limited sanctions in response to alleged Syrian involvement in many terrorist incidents, including a widely publicized bombing at London's Heathrow airport in 1986.

During 1987 Damascus adopted an essentially moderate position, as evidenced by its June decision to shut down the Syrian offices of the extremist Palestinian group led by Abu Nidal (see Revolutionary Council of Fatah in section on the Palestinian Liberation Organization). Normal relations were reestablished with most Western nations and, following the November summit of the Arab League, conservative Arab regimes reportedly agreed to increase their aid to Syria in return for President Assad's pledge to play "a constructive role" in attempts to resolve the Iran/Iraq war. Counterbalancing such developments was a report from Amnesty International late in the year that charged the government with widespread torture and abuse of political prisioners, including supporters of PLO Chairman Yasir 'Arafat, with whom Assad had been feuding since 1983 (see article on PLO).

On the economic front, continued decline led to the dismissal or resignation of several cabinet ministers in midyear amid charges of corruption and incompetence. At the end of October Prime Minister 'Abd al-Ra'uf al-KASM also resigned and a group of technical experts, expected to pursue a greater role for the private sector, were included in the new government of Mahmud al-ZUBI.

The economic outlook brightened somewhat in the first half of 1988 as Syria, with recently enhanced estimates of oil reserves, became, for the first time, a net exporter of crude. The dominant political development during that period was an April reconciliation between President Assad and the PLO's 'Arafat which was viewed as further extending Syrian influence in regional affairs.

POLITICAL PARTIES

The *Baath* Party has enjoyed de facto dominance of the Syrian political system since 1963, its long tenure being partly attributable to its influence among the military. The party system has operated in an unusual fashion, with the nominally illegal Communist Party, which has been formally linked with the first four groups below in the **National Progressive Front** (*al-Jibha al-Wataniyah al-Taqaddumiyah*) since its formation by President Assad in 1972, running separately from the NPF in the 1981 and 1986 elections.

National Progressive Front:

Baath Party. Formally known as the Regional Command of the Arab Socialist Renaissance Party (*Hizb al-Baath al-'Arabi al-Ishtiraki*), the *Baath* is the Syrian branch of an international political movement that began in 1940 and remains active in Iraq and other Arab countries. The contemporary party dates from a 1953 merger of the Arab Resurrectionist Party, founded in 1947 by Michel Aflak and Salah al-Din Bitar, and the Syrian Socialist Party, founded in 1950 by Akram al-Hawrani. The *Baath* philosophy stresses socialist ownership of the principal means of production, redistribution of agricultural land, secular political unity of the Arab world, and opposition to imperialism.

During the party's Eighth Regional Congress at Damascus from January 5–21, 1985, a new 90-member Central Committee was elected, which immediately redesignated President Assad as secretary general and named 20 other members to the Regional Command, including the president's brother, Col. Rif'at al-Assad.

Leaders: Gen. Hafiz al-ASSAD (President of the Republic, Secretary General of the Party, and Chairman of the National Progressive Front), 'Abdallah al-AHMAR (Assistant Secretary General), Zuhayr MASHARIQA, Sulayman QADDAH.

Arab Socialist Union (*al-Ittihad al-Ishtiraki al-'Arabi*). The Arab Socialist Union has long been a "Nasserite" group.
Leaders: Dr. Jamal ATASSI, Isma'il al-KADHI (Secretary General).

Socialist Unionist Movement (*al-Haraka at-Tawhidiyah al-Ishtiraki-yah*). The Socialist Unionist Movement has also been regarded as a "Nasserite" group.
Leaders: Sami SOUFAN, Fayiz ISMA'IL (Secretary General).

Arab Socialist Party (*al-Hizb al-Ishtiraki al-'Arabi*). The Arab Socialist Party is anti-Egyptian and seeks a revival of parliamentary competition.
Leader: 'Abd al-Ghani KANNUT.

Communist Party of Syria (*al-Hizb al-Shuyu'i al-Suriyah*). The consistently pro-Soviet Communist Party is technically illegal but is permitted to operate openly and has been represented in the cabinet since 1966.
Leaders: Khalid BAKDASH (Secretary General), Yusuf FAYSAL (Deputy Secretary General).

There is also an anti-Soviet **Communist Action Party**, whose 1983 linkage with Palestinian dissidents to form "people's committees" in a number of Syrian communities prompted the arrest of more than 70 persons during a government crackdown in 1986. The crackdown was also reportedly aimed at members of a small, recently-formed group, the **Nasserite Popular Organization**.

Extremist Opposition:

Muslim Brotherhood (*al-Ikhwan al-Muslimin*). The Brotherhood is a Sunni fundamentalist movement that has long maintained an active underground campaign against the *Baath* and its leadership, being charged, inter alia, with the massacres at Aleppo and Latakia in 1979 as well as the killing of a number of Soviet technicians and military advisers in 1980. In February 1982 it instigated an open insurrection at Hama which government troops were able to quell only after three weeks of intense fighting that resulted in the devastation of one-quarter of the city. Subsequently, it was announced that on March 11 the Brotherhood had joined with the **Islamic Front in Syria** and a number of other groups within the country and abroad in establishing a **National Alliance for the Liberation of Syria,** which in 1986 was reportedly headquartered at Cairo, Egypt.

LEGISLATURE

The **People's Council** (*Majlis al-Sha'ab*) is a directly elected, unicameral body presently consisting of 195 members serving four-year terms. At the most recent election of February 10–11, 1986, candidates running on a National Progressive Front joint list won 151 seats (Baath Party, 129; Arab Socialist Union, 9; Socialist Unionist Movement, 8; Arab Socialist Party, 5), while the Communist Party, running separately, won 9 seats, with independents capturing the remaining 35 seats.

Speaker: 'Abd al-Qadir QADDURAH.

CABINET

Prime Minister	Mahmau al-Zubi
Deputy Prime Minister	Lt. Gen. Mustafa Talas
Deputy Prime Minister for Economic Affairs	Dr. Salim Yasin
Deputy Prime Minister for Services Affairs	Mahmud Qaddur

Ministers

Agriculture and Agrarian Reform	Muhammad Ghabbash
Communications	Murad Quwatli
Construction	Marwan Farra
Culture and National Guidance	Dr. Najah al-'Attar
Defense	Lt. Gen. Mustafa Talas
Economy and Foreign Trade	Dr. Muhammad al-'Imadi
Education	Ghassan Halabi
Electricity	Kamil al-Baba
Finance	Dr. Khalid al-Mahanyani
Foreign Affairs	Farouk al-Shara'
Health	Dr. Iyad Statti
Higher Education	Dr. Kamal Sharaf
Housing and Utilities	Muhammad Nur Antabi
Industry	Antoine Jubran
Information	Muhammad Salman
Interior	Dr. Muhammad Harba
Irrigation	'Abd al-Rahman Madani
Justice	Khalid al-Ansari
Local Administration	Ahmad Diab
Oil and Mineral Wealth	Dr. Habib Matanyas
Religious Trusts	'Abd al-Majid Tarabulsi
Social Affairs and Labor	Haydar Buzu
Supply and Internal Trade	Hasan al-Saqqa
Tourism	'Adnan Quli
Transportation	Yusuf al-Ahmad
Governor, Central Bank	Hisham Mitwalli

NEWS MEDIA

Press. The press is strictly controlled, most publications being issued by government agencies or, under government license, by political, religious, labor, and professional organizations. In June 1978 ten journalists, including Adnan Baghajati, editor of *al-Baath,* were barred from press activity, thus bringing to 120 the number of journalists known to have been purged within a two-year period for leftist views. No newspaper has national circulation; the following are published daily at Damascus, unless otherwise noted: *al-Thawra* (55,000); *al-Baath* (50,000), organ of the Baath; *al-Jamahir al-'Arabiyah* (Aleppo, 10,000); *al-Shabab* (Aleppo, 9,000); *Barq al-Shimla* (Aleppo, 6,500); *al-Fida* (Hama, 4,000).

News agencies. *Agence Arabe Syrienne d'Information* issues Syrian news summaries to foreign news agencies; several foreign bureaus also maintain offices at Damascus.

Radio and television. Broadcasting is a government monopoly and operates under the supervision of the General Directorate of Broadcasting and Television. There were approximately 2.1 million radio and 405,000 television receivers in 1987.

INTERGOVERNMENTAL REPRESENTATION

Ambassador to the US: (Vacant).

US Ambassador to Syria: William L. EAGLETON, Jr.

Permanent Representative to the UN: Ahmad Fathi al-MASRI.

IGO Memberships (Non-UN): AFESD, AMF, BADEA, CCC, *EIB,* IC, ICAC, IDB, Intelsat, Interpol, IWTC, LAS, NAM, OAPEC.

TANZANIA

United Republic of Tanzania
Jamhuri ya Muungano wa Tanzania

Political Status: Independent member of the Commonwealth; established in its present form April 26, 1964, through union of the Republic of Tanganyika (independent 1961) and the People's Republic of Zanzibar (independent 1963); present one-party constitution adopted April 25, 1977.

Area: 364,898 sq. mi. (945,087 sq. km.), encompassing Tanganyika, 363,948 sq. mi. (942,626 sq. km.) and Zanzibar 950 sq. mi. (2,461 sq. km.).

Population: 17,512,611 (1978C), 22,628,000 (1988E).

Major Urban Centers (1978C): DAR ES SALAAM (757,346), Zanzibar (town, 110,669), Mwanza (110,611), Tanga (103,409). The transfer of government operations to a new capital at Dodoma is expected to be completed by 1990.

Official Languages: English, Swahili.

Monetary Unit: Shilling (market rate March 1, 1988, 93.73 shillings = $1US).

President: Ali Hassan MWINYI; appointed Vice President of Tanzania on January 30, 1984, and elected President of Zanzibar on April 19; sworn in as President of Tanzania on November 5, 1985, to succeed Julius Kambarage NYERERE, following election of October 27.

First Vice President and Prime Minister: Joseph S. WARIOBA; appointed First Vice President by the President on November 6, 1985; named Prime Minister on the same day, succeeding Salim Ahmed SALIM.

Second Vice President, President of Zanzibar, and Chairman of the Zanzibar Revolutionary Council: Idris Abdul WAKIL; elected President of Zanzibar (and thus Vice President of the Republic) on October 13, 1985, succeeding Ali Hassan MWINYI on October 17; became Second Vice President upon designation of Joseph S. Warioba as First Vice President on November 6.

THE COUNTRY

The United Republic of Tanzania combines the large territory of Tanganyika on the East African mainland and the two islands of Zanzibar and Pemba off the East African coast. Tanzania's people are overwhelmingly of African (primarily Bantu) stock, but there are significant Asian (largely Indian and Pakistani), European, and Arab minorities. In addition to the indigenous tribal languages, Swahili (Kiunguja is the Zanzibari form) serves as a lingua franca, while English and Arabic are also spoken. A majority of the population (over 60 percent on the mainland and over 90 percent on Zanzibar) is Muslim, the remainder adhering to Christianity or traditional religious beliefs. Females are estimated to comprise 50 percent of the labor force, with responsibility for over 70 percent of subsistence activities; Tanzanian women have a relatively high level of literacy and are significantly represented in all levels of government and party affairs.

The economy is primarily agricultural, benefiting from few extractive resources except diamonds. The most important crops on the mainland are coffee, cotton, and sisal, which collectively account for approximately two-fifths of the country's exports. The economies of Zanzibar and Pemba are based on cloves and coconut products. Industry, which accounts for about 15 percent of the gross domestic product, is primarily limited to the processing of agricultural products and the production of nondurable consumer goods, although there is an oil refinery that is dependent on imported crude. Modernization plans were enhanced by the completion in mid-1976, with Chinese financial and technical assistance, of the Tanzania-Zambia Railway (Tazara), which links Dar es Salaam and the Zambian copper belt.

Since 1979, the country has encountered serious economic difficulty, exacerbated by a drought-induced decline in cash-crop output and rapid population growth. Assistance from the International Monetary Fund was suspended in 1982, necessitating severe budget cutbacks. Four years later, faced with an external debt crisis, the government acceded to IMF demands for devaluation of the Tanzanian shilling, price increases for food producers, liberalization of export-import regulations, and privatization of state-run enterprises (see Current issues, below).

GOVERNMENT AND POLITICS

Political background. The former British-ruled territories of Tanganyika and Zanzibar developed along separate lines until their union in 1964. Tanganyika, occupied by Germany in 1884, became a British-administered mandate under the League of Nations and continued under British administration as a United Nations trust territory after World War II. Led by Julius K. NYERERE of the Tanganyika African National Union (TANU), it became independent within the Commonwealth in 1961 and adopted a republican form of government with Nyerere as president in 1962.

Zanzibar and Pemba, British protectorates since 1890, became independent in 1963 as a constitutional monarchy within the Commonwealth. However, little more than a month after independence, the Arab-dominated government of Sultan Seyyid Jamshid bin Abdullah bin KHALIFA was overthrown by African nationalists, who established a People's Republic with Sheikh Abeid Amani KARUME of the Afro-Shirazi Party (ASP) as president.

Following overtures by Nyerere, the two countries combined on April 26, 1964, to form the United Republic of Tanganyika and Zanzibar, renamed the United Republic of Tanzania later in the same year. Nyerere became president of the unified state and in September 1965 was overwhelmingly confirmed in that position by popular vote in both sections of the country. Karume, in addition to becoming first vice president of Tanzania, continued to head the quasi-independent Zanzibar administration until April 1972, when he was assassinated; Nyerere thereupon appointed Aboud JUMBE to succeed Karume as first vice president and as leader of the ASP.

On February 5, 1977, the mainland Tanganyika African National Union and the Zanzibar-based Afro-Shirazi Party merged to form the Revolutionary Party of Tanzania (CCM), while a new constitution, adopted on April 25, accorded the CCM a "dominant" role in the Tanzanian governmental system. On November 5, 1980, Prime Minister Edward SOKOINE announced his retirement for reasons of health, and the president, two days later, named Cleopa David MSUYA as his successor.

Sokoine returned as prime minister on February 24, 1983, but was killed in an automobile accident on April 12, 1984, and was succeeded 12 days later by Salim Ahmed SALIM. Earlier, on January 27, Vice President Jumbe had submitted his resignation in the wake of mounting secessionist agitation on Zanzibar, Ali Hassan MWINYI being named his replacement on January 30.

Although having announced in early 1984 his intention to step down as head of state upon the expiry of his current term, Nyerere surprised observers (who had predicted a change of heart after Sokoine's death) by withdrawing from contention at the 1985 CCM congress in favor of Vice President Mwinyi, who was overwhelmingly nominated as the sole candidate for the October presidential balloting. Because of a constitutional prohibition against Zanzibari occupying both presidential and prime ministerial offices, Prime Minister Salim was replaced following the October 27 poll by Justice Minister Joseph WARIOBA, who also assumed the post of first vice president; concurrently, Idris Abdul WAKIL, who had been elected president of Zanzibar on October 13, became second vice president, while Salim was named deputy prime minister and minister of defense.

Mwinyi's elevation to the presidency and his encouragement of private enterprise appeared to stem secessionist sentiment on Zanzibar although the island leadership continued its independent pursuit of economic recovery. The latter appeared to be threatened in early 1988 by evidence of a power struggle between Wakil and Chief Minister Shariff HAMAD, who came from the northern island of Pemba where 90 percent of the islands' cloves are produced. On January 23 Wakil, claiming that dissidents were plotting a coup, suspended the Zanzibari government and three days later replaced it with a new administration headed by Omar Ali JUMA.

Constitution and government. The "permanent" constitution of April 25, 1977, did not significantly alter the system of government prescribed by the "interim" document of 1965; however, a number of amendments were adopted prior to the 1985 election. Tanzania remains a one-party state, with controlling influence exercised by the Revolutionary Party at both national and regional levels. The president is nominated by the CCM and elected by universal suffrage for no more than two five-year terms. The vice president must come from Zanzibar if the president is from the mainland, and vice versa. The executive is headed by a presidentially appointed prime minister. The National Assembly, slightly more than two-thirds of whose members are at present directly elected, sits for a five-year term, subject to presidential dissolution (in which case the president himself must stand for reelection). The judicial system on the mainland is headed by a High Court and includes local and district courts. In August 1979, a Tanzanian Court of Appeal was established to assume, inter alia, the functions of the East African Court of Appeal, which had ceased to exist with the collapse of the East African Community in 1977. All judges are appointed by the president.

Tanzania's 25 administrative regions (20 on the mainland, 5 on Zanzibar) are each headed by a regional commissioner appointed by the central government. Below the regional level there are municipalities, town councils, and, in rural locations, area or district councils.

On October 13, 1979, a new constitution for Zanzibar was promulgated by its Revolutionary Council after having been approved by the CCM. Under the new system, designed to provide for "more democracy" without contravening the union constitution of Tanzania, the president of Zanzibar, upon nomination by the party, is directly elected for a five-year term and held to a maximum of three successive terms. There is also a directly elected House of Representatives endowed with the legislative authority previously exercised by the Revolutionary Council. The latter has, however, been retained as a "high executive council" of cabinet status, with members appointed by the president.

Foreign relations. Tanzania belongs to the United Nations and most of its Specialized Agencies, the Commonwealth, and the Organization of African Unity. In addition, it participated with Kenya and Uganda in the East African Community until the organization was dissolved in mid-1977. Under Nyerere's leadership, Tanzania has pursued a policy of international nonalignment and of vigorous opposition to colonialism and racial discrimination, particularly in southern Africa. It has given asylum to political refugees from African countries, and various liberation groups are headquartered at Dar es Salaam. The country maintains no relations with South Africa, and severed relations with Britain from 1965 to 1968 to protest London's Rhodesian policy. Relations with the United States have been strained at times by Tanzanian disagreement with US policies relating to Africa and, until Washington's rapprochement with Peking, by US uneasiness over Tanzanian acceptance of military and economic aid from China.

Long-standing friction with Uganda escalated into overt military conflict in late 1978 (see entry under Uganda). After a six-month campaign that involved the deployment of some 40,000 Tanzanian troops, the forces of Ugandan president 'Idi Amin were decisively defeated, Amin fleeing to Libya. Subsequently, under an agreement signed with the government of Godfrey Binaisa, approximately 20,000 Tanzanians remained in the country to man security points pending the training of a new Ugandan army. During 1980, Kenya and Sudan were among the regional states expressing concern over the continuing presence in Uganda of the Tanzanian troops, the last of which were finally withdrawn in May-June 1981.

Relations with Kenya improved measurably upon the conclusion of a November 1983 accord between the two and Uganda on the distribution of EAC assets and liabilities. On November 17, the border between Tanzania and Kenya, originally closed in 1977 in order to "punish" Kenya for allegedly dominating Tanzania's economy, was reopened and both countries reached agreement on a series of technical cooperation issues. Rapprochement was further enhanced on December 12, when the three former EAC members exchanged high commissioners in an effort "to facilitate expansion and consolidation in economic matters".

Current issues. Ali Hassan Mwinyi's election as president in October 1985 was hailed as a "rare peaceful transition of power" for Africa. However, the much-revered Nyerere is still considered to be the most influential person in the country, particularly in view of his reelection as CCM chairman in October 1987. Underscoring a lack of high-level consensus, the two leaders have differed over the appropriateness and effectiveness of policy changes that led to renewed IMF debt rescheduling in 1986. Nyerere, while accepting a need to "correct" past economic "mistakes", has charged that the IMF was "no friend of Tanzania". He has also expressed concern that changes in socialist structures could jeopardize past advances in literacy, health services, nutrition for the poor, and a more equitable distribution of income. Nevertheless, the administration pushed ahead in 1987 with its new economic policies and related campaigns against corruption and bureaucratic inefficiency. One immediate result was the approval in July of donor aid through the World Bank of $955 million for 1987 and $978 million for 1988.

There was little disagreement among Tanzanian leaders in regard to the country's other major issue—the regional impact of the South African policies. Declaring that Pretoria's destabilization efforts in neighboring countries represented a direct threat to Tanzania, the government acknowledged in 1987 that it had sent troops to Mozambique to assist Maputo in the fight against Renamo rebels.

Mwinyi also called for mandatory economic sanctions against Pretoria and lent support to the effort by Front-Line States to avoid South African trade routes. To that end, a new five-year plan for infrastructural development was expected to give Malawi greater access to Tanzanian highways; other programs called for rehabilitation and upgrading of the Tanzania-Zambia Railway and the port at Dar es Salaam.

POLITICAL PARTIES

Government Party:

Revolutionary Party of Tanzania (*Chama Cha Mapinduzi* — CCM). The CCM was formally launched on February 5, 1977, two weeks after a merger was authorized by a joint conference of the Tanganyika African National Union (TANU) and the Afro-Shirazi Party (ASP) of Zanzibar. During the January 24 conference at Dar es Salaam, (then) President Nyerere asserted that the new organization would be "supreme" over the governments of both mainland Tanzania and Zanzibar. Subsequently, a National Executive Committee (NEC) was named by a process of hierarchical (indirect) election and, in turn, appointed a smaller Central Committee, headed by President Nyerere.

Founded in 1954, TANU was instrumental in winning Tanganyika's independence from Britain in 1961 and served after independence as the nation's leading policymaking forum, nominating both the president and candidates for election to the National Assembly. Its program, as set forth in the 1967 Arusha Declaration and other pronouncements, called for the development of a democratic, socialist, one-party state.

The ASP, organized in 1956–1957 by Sheikh Abeid Amani Karume, played a minor role in Zanzibari politics until the coup of 1964. Subsequently, it became the dominant party in Zanzibar and the leading force in the Zanzibar Revolutionary Council. Communist and Cuban models influenced its explicitly socialist program.

At the second national conference of the CCM, held at Dar es Salaam on January 20–24, 1982, delegates approved a series of proposals advanced by the NEC that would reestablish a separation of powers between party and state, particularly at the regional and local levels. President Nyerere defended the proposals on the ground that the existing concentration of authority had led to subordination of the party to the state. On the other hand, in 1986 Nyerere, who retained his party chairmanship despite having relinquished the state presidency, questioned the advisability of one-party systems for African countries, suggesting that the absence of political challenge bred complacency. He was elected to another five-year term as chairman at the CCM's third congress on October 22–31, 1987.

Leaders: Julius K. NYERERE (Chairman), Ali Hassan MWINYI (President of the Republic and Vice Chairman of the Party), Salim Ahmed SALIM (former Prime Minister and Party Secretary for Defense and Security), Rashidi Mfaume KAWAWA (Secretary General).

LEGISLATURE

The unicameral **National Assembly** (*Bunge*), which serves a five-year term, barring dissolution, is currently composed of 244 directly elected, indirectly elected, appointed, and ex officio members. At the most recent election of October 27, 1985, 168 seats (including 50 on Zanzibar and Pemba) were contested by 328 candidates, all approved by the CCM. An additional 76 seats are allocated to the following: 5 designates of the islands' House of Representatives; 15 women elected by the Assembly; 15 representatives of mass organizations; 15 presidential nominees; and (serving ex officio) 25 regional commissioners (who are also party secretaries), and the president of Zanzibar.

Speaker: Chief Adam SAPI MKWAWA.

CABINET

Prime Minister	Joseph S. Warioba
Deputy Prime Minister	Salim Ahmed Salim
Ministers	
Agriculture and Livestock Development	Jackson Makweta
Communications and Works	Mustafa Nyang'anyi
Community Development, Culture, Youth and Sports	Fatma Saidi Ali
Defense and National Service	Salim Ahmed Salim
Finance, Planning and Economic Affairs	Cleopa David Msuya
Foreign Affairs	Benjamin Mkapa
Health and Social Welfare	Dr. Aaron D. Chiduo
Home Affairs	Brig. Muhiddin M. Kimario
Justice and Attorney General	Damian Lubova
Labor and Manpower Development	Christian Kisangi
Lands, Natural Resources and Tourism	Arcado Ntagazwa
Local Government and Cooperatives	Paul Bomani
Minerals and Energy	Al-Noor Kassum
National Education	Kighoma Ali Malima
Trade and Industry	Joseph Rwegasira
Water Development	Pius Ng'wandu
Without Portfolio	Rashidi Mfaume Kawawa
	Gertrude Mongella
Ministers of State	
Finance, Economic Affairs and Planning	Damas K. Mbogoro
International Cooperation	Amina Salum Ali
Planning and Economic Affairs	Damas K. Mbogoro
Prime Minister's Office	Anna Makinda
President's Office and Capital Development	Anna Abdallah
Regional Administration	Charles Kileo
Second Vice President's Office	Ali Salim Ahmed
Governor, Central Bank	Charles Nyirabu

NEWS MEDIA

Press. The Newspaper Ordinance of 1968 empowers the president to ban any newspaper if he considers such action to be in the "national interest". The following papers are published at Dar es Salaam: *Uhuru* (101,000), CCM daily in Swahili; *Mzalendo* (100,000), CCM weekly in Swahili; *News* (80,000 daily, 85,000 Sunday), formerly the *East African Standard*, in English.

News agencies. The domestic facility is the Tanzanian News Agency (*Shihata*); Reuters, *Xinhua*, and TASS are among foreign agencies maintaining bureaus at Dar es Salaam.

Radio and television. The two government-owned radio stations are Radio Tanzania, which broadcasts in Swahili and English, and Radio Tanzania Zanzibar, which broadcasts in Swahili. The two stations operate transmitters on approximately 20 different frequencies. There is no television service on the mainland, but a government-run noncommercial station on Zanzibar began operation in January 1974. There were approximately 1.5 million radio and 8,000 television receivers in 1987.

INTERGOVERNMENTAL REPRESENTATION

Ambassador to the US: Asterius M. HYERA.

US Ambassador to Tanzania: Donald K. PETTERSON.

Permanent Representative to the UN: Dr. Wilbert Kumalija CHAGULA.

IGO Memberships (Non-UN): ADF, AfDB, BADEA, CCC, CWTH, EADB, EEC(L), *EIB,* IACO, ICAC, ICO, IIC, Intelsat, Interpol, ITPA, NAM, OAU, SADCC.

THAILAND

Kingdom of Thailand
Prathet Thai

Political Status: Independent monarchy presently functioning under constitution approved December 18, 1978.

Area: 198,455 sq. mi. (514,000 sq. km.).

Population: 46,113,756 (1979C), 54,651,000 (1988).

Major Urban Center (1983E): BANGKOK (3,517,000; urban area, 5,018,000).

Official Language: Thai.

Monetary Unit: Baht (market rate March 1, 1988, 25.27 baht = $1US).

Sovereign: King BHUMIBOL Adulyadej (King RAMA IX); ascended the throne June 9, 1946; crowned May 5, 1950.
Heir Apparent: Crown Prince VAJIRALONGKORN.

Prime Minister: Gen. (Ret.) PREM Tinsulanonda (Independent); appointed by the King on March 3, 1980, following the resignation of Gen. KRIANGSAK Chamanan (National Democracy Party) on February 29; reappointed in 1983, and on August 5, 1986, following election of July 27; moved into caretaker status following legislative dissolution of April 29, 1988.

THE COUNTRY

Surrounded by Burma in the west, Laos in the north and northeast, Kampuchea in the southeast, and Malaysia in the deep south, the Kingdom of Thailand (known historically as Siam) is located in the heart of mainland Southeast Asia. It is a tropical country of varied mountainous and lowland terrain. About 75 percent of its population is of Thai stock; another 14 percent is composed of overseas Chinese, an urban group important in banking, mining, and commerce. Other minorities are of Malaysian, Indian, Khmer, and Vietnamese descent. Theravada Buddhism is professed by about 95 percent of the population, but religious freedom prevails and a number of other religions claim adherents. Women constitute approximately 40 percent of the labor force, primarily in agriculture, although they outnumber men in the manufacturing and informal trading sectors; female participation in government, while increasing somewhat in recent years, averages below 10 percent.

Like most countries in Southeast Asia, Thailand is predominantly rural, approximately three-fourths of its people being engaged in agriculture. One of the largest net exporters of rice in the world, Thailand also ships rubber, corn, and tin abroad. The country's mineral resources include cassiterite (tin ore), tungsten, antimony, coal, iron, lead, manganese, molybdenum, and gemstones. Industrial output includes textiles and refined petroleum as well as building materials, paper, jute, and tobacco products. Until quite recently, the Thai economy was both rapidly developing and stable, the government avoiding excessive deficit financing, husbanding its foreign-exchange reserves, and maintaining a strong currency readily convertible at free-market rates. However, by late 1979 a variety of factors, including rapidly rising oil prices, had contributed to diminished foreign-exchange reserves, a burdensome trade deficit, and a rate of inflation that had doubled over the preceding twelve months to nearly 20 percent. Limited recovery thereafter (including a drop in inflation to less than 2 percent by mid-1986) was attributed, in part, to the exploitation of recently discovered natural gas deposits, which were expected to yield a substantial reduction in the country's dependency on imported oil.

GOVERNMENT AND POLITICS

Political background. Early historical records indicate that the Thai people migrated to present-day Thailand from China's Yunnan Province about a thousand years ago. By the fourteenth century the seat of authority was established at Ayutthaya, a few miles from Bangkok. Toward the end of the eighteenth century, Burmese armies conquered the Kingdom but were eventually driven out by Rama I, who founded the present ruling dynasty and moved the capital to Bangkok in 1782. Upon the conquest of Burma by the British in 1826, Rama III began the process of accommodating European colonial powers by negotiating a treaty of amity and commerce with Britain. Subsequent monarchs, Rama IV and V, demonstrated great skill, by a combination of diplomacy and governmental modernization, in making it possible for their country to survive as the only Southeast Asian power free of European domination in the nineteenth and early twentieth centuries.

Thailand was ruled as an absolute monarchy until 1932, when a group of military and civilian officials led by Col. (later Field Mar.) Luang PIBULSONGGRAM (PIBUL Songgram) and PRIDI Phanomyong seized power in the first of what was to be a long series of military coups. A constitution, the first of 12 adopted to date, was promulgated by the king but never became fully effective, and the government continued to be controlled at most times by military cliques that succeeded each other by coup d'état. The Pibulsonggram dictatorship sided with the Japanese in World War II, but the anti-Japanese *Seri Thai* (Free Thai) movement, led by Pridi and SENI Pramoj, paved the way for reconciliation with the Allied powers at the war's end. Pridi dominated the first postwar government but was discredited and fled to Peking in 1947, after Pibulsonggram had again seized power. Pibulsonggram was overthrown a decade later by Field Marshal SARIT Thanarat, who appointed a constituent assembly in 1959 but continued to rule by martial law until his death in December 1963. Sarit's successor, Field Marshal THANOM Kittikachorn, likewise began his regime in authoritarian style, stressing economic over political development and working closely with Gen. PRAPAS Charusathira, the army commander and reputed national strongman.

Following promptings from the throne, the military regime agreed to the promulgation in June 1968 of a new constitution restoring limited parliamentary government, and an officially sponsored political party, the United Thai People's Party (UTPP), was organized to contest a lower-house election in February 1969. The opposition Democrat Party, led by Seni Pramoj, won all seats in the major urban centers of Bangkok and Thonburi, but the government, through the UTPP, mustered sufficient strength elsewhere to retain control and Thanom was reappointed prime minister.

The Thanom government decided in November 1971 that parliamentary inefficiency had placed the country in a position where outward forms of democracy could no longer be tolerated. The legislature was thereupon dissolved, the constitution suspended, and all political parties banned, except for a new government-sponsored Revolutionary Party.

In October 1973, as a result of widespread student demonstrations, the Thanom government fell and the rector of Thammasat University, SANYA Dharmasakti (Thammasak), was appointed prime minister. Following the adoption of a new constitution in October 1974 and a legislative election on January 26, 1975, Democrat Party leader Seni Pramoj formed a new government which, however, lasted only until March 6, when it was defeated on a confidence vote. Eleven days later, the retiring prime minister's younger brother, KUKRIT Pramoj, succeeded in organizing a coalition government based primarily on the Thai Nation Party and his own Social Action Party. Kukrit lost his legislative seat at an election on April 4, 1976, which returned a greatly increased plurality for the Democrat Party. Seni returned as prime minister on April 21 but resigned on September 23 after being criticized for not opposing the return from exile of former prime minister Thanom. Reappointed two days later, Seni was ousted on October 6 by a military coup nominally headed by Admiral SANGAD Chaloryu, who was designated chairman of a newly established Administrative Reform Council (ARC). On October 22, King BHUMIBOL approved the formation of a military-dominated government headed by a former Supreme Court justice, THANIN Kraivichien.

After surviving an attempted right-wing coup on March 26, 1977, the Thanin government was ousted on October 20 by the military, which established a 23-member Revolutionary Council (subsequently the National Policy Council) virtually identical in composition to the former ARC. On November 11 the Council designated Gen. KRIANGSAK Chamanan, the commander of the armed forces, as prime minister.

An election was held on April 22, 1979, to the lower house of a Parliament established under a new constitution adopted December 18, 1978. While Kukrit's Social Action Party secured an overwhelming plurality of the votes cast, Kriangsak's control of the appointive upper house permitted him to remain in office at the head of a new government

formed on May 24, the National Policy Council being dissolved. An economic crisis in late 1979 posed an increasingly grave threat to Kriangsak's leadership, however, forcing him to form a new government on February 11, 1980, and, in order to avoid a near-certain legislative vote of no confidence, to resign on February 29, Gen. PREM Tinsulanonda being designated as his successor on March 3.

In April 1981 a coup by a group of middle-ranked army officers (dubbed the "Young Turks" and characterized by *Le Monde* as "nationalist and vaguely socialist" in outlook) was narrowly averted by the loyalty of senior officers and the timely intervention of the monarch. By the end of 1982, General Prem, after 33 months in office, had become the longest-serving chief executive in a decade.

No clear parliamentary majority emerged at the election of April 18, 1983, and General Prem, who on April 26 announced his intention to retire from politics, was induced to return as nonpartisan head of a four-party coalition government on April 30.

A number of army and air force officers under the alleged leadership of Col. MANOON Roopkachorn, a former Young Turk, launched another attempted coup on September 9, 1985, while the prime minister and the armed forces commander, Gen. ARTHIT Kamlang-Ek, were both out of the country. Eight days later, former prime minister Kriangsak was arrested for complicity in the revolt, as were a number of senior officers, including the former armed forces commander, Gen. SIRM Na Nakorn, although it was subsequently alleged that the latter had acted under duress.

Cleavages within the Social Action Party, largest of the coalition partners, that turned in part on the issue of appointive versus elective claims to cabinet membership, weakened the government in the spring of 1986 and forced General Prem to call a premature election on July 27 at which the Democrats replaced Social Action as the dominant legislative grouping. On August 11 a new four-party government was installed under Prem's leadership. One month earlier, General Arthit, long viewed as a potential "knight on a white horse", had been effectively replaced by Gen. CHAOVALIT Yongchaiyut, pending formal retirement on August 11.

On April 29, 1988, facing a nonconfidence vote that most observers expected him to win, Prime Minister Prem called for dissolution of the Assembly and scheduled a new election for July 24.

Constitution and government. Thailand is a highly centralized constitutional monarchy traditionally functioning through a strong prime minister. In the modern era, the king has exercised little direct power but remains a popular symbol of national unity and identity. Under the 1978 constitution, the prime minister enjoys special powers (including authority to imprison or execute suspects) in national security cases, and neither he nor other members of the cabinet need hold elective office. Prior to April 21, 1983 (under transitional provisions of the basic law), he was confirmed and could only be dismissed by joint action of an appointed Senate and an elected House of Representatives. At present, under highly controversial deferred provisions, the Senate remains, but with greatly reduced powers (see

Legislature, below). The judicial system is patterned after European models. The Supreme Court, whose justices are appointed by the king, is the final court of appeal in both civil and criminal cases; an intermediate Court of Appeals hears appeals from courts of first instance located throughout the country.

Thailand is divided into 71 provinces, including the metropolis of Greater Bangkok. Provincial governors are appointed by the minister of the interior, who also appoints district officers to serve as subprovincial administrators. The larger towns are governed by municipal assemblies, while in rural areas popularly elected village headmen exercise limited authority.

Foreign relations. One of the few Asian countries to reject a neutralist posture, Thailand was firmly aligned with the United States and other Western powers after World War II and was a signatory of the Southeast Asia Collective Defense Treaty, which established the now-defunct Southeast Asia Treaty Organization (SEATO) in 1954. During the period 1952–1972 Thailand received almost $1.2 billion in US military aid, more than twice the economic assistance granted from 1946 to 1972. The Thanom government sanctioned the use of Thai air bases for US military operations in Laos and South Vietnam, and at its peak in 1969 the American buildup totaled 48,000 men. By the end of 1974, the number had been reduced to 27,000, and in compliance with a policy established by Prime Minister Kukrit when he assumed office in March 1975, all remaining US military installations were closed down in mid-1976.

Various UN bodies functioning in East and Southeast Asia maintain headquarters at Bangkok, and Thailand has played a leading role in the establishment of several regional organizations, such as the Association of Southeast Asian Nations (ASEAN). Its closest regional allies have been the Philippines and Malaysia. Relations with Kampuchea (Cambodia) have traditionally been antagonistic, although Thailand joined with other ASEAN nations in recognizing the Pol Pot regime in mid-1975 and in calling for "the immediate withdrawal of all foreign troops" following the Vietnamese invasion of December 1978.

While tacitly aiding *Khmer Rouge* forces in their opposition to the Vietnamese-backed regime of Heng Samrin, Thailand's major objective was to facilitate the acceptance by noncommunist Khmer resistance groups of the need for formation of a united front. Its efforts toward this end, coordinated with those of Malaysia and Singapore, were instrumental in the organization of the Coalition Government of Democratic Kampuchea in June 1982, although effective integration was never achieved and the ability of CGDK guerrillas to withstand search-and-destroy attacks by Phnom Penh-based forces had waned measurably by mid-1986 (see Kampuchea article).

The principal external concern in 1987 was an escalation of border tension with Laos in the wake of a major military effort to dislodge Lao troops from a contested area in northeastern Phitsanuloke province. The dispute stemmed from differing interpretations of a 1907 Franco-Siamese treaty that had been unresolved by a bitter diplomatic exchange between representatives of the two governments eight months earlier.

Current issues. A high degree of personalism and the pervasive influence of the military has continued to dominate Thai politics. Remaining aloof from direct involvement in the 1986 election by refusing to contest a parliamentary seat, General Prem was the principal beneficiary of the balloting, which resulted in the formation of a new four party government on August 11. Deep fissures had, however, emerged within the ranks of both the Social Action and Democrat parties, coupled with uncertainty as to the future political intentions of General Chaovalit, who on several occasions had displayed a desire to seek early retirement. Subsequently, the prime minister attempted to counter an apparent decline in personal popularity by mounting an unprecedented anti-corruption campaign centering on a scandal involving the forgery of royal decorations. His dissolution of the National Assembly in April 1988, while unexpected, was viewed as politically adroit, given increasing party fractionalization that seemed to ensure the likelihood of his returning to power after the July balloting. Significantly, the prime minister refused on May 2 to accept the resignation of General Chaovalit (the latter fulfilling a pledge made in accepting appointment two years earlier), thereby removing Chaovalit from immediate consideration as a potential successor.

POLITICAL PARTIES

Political party activity was suspended following the coup of October 6, 1976. The election of April 1976 had been called, in part, to reduce an excessively large number of parties represented in the legislature. No substantial reduction was, however, achieved, with the number of candidates rising from 1,630 in 1979 to 1,862 in 1983 and to 3,813 in 1986.

Parties Registered for the 1986 Election:

Of the 16 parties listed below, all but the last secured lower house parliamentary representation at the balloting of July 27. The first four participated in the Prem government inducted on August 11, while the United Democratic Party represented the largest opposition grouping.

Democrat Party (*Prachathipat*). Organized in 1946, the Democrats now constitute Thailand's oldest party. Traditionally a strong defender of the monarchy, the party has derived much of its support from urban professional and official groups. The largest legislative party after the 1975 and 1976 elections, it dropped to third place in 1983 before regaining a sizeable plurality of 100 seats in 1986. Coincident with the legislative dissolution of April 29, 1988, some 31 dissidents announced that they were withdrawing to form a new party to contest the election scheduled for July 24.

Leaders: BHICHAI Rattakul (Deputy Prime Minister), Lt. Col. SANAN Khachornprasat (Secretary General).

Thai Nation (*Chart Thai*). The largest political grouping in the Kukrit government coalition and the second largest in the lower house after the elections of 1976 and 1979, the Thai Nation includes a substantial number of military figures in its active membership and is regarded as the principal heir of the Thanom regime's United Thai People's Party. It fell to third place in legislative strength after formation of the National Democracy Party (below) in 1981. It placed second in the 1983 balloting, but claimed a plurality of House seats as the result of an announced merger with the Siam Democratic Party (*Prachathipat Siam*), then led by Col. Phol Rerngprasertvit and Dr. Mant Patanothai, and the Progressive Party (see below). It was runner-up in the 1986 balloting, with 63 seats.

Leaders: Maj. Gen. CHATCHAI Choonhavan (Deputy Prime Minister), BANHARN Silapaarcha (Secretary General).

Social Action Party (*Pak Kit Sangkhom*). An offshoot of the Democrat Party, the Social Action formation is somewhat more conservative than the parent group. The third largest party in 1975, it became second-ranked in 1976 and obtained a sizeable plurality in 1979, winning twice as many seats as its nearest competitor, the Thai Nation. It was the leading party in the 1983 balloting and was the core of the Prem government coalition prior to the emergence of internal fissures that prompted the resignation of longtime party leader Kukrit Pramoj in late 1985 and necessitated the legislative dissolution of May 1986.

Leaders: PHONG Sarasin (Deputy Prime Minister), Air Ch. Mar. SIDDHI Savetsila (Foreign Minister), THUNGYOD Chittaveera (Acting Secretary General).

People's Party (*Rashadorn*). *Rashadorn* was formed in May 1986 by a largely military group whose leader, Gen. Tienchai Sirisamphan, had played a prominent role in the counter-coup operation of September 1985.

Leaders: Gen. TIENCHAI Sirisamphan, Gen. MANA Rattanokoset (Secretary General).

National Democracy Party (*Pak Chart Prachathipatai*). Organized in June 1981 by former prime minister Kriangsak Chamanan, the NDP was formally registered as a party after its founder's return to politics in a runaway by-election victory the following August. Its ranks swelled by defectors from other parties, including the former Freedom and Justice (*Seritham*), which had won 29 seats in 1979, it became the second-largest group in the House of Representatives by the end of the year but was weakened thereafter by personal and policy disagreements among its members. A member of the government coalition after the 1983 balloting, at which it won 15 seats, it elected only three members in July 1986.

Leaders: Gen. KRIANGSAK Chamanan (former Prime Minister), WICHIT Sukuiriya (Secretary General).

Thai Citizens (*Prachakorn Thai*). *Prachakorn Thai* was launched prior to the 1979 election by the promilitary and charismatic populist Samak Sundaravej, who succeeded in routing the Democrats in their traditional stronghold of Bangkok. It participated in a quadripartite government coalition with the Democrat, National Democracy, and Social Action parties from 1983 to 1986.

Leaders: SAMAK Sundaravej, SAMAK Sirichan (Secretary General).

United Democratic Party (*Pak Saha Prachathipatai*). The largely anti-Prem UDP was organized by a number of Social Action and *Chart Thai* dissidents prior to the 1986 election. It ran fourth in the July 27 balloting, winning 38 lower house seats.

Leaders: BOONTHENG Thongsawasdi (former Deputy Prime Minister), Col. PHOL Rerngprasertvit, TAMCHAI Khamphato (Secretary General).

United Thai (*Ruam Thai*). *Ruam Thai* was organized by a number of Social Action dissidents prior to the 1986 balloting, at which it won 19 seats.

Leaders: NARONG Wongwan, PITYANAT Watcharaporn (Secretary General).

Community Action Party (*Kit Prachakom*). The CAP was formed prior to the 1986 balloting by former Social Action leader Boonchu Rojanasathien.

Leaders: BOONCHU Rojanastien (former Deputy Prime Minister), SIRA Pattamakom (Acting Secretary General).

Progressive Party (*Koa Nar*). Reportedly merged with *Chart Thai* after the 1983 election, *Koa Nar* ran separately in 1986, winning nine House seats.

Leaders: UTHAI Pimchaichon, BOONKERT Hitankam (Secretary General).

Mass Party (*Muan Chon*). *Muan Chon* was formally registered in June 1985 by a group of dissidents from both government and opposition ranks. It won three seats in the 1986 balloting.

Leaders: CHALERM Yoobamrung, Col. ADUL Kanchanapant (Secretary General).

New Force (*Palang Mai*). The reformist New Force, organized by a group of intellectuals who were opposed to the former military regime, supported the Prem government after the 1983 election, although failing to secure parliamentary representation. It obtained one seat in 1986.

Leaders: Dr. PRASAN Tangchai, SANTARN Suriyakham (Secretary General).

Democratic Labor Party (*Rang-Ngarn Prachathipatai*). The DLP also secured one House seat in 1986.

Leaders: PRASERT Sapsunthorn, HARN Linanond, YONGYUT Watanavikorn (Secretary General).

Liberal Party (*Sereeniyon*). The Liberal Party is a small business-oriented grouping that won its first legislative seat in 1986.

Leaders: PREEDA Pattanatabutra, MARUT Channarong (Secretary General).

Also participating in the 1986 balloting were the **Thai Mass** (*Puangchon Chao Thai*), which obtained one House seat, and the **Love Thai** (*Rak Thai*), which failed to secure representation.

Parties Not Participating in the 1986 Election:

Rural Development Party (*Phatthana Tchonnabot*). The *Phatthana Tchonnabot* was reported to have been officially registered as a new party in November 1985, but did not present candidates at the July 1986 balloting.

Leader: DIREK Direkwathana.

Social Democratic Party (*Pak Prachathipat Sangkhom*). Organized by members of the former Socialist Party and United Socialist Front (an amalgamation of six earlier leftist groups concentrated in the northeast region), the Social Democratic Party was the only left-wing group to put forward candidates at the 1979 election, none of whom were elected. It won two House seats in 1983.

Leaders: Col. SOMKID Srisangkom, KLAEW Norpati (Secretary General).

Thai People's Party (*Pak Chao Thai*). The Thai People's Party (not to be confused with *Prachakorn Thai,* which is sometimes rendered as Thai People's) is a monarchist party whose (then) sole legislator contested the 1983 election as an independent.

Leaders: Capt. SOMWONG Sarasart, Dr. SALAI Sookapantpotaram (Secretary General).

Thai People (*Prachathai*). A formation distinct from both the *Prachakorn Thai* and *Pak Chao Thai, Prachathai* won four House seats at the April 1983 election.

Leaders: THAWNEE Kraikupt, Gen. SUNTI Chairatana (Secretary General).

Moral Force (*Palang Dharma*). The Moral Force was organized in May 1988 by a retired major general, Chamlong Srimuang, who immediately attracted widespread attention at Bangkok for a "clean image" style that included screening potential party members for personal integrity. While Chamlong indicated that he would not personally contest the July 1988 balloting, a longtime relationship with Prem suggested that PDP members securing legislative seats would support the incumbent prime minister.

Leader: CHAMLONG Srimuang.

Illegal Groups:

The **Committee for the Coordination of Patriotic and Democracy-Loving Forces** (CCPDF) was formed in 1977 by the **Communist Party of Thailand** (CPT) and dissident members of the Socialist Party and United Socialist Front in support of guerrilla operations in the north, northeast, and south (where a **Thai Muslim People's Liberation Armed Forces**—MPLAF was also established under Communist leadership). Beginning in early 1979 the conflict between Kampuchean and Vietnamese forces had an adverse effect on the Thai insurgents along the Kampuchean border, a number of reports indicating that fighting had broken out between pro-Chinese and pro-Vietnamese factions within the CCPDF. Collaterally, China reduced its support of the CPT in order to secure Bangkok's aid in the transmission of supplies to Democratic Kampuchean forces. As a result, many of the rebels surrendered to Thai authorities, although a breakaway pro-Vietnamese group called the Thai People's Revolutionary Movement, popularly known as the **New Party** (*Pak Mai*), was formed at Vientiane, Laos, in early 1982. Meanwhile, sporadic insurgency continued in the south, with the Muslim **Pattani United Liberation Organization** (PULO) announcing in May 1986 that it had joined with other secessionist groups to form a **Mujahidin Pattani Movement**. In January 1988, on the other hand, some 300 southern CPT guerrillas were reported to have surrendered to army authorities.

LEGISLATURE

A partially elected bicameral **National Assembly** (*Ratha Satha*) was reestablished under the 1978 constitution, replacing a unicameral, military-dominated National Legislative Assembly that had been appointed in November 1977.

President: Dr. UKRIT Mongkolnavin.

Senate (*Woothi Satha*). The upper house currently consists of 261 members appointed for six-year terms by the king on recommendation of the prime minister. At present its functions are largely advisory, a deferred provision of the 1978 basic law (effective April 21, 1983) providing that it would no longer meet in joint session with the House of Representatives to appoint the prime minister, debate confidence motions, or adopt the budget. The present body, heavily weighted in favor of the military, was appointed on July 28, 1986.

President: UKRIT Mongkolnavin.

House of Representatives (*Satha Poothan*). The lower chamber presently contains 347 members elected by direct universal suffrage for four-year terms, subject to dissolution. The distribution of seats following the most recent general election on July 27, 1986, was as follows: Democrat Party, 100; Thai Nation, 63; Social Action Party, 51; United Democratic Party, 38; Thai Citizens, 24; United Thai, 19; People's Party, 18; Community Action Party, 15; Progressive Party, 9; Mass Party, 3; National Democracy Party, 3; New Force, Liberal Party, Thai Mass Party, Democratic Labor Party, 1 each. The distribution was essentially unchanged at dissolution on April 29, 1988.

C A B I N E T

[caretaker government, as of April 29, 1988]

Prime Minister	Gen. (Ret.) Prem Tinsulanonda
Deputy Prime Ministers	Maj. Gen. Chatchai Choonhawan
	Phong Sarasin
	Adm. Sonthi Bunyachai
	Gen. Thianchai Sirisamphan
Ministers	
Attached to Office of	
Prime Minister	Arun Phanuphong
	Chaisiri Ruangkanchanases
	Michai Ruchuphan
	Fl. Off. Suli Mahasanthana
Agriculture and Cooperatives	
(Acting)	Sano Thianthong
Commerce	Montri Phongphanit
Communications	Banhan Sinlapa-Acha
Defense	Air Ch. Mar. (Ret.) Phaniang
	Kantarat
Education (Acting)	Gen. Mana Rattanakoset
Finance	Suthi Singsaen
Foreign Affairs	Air Ch. Mar. (Ret.) Siddhi
	Savetsila
Industry	Pramuan Saphawasu
Interior	Gen. Prachuap Suntharangkun
Justice	Sa-at Piyawan
Public Health (Acting)	Maj. Gen. Chatchai Choonhawan
Science, Technology and Energy	
(Acting)	Phong Sarasin
State University Bureau	Subin Pinkhayan
Governor, Central Bank	Kamchon Sathirakun

N E W S   M E D I A

Press. Immediately after the 1976 coup all newspapers were banned. Subsequently, most were permitted to resume publication under strict censorship, which was formally lifted after the coup of October 1977. The following are dailies issued in Thai at Bangkok, unless otherwise noted: *Thai Rath* (600,000), sensationalist; *Daily News* (440,000); *Dao Siam* (142,000); *Daily Times* (140,000); *Siam Rath* (120,000); *Sing Sian Yit Pao* (88,000), in Chinese; *Siri Nakhorn* (78,000), in Chinese; *Ban Muang* (73,000); *Bangkok Post* (39,000), in English; *The Nation* (38,000), in English; *Bangkok World* (10,000), in English.

News agencies. There is no domestic facility; however, numerous foreign bureaus maintain offices at Bangkok.

Radio and television. There is a variety of radio and television services provided under government auspices; some are educational and some accept commercial advertising. Broadcasts are in Thai, English, French, and a number of other languages. There were approximately 7.8 million radio and 3.4 million television receivers in 1987.

INTERGOVERNMENTAL   REPRESENTATION

Ambassador to the US: ARSA Sarasin.

US Ambassador to Thailand: William Andreas BROWN.

Permanent Representative to the UN: Nitya PIBULSONGGRAM.

IGO Memberships (Non-UN): ADB, ANRPC, APCC, ASEAN, CCC, CP, ICM, ICO, INRO, Intelsat, Interpol, ISO, ITC, PCA.

T O G O

Republic of Togo
République Togolaise

Political Status: Independent republic since 1960; personal military rule imposed in 1967; one-party state established November 29, 1969; Third Republic proclaimed on January 13, 1980, under constitution adopted in referendum of December 30, 1979.

Area: 21,622 sq. mi. (56,000 sq. km.).

Population: 2,703,000 (1981C), 3,148,000 (1988E).

Major Urban Center (1978E): LOME (230,000).

Official Language: French.

Monetary Unit: CFA Franc (market rate March 1, 1988, 285.80 francs = $1US).

President: Gen. Gnassingbé EYADEMA; assumed power by coup d'état in 1967; proclaimed himself President in 1967 for an indefinite term; confirmed by referendum in 1972; elected, unopposed, to subsequent seven-year terms on December 30, 1979, and December 21, 1986.

T H E   C O U N T R Y

Wedged between Ghana and Benin on Africa's Guinea Coast, the small Republic of Togo extends inland from a 31-mile coastline for a distance of 360 miles. Eighteen major tribal groups are located in its hilly, hot, and humid territory, the best known being the culturally dominant Ewe in the south, whose traditional homeland extends into Ghana; the Mina, another southern people; and the Cabrais in the north, who supply the bulk of the country's small army. Although French has been accorded official status, most people use indigenous languages, with Ewe being predominant in the south and Twi in the north.

About 75 percent of the population adheres to traditional religious beliefs; the remainder embraces Christianity (20 percent, mainly Roman Catholics) and Islam (5 percent). Somewhat more than half of the adult female population is in the work force, predominately in the agricultural and trading sectors; however, female representation in government is minimal.

The economy depends primarily on subsistence agriculture, the two most important crops being cocoa and coffee, with cotton acreage quadrupling in recent years. Phosphate is the leading export earner, while oil refining, steel fabrication, and cement production are assuming increasing industrial importance. Smuggling has long been a source of contention with Ghana; as much as a third of Togo's cocoa exports originates in the neighboring state and is smuggled into Togo in exchange for luxury items that are much cheaper than in other parts of Africa. Current development focuses largely on tourism, agriculture, and a new free port at Lomé. The World Bank and other international institutions, encouraged by the government's commitment to budget austerity and the privatization of some state-run enterprises, have supported these and other efforts to recover from the fall of commodity prices on the world market.

GOVERNMENT AND POLITICS

Political background. The present Republic of Togo is the eastern section of the former German Protectorate of Togoland, which became a League of Nations mandate after World War I and was divided into separate zones of British and French administration. After World War II, France and Britain continued to administer the eastern and western sections as United Nations trust territories. Following a UN-supervised plebiscite, Western (British) Togoland became part of the new state of Ghana on the latter's accession to independence in 1957. Eastern (French) Togoland, which became a French-sponsored autonomous republic in 1956, achieved complete independence in agreement with France and the United Nations on April 27, 1960.

Sylvanus OLYMPIO, leader of the predominantly Ewe party then known as the Togolese Unity Committee (CUT), became the country's first chief executive. Olympio's somewhat dictatorial rule, coupled with his alienation of the army by the imposition of an austerity program, contributed to his assassination in 1963. Nicolas GRUNITZKY, Olympio's chief political rival, succeeded him as president and attempted to govern on a multiparty basis with northern support. Grunitzky failed, however, to establish firm control and was deposed in 1967 by (then) Maj. Etienne EYADEMA, a northerner who was chief of staff of the armed forces. Acting in the name of a National Reconciliation Committee, Eyadéma suspended the constitution, outlawed political activity, and instituted direct military rule. Later the same year, he dissolved the NRC and declared himself president, while stating that the army would surrender its powers to a civilian authority as soon as peace and reconciliation had been achieved. Subsequently, although a regime-supportive party, the Rally of the Togolese People (RPT), was established in 1969, pro forma

attempts the same year and in 1971 to return the nation to civilian rule were described as overruled by the "popular will".

A constitution, originally drafted ten years before, was accepted by a reported 98 percent of the registered electorate on December 30, 1979, in balloting at which General Eyadéma (whose first name had been "Africanized" to Gnassingbé in 1974) stood as the sole candidate for a seven-year term as president. Concurrently, a unicameral General Assembly was constituted on the basis of a single list of candidates presented by the RPT. In September 1986, the government reported it had withstood a coup attempt allegedly fomented in Ghana and Burkina Faso by supporters of the exiled sons of former president Olympio (see Current issues, below). On December 2, President Eyadéma was unopposed in election to a further seven-year term.

Constitution and government. The 1979 constitution provides for a highly centralized system of government headed by a strong executive who presides over a cabinet of his own selection and is empowered to dissolve the legislature after consulting the Political Bureau of the RPT. The single-chambered National Assembly is currently composed of 77 deputies, all of whom are popularly elected for five-year terms from an RPT-approved list of nominees. The judicial system is headed by a Supreme Court and includes a Court of Appeal and courts of the first and second instance. There are special courts for administrative, labor, and internal security matters.

The country is divided for administrative purposes into four provinces, each headed by an inspector appointed by the president. The provinces are subdivided into prefectures that were formerly administered by presidentially appointed chiefs and "special delegations" (councils). However, in July 1987, as part of a move toward "democratization", both prefectural and municipal elections were conducted on the basis of direct universal suffrage and multicandidature (but not multiparty) balloting.

Foreign relations. Togo's foreign policy has been characterized by nonalignment although historic links have provided a foundation for continued financial and political support from the West. Bowing to pressure from the Arab bloc, it severed diplomatic relations with Israel from 1973 until full restoration in 1987.

Although one of the smallest and poorest of the African states, Togo has played a leading role in efforts to promote regional cooperation. It was the host nation for negotiation of the first and second Lomé conventions between the European Community and developing African, Caribbean, and Pacific (ACP) countries, and worked closely with Nigeria in organizing the Economic Community of West African States (ECOWAS) in May 1975. Earlier, it had assumed observer status with the francophone West African Economic Community (CEAO) and in 1979 joined the CEAO states in a Non-Aggression and Defense Aid Agreement. Its major regional dispute concerns the status of Western Togoland, which was incorporated into Ghana in 1957. A clandestine "National Liberation Movement of Western Togoland" has been active in supporting Togo's claim to the 75-mile-wide strip of territory and has called for a new UN plebiscite on the issue. There have been numerous incidents along the Ghanaian border and the

Eyadéma and Rawlings regimes have regularly accused one another of destabilization efforts, including the "harboring" of each other's political opponents. Heated exchanges occurred with Ghana and, to a lesser degree, Burkina Faso, following the reported coup attempt in Togo in September, 1986, although Eyadéma avoided accusing Accra and Ouagadougou of direct involvement in the plot (see Ghana, Foreign relations).

Although not bordering states (being separated by Benin), Togo and Nigeria conducted a joint air parade at Lomé in January 1988, during which it was announced that they were working toward "integration" of their respective armed forces.

Current issues. In February 1987 General Eyadéma celebrated the 20th anniversary of his presidency with his control seemingly fortified in the wake of the 1986 coup attempt. Following Lomé's announcement that some 60 insurgents had been subdued following brief fighting, strong messages of support emanated from many African and Western governments. In addition, France's temporary deployment of troops and jet fighters to Togo was expected to discourage further overthrow attempts. By mid-1987 relations with Ghana had been largely normalized, with Lomé calling for help from regional organizations to resolve longstanding enmity between the two countries.

Some external observers questioned whether the coup attempt had been as serious as described by Lomé, suggesting that the government benefited from a shift of attention away from earlier reports of widespread torture and illegal detention of political prisoners. The government denied all such charges and in January 1987 Eyadéma announced the release of "the last political prisoner". In June he met for the first time with leaders of former political parties, saying that further talks would be held to promote national unity.

In another measure expected to generate popular support, the administration approved increases in wages and benefits, frozen for several years, for both public and private employees. Although careful to note that the new measures "do not mark the end of the policy of austerity", the government also launched a five-year program for infrastructural development. The World Bank endorsed the plan, congratulating Lomé for initiating economic recovery by having had "the courage and perseverance to implement [earlier] adjustment programs".

POLITICAL PARTIES

Political parties were banned after the 1967 coup. Two years later, the official Rally of the Togolese People was organized as the sole legitimate political party.

Official Party:

Rally of the Togolese People (*Rassemblement du Peuple Togolais* — RPT). Formed in 1969 under the sponsorship of President Eyadéma, the RPT is presently the only legal political organization; its auxiliary formations include women's, youth, and labor groups. Some 2,000 delegates to the fourth party congress, which convened at Lomé on Decem-

ber 4, 1986, approved an increase in the size of the RPT Politburo from 9 to 13 members and recommended that the country's capital be transferred to an unspecified inland site.

Leaders: Gen. Gnassingbé EYADEMA (President of the Republic and of the Party), Samon KORTHO (Permanent Director), Kunale EKLO (Administrative Secretary).

Expatriate Opposition:

Togolese Movement for Democracy (*Mouvement Togolais pour la Démocratie* — MTD). The MTD is a Paris-based organization which claimed in 1980 that 34 persons released from confinement on January 13 were "not real political prisoners" and that hundreds of others remained incarcerated. It disclaimed any responsibility for the wave of bomb attacks in 1985, while charging that the Eyadéma regime had "unleashed a wave of repression" in their wake. In mid-1986, MTD assistant secretary general Paulin Lossou fled France in the face of a decision by authorities to expel him to Argentina for his "partisan struggle" against the Eyadéma regime. Several reported MTD members were imprisoned in 1986 for distributing anti-Eyadéma pamphlets but all of their sentences were commuted by 1987. The government accused the MTD with complicity in the September 1986 coup attempt, alleging a plan to install Gilchrist Olympio, exiled son of the former president, if the overthrow had succeeded. Olympio described the charges as "preposterous", suggesting that internal dissent had generated the unrest.

Leaders: Richard da SILVEIRA (Secretary General), Paulin LOSSOU (Assistant Secretary General).

LEGISLATURE

A unicameral **National Assembly** (*Assemblée Nationale*) of 67 members was elected on a single list for a five-year term in December 1979. At the most recent balloting on March 24, 1985, 77 deputies were selected under a one-round, single vote system from 216 candidates approved by the RPT.

President: Mawupe VOVOR.

CABINET

President	Gen. Gnassingbé Eyadéma
Ministers	
Civil Service and Labor	Bitoktipou Yagninim
Commerce and Transport	N'Souwodji Kawo Ehe
Environment and Tourism	Yao Komlavi
Equipment and Telecommunications	Nassirou Ayeva
Finance and Economy	Komlan Alipui
Foreign Affairs and Cooperation	Yaovi Adodo
Industry and State Enterprises	Koffi Djondo
Information	Gbenyon Amegboh
Interior	Komlan Agbetiafa
Justice, Keeper of the Seal	Kpotivi Têvi Djidjogbé Laclé
National Defense	Gen. Gnassingbé Eyadéma
National Education and Scientific Research	Tchaa-Kozah Tchalim
Plan and Mines	Barry Moussa Barque
Public Health, Social Affairs and Women's Affairs	Ayissah Agbetra
Rural Development	Koffi Kadanga Walla
Rural Management	Samon Korto
Technical Education and Professional Training	Koffi Edoh
Youth, Culture and Sports	Komla Dometo Gnemegna
Director, Central Bank	Yao Messan Aho

NEWS MEDIA

News media are government owned and operated except

for a few independent publications, which are subject to sporadic press control.

Press. The following are French-language journals currently being published at Lomé: *La Nouvelle Marche* (10,000), government-owned daily; *Journal Officiel de la République du Togo,* government daily; *Bulletin d'Information de l'Agence Togolaise de Press,* official weekly.

News agencies. *Agence Togolaise de Presse* is the official facility; *Agence France-Presse* and *Deutsche Presse-Agentur* maintain bureaus at Lomé.

Radio and television. The government-operated *Radiodiffusion du Togo* broadcasts from Lomé in French, English, and indigenous languages to approximately 270,000 receivers. *Télévision Togolaise* began limited programming at Lomé in 1973; other transmitters are located at Alédjo-Kadara and Mont Agon. There were 23,000 TV sets in 1987.

INTERGOVERNMENTAL REPRESENTATION

Ambassador to the US: Ellam-Kodjo SCHUPPIUS.

US Ambassador to Togo: David A. KORN.

Permanent Representative to the UN: Koffi ADJOYI.

IGO Memberships (Non-UN): ACCT, ADF, AfDB, BADEA, BOAD, CENT, Copal, ECOWAS, EEC(L), *EIB,* IACO, ICO, Intelsat, Interpol, NAM, OAU, OCAM.

TONGA

Kingdom of Tonga
Pule'anga Fakatu'i 'o Tonga

Political Status: Constitutional monarchy; independent within the Commonwealth since June 4, 1970.

Area: 270 sq. mi. (699 sq. km.).

Population: 96,448 (1984C), 105,000 (1988E).

Major Urban Center (1984C): NUKU'ALOFA (27,700).

Official Languages: Tongan, English.

Monetary Unit: Pa'anga (market rate March 1, 1988, 1 pa'anga = $1.39US); the pa'anga is at par with the Australian dollar.

Head of State: King TAUFA'AHAU TUPOU IV; succeeded to the throne December 16, 1965, on the death of his mother, Queen SALOTE TUPOU; crowned July 4, 1967.

Prime Minister: Prince Fatafehi TU'IPELEHAKE, brother of the King; appointed at the time of the King's accession in December 1965.

THE COUNTRY

Located south of Western Samoa in the Pacific Ocean, Tonga (also known as the Friendly Islands) embraces some 200 islands that run north and south in two almost parallel chains. Only 45 of the islands are inhabited, the largest being Tongatapu, which is the seat of the capital and the residence of almost two-thirds of the country's population. Tongans (mainly Polynesian with a Melanesian mixture) constitute 98 percent of the whole, while Europeans and other Pacific islanders make up the remainder. The majority of the population is Christian, approximately 60 percent belonging to the Free Wesleyan Church of Tonga. The official female labor force participation rate is less than 14 percent, due, in part, to child-rearing demands in a society with an average of 5 children per family; female representation in government is virtually nonexistent.

Primarily an agricultural country, Tonga produces coconuts and copra, bananas, vanilla, yams, taro, sweet potatoes, and tropical fruits. Pigs and poultry are raised, while beef cattle (traditionally bred by Europeans) are beginning to assume added importance, thus reducing dependence on beef imports. The possibility of exporting premium quality red cedar timber to Australia is currently being explored. With the exception of some coconut-processing plants, no significant industries exist, though exploration for oil has been under way for several years.

GOVERNMENT AND POLITICS

Political background. Christianized by European missionaries in the early nineteenth century, Tonga became a unified kingdom in 1845. British protection began in 1900 with the conclusion of a treaty of friendship and alliance whereby a British consul assumed control of the islands' financial and foreign affairs. New treaties with the United Kingdom in 1958 and 1968 gave Tonga full internal self-government in addition to limited control over its external relations, with full independence within the Commonwealth occurring on June 4, 1970. The present king, TAUFA'AHAU TUPOU IV, has governed since late 1965 when he succeeded his mother, Queen SALOTE TUPOU, whose reign had begun in 1918.

Constitution and government. Tonga is a hereditary constitutional monarchy whose constitution dates back to 1875. The executive branch is headed by the king and his Privy Council, which includes (in addition to the monarch) a cabinet that encompasses a prime minister, a deputy prime minister, other ministers, and the governors of Ha'apai and Vava'u. Meeting at least once a year, the unicameral Legislative Assembly includes an equal number of hereditary nobles and elected people's representatives, plus the cabinet members sitting ex officio; when the legislature is not in session, the Privy Council is empowered to enact legislation which must, however, be approved by the Assembly at its next meeting. The judicial system is composed of a Supreme Court, magistrates' courts, and a Land Court. Ultimate judicial appeal is to the king, who appoints all judges.

Tonga is administratively divided into several groups of islands, the most important of which are the Tongatapu group, the Ha'apai group, and the Vava'u group.

Foreign relations. In 1900 Tonga and the United Kingdom signed a Treaty of Friendship and Protection, which provided for British control over financial and external affairs. Tonga became a member of the Commonwealth on independence and is affiliated with the European Economic Community under the Lomé Convention. Although not a member of the United Nations, it participates in a number of UN-related organizations, including the FAO, WHO, and UNESCO; it was admitted to the International Monetary Fund (IMF) in September 1985. Regionally, it belongs to the South Pacific Forum (SPF) and the South Pacific Commission (SPC).

In October 1986 Neiafu, in the northern Vava'u group, and Nuku'alofa, the capital, had served as twin venues for the concluding session of negotiations that, after 25 months, yielded agreement on a tuna treaty between the United States and members of the SPF Fisheries Agency. The local economy was reported to have benefitted substantially from the nine-day discussions, which, for approximately $60 million, permitted access by the US tuna fleet to nearly 8 million square miles of prime fishing grounds over a five-year period.

Current issues. Tonga's most controversial issue during 1986 was a private citizen's action against members of the Legislative Assembly late in the year for alleged misuse of public funds in connection with lodging and other expenses during public meetings (*fonos*) held to explain new tax laws; the expenses reportedly exceeded $2 million, more than twice an initial government projection of $758,000. Churchmen were prominently involved in the dispute, claiming that the scandal prejudiced traditional popular respect for the integrity of the country's leaders. The case had a profound impact on the legislative balloting of February 1987, with only three of the nine incumbent people's representatives being reelected. Subsequently, Tonga's Privy Council ruled that the charges were not subject to adjudication on the ground that the Assembly had exclusive authority in regard to allowances for members.

In mid-1987 it was reported that King Taufa'ahau Tupou had granted former Philippines president Ferdinand Marcos a Tongan passport in recognition of past friendship, though the action (which did not involve the diplomatic status that Marcos had sought) appeared largely symbolic because of US unwillingness to permit the ousted chief executive to leave Hawaii.

POLITICAL PARTIES

There are no political parties in Tonga.

LEGISLATURE

Following the most recent election of February 18–19, 1987, the unicameral **Legislative Assembly** consisted, apart from the speaker, of 9 nobles selected by the 33 hereditary nobles of Tonga and 9 people's representatives elected by universal suffrage, with 8 cabinet ministers and the governors of Ha'apai and Vava'u sitting ex officio.
Speaker: Kalaniuvalu FOTOFILI.

CABINET

Prime Minister	Prince Fatafehi Tu'ipelehake
Deputy Prime Minister	S.L. Tuita
Ministers	
Agriculture	Prince Fatafehi Tu'ipelehake
Civil Aviation and Disaster Relief	S. Langi Kavaliku
Defense	Prince Tupouto'a
Education	S. Langi Kavaliku
Finance	Cecil Cocker
Foreign Affairs	Prince Tupouto'a
Health	Dr. Sione Tapa
Industry, Trade and Commerce	Baron Vaea
Lands, Survey and Natural Resources	S.L. Tuita
Police	George Akau'ola
Works	S. Langi Kavaliku

NEWS MEDIA

Press. A government weekly, *Kalonikali Tonga/Tonga Chronicle,* is printed in Tongan (6,000) and English (1,200) editions. In late 1980, a daily, *Talanga/Speak Out,* with an initial circulation of 2,000, was launched at Aukland, New Zealand; aimed, in part, at some 25,000 expatriates, it also circulates in Tonga. The *Tongan Times* began publication in 1984, while a number of opposition papers including *Fetu'uesiafi* (Shooting Star) have recently been launched.

Radio and television. Radio broadcasting is the responsibility of the Tonga Broadcasting Commission, which transmits commercial programming in Tongan, English, Fijian, and Samoan to approximately 68,000 receivers. A "pirate" television station, ASTL-V3, began transmitting in mid-1984, while King Taufa'ahau announced in 1985 that an officially-approved system would shortly be installed by two US-based fundamentalist church groups.

INTERGOVERNMENTAL REPRESENTATION

Tonga has not as yet elected to apply for membership in the United Nations.

Ambassador to the US: Siaosi Taimani 'AHO (resident in the United Kingdom).

US Ambassador to Tonga: Leonard ROCHWARGER (resident in Fiji).

IGO Memberships (Non-UN): ADB, CWTH, EEC(L), *EIB,* Interpol, SPC, SPEC, SPF.

TRINIDAD AND TOBAGO

Republic of Trinidad and Tobago

Political Status: Independent member of the Commonwealth since August 31, 1962; republican constitution adopted August 1, 1976.

Area: 1,980 sq. mi. (5,128 sq. km.).

Population: 1,079,791 (1980C), 1,240,000 (1988E).

Major Urban Centers (1980C): PORT-OF-SPAIN (65,906); San Fernando (33,490).

Official Language: English.

Monetary Unit: Trinidad and Tobago Dollar (market rate March 1, 1988, 3.60 dollars = $1US).

President: Noor Mohammed HASANALI; elected to a five-year term by Parliament on February 16, 1987; sworn in on March 18, succeeding Ellis Emmanuel Innocent CLARKE.

Prime Minister: Arthur Napoleon Raymond ROBINSON (National Alliance for Reconstruction); appointed by the President on December 16, 1986, to succeed George Michael CHAMBERS (People's National Movement), following election of the previous day.

THE COUNTRY

Composed of a pair of scenic tropical islands off the northern coast of South America (see map, p. 22), the English-speaking state of Trinidad and Tobago forms the southern extremity of the island chain known as the Lesser Antilles. Trinidad is the larger and more highly developed of the two islands, accounting for nearly 95 percent of the country's area and population and by far the greater part of its national wealth. As in nearby Guyana, approximately 43 percent of the population encompasses descendants of African slaves, while another 40 percent embraces descendants of East Indian indentured laborers imported during the nineteenth century. Most of the former are presently concentrated in urban areas, while most of the latter are active as independent farmers. People of mixed ancestry, together with a few Europeans and Chinese, make up the rest of Trinidad's inhabitants, while Tobago's population is largely Negro. Roman Catholicism predominates, but Hinduism, Protestant Christianity, and Islam are also represented.

The economy is heavily dependent on refined petroleum and related products derived from both domestically extracted and imported crude oil. Although domestic reserves were thought to be approaching exhaustion in the late 1960s, natural gas and oil deposits subsequently discovered off Trinidad's southeast coast gave new impetus to the refining and petrochemical industries, which now account for over 90 percent of export earnings. Starting in 1973, soaring oil prices produced rapid growth, pushing per capita income by the early 1980s to about $7,000, the third highest in the Western Hemisphere. Since then, the country has been in economic decline as the result of falling prices and markets for its oil, reserves of which are not expected to last for more than another decade. Tourism is of growing importance, while agriculture plays a relatively minor role in the islands' economy. Sugar (the most important crop), cocoa, and other products are exported, and some progress has been made in developing a more balanced agricultural sector geared to domestic consumption.

GOVERNMENT AND POLITICS

Political background. Discovered by Columbus and ruled by Spain for varying periods, Trinidad and Tobago became British possessions during the Napoleonic wars and were merged in 1888 to form a single Crown Colony. Political and social consciousness developed rapidly during the 1930s, when the trade-union movement and socialism began to emerge as major influences. The People's National Movement (PNM), the country's first solidly based political party, was founded in 1956 by Dr. Eric WILLIAMS and controlled the government without interruption for the next 30 years. Following participation in the short-lived, British-sponsored Federation of the West Indies from 1958 to 1962, Trinidad and Tobago was granted full independence within the Commonwealth on August 31, 1962.

After an initial period of tranquillity, "Black power" demonstrations broke out, which led to the declaration of a state of emergency in April 1970 and subsequently to an attempted coup by elements of the military. Signs of continued political instability included an opposition boycott of the 1971 legislative election, at which only 33 percent of the registered voters cast ballots, and a fresh wave of labor unrest that resulted in the reimposition of a state of emergency in October 1971.

In October 1973, Prime Minister Williams announced his intention to retire from politics but reversed himself two months later, ostensibly at the request of his party, until steps had been taken to implement a republican constitution. In the legislative election of September 13, 1976, Williams' PNM won 24 of the 36 House seats. Williams died unexpectedly on March 29, 1981, and was succeeded as prime minister and party leader by George M. CHAMBERS, who led the PNM to a 26–10 victory in parliamentary balloting on November 9.

Severe economic decline and the formation for the first time of a solid coalition of opposition groups, the National Alliance for Reconstruction (NAR), led to reversal in 1986 of the PNM's theretofore uninterrupted control of the government, the NAR winning 33 of 36 House seats in balloting on December 15, with Arthur N.R. ROBINSON succeeding Chambers as prime minister.

Constitution and government. Under the 1976 constitution, Trinidad and Tobago became a republic, with a president (elected by a majority of both houses of Parliament) replacing the former governor general. The functions of the head of state remain limited, executive authority being exercised by a prime minister and cabinet appointed from among the members of the legislature. Parliament consists of an appointed Senate, a majority of whose members are proposed by the prime minister, and a House of Representatives elected by universal adult suffrage. The judicial system is headed by a Supreme Court, which consists of a High Court and a Court of Appeal, while district courts function at the local level. There is also an Industrial Court and a Tax Appeal Board, both functioning as superior courts of record. Judges are appointed by the president on the advice of the prime minister. An unusual feature of the constitution is retention of the right of ultimate appeal to the judicial committee of the UK Privy Council. The provision is designed to afford litigants access to a completely disinterested final court.

Local administration is carried out on the basis of 8 counties, which are subdivided into 30 electoral wards (1 embracing all of Tobago). Three municipalities (Port-of-Spain, San Fernando, and Arima) have elected mayors and city councils.

After three years of debate, the House of Representatives in September 1980 approved a bill establishing a 15-member House of Assembly for Tobago with primarily consultative responsibilities. In January 1987, Tobago was granted full internal self-government, its House being given control of revenue collection, economic planning, and provision of services.

Foreign relations. In 1967 Trinidad and Tobago, which had joined the United Nations at independence, became the first Commonwealth nation to be admitted to the Organization of American States. The country's anticolonial but democratic and pro-Western foreign policy is oriented chiefly toward the Western Hemisphere and includes active participation in such regional organizations as Caricom. However, since 1983 a number of disputes with fellow Caricom members over trade restrictions have tended to hinder regional cooperation. Port-of-Spain's objections to the US-led invasion of Grenada in October 1983 also cooled relations with a number of Eastern Caribbean states, most notably Barbados, and strained traditionally cordial relations with the United States, Prime Minister Chambers criticizing what he perceived as the US Reagan administration's attempt to "militarize" the region. However, efforts have subsequently been initiated to lower the government's profile both on trade and foreign policy issues. Relations with China and the Soviet Union were established in 1974, while a broad trade agreement signed in August 1984 with the PRC was hailed as a "major leap forward in China's relations with the Commonwealth Caribbean".

No major foreign policy changes have as yet been advanced under the NAR administration, the essentially moderate Prime Minister Robinson having set as an initial priority the elimination of trade barriers within Caricom.

Current issues. Given manifest economic difficulty, the NAR's success in the December 1986 election was not unexpected, although the magnitude of its victory (66 percent of the popular vote to the PNM's 32 percent and an 11–1 margin in House seats) surprised most observers. An unusually large voter turnout indicated rejection of Prime Minister Chambers' campaign assurance that the recession had "bottomed out" and his assertion that the opposition coalition, derided as a "shotgun marriage", could not hold together long enough to govern effectively.

Soon after taking office, Prime Minister Robinson, in a hastily assembled 1987 budget proposed a variety of tax increases and duty adjustments, the pruning of expenditures, and a halt to cost of living increments for public sector employees. The last elicited immediate criticism from the labor movement and the allowances were restored (on a flat-rate, rather than the earlier index basis) in July after a group of Tapia House members (see NAR entry under Political Parties, below) had withdrawn from the Alliance. A few weeks earlier, despite an official projection of continued net decline in GDP and a rise in unemployment to nearly 20 percent, Robinson had insisted that progress was being made toward "economic stabilization". The electorate responded at local balloting in mid-September by giving the NAR control of two of the main island's four

municipal councils, as well as an increased majority of borough and county council seats.

The new government's economic problems were accompanied by a controversy stemming from a number of senatorial and statutory board appointments made by Ellis Clarke immediately prior to his retirement from the presidency in March. After bitterly denouncing the "illegal appointments" as part of an effort to shackle his administration's policies, Robinson introduced a constitutional amendment bill that would mandate the resignation of presidential appointees at the conclusion of each presidential term. However, public protests forced withdrawal of the bill and the issue was referred to a recently established constitutional reform commission.

In February 1988 NAR unity was shattered by the dismissal from both party and government posts of a number of dissidents, including External Affairs Minister Basdeo PANDAY. The action came in the wake of a secret meeting that was allegedly aimed at the ouster of Robinson because of his "authoritarian" leadership. In mid-May the party's national council voted to suspend the membership of the dissidents, who were accused by the prime minister of "attempting to mash up the party and damage the country in a totally destructive manner." The net result was heightened polarization between the East Indian and Black communities (led by Panday and Robinson, respectively) that could conceivably force an early election.

POLITICAL PARTIES

Prior to 1976, Trinidad and Tobago's party system was based primarily on a long-standing rivalry between the ruling People's National Movement (PNM) and the opposition Democratic Labour Party (DLP), the PNM serving to some extent as a vehicle for African voters and the DLP mainly representing East Indians. Efforts toward a unified electoral opposition began in 1981, when the United Labour Front (ULF), which had emerged after the 1976 election as the principal opposition grouping, aligned itself with two smaller parties as the Trinidad and Tobago National Alliance; two years later, the Alliance and the Organization for National Reconstruction formed a temporary coalition (known as the "Accommodation") which gained 66 of the county council seats to the PNM's 54. The linkage was formalized in September 1985, with the organization of the National Alliance for Reconstruction (below).

Government Party:

National Alliance for Reconstruction (NAR). The NAR was launched in 1984 as a coalition of the United Labour Front (ULF), the Democratic Action Congress (DAC), and the Tapia House Movement (THM); all had participated in the 1981 campaign as members of the Trinidad and Tobago National Alliance (TTNA). In September 1985, the Organization for National Reconstruction (ONR) joined the new formation, which reorganized as a unified party in February 1986.

The ULF had grown out of labor unrest in the sugar, oil, and transport industries in early 1975, and campaigned in 1976 for the nationalization of these and other major industries. Its leadership consisted primarily of a somewhat uneasy coalition of longtime opponents of the late Prime Minister Williams, including Basdeo Panday, East Indian head of the sugar workers' union; George Weekes, head of the Black-dominated oil workers; and James Millette of the United National Independence Party

(UNIP). The small Liberal Action Party (LAP), led by Ivan Perot, also joined the ULF prior to the 1976 balloting. Panday resigned as both party and union head in the wake of a poor showing by the former in the 1980 local elections, but was subsequently returned to the posts by overwhelming majorities. The ULF obtained 8 House of Representatives seats in November 1981.

Headed by A.N.R. Robinson, a former PNM associate (and one-time heir apparent) of Prime Minister Williams, the DAC was a relatively conservative grouping that won the two seats from the island of Tobago in the 1976 parliamentary election, retaining both in 1981. In mid-1978, Winston Murray, one of the winners in 1976, repudiated Robinson's leadership and in 1980 withdrew from the party (see Fargo House Movement, below). Robinson himself resigned his seat to stand for reelection to the Tobago House of Assembly in 1980, subsequently being named chairman of the new body.

The Tapia ("mud wall") group emerged as an offshoot of the Black power movement at the University of the West Indies. It called for the nationalization of all foreign-controlled enterprises and a reconstituted, elected Senate with greater representation of ordinary citizens. In late 1974, four of its members were appointed opposition delegates to the Senate on the recommendation of Roy Richardson (see ULDP, below), who was then the sole recognized opposition member of the House of Representatives. The THM won no parliamentary seats in 1981 and many of its members, including Tapia leader Lloyd BEST, withdrew from the Alliance in June 1987 after accusing the Robinson administration of "drifting as aimlessly" as its predecessor.

The moderately left-of-center ONR was founded by Karl Hudson-Phillips following his withdrawal from the PNM in April 1980. Although failing to win any legislative seats in 1981, the group ran second in the popular vote (22.3 percent) and, given the ULF's largely ethnic base among sugar workers, was called "the only real claimant, other than the PNM, to national party status". Despite his group's steadily improving position in the polls, Hudson-Phillips declared in June 1985 that he would not stand for prime minister, thereby providing indirect support for Robinson's candidacy.

The NAR's success in coalescing behind Robinson and its leader's ability to attract support from diverse ethnic and labor groups were considered major factors in the group's stunning victory in the December 15, 1986, balloting. However, by early 1988 the Alliance had encountered severe internal stress, culminating in the suspension of a group of ULF dissidents led by Basdeo Panday, that threatened to divide its ranks along racial lines (see Current issues, above).

Leaders: Arthur N.R. ROBINSON (DAC, Prime Minister and Party Leader), Herbert ATWELL (Chairman), Karl HUDSON-PHILLIPS (ONR), Bhoendradatt TEWARIE (General Secretary).

Opposition Parties:

People's National Movement (PNM). Created in 1956 by historian-politician Eric Williams, the PNM was the first genuinely modern party in the country's history and owed much of its success to its early formation, its founder's gift for leadership, and its comparatively high degree of organization. Although its support is predominantly African, its progressive and internationalist programs have been distinguished by their emphasis on national unity irrespective of ethnic origin. Leadership problems within the PNM have involved A.N.R. Robinson and Karl Hudson-Phillips (see ONR, above). Following Williams' death on March 29, 1981, George M. Chambers was elected party leader.

After three decades of uninterrupted rule, the PNM was forced into opposition on December 15, 1986, when it retained only 3 of 36 House seats. The overwhelming reversal was attributed to the inability of the Chambers administration to halt steady economic decline since 1982. Following the defeat, Chambers resigned as party leader and announced his intention to retire from politics. Subsequently, the party's youth movement won its first battle with the "old guard" by the naming of 40-year-old Patrick Manning, one of the three successful House candidates, as interim political leader.

Leader: Patrick MANNING (Leader of the Opposition).

National Joint Action Committee (NJAC). The NJAC was organized by Geddes Granger, who played a leading role in the Black-power disturbances of 1970 and was under detention from October 1971 to June 1972 before changing his name to Makandal Daaga. The group contested elections in 1981, when it secured 3.3 percent of the popular vote, and in 1986, when it won 1.5 percent.

Leader: Makandal DAAGA.

Fargo House Movement (FHM). The Tobago-based FHM was formed in 1980 by DAC dissident Winston Murray, who (unlike A.N.R. Robinson) supported the government's Tobago House of Assembly Bill. The FHM won no seats in the Assembly election of November 24, Dr. Murray having chosen to retain his parliamentary seat and hence not to stand as a candidate. The Movement won no seats in either the 1981 or 1986 national balloting.

Leader: Dr. Winston MURRAY.

Social Democratic Party (SDP). The SDP emerged as the result of a 1972 split in the longtime opposition **Democratic Labour Party** (DLP) into an "official" DLP faction then led by Alloy LEQUAY and an "unofficial" faction (appealing mainly to Hindus) led by Vernon Jamadar. In early 1976 the "official" faction joined the UDLP coalition (below), leaving the "unofficial" faction as a rump group which subsequently organized as the SDP.

Leader: Vernon JAMADAR.

United Democratic Labour Party (UDLP). The UDLP was organized prior to the 1976 election as an opposition coalition embracing the "official" faction of the DLP, the **United Progressive Party** (UPP), and two smaller groups, the **Liberal Party** (LP) and the **African National Congress** (ANC). Roy Richardson of the UPP, who had defected from the PNM after his election to the House of Representatives in 1971, was named leader of the coalition. The UDLP presently holds no legislative seats.

Leaders: Roy RICHARDSON (UPP), Sinbhoonath CAPILDEO ("official" DLP), P.G. FARQUHAR (LP).

Minor opposition parties include the **West Indian National Party** (WINP), led by Ashford SINANAN; the **Democratic Liberation Party**, a breakaway faction of the WINP led by Bhadase S. MARAJ; the **United Freedom Party**, led by Ramdeo SAMPAT-MEHTA; and the People's Popular Movement, led by former trade union leader Michael ALS, which won .14 percent of the popular vote in the 1986 election.

LEGISLATURES

The national **Parliament** is a bicameral body consisting of an appointed Senate and an elected House of Representatives; Tobago has a unicameral **House of Assembly**.

Senate. The upper chamber consists of 31 members appointed by the president for a maximum term of five years: 16 are named on the advice of the prime minister; 6 on the advice of the leader of the opposition; and 9 at his own discretion from religious, economic, and social groups.

President: Michael WILLIAMS.

House of Representatives. The lower chamber has 36 members directly elected for five-year terms, subject to dissolution. At the election of December 15, 1986, the National Alliance for Reconstruction won 33 seats and the People's National Movement, 3.

Speaker: Nizam MOHAMMED.

Tobago House of Assembly. Tobago's legislature consists of 15 members, 12 directly elected and 3 named by the majority party; its term is four years. At the most recent balloting of November 26, 1984, the Democratic Action Congress (subsequently a founding component of the NAR) won 11 of the elective seats and the People's National Movement, 1. Arthur N.R. Robinson was chairman of the body, prior to being designated prime minister.

Chairman: Jeffrey DAVIDSON.

CABINET

Prime Minister	Arthur N.R. Robinson
Ministers	
Community Development, Welfare and the Status of Women	Gloria Henry
Decentralization	Brinsley Samaroo
Education	Clive Pantin
Energy, Labor, Employment and Manpower Resources	Dr. Albert Richards

External Affairs and International	
Trade	Sahedeo Basdeo
Finance and Economy	Arthur N.R. Robinson
Food Production, Forestry and Marine	
Exploitation	Lincoln Myers
Health, Welfare and Status of Women	Dr. Emmanuel Hosein
Industry, Commerce and Tourism	Kenneth Gordon
Legal Affairs	Selwyn Richardson
National Security and Immigration	Herbert Atwell
Planning and Reconstruction	Winston Dookeran
Public Utilities and Settlements	Pamela Nicholson
Sport, Culture, Creative Arts and Youth	
Affairs	Jennifer Johnson
Works and Infrastructure	Carson Charles
Without Portfolio	Bhoendradatt Tewarie
Attorney General	Selwyn Richardson
Governor, Central Bank	William Demas

NEWS MEDIA

Press. The following are privately owned and are published daily at Port-of-Spain, unless otherwise noted: *Trinidad and Tobago Express* (62,000 daily, 81,000 Sunday); *Trinidad Guardian* (53,000 daily, 82,000 Sunday); *Evening News* (34,000); *The Sun* (25,000).

Radio and television. Radio programming is provided by the government-controlled National Broadcasting Service (Radio 610) and by the commercial Trinidad Broadcasting Company. Commercial television is provided by the Trinidad and Tobago Television Company. There were approximately 554,000 radio and 345,000 television receivers in 1987.

INTERGOVERNMENTAL REPRESENTATION

Ambassador to the US: John Reginald DUMAS.

US Ambassador to Trinidad and Tobago: Sheldon J. KRYS.

Permanent Representative to the UN: D.H.N. ALLEYNE.

IGO Memberships (Non-UN): Caricom, CCC, CDB, Copal, CWTH, EEC(L), *EIB*, Geplacea, IADB, ICCO, ICO, Intelsat, Interpol, IWTC, NAM, OAS, OPANAL, SELA.

TUNISIA

Republic of Tunisia
al-Jumhuriyah al-Tunisiyah

Political Status: Independent state since 1956; republic proclaimed July 25, 1957; under one-party dominant, presidential regime.

Area: 63,170 sq. mi. (163,610 sq. km.).

Population: 6,975,450 (1984C), 7,341,000 (1988E).

Major Urban Centers (1984C): TUNIS (596,654); Sfax (Safaqis, 231,911); Djerba (92,269).

Official Language: Arabic; French is widely spoken as a second language.

Monetary Unit: Dinar (market rate March 1, 1988, 1 dinar = $1.24US).

President: Gen. Zine El-Abidine BEN ALI; appointed Prime Minister on October 2, 1987; assumed the presidency upon deposing Habib BOURGUIBA on November 7.

Prime Minister: Hedi BACCOUCHE; designated Prime Minister on November 7, 1987, succeeding Gen. Zine El-Abidine BEN ALI.

THE COUNTRY

Situated midway along the North African littoral between Algeria and Libya, Tunisia looks north and eastward into the Mediterranean and southward toward the Sahara Desert. Along with Algeria and Morocco, it forms the Berber-influenced part of North Africa known as the "Maghreb" (West) to distinguish it from other Middle Eastern countries, which are sometimes referred to as the "Mashreq" (East). Tunisia's terrain, well wooded and fertile in the north, gradually flattens into a coastal plain adapted to stock-raising and olive culture, and becomes semidesert in the south. The ethnically homogeneous population is almost exclusively of Arab-Berber stock, Arabic in speech, and Sunni Muslim in religion. Although most members of the former French community departed after Tunisia gained independence in 1956, French continues as a second language and small French, Italian, Jewish, and Maltese minorities remain. Women constitute a larger proportion of the labor force in rural than in urban areas, largely due to a conservative interpretation of Islam and high urban unemployment; however, in 1984 girls comprised over 40 percent of primary and secondary school students, a substantial increase over 1972. At a ruling party congress in March 1985, President Bourguiba praised his country's efforts in the emancipation of women.

Some 45 percent of the population is engaged in agriculture, the main products being wheat, barley, olive oil, wine, and fruits. Petroleum is the leading export, and there is some mining of phosphates, iron ore, lead, and zinc. Industry, though limited, is expanding, with steel, textiles, and chemicals firmly established. Most development is concentrated in coastal areas, unemployment and poverty being widespread in the subsistence farming and mining towns of the south.

GOVERNMENT AND POLITICS

Political background. Seat of the Carthaginian empire destroyed by Rome in 146 BC, Tunisia was successively conquered by Romans, Arabs, and Turks before being occupied by France in 1881 and becoming a French protectorate under a line of native rulers (beys) in 1883. Pressure for political reforms began after World War I and in 1934 resulted in establishment of the nationalist Neo-Destour (New Constitution) Party, which became the spearhead of a drive for independence under the leadership of Habib BOURGUIBA. Nationalist aspirations were further stimulated by World War II and an initial breakdown in independence negotiations led to the outbreak of guerrilla warfare against the French in 1952. Internal autonomy was conceded by France on June 3, 1955, and on March 20, 1956, the protectorate was terminated, with the country gaining full independence.

A national constituent assembly controlled by the Neo-Destour Party voted on July 25, 1957, to abolish the monarchy and establish a republic under Bourguiba's presidency. A new constitution was adopted on June 1, 1959, while Bourguiba's leadership and that of the party were overwhelmingly confirmed in presidential and legislative elections in 1959 and 1964. Subsequently, in the late 1960s, the regime's radical socialist strategies of economic development failed and were abandoned in favor of efforts to attract foreign investment.

Bourguiba was reelected in 1969, but his failing health precipitated a struggle for succession to the presidency. One-time front-runner Bahi LADGHAM, prime minister and secretary general of the party, was apparently too successful: the attention he received as chairman of the Arab Superior Commission on Jordan and as effective executive during the president's absences led to a falling-out with an eventually rejuvenated Bourguiba; he was dismissed in 1970 and replaced by Hedi NOUIRA. President Bourguiba encountered an additional challenge from Ahmed MESTIRI, interior minister and leader of the liberal wing of the party. The liberals succeeded in forcing democratization of the party structure during the Eighth Party Congress in October 1971, but Bourguiba subsequently reasserted his control of the party apparatus. Mestiri was expelled from the party in January 1972 and from his seat in the National Assembly in May 1973, while Bourguiba was named president for life on November 2, 1974.

In February 1980, Prime Minister Nouira suffered a stroke and on April 24 Acting Prime Minister Mohamed MZALI was asked to form a new government. Mzali was reappointed following a general election on November 1, 1981, in which three additional parties were allowed to participate, none of which secured legislative representation. Bourguiba dismissed Mzali on July 8, 1986, replacing him with Rachid SFAR, theretofore finance minister.

On October 2, 1987, reportedly because of presidential displeasure at recent personnel decisions and an aggrandizement of personal power, Sfar was replaced as prime minister by Gen. Zine El-Abidine BEN ALI. Five weeks later, after a panel of doctors had declared the aged leader medically unfit, Bourguiba was forced to step down in favor of Ben Ali, who designated Hedi BACCOUCHE as his prime ministerial successor.

Constitution and government. The constitution of June 1, 1959, endowed the Tunisian Republic with a presidential system backed by the dominant position of the (then) Destourian Socialist Party (PSD). The president was endowed with exceptionally broad powers, including the right to designate the prime minister and to rule by decree during legislative adjournments. The unicameral Chamber of Deputies (styled the National Assembly until 1981) is elected by universal suffrage for a five-year term; it has limited authority and in practice has been wholly dominated by the ruling party, whose highly developed, all-pervasive organization serves as a powerful support of presidential policies both nationally and locally. The judi-

cial system is headed by a Court of Cassation and includes 3 courts of appeal, 13 courts of the first instance, and 51 cantonal courts. Judges are appointed by the president.

Tunisia is administratively divided into 18 provinces, each headed by a governor appointed by the president. The governors are assisted by appointed government councils and elected municipal councils.

In March 1988 Prime Minister Baccouche presented the Chamber of Deputies with a Constitutional Reform Bill which would abolish the life presidency accorded to President Bourguiba in favor of a chief executive who could be elected to no more than three five-year terms. Other changes would require new elections within 60 days of a presidential vacancy and reduce the role of the prime minister to one of "coordinating" ministerial activities.

Foreign relations. Tunisia has been a nonaligned nation since independence; it maintains relations with both Eastern and Western countries, although it places particular emphasis on its relations with the West and with Arab governments. It has played an active role in seeking a solution to the Arab-Israeli problem, stressing the need for resolution of the Palestinian question as part of an overall settlement.

Beginning in 1979, a series of agreements were signed with Algeria, culminating in a March 1983 "Maghreb Fraternity and Co-Operation Treaty", to which Mauritania acceded the following December. Relations with Libya, though reestablished in 1982 after a 1980 rupture over seizure of a southern town by alleged Libyan-trained insurgents, have continued to be difficult: despite reciprocal visits by Colonel Qadhafi and (then) Prime Minister Mzali, Tunisian officials continued to suspect Libyan involvement in the 1983 sabotage of an Algerian oil pipeline and widespread "bread riots" in January 1984. Following charges that Tunisia had sanctioned transit for a group involved in a May 1984 gun battle in Tripoli, Mzali recalled his country's ambassador to Libya; in August, Tunisian spokesmen reacted to the treaty of federation between Morocco and Libya by stating that they regarded the approach embodied in the trilateral treaty as more conducive to the promotion of Maghreb unity. After President Bourguiba's visit to Washington in June 1985, relations with Libya deteriorated further, leading to a mass expulsion of Tunisian workers, as well as reported Libyan incursions into Tunisia and efforts to destabilize its government. The Libyan threat brought pledges of military support from Algeria, Egypt, France, and the United States, with Tunis again suspending relations with Tripoli in September 1986. Following a March 1987 pledge by Libya to reimburse the expelled workers, relations once more eased, with a resumption of relations at the consular level in October and at the ambassadorial level in December. In January 1988 relations were also reestablished with Egypt, after an eight-year lapse.

During 1987 tension with France, which flared briefly over "tolerance" of former prime minister Mzali's bitter denunciations of the Bourguiba government, lessened following the arrest of six allegedly Iranian-backed Tunisian terrorists at Paris in March and the August revocation of Mzali's residence permit. Meanwhile, evidence linking domestic fundamentalism to Iran had led to the severance of diplomatic ties with Teheran.

Tunisia became a member of the United Nations in 1956 and is active in all the UN-related agencies. It joined the Arab League in 1958 but boycotted its meetings from 1958 to 1961 and again in 1966 as a result of disagreements with the more "revolutionary" Arab states. Over strong Libyan objections, the League established its headquarters at Tunis in early 1979 after the expulsion of Egypt necessitated removal from Cairo.

Current issues. President Bourguiba's ouster in November 1987 was not (as widely termed) a "bloodless coup" in that the circumstances of his departure, including succession by Prime Minister Ben Ali, were in accord with relevant provisions of the Tunisian constitution. Even Bourguiba was reported to have asserted that "perhaps I should have turned over power before". Following the deposition, Prime Minister Baccouche indicated that the new administration was committed to domestic pluralism and a policy of continued cooperation with its Western allies, while seeking improved relations with other North African countries, including Libya.

Earlier, continued economic decline and political uncertainty had yielded mounting problems for Tunisia. By mid-1987 the arrest of over 1,800 dissidents had given rise to continued demonstrations against both "Westernization" and repressive governmental policies, necessitating the establishment of a ten-member "Higher Islamic Council" for the adjudication of religious issues, on the one hand, and the widely publicized release of leading dissidents on the other. On August 2 bombs were exploded at two resort towns, one of which, Monastir, was President Bourguiba's birthplace. While responsibility for the attacks was claimed by the outlawed Islamic *Jihad,* the government blamed the Islamic Tendency Movement (see Political Parties, below).

POLITICAL PARTIES

Although not constitutionally mandated, Tunisia was effectively a one-party state from the time the Communist Party (PCT) was banned in January 1963 until its return to legal status in July 1981. A month earlier, the government had announced that recognition would be extended to all parties obtaining at least 5 percent of the valid votes in legislative balloting on November 1. On September 9, the PCT indicated that it would participate in the election after receiving official assurances that the 5 percent requirement would not be imposed in its case, and in 1983 recognition was extended to the two major opposition parties, the MUP and the MDS (below). All three boycotted the 1986 election because of the rejection of many of their candidate lists and administrative suspension of their publications. In November 1987 the Ben Ali government announced that it would introduce legislation legalizing all parties — including previously banned militant Islamic groups — that accepted its principles; a bill to such effect was submitted to the Chamber of Deputies in April 1988.

Government Party:

Constitutional Democratic Rally (*Rassemblement Constitutionnel Démocratique* — RCD). Known until October 1964 as the Neo-Destour Party and thereafter as the Destourian Socialist Party (*Parti Socialiste Destourien* — PSD), Tunisia's ruling party was given its present name in February 1988 to provide new impetus to "the practice of democracy" within its ranks. The original party was formed in 1934 as a splinter from the old Destour (Constitution) Party. Its moderately left-wing tendency was of less political significance than its organizational strength, derived in large part from affiliated syndicates representing labor, agriculture, artisans and merchants, students, women, and youth. Party members have filled all major government positions since independence.

At the 12th party congress in June 1986, President Bourguiba personally selected a new 90-member Central Committee and 20-member Political Bureau, ignoring party statutes calling for election by delegates. By the end of the year, following a rift in 1985, the PSD returned to close alignment with the General Union of Tunisian Workers (*Union Générale des Traivailleurs Tunisiens* — UGTT). During 1987 there were a number of personnel changes both before and after Bourguiba's ouster on November 7, including a reduction in the size of the Political Bureau to 12 members.

Leaders: Gen. Zine El-Abidine BEN ALI (President of the Republic), Hedi BACCOUCHE (Prime Minister and Secretary General of the Party), Dr. Hamed KAROUI (Party Director).

Other Parties:

Democratic Socialist Movement (*Mouvement des Démocrates Socialistes* — MDS). Organized as the Democratic Socialist Group in October 1977 by a number of former PSD cabinet ministers who sought liberalization of the nation's political life, the MDS was refused formal recognition in 1978, although its leader, Ahmed Mestiri, had served as an intermediary between the government and the trade-union leadership in attempting to resolve labor unrest. In March 1980 the PSD Political Bureau invited the dissidents to return and was told that while the gesture seemed "to proceed from good intentions", it did not reflect a degree of political accommodation "responding to the aspirations of the people". Although runner-up at the 1981 election, the MDS obtained only 3.28 percent of the vote, thus failing to secure either legislative representation or legal status, the latter being granted by Bourguiba in November 1983. Mestiri was arrested in April 1986 and sentenced to four months in prison for leading demonstrations against the United States' bombing of Libya. The arrest automatically disqualified him from running for legislative office and the MDS was an early advocate of the November electoral boycott. During its second national congress on December 26–28, the MDS called for constitutional revision that would require a general election in the event of a presidential vacancy.

Leaders: Ahmed MESTIRI (Secretary General), Dali JAZI (Assistant Secretary General).

Popular Unity Movement (*Mouvement de l'Unité Populaire* — MUP). The MUP is a radical reform movement that sought unsuccessfully to secure legal representation upon reorganization as a political party in June 1978. In early 1981 a split developed within the MUP leadership after the government granted amnesty to all members theretofore subject to legal restriction, the sole exception being its titular secretary general, Ahmed Ben Salah, who had been living in exile since his escape from prison in 1973. Salah subsequently declared his opposition to the group's participating in the November 1 balloting, causing a split between his supporters and an "internal" faction, led by Mohamed Bel Hadj Amor, that garnered only 0.81 percent of the vote but was also recognized in 1983 as a legal party. The internal group, operating as the **Popular Unity Party** (*Parti de l'Unité Populaire* — PUP), initially offered candidates for the 1986 balloting but most were declared ineligible by the government and the PUP withdrew three days before the election, citing the same harassment that had led to boycott by the other opposition groups.

Leaders: Ahmed Ben SALAH ("external" faction), Mohamed Bel Hadj AMOR ("internal" faction).

Tunisian Communist Party (*Parti Communiste Tunisien* — PCT). Established in 1934 as an entity distinct from its parent organization, the French Communist Party, the pro-Soviet PCT was outlawed in 1963 and regained legality in July 1981. Historically of quite limited membership, the party secured only 0.78 percent of the vote at the 1981 legislative balloting. Prior to the opposition boycott, the PCT had intended to participate in the 1986 election in alliance with the RSP (below). The party's Ninth National Congress was held at Tunis in June 1987.

Leader: Mohamed HARMEL (General Secretary).

Progressive Socialist Assembly (*Rassemblement Socialiste Progressiste* — RSP). Founded in 1983, the RSP was tolerated by the Bourguiba government until mid-1986. The RSP formed a "Democratic Alliance" with the PCT and planned to field candidates for the 1986 balloting. However, the coalition boycotted the election after the government disqualified some of its candidates and sentenced 14 of its members to six-month jail terms for belonging to an illegal organization.

Leader: Nejib CHEDBI (Secretary General).

Islamic Tendency Movement (*Mouvement de la Tendance Islamique* — MTI). The MTI was formed in early 1981 by a group of Islamic fundamentalists inspired by the 1979 Iranian revolution. Charged with fomenting a number of violent disturbances by Tunisian students, its most prominent leaders were arrested and sentenced to prison terms of varying duration prior to the 1981 election. Arrests continued into 1984, with the MTI claiming responsibility for the January "bread riots". In August, on the other hand, the group's president and secretary general were released from custody after pledging that they would refrain from future violent activities. The MTI boycotted the November 1986 balloting, charging that it would be "neither free nor fair". In March 1987, following the antiterrorist action by French authorities (see Foreign relations, above), many MTI adherents were arrested, including the Movement's leader, Rachid Ghanouchi. The group was subsequently charged with complicity in the August bombings, despite an insistence that it rejected revolutionary activity.

Leaders: Rachid GHANOUCHI (President), Abdelfettah MOUR-ROU (Secretary General).

Progressive Islamic Movement (*Mouvement Islamique Progressiste* — MIP). The MIP is a small group similar in commitment to the MTI, but with a somewhat more radical orientation.

Leader: Slaheddine JORCHHI (under arrest).

National Arab Rally (*Rassemblement National Arabe* — RNA). Less fundamentalist in outlook than the MTI but also banned subsequent to its launching in May 1981, the RNA announced as its goal "the total unity of the Arab countries". Its overall platform was construed by *Le Monde* as being infused "with a Libyan resonance".

Leader: Bashir ASSAD.

Islamic Liberation Party (*Parti de Liberation Islamique* — PLI). The most radical of Tunisia's Islamic fundamentalist organizations, the PLI advocates the replacement of secular regimes with a caliphate patterned after the early Islamic policy established by the Prophet Muhammad. Founded in Jordan by the Palestinian Taqi al-Din al-Nabhani in 1952, the party operates clandestinely in all Arab countries; in Tunisia, a number of ILP members were tried and jailed in August 1983 and March 1985.

LEGISLATURE

The **Chamber of Deputies** (*Majlis an-Nouab/Chambre des Députés*) is a unicameral body presently consisting of 125 members elected by direct popular vote for five-year terms. Members of the ruling party have occupied all seats since the body was established in 1959. Opposition parties boycotted the most recent election of November 2, 1986.

President: Mahmoud MESSADI.

CABINET

[as of April 11, 1988]

Prime Minister	Hedi Baccouche
Minister of State for Justice	Slaheddine Baly
Ministers	
Agriculture	Lassad Ben Osman
Communications	Brahim Khouaja
Culture	Abdel Malak Laarif
Defense	Zine El-Abidine Ben Ali
Finance	Nouri Zourgati
Foreign Affairs	Mahmoud Mestiri
Higher Education and Scientific Research	Abdessalem M'Seddi
Information	Abdelwahab Abdallah
Interior	Habib Ammar
National Economy	Slaheddine Ben M'Barek
National Education	Hedi Khelil
Prime Minister's Office	Dr. Hamed Karoui
Prime Minister's Office in Charge of Civil Service and Administrative Reform	Houssine Cherif
Prime Minister's Office in Charge of Planning	Mohamed Ghannouchi
Public Health	Dr. Souad Lyagoubi
Social Affairs	Taoufik Cheikhrouhou
Supplies and Housing	Sadok Ben Jama
Transport and Tourism	Abderrazak Kefi
Youth and Sports	Abdelhamid Escheikh
Governor, Central Bank	Ismail Khelil

NEWS MEDIA

Although free in principle, the media during most of the Bourguiba era were subject to pervasive party influence.

Press. The following are published daily at Tunis: *As-Sabah* (the morning, 90,000), independent, in Arabic; *al-Amal* (Action, 50,000), PSD organ, in Arabic; *L'Action* (50,000), PSD organ, in French; *Le Temps* (42,000), in French; *La Presse de Tunisie* (40,000), government organ, in French.

News agencies. The domestic facility is *Tunis Afrique Presse* (TAP); a number of foreign bureaus maintain offices at Tunis.

Radio and television. *Radiodiffusion Télévision Tunisienne* is a government station broadcasting in Arabic, French, and Italian. It also operates a television network linking the country with European transmissions. There were approximately 1.4 million radio and 500,000 television receivers in 1987.

INTERGOVERNMENTAL REPRESENTATION

Ambassador to the US: Habib BEN YAHIA.

US Ambassador to Tunisia: Robert H. PELLETREAU, Jr.

Permanent Representative to the UN: Ahmed GHEZAL.

IGO Memberships (Non-UN): ACCT, ADF, AfDB, AFESD, AMF, BADEA, CCC, *EIB,* IC, IDB, ILZ, Intelsat, Interpol, IOOC, IWTC, LAS, NAM, OAU.

TURKEY

Republic of Turkey
Türkiye Cumhuriyeti

Political Status: Independent republic established in 1923; parliamentary system restored in 1961, after military interregnum; military regime installed following coup of September 12, 1980, and legitimized, on a transitional basis, by national referendum of November 7, 1982; civilian government restored following parliamentary election of November 6, 1983.

Area: 301,380 sq. mi. (780,576 sq. km.).

Population: 50,664,458 (1985C), 54,591,000 (1988E).

Major Urban Centers (1986E): ANKARA (2,800,000); İstanbul (4,790,000); İzmir (1,900,000); Adana (1,300,000).

Official Language: Turkish.

Monetary Unit: Turkish Lira (market rate March 1, 1988, 1179.39 liras = $1US).

President of the Republic and of the Presidential Council: Gen. Kenan EVREN; succeeded Acting President İhsan Sabri ÇAĞLAYANGİL as Head of State on September 12, 1980; assumed office as President for a seven-year term on November 9, 1982, following referendum of November 7.

Other Members of the Presidential Council: Gen. Sedat CELASUN, Gen. Nurettin ERSİN, Gen. Tahsin ŞAHİN-KAYA, Adm. Nejat TÜMER; sworn in September 18, 1980.

Prime Minister: Turgut ÖZAL (Motherland Party); assumed office December 13, 1983, following Grand National Assembly election of November 6, succeeding Adm. Bülent ULUSU; reappointed following election of November 29, 1987.

THE COUNTRY

Guardian of the narrow straits between the Mediterranean and Black seas, present-day Turkey occupies the compact land mass of the Anatolian Peninsula together with the partially European city of İstanbul and its Thracian hinterland. The country, which has Bulgaria, Greece, Syria, Iraq, Iran, Syria, and the USSR as its immediate neighbors, has a varied topography and is subject to extreme variation in climate. It supports a largely Turkish population (over 90 percent, in terms of language) and a Kurdish minority (close to three million in the east and southeast), plus such smaller groups as Arabs, Circassians, Greeks, Armenians, Georgians, Lazes, and Jews. Approximately 98 percent of the population, including both Turks and Kurds, adhere to the Sunni sect of Islam, which maintains a strong position despite the secular emphasis of government policy since the 1920s.

Women constitute over 51 percent of the official labor force, with 88 percent of their number agricultural workers (largely as unpaid workers on family farms). While only 10 percent of the urban labor force is female, there is extensive participation by upper-income women in the professions: 20 percent of all lawyers, 30 percent of all doctors, and 34 percent of all bankers and teachers were women in 1981. However, in June 1985 women protested a decision by the Council of State that they could not become local governors.

Turkey traditionally has been an agricultural country, with approximately 60 percent of the population still engaged in agricultural pursuits; yet the contribution of industry to GDP is now larger than that of agriculture (57.4 and 51.3 percent, respectively, in 1985). Grain (most importantly wheat), tobacco, cotton, nuts, fruits, and olive oil are the chief agricultural products; sheep and cattle are raised on the Anatolian plateau, and the country ranks second in the world in production of mohair. Natural resources include chrome, copper, iron ore, manganese, bauxite, borax, and petroleum. The most important industries are textiles, iron and steel, sugar, food processing, cement, paper, and fertilizer. State economic enterprises (SEEs) account for more than 60 percent of fixed investment, although the present government is committed to substantial privatization (see Current issues, below).

Economic growth during the 1960s was substantial but not enough to overcome severe balance-of-payments and inflation problems, which intensified following the oil price increases of 1973–1974. By 1975 the cost of petroleum imports had more than quadrupled and was absorbing nearly two-thirds of export earnings. A major devaluation of the lira in mid-1979 failed to resolve the country's economic difficulties, and in early 1980, with inflation exceeding 100 percent, a $1.16 billion OECD loan package was negotiated, followed in June by $1.65 billion in IMF credits. Subsequently, aided by improving export performance and a tight curb on foreign currency transactions, the economy registered substantial recovery, with inflation being reduced to a still unsatisfactory level of 40–50 percent by late 1987.

GOVERNMENT AND POLITICS

Political background. The present-day Turkish Republic is the surviving core of a vast empire created by Ottoman rule in late medieval and early modern times. After a period of expansion during the fifteenth and sixteenth centuries in which Ottoman domination was extended over much of central Europe, the Balkans, the Middle East, and North Africa, the empire underwent a lengthy period of contraction and fragmentation, finally dissolving in the aftermath of a disastrous alliance with Germany in World War I.

A secular nationalist republic was proclaimed in October 1923 by Mustafa Kemal ATATÜRK, who launched a reform program under which Turkey abandoned much of its Ottoman and Islamic heritage. Its major components included secularization (separation of religion and state), establishment of state control of the economy, and creation of a new Turkish consciousness. Following his death in 1938, Atatürk's Republican People's Party continued as the only legally recognized party under his close associate, İsmet İNÖNÜ. One-party domination was not seriously contested until after World War II, when the opposition Democratic Party was established by Celal BAYAR, Adnan MENDERES, and others. Winning the country's first free election in 1950, the Democratic Party ruled Turkey for the next decade, only to be ousted in 1960 by a military coup led by Gen. Cemal GÜRSEL. The coup was a response to increased corruption within the Democratic Party and growing authoritarian attitudes of its leaders. Numerous leaders of the Democratic Party, including President Bayar and Prime Minister Menderes, were tried and found guilty of violating the constitution, as a result of which Bayar was imprisoned and Menderes executed. Civilian government was restored under a new constitution in 1961, with Gürsel remaining as president until his incapacitation and replacement by Gen. Cevdet SUNAY in 1966. The 1961 basic law established a series of checks and balances to offset a concentration of power in the executive and prompted a diffusion of parliamentary seats among several parties. A series of coalition governments, most of them led by İnönü, functioned until 1965, when Süleyman DEMİREL's Justice Party (a partial reincarnation of the Democratic Party) won a sweeping legislative mandate.

Despite its victory, the Demirel regime soon became the target of popular discontent and demands for basic reform. Although surviving the election of 1969, it was subsequently caught between left-wing agitation and military insistence on the maintenance of public order, a critical issue because of growing economic and social unrest and the growth of political terrorism. The crisis came to a head in 1971 with an ultimatum from the military that resulted in Demirel's resignation and the formation of a "nonparty" government by Nihat ERİM, the declaration of martial law in 11 provinces, the arrest of dissident elements, and the outlawing of the left-wing Turkish Labor and right-extremist National Order parties. The period immediately after the fall of the Erim government in 1972 witnessed another "nonparty" administration under Ferit MELEN and the selection of a new president, (retired) Adm. Fahri KORUTÜRK. Political instability was heightened further by an inconclusive election in 1973 and by both foreign and domestic policy problems stemming from a rapidly deteriorating economy, substantial urban population growth, and renewed conflict on Cyprus that yielded Turkish intervention in the summer of 1974.

Bülent ECEVİT was appointed prime minister in January 1974, heading a coalition of his own moderately progressive Republican People's Party and the smaller, religiously oriented National Salvation Party. Although securing widespread domestic acclaim for the Cyprus action and for his insistence that the island be formally divided into Greek and Turkish federal regions, Ecevit was opposed by Deputy Prime Minister Necmettin ERBAKAN, who called for outright annexation of the Turkish sector and, along with his National Salvation colleagues, resigned, precipitating Ecevit's own resignation in September. Both Ecevit and former prime minister Demirel having failed to form new governments, Sadi IRMAK, an independent, was designated prime minister on November 17, heading an essentially nonparliamentary cabinet. Following a defeat in the National Assembly only 12 days later, Irmak also was forced to resign, although remaining in office in a caretaker capacity until Demirel succeeded in forming a new government on April 12, 1975.

At a premature general election on June 5, 1977, no party succeeded in gaining a lower-house majority, and the Demirel government fell on July 13. Following Ecevit's failure to organize a majority coalition, Demirel returned as head of a three-party administration that failed to survive a no-confidence vote on December 31. Ecevit thereupon formed a minority government that included the Republican People's Party, a new Democratic Party (organized in 1970 but eventually disbanded in May 1980), the

Republican Reliance Party (whose members withdrew in September 1978), and a group of Justice Party dissidents.

Widespread civil and political unrest throughout 1978 prompted a declaration of martial law in 13 provinces on December 25. The security situation deteriorated further during 1979 and, faced with a number of ministerial defections, Prime Minister Ecevit was on October 16 again obliged to step down, Demirel returning as head of a Justice Party minority government on November 12.

Despite extensive rescheduling of the country's foreign debt, little economic recovery was registered during the first half of 1980, while the legislative and internal security situations deteriorated markedly. Terrorism, which was blamed for some 1,500 deaths in 1979, continued to escalate, prompting former prime minister Ecevit to appeal, unsuccessfully, for a broad-based "government of reconstruction". Symptomatically, the National Assembly failed in over 100 ballots to elect a successor to Fahri Korutürk as president of the Republic, Senate President İhsan Sabri ÇAĞLAYANGİL being obliged to assume the office on an acting basis at the expiration of Korutürk's seven-year term on April 6. On August 29, Gen. Kenan EVREN, chief of the General Staff, publicly criticized the Assembly for its failure either to elect a new president or to promulgate more drastic security legislation, and on September 12 mounted a coup on behalf of a five-man National Security Council (NSC) that suspended the constitution, dissolved the Assembly, proclaimed martial law in all of the country's 67 provinces, and, on September 21, designated a military-civilian cabinet under (retired) Adm. Bülent ULUSU. The junta banned all existing political parties; detained many of their leaders, including Ecevit and Demirel; imposed strict censorship; and arrested several thousand people on political charges.

At a national referendum of November 7, 1982, Turkish voters overwhelmingly approved a new constitution, under which General Evren was formally designated as president of the Republic for a seven-year term. One year later, on November 6, 1983, the recently established Motherland Party of former deputy prime minister Turgut ÖZAL outpolled two competing groups, including the reportedly military-backed Nationalist Democracy Party led by retired general Turgut SUNALP, to win a majority of seats in a newly constituted, unicameral Grand National Assembly. Following the election, General Evren's four colleagues on the NSC resigned their military commands, continuing as members of a Presidential Council upon dissolution of the NSC on December 6. On December 7, Özal was asked to form a government and assumed office as prime minister on December 13. A number of party realignments followed, with the Motherland Party increasing its majority from 212 to 251 in the 400-seat Assembly by early 1987 and winning 55 of 84 mayoralties at municipal elections on June 7. In a national referendum on September 6, a provision of the 1982 basic law banning former politicians from public life was rescinded by a narrow 50.2 percent margin and in parliamentary balloting in November 29 the Motherland Party swept 292 seats in an expanded 450-member Assembly.

Constitution and government. The 1961 constitution provided for the following: (1) a unicameral, 400-member

Grand National Assembly elected for a five-year term (the membership being increased to 450 in 1987); (2) a president who, at the conclusion of General Evren's seven-year incumbency, will be elected by the Assembly for a non-renewable term of like duration, and who is advised by a State Consultative Council of 30 members (20 presidentially appointed); (3) a four-member Presidential Council of senior military figures (to be dissolved after the 1989 presidential balloting); and (4) an advisory Economic and Social Council. In addition, the president is empowered to appoint and dismiss the prime minister and other cabinet members; to dissolve the Assembly and call for a new election, with the concurrence of two-thirds of the deputies or if faced with a government crisis of more than 30 days' duration; to declare a state of emergency, during which the government may rule by decree; and to appoint a variety of leading government officials, including senior judges and the governor of the Central Bank. Political parties may be formed if they are not class based, linked to trade unions, or committed to communism, fascism, or religious fundamentalism. Strikes that exceed 60 days duration are subject to compulsory arbitration, while strict controls are exercised over the media.

The Turkish judicial system is headed by a Court of Cassation, which is the court of final appeal. Other judicial bodies include an administrative tribunal called the Council of State; a Constitutional Court; and a variety of military courts, before which most security cases since the 1980 coup have been prosecuted.

The country is divided into 67 provinces, which are further divided into subprovinces and districts. Mayors and municipal councils have been popularly elected since 1984.

Foreign relations. Neutral until the closing months of World War II, Turkey entered that conflict in time to become a founding member of the United Nations, and has since joined all of the latter's affiliated agencies. Concern for the protection of its independence, primarily against possible Soviet threats, made Turkey a firm ally of the Western powers and led it to maintain one of the largest standing armies in the non-Communist world. Largely on US initiative, Turkey was admitted to NATO in 1952 and joined, in 1955, in creation of the Baghdad Treaty Organization, later the Central Treaty Organization (CENTO), which was officially disbanded in September 1979 following Iranian and Pakistani withdrawal. Relations with a number of Western governments have cooled since the mid-1960s, partly because of a lack of support for Turkey's position on the question of Cyprus. The dispute, with the fate of the Turkish Cypriot community at its center, became critical upon the island's attaining independence in 1960 and nearly led to war with Greece in 1967. The situation assumed major international importance in 1974 following the Greek officers' coup that resulted in the temporary ouster of Cypriot President Makarios, and the subsequent Turkish military intervention on July 20 with Turkish occupation of the northern third of the island.

Relations with the United States, severely strained by a congressional ban on military aid following the Cyprus invasion, were further exacerbated by a Turkish decision in July 1975 to repudiate a 1969 defense cooperation agreement and force the closure of 25 US military installations.

However, a new accord was included in March 1976 that called for reopening of the bases under Turkish rather than dual control, coupled with substantially increased US military assistance. The US arms embargo was finally lifted in September 1978, with the stipulation that Turkey continue to seek a negotiated resolution of the Cyprus issue (see entries under Cyprus and Greece for subsequent developments).

As a non-Arab state, Turkey for some years maintained relatively cordial relations with Israel. However, beginning in 1976, when it hosted a meeting of the Islamic Conference, it progressively strengthened its ties with regional Islamic governments. In December 1980 it reduced its diplomatic contacts with Israel to a "symbolic level" and joined in condemning the extension of Israeli law to the western Golan Heights a year later. A subsequent easing of relations that included a three-day visit to Turkey by Israeli Industry and Trade Minister Ariel Sharon in July 1986 was followed in September by an attack on İstanbul's Neve Shalom Synagogue that resulted in the killing of 21 worshippers, including seven rabbis. The Özal government strongly condemned the action and launched a major security investigation amid allegations that both the Abu Nidal terrorist organization and the (Shi'ite) Islamic *Jihad* had been involved.

In October 1984, an agreement was concluded with Iraq that permitted security forces of each government to pursue "subversive groups" (interpreted primarily as Kurdish rebels) up to a distance of five kilometers on either side of the border and to engage in follow-up operations for five days without prior notification. Late in the same year, relations with Bulgaria worsened because of the latter's campaign to assimilate ethnic Turks, and plummeted further in 1985 because of a Bulgarian census that precluded registration by foreign nationality and sought no information on religious affiliation. As a result, an emphasis on shipping in a new trade agreement with Romania was construed as part of an effort to divert transit traffic from the more immediate neighbor. Meanwhile, Turkey attempted to maintain cordial relations with both Iran and Iraq, Ankara's foreign minister affirming his country's willingness to mediate between the two in the ongoing Gulf war.

While the Turkish government under Evren and Özal has consistently affirmed its support of NATO and its desire to gain full entry to the European Community (having been an associate member of the European Economic Community since 1964), relations with Western Europe deteriorated in the wake of the 1980 coup because of alleged human rights violations. In 1981, the EC imposed restrictions on the import of Turkish goods, while failing to authorize the disbursement of funds committed in a $600 million aid program. Collaterally, the credentials of Turkish delegates to the Parliamentary Assembly of the Council of Europe were suspended until May 1984, when the Assembly noted that progress had been made toward the restoration of democracy, while urging greater consideration for human rights and full freedom of action for political parties. Despite Greek protests, Turkey assumed the largely symbolic Council presidency for a six-month term in October 1986 and, in an action viewed as enhancing its prospects for EC membership, applied for admission to the Western European Union in April 1987.

During late January 1988 Prime Minister Özal and his Greek counterpart, Andreas Papandreou, met at Davos, Switzerland, pledging themselves to the initiation of a dialogue on common problems between their two countries. The leaders agreed to set up committees to review cultural and economic relations, and to promote contacts between businessmen, governmental officials, and the press; they further agreed to establish an Ankara-Athens hot line and to make reciprocal visits to the two capitals. Subsequently Turkey announced that Greek nationals could convert their holdings to cash (implying that the funds could be transferred out of the country), while Greece announced that it would lift its reservation to an Adjustment Agreement between Turkey and the European Community. The partial rapprochement with Greece was followed in late February by a meeting at Belgrade, Yugoslavia, between the foreign ministers of Turkey and Bulgaria, which yielded a protocol aimed at reducing frictions between their two governments, including the establishment of a commission to deal with the highly sensitive issue of the ethnic Turkish minority in Bulgaria.

Current issues. The principal beneficiaries of the September 1987 repeal of the constitutional ban on public activity by pre-1980 political leaders were former prime ministers Süleyman Demirel and Bülent Ecevit. The former immediately assumed leadership of the right-wing True Path Party, which retained its status as the third-ranked Assembly grouping after the November balloting; however, the latter's Democratic Left Party failed to obtain legislative representation, with Ecevit thereupon announcing his retirement from politics—an action that was subsequently retracted under pressure from the party rank and file. The arithmetic of the electoral law, specifically designed to inhibit the earlier party fractionalization, yielded a 64.9 percent majority for the Motherland Party, although it obtained only 39.3 percent of the vote.

While trials continued during 1987 for politically motivated offenses, the security situation appeared to have eased, and by March martial law continued only in four Kurdish-speaking provinces, after being replaced by less severe states-of-emergency in four others, plus İstanbul. In December the prime minister announced a plan designed to make Turkey a leading industrial power by the year 2000 "if political and economic stability continues". While including a relaxation of interest rates and a loosening of currency restrictions, much of the package centered on a policy, first announced in late 1986 and officially launched the following May, to privatize a substantial number of the state companies that currently provide some 40 percent of the country's goods and services. Without elaboration, Özal also pledged constitutional changes dealing with the centralized university system and both civil and criminal law.

POLITICAL PARTIES

Turkey's former multiparty system developed gradually out of the monopoly originally exercised by the historic Republican People's Party (*Cumhuriyet Halk Partisi*— CHP), which ruled the country without serious competi-

tion until 1950 and which, under Bülent Ecevit, was most recently in power from January 1978 to October 1979. The Democratic Party (*Demokrat Parti*—DP) of Celal Bayar and Adnan Menderes, founded by RPP dissidents in 1946, came to power in 1950, maintained control for the next decade, but was outlawed in consequence of the military coup of 1960, many of its members subsequently entering the conservative Justice Party (*Adalet Partisi*—AP). Other formations included an Islamic group, the National Salvation Party (*Milli Selâmet Partisi*—MSP); the ultra-conservative Nationalist Action Party (*Milliyetçi Hareket Partisi*—MHP); and the leftist Turkish Labor Party (*Türkiye İşçi Partisi*—TİP). All party activity was banned by the National Security Council on September 12, 1980, while the parties themselves were formally dissolved and their assets liquidated on October 16, 1981.

Approval of the 1982 constitution ruled out any immediate likelihood that anything resembling the earlier party system would reappear. In order to qualify for the 1983 parliamentary election, new parties were required to obtain the signatures of at least 30 founding members, subject to veto by the National Security Council. Most such lists were, without explanation, rejected by the NSC, with only three groups (the Nationalist Democracy, Populist, and Motherland parties) being formally registered for the balloting on November 6. Of the three, only the ruling Motherland Party remained by mid-1986: the Populist Party merged with the Social Democratic Party in November 1985 to form the Social Democratic People's Party, (subsequently the Social Populist Party, below), while the center-right Nationalist Democracy Party (*Milliyetçi Demokrasi Partisi*—MDP) dissolved itself in May 1986. Upwards of a dozen smaller groups also surfaced briefly during 1983–1987.

Government Party:

Motherland Party (*Anavatan Partisi*—Anap). Anap is a right-of-center grouping committed to the growth of private, rather than state-controlled business enterprise, while advocating closer links to the Islamic world. It won an absolute majority of 212 Assembly seats, one of which was subsequently disallowed by the NSC, in November 1983, increasing its representation to 237 at by-elections in September 1986. At the local elections of March 1984, it obtained control of municipal councils in 55 of the country's 67 provincial capitals. Its ranks augmented by most former deputies of the Free Democratic Party (*Hür Demokrat Partisi*—HDP), which was formed by a number of independents in May 1986, but dissolved the following December, Anap claimed 255 Assembly seats by May 1987 and won a commanding majority of 292 seats at the election of November 29.

Leaders: Turgut ÖZAL (Prime Minister), Mehmet KEÇECİLER, Mustafa TAŞAR (Secretary General).

Opposition Parties:

Social Democratic Populist Party (*Sosyal Demokrasi Halkçı Parti*— SHP. The SHP was formed initially, in late 1985, as the Social Democratic People's Party (*Sosyal Demokrat Halk Partisi*—SDHP) by merger of the Populist Party (*Halkçı Parti*—HP), a center-left formation that secured 117 seats in the 1983 Grand National Assembly election, and the Social Democratic Party (*Sosyal Demokrasi Partisi*—Sodep), which was not permitted to offer candidates for the 1983 balloting. A left-of-center grouping that drew much of its support from former members of the Republican People's Party, Sodep participated in the 1984 local elections, winning 10 provincial capitals. The SHP was runner-up to Anap in November 1987 winning 99 Assembly seats, despite the defection of 20 deputies from the SDHP on December 26, 1986, most of whom joined the Democratic Left Party (below).

Leaders: Erdal İNÖNÜ (President), Fikri SAĞLAR (Secretary General).

Democratic Left Party (*Demokratik Sol Parti* — DSP). Formation of the DSP, a center-left populist formation, was announced in March 1984 by Rahşan Ecevit, the wife of former prime minister Bülent Ecevit, who was barred from political activity prior to the constitutional referendum of September 1987. At the November election, the party attracted sufficient social democratic support to weaken the SHP, without itself winning the minimum 10 percent vote share required for parliamentary representation.

Leader: Bülent ECEVIT (former Prime Minister).

True Path Party (*Doğru Yol Partisi* — DYP). The center-right DYP was organized as a successor to the Grand Turkey Party (*Büyük Türkiye Partisi* — BTP), which was banned shortly after its formation in May 1983 because of links to the former Justice Party of Süleyman Demirel. The new group was permitted to participate in the local elections of March 1984, but won control in none of the provincial capitals. By early 1987, having been joined by most assemblymen elected at the September 1986 by-election by the subsequently dissolved Citizen Party (*Vatandaş Partisi* — VP), it was the third-ranked party in the Grand National Assembly. The DYP remained in third place by winning 59 seats at the November 1987 balloting.

Leader: Süleyman DEMİREL (former Prime Minister and President of the Party).

Welfare Party (*Refah Partisi* — RP). The Welfare Party was organized by former members of the Islamic fundamentalist National Salvation Party. It participated in the 1984 local elections, winning one provincial capital. It secured no Assembly seats in 1987.

Leaders: Necmettin ERBAKAN (former NSP leader), Ahmet TEKDAL.

Nationalist Work Party (*Milliyetçi Calışma Partisi* — MÇP). The MÇP is an extreme right-wing party formed in November 1985 by sympathizers of the pre-1980 Nationalist Action Party. It is unrepresented in the Grand National Assembly.

Leaders: Alpaslan TÜRKEŞ (President), Ali KOÇ.

Reformist Democratic Party (*Islahatçı Demokrasi Partisi* — IDP). The IDP is a recently organized and relatively ineffectual right-wing formation that has ideological affinities with both the RP and MCP, while standing apart from each.

Leader: Aykut EDİBALİ.

Turkish Communist Party (*Türkiye Komünist Partisi* — TKP). Proscribed since 1925, the pro-Soviet TKP long maintained its headquarters in Eastern Europe, staffed largely by exiles and refugees who left Turkey in the 1930s and 1940s. Although remaining illegal, its activities within Turkey revived in 1983, including, according to the conservative newspaper *Tercüman,* the convening of its first congress in more than 50 years. *Tercüman* also alleged that the designation of Haydar Kutlu as the party's new secretary general completed a takeover of the TKP by leaders of the former Turkish Labor Party, which had been formally dissolved in 1971 and again in 1980.

Leaders: Nihat SARGIN (President), Haydar KUTLU (Secretary General).

Extremist Groups:

Extremist and terrorist groups include the "Grey Wolves" youth wing of the banned ultrarightist MHP, the leftist **Revolutionary Path** (*Devrimci Yol* — Dev-Yol) and the more radical **Revolutionary Left** (*Devrimci Sol* — Dev-Sol), both derived from the Revolutionary Youth (*Dev Genç*), which operated in the late 1960s and early 1970s in partial linkage to the far leftist Turkish People's Salvation Army; the **Turkish People's Liberation Party Front** (*Türkiye Halk Kurtuluş Partisi Cephesi* — THKP-C), the **Turkish Workers' and Peasants' Liberation Army** (*Türkiye İşçi Köylü Kurtuluş Ordusu* — TİKKO), and the **Kurdish Workers' Party** (PKK or Apo'cular), all of which have experienced numerous arrests — often leading to executions — of members; and a variety of Armenian guerrilla units composed almost entirely of nonnationals and operating, variously, as the "Secret Army for the Liberation of Armenia" (Asala), including a so-called "Orly group"; the "Justice Commandos for the Armenian Genocide"; the "Pierre Gulmian commando"; the "Levan Ekmekciyan suicide commando"; and the "Armenian Revolutionary Army".

LEGISLATURE

The 1982 constitution replaced the former bicameral legislature with a unicameral **Turkish Grand National Assembly** (*Türkiye Büyük Millet Meclisi*) of 400 members elected for five-year terms. Of the three parties authorized to present candidates at the balloting of November 6, 1983, the Motherland Party obtained 212 seats (1 subsequently vacated by the NSC); the Populist Party, 117; and the Nationalist Democracy Party, 71. At the most recent election for a 450-member Assembly on November 29, 1987, the Motherland Party obtained 292 seats; the Social Populist Party, 99; and the True Path Party, 59.

Speaker: Yıldrım AKTÜRK.

CABINET

Prime Minister	Turgut Özal
Deputy Prime Minister	Kaya Erdem
Ministers	
Agriculture, Forests, and Village Affairs	Hüsnü Doğan
Communications and Transport	Ekrem Pakdemirli
Culture and Tourism	Mustafa Tınaz Titiz
Energy and Natural Resources	Fahrettin Kurt
Finance and Customs	Ahmet Kurtcebe Alptemoçin
Foreign Affairs	Mesut Yılmaz
Health and Social Assistance	Bülent Akarcalı
Industry, Trade and Technology	Şükrü Yürür
Interior	Mustafa Kalemli
Justice	Mahmut Oltan Sungurlu
Labor and Social Security	İmren Aykut
National Defense	Ercan Vuralhan
National Education, Youth and Sports	Hasan Celal Güzel
Public Works and Resettlement	Safa Giray
Ministers of State	
Economics	Yusuf Bozkurt Özal
European Community	Ali Bozer
Speaker of Government	Mehmet Yazar
Turkish Radio Television	Adnan Kahveci
Without Portfolio	Veysel Atasoy
	Cemil Çiçek
	Nihat Kitapçı
	Kazım Oksay
	Abdullah Tenekeci
Governor, Central Bank	Rustu Saraçoğlu

NEWS MEDIA

Formal censorship of the media in regard to security matters was imposed in late 1979 and was expanded under the military regime installed in September 1980. A new press law promulgated in November 1982 gave public prosecutors the right to confiscate any publication prior to sale, permitted the government to ban foreign publications deemed to be "a danger to the unity of the country", and made journalists and publishers liable for the issuance of "subversive" material.

Press. Recently launched papers include the rightist *Türkiye* and the liberal *Söz,* in addition to two others that reportedly sell over a million copies a day: *Tan,* an extremely sensationalist and questionably journalistic spin-off of *Günaydın,* and *Sabah,* published by the *Yeni Asır* group, which is at present somewhat more responsible than upon its founding in early 1986. By contrast, the circulation of most other papers has sharply declined, the following figures (for papers published at İstanbul, unless otherwise noted) being rough current estimates: *Hürriyet* (400,000), liberal-rightist; *Günaydın* (300,000), semisensationalist; *Güneş* (250,000), centrist; *Tercüman* (220,000), rightist; *Milliyet* (210,000), formerly liberal, now center-rightist; *Cumhuriyet* (100,000), influential leftist; *Barış* (Ankara, 50,000); *Yeni Asır* (İzmir, 50,000).

News agencies. The government-controlled Anatolian News Agency and the privately owned Turkish News Agency (*Türk Haberler Ajansı*) and *Hürriyet Haber Ajansı* are located in several cities. Foreign bureaus maintaining offices in Turkey include *Agence France-Presse, Agenzia Nazionale Stampa Associata* (ANSA), *Deutsche Presse-Agentur* (DPA), AP, UPI, and TASS.

Radio and television. The state-controlled Turkish Radio Television Corporation (*Türkiye Radyo Televizyon Kurumu*) broadcasts over two television channels: TV1 and TV2; in addition there are four radio programs, two of which are FM. There were approximately 8.3 million radio and 5.0 million television receivers in 1987.

INTERGOVERNMENTAL REPRESENTATION

Ambassador to the US: Dr. Sükrü ELEKDAĞ.

US Ambassador to Turkey: Robert STRAUSZ-HUPE.

Permanent Representative to the UN: İlter TÜRKMEN.

IGO Memberships (Non-UN): BIS, CCC, CEUR, EEC(A), *EIB,* IC, ICAC, IDB, IEA, INRO, Intelsat, Interpol, IOOC, IWTC, NATO, OECD, PCA.

TUVALU

Political Status: Former British dependency; independent with "special membership" in the Commonwealth since October 1, 1978.

Land Area: 10 sq. mi. (26 sq. km.).

Resident Population: 8,229 (1985C), 8,800 (1988E). Both figures are exclusive of more than 3,000 Tuvaluans living overseas.

Major Urban Center: None; the administrative center is located at Fongafale, on the island of Funafuti.

Official Language: English (Tuvaluan is widely spoken).

Monetary Unit: Australian Dollar (market rate March 1, 1988, 1.39 dollars = $1US). A Tuvaluan coinage (at par with the Australian) was introduced in 1977 but is circulated largely for numismatic purposes.

Sovereign: Queen ELIZABETH II.

Governor General: Sir Tupua LEUPENA, sworn in March 1, 1986, to succeed Sir Fiatau Penitala TEO.

Prime Minister: Dr. Tomasi PUAPUA; elected by Parliament on September 17, 1981, to succeed Toalipi LAUTI; reelected following legislative balloting of September 12, 1985.

THE COUNTRY

Formerly known as the Ellice Islands in the Gilbert group, Tuvalu consists of nine atolls stretching over an area of 500,000 square miles north of Fiji in the western Pacific. Only eight of the islands are considered inhabited for electoral purposes; activity on the ninth is confined to a copra plantation. With a total land area of 10 square miles, Tuvalu is one of the world's smallest countries, although its population density is the highest among South Pacific island nations. Its inhabitants are predominantly Polynesian and Protestant Christian. The soil is poor, and agricultural activity is confined largely to the coco palm and its derivatives, yielding a dependency on imported food. Women constitute 30 percent of the paid labor force, concentrated almost entirely in the service sector; female participation in politics and government is minimal.

Most of the islands' revenue has traditionally been derived from the sale of stamps and coins and from remittances by Tuvaluans working abroad, primarily as merchant seamen or as phosphate miners on Nauru and Kiribati's Banaba Island. In 1987 these resources were augmented by an agreement with Australia, New Zealand, and the United Kingdom for the establishment of a $19 million trust fund that is expected to cover more than one-third of the country's annual budget. Current economic plans include the development of handicraft industries and the exploitation of marine resources.

GOVERNMENT AND POLITICS

Political background. Proclaimed a protectorate with the Gilbert Islands (now independent Kiribati) in 1892 and formally annexed by Britain in 1915–1916, when the Gilbert and Ellice Islands Colony was established, the Ellice Islands were separated on October 1, 1975, and renamed Tuvalu. Independence on October 1, 1978, occurred only five months after the acquisition of full internal self-government, former chief minister Taolipi LAUTI becoming prime minister and Sir Fiatau Penitala TEO being designated Crown representative. On September 17, 1981, nine days after the country's first general election since independence, Lauti, on a 5–7 parliamentary vote, was obliged to yield office to Dr. Tomasi PUAPUA. Lauti's defeat was blamed largely on his controversial decision in 1979 to invest most of the government's capital with a California business which promised assistance in obtaining a $5 million development loan; the money, plus interest, was reported to have been returned by mid-1984.

Dr. Puapua remained in office as head of a largely unchanged administration following the most recent election of September 12, 1985.

Constitution and government. The 1978 constitution (a substantially revised version of a preindependence document adopted three years earlier) provides for a governor general of Tuvaluan citizenship who serves a four-year term and a prime minister who is elected by a unicameral Parliament of 12 members (2 members each from the more populous islands of Funafuti, Nanumea, Niutao, and Vaitupu, and 1 each from Nanumanga, Nui, Nukufetau, and Nukulaelae). Should the office of prime minister become vacant with Parliament unable to agree on a successor, the governor general may, at his discretion, name a chief executive or call for legislative dissolution. The government is collectively responsible to Parliament, whose normal term is four years. The judiciary consists of a High Court, which is empowered to hear appeals from courts of criminal and civil jurisdiction on each of the eight inhabited islands as well as from local magistrates' courts. Appeals from the High Court may be taken to the Court of Appeal in Fiji and, in last resort, to the Judicial Committee of the Privy Council at London. Island councils (most of whose members are reportedly wary of centralized government) continue to be dominant in local administration.

In accordance with the results of a 1986 public poll that rejected republican status, the government announced that the link with the Crown would be retained, although constitutional changes would be introduced that would limit the governor general to a largely ceremonial role. In August 1987 Parliament rescinded a constitutional requirement that the governor general retire at age 65, thus permitting the incumbent, Sir Tupua LEUPENA, to complete his full term.

Foreign relations. Upon independence Tuvalu elected to join Nauru as a "special member" of the Commonwealth, having the right to participate in all Commonwealth affairs except heads of government meetings. Not a member of the United Nations, it is affiliated at the regional level with the South Pacific Commission and the South Pacific Forum. Most of its contacts with other states are through representatives accredited to Fiji or New Zealand, although in 1984 formal relations, backdated to 1979, were established with Kiribati (the former Gilbert Islands, with which Tuvalu—then the Ellice Islands—had been joined under British colonial rule).

In early 1979 Tuvalu and the United States signed a treaty of friendship (ratified in June 1983) that included provision for consultation in the areas of defense and marine resources, with Washington acknowledging Tuvalu's sovereignty over four islands (Funafuti, Nukufetau, Nukulaelae, and Niulakita) originally claimed by the US Congress in the so-called Guano Act of 1856.

While sharing the antinuclear sentiments of most of its immediate neighbors (see Current issues, below), Tuvalu has exhibited a largely pro-Western posture, rejecting, in 1985, a bid from the Soviet Union for fishing rights in a 200-mile exclusive economic zone that had been declared in 1983.

Current issues. In February 1986, Tuvalu refused to sanction a "goodwill visit" by a French warship as a means of protesting continued nuclear testing in French Polynesia. Earlier, in August 1985, it had become one of the signatories of the South Pacific Forum's Treaty of Rarotonga, which declared the South Pacific a nuclear-free zone.

Domestically, the government continues to promote a family-planning program that had been introduced in March 1985 in response to concern that a rapidly growing population might overwhelm the country's limited economic capacity.

POLITICAL PARTIES

There are at present no political parties in Tuvalu.

LEGISLATURE

Known prior to independence as the House of Assembly, the unicameral **Parliament** consists of 12 members: 2 each from the four islands with population in excess of 1,000 and 1 each from the remaining inhabited islands. The legislative term, subject to dissolution, is four years. The most recent election was held on September 12, 1985, with 9 of 12 incumbent members being reelected.

Speaker: Vasa Vave FOUNUKU.

CABINET

Prime Minister	Dr. Tomasi Puapua
Ministers	
Commerce and Natural Resources	Lale Seluka
Finance	(Vacant)
Foreign Affairs	Dr. Tomasi Puapua
Local Government	Dr. Tomasi Puapua
Social Services	Solomona Tealofi
Works and Communications	Lale Seluka
Attorney General	John B. Aitkenson

NEWS MEDIA

Press. The only source of printed news is *Tuvalu Echoes/Sikuleo o Tuvalu* (200), published fortnightly in English and Tuvaluan by the government's Broadcasting and Information Division.

Radio and television. Radio Tuvalu broadcasts for about six hours daily from Funafuti to approximately 2,000 receivers. There is no television service.

INTERGOVERNMENTAL REPRESENTATION

As of July 1, 1988, Tuvalu had not applied for admission to the United Nations.

Ambassador to the US: Ionatana IONATANA (resident in Tuvalu).

US Ambassador to Tuvalu: Leonard ROCHWARGER (resident in Fiji).

IGO Memberships (Non-UN): *CWTH,* EEC(L), *EIB,* SPC, SPEC, SPF.

UGANDA

Republic of Uganda

Political Status: Independent member of the Commonwealth since October 9, 1962; republican constitution adopted September 8, 1967; personal military rule (instituted January 25, 1971) overthrown with establishment of provisional government on April 11, 1979; present military regime installed on January 29, 1986.

Area: 91,133 sq. mi. (236,036 sq. km.).

Population: 12,630,076 (1980C), 16,000,000 (1988E).

Major Urban Center (1980C): KAMPALA (458,400).

Official Language: English (Swahili and Luganda are widely used).

Monetary Unit: Uganda Shilling (market rate March 1, 1988, 59.10 shillings = $1US). On May 18, 1987, a new shilling was introduced worth 100 of the old.

President: Yoweri Kaguta MUSEVENI; sworn in January 29, 1986, following the overthrow of Lt. Gen. Tito OKELLO Lutwa on January 27.

Prime Minister: Dr. Samson (Sam) KISEKKA; appointed by the President on January 30, 1986, succeeding Abraham WALIGO.

THE COUNTRY

Landlocked Uganda, located in East Central Africa, is bounded on the east by Kenya, on the south by Tanzania and Rwanda, on the west by Zaire, and on the north by Sudan. The country is known for its lakes (among them Lake Victoria, the source of the White Nile) and its mountains, the most celebrated of which are the Mountains of the Moon (the Ruwenzori), lying on the border with Zaire. The population embraces a number of African tribal groups, including the Baganda, Iteso, Banyankore, and Basoga. For many decades a substantial Asian (primarily Indian) minority engaged in shopkeeping, industry, and the professions. In 1972, however, the government decreed the expulsion of all noncitizen Asians as part of a plan to put Uganda's economy in the hands of nationals, and at present only a scattering of Asians are still resident in the country. Approximately 50 percent of the population is Christian and another 15 percent is Muslim, the remainder adhering to traditional African beliefs. Women are primarily responsible for subsistence agriculture, most male rural labor being directed toward cash crops; women also dominate trade in rural areas, although not in the cities.

Agriculture, forestry, and fishing contribute about three-fourths of Uganda's gross domestic product, while industry, still in its infancy, accounts for less than 10 percent. Coffee, which has provided over 90 percent of exports by value since 1977, is the principal crop, followed by cotton, tea, peanuts, and tobacco.

Since the late 1960s Uganda has experienced a cycle of violence arising from tribal warfare, strongman governments, rebel activity, and coups that has left more than 800,000 dead, many of them reportedly victims of military atrocities. The resultant drop in agricultural and industrial output joined with heavy capital flight to produce severe economic distress. The present regime has attempted to kindle recovery through enhanced exploitation of resources and renegotiation of the external debt in light of improved internal security (see Current issues, below).

GOVERNMENT AND POLITICS

Political background. Uganda became a British protectorate in 1894–1896 and began its progress toward statehood after World War II, achieving internal self-government on March 1, 1962, and full independence within the Commonwealth on October 9, 1962. A problem involving Buganda and three other traditional kingdoms was temporarily resolved by granting the kingdoms semi-autonomous rule within a federal system. The arrangement enabled Buganda's representatives to participate in the national government, and the king (*kabaka*) of Buganda, Sir Edward Frederick MUTESA II, was elected president of Uganda on October 9, 1963. The issue of national unity versus Bugandan particularism led Prime Minister Apollo Milton OBOTE, leader of the Uganda People's Congress (UPC) and an advocate of centralism, to depose the president and vice president in February 1966. A constitution eliminating Buganda's autonomous status was ratified in April 1966 by the National Assembly, which consisted mainly of UPC members. Failing in an effort to mobilize effective resistance to the new government, the *kabaka* fled the country in May, and a new republican constitution, adopted in September 1967, eliminated the special status of Buganda and the other kingdoms. Earlier, on April 15, 1966, Obote had been designated president by the National Assembly for a five-year term. In December 1969, he banned all opposition parties and established a one-party state with a socialist program known as the Common Man's Charter.

On January 25, 1971, (then) Maj. Gen. 'Idi AMIN Dada, commander in chief of the army and air force, mounted a successful coup that deposed Obote while he was abroad at a Commonwealth heads of government meeting. In addition to continuing the ban on opposition political activity, Amin suspended parts of the constitution, dissolved the National Assembly, and secured his own installation as president of the Republic.

Following an invasion by Tanzanian troops and exile forces organized as the Uganda National Liberation Army (UNLA), the Amin regime, which had drawn worldwide condemnation for atrocities against perceived opponents, was effectively overthrown with the fall of Kampala on April 10–11, 1979, the former president fleeing to Libya. Concurrently, the National Consultative Council (NCC) of the Uganda National Liberation Front (UNLF) designated Professor Yusuf K. LULE, former vice chancellor of Makerere University, as president of the Republic and head of a provisional government. On June 20 the NCC announced that Godfrey Lukongwa BINAISA, a former attorney general under President Obote, had been named to succeed Lule in both capacities.

After a series of disagreements with both the NCC and the UNLF's Military Commission, including an attempted dismissal of UNLA's chief of staff, Binaisa was relieved of his authority on May 12, 1980, and placed under house arrest. On May 18 the chairman of the Military Commission, Paulo MUWANGA, announced that a three-member Presidential Commission had been established to exercise executive power through a cabinet of ministers on advice of its military counterpart, pending a national election later in the year.

Former president Obote returned from Tanzania on May 27, and in mid-June agreement was reached between party and UNLF representatives on four groups that would be permitted to participate in the presidential/legislative campaign. At balloting on December 10–11, the UPC won a majority of seats in the National Assembly, thus assuring Obote's reinvestiture as chief executive. During the next five years, while UNLA achieved some success in quelling armed resistance to the Obote regime, Yoweri MUSEVENI's National Resistance Army continued to hold the agriculturally important "Luwero triangle" north of Kampala, as well as its traditional strongholds in the Banyankore-dominated southwest. During the same period, many army actions against civilians were reported, including the harassment, wounding, or killing of opposition Democratic Party members; by mid-1985, over 200,000 were estimated to have died, either from army "excesses" or official counterinsurgency efforts.

On July 27, 1985, in a self-proclaimed attempt to "stop the killing", Brig. Basilio Olara OKELLO led a senior officers' coup against Obote who had lost much international support and was again forced into exile. Two days later, the constitution was suspended and Obote's army chief of staff, Lt. Gen. Tito OKELLO, was sworn in as chairman of a ruling Military Council. On August 6, General Okello called for all guerrilla groups, including former Amin soldiers, to join his army, while naming Obote's vice president, Paulo MUWANGA, as prime minister and Democratic Party leader Paul SSEMOGERERE as minister of the interior. Unlike most other resistance leaders, Museveni did not accede to Okello's call for "unity", citing continued abuses by army personnel who routinely failed to defer to Okello. In contrast, Museveni's NRA had a reputation of being well-disciplined, relatively free of tribal rivalries, and far less brutal toward civilians.

By September, when the first of a series of Kenyan- and Tanzanian-mediated peace talks began at Dar es Salaam, NRA forces had taken control of a number of strategic towns and supply routes, while Muwanga had been replaced by another Obote associate, Abraham WALIGO, as prime minister. In November, Museveni announced that "in order to provide services pending an agreement with the regime at Kampala", an "interim administration" was being established in rebel-held areas.

A peace pact signed at Nairobi on December 17 gave Museveni the vice-chairmanship of the Military Council, while providing for the dissolution of all existing armed units and the recruitment, under external supervision, of a new, fully representative force. However, the accord did not take effect: after failing to attend "celebrations" scheduled for January 4, Museveni, citing continuing human rights abuses, launched a drive on Kampala, which culminated in the overthrow of the six-month-old Okello regime on January 27, 1986. Two days later, while NRA forces consolidated their control, Museveni was sworn in as president, thereafter appointing a cabinet which included as prime minister Dr. Samson KISEKKA, formerly the NRA's external spokesman.

Although the new government contained members of a number of political groups, Museveni disappointed some supporters by concentrating power among his longtime southern aides. Meanwhile, UNLA units that had not disbanded fled to the north and east, where they and other rebel groups fought the NRA with dwindling effectiveness through 1987 (see Current issues, below).

In mid-1986 Museveni absolved his immediate predecessor, General Okello, of atrocities committed by troops under his command. No such tender was made to former presidents Amin and Obote, however, Museveni calling for their repatriation to face charges by a special commission of inquiry established to review the "slaughter" by their Nilotic followers of Bantu southerners.

Constitution and government. The 1962 constitution was suspended by Prime Minister Obote in February 1966. A successor instrument adopted in April 1966 terminated the federal system but was itself replaced in September 1967 by a republican constitution that established a president as head of state, chief executive, and commander in chief of the armed forces.

While he did not formally revoke the 1967 constitution when he came to power, President Amin in February 1971 ordered suspension of the legal system and assumed judicial as well as executive and legislative powers. Subsequently, though martial law was never declared, military tribunals tried both civil and criminal cases and authorized numerous public executions. With but minor modification, the 1967 constitution was reinstated by the UNLF as the basis of postmilitary government in 1980; in mid-1985, it was suspended by the Military Council and has since remained inoperative.

On February 1, 1986, while in the process of organizing an interim government dominated by, but not confined exclusively to, members of his National Resistance Movement (NRM), President Museveni announced the appointment of a National Resistance Council (NRC) to serve in a quasi-legislative capacity pending a national election in "three to five years".

Local government has assumed a variety of forms since 1971, the Amin and Lule governments both having reorganized the provincial and district systems. In May 1986, a further reorganization was announced by the Museveni administration, the traditional district commissioners thenceforth to be known as district secretaries reporting to centrally appointed special district administrators, rather than directly to Kampala. The special administrators, in turn, were charged with presiding over the formation of local NRM councils.

Foreign relations. Uganda has long based its foreign policy on a posture of nonalignment and anticolonialism. However, after being criticized by the Amin regime for its policies in Vietnam, Cambodia, and the Middle East, the United States terminated its economic assistance program in mid-1973 and subsequently closed its embassy because of public threats against officials and other Americans residing in the country. Three years later, in an event of major international impact, Israeli commandos raided Entebbe airport during the night of July 3–4, 1976, to secure the release of passengers of an Air France airliner that had been hijacked over Greece by Palestinian Arab guerrillas and flown to Uganda via Libya. While Amin denied allegations that he had cooperated with the hijackers, he protested Israel's action and accused Kenya of aiding in its implementation.

Tensions with both Kenya and Tanzania resulted not only in the collapse of the tripartite East African Community (once hailed as a model of regional cooperation) in June 1977 but, ultimately, in the Tanzanian military intervention of early 1979. The latter action came in the wake of an ill-conceived incursion into northern Tanzania in October 1978 by Ugandan troops, with effective Tanzanian withdrawal from Uganda not occurring until mid-1981 due to the retraining requirements of the post-Amin Ugandan army. The two neighbors were critically involved in discussions between the short-lived Okello regime and the NRA, Kenyan President Moi being credited with negotiating the December peace agreement between Okello and Museveni. Following Museveni's takeover in January 1986, both governments were quick to recognize the new regime, as was the United States, which was reported to have offered $12 million in development aid "as soon as internal security is assured". Relations with Kenya deteriorated in 1987, however, with a series of border incidents and mutual accusations over the harboring of political dissidents. Nairobi also expressed displeasure at Ugandan links with Libya, particularly as manifested in an April trade accord.

At midyear, Kampala concluded a security agreement with Sudan, despite charges that Khartoum was aiding anti-Museveni rebel forces. The new administration also accused former president Obote of training soldiers in Zambia, intimating that Lusaka was turning a blind eye to the activity.

Current issues. Despite continued military and economic challenges, the Museveni regime has generally been credited with having restored a measure of stability to Uganda. To the surprise of observers who had predicted more effective resistance, the NRA in 1986 and 1987 routinely routed UNLA and other rebel forces in the north and east. Although Museveni's mid-1987 announcement that the war was "over" may have been premature given ongoing tribal enmity, the fighting appeared to have diminished. Both internal and external observers applauded Museveni's apparent control of the army, which, with some exceptions, avoided terrorist acts against civilians. However, some critics accused the administration of human rights abuses, particularly in regard to the treatment of prisoners, and questioned its commitment to liberalization in light of uncertain relations with potential opposition groups.

As the military situation improved, the administration moved to rebuild the economy, where substantial improvement seemed possible. Shortly after assuming control, the NRM leaders had instituted a number of inappropriate policies, including heavy subsidies for gas, sugar, and other commodities and upward revaluation of the currency. During 1987, price controls and subsidies were eliminated and devaluation was ordered, the reversal winning substantial aid from the World Bank and the International Monetary Fund.

POLITICAL PARTIES AND GROUPS

Uganda was ruled by Milton Obote's Uganda People's Congress (UPC) from the country's independence until 1971 and again after the first post-Amin election in December 1980; the latter balloting was also contested by the Democratic Party, led by Paul Ssemogerere, which won 51 of 126 legislative seats, Yoweri Museveni's Uganda Patriotic Movement, which won 1, and the Conservative Party, led by Joshua Mayanja-Nkangi. In early 1981, Museveni dissolved his party to take up armed revolt against Obote, very little effective civilian opposition to the regime remaining, since the DP had been weakened by sizable defections to the UPC on the one hand and sporadic government harassment, killing and/or detention of its leadership on the other.

Although General Okello's Military Council released a number of political detainees and appointed Ssemogerere to its cabinet, most DP leaders supported Museveni's NRA in the civil war which followed the takeover. Other armed resistance groups, which had cooperated informally with Museveni prior to the coup, joined Okello, including Brig. Moses Ali's Uganda National Rescue Front and Andrew Kayira's Uganda Freedom Movement. Following the NRA's takeover at Kampala, components of these forces fled with former UNLA members into the largely uncontrolled north, although most of their leaders entered the Museveni government.

Upon his installation as president, Museveni announced plans for "the restoration of democracy", including new elections under a restructured constitution; meanwhile, political activity is to be suspended, though political parties, as such, are not proscribed and several maintain offices and small staffs.

Political Groups:

National Resistance Movement (NRM). The NRM was formed prior to the 1985 ouster of President Obote, its military wing, the National Resistance Army (NRA), winning government control in January 1986. NRM leader Yoweri Museveni declared upon his assumption of the presidency of the republic that the NRM was a "clear-headed movement" dedicated to the restoration of democracy in Uganda.

Leaders: Yoweri MUSEVENI (President of the Republic), Dr. Samson KISEKKA (Prime Minister), Moses KIKONGO (Chairman, National Resistance Council).

Uganda People's Congress (UPC). Formed in 1960 and the ruling party under former president Obote, the UPC was accorded token representation in the Museveni government. However, its internal leader, Paulo Muwanga, faced murder and kidnapping charges in 1987 as the result of events that occurred while he was Obote's vice-president. Although charges that Muwanga was involved in an alleged coup plot in October 1986 were eventually dropped, the government continued to accuse Obote and some exiled UPC members of plotting an overthrow through 1987.

Leaders: Dr. Apollo Milton OBOTE (in exile), Paulo MUWANGA, Anthony BUTELE.

Democratic Party (DP). An advocate of centralization and a mixed economy, the DP, drawing on a solid Roman Catholic base, enjoys strong support in southern Uganda. Banned in 1969, it ran second to the UPC in the post-Amin balloting of December 1980 and participated in the Okello government following Obote's ouster in 1985. Several members of the DP executive committee were included in President Museveni's first cabinet, although DP-NRM relations had deteriorated by 1987.

Leaders: Paul Kawanga SSEMOGERERE (President), Robert KITARIKO (Secretary General).

Nationalist Liberal Party (NLP). The NLP was organized in 1984 by a dissident faction of the DP.

Leader: Tiberio OKENY.

Conservative Party (CP). The CP is a small formation whose leader, prime minister of Buganda in 1964–1966, participated in the Okello government as minister of labor and was awarded the education portfolio by Museveni.

Leader: Joshua MAYANJA-NKANGI.

Uganda Freedom Movement (UFM). The UFM's former secretary general, Andrew Kayiira, participated in the Okello regime as a member of its Military Council, subsequently entering the Museveni government as minister of energy. Its chairman, a leading opponent of former president Obote, was released from prison following the July 1985 coup. In October 1986 Kayiira was among those arrested in an alleged coup plot although the charges were dropped in February 1987. Shortly after his release, Kayiira was killed in what the government said was an armed robbery. UFM officials intimated possible government involvement in the killing and withdrew their support of the administration. Earlier, some members of the UFM's former military wing, the **Uganda Freedom Army** (UFA), had been assimilated into the NRA.

Leader: Balaki K. KIRYA (Chairman).

Federal Democratic Movement of Uganda (Fedemu). Fedemu held two seats on General Okello's Military Council, its leader, David Lwanga, subsequently entering the Museveni government as minister of environmental protection. Along with members of other political groups, Lwanga was arrested in October 1986 for participating in a coup plot. Although charges against Lwanga were eventually dropped, the government charged Fedemu with further agitation, amid reports of its possible linkage with the UPDM (below).

Leader: David Livingstone LWANGA (Chairman).

Uganda National Rescue Front (UNRF). The UNRF's leader, Brig. Moses Ali, formerly served as finance minister in the Amin government and subsequently joined the Museveni cabinet as minister of tourism and wildlife, although UNRF forces, originating primarily from Amin's homeland west of the Nile River, had joined Okello troops in fighting the NRA.

Leader: Brig. Moses ALI.

Uganda People's Democratic Movement (UPDM). Formed in May 1986 by disparate anti-Museveni forces including retreating UNLA troops and former Amin supporters allegedly operating out of southern Sudan, the UPDM subsequently conducted military activity in the north and east of Uganda through the loosely-organized **United People's Democratic Army** (UPDA). UPDM leaders announced they were seeking "the restoration of democracy" and not the return of any leader. By mid-1987 the UPDA, highly factionalized from its inception, was reportedly disintegrating as the result of heavy losses inflicted by the NRA. It was unclear if a direct UPDA link existed with still-operating groups such as the **Uganda People's Army** (UPA) or the so-called **Holy Spirit Movement** led by "voodoo priestess" Alice LAKWEMA who reportedly promised recruits magical protection from bullets.

Leader: John OKELLO.

LEGISLATURE

The former National Assembly was dissolved following the July 1985 coup. On February 1, 1986, an appointed **National Resistance Council** of 23 members was sworn in to serve as an interim legislature. In September, President Museveni announced that all government ministers, including deputy and assistant ministers, would thenceforth sit as ex officio members of the Council, while earlier reports had indicated that its size might be increased to about 100, with the addition of representatives from NRM local bodies.

Chairman: Moses KIKONGO.

CABINET

Prime Minister	Dr. Samson Kisekka
First Deputy Prime Minister	Eriya Kategaya
Second Deputy Prime Minister	Paul Kawanga Ssemogerere
Third Deputy Prime Minister	Abubakar Mayanja

Ministers

Agriculture	Victoria Ssekitoleko
Animal Industry and Fisheries	George Mondo Kagonyera
Commerce	George Kanyeihamba
Constitutional Affairs	Dr. Sam Njuba
Cooperatives and Marketing	John Ssebana Kizito
Defense	Yoweri Museveni
Education	Joshua Mayanja-Nkangi
Energy	Jaberi Bidandi Ssali
Environmental Protection	Joseph Okune
Finance	Chrispus Kiyonga
Foreign Affairs	Paul Kawanga Ssemogerere
Health	Adoko Nekyon
Housing and Urban Development	James Wapakabulo
Industry and Technology	Stanley Elly Tumwine
Information and Broadcasting	Ali Kirunda Kivejinja
Internal Affairs	Paul Kawanga Ssemogerere
Justice	Joseph Mulenga
Labor	Stanislas Okurut
Lands and Surveys	Ben Okello Luwum
Local Government	Amanya Mushega
Planning and Economic Development	Yoweri Kyesimira
Public Service and Cabinet Affairs	Tom Rubale
Regional Cooperation	Paul Etiang
Relief and Social Rehabilitation	Chango Machyo
Tourism and Wildlife	Brig. Moses Ali
Transportation and Communications	Dr. Ruhakana Rugunda
Water and Mineral Development	Robert Kitariko
Works	Daniel Serwango Kigozi
Youth, Culture and Sports	Edward Kakonge
Without Portfolio	David Kibirango

Ministers of State

Defense	Daniel Omara-Atubo
Education	John Ntimba
Foreign Affairs	Tarsis Kabwegyere
Health	Dr. Ronald Bata
Internal Affairs	N. Katinda Otafiire
Office of the President (Karamoja)	Anthony Butele
Office of the President (Security)	Balaki Kirya
Office of the President (Special Duties)	Ateker Ejalu
Office of the President (Women's Development)	Joyce Mpanga
Office of the President and National Political Commissar	Dr. Kiiza Besigye
Attorney General	Joseph Mulenga
Governor, Bank of Uganda	Suleiman Kiggundu

NEWS MEDIA

Press. The press under the Amin regime was subject to very strict censorship and underwent an extremely high rate of attrition. Substantial relaxation occurred after the installation of President Binaisa in June 1979. In March 1981 the Obote government banned a number of papers that had been critical of the UPC and subsequently took additional measures against both foreign and domestic journalists who had commented unfavorably on the security situation within Uganda. Although the press now enjoys relative freedom, President Museveni threatened action in late 1986 against newspapers which "denigrate" the military. The following are currently published at Kampala: *New Vision,* NRM daily, in English (launched in March 1986 as successor to the *Uganda Times,* which had ceased publication in early 1985); *The Star,* in English; *Taifa Empya,* in Luganda; *Munnansi News Bulletin,* DP weekly in English.

News agencies. The domestic facility is the Uganda News Agency (UNA); *Novosti,* TASS, Reuters, and AP maintain bureaus at Kampala.

Radio and television. The Ministry of Information and Broadcasting controls the Uganda Broadcasting Corporation, which provides radio programs over two networks, and the Uganda Television Service, which initiated color transmissions in 1975. There were approximately 600,000 radio and 90,000 television receivers in 1987.

INTERGOVERNMENTAL REPRESENTATION

Ambassador to the US: Princess Elizabeth BAGAAYA Nyabongo.

US Ambassador to Uganda: Robert G. HOUDEK.

Permanent Representative to the UN: Wanume KIBEDI.

IGO Memberships (Non-UN): ADF, AfDB, BADEA, CCC, CWTH, EADB, EEC(L), *EIB,* IACO, IC, ICAC, ICO, IDB, IIC, Intelsat, Interpol, ISO, ITPA, NAM, OAU, PCA.

UNION OF SOVIET SOCIALIST REPUBLICS

Soyuz Sovyetskikh Sotsialisticheskikh Respublik

Short Name: **Soviet Union** (*Sovyetskii Soyuz*)

Political Status: Russian Soviet Federated Socialist Republic established July 10, 1918; federal union of 4 (subsequently 15) Soviet Socialist Republics established December 30, 1922; present constitution adopted October 7, 1977.

Area: 8,649,489 sq. mi. (22,402,200 sq. km.).

Population: 262,436,227 (1979C), 285,351,000 (1988E).

Major Urban Centers (1986E): MOSCOW (urban area, 8,739,000); Leningrad (urban area, 4,902,000); Kiev (2,486,000); Tashkent (2,076,000); Baku (1,726,000); Kharkov (1,572,000); Minsk (1,503,000); Gorky (1,406,000); Novosibirsk (1,400,000); Sverdlovsk (1,312,000); Kuibyshev (1,263,000); Odessa (1,139,000).

Official Language: Russian.

Monetary Unit: Ruble (noncommercial rate March 1, 1988, 1 ruble = $1.67US).

Chairman of the Presidium of the Supreme Soviet: Andrei Andreyevich GROMYKO, elected by the Supreme Soviet on July 2, 1985, the office having remained vacant since the death of Konstantin Ustinovich CHERNENKO on March 10.

First Deputy Chairman of the Presidium: Pyotr Nilovich DEMICHEV; designated by the Supreme Soviet on June 18, 1986, succeeding Vasily Vasilyevich KUZNETSOV.

Chairman of the Council of Ministers: Nikolai Ivanovich RYZHKOV; appointed September 27, 1985, upon the resignation of Nikolai Aleksandrovich TIKHONOV.

General Secretary of the Communist Party of the Soviet Union: Mikhail Sergeyevich GORBACHEV; appointed by the Central Committee of the CPSU on March 11, 1985, succeeding Konstantin Ustinovich CHERNENKO.

THE COUNTRY

Largest in area of the countries of the world, surpassed in population only by China and India, and exceeded only by the United States in industrial production, the Soviet Union stretches across half of Europe and all of Asia, from the Baltic and the Danube to the Bering Sea and the Pacific. The European portion, west of the Ural Mountains, is the older and more developed part of the country, and includes, in addition to the historical Russian territories, the separate Soviet Republics of the Ukraine and Byelorussia (White Russia); the three Baltic Republics of Estonia, Latvia, and Lithuania (all annexed in 1940); the Moldavian Republic in the southwest; and Armenia, Azerbaidzhan, and Georgia, which were components of the former Transcaucasian SFSR until each became a separate Republic in 1936. The much larger Asiatic part of the country was not opened up until the eighteenth and nineteenth centuries and has experienced large-scale industrial development only since World War II. The bulk of the eastern territory, Siberia and the Far East, is politically linked with European Russia as part of the Russian Soviet Federated Socialist Republic (RSFSR); the Central Asian sections, inhabited largely by non-Russian peoples, are organized as separate Kazakh, Kirghiz, Tadzhik, Turkmen, and Uzbek Soviet Republics.

Russians and other Eastern Slavs predominate among the more than 170 ethnic groups living within Soviet borders. At the time of the 1979 census, Russians numbered some 137 million and accounted for 51.9 percent of the total population, while 60 million Ukrainians and Byelorussians accounted for 22.5 percent. Other numerically significant groups included Uzbeks, Tatars, Kazakhs, Azerbaidzhanians, Armenians, Georgians, Lithuanians, and Jews. This composite ethnic structure has caused a degree of tension and instability, since the limited cultural and linguistic autonomy accorded to minority groups tends to run counter to the ideological and political uniformity ultimately expected of the population as a whole. Traditional religious attachments persist despite officially sponsored antireligious propaganda and practical restrictions on the functioning of religious bodies, while widespread resistance has met efforts to increase the use of Russian among non-Russian peoples.

Overall, 90 percent of adult women work full-time outside the home, with significantly less female participation in the Asian republics. Most work in manufacturing, clerical, and agricultural sectors; while some professions, such as medicine, are dominated by women, most managerial posts are held by men. Approximately one-third of the Supreme Soviet and Communist Party membership is female, but Alexandra Biryukova, named to the CPSU Secretariat in March 1986, is the first woman to occupy such a high-level post in more than two decades.

Still predominantly agricultural at the time of the 1917 Revolution, the Soviet Union reached its present position as the world's second-ranking industrial power through a policy of planned, forced industrialization, long sustained at the expense of agriculture and consumer needs. The annual average percentage rate of increase in industrial production has nonetheless receded steadily through all five-year plans completed since 1950 (13.1 in 1951–1955; 10.4 in 1956–1960; 8.6 in 1961–1965; 8.4 in 1966–1970; 6.5 in 1971–1975; 4.2 in 1976–1980; and 3.7 in 1981–1985).

Beginning in 1965, a series of management innovations was initiated in an effort to reverse the decline. Individual enterprises were given somewhat greater operational independence as well as control over the use of a specified share of profits. Central planning procedures were simplified, and profits and sales, rather than gross output, were made the primary criteria in evaluating performance; however, output assignments were retained for the most important products, as was the centralized system of supply.

The continued inability to reverse slackening growth in production was denounced by Secretary Gorbachev after his succession to leadership in 1985. Thus, as of January 1, 1988, some 60 percent of the country's enterprises were assigned powers of economic responsibility and self-financing. Under the new system, enterprises must cover all central-budget allocations, wages, costs of materials, and production development, with product output to be determined on the basis of contracts among enterprises themselves as suppliers and purchasers, as well as of contracts with government agencies.

Earlier, the declining industrial growth rate had been partly attributed to an increased emphasis on consumer-goods production, which led to lower overall investment levels. Production of such items as textiles, footwear, television sets, refrigerators, washing machines, and cars had been significantly increased, and the 1971–1975 plan for the first time provided for the output of consumer goods to increase proportionately faster than the production of capital goods. While no such provision was made in the 1976–1980 plan, it was repeated in those for both 1981–1985 and 1986–1991, despite periodic complaints of low-quality output.

Deficiencies in agricultural output have plagued the Soviet Union since the late 1920s and early 1930s, when forced collectivization herded small-scale peasant households into state and collective farms. Severe setbacks in grain production during the early 1960s forced the Soviets to purchase large quantities of wheat from the West and prompted a variety of reforms intended to raise farm output. Beginning in 1965, procurement prices for obligatory deliveries to the state were raised and targets stabilized, plans for sharply higher investment in agriculture and fertilizer production were announced, and collective farmers were granted assured monthly wages and old-age pensions. Previously, the burdensome restrictions on private plots and private livestock had been lifted. Although the small household plots left for the peasants' private use account for only 3 percent of the total sown area, they provide a disproportionately large share of gross agricultural production and are an important source of food for the urban population. The most recent innovation in regard to agricultural output has been the introduction of a contract between a family team and a farm administration in order to permit the private working of tracts larger than household plots.

Record total agricultural production in 1966 and 1968 was followed by a series of crop failures, again necessitating unusually large food and feed grain imports and causing a severe drain in the Soviet balance of payments. The 1975 grain harvest of 140 million tons was 75 million less than planned and represented the poorest performance by Soviet agriculture in a decade. While the 1976 harvest rebounded to a record 224 million tons and that of 1978 to 237 million (after a disappointing 196 million in 1977), the 1979 yield of 179 million tons represented another major reversal, with no immediate improvement thereafter: 189 million tons in 1980, 158 in 1981, 187 in 1982, 192 in 1983, 172 in 1984, 191 in 1985, 210 in 1986, and 211 in 1987.

Efforts to increase foreign trade, especially as a means of promoting technological transfer, continue to show indifferent results. In 1987 the physical volume of imports and exports rose 1.0 percent, but the monetary value (128 billion rubles) dropped 2.2 percent, largely because of lower world prices and reduced Western exports to the Soviet Union; during the year, 62 percent of Soviet foreign trade was with other members of the Council for Mutual Economic Assistance (CMEA). On the other hand, individual Soviet concerns, permitted for the first time to enter the world market, accounted for 12 percent of exports and 28 percent of imports. A further effort toward decentralized trade resulted in the establishment of 23 joint Soviet-foreign enterprises and 14 other international undertakings within the Soviet Union.

Total trade with the United States amounted to $220 million in 1971 but rose sharply to $1,375 million in 1973, embracing imports (largely grain) of $1,190 million and exports of $185 million. Total US-Soviet trade for 1976 reached a record $2,530 million (an increase of 19.7 percent over 1975), with 59.2 percent of the US shipment total of $2,310 million consisting of grain. A new US-Soviet trade record for 1980 had been anticipated on the basis of Soviet orders for more than 21 million metric tons of corn and wheat (compared to shipments of 15.7 million in 1978–1979). However, the Carter administration drastically curtailed deliveries in response to the Soviet invasion of Afghanistan in December 1979, resulting in an actual trade exchange of $1,967 million for 1980, only 44 percent of the year before. Comparable figures for 1981–1983, reflecting the decision of the Reagan Administration to encourage agricultural trade with the Soviet Union, were $2,779 million, $2,815 million and $2,350 million. In 1984 the volume surged to more than $3,838 million, with lower levels of $2,832 million, $1,814 million, and $1,940 million in 1985–1987.

GOVERNMENT AND POLITICS

Political background. Russia's national history prior to the Revolution of 1917 was that of a series of small medieval fiefs which gradually united under the leadership of the grand dukes of Moscow, expanding into the vast but unstable empire that collapsed midway through World War I. Military defeat and rising social unrest resulting from that conflict led directly to the "February" Revolution of 1917, the abdication of Tsar NICHOLAS II (March 15, 1917, by the Western calendar), and the formation of a Provisional Government whose best-remembered leader was Aleksandr F. KERENSKY. Unable to cope with the country's mounting social, political, economic, and military problems, the Provisional Government was forcibly overthrown in the "October" Revolution of November 7, 1917, by the Bolshevik wing of the Russian Social Democratic Party under Vladimir Ilyich LENIN. The new Soviet regime, so called because it based its power on the support of newly formed workers', peasants', and soldiers' councils, or "soviets", proceeded under Lenin's guidance to proclaim a dictatorship of the proletariat; to nationalize land, means of production, banks, and railroads; and to establish on July 10, 1918, a socialist state known as the Russian Socialist Federated Soviet Republic (RSFSR). Peace with the Central Powers was concluded at Brest-Litovsk on March 3, 1918, but civil war and foreign intervention lasted until 1922. Other Soviet Republics which had meanwhile been established in the Ukraine, Byelorussia, and Transcaucasia joined with the RSFSR by treaty in 1922 to establish the Union of Soviet Socialist Republics (USSR), whose first constitution was adopted on July 6, 1923.

Lenin's death in 1924 was followed by struggles within the leadership of the ruling Communist Party before Joseph Vissarionovich STALIN emerged in the later 1920s as the unchallenged dictator of party and country. There followed an era characterized by extremes: forced industrialization that began with the first five-year plan in 1928; all-out collectivization in agriculture commencing in 1929–1930; far-reaching political and military purges in 1936–1938; the conclusion in August 1939, on the eve of World War II, of a ten-year nonaggression pact with Nazi Germany; the use of Soviet military power during 1939–1940 to expand the Soviet frontiers at the expense of Poland, Finland, Romania, and the Baltic Republics of Estonia, Latvia, and Lithuania; and an abrupt end of Nazi-Soviet collaboration when German forces attacked the USSR on June 22, 1941. The subsequent years of heavy fighting, which cost the USSR an estimated 20 million lives and left widespread devastation in European Russia, served to eliminate the military power of Germany and ultimately enabled the USSR to extend its influence into the heart of Europe and to exercise a relatively free hand in the political reconstruction of the areas adjoining its western borders.

Within the Soviet Union, the end of World War II brought a return to the harsh conditions and oppressive policies of the 1930s. Using increasingly rigorous police methods to enforce conformity at home, Stalin employed the apparatus of international communism to impose a similar uniformity on the Communist-ruled states of Eastern Europe — except for Yugoslavia, whose defiance of Soviet authority led to its exclusion from the Soviet bloc in 1948. The wartime alliance with the Western powers meanwhile gave place to a "cold war" whose leading events included the Berlin blockade of 1948–1949 and the Korean War of 1950–1953.

Stalin's death on March 5, 1953, initiated a new period of political maneuvering among his successors. The post of chairman of the Council of Ministers, held successively by Georgy M. MALENKOV (1953–1955) and Nikolai A. BULGANIN (1955–1958), was assumed in March 1958 by Nikita S. KHRUSHCHEV, who had become first secretary of the Soviet Communist Party (CPSU) in September 1953. Khrushchev's denunciation of Stalin's despotism at the 20th CPSU Congress in February 1956 gave impetus to a policy of "de-Stalinization" in the USSR and Eastern Europe that involved the release and rehabilitation of millions of political prisoners, a curbing of the secret police, greater freedom of expression, more benefits to the consumer, and more relaxed relations with the West. Emphasis in Soviet foreign policy shifted from military confrontation to peaceful "competitive coexistence", symbolized by a growing foreign-aid program and by such achievements as the launching of the world's first artificial earth satellite, "Sputnik", in 1957. Khrushchev's policies nevertheless yielded a series of sharp crises within and beyond the Communist world. An incipient liberalization movement in Hungary was crushed by Soviet armed forces in 1956, relations with Communist China deteriorated from year to year, and recurrent challenges to the West culminated in a severe defeat for Soviet aims in the Cuban missile confrontation with the United States in October 1962.

Khrushchev's erratic performance resulted in his dismissal on October 14–15, 1964, and the substitution of collective rule, under which Leonid I. BREZHNEV became head of the CPSU and Aleksei N. KOSYGIN became chairman of the Council of Ministers. The new leadership rescinded some of Khrushchev's internal reforms, such as the establishment of parallel party hierarchies in agriculture and industry, and the system of regional economic councils. In 1965 Nikolai V. PODGORNY succeeded Anastas I. MIKOYAN as chairman of the Presidium of the Supreme Soviet and thereby as nominal head of state, while Leonid Brezhnev clearly emerged from the 24th Party Congress in 1971 as first among equals. His position as CPSU general secretary was reconfirmed at the 25th and 26th Congresses in 1976 and 1981.

On June 16, 1977, the Supreme Soviet designated Secretary Brezhnev to succeed Podgorny as chairman of the Presidium, concurrent with his service as party leader. A month earlier, the CPSU Central Committee had endorsed the essentials of a new constitution, the final version of which was ratified by the Supreme Soviet on October 7.

In October 1980 Aleksei Kosygin asked to be relieved of his duties as chairman of the Council of Ministers because of declining health, and was replaced by First Deputy Chairman Nicolai TIKHONOV. Of more far-reaching consequence was the death of Brezhnev on November 10, 1982, and his replacement as party secretary two days later by Yuri V. ANDROPOV, who had stepped down as head of the KGB, the Soviet intelligence and internal security agency, on May 26. Andropov was named chairman of the Presidium on June 16, 1983, but died on February 9, 1984, and was succeeded as CPSU general secretary (on February 13) and as head of state (on April 11) by Konstantin U. CHERNENKO.

Long reputed to be in failing health and widely viewed as having been elevated to the top leadership on a "caretaker" basis, Chernenko succumbed on March 10, 1985. As evidence that the succession had already been agreed upon, the relatively young (54) Mikhail S. GORBACHEV was named general secretary on the following day, the Presidium chairmanship remaining temporarily vacant.

During the ensuing year, wide-ranging personnel changes were effected in both the government and the party. On

July 2 the USSR's longtime foreign minister, Andrei A. GROMYKO, was named to succeed Chernenko as Presidium chairman, while Nikolai I. RYZHKOV replaced the aging Tikhonov as chairman of the Council of Ministers on September 27. However, the most numerous changes occurred among top party and ministerial officials, nearly one-third of the former and one-half of the latter being removed (typically in favor of younger technocrats) by the conclusion of the 27th CPSU Congress in March 1986.

Constitution and government. The present Soviet constitution is the result of work initiated by a constitutional commission appointed by Premier Khrushchev in 1962 and chaired from 1964 by Secretary Brezhnev. A preliminary draft was issued in June 1977 and submitted to national discussion and proposed revision until late September. A somewhat edited final version was adopted at a special session of the Supreme Soviet on October 7.

The essential content of the 1977 basic law does not depart significantly from that of its predecessor, the so-called Stalin constitution of 1936. Both provide for a nominally democratic system based on universal adult suffrage and embellished by guarantees of civil and political rights. The extent, however, to which particulars are elaborated is new. A total of 69 articles, as contrasted with 27 in 1936, delineate a wide range of principles, rights, liberties, and obligations in the political, economic, and social spheres. Most of this material, now assigned prominence in the opening section of the constitution, serves to make explicit selected components of prevailing Communist ideology, particularly as set forth in the 1961 party program. Thus the CPSU is, for the first time, identified as "the leading and guiding force of Soviet society"; the USSR is hailed as a "developed socialist society" having as its objective "the building of a classless communist society"; the nation's economy is described as a single entity "embracing all elements of social production, distribution, and exchange"; and Soviet foreign policy is described as being directed "at ensuring favorable international conditions for the building of communism in the USSR" within a framework of "socialist internationalism" and participation in the "international socialist division of labor". At the same time, an effort is made to strike a prescriptive balance. Party organs are exhorted to "act within the framework of the Constitution"; the intelligentsia are included with workers and peasants in defining the social base of the country; land is to be made available for the construction of individual dwellings as well as for small household farming; and Soviet foreign policy is to be directed to international disarmament, the peaceful coexistence of states, and observance of the Helsinki Final Act of 1975.

The current constitution thus exhibits both restrictive and liberalizing language while offering no mandate for basic change in either political or social conditions under a system which from its earliest days has operated without realization of constitutional rights and procedures as understood in the West. In pursuit of his campaign for radical reform, however, Gorbachev has reinterpreted the basic contours of the Soviet system in favor of openness (*glasnost*), restructuring (*perestroika*), and democracy (extensive citizen participation). The result has been a general relaxing of censorship accompanied by remarkably frank criticism of party and governmental organizations and administrators; widespread freedom in the arts; the founding of thousands of independent political and other interest groups; the release of a significant number of political prisoners; curbs on psychiatric imprisonments; permission for leading dissidents to emigrate; and experiments in free elections for legislative seats, party offices, and production management posts.

Formally, the Soviet Union is a federal state based on a voluntary union of 15 Soviet Socialist Republics, each with its own constitution and government and full powers of self-administration in all fields not expressly reserved to the central government. The Union Republics, with their capitals and most recent area and population figures, are given below.

Republic and Capital	Area (sq. mi.)	Population (1987E)
Russian Soviet Federated Socialist Republic — RSFSR (Moscow)	6,592,800	145,300,000
Armenian SSR (Yerevan)	11,500	3,412,000
Azerbaidzhan SSR (Baku)	33,400	6,811,000
Byelorussian SSR (Minsk)	80,100	10,078,000
Estonian SSR (Tallinn)	17,400	1,556,000
Georgian SSR (Tbilisi)	27,000	5,266,000
Kazakh SSR (Alma-Ata)	1,049,100	16,244,000
Kirghiz SSR (Frunze)	76,600	4,143,000
Latvian SSR (Riga)	25,600	2,647,000
Lithuanian SSR (Vilnius)	25,200	3,641,000
Moldavian SSR (Kishinev)	13,000	4,185,000
Tadzhik SSR (Dushanbe)	55,300	4,807,000
Turkmen SSR (Ashkhabad)	188,500	3,361,000
Ukrainian SSR (Kiev)	233,100	51,200,000
Uzbek SSR (Tashkent)	172,800	19,026,000

Despite its federal form, the USSR in practice is a centralized state in which the Union government has exceptionally wide powers and can count on the unquestioning obedience of the governments of the Union Republics, each of which is controlled by the Communist Party in the same manner as the Union government itself.

Nominally, the highest organ of state power is the Supreme Soviet of the USSR, a bicameral legislative body whose two coequal houses, the Soviet of the Union and the Soviet of Nationalities, are elected by universal suffrage every five years. Although the legislative activity of the Supreme Soviet has traditionally been limited to approving the budget and other measures submitted to it by the government, in recent years its authority has been increased somewhat by enlarging the number of its standing committees; by empowering them to subpoena officials, initiate and examine legislative drafts, and examine the work of executive agencies; and by permitting the body to make substantive amendments of the annual budget and economic plan.

Exercising authority between the two annual sessions of the Supreme Soviet is a 39-member Presidium, including, as ex officio deputy chairmen, the 15 chairmen of the Supreme Soviets of the Union Republics. The remaining 24 members, including the chairman, first deputy chairmen, and secretary, are elected by the Supreme Soviet. The chairman of the Presidium also serves as head of state. In addition, the Supreme Soviet appoints the chairman and the other members of the Council of Ministers, which bears direct responsibility for the operation of the national economy as well as for normal administrative functions. The operating responsibilities of the so-called "all-Union" ministries are exercised directly throughout the Soviet Union; those of the so-called "Union Republic" ministries are usually exercised indirectly through the corresponding ministries of the Union Republics. (The 1936 constitution specified the content of each list, which necessitated repeated constitutional amendments to validate actions by the Council of Ministers; under the present constitution changes in the lists are enacted by ordinary legislation.)

The Soviet Union's four-tiered judicial system comprises (1) local people's courts, consisting of judges and assessors directly elected for periods of five and two and one-half years, respectively; (2) regional and territorial courts, whose judges are appointed by the corresponding Soviets for five-year periods; (3) the Supreme Courts of the Union Republics, similarly appointed by the Union Republic Soviets; and (4) the Supreme Court of the USSR, which is appointed by the Supreme Soviet of the USSR and serves as the chief court and supervising organ for all courts of the Union Republics. The procurator general of the USSR, appointed by the Supreme Soviet for a five-year term, is responsible for watching over the legality of the acts of all institutions of the Soviet Union and seeing that the law is correctly interpreted and uniformly applied.

Government in the Union Republics is closely patterned on that of the USSR itself. Each has its own Supreme Soviet, Presidium, and Council of Ministers, whose chairman is an ex officio member of the USSR Council of Ministers. Each Union Republic is entitled to maintain direct relations with foreign states, and two of them — the Ukraine and Byelorussia — are separately represented in the United Nations and various related agencies.

Within the Union Republics there exist a number of smaller, nominally self-governing units set up for the accommodation of minority national groups and organized as Autonomous Republics (20), Autonomous Regions (8), and National Areas (10). Each of these units, a majority of which are located in the territory of the Russian Republic (RSFSR), has its own Supreme Soviet and Council of Ministers and is represented in the USSR Soviet of Nationalities.

Subnational government is conducted throughout the USSR by means of an elaborate network of legislative councils (soviets of people's deputies) extending down to territory, region, city, district, settlement and village levels. In a distinctly new departure, an experiment was conducted during the local elections of June 21, 1987, at which voters were given a choice among candidates (all party-approved) for seats in the soviets of 162 districts and their constituent cities, settlements, and villages.

Foreign relations. Soviet foreign policy has been shaped by the interaction of three main influences: the national interest and expansionist tradition of the Russian state; the revolutionary expectations enshrined in Communist ideology and associated particularly with Lenin, who saw the Soviet Union as the spearhead of world revolution; and the pragmatism introduced by Khrushchev during the 1950s in an attempt to adjust to the new conditions created by nuclear weapons — conditions that have prompted Sec-

retary Gorbachev to adopt even more flexible international policies.

A primary Soviet concern after World War II was to develop the strength and solidarity of the "camp of Socialism", making use of such instruments as the Warsaw Pact and the Council for Mutual Economic Assistance (CMEA). This effort was complicated by persistent centrifugal tendencies and pressures for greater autonomy within the Communist world, as manifested particularly in Yugoslavia's rejection of Soviet domination in 1948, the Hungarian uprising in 1956, the ill-fated liberalization movement in Czechoslovakia in 1968, and the short-lived acceptance of independent trade-unionism in Poland in 1980. Of equal concern was the independent posture adopted by the People's Republic of China (PRC), which, under Mao Zedong, vehemently condemned post-Stalin "revisionism" in the USSR and subsequently diminished Soviet influence within the international Communist movement by splitting many of the national Communist parties into pro-Soviet and pro-Chinese factions. Protracted Soviet efforts led in June 1969 to a conference in Moscow of 75 Communist parties, but attempts to bring about a formal condemnation of the PRC were unsuccessful. Further erosion of Moscow's leadership within the Communist world was evidenced by Soviet concessions to national aspirations at the long-delayed East Berlin conference of 29 European parties in mid-1976. By 1977 most of the leading West European parties had committed themselves, in varying degrees, to independent parliamentary activity under the banner of "Eurocommunism", although none was able to generate measurable electoral success thereby. Meanwhile, by the late 1970s, the slowed growth in Soviet national production yielded efforts to make CMEA members less economically dependent on the USSR. More recently, under Secretary Gorbachev, relations with China have significantly eased, while Soviet-bloc countries have been encouraged to emulate Moscow in undertaking sweeping economic reforms.

In relations with Western countries, the manifestations of ingrained hostility and suspicion that characterized Soviet policy at the height of the "cold war" have given place since the mid-1950s to a more temperate approach, apparently dictated by awareness of the risks implicit in any hostile encounter involving nuclear weapons and by an appreciation of the potential danger of China. A primary Soviet concern is the physical security of the USSR and the other Communist states through limitations on the military capabilities of potential opponents. Thus, Moscow strongly opposed the rearmament of West Germany; has urged the dissolution of NATO, the withdrawal of US military forces from Europe, and the organization of an all-European security system free of US influence; and has proposed the establishment of nuclear-free zones in the Baltic and the Mediterranean. In the area of arms control, the USSR has shown interest in limiting the scale and intensity of the arms race through such measures as the 1968 Treaty on the Non-Proliferation of Nuclear Weapons and the partial nuclear test-ban treaty of 1963, which was expanded in 1974 and 1976 to include the curtailment and on-site inspection of underground nuclear explosions. First-round talks with the United States on limiting strategic arms (SALT) were begun in November 1969 and ran for 30 months, to May 1972. The talks resulted in an antiballistic missile (ABM) treaty approved by the US Senate in August 1972, and a five-year executive agreement on offensive weapons that froze the number of land- and submarine-based missile launchers, limiting for the first time the strategic arsenals of the two military superpowers. Second-round talks were initiated in November 1972 and continued intermittently, without substantive result, until July 1974, when President Nixon and Secretary Brezhnev agreed to negotiate a new interim accord to succeed the agreement reached in 1972. Brezhnev and President Ford, meeting at Vladivostok on November 23–24, 1974, reaffirmed the intention to conclude an agreement to last through 1985 by means of further talks, originally scheduled for 1975 but postponed because of the impending US presidential election. Although major differences remained in October 1977, when the original accord expired, each side indicated a willingness to continue to abide by its terms in the expectation that a long-range agreement would be forthcoming. Ultimately, however, the SALT II accord signed at Vienna, Austria, by President Carter and Chairman Brezhnev in June 1979 was not acted upon by the US Senate, the Carter administration having, in effect, withdrawn it from consideration following the December 1979 Soviet intervention in Afghanistan. A collateral series of meetings between NATO and Warsaw Pact representatives on mutual and balanced force reductions (MBFR) in Central Europe was initiated in 1973 but has yielded little in the way of substantive agreement. US-Soviet negotiations on limiting intermediate-range nuclear forces (INF) began at Geneva on November 30, 1981, and were followed on June 29, 1982, by the opening of strategic arms reduction talks (START), neither of which had yielded measurable results prior to a meeting between Secretary Gorbachev and President Reagan at Reykjavik, Iceland, on October 11–12, 1986, that was to have defined the agenda for a substantive summit in the United States. During the Reykjavik talks, Gorbachev signalled a willingness to make significant concessions on a wide range of arms issues, but insisted that any such accord preclude further development of the US Strategic Defense Initiative (SDI), popularly known as "Starwars", save in a laboratory environment—a condition that the American chief executive vehemently rejected. Negotiations nonetheless continued through 1987, culminating in a historic disarmament treaty signed by Secretary Gorbachev and President Reagan at Washington in December. Although the SDI dispute remained unresolved, the treaty for the first time eliminated an entire class of offensive weapons — 1,752 Soviet and 859 American nuclear missiles, ranging from 300 to 3,400 miles — with inspection teams from each country to be stationed on the other's territory.

In the Middle East, the USSR avoided direct involvement in the 1967 Arab-Israeli conflict but used the opportunity to establish an expanded naval presence in the Mediteranean and to strengthen its position in the Arab world through postwar military aid to the defeated Arab states. It strongly supported the Arabs in the 1973 Arab-Israeli War and in November 1974 gave its diplomatic support to the creation of a separate Palestinian state. Although its influence was jarred by the expulsion of Soviet personnel from Egypt in 1972 and further impaired by ambivalence regarding Syria's military involvement in Lebanon, which began in 1976, the USSR is still prominently involved in the affairs of the region, most recently rearming Syria following the June 1982 invasion of Lebanon by Israel. In the wake of Iranian attacks on oil tankers in the Persian Gulf, the Soviet Union joined the other permanent members of the Security Council on July 20, 1987, in unanimous approval of a resolution calling for a cease fire and peace negotiations. In September the Soviet Union went on to suggest that the Security Council sponsor an international force to protect shipping in the Gulf; however, as the year concluded, the Soviets resisted appeals for a UN arms embargo on Iran.

For much of the past quarter-century, the USSR has attempted to counter Chinese as well as Western influences throughout the Third World. In Africa, where its attempts to gain a political foothold encountered a number of setbacks in the early 1960s, it now seeks to improve relations with the more moderate states while maintaining its links to the more radical regimes, particularly in the eastern Horn, where its abrupt transfer of support from Somalia to Ethiopia in 1977 was a major factor in the latter's Ogaden War victory a year later. In East Asia, the USSR has entered into a number of economic cooperation agreements with Japan, despite reluctance to conclude a post-World War II peace treaty because of political and territorial differences. In Southeast Asia, it has formally allied itself with Vietnam and Laos in a largely successful effort to preclude Chinese intrusion. In Latin America, it continues to provide crucial economic assistance to the Cuban regime of Fidel Castro but has not actively supported Havana's revolutionary program elsewhere in the continent, save for military and economic assistance to the *sandinista* government of Nicaragua, including a guarantee in April 1985 to supply up to 90 percent of Managua's oil needs (a tender that was substantially reduced in 1987).

At the United Nations, where its status as a permanent member of the Security Council confers a right of veto that has been used on more than 100 occasions, the USSR has tended to avoid major initiatives, cooperating with Byelorussia and the Ukraine (which were granted separate membership in the UN at its establishment in 1945) in the work of the organization only to the extent judged narrowly consistent with Soviet interests. On September 17 Secretary Gorbachev proposed to the General Assembly that the Security Council take a larger role in peacekeeping activities and in preserving military stability by verifying arms control agreements. In addition his plan called for other fresh departures: wider mandatory jurisdiction for the International Court of Justice; a new tribunal to investigate acts of terrorism; and the setting of international legal and humane standards for reuniting families and for facilitating international marriages and people's contacts generally. Subsequently, on October 5, the Soviet Union announced that it was paying all its outstanding debts to the UN, covering both regular budget ($28 million) and peacekeeping ($197 million) assessments.

Taking advantage of what was apparently perceived as the strategic disintegration of a historic buffer zone, Moscow became deeply involved in the affairs of neighboring

Afghanistan in the wake of a pro-Soviet coup in April 1978. Its involvement escalated into a military incursion and virtual occupation of the country on December 27, 1979, after two further changes of government — neither involving anti-Soviet principals — under circumstances that have not yet been completely explained (see entry under Afghanistan). The move was widely condemned by both Muslim and Western governments, although formal action by the UN Security Council was blocked by a Soviet veto on January 7, 1980. Despite continuous military action by some 115,000 Soviet troops in support of the Kabul government, the effort to rout Afghan guerrillas produced only stalemate at best, with growing concern among the Soviet people and leadership over its human and economic costs. In an effort to end what he called "one of the most bitter and painful regional conflicts", Secretary Gorbachev announced in February 1988 that the Soviet troops would be withdrawn over a ten-month period beginning May 15 if proximity talks at Geneva, Switzerland, between Afghan and Pakistani representatives yielded agreement by March 15. On May 15, in the wake of the accords concluded on April 14 (see Afghanistani Foreign relations), Soviet troops began leaving on a projected nine-month schedule.

Current issues. During 1987 Secretary Gorbachev's program of "restructuring" under conditions of "openness" ran an uneven course. On October 21 one of his reported opponents, Geidar A. ALIYEV, was retired from the Politburo. Subsequently, in mid-November, Boris N. YELTSIN, a strongly pro-Gorbachev candidate member of the Politburo, berated party officials before the Central Committee for recalcitrance in pursuing reform. Several days of seemingly confused maneuvering ended with the removal of Yeltsin from his post as Moscow party leader and assignment to the manifestly less distinguished position of first deputy chairman of the State Committee on Construction; in February he was dismissed from the Politburo as well.

In a move toward frankness about the past, the CPSU acknowledged the half-century-old injustice suffered by Nikolai I. Bukharin, Aleksei I. Rykov, and eight other prominent leaders who had perished in the Stalin purge trials of 1937. Noting such abuses as "admissions of guilt wrung from the accused through unlawful methods", a review commission absolved the victims of all charges and restored them to places of honor in the history of the party. Further exoneration of purged Old Bolsheviks occurred in June 1988 when the Soviet Supreme Court annulled the sentences of Lev B. Kamenev, Grigory L. Pyatkov, and Grigory Y. Zinoviev, all of whom had been executed, and of Karl B. Radek, who had been incarcerated in a labor camp.

Greater freedom for nationalities yielded a complex picture, one that eventually assumed serious proportions. In the wake of relaxed emigration restrictions some 8,155 Jews (the largest number since 1981) left the country, as did a record 14,488 ethnic Germans and a lesser, but progressively increasing number of the Armenians. Within several titular republics, particularly in the Baltic area, movements for greater autonomy gained ground. However, the most severe challenge to Gorbachev's leadership arose when the legislature of the Nagorno-Karabakh Au-

tonomous Region, situated in principally Muslim Azerbaidzhan but with a largely Armenian population, voted to annex the territory to predominantly Christian Armenia. Large-scale demonstrations by Armenians were followed by Azerbaidzhani riots, in the course of which at least 33 lives were lost. Eventually the general secretary himself was forced to intervene, apparently with an offer of Armenian control over schools and the establishment of an Armenian-language television station in Nagorno-Karabakh, but with no indication that borders would be changed.

At a February 1988 meeting of the Central Committee, Gorbachev called for the "free development" of national cultures in the Soviet Union, a subject that he termed the "most fundamental, vital question of our society." He also appealed for a reformulation of Marxist-Lenist principles in light of an evolving "socialist pluralism of views", although denying emphatically that this meant repudiating the legacy of the ideology's founding fathers. In another burst of candor, Gorbachev speculated that the Soviet economy may actually have declined in the early 1980s if one discounted revenues from alcoholic sales and from oil sold abroad.

The most remarkable evidence of Gorbachev's commitment to change occurred during a national party conference (the first since 1947), which met on June 28–July 1. In the course of a lengthy address to 5,000 delegates, the general secretary called for a wide range of constitutional reforms that would yield a chief executive with broad authority; a national legislature of approximately 400 members drawn from a larger body of popularly elected representatives, to which genuine law-making powers would be assigned; legal reforms to ensure the independence of the judiciary; competitive balloting for local and regional soviets; and withdrawal of the party from day-to-day managment of governmental bodies and economic enterprises.

POLITICAL PARTIES

The USSR is a one-party state in which the Communist Party of the Soviet Union (CPSU) holds a monopoly position and has heretofore directed the operations of government at all levels.

Communist Party of the Soviet Union — CPSU (*Kommunisticheskaya Partiya Sovyetskovo Soyuza* — KPSS). The party that now rules the USSR was founded by V.I. Lenin in 1903 when the long-established Russian Social Democratic Labor Party, meeting in exile at London, split into more militant majority (bolshevik) and more moderate minority (menshevik) factions. The Bolsheviks, antecedents of the present-day Communists, spearheaded the October Revolution of 1917 under Lenin's leadership and subsequently organized as the Russian Communist Party, joining in 1925 with the Communist parties of the other Soviet Republics to form the All-Union Communist Party of Bolsheviks. The present party name was adopted in 1952. With a membership of approximately 19 million in January 1986, the CPSU has an elaborate organization that extends into every community and every section of Soviet society. Under its operating principle of "democratic centralism", power theoretically flows upward through a hierarchy of representative bodies; in practice, however, these organizations serve as a transmission belt for instructions passed down from the top.

The supreme organ of the CPSU is the Party Congress, which normally meets every five years. (The 27th Party Congress, attended by nearly 5,000 delegates, met from February 25 to March 6, 1986.) In addition to approving the policies advanced by party leaders, the Congress elects the CPSU Central Committee, which meets at least twice a year to carry on the work of the party between congresses. The Central Committee in turn elects the two party bodies in which real authority is concentrated: the Politburo (consisting, as of March 1988, of 13 full and 7 candidate members), which is the party's supreme policymaking organ and directs the work of the Central Committee between its plenary meetings; and the Secretariat (currently 12 members including the general secretary), which directs the work of the entire party machine on a day-to-day basis. Membership in these bodies, though nominally elective, is actually determined by co-optation among party leaders, and the overlapping of membership among the Politburo, the Secretariat, and the Council of Ministers reflects the concentration of power in the hands of a comparatively small group. After a lengthy period of comparative stability, the 12 months following the accession of Mikhail Gorbachev witnessed a turnover of nearly one-third in the top leadership positions, the average age of the incumbents being reduced by nearly 20 years to 63, with Gorbachev, at 55, the second youngest member. Among the current full members of the Politburo, only three (Gromyko, Shcherbitsky, and Solomentsev) are of the now almost totally superseded Brezhnev age cohort.

General Secretary: Mikhail S. GORBACHEV

Other Members of Politburo: Gen. Viktor M. CHEBRIKOV (Chairman, State Security [KGB]), Andrei A. GROMYKO (Chairman of the Presidium, Supreme Soviet), Yegor K. LIGACHEV (Secretary, CPSU Central Committee), Victor P. NIKONOV (Secretary, CPSU Central Committee), Nikolai I. RYZHKOV (Chairman, Council of Ministers), Vladimir V. SHCHERBITSKY (First Secretary, Ukrainian Central Committee), Eduard A. SHEVARDNADZE (Foreign Minister), Nikolai N. SLYUNKOV (Secretary, CPSU Central Committee), Mikhail S. SOLOMENTSEV (Chairman, Party Control Committee), Vitaly I. VOROTNIKOV (Chairman, RSFSR Council of Ministers), Aleksandr N. YAKOVLEV (Secretary, CPSU Central Committee), Lev N. ZAIKOV (First Secretary, Moscow City Party Committee).

Candidates: Pyotr N. DEMICHEV (First Deputy Chairman of the Presidium, Supreme Soviet), Vladimir I. DOLGIKH (Secretary, CPSU Central Committee), Yuri D. MASLYUKOV (First Deputy Chairman, Council of Ministers), Georgy P. RAZYMOVSKY (Secretary, CPSU Central Committee), Yuri F. SOLOVYEV (First Secretary, Leningrad Province Party Committee), Nikolai V. TALYZIN (First Deputy Chairman, Council of Ministers), Dmitri T. YAZOV (Defense Minister).

Central Committee Secretariat: Oleg D. BAKLANOV (former Minister of General Machine Construction), Alexsandra P. BIRYUKOVA (Consumer Goods), Anatoly F. DOBRYNIN (International Affairs), Vladimir I. DOLGIKH (Heavy Industry), Mikhail S. GORBACHEV (General Secretary), Yegor K. LIGACHEV (Ideology and Cadres), Anatoly I. LUKYANOV (Chief of Central Committee General Department), Vadim A. MEDVEDEV (Science and Education), Viktor P. NIKONOV (Agriculture), Georgy P. RAZUMOVSKY (Party Appointments), Nicolai N. SLYUNKOV (Economics), Alexsandr N. YAKOVLEV (Propaganda), Lev N. ZAIKOV (Military-Industrial Affairs).

The **Komsomol,** or All-Union League of Communist Youth (*Kommunisticheskii Soyuz Molodyozhi*), is an auxiliary to the CPSU with its own Congress, Central Committee, Politburo, and Secretariat, and a membership in January 1987 of 40.4 million in the 14–28 age group. Komsomol members serve as leaders and advisers for the "Young Pioneers", an organization for children between 10 and 14.

First Secretary: Viktor I. MIRONENKO.

LEGISLATURE

The **Supreme Soviet of the USSR** (*Verkhovnyi Sovyet SSSR*) consists of two coequal houses, the Soviet of the Union, which is elected on the basis of undifferentiated population districts, and the Soviet of Nationalities, which is elected on the basis of territorial-nationality units. Elections to both houses, conducted by universal suffrage from single lists of CPSU-approved candidates running in single-member constituencies, are held at five-year intervals. The last elections were held March 4, 1984.

Chairman of the Presidium: Andrei A. GROMYKO.

Soviet of the Union (*Sovyet Soyuza*). The Soviet of the Union has 750 members elected on the basis of one deputy for every 300,000 inhabitants.

Chairman: Yuri N. KHRISTORADNY.

Soviet of Nationalities (*Sovyet Natsionalnostey*). The Soviet of Nationalities has a total membership of 750: 32 deputies from each of the 15 Union Republics, 11 from each of the 20 Autonomous Republics, 5 from each of the 8 Autonomous Regions, and 1 from each of the 10 National Areas.

Chairman: Augusts E. VOSS.

CABINET

[as of June 1, 1988]

The Council of Ministers, composed exclusively of CPSU members, which was inducted April 12, 1984, following the convening of the Supreme Soviet elected on March 4, was virtually identical with its predecessor, only a limited number of changes in the latter having been made after its initial installation in April 1979. By contrast, an overwhelming proportion of incumbent ministers were replaced in the period March 1985 to June 1988.

The 1977 constitution provides for a Presidium of the Council of Ministers, consisting of the chairman and deputy chairmen, mandated to resolve economic and other issues involving the state administration.

In the cabinet list that follows the names of full or candidate Politburo members are given in full capitals; last names are capitalized in the cases of ministers serving concurrently as Bureau, Commission, or State Committee chairmen.

For the distinction between All-Union and Union Republic ministries, see Constitution and government, above.

Chairman, USSR Council of Ministers	NIKOLAI I. RYZHKOV
First Deputy Chairmen	YURI D. MASLYUKOV
	Vsevolod S. MURAKHOVSKY
	NIKOLAI V. TALYZIN
Deputy Chairmen	Aleksei K. Antonov
	Yuri P. BATALIN
	Igor S. BELOUSOV
	Vladimir K. Gusev
	Vladimir M. KAMENTSEV
	Boris Y. SHCHERBINA
	Ivan S. SILAYEV
	Boris L. TOLSTYKH
	Gennady G. Vedernikov
	Lev A. VORONIN
Administrator of Affairs, Council of Ministers	Mikhail S. Smirtyukov
Chairman, People's Control Committee	Sergei I. Manyakin
Chief Arbitrator, State Board of Arbitration	Nicolai P. Malshakov
Board Chairman, State Bank (Gosbank)	Nikolai V. Garetovsky
Bureau Chairmen	
Fuel and Energy Complex	Boris Y. SHCHERBINA
Machine Building	Ivan S. SILAYEV
Social Development	NIKOLAI V. TALZIN
Commission Chairmen	
Improvement of Management, Planning and the Economic Mechanism	YURI D. MASLYUKOV

Military Industrial	Igor S. BELOUSOV
State Foreign Economic	Vladimir M. KAMENTSEV

All-Union State Committee Chairmen

Computer Technology and Information Science	Nikolai V. Gorshkov
Hydrometeorology and Environmental Control	Yuri A. Izrael
Inventions and Discoveries	Ivan S. Nayashkov
Material Reserves	Fedor I. Loshchenkov
Safety in the Atomic Power Industry	Vadim M. Malyshev
Science and Technology	Boris L. TOLSTYKH
Standards	Georgi D. Kolmogorov

All-Union Ministers

Agricultural Machine and Tractor Building	Aleksandr A. Yezhevsky
Atomic Power	Nikolai F. Lukonin
Automotive Industry	Nikolai A. Pugin
Aviation Industry	Apollon S. Systsov
Chemical Industry	Yuri A. Bespalov
Chemical and Petroleum Machine Building	Vladimir M. Lukyanenko
Civil Aviation	Col. Gen. Aleksandr N. Volkov
Coal Industry	Mikhail I. Shchadov
Communications Equipment Industry	Erlen K. Pervyshin
Construction in the Eastern Regions	Aleksandr A. Babenko
Construction in the Northern and Western Regions	Vladimir I. Reshetilov
Construction in the Southern Regions	Arkady N. Shchepetilnikov
Construction in the Urals and West Siberia Regions	Sergei V. Bashilov
Construction Materials Industry	Sergei F. Voyenushkin
Construction of Petroleum and Gas Industry Enterprises	Vladimir G. Chirskov
Construction, Road and Municipal Machine Building	Yevgeny A. Varnachev
Defense	Gen. DMITRI T. YAZOV
Defense Industry	Pavel V. Finogenov
Electrical Equipment Industry	Oleg G. Anfimov
Electronics Industry	Vladislav G. Kolesnikov
Ferrous Metallurgy	Serafim V. Kolpakov
Foreign Economic Relations	Konstantine F. Katushev
Gas Industry	Viktor S. Chernomyrdin
General Machine Building	Vitaly K. Doguzhiyev
Geology	Yevgeny A. Kozlovsky
Heavy, Power, and Transport Machine Building	Vladimir M. Velichko
Instrument Making, Automation Equipment and Control Systems	Mikhail S. Shkabardnya
Machine Building	Boris M. Belousov
Machine Tool and Tool Building Industry	Nikolai A. Panichev
Maritime Fleet	Yuri M. Volmer
Medical and Microbiological Industry	Valery A. Bykov
Medium Machine Building	Lev D. Ryabev
Mineral Fertilizer Production	Nikolai M. Olshansky
Nonferrous Metallurgy	Vladimir A. Durasov
Petroleum Industry	Vasily A. Dinkov
Petroleum Refining and Petrochemical Industry	Nikolai V. Lemayev
Radio Industry	Vladimir I. Shimko
Railways	Nicolai S. Konarev
Shipbuilding Industry	Igot V. Koksanov
Transport Construction	Vladimir A. Brezhnev

Union-Republic Committee Chairmen

Agro-Industrial (Gosagroprom)	Vsevolod S. MURAKHOVSKY
	Aleksandr I. Iyevlev (1st. Dep.)
	Yevgeni I. Sizenko (1st. Dep.)

Cinematography (Goskino)	Aleksandr I. Kamshalov
Environmental Protection	Fedor T. Morgun
Foreign Tourism	Vladimir Y. Pavlov
Forestry	Aleksandr C. Isayev
Labor and Social Problems	Ivan I. Gladky
Material and Technical Supply (Gossnab)	Lev A. VORONIN
Physical Culture and Sports	Marat V. Gramov
Planning (Gosplan)	YURI D. MASLYUKOV
	Anatoly A. Reut (1st. Dep.)
Prices	Valentin S. Pavlov
Public Education	Gennady A. Yagodin
Publishing	Mikhail F. Nenashev
State Construction (Gosstroy)	Yuri P. Batalin
	Leonid A. Bibin (1st. Dep.)
	Boris N. Yeltsin (1st. Dep.)
State Security (KGB)	Gen. VIKTOR M. CHEBRIKOV
Statistics	Mikhail A. Korolev
Supervision of Safe Working Practices in Industry and Mines	Ivan M. Vladychenko
Television and Radio Broadcasting	Aleksandr N. Aksenov

Union Republic Ministers

Communications	Vasily A. Shamshin
Culture	Vasily G. Zakharov
Finance	Boris I. Gostev
Fish Industry	Nikolai I. Kotlyar
Foreign Affairs	EDUARD A. SHEVARDNADZE
Grain Products	Aleksandr D. Budyka
Health	Yevgeny I. Chazov
Installation and Special Construction Work	Boris V. Bakin
Internal Affairs	Aleksandr V. Vlasov
Justice	Boris V. Kravtsov
Land Reclamation and Water Resources	Nikolai F. Vasilyev
Light Industry	Vladimir G. Klyuyev
Power and Electrification	Anatoly I. Mayorets
Timber Industry	Mikhail I. Busygin
Trade	Kondrat Z. Terekh

Chairmen of Councils of Ministers of Union Republics

Armenian SSR	Fadey T. Sarkisyan
Azerbaidzhan SSR	Gasan N. Seidov
Byelorussian SSR	Mikhail V. Kovalev
Estonian SSR	Bruno E. Saul
Georgian SSR	Otar Y. Cherkeziya
Kazakh SSR	Nursultan A. Nazarbayev
Kirghiz SSR	Apas D. Dzhumagulov
Latvian SSR	Yuri Y. Ruben
Lithuanian SSR	Vitautas V. Sakalauskas
Moldavian SSR	Ivan P. Kalin
RSFSR	VITALY I. VOROTNIKOV
Tadzhik SSR	Izatullo K. Khayeyev
Turkmen SSR	Annamurad Khodzhamuradov
Ukrainian SSR	Vitaly A. Masol
Uzbek SSR	Gayrat K. Kadyrov

NEWS MEDIA

Until Secretary Gorbachev's restructuring and openness efforts, newsgathering and the dissemination of news and opinion in the USSR were exclusively public functions performed largely in accordance with guidelines established by the government, the CPSU, and the latter's supporting organizations. Although freedom of speech and the press, as well as access to radio and television, are constitutionally guaranteed, government or party ownership and control of most media inhibited any significant deviation from established policy, save by the editors of clandestine publications issued by civil-rights or unlicensed religious groups, many of whom were prosecuted for "anti-Soviet agitation and propaganda". A major departure began in 1986, however: the rise of a strikingly free range of press reporting and expression of opinion. Most official censorship (including radio jamming of the Russian language services of the British Broadcasting Corporation and the Voice of America) was abandoned, being replaced by the self-censorship of increasingly bold editorial boards. Restraints on "irresponsibility" in the press have been counselled by more conservatively-minded leaders, Yegor Ligachev—the second most influential member in the Politburo—among them, and on occasion by Secretary Gorbachev himself. But through 1987 no evident curtailment of the remarkably freer press news and comment had been imposed. Virtually all larger newspapers are now eagerly read by Soviet citizens who can in fact often find a candor not exceeded by comparable publications in the West.

Press. The Soviet press is as voluminous and diversified in form as it is uniform in political content. More than 8,400 newspapers, including more than 4,000 house organs and rural and collective farm papers, are published, with an overall circulation of nearly 200 million. Newspapers, most of which appear six days a week, are printed in 55 Soviet and 9 foreign languages; periodicals are published in 44 Soviet and 25 foreign languages.

Listed below are the principal national and Union Republic dailies; all are published in Russian, unless otherwise indicated. In the case of the Union Republic dailies, unless otherwise indicated, all are published jointly by the Communist Party, the Supreme Soviet, and the Council of Ministers of the Union Republic in which they appear. Most circulation figures are for 1986. By early 1988 a virtual circulation war was being reported, with several of the more outspoken organs (including *Izvestiya* enjoying substantial sales increases and some of the more conservative (notably *Pravda*) experiencing modest declines.

USSR (Moscow): *Trud* (Labor, 18,200,000), published by All-Union Central Council of Trade Unions, printed in 44 cities, specializes in union affairs; *Komsomolskaya Pravda* (14,600,000), published by Komsomol Central Committee, youth appeal; *Pravda* (Truth, 11,000,000), most authoritative daily, published by CPSU Central Committee, printed in 44 cities; *Selskaya Zhizn* (Rural Life, 9,000,000), published by CPSU Central Committee, printed in 21 cities, primarily agricultural with some general news; *Izvestiya* (News, 6,900,000), published by Presidium of Supreme Soviet, printed in 40 cities, authoritative on foreign affairs and work of soviets; *Literaturnaya Gazeta* (Literary Gazette, 3,000,000), published by the Union of Soviet Writers, literary and social news; *Krasnya Zvezda* (Red Star, 2,400,000), published by Ministry of Defense, military and general news; *Nedelya* (The Week, 2,000,000), sold separately as Sunday tabloid supplement to *Izvestiya*.

Russian SFSR (Moscow): *Sovyetskaya Rossiya* (Soviet Russia, 3,600,000), published by the RSFSR Communist Party Bureau and Council of Ministers, printed in 16 cities of the Russian Republic; *Leningradskaya Pravda* (Leningrad Truth, Leningrad, 350,000), published by Leningrad Province and City Communist parties and soviets; *Moskovskaya Pravda* (Moscow Truth, 230,000), published by Moscow Province Communist Party and Soviet.

Armenian SSR (Yerevan): *Kommunist* (Communist); *Sovyetakan Ayastan* (Soviet Armenia), in Armenian.

Azerbaidzhan SSR (Baku): *Bakinski Rabochi* (Baku Worker); *Kommunist* (Communist), in Azerbaidzhanian.

Byelorussian SSR (Minsk): *Sovyetskaya Belorussia* (Soviet Byelorussia); *Zvyazda* (Star), in Byelorussian.

Estonian SSR (Tallinn): *Sovyetskaya Estonia* (Soviet Estonia); *Rahva Hääl* (People's Voice), published in Estonian by the Estonian and Tallinn Communist parties and soviets.

Georgian SSR (Tbilisi): *Kommunisti* (Communist), in Georgian; *Zarya Vostoka* (Dawn of the East).

Kazakh SSR (Alma-Ata): *Kazakhstanskya Pravda* (Kazakhstan Truth); *Sotsialistik Kazakhstan* (Socialist Kazakhstan), in Kazakh.

Kirghiz SSR (Frunze): *Sovyetskaya Kirgizia* (Soviet Kirghiz); *Sovyettik Kyrgyzstan* (Soviet Kirghizstan), in Kirghiz.

Latvian SSR (Riga): *Sovyetskaya Latvia* (Soviet Latvia); *Cina* (Struggle), published in Latvian by the Latvian Communist Party and Supreme Soviet.

Lithuanian SSR (Vilnius): *Sovyetskaya Litva* (Soviet Lithuania); *Tiesa* (Truth), in Lithuanian.

Moldavian SSR (Kishinev): *Moldova Socialiste* (Socialist Moldavia), published in Moldavian by the Moldavian Communist Party and Supreme Soviet; *Sovyetskaya Moldavia* (Soviet Moldavia).

Tadzhik SSR (Dushanbe): *Kommunist Tadzhikistana* (Tadzhikian Communist); *Tochikistoni Soveti* (Soviet Tadzhikistan), in Tadzhik.

Turkmen SSR (Ashkhabad): *Turkmanskaya Iskra* (Turkmenian Spark); *Sovyet Turkmenistany* (Soviet Turkmenia), in Turkmen.

Ukrainian SSR (Kiev): *Pravda Ukrainy* (Ukranian Truth); *Rabochaya Gazeta* (Workers' Gazette), published in Ukranian and Russian by the UCP Central Committee; *Radanska Ukraina* (Soviet Ukraine), in Ukrainian.

Uzbek SSR (Tashkent): *Pravda Vostoka* (Truth of the East); *Sovyet Uzbekistoni* (Soviet Uzbekistan), in Uzbek.

News agencies. The domestic agencies are the Telegraphic Agency of the Soviet Union (*Telegrafnoye Agentstvo Sovyetskogo Soyuza*—TASS) and the Novosti Press Agency (*Agentstvo Pechati Novosti*—APN). Most of the leading foreign agencies also maintain bureaus at Moscow.

Radio and television. Radio and television are state operated, under the jurisdiction of the State Committee for Television and Radio Broadcasting of the USSR Council of Ministers. Radio Moscow broadcasts five main programs daily for listeners in the Soviet Union, with special broadcasts for separate regions (the Urals, Siberia, Middle Asia, and the Soviet Far East) and overseas programs in 70 languages. More than 93 percent of the Soviet population now lives in areas with television reception, and programs are presented in both Russian and national languages. The ultramodern facilities at Ostankino on the outskirts of Moscow serve as the main programming center for Soviet Central Television and provide five channels for reception in major metropolitan areas. A chain of communications satellites transmits television programs between Moscow, Vladivostok, and other cities. Color programs are exchanged between Moscow and Paris by the Soviet-French SECAM system. There were more than 176 million radio and 90 million television receivers in 1987.

INTERGOVERNMENTAL REPRESENTATION

Ambassador to the US: Yuri V. DUBININ.

US Ambassador to Soviet Union: Jack F. MATLOCK, Jr.

Permanent Representatives to the UN: Aleksandr M. BELONOGOV (USSR), Lev I. MAKSIMOV (Byelorussian SSR), Gennady I. OUDOVENKO (Ukrainian SSR).

IGO Memberships (Non-UN): CMEA, IBEC, ICAC, ICCAT, ICCO, ICES, IIB, ILZ, Inmarsat, INRO, ISO, IWC, IWTC, PCA, WTO.

UNITED ARAB EMIRATES

al-Imarat al-'Arabiyah al-Muttahida

Political Status: Federation of six former Trucial States, Abu Dhabi, Dubai, Sharjah, Fujaira, 'Ajman, and Umm al-Qaiwain, established December 2, 1971; the seventh, Ras al-Khaima, joined in 1972.

Area: 32,278 sq. mi. (83,600 sq. km.).

Population: 1,622,464 (1985C), embracing Abu Dhabi (670,125), Dubai (419,104), Sharjah (268,722), Ras al-Khaima (116,470), 'Ajman (64,318), Fujaira (54,425), and Umm al-Qaiwain (29,229); 1,825,000 (1988E). Figures include noncitizens (approximately three-quarters of the total population).

Major Urban Center (1980C): ABU DHABI (242,975).

Official Language: Arabic.

Monetary Unit: Dirham (market rate March 1, 1988, 3.67 dirhams = $1US).

Supreme Council: Composed of the rulers of the seven Emirates (with dates of accession): Sheikh Zayid ibn Sultan Al NUHAYYAN (Abu Dhabi, 1966), Sheikh Rashid ibn Sa'id Al MAKTUM (Dubai, 1958), Sheikh Sultan ibn Muhammad al-QASIMI (Sharjah, 1972), Sheikh Saqr ibn Muhammad al-QASIMI (Ras al-Khaima, 1948), Sheikh Hamad ibn Muhammad al-SHARQI (Fujaira, 1974), Sheikh Humayd ibn Rashid al-NU'AYMI ('Ajman, 1981), and Sheikh Rashid ibn Ahmad al-MU'ALLA (Umm al-Qaiwain, 1981).

President: Sheikh Zayid ibn Sultan Al NUHAYYAN (Ruler of Abu Dhabi); elected by the six original Emirs and sworn in as first President of the Union on December 2, 1971; reelected in 1976, 1981, and on October 15, 1986.

Vice President and Prime Minister: Sheikh Rashid ibn Sa'id Al MAKTUM (Ruler of Dubai); elected Vice President in 1971, 1976, 1981, and 1986 for terms concurrent with those of the President; named Prime Minister by action of the Supreme Council on April 30, 1979, following the resignation on April 25 of Sheikh Maktum ibn Rashid Al MAKTUM (Crown Prince of Dubai).

THE COUNTRY

Formerly known as the Trucial States because of truces concluded with Britain in the nineteenth century, the United Arab Emirates extends some 400 miles along the Persian Gulf from the southeast end of the Qatar peninsula to a point just short of Ras Musandam. It encompasses a barren, relatively flat territory characterized by extreme temperatures and sparse rainfall. The majority of the indigenous population is Arab and adheres to the Sunni sect of Islam; there are also significant numbers of Iranians, Indians, Pakistanis, Baluchis, and Negro descendants of former slaves among the noncitizen population. Although Arabic is the official language, English and Persian are also spoken.

Traditionally, the area was dependent upon trading, fishing, and pearling. However, the discovery in 1958 of major oil reserves in Abu Dhabi and subsequently of smaller deposits in Dubai and Sharjah dramatically altered the federation's economy. In 1984 the UAE had the world's highest GNP per capita, nearly $22,000, although the figure was down from over $28,000 in 1980 due to declining oil revenue. Oil wealth led to rapid modernization of the infrastructure, advances in education and health services, and a construction boom requiring a massive inflow of foreign labor. New industrial cities were established at Jebel Ali in Dubai and Ruwais in Abu Dhabi as diversification efforts, while not as successful as planned, produced shipyards, cement factories, and other manufacturing sites. Since 1982, however, UAE has experienced progressive belt-tightening and a slowdown in economic growth. Dubai continues to perform its historical role as an entrepôt, while for the most part the northern emirates rely on traditional economic activity and development financing provided by the wealthier states.

GOVERNMENT AND POLITICS

Political background. Originally controlling an area known in the West as a refuge for pirates, the sheikhs first entered into agreements with the British in the early nineteenth century. After the failure of the initial treaty agreements of 1820 and 1835, a Perpetual Maritime Truce was signed in 1853. Relations with Britain were further strengthened by an Exclusive Agreement of 1892, whereby the sheikhs agreed not to enter into diplomatic or other foreign relations with countries other than Britain. In return, Britain guaranteed defense of the sheikhdoms against aggression by sea.

The treaty arrangements with Britain lasted until 1968, when the British announced their intention to withdraw from the Persian Gulf by 1971. An early attempt at unification, the Federation of Arab Emirates, was initiated in 1968 with British encouragement but collapsed when Bahrain and Qatar declared their separate independence in 1971. Subsequently, the leaders of the Trucial States organized a new grouping, the United Arab Emirates, which was formally constituted as an independent state on December 2, 1971, with Sheikh Zayid ibn Sultan Al NUHAYYAN as president; Ras al-Khaima, which initially rejected membership, acceded to the UAE two months later.

Apart from the death of Sheikh Khalid ibn Muhammad al-QASIMI (ruler of Sharjah) following an attempted coup in 1972, few major political developments occurred until the spring of 1979, when a series of disputes, principally between Abu Dhabi and Dubai over the extent of federal powers, led to the April 25 resignation of Prime Minister Sheikh Maktum ibn Rashid Al MAKTUM and his replacement five days later by his father, Sheikh Rashid ibn Sa'id Al MAKTUM, ruler of Dubai, who retained his position as vice president. In 1981 the emirs of 'Ajman, Sheikh Rashid ibn Humayd al-NU'AYMI, and of Umm al-Qaiwain, Sheikh Ahmad ibn Rashid al-MU'ALLA, both of whom had ruled for more than 50 years, died and were succeeded by their sons, Sheikh Humayd ibn al-NU'AYMI and Sheikh Rashid ibn Ahmad al-MU'ALLA, respectively.

On June 17, 1987, Sheikh 'Abd al-Aziz al-QASIMI seized power in Sharjah, accusing his brother, Sheikh Sultan Muhammad al-QASIMI, of fiscal mismanagement; however, on July 20 Sheikh Muhammad was reinstated by the Supreme Council, which decreed that Sheikh 'Abd al-

Aziz should thenceforth hold the title of crown prince and of deputy ruler, with substantial control of the emirate's economy.

Constitution and government. The institutions of the UAE were superimposed upon the existing political structures of the member states, which generally maintain their monarchical character. Under the federal constitution, the rulers of the constituent states are participants in a Supreme Council, which elects a president and vice president for five-year terms. The president in turn appoints a prime minister and a cabinet, while a consultative Federal National Council is made up of delegates appointed by the various rulers. In July 1976, the Council, following failure to reach agreement on a new constitutional draft, voted to extend the life of the existing constitution for another five years beyond December 2; further five-year extensions were voted in 1981 and 1986.

Judicial functions have traditionally been performed by local courts applying Muslim law and by individual decisions rendered by the ruling families. In June 1978, however, the president signed a law establishing four Primary Federal Tribunals (in Abu Dhabi, 'Ajman, Fujaira, and Sharjah) to handle disputes between individuals and the federation, with appeal to a federal Supreme Court. The basic administrative divisions are the constituent states, each of which retains local control over mineral rights, taxation, and police protection.

Foreign relations. The United Arab Emirates is a member of the United Nations, the Arab League, the Organization of Petroleum Exporting Countries, and various regional groupings. Relations have been cordial with most countries, including the United States, although there have been territorial disputes, now largely resolved, with Iran, Oman, Qatar, and Saudi Arabia.

In 1971 Iran occupied three small Persian Gulf islands: Abu Musa and the Greater and Lesser Tunbs. Abu Musa was occupied by agreement with Sharjah, but the Tunbs continued to be claimed by Ras al-Khaima. However, the dispute, which involved the delineation of the Gulf Median Line, became a relatively dormant issue following the establishment of diplomatic relations between Iran and the UAE in October 1972. A somewhat more serious dispute with Saudi Arabia and Oman concerned portions of Abu Dhabi, including the potentially oil-rich Buraimi Oasis, which is located at the juncture of the three states. Under the terms of an agreement reached in 1974, six villages of the oasis were awarded to Abu Dhabi and two to Oman; Saudi Arabia, in return for renouncing its claim, was granted a land corridor through Abu Dhabi to the Persian Gulf port of Khawr al-Udad.

In early 1981, the UAE joined with five neighbors (Bahrain, Kuwait, Oman, Qatar, and Saudi Arabia) in establishing the Cooperative Council of the Arab Gulf States (more commonly known as the Gulf Cooperation Council — GCC) as a means of coordinating members' policies bearing on security and stability in the area. Concern over the Iran-Iraq war has led the UAE to participate in the GCC's annual "Peninsula shield" joint military maneuvers. Although the hazards of the regional conflict have not precluded a recent increase in trade with Tehran, the UAE and the other GCC states have become increasingly aware of their vulnerability to Iranian aggression and to the potentially destabilizing effects of an Iranian-inspired Islamic revolution; thus, at the December 1987 GCC summit at Riyadh, Saudi Arabia, discussion centered on negotiations with Egypt for military aid and support. Meanwhile, in the wake of oilfield bombings by the Gulf combatants, including one by unidentified aircraft that killed eight people and destroyed two of five platforms in Abu Dhabi, the UAE took steps to purchase advance warning systems from Britain, France, and the United States.

Current issues. During 1986, plummeting oil revenues disrupted the UAE economy, with budget austerity halting many development projects and prompting large scale repatriation of foreign workers. In 1987, largely because of a highly independent oil production policy, the UAE became OPEC's fourth-largest oil exporter with almost $9 billion in revenue. On the other hand, the Emirates' petroleum minister agreed at a mid-December OPEC meeting to curtail oil production to half of the previous six-month average.

Earlier, many foreign banks reportedly were considering withdrawing from the UAE, described as the "world's most overbanked country", because of plunging profits. The banks pressed the government for changes in the authority of *shari'a* law which, because of its strict construction of usury, hampers legal recourse against defaulting debtors; as a result, the National Consultative Council in December 1987 approved a decree liberalizing the payment of interest.

POLITICAL PARTIES

There are no political parties in the United Arab Emirates, though several small clandestine groups exist.

LEGISLATURE

The 40-member consultative assembly, or **Federal National Council,** consists of delegates appointed by the rulers of the constituent states for two-year terms. There are 8 delegates each from Abu Dhabi and Dubai, 6 each from Sharjah and Ras al-Khaima, and 4 each from the other emirates.

Speaker: Hilal ibn Ahmad LUTAH.

CABINET

Prime Minister	Sheikh Rashid ibn Sa'id Al Maktum
Deputy Prime Ministers	Sheikh Maktum ibn Rashid Al Maktum
	Sheikh Hamdan ibn Muhammad Al Nuhayyan
Ministers	
Agriculture and Fisheries	Sa'id Muhammad al-Raqbani
Communications	Muhammad Sa'id al-Mulla
Defense	Sheikh Muhammad ibn Rashid ibn Sa'id Al Maktum

Economy and Commerce   Sayf 'Ali al-Jarwan
Education and Youth   Faraj Fahdil al-Mazrui
Electricity and Water   Humayd Nasir al-'Uways
Finance and Industry   Sheikh Hamdan ibn Rashid
                                       ibn Sa'id Al Maktum
Foreign Affairs   (Vacant)
Health   Hamad 'Abd al-Rahman
                                       al-Madfa
Information and Culture   Sheikh Ahmad ibn Hamid
                                       Al Nuhayyan
Interior   Sheikh Mubarak ibn
                                       Muhammad Al Nuhayyan
Islamic Affairs and Religious   Sheikh Muhammad ibn Hasan
   Endowments   al-Khazraji
Justice   Abdallah Humayd al-Mazrui
Labor and Social Affairs   Khalfan Muhammad al-Rumi
Petroleum and Mineral Resources   Mani ibn Sa'id al-'Utayba
Planning   Sheikh Humayd ibn Ahmad
                                       al-Mu'alla
Public Works and Housing   Muhammad Khalifa al-Kindi

Governor, Central Bank   'Abd al-Malik Hamar

NEWS MEDIA

Press. The following are published daily in Arabic, unless otherwise noted: *al-Ittihad* (Abu Dhabi, 63,000), designated as the official daily of the UAE; *al-Khalij* (Sharjah, 59,000), independent daily; *Khalij Times* (Dubai, 48,000), English daily; *Gulf News* (Dubai, 21,000), English daily; *Emirates News* (Abu Dhabi, 21,000), English daily; *al-Wahdah* (Abu Dhabi, 10,000), independent daily; *al-Dhafra* (Abu Dhabi), independent weekly.

News agencies. The Emirates News Agency was founded in 1977; Reuters maintains an office at Dubai.

Radio and television. The Voice of the United Arab Emirates maintains radio stations in Abu Dhabi, Dubai, Ras al-Khaima, and Sharjah; the United Arab Emirates Television Service operates at Abu Dhabi, Dubai, and Ras al-Khaima. In addition, Dubai Radio and Colour Television operates several radio and television stations. There were approximately 436,000 radio and 150,000 television receivers in 1987.

INTERGOVERNMENTAL REPRESENTATION

Ambassador to the US: Ahmad S. al-MOKARRAB.

US Ambassador to the United Arab Emirates: David Lyle MACK.

Permanent Representative to the UN: Muhammad Hussain al-SHAALI.

IGO Memberships (Non-UN): AFESD, AMF, BADEA, CCC, GCC, IC, IDB, Intelsat, Interpol, LAS, NAM, OAPEC, OPEC.

UNITED KINGDOM

United Kingdom of Great Britain and Northern Ireland

Political Status: Constitutional monarchy, under democratic parliamentary regime.

Area: 94,249 sq. mi. (244,104 sq. km.), embracing England and Wales, 58,382 sq. mi. (151,209 sq. km.); Scotland, 30,415 sq. mi. (78,775 sq. km.); Northern Ireland, 5,452 sq. mi. (14,120 sq. km.).

Population: 55,775,650 (1981C), including England and Wales, 49,082,758; Scotland, 5,130,735; Northern Ireland, 1,562,157; 56,775 (1988E).

Major Urban Centers (1985E): *England:* LONDON (urban area, 6,767,500); Birmingham (1,007,500); Leeds (710,500); Sheffield (538,700); Liverpool (491,500); Manchester (451,100); Bristol (393,800); Coventry (312,200); *Wales:* CARDIFF (278,900); *Scotland:* EDINBURGH (439,700); Glasgow (733,800); *Northern Ireland:* BELFAST (301,600).

Principal Language: English (Scottish and Irish forms of Gaelic are spoken in portions of Scotland and Northern Ireland, respectively, while Welsh is spoken in northern and central Wales).

Monetary Unit: Pound Sterling (market rate March 1, 1988, 1 pound = $1.77US).

Sovereign: Queen ELIZABETH II; proclaimed Queen on February 6, 1952; crowned June 2, 1953.
  Heir Apparent: CHARLES Philip Arthur George; invested as Prince of Wales on July 1, 1969.

Prime Minister: Margaret THATCHER (Conservative Party); appointed by the Queen on May 4, 1979, to succeed James CALLAGHAN (Labour Party) following general election of May 3; continued in office following elections of June 9, 1983, and June 11, 1987.

THE COUNTRY

The United Kingdom of Great Britain and Northern Ireland occupies the major portion of the British Isles, the largest island group off the European coast. The individual identity of its separate regions, each with distinctive ethnic and linguistic characteristics, is reflected in the complex governmental structure of the country as a whole. England, the heart of the nation, comprises over half the total area and 80 percent of the total population. Wales, conquered in the Middle Ages, has been integrated with England in both law and administration (Welsh affairs are administered by a cabinet minister advised by a Council for Wales) but has its own capital, Cardiff, and a national language, Welsh, which is spoken by some 26 percent of the population. Scotland, ruled as a separate kingdom until 1707, has its own legal, educational, and local government systems, but not its own parliament. Northern Ireland became part of the United Kingdom in 1800 but was accorded home rule in 1920, mainly because of its special position vis-à-vis the Irish Republic. Varieties of the Gaelic language are spoken in both Scotland and Northern Ireland. The existence of two established churches, the Church of England (Episcopal) and the Church of Scotland (Presbyterian), imposes no limit on religious freedom. In 1982, women comprised 42 percent of the paid work force, concentrated in the retail, clerical and human services sectors, and earned approximately 74 percent of men's wages; female representation in government, the currrent prime minister notwithstanding, averages less than 10 percent.

Great Britain was the seat of the industrial revolution of the eighteenth century, and most of its urbanized and highly skilled population is engaged in manufacturing and service industries, mainly transport, commerce, and finance. Machinery, basic manufactures, and agricultural products constitute the bulk of British imports; machinery and transport equipment, basic manufactures, chemicals, and mineral fuels are the chief exports. Despite land scarcity, British agriculture still supplies half the nation's food requirements, chiefly in high-value foodstuffs.

The British economy has experienced intermittent crises since World War II as the result of factors that have included the liquidation of most of the country's overseas assets, the requirements of a domestic full-employment policy that has only recently been revised, and difficulties encountered in applying the drastic measures needed to increase productivity and exports. The pound sterling has been devalued several times, while resistance to change and lack of flexibility in management and labor practices have limited economic growth and delayed the achievement of equilibrium. Immigration and emigration, featuring the so-called "brain drain" of skilled professional personnel (mainly to the United States) and a concurrent influx of non-White labor from Nigeria, Pakistan, the West Indies, and elsewhere, have also produced unsettling economic and social effects. The oil crisis of 1973–1974 was particularly damaging to an economy which a year earlier had been beset by strikes following the imposition of price and income curbs and had just experienced its worst trade deficit in history. In early 1976 a government report indicated that public expenditure had grown by almost 20 percent in three years. Most leading indicators thereafter were mixed. In 1978 policies of fiscal constraint and increased exploitation of North Sea oil reserves yielded an unanticipated increase of 3 percent in gross domestic product and a halving of the inflation rate to 8 percent. However, by mid-1980 real GDP was declining at an annual rate of more than 2 percent, while inflation had reescalated to nearly 18 percent, before again receding to less than 5 percent in 1983. A longtime imbalance in foreign trade was reversed in 1980, the net figures remaining positive through 1982; domestic unemployment, on the other hand, increased marginally through the same period to nearly 14 percent, save in some areas of the north, where the figure had risen to as much as 50 percent by 1984. By early 1987, although the balance of trade remained in deficit and unemployment had dipped only marginally to 11 percent, most indicators were distinctly encouraging: corporate profits had risen, productivity was second only to that of Japan, and inflation had receded further to 4.1 percent.

GOVERNMENT AND POLITICS

Political background. After reaching its apogee of global influence in the closing decades of the Victorian era, the United Kingdom endured the strains of the two world wars with its political institutions unimpaired but with sharp reductions in its relative economic strength and military power. The steady erosion of the British imperial position, particularly since World War II, has been only partially offset by the concurrent development and expansion of the Commonwealth, a grouping that continues to reflect an underlying British philosophy but whose center of gravity has increasingly shifted to non-White, non-English-speaking members. The shrinkage of British military and economic resources has been accompanied by sharp readjustments in policies and attitudes toward Europe, the United States, and the Soviet Union. Despite continuing differences on many issues, the three traditional parties—Conservative, Labour, and Liberal (now the Social and Liberal Democrats)—have in some respects drawn closer together in the face of recurrent domestic malaise and declining international status.

The Labour Party, after winning the postwar elections of 1945 and 1950 under the leadership of Clement R. ATTLEE, went into opposition for 13 years while the Conservative Party governed under prime ministers Winston CHURCHILL (1951–1955), Anthony EDEN (1955–1957), Harold MacMILLAN (1957–1963), and Sir Alexander DOUGLAS-HOME (1963–1964). A Conservative defeat in the general election of October 1964 returned Labour to power under Harold WILSON, who had succeeded Hugh GAITSKELL as party leader in 1963. Initially holding only a four-seat majority in the House of Commons, Labour substantially improved its position in the election of March 1966, winning an overall majority of 96 seats. At the election of June 1970, the tide swung back to the Conservatives, who under Edward HEATH obtained an overall majority of 15 seats in the House. In February 1974 the Conservatives outpolled Labour but fell three seats short of a plurality, Wilson returning to head the first minority government since 1929. Eight months later, Labour substantially improved its position by winning a plurality of 43 seats and an all-party majority of three. In April 1976, Wilson, who had earlier signaled his intention to resign, was succeeded as prime minister by Foreign Secretary James CALLAGHAN following the latter's election to leadership of the Parliamentary Labour Party. Callaghan was not able to reverse a subsequent swing to the Conservatives, who in May 1979 obtained 339 seats (an all-party majority of 44) in the House of Commons, Margaret THATCHER (designated party leader four years earlier) becoming the first female prime minister in British (and European) history. Benefiting from popular response to Mrs. Thatcher's handling of the Falklands war (see Foreign relations, below), the Conservatives increased their majority to 72 at the election of June 1983. The Conservatives retained control of Commons with a somewhat diminished, but still comfortable majority on June 11, 1987, Mrs. Thatcher becoming the first prime minister in modern British history to win three consecutive terms.

For nearly two decades, the viability of the United Kingdom as a political entity has been a matter of major concern. The most intractable problem has been that of deep-rooted conflict in Northern Ireland between Protestants committed to majority rule and a Catholic minority, substantial elements of which seek union with the Republic of Ireland. In the wake of widespread public disorder, direct rule from London was imposed in 1972 and reimposed in 1974, following the collapse of an attempt to establish an executive comprising representatives of both factions. The most recent effort to resolve the impasse was the election in October 1982 of a 78-member Northern Ireland Assembly to which the Thatcher government had hoped to turn over power by means of a process of "rolling devolution". However, the plan met with no success (for further details, see following article on Northern Ireland). Earlier, alarmed by the growing influence of the Scottish National Party, which won a third of the Scottish votes in the October 1974 general election, the Labour leadership, in a 1975 government paper, proposed the establishment of local assemblies for both Scotland and Wales. In 1976 a bill to such effect was introduced in the House of Commons and was given a second reading, despite Conservative criticism that the departure would prove costly and contain "the danger of a break-up of Britain". Action on the legislation (in the form of separate bills for the two regions) was completed in mid-1978 but rendered moot by referenda in March 1979 that yielded rejection of devolution in Wales and approval by an insufficient majority in Scotland.

Constitution and government. The United Kingdom is a constitutional monarchy which functions without a written constitution on the basis of long-standing but flexible traditions and usages. Executive power is wielded on behalf of the sovereign by a cabinet of ministers drawn largely from the majority party in the House of Commons and, to a lesser degree, from the House of Lords. The prime minister is the leader of the majority party in the Commons and depends upon it for support.

Elected by universal adult suffrage, the House of Commons has become the main repository of legislative and financial authority. The House of Lords retains the power to review, amend, or delay for a year legislation other than financial bills and takes a more leisurely overview of legislation, sometimes acting as a brake on the Commons. The lower house has a statutory term of five years but may be dissolved by the sovereign on recommendation of the prime minister if the latter's policies should encounter severe resistance or if the incumbent feels that new elections would increase the ruling party's majority.

The judicial system of England and Wales centers in a High Court with three divisions (Chancery; Probate, Divorce, and Admiralty; Queen's Bench); a Court of Appeal; and as final arbiter, the House of Lords. Scotland has its own High Court of Justiciary (criminal) and Court of Session (civil), with a similar right of appeal to the House of Lords. Northern Ireland has a separate Supreme Court of Judicature and Court of Criminal Appeal, both of which are under the jurisdiction of the UK Parliament.

Local government in England, Wales, and Northern Ireland is conducted through administrative counties (subdivided into districts) and county boroughs, while Scotland, under a system introduced in 1975, is divided into 9 mainland regions (embracing 53 districts) and 3 island areas. Greater London, with almost one-third of the country's population, is subdivided into 32 London boroughs, each with its own elected council operating under powers conferred by Parliament.

Foreign relations. Reluctantly abandoning its age-long tradition of "splendid isolation", the United Kingdom became a key member of the Allied coalitions in both world wars and has remained a leader in the Western group of nations, as well as one of the world's nuclear powers. Postwar British governments have sought to retain close economic and military ties with the United States while maintaining an independent British position on most international issues. On questions of East-West relations, British attitudes have generally paralleled those of the United States while reflecting somewhat less antipathy to communism on ideological grounds. Despite financial stringencies and the resultant curtailment of military commitments, Britain has continued to play an important role in the United Nations and in collective security arrangements, such as NATO, but its decision not to create an independent nuclear striking force and its general withdrawal of military forces from the Far East and the Persian Gulf substantially diminished its weight in the global balance of power.

The UK's participation in the work of such institutions as the IMF, GATT, OECD, and the Colombo Plan reflects its continued central position in international financial and economic affairs as well as its commitment to assist in the growth of less-developed countries. Unwilling to participate in the creation of the European Communities (EEC, ECSC, Euratom), it took the lead in establishing the European Free Trade Association in 1960. Subsequently, Conservative and moderate Labour leaders began to urge British entry into the Common Market despite anticipated problems for the UK and other Commonwealth members. France, however, vetoed the British application for admission in 1963 and subsequently maintained its opposition to British entry on the ground that the country remained too closely tied to the United States and was insufficiently "European" to justify close association with the continental nations. Following the resignation of French President de Gaulle in 1969, British leaders signaled their intention of making a renewed effort to obtain membership. A bill sanctioning entry was approved by the House of Commons on October 29, 1971, and Britain was formally admitted to the EC grouping on January 1, 1973. Opposition to membership remained, however, as reflected by a 33 percent "no" vote cast in a referendum held June 5, 1975.

In late 1979 the Thatcher government won worldwide plaudits for its resolution of the seven-year Rhodesian civil war through a lengthy process of negotiation that commenced at the annual Commonwealth Conference at Lusaka, Zambia, on August 1–7 and continued for more than three months at London, culminating in a ceasefire accord on December 5, agreement on a new constitution, and independence under Black majority rule on April 18, 1980 (see entry under Zimbabwe). In September 1981, Belize (formerly British Honduras) was also granted independence, following a breakdown in talks with Guatemala over obligations under an 1859 treaty that Britain had been charged with failing to honor (see entry under Belize).

The Falkland Islands war that erupted in April 1982 followed nearly two decades of sporadic negotiations between Britain and Argentina in a fruitless effort to resolve a dispute that had commenced in the late eighteenth century with the establishment of British and Spanish settlements on West and East Falkland, respectively. In 1774, under circumstances that have never been completely explained, the British withdrew, while the Spaniards departed in the wake of Argentine independence some 50 years later. Britain returned to the islands in 1833, two years after a group of Argentinian settlers had been evicted by an American naval commander in a controversy over maritime jurisdiction. Subsequently, Argentina pressed its claim on the basis of legal succession, while Britain appealed to the principle of uninterrupted occupation and its colonists' right to self-determination. Insisting that further diplomatic efforts were useless, Argentina mounted an invasion of the islands on April 2, 1982, quickly overcoming resistance by a small force of British Marines. Britain responded by dispatching a sizable armada that reached the area in late May and succeeded, through the efforts of some 5,000 troops, in defeating the main Argentinian force at the capital, Stanley, on June 14. In the wake of the action, London announced that a substantial military garrison would be retained on the Falklands for an indefinite period, while no substantive progress was reported by early 1988 in response to UN General Assembly appeals for a negotiated solution to the sovereignty issue.

In September 1984 Britain and China agreed that the latter would regain possession of Hong Kong in 1997, although the Thatcher government continued to rebuff Spanish appeals for the reversion of Gibraltar, given manifest opposition to such a move by its inhabitants (see Related Territories, below).

Current issues. Although not only Labour, but the Liberal-Social Democratic Alliance had pulled ahead of the Conservatives in opinion polls in mid-1986, the Tories had regained the lead by March 1987, prompting Mrs. Thatcher to call a general election, one year early, for June 11. A variety of factors had contributed to the revival in Conservative prospects. Unemployment was falling, strikes were at their lowest level in nearly a quarter-century, manufacturing output and productivity were on the rise, and the economy, overall, was expanding, despite continued revenue shortfall because of depressed prices for North Sea oil. Within the Labour Party, new fissures had emerged following a decision by opposition leader Neil KINNOCK to press for unilateral nuclear disarmament—a position that fully a third of Labour supporters reportedly opposed—while heightened international visibility was anticipated from a forthcoming visit by the prime minister to Moscow (the first for a British cabinet head in 12 years). Possibly of greatest consequence, however, was the changed nature of the British polity. The historic polarization between privileged and working classes had been significantly disrupted by the "Thatcher revolution" based, in the words of a *New York Times* correspondent, on the suggestion that "market economics could democratize opportunity in a class-ridden nation and produce a more humane society than the traditional welfare mechanisms of the 'nanny state' ". While Labour bitterly denounced the Thatcher prescription as a "glorification of selfishness", it commanded widespread middle class appeal, while defining a new anchor point for the Conservatives at the center of the political spectrum.

Despite continued high unemployment, a deteriorating National Health Service, and opposition warnings of the "Americanization of Britain" (in part because of the prime minister's close ties to US President Reagan), the Conservatives obtained the second-highest majority since World War II at the June balloting. In large part, the outcome was interpreted as an endorsement of free-market "Thatcherism" (the government having sold a total of some $30 billion of state properties and enterprises to the private sector, with the nation's stockholders increasing from 2 to 8 million, during the prime minister's two previous terms.

POLITICAL PARTIES

Government Party:

Conservative Party. Although in opposition during 1964–1970 and 1974–1979, the Conservative Party (formally the Conservative and Unionist Party) has dominated British politics through most of this century, and returned to power by winning a comfortable majority in the House of Commons at the election of May 1979, with an improved showing in June 1983, when it won 397 of 650 seats. It retained power in June 1987, with a somewhat reduced majority of 375 seats.

Rooted in tradition, Conservative policies are generally congenial to business and the middle class, but also draw support from farmers and a segment of the working class. The party has suffered internal dissension, as exemplified by a right-wing movement formerly led by Enoch Powell, who renounced his parliamentary seat in February 1974 to support the Labour position on immigration and the EEC, and who was returned the following October as an Ulster Unionist. In February 1975 Margaret Thatcher, former secretary of state for education and science, was elected leader in the House of Commons, succeeding Edward Heath, under whom the Conservatives had lost three of the previous four elections. Following the party's return to power, a rift developed between moderate members (styled "wets") and those supporting Mrs. Thatcher's stringent monetary and economic policies, a number of the former being dismissed from government posts in a major cabinet reshuffle in September 1981. The party's 1983 campaign manifesto called, inter alia, for tough laws to curb illegal strikes and continued "privatization" of government-controlled industry. The emphasis in 1987 was on continued "positive reform" in areas such as sound fiscal management, control of inflation, greater financial independence for individuals, and improved health care.

Leaders: Margaret THATCHER (Prime Minister and Leader of the Party), Viscount WHITELAW (Deputy Leader), John WAKEHAM (Leader of the House of Commons), Lord BELSTEAD (Leader of the House of Lords), Sir Geoffrey HOWE (Foreign Minister), Norman TEBBIT (Chairman).

Opposition Parties:

Labour Party. An evolutionary socialist party in basic doctrine and tradition, the Labour Party has moved somewhat rightward in recent decades but continues to reflect the often conflicting views of trade unions, doctrinaire socialists, and intellectuals, while seeking to broaden its appeal to the middle classes and white-collar and managerial personnel. The trade unions, which constitute the basis of the party's organized political strength, have strongly opposed policies advanced by both Conservative and Labour governments to limit wage increases, and successfully resisted Labour government plans for legal restrictions on unofficial strikes in the spring of 1969. Minority criticism within the party also arose when the leadership failed to oppose US policy in Vietnam and when Prime Minister Wilson attempted to reach accommodation with the insurgent regime in Rhodesia. The party condemned the 1968 Soviet intervention in Czechoslovakia but has been unenthusiastic in supporting British participation in NATO and divided on the merits of British involvement in the European Communities. Present Labour policy supports further cuts in defense spending, government control of oil operations in the North Sea, and the importance of an unwritten "social contract", under which the unions will curtail inflationary wage demands in return for programs of greater social equity.

As a result of a series of resignations and defections, including the adherence of two former Labour MPs to a new Scottish Labour Party (below), the Labour government lost its parliamentary majority in 1976 and retained office only by concluding a legislative pact with the Liberals in early 1977. The agreement was terminated at the conclusion of the 1977–1978 session, and Labour went into opposition after the May 1979 election, at which it secured 268 seats in the House of Commons, as contrasted with 319 in 1974. Its representation declined further to 209 in 1983, but rose to 229 in 1987.

A major dilemma surfaced in 1980 when the party's conference at Blackpool on September 29–October 3 voted that designation of its leader should be by a partywide electoral college procedure, rather than by its parliamentary delegation, but failed to agree on how the voting should be weighted. As a result, Michael Foot was elected by the parliamentary group to succeed James Callaghan as party leader upon the latter's resignation on October 15. The procedural issue was seemingly resolved at a special party conference in January 1981 with a decision to award 40 percent of the voting strength to the trade unions and 30 percent each to the parliamentary and constituency parties. However, this was unacceptable to a number of parliamentary members, who subsequently withdrew to form the Social Democratic Party (see under Social and Liberal Democrats, below). The party's 1983 manifesto called for full nationalization of British Petroleum; cancellation of cruise and Pershing missile deployments, as well as the Trident submarine program; less restrictive immigration laws; and reversal of cutbacks in the National Health Service. The 1987 manifesto called for nuclear disarmament and efforts to reduce unemployment in a context of industrial modernization and expansion.

Leaders: Neil KINNOCK (Leader of the Party and of the Opposition), Roy HATTERSLEY (Deputy Leader), Stanley ORME (Chairman, Parliamentary Party), Lawrence WHITTY (General Secretary).

Co-operative Party. The Co-operative Party operates largely through some 200 affiliated cooperative societies throughout Britain. Under an agreement with the Labour Party, it cosponsors candidates at national, local, and European Parliament elections.

Leaders: B. HELLOWELL (Chairman), D. WISE (Secretary.)

Social and Liberal Democrats (SLD). The SLD was formed by merger of the former Liberal and Social Democratic parties, as approved at conferences of the two groups on January 23 and 31, 1988, respectively.

Reduced to a minority position by the rise of Labour after World War I, the Liberal Party continued to uphold the traditional values of European liberalism and sought, without notable success, to attract dissident elements in both of the main parties by its nonsocialist and reformist principles. Despite having won only 13 seats in the election of October 1974, the party embarked on a crucial role in March 1977 by entering into a parliamentary accord with Labour, thus, for the first time in nearly 50 years, permitting a major party to continue in office by means of third-party support. It returned to formal opposition at the beginning of the 1978–1979 session. In September 1982 the party voted to form an electoral alliance with the Social Democratic Party, which yielded an aggregate of only 23 parliamentary seats, despite a 25.4 percent share of the vote, at the election of June 1983. At the 1984 balloting the alliance won 23 seats with a 22.6 percent vote share.

The SDP was formally organized on March 26, 1981, as an outgrowth of a Council for Social Democracy that had been established under the joint leadership of Roy Jenkins, Dr. David Owen, William Rodgers, and Shirley Williams, all former Labour cabinet members who opposed the procedure for leadership selection adopted by the parent party two months earlier. Jenkins, a moderate who had headed the European Common Market from 1977 to 1981, also regarded Labour policy in a number of areas, including European unity and disarmament, as being extremist, while Owen sought to cast the new party in an essentially radical image. In July 1982 Jenkins defeated Owen for the SDP leadership in a mail ballot of some 65,000 adherents. Subsequently, in the SDP/Liberal electoral alliance, Liberal leader David Steel agreed to serve under Jenkins should the coalition succeed in defeating the two leading contenders at the next election. While impressing observers with its showing in a series of by-elections in 1981–1982, the SDP appeared to founder in the wake of Prime Minister Thatcher's handling of the Falklands crisis. The party disappointed supporters by securing only six of the 23 seats won by the alliance in 1983, Owen succeeding Jenkins as party leader on June 15. Objecting strenuously to the proposed merger with the Liberals, Owen resigned from the leadership in August 1987 and in February 1988 announced that he would participate in the formation of a "new" SDP.

Leaders: Robert MACLENNAN and David STEEL (Joint Interim Leaders).

Ulster Unionists. The bulk of the Northern Ireland delegation to Parliament consists of Unionists, who are committed to the maintenance of Ulster's tie with Great Britain and continued separation from the Irish Republic. Following the establishment of a coalition government for Northern Ireland on December 31, 1973, the Unionist Party split into several factions, of which three are presently represented in the House of Commons. (For other Ulster parties, see separate section on Northern Ireland.)

Leaders: James MOLYNEAUX (Official Unionist), Rev. Ian PAISLEY (Democratic Unionist), James KILFEDDER (Ulster Popular Unionist).

Scottish National Party (SNP). The SNP advocates home rule "as a step toward Scottish independence", its 1987 manifesto calling for an independent Scottish parliament elected by proportional representation. At the 1979 election, it lost nine of its eleven seats, the two remaining being retained in 1983 and augmented to three in 1987.

Leaders: Gordon WILSON (Chairman), Donald STEWART (President), John SWINNEY (National Secretary).

Welsh Nationalist Party (*Plaid Cymru*). Founded in 1925, the *Plaid Cymru* (literally "Party of Wales") seeks greater autonomy for Wales within the United Kingdom. In May 1987 it entered into a parliamentary alliance with the SNP to work for constitutional, economic, and social reform in both regions. It elected two MPs in 1983 and three in 1987.

Leaders: Dafydd Elis THOMAS (President), Dafydd WILLIAMS (Secretary).

National Front. The National Front was organized in 1967 by merger of a number of radical groups of the extreme Right. Descended from the interwar British Union of Fascists, the Front has exploited White anxieties stemming from the postwar influx of Asian and African immigrants, urging that they be deported to their countries of birth. During 1977 the organization became increasingly involved in acts of violence in non-White urban areas, including clashes with left-wing demonstrators in London and Birmingham. Although unrepresented in Parliament, the Front has won a number of city council seats in racially mixed neighborhoods.

Leader: Nick GRIFFIN (Chairman).

National Party (NP). The NP was formed in 1974 by a moderate National Front faction that was ousted after having temporarily taken over the leadership of the parent party.

Leader: John Kingsley READ (Chairman).

Green Party. Organized in 1973 as the Ecology Party, the Greens adopted their present name in 1985. The party addresses itself to human rights issues in addition to problems affecting the environment. It obtained less than 0.3 percent of the vote in 1987, winning no parliamentary representation.

Leaders: Brig OUBRIDGE, Jo ROBBINS, Lindy WILLIAMS (Co-Chairpersons); Gundula DOREY (Secretary).

Communist Party of Great Britain. Numerically and practically insignificant in national politics, the Communist Party holds no seats in the Commons and has lost much strength even in its few trade-union strongholds. It adopted an essentially Eurocommunist posture in May 1985, following an intense 18-month internal struggle.

Leader: Gordon McLENNAN (General Secretary).

Socialist Party of Great Britain (SPGB). The SPGB is a small Marxist party originally founded in 1904.

Leader: A. ATKINSON (General Secretary).

Socialist Workers' Party (SWP). The SWP, a Trotskyite organization, has occasionally been involved in street clashes with the National Front.

Leader: Duncan HALLAS (Chairman).

Workers' Revolutionary Party (WRP). The WRP is a Trotskyite formation that is active in the automobile, mining, and theatre industries. A splinter group, including the actress Vanessa Redgrave, that opposed cooperation with other left-wing groups, was expelled in October 1985.

Leader: Mike BANDA (General Secretary).

LEGISLATURE

The **Parliament** of the United Kingdom serves as legislative authority for the entire Kingdom. Meeting at Westminster (London) with the queen as its titular head, it consists of a partly hereditary, partly appointed House of Lords and an elected House of Commons, which is the real locus of power. (Until March 1972, Northern Ireland had a separate bicameral legislature whose competence was limited to local matters; for subsequent developments, see following article.)

House of Lords. The House of Lords consists of approximately 1,100 members, of whom about four-fifths are hereditary peers, either by succession or of first creation. The remaining members include the 24 senior bishops of the Church of England, serving and retired Lords of Appeal in Ordinary (who constitute the nation's highest body of civil and criminal appeal), and other life peers. Since passage of the 1963 Peerage Act, all Scottish peers (instead of the former representative group of 16) and all peeresses in their own right may claim seats in the House; in addition, hereditary peerages may be disclaimed for the lifetimes of the holders, thus permitting them to stand for election to the House of Commons.

Despite its size, only about 200–300 members of the Lords attend sessions with any degree of regularity. Under a Labour government proposal advanced in 1968, hereditary peers would have been gradually eliminated in favor of created peers divided into voting and nonvoting members, depending on their willingness to engage fully in the work of the House. The proposal was ultimately withdrawn because of back-bench resistance; in any event, it would have had little practical effect on parliamentary procedure, since the upper chamber has been precluded since 1911 from vetoing money bills and was restricted in 1949 to a suspensive veto of one year on all other bills.

Lord Chancellor: Lord MACKAY.

House of Commons. As of 1988, the House of Commons consisted of 650 members directly elected from single-member constituencies for terms of five years, subject to dissolution. The strength of the parties, exclusive of the speaker, following the election of June 11, 1987, was as follows (the distribution after the previous general election on June 9, 1983, being given in parentheses): Conservative Party, 375 (396); Labour Party, 229 (209); Liberal/Social Democratic Alliance, 22 (23), encompassing Liberal Party, 17 (17) and Social Democratic Party, 5 (6); Ulster Unionists, 13 (15), encompassing Official Unionist Party, 9 (11), Democratic Unionist Party, 3 (3), Ulster Popular Unionist Party, 1 (1); Scottish National Party, 3 (2); Welsh Nationalist Party, 3 (2); Ulster Social Democratic and Labour Party, 3 (1); *Sinn Féin*, 1 (1).

Speaker: Bernard WEATHERILL.

CABINET

Prime Minister and First Lord of the Treasury	Margaret Thatcher
Secretaries of State	
Defense	George Younger
Education and Science	Kenneth Baker
Employment	Norman Fowler
Energy	Cecil Parkinson
Environment	Nicholas Ridley
Foreign and Commonwealth Affairs	Sir Geoffrey Howe
Home Department	Douglas Hurd
Northern Ireland	Thomas King
Scotland	Malcolm Leslie Rifkind
Social Services	Norman Fowler
Trade and Industry	Lord Young
Transport	Paul Channon
Wales	Peter Walker
Minister of Agriculture, Fisheries and Food	John McGregor
Chancellor of the Duchy of Lancaster	Kenneth Clarke
Chancellor of the Exchequer	Nigel Lawson
Chief Secretary to the Treasury	John Major
Lord Chancellor	Lord MacKay
Lord President of the Council and Leader of the House of Commons	John Wakeham
Lord Privy Seal and Leader of the House of Lords	Lord Belstead
Paymaster General	Peter Brooke
Governor, Bank of England	Robert Leigh-Pemberton

NEWS MEDIA

Freedom combined with responsibility represents the British ideal in the handling of news and opinion, as developed first in the press and later extended to radio and television. The press, while privately owned and free from censorship, is subject to strict libel laws and is often made aware of government preferences with regard to the handling of news reports. Responsibility for the oversight and management of radio and television is vested in autonomous public bodies.

Press. Per capita consumption of newspapers in the United Kingdom, once the highest in the world, has fallen off substantially in recent years but is still close to 30 issues per 100 inhabitants. During 1980, faced with mounting costs and continuing labor problems, the principal shareholder in the Times Newspapers announced that *The Times, The Sunday Times,* and a number of related organs would cease publication in early 1981 if new owners could not be found, while publication of *The Observer* and the *Financial Times* was interrupted and the *Evening News* and *Evening Standard* merged. In February 1981 the *Times* group was sold to News International, a UK subsidiary of the Australian-based News, Ltd., controlled by Rupert Murdoch. Subsequently, the unions and management engaged in a prolonged and bitter controversy over the introduction of labor-saving printing equipment, in the course of which Murdoch discharged some 5,500 striking unionists and moved his printing operation to the London suburb of Wapping, which during 1986 was the scene of much labor violence. Other publishers also left Fleet Street prior to abandonment of the work action (made difficult by tough labor legislation introduced by the Thatcher government) in February 1987. Meanwhile, a number of new papers were launched, including *Today* in March 1986 and the more immediately successful *Independent* in October, while virtually all moved to take advantage of the new computer-based technology. One of the most successful among the "quality" papers has been the *Telegraph,* which under new ownership has defied British press tradition by refusing to participate in the "lobby", a self-regulated club of parliamentary correspondents who are given daily government news briefings on condition that the source not be identified.

The following papers (circulation figures for 1987) are dailies and, in the case of England, are published at London, unless otherwise indicated:

England: *News of the World* (4,942,000), Sunday, sensationalist; *The Sun* (3,993,000), sensationalist; *Daily Mirror* (3,121,500), pro-Labour; *Sunday Mirror* (3,018,900), pro-Labour; *The Sunday People* (2,932,500), independent; *Sunday Express* (2,214,600), independent; *Daily Mail* (1,759,500), independent; *Daily Express* (1,697,200), pro-Conservative; *The Mail on Sunday* (1,688,000); *The Star* (1,288,600); *The Sunday Times* (1,220,000), independent; *Daily Telegraph* (1,147,000), Conservative; *The Observer* (773,500), Sunday, independent; *Sunday Telegraph* (720,900), Conservative; *London Standard* (522,400), Conservative, launched in 1980 by merger of *Evening News* and *Evening Standard; The Guardian* (London and Manchester, 493,600), independent; *The Times* (442,400), founded 1785, moderate Conservative; *Today* (307,300), independent; *The Independent* (292,700); *Financial Times* (279,800), independent; *Birmingham Evening Mail* (Birmingham, 275,000), independent; *Liverpool Daily Post* (Liverpool, 72,000), independent; *The Journal* (Newcastle, 66,000), independent.

Wales: *South Wales Echo* (Cardiff, 103,100), independent; *Western Mail* (Cardiff, 81,100), independent.

Scotland: *Sunday Post* (Glasgow, 1,510,000); *Daily Record* (Glasgow, 759,000), independent; *Scottish Daily Express* (Glasgow, 215,000); *Evening Times* (Glasgow, 192,600); *Courier and Advertiser* (Dundee, 128,000); *Evening News* (Edinburgh, 127,700); *Glasgow Herald* (Glasgow, 122,200), independent; *The Press and Journal* (Aberdeen, 110,800), independent; *The Scotsman* (Edinburgh, 98,900), independent.

Northern Ireland: (see next article).

News agencies. Britain boasts the world's oldest news agency, Reuters, founded by the pioneer German newsgatherer Paul von Reuter, who established his headquarters at London in 1851. The company is now a worldwide service controlled by press interests in Britain, Australia, and New Zealand, which in May 1984 made a public tender of a portion of their holdings. The other leading agencies are the Associated Press, Ltd., a British subsidiary of the Associated Press of the United States; the Exchange Telegraph Co., Ltd.; the Press Association, Ltd., founded in 1868; and the United Press International (U.K.), Ltd., a British subsidiary of the United Press International.

Radio and television. Broadcasting services are provided by the semi-official British Broadcasting Corporation (BBC), founded in 1922, and by the Independent Broadcasting Authority (IBA), organized as a public corporation in 1954. The BBC, which is financed by license fees, operates two color television services (BBC-1 and BBC-2) and four domestic radio services. The IBA, which is supported by paid advertising, offers television services through a variety of program contractors and began independent radio operations in 1973; in 1980 it was authorized to initiate a "fourth channel" on condition that a suitable proportion of its transmissions in Wales be in Welsh and that broadcasts elsewhere be in the form of "national service" provided otherwise than by independent contractors. Both organizations are subject to government control but are independent in the conduct of their daily programming. There were approximately 63.7 million radio and 18.8 million television receivers in 1987.

INTERGOVERNMENTAL REPRESENTATION

Ambassador to the US: Sir Antony ACLAND.

US Ambassador to the UK: Charles H. PRICE II.

Permanent Representative to the UN: Sir Crispin TICKELL.

IGO Memberships (Non-UN): ADB, ADF, AfDB, BIS, CCC, CDB, CERN, CEUR, CP, CWTH, EC, EIB, ESA, Eurocontrol, G10, IADB, ICAC, ICCO, ICES, ICO, IEA, ILZ, Inmarsat, INRO, Intelsat, Interpol, IOOC, ISO, ITC, IWC, IWSG, IWTC, NATO, OECD, PCA, SPC, WEU.

RELATED TERRITORIES

All major, and many minor, territories of the former British Empire have achieved full independence in the course of the last century, and most are now members of the Commonwealth, a voluntary association of states held together primarily by a common political and constitutional heritage (see "The Commonwealth" in Intergovernmental Organizations section). In conventional usage, the term Commonwealth also includes the territories and dependencies of the United Kingdom and other Commonwealth member countries. As of 1987, the United Kingdom itself retained a measure of responsibility, direct or indirect, for 17 political entities linked to Britain through a variety of constitutional and diplomatic arrangements. These territories include 3 Crown Fiefdoms, 12 Colonies, and 2 essentially uninhabited territories.

Crown Fiefdoms:

Though closely related to Great Britain both historically and geographically, the Channel Islands and the Isle of Man are distinct from the United Kingdom and are under the jurisdiction of the sovereign rather than the state.

Channel Islands. Located in the English Channel off the northwest coast of France, the Channel Islands have been attached to the British Crown since the Norman Conquest. The nine islands have a total area of 75 square miles (194 sq. km.) and a population (1986E) of 139,000. The two largest and most important are Jersey and Guernsey, each of which has its own parliament but is linked to the British Crown through a representative who serves as lieutenant governor and commander in chief. St. Helier on Jersey and St. Peter Port on Guernsey are the principal towns. The small islands of Alderney, Sark, Herm, and Jethou have their own constitutional arrangements but are usually classified as dependencies of Guernsey. Because of their mild climate and insular location, the islands

are popular tourist resorts, and their low tax rate has attracted many permanent residents from the UK.

Lieutenant Governor and Commander in Chief of Jersey: Adm. Sir William PILLAR.

Bailiff of Jersey and President of the States: Sir Peter J. CRILL.

Lieutenant Governor and Commander in Chief of Guernsey and its Dependencies: Lt. Gen. Sir Alexander BOSWELL.

Bailiff of Guernsey and President of the States: Sir Charles FROSSARD.

Isle of Man. Located in the Irish Sea midway between Northern Ireland and northern England, the Isle of Man has been historically connected to Great Britain for almost 400 years but remains politically distinct. It has an area of 227 square miles (588 sq. km.) and a population (1986C) of 64,282. The principal town is Douglas, with a population of 20,370. The island's self-governing institutions include the Tynwald, a parliamentary body consisting of a 12-member Legislative Council and a 24-member House of Keys (which for most matters sit together), and an Executive Council comprising two members of the Legislative Council and five members of the House. There is a Crown-appointed lieutenant governor, who is a member of the Legislative Council. The island levies its own taxes and has a special relationship with the European Community (EC).

Lieutenant Governor: Maj. Gen. Laurence A.W. NEW.

Chief Minister: M.R. WALKER.

Colonies:

The territories described below remain directly subordinate to the United Kingdom although a number of them enjoy almost complete autonomy in internal affairs.

Anguilla. One of the most northern of the Caribbean's Leeward Islands (see map, p. 22), Anguilla was first settled by the British in 1632 and became part of the Territory of the Leeward Islands in 1956. Following establishment of the Associated State of St. Kitts-Nevis-Anguilla in early 1967, the Anguillans repudiated government from Basseterre, and a British commissioner was installed following a landing by British security forces. The island was subsequently placed under the direct administration of Britain, while a separate constitution that was provided in February 1976 gave the resident commissioner (subsequently governor) authority over foreign affairs, defense, civil service, and internal security, all other functions being the responsibility of a seven-member House of Assembly. An act of December 1980 formally confirmed the dependent status of the territory, which also encompasses the neighboring island of Sombrero.

Anguilla has a land area of 35 square miles (91 sq. km.), exclusive of Sombrero's 2 square miles (5 sq. km.), and a resident population (1984E) of 7,019. A leading source of income is provided by remittances from some 2,000 Anguillans living overseas. The island has no clearly defined capital, apart from a centrally located sector known as The Valley.

Governor: G.O. WHITTAKER.

Chief Minister: Emile R. GUMBS.

Bermuda. A British Crown Colony since 1684, Bermuda consists of 150 islands and islets in the western Atlantic and is largely devoid of economic resources other than its tourist potential. It has a total land area of 21 square miles (53 sq. km.) and a population (1987E) of 58,100, concentrated on some 20 islands. Blacks make up approximately 60 percent of the total population. The capital is Hamilton, with a population of approximately 1,700. Under a constitution approved in mid-1967 (amended, in certain particulars, in 1979), Bermuda was granted a system of internal self-government whereby the Crown-appointed governor exercises responsibility for external affairs, defense, internal security, and police, while the premier and cabinet, though appointed by the governor, are responsible to a popularly elected 40-member House of Assembly for all internal matters. The 11 members of the upper house, or Senate, are likewise appointed by the governor, in part on the advice of the premier and the leader of the opposition. The first general election under the new constitution, held in May 1968 against a background of Black rioting, resulted in a decisive victory for the moderately right-wing, multiracial **United Bermuda Party** (UBP), whose leader, Sir Henry TUCKER, became the Colony's first premier. The left-wing **Progressive Labour Party** (PLP), led by Walter ROBINSON and mainly Black in membership, had campaigned for independence and an end to British rule, and its unexpectedly poor showing was generally interpreted as a popular endorsement of the existing constitutional arrangements. At the most recent election of

October 29, 1985, the UBP returned 26 members to the House of Assembly, while the PLP returned 7 and the fledgling National Liberal Party (NLP), 2.

Governor: Viscount DUNROSSIL.
Premier: John W. SWAN.

British Indian Ocean Territory. At the time of its establishment in 1965, the British Indian Ocean Territory consisted of the Chagos Archipelago, which had previously been a dependency of Mauritius, and the islands of Aldabra, Farquhar, and Desroches, which had traditionally been administered from the Seychelles. The Territory was created to make defense facilities available to the British and US governments and was legally construed as being uninhabited, although a transient population was relocated to Mauritius from Diego Garcia in the Chagos group to make way for the construction of US air and naval installations. Upon the granting of independence to the Seychelles in June 1976, arrangements were made for the reversion of Aldabra, Farquhar, and Desroches, the Territory thenceforth to consist only of the Chagos Archipelago, with its administration taken over by the Foreign and Commonwealth Office. The total land area of the archipelago, which stretches over some 21,000 square miles of the central Indian Ocean, is 20 square miles (52 sq. km.).

Commissioner: William MARSDEN (resident in United Kingdom).
Administrator: Clive STITT (resident in United Kingdom).

British Virgin Islands. A Caribbean group of 36 northern Leeward Islands located some 60 miles east of Puerto Rico, the British Virgin Islands have a total area of 59 square miles (153 sq. km.) and a population (1987E) of 12,226. The largest island, Tortola, is the site of the chief town and port of entry, Road Town. The administration is headed by a governor. Representative institutions include a largely elected Legislative Council and an appointed Executive Council. A chief minister is chosen from the legislature by the governor. The islands, which have strong ties with the adjacent US Virgin Islands, declined to become one of the West Indies Associated States. At the most recent election of September 30, 1986, the Virgin Islands Party (VIP) won 5 of 9 Council seats, ousting the administration headed by independent member Cyril B. ROMNEY, who had been involved with a company undergoing investigation for money-laundering activities.

Governor: John Mark Ambrose HERDMAN.
Chief Minister: H. Lavity STOUTT.

Cayman Islands. Located in the Caribbean, northwest of Jamaica, the Caymans (Grand Cayman, Little Cayman, and Cayman Brac) cover 100 square miles (259 sq. km.) and have a population (1987E) of 22,700. George Town, on Grand Cayman, is the capital. Previously governed from Jamaica, the Caymans were placed in 1962 under a British administrator (later governor), who is assisted by an Executive Council and a largely elected Legislative Assembly, over which he presides. The traditional occupations of seafaring and turtle and shark fishing have largely been superseded by tourism and other services, and the islands have recently become a significant offshore banking center and corporate tax haven. By 1980, some 325 banks and 12,000 companies were registered in the Caymans and in July 1986 the government agreed to extend a 1984 agreement with the United States providing for the exchange of information on illegal drug and money-laundering activities.

Governor and President of Executive Council: Alan James SCOTT.

Falkland Islands. Situated some 480 miles northeast of Cape Horn in the South Atlantic (see map, p. 26), the Falkland Islands Colony currently encompasses the East and West Falklands in addition to some 200 smaller islands; the South Georgia and the South Sandwich islands (below) ceased to be governed as dependencies of the Falklands in October 1985. The total area is 4,700 square miles (12,173 sq. km.) and the resident population, almost entirely of British extraction, is 1,919 (1986C). The economy, traditionally dependent on wool production, has suffered from a declining export market in recent years. Stanley, on East Falkland Island, is the chief town. The governor is also the high commissioner of the South Georgia and South Sandwich islands and of the British Antarctic Territory. Under a constitution introduced in 1964, he is assisted by Executive and Legislative councils. The separate post of chief executive (responsible to the governor) was created in 1983.

The Colony is the object of a long-standing dispute between Britain and Argentina, which calls it the Malvinas Islands (*Islas Malvinas*). Argentina's claim to sovereignty is based primarily on purchase of the islands by Spain from France in 1766; Britain claims sovereignty on the basis of a 1771 treaty, although uninterrupted possession commenced only in

1833. The Argentine claim has won some support in the UN General Assembly, and the two governments engaged in a lengthy series of inconclusive talks on the future disposition of the territory prior to the Argentine invasion of April 2, 1982, and the eventual reassertion of British control ten weeks later (see Foreign relations, above). The issue is complicated by evidence that large-scale oil and gas deposits may lie beneath the islands' territorial waters. In addition, Britain has taken the position that any solution must respect the wishes of the inhabitants, who were described in an official 1976 report as being "generally dispirited and divided" except in their desire to remain British. Thus, a revised basic law, promulgated in 1985, refers explicitly to the islanders' right of self-determination.

In the wake of the 1982 war, Britain imposed a 150-mile protective zone, measured from the islands' center. In October 1986 it added a 200-mile economic zone, effective February 1, 1987, overlapping a similar zone declared by Argentina off its continental mainland. There were indications, however, that British authorities would not attempt to police the area beyond the 150-mile limit, thus averting direct conflict between fisheries protection vessels of the two governments.

In March 1988 military maneuvers termed "Operation Fire Focus" were held to test Britain's rapid deployment strategy for defending the islands, drawing protests from several Latin governments and an Argentine "defensive" alert.

Governor: Gordon Wesley JEWKES.
Chief Executive: Brian CUMMINGS.

Gibraltar. The Crown Colony of Gibraltar, a rocky promontory at the western mouth of the Mediterranean, was captured by the British in 1704 and ceded by Spain to the United Kingdom by the Treaty of Utrecht in 1713. The Colony has an area of 2.5 square miles (6.5 sq. km.), and its population numbers 28,900 (1987E), of whom about 20,000 are native Gibraltarians. The economy is supported mainly by expenditures in support of its air and naval facilities. British authority is represented by a governor. Substantial self-government was introduced in 1964 and further extended by a new constitution, introduced May 30, 1969, that provided for an elected 15-member House of Assembly.

Gibraltar has been the subject of a lengthy dispute between Britain and Spain, which has pressed in the United Nations and elsewhere for "decolonization" of the territory and has impeded access to it by land and air. A referendum conducted by the British on September 10, 1967, showed an overwhelming preference for continuation of British rule, but Spain rejected the results and declared the referendum invalid. Spain's position was subsequently upheld by the UN General Assembly, which called in December 1968 for the ending of British administration by October 1, 1969. A month after promulgation of the 1969 constitution, which guarantees that the Gibraltarians will never have to accept Spanish rule unless the majority so desires, Spain closed its land frontier with the Colony. In January 1978 Spain agreed to the restoration of telephone links to the city, while discussions between British and Spanish representatives at London in April 1980 yielded an agreement to reopen the border to Spanish transients and British residents by midyear. However, the action was delayed until December 14, 1982, partly because of problems regarding the status of Spanish workers in the Colony. The border was fully reopened in February 1985, following an agreement in November to provide equality of rights for Spaniards in Gibraltar and Gibraltarians in Spain; in addition, Britain agreed, for the first time, to enter into discussions on the sovereignty issue, although Prime Minister Thatcher responded to an April 1986 appeal from Spain's King Juan Carlos by reaffirming her government's commitment to abide by the wishes of the colony's inhabitants.

At the most recent election of March 25, 1988, the Gibraltar Socialist Labour Party won a bare majority of eight legislative seats, its leader, Joe Bossano, becoming chief minister. Upon assuming office Bossano declared that most of the residents opposed the 1984 accord with Spain. Earlier, in December 1987, the Assembly had rejected a UK-Spanish agreement on cooperative administration (particularly in regard to customs and immigration procedure) of the Colony's airport. Quite apart from the impact of exclusive British control on the sovereignty issue, Spain has argued that the isthmus to the mainland (on which the airport is located) was not covered by the 1713 treaty.

Governor: Air Chief Mar. Sir Peter TERRY.
Chief Minister: Joe BOSSANO.

Hong Kong. The Crown Colony of Hong Kong, situated on China's southeastern coast, consists of (1) Hong Kong Island and Kowloon Peninsula, both ceded by China to Great Britain "in perpetuity" in the mid-nineteenth century, and (2) the mainland area of the New Territories, leased for 99 years in 1898. The total area of the Colony is 410 square miles (1,062 sq. km.), the New Territories alone occupying 365 square miles. The population, concentrated on Hong Kong Island and Kowloon, is 5,542,000 (1987E), of which 98 percent is Chinese and nearly one-quarter is from the People's Republic of China. The capital is Victoria, on Hong Kong Island. The economy is based primarily on exported industrial products, especially cotton textiles, and has maintained its viability, despite rising production costs, largely because of a consistently favorable balance of trade.

Responding to mounting indications of uneasiness on the part of the business community, Britain and China embarked in October 1982 on talks at the diplomatic level on transition to a reassumption of Chinese sovereignty. The talks yielded the initialing on September 26, 1984, of a "Sino-British Declaration of the Question of Hong Kong". Under the slogan "one country and two systems", China will regain title to the entire area in 1997, when the lease of the New Territories expires, while agreeing to maintain the enclave as a capitalist "Special Administrative Region" for 50 years thereafter.

The Colony's constitution provides for a governor who presides over Executive and Legislative councils, the latter currently consisting of 56 members, of whom 12 are elected by regional and local governing units, 12 are designated by "functional constituencies", 22 are appointed by the governor, and 10 are government officials.

Governor and President of Executive Council: Sir David WILSON.

Montserrat. A West Indian dependency in the Leeward Island group (see map, p. 22) with an area of 38 square miles (98 sq. km.), Montserrat has a population (1987E) of 11,900. Its chief town is Plymouth and its principal exports are Sea Island cotton, fruits, and vegetables. Ministerial government was introduced in 1960, and the Colony is controlled by an appointed Executive Council presided over by a governor. The Legislative Council is largely elected. Montserrat was a member of the former West Indies Federation but chose not to become one of the West Indies Associated States. It is a member of the Caribbean Community and Common Market.

Governor: Christopher J. TURNER.
Chief Minister: John A. OSBORNE.

Pitcairn Islands. Isolated in the eastern South Pacific and known primarily for its connection with the *Bounty* mutineers, Pitcairn has been a British possession since 1838. Juridically encompassing the adjacent islands of Ducie, Henderson, and Oeno, the dependency has a total area of 1.75 square miles (4.53 sq. km.) and a declining population, which in 1983 totaled 59 persons. The British high commissioner to New Zealand serves as governor. Locally, the island is administered by an Island Council consisting of four elected island officers, an island secretary, and five nominated members.

Governor: Terence D. O'LEARY (resident in New Zealand).
Island Magistrate: Brian YOUNG.

St. Helena. St. Helena and its dependencies, Ascension Island and the Tristan da Cunha island group, occupy widely scattered positions in the South Atlantic between the west coast of Africa and the southern tip of South America. St. Helena, the seat of government, has an area of 47 square miles (122 sq. km.) and a population (1985E) of 6,258. Its principal settlement is Jamestown. The Colony is administered by a governor, who is assisted by an Executive Council, and by a Legislative Council introduced in January 1967.

Governor: Francis E. BAKER.

Ascension Island. Encompassing an area of 34 square miles (88 sq. km.) and with a 1985 population (excluding British military personnel) of 1,196, Ascension Island was annexed to St. Helena in 1922 and is presently the site of a BBC relay station, a US space-tracking station, and a major sea-turtle hatching ground.

Administrator: M.T. BLICK.

Tristan da Cunha. Tristan da Cunha has an area of 40 square miles (104 sq. km.) and a population (1985) of 313. The island's entire population was evacuated when the main volcanic island erupted in 1961, but was returned in 1963.

Administrator: R. PERRY.

Turks and Caicos Islands. The Turks and Caicos Islands, a southeastward extension of the Bahamas, consists of 30 small cays (6 of which are inhabited) with a total area of 166 square miles (430 sq. km.) and a population (1980C) of 7,413. The capital is at Grand Turk. Linked to Britain since 1766, the Turks and Caicos became a Crown Colony in 1962 following Jamaica's independence. A constitution adopted in 1976 provides for a governor, an eight-member Executive Council, and a Legislative Council of eleven elected, four ex-officio, and three nominated members. The former chief minister, Norman B. SAUNDERS, was obliged to resign after his arrest on drug trafficking charges at Miami, Florida, in March 1985, Deputy Chief Minister Nathaniel J.S. FRANCIS being elected as his successor on March 28. Francis was also forced to resign following the issuance of a commission of inquiry report on arson, corruption, and related matters, the British government deciding on July 25, 1986, to impose direct rule under the governor, with assistance from a four-member advisory council. Subsequently, a three-member constitutional commission was appointed to draft revisions in the basic law to inhibit corruption and patronage and promote "fair and effective administration". At an election marking the islands' return to constitutional rule on March 3, 1988, the People's Democratic Movement, previously in opposition, won all but two Legislative Council seats.

Governor: Michael J. BRADLEY.
Chief Minister: Oswald SKIPPINGS.

Uninhabited Territories:

South Georgia and the South Sandwich Islands. South Georgia is an island of 1,387 square miles (3,592 sq. km.) situated approximately 800 miles east-south-east of the Falklands; it was inhabited only by a British Antarctic Survey team at the time of brief occupation by Argentine forces in April 1982. The South Sandwich Islands lie about 470 miles southeast of South Georgia and were uninhabited until occupied by a group of alleged Argentine scientists in December 1976, who were forced to leave in June 1982. Formerly considered dependencies of the Falklands, the islands were given separate status in October 1985.

Commissioner: Gordon Wesley JEWKES (resident in the Falkland Islands).

British Antarctic Territory. Formerly the southern portion of the Falkland Islands Dependencies, the British Antarctic Territory was separately established in 1962. Encompassing that portion of Antarctica between 20 degrees and 80 degrees West Longitude, it includes the South Shetland and South Orkney islands as well as the Antarctic Peninsula (see map, p. 19). Sovereignty over the greater portion of the Territory is disputed by Great Britain, Argentina, and Chile, and its legal status remains in suspense in conformity with the Antarctic Treaty of December 1, 1959. The responsible British authority is a high commissioner, who is also governor of the Falkland Islands.

High Commissioner: Gordon Wesley JEWKES (resident in the Falkland Islands).

UNITED KINGDOM: NORTHERN IRELAND

Political Status: Autonomous province of the United Kingdom under separate parliamentary regime established in 1921 but suspended March 30, 1972; coalition executive formed January 1, 1974; direct rule reimposed May 28, 1974; consultative Northern Ireland Assembly elected October 20, 1982; consultative role for the Republic of Ireland established in Dublin-London agreement of November 15, 1985; Assembly dissolved by United Kingdom June 19, 1986.

Area: 5,452 sq. mi. (14,120 sq. km.).

Population: 1,562,157 (1981C), 1,609,000 (1988E).

Major Urban Center (1985E): BELFAST (301,600).

Official Language: English.

Government: Direct rule under UK Secretary of State for Northern Ireland (currently Thomas KING) reimposed following resignation of Brian FAULKNER as Chief Executive and collapse of coalition regime on May 28, 1974.

THE COUNTRY

Geographically an integral part of Ireland, the six northern Irish counties (collectively known as "Ulster") are politically included within the United Kingdom for reasons rooted in the ethnic and religious divisions introduced into Ireland by English and Scottish settlement in the seventeenth century. As a result of this colonization effort, which set the pattern of Northern Ireland's still partly agrarian economy, the long-established Roman Catholic population of the northern counties came to be heavily outnumbered by adherents of Protestant denominations, who assumed a dominant political, social, and economic position and insisted upon continued association of the territory with the United Kingdom when the rest of Ireland became independent after World War I. Roman Catholics, while strongly represented throughout Northern Ireland and particularly in the city of Londonderry, constitute only about one-third of the total population. Catholic complaints of discrimination, especially in regard to the allocation of housing and jobs and to limitation of the franchise in local elections, were the immediate cause of the serious disturbances that commenced in Northern Ireland during 1968–1969.

GOVERNMENT AND POLITICS

Political background. Governed as an integral part of the United Kingdom throughout the nineteenth and twentieth centuries, Northern Ireland acquired autonomous status in 1921 as part of a general readjustment necessitated by the success of the Irish independence movement in the rest of Ireland. The Government of Ireland Act of 1920 provided for a division of Ireland as a whole into separate northern and southern sections, each with its own legislature plus a continuing right of representation in the British Parliament at Westminster. This arrangement was rejected by the Irish nationalist authorities in Dublin but was reluctantly accepted in Northern Ireland as the best available alternative to continuing as an integral part of the United Kingdom. The new government of Northern Ireland was dominated from the beginning by the pro-British, Protestant interests controlling the Ulster Unionist Party (UUP). Ties with Britain were sedulously maintained, both for religious and historic reasons and because of accompanying economic benefits, including social services and agricultural subsidies. Opposition sentiment in favor of union with the Irish Republic represented a continuing but long-subdued source of tension.

Catholic-led "civil rights" demonstrations against political and social discrimination erupted during 1968, evoking counterdemonstrations by Protestant extremists and lead-

ing to increasingly serious disorders, particularly in Londonderry. In November 1968 the government of Prime Minister Terence O'NEILL proposed a number of reform measures that failed to halt the disturbances and occasioned a lessening of support for the prime minister within his own government and party. Parliament was accordingly dissolved, with a new election in February 1969 producing the usual Unionist majority but failing to resolve the internal Unionist Party conflict. In April mounting disorders and acts of sabotage led the Northern Ireland government to request that British army units be assigned to guard key installations. Although O'Neill persuaded the Unionist Parliamentary Party to accept the principle of universal adult franchise at the next local government elections, he resigned as party leader on April 28 and as prime minister three days later. His successor in both offices was Maj. James D. CHICHESTER-CLARK, an advocate of moderate reform who was chosen by a 17–16 vote of the Unionist Parliamentary Party over Brian FAULKNER, an opponent of the O'Neill reform program who nevertheless was given a seat in the new cabinet. The government promptly announced an amnesty for all persons involved in the recent disturbances and received a unanimous vote of confidence on May 7.

Renewed rioting at Belfast, Londonderry, and elsewhere during the first half of August exacted a toll of 8 killed and 758 wounded before order was restored. Following a meeting at London with Prime Minister Wilson, Chichester-Clark agreed on August 19 that all security forces in Northern Ireland would be placed under British command, that Britain would assume ultimate responsibility for security, and that steps would be taken to ensure equal treatment of all citizens in Northern Ireland in regard to voting rights, housing, and other issues.

Opinions differ as to responsibility for the increasingly violent character of the struggle that developed after 1969, when Protestant incursions into Catholic communities necessitated a far more widespread deployment of British army units. To a large extent, the initiative has clearly lain with the illegal Provisional Irish Republican Army (see Provisional IRA under Political Parties and Groups, below, and *Sinn Féin* under Political Parties in Ireland article), whose sustained campaign of bombing has avowedly been aimed at forcing the full withdrawal of Britain, although "loyalist" paramilitary organizations have also engaged in terrorist acts. The situation in the strife-torn province turned sharply worse on "Bloody Sunday", January 30, 1972, when a prohibited Catholic civil-rights march at Londonderry was infiltrated by hooligan elements and 13 civilians were killed in clashes with British troops. A wave of violence and hysteria followed, but Prime Minister Brian Faulkner, who had succeeded Chichester-Clark on March 23, 1971, and the Northern Ireland government turned a deaf ear to London's increasingly insistent demands that the responsibility for maintaining law and order in Northern Ireland be formally transferred to the United Kingdom. Unable to act in agreement with the Belfast regime, British Prime Minister Heath decided to remove it from power and reimpose direct rule. On March 24, 1972, he announced that all legislative and executive powers vested in the Northern Ireland Parliament and government were to be transferred to the United Kingdom until a political solution to the problems of the province could be worked out in consultation with all concerned. William (subsequently Viscount) WHITELAW, a leading member of the British government, was designated to exercise necessary authority through the newly created office of secretary of state for Northern Ireland. With the backing of the three leading British parties, these changes were quickly approved by the British Parliament and became effective, initially for a period of one year, on March 30, 1972. The Northern Ireland Parliament was prorogued rather than dissolved, the new act explicitly reaffirming past promises that neither all nor part of Ulster would cease to be part of the United Kingdom without its consent.

A plebiscite on the future of Northern Ireland was held March 8, 1973, but was boycotted by the Catholic parties. An unimpressive 57.4 percent of the electorate voted for Ulster's remaining within the United Kingdom, while 0.6 percent voted for union with the Republic of Ireland, the remainder abstaining. Twelve days later, the British government issued a White Paper stating that (1) direct rule would be continued until agreement on a workable structure of government could be obtained, (2) Northern Ireland would remain part of the United Kingdom "for as long as that is the wish of its people", (3) Northern Ireland would continue to elect 12 members to the UK House of Commons, and (4) a Northern Ireland Assembly of 80 members would be elected as soon as possible for a four-year term. The last provision was formalized on July 18 by passage of a parliamentary bill permitting the devolution of powers to an Assembly and executive, and on November 27 Brian Faulkner was named chief of an executive-designate that included representatives of both Protestant and Catholic factions.

In a meeting at Sunningdale, England, on December 6–9, 1973, that was attended by members of the Irish Republican and UK governments as well as the executive-designate of Northern Ireland, agreement was reached on the establishment of a tripartite Council of Ireland to oversee changes in the relationship between the northern and southern Irish governments, and on January 1, 1974, direct rule was terminated. The bulk of Faulkner's Unionist Party rejected the agreement, however, forcing his resignation as party leader and, on May 28, as chief executive. Concurrently, the government itself collapsed and direct rule was reimposed.

In July 1974 the UK Parliament passed the Northern Ireland Act of 1974, which authorized the election of a Constitutional Convention to speak for public sentiment on future government institutions, with the provision that any proposals must include the sharing of power between the religious communities. At balloting on May 1, 1975, the United Ulster Unionist Coalition (UUUC), a grouping of largely "anti-Sunningdale" parties, won 45 of 78 Convention seats. In a manifesto issued prior to the election, the UUUC had called for the retention of Northern Ireland's link with the Crown, increased representation in the UK Parliament, and the restoration of local government, while rejecting any form of imposed association with the Irish Republic. In September, following talks between William CRAIG of the UUUC's Vanguard Unionist Party (VUP)

and representatives of the "pro-Sunningdale" Social Democratic and Labour Party (SDLP), a difference of opinion emerged regarding the participation of republicans in a future cabinet for Northern Ireland. On September 8 the UUUC Convention members voted 37–1 against such participation, and on November 20 the Convention concluded its sitting with a formal report that embraced only UUUC proposals. The Convention was reconvened on February 3, 1976, in the hope of reaching agreement with the SDLP and other opposition parties, but registered no further progress and was dissolved a month later.

The UUUC was itself dissolved on May 4, 1977, following the failure of a general strike called by its more intransigent components, the Democratic Unionist Party (DUP) and the United Ulster Unionist Party (UUUP), acting in concert with the Ulster Workers' Council (UWC) and the Ulster Defense Association (UDA), the largest of the Protestant paramilitary groups. For the year as a whole, the level of violence fell to its lowest since 1970, with only 111 deaths attributed to extremist activity, as contrasted with 296 the year before. In view of the improvement, (then) Secretary of State for Northern Ireland Roy MASON proposed in late November that a new attempt be made to restore local rule. The effort was abandoned, however, because of an intensification of violence in the first quarter of 1978, which prompted the House of Commons in late June to extend the period of direct rule for another year, as of July 16. In the wake of continued outbreaks, the order was again renewed on July 2, 1979.

In November 1979 the new secretary of state for Northern Ireland, Humphrey ATKINS, issued a call to the Official Unionist, Democratic Unionist, Social Democratic and Labour, and Alliance parties (see below) to attend a conference on development of a mechanism to "transfer as wide a range of powers as can be agreed" on a basis that would not alter the existing constitutional status of the province. Although the Official Unionists declined to attend, the conference opened on January 7, 1980, with representatives of the other three groups present. The proposals offered were, however, widely divergent, and the conference adjourned on March 24 with little accomplished.

Amid growing violence, a hunger strike was initiated on October 27 by seven persons confined in Maze prison near Belfast. While the strike was called off on December 18 following government promises of improvement in prison conditions, the action was widely publicized and was renewed in March 1981, with ten prisoners ultimately dying. The only significant development for the remainder of the year was a meeting at London on November 6 between UK Prime Minister Margaret Thatcher and (then) Irish Prime Minister Garret FitzGerald, at which the two leaders agreed to set up an Anglo-Irish Intergovernmental Council (AIIC) to meet on a periodic basis to discuss matters of common concern.

In early 1982, the Thatcher government secured parliamentary approval for the gradual reintroduction of home rule under a scheme dubbed "rolling devolution". The initiative assumed substantive form with balloting on October 20 for a new 78-member Northern Ireland Assembly, in which the Provisional *Sinn Féin* (the political wing of the

Provisional IRA) for the first time participated, obtaining 5 seats. The poll was accompanied, however, by an upsurge of terrorist activity, with both the Provisional *Sinn Féin* and the SDLP boycotting the Assembly session that convened on November 11 to formulate devolution recommendations. Subsequently, on December 20, the UK Parliament approved an order increasing from 12 to 17 the number of lower-house seats allocated to Ulster at the next general election (held June 9, 1983).

Following an initiative from SDLP leader John HUME in March 1983, the Belfast government announced the formation of a cross-frontier New Ireland Forum to discuss the impact of island unification on church-state and interfaith relations, as well as its implications for economic development. Talks between a number of groups commenced in mid-April, but neither the Unionist nor Alliance parties in the north nor the Workers' Party in the Republic chose to attend, while no invitation was extended to the *Sinn Féin* (the term "Provisional" being generally abandoned with the relinquishment of competing *Sinn Féin* identification by the Worker's Party [see Political Parties and Groups, below] in April 1982). The Forum's report, issued in May 1984, offered a number of suggestions for moving toward a solution of the Northern Ireland problem, none of which proved acceptable to the British government.

During a meeting at Hillsborough Castle, Northern Ireland, on November 15, 1985, prime ministers Thatcher and FitzGerald concluded an Anglo-Irish agreement that established an Intergovernmental Conference within the context of the AIIC to deal on a regular basis with political and security issues affecting the troubled region. Subsequently, in reaction to Unionist maneuvering, the nonsectarian Alliance Party joined the *Sinn Féin* and SDLP in boycotting the Northern Ireland Assembly, while the three Unionist parties resigned their seats in the UK House of Commons. In by-elections to refill the vacancies on January 23, 1986, the earlier distribution (OUP, 11; DUP, 3; UPUP, 1) was unchanged, save for the loss of one Official Unionist seat to the SDLP. (At the most recent UK balloting of June 11, 1987, the OUP lost an additional seat, the other parties retaining their previous representation). On June 19, 1986, the UK government dissolved the Assembly, which had become little more than an anti-accord forum for Unionists. The dissolution, which signalled the conclusion of London's seventh major peace initiative in 14 years, did not, however, abolish the body, leaving open the possibility of future electoral replenishment.

Constitution and government. The Government of Ireland Act of 1920 gave Northern Ireland its own government and a Parliament empowered to act on all matters except those of "imperial concern" (finance, defense, foreign affairs, etc.) or requiring specialized technical input. The royal authority was vested in a governor appointed by the Crown and advised by ministers responsible to Parliament; in practice, the leader of the majority party was invariably designated as prime minister. Parliament consisted of a 52-member House of Commons, directly elected from single-member constituencies, and a Senate, whose 26 members (except for 2 serving ex officio) were elected by the House of Commons under a proportional representation system. Voting for local government bodies was subject to a prop-

erty qualification that excluded an estimated 200,000 adults, including a disproportionate number of minority Catholics.

The effective disenfranchisement of a substantial portion of the Catholic population precipitated the original disturbances in 1968–1969. Since then, British efforts to bring about agreement on a form of coalition government acceptable to both Protestants and Catholics have yet to bear fruit, while direct rule, in effect since 1972 (save for January–May 1974), continues through the UK secretary of state for Northern Ireland.

Recent developments. Although the Anglo-Irish agreement of November 1985, which acknowledged British sovereignty over Northern Ireland while granting Dublin a consultative role in the territory's affairs, was intended to curtail unrest, its immediate results were not only the effective loss of the Northern Ireland Assembly, but an outbreak of protest by Unionists, many of whom considered the accord as an initial step toward Irish unity. A "loyalist strike" on March 3, 1986, paralyzed commerce and transportation throughout Ulster, and Unionist civil disobedience, accompanied by acts of violence, continued throughout the year.

During 1987 the Unionist position softened (see OUP and UDA, below) as moderates called for "politics over protest". The theretofore hardline James MOLYNEAUX of the OUP and Rev. Ian R.K. PAISLEY of the DUP called off an 18-month boycott of the House of Commons and indicated a willingness to resume negotiations toward a political settlement that would provide power-sharing with Catholics, possibly in the context of an independent Northern Ireland state. However, the Unionists remained steadfast in their opposition to the 1985 agreement, which the SDLP as the major voice of Catholic sentiment continued to support. Consequently, at the second anniversary of the accord in November 1987 it was apparent that no effective Protestant-Catholic "bridge" had been established as envisioned by the UK and Irish governments. As a result, there was no respite in 1987 from the political violence that had left more than 2600 dead since 1969. The Provisional IRA took responsibility for 60 of the year's 93 deaths, including 11 civilians killed in a bomb explosion at Enniskillen on November 8 that generated widespread condemnation within Northern Ireland and throughout the world. In January 1988 the UK government announced it was strengthening its security forces in light of evidence that the Provisional IRA had received "substantial" arms shipments, including surface-to-air missiles, from Libya in recent years.

POLITICAL PARTIES AND GROUPS

Prior to the outbreak of violence in 1968–1969, the dominant party in Northern Ireland was the Ulster Unionist Party (UUP), which controlled both houses of Parliament and most local government bodies, while providing most of Northern Ireland's delegates to the UK Parliament. At the UK level, its policies were in most respects similar to those of the Conservative Party. Following the collapse of the Sunningdale Agreement, it split into pro- and anti-

Faulkner groups, the Official Unionist Party, the Democratic Unionist Party, and the United Ulster Unionist Party constituting the core of the United Ulster Unionist Coalition (UUUC) prior to its dissolution in May 1977.

Official Unionist Party (OUP). The Official Unionist Party comprises the bulk of Ulster Unionists who were opposed to the Sunningdale Agreement. On February 25, 1978, the Vanguard Unionist Party (VUP), which had been organized in 1973 and was a member of the UUUC until just before the 1975 Constitutional Convention, voted to disband, its sole representative at Westminster, William Craig, joining the Official Unionists. The OUP secured a plurality of 26 seats at the Northern Ireland Assembly election of October 1982 and 11 of the 15 House of Commons seats won by Unionists in June 1983. The formation of a "joint working party" between the OUP and the DUP was announced in August 1985 to plan strategy to protect "Ulster's interests within the UK". Throughout 1986 the Unionist joint working party attempted to disrupt local government in protest of the Anglo-Irish accord, the OUP expelling seven people from the party in October for ignoring a directive to boycott local council business. By contrast, joint OUP/DUP publications in 1987 called for all Northern Ireland parties to negotiate an alternative to the 1985 accord in a spirit of "friendship, cooperation, and consultation". In addition, the OUP, DUP and UPUP agreed to present only one Unionist candidate from each constituency in the 1987 House of Commons elections, retaining 13 of the 14 seats held by Unionists at dissolution.

Leaders: James MOLYNEAUX, Harold McCUSKER, Frank MILLAR (General Secretary).

Democratic Unionist Party (DUP). The DUP split from the Ulster Unionist Party in 1971 in support of a strongly right-wing, anti-Catholic position. It has consistently been runner-up to the OUP, winning 21 seats in the 1982 Assembly election and 3 House of Commons seats in June 1983, all of the latter being retained in 1987.

Leaders: Rev. Ian R.K. PAISLEY (Parliamentary Leader), Peter ROBINSON (Deputy Leader), James McCLURE (Chairman), Rev. Alan KANE (Secretary).

Ulster Popular Unionist Party (UPUP). The UPUP was organized (initially as the Ulster Progressive Unionist Party) in January 1980 by James Kilfedder, who had left the former UUUC after the 1974 balloting and subsequently sat in the Commons as an independent until the 1979 election, when he was returned under the designation of Ulster Unionist (not to be confused with the OUP). He retained his seat in 1983, 1986, and 1987. The party, essentially Kilfedder's personal vehicle, is primarily interested in devolved government in Northern Ireland, with proportional representation in the Commons.

Leader: James KILFEDDER.

Ulster Liberal Party (ULP). The ULP is an Ulster affiliate of the British Liberal Party. At present, it has no parliamentary representation.

Leaders: Michael WARDEN (Chairman), Tony COGHLAN (Secretary).

Alliance Party. A nonsectarian and nondoctrinaire group founded in 1970 in reaction to growing civil strife, the Alliance Party, like the SDLP, participated in the post-Sunningdale Faulkner government. It won 10 Assembly seats in 1982 and was the only non-Unionist party to participate in that body's subsequent proceedings. For lack of alternative proposals, the party in 1987 announced continued support of the 1985 agreement, although it called for the additional enactment of a bill of rights for Northern Ireland. It has achieved occasional success in local elections but has never won a seat in the House of Commons.

Leaders: John CUSHNAHAN, Gordon MAWHINNEY, Dr. John ALDERDICE, Susan EDGAR (General Secretary).

Social Democratic and Labour Party (SDLP). The SDLP is a largely Catholic, left-of-center party that endorses the eventual reunification of Ireland by popular consent. Its longtime leader, Gerard Fitt, participated in the post-Sunningdale Faulkner government and subsequently became the only non-Unionist to hold a seat in the UK House of Commons. Fitt resigned as leader in November 1979, after the SDLP constituency representatives and executive had rejected the government's working paper for the 1980 devolution conference. The party won 14 Assembly seats in 1982, but joined *Sinn Féin* (below) in boycotting sessions. It won three House of Commons seats in 1987, its candidates supporting the 1985 Anglo-Irish accord but attacking the Thatcher government on employ-

ment, housing, education, and agricultural policies.

Leaders: John HUME, Seamus MALLON, Eamon HANNA (General Secretary).

Workers' Party (WP). The WP, formerly known as the Workers' Party Republican Clubs, is the Northern Irish wing of the Workers' Party in the Irish Republic (see Ireland: Political Parties). It supports the parent organization's goal of a "socialist republic" for a unified Ireland but most of its activity is devoted to local issues affecting the working class in Belfast and border areas. The WP presented 14 candidates, none of whom was successful, in the 1987 general election.

Leader: Seamus LYNCH (Chairman of Northern Ireland wing).

Sinn Féin. The islandwide *Sinn Féin* (see Ireland: Political Parties) serves as the legal political wing, of the outlawed Provisional Irish Republican Army (see Paramilitary groups, below). It contested the 1982 Assembly election but, in accordance with long-standing practice in the south, indicated that none of its successful candidates would claim their seats. (In November 1986 *Sinn Féin* voted to reverse its policy of boycotting the Irish Parliament and to take seats won in local elections in the south.) The 1987 *Sinn Féin* manifesto demanded improvement in living and working conditions for its primarily Catholic, working class constituency. It also called for the disbanding of British security forces, the withdrawal of Britain from Northern Ireland government, and negotiation of a political settlement through an all-Ireland constitutional conference. Its president, Gerard Adams, was *Sinn Féin*'s only successful candidate in 1987, but, as in 1983, he refused to occupy his seat in the Commons.

Leader: Gerard ADAMS (President).

Other minor groups include the **Progressive Unionist Party** (PUP), widely considered the successor to the Volunteer Political Party, the former political wing of the Ulster Volunteer Force (see UVF, below); the **Irish Independence Party** (IIP), an anti-Unionist group which plays a minor role in local politics; the **United Ulster Unionist Party** (UUUP), organized in 1975 by VUP members opposed to inclusion of Catholic representation in a future government; the **Ulster Loyalist Democratic Party** (ULDP), the political wing of the Ulster Defence Association (see UDA, below) which has lobbied for an independent Northern island state; and the Ulster Loyalist Democratic Front, whose formation by members of the OUP, DUP, and UDA was announced in 1985.

Paramilitary groups:

Provisional Irish Republican Army (Provisional IRA). The outlawed Provisional IRA was formed in December 1969 as a breakaway group of the Irish Republican Army (IRA — see *Sinn Féin* under Ireland: Political Parties). The "Provisionals", whose name derived from the "Provisional Government of the Irish Republic" in 1916, committed themselves to an "anticolonial" armed struggle and have taken responsibility for many anti-British, anti-Unionist bombings and shootings in Northern Ireland and Great Britain. A 1977 reorganization led to the formation of a political front (see *Sinn Féin,* above) and the creation of largely autonomous "cells" of as few as four or five persons in furtherance of its guerrilla campaign. It is estimated that there are only about 300 Provisional IRA "soldiers", although active sympathizers are believed to number well into the thousands.

Irish National Liberation Army (INLA). Also illegal, the INLA was formed in 1975 by a small group of hardline Marxists who split from *Sinn Féin* and the "Official" IRA because of the adoption by those groups of a policy of nonviolence (see *Sinn Féin* under Ireland: Political Parties). The INLA subsequently took responsibility for shootings and bombings in Northern Ireland and the Irish Republic but was in disarray by 1987: 11 members were reported to have died in internecine fighting over a proposal to disband, while its political wing, the Irish Republican Socialist Party, had become essentially inoperative.

Ulster Defence Association (UDA). The 10,000-member UDA, the largest Protestant paramilitary organization, was formed as an umbrella organization for many long-standing local defense associations in Belfast and Londonderry shortly after the creation of the Provisional IRA. Like *Sinn Féin,* it has retained legal status by disavowing direct involvement in violent acts. The UDA has sponsored political activity through the Ulster Loyalist Democratic Party (above) and in 1987 its leaders presented a "Common Sense" plan for Unionists to shift from a policy of "just saying no" to proposals for constitutional settlement with the Catholic minority.

Ulster Freedom Fighters (UFF). The UFF has taken responsibility for a number of sectarian killings since its formation in 1973 to defend loyalist areas and combat the Provisional IRA. Allegations have been made but not proven of links between the illegal UFF and the legal UDA (above).

Ulster Volunteer Force (UVF). Following its formation in 1966, the illegal UVF took responsibility for a number of anti-Catholic car bombings and assassinations. However, its membership has reportedly dropped sharply in recent years, partly because of arrests stemming from infiltration by security forces.

LEGISLATURE

The former bicameral Northern Ireland Parliament, consisting of an indirectly elected Senate of 26 members and a directly elected House of Commons of 52 members, was to have been replaced by a unicameral Northern Ireland Assembly under the British Parliamentary Act of July 18, 1973. The plan was abandoned after the fall of the Faulkner government in May 1974, when direct rule was reimposed.

The 78-member **Northern Ireland Assembly** elected on October 20, 1982, was endowed with only consultative responsibilities and both the SDLP and *Sinn Féin* refused to take up their seats. The Assembly was dissolved in June 1986 (see Political background, above).

NEWS MEDIA

Press, radio, and television are organized along the same lines as in Great Britain.

Press. The following newspapers are published at Belfast: *Belfast Telegraph* (152,000), independent daily; *Sunday News* (61,000), independent; *News Letter* (44,000), Unionist daily; *Irish News* (43,000), nationalist daily.

UNITED STATES

United States of America

Political Status: Independence declared July 4, 1776; federal republic established under constitution adopted March 4, 1789.

Area: 3,615,122 sq. mi. (9,363,166 sq. km.); includes gross area (land and water) of the 50 states, excluding Puerto Rico and other territories.

Population: 226,545,805 (1980C), 245,604,000 (1988E), excluding Puerto Rico and other territories. (The 1988 estimate is for April 1 to accord with dating of the 1980 census result. Both figures are subject to possible underenumeration of 6–12 million illegal aliens.)

Major Urban Centers (1986E):

	Population	
	City Proper	*Urban Area*
WASHINGTON, D.C.	626,000	3,563,000
New York, N.Y.	7,263,000	8,473,000
Los Angeles, Calif.	3,259,000	8,296,000
Chicago, Ill.	3,010,000	8,116,000
Houston, Texas	1,729,000	3,231,000
Philadelphia, Penn.	1,643,000	4,826,000
Detroit, Mich.	1,086,000	4,335,000
San Diego, Calif.	1,015,000	2,201,000
Dallas, Texas	1,004,000	2,401,000
San Antonio, Texas	914,000	1,276,000
Phoenix, Ariz.	894,000	1,900,000
Baltimore, Md.	753,000	2,280,000
San Francisco, Calif.	749,000	1,588,000
Indianapolis, Ind.	720,000	1,213,000
Memphis, Tenn.	653,000	960,000
Jacksonville, Fla.	610,000	853,000
Milwaukee, Wisc.	605,000	1,380,000
Boston, Mass.	574,000	2,824,000
Columbus, Ohio	566,000	1,299,000
New Orleans, La.	554,000	1,334,000
Cleveland, Ohio	536,000	1,850,000
Denver, Colo.	505,000	1,633,000
Seattle, Wash.	486,000	1,751,000
Kansas City, Mo.	441,000	1,518,000
St. Louis, Mo.	426,000	2,438,000
Pittsburgh, Penn.	387,000	2,123,000

Principal Language: English.

Monetary Unit: Dollar (selected market rates March 1, 1988, $1US = 0.56 UK pounds sterling, 5.72 French francs, 1.69 FRG Deutsche marks, 1.39 Swiss francs, 128.00 Japanese yen).

President: Ronald Wilson REAGAN (Republican Party); elected November 4, 1980, and inaugurated January 20, 1981, succeeding Jimmy (James Earl) CARTER (Democratic Party); reelected November 6, 1984, and inaugurated January 20, 1985, for a second four-year term.

Vice President: George Herbert Walter BUSH (Republican Party); elected November 4, 1980, and inaugurated January 20, 1981, succeeding Walter Frederick MONDALE (Democratic Party); reelected November 6, 1984, and inaugurated January 20, 1985, for a term concurrent with that of the President.

THE COUNTRY

First among the nations of the world in economic production, the United States ranks fourth in area (behind the USSR, Canada, and China) and also fourth in population (after China, India, and the USSR). Canada and Mexico are the country's only contiguous neighbors, most of its national territory ranging across the North American continent in a broad band that encompasses the Atlantic seaboard; the Appalachian Mountains; the Ohio, Mississippi, and Missouri river valleys; the Great Plains; the Rocky Mountains and the deserts of the Southwest; and the narrow, fertile coastland adjoining the Pacific. Further contrasts are found in the two noncontiguous states: Alaska, in northwestern North America, where the climate ranges from severe winters and short growing seasons in the north to equable temperatures in the south; and Hawaii, in the mid-Pacific, where trade winds produce a narrow temperature range but extreme variations in rainfall.

Regional diversity is also found in economic conditions. Industrial production is located mainly in the coastal areas and in those interior urban centers with good transportation connections, as in the Great Lakes region. Agricultural products come primarily from the Mountain, Plains, Midwestern, and Southeastern states. Per capita income varies considerably from region to region, ranging in 1985 from $11,243 in the Central Southeast to $17,163 in New England.

The nation's ethnic diversity is a product of large-scale voluntary and involuntary immigration, much of which took place before 1920. At the time of the 1980 census, the population was over 94 percent native born and was classified as 83.1 percent White and 11.7 percent Black; in addition, there were 1,420,400 American Indians, 806,000 Chinese, 774,700 Filipinos, 701,000 Japanese, 354,600 Koreans, 261,700 Vietnamese, and 6,999,200 others (including, principally, Spanish Americans, who are presumed to have been unwilling or unable to identify themselves as either White or Black on the census forms). Religious diversity parallels, and is in part caused by, ethnic diversity. Roman Catholics constitute 37 percent of formal church members; people of a wide variety of Protestant affiliations, 55 percent; and Jews, 4 percent. While English is the principal language, Spanish is the preferred tongue of sizable minorities in New York City (largely migrants from Puerto Rico), in Florida (mainly Cuban refugees), and near the Mexican border. Various other languages are spoken among foreign-born and first-generation Americans.

In 1986, women constituted 44 percent of the full-time labor force and 68 percent of part-time workers; concentrated in clerical, retail and human service occupations, women earn approximately 69 percent of the average male wage. Females currently hold 21 seats (4.8 percent) in the US House of Representatives and 2 (.02 percent) in the Senate; by contrast, their representation in state legislatures has grown steadily in recent years from 8.0 percent in 1975 to 14.8 percent in 1986. In addition, a number of autonomous women's organizations serve as influential nonelectoral political forces, including the National Women's Political Caucus (NWPC) and the National Organization for Women (NOW).

Owing to a historic transfer of population from farm to city (now virtually at an end, with some reverse migration from urban areas), only a small proportion of the population is engaged in agriculture, which nevertheless yields a substantial proportion of US exports. In 1986, agriculture employed 3.2 million workers out of a total civilian labor force of 109.6 million, excluding 6.9 million unemployed. By contrast, approximately 27 percent of the labor force was engaged in mining, manufacturing, and construction; 21 percent in wholesale and retail trade; and 36 percent in government and service activities. Of increasing importance to the administration of the nation's social-security system is the aging of the population, the percentage of those 65 and older having risen from approximately 4.0 in 1900 to 11.5 in 1986.

The United States has experienced long-term economic growth throughout most of its history, with marked short-term fluctuation in recent years. During 1961–1965 the real annual per capita change in gross national product averaged +3.2 percent; it dropped to +1.9 percent in 1966–1970, dipped further to +1.7 percent during the recession of 1973–1975, rose to +3.8 percent in 1976–1980, fell sharply to −2.5 percent in 1982, surged to +6.8 percent (the highest since 1951) in 1984, and again retreated to +2.9 percent in 1986. During the period 1967–1985 the domestic purchasing power of the US dollar, as measured by the consumer price index, declined steadily from 1.00 to 0.31, the annual rate of inflation reaching a high of 13.5 percent in 1980, but declining thereafter to 2.0 in 1986. Of considerable recent significance has been a decline in the exchange value of the dollar, which stood at $0.71 per European Currency Unit (ECU) in late December 1984, but had fallen to $1.38 per ECU by December 1987, with marginal recovery thereafter.

GOVERNMENT AND POLITICS

Political background. Beginning as a group of 13 British colonies along the Atlantic seaboard, the "united States of America" declared themselves independent on July 4, 1776, gained recognition as a sovereign nation at the close of the Revolutionary War in 1783, and in 1787 adopted a federal constitution which became effective March 4, 1789, George WASHINGTON taking office as first president of the United States on April 30. A process of westward expansion and colonization during the ensuing hundred years found the nation by 1890 in full possession of the continental territories that now comprise the 48 contiguous states. Alaska, purchased from Russia in 1867, and Hawaii, voluntarily annexed in 1898, became the 49th and 50th states in 1959. The constitutional foundation of the Union has been severely threatened only by the Civil War of 1861–1865, in which the separate confederacy established by 11 southern states was defeated and reintegrated into the Federal Union by military force. The US political climate has been characterized by the alternating rule of the Republican and Democratic parties since the Civil War, which initiated a period of industrial expansion that continued without major interruptions through World War I and into the great depression of the early 1930s.

The modern era of administrative centralization and massive federal efforts to solve economic and social problems began in 1933 with the inauguration of Democratic President Franklin D. ROOSEVELT, while the onset of direct US involvement in World War II brought further expansion of governmental power. Following the defeat of the Axis powers, efforts supporting European reconstruction and attempting to meet the challenge posed by the rise of the Soviet Union as a world power dominated the administration of Harry S TRUMAN, the Democratic vice president who succeeded Roosevelt upon his death on April 12, 1945, and won election in 1948 to a full four-year term. Newly armed with atomic weapons, the United States abandoned its traditional isolation to become a founding member of the United Nations and the leader of a worldwide coalition directed against the efforts of the Soviet Union and, after 1949, the People's Republic of China to expand their influence along the periphery of the Communist world. A series of East-West confrontations over Iran, Greece, and Berlin culminated in the Korean War of 1950-1953, in which US forces were committed to large-scale military action under the flag of the United Nations.

Dwight D. EISENHOWER, elected president on the Republican tickets of 1952 and 1956, achieved a negotiated settlement in Korea and some relaxation of tensions with the Soviet Union, but efforts to solve such basic East-West problems as the division of Germany proved unavailing. While Eisenhower's attempts to restrict the role of the federal government met only limited success, his eight-year incumbency witnessed a resumption of progress toward legal equality of the races — after a lapse of some 80 years — pursuant to the 1954 Supreme Court decision declaring segregation in public schools unconstitutional. An economic recession developed toward the end of Eisenhower's second term, which also saw the beginning of a substantial depletion of US gold reserves. In spite of a resurgent economy, balance-of-payments problems persisted throughout the succeeding Democratic administrations of presidents John F. KENNEDY (January 20, 1961, to November 22, 1963) and Lyndon B. JOHNSON (November 22, 1963, to January 20, 1969).

The assassinations of President Kennedy in 1963 and of civil-rights advocate Martin Luther KING, Jr., and Senator Robert F. KENNEDY in 1968 provided the most dramatic evidence of a deteriorating domestic climate. To counter sharpening racial and social antagonisms and growing violence on the part of disaffected groups and individuals, the Congress, at President Johnson's urging, passed laws promoting equal rights in housing, education, and voter registration, and establishing programs to further equal job opportunities, urban renewal, and improved education for the disadvantaged. These efforts were in part offset by the negative domestic consequences of US involvement in the Vietnam War, which had begun with limited economic and military aid to the French in the 1950s but by the mid-1960s had become direct and massive. Disagreement over Vietnam was also largely responsible for halting a trend toward improved US-Soviet relations that had followed the Cuban missile confrontation of 1962 and had led in 1963 to the signing of a limited nuclear test-ban treaty. Moved by increasing public criticism of the government's Vietnam policy, President Johnson on March 31, 1968, announced the cessation of bombing in most of North Vietnam as a step toward direct negotiations to end the war, and preliminary peace talks with the North Vietnamese began at Paris on May 13.

Richard M. NIXON, vice president during the Eisenhower administration and unsuccessful presidential candidate in 1960, was nominated as the 1968 Republican candidate for president, while Vice President Hubert H. HUMPHREY became the Democratic nominee and former Alabama governor George C. WALLACE, a dissident Democrat, ran as the candidate of the American Independent Party, which sought to capitalize primarily on sectional and segregationist sentiments. Nixon won the election on November 5 with 43.4 percent of the national popular vote, the poorest showing by any victorious candidate since 1912. Humphrey captured 42.7 percent and Wallace won 13.5 percent — the largest total for a third-party candidate since 1924.

Following his inauguration on January 20, 1969, President Nixon embarked on a vigorous foreign-policy role while selectively limiting the nation's external commitments in Southeast Asia and elsewhere. Domestically, the Nixon administration became increasingly alarmed at the growing antiwar movement and reports of radical extremist activity, and in April 1970 initiated a program of surveillance of militant left-wing groups and individuals. In May the president's decision to order Vietnamese-based US troops into action in Cambodia provoked an antiwar demonstration at Kent State University, in the course of which four students were killed by members of the Ohio National Guard. Final agreement on a peace treaty in Vietnam was not obtained until January 27, 1973 (see Foreign relations, below), by which time the "youth rebellion" that had characterized the late 1960s was in pronounced decline.

Nixon was reelected in a landslide victory over an antiwar Democrat, Senator George S. McGOVERN of South Dakota, on November 7, 1972. Winning a record-breaking 60.7 percent of the popular vote, Nixon swept all major electoral units except Massachusetts and the District of Columbia, though the Democrats easily retained control of both houses of Congress. Within a year, however, the fortunes of Republican executive leaders were almost unbelievably reversed. On October 10, 1973, Spiro T. AGNEW resigned as vice president after pleading nolo contendere to having falsified a federal income-tax return. He was succeeded on December 6 by longtime Michigan Congressman Gerald R. FORD, the first vice president to be chosen, under the 25th Amendment of the Constitution, by presidential nomination and congressional confirmation. On March 1, 1974, seven former White House and presidential campaign aides were charged with conspiracy in an attempted cover-up of the Watergate scandal (involving a break-in at Democratic National Committee headquarters on June 17, 1972), while President Nixon, because of the same scandal, became on August 9 the first US chief executive to tender his resignation. Vice President Ford, who succeeded Nixon on the same day, thus became the first US president never to have participated in a national election.

At the election of November 2, 1976, the Democratic candidate, former Georgia governor Jimmy CARTER, defeated President Ford by a bare majority (50.6 percent) of the popular vote, Ford becoming the first incumbent since 1932 to fail in a bid for a second term. Carter also became a one-term president on November 4, 1980, his Republican opponent, Ronald REAGAN, sweeping all but six states and the District of Columbia with a popular vote margin of 10 percent and a nearly ten-to-one margin in the electoral college. In congressional balloting, the Republicans won control of the Senate for the first time since 1952 and registered substantial gains in the House of Representatives, the two houses for the first time since 1916 being controlled by different parties.

The 1980 outcome was hailed as a "mandate for change" unparalleled since the Roosevelt landslide of 1932. Accordingly, President Reagan moved quickly to address the nation's economic problems by a combination of across-the-board fiscal retrenchment and massive tax cuts, with only the military establishment receiving significant additional funding in an attempt to redress what was portrayed as a widening gap between US and Soviet tactical and strategic capabilities. An important component of what was billed as the "New Federalism" was sharply curtailed aid to the states, which were invited to accept responsibility for many social programs that had long been funded directly from Washington. While most liberals decried the new administration's commitment to economic "realism", significant progress was achieved by late 1982 in lowering interest rates and slowing inflation, two of the more visible signs of recovery.

Despite the onset of severe economic recession that the administration sought to counter with a series of "hard-line" fiscal and monetary policies, the midterm elections of November 2, 1982, yielded no significant alteration in the domestic balance of power. The Democrats realized a net gain of 7 governorships (the resultant distribution being 34 Democratic incumbents to 16 Republican) and increased their majority in the House of Representatives by 26 seats to 269–166. However, Republican control of the Senate remained unchanged at 54–46.

On November 6, 1984, President Reagan won reelection by the second largest electoral college margin (97.6 percent) in US history, nearly equalling the record of 98.5 percent set by President Roosevelt in 1936. His Democratic opponent, Walter F. MONDALE, won only in his home state of Minnesota and in the District of Columbia. The Republicans also retained control of the Senate (53–47), despite a net loss of two seats, while the Democrats retained control of the House with a reduced majority of 253–182. The gubernatorial balloting yielded a net gain of one for the Republicans, who, as in 1982, could thereafter claim incumbents in 16 states, as contrasted with 34 for the Democrats.

During the 1984 campaign, Reagan had promised no increase in personal income taxes and in his inaugural address on January 21, 1985, called for a simplified tax system and drastic limitations on federal spending, from which the military would, however, be partially exempt. Over the ensuing 18 months, sweeping changes were made in what ultimately emerged as the Tax Reform Act of 1986, particularly in a reduction in the number of tax brackets and a lowering of the top rate, with families at or below the poverty line freed of any obligation; the package was to be paid for, in part, by the elimination of many deductions and loopholes, with little measurable gain for individuals in the middle-income range. During the same period, while inflation and unemployment remained at acceptable levels, massive trade deficits were recorded, despite steady erosion in the value of the US dollar, which declined by more than 20 percent in trade-weighted terms from December 1984 to March 1986. As a result, the Reagan administration, steadfastly maintaining its commitment to free trade, called for measures to counter what it perceived as a "protectionist upsurge" on the part of many of its trading partners.

At the nonpresidential balloting of November 4, 1986, the Democrats maintained their control of the House by an increased margin of 258–177, while regaining control of the Senate, 55–45. At the state level they suffered a net loss of 8 governorships, retaining a bare majority of 26.

Constitution and government. The Constitution of the United States, drafted by a Constitutional Convention at Philadelphia in 1787 and declared in effect March 4, 1789, established a republic in which extensive powers are reserved to the states, currently 50 in number, that compose the Federal Union. The system has three distinctive characteristics. First, powers are divided among three federal branches—legislative, executive, and judicial—and between the federal and state governments, themselves each divided into three branches. Second, the power of each of the four elements of the federal government (the presidency, the Senate, the House of Representatives, and the federal judiciary) is limited by being shared with one or more of the other elements. Third, the different procedures by which the president, senators, and members of the House of Representatives are elected make each responsible to a different constituency.

Federal executive power is vested in a president who serves for a four-year term and, by the 22nd Amendment (ratified in 1951), is limited to two terms of office. The president and vice president are formally designated by an Electoral College composed of electors from each state and the District of Columbia. Selected by popular vote in numbers equal to the total congressional representation to which the various states are entitled, the electors are pledged to vote for their political parties' candidates and customarily do so. The president is advised by, and discharges most of his functions through, executive departments headed by officers whom he appoints but who must have Senate approval. He may, if he desires, use these officers collectively as a cabinet having advisory functions. In addition, he serves as commander in chief, issuing orders to the military through the secretary of defense and the Joint Chiefs of Staff of the Army, Navy, and Air Force, who also serve him collectively as an advisory body.

Legislative power is vested in the bicameral Congress: the Senate, which has two members from each state, is chosen by popular vote for six-year terms and is renewed by thirds every two years; the House of Representatives, elected by popular vote every two years, has a membership based on population, each state being entitled to at least one representative. The two houses are further differentiated by their responsibilities: e.g., money bills must originate in the House; the advice and consent of the Senate is required for ratification of treaties. In practice, no major legislative or financial bill is considered by either chamber until it has been reported by, or discharged from, one of many standing committees. By custom, the parties share seats on the committees on a basis roughly proportional to their legislative strength, and within the parties preference in committee assignments has traditionally been accorded primarily on the basis of seniority (continuous service in the house concerned), although departures from this rule are becoming more common. The Senate (but not the House) permits "unlimited debate", a procedure under which a determined minority may, by filibustering, bring all legislative action to a halt unless three-fifths of the full Senate elects to close debate. Failing this, the bill objectionable to the minority will eventually be tabled by the leadership. A presidential veto may be overridden by separate two-thirds votes of the two houses.

Congress has created the General Accounting Office to provide legislative control over public funds and has established some 60 agencies, boards, and commissions—collectively known as "independent agencies"—to perform specified administrative functions.

The federal judiciary is headed by a nine-member Supreme Court and includes courts of appeal, district courts, and various special courts, all created by Congress. Federal judges are appointed by the president, contingent upon approval by the Senate, and serve during good behavior. Federal jurisdiction is limited, applying, most importantly, to cases in law and equity arising under the Constitution, to US laws and treaties, and to controversies arising between two or more states or between citizens of different states. Jury trial is prescribed for all federal crimes except those involving impeachment, which is voted by the House and adjudicated by the Senate.

The federal constitution and the institutions of the federal government serve generally as models for those of the states. Each state government is made up of a popularly elected governor and legislature (all but one bicameral) and an independent judiciary. The District of Columbia, as the seat of the national government, has traditionally been administered under the direct authority of Congress; however, in May 1974 District voters approved a charter giving them the right to elect their own mayor and a 13-member City Council, both of which took office on January 1, 1975. Earlier, under the 23rd Amendment to the Constitution (ratified in 1961), District residents had won the right to participate in presidential elections and in 1970 were authorized by Congress to send a nonvoting delegate to the House of Representatives. An amendment to give the District full congressional voting rights was approved by both houses of Congress in 1978, but has not yet been ratified by the requisite 38 of the 50 state legislatures.

In practice, the broad powers of the federal government, its more effective use of the taxing power, and the existence of many problems transcending the capacity of individual states have tended to make for a strongly centralized system of government. Local self-government, usually through municipalities, townships, and counties, is a well-established tradition, based generally on English models. Education is a locally administered, federally subsidized function.

State and Capital	Area (sq. mi.)	Population (1987E)
Alabama (Montgomery)	50,708	4,086,000
Alaska (Juneau)	566,432	544,000
Arizona (Phoenix)	113,417	3,432,000
Arkansas (Little Rock)	51,945	2,386,000
California (Sacramento)	156,361	27,531,000
Colorado (Denver)	103,766	3,308,000
Connecticut (Hartford)	4,862	3,212,000
Delaware (Dover)	1,982	641,000
Florida (Tallahassee)	54,090	11,962,000
Georgia (Atlanta)	58,073	6,244,000
Hawaii (Honolulu)	6,425	1,081,000
Idaho (Boise)	82,677	1,006,000
Illinois (Springfield)	55,748	11,569,000
Indiana (Indianapolis)	36,097	5,518,000
Iowa (Des Moines)	55,941	2,826,000
Kansas (Topeka)	81,787	2,469,000
Kentucky (Frankfort)	39,650	3,733,000
Louisiana (Baton Rouge)	44,930	4,504,000
Maine (Augusta)	30,920	1,184,000
Maryland (Annapolis)	9,891	4,532,000
Massachusetts (Boston)	7,826	5,838,000
Michigan (Lansing)	56,817	9,191,000
Minnesota (St. Paul)	79,829	4,243,000
Mississippi (Jackson)	47,296	2,643,000
Missouri (Jefferson City)	68,995	5,100,000
Montana (Helena)	145,587	814,000
Nebraska (Lincoln)	76,483	1,595,000
Nevada (Carson City)	109,889	993,000
New Hampshire (Concord)	9,027	1,058,000
New Jersey (Trenton)	7,521	7,687,000
New Mexico (Santa Fe)	121,412	1,518,000
New York (Albany)	47,831	17,759,000
North Carolina (Raleigh)	48,798	6,422,000
North Dakota (Bismarck)	69,273	674,000
Ohio (Columbus)	40,975	10,767,000
Oklahoma (Oklahoma City)	68,782	3,295,000
Oregon (Salem)	96,184	2,716,000
Pennsylvania (Harrisburg)	44,966	11,874,000
Rhode Island (Providence)	1,049	982,000
South Carolina (Columbia)	30,225	3,420,000
South Dakota (Pierre)	75,955	707,000
Tennessee (Nashville)	41,328	4,848,000
Texas (Austin)	262,134	16,937,000
Utah (Salt Lake City)	82,096	1,694,000
Vermont (Montpelier)	9,267	547,000
Virginia (Richmond)	39,780	5,883,000
Washington (Olympia)	66,570	4,514,000
West Virginia (Charleston)	24,070	1,902,000
Wisconsin (Madison)	54,464	4,791,000
Wyoming (Cheyenne)	97,203	506,000

Federal District

District of Columbia	61	621,000

Foreign relations. US relations with the world at large have undergone a continuing adjustment to the changing conditions created by the growth of the nation and the multiplication of its foreign contacts. An initial policy of noninvolvement in foreign affairs, which received its classical expression in President Washington's warning against "entangling alliances", has gradually given place to one of active participation in all phases of international life. At the same time, the nation has been gradually transformed from a supporter of revolutionary movements directed against the old monarchical system into a predominantly conservative influence, with a broad commitment to the support of traditional democratic values against challenges from either the Right or, more especially, the Communist or pseudo-Communist Left.

US policy in the Western Hemisphere, the area of most long-standing concern, continues to reflect the preoccupations that inspired the Monroe Doctrine of 1823, in which the US declared its opposition to European political involvement and further colonization in the Americas and in effect established a political guardianship over the states of Latin America. Since World War II, this responsibility has become largely multilateral through the development of the Organization of American States, and direct US intervention in Latin American affairs has typically been limited to a few instances where a Central American or Caribbean country appeared in immediate danger of falling under leftist control.

Overseas expansion during the late nineteenth and early twentieth centuries resulted in the acquisition of American Samoa, Hawaii, and, following the Spanish-American War of 1898, the Philippines, Puerto Rico, and Guam; in addition, the US secured a favored position in Cuba in 1902–1903, obtained exclusive rights in the Panama Canal Zone in 1903, and acquired the US Virgin Islands by purchase in 1917. It did not, however, become an imperial power in the traditional sense and was among the first to adopt a policy of promoting the political evolution of its dependent territories along lines desired by their inhabitants. In accordance with this policy, the Philippines became independent in 1946; Puerto Rico became a free commonwealth associated with the US in 1952; Hawaii became a state of the Union in 1959; measures of self-government have been introduced in the Virgin Islands, Guam, and American Samoa; and the Canal Zone was transferred to Panama on October 1, 1979, although the United States is to retain effective control of 40 percent of the area through 1999. Certain Japanese territories occupied during World War II were provisionally retained under US control for strategic reasons, with those historically of Japanese sovereignty, the Bonin and Ryukyu islands, being returned in 1968 and 1972, respectively. The greater part of Micronesia (held by Japan as a League of Nations mandate after World War I) became, by agreement with the United Nations, the US Trust Territory of the Pacific. In 1986, following the conclusion of a series of compacts of association with the Commonwealth of the Northern Mariana Islands, the Federated States of Micronesia (Yap, Truk, Pohnpei, and Kosrae), the Republic of the Marshall Islands, and the Republic of Belau (Palau), the UN Trusteeship Council indicated that it would be appropriate to terminate the trusteeship and under US law (not yet endorsed by the Security Council) only Belau remains, for technical reasons, within the strategic framework (see Related Territories, below).

Globally, US participation in the defeat of the Central powers in World War I was followed by a period of renewed isolation and attempted neutrality, which, however, was ultimately made untenable by the challenge of the Axis powers in World War II. Having played a leading role in the defeat of the Axis, the US joined with its allies in assuming responsibility for the creation of a postwar order within the framework of the United Nations. However, the subsequent divergence of Soviet and Western political aims, and the resultant limitations on the effectiveness of the UN as an instrument for maintaining peace and security, impelled the US during the late 1940s and the 1950s to take the lead in creating a network of special mutual security arrangements that were ultimately to involve commitments to over four dozen foreign governments. Some of these commitments, as in NATO, the ANZUS Pact, and the Inter-American Treaty of Reciprocal Assistance (Rio Pact), are multilateral in character; others involve defense obligations toward particular governments, such as those of Thailand, the Philippines, and the Republic of Korea.

Concurrently, the US has exercised leadership in the field of international economic and financial relations through its cosponsorship of the World Bank and the International Monetary Fund, its promotion of trade liberalization efforts, and its contributions to postwar relief and rehabilitation, European economic recovery, and the economic progress of less-developed countries. Much of this activity, like parallel efforts put forward in social, legal, and cultural fields, has been carried on through the UN and its related agencies.

The US has actively pursued international agreement on measures for the control and limitation of strategic armaments. First-round strategic arms limitation treaty (SALT) talks were initiated with the Soviet Union in late 1969 and ran until May 1972, resulting in a five-year agreement to limit the number of certain offensive weapons. Though second-round talks, held from November 1972 until early 1974, produced few substantive results, President Nixon and Soviet Chairman Brezhnev agreed in July 1974 to negotiate a new five-year accord, and the intention was reaffirmed during a meeting between Brezhnev and President Ford at Vladivostok in November 1974. Progress again slowed until late 1978, President Carter and Brezhnev finally signing the SALT II treaty at Vienna on June 18, 1979. However, the treaty remained unratified following the Soviet invasion of Afghanistan on December 27. A collateral series of meetings between NATO and Warsaw Pact representatives on mutual and balanced force reductions (MBFR) in Central Europe was initiated in 1973 but has yielded little in the way of substantive agreement. More recently, US-Soviet negotiations on limiting intermediate-range nuclear forces (INF) began at Geneva in November 1981 and were followed in June 1982 by the initiation of strategic arms reduction talks (START). While the START talks continued without visible closure, a precedent-shattering breakthrough was registered in 1987 with the conclusion of an INF accord that for the first time provided for the elimination of an entire category of nuclear weapons. Following an impasse generated by Soviet insistence during a summit at Reykjavik, Iceland, in October 1986 that limitations on development of the US Strategic Defense Initiative ("Star Wars") be included in any major arms agreement, the USSR called in February 1987 for the withdrawal from Europe of both longer-range (600–3,400 mile) intermediate weapons (LRINF) and shorter-range (300–600 mile) weapons (SRINF). The United States responded in March by proposing a global limit of 100 LRINF warheads (none in Europe) and parity in SRINF-category missiles (an existing imbalance favoring the Soviet Union), while expressing a preference for total elimination of both. In late July Secretary Gorbachev agreed to the "global double-zero option", but insisted that shorter-range Persing 1As controlled by West Germany also be destroyed. In September, following Chancellor Khol's approval of the condition, agreement was reached in principal on the historic treaty signed on December 8, during a Reagan-Gorbachev summit at Washington.

US military forces, operating under a UN mandate, actively opposed aggression from Communist sources in the Korean War of 1950–1953. Other US forces, together with those of a number of allied powers, assisted the government of the Republic of Vietnam in combating the insurgent movement that was actively supported by North Vietnamese forces for nearly two decades. Beginning in 1965, this assistance reached the proportions of a major

US military effort, which continued after the initiation of peace talks in 1968. The lengthy discussions, involving US Secretary of State Henry A. KISSINGER and North Vietnamese diplomat Le Duc Tho as the most active participants, resulted in the conclusion of a four-way peace agreement on January 27, 1973, that called for the withdrawal of all remaining US military forces from Vietnam, the repatriation of American prisoners of war, and the institution of political talks between the Republic of Vietnam and its domestic (Viet Cong) adversaries. The US withdrawal was followed, however, by a breakdown in talks, renewed military operations in late 1974, and the collapse of the Saigon government on April 30, 1975.

In a move of major international significance, the United States and the People's Republic of China announced on December 15, 1978, that they would establish diplomatic relations as of January 1, 1979. Normalization was achieved essentially on Chinese terms, with the US meeting all three conditions that the PRC had long insisted upon: severance of US diplomatic relations with Taipei, withdrawal of US troops from Taiwan, and abrogation of the Republic of China defense treaty. On the other hand, Washington indicated that it would maintain economic, cultural, and other unofficial relations with Taiwan, such ties being presumed sufficient to ensure the immediate welfare of the Taiwanese people.

In the Middle East, Secretary Kissinger embarked on an eight-month-long exercise in "shuttle diplomacy" following the Arab-Israeli "October War" of 1973, which involved the heaviest fighting since 1967 on both the Sinai and Syrian fronts. US economic interests were, for the first time, directly involved as a result of an Arab embargo, instituted in October 1973, on all oil shipments to both the United States and Western Europe. The embargo was terminated by all but two of the producing nations, Libya and Syria, in March 1974, following the resumption of full-scale diplomatic relations (severed since 1967) between the United States and Egypt. On May 31, 1974, after a marathon 32-day period of negotiations by Secretary Kissinger, representatives of Israel and Syria met at Geneva to sign an agreement covering a ceasefire, troop disengagement, and exchange of prisoners on the Golan Heights. The following month, a renewal of diplomatic relations between the US and Syria (also suspended since 1967) was announced. In September 1978, President Carter, hosting the Camp David summit, was instrumental in negotiating accords that led to the signing of a treaty of peace between Egypt and Israel at Washington on March 26, 1979.

Despite a recognized danger to US diplomatic personnel, the Carter administration permitted the deposed shah of Iran to enter the United States in October 1979 for medical treatment and, on November 4, militants occupied the US Embassy compound at Teheran, taking 66 hostages. Thirteen Blacks and women were released within days, with the militants, supported by Iranian leader Ayatollah Khomeini, demanding the return of the shah in exchange for the remainder. Although condemnations of the seizure were forthcoming from the UN Security Council, the General Assembly, and the World Court, neither they nor personal pleas by international diplomats were heeded by the Islamic Republic's leadership prior to negotiations that commenced immediately prior to the 1980 US election and culminated in the freeing of the hostages on presidential inauguration day 1981.

The Reagan administration has been active in a wide range of foreign contexts. It views conclusion of the 1987 INF treaty as the result of consistent (and largely successful) pressure on its European allies to maintain a high level of military preparedness vis-à-vis the Soviet Union. In the Middle East, it attempted to negotiate a mutual withdrawal of Israeli and Syrian forces from Lebanon in the wake of the Israeli invasion of June 1982 and the subsequent evacuation of PLO forces from Beirut, for which it provided truce-supervision assistance. During 1987, despite the risk of a major confrontation with Iran, it mounted a significant naval presence in the Persian Gulf to protect oil tankers from sea-borne mines and other threats stemming from the Iran-Iraq conflict. In Asia, it has provided substantial military assistance to Pakistan and Thailand in response to Communist operations in Afghanistan and Kampuchea, respectively, while strongly supporting the post-Marcos regime in the Philippines. In the Caribbean, it provided the bulk of the forces that participated in the 1983 post-coup intervention in Grenada and welcomed the 1986 ouster of Haitian dictator François Duvalier. In Central America, it has attempted to contain alleged Soviet-Cuban involvement in Nicaragua and to assist the Salvadoran government in its efforts to defeat leftist guerrilla forces. Overall, in keeping with a 1980 campaign pledge, the present chief executive has sought to restructure both the military and civilian components of the nation's foreign-aid program so as to reward "America's friends", whatever their domestic policies, in an implicit repudiation of his predecessor's somewhat selective utilization of aid in support of global human-rights objectives.

A major foreign as well as domestic embarrassment to President Reagan in the waning months of his administration was the dramatic and complex "Irangate" scandal that erupted in November 1986, when a Beirut newspaper reported that former US national security advisor Robert McFARLANE and others had secretly visited Iran in October to discuss the release of American hostages, presumed held by Shi'ite terrorists in Lebanon, in exchange for military equipment needed by Iran in the course of its war with Iraq. Subsequently, it was revealed that shipments of "spare parts" had been made during the previous year as part of a covert operation involving Adm. John POINDEXTER (McFarlane's successor as national security advisor) and Marine Lt. Col. Oliver NORTH, a member of the NSC staff, who had played a central role in providing aid to the *contra* rebels in Nicaragua. When it became known that proceeds from the sales had been diverted (in apparent violation of US law) to the *contras,* Admiral Poindexter resigned and Colonel North was dismissed from their NSC posts. Others implicated in the affair included retired Air Force general Richard V. SECORD, who reportedly coordinated the *contra* aid effort; White House chief of staff Donald T. REGAN, who ultimately resigned in February 1987; and CIA director William J. CASEY, who resigned for health reasons on January 29 and died on May 6.

Current issues. Buffeted by the Iran-*contra* affair, but buoyed by the signing of the INF treaty, President Reagan travelled to Moscow in late May 1988 for a fourth and presumably concluding summit with Secretary Gorbachev that received wide publicity but was of little substantive significance. Meanwhile, domestic attention had turned to the contest between Republican George BUSH and Democratic Michael DUKAKIS for election as Reagan's successor on November 8. While early polls showed Bush trailing Dukakis, the race had tightened by midyear. Bush did not seem capable of generating the degree of broad-based support that had characterized much of the Reagan incumbency, while his party suffered from a number of recent scandals involving close associates of the president; in addition, evidence surfaced in June of massive fraud in Defense Department procurement. Other problems that were also seen as damaging the Republicans included a health crisis generated by the Acquired Immune Deficiency Syndrome (AIDS); evidence of a losing war against illegal drugs (particularly cocaine); an inability to staunch the influx of aliens (largely Mexican), despite passage of a new Immigration Reform and Control Act; and an impressive array of economic challenges, including massive trade deficits (despite a significantly weakened US dollar); an international debt crisis (the United States having become the world's leading net debtor); and uncertainty following a major stock market crash in October 1987. Internationally, the administration had been unable to force the ouster of Panama's General Noriega and remained uncertain of its role elsewhere in Central America; it had been embarrassed not only by the revelation that the Soviets had implanted listening devices in a partially constructed US embassy in Moscow, but also by evidence that it had attempted the same at a new Soviet complex in Washington; perhaps most importantly, it had been largely unsuccessful in influencing the course of events in the Middle East, where a deep-rooted Palestinian uprising in Israel had been added to the continuing crisis in the Lebanon and the protracted conflict in the Gulf.

POLITICAL PARTIES

Although the US Constitution makes no provision for political parties, the existence of two (or occasionally three) major parties at the national level has been a feature of the American political system almost since its inception. The present-day Democratic Party traces its origins directly back to the "Republican" Party led by Thomas Jefferson during George Washington's administration, while the contemporary Republican Party, though not formally constituted until the 1850s, regards itself as the lineal descendant of the Federalist Party led by Alexander Hamilton during the same period.

The two-party system has been perpetuated by tradition, by the practical effect of single-member constituencies as well as a single executive, and by the status accorded to the second main party as the recognized opposition in legislative bodies. The major parties do not, however, constitute disciplined doctrinal groups. Each is a coalition of autonomous state parties — themselves coalitions of county and city parties — which come together chiefly in presidential election years to formulate a general policy statement, or platform, and to nominate candidates for president and vice president. Control of funds and patronage is largely in the hands of state and local party units, a factor that weakens party discipline in Congress. Policy leadership is similarly diffuse, both parties searching for support from as many interest groups as possible and tending to operate by consensus.

As contrasted with patterns in most other countries with bi- or multiparty systems, popular identification with the two major parties has been remarkably stable in recent years. From 1960 to 1984, according to surveys by the University of Michigan, between 40 and 46 percent of the voters considered themselves Democrats, while 22 to 29 percent identified with the Republicans. During the same period, 23 to 35 percent viewed themselves as independents (the higher figure occurring in the mid-1970s, when younger voters tended to dissociate themselves from partisan politics).

Since 1932, the rate of voter participation has averaged 56.8 percent in presidential elections, ranging from 51.1 percent in 1948 to 62.8 percent in 1960. The turnout in nonpresidential years has been much lower, averaging 40.3 percent, with a range of from 32.5 percent in 1942 to 45.4 percent in 1962 and 1964.

Presidential Party:

Republican Party. Informally known as the "Grand Old Party" (GOP), the present-day Republican Party was founded as an antislavery party in the 1850s and includes Abraham Lincoln, Theodore Roosevelt, Herbert Hoover, and Dwight D. Eisenhower among its past presidents. Generally more conservative in outlook than the Democratic Party, it normally draws its strength from the smaller cities and from suburban and rural areas, especially in the Midwest and parts of New England. In recent years Republicans have tended to advocate welfare and tax reforms, including a simplified tax system and revenue-sharing to relieve the burden of local property taxes; the achievement of a "workable balance between a growing economy and environmental protection"; the defeat of "national health insurance" in favor of a program financed equally by employers, employees, and the federal government; increased defense spending; and the maintenance of US forces in Europe and elsewhere at sufficient strength to preclude the nation's becoming a "second-class power".

Leaders: Ronald REAGAN (President of the US), George BUSH (Vice President of the US), Robert J. DOLE (Senate Minority Leader), Robert MICHEL (House Minority Leader), Frank J. FAHRENKOPF (National Chairman).

Opposition Party:

Democratic Party. Originally known as the Republican Party and later as the Democratic Republican Party, the Democratic Party counts Thomas Jefferson, Andrew Jackson, Grover Cleveland, Woodrow Wilson, Franklin D. Roosevelt, John F. Kennedy, and Lyndon B. Johnson among its past leaders. Its basis is an unstable coalition of conservative politicians in the Southeastern states, more liberal political leaders in the urban centers of the Northeast and the West Coast, and populists in some towns and rural areas of the Midwest. The party was weakened in 1968 by such developments as the conservative secessionist movement led by George C. Wallace and the challenge to established leadership and policies put forward by senators Eugene J. McCarthy and Robert F. Kennedy, both of whom had sought the presidential nomination ultimately captured by Hubert H. Humphrey. It was further divided by the nomination of Senator George S. McGovern, a strong critic of the Vietnam policies of both presidents Johnson and Nixon, as Democratic presidential candidate in 1972. On the other hand, the party benefited from the circumstances surrounding the resignations of Vice President Agnew in 1973 and of President Nixon in 1974, scored impressive victories in both the House and Senate in 1974, recaptured the presidency in 1976, and maintained its substantial congressional majorities in 1978. In 1980, it retained control of the House by a reduced majority while losing the Senate and suffering decisive rejection of President Carter's bid for reelection. Its strength in Congress was largely unchanged in 1984, despite the Reagan presidential landslide and in 1986 it regained control of the Senate.

Leaders: Robert C. BYRD (Senate Majority Leader), James WRIGHT (Speaker of the House), Thomas S. FOLEY (House Majority Leader), Paul KIRK (National Committee Chairman).

Other Parties:

While third parties have occasionally influenced the outcome of presidential balloting, the Republican Party in 1860 was the only such party in US history to win a national election and subsequently establish itself as a major political organization. The third parties having the greatest impact have typically been those formed as largely personal vehicles by prominent Republicans or Democrats who have been denied nomination by their regular parties, such as Theodore Roosevelt's Progressive ("Bull Moose") Party of 1912 and the American Independent Party organized to support the 1968 candidacy of George C. Wallace.

The only nonparty candidates in recent history to attract significant public attention were former Democratic senator Eugene J. McCARTHY, who secured 751,728 votes (0.9 percent of the total) in 1976, and former Republican congressman John B. ANDERSON, who polled 5,719,722 (6.6 percent) in 1980. The only minor party candidate to receive more than 100,000 votes in 1984 was David BERGLAND of the **Libertarian Party,** for whom approximately 250,000 ballots (0.3 percent) were cast. Other contestants (receiving a combined total of 0.3 percent) were advanced by the rightist **American Party,** the social democratic **Citizens Party,** the **Communist Party,** the **Populist Party,** and the **Socialist Workers Party.**

LEGISLATURE

Legislative power is vested by the constitution in the bicameral **Congress of the United States.** Both houses are chosen by direct popular election, one-third of the Senate and the entire House of Representatives being elected every two years. Congresses are numbered consecutively, with a new Congress meeting every second year. The last election (for the 100th Congress) was held November 4, 1986.

Senate. The upper chamber consists of 100 members—two from each state—elected on a statewide basis for six-year terms. Following the 1984 election, the Democratic Party held 55 seats and the Republican Party held 45.

President: George BUSH (Vice President of the US).
President Pro Tempore: Strom THURMOND.

House of Representatives. The lower house consists of 435 voting representatives, each state being entitled to at least one representative and the actual number from each state being determined periodically according to population. The size and shape of congressional districts are determined by the states themselves; however, the Supreme Court has ruled that such districts must be "substantially equal" in population and must be redefined when they fail to meet this requirement. A resident commissioner from Puerto Rico, elected for a four-year term, takes part in discussions of the House but has no vote. Since 1970, the District of Columbia and, since 1973, Guam and the Virgin Islands have also been represented by nonvoting delegates. Following the 1986 election, the Democratic Party held 258 of the voting seats and the Republican Party held 177.

Speaker: James WRIGHT.

CABINET

President	Ronald Reagan
Vice President	George Bush
Secretaries	
Agriculture	Richard E. Lyng
Commerce	C. William Verity
Defense	Frank Carlucci
Education	William J. Bennett
Energy	John S. Herrington
Health and Human Services	Dr. Otis R. Bowen
Housing and Urban Development	Samuel R. Pierce, Jr.
Interior	Donald P. Hodel
Labor	Ann Dore McLaughlin
State	George P. Shultz
Transportation	James H. Burnley IV
Treasury	James A. Baker III
Attorney General	Edwin Meese III

NEWS MEDIA

The press and broadcasting media are privately owned and enjoy editorial freedom within the bounds of state libel laws. There is no legal ban on the ownership of broadcasting facilities by the press, and in 1950 some 43 percent of the commercial television stations were so owned. The Federal Communications Commission (FCC) has, however, been under some pressure to deny relicensing under potentially monopolistic circumstances, and only 29 percent of the television outlets were cross-owned as of 1985.

Press. There were 9,031 newspapers, excluding house organs and special-purpose publications, issued in the United States as of January 1, 1987. Weeklies outnumbered dailies by more than four to one; in addition, there were more than 120 Black and 200 foreign-language newspapers, the latter published in a total of 36 languages. Until quite recently only a few papers have sought national distribution, the most important of the dailies being the New York-based *Wall Street Journal,* published in four regional editions; the Boston-based *Christian Science Monitor,* published in three domestic editions plus an international edition; *The New York Times,* whose national edition is transmitted by satellite for printing in eight locations throughout the country; and *USA Today,* which, after a phased market-by-market expansion beginning in 1982, reached a nationwide circulation of 1.6 million in early 1988.

After a lengthy period of decline, due in part to the impact of television on the printed media, both the number and circulation of daily newspapers appeared to have stabilized in 1979–1980, with no suspensions and a net shrinkage in circulation of only 0.03 percent for the year. During 1981–1986, on the other hand, the number issued fell from 1,747 to 1,646, while circulation rose marginally from 61.4 million to 63.8 million. Significantly, some of the country's leading papers, including the *Buffalo Courier Express,* the *Cleveland Press,* the *Des Moines Tribune,* the *Minneapolis Star,* the *Philadelphia Bulletin,* the *Seattle Times,* and the *Washington Star,* were among the casualties. In addition, an ever-growing number of formerly independent papers are being brought under the control of publishing groups. There were more than 150 such groups in 1987, including Gannett newspapers (90 dailies), Thompson newspapers (82 dailies, in addition to 38 Canadian papers), Donrey Media (48 dailies), Ingersall Publications (40 dailies), Knight-Ridder newspapers (33 dailies), Newhouse/Booth newspapers (25 dailies), Cox Enterprises (19 dailies), Scripps-Howard newspapers (18 dailies), and Hearst newspapers (12 dailies); in addition, 29 papers with a combined circulation of 1.3 million are controlled by Texas entrepreneur William Dean Singleton through a number of private companies.

The principal guides to the following selection are size of circulation and extent of foreign-affairs news coverage. Ordinarily, where two dailies are published in the same city by one firm, only the larger is referenced. A few newspapers with relatively low circulation are included because of their location, special readership character, etc. The list is alphabetical according to city of publication, city designations as components of formal names being omitted. Circulation figures are for 1987 (Monday-Friday and/or Sunday editions only).

Akron, Ohio: Beacon Journal (155,023 evening, 225,741 Sunday), independent.

Atlanta, Georgia: Constitution (264,812 morning, 645,916 Sunday in comb. ed. with *Journal*), independent Democratic.

Baltimore, Maryland: Sun (223,334 morning, 187,304 evening, 489,771 Sunday), independent (the *News American,* one of the nation's oldest continuously published dailies, ceased publication in May 1986).

Birmingham, Alabama: *News* (169,059 evening, 210,805 Sunday), independent.

Boston, Massachusetts: *Globe* (500,106 all day, 798,118 Sunday), independent; *Herald* (355,494 morning), independent; *Christian Science Monitor* (186,195), independent daily.

Buffalo, New York: *News* (321,301 evening, 375,897 Sunday), independent.

Charlotte, North Carolina: *Observer* (218,501 morning, 275,180 Sunday), independent.

Chicago, Illinois: *Tribune* (758,464 all day, 1,126,293 Sunday), independent Republican; *Sun-Times* (612,686 morning, 625,935 Sunday), independent.

Cincinnati, Ohio: *Enquirer* (191,645 morning, 323,390 Sunday), independent.

Cleveland, Ohio: *Plain Dealer* (452,343 morning, 429,783 Sunday), independent.

Dallas, Texas: *Morning News* (390,987 morning, 531,417 Sunday), independent Democratic; *Times Herald* (246,370 all day, 338,963 Sunday), independent.

Dayton, Ohio: *Daily News/Journal Herald* (196,417 evening, 228,680 Sunday), independent Democratic.

Denver, Colorado: *Post* (227,105 evening, 425,454 Sunday), independent.

Des Moines, Iowa: *Register* (221,869 morning, 364,727 Sunday), independent.

Detroit, Michigan: *Free Press* (639,720 morning, 724,342 Sunday), independent; *News* (678,399 all day, 839,319 Sunday), independent.

Fort Worth, Texas: *Star-Telegram* (136,305 morning, 130,606 evening, 318,936), independent Democratic.

Grand Rapids, Michigan: *Press* (136,511 evening, 182,388 Sunday), independent.

Hartford, Connecticut: *Courant* (221,962 morning, 309,329 Sunday), independent.

Honolulu, Hawaii: *Star-Bulletin* (99,963 evening, 196,092 Sunday in comb. ed. with *Advertiser*), independent.

Houston, Texas: *Chronicle* (406,084 all day, 531,528 Sunday), independent Democratic; *Post* (305,375 morning, 365,303 Sunday), independent.

Indianapolis, Indiana: *Star* (229,595 morning, 400,150 Sunday), independent.

Jacksonville, Florida: *Florida Times-Union* (160,405 morning, 228,584 Sunday), independent.

Kansas City, Missouri: *Star* (223,134 evening, 433,480 Sunday), independent.

Little Rock, Arkansas: *Arkansas Gazette* (136,814 morning, 185,311 Sunday), independent Democratic.

Los Angeles, California: *Times* (1,117,952 morning, 1,397,192 Sunday), independent; *Herald-Examiner* (240,232 evening, 200,377 Sunday), independent.

Louisville, Kentucky: *Courier-Journal* (267,123 morning, 322,557 Sunday), independent Democratic.

Memphis, Tennessee: *Commercial Appeal* (223,926 morning, 291,275 Sunday), independent.

Miami, Florida: *Herald* (437,233 morning, 546,980 Sunday), independent.

Milwaukee, Wisconsin: *Journal* (289,254 evening, 516,890 Sunday), independent.

Minneapolis, Minnesota: *Star & Tribune* (382,832 all day, 625,504 Sunday), independent.

Nashville, Tennessee: *Tennessean* (119,120 morning, 255,318 Sunday), Democratic.

New Orleans, Louisiana: *Times-Picayune* (280,889 all day, 351,525 Sunday), independent Democratic.

New York, New York: *Daily News* (1,278,118 morning, 1,631,688 Sunday), independent; *Post* (740,123 evening), independent; *Times* (1,056,924 morning, 1,645,060 Sunday), independent; *Wall Street Journal* (2,026,276 morning), independent; *Amsterdam News* (34,915), Black weekly.

Newark, New Jersey: *Star-Ledger* (461,080 morning, 681,802 Sunday), independent.

Oakland, California: *Oakland Tribune* (151,669 evening, 156,343 Sunday).

Oklahoma City, Oklahoma: *Oklahoman* (242,214 morning, 336,518 Sunday), independent.

Omaha, Nebraska: *World-Herald* (120,062 morning, 101,991 evening, 290,197 Sunday), independent.

Philadelphia, Pennsylvania: *Inquirer* (494,844 morning, 989,250 Sunday), independent.

Phoenix, Arizona: *Gazette* (92,814 evening), independent.

Pittsburgh, Pennsylvania: *Press* (232,887 evening, 564,987 Sunday), independent; *Post-Gazette/Sun Telegraph* (170,242 morning), independent.

Portland, Oregon: *Oregonian* (321,677 morning, 404,186 Sunday), independent.

Providence, Rhode Island: *Bulletin* (110,180 evening), independent.

Raleigh, North Carolina: *News and Observer* (139,432 morning, 182,891 Sunday), independent Democratic.

Richmond, Virginia: *Times-Dispatch* (139,048 morning, 237,525 Sunday), independent.

Rochester, New York: *Democrat and Chronicle* (128,869 morning, 256,933 Sunday), independent.

Sacramento, California: *Union* (90,888 morning, 89,561 Sunday), independent.

St. Louis, Missouri: *Post-Dispatch* (357,314 evening, 548,955 Sunday), liberal.

St. Petersburg, Florida: *Times* (285,549 morning, 350,400 Sunday), independent.

Salt Lake City, Utah: *Tribune* (112,625 morning, 142,644 Sunday), independent.

San Diego, California: *Union* (252,686 morning, 415,588 Sunday), Republican.

San Francisco, California: *Chronicle* (557,934 morning), independent Republican; *Examiner* (142,335 evening, issued Sunday in comb. ed. with *Chronicle*), independent Republican.

Seattle, Washington: *Post-Intelligencer* (203,726 morning, 500,781 Sunday), independent.

Toledo, Ohio: *Blade* (160,835 evening, 219,293 Sunday), independent.

Washington, DC: *Post* (796,659 morning, 1,112,802 Sunday), independent.

Wichita, Kansas: *Eagle-Beacon* (128,865 morning, 193,502 Sunday), independent.

News agencies. The two major news agencies are the Associated Press (AP), an independent news cooperative serving more than 1,300 newspapers and 3,700 radio and television stations in the United States, and the financially plagued United Press International (UPI), which was rescued from bankruptcy by Mexican publisher Mario Vázquez Raña in 1986 and whose operating rights were sold to an investment group associated with Financial News Network in early 1988. In addition, a number of important newspapers which maintain large staffs of foreign correspondents sell syndicated news services to other papers. Among the larger of these are the *New York Times,* the *Chicago Tribune,* the *Los Angeles Times,* and the *Washington Post.*

Radio and television. Domestic radio and television broadcasting in the United States is a private function carried on under the oversight of the Federal Communications Commission (FCC), which licenses stations on the basis of experience, financial soundness, and projected program policy. Under a "fairness doctrine" embodied in FCC rules and upheld by the Supreme Court, radio and television broadcasters are required to present both sides of important issues. However, the so-called "equal time" legislation, which required a broadcaster who gave free time to a political candidate to do the same for his opponent, was amended on September 25, 1975, by the FCC, which stated that candidates' news conferences and political debates are news events and thus are not subject to the equal-time ruling. The National Association of Broadcasters (NAB) is a private body which sets operating rules for radio and television stations and networks.

There were approximately 480 million radio and 164 million television receivers in use in the United States in 1987. Of the 8,807 commercial radio stations in operation in 1986, 4,863 were AM and 3,944 were FM outlets. Approximately one-third of the total were owned by or affiliated with one of the four major commercial radio networks: American Broadcasting Company (ABC), Columbia Broadcasting System (CBS), Mutual Broadcasting System (MBS), and National Broadcasting Company (NBC). Supported primarily by paid advertising, most stations carry frequent news summaries; a few, in the larger cities, now devote all of their air time to such programming. Noncommercial programming was offered by an additional 1,194 FM outlets.

There were 1,290 commercial television stations in operation during 1987, most of them owned by or affiliated with one of three commercial television networks headquartered at New York City: American Broadcasting Company (ABC), Columbia Broadcasting System (CBS), and National Broadcasting Company (NBC). Supported primarily by paid advertising, most stations present news highlights, evening news summaries, and programs of comments and analysis. There is also a nonprofit Public Broadcasting Service (PBS), which services approximately 300 affiliated noncommercial television stations. In addition, more than 7,900 commercial cable TV systems are in operation, servicing 45 million subscribers.

Foreign radio broadcasting is conducted under governmental auspices by the Voice of America (VOA), a division of the International Communication Agency (ICA) that broadcasts in nearly four dozen languages throughout the world. (The ICA was created by the April 1978 merger of the US Information Agency and the US State Department Bureau of Educational and Cultural Affairs.) In addition, the private, though federally funded, Board for International Broadcasting sponsors both Radio Free Europe, which broadcasts from Western Europe in six Eastern European languages, and Radio Liberty, which broadcasts to the peoples of the Soviet Union in 15 languages from transmitters in Europe and the Far East. The somewhat controversial Florida-based Radio Martí, a VOA affiliate, commenced Spanish-language transmissions to Cuba on May 20, 1985.

INTERGOVERNMENTAL REPRESENTATION

The various US ambassadors to foreign governments, as well as the various foreign ambassadors accredited to the US, are given at the end of the relevant country articles.

Permanent Representative to the UN: Vernon A. WALTERS.

IGO Memberships (Non-UN): ADB, ADF, AfDB, ANZUS, BIS, CCC, CP, G10, IADB, IATTC, ICAC, ICCAT, ICES, ICM, ICO, IEA, IIC, ILZ, Inmarsat, INRO, Intelsat, Interpol, ISO, IWC, IWSG, IWTC, NATO, OAS, OECD, PCA, SPC.

RELATED TERRITORIES

The United States never acquired a colonial empire of significant proportions. Among its principal former overseas dependencies, the Philippines became independent in 1946, Puerto Rico acquired the status of a commonwealth in free association with the US in 1952, and Hawaii became the 50th state of the Union in 1959. In addition to Puerto Rico, the US now exercises sovereignty in the US Virgin Islands, Guam, American Samoa, and an assortment of smaller Caribbean and Pacific islands. Until October 1, 1979, it held administrative responsibility for the Panama Canal Zone (see Panama: Related Territory), while US administration of the Trust Territory of the Pacific is in the process of termination.

Puerto Rico. Situated in the Caribbean between the island of Hispaniola in the west and the Virgin Islands in the east (see map, p. 22), the Commonwealth of Puerto Rico comprises the large island of Puerto Rico together with Vieques, Culebra, and many smaller islands. Its area is 3,435 square miles (8,897 sq. km.), and its population (1986E) is 3,274,000. Since 1972, "reverse emigration" has more than offset relocation to the mainland. Despite a falling birth rate, population density remains among the highest in the world, amounting in 1986 to 953 persons per square mile (368 per sq. km.). San Juan, with a population of 434,849 (1980C), is the capital and principal city. Spanish blood and culture are dominant, with an admixture of American Indian, African, and other immigrant stock, largely from Western Europe and the United States. Most Puerto Ricans are Spanish-speaking and Roman Catholic, although religious freedom prevails and both English and Spanish serve as official languages. The economy, traditionally based on sugar, tobacco, and rum, advanced dramatically after 1948 under a self-help program known as "Operation Bootstrap" that stressed diversification and the use of incentives to promote industrialization through private investment, both local and foreign. Subsequently, industry surpassed agriculture as a source of income, with per capita income between 1965 and 1975 more than doubling, from $1,069

to $2,222, and reaching $4,565 in 1986. Despite marked economic and social gains, however, the Commonwealth is burdened by inflation, high public debt, and unemployment that has ranged between 14 and 23 percent of the work force since 1975.

Ceded by Spain to the US under the 1898 Treaty of Paris, Puerto Rico was subsequently governed as an unincorporated US territory. The inhabitants were granted US citizenship in 1917, obtaining in 1947 the right to elect their own chief executive. The present commonwealth status, based on a US congressional enactment of 1950 approved by plebiscite in 1951, entered into effect on July 25, 1952; under its terms, Puerto Rico now exercises approximately the same control over its internal affairs as do the 50 states. Residents, though US citizens, do not vote in national elections and are represented in the US Congress only by a resident commissioner, who has a voice, but no vote, in the House of Representatives. Federal taxes do not apply in Puerto Rico except by mutual consent (e.g., social-security taxes). The Commonwealth constitution, modeled on that of the United States but incorporating a number of progressive social and political innovations, provides for a governor and a bicameral Legislative Assembly (consisting of a Senate and a House of Representatives) elected by universal suffrage for four-year terms. An appointed Supreme Court heads the independent judiciary.

Puerto Rican politics was dominated from 1940 through 1968 by the **Popular Democratic Party** (*Partido Popular Democrático* – PPD) of Governor Luis MUÑOZ Marín, the principal architect of "Operation Bootstrap" and of the commonwealth relationship with the US. While demands for Puerto Rican independence declined sharply after 1952, a substantial movement favoring statehood continued under the leadership of Luis A. FERRE and others. In a 1967 plebiscite 60.4 percent opted for continued commonwealth status, 39 percent for statehood, and 0.6 percent for independence. Following shifts in party alignments in advance of the 1968 election, Ferré was elected governor as head of the pro-statehood **New Progressive Party** (*Partido Nuevo Progresista* – PNP), which also gained a small majority in the House of Representatives. Four years later, the PPD, under Rafael HERNANDEZ Colón, regained the governorship and full control of the legislature, while the PNP, under San Juan Mayor Carlos ROMERO Barceló, returned to power in 1976.

The traditionally antistatehood PPD officially boycotted the October 1978 primary for selection of delegates to the US Democratic Party national convention and a pro-statehood faction, styling itself the New Democratic Party, easily won. With PPD head Hernández Colón having been succeeded in July by Miguel HERNANDEZ Agosto, and despite octogenarian Muñoz Marín's return to politics as an advocate for continued commonwealth status, "statehooders" thus held control, for the first time, of both the PPD and the PNP.

In 1979 former governor Hernández Colón, leader of the pro-commonwealth *autonomista* wing of the PPD, was designated as his party's 1980 gubernatorial candidate. With the campaign largely focused on the issue of the island's status, the "new thesis" of the PPD called for Commonwealth administration of most transferred federal funds, authority to negotiate international trade agreements, and creation of a 200-mile economic zone to ensure local control of marine resources and potential offshore petroleum deposits. Governor Romero Barceló, meanwhile, was expected to call for a 1981 plebiscite on statehood, should he win reelection. At the November 4 balloting, the PNP won the governorship by an extremely narrow margin of 0.3 percent of the votes cast, while losing the Senate to the PPD (15–12) and tying the opposition in the House (25–25). In view of the outcome, Governor Romero Barceló subsequently announced that he would defer plans for the plebiscite on statehood.

At the 1984 election, Romero Barceló was defeated in his bid for another term by Hernández Colón, thereby ensuring that the statehood issue would, for the moment, recede in importance. The PPD victory was attributed, in part, to an active campaign waged by the **Puerto Rican Renewal Party** (*Partido Renovación Puertorriqueño* – PRP), a group organized by dissident PNP leader and mayor of San Juan, Dr. Hernán PADILLA in August 1983.

A comparatively small, but frequently violent, independence movement has been active since the 1920s, when the radical Nationalist Party was formed by Pedro ALBIZU Campos. On November 1, 1950, a group of *nacionalistas* attempted to assassinate President Truman, while on March 1, 1954, another group wounded five US congressmen on the floor of the House of Representatives; on September 6, 1979, President Carter commuted the sentences of the four Puerto Ricans still serving sentences for the two attacks, despite Romero Barceló's strong objection. Currently, the separatist movement is directed by the Marxist **Puerto Rican Socialist Party** (*Partido Socialista Puertorriqueño* – PSP), led by Juan MARI Bras and Carlos GALLISA, and the socialist **Puerto Rican Independence Party** (*Partido Independentista Puertorriqueño* — PIP), led by Rubén BERRIOS Martínez. The PSP and PIP have won no more than a combined 6 percent of the vote in recent elections. The most prominent far-left organization advocating independence is the **Armed Forces for National Liberation** (*Fuerzas Armadas de Liberación Nacional* — FALN), which has engaged in terrorist activities in New York City as well as in San Juan. On December 3, 1979, three other terrorist groups — the **Volunteers of the Puerto Rican Revolution**, the **Boricua Popular Army** (also known as the *Macheteros*), and the **Armed Forces of Popular Resistance** — claimed joint responsibility for an attack on a busload of US military personnel that killed two and left ten injured. Internationally, the independence movement had received support in September 1978, when the UN Decolonization Committee endorsed a Cuban resolution that labeled Puerto Rico a "colony" of the United States and called for a transfer of power prior to any referendum on statehood.

Newspapers in Puerto Rico are free of censorship; the largest circulations are those of San Juan's *El Vocero de Puerto Rico* (206,200), *El Nuevo Dia* (195,000 daily, 203,000 Sunday), and *El Mundo* (100,000 daily, 120,000 Sunday). There are 66 commercial radio stations and 10 commercial television stations; in addition, the Commonwealth Department of Education sponsors a radio and a television network, while the US Armed Forces operates four radio and four television stations. There were more than 2 million radio and 830,000 television receivers in 1987.

Governor: Rafael HERNANDEZ Colón.

Virgin Islands. Situated 40 miles east of Puerto Rico and just west and south of the British Virgin Islands (see map, p. 22), the US Virgin Islands (formerly known as the Danish West Indies) include the large islands of St. Croix, St. Thomas, and St. John, and some four dozen smaller islands. The total area, including water surfaces, is 133 square miles (344 sq. km.); the population (1986E) numbers about 110,000. The capital and only large town is Charlotte Amalie on St. Thomas. Two-thirds of the people are of African origin, and approximately one-quarter are of Puerto Rican descent. Literacy is estimated at 90 percent and English is the principal language, although Spanish is widely spoken. The people are highly religious and belong to a variety of sects, predominantly Protestant. The island's relatively prosperous economy is based largely on a flourishing tourist industry.

Purchased by the US from Denmark in 1917, the Virgin Islands are governed as an unincorporated territory of the US and administered under the Department of the Interior. The inhabitants were made US citizens in 1927 and were granted a considerable measure of self-government in the Revised Organic Act of 1954, which authorized the creation of an elected 15-member Senate. Under a New Organic Act of 1968, executive authority was vested in a governor and a lieutenant governor, both of whom since 1970 have been popularly elected. Since 1973, the territory has sent one nonvoting delegate to the US House of Representatives.

There is no visible sentiment for independence, a formal constitution for the islands having been rejected in 1964, in 1971, and in March 1979, when 56 percent of the electorate voted against a proposal that would have authorized elective local governments for each of the three main islands. Nonetheless, President Reagan in July 1981 signed into law a resolution approving a basic law for the territory, but the document was also rejected in a referendum the following November.

Juan F. LUIS of the **Independent Citizens' Movement** (a breakaway faction of the dominant Democratic Party) was sworn in as governor on January 2, 1978, upon the death of Gov. Cyril E. KING, and was elected to a full four-year term the next November; he was reelected to an additional term in 1982. Alexander Farrelly, a Democrat, defeated the ICM's Adelbert BRYAN at gubernatorial run-off balloting in November 1986.

Governor: Alexander FARRELLY.

Guam. Geographically the southernmost and largest of the Mariana Islands, the unincorporated US territory of Guam now forms an enclave of US sovereignty within the US-administered Trust Territory of the Pacific Islands (below). Its area of 212 square miles (549 sq. km.) supports a population that numbers (1986E) approximately 127,000, exclusive of some 22,000 US servicemen and their dependents. Agaña, the capital, has a civilian population of about 2,600. The islanders, predominantly of Chamorro (Micronesian) stock and Roman Catholic faith, have a high level of education, with a literacy rate of over 90 percent. The economy is largely dependent on military spending (Guam is the site of a major US air base) and tourism (some 350,000 arrivals a year, almost entirely from Japan).

Originally acquired from Spain by the 1898 Treaty of Paris, Guam is currently under the jurisdiction of the US Department of the Interior.

Guamamians were made US citizens by an Organic Act of 1950; although they do not vote in national elections, they have sent a nonvoting delegate to the US House of Representatives since 1973. Under the Guam Elective Governor Act of 1968, both the governor and lieutenant governor have, since 1970, been popularly elected. A District Court heads the judicial system. Local government in 19 municipalities is headed by elected district commissioners.

At the election of November 2, 1982, the Democratic nominee, Ricardo J. BORDALLO, narrowly defeated the Republican gubernatorial incumbent, while the Republicans won control of the 21-member Legislature. On September 6, 1986, Bordallo won the Democratic primary in a bid for reelection, despite having been indicted three days earlier for influence peddling, but lost in the November balloting to the Republican candidate, Joseph Ada; concurrently, completing a reversal of the 1982 outcome, the Democrats, although deeply divided between pro- and anti-Bordallo factions, captured the Legislature. Bordallo was ultimately convicted in February 1987.

In 1982, voters, by a three-to-one margin, had expressed a preference for commonwealth status, rather than statehood, and on August 15, 1987, are scheduled to participate in an advisory referendum on a Commonwealth Act. If endorsed, the Act is expected to encounter stiff resistance in the US Congress because of a section specifying that the indigenous Chamorro people (rather than all residents or citizens of Guam) would be entitled to change the island's future status, not excluding the possibility of independence.

Governor: Joseph F. ADA.

American Samoa. Located in the South Pacific just east of the independent state of Western Samoa, the unincorporated territory of American Samoa includes (1) the six Samoan islands (Annuu, Ofu, Olosega, Rose, Tau, Tutuila) annexed by the United States pursuant to a treaty with Britain and Germany in 1899 and (2) the separate Swain's Island, some 200 miles to the north and west, which was annexed in 1925. American Samoa has a total land area of 76 square miles (197 sq. km.) and a population almost entirely of Polynesian stock that numbers (1986E) approximately 37,000. Pago Pago, the capital, is situated on the island of Tutuila. The social structure is based on the same *matai* (family chief) system that prevails in Western Samoa. Although educational levels are comparatively high, subsistence farming and fishing remain the predominant way of life. US government spending, fish canning, and tourism are the main sources of income, and the government is the territory's largest single employer. About one-third of all high-school graduates leave Samoa for the US mainland.

Constitutionally, American Samoa is an unorganized, unincorporated territory whose indigenous inhabitants are nationals but not citizens of the United States. Administered since 1951 by the Department of the Interior, the territory voted for its first elected governor in November 1977. Its bicameral legislature (*Fono*) consists of an 18-member Senate chosen by clan chiefs and subchiefs, and a popularly elected, 20-member House of Representatives. The judiciary consists of a High Court and five district courts. Appointed district governors head the territory's three political districts.

Governor: A.P. LUTALI.

Other Insular Possessions:

Howland, Baker, and Jarvis Islands. Uninhabited, with a combined area of about 3 square miles (7.77 sq. km.), Howland, Baker, and Jarvis are widely scattered islands situated more than 1,300 miles south of Honolulu. Claimed by the United States in 1936, they are under the administration of the Department of the Interior.

Johnston and Sand Islands. Known also as Johnston Island or Johnston Atoll, the Johnston and Sand Islands lie 700 miles southwest of Hawaii and have a combined area of less than 0.5 square miles (1.3 sq. km.). The population of Johnson Island was 327 in 1980; Sand Island is uninhabited. The islands were annexed in 1858 and are under the administration of the US Defense Nuclear Agency.

Kingman Reef. The uninhabited Kingman Reef, surrounding a lagoon some 1,100 miles south of Honolulu, was annexed in 1922 and is administered by the Department of the Navy.

Midway Islands. Consisting of Eastern and Sand islands (not to be confused with Sand Island, above), the Midway Islands have a combined area of 2 square miles (5.2 sq. km.) and a population (1980) of 2,453. Located at the western end of the Hawaiian chain, they were annexed in 1867 and are administered as an unincorporated territory by the Department of the Navy.

Navassa. Situated between Jamaica and Haiti and claimed by the United States in 1916, Navassa is a small island of 2 square miles (5 sq. km.) that serves as the site of a lighthouse maintained by the US Coast Guard.

Palmyra Island. An uninhabited group of islets with an area of 4 square miles (10.4 sq. km.), Palmyra lies about 1,000 miles south of Honolulu and is administered by the Department of the Interior.

Wake Island. Consisting of three islets with a combined area of 3 square miles (7.8 sq. km.) and a population in 1980 of 1,302, Wake Island lies roughly midway between Hawaii and Guam. It was formally claimed by the United States in 1900. The site of an important air base, it is administered by the Department of the Air Force.

Numerous other small insular territories have historically been claimed by the United States, including Christmas Island in the Indian Ocean, which passed from British to Australian administration in 1958; and Quita Sueño, Roncador, Serrana, and Serranilla, a group of uninhabited islets in the western Caribbean that was turned over to Colombia under a 1972 treaty that the US Senate failed to ratify until 1981 because of conflicting claims by Nicaragua. Most attention focused, however, on the so-called "Guano Act" of 1856, under which the United States claimed jurisdiction over some 58 Pacific islands ostensibly discovered by American citizens and presumed to contain extractable resources, principally phosphate. As of 1978, 25 such claims were extant.

In April 1979 it was reported that the United States had concluded a treaty with the newly independent state of Tuvalu whereby it renounced all claims under the Act to the four southernmost of the country's nine islands. The following September, it concluded a similar treaty with Kiribati under which, in addition to surrendering Canton and Enderbury (theretofore under joint British and American administration) it relinquished claims, under the 1856 legislation, to the eight Phoenix Islands, the five Southern Line Islands, and Kiritimati (Christmas) Island in the Northern Line group. In June 1980 a treaty was concluded with New Zealand whereby US claims to four islands in the northern Cook group were also abandoned.

Micronesia (excluding Guam):

Spread over some 3 million square miles of the Western Pacific north of the equator, Micronesia's more than 2,140 islands and atolls encompass the three major archipelagos of the Caroline Islands, the Mariana Islands, and the Marshall Islands, with a combined area of about 700 square miles (1,813 sq. km.). The inhabitants of the approximately 90 inhabited islands belong to a variety of linguistic and cultural groups. Christianity is widespread, and missionaries have played an important cultural role. Subsistence farming and fishing remain the basis of the economic structure, which retains its largely indigenous character despite recent modernization efforts. Imports far exceed exports (principally copra).

Held by Germany before World War I, the three archipelagos (apart from the Mariana enclave of Guam) were administered by Japan under a League of Nations mandate during the interwar period and came under US occupation in World War II. Under an agreement approved by the UN Security Council on April 27, 1947, the islands were organized as the strategic Trust Territory of the Pacific Islands under the UN trusteeship system, with the United States as administering authority. Governing responsibility, originally vested in the Department of the Navy, was transferred to the Department of the Interior in 1951.

Prior to 1977 the Territory was divided into the six districts of the Marianas, the Marshalls, Palau, Ponape, Truk, and Yap, with executive authority vested in a high commissioner appointed by the president with the advice and consent of the Senate. Limited legislative authority was conferred in 1965 on a Congress of Micronesia, consisting of a 12-member Senate (2 senators from each district) and a 21-member House of Representatives (3 representatives from the Marianas, 4 from the Marshalls, 3 from Palau, 4 from Ponape, 5 from Truk, and 2 from Yap). Each district was provided with its own legislative body and with a district administrator responsible to the high commissioner.

Following acceptance of a 1975 covenant authorizing creation of the Commonwealth of the Northern Mariana Islands (CNMI), the rest of the Trust Territory was regrouped, Kosrae (formerly Kusaie in Ponape District) becoming the new sixth district and the lower house of the Congress of Micronesia being reduced to 20 members, Kosrae having 2. In July 1978, voters in four of the six districts approved a constitution for a Federated States of Micronesia (FSM) in "free association" with the United States, the Federated States to have full internal self-government

and responsibility for foreign affairs, with the United States retaining defense responsibilities for 15 years. Only the Marshall Islands and Palau rejected the proposal, and on October 31 both houses of the Congress of Micronesia unanimously agreed to dissolve, with representatives from Kosrae, Ponape, Truk, and Yap serving as an interim congress prior to the establishment of the Federated States on May 15, 1979.

Negotiations regarding the future status of the Federated States, the Marshalls, and Palau took place throughout 1979–1980, culminating with the initialing at Washington of compacts of "free association" by representatives of the Federated States and the Marshall Islands on October 31, 1980, and by representatives of Palau (which subsequently adopted the name Republic of Belau) on November 17. The compacts were approved by plebiscites in each of the three regions during 1983, with the US Congress approving the FSM and Marshall Islands instruments in December 1985 and the Belau pact in September 1986.

In June 1986 the Trusteeship Council endorsed by a 3–1 vote the position that the United States had satisfactorily discharged its obligations and that it was appropriate to terminate the trusteeship. The majority noted that UN missions sent to observe the plebiscites had concluded that the results constituted a free and fair expression of the wishes of the inhabitants; the Soviet Union, casting the negative vote, was highly critical of US policy regarding economic development and potential military use of the Territory. Subsequently, although the UN Charter provides that "alteration or amendment" of a strategic trust "shall be exercised by the Security Council" (where the Soviets hold veto power), Washington declared the compacts with the Marshall Islands and the Federated States to be in effect from October 21 and November 3, 1986, respectively, with CNMI inhabitants acquiring US citizenship on the latter date. A collateral declaration in respect of the Belau compact had been anticipated, but was deferred because of a territorial appellate court ruling on September 17 that a provision amending the Belau constitution to permit facilities for US conventional and nuclear forces had not obtained a requisite (75 percent) majority. Thus, Belau remained, under US law, the one remaining component of the Trust Territory, with no conclusive resolution of its status as of July 1, 1988 (see Republic of Belau, below). The situation is further clouded by the fact that Security Council approval for termination of the strategic trust has not yet been secured.

Commonwealth of the Northern Mariana Islands. Located north of the Caroline Islands and west of the Marshalls in the Western Pacific, the Marianas (excluding Guam) are an archipelago of 16 islands with a land area of 185 square miles (479 sq. km.). The population of 20,000 (1986E) resides on six islands, including Saipan (the administrative center), Tinian, and Rota. Classed as Micronesian, the people are largely Roman Catholic.

In 1972 a Marianas Political Status Commission initiated negotiations with Washington that resulted in the 1975 signing of a covenant to establish a Commonwealth of the Northern Mariana Islands in political union with the United States. The covenant was approved by the US Senate on February 24, 1976, and signed by President Ford on March 24, 1976. In December 1977 the Commonwealth's first governor and a Northern Marianas Commonwealth Legislature, which consists of a 9-member Senate elected for a four-year term and a 14-member House of Representatives elected biennially, was constituted, the legislators assuming office on January 9, 1978. Under US and local law, the CNMI ceased to be a component of the Trust Territory on November 3, 1986, with its residents becoming US citizens on the same day.

Governor: Pedro P. TENORIO.

Federated States of Micronesia. With a total land area of some 267 square miles (692 sq. km.) and a population of 73,755 (1980C), the Federated States consists of the districts of Kosrae; Pohnpei (formerly Ponape), site of the capital, Kolonia; Truk, where half the total population resides; and Yap. Together with Belau, they constitute, geographically, the Caroline Islands. As of May 10, 1979, each of the four districts became internally self-governing, with their own legislatures and executives, under a constitution approved by referendum on July 18, 1978. Elections to a federal Congress were held on March 27, 1979, and the first president of the federation (selected by the Congress) was sworn in on May 15. The present incumbent was elected on May 11, 1987. Micronesia's compact of free association with the United States was approved by the US Congress on December 13, 1985, and declared to be in effect as of November 3, 1986. Under the compact residents are not US citizens and do not have an unrestricted right of emigration to the United States.

President: John HAGLELGAM.

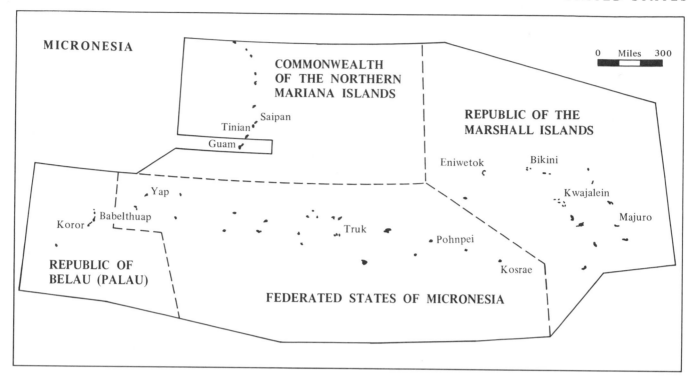

Marshall Islands. The Marshalls include 29 atolls and 5 coral islands encompassing approximately 70 square miles (181 sq. km.) and a population of 31,041 (1980C). The administrative center, Majuro Atoll, is located at the eastern end of the Trust Territory, while the largest atoll, Kwajalein, is the site of a US missile-testing range. A continuing source of controversy has been the status of Eniwetok and Bikini atolls, both of which were evacuated and used as sites for nuclear-bomb tests after World War II. Following a three-year decontamination program, Eniwetok was returned to the islanders in 1980, but Bikini remained largely uninhabitable because of residual radiation. While an overall majority of the Marshall Islanders had previously approved the compact of free association with the United States, Bikinians withheld their assent until the conclusion, in early 1985, of a $75 million settlement in compensation for damage to their health and property. Following the settlement, the US Congress approved the compact, which was declared to be in effect as of October 21, 1986. As in the case of the FSM, residents are not US citizens. Since May 1, 1979, the government has been headed by a president and a 33-member Parliament (*Nitijela*).

President: Amata KABUA.

Republic of Belau. Encompassing an area of some 178 square miles (461 sq. km.) at the western extremity of the Caroline Islands, Belau (the Paluan word for Palau) has a population of 12,177 (1980C). The administrative center is currently Koror, although a permanent capital is to be established on the largest island, Babelthuap, by 1990. A republican constitution was adopted by referendum in October 1979, with the district's first presidential and legislative elections under the basic law being held November 4, 1980. The bicameral Parliament consists of an 18-member Senate, elected on a population basis, and a 16-member House of Delegates, with one representative from each of the Republic's states. The president and vice president, elected on separate tickets, were first inaugurated on January 1, 1981, at which time Palau became the Republic of Belau. On November 30 Haruo I. REMELIK was elected to a second four-year term as chief executive on a platform that called for early implementation of the 1980 agreement on free association with the United States. In an act that did not appear to have been politically motivated, Remelik was assassinated on June 30, 1985, and at a special election on August 28 Lazarus Salii defeated Acting President Alfonso OITERONG as Remelik's successor.

The Belauan compact, including provision for substantial US aid, but requiring that the Republic provide facilities for US conventional and nuclear forces, was approved by 60 percent of the voters in a 1983 plebiscite, with only 50 percent agreeing to an accompanying proposal to override a constitutional ban on the entry, storage, or disposal of nuclear, chemical, or biological weapons and waste. A second plebiscite on September 4, 1984, also failed to secure the 75 percent majority for the override. A third plebiscite, held on February 21, 1986, in the wake of an enhanced US aid commitment, yielded a favorable vote of 72 percent. President Salii, who had received assurances that Washington would not "use, test, store, or dispose of nuclear, toxic, chemical, gas, or biological weapons on the islands", then suggested that only a simple majority was needed for compact approval. His position was challenged by the islands' ranking chief, who obtained a favorable appellate ruling by the Belau Supreme Court on September 17. Congressional endorsement of the compact immediately prior to the decision notwithstanding, the US government responded by declaring that it would "respect the judicial process of Belau" and the agreement was not implemented. Subsequent plebiscites on December 2 and June 30, 1987, yielded approval by 66 percent and 68 percent, respectively. A referendum on amending the constitution to suspend the applicability of its antinuclear clause to the compact was then held on August 4, which resulted in 71 percent approval, with majorities in 14 of the 16 states. The vote was hailed by the government, which contended that amendment (as distinguished from overriding a constitutional proscription) required only a simple majority overall, coupled with majorities in at least twelve states. The constitutional issue seemingly having been resolved, a sixth plebiscite (yielding 73 percent approval) was held on August 21, with the Belauan legislature voting on August 27 to approve the compact. Meanwhile, a suit had been filed contending that constitutional revision could occur only in conjunction with a presidential election, but was withdrawn (apparently as the result of duress) on the day of the plebiscite. On March 28, 1988, the US Senate endorsed the compact, although strong opposition continued to block action in the House of Representatives. On April 22, acting on a refiled opposition suit, the islands' Supreme Court ruled that the August 4 referendum was invalid. President Reagan responded by urging the House to proceed with its vote on the ground that the legislation contained safeguards that would preclude implementation of the pact until the court's decision had been appealed. Subsequently, Moses ULUDONG, an announced candidate for the Belauan presidency in November, proposed that the pending compact be scrapped in favor of a commonwealth arrangement. Thus, as of July 1, 1988, Belau remained the sole US-recognized component of the Trust Territory.

High Commissioner of the Trust Territory: Janet McCOY.
President of the Republic of Belau: Lazarus E. SALLI.

URUGUAY

Oriental Republic of Uruguay
República Oriental del Uruguay

Political Status: Independent state proclaimed in 1825; republic established in 1830; presidential-congressional system reinstated on March 1, 1985, supplanting military-controlled civilian government in power since February 1973.

Area: 68,037 sq. mi. (176,215 sq. km.).

Population: 2,921,798 (1985C), 2,963,000 (1988E). The 1985 census figure is preliminary.

Major Urban Center (1985E): MONTEVIDEO (1,508,000).

Official Language: Spanish.

Monetary Unit: New Peso (market rate March 1, 1988, 303.50 pesos = $1US).

President: Dr. Julio María SANGUINETTI Cairolo (Colorado Party); elected November 25, 1984, and inaugurated March 1, 1985, for a five-year term, succeeding Rafael ADDIEGO Bruno, who had become Acting President on February 12, following the resignation of Transitional President Gregorio Conrado ALVAREZ Armellino.

Vice President: Enrique TARIGO (Colorado Party); elected in balloting of November 25, 1984, and sworn in March 1, 1985, for a term concurrent with that of the President, succeeding Dr. Hamlet REYES.

THE COUNTRY

Second smallest of the independent countries of South America, Uruguay was historically among the foremost in terms of education, per capita income, and social welfare. Its official designation as the Oriental Republic of Uruguay derives from its position on the eastern bank of the Uruguay River, which forms its frontier with Argentina and opens into the great estuary of the Rio de la Plata, on which both Montevideo and the Argentine capital of Buenos Aires are situated. From its 120-mile Atlantic coastline, Uruguay's rolling grasslands gently climb to the Brazilian boundary in the northeast. More than half of the population, which is almost entirely of Spanish and Italian origins, is concentrated in Montevideo, the only large city.

Although cattle- and sheep-raising were the traditional basis of the economy, crop farming has increased in recent years and a sizable industrial complex (primarily food processing) has developed around the capital. Textiles, meat, wool, and leather goods are currently the leading exports, while industrial promotion and foreign investment laws instituted in the early 1980s have encouraged production of electrical equipment and minerals. The gross domestic product rose at an average rate of 4.8 percent during 1974–1980 but was accompanied by massive inflation that ranged between 45 and 80 percent annually. After 1980, inflation fell dramatically (to a low of 19 percent in 1982) but was coupled with a severe recession induced, in part, by devaluation of the Argentine peso in 1981, followed by disruptions attributed to the Falklands war the following year. During 1987 inflation returned to more than 60 percent, although unemployment fell from upwards of 30 percent in 1983 to a more acceptable 8.3 percent. By early 1988 the economic picture, brightened by a rise in exports, showed further signs of improvement, although the external debt had grown to more than $5 billion, prompting a round of rescheduling with more than 100 creditor banks in March.

GOVERNMENT AND POLITICS

Political background. Before 1900, Uruguay's history was largely determined by the bufferlike position that made it an object of contention between Spain and Portugal and, later, between Argentina and Brazil. Uruguayan independence, proclaimed in 1825, was recognized by the two neighboring countries in 1828, but both continued to play a role in the internal struggles of Uruguay's Colorado and Blanco parties following proclamation of a republic in 1830. The foundations of modern Uruguay were laid during the presidency of José BATLLE y Ordóñez, who took office under the Colorado banner in 1903 and initiated the extensive welfare program and governmental participation in the economy for which the nation was subsequently noted. Batlle y Ordóñez and the Colorado Party were also identified with the method of government by presidential board, or council, a system employed from 1917 to 1933 and again from 1951 to 1967. The Colorados, who had controlled the government continuously from 1865, were finally ousted at the election of 1958 but were returned to power in 1966, when voters also approved a constitutional amendment returning the country to a one-man presidency.

The first of the presidents under the new arrangement, Oscar Diego GESTIDO (Colorado), took office in March 1967 but died nine months later and was succeeded by Vice President Jorge PACHECO Areco (Colorado). Faced with a growing economic crisis, rising unrest among workers and students, and increasinging activity by *Tupamaro* guerrillas, both presidents sought to enforce economic austerity and resorted to emergency security measures. The election of Juan María BORDABERRY Arocena (Colorado) in November 1971 did little to alleviate the country's problems. Continuing economic and political instability, combined with opposition charges of corruption, culminated in military intervention on February 8, 1973. Under the direction of generals César Augusto MARTINEZ, José PEREZ Caldas, and Esteban CRISTI, the military presented a 19-point program that placed emphasis on economic reform, reducing corruption by officials, and greater military participation in political life. The program was accepted by President Bordaberry on February 13, and governmental reorganization began almost immediately. A National Security Council was created to oversee the administration, Congress was dissolved on June 27 and replaced by a Council of State, and municipal and local councils were supplanted by appointed bodies. Opposition to the increasing influence of the military was met by coercion: a general strike by the National Confederation of Workers (*Confederación Nacional de Trabajadores* — CNT) resulted in the group's proscription, while several opposition political leaders were placed in temporary detention during July and August. The National University of Montevideo was closed in October, and the Communist-led *Frente Amplio,* in addition to numerous minor leftist groups, was banned in December. Subsequently, as many as 400,000 Uruguayans were reported to have fled the country.

In early 1976 a crisis shook the uneasy alliance between President Bordaberry and the armed forces. The president, whose constitutional term was due to expire, wished to remain indefinitely in office as head of a corporativist state within which normal political activity would be prohibited. The military, on the other hand, preferred a Brazilian-style "limited democracy", with the traditional parties gradually reentering the political process over the ensuing decade. On June 12 the military view prevailed: Bordaberry was deposed and Vice President Alberto DEMICHELLI was named as his interim successor. On July 14 a newly constituted Council of the Nation (incorporating the Council of State, the three heads of the armed services, and other high-ranking officers) designated Dr. Aparicio MENDEZ Manfredini as president for a five-year term commencing September 1.

In August 1977, the government announced that President Méndez had accepted a recommendation by the military leadership that a general election be held in 1981, although only the Colorado and National (Blanco) parties would be permitted to participate. Subsequently, it was reported that a new constitution would be promulgated in 1980, while all parties would be permitted to resume their normal functions by 1986.

The proposed basic law, which would have given the military effective veto power within a context of "restricted democracy", was rejected by more than 57 percent of those participating in a referendum held November 30, 1980. The government promptly accepted the decision while announcing that efforts toward "democratic institutionalization" would continue "on the basis of the current regime".

On September 1, 1981, following designation a month earlier by the Council of the Nation, the recently retired army commander, Lt. Gen. Gregorio Conrado ALVAREZ Armellino, assumed office as "transition" president for a term scheduled to end upon reversion to civilian rule in March 1985. Fourteen months later, on November 28, 1982, a nationwide election was held to select delegates to conventions of three legally recognized groups, the Colorado and Blanco parties and the Civic Union, whose leaders were to be charged with participation in the drafting of a constitution to be presented to the voters in November 1984. The balloting, in which antimilitary candidates outpolled their promilitary counterparts within each party by almost five to one, was followed by a series of talks between the regime and the parties, which broke down in July 1983 over the extent of military power under the new basic law. The impasse yielded a period of instability through mid-1984, with escalating public protests (including Chilean-style "banging of the pots"), increased press censorship, and arrests of dissidents (most prominently the respected Blanco leader, Wilson FERREIRA Aldunate, upon his return from exile on June 16). Government statements that adherence to the declared electoral timetable (which called for balloting on November 25) would be "conditional" upon the cooperation of the civilian parties yielded further protests, while deteriorating economic conditions prompted a series of work stoppages.

Following the resumption of talks in late July between the army and a multiparty grouping (*Multipartidaria*) consisting of the legal parties (excluding the Blancos, who had quit the group in protest at the imprisonment of their leader) and a number of formations that were still nominally illegal, an agreement was reached confirming the November 25 election date and establishing a transitional advisory role for the military until late 1985. The signing of the pact was followed by a relaxation of press censorship and the legalization of bans on a number of additional parties which, in concert with the still-outlawed Communist Party, reactivated the 1971 *Frente Amplio* coalition.

Despite their condemnation of the August agreement as an "acceptance of dictatorship", the Blanco party rejoined the *Multipartidaria* in early November, after the group had initiated talks with business and union leaders on a peaceful transition to civilian rule.

Due to the continued proscription of both the Blanco leader and *Frente Amplio* spokesman, Gen. Liber SEREGNI, the Colorado candidate, Julio María SANGUINETTI Cairolo, enjoyed a considerable advantage in the presidential race, gaining a 38.6 percent vote share at the November balloting while his party won a slim plurality in both houses. The new Congress convened on February 15, 1985, followed by Sanguinetti's inaugural in March 1.

To avoid public embarassment at the swearing-in ceremony (the president-elect having indicated an aversion to accepting the presidential sash from a military ruler), President Alvarez had resigned on February 12, Supreme Court President Rafael ADDIEGO Bruno being named his interim replacement. In further attempts to remove the legacy of the military regime, the Sanguinetti government, with broad support from the public and opposition parties, released all political prisoners, including former Tupamaro guerrillas, and permitted the return of an estimated 20,000 exiles. On the other hand, a decision in 1986 to declare an amnesty for military members charged with human rights abuses generated strong dissent (see Current issues, below).

Constitution and government. The present governmental structure is modeled after that of the 1967 constitution. Executive power is vested in the president, assisted by a cabinet that he appoints, while legislative authority is lodged in a bicameral Congress. Both the president and the Congress are elected through a complex system of electoral lists that allows political parties to present multiple candidates. The judicial system includes justices of the peace, courts of first instance, courts of appeal, and a Supreme

Court. Subnationally, Uruguay is divided into 19 departments, which were returned to administration by elected officials at the balloting of November 1984.

In accordance with "Institutional Act No. 19" (the August 1984 agreement between the Alvarez regime and the *Multipartidaria*), the army, navy, and air force commanders participate in an advisory National Defense Council, which also includes the president, the vice president, and the defense, foreign, and interior ministers. The Council's actions are subject to the approval of Congress. Other provisions of the Act require the president to appoint military commanders from a list presented by the armed forces, limit the scope of military justice to crimes committed by members of the armed forces, and preclude the declaration of a state of siege without congressional approval.

Foreign relations. A member of the United Nations, the Organization of American States, the Latin American Free Trade Association, and other Western Hemisphere organizations, Uruguay has been a consistent supporter of international and inter-American cooperation and of nonintervention in the affairs of other countries. Not surprisingly, the former military government maintained particularly cordial relations with neighboring rightist regimes, while vehemently denying accusations of human rights violations by a number of international organizations. As a result, military and economic aid was substantially reduced under US President Carter. Although marginal increases were permitted during the first Reagan administration, a campaign led by the exiled Ferreira Aldunate tended to isolate the Méndez and Alvarez regimes internationally, while the January 1984 accession of Raúl Alfonsín in Argentina substantially inhibited relations with Buenos Aires.

Prior to his assumption of office, Sanguinetti met with Alfonsín and other regional leaders. His inauguration, attended by some 500 representatives of over 73 countries, featured a carefully staged, but largely unproductive meeting between US Secretary of State Shultz and Nicaraguan President Ortega. Diplomatic relations with Cuba, broken in 1974 at the request of the OAS, were restored in late 1985, while the new government, in an effort to stimulate economic revitalization, has negotiated trade accords with Argentina, Brazil, Mexico, Paraguay, and the Soviet Union. During a February 1988 regional summit near Colonia, Uruguay, with Presidents Alfonsín of Argentina and Sarney of Brazil, President Sanguinetti pledged his government's accession to protocols of economic integration adopted by the neighboring states in December 1986 (see Argentina: Foreign relations).

Current issues. In early 1986, the Sanguinetti government negotiated a "national accord", under which opposition parties agreed to support a variety of economic and political initiatives, some being accorded cabinet representation in return. However, the agreement was subsequently strained, particularly in regard to the issue of amnesty for military personnel charged with human rights abuses during the previous regime. After heated congressional and public debate (opinion polls showed overwhelming opposition), the amnesty was approved in the form of a *Punto Final* ("Full Stop") law on December 22. Leftist opponents

thereupon launched a campaign to collect the more than 500,000 signatures (representing one-quarter of the electorate) needed to force a national referendum on the question. By early 1988 more than 600,000 signatures had been obtained, although official verification of their authenticity was expected to take several months. While viewed as an overall victory for the military, the amnesty bill also contained a number of provisions (such as transferring the intelligence services to the civilian-controlled Defense Ministry) that were designed to limit future excesses by the armed services. Subsequently, the government was studying a draft organic law that would override portions of Institutional Act No. 19 and restore to the president sole authority to appoint senior officers.

POLITICAL PARTIES

Uruguay's two traditional parties, the historically liberal Colorado Party and the more conservative Blanco (National) Party, take their names from flags utilized by their respective factions in the 1836 civil war. Prior to the "temporary" proscription of all party activity in June 1976, both principal parties had included innumerable factions, which were not subject to overall party discipline and were permitted to run their own candidates at election time. In the party delegate balloting of November 28, 1982, Colorado factions presented 45 lists of candidates and Blanco factions presented 21, although most of the votes were won by a quite limited number of groups or coalitions representing both pro- and antigovernment sentiment. A third legal participant, the ultraconservative Civic Union, obtained only 1.2 percent of the vote.

The *Multipartidaria*, a grouping formed in late 1983 to mobilize and solidify opposition to the military regime, was composed of all three groups plus the proscribed Communist, Socialist, and Christian Democratic parties. The legalization of the last two in August 1984 yielded the rebirth of the 1971 coalition, the Broad Front (*Frente Amplio*), which presented a tripartisan candidate in the November 1984 election. All parties were legalized following President Sanguinetti's inauguration in March 1985.

While most opposition parties formally refused to join the Colorados in the "National Unity Government" proposed by Sanguinetti in late 1984 (the Blancos and Broad Front together holding more legislative seats than the Colorados), some Blanco and Civic Union members were allowed by their parties to join the cabinet as individuals. Given the post-military importance of the country's labor unions, a number of parties or party groups have adopted the practice of entering lists in union elections as a means of influencing or coopting leaders of the several labor federations.

Government Party:

Colorado Party (*Partido Colorado* – PC). In power continuously from 1865 to 1958, the PC again won control of the executive in 1966. Appealing mainly to the urban population, its program has emphasized liberal and progressive principles, social welfare, government participation in the economy, and inter-American cooperation. The party's leading faction, the Batllist *Unidad y Reforma*, is named after former president José Batlle y Ordóñez and is led by Jorge Batlle Ibáñez, a longtime opponent of the military establishment. Formally headed by Julio María Sanguinetti because of the personal proscription of Batlle Ibáñez under the military regime, the faction obtained 45 percent of the party vote at the November 1982 balloting and successfully advanced Sanguinetti as its presidential candidate in 1984. Other factions include the promilitary *Unión Colorado Battlista* (*pachequista*) group led by former president Jorge Pacheco Areco, who ran as a minority presidential candidate in 1984; the *Libertad y Cambio,* led by Vice President Tarigo; and the antimilitary *Batllismo Radical* and *Corriente Batllista Independiente.* In 1986 the party strongly endorsed the military amnesty urged by President Sanguinetti, while continuing to promote coalition efforts with elements of the Blanco Party.

Leaders: Julio María SANGUINETTI Cairolo (President of the Republic, *Unidad y Reforma*), Jorge BATTLE Ibáñez (*Unidad y Reforma*), Jorge PACHECO Areco (*Unión Colorado Battlista*), Enrique TARIGO (Vice President of the Republic, Secretary General of the Party, and leader of *Libertad y Cambio*), Manuel FLORES Mora (*Batllismo Radical*), Manuel FLORES Silva (*Corriente Batllista Independiente*).

Opposition Parties:

Blanco Party (*Partido Nacional* — PN). Traditionally representing conservative, rural, and clerical elements but now largely progressive in outlook, the Blancos won the elections of 1958 and 1962, subsequently failing to win control of either the executive or legislature. Its principal grouping, the centrist *Por la Patria,* was led, prior to his death in March 1988, by Wilson Ferreira Aldunate, who was in exile at the time of the 1982 balloting. His absence did not prevent the *ferreiristas* from obtaining 70 percent of the party vote in 1982; other antimilitary factions in 1982 included the *Consejo Nacional Herrerista,* heir to a tendency formed in 1954 by Luis Alberto de Herrera, and the conservative *Divisa Blanca,* led by Eduardo Pons Etcheverry.

Ferreira returned to Uruguay in June 1984 and was promptly arrested, along with his son, Juan Raúl, who had led an exile opposition group known as the Uruguayan Democratic Convergence. After officially rejecting the August "Institutional Act No. 19" and refusing to participate in the election campaign, the main faction, at Ferreira's urging, offered Alberto Zumarán as its presidential candidate. Zumarán won 32.9 percent of the vote, while the Blancos obtained 35 seats in the Chamber of Deputies and 11 Senate seats. Released from prison 5 days after the November balloting, Ferreira was elected party president in February 1985. Although he initially criticized the reported "deal" between the military and the Colorados to thwart the initiation of human rights trials, he vowed to "let the president govern" and supported the military amnesty program in 1986. The issue split the party, however, as the left-leaning *Movimiento de Rocha* faction, led by Carlos Julio Pereira, called for a referendum to defeat the measure. The smaller, right-leaning *Divisa Blanca* not only supported the amnesty but also reportedly urged coalition with the Colorados.

Leaders: Juan Raúl FERREIRA Sienra, Alberto ZUMARAN, Carlos Julio PEREIRA (*Movimiento de Rocha*), Luis Alberto LANCALLE (*Consejo Nacional Herrerista*), Eduardo Pons ETCHEVERRY (*Divisa Blanca*).

Broad Front (*Frente Amplio*). Originally a Communist-led grouping that included the Christian Democrats, the Socialists, and a pro-Cuban group styled the Oriental Revolutionary Movement (*Movimiento Revolucionario Oriental* — MRO), the Front contested the 1971 election but was subsequently proscribed by the military regime, while its presidential candidate, retired general Liber Seregni, was imprisoned and stripped of his military rank. Seregni was released in March 1984 but was banned from political activity, thus unable to serve as nominee of the Front, which included the PDC and the PCU (below), the **Socialist Party,** led by Juan CARDOZO, and dissidents from the Colorado and Blanco parties. In the November 1984 balloting, Front candidate Juan Crottogini won 20.4 percent of the vote, while the coalition won 21 Chamber seats (almost as many as the Blancos) and 6 Senate seats. In the spring of 1985 there were reports of a split between social-democratic and Marxist ("Lista 99") legislators over the degree of support to be given to the Sanguinetti administration, although in May the president, in a gesture to the Front, decreed that Seregni's military rank be restored. In 1985, the "Lista 99" faction joined with elements of the Christian Democratic and Socialist parties in a "Triple Alliance" which contested elections in student and labor organizations, winning the leadership of the leading student federation in July. Throughout 1986 the Front was solidly opposed to the military amnesty program, joining the call for a plebiscite to decide the issue, although

it rejected a membership bid by the like-minded MLN (below).

Leaders: Gen. Liber SEREGNI Mosquera (Chairman), Dr. Juan José CROTTOGINI.

People's Government Party (*Partido por el Gobierno del Pueblo* — PGP). Formed in mid-1986 by an apparent majority of Broad Front participants, the PSD indicated that it would remain within the alliance, while the designation of "Lista 99" leader Sen. Hugo Batalla as the new group's leader suggested a reconciliation of previously antagonistic elements.

Leader: Hugo BATALLA.

Christian Democratic Party (*Partido Demócrata Cristiano* — PDC). Currently left-democratic in orientation, the PDC was founded in 1962 by dissidents from the predecessor of the current Civic Union (below). Banned in November 1982, the PDC operated negatively as a "fourth party" by calling on its followers for blank ballots, some 84,000 of which were cast. The ban was lifted in August 1984; subsequently, the PDC has operated as the "moderate" tendency within the *Frente Amplio,* although some members joined the Triple Alliance.

Leaders: Héctor LESCANO, Francisco ONTONELLI, Juan Pablo TERRA, Carlos VASSALLO (Secretary General).

Communist Party of Uruguay (*Partido Comunista del Uruguay* — PCU). Although it remained banned until after Sanguinetti assumed office, the small PCU entered the *Frente Amplio* under the name Advanced Democracy (*Democracia Avanzada*). Its secretary general, resident in Moscow for many years, returned to Uruguay in November 1984.

Leaders: Alberto ALTESOR, Jaime PEREZ, Rodney ARISMENDI (Secretary General).

Civic Union (*Unión Cívica*). The original *Unión Cívica* was a conservative Catholic action party from which the left-of-center Christian Democrats withdrew in 1962. The present party is composed of right-wing Christian Democrats who withdrew from the PDC in 1971. A distinctly minor grouping, the party obtained only 14,244 votes out of nearly 1.1 million cast in 1982, and won only 2 lower house seats in 1984, with 5.8 percent of the presidential vote going to its candidate, Juan Chiarino. Nonetheless, Chiarino was included in Sanguinetti's cabinet as Defense Minister.

Leaders: Juan Vicente CHIARINO, Humberto CIGANDA.

Also contesting the November 1984 elections were the **Socialist Convergence** (*Convergencia Socialista*), whose presidential candidate, Carlos CERROTTI Frioni, subsequently joined the Triple Alliance; the **Workers' Party** (*Partido de los Trabajadores*), with Juan Carlos VITAL Andrade and Alicia SANTAMARIA as its presidential and vice-presidential candidates, respectively; and the **Patriotic Union** (*Unión Patriótica*), a promilitary grouping founded in August 1984 by Colonel Nestor BOLENTINI, who became its presidential candidate, but died three days before the election, contributing to the party's dismal showing of less than 1,000 votes. None of the fringe parties obtained congressional representation.

Extraparliamentary Opposition:

National Liberation Front (*Movimiento de Liberación Nacional* — MLN). Commonly referred to as the *Tupamaros* (after Túpac Amaru, an eighteenth-century Inca chief who was burned at the stake by the Spaniards), the MLN was long a clandestine guerrilla group, utilizing both violence and charges of political corruption in an attempt to radically alter Uruguayan society. Its last recorded clash with the police was at Montevideo in April 1974; six years later, in 1980, MLN founder Raúl SENDIC was sentenced to 45 years imprisonment after having been held without trial since 1972. A number of others were sentenced for "subversion" in late 1983 at the height of the anti-dissident campaign. Many Tupamaros were among the hundreds who returned to Uruguay at the end of 1984, while the core of the group, including Sendic, was released when all political prisoners were freed in March 1985. At the MLN's first legal convention in December 1985, an estimated 1500 delegates established a 33-member central committee and endorsed the abandonment of armed struggle in favor of nonviolent electoral politics. However, its bid to join the Broad Front was rebuffed in 1986, reportedly due to PDC objection, although the MLN's Marxist-nationalist support for labor and land reform appeared well-suited to the Front's political program. The MLN was one of the leading opponents of the government's controversial military amnesty program (see Current issues, above), attracting an estimated 17,000 for its first political rally in December 1986.

Leader: Raúl SENDIC Antonaccio.

LEGISLATURE

The bicameral **Congress** (*Congreso*), dissolved in June 1973 and replaced under the military regime with an appointive Council of State, reconvened for the first time in 12 years on February 15, 1985, following the election of November 25, 1984. The houses are elected simultaneously, both for five-year terms.

President: Enrique TARIGO.

Senate (*Senado*). The Senate consists of 30 members, distributed after the 1984 balloting as follows: Colorado Party, 13 seats; Blanco Party, 11; Broad Front, 6.
President: Enrique TARIGO.

Chamber of Deputies (*Camera del Diputados*). The 99-member Chamber of Deputies is elected from national lists. At the 1984 election, the Colorado Party won 41 seats; the Blanco Party, 35; the Broad Front, 21; and the Civic Union, 2.
Speaker: Luis ITUNO.

CABINET

President	Dr. Julio María Sanguinetti Cairolo
Vice President	Enrique Tarigo
Ministers	
Agriculture and Fisheries	Pedro Bonino
Economy and Finance	Ricardo Zerbino
Education and Culture	Dr. Adela Reta
Foreign Affairs	Luis Barrios Tassano
Industry and Energy	Jorge Presno
Interior	Antonio Marchesano
Justice	Dr. Adela Reta
Labor and Social Welfare	Hugo Fernández Faingold
National Defense	Hugo Medina
Public Health	Dr. Raúl Ugarte
Tourism	Jorge Villar
Transport and Public Works	Jorge Sanguinetti
Secretary of Planning, Coordination and Information	José María Puppo Riveiro
President, Central Bank	Ricardo Pascale

NEWS MEDIA

The press is privately owned and edited; broadcasting is conducted under both private and governmental auspices.

Press. Uruguay's long tradition of press freedom was severely curtailed during the military interregnum of 1973–1984. During this period, subject to intermittent suspension, the following dailies appeared at Montevideo: *El País* (130,000), Blanco conservative; *El Diario* (100,000), Colorado independent; *El Día* (90,000 daily), Colorado-*batllista*; *El Mañana* (40,000), Colorado; *El Diario Español* (20,000); *Diario Oficial,* official bulletin.

In late 1984, *La Hora/Diario Cooperativo*, representing the *Frente Amplio*, and *El Nuevo Tiempo*, representing the Blanco *corriente popular* tendency, commenced daily publication, as did a number of weeklies, including the following: *Jaque*, independent Colorado-*battlista*; *Opinar*, Colorado-*Libertad y Cambio*; *El Correo de los Viernes* and *La Semana Uruguaya,* Colorado-*battlista*; *Democracia*, Blanco-*Por la Patria*; *Sin Censura*, Blanco-*ferreirista*; *Aquí*, Christian Democratic.

News agencies. There is no domestic facility; numerous foreign bureaus, including Reuters and UPI, maintain offices at Montevideo.

Radio and television. The *Administración Nacional de Telecomunicaciones* (Antel) and the *División Control Servicios Radio-Eléctricos* supervise radio and television transmissions, which originate under both governmental and commercial sponsorship. There were approximately 1.8 million radio and 510,000 television receivers in 1987.

INTERGOVERNMENTAL REPRESENTATION

Ambassador to the US: Hector LUISI.

US Ambassador to Uruguay: Malcolm Richard WILKEY.

Permanent Representative to the UN: Dr. Felipe Héctor PAOLILLO.

IGO Memberships (Non-UN): ALADI, CCC, IADB, ICM, Intelsat, Interpol, IWC, OAS, OPANAL, PCA, SELA.

VANUATU

Republic of Vanuatu
République de Vanuatu (French)
Ripablik blong Vanuatu (Bislama)

Political Status: Formerly the New Hebrides; became the Anglo-French Condominium of the New Hebrides in 1906; present name adopted upon becoming an independent member of the Commonwealth on July 30, 1980.

Area: 4,647 sq. mi. (12,035 sq. km.).

Population: 111,251 (1979C), 149,000 (1988E).

Major Urban Center (1985E): VILA (Port Vila, 14,200).

Official Languages: English, French. Bislama (a pidgin dialect) is recognized constitutionally as the "national language", and efforts are currently under way to accord it equal status as a medium of instruction.

Monetary Unit: Vatu (market rate March 1, 1988, 103.85 vatu = $1US). The vatu was introduced in January 1981 to replace both French- and Australian-issued notes and coins.

President: Ati George SOKOMANU (formerly George KALKOA); designated for a five-year term on July 4, 1980, by an electoral college consisting of the preindependence Representative Assembly and the presidents of the Regional Councils of Santo and Tanna; resigned February 17, 1984; redesignated by electoral college on March 8.

Prime Minister: Fr. Walter Hayde LINI (*Vanuaaku Pati*), former Chief Minister, sworn in as Prime Minister on July 30, 1980; reconfirmed following general elections of November 2, 1983 and November 30, 1987.

THE COUNTRY

An 800-mile-long archipelago of some 80 islands, Vanuatu is situated in the western Pacific southeast of the Solomon Islands and northeast of New Caledonia. The larger islands of the group are Espiritu Santo, Malekula, Tanna, Ambrym, Pentecost, Erromanga, Aoba, Epi, and Efate, on which the capital, Vila, is located. Over 90 percent of the inhabitants are indigenous Melanesians; the remainder encompasses small groups of French, English, Vietnamese, Chinese, and other Pacific islanders. Approximately 85 percent are Christian, Presbyterians constituting the largest single denomination, followed by Roman Catholics and Anglicans. Approximately three-quarters of adult women have been described as "economically active", most of them in agricultural pursuits; female participation in government, on either the village or national level, is minimal.

The bulk of the population is engaged in some form of agriculture: coconuts, taro, and yams are grown for subsistence purposes, with copra, frozen fish, and beef constituting the principal exports. In 1981 a national airline was established, while maritime legislation was enacted to promote Vanuatu as "a flag of convenience". The country is also being developed as an offshore financial center, with well over a thousand companies incorporated at Port Vila yielding close to $1.5 million annually in revenue. Although Vanuatu has been formally characterized by the United Nations as a "least developed country", tourism, forestry projects, and the discovery of promising mineral deposits, including gold, offer potential for long-term economic growth.

GOVERNMENT AND POLITICS

Political background. Settled during the first half of the nineteenth century by a variety of British and French nationals, including a sizable contingent of missionaries, the New Hebrides subsequently became the scene of extensive labor recruitment by plantation owners in Fiji and Queensland. Following a series of unsuccessful efforts to stem the frequently inhumane practice of "blackbirding", Britain and France established a Joint Naval Commission in 1886 to safeguard order in the archipelago. Two decades later, faced with competition by German interests, the two governments agreed to form a cumbersome but reasonably serviceable condominium structure that entailed dual instruments of administration at all levels, including two police forces, two resident commissioners, and two local commissioners in each of the territory's four districts.

A 42-member Representative Assembly (replacing an Advisory Council established in 1957) convened for the first time in November 1976 but immediately became embroiled in controversy as to whether 13 members not elected by universal suffrage (4 representing tribal chiefs and 9 representing economic interests) should be required to declare party allegiance. Condemning what they termed the "present unworkable system of government", the 21 representatives of the Party of Our Land (*Vanuaaku Pati*) boycotted the second Assembly session in February 1977, prompting the colonial administrators to call a new election, the results of which were voided because of another *Vanuaaku Pati* boycott.

At the Assembly election of November 14, 1979, *Vanuaaku Pati* won 26 of 39 seats, and on November 29 party leader Fr. Walter LINI was designated as chief minister. Earlier, the colonial powers had agreed to independence in 1980, a constitution having been drafted in September and approved in a series of notes between London and Paris in October.

The attainment of independence on July 30, 1980, was clouded by secessionist movements on a number of islands, most importantly Espiritu Santo, whose principal town had been seized, with indirect support from the local French community, by the cultist *Na-Griamel* movement under the leadership of Jimmy Tupou Patuntun STEVENS. The Vanuatu flag was, however, raised at Santo on July 30 by an emissary of the Lini government in the presence of a contingent of British and French troops that was withdrawn on August 18 upon the arrival of a Papua New Guinean force backed by central government police. Most of the insurgents subsequently surrendered, Stevens being sentenced on November 21 to a prison term of fourteen and one-half years. The aftermath of the revolt continued well into 1981, with over 700 eventually convicted of crimes related to it. Stevens' trial had revealed that the insurgency was supported by both the former French resident commissioner (subsequently declared *persona non grata* by the Lini government) and the Phoenix Foundation, a right-wing group based in Carson City, Nevada. By late 1981 the security situation had improved substantially, and all of the imprisoned rebels except Stevens and his principal lieutenant, Timothy WELLES, were released.

The Lini government was returned to office in the islands' first post-independence election on November 2, 1983. Three months later, following his conviction on a charge of nonpayment of a road tax, President Sokomanu resigned. While voicing his frustration with Father Lini and offering to lead a new "national unity" government as prime minister, Sokomanu was reappointed to his former post by the electoral college on March 8.

Lini was returned to office following the balloting of November 30, 1987, at which *Vanuaaku Pati*'s vote share fell, for the first time, below 50 percent, while the opposition Union of Moderate Parties (UMP) increased its showing to 42 percent, as contrasted with 33 percent in 1983.

Constitution and government. Under the independence constitution, Vanuatu's head of state is a largely titular president designated for a five-year term by an electoral college consisting of the Parliament and Regional Council presidents. Executive power is vested in a prime minister elected by secret legislative ballot; both the prime minister and other ministers (whom the prime minister appoints) must hold legislative seats. Members of the unicameral Parliament are elected from multimember constituencies through a partially proportional system intended "to ensure fair representation of different political groups and opinions". The legislative term is four years, subject to dissolution. There is also a National Council of Chiefs, whose members are designated by peers sitting in District Councils of Chiefs, which is empowered to make recommendations to the government and Parliament on matters relating to indigenous custom and language. A national ombudsman is appointed by the president after consultation with the prime minister, party leaders, the president of the National Council of Chiefs, and others. The judicial system is headed by a four-member Supreme Court, the chief justice being named by the president after consultation with the prime minister and the leader of the opposition; of the other three justices, one is nominated by the speaker of Parliament, one by the president of the National Council of Chiefs, and one by the presidents of the Regional Councils. A Court of Appeal is constituted by two or more Supreme Court justices sitting together, while Parliament is authorized to establish village and island courts, as deemed appropriate. Each region is entitled to elect a Regional Council that may negotiate with the central government regarding administrative devolution, subject to parliamentary approval of the particulars.

Foreign relations. Although Vanuatu was not admitted to the United Nations until the fall of 1981, it became, at independence, a member of the Commonwealth and the *Agence de Coopération Culturelle et Technique* (ACCT), an organization established in 1969 to promote cultural and technical cooperation within the French-speaking world. Regionally, it is a member of the South Pacific Commission (SPC) and the South Pacific Forum (SPF), while in 1984 both the Asian Development Bank (ADB) and the Economic and Social Commission for Asia and the Pacific (ESCAP) established regional headquarters at Port Vila. Diplomatic relations were established with the Soviet Union in July 1986, and with the United States the following October, although the country maintains no embassies abroad.

Vanuatu is an outspoken member of the region's left-leaning "Melanesian bloc", displaying a strong antinuclear posture and contributing to debate on sensitive "decolonization" issues, such as Indonesian claims in East Timor and the independence movement in New Caledonia. In 1986, Lini asked the SPF to speak out on global issues as well, including support and recognition for the Palestine Liberation Organization (PLO) and the South West African People's Organization (SWAPO).

Vanuatu's commitment to a nonaligned foreign policy and its tendency to vote with radical Third World nations in international organizations has strained relations with all three of its major aid donors: the United Kingdom, Australia, and France. Port Vila's establishment of diplomatic relations with Cuba in 1983 and Libya in 1986 also generated concern among Western governments as did its signing of a major fishing treaty with the Soviet Union in early 1987.

Current issues. *Vanuaaku Pati's* relatively poor showing at the November 1987 election was attributed to the posture of the Lini government in a variety of interrelated foreign and domestic issues. The prime minister's cultivation of a "Libyan connection" in the wake of the US attack on Tripoli and Benghazi in April 1986 and his anti-French position on New Caledonia yielded a sharp decline in foreign aid and may have alienated investors in the country's offshore banks. Pro-Western groups also questioned the political wisdom of the Soviet fishing agreement (the first to grant Moscow the use of shore facilities in the South Pacific), despite the pact's short-term economic benefit of $1.5 million.

Relations with France were further strained immediately prior to the November balloting by the expulsion of the French ambassador on charges of illicitly funding the francophone UMP — an action termed by the *Pacific Islands Monthly* as "quixotic", given the country's sizeable French minority.

POLITICAL PARTIES

Government Party:

Party of Our Land (*Vanuaaku Pati*). Long at the forefront of the drive for independence and the return of indigenous lands, *Vanuaaku Pati* was formed in 1972 as the New Hebrides National Party. Its boycott of a Representative Assembly election in 1977 led to cancellation of the results. It won 26 of 46 legislative seats in November 1987, a reduction, proportionally, from 24 of 39 in 1983. In an unexpected contest in December 1987, Secretary General Barak Sope challenged Fr. Walter Lini for the party leadership, but was defeated by a near 2–1 vote despite serious health problems reportedly encountered by the prime minister in the wake of a "mild" stroke early in the year.

Leaders: Fr. Walter Hayde LINI (Prime Minister of the Republic and President of the Party), Barak SOPE (Secretary General).

Opposition Parties:

Union of Moderate Parties (UMP). The UMP is the successor to the New Hebrides Federal Party (NHFP), which was organized in early 1979 as an alliance of predominantly pro-French groups, including Jimmy Stevens's *Na-Griamel*. Following the deportation of two NHFP MPs to New Caledonia in 1982 for involvement in the Santo rebellion, the nonsecessionist elements of the party regrouped under the present label, winning 12 seats at the 1983 election and 19 in 1987. Party leader Vincent Boulekone was ousted from the Parliament in 1986 for missing meetings but ordered reinstated by the Supreme Court, which ruled that ill health excused the absences. Following the 1987 balloting, he was replaced by Maxime Carlot.

Leaders: Maxime CARLOT (Leader of the Opposition), Vincent BOULEKONE Vihresanial.

Vanuatu Independent Alliance Party (VIAP). The VIAP is a Santo-based group formed in June 1982 by two dismissed *Vanuaaku Pati* ministers, Thomas Reuben Seru and George Worek. It announced its intention to adopt a posture midway between the government and the parliamentary opposition "to try to give new directions in the functioning of the government". For the 1983 campaign it adopted a platform based on "free enterprise capitalism and anti-communism", losing all three of its existing parliamentary seats.

Leaders: Thomas Reuben SERU, George WOREK, Kalmer VOCOR.

National Democratic Party (NDP). The NDP was formed in late 1986 in preparation for the 1987 election. Led by John Naupa, transport minister in the Lini government from 1980 to 1983, the NDP attacked the administration's handling of the economy and insisted that foreign policy should concentrate on the maintenance of good relations with Britain and France.

Leader: John NAUPA.

Vanuatu Labour Party (VLP). The VLP was formed in late 1986 by a group of trade unionists who reportedly had intended to support the NDP, but withdrew several weeks prior to the latter's formal launching.

Leader: Kenneth SATUNGIA.

New People's Party (NPP). Reportedly drawing support from young, urban, and educated ni-Vanuatu, the NPP was also formed in late 1986, primarily in opposition to the Lini administration's economic policies.

Leaders: Frazer SINE, Jimmy TASSO.

Minor parties include the secessionist *Na-Griamel* (which, although a member of NHFP, chose not to join the UMP) and the *Namake Auti* and *Fren Melanesia*, two small groups representing "bush" interests on the islands of Santo and Malakula; another regional group, the **Efate Laketu Party,** was formed at Vila in 1982.

LEGISLATURE

The Vanuatu **Parliament** is a unicameral body currently consisting of 46 members elected for four-year terms, subject to dissolution. At the election of November 30, 1987, *Vanuaaku Pati* won 26 seats; the Union of Moderate Parties, 19; and an independent, 1.

Speaker: Bereteitari NEETI.

CABINET

Prime Minister	Fr. Walter Lini
Ministers	
Agriculture and Livestock	Jack Hopa
Civil Aviation, Telecommunications, Forestry and Energy	Harold Qualao
Education	Sethy J. Regenvanu
Finance and Housing	Sela Molisa
Foreign Affairs and Judicial Services	Donald Kalpokas
Health	Fred Timakata
Home Affairs	Iolu Abbil
Lands, Minerals and Fisheries	William Mahit
Planning, Information and Public Services	Fr. Walter Lini
Trade, Commerce and Industry	Edward Nipake Natebei
Transport, Tourism, Public Works and Water Supply	Barak Sope

NEWS MEDIA

Press. The *Vanuatu Weekly* (1,700) is published at Port Vila in English, French, and Bislama.

Radio and television. The government-operated Radio Vanuatu broadcasts from Vila to approximately 18,000 receivers. There is no television service.

INTERGOVERNMENTAL REPRESENTATION

Ambassador to the US: Vanuatu does not maintain an embassy at Washington.

US Ambassador to Vanuatu: Everett E. BIERMAN (Resident in Papua New Guinea).

Permanent Representative to the UN: Nikenike VUROBARAVU.

IGO Memberships (Non-UN): ACCT, ADB, APCC, CWTH, EEC(L), *EIB,* SPC, SPEC, SPF.

VATICAN CITY STATE

Stato della Città del Vaticano

Note: We have discontinued the practice of placing the title "Cardinal" after the given name, as in "Agostino Cardinal Casaroli". This style, which derives from the old British custom of referring to nobility in the form "Richard, Duke of York", is no longer favored by modern press sources.

Political Status: Independent sovereign state, under papal temporal government; international status governed by the Lateran Treaty with Italy of February 11, 1929.

Area: 0.17 sq. mi. (0.44 sq. km.).

Population: 1,250 (1988E).

Official Languages: Italian, Latin.

Monetary Unit: By agreement with the Italian government, the Vatican has the right to issue papal coinage (its total value not to exceed 100 million lire, except in holy years and in the year a Council is convened). The lira is, however, normally used as the medium of exchange (market rate March 1, 1988, 1244.40 lire = $1US).

Sovereign (Supreme Pontiff): Pope JOHN PAUL II (Karol WOJTYŁA); elected to a life term by the College of Cardinals on October 16, 1978, succeeding Pope JOHN PAUL I (Albino LUCIANI), who died September 28, 1978.

Secretary of State: Cardinal Agostino CASAROLI (Italy); appointed Acting Secretary by Pope John Paul II on April 30, 1979, following the death of Cardinal Jean VILLOT (France) on March 9; confirmed as Secretary of State and President of the Pontifical Commission for the Vatican City State on July 1; relinquished the latter position on April 9, 1984.

President of the Pontifical Commission for the Vatican City State: Cardinal Sebastiano BAGGIO (Italy); appointed by the Pope on April 9, 1984.

THE COUNTRY

An enclave within the city of Rome, the Vatican City State, the smallest independent entity in the world, derives its principal importance from its function as the seat of the Roman Catholic Church and official residence of its head, the pope. The central administration of the Church is customarily referred to as the Holy See (*Santa Sede*), or more informally as "the Vatican". The Vatican City State is simply the territorial base from which the leadership of the Church exercises its worldwide religious and ecclesiastical functions. The population, predominantly of Italian and Swiss extraction, is mainly limited to Vatican officials and employees and their families. Italian is the language of common use, although Latin is employed in the official acts of the Holy See.

The Vatican's income is based on contributions from Roman Catholic congregations around the world as well as on substantial investments in real estate, bonds, and securities. The Administration of the Patrimony of the Holy See manages its holdings, while the Institute for Religious Works acts as a bank for moneys held by affiliated religious orders. The Vatican's financial status remains the subject of perennial speculation, although an unprecedented announcement in November 1979 revealed that the Church's operations would be $20 million in deficit for the year; a similar announcement in March 1987 projected a record shortfall of $67 million, due mainly to increased personnel costs and the fall of the dollar against the lira, although the projection was reduced to $59.3 million in October because of cost-cutting measures and improved fund raising.

GOVERNMENT AND POLITICS

Political background. The recognition of the Vatican City State by Italy in the Lateran Treaty of 1929 terminated a bitter political controversy which had persisted ever since the unification of Italy in 1860–1870. Prior to that time, the popes had exercised political sovereignty over the city of Rome and substantial portions of the Italian peninsula, where they ruled as territorial sovereigns in addition to their spiritual and administrative functions as heads of the Catholic Church. The absorption of virtually all territorial holdings by the new Italian state and the failure of Pope PIUS IX to accept the legitimacy of the compensation offered by the Italian Parliament left the Holy See in an anomalous position that was finally regularized, after a lapse of two generations. In addition to the Lateran Treaty, by which Italy recognized the independence and sovereignty of the Vatican City State, a concordat was concluded that regulated the position of the Church within Italy, while a financial convention compensated the Holy See for its earlier losses. The status of the Vatican City State as established by the Lateran Treaty has since been recognized, formally or tacitly, by a majority of the world's governments.

Pope PAUL VI (Giovanni Battista MONTINI), who had been elected on June 21, 1963, died on August 6, 1978, and was succeeded on August 26 by Pope JOHN PAUL I (Albino LUCIANI), who in turn succumbed on September 28 after the shortest pontificate since that of Pope Leo XII in 1605. His successor, Cardinal Karol WOJTYŁA, archbishop of Kraków, Poland, who assumed the title Pope JOHN PAUL II, became on October 16 the first non-Italian to be elected since Pope Adrian VI in 1522.

Thereafter, there were two attempts on the pontiff's life. On May 13, 1981, he was shot and seriously wounded en route to a general audience in St. Peter's Square, Rome, by Mehmet Ali AGCA, who had escaped from a Turkish prison after having confessed to the January 1979 murder of a prominent Istanbul newspaper editor; subsequently, on May 12, 1982, a dissident priest, Fr. Juan FERNANDEZ Krohn, attempted unsuccessfully to attack him with a bayonet at Fatima, Portugal.

One of the Church's most vexing recent problems stemmed from links between the Institute for Religious Works (*Istituto per le Opere di Religione* — IOR), otherwise known as the Vatican bank, and Italy's Banco Ambrosiano, which collapsed on August 6, 1982. Italian banking officials attributed part of the failure to letters of patronage provided by the president of the Vatican bank, American Archbishop Paul MARCINKUS, to the former president of Banco Ambrosiano, Roberto CALVI, who was found hanged from a London bridge, an apparent suicide, in June. The Vatican and the Italian government subsequently appointed a joint commission to investigate the matter and in May 1984 the IOR agreed "in recognition of moral involvement", but without admission of culpability, to pay 109 creditor banks up to $250 million of a $406 million settlement against Banco Ambrosiano's successor institution. The scandal resurfaced in March 1987, when Italian press sources reported the existence of arrest warrants for Marcinkus and two other IOR officials. Vatican authorities responded by pointing out that the Lateran Treaty exempted "the central entities of the Church . . . from any interference by the Italian state" and in late July Italy's Court of Cassation cited the exemption in voiding the warrants.

Earlier, in February 1984, negotiations were concluded on a new concordat governing relations between Italy and the Vatican, which had commenced in 1976 but had been stalled by the Banco Ambrosiano controversy. The agreement provided, *inter alia,* for the abandonment of Roman Catholicism as Italy's state religion and of mandated religious instruction in public schools; on the other hand, secular authorities would continue to accord automatic recognition to church marriages and full freedom to Catholic schools.

Constitution and government. The Apostolic Constitution (*Regimini Ecclesiae Universae*) of 1967 is the constitution of the Vatican City State, which retains the form of an absolute monarchy. Supreme legislative, executive, and judicial power is vested in the pope, who is elected for life and serves concurrently as bishop of Rome, supreme pontiff of the Universal Church, primate of Italy, archbishop and metropolitan of the Province of Rome, and sovereign of the Vatican City State.

Assisting the pope in the exercise of his varied responsibilities are the members of two major organs, the College of Cardinals and the Roman Curia (*Curia Romana*). Members of the College, whose number reached an all-time high of 161 in May 1988, are named by the pope and serve as his chief advisers and coadjutors during his lifetime; upon his death, those under the age of 80 (set at a maximum of 120 in 1973) meet in secret conclave to elect his successor. A number of cardinals also hold positions on the various bodies that constitute the Curia, which serves as the Church's central administrative organ. Political responsibilities devolve primarily on the Secretariat of State, which is responsible for the diplomatic relations of the Holy See, and on the Council for the Public Affairs of the Church, which concerns itself with foreign affairs. Both bodies are headed by a cardinal secretary of state who also served as president of a Pontifical Commission overseeing civil administration of the Vatican until reassignment of the office in April 1984.

The Vatican City State has its own guard force, postal service, coinage, utilities, communication system, and local tribunal with a right of appeal to higher ecclesiastical courts.

Foreign relations. The foreign relations of the Holy See are primarily centered on its international status as seat of the Church, rather than on its status as a sovereign entity. Its relations as a sovereign state continue to be governed by the Lateran Treaty and related agreements with the Italian government.

The historic breach with Protestant Christendom was partly overcome in 1982. Early in the year, Britain and the Vatican moved toward resolution of a centuries-old dispute by establishing full diplomatic relations for the first time since Henry VIII broke with the Roman Church in 1532. Seven months later, on August 2, the Vatican announced that the Holy See and the Lutheran countries of Denmark, Norway, and Sweden (who had also broken with Rome during the sixteenth century) would exchange ambassadors in an effort "to promote and develop mutual friendly relations". Subsequently, on January 10, 1984, formal relations at the ambassadorial level were reestablished, after a lapse of 117 years, with the United States. Worldwide, such linkages now total well over 100 with unofficial representation by apostolic delegates in a number of other countries. In addition, the Holy See maintains a permanent observer at the United Nations and some of its associated agencies; it is also a member of the Universal Postal Union, the International Telecommunication Union, and the International Atomic Energy Agency.

While in principle the Holy See maintains a neutral posture in secular matters, recent popes have taken an active interest in international affairs. A manifestation of this orientation was the sending of representatives to the Conferences on Security and Cooperation in Europe held at Helsinki in 1975, Belgrade in 1977–1978, and Madrid in 1980–1983. A somewhat more specific issue was addressed by Pope Paul VI in April 1974, when he announced the dropping of earlier demands for internationalization of Jerusalem and called upon the United Nations to develop a new formula that would include the Vatican's right to be consulted in any settlement between Israel and the Arab states regarding the status of the city. In an equally specific vein, Pope John Paul II departed from tradition in strongly endorsing the Egyptian-Israeli peace treaty immediately prior to its signing at Washington on March 26, 1979.

Current issues. Having embarked on nearly three dozen foreign tours since his election in 1978, John Paul II has been described as the "most peripatetic pontiff in history". While most frequently speaking to the ecclesiastical rather than the secular aspects of such social issues as birth control, abortion, and divorce, the pope on numerous occasions has explicitly addressed political concerns, including, during a 1979 speech to the UN General Assembly, human rights, peace, and disarmament. In May 1980, the pontiff told assembled diplomats at Nairobi, Kenya, that "political independence and national sovereignty demand . . . that there be also economic independence and freedom from ideological domination". The pope concluded his third African tour on August 10–19, 1985, in Morocco, the first Arab country that he had visited; subsequently, on April 13, 1986, in an act without recorded precedent, he was received by the chief rabbi of Rome at the city's central synagogue, where he condemned all forms of anti-Semitism and deplored the genocide of the Jewish people during World War II.

While John Paul II has frequently cautioned churchmen against overt social activism at the expense of their pastoral duties, he has strongly supported Nicaraguan clerics in a lengthy dispute with the *sandinista* government and during a 1986 meeting with Brazilian President José Sarney endorsed a position taken by the country's National Conference of Bishops in favor of land reform.

In early 1987, in its first attempt to address a global policy issue, the Pontifical Commission for Justice and Peace urged, in the interest of "international solidarity", the rescheduling of Third World debts, including total remission in "emergency situations" so as not to burden insolvent governments with "immediate and intolerable demands which [they] cannot meet". A year later, in a major document on homelessness, the Commission called on governments to insure a just distribution of housing by condemning real estate practices that permit speculation without consideration of the social value of property.

In June 1987, amid worldwide protests from both Jewish and non-Jewish groups, Pope John Paul granted an audience to Austrian President Kurt Waldheim, who had been accused of complicity in war crimes while serving in the German army during World War II. A few days before the visit, at which Waldheim's wartime activities reportedly were not discussed, the Vatican took the unusual step of responding to the criticism by issuing a terse communiqué reiterating its opposition to "the terrible reality of extermination" that had been inflicted upon Jews by the Nazis; the critics were further mollified by an audience granted to American Jewish leaders in September on the eve of a papal visit to the United States.

NEWS MEDIA

As the seat of the central organization of the Roman Catholic Church, Vatican City is also the center of a worldwide communications network and of a variety of publicity media directed to both Italian and international audiences. All publications and broadcasting are conducted under Church auspices and generally reflect a clerical point of view, though with varying degrees of authority.

Press. *L'Osservatore Romano* and related publications are the principal media for Vatican comment on secular affairs; other publications are primarily concerned with ecclesiastical matters. The leading publications are *L'Osservatore Romano* (70,000), semiofficial Vatican daily, weekly editions published in English, French, German, Italian, Polish, Portuguese, and Spanish; *Bollettino Ufficiale della Santa Sede/Acta Apostolicae Sedis* (6,000), official monthly in Italian and Latin; *Annuario Pontificio*, official annual, edited by the Central Statistics Office.

News agency. *Agenzia Internazionale Fides* (AIF) services news of mission countries throughout the world.

Radio and television. Radio Vatican, located in Vatican City and at Santa Maria di Galeria outside Rome, broadcasts in 35 modern languages and in Latin. There is no television service.

INTERGOVERNMENTAL REPRESENTATION

Apostolic Pro-Nuncio to the US: Archbishop Pio LAGHI.

US Ambassador to the Holy See: Frank SHAKESPEARE.

Permanent Observer to the UN: Archbishop Renato Raffaele MARTINO.

IGO Memberships (Non-UN): Intelsat, IWTC.

VENEZUELA

Republic of Venezuela
República de Venezuela

Political Status: Independence originally proclaimed in 1811 as part of Gran Colombia; independent republic established in 1830; federal constitutional system restored in 1958.

Area: 352,143 sq. mi. (912,050 sq. km.).

Population: 14,516,735 (1981C), 17,616,000 (1988E).

Major Urban Centers (urban areas, 1986E): CARACAS (3,185,000); Maracaibo (1,261,000); Valencia (1,089,000); Barquisimeto (696,000).

Official Language: Spanish.

Monetary Unit: Bolívar (principal rate March 1, 1988, 14.50 bolívares = $1US).

President: Dr. Jaime LUSINCHI (Democratic Action); elected December 4, 1983, and inaugurated February 2, 1984, for a five-year term, succeeding Dr. Luis HERRERA Campíns (Christian Social Party).

THE COUNTRY

Situated on the northern coast of South America between Colombia, Guyana, and Brazil, the Republic of Venezuela is made up of alternating mountainous and lowland territory drained, for the most part, by the Orinoco River and its tributaries. Two-thirds or more of the rapidly growing population, most of it concentrated in coastal and northern areas, is of mixed descent, the remainder being Caucasian, Negro, and Amerindian. Roman Catholicism is the dominant faith, but other religions are tolerated. Women constitute about one-third of the paid labor force, concentrated in the clerical and service sectors; in government, women comprise less than 3 percent of elected representatives.

One of the world's leading oil producers, Venezuela has the highest per capita income in Latin America, though national wealth is very unevenly distributed. The industrial sector, which includes iron and natural gas, employs about one-fourth of the labor force and contributes nearly one-half of the GDP. By contrast, agriculture accounts for only about 6 percent of GDP; rice, corn, and beans are the principal subsistence crops, while coffee and cocoa are exported, along with some sugar, bananas, and cotton. Under government sponsorship Venezuela has been attempting to regain its historic position as a major stock-raising country, while diversification has become the keynote of economic planning, in part to reduce a dependence on oil sales that in recent decades have accounted for more than 90 percent of export revenue. During the boom years of the 1960s and 1970s Venezuelans earned a worldwide reputation for "conspicuous consumption"; subsequently, negative growth has prevailed, threatening fiscal stability and prompting the implementation of wide-ranging austerity measures.

GOVERNMENT AND POLITICS

Political background. Homeland of Simón BOLIVAR, "the Liberator", Venezuela achieved independence from Spain in 1821 and became a separate republic in 1830. A history of political instability and lengthy periods of authoritarian rule culminated in the dictatorships of Gen. Juan Vicente GOMEZ in 1908–1935 and Gen. Marcos PEREZ Jiménez in 1952–1958, the interim being punctuated by unsuccessful attempts to establish democratic government. The overthrow of the Pérez Jiménez regime by a military-backed popular movement in January 1958 prepared the way for the elected regimes which have since prevailed.

The return to democratic rule was marked by the December 1958 election of Rómulo BETANCOURT, leader of the Democratic Action (AD) party and of the non-Communist Left in Latin America. Venezuela made considerable economic and political progress under the successive AD administrations of Betancourt (1959–1964) and Raúl LEONI (1964–1969), with Cuban-supported subversive and terrorist efforts being successfully resisted. The election and inauguration of Dr. Rafael CALDERA Rodríguez of the Christian Social Party (COPEI) in 1969 further institutionalized the peaceful transfer of power. As the first Christian Democratic president in Venezuela and the second in Latin America (following Eduardo Frei Montalva of Chile), Caldera adhered to an independent pro-Western policy, while seeking to "normalize" Venezuelan political life through such measures as legal recognition of the Communist Party, appeals to leftist guerrilla forces to lay down their arms, and the broadening of diplomatic contacts with both Communist and non-Communist regimes.

Caldera was succeeded by AD candidate Carlos Andrés PEREZ following the election of December 1973, which was highlighted by challenges from the rightist Nationalist Civic Crusade of former dictator Pérez Jiménez and the New Force, an alliance of left-wing parties. Following his inauguration in March 1974, President Pérez concentrated his energies on plans to equalize distribution of Venezuela's substantially increased petroleum revenue.

In a minor upset at the election of December 1978, COPEI presidential candidate Luis HERRERA Campíns defeated AD candidate Luis PIÑERUA Ordaz. The two parties won an identical number of elective seats in both houses of Congress, but the AD secured a one-member plurality in the Senate because of a seat constitutionally reserved for outgoing President Pérez.

Capitalizing on disillusionment with COPEI's inability to cope with the impact of declining oil revenue, the AD won 50 percent of the vote at the election of December 4, 1983, COPEI polling less than 30 percent; AD presidential candidate Jaime LUSINCHI, having defeated former president Caldera and 6 other candidates, was inaugurated on February 2, 1984.

Constitution and government. Under its constitution of January 23, 1961, Venezuela is a federal republic composed of 20 states, a Federal District (Caracas), 2 Federal Territories (Amazonas and Delta Amacuro), and 72 Federal Dependencies (islands in the Antilles). The states enjoy substantial autonomy but must comply with the constitution and laws of the Republic. Executive power is vested in a president who is elected by universal suffrage for a five-year term and cannot be reelected for ten years thereafter. He appoints and presides over the cabinet. The legislative body (Congress) consists of a Senate and a Chamber of Deputies, both elected by universal suffrage for five-year terms concurrent with that of the president. Voting is compulsory for those over 18, including illiterates. Heading the judicial system is a Supreme Court, whose members are elected for nine-year terms by a joint session of Congress. The states and territories are administered by presidentially appointed governors. States have their own elected, unicameral legislative assemblies and are divided into county-type districts with popularly elected municipal councils; elected councils also exist in the Federal District and the Federal Territories.

State and Capital	Area (sq. mi.)	Population (1985E)
Anzoátegui (Barcelona)	16,720	747,100
Apure (San Fernando)	19,500(E)	213,300
Aragua (Maracay)	2,160	972,800
Barinas (Barinas)	15,000(E)	355,800
Bolívar (Ciudad Bolívar)	91,868	750,200
Carabobo (Valencia)	1,800	1,159,000
Cojedes (San Carlos)	5,700	146,200
Falcón (Coro)	9,575	549,700
Guárico (San Juan)	20,000(E)	429,300
Lara (Barquisimeto)	7,640	1,031,100
Mérida (Mérida)	5,000(E)	501,200
Miranda (Los Teques)	3,070	1,550,800
Monagas (Maturín)	28,904	426,300
Nueva Esparta (La Asunción)	444	215,100
Portuguesa (Guanare)	5,870	463,700
Sucré (Cumaná)	4,560	639,500
Táchira (San Cristóbal)	4,285	720,300
Trujillo (Trujillo)	2,860	473,200
Yaracuy (San Felipe)	2,740	328,000
Zulia (Maracaibo)	24,360	1,830,100

Federal District

Caracas	745	2,259,200

Federal Territory and Capital

Amazonas (Puerto Ayacucho)	67,063	47,800
Delta Amacuro (Tucupita)	15,520	81,642

Foreign relations. A member of the United Nations and its related agencies, the Organization of Petroleum Exporting Countries, the Organization of American States, the Latin American Integration Association, and other hemispheric organizations, Venezuela has consistently been aligned with the Western, anti-Communist position in both inter-American and world affairs. During the presidencies of Betancourt and Leoni, it was subjected by the regime of Cuban Premier Castro to repeated propaganda attacks and armed incursions. Although it consequently took a particularly harsh line toward Cuba, it was equally critical of right-wing dictatorships in the Americas and for some years refused to maintain diplomatic relations with governments formed as a result of military coups. This policy was modified during the 1960s by the establishment of diplomatic relations with Argentina, Panama, and Peru as well as with Czechoslovakia, Hungary, the Soviet Union, and other Communist countries, while in December 1974, despite earlier differences, a normalization of relations with Cuba was announced.

A long-standing territorial claim to the section of Guyana west of the Essequibo River (see map, p. 242) has caused intermittent friction with that country, Venezuela declining in June 1982 to renew a 12-year moratorium on unilateral action in the dispute and refusing in December to sanction submission of the controversy to the International Court of Justice. Although the parties ultimately agreed to submit the issue to arbitration by the UN secretary general, no resolution had been achieved as of early 1988. Caracas has also been engaged in a 30-year dispute with Colombia regarding sovereignty over the Gulf of Venezuela (Gulf of Guajira), with tension escalating to the

level of high military alert following the unauthorized intrusion of a Colombian ship into Venezuelan territorial waters in August 1988. Other disagreements have arisen over the smuggling of food-stuffs, drug trafficking, and alleged attacks by Colombia's *Ejercito de Liberación Nacional* guerrillas on the Venezuelan national guard.

Convinced that recent Central American unrest had stemmed from socio-economic inequities rather than from East-West controversy, Venezuelan leaders met with representatives from Colombia, Mexico, and Panama on the Panamanian island of Contadora in January 1983 to initiate a series of multilateral negotiations aimed at promoting peace in the region. The current Venezuelan administration appears to have withdrawn somewhat from the Contadora initiative, shifting its previously neutral posture toward Nicaragua to one of "deep freeze" by refusing to send observers to the November 1984 Nicaraguan elections, suspending oil shipments in early 1985, and granting asylum to rebel leader Eden Pastora Gomez. Concurrently, the Lusinchi administration has moved to strengthen its role in the Caribbean, concluding economic and cultural cooperation accords with Trinidad and Tobago, and promoting trade links with Barbados.

Apart from its strong support of Argentina during the 1982 Falklands conflict, relations with the United States have been generally close, although Venezuela receives little US aid in view of its high national income and has occasionally objected to what it considers detrimental US trade policies.

Current issues. Inheriting from his predecessor a $34 billion foreign debt, fiscal overcommitment, and mounting capital flight, President Lusinchi launched a highly restrictive program that included currency devaluations, debt rescheduling negotiations, budget cutbacks, import restrictions, and encouragement of a "more austere" lifestyle. Sporadic successes were achieved, such as significant increases in agricultural production, which in 1986 contributed to measurable economic growth for the first time in eight years. However, the plunge in oil profits (44 percent in 1986) continued to limit recovery; unemployment reached 16 percent in early 1987 and the spiraling inflation rate was at least the precipitating factor behind student demonstrations that erupted periodically throughout the spring and summer.

In May 1987, the Lusinchi government announced a series of measures designed to increase purchasing power and placate the nation's increasingly restive labor confederation. The measures, including wage increases for public- and private-sector employees, a 120-day ban on dismissal of workers, and a 120-day freeze on prices, were extended for an additional two months in September in an effort to curb an inflation which had reached 36 percent. Concurrently, Caracas signed a $20.3 billion rescheduling agreement on public-sector debts to creditor banks. The accord not only allowed payments to be stretched out until 1999, but also reduced the total amount of principal to be repaid. In February 1988 the government announced that it would attempt to further ease the burden of debt servicing, thereby encouraging industrial growth. A month later it also acknowledged that in order to compensate for a substantial decline in foreign reserves it had begun selling gold, with an expected total return of $300 million.

POLITICAL PARTIES

Prior to its 1983 victory, the Democratic Action party controlled the presidency during 1958–1968 and 1973–1978, the 1968 and 1978 contests being won by Christian Socialists. Early threats to the democratic regime were posed by two left-wing groups, the Movement of the Revolutionary Left (MIR) and the Communist Party of Venezuela (PCV); both were banned in 1962, but the PCV was legalized in March 1969 following its renunciation of the use of force for political ends, while the MIR was legalized in 1973. In 1981, a National Leftist Coordinating Committee (*Coordinadora Nacional de la Izquierda*) attempted, unsuccessfully, to agree on a common leftist presidential candidate for the 1983 election; the lack of agreement persisted into 1988, with three leftist candidates being presented for the presidential balloting in December.

Leading Parties:

Democratic Action (*Acción Democrática* — AD). Founded in 1937, the AD was forced underground by the Pérez Jiménez dictatorship but regained legality in 1958 and held power for ten years thereafter. An advocate of rapid economic development, welfare policies, and Western values, it has experienced three splits since 1960 but won an overwhelming victory in 1973, capturing the presidency and both houses of Congress. Although losing the presidency in 1978, it remained the largest party in the Senate and secured the same number of seats as the Christian Socialists in the Chamber of Deputies. It regained the presidency in December 1983, while winning majorities in both houses of Congress; it further consolidated its position with a decisive victory at municipal balloting in May 1984. By 1987, with its popularity waning because of continued economic crisis, the AD was deeply divided in the selection of a candidate for the 1988 presidential poll, former interior minister Octavio Lepage Barretto, handpicked by President Lusinchi as his successor, ultimately being defeated for the nomination by former president Carlos Andrés Pérez at party electoral college balloting on October 11.

Leaders: Dr. Jaime LUSINCHI (President of the Republic), Carlos Andrés PEREZ (former President of the Republic), Dr. Gonzalo BARRIOS (President of the Party), David MORALES Bello, Octavio LEPAGE Barretto, Alejandro IZAGUIRRE (Secretary General).

Christian Social Party (*Partido Social-Cristiano/Comité de Organización Politica Electoral Independiente* — COPEI). Founded in 1946, COPEI offers a moderately conservative reflection of the social doctrines of the Roman Catholic Church. It nonetheless spans a wide range of opinion, from a clerical right wing to an ultraprogressive, youthful left wing. The party won the presidency by a narrow margin in 1968, and recaptured the office in 1978, without, however, winning control of the Congress. Although it secured 14 Senate and 61 Chamber seats in 1983, it ran a poor second to the AD at the 1984 municipal elections. Subsequently the party was torn by a bitter presidential nomination race between COPEI founder Rafael Caldera Rodríguez and his one-time protege Eduardo Fernández, whose nearly 3–1 victory late in the year was termed a "patricidal" embarrassment for the veteran party leader.

Leaders: Dr. Rafael CALDERA Rodríguez and Dr. Luis HERRERA Campíns (former Presidents of the Republic), Dr. Godofredo GONZALEZ (Acting President of the Party), Eduardo FERNANDEZ (Secretary General).

Lesser Groups:

National Opinion (*Opinión Nacional* — Opina). Formed in 1961, Opina won three Chamber seats in 1983, while placing fifth in the presidential balloting.

Leaders: Jorge OLAVARRIA (1983 presidential candidate), Pedro Luis BLANCO Peñalver (President), Amado CORNEILLES (Secretary General).

Democratic Republican Union (*Unión Republicana Democrática* — URD). Founded in 1946 and once Venezuela's second-largest party, the URD champions principles similar to those of the AD and has, in the past, supported AD governments. It won three Chamber seats in 1983. In 1987 the party, for the first time, put forward a woman, Ismenia VILLALBA, as its presidential nominee.

Leaders: Dr. Jóvito VILLALBA, Simón Antonio PAVAN (Secretary General).

New Generation (*Nueva Generación* — NG). The NG is a right-wing group formed in 1979.

Leader: Gen. Arnaldo CASTRO Hurtado (1983 presidential candidate).

National Redemption (*Rescate Nacional* — RN). The RN is a personalist grouping organized prior to the 1983 election to support the presidential candidacy of retired general Luis Enrique Rangel Bourgoin.

Leader: Gen. Luis Enrique RANGEL Bourgoin.

National Integration Movement (*Movimiento de Integración Nacional* — MIN). Formed in 1977, the MIN retained its single Chamber seat in 1983.

Leader: Gonzalo PEREZ Hernández (Secretary General).

Movement to Socialism (*Movimiento al Socialismo* — MAS). Originating as a radical left-wing group that split from the PCV (below) in 1971, the MAS subsequently adopted a "Eurocommunist" posture and became the dominant legislative party of the Left by capturing 2 Senate and 11 Chamber seats in 1978. It supported José Vicente Rangel for the presidency in 1978, but with the exception of a small group of dissidents, was deeply opposed to his 1983 bid as leader of a left-wing coalition that included the NA (below). Having responded positively to a mid-1981 appeal from AD leader Carlos Andrés Pérez for a "synchronization of the opposition", it appeared to be adopting a democratic-socialist rather than a rigidly Marxist orientation. At the 1983 balloting, it secured two Senate and 10 Chamber seats, while its nominee, Teodoro Petkoff, placed third in the presidential race. The party, joined by the MIR (below), has renominated Petkoff as its 1988 candidate.

Leaders: Pompeyo MARQUEZ (President), Teodoro PETKOFF (1988 presidential candidate), German LAIRET, Freddy MUNOZ (Secretary General).

Movement of the Revolutionary Left (*Movimiento de Izquierda Revolucionaria* — MIR). Organized in 1960 by a group of student radicals, the MIR engaged in urban terrorism in 1961–1964, while subsequently operating as a guerrilla force from a rural base. Having captured one Chamber seat following its legalization as a political party in 1973, it increased its representation to four in 1978. In 1980, it split into two factions, an anti-Moscow group led by Moisés Moliero that in subsequent adjudication was awarded its party name and supported MAS presidential candidate Teodoro Petkoff, and a pro-Moscow-group led by party founder and 1978 presidential candidate, Américo MARTIN, that supported José Vicente Rangel (see NA, below). In late 1987 the party was reported to have "merged" with MAS in support of Petkoff's 1988 candidacy.

Leaders: Héctor PEREZ Marcano (President), Moisés MOLIERO (Secretary General).

New Alternative (*Nueva Alternative* — NA). The NA was formed by José Vicente Rangel in 1982 as an anti-MAS coalition that included the pro-Moscow faction of the MIR and the groups listed below. In a move that was reportedly viewed with "scepticism" by other leftist formations, the NA nominated Leopoldo DIAZ Bruzual, former COPEI militant and former president of the Central Bank, as its 1988 presidential candidate.

Leaders: José Vicente RANGEL (1983 presidential candidate), Guillermo GARCIA Ponce (Secretary General).

United Vanguard (*Vanguardia Unida* — VU). Also known as the Revolutionary Communist Vanguard (*Vanguardia Revolucionaria Comunista* — VRC) and previously styled the United Communist Vanguard (*Vanguardia Unitaria Comunista* — VUC), the VU split from the PCV (below) in 1974 and won one Chamber seat in 1978.

Leaders: Eduardo MACHADO, Guillermo GARCIA Ponce (Secretary General).

Revolutionary Action Group (*Grupo de Acción Revolucionaria* — GAR). Of left-wing Catholic origin, the GAR is led by a former member of COPEI.

Leader: Rafael IRRIBARREN.

Radical Cause (*Causa R*). *Causa R* is a far-Left group whose founder, Alfredo Maneiro, died in 1983.

Leader: Andrés VELASQUEZ.

People's Electoral Movement (*Movimiento Electoral del Pueblo*— MEP). The MEP was founded in 1967 by a left-wing faction of the AD that disagreed with the party's choice of a presidential candidate for the 1968 election. It won three Chamber seats in 1978, none in 1983. In 1987 the party selected Edmundo CHIRINOS, rector of the Central University of Venezuela, as its 1988 presidential nominee, who, in addition to being supported by the Communist Party (below), received the endorsement of the **Independent Moral Movement** (*Movimiento Moral Independiente* —MMI), a small left-wing group formed in 1986.

Leaders: Dr. Luis Beltrán PRIETO Figueroa (President), Dr. Jesús PAZ Galárraga (Vice President), Salom MESA Espinoza, Adelso GONZALEZ Urdaneta (Secretary General).

Communist Party of Venezuela (*Partido Comunista de Venezuela*— PCV). Founded in 1931, the PCV was proscribed in 1962 but restored to legality in 1969. Although the official leadership adheres to the Soviet line and rejects revolutionary violence in favor of political action, there have been recent reports of "dissidence" within its ranks. The party currently holds three seats in the Chamber of Deputies and has endorsed the 1988 presidential candidacy of Edmundo Chirinos.

Leaders: Jesús FARIA (President), Héctor MUJICA, Alonso OJEDA Olaechea (Secretary General).

The People's Advance (*El Pueblo Avanzar*—EPA). The EPA is an outgrowth of a faction of radical students and faculty at the Andrés Bello Catholic University.

Leader: Edwin ZAMBRANO.

Socialist League (*Liga Socialista*—LS). Founded in 1974, the LS retained its one Chamber seat in 1983.

Leaders: Carmelo LABORIT (President), Julio ESCALONA, David NIEVES.

Party of the Venezuelan Revolution (*Partido de la Revolución Venezolana*—PRV). The PRV is headed by Douglas Bravo, leader of the Armed Forces of National Liberation (*Fuerzas Armadas de Liberación Nacional*—FALN), one of the most active of the guerrilla groups of the mid-1960s.

Leader: Douglas BRAVO.

Clandestine Groups:

Very few of the once numerous guerrilla groups are now active. Among those refusing to take advantage of the government's pacification program were the Maoist-oriented **América Silva Guerrilla Front of the Red Flag** (*Frente Guerrillero América Silva de Bandera Roja*), which had been active in the eastern state of Anzoátegui. In December 1983, the government reported that the front was virtually destroyed with the capture of 24 of its members, including its alleged leader, Juan Pablo MIRANDA Herrera, although Red Flag adherents claimed responsibility for two bomb attacks in September 1984. Another guerrilla group, the **Argimiro Gabaldón Revolutionary Command** (*Comando Revolucionario Argimiro Gabaldón*), was charged with the kidnapping of US businessman William Niehous in 1976, but a number of the Command's leaders were captured in March 1977 and Niehous was rescued, unharmed, in June 1979. A new left-wing guerrilla group, **We Shall Overcome** (*Venceremos*), was reportedly responsible for planting a bomb outside of the Ministry of the Interior in April 1987.

LEGISLATURE

The bicameral **National Congress** (*Congreso Nacional*) consists of a Senate and a Chamber of Deputies, both sitting for five-year terms. Under the present system of representation, most members are elected directly, with additional seats being awarded to minority parties.

Senate (*Senado*). The Senate has at least two members from each state and two from the Federal District, with former presidents accorded life tenure. Following the election of December 4, 1983, the Democratic Action held 28 elective seats; the Christian Social Party, 14; and the Movement to Socialism, 2.

President: Reinaldo Leandro MORA.

Chamber of Deputies (*Cámara de Diputados*). The Chamber has at least two deputies from each state and one from the Federal District.

Following the December 1983 election, the Democratic Action held 112 seats; the Christian Social Party, 61; the Movement to Socialism, 10; the National Opinion, the Democratic Republic Union, and the Communist Party of Venezuela, 3 each; and the National Integration Movement, the Union for the New Alternative, and the Socialist League, 1 each.

President: Leonardo FERRER.

CABINET

President	Jaime Lusinchi
Ministers	
Agriculture and Livestock	Wenceslao Mantilla
Coordination and Planning	Modesto Freites Pinate
Development	Héctor Meneses
Education	Pedro Cabello Poleo
Energy and Mines	Arturo Hernández Grisanti
Environment and Natural Resources	Guillermo Colmenares Finol
Family Affairs	Virginia Olivio de Celli
Finance	Héctor Hurtado Navarro
Foreign Affairs	Germán Nava Carillo
Health and Social Welfare	Francisco Montbrun
Interior	José Angel Ciliberto
Justice	José Manzo González
Labor	Simón Antoni Paván
National Defense	Gen. Eliodoro Guerrero Gómez
Secretariat of the Presidency	Dr. Carmelo Lauría Lesseur
Transport and Communications	Vicente Pérez Cayena
Urban Development	César Quintana Romero
Ministers of State	
Guyana Development	Leopoldo Sucre Figarella
Investment Fund	Herberto Urdaneta (Acting)
Science and Technology	Dr. Julio Arends
Advisers to the Presidency	
International Economic Affairs	(Vacant)
Marine, River and Lake Affairs	Vice Adm. Andrés Eduardo Brito Martínez
State Enterprises	(Vacant)
Comptroller General	Zoraida García Vara
Governor, Federal District	Adolfo Ramírez Torres
President, Central Bank	Mauricio García Araujo

NEWS MEDIA

The media are free in principle but are subject to censorship in times of emergency.

Press. The following are Spanish dailies published at Caracas, unless otherwise noted: *Ultimas Noticias* (235,000), independent; *El Mundo* (196,000), independent; *Diario 2001* (160,000), independent; *El Nacional* (140,200), independent; *El Universal* (138,000); *La Crítica* (Maracaibo, 83,000); *Panorama* (Maracaibo, 75,000); *El Diario de Caracas* (50,000). *The Daily Journal* (18,000), in English.

News agencies. There is no domestic facility; foreign agencies with offices at Caracas include ANSA, AP, Reuters, TASS, and UPI.

Radio and television. Broadcasting is controlled by the *Ministerio de Comunicaciones* and supervised by the *Cámara Venezolana de la Industria Radio y Televisión,* an association of broadcasters. All of the country's approximately 145 radio stations are commercial, with the exception of 1 governmental (*Radio Nacional*) and 5 cultural stations. There were 6.7 million radio receivers in 1986; television, received by approximately 2.8 million sets, is operated by the government and by commercial companies.

INTERGOVERNMENTAL REPRESENTATION

Ambassador to the US: Valentin HERNANDEZ.

US Ambassador to Venezuela: Otto J. REICH.

Permanent Representative to the UN: Dr. Andrés AGUILAR.

IGO Memberships (Non-UN): ALADI, Ancom, APEF, CDB, Geplacea, IADB, ICCO, ICM, ICO, Intelsat, Interpol, ISO, IWTC, NAM, OAS, OPANAL, OPEC, PCA, SELA.

VIETNAM

Socialist Republic of Vietnam
Công-Hòa Xã-Hôi Chu-Nghĩa Viêt Nam

Political Status: Communist republic originally proclaimed September 2, 1945. Democratic Republic of Vietnam established in the North on July 21, 1954; Republic of Vietnam established in the South on October 26, 1955. Socialist Republic of Vietnam proclaimed July 2, 1976, following surrender of the southern government on April 30, 1975; present constitution adopted December 18, 1980.

Area: 128,402 sq. mi. (332,561 sq. km.).

Population: 52,741,766 (1979C), 62,430,000 (1988E).

Major Urban Centers: HANOI (1983E, 2,674,000); Ho Chi Minh City (formerly Saigon, 1979C, 3,420,000); Haiphong (1979C, 1,279,100); Da Nang (1973E, 492,000); Nha Trang (1973E, 216,000); Qui-Nhon (1973E, 214,000); Hué (1973E, 209,000).

Official Language: Vietnamese.

Monetary Unit: Dông (official rate March 1, 1988, 368.00 dông = $1US).

Chairman of the Council of State: VO CHI CONG; elected by the National Assembly on June 18, 1987, to succeed TRUONG CHINH.

Chairman of the Council of Ministers (Premier): DO MUOI; elected by the National Assembly on June 22, 1988, to succeed VO VAN KIET, who had held office on an acting basis since the death of PHAM HUNG on March 11.

THE COUNTRY

A tropical land of varied climate and topography, Vietnam extends for roughly 1,000 miles along the eastern face of the Indochina Peninsula between the deltas of its two great rivers, the Red River in the North and the Mekong in the South. To the east, the country borders on the Gulf of Tonkin and the South China Sea; in the west, the mountains of the Annamite Chain separate it from Kampuchea (Cambodia) and Laos. A second mountainous region in the North serves as a partial barrier between Vietnam and China, which historically has exercised great influence in Vietnam and provided its name, "Land of the South".

The Vietnamese population is of mixed ethnic stock and includes substantial groups of highland tribes as well as Chinese, Khmer, and other non-Vietnamese peoples. Although religion is not encouraged by the state, a majority of the Vietnamese are nominally Buddhists and Taoists, with a significant Roman Catholic minority, particularly in the South. Vietnamese is the national language, while French has long been the preferred second language. Women constitute close to one-half the paid labor force, concentrated in agriculture, health, and education. Their participation in party and governmental affairs is proportionally less, with a decline in influence at the local level since reunification because of reported cultural "backlash".

Northern Vietnam has traditionally been a food-deficient area, dependent on supplementary rice and other provisions from the South. It has, on the other hand, a considerable industrial economy based on substantial resources of anthracite coal, chromite, iron, phosphate, tin, and other minerals, which are processed by an infrastructure introduced during the years of French rule. In southern Vietnam over three-fourths of the labor force is engaged in farming and fishing. Rubber and rice have traditionally been the area's major exports, while industry has been limited for the most part to the production of light consumer goods and the processing of agricultural commodities.

A key component of the Socialist Republic's 1976–1980 Five-Year Plan was large-scale redistribution of the population, including resettlement of many residents of southern cities into "new economic zones" in rural areas, and the shifting of surplus labor northward. Midway through the plan the government announced that it intended to nationalize all land beyond what was needed by individual families to meet basic requirements, but the adverse impact on production led to new decrees in September 1979 permitting greater freedom to cultivate reclaimed and virgin land. Since that time, food self-sufficiency has largely been achieved, in part because of a product contract system whereby farmers are allowed free use of goods after meeting state quotas. Incentives for industrial export production, foreign investment, and expansion of such nonsocialist components as handicraft industries have also been initiated, while decentralization of economic planning since 1982 has yielded modest overall growth; however, such improvement has failed to match population increase, estimated at 2.2 percent in 1985. In late 1986, it was reported that aid from the Soviet Union, theretofore estimated at $1 billion a year, would be increased to more than $2 billion annually over the next five years.

GOVERNMENT AND POLITICS

Political background. Vietnam's three historic regions of Tonkin in the north, Annam in the center, and Cochin-China in the south came under French control in 1862–1884 and were later joined with Cambodia and Laos to form the

French-ruled Indochinese Union, more commonly called French Indochina. The Japanese, who occupied Indochina in World War II, permitted the establishment in Vietnam on September 2, 1945, of the Democratic Republic of Vietnam (DRV) under HO CHI MINH, the Communist leader of the nationalist resistance movement then known as the Vietminh (*Viêt Nam Duc-Lap Don Minh Hoi,* or Vietnamese Independence League). Although the French on their return to Indochina accorded provisional recognition to the DRV, subsequent negotiations broke down, and in December 1946 the Vietminh initiated military action against French forces. While fighting with the Vietminh continued, the French in 1949 recognized BAO DAI, former emperor of Annam, as head of state of an independent Vietnam within the French Union. Treaties conceding full Vietnamese independence in association with France were initialed at Paris on June 4, 1954; in practice, however, the jurisdiction of the Bao Dai government was limited to South Vietnam as a consequence of the military successes of the Vietminh, the major defeat suffered by French forces at Dien Bien Phu in May 1954, and the armistice and related agreements concluded at Geneva on July 20–21, 1954. Those agreements provided for a temporary division of Vietnam near the 17th parallel into two separately administered zones—Communist in the North and non-Communist in the South—pending an internationally supervised election to be held in 1956. These arrangements were rejected, however, by the Bao Dai government and by the republican regime that succeeded it in South Vietnam in 1955. Vietnam thus remained divided between a northern zone administered by the Communist-ruled DRV and a southern zone administered by the anti-Communist government of the Republic of Vietnam.

Within North Vietnam, the years 1954–1958 were devoted to economic recovery, establishment of a socialist society, and industrialization. A new constitution promulgated in 1960 consolidated the powers of the central government, and elections in 1960 and 1964 reaffirmed the preeminence of Ho Chi Minh, who continued as president of the DRV and chairman of the Vietnam Workers' Party (successor to the Indochinese Communist Party). Ho Chi Minh died in 1969, his party position remaining unfilled in apparent deference to his memory, with the political leadership passing to LE DUAN, who had been named first secretary nine years earlier.

Communist-led subversive and terrorist activity against the government of South Vietnam had been resumed in the late 1950s by so-called Vietcong (Vietnamese Communist) resistance elements in a continuation of the earlier anti-French offensive, now supported and directed by the Communist North. Within the South, these operations were sponsored from 1960 onward by a Communist-controlled political organization called the National Front for the Liberation of South Vietnam (NLF). Despite the initiation of US advisory assistance to South Vietnamese military forces in 1954, guerrilla operations by Vietcong and regular North Vietnamese units proved increasingly disruptive, and by early 1965 the Republic of Vietnam appeared threatened with military defeat. The United States therefore intensified its efforts by initiating air operations against selected military targets in the North and by ordering large contingents of its ground force into action in the South.

Earlier, in 1961, the growth of the Communist-supported insurgency forced NGO DINH DIEM (who had assumed the South Vietnamese presidency following the ouster of Bao Dai in 1955) to assume emergency powers. Popular resentment of his increasingly repressive regime led, however, to his death in a coup d'état directed by Gen. DUONG VAN MINH ("Big Minh") on November 1, 1963. A period of unstable military rule followed, power being held successively by General Minh (November 1963 to January 1964), Gen. NGUYEN KHANH (January 1964 to February 1965), and Gen. NGUYEN VAN THIEU, who took control in February 1965 and assumed the functions of head of state in June, leaving the more powerful post of prime minister to Air Marshal NGUYEN CAO KY. In response to US pressure, a new constitution was promulgated on April 1, 1967, and Thieu and Ky were elected president and vice president, respectively, on September 3.

Following the large-scale "Tet offensive" by Communist forces in South Vietnam in January-February 1968, the United States on March 31 announced a cessation of bombing in all but the southern area of North Vietnam, adjacent to the demilitarized zone on both sides of the 17th parallel. The action proved more successful than a number of earlier bombing halts in paving the way for peace talks. Preliminary discussions between US and North Vietnamese representatives were initiated at Paris on May 13, while expanded talks began at Paris on January 18, 1969, although it was not until September 1972, following major US troop withdrawals and the failure of another major Communist offensive, that Hanoi agreed to drop its insistence on imposing a Communist regime in the South and accepted a 1971 US proposal for a temporary ceasefire. A peace agreement was subsequently concluded on January 27, 1973, on the basis of extensive private discussions between US Secretary of State Kissinger and DRV negotiator LE DUC THO. Its provisions called for a withdrawal of all remaining US forces and an institution of political talks between the South Vietnamese and the Vietcong aimed at the establishment of a National Council of National Reconciliation and Concord (NCNRC). The Saigon government and the Provisional Revolutionary Government of South Vietnam failed, however, to reach agreement on the Council's composition. Moreover, despite the US withdrawal and North Vietnam's formal support of the peace accord, it was estimated that as of May 1974 some 210,000 North Vietnamese troops were fighting in the South, as compared to 160,000 at the time of the 1972 ceasefire.

A new Communist offensive, launched in late 1974, resulted in the loss of Phuoc Long Province, 70 miles north of Saigon, in early January 1975. By late March, in the wake of a near total collapse of discipline within the South Vietnamese army, the cities of Hué and Da Nang had fallen. On March 25, President Thieu ordered Prime Minister TRAN THIEN KHIEM to organize a broadly representative government to deal with the emergency, but by early April demands were being advanced for Thieu's resignation. On April 4 the Khiem government resigned and NGUYEN BA CAN, the speaker of the House of Representatives, was named to head a new cabinet that was installed on April 14. Seven days later, as the Communist forces neared Saigon, President Thieu announced his resignation and Vice President TRAN VAN HUONG was sworn in as his successor. Huong himself resigned on April 28 in favor of Gen. Duong Van Minh, who called for a ceasefire and immediate negotiations with North Vietnamese and People's Liberation Armed Forces (PLAF) representatives. The appeal was rejected, and on April 30 Communist forces entered Saigon to receive the surrender of the South Vietnamese government.

Upon the fall of Saigon, a Military Management Committee under PLAF Lt. Gen. TRAN VAN TRA was established to govern the city. On June 6 the Provisional Revolutionary Government under the nominal presidency of HUYNH TAN PHAT was invested as the government of South Vietnam, although real power appeared to be exercised by PHAM HUNG, fourth-ranked member of the Politburo of the North Vietnamese Workers' Party and secretary of its South Vietnamese Committee. At a conference held at Saigon on November 5–6, a delegation headed by Hung was named to negotiate with northern representatives on an election to a National Assembly that would appoint a government for all of Vietnam. Talks between the two delegations on November 15–21 ended with an announcement that the election would be held prior to the first anniversary of the conquest of the South.

The enlarged legislature was elected on April 25, 1976, and convened for the first time at Hanoi on June 24. On July 2 it proclaimed the reunification of the country, which was to be styled the Socialist Republic of Vietnam. On the same day, it named TON DUC THANG, the incumbent president of North Vietnam, as head of state. It also announced the appointment of two vice presidents: NGUYEN LUONG BANG, theretofore vice president of the DRV, and NGUYEN HUU THO, leader of the southern National Liberation Front. DRV Premier PHAM VAN DONG was designated to head a cabinet composed largely of former North Vietnamese ministers, with the addition of six South Vietnamese. On December 20, at the conclusion of a congress of the Vietnam Workers' Party held at Hanoi, the party changed its name to the Vietnamese Communist Party (VCP) and adopted a series of guidelines designed to realize the nation's "socialist goals".

Vice President Nguyen Luong Bang died on July 19, 1979, no successor being named, while President Ton Duc Thang's death on March 30, 1980, resulted in Nguyen Huu Tho's appointment as acting president on April 1. A new National Assembly was elected on April 26, 1981, and, under a revised constitution adopted the preceding December, designated a five-member collective presidency (Council of State) on July 4. The second-ranked member of the VCP Politburo, TRUONG CHINH, was named Council chairman (thus becoming nominal head of state), the third-ranked Pham Van Dong continuing as chairman of the Council of Ministers.

Longtime party leader Le Duan died at Hanoi on July 10, 1986, the VCP Central Committee naming Truong Chinh as his successor four days later. However, the designation proved temporary; in a remarkable change of leader-ship at the Sixth VCP Congress in December, NGUYEN VAN LINH was named general secretary, with Truong Chinh (who remained State Council Chairman), Pham Van Dong (who continued as premier), Le Duc Tho, and three others (Defense Minister VAN TIEN DUNG, army political commissar CHU HUY MAN, and former vice premier TO HUU) all being retired from the Politburo. A major governmental reorganization ensued in February 1987, while in mid-June, following a National Assembly election in April, VO CHI CONG succeeded Truong Chinh as chairman of the Council of State and Pham Hung replaced Pham Van Dong as chairman of the Council of Ministers. Senior Gen. VO VAN KIET, theretofore a deputy chairman of the Council of Ministers, was named acting chairman following Pham Hung's death in March 1988, the currently third-ranked Politburo member, DO MUOI, being designated his permanent successor on June 22.

Constitution and government. Upon reunification in 1976, the DRV constitution of January 1, 1960, was put into effect throughout the country pending adoption of a new basic law that on December 18, 1980, received unanimous legislative approval. The present document defines the Socialist Republic as a "state of proletarian dictatorship" advancing toward socialism, and identifies the Communist Party as "the only force leading the state and society". All power ostensibly belongs to the people and is exercised through their elected representatives, the highest organ of state authority being a unicameral National Assembly elected by universal adult suffrage. Its normal five-year term may be prolonged in the event of war and other exceptional circumstances. The Assembly elects, for a term of office corresponding to its own, a Council of State, which is the highest legislative organ and the state's collective presidency; the Council chairman also chairs the National Defense Council. Administrative functions are directed by the chairman and other members of a Council of Ministers (none of whom may be members of the Council of State), all appointed by and responsible to the Assembly. The judicial system is headed by the chief justice of the Supreme People's Court and the procurator general of the Supreme People's Organ of Control, both being Assembly appointees. People's Courts, Military Tribunals, and People's Organs of Control operate at the local level.

For administrative purposes the country is divided into provinces (16 in the North, 20 in the South) and municipalities; provinces are further divided into districts (subdivided into villages and townships), and towns and provincial capitals (subdivided into villages and wards), while municipalities are divided into precincts (subdivided into wards). Each unit elects a People's Council, which then selects a People's Committee to serve as an executive.

Foreign relations. For many years prior to reunification, North Vietnamese external policy combined traditional Vietnamese nationalism with Communist ideology and tactics. Relations with most other Communist nations were close, and aid from the People's Republic of China, the Soviet Union, and Eastern Europe was essential both to the DRV's industrial development and to its military campaigns in the South. Largely because of this dependence, the DRV avoided commitments to either side in the Sino-Soviet dispute, although it disregarded Peking's objections by participating in the Paris peace talks in 1968, as a result of which some 40,000 to 50,000 Chinese military personnel who had been helping to maintain North Vietnam's transportation network were reported to have been withdrawn.

The DRV had long been involved in the internal affairs of both Laos and Kampuchea, where for many years it supported insurgent movements, partly as a means of keeping open its supply routes to South Vietnam. Subsequent to reunification, Hanoi concluded a number of mutual cooperation agreements with Laos which some observers viewed as leaving that country little more than a province of Vietnam. Collaterally, relations with Kampuchea deteriorated sharply, yielding numerous military encounters along the two countries' common frontier and a severance of diplomatic relations in December 1977. The clashes continued throughout 1978, escalating into full-scale border warfare and a Vietnamese invasion of its neighbor at the end of the year. On January 7, 1979, Phnom Penh fell to the Vietnamese, supported by a small force of dissident Khmers styling themselves the Kampuchean National United Front for National Salvation, and on January 8 a pro-Vietnamese "People's Republic of Kampuchea" was proclaimed under Heng Samrin, a former member of the Kampuchean General Staff. Continued fighting during the remainder of the year caused massive human and physical destruction and generated a new flood of Southeast Asian refugees (primarily into Thailand) without, however, eliminating remnants of the former Democratic Kampuchean regime, who continued guerrilla operations near the western border (see article on Kampuchea). Meanwhile, some 200,000 Vietnamese troops remained in the country.

In reaction to the drive into Kampuchea, Chinese forces invaded northern Vietnam on February 17, 1979, and occupied a number of border towns, suffering heavy casualties before withdrawing in mid-March. The incursion was described by Beijing as a "limited operation" designed to teach Hanoi "a lesson" after failure to resolve a number of long-standing disputes — primarily, the validity of late nineteenth-century border agreements between France and the Chinese Empire, sovereignty over the Paracel and Spratly islands in the South China Sea, and jurisdiction over territorial waters in the Gulf of Tonkin. Peace talks undertaken by Hanoi and Beijing in April 1979 were broken off by the Chinese in March 1980. Intermittent border conflicts continued thereafter, usually subsequent to or concurrent with Vietnamese offensives against Kampuchean rebels. In February 1986 the New China News Agency (*Xinhua*) charged Hanoi with having launched 33 attacks into Yunnan Province during the previous month, causing the death or injury of 65 Chinese soldiers and civilians. Eleven months later, in early January 1987, China mounted a three-day incursion into Vietnam's Ha Tuyen province; while falling short of an attempt to teach Hanoi a "second lesson", it was the bloodiest encounter since 1979, with casualty claims of nearly 2,000 killed or wounded.

Prior to the end of the Vietnam War, Hanoi had evidenced no interest in joining the United Nations. An application was eventually submitted in July 1975, but was rejected by US action in the Security Council, as was a second application submitted on behalf of the newly uni-

fied state in August 1976. In May 1977 the United States withdrew its objection after Vietnamese representatives at Paris had agreed to provide additional information on the fate of missing US servicemen and the Socialist Republic was admitted to the world body at the General Assembly session that convened on September 20. By contrast, Vietnam followed Poland in withdrawing (effective May 31, 1985) from the International Labour Organisation, after have charged the ILO with bias against socialist and developing countries.

In June 1978, as relations with the People's Republic of China became increasingly hostile, Vietnam signaled its mounting dependence on the Soviet Union by joining the Soviet-led Council for Mutual Economic Assistance as the organization's second Asian member; five months later, just prior to the invasion of Kampuchea, Hanoi and Moscow concluded a treaty of friendship and cooperation.

Current issues. During the second half of 1986, the VCP experienced the most dramatic leadership changes in its 56-year history. Le Duan, who had served as general secretary since 1960, died on July 10 and was succeeded by the 80-year-old head of state, Truong Chinh. Subsequently, at the conclusion of the Sixth Party Congress in mid-December, Truong Chinh and five other senior leaders were removed from the Politburo, with Nguyen Van Linh, theretofore Ho Chi Minh City party leader, assuming the post of general secretary. Even more drastic were changes in the party secretariat, where nine new members were appointed and only three individuals named in 1982 were retained. At the Central Committee level, one-third of those appointed at the Fifth Congress were ousted, nearly half of whom had been government officials dealing with some aspect of the nation's economy. Earlier, a purge of the economic bureaucracy had yielded the dismissal, among others, of two deputy prime ministers, the ministers of both internal and foreign trade, and the director general of the State Bank. Echoing the party changes was a major governmental restructuring in mid-February 1987, in the course of which a number of new ministries were created, others were consolidated, and six new deputy chairmen of the Council of Ministers were appointed. The reorganization was completed in mid-June, when Truong Chinh and Pham Van Dong stepped down as heads of state and government, respectively.

The personnel changes at the Sixth Congress had reportedly been preceded by intense debate within the party leadership on how best to respond to a wide variety of economic problems that manifestly called for reform. While food production in both 1985 and 1986 was relatively satisfactory, it was by no means certain that increases during the next four years would be adequate to feed a population expected to grow by nearly 14 percent through the period. Meanwhile, problems in other sectors were nearing conditions of crisis, with both light and heavy industry falling far short of needs and a currency reform, launched in late 1985 to generate fiscal stability, yielding quite the opposite: by November, inflation had escalated to 700 percent, necessitating an 80 percent devaluation of the dông. In addition, a five-year work force "redistribution" of some 1.3 million individuals had not noticeably reduced large scale migration to the cities — particularly in the south — where desperate conditions for poorer families were widespread. Burdened by these difficulties, Vietnam (with substantially less enthusiasm than either China or the Soviet Union) moved by mid-1987 to adopt a number of capitalist-style measures that included the encouragement of privately owned production, the creation of the nation's first commercial bank, and an "opening to foreign business" aimed primarily at the launching of joint ventures, but not excluding totally foreign-owned enterprises. These tendencies, seemingly strengthened by the designation of Vo Van Kiet as acting chairman of the Council of Ministers in March 1988, appeared to be threatened by the appointment of Do Muoi in late June. The new chairman had reportedly directed the recent purges against party members and was believed to be associated with the hard-liners previously allied with Le Duan.

In foreign affairs, Hanoi has responded warily to Moscow's improved relations with Beijing—particularly since Soviet leader Gorbachev's Vladivostok speech in July 1986 did not contain a ritual assurance that normalization with China "would not be at the expense of any third country". However, such an assurance was tendered by the leader of the Soviet delegation to the Sixth Party Congress, who pointedly added that "if Vietnam and China want to restore normal relations, they should talk directly with each other". In regard to Kampuchea, party officials have indicated on a number of occasions that "we stand for continued withdrawal of Vietnamese volunteers", while reiterating an earlier pledge that such withdrawal would be completed by 1990. In keeping with such assurances, Hanoi formally turned over control of the anti-insurgent campaign to Kampuchean commanders on June 30, 1988, and announced a partial troop withdrawal.

POLITICAL PARTIES

The Communist party apparatus of North Vietnam operated for many years as the Vietnam Workers' Party— VWP (*Dang Lao Dong Viêt Nam*). The VWP was formed in 1954 as successor to the Indochinese Communist Party (founded in 1930 and ostensibly dissolved in 1954) and was the controlling party of North Vietnam's National Fatherland Front (NFF). In South Vietnam, the core of the Provisional Revolutionary Government formed in 1969 was the National Liberation Front (NLF), which had been organized in 1960 by some 20 groups opposed to the policies of President Diem. On July 6, 1976, representatives of the NFF, the NLF, and other organizations met at Hanoi to organize an all-inclusive **Vietnam Fatherland Front** (VFF), which was formally launched during a congress held at Ho Chi Minh City on January 31–February 4, 1977. In addition to the parties listed below, the Front includes various trade-union, peasants', women's, youth, and other mass organizations. Under an electoral law approved by the National Assembly on December 22, 1980, the VFF is responsible for nominating candidates in all constituencies, in consultation with local groups.

Leading Party:

Vietnamese Communist Party—VCP (*Dang Cong San Viêt Nam*). Its present name was adopted by the VWP at its Fourth Congress in 1976. The 1,129 delegates to the Sixth Congress, held at Hanoi on December 15–18, 1986, approved expansion of the party's Central Committee from 116 full and 36 alternate members to 124 full and 49 alternate members, in addition to a drastic restructuring of the Politburo that included retirement of five of its six most senior leaders (see Current issues, above).

General Secretary: NGUYEN VAN LINH.

Other Members of Politburo: DO MUOI (Chairman, Council of Ministers), Lt. Gen. DOAN KHUE (former First Deputy Defense Minister), Senior Gen. DONG SY NGUYEN (Deputy Chairman, Council of Ministers), Senior Gen. LE DUC ANH (Commander, Vietnamese forces in Kampuchea), Maj. Gen. MAI CHI THO (former Mayor and Party Secretary, Ho Chi Minh City), NGUYEN CO THACH (Foreign Minister), NGUYEN DUC TAM (Secretary, Central Committee), NGUYEN THANH BINH (Secretary, Hanoi Party Committee), TRAN XUAN BACH (Member, Secretariat), VO CHI CONG (Chairman, State Council), Senior Gen. VO VAN KIET (former Acting Chairman, Council of Ministers).

Alternate: DAO DUY TUNG (Chairman, VCP Propaganda Department).

Central Committee Secretariat: Lt. Gen. DAM QUANG TRUNG, DAO DUY TUNG, LE PHUC THO, NGUYEN DUC TAM, NGUYEN KHANH, Lt. Gen. NGUYEN QUYET, NGUYEN VAN LINH, PHAM THE DUYET, TRAN KIEN, TRAN QUOC HUONG, Lt. Gen. TRAN QUYET, TRAN XUAN BACH, VU OANH.

Other Parties:

Socialist Party (*Dang Xa Hoi*). Organized at Hanoi in 1951 as a grouping of intellectuals, the Socialist Party has recently testified to Communist leadership as "an organizational principle of the state".

Leader: NGUYEN XIEN (Secrtary General).

Democratic Party (*Dang Dan Chu*). The Democratic Party was formed in North Vietnam in 1944 as a Communist-affiliated group appealing to intellectuals, businessmen, and the petite bourgeoisie.

Leader: NGHIEM XUAN YEM (Secretary General).

LEGISLATURE

The present **National Assembly** (*Quoc Hoi*) is a unicameral body of 496 members representing 93 constituencies. At the most recent election of April 19, 1987, 829 candidates were nominated by approved political parties and "revolutionary mass organizations".

Chairman: LE QUANG DAO.

CABINET

[as of June 22, 1988]

Chairman, Council of Ministers	Do Muoi
Deputy Chairmen	Senior Gen. Dong Sy Nguyen
	Nguyen Co Thach
	Nguyen Khanh
	Tran Duc Luong
	Senior Gen. Vo Nguyen Giap

State Commission Chairmen

Inspection	Huynh Cong To
Law	Tran Quang Huy
Planning	Senior Gen. Dau Ngoc Xuan
Prices	Phan Van Tien
Science and Technology	Dang Huu

Ministers

Agriculture and Food Industry	Nguyen Cong Tan
Communications and Transportation	Bui Danh Luu
Construction	Phan Ngoc Tuong
Culture	Tran Van Phac
Education	Pham Minh Hac
Energy	Vu Ngoc Hai
Engineering and Metals	Phan Thanh Liem

Finance	Hoang Quy
Foreign Affairs	Nguyen Co Thach
Foreign Trade	Doan Duy Thanh
Forestry	Phan Xuan Dot
Higher and Vocational Education	Tran Hong Quan
Home Trade	Hoang Minh Thang
Information	Tran Hoan
Interior	Mai Chi Tho
Justice	Phan Hien
Labor	Nguyen Ky Cam
Light Industry	Vu Tuan
Marine Products	Nguyen Tan Trinh
National Defense	Senior Gen. Le Duc Anh
Public Health	Dang Hoi Xuan
Supply	Hoang Duc Nghi
War Invalids and Social Welfare	Nguyen Ky Cam
Water Conservancy	Nguyen Canh Dinh
Director General, State Bank	Lu Minh Chau

NEWS MEDIA

All communications media are controlled and operated by the government, the Vietnamese Communist Party, or subordinate organizations.

Press. The following are published daily at Hanoi, unless otherwise noted: *Nhan Dan* (The People, 305,000), official VCP organ; *Quan Doi Nhan Dan* (People's Army, 200,000), army organ; *Giai Phong* (Liberation, Ho Chi Minh City, 45,000), local VCP organ; *Lao Dong* (Labor, 37,000), weekly trade-union publication; *Hanoi Moi* (New Hanoi), local VCP organ; *Dai Doan Ket* (Great Union, Ho Chi Minh City), weekly organ of Fatherland Front; *Doc Lap* (Independence), weekly VDP organ; *To Quoc* (Fatherland), monthly VSP organ. The last remaining independent paper at Ho Chi Minh City, *Tin Sang* (Morning News), was closed down in mid-1981.

News agencies. The domestic facility is the Vietnam News Agency (VNA). *Agence France-Presse* (AFP), *Novosti,* and TASS are among the foreign agencies maintaining offices at Hanoi.

Radio and television. Under supervision of the Vietnam Radio and Television Commission, the Voice of Vietnam broadcasts to approximately 6 million receivers. Television service was available to some 2.4 million receivers in eight cities in 1986.

INTERGOVERNMENTAL REPRESENTATION

As of July 1, 1988, the United States and the Socialist Republic of Vietnam did not maintain diplomatic relations.

Permanent Representative to the UN: (Vacant).

IGO Memberships (Non-UN): ADB, ANRPC, CMEA, IIB, Intelsat, NAM.

WESTERN SAMOA

Independent State of Western Samoa
Malo Sa'oloto Tuto'atasi o Samoa i Sisifo

Note: The capitalized portions of personal names in this article are, in most cases, not family but (usually abbreviated) given names, preceded by honorifics.

Political Status: Independent state since January 1, 1962; member of the Commonwealth since 1970; under mixed political system approximating a constitutional monarchy.

Area: 1,097 sq. mi. (2,842 sq. km.).

Population: 158,940 (1986C), 160,000 (1988E).

Major Urban Center (1981C): APIA (33,170).

Official Languages: English, Samoan.

Monetary Unit: Tala (market rate March 1, 1988, 2.03 tala = $1US).

Head of State: Susuga Malietoa TANUMAFILI II; assumed office as Joint Head of State for Life on January 1, 1962, becoming sole Head of State on the death of his associate, Tupua TAMASESE Meaole, on April 5, 1963.

Prime Minister: Tofilau ETI Alesana (Human Rights Protection Party); succeeded Va'ai KOLONE (Independent) on April 7, 1988, following election of February 26.

THE COUNTRY

Western Samoa consists of two volcanic islands (Savai'i and Upolu) and several minor islets located east of Fiji and west of American Samoa, in the south central Pacific. The country enjoys a tropical climate and good volcanic soils, but rugged topography limits the cultivated and populated areas to the lowlands and coastal fringes. The Christian, highly literate Samoans are representatives of the second-largest ethnic group of Polynesia. They have had lengthy contact with the West but retain their traditional social structure based on an extended family grouping known as the *aiga,* whose chief, or *matai,* serves also as the group's political representative. Although women are officially counted as 16 percent of the labor force, evidence points to much higher involvement in subsistence activities.

The economy is largely based on subsistence agriculture and fishing, supplemented by the production of copra, cocoa, and bananas for export. Basic raw materials are, however, lacking, and despite increased utilization of timber resources the country suffers from a chronic trade deficit, part of which is offset by overseas remittances from Samoans living in New Zealand and the United States. In recent years, tourism has been making an increasingly important contribution to the islands' economy and construction on the country's first international hotel, the Royal Samoan, is now under way.

GOVERNMENT AND POLITICS

Political background. An object of missionary interest since the 1830s, the Samoan Islands came under joint British, German, and American supervision in 1889 but were politically divided as a consequence of an 1899 treaty whereby the United States annexed Eastern (American) Samoa, while Western Samoa became a German protectorate. New Zealand occupied Western Samoa during World War I and acquired subsequent control of the territory under a League of Nations mandate. Opposition to the

New Zealand administration resulted in the formation of a nationalist organization known as the "Mau", which was active between 1927 and 1936.

Following World War II, a Samoan request for independence was rejected, and Western Samoa continued under New Zealand administration as a United Nations Trust Territory. Political evolution, however, gained momentum. Cabinet government was introduced in 1959; a new constitution, adopted in 1960, was approved by plebiscite in 1961; and Western Samoa became fully independent by agreement with New Zealand and the United Nations on January 1, 1962. The largely ceremonial position of head of state was at first held jointly by the representatives of two of the four royal lines (the Tuiaana/Tuiatua and the Malietoa), but one of the incumbents died in 1963 and the other continues in an individual capacity.

Political life since independence has seen a number of changes as well as a series of recent challenges to certain aspects of the country's constitutional structure. The initial government under Prime Minister Fiame MATA'AFA Mulinu'u lasted through 1970, when it was replaced by an administration headed by Tupua Tamasese LEALOFI IV. The Tamasese regime was in turn succeeded in 1973 by another Mata'afa government, although Lealofi returned as acting prime minister to serve the remainder of Mata'afa's term upon the latter's death in May 1975. In March 1976, following a legislative election in which over half of the incumbents lost their seats, Taisi Tupuola EFI became the first prime minister not a *Tama Aiga* ("Royal Son") from one of the four leading families. In the wake of balloting on February 24, 1979, that again saw over half the Assembly members defeated, Tupuola Efi was redesignated prime minister after legislative endorsement by a narrow vote of 24–23.

At the election of February 27, 1982, the islands' first formally constituted political group, the Human Rights Protection Party (HRPP), won a plurality of 22 parliamentary seats and after a lengthy period of consultation with independent members succeeded, on April 13, in organizing a government under Va'ai KOLONE. However, the party lost its one-seat majority in late June upon the ouster of a member found guilty of electoral malpractice, and on September 18 Kolone's own seat was vacated by the Supreme Court on similar grounds. Former prime minister Tupuola Efi was thereupon returned to office, although his attempt to form a coalition government was rebuffed by the HRPP, which argued that the court had acted *ultra vires* in its expulsion orders. Upon rejection of a budget bill, Efi was again forced to resign, and the new HRPP leader, Tofilau ETI Alesana, succeeded him on December 30, the party having regained its majority in by-elections to refill the vacated seats. In mid-1984, opposition leader Tupuola Efi was designated a *Tama Aiga* in succession to his cousin, former prime minister Tupua Tamasese Leolofi IV, thenceforth being addressed as Tupua Tamasese EFI.

The HRPP captured 31 of 47 Assembly seats at the election of February 22, 1985, Tofilau Eti being redesignated prime minister after former prime minister Va'ai Kolone had withdrawn a bid to recover the party leadership.

Despite his party's technical majority, Eti was forced to resign on December 27 after members of the HRPP had joined with the opposition (now including Va'ai Kolone) to defeat the 1986 budget bill by a 27–19 vote. During the following week, a new coalition government headed by Kolone was formed, the head of state having rejected a request to dissolve the Assembly.

The results of the extremely close election of February 26, 1988, were not announced until the new Assembly convened on April 7, at which time the HRPP was declared to have obtained a bare majority of 24 seats, with Tofilau Eti returning as prime minister. By late June, following a number of Supreme Court rulings on electoral challenges, the HRPP held a 25–19 majority, with three seats to be refilled in by-elections.

Constitution and government. As defined by the constitution of October 28, 1960, Western Samoa's political institutions combine the forms of British-style parliamentary democracy with elements of the traditional Samoan social structure. The head of state (*O le Ao o le Malo*), who performs the duties of a constitutional sovereign, has been and presumably will continue to be recruited from among the four paramount island chiefs. Although the present incumbent has been designated for life, future heads of state will be elected by the Legislative Assembly for five-year terms. The head of state appoints the prime minister and, on the latter's advice, members of the cabinet, who are drawn from the Assembly and are responsible to that body. Most members of the Assembly, which sits for a three-year term (subject to dissolution), are indirectly elected by *matai,* or family heads, whose number was increased by one-third to 16,000 in a series of controversial appointments prior to the 1985 balloting; direct election is limited to two special representatives chosen by universal adult suffrage of persons outside the *matai* system. The judicial system is headed by a Supreme Court and includes a Court of Appeal, magistrates' courts, and a special Land and Titles Court for dealing with disputes over customary land and Samoan titles.

For the most part, local government is carried out through the *matai* system and includes the institution of the village *fono,* or council. There are some part-time government officials who operate in rural areas.

Foreign relations. Western Samoa has established diplomatic relations with over two dozen other countries (including the People's Republic of China), most of which conduct relations with Apia through diplomats accredited to New Zealand. Although not choosing to apply for United Nations membership until 1976, it had previously joined a number of UN subsidiary agencies and other international organizations, including the World Health Organization, the International Monetary Fund, and the World Bank group, In addition to such regional organizations as the South Pacific Commission.

Relations with the country's principal trading partner, New Zealand, which had been cordial since independence, cooled in 1978–1979 as a result of Wellington's attempt to expel some 200 Samoan "overstayers" who had been assured New Zealand citizenship. Subsequently, the Judicial Committee of Privy Council at London ruled that all Western Samoans born between 1928 and 1949 (when New Zealand passed legislation separating its own citizenship from that of Britain), as well as their children, were entitled to such rights. However, the decision was effectively invalidated by an agreement concluded in mid-1982 by prime ministers Va'ai Kolone and Robert Muldoon whereby only the estimated 50,000 Samoans resident in New Zealand could claim citizenship. The accord was widely criticized within Western Samoa, (then) opposition leader Tupuola Efi chastising the government for abrogating "a basic tenet of the Anglo-Saxon legal heritage that the right to legal citizenship can only be surrendered by personal choice".

Current issues. After assuming office in December 1982, the essentially conservative Tofilau Eti pursued a carefully constructed austerity policy that, after two devaluations of the tala accompanied by relatively modest expressions of popular discontent, succeeded in substantially curbing both foreign and domestic debt, reducing inflation from 20.5 percent in 1980 to 10.3 percent by mid-1985, and earning praise from the World Bank as a model for Third World economic recovery.

During 1986, with copra and cocoa prices in decline and confronted with an annual trade deficit estimated at $10 million, the Va'ai Kolone government recommitted itself to expansion of tourism and explored the possibility of withdrawing from certain types of public sector activity, including the transfer of some 30,000 acres of prime agricultural land to private ownership.

Accompanying the electoral challenges that initially clouded Tofilau Eti's return to office in April 1988 was an appeal from Western Samoa's National Council of Women to change the voting system in favor of a universal franchise for all individuals over the age of 21. An earlier such proposal (which would have limited actual office-holding to *matais*) had been rejected by the Assembly in 1981, while an amended version that would have given the vote to all persons 25 years or older upon approval of their constituency chiefs had been defeated in 1984. In June the *Washington Pacific Report* stated that Eti had pledged to hold a national referendum on the issue.

POLITICAL PARTIES

Traditionally, there were no political parties in Western Samoa. Following the 1979 election, the Human Rights Protection Party (HRPP) was organized by Va'ai Kolone to oppose the reconfirmation of Taisi Tupuola as prime minister. Following his expulsion from the Assembly in 1982, Va'ai turned the party leadership over to Tofilau Eti and, upon his return, sat as an opposition independent.

Human Rights Protection Party (HRPP). One seat short of a legislative majority after its formation in 1979, the HRPP won 22 of 47 seats at the February 1982 balloting and, after protracted negotiation with independent members, secured a one-seat majority that permitted the installation of a Va'ai Kolone government on April 13. As a result of legal actions in late June and mid-September, two seats, including the prime minister's, were lost, Va'ai turning the party leadership over to Tofilau Eti, who was able to form a new HRPP government at the end of the year. Tofilau subsequently led the HRPP to a landslide 31–16 victory at the election of February 22, 1985, but lost control of the government in December by defection of HRPP members to the opposition. He was redesignated prime minister with the barest possible legislative majority in April 1988.

Leader: Tofilau ETI Alesana (Prime Minister).

Samoan National Development Party (SNDP). The SNDP was formed by opposition leader Tupua Tamasese Efi following the 1988 election.

The new group was reportedly backed by members of the former Christian Democratic Party (organized by Efi prior to the 1985 balloting, at which it won 16 seats), in addition to defectors from the HRPP.

Leader: Tupua Tamasese EFI (Leader of the Opposition).

LEGISLATURE

The unicameral **Legislative Assembly** (*Fono*) is elected for a three-year term (subject to dissolution). It encompasses 45 members chosen from territorial constituencies by the *matai*, in addition to 2 members elected by universal suffrage of persons outside the *matai* system and registered on the individual voters' roll. At the most recent general election on February 26, 1988, the results of which were not reported until the Assembly convened on April 7, the Human Rights Protection Party was credited with winning a bare majority of 24 seats. The Supreme Court subsequently awarded an additional seat to the HRPP and called for new balloting in three constituencies, leaving the newly formed Samoan National Development Party with an apparent potential of no more than 22 seats.

Speaker: Aeau PENIAMINA.

CABINET

[as of April 15, 1988]

Prime Minister	Tofilau Eti Alesana
Ministers	
Agriculture, Forests and Fisheries	Pule Lakemo
Broadcasting	Tofilau Eti Alesana
Economic Affairs	Tanuvafa Livi
Education	Patu Afaese
Finance	Tuilaepa Sailele Malielegaoi
Foreign Affairs	Tofilau Eti Alesana
Health	Polataivao Fosi
Justice	Tofilau Eti Alesana
Labor	Tofilau Eti Alesana
Lands and Surveys	Sifuiva Sione
Police and Prisons	Tofilau Eti Alesana
Post Office	Jack Netzler
Public Works	Leiataua Vaiao Alailima
Transportation and Civil Aviation	Jack Netzler
Youth, Sports and Culture	Patu Afaese
Attorney General	Tofilau Eti Alesana
Governor, Central Bank	John Howard

NEWS MEDIA

Press. Freedom of the press is constitutionally guaranteed, although instances of implicit censorship or of contempt citations against journalists are not unknown. The following are issued at Apia in English and Samoan: *Savali* (11,000), government fortnightly; *Samoa Weekly* (4,500); *The Samoa Times* (3,000), weekly; *The Observer* (3,000), weekly; *Samoa Sun,* weekly, founded 1980.

Radio and television. The Western Samoa Broadcasting Service is a government-controlled body which provides commercial radio service in English and Samoan to the country's approximately 72,000 sets. Television is received from American Samoa by some 2,800 sets.

INTERGOVERNMENTAL REPRESENTATION

Ambassador to the US and Permanent Representative to the UN: Maiava Iulai TOMA.

US Ambassador to Western Samoa: There is no mission at Apia, although one is to be established in late 1988. Relations are conducted through the US Ambassador to New Zealand (currently Paul Matthews CLEVELAND).

IGO Memberships (Non-UN): ADB, APCC, CWTH, EEC(L), *EIB*, ICCO, SPC, SPEC, SPF.

YEMEN ARAB REPUBLIC

al-Jumhuriyah al-'Arabiyah al-Yamaniyah

Political Status: Independent Islamic Arab republic established in 1962; first permanent constitution established December 1970; presently operating under provisional constitution proclaimed June 19, 1974.

Area: 75,290 sq. mi. (195,000 sq. km.).

Population: 9,274,173 (1986C), 9,425,000 (1988E), including those living abroad (approximately 1,400,000 in 1981).

Major Urban Centers (1981C): SAN'A (277,818); Hodeida (al-Hudaydah, 126,386); Ta'iz (119,573).

Official Language: Arabic.

Monetary Unit: Yemeni Rial (principal rate March 1, 1988, 9.76 rials = $1US).

President: Col. 'Ali 'Abdallah SALIH; elected by the Constituent People's Assembly on July 17, 1978, following the assassination of Lt. Col. Ahmad Husayn al-GHASHMI on June 24; reelected on May 23, 1983.

Vice President: Qadi 'Abd al-Karim al-ARASHI; elected by the Constituent People's Assembly on July 20, 1978; reappointed by the President on October 15, 1980.

Prime Minister: 'Abd al-'Aziz 'Abd al-GHANI; served as Prime Minister 1975–1980 and as co-Vice President from October 1980 to November 1983; reappointed as Prime Minister on November 12, 1983, succeeding Dr. 'Abd al-Karim 'Ali al-IRYANI.

THE COUNTRY

Located at the southwestern corner of the Arabian peninsula, north of the passage between the Red Sea and the Gulf of Aden, the Yemen Arab Republic (also known as North Yemen) borders on Saudi Arabia and the People's Democratic Republic of Yemen (South Yemen). The Tihama, a hot, semidesert strip, separates the Red Sea coast from the generally well-watered mountainous area of the interior. The people are predominantly Arab, although Negroid strains are present in the coastal region, and are divided into two Muslim religious communities: the Zaidi of the Shi'a sect in the north, center, and east; and the Shafi'i community of the Sunni sect in the south and the southwest.

Over a million Yemeni men work outside the country, primarily in Saudi Arabia and other oil-rich Arab states. Their exodus has created an internal labor shortage and increased female responsibility for the bulk of subsistence agricultural production. However, the requirements of purdah have precluded any substantial female participation outside the household, women being unrepresented in government and girls constituting only one-third of all primary and secondary school students.

As a result of its topographical extremes, a variety of crops is produced, including cotton (the leading export), grains, fruits, coffee, and *qat* (a mild narcotic leaf which is chewed daily by an estimated 90 percent of the population). Remittances from Yemenis working abroad, along with foreign assistance, yielded most of the financing for two Five-Year Development Plans (1977–1981 and 1982–1986) that focused on transport, communications, agriculture, housing, manufacturing, and utilities. However, a major earthquake in December 1982 and worldwide recession in the petroleum industry hampered the effectiveness of the second plan; as a result, the YAR remains one of the region's poorest countries as it struggles to combat 75 percent illiteracy and a high infant mortality rate. The recent discovery of major oil deposits gives some promise of long-term economic relief and accompanying social change, although the government is approaching the prospect cautiously (see Current issues, below).

GOVERNMENT AND POLITICS

Political background. Former site of the Kingdom of Sheba and an early center of Near Eastern civilization, Yemen fell under the rule of the Ottoman Turks in the sixteenth century. The withdrawal of Turkish forces in 1918 made it possible for Imam YAHYA, the traditional ruler of the Zaidi religious community, to gain political supremacy. Yahya remained as theocratic ruler until 1948, when he was murdered in an attempted coup and succeeded by his son, Sa'if al-ISLAM Ahmad. The new leader instituted a more outward-looking policy: diplomatic relations were established with the Soviet Union in 1956, and in 1958 Yemen joined with the United Arab Republic (Egypt and Syria) in an abortive federation known as the United Arab States.

A series of unsuccessful risings against the absolute and antiquated regime of the imams culminated on September 26, 1962, in the ouster of the newly installed Iman Muhammad al-BADR by a group of army officers under Col. (later Field Marshal) 'Abdallah al-SALAL, who established a republic with close ties to the UAR. Although the new regime was recognized by the United States and many other governments, resistance by followers of the imam precipitated a civil war that continued intermittently until early 1969. Saudi Arabian support for the royalists was more than offset by Egyptian aid to the republicans that included an estimated 70,000 troops.

The external forces were withdrawn in late 1967, following the UAR's defeat in the June war with Israel and the conclusion of an agreement with Saudi Arabia at an Arab summit at Khartoum, Sudan. President Salal was subsequently ousted in favor of a three-man Presidential Council headed by 'Abd al-Rahman al-IRYANI. Internal factional rivalry continued, but in May 1970 an informal compromise was reached whereby royalist elements were assimilated into the regime. The rudiments of modern governmental institutions were established with the adoption of a new constitution in late 1970 and the election of a Consultative Council in early 1971, although political stability continued to depend on the personal fortunes of such leaders as prime ministers Hassan al-'AMRI and Muhsin Ahmad al-'AYNI. On June 13, 1974, in another, apparently bloodless coup, the Iryani regime was superseded by a seven-man Military Command Council (MCC) led by Lt. Col. Ibrahim Muhammad al-HAMADI. In January 1975, Prime Minister 'Ayni, who had been appointed only seven months earlier, was replaced by 'Abd al-'Aziz 'Abd al-GHANI.

On October 11, 1977, Colonel Hamadi was assassinated at San'a by unknown assailants, and the MCC immediately established a three-man Presidential Council headed by Lt. Col. Ahmad Husayn al-GHASHMI, with Prime Minister Ghani and Maj. 'Abdallah 'Abd al-'ALIM, commander of the paratroop forces, as the other members. Ghashmi was also assassinated on June 24, 1978, by a bomb carried by a "special emissary" of the South Yemeni government. A new four-member provisional Presidential Council was thereupon organized, including Prime Minister Ghani, Constituent Assembly Speaker 'Abd al-Karim al-ARASHI, Armed Forces Commander 'Ali al-SHIBA, and Maj. (subsequently Col.) 'Ali 'Abdallah SALIH. On July 17, the Assembly elected Colonel Salih president of the Republic and three days later named Arashi to the newly created office of vice president, Ghani being continued as prime minister.

Attempts to overthrow Salih were reported in July and October 1978, while a prolonged delay in reaching agreement on constitutional issues was attributed to continuing conflict between republican and traditionalist groups. The situation was further complicated in early 1979 when South Yemeni forces crossed into North Yemen and were joined by rebels of the leftist National Democratic Front (NDF), led by Sultan Ahmad 'UMAR. Following mediation by the Arab League, a ceasefire was implemented on March 16, the southern troops being withdrawn. On March 30, talks in Kuwait between President Salih and Chairman Isma'il of the People's Democratic Republic concluded with a mutual pledge to reopen discussions on eventual unification of the two Yemens. Toward that end, a number of high-level meetings between San'a and Aden took place during the next 18 months, while on October 15, 1980, in a significant internal reorganization, Prime Minister Ghani was replaced by Dr. 'Abd al-Karim 'Ali al-IRYANI and named co-vice president.

In the fall of 1981, unification talks resumed between President Salih and his South Yemen counterpart, 'Ali Nasir Muhammad, culminating in an agreement signed at Aden on December 2 to establish a Yemen Council, embracing the two chief executives, and a Joint Ministerial Council to promote integration in the political, economic, and social spheres. On December 30, the Aden News Agency reported that a draft constitution of a unified Yemeni Republic had been prepared and would be submitted to referenda in the two states at an unspecified future date.

On May 22, 1983, the Assembly reelected Salih for a second five-year term, while, on November 12, Vice President Ghani was reappointed prime minister, with Iryani assigned to directing the reconstruction of earthquake-damaged areas.

Constitution and government. Yemen is an Islamic Arab republic whose contemporary constitutional development did not begin until 1962 and has since been impeded by civil war and internal political instability. Various interim constitutions preceded announcement of the constitution of December 28, 1970, which was suspended by the leaders of the June 1974 coup.

A 99-member Constituent People's Assembly was established by the Military Command Council in February 1978, the Council itself being dissolved two months later. The current president, named by the Assembly in July 1978, was initially assisted by a vice president and a prime minister, a second vice president being added in 1980. In May 1979, by presidential decree, the Assembly was expanded to 159 members and a 15-member Consultative Council was created, while a 1,000-member General People's Congress, composed of both elected and appointed representatives, was convened in August 1982. The judicial system is based on Islamic religious law (*shari'a*), which is administered in each district by a *hakim;* it also includes a People's Tribunal and a State Security Court, the latter established to hear political cases.

The country is divided into seven provinces (*alwiyah*), each headed by a governor or area commander of the armed forces. The provinces are subdivided into districts, and both provincial and district officials are directly responsible to the central government. In July 1985 elections were held for some 17,500 seats on local congresses, constituted to direct village development projects.

Foreign relations. Yemen broke out of its age-long, largely self-imposed isolation in the mid-1950s, when the imam's government accepted economic and military aid from the Soviet Union, the People's Republic of China, the United Arab Republic, and the United States. Diplomatic relations with Washington were broken off in June 1967 during the Arab-Israeli war, but a reconciliation was effected in July 1972.

North Yemeni foreign concerns turn primarily on the country's relationship to its two immediate neighbors, conservative Saudi Arabia and Marxist South Yemen. Despite the former's previous record of support for Yemen's defeated royalists, Saudi money and arms were instrumental during intermittent border warfare with South Yemen in 1971–1972 and again in February-March 1979. However, subsequent reaffirmation of the two Yemens' intention to merge (originally announced in 1972) was cooly received by Riyadh, which withheld several hundred million dollars in military supplies. In turn, North Yemen renewed its military dealings with the Soviet Union, and in October 1979 the Saudis were reported to have cut off their annual budgetary supplement of $250 million. Assistance was restored in early 1980, following a pledge by San'a that Soviet aid and advisers would be phased out, but the level of Soviet support did not noticeably diminish thereafter and in 1984 the YAR signed a 20-year friendship treaty with Moscow.

In a matter of both domestic and regional significance, the YAR serves as the home base of an estimated 3,000 Palestinian guerrillas, San'a having been chosen as the military headquarters of Yasir 'Arafat's Palestine National Liberation Movement (*Fatah*), the core PLO component.

Current issues. As the YAR drew near to becoming a significant oil exporter, government attention focused as much on possible problems from the transition as on the ultimate economic and social benefits. Tight controls were placed on information about developments in the oil fields, lest news of potential wealth jeopardize much-needed foreign aid and cause a disruptive influx of Yemeni workers from jobs in other countries. Despite the prospect of oil revenue, the government, faced with 30 percent inflation and growing deficits, maintained its austerity program of expenditure cuts, import reductions, and currency devaluation. Although oil exports were expected to begin by early 1988, government estimates of exploitable reserves were much lower than those of foreign experts, who judged the potential to be upwards of 500 million barrels, exclusive of "promising deposits" along the border with the People's Democratic Republic. Meanwhile, the presence in North Yemen of the ousted PDRY leader, 'Ali Nasir Muhammad, caused a strain in relations with the south, despite a continuance of periodic unity talks. Throughout 1987 President Salih repeatedly called for reconciliation, insisting that since there was "no difference between the northern and southern parts" Mohammad was "staying in his homeland".

POLITICAL PARTIES

Under the imams, political parties were banned. Historically, political alignments have been determined by tribal and religious loyalties. The supporters of former president Salal formed a group known as the Popular Revolutionary Union, and in 1973 former president Iryani formed a group known as the Yemeni Union; however, neither group still exists. Foreign-based parties, such as the *Baath* and the Arab Nationalist Movement, have had few adherents in North Yemen.

Guerrilla Opposition:

National Democratic Front (NDF). Formed in 1976 by an assortment of Baathists, Marxists, Nasserites, and disaffected Yemenis, the NDF has engaged in sporadic military action against the San'a government. Its strongest effort, supported by units of the South Yemen army, was a January 1979 invasion of North Yemen that was terminated as the result of a ceasefire negotiated by the Arab League. Following announcement of the Yemeni merger agreement in December 1981 and a major government offensive against NDF strongholds in the north during the ensuing spring and summer, its effectiveness was presumed to be greatly reduced, one observer stating at the end of the year that the group was largely "dormant".

Leader: Sultan Ahmad 'UMAR.

LEGISLATURE

In February 1978, a 99-member **Constituent People's Assembly** was appointed by the Military Command Council to pave the way for "the return of democracy to public life"; in May 1979, following dissolution of the Command Council, its membership was increased to 159, the new members being appointed by the president.

In October 1981, the government called for the establishment of a **General People's Congress** of 700 elected members and 300 presidential appointees, which first assembled in August 1982. The Congress is mandated to meet every two years, with reelection scheduled every four years; however, the Third Congress convened on August 25, 1986, with no report of an intervening election.

Speaker of Constituent People's Assembly: Qadi 'Abd al-Karim 'Abdallah al-ARASHI.

Secretary General of General People's Congress: Col. 'Ali 'Abdallah SALIH.

CABINET

Prime Minister	'Abd al-'Aziz 'Abd al-Ghani
Deputy Prime Ministers	Muhammad Sa'id al-'Attar
	'Abd al-Karim al-Iryani
	Hasan Muhammad Makki
Deputy Prime Minister for Domestic Affairs	Lt. Col. Mujahid Yahya Abu Shawarib
Ministers	
Agriculture and Fisheries	Husayn 'Abdallah al-'Amri
Awqaf and Guidance	Qadi 'Ali ibn 'Ali Samman
Civil Service and Administrative Reform	Isma'il Ahmad al-Wazir
Communications and Transport	Ahmad Muhammad al-Ansi
Development	Muhammad Sa'id al-'Attar
Economy, Supply and Trade	Muhammad al-Khaddam al-Wajih
Education	'Abdallah al-Jayfi
Electricity, Water and Sewage Works	Muhammad Hasan Sabra
Finance	'Alawi Salih al-Salami
Foreign Affairs	'Abd al-Karim al-Iryani
Health	Dr. Muhammad Ahmad al-Kabab
Information and Culture	Hasan Ahmad al-Lawzi
Interior	Maj. 'Abdallah Husayn Barakat
Justice	Ahmad Muhammad al-Jubi
Labor, Social Affairs and Youth	Lt. Col. Muhsin Muhammad al-'Ulufi
Local Government	Muhammad 'Abdallah al-Jayfi
Municipalities and Housing	Ahmad Muhammad Luqman
Petroleum and Mineral Resources	Ahmad 'Ali Muhani
Public Works	'Abdallah Husayn al-Kurshumi
Ministers of State	
Affairs of Yemeni Unity	Yahya Husayn al-'Arashi
Cabinet Affairs	Ahmad Salih al-Ru'ayni
Youth and Sports	'Abdallah Nasir al-Darafi
Without Portfolio	Husayn 'Ali al-Hubayshi
Governor, Central Bank	Muhammad al-Junayd

NEWS MEDIA

Press. The following are published in Arabic: *al-Jumhuriyah* (Ta'iz), government daily; *al-Thawra* (San'a), government daily; *al-Bilad* (San'a), rightist weekly; *Marab* (Ta'iz), Nasserite weekly; *al-Sabah* (Hodeida), reformist weekly; *San'a* (San'a), leftist fortnightly; *al-Yaman* (San'a), rightist fortnightly.

News agency. The Saba News Agency is located at the capital.

Radio and television. There are government-controlled radio stations at San'a, Ta'iz, and Hodeida broadcasting to approximately 320,000 receivers. Television service, introduced in 1975, was received by some 150,000 sets in 1987.

INTERGOVERNMENTAL REPRESENTATION

Ambassador to the US: Muhsin Ahmad ALAINI.

US Ambassador to the Yemen Arab Republic: Charles Franklin DUNBAR.

Permanent Representative to the UN: Muhammad Salem BASENDWAH.

IGO Memberships (Non-UN): AFESD, AMF, IC, IDB, Intelsat, Interpol, LAS, NAM.

PEOPLE'S DEMOCRATIC REPUBLIC OF YEMEN

Jumhuriyat al-Yaman al-Dimuqratiyah al-Sha'biyah

Political Status: Independent republic since 1967; Marxist-Leninist constitutional system adopted December 27, 1978.

Area: 130,065 sq. mi. (336,869 sq. km.).

Population: 1,590,275 (1973C), 2,506,000 (1988E).

Major Urban Center (1977E): ADEN (291,600).

Official Language: Arabic.

Monetary Unit: Yemeni Dinar (market rate March 1, 1988, 1 dinar = $2.90US).

Chairman of the Presidium of the People's Supreme Council: Haydar Abu Bakr al-'ATTAS; named Chairman of the Council of Ministers on February 14, 1985; named Interim Chairman of the Presidium of the PSC on January 24, 1986, following attempted military purge by the former Chairman, 'Ali Nasir Muhammad al-HASANI on January 13; confirmed as Head of State on February 8; reconfirmed for a five-year term on November 6, 1986, following legislative election of October 28–30.

Chairman of the Council of Ministers (Prime Minister): Dr. Yasin Sa'id NU'MAN; designated by the Supreme People's Council on February 8, 1986, succeeding Haydar Abu Bakr al-'ATTAS; redesignated on November 6, 1986.

THE COUNTRY

Located at the southern end of the Arabian Peninsula, the People's Democratic Republic of Yemen (also known as South Yemen) is an arid, extremely hot country that en-compasses large tracts of mountainous and desert terrain. It also includes the islands of Socotra in the Gulf of Aden, Perim in the narrow Bab el Mandeb strait, and Kamaran in the Red Sea. The principal city is the important port of Aden, once the leading seat of British military power in the Middle East and still a commercial center for South Arabia and the nearby African Coast. The population, partly urbanized and partly adhering to tribal customs, is predominantly Arab and Sunni Muslim. As an Arab state with a Marxist government, the PDRY has emphasized women's rights, reversing the earlier feudal attitude of total female subservience.

Since 1969, the government has assumed control of much of the economy. Most agricultural output (cotton, coffee, grains, and tobacco as well as a variety of fruits and vegetables) is produced by cooperatives and state farms; fishing, which contributes significant foreign-exchange earnings, is also state controlled, while the principal industry, the Aden petroleum refinery, was nationalized in 1977. Once one of the world's leading oil bunkering and entrepôt centers, the port of Aden was severely crippled by the 1967–1975 closure of the Suez Canal and has since failed to return to its earlier level of activity.

GOVERNMENT AND POLITICS

Political background. British control of what is now South Yemen began with the occupation of Aden in 1839 and, through treaties with numerous local rulers, was gradually extended north and eastward to include what came to be known as the Western and Eastern Protectorates. Aden was ruled as part of British India until 1937, when it became a separate Crown Colony. In preparation for eventual independence, the British established the Federation of South Arabia, in which the colony of Aden was associated with 16 dependent states that had previously belonged to the Protectorates. Plans for a transfer of power to the rulers of the Federation were frustrated, however, by increasing nationalist agitation and terrorist activity on the part of radical elements. By 1967, a power struggle among rival nationalist groups had resulted in the emergence of the left-wing National Liberation Front (NLF) as the area's strongest political organization. Control of the territory was accordingly handed over by Britain to representatives of the NLF on November 30, 1967.

Qahtan al-SHAABI, the principal NLF leader, became president and prime minister of the new republic, which, though beset by grave internal problems and attempted revolts, rapidly emerged as a center of left-wing revolutionary nationalist agitation in South Arabia. The position of the comparatively moderate Shaabi became progressively weaker and, as the result of a continuing power struggle between the moderate and radical wings of the NLF, he was forced from office in June 1969, the country's name being changed in December 1970 to the People's Democratic Republic of Yemen. In August 1971, another change of government brought into power Salim Rubay'i 'ALI and 'Abd al-Fattah ISMA'IL, heads of the pro-Chinese and pro-Soviet factions of the National Front, respectively; both participated in a three-member Presidential Council, chaired by 'Ali as head of state.

In the course of a leadership struggle that erupted into street fighting at the capital on June 26, 1978, 'Ali was removed from office and executed, after allegations (largely discounted by foreign observers) that he had been involved in the assassination two days earlier of President Ghashmi of North Yemen. Following 'Ali's ouster, Prime Minister 'Ali Nasir Muhammad al-HASANI was designated chairman of the Presidential Council, with Isma'il and Defense Minister 'Ali Ahmad Nasir ANTAR al-Bishi as the other members. Although expanded to five members on July 1, the presidential collegium was superseded on December 27 by an 11-member Presidium of a recently elected Supreme People's Council, Isma'il serving as chairman. Earlier, in mid-October, the Yemen Socialist Party (YSP) had been organized, in succession to the National Front, as the country's controlling political organization.

On March 30, 1979, Chairman Isma'il and President Salih of North Yemen concluded a three-day meeting at Kuwait that had been called in the wake of renewed hostilities between their two countries in February-March (see Yemen Arab Republic: Political background). Despite obvious ideological differences between the conservative North and the Marxist-Leninist South, the leaders pledged that they would renew efforts first broached in 1972, but suspended in 1975, to unify the two Yemens.

On April 21, 1980, Chairman Isma'il, ostensibly for reasons of ill health, resigned his government and party posts, with 'Ali Nasir Muhammad being named by the YSP Central Committee as his successor in both capacities. Five days later, the Supreme People's Council confirmed Muhammad (who retained the prime ministership) as head of state. His position was further consolidated at an extraordinary party congress on October 12-14, when a Politburo and a Secretariat dominated by his supporters were named, and at an extraordinary session of the SPC on October 16, when a revamped cabinet was approved.

In the fall of 1981, unification talks were resumed between the leaders of North and South Yemen, culminating in an agreement signed at Aden on December 2 to establish a Yemen Council, consisting of President Salih and Chairman Muhammad, and a Joint Ministerial Council to promote integration in the political, economic, and social spheres. On December 30, the Aden News Agency reported that a draft constitution of a unified Yemeni Republic had been prepared and would be submitted to referenda in the two states at an unspecified future date.

At the conclusion of an SPC session on February 14, 1985, Muhammad resigned as chairman of the Council of Ministers, while retaining his position as head of state. Concurrently, a new cabinet was approved, headed by former construction minister Haydar Abu Bakr al-'ATTAS. In October, Muhammad was reelected secretary general of the YSP, albeit as part of a political compromise that necessitated enlargement of the Central Committee from 47 to 77 members and the Politburo from 13 to 16. In particular, the reinstatement of former chairman Isma'il indicated that there would be increased opposition to the policies of the incumbent state and party leader.

On January 13, 1986, Chairman Muhammad mounted a "gangland style massacre" of YSP opponents, in the course of which Isma'il and a number of others, including

Defense Minister Salih Muslih QASIM, were killed. However, the chairman's opponents regrouped and, after more than a week of bitter fighting at the capital, succeeded in defeating "the 'Ali Nasir clique". On January 24, ministerial chairman 'Attas, who had been in India at the time of the attempted purge, was designated interim head of state. On February 6, the YSP Central Committee named 'Ali Salim al-BIEDH to succeed Muhammad as its secretary general, while the SPC on February 8 confirmed 'Attas as Presidium chairman and appointed a new government headed by Dr. Yasin Sa'id NU'MAN; both were reconfirmed on November 6, 1986, by a new Council elected on October 28-30.

Constitution and government. The constitutional changes introduced in December 1978 were based on the communist model. The highest organ of state power is the Supreme People's Council which elects a Presidium of 11-17 members, whose chairman serves as titular head of state. Executive functions are performed by a Council of Ministers whose membership is subject to pro forma SPC approval. The judicial system includes a Supreme Court and magistrates' courts. In some areas, Islamic law (*shari'a*) and tribal customs are applied.

South Yemen is divided for administrative purposes into 6 governorates, each headed by a centrally appointed governor, and 28 provinces.

Foreign relations. The People's Democratic Republic of Yemen professes a policy of nonalignment in foreign affairs, but its relations with other Arab countries have been mixed because of its long-standing opposition to all conservative regimes and its recent close association with the Soviet Union. It voted against the admission of the Persian Gulf sheikhdoms to the Arab League, while numerous border clashes have resulted from tensions with Saudi Arabia and the Yemen Arab Republic. The establishment in March 1976 of diplomatic and economic relations with the former suggested a partial shift in foreign policy, but assistance continued to be extended to the radical Dhofar guerrillas in southwestern Oman and the antigovernment National Democratic Front (NDF) rebels in southern North Yemen. Support for the latter group subsequently waned, however, in the context of revived North-South unification discussions, while the first high-level meeting in 15 years with Omani representatives was convened in Kuwait on October 25, 1982. The "reconciliation" talks were held under the auspices of the Gulf Cooperation Council and represented the fruition of several months of mediation by Council members. Elsewhere, as a member of the hard-line Arab "steadfastness front", Aden has rejected any partial settlement of the Middle East question, particularly the 1979 Egyptian-Israeli peace treaty. In March 1985, the PDRY joined Libya, Syria, and Algeria in forming a Pan-Arab Command, with the announced goal of liquidating Israel.

The presence in South Yemen of 300-1,000 Soviet, 300-700 Cuban, and 100 East German military and security personnel has been of concern not only to the West but to more moderate Arab states. The October 25, 1979, signing at Moscow by chairmen Brezhnev and Isma'il of a 20-year treaty of friendship between their states was a further indication of the PDR's move into the Soviet camp, although the treaty specifically recognized South Yemen's nonaligned status. Earlier, there were reports that the USSR had installed surface-to-air missiles and was constructing submarine pens on Socotra Island, having already developed facilities for surface naval vessels. On the other hand, for some years prior to his overthrow, there were indications that 'Ali Nasir Muhammad had become somewhat disenchanted with the benefits to his regime of the "Moscow connection". Thus, he had engaged in lengthy unification talks with non-Communist North Yemen, had attempted to end a long-standing border dispute with conservative Oman, and had made overtures to potential Western investors.

Current issues. The government that emerged after the brief, but destructive civil war in January 1986 did little to change foreign or domestic policies, concentrating on consolidating internal power and assuring neighboring countries of its potential for stability. Although not perceived as a strong political figure when first appointed Presidium chairman, Haydar Abu Bakr al-'Attas gained enough confidence to call for a general election in October, the new Supreme People's Council reconfirming the existing leadership on November 6.

Amnesty was granted to a majority of the participants in the January fighting, except for 'Ali Nasir Muhammad and a group of close supporters, most of whom had fled to North Yemen. For his part, the former chairman travelled freely in nearby countries, soliciting support from old allies and generating speculation that a counter coup might be attempted. The government declared that reconciliation with Muhammad, as proposed by some foreign mediators, was impossible, decrying his instigation of the January struggle that had caused an estimated 4,000 deaths and upwards of $100 million in damage.

By early 1987 there were reports of division within the post-Muhammad leadership, with the relatively moderate 'Attas and YSP Secretary General Biedh apparently being opposed by Sa'id Salih SALIM, the national security minister, and Salim Salih MUHAMMAD, the YSP deputy secretary general. On the other hand, Biedh had a February meeting at Moscow with Soviet leader Mikhail Gorbachev, in the wake of a series of economic agreements that had been concluded with the Soviets by Council of Ministers chairman Nu'man.

In December 1987 five of Muhammad's followers were executed for treason, while 30 others, including the former head of state, received death sentences in absentia.

POLITICAL PARTIES

Prior to independence, the National Liberation Front (NLF) and the Front for the Liberation of Occupied South Yemen (FLOSY) fought for control, with adherents of the latter subsequently going into exile. In October 1975, the NLF joined with the Popular Vanguard Party (a *Baath* group) and the Popular Democratic Union (a pro-Moscow Communist party) to form the United Political Organization of the National Front (UPONF). The latter was supplanted in 1978 by the Yemen Socialist Party, within which the PDU continues to enjoy organizational autonomy.

Government Party:

Yemen Socialist Party (YSP). Modeled on the Communist Party of the Soviet Union, the YSP was constituted on October 11–14, 1978, as a Marxist-Leninist "vanguard party". Its supreme organ is a Congress, which meets every five years, though extraordinary sessions may be called by the Central Committee or by one-third of all party members. The Central Committee, which is elected by the Congress, in turn elects functional committees, a Secretariat, and a Politburo, where effective power resides.

Although 'Abd al-Fattah Isma'il was named "honorary chairman" of the YSP upon resigning as secretary general in April 1980, no mention of his role was made during the party's October 12–14, 1980, extraordinary congress. In early 1985, he returned to South Yemen after several years in the Soviet Union and was among those killed in the massacre of January 13, 1986.

Secretary General: 'Ali Salim al-BIEDH.

Deputy Secretary General: Salim Salih MUHAMMAD.

Other Members of Politburo: Fadl Mushin 'ABDALLAH, Haydar Abu Bakr al-'ATTAS, Dr. 'Abd al-'Azziz al-DALI, 'Ali 'Abd al-Razzak Ba DHIB, Muhammad Sa'id 'Abdallah MUSHIN, Dr. Yasin Sa'id NU'MAN, Sa'id Salih SALIM, Salih Munassir al-SIYAYLI, 'Ali Salim Abu ZAYD.

Candidates: Salih 'Ubaid AHMAD, Dr. 'Abdallah Ahmad al-KHAM-RIRI, Muhammad Hayder MASDUS.

Secretariat: 'Ali Salim al-BIEDH, Salim Salih MUHAMMAD, Salih 'Abdallah MUTHANNA, Salih Munassir al-SIYAYLI.

Exile Grouping:

The formation was reported in 1983 of a **National Assembly of Patriotic Forces** (NAPF), an anti-Marxist movement led by former prime minister Muhammad 'Ali HAITHEM and 'Abd al-Kawi MAKKOUI, former chief minister of Aden. In February 1986, Haithem appealed from Paris for the establishment of a government of national unity encompassing all political forces inside and outside the country.

LEGISLATURE

Legislative authority is vested in a 111-member **Supreme People's Council,** which replaced a provisional body of the same name following the 1978 election. A majority of the councillors are members of the Yemen Socialist Party; the rest are independents acceptable to the party. Although the constitution calls for a five-year mandate, political uncertainty delayed the most recent election until October 28–30, 1986. The Council elects a Presidium of 11–17 members, whose chairman serves as head of state.

Chairman of Presidium: Haydar Abu Bakr al-'ATTAS.

CABINET

Chairman, Council of Ministers	Dr. Yasin Sa'id Nu'man
Deputy Chairmen	Salih Abu Bakr bin Husaynun
	Salih Munassir al-Siyayli
Ministers	
Agriculture and Agrarian Reform	Ahmad 'Ali Muqbil
Culture and Information	Muhammad Ahmad Jirghum
Defense	Col. Salih 'Ubayd Ahmad
Education	Salim Ba Salim
Energy and Mineral Resources	Salih Abu Bakr bin Husaynun
Finance	Dr. Ahmad Nasir al-Danani
Fisheries	Salim Muhammad Jibran
Foreign Affairs	Dr. 'Abd al-'Aziz al-Dali
Health	Sa'id Sharaf
Industry, Trade and Supply	'Abdallah Muhammad 'Uthman
Installations and Housing	'Abd al-Qawi Muthanna Hadi

Interior	Salih Munassir al-Siyayli
Justice and Religious Trusts	'Abd al-Wasi Salim
Labor and Civil Service	'Abd al-Jabir Rashid 'Uthman
Planning	Dr. Faraj bin Ghanim
State Security	Sa'id Salih Salim
Transport and Communications	Salih 'Abdallah Muthanna
Minister of State for Union Affairs	Rashid Muhammad Thabit
Director General, Secretariat of the Council of Ministers	Khalid 'Umar Ba Junayd

NEWS MEDIA

All news media are controlled by the government.

Press. The following are published at Aden: *al-Rabi Ashar Min Uktubar* (14 October, 20,000), government daily; *Ash-Sharara* (The Spark, 5,000), daily; *al-Thaqafa al-Jadida* (3,000), monthly organ of the Ministry of Culture and Tourism; *al-Thawra,* YSP weekly; *al-Rayah,* weekly.

News agencies. The domestic service is the government-owned Aden News Agency; *Novosti* maintains an office at Aden.

Radio and television. The Democratic Yemen Broadcasting Service is a government-controlled body that provides commercial radio and television service. There were approximately 310,000 radio and 47,000 television sets in 1987.

INTERGOVERNMENTAL REPRESENTATION

As of March 15, 1988, the United States and the People's Democratic Republic of Yemen had not established diplomatic relations.

Permanent Representative to the UN: 'Abdallah Salih al-ASHTAL.

IGO Memberships (Non-UN): AFESD, AMF, IC, IDB, LAS, NAM.

YUGOSLAVIA

Socialist Federal Republic of Yugoslavia
Socijalistička Federativna Republika Jugoslavija

Political Status: Independent monarchy constituted December 1, 1918; Communist People's Republic, with federal system of government, instituted November 29, 1945; Socialist Federal Republic proclaimed April 7, 1963; under collegial Presidency instituted July 29, 1971; present constitution adopted February 21, 1974.

Area: 98,766 sq. mi. (255,804 sq. km.).

Population: 22,424,711 (1981C), 24,229,000 (1988E).

Major Urban Centers (1981C): BELGRADE (1,470,073); Zagreb (768,700); Skopje (506,547); Sarajevo (448,500); Ljubljana (305,200).

Official Languages: The principal languages are Serbo-Croatian, Slovenian, and Macedonian; however, under the 1974 constitution all languages of the peoples and nationalities of Yugoslavia are accorded official status.

Monetary Unit: Yugoslav Dinar (market rate March 1, 1988, 1352.93 dinars = $1US).

President of the Presidency: Raif DIZDAREVIĆ (Bosnia-Herzegovina); elected to the Presidency on November 26, 1987, to fill the duration of the five-year term (from May 15, 1984) of Hamdija POZDERAC, who resigned on September 12; became President for a one-year term on May 15, 1988, succeeding, by rotation, Lazar MOJSOV (Macedonia).

Vice President of the Presidency: Stane DOLANC (Slovenia); elected to the Presidency for a five-year term on May 15, 1984; became Vice President for a one-year term on May 15, 1988, succeeding, by rotation, Raif DIZDAREVIC (Bosnia-Herzegovina).

Other Members of the Presidency: Gen. Nikola LJUBIČIĆ (Serbia), Josip VRHOVEC (Croatia), Veselin DJURANOVIĆ (Montenegro), Radovan VLAJKOVIĆ (Vojvodina), Sinan HASINI (Kosovo), Lazar MOJSOV (Macedonia), Stipe ŠUVAR (President of the Presidium of the Central Committee of the League of Communists of Yugoslavia, ex officio). The constituency members are listed in rotational sequence.

President of Federal Executive Council (Prime Minister): Branko MIKULIĆ; nominated by the Presidency on January 6, 1986, and elected for a four-year term by the Federal Assembly on May 16, succeeding Milka PLANINC.

THE COUNTRY

Situated on the Western side of the Balkan Peninsula between the Adriatic and the Danube, Yugoslavia extends in a southeasterly direction from the Austrian Alps to the upper Vardar Valley, which it shares with Greece. The northeastern section of the country, comprising portions of Serbia and Croatia, forms part of the Danubian Plain. This region, together with the more rugged Slovenia in the northwest, is more highly developed agriculturally and industrially than are the mountainous republics of Bosnia-Herzegovina in the southwest, Montenegro in the south, and Macedonia in the southeast. The predominantly South Slav population includes a number of distinct peoples with kindred but separate languages and cultures, the 1981 census identifying the primary ethnic groups as Serbs (37 percent), Croats (20 percent), Bosnian Muslims (9 percent), Slovenes and Albanians (8 percent each), Macedonians (6 percent), Montenegrins (3 percent), and Hungarians (2 percent). The country's main religious groups are the Serbian Orthodox (Serbs and Macedonians), Roman Catholic (Croats, Slovenes, and Hungarians), and Muslim (Bosnians, Herzegovinians, Albanians, and Turks). In 1980, women constituted 36 percent of the paid labor force, although this share has been described as declining during the recent period of economic difficulty; women average 25 percent representation in governmental and party bodies.

Largely underdeveloped before World War II, Yugoslavia made rapid advances after 1945 under a Communist regime remarkable for its pragmatic and flexible methods of economic management. Initial policies of forced agricultural collectivization were progressively modified following Yugoslavia's rupture with the USSR in 1948, and private farms currently account for about two-thirds of agricultural output. In industry, worker participation in the "social self-management" of enterprises was initiated as early as 1950, with later reforms further institutionalizing decentralization while moving the country toward a Western-style market economy. Close trading relations with the West were established during a 1949–1953 economic boycott by the Soviet bloc, and in 1966 Yugoslavia became the first Communist state to conclude a trade agreement with the European Economic Community. Recent economic growth has been sluggish, a targeted annual increase of 2.5 percent not proving attainable under the 1981–1985 Five-Year Plan. Both inflation and unemployment are also chronic problems, the former climbing to nearly 90 percent and the latter to more than 15 percent in 1986, although austerity measures succeeded in converting a current account deficit of $1.6 billion in 1982 to substantial surpluses in each of the following four years.

GOVERNMENT AND POLITICS

Political background. Following centuries of national struggle against the Turkish and Hapsburg empires, Yugoslavia emerged as a unified state with the formation on December 1, 1918, of the Kingdom of the Serbs, Croats, and Slovenes under the Serbian House of Karadjordjević. Uniting the former independent kingdoms of Serbia and Montenegro with the Croatian, Dalmatian, and Bosnian-Herzegovinian territories previously ruled by Austria-Hungary, the new entity (formally styled Yugoslavia on October 3, 1929) was ruled between World Wars I and II as a highly centralized, Serb-dominated state in which the Croats became an increasingly disaffected minority. The Serb-Croat antagonism, which caused many Croats to sympathize with Nazi Germany and Fascist Italy, continued even after the two Axis powers attacked and occupied the country on April 6, 1941. Wartime resistance to the Axis was led by two rival groups, the proroyalist Chetniks, under Gen. Draža MIHAILOVIĆ, and the Communist-inspired Partisans, led by Marshal Josip Broz TITO, a Croat who sought to enlist all the country's national groups in the liberation struggle. The Partisans' greater effectiveness in opposing the occupation forces and securing Allied aid paved the way for their assumption of power at the end of the war. In March 1945, Tito became prime minister in a "Government of National Unity", and on November 29, 1945, the monarchy was abolished, and a Federal People's Republic of Yugoslavia, based on the equality of the country's principal national groups, was proclaimed. On January 14, 1953, under a new constitution, Tito was elected president of the Republic.

Yugoslavia developed along orthodox Communist lines until 1948, when its refusal to submit to Soviet directives led to its expulsion from the Communist bloc and the imposition of a political and economic blockade by the USSR and its East European allies. Aided by Western arms and economic support, Yugoslavia maintained its autonomy throughout the Stalin era and by the late 1950s had achieved a partial reconciliation with the Warsaw Pact states, although it still insisted on complete independence and the right to find its own "road to socialism". Internally, Yugoslavia had become the first East European country to evolve institutions that moderated the harsher features of Communist rule and encouraged the development of a democratic form of communism based on new interpretations of Marxism. A federal constitution promulgated in 1963 consolidated the system of "social self-management" by attempting to draw the people into economic and administrative decision-making at all levels; it also expanded the independence of the judiciary, increased the responsibilities of the federal legislature and those of the country's six constituent republics and two autonomous provinces, and widened freedom of choice in elections. Although Communist control remained firm and ideological deviations were sternly repressed, the ouster in July 1966 of Vice President Aleksandar RANKOVIĆ, the leading opponent of the new trend, indicated Tito's determination to proceed with further reforms. Soviet intervention to halt a similar trend in Czechoslovakia in 1968 failed to dampen this resolve. Rejecting the so-called Brezhnev doctrine of "limited sovereignty" among members of the "Socialist commonwealth", Yugoslavia reaffirmed its readiness to fight for its independence if necessary and proceeded with further applications of the "self-management" principle. These efforts culminated in the adoption of the nation's fourth postwar constitution on February 21, 1974.

On May 4, 1980, after a four-month illness, Marshal Tito, president for life of the Republic and of the League of Communists of Yugoslavia (LCY), died at the age of 87, the leadership of state and party thereupon passing to collegial executives—the state Presidency and the Presidium of the LCY Central Committee, respectively. The administrative machinery assembled during the 1970s under Tito and his close associate Edvard KARDELJ (who had died in February 1979) continued to run smoothly: on May 15, Cvijetin MIJATOVIĆ succeeded Lazar KOLIŠEVSKI as president of the state Presidency for a one-year term, while on October 20 the presidency of the party Presidium rotated, also for a one-year term, to Lazar MOJSOV. On May 15, 1987, Mojsov, as a member of the presidency from Macedonia, assumed, in accordance with the principle of rotation, the position of titular head of state, with Hamdija POZDERAC (Bosnia-Herzegovina), on a similar basis, designated as his deputy. Pozderac resigned as vice president in September amid allegations of involvement in a financial scandal, the Bosnia-Herzegovina seat on the collegium being refilled in November by the (theretofore) foreign minister, Raif DIZDAREVIĆ, who succeeded to the state presidency on May 15, 1988.

Constitution and government. Yugoslavia under successive postwar constitutions has remained a Communist one-party state. Political control is exercised throughout the governmental structure by the Communist Party, known since 1952 as the League of Communists of Yugoslavia (LCY), and by its "front" organization, the Socialist Alliance of the Working People of Yugoslavia (SSRNJ).

The distinctive feature of the postwar Yugoslav state is

its federal structure, which accords national status to and permits a substantial measure of self-government in its six constituent Socialist Republics: Serbia, Croatia, Slovenia, Bosnia-Herzegovina, Macedonia, and Montenegro; autonomous status is also conceded to the two Socialist Autonomous Provinces of Vojvodina and Kosovo (formerly Kosovo-Methohija), both of which are geographically situated within the Serbian Socialist Republic. Each Republic has its own governmental apparatus, with an indirectly elected assembly, an executive, and a judiciary; similar institutions exist in the two provinces.

Republic and Capital	Area (sq. mi.)	Population (1981C)
Bosnia and Herzegovina (Sarajevo)	19,741	4,116,439
Croatia (Zagreb)	21,829	4,578,109
Macedonia (Skopje)	9,928	1,913,571
Montenegro (Titograd)	5,333	583,475
Serbia (Belgrade)	21,609	5,666,060
Slovenia (Ljubljana)	7,819	1,883,764
Autonomous Province and Capital		
Kosovo (Priština)	4,203	1,584,558
Vojvodina (Novi Sad)	8,303	2,028,239

Supreme state power is vested in the Federal Assembly, which comprises a Federal Chamber and a Chamber of Republics and Provinces. The electoral process is relatively complex. At the first stage, delegates are elected by "Basic Organizations of Associated Labor" (the fundamental units of the nation's self-management system) to some 12,000 local assemblies. These representatives then elect delegates to about 510 communal assemblies, which in turn elect delegates to assemblies of the republics and autonomous provinces. At the final stage, delegates to the Federal Chamber are elected by the communal assemblies, while those to the Chamber of Republics and Provinces are elected by the assemblies of the eight federal units. All candidates are screened by the Socialist Alliance, and federal electoral law stipulates that at least half of the members of the Federal Chamber must be drawn from the Organizations of Associated Labor.

The state Presidency is a collegial body composed of (1) a member from each republic and autonomous province, elected for a term of five years by the Federal Assembly, and (2) the president of the Presidium of the League of Communists of Yugoslavia, ex officio. The constitution provided additionally for the Federal Assembly to elect Josip Broz Tito to an unlimited term as president of the Republic, the office ceasing to exist upon Tito's death; thus on May 4, 1980, the duties of head of state formally devolved to the collective Presidency, with the positions of president and vice president of the Presidency to rotate annually. Members of the Federal Executive Council (cabinet), which is designated as the executive body of the Federal Assembly, are nominated by the state Presidency and elected by the Assembly for four-year terms; councillors may not be elected for more than two consecutive terms.

The judiciary is headed by a Constitutional Court and a Federal Court, the latter hearing appeals from the six republican and two provincial supreme courts. At lower levels there are communal and county courts as well as economic and military tribunals.

Foreign relations. Since 1948, Yugoslavian foreign policy has concentrated on maintaining the country's independence from both major power blocs. Though highly critical of US policy in Vietnam and the Middle East, Yugoslavia was equally critical of the Warsaw Pact intervention in Czechoslovakia in 1968, the Moscow-supported Vietnamese invasion of Kampuchea in 1978–1979, and the Soviet intervention in Afghanistan in December 1979.

The Tito regime consistently advocated peace, disarmament, détente, and aid to anticolonial and developmental struggles of Third World countries. Along with Egypt's Nasser and India's Nehru, Tito was considered a founder of the Nonaligned Movement and consistently championed its cause. At the sixth conference of nonaligned states, held September 3–8, 1979, at Havana, Cuba, President Tito, responding to Fidel Castro's call for the Movement to draw closer to the Soviet Union, asserted that it should reject "all forms of political and economic hegemony".

Regionally, relations with Bulgaria continue to be impeded by Sofia's insistence that all Macedonians be recognized as ethnically Bulgarian, while nationalist sentiments among ethnic Albanians in Kosovo, where they constitute a majority of the population, have complicated Yugoslavian-Albanian relations. Long bitterly hostile to the "revisionists" in Belgrade, Tirana did not agree to establish diplomatic relations until 1971. In the wake of Albania's mid-1978 falling-out with Peking, trade between the two countries more than doubled, although the unrest in Kosovo continues to fuel mutual hostility.

Current issues. In addition to continued economic difficulty, 1987 witnessed a major financial scandal and continued unrest in the largely Albanian-populated province of Kosovo. The scandal involved the issuance of unsecured promissory notes for upwards of $500 million to nearly 60 banks in four republics by Agrokomerc, a leading Bosnian agro-industrial complex. One of those ultimately arrested in the affair was the brother of federal Vice President Hamdija Pozderac, who was obliged to resign after the intervention of Branko Mikulić, the president of the Federal Executive Council and a fellow Bosnian.

The ethnic turmoil in Kosovo had been characterized by a government spokesman in early 1986 as "Yugoslavia's single greatest problem". Leaders of the Albanian majority had long demanded that the province ("autonomous" under the constitution) be accorded republic status—a concession that the existing republics were unwilling to grant because the territory would then be in a position to exercise a right of secession from the federation. In mid-1986 Belgrade felt obliged to adopt measures intended to halt an exodus of Serbs and Montenegrins, who had come under increased ethnic harassment, including terrorist acts by clandestine separatist groups. Included were penalties for the sale of homes to Albanians by minority individuals, as well as employment and other incentives to encourage the return of those who had left. Such efforts were deemed insufficient by the affected minorities, who mounted a major demonstration outside the Federal Assembly late in the year for more concerted action on their behalf. The crisis subsequently exposed a long-rumored feud between Serbian party leader Slobodan MILOSEVIĆ and the republic's president, Ivan STAMBOLIĆ, who was dismissed from office in December 1987 after being accused of excessive leniency toward the Albanians.

POLITICAL PARTIES

Since the establishment of full Communist rule shortly after World War II, Yugoslavia's only authorized political party has been the Communist Party, which was redesignated as the League of Communists of Yugoslavia (LCY) in 1952. Political control is exercised largely through a "popular front" grouping known until 1952 as the People's Front and subsequently as the **Socialist Alliance of the Working People of Yugoslavia** (*Socijalistički Savez Radnog Naroda Jugoslavija*—SSRNJ). With a membership of about 14 million, the SSRNJ controls the electoral procedure and much of the press, and plays a much less subservient role than do comparable organizations in other East European countries. Its highest organ is the Federal Conference, headed by a Presidium of 32 members, whose president is rotated annually.

League of Communists of Yugoslavia—LCY (*Savez Komunista Jugoslavija*—SKJ). Founded in 1919 and led by Marshal Tito from 1937 until his death, Yugoslavia's Communist party has been increasingly democratized over the past generation, although it has stopped short of permitting any organized opposition. Elaborately structured at the communal, republican, and federal levels, the party's membership in March 1985 was 2.2 million. Its supreme organ is the party Congress, which is elected by units at the communal level.

The party structure was extensively reorganized beginning with the Ninth Party Congress in March 1969, when, most importantly, the Central Committee was abolished in favor of annual party conferences; however, the Committee was restored at the next congress, held in May 1974. At the Eleventh Congress, held at Belgrade on June 20–23, 1978, the Presidium, which is selected by the Central Committee, was reduced from 39 members to 24 (including Marshal Tito) and its 12-member Executive Committee was dissolved. The new Presidium, which elected 9 executive secretaries from within the Central Committee at its first meeting on June 23, thus became the major LCY policy-making organ. Under a standing rule adopted the following October, the Presidium decreed that its president would be selected annually on a rotation basis among the republics and provinces. In May 1979 it was further decided that the position of Presidium secretary would be similarly filled, though on a biennial basis.

Following the death of Marshal Tito in May 1980, the post of party president was abolished, the right to represent the LCY on the state Presidency being assigned to the president of the Presidium; in addition, authority to propose the membership of the Presidium was given to a special commission of the Central Committee, while the Presidium was authorized to convene Central Committee sessions.

In a context of remarkably frank and open discussion, delegates to the Twelfth Congress, held at Belgrade on June 26–29, 1982, approved a variety of amendments to the LCY statutes, including those that had been enacted on a provisional basis since the previous congress. The president of the Presidium was, for the first time, elected by secret ballot, although there was no competing candidate and an appeal for the future election of all party officials by secret ballot on a multicandidature basis was rejected.

At the Thirteenth Congress, held at Belgrade on June 25–28, 1986, a new Central Committee of 165 full members was named, as was a Presidium of 23 members: 3 representing each of the six republics, 2 representing each of the two autonomous provinces, and 1 representing the army. Of the Presidium members, 14 were elected (2 from each republic and 1 from each autonomous province), while 9 were designated ex officio (the presidents of the republican, provincial, and army LCY organizations). Immediately thereafter, the new Presidium held its first session, at which

it designated a president, secretary, and 6 executive secretaries (as compared with 3 in 1982). In what was formally styled a "change of generations", only 38 members of the preceding Central Committee were reelected, while all but one member each of the Presidium and Executive Secretariat were new appointees.

President of the Presidium (1988–1989): Stipe ŠUVAR (Croatia).

Secretary of the Presidium (1988–1989): Stefan KOROSEČ (Slovenia).

Other Elected Members of the Presidium: Ivan BRIGIĆ and Milanko RENOVICA (Bosnia-Herzegovina), Ivica RAČAN (Croatia), Milan PANČEVSKI and Vasil TUPURKOVSKI (Macedonia), Marko ORLANDIĆ and Vidoje ŽARKOVIĆ (Montenegro), Dusan CKREBIĆ and Radiša GAČIC (Serbia), Franc ŠETINĆ (Slovenia), Kolj SIROKA (Kosovo), Bošco KUNIĆ (Vojvodina).

Ex Officio Members of the Presidium: Milan UZELAC (Bosnia-Herzegovina), Stanko STOJČEVIĆ (Croatia), Jakov LAZAROSKI (Macedonia), Miljan RADOVIĆ (Montenegro), Slobodan MILOŠEVIĆ (Serbia), Milan KUČAN (Slovenia), Azem VLASI (Kosovo), Djordje STOJŠIĆ (Vojvodina), Gen. Georgije JOVIČIĆ (People's Army).

Presidium Executive Secretaries: Slobodan FILIPOVIĆ, Marko LOLIĆ, Vukasin LONČAR, Boris MUŽEVIĆ, Stanislav STOJANOVIĆ, Uglješa UZELAC, Ljubomir VAROŠLIJA.

LEGISLATURE

Under the 1974 constitution, the **Federal Assembly** (*Savezna Skupština*) is a bicameral body consisting of a Federal Chamber and a Chamber of Republics and Provinces, both sitting for four-year terms. The most recent final stages of election to these bodies occurred in May 1986. The presidents of the Assembly and both chambers are elected on an annual basis, with rotation among representatives of the republics and provinces.

President of the Federal Assembly (1988–1989): Dusan POPOZSKI (Macedonia).

Federal Chamber. The Federal Chamber is composed of 30 delegates from each of the six constituent republics and 20 from each of the two autonomous provinces (all nominated by the Socialist Alliance of the Working People).

President (1988–1989): Stjepan NOVAKOVIĆ (Vojvodina).

Chamber of Republics and Provinces. The Chamber of Republics and Provinces is composed of 12 delegates from each republican assembly and 8 delegates from each provincial assembly, all elected by secret ballot of the chambers of the eight assemblies sitting in joint session.

President (1988–1989): Abaz KAZAZI (Kosovo).

CABINET

The **Federal Executive Council,** which serves for a four-year term as the country's highest political-executive organ and is headed by a president with functions comparable to those of a prime minister, was last elected by the Federal Assembly on May 16, 1986. In addition to the president and 2 vice presidents, it currently has 28 members: 12 without portfolio, 8 who serve as federal secretaries, and 8 who serve as federal committee chairmen. All are affiliated with the LCY and act collectively as a governmental steering committee.

President, Federal Executive Council	Branko Mikulić
Vice Presidents, Federal Executive Council	Milos Milosavljević
	Janez Zemljaric
Members, Federal Executive Council	Dr. Dragi Danev
	Franciska Herga
	Dr. Radoje Kontić

Dr. Oskar Kovac
Radovan Makić
Dr. Muhamet Mustafa
Nevenka Neralić-Milivojević
Egon Padovan
Mito Pejovski
Tibor Salma
Dr. Ibrahim Tabaković
Momcilo Vučinić

Federal Secretaries

Finance	Svetozar Rikanović
Foreign Affairs	Budimir Lončar
Foreign Trade	Nenad Krekić
Information	Svetozar Duratović
Internal Affairs	Dobroslav Čulafić
Justice and General Administration	Dr. Petar Vajović
Markets and General Economic Affairs	Aleksander Donev
National Defense	Veljko Kadijević

Federal Committee Chairmen

Agriculture	Savo Vujkov
Energy and Industry	Dr. Andrej Ocvirk
Labor, Public Health and Social Security	Dr. Janko Obocki
Legislation	Dr. Lojze Ude
Scientific and Technological Development	Dr. Bozidar Matić
Tourism	Miodrag Mirović
Transport and Communications	Branko Mamula
Veterans and Disabled Persons	Ilija Vakić
Governor, National Bank of Yugoslavia	Dusan Vlatković

NEWS MEDIA

Originally operated directly by the government, postwar Yugoslavia's information media have functioned since the mid-1950s under a system of "social self-management" that gives a voice to the employees of an enterprise but reserves the principal role to a political sponsor, in most cases the Socialist Alliance of either the federal republic (SSRNJ) or of a constituent republic. Freedom of the press and other media was formally introduced in 1960 but does not extend to attacks on the basic principles of the regime. On November 25, 1980, the SSRNJ turned down a request by several intellectuals to publish a new political journal; an earlier letter soliciting contributions for the proposed "free and democratic magazine" had called for greater freedom of expression and a loosening of state control over the press and broadcasting. Since 1981, press criticism of the Kosovo unrest and the declining economic situation has become increasingly strident. As a result, by 1987 the government had investigated a number of youth publishing houses for carrying provocative articles, banned various issues of intellectual periodicals, and jailed several persons for distributing anti-state propaganda.

Press. Newspapers are published in the languages of all Yugoslav nationalities and national minorities. The following are dailies published at Belgrade in Serbo-Croatian, unless otherwise noted: *Večernje Novosti* (340,000), SSRNJ organ; *Večernje List* (Zagreb, 295,000); *Politika* (260,000), Yugoslavia's principal prewar journal, founded in 1901; *Politika Ekspres* (250,000), evening paper published by *Politika* since 1963; *Delo* (Ljubljana, 100,000), organ of the Slovenian SSRN, in Slovenian; *Vjesnik* (Zagreb, 77,000), organ of Croatian SSRN; *Oslobodjenje* (Sarajevo, 69,000), organ of Bosnia-Herzegovinian SSRN; *Slobodna*

Dalmacija (Split, 68,000), organ of Dalmatian SSRN; *Borba* (35,000), SSRNJ organ, Cyrillic and Roman editions published at Belgrade and Zagreb, respectively; *Dnevnik* (Novi Sad, 30,000), organ of Vojvodinan SSRN; *Nova Makedonija* (Skopje, 24,000), organ of Macedonian SSRN; *Pobjeda* (Titograd, 19,000), organ of Montenegrin SSRN.

News agencies. The domestic facility is the Yugoslav Telegraph Agency (*Telegraska Agencija Nove Jugoslavija* — Tanjug), which for more than a decade has been a leader in the attempt to forge a "new world information order" by processing radio-transmitted Third World news through a computer-based system known as "Pool".

Radio and television. The Association of Yugoslav Radio and Television Stations (*Jugoslovenska Radio-Televizija Udruženje Radiostanica*) is government operated. The main stations are located at Belgrade, Zagreb, and Ljubljana. There were approximately 6.0 million radio and 4.1 million television receivers in 1987.

INTERGOVERNMENTAL REPRESENTATION

Ambassador to the US: Zivorad KOVACEVIĆ.

US Ambassador to Yugoslavia: John Douglas SCANLAN.

Permanent Representative to the UN: Dragoslav PEJIĆ.

IGO Memberships (Non-UN): ADF, AfDB, BIS, CCC, *CIPEC*, *CMEA*, *EIB*, IADB, IBA, ICAC, ICCO, ICO, ILZ, Intelsat, Interpol, IOOC, ISO, NAM, *OECD*, PCA.

ZAIRE

Republic of Zaire
République du Zaïre

Political Status: Independent republic established June 30, 1960; present one-party constitution promulgated February 15, 1978.

Area: 905,562 sq. mi. (2,345,409 sq. km.).

Population: 34,671,607 (1985C), 38,347,000 (1988E). The 1985 figure (reported in 1987) does not accord with a 1984 census figure of 29,671,407.

Major Urban Centers (1976E): KINSHASA (2,443,900); Kananga (704,200); Lubumbashi (451,300); Mbuji-Mayi (382,600); Kisangani (339,200).

Official Languages: French, local languages (principally Kikongo, Kingawa, Kiswahili, Lingala, Tshiluba).

Monetary Unit: Zaïre (market rate March 1, 1988, 143.05 zaïre = $1US).

President of the Republic and of the Popular Movement of the Revolution: Field Marshal MOBUTU Sese Seko Kuku Ngbendu Wa Za Banga (Joseph Désiré MOBUTU); became Head of State by military coup in 1965; named President of the Popular Movement of the Revolution in 1967; elected President of the Republic by popular vote in 1970; reelected in 1977 and on July 29, 1984; inaugurated for a third seven-year term on December 5.

First State Commissioner (Prime Minister): SAMBWA Pida Nbagui; appointed by the President to succeed MABI Mulumba on March 7, 1988.

THE COUNTRY

Formerly known as the Belgian Congo and subsequently as the Democratic Republic of the Congo, Zaire is situated largely within the hydrographic unit of the Congo River basin, in west-central Africa. The second-largest of the Sub-Saharan nations, the equatorial country is an ethnic mosaic of some 200 different groups. Bantu tribes (Bakongo, Baluba, and others) represent the largest element in the population, about half of which is Christian. Among the rural population, women are responsible for most subsistence agriculture, with men the primary cash crop producers; in urban areas, women constitute more than a third of wage earners, most of whom also engage in petty trade on the black market to supplement family income.

Zaire has a potentially sound economic infrastructure buttressed by great natural wealth in mineral resources, agricultural productivity sufficient for both local consumption and export, and a system of inland waterways that provides access to the interior and is the foundation for almost half of the total hydroelectric potential of Africa. Mineral extraction—most of it by the state-owned *La Générale des Carrières et des Mines* (Gecamines)—dominates the economy: cobalt and copper (the leading exports), diamonds, tin, manganese, zinc, silver, cadmium, gold, and tungsten are among the commercially exploited reserves. Offshore oil began flowing in late 1975, while important agricultural products include coffee, rubber, palm oil, cocoa, and tea. Despite these assets Zaire's per capita income is one of the lowest in Africa, and the economy has for some years hovered on the brink of disaster because of corruption, depressed prices for major exports, massive foreign indebtedness, and an inflation rate that has often exceeded 100 percent. While austerity measures mandated by the IMF helped to buttress exports and cut inflation to 20 percent by mid-1985, the latter again accelerated, reaching more than 125 percent by early 1987. Collaterally, the standard of living remained low, with half of the country's food being imported and the average monthly wage equal to a week's family expenses.

GOVERNMENT AND POLITICS

Political background. The priority given to economic rather than political development during Belgium's 75-year rule of the Congo contributed to an explosive power vacuum when independence was abruptly granted in June 1960. United Nations intervention, nominally at the request of the central government headed by President Joseph KASAVUBU, helped to check the centrifugal effects of factionalism and tribalism and to preserve the territorial integrity of the country during the troubled early years, which witnessed the removal and death of its first prime minister, Patrice LUMUMBA, and the gradual collapse of separatist regimes established by Albert KALONJI

in Kasai, Moïse TSHOMBE in Katanga (now Shaba Region), and Antoine GIZENGA in Stanleyville (now Kisangani). The withdrawal of UN peacekeeping forces in 1964 did not mark the end of political struggle, however, with Tshombe, who was appointed interim prime minister in July, and Kasavubu subsequently vying for power of what became the Democratic Republic of the Congo in August. On November 24, 1965, the commander of the army, (then) Maj. Gen. Joseph D. MOBUTU, who had previously held control of the government from September 1960 to February 1961, dissolved the civilian regime and proclaimed himself president of the "Second Republic".

During 1966 and 1967, Mobutu put down two major challenges to his authority by White mercenaries and Katangan troops associated with the separatist activities of former prime minister Tshombe. Pierre MULELE and Gaston N'GALO, leaders of the rebellion against the central government in 1963–1964, were executed in 1968 and 1969, respectively; Tshombe died in captivity in Algeria in June 1969. Other plots were reported in 1971, one of them involving former associates of Mobutu, who in 1970 had been directly elected (albeit as sole candidate) to the presidency following establishment of the Popular Movement of the Revolution (MPR). Shortly thereafter, in an effort to reduce tension and to solidify national unity, Mobutu embarked upon a policy of "authenticity", which included the general adoption of African names.

The country's Shaba Region was the scene of attempted invasions in March 1977 and May 1978, by rebel forces of the Congolese National Liberation Front (FLNC) directed by a former Katangan police commander, Nathanael MBUMBA. The first attack, repulsed with the aid of some 1,500 Moroccan troops airlifted to Zaire by France, was said to have failed because of Mbumba's inability to enlist the aid of other groups opposed to the Mobutu regime, particularly the Popular Revolutionary Party (PRP) of eastern Zaire, led by Laurent KABILA. In 1978, government forces were initially assisted by French and Belgian paratroops, whose presence was defended as necessary to ensure the orderly evacuation of Europeans, and subsequently by a seven-nation African security force that was not withdrawn until July-August 1979.

The 1977 Shaba invasion was followed by a series of government reforms that included the naming in July of MPINGA Kasenda to the newly created post of first state commissioner (prime minister) and the holding of direct elections in October to urban councils, to the National Legislative Council, and for 18 seats on the MPR Political Bureau. Having been reconfirmed by referendum as MPR president, Mobutu was invested for a second seven-year term as head of state on December 5.

In March 1979, the National Executive Council (cabinet) was reorganized, with BO-BOLIKO Lokonga being named to replace Mpinga, who became permanent secretary of the MPR. A secret session of the party Political Bureau on July 31–August 4, 1980, when an MPR Central Committee and an Executive Secretariat were created, preceded another leadership change, NGUZA Karl-I-Bond being designated first state commissioner on August 27 and Bo-Boliko assuming the new position of party executive secretary. In April 1981, Nguza resigned while on a trip to Belgium, declaring that he would have been imprisoned had the announcement been made prior to his scheduled departure; NSINGA Udjuu Ongwakebi Untube was named as his successor. Nsinga was in turn replaced by KENGO Wa Dondo in a major government reorganization on November 5, 1982, following a single-party (but multiple-candidature) election to the National Legislative Council on September 18–19.

Again presenting himself as the sole candidate, President Mobutu was reelected for a third seven-year term on July 27, 1984. Fifteen months later, on October 31, 1986, Mobutu announced that the post of first state commissioner had been abolished, Kengo being redesignated as foreign minister; however, the office (frequently rendered in English as that of prime minister) was restored in the course of a major ministerial reshuffling in January 1987, with former finance minister MABI Mulumba being designated its incumbent. Mabi was in turn succeeded on March 7, 1988, by SAMBWA Pida Nbagui.

Constitution and government. A constitution drafted under Mobutu's direction and approved by popular referendum in 1967 established a strong presidential system, certain features of which were drastically modified by amendments enacted in August 1974. Decisions of the Political Bureau of the Popular Movement of the Revolution were made binding upon both executive and legislative branches, thus making the Political Bureau the supreme state organ, while the president of the MPR was also designated president of the Republic. The trend toward synthesis of government and party institutions was further exemplified by the creation of a National Executive Council (whose members were restyled state commissioners), in effect a fusion of the former cabinet with the Executive Council of the MPR. These changes were affirmed in a new constitution promulgated on February 15, 1978, in which the MPR was characterized as "the Zairean Nation organized politically" with an ideological commitment to "Mobutism". The president, who "represent[s] the Nation", presides over all organs of government, including the MPR Political Bureau, the National Executive Council, and the legislature.

Members of the National Legislative Council (people's commissioners) are elected every five years from a list of candidates approved by the MPR. An electoral code promulgated on July 18, 1977, authorized multiple contestants for legislative seats and the direct election of 18 of the 30 (subsequently 38) members of the MPR's Political Bureau, the remaining members being designated by the president. However, under a constitutional amendment adopted in February 1980, the president was empowered to name all 38 Political Bureau members, effective in 1982. In November 1980 an additional draft amendment bill was passed by the legislature to accommodate other party reforms introduced in August (see Political Parties, below). The judicial system, which is supervised by a Justice Department established in January 1980, includes a Supreme Court, 9 courts of appeal, and 32 tribunals of first instance.

Zaire is divided administratively into eight regions (formerly known as provinces) and the capital district of Kinshasa, each headed by a presidentially appointed regional commissioner. The regions are divided into sub-regions (formerly known as districts). At the local level, directly elected councils have been introduced in urban areas.

Foreign relations. Zaire has generally pursued a moderate line in foreign policy while avoiding involvement in non-African issues. Relations with its former colonial ruler have been periodically strained, partly because vocal anti-Mobutu factions are based in Brussels, although Belgium remains a major aid donor. Recent development efforts have led to enhanced economic ties with Japan, the United States, and West European countries, especially France, which Kinshasa in 1986 called its new European "fountainhead". Relations with former French territories in central Africa have fluctuated. The Union of Central African States was formed with Chad in 1968 and over 3,000 Zairian troops were sent to Chad in support of President Habré in 1983. In addition, Burundi and Rwanda have joined Zaire in establishing the Economic Community of the Great Lakes Countries (CEPGL), the object being an eventual common market. Relations with Zambia have remained cordial despite a Zairian claim to part of that country's northern Kaputa and Lake Mweru districts; an agreement was reached in 1986 to settle the dispute through a joint commission scheduled to complete a boundary demarcation within two years. In the west, border incidents involving the People's Republic of the Congo have periodically erupted, while in the east Zairian troops were given permission by Kampala in July 1987 to cross into Ugandan territory to engage rebels associated with the Congolese National Movement (see Political Parties, below).

A lengthy cold war between Zaire and Angola was formally terminated by Angolan President Neto's visit to Zaire in August 1978 and a reciprocal visit by President Mobutu to Angola the following October. The latter visit concluded with the signing of a cooperation agreement between the two governments and a mutual pledge to proceed with the establishment of a commission under the Organization of African Unity to guard against rebel violations from either side of the 1,250-mile common border. By 1987, however, it had become apparent that the United States was deeply involved in covert activities in the vicinity of the Belgian-built air base at Kamina in southern Zaire, including plans to remodel the facility for delivery of supplies to the Angolan rebel forces led by Jonas Savimbi. Such collusion notwithstanding, President Mobutu joined in April with the heads of state of Angola, Mozambique, and Zambia in concluding, at Luanda, a declaration of intent to reopen the Benguela railroad, which had been effectively closed by Angolan guerrilla operations since 1976 (see Angola: Current issues).

In May 1982, Kinshasha announced that it was resuming diplomatic relations with Israel, reversing a rupture that had prevailed since the 1973 Arab-Israeli war. Earlier, President Mobutu had stated that the suspension was originally intended as a gesture of support for Egypt, but was no longer justified in view of the return of the last of the occupied Egyptian territories in April, as provided by the 1979 peace treaty. In response, a number of Arab governments severed relations with Zaire, while regional leaders expressed concern at the Israeli "reentry" into Africa. In November, Israel's defense minister, Ariel Sharon, flew to Zaire to conclude arrangements for the supply of arms and the training of Zairian forces, particularly a "presidential battalion" under Mobutu's direct command. Further military aid commitments were secured by Mobutu during a May 1985 visit to Israel, the regional backlash being tempered in 1986 by Zaire's resumption of participation in the Organization of African Unity after a two-year hiatus occasioned by OAU's admission of the Saharan Arab Democratic Republic.

Current issues. A presidential decree of January 13, 1987, established a timetable for the election of community, district, and town councilors, as well as regional and national legislators, between May 31 and September 6. In late August, however, the MPR Central Committee voided the local results because of "foul play" in both rural and urban areas, and extended the mandates of the regional assemblies and lesser bodies elected in 1982 to February 1988, with new elections to be mounted in March. The national poll proceeded as scheduled in September, with extraordinary precautions taken to avoid the irregularities claimed in the earlier balloting and with results announced on a region-by-region basis to avoid countrywide "manipulation and fraud".

In economic affairs, the government during 1987 continued its efforts to revive Zaire's faltering economy by liberalizing the investment code, easing controls on foreign exchange, and adopting its first five-year development plan. Austerity measures previously mandated by the International Monetary Fund continued in effect, although the country remained a net exporter of capital. Early in the year the IMF agreed to provide $126 million in new loans, with debt service obligations not to exceed 10 percent of export earnings. In addition, the World Bank agreed at midyear to a structural adjustment loan package.

POLITICAL PARTIES

All existing parties were outlawed in 1965. Subsequently, the only legal grouping has been the Popular Movement of the Revolution (MPR). Established under General Mobutu's auspices in April 1967, the MPR has progressively integrated itself with the governmental infrastructure. An attempt in 1980 by a number of parliamentarians to form a de facto opposition party, the Union for Democracy and Social Progress, was effectively countered by the MPR in effectively co-opting most of its domestic leadership. Numerous exile opposition groups, most of them based in either Belgium or France, are also known to exist; in September 1987 it was announced that 13 such groups had formed a government in exile with the "sole aim" of overthrowing Mobutu.

Government Party:

Popular Movement of the Revolution (*Mouvement Populaire de la Révolution* — MPR). With a program stressing indigenous nationalism, or "authenticity", the MPR serves as the political base of the Mobutu regime. Legally, each Zairian becomes a member of the party at birth. Party organs include a Congress; a Political Bureau, which consists exclusively of presidential appointees; and Legislative, Executive, and Judicial councils. In August 1980, three additional organs were created: a Central Committee, whose membership was reduced from 114 to 80 in

early 1985; an Executive Secretariat; and a party chairmanship, which is held by the party president and is considered the central organ of control and decisionmaking.

Leaders: Fld. Mar. MOBUTU Sese Seko (President of the Republic and Chairman of the Party), KITHIMA bin Ramazani (Secretary General), KAMANDA wa Kamanda (Deputy Secretary General).

Union for Democracy and Social Progress (*Union pour la Démocratie et le Progrès Social* — UDPS). The UDPS was the outgrowth of an effort in late 1980 to establish an opposition party within Zaire dedicated to the end of President Mobutu's "arbitrary rule". Subsequently, the government arrested, sentenced and eventually amnestied various of its members including 13 former people's commissioners. An apparent split in the leadership was reported in April 1986 when local UDPS officials declared that DIKONDA wa Lumanyisha, a Brussels-based founder of the party, no longer represented them, while the former UDPS secretary general Etienne Tshisekedi wa Malumba declared in September 1987 that an agreement had been concluded with President Mobutu whereby the group would be accorded the status of a "tendency" within the MPR.

Leaders: KIBASA Maliba, Etienne TSHISEKEDI wa Malumba.

Clandestine and Exile Groups:

In recent years a number of umbrella exile groups have been formed, most subsequently becoming moribund. They include the Organization for the Liberation of the Congo-Kinshasa (*Organisation pour la Libération du Congo-Kinshasa* — OLC), established in 1978; the Council for the Liberation of the Congo (*Conseil pour la Libération du Congo* — CLC), formed in 1980; and the Congolese Front for the Restoration of Democracy (*Front Congolaise pour la Restauration de la Démocratie* — FCD), established in 1982 by former prime minister Nguza Karl-I-Bond after his flight to Belgium in 1981. In June 1985, Nguza returned to Kinshasa, offering "national reconciliation" to President Mobutu, who named him ambassador to the United States in July 1986. The action was bitterly denounced by opposition groups both in and out of the former FCD, a number of which participated in formation of the exile shadow government proclaimed at Bex, Switzerland, in 1987.

Congolese National Movement (*Mouvement National du Congolais* — MNC). The MNC is an exile group with at least two discernible current factions, the **Congolese National Movement–Lumumba** (*Mouvement National Congolais–Lumumba* — MNCL) and the **Reformed Congolese National Movement** (*Mouvement National Congolais Rénové* — MNCR). The MNC became visible in 1978, when its president was detained by Belgian authorities and expelled to France, with similar action taken against its secretary general in 1984 after the group claimed responsibility for a series of March bombings at Kinshasa. In 1985, the MNC emerged as the most active of the external groups: in April it issued a statement listing those allegedly killed by government troops during disturbances in eastern provinces in late 1984, and calling Mobutu "an element of instability in central Africa". Following the repatriation of Nguza Karl-I-Bond and the collapse of the FCD, it issued a joint communique with the FLNC (below), accusing the former leader not of "reconciliation" but "of unconditional rallying to Mobutu". In September 1985 leaders of both the MNCL and the MNCR joined with the Swiss-based **Congolese Democratic and Socialist Party** (*Parti Démocratique et Socialiste Congolaise* — PDSC), led by Allah Fior MUYINDA, in inviting other opposition groups to participate in a joint working commission to oversee "activities [to be launched] over the whole country in coming days". MNCR leader Paul-Roger Mokede was named president of the exile provisional government at a meeting in Switzerland in September 1987, but rejected the designation on the ground that Zaire could not "afford the luxury" of a parallel regime. Other groups represented at the 1987 meeting included the **Avante-guarde Zairean Labor Party** (*Parti d'Avant-garde Zaïrois du Travail*); the **Community of Zairean Exiles of France** (*Communauté d'Exiles Zaïrois de France*); the **Congolese Liberation Party** (*Parti de Libération Congolais*), led by Antoine MARANDURA; the **Democratic Alternative on the Horizon** (*Alternative Démocratique à l'Horizon*); the **January 17 Movement** (*Mouvement du 17 Janvier*); and the **Zairean Social-Liberal Party** (*Parti Social-Libéral Zaïrois*), led by Dieudonne KILINGA.

Leaders: Paul-Roger MOKEDE (MNCR), Albert-Jerry MEHELE and Albert ONAWELHO (MNCL).

Congolese National Liberation Front (*Front de la Libération Nationale Congolaise* — FLNC). A former CLC constituent group, the FLNC is composed largely of Katangese expatriates, some of whom became foreign mercenaries after the fall of the Tshombe regime in 1963. It mounted unsuccessful invasions of Zaire's Shaba Region from bases in Angola in March 1977 and May 1978 (see Political background, above).

Leader: Nathanael MBUMBA.

Popular Revolutionary Party (*Parti de la Révolution Populaire*— PRP). The PRP, a Marxist-oriented group, has mounted sporadic anti-government guerrilla operations in eastern Zaire. Prior to joining the FCD, its exile leadership had participated in formation of the CLC. In early 1986 it was reported that some 500 PRP rebels had surrendered to the government.

Leader: Laurent KABILA.

Other dissident groups include the **National Movement for Union and Reconciliation in Zaire** (*Mouvement pour l'Union et la Reconciliation au Zaïre*—MURZ), a former constituent group of the CLC led by Mbeka MAKOSSO, who had been secretary general of the OLC; the **Socialist Party of Zaire** (*Parti Socialiste Zaïrois*—PSZ), six of whose members were arrested in mid-1985 following disturbances in the Shaba region, with the PSZ's secretary general, Aimé BETOU, declaring from Paris that they had been "wrongly accused"; and the Marxist **Worker and Peasant Party** (*Parti Ouvrier et Paysan*—POP), founded by Simon-Pierre KWENGE in November 1986.

LEGISLATURE

The **National Legislative Council** (*Conseil Législatif National*) is a unicameral body currently consisting of 210 "people's commissioners" elected for five-year terms on September 6, 1987, from a list of 1,075 candidates approved by the Popular Movement of the Revolution.

Speaker: KALUMA Mwana Kahambwe.

CABINET

President	Field Mar. Mobutu Sese Seko
First State Commissioner	Sambwa Pida Nbagui
Deputy First State Commissioner for Economic and Financial Affairs	Nyembo Shabani
Deputy First State Commissioner for Political, Administrative and Social Affairs	Nimy Mayidika Ngimbi
State Commissioners	
Agriculture	Nyembo Shabani
Budget	Kinzonzi Mvutukidi Ngindu
Citizens Rights and Liberties	Nimy Mayidika Ngimbi
Civil Service	Mwando Nsimba
Culture, Arts and Tourism	Beyeye Djema
Finance	Kamitatu Massamba
Foreign Affairs and International Cooperation	Nguza Karl-I-Bond
Foreign Trade	Kanumubadi Badibanga Mbakese
Higher and University Education and Scientific Research	Luhahi a Niama
Information and Press	Ekila Liyonda
Labor and Social Security	Kisolokele Wamba
Mines and Energy	Kisanga Kabongelo
National Defense, Territorial Security and Veteran's Affairs	Field Mar. Mobutu Sese Seko
National Economy and Industry	Mokonda Bonza
Parastatals	Mulumba Lukoji
Planning	Kasereka Kasai
Post, Telephone and Telecommunications	Ileo Itambala
Primary and Secondary Education	Nzege Aliaziambina
Public Health	Dr. Ngandu Kabeya
Public Works	Mokolo wa Mpombo
Real Property, Environment and Conservation	Pendje Demodetdo Yako
Rural Development	Kayinga Onsi Ndal
Social Affairs	Muduka Inyanza
Sports and Leisure	Tshimbombo Mukuna
Territorial Administration and Decentralization	Mandungu Bula Nyati
Transport and Communications	Sampassa Kaweta Milombe
Urbanism and Housing	Kibangula Kia Makonga
Governor, Central Bank	Pay Pay wa Syakassighe

NEWS MEDIA

Newspapers in Zaire have been increasingly subject to government control. In recent years a "restructuring" of the press has reduced the number of papers being issued.

Press. The following are dailies published at Kinshasa, unless otherwise noted: *Elima* (12,000); *Salongo* (10,000); *Boyoma* (Kisangani); *Mjumbe* (Lubumbashi).

News agencies. The domestic facility is *Agence Zaïre-Presse* (AZaP); *Agence France-Presse, Xinhua,* and Reuters also maintain bureaus at Kinshasa.

Radio and television. Radio broadcasting is provided by the government over the national station, *La Voix du Zaïre,* and regional stations. Commercial television is provided by the government-operated, commercial Zaire Television. There were approximately 530,000 radio and 16,000 television receivers in 1987.

INTERGOVERNMENTAL REPRESENTATION

Ambassador to the US: MUSHOBEKWA Kalimba wa Katana.

US Ambassador to Zaire: William Caldwell HARROP.

Permanent Representative to the UN: BAGBENI ADEITO Nzengeya.

IGO Memberships (Non-UN): ACCT, ADF, AfDB, BADEA, CCC, CEPGL, CIPEC, EEC(L), *EIB,* IACO, ICO, Intelsat, Interpol, NAM, OAU, PCA.

ZAMBIA

Republic of Zambia

Political Status: Independent republic within the Commonwealth since October 24, 1964; under one-party, presidential-parliamentary system.

Area: 290,584 sq. mi. (752,614 sq. km.).

Population: 5,661,801 (1980C), 7,568,000 (1988E).

Major Urban Centers (1980C): LUSAKA (538,469); Kitwe (314,794); Ndola (282,439).

Official Language: English.

Monetary Unit: Kwacha (market rate March 1, 1988, 8.00 kwachas = $1US).

President: Dr. Kenneth David KAUNDA; first elected by the National Assembly on January 21, 1964, assuming office on October 24; popularly reelected for five-year terms in 1968, 1973, 1978, and on October 27, 1983.

Secretary General of the United National Independence Party: Alexander Grey ZULU; appointed by the President on April 24, 1985, to succeed Humphrey MULEMBA.

Prime Minister: Kebby MUSOKOTWANE; appointed by the President on April 24, 1985, to succeed Nalumino MUNDIA.

THE COUNTRY

Landlocked Zambia, the former British protectorate of Northern Rhodesia, is bordered by Zaire, Tanzania, and Malawi on the north and east, and by Angola, Namibia (South West Africa), Zimbabwe, and Mozambique on the west and south. Its terrain consists primarily of a high plateau with abundant forests and grasslands. The watershed between the Congo and Zambezi river systems crosses the northern part of the country. The bulk of the population belongs to various Bantu tribes, the most influential being the Bemba in the north and the Lozi, an offshoot of the Zulu, in the southwest. Nonindigenous groups include a small number of Whites (mainly British and South African), Asians, and Coloureds (persons of mixed descent) concentrated in the "copper belt" in the north. Nearly three-quarters of native Zambians are nominally Christian, almost equally divided between Catholics and Protestants; the remainder adhere to traditional African beliefs. The official language is English, but Afrikaans and more than 70 local languages and dialects are spoken. Women comprise approximately one-third of the labor force, not including unpaid agricultural workers. Although a number of women involved in the independence struggle have achieved positions of influence in the ruling party, their representation does not extend to local levels, females still being considered minors under the law.

Zambia is one of the world's five largest producers of copper, which has recently accounted for 80–95 percent of total exports, and is second only to Zaire in cobalt output; lead, manganese, sulphur, and zinc are among other minerals being extracted. Agriculture employs two-thirds of the labor force, with maize, peanuts, tobacco, and cotton constituting the chief commercial crops. Because of a booming copper industry, Zambia, until the early 1970s, enjoyed one of Africa's highest standards of living, with rapid development of schools, hospitals, and highways. However, a subsequent decline in copper prices (currently less than one-third of the 1975 level) has yielded infrastructural decay, rising unemployment among a rapidly growing and highly urbanized population, a foreign exchange shortage, and an external debt of more than $5 billion. In accordance with agreements with the International Monetary Fund dating back to the mid-1970s, the government has practiced budgetary restraint while relaxing government control of the economy. Since copper reserves may be exhausted within 15 years, current development efforts focus on the country's long-neglected agricultural potential, a slump in food production having contributed to growing unrest over austerity measures (see Current issues, below).

GOVERNMENT AND POLITICS

Political background. Declared a British sphere of influence in 1888, Northern Rhodesia was administered jointly with Southern Rhodesia until 1923–1924, when it became a separate British protectorate. From 1953 to 1963, it was linked with Southern Rhodesia and Nyasaland (now Malawi) in the Federation of Rhodesia and Nyasaland, which was dissolved at the end of 1963 in recognition of the unwillingness of the Black majority populations in Northern Rhodesia and Nyasaland to continue under the political and economic domination of White-ruled Southern Rhodesia. A drive for Northern Rhodesia's complete independence, led by Harry NKUMBULA and Kenneth D. KAUNDA, concluded on October 24, 1964, when the territory became an independent republic within the Commonwealth under the name of Zambia (after the Zambezi River). Kaunda, as leader of the majority United National Independence Party (UNIP), became head of the new state; Nkumbula, whose African National Congress (ANC) had trailed in the preindependence election of January 1964, became leader of the opposition. The political predominance of Kaunda and his party was strengthened at the general election of December 1968, Kaunda winning a second five-year term as president and the UNIP again capturing an overwhelming legislative majority. In December 1972, Kaunda promulgated a law banning all parties except the UNIP and introducing what was termed "one-party participatory democracy". On December 12, 1978, he was reelected for a fourth term following disqualification of Nkumbula and former vice president Simon M. KAPWEPWE.

On August 27, 1983, the president dissolved the National Assembly to pave the way for an October 27 election, in which, as sole presidential candidate, he garnered 93 percent of the vote and was returned to office for a fifth five-year term. Two years later, in a cabinet reshuffle interpreted as reflecting a desire to clear the way for a stable presidential succession, Kaunda transferred to diplomatic posts both the prime minister and the UNIP secretary general; Defense Minister Alexander Grey ZULU was chosen to head the party, while Prime Minister Nalumino MUNDIA was replaced by Minister of Education and Culture Kebby MUSOKOTWANE.

Constitution and government. At a UNIP national conference in August 1973, the 1964 basic law was replaced by a constitution of the "second republic". The 1973 document provides for the sharing of authority between the party and traditional organs of government, with the 25-member Central Committee of the UNIP bearing primary responsibility for the formulation of national policy, the execution of which lies with the cabinet. As amended in 1978, the constitution further stipulates that candidates for the presidency must have been UNIP members for five years. To further emphasize the role of the party, its secretary general (rather than the prime minister) is designated the nation's second-ranking official. Formally elected by universal suffrage for a five-year term, the president is empowered to veto legislation. Should the National Assembly override a veto, the president may dissolve the legislature. In addition, he names the secretary general of the UNIP from the members of its Central Committee and appoints the prime minister and other cabinet officials from the National Assembly, all of whose members must belong to the UNIP. The possibility of independent candidature was raised following the 1983 Assembly balloting, but no action had been taken in the matter by early 1988. There is also an advisory House of Chiefs, composed of leading tribal authorities. The judiciary embraces a Supreme Court, a High Court, and various local courts. All judges are appointed by the president.

Administratively, the country is divided into nine provinces, including the city of Lusaka and its environs. Each province is subdivided into districts. All leading provincial and district officials are appointed by the central government.

Foreign relations. While pursuing a generally nonaligned foreign policy (an 18-year coolness with Britain having been ended by a Kaunda state visit to London in 1983), Zambia has long opposed racial discrimination in southern Africa and has provided sanctuary for numerous exile groups engaged in guerrilla operations against White-controlled territories. During 1984–1986, its prestige among Front-Line States was visibly enhanced. In the wake of treaties concluded by Angola and Mozambique with South Africa, Lusaka became the headquarters of the African National Congress (ANC), making it a target for bomb attacks in May 1986 by South Africa forces, who also crossed the border on a "reconnaissance mission" in April 1987 that left several persons dead. Kaunda assumed chairmanship of the Front-Line grouping in early 1985, vowing to promote increased mutual support among member governments. In 1986 he denounced the United States and the United Kingdom for "conspiring" to support the South African government, warning they would share responsibility for the impending antiapartheid "explosion". Zambia has also been in the forefront of a regional plan to reduce the use of South African trade routes, recently concluding agreements to participate in the rehabilitation of the Benguela Railway in Angola and the Tanzania-Zambia (Tanzam) link to Dar es Salaam. In other regional affairs, troops have at times been deployed in border clashes with Malawi and Zaire, the latter agreeing in 1986 to a two-year joint review and demarcation of disputed territory.

Current issues. In December 1986 riots spread throughout the northern copper belt as prices for corn meal doubled upon the withdrawal of subsidies to stimulate a freer market. President Kaunda restored the subsidies and, in the face of a wave of strikes and other unrest, declared in May 1987 that demands from the IMF had "become completely unbearable". The government rejected the IMF's latest financing proposal in favor of an independent economic recovery program. Coming as it did from one of Africa's most respected "elder statesmen", the move attracted worldwide attention, Third World countries in particular studying the response of Western donors. Some observers expected Kaunda would eventually be forced back into the IMF fold, probably following the 1988 election.

Although the economic and social difficulties produced a call from reformists for a multiparty political system, Kaunda dismissed the idea as unworkable because of "too many tribal conflicts". He continued to blame many of his country's ills on South Africa, whose leaders were accused of regional destabilization policies.

POLITICAL PARTIES

As a result of legislation enacted in December 1972, the United National Independence Party became the country's sole legal political party.

United National Independence Party (UNIP). Zambia's present ruling party was formed as a result of the 1958 withdrawal of Kenneth D. Kaunda, Simon M. Kapwepwe, and others from the older African National Congress (ANC), led by Harry Nkumbula. The UNIP, which was banned by the British in March 1959 and was reconstituted in October 1959, has ruled Zambia since independence. The principal party organ is the General Conference, which convenes every five years. Under the 1973 constitution, the members of the party's Central Committee are responsible for the formulation of overall national policy, while the president of Zambia is also the party president. All candidates for election to the National Assembly must be members of the UNIP.

Leaders: Dr. Kenneth David KAUNDA (President of the Republic and of the Party), Alexander Grey ZULU (Secretary General).

LEGISLATURE

The **National Assembly** is a unicameral body consisting of a maximum of 136 members: 125 elected by universal suffrage for five-year terms, up to 10 presidential appointees, and the speaker. Candidates for the Assembly must be members of the UNIP and must be approved by the party's Central Committee. The most recent election was held on October 27, 1983.

Speaker: Dr. Robinson NABULYATO.

CABINET

Prime Minister	Kebby Musokotwane
Secretary of State for Defense and Security	Alex Shapi
Ministers	
Agriculture and Water Development	Fitzpatrick Chuula
Commerce and Industry	K.M. Jameson Kalaluka
Cooperatives	Justin Mukando
Decentralization	Rajah Kunda
Defense	Gen. Malimba Masheke
Finance and Development Planning	Gibson Chigaga
Foreign Affairs	Luke J. Mwananshiku
General Education and Culture	Basil Kabwe
Health	Rodger C. Sakuhuka
Higher Education	Lameck K.H. Goma
Home Affairs	Paul Mulukutila
Labor and Social Services	Uniah Mwila
Lands and Natural Resources	Ben Kakoma
Legal Affairs	Frederick Chomba
Mines	Pickson Chitambala
National Guidance, Information and Broadcasting Services	Milimo Punabantu

Power, Transport and Communications	Gen. Kingsley Chinkuli
Presidential Affairs	Arnold K. Simuchimba
Tourism	Leonard S. Subulwu
Works and Supply	Haswell Y. Mwale
Youth and Sports	Frederick Shumba Hapunda
Attorney General	Frederick Chomba
Governor, Central Bank	Francis Nkhoma

NEWS MEDIA

Rigid control is exercised over the news media.

Press. In April 1980, following publication in the *Times of Zambia* of an article critical of the government, President Kaunda warned that press freedoms might be curtailed. Subsequently, on October 1, 1982, the *Times,* which had long been dominated by the UNIP, was acquired outright from the British conglomerate Lonrho. The following are English-language newspapers: *Times of Zambia* (Ndola, 60,000 daily, 58,000 Sunday), UNIP organ; *Zambia Daily Mail* (Lusaka, 45,000), government owned; *Sunday Post,* independent, launched in October 1982.

News agencies. The Zambia News Agency (Zana) is the domestic facility; *Agence France-Presse, Deutsche Presse-Agentur,* Reuters, and TASS are among those maintaining bureaus at Lusaka.

Radio and television. The government controls the radio and television networks. Zambia Broadcasting Services transmits in English and seven Zambian languages to the nation's 250,000 radio receivers, while Television-Zambia provides programming for the nation's 200,000 television receivers.

INTERGOVERNMENTAL REPRESENTATION

Ambassador to the US: Nalumino MUNDIA.

US Ambassador to Zambia: Paul Julian HARE.

Permanent Representative to the UN: Lt. Gen. Peter Dingi ZUZE.

IGO Memberships (Non-UN): ADF, AfDB, BADEA, CCC, CIPEC, CWTH, EEC(L), *EIB,* ILZ, Intelsat, Interpol, NAM, OAU, SADCC.

ZIMBABWE

Republic of Zimbabwe

Political Status: Became self-governing British Colony of Southern Rhodesia in October 1923; unilaterally declared independence November 11, 1965; White-dominated republican regime proclaimed March 2, 1970; biracial executive established on basis of transitional government agreement of March 3, 1978; returned to interim British rule on basis of ceasefire agreement signed December 21, 1979; achieved de jure independence as Republic of Zimbabwe on April 18, 1980; became de facto one-party state on December 22, 1987.

Area: 150,803 sq. mi. (390,580 sq. km.).

Population: 7,539,000 (1982C), 8,785,000 (1988E). The 1982 census result is provisional.

Major Urban Centers (1982C): HARARE (formerly Salisbury, 656,000); Bulawayo (413,800).

Official Language: English (Shona and Sindebele are the principal African languages).

Monetary Unit: Zimbabwe Dollar (market rate March 1, 1988, 1 dollar = $1.74US).

President: Robert MUGABE; sworn in as Prime Minister on April 18, 1980, following legislative election of February 14 and 27–29; reconfirmed following election of June 30 and July 1–2, 1985; elected President by Parliament on December 30, 1987, and inaugurated for a six-year term on December 31, succeeding the former head of state, Rev. Canaan Sodindo BANANA.

Vice President: Simon Vengai MUZENDA; elected on December 30, 1987, and inaugurated on December 31 for a term concurrent with that of the President.

THE COUNTRY

Bordered by Botswana, Zambia, Mozambique, and South Africa, Zimbabwe occupies the fertile plateaus and mountain ranges between southeastern Africa's Zambezi and Limpopo rivers. The population includes nearly 8 million Africans, mainly Bantu in origin; approximately 200,000 Europeans; and smaller groups of Asians and people of mixed race. The Africans may be classified into two multitribal groupings, the Shona (about 75 percent, overall) in the north and the Ndebele, concentrated in the southern area of Matabeleland. Shona-Ndebele rivalry dates back to the nineteenth century and has contributed to a pronounced north-south cleavage in the current Parliament. The majority of the European population is Protestant, although there is a substantial Catholic minority; the Africans include both Christians and followers of traditional religions; the Asians are divided between Hindus and Muslims.

In 1980, one-third of the paid labor force was estimated to be female; Black women are responsible for most subsistence agriculture (cash-crop production being undertaken mainly by White farmers), with White and Asian women concentrated in the clerical and service sectors. A Legal Age of Majority Act, passed in 1982, significantly enhanced the legal status of women (including the right of personal choice in selecting a marital partner, the right to own property outright, and the ability to enter into business contracts); it has, however, been unevenly utilized because of its conflict with traditional law. Following the 1985 election, there were two female cabinet members, with female representation in both local and national elective bodies averaging about 5 percent.

Zimbabwe is well endowed with natural resources that have yielded a relatively advanced economy oriented toward foreign trade and supported by a sophisticated infrastructure. The country exports asbestos, chrome, copper, and other mineral products to a wide variety of foreign markets, while agricultural self-sufficiency permits export of maize and other food crops to shortage-plagued neighbors. Although international trade sanctions were imposed on Zimbabwe (then Rhodesia) from 1965 to 1979, its economy prospered for much of the period because of continued access to trade routes through Mozambique (until 1976) and South Africa, which became the conduit for up to 90 percent of Zimbabwean imports and exports. The economy was further stimulated by the lifting of sanctions at the end of 1979, although drought and falling commodity prices have since contributed to fiscal difficulties, including budget deficits and persistent inflation. In addition, unemployment has been aggravated by a growing pool of workers seeking better jobs as the result of rapid educational advances for Blacks. Despite continued Marxist-Leninist rhetoric, the government has relaxed its control of the economy in favor of private business, industry, and agriculture, although a lack of enthusiasm for foreign investment has drawn increasing criticism from the business community.

GOVERNMENT AND POLITICS

Political background. Originally developed and administered by the British South Africa Company, Southern Rhodesia became an internally self-governing British colony in 1923 under a system that concentrated political power in the hands of its White minority. In 1953 it joined with Northern Rhodesia (now Zambia) and Nyasaland (now Malawi) in the so-called Federation of Rhodesia and Nyasaland, reverting to separate status in 1963 when the Federation was dissolved and its two partners prepared to claim their independence. A new constitution granted to Southern Rhodesia by Britain in December 1961 conferred increased powers of self-government and contained various provisions for the benefit of the African population, including a right of limited representation in the Legislative Assembly. The measure failed, however, to resolve a sharpening conflict between African demands for full political equality based on the principle of "one-person, one-vote" and White Rhodesian demands for permanent White control.

In view of the refusal of Britain to agree to independence on terms that would exclude majority rule, the colonial government under Prime Minister Ian D. SMITH issued on November 11, 1965, a Unilateral Declaration of Independence (UDI) purporting to make Rhodesia an independent state within the Commonwealth, loyal to the queen but free of external constraints. Britain repudiated the action, declared the colony to be in a state of rebellion, invoked financial and economic sanctions, but refused to use force against the Smith regime. British Prime Minister Harold Wilson held personal meetings with Smith in December 1966, after which UN sanctions were imposed, and in October 1968, but no agreement was reached and the Rhodesian authorities continued their efforts to consolidate the territory's independent posture.

Rhodesia approved a new constitution on June 20, 1969, declaring itself a republic; subsequently, Britain suspended formal ties with the separatist regime. However, further British initiatives under Conservative leadership resulted in a set of proposals for settlement of the dispute in November 1971. These proposals were declared unacceptable by independent African leaders at the United Nations

and were dropped in May 1972 after a 15-man British commission under Lord PEARCE found that they were equally unacceptable to the majority of Rhodesia's African population.

On December 8, 1974, an agreement was concluded at Lusaka, Zambia, by Bishop Abel MUZOREWA of the African National Council (ANC), Joshua NKOMO of the Zimbabwe African People's Union (ZAPU), Ndabaningi SITHOLE of the Zimbabwe African National Union (ZANU), and James CHIKEREMA of the Front for the Liberation of Zimbabwe (Frolizi), whereby the latter three, representing groups that had been declared illegal within Rhodesia, would join an enlarged ANC executive under Bishop Muzorewa's presidency for a period of four months to prepare for negotiations with the Smith regime aimed at "the transfer of power to the majority". Three days later, Prime Minister Smith announced that upon the receipt of assurances that a ceasefire would be observed by insurgents within Rhodesia, all Black political prisoners would be released and a constitutional conference held "without any preconditions". Four days later, however, Smith again reiterated his government's opposition to the principle of majority rule.

On March 4, 1975, Sithole, who had returned to Salisbury in December, was arrested by Rhodesian authorities on charges of plotting to assassinate his rivals in order to assume the ANC leadership. He was released a month later, following the intervention of Prime Minister Vorster of South Africa. A few days earlier, the Zambian government had announced that the Lusaka offices of ZANU, ZAPU, and Frolizi would be closed in accordance with its interpretation of the December 1974 agreement and the subsequent recognition of the ANC by the Organization of African Unity. ZANU spokesmen responded by charging that the presidents of Botswana, Tanzania, and Zambia had secretly agreed at the December talks to reconstitute the ANC leadership under the presidency of Nkomo without consulting Rhodesian African leaders.

During an ANC executive committee meeting at Salisbury on June 1, fighting broke out between ZANU and ZAPU representatives, and ZANU announced that it would not send delegates to an ANC congress scheduled for June 21–22. Frolizi also indicated that it would be unrepresented because the government had refused to grant its delegates an amnesty to return to Rhodesia. On June 16, Bishop Muzorewa announced that the proposed congress would not take place "due to serious administrative and other extreme difficulties".

Following an inconclusive meeting at Victoria Falls (on the Rhodesia-Zambia border) on August 25–26 between the leaders of Rhodesia, South Africa, Zambia, and the ANC, the Nkomo faction, meeting at Salisbury on September 27–28, elected Nkomo president of the ANC within Rhodesia. On December 1, Nkomo and Prime Minister Smith concluded a series of meetings by signing a "Declaration of Intention to Negotiate a Settlement" of the Rhodesian issue. Under the agreement, which was repudiated by external ANC leader Bishop Muzorewa (then resident in Zambia) and by ZANU leader Sithole, all members of the ANC negotiating team were guaranteed freedom to enter Rhodesia to attend the projected talks. Early 1976 witnessed an intensification of guerrilla activity by Mozambique-based insurgents under the leadership of former ZANU secretary general Robert MUGABE, the closing of the Mozambique border on March 3, and a breakdown in the talks between Nkomo and Smith on March 19.

In early September it was reported that South African Prime Minister Vorster had agreed to a US-British offer to provide upwards of $2 billion in financial guarantees to Rhodesia's White settlers, contingent upon Salisbury's acceptance of majority rule. Prime Minister Smith subsequently announced that he had accepted a comprehensive "package" tendered by US Secretary of State Kissinger in a meeting at Pretoria, South Africa, on September 19 that called for a biracial interim government and the establishment of majority rule within two years. Britain responded to the Kissinger-Smith accord by convening a conference at Geneva between a White delegation led by Smith and a Black delegation that included Nkomo, Mugabe, Muzorewa, and Sithole. The conference, which ran from October 28 to December 14, failed, however, to yield a settlement, the Black leaders rejecting the essentials of the Kissinger plan by calling for an immediate transfer to majority rule and the replacement of the all-White Rhodesian army by contingents of the nationalist guerrilla forces.

Alternative proposals advanced by the Black leadership pointed to major differences between the various factions, Mugabe and Nkomo demanding a "British presence" in Rhodesia (rejected by Sithole) while refusing to accept Sithole and Muzorewa's proposals for an election prior to the transfer of power. Earlier, on September 9, Sithole had announced the withdrawal of ZANU from the ANC, which since its formation in December 1974 had been split into two wings led by Bishop Muzorewa and ZAPU leader Nkomo. Collaterally, Mugabe claimed the leadership of ZANU and the Sithole group within Rhodesia became known as ANC-Sithole, while the Muzorewa group became known as the United African National Council (UANC).

On September 28, Mugabe called for a unified military command of all guerrilla forces, and on October 9 announced the formation of a Patriotic Front linking ZANU and ZAPU military units. Although subsequently endorsed both by the Organization of African Unity and the Front-Line States (Angola, Botswana, Mozambique, Tanzania, and Zambia), the Front failed to achieve full integration because of the Soviet orientation of ZAPU, many of whose recruits were trained by Cubans in Angola, and the Chinese orientation of ZANU, most of whose recruits were trained in Tanzania. To complicate matters further, a dissident ZANU group withdrew its cadres from Mugabe's leadership on October 11 and formally redesignated Sithole as party president; however, Sithole and Muzorewa continued to assume a relatively moderate posture during 1977, engaging in sporadic negotiations with the Smith regime, while Nkomo and Mugabe constituted the core of a more radical external leadership.

In January 1977 three moderate White groups—the Rhodesian Party, the Centre Party, and the National Pledge Association—joined in a "National Unifying Force" to campaign for the effective removal of discriminatory legislation and a meaningful accord with the Black majority. However, more crucial pressure was exerted by rightist elements within the ruling Rhodesian Front following an RF decision in March to liberalize constitutional provisions regarding land tenure. The dissidents were expelled from the RF on April 29 and organized themselves as the Rhodesian Action Party (RAP) on July 4. Since the RF thus lost the majority required for constitutional amendment, a new election was called for August 31, at which the Front regained all 50 seats on the European roll.

During the year, a number of British proposals were advanced in hopes of resolving the impasse on interim rule. On January 11, concurrent with an announcement that resumption of the Geneva discussions would be indefinitely postponed, Ivor RICHARD, British representative to the UN and chairman of the Geneva Conference, called for the appointment of a British resident commissioner at Salisbury who would play a "balancing role" in the negotiations with "a great deal of constitutional power". He further proposed an interim Rhodesian Council embracing 20 Blacks (5 from each of the leading nationalist factions) and 10 Whites (5 British and 5 Rhodesian). The proposal was immediately rejected by Prime Minister Smith, who conveyed his government's opposition to "any British presence in any form". In September, however, a revised version of the proposal was endorsed by the UN Security Council. Under the new plan, a British resident commissioner (Field Marshal Lord CARVER) would be appointed for a period of six months, during which arrangements would be made for a new constitution and a one-person, one-vote general election. The plan also called for the creation of a new Rhodesian army containing mixed Black-White units, and the appointment of a UN special representative (Indian Lt. Gen. Prem CHAND, former commander of the UN Force in Cyprus, who was named to the new post on October 4). While the initial reaction by all parties was encouraging, both Nkomo and Mugabe subsequently insisted that transitional control be exercised by the Patriotic Front rather than by the British commissioner. The change in attitude was occasioned largely by a dispute regarding the timing of a general election, Front leaders insisting, because of Bishop Muzorewa's apparent widespread popularity, that the election be deferred for as long as three years after independence. Subsequently, Prime Minister Smith declared that the British settlement plan had "clearly failed" and resumed discussions, based on a revision of the earlier "Kissinger package", with Muzorewa and Sithole. On December 10, Nkomo declared in a press conference at Lusaka, Zambia, that Front leaders would not join the "fake so-called internal settlement talks by Smith and his puppets".

Despite the intransigence of the Patriotic Front, agreement was reached on March 3, 1978, by Smith, Muzorewa, Sithole, and Mashona Chief Jeremiah S. CHIRAU of ZUPO (see Political Parties, below) to form a transitional government that would lead to Black rule by the end of the year. Accordingly, an Executive Council comprising the four was established on March 21, while a multiracial Ministerial Council to replace the existing cabinet was designated on April 12. On May 16 the Executive Council released preliminary details of a new constitution that would feature a titular president elected by members of Parliament, sitting as an electoral college. In the face of escalating guerrilla activity, however, the existing House of Assembly voted on June 26—despite the unanimous objection of its Black members—to renew for another year the state of emergency that had been in effect since 1965. More important, although all racial discrimination was formally abolished on October 10, the projected national election was, in early November, postponed until April 1979, following the failure of a renewed effort to convene an all-party conference.

A new constitution was approved by the Assembly on January 20, 1979, and endorsed by 84 percent of the White voters in a referendum on January 30. Although condemned by the UN Security Council by a 12–0 vote (with 3 abstentions) on March 8, a lower-house election was held on April 10 and 17–20 for 20 White and 72 Black members, respectively, at which the UANC won 51 seats in the face of a boycott by the Patriotic Front parties. Following a Senate election on May 23, Josiah GUMEDE of the UANC was elected president of Zimbabwe/Rhodesia and, on May 29, requested Bishop Muzorewa to accept appointment as prime minister.

On June 7, US President Carter rejected an appeal for recognition of the new government, expressing doubt that the election had been either free or fair since "the Black citizens . . . never had a chance to consider or to vote against the Constitution", while the White minority retained "control over the Army, the police, the system of justice and the civil service". Earlier, the newly appointed British prime minister, Margaret Thatcher, had stated that responsibility for deciding on the legality of the Muzorewa government lay with the UK Parliament, although Foreign and Commonwealth Secretary Lord Carrington argued in the House of Lords that it would be "morally wrong to brush aside an election in which 64 percent of the people of Rhodesia cast their vote".

Following renewed guerrilla activity by Patriotic Front forces at midyear, British and other Commonwealth leaders, meeting at Lusaka, Zambia, on August 1–7, issued a call for talks at London in mid-September between representatives of the Muzorewa government and the Patriotic Front. The discussions, which commenced on September 10 and ran for 14 weeks, yielded a ceasefire agreement on December 5 whereby Britain would reassume full authority for administering the country for an interim period, during which a new and carefully monitored election would be held, prior to the granting of legal independence. On December 7 the terms of the agreement (which was not formally signed by the principals until December 21) were approved by Parliament and Lord SOAMES was appointed colonial governor, with Sir Anthony DUFF as his deputy. On December 12, Lord Soames arrived at Salisbury, where he was welcomed by members of the former government of Zimbabwe/Rhodesia, who, one day earlier, had approved a parliamentary bill terminating the Unilateral Declaration of Independence and transferring authority to the British administration.

White and common roll elections were held in February 1980, the Rhodesian Front winning all 20 White seats and Mugabe's ZANU-PF winning a substantial overall majority in the House of Assembly. Accordingly, Mugabe was asked by Lord Soames on March 4 to form a cabinet that included 16 members of ZANU-PF, 4 members of Nkomo's Patriotic Front–ZAPU, and 2 members of the RF. The new government was installed during independence day ceremonies on April 18 following the inauguration of Rev. Canaan Sodindo BANANA, a Mugabe supporter, as president of the Republic.

The period immediately after independence was characterized by persistent conflict between ZANU-PF and PF-ZAPU armed forces (units of Mugabe's Zimbabwe African National Liberation Army—ZANLA and Nkomo's Zimbabwe People's Revolutionary Army—ZIPRA, respectively). To some extent the difficulties were rooted in tribal loyalties, most ZANLA personnel having been recruited from the northern Shona group, while ZIPRA had recruited primarily from the Ndebele people of Matabeleland. During 1981 the level of overt violence subsided, the government announcing on November 7 that merger of the two guerrilla organizations and the former Rhodesian security force into a 50,000-man Zimbabwean national army had been completed. However, personal animosity between Mugabe and Nkomo continued, threatening the viability of the coalition regime. In January 1982 a substantial arms cache was discovered on a ZAPU-owned farm, reportedly the yield from a hijacking by ZIPRA forces in late 1980 of three trains of weapons confiscated from guerrillas and consigned to the army. On February 17, Nkomo and three other ZAPU government members were dismissed in a major cabinet reorganization, Nkomo declaring that his group should thenceforth be construed as an opposition party. By 1984 violence by dissident Nkomo supporters had produced major confrontations with government forces in Matabeleland, while defections from Ian Smith's party, renamed the Conservative Alliance of Zimbabwe (CAZ), had reduced its strength in the Assembly to 7.

After a series of postponements attributed to a need to redraw electoral districts and prepare new voter lists, the first post-independence legislative elections were held in mid-1985. Smith's Conservative Alliance rallied to regain 15 of the 20 White seats on June 27, while in common roll balloting on July 1–4, Mugabe's ZANU-PF won all but one of the non-Matabeleland constituencies, raising its Assembly strength to 64 as contrasted with ZAPU's 15. Although the results fell short of the mandate desired by Mugabe for introduction of a one-party state, ZAPU members, including Nkomo, responded to overtures for merger talks, which continued sporadically during the next two years, eventually yielding an agreement on December 22, 1987, whereby the two parties would merge, with Nkomo becoming one of two ZANU-PF vice presidents. Three months earlier, following expiration of a constitutionally mandated seven-year entrenchment, the White seats in both houses of Parliament had been vacated and refilled on a "non-constituency" basis by the Assembly. On December 31 Mugabe, having secured unanimous Assembly endorsement the day before, was sworn in as executive president; concurrently, Simon MUZENDA was inaugurated as vice president, the post of prime minister being dropped.

Constitution and government. The constitution that issued from the 1979 London talks provided for a president designated for a six-year term by the two houses of Parliament sitting as an electoral college. Executive authority was vested a cabinet headed, as prime minister, by the person best able to command a legislative majority. However, in late 1987 the post of prime minister was abolished in favor of an executive presidency. Parliament currently consists of a 40-member Senate and a 100-member House of Assembly (for electoral details, see Legislature, below), although in 1985 government officials announced plans to abolish the appointed Senate, no provision for it being made in a new House of Parliament that is currently under construction. There is also an Advisory Council of Chiefs and an ombudsman, appointed by the president, to investigate complaints against actions by political authorities. The judicial system is headed by a High Court (with both general and appellate divisions) and includes magistrates' courts at the local level. Constitutional amendments require the support of at least 27 senators and 70 assemblymen.

The country is administratively divided into eight provinces: Mashonaland (West, Central, East), Matabeleland (North, South), Midlands, Manicaland, and Victoria. Each is headed by a centrally appointed provincial commissioner and serves, additionally, as an electoral district.

Foreign relations. Upon independence, Zimbabwe became a member of the Commonwealth; it was admitted to the Organization of African Unity the following July and to the United Nations in August. In January 1983 it was elected to a seat on the UN Security Council, where its representatives assumed a distinctly anti-American posture: in September 1983, Zimbabwe abstained from a US-sponsored resolution condemning the Soviet destruction of a South Korean jetliner, while co-sponsoring two months later a resolution against the US invasion of Grenada. The growing strain in relations with the United States culminated in 1986 with Washington's withdrawal of all aid in response to strongly worded attacks from Harare on US policy regarding South Africa. Prime Minister Mugabe refused to apologize for the verbal onslaughts, saying Zimbabwe would accept the loss of the $20 million-per-year aid rather than be "coerced" into "toeing the US line".

In regional affairs, Harare has taken a leading position among the Front-line States bordering South Africa, concluding a mutual security pact with Mozambique in late 1980 and hosting several meetings of the Southern African Development Coordination Conference (SADCC). In recent years it has provided active support for the Maputo government's anti-insurgency campaign, approximately 10,000 troops being stationed in Mozambique in 1986, primarily to defend the transport corridor to Beira on the Indian Ocean, which the Front-line States view as crucial to diminish reliance on South African trade routes. While initially declining, for the sake of "the process of [domestic] reconciliation", to provide bases for Black nationalist attacks on South Africa, Harare has been placed in a delicate position by a number of African National Congress (ANC) actions apparently originating from Zimbabwean

territory, which have yielded a number of cross-border incursions by South African troops.

Zimbabwe's international status was heightened in 1985 by Mugabe's election to a three-year term as chairman of the Nonaligned Movement, which held its triennial summit at Harare in September 1986.

Current issues. The decision in late 1987 to proceed toward the establishment of a one-party state was by no means unexpected or universally condemned. Zimbabwe had been afflicted since independence by ethnic tension between its northern Shona-speaking majority and a southern Ndebele-speaking minority, from which the Mugabe and Nkomo parties, respectively, drew most of their political support. A series of killings at midyear (attributed to ZAPU militants though disavowed by Nkomo) had led to a ban on opposition party rallies or meetings, while the government ordered the closing of all ZAPU offices in September. Both actions were seen, in part, as designed to heighten the pressures for merger, to which Nkomo eventually acceded with a public display of remarkably good grace. Somewhat surprisingly, in a January 1988 cabinet reshuffle designed to accommodate a number of Nkomo supporters, no incumbent ministers were dropped, although several were manifestly demoted. The result was one of the developing world's largest governments (53 members, including deputy ministers and ministers of state).

POLITICAL PARTIES

Prior to the "internal settlement" agreement of March 1978, Rhodesian parties could be broadly grouped into (1) the all-White Rhodesian Front (RF), which maintained overwhelming predominance in the elections of 1965, 1970, 1974, and 1977; (2) a number of small White opposition groups on the right and left of the ruling Front; and (3) a variety of Black opposition parties ranging from relatively moderate formations under such leaders as Bishop Muzorewa, Reverend Sithole, and Chief Chirau, to the more radical and overtly insurgent groups led by Robert Mugabe and Joshua Nkomo. The principal African leaders agreed during a summit conference at Lusaka, Zambia, in December 1974 to work together under Bishop Muzorewa of the African National Council (ANC) to achieve majority rule in Rhodesia, but disagreements precluded the creation of a unified Black movement. The moderate leaders thereupon joined the RF's Ian Smith in establishing a transitional government to prepare for a one-person, one-vote election originally scheduled for December 1978 but subsequently postponed to April 1979, while Mugabe and Nkomo entered into a somewhat tenuous Patriotic Front committed to the military overthrow of the biracial regime.

Although Nkomo expressed a desire to continue the alliance, Mugabe's Zimbabwe African National Union–Patriotic Front (ZANU-PF) and Nkomo's Patriotic Front–Zimbabwe African People's Union (PF-ZAPU) contested the common roll election of February 27–29, 1980, as separate entities, ZANU-PF winning 57 of 80 Assembly seats and PF-ZAPU winning 20.

Nkomo's Patriotic Front revived its earlier ZAPU designation following the government rupture of February 1982, while ZANU-PF moved toward the establishment of a one-party state which was consummated, on a de facto basis, with the signature of a merger agreement by Mugabe and Nkomo on December 22, 1987.

Government Party:

Zimbabwe African National Union–Patriotic Front (ZANU-PF). ZANU, formed in 1963 as a result of a split in ZAPU, organized a common front with the latter in 1973. Ndabaningi Sithole, then ZANU president, agreed to participate in the ANC coalition in December 1974 but withdrew in mid-1975. In 1976 Robert Mugabe claimed the leadership of the organization and concluded a tactical (Patriotic Front) agreement with Joshua Nkomo of ZAPU, although a minority of the membership apparently remained loyal to Sithole. The alliance broke down prior to the 1980 Assembly election, Nkomo's group campaigning as PF-ZAPU and Mugabe's as ZANU-PF. Both parties participated in the government formed at independence, although ZANU-PF predominated with 16 of 22 ministerial appointments.

On August 8–12, 1984, ZANU-PF held its first congress in over 20 years, at which it affirmed a commitment to Marxist-Leninist principles and appointed a 15-member politburo and a 90-member central committee. It also committed itself to the establishment of a one-party system if (as occurred) it succeeded in retaining a majority in the 1985 legislative balloting. Such a system effectively resulted from the merger agreement of December 1987, with Nkomo being named a ZANU-PF vice president and second secretary.

Leaders: Robert MUGABE (President of the Republic and of the Party), Simon MUZENDA (Vice President of the Republic and of the Party), Joshua NKOMO (Senior Minister and Vice President of the Party).

Other Parties:

Following abolition of the theretofore entrenched White seats in October 1987 and the ZANU-ZAPU merger agreement in December, formal parliamentary opposition was reduced to the single seat that had been won, apparently as the result of a local squatter controversy in Manicaland, by the Zimbabwe African National Union — Sithole (ZANU-S). By contrast, upwards of a dozen parties had been active at the time of the 1985 balloting (for details on their composition and leadership, see the 1987 edition of the *Political Handbook*).

LEGISLATURE

Zimbabwe/Rhodesia has had three legislatures since 1978. The UDI Parliament consisted of a Senate of 23 members (10 directly elected European, 10 indirectly elected African, 3 presidentially appointed) and a House of Assembly of 66 members (50 directly elected European, 8 directly elected and 8 indirectly elected African). The constitution of January 1979 provided for a Senate of 30 members (10 directly elected European, 10 directly elected and 10 indirectly elected African) and a House of 100 members (20 directly elected and 8 indirectly elected European, and 72 directly elected African). The body's authority formally ceased on December 11, when it unanimously approved a bill returning the country to "Her Majesty's dominions".

Under the present constitution, **Parliament** consists of a Senate and a House of Assembly, as described below.

Senate. The upper house contains 40 members, which prior to expiration of the constitutional entrenchment of White seats were distributed as follows: 14 indirectly elected by the common roll membership of the House of Assembly, 10 by Assembly members elected on the White roll, 5 each by Mashonaland and Matabeleland chiefs as representatives of the Council of Chiefs, and 6 appointed by the president of the Republic. On October 30, 1987, following abolition of the White roll, the Assembly elected 10 replacement senators, of whom 4 were White.

President: Nollan MAKOMBE.

House of Assembly. The lower house contains 100 members elected for five-year terms, subject to dissolution. Prior to the expiration of White retrenchment, 80 were from common roll and 20 from White roll constituencies. After the White election on June 27, 1985, and common roll balloting on July 1–4, the distribution of seats was as follows: Zimbabwe African National Union-Patriotic Front, 64; Zimbabwe African People's Union, 15; Conservative Alliance of Zimbabwe, 15; Independent Zimbabwe Group, 4; Zimbabwe African National Union-Sithole, 1; independent, 1. The ZANU-PF majority rose to 66 in 1986 with the defection of one ZAPU and one CAZ member. On October 23, 1987, following abolition of the White roll, the Assembly elected 20 new members (including 11 Whites) to fill the "non-constituent" seats, thereby increasing ZANU-PF's majority to 77. Upon merger of ZANU-PF and ZAPU on December 22, the ZANU-S assemblyman became the only opposition member.

Speaker: Didymus MUTASA.

CABINET

President	Robert Mugabe
Vice President	Simon Vengai Muzenda

Senior Ministers

Finance, Economic Planning and Development	Dr. Bernard Chidzero
Local Government, Rural and Urban Development	Joshua Nkomo
Political Affairs	Maurice Nyagumbo

Ministers

Cooperatives, Community Development and Women's Affairs	Joyce Mujuru (Teurai Ropa Nhongo)
Defense	Enos Nkala
Energy, Water Resources and Development	Kumbirai Kangai
Foreign Affairs	Nathan Shamuyarira
Health	Felix Muchemwa
Higher Education	Dzingai Mutumbuka
Home Affairs	Moven Mahachi
Industry and Technology	Dr. Callistus Ndlovu
Information, Posts and Telecommunications	Dr. Witness Mangwende
Justice, Legal and Parliamentary Affairs	Emmerson Munangagwa
Labor, Manpower Planning and Social Welfare	John Nkomo
Lands, Agriculture and Rural Settlement	David Karimanzira
Local Government, Rural and Urban Development	Enos Chikowore
Mines	Richard Hove
National Supplies	Simbi Mubako
Natural Resources and Tourism	Victoria Chitepo
Primary and Secondary Education	Fay Chung
Public Construction and National Housing	Joseph Msika
Trade and Commerce	Dr. Oliver Munyaradzi
Transport	Simbarashe Mubengegwi
Youth, Sport and Culture	David Kwindini

Ministers of State in President's Office

National Scholarships	Joseph Culverwell
National Security	Sydney Sekeramayi
Political Affairs	Ernest Kadungure
	Naomi Nhiwatiwa
	Frederick Shava
	Herbert Ushewokunze
	Eddison Zrobgo
Public Service	Chris Anderson
Governor, Central Bank	Dr. K.J. Moyana

NEWS MEDIA

Press. In early 1981 it was reported that the government had purchased 42 percent of the shares of the (South African) Argus group, thereby acquiring control of the largest newspapers in Zimbabwe, which, unless otherwise noted, are English-language dailies published at Harare: *Sunday Mail* (150,000); *The Herald* (130,000); *The Chronicle* (Bulawayo, 65,000); *Sunday News* (Bulawayo, 59,000).

News agencies. It was announced in October 1980 that the South African Press Association had relinquished its interest in the Salisbury-based Inter-African News Agency, the latter being reorganized as the Zimbabwe Inter-African News Agency (ZIANA). *Agence France-Presse,* AP, Reuters, and UPI are among the foreign agencies that maintain bureaus at Harare.

Radio and television. The Zimbabwe Broadcasting Corporation, an independent statutory body, regulates radio and television stations; service is in English and three African languages. There were approximately 318,000 radio and 112,000 television receivers in 1987.

INTERGOVERNMENTAL REPRESENTATION

Ambassador to the US: (Vacant).

US Ambassador to Zimbabwe: James Wilson RAWLINGS.

Permanent Representative to the UN: Dr. Isack Stanislaus Gorerazvo MUDENGE.

IGO Memberships (Non-UN): ADF, AfDB, BADEA, CCC, CWTH, EEC(L), *EIB,* IACO, ICO, Interpol, ISO, NAM, OAU, SADCC.

PALESTINE LIBERATION ORGANIZATION

Munathamat al-Tahrir al-Falistiniyya

Establishment of the PLO was authorized on January 17, 1964, during an Arab summit held at Cairo, Egypt. Largely through the efforts of Ahmad SHUQAIRI, the Palestinian representative to the Arab League, an assembly of Palestinians met at (East) Jerusalem the following May 28–June 2 to draft a National Covenant and General Principles of a Fundamental Law, the latter subsequently serving as the constitutional basis of a government-in-exile. Under the Fundamental Law, the assembly became a 315-member Palestinian National Council (PNC) composed primarily of representatives of the leading *fedayeen* (guerrilla) groups, various Palestinian mass movements and trade unions, and Palestinian communities throughout the Arab world. A 15-member Executive Committee was established as the PLO's administrative organ, while an intermediate Central Council (initially of 21 but subsequently 55 members), with combined legislative-executive responsibilities, was created in 1973.

In its original form, the PLO was a quasi-governmental entity designed to act independently of the various Arab states in support of Palestinian interests. Its subordinate organs encompassed a variety of political, cultural, and fiscal activities as well as a Military Department, under which a Palestine Liberation Army (PLA) was established as a conventional military force of recruits stationed in Egypt, Iraq, and Syria.

In the wake of the 1967 Arab-Israeli war, the direction of the PLO underwent a significant transformation. Shuqairi resigned as chairman of the Executive Committee and was replaced in December 1967 by Yahia HAMMUDA, who was in turn succeeded in February 1969 by Yasir 'ARAFAT, leader of *Fatah* (below). At that time the PNC adopted a posture more favorable to guerrilla activ-ities against Israel; insisted upon greater independence from Arab governments; and for the first time called for the establishment of a Palestinian state in which Muslims, Christians, and Jews would have equal rights. In effect, the PLO thus tacitly accepted a Jewish presence in Palestine, although it remained committed to the eradication of any Zionist state in the area.

In 1970–1971 the PLO and the *fedayeen* groups were expelled from Jordan, and as a result Lebanon became their principal base of operations. The Israeli victory in the October 1973 war, and the fear that Jordan might negotiate on behalf of Palestinians from the occupied territories, resulted in another change in the PLO's strategy: in June 1974 it formally adopted a proposal which called for the creation of a "national authority" in the West Bank and Gaza as a first step toward the liberation of historic Palestine. This tacit recognition of Israel precipitated a major split among the PLO's already ideologically diverse components, and on July 29 a leftist "rejection front" was formed in opposition to any partial settlement in the Middle East. In December 1976 the PLO Central Council voiced support for establishment of an "independent state" in the West Bank and Gaza, which was widely interpreted as implying acceptance of Israel's permanent existence. Shortly thereafter, contacts were established between the PLO and the Israeli Left.

On September 1, 1982, immediately after the PLO withdrawal from West Beirut (see Lebanon article), US President Reagan proposed the creation of a Palestinian "entity" in the West Bank and Gaza, to be linked with Jordan under King Hussein. The idea was bitterly attacked by pro-Syrian radicals during a PNC meeting at Algiers in February 1983, with the Council ultimately calling for a "confederation" between Jordan and an independent Palestinian state, thus endorsing an Arab League resolution five months earlier that implicitly entailed recognition of Israel. Over radical objections, the Algiers meeting also sanctioned a dialogue with "progressive and democratic" elements within Israel, i.e., those favoring peace with the PLO. This position, however, was also unacceptable to the group's best-known moderate, Dr. Issam SARTAWI, who resigned from the Council after being denied an opportunity to deliver a speech calling for formal discussions with Israeli leaders on the possibility of a clear-cut "two-state" solution. Subsequently, in an apparent trial balloon, *Fatah*'s deputy chairman, Salah KHALAF, declared that the group would support the Reagan peace initiative if the United States were to endorse the principle of Palestinian self-determination; the meeting's final communique, on the other hand, dismissed the Reagan proposal "as a sound basis for a just and lasting resolution of the Palestinian problem".

In early April, 'Arafat met for three days with King Hussein, without reaching agreement on a number of key issues, including the structure of a possible confederation, representation of Palestinians in peace negotiations with Israel, and removal of PLO headquarters to 'Amman. As the discussions concluded, Dr. Sartawi was assassinated at Albufeira, Portugal, by a member of an extremist *Fatah* splinter, headed by the Damascus-based Sabry Khalil al-BANNA (also known as Abu Nidal). A week later, amid evidence of growing restiveness among Palestinian guerrillas in eastern Lebanon, the PLO Executive Committee met at Tunis to consider means of "surmounting the obstacles" that had emerged in the discussions with Hussein.

In mid-May, 'Arafat returned to Lebanon for the first time since the Beirut exodus to counter what had escalated into a dissident rebellion led by Musa AWAD (also known as Abu Akram) of the Libyan-backed Popular Front for the Liberation of Palestine — General Command (PFLP — GC), a splinter of the larger PFLP (see below) led by Georges HABASH. In late June, he convened a meeting of *Fatah*'s Revolutionary Council at Damascus to deal with the mutineers' insistence that he abandon his flirtation with the Reagan peace plan and accord greater priority to military confrontation with Israel. The rebels also called for "collective leadership [of *Fatah*] and elimination of singular rule".

On June 24, President Assad ordered 'Arafat's expulsion from Syria after the PLO leader had accused him of fomenting the rebellion and a month later 'Arafat ousted two senior commanders whose earlier promotions had precipitated tension within the ranks of the Bekka Valley guerrillas. The fighting nonetheless continued, and in early November one of 'Arafat's two remaining Lebanese strongholds north of Tripoli fell to the insurgents. Late in the month, the PLO leader agreed to withdraw from an increasingly untenable position within the city itself, exiting from Lebanon for the second and possibly last time on December 20 in a Greek ferry escorted by French naval vessels.

Following a series of Moscow-backed meetings at Aden, South Yemen, 'Arafat announced in July 1984 that the PLO rift had been healed. However, most of the radical factions had refused to take part in the Aden talks. Their absence notwithstanding 'Arafat was forced to accept two, presumably pro-Syrian, policy advisors, while a "unity" meeting of the PNC, scheduled to meet at Algiers in November, was forced, because of Syrian pressure, to convene instead at 'Amman. Subsequently, in late December, evidence of continued deep division within the movement was provided by the assassination (carried out by the splinter terrorist organization Black September) of another leading PLO moderate, Fahd KAWASMEH, former mayor of the Israeli-occupied West Bank town of Hebron.

In early 1985, 'Arafat strengthened and formalized his ties with Jordan's King Hussein in an accord signed by both leaders on February 11. The agreement, described as "a framework for common action towards reaching a peaceful and just settlement to the Palestine question", called for total withdrawal by Israel from the territories it had occupied in 1967 in exchange for comprehensive peace; the right of self-determination for the Palestinians within the context of a West Bank-Gaza/Jordan confederation; resolution of the Palestinian refugee problem in accordance with United Nations resolutions; and peace negotiations under the auspices of an international conference to be attended by the five permanent members of the UN Security Council and representatives of the PLO, the latter being part of a joint Jordanian-Palestinian delegation.

The agreement prompted a flurry of diplomatic activity involving Jordan, the PLO, the United States, and Israel aimed at constituting a Jordanian-Palestinian negotiating team whose members would be acceptable to all parties. However, by the end of 1985, there was little progress toward selecting Palestinian delegates acceptable to the United States and Israel.

'Arafat's peace overtures deepened divisions within the ranks of the Palestine national movement. In reaction to the February pact with Jordan, six PLO affiliated organizations formed a Palestine National Salvation Front (PNSF) at Damascus to oppose 'Arafat's policies. They included the Palestine Liberation Front, the PFLP, the PFLP-General Command, *al-Sa'iqa,* the Palestine Popular Struggle Front, and a dissident faction of *Fatah.* All six factions supported Syria's efforts to undermine 'Arafat's leadership of the PLO.

Differences over peace initiatives also erupted during a November meeting at Baghdad of the Palestine Central Council, the 70-member interim "parliament" of the Palestine National Council. Disagreement turned mainly on whether to accept UN Security Council Resolutions 242 and 338 calling for withdrawal from the occupied territories and peaceful settlement of the Palestine dispute in a manner that would imply recognition of Israel.

In November, 'Arafat attempted to reenforce his image as "peace-maker" with a declaration denouncing terrorism. The "Cairo Declaration" was issued after lengthy discussions with Egyptian President Husni Mubarak on ways to speed up peace negotiations. 'Arafat cited a 1974 PLO decision "to condemn all outside operations and all forms of terrorism". He promised to take "all punitive measures against violators" and stated that "the PLO denounces and condemns all terrorist acts, whether those involving countries or by persons or groups, against unarmed innocent civilians in any place".

Meanwhile, relations between 'Arafat and Hussein had again been strained by a number of incidents that displeased the king. The PLO was involved in the October hijacking of the Italian cruise ship, *Achille Lauro,* which resulted in the murder of an American tourist, while talks were broken off between the British government and a joint Palestinian-Jordanian delegation because of PLO refusal to sign a statement recognizing Israel and renouncing the use of terrorism.

In Lebanon, the PLO sustained both military and political defeats at the hands of the Shi'ite *al-Amal* forces which besieged two Palestine Arab refugee camps during May and June. Fighting between Palestinians and Lebanese Shi'ites continued for several weeks with hundreds of Palestinian casualties. At the request of 'Arafat an extraordinary session of the Arab League Council was convened at Tunis to intercede. The Council called on all parties to end the siege, which was accomplished by Syrian mediation in mid-June. One effect of the action was to temporarily heal the rift between pro-and anti-'Arafat Palestinian factions.

Earlier, a PLO diplomatic coup had been achieved with the May release by Israel of 1,150 Palestinians prisoners in exchange for three Israeli soldiers captured by Palestinian forces in the Lebanese war. Since the prisoners included many prominent terrorists, a political furor ensued within Israel.

By early 1986, it had become apparent that the Jordanian-PLO accord had stalled over 'Arafat's refusal, despite strong pressure from King Hussein and other Arab moderates, to endorse UN Resolutions 242 and 338 as the basis of a solution to the Palestinian issue. Among the PLO's objections were references to Palestinians as refugees and a failure to accord them the right of self-determination. On the latter ground, 'Arafat rejected a secret US tender of seats for the PLO at a proposed international Middle East peace conference. In February Hussein announced that the peace effort had collapsed and encouraged West Bank and Gaza Strip Palestinians to select new leaders. He underscored the attack on 'Arafat during the ensuing months by proposing an internationally financed, $1.3 billion development plan for the West Bank, which he hoped would win the approval of its "silent majority". The PLO denounced the plan, while terming Israeli efforts to appoint Arab mayors in the West Bank as attempts to perpetuate Israeli occupation. The rupture culminated in Hussein's ordering the closure of *Fatah*'s Jordanian offices in July.

Hussein's overture elicited little support from the West Bank Palestinians and by late 1986 it was evident that 'Arafat still commanded the support of his most important constituency. Rather than undercutting 'Arafat's position, Hussein's challenge paved the way for unification talks between *Fatah* and other PLO factions that had opposed the accord from the outset. Following initial opposition from the PNSF in August, the reunification drive gained momentum in early 1987 with indications that Habash's PFLP, the Front's largest component, might join the Democratic Front for the Liberation of Palestine (DFLP, below) and other groups in trying to rescue the PLO from its debilitating fractionalization. Support was also received from PLO factions in Lebanon that had recently coalesced under *Fatah* leadership to withstand renewed attacks by

al-Amal forces. Indeed, Syria's inability to stem the mass return of heavily armed *Fatah* guerrillas to Lebanon was viewed as a major contributor to 'Arafat's resurgency within the PLO. Meanwhile, King Hussein also attempted to mend relations with the PLO by announcing that the Jordanian-PLO fund for West Bank and Gaza Strip Palestinians, suspended at the time of the February breach, would be reactivated. Subsequently, the fund was bolstered by new pledges totalling $14.5 from Saudi Arabia and Kuwait.

Although hard-line factions still urged 'Arafat's ouster, the PLO leader's more militant posture, particularly his formal repudiation in early April of the accord with Jordan, opened the way for convening the long-delayed 18th session of the PNC (its membership reportedly having been expanded to 426) at Algiers on April 20–26. Confounding critics who had long predicted his political demise, 'Arafat emerged from the meeting with his PLO chairmanship intact, thanks in part to a declared willingness to share the leadership with representatives of non-*Fatah* factions. Thus, despite the fact that several Syrian-based formations boycotted the Algiers meeting, 'Arafat's appearance at its conclusion arm-in-arm with former rivals Georges Habash of the PFLP and Nayif HAWATMEH of the DFLP appeared to symbolize the success of the unity campaign. Habash took the occasion to announce disbandment of the PNSF, although factions outside the unity group challenged his right to do so.

Final PNC resolutions pledged continued armed struggle against Israel, rejected the UN resolutions, and called for the establishment of a Palestinian state encompassing the West Bank and Gaza Strip, with Jerusalem as its capital. A complication was a resolution implying condemnation of Egypt for its peace treaty with Israel. Although 'Arafat had succeeded in having the resolution's language softened, Egypt responded by closing local PLO offices.

During the last half of the year there were reports of secret meetings between the PLO and left-wing Israeli politicians to forge an agreement based on a cessation of hostilities, a halt to Israeli settlement in the Gaza Strip and West Bank, and mutual recognition by the PLO and Israel. However, nothing of substance was achieved and by November it appeared that interest in the issue had waned, as evidenced by the far greater attention given to the Iran/Iraq war at an Arab League summit in November.

The Palestinian question returned to the forefront in December with the outbreak of violence in the occupied territories (see Israel: Current issues). Although the disturbances were believed to have started spontaneously, the PLO, by mobilizing grassroots structures it had nurtured throughout the 1980s, helped to fuel their transformation into an ongoing *intifada* (uprising).

In an apparent effort to heighten PLO visibility, 'Arafat demanded in March 1988 that the formation be accorded full representation (rather than participation in a joint Jordanian/Palestinian delegation) at any Middle Eastern peace conference. However, the prospects for such a conference dimmed in April when the PLO's military leader, Khalil al-WAZIR (also known as Abu Jihad), was killed by an apparent Israeli assassination team. Whatever the motive for the killing, its most immediate impact was to enhance PLO solidarity and provide the impetus for a dramatic "reconciliation" between 'Arafat and Syrian President Assad. On the other hand, the intrinsic fragility of the rapprochement was soon demonstrated by bloody clashes between *Fatah* and Syrian-backed *Fatah* dissidents (see Fatah Uprising, below) for control of the Beirut refugee camps in May and June.

Leaders: Yasir 'ARAFAT (Chairman), Faruk QADDUMI (Political Affairs), Mahmud ABBAS (International Relations), Jamal al-SURANI (Secretary).

Groups Participating in the April 1987 PNC Meeting at Algiers:

Fatah. The term *Fatah* is a reverse acronym of *Harakat Tahrir Filastin* (Palestine Liberation Movement), established mainly by Gulf-based Palestinian exiles in October 1959. The group initially adopted a strongly nationalist but ideologically neutral posture, although violent disputes have subsequently occurred between traditional (rightist) and leftist factions. While launching its first commando operations against Israel in January 1965, it remained aloof from the PLO until the late 1960s, when divisiveness within the Organization, plus *Fatah*'s staunch (though unsuccessful) defense in March 1968 of the refugee camp at Karameh, Jordan, contributed to the emergence of Yasir 'Arafat as a leading Palestinian spokesman. Since his election as PLO chairman in 1969, *Fatah* has been the PLO's core component.

Commando operations have been a primary responsibility of *al-'Asifa*, the formation's military wing. Following expulsion of the *fedayeen* from Jordan, a wave of "external" (i.e., non-Middle Eastern) operations were conducted by "Black September" terrorists, although *Fatah* has never acknowledged any association with such extremist acts as the September 1972 attack against Israeli athletes at the Munich Olympics. By early 1973 the number of "external" incidents had begun to diminish, and during the Lebanese civil war of 1975-1976 *Fatah*, unlike most other Palestinian organizations, attempted to play a mediatory role.

As the result of a leadership decision in October 1973 to support the formation of a "national authority" in any part of the West Bank it managed to "liberate", a hard-line faction supported by Syria broke from *Fatah* under the leadership of Sabry Khalil al-Banna (see Revolutionary Council of *Fatah*, below). Smaller groups defected after the defeat at Beirut in 1982.

Internal debate in 1985-1986 as to the value of diplomatic compromise was resolved in early 1987 by the adoption of an essentially hard-line posture, a decision apparently considered necessary to ensure continuance of the group's preeminence within the PLO.

In April 1988 PLO military chief Khalil al-Wazir (alias Abu Jihad), long considered second only to 'Arafat within *Fatah* and the PLO, was assassinated at his home near Tunis. Despite his alleged long-standing involvement in anti-Israeli violence, Wazir was perceived as a moderate whose ability to bridge ideological gulfs was instrumental in the 1987 PLO reconciliation. Many analysts concluded that his death created a serious "power vacuum" within *Fatah* and the PLO.

Leaders: Yasir 'ARAFAT (Chairman), Salah KHALAF (alias Abu Iyad, Deputy Chairman).

Democratic Front for the Liberation of Palestine (DFLP). Established in February 1969 as a splinter from the PFLP (below), the DFLP was known as the Popular Democratic Front (PDFLP) until adopting its present name in 1974. A year earlier, the Front had become the first Palestinian group to call for the establishment of a democratic state—one encompassing both banks of the Jordan—as an intermediate step toward founding a national entity that would include all of historic Palestine. Its ultimate goal, therefore, has been the elimination of Hashemite Jordan as well as Zionist Israel. The DFLP has advocated a form of secular nationalism rooted in Marxist-Leninist doctrine, whereas *Fatah* initially envisaged a state organized on the basis of coexistent religious communities. Despite their political differences, the DFLP and *Fatah* tended to agree on most issues after their expulsion from Jordan in 1971. The DFLP did, however, support the Muslim Left in the Lebanese civil war of 1975-1976.

The Front, which since 1984 had taken a middle position between pro- and anti-'Arafat factions, played a major role in the recent PLO reunification. Its close ties with the PFLP, reduced in 1985 when the DFLP opted not to join the PFLP-led Palestine National Salvation Front (PNSF), were reestablished during the 1987 unity campaign.

Leader: Nayif HAWATMEH (Secretary General).

Popular Front for the Liberation of Palestine (PFLP). The leftist PFLP was established in 1967 by merger of three main groups: an early Palestine Liberation Front, led by Ahmad Jabril; and two small offshoots of the Arab Nationalist Movement, the Youth for Revenge and Georges Habash's Heroes of the Return. The PFLP has long favored a comprehensive settlement in the Middle East and has resisted the establishment of a West Bank state as an intermediate strategy. Its ultimate goal is the formation of a Palestinian nation founded on scientific socialism, accompanied by its own evolution into a revolutionary proletarian party.

After the failure of efforts to achieve PLO unity in 1984, the PFLP played a key role in formation of the anti-'Arafat Palestine National Salvation Front. However, after some initial hesitation, it endorsed the 1987 reunification in light of *Fatah*'s increased militancy. Habash was reported to have been instrumental in negotiating the 'Arafat/Hassad "reconciliation" in April 1988.

Leader: Georges HABASH (General Secretary).

Palestine Liberation Front (PLF). The PLF emerged as an Iraqi-backed splinter from the PFLP-GC. The group itself subsequently split into two factions—a Damascus-based group led by Talaat Yacoub and a Tunis-based group led by Abul Abbas (the latter sentenced in absentia to life imprisonment by Italian courts for his alleged role in masterminding the hijacking of the cruise ship *Achille Lauro* in 1985). Although Yasir 'Arafat had vowed that he would be removed from his seat on the PLO executive committee because of the conviction, Abbas was granted "provisional" retention of the position at the 1987 PNC unity meeting, which was supported by both PLF factions. Reconciliation within the PLF was subsequently achieved, Yacoub being named general secretary and Abbas accepting a position as his deputy.

Leaders: Talaat YACOUB (General Secretary), Abul ABBAS (Deputy General Secretary).

Palestine Communist Party (PCP). The Soviet-backed PCP was formed in 1982 to encompass Palestinian Communists in the West Bank, Gaza Strip, Lebanon, and Jordan with the approval of parent Communist organizations in those areas. Although it had no formal PLO affiliation, the PCP in 1984 joined the Democratic Alliance's campaign to negotiate a settlement among sparring PLO factions. As part of the reunification program approved in April 1987, the PNC officially embraced the PCP, granting it representation on PLO leadership bodies. The PCP, which is technically illegal but generally tolerated in the occupied territories, endorses the creation of a Palestinian state adjacent to Israel following withdrawal of Israeli troops from occupied territories.

Leaders: Bashir al-BARGHUTI, Sulayman al-NASHSHAB.

Palestine Popular Struggle Front (PPSF). The PPSF also broke from the PFLP while participating in the Lebanese civil war on behalf of the Muslim Left.

Leader: Samir GHOSHE.

Arab Liberation Front (ALF). The ALF has long been closely associated with the Iraqi branch of the *Baath*. Its history of terrorist activity included an April 1980 attack on an Israeli kibbutz. Subsequently, there were reports of fighting at Beirut between the ALF and pro-Iranian Shi'ites.

Leaders: 'Abd al-Wahab KAYYALI, Ahmed ABDERRAHIM.

Groups Boycotting the April 1987 PNC Meeting:

Popular Front for the Liberation of Palestine–General Command (PFLP-GC). Although the General Command broke from the parent front in late 1967, both organizations fought on the side of the Muslim Left in the Lebanese civil war. The GC was reported to have influenced the uprisings in the West Bank and Gaza Strip in late 1987 and 1988, having established a clandestine radio station, the Voice of Jerusalem, that attracted numerous listeners throughout the occupied territories.

Leaders: Talal NAJI, Musa AWAD, Ahmad JABRIL (Secretary General).

al-Sa'iqa. Dominated by Syria, *al-Sa'iqa* ("Thunderbolt") came into conflict with *Fatah* as a result of its active support for Syrian intervention during the Lebanese civil war. The group's longtime leader, Zuheir Mohsen, who served as the PLO's chief of military operations, was assassinated at Paris in July 1979, his successor being a former Syrian air force general.

Leader: Issam al-KADE.

Revolutionary Council of Fatah. The Revolutionary Council has been held responsible for more than 100 terrorist incidents since it broke away from its parent group in 1974. Targets have included Palestinian moderates as well as Israelis and other Jews. The group's predilection for attacks in public places in Europe and Asia led to allegations of its involvement in the assaults on the Vienna and Rome airports in December 1985. The shadowy organization, which has operated under numerous names, is led by Sabry Khalil al-Banna, better known as Abu Nidal, one of the first PLO guerrillas to challenge the leadership of Yasir 'Arafat. Nidal reportedly plotted to have 'Arafat killed soon after their split, prompting a trial in absentia by the PLO, which issued a death sentence. Somewhat surprisingly, the group sent representatives to the preparatory meeting for the April 1987 PNC session, although they walked out during the first day of the regular session. Reports subsequently surfaced that the Council had agreed to halt terrorist acts against Palestinian supporters of 'Arafat, raising the possibility of a more formal rapprochement in the future. In June 1987 it apparently moved its base of operations to Lebanon's Bekaa Valley after its Syrian offices had been closed by President Assad. (This group should not be confused with the Fatah Revolutionary Council, a political organ of *Fatah* referenced in the main section, above).

Leader: Sabry Khalil al-BANNA (Abu Nidal).

Fatah Uprising. An outgrowth of the internal PLO fighting of 1983 in Lebanon, the Uprising is a *Fatah* splinter group which, headquartered at Damascus, draws its membership from PLO dissidents who remained in Beirut following the departure of Yasir 'Arafat. One of the most steadfast of the anti 'Arafat formations, it waged a bitter (and largely successful) struggle with mainstream adherents for control of Beirut's refugee camps in May-June 1988.

Leader: Saed MUSA (Abu Musa).

INTERGOVERNMENTAL
ORGANIZATIONS

AGENCY FOR CULTURAL AND TECHNICAL COOPERATION (ACCT)

Agence de Coopération Culturelle et Technique

Established: By convention signed March 21, 1970, at Niamey, Niger, during the Second International Conference of Francophone Countries.

Purpose: To facilitate the exchange of culture, education, science, and technology among French-speaking countries.

Headquarters: Paris, France.

Principal Organs: General Conference (all members), Secretariat.

Secretary General: Paul Okumba d'Okwatseque (Gabon).

Membership (30): Belgium, Benin, Burkina Faso, Burundi, Canada, Central African Republic, Chad, Comoros, Congo, Djibouti, Dominica, France, Gabon, Guinea, Haiti, Ivory Coast, Lebanon, Luxembourg, Mali, Mauritius, Monaco, Niger, Rwanda, Senegal, Seychelles, Togo, Tunisia, Vanuatu, Vietnam, Zaire.
Associate Members (7): Cameroon, Egypt, Guinea-Bissau, Laos, Mauritania, Morocco, St. Lucia.
Participating Governments (2): New Brunswick, Quebec.

Working Language: French.

Origin and development. Creation of the ACCT was proposed at the First International Conference of Francophone Countries, which met at Niamey, Niger, on February 17–20, 1969. Arising in response to a perceived lack of formal cooperation among French-speaking states, the Agency was designed to act as a clearinghouse for members in the areas of culture, education, and technology. Subsequently, it adopted a program of financial assistance to projects in member states, especially those efforts directed toward the needs of the rural poor. Membership in the ACCT has grown to encompass all major French-speaking states except Algeria, as well as several in which French culture is important, though not dominant.
Structure. The General Conference, which usually meets every two years, comprises ministerial level representatives of all members and is the ACCT's highest authority. The General Conference elects its president; nine vice presidents, who sit on a policy-reviewing Bureau; and an ACCT secretary general who directs a staff of about 100 persons.
Activities. In 1983, the ACCT signed a cooperation agreement with the 21-member Council of Europe, the two organizations pledging to coordinate activities in the areas

of culture, education, and science and technology, primarily by means of information exchanges. During 1984–1985, the Agency was involved in a number of activities promoting French culture and education; among these were the Conference of Communication Ministers at Cairo, the 18th Congress of the International Institute of Correct French Expression (*Congrès de l'Institut International de Droit d'Expression Français*), the French Festival of Quebec, and researching and classifying traditional medicines of member countries.

The establishment of a full-fledged Francophone Commonwealth was first suggested to ACCT members in 1980. However, disputes both within Canada and between Canada and France over the issue of Quebec separatism delayed the convening of a francophone summit until February 17–19, 1986. The summit, held outside Paris, was attended by delegations from 42 countries and regions. A 13-point program of action was adopted which called, *inter alia,* for the formation of a francophone television network, the provision of linguistic data to the francophone world by means of videotext, and the strengthening of cooperation between francophone delegations at the United Nations. Responsibility for a number of the summit's proposals was given to the ACCT, whose General Conference met in a extraordinary session in December to consider structural and financial reforms that would permit it to assume greater francophone authority. Concurrently, Canada, already the ACCT's leading financial contributor, announced it was doubling its level of support.

A second summit, attended by 43 delegations from 37 countries (including all ACCT members except Cameroon and Vanuatu), was held September 2–4, 1987, in Quebec City, Canada. African economic issues, particularly the external debt crisis and falling world commodity prices, dominated the meeting, during which Canada announced that it was forgiving about $330 million in debts owned by seven African countries. Discussion also continued on the future role of the ACCT in whatever francophone structure might emerge from the summits, the next of which is scheduled for 1989 in Dakar, Senegal.

AGENCY FOR THE PROHIBITION OF NUCLEAR WEAPONS IN LATIN AMERICA AND THE CARIBBEAN (OPANAL)

Organismo para la Proscripción de las Armas Nucleares en la América Latina y el Caribe

Established: By Treaty of Tlatelolco (Mexico), signed February 14, 1967. The inaugural meeting of OPANAL was held September 2, 1969.

Purpose: To administer the Treaty for the Prohibition of Nuclear Weapons in Latin America, without prejudice to peaceful uses of atomic energy. Designed to make Latin America a nuclear-free zone, the Treaty prohibits all testing, manufacture, acquisition, installation, and development of nuclear weapons.

Headquarters: Mexico City, Mexico.

Principal Organs: General Conference of Contracting Parties, Council (5 members), Secretariat.

Secretary General: Dr. Antonio Stemel París (Venezuela).

Membership (25): Antigua and Barbuda, Bahamas, Barbados, Bolivia, Brazil, Chile, Colombia, Costa Rica, Dominican Republic, Ecuador, El Salvador, Grenada, Guatemala, Haiti, Honduras, Jamaica, Mexico, Nicaragua, Panama, Paraguay, Peru, Suriname, Trinidad and Tobago, Uruguay, Venezuela.

Working Language: Spanish.

Origin and development. The idea of making Latin America a nuclear-free zone was broached in the early 1960s, with the Cuban missile crisis of October 1962 serving as a catalyst. In April 1963 the presidents of Bolivia, Brazil, Chile, Ecuador, and Mexico announced that they were prepared to sign a multilateral agreement to that end, and the following November their declaration gained the support of the UN General Assembly. During a conference at Mexico City on November 23–27, 1965, a Preparatory Commission on the Denuclearization of Latin America was created, with instructions to prepare a draft treaty. Differences regarding transit, guarantees, boundaries, and safeguards on peaceful nuclear activities were eventually resolved, and on November 14, 1967, a treaty was signed at Tlatelolco, Mexico City. Of the 25 Latin American states that have thus far ratified the document, 23 have done so without reservations, the exceptions being Brazil and Chile (see Activities, below). Argentina has signed but not ratified the treaty while Belize and Guyana are ineligible to sign until their territorial disputes with Guatemala and Venezuela, respectively, are settled. Cuba, Dominica, St. Christopher and Nevis, St. Lucia, and St. Vincent and the Grenadines have declined to sign, Havana stating it will withhold adherence until the United States relinquishes its military base at Guantánamo.

Structure. The General Conference, the principal political organ of OPANAL, comprises representatives of all member states, who attend regular sessions every two years. The Conference, which may also hold special sessions, elects the members of the Council. The latter, composed of five members elected for four-year terms (equitable geographic distribution being a consideration), functions continuously (the current Council members are Costa Rica and Uruguay, until 1989, and Colombia, Mexico, and Peru, until 1991); its responsibilities include maintaining a control system for verifying the absence of tests and manufacture of nuclear weapons in Latin America. The secretary general, the chief administrative officer of the Agency, is elected by the Conference for a maximum

of two four-year terms. He may not be a national of the country where the Agency is headquartered.

Activities. OPANAL's primary functions are to ensure the absence of nuclear weapons in Latin America and to encourage peaceful uses of atomic energy. For example, OPANAL attempts to prevent the diversion of economic resources into nuclear armament technology and to guard against possible nuclear attacks. In the latter regard, it has been active in seeking ratifications of Additional Protocols I and II of the Treaty, the former designed for ratification by external powers controlling territory in Latin America (Britain, France, the Netherlands, the United States), and the latter for ratification by powers agreeing to respect the nuclear-free status of the zone by not using or threatening to use nuclear weapons against a party to the Treaty. The Netherlands, the United Kingdom, and the United States have ratified Protocol I; France has accepted it in spirit but has been constrained from definitive action by a constitutional provision whereby French territories, such as Martinique, are accorded the same status, for certain purposes, as provinces within France. Thus, ratification of Protcol I would require application of its provisions not only with regard to Caribbean territories but throughout France. Protocol II has been ratified by Britain, France, the People's Republic of China, the Soviet Union, and the United States.

The full adherence of regional states to the Treaty has been delayed by national ambitions and regional rivalries. Although Brazil and Chile have both signed and ratified the document, they have not brought it into force, in accord with a provision specifying that the Treaty does not enter into effect until all regional states have adhered to it; the other signatories have waived this provision. Argentina has cited a number of technical reservations for withholding ratification, while insisting that Brazil implement the Treaty first. Argentina and Brazil have also sought reassurances regarding peaceful nuclear projects planned or already under way in both countries, while expressing mutual concern over the stationing of Soviet nuclear weapons in Cuba.

Following the Falklands (Malvinas) dispute in 1982, Argentina charged that Britain had violated Protocol II by operating warships equipped with nuclear weapons within the Latin American nuclear-free zone. This incident, along with the claim that the agreement hampers less-developed countries' utilization of nuclear technology for peaceful purposes, led Argentina to announce in June 1984 that it did not intend to proceed toward ratification.

Further negotiations with Argentina over the use of nuclear explosions for peaceful purposes were reported at the 10th Regular Session of the General Conference, held April 27–30, 1987, at Montevideo, Uruguay. The Conference directed Secretary General París to draft a proposed additional protocol that would govern such explosions, "following the rules of radiological protection accepted by the international community". In a related area, París reported that 18 members had completed treaty-mandated negotiations with the International Atomic Energy Agency (IAEA) for the application of IAEA safeguards, including periodic inspections, to their nuclear activities. The Conference also called for the drafting of an additional protocol to ban the dumping of radioactive material in the region; suggested increased cooperation with the South Pacific Forum, whose members concluded a nuclear-free treaty in 1985; and expressed its disappointment over "insufficient dynamics in international nuclear cooperation".

ANDEAN GROUP

Grupo Andino

Established: By Agreement of Cartagena (Colombia), dated May 26, 1969 (effective October 16, 1969), as modified by the Protocol of Lima, dated October 30, 1976; Decision 117, dated February 14–17, 1977; and the Arequipa (Peru) Protocol, dated April 21, 1978.

Purpose: To promote the balanced, harmonious development of the member countries, to accelerate their growth through economic integration, and to establish conditions favorable for developing a subregional common market.

Headquarters: Lima, Peru.

Principal Organs: Commission (all members), Andean Council (foreign ministers of member countries), Board (3 members), Parliament, Court of Justice.

Coordinator of the Board: Jaime Salazar Montoya (Colombia).

Membership (5): Bolivia, Colombia, Ecuador, Peru, Venezuela.
   Associate Member: Panama.
   Observers (26): Argentina, Australia, Austria, Belgium, Brazil, Canada, Costa Rica, Denmark, Egypt, Finland, France, Federal Republic of Germany, India, Israel, Italy, Japan, Mexico, Netherlands, Paraguay, Spain, Sweden, Switzerland, United Kingdom, United States, Uruguay, Yugoslavia.

Official Language: Spanish.

Origin and development. Officially known as the *Junta del Acuerdo de Cartagena* after its founding instrument, the Andean Group is also identified as the Andean Subregional Group or the Andean Common Market — Ancom. It was formed to speed economic integration among those countries whose economies were more compatible with each other than with the rest of the Latin American states. Venezuela became a full member in 1973, while Mexico has considered itself a "working partner" since 1972.

The controversial Andean Foreign Investment Code (Decision 24), under which foreign-owned enterprises must become "mixed companies" of less than 50 percent foreign capital to benefit from the Group's tariff concessions, was adopted in 1971. In 1974 Chile, then a member, introduced a very liberal foreign investment law in contravention of

Decision 24; after intense negotiation, it withdrew from membership in 1976 because of its partners' refusal to rescind the Code. Panama joined as an associate member in 1979, and in late 1983 announced its intention to open negotiations leading to full membership.

Structure. The Commission, the principal political organ of the Group, formulates general policy and adopts implementary measures; approves procedures for coordinating development plans and harmonizing economic policies; appoints and removes members of the Board, to which it delegates powers; approves, disapproves, or amends Board proposals; and approves the annual budget submitted by the Board. The Commission holds regular sessions three times a year, but special meetings may be convened when requested by member states or the Board. The latter, the principal technical organ, comprises three members who "act only with reference to the interests of the subregion as a whole".

As a means of accelerating the integration process, the members agreed on October 28, 1979, to establish an Andean Parliament, and on November 13, 1979, announced the formation of a consultative Andean Council of Foreign Ministers to coordinate external policy for the region. In order to address disputes among members regarding compliance with the Cartagena Agreement, member heads of state established the Andean Court of Justice at Quito, Ecuador, on July 20, 1983.

Activities. In 1985 and 1986 the Group's work programs emphasized agricultural modernization and research, industrial development, and expanded market and commercial activities. Among the Group's major foreign relations objectives are improving relations with Argentina; strengthening economic relations with Panama; expanding economic cooperation with Brazil and Mexico; increasing cooperation with Caricom, SELA, and ECLAC; improving relations with developing countries, particularly in concert with ASEAN, ECOWAS, the Nonaligned Movement, and the Group of 77; and, of particular importance, enhancing cooperation with the European Community (EC). Another focus of recent attention has been the external debt crisis, the Group joining other Latin American countries in calling for "constructive dialogue" with global creditors and development of a multilateral strategy to replace the case-by-case negotiations favored by the United States.

In practical terms, the Group has failed to achieve most of its major long-term goals. As a result, negotiations began in 1982 to modify the original accord to reflect the Group's true role more accurately and to ease the terms of Decision 24 to permit a greater flow of capital to the region. After numerous disputes and delays over proposed changes, the "Quito Protocal", signed at Quito, Ecuador, on May 12, 1987, rescinded nearly all of Decision 24. Members became free to establish their own regulations on foreign investment, with the proviso that major ownership of enterprises be sold to local investors within 30 or 37 years, depending on the country involved. However, despite the Group's new philosophy that "foreign investment is better than foreign debt", political and economic turmoil in the individual countries continued to restrain investment except in the petroleum and tourism sectors.

The 1987 agreement also appeared to undercut or eliminate many of the Group's former aims, particularly the establishment of a genuine customs union with a common external tariff, now described as "quietly forgotten". In addition, a number of industrial development programs, effectively moribund for several years, were officially scrapped. While some observers argued that the changes left the Group "as good as dead", others responded that effective economic, political, cultural, and social cooperation remained possible. Thus, work proceeded on the implementation of an economic agreement in force since the beginning of the year with the EC, while the Group agreed in November to lower tariffs and gradually eliminate other barriers to intraregional trade.

ANZUS

Official Name: Tripartite Security Treaty Between the Governments of Australia, New Zealand, and the United States (ANZUS Pact).

Established: By Treaty signed September 1, 1951, at San Francisco, United States, effective April 29, 1952.

Purpose: "Each Party recognizes that an armed attack in the Pacific Area on any of the Parties would be dangerous to its own peace and safety and declares that it would act to meet the common danger in accordance with its constitutional processes."

Principal Organ: ANZUS Council.

Membership (3): Australia, New Zealand, United States.

Official Language: English.

Origin and development. The ANZUS Pact was concluded at the time of the 1951 peace settlement with Japan as part of a complex of US-supported mutual security arrangements in the Pacific. Subsequent realignments in international and regional politics reduced the effectiveness of the treaty, while its trilateral character is now in de facto suspense because of disagreement between the United States and New Zealand over the latter's ban on nuclear vessels (see below).

Structure. ANZUS lacks both a headquarters and a permanent staff, its only political organ being the ANZUS Council, which consists of the members' foreign ministers or their deputies. The Council is empowered to consider any matter which a Treaty partner views as relevant to the security of individual members or of the alliance. In the past, it met annually at Canberra, Wellington, or Washington, with most costs borne by the host government. Council meetings were attended by military advisers, who also meet separately. At its first meeting in 1952, the Council decided that responsibility for coordination between

meetings would be given to the member states' representatives in Washington.

Activities. In the absence of a comprehensive Pacific security system, the ANZUS treaty has served primarily as a vehicle for political/strategic consultation. The Council has monitored and discussed significant political and economic developments considered by the partners to be relevant to their security interests. In recent years, ANZUS has concerned itself with an increased Soviet presence in the South Pacific and South Asian areas. This concern was overshadowed in 1985 by New Zealand's refusal to permit US warships to dock at its ports without formal notification that they were neither nuclear-powered nor nuclear-armed. The action prompted the United States, which has a firm policy of not announcing which of its ships carry nuclear weapons, to postpone all ANZUS meetings and military exercises until further notice. David Lange, New Zealand's prime minister, affirmed his commitment to the security pact, but his stand on the nuclear issue left the future of ANZUS in doubt.

The controversy between New Zealand and the United States continued in 1986, following the introduction by the Lange government of legislation banning nuclear-armed and nuclear-powered ships and aircraft from its territory and declaring New Zealand a nuclear-free zone. In a communiqué issued at the conclusion of a US-Australian ministerial meeting at Sydney on June 22, 1987, the two governments declared "that the Treaty would remain in place and would provide the underlying framework for a resumption of full trilateral cooperation when that became feasible". However, Washington, reaffirming the abrogation of its responsibilities to New Zealand, rescinded the latter's rights to discount prices on US military equipment. Australia stated that its bilateral security relationship with New Zealand would be maintained, although Wellington had insisted earlier that bilateral action would be the equivalent of Treaty abrogation. The situation remained unchanged through 1987, New Zealand's defense minister stating there was "no pressure which will force us to accept nuclear weapons".

ARAB LEAGUE

al-Jami'a al-'Arabiyah

Official Name: League of Arab States.

Established: By treaty signed March 22, 1945, at Cairo, Egypt.

Purpose: To strengthen relations among member states by coordinating policies in political, cultural, economic, social, and related affairs; to mediate disputes between members, or between members and third parties.

Temporary Headquarters: Tunis, Tunisia.

Principal Organs: Council of the League of Arab States (all members), Economic Council (all adherents to the 1950

Collective Security Treaty), Joint Defense Council (all adherents to the 1950 Collective Security Treaty), Council of Arab Information Ministers (all members), Permanent Committees (all members), Arab Summit Conferences, General Secretariat.

Secretary General: Chedli Klibi (Tunisia).

Membership (22): Algeria, Bahrain, Djibouti, Egypt, Iraq, Jordan, Kuwait, Lebanon, Libya, Mauritania, Morocco, Oman, Palestine Liberation Organization, Qatar, Saudi Arabia, Somalia, Sudan, Syria, Tunisia, United Arab Emirates, Yemen Arab Republic, People's Democratic Republic of Yemen. Egyptian membership was suspended in April 1979.

Official Language: Arabic.

Origin and development. A long-standing project that reached fruition late in World War II, the League was founded primarily on Egyptian initiative following a promise of British support for any Arab organization that commanded general support. In its earlier years the organization focused mainly on economic, cultural, and social cooperation, but in 1950 a Convention on Joint Defense and Economic Cooperation was concluded that obligated the members in case of attack "immediately to take, individually and collectively, all steps available, including the use of armed force, to repel the aggression and restore security and peace". In 1976 the Palestine Liberation Organization (PLO), which had participated as an observer at all League conferences since September 1964, was admitted to full membership. Egypt's membership was suspended in the wake of its 1979 peace agreement with Israel.

Structure. The principal political organ of the League is the Council, which meets twice a year, normally at the foreign ministers level. Each member has one vote in the Council; decisions bind only those states which accept them. The Council's main functions are to supervise the execution of agreements between members, to mediate disputes, and to coordinate defense in the event of attack. There are, at present, 16 committees and other bodies attached to the Council, six of which, dealing with communications, cultural, economic, health, legal, and social issues are mandated by the League treaty.

Three additional bodies were established by the 1950 Convention: a Joint Defense Council to function in matters of collective security and to coordinate military resources; a Permanent Military Commission, composed of representatives of the general staffs, to draw up plans for joint defense; and an Economic Council, composed of the ministers of economic affairs, to coordinate Arab economic development. An Arab Unified Military Command, charged with the integration of strategy for the liberation of Palestine, was formed in 1964.

The General Secretariat is responsible for internal administration and the execution of Council decisions. It also administers several agencies, including the Bureau for Boycotting Israel (headquartered at Damascus, Syria).

Membership in the League carries with it membership in a number of Specialized Agencies, including the Arab Bank for Economic Development in Africa (BADEA), the Arab Monetary Fund (AMF), and the Organization of Arab Petroleum Exporting Countries (OAPEC) [see separate listings] and a variety of other bodies dealing with economic, social, and technical matters.

Activities. During 1985, the PLO requested two emergency meetings of the League to recommend a solution to the problem of massacres of Palestinians in Lebanese refugee camps. The first meeting dealt with the problem, but made no recommendations. The second meeting acquired important overtones when the question of a regular summit meeting, which had not been held in three years because of ideological differences between members, was included in the agenda. However, since Algeria, Lebanon, Libya, South Yemen, and Syria had decided to boycott the meeting, the final communiqué dealt only with the Palestinian question. The League rejected a Jordanian-PLO proposal to create a Palestinian state "federated" with Jordan, reiterating its support of the Fez plan, which calls for a Palestinian state with Israeli-occupied East Jerusalem as its capital.

On January 5, 1986, at a special Council meeting, the League "vigorously condemned" the US threat of military action against Libya; the threats came after the alleged Libya-backed terrorist attacks on the Rome and Vienna airports nine days earlier. A meeting of League foreign ministers on March 27 again condemned Washington for hostilities resulting from US naval manuevers in the Gulf of Sirte, while members subsequently participated in the general Arab denunciation of US airstrikes on Tripoli and Benghazi on April 15 (see entry under Libya).

After many years of preoccupation with Arab-Israeli issues, the League's attention in 1987 turned to the Iraq-Iran conflict as Arab moderates sought a united front against Iran and the potential spread of militant Islamic fundamentalism. An extraordinary summit conference held November 8-11 at 'Amman, Jordan, condemned "the Iranian regime's intransigence, provocations, and threats to the Arab Gulf States" and called for international "pressure" to encourage Iran to accept a UN-sponsored ceasefire. Although Syrian and Libyan opposition blocked a proposed restoration of membership privileges to Egypt, the summit declared that members could establish relations with Cairo individually. A number of countries, including the Gulf states, quickly did so, apparently in the hope that Egypt's military strength would provide additional protection against expanded confrontation in the Gulf.

Palestinian issues quickly returned to the forefront of the League's agenda in early 1988 because of the uprising (*intifada*) in the Gaza Strip and West Bank. A summit held at Algiers on June 7-9 affirmed "moral, political, and diplomatic" support for the *intifada* but resisted reported PLO pressure for monetary support, leaving such aid up to the individual members.

ARAB MONETARY FUND (AMF)

Established: By Articles of Agreement signed April 27, 1976, at Rabat, Morocco, with effect from February 2, 1977.

Purpose: To correct disequilibria in the balance of payments of member states; to promote the stability of exchange rates among Arab currencies, rendering them mutually convertible; to promote Arab economic integration and development; to encourage the creation of a unified Arab currency; and to coordinate policies in other international monetary and economic forums.

Headquarters: Abu Dhabi, United Arab Emirates.

Principal Organs: Board of Governors (all members), Board of Executive Directors (9 members), Loan and Investments Committees.

Managing Director: Dr. Abdullah Ibrahim al-Kuwaiz (Saudi Arabia).

Membership (21): Algeria, Bahrain, Egypt, Iraq, Jordan, Kuwait, Lebanon, Libya, Mauritania, Morocco, Oman, Palestine Liberation Organization, Qatar, Saudi Arabia, Somalia, Sudan, Syria, Tunisia, United Arab Emirates, Yemem Arab Republic, People's Democratic Repubic of Yemen. Egyptian membership was suspended in April 1979.

Official Language: Arabic.

Origin and development. Although a proposal to form an Arab Payments Union was made by the Arab Economic Council in the 1960s and a meeting was subsequently held for that purpose, the idea was discarded as attention was drawn to more pressing political issues. With the quadrupling of oil prices in 1974, however, concern once again focused on the issue of monetary problems. The objective was now more ambitious: an organization to deal with recycling, or investing, Arab "petrodollars" in order to decrease dependence upon foreign handling of surplus funds. This goal is clearly implicit in the Articles of Agreement signed in April 1976.

Structure. The Board of Governors, comprising one governor and one deputy governor from each member state, serves as the Fund's general assembly and holds all administrative powers. Meeting at least once a year, it is responsible for capitalization, income distribution, and the admission and suspension of members. The Board of Executive Directors, consisting of the Fund's managing director and eight experts elected for three-year terms from the member states, performs tasks assigned it by the Board of Governors.

Activities. Unlike the International Monetary Fund, the AMF's principal aim is to foster the economic integration of member states. Thus the Fund guarantees loans to Arab countries to correct payment imbalances resulting from unilateral or pan-Arab development projects, while using its capital as a catalyst to advance Arab financial instruments and to promote creation of a unified Arab currency. It provides technical assistance to the monetary and banking agencies of member countries, largely through training seminars in such areas as branch banking and accounting, bank supervision and internal auditing, and documentary credit. It also cooperates with other Arab and international organizations to discuss and promote areas of common interest.

From the beginning of lending operations in 1978 through 1986, the Fund approved 64 loans totalling about 333 million Arab Accounting Dollars (AAD) to 11 countries. In 1986 11 new loans worth 33.9 million AAD were approved for six countries, Tunisia becoming a recipient for the first time. One of the loans was made to Morocco in connection with the Inter-Arab Trade Facility, established in 1981 to provide concessional interest rates to members with balance of trade deficits with other members. In accordance with a 1985 decision that members requesting loans must be current on payment of principal and interest on outstanding loans, the Fund in 1986 suspended lending to Iraq, Somalia, and Sudan.

In late 1987 the AMF launched a restructuring program under recently appointed chairman Abdullah al-Kuwaiz, apparently with widespread support from Arab bankers. The AMF's "fresh priorities" included the creation of a regional securities market and the strengthening of securities markets in member states to provide long-term financing for development. The chairman also called on commercial banks to aid in the creation of a "regional framework" of financing for enhanced inter-Arab trade.

ASSOCIATION OF SOUTHEAST ASIAN NATIONS (ASEAN)

Established: By foreign ministers of member states at Bangkok, Thailand, August 9, 1967.

Purpose: ". . . to accelerate economic growth, social progress and cultural development in the region . . . to promote active collaboration and mutual assistance on matters of common interest in the economic, social, cultural, technical, scientific, and administrative fields . . . to collaborate more effectively for the greater utilization of [the member states'] agriculture and industries, the expansion of their trade, including the study of problems of international commodity trade, the improvement of their transport and communication facilities and raising the living standards of their people."

Headquarters: Djakarta, Indonesia.

Principal Organs: ASEAN Heads of Government (all members), ASEAN Ministerial Meeting (all members), Standing Committee (all members), nine Permanent Committees, eight Ad Hoc Committees, ASEAN Subcommittee on Women, Secretariat.

Secretary General: Roderick Yong Yin Fatt (Brunei).

Membership (6): Brunei, Indonesia, Malaysia, Philippines, Singapore, Thailand. (Sri Lanka was denied admission, on geographic grounds, in 1982, while Brunei was admitted following independence in 1984.)
  Observer: Papua New Guinea.

Official Language: English.

  Origin and development. ASEAN was part of a continuing effort during the 1960s to create a framework for regional cooperation among the non-Communist states of Southeast Asia. Earlier efforts included the Association of Southeast Asia (ASA), established in 1961 by Malaya, the Philippines, and Thailand; and the short-lived "Maphilindo" association, created in 1963 by Indonesia, Malaya, and the Philippines. The change of government in Indonesia in 1966 opened the way to a somewhat broader association, plans for ASEAN being broached at a conference at Bangkok, Thailand, in August and implemented a year later. A further widening of ASEAN's sphere of concerns occurred with the first ASEAN-sponsored regional summit conference held at Pattaya, Thailand, in early February 1976. In the wake of these discussions as well as more recent talks with the United States, Canada, India, and the European Communities, ASEAN began to adopt a more global posture, its leaders calling for a "more constructive" North-South dialogue and offering to play a mediary role in the establishment of a new international economic order (NIEO).
  Structure. While the ASEAN Heads of Government is the organization's highest authority, the annual Ministerial Meeting, composed of the foreign ministers of the member states, ordinarily sets general policy. Continuing supervision of ASEAN activities is the responsibility of the Standing Committee which, located in the country hosting the Ministerial Meeting, consists of the foreign minister of the host country as chairman, the accredited ambassadors of the other five members, the ASEAN directors general, and the ASEAN secretary general. There are eight technical committees, five of which deal with economic cooperation: Finance and Banking; Food, Agriculture and Forestry; Industry, Minerals and Energy; Trade and Tourism; Transportation and Communication. The three noneconomic committees are concerned with Culture and Information, Science and Technology, and Social Development. In addition, there are numerous subcommittees, expert/working groups, and private-sector organizations that typically engage in upwards of 300 meetings or project activities per year.
  Activities. Although economic cooperation has long been a principal ASEAN concern, progress has been slowed by differing levels of development and similarity of exports.

By contrast, the Association has consistently demonstrated political solidarity, primarily through an anticommunist posture that in recent years has yielded strong condemnation of Vietnam's military involvement in Kampuchea.
  In an effort to alter its "single-issue" image, ASEAN convened its first summit in a decade on December 14–15, 1987. Meeting at Manila, Philippines, the heads of state called for a reduction in tariff barriers between members and a rejuvenation of regional economic projects, observers noting that concerted action seemed more likely than in the past because of an increasingly hostile global trading environment and concern over growing Western protectionism. A protocol was also signed permitting regional enlargement of the Association, presumably by the inclusion of Southern and Western Pacific states. The latter prospect was seemingly enhanced by an agreement to "intensify" efforts to create a regional nuclear-free zone, although the related issue of US military bases in the Philippines was not discussed. The other major development of the summit was an announcement from Japan that it was offering the ASEAN countries $2 billion in low-interest loans and investments over the next three years to finance private sector projects.

BANK FOR INTERNATIONAL SETTLEMENTS (BIS/BIZ)

Banque des Réglements Internationaux
Bank für Internationalen Zahlungssausgleich
Banca del Regolamenti Internazionali

Established: By Agreement of Incorporation with the Swiss government dated January 20, 1930, with operations commencing March 17, 1930.

Purpose: ". . . to promote the cooperation of central banks and to provide additional facilities for international financial operations; and to act as trustee or agent in regard to international financial settlements. . . ."

Headquarters: Basel, Switzerland.

Principal Organs: Board of Directors (13 members; 2 each from Belgium, France, Federal Republic of Germany, Italy, United Kingdom, and 1 each from the Netherlands, Sweden, Switzerland), General Meeting, Management.

President and Chairman of the Board: Dr. W.F. Duisenberg (Netherlands).

Membership (29): Australia, Austria, Belgium, Bulgaria, Canada, Czechoslovakia, Denmark, Finland, France, Federal Republic of Germany, Greece, Hungary, Iceland, Ireland, Italy, Japan, Netherlands, Norway, Poland,

Portugal, Romania, South Africa, Spain, Sweden, Switzerland, Turkey, United Kingdom, United States (American shareholders are a group of commercial banks), Yugoslavia.

Official Languages: English, French, German, Italian.

Origin and development. The BIS was created to handle post-World War I reparations payments. Though the worldwide economic depression of the 1930s resulted in a moratorium on these payments, the BIS continued to function as the "central banker's central bank". Its existence was threatened at the end of World War II, when the United States at Bretton Woods proposed its dissolution, but by the 1960s the BIS had regained an important role in international monetary affairs. This was a by-product of both the increased importance of monetary policy in international financial relations and the US reliance on "swap arrangements" to finance its balance-of-payments deficit. Furthermore, the role of the BIS was enhanced when the Eurocurrency market emerged as an independent force in world politics. Not only was the BIS an active participant in the market, but its annual reports contained valuable data on market size and fluctuations. While the BIS was traditionally identified as a European bankers' association, the designation became less appropriate as US, Canadian, and Japanese banks took an increasingly active role in its policymaking. In 1970 the central bank of Canada became a member, and Japan rejoined after having had its membership lapse from 1952 to 1970 as part of the World War II peace settlement.

Structure. Administration is vested in three organs: the General Meeting, the Board of Directors, and the Management. The General Meeting is held annually on the second Monday in June. The Board of Directors is responsible for the conduct of the Bank's operations at the highest level; the United States, although regularly represented at the Bank's meetings, has not occupied the two seats to which it is entitled on the Board since World War II.

Working closely with the Bank is the privately funded Group of Thirty, made up of leading central and commercial bankers, who meet periodically to discuss trends within the international banking community.

Activities. Although created to play a role in international settlements, the Bank today functions in a variety of capacities. First, it aids member central banks in managing and investing their monetary reserves. Second, it is a major research center, as evidenced by the influence of its annual report in international monetary circles and by its role in collecting and distributing statistical data on international banking and monetary trends. Third, it provides a cooperative forum for central bankers and representatives of international financial institutions. In addition, the BIS acts as a secretariat for the Committee of Governors of the Central Banks of the Member States of the European Economic Community, the Board of Governors of the European Monetary Cooperation Fund, the Committee on Banking Regulations and Supervisory Practices of the Group of Ten, the Group of Experts on Payment Systems, and the Group of Experts on Monetary and Data-Bank Questions.

In its capacity as Secretariat for the Board of Governors of the European Monetary Cooperation Fund, the Bank is primarily concerned with administration of the European Monetary System (EMS). In addition to ensuring that EMS governing arrangements are properly enforced, the BIS directs its attention to strengthening coordination of EC members' exchange-rate, interest-rate, and domestic marketing policies, with a view toward preparing for the planned "institutional phase" of the EMS.

In the course of monitoring international banking trends, the Bank noted that loan commitments to Eastern European and non-oil-exporting countries declined during 1982–1983. Lending to these high-risk groups continued to be sporadic and at low levels during 1984–1985. International private banks shunned making new loans to such countries due to their heavy indebtedness and threats of default, while increasing commitments in the industrialized countries. The BIS warned that a reduction of credit available to the developing countries would adversely affect their ability to buy Western manufactured goods and thus would slow global recovery, while a lending focus on the West would keep interest rates artificially high.

In its 1985–1986 Annual Report, the Bank noted the salutary impact of a decline in commodity prices, particularly oil, on developed countries' economies. It commented favorably on the US "employment miracle" and Washington's success in reducing inflation, while pointing out that "the high geographical and occupational mobility of labor and the differentiation of wage levels in the United States stand in marked contrast to ingrained patterns in Europe."

The 1986–1987 Report was substantially less sanguine, arguing that "the challenges facing policymakers" were, in some respects, "more formidable" than they had been twelve months earlier. It found the leading industrial countries faced with three disquieting facts: an enhanced risk of trade war, a slowdown in economic growth in response to exchange rate realignments, and increased difficulty in stabilizing exchange rates through exchange market intervention. It also found that balance-of-payments problems for debtor nations had heightened either for external reasons "or as a consequence of domestic policy mismanagement". Overall, relatively low inflation rates, low nominal interest rates, and low oil prices had "not given the boost to economic growth" that forecasters had anticipated.

In view of such worldwide economic problems, the BIS recently has coordinated efforts to make the international banking system "safer" by requiring banks to maintain larger cash reserves. In December 1987 the US Federal Reserve Bank and central banks from 11 other countries announced a preliminary agreement, under BIS auspices, that would gradually increase the capitalization of most banks through 1992, thus providing high-risk loans with bigger cash "cushions". Final approval of the plan was scheduled for mid-1988 after a six-month review by the global banking community.

In its 1987–1988 report the Bank said that "neither gloom nor exuberance" was called for although many of the major problems from previous years, most notably large trade imbalances, were "still awaiting solution". For the developing countries, growth declined and inflation remained high, although a few "hopeful signs" were seen on the debt front. For the industrialized world, "some progress" had been achieved in coordinating fiscal policies but protectionist pressure continued and a return to higher inflation appeared possible. While the October 1987 stock market crash—the year's dominant financial event—was "alarmingly sharp and widespread", the world's markets and financial institutions displayed "a remarkable resilience", aided by "swift and efficient response" from monetary authorities.

The Bank's assets, as of March 31, 1988, were 38.2 billion gold francs (approximately $74.1 billion).

BENELUX ECONOMIC UNION

Union Economique Benelux
Benelux Economische Unie

Established: By Customs Convention signed at London, England, September 5, 1944, effective January 1, 1948; present organization created by Treaty signed February 3, 1958, at The Hague, Netherlands, effective November 1, 1960.

Purpose: To develop closer economic links among member states; to assure a coordinated policy in economic, financial, and social fields; and to promote a common policy in foreign trade, particularly with regard to the exchange of goods and services with developing countries.

Headquarters: Brussels, Belgium.

Principal Organs: Committee of Ministers, Interparliamentary Consultative Council, Council of the Economic Union, Economic and Social Advisory Council, College of Arbitration, Benelux Court of Justice, Secretariat.

Secretary General: Dr. Egbert Diederik Jan Kruijtbosch (Netherlands).

Membership (3): Belgium, Luxembourg, Netherlands.

Official Languages: French, Dutch.

Origin and development. The origins of the Benelux Economic Union can be dated from 1930, when Belgium, Luxembourg, and the Netherlands concluded a convention with Denmark, Norway, Sweden, and Finland setting forth a joint intention to reduce customs autonomy. In 1932 the Belgium-Luxembourg Economic Union and the Netherlands concluded the Convention of Ouchy, by which the three governments agreed not to increase reciprocal customs duties, to reduce import duties, and to eliminate as soon as possible existing commercial restrictions. An impasse of ten years followed, largely because of international tensions and the opposition of several countries to the loss of most-favored-nation status, but in October 1943 the

three governments-in-exile concluded at London, England, an agreement designed to regulate payments and strengthen economic relations after the war. In September 1944 the same three signed the Dutch-Belgium-Luxembourg Customs Convention, but economic disparities caused by the war delayed implementation until 1947. In June 1953 the governments adopted a protocol embracing social as well as economic policies, while an additional protocol setting forth a common commercial policy soon followed. Thus the Benelux Treaty of 1958 served primarily to codify agreements that had already been concluded.

Structure. The governing body of the Union is the Committee of Ministers, which comprises at least three ministers from each member state and normally includes the ministers of foreign affairs, foreign trade, economic affairs, finance, and agriculture. Meeting at least once every quarter, it supervises application of the Treaty and is responsible for ensuring that Treaty aims are pursued. Decisions are made unanimously. Ministerial working parties facilitate Committee tasks.

The Benelux Interparliamentary Consultative Council, established by a convention signed November 5, 1955, predates the establishment of the present organization. The Council's 49 members—21 each from Belgium and the Netherlands and 7 from Luxembourg—are chosen from the respective national parliaments. Recommendations by the Council to the member states require a two-thirds majority vote; other decisions need only a simple majority.

The Council of the Economic Union, comprising senior officials from the member governments, is responsible for ensuring implementation of decisions made by the Committee of Ministers and for recommending to the Committee any proposals necessary for the functioning of the Union. It also coordinates the activities of the Union's numerous committees and special committees and transmits their proposals, with its own comments, to the Committee of Ministers.

The Economic and Social Advisory Council consists of 27 members (plus an equal number of deputies), one-third from representative social and economic institutions in each country. It may advance proposals on its own initiative to the Committee of Ministers and also renders advisory opinions on matters referred to it by the Committee.

Settlement of any disputes between members over application of the Treaty is the responsibility of the College of Arbitration, which is composed of six members (two from each member state) appointed by the Committee of Ministers. To date, no disputes have been referred to the College.

The Benelux Court of Justice was established at Brussels, Belgium, on May 11, 1974. Composed of senior judges from the member countries, it interprets common legal rules, either at the request of a national court, in which case the Court's decisions are binding, or at the request of a member government, in which case the Court serves only in a consultative capacity.

The Secretariat is headed by a secretary general, always of Dutch nationality, and two deputy secretaries general, one from Belgium and the other from Luxembourg.

Activities. Benelux facilitates the free movement of persons, services, goods, and capital between the member states by such measures as the abolition of passport controls and labor permits; the elimination of discrimination in regard to working conditions, social benefits, and the right to practice a profession; the removal of import duties and most quotas; and the banning of national discrimination in purchases by public bodies. It also levies uniform customs duties on products imported from non-EC countries; acts as a single unit in concluding trade, immigration, and patent agreements with such countries; and operates as a caucus for the member countries, particularly prior to meetings of such intergovernmental economic organizations as the EC and the OECD. To further disencumber intra-Benelux trade, all internal border formalities have been conducted since 1984 through the use of a shortened form, the so-called Single Administrative Document (SAD), which was subsequently adopted throughout the European Community.

In recent years Benelux has concluded accords with France and West Germany permitting easier border crossing for both individuals and merchandise, while providing for enhanced cooperation in police and security matters. The goal is the elimination of nearly all controls at the French and German borders by 1990 as a precursor to the similar frontier arrangements throughout the EC.

Internally, Benelux has recently focused on environmental concerns, including noise abatement, reduction in water and air pollution, and the creation of union-wide zoning maps. Cross-border cooperation between local authorities in other areas, such as fire, sewer, water, and telecommunication services, was also authorized by a convention that went into effect in 1987.

CARIBBEAN COMMUNITY AND COMMON MARKET (CARICOM)

Established: August 1, 1973, pursuant to the July 4, 1973, Treaty of Chaguaramas (Trinidad), as successor to the Caribbean Free Trade Association.

Purpose: To deepen the integration process prevailing within the former Caribbean Free Trade Association, to enable all member states to share equitably in the benefits of integration, to operate certain subregional common services, and to coordinate the foreign policies of the member states.

Headquarters: Georgetown, Guyana.

Principal Organs: Heads of Government Conference (all members), Common Market Council (all members), Conference of Ministers Responsible for Health, Standing Committees, Secretariat.

Secretary General: Roderick Rainford (Jamaica).

Membership (13): Antigua and Barbuda, Bahamas, Barbados, Belize, Dominica, Grenada, Guyana, Jamaica, Montserrat, St. Kitts-Nevis, St. Lucia, St. Vincent, Trinidad and Tobago.

Observers (3): Anguilla, Bermuda, British Virgin Islands, Dominican Republic, Haiti, Suriname.

Official Language: English.

Origin and development. The formation of the Caribbean Free Trade Association (Carifta) in 1968 followed several earlier attempts to foster economic cooperation among the Commonwealth countries and territories of the West Indies and Caribbean. The initial agreement was signed by Antigua, Barbados, and Guyana on December 15, 1965, at Antigua, while an amended accord was approved at Georgetown, Guyana, on February 23, 1968, by those governments, Trinidad and Tobago, and the West Indies Associated States. Jamaica joined in June 1968 and was followed later in the month by the remaining British-associated islands, which meanwhile had agreed to establish their own Eastern Caribbean Common Market. Belize was accepted for membership in June 1970.

At an eight-member conference of heads of state of the Caribbean Commonwealth Countries at Georgetown in April 1973, the decision was taken to replace Carifta with a new Caribbean Community and Common Market (Caricom) that would provide additional opportunities for economic integration, with an emphasis on obtaining greater benefits for the less-developed members. The new grouping was formally established at Chaguaramas, Trinidad, on July 4, 1973, by the prime ministers of Barbados, Guyana, Jamaica, and Trinidad. Although the Treaty came into effect August 1, 1973, Carifta was not formally superseded until May 1, 1974, by which time all former Carifta members except Antigua and St. Kitts-Nevis-Anguilla had acceded to the new grouping. Antigua joined on July 5, 1974, and St. Kitts-Nevis-Anguilla acceded on July 26, with St. Kitts-Nevis continuing the membership after the United Kingdom, in late 1980, resumed responsibility for the administration of Anguilla. After a lengthy period of close cooperation with the grouping, the Bahamas formally acceded to membership in July 1983.

The 1973 Treaty provided for a common external tariff and a common protective policy vis-à-vis Community trade with nonmembers, a scheme to harmonize fiscal incentives to industry and development planning, and a special regime for the less-developed members of the Community.

In the wake of unfavorable economic developments during the mid-1970s, the progress of the Caricom members toward economic coordination and integration stagnated. Cooperation in finance and joint development projects was virtually halted and members resorted to developing separate, often conflicting, policies; the problem was most acute in the area of trade, where Guyana and Jamaica adopted protectionist policies in an effort to offset severe foreign-exchange shortages. The eight least-developed members were especially affected by this development, causing the World Bank to assert in April 1979 that Caricom's biggest failure was the lack of any major economic improvement in these countries.

Structure. Policy decisions under the Treaty of Chaguaramas are assigned to a Heads of Government Conference, which meets annually and is the final authority for all Caricom organs. Each participating state has one vote and most decisions are taken unanimously. A Common Market Council deals with operational aspects of common market activity, while general administration is entrusted to a Secretariat consisting of five chief divisions: Sectoral Policy and Planning; Legal; Trade, Economics, and Statistics; Functional Cooperation; and General Services and Administration. Standing Committees include Education, Industry, Labor, Foreign Affairs, Finance, Agriculture, and Mines.

In accord with the 1973 Treaty, the following are "associate institutions" of Caricom: the Caribbean Development Bank (see separate entry under Regional and Subregional Development Banks), the Caribbean Examinations Council, the Caribbean Investment Corporation, the Council of Legal Education, the Caribbean Meteorological Council, the Organization of Eastern Caribbean States (see separate entry), the Regional Shipping Council, the University of Guyana, and the University of the West Indies.

Activities. Efforts to stimulate intraregional trade have been ineffective despite the 1984 "Nassau Agreement" which called for the dismantling of trade barriers between Caricom members. However, in light of a 33 percent decline in such trade in 1986 alone, the 8th Conference of Caricom Heads of Government in July 1987 pledged to remove all intraregional protectionist measures by September 30, 1988. To that end, Trinidad and Tobago in August eliminated its 12 percent stamp duty on imports from eight other Caricom partners and in December Caricom announced unrestricted trade for certain products, including processed foods, garments, footwear, and chemicals.

The Conference also agreed that the Caribbean Export Credit Facility, originally assigned a start-up date of July 1, 1987, would begin operations in 1988. The facility will provide a wide range of trade and investment financing, including pre-and post-shipping credit for regional exporters. A beginning equity of about $70 million is planned — $16 million from Caricom governments and the Caribbean Development Bank, the rest from international financial institutions.

In other action, the 1987 Conference called for completion by the end of 1987 of a framework for regional economic ventures; declared 1988 the "Year of Small Business"; ordered feasibility studies on proposed region-wide shipping and air transport systems; endorsed regional anti-drug efforts; and directed Caricom finance ministers to develop a joint strategy for dealing with the external debt crisis. The Conference deferred action on the proposed creation of a Caricom human rights commission but declared that Haiti and Suriname would have no further access to Caricom institutions until "the democratic process" in those countries gets "back on track" and "proper elections" are held.

The Conference also criticized "growing protectionism" on the part of Washington, which it argued had contributed to the failure of the Caribbean Basin Initiative (CBI), launched in 1983 to stimulate trade with the United States. In international political affairs, it condemned apartheid and supported economic sanctions against South Africa; approved the Central American peace initiative for resolution of the Nicaraguan conflict; and endorsed the proposal for a UN-sponsored peace conference to settle the Iran-Iraq war.

Caricom held an emergency summit meeting in Barbados on January 6, 1988, to discuss the Haitian political situation. While no direct action was taken, summit participants again criticized the Namphy regime and attacked the elections scheduled for later that month as "not credible".

CENTRAL AFRICAN CUSTOMS AND ECONOMIC UNION (UDEAC)

*Union Douanière et Economique
de l'Afrique Centrale*

Established: By treaty signed December 8, 1964, at Brazzaville, Congo, effective January 1, 1966.

Purpose: ". . . to promote the gradual and progressive establishment of a Central African Common Market . . . [which will] greatly contribute to the improvement of the living standard of [the member states'] peoples. . . ."

Headquarters: Bangui, Central African Republic.

Principal Organs: Council of Heads of State (all members), Consultative Committee (all members), General Secretariat.

Secretary General: Ambroise Foalem (Cameroon).

Membership (6): Cameroon, Central African Republic, Chad, Congo, Equatorial Guinea, Gabon.

Official Language: French.

Origin and development. Prior to attaining independence, the Central African Republic, Chad, the Congo, and Gabon were joined in the Equatorial Customs Union (*Union Douanière Equatoriales* — UDE), which sought to harmonize the fiscal treatment of industrial investments — a unique feature retained by the UDEAC. In June 1961 Cameroon joined the UDE, and by mid-1962 an external common tariff had been established. In 1964, having agreed to form the UDEAC by 1966, the members began more comprehensive economic cooperation, including coordination of development policies, especially in the fields of infrastructure and industrialization. In early 1968 Chad and the Central African Republic announced their intention to withdraw from the UDEAC, but the latter reversed itself later in the year. Chad's withdrawal became effective

January 1, 1969, although N'Djamena continued to participate in some activities. In December 1975 it was granted observer status in the Council of Heads of State and ultimately rejoined the grouping in December 1984. Equatorial Guinea joined the UDEAC in December 1983, while Sao Tome and Principe attended the 1986 and 1987 summits as an observer.

Structure. The Council of Heads of State meets at least once a year to coordinate the general customs and economic policies of the participating states. The Consultative Committee, composed of finance ministers or ministers concerned with economic development, meets at least twice a year to deal with operational matters.

Activities. The UDEAC adjusts common external customs tariffs; coordinates legislation, regulations, and investment codes; harmonizes internal taxes; and develops common industrialization projects, development plans, and transport policies. In 1973 the *Banque des Etats de l'Afrique Centrale*—BEAC was established as a central bank for all UDEAC members and Chad.

In January 1978 the UDEAC heads of state adopted additional measures designed to facilitate economic unity. These included a projected common income tax, community administration of waterways between Bangui and Brazzaville, and harmonization of legislation dealing with migration and industrialization. In addition, members agreed to increase cooperation in business and civil service administration, to standardize customs procedures, and to establish common structures for scientific and technical research, transportation, communications, and tourism. UDEAC was also a major actor in the formation of the Economic Community of Central African States (*Communauté Economique des Etats de l'Afrique Centrale*—CEEAC). The new association of ten French- and Portuguese-speaking states, established in October 1983, was originally proposed at the 17th UDEAC summit in 1981.

The long-standing debate on eliminating obstacles to trade, communication, and free circulation of people continued at the 22nd summit, held at Bata, Equatorial Guinea, on December 18–19, 1986. Participants decried the fact that preoccupation with internal security matters prevented some members from making more positive contributions to the realization of UDEAC goals.

The 23rd summit was held at N'Djamena, Chad, on December 19, 1987. Only three heads of state (the presidents of Chad, Gabon, and Equatorial Guinea) were in attendance, the others reported to have been absent because of domestic problems. In view of the attendance, the meeting was brief, with no major action taken save for reappointment of the incumbent secretary general, approval of a substantially reduced budget for 1988, and agreement to reorganize the BEAC, which the finance ministers at a subsequent meeting on December 29 described as needing "vigorous recovery measures of a monetary nature". The financial condition of the BEAC was further discussed during an "informal" summit of all six UDEAC heads of state at Libreville, Gabon, on January 8, 1988.

CENTRAL AMERICAN COMMON MARKET (CACM/MCCA)

Mercado Común Centroamericano

Established: By General Treaty of Central American Economic Integration, signed December 13, 1960, at Managua, Nicaragua, effective June 3, 1961.

Purpose: "The Contracting States agree to set up among themselves a common market which should be fully established in not more than five years from the date of the entry into force of [the] Treaty. They also undertake to set up a customs union among their territories."

Headquarters: Guatemala City, Guatemala.

Principal Organs: Central American Economic Council (all members), Executive Council (all members), Permanent Secretariat.

Secretary General: Raúl Sierra Franco (Guatemala).

Members (5): Costa Rica, El Salvador, Guatemala, Honduras, Nicaragua.

Official Language: Spanish.

Origin and development. The Central American Economic Integration Program was formally established on August 17, 1952, when the economic ministers of five states organized a Committee for Economic Cooperation of the Central American Isthmus. The primary instrument of the CACM is the General Treaty of Central American Economic Integration, which was signed by El Salvador, Guatemala, Honduras, and Nicaragua in December 1960 and became effective in June 1961, after deposit of the required instruments of ratification. Costa Rica acceded to the Treaty on June 23, 1962. The General Treaty incorporates the Agreement on the Regime for Central American Integration Industries, signed June 10, 1958, and also keeps in force several other agreements: the Multilateral Treaty of Central American Free Trade and Economic Integration, also concluded June 10, 1958; the Central American Agreement on the Equalization of Import Duties and Charges and its accompanying Protocol on Central American Preferential Tariff, adopted September 1, 1959; and six additional protocols signed after that time but not ratified by all five countries. While not affecting the validity of these agreements, the General Treaty takes precedence.

The CACM suffered the de facto withdrawal of Honduras in 1969 as a result of its war with El Salvador. Although Honduras continued to view itself as a de jure member, it suspended participation in the CACM in December 1970 by imposing tariffs on all imports from the region. In October 1980, however, Honduras and El Salvador concluded a peace treaty and agreed to restore bilateral trade. This development, along with the restoration of relations with Nicaragua in April 1981, led to Honduras' pledge to participate in the restructuring of the Common Market.

The CACM was to have been replaced by the Economic and Social Community of Central America (*Communidad Económica y Social Centroamericana* – CESC), with some expectation that the largely inactive Organization of Central American States (*Organizatión de Estados Centroamericanos* – ODECA),whose charter had come into effect in 1952, would also be thereby superseded. However, the new organization's draft treaty, published on March 23, 1976, was not ratified by any of the potential members. During 1978 a number of alternative treaties were prepared, but none proved acceptable in advance of the resolution of the differences between El Salvador and Honduras. Although negotiations held throughout 1980–1981 achieved some progress, a new accord could not be completed prior to the June 3, 1981, expiration of the General Treaty, which will, however, remain in effect unless one of the members chooses to withdraw, necessitating dissolution within five years.

Structure. The Central American Economic Council, which meets about every three months, is the CACM policy-making organ. It consists of the economic ministers of the member states and has general responsibility for the integration and coordination of the members' economies. The Executive Council, comprising deputies to the ministers and their alternates, exercises continuing supervision over the course of economic integration and prescribes steps required to fulfill the provisions of the General Treaty. The secretary general is elected for a three-year term by the Economic Council.

Activities. The General Treaty envisaged the dismantling of internal tariffs and other trade barriers between the member states and the establishment of a common external tariff for imports from outside the area. Over a period of years, most internal barriers were removed from within the de facto four-member group, and agreement was reached on 98 percent of the items in the regional customs classification.

Disagreements among members coupled with mounting debt and protectionist pressures have recently halted progress toward the realization of CACM's goals. The most serious breach occurred in December 1983, when Guatemala imposed licensing and other restrictions on trade with its regional partners. Although the action provoked strong reaction by other members, the issue has not yet been resolved within the Common Market forum, necessitating the adoption of what were intended to be a series of temporary trade agreements on a bilateral basis.

In mid-1984, an effort was made to "reactivate" the CACM, talks being held in September with European Community representatives to generate EC aid, which yielded an economic cooperation agreement with the EC in November 1985. However, continued instability in the region left the organization essentially moribund, although the economic ministers succeeded in negotiating an intraregional instrument of payment (*Derecho de Importación*

Centroamericano – DICA) in July 1986 and a parliament to serve as a catalyst for increased regional cooperation has been proposed.

In a move seen as reflecting a desire to strengthen the CACM despite the apparent lack of US enthusiasm for such an effort, the EC in February 1987 agreed to increase its assistance to members in the form of direct aid to community development programs, especially those promoting food self-sufficiency. Prospects for revitalizing the CACM may also have been enhanced by the subsequent negotiations on the Central American Peace Plan spearheaded by Costa Rican President Arias. Although the agreements reached by the Central American leaders were directed primarily at ending the fighting in the region, they included a proposal that elections to a 100-member Central American Parliament be conducted simultaneously in all five countries in 1988.

COLOMBO PLAN FOR COOPERATIVE ECONOMIC AND SOCIAL DEVELOPMENT IN ASIA AND THE PACIFIC

Established: July 1, 1951, pursuant to an initiative by Commonwealth foreign ministers at Colombo, Sri Lanka, January 9–14, 1950.

Purpose: To facilitate economic and social development, and to coordinate technical assistance and capital aid to the countries of Asia and the Pacific.

Headquarters: Colombo, Sri Lanka.

Principal Organs: Consultative Committee (all members), Colombo Plan Council (all members), Colombo Plan Bureau.

Bureau Director: Gilbert H. Sheinbaum (United States).

Membership (26):
Major Donors (6): Australia, Canada, Japan, New Zealand, United Kingdom, United States.
Regional Members (20): Afghanistan, Bangladesh, Bhutan, Burma, Fiji, India, Indonesia, Iran, Kampuchea, Republic of Korea, Laos, Malaysia, Maldives, Nepal, Pakistan, Papua New Guinea, Philippines, Singapore, Sri Lanka, Thailand.

Origin and development. What was initially styled the "Colombo Plan for Cooperative Economic Development in South and Southeast Asia" was conceived at a meeting of the Commonwealth foreign ministers at Colombo, Sri Lanka, in January 1950. The decision to form a Consultative Committee resulted in meetings at Sydney, Australia, and London, England, the same year, while technical co-operation began in March 1951, after the commencement of capital aid operations in support of national development plans. Soon after its inception the Plan began to lose its exclusively anglophone character, and Commonwealth countries now constitute a minority of the membership. The present name was adopted following the December 1977 implementation of a new constitution intended to reflect more accurately the Plan's extended geographic composition and scope of activity.

Structure. The Colombo Plan is multilateral in approach but bilateral in operation: multilateral in that the Plan takes cognizance of the problems of Asia and the Pacific as a whole and endeavors to deal with them in a coordinated way; bilateral because negotiations for assistance are made directly between a donor and a recipient country.

The Consultative Committee, the highest deliberative body, consists of ministers representing the member governments. It meets biennially to survey the development of the region, assess needs, and examine how international cooperation can help fill gaps in national resources and accelerate development. The Colombo Plan Council, which generally consists of the heads of members' diplomatic missions at Colombo, meets several times a year to direct activity of the Colombo Plan Bureau and the Drug Advisory Program (DAP) and to prepare recommendations on current issues for consideration by the Consultative Committee. The Bureau serves as the Plan's secretariat, conducts research, records aid flow to the region, and disseminates information on the Plan as a whole. The DAP, launched in 1973 to help ameliorate the causes and consequences of drug abuse in member states, has become one of the Plan's most active components. It is funded by voluntary contributions from several members.

Activities. Apart from the DAP agenda (supervised by an advisor to the Bureau director), current activities take two principal forms: capital aid in the form of grants and loans or commodities, including food-grain fertilizers, consumer goods, and specialized equipment; and technical cooperation, represented by services of experts and technicians, facilities for study abroad in advanced technology, and intraregional training opportunities. A Colombo Plan Staff College for technician education, established in 1974, was relocated from Singapore to Manila in 1987.

The 31st meeting of the Consultative Committee, held November 24–29, 1986, at Sydney, Australia, called for special emphasis on human resources development with particular attention to women's programs. In response to other Committee directives, the Plan in 1987 also initiated programs to promote entrepreneurship in agriculture and fisheries and to expand technical and vocational training in the private sector. The next Consultative Committee session is scheduled for Dhaka, Bangladesh in late 1988, with the role of foreign investment in economic and social development as a principal agenda item.

Figures released in 1987 showed that bilateral development aid from the six donor members surged, after a period of marginal decline, from $3.6 billion in 1985 to more than $5 billion in 1986. The total disbursements by country were: Japan—$2,696 million (up 55 percent); United States—$1,224 million (up 35 percent); United Kingdom—$434 million (up 47 percent); Australia—$384 million (down 4 percent); Canada—$270 million (down 6 percent); New Zealand—$9 million (down 11 percent).

THE COMMONWEALTH

Established: By evolutionary process formalized December 31, 1931, in the Statute of Westminster.

Purpose: To give expression to a continuing sense of affinity and to foster cooperation among states presently or formerly owing allegiance to the British Crown.

Commonwealth Center: The Secretariat is located at Marlborough House, London, which also serves as the site of Commonwealth meetings in the United Kingdom.

Principal Organs: Meeting of Heads of Government, Secretariat.

Head of the Commonwealth: Queen Elizabeth II.

Secretary General: Sir Shridath Surendranath Ramphal (Guyana).

Membership (46, with years of entry): Antigua and Barbuda (1981), Australia (1931), Bahamas (1973), Bangladesh (1972), Barbados (1966), Belize (1981), Botswana (1966), Brunei (1984), Canada (1931), Cyprus (1961), Dominica (1978), Gambia (1965), Ghana (1957), Grenada (1974), Guyana (1966), India (1947), Jamaica (1962), Kenya (1963), Kiribati (1979), Lesotho (1966), Malawi (1964), Malaysia (1957), Maldives (1982), Malta (1964), Mauritius (1968), New Zealand (1931), Nigeria (1960), Papua New Guinea (1975), St. Kitts-Nevis (1983), St. Lucia (1979), St. Vincent and the Grenadines (1979), Seychelles (1976), Sierra Leone (1961), Singapore (1965), Solomon Islands (1978), Sri Lanka (1948), Swaziland (1968), Tanzania (1961), Tonga (1970), Trinidad and Tobago (1962), Uganda (1962), United Kingdom (1931), Vanuatu (1980), Western Samoa (1970), Zambia (1964), Zimbabwe (1980). During their 1987 meeting at Vancouver, Canada, the heads of government announced that the membership of Fiji had "lapsed" as of the country's declaration of a republic on October 15. (see Activities, below).

Special Members (2): Nauru (1968), Tuvalu (1978). Both participate in functional meetings and activities and are eligible for Commonwealth technical assistance, but do not participate in the Meeting of Heads of Government.

Working Language: English.

Origin and development. A voluntary association that gradually superseded the British Empire, the Commonwealth traces its origins back to the mid-1800s, when internal self-government was first introduced in the colonies of Australia, British North America (Canada), New Zealand, and part of what was to become the Union of South Africa. The increasing maturity and independence of these overseas communities, particularly after World War I, eventually created a need to redefine the mutual relationships between the United Kingdom and the self-governing "dominions" that were collectively coming to be known as the "British Commonwealth of Nations". The Statute of Westminster, enacted by the British Parliament in 1931, established the principle that all members of the association were equal in status and in no way subordinate one to another, though united by allegiance to the Crown.

The original members of the Commonwealth, in addition to the United Kingdom, were Australia, Canada, the Irish Free State, Newfoundland, New Zealand, and the Union of South Africa. In 1949 Newfoundland became a province of Canada and the Irish Republic became an independent state outside the Commonwealth; South Africa ceased to be a member upon becoming a republic in 1961. Pakistan withdrew in 1972.

The ethnic, geographic, and economic composition of the Commonwealth has been modified fundamentally by the accession of former colonial territories in Asia, Africa, and the Western Hemisphere. This infusion of racially non-White and economically less-developed states involved significant political implications, including modification of the Commonwealth's unwritten constitution to accommodate the desire of many new members to renounce allegiance to the British Crown and adopt a republican form of government. The pattern was set when the Commonwealth prime ministers in 1949 accepted India's formal declaration that on becoming a republic it would accept the Crown as a symbol of the Commonwealth association and recognize the British sovereign as head of the Commonwealth. The new thrust was further evidenced by a North-South summit in October 1981, which reflected the fact that a majority of Commonwealth members were developing countries. Subsequently, a 1982 report, *The North-South Dialogue: Making it Work*, proposed a number of institutional and procedural reforms to facilitate global negotiations on development and related issues, while a 1983 document, *Towards a New Bretton Woods*, proposed short-, medium-, and long-range changes to enhance the efficiency and equity of the international trading and financial system.

Structure. One of the least institutionalized intergovernmental organizations, the Commonwealth was virtually without permanent machinery until the establishment of its Secretariat in 1965. The symbolic head of the organization is the reigning British monarch, who serves concurrently as constitutional sovereign in those member states that still maintain their traditional allegiance. Since World War II, the heads of government have held biennial meetings, while specialized consultations occur periodically among those national ministers responsible for such fields as foreign affairs, defense, and finance. The Secretariat organizes meetings and conferences, collects and disseminates information on behalf of the membership, and is responsible for implementing collective decisions.

Within the Secretariat, the Commonwealth Fund for Technical Cooperation (CFTC) channels technical assistance to less-developed states. The Fund is financed by all Commonwealth countries on a voluntary basis, and its governing body includes representatives of all contributors. Also within the Secretariat is a recently established Industrial Development Unit and an Adviser on Women and Development.

Activities. Cooperation in economic affairs is a vital Commonwealth activity, and the national finance ministers, meeting in the nearest convenient Commonwealth site, normally convene on the eve of the annual fall meetings of the International Monetary Fund and World Bank to discuss international monetary and economic issues. In support of their efforts, a Consultative Group on International Economic Issues was formed in 1983.

During their biennial meeting at Nassau, Bahamas, in October 1985, the heads of government issued a call for international cooperation in combating both drug trafficking and international terrorism. They also urged a ban on nuclear testing and any use of chemical weapons. As part of their continuing condemnation of South African racial policies, they appointed a Commonwealth Group of Eminent Persons (COMGEP), charged with encouraging a dialogue toward democracy and ending apartheid. In accordance with its mandate, the Group carried out an extensive program of visits to South Africa and the Frontline States in March and April 1986, subsequently issuing a report that called for coordinated sanctions against Pretoria as the only peaceful way to effect change in its racial policies.

The Thirteenth Commonwealth Games, held at Edinburgh, Scotland, on July 24-August 2, 1986, was adversely affected by Britain's stand on South Africa. In protest at the reluctance of the Thatcher government to adopt meaningful antiapartheid measures, 31 of the member countries boycotted the Games. Britain's isolation on the sanctions issue continued at a London mini-summit on August 3–5, the participants ultimately settling on an agreement to disagree. It was the first public failure on the part of Commonwealth members to achieve consensus on a major policy question.

The disagreement over South Africa continued at the Vancouver, Canada, summit on October 13–17, 1987, Prime Minister Thatcher again refusing to join the call for sanctions, although urging increased support for the Frontline States. The British position had triggered a "parallel Commonwealth conference on southern Africa" at Vancouver on October 12, during which President Kaunda of Zambia asked how "people who fought Nazi Germany [could] conspire with the Nazis of today".

A declaration on October 16 that Fiji's Commonwealth status had lapsed was in accordance with established practice regarding members who had adopted republican constitutions. However, the eligibility of such states to apply for readmission was expected to be challenged in the case of Fiji by the government of India on the ground that the new Fijian regime was blatantly racist in refusing to extend appropriate constitutional recognition to the island's Indian majority.

The next summit is scheduled for 1989 at Kuala Lumpur, Malaysia.

COUNCIL FOR MUTUAL ECONOMIC ASSISTANCE (CMEA/COMECON)

Sovet Ekonomicheskoi Vzaimopomoshchi

Established: April 1949, based on an agreement concluded at Moscow, Union of Soviet Socialist Republics, January 25, 1949; present Charter adopted December 14, 1959, with effect from April 13, 1960.

Purpose: "The Council for Mutual Economic Assistance shall have as its aim contributing, through the union and coordination of the forces of member countries of the Council, to the planned development of the national economy and an acceleration of the economic and technical progress of these countries; raising the level of industrialization of the underdeveloped countries; an uninterrupted growth in labor productivity; and a steady rise in the well-being of the peoples of the member countries."

Headquarters: Moscow, Union of Soviet Socialist Republics.

Principal Organs: Session of the Council (all members), Executive Committee (all members), Standing Commissions (all members), Secretariat.

Executive Secretary: Vyacheslav V. Sychev (USSR).

Membership (11): Albania (has not participated since 1961), Bulgaria, Cuba, Czechoslovakia, German Democratic Republic, Hungary, Mongolia, Poland, Romania, Union of Soviet Socialist Republics, Vietnam.
    Associate Member: Yugoslavia.
    Cooperating Countries (3): Finland, Iraq, Mexico.
    Observers (7): Afghanistan, Angola, Ethiopia, Laos, Mozambique, Nicaragua, People's Democratic Republic of Yemen.

Official Languages: All member countries' languages; the working language is Russian.

Origin and development. The CMEA (or Comecon) was ostensibly established as a Communist response to the Marshall Plan and the accompanying steps toward economic integration in Western Europe. Albania, Bulgaria, Czechoslovakia, Hungary, Poland, Romania, and the USSR were the original members. Albania withdrew from participation in 1961, following its break with the USSR, but has not formally withdrawn from the Charter; Yugoslavia was not an initial participant and has never become a full member. The German Democratic Republic joined in September 1950, as did the Mongolian People's Republic in June 1962 following a Charter modification permitting

membership of non-European states. Cuba joined in 1972, while Vietnam became the second Asian member in 1978. In 1973, after two years of negotiation, Finland signed an agreement for economic, scientific, and technological cooperation, thus becoming the first free-market economy to be associated with the organization; in July 1975 Iraq became the first developing country to sign such an agreement, while similar ties were established with Mexico that August. Delegations from a number of nonmember socialist states (including, most recently, those listed under Membership, above) have attended Council meetings as observers.

Between 1949 and 1955 the Council contributed little to the economic progress of the socialist bloc, serving mainly as an instrument of Soviet control over the economies of Eastern Europe. During the period of Nikita Khrushchev's ascendancy, however, the organization was accorded a more significant role. Its revised Charter, adopted in December 1959, emphasized "the many-sided economic and scientific-technical cooperation of the member countries". Areas identified as suitable for CMEA-directed planning included agriculture, transport, capital investment, trade relations, and the exchange and utilization of advanced technology.

At an April 1969 special summit conference, members agreed that greater emphasis should be placed on "socialist integration and division of labor". It was not until July 1971, however, that a comprehensive integration program emphasizing specialized production among members was adopted. Although the program included specific assurances against the creation of a supranational organization, the issue resurfaced at the 32nd Session in June 1978, when a Soviet proposal to make majority decisions binding on all members was rejected. Had it passed, the proposal would have most significantly affected Romania, which often shuns Council projects. In addition, East Germany complained that economic integration had brought increasing specialization of production and a concomitant transfer of certain elements of production from East Germany to other CMEA members. The German position appeared to be but one example of the common complaint that most of the benefits of membership go to the Soviet Union.

Structure. The Session of the Council, CMEA's principal political organ, has authority to discuss all matters within the domain of the organization and to make recommendations and decisions. All members are represented at Session meetings, which are held at least once a year (alternately in the capitals of member states) and are presided over by the head of the delegation of the host country. All decisions must be unanimous. The Executive Committee, created in June 1962, is CMEA's principal executive body; it normally meets every two months to review the organization's work and to further the coordination of national economic plans, investment programs, and trade policies.

Most of the organization's regular business is assigned to Standing Commissions, each of which is composed of experts from all member states and focuses on a particular area of responsibility, such as the chemical, power, machine-building, and electronics industries; agriculture; health;

and peaceful uses of atomic energy. In addition, the Council has established two banks, the International Bank for Economic Cooperation (IBEC) and the International Investment Bank (IIB), as well as the CMEA Institute of Standardization and the International Institute for Economic Problems of the World Socialist System.

Activities. The CMEA has recently been adversely affected by stagnation in East-West trade, a growing hard-currency debt on the part of its members, and increasing disagreement as to means of overcoming these and other economic difficulties. Disputes involving the degree to which members should decentralize their economies, introduce economic reforms, and react to Western economic sanctions resulting from events in Afghanistan and Poland figured in the delay of a planned 1983 CMEA summit. The meeting that finally convened at Moscow in June 1984 was accompanied by a complete news blackout. However, pre- and post-summit news conferences disclosed that members had agreed to formulate their future five-year plans in an integrated fashion, to increase intra-CMEA trade, and to conduct joint research and development programs in high-technology areas.

Despite outward signs of cooperation, tension was discernible among CMEA members during their 40th Session at Warsaw, Poland, in June 1985. Bulgaria, Hungary, and Romania maintained their need for increased food prices while the Soviet Union continued to complain about the inferior quality of manufactures imported from other Eastern Bloc countries. Accords were signed to develop computerized systems for industrial production and to better define the legal status, privileges, and immunities of CMEA members, and a cooperation agreement between CMEA and Mozambique was ratified. In addition, a proposal was advanced for the establishment of formal relations between CMEA and the European Community (EC). In early 1986 EC officials responded positively to the proposal and exploratory talks between representatives of the two blocs were held at Geneva, Switzerland, in September. The EC had previously rebuffed overtures by the CMEA on the ground that the latter's lack of a common commercial policy precluded its negotiating trade agreements on behalf of its members. This position remained essentially unchanged as a result of the Geneva meeting, the Western representatives continuing to argue that the Community's trade relations should be on a bilateral basis with individual CMEA countries.

The first formal summit of CMEA party leaders since 1984 convened at Moscow on November 10, 1986. The session came a week after the heads of government had met at Bucharest, Romania, to sign accords for joint production enterprises and other activities designed to heighten cooperation among members by reducing bureaucratic barriers. Observers attributed its timing to the urgency that Soviet leader Gorbachev attributed to the infusion of new dynamism into the East European economies. However, an official description of the talks as "frank", coupled with unusual secrecy surrounding them, seemed to suggest that disagreement continued among CMEA members. Significantly, little CMEA activity was reported during 1987 prior to a special session at Moscow on October 13–14, during which support was again voiced for formal ties with the EC, aid increases to non-European members, development of currency convertibility, and restructuring of CMEA "machinery".

COUNCIL OF ARAB ECONOMIC UNITY (CAEU)

Established: By resolution of the Arab Economic Council of the League of Arab States at Cairo, Egypt, June 3, 1957, effective at its first meeting May 30, 1964.

Purpose: To provide a flexible framework for achieving economic integration of Arab states.

Headquarters: 'Amman, Jordan.

Principal Organs: Council (all members), General Secretariat.

Secretary General: Mahdi M. al-Obaidi.

Membership (13): Egypt, Iraq, Jordan, Kuwait, Libya, Mauritania, Palestine Liberation Organization, Somalia, Sudan, Syria, United Arab Emirates, Yemen Arab Republic, Yemen People's Democratic Republic. Egypt's membership was suspended in 1979.

Official Language: Arabic.

Origin and development: In January 1956, the Arab League agreed on the necessity for an organization that would deal specifically with the economic problems of Arab countries. As a result, on June 3, 1957, a resolution was passed creating the Council of Arab Economic Unity. The organization officially came into existence on May 30, 1964.

Structure: The Council, consisting of the economic, finance, and trade ministers of member states, meets twice a year to discuss and vote on the organization's agenda. The Secretariat oversees implementation; it also has the duty of drawing up the work plans which are presented to the Council.

Activities: Since its inception, activities have focused on furthering economic development and encouraging economic cooperation between Arab countries. To promote these ends, an Arab Common Market was established by the Council in 1964. The Market's initial aim to abolish all taxes and other duties levied on items of trade between Arab countries was achieved in 1971. The second part of the plan, a customs union of all members, formed part of the Council's 1981–1985 work plan, but has not yet been fully implemented. In June 1985 an agreement was concluded with the Council for Mutual Economic Assistance (CMEA) for cooperation in a variety of scientific and technical areas.

The 1986–1990 work plan retained most of the emphasis of recent years, including study of ways to form joint Arab companies and federations, to coordinate agricultural and industrial programs, and to improve existing road and railway networks.

COUNCIL OF EUROPE

Conseil de l'Europe

Established: By statute signed at London, England, May 5, 1949, effective August 3, 1949; structure defined by General Agreement signed September 2, 1949.

Purpose: "To work for greater European unity, to improve the conditions of life and develop human values in Europe, and to uphold the principles of parliamentary democracy, the rule of law and human rights."

Headquarters: Strasbourg, France.

Principal Organs: Committee of Ministers (all members), Parliamentary Assembly (170 parliamentary delegates are authorized, although 3 seats allocated to Cyprus have been vacant since 1965), Conference of Local and Regional Authorities, Secretariat.

Secretary General: Marcelino Oreja Aguirre (Spain).

Membership (21): Austria, Belgium, Cyprus, Denmark, France, Federal Republic of Germany, Greece, Iceland, Ireland, Italy, Liechtenstein, Luxembourg, Malta, Netherlands, Norway, Portugal, Spain, Sweden, Switzerland, Turkey, United Kingdom. (Accession procedures have begun for San Marino and in early 1988 Finland announced its intention to apply for membership.)
Observer for Parliamentary Assembly: Israel.

Official Languages: English, French. German and Italian are also working languages in the Parliamentary Assembly.

Origin and development. In 1946 Winston Churchill put forward at Zürich, Switzerland, his plan for a "United States of Europe", and an implementing program was subsequently drawn up at Hertenstein, Switzerland, by former European resistance fighters. International groups were quickly established, and one of the most important of these, the Union of European Federalists, joined Churchill's United Europe Movement, the Economic League for European Cooperation, and the French Council for United Europe to form an International Committee of Movements for European Unity. Under the leadership of the Englishman Duncan Sandys, the Committee organized the first Congress of Europe at The Hague, Netherlands, in May 1948, and called for the establishment of a European Assembly and other measures to unite Western Europe. Meanwhile, the signatories of the five-power Brussels Treaty of March 17, 1948, took up the proposals at the governmental level. These combined efforts came to fruition on May 5, 1949, when the foreign ministers of Belgium, Denmark, France, Ireland, Italy, Luxembourg, Netherlands, Norway, Sweden, and the United Kingdom met at London to sign the Statute of the Council of Europe.

The organization was conceived essentially as an instrument for promoting increased unity in Western Europe through discussion and, where appropriate, common action in the economic, social, cultural, scientific, legal, and administrative areas, and in the protection of human rights. Matters relating to national defense were specifically excluded from its scope. Greece, admitted in 1949, was obliged to withdraw in 1969 because of alleged violations of human rights by the Papadopoulos government; it was readmitted on November 28, 1974, after a change of government in July and the holding of parliamentary elections on November 17. The newest member, Liechtenstein, was admitted on November 23, 1978. Turkey's credentials were suspended in May 1981, in response to the military coup of the previous September. In September 1983, the Assembly also voted to bar members from the new Turkish legislature because of the unrepresentative character of their election. However, the action was rescinded in May 1985, following a report by the Council's Political and Legal Affairs Committee that progress had been made over the last year in the restoration of democracy and respect for human rights.

Structure. The Committee of Ministers, composed of the foreign ministers of all member states, considers all actions required to further the aims of the Council and makes recommendations, which are based on the rule of unanimity, to member governments. The Committee normally meets twice a year at the ministerial level, at the headquarters or at Paris, France. Most of its current work, however, is performed by deputies who meet about ten times a year at Strasbourg, France.

The Parliamentary Assembly, the deliberative organ, can consider any matter within the competence of the Council. Its conclusions, if they call for action by governments, take the form of recommendations to the Committee of Ministers. The members of the Assembly are drawn from national parliaments and apportioned according to population, the states with the smallest populations having 2 seats and those with the largest, 18. The method of delegate selection is left to the national parliaments. Within the Assembly all members participate not as state representatives but as individuals or as representatives of political groups; each delegation includes spokesmen from both the government and the opposition. The president of the Parliament is elected for a renewable term of one year; normally he is reelected and serves a total of three years.

Part of the Council's work is carried out by specialized institutions, such as the European Commission of Human Rights, the European Court of Human Rights, the European Youth Foundation, and the Conference of Local and Regional Authorities. The last, comprising local and regional representatives of member states, serves as a liaison between the Council and the European Community (EC).

The Council's parliamentary, ministerial, and governmental committees are serviced by some 800 officials recruited from all member countries and divided among eight directorates and the Office of the Clerk of the Assembly. The secretary general, deputy secretary general, and clerk of the assembly are elected for renewable, five-year terms by the Assembly from a list of candidates proposed by the Committee of Ministers.

Activities. Possibly the most significant achievements of the Council have been the drafting and implementation of the European Convention for the Protection of Human Rights and Fundamental Freedoms (together with protocols) and the establishment of the European Commission of Human Rights and the European Court of Human Rights. Dissatisfied with the declaratory character of the Universal Declaration of Human Rights adopted by the UN General Assembly in 1948, the Parliamentary Assembly at its first session in 1949 recommended the adoption of a specifically European Convention. Signed in November 1950 and entering into force in September 1953, the Convention set up the European Commission, composed of one independent lawyer from each member state, to examine alleged violations by signatory states.

In April 1983 a protocol calling for the abolition of capital punishment was signed by 12 Council members; it entered into force in February 1985, following ratification by five signatories who had abolished, or promised to abolish, the death penalty. An additional protocol, approved in November 1984, seeks to protect the rights of aliens in cases of expulsion, the right of appeal in trial cases, the right of compensation for miscarriage of justice, the right not to be tried twice for the same offense, and the equality of spouses. A further development in the area of human rights was the signature by ten members (plus Canada and the United States) of a pact to allow persons convicted abroad to serve their sentences in prisons in their home countries, with a possibility of penalty reduction without the consent of the sentencing authorities. Most recently, a protocol for the prevention of torture or other abuse of prisoners was opened for signature in November 1987.

Following a recommendation of the Parliamentary Assembly, a Commission of Eminent European Personalities, headed by former Italian Prime Minister Emilio Colombo, convened in January 1985 to examine "perspectives for European cooperation beyond the present decade". Subsequently, with particular reference to the European Community. The group urged increased dialogue in such areas as culture, education, human rights, and science and technology.

During its 1987 meetings the Committee of Ministers reviewed East-West relations, exchanged views on the Middle East, and pledged further cooperation with the EC. It also explored ways to promote the cultural sector, in light of dwindling government resources for that purpose, and adopted recommendations for a common European AIDS-prevention program.

Topics addressed by the 1987 Assembly included the breakdown of "social cohesion" as the result of drug use; "xenophobia" over refugees and migrants; nuclear accidents and the related issue of the potential negative impact on society of scientific and technological change; proposed increased economic cooperation with Africa; and projected expansion of the European high-speed train network. In response to committee reports which described the organization as "extremely ill-equipped and staffed" and suffering from governmental and public apathy, the Assembly called on member states to increase their financial contributions and to be more receptive to Council proposals.

COUNCIL OF THE ENTENTE

Conseil de l'Entente

Established: May 29, 1959, at Abidjan, Côte d'Ivoire, by convention signed by representatives of states formerly forming part of French West Africa.

Purpose: To promote political, economic, and social coordination among the member states.

Headquarters: Abidjan, Côte d'Ivoire.

Principal Organs: Council (all members), Ministerial Council (all members), Mutual Aid and Loan Guarantee Fund (all members), Secretariat.

Administrative Secretary: Paul Kaya (Côte d'Ivoire).

Membership (5): Benin, Burkina Faso, Côte d'Ivoire, Niger, Togo.

Official Language: French.

Origin and development. The Council was formed in 1959 by Benin (then Dahomey), Burkina Faso (then Upper Volta), Côte d'Ivoire, and Niger; Togo joined in 1966. In its early years the Council was seen as a vehicle for Côte d'Ivoire, by far the most economically and politically powerful member, to promote its preeminence in the face of other actual and proposed West African groupings. In 1965, however, Ivorian President Houphouët-Boigny's proposal to grant dual nationality to resident nationals from the other member states was dropped because of strong domestic opposition. The Council has had little political impact since, confining most of its activity to the economic sphere. Thus, as part of a 1966 reorganization, the Council adopted a convention establishing the Mutual Aid and Loan Guarantee Fund. The Fund seeks to promote economic development and regional integration; to assist in preparing specific economic projects; to obtain assistance from donor organizations; and to promote increased trade, commerce, and investment both among the members of the Entente and with their neighbors. In 1970 an associated Economic Community of Livestock and Meat (*Communauté Economique du Bétail et de la Viande*—CEBV) was established to provide technical and financial support for the region's cattle industry.

Structure. The organization's principal organ, the Council, encompasses the members' heads of state. It meets periodically, the location of meetings rotating among the capitals of the members. Council sessions are preceded by meetings of a Ministerial Council composed of representatives of the five governments.

In accordance with a modified structure adopted in December 1973, the Mutual Aid and Loan Guarantee Fund is governed by a Board of Directors composed of the five heads of state. Its Management Committee, which meets twice a year, handles administrative and financial matters, including the approval of guarantees. An administrative Secretariat considers applications for guarantees, the reduction of interest rates, and the extension of loan repayment periods, as well as providing various regional centers with support for technical assistance, development, and cooperation.

Activities. Over the past two decades, the member states have set up a number of institutional arrangements to cover various aspects of development. Thus, the Council has established a port and harbor administration, a railway and road traffic administration, and a unified quarantine organization. In early 1976, a draft agreement was initialed guaranteeing further cooperation in land transport, telecommunications, tourism, water prospecting, and surveying.

Recent programs have concentrated on food production and village water projects, as well as expansion of the energy and tourism sectors. In addition, the CEBV has become increasingly active, inaugurating a campaign in early 1987 against an "invasion" of heavily subsidized non-African meat.

In February 1987 several French banks signed a deposit agreement for 268 million French francs (approximately $44 million) with the Mutual Aid and Loan Guarantee Fund which was expected to strengthen Council operations. The Council's budget, however, has been declining regularly in the 1980s, the 1987 total being set at 1.1 billion CFA francs ($3.6 million), as contrasted with 1.24 billion in 1986.

Regional security issues have also been the object of recent Council attention, prompting a summit in September 1985 in the wake of "sabotage and terrorism" in Niger in June and in Togo in August. The meeting yielded a resolution pledging cooperative action to counter destabilization. However, President Sankara of Burkina Faso expressed reservations on the "sincerity" of the resolution, apparently because of the harboring of Burkinabe dissidents by other member states. Following Sankara's death in an October 1987 coup, his successor, Capt. Blaise Compaoré, pledged to "try to go as far as possible" in strengthening relations with other Council members.

CUSTOMS CO-OPERATION COUNCIL (CCC)

Conseil de Coopération Douaniere

Established: By convention signed by the 13 governments comprising the Committee for European Economic Co-operation on December 15, 1950.

Purpose: To study questions relating to cooperation in customs matters among members; to examine political and economic aspects of customs systems with the hope of achieving harmony and uniformity; to promote international cooperation in customs matters.

Headquarters: Brussels, Belgium.

Principal Organs: Council (all members), Subordinate Committees (Customs Valuation, Enforcement, Finance, Interim Harmonized System, Nomenclature, Permanent Technical, Staff Appeals, Valuation), Secretariat.

Secretary General: Glenn Robert Dickerson (United States).

Membership (102): Algeria, Argentina, Australia, Austria, Bahamas, Bangladesh, Belgium, Botswana, Brazil, Bulgaria, Burkina Faso, Burundi, Cameroon, Canada, Central African Republic, Chile, China, Congo, Côte d'Ivoire, Cyprus, Czechoslovakia, Denmark, Egypt, Ethiopia, Finland, France, Gabon, Federal Republic of Germany, Ghana, Greece, Guatemala, Guyana, Haiti, Hong Kong, Hungary, Iceland, India, Indonesia, Iran, Ireland, Israel, Italy, Jamaica, Japan, Jordan, Kenya, Republic of Korea, Lebanon, Lesotho, Liberia, Libya, Luxembourg, Madagascar, Malawi, Malaysia, Mali, Malta, Mauritania, Mauritius, Mexico, Morocco, Mozambique, Nepal, Netherlands, New Zealand, Niger, Nigeria, Norway, Pakistan, Paraguay, Peru, Philippines, Poland, Portugal, Romania, Rwanda, Saudi Arabia, Senegal, Sierra Leone, Singapore, South Africa, Spain, Sri Lanka, Sudan, Swaziland, Sweden, Switzerland, Syria, Tanzania, Thailand, Trinidad and Tobago, Tunisia, Turkey, Uganda, United Arab Emirates, United Kingdom, United States, Uruguay, Yugoslavia, Zaire, Zambia, Zimbabwe.

Official Languages: English, French.

Origin and development. In an effort to facilitate the movement of goods within Western Europe and thereby aid in post-World War II reconstruction, the 13 governments comprising the Committee for European Economic Co-operation issued a joint declaration in September 1947 establishing a study group to consider the feasibility of a European customs union. A year later the group created an Economic Committee (disbanded following the formation of the Organization for European Economic Co-operation, predecessor of the OECD) and a Customs Committee, the latter to be assisted by a Permanent Tariff Bureau. In 1949, however, the study group abandoned the concept of a customs union as an immediate priority, choosing instead to standardize customs definitions and procedures. As a result, three conventions were signed on December 15, 1950, establishing the Customs Co-operation Council and adopting the Brussels Definition of Value and the Brussels Nomenclature. Participation in the Council does not oblige members to adopt regulations and recommendations incompatible with their existing policies.

Structure. Of the CCC's eight subsidiary committees, the Valuation Committee is responsible for the operation of the Convention on the Valuation of Goods for Customs Purposes, while the Nomenclature Committee supervises the Convention on Nomenclature for the Classification of Goods in Customs Tariffs. The Harmonized Systems Committee studies methods for harmonizing the disparate instruments now being used in international trade. Administrative functions are directed by the Secretariat.

Activities. In the interest of liberalizing international trade, the CCC continues to discuss and propose practical means for harmonizing and standardizing customs systems. The Council also disseminates information on customs procedures and advises members on matters of nomenclature and valuation. In recent years, various services and technical assistance have been extended to non-member developing countries.

During 1985–1986 the Council's Enforcement Committee sought to promote more effective action by members to combat customs offences, including piracy and counterfeiting, while an exhibition of technical aids to enforcement was presented at the 67th/68th annual sessions at Brussels on June 23–27, 1986. In 1987 the Council intensified its efforts to combat drug smuggling in cooperation with other international organizations; studied the application of computers to the customs field; initiated a public relations campaign to gain wider public awareness of Council activities; and reviewed the growing problem of the smuggling of endangered wildlife. In what was expected to be a major step forward in the achievement of CCC goals, the Harmonized Commodity Description and Coding System, providing universal customs nomenclature, went into force on January 1, 1988. By midyear 43 countries, accounting for more than 50 percent of world trade, were applying the system.

ECONOMIC COMMUNITY OF CENTRAL AFRICAN STATES (CEEAC)

Communauté Economique des Etats de l'Afrique Centrale

Established: By treaty signed by the heads of state of the member countries on October 18, 1983, at Libreville, Gabon.

Purpose: To end customs duties and other restrictions on trade between the member countries and establish a common market by the year 2000.

Headquarters: Libreville, Gabon.

Principal Organs: Conference of the Heads of State and Government (all members), Council of Ministers (all members), Directorates, Secretariat.

Secretary General: Lunda Bululu (Zaire).

Membership (10): Burundi, Cameroon, Central African Republic, Chad, Congo, Equatorial Guinea, Gabon, Rwanda, Sao Tome and Principe, Zaire.
Observer: Angola.

Official Languages: French, Portuguese.

Origin and development. In 1977 President Mobutu Sese Seko of Zaire proposed a merger of the three-member Economic Community of the Great Lakes Countries (CEPGL, below), with the four-member Central African Customs and Economic Union (UDEAC) to form a francophone Central African grouping. The proposal resurfaced in 1981 yielding, in December, the UDEAC Libreville Declaration, which called for the establishment of a group comprising the members of CEPGL and UDEAC plus Angola, Chad, Equatorial Guinea, and Sao Tome and Principe. The resulting CEEAC was formally inaugurated at Libreville, Gabon, on December 21, 1985, in accordance with a treaty concluded at Libreville on October 18, 1983.

At a summit meeting of the founding states at Brazzaville, Congo, on December 17, 1984, Congolese President Denis Sassou-Nguesso reiterated the need for a Central African common market as "the African reply to the total failure of attempts to establish a new economic world order". He added that "Inter-African trade, which represented 5.2 percent of continental trade in 1970, is at present about 2.9 percent". At the summit, the initial budget for the organization was set at $1.9 million, with member contributions varying from 18 to 3.8 percent.

Structure. The principal government body of the CEEAC is the Conference of Heads of States and Government, which meets annually. There is also a Council of Ministers, a number of standing directorates, and a Secretariat.

Activities. At the formal launching of the CEEAC, Secretary General Bululu declared that the aim of the organization was to "promote and reinforce cooperation and a sustained and balanced development in all areas of both economic and social activity between member states".

At the second CEEAC summit, held at Yaounde, Cameroon, on January 23–24, 1986, the Conference received a report from the Council of Ministers and adopted a number of standing regulations governing the organization's activities. It approved a 1986 budget of $3.2 million and charged the secretary general with the drafting of a program of action aimed at increasing intra-Community trade, also requesting that he prepare a study on Community transport and communications infrastructure. In July, the central bank governors of the member states met at Libreville, Gabon, to consider the establishment of a clearing house for the diverse national currencies in use in the area, while in January 1987 the governors announced plans to establish an Association of Commercial Banks for Central Africa. Subsequently, the CEEAC Committee for Trade, Customs, and Immigration recommended the progressive elimination of tariff barriers between members. These and other economic goals were reaffirmed at the third CEEAC summit, held at Libreville, Gabon, in August 1987, although there was little reported discussion as to their implementation.

At the fourth CEEAC summit, held at Kinshasa, Zaire, on February 26–27, 1988, a $3.6 budget was adopted for

1988, even though significant arrears were reported in members' contributions to the $2.5 million 1987 budget.

ECONOMIC COMMUNITY OF THE GREAT LAKES COUNTRIES (CEPGL)

Communauté Economique des Pays des Grands Lacs

Established: By convention signed by the heads of state of the member countries on September 26, 1976, at Gisenyi, Rwanda.

Purpose: To promote regional economic integration; to increase security and welfare for the region; to facilitate political, cultural, technical, and scientific cooperation among the members; and to contribute to the strengthening of national sovereignty and African unity.

Headquarters: Gisenyi, Rwanda.

Principal Organs: Conference of Heads of States (all members), Council of Ministers and State Commissioners (all members), Arbitration Commission, Specialized Technical Commissions, Permanent Executive Secretariat.

Executive Secretary: Antoine Nduwayo (Burundi).

Membership (3): Burundi, Rwanda, Zaire.

Official Language: French.

Origin and development. The first proposal for the creation of an organization concerned with the social, cultural, economic, and political problems of the Central African subregion emerged from discussions held during a 1966 summit meeting of the heads of state of Burundi, Rwanda, and Zaire (then the Democratic Republic of the Congo). On August 29, at the conclusion of their four-day summit at Kinshasa, the three leaders signed a mutual security pact, while Burundi and the DRC signed trade and cultural agreements that contained provisions for closer policy coordination and cooperation. The Kinshasa agreement was reaffirmed during a tripartite summit in 1974 and was strengthened with the addition of clauses on refugees, undesirable aliens, and joint promotion of tourism, communication, and social security measures. In May 1975 the three states' foreign ministers met to discuss a draft general convention on economic, technical, scientific, and cultural cooperation, the final version of which, establishing the Economic Community of the Great Lakes Countries, was signed by the heads of state of Burundi, Rwanda, and Zaire on September 20, 1976. In 1980 the Development Bank of the Great Lakes States (*Banque de Développement des Etats des Grands Lacs*—BDEGL) was inaugurated at Goma, Zaire, to finance Community projects. The subse-

quent Economic Community of Central African States (*Communauté Economique des Etats de l'Afrique Centrale*—CEEAC, above) was formally launched in October 1983 by a treaty signed at Libreville, Gabon, to which all three CEPGL states were signatories. Although left open to "any country in the region which wished to join it in order to contribute to the strengthening of African unity", CEPGL's own membership has remained at three.

Structure. The legal authority of CEPGL is vested in the Conference of the Heads of State, which normally meets once a year to approve the Community's budget and action program. Preparation for the annual summits and the implementation of CEPGL resolutions are responsibilities of the Council of Ministers and State Commissioners. Technical and administrative assistance for both groups is provided by the Permanent Executive Secretariat.

Activities. Although emerging from a mutual security pact and spurred in part by the member states' proximity to South Africa, Community activities have focused on economic issues. To promote economic development and integration, the Community has proposed a number of projects, including development of the Ruzizi River Valley for hydroelectric power, methane gas extraction from Lake Kivu, coordination of members' transportation and communications networks, and joint cement, bottling, and agricultural materials production. The CEPGL has also acted to harmonize regulation in car insurance and investment, to increase freedom of movement of goods and people, and to coordinate health, agricultural, and other basic research. The Community's current five-year plan (1987–1991) calls for community projects in agriculture, industry, energy, tourism, and communications, with additional provision for monetary cooperation and the harmonization of pricing policies.

During their ninth summit at Gbadolite, Zaire, in November 1986, the CEPGL heads of state authorized the BDEGL to finance construction of five radio relay stations to link telecommunications among the member states. In addition, the heads of state endorsed the creation of a regional dairy industry and called for a study of the impact of proposed preferential tariffs for industrial products on the customs earnings of regional states. A decision on the imposition of the tariffs was delayed for at least one more year at the tenth summit in January 1988 at Bujumbura, Burundi.

ECONOMIC COMMUNITY OF WEST AFRICAN STATES (ECOWAS/CEDEAO)

Communauté Economique des Etats de l'Afrique de l'Ouest

Established: By Treaty of Lagos (Nigeria), signed May 28, 1975.

Purpose: The ending of customs duties and other restrictions on trade between member states; the establishment of a common external tariff and commercial policy; and the "harmonization of the economic and industrial policies of the Member-states and the elimination of the disparities in levels of development of the Member-states".

Headquarters: Lagos, Nigeria.

Principal Organs: Supreme Authority of Heads of State and Government (all members); Council of Ministers (all members); Specialized Commissions; Community Tribunal; Fund for Cooperation, Compensation, and Development (FCCD); Executive Secretariat.

Executive Secretary: Momadu Munu (Sierra Leone).

Membership (16): Benin, Burkina Faso, Cape Verde Islands, Côte d'Ivoire, Gambia, Ghana, Guinea, Guinea-Bissau, Liberia, Mali, Mauritania, Niger, Nigeria, Senegal, Sierra Leone, Togo.

Official Languages: English, French.

Origin and development. The Economic Community of West African States received its greatest impetus from discussions in October 1974 between General Yakubu Gowon of Nigeria and President Gnassingbé Eyadéma of Togo, who advanced plans for a more comprehensive economic grouping than the purely francophone West African Economic Community (see separate entry). The Treaty establishing ECOWAS was signed by representatives of 15 West African states at Lagos, Nigeria, May 28, 1975, and by the end of June had been formally ratified by enough signatories (7) to become operative. However, it took until November 1976 for an agreement to be worked out on protocols to the Treaty. The long delay resulted in part from Senegal's effort to make its ratification dependent upon a broadening of the Community to include Zaire and several other francophone states of Central Africa. Ultimately, it was decided that any such expansion would be unrealistic.

After five years of negotiation, the ECOWAS heads of state and government agreed, at their May 1980 summit conference, to initiate a trade liberalization program, with customs duties on local raw materials and handicrafts to be eliminated as of May 1981. The sixth ECOWAS summit, held in 1981, marked the implementation of the first stage of the program, during which the more developed members reduced internal tariffs over a four-year period, less developed members being given an eight-year timetable. In addition, the summit participants agreed in principle to a mutual defense pact under which defense units would carry out joint maneuvers that would be mobilized to defend a member under external attack or to act as a peacekeeping force in the event of intra-Community conflict. In response to constraints on the free movement of people among member countries, ECOWAS has approved protocols permitting three-month stays without visas and endorsing the right of individuals to employment anywhere in the community. However, the latter protocol has yet to be ratified by the required minimum of seven members.

Structure. The basic structure of ECOWAS consists of a Supreme Authority of Heads of State and Government with a rotating chairmanship; a Council of Ministers with two representatives from each member; an Executive Secretariat appointed for a four-year period; a Community Tribunal to settle disputes arising under the Treaty; and four Specialized Commissions: Trade, Industry, Transport, and Social Affairs.

A Fund for Cooperation, Compensation, and Development (FCCD) is supported by members' contributions and the revenues of Community enterprises. In addition to financing mutually approved projects, the Fund, headquartered at Lomé, Togo, compensates members who suffer losses due to the establishment of Community enterprises or to the liberalization of trade.

Activities. ECOWAS has been criticized for failing to meet expectations because of inadequate implementation of numerous summit decisions. The Community's image has also been weakened by internal discord (including disputes between Liberia and Sierra Leone and between Burkina Faso and Mali), financial delinquencies, expulsions of foreign nationals (most importantly by Nigeria in 1984–1985), and occasional border closings.

During the ninth summit, held at Abuja, Nigeria, on June 30–July 2, 1986, Nigerian President Babangida urged member states not to permit ECOWAS to "sink", his country's apparent rededication to the organization raising hopes that its effectiveness would increase. The subsequent summit, held at Abuja in July 1987, formally approved a four-year, $926 million economic recovery program involving 136 regional and national projects, many of them relating to food production and processing. About 70 percent of the funding was expected to come from outside ECOWAS, leaders hoping that Western donors particularly would begin to view the Community in a more positive light. In other action the summit leaders authorized the creation of a West African Health Organization to reduce duplication of efforts by separate anglophone and francophone groups; created a West African Women's Association; called for a special conference on the external debt crisis; endorsed regional tourism and telecommunications projects; and attended groundbreaking ceremonies for a new $16.6 million ECOWAS secretariat building at Abuja. The summit also endorsed monetary cooperation as the first step toward a single monetary zone using a common currency (observers noting that formidable barriers stood in the way of the plan's realization).

Further underlining continued political discord among members and the preeminence of Nigeria within the community, President Babangida of Nigeria was elected for a third year as chairman after the nomination of (then) President Sankara of Burkina Faso had been blocked by objections from Togo and Côte d'Ivoire.

THE EUROPEAN COMMUNITIES

The European Communities (EC) is the collective designation of the twelve-state European Coal and Steel Community (ECSC), European Economic Community (EEC, also known as the Common Market), and European Atomic Energy Community (Euratom). Because all three have been serviced for the past two decades by Common Institutions, without separate bureaucracies, reference to a singular "European Community" has been formally encouraged by the European Parliament (below) and is the style most frequently employed by the Commission of the European Communities and much of the world's press.

Common Institutions

The Common Institutions of the European Communities were established by treaty signed at Brussels, Belgium, April 8, 1965, effective July 1, 1967. Each of the three component organizations has its own treaty origins, as discussed below.

Headquarters: Brussels, Belgium.

Principal Organs: European Council (heads of state or government of all members), Council of Ministers (all members), Commission (17 members, appointed by the member governments), European Parliament (518 representatives), Court of Justice (13 judges).

Presidency of the Council of Ministers: Rotates every six months by alphabetical order of member states.

President of the Commission: Jacques Delors (France).

President of the Parliament: Sir Henry Plumb (United Kingdom).

President of the Court: Lord MacKenzie Stuart (United Kingdom).

Members of the Three Communities (12): Belgium, Denmark, France, Federal Republic of Germany, Greece, Ireland, Italy, Luxembourg, Netherlands, Portugal, Spain, United Kingdom.

Official Languages: Danish, Dutch, English, French, Gaelic, German, Greek, Italian, Portuguese, Spanish.

Origin and development. A treaty fusing the Communities' institutions and establishing a single Council of Ministers, Commission, Parliament, and Court of Justice was signed by the (then) six member governments (Belgium, France, Federal Republic of Germany, Italy, Luxembourg, Netherlands) at Brussels, Belgium, on April 8, 1965, but its application was delayed by prolonged disagreement over the selection of a president to head the newly merged Commission. The choice of Jean Rey of Belgium was ultimately approved, and the new institutions were formally established as of July 1, 1967. Denmark, Ireland, and the United Kingdom joined the grouping on January 1, 1973; Greenland, having become internally independent of Danish rule in 1979, was permitted, on the basis of a 1982 referendum, to terminate its relationship on February 1, 1985; Portugal and Spain were admitted to membership on January 1, 1986.

Structure. The shared institutional framework of the EC has the same basic components as those originally allotted to the individual Communities: a Council of Ministers to provide overall policy direction, an expert Commission charged with guidance and management responsibilities, a European Parliament to represent the public, and a Court of Justice to adjudicate legal issues.

The Council of Ministers is the only EC institution that directly represents the member governments. Depending on the subject under discussion, they may be represented by their foreign ministers, as is usually the case for major decisions, or by other ministers. In dealing with ECSC matters, the Council is mainly limited to voicing an opinion before the Commission makes a decision, although Council approval (usually by majority vote) is required on certain fundamental issues before Commission decisions become binding. On matters relating to the EEC and Euratom, the Council makes the final policy decision, but it does so on the basis of Commission proposals that can be modified only by unanimous vote. As a result of the Luxembourg compromise in 1966, the principle of unanimity was also retained for issues in which a member feels it has a "vital interest".

The Commission of the European Communities consists of 17 members, 2 each from France, the Federal Republic of Germany, Italy, Spain, and the United Kingdom, and 1 each from the other seven states. In general, the Commission mediates between the member governments in Community matters, exercises a broad range of executive powers, and initiates Community action. Its members are completely independent and are forbidden by treaty to accept instructions from any national government. Decisions are made by majority vote.

The European Parliament is responsible for advising the Commission and, save for deference to the Council in regard to agricultural spending, participates in formulation of the annual EC budget, a draft of which, by a two-thirds vote, it may reject. It may also dismiss the Commission by vote of censure. The first direct elections to the Parliament were completed in June 1979, its (then) 410 seats being divided as follows: France, the Federal Republic of Germany, Italy, and the United Kingdom, 81 each; Netherlands, 25; Belgium, 24; Denmark, 16; Ireland, 15; and Luxembourg, 6. On January 1, 1981, 24 Greek representatives were added, bringing the total seats to 434. Upon the admission of Portugal and Spain, with 24 and 60 representatives, respectively, the total number of seats rose to 518. Each country determines how it will organize constituencies and voting, and whether European Parliament delegates may be members of national legislatures.

The Court of Justice has the power to decide whether acts of the Commission, the Council of Ministers, the member governments, and other bodies are compatible with the governing treaties. Thus, it ruled in 1986 that the budget approved in December 1985 was invalid because of spending increases voted by the Parliament without Council concurrence. It also may rule in cases submitted by national courts regarding interpretation of the treaties and implementing legislation. In a seminal decision, the Court ruled in October 1979 that the Commission had the authority to represent the EC in global commodity agreement negotiations, with participation by individual member states being dependent on considerations such as whether the EC as a whole or the separate states were to be responsible for financial arrangements (particularly in regard to buffer stocks).

In addition to the institutions established by the 1965 treaty, a number of other influential organs have evolved, the most important being the European Council. Comprising the heads of state or government of the participating countries, the Council resulted from a December 1974 summit conference agreement that EC leaders should convene regularly (at present twice a year) not only to address questions of European policy but to provide overall guidance to foreign ministers who meet quarterly to coordinate their respective foreign policies.

In late 1985 the Council approved a number of reforms, most of which were ultimately included in The Single European Act, which amended the Treaty of Rome in ways intended to streamline the decision-making process, open up more areas to EC jurisdiction, and reinvigorate the movement toward European economic and political cooperation. The Act, which went into effect July 1, 1987, following ratification by each EC member, calls for the establishment of a wholly integrated internal market by 1992 with increased use of majority voting within the Council of Ministers in this and other areas. The powers of the European Parliament were also expanded and, in what many observers consider one of the Act's most important provisions, a permanent secretariat, headquartered at Brussels, Belgium, was established to assist the presidency of the Council of Ministers in implementing a framework of European political cooperation.

Activities. All EC activities are now carried out by personnel of the Common Institutions although most are discussed under the treaty groupings listed below. Issues not officially within the purview of a specific Community can be addressed by means of a "gap-filling" provision (Art. 235) of the Treaty of Rome intended to avoid excessive recourse to treaty amendment. The Single European Act addressed some of those issues, including foreign policy (an area in which the EC has been seeking a more unified position). In particular, measures to combat terrorism have been a focus of recent debate, although EC members have thus far been able to agree on little more than the sharing of intelligence information. In 1986 Britain, convinced that the Syrian government had been involved in a bomb attempt at Heathrow Airport, called for extensive EC retaliatory measures against Damascus. After initial hesitation, 10 of the 11 other EC members (Greece dissenting) banned

new arms sales to Syria and suspended high-level contacts with the Assad government. Except for Britain, however, the EC members in July 1987 decided to reestablish ministerial contacts with Syria as part of a revived Middle Eastern peace initiative.

In recent years the Community has also attempted to formulate common policy in regard to South Africa although opposition from Britain and Portugal in May 1987 blocked a proposed "charter of principles" that would have governed EC anti-apartheid measures.

In July 1987 the EC announced that Morocco's application for membership had been rejected "on a geographic basis". Earlier in the year Turkey's membership application was referred to the Commission for a review that was expected to take at least several years in view of EC concerns over Turkey's human rights record, its underdeveloped economy, and its strained relationship with Greece.

EUROPEAN COAL AND STEEL COMMUNITY
(ECSC)
*Communauté Européenne du Charbon
et de l'Acier*
(CECA)

Established: By treaty signed at Paris, France, on April 18, 1951, effective July 25, 1952.

Purpose: To ensure adequate supplies of coal and steel, to establish the lowest reasonable prices, to equalize access to coal and steel by all consumers within the customs union, to regulate the industries in order to ensure rational utilization of resources, to expand production and international trade, and to improve the living and working conditions of the work force of the industries.

Membership: (See Common Institutions).

Origin and development. The formation of the European Communities was one of the most significant expressions of the movement toward European unity that grew out of the moral and material devastation of World War II. For many Europeans, the creation of a United States of Europe seemed to offer the best hope of avoiding a repetition of that catastrophe. Other influences included the fear of Soviet aggression and the practical experience in economic cooperation gained by administering Marshall Plan aid through the Organization for European Economic Cooperation (OEEC).

These elements converged in a 1950 proposal by French Foreign Minister Robert Schuman envisaging the establishment of a common market for coal and steel that would, among other things, serve as a lasting guarantee of European peace by forging an organic link between France and Germany. Although the United Kingdom declined to participate in the project, the governments of France, the Federal Republic of Germany, Italy, Belgium, the Netherlands, and Luxembourg agreed early in 1951 to put the "Schuman Plan" into effect. The original institutional structure of the ECSC, whose headquarters was established in Luxembourg, included a Council of Ministers, an executive High Authority, a parliamentary Assembly, and a Court of Justice.

As the first of the three Communities, the ECSC pioneered the concept of a European common market by abolishing price and transport discrimination and eliminating customs duties, quota restrictions, and other trade barriers on coal, steel, iron ore, and scrap. A common market for coal, iron ore, and scrap was established on February 1, 1953; for steel, on May 1, 1953; and for special steels, on August 1, 1954. Concurrently, steps were taken to harmonize external tariffs on these products. In addition, Communitywide industrial policy has been facilitated through short- and long-term forecasts of supply and demand, investment guidance and coordination, joint research programs, and regional development assistance. These activities are financed by a direct levy on Community coal and steel, the level being fixed by the Commission in consultation with the European Parliament.

A global economic slowdown and a declining market for European steel, having generated problems of overcapacity and financial difficulty, caused the declaration of a "manifest crisis" in late 1980. Under this provision of the ECSC treaty, production quotas and a market regulation scheme were imposed and restructuring aid was provided for those adversely affected by the declaration. A successor agreement, ratified July 3, 1981, was the result of a compromise between those members favoring a continuation of aid to avoid social upheavals and those desiring an early end to the crisis program. The 1981 accord called for the cessation of all aid, except for purposes of restructuring, by July 1, 1982, with restructuring assistance to be terminated by December 31, 1985.

Beginning in 1982, the Community and the United States became involved in a number of trade disputes. The first concerned US duties levied in response to subsidies given to European steel manufacturers. It was followed by the prospect of a full-scale trade war in 1983–1984. The larger controversy was triggered by the US imposition of both tariffs and quotas for EC steel imports because of evidence that its domestic industry was being harmed by the imports. A negotiated settlement was eventually reached after the Community had taken the dispute to GATT and the OECD. However, problems again surfaced in November 1984, the United States threatening to ban all imports of EC steel pipe and tube until the end of the year in an effort to force the acceptance of export ceilings. In late December, the Community agreed to limit its shipments to 7.6 percent of the US market.

An agreement was reached in November 1985 between the Community and the United States which regulated exports of 21 categories of steel, excluding semifinished products, for the period 1986–1989. In December, a quota of 600,000 tons was imposed by the United States on semifinished imports, of which 200,000 tons were to be allowed at the discretion of the US Special Trade Representative. (EC shipments had amounted to some 900,000 tons annually over the preceding two years.) On February 19, 1986, Washington invoked a rigid interpretation of the terms of both the general steel agreement and the semifinished steel quota system, after the announcement, two days earlier, of retaliatory EC quotas on US imports.

In September 1987 EC industry ministers agreed that substantial reduction in steel production was required,

although strong pressure from steel companies and labor unions precluded agreement on how cuts should be made. A special committee of experts appointed to study the matter recommended that quotas for most steel products be lifted by July 1988 to permit free-market determination of output. The European Commission, which estimates the EC steel production surplus at about 20 million tons per year, endorsed the panel's proposals and submitted them for consideration by the Council of Ministers.

EUROPEAN ECONOMIC COMMUNITY
(EEC)
Communauté Economique Européenne
(CEE)

Established: By Treaty of Rome (Italy), signed March 25, 1957, effective January 1, 1958.

Purpose: "It shall be the aim of the Community, by establishing a Common Market and progressively approximating the economic policies of Member States, to promote throughout the Community a harmonious development of economic activities, a continuous and balanced expansion, an increased stability, an accelerated raising of the standard of living and closer relations between its Member States."

Full Members: (See Common Institutions).

Associate Members (3): Cyprus, Malta, Turkey.

African, Caribbean, and Pacific (ACP) Countries Affiliated under Lomé Convention (66): Angola, Antigua and Barbuda, Bahamas, Barbados, Belize, Benin, Botswana, Burkina Faso, Burundi, Cameroon, Cape Verde Islands, Central African Republic, Chad, Comoro Islands, Congo, Côte d'Ivoire, Djibouti, Dominica, Equatorial Guinea, Ethiopia, Fiji, Gabon, Gambia, Ghana, Grenada, Guinea, Guinea-Bissau, Guyana, Jamaica, Kenya, Kiribati, Lesotho, Liberia, Madagascar, Malawi, Mali, Mauritania, Mauritius, Mozambique, Niger, Nigeria, Papua New Guinea, Rwanda, St. Christopher and Nevis, St. Lucia, St. Vincent, Sao Tome and Principe, Senegal, Seychelles, Sierra Leone, Solomon Islands, Somalia, Sudan, Suriname, Swaziland, Tanzania, Togo, Tonga, Trinidad and Tobago, Tuvalu, Uganda, Vanuatu, Western Samoa, Zaire, Zambia, Zimbabwe.

Origin and development. The most decisive stage in the development of the Communities was reached with the signature at Rome, Italy, in March 1957 of the two treaties establishing the European Economic Community (EEC) and the European Atomic Energy Community (Euratom), both of which entered into force January 1, 1958. The institutions of the EEC, headquartered at Brussels, Belgium, were broadly fashioned on those of the ECSC, comprising a Council of Ministers, an executive Commission, and the Assembly and Court of Justice already operating under the earlier treaty. Two types of national linkage to the EEC were detailed: full membership, under which an acceding state agreed to the basic principles of the Treaty of Rome; and associate membership, involving the establishment of agreed reciprocal rights and obligations in regard to such matters as commercial policy.

The central issues of the Communities—expansion through admission of additional European states, and the sharing of authority by member governments and the Communities' main administrative organs—have been most acute in the case of the EEC, whose rapid development included a series of crises in which the French government, with its special concern for national sovereignty and its mistrust of supranational endeavors, frequently opposed the other members.

The crucial issue of national sovereignty versus Community authority was initially posed in 1965. Ostensibly to protest EEC failure to reach timely agreement on agricultural policy, the French government instituted a boycott of all three Communities that was maintained from July 1, 1965, to January 30, 1966, and was ended through an intergovernmental understanding that tended to restrict the independent authority of the Commission to establish and execute Community policy.

The membership issue was first brought to the forefront by the decision of the United Kingdom, announced July 31, 1961, to apply for admission to the EEC on condition that arrangements could be made to protect the interests of other Commonwealth states, the other members of the European Free Trade Association (EFTA), and British agriculture. Preliminary discussion of the British bid continued through 1962 but was cut short by France in early 1963 on the general ground that the United Kingdom was too close to the United States and not sufficiently European in outlook. A formal application for membership in the three Communities was submitted on May 11, 1967, with similar bids subsequently being advanced by Ireland, Denmark, and Norway. Action was again blocked by French opposition, despite support for British accession by the Commission and the other five member states. Further negotiations for British, Irish, Danish, and Norwegian membership opened in June 1970, and on January 22, 1972, the treaty of accession and accompanying documents, which provided for expansion to a ten-state organization, were signed at Brussels. However, Norwegian voters, not entirely satisfied with concessions offered for the benefit of their state's agricultural and fishing interests, rejected accession in a national referendum held September 24–25. On the other hand, accession was approved by referendum in Ireland on May 11 and in Denmark on October 2. In the case of the United Kingdom, legislation permitting entry was approved by Parliament and entered into force October 17, the three accessions becoming effective January 1, 1973. On February 9, 1976, the Council of the European Communities stated that, in principle, it endorsed Greece's request for full membership (an agreement of association having been approved in 1962) and a treaty of admission was signed on May 28, 1979. Accordingly, Greece became the Communities' tenth member on January 1, 1981.

Negotiations concerning Portuguese and Spanish membership began in October 1978 and February 1979, respectively, but apprehension over the ability of the Iberian states to speed industrial diversification and the projected impact of the two heavily agricultural economies on the EC's Common Agricultural Policy (see below) caused delays. Thus, Portugal and Spain were not formally admitted until January 1, 1986. An association agreement with Turkey was promulgated in 1964, while in February 1980 Community representatives met with the Turkish foreign minister and agreed to strengthen political and commercial ties "with a view to facilitating the accession of Turkey to the Community at a later date." Following the September 1980 military coup in Turkey, the association agreement was suspended briefly, but an expanded set of accords was subsequently negotiated and entered into effect on January 1, 1981. (See Common Institutions, above, for the current status of Turkey's application for full EC membership.)

Following the declaration of the establishment of the "Turkish Republic of Northern Cyprus", the Commission reaffirmed its support for the unity of the Republic of Cyprus and the Community's 1973 association agreement with the Greek-dominated government.

Earlier, an agreement of association was concluded with Malta (1971), while a Convention of Association linking the EEC with 17 African states and Madagascar (then the Malagasy Republic) had been signed at Yaoundé, Cameroon, on July 20, 1963. A similar agreement was concluded with Kenya, Tanzania, and Uganda at Arusha, Tanzania, on July 26, 1968. Under the UK treaty of accession, all independent Commonwealth states became eligible for association with the Community through the Yaoundé Convention, through aid and institutional ties, or through special trade agreements. Both the Yaoundé and Arusha conventions were, however, superseded with the signing at Lomé, Togo, on February 28, 1975, of a Convention establishing a comprehensive trading and economic cooperation relationship between the EC and 46 (subsequently 66) developing African, Caribbean, and Pacific (ACP) countries. Included in the Lomé Convention's provisions were (1) the granting by the EC of duty-free access on a nonreciprocal basis to all industrial and to 96 percent of agricultural products exported from ACP countries; (2) the setting up of a comprehensive export stabilization program (Stabex) guaranteeing income support to the ACP countries for their primary products; (3) increased development assistance to the ACP countries from EC sources; (4) industrial cooperation between the full members and the associated countries; and (5) the creation of a Council of Ministers, a Committee of Ambassadors, and a Consultative Assembly to implement the agreement.

A second such Convention (Lomé II), which entered into force January 1, 1981, increased Community aid by 62 percent and included a plan to assist ACP producers of copper and tin. In addition, ACP workers in the Community were guaranteed the same working conditions, social-security benefits, and earnings rights as the labor force of EC members. ACP members complained, however, that the new Convention was little different from its predecessor, that inflation would consume most of the new aid, and that trade concessions were marginal. Indeed, the conclusion of a September 1980 conference in Luxembourg on the impact of Lomé II was that "trade relations had not dramatically improved and in fact had deteriorated for many ACP nations, although those countries as a group had moved back into an overall [trade] surplus with the Community."

Following two years of decline, commodity prices stabilized somewhat during 1982 and 1983. Thus, the negotiations for Lomé III, which opened in October 1983, were less acrimonious than the earlier meetings between the EC and the ACP countries. Under the new five-year pact, concluded on December 8, 1984, the Community agreed to expand the volume of financial resources by 60 percent in nominal terms (to $5.96 billion) over that of its predecessor; in real terms, however, the expansion was expected to do little more than maintain the value of the Lomé II endowment. The new funds were to be used largely to encourage "self-reliant and self-sustained development", with an emphasis on improving the living standards of the poorest people in the ACP countries. The proportion of the endowment set aside to help stabilize earnings from exports of certain agricultural products (STABEX) was increased from 11.99 percent under Lomé II to 12.50 percent, while the list of products covered was extended to 48 with the addition of dried bananas, mangoes, and shea nut oil.

After nearly four years of effort by Prime Minister Pierre Trudeau's government to establish a "contractual relationship" between Canada and the EC, a Framework Agreement for Commercial and Economic Cooperation was signed July 6, 1976 — the first such accord between the Community and an industrialized country. A set of accords based on the Canadian model was concluded with Japan in July 1980. Other cooperation agreements have been signed with Algeria (1976), Bangladesh (1976), Brazil (1980), China (1978), Egypt (1977), India (1973 and 1981), Israel (1975), Jordan (1977), Lebanon (1977), Mexico (1975), Morocco (1976), Pakistan (1976), Sri Lanka (1975), Syria (1977), Tunisia (1976), and Yugoslavia (1980). A joint cooperation agreement was signed with the five members of the Association of Southeast Asian Nations (ASEAN) in March 1980, and with the Andean Group in December 1983.

Building on the experience of the ECSC, the EC assumed the task of creating a Communitywide customs union that would abolish all trade restrictions and establish freedom of movement for all goods, services, labor, and capital. A major part of this task was accomplished by July 1, 1968, a year and a half ahead of the schedule laid down in the Treaty of Rome. All customs duties on Community internal trade had been gradually removed, and a common external tariff, likewise arrived at by stages, was ready to be applied. The level of the tariff took into account reductions agreed upon in the 1964–1967 "Kennedy Round" negotiations under the General Agreement on Tariffs and Trade (GATT), at which the EC had negotiated as a unit. At the end of the Community's "transition period" (December 31, 1969), workers became legally free to seek employment in any member state, although in practice the freedom had already existed.

The Treaty of Rome provides for steps leading toward a full economic union of the member states. To this end, it stipulates that common rules shall be applied to ensure fair competition and that common policies shall govern agriculture, transport, and foreign trade. Consequently,

a Common Agricultural Policy (CAP), centrally financed from a conjoint fund, was put into effect July 1, 1968. The product of extremely complex negotiations, it involves common marketing policies with free trade throughout the Community, common price levels for major products, a uniform policy for external trade in agricultural products (including export subsidies), and a program to increase the efficiency of Community farming. The CAP has, however, been a constant source of controversy. ACP members and other major food exporters have charged that the CAP, by permitting inefficiency and encouraging production of surpluses, has lowered international agricultural prices and has led the EC to "dump" such farm commodities as sugar and butter on the world market. The problem was only partially resolved by a Commission "Green [consultation] Paper" which recommended that a market-oriented pricing policy replace farm subsidies.

Within the Community itself, an inequitable burden of CAP financing and the escalating cost of the policy caused dissension and spurred the drafting of a 1981 "agenda for the future" designed to reform the budget by increasing emphasis on social and regional policies and proportionally decreasing agricultural funding. The spiraling cost of CAP subsidies and EC revenue shortfalls forced the Community to freeze some CAP payments in October 1983. The problem of finding a compromise package of agricultural and budgetary policy reforms — including budget rebates demanded by the UK — caused the breakup of both the December 1983 Athens and the March 1984 Brussels meetings of the Council of Ministers. The main division between members concerned the extent and speed of reforms of CAP and the linking of members' contributions to the Community budget to their individual wealth and EC benefits.

European leaders meeting at Fontainebleau, France, on June 25–26, 1984, finally reached accord on budgetary policy. For 1984, Britain was accorded a budget rebate of $800 million and was guaranteed a rebate of two-thirds of its net contribution to the Community in future years, with EC revenues being enhanced by an increase from 1 percent to 1.4 percent of the value-added tax received from member states. Concessions were also made to limit West Germany's financial burden, officials expressing the hope that progress would thenceforth be made on "relaunching" the Community.

The goal of a complete economic and monetary union has not yet been realized; however, agreement was reached in July 1978 for the establishment of a European currency association that would include a joint reserve fund to prevent intermember currency fluctuations and a mechanism by which intra-Community accounts can be settled by use of European Currency Units (ECUs). The resultant European Monetary System (EMS) came into effect March 13, 1979. In its nine years of existence, the ECU has become an attractive medium for the issue of bonds by private and public financial institutions, placing the ECU behind only the US dollar and the German deutschmark in popularity on the international bond market. In May 1983, the Community authorized a loan of ECU 4 billion ($3.7 billion) to help France defend its faltering franc until a domestic austerity policy became effective; France had threatened to leave the EMS if the loan was not granted.

Since 1985 proponents of unity have won a series of endorsements from EC organs and member states for measures designed to create a true internal common market by 1992. New rules have been approved to liberalize capital movement across community borders while other plans range from minimizing frontier transport checks to standardizing national tax laws. On January 1, 1988, a lone, shortened customs document, known as the Single Administrative Document, went into effect at all intra-EC borders as well as at those with members of the European Free Trade Association. Common transit procedures were also implemented to facilitate the movement of goods.

Despite progress toward full integration, the EC has remained seriously divided on many economic issues, particularly CAP subsidies, the resolution of budget crises, and pressure for the wealthier northern EC members to increase aid to the poorer southern members. Summits in July and December 1987 broke up without resolution of the spending deficit, yearly outlay running about $6 billion over the members' total budgeted contributions of $35 billion. Disagreement continued to center on the controversial CAP subsidies and large-scale storage of surplus food, which accounted for some 70 percent of EC spending despite recent cutbacks in beef and dairy products. Britain refused to increase its EC contribution until "financial discipline" had been instituted, including subsidy cuts to allow the free market to control agricultural production. West Germany, whose farming industry is relatively inefficient, opposed broad subsidy cuts while France assumed a middle ground. The southern countries, on the other hand, appeared ready to compromise on subsidies in return for extra development aid.

In view of the problems involved, an emergency summit at Brussels, Belgium, on February 12–13, 1988, achieved remarkable results. After marathon negotiations, the participants established a budget ceiling of 1.3 percent of the EC's GNP, set a cap on future growth of agricultural subsidies of no more than three-quarters of increased GNP, approved cuts in the intervention price for surplus farm commodities, and agreed to double aid to the southern members over a five-year period. While most of the cost was expected to be borne by West Germany, observers were persuaded that meaningful progress had finally been made toward meeting the Community's 1992 integration deadline.

The economic success of the EC has aroused both admiration and anxiety among nonmember states. Members of EFTA who chose not to join the enlarged grouping have concluded industrial free-trade agreements with it, and on January 1, 1984, all duties on manufactured and processed goods were formally eliminated. Similarly, the hostility of the socialist bloc toward the EC has diminished in recent years. In January 1976, Sir Christopher Soames traveled to Romania, becoming the first European commissioner to visit a CMEA member country in an official capacity. The purpose of Soames' visit was to continue the EC-CMEA dialogue, which was expected to lead to an institutionalized trading relationship between the members of Europe's two leading economic entities. Although no such arrangement has yet materialized, a cooperation agreement was concluded in February 1980 with Yugoslavia, an associate member of the CMEA. Most Yugoslav industrial exports and selected primary products were granted trade concessions, while Belgrade in turn extended most-favored-nation status to EC exports. The agreement further provided for the establishment of a Cooperation Council to facilitate mutual objectives and promote interaction in such areas as agriculture, energy, industry, science and technology, tourism, and transport. In mid-1980 the EC and Romania signed a trade accord on industrial products that was expected to serve as a model for similar agreements with other CMEA members, negotiations continuing into mid-1988 on proposed full "normalization of relations".

While trade with the United States is of major importance ($132 billion in 1986), numerous disputes have resulted in actual and threatened tariff measures. A January 1987 agreement providing compensation for American farmers assuaged US complaints over the loss of grain markets following the entry of Spain and Portugal into the Community. However, Washington continued to seek access to European agricultural, telecommunications, and aviation markets with an "aggressiveness" that generated manifest EC resentment. For its part, the EC decried US "protectionist predilictions" promising, if needed, retaliatory tariff increases and calling for intervention by the Reagan administration to halt the fall of the dollar in world money markets.

Relations with Japan, another major trading partner, have been even more strained in recent years, the EC insisting that Tokyo take steps to reduce the large and steadily growing trade imbalance by opening up Japanese markets further to European goods. Concurrently, the EC has imposed numerous duties to combat what it alleges has been the widespread "dumping" of Japanese exports, particularly electronic equipment, in Europe.

EUROPEAN ATOMIC ENERGY COMMUNITY
(Euratom)
Communauté Européenne de l'Energie Atomique
(CEEA)

Established: By Treaty of Rome (Italy), signed March 25, 1957, effective January 1, 1958.

Purpose: To develop research, to disseminate information, to enforce uniform safety standards, to facilitate investment, to ensure regular and equitable distribution of supplies of nuclear material, to guarantee that nuclear materials are not diverted from their designated uses, to exercise certain property rights in regard to such materials, to create a common market for the free movement of investment capital and personnel for nuclear industries, and to promote the peaceful uses of atomic energy.

Membership: (See Common Institutions).

Origin and development. Euratom was established in response to the assessment that atomic power on a large scale would be urgently needed to meet the growing energy requirements for economic expansion. The original six ECSC member states also sought to reduce the lead that

Britain, the Soviet Union, and the United States had acquired in the field of peaceful uses of nuclear energy. To this end, the members decided to pool their efforts, the area being too complex and expensive to be dealt with nationally. Structurally, the Treaty of Rome provided for a Council, a Commission, and the sharing of the Assembly and Court of Justice already operating under the ECSC.

In December 1969 it was agreed to reshape Euratom so that it could conduct nuclear research under contract for Community clients and extend its activities to nonnuclear scientific research projects, especially those involving other European states. The Council also resolved to streamline the Community's management, making its operations more flexible and ensuring more effective coordination of its nuclear activities. These reforms took effect in 1971. In 1981, an agreement came into force between the Community, France, and the International Atomic Energy Agency (IAEA) regarding safeguards on certain nuclear materials, while officials signed long-term agreements establishing conditions for the sale and security within the EC of nuclear materials supplied by Australia and Canada.

Much effort has been expended on furthering the development of peaceful European nuclear industry, primarily by supplementing and coordinating national nuclear research programs. In 1981, in order to reduce dependence on external fuel supplies, the European Commission nearly doubled its request for Community funding for the 1982–1986 nuclear energy research plan, primarily to develop the Joint European Torus (JET), which would produce energy from a controlled thermonuclear fusion process.

The safety of nuclear energy production for both plant workers and the general public has been of growing concern. Research has focused on improving reactor design and safeguards, establishing joint safety criteria for intraregional nuclear material trade, and assessing the environmental impact of radioactive waste handling. The Commission also operates a supply agency for fissionable material and conducts inspections of nuclear installations that use such supplies, in order to ensure that nuclear material is not diverted from peaceful uses. A set of amendments to the Treaty of Rome proposed by the Commission in 1983 was aimed at the creation of a "nuclear common market" by facilitating intra-EC trade in non-military nuclear materials and services. The proposed reforms include a prohibition against national barriers to trade in nuclear materials originating in member states, the abolition of the Community Supply Agency's supply monopoly in nuclear fuels, and an affirmation of the Commission's preeminent position in concluding supply and other agreements with third countries. Efforts are also being made to protect the Community from a disruption of nuclear fuel supplies, in view of the fact that nuclear energy provides approximately 20 percent of its energy production.

A controversy arose in 1986 over the proposed inspection of a building at the Sellafield nuclear plant in Britain, where spent fuel from both civilian and military Magnox reactors was being reprocessed. Britain initially rejected inspection on the ground that the Euratom treaty did not apply to military installations, while EC officials argued that the treaty applied to "mixed installations" where civil and military materials are handled together. An agreement announced in June gave Euratom inspectors full access to the site, with reprocessing activity being closed down in February 1987 after the discovery of several radioactive leaks.

EUROPEAN FREE TRADE ASSOCIATION (EFTA)

Established: By convention signed at Stockholm, Sweden, January 4, 1960, effective May 3, 1960.

Purpose: To promote economic expansion, full employment, and higher standards of living through elimination of barriers to nonagricultural trade among member states.

Headquarters: Geneva, Switzerland.

Principal Organs: Council (all members), EFTA Council Committees (all members), Consultative Committee (all members), Secretariat.

Secretary General: Georg Reisch (Austria).

Membership (6): Austria, Finland, Iceland, Norway, Sweden, Switzerland. Liechtenstein is also a participant by virtue of its customs union with Switzerland.

Working Language: English.

Origin and development. EFTA was established under British leadership in 1959–1960 as the response of Europe's so-called "outer seven" states to the creation of the original six-state European Economic Community (EEC). With the breakdown of negotiations to establish a single, all-European free-trade area encompassing both groups, the seven decided to set up a separate organization that would enable the non-EEC states both to maintain a unified position in further bargaining with the "inner six" and to carry out a modest liberalization of trade within their own group. Unlike the EEC, EFTA was not endowed with supranational features and was not designed to effect a common market or common external tariff, but merely the elimination of internal trade barriers on nonagricultural goods. This objective was met in 1967, three years ahead of schedule.

Finland became an associate member of EFTA in 1961; Iceland joined as the eighth full member in 1970. Denmark and the United Kingdom withdrew on January 1, 1973, when they joined the European Communities; Portugal withdrew for the same reason on January 1, 1986. On the latter date, Finland, on the basis of a request submitted in September 1985, was admitted to full membership.

Structure. The Council of Ministers, EFTA's principal political organ, consists of one representative from each member state and normally meets three times a year at the ministerial level, more often at lower levels. Its responsibilities include supervising the implementation and operation of the tariff reduction system. Decisions must be unanimous when they involve increased obligations for member states. Assisting the Council are nine standing committees composed of national officials: the Committee of Origin and Customs Experts, the Consultative Committee, the Committee of Trade Experts, the Committee on Technical Barriers to Trade, the Budget Committee, the Committee on Agriculture and Fisheries, the Economic Committee, the Economic Development Committee, and the Committee of Members of Parliament of EFTA countries. An EFTA-Yugoslav Joint Committee was established in 1978. The EFTA Secretariat is quite small, reflecting the comparatively limited scope of the organization.

Activities. EFTA's initial main objectives were to establish free trade among the member states in nonagricultural products and to negotiate a comprehensive agreement that would permit limited access to EC markets. The first goal was achieved in 1966, while a series of trade pacts with the European Community, the first of which became effective January 1, 1973 (concurrent with the Community's expansion), has gone far toward fulfilling the second. On January 1, 1984, the last duties on most industrial trade between EFTA and the EC were removed, thereby creating a 17-member free trade area with 310 million consumers.

Following enlargement of the European Community, a further range of activity was unofficially added to the EFTA agenda and cooperation was extended to more diverse economic matters than the trade concerns specified in the Stockholm convention. Explicitly recognized by the Ministerial Council at its meeting of May 1975, these concerns involved cooperation among EFTA countries in such subjects as raw materials, monetary policy, inflation, and unemployment. The last two were foci of a special Consultative Committee meeting at Stockholm, Sweden, in February 1977. The trade-union leaders who convened the session intended it as a forum for reaching consensus about the economic policy objectives of member countries; however, some government and employer association representatives displayed notable lack of enthusiasm for embarking on such a course. Similar tension was evident during a summit meeting at Vienna, Austria, in May 1977. Organized outside EFTA's institutional framework, the first summit in 11 years adopted the so-called Vienna Declaration, which prescribed a broad framework for future activities. It included, for example, a resolution calling upon EFTA to become a "forum for joint consideration of wider European and world-wide economic problems in order to make a constructive contribution to economic cooperation in international fora". In pursuit of this goal, a multilateral free-trade agreement between the EFTA countries and Spain was signed at Madrid on June 26, 1979, while in 1982 concessions were extended to permit Portugal to expand its industrial base prior to joining the EC. Upon their accession to the larger grouping, it was agreed that Spain and Portugal would conclude special arrangements with EFTA countries. Both have agreed to a seven-year transitional period for the phaseout of obstacles to full trade and have been extended protocols for agricultural products.

Cooperation between EFTA and the EC has continued to grow, based on general guidelines promulgated in the 1984 Luxembourg Declaration. The accord called for the reduction of nontariff barriers, more joint research and development projects, and exploratory talks in areas such as transportation, agriculture, fishing, and energy. In an effort to disencumber border formalities, EFTA reached agreement with the EC on the use of a lone, simplified customs form, the Single Administrative Document (SAD), to cover trade within and between the two groups. The SAD convention was the first multilateral agreement between EFTA and the EC, previous pacts having taken the form of similar but separate agreements between each EFTA member and the EC; both the SAD agreement and another multilateral convention on common transit procedures became effective on January 1, 1988.

Another recent priority for EFTA has been to encourage use of the General Agreement on Tariffs and Trade (GATT) to combat deterioration in world trade and overcome protectionist sentiment on the part of some leading industrialized nations. The EFTA Council of Ministers at its May 1987 meeting called for strengthening GATT's regulatory framework and "unremitting efforts" by all GATT members to assure the success of the current "Uruguay Round" negotiations.

EFTA figures showed that export volume was up only 2.2 percent for 1986, less than half the average annual growth since 1972. Meanwhile, Japanese exports to EFTA countries continued to soar, helping to push the overall EFTA trade deficit up from $.7 billion in 1985 to $4.4 billion in 1986. Preliminary reports released in early 1988 indicated that the trade deficit grew to about $8.4 billion in 1987.

EUROPEAN ORGANIZATION FOR NUCLEAR RESEARCH (CERN)

Organisation Européenne pour la Recherche Nucléaire

Established: By convention signed at Paris, France, on July 1, 1953, effective September 29, 1954.

Purpose: "To provide for collaboration among European States in subnuclear research of a pure scientific and fundamental character, and in research essentially related thereto. The Organization shall have no concern with work for military requirements and the results of its experimental and theoretical work shall be published or otherwise made generally available."

Headquarters: Geneva, Switzerland.

Principal Organs: Council (all members), Committee of the Council (all members), Scientific Policy Committee, Finance Committee, Experiments Committees.

Director General: Herwig Schopper (Federal Republic of Germany); to be succeeded by Carlo Rubbia (Italy) on January 1, 1989.

Membership (14): Austria, Belgium, Denmark, France, Federal Republic of Germany, Greece, Italy, Netherlands, Norway, Portugal, Spain, Sweden, Switzerland, United Kingdom.

Observers (4): European Community, Poland, Turkey, Yugoslavia.

Official Languages: English, French.

Origin and development. The European Organization for Nuclear Research was established September 29, 1954, upon ratification of a convention drawn up at Paris, France, the preceding July. The convention followed a resolution of the United Nations Educational, Scientific and Cultural Organization (UNESCO) general conference held at Florence, Italy, in 1950 and an intergovernmental conference convened by UNESCO in December 1951. The Organization replaced the *Conseil Européen pour la Recherche Nucléaire* (CERN), which had come into being February 15, 1952, but retained its predecessor's acronym, CERN. Spain withdrew from membership in 1968, but returned in 1982.

Structure. The Council of CERN, which normally meets twice a year, is composed of two representatives from each member state and their advisers. Heading the Council are a president and two vice presidents. The Committee of the Council, consisting of one representative per member state plus the chairmen of the Scientific Policy Committee, the Finance Committee, and the European Committee for Future Accelerators, is an informal forum where members can present their individual viewpoints and confidentially discuss difficult questions. The Scientific Policy Committee, composed of 21 scientists elected without regard to geographical distribution, provides the Council with advice on scientific developments and their implications for the Organization. The Finance Committee consists of one representative from each member state. The four Experiments Committees—one for each of the CERN facilities—are chaired by scientists from outside CERN and are charged with studying the proposals made by physicists in member states for experiments to be conducted on CERN equipment.

Activities. From a relatively low level in the early years, the use of CERN's experimental facilities has now grown to involve some 2,000 experimental physicists from over 160 European universities and research institutes. Recently, CERN researchers have been involved in the design and creation of a large electron-positron storage ring, usually referred to as an LEP. The ring, scheduled to be operational in 1989, will allow intense beams of electrons and positrons to be collided at very high energies, thus providing European scientists with unique capacity for investigating nature's most fundamental particles and forces. In 1981 CERN researchers succeeded in producing collisions between protons and their antimatter counterparts, antiprotons; in 1983, they discovered three subatomic force-transmitting particles called weak intermediate bosons and

in mid-1984 announced that they had found evidence of a yet smaller particle, the theretofore theoretically defined quark.

During 1985, CERN participated in conferences on many scientific subjects including electron cooling, electronuclear physics, and particle physics. Major research efforts continued on the use of the new LEP electron-positron storage ring, and a "Working Group on the Scientific and Technological Future of CERN" was established to look into the possible construction of other accelerators, such as a proton-proton collider which could be added to the same 27-kilometer tunnel currently housing the LEP. In addition, an inquiry was launched on CERN's impact on industry. The study demonstrated benefits from CERN's technological discoveries in areas such as methods for strengthening glass, new epoxy-resin mouldings, and high quality electrical insulation for low temperatures. An additional study explored the "economic utility" of contracts with European industries, such activity being found to pay back 60 percent of CERN's annual budget in the form of added value.

Debate over the future of CERN's financing dominated the organization's activities in 1986. In March, the Council unanimously approved a British proposal to set up an independent review committee to investigate the future development of human and material resources for maximum cost effectiveness and the implications of alternative levels of funding by the member states, many of which are under pressure to increase spending in other research areas. The resolution followed a 1985 report from a special UK commission headed by Sir John Kendrew that recommended a British reduction of 25 percent in overall expenditure on high energy physics by 1991, allowing time for the completion of the LEP collider. The decision met with disapproval from the physics community due to a concern that such cuts might cause the group's experimental activities to cease. CERN physicists, worried that resources will not be available after the completion of LEP's first phase in 1989, began attempts to secure additional funding for the Organization, including the possibility of contributions from nonmembers such as Canada, Japan, and the United States. In addition, to meet costs associated with the LEP (described as the "largest scientific instrument in the world"), some CERN members have paid annual contributions in advance. The 1988 budget has been set at 782 million Swiss francs (approximately $560 million).

During its regular session at Geneva on June 23–24, 1988, the Council decided to implement staff cuts and introduce more accurate methods for calculating the budget as part of a new long-term financial strategy recommended by the review committee.

EUROPEAN ORGANIZATION FOR THE SAFETY OF AIR NAVIGATION (EUROCONTROL)

Established: By convention signed at Brussels, Belgium, on December 13, 1960, effective March 1, 1963; and amended by protocol signed February 12, 1981, effective January 1, 1986.

Purpose: To strengthen the cooperation of the contracting parties and to develop their joint activities in the field of air navigation, making due allowance for defense needs and providing maximum freedom for all airspace users consistent with the required level of safety.

Headquarters: Brussels, Belgium.

Principal Organs: Permanent Commission for the Safety of Air Navigation (all members); Agency for the Safety of Air Navigation (all members), consisting of a Committee of Management and a Director General.

Director General: Horst Flentje (Federal Republic of Germany).

Membership (8): Belgium, France, Federal Republic of Germany, Ireland, Luxembourg, Netherlands, Portugal, United Kingdom.

Official Languages: Dutch, English, French, German, Portuguese.

Origin and development. As early as 1957, governments were exploring the possibility of formulating an air traffic control procedure for their airspace which disregarded national frontiers. The growing number of aircraft travelling at ever-higher speed and altitude, the pace at which the aeronautical sciences were advancing, and the greater interdependence of the industrialized states of Western Europe all pointed toward the need for such a joint venture. However, it was not until January 1958, at the Fourth European Mediterranean Regional Air Navigation Convention of the International Civil Aviation Organization (ICAO) at Geneva, Switzerland, that the idea was officially discussed. Subsequently, several meetings were held by concerned directors general of civil aviation, and on June 9, 1960, the ministers responsible for civil and military aviation in Belgium, France, the Federal Republic of Germany, Italy, Luxembourg, the Netherlands, and the United Kingdom met at Rome, Italy, to consider a draft convention. Two diplomatic conferences followed (the Italians being

no longer participating), and the convention was signed at the second of these, in December 1960. Ireland acceded to the convention in 1965; Portugal became an associate member in 1976 and a full member in 1986. In 1987 the Permanent Commission unanimously accepted the applications of Greece and Turkey to accede to the amended convention subject to national ratification procedures in those two states.

Structure. Eurocontrol comprises two bodies: the Permanent Commission for the Safety of Air Navigation, a governing body composed of delegates from each member state representing the interests of both civil aviation and national defense; and an executive body, the Agency for the Safety of Air Navigation. The latter is administered by a Committee of Management (two delegates from each state) and a director general, who heads four Directorates at Brussels and five External Services.

The Agency's central administration is financed by means of contributions from each member state assessed on the basis of the following formula: an initial 30 percent of the contribution in proportion to the value of the state's Gross National Product and a further 70 percent in proportion to the value of the state's route facility cost-base.

Activities. The Organization is required to analyze future needs of air traffic and new techniques to meet them; to establish common long-term objectives in the field of air navigation and to establish a common medium-term plan for air traffic services taking account of the long-term objectives; to coordinate the research and development programs of the member states; and to assist, on request, in the performance of specific air navigation tasks or in the provision and operation of air traffic services.

Specifically, the Organization provides air traffic control services, from its Maastricht center in the Netherlands, to aircraft operating in the upper airspace of the three Benelux states and the northern part of the Federal Republic of Germany on behalf of and at the request of these states. In addition, the Organization prepares and executes studies, tests and trials at its Experimental Centre at Brétigny-sur-Orge, near Paris; trains air traffic services personnel at the Institute of Air Navigation Services in Luxembourg; calculates, bills and collects air navigation route charges at the Central Route Charges Office in Brussels; and provides an international air traffic flow management system through its Central Data Bank in Brussels.

EUROPEAN SPACE AGENCY (ESA)

Established: On a de facto basis by agreement signed at a meeting of the European Space Conference at Brussels, Belgium, on July 31, 1973, effective May 1, 1975; de jure establishment achieved upon ratification of convention on October 30, 1980.

Purpose: To provide for and promote, for exclusively peaceful purposes, cooperation among European states in space research and technology, with a view to their being used for scientific purposes and for operational space applications; to elaborate and implement a long-term European space policy; and to progressively "Europeanize" national space programs.

Headquarters: Paris, France.

Principal Organs: Council (all members), Science Programme Committee, Programme Boards, Directorate.

Director General: Reimar Lüst (Federal Republic of Germany).

Membership (13): Austria, Belgium, Denmark, France, Federal Republic of Germany, Ireland, Italy, Netherlands, Norway, Spain, Sweden, Switzerland, United Kingdom.
Associate Member: Finland. In addition, Canada participates in some ESA projects.

Origin and development. The decision to form the ESA was made at meetings of the European Space Conference in December 1972 and July 1973, culminating 14 years of persistent effort by the Consultative Assembly of the Council of Europe to establish a single European space organization and a common European satellite and launcher program. The long gestation period was due in part to delicate negotiations over which projects of the European Space Research Organization (ESRO) and the European Space Vehicle Launcher Development Organization (ELDO) would be continued upon their consolidation into the ESA, and in part to disagreement between France and the Federal Republic of Germany as to the naming of a director general. Austria and Norway, having initially been observers and subsequently associate members, acceded to full membership on January 1, 1987. On the same date, Finland became an associate member.

Structure. The ESA structure was patterned essentially after that of ESRO, having as its governing body a Council in which each member state has one vote. The staffs of both ESRO and ELDO were absorbed into the ESA Directorate, with six group directors—for scientific programs, technical direction, space transportation systems, spacecraft operations, applications programs, and administration—constituting a management board under the director general. The Agency also has a number of national program facilities and three technical establishments: the European Space Research and Technology Centre (ESTEC), at Noordwijk, Netherlands; the European Space Operations Centre (ESOC), at Darmstadt, West Germany; and the Space Documentation Centre (ESRIN, from the facility's previous name, the European Space Research Institute), at Frascati, Italy. The member states finance the Agency, contributing on the basis of a percentage of gross national product to the general and scientific budgets, and on an ad hoc basis to other programs. Contributions are also made by observer nations that participate in specific programs.

Activities. The ESA has developed or contributed to a wide range of satellite programs in many fields, including telecommunications and earth and space observation,

while promoting experiments on the potential for scientific and commercial exploitation of space. Initially a "junior partner" with the United States' National Aeronautics and Space Administration (NASA) on projects such as Spacelab, the Agency, through its commercial affiliate Arianespace, now competes directly with NASA in the satellite-launching business. However, ESA-NASA cooperation continues in other areas such as the proposed permanently manned Space Station.

Central to the overall ESA program was the development of the Ariane rocket to propel independent launches from facilities at Kourou, French Guiana. Since the ESA convention prohibits the Agency from engaging in profit-making activities, the launches are conducted by Arianespace, established in 1980 by European aerospace industries and banks in conjunction with the French Space Agency. In February 1986 Arianespace offered to expand its schedules for 1987 and 1988 to accommodate companies and governments whose launches were cancelled by NASA following the explosion of the space shuttle Challenger in January. However, Arianespace was forced to suspend its own schedule in May after the fourth Ariane failure in its 18-launch history. Thus, the West was left without immediate launch capability.

Following redesign of Ariane's third state rocket ignition system and other components, Arianespace resumed activity with the successful launch and deployment of two communication satellites, via an Ariane-3 rocket, on September 15, 1987. At that time a backlog existed of more than 40 satellites with a total value of $2.4 billion, which were expected to be included in multiple-satellite payloads launched at the rate of eight or nine per year.

In light of the September success, the ESA Council at a meeting November 9–10 at The Hague, Netherlands, again endorsed expansion of the program, despite calls for retrenchment from British and other government leaders. Included are the development of Hermes, the French manned space shuttle; Columbus, the European component of the international Space Station; and Ariane-5, a more powerful rocket incorporating a new cryogenic propulsion system. Current schedules call for Ariane-5 launching and Columbus deployment in 1995 and an initial Hermes flight in 1998.

In other 1987 activity, the ESA inaugurated a Large Space Simulator with a high-power artificial sun to better simulate in-orbit environmental conditions. The Agency also received an October 1990 launch date from NASA for the joint "Ulysses" mission to probe the sun and Jupiter. Analysis continued of data and photographs received during the Giotto probe's successful close encounter with Halley's Comet in March 1986, while work proceeded on Eureca, a retrievable space platform slated for experiments in communications as well as in life and material sciences.

On June 15, 1988, ESA inaugurated the Ariane-4 rocket, estimated to be about twice as powerful as Ariane-3, with the successful launch of three satellites from Kourou.

GROUP OF TEN

Established: As the group of contributing countries to the General Arrangements to Borrow (GAB), negotiated at Paris, France, in 1962 by the Executive Board of the International Monetary Fund.

Purpose: To discuss problems relating to the functioning and structure of the international monetary system.

Principal Organs: None; communication within the Group occurs at regular and ad hoc meetings of ministers, ministerial deputies, and governors or other representatives of the members' central banks.

Chairman: Kjell-Olof Feldt (Sweden).

Membership (11): Belgium, Canada, France, Federal Republic of Germany, Italy, Japan, Netherlands, Sweden, Switzerland, United Kingdom, United States.

Nonstate Participants (4): International Monetary Fund (IMF), Organization for Economic Cooperation and Development (OECD), Bank for International Settlements (BIS), Commission of the European Communities (EC).

Origin and development. The Group of Ten (G-10), also sometimes known as the Group of Eleven since Switzerland's accession to membership in 1984, consists of those states which contribute to the General Arrangements to Borrow (GAB), a supplementary loan agreement negotiated to increase the lending resources of the IMF. The GAB was formally launched in October 1962, although prospective members had been meeting earlier to examine the international monetary system. Never limited to discussion of loan requests under the GAB, the G-10 in 1966 recommended the establishment of special drawing rights (SDRs) as a supplementary IMF liquidity resource. With the approval of G-10 members and the IMF's board of governors, the GAB was substantially restructured in 1983 to deal with the potential default of heavily indebted countries. The new provisions extended the IMF's lines of GAB credit from SDR 6.4 billion to SDR 17 billion, allowed the use of some GAB resources by non-GAB participants, and extended GAB association to certain borrowing arrangements between the IMF and non-GAB participants.

Structure. One of the least institutionalized intergovernmental organizations, the G-10 holds meetings at several levels. Ministerial sessions are attended by the finance ministers and central-bank governors of each member state, the president of the Swiss National Bank, the managing director of the IMF, the secretary general of the OECD, the general manager of the BIS, and the president of the EC Commission. Meetings are held in the spring and fall of each year immediately prior to meetings of the IMF's Interim Committee, with ad hoc sessions called as needed.

In addition, the central bank governors meet monthly. At the official "deputy" level, each member state is represented by high-level civil servants from its finance ministry and central bank, along with senior staff members of the IMF, the OECD Secretariat, the BIS and the EC Commission.

Activities. The G-10 addresses a wide range of problems relating to international liquidity, bank lending, monetary policy, trade balances, and other economic issues. Meetings are private and detailed information on decisions is often not made public. However, broadly-worded communiqués are sometimes issued prior to IMF meetings or at times of international economic unrest. The G-10 also continues to be responsible for approving loan requests under the GAB; such loans are financed only by those states that approve the particular requests, but G-10 members provide "multilateral surveillance" over loan recipients.

G-10 activity has been intertwined with and sometimes supplanted by several subgroups. In 1967 the finance ministers and central bank governors of five G-10 members (France, Federal Republic of Germany, Japan, United Kingdom, United States) began to meet regularly as an additional informal caucus on international economic monetary developments. They became known as the Group of Five (G-5). In 1975 the G-5 promoted still another forum, comprising the heads of state or government of its members who began to meet at yearly summits. Following the addition of Italy and Canada, the group became known as the Group of Seven (G-7), its summits also being attended by the president of the EC Commission and the president of the EC Council of Ministers (if not someone from a G-7 country). In general, the G-5 continued to operate in confidence while the G-7 summits generated wide publicity on a broad agenda that grew to include issues well beyond the G-10's purview, such as terrorism and arms control. To bring the goal of economic cooperation more sharply into focus, the G-7 directed in May 1986 that regular meetings of the G-7 finance ministers be held between summits.

A continuing concern of the G-10 has been the promotion of global economic recovery, viewed by members as the only solution to the debt crisis. In 1985, the Group reviewed the existing system of floating exchange rates and, following recommendations by its study group, declared the system to be in need of modification. Suggestions were made for enhancing the stability of the international economic order, while a fiscal strategy to increase the value of the yen was adopted as a means of reducing Japanese trade imbalances. The Group also requested that directors of the IMF undertake a comprehensive review of the future role of SDRs.

In early 1986 the Group of Five urged the Reagan administration to drive down the dollar's value to make American goods more competitive in the world market and to correct imbalances in the world economy. A French proposal to create "target zones" under which a government would attempt to keep its currency within a certain range was rejected, the Group declaring that exchange market intervention could have only a limited global impact. During a G-10 ministerial meeting at London in January, the central banks were charged with considering a reduction in interest rates to create lower loan payments for developing countries, more investment opportunities for European industries, and a decrease in the US budget deficit. However, no formal commitment to lower rates was made because of concern that inflation might undermine the effort to depreciate the dollar. During an April meeting at Washington, governments were urged to coordinate economic policies for further reform of the monetary system within the framework of the IMF. Tension emerged at the meeting as a result of the feeling by some members that the Group was being overshadowed by the recent activity of the more exclusive G-5.

In September 1986 G-5 and G-7 meetings ended with West Germany and Japan rejecting US demands to lower their interest rates and Washington disagreeing with efforts to halt the fall of the dollar. At a Paris meeting in February 1987 six of the G-7 members agreed to try to stabilize their currencies at prevailing levels, Italy withdrawing from the meeting because some aspects of the accord had been negotiated at a G-5 meeting to which it had not been invited. Although Japan and West Germany proceeded with reforms in connection with the February accord, disagreement again broke out following the October stock market crash. Subsequently, the United States was criticized by its allies for its huge trade and budget deficits and the continued decline in the value of the dollar.

In a rare public statement, apparently designed to reassure nervous financial markets, the G-10 central bank governors called in November for fiscal moves by the major industrialized countries to reduce trade imbalances and stabilize exchange rates. While noting that policies already implemented were producing gradual benefits, the G-7 finance ministers and central bank governors released a statement in December calling for intensified cooperation to combat protectionism, avoid excessive exchange rate fluctuations, and correct trade imbalances.

In other 1987 activity, the G-10 endorsed renewal of the GAB for a five-year period beginning December 24, 1988, reviewed debt problems facing developing countries, stressed the need for policies conducive to noninflationary growth in the world economy, and supported measures for increased capitalization requirements for banks (see article on Bank for International Settlements).

During a generally harmonious summit at Toronto, Canada, on June 19–21, 1988, the G-7 leaders reaffirmed their commitment to the maintenance of a stable dollar and agreed to relax debt-repayment pressure on the world's poorest countries. The leaders expressed confidence in the current status of the world economy, attributing its resuscitation to wider free market activity, including deregulation, throughout much of the world.

GULF COOPERATION COUNCIL (GCC)

Formal Name: Cooperation Council for the Arab States of the Gulf.

Established: Initial agreement endorsed on February 4–5, 1981, at Riyadh, Saudi Arabia; constitution formally adopted at Abu Dhabi, United Arab Emirates, on May 25–26, 1981.

Purpose: "(i) To achieve coordination, integration and cooperation among the member states in all fields in order to bring about their unity; (ii) to deepen and strengthen the bonds of cooperation existing among their peoples in all fields; (iii) to draw up similar systems in all fields . . . ; and (iv) to promote scientific and technical progress in the fields of industry, minerals, agriculture, sea wealth and animal wealth . . . for the good of the peoples of the member states."

Headquarters: Riyadh, Saudi Arabia.

Principal Organs: The Supreme Council; Ministerial Council; General Secretariat; various economic, social, industrial and trade, and political committees.

Secretary General: 'Abdallah Yacoub Bisharah (Kuwait).

Membership (6): Bahrain, Kuwait, Oman, Qatar, Saudi Arabia, United Arab Emirates.

Official Language: Arabic.

Origin and development. The formal proposal for an organization designed to link the six Arabian Gulf states on the basis of their special cultural and historical ties emerged from a set of plans formulated by the Kuwaiti government. At a meeting on February 4–5, 1981, the Gulf foreign ministers codified the Kuwaiti proposals and issued the Riyadh Agreement, which proposed cooperative efforts in cultural, social, economic, and financial affairs. On March 10, after settling on legal and administrative provisions, the ministers initialed a constitution for the GCC at Muscat, Oman; the Council came into formal existence with the signing of the constitution by the Gulf heads of state during the first Supreme Council meeting on May 25–26, 1981, at Abu Dhabi, United Arab Emirates.

Structure. The Supreme Council, composed of the six members' heads of state, convenes annually and is the highest authority of the GCC, directing the general course and policies of the organization. The foreign ministers of the member states comprise the Ministerial Council, which meets four times a year and is assisted by a number of substantive committees. The Secretariat, headquartered at Riyadh, Saudi Arabia, supplements the work of several bodies including the secretary general's office, the Commission for Settlement of Disputes, and Economic, Political, Legal, Financial, Environmental, and Information centers. Permanent ministerial councils exist in the areas of agriculture, oil, communications and trade.

In the economic sphere, the first Supreme Council meeting convened in May 1981 and established a $6 billion fund to finance joint-venture projects, the resultant Gulf Investment Corporation holding its first board of directors' meeting in November 1983. In June 1981, a Unified Economic Agreement was signed to provide coordination in commerce, industry, and finance, and to prepare the way for a common market. The first stage of the Agreement, implemented in March 1983, provided for the free movement of all agricultural, animal, industrial and natural resource products between member states. At the second meeting of heads of state in November 1981 at Riyadh, agreement was reached on further harmonization of investment and trade regulations.

Although members had earlier denied that the GCC was intended as a military grouping, events in the Middle East prompted Gulf leaders to consider joint security measures, leading to the first GCC joint military exercises in late 1983 and the formation of a defense force called the "Peninsula Shield". These attempts at regional coordination have been tenuous, however, because of political differences among the participants.

Activities. Since GCC members control a third of the world's oil reserves, oil and oil-related issues are among its major concerns. In 1983 the Council demonstrated its solidarity in drafting production quotas for the January 1983 OPEC ministerial meeting, considering but quickly rejecting any price cuts. The GCC member states, with Iran and Iraq, also constitute the Regional Organization for the Protection of the Marine Environment, which became concerned with a massive oil spill that dumped 4–5,000 barrels of oil a day into the Gulf following Iraq's bombing of Iran's oil fields in January 1983. While unable to arrange a cease-fire between Iran and Iraq to cap the wells, GCC foreign ministers approved the use of a special ship to sweep up the spilled oil and prevent the pollution of member states' waters and shores.

The Iran-Iraq conflict occupied the Council throughout 1983–1984. In May 1983 the foreign ministers proposed a peace plan whereby both states would withdraw their troops to prewar positions, exchange prisoners, and be eligible for war reparations from a GCC-financed reconstruction fund; the plan, along with other Council ceasefire proposals, was rejected. Following the escalation of attacks by both Iran and Iraq upon oil tankers in the Strait of Hormuz in May–June 1984, a foreign ministers' meeting in Saudi Arabia yielded an announcement that Council members would reimburse customers for oil lost in such assaults, as well as an agreement on collective air defense for tanker routes. These actions were prompted by a steep rise in war-risk insurance on tankers in the Gulf, which threatened the competitiveness of Gulf oil in the world market.

In 1985 the GCC emphasized greater economic and defense cooperation. At various ministerial meetings, programs to coordinate currency exchange rates, protect local trade, establish food and oil reserves, and promote industrial self-sufficiency were discussed. The sixth summit on November 3–6, 1985 at Muscat, Oman, opened with an appeal from Sultan Qabus of Oman for members to join in combatting terrorism and concluded with a warning that the "recent escalation" of the Iran-Iraq war threatened the stability of the region and freedom of navigation in its waters. The final communiqué confirmed the willingness of the GCC to assist in finding a peaceful solution to the Gulf conflict, with appropriate regard to the "legitimate interests of both parties". The heads of state also supported the development of a strategy of security cooperation and

expressed continued support for the Palestine Liberation Organization as the sole representative of the Palestine people.

Similar issues dominated the seventh summit meeting on November 2–5,1986,at Abu Dhabi, United Arab Emirates. The members called for an immediate ceasefire in the Iran-Iraq conflict and an end to attacks on shipping in the Gulf.

In February 1987 the GCC foreign ministers approved a comprehensive security strategy to be presented at the summit scheduled for December. Although details of the plan were not released, observers agreed that a GCC military force would at best only offer limited deterrence. Therefore, throughout the year the GCC states pressed for additional regional and global support to guard against future Iranian aggression or extension of militant Islamic fundamentalism. In June the GCC foreign ministers endorsed Kuwait's call for US warships in the Gulf to protect oil tankers that had been reflagged under American auspices. In November the GCC joined other Arab states in making the war the main issue at the long-delayed Arab League summit which condemned Iranian "provocation and threats" against the Gulf states.

During the eighth session of the Supreme Council, held on December 26–29, 1987, at Riyadh, Saudi Arabia, the GCC urged Teheran to accept the peace plan being advanced by the UN Security Council. It also reportedly endorsed the GCC regional security plan although specifics again were not revealed.

INTERGOVERNMENTAL COMMITTEE FOR MIGRATION (ICM/CIM)

Comité Intergouvernemental pour les Migrations
Comité Intergubernamental para las Migraciónes

Established: At Brussels, Belgium, in 1951 as a provisional movement to facilitate migration from Europe; formal constitution effective November 30, 1954; present name adopted in November 1980.

Purpose: To effect the orderly movement of migrants and refugees to countries offering resettlement; to assist, through selective migration, the social and economic advancement of less-developed countries.

Headquarters: Geneva, Switzerland.

Principal Organs: Council (all members), Executive Committee (nine members, elected annually), Secretariat.

Director: James L. Carlin (United States); to be succeeded by James Purcell (United States) on October 1, 1988.

Membership (33): Argentina, Australia, Austria, Belgium, Bolivia, Chile, Colombia, Costa Rica, Cyprus, Denmark, Dominican Republic, Ecuador, El Salvador, Federal Republic of Germany, Greece, Guatemala, Honduras, Israel, Italy, Kenya, Luxembourg, Netherlands, Nicaragua, Norway, Panama, Paraguay, Peru, Portugal, Switzerland, Thailand, United States, Uruguay, Venezuela.

Observers (18): Brazil, Canada, Cape Verde, Egypt, Guinea-Bissau, Holy See, Japan, Republic of Korea, Partnership with the Children of the Third World (*Partage avec les Enfants du Tiers Monde*), Philippines, Presiding Bishop's Fund for World Relief/Episcopal Church, Refugee Council of Australia, San Marino, Sovereign Order of Malta, Spain, Sweden, Turkey, United Kingdom.

Official Languages: English, French, Spanish.

Origin and development. A Provisional Intergovernmental Committee for the Movement of Migrants from Europe was established by delegates to a 16-nation International Migration Conference at Brussels, Belgium, in 1951. The Intergovernmental Committee for European Migration (ICEM) was based on a constitution that came into force November 30, 1954, while in November 1980 the organization decided to delete "European" from its name due to the inappropriateness of the designation in describing the ICM's prevailing scope of activities. On May 20, 1987, a number of formal amendments to the ICM constitution were approved, including a change of name to the International Organization for Migration (IOM); the amendments are to come into effect when approved by two-thirds of the organization's member states.

Structure. The Council, normally meeting once a year, is composed of representatives of all countries subscribing to the Committee's principles and contributing to its administrative budget. The nine-member Executive Committee, which meets twice a year, is elected annually. There are subcommittees on Budget and Finance (five members, elected annually) and Coordination of Transport (all members), in addition to a Secretariat headed by a director.

Activities. Since February 1952, when ICEM operations began, more than 3.7 million migrants and refugees have been given relocation assistance, with orientation, placement, vocational and language training, and other resettlement services made available when needed. The ICM also maintains an emergency operations program, providing transportation and resettlement assistance in periods of sudden refugee activity. Since 1965, the Committee has carried out a Selective Migration Programme to facilitate a transfer of technology from Europe to Latin America through the migration of highly qualified individuals. Over 26,000 European professionals, technicians, and skilled workers have been relocated since the Programme's inception. Since 1971, the Committee has also participated in the emigration of over 250,000 Jews from the Soviet Union.

The ICM has assisted in the resettlement of nearly 1 million refugees from Indochina since 1975. It has also been active in Latin America, where it has assisted intraregional migration and the resettlement of nationals returning to El Salvador. With involvement of such magnitude, the Committee has expanded the scope of its activities, including cultural and language training. It also provides medical examinations to determine the refugees' fitness for travel and their freedom from infectious diseases that could be transmitted to their countries of resettlement. In addition, special programs have been established to assist handicapped refugees.

In recent years the ICM has participated in numerous efforts to address the "brain-drain" problem of developing countries by encouraging their citizens to return following overseas education or job training, while an Integrated Experts Program has provided highly skilled personnel from developed countries for projects in developing countries throughout the world.

In November 1986 the Council agreed to coordinate a one-year Afghan Medical Program to provide, in conjunction with both private and international medical organizations, specialized treatment and rehabilitation for wounded Afghan refugees.

Several ICM members agreed in 1987 to make special contributions to help cover shortfalls in underfinanced programs, while urging the solicitation of private donations. Thus, the United States Association for International Migration was organized in June to raise private funds to supplement ICM work. During the year agreements were signed with the EC and the United States to extend a "Return of Talent to Africa" program; in addition, the Afghan Medical Program, the subject of widespread publicity in many Western countries, was extended under a grant from USAID. At its December meeting the Council adopted a 1988 budget of $105.7 million.

INTERNATIONAL BANK FOR ECONOMIC COOPERATION (IBEC)

Myezhdoonarodne Bank Ekonomechyeskova Sotroodnechyestva

Established: In October 1963, commencing operations in January 1964.

Purpose: To assist in the economic cooperation and development of member countries.

Headquarters: Moscow, USSR.

Principal Organs: Council (all members), Board (all members).

Chairman: Vaja G. Djindjikhadze (USSR).

Membership (10): Bulgaria, Cuba, Czechoslovakia, German Democratic Republic, Hungary, Mongolia, Poland, Romania, Union of Soviet Socialist Republics, Vietnam.

Official Languages: All member countries' languages; the working language is Russian.

Origin and development. Sometimes identified as "the Eastern bloc counterpart to the IMF", the IBEC was established as an adjunct to the Council for Mutual Economic Assistance (CMEA). Its original membership encompassed the East European communist states, exclusive of Albania and Yugoslavia, plus Mongolia. Cuba and Vietnam joined the Bank in 1974 and 1977, respectively.

Structure. Administratively, the IBEC is governed by a Council that meets twice yearly. Although various executive officers of the member states' national and trading banks, as well as deputy ministers of finance and trade, participate in Council deliberations, each country has a single vote irrespective of its share in the capital of the Bank. Other organs include a ten-member Board of permanent representatives that reports to the Council; a six-member Auditing Committee; and four Departments: Convertible Currency, Transferable Rouble, Economic and Research, and Operations.

Activities. Despite its stated purpose, the Bank's activities focus primarily on financial credits and settlements in facilitation of trade between the participants. It also serves as a center for members' financial transactions with external banking institutions, reportedly including substantial amounts of hard-currency borrowing. The Bank relies on the Council for Mutual Economic Assistance to set its agenda.

According to an unclassified report issued by the US Central Intelligence Agency in mid-1980, the Bank's hard-currency lending had closely paralleled overall East European indebtedness to the West, rising steadily in the mid-1970s from $0.7 billion in 1971 to $3.7 billion in 1978. During its first 20 years of operations, direct lending by the Bank exceeded TR 100.8 billion, with a steady increment in preferential credit shares granted to Cuba, Mongolia, and Vietnam. In 1986 credits extended to the banks of member countries totaled TR 18 billion.

INTERNATIONAL CRIMINAL POLICE ORGANIZATION (ICPO/INTERPOL)

Organisation Internationale de Police Criminelle

Established: As the International Criminal Police Commission (ICPC) by the Second International Criminal Police Congress at Vienna, Austria, in 1923; present name and constitution adopted by the 25th Congress, with effect from June 13, 1956.

Purpose: ". . . to ensure and promote the widest possible mutual assistance between all criminal police authorities within the limits of the law existing in the different countries and in the spirit of the Universal declaration of Human Rights".

Headquarters: Saint-Cloud, France. A new headquarters at Lyon, France, is scheduled for completion by late 1988.

Principal Organs: General Assembly (all members), Executive Committee (15 members), General Secretariat.

Secretary General: Raymond E. Kendall (United Kingdom).

Membership (146): Algeria, Angola, Andorra, Antigua and Barbuda, Argentina, Aruba, Australia, Austria, Bahamas, Bahrain, Bangladesh, Barbados, Belgium, Belize, Benin, Bolivia, Botswana, Brazil, Brunei, Burkina Faso, Burma, Burundi, Cameroon, Canada, Central African Republic, Chad, Chile, China, Colombia, Congo, Costa Rica, Côte d'Ivoire, Cuba, Cyprus, Denmark, Djibouti, Dominica, Dominican Republic, Ecuador, Egypt, Equatorial Guinea, Ethiopia, Fiji, Finland, France, Gabon, Gambia, Federal Republic of Germany, Ghana, Greece, Grenada, Guatemala, Guinea, Guyana, Haiti, Honduras, Hungary, Iceland, India, Indonesia, Iran, Iraq, Ireland, Israel, Italy, Jamaica, Japan, Jordan, Democratic Kampuchea, Kenya, Kiribati, Republic of Korea, Kuwait, Laos, Lebanon, Lesotho, Liberia, Libya, Liechtenstein, Luxembourg, Madagascar, Malawi, Malaysia, Maldives, Mali, Malta, Mauritania, Mauritius, Mexico, Monaco, Morocco, Nauru, Nepal, Netherlands, Netherlands Antilles, New Zealand, Nicaragua, Niger, Nigeria, Norway, Oman, Pakistan, Panama, Papua New Guinea, Paraguay, Peru, Philippines, Portugal, Qatar, Romania, Rwanda, St. Kitts-Nevis, St. Lucia, St. Vincent, Saudi Arabia, Senegal, Seychelles, Sierra Leone, Singapore, Somalia, Spain, Sri Lanka, Sudan, Suriname, Swaziland, Sweden, Switzerland, Syria, Tanzania, Thailand, Togo, Tonga, Trinidad and Tobago, Tunisia, Turkey, Uganda, United Arab Emirates, United Kingdom, United States, Uruguay, Venezuela, Yemen Arab Republic, Yugoslavia, Zaire, Zambia, Zimbabwe. There are also national central subbureaus in Bermuda, Cayman Islands, Gibraltar, and Hong Kong.

Official Languages: English, French, Spanish, Arabic.

Origin and development. Interpol's origins lie in the First International Criminal Police Congress convened at Monte Carlo, Monaco, in 1914 by Prince Albert I, who felt that an international effort was required to combat crime. However, World War I intervened, and it was not until a Second Congress at Vienna, Austria, in 1923 that what was known as the International Criminal Police Commission (ICPC) was formally launched. It was agreed from the outset that the Commission would not be a working police force, but would serve as an information center based on respect for each member's national sovereignty; in addition, it would focus entirely on common criminal activity, avoiding involvement in political, military, racial, or religious matters. By 1930, a Secretariat had been established at Vienna with a number of specialized departments that included international criminal records, counterfeiting, fingerprinting, and passport forgery; an international police radio network was set up in 1935. Following the 1938 *Anschluss,* an Austrian Nazi was named Viennese police commissioner, hence president of the ICPC under its existing constitution. As a result, the 1938 Congress at Bucharest, Hungary, was the last to be convened prior to World War II.

The Commission was revived at Brussels, Belgium, in 1946, the members agreeing to establish permanent headquarters at Paris, France (relocation to the Paris suburb of Saint-Cloud occurring in 1967). During the 25th Congress at Vienna in 1956, it was decided to change the name from "Commission" to "Organization", in accordance with prevailing multinational practice; concurrently the acronym "Interpol" was formally adopted, having previously been introduced as part of the body's on-the-air radio signature.

Under its 1956 constitution, Interpol was authorized to establish relations with the Customs Co-operation Council (CCC), the UN's Economic and Social Council (ECOSOC) and other international bodies; however, it was not until 1971 that the Organization was accorded recognized intergovernmental status through an agreement of cooperation with the Council of Europe and regularized linkage with ECOSOC.

Structure. Interpol's governing body is its General Assembly, which meets in ordinary session at least once a year in a different member country. Extraordinary sessions, which may be called by the Executive Committee or a majority of the membership, are held at Saint-Cloud. The Assembly decides general policy, rules on the work program submitted by the secretary general, approves the budget, elects the Executive Committee, and adopts resolutions on matters of international police concern. The 15-member Executive Committee, which meets twice a year, is composed of a president (serving a four-year term), three vice presidents and nine delegates (serving three-year terms), and two auditors. The secretary general, who is appointed for a five-year term by the Assembly on recommendation of the Executive Committee, supervises a staff of 250–300 persons, most of whom are employed in the Secretariat's four main divisions (General Administration, International Criminal Police Coordination, Research, Publication) and seven specialized groups. A large part of the work is coordinated, on a day-to-day basis, with national central bureaus or other police bodies designated by member states. Rapid communication with the national agencies is facilitated by an international radio network, operating through a dozen remote-controlled transmitters, and a telex system for the relay of hard-copy messages. A Standing Committee on Information Technology was established in 1984 to oversee the modernization and expansion of the communications network.

Activities. Most of Interpol's activities deal with the exchange of information on counterfeiting, bank and other financial fraud, drug trafficking, art theft, and related forms of common criminal activity across national frontiers. In this endeavor, it maintains close relations with a number of specialized international bodies, such as the UN Commission on Narcotic Drugs, the International Civil Aviation Organization (ICAO), and the International Air Transport Association (IATA).

Until quite recently, Interpol was reluctant to participate in measures to combat international terrorism because such acts are often politically motivated and the Organization's constitution prohibits investigation of political matters. However, at the 1984 Assembly, members agreed that it could become involved if the criminal element of a violent act, such as murder, kidnapping, or bombing, outweighed the political aspect. Subsequently, the 1985 Assembly approved the creation of an International Terrorism Group, which commenced informational and analytical services in January 1986. At the same Assembly a British citizen, Raymond Kendall, was elected secretary general, the first time that such an appointment had not gone to a national of the Organization's host country.

The 56th General Assembly, held on November 23–27, 1987, at Nice, France, called for increased cooperation with the banking and financial communitites to combat the rapid increase in fraud in those areas. Other resolutions reflected Interpol's growing attention to the problems of fraudulent travel documents and trafficking in weapons and explosives.

INTERNATIONAL ENERGY AGENCY (IEA)

Established: By the OECD Council of Ministers at Paris, France, November 15, 1974.

Purpose: To coordinate the responses of participating states to the world energy crisis and to develop an oil-sharing mechanism for use in times of supply difficulties.

Headquarters: Paris, France.

Principal Organs: Governing Board (all members), Management Committee, Secretariat.

Executive Director: Helga Steeg (Federal Republic of Germany).

Membership (21): Australia, Austria, Belgium, Canada, Denmark, Federal Republic of Germany, Greece, Ireland, Italy, Japan, Luxembourg, Netherlands, New Zealand, Norway, Portugal, Spain, Sweden, Switzerland, Turkey, United Kingdom, United States.

Observers: All other OECD members, as well as the Commission of the European Communities, may participate as observers.

Origin and development. Created as a response by OECD member states to the energy crisis of 1973–1974, the IEA began provisional operation on November 18, 1974, with signatory governments given until May 1, 1975, to deposit instruments of ratification. The agreement establishing the Agency was to remain in force for ten years. Norway, one of the original sponsors, did not immediately participate as a full member because of fear that sovereignty over its own vast oil resources might be impaired.

Subsequently, Spain, Austria, Sweden, and Switzerland applied for membership, although the last three reserved the right to withdraw if IEA operations interfered with their neutrality. At a meeting of the Governing Board on February 5–7, 1975, New Zealand was admitted, and a later agreement with Norway raised it from an associate to a full member. More recently, Australia, Greece, and Portugal have joined. France has cooperated with the Agency as a nonmember.

Structure. The IEA's Governing Board is composed of ministers of member governments. The Board is assisted by four Standing Groups concerned with emergency questions, long-term cooperation, the oil market, and relations between energy producers and consumers. Decisions of the Governing Board are made by a weighted majority except in the case of procedural questions, where a simple majority suffices. In the event of an oil shortfall of 7 percent or more, the Secretariat is to report that fact to the intermediate Management Committee, which in turn will report to the Governing Board. Only the latter, which must reach a decision in 48 hours, can invoke oil-sharing contingency plans. Participating countries agreed initially to maintain oil stocks equal to 60 days' normal consumption, with the period to be extended at a later date. The IEA also maintains an import-monitoring system and a "quick response" mechanism. The former commits members' energy ministers to participate in quarterly reviews of the IEA's import targets, while the latter provides a framework for the imposition of legal ceilings on members' oil imports in the case of a market crisis.

Activities. Global recession, an oil glut, and increased energy efficiency on the part of the OECD membership have combined to reduce the threat of a new energy crisis, although IEA officials have consistently warned against energy conservation "complacency". Energy surveys in 1983 were encouraging: member oil reserves of over 100 days, a global spare oil capacity of 7–10 million barrels a day through 1986–1987, and a 31 percent improvement in members' industrial energy efficiency during the 1973–1982 period.

In 1984 IEA members discussed plans to be implemented should the Strait of Hormuz be closed because of the Gulf war. Although one-third of West Europe's oil is carried through the Strait, existing reserves and slackened demand have lessened the potential impact of such an eventuality. In addition, members agreed to early use of government-owned or controlled oil supplies to calm the market in cases of disruption. Major studies were undertaken on the production and use of electricity in IEA countries to the year 2000 and on the lessons learned from conservation programs in the last ten years. Currently, more than sixty collaborative projects spanning the spectrum of energy technologies are under way.

During a meeting on April 10, 1986, at Paris, France, energy ministers from member countries ruled out joint action with the Organization of the Petroleum Exporting Countries (OPEC) to stabilize oil prices. They also reaffirmed a 1985 commitment not to impose new duties or other protective measures on oil imports that would lead to higher domestic energy prices.

A major report published by the Agency in early 1987, *Energy Conservation in IEA Countries,* stated that the amount of energy used per unit of member countries' GDP fell by 20 percent between 1973 and 1985, with considerable potential remaining for added efficiency in energy utilization, given appropriate further action by government policymakers. By contrast, IEA figures released in March showed that OECD oil consumption had risen 2.5 percent in 1986 with a further one percent increase predicted for 1987. Nonetheless, the IEA indicated that oil stocks were high enough to deal with any drawdown that might occur should higher prices be established by OPEC. At the May ministerial meeting US Energy Secretary John S. Herrington warned IEA members not to relax their guard as indications pointed to a tightening in the world oil market.

INTERNATIONAL MARITIME SATELLITE ORGANIZATION (INMARSAT)

Established: On the basis of convention and operating agreement adopted September 3, 1976, with effect from July 26, 1979. Actual operations commenced February 1, 1982.

Purpose: To make provision for the satellites and their control systems necessary for improving maritime communications, subject to usage for peaceful purposes only.

Headquarters: London, United Kingdom.

Principal Organs: Assembly (all parties to convention), Council (representatives of 18 signatories or groups of signatories with largest investment shares, plus representatives of 4 signatories elected by the Assembly on basis of equitable geographic distribution), Directorate.

Director General: Olof Lundberg (Sweden).

Membership (54, investment share percentages as of January 31, 1988, in parentheses): United States (27.50); United Kingdom (15.16); Norway (14.00); Japan (9.48); France (3.42); Union of Soviet Socialist Republics (including Byelorussian SSR and Ukrainian SSR, 3.30); Singapore (2.70); Greece (2.69); Netherlands (2.20); Spain (2.00); Denmark (1.88); Federal Republic of Germany (1.83); Brazil (1.81); Italy (1.56); Canada (1.50); Australia (1.30); Saudi Arabia (1.07); Kuwait (0.90); Sweden (0.75); Republic of Korea (0.54); Belgium (0.49); India (0.44); Poland (0.37); Finland (0.35); People's Republic of China (0.30); Indonesia (0.28); Bulgaria (0.24); Egypt (0.15); Portugal (0.14); Liberia (0.13); Argentina, United Arab Emirates, Philippines (0.12 each); New Zealand, Iran (0.11 each);

Bahrain (0.09); German Democratic Republic, Malaysia, Panama (0.08 each); Gabon, Tunisia (0.06 each); Sri Lanka, Algeria, Chile, Colombia, Iraq, Israel Oman, Pakistan, Peru, Qatar (0.05 each). Nigeria became a member in February 1988, its investment share yet to be announced.

Official Languages: English, French, Russian, Spanish.

Origin and development. The need for an organization to establish and maintain satellite communication for maritime purposes was first broached at a 1971 World Administrative Radio Conference for Space Telecommunications held under the auspices of the International Telecommunication Union (ITU). The development of Inmarsat's convention and operating agreement took place in three sessions of a conference organized by the Inter-Governmental Maritime Consultative Organization (IMCO) held April 23–May 9, 1975; February 9–28, 1976; and September 1–3, 1976. For the initial phase of its activity, Inmarsat leased service from the US Communications Satellite Organization (Comsat) on three *Marisat* satellites positioned over the Atlantic, Indian, and Pacific oceans.

Structure: The Assembly, which establishes general policy for the Organization, meets every two years; the Council meets three times a year. Membership shares, which determined levels of financial contribution, were initially based on estimated utilization of the system by ships of signatory registry. The distribution of shares is revised on the basis of actual utilization on February 1 of each year.

Activities. Inmarsat operates a system of nine leased satellites to provide telephone, telex, data and facsimile, distress and safety, and some television communication services to the shipping, offshore, and aviation industries. With the current generation of geostationary satellites, virtually all of the globe between 75 degrees north and south is now covered by the system, which provides more than 6,500 ships with a variety of services, including weather and navigational reports and warnings, medical advice and assistance, and ship position reports. Included in the system are coastal earth stations which provide linkage between the satellites and the international telecommunications network. As of October 1987, there were 20 such stations: four in the Soviet Union; two each in Japan, Poland, and the United States; and one each in Brazil, Egypt, France, Greece, Italy, Kuwait, Norway, Saudi Arabia, Singapore, and the United Kingdom. Inmarsat also provides emergency transportable communications at times of human disaster and natural catastrophe.

In April 1985, Inmarsat signed a contract with British Aerospace Dynamics Group to build three new Inmarsat-2 satellites, which will triple communications capacity in the Atlantic. The new satellites were originally set for launching in late 1988, but shutdowns by both the US Space Shuttle and the European Arianespace programs forced changes in Inmarsat's schedule. The next launch is currently scheduled for December 1989 via a US Delta-2 rocket.

Inmarsat has recently moved to expand its services in several areas. At its biennial meeting in October 1985 the Assembly voted to alter the Organization's convention to permit it to provide services to the aeronautical community.

The services, will include data links for transmission of essential information such as airline operation, performance, in-flight location, and weather conditions. In addition, in-flight telephone service for passengers will be provided, which will enable them to call or be called anywhere in the world. Trials of the new services are set for 1988 with full operations planned by the end of 1989.

Inmarsat has been involved in the formulation of a new international agreement to permit vessels operating in ports and territorial seas to use Inmarsat satellite terminals. The agreement, which is restricted to Inmarsat members, opened for signature on January 1, 1986, and will enter into force upon the accession of 25 countries.

Other projected activity includes the use of satellites for data transmission to and from mobile units on land, proposed amendments to the Inmarsat convention to permit such expansion of its program being introduced in 1987. During the year Inmarsat announced final specifications for a very lightweight, but low-cost terminal that would allow a new range of small ships and personal boat operators access to satellite communications. It also cooperated in trials of an international paging system expected to be of particular use to long-distance trucking firms and investigated proposals for further research on the use of its satellites for navigation and position determination.

INTERNATIONAL TELECOMMUNICATIONS SATELLITE ORGANIZATION (INTELSAT)

Established: By two international agreements concluded at Washington, DC, on August 20, 1971, effective February 12, 1973. The Agreement Relating to the International Telecommunications Satellite Organization—Intelsat, with four annexes, was concluded among participating states; the Operating Agreement Relating to the International Telecommunications Satellite Organization—Intelsat, with one annex, was signed by states and public or private telecommunications entities designated by participating states.

Purpose: ". . . to carry forward on a definitive basis the design, development, construction, establishment, operation and maintenance of the space segment of the global commercial telecommunications satellite system. . . ."

Headquarters: Washington, DC, United States.

Principal Organs: Assembly of Parties (all state members), Meeting of Signatories (all signatories to the Agreements), Board of Governors (27 members), Executive Organ.

Director General: Dean Burch (United States).

Membership (114): Afghanistan, Algeria, Angola, Argentina, Australia, Austria, Bangladesh, Bahamas, Barbados, Belgium, Benin, Bolivia, Burkina Faso, Brazil, Cameroon, Canada, Central African Republic, Chad, Chile, China, Colombia, Congo, Costa Rica, Côte d'Ivoire, Cyprus, Denmark, Dominican Republic, Ecuador, Egypt, El Salvador, Ethiopia, Fiji, Finland, France, Gabon, Federal Republic of Germany, Ghana, Greece, Guatemala, Guinea, Haiti, Honduras, Iceland, India, Indonesia, Iran, Iraq, Ireland, Israel, Italy, Jamaica, Japan, Jordan, Kenya, Republic of Korea, Kuwait, Lebanon, Libya, Liechtenstein, Luxembourg, Madagascar, Malawi, Malaysia, Mali, Mauritania, Mauritius, Mexico, Monaco, Morocco, Netherlands, New Zealand, Nicaragua, Niger, Nigeria, Norway, Oman, Pakistan, Panama, Papua New Guinea, Paraguay, Peru, Philippines, Portugal, Qatar, Rwanda, Saudi Arabia, Senegal, Singapore, Somalia, South Africa, Spain, Sri Lanka, Sudan, Sweden, Switzerland, Syria, Tanzania, Thailand, Togo, Trinidad and Tobago, Tunisia, Turkey, Uganda, United Arab Emirates, United Kingdom, United States, Uruguay, Vatican City, Venezuela, Vietnam, Yemen Arab Republic, Yugoslavia, Zaire, Zambia.

Nonsignatory Users (38): Antigua and Barbuda, Bahrain, Belize, Botswana, Brunei, Burma, Burundi, Cape Verde, Cook Islands, Cuba, Djibouti, Equatorial Guinea, Gambia, Guyana, Kiribati, Democratic People's Republic of Korea, Lesotho, Liberia, Maldives, Malta, Mozambique, Nauru, Nepal, Poland, Romania, Sao Tome and Principe, Seychelles, Sierra Leone, Solomon Islands, Suriname, Swaziland, Tonga, Union of Soviet Socialist Republics, Vanuatu, Western Samoa, People's Democratic Republic of Yemen, Zimbabwe.

Official Languages: English, French, Spanish.

Origin and development. The first worldwide satellite communications system dates from 1964, when the interim International Telecommunications Satellite Consortium was set up. All state members of the International Telecommunication Union (ITU) wishing to share in the costs of designing, establishing, and operating global communications satellite facilities were permitted to invest, although access to the system was open to all states that agreed to assume prorated costs of the actual use of the facilities. The administrative and technological management of the consortium, as well as the predominant voting power, resided in Comsat, a United States corporation established by Congress in 1962. However, the increasing importance of satellite telecommunications and the growth in membership — including an expanding proportion of less-developed states — generated resistance to the role of Comsat, with members challenging its monopoly and calling for greater decisionmaking input by users. Thus the new Intelsat organization was established. More recently, pressure has developed within Intelsat itself for increased technical and financial assistance to less-developed member states.

Structure. The Assembly of Parties, which meets every two years, gives "consideration to those aspects of Intelsat which are primarily of interest to the parties as sovereign states"; the Meeting of Signatories is primarily concerned with financial and operational matters and establishes the minimum investment share required for membership on the Board of Governors. The latter is composed of those signatories who, individually or in groups, have contributed not less than a specified investment share, plus up to five governors, each representing a group of at least five signatories located within the same ITU region. Meeting on an average of five times a year, the Board provides continuous management policy direction. The Executive Organ, with a staff of about 600, is headed by a director general.

Activities. Intelsat's 13-satellite system provides about two-thirds of the world's international telecommunication services, including telephone, television, facsimile, data, and telex transmissions between earth stations in more than 140 countries. Its facilities are also used for domestic telecommunications by 25 countries, now allowed to purchase transponders on Intelsat satellites or lease them on a long-term, non-preemptible basis.

The Intelsat I, II, and III series of satellites, which operated during most of the Organization's first decade, have been supplanted by larger and more effective spacecraft — Intelsat IV, IV-A, and V, the last having a capacity of 12,000 voice circuits and two television channels. In comparison, Intelsat VI, now scheduled for its first deployment in 1989 (see below), will be able to carry 120,000 telephone calls simultaneously in addition to three television channels. Work on the next level of satellite sophistication, Intelsat VII, was scheduled to begin in 1988.

The deployment of new satellites has been delayed because of recent failures within the US space shuttle and European Arianespace programs. Intelsat satellites were initially scheduled for launch on shuttle missions in 1987, 1988, and 1989. However, after the January 1986 explosion of the space shuttle Challenger, Intelsat announced it would use Arianespace to launch the first three Intelsat VI satellites. Then, in May 1986 an Ariane rocket launching an Intelsat V satellite failed and the Arianespace program was itself suspended until September 1987. In August 1987 Intelsat signed a contract for the launch of 2 Intelsat VI satellites by a private US firm, Martin Marietta, via Titan III rockets in 1989 and 1990. The specifications for the new Intelsat VII satellite call for compatibility with both the Ariane and Titan rockets, launches being currently planned for 1992 and 1993.

With the demand for satellite telecommunications facilities growing at more than 15 percent annually, Intelsat in recent years has faced the issue of direct competition from private and other government-owned or government-supported providers. In 1985 the US Federal Communications Commission (FCC) agreed to permit limited international transmissions by non-Intelsat satellites and numerous proposals followed from private and government-affiliated operations. Intelsat initially objected strongly to the US action on the ground that it would suffer "economic harm" from the competition. However, mutual accommodations, which reportedly will protect most of Intelsat's revenues and operations, have lessened concern over the issue. In April 1987 the Intelsat Assembly of Parties approved PanAmSat, a separate international satellite system which will provide service between the United States and Peru, seven other international "coordinations" between previously established domestic systems were also approved.

In September 1987 Richard R. Colino, the former director general of Intelsat, was sentenced at Washington DC to six years in prison and fined $865,000 after pleading guilty to fraud and conspiracy charges connected with the siphoning of an estimated $5.4 million from the agency. Colino and Jose L. Alegrett, deputy director general for business planning and external development, had been dismissed by the Board of Governors in December 1986 after independent auditors raised questions about possible financial irregularities. Dean Burch, former chairman of the US FCC, was named as the new director general in April 1987.

ISLAMIC CONFERENCE

Mujtana' al-Islamiyah

Official Name: Organization of the Islamic Conference.

Established: By agreement of participants of the summit meeting of Muslim Heads of State at Rabat, Morocco, September 22–25, 1969; first conference convened at Jiddah, Saudi Arabia, March 23–26, 1970.

Purpose: To promote Islamic solidarity and further cooperation among member states in the economic, social, cultural, scientific, and political fields.

Headquarters: Jiddah, Saudi Arabia.

Principal Organs: Islamic Conference of Foreign Ministers (all members), Islamic Countries' Conference for Economic Cooperation (all members), Secretariat.

Secretary General: Sayed Sharifuddin Pirzada (Pakistan).

Membership (46): Afghanistan, Algeria, Bahrain, Bangladesh, Benin, Brunei, Burkina Faso, Cameroon, Chad, Comoro Islands, Djibouti, Egypt, Gabon, Gambia, Guinea, Guinea-Bissau, Indonesia, Iran, Iraq, Jordan, Kuwait, Lebanon, Libya, Malaysia, Maldives, Mali, Mauritania, Morocco, Niger, Nigeria, Oman, Pakistan, Palestine Liberation Organization, Qatar, Saudi Arabia, Senegal, Sierra Leone, Somalia, Sudan, Syria, Tunisia, Turkey, Uganda, United Arab Emirates, Yemen Arab Republic, People's Democratic Republic of Yemen. Afghanistan's membership was suspended in January 1980; Egypt's membership, suspended in May 1979, was restored in April 1984.
Observer: Turkish Republic of Northern Cyprus.

Official Languages: Arabic, English, French.

Origin and development. Although the idea of an organization for coordinating and consolidating the interests of Islamic states originated in 1969 and meetings of the Conference were held throughout the 1970s, the Islamic Conference has only recently achieved worldwide attention. Throughout its history, economics has played a prominent role in the Organization's activities. Thus it was the Conference which was responsible for establishing the Islamic Development Bank and the Islamic Solidarity Fund.

Structure. A relatively unstructured organization, the body's main institution is the Conference of Foreign Ministers, although a conference of members' heads of state is held every three years. A Committee for Economic and Trade Cooperation has recently been organized, as well as a Secretariat with Political, Cultural, Administrative, and Financial divisions, each headed by a deputy secretary general. Various other bodies have been established within the Organization, including the International Islamic Press Agency (1972), the Islamic Development Bank (1974), the Islamic States Broadcasting Organization (1975), the Islamic Solidarity Fund (1977).

Activities. The foci of concern since 1980 have been wars involving member countries. The first extraordinary meeting of the Conference of Foreign Ministers, held at Islamabad, Pakistan, on January 27–29, 1980, condemned the Soviet invasion of Afghanistan and suspended Kabul's membership. The "Mecca Declaration", issued at the third Islamic Summit in 1981, called for the immediate withdrawal of all foreign troops from the country and for a political solution that would guarantee Afghanistan's international status.

The major decision taken at the 1984 Morocco summit was the lifting of Egypt's suspension of membership. The conferees were unable to reach consensus on continued fighting in Afghanistan and Lebanon, and between Iran and Iraq. A Casablanca Charter, which called for greater Islamic solidarity and regional reconciliation was adopted, while applications for membership from Benin and Brunei were approved.

At their sixteenth annual meeting in 1986, the foreign ministers condemned the imposition of US sanctions against Libya in retaliation for its alleged support of terrorism. Subsequently, the Organization arranged for talks in September between the new Philippines government and Moslem separatists of the Moro National Liberation Front in an attempt to end the Front's 14-year-old insurgency.

The fifth Islamic summit was held under heavy security on January 26–28, 1987, at Kuwait City, Kuwait, in a $400 million conference facility specially built for the meeting. The Iran-Iraq war, raging only 50 miles away, was the summit's main focus. However, since Iran failed to attend on the ground that Kuwait supported Iraq in the war, little was accomplished save for the passing of a resolution calling for an immediate ceasefire. Other resolutions condemned terrorism while endorsing the Syrian-backed distinction between terrorism and the acts of a "legitimate national liberation movement"; urged the Soviet Union to withdraw its troops from Afghanistan, calling their presence a major obstacle to relations between Moscow and Muslim countries; condemned the "strategic alliance" between Israel and the United States; and supported the Palestinian Liberation Organization in its contention that UN resolutions were "insufficient" to resolve the conflict in the Middle East. Numerous unofficial meetings at the summit were also reported, those involving previously estranged Arab leaders apparently helping to lay the groundwork for the long-delayed Arab League summit in November.

LATIN AMERICAN ECONOMIC SYSTEM (LAES/SELA)

Sistema Económico Latinoamericana

Established: By treaty signed at Panama City, Panama, October 17, 1975.

Purpose: To create and promote Latin American multinational enterprises, to protect the prices of basic commodities while ensuring markets for regional exports, and to reinforce technological and scientific cooperation among member states.

Headquarters: Caracas, Venezuela.

Principal Organs: Latin American Council (all members), Action Committees, Secretariat.

Permanent Secretary: Sebastián Alegrett (Venezuela).

Membership (26): Argentina, Barbados, Bolivia, Brazil, Chile, Colombia, Costa Rica, Cuba, Dominican Republic, Ecuador, El Salvador, Grenada, Guatemala, Guyana, Haiti, Honduras, Jamaica, Mexico, Nicaragua, Panama, Paraguay, Peru, Suriname, Trinidad and Tobago, Uruguay, Venezuela.

Origin and development. SELA received its strongest impetus from discussions between Venezuelan President Carlos Andrés Pérez and Mexican President Luis Echeverría during the former's visit to Mexico in March 1975. It has been suggested that the two became convinced of the need for a purely Latin American economic organization after passage of the 1974 United States Trade Reform Act. The new agency succeeded the Latin American Economic Coordination Commission (CECLA), which had attempted to provide linkage between Latin economic policies and those of more developed states.

Structure. The governing Latin American Council, composed of ministers from each member state, convenes at least once a year. To facilitate its work, the Council may designate Action Committees; thus far, committees have been established for (1) channeling funds for earthquake recovery in Guatemala, (2) studying projects aimed at the production of high-protein foodstuffs, (3) accelerating housing construction and other social-welfare projects, (4) creating an authority responsible for information on production surpluses and shortfalls, and (5) designing an agency to disseminate information on technical and scientific issues that have application to Latin American development. The Secretariat is headed by a permanent secretary whose term of office is four years.

Activities. While many observers still believe that SELA has the potential to further regional integration in Latin America, progress has been much slower than expected. Nevertheless, a number of cooperative agreements were signed in 1980, including accords to establish a regional monetary system, to work with the UN Industrial Development Organization (UNIDO) and the UN Development Programme (UNDP) on projects in energy and capital goods, and to join with the UN Economic Commission for Latin America and the Caribbean (ECLAC) in increasing joint projects in finance and the exchange of technical information. In January 1982, SELA and the Economic Community of West African States (ECOWAS) concluded an agreement at Caracas, Venezuela, to promote trade between member countries of the two organizations.

SELA has also been striving to increase its role as a Latin American representative in extraregional forums, as evidenced by recent overtures to the European Community. Concerned with the decline of Latin America as an EC trade partner, SELA has proposed a number of measures to enhance trade between the regions. Latin American countries have been particularly hurt by the EC's Common Agricultural Policy, steel and textile restrictions, and a reduction in the Community's generalized system of preferences. Thus, SELA has called for the establishment of a permanent dialogue mechanism and extention of most-favored nation status to all Latin American countries.

With Latin American debt reaching crisis proportions, SELA and the United Nations Economic Commission for Latin America responded to a request by Ecuador's President Hurtado Larrea in February 1983 to propose a debt and development strategy. The subsequent report called for increased regional cooperation among debtors in order to face creditors with an institutionalized rescheduling process, more equitable terms and conditions for rescheduling, and increased intraregional trade to spur development.

Discussion of the debt crisis has continued within SELA and other regional organizations, albeit with little apparent impact. A regional economic conference sponsored by SELA in October 1986 endorsed the concept of linking a country's debt service to its real capacity to pay. In a further toughening of SELA's stance on the issue, the economic ministers of its member states in January 1987 singled out external debt as one of the region's greatest obstacles to development. In May a group of prominent Latin American leaders, led by former Venezuelan president Carlo Andrés Pérez, signed a document outlining plans for regional negotiations with creditors in place of the "case-by-case" approach then in effect. SELA's foreign and finance ministers were asked to review and endorse the plan, which calls for either linking debt payments to exports or limiting them to two percent of GNP. In September, Argentina, Brazil, and Mexico formed the "Group of Three" to coordinate their debt negotiations, although observers suggested that effective action by it or any other grouping of Latin American states remained doubtful in view of widespread political instability and the reluctance of many countries to relinquish economic autonomy.

LATIN AMERICAN INTEGRATION ASSOCIATION (LAIA/ALADI)

Asociación Latinoamericana de Integración

Established: By treaty signed at Montevideo, Uruguay, August 12, 1980, effective March 18, 1981, as successor to the Latin American Free Trade Association.

Headquarters: Montevideo, Uruguay.

Principal Organs: Council of Ministers of Foreign Affairs (all members), Committee of Representatives (all members), Evaluation and Convergence Conference (all members), Secretariat.

Secretary General: Norberto Bertaina (Uruguay).

Membership (11): Argentina, Bolivia, Brazil, Chile, Colombia, Ecuador, Mexico, Paraguay, Peru, Uruguay, Venezuela.

Observers (12): Andean Group, Costa Rica, Cuba, Dominican Republic, Guatemala, Honduras, Inter-American Development Bank, Organization of American States, Portugal, Spain, United Nations Development Program, United Nations Economic Commission for Latin America and the Caribbean.

Official Languages: Spanish, Portuguese; Spanish is the working language.

Origin and development. The decision to establish ALADI resulted from an 11-day meeting at Acapulco, Mexico, in June 1980, of the members of the then extant Latin American Free Trade Association (LAFTA), an organization whose membership was identical to the present organization but whose charter was somewhat more ambitious. At the Acapulco meeting it was argued that a new organization was needed which would be more modest in its goals than LAFTA, without a specific timetable for the achievement of a free-trade zone, and which would explicitly take into account the considerable national differences in economic development that made undesirable the reciprocal trade concessions on which LAFTA had focused. The opposition to ALADI was led by the Brazilian and Mexican foreign ministers, who claimed that all that was necessary was a new protocol to the LAFTA charter. The majority, however, followed the lead of the Andean Group (see separate entry) and agreed to establish a new organization.

While the aim of ALADI is to decrease trade barriers among its member states, no deadline has been set for the achievement of a free-trade zone and flexibility is allowed for members to enter into bilateral tariff, trade, and tech-nology agreements. Moreover, members have been classi-fied according to their levels of economic development and all tariff concessions which are negotiated are to take into account these relative assessments: the less-developed members are Bolivia, Ecuador, and Paraguay; the medium-developed are Chile, Colombia, Peru, Uruguay, and Venezuela; the more-developed are Argentina, Brazil, and Mexico. Existing tariff concessions, largely negotiated under the auspices of LAFTA, were renegotiated during the period 1980–1983 and, in some cases, suspended. New tariff negotiations are to include both reciprocal and preferential accords.

Structure. The Council, composed of the foreign ministers of the member states, is ALADI's principal political organ. Its annual meetings provide a means for reviewing the work of the organization and determining policy. The Committee of Representatives is the Association's permanent political body and meets regularly to ensure that the provisions of the treaty are being implemented. The Evaluation and Convergence Conference, composed of plenipotentiaries of the member states, has the broad task of reviewing integration efforts and promoting new endeavors.

Activities. The transitional period of LAFTA agreement renegotiation ended on April 30, 1983, with a total of 65 "partial scope" (bi- or multilateral) trade agreements having been concluded by members. On the same date, ALADI members signed the first three "regional scope" agreements which provide for preferential treatment for products imported from Bolivia, Ecuador, and Paraguay.

During the first meeting of the Council of Ministers of Foreign Affairs, held November 16, 1983, at Washington, DC, a new secretary general was appointed and work was completed on the Regional Tariff Preference (RTP) scheme. The RTP, subsequently approved during the April 26–27, 1984, Council meeting at Montevideo, Uruguay, established a system of tariff cuts from July 1, 1984, for all ALADI members on the basis of their level of development. The Council also approved resolutions aimed at strengthening financial and monetary cooperation mechanisms; providing special aid measures for less-developed members; ending nontariff barriers to trade; and extending ALADI cooperative measures, including the RTP, to other Latin American and Caribbean states.

In late 1984, a Regional Trade System for ALADI was proposed on the basis of two objectives and two targets. The objectives were expanding and liberalizing intraregional trade while providing measures for regulating bilateral and multilateral commitments in a timely fashion. The targets were removing trade barriers, promoting reciprocal exchanges, and reducing tariff preferences; and introducing measures to ensure the permanence of trade partnerships and the growth of harmonious trade within the region.

In 1984–1985, ALADI decided to specialize in trade and payments. Thus, its attention was directed to promoting the relationship between financing and reciprocal payments and on improving trade within the current financial environment. The final declaration of a special March 2, 1985, summit meeting stated ALADI's intent to use regional integration and cooperation to counteract the negative effects of the current economic and social crisis. At the regular meeting later in the month, it was decided that beginning January 1, 1986, ALADI would have a new Tariff Nomenclature (*Nomenclatura Arancelaria de la ALADI—NALADI)* to ensure appropriate comparability among the national tariffs of members.

High-level representatives from member countries met at Buenos Aires, Argentina, on April 7–9, 1986, in the first stage of a regional round of negotiations to revive sluggish Latin American economies. They issued a "Buenos Aires Letter" that provided cooperation guidelines, in addition to an agenda addressing four main fields of negotiation: trade expansion and regulation, cooperation and economic complementarity, payments and export financing, and preferential measures for the less developed countries of the area. During a subsequent negotiating round at Acapulco, Mexico, on July 21–25, members agreed to a regional import-substitution program, the removal of nontariff barriers, enlargement of the market opening lists in favor of the less-developed countries, and the establishment of regional origin and safeguard rules as of April 27, 1987.

During a meeting at Montevideo, Uruguay, on March 11–12, 1987, the Council of Ministers of Foreign Affairs reaffirmed its "integrationist will" and dedication to the "reinvigoration" of ALADI. In support of that goal, the Council approved on expansion of the RTP, endorsed the proposed elimination of non-tariff barriers by March 1988, established a plan of action to assist the region's less-developed countries, and announced an agreement designed to yield a 40 percent increase in intraregional trade by 1991.

MANO RIVER UNION

Union du Fleuve Mano

Established: By Mano River Declaration issued by the presidents of Liberia and Sierra Leone on October 3, 1973, and accompanying protocols signed in 1974.

Purpose: To promote the economic development of member states by the elimination of tariff barriers and the creation of new productive capacity, with particular emphasis on the hydroelectric potential of the Mano River.

Headquarters: Freetown, Sierra Leone.

Principal Organs: Ministerial Council, Secretariat.

Secretary General: Dr. Abdoulaye Diallo (Guinea).

Members: Guinea, Liberia, Sierra Leone.

Working Languages: English, French.

Origin and development. The Mano River Union was founded in the hope that it might lead to the economic integration of a number of West African states. Guinea joined the group on October 3, 1980, and on May 28, 1981, a customs union was established, with tariff barriers eliminated between the original members and transitional arrangements established for Guinea. However, political conflicts between members, financial problems within the Union, and political and economic turmoil within the three member states have precluded the attainment of many of the organization's original objectives.

Structure. General policy, including approval of the Union's budget, is normally established by the Ministerial Council, which meets yearly. Day-to-day administration is the responsibility of the Secretariat, which maintains offices at Monrovia, Liberia, as well as at Freetown, Sierra Leone; in 1980 an Industrial Development Unit was formed within the Secretariat.

Activities. A two-day summit at Freetown in January 1983 yielded agreement on extradition of criminals and free movement of nationals across member states' boundaries. Nine months later, at the Union's tenth anniversary celebration, groundbreaking ceremonies were held for the Monrovia/Freetown highway, West Germany, AEB, OPEC, BADEA, and the Nigerian Trust Fund having covered 80 percent of the project's cost.

In November 1985 Liberian President Samuel K. Doe recalled (then) Secretary General Augustus Caine from the Union's headquarters after accusing Sierra Leone of involvement in an attempted coup by an opposition group. Guinea was also charged with complicity and, despite denials by both governments, borders with the two countries were closed. The tension caused virtually all activities to cease and left the organization without an approved budget.

Dr. Caine returned to his post in March 1986 and, with the assistance of the Organization of African Unity (OAU), convinced Guinea President Lansana Conté to mediate the dispute. On July 12 President Momoh of Sierra Leone joined Doe and Conté in the first summit since 1983 at Conakry, Guinea, the three agreeing to end their differences "in the spirit of the Mano River Union". Liberia's borders with Sierra Leone were reopened immediately, those with Guinea having previously reopened on January 14.

With the potential for revitalization established, the 11th Ministerial Meeting at Conakry in early September sought ways to return the Union to financial solvency, the lengthy failure of the members to meet budgeted contributions having halted work on the Monrovia/Freetown highway, a hydroelectric power station, and other projects. The members agreed to make payments on arrears, with sharp reductions ordered in the size of staff and scope of programs.

In November the three heads of state concluded a treaty of nonaggression and security cooperation which prohibited subversive activities by one member against another and called for the creation of a joint committee for settling disagreements within the framework of the OAU. Existing bilateral defense cooperation agreements between Sierra Leone and Guinea and between Liberia and Guinea were incorporated into the agreement.

The security pact was upheld during 1987 with reported coup attempts in Sierra Leone and Liberia failing to generate intraregional accusations. However, little progress was registered in economic cooperation and development projects because of low staff morale and continued insolvency. Nonetheless, further budget reductions were ordered during the 12th Ministerial Meeting at Freetown in November, with replacements named for Dr. Caine and other top officials. During a summit meeting at Freetown on March 2, 1988, presidents Conté, Doe, and Momoh endorsed the restructuring and vowed to hasten development of a monetary union for their states.

NONALIGNED MOVEMENT

Established: In the course of an increasingly structured series of nonaligned conferences, the first of which met at Belgrade, Yugoslavia, September 1–6, 1961, and the most recent at Harare, Zimbabwe, September 1–7, 1986.

Purpose: To ensure "the national independence, sovereignty, territorial integrity and security of nonaligned countries" in their "struggle against imperialism, colonialism, neocolonialism, apartheid, racism, including Zionism, and all forms of foreign aggression, occupation, domination, interference or hegemony, as well as against great power and bloc politics" (*Final Declaration,* Havana, 1979).

Headquarters: None.

Principal Organs: Conference of Heads of State (all members), Meeting of Foreign Ministers (all members), Political and Economic Committees, Coordinating Bureau (36 members).

President: Robert Mugabe (Zimbabwe).

Membership (101): Afghanistan, Algeria, Angola, Argentina, Bahamas, Bahrain, Bangladesh, Barbados, Belize, Benin, Bhutan, Boliva, Botswana, Burkina Faso, Burundi, Cameroon, Cape Verde Islands, Central African Republic, Chad, Colombia, Comoro Islands, Congo, Côte d'Ivoire, Cuba, Cyprus, Djibouti, Ecuador, Egypt, Equatorial Guinea, Ethiopia, Gabon, Gambia, Ghana, Grenada, Guinea, Guinea-Bissau, Guyana, India, Indonesia, Iran, Iraq, Jamaica, Jordan, Kampuchea, Kenya, Democratic People's Republic of Korea, Kuwait, Laos, Lebanon, Lesotho, Liberia, Libya, Madagascar, Malawi, Malaysia, Maldives, Mali, Malta, Mauritania, Mauritius, Morocco, Mozambique, Nepal, Nicaragua, Niger, Nigeria, Oman, Pakistan, Palestine Liberation Organization, Panama, Peru, Qatar, Rwanda, St. Lucia, Sao Tome and Principe, Saudi Arabia, Senegal, Seychelles, Sierra Leone, Singapore, Somalia, South West African People's Organisation, Sri Lanka, Sudan, Suriname, Swaziland, Syria, Tanzania, Togo, Trinidad and Tobago, Tunisia, Uganda, United

Arab Emirates, Vanuatu, Vietnam, Yemen Arab Republic, People's Democratic Republic of Yemen, Yugoslavia, Zaire, Zambia, Zimbabwe. The 1979 Conference refused to seat either delegation (representing the Khieu Samphan and Heng Samrin regimes) from Kampuchea; subsequently Burma, a founding member, announced its withdrawal, while Venezuela shifted from full-member to observer status because of a boundary dispute with Guyana.

Observers (11): Antigua and Barbuda, Brazil, Costa Rica, Dominica, El Salvador, Mexico, Papua New Guinea, Philippines, the United Nations, Uruguay, Venezuela.

Guests (9): Austria, Dominican Republic, Finland, Portugal, Romania, San Marino, Sweden, Switzerland, the Vatican.

Origin and development. The first Conference of Nonaligned Heads of State, at which 25 countries were represented, was convened at Belgrade in September 1961, largely through the initiative of Yugoslavian President Josip Tito, who had expressed concern that an accelerating arms race might result in war between the Soviet Union and the United States (Yugoslavia has since remained the only full member from continental Europe). Subsequent Conferences, involving ever-increased participation by Third World countries, were convened at Cairo, Egypt, in 1964; Lusaka, Zambia, in 1970; Algiers, Algeria, in 1973; Colombo, Sri Lanka, in 1976; Havana, Cuba, in 1979; New Delhi, India, in 1983; and Harare, Zimbabwe, in 1986.

The 1964 Conference at Cairo, with 47 countries represented, featured widespread condemnation of Western colonialism and the retention of foreign military installations. Thereafter, the focus shifted away from essentially political issues, such as independence for dependent territories, to the advocacy of occasionally radical solutions to global economic and other problems. Thus, at Algiers in 1973 there was an appeal for concerted action by the "poor nations against the industrialized world"; this became a basis of debate within the United Nations for a new international economic order (NIEO) and led to the convening of an inconclusive Conference on International Economic Cooperation at Paris, France, in late 1975.

At Colombo in 1976 the changed outlook was summed up by the foreign minister of Singapore, who, after pointing out that the Nonaligned Movement (NAM) was founded on anticolonialism, stated that "the new thrust . . . is economic" and that economic issues would henceforth "be the major concern of international politics". Col. Mu'ammar al-Qadhafi of Libya went so far as to demand that the nonaligned nations press for compensation from former colonial rulers for the "international robberies" they had committed, while others, using OPEC as a model, called for the formation of effective producers' associations in such commodities as bauxite, copper, and aluminum.

At the 1979 Havana meeting, political concerns resurfaced in the context of an intense debate between Cuban President Castro, who was charged with attempting to "bend" the movement in the direction of the "socialist camp", and Yugoslavian President Tito, who urged that it remain true to its genuinely nonaligned origins. In search of a compromise, the Final Declaration of the Havana Conference referred to the movement's "non-bloc nature" and its opposition to both "hegemony" (a euphemism used in reference to presumed Soviet ambitions) and all forms of "imperialism, colonialism, and neocolonialism". In addition, the Conference reiterated an earlier identification of "Zionism as a form of racism", called for withdrawal of all foreign troops from Cyprus and South Korea, and declared its support for resistance movements in Namibia and Zimbabwe (then Rhodesia). It also referred to the Coordinating Bureau the question of whether Egypt should be excluded from membership because of "the damage caused to the Arab countries" by having concluded a peace treaty with Israel.

At the 1983 New Delhi conference, delegates focused on the precarious financial condition of Third World countries. The conference's declaration stated, in part, that developed countries should meet with developing countries to discuss debt relief, reduced trade barriers, increased aid for development, and increased cash flow. Its economic proposals, already widely accepted by the world banking community, called for the rescheduling of Third World debt and an increase in Special Drawing Rights by the International Monetary Fund. Other major points in the declaration included appeals for a halt in the arms race and demilitarization of the Indian Ocean, a tribunal to try Israel on charges of war crimes against the Palestinian people, and support to the Argentinians in their dispute with Britain over the Falklands (Malvinas) Islands. In addition, the actions of the Soviet Union in Kampuchea and Afghanistan and of the United States in El Salvador were implicitly condemned.

Structure. By convention, the chief executive of the country hosting the most recent Conference of Heads of State serves as the NAM's president. Foreign ministers' meetings are convened irregulary between Conferences, which are held every three years. A 25-member Coordinating Bureau, established at the 1973 Conference, was expanded to 36 members in 1979, the regional distribution being as follows: Africa, 17 seats; Asia, 12; Latin America, 5; Europe, 1; with 1 seat being shared between Europe and Africa.

Activities. A special meeting held April 25, 1985, at Bandung, Indonesia, commemorated the thirtieth anniversary of the Asia-Africa Conference, which had laid the foundation for the NAM. The meeting's final declaration stated that the world was in more desperate straits than in 1955 because of increased tension, violence, and insecurity. During a conference at Luanda, Angola, on September 4–9, 1985, foreign ministers demanded economic sanctions against South Africa, condemned US involvement in Nicaragua, endorsed self-determination for New Caledonia, and called for negotiations between Morocco and Polisario guerrilla forces in the Western Sahara.

The eighth summit was held at Harare, Zimbabwe, on September 1–7, 1986, the 25th anniversary of the Movement. The site was chosen to underscore the group's main concern: the South African government's policy of forced racial segregation. A final declaration called on nonaligned nations to adopt selective, voluntary sanctions against South Africa pending the adoption of comprehensive, mandatory measures, including the termination of air links and restrictions on trade and investment, by the UN Security Council. The members demanded international pressure to eliminate apartheid, Pretoria's withdrawal from Namibia (South-West Africa), and an end to its aggression against neighboring states. Plans were made to send a team of foreign ministers to South Africa's major trading partners, the United States, the United Kingdom, West Germany, and Japan, to encourage the imposition of immediate sanctions. In addition, an African Fund was authorized to assist Black liberation movements in Namibia and South Africa and to aid the infrastructures of the six Front-Line States.

With Liberia, Singapore, and a number of other members dissenting, the United States was severely criticized for its lack of sanctions against Pretoria, as well as for its policies toward Angola, Libya, and Nicaragua. Zimbabwe's prime minister, Robert Mugabe, in his opening remarks, charged the United States with "international bullyism" by its attacks on Libya. In implicit criticism of the Soviet Union, the withdrawal of foreign forces from Afghanistan was also urged. The superpowers were called upon to create a moratorium on all nuclear testing and development and, in what was named the "Harare Appeal", the heads of state agreed to send letters to the leaders of the two countries asking them to work together to end the arms race.

In other areas, the group denounced Israel for its occupation of Arab territory and its activities in Lebanon, while reiterating support for the Palestinians' "just struggle". An appeal was made for the end of interference by unspecified outsiders in the Kampuchean conflict, and both sides were encouraged to negotiate for peace in the Iran-Iraq war. In recognition of a commitment to end structural imbalances in the world economy and the increasing debt problem of the Third World, a plea was made for a new international economic order aimed at reform of the monetary system, fairer trade practices, and a renewal of the North-South dialogue. A special ministerial committee for economic cooperation among the nonaligned was formed, and a call was issued for a new round of multilateral trade negotiations, in which the United Nations Conference on Trade and Development (UNCTAD) would play an enhanced role. In addition, an Independent Commission of the South on Development Issues, chaired by former Tanzanian president Julius Nyerere, was established to study the causes of underdevelopment and produce common strategies to combat it.

The hope of emerging from the summit as a united front with greater influence in world affairs was thwarted by quarrels and disputes. Libya's Mu'ammar al-Qadhafi branded the organization useless and suggested that members align themselves with the Warsaw Pact. He also attacked several countries for their association with the United States and recognition of Israel. Iran's president, Hojatolislam Ali Khamenei, demanded that Iraq be branded an aggressor and expelled from the group for starting the Gulf war. Further tension emerged when India and Pakistan disagreed over the handling of the September 1986 hijacking of a Pan American airliner at Karachi, Pakistan.

Because of controversy over a Nicaraguan bid, final decision on the choice of venue for the 1989 summit has been delayed. Some members feel that Nicaragua, perceived by many as aligned, would impair the Movement's image of neutrality.

In November 1986 the NAM sponsored the Lima Conference on Third World Indebtedness, which called for multilateral rather than case-by-case negotiations between developing countries and their creditors. In 1987 activity, the Committee of Nine on Palestine, appointed at the 1986 summit, called on NAM President Mugabe to convene a conference to seek a settlement that would enable "all states in the region, including the State of Palestine, to live in amity and within secure borders". At a June meeting of NAM information ministers, Mugabe accused Western news agencies of "distorting information" by wearing "ideological blinkers", while the ministers encouraged further expansion and use of the Nonaligned Countries News Agency Pool (NANAP), established to reduce the Third World's dependence on Western news services.

NORDIC COUNCIL

Established: By enabling legislation passed by the parliaments of the member states (excluding Finland, which joined in 1955), following agreement at a foreign ministers' meeting at Copenhagen, Denmark, March 16, 1952, with effect from February 12, 1953.

Purpose: To provide a forum for consultation among the legislatures and governments of the member states on matters of common interest.

Headquarters: Stockholm, Sweden.

Principal Organs: Council (all members), Presidium (all members), Standing Committees, Secretariats.

President of the Presidium (1987–1988): Elsi Hetemäki-Olander (Finland).

Membership (5): Denmark (including Faroe Islands and Greenland), Finland (including Åland), Iceland, Norway, Sweden.

Official Languages: Danish, Norwegian, Swedish.

Origin and development. First advocated by Denmark in 1938, the Nordic Council grew out of an unsuccessful attempt in 1948–1949 to negotiate a Scandinavian defense union. A drafting committee set up by the Nordic Interparliamentary Union in 1951 developed the legal basis of the organization, which was established not by treaty but by identical laws adopted by the parliaments of Denmark, Ireland, Norway, and Sweden. A supplementary Treaty of Cooperation (since subject to several amendments) was signed at Helsinki, Finland, on March 23, 1962, to further develop legal, cultural, social, economic, and communica-

tions cooperation. In 1970 the Faroe Islands and the Åland Islands were granted separate representation within the Danish and Finnish delegations, respectively. In 1971 a Council of Ministers was created as a separate forum for cooperation among the Nordic governments. In 1984 Greenland was granted separate representation within the Danish delegation.

Structure. The Council encompasses 87 members elected by national or territorial parliaments. The Swedish and Norwegian parliaments select 20 representatives each; Iceland's parliament selects seven. Of Denmark's 20 representatives, 16 are selected by the national parliament and two each by the parliaments of the Faroe Islands and Greenland. Of Finland's 20 representatives, 18 are selected by the national parliament and two by the parliament of the Åland Islands. In principle each delegation reflects the distribution of parties within its parent legislature. Since 1982 there have also been four political groups (Social Democratic, Conservative, Center, and Socialist Left) within the Council itself.

The Council, augmented by nonvoting representatives, normally meets once a year. Its influence emanates primarily from recommendations and statements of opinion addressed to the Council of Ministers or one or more of the member governments. Reporting to the Council are six Standing Committees: Economic, Communications, Legal, Cultural, Social and Environment, and Budget and Control.

A Presidium, consisting of a president and nine vice presidents, is appointed by the plenary assembly from among its elected members. It presides over the assembly session and supervises the Council's work between meetings, assisted by a Secretariat under the direction of a secretary general. The Secretariat is also responsible for day-to-day contact with the Council of Ministers and other international organizations.

The Council of Ministers, whose composition varies according to the subject under consideration, reviews Nordic Council recommendations and serves as a regional decision-making body. Its decisions, which must be unanimous, are binding on the member states save in matters subject to ratification by the national parliaments. The Council of Ministers is assisted by its own Secretariat, located at Copenhagen, Denmark.

Activities. The Nordic Council has provided a forum for consultation among the Scandinavian parliaments on questions of economic, cultural, and legal cooperation. Cultural cooperation has taken many forms, including joint research into problems in reading and writing, the establishment of institutions to promote mutual understanding of Nordic languages, and the establishment of common academies for folk art, urban and regional planning, and public health. In some areas the laws of the Nordic countries have been almost completely harmonized, while in other areas agreement has been reached on common principles or basic legal rules. Particularly impressive results have been obtained in civil and family law. In the commercial field, laws bearing on contracts, installment purchases, instruments of debt, commercial agents, insurance, bills of exchange, and checks are now almost identical, as are those governing copyrights, patents, trademarks, and industrial designs. In 1981, a Nordic Language Convention allowed citizens of one Nordic country to use their native language in court proceedings in another Nordic jurisdiction. An agreement on voting rights was concluded in October 1975, with subsequent revisions allowing all Nordic citizens reciprocal rights of voting and of contesting municipal elections in the country in which they are resident.

Cooperation in social and health policy was formalized in the 1955 Convention on Social Security, augmented in 1975 by an agreement on rights relating to sickness, pregnancy, and birth. A new Convention on Social Security, signed on March 5, 1981, extended additional coverage to individuals temporarily resident in a Nordic country other than their own. In 1973 a Nordic Transport Agreement was enacted to increase efficiency in transportation and communications. Between 1979 and 1983, cooperation in the area of transport increased further with the construction of an interstate highway system, harmonization of road traffic rules, agreements for the development of a rational and efficient traffic system, and establishment of a common Scandinavian Airline System. In the economic field, a Nordic Investment Bank became operative June 1, 1976 (see section on Regional Development Banks). Additional conventions include a 1974 accord on protection of the environment, a 1981 treaty on Nordic cooperation in development assistance, and a 1982 common labor market agreement which guarantees the right to seek work and residence within all member states. A Nordic Research Policy Council was established in 1983 to coordinate research in a number of scientific areas, while a Development Fund was inaugurated in 1987 to expand railway and highway construction in the West Nordic region.

In recent years much attention has been paid to the promotion of intraregional economic growth as well as heightened extraregional trade. During its 35th plenary session at Helsinki, Finland, in February 1987, the Council endorsed recommendations from the Council of Ministers for the removal of technical and other nontariff barriers to trade between members and for increased cooperation with other international groupngs, especially the European Community. In other activity, the Council asked the Council of Ministers to study alternatives for increasing the budget for Nordic projects, to draw up a regional plan to combat air and water pollution, to extend cooperation in broadcasting, to emphasize consumer protection programs, and to conduct research projects on drug abuse and control policies.

NORTH ATLANTIC TREATY ORGANIZATION (NATO/OTAN)

Organisation du Traité de l'Atlantique Nord

Established: September 17, 1949, by action of the North Atlantic Council pursuant to the North Atlantic Treaty signed at Washington, DC, on April 4, 1949, and effective August 24, 1949.

Purpose: To provide a system of collective defense in the event of armed attack against any member by means of a policy based on the principles of credible deterrence and genuine détente; to work towards a constructive East-West relationship through dialogue and mutually advantageous cooperation, including efforts to reach agreement on militarily significant, equitable, and verifiable arms reduction; to cooperate within the alliance in economic, scientific, cultural, and other areas.

Headquarters: Brussels, Belgium.

Principal Organs: North Atlantic Council (all members), Defense Planning Committee and Nuclear Planning Group (all members except France), Military Committee (all members except France and Iceland).

Chairman of the North Atlantic Council and Secretary General: Manfred Wörner (Federal Republic of Germany).

Membership (16): Belgium, Canada, Denmark, France, Federal Republic of Germany, Greece, Iceland, Italy, Luxembourg, Netherlands, Norway, Portugal, Spain, Turkey, United Kingdom, United States.

Official Languages: English, French.

Origin and development. The postwar consolidation of Western defenses was undertaken in light of the perceived hostility of the Soviet Union as reflected in such actions as the creation of the Communist Information Bureau (Cominform) in October 1947, the February 1948 coup in Czechoslovakia, and the June 1948 blockade of West Berlin. American willingness to join Western Europe in a common defense system was expressed in the Vandenberg Resolution adopted by the US Senate on June 11, 1948, and subsequent negotiations culminated in the signing of the North Atlantic Treaty on April 4, 1949, by representatives of Belgium, Canada, Denmark, France, Iceland, Italy, Luxembourg, Netherlands, Norway, Portugal, the United Kingdom, and the United States.

The Treaty did not prescribe the nature of the organization that was to carry out the obligations of the signatory states, stipulating only that the parties should establish a council which, in turn, would create a defense committee and any necessary subsidiary bodies. The outbreak of the Korean War on June 25, 1950, accelerated the growth of the alliance and led to the appointment in 1951 of Gen. Dwight D. Eisenhower as the first Supreme Allied Commander in Europe. Emphasis on strengthened military defense of a broad area, reflected in the accession of Greece and Turkey to the Treaty on February 18, 1952, reached a climax at a meeting of the North Atlantic Council at Lisbon, Portugal, on February 20–25, 1952, with the adoption of goals calling for a total of 50 divisions, 4,000 aircraft, and strengthened naval forces. Subsequent plans to strengthen the alliance by rearming the Federal Republic of Germany (as part of the European Defense Community) collapsed, with the result that the FRG was permitted to establish its own armed forces and, in May 1955, to join NATO.

NATO's gravest problem during the mid-1960s was the estrangement of France over matters of defense. French resistance to military "integration" under NATO reached a climax in 1966 when President de Gaulle announced the removal of French forces from consolidated commands and gave notice that all allied troops not under French command had to be removed from French soil by early 1967. These stipulations necessitated the rerouting of supply lines for NATO forces in Germany; transfer of the alliance's European command from Paris, France, to Casteau, Belgium; and relocation of other allied commands and military facilities. Since its withdrawal from the integrated military command structure, France has participated selectively in NATO's activities.

During the 1970s, NATO suffered from additional internal strains. Early in 1976 Iceland threatened to leave the Organization because of a dispute with Britain over fishing rights off the Icelandic coast. Disputes between Greece and Turkey, initially over Cyprus and subsequently over offshore oil rights in the Aegean Sea, resulted in Greece's withdrawal from NATO's integrated military command and a refusal to participate in NATO military exercises. In October 1980, five months after Greece threatened to close down US bases on its territory, negotiations yielded an agreement on its return as a full participant. In 1981, however, Greece's status was again put in doubt by the election of a Socialist government that had called for a second withdrawal. Indicatively, Athens delayed issuance of a final communiqué at the December 1981 meeting of defense and foreign ministers because of the dispute with Ankara. Although Greece has not yet carried through on its threat, relations with its neighbor have remained tenuous.

In 1977, US representatives attempted to convince their European allies to increase defense spending and to expand cooperation in weapons development programs. As a result, the NATO defense ministers agreed to seek a real increase in defense spending of 3 percent per year, a commitment repeated in subsequent years and still the alliance's official, albeit unachieved, target. Much subsequent discussion within NATO focused on US exhortations that the European members live up to the 1977 agreement; this was viewed as particularly critical in light of the Soviet invasion of Afghanistan, the Iran-Iraq war, unrest in Poland, and the Reagan administration's perception of a massive Soviet military buildup. Offsetting the US demands for increased defense spending were the joint pressures of economic recession, budget limitations, and a growing antinuclear movement in Western Europe.

In June 1980 US President Jimmy Carter reaffirmed his administration's conviction that Spanish membership in NATO would significantly enhance the Organization's defensive capability. The Spanish government originally made its application contingent upon Britain's return of Gibraltar and the admission of Spain to the European Community, but Madrid later decided that it could negotiate both issues subsequent to entry. Therefore, following approval in late October by the Spanish *Cortes,* the government formally petitioned for NATO membership, with

a protocol providing for Spanish accession being signed by the members on December 10, 1981. Spain's Socialist Party had long opposed entry, although its leader, Felip González, appeared to waver on the issue after being designated prime minister in December 1982. Two years later, he indicated that he would not attempt to influence the outcome of an accession referendum in March 1986, the results of which, by a 53 percent margin, ensured Spain's continued participation with three domestic stipulations: the maintenance of Spanish forces outside NATO's integrated command; a ban on the installation, storage, and introduction of nuclear weapons; and a progressive reduction in the US military presence.

Structure. NATO possesses a dual military-civilian institutional structure that has developed to meet its unique combination of military and civil responsibilities.

The Military Committee, consisting of permanent military representatives from all members except France and Iceland, is the highest military authority under the Council and Defense Planning Committee (DPC), with responsibility for furnishing guidance on military questions both to the Council and to subordinate commands. The NATO military structure embraces three main regional commands: Allied Command Europe, Allied Command Atlantic, and Allied Command Channel. Each is responsible for developing defense plans for its area, for determining force requirements, and for the deployment and exercise of its forces. Except for certain air defense forces in Europe, however, the forces assigned to the various commands remain under national control in peacetime. The headquarters of Allied Command Europe, known formally as Supreme Headquarters Allied Powers Europe (SHAPE), is located at Casteau. The Supreme Allied Commander Europe (Saceur) has traditionally been designated by the United States and serves concurrently as Commander in Chief of US forces in Europe (Cinceur). Allied Command Atlantic, with headquarters at Norfolk, Virginia, is headed by the Supreme Allied Commander Atlantic (Saclant), who is also designated by the United States. Allied Command Channel (Acchan), with headquarters at Northwood (Middlesex), England, is directed by the Allied Commander in Chief Channel (Cinchan). The Canada–United States Regional Planning Group, originally created in 1940, was incorporated into the NATO command structure in 1949. Its task is to recommend plans for the defense of the US-Canada region.

On the civilian side, the North Atlantic Council is the principal political organ. It normally meets twice a year at the ministerial level to consider major policy issues, with the participation of the member states' ministers of foreign affairs. Between ministerial meetings the Council remains in permanent session at NATO headquarters, where member governments are represented by permanent delegates holding ambassadorial rank. All policy decisions of the Council must be unanimous. The DPC was organized in 1963 primarily to analyze national defense expenditures of NATO members and to coordinate military planning, forces, and weapons with these projections. The Committee meets periodically in Permanent Representative sessions and twice a year at the ministerial level.

Subject to policies established by the Council and the Defense Planning Committee, the work of NATO is conducted by specialized committees organized to deal with political, economic, military, and a variety of other matters. The Committee on the Challenges of Modern Society, for example, was formed in response to a proposal made by US President Nixon on the 20th anniversary of NATO that the alliance should seek solutions to common environmental problems.

The secretary general, who is designated by the Council, is responsible for implementing Council and DPC decisions and providing them with expert advice. He has an important political role in achieving consensus among member governments and can offer his services in seeking solutions to bilateral disputes.

The North Atlantic Assembly, founded in 1955 as the NATO Parliamentarians' Conference, is completely independent of NATO but constitutes an unofficial link between it and parliamentarians of member states. By keeping under constant review the alliance's major political problems and disseminating knowledge of its policies and activities, the Assembly encourages political discussion of NATO matters. It meets each autumn in plenary session.

Activities. In accord with a 1979 agreement among the NATO members, deployment of intermediate-range nuclear forces was begun in Britain, Italy and West Germany in November 1983. The parliaments of Belgium and the Netherlands continued to debate the deployment scheduled for their countries, Belgium ultimately approving deployment in March 1985 and the Netherlands following suit in November. As an immediate consequence of the deployment, Soviet representatives walked out of the negotiations on intermediate-range nuclear forces (INF) and strategic arms reduction (START) on November 23 and December 8, 1983, respectively, with talks being suspended thereafter until March 1985.

During 1985 discussion within NATO centered on new US weapons research, with particular emphasis on the Strategic Defense Initiative (SDI), known as "Star Wars" because of its space-based laser configuration. Other NATO countries were asked to participate in research on SDI weapons and to consider areas in which they might wish to contribute their efforts. However, France refused any role and the development of SDI remained a source of contention within the alliance. Thus, the final communiqué of a foreign ministers' meeting in December made no reference to the Initiative, participants expressing support instead for American arms-control efforts. Although disappointed with the failure of the US-USSR arms summit at Reykjavik, Iceland, in October 1986 (see US and USSR articles), the ministers again failed to criticize publicly the Reagan administration's posture on SDI. NATO's Nuclear Planning Group, meeting at Gleneagles, Scotland, on October 21–22, played down reports of disagreement over Star Wars and voiced objection to the elimination of European nuclear capabilities without adequate reductions in chemical and conventional forces.

Three major agreements were reached by the NATO allies from late 1985 to mid-1986. Ending a long-running battle, formal plans for cooperation in the development of new conventional weapon systems were approved by the foreign ministers on December 12, 1985 at Brussels, Belgium, with a commitment to review several joint projects, ranging from research to production and testing, aimed at eliminating deficiencies and duplication in nonnuclear equipment. In May 1986, NATO defense ministers endorsed a proposal for the production of new chemical weapons by the United States. The accord sanctioned the removal of existing stockpiles from West Germany by 1992 and for storage of the new binary weapons in the eastern United States, except in times of crisis or war. Some members, however, opposed the program, which they felt could undermine efforts by the 40-nation Disarmament Conference at Geneva to negotiate a worldwide ban on such weapons. NATO also participated in the tenth round of the 35-nation Conference on Security and Cooperation in Europe at Stockholm, Sweden, which led to the historic adoption of confidence- and security-building measures aimed at decreasing the risk of accidental war. After concessions by both sides, rules of conduct were developed to provide a framework for notification and verification of troop movements and military maneuvers by NATO and Warsaw Pact nations.

Division between NATO allies erupted with the US bombing of Libya in April 1986. Most West European governments apart from Britain were critical of the attack, with France and Spain refusing to allow the use of their airspace for the action. Questions regarding the limits of NATO's mandate prompted the secretary general, Lord Carrington, to recommend the creation of an outside forum for such controversial issues as international terrorism. US actions were also assailed by the foreign ministers during a May 1986 meeting at Halifax, Nova Scotia, after the Reagan administration had announced its plans to abandon the 1979 SALT II treaty because of the Soviet Union's failure to adhere to its terms. The allies were disturbed because the decision had been made without consultation and felt it illustrated disdain for efforts to obtain new arms-control agreements.

Earlier conflict within the alliance had arisen when Greece asserted that Turkey, not the Soviet Union, was the greatest threat to its security. The Papandreou government went on to declare that it would not participate in NATO military exercises in the Aegean if Greece's claims vis-à-vis Ankara went unrecognized. At a December 5, 1984, meeting at Brussels, Belgium, both Greece and Turkey vetoed each other's defense plans, with the result that neither committed forces for 1985. Subsequently, Greece withdrew from NATO's Defense College upon the scheduling of an exercise in which a hypothetical government, with foreign help, overthrows a "leftist" regime. In April 1986, on the other hand, Greece participated in a naval exercise for testing NATO's methods of supervising civil shipping.

When it became apparent in 1987 that the superpowers were moving toward a treaty eliminating intermediate-range nuclear weapons, concern was voiced within NATO over the impact on deterrence capability, given the Warsaw Pact's superiority to NATO in conventional forces. Some members also seemed to feel that the treaty might represent a "decoupling" of the United States from its extensive military presence in Europe. However, NATO defense ministers ultimately announced their countries' "unanimous and full support" for the agreement signed in December by Soviet General Secretary Gorbachev and US President

Reagan. The ministers also encouraged further discussions regarding conventional arms and so-called "battlefield" (very short-range) nuclear weapons. Some leaders in West Germany, where a "tactical" nuclear war is most likely to be fought, supported the elimination of battlefield weapons, a move opposed by most other NATO members.

In June 1987 Gen. John R. Galvin, theretofore responsible for overseeing US military forces in Latin America, was installed as Supreme Allied Commander Europe. Galvin succeeded Gen. Bernard W. Rogers, who was popular among NATO associates for his predominately "European point of view" and had been critical of the Soviet-US missile treaty. In addition, NATO's top civilian official, Lord Carrington, announced his retirement, Manfred Wörner, for five years West Germany's defense minister, becoming the first person from his country to be named secretary general, effective July 1, 1988. The appointment was seen as recognition of West Germany's critical "frontline" geographic position vis-à-vis the Soviet bloc and of its role as the leading European contributor of NATO funds and personnel.

During their first summit in six years, held at Brussels on March 2–3, 1988, the 16 NATO heads of state and government again called for a reduction in Warsaw Pact conventional arms and dedicated NATO to an "appropriate mix of adequate and effective nuclear and conventional arms which will continue to be kept up to date where necessary". In effect, the vagueness of the statement permitted the summit leaders to emphasize their solidarity on NATO's future role while postponing action on the potentially divisive issue of battlefield nuclear weapons.

ORGANIZATION FOR ECONOMIC COOPERATION AND DEVELOPMENT (OECD/OCDE)

Organisation de Coopération et de Développement Economique

Established: By convention signed at Paris, France, December 14, 1960, effective September 30, 1961.

Purpose: ". . . to help member countries promote economic growth, employment, and improved standards of living through the coordination of policy [and] . . . to help promote the sound and harmonious development of the world economy and improve the lot of the developing countries, particularly the poorest."

Headquarters: Paris, France.

Principal Organs: Council (all members), Executive Committee (14 members), Economic Policy Committee, Development Assistance Committee, Secretariat.

Secretary General: Jean-Claude Paye (France).

Membership (24): Australia, Austria, Belgium, Canada, Denmark, Finland, France, Federal Republic of Germany, Greece, Iceland, Ireland, Italy, Japan, Luxembourg, Netherlands, New Zealand, Norway, Portugal, Spain, Sweden, Switzerland, Turkey, United Kingdom, United States.

Limited Participants: Commission of the European Communities, Yugoslavia.

Official Languages: English, French.

Origin and development. The OECD replaced the Organization for European Economic Cooperation (OEEC), whose original tasks—the administration of Marshall Plan aid and the cooperative effort for European recovery from World War II—had long been completed, though many of its activities had continued or had been adjusted to meet the needs of economic expansion. By the 1960s the once seemingly permanent dollar gap had disappeared, many quantitative restrictions on trade within Europe had been eliminated, and currency convertibility had been largely achieved. This increased economic interdependence suggested the need for an organization in which North American states would participate on an equal footing. Thus the OEEC, of which Canada and the United States had been only associate members, was transformed into the OECD. The new grouping was also viewed as a means of overseeing foreign aid contributions to less-developed states. It later expanded to include virtually all the economically advanced free-market states: Japan became a full member in 1964, followed by Finland in 1969, Australia in 1971, and New Zealand in 1973.

Structure. The Council, the principal political organ, convenes at least once a year at the ministerial level, though regular meetings are held by permanent representatives. Generally, acts of the Council require unanimity, although different voting rules may be adopted in particular circumstances. Supervision of OECD activities is the responsibility of the 14-member Executive Committee, whose members are elected annually by the Council and normally meet once a week. The secretary general, who chairs the regular Council meetings, is responsible for implementing Council and Executive Committee decisions.

Probably the best known of OECD's subsidiary organs is the Development Assistance Committee (DAC), which evolved from the former Development Assistance Group and now includes most of the world's economically advanced states as well as the Commission of the European Communities. The DAC oversees members' official resource transfers. The Economic Policy Committee, another major OECD organ, is responsible for reviewing economic activities in all member states; its Working Party 1 (WP-1) is a forum for the analysis of macroeconomic and structural policies, while Working Party 3 (WP-3) is a center for examining balance-of-payments problems. A Working Party on Long-Term Problems of Turkey was formed in 1979 to review Turkish policies and to facilitate assistance from other OECD members. Other committees have been established to deal with Agriculture, Consumer Policy, Economic and Development Review, Education, Energy, Environment, Financial Markets, Fiscal Affairs,

Industry, International Investment and Multinational Enterprises, Invisible Transactions, Manpower and Social Affairs, Maritime Transport, Restrictive Business Practices, Scientific and Technological Policy, Tourism, and Trade. The Committee on International Investment and Multinational Enterprises was responsible for formulating a voluntary code of conduct for multinational corporations that was adopted by the OECD in 1976. In addition, "high-level groups" have been organized to investigate Commodities, Positive Adjustment Policies, and Employment of Women. There is also an Executive Committee Group on North-South Economic Issues.

To complement the work of the DAC, an OECD Development Center was established in 1962. Its current priorities emphasize the problems of meeting the basic needs of the world's poorest people, with a focus on rural development and appropriate technology. The Center for Educational Research and Innovation (CERI), established in 1968, works toward similar goals.

The OECD Nuclear Energy Agency (NEA), established in December 1957, supplements national efforts toward peaceful nuclear development, while the Organization's Energy Committee has sought to assist with the energy needs of the member states. The secretary general participated in the 1974 Washington Energy Conference, and representatives of the United States, Canada, and all of the members of the European Communities except France subsequently agreed to establish a new International Energy Agency (IEA) under OECD auspices (see separate entry). In 1976 the Research Project on the Future Development of Advanced Industrial Societies in Harmony with That of the Developing Countries (Interfutures) was established within the OECD framework, but with its own governing committee. All OECD members except New Zealand participate in the activities of the Development Center and the Nuclear Energy Agency.

Activities. The key to the OECD's major role in international economic cooperation is its continuous review of economic policies and trends in member states, each of which submits information annually on its economic status and policies and is required to answer questions prepared by the Secretariat and other members. This "confrontation" review procedure has led to very frank exchanges, often followed by recommendations for policy changes. OECD analyses, generated in part through the use of a highly sophisticated computerized model of the world economy, are widely respected for being free of the political concerns that often skew forecasts issued by individual countries.

In the early 1980s, the OECD turned to a consideration of supply-side economic policies to augment existing anti-inflation measures. In addition, members examined the social problems inherent in structural adjustments required of mature economies. With the appearance of economic recovery within the OECD, members began consideration of policies to achieve sustainable growth and reduction of unemployment along with more specialized concerns such as liberalization of trade in services and management of the international debt crisis.

In recent years the OECD has been in the forefront of efforts to combat unstable currencies, massive trade imbalances, Third World indebtedness, and high unemployment in industrialized countries. Success has been limited, however, and in early 1987 the OECD leadership described prevailing policies as insufficient to deal with the world's economic turmoil. In particular the OECD urged the United States to reduce its large budget deficit and try to halt the fall of the value of the dollar in world money markets. In contrast, Japan and West Germany were encouraged to cut taxes, increase public spending, and take other measures to stimulate their domestic economies and reduce their trade surpluses.

At the annual Council meeting in May 1987 the ministers issued a broad statement on the need for cooperation to overcome obstacles to global prosperity. Although few specific proposals emerged, agreement was reached on world agricultural production, the ministers surprising observers by endorsing a set of principles that called for reducing government subsidies and permitting wider free-market influence.

In its December 1987 forecast, the OECD predicted that the economic growth rate among Western industrialized nations would decline to 2.25 percent in 1988 and to 1.75 percent in 1989. While Japan was praised for recent policy changes, the United States was urged to increase the pace of its budget deficit reduction and West Germany was criticized in uncharacteristically harsh language for inadequate stimulation of its economy. Subsequently, during a Council meeting at Paris on May 18–19, 1988, the ministers noted "encouraging features in the current economic situation" as far as growth, trade balances, and inflation were concerned.

ORGANIZATION OF AFRICAN UNITY (OAU/OUA)

Organisation de l'Unité Africaine

Established: By Charter of the Organization of African Unity, adopted at Addis Ababa, Ethiopia, May 25, 1963.

Purpose: ". . . to promote the unity and solidarity of the African states; to coordinate and intensify their cooperation and efforts to achieve a better life for the peoples of Africa; to defend their sovereignty, their territorial integrity and independence; to eradicate all forms of colonialism from Africa; and to promote international cooperation having due regard to the Charter of the United Nations and the Universal Declaration of Human Rights."

Headquarters: Addis Ababa, Ethiopia.

Principal Organs: Assembly of Heads of State and Government (all members), Council of Ministers (all members), General Secretariat.

Secretary General: Ide Oumarou (Niger).

Membership (50): Algeria, Angola, Benin, Botswana, Burkina Faso, Burundi, Cameroon, Cape Verde Islands, Central African Republic, Chad, Comoro Islands, Congo, Côte d'Ivoire, Djibouti, Egypt, Equatorial Guinea, Ethiopia, Gabon, Gambia, Ghana, Guinea, Guinea-Bissau, Kenya, Lesotho, Liberia, Libya, Madagascar, Malawi, Mali, Mauritania, Mauritius, Mozambique, Niger, Nigeria, Rwanda, Sahrawi Arab Democratic Republic, Sao Tome and Principe, Senegal, Seychelles, Sierra Leone, Somalia, Sudan, Swaziland, Tanzania, Togo, Tunisia, Uganda, Zaire, Zambia, Zimbabwe.

Official Languages: English, French, and "if possible, African languages".

Origin and development. The OAU is the most conspicuous result of the search for unity among the emerging states of Africa, a number of whose representatives participated in the first Conference of Independent African States at Accra, Ghana, in April 1958. However, common action had been seriously impaired by the division of the newly independent states into rival blocs, notably the "Casablanca group" led by Ghana and Guinea, which stressed left-wing socialism, radical anticolonialism, and pan-Africanism; and the more moderate "Monrovia group", which favored a cautiously evolutionary and more subregional approach to African problems. In an attempt to heal this split, a 20-state summit conference of African leaders met at Addis Ababa on May 22–25, 1963, at the invitation of Emperor Haile Selassie of Ethiopia. The OAU resulted from that conference. With a view toward expanding the range of the Organization's activities, ministers at the first OAU economic summit, held at Lagos, Nigeria, in April 1980 agreed to establish an African common market by the year 2000.

A recent series of conflicts have made it difficult for the OAU to live up to its name. In 1981, acting upon a request from the president of Chad, the OAU agreed to send a pan-African peacekeeping force to that country. Following several months of negotiation on the composition, financing, and leadership of the force, OAU troops arrived in Chad in December 1981. The contingent was unable to enforce a political settlement, and the Organization decided in 1982 that it would be unable to continue its support of the undertaking due to lack of funds, although continuing thereafter as a participant in attempted mediation of the conflict.

Intense controversy erupted in February 1982 over the seating of a delegation from the Sahrawi Arab Democratic Republic (SADR)—the national name adopted by the Polisario Front guerrillas in the Western Sahara. The 19th Assembly of Heads of State was unable to convene at Tripoli, Libya, in August because of Moroccan-led opposition to SADR attendance. An effort was made to reconvene the meeting in November, after the SADR had been induced to "voluntarily and temporarily" withdraw from participation; however, a new boycott resulted from Libya's refusal to admit Chadians representing the Hissein Habré government. The summit was finally convened in June 1983 at Addis Ababa with Libya's boycott still in effect and the SADR seat remaining vacant. Morocco withdrew from the Organization following the return of the SADR in October

1984; in support of Morocco, Zaire suspended its membership, but returned as a participant in the 1986 summit.

Structure. The Assembly of Heads of State and Government, the principal political organ, meets annually to define overall OAU policy and to supervise the activities of other OAU agencies. Each member state is entitled to one vote, with decisions on all but procedural matters requiring a two-thirds majority.

The Council of Ministers, comprising the foreign ministers or other designated representatives of all member states, meets at least twice a year to confer on preparation for meetings of the Assembly, the implementation of its decisions, the OAU budget, and matters of intra-African cooperation and general international policy. Each member has one vote; all decisions are by simple majority.

The Commission of Mediation, Conciliation, and Arbitration, which functions under Assembly direction, is composed of 21 professionally qualified members, who act in their private capacities; nominated by member governments, they are elected by the Assembly for five-year terms. The Commission may consider any interstate dispute brought to it by the parties concerned, the Council, or the Assembly. However, a party to a dispute may refuse to submit to the jurisdiction of the Commission.

Specialized commissions have been established for defense; economic and social concerns; and educational, scientific, cultural, and health matters. Related agencies include the African Civil Aviation Commission (AFCAC), the Pan-African News Agency (PANA), the Pan-African Postal Union (PAPU), the Pan-African Telecommunications Union (PATU), and the Union of African Railways (UAR).

Activities. The OAU has long functioned as a sounding board for African opinion on such problems as colonialism and racial discrimination; thus, it continues to be an active observer of attempts to resolve the Namibian situation and to end apartheid in South Africa. Concern has also grown over human rights and refugee problems throughout the continent. The African Commission on Human and Peoples' Rights held its first meeting in November 1987 to develop procedures for implementing the OAU charter on the subject, adopted in 1981 but only recently ratified by the required majority of members.

Southern Africa was the main agenda item at the 22nd Assembly meeting held at Addis Ababa on July 28–30, 1986. A resolution was passed to set up a consultative committee composed of the OAU chairman, leaders of the six Front-Line States, five other OAU members, and the southern African liberation movements. Resolutions were passed calling for intensification of the liberation struggle in South Africa and describing US military aid to the UNITA movement in Angola as "undeclared war in violation of the UN charter". The Assembly condemned (with reservations by five members) the April US bombing raids on Libya and appealed to France to return the island of Mayotte to the Comoros. A call was also issued for the inclusion of an international conference on debt in an action program approved by the recently concluded UN special session on Africa.

Heated debate over OAU finances was reported at the Council of Ministers meeting in February 1987. With 40 of the 50 members in arrears by a total of $47 million, the Council, over the objections of Secretary General Oumarou, reduced the yearly budget from $25 million to $23.2 million.

The financial problems contributed to an ongoing perception that the Organization had become what one correspondent called "an ineffective political forum with illusory continental unity". Lending credence to that view, only 19 heads of state attended the 23rd Assembly held on July 27–30 at Addis Ababa. The Assembly again evidenced consensus on southern African issues, although most of its resolutions (such as one calling for members to impose mandatory sanctions against Pretoria) remained largely symbolic. Unanimity regarding the continent's external debt proved unobtainable, with some states pressing for repayment moratoriums and others calling for at least partial repayments. Although the Assembly elected Zambian President Kenneth Kaunda, a strong critic of Western creditors, as the OAU's new chairman, a special summit at Addis Ababa in December adopted a relatively moderate position, calling for the conversion of some loans to grants and liberalized repayment schedules for others.

In other 1987 activity, the OAU called for an international conference on refugees and displaced persons in southern Africa and endorsed programs to guarantee "protection and basic rights" for children throughout the continent. Under Kaunda's leadership, the Organization again moved to the forefront of mediation between Chad and Libya, brokering a September ceasefire that was seen as a possible forerunner to permanent resolution of the conflict.

ORGANIZATION OF AMERICAN STATES (OAS/OEA)

Organisation des Etats Américains
Organizaçã o dos Estados Americanos
Organización de los Estados Americanos

Established: By Charter signed at Bogotá, Colombia, April 30, 1948, effective December 13, 1951; reorganized by a Protocol of Amendment signed at Buenos Aires, Argentina, February 27, 1967, effective February 27, 1970.

Purpose: To achieve "an order of peace and justice, promoting solidarity among the American states; [to strengthen] their collaboration and [defend] their sovereignty, their territorial integrity, and their independence . . . as well as to establish . . . new objectives and standards for the promotion of the economic, social, and cultural development of the peoples of the Hemisphere, and to speed the process of economic integration".

Headquarters: Washington, DC, United States.

Principal Organs: General Assembly (all members); Meeting of Consultation of Ministers of Foreign Affairs (all members); Permanent Council (all members); Inter-American Economic and Social Council (all members); Inter-American Council for Education, Science, and Culture (all members); Inter-American Juridical Committee (11 jurists from member states); Inter-American Nuclear Energy Commission (all members); Inter-American Commission on Human Rights; Inter-American Drug Abuse Control Commission; General Secretariat.

Secretary General: João Clemente Baena Soares (Brazil).

Membership (32): Antigua and Barbuda, Argentina, Bahamas, Barbados, Bolivia, Brazil, Chile, Colombia, Costa Rica, Cuba (excluded from formal participation in OAS activities since 1962), Dominica, Dominican Republic, Ecuador, El Salvador, Grenada, Guatemala, Haiti, Honduras, Jamaica, Mexico, Nicaragua, Panama, Paraguay, Peru, St. Christopher and Nevis, St. Lucia, St. Vincent, Suriname, Trinidad and Tobago, United States, Uruguay, Venezuela.

Permanent Observers (24): Algeria, Austria, Belgium, Canada, Cyprus, Egypt, Equatorial Guinea, Finland, France, Federal Republic of Germany, Greece, Guyana, Holy See, Israel, Italy, Japan, Republic of Korea, Morocco, Netherlands, Pakistan, Portugal, Saudi Arabia, Spain, Switzerland.

Official Languages: English, French, Portuguese, Spanish.

Origin and development. The foundations of the OAS were laid in 1890 at an International Conference of American States at Washington, DC, where it was decided to form an International Union of American Republics to serve as a permanent secretariat. The name of the Organization was changed in 1910 to Union of American Republics, and the Bureau was renamed the Pan American Union.

The experience of World War II encouraged further development of the still loosely organized "inter-American system". An Inter-American Conference on Problems of War and Peace, meeting at Mexico City in February-March 1945, concluded that the American republics should consider the adoption of a treaty for their mutual defense. By the Inter-American Treaty of Reciprocal Assistance (Rio Treaty), which was opened for signature at Rio de Janeiro, Brazil, on September 2, 1947, they agreed that an armed attack originating either within or outside the American system would be considered an attack against all of them, and each would assist in meeting such an attack. Organizational streamlining was undertaken by the Ninth International Conference of American States, which met at Bogotá, Colombia, in March-May 1948 and established the Organization of American States.

The adoption by Cuba of a Marxist-Leninist ideology generally was viewed by other American governments as incompatible with their fundamental principles, and the Eighth Meeting of Consultation of Ministers of Foreign Affairs, held at Punta del Este, Uruguay, on January 23-31, 1962, determined that Cuba in effect had excluded itself from participation in the inter-American system due to its violation of Rio Treaty provisions. Over time, however, several members began to question the value of continued ostracism of the Castro regime. The trade and diplomatic quarantine against Cuba was ultimately lifted at a special consultative meeting on July 29, 1975, at San José, Costa Rica, although the "freedom of action" resolution did not constitute termination of Cuba's exclusion from formal participation in OAS activities. Some members supported the invocation of Rio Treaty sanctions against Nicaragua in 1980–1981 because of accusations that it had been involved in militarism and interference in other American states, but no action was taken by members meeting in formal session.

Evidence of the Organization's increasing economic and social concern was manifested by the adoption of the Act of Bogotá, a program of social development, by a special OAS conference on September 30, 1960. On August 17, 1961, an Inter-American Economic and Social Conference adopted the Charter of Punta de Este, a ten-year program designed to implement the provisions of the Alliance for Progress, while a code of conduct for transnational corporations was approved in July 1978.

On July 18, 1978, the nine-year-old Convention on Human Rights entered into force. The agreement provided for an Inter-American Court of Human Rights composed of seven judges who are elected by the OAS Assembly and serve in a private capacity. Most members have ratified the Convention with reservations, however, and the Court's impact has been limited. On the other hand, the Inter-American Commission on Human Rights has become more active, devoting, for example, two weeks in September 1979 to an on-site investigation of alleged human-rights violations in Argentina. The results of that investigation became the focus of the November 1980 General Assembly meeting, which concluded a compromise accord whereby the Assembly deplored every form of human-rights infringement, without passing judgment on the specific cases enumerated in the Commission report. Chile, following criticism of its human-rights policy by the Commission's President, suspended its participation in Commission activities and accused the body of exceeding its powers.

The changing character of the OAS has led to calls for reassessment and reform of the Organization, its structure, and its budget, although little formal action has occurred. At the same time, a dramatic increase in the number of newly independent Caribbean members has been accompanied by a call for additional OAS attention to the islands' special trade and economic problems.

Structure. The principal political organ of the OAS, the General Assembly, meets annually to discuss the budget and to supervise the work of the Organization's specialized agencies. Other organs include the Inter-American Economic and Social Council (IA-Ecosoc); the Permanent Council, which serves as the Organ of Consultation under the Rio Treaty in cases of aggression; the Inter-American Council for Education, Science, and Culture, which, like IA-Ecosoc, is responsible to the General Assembly; and the Inter-American Juridical Committee, the Inter-American Nuclear Energy Commission, and the Pan-American Highway Congress, which meet twice a year, biennially, and every four years, respectively. The Meeting of Consultation of Ministers of Foreign Affairs discharges the Orga-

nization's security functions and is convened to consider urgent problems.

Activities. Political and security functions, although increasingly supplemented by economic and social considerations, continue to hold a prominent place in OAS activities. In part because of the Falkland Islands crisis, 1982 witnessed a marked increase in tension between the OAS and the United States, raising doubts as to the capacity of the Organization to serve the diverse needs of its members. The crisis, which began with the Argentinian invasion of the islands on April 2, yielded an extended special session of the OAS at Washington during April and May. The participants considered a possible US breach of the 1947 Rio pact and passed a resolution supporting Argentina's claim to sovereignty over the territory. At the conclusion of the session, the British effort to regain the Falklands was condemned, the United States was asked to cease providing Britain with weapons, and members were invited to tender assistance to Argentina. Following the termination of hostilities on June 14, efforts to resolve the sovereignty issue continued through UN channels.

Subsequently, the Organization entered a period of scandal, rifts between members, and charges of ineffectiveness. The situation in Central America continued to be contentious, with Nicaragua and the United States sparring within the Organization as well as at the United Nations. The conflict reflected a deeper cleavage that had developed between the US and English-speaking Caribbean members and the bulk of the Central and Latin American members — a rift that widened following the intervention in Grenada in October 1983. A majority of members attending a special OAS session on October 26 condemned the action, with the United States and its Caribbean allies countering that, as an effort to resolve a condition of anarchy, it did not violate the Rio treaty.

Further shock came with the unexpected resignation of Secretary General Alejandro Orfila during the 13th Assembly, held November 14–16, 1983, at Washington, DC. Orfila's resignation, effective March 31, 1984, was spurred by his dissatisfaction over the role of the Organization in regional problems and the limited powers of the secretary general. In early April 1984 it was revealed that Orfila had accepted outside wages in violation of his OAS contract and that he and other officials had made questionable use of OAS discretionary funds and contracts. Following an investigation, the Council on April 12 unanimously passed a motion of censure against Orfila.

A special foreign ministers' meeting convened at Cartagena, Colombia, on December 2, 1985, to consider proposed amendments to the OAS charter. The Protocol of Cartagena, adopted three days later, would modify admission rules to open the possibility of membership after 1990 for Belize and Guyana (currently ineligible because of territorial disputes with OAS members Guatemala and Venezuela, respectively). Under the new criteria, all regional states that were members of the United Nations as of December 10, 1985, plus specified nonautonomous territories (Bermuda, French Guiana, Guadaloupe, Martinique, and Montserrat, but not the Falkland/Malvinas Islands) would be permitted to apply. The Protocol also provided for increasing the authority of the secretary general, permitting him, on its own initiative, to bring to the attention of the Assembly any matter which "could affect the peace and security of the continent and development of its member countries". A further reform would allow the Permanent Council to provide peacekeeping services to help ameliorate regional crises. The 15th General Assembly, convening immediately after the foreign ministers meeting, approved the Protocol, which by early 1988 it had not yet entered into force because instruments of ratification had not been received from 21 members.

Despite initial opposition from the United States, the OAS played an active role throughout 1987 and early 1988 in the Central American peace plan negotiations initiated by Costa Rica's President Arias. Although progress in the talks was a primary topic at the 17th General Assembly, held at Washington in November 1987, attention also focused on an "extremely grave" financial crisis stemming from shortfalls in budgetary contributions for the previous three years. In other activity, the Assembly again expressed concern over human rights violations in the region, called for a plan of action for agricultural revitalization, charged the Permanent Council with preparing for a Special General Assembly on Inter-American Cooperation for Development, and noted its objection to proposed protectionist legislation in the US Congress.

In late November the leaders of eight major Latin American countries met at Acapulco, Mexico, to appeal for extensive restructuring of the OAS, which they described as not carrying out its function effectively. Among the issues expected to be discussed in 1988 was their recommendation that Cuba be permitted to resume its participation in the Organization's activities.

In early 1988 OAS officials reported that, despite a 25 percent cutback in staff size, the ongoing fiscal crisis threatened the future of the Organization. Over two-thirds of the members were reportedly in arrears, with the United States, already behind $27 million in its payments, seemingly prepared to pay only about one-fifth of its scheduled $42 million contribution for 1988.

ORGANIZATION OF ARAB PETROLEUM EXPORTING COUNTRIES (OAPEC)

Established: By agreement concluded at Beirut, Lebanon, on January 9, 1968.

Purpose: To help coordinate members' petroleum policies, to adopt measures for harmonizing their legal systems to the extent needed for the group to fulfill its mission, to assist in the exchange of information and expertise, to provide training and employment opportunities for their citizens, and to utilize members' "resources and common potentialities" in establishing joint projects in the petroleum and petroleum-related industries.

Headquarters: Kuwait City, Kuwait.

Principal Organs: Council of Ministers (all members), Executive Bureau (all members), Judicial Board, Secretariat.

Acting Secretary General: 'Abd al-Aziz al-Waittari (Iraq).

Membership (11): Algeria, Bahrain, Egypt (membership suspended in 1979), Iraq, Kuwait, Libya, Qatar, Saudi Arabia, Syria, Tunisia (withdrew from active membership in 1986), United Arab Emirates.

Official Language: Arabic.

Origin and development. Established by Kuwait, Libya, and Saudi Arabia in early 1968 in recognition of the need for further cooperation among Arab countries which relied on oil as their principal source of income, OAPEC was expanded in May 1970 by the accession of Algeria, Bahrain, Qatar, and Abu Dhabi and Dubai, the last two subsequently (in May 1972) combining their membership as part of the United Arab Emirates. In December 1971 the founding Agreement was liberalized to permit membership by any Arab country having oil as a significant — but not necessarily the major — source of income, with the result that Syria and Egypt joined in 1972 and 1973, respectively. Also in 1972, Iraq became a member. A Tunisian bid for membership failed at the December 1981 ministerial meeting because of Libyan opposition stemming from a dispute with Tunis over conflicting claims to offshore oil deposits, but was approved in 1982. In 1986, however, Tunisia withdrew from active membership because of a change in status from that of a net exporter to a net importer of energy and its inability to make its OAPEC contributions.

OAPEC joint ventures and projects include the Arab Maritime Petroleum Transport Company (AMPTC), founded in 1973 with headquarters at Kuwait; the Arab Shipbuilding and Repair Yard Company (ASRY), established in Bahrain in 1974; the Arab Petroleum Investments Corporation (Apicorp), set up in 1975 at Damman, Saudi Arabia; the Arab Petroleum Services Company (APSC), founded in 1977 and operating from Tripoli, Libya; the Arab Petroleum Training Institute (APTI), formed in 1979 at Baghdad, Iraq; and the Arab Engineering Company (Arec), established in 1981 in Abu Dhabi. Shareholders in these ventures are typically either the member governments themselves or state-owned petroleum enterprises.

Structure. The Council of Ministers, OAPEC's supreme authority, is composed of the members' petroleum ministers and convenes at least twice a year to draw up policy guidelines and direct ongoing activities. An Executive Bureau, which meets at least three times a year, assists the Council in management of the Organization. The protocol establishing the Judicial Tribunal entered into effect on May 8, 1980, following ratification by all member states; the Tribunal serves as an arbitration council between OAPEC members or between a member and a petroleum company operating in that country, with all decisions final and binding. The Secretariat, headed by a secretary general and no more than three assistant secretaries general, encompasses four Departments: Administrative and Financial, Economic, Information and Library, and Technical Affairs.

Activities. During 1986, the Organization, prompted by the effects of declining world oil prices, urged industrialized nations to redistribute some of their accrued savings to aid developing countries. Due to the decrease in oil revenue, OAPEC members have reduced their own assistance to the Third World.

In early 1987 OAPEC called for increased cooperation between its members and their worldwide consumers, suggesting that particular attention be given to ties with the European Community, which buys 40 percent of OAPEC oil exports. (Relations with the EC have been strained by a still unresolved dispute over EC tariffs on Arab petrochemical exports to Western Europe.) OAPEC also endorsed greater "flexibility and simplicity" in contracts between oil exploration companies and developing countries to protect both sides from the effects of sharp price fluctuations.

At a June ministerial meeting it was announced that members' contributions were in arrears by $14.4 million at the end of 1986. As a result, the "cash-strapped" Organization ordered deep budget cuts in its 1987–1991 five-year program.

ORGANISATION OF EASTERN CARIBBEAN STATES (OECS)

Established: By treaty signed at Basseterre, St. Kitts, on June 18, 1981, effective July 4, 1981.

Purpose: To increase cooperation among members in foreign relations; to harmonize economic, trade, and financial policies; and to coordinate defense and security arrangements, ultimately leading to a deepening of subregional integration.

Headquarters: Castries, St. Lucia.

Principal Organs: Authority of Heads of Government of the Member States, Foreign Affairs Committee, Defense and Security Committee, Economic Affairs Committee and Secretariat, Central Secretariat.

Director General: Dr. Vaughan Lewis (former director of the Institute of Social and Economic Research, University of the West Indies).

Membership (7): Antigua and Barbuda, Dominica, Grenada, Montserrat, St. Lucia, St. Kitts-Nevis, St. Vincent and the Grenadines.
Associate Member: British Virgin Islands.

Official Language: English.

Origin and development. The seven participants in the OECS were formerly members of the West Indies Associated States, a preindependence grouping established in 1966 to serve various common economic, judicial, and diplomatic needs of British Caribbean territories. The attainment of independence of four of the members—Dominica, Grenada, St. Lucia, and St. Vincent—during 1974–1979 and the impending independence of Antigua on November 1, 1981, gave impetus to the formation of a new organization.

Meeting at Castries, St. Lucia, in 1979, the prospective members called for establishment of the OECS as a means of strengthening the subregional association of seven least-developed members of the Caribbean Community (Caricom, see separate entry). Following nearly a year and a half of negotiations, an OECS treaty was concluded that came into force on July 4, 1981, Caricom's eighth anniversary. A dispute over location of the new Organization's headquarters was settled by agreement that its Central Secretariat would be located at Castries, St. Lucia (administrative center of the former Associated States), while its Economic Affairs Secretariat would be located at St. Johns, Antigua, where the Secretariat of the Eastern Caribbean Common Market (ECCM) was sited.

Structure. Final authority within the OECS is reserved for the meeting of heads of government of the member states. The Foreign Affairs Committee and the Defense and Security Committee supervise the coordination of members' external relations and the formulation of a common OECS position in world forums. Authority over the ECCM rests with the Economic Affairs Committee and Secretariat, while the Central Secretariat prepares reports, assists the work of the other organs, and provides administrative and legal expertise.

Activities. In order to facilitate the process of regional integration, the OECS engages in a variety of activities. The ECCM promotes economic integration by coordinating members' economic and trade policies, while additional technical expertise is to be provided through the creation of a pool of experts within the Economic Affairs Secretariat. The strengthening of cooperation in such common areas as tourism, security, the judiciary, currency, and civil aviation is another major concern of the Organization.

To further cooperation and integration in the Caribbean, OECS established the Eastern Caribbean Central Bank (ECCB) on October 1, 1983, in accordance with its decision in July 1982 to upgrade the Eastern Caribbean Currency Authority. The major functions of the ECCB are the administration of the EC dollar currency used by members, exchange control, currency rate adjustment, regulation of credit policies, fixing interest rates, and establishing reserve requirements for members' commercial banks.

In response to political unrest in Grenada in October 1983, the OECS formally requested the intervention of troops from the United States, member countries, and other Caribbean states, which succeeded in restoring order on the island. Following the intervention, a Regional Security System (RSS) was established in cooperation with the United States to ensure the political stability of the seven members and in September 1985 RSS military exercises were held on St. Lucia. During 1986 the participants failed to reach a security consensus, thus threatening the system's continuation; however, all seven OECS members joined British, Jamaican, and US units in RSS exercises on Dominica in May 1987.

While the heads of government meeting on June 13–14, 1985, at St. George's, Grenada, focused primarily on economic issues, the twin problems of poverty and underdevelopment prompted St. Lucia's prime minister, John Compton, to call on the OECS to consider formation of a political union to counter regional nationalism and promote integration. The May 1987 summit in the British Virgin Islands ended with apparent agreement to work towards such a union. However, in August Prime Minister Bird of Antigua and Barbuda rejected the proposal as of no benefit to his country, insisting that it would be "overrun" by people from less prosperous islands if freedom of movement was implemented. Nonetheless, the other OECS leaders reaffirmed their support for the plan at a November summit in St. Lucia. They approved the creation of several task forces to develop specific recommendations and called for accelerated education of the population on the effects of the union. Supporters of unification said they still hoped that referenda could be held on the question in individual OECS countries by the end of 1988, following the establishment of a Regional Consultative Committee which would draft the final proposal.

Possibly giving impetus to the unity plan, the ECCB reported in December 1987 that the growth rate within OECS had slowed to about 2 percent for the year in comparison to 5.5 percent in 1986. To promote economic stimulation in several areas, including intraregional trade, the OECS called for the establishment of "full trade liberalization", including harmonized customs procedures, during 1988. The region has also submitted numerous agriculture, education, and transportation projects to the European Community for financing through the Lomé III convention. In addition, OECS is seeking "functional cooperation" and an "institutional relationship" with the US Virgin Islands, whose governor attended the November 1987 summit for informal discussions on how such linkage could be established.

ORGANIZATION OF THE PETROLEUM EXPORTING COUNTRIES (OPEC)

Established: By resolutions adopted at Baghdad, Iraq, on September 14, 1960, and codified in a Statue approved by the Eighth (Extraordinary) OPEC Conference, held April 5–10, 1965, at Geneva, Switzerland.

Purpose: To coordinate and unify petroleum policies of member countries; to devise ways to ensure stabilization of international oil prices in order to eliminate "harmful and unnecessary" price and supply fluctuations.

Headquarters: Vienna, Austria.

Principal Organs: Conference (all members), Board of Governors (all members), Economic Commission Board, Secretariat.

Secretary General (Acting): Dr. Fadhil J. al-Chalabi (Iraq).

Membership (13, with years of entry): Algeria (1969), Ecuador (1973), Gabon (1973 as an associate member and 1975 as a full member), Indonesia (1962), Iran (1960), Iraq (1960), Kuwait (1960), Libya (1962), Nigeria (1971), Qatar (1961), Saudi Arabia (1960), United Arab Emirates (Abu Dhabi in 1967, with the membership being transferred to the UAE in 1974), Venezuela (1960).

Official Language: English.

Origin and development. A need for concerted action by petroleum exporters was first broached in 1946 by Dr. Juan Pablo Pérez Alfonso of Venezuela. His initiative led to a series of contracts in the late 1940s between oil-producing countries, but it was not until 1959 that the first Arab Petroleum Conference was held. At that meeting Dr. Pérez Alfonso convinced the Arabs, in addition to Iranian and Venezuelan observers, to form a union of producing states, with OPEC being formally created by Iran, Iraq, Kuwait, Libya, Saudi Arabia, and Venezuela on September 14, 1960, during a conference at Baghdad, Iraq.

The rapid growth of energy needs in the advanced industrialized states throughout the 1960s and early 1970s provided OPEC with the basis for extracting ever-increasing oil prices, but OPEC demands were not limited to favorable prices; members demanded the establishment of an infrastructure for future industrialization including petrochemical plants, steel mills, aluminum plants, and other high-energy industries as a hedge against the anticipated exhaustion of their oil reserves in the twenty-first century.

With the global recession of the mid-1970s and the implementation of at least rudimentary energy conservation programs by many advanced industrialized countries, OPEC demands temporarily moderated. After a series of price freezes, however, inflation and continued decline in the value of the US dollar prompted reconsideration of the moratorium. Thus in December 1978, with a view toward civil unrest and curtailed petroleum output in Iran, the OPEC ministers agreed to raise the price per barrel by 14.5 percent in four steps, the first time the OPEC had agreed to a staggered price-rise policy. By contrast, at a meeting in December 1979 no agreement could be reached on a coordinated price structure, yielding intense intra-OPEC competition thereafter, with an effort launched in 1981 to impose an overall production ceiling giving rise to quota as well as price disputes.

Structure. The OPEC Conference, which normally meets twice a year, is the supreme authority of the Organization. Comprising the oil ministers of the member states, the Conference formulates policy, considers recommendations from the Board of Governors, and approves the budget. The Board consists of governors nominated by the various member states and approved by the Conference for two-year terms. In addition to submitting the annual budget, various reports, and recommendations to the Conference, the Board directs the Organization's management, while the Secretariat performs executive functions. Operating within the Secretariat are a Division of Research, including departments for Energy Studies, Economics and Finance, and Information Services; a Department of Personnel and Administration; a Public Relations Department; an Office of the Secretary General; and a Legal Affairs Unit. In addition, an Economic Commission Board, established as a specialized body in 1964, works within the Secretariat framework to promote equitable and stable international oil prices.

The OPEC Fund for International Development has made significant contributions to developing countries, mostly Arabian and African, in the form of balance-of-payments support, direct financing of imports, and project loans in such areas as energy, transportation, and food production. By November 1986, the number of loans approved by the fund totaled 401, valued at $1,975.75 million. Lending in 1987 rose more than 50 percent over the previous year to $140 million, the Organization announcing its intention to continue the increase at a rate of 10 percent every two years with an emphasis on small development projects.

Recent developments. In December 1985, as spot market prices dropped to $24 a barrel and production dipped to as low as 16 million barrels a day, OPEC abandoned its formal price structure in an effort to secure a larger share of the world's oil market. By mid-1986, however, oil prices had dropped by 50 percent or more to their lowest level since 1978, generating intense concern among OPEC members with limited oil reserves, large populations, extensive international debts, and severe shortages of foreign exchange. However, Saudi Arabia increased its output by 2 million barrels a day in January 1986 to force non-OPEC producers to cooperate with the cartel in stabilizing the world oil market.

During a total of 31 days over the ensuing six months, OPEC met at Geneva to formulate strategy aimed at raising prices. At a nine-day meeting in March, ministers agreed only on an effort to revise the existing $28 benchmark price on the basis of a projected overall output of 14 million barrels a day; consensus on individual national quotas could not be obtained. As a result, five non-OPEC producers, Angola, Egypt, Mexico, Malaysia, and Oman, rejected a request that they cut production by 20 percent.

A continuation of the meeting in April brought the group no closer to agreement on individual quotas; however all delegations, except those of Algeria, Iran, and Libya, approved a cumulative limit of 16.3 million barrels a day for the second and third quarters of 1986 and 17.3 million for the last quarter. Two further meetings, one at the Yugoslav island of Brioni on June 25th and the other at Geneva on July 28th, resulted in a unanimous decision to reintroduce earlier production quota ceilings for all members, excluding Iraq, for the months of September and October.

The acceptance of production ceilings appeared to signify a relaxation of conflict within OPEC. Iran, which had previously insisted that any increase in Iraq's quota be matched by an increase in its own allocation, reversed its position. Saudi Arabia, while maintaining that the ceilings did not preclude OPEC's attainment of a fair market share, relaxed its request that quotas be completely overhauled and appeared to have realigned itself with Algeria, Iran, and Libya, all of whom had long supported an end to the price war. In response to the renewed cohesiveness of the Organization, oil prices increased slightly. Furthermore, Mexico and Norway promised to cut their production by 10 percent. The United Kingdom, on the other hand, refused to cooperate, reaffirming its position not to interfere with the policies of independent North Sea oil companies.

At the 79th Extraordinary Conference in October, the ministers further limited output until December 31, 1986, and pledged to return to a fixed-price method of setting oil production limits. On December 11–20, 1986, members agreed to cut combined oil production by one million barrels per day beginning January 1, 1987, and to institute fixed prices averaging $18 per barrel by February 1, 1987. All members were to reduce production by 5 percent, except Iran and Iraq, who were given nominal ceiling limitations. However, in a renewed blow to OPEC unity, Iraq, demanding parity with Iran, failed to endorse the proposal; Iran reacted by requesting Iraq's suspension from the group.

Relative calm prevailed within the organization during the first half of 1987, with prices ranging from $18 to $21 per barrel. By midyear, however, overproduction by most members and a weakening of world oil demand began to push prices downward. At the end of June OPEC had adjusted its quota down to 16.6 million barrels a day but individual quotas were largely ignored and production approached 20 million barrels a day later in the year. Consequently, Saudi Arabia warned its partners that if the "cheating" continued it would no longer serve as the oil market's stabilizer by reducing its own production to support higher prices.

During their December meeting at Vienna, OPEC oil ministers attempted to reimpose discipline but the talks became embroiled in political considerations stemming from the Gulf War. Iraq again refused to accept quotas lower than those of Iran, while Teheran accused Gulf Arab states of conspiring with Baghdad against Iranian interests. For their part, non-Arab states protested that war issues were inhibiting the adoption of sound economic policies. The meeting concluded with twelve members endorsing the $18 per barrel fixed-price concept and agreeing to a 15 million barrel per day production quota, Iraq's nonparticipation leaving it free to produce at will. However, widespread discounting quickly forced prices down to about $15 a barrel. Subsequently, in the wake of a report that OPEC's share of the oil market (66 percent in 1979) had fallen below 30 percent, an appeal was issued to nonmember states to assume a greater role in stabilizing prices and production.

A sharp drop in oil prices to between $13 and $14 per barrel in early 1988 prompted OPEC to meet with non-OPEC oil exporting countries for the first time to formulate joint strategies for control of the oil market. Although six non-OPEC contries agreed to a 5 percent cut in exports, OPEC subsequently was unable to reach consensus on a reciprocal 5 percent decrease; as a result, the agreement collapsed and disarray continued within OPEC.

PERMANENT COURT OF ARBITRATION

Cour Permanente d'Arbitrage

Established: By the First International Peace Conference held at The Hague, Netherlands, in 1899. The Convention for the Pacific Settlement of International Disputes was signed July 29, 1899, and entered into force September 4, 1900. The Convention was revised October 18, 1907, by the Second International Peace Conference at The Hague and entered into force January 26, 1910.

Purpose: To facilitate the arbitration of international disputes.

Headquarters: The Hague, Netherlands.

Principal Organs: Administrative Council, International Bureau.

Secretary General: Jacob Varekamp (Netherlands).

Membership (76): Argentina, Australia, Austria, Belgium, Bolivia, Brazil, Bulgaria, Burkina Faso, Byelorussian Soviet Socialist Republic, Cameroon, Canada, Chile, China, Colombia, Cuba, Czechoslovakia, Denmark, Dominican Republic, Ecuador, Egypt, El Salvador, Fiji, Finland, France, German Democratic Republic, Federal Republic of Germany, Greece, Guatemala, Haiti, Honduras, Hungary, Iceland, India, Iran, Iraq, Israel, Italy, Japan, Kampuchea, Laos, Lebanon, Luxembourg, Malta, Mauritius, Mexico, Netherlands, New Zealand, Nicaragua, Nigeria, Norway, Pakistan, Panama, Paraguay, Peru, Poland, Portugal, Romania, Senegal, Spain, Sri Lanka, Sudan, Swaziland, Sweden, Switzerland, Thailand, Turkey, Uganda, Ukrainian Soviet Socialist Republic, Union of Soviet Socialist Republics, United Kingdom, United States, Uruguay, Venezuela, Yugoslavia, Zaire, Zimbabwe. The People's Republic of China, a de jure member, was requested on June 2, 1972, to clarify its position toward the Hague Conventions. The request is still under consideration in Peking and there are presently no Chinese representatives on the panel of arbitration.

Origin and development. A product of the Hague Peace Conference of 1899, the Convention for the Pacific Settlement of International Disputes contained — in addition to provisions on good offices, mediation, and inquiry — a number of articles of international arbitration, the object of which was "the settlement of differences between States by judges of their own choice, and on the basis of respect of law". The Convention did not impose any obligation to arbitrate, but attempted to set up a structure that could be utilized when two or more states desired to submit a dispute. Detailed procedural rules were therefore set out in the Convention, and the Permanent Court of Arbitration was established. The revised Convention of 1907 included a method for selecting arbitrators.

Structure. The so-called Permanent Court of Arbitration is in no sense a "permanent court"; instead, a Court is selected from among a permanent panel of arbitrators. Each party to the Convention is eligible to nominate a maximum of four persons "of known competency in questions of international law, of the highest moral reputation, and disposed to accept the duties of Arbitrator". When two states decide to refer a dispute to the Court, they can select two arbitrators from among those nominated by the signatory states. Only one of those selected can be a national or nominee of the selecting state. The four arbitrators then choose an umpire. Detailed provision is made in the Convention for selection of an umpire if the arbitrators are unable to agree.

The International Bureau is the administrative arm of the Court and serves as its registry. It channels communications concerning the meetings of the Court, maintains archives, conducts administrative business, and receives from contracting parties reports on the results of arbitration proceedings. The Administrative Council of the Bureau is composed of diplomatic representatives of contracting parties accredited to The Hague; the Netherlands' minister of foreign affairs acts as president of the Council.

Activities. Although the United Nations Charter expressly preserves the freedom of states to submit their differences to tribunals other than the International Court of Justice (ICJ), arbitration has become a relatively infrequent means of resolving international disputes. The post–World War II activity of the Permanent Court has included one Commission of Enquiry, the "Red Crusader" incident involving Denmark and Great Britain; three cases of conciliation, two involving France and Switzerland and one involving Greece and Italy; and a singular arbitration, which concerned the breaking of a contract by an English company dealing with the Sudanese government.

In 1981, the Court provided facilities for the Iran–United States Claims Tribunal, established under Algerian auspices, to resolve claims against Iranian assets frozen in the wake of the 1979 hostage crisis.

Under the standard rules for commercial arbitration established by the United Nations Commission for International Trade Law (UNCITRAL), the court's secretary general may be requested to designate an appointing authority to select a second or a third arbitrator when one of the parties in a dispute fails to appoint an arbitrator or when the party-appointed arbitrators cannot reach agreement on the choice of the third arbitrator. In addition, under many private contracts and international bilateral or multilateral agreements, the secretary general is mentioned as an authority competent to designate arbitrators, a function he has performed frequently in recent years.

The members of the International Court of Justice (ICJ) are elected by the UN General Assembly and the Security Council from a list of nominees chosen by the members of the Permanent Court of Arbitration. Members of the Permanent Court may also select and present candidates for the Nobel Peace Prize.

PERMANENT INTER-STATE COMMITTEE ON DROUGHT CONTROL IN THE SAHEL (CILSS)

Comité Inter-Etats de Lutte contre la Sécheresse dans le Sahel

Established: During 1973, in cooperation with the United Nations Sudano-Sahelian Office.

Purpose: To overcome drought and promote cooperative development in the Sahel region.

Headquarters: Ouagadougou, Burkina Faso.

Principal Organs: Conference of Heads of State (all members), Council of Ministers (all members), Executive Council, Executive Secretariat.

Executive Secretary: Brah Mahamane (Niger).

Membership (9): Burkina Faso, Cape Verde, Chad, Gambia, Guinea-Bissau, Mali, Mauritania, Niger, Senegal. Guinea and Nigeria applied for membership in 1983.

Working Language: French. (The introduction of Portuguese and Arabic as working languages has been approved in principle, although study continues on implementation.)

Origin and development. The CILSS was formed to augment efforts of the UN's Sudano-Sahelian Office in combating drought and promoting economic development in the Sahelian region of Africa. One of its principal objectives in recent years has been to overcome the effects of endemic shortfalls of cereal by the creation of a regional grain reserve. By early 1981 it had also approved a strategy for improving food management, livestock, and the development of infrastructure. In 1984, ministers approved the establishment of the Sahel Fund to finance and coordinate national food strategies to mitigate the effects of permanent drought in the area. During its first five years, the organization managed over 600 projects valued at approximately $5 billion.

Structure. The CILSS is a relatively unstructured organization that meets in plenary session at least once a year to approve an annual budget and discuss major undertakings. At other times it holds joint meetings with such bodies as the UN Food and Agriculture Organization (FAO) to address matters of common concern.

A reorganization of the Executive Secretariat in May 1985 abolished its earlier function of overseeing specific programs, concurrent with the formation of a new Executive Council comprised of the executive secretary and the directors of the Sahel Institute at Bamako, Mali, and the Agrometeorology and Operational Hydrology Center (*Agrhyment*) at Naimey, Niger. The Council was charged with monitoring overall CILSS operations, including budget preparation.

Activities. In January 1985, the Council of Ministers decided that it was necessary to restructure the CILSS at both the organizational and strategic levels in order to better achieve its goals in drought control and grain production. The ministers also urged the adoption of a new regional strategy to fight drought and desertification. At an extraordinary Council meeting in May 1985, the main focus was on coordination of national policies in the areas of rural development and desertification, including cooperation between the international community and member states in enhancing program resources and publicizing regional needs.

During the seventh Conference of the Heads of State at Dakar, Senegal, on January 29, 1986, an appeal was made for renewed efforts to reduce desertification and make the Sahel subregion self-sufficient in food production. Warning of desert encroachment and a decrease in fertility, the leaders called for the support of the world community in their struggle. While seasonal rains resulted in a 55 percent improvement in projected harvests for the year, the danger of famine still necessitated the need for programs such as improved distribution of seeds, increased availability of medical care, and enforcement of an early warning system for food shortages. Projects for 1986 included cereal production, water supply, afforestation, and plans for a trans-Sahelian railroad for landlocked members.

During its January 1987 meeting the Council of Ministers called for the establishment of a four-year program to protect plant life. It also endorsed a program to educate children on measures to counter the effects of drought and desertification in everyday life. In December it was reported that cereal production had fallen 12 percent during the year, largely because of insufficient rainfall. As a result, Executive Secretary Mahamane appealed to external donors to help facilitate intraregional food transfers.

In addition to the issues of food self-sufficiency and desertification, the eighth Conference of the Heads of State at N'Djamena, Chad, on January 28–29, 1988, addressed the region's economic difficulties, calling the Sahel's "financial dependency" an intrinsic element of its food problems. The summit leaders also called for expanded regional activity in the fight against crop-damaging pests.

REGIONAL AND SUBREGIONAL DEVELOPMENT BANKS

Regional development banks are intended to accelerate economic and social development of member states by promoting public and private investment. The banks are not meant, however, to be mere financial institutions in the narrow sense of the term. Required by their charters to take an active interest in improving their members' capacities to make profitable use of local and external capital, they engage in such technical-assistance activities as feasibility studies, evaluation and design of projects, and preparation of development programs. The banks also seek to supplement their activities with the work of other national and international agencies engaged in financing international economic development. Subregional banks have historically concentrated more on integration projects than have regional development banks.

African Development Bank
(AfDB)
Banque Africaine de Développement
(BAD)

The Articles of Agreement of the AfDB were signed on August 4, 1963, at Khartoum, Sudan, with formal establishment of the institution occurring in September 1964, after 20 signatories had deposited instruments of ratification. Lending operations commenced in July 1966 at the Bank's headquarters at Abidjan, Ivory Coast.

Until 1982, membership in the AfDB was limited to states within the region. At the 1979 Annual Meeting the Board of Governors approved an amendment to the Bank's statutes permitting nonregional membership as a means of augmenting the institution's capital resources; however, it was not until the 17th Annual Meeting, held in May 1982 at Lusaka, Zambia, that Nigeria announced withdrawal of its objection to the change. Non-African states became eligible for membership on December 20, 1982, and by the end of 1983 over 20 such states had joined the Bank.

The Bank's leading policymaking organ is its Board of Governors, encompassing the finance or economic ministers of the member states; the governors elect a Bank president, who serves a five-year term and is chairman of a Board of Directors. The governors are empowered to name 18 directors, each serving a three-year term, with 12 seats to be held by Africans. The Bank's African members are the same as for the Organization of African Unity (OAU), save the inclusion of Morocco (no longer a member of the OAU) and the exclusion of the SADR.

While limiting the Bank's membership to African countries was initially viewed as a means of avoiding practical difficulties and undesirable political complications, it soon became evident that the major capital-exporting states were unwilling to loan funds without having a continuous voice in their use. In response to this problem, an African Development Fund (ADF) was established in November 1972 as a legally distinct intergovernmental institution in which contributing countries would have a shared managerial role. The ADF Board of Governors encompasses one representative from each state as well as the AfDB governors, ex officio; the 12-member Board of Directors includes 6 nonregional designees. Nonregional contributing countries — all of whom are now AfDB members — are Argentina, Austria, Belgium, Brazil, Canada, China, Denmark, Finland, France, Federal Republic of Germany, India, Italy, Japan, Republic of Korea, Kuwait, Netherlands, Norway, Portugal, Saudi Arabia, Spain, Sweden, Switzerland, United Kingdom, United States, and Yugoslavia. In addition, in February 1976 (with effect from April 1976),

an agreement was signed by the Bank and the government of Nigeria establishing a Nigeria Trust Fund (NTF) with an initial capitalization of 50 million Nigerian naira (about $80 million). Unlike the ADF, the NTF is directly administered by the AfDB. Together, the AfDB, the ADF, and the NTF constitute the African Development Bank group.

Earlier, in November 1970, the AfDB had participated in the founding of the International Financial Society for Investments and Development in Africa (*Société Internationale Financière pour les Investissements et le Développement en Afrique* — SIFIDA). Headquartered at Geneva, Switzerland, with the International Finance Corporation (IFC) and a large number of financial institutions from advanced industrial countries among its shareholders, SIFIDA is authorized to extend loans for the promotion and growth of productive enterprises in Africa. Another related agency, the Association of African Development Finance Institutions (AADFI), inaugurated in March 1975 at Abidjan, was established to aid and coordinate African development projects, while the African Reinsurance Corporation (Africare), formally launched in March 1977 at Lagos, Nigeria, promotes the development of insurance and reinsurance activity throughout the continent. The AfDB holds 10 percent of Africare's authorized capital of $15 million. Shelter-Afrique, established to facilitate lending which would improve Africa's housing situation, began operations in January 1984 at its Nairobi, Kenya, headquarters.

In 1985, after more than twenty years of operation, the Group's one-year lending commitments for the first time exceeded $1 billion. Lending continued to rise in 1986 with $1,639 million being approved for 90 projects, the AfDB accounting for $1,034 million, the ADF for $585 million, and the NTF for $20 million. Agricultural projects received the greatest percentage of the loans, about 37 percent, in line with recent AfDB policy to give them highest priority. The 1986 lending commitments brought the AfDB cumulative total to $8.4 billion for 963 projects. However, more than half of the money has not been expended, in part because of disbursement procedures that until recently were quite cumbersome.

To provide for increased lending, the Bank in 1987 announced plans to raise its capital from $6.3 billion to $19.6 billion, nonregional members being given five years and African countries 10 years to make their additional contributions.

During the June 9–11, 1987, annual meeting at Cairo, Egypt, a feasibility study for an African Export/Import Bank was approved in support of the Bank's recent emphasis on the private sector, which has "tended to be neglected in the post-colonial era". Despite opposition from the United States, the meeting also endorsed a call for a conference of African countries to discuss the continent's external debt crisis and possible multilateral approaches to its resolution. Bank leaders warned, however, that members should not become excessively preoccupied with debt forgiveness, since it might inhibit the flow of new money from creditor nations and institutions. Subsequently, nonregional members agreed in November to a $2.7 billion finance package for "soft" loans through the ADF from 1988–1991, an increase of more than $1 billion over the previous three-year package.

Arab Bank for Economic Development in Africa

*Banque Arabe de Développement
Economique en Afrique*
(BADEA)

The idea of an Arab bank to assist in the economic and social development of all non-Arab African states was first discussed by the Arab heads of state during the Sixth Arab Summit at Algiers, Algeria, in November 1973. BADEA, with headquarters at Khartoum, Sudan, began operations in March 1975. Its main functions include the provision of financing required for development projects, promoting and stimulating private Arab investment in Africa, and supplying technical assistance. BADEA financing is generally limited to 40 percent of the total cost of a project or $10 million, whichever total is smaller, although both ceilings can be raised to account for "exceptional conditions". Technical assistance is usually provided in grant form. All member states of the Organization of African Unity, except Liberia and Zaire (because of links with Israel), and Arab League participants, are eligible for funding. To date the preponderance of aid has been devoted to infrastructural improvements although the Board of Directors has recently accorded additional priority to projects promoting increased food production. The Bank has traditionally favored the least-developed countries in its disbursements, many of which have been in the form of outright grants.

The Bank's highest authority is the Board of Governors (one governor for each member), with day-to-day administration assigned to a Board of Directors, one of whose 11 members serves as Board chairman and Bank president. The subscribing members of the Bank, listed in descending order of contribution, are: Saudi Arabia, Libya, Kuwait, Iraq, United Arab Emirates, Qatar, Algeria, Morocco, Oman, Tunisia, Lebanon, Jordan, Bahrain, Sudan, Palestine Liberation Organization, Egypt, Mauritania, and Syria. Egypt's membership was suspended in 1979.

BADEA's subscribed capital is currently $1,048 million. In the 1986–1987 biennium the Bank approved $128.48 million for 31 projects, bringing cumulative totals to $829.84 million for 176 projects. In addition BADEA administers 37 "soft" loans totaling $214.24 million extended through the Special Arab Aid Fund for Africa (SAAFA) from its beginning of operations in 1974 until 1977, at which time SAAFA capital was incorporated into that of BADEA. The cumulative distribution of loans by sector in 1986–1987 was as follows: infrastructure development, 49.7 percent; agriculture, 25.8 percent; industry, 13.3 percent; energy, 9.2 percent; special programs, 1.8 percent; and technical assistance, 0.2 percent.

In recent years, the Bank's leadership has called for consolidation of projects in view of decreasing Arab oil revenues and the African states' external debt problems. In July 1987 the Bank hosted a meeting of aid agencies from individual Arab countries, including the highly active Kuwait Fund for Arab Economic Development (which has assisted non-Arab developing countries since 1974), to discuss ways of further coordinating participation in African development.

Arab Fund for Economic and Social Development
(AFESD)

The Arab Fund for Economic and Social Development, which originated in an accord reached on May 16, 1968, and began functioning in December 1971, is headquartered in Kuwait. Its aim is to assist in the financing of development projects in Arab states by offering loans on concessional terms to governments, particularly for joint ventures, and by providing technical expertise. The chief policymaking organ of the Fund is the Board of Directors (one representative from each participating country), which elects a six-member Board of Directors chaired by a director general. Members include Algeria, Bahrain, Djibouti, Egypt (suspended since 1979), Iraq, Jordan, Kuwait, Lebanon, Libya, Mauritania, Morocco, Oman, the Palestine Liberation Organization, Qatar, Saudi Arabia, Somalia, Sudan, Syria, Tunisia, United Arab Emirates, Yemen Arab Republic, and People's Democratic Republic of Yemen.

During the 11th Arab League summit at 'Amman, Jordan, in November 1980, a new $5 billion fund was announced to provide additional aid to the six least-developed Arab countries: Djibouti, Mauritania, Somalia, Sudan, Yemen Arab Republic, and Yemen People's Democratic Republic. Initially, it was projected that the AFESD would distribute approximately $500 million annually from the new fund in the form of 30-year loans, with a 1 percent interest rate after a 10-year grace period. Although difficulty arose over the contention of the facility's founders — Iraq, Kuwait, Qatar, Saudi Arabia, and the United Arab Emirates — that they, and not the AFESD as a whole, should control disbursement, a Secretariat and an implementation procedure for the 'Amman Fund were created within the AFESD in December 1980.

The AFESD serves as the secretariat for the Coordination Group of the Arab and Regional Development Institutions and in 1985 contributed $105.10 million in disbursements, as well as $336.93 million in commitments to the Group's projects. The annual *Unified Arab Economic Report,* covering current economic issues and prospects, is prepared by the Fund in cooperation with the AMF, the Arab League, and OAPEC.

In mid-1987 the AFESD reported that it had provided $361 million in development aid during 1986. Although final figures were not yet available, AFESD lending activity was believed to have declined in 1987. In December the AFESD met with other Arab financial institutions to consider proposals from the Arab Monetary Fund to promote greater inter-Arab trade.

Asian Development Bank
(ADB)

Launched under the auspices of the UN Economic Commission for Asia and the Far East (ESCAFE), subsequently the Economic and Social Commission for Asia and the Pacific (ESCAP), the ADB began operations at its Manila, Philippines, headquarters on December 19, 1966, as a means of aiding economic growth and cooperation among regional developing countries. Its original membership of

31 has since expanded to 47, including 32 regional members: Afghanistan, Australia, Bangladesh, Bhutan, Burma, China, Cook Islands, Fiji, Hong Kong, India, Indonesia, Japan, Kampuchea, Kiribati, Republic of Korea, Laos, Malaysia, Maldives, Nepal, New Zealand, Pakistan, Papua New Guinea, Philippines, Singapore, Solomon Islands, Sri Lanka, Taiwan ("Taipei, China"), Thailand, Tonga, Vanuatu, Vietnam, and Western Samoa; and 15 nonregional members: Austria, Belgium, Canada, Denmark, Finland, France, Federal Republic of Germany, Italy, Netherlands, Norway, Spain, Sweden, Switzerland, United Kingdom, and United States. The People's Republic of China acceded to membership on March 10, 1986, after the ADB agreed to change Taiwan's membership title from "Republic of China" to "Taipei, China". In protest, Taiwan withdrew from participation in Bank meetings, although continuing its financial contributions. Each member state is represented on the Board of Governors, which selects a twelve-member Board of Directors (eight from regional states) and a Bank president who chairs the latter Board.

The ADB's resources are generated through subscriptions, borrowings on capital markets, and income from a variety of sources, including interest on undisbursed assets. The vast majority of funds are in the form of country subscriptions, which totaled $19.5 billion in December 1986. Leading subscribers were Japan (15.1 percent), the United States (14.9 percent), China (7.2 percent), India (7.0 percent), Australia (6.4 percent), Indonesia (6.1 percent), Canada (5.8 percent), the Republic of Korea (5.6 percent), and the Federal Republic of Germany (4.8 percent). In all, more than 64 percent of subscribed capital has been provided by regional members.

In June 1974 an Asian Development Fund (ADF) was established to consolidate the activities of two earlier facilities, the Multi-Purpose Special Fund (MPSF) and the Agricultural Special Fund (ASF), whose policies had been criticized because of program linkages to procurement in donor countries. The ADF, which provides soft loans, receives most of its funding from voluntary contributions by the industrialized ADB members who also endow a Technical Assistance Special Fund (TASF).

In recent years there has been intense debate within the ADB in regard to proposed changes in lending policies. Western contributors have called on the Bank, which in the past has provided loans almost exclusively for specific development projects, to provide more "policy-based" loans. With such loans the recipient country has discretion in spending the money as long as certain economic reforms are implemented. Also in partial response to Western demands, the ADB in 1986 established a private sector division to provide private enterprise loans that would not require government guarantees. Subsequently, after potential loan recipients complained that ADB requirements were too stringent, the ADB adopted an adjustable lending rate system and by January 1, 1988, the Bank's average interest charge was down to 6.59 percent, the lowest in its history.

Bank lending in 1987 amounted to $2.4 billion (up from $2.0 billion in 1986) for 48 projects in 17 countries. Lending for transport and communications accounted for about 33 percent, followed by industry and nonfuel minerals (26.5 percent), agriculture and agro-industry (21.7 percent), energy (13.6 percent), and social infrastructure (5.6 percent). Cumulative lending reached $21.8 billion — $14.7 billion from ordinary capital resources and $7.1 billion from the ADF.

Caribbean Development Bank
(CDB)

The origins of the CDB can be traced to a July 1966 conference of Canada and the anglophone Caribbean states at Ottawa, where it was decided to study the possibility of creating a development-oriented financial institution for the Commonwealth Caribbean territories. An agreement formally establishing the CDB was signed at Kingston, Jamaica, on October 18, 1969. From the time it commenced operations in January 1970, the Bank's activities have included assistance in coordinating development among members, promoting trade, mobilizing public and private financing for developmental purposes, and providing technical assistance. The Commonwealth Caribbean members are Anguilla, Antigua and Barbuda, Bahamas, Barbados, Belize, British Virgin Islands, Cayman Islands, Dominica, Grenada, Guyana, Jamaica, Montserrat, St. Kitts and Nevis, St. Lucia, St. Vincent, Trinidad and Tobago, and Turks and Caicos Islands; Colombia, Mexico, and Venezuela also participate, as do three nonregional members, Canada, France, and the United Kingdom. Italy's application for membership was approved by the Board of Governors in 1985 and referred to the Italian Parliament, which by late 1987 had yet given its approval. Membership negotiations are also presently under way with the Federal Republic of Germany.

The principal policymaking body is the Board of Governors, to which each CDB member names a member, except for the British Virgin Islands, the Cayman Islands, Montserrat, and the Turks and Caicos Islands, which are collectively represented. An 11-member Board of Directors (including two nonregional directors) is elected by the Board of Governors, as is the Bank president. Voting on both bodies is weighted on the basis of capital subscriptions, of which regional members must hold 60 percent. The Bank is headquartered at St. Michael, Barbados.

In 1986 the Bank approved 19 loans valued at $59 million — $31 million for governments and government-owned corporations, $24 million in the form of lines of credit to development finance corporations, and $4 million for a private sector tourism loan. The total was up about 42 percent from 1985. However, cancellations of loans approved in previous years reached $22.2 million in 1986, compared with $8.6 million in 1985.

About 60 percent of the 1986 approvals were for "soft" concessionary loans through the Special Development Fund, up from 45 percent in 1985. In view of "difficult economic conditions" in many member countries and planned cutbacks by international and national aid agencies, the CDB sought to expand its emphasis on such loans even further in 1987. In addition, at the end of the year, the Bank made its first structural adjustment loan under a new program designed to "eliminate impediments to growth and development" by tying loans to economic policy reforms by recipients.

The Bank reported that 19 loans totaling $40.1 million were approved in 1987 with cancellations on previous loans declining substantially from the 1986 level to about $4.4 million. Cumulative lending approval reached $636 million with disbursements of $491 million. At the end of the year the Bank's resources stood at $633 million.

Central African States Development Bank
Banque de Développement des Etats de l'Afrique Centrale
(BDEAC)

The Central African States Development Bank was established on December 3, 1975, as a joint venture of Cameroon, the Central African Republic, Chad, Congo, and Gabon, with Equatorial Guinea, theretofore an observer, joining as a sixth full member in 1986. The Bank commenced operations on January 2, 1977. It is governed by an annual General Assembly, composed of representatives of the regional states and of the African Development Bank, the Central African States Bank, and the governments of France, the Federal Republic of Germany, and Kuwait, all of whom are shareholders and are represented on a 16-member Board of Directors that meets three times a year.

From its inception through June 1986, the Bank approved 58 loans involving a total of 30.9 billion CFA francs. Cumulative disbursements were 11.9 billion CFA francs. During the 1985–1986 financial year, five requests were approved in the amount of 7.1 billion CFA francs. Projects included the creation of rubber complexes in Gabon and the Congo, the completion of an oil-palm facility and construction of a pier in the Congo, and the renovation of a cotton mill in Cameroon. Agriculture and rural development, which previously attracted little Bank support, accounted for nearly 75 percent of the disbursements in 1985–1986. In the five-year period ending June 30, 1986, the geographic distribution of loans was: Congo, 32 percent; Cameroon, 23 percent; Central African Republic, 20 percent; Gabon, 19 percent; and Chad, 6 percent (the rate of loans to Chad being depressed because of unsettled conditions in that country).

Central American Bank for Economic Integration
Banco Centroamericano de Integración Económico
(BCIE)

The BCIE was established on December 13, 1960, as the result of an initiative originating in the Central American Economic Cooperation Committee of the UN Economic Commission for Latin America (ECLA). In 1959 the Committee had called for the preparation, in conjunction with national and other international agencies, of a draft charter for a Central American institution dedicated to financing and promoting integrated economic development. The charter was drafted concurrently with the General Treaty on Central American Economic Integration, which established the Central American Common Market (CACM)

of Costa Rica, El Salvador, Guatemala, Honduras, and Nicaragua. The latter four states signed the Bank's constitutive agreement on December 12, 1960, while Costa Rica became a signatory on July 27, 1963. The BCIE document provides that only adherents to the General Treaty are eligible for loans and guarantees. The Board of Governors, which meets formally once a year, constitutes the highest authority of the Bank and consists of the finance minister and central bank president of each member country. The Board of Directors, responsible for BCIE's management, is comprised of five members, one from each country.

Headquartered at Tegucigalpa, Honduras, the Bank began operations on May 31, 1961, and continued to function, with minimal structural changes, in the aftermath of the 1969 war between El Salvador and Honduras. As an institution of the CACM, the Bank administers various special funds while focusing its lending on infrastructural projects (roads, water supplies, electrification, industrial development, housing, and technical education programs). Resources are conveyed through the following major funds: the Ordinary Fund, the Central American Fund for Economic Integration, the Housing Fund, and the Social Development Fund. In May 1981, the Board of Governors created the Central American Common Market Fund, independent of the Bank's general resources, to finance unpaid balances derived from intraregional transactions. Initial capitalization was set at $50 million, while the loan portfolio as of June 30, 1986, totalled $20.0 million.

In 1985 the Bank authorized the creation of a Fund for the Economic and Social Development of Central America (FESDCA) as a temporary mechanism to permit participation by extraregional countries independent of the Bank's general resources. Mexico and the European Community registered as contributors to the Fund in 1986, with Argentina, Colombia, and the Dominican Republic expressing interest in its operations. The absorption of the FESDCA into the Bank's regular activity was planned following the expected approval of BCIE charter changes that would extend full BCIE membership to extraregional countries.

Following the members' 1976 decision to undertake "special capital contributions", the Bank's resources multiplied and its loans reached a peak annual authorization of $185 million in the 1980–1981 fiscal year. Subsequently, Bank activity plummeted because of economic, social, and political turmoil in the region, loan authorizations totalling only $11 million in 1983–1984 and $34 million in 1984–1985. In 1985–1986 eight public sector loans totalling $29 million were authorized, bringing cumulative commitments to $1.7 billion for 938 loans.

East African Development Bank
(EADB)

The charter of the East African Development Bank was contained in an annex to the December 1967 treaty establishing the East African Community (EAC), which collapsed in June 1977 because of tensions among its members: Kenya, Tanzania, and Uganda. Since the Bank was not supported by EAC general funds, it remained formally in existence, with headquarters at Kampala, Uganda. Subsequently, a mediator responsible for dividing the Community's assets among its former members was charged with making recommendations concerning the Bank's future, and in late 1979 a new tripartite treaty providing for a revival of EADB activity was drafted. The Bank's new charter, completed during the first half of 1980 and signed by the three members in July, seeks to rechannel the thrust of Bank lending toward agricultural, infrastructural, and technical-assistance support efforts.

In early 1984, the International Monetary Fund granted the EADB permission to hold Fund special drawing rights (SDRs), further enhancing the Bank's financial base and flexibility. Since then, the Bank has been actively seeking new sources of finance, while calling upon external consultants to examine problems facing the public and private sectors in the member states.

In 1986 the Bank approved 22 loans totalling $16 million, down from $22 million in 1985. Available resources rose from $22.5 million to $66.4 million, although only $41.4 million was committed by the end of the year. Income from undisbursed resources permitted the bank to realize a profit of $2.2 million despite repayment arrears. Soft loans and grants from European donors provided most of the additional resources in 1986.

The Bank announced its intention in 1987 to augment its authorized capital through additional member contributions and the issuance of shares to nonregional donors. In May the African Development Bank announced that it would lend the EADB $36 million to finance a variety of small-scale projects in the three member countries, while in December the European Investment Bank approved loans of $15.2 million, half to be used to strengthen the EABD capital base and the other half for project lending.

European Investment Bank
(EIB)

The EIB is the European Community's bank for long-term finance. It was created by the Treaty of Rome, which established the European Economic Community (EEC) on January 1, 1958. The Bank, headquartered at Luxembourg, has as its basic function the balanced and steady development of EC member countries, with the greater part of its financing going to projects that favor the development of less-advanced regions, serve the common interests of several members or the whole community, and promote industrial modernization and conversion. The EIB membership is identical to that of the EC: Belgium, Denmark, France, Federal Republic of Germany, Greece, Ireland, Italy, Luxembourg, Netherlands, Portugal, Spain, and the United Kingdom, each of which has subscribed part of the Bank's capital, although most funds required to finance its operations are borrowed by the Bank on international and national capital markets. In June 1985 the Board of Governors agreed to increase the Bank's subscribed capital from 14.4 billion ECUs ($15.4 billion) to 26.5 billion ECUs ($28.4 billion), and with the accession of Spain and Portugal in 1986, the amount was further increased to $28.8 billion ECUs ($30.8 billion), with Germany, France, Italy, and the United Kingdom providing the largest shares at 5.5 billion ECUs ($5.9 billion) each. The EIB borrowed

5.7 billion ECUs ($6.1 billion) in 1985 and 6.9 billion ECUs ($7.4 billion) in 1986 from capital markets, raising the total amount from 1961 to 1986 to 39.0 billion ECUs ($41.7 billion). [Note: the December 1986 conversion rate of $1.07 per ECU is used throughout.]

EIB activities were initially confined to the territory of member states but have gradually been extended to many other countries under terms of association or cooperation agreements. Current participants include 12 countries in the Mediterranean region (Algeria, Cyprus, Egypt, Israel, Jordan, Lebanon, Malta, Morocco, Syria, Tunisia, Turkey, Yugoslavia) and the 66 African, Caribbean, and Pacific (ACP) signatories of the current Lomé Convention.

The Bank is administered by a 12-member Board of Governors (1 representative—usually the finance minister—from each EC state) and a 22-member Board of Directors (3 each from France, Federal Republic of Germany, Italy, and the United Kingdom; 2 from Spain; 1 each from Belgium, Denmark, Greece, Ireland, Luxembourg, the Netherlands, and Portugal; and 1 representing the European Commission). The president of the Bank, appointed by the Board of Governors, chairs the Board of Directors and heads a Management Committee that encompasses six vice presidents. Other organs include a three-member Audit Committee, six directorates, various subsidiary departments, and a Technical Advisory Service.

Total EIB lending in 1986 reached nearly $7.5 billion ECUs ($8.0 billion), up from $7.2 billion ECUs ($7.7 billion) in 1985. The New Community Instrument (NCI), established in 1979, provided 393 million ECUs ($421 million) for the promotion of priority objectives in energy, infrastructure, and other productive sectors. Of the total financing, 7.1 billion ECUs ($7.6 billion) was provided for the members of the EC, while 474 million ECUs ($507 million) went to projects outside the Community. Funds in the amount of 3.7 billion ECUs ($4.0 billion) were channeled toward regional development projects to enhance the economic progress of less-favored regions within the Community. The bulk of the loans went to industry, 1.9 billion ECUs ($2.0 billion). Lesser amounts were extended in support of energy, infrastructure, and environmental protection. Actual disbursements for the year came to 7.0 billion ECUs ($7.5 billion) compared to $5.9 billion ECUs ($6.3 billion) in 1985.

At its annual meeting in July 1987 the Board of Governors reaffirmed the Bank's commitment to continue to be a source of financing for Europe's major infrastructural projects. Toward that end, the Bank approved a six-year financing arrangement for $1.4 billion ECUs ($1.6 billion), the largest agreement in the Bank's history, toward the construction of the Eurotunnel under the English Channel. Total lending for 1987 was $7.8 billion ECUs ($10.2 billion at the December 31, 1987 exchange rate).

Inter-American Development Bank
Banco Interamericano de Desarrollo
(IADB/BID)

Following a reversal of long-standing opposition by the United States, the IADB was launched in 1959 upon acceptance of a charter drafted by a special commission to the

Inter-American Economic and Social Council of the Organization of American States (IA-Ecosoc). Operations began on October 1, 1960, with permanent headquarters at Washington, DC.

The purpose of the IADB is to accelerate economic and social development in Latin America, in part by acting as a catalyst for public and private external capital. In addition to helping regional states to coordinate development efforts, the Bank provides technical assistance, conducts borrowings on international capital markets, and participates in cofinancing with other multilateral agencies, national institutions, and commercial banks. Loans cannot exceed 50 percent of project cost. In the wake of criticism that the Bank had not supported regional integration and had neglected the area's poorest nations, major contributors agreed in December 1978, after eight months of intense negotiations, to adopt a US-sponsored policy that would allocate less assistance to wealthier developing nations — such as Argentina, Brazil, and Mexico — and, within such countries, would focus primarily on projects aimed at benefiting the neediest economic sectors.

The current members of the IADB are Argentina, Austria, Bahamas, Barbados, Belgium, Bolivia, Brazil, Canada, Chile, Colombia, Costa Rica, Denmark, Dominican Republic, Ecuador, El Salvador, Finland, France, Federal Republic of Germany, Guatemala, Guyana, Haiti, Honduras, Israel, Italy, Jamaica, Japan, Mexico, Netherlands, Nicaragua, Norway, Panama, Paraguay, Peru, Portugal, Spain, Suriname, Sweden, Switzerland, Trinidad and Tobago, United Kingdom, United States, Uruguay, Venezuela, and Yugoslavia. (Norway was admitted as the 17th nonregional member in January 1986, pledging $29 million in capital subscriptions and another $13 million for Special Operations.) Each member is represented on the Board of Governors, the Bank's policymaking body, by a governor and an alternate, who convene at least once a year. Administrative responsibilities are exercised by 12 executive directors (1 appointed by the United States, the others by country groupings ranging in number from one to eight). The Bank president, elected by the governors, presides over sessions of the Board of Executive Directors and, in conjunction with an executive vice president, is responsible for the daily management of eight IADB departments and two offices. In addition, the Institute for Latin American Integration (*Instituto para la Integración de América Latina* — Intal), founded in 1963 and headquartered at Buenos Aires, Argentina, functions as a permanent Bank department. Voting is on a weighted basis according to a country's capital subscription; leading subscribers are the United States (34.7 percent), Argentina (11.6 percent), Brazil (11.6 percent), Mexico (7.5 percent), and Venezuela (6.2 percent). Nonregional members hold less than 6 percent of the voting shares.

In November 1984 the Inter-American Investment Corporation (IAIC) was established as an affiliate of the IADB to "encourage the establishment, expansion, and modernization of small- and medium-sized private enterprises". Following the first joint meeting of the Boards of Governors of the IADB and the IAIC in March 1987, it was announced that IAIC operations would begin "in the near future".

In 1986 the IADB approved loans for 56 projects totalling $3.0 billion, bringing cumulative lending approval to $35.4 billion. Disbursements in 1986 totalled $2.3 billion while 1987 lending was reported as $2.4 billion.

The Bank has called for a $25 billion capital replenishment that would allow its lending to nearly double to $5 billion annually for the next five-year period. However, the replenishment remained in question in early 1988 after a year-long dispute over demands by the United States, the major projected contributor, for greater influence at the Bank, including virtual veto power over loans. Latin American and Caribbean members, although willing to accept the US request to link some loans to economic reform, have objected to the veto. The conflict was seen as central to the February 1988 resignation of Antonio Ortiz Mena of Mexico after 17 years as IADB president. Uruguay's Foreign Minister Enrique Iglesias was named president effective April 1, observers suggesting his appointment could have a salutary effect on the replenishment impasse.

International Investment Bank
Myezhdoornarodne Investetzeonne Bank
(IIB)

Playing a Soviet-bloc regional role somewhat analogous to that of the UN's World Bank, the IIB began operations on January 1, 1971, following an agreement concluded at Moscow, USSR, in July 1970. The original signatories were Bulgaria, Czechoslovakia, German Democratic Republic, Hungary, Mongolia, Poland, and Union of Soviet Socialist Republics. Cuba and Romania adhered to the agreement in 1971, as did Vietnam in 1977. All members are represented on the IIB Council, which is the Bank's highest authority, with each country having one vote. The principal executive body is a four-member Board, which oversees the operations of eight departments.

The IIB grants long-term (up to 15-year) and medium-term (up to 5-year) credits for projects designed to enhance the economies of member states, as well as for other projects approved by the Council. The credits may be granted either in hard currency or in transferable roubles (TRs), the Bank's unit of account. At the beginning of 1986, authorized capital totaled TR 1.07 billion, of which the largest shares were allocated to the Soviet Union (37 percent), the German Democratic Republic (16 percent), Czechoslovakia (12 percent), and Poland (11 percent).

As with the International Bank for Economic Cooperation (IBEC), each IIB member is granted a credit quota, denominated in transferable roubles in proportion to its share of trade within the Council for Mutual Economic Assistance (CMEA). Emphasis is given to projects in compliance with the Long-Term Purpose-Oriented Cooperation Programs (LPCP) of the CMEA, which are directed toward improving supplies of energy and raw materials, developing machine-building industry, facilitating transport improvement, and meeting demand for foodstuffs and consumer goods. Close relations are maintained not only with the CMEA but with the IBEC, the three having cooperated to improve payment and credit relations among their member countries.

From its inception to the end of 1986, the IIB authorized financing of TR 12 billion for 103 projects. Sectoral credit shares during that period were: fuel industry and energetics, 64 percent; machine-building (including electrical engineering and the electronics industry), 23 percent; metallurgy, 5 percent; chemical industries, 4 percent; and transportation, food, and other industries, 4 percent.

Credits totalling TR 900 million were approved in 1986 for nine projects, the largest being the construction of a 4600 kilometer pipeline to facilitate natural gas deliveries from the Soviet Union to other CMEA members. Other projects included renovation and expansion of textile and washing machine plants in East Germany and metal-working and steel pipe plants in Bulgaria. As of January 1, 1987, the Bank's balance stood at TR 2.57 billion, with a net income for 1986 of TR 24.3 million being reported.

Islamic Development Bank
(IDB)

The IDB originated in a Declaration of Intent issued by the Conference of Finance Ministers of Islamic Countries during their December 15, 1973, meeting at Jiddah, Saudi Arabia. The Bank's Articles of Agreement were approved and adopted by the Second Conference of Finance Ministers on August 10, 1974, with the Bank commencing activities in October 1975. The purpose of the IDB, which is headquartered at Jiddah, is to "foster the economic development and social progress in member countries and Muslim communities individually as well as jointly", guided by the tenets of *shari'a* (Islamic law). In addition to providing assistance for feasibility studies, infrastructural projects, development of industry and agriculture, import financing, and technology transfers, the IBD operates several special funds, including one to aid Muslim populations in non-member countries. Since *shari'a* proscriptions include the collection of interest, various alternative financing methods, such as leasing and profit-sharing, are pursued, with service charges for loans being based on the expected administrative costs of the loan operations. The IDB also attempts to promote cooperation with Islamic banks as well as with national development institutions and other international agencies. The Bank uses as its unit of account the Islamic dinar (ID), which is at par with the special drawing right (SDR) of the International Monetary Fund. Authorized capital of the IDB is ID 2 billion, encompassing 200,000 shares of ID 10,000 each. Subscribed capital in 1986 totaled ID 1.9 billion ($2.3 billion), and paid-up capital amounted to ID 1.5 billion ($1.9 billion).

The Bank's primary decisionmaking and administrative organs are a Board of Governors and a Board of Executive Directors, the former composed of the member countries' ministers or their designees. Of the ten executive directors, four are appointed by the largest subscribers to the Bank's capital (Saudi Arabia, 28 percent; Libya, 17 percent; Kuwait, 14 percent; and the United Arab Emirates, 11 per cent), while six are elected by the governors of the other member states.

A prerequisite to joining the Bank is membership in the Islamic Conference. Present members include Afghanis-tan, Algeria, Bahrain, Bangladesh, Benin, Brunei, Burkina Faso, Cameroon, Chad, Comoro Islands, Djibouti, Egypt, Gabon, Gambia, Guinea, Guinea-Bissau, Indonesia, Iraq, Jordan, Kuwait, Lebanon, Libya, Malaysia, Maldives, Mali, Mauritania, Morocco, Niger, Oman, Pakistan, Palestine Liberation Organization, Qatar, Saudi Arabia, Senegal, Sierra Leone, Somalia, Sudan, Syria, Tunisia, Turkey, Uganda, United Arab Emirates, Yemen Arab Republic, and People's Democratic Republic of Yemen. The Bank governors voted to suspend Afghanistan's membership at their 1981 annual meeting.

During its eleventh fiscal year, from September 1985–August 1986, the Bank financed 104 projects totaling ID 756.92 million ($848.95 million). Ordinary operations accounted for ID 175.73 million ($192.53 million) of the total, while foreign trade financing operations received ID 572.84 million ($647.28 million), and special operations amounted to ID 8.35 million ($9.24 million). A decreased demand for development funds and a paucity of viable projects led to a decline in overall financing from the previous year's figure of ID 1001.47 million ($988.92 million). Sectoral distribution of financing for the period was as follows: industry, 42.0 percent; transport and communication, 23.1 percent; agriculture, 18.8 percent; social sectors, 8.9 percent; and utilities, 7.3 percent. Cumulative commitments, net of cancellations, through October 1986 for 661 projects amounted to ID 5.55 billion ($6.21 billion), of which 32 percent financed loans for less-developed countries (LDCs). Disbursements for the fiscal year totaled ID 557.16 million ($635.25 million), raising the cumulative total at the end of 1986 to ID 4.1 billion ($4.5 billion).

The Board of Governors, during their tenth annual meeting on March 23, 1986, at 'Amman, Jordon, approved the establishment of a Longer-term Trade Financing Scheme as a strategy to increase member countries' exports; contributions for the Scheme will be made to a trust fund within the IDB. In July, the Board of Directors endorsed the creation of a fund, tentatively titled the IDB Unit Trust, to serve as a secondary market for mobilizing additional financial resources. Throughout the year, the Bank continued its implementation of the Special Program for Sahelian members, which granted $50 million in emergency aid to alleviate problems caused by drought.

In March 1987 the IDB was selected to manage the new Islamic Banks' Portfolio, a fund established by 21 Islamic banks to finance trade between Islamic countries. The IDB contributed $25 million to the $65 million initial capital of the Portfolio, which was also authorized to issue up to $650 million in public shares. In December IDB financing approval for the 1986–1987 fiscal year was reported to have totalled $741 million.

Nordic Investment Bank
(NIB)

A Nordic investment bank was first proposed in June 1957, but its creation was postponed by the founding of the European Free Trade Association. Though further discussed in 1962 and 1964, it was not until June 1, 1976, that an agreement establishing the Bank came into force. It is headquartered at Helsinki, Finland.

The members of the NIB are the same as those of the Nordic Council: Denmark, Finland, Iceland, Norway, and Sweden. Each country appoints two members to the ten-member Board of Directors which heads the Bank under a rotating chairmanship. In addition, a Control Committee, on which all five countries are represented, oversees Bank audits and ensures that the Bank is managed according to its statutes.

The purpose of the Bank is to provide financing "on normal banking terms, taking socio-economic considerations into account", for projects that will expand Nordic production and exports while strengthening economic cooperation among member countries. The bulk of NIB loans have gone to projects jointly undertaken by companies or institutions in two or more member countries. Such loans are always issued in conjunction with cofinancing from domestic banks and credit institutions, NIB participation being limited to no more than 50 percent of the total.

In the 1980s the NIB has also become an international lender. In 1981 the first loans for joint Nordic projects outside the region were issued after Norway had lifted its objection to them. Subsequently, in 1982, the Nordic Council of Ministers established a new supplemental facility, Nordic Project Investment Loans (NPIL), to be administered by the NIB to provide loans for projects "of Nordic interest" in developing countries as well as certain state-trading countries. In conjunction with the Nordic Council, the Bank is also currently considering the establishment of a "soft window" for distribution of grants and concessionary loans to developing countries.

Both regional and international lending have recently accelerated. NPIL lending authorization, originally set at SDR 350 million, was raised to SDR 700 million ($900 million) on January 1, 1987, to accommodate increased demand. NIB authorized capital, excluding the NPIL, was raised to SDR 1.6 billion ($2.1 billion) on August 1, 1987, after the Bank had nearly reached the previous lending limit of SDR 800 million.

In 1986 the Bank disbursed 88 loans totalling SDR 533 million ($652 million). At the end of the year the total of outstanding loans stood at SDR 1.4 billion ($1.7 billion), SDR 1,277 million for regional projects and SDR 150 million for nonregional projects. The sectoral distribution of regional loans was: energy and oil, 34 percent; chemical industry, 16 percent; engineering industry, 14 percent; mining and raw materials processing industry, 11 percent; communications, 8 percent; forestry, 3 percent; electronics and data processing, 1 percent; others, 13 percent.

The Bank reported continued growth in 1987, loan disbursements for the year amounting to SDR 571 million ($811 million) and total assets increasing to SDR 3.1 billion ($4.4 billion).

West African Development Bank
Banque Ouest-Africaine de Développement
(BOAD)

An agreement to establish a West African Development Bank was initialed at a Paris, France, summit meeting of French-speaking African states on November 13–14, 1973.

The Bank formally commenced operations on January 1, 1976, with headquarters at Lomé, Togo. The BOAD provides regional financing for the seven members (Benin, Burkina Faso, Côte d'Ivoire, Mali, Niger, Senegal, Togo) of the West African Monetary Union (*Union Monetaire Ouest-Africaine* — UMOA), the object being to promote equitable development and achieve economic integration through priority development projects. The unit of account is the CFA franc, valued as of March 1, 1988 at CFA 285.80 per US dollar.

The organs of the Bank include the Council of Ministers of the UMOA and a Directors Committee, the latter encompassing not only representatives of the six member states but of the UMOA's Central Bank of West African States (*Banque Centrale des Etats de l'Afrique de l'Ouest* — BCEAO), in addition to a group of French and West German experts. The president of the Directors Committee also serves as president of the Bank.

A meeting of member ministers on October 30–31, 1983, at Niamey, Niger, yielded approval of a Bank proposal to implement regional integration projects, harmonize national development policies, and facilitate maximum utilization of internal and external resources. In order to strengthen its lending profile, the BOAD has received a $6 million, 12-year line of credit from the Arab Bank for Economic Development in Africa (BADEA) and lines of $6.1 million and $14 million, respectively, from the International Bank for Reconstruction and Development (IBRD) and the International Development Association (IDA). In addition, cooperative agreements with the International Fund for Agricultural Development (IFAD), the International Bureau for Information, and the African Regional Centre for Technical Design and Building were approved during the 1985–1986 fiscal year.

In 1986 and 1987 BOAD expanded its association with the international banking community, reaching credit agreements with, among others, the European Investment Bank and financial institutions in Canada, Japan, and India. By January 1988 the Bank's cumulative commitments to its seven members had reached 86.5 billion CFA. Projects covered by 1986 and 1987 loans included airport rehabilitation in Burkina Faso; rural development in Côte d'Ivoire; telecommunications, energy, and hydroagricultural programs in Senegal; and rural water programs in Niger.

SOUTH ASIAN ASSOCIATION FOR REGIONAL COOPERATION (SAARC)

Established: By charter signed at Dhaka, Bangladesh, on December 8, 1985.

Purpose: ". . . to promote the welfare of the peoples of south Asia and to improve their quality of life; . . . to promote and strengthen collective self-reliance among the countries of south Asia; . . . to promote active collaboration and mutual assistance in the economic, social, cultural, technical and scientific fields; . . . and to co-operate with international and regional organizations with similar aims and purposes."

Headquarters: Kathmandu, Nepal.

Principal Organs: Meeting of Heads of State or Government (all members), Council of Ministers (all members), Standing Committee of Foreign Secretaries (all members), Program Committee (all members), Secretariat.

Secretary General: Abul Ahsan (Bangladesh).

Membership (7): Bangladesh, Bhutan, India, Maldives, Nepal, Pakistan, Sri Lanka.

Origin and development. Prior to formation of the SAARC, South Asia had been the only major world region without a formal venue for multigovernmental cooperation. The organization was launched at Dhaka, Bangladesh, on December 8, 1985, during the first high-level meeting of the participating governments' political leaders. The summit was convened on recommendation of the ministerial South Asian Regional Cooperation Committee (SARC), formed at New Delhi, India, in August 1983, with subsequent meetings at Male, Maldives, in July 1984 and Thimbu, Bhutan, in May 1985. At the conclusion of SAARC's founding session, the participants issued a charter setting forth the objectives of the new grouping, in addition to a "Dhaka Declaration" that called upon states to conclude a comprehensive Nuclear Test Ban Treaty. It was agreed that future summits would be convened annually, that foreign ministers would meet twice a year, that decisions would be by unanimous vote, and that "bilateral and contentious" issues would be avoided.

The second summit at Bangalore, India, on November 16–17, 1986, was preceded by meetings of the organization's Program Committee and Standing Committee of Foreign Secretaries, which discussed norms and procedures for projected SAARC institutions, as well as priorities for projects to be undertaken by member countries. The "Bangalore Declaration", issued at the summit's conclusion, noted that considerable progress had been made in implementing an integrated program of action (IPA), welcomed the signing of a ministerial memorandum of understanding on the establishment of a Secretariat, and addressed a number of international issues, such as action against terrorism, the crisis facing the UN system, the lack of visible movement on arms control during the Reagan-Gorbachev meeting at Reykjavik, Iceland, and the need for a new round of multilateral trade negotiations to help ease the global economic crisis.

Structure. General policies are formulated at the annual meeting of heads of state and, to a lesser extent, at the semiannual meetings of the Council of Ministers. A Secretariat was established in January 1987 at Kathmandu, while technical committees have been formed in several areas including aviation and the prevention of drug abuse and trafficking. The latter report to the Standing Committee of Foreign Secretaries which prepares recommendations for the Council of Ministers.

Activities. The record of the first three regional summits, coupled with SAARC's repudiation of involvement in purely bilateral concerns, affords little hope that the grouping can serve as a forum for resolving major conflicts within the subcontinent, such as the Himalayan river waters dispute between India and Bangladesh, the confrontation between ethnically South Indian Tamil guerrillas and the Sri Lankan government, and the variety of problems affecting relations between India and Pakistan. SAARC meetings have, however, provided opportunities for informal discussions between regional leaders on a wide range of such issues. More immediate benefit is sought by reducing tension through cooperation in areas such as communications, transport, and rural development. Thus, a Group of Experts that convened at New Delhi on February 23, 1987, attempted to facilitate "people-to-people contacts" through the establishment of an SAARC documentation center, the institution of academic programs that would inculcate a sense of South Asian community, the promotion of tourism, the creation of a South Asian broadcasting network, and the formation of organized volunteer programs in reforestation, wasteland development, and agricultural extension.

The Association's third summit, held at Kathmandu on November 2–4, 1987, yielded agreements for cooperation in several other areas, including the stockpiling of emergency food supplies and the suppression of terrorism. The convention on terrorism must be ratified by member states and requires the conclusion of bilateral treaties for certain of its provisions, such as the extradition of terrorists, to come into effect. A declaration issued at the end of the summit also urged study of potential economic cooperation and the consequences of natural disasters.

Despite the apparent cordiality of the summit, some behind-the-scenes tension was reported, particularly between India and Pakistan. One source of conflict was a membership application from Afghanistan, sponsored by New Delhi but rejected by the other SAARC members because of the Soviet military presence. There was also disagreement over a Pakistani proposal for a South Asian treaty banning nuclear weapons, the final declaration simply noting SAARC's resolve to "contribute" to nuclear disarmament.

SOUTH PACIFIC COMMISSION (SPC/CPS)

Commission du Pacifique Sud

Established: By Agreement signed at Canberra, Australia, February 6, 1947, effective July 29, 1948; structure modified by Memoranda of Understanding signed at Rarotonga, Cook Islands, October 2, 1974, and at Nouméa, New Caledonia, October 20, 1976.

Purpose: ". . . to provide a common forum within which the Island peoples and their governments can express themselves on issues, problems, needs and ideas common to the region; . . . to assist in meeting the basic needs of the peoples of the region; . . . to serve as a catalyst for the development of regional resources . . . ; to act as a centre for collection and dissemination of information on the needs of the region . . ."

Headquarters: Nouméa, New Caledonia.

Principal Organs: South Pacific Conference (all members), Committee of the Whole (all members), Committee of Representatives of Participating Governments and Administrations (all members), Secretariat.

Secretary General: Palauni M. Tuiasosopo (American Samoa).

Members (27): American Samoa, Australia, Belau (formerly Palau), Cook Islands, Federated States of Micronesia, Fiji, France, French Polynesia, Guam, Kiribati, Marshall Islands, Nauru, New Caledonia, New Zealand, Niue, Northern Mariana Islands, Papua New Guinea, Pitcairn Islands, Solomon Islands, Tokelau, Tonga, Tuvalu, United Kingdom, United States, Vanuatu, Wallis and Futuna Islands, Western Samoa.

Official Languages: English, French.

Origin and development. The South Pacific Commission was organized in 1947–1948 to coordinate the economic and social development policies of states administering dependent South Pacific territories. The Netherlands, an original member, withdrew in 1962 when it ceased to administer the former colony of Dutch New Guinea. The Commission's retention of elements of its earlier tutelary character was called into question by participants in the original South Pacific Conference, which was composed exclusively of dependent territories. Thus the members of the Conference proposed in 1973 that joint sessions of the Commission and Conference be held. In this manner the representatives of the dependent South Pacific territories hoped to influence the aid policies of the administering states. Under the 1974 Memorandum of Understanding, the Commission and Conference meet once a year in a joint session known as the South Pacific Conference. The Memorandum also established a Planning and Evaluation Committee to meet annually to evaluate the preceding year's work program, to examine the draft work program and budget for the coming year, to prepare an agenda for the Conference, and to report to the Conference. Until 1976, each participating government was entitled to one vote for itself and one for each territory it administered; the Memorandum abolished this multiple procedure, giving each delegation one vote in the Committee.

Under a 1980 amendment to the Canberra Agreement, any territory in the region, if invited, might become a full member of the Commission. Thus, the Cook Islands and Niue, both dependencies of New Zealand, were admitted, as were the Federated States of Micronesia, the Marshall Islands, and the Northern Mariana Islands, whose de jure separation from the US Trust Territory of the Pacific was not yet complete. Australia, on the other hand, objected to the seating at the 1980 meeting of a representative of Norfolk Island (a member of the original South Pacific Conference), who was obliged to attend as a member of the Australian delegation. The other component of the US Trust Territory of the Pacific, Belau, was admitted to full participation in 1981.

With the inclusion of Micronesian territories (all located north of the equator) to Commission membership, it has been suggested that the designations "South Pacific Commission" and "South Pacific Conference" are now outdated, although no formal effort to change them has yet been broached.

Structure. The Conference scrutinizes the Commission's budget and work program and is empowered to discuss any matter within the purview of the Commission. As authorized by the 1974 Memorandum, the October 1983 Conference established a Committee of Representatives of Participating Governments and Administrations to approve the administrative budget and to report on it to the Conference. Also created was a Committee of the Whole to meet annually four months prior to the Conference to evaluate the preceding year's work program, to examine the draft work program and budget for the coming year, to agree on topics to be discussed by the Conference, to nominate the Conference's principal officers, and to report to the Conference on its work. These two bodies replaced the earlier Planning and Evaluation Committee and the Committee of Representatives of Participating Governments.

In recent years, a number of proposals have been advanced for expanding the SPC mandate, including an appeal by Papua New Guinea at the 1980 and 1981 Conference sessions for the formation of a Pacific Island political alliance that would seek observer status at the United Nations and elsewhere as a "lobby" on behalf of regional interest. No action was taken on the proposal, while action on a more modest recommendation that the SPC amalgamate with the South Pacific Bureau for Economic Cooperation —and, by implication, with its parent body, the South Pacific Forum (below)—has been deferred until completion of feasibility studies. This position was maintained even after the SPF had, in 1983, expressed interest in the merger proposal.

Activities. At the 16th Conference in 1976, members adopted a Review Committee recommendation that the SPC engage in the following specific activities: (a) rural development; (b) youth and community development; (c) ad hoc expert consultancies; (d) cultural exchanges (in arts, sports, and education); (e) training facilitation; (f) assessment and development of marine resources and research; and that special consideration should be given to projects and grants-in-aid which do not necessarily fall within these specific activities, but which respond to pressing regional or subregional needs or to the expressed needs of the smaller Pacific countries.

Much of this agenda remained current a decade later at the 26th Conference, which met at Papeete, French Polynesia, on November 3–5, 1986. A general review of activities by the outgoing secretary general included reference to such matters as an expanded Community Education Training Center in Fiji, advances in agricultural cultivation techniques suitable to atoll situations, the Conference's Deep Sea Fisheries Development Project, the status of a South Pacific Regional Environmental Program, and the development of a statistical training package for island members.

During the 27th Conference, held at Nouméa, New Caledonia, November 10–14, 1987, the five major contributing members — Australia, France, New Zealand, the United Kingdom, and the United States — promised extrabudgetary contributions to enhance SPC activities. The Conference also decided to seek additional funds from international organizations and nonmember countries, particularly Japan. In other activity, the Conference called for additional priority to be given to health and women's programs and expressed its confidence in the ability of the Commission "to continue adjusting to the changing needs of the region". Vanuatu, the Marshall Islands, and Papua New Guinea were absent from the session, Papuan officials reportedly urging that the SPC be "scrapped" because of its "colonial" nature. The next Conference is scheduled for October 10–12, 1988, at Rarotonga, Cook Islands.

SOUTH PACIFIC FORUM (SPF)

Established: At meeting of a subgroup of the South Pacific Commission at Wellington, New Zealand, in August 1971.

Purpose: To facilitate cooperation among member states, to coordinate their views on political issues of concern to the subregion, and to accelerate member states' rates of economic development.

Headquarters: Suva, Fiji.

Principal Organs: South Pacific Forum, South Pacific Bureau for Economic Cooperation (SPEC), SPEC Committee, SPEC Secretariat.

Director of SPEC Secretariat: Mahe Tupouniua (Tonga).

Membership (15): Australia, Cook Islands, Federated States of Micronesia, Fiji, Kiribati, Marshall Islands, Nauru, New Zealand, Niue, Papua New Guinea, Solomon Islands, Tonga, Tuvalu, Vanuatu, Western Samoa.
Observer: Belau (formerly Palau).

Official Language: English.

Origin and development. Since the South Pacific Commission (above) was barred from concerning itself with political affairs, representatives of several South Pacific governments and territories decided in 1971 to set up a

separate organization where they might speak with a common voice on a wider range of issues. At the meeting of the Forum in April 1973, representatives of Australia, Cook Islands, Fiji, Nauru, New Zealand, Tonga, and Western Samoa signed the Apia Agreement, which established the South Pacific Bureau for Economic Cooperation (SPEC) as a technical subcommittee of the committee of the whole. The Gilbert Islands (now Kiribati), Niue, Papua New Guinea, Solomon Islands, Tuvalu, and Vanuatu subsequently acceded to the Agreement. The Marshall Islands and the Federated States of Micronesia, formerly observers, were granted membership in 1987 after Washington, in late 1986, had declared their compacts of free association with the United States to be in effect. Belau retained its SPF observer status pending resolution of its compact status (see United States: Related Territories and United Nations: Trusteeship Council).

In 1975, the Bureau was officially designated as the Forum's secretariat, with the SPEC Secretariat responsible for administration of the parent group. A Forum-sponsored South Pacific Regional Trade and Cooperation Agreement (Sparteca), providing for progressively less restricted access to the markets of Australia and New Zealand, came into effect in 1981; the process reached a conclusion in 1985 with the approval of measures by Canberra and Wellington eliminating all duties for most products from other SPF members.

Structure. The SPF meets annually at the ministerial or summit level. The SPEC Committee, comprising ministers of departments in areas related to the specific issues under discussion, usually meets twice a year. The SPEC Secretariat operates continuously, its director reporting to the SPF whenever the latter is convened. Affiliated with SPEC are the Association of South Pacific Airlines (ASPA); the Pacific Forum Line, a shipping agency formed by 10 SPF members in 1977; the South Pacific Forum Fisheries Agency (FFA); the South Pacific Trade Commission, which is financed by Australia to help other SPF members develop new markets; and the South Pacific Tourism Council, which is funded by a grant from the European Community.

Activities. Following a decision at the 15th annual SPF meeting, the delegates to the 16th annual meeting in 1985 concluded the Treaty of Rarotonga (Cook Islands), which declared the South Pacific to be a nuclear-free zone. The Treaty forbids manufacturing, testing, storing, dumping, and using nuclear weapons and materials in the region. It does, however, allow each country to make its own defense arrangements including whether or not to host nuclear warships. The Treaty became operative in December 1986 when Australia became the eighth SPF member to tender its ratification. Those countries known to possess nuclear weapons were asked to sign the Treaty's protocols, the SPF having added an "opt-out" provision which would permit adherents to withdraw if they believed their national interests were at stake. Subsequently, the Soviet Union and China signed the protocols, while France, the United Kingdom, and the United States declined to do so.

Controversy has also arisen in recent years regarding US tuna fishing in the region, Washington and the Forum Fisheries Agency (FFA) eventually concluding a five-year agreement in April 1987 under which the US government and the tuna industry will pay $12 million annually in cash grants and development aid for the rights (ratification by ten FFA members and the US Congress, expected to be forthcoming in 1988, is required for implementation of the accord). The fishing agreement is of political importance since US tuna boats have periodically been charged with "poaching" by SPF members, several of whom have signed bilateral fishing pacts with the Soviet Union.

The 18th annual meeting was held at Apia, Western Samoa, on May 29–30, 1987, scarcely more than two weeks after the region's first military coup had overthrown the government of Fiji. Delegates were manifestly divided over the action, Australia and New Zealand being deeply opposed to the ouster of an elected government, while many island leaders sympathized with the desire of indigenous Fijians to protect their traditional rights. A diplomatic impasse was averted by word from Fijian Governor General Ganilau that the crisis would make it impossible for his interim administration to participate and the SPF leaders finally agreed on a statement expressing "deep concern and anguish" over the situation.

The other major topic at the meeting was the political situation in New Caledonia (see France: Related Territories). Reflecting the strong feelings of the Melanesian "Spearhead Group" (Papua New Guinea, the Solomon Islands, and Vanuatu), the Forum expressed "grave disquiet" over French policies in New Caledonia and called for a settlement that would guarantee "the rights and interests of all inhabitants . . . with special recognition of Kanak rights". However, the Forum rejected a proposal from the Spearhead Group to seek SPF observer status in New Caledonia's Kanaka Socialist National Liberation Front (FLNKS).

SOUTHERN AFRICAN DEVELOPMENT COORDINATION CONFERENCE (SADCC)

Established: During a summit meeting of Black southern African countries at Lusaka, Zambia, on April 1, 1980.

Purpose: To promote economic cooperation among independent Southern African states by synchronizing development plans and reducing economic dependence upon the Republic of South Africa.

Headquarters: Gaborone, Botswana.

Principal Organs: Meeting of Heads of State or Government (all members), Council of Ministers (all members), Executive Secretariat, Southern African Transport and Communications Commission.

Executive Secretary: Dr. Simbarashe H.S. Makoni (Zimbabwe).

Membership (9): Angola, Botswana, Lesotho, Malawi, Mozambique, Swaziland, Tanzania, Zambia, Zimbabwe.

Origin and development. The SADCC traces its origin to a "Southern African Development Coordination Conference" held at Arusha, Tanzania, in July 1979 and attended by Angola, Botswana, Mozambique, Tanzania, and Zambia — the "Front-Line States" allied in opposition to White rule in southern Africa — as well as by potential bilateral and multilateral donors. A draft declaration entitled "Southern Africa: Towards Economic Liberation" was drawn up proposing a program of action to improve regional transportation, agriculture, industry, energy, and development planning, with a view toward reducing economic dependence on the Republic of South Africa. As a follow-up to the Arusha meeting, the SADCC was formally established during a summit of the heads of state or government of nine countries (the original five plus Lesotho, Malawi, Swaziland, and Zimbabwe) that convened on April 1, 1980, at Lusaka, Zambia.

Structure. A Meeting of Heads of State or Government is convened annually. In addition, ministerial representatives attend an annual Council of Ministers meeting, with special sessions called during the year to discuss specific regional policies. The Conference's first operational body, the Southern African Transport and Communications Commission (SATCC), was established at Maputo, Mozambique, in July 1980, while an Energy Commission, based at Luanda, Angola, became, in 1982, the second operational body to receive authorization. The Secretariat, located at Gaborone, Botswana, has been deliberately kept small to avoid the bureaucratic entanglements that SADCC members believe have hamstrung most African regional groupings. Consequently, under the terms of the "Lusaka Declaration" issued in 1980, SADCC members have been assigned a coordinating role over specified economic concerns. Thus the SATCC was formed under Mozambique's leadership and the Energy Commission has been sponsored by Angola, while other states have received the following assignments: Botswana, livestock production, animal disease control, and crop production research; Lesotho, soil and water conservation, land utilization, and tourism; Malawi, fisheries, forestry, and wildlife; Swaziland, manpower development and training; Tanzania, industry and trade; Zambia, development funding and mining; and Zimbabwe, regional food security.

Activities. The SADCC is considered one of the most viable of the continent's regional groupings although its actual accomplishments have been modest compared to the development needs of its members. During its first six years the SADCC concentrated on the rehabilitation and expansion of transport corridors to permit the movement of goods from the interior of the region to ocean ports without being dependent on routes through South Africa. However, rebel activity, primarily in Mozambique, and alleged destabilization efforts by Pretoria limited the success of the effort. Thus, beginning in 1986, the SADCC placed increased emphasis on production within the private and parastatal sectors in order to produce the broad, long-term growth that could significantly reduce members' economic dependence on South Africa. In furtherance of the new thrust, the SADCC met with 120 representatives of the regional and international business communities to discuss the expansion of private industry. Concurrently, substantial funding increases were promised by the United States, the United Kingdom, West Germany, the Netherlands, and the Nordic states.

During the 7th summit at Lusaka on July 24, 1987, the heads of government condemned the "continuation and intensification" of South Africa's "acts of aggression and destabilization" against SADCC members. The conference has called for the international community to impose comprehensive, mandatory sanctions against Pretoria to protest apartheid. However, consensus has not been attained on proposed regional action, such as the severance of air links with Pretoria, primarily because of objections from Lesotho and Swaziland, the SADCC members whose economies are most directly linked to South Africa. In other action at the 1987 summit, the SADCC leaders pledged to create food stockpiles to deal with widespread food shortages and called on international creditors to ease the region's debt burden.

The SADCC's current program of action encompasses some 400 projects ranging from small feasibility studies to large port and railway construction projects. They are valued at $5.4 billion, with about half of the funding provided by donor countries and organizations. At a meeting in January 1988, donors reportedly pledged an additional $1 billion to the SADCC over the next four years.

UNITED NATIONS (UN)

Established: By Charter signed at San Francisco, United States, June 26, 1945, effective October 24, 1945.

Purpose: To maintain international peace and security; to develop friendly relations among states based on respect for the principle of equal rights and self-determination of peoples; to achieve international cooperation in solving problems of an economic, social, cultural, or humanitarian character; and to harmonize the actions of states in the attainment of these common ends.

Headquarters: New York, United States.

Principal Organs: General Assembly (all members), Security Council (15 members), Economic and Social Council (54 members), Trusteeship Council (5 members), International Court of Justice (15 judges), Secretariat.

Secretary General: Javier Pérez de Cuéllar (Peru).

Membership (159): See Appendix B.

Official Languages: Arabic, Chinese, English, French, Russian, Spanish.

Working Languages: Chinese, English, French, Russian, Spanish.

Origin and development. The idea of creating a new intergovernmental organization to replace the League of Nations was born early in World War II and first found public expression in an Inter-Allied Declaration signed at London, England, on June 12, 1941, by representatives of five Commonwealth states and eight European governments-in-exile. Formal use of the term United Nations first occurred in the Declaration by United Nations, signed at Washington, DC, on January 1, 1942, on behalf of 26 states that had subscribed to the principles of the Atlantic Charter (August 14, 1941) and had pledged their full cooperation for the defeat of the Axis powers. At the Moscow (USSR) Conference on October 30, 1943, representatives of China, the Union of Soviet Socialist Republics, the United Kingdom, and the United States proclaimed that they "recognized the necessity of establishing at the earliest practicable date a general international organization, based on the principle of the sovereign equality of all peace-loving states, and open to membership by all such states, large and small, for the maintenance of international peace and security". In meetings at Dumbarton Oaks, Washington, DC, between August 21 and October 7, 1944, the four powers reached agreement on preliminary proposals and determined to prepare more complete suggestions for discussion at a subsequent conference of all the United Nations.

Meeting at San Francisco, California, from April 25 to June 25, 1945, representatives of 50 states participated in the drafting of the United Nations Charter, which was formally signed on June 26. Poland was not represented at the San Francisco Conference but later signed the Charter and is counted among the 51 "original" United Nations members. Following ratification by the five permanent members of the Security Council and a majority of the other signatories, the Charter entered into force October 24, 1945. The General Assembly, convened in its first regular session on January 10, 1946, accepted an invitation to establish the permanent home of the organization in the United States; privileges and immunities of the United Nations headquarters were defined in a Headquarters Agreement with the United States government signed June 26, 1947.

The membership of the UN, which increased from 51 to 60 during the period 1945–1950, remained frozen at that level for the next five years as a result of US-Soviet disagreements over admission. The deadlock was broken in 1955 when the superpowers agreed on a "package" of 16 new members: four Soviet-bloc states, four Western states, and eight "uncommitted" states. Since then, states have normally been admitted with little delay. The exceptions are worth noting. The admission of the two Germanies in 1973 led to proposals for admission of the two Koreas and of the two Vietnams. Neither occurred, formal application of the Democratic Republic of Vietnam and the post-Thieu Republic of Vietnam being rejected by the Security Council on August 18, 1975. On November 16, 1976, the United States used its 18th veto in the Security Council to prevent the admission of the recently united Socialist Republic of Vietnam, having earlier in the same session, on June 23, 1976, employed its 15th veto to prevent Angola from joining. Later in the session, however, the United States relented and Angola gained admission. In July 1977 Washington dropped its objection to Vietnamese membership as well. With the admission of Brunei, the total membership during the 39th session of the General Assembly in 1984 rose to 159, a figure still short of the organization's goal of universality. As of July 1, 1988, fully independent states that remained outside the organization (though participating in certain of its associated bodies) included Kiribati, Democratic People's Republic of Korea, Republic of Korea, Nauru, Switzerland, Tonga, and Tuvalu.

Structure. The UN system can be viewed as comprising (1) the principal organs, (2) subsidiary organs established to deal with particular aspects of the organization's responsibilities, (3) a number of specialized and related agencies, and (4) a series of ad hoc global conferences to examine particularly pressing issues.

The institutional structure of the principal organs resulted from complex negotiations that attempted to balance both the conflicting claims of national sovereignty and international responsibility, and the rights of large and small states. The principle of sovereign equality of all member states is exemplified in the General Assembly; that of the special responsibility of the major powers, in the composition and procedure of the Security Council. The other principal organs included in the Charter are the Economic and Social Council (ECOSOC), the Trusteeship Council, the International Court of Justice (ICJ), and the Secretariat.

The bulk of intergovernmental bodies related to the UN consists of a network of Specialized Agencies established by intergovernmental agreement as legal and autonomous international entities with their own memberships and organs and which, for the purpose of "coordination", are brought "into relationship" with the UN. While sharing many of their characteristics, the General Agreement on Tariffs and Trade (GATT) and the International Atomic Energy Agency (IAEA) remain legally distinct from the Specialized Agencies.

The proliferation of subsidiary organs can be attributed to many complex factors, including new demands and needs as more states attained independence; the effects of the "cold war"; a gradual diminution of East-West bipolarity; a greater concern with promoting economic and social development through technical-assistance programs (almost entirely financed by voluntary contributions); and a resistance to any radical change in international trade patterns. For many years, the largest and most politically significant of these subordinate organs were the United Nations Conference on Trade and Development (UNCTAD) and the United Nations Industrial Development Organization (UNIDO), both of which were initially venues for debates, for conducting studies and presenting reports, for convening conferences and specialized meetings, and for mobilizing the opinions of nongovernmental organizations. They also provided a way for less-developed states to formulate positions vis-à-vis the industrialized states. During the 1970s both became intimately involved in activities related to program implementation and on January 1, 1986, UNIDO became the UN's 16th Specialized Agency.

One of the most important developments in the UN system has been the expanded use of ad hoc conferences to deal with major international problems. The first of these, the 1972 UN Conference on the Human Environment (UNCHE), resulted in the establishment of the United Nations Environment Programme (UNEP), which became the first major UN organ to be headquartered in the Southern Hemisphere (Nairobi, Kenya). The August 1974 World Population Conference drafted a set of guidelines for states to consider when formulating population policies, while delegates to the November 1974 World Food Conference agreed on the establishment of a new UN agency, the World Food Council, to coordinate programs to give the world (particularly less-developed states) more and better food.

In the wake of the UN-sponsored World Conference of the International Women's Year at Mexico City in June-July 1975, the General Assembly proclaimed 1976–1985 the UN Decade for Women: Equality, Development and Peace, and convened a conference on the subject at Copenhagen, Denmark, in July 1980. A follow-up conference to review the Decade's achievements was held in July 1985 at Nairobi, Kenya, concurrent with a meeting of nongovernmental organizations and women's groups called Forum 85.

Three 1987 conferences yielded mixed results. Participants in the Conference for the Promotion of International Cooperation in the Peaceful Uses of Nuclear Energy, which convened at Geneva, Switzerland, in March, could not reach agreement on proposed recommendations. Delegates to the Conference on the Relationship between Disarmament and Development, which concluded at New York in September, recommended that a portion of resources released by disarmament be allocated to social and economic development; however, the United States was not represented, arguing that disarmament and development were separate issues. Moreover, because of reservations by other Western nations, the Conference's final document was substantially weaker than desired by Third World and Communist bloc countries.

The most successful 1987 conference was the Conference on Drug Abuse and Illicit Trafficking, held at Vienna, Austria, in June, with most of the World's intergovernmental and nongovernmental anti-drug organizations in attendance. By acclamation the Conference adopted a declaration committing all participants to "vigorous action" to reduce drug demand as well as supply. In addition, it approved a comprehensive handbook of guidelines to assist governments and organizations in reaching a total of 35 "action targets" during the ensuing decade. (Other UN conferences are discussed under General Assembly: Activities, below, or within entries for various sponsoring UN bodies.)

GENERAL ASSEMBLY

Membership (159): All members of the United Nations (see Appendix B), although South Africa has been excluded from participation since 1974.

Observers (17): Agency for Technical and Cultural Cooperation, Asian-African Legal Consultative Committee, Commonwealth Secretariat, Council for Mutual Economic Assistance, European Community, Holy See,

Islamic Conference, Democratic People's Republic of Korea, Republic of Korea, Latin American Economic System, League of Arab States, Monaco, Organization of African Unity, Organization of American States, Palestine Liberation Organization, South West Africa People's Organization of Namibia, Switzerland.

Origin and development. The prominence today of the General Assembly in the UN system cannot simply be traced to the Charter but rather to the Assembly's vigorous exercise of its clearly designated functions and to its assertion of additional authority in areas, most notably the maintenance of peace and security, in which its Charter mandate is ambiguous.

Since all members of the UN participate in the Assembly on a one-country, one-vote basis, the kinds of resolutions passed in the Assembly have varied considerably as the membership has changed. Thus while the Assembly's early history was dominated by "cold war" issues, the rapid expansion of the membership to include less-developed countries — now comprising an overwhelming majority — has led to a focus on issues of decolonization and development. A Declaration on the Granting of Independence to Colonial Countries and Peoples, adopted on December 14, 1960, proclaimed the "necessity of bringing to a speedy and unconditional end colonialism in all its forms and manifestations". A special committee on the implementation of this declaration, known informally as the Special Committee of Twenty-four, has maintained continuous pressure for its application to the remaining non-self-governing territories.

As the end of colonialism in the world at large approached, UN attention focused increasingly upon the problems of colonialism and racial discrimination in certain southern African territories: the Portuguese dependencies of Angola, Mozambique, and Portuguese Guinea; Southern Rhodesia; and Namibia. In the course of the 1960s, the General Assembly moved from general assertions of moral and legal rights in this area to condemnations of specific governments, accompanied by requests for diplomatic and economic, and threats of military, sanctions. In 1972 the Assembly "condemned", for the first time, violations by the United States of Security Council sanctions against importing chrome and nickel from Southern Rhodesia. In December 1976 the Assembly took the unprecedented action of passing a resolution endorsing "armed struggle" for Namibian independence. An accompanying UN plan to such effect called for a ceasefire between South African and indigenous forces — essentially, guerrillas of the South West African People's Organisation (SWAPO) — UN supervision of the truce, a gradual withdrawal of all troops in Namibia, and, seven months after the ceasefire, UN-supervised elections for a Namibian constitutional assembly. Subsequent negotiations on Namibian independence centered on a five-country Transitional Assistance Group (TAG) — Canada, France, the Federal Republic of Germany, the United Kingdom, and the United States — rather than in the UN Council for Namibia, in view of South African opposition to the latter's mandate. However, settlement remained elusive, primarily because of a schism between South Africa and SWAPO over Pretoria's

linking Namibian independence with the withdrawal of Cuban and Eastern European troops stationed in Angola. The stalemate persisted through 1987, with the Council for Namibia, meeting at the ministerial level for the first time in 20 years, condemning the "Transitional Government of National Unity" installed by South Africa in June 1985 and calling for the "unconditional and speedy" implementation of the 1974 plan.

The Assembly's work in the area of development formally began with a proposal by US President John F. Kennedy that the 1960s be officially designated as the UN Development Decade. The overall objective of the Decade was the attainment in each less-developed state of a minimum annual growth rate of 5 percent in aggregate national income. To this end, the developed states were asked to make available the equivalent of 1 percent of their income in the form of economic assistance and private investment. By 1967 it had become clear that not all of the objectives would be achieved by 1970, and a 55-member Preparatory Committee for the Second UN Development Decade was established by the General Assembly in 1968 to draft an international development strategy (IDS) for the 1970s. While the publicity surrounding the demand for a new international economic order (NIEO), particularly at the 1974, 1975, and 1980 special sessions of the General Assembly, tended to overshadow the IDS, the latter maintained its effectiveness, establishing quantitative targets for the Second Development Decade and on some issues, such as human development, remaining the single most comprehensive program of action for less-developed states. Targets for the Third Development Decade, which began January 1, 1981, include the following: an average annual growth rate of 7 percent in gross domestic product; expansion of exports and imports of goods and services by not less than 7.5 and 8.0 percent, respectively; gross domestic savings of approximately one-quarter of GDP by 1990; expansion of agricultural production at an average annual rate of at least 4 percent; expansion of manufacturing output at an average yearly rate of 9 percent; reduction of infant mortality in the poorest countries to less than 120 per 1,000 live births; and life expectancy in all countries of at least 60 years.

The General Assembly has increasingly concentrated on North-South relations, with an emphasis on economic links between advanced industrialized countries (often excluding those having centrally planned economies) and less-developed countries. Major discussion topics, all of them integral to the NIEO, have included the following: international monetary reform and the transfer of real resources for financing development; transfer of technological and scientific advances, with specific emphasis on the reform of patent and licensing laws; restructuring of the economic and social sectors of the UN system; expansion of no-strings-attached aid; preferential and non-reciprocal treatment of less-developed states' trade; recognition of the full permanent sovereignty of every state over its natural resources and the right of compensation for any expropriated foreign property; the regulation of foreign investment according to domestic law; supervision of the activities of transnational corporations; a "just and equitable relationship" between the prices of imports from and exports to less-developed states ("indexation"); and an enhancement of the role of commodity-producers' associations. In recent years, efforts have been made to conduct an all-encompassing discussion of development issues in the form of global negotiations. Although a UN special session has been held on this topic, advanced and developing countries still disagree on the necessity, scope, and utility of the proposed negotiations.

Structure. All members of the UN, each with one vote, are represented in the General Assembly, which meets once a year in regular session, normally commencing the third Tuesday in September. Special sessions may be called at the request of the Security Council, of a majority of the member states, or of one member state with the concurrence of a majority. Fourteen such sessions have thus far been convened: Palestine (1947 and 1948), Tunisia (1961), Financial and Budgetary Problems (1963), Review of Peace-Keeping Operations and Southwest Africa (1967), Raw Materials and Development (1974), Development and International Economic Cooperation (1975 and 1980), Disarmament (1978 and 1982), Financing for UN Forces in Lebanon (1978), Namibia (1978 and 1986), and the Economic Crisis in Africa (1986). The main item for discussion at the 1980 special session, a proposed text on "Procedures and Time-Frame for the Global Negotiations", was merely "noted" by the delegates. The chief controversy involved the preference of the less-developed countries for a global development conference, with a one-state, one-vote rule of decisionmaking, whereas the industrialized countries favored assigning aspects of the agenda to the appropriate Specialized Agencies, with weighted voting. The twelfth special session, held June 7–July 10, 1982, was the second to be concerned with disarmament, the 1980s having been declared the Second Disarmament Decade by the General Assembly. The thirteenth special session, called at the request of the Organization of African Unity, was held May 27–June 1, 1986, and was the first to deal with the economic problems of a single world region; it concluded with unanimous agreement on the need for African governments to institute structural reforms in their economic systems, with Western nations pledging to "provide sufficient resources" in support of the continental recovery program. The fourteenth special session, held September 17–20, 1986, to discuss the status of the Namibian independence plan, yielded little more than a reaffirmation of the UN's longstanding positions on the issue (see Origin and development, above).

Under the "Uniting for Peace" resolution of November 3, 1950, an emergency special session may be convened by nine members of the Security Council or by a majority of the UN members in the event that the Security Council is prevented, by lack of unanimity among its permanent members, from exercising its primary responsibility for the maintenance of international peace and security. The seventh, eighth, and ninth such sessions dealt, respectively, with the question of Palestine (July 22–29, 1980), negotiations for Namibian independence (September 3–14, 1981), and the occupied Arab territories (January 29–February 5, 1982).

The seventh emergency special session was resumed on four separate occasions during 1982. On April 27–28

Assembly members reviewed a Syrian proposal to expel Israel because of its alleged violations of the UN Charter and branded the Jewish state as a "non-peaceloving nation". A second meeting was held after Israel's June 6 invasion of Lebanon, while a third, on August 16–19, reviewed the Lebanese situation, established June 4 as the International Day of Innocent Children Victims of Aggression, and set August 16–27, 1983, for an International Conference on the Question of Palestine. The session convened again on September 24 to urge Security Council action and an investigation following the massacre of hundreds of Palestinians in the Beirut refugee camps of Chatila and Sabra. Meanwhile, the ninth emergency special session had concluded its work with the approval of a resolution condemning Israel's December 1981 decision to annex the Golan Heights as an "act of aggression" and calling upon member states to sever military, trade, diplomatic, and cultural relations with Israel.

The General Assembly elects the 10 nonpermanent members of the Security Council; the 54 members of ECOSOC; the elected members of the Trusteeship Council; and, together with the Security Council (but voting independently), the judges of the International Court of Justice. On recommendation of the Security Council, it appoints the secretary general and is empowered to admit new members. The Assembly also approves the UN budget, apportions the expenses of the organization among the members, and receives and considers reports from the other UN organs.

At each session the General Assembly elects its own president and 21 vice presidents, approves its agenda, and distributes agenda items among its committees, which are grouped by its rules of procedure into three categories: Main, Procedural, and Standing.

All member states are represented on the seven Main Committees: First Committee (Political and Security), Special Political Committee (shares the work of the First Committee), Second Committee (Economic and Financial), Third Committee (Social, Humanitarian, and Cultural), Fourth Committee (Trusteeship, including Non-Self-Governing Territories), Fifth Committee (Administrative and Budgetary), and Sixth Committee (Legal). Each member has one vote; decisions are taken by a simple majority. Resolutions and recommendations approved by the Main Committees are returned for final action by a plenary session of the General Assembly, where each member again has one vote but where decisions on "important questions" — including recommendations on peace and security questions; election of members to UN organs; the admission, suspension, and expulsion of member states; and budget matters — require a two-thirds majority of the members present and voting. Agenda items not referred to a Main Committee are dealt with directly by the Assembly in plenary session under the same voting rules.

There are two Procedural (Sessional) Committees. The General Committee, which is composed of 29 members (the president of the General Assembly, the 21 vice presidents, and the chairmen of the seven Main Committees), draws up the agenda of the plenary meetings, determines agenda priorities, and coordinates the proceedings of the Committees. The Credentials Committee, which consists of nine members, is appointed at the beginning of each Assembly session and is responsible for examining and reporting on credentials of representatives.

The two Standing Committees deal with continuing problems during and between the regular sessions of the General Assembly. The Advisory Committee on Administrative and Budgetary Questions (13 members) handles the budget and accounts of the UN as well as the administrative budgets of the Specialized Agencies; the Committee on Contributions (18 members) makes recommendations on the scale of assessments to be used in apportioning expenses. The members of each Standing Committee are appointed on the basis of broad geographical representation, serve for terms of three years, retire by rotation, and are eligible for reappointment.

The General Assembly is also empowered to establish subsidiary organs and ad hoc committees. Apart from the Special Bodies (see below), some three dozen such entities of varying size presently deal with political, legal, scientific, and administrative matters. Among those of an essentially political character (with dates of establishment) are the Special Committee on the Implementation of the Declaration on Decolonization (1961), the Special Committee against Apartheid (1962), the Special Committee on Peace-Keeping Operations (1965), the Ad Hoc Committee on the Indian Ocean (1972), the UN Council for Namibia (1967), and the Disarmament Commission (1978). Subsidiary groups dealing with legal matters include the International Law Commission (1947), the Advisory Committee on the UN Programme of Assistance in Teaching, Study, Dissemination, and Wider Appreciation of International Law (1965), and the UN Commission on International Trade Law (1966). Those dealing with scientific matters include the Committee on the Peaceful Uses of Outer Space (1959), the UN Scientific Advisory Committee (1954), and the UN Scientific Committee on the Effects of Atomic Radiation (1955). Among the subsidiary groups dealing with administrative and financial matters are the Investments Committee (1947), the International Civil Service Commission (1948), the UN Administrative Tribunal (1949), the UN Joint Staff Pension Committee (1948), the Committee of Trustees of the UN Trust Fund for South Africa (1965), and the Advisory Committee on the UN Educational and Training Programme for Southern Africa (1968).

Activities. Endowed with the broadest powers of discussion of any UN organ, the Assembly may consider any matter within the scope of the Charter or relating to the powers and functions of any organ provided for in the Charter. It may also make corresponding recommendations to the members or to the Security Council; however, it may not make recommendations on any issue which the Security Council has under consideration, unless requested to do so by that body.

Both the General Assembly and the Security Council are entrusted by the Charter with responsibilities concerning disarmament and the regulation of armaments. Disarmament questions have been before the organization almost continuously since 1946, and a succession of specialized bodies has been set up to deal with them. Among those currently in existence are the all-member Disarmament Commission, established in 1952 and reconstituted in 1978,

and the 40-member Conference on Disarmament (known until 1984 as the Committee on Disarmament), which meets at Geneva, Switzerland, under joint US-USSR chairmanship. The UN played a role in drafting the Treaty Banning Nuclear Weapon Tests in the Atmosphere, in Outer Space, and under Water (effective October 10, 1963), as well as the Treaty on the Non-Proliferation of Nuclear Weapons (effective March 5, 1970). The Second Special Session on Disarmament, held June 7–July 10, 1982, at UN headquarters, had as its primary focus the adoption of a comprehensive disarmament program based on the draft program developed in 1980 by the Committee on Disarmament. Although the session heard messages from many of the world's leaders, two-thirds of the delegations, and almost 80 international organizations, no agreement was reached on the proposal. At the 37th regular session of the General Assembly, which opened in September 1982, some 60 resolutions concerning disarmament were discussed. Of those adopted, three called for negotiation of new nuclear test-ban treaties. Additional resolutions, adopted over Western opposition, called for a freeze on the production and deployment of nuclear weapons.

The General Assembly has also endorsed US-Soviet bilateral agreements on the limitation of offensive and defensive strategic weapon systems; has urged wide adherence to the Convention on the Prohibition of the Development, Production, and Stockpiling of Bacteriological (Biological) and Toxin Weapons and on Their Destruction (opened for signature April 10, 1972); and in April 1981 opened for ratification a Convention on Prohibition or Restrictions on the Use of Certain Conventional Weapons which may be deemed to be Excessively Injurious or to have Indiscriminate Effects, the intention being to protect civilians from such weapons as napalm, land mines, and booby traps. The following November, a UN group of experts issued a report stating that they had been unable to verify allegations that the Soviet Union was using chemical or biological weapons in Afghanistan, Kampuchea, or Laos. A second report on the alleged use of illegal chemical and toxic weapons in Afghanistan and Southeast Asia, published in December 1982, stated that although direct evidence and conclusive proof had not been found, circumstantial evidence tended to indicate that chemical warfare was being conducted. The United States objected to the group's inability to offer conclusive evidence of chemical weapons, while the Soviet Union, Vietnam, and their allies not only denied the allegation but countered that an increased rate of congenital defects in Vietnamese children stemmed from US use of dioxins (the defoliant Agent Orange) during the Vietnam War.

UN activity in regard to human rights also dates virtually from the organization's founding. The Assembly's adoption in 1948 of the Universal Declaration of Human Rights marked what was perhaps the high point of UN action in this field. Subsequently, the Human Rights Commission directed efforts to embody key principles of the Declaration in binding international agreements. These efforts culminated in two human-rights covenants—one dealing with economic, social, and cultural rights, and the other with civil and political rights—both of which came into force in January 1976.

On October 3, 1975, concern for human rights was, for the first time, explicitly linked with nationalism in the form of a resolution contending "that Zionism is a form of racism and racial discrimination". After considerable parliamentary maneuvering, the resolution passed on November 10 by a vote of 72–35–32. Two days later, US Ambassador to the UN Daniel P. Moynihan launched what appeared to be a counterattack. He presented a draft resolution appealing to "all governments to proclaim an unconditional amnesty by releasing . . . persons deprived of their liberty primarily because they have sought peaceful expression of beliefs at variance with those held by the governments". While the US proposal was quickly withdrawn in the face of hostile amendments, both it and the Zionism resolution suggested that a new phase was opening in what had for some years been a relatively dormant issue on the UN calendar.

During 1981 the General Assembly approved a number of resolutions concerned with eliminating racism, racial discrimination, and South African apartheid. The Assembly also extended its concern to Latin America, urging Bolivia to ensure fundamental freedoms for its people, and chastising Chile and El Salvador for permitting deterioration of human rights. With respect to the grave refugee situation in Somalia, the Sudan, and Djibouti, and the displaced peoples in Ethiopia and South Africa, the General Assembly on December 15, 1981, called for additional international assistance. Another resolution condemned totalitarian ideologies.

Questions relating to outer space are the province of a 47-member Committee on the Peaceful Uses of Outer Space, established by the General Assembly in 1960 to deal with the scientific, technical, and legal aspects of the subject. In addition to promoting scientific and technical cooperation on a wide range of space endeavors, the Committee was responsible for the adoption of the Treaty on Principles Governing the Activities of States in the Exploration and Use of Outer Space, Including the Moon and Other Celestial Bodies (entered into force October 10, 1967) and the Agreement on the Rescue of Astronauts, the Return of Astronauts, and the Return of Objects Launched into Outer Space (entered into force December 3, 1968). In July 1979 the Committee produced a new draft treaty proclaiming that the moon's resources were "the common heritage of mankind". In addition, the Committee's legal subcommittee has been drafting a treaty on direct television broadcasting via satellite and home receivers, and another on satellite sensing of the earth's minerals and living resources.

The Second Conference on the Exploration and Peaceful Uses of Outer Space was held August 9–21, 1982, at Vienna, Austria, where the first space conference had convened in 1968. In addition to reiterating a call for adherence to the 1967 Treaty and for improved UN monitoring of compliance, the Conference recommended that the General Assembly adopt measures designed to accelerate the transfer of peaceful space technology, to expand access to space and its resources for developing countries, and to establish a UN information service on the world's space programs.

Oceanic policy has become a major UN concern. In 1968 the General Assembly established a 42-member Committee on the Peaceful Uses of the Sea-Bed and the Ocean Floor and in 1970 advanced a Treaty on the Prohibition of the Emplacement of Nuclear Weapons and Other Weapons of Mass Destruction on the Sea-Bed and the Ocean Floor and in the Subsoil Thereof. Detailed and controversial negotiations in this area have since ensued, most notably in conjunction with the Third UN Conference on the Law of the Sea (UNCLOS), which held 11 sessions, the first at Caracas, Venezuela (August 1974), and the last at UN headquarters (March–April 1982). Delegates to the tenth session (August 1981), at Geneva, Switzerland, reluctantly agreed to discuss several sensitive issues about which the US Reagan administration had expressed reservations. Although the 440 articles of the proposed treaty had received consensual approval during previous UNCLOS sessions, the United States demanded that items such as the regulation of deep-sea mining and the distribution of members for a proposed International Seabed Authority be reexamined before it would consider approving the document.

Following a year-long review of the proposed treaty, Washington ended its absence from the Conference with the presentation of a list of demands and revisions to be discussed at the eleventh session. Although compromises were reached in a number of disputed areas, other differences remained unresolved, including the rights of retention and the entry of private enterprises to seabed exploration and exploitation sites, mandatory technology transfers from private industry to the Seabed Authority, and amending procedures. On April 30, 1982, the treaty was approved by 130 Conference members, with 17 abstentions and 4 voting against: Israel, Turkey, the United States, and Venezuela. The treaty was opened for ratification and signed by 117 countries in a ceremony held at Caracas, Venezuela, on December 10, and will enter into force one year after ratification by 60 states. On December 30 the Reagan administration informed the UN that it would not pay its 25 percent share of the costs for the Preparatory Commission established under the treaty. UN officials responded that the United States was obligated to meet its assessment because the Commission is a subsidiary organ of the General Assembly, while Washington asserted that since the Commission was established by treaty, only treaty signatories were legally bound to pay the Commission's expenses.

The Preparatory Commission has been charged with establishing the two main organs of the Convention—the International Sea-Bed Authority and the International Tribunal for the Law of the Sea. In addition, the General Assembly in 1983 created the Office of the Special Representative of the Secretary-General for the Law of the Sea, a permanent body whose functions include carrying out the central program on law of the sea affairs, assisting states in consistently and uniformly implementing the Convention's provisions, and providing general information concerning the treaty.

By December 9, 1984, the deadline for signing the Convention, 159 nations had become signatories; by late 1987, instruments of ratification had been deposited by 34 countries and the UN Council for Namibia. Meanwhile, the UN announced that many countries were already complying with the provisions of the Convention.

By mid-1988 France, Japan, India, and the Soviet Union had been registered by the Preparatory Commission as "pioneer investors" under a program established to recognize national investments already made in exploration, research, and development work related to sea-bed mining. Pioneer investors are entitled to explore allocated portions of the international sea-bed but must wait until the Convention enters into force to begin commercial exploitation.

1986 and 1987 Sessions

In 1986 the General Assembly focused much of its attention on a financial crisis generated by drastic reductions in contributions by several countries, including the United States, which withheld $110 million of its $210 million assessment to protest what it termed a bloated and inefficient organization that did not accord sufficient influence to major contributors in spending decisions. Calling the impending deficit a threat to the viability of the United Nations, Secretary General Pérez de Cuéllar proposed sweeping savings measures that were endorsed by the reconvened 40th Assembly in April and expanded by the 41st Assembly late in the year. An estimated $70 million was saved by the short-term changes, which included a recruiting freeze, the delay of planned construction, deferred promotions, and reductions in spending for travel, consultants, overtime, and temporary help.

The 41st Assembly also endorsed most of the longer-term proposals advanced by an 18-member Group of High-Level Intergovernmental Experts, which agreed that the United Nations had become "too complex, fragmented and top-heavy" and was hampered by a proliferation of internal bodies with overlapping agendas. In response, a variety of measures, such as staff reductions and the consolidation of departments, were scheduled for immediate implementation, while the Economic and Social Council (ECOSOC) was directed to complete a study by 1988 on further restructuring, including possible changes in the budgetary decision process.

Although he described the retrenchment as "a blueprint for a more efficient United Nations", Pérez de Cuéllar, who had been persuaded to accept a new five-year term, declared in early 1987 that the organization remained "on the verge of bankruptcy". He called for full financial participation by all members, particularly the United States, which welcomed the reforms but cautioned that they represented only "a beginning".

Maintaining its strongly anti-apartheid posture during its regular session from September 16 to December 19, the 41st Assembly called, unsuccessfully, for the Security Council to impose economic sanctions, including an oil embargo, on South Africa. Another long-standing position was reaffirmed with resolutions condemning Israeli actions in the Middle East. In addressing new concerns, the Assembly condemned the US bombing of Libyan cities in April and urged immediate compliance with the International Court's ruling against US involvement in Nicaraguan affairs. Resolutions were also adopted calling for worldwide cooperation in dealing with the growing drug problem, negotiations to ease the external debt difficulties of developing countries, the creation of a "zone of peace and cooperation" in the South Atlantic, and expanded discussion of disarmament and other nuclear issues.

At its regular session from September 15 to December 21, 1987, the 42nd Assembly adopted a $1.77 billion budget for the 1988–1989 biennium. Despite the payment of arrears by the Soviet Union (Moscow having called throughout the year for enhanced UN activity and authority in peacekeeping and other areas), the financial status of the organization remained precarious. By December arrears totaled some $450 million, more than half owed by the United States, with Pérez de Cuéllar declaring that the organization might be forced to borrow money to avoid insolvency unless increased contributions were forthcoming.

Much of the 42nd Assembly's attention focused on highly visible UN participation in peace negotiations involving Afghanistan, Central America, the Persian Gulf, and southern Africa. The Assembly also reiterated its appeal for a UN-sponsored Middle East peace conference, reaffirming its condemnation of Israeli policies and practices in the region. Other resolutions denounced the continued Soviet presence in Afghanistan, deplored cuts in foreign aid to Africa and the lack of success in the continent's recovery program, appealed again for sanctions against South Africa, and committed the United Nations to a leadership role in an campaign to halt the spread of AIDS. The Assembly also approved lengthy documents drafted by subsidiary bodies on long-term environmental concerns and measures to inhibit the threat or use of force in international relations.

GENERAL ASSEMBLY:
SPECIAL BODIES

Over the years, the General Assembly has created a number of semiautonomous special bodies, two of which (UNCTAD, UNDP) deal with development problems, four (UNDRO, UNHCR, UNICEF, UNRWA) with relief and welfare problems, and two (UNEP, UNFPA) with demographic and environmental problems, while three (UNITAR, UNRISD, UNU) are research and training bodies. The most recent, the World Food Council, is designed to carry forward the work of the 1974 World Food Conference. A former special body, the United Nations Industrial Development Organization (UNIDO) became a Specialized Agency on January 1, 1986.

United Nations Children's Fund
(UNICEF)

Established: By General Assembly resolution of December 11, 1946, as the United Nations International Children's Emergency Fund. Initially a temporary body to provide emergency assistance to children in countries ravaged by war, the Fund was made permanent by General Assembly resolution on October 6, 1953, the name being changed to United Nations Children's Fund while retaining the abbreviation UNICEF.

Purpose: To give assistance, particularly to less-developed countries, in the establishment of permanent child health and welfare services.

Headquarters: New York, United States.

Principal Organs: Executive Board (41 members), Program Committee (Committee of the Whole), Committee on Administration and Finance (18 members), National Committees, Secretariat. Membership on the Executive Board is on the following geographical basis: Africa, 9 seats; Asia, 9; Latin America, 6; Eastern Europe, 4; Western Europe and other, 12; with 1 additional seat rotating among the five groupings.

Executive Director: James P. Grant (United States).

Recent activities. UNICEF is actively involved in broadening its support of maternal and child health, nutrition, education, and social-welfare programs. To improve child health and nutrition, UNICEF has formulated four strategies: the use of oral rehydration therapy (giving the child a mixture of salt, sugar, and water during bouts of intestinal infection instead of withholding food and drink), the immunization of children against childhood diseases, the use of breastfeeding instead of artificial infant formulas, and the employment of child-growth charts by which a mother can follow her child's progress and determine when more food intake is necessary. UNICEF determined that before any of these could be truly effective, there had to be basic changes in the life style of the poor: an increased income would be required to improve maternal and child nutrition, health, and education. A number of agricultural solutions have been suggested, including an increase in the number of small labor-intensive farms (producing both food and cash income for families). An increase in food subsidies for pregnant women and children has also been recommended. UNICEF stated that these measures, as well as others already in use, could help break the cycle of "ill-health, low energy, low productivity, low incomes and a low level of financial and energy investment in improving family and community life".

Much of UNICEF's activity is carried out under the Child Survival and Development Revolution (CSDR), adopted in 1983 to provide "a creative and practical approach" to accelerating progress for children. Programs have been extended recently to deal with the problems of children affected by armed conflicts, exploitation, abuse, and neglect. Increased attention has also been given to the role of women in economic development, the need for family "spacing", and the provision of better water and sanitation facilities. In all the areas it covers, UNICEF's goal is to foster community-based services provided by workers selected by the community and supported by existing networks of government agencies and nongovernment organizations.

During the celebration of its 40th anniversary in 1986 UNICEF noted that extraordinary progress had been made in basic areas: infant and child mortality rates were less than half what they were in 1950 and life expectancy and literacy rates were up substantially. UNICEF estimated

that over 1.5 million children were being saved annually in developing countries through oral rehydration therapy and immunization. Projections suggested that the figure could rise to 3–5 million by 1990.

Nevertheless, in UNICEF's 1987 and 1988 *State of the World's Children* reports, Executive Director James P. Grant called for a "new political, economic, and moral ethic" to address the fact that more than 14 million children die "almost without notice" each year. The report noted that advances had been made in recent years, due in part to the attention of the mass media, in preventing large-scale deaths from emergencies such as famine; however, similar public attention has not been given to the "silent emergencies" of frequent infection and undernutrition. In addition, UNICEF warned of the adverse effects that economic adjustment policies in developing countries were having on the poor and called for "adjustment with a human face" in addition to debt rescheduling and improved aid flows.

United Nations Conference on Trade and Development (UNCTAD)

Established: By General Assembly resolution of December 30, 1964.

Purpose: To promote international trade with a view to accelerating the economic growth of less-developed countries, to formulate and implement policies related to trade and development, to review and facilitate the coordination of various institutions within the United Nations system in regard to international trade and development, to initiate action for the negotiation and adoption of multilateral legal instruments in the field of trade, and to harmonize trade and related development policies of governments and regional economic groups.

Headquarters: Geneva, Switzerland.

Principal Organs: Trade and Development Board (131 members); six Main Committees: Commodities (101 members), Invisibles and Financing Related to Trade (100 members), Manufactures (89 members), Shipping (90 members), Transfer of Technology (86 members), and Economic Cooperation among Developing Countries (95 members); Special Committee on Preferences (open to all members).

Secretary General: Kenneth K.S. Dadzie (Ghana).

Membership (168): All UN members, plus Democratic People's Republic of Korea, Holy See (Vatican City State), Republic of Korea, Liechtenstein, Monaco, Namibia (represented by the UN Council for Namibia), San Marino, Switzerland, Tonga.

Recent activities. UNCTAD's quadrennial meeting of governmental, intergovernmental, and nongovernmental representatives is considered the world's most comprehensive forum on North-South economic issues. However, staff reports and other analyses issued prior to UNCTAD

VII, held at Geneva, Switzerland, July 9–August 3, 1987, painted a gloomy picture both of UNCTAD's past accomplishments and of its prospects for aiding developing countries in the immediate future.

A major area of concern was negligible activity within UNCTAD's Integrated Programme for Commodities (IPC), established in the mid-1970s to secure fair and stable prices for 18 commodities crucial to developing countries' foreign exchange. The relatively few agreements negotiated by producers through the IPC had failed to counter the collapse of commodity prices in the early 1980s. In addition, the IPC's $750 million Common Fund for Commodity Stabilization, approved in 1980 to combat extreme price fluctuations through buffer stocks, had failed to secure ratification by the required number of UNCTAD members.

UNCTAD reports also despaired of the global debt crisis that continued to yield a net transfer of resources from developing to developed countries. Despite the efforts of UNCTAD's Substantial New Program of Action for the 1980s for the Least Developed Countries, the latter were experiencing high unemployment, declining living standards, and falling levels of per capita output.

Overall, efforts to stimulate economic activity and promote exports were being hindered by declining access to external investment and concessional aid, as well as by fragmentation in world trading systems and growing protectionism among industrialized nations.

In April 1987 the Group of 77, which represents 127 developing countries within UNCTAD, condemned "the current crisis in international economic relations and the state of disarray and disequilibrium which characterizes these relations". The Group also criticized the International Monetary Fund and the World Bank as "being designed exclusively to protect the interests of creditor nations". However, at UNCTAD VII the Group adopted a less strident tone than at UNCTAD VI in 1983. The softening of rhetoric was deemed partially responsible for UNCTAD VII's adoption of a Final Act declaring consensus on debt, trade, development, and monetary issues. In general, the developing countries agreed to place more emphasis on private enterprise and free market activity, while the West endorsed "flexibility" on debt repayments. The Final Act also stressed the "complementarity" between UNCTAD and the General Agreement on Trade and Tariffs (GATT) and strongly endorsed the UN's Program of Action for African Economic Recovery and Development 1986–1990. While some observers suggested that the document signalled a "new spirit" in North-South relations, a pronounced lack of enthusiasm from the United States for UNCTAD VII remained a concern. On the other hand, the Soviet Union and its allies underscored their growing support for UN operations by ratifying the IPC's Common Fund and agreeing to contribute to its capital; as a result, the long-delayed implementation of the Fund was expected by the end of 1988.

United Nations Development Programme
(UNDP)

Established: By General Assembly resolution of November 22, 1965, which combined the United Nations Expanded Programme of Technical Assistance (UNEPTA) with the United Nations Special Fund (UNSF).

Purpose: To coordinate and administer technical assistance provided through the UN system, in order to assist less-developed countries in their efforts to accelerate social and economic development.

Headquarters: New York, United States.

Principal Organs: Governing Council (48 members), Committee of the Whole, Executive Management Committee, Office for Projects Execution, Inter-Agency Procurement Services Unit. Membership on the Governing Council rotates on the following geographical basis: developing countries, 27 seats (Africa, 11; Asia and Yugoslavia, 9; Latin America, 7); economically more-advanced countries, 21 seats (Eastern Europe, 4; Western Europe and other, 17).

Related Organs: The following special funds and activities are administered by the UNDP: the UN Capital Development Fund (UNCDF), established in 1960 but administered by the UNDP since 1972; the United Nations Volunteers (UNV), formed in 1971; the UN Revolving Fund for Natural Resources Exploration (UNRFNRE), founded in 1974; Development Assistance for National Liberation Movements (DANLM), formed in 1974 as the UN Trust Fund for Colonial Countries and Peoples and renamed in 1982; the UN Sudano-Sahelian Office (UNSO), placed under the UNDP in 1976; the UN Special Fund for Landlocked Developing Countries, administered by the UNDP since 1977; the UN Fund for Science and Technology for Development (UNFSTD), established as an Interim Fund in 1979 and redesignated as of January 1982; the Energy Account, authorized by the Governing Council in 1980; the UN Development Fund for Women (UNDFW), formerly the Voluntary Fund for the UN Decade for Women, established in 1980 and renamed in 1985; and the UN Office for Emergency Operations in Africa (UNOEOA), set up in 1985.

Administrator: William H. Draper, 3rd (United States).

Recent activities. The UNDP works with over 150 governments and over 30 intergovernmental agencies to promote more rapid economic growth and better standards of living throughout Africa, Asia, Latin America, the Arab World, and parts of Europe. To this end, the UNDP currently supports over 5,300 operational projects in five main fields: (1) surveying and assessing natural resources having industrial, commercial, or export potential; (2) stimulating capital investments; (3) training in a wide range of vocational and professional skills; (4) transferring appropriate technologies and stimulating the growth of local technological capabilities; and (5) aiding economic and social planning. In addition, the General Assembly has assigned the UNDP three special mandates for the 1980s: the International Drinking Water Supply and Sanitation Decade (1981–1990), the Women in Development program, and implementation of the new international economic order

(NIEO). The UNDP operates 112 field offices in support of programs in more than 150 countries.

Funding for UNDP activities is provided by country contributions and pledges. After suffering financial setbacks in 1983–1984, the Governing Council's Intersessional Committee recommended that United Nations members should maintain the real value of contributions from year to year, with the UNDP administrator holding informal talks with governments to assure additional funds. The UNDP financial situation subsequently improved and in 1986 contributions exceeded $1 billion for the first time. The leading donors were the United States ($143.9 million), Sweden ($81.4 million), and the Netherlands ($76.4 million). Preliminary figures indicated another record in contributions would be reached in 1987.

Distributions are determined by indicative planning figures (IPFs) which project the amount available for a given country over a five-year period. Criteria include factors such as population, per capita gross national product (GNP), geographic constraints, debt services costs, and terms of trade. Total outlay for 1982–1986 was $2.7 billion with 42 percent providing financing for projects in least-developed countries; $3.2 billion is projected for 1987–1991 with 64 percent going to those countries with a per capita GNP equal to or less than $375.

During its annual session held May 26–June 19, 1987, at New York, the Governing Council recommended that more assistance be given to the private sector to combat faltering economic conditions in many developing countries. In support of that approach, the Council pointed to the success of UNDP programs which help small- and medium-sized businesses in the Caribbean and Africa obtain private financing for initiating or expanding operations. In other activity, the Council asked UNDP administrators to assist governments in formulating debt-managing strategies, pledged $3 million to the World Health Organization's Special Program on AIDS, reaffirmed the UNDP's concern over environmental issues, again stressed the need for expanded integration of women in development, and called for additional implementation of projects within the ten-year-old Technical Cooperation among Developing Countries (TCDC).

United Nations Disaster Relief Coordinator's Office (UNDRO)

Established: By General Assembly resolution of December 14, 1971, becoming operational March 1, 1972.

Purpose: To coordinate and help mobilize aid to disaster areas by other bodies, to raise the level of predisaster planning and preparedness, and to encourage research and the dissemination of information about the causes of disaster.

Headquarters: Geneva, Switzerland.

Field Officers: UNDRO is represented in over 110 less-developed countries by Resident Representatives of the United Nations Development Programme.

Coordinator: M'Hamed Essaafi (Tunisia).

Recent activities. UNDRO is a worldwide information and action center on disaster situations and relief measures, rather than a body which responds to disasters per se. In fact, the agency is restricted to contributing no more than $50,000 from its regular budget toward relief of a particular disaster. Thus assistance projects are dependent on cooperation with other international agencies. For example, during late 1983 and early 1984 UNDRO collected $4 million for famine relief in Benin, Chad, Ethiopia, Mauritania, Mozambique, and Somalia, and over $87 million for victims of natural disasters in Bolivia, Ecuador, and Peru. After the November 1985 volcano eruption in Colombia, UNDRO reported contributions of $13 million from intergovernmental organizations, individual governments, the Red Cross and Red Crescent, as well as various private donors. Its own allocation consisted of a $30,000 cash grant and the dispatch of staff members to the area.

In recent years, UNDRO has sponsored seminars on disaster-preparedness strategies and participated in the founding of national and regional disaster coordination centers such as the Coordination and Information Centre for Emergencies in Chad. It has also participated in programs for the development of disaster prevention, including earthquake prevention in the Balkan and Ibero-Maghrebian regions and flood prevention in Argentina, Eqypt, Mozambique, and Poland.

In 1984–1985, UNDRO arranged for a total of $2.1 billion in aid for nearly 100 disaster situations, a 200 percent increase over the $700 million raised during the previous biennium. Sixty-five countries contributed $1.5 billion for the period, the largest being the United States at $654 million, Italy at $154 million, and the Federal Republic of Germany at $56 million, while the European Community provided $284 million. From 1984 through 1986 UNDRO cooperated with the UN's Office for Emergency Operations in Africa in combatting critical situations arising from famine and other disasters. In May 1987 donors at a special meeting organized by UNDRO pledged $200 million for humanitarian assistance to Mozambique after a mission sent by UN Secretary General Pérez de Cuéllar had reported on the effects of the country's continuing guerrilla war.

United Nations Environment Programme (UNEP)

Established: By General Assembly resolution of December 15, 1972, as the outgrowth of a United Nations Conference on the Human Environment held at Stockholm, Sweden, June 6–16, 1972.

Purpose: To facilitate international cooperation in all matters affecting the human environment; to ensure that environmental problems of wide international significance receive appropriate governmental consideration; and to promote the acquisition, assessment, and exchange of environmental knowledge.

Principal Organs: Governing Council (58 members), Bureau of the Programme, Bureau of the Environmental Fund and Administration, Secretariat. Membership on the

Governing Council rotates on the following geographical basis: Africa, 16 seats; Asia, 13; Latin America, 10; Eastern Europe, 6; Western Europe and other, 13.

Headquarters: Nairobi, Kenya.

Executive Director: Dr. Mostafa Kamal Tolba (Egypt).

Recent activities. In addition to distributing both technical and general information, notably through its "state of the environment" reports, UNEP acts as a catalyst within the UN system on environmental matters. Its operations encompass a Global Environmental Monitoring System (GEMS), a Global Resource Information Data Base (GRID), a global information network on the environment (Infoterra), an International Register of Potentially Toxic Chemicals, various advisory services, and a clearinghouse, established in 1982, to mobilize additional resources from governments, private groups, and intergovernmental and nongovernmental organizations to address environmental concerns. Since its inception UNEP has implemented more than 1,000 projects. Among the areas of current concern are desertification, depletion of the ozone layer, the "greenhouse" warming trend in the earth's atmosphere, water and air pollution, the protection of wildlife and flora, the development of safe nuclear power and other alternate sources of energy, and the handling of hazardous materials. UNEP also supports a broad range of public education programs designed to combat the mismanagement of natural resources and to build environmental considerations into development planning.

UNEP has been in the forefront of efforts to negotiate international agreements on environmental issues, achieving particular success in heightened support for its regional seas program. Nine conventions involving more than 130 countries have been adopted to control land-based sources of sea pollution, reduce the frequency and limit the consequences of oil spills, and protect fragile coastal ecosystems. In addition, UNEP was instrumental in the creation of multilateral African (1985) and Arab (1986) programs to promote overall environmental cooperation.

The *1987 State of the World Environment* report, covering 1981–1986, described conditions as "mixed": improvement or stability had been achieved in some areas, such as water and air quality, while deterioration continued in others, such as desertification. The report noted that although environmental issues had drawn increased public awareness, many governments had become less willing and able to deal with them because of difficult economic conditions. As part of UNEP's recent strategy of assessing the influence of political factors on environmental progress, the report also called for a slowdown in the world arms race and alleviation of the debt burdens of developing countries so that more resources could be allocated to the environment.

At its biennial meeting in June 1987 UNEP's Governing Council approved "An Environmental Perspective Until the Year 2000" which was subsequently endorsed by the UN General Assembly. The Perspective contains numerous recommendations and guidelines to assure that future economic growth is achieved in conjunction with "prudent management of natural resources". It also stresses the importance of the private sector and nongovernmental organizations in protecting the environment and endorses closer relations between UNEP and the UN Development Program (UNDP). In other activity, the Council selected the first 90 individuals and organizations for inclusion in what will eventually be a 500-member environmental "roll of honor". UNEP Executive Director Mostafa Kamal Tolba had suggested such recognition of "success stories" as a means of counterbalancing the "gloom and impending doom" emphasis of most environmental forecasts.

In September, after several years of negotiation sponsored by UNEP, 24 countries signed a treaty at Montreal, Canada, on chlorofluorocarbons, which are believed to be the major contributors to recent depletion of the ozone layer in the earth's atmosphere. The signatories agreed that production of chlorofluorocarbons would initially be frozen at existing levels and subsequently reduced. UNEP was allocated $10.1 million from the 1986–1987 UN budget, with additional funding provided by a variety of public and private sources.

United Nations Institute for Training and Research (UNITAR)

Established: By General Assembly resolution of December 11, 1963. The inaugural meeting of the Board of Trustees was held March 24, 1965, the Institute becoming operational the following year.

Purpose: "To enhance the effectiveness of the United Nations through training and research in the maintenance of peace and security and in the promotion of economic and social development."

Headquarters: New York, United States.

Principal Organ: Board of Trustees of 20 members, of whom one or more may be officials of the UN Secretariat and the others governmental representatives; the UN Secretary General, the President of the General Assembly, the President of the Economic and Social Council, and the Institute's Executive Director are ex officio members.

Executive Director: Michel Doo Kingué (Cameroon).

Recent activities. UNITAR has continued to provide practical assistance to the UN system, with particular emphasis on the problems of less-developed countries and on the creation of a new international economic order (NIEO). The Institute is also concerned with the professional enrichment of national officials and diplomats dealing with UN-related issues, and provides training for officials within the UN system. Seminars, courses, and symposia have dealt with multilateral diplomacy, economic development, international law, and UN documentation.

Despite worldwide praise for the organization, contributions to UNITAR's budget have been less than desired, including a refusal by the General Assembly to provide a $50 million endowment fund that would assure its survival.

In 1985, the UN Secretary General proposed a reorientation of the Institute's program and activities, on the basis of which long-term financial arrangements might be considered. UNITAR's Executive Director was invited to draw up a medium-term integrated research and training program that would aim at enhancing the knowledge and experience of diplomats and national officials with regard to multilateral cooperation. At the 1985 UN Pledging Conference for Development, only $639,000 was raised for UNITAR, with a further decline to $600,000 in 1986. Subsequently, at its fall 1986 session, the General Assembly endorsed a recommendation that UNITAR continue with a retrenched program, while attempting to mobilize additional support by voluntary contributions.

In April 1987 the Board of Trustees adopted a tentative program for 1988 and 1989 even though major shortfalls were again occurring in members' contributions to the 1987 budget. UN Secretary General Pérez de Cuéllar said later in the year that, although he personally supported continuation of the Institute, he might propose that it be phased out if its financial crisis could not be resolved. However, such action was postponed for at least a year, with UNITAR continuing to function with a skeletal staff in 1988 pending an emergency Board meeting scheduled for September.

United Nations Office of High Commissioner for Refugees (UNHCR)

Established: By General Assembly resolution of December 3, 1949, with operations commencing January 1, 1951, for a three year period; extensions subsequently approved through December 31, 1988.

Purpose: To provide protection, emergency relief, and resettlement assistance to refugees, and to promote permanent solutions to refugee problems.

Headquarters: Geneva, Switzerland.

Principal Organs: Executive Committee, Administration (embracing Divisions of External Affairs, Protection, Assistance, and Administration and Management).

High Commissioner: Jean-Pierre Hocké (Switzerland).

Membership of Executive Committee (43): Algeria, Argentina, Australia, Austria, Belgium, Brazil, Canada, China, Colombia, Denmark, Finland, France, Federal Republic of Germany, Greece, Holy See (Vatican City State), Iran, Israel, Italy, Japan, Lebanon, Lesotho, Madagascar, Morocco, Namibia (represented by the UN Council for Namibia), Netherlands, Nicaragua, Nigeria, Norway, Pakistan, Somalia, Sudan, Sweden, Switzerland, Tanzania, Thailand, Tunisia, Turkey, Uganda, United Kingdom, United States, Venezuela, Yugoslavia, Zaire. Membership on the Executive Committee is permanent following approval by the Economic and Social Council and the General Assembly.

Recent activities. The UNHCR, financed by a limited UN subsidy for administration and contributions from governments, nongovernmental organizations, and individuals, attempts to ensure the treatment of refugees according to internationally accepted standards. It promoted the adoption of the UN Convention on the Status of Refugees in 1951 and an additional protocol in 1967 which provide a universally applicable definition of the term "refugee", establish minimum standards for treatment of refugees, grant favorable legal status to refugees, and accord refugees certain economic and social rights. (As of July 1987, 103 countries had signed at least one of the documents.) In addition, the office conducts material assistance programs that provide emergency relief (food, medicine) and supplementary aid while work proceeds on the durable solutions of, in order of priority, the voluntary repatriation of refugees, their integration into the country where asylum was first sought, or their resettlement to a third country. Activities are often conducted in cooperation with other UN agencies, national governments, regional bodies such as the Organization of African Unity and the Council of Europe, and private relief organizations.

The growth in number and magnitude of refugee problems in recent years has resulted in a corresponding increase in the responsibilities entrusted to the UNHCR. Concurrently, the Office has experienced fiscal problems which forced program cuts in 1985 and 1986 in areas such as education, housing, and employment. In 1986 UNHCR High Commissioner Jean-Pierre Hocké criticized donor countries for "compassion fatigue" and accused some recipient countries of manipulating their refugee aid for political purposes. In addition, as part of overall UN belt-tightening, Hocké initiated a restructuring of the UNHCR to make it more of a "field-based, performance-oriented" operation.

Donor response subsequently improved, with the program budget reaching $349 million in 1987. However, the UNHCR expressed concern over what it considered deterioration of attitudes throughout the world toward refugees. In particular, status reports decried the tightening of borders by Western countries in the wake of economic slowdown, disregard of refugee protocol by some signatories to UN agreements, and the inability of the world community to mitigate the underlying causes of refugee movements. The report also strongly condemned the increase in armed attacks on refugee camps, the detention-like setting of many of the camps, and the widespread abuse of and discrimination against female refugees.

During its 38th session October 5–12, 1987, at Geneva, the UNHCR's Executive Committee once again called for the strengthening of UNHCR's protective function as attacks on refugee camps and settlements continued. The Committee also approved an agreement with the UN Development Program to promote development among refugees and returnees. The UNHCR estimated the existing number of refugees in the world to be 12 million, 9.5 million of whom have sought asylum in developing countries where they were "eating from an empty table". Major problems stem from the fighting in Afghanistan, which has generated the flight, largely to Pakistan and Iran, of approximately four million people; unrest in Southeast Asia, where UNHCR in recent years has spearheaded a campaign to protect and assist "boat people" refugees; and protracted civil wars and other violence in Africa and Central America.

United Nations Population Fund
(UNFPA)

Established: By the Secretary General in July 1967 as the Trust Fund for Population Activities; name changed in May 1969 to United Nations Fund for Population Activities (UNFPA), with administration assigned to United Nations Development Programme (UNDP); became operational in October 1969; placed under authority of the General Assembly in December 1972; became a "subsidiary organ" of the Assembly in December 1979; name changed to United Nations Population Fund in December 1987, with the UNFPA designation being retained.

Purpose: To enhance the capacity to respond to needs in population and family planning, promote awareness of population problems in both developed and developing countries and possible strategies to deal with them, assist developing countries in dealing with their population problems in the forms and means best suited to their needs, and play a leading role in the UN system in promoting population programs.

Principal Organ: Governing Council (same membership as the UNDP Governing Council).

Headquarters: New York, United States.

Field Officers: 34 Deputy Representatives and Senior Advisors on Population attached to offices of UNDP Resident Representatives.

Executive Director: Dr. Nafis Sadik (Pakistan).

Recent activities. The UNFPA continues to be the largest source of multilateral population assistance to less-developed areas. Although the global population growth rate has been declining in recent years, the UNFPA in 1987 estimated that population was still increasing by 80 million annually with nine out of ten births occurring in Third World countries. Total population reached five billion in 1987 and is expected to reach six billion in 2000 and seven billion in 2010.

The UNFPA sponsored the United Nations Second International Conference on Population, held August 6–13, 1984, with an agenda that included revision of the World Population Plan of Action adopted at Bucharest, Romania, in August 1974. After much controversy and debate the final declaration, entitled The Mexico City Declaration on Population and Development, was adopted by consensus. Its numerous proposals included the following: that population and development policies should strive for community backing to achieve the best results; that the complete equality of women in social, economic, and political life, regardless of cultural, religious, or economic barriers, must be hastened, by government action if necessary; that universal access to family planning information must be provided; and that special attention be given to maternal and child health services within primary health care systems, as well as to means of dealing with increasingly youthful populations in developing countries and increasingly elderly populations in developed countries.

Recently, a powerful anti-abortion coalition in Washington gained sufficient influence to cause the United States, previously the UNFPA's largest donor, to withhold $10 million from its $46 million pledge in 1985 and all of its $25 million pledges in 1986 and 1987. The US agency for International Development said the action was taken because of the UNFPA's continued activity in China despite allegations that its population policies result in coerced abortions and sterilizations. The UNFPA strongly denied that it supported abortion anywhere "in policy or practice", pointing out that its programs in China involve census assistance, training for family planning experts, and the production and importation of contraceptives.

Despite the loss of US funds, the UNFPA reached a record funding level in 1987 of $155 million for projects in 133 countries. Contributions in 1988 were expected to total about $168 million. Much of the additional revenue was slated for programs in sub-Saharan Africa, which the UNFPA describes as the last region in the world with an increasing rate of population growth. The UNFPA has recently shifted its emphasis in that region from the collection of population data to direct family planning activity and the provision of maternal and child health services.

The UNFPA's *1987 State of World Population* report focused on the Fund's contention that economic growth in developing countries is often linked to reduction in population growth rates. The report argued that inappropriate population growth "sucks the lifeblood from the development process", depletes the environment, and exacerbates health, education, food, and other social problems. In other 1987 activity, the UNFPA coordinated worldwide observation of the "Day of Five Billion" in July, called for more programs to elevate the status of women as a means of reducing population growth, announced a reorganization of internal UNFPA bodies and the creation of a task force to review program efficiency, and agreed to participate in international programs to combat the spread of AIDS.

United Nations Relief and Works Agency for Palestine Refugees in the Near East
(UNRWA)

Established: By General Assembly resolution of December 8, 1949; mandate most recently extended through June 30, 1990.

Purpose: To provide relief, education, and welfare services to Palestinian refugees (i.e., persons or the descendants of persons whose normal residence was Palestine for a minimum of two years preceding the Arab-Israeli conflict in 1948 and who, as a result of that conflict, lost both their homes and their means of livelihood).

Headquarters: Vienna, Austria, and 'Amman, Jordan.

Commissioner General: Georgio Giacomelli (Italy).

Advisory Commission: Composed of representatives of the governments of Belgium, Egypt, France, Japan, Jordan, Lebanon, Syria, Turkey, United Kingdom, United States.

Recent activities. Of the persons who fell under the established definition of Palestinian refugee in 1987, more than 2.1 million were registered with the Agency. About 767,000 of that number lived in 61 refugee "camps", many of which have in effect become permanent towns, while the remainder lived in previously established towns and villages in the area served by the UNRWA — Jordan, Lebanon, Syria, and the Israeli-occupied West Bank and Gaza Strip. UNRWA's original priority was to provide direct humanitarian relief to refugees uprooted by fighting that followed the creation of Israel. In the absence of a peaceful settlement to the Palestinian question as initially envisioned by the United Nations, UNRWA's attention has shifted to education (it runs about 635 schools attended by nearly 350,000 students) and the provision of public health services to a basically self-supporting population. Only about five percent of the Agency's clientele currently receives direct aid, with the distribution of food being limited to Lebanon.

Strife in Lebanon posed the most serious operational problem to UNRWA during 1986 and 1987, leading to administrative problems, curtailment of services in some areas, and threats to UNRWA personnel through death (seven staff members were killed in the course of the year), injury, or kidnapping. Officials also reported the strong potential for disruption of UNRWA services in the Gaza Strip and West Bank where overcrowding and a receding labor market were exacerbating refugee discontent.

In December 1986 the UN General Assembly endorsed a three-year plan for UNRWA under which the Agency's General Fund budget would increase from $178 million in 1987 to $201 million in 1990. The increases are designed to meet the demands of population growth and an increase in the number of refugees qualifying for "special hardship" assistance as the result of economic decline in the Middle East. Of the proposed $188 million General Fund budget for 1988, 56 percent has been earmarked for education, 15 percent for health services, 11 percent for relief sevices, and the remainder for operational services and administration.

In addition to its General Fund activities, the UNRWA operates a Project Fund, under which donors make special contributions for specific projects, and a Capital Construction Fund for UNRWA facilities. In his 1987 report to the General Assembly, UNRWA Commissioner Georgio Giacomelli said that austerity measures in effect since 1985 had forced the Agency to neglect building construction and rehabilitation, resulting in overcrowded and deteriorating schools. He called for a "widening" of UNRWA's circle of contributors to support $50 million in construction projects over the next three years. As an example of the "endurance test" the UNRWA and Palestinian refugees have faced, Giacomelli noted that the Agency had recently initiated special services for elderly persons, some of whom were approaching their fortieth year in refugee status. He also reported that the region's economic recession had increased pressure on the Agency to boost nutrition, sanitation, and medical programs.

United Nations Research Institute for Social Development (UNRISD)

Established: July 1, 1964, by means of an initial grant from the government of the Netherlands, in furtherance of a General Assembly resolution of December 5, 1963, on social targets and social planning.

Purpose: To conduct research into the "problems and policies of social development and relationships between various types of social and economic development during different phases of economic growth".

Headquarters: Geneva, Switzerland.

Principal Organ: Board, consisting of a Chairman appointed by the UN Secretary General; a representative of the UN Secretariat; two representatives (in rotation) from the ILO, FAO, WHO, and UNESCO; the Executive Secretary of the Economic Commission for Western Asia; the Directors of the Latin American Institute for Economic and Social Planning, and the Asian and African Institutes for Economic Development and Planning; the Institute Director; and seven social scientists nominated by the UN Commission for Social Development and confirmed by the Economic and Social Council.

Director: Dharam Ghai (Kenya).

Recent activities. Following the adoption of a "research perspective" in 1979, the Institute's work covered four main areas: Food Systems and Society, in which the flow of food from producers to consumers in ten countries was analyzed to gain insight on reducing hunger and malnutrition; Popular Participation, in which "organized efforts on the part of less privileged social groups to increase control over resources and regulative institutions" were studied; Improvement of Development Data and Methods of Analysis and Monitoring; and Social Conditions of Refugees.

As it began preparation of a new research perspective in 1986, the Board warned that social conditions were deteriorating in much of the developing world, partly because social issues were accorded lower priority as the result of economic decline. To obtain maximum value from scarce resources, the Board called for the Institute to expand its already extensive cooperation with other UN bodies and existing research organizations in developing countries. In addition, the Board urged that emphasis be given to research in which findings were most likely to produce practical applications.

Discussion and revision of the parameters of the new research perspective continued into mid-1988, final decisions being expected at a Board meeting scheduled for July. The proposed redefinition of research areas immediately prior to the meeting were: food policy in the world recession (social, economic, and policy implications of pricing and marketing reform); refugees, returnees, and local society (interaction and livelihood); patterns of consumption (qualitative aspects of development); and adjustment, livelihood, and power (social impact of the economic crisis).

In addition, the Board was expected to continue its support of the Research Data Bank, an outgrowth of the previous development data program.

Annual funding for the UNRISD recently has averaged about $1.6 million, primarily in the form of government contributions.

United Nations University
(UNU)

Established: By General Assembly resolution of December 11, 1972; Charter adopted December 6, 1973; began operations September 1, 1975.

Purpose: To conduct action-oriented research in fields related to development, welfare, and human survival, and to train young scholars and research workers.

Headquarters: Tokyo, Japan.

Principal Organs: University Council (comprising 24 educators, each from a different country, in addition to the UN Secretary General, the Directors General of UNESCO and UNITAR, and the University Rector, ex officio); Advisory Committees on the World Hunger Programme, the Human and Social Development Programme, and the Programme on the Use and Management of Natural Resources.

Rector: Gurgulino de Souza (Brazil).

Recent activities. Scholars affiliated with and contracted by the UNU, working at more than one hundred research centers and universities throughout the world, conduct research on peace and conflict resolution, the global economy, energy systems and policy, resource policy and management, the food-energy nexus, food and nutrition, biotechnology, information retrieval, laser physics, and human and social development.

In 1985, the UNU established the World Institute for Development Economics Research (WIDER). WIDER is a research and training center located in Finland, which has provided a $25 million endowment fund. The major themes of the Institute's program are hunger and poverty; money, trade and finance; and technology transformation.

During its 27th session on July 7–11, 1986, at Tokyo, the UNU Council discussed items for inclusion in its second Medium Term Perspective (MTP), covering the period 1987–1993. The Council approved a proposal for an external evaluation of University activities over its first ten years and heard progress reports regarding its permanent Tokyo headquarters and its proposed Research and Training Center (RTC) in Japan.

In 1987 the Council approved the creation of the Institute for Natural Resources in Africa (INRA) in Yamassoukro, Côte d'Ivoire, with the goal of strengthening scientific and technological capacities in areas such as land use, water management, energy resources, and minerals development. In addition to the work of its core academic staff, the institute will support work by research associates at universities across the continent. The Council also

reviewed progress on two projects initiated in 1983 which were about to publish extensive findings and recommendations. One studied the past relationship between development planning and actual development progress in seven countries in the hope of determining the social and political conditions necessary for effective national planning. The other examined questions of peace and conflict resolution in the context of recent shifts in global strategies.

Gurgulino de Souza, who became UNU rector in September 1987, called for an intensive dialogue with current and potential donors to overcome a financial shortfall. Cost-cutting measures have been introduced as declining interest rates, the rise of the yen and concurrent fall in the dollar, and the high cost of living in Tokyo have undercut the UNU's endowment status.

World Food Council
(WFC)

Established: By General Assembly resolution of December 17, 1974, on recommendation of the World Food Conference held at Rome, Italy, November 5–16, 1974. The first meeting of the Council was held at Rome on June 23–28, 1975.

Purpose: To act as a coordinating mechanism for food production, nutrition, food security, food aid and trade, and related concerns of the UN system.

Headquarters: Rome, Italy.

Executive Director: Gerald I. Trant (Canada).

Membership: The 36 states represented on the Council are selected on the following geographical basis: Africa, 9 seats; Asia, 8; Latin America, 7; Eastern Europe, 4; Western Europe and other, 8.

Recent activities. In 1985 the WFC's attention focused on issues raised by emergency food shortages in Africa—famine-induced infant mortality, aid effectiveness, the need to increase food production, and lack of access to food for the undernourished. As conditions eased, the Council in 1986 endorsed the General Assembly's five-year program to promote African recovery and long-term development as a solution to the continent's cyclical food problems.

During the WFC's 13th ministerial session on June 8–11, 1987, at Beijing, China, it was estimated that there were as many as 730 million food-deprived people in the world —60 percent of them in Asia, 25 percent in Africa, 10 percent in Latin America, and 5 percent in the Middle East. The Council noted that despite record global food surpluses, the number of hungry or malnourished people exceeded the number that existed at the time of the 1974 World Food Conference. Problems have accelerated in the 1980s, the ministers reported, as the result of economic decline, trade deterioration, rising external debts for Third World countries, and subsequent adjustment policies that have constrained resource allocation.

The Council urged governments and international organizations to exhibit the "political will" necessary to eliminate "the scourge of hunger", calling in particular for extended regional and South-South cooperation to boost food production and rural development. In response to recent calls for consolidation of UN and other international operations to curtail duplication of effort, the Council argued that it should continue to serve as the major organ for review and analysis of food policies while staying clear of the operational activities provided by numerous other agencies.

SECURITY COUNCIL

Permanent Membership (5): China, France, Union of Soviet Socialist Republics, United Kingdom, United States.

Nonpermanent Membership (10): Argentina, Federal Republic of Germany, Italy, Japan, Zambia (to December 1988); Algeria, Brazil, Nepal, Senegal, Yugoslavia (to December 1989).

Origin and development. In declaring the primary purpose of the UN to be the maintenance of international peace and security, the Charter established a system for collective enforcement of the peace whose salient characteristic was its dependence on unity among the five permanent members of the Security Council. Since this has seldom proved attainable in practice, the peace efforts of the Council have been effective only to the degree that political accord has been possible in relation to specific international disputes, and only when the parties to such conflicts have been willing to allow the UN to play its intended role.

The only instance of an actual military operation undertaken under UN auspices in response to an act of aggression was the Korean involvement of 1950–1953. The action was possible because the Soviet Union was boycotting the Security Council at the time and was thus unable to exercise a veto. The United States, which had military forces readily available in the area, was in a position to assume direction of a UN-established Unified Command, to which military forces were ultimately supplied by 16 member states. The UN Command remains in South Korea, but with troops from the United States constituting the only foreign contingent. On June 27, 1975, the US representative to the UN proposed, in a letter to the president of the Security Council, that the Command be dissolved, with US and South Korean officers as "successors in command," if North Korea and China would first agree to continue the armistice. By mid-1988, no such agreement had yet been signed.

In certain other instances, as in the India-Pakistan War of 1965 and the Arab-Israeli War of 1967, the positions of the major powers have been close enough to lend weight to Security Council resolutions calling for ceasefires.

Structure. Originally composed of five permanent and six nonpermanent members, the Council was expanded as of January 1, 1966, to a membership of 15, including ten nonpermanent members elected by the Assembly for two-year terms. The Charter stipulates that in the election of the nonpermanent members due regard is to be paid to the contribution of members to the maintenance of interna-

tional peace and security and to the other purposes of the organization, and also to equitable geographic distribution. The presidency of the Security Council rotates monthly.

Council decisions on procedural matters are made by an affirmative vote of any nine members. Decisions on all other matters, however, require a nine-member affirmative vote that must include the concurring votes of the permanent members; the one exception is that in matters involving pacific settlement of disputes, a party to a dispute must abstain from voting. It is the requirement for the concurring votes of the permanent members on all but procedural questions that enables any one of the five to exercise a "veto", no matter how large the affirmative majority.

In discharging its responsibilities the Security Council may investigate the existence of any threat to peace, breach of the peace, or act of aggression, and in the event of such a finding, may make recommendations for resolution or decide to take enforcement measures to maintain or restore international peace and security. Enforcement action may include a call on members to apply economic sanctions and other measures short of the use of armed force. Should these steps prove inadequate, the Security Council may then take such military action as is deemed necessary.

The Charter established a Military Staff Committee, composed of the permanent members' chiefs of staff (or their representatives), to advise and assist the Security Council on such questions as the Council's military requirements for the maintenance of peace, the regulation of armaments, and possible disarmament. In the absence of agreements to place armed forces at the Council's disposal, as envisaged by the Charter, the Committee has not assumed an important operational role.

In addition to the Military Staff Committee, the Security Council currently has two Standing Committees—the Committee on the Admission of New Members and the Committee of Experts in Rules of Procedure—as well as a Sub-Committee on Namibia, all composed of the five permanent Council members.

Activities. Peacekeeping activities include observation, fact-finding, mediation, conciliation, and assistance in maintaining internal order. UN observer groups to supervise ceasefire lines, truce arrangements, and the like have functioned in the Balkans, Indonesia, Irian Jaya (West New Guinea), Israel, Kashmir, Lebanon, and the Yemen Arab Republic. On a larger scale, the UN Operation in the Congo (UNOC) was initiated in 1960 and continued until 1964 in an attempt to stabilize the chaotic situation in that state (now Zaire). Since 1964 the UN Force in Cyprus (UNFICYP) has attempted to alleviate conflict between the Greek and Turkish elements in the Cypriot population under a mandate subject to semiannual renewal.

Several peacekeeping operations have been located in the Middle East. A UN Emergency Force (UNEF) was interposed between the military forces of Egypt and Israel in the Sinai and Gaza areas from early 1957 until its withdrawal on the insistence of Egypt in 1967. The UNEF was reconstituted in October 1973 to supervise a ceasefire along the Suez Canal and to ensure a return of Israeli and Egyptian forces to the positions which they held on October 22, 1973. Soon after the signing of the Egyptian-Israeli peace

treaty in March 1979, it became clear that the Soviet Union
—on behalf of its Arab friends—would veto an extension
of the force when its mandate expired on July 25. Faced
with this prospect, the United States concluded an agreement with the Soviet Union to allow monitoring of the
treaty arrangements by the UN Truce Supervision Organization (UNTSO), established in 1948 to oversee the Arab-
Israeli ceasefire. Other forces currently serving in the
Middle East are the UN Interim Forces in Lebanon (UNI-
FIL), established in 1978, and the UN Disengagement Observer Force (UNDOF), the latter deployed in Syria's Golan
Heights since 1974. (For organizational details on existing
peacekeeping forces, see the next section.)

As a body that meets year round and is frequently called
upon to respond to world crises, the Security Council is
often the most visible of the UN organs. Given its composition and the nature of its duties, political considerations typically dominate its deliberations. In the 1980s, the
Council has tended to focus on conditions in the Middle
East, Central America, and South Africa. During 1986,
it debated resolutions condemning Israel for continued
military activity in southern Lebanon, the alleged violation
of the sanctity of a Jerusalem mosque, and the interception
of a Libyan airliner in the search for suspected terrorists.
The resolutions failed as the result of vetoes by the United
States, itself the subject of condemnation resolutions later
in the year. Other Western-bloc Council members joined
the United States in defeating a measure denouncing the
US bombing of Libya in April, while the United States cast
the only vote against a resolution seeking to ban military
and financial aid to *contra* rebels fighting the government
of Nicaragua, which has repeatedly brought the issue of
US involvement in its affairs to the Council floor in recent
years.

The major topics of debate in 1987 were the Iran-Iraq
war, the proposed imposition of mandatory sanctions
against South Africa for its apartheid and Namibian policies, and Israeli actions in the Gaza Strip and West Bank.
In July the Council approved a peace plan that initially
showed promise for halting the Gulf war. However, negotiations conducted by UN Secretary General Javier Pérez
de Cuéllar at the Council's request ultimately stalled and
the Council by mid-1988 was reportedly considering the
imposition of an arms embargo against Iran for its failure
to endorse the plan. US and UK vetoes continued to block
the imposition of sanctions against South Africa although
the Council late in 1987 unanimously condemned the "illegal entry" of its troops into Angola. In December the
Council approved (with the United States abstaining) a
resolution deploring Israeli "practices and policies" during
recent outbreaks in the occupied territories. The Council
also urged a reactivation of UN leadership in Middle East
peace negotiations.

SECURITY COUNCIL:
PEACEKEEPING FORCES

Note: In addition to the forces listed below, the United Nations Command
in Korea (established on June 25, 1950) remains technically in existence.
The only UN member now contributing to the Command is the United
States, which proposed in June 1975 that it be dissolved. As of July 1,
1988, no formal action had been taken on the proposal (see Security
Council: Origin and development).

United Nations Military Observer Group
in India and Pakistan
(UNMOGIP)

Established: By resolutions adopted by the United Nations
Commission for India and Pakistan on August 13, 1948,
and January 5, 1949; augmented and brought under the
jurisdiction of the Security Council by resolution of September 6, 1965, in view of a worsening situation in Kashmir.
Current activities are restricted to the Indian side of the
line of control established by India and Pakistan in July
1972.

Purpose: To assist in implementing the ceasefire agreement
of January 1, 1949.

Commander: Brig. Gen. James Parker (Ireland).

Composition: As of April 1988, the UNMOGIP had an
authorized strength of 37 military observers, provided by
Belgium, Chile, Denmark, Finland, Italy, Norway, Sweden, and Uruguay.

United Nations Truce Supervision Organization
(UNTSO)

Established: By Security Council resolution of May 1948.

Purpose: To supervise the ceasefire arranged by the Security Council following the 1948 Arab-Israeli War. Its mandate was subsequently extended to embrace the armistice
agreements concluded in 1949, the Egyptian-Israeli peace
treaty of 1979, and assistance to other UN forces in the
Middle East. Since August 1982, UNTSO has also monitored events in and around Beirut, Lebanon.

Headquarters: Jerusalem, Israel.

Chief of Staff: Lt. Gen. Martin Vadset (Norway). Lt. Gen.
Ensio Siilasuuo (Finland) serves as chief coordinator of UN
peacekeeping missions in the Middle East.

Participating Countries (16): Argentina, Australia, Austria, Canada, Chile, Denmark, Finland, France, Ireland,
Italy, Netherlands, New Zealand, Norway, Sweden, Union
of Soviet Socialist Republics, and United States.

Composition: As of March 1988, the UNTSO had an
authorized strength of 294 military observers from the
participating countries.

United Nations Disengagement Observer Force
(UNDOF)

Established: By Security Council resolution of May 31,
1974.

Purpose: To observe the ceasefire between Israel and Syria
following the 1973 Arab-Israeli War.

Force Commander: Maj. Gen. Gustaf Welin (Sweden).

Composition: As of November 1987, 1,323 volunteers from the Austrian, Canadian, Finnish, and Polish armed forces, plus 7 observers assigned from UNTSO.

United Nations Force in Cyprus
(UNFICYP)

Established: By Security Council resolution of March 4, 1964, after consultation with the governments of Cyprus, Greece, Turkey, and the United Kingdom.

Purpose: To serve as a peacekeeping force between Greek and Turkish Cypriots.

Force Commander: Maj. Gen. Günther Greindl (Austria).

Composition: As of November 1987, 2,122 volunteers from the armed and civilian police forces of Australia, Austria, Canada, Denmark, Finland, Ireland, Sweden and the United Kingdom.

United Nations Interim Force in Lebanon
(UNIFIL)

Established: By Security Council Resolution of March 19, 1978.

Purpose: To confirm the withdrawal of Israeli troops from Lebanon and to restore peace and help ensure the return of Lebanese authority to southern Lebanon.

Force Commander: Maj. Gen. Lars-Eric Wahlgren (Sweden).

Composition: As of January 1988, approximately 5,800 troops from Fiji, Finland, France, Ghana, Ireland, Italy, Nepal, Norway, and Sweden. Although the Security Council approved a resolution on February 25, 1982, expanding UNIFIL from 6,000 to 7,000 troops, it was weakened by the withdrawal of Nigerian and some Nepalese troops in the wake of Israel's June 2 reentry into southern Lebanon. UNIFIL is also assisted by unarmed observers (76 as of January 1988) from UNTSO.

ECONOMIC AND SOCIAL COUNCIL
(ECOSOC)

Membership (54): *Australia, Belgium,* Belize, Bolivia, Bulgaria, *Byelorussian Soviet Socialist Republic,* Canada, China, Colombia, Cuba, Denmark, *Djibouti, Egypt,* France, *Gabon, German Democratic Republic,* Federal Republic of Germany, Ghana, Greece, Guinea, India, Iran, *Iraq,* Ireland, *Italy, Jamaica,* Japan, Lesotho, Liberia, Libya, *Mozambique,* Norway, Oman, *Pakistan, Panama, Peru, Philippines,* Poland, Portugal, Rwanda, Saudi Arabia, *Sierra Leone,* Somalia, Sri Lanka, Sudan, *Syria,* Trinidad and Tobago, Union of Soviet Socialist Republics, United Kingdom, *United States,* Uruguay, Venezuela, Yugoslavia, Zaire. One third of the members rotate annually on the following geographical basis: Africa, 14 seats; Asia, 11; Latin America, 10; Eastern Europe, 6; Western Europe and other, 13; those with terms ending December 31, 1988, are italicized.

President of the 1988 Sessions: Dr. Andrés Aguilar (Venezuela).

Origin and development. Initially, the activities of ECOSOC were directed primarily to the twin problems of relief and reconstruction in war-torn Europe, Asia, and, after 1948, Israel. By the mid-1950s, however, the problems of less-developed states of Africa, Asia, and Latin America had begun to claim the primary attention they receive today.

Substantially increased activity has occurred under the auspices of ECOSOC subsidiary organs as UN operations have proliferated in the economic and social fields. At the direction of the General Assembly, ECOSOC in 1987 established a special commission to identify ways to simplify UN structures and functions in those areas. The Commission's report was due in mid-1988, initial discussions indicating it would recommend enhanced policymaking and oversight roles for ECOSOC.

Structure. By a Charter amendment that entered into force August 31, 1965, the membership of ECOSOC was increased from 18 to 27 in order to provide wider representation to new states in Africa and Asia. Similarly, membership was raised to 54 as of September 24, 1973. One-third of the members are elected each year for three-year terms, and all voting is by simple majority; each member has one vote.

Much of ECOSOC's activity is carried on through its six Functional and five Regional Commissions (described in separate sections, below) and eight Standing Committees and Commissions: Commission on Human Settlements (established in 1977), Commission on Transnational Corporations (1974), Committee on Natural Resources (1970), Committee on Negotiations with Intergovernmental Agencies (1946), Committee on Non-Governmental Organizations (1946), Committee for Programme and Coordination (1962), Committee on Review and Appraisal (1971), and Committee on Science and Technology for Development (1971). In addition, there are assorted Expert Bodies (Advisory Committee on the Application of Science and Technology to Development, Committee for Development Planning, Committee of Experts on the Transport of Dangerous Goods, Committee on Crime Prevention and Control, Group of Experts on Tax Treaties between Developed and Developing Countries, United Nations Group of Experts on Geographical Names) and ad hoc groups. Because of the scope of its responsibilities, ECOSOC also has complex relationships with a number of UN subsidiary and related organs. It participates in the Administrative Committee on Coordination (ACC), which is composed of the secretary general and the heads of the Specialized Agencies and the International Atomic Energy Agency (IAEA), and elects the members of the International Narcotics Control Board (INCB) on the recommendation of various UN bodies. It also elects the Governing Council of the United Nations Development Programme, the Executive Board of the United Nations Children's Fund, the

Executive Committee of the United Nations Office of High Commissioner for Refugees, half of the members of the UN/FAO Intergovernmental Committee of the World Food Programme, and seven Board members of the United Nations Research Institute for Social Development.

Activities. ECOSOC produces or initiates studies, reports, and recommendations on international economic, social, cultural, educational, health, and related matters; promotes respect for, and observance of, human rights and fundamental freedoms; negotiates agreements with the UN Specialized Agencies to define their relations with the UN; and coordinates the activities of the Specialized Agencies through consultations and recommendations.

In 1986 and 1987 ECOSOC called for increased consultation and cooperation among UN bodies, other intergovernmental and nongovernmental organizations, governments, and the private sector to deal with the world's growing economic and social turmoil. Among the problems the Commission considered of most pressing concern were the flow of resources from developing to developed countries, the external indebtedness of Third World countries, rising crime rates, widespread hunger and malnutrition, insufficient economic integration of women, human rights violations, housing shortages, population growth, drug abuse, and the spread of AIDS. In other 1987 activity, ECOSOC called for "perseverance" by its Commission on Transnational Corporations, which, despite several years of negotiations, had failed to reach agreement on a code of conduct for transnational business activity.

ECONOMIC AND SOCIAL COUNCIL: FUNCTIONAL COMMISSIONS

ECOSOC's Functional Commissions prepare reports, evaluate services, and make recommendations to the Council on matters of economic and social concern to member states. Participants are elected for terms of three or four years, depending on the particular Commission. Selection is made with due regard for geographical distribution; in the case of the Commission on Narcotic Drugs, emphasis is also given to countries producing or manufacturing narcotic materials.

The Commission on Human Rights has a Subcommission on Prevention of Discrimination and Protection of Minorities, while the Commission on Narcotic Drugs has a Subcommission on Illicit Drug Traffic and Related Matters in the Near and Middle East.

In the membership lists below, countries with terms expiring on December 31, 1988, are italicized.

Commission on Human Rights

Established: February 18, 1946.

Purpose: To prepare reports and submit recommendations on (1) an international bill of rights; (2) civil liberties; (3) the status of women; (4) the protection of minorities; (5) the prevention of all forms of discrimination based on race, sex, language, and religion; and (6) all other matters related to human rights.

Membership (43): *Algeria,* Argentina, Austria, Bangladesh, Belgium, Botswana, Brazil, Bulgaria, *Byelorussian Soviet Socialist Republic,* China, Colombia, *Costa Rica,* Cyprus, Ethiopia, France, Gambia, German Democratic Republic, Federal Republic of Germany, India, Iraq, *Ireland,* Italy, Japan, Mexico, *Mozambique, Nicaragua,* Nigeria, *Norway,* Pakistan, Peru, Philippines, Rwanda, Sao Tome and Principe, Senegal, Somalia, Spain, Sri Lanka, Togo, Union of Soviet Socialist Republics, United Kingdom, United States, Venezuela, Yugoslavia.

New Members as of January 1, 1989: Canada, Cuba, Morocco, Panama, Swaziland, Sweden, Ukrainian Soviet Socialist Rpublic.

Commission on Narcotic Drugs

Established: February 16, 1946.

Purpose: To advise the Council on matters related to the control of narcotic drugs.

Membership (40): Algeria, Argentina, Australia, Belgium, Bolivia, Brazil, Bulgaria, Canada, China, Côte d'Ivoire, Denmark, Ecuador, Egypt, France, Federal Republic of Germany, Hungary, India, Indonesia, Italy, Japan, Lebanon, Madagascar, Malaysia, Mali, Mexico, Netherlands, Nigeria, Pakistan, Peru, Poland, Senegal, Spain, Switzerland, Turkey, Union of Soviet Socialist Republics, United Kingdom, United States, Venezuela, Yugoslavia, Zambia.

There are no members with terms expiring in 1988.

Commission for Social Development

Established: June 21, 1946, as the Social Commission; renamed the Commission for Social Development on July 29, 1966.

Purpose: To advise the Council on all aspects of social development policies; recently this has included an increased emphasis on policies aimed at increasing the equitable distribution of national income.

Membership (32): Argentina, Austria, Bangladesh, Chile, Cyprus, *Denmark,* Dominican Republic, France, Federal Republic of Germany, German Democratic Republic, Ghana, Guatemala, Haiti, *Indonesia,* Iraq, *Italy,* Liberia, Libya, *Mali, Netherlands,* Norway, Pakistan, *Panama, Poland,* Romania, Sudan, *Thailand,* Togo, Union of Soviet Socialist Republics, Uganda, United States, Zimbabwe.

New Members as of January 1, 1989: Cameroon, China, Ecuador, Finland, Malta, Philippines, Poland, Spain.

Commission on the Status of Women

Established: June 21, 1946.

Purpose: To report to the Council on methods to promote women's rights; to develop proposals giving effect to the principle that men and women should have equal rights.

Membership (32): Australia, Bangladesh, Brazil, Burkina Faso, *Byelorussian Soviet Socialist Republic,* Canada, China, Costa Rica, Côte d'Ivoire, Cuba, Czechoslovakia, France, Gabon, German Democratic Republic, *Greece,* Guatemala, *India,* Italy, Japan, Lesotho, *Mauritius,* Mexico, Pakistan, Philippines, Sudan, Sweden, *Tunisia,* Turkey, Union of Soviet Socialist Republics, United States, *Venezuela,* Zaire.

New Members as of January 1, 1989: Austria, Colombia, Morocco, Poland, Thailand, Tanzania.

Population Commission

Established: October 3, 1946.

Purpose: To study and advise the Council on population and immigration; to improve the quality and broaden the scope of national censuses.

Membership (27): Boliva, Brazil, Burundi, *Cameroon,* China, Colombia, Cuba, France, Federal Republic of Germany, Iran, Iraq, Japan, Malawi, *Mauritius,* Mexico, *Netherlands,* Nigeria, Poland, Rwanda, Sweden, *Thailand,* Togo, Turkey, Ukrainian Soviet Socialist Republic, Union of Soviet Socialist Republics, United Kingdom, United States.

New Members as of January 1, 1989: Bangladesh, Belgium, Egypt. (As of July 1, 1988, there had been no election for one African seat scheduled to become vacant January 1, 1989).

Statistical Commission

Established: June 21, 1946.

Purpose: To develop international statistical services; to promote the development of national statistics and to make them more readily comparable.

Membership (24): Argentina, Brazil, Bulgaria, China, Czechoslovakia, Egypt, *Finland,* France, Federal Republic of Germany, Ghana, *India,* Japan, Mexico, Morocco, *New Zealand,* Pakistan, Panama, Spain, Togo, *Ukrainian Soviet Socialist Republic,* Union of Soviet Socialist Republics, United Kingdom, United States, Zambia.

New Members as of January 1, 1989: Canada, Hungary, Iran, Norway.

ECONOMIC AND SOCIAL COUNCIL: REGIONAL COMMISSIONS

The primary aim of the five Regional Commissions, which report annually to ECOSOC, is to assist in raising the level of economic activity in their respective regions and to maintain and strengthen the economic relations of the states in each region, both among themselves and with others. The Commissions adopt their own procedural rules, including how they select officers. Each Commission is headed by an executive secretary, who holds the rank of under secretary of the UN, while their Secretariats are integral parts of the overall United Nations Secretariat.

The Commissions are empowered to make recommendations directly to member governments and to Specialized Agencies of the United Nations, but no action can be taken in respect to any state without the agreement of that state.

Economic Commission for Africa (ECA)

Established: April 29, 1958.

Purpose: To "initiate and participate in measures for facilitating concerted action for the economic development of Africa, including its social aspects, with a view to raising the level of economic activity and levels of living in Africa, and [to maintain and strengthen] the economic relations of countries and territories of Africa, both among themselves and with other countries of the world".

Headquarters: Addis Ababa, Ethiopia.

Subsidiary Organs: Conference of Ministers; Intergovernmental Committee of Experts for Science and Technology Development; Intergovernmental Regional Committee on Human Settlements; Joint Conference of African Planners, Statisticians, and Demographers; Conference of Ministers of African Least Developed Countries; Secretariat. The Secretariat comprises a Cabinet Office of the Executive Secretary and ten Divisions: Socio-Economic Research and Planning; International Trade and Finance; Joint ECA/FAO Agriculture; Joint ECA/UNIDO Industry; Social Development; Natural Resources; Transport, Communication, and Tourism; Public Administration, Management, and Manpower; Statistics; and Population.

Executive Secretary: Dr. Adebayo Adedeji (Nigeria).

Membership (51): Algeria, Angola, Benin, Botswana, Burkina Faso, Burundi, Cameroon, Cape Verde Islands, Central African Republic, Chad, Comoro Islands, Congo, Côte d'Ivoire, Djibouti, Egypt, Equatorial Guinea, Ethiopia, Gabon, Gambia, Ghana, Guinea, Guinea-Bissau, Kenya, Lesotho, Liberia, Libya, Madagascar, Malawi, Mali, Mauritania, Mauritius, Morocco, Mozambique, Niger, Nigeria, Rwanda, Sao Tome and Principe, Senegal, Seychelles, Sierra Leone, Somalia, South Africa, Sudan, Swaziland, Tanzania, Togo, Tunisia, Uganda, Zaire, Zambia, Zimbabwe. The membership of South Africa was suspended in 1963 as a result of its racial policies.

Associate Members (3, representing non-self-governing territories in Africa including African islands): France, Namibia (represented by the UN Council for Namibia), United Kingdom. Switzerland also participates in a consultative capacity.

Recent activities. To the four traditional methods by which the ECA has carried out its technical-assistance activities—advisory services; studies; meetings, seminars, training workshops, and conferences; and collection and dissemination of information—a fifth was added in the late 1970s: analysis and implementation of intercountry projects. Inclusion of the last reflected the Commission's status as executing agency of UNDP-sponsored and other projects, as well as a desire to overcome criticism that it had been excessively research-oriented. As part of its added responsibility, the ECA introduced an evaluation of the agricultural development plans and projects of 40 African intergovernmental organizations in line with the objectives of the Regional Food Plan for Africa (Afplan) and the "Lagos Plan of Action".

The Lagos Plan, largely based on ECA recommendations for coordinated economic development in Africa, calls for, inter alia, establishment of an African common market by the end of the century; continental self-sufficiency in food, energy, and various raw materials and manufactured goods; and coordination of such services as transportation and communication. Toward these goals, a UN Trust Fund for African Development was established in April 1981, while in May, after several years of ECA-sponsored discussions, ministers from Eastern and Southern African countries approved plans for a 12-member East and Southern African Preferential Trade Area, which was established by a treaty signed on December 21.

The ECA has also sponsored or undertaken activities in areas such as industrial development, food and agriculture, population, natural resources, science and technology, international trade and finance, economic cooperation and integration, and social development. Most recently, during the second half of 1986, a blueprint was formulated for the creation of an African Monetary Fund.

The ECA continues to coordinate and participate in conferences dealing with the full range of economic issues confronting Africa during the Third UN Development Decade. In addition, it is involved in a host of continental and subregional ventures, including five trans-African highway construction projects; a plan to construct a bridge to link Africa and Europe; the Pan-African Telecommunication Network (Paneftel), undertaken in cooperation with the International Telecommunication Union (ITU), and the OAU; and assorted subregional food and mineral development projects. Five ECA Multinational Programming and Operational Centres (Mulpocs) are helping to implement various regional development plans, while recent institutional activities have included the establishment of the African Centre for Applied Research and Training in Social Development at Tripoli, and the African Institute for Higher Technology Training at Nairobi, Kenya.

In light of widespread famine in the first half of the 1980s, much of the Commission's work in recent years has concentrated on agriculture—particularly the relationship between government policies and food shortages—and the five-year UN Programme of Action for African Economic Recovery and Development, adopted in 1986. Despite those efforts, the participants in the 13th Ministerial Conference, held at Addis Ababa, Ethiopia, in April 1987, concluded that the flow of resources to the continent was diminishing and that little headway was being made in resolving the external debt crisis. In his end-of-the-year message, Executive Secretary Adebayo Adedeji put much of the blame on industrialized donor nations, charging them with failing to make the investments promised under the UN recovery program in return for the implementation

of stringent economic adjustment policies by African nations.

Economic Commission for Europe
(ECE)

Established: March 28, 1947.

Purpose: To strengthen economic relations among Eastern and Western European countries and to raise the level of their economic activities.

Headquarters: Geneva, Switzerland.

Subsidiary Organs: Chemical Industry Committee; Coal Committee; Committee on Agricultural Problems; Timber Committee; Committee on the Development of Trade; Committee on Electric Power; Conference of European Statisticians; Committee on Gas; Committee on Housing, Building, and Planning; Inland Transport Committee; Steel Committee; Senior Economic Advisers to ECE; Senior Advisers to ECE Governments on Science and Technology; Senior Advisers to ECE Governments on Environmental Problems; Senior Advisers to ECE Governments on Energy; Secretariat.

Executive Secretary: Gerald Hinteregge (Austria).

Membership (34): Albania, Austria, Belgium, Bulgaria, Byelorussian Soviet Socialist Republic, Canada, Cyprus, Czechoslovakia, Denmark, Finland, France, German Democratic Republic, Federal Republic of Germany, Greece, Hungary, Iceland, Ireland, Italy, Luxembourg, Malta, Netherlands, Norway, Poland, Portugal, Romania, Spain, Sweden, Switzerland, Turkey, Ukrainian Soviet Socialist Republic, Union of Soviet Socialist Republics, United Kingdom, United States, Yugoslavia. (Israel's application for membership, based on its "fundamental economic relations" with the European Community and the United States, is under review by ECOSOC).

Recent activities. In recent years ECE activities have increasingly focused on cooperation in the areas of energy, transportation, and environmental protection. Ongoing projects in which the Commission is participating include the interconnection of Balkan power grids, construction of a Trans-European North-South Motorway, and the abatement of air and water pollution. A Convention on Long-Range Transboundary Air Pollution was adopted in November 1979, with a Protocol on the reduction of sulphur emissions (the primary cause of "acid rain") adopted in 1985 and implemented in September 1987. A Declaration of Policy on the Prevention and Control of Water Pollution was issued in 1980 and implemented in 1983. In addition, the Commission participated in the Conference on the Causes and Prevention of Damage to Forests and Waters By Air Pollution in Europe, held at Munich, West Germany, in June 1984, where damage to man-made structures by sulfur emissions was also considered. October 1985 witnessed the implementation of the International Convention on the Harmonization of Controls of Goods at

Frontiers, as part of an effort to make uniform border regulations for the shipment of goods in Europe.

During the 42nd session of the ECE, held March 31–April 10, at Geneva, Switzerland, delegates once again stressed the promotion of East-West trade, industrial and scientific cooperation, environmental protection, and measures to govern the transport of dangerous goods. The Commission also created an ad hoc committee to review ECE structures and functions as part of the UN streamlining campaign. At a special session (the first of its kind), held November 9–10, at Geneva, the Commission adopted the committee's recommendations for substantial cuts in the number of ECE subsidiary bodies, reduction in documentation levels, and consolidation or elimination of lower priority programs. The current major fields of ECE study were listed as agriculture and timber, economic projections, energy, environment, human settlements, industry, inland transport, science and technology, statistics, and trade.

Economic Commission for
Latin America and the Caribbean
(ECLAC)
Comisión Económica para America Latina y el Caribe
(CEPAL)

Established: February 25, 1948, as the Economic Commission for Latin America; current name adopted in 1984.

Purpose: To "initiate and participate in measures for facilitating concerted actions for . . . raising the level of economic activity in Latin America and for maintaining and strengthening the economic relations of the Latin American countries, both among themselves and with other countries of the world".

Headquarters: Santiago, Chile.

Subsidiary Organs: Central American Economic Cooperation Committee, Trade Committee, Latin American Center for Economic and Social Documentation, Latin American Institute for Social and Economic Planning, Latin American Center for Demography, Caribbean Development and Cooperation Committee, Committee of High-Level Government Experts, Presiding Officers of the Regional Conference on the Integration of Women into the Economic and Social Development of Latin America and the Caribbean, Secretariat.

Executive Secretary: Gert Rosenthal (Guatemala).

Membership (40): Antigua and Barbuda, Argentina, Bahamas, Barbados, Belize, Bolivia, Brazil, Canada, Chile, Colombia, Costa Rica, Cuba, Dominica, Dominican Republic, Ecuador, El Salvador, France, Grenada, Guatemala, Guyana, Haiti, Honduras, Jamaica, Mexico, Netherlands, Nicaragua, Panama, Paraguay, Peru, Portugal, St. Christopher-Nevis, St. Lucia, St. Vincent, Spain, Suriname, Trinidad and Tobago, United Kingdom, United States, Uruguay, Venezuela.
Associate Members (4): British Virgin Islands, Montserrat, Netherlands Antilles, United States Virgin Islands. The

Federal Republic of Germany and Switzerland participate in a consultative capacity.

Recent activities. Most of ECLAC's work agenda is conducted through various operational programs: Food and Agriculture, Development Issues and Policies, Environment, Human Settlements, Industrial Development, International Trade, Natural Resources and Energy, Demographics (through the Latin American Center for Demography—CELADE), Transnational Corporations, Science and Technology, Social Development and Humanitarian Affairs, Statistics, Transport, Economic and Social Documentation (through the Latin American Center for Economic and Social Documentation-CLADES), and the Administration of Technical Cooperation.

A relatively new area of concern for ECLAC is technical and economic cooperation among developing countries. The Commission is providing preparation, evaluation, and technical assistance for "horizontal development" projects among its members in the areas of agro-industrial and energy planning, and transportation. In addition, the Secretariats of ECLAC and the Economic Commission for Africa met in February 1982 to discuss a work agenda, partially supported by the United Nations Development Programme, for their organizations' cooperation in human resource development and in scientific, technical, and trade projects. With a view toward expanding both work programs, secretariats from ECLAC and the other ECOSOC regional commissions prepared a joint report on technical and economic cooperation among developing countries which was presented to the parent group in 1983.

The economic crisis in Latin America has been of major concern to ECLAC whose 1983–1984 annual survey described the situation as the most severe since the 1930s. A report on "Bases for a Latin America Response to the International Economic Crisis", prepared in cooperation with the Latin American Economic System (SELA), served as the focus of a Latin American Economic Conference held at Quito, Ecuador, on January 9–13, 1984. At its conclusion, the 26 Latin American participants adopted a Declaration of Quito and a plan of action to revitalize their economies and reduce external debt. In late 1985, recognizing the impact of foreign policy on development processes, the UNDP joined with ECLAC in launching a program of consultation and research in cooperation with the region's foreign ministers, 15 of which had joined the project by mid-1987.

During the 21st session of ECLAC on April 17–25, 1986, at Mexico City, Mexico's President Miguel de la Madrid called for a restructuring of world economic relations, insisting that debtor countries had experienced a "significant loss of social progress" as the result of the global downturn in the 1980s. Many delegates blamed the region's economic "crumbling" on austerity adjustments "imposed" by the International Monetary Fund. Continued pressure for change yielded an extraordinary session of ECLAC at Mexico City on January 19–23, 1987, with (then) Executive Secretary Norberto González describing the region's external debt as "not payable" and predicting unilateral withholding of payments if restructuring was not achieved.

In his 1987 year-end report, González noted that the external debt had risen to $410 billion, reflecting an overall "worsening" of economic affairs that had also produced a decline in the growth rate and accelerated inflation. Delegates to ECLAC's 22nd session, held at Rio de Janeiro, Brazil, in April 1988, again called for more regional coordination to "confront" creditors. However, there was less denunciation of "external factors" than in previous years, the Commission emphasizing its long-standing support of industrialization and regional integration to cure economic malaise.

Economic and Social Commission for Asia and the Pacific (ESCAP)

Established: March 28, 1947, as the Economic Commission for Asia and the Far East; current name adopted in 1974.

Purpose: To facilitate cooperation in economic and social development within the region, while providing technical assistance and serving as a forum for debate.

Headquarters: Bangkok, Thailand. A Pacific Operations Centre opened in Vanuatu in 1984.

Subsidiary Organs and Related Bodies: Committee for Coordination of Joint Prospecting for Mineral Resources in Asian Offshore Areas, Committee for Coordination of Joint Prospecting for Mineral Resources in the South Pacific Area, Regional Mineral Resources Development Center, South-East Asia Tin Research and Development Center, Special Body on Land-Locked Countries, Regional Center for Technology Transfer, Regional Network for Agricultural Machinery, Interim Committee for Coordination of Investigations of the Lower Mekong Basin, Asia-Pacific Telecommunity, Asian Highway Network Project, Statistical Institute for Asia and the Pacific, ESCAP/WMO Typhoon Committee, WMO/ESCAP Committee on Tropical Cyclones, Asia and Pacific Coconut Community, Asian Clearing Union, Asian Free Trade Zone, Asian Reinsurance Corporation, International Pepper Community, Asian and Pacific Development Center, Regional Coordinating Center for Research and Development of Coarse Grains, Pulses, Roots, and Tuber Crops. There are also the following legislative committees: Agricultural Development; Development Planning; Industry, Technology, Human Settlements, and the Environment; Natural Resources; Population; Shipping, Transport, and Communications; Social Development; Statistics (incorporating the Conference of Asian Statisticians); Trade.

Executive Secretary: Shah A.M.S. Kibria (Bangladesh).

Membership (38): Afghanistan, Australia, Bangladesh, Bhutan, Brunei, Burma, China, Fiji, France, India, Indonesia, Iran, Japan, Kampuchea, Republic of Korea, Laos, Malaysia, Maldives, Mongolia, Nauru, Nepal, Netherlands, New Zealand, Pakistan, Papua New Guinea, Philippines, Singapore, Solomon Islands, Sri Lanka, Thailand, Tonga, Tuvalu, Union of Soviet Socialist Republics, United Kingdom, United States, Vanuatu, Vietnam, Western Samoa.
Associate Members (9): Belau (Pelau), Commonwealth of the Northern Mariana Islands, Cook Islands, Federated States of Micronesia, Guam, Hong Kong, Kiribati, Marshall Islands, Niue. American Samoa's application for associate membership was endorsed by ESCAP in 1988 and forwarded to ECOSOC for final approval. Switzerland participates in a consultative capacity.

Recent activities. ESCAP, operating through numerous committees and associated bodies, has increasingly become an executing agency for research and development projects in areas that include food and agriculture, integrated rural development, the transfer of technology and financial resources, trade, energy, and primary commodities. Following an in-depth reassessment of its development activities in 1983, the Commission directed that current priority be given to combating poverty, correcting rural-urban disparities (in part by encouraging the dispersal of industries away from metropolitan areas), and assisting the region's least developed countries. To strengthen its role in helping South Pacific island nations and territories, ESCAP inaugurated a Pacific Operations Centre in Vanuatu in 1984. In conjunction with overall UN policy, recent ESCAP programs have also emphasized environmental concerns and human resources development, particularly the economic integration of women. In addition, ESCAP remains a source of highly respected economic analyses, including its annual *Economic and Social Survey of Asia and the Pacific.*

In 1986 ESCAP completed a study of the region's vulnerability to natural disasters (particularly volcanic eruptions, earthquakes, and floods), urging member governments to assess geological and hydrological constraints in attempting to deal with "explosive" urban growth. A five-year ESCAP project was authorized to train government engineers, collect information, and map the expansion of cities to minimize damage and loss of life from future disasters. During the year ESCAP also discussed logging limits to avert deforestation, stricter laws to reduce traffic accidents, training to maximize the use of technological advances, and increased aid for the region's least developed countries. In addition, the Commission sponsored a trade ministers' meeting, the first in eight years, at Bangkok, Thailand, on June 16–18 to examine strategies for combating protectionism, uncoordinated trade agreements, and unstable commodity prices.

Among the issues under review in 1987 were the need for greater regional cooperation in developing insurance markets and in addressing a potential energy crisis. In October, the ESCAP Committee on Natural Resources, estimating that the region's known oil reserves would be exhausted in about 16 years at the current rate of extraction, approved a regional energy plan for 1990–1995 that calls for stringent oil conservation measures and the development of alternative energy sources.

Economic and Social Commission for Western Asia (ESCWA)

Established: August 9, 1973, as the Economic Commission for Western Asia; current name adopted in 1985.

Purpose: To "initiate and participate in measures for facilitating concerted action for the economic reconstruction and development of Western Asia, for raising the level of economic activity in Western Asia, and for maintaining and strengthening the economic relations of the countries of that area, both among themselves and with other countries of the world".

Headquarters: Baghdad, Iraq.

Subsidiary Organs: Arab Center for the Study of Arid Areas and Dry Lands, Arab Planning Institute, Arab Institute for Training and Research Statistics, Secretariat.

Executive Secretary: Mohamed Said Nabulsi (Jordan).

Membership (14): Bahrain, Egypt, Iraq, Jordan, Kuwait, Lebanon, Oman, Palestine Liberation Organization, Qatar, Saudi Arabia, Syria, United Arab Emirates, Yemen Arab Republic, Yemen People's Democratic Republic.

Recent activities. The most important procedural event in the Commission's history was the 1977 decision to grant full membership to the Palestine Liberation Organization (PLO)—the first nonstate organization to achieve such standing in a UN agency—despite a fear on the part of some UN members that the PLO would use its status in the Commission as a precedent for launching an effort to gain full membership in the General Assembly.

The ESCWA work agenda is largely carried out through a variety of operational programs: Food and Agriculture; Development Issues and Policies; Human Settlements; Industrial Development; International Trade and Development; Labor, Management, and Employment; Natural Resources; Population; Development Finance and Administration; Science and Technology; Social Development; Statistics; Transport, Communications, and Tourism; and Transnational Corporations. Many ESCWA projects are conducted in conjunction with other UN organizations such as the UN Development Program, the Food and Agriculture Organization, the UN Environmental Program, and the UN Industrial Development Organization.

In 1985, ESCWA, following the lead of other ECOSOC regional commissions, moved to establish a standing committee on statistics to coordinate statistical activity within the region, beginning with the harmonization of standards and definitions. During its 13th annual session in April 1986 at Baghdad the primary topic was the economic recession that had begun in 1983 and its adverse effect on the region's foreign debt. Delegates also urged further efforts to coordinate ESCWA programs with various Arab economic organizations and directed that priority be given to telecommunications projects and analyses of the impact of oil market changes on regional economic health. The Commission formally protested UN budget constraints that forced curtailment of some ESCWA programs and left many professional positions vacant. However, at its 1987 session the Commission agreed, as a budget saving measure, to hold its meetings biennially rather than annually.

TRUSTEESHIP COUNCIL

Membership (5):
Administering Member: United States.
Other Permanent Members of the Security Council: China, France, Union of Soviet Socialist Republics, United Kingdom. China does not participate in Trusteeship activity.

President (1987): John A. Birch (United Kingdom).

Structure. Under the UN Charter the membership of the Trusteeship Council includes (1) those UN member states administering Trust Territories, (2) those permanent members of the Security Council that do not administer Trust Territories, and (3) enough other members elected by the General Assembly for three-year terms to ensure that the membership of the Council is equally divided between administering and nonadministering members. These specifications became increasingly difficult to meet as the number of Trust Territories dwindled. In consequence, no members have been elected to the Council since 1965.

Activities. The Trusteeship Council is the organ principally responsible for the supervision of territories placed under the International Trusteeship System. Originally embracing 11 territories that had been either League of Nations mandates or possessions of states defeated in World War II, the System was explicitly designed to promote advancement toward self-government or political independence. Ten of the former 11 Trust Territories (British Togoland, French Togoland, British Cameroons, French Cameroons, Ruanda-Urundi, Somaliland, Tanganyika, Nauru, northern New Guinea, and Western Samoa) have since become independent, either as sovereign states or through division or merger with neighboring states, in accordance with the wishes of the inhabitants.

The only Trust Territory now remaining is the US-administered Trust Territory of the Pacific Islands, which has undergone several administrative reorganizations, the most recent yielding four groupings: the Northern Mariana Islands, the Federated States of Micronesia, the Marshall Islands, and Belau (formerly Palau). In 1975, the Northern Mariana Islands voted for commonwealth status in political union with the United States. In 1983, the Federated States of Micronesia and the Marshall Islands approved "compacts of free association" providing for internal sovereignty combined with continued US economic aid and control of defense. A similar compact was endorsed by majorities in several plebescites in Belau, but the Belauan Supreme Court ruled in 1986 that a collateral revision of the Belauan constitution to permit facilities for nuclear-armed US forces must first secure (as yet, unattained) 75 percent approval.

In addition to the Belauan question, termination of the Territory's trust status remained clouded by opposition from the Soviet Union, a permanent member of both the Trusteeship and Security councils. Since the Trust Territory of the Pacific Islands, unlike other trust territories, was designated a "strategic area" at its inception, a supervisory role, according to the UN Charter, is "exercised" by the Security Council, implying that its approval is required for termination of the trusteeship. Advocates of the agreements, aware that Soviet intransigence could forestall Security Council action indefinitely, have argued that the Security Council need only to be informed of termination by the Trusteeship Council.

At its 53rd session on May 12-June 30, 1986, the Trusteeship Council endorsed by a three-to-one vote the position that the United States had satisfactorily discharged its obligations and that it was appropriate to terminate the trusteeship. The majority argued that UN missions sent to observe the plebescites had concluded that the results constituted a free and fair expression of the wishes of the people. In casting its negative vote, the Soviet Union was highly critical of US policy regarding economic development and potential military use of the Territory. Subsequently, Washington declared the compacts with the Marshall Islands and the Federated States to be in effect from October 21 and November 3, 1986, respectively, with inhabitants of the Commonwealth of the Northern Mariana Islands acquiring US citizenship on the latter date. Thus, Belau remained — under US law — the one remaining component of the Trust Territory.

Amid growing violence and political turmoil, referenda were held in Belau in August 1987 which led the Belauan government to declare the constitutional issue resolved and the compact approved (for details, see section on Belau under United States: Related Territories). However, questions remained as to the legitimacy of the referenda and the US Congress had yet to approve the compact by mid-1988. Meanwhile, within the Trusteeship Council, the Soviet Union continued to charge the United States with "anti-Charter" activity in the handling of the Trust Territory.

Upon formal resolution of the Micronesian issue, the mandate of the Trusteeship Council will presumably be exhausted.

INTERNATIONAL COURT OF JUSTICE
(ICJ)

Established: By Statute signed as an integral part of the United Nations Charter at San Francisco, United States, June 26, 1945, effective October 24, 1945.

Purpose: To adjudicate disputes referred by member states and to serve as the principal judicial organ of the United Nations; to provide advisory opinions on any legal question requested of it by the General Assembly, Security Council, or other organs of the United Nations and Specialized Agencies that have been authorized by the General Assembly to make such requests.

Headquarters: The Hague, Netherlands.

Composition (15 Judges, elected by the UN General Assembly and Security Council for terms ending on February 5 of the years indicated):

José-María Ruda (President)	Argentina	1991
Kéba Mbaye (Vice President)	Senegal	1991
Roberto Ago	Italy	1997
Mohammed Bedjaoui	Algeria	1997
Taslim Olawale Elias	Nigeria	1994
Jens Evensen	Norway	1994
Gilbert Guillaume	France	1991
Sir Robert Y. Jennings	United Kingdom	1991
Manfred Lachs	Poland	1994
Ni Zhengyu	China	1994
Shigeru Oda	Japan	1994
Stephen M. Schwebel	United States	1997
Mohamed Shahabuddeen	Guyana	1997
Nagendra Singh	India	1991
Nikolai K. Tarassov	USSR	1997

Parties to the Statute (163): All members of the United Nations (see Appendix B), plus Liechtenstein, Nauru, San Marino, and Switzerland.

Official Languages: English, French.

Origin and development. The International Court of Justice, often called the World Court, is the direct descendant of the Permanent Court of International Justice (PCIJ). Created in 1920 under the Covenant of the League of Nations, the PCIJ, which between 1922 and 1938 had 79 cases referred to it by states and 28 by the League Council, was dissolved on April 19, 1946, along with the other organs of the League.

The Statute of the International Court of Justice, which was adopted at the San Francisco Conference in June 1945 as an integral part of the Charter of the UN, entered into force with the Charter on October 24, 1945. Except for a few essentially formal changes, the Statute is identical to that of the PCIJ. All members of the UN are automatically parties to the Statute, as are three nonmember states, Liechtenstein, San Marino, and Switzerland. Only states may be parties to cases before the Court, whose jurisdiction extends to all cases which the parties refer to it and all matters specifically provided for in the UN Charter or other existing treaties. In the event of a dispute as to whether the Court has jurisdiction, the matter is settled by a decision of the Court itself. The General Assembly or the Security Council may request the ICJ to give an advisory opinion on any legal question; other UN organs or Specialized Agencies, if authorized by the General Assembly, may request advisory opinions on legal questions arising within the scope of their activities.

States adhering to the Statute are not required to submit disputes to the Court, whose jurisdiction in a contentious case depends upon the consent of the disputing states. In accordance with Article 36 of the Statute, states may declare that they recognize as compulsory, in relation to any other country accepting the same obligation, the jurisdiction of the Court in all legal disputes concerning (1) the interpretation of a treaty; (2) any question of international law; (3) the existence of any fact which, if established, would constitute a breach of an international obligation; and (4) the nature or extent of the reparation to be made for the breach of such an obligation. However, declarations under Article 36 have often been qualified by conditions relating, for example, to reciprocity, the duration of the obligation, or the nature of the dispute. The

United States, in accepting the Court's compulsory jurisdiction in 1946, excluded matters of domestic jurisdiction "as determined by the United States of America". This exception, often called the Connally Amendment, has been something of a model for other states.

Structure. The ICJ consists of 15 judges elected for renewable nine-year terms by separate majority votes of the UN General Assembly and the Security Council, one-third of the judges being elected every three years. Candidates are nominated by government-appointed national groups of highly reputed international law bodies, with the General Assembly and Security Council assessing the nominees according to the qualifications required for appointment to the highest judicial offices of their respective states. Due consideration is also given to ensuring that the principal legal systems of the world are represented. No two judges may be nationals of the same state, and no judge while serving on the ICJ may exercise any political or administrative function or engage in any other occupation of a professional nature. As a protection against political pressure, no judge can be dismissed unless in the unanimous opinion of the other judges he has ceased to fulfill the required conditions for service. If there are no judges of their nationality on the Court, the parties to a case are entitled to choose ad hoc or national judges to sit for that particular case. Such judges take part in the decision on terms of complete equality with the other judges.

The procedural rules of the ICJ have been adopted without substantial change from those of the PCIJ, the court itself electing a president and a vice president from among its members for three-year terms. In accordance with Article 38 of the Statute, the Court in deciding cases applies (1) international treaties and conventions; (2) international custom; (3) the general principles of law "recognized by civilized nations"; and (4) judicial decisions and the teachings of the most highly qualified publicists, as a subsidiary means of determining the rules of law. All questions are decided by a majority of the judges present, with nine judges constituting a quorum. In the event of a tie vote, the president of the Court may cast a second, deciding vote.

The Registry of the Court, headed by a registrar (currently Eduardo Valencia-Ospina of Colombia), maintains the list of cases submitted to the court and is the normal channel to and from the Court.

Activities. Among the most celebrated of the advisory opinions thus far rendered by the ICJ was its determination on July 20, 1962, that the expenses of the UN Operation in the Congo and the UN Emergency Force in the Middle East were "expenses of the Organization" within the meaning of Article 17 of the UN Charter, which stipulates that such expenses "shall be borne by the members as apportioned by the General Assembly".

Of special importance have been Court actions with respect to South Africa's administration of the former League of Nations mandate of South West Africa (Namibia) and the extension of apartheid to that territory. In an advisory opinion rendered in 1950, the Court held that South Africa's administration was subject to supervision and control by the UN General Assembly, and in 1962 it declared itself competent to adjudicate a formal complaint against South Africa that had been instituted by Ethiopia and Liberia. On July 18, 1966, however, the Court by an 8–7 vote dismissed the Ethiopian and Liberian complaints on the ground that those two states had not established "any legal right or interest appertaining to them in the subject matter of their claims". Because of this decision, confidence in the ICJ decreased, especially among African states. Thus the number of cases heard by the Court has not grown in proportion to the increase in the number of states adhering to the Court's Statute.

In 1970 the ICJ again rendered an advisory opinion concerning Namibia. This opinion stated that South Africa was obligated to withdraw its administration from the territory immediately, that members of the UN were under an obligation to recognize the illegality of the South African presence and the invalidity of any actions taken by South Africa on behalf of Namibia, and that members were to refrain from any dealings with South Africa that might imply recognition of the legality of its presence there. States not belonging to the UN were also requested to follow these recommendations.

More recently, in a decision handed down in April 1977 after six years of deliberation, a tribunal of five judges from the Court ruled in favor of Chile in a case involving the long-standing dispute between that country and Argentina over three islands near the Beagle Channel. With implementation scheduled for May 2, 1978, Argentina formally notified the Court on January 25 that it had decided to reject the ruling. After much subsequent negotiation, a bilateral treaty ending the dispute was concluded by the principals on January 23, 1984 (see articles on Argentina and Chile).

On November 28, 1979, the United States asked the Court to order Iran to release the 53 US hostages who were being held in the US Embassy at Teheran. The United States claimed violation of the Vienna Convention on Diplomatic Relations and on Consular Relations; the Treaty of Amity, Economic Relations, and Consular Rights between the United States and Iran; and the Convention on the Prevention of Crimes Against Internationally Protected Persons, Including Diplomatic Agents. On December 15 the Court unanimously upheld the US complaint. On May 24, 1980, the Court issued its formal holdings in the case. The six-part decision ordered Iran to release all of the hostages immediately and warned its government not to put them on trial; the Court also held that Iran was liable to pay reparations for its actions. However, on April 7, 1981, following the release of the hostages, the United States requested that the Court dismiss its claim against Iran for payment of damages. The Court approved the petition, and in October began to receive approximately 3,000 cases from US companies and individuals filing for damages from Iran's current government.

Among the Court's more recent rulings was an October 1984 decision in a dispute between the United States and Canada over possession of about 30,000 square nautical miles of the Gulf of Maine southeast of New England and Newfoundland. The ruling awarded about two-thirds of the area in question to the United States and the remainder to Canada. The Court also settled a long-standing border dispute between Mali and Burkina Faso with a decision in December 1986 which divided the contested area into roughly equal parts.

The Court's most publicized recent case involved a suit brought by Nicaragua challenging US involvement in the mining of its harbors. During preliminary hearings, begun in April 1984, Nicaragua charged that the action was a violation of international law and asked for reparations. The United States sought, unsuccessfully, to have the case dismissed on the ground that Nicaragua's failure to submit an instrument of ratification of the Court's statutes prevented it from appearing before the Court. On May 10, the ICJ rendered an interim decision that directed the defendant to cease and refrain from mining operations and to respect Nicaraguan sovereignty. On November 26, the Court ruled that it had a right to hear the case, and in early 1985, Washington, anticipating an adverse ruling, stated it would not participate in further proceedings on the ground that it was a "political case" over which the Court lacked jurisdiction. On June 27, 1986, citing numerous military and paramilitary activities, the Court ruled the United States had breached international law by using force to violate Nicaragua's sovereignty. In a series of 16 rulings, each approved by a substantial majority, the Court directed the United States to cease the activity cited and to pay reparations to Nicaragua. The judgement was nonenforceable, however, as the United States had previously informed the Court that it would not submit to ICJ jurisdiction regarding conflicts in Central America.

In 1986, Nicaragua also filed suit against Honduras and Costa Rica for frontier incidents and attacks allegedly organized by anti-*Sandinista contra* forces. Honduras announced it did not consent to the Court's jurisdiction in the matter, although in February 1987 it agreed to refer to the ICJ a dispute with El Salvador involving both land border demarcation and maritime jurisdiction. Later in the year, as negotiations on a proposed Central American peace plan proceeded, Nicaragua dropped the suit against Costa Rica and "postponed" its action against Honduras.

In April 1988, at the request of the General Assembly, the Court was brought into the dispute between the United Nations and the United States over US attempts to close the UN observer mission of the Palestine Liberation Organization (PLO). The United States had ordered the closing because recent legislation classified the PLO as a "terrorist" organization but the General Assembly strongly denounced the US action as a violation of the 1947 "host country" treaty. The Court ruled that the United States must submit the issue to binding international arbitration, although it was unclear whether the United States would accept the decision.

SECRETARIAT

Secretary General	Javier Pérez de Cuéllar (Peru)
Director General for Development and International Economic Cooperation	Jean Louis Ripert (France)
Executive Office of the Secretary General (Chef de Cabinet)	Virendra Dayal (India)

Under Secretaries General

Special Political Affairs	Diego Cordóvez (Ecuador)
	Marrack I. Goulding (United Kingdom)
Special Political Questions, Regional Cooperation, Decolonization and Trusteeship	Abdulrahim A. Farah (Somalia)
Political and General Assembly Affairs	Joseph W. Reed (United States)
Political and Security Council Affairs	Vasily Safronchuk (USSR)
Disarmament Affairs	Yasushi Akashi (Japan)
International Economic and Social Affairs, Special Representative for Humanitarian Affairs in Southeast Asia	Rafeeuddin Ahmed (Pakistan)
Technical Cooperation for Development	Xie Qimei (China)
Legal Affairs	Carl August Fleischhaver (Federal Republic of Germany)
Administration and Management, Special Representative for Namibia	Martti Ahtisaari (Finland)
Conference Services	Eugeniusz Wyzner (Poland)
Public Information	Thérese P. Sevigny (Canada)
Special Representative for the Law of the Sea	Satya N. Nandan (Fiji)
UN Office at Geneva (Director General)	Jan Martenson (Sweden)
UN Office at Vienna (Director General)	Margaret Joan Anstee (United Kingdom)

Assistant Secretaries General

Co-ordinator for the Improvement of the Status of Women	Mercedes Pulido de Briceño (Venezuela)
Center Against Apartheid	Sotirios Mousouris (Greece)
Comptroller, Office of Program Planning, Budget, and Finance	Louis M. Gómez (Argentina)
Financial Services	J. Richard Foran (Canada)
Human Resources Management	Kofi A. Annan (Ghana)
Research and the Collection of Information	James O.C. Jonah (Sierra Leone)

Structure. The Secretariat consists of the secretary general and the UN staff. The secretary general, who is appointed for a five-year term by the General Assembly on recommendation of the Security Council, is designated chief administrative officer by the Charter, which directs him to report annually to the General Assembly on the work of the UN, to appoint the staff, and to perform such other functions as are entrusted to him by the various UN organs. Under Article 99 of the Charter, the secretary general may bring to the attention of the Security Council any matter which in his opinion may threaten international peace and security.

The Charter defines the "paramount consideration" in employing staff as the necessity of securing the highest standards of efficiency, competency, and integrity, with due regard to the importance of recruiting on as wide a geographical basis as possible. In the performance of their duties, the secretary general and the staff are forbidden to seek or receive any instructions from any government or any other authority external to the UN. Each member of the UN, in turn, is bound to respect the exclusively international character of the Secretariat's responsibilities and not to seek to influence it in the discharge of its duties.

In December 1977 the UN General Assembly adopted, without a vote, Resolution 32/97, which gave the secretary general authority to appoint a director general for development and international economic cooperation. Responsibilities of the UN's "second-in-command" include providing leadership to the relevant components of the UN system and ensuring coherence, coordination, and efficient management of all UN activities in the economic and social fields.

In addition to its New York headquarters, the UN maintains European offices at Geneva, Switzerland, and Vienna, Austria, whose staffs include the personnel of various specialized and subsidiary organs.

The regular budget of the organization is financed primarily by obligatory contributions from the member states, as determined by a scale of assessments that is based on capacity to pay and varies from 0.01 percent of the total for the smallest members to 25.00 percent for the United States. Collectively, seven Western industrialized countries (Canada, France, Federal Republic of Germany, Italy, Japan, United Kingdom, United States) contribute approximately 60 percent of the budget, the only other significant contributor being the Soviet Union (10.54 percent). Activities outside the regular budget, including most peacekeeping activities and technical cooperation programs, are separately financed, partly through voluntary contributions.

Activities. Other functions of the secretary general include acting in that capacity at all meetings of the General Assembly, the Security Council, the Economic and Social Council, and the Trusteeship Council, and presenting any supplementary reports on the work of the UN that are necessary to the General Assembly.

The level of international political activity undertaken by a secretary general depends as much on the contemporary political environment and his own personality as on Charter provisions. The most important factor has often been the acquiescence of the superpowers. This was most vividly demonstrated by the Soviet challenge to the Secretariat during the Belgian Congo crisis of 1960. UN intervention in the Congo, initiated on the authority of the Security Council in the summer of 1960, led to sharp Soviet criticism of Secretary General Dag Hammarskjöld and a proposal by Soviet Chairman Nikita Khrushchev on September 23, 1960, to abolish the Secretariat and substitute a tripartite executive body made up of Western, Communist, and neutral representatives. Although the proposal was not adopted, the USSR maintained a virtual boycott of the Secretariat up to the time of Hammarskjöld's death on September 18, 1961, and imposed a number of conditions before agreeing to U Thant of Burma as his successor. U Thant was in turn succeeded in 1971 by Kurt Waldheim of Austria.

On December 11, 1981, in the wake of decisions by Kurt Waldheim and Salim A. Salim of Tanzania to withdraw from consideration, Javier Pérez de Cuéllar of Peru was selected by a closed session of the UN Security Council as the recommended candidate for UN secretary general (see Security Council, above). The full UN General Assembly unanimously elected Pérez de Cuéllar on December 15, and

his five-year term as the fifth secretary general began January 1, 1982.

During his third year as secretary general, Pérez de Cuéllar continued his brand of "quiet diplomacy" in addressing new and continuing problems facing the UN and the Secretariat. He made several trips to the Middle East in an effort to find a peaceful solution to the Iran-Iraq war and travelled to Southeast Asia for discussions between Kampuchean, Thai, and Vietnamese leaders, in an effort to ease tensions in the area. Other visits were made to all parts of the world in efforts to promote peace, economic development, and civil rights.

Of special interest to Peréz de Cuéllar in 1985 was the worsening famine in 21 African countries. On January 21, he set up, under the direct supervision of his office, the Office of Emergency Operations in Africa (OEOA). It was intended as a short-term agency for the purpose of coordinating UN assistance and support to the continent and providing ". . . all needed assistance requested by affected countries and the international community at large . . ." The OEOA held its first world conference in March 1985 to discuss its preliminary findings, issued the month before, outlining the needs of drought-stricken African countries.

In 1986, with the easing of immediate food shortages, Pérez de Cuéllar urged that attention be focused on improvements in the social and economic infrastructures of African countries. Asserting that the continent's recurrent crises "do not stem primarily from drought" but from underdevelopment, he tendered proposals in five priority areas to a special session of the General Assembly.

Throughout the year, the secretary general continued his efforts to negotiate settlements in Central America, Lebanon, the Persian Gulf, and the Western Sahara. While lamenting a lack of "political will" for resolving most such conflicts, he was able in July to arbitrate the "Rainbow Warrior" dispute between France and New Zealand (see New Zealand: Foreign relations).

Despite earlier hints that he might not seek a second term because of budget problems (see General Assembly, above), Pérez de Cuéllar, upon the unanimous recommendation of the Security Council, was reelected secretary general by the General Assembly on October 10, 1986, for an additional five years beginning January 1, 1987.

In September 1987 Pérez de Cuéllar launched an intensive campaign to win support from Iran and Iraq for a Security Council plan to settle the Gulf War. Further underscoring his heightened visibility in international diplomacy, the secretary general in October was selected to serve on the committee charged with verifying compliance with the recently negotiated Central American peace plan. In addition, Under Secretary General for Special Political Affairs Diego Cordóvez played a prominent role in the lengthy negotiations which led to the April 1988 agreement for the withdrawal of Soviet troops from Afghanistan.

UNITED NATIONS: SPECIALIZED AGENCIES

FOOD AND AGRICULTURE ORGANIZATION OF THE UNITED NATIONS
(FAO)

Established: By constitution signed at Quebec, Canada, October 16, 1945. The FAO became a UN Specialized Agency by agreement with the Economic and Social Council (approved by the General Asembly on December 14, 1946).

Purpose: ". . . to promote the common welfare by furthering separate and collective action . . . for raising levels of nutrition and standards of living . . . securing improvements in the efficiency of the production and distribution of all food and agricultural products, bettering the condition of rural populations, and thus contributing toward an expanding world economy."

Headquarters: Rome, Italy.

Principal Organs: General Conference (all members), Council (49 members), Secretariat.

Director General: Dr. Edouard Saouma (Lebanon).

Membership (158): See Appendix B.

Official Languages: Chinese, English, French, Spanish.

Working Languages: English, French, Spanish (Arabic is a working language for limited purposes).

Origin and development. The 34 governments represented at the UN Conference on Food and Agriculture held at Hot Springs, Virginia, May 18–June 3, 1943, agreed that a permanent international body should be established to deal with problems of food and agriculture, and recommended that detailed plans be drawn up by an Interim Commission on Food and Agriculture. The Interim Commission submitted a draft constitution that was signed at Quebec, Canada, on October 16, 1945, by the 30 governments attending the first session of the FAO Conference. The Organization, which inherited the functions and assets of the former International Institute of Agriculture at Rome, Italy, was made a Specialized Agency of the United Nations effective December 14, 1946.

After extensive discussion at its July 1976 meeting, the FAO Council adopted a major reform proposal that called for a cutback in personnel, publications, and meetings, and the creation, from the resultant savings, of an $18.5 million Trust Fund for direct technical assistance to member states. Several of the leading donor nations, notably Japan and the United Kingdom, had expressed reservations over the creation of the Fund — the first such in the FAO's history — because it would use compulsory contributions to benefit individual states. Such aid had previously been provided on a voluntary basis.

On November 14, 1977, Namibia (South West Africa), which had previously joined several UN Specialized Agencies as an associate member, was admitted to the FAO as a full member. The action was taken despite US objections that the Organization was setting a dangerous precedent in admitting a territory that was not yet self-governing.

Structure. The General Conference, which normally meets at Rome once every two years, is the Organization's major policymaking organ; each member has one vote. Its responsibilities include approving the FAO budget and program of work, adopting procedural rules and financial regulations, formulating recommendations on food and agricultural questions, and reviewing the decisions of the FAO Council and subsidiary bodies.

The FAO Council, whose 49 members are elected by the Conference for three-year terms, meets between sessions of the Conference and acts in its behalf as an executive organ responsible for monitoring the world food and agriculture situation and recommending any appropriate action. Committees of the Council, including the Program and Finance committees and the Committees on Commodity Problems, Fisheries, Agriculture, and Forestry, address specialized issues.

Responsibility for implementing the FAO program rests with the Secretariat, headed by a director general with a six-year term of office. Its headquarters staff embraces some 4,500 individuals, while more than 2,800 are assigned to regional offices and field projects. The regional offices are located at Accra, Ghana (West Africa); Arusha, Tanzania (East Africa); Bangkok, Thailand (Asia and the Pacific); and Santiago, Chile (Latin America). There is also a regional representative for Europe. Liaison offices are maintained at UN headquarters and at Washington, DC.

Activities. To fulfill its stated purposes of raising living standards and securing improvement in the availability of agricultural products, the FAO collects, analyzes, interprets, and disseminates information relating to nutrition, food, and agriculture. It recommends national and international action in these fields, furnishes such technical assistance as governments may request, and cooperates with governments in organizing missions needed to help them meet their obligations. To provide a focus for the Organization's activities, the director general prepares an annual report, *The State of Food and Agriculture,* which is reviewed by the FAO Council as a basis for making recommendations to members.

FAO operations conducted with other international bodies include a Joint FAO/WHO/OAU Regional Food and Nutrition Commission for Africa, a Joint FAO/OAU Nationhood Programme for Namibia, and a joint FAO/IAEA program dealing with the problems of food production and protection through nuclear techniques of least harm to the environment.

FAO activities were significantly broadened in 1963 when, following a suggestion by the United States, a

UN/FAO **World Food Programme** (WFP) began operations to promote economic and social development and provide relief services in the event of natural and man-made disasters. In recent years the WFP's services and advice have been increasingly used to purchase and ship food with funds provided by governments and various UN agencies. More than $400 million was pledged for the WFP for the 1986–1987 biennium.

Drought-induced famine in Africa became a major concern of the FAO in 1982. Subsequently, the Organization also became involved in the search for long-term solutions to the continent's cyclical food shortages. In 1986, while noting that food production in Africa had recovered somewhat, the FAO called for substantial changes in agricultural policies that would give higher priority to food production, increase assistance to small-scale farmers, boost price incentives, and promote environmental conservation. The Organization also urged donor governments to pursue international trade policies that would encourage broad economic development of African countries.

FAO activity in 1987 included the drafting of a proposed international agreement on permissible levels of radioactive contamination in food, an issue spawned by the accident at the Chernobyl, USSR, nuclear power plant in 1986. The Organization also participated in the UN antidrug campaign, promoting the substitution of legitimate food crops for those that serve as raw materials for illegal drugs. In addition, the FAO expanded its successful antilocust spraying campaign in Africa.

In May 1987 FAO Director General Edouard Saouma told the WFP's Committee on Food Aid Policies and Programs that the use of food from surpluses in the North to feed hungry people in the South was not a lasting remedy for either hunger or surpluses. He cautioned delegates to remember that food aid programs should be designed to solve "the problems of recipients, not those of the donors".

During the 24th biennial General Conference, held in November 1987 at Rome, Dr. Saouma was reelected for a third six-year term despite an intense campaign by the United States, Canada, and other Western countries against him. Saouma's critics charged that the FAO was poorly managed, evinced an anti-Western tone, and lacked adequate planning, review, and accounting procedures. In early 1988 the United States announced it was cutting its FAO contributions sharply and the United Kingdom and Italy threatened "delays" in their contributions. Dr. Saouma reacted by suggesting that it was such action by major donors, not mismanagement, that had caused the organization's fiscal crisis.

INTERNATIONAL BANK FOR RECONSTRUCTION AND DEVELOPMENT (IBRD)

Established: By Articles of Agreement signed at Bretton Woods, New Hampshire, July 22, 1944, effective December 27, 1945; began operation June 25, 1946. The IBRD became a UN Specialized Agency by agreement with the Economic and Social Council (approved by the General Assembly on November 15, 1947).

Purpose: To promote the international flow of capital for productive purposes, initially the rebuilding of nations devastated by World War II. The main objective of the Bank at present is to offer loans at reasonable terms to member developing countries willing to engage in projects that will ultimately increase their productive capacities.

Headquarters: Washington, DC, United States.

Principal Organs: Board of Governors (all members), Executive Directors (21).

President: Barber B. Conable, Jr. (United States).

Membership (151): See Appendix B.

Working Language: English.

Origin and development. The International Bank for Reconstruction and Development was one of the two main products of the United Nations Monetary and Financial Conference held at Bretton Woods, New Hampshire, July 1–22, 1944. The Bank was conceived as a center for mobilizing and allocating capital resources for the reconstruction of war-torn states and the expansion of world production and trade; its sister institution, the International Monetary Fund (IMF), was created to maintain order in the field of currencies and exchange rates and thus to prevent a repetition of the financial chaos of the 1930s. The Articles of Agreement of the two institutions were annexed to the Final Act of the Bretton Woods conference and went into effect December 27, 1945, following ratification by the required 28 states.

With the commencement of the US-sponsored European Recovery Program in 1948 and the enunciation in 1949 of the US "Point Four" program of technical assistance to less-developed areas, the focus of IBRD activities began to shift toward economic development. Accordingly, two affiliated institutions—the International Finance Corporation (IFC) and the International Development Association (IDA), created in 1956 and 1960, respectively (see separate entries)—were established within the IBRD's framework to undertake developmental responsibilities for which the IBRD itself was not qualified under its Articles of Agreement. (The IBRD and IDA are often called the World Bank, or, in conjunction with the IFC, the World Bank group.) In addition, on July 29, 1975, the Bank's executive directors voted to establish the Intermediate Financing Facility, more commonly known as the Third Window, to provide an additional source of bank financing for fiscal years 1976 and 1977. Loans under the auspices of the Third Window were on terms intermediate between the standard terms of the Bank and the concessional terms of the IDA. In May 1976, in what (then) Bank President Robert McNamara termed a "useful and necessary first step" to ensure the further growth of the Bank's lending capacity, the executive directors approved a Special Capital Increase of $8.3 billion; this was followed in January 1980 by the adoption by the Board of Governors of a resolution increasing the Bank's authorized capital stock by an equivalent of $40 billion—a virtual doubling of resources. An additional proposal by President McNamara to increase available lending capital by establishing an energy affiliate was rejected in mid-1981 by the United States and other member countries.

Structure. All powers of the IBRD are formally vested in the Board of Governors, which consists of a governor and an alternate appointed by each member state. The IBRD governors, who are usually finance ministers or equivalent national authorities, serve concurrently as governors of the IMF as well as of the IFC and IDA. The Board meets each fall to review the operations of these institutions within the framework of a general examination of the world financial and economic situation. One meeting in three is held away from Washington.

Most powers of the Board of Governors are delegated to the IBRD's 22 executive directors, who meet at least once a month at the Bank's headquarters and are responsible for the general conduct of the Bank's operations. Five of the directors are separately appointed by those members holding the largest number of shares of capital stock (France, the Federal Republic of Germany, Japan, the United Kingdom, and the United States). The others are individually elected for two-year terms by the remaining IBRD members, who are divided into 17 essentially geographic groupings each of which selects one director. (Since Saudi Arabia by itself constitutes one of the geographic entities, its "election" of a director amounts, in practical terms, to an appointment. The same has been true for the People's Republic of China since 1980, when it replaced Taiwan as a member of the IBRD and agreed to a 60 percent increase in the country's capital subscription.) Each director is entitled to cast as a unit the votes of those members who elected him.

The Bank operates on a weighted voting system that is largely based on individual country subscriptions (themselves based on IMF quotas), but with poorer states being accorded a slightly disproportionate share. As of mid-1987, the leading subscribers were the United States, with 20.42 percent (19.42 percent of voting power); Japan, 5.78 (5.52); Federal Republic of Germany, 5.75 (5.49); United Kingdom, France, 5.51 (5.27) each; China, 3.56 (3.41); India, 3.37 (3.24); Canada, 3.36 (3.23); Saudi Arabia, 3.17 (3.04); and Italy, 2.81 (2.70). Total subscriptions amounted to SDR 66.6 billion ($85.2 billion at the June 30 rate of $1.28 per SDR).

The president of the IBRD is elected to a five-year renewable term by the executive directors, serves as their chairman, and is responsible for conducting the business of the Bank as well as that of the IDA and IFC. In accordance with the wishes of the US government, McNamara was replaced, upon his retirement in June 1981, by Alden W. Clausen, a former president of the Bank of America, who restructured the Bank's upper echelon to reflect his preference for collegial management and delegation of authority. On June 30, 1986, Clausen was succeeded by Barber B. Conable, Jr., who had served on a number of financial committees in the course of ten consecutive terms in the US House of Representatives. In May 1987 Conable announced a major reorganization within the Bank to clarify and strengthen the roles of the president and senior management. Bank operations were rearranged into four broad groups, each headed by a senior vice president reporting directly to the president. Other changes included the creation of country departments to oversee all aspects of individual lending projects, thereby eliminating previous cross-departmental responsibilities for various parts of projects. In response to criticism that the Bank had developed a "bloated" bureaucracy, Conable also ordered a controversial review of all Bank positions which ultimately yielded about 400 redundancies.

Activities. The activities of the IBRD are principally concerned with borrowing, lending, aid coordination, and technical assistance and related services.

Most funds available for lending are obtained by direct borrowing on world financial markets. Only about 9.5 per cent of the capital subscription of the member states represents paid-in capital in dollars, other currencies, or demand notes; the balance is "callable capital" that is subject to call by the Bank only when needed to meet obligations incurred through borrowing or through guaranteeing loans. Most of the Bank's operating funds are obtained by issuing interest-bearing bonds and notes to public and private investors.

The Articles of Agreement state that the IBRD can make loans only for productive purposes for which funds are not obtainable in the private market on reasonable terms. Loans are long-term (generally repayable over as much as 20 years, with a five-year grace period) and are available only to member states, to their political subdivisions, and to enterprises located in the territories of member states (in which case states involved must guarantee the projects).

In order to maintain the Bank's financial strength and integrity as a borrower in the world capital markets, the executive directors agreed on July 2, 1982, to switch from the Bank's traditional fixed-interest policy to a variable-interest policy. This action, taken in conjunction with the Bank's borrowing operations in short-term capital markets, was intended to enable the Bank to charge interest rates that more accurately reflect the institution's current capital costs. Under the new system, interest rates are adjusted each January 1 and July 1 to reflect the cost of funds in a pool of Bank borrowings from the preceding six-month period, plus a 0.5 percent surcharge. The Bank has also initiated currency swap arrangements as an additional method of reducing its overall borrowing costs.

In the field of aid coordination, the Bank has taken the lead in promoting a multilateral approach to the development problems of particular states by organizing groups of potential donors to work out long-range comprehensive plans for assistance. In addition, the Bank has worked on projects with a large number of multilateral financial agencies, including the African Development Bank, the Asian Development Bank, the Inter-American Development Bank, the European Development Fund, and the Arab Fund for Economic and Social Development.

IBRD technical-assistance activities are directed toward overcoming the shortage of skills that tends to hamper economic growth in less-developed states. The Bank finances and organizes numerous preinvestment studies, ranging from those aimed at determining the feasibility of particular projects to sector studies directed toward formulating investment programs in such major fields as power and transport. It also sends expert missions to assist members in designing development programs and adopting policies conducive to economic growth, while the Economic Development Institute, the IBRD staff college, helps train senior officials of less-developed states in development techniques.

In 1984, a time of review and reappraisal which some critics described as a "mid-life crisis", the IBRD implemented new mechanisms to boost central bank borrowing as well as borrowing in floating-rate notes. However, despite pressures arising from recession and indebtedness in the Third World, donor members—especially the United States—opposed any increase in the Bank's general resources.

In 1985 activity, the Bank approved a charter for a Multilateral Investment Guarantee Agency (MIGA—see below regarding implementation), approved a $3 million contribution to assist emergency food deliveries to Africa, and joined 13 industrialized nations in pledging more than $1 billion for long-term economic aid to African countries. In October the United States, in a significant policy shift, announced it was willing to support an increase in capital resources. Negotiations in that regard intensified in 1986 as the worsening debt crisis increased pressure on the Bank for new and expanded strategies for helping developing countries.

In May 1987 the Bank entered an unusually turbulent period when President Conable launched a structural reorganization and staff retrenchment (see Structure, above). Some critics suggested the Bank subsequently became "too preoccupied with itself" to the detriment of pending loan projects. On the other hand, response was widely favorable to policy statements by Conable "rededicating" the Bank to alleviating poverty in the Third World while expanding emphasis on environmental protection, debt-front action, and the integration of women in development.

During the 42nd annual meeting, held at Washington on September 29–October 1, 1987, the Board of Governors broadly endorsed Conable's initiatives, indicating the stage was set for quick approval of the proposed capital increase. In other action, the Governors praised Bank efforts to expand lending to sub-Saharan African and poor Asian countries, called for greater policy coordination among industrialized countries, urged resolve in resisting protectionist impulses, and supported expanded World Bank/IMF collaboration, particularly in regard to structural adjustment loans. It was reported that during the fiscal year July 1, 1986, through June 30, 1987, the IBRD approved loans totaling $14.2 billion for 127 operations in 39 countries, more than $4 billion of the total being earmarked for sectoral or structural adjustment.

On April 12, 1988, the Multilateral Investment Guarantee Agency (MIGA) formally came into being with about 54 percent of its initial $1.1 billion in authorized capital having been subscribed by 29 countries, including nine capital-exporting nations. The Agency was established to provide borrowers with protection against noncommercial risks such as war, uncompensated expropriations, or repudiation of contracts by host governments without adequate legal redress for affected parties. MIGA will provide coinsurance or reinsurance to complement political risk insurance already provided by regional, national, and private

entities. Although affiliated with the World Bank, MIGA will operate legally and financially as a separate body. In keeping with its mandate to promote the flow of investment to developing countries, the Agency was also expected to extend a wide range of advisory and technical services.

On April 27, 1988, the Board of Governors approved the expansion of the Bank's authorized capital by nearly $75 billion, bringing the total to $171 billion. It has been estimated that the increase will permit lending to reach annual levels above $20 billion in the early 1990s.

INTERNATIONAL CIVIL AVIATION ORGANIZATION
(ICAO)

Established: By Convention signed at Chicago, United States, December 7, 1944, effective April 4, 1947. The ICAO became a UN Specialized Agency by agreement with the Economic and Social Council (approved by the General Assembly on December 14, 1946, with effect from May 13, 1947).

Purpose: To promote international cooperation in the development of principles and techniques of air navigation and air transport.

Headquarters: Montreal, Canada.

Principal Organs: Assembly (all members), Council (33 members), Air Navigation Commission (15 members), Air Transport Committee (30 members), Legal Committee (all members), Committee on Joint Support of Air Navigation Services (9–11 members), Committee on Unlawful Interference (15 members), Finance Committee (9–13 members), Secretariat.

Secretary General: Yves Lambert (France).

Membership (157): See Appendix B.

Official Languages: English, French, Russian, Spanish.

Origin and development. The accelerated development of aviation during World War II provided the impetus for expanding international cooperation begun in 1919 with the establishment of an International Commission for Air Navigation (ICAN) under the so-called Paris Convention drafted at the Versailles Peace Conference. The main result of the International Civil Aviation Conference held at Chicago, Illinois, in November-December 1944 was the adoption of a 96-article Convention providing, inter alia, for a new international organization that would supersede both ICAN and the Pan-American Convention on Commercial Aviation (concluded in 1928). Responsibilities assigned to the new organization included developing international air navigation; fostering the planning and orderly growth of safe international air transport; encouraging the development of airways, airports, and air navigation facilities; preventing economic waste caused by unreasonable competition; and promoting the development of all aspects of international civil aeronautics.

An interim agreement, also signed at Chicago on December 7, 1944, established the Provisional International Civil Aviation Organization (PICAO), which functioned from June 1945 until the deposit of ratifications brought the ICAO itself into existence in April 1947. Its status as a UN Specialized Agency was defined by an agreement approved during the first session of the ICAO Assembly.

At the 1971 meeting of the Assembly, a resolution was passed limiting both South African participation in ICAO meetings and its access to ICAO documents and other communications.

Structure. The Assembly, in which each member state has one vote, is convened at least once every three years to determine general policy, establish a budget, elect the members of the Council, and act on any matter referred to it by the Council.

Continuous supervision of the ICAO's operation is the responsibility of the Council, which is composed of 33 states elected by the Assemby for three-year terms on the basis of their importance in air transport, their contribution of facilities for air navigation, and their geographical distribution. Meeting frequently at Montreal, the Council implements Assembly decisions; appoints the secretary general; administers ICAO finances; collects, analyzes, and disseminates information concerning air navigation; and adopts international standards and recommended practices with respect to civil aviation. The Council is assisted by, and appoints the members of, the Air Navigation Commission and the various standing committees. Regional offices are maintained at Cairo, Egypt (Middle East); Nairobi, Kenya (Eastern Africa); Neuilly-sur-Seine, France (Europe); Mexico City, Mexico (North America and Caribbean); Lima, Peru (South America); Dakar, Senegal (Africa); and Bangkok, Thailand (Asia and the Pacific).

Activities. The ICAO has been instrumental in generating international action in such areas as meteorological services, air traffic control, communications, and navigation facilities. It also has an impressive record of advancing uniform standards and practices to ensure safety and efficiency. Any member unable to implement an established civil aviation standard must notify the ICAO, which in turn notifies all other members. Standards and practices are constantly reviewed and, when necessary, amended by the Council. Other areas of involvement have included the leasing and chartering of aircraft, the fight against hijacking and air piracy, and minimizing the effects of aircraft noise on the environment. The ICAO's intensified efforts to devise effective deterrents to hijacking and air piracy resulted in a series of international conventions developed under its auspices at Tokyo, Japan, in 1963; at the Hague, Netherlands, in 1970; and at Montreal in 1971.

The ICAO provides technical assistance to over 100 less-developed countries. Among the most important recent technical-assistance activities have been analyses of long-term civil aviation requirements and the preparation of national civil aviation plans, as well as the development and updating of aviation skills.

In addition to its usual activities in the fields of air traffic safety, technical assistance, and harmonization of air transport regulations, the ICAO considered the issue of the interception of civil aircraft following the September 1, 1983, destruction by Soviet fighters of a Korean Air Lines Boeing 747 carrying 269 civilians. The ICAO Council, meeting in extraordinary session at Montreal, Canada, on September 16, condemned the downing and appointed an eight-member team to conduct an independent inquiry into the incident. The team's draft report, released by Council vote on December 13, found no evidence to support Soviet claims that the aircraft had intentionally strayed over Soviet airspace in order to conduct intelligence operations. The report concluded that the aircraft deviated from its course as a result of a navigational error probably caused by an improperly programmed flight computer and that the crew was unaware that they were off course. The report was submitted to the ICAO's Air Navigational Committee, whose own report, issued in early 1984, was the basis of an amendment to the Chicago Convention recognizing the duty to refrain from the use of weapons against civil aircraft in flight. The amendment, approved on May 10, 1984, at a special Assembly session at Montreal, awaits ratification by two-thirds of the membership.

During 1984–1985, emphasis continued to be placed on improving the operating characteristics of transport aircraft by increasing engine efficiency, reducing airframe and systems mass, improving maintainability, and optimizing operating profiles. Attention was also given to instrument procedure design training, control of aircraft noise and aircraft engine emissions, international standards for helicopter operations, and the experimental search and rescue satellite-aided tracking system (SARSAT).

The ICAO Council, on December 19, 1985, adopted an amendment to Annex 17 (Aviation Security) of the Convention on International Civil Aviation which would require all contracting states of the Organization to apply more stringent security measures for international flights. The measures would involve tighter controls on baggage, transfer and transit passengers, the denial of access to aircraft by unauthorized personnel, and a ban on contact between screened and unscreened passengers. Each state would be required to implement measures to protect cargo, baggage, mail, and operator's supplies and to establish procedures for inspecting an aircraft likely to be the subject of unlawful interference.

On February 28, 1986, the ICAO Council condemned the action of Israel, two weeks earlier, in intercepting a Libyan civilian airplane in international airspace and forcing it to land in Israel. In its 1986 annual review, the ICAO reported that the incidence of unlawful interference with aircraft had declined although there was "a disturbing continuation" of the recent trend for such incidents to be of a violent nature. According to the report, the ICAO conducted 187 projects in 1986, with spending on technical assistance to developing countries reaching about $52 million.

In June 1987 the Council decided to convene an International Conference on Air Law at Montreal in February 1988 to review a proposed protocol that would make acts of violence at international airports subject to universal jurisdiction and severe penalties.

INTERNATIONAL DEVELOPMENT ASSOCIATION
(IDA)

Established: By Articles of Agreement concluded at Washington, DC, January 26, 1960, effective September 24, 1960. The IDA became a UN Specialized Agency by agreement with the Economic and Social Council (approved by the General Assembly on March 27, 1961).

Purpose: To assist in financing economic development in less-developed member states by providing development credits on special terms, with particular emphasis on projects not attractive to private investors.

Headquarters: Washington, DC, United States.

Membership (136): See Appendix B.

Working Language: English.

Origin and development. The IDA was established in response to an increasing awareness during the latter 1950s that the needs of less-developed states for additional capital resources could not be fully satisfied through existing lending institutions and procedures. This was particularly true of the very poorest states, which urgently needed finance on terms more concessionary than those of the International Bank for Reconstruction and Development (IBRD). Thus the United States proposed in 1958 the creation of an institution with authority to provide credits on special terms in support of approved development projects for which normal financing was not available. Following approval by the Board of Governors of the IBRD, the IDA was established as an affiliate of that institution and was given a mandate to provide development financing, within the limits of its resources, on terms more flexible than those of conventional loans and less burdensome to the balance of payments of recipient states.

The authorized capital of the IDA was initially fixed at $1 billion, of which the United States contributed $320 million. Members of the institution were divided by the IDA Articles of Agreement into two groups, in accordance with their economic status and the nature of their contributions to the institution's resources. Part I (high-income) states pay their entire subscription in convertible currencies, all of which may be used for IDA credits; Part II (low-income) states pay only 10 percent of their subscriptions in convertible currencies and the remainder in their own currencies. Part I countries account for about 96 percent of total subscriptions and supplementary resources (special voluntary contributions and transfers from IBRD net earnings). As of June 30, 1987, leading Part I contributors were the United States, with $11.9 billion in subscriptions and contributions (18.4 percent of voting power under the IDA's weighted system); Japan, $7.5 billion (8.8); Federal Republic of Germany, $4.8 billion (7.1); United Kingdom, $3.7 billion (6.3); France, $2.4 billion (3.8); Canada, $1.8 billion (3.3); Netherlands, $1.3 billion (2.0); Italy, $1.3 billion (2.6); Sweden, $1.1 billion (2.2); and Australia, $735 million (1.4). Leading Part II contributors were Saudi Arabia,

$1.2 billion (2.9); Spain, $118 million (1.3); Brazil, $65 million (1.7); India, $53 million (3.2); Argentina, $49 million (1.5); and China, $39 million (1.9).

Significant increases in the IDA's lending capital were agreed upon in 1964, 1968, 1972, 1977, and 1979. The sixth replenishment (IDA-VI), agreed to in January 1980, was to provide for legal commitments of $12 billion for the three-year period beginning July 1, 1981. However, with formal approval requiring adherence by members representing 80 percent of the new subscriptions, the replenishment was delayed due to inaction by the United States, which was to provide 27 percent of the increase. Although the replenishment was finally authorized in August, a decision of the US Congress to divide the US share into four contributions during 1981–1983 caused deep concern at the World Bank group annual meeting in September, since it threatened loan credits already approved by the IDA in advance of the increase. The seventh replenishment (for 1984–1987) was also adversely affected by US action, only $9 billion of a target of $16 billion becoming available after Washington had decided to cut its annual contributions by 20 percent.

Structure. As an affiliate of the IBRD, the IDA has no separate institutions; its directors, officers, and staff are those of the IBRD.

Activities. The IDA is the single largest multilateral source of concessional assistance for low income countries. Although current criteria permit lending to any country whose 1986 per capita income was $835 or less, most IDA commitments (96 percent in 1984–1986) are made to countries with annual per capita incomes of less than $400. Under conditions revised as part of the IDA's eighth replenishment (see below), credits are extended for terms of 40 years for least developed countries and 35 years for other countries. Credits are free of interest but there is a 0.75 percent annual service charge on disbursed credits (a 0.50 percent "commitment fee" on undisbursed credits was eliminated effective July 1, 1988). All credits carry a ten-year grace period with complete repayment of principal due over the remaining 30 or 25 years of the loans.

The vast majority of IDA credits have been provided for projects to improve physical infrastructure: road and rail systems, electrical generation and transmission facilities, irrigation and flood-control installations, educational facilities, telephone exchanges and transmission lines, and industrial plants. Increasingly, however, loans have been extended for rural development projects designed specifically to raise the productivity of the rural-dwelling poor. These credits cut across sectoral lines and also include provision for feeder roads, rural schools, and health clinics.

After lengthy neogtiations in 1986 an agreement (formally approved by the Board of Governors in June 1987) was reached on an eighth replenishment: a basic replenishment of $11.5 billion was established with an additional $.9 billion promised in supplemental contributions from a number of countries, led by Japan ($450 million) and the Netherlands ($126 million). About 45–50 percent of the additional resources were to be allocated to countries in Sub-Saharan Africa, 30 percent to China and India, and the rest to other Third World recipients. Donors earmarked $3–3.5 billion for support of structural adjustment policies, particularly in Africa. In addition, the Governors shortened repayment schedules somewhat to promote earlier and more extensive reflow of credits back through the Association.

For the fiscal year July 1, 1986, to June 30, 1987, the IDA approved $3.5 billion in credits with cumulative disbursements since its establishment reaching $28.9 billion.

INTERNATIONAL FINANCE CORPORATION
(IFC)

Established: By Articles of Agreement concluded at Washington, DC, May 25, 1955, effective July 20, 1956. The IFC became a UN Specialized Agency by agreement with the Economic and Social Council (approved by the General Assembly on February 20, 1957).

Purpose: To further economic development by encouraging the growth of productive private enterprise in member states, particularly the less-developed areas. Its investment is usually in private or partially governmental enterprises.

Headquarters: Washington, DC, United States.

Membership (133): See Appendix B.

Working Language: English.

Origin and development. The International Finance Corporation was established in 1956 to promote the growth of productive private enterprise in less-developed states. A suggestion that an international agency might be formed to extend loans to private enterprises without government guarantees and to undertake equity investments in participation with other investors was made in 1951 by the US International Development Advisory Board. That summer the UN Economic and Social Council requested that the International Bank for Reconstruction and Development (IBRD) investigate the possibility of creating such an agency, and a staff report was submitted to the UN secretary general in April 1952. The General Assembly in late 1954 requested the IBRD to draw up a charter, and the following April the Bank formally submitted a draft for consideration. The IFC came into being on July 20, 1956, when the Articles of Agreement had been accepted by 31 governments representing a sufficient percentage of total capital subscriptions.

Structure. As an affiliate of the IBRD, the IFC shares the same institutional structure. The president of the IBRD is also president of the IFC, and those governors and executive directors of the IBRD whose states belong to the IFC hold identical positions in the latter institution. The Corporation has its own operating and legal staff but draws on the Bank for administrative and other services. Daily operations are directed by an executive vice president.

As is true of the IBRD and the IDA, the IFC employs a weighted voting system based on country subscriptions, but with less-developed states holding a disproportionate share of voting power.

Activities. The IFC concentrates its efforts in five principal areas: investments, promotion, a capital markets program, syndications, and technical assistance. It conducts its own investment program, investigates the soundness of proposed projects in order to furnish expert advice to potential investors, and generally seeks to promote conditions conducive to the flow of private investment into development tasks. Investments, in the form of share subscriptions and long-term loans, are made in projects of economic priority to less-developed member states where sufficient private capital is not available on reasonable terms and when the projects offer reasonable prospects of adequate returns. The IFC also carries out standby and underwriting arrangements, and under a policy adopted in July 1968 may give support in the preinvestment stage of potential projects by helping to pay for feasibility studies and for coordinating industrial, technical, and financial components, including the search for business sponsors. In addition, the IFC may join other investment groups interested in backing pilot or promotional companies, which then carry out the necessary studies and negotiations needed to implement the projects. The Corporation neither seeks nor accepts government guarantees in its operations.

Supported by nine increases in its equity capital, the IFC has continued to expand the volume of its investment activities in real terms and to reorient its program by increasing its emphasis on the least-developed regions and lower-income countries, expanding operations into a greater number of member countries, and broadening the sector composition of its investments, especially into natural resource development, agribusiness, and financial operations.

On June 21, 1984, the Board of Directors approved a resolution to increase the IFC's capital by $650 million. This action was followed by an agreement for an additional $750 million increase in capital. The extra money was needed to support investments of $8.1 billion for developing countries in their new five-year program. The new program included responses to high-priority private sector development needs, assistance in corporate restructuring, creation of a bonding facility for construction firms operating internationally, and establishment of a secondary mortgage-market institution.

In late 1985, the IFC announced the creation of a special mutual fund, the Emerging Markets Growth Fund; its purpose is to invest in securities of companies listed on Third World stock exchanges, with the intention of accelerating capital investment. The Fund commenced operations in early 1986 with a capital base of $50 million for investment in developing countries with relatively open securities markets. Other recent initiatives include the Africa Project Development Facility (APDF), launched in May 1986 in conjunction with the UN Development Program and the African Development Bank to assist African entrepreneurs in project preparations; the Guaranteed Recovery of Investment Principal (GRIP) program, designed to give investors guaranteed protection of their principle in equity investments made through the IFC in developing countries; and the Foreign Investment Advisory Service, established to provide investment counsel to developing countries.

During the fiscal year July 1, 1986, through June 30,

1987, the IFC approved $790 million in investments for 92 business ventures. The period marked the third year of a five-year program devoted to extensive expansion of IFC activity, officials noting that while approvals were meeting program objectives, actual disbursements were lagging significantly.

INTERNATIONAL FUND FOR AGRICULTURAL DEVELOPMENT
(IFAD)

Established: By the World Food Conference held at Rome, Italy, in November 1974. IFAD became a UN Specialized Agency by an April 1977 decision of the Committee on Negotiations with Intergovernmental Agencies of the Economic and Social Council (approved by the General Assembly on December 29, 1977).

Purpose: To channel investment funds to the developing countries to help increase their financial commitments to food production, storage, and distribution, and to nutritional and agricultural research.

Headquarters: Rome, Italy.

Principal Organs: Governing Council (all members), Executive Board (18 members), Secretariat.

President: Idriss Jazairy (Algeria).

Membership (142): See Appendix B.

Origin and development. The creation of the International Fund for Agricultural Development is regarded as one of the most significant recommendations approved by the November 1974 World Food Conference, which set a 1980 target for agricultural development of $5 billion, to be disbursed either directly or indirectly through the Fund. At the Seventh Special Session of the General Assembly, held in September 1975, it was agreed that the Fund should have an initial target of 1 billion special drawing rights (SDRs), or about $1.25 billion. Until that sum was pledged and the IFAD agreement was ratified by 36 states — including six developed, six oil-producing, and 24 other developing states — the Fund took the form of a Preparatory Commission. Meeting periodically from September 1976 through July 1977, the Commission worked out detailed arrangements for the Governing Council's first meeting and for the formal commencement of the Fund's activities. The Council first convened on December 13, 1977, and IFAD approved its first projects in April 1978.

Structure. The Governing Council, which normally meets annually but can convene special sessions, is the Fund's policymaking organ, with each member state having one representative. The Council may delegate certain of its powers to the 18-member Executive Board, composed of delegates from six developed (Category I), six oil-producing (Category II), and six non-oil developing (Category III) states. Decisions of the Council are made on the basis of a weighted voting system under which donor countries (those in the first two categories) cast votes based primarily on the size of their contributions, while recipient states share equally in Category III voting power. The Fund also has a small Secretariat and six operational bodies: the Financial Services Division, Personal Services Division, Project Management Department, Economic and Planning Department, General Affairs Department, and Legal Services Division.

Activities. The Fund is the first international institution established exclusively to provide multilateral resources for agricultural development of rural populations. IFAD-supported projects combine three interrelated objectives: raising food production, particularly on small farms; providing employment and additional income for poor and landless farmers; and reducing malnutrition by improving food distribution systems and enhancing cultivation of the kinds of crops the poorest populations normally consume.

The bulk of the Fund's resources are made available in the form of highly concessional loans repayable over 50 years (including a 10-year grace period), with a 1 percent service charge. Those loans are extended only for projects in countries where the 1976 per capita income was under $300. For projects in relatively more developed countries, loans are extended on ordinary terms, at 8 percent for 15–18 years with a three-year grace period, or on intermediate terms, at 4 percent for 20 years with a five-year grace period. Many projects receiving IFAD assistance have been cofinanced with the Asian Development Bank, the African Development Bank, the Inter-American Development Bank, the World Bank, the UN Development Programme, and other international funding sources. The countries in which the projects are located also often contribute financially.

In 1981 the Fund approved its first replenishment in the amount of $1.07 billion, $620 million from members of the Organization for Economic Cooperation and Development (OECD) and $450 million from members of the Organization of Petroleum Exporting Countries (OPEC). However, falling oil prices, the general slowdown in the world economy, and the issue of OECD/OPEC "burden sharing" within the Fund led to contentious negotiations on a second replenishment. Agreement was finally reached on a 1985–1987 replenishment of nearly $466 million, $273 million from OECD members, $184 million from OPEC countries, and $28 million from non-oil developing countries.

Although about $166 million was still in arrears on second replenishment contributions, negotiations began at the 11th annual Council meeting, held at Rome on January 26–29, 1988, on a third replenishment that would permit significantly accelerated lending. The Council members launched the talks after hearing from a high-level committee, established in 1986 to study IFAD resources and lending arrangements, that IFAD members and the rest of the international community remained "strongly committed" to the Fund. However, the committee also proposed policy changes designed to improve the IFAD's long-term financial situation. During the meeting, the Council was informed that pledges to the Special Program for Sub-Saharan African Countries Affected by Drought and Desertification, established in 1986 to provide additional help for small farmers in 24 countries, had surpassed its $300 million target.

A review of the Fund's first decade of activity reported that the IFAD had extended about $2.3 billion in loans for 221 projects in 89 countries. The projects attracted an additional $3.4 billion in cofinancing from other institutions and $4.2 billion from the governments of countries in which the projects were located.

The ten-year report noted that the IFAD had moved away from costly infrastructure, large-scale irrigation, and massive resettlement schemes to smaller and simpler projects emphasizing low-cost technologies. Additional emphasis was to be given to the Fund's highly successful program of small loans to poor persons in rural areas. Although other institutions had labeled such persons as uncreditworthy, the Fund reported that it had achieved a repayment level well over 90 percent, thanks in part to the formation by the loan recipients of village groups to oversee "banking" operations. The report concluded that priorities for the next decade should include the greater involvement of women in Fund loans, attention to environmental protection, the development of livestock and fisheries projects, and the extension of applied research and training.

INTERNATIONAL LABOUR ORGANISATION
(ILO)

Established: By constitution adopted April 11, 1919; instrument of amendment signed at Montreal, Canada, October 9, 1946, effective April 20, 1948. The ILO became a UN Specialized Agency by agreement with the Economic and Social Council (approved by the General Assembly on December 14, 1946).

Purpose: To promote international action aimed at achieving full employment, the raising of living standards, and improvement in the conditions of labor.

Headquarters: Geneva, Switzerland.

Principal Organs: International Labour Conference (all members), Governing Body (28 governmental, 14 employer, and 14 employee representatives), International Institute for Labour Studies, International Centre for Advanced Technical and Vocational Training, International Labour Office (Director General and staff).

Director General: Francis Blanchard (France).

Membership (150): See Appendix B.

Official Languages: English, French.

Origin and development. The International Labour Organisation's original constitution, drafted by a commission representing employers, employees, and governments, formed an integral part of the 1919 peace treaties and established the Organisation as an autonomous intergov-

ernmental agency associated with the League of Nations. The ILO's tasks were significantly expanded by the 1944 International Labour Conference at Philadelphia, which declared the right of all human beings "to pursue their material well-being and their spiritual development in conditions of dignity, of economic security and equal opportunity". The declaration was subsequently appended to the ILO's revised constitution, which took effect June 28, 1948.

In 1946 the ILO became the first Specialized Agency associated with the United Nations. Since then, the Organisation's considerable growth (the regular budget has risen from $4.5 million in 1948 to $325 million for the 1988–1989 biennium) has been accompanied by numerous changes in policy and geographical representation. While improved working and living conditions and the promotion of full employment remain central aims, the ILO also deals with such matters as migrant workers, multinational corporations, the working environment, and the social consequences of monetary instability. Moreover, the initial dominance of industrial countries with market economies has given way to a more varied membership, with important parts now played by the centrally planned economies of Eastern Europe, many newly independent states, and the Third World in general.

In 1970 one of the first official acts of Director General Wilfred Jenks of the United Kingdom was to appoint a Soviet assistant director general. The hostile reaction of the American Federation of Labor–Congress of Industrial Organizations (AFL-CIO) led the US Congress to suspend temporarily payment of US contributions to the Organisation. The ire of the Congress and the AFL-CIO was again aroused in 1975 when the ILO granted observer status to the Palestine Liberation Organization (PLO). Finally, on November 5, 1975, the United States filed its intention to withdraw from the ILO, objecting to a growing governmental domination of workers' and employers' groups, what it considered the ILO's "appallingly selective concern" for human rights, and other philosophical differences. On November 1, 1977, US President Carter formally announced his country's withdrawal, effective November 5. Shortly thereafter, however, US Secretary of Labor F. Ray Marshall strongly hinted that Washington might reconsider. Thus, the Carter administration carefully watched events at subsequent annual Conferences. The June 1979 Conference was marked by the absence of any anti-Israel motions. Moreover, the ILO responded to the complaints of Amnesty International by asking the Soviet government if it were possible for free trade unions to exist in the USSR. Such events led Carter to announce in February 1980 that the United States would return to the Organisation.

Structure. The ILO is unique among international organizations in that it is based on a "tripartite" system of representation that includes not only governments but employer and employee groups as well.

The International Labour Conference, which meets annually, is the ILO's principal political organ; all member states are represented. Each national delegation to the Conference consists of two governmental delegates, one employer delegate, and one employee delegate. Each delegate has one vote, and split votes within a delegation are common. Conference duties include approving the ILO budget, electing the Governing Body, and setting labor standards through the adoption of conventions. Most important items require a two-thirds affirmative vote.

The Governing Body normally meets three or four times a year. Of the 28 governmental delegates, 10 represent the 11 "states of chief industrial importance"; the other 18 are elected for three-year terms by the governmental representatives in the Conference. The 14 employer and 14 employee representatives are similarly elected by their respective groups. (See Activities, below, for proposed restructuring of the Governing Body.) The Governing Body reviews the budget before its submission to the Conference, supervises the work of the International Labour Office, appoints and reviews the work of the various industrial committees, and appoints the director general.

The International Labour Office, headed by the director general, is the secretariat of the ILO. Its responsibilities include preparing documentation for the numerous meetings of ILO bodies, compiling and publishing information on social and economic questions, conducting special studies ordered by the Conference or the Governing Body, and providing advice and assistance, on request, to governments and to employer and employee groups.

Activities. The ILO is charged by its constitution with advancing programs to achieve the following: full employment and higher standards of living; the employment of workers in occupations in which they can use the fullest measure of their skill and make the greatest contribution to the common well-being; the establishment of facilities for training and the transfer of labor; policies (in regard to wages, hours, and other conditions of work) calculated to ensure a just share of the fruits of progress to all; the effective recognition of the right of collective bargaining; the extension of social-security benefits to all in need of such protection; the availability of comprehensive medical care; the provision of adequate nutrition, housing, and facilities for recreation and culture; and the assurance of equality of educational and vocational opportunity. In addition, the ILO has established an International Programme for the Improvement of Working Conditions and Environment — PIACT (its French acronym). PIACT activities include standard-setting, studies, tripartite meetings, and clearinghouse and operational functions.

The ILO's chief instruments for achieving its constitutional mandates are the adoption of conventions and recommendations. Conventions are legal instruments open for ratification by governments; while not bound to ratify a convention adopted by the Conference, member states are obligated to bring it to the attention of their national legislators and also to report periodically to the ILO on relevant aspects of their own labor law and practice. Typical subjects covered by ILO conventions include Hours of Work, Industry (1919); Underground Work, Women (1935); Shipowners' Liability, Sick and Injured Seamen (1936); Abolition of Forced Labor (1957); and Indigenous and Tribal Populations (1957). Recommendations differ from conventions in that the former only suggest guidelines and therefore do not require ratification by the member states. In both instances, however, governments are subject to a supervisory procedure — the estab-

lishment of a commission of inquiry — that involves an objective evaluation by independent experts and an examination of cases by the ILO's tripartite bodies to ensure that the conventions and recommendations are being applied. There is also a widely-used special procedure whereby the Governing Body investigates alleged violations by governments of trade-unionists' right to "freedom of association".

Many ILO conventions and recommendations are based on research conducted at the International Centre for Advanced Technical and Vocational Training, established by the ILO in 1965 at Turin, Italy. The Centre provides residential training programs to those in charge of technical and vocational institutions, most of which are located in developing countries.

In 1969 the International Labour Conference launched the ILO's World Employment Programme to help national and international efforts to provide jobs for the world's rapidly expanding population. Activity in this area was highlighted by the Tripartite World Conference on Employment, Income Distribution, and Social Progress and the International Division of Labour, held at ILO headquarters June 4–17, 1976. The Conference produced a declaration of principles and a program of action aimed at creating tens of thousands of new jobs, largely in less-developed countries, by the year 2000. An ILO report, released in June 1984, predicted that at least 1 billion new jobs will have to be created world wide by then to meet current and future demands for employment.

At its 1984 annual session the Conference accepted a report from a special commission of inquiry which concluded that Poland had violated ILO conventions regarding union and workers' rights in suppressing the Solidarity labor movement. Soviet bloc countries protested the report and Warsaw announced its decision (unimplemented and apparently effectively withdrawn as of mid-1988) to leave the Organisation. Socialist members continued their criticism at the 1985 Conference, asserting that ILO structures and procedures were biased against socialist and developing countries.

The discord diminished following the 1986 Conference's decision to double the Governing Body's membership to 112 (56 governmental, 28 employer, and 28 employee representatives) and to abolish the 10 nonelective government seats reserved for states of "chief industrialized importance". Other parts of the restructuring called for the creation of a tripartite Committee of Thirteen to assess the validity of resolutions involving the condemnation of member states and for the Conference to be given the right to approve the Governing Body's appointment of the director general. The changes will be implemented upon their ratification of two-thirds of the members, including at least five states of chief industrial importance.

In other 1986 activity the Conference adopted new standards to protect workers from the hazards of asbestos, endorsed a safety and health code for coal miners, and reaffirmed its strong opposition to apartheid policies in South Africa. The ILO also issued reports throughout the year on child and youth labor, the adverse effects on employment of the Third World's heavy external debt, the need for further integration of workers in managerial decisionmaking, the growing role of "indirect benefits" in collective bargaining agreements, and the desirability of establishing a link between disarmament and development.

At its 73rd annual session, held at Geneva on June 3–24, 1987, the Conference approved draft texts on two new sets of international standards. The first will extend the protection given by national employment policies to the involuntarily unemployed and the second will provide safety and health regulations for the construction industry. The Conference also endorsed the creation of a "central mechanism" to monitor the observance of ILO standards, despite disagreement as to how it might function.

Among the issues covered by 1987 ILO reports were high unemployment in the shipping industry, the growing influence on employment of computers and other technological devices, drug and alcohol abuse among workers, and the need to protect the work of performing artists from electronic "piracy". Also in 1987 the ILO published guidelines to protect workers from potential dangers from radiation exposure.

Late in the year the ILO published the third and final volume of its *World Labor Report*—an exhaustive survey, supported by extensive statistical analysis, of the current employment situation and pending world labor issues. The new volume described conditions as "generally dark" with real-work incomes having fallen for several decades in many parts of the world. In particular, the report decried the "growing impoverishment of the Third World" where an estimated 90 million people are unemployed and 300 million underemployed.

INTERNATIONAL MARITIME ORGANIZATION
(IMO)

Established: March 17, 1958, as the Inter-Governmental Maritime Consultative Organization (IMCO) on the basis of a convention opened for signature on March 6, 1948. IMCO became a UN Specialized Agency as authorized by a General Assembly resolution of November 18, 1948, with the present designation being assumed on May 22, 1982, upon entry into force of amendments to the IMCO convention.

Purpose: To facilitate cooperation among governments "in the field of governmental regulation and practices relating to technical matters of all kinds affecting shipping engaged in international trade; to encourage the general adoption of the highest practicable standards in matters concerning maritime safety, efficiency of navigation and the prevention and control of marine pollution from ships; and to deal with legal matters" related to its purposes.

Headquarters: London, United Kingdom.

Principal Organs: Assembly (all members), Council (32 members), Facilitation Committee (all members), Legal Committee (all members), Maritime Safety Committee (all members), Marine Environment Protection Committee (all members), Committee on Technical Cooperation (all members), Secretariat.

Secretary General: Chandrika Prasad Srivastava (India).

Membership (131, plus 1 Associate Member): See Appendix B.

Official Languages: English, French, Russian, Spanish.

Working Languages: English, French, Spanish.

Origin and development. Preparations for the establishment of the Inter-Governmental Maritime Consultative Organization were initiated shortly after World War II but were not completed for well over a decade. Meeting at Washington, DC, in 1946 at the request of the UN Economic and Social Council, representatives of a group of maritime states prepared a draft convention that was further elaborated at a UN Maritime Conference held at Geneva, Switzerland, in early 1948. Despite the strictly limited objectives set forth in the convention, the pace of ratification was slow, primarily because some signatory states were apprehensive about possible international interference in their shipping policies. Canada accepted the convention in 1948 and the US Senate approved it in 1950, but the necessary 21 ratifications were not completed until Japan deposited its ratification on March 17, 1958. Additional difficulties developed at the first IMCO Assembly, held at London, England, in January 1959, over claims by Panama and Liberia that, as "major shipowning nations", they were eligible for election to the Maritime Safety Committee. An affirmative ruling by the International Court of Justice paved the way for a resolution of the issue at the second IMCO Assembly, held in April 1961.

The thrust of IMCO activities during its first decade involved maritime safety, particularly in regard to routing schemes. Adherence was on a voluntary basis until July 1977, when a Convention on the International Regulations for Preventing Collisions at Sea (1972) went into force. In 1979 the (1974) International Convention on the Safety of Life at Sea (SOLAS), specifying minimum safety standards for ship construction, equipment, and operation, received the final ratification needed to bring it into force, effective May 25, 1980. In terms of individual safety, the first International Convention on Maritime Search and Rescue was adopted on April 27, 1979, although not coming into effect until June 22, 1985; it requires each contracting government "to ensure that any necessary arrangements are made for coast watching and for the rescue of persons in distress round its coasts."

Problems of maritime pollution, highlighted by the *Torrey Canyon* disaster of March 1967, were the subject of a November 1968 special session of the Assembly, which led to the establishment of a Legal Committee and the scheduling of the first of several major conferences on marine pollution. On January 20, 1978, sufficient ratifications were finally received for the 1969 amendments to the International Convention for the Prevention of Pollution of the Sea by Oil (1954) to come into force, while the International Convention on Civil Liability for Oil Pollution Damage (1969) and the International Convention on the Establishment of an International Fund for Compensation for Oil Pollution Damage (1971) entered into force in 1975 and

1978, respectively. In January 1986, amendments formulated in 1984 to the International Convention for the Prevention of Pollution from Ships (1973), as modified by a 1978 Protocol, become binding. This treaty is regarded as the most important in the area of maritime pollution as it is concerned with both accidents and spills resulting from normal tanker operations.

Of importance in the area of maritime travel and transport was the entry into force on July 16, 1979, of a convention establishing the International Maritime Satellite Organization (Inmarsat, see separate entry). The new body is responsible for operating a worldwide communications system for merchant shipping based on space technology and the use of satellites.

By 1974 the tasks of the Organization had so expanded beyond those originally envisioned that the Assembly proposed a number of amendments to the original IMCO convention (see below), including a new statement of purpose and a new name, the International Maritime Organization (IMO). Bolivia joined the IMO in 1987, raising its membership to 131.

Structure. The Assembly, in which all member states are represented and have an equal vote, is the principal policy-making body of the Organization. Meeting in regular session every two years (occasional extraordinary sessions are also held), the Assembly decides upon the work program of IMO, approves the budget, elects the members of the Council, and approves the appointment of the secretary general. The Council normally meets twice a year and is responsible, between sessions of the Assembly, for performing all IMO functions except those under the purview of the Maritime Safety Committee, which meets at least once a year. Amendments to the original convention have increased the Council's membership to 32, comprising three groups: eight members representing "states with the largest interest in providing international shipping services", eight having "the largest interest in seaborne trade", and 16 elected from other countries with "a special interest in maritime transport and navigation and whose election . . . will ensure the representation of all major geographic areas of the world".

The Organization's technical work is largely carried out by a number of subcommittees of the Maritime Safety Committee, membership in which has been open to all IMO members since 1978. The subcommittees deal with such matters as navigation, radiocommunications, life-saving appliances, training, search and rescue, ship design and equipment, fire protection, stability and load lines, fishing vessels, containers and cargoes, dangerous goods, and bulk chemicals.

Because of both the importance of pollution problems and the dissatisfaction of some member states (particularly those that were not major maritime powers) with the restrictions on Council membership, the Maritime Environment Protection Committee, which is not subordinate to the Council, was established in late 1973.

The IMO also conducts a Technical Cooperation Program which provides training and advisory services to help developing countries establish and operate their maritime programs in conformity with international standards. The program is supported by voluntary funding amounting to

$8–10 million annually, a portion of which goes to the World Maritime University, established by the IMO at Malmo, Sweden, in 1983 to train high-level administrative and technical personnel.

A new procedure was introduced in 1986 to facilitate the adoption of most amendments to conventions. Originally positive action by two-thirds of the Contracting Parties to a convention was required. Under the new "tacit acceptance" procedure, amendments are deemed to be accepted if less than a third take negative action for a period generally set at two years (in no case less than one), assuming that rejections are not forthcoming from Parties whose combined fleets represent 50 percent of the world's gross tonnage of merchant ships.

Activities. The IMO's programs fall under five major rubrics: maritime safety, technical training and assistance, marine pollution, facilitation of maritime travel and transport, and legal efforts to establish an international framework of maritime cooperation. In most of these areas, IMO activity is primarily devoted to extensive negotiation, review, and revision of highly technical conventions, recommendations, and guidelines.

Recent amendments to existing conventions have reduced unnecessary paperwork and other delays to ships, passengers, crews, and cargoes; ordered expanded use on ships and offshore platforms of advanced lifesaving devices, such as enclosed lifeboats and individual immersion suits; and established new regulations for the discharge of noxious liquid chemical wastes at sea and at unloading sites. Also, in conjunction with the intensive UN-wide anti-drug campaign, the IMO has published guidelines to combat the use of international shipping to smuggle drugs. The Organization is also working on a global maritime distress and safety system (scheduled for introduction in 1991), regulations for dealing with abandoned offshore oil and gas platforms, and measures to suppress unlawful acts against ships.

At its 15th biennial session, held at London on November 9–20, 1987, the Assembly approved a budget for 1988–1989 of £21.6 million (about $40.4 million at the January 1,1988,exchange rate). Among other resolutions approved by the Assembly was one directing that measures be developed to improve the safety of "roll-on, roll-off" vehicle ferries in light of the *Herald of Free Enterprise* disaster in which 188 persons died off the coast of Belgium the previous March.

INTERNATIONAL MONETARY FUND
(IMF)

Established: By Articles of Agreement signed at Bretton Woods, New Hampshire, July 22, 1944, effective December 27, 1945; formal operations began March 1, 1947. The IMF became a UN Specialized Agency by agreement with the Economic and Social Council (approved by the General Assembly on November 15, 1947).

Purpose: "To promote international monetary cooperation through a permanent institution which provides the machinery for consultation and collaboration on international monetary problems. To facilitate the expansion and balanced growth of international trade, and to contribute thereby to the promotion and maintenance of high levels of employment and real income and to the development of the productive resources of all members as primary objectives of economic policy. To promote exchange stability, to maintain orderly exchange arrangements among members, and to avoid competitive depreciation. To assist in the establishment of a multilateral system of payments in respect of current transactions between members and in elimination of foreign exchange restrictions which hamper the growth of world trade. To give confidence to members by making the Fund's resources temporarily available to them under adequate safeguards, thus providing them with the opportunity to correct maladjustments in their balance of payments without resorting to measures destructive of national or international prosperity . . . [and] to shorten the duration and lessen the degree of disequilibrium in the international balance of payments of members."

Headquarters: Washington, DC, United States.

Principal Organs: Board of Governors (all members), Board of Executive Directors (22 members), Interim Committee on the International Monetary System (22 members), Managing Director and Staff.

Managing Director: Michel Camdessus (France).

Membership (151): See Appendix B.

   Origin and development. The International Monetary Fund is one of the two key institutions that emerged from the United Nations Monetary and Financial Conference at Bretton Woods, New Hampshire, July 1–22, 1944: the International Bank for Reconstruction and Development (IBRD) was established to mobilize and invest available capital resources for the reconstruction of war-damaged areas and the promotion of general economic development where private capital was lacking; the IMF was created with the complementary objectives of safeguarding international financial and monetary stability and of providing financial backing for the revival and expansion of international trade.

   Following ratification by the required 28 states, the Articles of Agreement of the Bank and Fund went into effect December 27, 1945, and formal IMF operations commenced March 1, 1947, under the guidance of Managing Director Camille Gutt (Belgium). While the membership of the IMF has greatly expanded, most Communist countries, including the Soviet Union, remain nonmembers. However, the pressures of external debt to the West mounted rapidly for some participants in the Soviet-bloc Council for Mutual Economic Assistance (CMEA) in the late 1970s, and in 1981 Hungary and Poland, both CMEA members, applied for IMF membership (Romania theretofore being the only East European participant). Hungary became a member in 1982, but Poland's admission was deferred pending resolution of questions regarding its existing debt and international payments obligations. In December

1984, the United States, with the largest proportion of voting power, lifted all objections concerning Poland, thus opening the way for its entry in June 1986.

   The development of the IMF has occurred in four phases, the first running from Bretton Woods until about 1957. Under the managing directorships of Camille Gutt and Ivor Rooth (Sweden), the Fund was seldom in the news and its activity, in the form of "drawings" or borrowings, was light. During much of this period the US Marshall Plan was providing the needed balance-of-payments support to the states of Europe because the IMF lacked the capital to perform such a massive task.

   At the end of 1956, when Per Jacobsson (Sweden) was named managing director, the Fund entered a more active phase, the outstanding example being large drawings by the United Kingdom, partly as a result of the 1956–1957 Suez crisis. While Jacobsson was a major participant in discussions concerning reform of the international monetary system, the IMF was not the primary institutional forum for these discussions.

   The third phase of development can be dated from Jacobsson's death in 1963. His successor, Pierre-Paul Schweitzer (France), managed the IMF during a period in which its activities were directed increasingly toward the needs of developing states. Also, by the mid-1960s the need for reform of the international monetary system had become more evident. Thus, beginning in 1965, the IMF participated in discussions looking toward the creation of additional "international liquidity" to supplement existing resources for financing trade. Discussion between the Group of Ten (see separate entry) and the Fund's executive directors led in 1967 to the development of a plan for creating new international reserves through the establishment of special drawing rights (SDRs) over and above the drawing rights already available to Fund members. Following approval in principle by the IMF Board of Governors in September 1967, an amendment to the Articles of Agreement was submitted by the Board of Executive Directors and approved by the Board of Governors in May 1968, preparatory to consideration by the member governments. On July 28, 1969, with three-fifths of the IMF members (with four-fifths of the voting power) having accepted it, the amendment was added to the Articles. In general, SDRs may be allocated to Fund members proportionate to their Fund quotas, subject to restrictions relating to the allocation and use of such rights. Also in 1969, the IMF established a special facility to aid buffer stock financing.

   The US suspension of the convertibility of the dollar into gold in August 1971 compounded the previous need for reform. By 1972 many states were "floating" their currencies and thus fundamentally violating the rules of the Fund, which were based on a system of fixed exchange rates normally pegged to the US gold price. That year, the United States decided not to support Schweitzer's reelection bid, largely because of his outspoken criticism of Washington's failure to "set its own economic house in order" and control its balance-of-payments deficits.

   When H. Johannes Witteveen (Netherlands) took over as managing director in 1973, his chief task was to continue reform of the international monetary system while enhancing the role of the IMF. Consequently, Witteveen proposed creation of an IMF oil facility that was established in June 1974 and served, in effect, as a separate borrowing window through which members could cover that portion of their balance-of-payments deficits attributable to higher imported oil prices. This facility provided 55 members with SDR 802 million until its termination in 1976. Three months later the Fund set up an "extended facility" to aid further those members with payments problems attributable to structural difficulties in their economies. In addition, as part of the accords reached at the fifth session of the Interim Committee, which met in Jamaica in January 1976, one-sixth of the Fund's gold was auctioned for the benefit of less-developed countries. The sales, which began in June 1976, continued until April 1980, with profits of $1.3 billion transferred directly to 104 countries and with another $3.3 billion placed in a Trust Fund to assist poorer countries. The final loan disbursement from the Fund upon the latter's discontinuance in March 1981 yielded a cumulative total of SDR 2.9 billion committed to 55 members. Trust Fund repayments have been used to support other IMF assistance programs.

Another plateau was reached when, at the end of April 1976, the Board of Governors approved its most comprehensive package of monetary reforms since the IMF's establishment. Taking the form of a second amendment to the Articles of Agreement, the reforms entered into force April 1, 1978. Their effect was to legalize the system of "floating" exchange arrangements, end the existing system of par values based on gold, and impose upon members an obligation to collaborate with the Fund and with each other in order to promote better surveillance of international liquidity. In addition, the requirement that gold be paid into the Fund was lifted, and the Fund's governors were given the authority to decide, by an 85 percent majority, to create a new Council that would be composed of governors, finance ministers, and persons of comparable rank, and would concern itself with the adjustment process and global liquidity.

The fourth phase of development was initiated with the entrance into office on June 17, 1978, of Jacques de Larosière (France). Committed to continuing Witteveen's active role and aided by a massive increase in IMF funds, Larosière addressed the major problems of the Fund's members: burdensome debts for non-oil developing countries, inflation and stagnant economic growth among the developed members, and balance-of-payments disequilibria for virtually all. In order to assist the non-oil-producing Third World countries, the Fund further liberalized its "compensatory facility" (established in 1963) for financing temporary export shortfalls, extended stand-by arrangements through the creation in 1979 of a "supplementary financing facility", and expanded the activities of the Trust Fund to provide additional credits on concessional terms.

To support the drain on its resources, the IMF has relied on frequent quota increases; the most recent, the Eighth General Review of Quotas, came into effect in January 1984 and raised the Fund's capital from SDR 61.1 billion to SDR 90 billion. Faced with growing pressure from the Fund's largest subscriber, the United States, to limit future increases, the IMF has pursued alternative means to augment its liquidity. These include borrowings from the mem-

bers of the Bank for International Settlements and Saudi Arabia and the possibility of issuing IMF bonds on the private market.

Structure. The IMF operates through a Board of Governors, a Board of Executive Directors, an Interim Committee on the International Monetary System, and a managing director and staff. Upon joining the Fund, each country is assigned a quota that determines both the amount of foreign exchange a member may borrow under the rules of the Fund (its "drawing rights") and its approximate voting power on IMF policy matters. As of April 1, 1988, the largest contributor, the United States, had 19.14 percent of the voting power, while the smallest contributors held considerably less than 1 percent each.

The Board of Governors, in which all powers of the Fund are theoretically vested, consists of one governor and one alternate appointed by each member state. In practice, its membership is virtually identical with that of the Board of Governors of the IBRD, and its annual meetings are actually joint sessions (which similarly include the governing boards of the Bank's two affiliated institutions, the International Development Association and the International Finance Corporation). One meeting in three is held away from Washington, DC.

The Board of Executive Directors, which has 22 members and generally meets at least once a week, is responsible for day-to-day operations and exercises powers delegated to it by the Board of Governors. Each of the five members having the largest quotas (currently the United States, the United Kingdom, the Federal Republic of Germany, France, and Japan) appoints a director. Appointment privilege is also extended to each of the two largest lenders to the Fund, providing they are not among the countries with the five largest quotas. Consequently, Saudi Arabia, the largest lender to the Fund, has appointed a director since 1978. The other directors are elected biennially by the remaining IMF members, who are divided into 16 geographic groupings, each of which selects one director. (The People's Republic of China constitutes one of the geographic entities by itself and therefore its "election" of a director, in practical terms, amounts to an appointment.) Each elected director casts as a unit all the votes of the states that elected him.

Pending establishment of a new Council at the ministerial level, an Interim Committee on the International Monetary System was established by a resolution adopted at the 1974 annual meetings. The Committee's 22 members represent the same countries or groups of countries as represented on the Board of Executive Directors. The Committee advises the Board of Governors as to the management and adaptation of the international monetary system and makes recommendations to the Board on how to deal with sudden disturbances that threaten the system.

The managing director, who is appointed by the Board of Executive Directors and serves as its chairman, conducts the ordinary business of the Fund and supervises the staff.

There are several other ministerial-level committees and groups which routinely interact with the Fund, usually in conjunction with joint IMF/World Bank sessions. One is the Development Committee, which was established in 1974 by the IMF and the World Bank to report on the global development process and to make recommendations to promote the transfer of real resources to developing countries. The committee, whose structure mirrors that of the Interim Committee, generally issues extensive communiqués prior to IMF/World Bank meetings.

Regular statements are similarly issued by the Group of Ten, the Group of Seven (for details on both see article on the Group of Ten), and the Group of 24. The latter group, which receives secretariat support from the Fund, represents the interests of the developing countries in negotiations on international monetary matters.

Activities. The IMF's central activity is to assist members in meeting short-term balance-of-payments difficulties by permitting them to draw temporarily upon the Fund's reserves, subject to established limits and conditions with respect to the amount of drawing rights, terms of repayment, etc. Assistance may take the form of "stand-by credits" (credits approved in advance), which may or may not be fully utilized. A member can also arrange to buy the currency of another member from the Fund in exchange for its own.

A second major IMF responsibility has been to supervise the operation of the international exchange-rate system in order to maintain stability among the world currencies and prevent competitive devaluations. In part because stable exchange-rate patterns depend upon economic stability, particularly the containment of inflationary pressures, the Fund since 1952 has regularly consulted with member states about their economic problems, the formulation and implementation of economic stabilization programs, and the preparation of requests for stand-by IMF assistance.

In the area of assistance to less-developed states, the Fund participates in many of the consultative groups and consortia organized by the IBRD. It also conducts a separate program of technical assistance — largely with reference to banking and fiscal problems — through its own staff and outside experts and through a training program organized by the IMF Institute at Washington, DC.

The Fund has recently encountered growing demands from the developing world for reform in its procedures. In particular, a number of states have objected to the imposition of the IMF's so-called "standard package" of conditionality, which often requires, for example, that a country reduce consumer imports, devalue its currency, and tighten domestic money supplies in return for stand-by credit. The issue continues to be a constant center of controversy for the IMF. Non-oil developing countries struggling under massive balance-of-payments deficits have called for greater Fund access but with fewer domestically unpopular restrictive conditions attached. At the same time, industrialized countries, adversely affected by high unemployment, inflation, and economic stagnation, have demanded stricter structural adjustment clauses and have called for increased reliance on the private sector as a source of aid and development capital for all but the poorest of the developing countries. As the extent of the Third World's debt crisis became more apparent in 1983, developed countries also began to exert pressure for a relaxation of some IMF conditions in order to encourage expansion and increase trade to reduce developing countries' deficits.

With the debt crisis worsening, the Board of Governors in October 1985 approved the creation of a Structural Adjustment Facility (SAF) to provide low-income countries with concessional loans in support of national policy changes designed to resolve persistent balance of payments problems. The SAF, funded by SDR 2.7 billion in reflows from the discontinued Trust Fund, was formally established in March 1986, offering ten-year loans with a 0.5 percent interest charge and a 5½-year grace period.

Pressure for further IMF initiatives continued throughout 1986 and 1987 in light of what many observers described as a "wrong-way" flow of resources that often yielded payback obligations to the IMF in excess of funds received in new loans. In addition, many national leaders, particularly in Africa, mounted a challenge to the "rigidity and austerity" of IMF lending conditions which, in the words of one critic, had driven governments "far beyond the limit of social tolerance".

Soon after his appointment as IMF managing director in January 1987, Michel Camdessus called for a complete review of IMF conditionality and a tripling of SAF funding. Following endorsement of the latter at the October 1987 joint IMF/World Bank annual meeting, the Fund announced the establishment of an Enhanced Structural Adjustment Facility funded by SDR 6 billion from 20 countries, led by Japan (SDR 2.8 billion) and West Germany (SDR 1 billion), but not including the United States. The new facility will generally offer the same terms and follow the same procedures as the SAF, which it is expected eventually to absorb.

Additional changes were approved at the Interim Committee meeting in April 1988, including the launching of an "external contingency mechanism" to assist borrowers in case of external "shocks", such as collapsing commodity prices or higher interest rates in world markets. The new mechanism will subsume the "compensatory facility" established in 1963, although the industrialized nations insisted on tightening previous conditions. Most importantly, borrowers facing unforeseen sharp drops in export earnings must henceforth engage in rigorous domestic action to qualify for relief.

Although Camdessus endorsed the proposal from the Group of 24 for a new SDR allocation, the April meeting yielded "insufficient support" for such action. The influence of the Fund's most conservative members, led by the United States, could also be seen in the managing director's assessment that, while study will continue on additional debt initiatives, the basic elements of the Fund's debt strategy "remain valid".

INTERNATIONAL TELECOMMUNICATION UNION
(ITU)

Established: By International Telecommunication Convention signed at Madrid, Spain, December 9, 1932, effective January 1, 1934. The ITU became a UN Specialized Agency by agreement with the Economic and Social Council (approved by the General Assembly on November 15, 1947).

Purpose: To foster international cooperation for the improvement and rational use of telecommunications.

Headquarters: Geneva, Switzerland.

Principal Organs: Plenipotentiary Conference (all members), World and Regional Administrative Conferences (all relevant members), Administrative Council (41 members), International Frequency Registration Board (5 members), Consultative Committees, General Secretariat.

Secretary General: Richard E. Butler (Australia).

Membership (162): See Appendix B.

Official Languages: Chinese, English, French, Russian, Spanish.

Working Languages: English, French, Spanish.

Origin and development. The beginnings of the International Telecommunication Union can be traced to the International Telegraph Union founded at Paris, France, on May 17, 1865. The International Telegraph Convention concluded at that time, together with an International Radiotelegraph Convention concluded at Berlin in 1906, was revised and incorporated into the International Telecommunication Convention signed at Madrid, Spain, on December 9, 1932. Entering into force January 1, 1934, the Madrid Convention established the ITU as the successor to previous agencies in the telecommunications field. A new convention adopted in 1947 took account of subsequent advances in telecommunications and also of the new position being acquired by the ITU as a UN Specialized Agency. Further conventions were adopted at Buenos Aires, Argentina, in 1952; at Geneva, Switzerland, in 1959; at Montreux, Switzerland, in 1965; at Málaga-Torremolinos, Spain, in 1973, and Nairobi, Kenya in 1982. The ITU lacks a permanent constitution; members meet at intervals of five to ten years to decide whether to renew the conventions.

The ITU has excluded South Africa from participation in current activities without, however, barring it from membership.

Structure. The ITU has a complicated structure, which is a reflection of its long history and growth: as international telecommunications has developed, new organs and functions have been grafted onto the preexisting ITU structure. The result is a plethora of conferences, assemblies, organs, and secretariats.

The Plenipotentiary Conference, the principal political organ of the ITU, normally meets about every six years to make any necessary revisions in the conventions, determine general policy, establish the organization's budget, and set a limit on expenditures until the next Conference. Each member has one vote on the Conference, which elects the Administrative Council and the International Frequency Registration Board (IFRB) as well as the secretary general and the deputy secretary general.

The Administrative Council, composed of 41 members, supervises the ITU's administration between sessions of the parent body. Meeting annually at the organization's headquarters, it reviews and approves the annual budget and coordinates the work of the ITU with other international organizations. The IFRB, a corporate body of five independent radio experts from different regions of the world, is supported by its own specialized secretariat. The Board examines and records frequency assignments, handles interference disputes, and otherwise furthers the use of the radio frequency spectrum. The General Secretariat, headed by the secretary general, administers the budget and directs the ITU's sizable research and publishing program.

World and Regional Administrative Conferences meet irregularly and deal largely with technical questions, while the International Radio Consultative Committee and the International Telegraph and Telephone Consultative Committee produce a mass of highly detailed reports and recommendations which, though not binding, carry great weight and are widely observed. Each committee has its own plenary Assembly and a small secretariat headed by a director elected by the respective Assembly.

Activities. The general aims of the ITU are to maintain and extend international cooperation for the improvement and rational use of telecommunications, to promote the development and efficient operation of technical facilities, and to increase the usefulness of telecommunication services. Within this framework the ITU has five main functions: (1) allocating radio frequencies and registering frequency assignments; (2) coordinating efforts to eliminate harmful interference between radio stations of different states; (3) aiding in establishing the lowest possible charges for telecommunication services; (4) undertaking studies, issuing recommendations and opinions, and collecting and publishing information for the benefit of its members; and (5) fostering the creation, development, and improvement of telecommunications in newly independent states. In the last regard, representatives from less-developed member states have demanded a greater voice in ITU policymaking.

The problems and opportunities presented by space telecommunications have become a particular ITU concern. An Extraordinary Administrative Radio Conference on Space Radiocommunications was held in October 1963 to allocate radio frequencies for space communications. On January 1, 1973, a partial revision of international regulations governing radio communication in outer space, approved in 1971 at the ITU-sponsored World Administrative Radio Conference for Space Telecommunications, entered into force.

A highpoint of the ITU's activities in the 1970s was the World Administrative Radio Conference (WARC), which met for ten weeks beginning September 24, 1979. The Conference, the first of its kind in 20 years, was charged with reviewing all uses of the radio frequency spectrum, related technical questions, and regulatory procedures.

During its September 28–November 5, 1982, Plenipotentiary Conference at Nairobi, Kenya, the ITU was faced with a threatened withdrawal of US financial support if it approved a resolution calling for the expulsion of Israel. Members eventually agreed on a milder resolution that criticized Israel for its June invasion of Lebanon.

The first session of the World Administrative Radio Conference (WARC) for the planning of high frequency bands allocated to the broadcasting services was held at Geneva from January 10 to February 11, 1984. The session focused primarily on establishing the technical parameters to be used for purposes of the plan.

In its celebration of World Telecommunication Day on May 17, 1987, the ITU concentrated on the role telecommunications play in the social, cultural, and economic development of nations. ITU Secretary General Richard E. Butler called for measures that would assure by the year 2000 that basic telecommunication facilities would be accessible to every inhabitant of our planet".

The next Plenipotentiary Conference is scheduled for 1989 at Nice, France.

UNITED NATIONS EDUCATIONAL, SCIENTIFIC AND CULTURAL ORGANIZATION (UNESCO)

Established: By constitution adopted at London, England, November 16, 1945, effective November 4, 1946. UNESCO became a UN Specialized Agency by agreement concluded with the Economic and Social Council (approved by the General Assembly on December 14, 1946).

Purpose: To contribute to peace and security by promoting collaboration among states in education, the natural and social sciences, communications, and culture.

Headquarters: Paris, France.

Principal Organs: General Conference (all members), Executive Board (51 members), Secretariat.

Director General: Federico Mayor Zaragoza (Spain).

Membership (158, plus 3 Associate Members): See Appendix B.

Official Languages: Arabic, English, French, Russian, Spanish. All five are also working languages.

Origin and development. UNESCO resulted from the concern of European governments-in-exile with the problem of restoring the educational systems of Nazi-occupied territories after World War II. Meetings of the Allied Ministers of Education began at London, England, in 1942, and proposals for a postwar agency for educational and cultural reconstruction were drafted in April 1944; the constitution of UNESCO, adopted at a special conference at London, November 1–16, 1945, came into force a year later, following ratification by 20 states.

The 1974 General Conference voted to exclude Israel from the European regional grouping of UNESCO, thus making it the only member to belong to no regional grouping. At the same session a motion was passed to withhold UNESCO aid from Israel on the ground that it had persisted "in altering the historical features" of Jerusalem during archaelogical excavations. At the 1976 General Conference, Israel was restored to full membership in the Organization; however, the Conference voted to condemn Israeli educational and cultural policies in occupied Arab territories, charging that the latter amounted to "cultural assimilation". The adoption of this resolution was reported to be part of the price demanded by Arab and Soviet-bloc

member countries for agreeing to Israel's return to the regional group. In November 1978 the Organization again voted to condemn and cut off funds to Israel on the ground that Arab monuments in Jerusalem had been destroyed in the course of further archaelogical activity.

Structure. The General Conference, which usually meets every even-dated year, has final responsibility for approving the budget, electing the Executive Board and (upon recommendation of the Board) the director general, and deciding overall policy. Each member state has one vote; decisions are usually made by a simple majority, although some questions, such as amendments to UNESCO's constitution, require a two-thirds majority.

The Executive Board, composed of 51 members elected by the Conference, is charged with general oversight of the UNESCO program and the budget; the Board examines drafts of both covering the ensuing two-year period and submits them, with its own recommendations, to the General Conference.

The Secretariat, which is headed by a director general selected for a six-year term by the General Conference (on recommendation of the Executive Board), is responsible for executing the program and applying the decisions of those two bodies.

A distinctive feature of UNESCO's constitutional structure is the role of the National Commissions. Comprising representatives of governments and nongovernmental organizations in the member states, the Commissions were initially intended to act as advisory bodies for UNESCO's program. However, they have also come to serve as liaison agents between the Secretariat and the diverse educational, scientific, and cultural activities in the participant states.

Activities. UNESCO's program of activities derives from its broad mandate to "maintain, increase and diffuse knowledge"; to "give fresh impulse to popular education and to the spread of knowledge"; and to "collaborate in the work of advancing the mutual knowledge and understanding of peoples". Within this mandate it (1) holds international conferences, conducts expert studies, and disseminates factual information concerning education, the natural and social sciences, cultural activities, and mass communication; (2) promotes the free flow of ideas by word and image; (3) encourages the exchange of persons and of publications and other informational materials; (4) attempts to ensure conservation and protection of books, works of art, and monuments of historical and scientific significance; and (5) collaborates with member states in developing educational, scientific, and cultural programs.

To promote intellectual cooperation, UNESCO has granted financial assistance to a vast array of international nongovernmental organizations engaged in the transfer of knowledge. It has also attempted to encourage the exchange of ideas by convening major conferences on such topics as life-long education, oceanographic research, problems of youth, eradication of illiteracy, and cultural and scientific policy. To further cooperation in science and technology, UNESCO was instrumental in the establishment of the European Organization for Nuclear Research (see separate entry) in 1954, the International Brain Research Organization (IBRO) in 1960, the International Cell Research Organization in 1962, a program on Man and the Biosphere that currently encompasses some 900 projects in 90 countries, the International Geological Correlation Programme, and the International Hydrological Programme. In addition, UNESCO provides the secretariat for the Intergovernmental Oceanographic Commission.

UNESCO's developmental efforts also focus on modernizing educational facilities, training teachers, combating illiteracy, improving science and social science teaching, and training scientists and engineers. The International Bureau of Education (IBE), which dates from 1925, became part of UNESCO in 1969, while the International Institute for Educational Planning (ITEP) and the Intergovernmental Committee for Physical Education and Sport (ICPES) were established by the Organization in 1963 and 1978, respectively.

UNESCO attempts to promote understanding among different cultures and the transformation of man's moral environment into one based on tolerance and cooperation. In its quest for better understanding, UNESCO has actively engaged in the preservation of museums and monuments; to this end the Organization promoted the adoption of a convention on the protection of cultural and historical sites of universal value and has organized fund-raising campaigns for such projects as preserving buildings in Venice, Italy, and reconstructing cultural and educational institutions in Montenegro, Yugoslavia. An International Fund for the Promotion of Culture became operational in 1976, while an ongoing project is preparation of a multi-volume *General History of Africa*. Although only a few countries have ratified the 1972 cultural property convention, UNESCO has been active in the campaign for the repatriation of cultural artifacts through its organization of committees to support individual countries' efforts.

In the social sciences, UNESCO has focused its attention on such areas as human rights, peace and disarmament, the environment, population issues, and socioeconomic conditions. The 1978 General Conference adopted a Declaration on Race and Racial Prejudice that rejected the concept that any racial or ethnic group is inherently inferior or superior, asserting that any such theory is without "scientific foundation and is contrary to the moral and ethical principles of humanity". UNESCO has also participated in activities related to the UN Decade for Women (1976–1985) and various other UN-designated years and decades while also undertaking socioeconomic studies intended to facilitate establishment of a new international economic order (NIEO).

Communications has proved a very controversial topic for UNESCO, which has attempted to advance the free flow of information and book development, expand the use of media, assist countries in developing the media they need, and disseminate the ideals of the United Nations. In 1976 heated argument erupted over a Soviet-sponsored resolution, which the United States perceived as a potential threat to the free flow of information; the problem was eventually resolved by recourse to textual vagueness. Debate at the 21st General Conference in 1980 raged over a resolution calling for the establishment of a New World Information and Communication Order (NWICO). Western delegates objected to the proposal, which called for an international code of journalistic ethics, on the ground that

it might restrict freedom of the press. The 1980 Conference did, however, approve resolutions creating an International Programme for the Development of Communications (IPDC). At the fourth extraordinary session of the General Conference, held at Paris in late 1982, the NWICO was included as a major component of the proposed medium-term UNESCO work plan for 1985–1989. A compromise plan for the NWICO was finally adopted that entailed the deletion of passages unacceptable to the industrialized countries, the rejection of a proposed study of Western news agencies, and the addition of material calling for freedom of the press and referencing its role as a "watchdog against abuses of power".

Debate over the NWICO continued in 1983. Despite the compromise seemingly accepted at the 1982 Paris meeting, the document presented at a symposium on the news media and disarmament at Nairobi, Kenya, on April 18–22, called for "national news agencies" and "codes of conduct" for journalists, with no mention of the right of news organs to operate freely. It also called for a study of the obstacles to circulation in industrialized countries of information produced in developing countries. In response, a number of industrial nations, including the United States, indicated that they would withhold funds from the Organization, forcing it to appeal to external sources to meet its projected 1984–1985 budget of $328.8 million.

Subsequently, the Organization came under even greater attack from members alleging unnecessary politicization of UNESCO activities and mismanagement by (then) Director General Amadou Mahtar M'Bow of Senegal. The United States, in the forefront of the critics, called for major reforms in 1984. Rebuffed in the effort, it withdrew from membership, with the United Kingdom and Singapore following suit in 1985.

The US withdrawal precipitated public attacks by M'Bow against Washington and its representatives; he further angered Western members by seeking voluntary contributions to cover the US assessment. Discord continued throughout 1986 although the Executive Board at its fall meeting expressed satisfaction with reform measures and personnel reductions implemented by M'Bow.

The controversial secretary general announced in late 1986 that he would not seek reelection upon expiration of his second term in November 1987 but, at the urging of the Organization of African Unity, subsequently reversed his position. Several additional Western nations threatened to withdraw from UNESCO in the event of M'Bow's reelection and acrimony dominated efforts by the October meeting of the Executive Board to determine its nominee for the post. Although he led his challengers through four ballots, M'Bow failed to attain the majority needed for victory. As the fifth and final ballot loomed, in which only the two leaders from the fourth ballot would be considered, M'Bow withdrew after it had become apparent that the Soviet bloc planned to cast its decisive votes for his opponent, Federico Mayor Zaragoza of Spain. The Board thereupon nominated Mayor although 20 (mostly African) members voted against him, reflecting a bitterness that some observers predicted could have lingering effects on UNESCO activity.

The General Conference in November formally elected Mayor, who promised to restructure and reinvigorate the

Organization in the hope of bringing the United States and the United Kingdom back into its fold. For their part, Washington and London expressed satisfaction with Mayor's selection but said reconsideration of their membership status would be contingent upon actual implementation of fiscal reform and a reorientation of UNESCO policy away from controversial areas such as the NWICO in favor of the earlier emphases on literacy development and scientific cooperation.

UNITED NATIONS INDUSTRIAL DEVELOPMENT ORGANIZATION (UNIDO)

Established: By General Assembly resolution of November 17, 1966, effective January 1, 1967. UNIDO became a UN Specialized Agency January 1, 1986, as authorized by a resolution of the Seventh Special Session of the General Assembly on September 16, 1975, based upon a revised constitution adopted April 8, 1979.

Purpose: To review and promote the coordination of UN activities in the area of industrial development, with particular emphasis on industrialization in less-developed countries, including both agro-based or agro-related industries and basic industries.

Headquarters: Vienna, Austria.

Principal Organs: General Conference (all members), Industrial Development Board (53 members), Program and Budget Board (27 members), Project Divisions (Policy Coordination, Assistance to Least-Developed Countries, Energy, System of Consultations), United Nations Industrial Development Fund, Secretariat.

Director General: Domingo L. Siazon, Jr. (Philippines).

Membership: (144): See Appendix B.

Origin and development. The creation of a comprehensive organization responsible for UN efforts in the field of industrial development was proposed to the General Assembly in 1964 by the first UN Conference on Trade and Development (UNCTAD). The General Assembly endorsed the proposal in 1965 and, through a 1966 resolution effective January 1, 1967, established UNIDO as a semi-autonomous special body of the General Assembly with budgetary and programmatic ties to other special bodies, such as UNCTAD and the UN Development Program (UNDP).

During its first General Conference at Vienna in 1971, UNIDO appealed for greater independence, particularly in light of the UNDP's extensive budgetary control. The plea was reiterated at the second General Conference at Lima, Peru, in 1975 and later that year the General Assembly, in an unprecedented move, authorized the change in status from that of a special body to a specialized agency, subject to the development and ratification of a UNIDO constitution. After extensive negotiations, representatives from 82 countries participating in a Conference of Pleni-

potentiaries at Vienna on March 19–April 8, 1979, adopted such a document and the ratification process, which was to take six years, began.

The third Conference, held at New Delhi, India, in January–February 1980, proved to be highly confrontational, with the industrialized countries objecting not only to the call for the establishment of a 20-year $300 billion global development fund, but to what they considered political provisions—including statements condemning colonialism and racism—in the New Delhi Declaration drafted by the developing countries' Group of 77. The controversy between rich and poor continued at the fourth Conference, which met at Vienna on August 2–19, 1984, little being achieved apart from a renewed call for capital mobilization in support of industrial progress in the Third World.

Although 120 governments had ratified the UNIDO constitution by March 1985, it was not until June 21 that the minimum of 80 formal notifications of such action had been tendered, in part because of an insistence by Eastern European countries that they be guaranteed a deputy director-generalship. Subsequently, a General Conference met at Vienna on August 12–17 and December 9–13 to pave the way for launching the organization as the United Nations' 16th Specialized Agency.

Structure. The General Conference, which meets every two years, establishes UNIDO policy and is responsible for final approval of its biennial budgets. The Industrial Development Board (IDB), which meets annually, exercises wide-ranging "policy review" authority and its recommendations exert significant influence on the decisions of the Conference. The IDB is presently composed of 33 members from developing countries, 15 from Western industrialized countries, and 5 from socialist-bloc countries. In practice, each sub-group selects its own members, although formal designation rests with the Conference. The 27 members of the Program and Budget Committee, which conducts extensive preliminary budget preparation, are distributed in a 19–9–3 ratio.

The Secretariat, comprising more than 1400 staff members, is headed by a director general appointed by the General Conference upon the recommendation of the IDB. In addition, at the second session of the 1985 General Conference it was decided to name five deputy directors general, thus permitting the designation of a director general or deputy each from Africa, Asia, and Latin America; two from the Western industrialized countries; and one from the socialist bloc. Accordingly, deputy director generals were named in May 1986 to head the following departments: external relations, public information, language and documentation; administration; program and project development; industrial operations; and industrial promotion, consultations, and technology.

UNIDO activity in most developing countries is coordinated by a resident Senior Industrial Development Field Advisor, of which there are about 30, or a resident Junior Professional Officer, of which there are about 65. In addition, expert advisors or consultants, numbering more than 1,100 in recent years, are hired from throughout the world to work temporarily on many of the development projects administered by UNIDO.

Activities. UNIDO research, analysis, statistical compilation, dissemination of information, and training provide general support for industrial development throughout the world. In addition, the Organization operates (usually in conjunction with other UN affiliates and national governments) nearly 2,000 field projects a year in areas such as planning, feasibility study, research and development for specific proposals, and installation of pilot industrial plants. UNIDO facilities include an Investment Promotion Service, which encourages contacts between businessmen and governments in developing countries and industrial and financial leaders in developed countries; a $9 million Working Capital Fund, established in 1986; and the Industrial Development Fund (IDF), established in 1978 to provide financing for innovative development projects outside the criteria of existing financial services. UNIDO was also instrumental in the creation of the International Center for Genetic Engineering and Biotechnology, established in 1987 with bases in Trieste, Italy, and New Delhi, India.

UNIDO sponsors numerous seminars, training sessions, and other symposia throughout the world: recent topics have included human resource development (with particular attention to the integration of women into the industrial process), hazardous waste management, transfer of industrial technology, solar energy, desertification, industrial safety, and the environmental impact of industry. In addition, UNIDO regularly conducts international "consulations" on basic industries of special concern to developing countries, most recently the fisheries, metallurgy, agricultural machinery, and food-processing industries.

For several years UNIDO operations have been constrained by financial difficulties arising from shortfalls in members' contributions and the falling value of the US dollar in relation to the Austrian schilling. Some programs were cut back in 1986 and officials predicted more drastic measures might be required. However, the situation eased somewhat in 1987 as the General Assembly extended the repayment schedule for a $16 million loan, with France, the two Germanies, and the Soviet Union providing $4.2 million in increased IDF contributions. During the most recent General Conference at Bangkok, Thailand, on November 9–13, 1987, it was decided to split budget contributions between US dollars and Austrian schillings to reduce the impact of dollar fluctuation. The 1988–1989 two-year budget was set at $57 million and AS 1800 million while 38 countries pledged $25.4 million for the IDF for 1988. The conference, attended by about 550 delegates from 118 countries, also endorsed UNIDO's recent emphasis on the promotion of small-and medium-scale industrial projects, cooperation with the private sector, and encouragement of entrepreneurship.

UNIVERSAL POSTAL UNION
Union Postale Universelle
(UPU)

Established: By Treaty signed at Berne, Switzerland, on October 9, 1874; present name adopted in 1878. The UPU became a UN Specialized Agency by agreement with the Economic and Social Council (approved by the General Assembly on November 15, 1947, with effect from July 1, 1948).

Purpose: To organize and improve world postal services and to promote the development of international postal collaboration.

Headquarters: Berne, Switzerland.

Principal Organs: Universal Postal Congress (all members), Executive Council (40 members), Consultative Council for Postal Studies (35 members), International Bureau.

Director General: A.C. Botto de Barros (Brazil).

Membership (168): See Appendix B.

Official Language: French.

Origin and development. The oldest of the UN Specialized Agencies, the Universal Postal Union traces its origins to a 15-state international conference held at Paris, France, in 1863 in recognition of the growing need to establish principles governing international postal exchange. The first International Postal Congress was convened at Berne, Switzerland, in 1874 and yielded a Treaty Concerning the Establishment of a General Postal Union, commonly known as the Berne Treaty. This was the forerunner of a multilateral convention that governed international postal service as of July 1, 1875; three years later, at the Second International Postal Congress, held at Paris, the name of the organization was changed to Universal Postal Union. By an agreement signed at Paris in 1947 and effective July 1, 1948, the UPU was recognized as the UN Specialized Agency responsible for international postal activity. A revision of the basic acts of the UPU to make them more compatible with the structure of other UN Specialized Agencies was carried out by the 15th Universal Postal Congress at Vienna, Austria, in 1964. The revised constitution, general regulations, and Convention (dated July 10, 1964) entered into force January 1, 1966. Due to its utility and historically nonpolitical character, the UPU has the largest membership of any of the UN Specialized Agencies; virtually all UN members, various dependent territories, and a number of nonmember states participate.

Despite the Union's nonpolitical tradition, South Africa was prevented from participating in the first week of the 1979 Congress at Rio de Janeiro, Brazil. Permanent exclusion of South Africa from the organization was precluded, however, because the UPU constitution contains no provision for such an action.

Structure. The Universal Postal Congress, composed of all UPU members and usually meeting at five-year intervals, is the principal organ of the Union. It establishes the UPU's work program and budget, and reviews its acts and subsidiary agreements. The Executive Council, consisting of 40 members elected by the Congress, maintains continuity between Congresses and normally meets yearly at Berne. Its responsibilities include maintaining relations with the rest of the UN system and other international organizations, preparing technical postal studies as a basis for recommendations to the Congress, and appointing the director general.

The Consultative Committee for Postal Studies, a committee of the Congress, was established in 1957 to conduct studies and give advice on technical, operational, and economic questions affecting postal service. The operations of the Committee, which is open to all UPU members, are directed by a Management Council that carries on the work of the Consultative Committee in the periods between Congresses.

The International Bureau, the permanent secretariat of the UPU, is headed by a director general appointed by the Executive Council. In addition to serving as a liaison for the member governments, it acts as a clearinghouse for the settlement of accounts resulting from international postal services.

Activities. The basic aims of the UPU are the improvement of the world's postal services and the maintenance of "a single territory for the reciprocal exchange of correspondence". This single-territory principle means that, in general, uniform postal rates must be charged for ordinary mail sent to any address in UPU territory, and that the postal authorities of all member states are pledged to expedite mail originating in other member states by the best means used to expedite their own mail. In addition, the UPU participates in UN technical cooperation programs for less-developed states; related activities have included recruiting and supplying experts, awarding fellowships for vocational training, and furnishing minor equipment as well as training and demonstration material.

Much of the work undertaken by the Union during 1983–1984 was in furtherance of resolutions adopted during the UPU's 18th Congress, held at Rio de Janerio, Brazil, in 1979. During its annual session, held at Berne on April 28–May 13, 1983, the Executive Committee concentrated on final implementation of the Rio resolutions on international high-speed mail, customs treatment of postal items, and shipment of dangerous substances by mail; the Consultative Council for Postal Services, meeting in conjunction with the Executive Council, stated that the projects in question would be largely completed by late 1984. Implementation of technical assistance, country and regional programs, and specific projects, such as electronic mail applications, were to be continued by the Union in cooperation with the UN Development Programme (UNDP), UNESCO, the International Telecommunication Union, and other organizations. Concurrently, the UPU was active in the World Communications Year (WCY), whose purpose was to provide a starting point for the establishment and strengthening of communication infrastructures in developing countries. Its accomplishments during the WCY and progress made in implementing the Rio resolutions were discussed at the 19th UPU Congress, held at Hamburg, Federal Republic of Germany, on June 18–July 26, 1984. During 1985, the UPU concentrated its efforts on international expedited mail (EMS), air transport of mail, speeding up customs treatment of mail, and further developing parcel post services.

In conjunction with UN-wide fiscal review aimed at budget retrenchment, the UPU recently conducted a study of the International Bureau's work methods and implemented "streamlining" measures. The 1987 budget ceiling was set at 22.5 million Swiss francs (about $13.9 million at the January 1, 1987 exchange rate), a decrease of over 2 million Swiss francs from the previous year.

The 20th UPU Congress is scheduled to to be held at Washington, DC, in 1989.

WORLD HEALTH ORGANIZATION (WHO)

Established: By constitution signed at New York, United States, July 22, 1946, effective April 7, 1948. WHO became a UN Specialized Agency by agreement with the Economic and Social Council (approved by the General Assembly on November 15, 1947, with effect from September 1, 1948).

Purpose: To aid in "the attainment by all peoples of the highest possible levels of health".

Headquarters: Geneva, Switzerland.

Principal Organs: World Health Assembly (all members), Executive Board (31 experts), Regional Committees (all regional members), Secretariat.

Director General: Dr. Hiroshi Nakajima (Japan).

Membership (166, plus 1 Associate Member): See Appendix B.

Official Languages: Arabic, Chinese, English, French, Russian, Spanish.

Origin and development. Attempts to institutionalize international cooperation in health matters originated as early as 1851 but reached full fruition only with establishment of the WHO. The need for a single international health agency was emphasized in a special declaration of the UN Conference on International Organization at San Francisco, California, in 1945, and the constitution of the WHO was adopted at a specially convened International Health Conference at New York in June-July 1946. Formally established on April 8, 1948, the WHO also took over the functions of the International Office of Public Health, established in 1907; those of the League of Nations Health Organization; and the health activities of the UN Relief and Rehabilitation Administration (UNRRA).

A turning point in the WHO's evolution occurred in 1976. As a result of decisions reached during that year's World Health Assembly, it began to reorient its work so that by 1980 a full 60 percent of its regular budget would be allocated for technical cooperation and for the provision of services to member states. In addition, all nonessential expenditures were to be eliminated, resulting in a reduction of 363 established administrative positions and a savings of over $41 million between 1978 and 1981. A further step in this process was taken in May 1979, when the 32nd World Health Assembly adopted the Alma-Ata report and declaration on primary health care and its relationship to socioeconomic development. Members were asked to submit collective, regional, and individual health care strategies to be used as the basis for the Global Strategy for Health for All by the Year 2000. The Global Strategy was adopted by the 34th Assembly in 1981, and a plan of action for its implementation followed in 1982.

Controversy at the 32nd World Health Assembly was generated by an abortive attempt by Arab representatives to suspend Israeli membership. The United States, objecting to politicization of the Organization, warned that it would probably withdraw from the WHO if the proposal were adopted. At the 33rd Assembly in May 1980, Arab members succeeded in gaining approval of a resolution that declared "the establishment of Israeli settlements in the occupied Arab territories, including Palestine", a source of "serious damage on the health of the inhabitants". Moreover, the conferees condemned the "inhuman practices to which Arab prisoners and detainees are subject in Israeli prisons". A clause that would have denied Israel's membership rights was deleted from a resolution before the 35th Assembly in May 1982 after the United States declared that it would withdraw from the meeting if the clause remained.

Structure. The World Health Assembly, on which all members are represented, is the principal political organ of the WHO. At its annual sessions, usually held at WHO headquarters in May, the Assembly approves the Organization's long-range work program as well as its annual program and budget. International health conventions may be approved and recommended to governments by a two-thirds majority vote. The Assembly similarly adopts technical health regulations that come into force immediately for those governments that do not specifically reject them.

The Executive Board is composed of 31 members who, although designated by governments selected by the Assembly, serve in an individual expert capacity rather than as governmental representatives. Meeting at least twice a year, the Board prepares the Assembly agenda and oversees implementation of Assembly decisions.

The Secretariat is headed by a director general designated by the Assembly on recommendation of the Board.

The WHO is the least centralized of the UN Specialized Agencies, much of its program centering upon six regional organizations: Southeast Asia (headquartered at New Delhi, India), the Eastern Mediterranean (Alexandria, Egypt), the Western Pacific (Manila, Philippines), the Americas (Washington, DC), Africa (Brazzaville, Congo), and Europe (Copenhagen, Denmark). Each of the six has a Regional Committee of all members in the area, and an office headed by a regional director.

Activities. The WHO acts as a coordinating authority on international health work and actively promotes cooperation in health matters. Its work program falls into six broad categories: development of health services, disease prevention and control, promotion of environmental health, health manpower development, promotion and development of biomedical and health services research, and health program development and support.

Cooperation with member governments primarily involves the following: development of services that will make primary health care available to the entire population, maternal and child health, family planning, nutrition, health education, health engineering, rural water supply and sanitation, control of communicable diseases, pro-

duction and quality control of drugs and vaccines, and promotion of research. The WHO also cooperates in the collection, analysis, and dissemination of health data, and sponsors comparative studies in cancer and heart diseases, mental illness, dental ailments, and other maladies.

The WHO has been particularly successful with immunization programs, beginning with its coordination of the worldwide smallpox vaccination campaign which eliminated the disease by the late 1970s. In 1974 the WHO also embarked, in conjunction with the UN Children's Fund (UNICEF), on a campaign to immunize all the world's children by 1990 against measles, poliomyelitis, diptheria, pertussis (whooping cough), tetanus, and tuberculosis.

Other WHO prevention programs combat the high incidence of life-threatening attacks of diarrhea among Third World children and diseases transmitted by insects and parasites, such as malaria and "river blindness" (onchocerciasis), the focus of an effective larvacide-spraying campaign in West Africa since 1977. Recently, WHO research and symposia have also addressed child abuse, smoking, worldwide economic decline in the 1980s and its negative impact on national health budgets, regulations on the international marketing of breast milk substitutes, the demographic imbalance of doctors, shortages of nurses and other health care professionals, drug abuse, food safety, travellers' health, sanitation, development of water resources, and the health problems of the homeless.

The most publicized aspect of WHO activity in recent years has been its coordination of international anti-AIDS efforts. Relying on voluntary contributions from many countries, the WHO in 1987 launched a global public information campaign to halt the transmission of AIDS and to promote better care for AIDS patients. At that time, the WHO estimated that 5–10 million persons were infected by the AIDS virus, which could mean up to 3 million new AIDS cases by 1992.

Resources for the AIDS campaign and other programs has been a major problem for the WHO for several years. The 40th World Health Assembly, held at Geneva on May 4–15, 1987, approved a 1988–1989 two-year budget of $634 million, exclusive of a projected $63 million anti-AIDS fund. However, WHO officials warned that many programs would be compromised if countries, in particular the United States, continued to pay less than their full assessed contributions.

At the 41st World Health Assembly, held at Geneva on May 2–13, 1988, Dr. Hiroshi Nakajima of Japan, previously the director of the WHO's Western Pacific region, was elected as the Organization's director general.

WORLD INTELLECTUAL PROPERTY ORGANIZATION (WIPO)

Established: By a Convention signed at Stockholm, Sweden, July 14, 1967, entering into force April 26, 1970. WIPO became a UN Specialized Agency by a General Assembly resolution of December 17, 1974.

Purpose: To promote, by means of cooperation among states and international organizations, the protection of "intellectual property", including literary, artistic, and scientific works; the contents of broadcasts, films, and photographs; and all types of inventions, industrial designs, and trademarks; and to ensure administrative cooperation among numerous intellectual property "unions".

Headquarters: Geneva, Switzerland.

Principal Organs: General Assembly (96 members), Conference (all members), Coordination Committee (47 members), Budget Committee (12 members), Permanent Committee for Development Cooperation Related to Industrial Property (96 members), Permanent Committee for Development Cooperation Related to Copyright and Neighboring Rights (80 members), Permanent Committee on Industrial Property Information (69 members), International Patent Documentation Center, International Bureau.

Director General: Dr. Arpad Bogsch (United States).

Membership: (119): See Appendix B.

Working Languages: Arabic, English, French, Russian, Spanish.

Origin and development. The origins of WIPO can be traced to the establishment of the Paris Convention on the Protection of Industrial Property in 1883 and the Berne Convention for the Protection of Literary and Artistic Works in 1886. Both conventions provided for separate international bureaus, or secretariats, which were united in 1893 and functioned under various names, the last being the United International Bureau for the Protection of Intellectual Property (BIRPI). BIRPI still has a legal existence for the purposes of those states that are members of the Paris or Berne unions but have not yet become members of WIPO; in practice, however, BIRPI is indistinguishable from WIPO. The Organization also assumed responsibility for administering a number of smaller unions based on other multilateral agreements and for coordinating subsequent negotiations on additional agreements. In December 1974, WIPO became the UN's 14th Specialized Agency.

In September 1977 the Coordination Committee agreed to ban South Africa from future meetings, but a move to exclude it from the Organization was narrowly defeated in 1979.

Structure. The General Assembly, comprising states which are parties to the WIPO Convention and are also members of any of the unions serviced by WIPO, is the Organization's highest authority. In addition, a Conference, comprising all parties to the WIPO Convention, serves as a forum for discussion of all matters relating to intellectual property and has authority over the activity and budget of WIPO's technical legal assistance program. Both organs meet biennially in odd-numbered years.

The International Bureau is the WIPO secretariat, which also services the Paris, Berne, and other such unions. With regard to WIPO, the International Bureau is controlled by the General Assembly and the Conference, while as far as the unions are concerned, the Bureau is governed by the

separate Assemblies and Conferences of Representatives of each. The Paris and Berne unions elect Executive Committees, whose joint membership constitutes the Coordination Committee of WIPO, which meets annually.

To aid in the transfer of technology from highly industrialized to developing countries, a WIPO Permanent Program for Development Cooperation Related to Industrial Property was established. In addition, a WIPO Permanent Program for Development Cooperation Related to Copyright and Neighboring Rights has been created to promote and facilitate the dissemination, in developing countries, of literary, scientific, and artistic works protected under the rights of authors and of performing artists, producers, and broadcasting organizations. Each program is directed by a Permanent Committee, membership of which is open to all WIPO states. There is also a WIPO Permanent Committee on Industrial Property Information which is responsible for intergovernmental cooperation regarding patent information (such as the standardization and exchange of patent documents) and the protection of industrial designs and trademarks.

Activities. WIPO administers more than 15 treaties dealing with the two main categories of intellectual property: copyright (involving written material, film, recording, and other works of art) and industrial property (covering inventions, patents, trademarks, and industrial designs). The most important treaty in the copyright field is the 77-member Berne Convention (see Origin and Development, above), most recently amended in 1979. It requires signatories to give copyright protection to works originating in other member states and establishes minimum standards for such protection.

The principal treaty affecting industrial property is the 98-member Paris Convention (see above), under which a member state must give the same protection to nationals of other contracting states as it gives to its own nationals. The Convention contains numerous additional regulations, some of which have been the subject of often contentious revision conferences during the 1980s. Discord has most frequently involved attempts by developing countries to shorten protection periods in order to facilitate the transfer of technology and speed up the development of product manufacturing.

In addition to its administrative function, WIPO also spearheads the review and revision of treaties already under its jurisdiction, while encouraging the negotiation of new accords where needed. Among the issues currently under study are the piracy and counterfeiting of sound and audiovisual recordings; proposed standards for regulating the cable television industry; proposed expansion of copyright protection for dramatic, choreographic, and musical works; and protection in new fields such as biotechnology and integrated circuits.

During the 18th Series of Meetings of the Governing Bodies of WIPO and its Unions, held at Geneva on September 21–30, 1987, delegates agreed to devote more of WIPO's resources to developing countries and called for another consultative meeting on possible revision of the Paris Convention. During the meetings, WIPO reported that activity was expanding under the Patent Cooperation Treaty (PCT), established to help inventors and industry obtain patent protection in foreign countries by filing single international applications rather than separate applications for each country. More than 8,000 applications were filed with the PCT in 1986 with the final 1987 figure expected to be 15–20 percent higher.

WORLD METEOROLOGICAL ORGANIZATION
(WMO)

Established: April 4, 1951, under authority of a World Meteorological Convention signed at Washington, DC, October 11, 1947. The WMO became a UN Specialized Agency by agreement with the Economic and Social Council (approved by the General Assembly on December 20, 1951).

Purpose: To coordinate, standardize, and improve world meteorological activities and encourage an efficient exchange of meteorological information between states.

Headquarters: Geneva, Switzerland.

Principal Organs: World Meteorological Congress (all members), Executive Committee (36 members), Regional Associations (all regional members), Technical Commissions, Secretariat.

Secretary General: Olu Patrick Obasi (Nigeria).

Membership (160): See Appendix B.

Official Languages: English, French, Russian, Spanish.

Origin and development. The World Meteorological Organization is the successor to the International Meteorological Organization (IMO) established in 1878 in a pioneering attempt to organize cooperation in meteorology. Technically, the IMO was not an intergovernmental organization, its members being the directors of various national meteorological services rather than the states themselves. Upon establishment of the UN, the IMO decided to restructure itself as an intergovernmental body. The World Meteorological Convention, drafted in 1947, entered into force March 23, 1950; formal establishment of the WMO took place April 4, 1951, at its first World Meteorological Congress. A Specialized Agency of the UN under an agreement approved in 1951, the WMO includes in its membership the great majority of UN members as well as several nonmember states and territories.

Structure. The World Meteorological Congress, in which all WMO members have one vote, is the Organization's main political organ. It meets at least once every four years to elect its officers and the members of the Executive Committee, to adopt technical regulations on meteorological practices and procedures, and to determine general policies. Decisions are made by a two-thirds majority except for the election of officers, which requires only a simple majority.

The Executive Committee, comprising 36 directors of national meteorological services, meets at least once a year to prepare studies and recommendations for the Congress, supervise the implementation of the Congress' decisions, assist members on technical matters, and approve the annual financial appropriation within the overall budget set by the Congress.

Six Regional Associations have been established by the Congress, for Africa, Asia, Europe, North and Central America, South America, and the South West Pacific. Composed of those member states whose meteorological networks lie in or extend into the given area, each Association meets once every four years and is responsible for coordinating regional meteorological activities and for examining, from a regional point of view, questions referred by the Executive Committee. The Congress has also established eight Technical Commisssions to provide expert advice in aeronautical meteorology, agricultural meteorology, atmospheric sciences, basic systems, climatology, hydrology, instruments and methods of observation, and marine meteorology. All members may be represented on the Commissions, which meet every four years.

The WMO Secretariat is headed by a secretary general, who is appointed by the Congress and is responsible for conducting technical studies, preparing and publishing the results of the WMO's activities, and generally supervising Organization activities.

Activities. The WMO facilitates worldwide cooperation in the establishment of meteorological observation stations; promotes the establishment and maintenance of systems for the rapid exchange of weather information; fosters standardization of meteorological observations and ensures the uniform publication of observations and statistics; furthers the application of meteorology to aviation, shipping, agriculture, and other activities; and encourages research and training in meteorology.

An expanded program of global weather observation and reporting, involving the use of earth-orbiting satellites, high-speed telecommunications, and computers, was approved in April 1967 by the Fifth World Meteorological Congress. In addition, a suggestion advanced by US President Kennedy in 1961, and subsequently elaborated by the UN and the WMO, resulted in creation of the World Weather Watch (WWW). Closely coordinated with the World Climate Research Program developed by the International Council of Scientific Unions (ICSU), the WWW keeps the global atmosphere under continuous surveillance with the aid of some 9,300 ground observation stations, 7,500 merchant ships, 3,000 aircraft, over 100,000 climatological stations in all parts of the world, and meteorological satellites operated by several members. Complementing this effort is a WMO program initiated in 1969 for global measurement of atmospheric pollutants in order to identify changes that might lead to climatic modifications. Still other environmental projects of the WMO include the monitoring of water pollution and water quality, and the development with other agencies of an Integrated Global Oceans Stations System (IGOSS) to do for the oceans what the WWW is doing for the atmosphere. A Weather Modification Programme has also been undertaken, the main focus of activity being a Precipitation Enhancement Project (PEP).

The Eighth World Meteorological Congress, held at Geneva in April-May 1979, adopted a World Climate Programme (WCO) that, in cooperation with a number of other UN-related agencies, encompasses projects in data gathering, practical application of climatic information to economic and social activities, and basic research.

A new WWW project came into operation in 1982: the Typhoon Operational Experiment (Topex) seeks to investigate various types of typhoon forecasting and warning systems under actual storm conditions. While the first phase of Topex is primarily an international venture utilizing the WMO's global network of geostationary satellites, remote-sensing technology, and typhoon modeling and statistical techniques for forecasting, a second phase is to establish a number of national programs in hydrology and disaster prevention and preparedness.

More than 400 delegates attended the Tenth World Meteorological Congress, held at Geneva in May 1987. The Congress approved the 1988–1991 World Weather Watch plan and established a four-year budget, exclusive of projects implemented by WMO for other agencies, of 170 million Swiss francs (about $133 million at the January 1, 1988, exchange rate).

UNITED NATIONS: RELATED ORGANIZATIONS

GENERAL AGREEMENT ON TARIFFS AND TRADE
(GATT)

Established: By General Agreement signed at Geneva, Switzerland, October 30, 1947, effective January 1, 1948.

Purpose: To promote the expansion of international trade on a nondiscriminatory basis in accordance with an agreed body of reciprocal rights and obligations.

Headquarters: Geneva, Switzerland.

Principal Organs: Session of the Contracting Parties (all members), Council of Representatives (all members), Trade Negotiations Committee, Standing Committees, International Trade Centre (administered jointly with UNCTAD), Secretariat.

Director General: Arthur Dunkel (Switzerland).

Contracting Parties (96): See Appendix B. (In addition to the Contracting Parties, one state has acceded provisionally and 28 other states are maintaining de facto application of the Agreement pending determination of their future commercial policies.)

Official Languages: English, French.

Origin and development. The General Agreement on Tariffs and Trade, signed in 1947, was not designed to set up a permanent international organization but merely to provide a temporary framework for tariff negotiations, pending the establishment of a full-fledged International Trade Organization (ITO) under UN auspices. A charter establishing an ITO in the form of a UN Specialized Agency responsible for developing and administering a comprehensive international commercial policy was drafted at the UN Conference on Trade and Employment, which met at Havana, Cuba, November 1947–March 1948; however, the so-called Havana Charter never went into effect, principally because opposition within the United States blocked the required approval by the US Senate. Delay in creating the ITO left GATT as the only available instrument for seeking agreement on rules for the conduct of international trade; furthermore, since the General Agreement was not cast as a treaty, it did not require formal ratification by the United States but could be implemented solely by executive action. Since 1950, when it became apparent that the ITO would be indefinitely postponed, GATT has attempted to fill a part of the resultant vacuum through a series of ad hoc arrangements.

Reducing tariffs through multilateral negotiations and agreements has been one of the principal techniques employed by GATT. Seven major tariff-negotiating conferences have been held under GATT auspices: at Geneva in 1947; at Annecy, France, in 1949; at Torquay, England, in 1951–1952; at Geneva in 1955–1956, 1961–1962 (the "Dillon Round", named for US Secretary of the Treasury Douglas Dillon), and 1963–1967 (the "Kennedy Round", named for US President John F. Kennedy); and at Tokyo and Geneva in 1973–1979 (the "Tokyo Round"). An eighth round commenced in September 1986 (see Activities, below).

The Kennedy Round far outdistanced its predecessors in magnitude and scope. For the first time, tariff reductions were negotiated on an "across-the-board" basis, involving whole categories of products rather than single items. Although failing to fulfill the announced objective of a 50 percent overall reduction on industrial tariffs, the conferees agreed upon reductions that, when fully implemented, averaged about 33 percent and attained the 50 percent level in many instances. Efforts to reduce trade barriers for agricultural products and with regard to less-developed states were much less successful, although an antidumping code and an extension of an earlier agreement regulating trade in cotton textiles were approved.

GATT has devoted particular attention to two matters left over from the Kennedy Round negotiations: the trade needs of less-developed states and the problem of nontariff barriers to trade (NTBs), particularly among industrialized states. Efforts to assist less-developed states in increasing their exports date back at least to 1964, when GATT established the International Trade Centre for this purpose in Geneva; in 1967 GATT and the UN Conference on Trade and Development (UNCTAD) agreed to merge their trade promotion activities under the Centre. Meanwhile, in 1965 the contracting parties formally added to the General Agreement a new Part IV on Trade and Development, which provided a formal basis for augmenting the participation of less-developed states in international trade and promoting the sustained growth of their export earnings. Continuous review of the implementation of these provisions has been entrusted to a Committee on Trade and Development and two subcommittees specifically mandated to investigate trade problems of the developing countries and the least-developed countries.

The 28th Session of the Contracting Parties, held at Geneva, November 1–14, 1972, adopted a timetable for new multilateral trade negotiations of even wider scope than the Kennedy Round. The aim of the new negotiations was nothing less than a broad restructuring of international trade to complement the reconstruction of the international monetary system as undertaken through the International Monetary Fund. The result, the Tokyo Round of Multilateral Trade Negotiations, was the most comprehensive agreement concluded during the seven rounds held under GATT auspices. Some of the Tokyo accords, providing for an improved framework for the conduct of world trade, took effect in November 1979. Most of the other agreements — covering not only tariff reductions (averaging 35–38 percent in a series of eight annual rounds) but also subsidies and countervailing duties, technical barriers to trade, import licensing procedures, a revised GATT antidumping code, bovine meat, dairy products, and civil aircraft — took effect on January 1, 1980. Agreements covering government procurement and customs valuation entered into effect January 1, 1981.

Structure. In keeping with its originally provisional character, GATT's institutional structure is in many ways less developed than that of the UN Specialized Agencies. The periodic Sessions of the Contracting Parties, at which all members are represented, constitute GATT's principal political organ. Meeting usually once a year, the contracting parties review progress under the General Agreement and decide on further measures. The Council of Representatives, composed of delegates from all member states, was established in 1960 to serve between Sessions of the Contracting Parties; it usually meets nine times a year. Of GATT's committees, the Trade Negotiations Committee, which serves as the steering group for multilateral trade negotiations, is clearly the most important. In addition, a Secretariat, headed by a director general, administers GATT activities.

Activities. The broad objective of GATT is to contribute to general economic progress through the acceptance by the contracting parties of agreed rights and obligations governing the conduct of their trade relations. Four main principles, from which detailed rules have emerged, underlie the General Agreement: (1) since trade should be conducted on a nondiscriminatory basis, all contracting parties are bound by the most-favored-nation clause in the application of import and export duties; (2) protection of domestic industries should be achieved through customs tariffs and not through other commercial measures (thus protective import quotas are prohibited); (3) consultations should be undertaken to avoid damage to the trading interests of other contracting parties; and (4) GATT should provide a framework for negotiating the reduction of tariffs and other barriers to trade, as well as a structure for embodying the results of such negotiations in a legal instrument.

Meeting regularly throughout the year, supervisory committees continue to review adherence to specific Tokyo Round agreements as well as the progress of national implementing legislation. In addition, committees have undertaken numerous studies, technical inquiries, and investigations of possible nonapplication of GATT provisions. At the same time, GATT has greatly increased its activities in the area of conciliation and settlement of disputes. GATT also administers the Arrangement Regarding International Trade in Textiles — the Multifibre Arrangement (MFA) — which was first negotiated in 1973 and most recently extended for a five-year period from July 1986 to resolve friction between expanding textile producers in developing countries and established producers in the West.

GATT is currently midway in its eighth round of negotiations, launched at the 42nd session of the Contracting Parties in September 1986 at Punta del Este, Uruguay. Pending formal completion (scheduled for 1990) of the "Uruguay Round", members agreed not to extend current levels of protection, with GATT serving as a "surveillance body" to address breaches of discipline.

In addition to tariffs, non-tariff measures, tropical products, natural resource-based products, and textiles and clothing, the Uruguay Round was authorized to consider a number of controversial topics. They include the potentially trade-restricting effects of investment measures, trade-related aspects of intellectual property rights (including trade in counterfeit goods), and agriculture, an area in which domestic subsidies in the United States and the European Community (EC) have been sharply attacked by other food exporters. Difficult negotiations were also expected in regard to trade in services (such as banking, data processing, and insurance), which the Contracting Parties, after lengthy debate, agreed to consider outside the legal framework of GATT, although utilizing GATT practices and procedures. The United States, in particular, had pushed for inclusion of trade in services on the GATT agenda, despite resistance from developing countries concerned about the possibility of compromising their own emerging service economies.

During the 43rd session of the Contracting Parties, held at Geneva on December 1–3, 1987, mixed reviews were issued on developments in the Uruguay Round: some delegates and GATT officials attributed a lack of progress in certain areas to a rising disregard for GATT precepts. The Session was also informed that nearly $20 million in members' arrears had created a fiscal crisis within the organization.

Several positive signs nonetheless emerged in early 1988. EC trade ministers reportedly agreed to give GATT more authority to monitor agreements and assess penalties for noncompliance measures which the EC in the past has opposed, despite pressure from most of the world's other industrialized nations. Observers also noted that GATT could be strengthened significantly in the near future as decisions are reached on accession requests from a number of states, including several major Latin American countries and the People's Republic of China, which suspended its membership in 1950 but now seeks readmission. In addition, it was reported that membership overtures from the

Soviet Union, rebuffed in 1986 primarily due to US opposition, were now receiving a warmer reception in Washington.

INTERNATIONAL ATOMIC ENERGY AGENCY (IAEA)

Established: By Statute signed at New York, United States, October 26, 1956, effective July 29, 1957. A working relationship with the United Nations was approved by the General Assembly on November 14, 1957.

Purpose: To "seek to accelerate and enlarge the contribution of atomic energy to peace, health and prosperity throughout the world" and to ensure that such assistance "is not used in such a way as to further any military purposes".

Headquarters: Vienna, Austria.

Principal Organs: General Conference (all members), Board of Governors (35 members), Scientific Advisory Committee, Secretariat.

Director General: Hans Blix (Sweden).

Membership (113): See Appendix B.

Official Languages: Chinese, English, French, Russian, Spanish.

Working Languages: English, French, Russian, Spanish.

Origin and development. In a 1953 address before the UN General Assembly, US President Dwight Eisenhower urged the establishment of an international organization devoted exclusively to the peaceful uses of atomic energy. The essentials of the US proposal were endorsed by the General Assembly on December 4, 1954, and the Statute of the IAEA was signed by 70 governments on October 26, 1956. Following ratification by 26 governments, the Statute entered into force July 29, 1957.

Although the Statute makes no provision for expelling member states, a two-thirds majority may vote suspension upon recommendation of the Executive Board. This procedure was followed in 1972, when the membership of the Republic of China was suspended and the People's Republic of China took its place. (International safeguards on the Republic of China's subsequent extensive atomic development have been possible only because that government still allows Agency controls.) In September 1976 a large group of Black African countries, led by Nigeria, initiated an abortive attempt to eject South Africa from the Agency. While still not excluded from membership, South Africa was barred from participation in the 23rd General Conference at New Delhi, India, in December 1979. A decision at the 26th General Conference, in September 1982, to reject the Israeli delegation's credentials led to a walkout by the United States and 15 other countries. The Conference charged that Israel had violated IAEA principles and

undermined the Agency's safeguards with its preemptive attack on Iraq's Osirak nuclear facility in June 1981. The United States, which supplies nearly 26 percent of the Agency's regular budget, announced that it would suspend its payments and contributions while reassessing its membership. Subsequently, following Director-General Blix's certification of Israel's continued membership in March 1983, Washington paid $8.5 million in back dues and resumed full participation in the Agency.

Structure. The General Conference, at which all members are entitled to be represented, meets annually at the organization's headquarters, usually in the latter part of September. Conference responsibilities include final approval of the Agency's budget and program, approval of the appointment of the director general, and election of 22 members of the Board of Governors. Decisions on financial questions, amendments to the Statute, and suspension from membership require a two-thirds majority; other matters are decided by a simple majority.

The Board of Governors, which normally meets four times a year, is vested with general authority for carrying out the functions of the IAEA. Of its 35 members, 22 are elected by the General Conference with due regard to equitable representation by geographic areas, while 13 are designated by the outgoing Board of Governors as the leaders in nuclear technology and production of atomic source material. Decisions are usually by simple majority, although budget approval and a few other matters require a two-thirds majority.

The IAEA's Secretariat is headed by a director general appointed for a four-year term by the Board of Governors with the approval of the General Conference. The director general is responsible for the appointment, organization, and functioning of the staff, under the authority and subject to the control of the Board. He also prepares the initial annual budget estimates for submission by the Board to the General Conference.

A Scientific Advisory Committee was set up in 1958 to advise the Board of Governors and the director general on matters of a scientific and technical character; Committee members are named on an individual basis for three-year terms. Similarly, in 1975 the Board of Governors established an Intergovernmental Advisory Group on Nuclear Explosions for Peaceful Purposes, with membership open to all IAEA participant states.

Activities. The IAEA differs from President Eisenhower's original concept in that it has not become a major center for distributing fissionable material. Its activities in promoting the peaceful uses of atomic energy fall into four main areas: (1) establishment of health and safety standards, (2) administration of a safeguards program to ensure that atomic materials are not diverted from peaceful to military uses, (3) technical assistance, and (4) aid in nuclear research and development.

Included in IAEA operations are the International Laboratory of Marine Radioactivity in Monaco; the International Centre for Theoretical Physics at Trieste, Italy (administered jointly with the UN Educational, Scientific, and Cultural Organization); the International Nuclear Information System, which provides a comprehensive bibliographic data base on peaceful applications of nuclear science and technology; and a large multidisciplinary nuclear research laboratory at Seibersdorf, Austria. The IAEA also coordinates the work of physicists from the European Community, Japan, the United States, and the Soviet Union, on a planned thermonuclear fusion reactor. In addition, the IAEA administers several multilateral conventions on nuclear matters, including civil liability for nuclear damage and the protection of nuclear material from theft, sabotage, and other hazards, such as those posed during international transport.

With the rapid increase in the number of Third World members, technical assistance has become important. This involves not only offering training programs and technical-assistance fellowships but also bringing together customers and suppliers of such specialized services as plant maintenance and oversight safety. More than one-half of the funds for such activities come in the form of voluntary contributions, despite complaints from poorer states, who believe that such funding should come from the IAEA's regular budget.

The importance of the Agency's role as administrator of the safeguards system has reflected world concern about the proliferation of nuclear weapons. The Treaty on the Non-Proliferation of Nuclear Weapons (NPT), signed July 1, 1968, and effective March 5, 1970, obligates signatory states (135 as of December 1987) possessing no nuclear weapons to accept safeguards to be set forth in an agreement concluded with the Agency. After the May 1974 surprise nuclear explosion by India, the IAEA initiated a major effort to tighten controls. Specifically, the director general called upon the governments of states possessing nuclear weapons to accept outside inspection when they conduct nuclear tests for peaceful purposes. Subsequently, the United Kingdom (1978), the United States (1980), France (1981), the Soviet Union (1985) and China (1985) concluded agreements with the IAEA regarding application of safeguards and inspection of certain civilian nuclear facilities.

Critics of the safeguards system have nonetheless asserted that the Agency's lack of manpower, reliable monitoring instruments, and aggressive tactics have prevented the verification of violations, and that a lack of political influence, particularly in imposing effective sanctions, has rendered it impotent in the face of safeguard violations. Harsher critics point to four countries—India, Israel, Pakistan and South Africa—suspected of the diversion of nuclear materials from peaceful to military uses, as indicated in February 1983 when the IAEA revealed that India was reprocessing and stockpiling weapons-grade plutonium.

In the wake of the world's worst-ever nuclear accident at Chernobyl, USSR, in April 1986, nuclear safety became the paramount focus of IAEA activities. Special IAEA sessions evaluated the immediate implications of the accident and laid the groundwork for full assessment of its long-term radiological consequences. Subsequently, a new convention establishing an "early warning system" for such accidents went into force in October 1986, while a convention for the provision of assistance in the case of nuclear or radiological emergency went into force in February 1987. As of early 1988 the conventions had been signed by 72 and 70 states, respectively.

In addition to nuclear power plant safety, recent IAEA symposia have addressed the management of spent fuel and radioactive waste, a proposed global radiation monitoring system, issues specific to "aging" nuclear plants, and new uranium mining techniques. The IAEA has also continued its extensive involvement in research and development projects in areas such as nuclear medicine, radiation-induced plant mutation to increase crop yield and resistance to disease; and insect control through large-scale release of radioactively sterilized male insects.

At the 31st General Conference, held on September 21–25, 1987, member states approved a $151 million budget for 1988, with 47 countries pledging $17 million in additional contributions to the technical assistance and cooperation fund. In other activity, after hearing from South African officials that they were considering signing the Treaty on the Non-Proliferation of Nuclear Waapons, the Conference deferred action for one year on a proposal, supported by many Third World countries, to suspend Pretoria's "rights and privileges" within IAEA.

In early 1988 the IAEA reported that 23 new nuclear reactors began operations in eight countries in 1987, bringing the total to 417 reactors, supplying more than 16 percent of the world's electricity, in 26 countries.

WARSAW TREATY ORGANIZATION (WTO)

Established: By Treaty of Warsaw (Poland), signed May 14, 1955, effective June 5, 1955.

Purpose: "In the event of armed attack in Europe on one or more of the Parties to the Treaty by any state or group of states, each of the Parties to the Treaty, in the exercise of its right to individual or collective self-defense in accordance with Article 51 of the Charter of the United Nations Organization, shall immediately, either individually or in agreement with other Parties to the Treaty, come to the assistance of the state or states attacked with all such means as it deems necessary, including armed force. The Parties to the Treaty shall immediately consult concerning the necessary measures to be taken by them jointly in order to restore and maintain international peace and security."

Headquarters: Moscow, Union of Soviet Socialist Republics.

Principal Organs: Political Consultative Committee (all members), Permanent Committee of Foreign Ministers (all members), Committee of Defense Ministers (all members), Joint Command of the Armed Forces, Military Council, Joint Secretariat.

Supreme Commander in Chief of the Joint Armed Forces: Marshal Viktor G. Kulikov (USSR).

Membership (7): Bulgaria, Czechoslovakia, German Democratic Republic, Hungary, Poland, Romania, Union of Soviet Socialist Republics.

Origin and development. The Warsaw Treaty Organization, also known as the Warsaw Pact, was established by the Soviet Union and its Eastern European allies as a direct response to measures taken by the governments of Western Europe and the United States to bring about the rearmament of the Federal Republic of Germany and its inclusion in the Western European Union and NATO. The Treaty of Friendship, Cooperation, and Mutual Assistance signed at Warsaw, Poland, on May 14, 1955, was conceived as an Eastern counterpart to the North Atlantic Treaty of April 4, 1949, and many of its provisions are patterned on that document. A protocol extending the Treaty for an additional 20 years was signed on April 26, 1985.

The eight original signatories were the USSR and all the Communist states of Eastern Europe except Yugoslavia. Albania, however, ceased to participate in 1962 and formally withdrew from membership on September 12, 1968. In the absence of military conflict in Europe, the mutual defense provisions of the Warsaw Treaty have never been invoked, and the Pact's main function has appeared to be that of providing a basis for the continued stationing of Soviet forces in Eastern Europe. Although members of the Pact have frequently held joint military exercises, their only actual joint operation was the occupation of Czechoslovakia by forces of six members on August 21, 1968. Ostensibly, this concerted move against one of the Pact's own members was dictated by concern for the military security of Eastern Europe, in view of Czechoslovakia's avowed intention to establish closer ties with the Federal Republic of Germany and other Western states. Of the active members of the alliance, Romania alone refused to participate in the Czech occupation. While the forces of other Eastern European members were soon withdrawn, Soviet forces remained, under a bilateral treaty with Czechoslovakia concluded October 16, 1968. Romania has since resisted closer integration and has advocated concurrent dissolution of the WTO and NATO. Various organizational changes instituted in March 1969 were interpreted as a partial concession to Romania's demand for a greater measure of equality among the signatory states.

Structure. Like NATO, the WTO has a dual structure of civilian and military institutions headed by a Political Consultative Committee and a Committee of Defense Ministers, respectively. The former, the Pact's principal political organ, is charged with coordinating all activities apart from purely military matters. In full session the Committee consists of the first secretaries of the Communist parties, heads of government, and foreign and defense ministers of member states. Its Joint Secretariat is headed by a Soviet official and composed of a specially appointed representative from each member, while a Permanent Commission makes recommendations on general questions of foreign policy. Since the 1969 reorganization the non-Soviet ministers of defense have not been directly subordinate to the commander in chief of the WTO but form, together with the Soviet minister, the Committee of Defense Ministers.

The Joint Command is required by the Treaty "to strengthen the defensive capability of the Warsaw Pact, to prepare military plans in case of war, and to decide on the deployment of troops". The Command consists of a commander in chief and a Military Council. The Council, which meets under the chairmanship of the commander, includes the chief of staff and permanent military representatives from each of the allied armed forces. The positions of commander in chief and chief of staff have invariably been held by Soviet officers. The Council appears to be the main channel through which the Eastern European forces are able to express their point of view to the commander in chief.

In the event of war, the forces of the other WTO members would be operationally subordinate to the Soviet High Command. The command of the air defense system covering the whole WTO area is now centralized at Moscow and directed by the commander in chief of the Soviet air defense forces. Among the Soviet military headquarters in the WTO area are the Northern Group of Forces at Legnica (Poland); the Southern Group of Forces at Budapest (Hungary); the Group of Soviet Forces in the German Democratic Republic at Zossen-Wünsford, near Berlin; and the Central Group of Forces at Milovice, north of Prague (Czechoslovakia). Soviet tactical air forces are stationed in Czechoslovakia, the German Democratic Republic, Hungary, and Poland.

In 1977 the WTO established a Permanent Committee of Foreign Ministers, with a joint secretariat under a Soviet director general. The Committee, the first structural change in the WTO since 1969, serves mainly as a political consultative organ; all decisions are reached by consensus.

Activities. The WTO has played a role in the ongoing international discussion of European security and the possible reduction of military forces in Europe. While frequent maneuvers enhance the preparedness of the combat-ready WTO forces, the Pact's political leaders have adjusted their posture to the shifting climate of East-West détente. The communiqué issued after the October 1985 pre-summit meeting of the Political Consultative Committee reflected both Soviet policy and Soviet leader Mikhail Gorbachev's style. For the first time, it was presented at a Western-style press conference. While retaining much earlier rhetoric about nuclear arms reduction and a nonaggression pact between the Eastern and Western alliances, it called for a "fresh approach" to the arms race and a "positive" response to Soviet proposals on space weapons and cuts in nuclear arsenals. The WTO also proposed that both superpowers freeze the size of their armed forces beyond national borders at levels reached in January 1986. Gorbachev's impact was even more evident in the communiqué following the March 1986 foreign ministers meeting, the overall tone being largely nonconfrontational and nonjudgmental.

During the annual Warsaw Pact summit held at Budapest, Hungary, on June 10–11, 1986, the Soviet Union and its allies proposed a reduction by both NATO and the WTO in manpower levels (of up to 500,000 by the early 1990s), tactical aircraft, and conventional and tactical nuclear weapons, with eventual elimination and prohibition of chemical weapons. At a meeting in Sweden on September 22 the WTO members joined NATO countries and European states not affiliated with either group in signing the path-breaking "Stockholm Declaration", the culmination of three years of negotiations through the Conference on Confidence- and Security-Building Measures and Disarmament in Europe. The WTO and NATO agreed to give each other advanced warning of all significant military exercises in Europe while also providing, for the first time in an East-West accord, for mutual, obligatory inspections of military activities.

In April 1987 the WTO announced proposals for a two-year freeze on military spending by itself and NATO. Not surprisingly, the WTO summit at East Berlin on May 28–29 endorsed all of the Soviet proposals under consideration in the ongoing US-Soviet Union talks on missile reductions in Europe. The summit, calling for direct talks with NATO (past discussions having always been conducted under the auspices of previously established institutions), said the anticipated missile treaty should be followed by reductions in conventional arms and forces, as well as in so-called "battlefield" nuclear weapons. The summit also reaffirmed its "military doctrine" — that nuclear weapons should only be used for defensive purposes — and asked NATO, which does not preclude first-strike use of nuclear weapons, for a similar declaration.

The WTO hailed the INF treaty of December 1987 (see US and USSR articles) as a "step of historical dimension". In deference to NATO's request, the WTO also agreed that future talks on reducing conventional arms could continue without reference to battlefield nuclear weapons, although it continued to press for their elimination.

WEST AFRICAN ECONOMIC COMMUNITY (CEAO)

Communauté Economique de l'Afrique de l'Ouest

Established: By treaty adopted at Bamako, Mali, on June 3, 1972, by the Heads of State of the six member states and the Foreign Minister of Benin (then Dahomey), and by protocols annexed to the treaty and signed by the Heads of State at Abidjan, Côte d'Ivoire, April 16–17, 1973.

Purpose: ". . . to promote the harmonized and balanced development of the economic activities of the member States with a view to achieving as rapidly as possible an improvement in the level of living of their populations."

Headquarters: Ouagadougou, Burkina Faso.

Principal Organs: Conference of Heads of State, Council of Ministers, General Secretariat, Solidarity and Intervention Fund for Community Development, Court of Arbitration.

Secretary General: Mamadou Haidara (Mali).

Membership (7): Benin, Burkina Faso, Côte d'Ivoire, Mali, Mauritania, Niger, Senegal.
   Observers (2): Guinea, Togo.

Official Language: French.

Origin and development. The West African Economic Community originated in a protocol of agreement signed at Bamako, Mali, in May 1970 by the heads of state of the now dissolved West African Customs and Economic Union (UDEAO). The signatories sought to establish an organization that would go beyond the limited goals for economic integration represented by the earlier Union and, as a result, adopted the CEAO treaty at Bamako on June 3, 1972. Meeting again on April 16–17, 1973, at Abidjan, Côte d'Ivoire, the signatories approved protocols annexed to the treaty, elected officers, and agreed on a site for the Secretariat. Although the Community came into formal existence on January 1, 1974, detailed consultations and a meeting of the Council of Ministers, held in late 1974, were required before the Community became fully operational. Subsequently, the CEAO secretary general sought to expand the organization's membership but found it impossible to convince anglophone states to join following establishment of the Economic Community of West African States (ECOWAS) in May 1975.

Structure. The Conference of Heads of State, the Community's principal political organ, meets biennially, the site rotating among the member states. The president of the Conference is the head of state of the host country; all decisions must be unanimous. The Conference is responsible for the appointment of the Community's secretary general, accountant, financial comptroller, and the president and members of the Court of Arbitration. The Council of Ministers, which meets at least twice a year and always convenes at least a month before sessions of the Conference, consists of each state's minister of finance or another member of government, depending on the subject under discussion. Decisions of the Council also must be unanimous. The General Secretariat, headed by a secretary general with a four-year renewable term of office, supervises the implementation of Conference and Council decisions. It also oversees the Community Development Fund, which compensates member states for trade losses and finances development projects, and the Solidarity and Intervention Fund (Fosidec), created in 1977 to aid development in the poorer member states.

Activities. The CEAO promotes the integration of member states in agriculture, animal husbandry, fishing, industry, transport, communications, and tourism. Members have agreed not to levy internal taxes within the Community on nonmanufactured, crude products. Industrial products, when exported to other member states, benefit from a special preferential system based on the substitution of a regional cooperation tax for all import taxes. The population of CEAO member states are accorded freedom on movement and the right to establish residency anywhere within the region. However, the Community has fallen short of the long-discussed establishment of a true common market, members acknowledging that trade barriers have proliferated rather than diminished in the face of continued economic disparity among member states.

Recognizing that a substantial majority of the Community's energy consumption is in the form of oil, the CEAO has set as one of its highest priorities the formation of an oil-distribution supply company. Other high-priority endeavors include the creation of a regional solar energy center, a management school, and a school of mining and technology. In 1985 the regional solar energy center received permission for a renewable energy equipment program, while a proposal to establish a Regional Center for Commercial Information and Documentation was approved.

The principal achievements of the 11th summit meeting, held March 26–27, 1986, at Ouagadougou, Burkina Faso, were improved relations among members and renewed credibility for an organization that had recently been rocked by scandal. In April a Burkinabe court convicted Moussa N'Gom, former CEAO secretary general, Moussa Diakite, former director of Fosidec, and Mohamed Diawara, former minister of planning for Côte d'Ivoire, of embezzling Fosidec funds. As a result of the scandal, the 12th summit, held April 21–22, 1987, at Nouakchott, Mauritania, placed Fosidec, theretofore largely autonomous, under the direct supervision of the CEAO secretary general. In other action, the annual budget was reduced by 10 percent to 1.1 billion CFA.

Thomas Sankara, (then) president of Burkina Faso, was chosen as the CEAO nominee for the presidency of ECOWAS. However, his candidacy failed at the ECOWAS summit in June, underlining continued regional discord and possible concern among conservative CEAO members over Sankara's zealous prosecution of the Community's recent financial scandal. Following Sankara's death in a September coup, his successor, Blaise Compaoré, was reported to have established closer relations with many other regional leaders, particularly Ivorian President Houphouët-Boigny, who had been instrumental in the creation of the CEAO and remained one of its dominant figures.

WESTERN EUROPEAN UNION (WEU)

Established: By protocols signed at Paris, France, October 23, 1954, effective May 6, 1955.

Purpose: Collective self-defense and political collaboration in support of European unity.

Headquarters: London, United Kingdom.

Principal Organs: Council (all members), Assembly (89 parliamentary representatives and 89 substitutes), Secretariat.

Secretary General: Alfred Cahen (Belgium).

President of the Assembly: Jean-Marie Caro (France).

Membership (7): Belgium, France, Federal Republic of Germany, Italy, Luxembourg, Netherlands, United Kingdom. Portugal applied for membership in 1984 as did Turkey in 1987.

Official Languages: English, French.

Origin and development. The WEU is the direct successor of the five-power Brussels Treaty Organization, which was established by the United Kingdom, France, and the Benelux states through the Treaty of Economic, Social, and Cultural Collaboration and Collective Self-Defense, signed at Brussels, Belgium, on March 17, 1948. The Brussels Pact had included provisions for automatic mutual defense assistance and envisioned coordination of military activity. However, de facto responsibilities in those areas were transferred to the 12-power North Atlantic Treaty Organization (NATO) following its creation in 1949. Shortly thereafter, the call for West German rearmament to permit FRG participation in NATO led to a revival of interest in a European army. In 1952 the six countries which had recently established the European Coal and Steel Community (ECSC)—France, West Germany, Italy, and the Benelux countries—signed a treaty to institute a European Defense Community which would have placed their military forces under a single authority. Following rejection of the EDC by the French Parliament in 1954, the United Kingdom invited the ECSC countries to revive the 1948 Treaty, which was modified and expanded to provide a framework for the rearming of West Germany and its admission to NATO. Under a series of protocols effective May 6, 1955, the Brussels organization was enlarged to include Italy and West Germany and was renamed the WEU.

The protocols redefined the purposes of the organization by including a reference to the unity and progressive integration of Europe; remodeled its institutional structure; established norms for member states' contributions to NATO military forces; provided for limitation of the strength and armaments of forces maintained under national command; took note of the United Kingdom's pledge to maintain forces on the mainland of Europe; acknowledged West Germany's intention to refrain from manufacturing atomic, chemical, biological, and certain other types of weapons; and established an Agency for the Control of Armaments in order to police restrictions on the armaments of all WEU members. However, the exercise of military responsibilities remained subordinate to NATO and the WEU has never established its own military force or armaments, although its binding defense alliance is still in force.

The concern over duplication of efforts also caused the WEU to transfer many of its social and cultural activities in 1960 to the Council of Europe. The Union remained active in economic affairs, serving after French President Charles de Gaulle's first veto of British entry into the European Economic Community (EEC) in 1963, as a link between the EEC and the United Kingdom. Activity in that area effectively ceased as well in the wake of UK admission to the European Communities (EC) in 1973; collaterally, WEU activity in the political field diminished in proportion to the growth of political consultation within the EC. Only in 1984, after a lengthy period of relative inactivity, did members call for a "reactivation" and restructuring of the WEU to foster the "harmonization" of views on defense, security, and other military issues precluded from EC debate.

Structure. The WEU's decision-making body is the Council which, in view of imprecise organizational language in the Brussels Treaty, has traditionally operated through two distinct groupings — the Council of Ministers and the Permanent Council. The Council of Ministers, composed of foreign and defense ministers of WEU countries, normally meets twice a year. However, separate meetings of the foreign and/or defense ministers may take place if the members so desire. The presidency of the Council is held by each member state for a one-year term. Council sessions are usually held in the country holding the presidency.

The Permanent Council, located in London, is mandated "to discuss in greater detail the views expressed by the Ministers and to follow up their decisions". It comprises the ambassadors of member countries to the United Kingdom and a senior official from the British Foreign and Commonwealth Affairs Office. Under the 1984 reactivation, the Permanent Council, which is chaired by the WEU secretary general, has been given greater authority. One of its current responsibilities is to oversee restructuring progress in conjunction with the Secretariat staff and to recommend further changes, if necessary, in WEU operations.

Much of the recent WEU reorganization has concentrated on two Paris-based subsidiary bodies — the Standing Armaments Committee (SAC) and the Agency for the Control of Armaments (ACA). The SAC had been mandated by the 1955 protocols with facilitating the joint production of armaments, while the ACA had been created to ensure, in liaison with NATO, that stocks of armaments in Europe did not exceed prescribed levels and that prohibited weapons were not manufactured. In 1985, however, the WEU decided to reduce SAC and ACA activity in favor of three new agencies which would more accurately reflect the Union's new emphasis: the Agency for the Study of Arms Control and Disarmament Questions, the Agency for the Study of Security and Defense Questions, and the Agency for the Development of Cooperation in the Field of Armament.

The WEU's other main organ is the Assembly, which encompasses the 89 representatives (18 each from France, West Germany, Italy, and United Kingdom; 7 each from Belgium and the Netherlands; and 3 from Luxembourg) of the WEU member countries to the Parliamentary Assembly of the Council of Europe. There are also 89 substitutes appointed to the WEU Assembly from members' national parliaments in general proportion to the strength of government and opposition parties. Representatives and substitutes may join political groups within the Assembly, of which there were four as of December 1986: the Federated Group of Christian Democrats and European Democrats (83 members), the Socialist Group (54 members), the Liberal Group (20 members), and the Communist Group (12 members).

The Assembly's regularly scheduled annual meeting is divided into two sessions, the first held in May or June and the second in November or December. The Assembly, which draws up its own agenda, functions as an independent consultative body, making recommendations to the WEU Council and to other intergovernmental organizations, sending resolutions to governments and national parliaments, and rendering its opinion on the annual reports of the Council. Its subordinate organs include a General Affairs Committee, which deals with the evolution of intra-European relations and the political aspects of European security; a Committee on Scientific, Technological, and Aerospace Questions, set up in July 1965 to consider the military aspects of European union in the field of advanced technology; and a Committee on Defense Questions and Armaments, whose reports have been considered among the most authoritative and incisive published analyses of Western European security needs and developments.

Activities. The WEU's Council of Ministers met at Rome, Italy, on October 26–27, 1984, prior to a parliamentarians' meeting on October 28–30. A "Statement of Rome" was issued which stated the "tasks" of the revived Union: an assessment of the Soviet threat, increased European arms collaboration, and the formulating of European views on arms control and East-West dialogue. Perceived as advantages of a revived WEU were the assurance of military aid in case of attack, security cooperation between France and West Germany, and an enhanced capacity to respond to public opinion on European defense issues.

Although the WEU seemed to lose some of its enthusiasm for revitalization in 1985, the movement subsequently regained momentum; in early 1987 the United Kingdom, which traditionally has relied more heavily on its security connections with the United States, called for its "strengthening". In August, Britain and France persuaded Belgium, Italy, and the Netherlands to join them in sending naval forces to the Persian Gulf to assist in the US-led escort of oil tankers. Adding to the heightened WEU posture, a Council of Ministers meeting at The Hague, Netherlands, in October approved a strongly-worded "Platform on European Security Interests" that stressed the need for the retention of some nuclear forces and an increase in conventional forces in Western Europe to maintain deterrence vis-à-vis the Warsaw Treaty forces. The ministers also reaffirmed the mutual defense pledges of WEU members and noted the growing importance of British and French independent nuclear forces. Although the WEU was careful not to suggest an intention to supplant NATO as the "pillar of Western European security", the new platform was generally interpreted as a response to the pending intermediate nuclear missile pact between the United States and the Soviet Union.

European concern over a possible reduction in the US military commitment in Europe was also expected to lead the WEU to act soon on proposals for expansion. The Union is currently in receipt of membership applications from Portugal and Turkey, with Greece, Norway, and Spain also expressing an interest in joining the group.

APPENDICES

APPENDIX A
CHRONOLOGY OF MAJOR
INTERNATIONAL EVENTS: 1945-1987

1945, February 7–22. Churchill, Roosevelt, Stalin meet at Yalta, USSR.

March 22. Treaty establishing Arab League signed at Cairo, Egypt.

May 7. Surrender of Germany.

May 8. Proclamation of end of the war in Europe.

June 5. US Secretary of State Marshall calls for European Recovery Program (Marshall Plan).

June 26. United Nations Charter signed at San Francisco, USA.

July 17–August 2. Churchill, Stalin, Truman meet at Potsdam, East Germany.

August 6. US drops atomic bomb at Hiroshima, Japan.

September 2. Surrender of Japan.

1946, July 29–October 15. Peace Conference meets at Paris, France.

December 30. UN Atomic Energy Commission approves US proposal for world control of atomic weapons.

1947, February 10. Peace treaties signed with Bulgaria, Finland, Hungary, Italy, Romania.

June 5. Marshall Plan inaugurated.

October 5. Communist Information Bureau (Cominform) established.

October 29. Customs union between Belgium, Netherlands, Luxembourg (Benelux) ratified.

October 30. General Agreement on Tariffs and Trade (GATT) negotiated at Geneva, Switzerland.

1948, March 17. Brussels Treaty signed by Belgium, France, Luxembourg, Netherlands, United Kingdom.

March 20. Soviet representatives walk out of Allied Control Council for Germany.

April 16. Organization for European Economic Cooperation (OEEC) established at Paris, France.

April 30. Organization of American States (OAS) Charter signed at Bogotá, Colombia.

May 14. State of Israel proclaimed.

June 28. Cominform expels Yugoslavia.

July 24–1949, May 12. Berlin blockade.

December 10. UN General Assembly adopts Universal Declaration of Human Rights.

1949, January 25. Council for Mutual Economic Assistance (CMEA) established at Moscow, USSR.

April 4. Treaty establishing North Atlantic Treaty Organization (NATO) signed at Washington, USA.

May 4. Statute establishing Council of Europe signed at London, United Kingdom.

1950, January 31. US President Truman orders construction of hydrogen bomb.

May 9. Schuman Plan for integration of Western European coal and steel industries proposed.

June 27. US intervenes in Korean War.

November 3. "Uniting for Peace" Resolution passed by UN General Assembly.

1951, April 18. Treaty establishing European Coal and Steel Community signed by Belgium, France, Federal Republic of Germany, Italy, Luxembourg, Netherlands.

September 1. Anzus Pact signed at San Francisco, USA, by Australia, New Zealand, United States.

September 8. Peace Treaty signed by Japan and non-Communist Allied powers at San Francisco, USA.

1952, May 27. European Defense Community (EDC) Charter signed by Belgium, France, Federal Republic of Germany, Italy, Luxembourg, Netherlands.

November 1. US explodes hydrogen bomb at Eniwetok Atoll.

1953, March 5. Death of Joseph Stalin.

December 8. US President Eisenhower proposes international control of atomic energy.

1954, January 21–February 18. Four-Power Foreign Ministers' Conference at Berlin, Germany.

April 26–July 21. Geneva (Switzerland) Conference on Southeast Asia.

April 28–May 2. Colombo (Ceylon) Conference of Asiatic powers.

August 30. French National Assembly rejects European Defense Community (ECD) treaty.

September 8. Treaty establishing Southeast Asia Treaty Organization (SEATO) signed at Manila, Philippines.

September 28–October 3. Nine-Power Conference at London, United Kingdom.

October 23. Allied occupation of West Germany ends.

November 29–December 2. Moscow (USSR) Conference of Communist nations on European security.

1955, February 18. Baghdad (Iraq) Pact signed by Iraq and Turkey.

May 6. Western European Union (WEU) inaugurated by admitting Italy and Federal Republic of Germany to Brussels Treaty.

April 18–24. Asian-African Conference at Bandung, Indonesia.

May 9. Federal Republic of Germany admitted to NATO.

May 14. Warsaw Pact signed by East European Communist governments.

1956, April 17. Cominform disbanded.

July 26. Egypt nationalizes Suez Canal.

August 16–23. Suez Conference at London, United Kingdom.

October 23–November 22. Anti-Communist rebellion in Hungary suppressed by Soviet troops.

October 29–November 6. Suez crisis.

1957, March 25. Rome (Italy) Treaty establishing European Economic Community (EEC) and European Atomic Energy Community (Euratom) signed.

December 26–1958, January 1. Asian-African Conference meets at Cairo, Egypt.

1958, February 24–April 27. First UN Conference on the Law of the Sea held at Geneva, Switzerland.

September 1–14. Geneva (Switzerland) Conference on Peaceful Uses of Atomic Energy.

1960, March 15–April 29, June 7–27. Ten-Power Disarmament Conference meets at Geneva, Switzerland.

May 1. U-2 incident.

May 3. European Free Trade Association (EFTA) of "Outer Seven" (Austria, Denmark, Norway, Sweden, Switzerland, Portugal, United Kingdom) established.

May 14. Beginning of Sino-Soviet dispute.

December 14. Charter of Organization for Economic Cooperation and Development (OECD) to replace OEEC signed at Paris, France.

1961, April 17–20. Bay of Pigs invasion of Cuba.

August 15. Start of construction of Berlin Wall between East and West Germany.

September 1–6. Conference of Nonaligned Nations at Belgrade, Yugoslavia.

1962, March 14. Opening of 17-nation Disarmament Conference at Geneva, Switzerland.

October 22–28. Cuban missile crisis.

1963, January 29. France vetoes British bid for admission to EEC.

May 25. Organization of African Unity (OAU) Charter adopted at Addis Ababa, Ethiopia.

August 5. Limited Nuclear Test-Ban Treaty signed at Moscow, USSR.

1964, March 23–June 15. UN Conference on Trade and Development meets at Geneva, Switzerland.

May 28. Palestine Liberation Organization (PLO) established.

October 5–11. Conference of Nonaligned Nations at Cairo, Egypt.

1965, February 21. Decision to merge European Economic Community (EEC), European Coal and Steel Community (ECSC), and European Atomic Energy Community (Euratom).

1966, March 11. France withdraws troops from NATO.

1967, January 27. Treaty governing exploration and use of outer space signed by US, USSR, and 60 other nations.

June 5. Beginning of Arab-Israeli War.

June 17. China explodes its first hydrogen bomb.

1968, January 16. Britain announces withdrawal of forces from Persian Gulf and Far East.

May 13. Beginning of Vietnam peace talks at Paris, France.

June 4. Nuclear Non-Proliferation Treaty approved by UN General Assembly.

August 20–21. Warsaw Pact forces occupy Czechoslovakia.

August 25. France explodes its first hydrogen bomb.

September 12. Albania withdraws from Warsaw Pact.

October 5. Outbreak of civil rights violence at Londonderry, Northern Ireland.

1969, March 2. Clash between Chinese and Soviet troops along Ussuri River.

April 28. Resignation of French President de Gaulle.

July 21. US lands first men on moon.

November 17–December 22. Initiation of Strategic Arms Limitation Talks (SALT) between US and USSR.

1970, March 2. Rhodesia issues unilateral declaration of independence from Britain.

August 12. Negotiation of European boundary treaty between Federal Republic of Germany and Soviet Union.

September 8–10. Conference of Nonaligned Nations at Lusaka, Zambia.

December 7. Boundary recognition treaty signed by Federal Republic of Germany and Poland.

1971, February 11. Treaty banning firing of atomic weapons from seabed signed by US, USSR, and 40 other nations.

November 12. President Nixon announces end of US offensive action in Vietnam.

1972, February 21–28. US President Nixon visits China.

May 22–29. President Nixon visits Soviet Union.

1973, January 1. Denmark, Ireland, United Kingdom enter European Communities.

February 12. Last US ground troops leave Vietnam.

September 5–9. Conference of Nonaligned Nations at Algiers, Algeria.

October 6–22. Fourth Arab-Israeli War.

October 17–1974, March 18. Arab embargo on oil shipments to US and other Western nations.

1974, January 18. Egypt and Israel sign agreement on disengagement of forces along Suez Canal.

May 20. Third UN Conference on Law of the Sea opens at Caracas, Venezuela.

July 20. Turkish intervention in Cyprus.

August 19–30. UN World Population Conference held at Bucharest, Romania.

November 5–16. UN World Food Conference held at Rome, Italy.

1975, February 28. First Lomé (Togo) Convention signed between EEC and developing African, Caribbean, and Pacific (ACP) states.

May 28. Treaty establishing Economic Community of West African States (ECOWAS) signed at Lagos, Nigeria.

June 5. Suez Canal reopened to international shipping.

July 30–August 1. Conference on Security and Cooperation in Europe (CSCE) holds final session at Helsinki, Finland.

September 4. Agreement between Egypt and Israel providing for Israeli withdrawal in Sinai and establishment of UN buffer zone.

October 17. Treaty establishing Latin American Economic System (SELA) signed at Panama City, Panama.

November 20. Death of Gen. Francisco Franco.

December 16–19. Conference on International Economic Cooperation meets at Paris, France.

1976, June 17. Outbreak of racial violence at Soweto, South Africa.

June 29–30. Conference of European Communist parties held at Berlin, East Germany.

July 3–4. Israeli raid on Entebbe Airport, Uganda.

August 16–19. Conference of Nonaligned Nations at Colombo, Sri Lanka.

September 9. Death of Mao Zedong.

1977, June 30. Southeast Asia Treaty Organization (SEATO) dissolved.

October 4–1978, March 9. Belgrade (Yugoslavia) Review Conference on Security and Cooperation in Europe.

November 19–21. Egyptian President Sadat visits Israel.

December 25. Israeli Prime Minister Begin confers with President Sadat at Ismailia, Egypt.

1978, September 9–17. President Sadat and Prime Minister Begin meet with US President Carter at Camp David, Maryland, USA.

1979, January 1. People's Republic of China and United States establish diplomatic relations.

January 16. Shah of Iran goes into exile.

March 26. Egyptian-Israeli peace treaty signed at Washington, USA.

September 3–8. Conference of Nonaligned Nations at Havana, Cuba.

September 26. Central Treaty Organization (CENTO) dissolved.

November 4. Iranian students seize US Embassy at Teheran.

December 27. Soviet military forces support coup in Afghanistan.

1980, April 18. Zimbabwe (formerly Rhodesia) declared legally independent.

May 4. Death of Yugoslavian President Josip Broz Tito.

September 22. Iraqi invasion of Iran initiates Persian Gulf war.

October 24. Independent trade union (Solidarity) officially registered in Poland.

November 11–December 19. First session of Madrid (Spain) Conference on Security and Cooperation in Europe.

1981, January 1. Greece enters European Communities.

January 20. Iran frees remaining US hostages.

October 6. Egyptian President Sadat assassinated.

December 13. Martial law declared in Poland.

December 14. Occupied Golan Heights placed under Israeli law.

1982, April 2–July 15. Falkland Islands (*Islas Malvinas*) war between Argentina and the United Kingdom.

April 30. Law of the Sea Convention adopted despite US objections.

June 6. Israeli invasion of Lebanon.

August 21–September 1. PLO forces evacuate Beirut, Lebanon.

October 8. Polish *Sejm* formally dissolves all existing trade unions.

November 10. Soviet leader Leonid Brezhnev dies; succeeded as CPSU general secretary by Yuri Andropov (November 12).

December 18. Martial law in Poland suspended.

1983, March 7–12. Conference of Nonaligned Nations at New Delhi, India.

September 1. USSR shoots down Korean Air Lines Boeing 747 passenger plane.

October 25. United States, in concert with six Caribbean states, invades Grenada (last troops withdrawn, December 12).

1984, February 9. Soviet leader Yuri Andropov dies; succeeded as CPSU general secretary by Konstantin Chernenko (February 13).

October 31. Indian Prime Minister Indira Gandi assassinated.

November 6. US President Reagan wins reelection by record margin.

1985, March 10. Soviet leader Konstantin Chernenko dies; succeeded as CPSU general secretary by Mikhail S. Gorbachev (March 11).

October 7. Palestinian terrorists seize Italian cruise ship, *Achille Lauro.*

November 15. Ireland and the United Kingdom sign accord granting Irish Republic consultative role in governance of Northern Ireland.

November 19–21. US President Reagan and Soviet leader Gorbachev hold summit meeting at Geneva.

1986, January 1. Spain and Portugal enter European Communities.

January 28. US space shuttle *Challenger,* on 25th shuttle mission, explodes after lift-off.

February 7. Jean-Claude Duvalier flees from Haiti to France, ending nearly three decades of his family's rule.

February 25. General Secretary Gorbachev calls for sweeping reforms in Soviet economic system.

February 25. Corazon Aquino inaugurated as Philippines president following disputed election on February 7; after holding rival inauguration, Ferdinand Marcos flies to Hawaii.

April 10. John Paul II makes first recorded papal visit to a Jewish synagogue.

April 15. US aircraft bomb Tripoli and Benghazi in response to alleged Libyan-backed terrorist activity in Europe.

April 26. Explosion at Chernobyl, USSR, power plant reults in worst nuclear accident in history.

September 1–7. Nonaligned Movement holds eighth summit at Harare, Zimbabwe.

September 15. Eighth round of GATT negotiations opens at Punta del Este, Uruguay.

October 11–12. US President Reagan and Soviet General Secretary Gorbachev hold inconclusive summit at Reykjavik, Iceland.

November 3. Former US Security Advisor Robert McFarlane reported to have secretly visited Teheran to negotiate an end to Iranian support for terrorism in return for spare parts for military equipment.

November 25. Attorney General Edwin Meese states that $10–30 million paid by Iran for US arms were diverted by Lt. Col. Oliver North to Nicaraguan insurgents.

1987, June 11. Margaret Thatcher becomes first prime minister in modern British history to lead her party to a third consecutive electoral victory.

July 22. Three US warships escort two reflagged Kuwaiti oil tankers into the Persian Gulf, in first test of reflagging program announced in May.

July 31. Iranian pilgrims clash with Saudi police in Mecca riot; 402 persons killed.

August 7. Five Central American presidents sign regional peace plan proposed by Oscar Arias of Costa Rica.

September 1. Erich Honecker becomes first East German head of state to visit West Germany.

October 19. US stock market crashes, with Dow Jones Industrial Average falling 508.32 in one session; foreign markets plummet the next day.

December 8. US President Reagan and Soviet General Secretary Gorbachev sign INF treaty calling for elimination of entire class of nuclear weapons.

December 9. Uprising (*intifada*) begins among Palestinians in the Gaza Strip, spreading to the West Bank the following day.

APPENDIX B
MEMBERSHIP OF THE UNITED NATIONS
AND ITS SPECIALIZED AND RELATED AGENCIES

ORGANIZATION[a]	UN[b]	FAO	GATT	IAEA	IBRD	ICAO	IDA	IFAD	IFC	ILO	IMF	IMO	ITU	UNESCO	UNIDO	UPU	WHO	WIPO	WMO
Members[c]	159	158[d]	96[e]	113[f]	151[g]	157[h]	136[i]	142[j]	133[k]	150[l]	151[m]	131[n]	162[o]	158[p]	144[q]	168[r]	166[s]	119[t]	160[u]
COUNTRIES																			
Afghanistan	1946	x		x	x	x	x	3	x	x	x		x	x	x	x	x		x
Albania	1955	x		x										x	x		x	x		x
Algeria	1962	x	(e)	x	x	x	x	2		x	x	x	x	x	x	x	x	x	x
Angola	1976	x	(e)			x		3		x		x	x	x	x	x	x	x	x
Antigua and Barbuda	1981	x	x		x	x		3	x	x	x	x	x	x			x		
Argentina	1945	x	x	x	x	x	x	3	x	x	x	x	x	x	x	x	x	x	x
Australia	1945	x	x	x	x	x	x	1	x	x	x	x	x	x	x	x	x	x	x
Austria	1955	x	x	x	x	x	x	1	x	x	x	x	x	x	x	x	x	x	x
Bahamas	1973	x	(e)		x	x		x	x	x	x	x	x	x		x	x	x	x
Bahrain	1971	x	(e)		x	x				x	x	x	x	x	x	x	x		x
Bangladesh	1974	x	x	x	x	x	x	3	x	x	x	x	x	x	x	x	x	x	x
Barbados	1966	x	x		x	x		3	x	x	x	x	x	x	x	x	x	x	x
Belgium	1945	x	x	x	x	x	x	1	x	x	x	x	x	x	x	x	x	x	x
Belize	1981	x	x		x			3	x	x	x		x	x	x	x	x		x
Benin	1960	x	x		x	x	x	3	x	x	x	x	x	x	x	x	x	x	x
Bhutan	1971	x			x		x	3			x		x	x	x	x			
Bolivia	1945	x		x	x	x	x	3	x	x	x	x	x	x	x	x	x		x
Botswana	1966	x	x		x	x	x	3	x	x	x		x	x	x	x	x		x
Brazil	1945	x	x	x	x	x	x	3	x	x	x	x	x	x	x	x	x	x	x
Brunei	1984	x	(e)			x							x	x			x	x	x

[a] The following abbreviations are used: UN—United Nations; FAO—Food and Agriculture Organization; GATT—General Agreement on Tariffs and Trade; IAEA—International Atomic Energy Agency; IBRD—International Bank for Reconstruction and Development; ICAO—International Civil Aviation Organization; IDA—International Development Association; IFAD—International Fund for Agricultural Development; IFC—International Finance Corporation; ILO—International Labour Organisation; IMF—International Monetary Fund; IMO—International Maritime Organization; ITU—International Telecommunication Union; UNESCO—United Nations Educational, Scientific and Cultural Organization; UNIDO—United Nations Industrial Development Organization; UPU—Universal Postal Union; WHO—World Health Organization; WIPO—World Intellectual Property Organization; WMO—World Meterological Organization.

[b] Dates are those of each member's admission to the United Nations.

[c] Totals for all columns beginning with FAO include non-UN members.

[d] The 158 members of FAO include the following not listed in the table: Democratic People's Republic of Korea, Republic of Korea, Namibia (represented by the UN Council for Namibia), Switzerland, Tonga.

[e] The 96 contracting parties to GATT include the following not listed in the table: Hong Kong, Republic of Korea, Switzerland. Of the 26 states marked (e) in the table, Tunisia has acceded provisionally, while the remaining 25 (plus Kiribati, Tonga, and Tuvalu, which are not listed) are territories to which GATT applied before independence and which now as independent states maintain de facto application of the Agreement pending final decisions as to their commercial policies.

[f] The 113 members of IAEA include the following not listed in the table: Holy See (Vatican City State), Democratic People's Republic of Korea, Republic of Korea, Liechtenstein, Monaco, Namibia (represented by the UN Council for Namibia), Switzerland.

[g] The 151 members of IBRD include the following not listed in the table: Kiribati, Republic of Korea, Tonga.

[h] The 157 members of ICAO include the following not listed in the table: Cook Islands, Kiribati, Democratic People's Republic of Korea, Republic of Korea, Monaco, Nauru, Switzerland, Tonga. USSR membership includes the Byelorussian and Ukrainian SSRs.

[i] The 136 members of IDA include the following not listed in the table: Kiribati Republic of Korea, Tonga.

[j] The 142 members of IFAD are divided into three categories: (1) developed states, (2) oil-producing states, and (3) developing states. Members include the following not listed in the table: Switzerland (1), Democratic People's Republic of Korea (3), Republic of Korea (3), Tonga (3).

[k] The 133 members of IFC include the following not listed in the table: Kiribati, Republic of Korea, Tonga.

[l] The 150 members of ILO include the following not listed in the table: Namibia (represented by the UN Council for Namibia), San Marino, Switzerland.

[m] The 151 members of IMF include the following not listed in the table: Kiribati, Republic of Korea, Tonga.

[n] The 131 members of IMO include the following not listed in the table: Democratic People's Republic of Korea, Republic of Korea, Switzerland. IMO also has one associate member: Hong Kong.

[o] The 162 members of ITU include the following not listed in the table: Holy See (Vatican City State), Kiribati, Democratic People's Republic of Korea, Republic of Korea, Liechtenstein, Monaco, Namibia (represented by the UN Council for Namibia), Nauru, San Marino, Switzerland, Tonga.

[p] The 158 members of UNESCO include the following not listed in the table: Democratic People's Republic of Korea, Republic of Korea, Monaco, Namibia (represented by the UN Council for Namibia), San Marino, Switzerland, Tonga. UNESCO also has three associate members: Aruba, British Virgin Islands, Netherlands Antilles.

[q] The 144 members of UNIDO include the following not listed in the table: Democratic People's Republic of Korea, Republic of Korea, Namibia (represented by the UN Council for Namibia), Switzerland, Tonga.

[r] The 168 members of UPU include the following not listed in the table: Holy See (Vatican City State), Kiribati, Democratic People's Republic of Korea, Republic of Korea, Liechtenstein, Monaco, Nauru, Netherlands Antilles, Overseas Territories of the United Kingdom, San Marino, Switzerland, Tonga, Tuvalu. South Africa was expelled in 1984.

[s] The 166 members of WHO include the following not listed in the table: Cook Islands, Kiribati, Democratic People's Republic of Korea, Republic of Korea, Monaco, San Marino, Switzerland, Tonga. WHO also has one associate member: Namibia (represented by the UN Council for Namibia).

[t] The 119 members of WIPO include the following not listed in the table: Holy See (Vatican City State), Democratic People's Republic of Korea, Republic of Korea, Liechtenstein, Monaco, Switzerland.

[u] The 160 members of WMO include the following not listed in the table which maintain their own meteorological services: British Caribbean Territories, French Polynesia, Hong Kong, Democratic People's Republic of Korea, Republic of Korea, Netherlands Antilles, New Caledonia, Switzerland. South Africa's membership has been suspended since 1975.

[v] In addition to expulsion from the UPU, certain of South Africa's rights of membership in ICAO, IAEA, ITU, UPU, WHO, WIPO, and WMO have been suspended or restricted.

ORGANIZATION	UN	FAO	GATT	IAEA	IBRD	ICAO	IDA	IFAD	IFC	ILO	IMF	IMO	ITU	UNESCO	UNIDO	UPU	WHO	WIPO	WMO
COUNTRIES (cont.)																			
Bulgaria	1955	x	x		x					x		x	x	x	x	x	x	x	x
Burkina Faso	1960	x	x	x	x	x	x	3	x	x	x		x	x	x	x	x	x	x
Burma	1948	x	x	x	x	x	x		x	x	x	x	x	x		x	x		x
Burundi	1962	x	x		x	x	x	3	x	x	x		x	x	x	x	x	x	x
Byelorussian Soviet Socialist Republic	1945			x							x			x	x	x	x	x	x	x
Cameroon	1960	x	x	x	x	x	x	3	x	x	x	x	x	x	x	x	x	x	x
Canada	1945	x	x	x	x	x	x	1	x	x	x	x	x	x	x	x	x	x	x
Cape Verde Islands	1975	x	(e)			x	x	x	3		x	x	x	x	x	x	x	x		x
Central African Republic	1960	x	x			x	x	x	3		x	x		x	x	x	x	x	x	x
Chad	1960	x	x			x	x	x	3		x	x		x	x		x	x	x	x
Chile	1945	x	x	x	x	x	x	3	x	x	x	x	x	x	x	x	x	x	x
China, People's Republic of	1945	x		x	x	x	x	3	x	x	x	x	x	x	x	x	x	x	x
Colombia	1945	x	x	x	x	x	x	3	x	x	x	x	x	x	x	x	x	x	x
Comoro Islands	1975	x			x	x	x	3		x	x		x	x	x	x	x		x
Congo	1960	x	x		x	x	x	3	x	x	x	x	x	x	x	x	x	x	x
Costa Rica	1945	x			x	x	x	x	3	x	x	x	x	x	x		x	x	x	x
Côte d'Ivoire	1960	x	x	x	x	x	x	3	x	x	x	x	x	x	x	x	x	x	x
Cuba	1945	x	x	x			x		3		x			x	x	x	x	x	x	x
Cyprus	1960	x	x	x	x	x	x	3	x	x	x	x	x	x	x	x	x	x	x
Czechoslovakia	1945	x	x	x		x					x		x	x	x	x	x	x	x	x
Denmark	1945	x	x	x	x	x	x	1	x	x	x	x	x	x	x	x	x	x	x
Djibouti	1977	x			x	x	x	3	x	x	x	x	x	x			x	x		x
Dominica	1978	x	(e)		x		x	3		x	x	x	x	x			x	x		x
Dominican Republic	1945	x	x	x	x	x	x	3	x	x	x	x	x		x	x	x	x		x
Ecuador	1945	x			x	x	x	x	3	x	x	x	x	x	x	x	x	x	x	x
Egypt	1945	x	x	x	x	x	x	3	x	x	x	x	x	x	x	x	x	x	x
El Salvador	1945	x			x	x	x	x	3	x	x	x	x	x	x		x	x	x	x
Equatorial Guinea	1968	x	(e)		x	x	x	3		x	x	x	x	x	x	x	x			
Ethiopia	1945	x			x	x	x	x	3	x	x	x	x	x	x	x	x	x		x
Fiji	1970	x	(e)		x	x	x	3	x	x	x	x	x	x	x	x	x	x	x	x
Finland	1955	x	x	x	x	x	x	1	x	x	x	x	x	x	x	x	x	x	x
France	1945	x	x	x	x	x	x	1	x	x	x	x	x	x	x	x	x	x	x
Gabon	1960	x	x	x	x	x	x	2	x	x	x	x	x	x	x	x	x	x	x
Gambia	1965	x	x		x	x	x	3	x		x	x	x	x	x	x	x	x	x	x
German Democratic Republic	1973			x							x			x	x	x	x	x	x	x
Germany, Federal Republic of	1973	x	x	x	x	x	x	1	x	x	x	x	x	x	x	x	x	x	x
Ghana	1957	x	x	x	x	x	x	3	x	x	x	x	x	x	x	x	x	x	x
Greece	1945	x	x	x	x	x	x	3	x	x	x	x	x	x	x	x	x	x	x
Grenada	1974	x	(e)		x	x	x	3	x	x	x			x	x	x	x	x		
Guatemala	1945	x			x	x	x	x	3	x	x	x	x	x	x	x	x	x	x	x
Guinea	1958	x			x	x	x	3	x	x	x	x	x	x	x	x	x	x	x	x
Guinea-Bissau	1974	x	(e)		x	x	x	3	x	x	x	x	x	x	x	x	x	x	x	x
Guyana	1966	x	x		x	x	x	3	x	x	x	x	x	x	x	x	x			x
Haiti	1945	x	x	x	x	x	x	3	x	x	x	x	x	x	x	x	x	x	x	x
Honduras	1945	x			x	x	x	3	x	x	x	x	x	x	x	x	x	x	x	x
Hungary	1955	x	x	x	x	x	x			x	x	x	x	x	x	x	x	x	x	x
Iceland	1946	x	x	x	x	x	x			x	x	x	x	x	x	x	x	x	x	x
India	1945	x	x	x	x	x	x	3	x	x	x	x	x	x	x		x	x	x	x
Indonesia	1950	x	x	x	x	x	x	2	x	x	x	x	x	x	x	x	x	x	x	x
Iran	1945	x			x	x	x	x	2	x	x	x	x	x	x	x	x	x		x
Iraq	1945	x			x	x	x	x	2	x	x	x	x	x	x	x	x	x	x	x
Ireland	1955	x	x	x	x	x	x	1	x	x	x	x	x	x	x	x	x	x	x
Israel	1949	x	x	x	x	x	x	3	x	x	x	x	x	x	x	x	x	x	x
Italy	1955	x	x	x	x	x	x	1	x	x	x	x	x	x	x	x	x	x	x
Jamaica	1962	x	x	x	x	x	x	3	x	x	x	x	x	x	x	x	x	x	x
Japan	1956	x	x	x	x	x	x	1	x	x	x	x	x	x	x	x	x	x	x
Jordan	1955	x			x	x	x	x	3	x	x	x	x	x	x	x	x	x	x	x
Kampuchea	1955	x	(e)	x	x	x	x				x	x	x	x	x		x	x		
Kenya	1963	x	x	x	x	x	x	3	x	x	x	x	x	x	x		x	x	x	x
Kuwait	1963	x	x	x	x	x	x	2	x	x	x	x	x	x	x		x	x		x
Laos	1955	x			x	x	x	3		x	x		x	x	x	x	x			x
Lebanon	1945	x		x	x	x	x	3	x	x	x	x	x	x	x	x	x	x	x	x
Lesotho	1966	x	x		x	x	x	3	x	x	x		x	x	x	x	x	x	x	x

ORGANIZATION	UN	FAO	GATT	IAEA	IBRD	ICAO	IDA	IFAD	IFC	ILO	IMF	IMO	ITU	UNESCO	UNIDO	UPU	WHO	WIPO	WMO
COUNTRIES (cont.)																			
Liberia	1945		x	x	x	x	x	3	x	x	x	x	x	x		x	x		x
Libya	1955		x	x	x	x	x	2	x	x	x	x	x	x	x	x	x	x	x
Luxembourg	1945	x	x	x	x	x	x	1	x	x	x		x	x	x	x	x	x	x
Madagascar	1960	x	x	x	x	x	x	3	x	x	x	x	x	x	x	x	x		x
Malawi	1964	x		x	x	x	x	3	x	x	x		x	x	x	x	x	x	x
Malaysia	1957	x	x	x	x	x	x		x	x	x	x	x	x	x	x	x		x
Maldives	1965	x		x	x	x		3	x		x	x	x	x		x	x	x	x
Mali	1960	(e)	x	x	x	x	x	3	x	x	x		x	x	x	x	x	x	x
Malta	1964	x		x	x			3		x	x	x	x	x	x	x	x	x	x
Mauritania	1961	x		x	x	x		3	x	x	x	x	x	x	x	x	x	x	x
Mauritius	1968	x	x	x	x	x	x	3	x	x	x	x	x	x	x	x	x	x	x
Mexico	1945	x	x	x	x	x	x	3	x	x	x	x	x	x	x	x	x	x	x
Mongolia	1961			x						x				x	x	x	x	x	x
Morocco	1956	x	x	x	x	x	x	3	x	x	x	x	x	x	x	x	x	x	x
Mozambique	1975	(e)		x	x	x	x	3	x	x	x	x	x	x	x	x	x		x
Nepal	1955			x	x	x	x	3	x	x	x	x	x	x	x	x	x		x
Netherlands	1945	x	x	x	x	x	x	1	x	x	x	x	x	x	x	x	x	x	x
New Zealand	1945	x	x	x	x	x	x	1	x	x	x	x	x	x	x	x	x	x	x
Nicaragua	1945	x	x	x	x	x	x	3	x	x	x	x	x	x	x	x	x	x	x
Niger	1960	x	x	x	x	x	x	3	x	x	x		x	x	x	x	x	x	x
Nigeria	1960	x	x	x	x	x	x	2	x	x	x	x	x	x	x	x	x		x
Norway	1945	x	x	x	x	x	x	1	x	x	x	x	x	x	x	x	x	x	x
Oman	1971			x	x	x	x	3	x		x	x	x	x	x	x	x		x
Pakistan	1947	x	x	x	x	x	x	3	x	x	x	x	x	x	x	x	x	x	x
Panama	1945		x	x	x	x	x	3	x	x	x	x	x	x	x	x	x	x	x
Papua New Guinea	1975	(e)		x	x	x	x	3	x	x	x	x	x	x	x	x	x		x
Paraguay	1945		x	x	x	x	x	3	x	x	x	x	x	x	x	x	x	x	x
Peru	1945	x	x	x	x	x	x	3	x	x	x	x	x	x	x	x	x	x	x
Philippines	1945	x	x	x	x	x	x	3	x	x	x	x	x	x	x	x	x	x	x
Poland	1945	x	x	x	x	x				x	x	x	x	x	x	x	x	x	x
Portugal	1955	x	x	x	x	x		3	x	x	x	x	x	x	x	x	x	x	x
Qatar	1971	(e)		x	x	x		2		x	x	x	x	x	x	x	x	x	x
Romania	1955	x	x	x	x			3		x	x	x	x	x	x	x	x	x	x
Rwanda	1962	x		x	x	x	x	3	x	x	x		x	x	x	x	x	x	x
St. Christopher and Nevis	1983	(e)		x		x		3			x			x	x				
St. Lucia	1979	(e)		x	x	x		3	x	x	x		x		x		x	x	x
St. Vincent	1980	(e)		x	x	x					x	x	x		x		x	x	
Sao Tome and Principe	1975	(e)		x	x	x		3		x				x	x		x	x	x
Saudi Arabia	1945		x	x	x	x	x	2	x	x	x	x	x	x	x	x	x	x	x
Senegal	1960	x	x	x	x	x	x	3	x	x	x	x	x	x	x	x	x	x	x
Seychelles	1976	(e)		x	x			3		x	x	x	x	x		x	x	x	x
Sierra Leone	1961	x	x	x	x		x	3	x	x	x	x	x	x	x	x	x		x
Singapore	1965	x	x	x	x					x	x	x	x			x	x		x
Solomon Islands	1978	(e)		x	x	x		3	x	x	x					x	x		x
Somalia	1960			x	x	x	x	3	x	x	x	x	x	x	x	x	x	x	x
South Africa[v]	1945	x	x	x	x	x			x		x		x			x	x	x	x
Spain	1955	x	x	x	x	x	x	1	x	x	x	x	x	x	x	x	x	x	x
Sri Lanka	1955	x	x	x	x	x	x	3	x	x	x	x	x	x	x	x	x	x	x
Sudan	1956		x	x	x	x	x	3	x	x	x	x	x	x	x	x	x	x	x
Suriname	1975	x		x	x			3		x	x	x	x	x	x	x	x	x	x
Swaziland	1968	(e)		x	x	x		3	x	x	x		x	x	x	x	x	x	x
Sweden	1946	x	x	x	x	x	x	1	x	x	x	x	x	x	x	x	x	x	x
Syria	1945		x	x	x	x	x	3	x	x	x	x	x	x	x	x	x	x	x
Tanzania	1961	x	x	x	x	x	x	3	x	x	x	x	x	x	x	x	x	x	x
Thailand	1946	x	x	x	x	x	x	3	x	x	x	x	x	x	x	x	x		x
Togo	1960	x		x	x	x	x	3	x	x	x	x	x	x	x	x	x	x	x
Trinidad and Tobago	1962	x		x	x	x	x	3	x	x	x	x	x	x	x	x	x		x
Tunisia	1956	(e)	x	x	x	x	x	3	x	x	x	x	x	x	x	x	x	x	x
Turkey	1945	x	x	x	x	x	x	3	x	x	x	x	x	x	x	x	x	x	x
Uganda	1962	x	x	x	x	x	x	3	x	x	x		x	x	x	x	x	x	x
Ukrainian Soviet Socialist Republic	1945		x								x				x	x	x	x	x	x
Union of Soviet Socialist Republics	1945			x		x					x		x	x	x	x	x	x	x	x

ORGANIZATION	UN	FAO	GATT	IAEA	IBRD	ICAO	IDA	IFAD	IFC	ILO	IMF	IMO	ITU	UNESCO	UNIDO	UPU	WHO	WIPO	WMO
COUNTRIES (cont.)																			
United Arab Emirates	1971	x	(e)	x	x	x	x	2	x	x	x	x	x	x	x	x	x	x	x
United Kingdom	1945	x	x	x	x	x	x	1	x	x	x	x	x		x	x	x	x	x
United States	1945	x	x	x	x	x	x	1	x	x	x	x	x		x	x	x	x	x
Uruguay	1945	x	x	x	x	x		3	x	x	x	x	x	x	x	x	x	x	x
Vanuatu	1981	x			x	x	x		x		x	x				x	x		x
Venezuela	1945	x		x	x	x		2	x	x	x	x	x	x	x	x	x	x	x
Vietnam	1977	x		x	x	x	x	3	x		x	x	x	x	x	x	x	x	x
Western Samoa	1976	x			x		x	3	x		x			x			x		
Yemen Arab Republic	1947	x			x	x	x	3	x	x	x	x	x	x	x	x	x	x	x
Yemen, People's Democratic Republic of	1967	x	(e)		x	x	x	3		x	x	x	x	x	x	x	x		x
Yugoslavia	1945	x	x	x	x	x	x	3	x	x	x	x	x	x	x	x	x	x	x
Zaire	1960	x	x	x	x	x	x	3	x	x	x	x	x	x	x	x	x	x	x
Zambia	1964	x	x	x	x	x	x	3	x	x	x		x	x	x	x	x	x	x
Zimbabwe	1980	x	x	x	x	x	x	3	x	x	x		x	x	x	x	x	x	x

INDEX

Part I (Geographical and Organizational Names) includes names of regions, countries, and territories; and intergovernmental organizations and affiliated institutions by full names and abbreviations. Part II (Personal Names) lists the heads of state and government of all countries as well as other individuals of special prominence. *Not* indexed are names of cabinet members (other than heads of government) and names which appear incidentally in the course of an article on another subject. When a name appears more than once within a single article, the index reference is to its first appearance.

PART I

(Geographical and Organizational Names)

PART II

(Personal Names)

862

ARCTIC

OCEAN

Greenland

Iceland   United Kingdom   Norway   Sweden   Finland

Monaco
German Democratic R
Liechtenstein
Northern Ireland   Denmark   Czechoslovakia
Ireland   Austria
Netherlands   Hungary
Belgium   Poland   Yugoslavia
Luxembourg   Romania
Federal Republic of Germany   Bulgaria
Switzerland   E   France   U   R
Andorra   Italy
Vatican City State   San Marino   Turkey
Portugal   Spain   Malta   Albania   Cyprus   Syria   Kuwa
                                 Greece   Lebanon   Iraq
Morocco   Tunisia   Israel   Jordan
                   Libya   Egypt   Bahrain
Algeria   Saudi Ara

Canada

NORTH

AMERICA

United

States

A
T
L
A
N
T
I
C

Senegal
Gambia   Mauritania
Cape Verde Is.   Mali   Niger   Sudan
Guinea-Bissau   Djibouti
Guinea   Benin   Chad   Central
Sierra Leone   Nigeria   African   Uganda   Ethiopia
Burkina Faso   Cameroon   Republic
Liberia   Togo   Gabon   Rwanda   Kenya   Somali
Côte d'Ivoire   Congo   Burundi
Ghana   Republic   Zaire   Tanzania   Comoro Is
Sao Tome   Angola   Malawi
and Principe   Zambia   Madagasca
Equatorial Guinea

Bahamas
Dominican
Mexico   Cuba   Haiti   Republic   St. Kitts-Nevis
                                      Antigua
Jamaica   Dominica
Belize   St. Vincent   St. Lucia
Guatemala   Grenada   Barbados
El Salvador   Panama   Trinidad and Tobago
Honduras   Venezuela   Guyana
Nicaragua   French Guiana
Costa Rica   Colombia
Ecuador   Suriname

AFRICA

O
C
E
A
N

Namibia
(South West Africa)   Botswan

Bophuthatswana

Mozambiqu
Zimbabwe
South   Venda
Africa   Swaziland
Lesotho
Transkei
Ciskei

SOUTH   AMERICA

Peru   Brazil

PACIFIC   Bolivia

Paraguay

Chile

OCEAN

Argentina   Uruguay

P

E